THE
PULPIT COMMENTARY

Edited by

H. D. M. Spence

and

Joseph S. Exell

————————

Volume 2
LEVITICUS
NUMBERS

Wm. B. Eerdmans Publishing Company, Grand Rapids, Michigan

THE PULPIT COMMENTARY

Edited by

H. D. M. Spence *and* Joseph S. Exell

This large-type edition republished
from new plates by

WM. B. EERDMANS PUBLISHING COMPANY
Grand Rapids, Michigan

ISBN 0-8028-8059

Reprinted September 1980

PHOTOLITHOPRINTED BY EERDMANS PRINTING COMPANY
GRAND RAPIDS, MICHIGAN, UNITED STATES OF AMERICA

LEVITICUS

INTRODUCTIONS BY

R. COLLINS   A. CAVE

EXPOSITION AND HOMILETICS BY

F. MEYRICK

HOMILIES BY VARIOUS AUTHORS

R. A. REDFORD   R. M. EDGAR
W. CLARKSON   J. A. MACDONALD

S. R. ALDRIDGE

AN ESSAY ON SACRIFICE

BY THE

REV. RICHARD COLLINS, M.A.

WHAT is the origin, true character, and proper place of sacrifice as a part of religion? Half a century ago, when many of us were schoolboys, there was certain definite teaching on this subject. Probably nine hundred and ninety-nine out of every thousand educated Englishmen, who had seriously turned their thoughts to the matter, were perfectly satisfied with the view, and regarded it as almost axiomatic, that sacrifice was a divinely appointed religious rite, intended to typify and educate the world for one Great Sacrifice, which Great Sacrifice having been accomplished, there was no need for, or even place for, any future sacrifice, truly so called, in the Christian Church. I do not put the matter thus under the idea that the consensus of antiquity is necessarily any warrant for the truth of a doctrine, but only because the view of sacrifice that I have alluded to has seemed to multitudes so scriptural, so simple, so fully to account for the peculiarities and mysteries of the subject, that in reconsidering it we should be led to use the utmost diligence in finally satisfying our minds as to its true place and character.

For we must reconsider it, if not for our own satisfaction, at least for the satisfaction of those we may have to teach. This duty is forced upon us by the fact that the waves of modern opinion have rudely shaken our ancient, and what perhaps we considered our orthodox, notions about sacrifices; and, indeed, it has been not merely a shaking, but a complex shaking—one wave rolling the notion in one direction and another in an opposite one, so that we feel that we must first secure the notion before we can assign it its true place in history and in reference to the Christian religion.

Men, probably equals in intellectual force and learning, have lately propounded views as to the nature and office of sacrifice so diametrically contradictory the one to the other that both cannot be true: the truth must either reside in the one, to the total exclusion of the other, or it must be found between the two, or beyond either. According to one view, sacrifice is a mistake of man's still undeveloped reason in the days of his ignorant wonder. The inexorable laws of nature pressed upon man's infant intelligence, so that he worshipped them in fear, and exalted them into gods. The inevitable begat the idea of an inflexible, exacting justice which must be satisfied or appeased. Hence arose the idea of propitiation before the presence of this rigorous justice, at length personified, by the immolation of the best a man had—the fruit of his body, or some other costly human sacrifice; a sacrifice which was, as human reason became more highly developed, commuted by the offering of animal instead of human life. A further development, as human reason grew, was a mere self-sacrifice, not of blood, but of service, as in the case of the Buddhist. And the last stage of development, according to this teaching, is the elimination from mankind of every sacrificial altar and every dogma having a sacrificial aspect.

According to the other view, not only were animal sacrifices of Divine institution, prospective to the Great Sacrifice, but tho duty of offering a sacrifice is still the central duty of the Christian Church. The Catholic Church is truly Christ's body only so long as it contains a sacrificing priesthood, and a sacrifice as truly such as were the sacrifices of Aaron. The offering of the Holy Eucharist is not a commemorative sacrifice in the sense of its being a commemoration of a sacrifice, but in the sense of its being a true oblation of that which shall plead for the quick, and even, as some hold, for the dead. In short, according to this school of thought, the highest development of human reason in respect to this matter is the exact converse of that previously stated. It is that the life of the Church absolutely depends upon its enshrinement of a true sacrificial altar and upon a continually sacrificing priesthood.

Where lies the truth?

As an exponent of the former view, we may take a recent article in the *Nineteenth Century*, on Shylock's bond, 'The Pound of Flesh,' by Mr. Moncure D. Conway. According to the argument pursued in that article, it is maintained that the idea of sacrifice arose from "non-human nature;" that it was the outgrowth of "nature-worship," the remorselessness of hard "natural" law calling for recompense; and that forgiveness is the highest development of "human nature"—that mercy is the basis of "purely human religion."

As an exponent of the other extreme, we may take the writings of Mr. Orby Shipley, who states that Christ becomes "incarnate in the hands of the priest" at the consecration of the elements in the Holy Eucharist, and that there and then a sacrifice is offered for the sins of mankind.

I propose to consider the subject of sacrifice

I. In its origin;

II. In its limits.

I.

The doctrine that sacrifices were originally the offspring of human ignoranco reflected on the Deity, is fairly summed up in the following extract from Mr. Conway's article to which I have alluded:[1] "Side by side," Mr. Conway writes, "in all ages and races, have struggled with each other the principle of retaliation and that of forgiveness. In religion the vindictive principle has euphemistic names; it is called law and justice. The other principle, that of remission, has had to exist by sufferance, and in nearly all religions has been recognized only in subordinate alliance with its antagonist. An eye for an eye, a tooth for a tooth, blood for blood, is primitive law. Projected into heaven, magnified into the Divine majesty, it becomes the principle that a Deity cannot be just, and yet a Justifier of offenders. 'Without the shedding of blood there is no remission of sins.' Since finite man is naturally assumed to be incapable of directly satisfying an infinite law, all religions, based on the idea of a Divine Lawgiver, are employed in devising schemes by which commutations may be secured and vicarious satisfactions of Divine law obtained. No Deity inferred from the always relentless forces of nature has ever been supposed able to forgive the smallest sin until it was exactly atoned for. For this reason, the Divine mercifulness has generally become a separate personification. The story of the 'pound of flesh' is one of the earliest fables concerning these conflicting principles."

Thus, then, if I understand this line of reasoning clearly, we are brought to the theory that all religions have been the imputations of human feelings and experiences to the Deity. And whether the Deity exist as the Great Unknown or be merely a

[1] *Nineteenth Century*, May, 1880, p. 830.

figment of man's brain, Mr. Conway's argument remains the same. According to this theory, as the principle of retaliation and that of forgiveness have struggled for ascendency in man's moral development, so in parallel lines have the god or gods, real or imaginary, been vindictive or forgiving. In this way, the history of the religions of mankind is merely the history of man's moral growth reflected on another sphere— where we see the survival of the moral fittest, human mercy, as a purely human force, gradually supplanting human vindictiveness. And thus Divine law, or justice, is translated by human vindictiveness; and the offering of sacrifices, animal or other, is a human scheme by which "commutations may be secured and vicarious satisfactions obtained" to propitiate, or appease, the supposed Divine vindictiveness.

Mr. Conway illustrates and supports his theory by reference to Brahmanic, Buddhistic, and Semitic examples.

"The following legend," he writes, "was related to me by a Hindu, as one he had been told in his childhood. The chief of the Indian triad, Indra, pursued the god Agni. Agni changed himself to a dove in order to escape; but Indra changed himself to a hawk, to continue the pursuit. The dove took refuge with Vishnu, second person of the triad, the Hindu saviour. Indra, flying up, demanded the dove; Vishnu, concealing it in his bosom, refused to give up the dove. Indra then took an oath that, if the dove were not surrendered, he would tear from Vishnu's breast an amount of flesh equal to the body of the dove. Vishnu still refused to surrender the bird, but bared his breast. The divine hawk tore from it the exact quantity, and the drops of blood— the blood of a saviour—as they fell to the ground, wrote the scriptures of the Vedas.

"We may see," Mr. Conway goes on to remark, "in the fable reflection of a sacrificial age; an age in which the will and word of a god became inexorable fate, but also the dawning conception of a divineness in the mitigation of the law, which ultimately adds saving deities to those which cannot be appeased." Versions of this story are traced in some of the Hindu writings; and advancing to the discussion of Buddhism, Mr. Conway says, " With Buddha the principle of remission supersedes that of sacrifice. His argument against the Brahmanic sacrifice of life was strong. When they pointed to these predatory laws of nature in proof of their faith that the gods approved the infliction of pain and death, he asked them why they did not sacrifice their own children; why they did not offer to the gods the most valuable lives. The fact was that they were outgrowing direct human sacrifices—preserving self-mortifications—and animals were slain in commutation of costlier offerings." The Semitic story adduced is, of course, that of Abraham and Isaac. "In the case of Abraham and Isaac," Mr. Conway writes, "the demand is not remitted, but commuted. The ram is accepted instead of Isaac. But even so much concession could hardly be recognized by the Hebrew priesthood as an allowable variation from a direct demand of Jahve, and so the command is said to have been given by Elohim, its modification by Jahve. The cautious transformation is somewhat in the spirit of the disguises of the Aryan deities, who may partially revoke as gods the orders they gave as hawks. It would indicate a more advanced idea if we found Jahve remitting a claim of his own instead of one made by Elohim."

Thus too the Jewish religion and the Christian religion are brought under the same category with Hinduism and Buddhism, and are made to illustrate the same human principles. The idea, possibility, probability, or claims of revelation are untouched.

I do not enter the arena of controversy to discuss with Mr. Conway the character and revelation of Jehovah; that would be quite beside the mark in this commentary. But standing on the platform of Holy Scripture, I wish thence to consider some portions of his theory.

Now, while Jew and Christian have sufficient reason for believing that certain sacrifices were commanded or sanctioned by Divine revelation, as a part of the religious observances of the Jewish people; yet we find sacrifices of one kind or another common to almost all ancient nations, and practised long before the Israelites were under Mount Sinai. Leaving out of sight, for the present, the object of the Mosaic sacrifices, and the possible question whether Jehovah sanctioned and regulated for the Jewish worship something which was already a part, as it were, of human nature, let us test the question, whether the practice of offering sacrifice can have had any such origin as that suggested by Mr. Conway.

First, take the central idea, if I understand Mr. Conway aright, that the principle of forgiveness, mercy, is a purely human attribute, and that it has been winning its way against the principle of vindictiveness by a kind of natural selection, in the struggle of the noble against the ignoble in the moral world. I fail to read this fact in the history either of the race or of the individual. The principle of retaliation, vindictiveness, we find to-day as robust as when the earliest pages of history were penned. Purely human, it has its origin in the instinct of self-preservation, and seems to be an echo in man of what can be traced through the brute creation. But is mercy, as expressed by the forgiveness of the injurious by the injured, of human origin at all? Is it anywhere to be traced in man's history apart from the influence of the religion of Jehovah? That there is a germ of mercy in the human constitution, there is no doubt; otherwise we could not understand, appreciate, or practise the principle of forgiveness at all. But where in the history of the human race do we find the principle contained in the words, "Forgive your enemies," asserting itself, except in what Christians hold to be a Divine revelation? It is undoubtedly true that Koong-foo-tse taught that men should "do as they would be done by." But we do not know whence he received his philosophy; possibly, in common with Gautama Buddha, from the teaching of pious Jews at the court of Babylon—an influence which may well have had a worldwide character (see Dan. vi. 25—28). And "Do as you would be done by" comes very far short of "Love your enemies." Buddhism, again, contains no teaching, so far as I have been able to discover, on the subject of forgiveness. The nearest approach to it that I have met with, is a story of the queen Sâmawati, who, when her enraged husband was about to shoot her with a poisoned arrow, looked at him with a smile of affection, and so paralyzed his arm that he could not draw the bow; an act that was followed by this wise piece of advice, "When you desire to pacify anger, look upon the angered person with love." But this could only be in the case, like her own, when love pre-existed. And this story is not related by the Buddhists to enforce forgiveness for its own sake, but to illustrate their doctrine that there is a supernatural power, derived from merit in a former state of existence, which preserves its possessor from danger. Mr. Conway states that "in Buddhism the principle of remission supersedes that of sacrifice." I do not know upon what quotations from Buddhistic writings he would verify this statement. Certainly sacrifice is impossible in Buddhism, since it forbids the taking of all life. But I have no evidence that that peculiar law of Buddha has any especial reference to the sacrifice of animals as a religious observance. And with respect to the principle of remission, or forgiveness, I am not aware of a word—though it may be that I have not exhausted the Buddhistic lore—in the teachings of Buddha relating to it, either as a duty of man towards man, or as something to be desired from a higher power. Indeed, Buddhism acknowledges no higher power than man, and seeks not forgiveness, but merit, by which the individual man may be freed from the curse of mortality. That the idea of merit, that underlies all Buddhistic teaching, may originally have been connected with the idea of the remission of sins, is not only possible but probable. But in our present ignorance of the true historical origin of the teachings of Buddha, this is a subject, the discussion of which would be without the scope of this essay. The fact with regard to Buddhism as now known is that, while the idea of sacrifice is historically present, it has no reference to remission or forgiveness. Self-sacrifice, which is so essential a part of Buddhism, is nowhere connected with remission, but merit; as when Gautama, while a Bōdhisat (*i.e.* a candidate for the Buddhahood), voluntarily allowed a hungry tigress to devour him, in order to save her life and that of her cubs, as a step towards becoming a Buddha.

In Hinduism, again, there is no teaching on the subject of forgiveness, either as between man and man, or the deity and man, except in a very few passages in some of the earliest hymns of the Rig Veda: as Hinduism progresses, the idea is lost, not developed. When the head of the cock is cut off before the altar of Kāli, there is no thought of obtaining forgiveness of the deity ; the general idea is, as with the Buddhist, that merit will accrue on the performance of a prescribed act of religion which they have learned from their forefathers. There are whole races of men in whose vocabulary there is no word for forgiveness. The spirit of retaliation seems to be still as potent as ever, apart from the spirit of Christianity. The successful struggle of the principle of forgiveness, as a purely human attribute, against the principle of retaliation, does not appear to me to be made out. There must, therefore, be some other reason why the virtue of forgiveness, theoretically at all events, holds so influential a position in the ethics of the learned men of Europe. The Christian would maintain that this virtue has been learned solely from Holy Scripture by the moderns, and from anterior Divine revelation by the ancients.

Then, again, we have to confront the theory that man, under the influence of a religious instinct (and, of course, the case of the Christian religion is here included), has formed no higher ideal of Divine justice than such as is a reflection of his own innate sense of retaliation or vindictiveness. This, I suppose, to be the meaning of the passages quoted before : " In religion the vindictive principle has euphemistic names; it is called law and justice. . . . An eye for an eye, a tooth for a tooth, blood for blood, is primitive law. Projected into heaven, magnified into the Divine majesty, it becomes the principle that a Deity cannot be just, and yet a Justifier of offenders."

Now, this is a subject that requires extremely nice discrimination. For that the idea of vindictiveness, or retaliation, has been " projected," so to speak, on the Divine justice by the short-sightedness of man, there is no doubt. But that the idea of the Divine justice that underlies the Christian religion is the offspring of such a principle in man's heart, is a theory which entirely subverts the truth of Christianity.

We may begin by remarking that our natural views of justice, equity, are not, of course, in any degree the children of our natural impulse towards retaliation. Nor can Mr. Conway be supposed to suggest this. Equity, human justice, represented by the ancients under the symbol of an even balance, so far from being the child of the principle, or spirit, of vindictiveness, is that which alone controls it. Justice determines whether the " pound of flesh " and the debt are really in equipoise ; justice stops a man when his instinctive vindictiveness sends him in pursuit of his enemy ; the laws of England do not allow a man to retaliate, but endeavour to put him into the hands of justice ; and so when our Saviour said, " Ye have heard that it hath been said, An eye for an eye, and a tooth for a tooth : but I say unto you, That ye resist not evil," he evidently meant that men should curb the impetuosity of personal vindictiveness, and leave their case in the hands of a more perfect justice.

Man has the power of realizing a perfect, even-handed justice, however often and however far he may have abused the principle in practice. And although he may have reflected his own imperfections on false gods, and may have made them vindictive, the Divine justice that underlies the Christian religion owns none of this imperfection, but is in accordance with that perfect ideal that man is capable of forming, though not always of practising.

How, then, does the Christian religion regard the Divine justice in relation to the forgiveness of sins? Does it impute to that justice vindictiveness, or retaliation, and then " devise a scheme by which a commutation may be secured, and a vicarious satisfaction obtained," to meet the inexorable demands of that Divine retaliation? The Scripture does indeed say that " by the deeds of the Law there shall no flesh be justified in his sight." But this is no threat of retaliation; for it simply states a self-evident fact, that a man cannot be both guilty and guiltless. And there is no part of Holy Scripture which says that " the Deity cannot be just, and yet a Justifier of offenders." On the contrary, it says that " God *can* be just, and yet the Justifier of the ungodly; " and it makes it a part of the justice of God that he does forgive offences, for " He is faithful and just to forgive us our sins." But it will be said, this act of God's justice, in forgiving offenders, is only extended, according to the Christian Scriptures, in view of the " satisfaction " made to the Divine justice in the death of the Saviour Jesus Christ as a vicarious offering; and that a satisfaction implies something to be satisfied. This is in a certain sense true; but there is no word in the New Testament which represents the satisfaction as made to any principle of retaliation. And I may note, in passing, that the word itself, " satisfaction," though occurring in the Prayer of Consecration in the English Prayer-book, does not anywhere occur in that connection in the New Testament. The utmost care is needed in enforcing the doctrine of the atonement from the pulpit, lest the idea of retaliation should be inferred. The spirit of retaliation would make God thirst for the blood of the sinner, whereas God " willeth not the death of a sinner; " it would represent the Deity as injured, whereas God cannot be injured. We cannot shut up the doctrine of the atonement under the naked formula, that man must be punished on account of his sins unless some one else can be found to be punished for him; that the justice of God must have suffering somewhere, if man is not to suffer. To provide suffering was not the one only object of the atonement; it was not merely to balance suffering against suffering that the one Great Sacrifice was offered.

To what, then, was satisfaction made? It is made to absolute justice, to the truth of God; and it is made not only by the sufferings, but by the perfect life of Jesus, as the perfect man, in obedience to the Law. Justice—not retaliation—demands that what a man sows, that shall he reap. Man sows sin, and reaps the necessary results—death, the forfeiture of God's presence. Man cannot be pardoned and restored on his own merits. The merits of another are offered to him. The picture of atonement in the Old Testament is that of a covering of sins, and in the New Testament is reconciliation of man to God. In the English version of the New Testament the word "atonement" occurs once, and translates the word which is elsewhere translated "reconciliation" (*katallage*). The satisfaction on which this covering of sins and reconciliation of man to God is based embraces the life, death, resurrection, ascension, and mediation of the Saviour God-man. The object in view of the life, death, and resurrection of Jesus was not one, but manifold. It was to manifest God (" God manifest in the flesh"); to reconcile man's heart (" You, that were sometimes alienated and enemies in your mind by wicked works, yet now hath he reconciled in the body of his flesh through death, to present you holy and unblameable and unreproveable in his sight "); to show man that he has a Mediator (" the one Mediator between God and man, the man Christ Jesus "); to prove his love (" Greater love hath no man than this, that a man lay down his life for his friends "); to enter death that he might show man that he is the victor over it, as the Firstfruits from the dead ("If Christ be not raised, then is our hope in vain"); to read a lesson to other spheres ("To the intent that now unto the principalities and powers in heavenly places might be known by the Church the manifold wisdom of God, according to the eternal purpose which he purposed in Christ Jesus our Lord"). In all this he stood in man's place to suffer; the "chastisement of our peace was upon him; and with his stripes we are healed;" "he redeemed us from the curse of the Law, being made a curse for us." His merits were so perfect that they outweighed all man's demerits, so that for his sake man can be justified and accepted according to the covenant of grace. Nay, this doctrine of the atonement is too wonderful, too mysteriously great, too deep to be gauged by man; we have not yet fathomed its depths; nor had even the inspired apostle, who wrote, "Oh the depth of the riches both of the wisdom and knowledge of God! how unsearchable are his judgments, and his ways past finding out!" But to introduce the spirit of vindictiveness, or retaliation, on the part of the Jehovah of the sacred Scriptures, as thirsting for the blood of the sinner, and demanding the sufferings of Christ from any principle analogous to the human principle of retaliation—as though he would demand the pound of flesh because he could not obtain the sheltered dove—is one of the greatest insults ever offered to the Christian religion, which declares that the whole motive power towards salvation was love. "God so loved the world, that he gave his only begotten Son, that whosoever believeth in him should not perish, but have everlasting life."

The fact, however, remains, that the Christian religion does centre round a Sacrifice; and the further fact remains, that not only was the Jewish religion a religion of sacrifices, but that in almost all, if not all, nations sacrifices have been offered from the earliest days of historical man, and in many cases up to the present moment. What has originally given birth to the idea of sacrifices? It is asked, "Are they not substitutions, that have suggested themselves to man, by which to propitiate and avert from himself the supposed Divine vindictiveness, which he has euphemized as Divine law and justice?" The answer must be, first, that it seems impossible that man could invent the system of sacrifice. Suppose a man, in the dawn of human reason, who should have no better idea of Divine justice than as interpreted by his own innate vindictiveness. We may even suppose him to have reasoned up to the conclusion, that the deity cannot be just, and yet the justifier of the guilty; that is, that a man cannot be held to be guiltless unless his complete innocence is manifest. And to this he adds, from his own nature, that Nemesis must overtake him. But what is there in human nature to suggest to him to make an offering in blood, whether human or animal? He fears, it may be, the vengeance, the vindictiveness, or even the malignity of an unseen deity on himself. But what is there in that to suggest the idea of a propitiatory offering, a commutation, a vicarious satisfaction, in lieu of his own person, in blood? Nay, what is there to suggest any offering of any kind? Human vindictiveness might lead him to hurl a dart at the imagined deity, could he hope to reach him; but of what avail would any kind of offering be? Would he think of bribing the deity not to injure him, as he might bribe an earthly judge? Should such a thought arise in his mind, it would perish at the first attempt; for what man would try twice to bribe an earthly judge who persistently refused the bribe? And what man, in fear of an earthly judge, would think of going to his door with the life-blood of his son, or of the best of his flock?

We will suppose the case of such a primitive man, totally unacquainted, from whatsoever cause, with any portion of a Divine revelation. He embodies in his imagination the phenomena of the atmosphere as the attributes of a personal deity, whom we may call Indra. From Indra he receives the bounties of the sun and rain which mature his harvests, and also the floods, torrents, tempests, and thunder and lightning, which make him fear. He surrounds this deity with a moral atmosphere of inflexible, uncompromising remorselessness—the moral shadow, we may say, of the character he attaches to the physical heavens. Suppose, then, that one day, when he and his sons are reaping their harvest, their great desire being for a cloudless heaven to dry their sheaves, an ominous cloud gathers; the heavens are soon black, the forked lightning darts with angry quiver from cloud to cloud, and from cloud to earth; the thunder seems to split the firmament in rage; till out darts a forked tongue of flame, and slays his youngest son at his feet. Will he regard this as Indra's retaliation on account of some offence he has been guilty of? Suppose it is so. What would human nature suggest to him to do in order to escape, if possible, Indra's further vindictiveness? Is there anything in his nature that would lead him to cut the throat of his eldest son, and, hurling him on a pile of faggots, to consume his body with fire, as a holocaust, to appease the supposed wrath of Indra, and so, under the idea of sacrificing a substitute of the greatest worth in his estimation, to ward off danger from himself? Would he be likely to fling the blood of his lamb or his kid towards the heavens, under the idea of sheltering himself from Indra's retaliative stroke? Or could anything in his own nature suggest to him that Indra required some voluntary sacrifice? We cannot touch even the elements of such a thought in man's nature, much less trace their development. There is nothing whatever, surely, in human nature to suggest such thought or action.

But there is a kind of sacrifice which man has always understood—self-sacrifice for the sake of another. Mr. Conway's illustrations would seem to me to touch this thought rather than the idea of commutation by sacrifice. History is full of this phase of sacrifice. When Gautama Buddha, as related above, was pictured as giving his body as food to the tigress, the idea was self-sacrifice for the sake of the starving animal and her young. The bravery of Horatius Cocles, though his life was spared, is an illustration of the same thought. There *is* the idea of substitution: but it is a substitution in the sacrifice of one's self at one's own hands for the salvation of another. This is a doctrine which man can understand. But the idea of thrusting forward a substitute for the sake of guarding one's self is foreign to man's innate nobility.

Turn the matter as we will, nothing is more difficult than to try to realize what there is in man that would lead him of his own accord to offer the life of a bullock, a sheep, a goat, or a dove, to propititate the Divine justice. But it has been done in all ages. How has the custom originated?

It has arisen about the world-sacrifice of Jesus Christ. That was a self-sacrifice of the highest conceivable import; but it involved the shedding of a life. And that one Sacrifice, coupled with the life, resurrection, and ascension of Jesus Christ, was in all its bearings the most significant event that ever happened in the history of the human race. Should not, then, the world of all time be educated for that one great central " mystery of godliness," the reconciliation of the world by " God manifest in the flesh," the outward circumstance of which was the life-shedding of Jesus on Calvary?

The world has often been divinely taught by signs; and the deeper the degradation of man, the simpler and more pointed the sign. Jeremiah, with his " marred girdle," his " potter's clay," his " good and evil figs; " Ezekiel, with his " tile," his " razor," his " staff upon his shoulder," and his " seething-pot," are familiar examples. In these days of the Christian Church we are taught by a very significant symbol to realize, as we look upon it, the offering of Jesus Christ on the cross; a symbol appointed by his own words and acts—" This do in remembrance of me." The breaking of bread and the eating it, the pouring out of wine and the drinking it, are the symbol under which we are to " show the Lord's death till he come."

But how was the world to be educated in prospect of that Sacrifice? The great central fact to be taught was—the shedding of a life the salvation and life of the world. We are taught now to look upon that Sacrifice at a meal, because the atoning power must always be connected with the life-giving power. The eating of bread and the drinking of wine are signs distinct enough to keep the world in memory of the fact and character of the death of Christ, the Life of the world. The Lord's Supper is, moreover, a bridge of history, taking us back by unerring steps to the hour of its institution, and the hour of Christ's agony. But to prepare the world for this great idea, to perpetuate through succeeding generations, before the event, an expectation of the coming "mystery," something more distinct was appointed.

To take the Mosaic dispensation as a starting-point, we find under that dispensation the great analogue to the Lord's Supper in the system of sacrifice. And we have the authority of the Epistle to the Hebrews for saying that the Jewish sacrifices were a figure of Christ. Then also the symbol was connected with a meal; or had in every case at least some reference to food. Except in the case of the whole burnt offering, either the priests and the offerers of the sacrifice, or the priests alone, solemnly ate the offering, and that for the most part, in "the holy place." Nor was the animal sacrifice the only sacrifice: the "meat offering" (*minchah*) was as truly a sacrifice as the lamb, part being also consumed in the holy fire, and part eaten by the priest. Every animal sacrifice was an animal or bird used for food. But to the ritual of the animal sacrificial meal was added a most elaborate ritual as to the previous slaying of the animal itself, and the sprinkling of its blood, the offerer putting his hand on the head of the victim, and being taught to regard the sacrifice as a picture of atonement, the Hebrew idea of which was a covering, or a hiding of sin; and the blood was called the blood of the covenant. Thus, while the lesson of life by food is the same in the Lord's Supper and the sacrificial feast, the symbol of breaking of bread in token of the death of the Lord's body is replaced by a much more powerful symbol in the slaying of the animal that supplies the feast, and the solemn sprinkling of its blood. The two ordinances are from the same hand; and while we see the exquisite beauty of the symbolism in the commemorative Supper of the Lord, we cannot fail to see the beauty of power in the parallel symbolism of the shedding of blood in the prospective Old Testament dispensation.

But for the Jews to realize that power they must have been instructed in the fact that God would provide a greater, a perfect atonement in the person of the long-promised Messiah. They must have had an intelligent knowledge of what the "covenant" meant. The Eucharistic service of the Church of the Christian dispensation could have no meaning for the man who was unacquainted with the atonement of Christ. Nor can we conceive the intelligent and devout Jew seeing in the mere blood and death of an animal a covering for his sin. The Jew was not taught that the death of the animal was accepted instead of his punishment; but he was instructed to look upon it as a foreshadowing of a perfect Offering to come. This may not be apparent on a cursory glance at the Pentateuch; but the New Testament commentary leaves no doubt on the question. "It is not possible that the blood of bulls and of goats should take away sins;" the first tabernacle was "a figure for the time then present;" "the Law having a shadow of good things to come, and not the very image" (or full revelation) "of the things, can never with those sacrifices which they offered year by year continually make the comers thereunto perfect." This is not a contradiction of the Old Testament, but an explanation of the Mosaic dispensation. Of Moses we know, through our Saviour's own words, that he saw through and beyond the type to the Antitype: "Had ye believed Moses, ye would have believed me: for he wrote of me;" as of Abraham, that he "saw Christ's day, and was glad." That the sacrifices were nothing in themselves is a lesson constantly brought before the Jews. "To what purpose is the multitude of your sacrifices unto me? saith the Lord: I am full of the burnt offerings of rams, and the fat of fed beasts; and I delight not in the blood of bullocks, or of lambs, or of he goats." That the offering of the sacrifice was efficacious in itself for atonement as an *opus operatum*, was man's perversion of the truth; a perversion that is consonant with all that we know of human nature, of which every age testifies that it will hold tenaciously to the outward forms of religion, and with difficulty maintain its spirit. The Jew was never taught that the slaying or offering of the animal was an atonement in itself. Neither the animal nor the *minchah* was a substitute for something else—a commutation, but a foreshadowing, an educating of the world for the appreciation of the one atonement. As the sabbatical divisions of days and years were to familiarize Israel with the idea of a final rest; as the cities of refuge were to familiarize them with the idea of salvation; as the most remarkable institution of the goel, the kinsman-redeemer, was to familiarize them with the idea of redemption;—so the most elaborate ritual of sacrifice was to train them for the expectation of the offering of Jesus Christ once for all on the cross, for the reconciliation of the world. It was the great sacrament of the old world.

Thus, then, the nature and the object of the Mosaic sacrifice seems very evident; and its origin, with that of all its most remarkable accompaniments, was Divine. The further question now arises, What was the origin of other and previous sacrifices? First of all, the idea of sacrifice, as connected with the worship of Jehovah, was not originated under the Mosaic dispensation. Jethro, before the institutions of Mount Sinai, "took a burnt offering (*olah*) and sacrifices (*zebachim*) for God." These are the same words that are in use afterwards under the Mosaic dispensation, "And Aaron came, and all the elders of Israel, to eat bread with Moses' father-in-law before God" (Exod. xviii. 12) —not an ordinary, but, no doubt, the sacrificial feast, the old-world sacrament. Again, Jacob, on the eve of his memorable parting with Laban, "offered sacrifice upon the mount, and called his brethren to eat bread." The sacrifice here, again, was the *zebach*; and was not the "eating bread" the same sacrificial feast? Noah also on coming out of the ark "builded an altar" (*mizbeach*, from *zabach*, to slay), "and took of every clean beast, and of every clean fowl" (*i.e*, such as were *eaten*), "and offered burnt offerings (*oloth*) on the altar." Of Abel also, in the very first generation of historical men, we know that he "brought of the firstlings of his flock and of the fat thereof," as an offering unto the Lord; and why was his offering acceptable but that it was brought in obedience to God's own express direction?

The animals sacrificed were always food animals. Twice the sacrifice is mentioned in connection with a meal. And in Exodus, "to hold a feast" and "to sacrifice" seem to refer to the same event. The inference, therefore, is by no means extravagant, that the pre-Mosaic sacrifices were of precisely the same kind as those of the Mosaic dispensation. The "clean" animals used for sacrifice were so used *because* they were the animals used for food. (The theory, it may be observed, that animal food was not used before the Deluge seems to rest on no foundation whatever.) And if food was consecrated to the worship of Jehovah from the days of Adam, as food is now consecrated by the words of Jesus himself to the same worship in the Lord's Supper, where shall we seek for the origin of that significant feast, and the ritual of its observance, but in Jehovah himself?

It may not be unimportant, as a confirmation of such a view of the matter, to note here that the Mosaic dispensation, in probably every point, would seem to have been a *renewal* of former Divine directions as to the externals of worship. The leading features of the Mosaic dispensation wear the appearance rather of a reformation than of an initial institution. Thus the very form and character of the tabernacle itself, and after it of the temple of Solomon, were precisely the same as we now find in many Hindu temples. We cannot think that the Hindus copied at any time the form of the tabernacle in the wilderness or of the temple on Mount Moriah. Rather we must suppose that the Hindus still perpetuate what was the most primitive form of a temple for Divine worship, the fane with its two rooms and the surrounding court; and that that form was reinstituted under Mount Sinai. Nor was there anything new in the Aaronic priesthood: Melchizedek was a *cohen;* Jethro was a *cohen.* Then, again, as to the sacrifices, the *minchah* is still the daily offering in the Hindu temple; food is offered before the idol in the inner room of the fane, a handful is consumed on the sacrificial fire, and the meal is eaten by the priests. The same kind of food offering was made both by Greeks and Romans. The sacrifice of food animals has also been perpetuated by various other nations. Such were the principal sacrifices among the Greeks and Romans, and among the Hindus there is still the sacrifice of the lamb. Some even of the minutiæ too of the more ancient rites evidently remained intact for ages; as, for instance, compare Numb. xix, 2, "They shall bring thee a red heifer . . , upon which never came yoke," with Ovid ('Fasti,' iii. 375, 376)—

> "Tollit humo munus cæsa prius ille juvenca,
> Quæ dederat nulli colla premenda jugo,"

We cannot account for these things by supposing that the heathen nations learned the rules of sacrifice from the Jews. The only rational supposition is that they retained many of the externals of primitive worship, while the worship of the Jews was truly the primitive worship divinely restored. Heathen religious rites and sacrifices are fossils of the old-world Church history, the *exuviæ* of dead faiths. Incrusted, indeed, they are with superstitions many and grievous, petrified, the true primitive life long since crushed out of them; but yet unmistakably the remains of an ancient garden of the Lord's, of a primitive sacrificial and sacramental worship, the analogue of that which was again seen in the days of Moses, David, and Solomon.

If such be the case, we cannot hesitate to conclude that the whole system of heathen sacrifice, however degraded and distorted in its present application, bears ample witness to a Divine origin. The theory that sacrifice is an outcome of human nature does not bear examination. The fact that man will cling to the externals of religion while losing its spirit, is attested by all history. The very existence, therefore, of priest and sacrifice as worldwide facts would seem to point back infallibly to a day of pure religion and a God-appointed worship.

II.

Is there a sacrifice, a priesthood, and an altar in the Christian Church?

This question is so suggestive, and related to so much that is collateral, that only salient points must here be touched upon, and such as have reference to what has gone before, or this essay would very soon exceed its due limits.

First, perhaps, it is well to guard one's self against an idea too commonly expressed, that the Mosaic dispensation was "imperfect." The thought has arisen around the expression in the Epistle to the Hebrews of the "greater and more perfect tabernacle." The Mosaic dispensation *was* imperfect, as all human things must be, even when of Divine appointment, when compared with Christ; but it was not imperfect as a dispensation. No ordinance from God's hands can be imperfect. The sacrificial system must have been the very best method of teaching the ways of God to man, or it would not have been instituted. We must not, therefore, approach the words, "sacrifice," "priest," "altar," with a prejudice. They were once God's ordinance. Are they so still?

The Lord's Supper is manifestly a modification of the ancient prospective sacrificial system, for the edification of the Church in retrospect. In what particulars, as regards directions actually recorded, does the institution given under Mount Sinai differ from the Saviour's institution? In both the Saviour is typified by food at a meal. But in the latter there is no direction as to an "offering;" neither is the Church nor the individual instructed to "present" the bread and the wine before God, as under the former sacrificial system. There is no direction as to animal food; indeed, practically it is prohibited. There is, therefore, no ritual of blood. There is no command to confess sins in connection with an offering, as when under the older dispensation the offerer laid his hand on the head of the victim. There is no command to burn a portion of the food in the sacred fire; no sacred fire is vouchsafed. Hence no altar, of the same character as the Jewish altar, is required; nor is one mentioned by the Saviour. There is no mention made of a priest; those who were commanded to perpetuate the ordinance were not called *cohens* by Christ, but "apostles," missionaries. Nearly all the actual ancient sacrificial duties, both of priest and people, were practically abrogated at the institution of the Lord's Supper, the only point authoritatively preserved being the partaking of the *minchah* with wine. The Lord's Supper, then, in that it is a typical feast, a part of the ancient feast, picturing the blessed Redeemer in his sacrifice for the life of the world—"This is my body, which is given for you;" "This is my blood of the new covenant"—has most distinctly a sacrificial aspect; but it is denuded of almost all the observances peculiar to the ancient sacrificial feast. It points to the same *offering* as the old-world sacrifices, and by the same method, but accompanied, as it is apparently intended to be, with much less elaborate circumstance. An adaptation, however, of the more ancient sacrificial system it most manifestly is; such an adaptation as seemed to him, who is the All-wise, best fitted for the edification of the future Church.

But is it not evident that, by the method of our Saviour's institution, many details were left to be otherwise determined? Nothing can be more distinct than the matter, the form, and the intention of the Lord's Supper; but there is no direction as to the how, the when, or the where. Under the Mosaic dispensation every, the most minute, particular was provided for by Divine ordinance. Time, place, person, and manner are most exhaustively described. But our Saviour did not in like manner appoint the priest, the vestments, the accompaniments, the ritual of the Holy Meal. The commission, "Do this in remembrance of me," was given to the sacred society of apostles, or missionaries, who afterwards received that further commission, "Go ye into all the world, and preach the gospel to every creature." They, therefore, were the first celebrants; but their exact method of procedure has not been handed down to us. They were inspired men; had they subsequently any Divine directions? All we know on this matter is found in 1 Cor. xi. Were the apostles left to their private judgments as to the arrangements necessary for the suitable celebration of the Lord's Supper? or were they divinely directed? We cannot know. But we do know that very early in the history of the Church the Lord's Supper was separated from the agapæ, and administered at a special service; that at this service there were customs which seem to be a modified revival of the customs of the ancient sacrificial system, notably the confession of sins by the congregation, and the public declaration of God's acceptance on repentance. It could not have escaped the early Christians, especially the Jewish converts, that the Lord's Supper (established, too, as it had been, during the observance of the most significant and important of the Jewish sacrificial feasts) was a retrospective adaptation of the once prospective sacrifice. We cannot wonder, there-fore—though we know not the exact customs of the apostles themselves—that we should early read of the Christian sacrifice, the Christian priest, the Christian altar. The " elements " of the feast were a continuation of the " meat offering," the *minchah*, part of every former sacrifice; the presbyter, elder, or president, who served at the table, though not a priest of the Aaronic line, yet might well be called, in a certain though modified sense, a priest; and the table at which he served, though no longer the seat of the sacred fire, or sprinkled with blood, was to the Christian what the altar had been to the Jew—that from which he fed on the picture of Christ. And I cannot doubt, on a candid examination of the expression, though I once held to the contrary, that there is a reference to the table of the Lord's Supper in Heb. xiii. 10, " We (Christians) have an altar, whereof they have no right to eat which serve the taber-nacle." True it is that Christ's divinity is the actual altar of the universe, which upheld, sustained, and sanctified the humanity of Jesus in his sacrifice of himself; yet, as the Jewish altar was that which held the picture of the Sacrifice to come, and from which the Jew ate the emblematic feast, so the holy table from which we Christians feed in memory of Christ's death, is, in a parallel though modified sense, an altar. To refuse to the Christian Church, then, the very names of sacrifice, priest, and altar would seem almost to be to deny the propriety and solemnity of the words under the earlier dispensation, and to interfere materially with our understanding the real signifi-cance of our Saviour's institution as an adaptation of the divinely appointed sacrificial system to the Christian dispensation.

Yet as different views may, no doubt, lawfully be taken as to the intention of our blessed Saviour's silence at the moment of the institution of the Lord's Supper, we should surely allow that latitude of thought to others who, like ourselves, love the Lord Jesus in sincerity.

What is the error that has grown up about the words " sacrifice," " priest," and " altar"? It is idolatry; that is, making the picture more than a picture. When the Jew believed that the blood of bulls and of goats *could* take away sin, he perverted the truth and the ordinance of God; and when the Christian holds that there is in the Lord's Supper a propitiatory sacrifice for the quick and the dead for the remission of sins, he equally abuses the truth of God and the beauty of the ordinance. It is the confounding of the inward spiritual grace in the sacraments with the rite itself that has been at the root of the chief of the religious errors of mankind. The inward spiritual grace is the apprehension and appropriation by the intelligence and the affections of that which the outward observance typifies, and therefore to the faithful the actual reception of its benefit; and the observance itself, when rightly understood, becomes an instrument in arousing that apprehension, as well as a pledge and means, by virtue of its institution, of our receiving that grace. But to make a sacrament an *opus operatum*, to convert the image into that which it represents, is idolatry. It is this astounding, though truly human, error that plunged the ancient world into heathenism, the Jewish world into Pharisaism, and the Christian world into what is now commonly called Popery. The fall of the intelligence when the floods of superstition are let in upon the soul, is great indeed; so that a man can even hold the blasphemous doctrine that the blessed Redeemer can become incarnate in the sacramental elements of bread and wine in the hands of the priest, and that it is necessary for salvation that the body, soul, and divinity of Jesus Christ should be digested in the human stomach. This is a fall sorer than any fall on record of the Jews; however much we may pity their unbelief, we have no evidence that any Jew ever taught that every Passover lamb and every victim brought to the altar was God incarnate; and yet, if it be true of the Christian element of sacrifice, it must have been true of the Jewish. We cannot wonder at the reformers of the English Church expunging the word "altar" from the Prayer-book, when we know how the idea of the Christian altar was perverted to serve the purposes of the grossest idolatry. But in meeting the doctrinal errors that have entwined themselves, like Laocoon's snakes, around the Christian altar, it is surely not necessary for us to blind ourselves to the fact that our Saviour did perpetuate for the Church the principle and method of the ancient sacrificial feast; and that, therefore, in some sense at least, we have, as the Church seems from very early times to have expressed herself, a sacrifice, a priest, and an altar; always remembering that, in reference to sacrifice, that sense, as defined by St. Chrysostom and others in the early Church, who speak of the Eucharist as a sacrifice, is that it is a "*commemoration* of a sacrifice" (*vide* St. Chrysostom on Heb. x. 9).

The points to be kept, then, constantly and prominently before the Church are: first, that we must not misinterpret the character of the Jewish sacrifice itself; second, that we must maintain, as a truth for all time, that an image of a thing cannot be the thing itself; and third, that as the Jewish sacrifice was not truly in itself propitiatory, but only the figure and pledge of propitiation and spiritual life, so there is no propitiation, but only a figure and pledge of the propitiatory and life-giving office of Christ in the Holy Eucharist. And then we need not fear to use the Old Testament terms, as in one instance appears to me to have been done in the Epistle to the Hebrews, for designedly parallel Christian ordinances.

And the conclusion of the whole matter seems to be, that the Church still has, in a reasonable though modified sense, not an offering for sin, but still a sacrifice, which the Church of England calls a "sacrifice of praise and thanksgiving."

THE LEVITICAL SACRIFICES LITERALLY CONSIDERED

BY THE

REV. PROFESSOR ALFRED CAVE, B.A.

THAT man of steel, as he was called, Origen, the greatest of the great Fathers of Alexandria, had, to judge from his Eclogues and his Homilies on Leviticus, a very poor opinion of the literal interpretation of the ritualistic sections of the Book of the Law. The circumstantial and realistic observances of the Jew, based upon an unquestioning acceptance of the Levitical injunctions, were considered by Origen both inappropriate and useless. Nay, the literal interpretation of this diversified rubric made, he thought, cavillers and infidels; for it led some, to use his own words, to "despise the Law as a vile thing unworthy of the Creator," and others to "impiously condemn the Creator himself who could ordain such vile commands." Hence his so-called *spiritual* sense— a gross misnomer, unless the *spiritual* is synonymous with the *imaginative*—was Origen's great panacea for all the apparent inanities of the sacred records, the infallible harmonizer of all its seeming contradictions. And his talented lead has, alas! been followed by only too many eminent successors. It was but an application of the same method of forcibly squaring Law with Gospel, when in the next age such moulders of opinion as Augustine and Ambrose descended—the former to expound in his treatise, 'De Isaak et Anima,' the simple fact of Rebekah's filling her pitcher at the well, as "the soul descending to the fountain of wisdom to draw the discipline of pure knowledge," and the latter to find a reference in circumcision to the resurrection of Christ, *quæ desideria carnalia aufert.* Even when the reign of Augustine in Biblical hermeneutics gave way before the influence of that delicate exegete, Isidore of Hispala, whose work, 'De Allegoriis,' became a type of scriptural exposition in the Middle Ages, it was virtually the same allegorizing principle which was advocated and exemplified. Nor was the case different at the Reformation. When, at that epoch, the close study of Scripture became a vital necessity for the consolidation of belief, the writings of Melancthon and Luther, Zwingli and Calvin, abundantly testify to the predominant fondness for "spiritualizing;" whilst the subsequent history of the Lutheran and Reformed Churches further witnesses to the potency of these revered leaders, until *spiritualizing* blossomed into such amusing, if not appalling, extravagances as are to be found in Coccejus and his school. To Lund, for example, Aaron's rod that budded was a type of the rod out of the stem of Jesse; its supernatural greenness was a type of Christ's supernatural conception; the mystery of its sprouting a type of the mystery of the birth of the Son of the Virgin; the night of its blossoming was a type of the night in which the miraculous birth of Christ occurred; there were three things on the rod, after the miracle, which were not there before—leaves, flowers, and fruits, whereby the threefold work of the Redeemer is prefigured; and, not to linger further upon this illustration, in the preservation of the rod within the holy of holies we have foreshadowed, he supposed, the passing of the risen Christ into the heavens, there to await the advent of his elect.[1] Could exegetical caprice go further?

That this "spiritualizing" method of interpretation has fallen somewhat into disrepute is due to an unexpected source of enlightenment. "It is an ill wind that blows no one good," and a more vivid conception of the historical character of the Old Testament has been one of the good things which the ill wind of rationalism, with its microscopic and carping criticism of the letter, has blown to the Christian Church. When the rationalists frigidly maintained that the Old Testament was but a collection of the historical records of Judaism, to be regarded in the same light as a collection of the archives of Greece say, or Rome, the Church could at least cheerfully accept one part of the contention, and believe that the Old Testament was a historical record. Thus the Old Testament came to be studied for itself, as well as for its connection with the New. Thus the Old Testament came to be considered at least as worthy of examination for its own sake, and apart from its relation to Christianity, as the sacred books of Mahomet or Zoroaster, Kakya-Mouni or Buddha. In fact, it is now readily acknowledged that the most repulsive details of the ceremonial law, to say nothing of the splendid eloquence of the prophets, are facts in religious history deserving of close investigation as such. Largely thanks to the indirect influence of the rationalistic movement, the Jews are now seen to have had a distinctive religion of contemporary as well as prospective value.

To trace the outline of that Old Testament faith, to authenticate the credibility and the historical character of its records, to contrast that faith with the other religions of the world, to demonstrate its advance upon the creeds of heathendom and towards the creed of Christ,—such a task of elucidation, comparison, and defence is one of the pressing needs of our day, to be satisfied only by the use of all modern appliances, and in view of all modern scholarship. One prominent phase of that Old Testament religion is that of Mosaism, or the religion of the Hebrews as far as it can be deduced from the Pentateuch. Further, of Mosaism the Levitical sacrifices form no unimportant section. To study the nature and significance of these Levitical sacrifices, as they are in themselves, rather than in their connection with Christianity, is the aim of this introduction. In other words, our purpose is to prosecute the literal interpretation of the injunctions of the Law which bear upon these sacrifices, and to see whither such interpretation will conduct us. The Levitical sacrifices will approve themselves a religious cultus not unworthy to be designated Divine.

The course which will be pursued is as follows. A classification of the Levitical sacrifices will *first* be given. *Next*, some principles will be deduced from the letter of Scripture by which the comprehension of the Levitical sacrifices will be facilitated. *Thirdly*, an application will be made of the principles thus deduced to the elucidation of the entire scheme of the Levitical sacrifices. *Fourthly*, the relation of this sacrificial worship to that of the patriarchal age will be pointed out. *Fifthly*, the relation of this sacrificial worship to the sacrificial views of the New Testament will call for some remark. And *lastly*, a few words may be bestowed upon the bibliography of the subject.

And at this point the writer may advisedly call attention to the different standpoint he here assumes to that occupied in his work upon 'The Scriptural Doctrine of Sacrifice.' To put that standpoint briefly, he would say that, whereas his view of the Jewish sacrifices was previously more analytic, he aims in this introduction at a synthesis, at building up into a consistent whole the numerous details of the Mosaic ritual, and dis-

---

[1] Lundius, 'Die alten judischen Heiligthümer, Gottesdienste und Gewohnheiten dargestellet.' Hamburg, 1695, 1698, 1704, 1712; edited and annotated by Wolf, in a new edition, issued in 1738.

playing thereby the salient and instructive characteristics of the Levitical sacrificial cultus. Let the writer state, however, once for all, that where he has expressed any details of that cultus in as fitting and accurate language as he is capable of in his earlier work, he has not gone about to seek a new dress for old facts, but has freely used his previous materials. Where, therefore, passages occur in inverted commas, without the mention of the name of an author, it will be understood that the writer quotes from his earlier work.

A. The Classification of the Levitical Sacrifices.

At the outset it is necessary to classify the numerous sacrificial rites of the old covenant with some accuracy. An indispensable preliminary to such a classification is a precise definition of "sacrifice." According to the usage of the Old Testament, the most general term for sacrifice is *qorban*. This word was employed in the Law to describe the genus of which sacrifices of all kinds were species. It is expressly predicated of the burnt offering, the peace offering, the thank offering and the votive offering, the sin offering, the trespass offering, the Passover, the sacrifice of the Nazarite on the expiry or breach of his vow, the whole range of national sacrifices, the firstfruits, and even offerings made to Jehovah of the spoils of battle. *Qorban* is manifestly the generic Hebrew term, equivalent to our English term *sacrifice*. The important thing, therefore, in defining "sacrifice" in a scriptural sense is to ascertain the customary Biblical significance of this term. Not to delay upon philological considerations, which may be studied by the curious in the Appendix to the writer's previously mentioned work, suffice it to say that this Hebrew word is expressly used and translated by an unequivocal Greek word in a passage in the seventh chapter of St. Mark's Gospel. That passage runs thus: " Ἐὰν εἴπῃ ἄνθρωπος τῷ πατρὶ ἢ τῇ μητρί· Κορβᾶν, ὅ ἐστιν δῶρον, ὃ ἐὰν ἐξ ἐμοῦ ὠφεληθῇς : " " If a man shall say to his father or his mother, *Qorban*, that is to say, a gift, by whatsoever thou mightest be profited by me " (Mark vii. 11). This " κορβᾶν, ὅ ἐστιν δῶρον " settles the meaning of the Hebrew sacrificial technicality once for all, at the same time as the insertion of the Hebrew word throws light upon the unfilial pleading alluded to. *Qorban*, the equivalent of the English word *sacrifice* in general, is *a gift to God*. The usage of the LXX. is identical. A sacrifice in the Levitical sense was a gift, or offering, or presentation made to Jehovah. Ewald was, therefore, perfectly at liberty to call abstinence from labour upon the sabbath a sacrifice of rest ; nor would it be inconsistent with the usage of the Pentateuch to call obedience to the legal injunctions concerning the seventh year and the year of jubilee by the name of sacrifice, or to regard a scrupulous adherence to the Levitical laws of food a self-denial of the nature of a sacrifice. In the large majority of cases, however, a distinction was perceptible. A sacrifice, in the legal sense, was, it is true, a presentation to Jehovah. But in the stricter sense of the word a presentation could not be indiscriminately made either as regards time or place. Especially is emphasis laid in the Law upon the place of presentation. It is at the place where Jehovah consents to record his Name, at the one appointed place for Divine worship, that sacrifices in the stricter sense can alone be made. Whilst, therefore, Ewald is etymologically correct, it is doubted by many whether he is not inconsistent with the usage of the Law when he designates those offerings sacrifices which were not presented at the one appointed place where man might meet with his Maker. It is true that the usage for which Ewald contends, according to which prayers, and charity, and abstinence, and obedience, may be termed sacrifices, is common to the books of the prophets and of the New Testament, whereas, on the other hand, the legal application of sacrifice seems to be almost restricted to offerings associated with the courts of the Lord. Kurtz avoids the difficulty by dividing the Levitical sacrifices into sacrifices in general and altar sacrifices—an unnecessary distinction, apt to conceal their common significance.

Defining sacrifice, then, in accordance with both usage and etymology, as a gift, a presentation to God, a surrender to God of what has cost the offerer something, a material embodiment of the self-sacrificing spirit, and remembering that in the large majority of cases at least these sacrifices were associated with the holy places,—the several ordinances of the Mosaic Law in reference thereto will arrange themselves under the following classes. There were the *national* sacrifices, or those presented in the name of the entire Jewish people by their representatives. There were the *official* sacrifices, or the specific acts of worship by presentation prescribed for the ecclesiastical and political orders. And there were the *personal* sacrifices, which were made by individual suppliants of the Heavenly Majesty. To the enumeration of the several varieties under each of these three divisions we now proceed, after uttering a proviso. When we speak of the Levitical sacrifices we do not mean those which are recorded in Leviticus simply, but those contained in any of the legal portions of the Pentateuch. The Book of Leviticus does not contain the entire Mosaic ritual; its legal provisions are supplemented by parts of Exodus and Numbers. Indeed, it is doubtful whether the sharp separation of the Leviticus from the other parts of the Pentateuch is not of very late date. Apparently, to judge from the Jewish rolls of the Law, what we now call the Book of Leviticus was simply sections twenty-four to thirty-three of the Torah,[1] the first division of the Hebrew Scriptures.

I. THE NATIONAL SACRIFICES. Sacrifice, as a form of Divine worship, was not confined under the Law to individuals, whether among the priests or the populace. The nation as such was identified with sacrificial observances. A national rejoicing was regarded as possible, and therefore a national thank offering. The chosen people were supposed to be collectively capable of humiliation and confession of sin, and therefore of a national atonement. Similarly, a national self-surrender to the will of Jehovah was deemed to be frequently appropriate, and hence national burnt offerings were consumed in the national behalf. This national identification with the Levitical sacrifices is a prominent characteristic of the Jewish Church.

The *national* offerings consisted: 1. Of the *serial* offerings, or those daily, weekly, and monthly sacrifices ordered to be presented in the nation's behalf. 2. Of the *festal* offerings, or the ceremonial appropriate to the several exceptional days of sacrificial observance. 3. Of the offerings for the service of the holy place; and 4. Of some extraordinary offerings instituted in response to a widely felt need for worship or humiliation at extraordinary seasons.

1. *The serial offerings.* Every day, morning and evening, the priests were bidden to effect, in the name of the congregation, the burnt offering of a lamb of a year old, and to present therewith its appropriate meal offering and drink offering (Exod. xxix. 38—42; ch. vi. 1—4; Numb. xxviii. 3—8). The presentation was made according to the customary ritual for burnt offering. From the regularity of its succession this daily burnt offering is also called the "continual" or "continuous" burnt offering (Exod. xxix. 42; Numb. xxviii. 6; comp. Dan. viii. 11). The only additional feature of this daily offering to which attention need be called is the probability of a direct association with the people at large by a peculiarity of ritual. According to rabbinic tradition, the nation was expressly represented in the court of the Lord's house by certain אַנְשֵׁי מַעֲמָד, or permanent officials, who performed the customary rites of the imposition of their hands upon the victim, and its slaughter. Should this tradition

---

[1] See 'Commentary upon the Holy Bible,' edited by Canon Cook, 'Leviticus,' vol. i. p. 493.

simply refer to the days of Zerubbabel's temple, still that later practice must point back to some earlier form of national representation.[1]

Every sabbath the daily burnt offering was doubled night and morning (Numb. xxviii. 9, 10).

On the first day of every month, or on the new moon as it was called, two young bullocks, a ram, and seven lambs, with the prescribed meal and drink offerings, were ordered to be offered, in addition to the continuous burnt offering; a kid was also to be killed for a sin offering (Numb. xxviii. 11—15). The new moon was also emphasized by a rousing blast upon the silver trumpets (Numb. x. 10). Further, on the new moon of the seventh month, dignified pre-eminently with the name of the Feast of the Blast of Trumpets, an additional burnt offering was to be made of a bullock, a ram, and seven lambs, in addition, that is, to the offering of the month and the daily burnt offering (ch. xxiii. 23—25; Numb. xxix. 1—6).

2. *The festal offerings.* Following the order of the Levitical calendar, the several festal or solemn seasons were Passover, the Paschal Feast, and Pentecost (or the Passover cycle), and the Day of Atonement, followed by the Feast of Tabernacles (or the cycle of the seventh month).

The Passover cycle. Even in the first celebration of the Passover, amidst all the idolatry and hardship of Egypt, there were features of sacrificial import. It was by Divine command that a lamb or kid, a male and physically immaculate, had been slain at sunset in every household, the sacred blood having been sprinkled with hyssop upon the posts and lintels of the front door. Also it was by Divine command that the victim was roasted whole, and hastily partaken of with loins girt and staff in hand Thus two features—the blood ritual and the sacred feast—were not without their sacrificial reference. And this reference was made yet more distinct when the perpetual celebration of the Passover was enjoined under altered conditions, and when the solemn feast of expectation became the solemn feast of reminiscence. Instead of being slain at home, the Paschal lamb was to be slain in the court of the tabernacle, and instead of being sprinkled upon the doorway of the offerer, it was to be sprinkled upon the altar of burnt offering (comp. Exod. xii.; Deut. xvi. 1—8; 2 Chron. xxx. 16; xxxv. 11; also Exod. xiii. 3—10; xxxiv. 18—21; ch. xxiii. 4—8; Numb. ix. 1—14; xxviii. 16—25).

On the morning after the Paschal Supper, namely, on the fifteenth of the first month, the Paschal Feast commenced. It lasted seven days, the first day and the last partaking of the character of a sabbath; that is to say, work being interdicted, and a public assembly of the people at the one place of worship enjoined. This feast is known under two names. It is most frequently called in the Pentateuch the Feast of Unleavened Bread, from the circumstance that none but such bread was eaten by command throughout its course. It is once designated the Feast of the Passover in the Pentateuch. In after times these names were retained. At this feast, in addition to the abstention from leaven—itself of sacrificial significance—a peculiar ritual was ordered to be observed. Every day, after the offering of the customary burnt offering, a further offering by fire was made. Two bullocks, a ram, and seven lambs, with their accompanying meal and drink offerings, were to constitute the festal burnt offering, and one goat the sin offering; these offerings being repeated every day of the feast. The second day of the feast was also characterized by an additional act, not a little curious. Being the time of early harvest, a sheaf of the firstfruits was brought to the priest, who "waved" it before the Lord, presenting at the same time a lamb for a burnt offering,

---

[1] See Carpzov, 'Apparatus Historico-Criticus Antiquitatum Gentis Hebraicæ' (1748), pp. 109, 110. Comp. Keil, 'Handbuch der Bibl. Archäologie,' sect. 76, 1.

together with a fifth of an ephah of meal and a quarter of a hin of wine (comp. ch. xxiii. 9—14; Numb. xxviii. 17—25).

Fifty days after the Paschal Supper came the Feast of Harvest—to use one of the several designations of the final feast of the Passover cycle—so called from the time of its observance. Another name for this feast was that of Firstfruits, a designation which is self-explanatory. From the fact that seven full weeks were allowed to elapse after the Passover before its celebration, it was also named the Feast of Weeks, or possibly this name refers to the whole period between Passover and Pentecost. The date of its occurrence also explains its later name, just mentioned, of Pentecost. The feast lasted but a day, and partook of the nature of a sabbath. This feast again has a special sacrificial ritual peculiar to itself, consisting of a meal offering, a burnt offering, a sin offering, and a peace offering: the meal offering being two loaves of leavened bread, to be offered as firstfruits; the burnt offering consisting of seven lambs, one ram, and a bullock, together with meal offerings and drink offerings; a kid constituting the sin offering, and two lambs the peace offering. The common details of the ritual of presentation were observed with two exceptions—the two loaves and the two lambs were simply waved before the Lord, and were not consumed by fire; they were "holy to the Lord for the priest" (comp. ch. xxiii. 15—21; Numb. xxviii. 26—31; Deut. xvi. 9—12).

The cycle of the seventh month. The seventh month stood out in strong relief in the Jewish calendar. It opened, as we have seen, with the Feast of Trumpets, as if to awaken the nation year by year to the high importance of the days in which its lot was cast, and continued with blended solemnity and rejoicing, bringing in due course the great Day of Atonement, upon the tenth of the month, and the Feast of Tabernacles, or Ingathering, upon the fifteenth.

The ritual of the Day of Atonement was peculiarly sacrificial, and although there is combined therein not only offerings referring to national sins, but those of an official nature, it may tend to clearness if that ritual be described in order once for all. "The law concerning the Day of Atonement contains instruction as to the performance of the appropriate ritual, and as to its performance annually. The prescribed ritual was as follows: As a sacrifice for the priesthood, the high priest was to bring a sin offering of a bullock and a burnt offering of a ram; and as a sacrifice for the congregation, a sin offering of two he-goats and a burnt offering of a ram. The priest was to be clothed, not in his state costume, but in a dress entirely of white, to be put on after bathing the whole body, and not simply the hands and feet as customarily. This dress of white was not even the plain official dress of the ordinary priesthood, for that had a coloured girdle. Lots were then cast upon the two he-goats—one lot for Jehovah and one for Azazel; and, according as the lots fell, so were they presented as living sacrifices before the altar. The ceremony of the expiation of the priesthood and the holy places then commenced. The bullock having been slain as a sin offering for himself and his house, the high priest filled the censer with embers from the altar of burnt offering and with incense, and placed the censer within the vail. Some of the blood of the ox was then sprinkled upon the mercy-seat and seven times upon the ground. Atonement was afterwards made for the nation. The he-goat was slain, and its blood, having been taken into the holiest, was sprinkled as the blood of the ox had previously been. The floor of the holy place was next sprinkled with blood, and the altars of incense and burnt offering. The expiation of the priesthood, tabernacle, and nation being now performed, an exquisitely symbolic act of forgiveness was gone through. The high priest placed both his hands upon the head of the live goat, confessed over it all the sins and transgressions of the people, and sent it away by a man who was standing ready into the desert. The high priest then removed his white garments, purified himself at the laver, and, having donned his official robes, offered the burnt offerings for himself and the people."

Further, the Feast of Tabernacles, time of wild and often libidinous rejoicing as it was, had its specific ritual of gifts and atonement, adjusted to the several days during which it lasted. Seven days long were the booths standing in the sacred court, and a kind of retrogression was observed in the sacrificial procedure. As on the other fast days, a goat was daily offered as a sin offering. The number of rams and lambs was doubled, being two and fourteen respectively. But it was in the number of bullocks that the distinguishing feature of the feast appeared. Seventy bullocks in all were offered, these being so distributed that, on the last day of the feast, seven were slain, eight on the day preceding, nine on the day previous to that, and so on, daily increasing by one until the total reached thirteen, the proportion slaughtered on the first day (comp. Exod. xxiii. 16; ch. xxiii. 34—43; Numb. xxix. 12—38; Deut. xvi. 13—16; xxxi. 10—13).

3. *The offerings for the service of the holy place.* These offerings consisted of the holy oil for the daily replenishing of the lamps of the golden candlesticks, arranged "from evening to morning" by the priesthood; of the incense, peculiarly compounded, and daily burnt upon the golden altar; and of the twelve loaves, arranged in rows, with frankincense and libations of wine, to judge from the furniture of the table of shewbread, which were laid before the Lord as a memorial at the beginning of every week, and eaten by the priests as "a most holy thing" at the close. In the present reference, the significant fact in connection with these offerings is that they were national rather than official, to say nothing of personal. For the materials thereof were selected from offerings representatively made by the people. Thus it is the children of Israel, and not the priests, who are bidden to bring pure olive oil for the lamps of the sanctuary. It would seem also that the constituents of the sacred incense were the gift of the people, seeing that in the first instance they were ordered to be provided by Moses, the representative of the tribes at large rather than of Levi. And, as regards the shewbread, conceding that the number of its loaves did not point to the number of the tribes, as seems probable, it is expressly said, "every sabbath it shall be presented before Jehovah continually *on the part of the sons of Israel,* an eternal covenant" (ch. xxiv. 8). Compare on the above statements, Exod. xxvii. 20; ch. xxiv. 2; Exod. xxx. 34—38; xxv. 30; ch. xxiv. 5—8; Numb. iv. 7; Exod. xxvii. 12.

4. *The extraordinary offerings.* Amongst these offerings, in which we see the general theory of Old Testament sacrifice applied to unlooked-for waves of national sentiment, whether penitential or eucharistic, may be classed such abnormal offerings as those for the erection of the tabernacle; those at the consecration of Aaron; the surrender of their mirrors by the Hebrew women for the manufacture of the brazen laver; the sin offerings presented by the congregation in acknowledgment of some special sin of national bearing, such as the crimes of Korah and Achan; or the multitude of sacrifices slaughtered at the consecration of the temple. A very interesting series of instances, showing as they do a trial of old ordinances in new conditions, an application of the Law to changed circumstances, an apprehension of the spirit which is nobler than an obedience to the letter; and suggesting, as they undoubtedly do suggest, a variety of possible adaptations of the Law to religious ends not expressly contemplated.

II. THE OFFICIAL SACRIFICES. Not only did the officials of the Jewish nation act as the religious representatives of the tribes in the manner just described, not only did they approach the Majesty on high as individual suppliants in the manner about to be described, but, according to the dictates of the Mosaic Law, there were sacrificial rites administered by them, neither in their representative nor in their individual capacity, but purely as officials. These rites pertained to the officials of Church and State and society at large, and may be conveniently classified according as they attached to the priests, the kings, the elders, and the ministering women.

1. *The priestly offerings.* Quite apart from their almost endless duties as the religious executive of the Israelites, there was a distinctive sacrificial cultus which belonged to the priests in their exceptional official functions. The following enumeration is exhaustive. There were special sin offerings to be made by any priest who had inadvertently erred in the discharge of his holy calling (ch. iv. 3). There was a specific offering of meal to be made by the high priest daily, morning and evening, within the outer vail (ch. vi. 14). The solemn expiation of the great Day of Atonement opened, as we have seen, with an atonement for the officiator and the whole priestly order. At the consecration of any high priest, priest, or Levite, characteristic offerings were enjoined, varying in costliness and manner in each case. Thus at the consecration of a Levite, the lowest grade in the hierarchy, there was a consecration itself called a sacrifice (Numb. viii. 13); after a process of purification, two young bullocks were offered, the one for a sin offering and the other for a burnt offering (Numb. viii. 5—26). At the consecration of a priest, the intermediate ecclesiastical grade, two sets of three acts were performed: in the first place, the novice was specially purified, solemnly invested, and religiously anointed; and in the second place, a triple sacrifice was presented in his behalf, consisting of a bullock for a sin offering, a ram for a burnt offering, and a ram for a peace offering (Exod. xxiv. 1—37; xl. 12—15; ch. viii. 1—36). At the consecration, however, of the "anointed priest," or "the priest" *par excellence*, afterwards called the "high priest," a more elaborate ceremonial still was ordained, occupying seven days instead of one, and, whilst consisting of the same series of acts—purification, investiture, anointing, and sacrifice, this last act showing as clearly as the investiture with the "golden garments" the exalted rank of the person concerned—whereas for an ordinary priest one bullock formed a sin offering, for a high priest seven bullocks were offered on successive days. A further evidence of his exalted position may be seen in the sin offering to be made by the high priest upon any infringement of his official duty. "He was to offer an ox without blemish. Having performed the presentation, the imposition of the hand, and the slaughtering in the customary manner, he took a part of the blood into the tabernacle, and sprinkled it seven times 'in the face of the vail of the holy,' and having put some of the blood upon the horns of the altar of incense, he poured out the remainder at the bottom of the altar of burnt offering. The same fatty portions which were removed in the case of the peace offerings were afterwards lifted off the carcase and consumed above the daily burnt offering, the high priest carrying the rest of the carcase to a clean place before the camp, and burning it on wood with fire." A ceremonial of highly significant variations!

2. *The offerings of the princes and the ruler.* Express mention is made of elaborate offerings made at the dedication of the tabernacle "by the princes of Israel, heads of the house of their fathers"—gold and silver utensils, a goat apiece for a sin offering, and large burnt offerings and peace offerings (Numb. vii. 10—89). Express mention is also made of a sin offering for a ruler, whether judge or king (ch. iv. 22—26). Remembering, however, the special offerings of David and Solomon on set occasions, it would appear that the offerings just mentioned are simply instances of an adaptation of the sacrificial cultus to the sanctification of the chief officers of the State, and instances which any occasion of great penitence or gratitude might constitute into an inspiring precedent.

3. *The offerings of the holy women.* In this case again we seem merely to have an instance of a class of presentations capable of infinite repetition by sections of Jewish society. These holy women "served at the door of the tabernacle" (Exod. xxxviii. 8; 1 Sam. ii. 22), not assisting, of course, in any of the ritual prescribed for the priests or Levites, but abiding apparently in a holy ministration of prayer and praise, fasting and sacrifice, like the saintly daughter of Phanuel; at least, such is the interpretation of these holy attendants suggested by the Septuagint, the Targum of Onkelos, Jerome, and many rabbis, as shown by Münster and Fagius in the 'Critici Sacri.'

III. THE PERSONAL OFFERINGS. These are divisible into two classes—the *blood* and the *bloodless* sacrifices, the former including the burnt offerings, the peace offerings, the sin and the trespass offerings; and the latter including the meat, or the meal, offerings, as they are better termed, the libations, the offerings of oil and incense, and a variety of oblations, such as the redemption moneys for every Israelite, the tithes, the firstlings, and the vows. Of these two classes in order; certain modifications of the blood and bloodless sacrifices under special circumstances may then be appended.

1. *The blood sacrifices. The burnt offerings.* Two points call for notice, namely, the injunctions concerning the victims to be slain, and those concerning the ritual to be observed in slaying. The victims varied with the wealth of the offerers. If the offerer was poor, a turtle-dove or pigeon sufficed to neutralize the command not "to appear before the Lord empty," and in the presentation of this humblest offering the officiating priest simply cleaned the birds and burnt them upon the accustomed altar. Richer offerings were such as an ox, a ram, or a goat, in the transformation of either of which into a sweet savour a more elaborate ritual was observed. This ritual is described at length because it was adopted in all burnt offerings, whether national, official, or personal. "The victim was brought to the altar by the offerer, who then forcibly laid his hand upon the animal's head, and slaughtered it upon the north side. In the act of slaughtering, the blood was caught by the priest and swung against the four walls of the altar. The offerer then flayed the slaughtered animal, divided it, cleansed the intestines and the lower parts of the legs; whereupon the officiating priest, appropriating the skin, placed the several parts, with the head and fat, in order upon the wood, which had been previously arranged upon the ever-burning fire, and the whole sacrifice rose 'as an offering of fire of a sweet savour unto Jehovah.'" A meal offering and a drink offering always accompanied this form of sacrifice (comp. ch. i.).

The peace offerings. In this case also emphasis must be laid upon the victims and the mode. With respect to the former, it might be a bull, a cow or a calf, a ram, a sheep or a lamb, a he-goat or a she-goat, the selection being regulated by the purse and the inclination of the offerer. As for the ritual, which *mutatis mutandis* was also observed in all the varieties of the peace offering, national, official, or individual, it in part resembled and in part differed from that of the burnt offering. "The victim having been brought to the altar, the offerer laid his hand upon its head, slaughtered it (but apparently not on the north side)—the priest meanwhile catching the blood and sprinkling it upon the altar—flayed, divided, and cleansed it. The course subsequently followed was essentially different from that employed for the burnt offering. Instead of burning the animal entire, the offerer detached all the separable portions of fat, such as the flare, and that in which the intestines, kidneys, and liver are embedded; and in the case of sheep severed the fat tail; these portions were then burnt with the daily burnt offering. The breast was afterwards 'waved' by a kind of horizontal movement, and given to the Aaronites, and the right leg was lifted or 'heaved off' as a gift to the officiating priest. The remains of the carcase were carried away by the offerer, and a meal made of it in the sacred precincts of the tabernacle.

Meat and drink offerings accompanied this form of sacrifice, one of the cakes of the meal offering always falling to the priest." Three occasions for the presentation of peace offerings are expressly mentioned : they might be made at special seasons of gratitude, and were then called thank offerings; they were presented when vows were made before the Lord, and were then called votive offerings ; or they were voluntarily made at any time when there was a longing for the fellowship of Jehovah, being then called voluntary offerings. The laws of the peace offering are given in chs. iii. and vii. 11—36.

The sin offerings. Some of the characteristic features of the sin offering have been already passed under review in connection with the national and official offerings, and it has already become evident that the *differentia* of this class of sacrifices was to be found in a peculiar manipulation of the blood of the animal slaughtered. This fact becomes very evident indeed when we turn to the regulations concerning the individual sin offerings. "When a ruler or common Israelite sinned through ignorance, they were ordered to bring, on becoming conscious of their fault, the ruler an immaculate he-goat, and the Israelite an immaculate shaggy she-goat; in both cases the offerer then went through the customary process of laying on the hand and slaying, upon which the priest, having collected the blood, smeared some upon the horns of the altar, poured out the rest at the foot, and burnt the whole of the fat upon the hearth; the carcase fell to the priest. The sin offerings were slain where the burnt offerings were. It is also noteworthy that, whilst many victims might be offered as a burnt offering, the sin offering might never consist of more animals than one." It will be perceived upon a comparison of the several forms of sin offering, that the ritual observed was always the same in certain important points, such as the manipulation with the blood, the burning of the fatty portions, and the destination of the carcase (which always fell to the priest, either for his own use or to burn without the camp). For the law of the sin offering, consult ch. iv.

The trespass offerings. However similar in name, these formed a class quite distinct from the preceding class, and this distinction must be considered later on. At present it is sufficient to tabulate, as has been done in the other three classes, the sort of victims presented and the manner of their presentation. "In all cases the offering consisted of a ram, the blood of which, after the customary presentation, imposition of hands, and slaughtering, instead of being smeared upon the horns of the altar or taken into the holy place like the blood of the sin offerings, was simply swung against the side of the altar, the ritual being thenceforth the same as for the sin offering either of a ruler or common Israelite. This class of sacrifice was always accompanied by a recompense, which was considered as due to God and man ; the discharge of the debt to God being effected by the placing by the priest of a fancy value upon the offered ram equivalent to the wrong done; and the human liability being discharged by the payment to the party wronged of the whole amount of the fraud, *increased by a retri- butory fifth.*" The laws of the trespass offerings are given in chs. v. 14, etc., and vi. 1—7.

2. *The bloodless sacrifices.* These include the so-called meat offerings, the tithes and the firstfruits, both of which were solemnly presented before the Lord at the altar of burnt offering and consecrated by a solemn dedication by fire of part to the Lord, and the other bloodless sacrifices which were not presented at the altar. Of these only the first class call for any further remarks.

The *meat offerings* were so called in the Authorized Version because meal was the staple food of the sixteenth century. Times and customs have now changed, and the word "meat" refers now to animal rather than vegetable food. It is now, therefore, advisable to speak of *meal* offerings, not *meat* offerings. These offerings were the Levitical vegetable sacrifices, and were preceded, with two exceptions—the daily offering of the high priest and that which was substituted by the poor for the burnt offering—by some form of blood sacrifice, either a burnt offering or a peace offering. "They consisted of fine wheaten flour, or of cakes of the same, variously prepared with oil, according to the culinary arts of the Jews, some being baked in a small oven like the Arab's *tannur*, some being prepared on plates, and some in a skillet; they also occasionally consisted of roasted ears of corn. To all these 'meat offerings' oil and salt were added, and to those which consisted of flour or grain incense also. . . . The ritual of presentation was very simple. The offerer brought the offering to the priest, who took a handful of the meal and oil with the incense, and burnt them on the altar, the remainder falling to the priest as 'a thing most holy.'"

3. *Certain modifications of the two previous classes enjoined under special circumstances.* Not merely did the Law contain directions for individual sacrifices such as have been already described, but some specific adaptations were enjoined of the sacrificial ritual, in order to expressly connect certain states of mind and body with the scenic worship of the sanctuary. The occasion for these modified forms of ritual were the following; they are simply named for the most part, and the references given to the Law for fuller details:—

Upon contact with a corpse (see Numb. xix. and comp. 'Scriptural Doctrine of Sacrifice,' p. 74).

Upon the cure of a leper. The purification of a restored leper was divided into two series of acts performed after an interval of seven days, being at both times a modified sacrificial ritual (comp. ch. xiv. and 'Scriptural Doctrine of Sacrifice,' p. 75).

After parturition. The mother who had recovered from childbirth must present herself with a sacrifice at the altar (see ch. xii. 1—8).

After cessation of derangement of sexual organs (see ch. xv. 1—15; 25—30).

In connection with the Nazarite vow. This vow of abstinence and continency was itself a form of sacrifice. It was also directly associated with the sacrificial ritual. Upon any unintentional defilement of a Nazarite by sudden death in his company, an offering was to be made of two doves, or pigeons, by way of atonement, and a lamb was to be brought as a trespass offering. There was also a peculiar rite to celebrate the expiry of his vow (comp. Numb. vi. 13—21).

At the so-called trial of jealousy, a solemn ordeal, by which conjugal infidelity was submitted to an awful sacrificial test. The suspicious husband brought the wife to the priest, together with an offering of barley meal, without oil or incense. The ordeal was this. The priest, taking some holy water from the laver, apparently in an earthen vessel in which he had mixed a little dust from the sacred court, and placing the meal in the woman's hand, sware the woman according to an appalling formula, to which he says, "Amen, amen." Further, he wrote the formula in a book, and, having blotted it out with the holy water, caused the woman to drink the water. Nor was the ordeal even yet complete. There was a subsequent waving of the meal before the Lord, a burning of it upon the altar, and a second potation of the holy water. With this result, the thigh of the perjured woman rotted (see Numb. v. 11—31).

B. SCRIPTURAL PRINCIPLES APPLICABLE TO THE ELUCIDATION OF THE LEVITICAL
SACRIFICES.

To the Christian mind, accustomed to accept instinctively as fundamental postulates the spirituality and universality of worship, it might well seem at first sight that so costly and complicated a ritual as has just been described was something less than

Divine. Origen's dilemma, that this cultus by presentation is either unworthy of its Creator, or its Creator is himself unworthy, seems to have some reason on its side. Nor does his escape from the dilemma appear at first blush irrational; it may seem better to some to inquire as to what these laws may be made to mean, rather than to investigate minutely what they seem to mean. Nevertheless, in real truth, it is needless to constitute one's self a pupil of the philosophical eunuch of Alexandria. Ascetic rebellion against the actual condition of life providentially arranged for us is not the highest mark of sanctified wisdom, and quite another method of escape than Origen's from the danger of the flesh may be pursued both in morals and in religion. As marriage may afford finer scope for the spiritual culture of life than celibacy, so a patient study of the reputed materialism of the Levitical sacrifices may issue in a more spiritual view of the Divine dealings than spiritualizing falsely so called. A little care and attention bestowed upon the actual teachings of Scripture show an exquisite adaptation to the needs of the Jew in the process of discipline to which he was divinely submitted. Indeed, a rational interpretation of the language of Scripture will elevate the Levitical cultus into so splendid an agent in the religious development of the chosen people, as not to be derogatory to Deity himself. At least, so we hope to show by an examination into the early records of the Pentateuch. By the sacrifice and offering which Jehovah did not for himself desire, he yet satisfactorily educated, as we shall see, a people to whom the higher revelation in the body could be made. Nay, however Judaism may fall short of Christianity, it is beyond all comparison with any other religious system developed during the world's course. A worship which could train and satisfy a David and an Isaiah, a Jeremiah and an Ezekiel, must be pre-eminent amongst the non-Christian faiths. The task we now place before ourselves, therefore, is to educe from the Old Testament certain general principles which may be applied to the comprehension of the Levitical sacrifices. What light the Jew had upon the rites he was bidden to perform, we are now to gather into a focus. If the labour be great, it will not be unremunerative; in this toil, too, there will be profit. The inquiry will conveniently range itself under the following heads: We shall first elicit from Scripture some fundamental ideas common to the whole of the Levitical sacrifices; we shall next investigate the significance attached by Scripture to the varied, yet ordained, ritual of those sacrifices; thirdly, we shall ascertain the meaning associated by Scripture with the several varieties of these sacrifices; and lastly, we shall consider the significance of the several feasts and fasts to the celebration of which the sacrificial ritual was accommodated. These details settled, it will then be possible to regard the Levitical sacrifices as a whole. The application of these leading principles to the multitudinous injunctions previously classified will then be easy, and the result, it is believed, will be at once stimulating to faith and evocative of devout thankfulness.

Here a caution may be not unwisely interpolated. It possibly calls for explicit statement that, when we speak of scriptural principles of sacrifices and of principles deducible from the Scriptures, we do not refer to proof texts merely. The interpretation and application of Scripture is not so facile. However poorly the writer has succeeded in his aim, that aim itself is to base the interpretation of the Levitical sacrifices upon a series of complete inductions from the scriptural data, including, as they do, the implications of philology and the suggestions of general usage, possibly the hints derivable from a trained sense, as well as the numerous passages for which chapter and verse can be given. Scriptural archæology is only inexpugnable when it consists of perfect inductions from Scripture, and perfect inductions must summarize tenor in addition to positive statements of facts.

1. *Certain fundamental ideas common to the Levitical sacrifices. The idea underlying*

the generic term "qorban." After what has been already said upon the meaning and Biblical usage of this term for all forms of sacrifice, whether bloodless or marked by the effusion of blood, whether presented at the altar or without discrimination of place, little further need be added. All the Levitical sacrifices were gifts to Jehovah. They gave tangible expression to the innate sentiments of every worshipper down to the lowest grade of the fetichist, that it is necessary to attest the self-denial of his soul by some gift which the hand can bring; a sentiment which Jehovah not only sanctioned in the Jew, but demanded when he said, "Thou shalt not appear before me empty." He who brought a *qorban* made a *presentation.* Undoubtedly the problem of the Levitical sacrifices is like one of those intricate locks which only a combination of keys can open. One master-key has been discovered in this idea of *qorban.* Whatever else the Levitical sacrifices were, they were presentations to Jehovah, sacrifices symbolic of self-sacrifice.

The idea underlying the term "kipper" and its several forms. This technical term and its derivatives are translated in the Authorized Version by *atone* and its derivatives. Without discussing the primary significance of the word,[1] suffice it to say that "atone" in its scriptural sense means "to cover sin," in other words, to neutralize or conceal sin so that it should not offend the Deity—to render the Divine wrath inoperative. To make an atonement, if we probe the Hebrew figure, "was to throw, so to speak, a veil over sin so dazzling that the veil and not the sin was visible, or to place side by side with sin something so attractive as to completely engross the eye. The figure which the New Testament uses when it speaks of the 'new robe,' the Old Testament uses when it speaks of atonement. When an atonement was made under the Law, it was as though the Divine eye, which had been kindled at the sight of sin and foulness, was now quieted by the garment thrown around it; or, to use a figure much too modern, yet equally appropriate, it was as if the sinner, who had been exposed to the lightning of the Divine wrath, had been suddenly wrapped round and insulated." So much for the idea of the word. In addition, let the precise association of the idea be remembered. This idea of *atonement* is expressly associated with the *blood* of the sacrifices in an important passage: "For the soul," it is said, in ch. xvii. 11, "of the flesh is in the blood, and I (the Lord) have given it you upon the altar to be an atonement for your souls: for the blood it atones by the soul." In other words, to avoid the lengthy controversy connected with this passage, it is at least alleged that the blood of every animal sacrifice has been appointed by God, for some reason of his own, as a means of neutralizing the sin of the Jew, because the blood is the life of the animal sacrificed. Four truths thus emerge, viz. first, the Levitical sacrifices had a power of atonement; secondly, that atonement was connected only with the blood sacrifices; thirdly, it was the effusion of blood which was declared to be a neutralizing of sin; and fourthly, this act of atonement was an act of substitution, that is to say, a forfeited human life was spared because of an animal life surrendered. Of course, we are not arguing either the reasonableness or irrationality of this fact; it is our present purpose simply to state it. Thus the second master-key to the Levitical sacrifices has been obtained. But although, to continue the figure, the door into the mysterious chamber is opened, the only available light is that which has followed our entrance; there are many windows to be unbarred and blinds to be lifted before the entire chamber is visible to its remotest corner and most secret recess. To this unbarring and illuminating we must now proceed.

The significance of the materials used in sacrifice. As our previous classification has shown, these materials were divisible into animal and non-animal offerings, or, to adopt

---

[1] 'Scriptural Doctrine of Sacrifice,' pp. 482—486.

the yet more significant technicalities, into blood and bloodless offerings. The ideas already educed render the interpretation of these two classes of material easy. The bloodless offerings were presentations simply; they were gifts made to Jehovah upon approach to him in worship; they were this and nothing more. The blood sacrifices were this *and* something more; they were both presentations and instruments of atonement; in addition to being the gifts of the offerer to Jehovah, they possessed the all-important blood which testified to the substituted life. In every case of animal sacrifice the blood spilt spoke of a substituted life, whilst in every case also the animal itself, of some value to the offerer, spoke of a presentation made. And it is this latter fact which elucidates another point in the ceremonial of animal sacrifice, namely, the variety and the kind of victims enjoined. Offerings were only to be made of such animals as did not contradict the Levitical laws of food—of such animals, therefore, as Jehovah could receive. Further, the victims were of very different value; a bullock was worth more than a cow, a cow than a calf, a calf than a ram, a ram than a sheep, a sheep than a lamb, a lamb than a pigeon, and a pigeon than a handful of meal; the gradation of animal became a gradation of gift. The more costly the gift the more self-sacrificing the offering.

The significance of the place of sacrifice. In the patriarchal age, it would appear, any place might be a place of special Divine revelation, and therefore a place where an altar might be erected; in the Levitical code, the legitimate place of sacrifice was more restricted. The large majority of offerings, as our previous description has already made evident, were ordered to be presented within the precincts of the one spot which Jehovah had consecrated by his presence. As it is said in Deut. xii. 5, 6, "But unto the place which the Lord your God shall choose out of all your tribes to put his Name there, even unto his habitation shall ye seek, and thither thou shalt come: and thither ye shall bring your burnt offerings, and your sacrifices, and your tithes, and heave offerings of your hand, and your vows, and your freewill offerings, and the firstlings of your herds and of your flocks." And yet again, in vers. 13, 14, "Take heed to thyself that thou offer not thy burnt offerings in every place that thou seest: but in the place which the Lord shall choose in one of thy tribes, there thou shalt offer thy burnt offerings, and there thou shalt do all that I command thee." And still more solemnly is the same injunction conveyed in ch. xvii. 3—9, "What man soever there be of the house of Israel, that killeth an ox, or lamb, or goat, in the camp, or that killeth it out of the camp, and bringeth it not unto the door of the tabernacle of the congregation, to offer an offering unto the Lord before the tabernacle of the Lord; blood shall be imputed unto that man; he hath shed blood; and that man shall be cut off from among his people: to the end that the children of Israel may bring their sacrifices, which they offer in the open field, even that they may bring them unto the Lord, unto the door of the tabernacle of the congregation, unto the priest, and offer them for slain offerings unto the Lord," etc. If apparent exceptions are seen in the case of Gideon, Manoah, David, and Elijah, it needs to be remembered that their aberrant practice was sanctioned by express Divine revelations; and so little was their example regarded as a type of permissible action, that when the Reubenites wished to build a second altar, all Israel grew furious, and was ready to put two tribes and a half to the sword. It is therefore evident that immense importance was attached under the Law to the place of sacrifice. That place was ordered in such a way that it always fell somewhere within the one sanctuary; and very significantly so, for there Jehovah was supposed and stated to be peculiarly present and approachable. There was a certain localization of the Deity according to the Mosaic Law, and the neighbourhood of the Shechinah was holy ground, as the Law itself represents Jehovah as saying. "And there I will meet" are the words of the Lord at the ordinance of the perpetual burnt offering at the door of tabernacle, "And there I will meet with the children of Israel, and the tabernacle shall be sanctified by my glory. And I will sanctify the tabernacle of the congregation, and the altar: I will sanctify also both Aaron and his sons, to minister to me in the priest's office. And I will dwell among the children of Israel, and will be their God" (Exod. xxix. 43, 44). Let it be noted, however, that, whilst the whole sanctuary was the abode of Jehovah, approach to him was limited by two conditions: first, certain sections of the sanctuary were allotted to certain sections of the people, the high priest alone being allowed to enter the holy of holies, the priests' peculiar portion being the holy place, and the court being apportioned to the Jew; and secondly, the altars were, so to speak, the centres of the several sections, in which their significance was concentrated and from which their power radiated.

Thus we have express scriptural authority for saying that the various offerings were to be presented within the precincts of the holy place, each according to the status of the worshipper, because there Jehovah, the covenant God, had consented to reveal his Name, and be peculiarly present.

The significance of the officiating priests. Not only was the large majority of sacrifices ordered to be made at a certain place, but by the mediation of a certain ecclesiastical executive. The Jews at large were not priests unto God, they did their priestcraft by deputy; and from the days of their unanimous refusal of the more exalted office of Divine administration, the tribe of Levi was set apart for holy service. The preceding description of the legal commands has already shown how large a part the priest played in sacrificial worship, how minute a rubric instructed the priest in the dutiful discharge of his sacred functions. For our present purpose, the tribe of Levi as a whole may be ignored; it is simply needful to concentrate attention upon the priests proper, the descendants of Aaron, and their official head, the so-called high priest. Had the fact of the mediation of priests any doctrine to convey to the reverent and thoughtful worshipper? Most assuredly. The priests were middle-men; they had an exceptional privilege of Divine approach; they represented God to man, and man to God. Every sacrifice presented through the priest was presented to Jehovah by the appointed medium of legal access.

2. *The significance of the several details of the sacrificial ritual.* It is next necessary to consider the significance of the curious and precise ritual ordered to be adopted in sacrificial worship, and to see whether and how far religious truths were taught thereby. It will be seen that no prescribed act was meaningless, and that each stage in the elaborate act of worship had its own message to convey.

The act of presentation. The first stage in every act of sacrifice was the deliberate presentation of the offerer and his gift at the appropriate altar. Entrance into the court of the Lord's house was not casual or heedless, but of set purpose. The offerer presented himself and his offering solemnly before the priest. Nor was this presentation a mere opportunity for an official examination into the fulfilment of the legal conditions of valid sacrifice, although the officiating priest was unquestionably bound to see that the victim had neither spot nor blemish nor any such thing. The presentation was itself a thoughtful religious act. Of what nature? Without entering upon the various replies which have been returned by Neumann, Keil, Kliefoth, Kurtz, and Wangemann, suffice it to say that the *thebiah* was a symbolical prayer for the privileges accruing to legal sacrifice. To come to the altar was to come to the Lord; to come with a willing and obedient mind, fulfilling the conditions of the Law, was to ask for a share in the promises thereto attached.

The imposition of the hand. The victim having been solemnly presented, "the offerer forcibly laid his hand upon its head; his hand, not his slave's; his hand, not his substitute's, nor his wife's, but his own hand "—to retranslate what Outram extracted from the Talmud. There was a forcible imposition of the hand upon the head of the victim by the offerer, whoever he might be, whether priest or layman, king or elder. And this act was singularly eloquent. Again refraining from entering into the protracted controversy as to the meaning of the rite (discussed in the writer's previous work), suffice it to say that this act was a dedication of the victim to the purpose for which it was brought. Perfunctory worship Jehovah would not have, and as the deliberate act of presentation kept the mind of the offerer awake to the importance of the rite in which he was engaging, so the deliberate act of the imposition of the hand kept the mind awake to the same great object. Just as the presentation said, " This is my deliberate act," so the imposition of the hand implied, " This is my deliberate gift."

The act of slaughter. This, be it observed, was always performed by the offerer (possibly assisted or guided by the Levites), and hence its significance. In offering an animal, he was bringing before God an atonement as well as a presentation. But atonement was by the blood, not by the living animal. Whilst, therefore, sacrifice as a gift was complete when the victim was dedicated to sacred purposes in the two first ritual acts already described and explained, sacrifice as an atonement was not complete until the blood was given to the priest. In the act of slaughter by his own hand, the offerer obediently brought before God the blood of atonement. The slaughtering was important as the consummation of the act of sacrifice by the presentation of the atoning blood before the Lord.

The heaving and waving. Sometimes a peculiar swinging of the offering was appended to the other acts of presentation, called "heaving" and "waving" (*therumah* and *thenupha*). This detail was enjoined in the consecration of the Levites and priests, in the vow of the Nazarite, in the offering of jealousy, in the cleansing of the leprous, in the thank offerings and the tithes. Nor are the movements themselves difficult to trace. " Heaving " was a perpendicular motion from below upwards, a swinging from earth towards heaven. " Waving " has been very differently understood. Some of the early Protestant exegetes regarded " waving " as making the sign of the cross, in which they found some mysterious reference to the crucifixion of Jesus; Hengstenburg and Bähr accept this interpretation whilst rejecting the inference. Gesenius, Thalhofer, Keil, Knobel, Schultz, and Oehler seem to regard *thenupha* as a mere synonym of *thebiah*, and as forming no distinct part of the ceremonial; in which view there is both truth and falsity, the " waving " being assuredly a part of the act of presentation, but a part of the ritual distinctly emphasized. As Wangemann has pointed out, the compilers of the Mishna—no mean authorities on the details of ancient worship—regard this movement of *heniph* as a " going and coming," as if " waving " were a horizontal movement backwards and forwards. With this certain passages in the Old Testament coincide. Thus Isaiah calls the swinging of an axe " waving," as also the angry shake of the threatening finger. On the whole, therefore, this significant act of the officiator would seem to be a more emphatic presentation. The priest took the offering and " heaved " it towards heaven, as if presenting it to the Deity who had made the heavens his throne, and then returned the gift to the altar by a " waving " process, which only differed from the reverse of " heaving " by the exercise of force to counteract gravity, and place the limb or the firstfruits, for example, upon the altar.

The significance of the manipulations with the blood. Although this act varied in the several kinds of sacrifice, it was nevertheless invariably a more or less complete pouring forth of the life-blood before the Lord. The rabbinical interpreters of the Law divided the manipulation in question into three acts—*lekicha, serika,* and *shepicha.* To the collection of the blood in a silver bowl they gave the name of *lekicha*; the application of the blood so reserved to the altar they called *serika*; and the pouring out of the superfluous blood at the runnel of the altar, whence it flowed into the brook Kedron, they designated *shepicha*. This triple division is useful as showing the stages of the customary procedure. It was the second stage which was manifestly the important one, the first being a mere preliminary, and the third a mere consequent thereto. This *serika*, or sprinkling, varied with the sacrifice, sometimes being a sprinkling of the surface of the brazen altar, sometimes a smearing of the horns, and sometimes a general aspersion of all the holy places and their sacred utensils. It was always, however, a bringing of blood in contact with the altar, and thus before Jehovah. Upon the significance of this repulsive proceeding to modern eyes we are left in no doubt. The interpretation thereof is given in the passage which has already been quoted (ch. xvii. 11), and concerning which, however interpreters may vary as to its exact purport, all are agreed that it defines the use of blood in the Law. " For the soul of the flesh," it runs, " is in the blood : and I (the Lord) have given it you upon the altar to be an atonement for your souls : for the blood atones by the soul." In other words, this verse asserts that the blood of the animal legally presented has been appointed by God as a means of atonement for human life, because that blood is really the life of the animal sacrificed, or, to put the same thing in other words, the blood or life of an animal has been graciously accepted by Jehovah (for some reason or other, and by some means or other) as a valid substitute for the life or blood of the sinful offerer. As Kahnis puts it, blood is life *in compendio*. By the blood manipulation one part of the twofold aim of animal sacrifice was completed, and a legal atonement was made for human sin.

The significance of the combustion upon the altar. In the blood manipulation, as has just been observed, the atoning aspect of animal sacrifices was complete ; the two remaining rites were connected with the offerings as gifts to God. There was in every case a burning of the carcase, wholly or in part ; this was the first of the remaining acts. The symbolism of this combustion is manifest. It was a sending of the gift to God. After arranging the divided or the selected portions of the carcase in the heaven-born fire, which had issued forth from the Divine presence at the consecration of the tabernacle, and had never been permitted to altogether expire, they were burned, that is to say, they were etherealized, and they rose to heaven as " a sweet savour." The rite bore a similar interpretation when it had reference to any of the bloodless offerings. To burn was to effectually present.

The significance of the concluding meal. In all offerings but the holocausts and certain forms of the sin offerings, the ritual ended in a sacrificial meal, enjoyed for the most part by the priesthood, but occasionally—that is to say, in the case of peace offerings—shared by the laity. Of necessity, when there was a consummating feast, the entire gift was not burnt; part was consumed by fire in symbolical gift to God, and part was retained. That this remnant commonly fell to the priesthood points to the significance of this closing act. The priests were the representatives of Jehovah ; consumption by the priest was as much giving to God as consumption on the altar. There was a mystical union between Jehovah and his priests, and participation by the latter was participation by the former. In the peace offering there was a continuation of the same idea. For a time, the sacrificing family was admitted to the privileges of the priesthood. It consisted for a gracious season of priests unto God. As Kurtz has strikingly said, " Just as the effusion of blood betokened justification, . . . so the sacrificial meal told its tale of the *unio mystica*."

3. *The significance of the several species of sacrifice.* It will be convenient to reverse our previous order of exposition, and begin with—

The bloodless offerings. In these, as their name *minchoth* implies, the fact of presentation is alone emphasized. They were gifts to God simply; they were not a means of atonement. The whole ritual of their offering was adapted to express that they were presentations alone. Their further significance varied with their material. They consisted always of the products of labour; they were therefore objective representations of so much self-sacrifice; and it is interesting to see how these pure gifts might be made from all the branches of human activity—agriculture, stock-farming, arboriculture, merchandise, luxuries, even the spoils of battle and the titles of property.

The several blood sacrifices. These conveyed both the leading elements of Jewish worship. They were at once gifts and means of atonement. The ritual enjoined accentuated both features of blood manipulation and presentation. Further, whilst every blood sacrifice made both the aspects of sacrifice prominent, the materials ordered and the ritual enjoined adapted these fundamental facts to varying states of mind and inclination. The burnt offerings, and sin offerings, and trespass offerings, and peace offerings, were all means of adoring God, and covering sin as well; but in each species there was a special adaptation to the more vivid expression and satisfaction of some religious state.

The *burnt offering* is most nearly allied to the bloodless sacrifices. As its ritual shows most clearly, and as its name of holocaust implies, presentation is its leading characteristic; so far from the blood manipulation constituting a prominent feature, it seems to be, what it is in fact, a mere means to an end, a recognition of sinfulness lest the gift of man be despised. The variation too in the victims allowed points to the same fact—to the relative value of gifts, and is a kind of Old Testament proclamation of the duty of proportionate giving; the poor man's handful of meal, or pigeon, tells the same story as the widow's mite. On the other hand, the swinging of the blood collected by the priest against the altar is the least emphatic manner of procedure in atonement, whereas the burning of the whole carcase pointed most conclusively to the animal as a presentation to God.

In the *sin offering*, on the contrary, it is just the blood manipulation which is strongly emphasized. If the burnt offering was an atonement that it might be a gift, the sin offering was a gift that it might be an atonement. This inference is suggested by the name as well as the ritual. A sin offering was an offering for sin—for sin of an accurately defined nature, sin *bishgagah*, sin of error, and not deliberate sin. As for the ritual, there is as distinct an accentuation of the blood manipulation as there is an evident withdrawal into the background of the ritual of gift, the carcase simply falling to the priest, or being unostentatiously burnt without the camp, as a thing which has performed its purpose elsewhere. Further, in connection with the ritual of the making a substitute for sin, it is important to notice the increase in the value of the substitute as the status of the offerer rose. There is a well-marked gradation in the victims commanded, from the comparatively worthless she-goat of the common Israelite to the more valuable he-goat of the ruler, and thence to the ox for the priest or the congregation. Again, be it observed that the sin offerings of individuals were not presentable for any sin, but only for the so-called sins of ignorance, error, weakness, whichever word may be most suitably employed for the frequent lapses of sanctified but depraved human nature. Sharply defined, therefore, sin offerings were gifts which were made for atonement of sins of ignorance, sins of ignorance, according to the Levitical conception, being any sins which did not wilfully contravene the dictates of Jehovah.

Similarly, the significance of the *trespass offerings* may be inferred from the ritual and the law of their presentation. From the former it is manifest that neither the element of gift nor of atonement was the prominent feature, but the element of restitution. In this class of sacrifice there was always an accompanying recompense, which was paid both to God who has been offended by the trespass, and to man who has been defrauded. It was the fancy value which was put upon the ram and which expiated the wrong-doer before the Great Giver of all things, and it was the monetary indemnity which expiated the human fraud, which gave to this offering its peculiar place and value. And this inference is strengthened by noting certain special cases in which this form of offering was ordained. Trespass offerings were to be made upon unconscious negligence in such dues as tithes or firstfruits, upon an unintentional infringement of a Divine command, and upon any deceitful violation of the rights of property; thus, to translate the injunctions into more general terms, trespass offerings were to be made upon any forgetfulness of duty to God or duty to our neighbour. There was always present in this class of sacrifices the idea of retribution.

Similarly, *in the peace offerings,* it is again manifest that it is neither the fact of gift nor that of atonement which is uppermost, but that of the sacrificial meal. In this class, as in the preceding, the elements of presentation and atonement are but means to an end. The peace offerings were gifts and expiations that they might be feasts. The peace offering was the social offering, the sacrifice of friendship, where a man and his kindred might have loving fellowship with Jehovah and his priests. The burnt offering was the act of one in *union* with Jehovah, the peace offering of one who would cement *union* by *communion.* The peace offering was the Lord's Supper of the old covenant.

4. *The significance of the several feasts and fasts.* The several feasts and fasts now call for consideration before we proceed to build up these numerous details into one consistent and instructive synthesis. The significance of these festal or penitential seasons must again be inferred from the scriptural records by means of a careful induction in each case.

The general import of these exceptional times and seasons in the Jewish calendar may be gathered from the name so frequently applied to them. They are called "holy convocations;" whereby is signified that they were not simply seasons of rest, a kind of *Décadi,* or *Sansculottide,* an atheistic day of rest, or popular festival; they were holy days as well as holidays. Nor were they, this name implies, like birth and marriage days, like Waterloo memorials and American Days of Independence, like Foundation Days and remembrances of a pious benefactor—mere jubilant or regretful reminiscences of past events, such as the Divine pause after Creation, or the flight from Egypt, or the tenting-out at Succoth; they were religious in the sense of present participation in spiritual privilege; they were sacramental memorials. In short, the Jewish festivals (to use a convenient term not to be understood as excluding days of humiliation), whatever else they were, whether holidays or days of rest, were dedicated to religious exercises, and therefore became media for new experimental participation in the blessings of religious truth.

The *sabbaths* were times of holy convocation, and nothing more. They were pauses authoritatively demanded in the busy life of the world for spiritual as well as physical ends. They stood out amidst the days of the week as the Lord's days, and as peremptorily as the fourth commandment bade " Remember the sabbath day to keep it holy," did prophets take up the strain, saying, " Moreover, I gave them my sabbaths, to be a sign between me and them, that they might know that it is I the Lord that sanctify them." Of the same general sabbatic character the new moons partook, and the sabbatic and jubilee year also. They were times for holiness and congregation in addition to being seasons of rest. Without calling any special historical event to mind, they were "holy convocations," labour being remitted that religion might be the more engrossing.

The remaining festal times and seasons had an additional characteristic. Besides being "holy convocations," when there might be a general adoration of Jehovah, and a general remembrance of his goodness, and a general participation in the blessedness which the truths he had graciously revealed were calculated to impart, there was in these other feasts and fasts a particular remembrance of some special religious crisis in the national history, a particular celebration of some special act of Divine goodness, and a particular reception of some special Divine blessing. It was as though each year there was again a remembrance of the principal needs of the religious life, together with the special Divine methods for ministering to those needs. In fact, as the sabbatic cycle of festivals was fitted to keep alive in the soul the general relations of the Jew to his covenant God, so the remaining festivals were individually adapted to fan the flickering embers of some single spiritual sense only too liable to expire. The several exceptional festivals were ordained to be at once holy convocations, sacred memorials, and blessed sacraments, and both history and precept are inadequately estimated if either element is disregarded.

Thus it is an insufficient interpretation of the *Passover* if it is spoken of simply as a remembrance of the first constitution of the released Hebrews. The *Passover*, as it was celebrated from year to year, was a re-enactment, a reiteration, a renewal of that ancient rite which inaugurated the Divine adoption of Israel as "a peculiar treasure, a kingdom of priests, and a holy nation," as Jehovah himself described the liberated Egyptian slaves. Passover was a time of solemn convocation and sacred reminiscence; it was also a repetition of that symbolic ritual by which the children of Israel were admitted into their peculiar relationship to the Deity, wherein they may feast as the ransomed sons of God. Briefly, Passover was a holy convocation, when the first Passover was recapitulated, and the nation again entered upon the amenities of Divine forgiveness and adoption. Or, yet more briefly, Passover was the Feast of Justification, "made year by year continually."

The days succeeding the Passover constitute one long festal season, commencing with the days of Unleavened Bread, and ending with the Feast of Firstfruits. Again we have an addition to the general significance of a festival for a special end. The justified nation is now submitting itself to rules of abstinence and habits of self-sacrifice. A not unsuitable name for this season would be the Feast of Consecration; or, to modify our previous form of speech, the Feast of Weeks, by which name the Old Testament seems sometimes to designate the whole period from Passover to Pentecost, was marked by special days of holy convocation, in which the first joys of national obedience and deliverance were reiterated, and the people admitted to the privileges of the Divine adoption testified to its blessedness by willing consecration of self and substance to Divine purposes. More briefly, the Feast of Weeks was the Feast of Consecration, "made year by year continually."

A similar line of remark is applicable to the great *Day of Atonement*. This day of humiliation was by no means a repetition of the Passover, as some have thought. It does not celebrate the entrance of the people upon covenant rights, nor the beneficial remembrance of that entrance; it is a fast and a penitential season for those who have been already admitted to the Divine intimacy. What else, then, could the Day of Atonement signify than the atonement demanded by the sinfulness inseparable even from the reconciled? What else could the Day of Atonement suggest than the permanent need of atonement even by a nation of priests? And what else did that day proclaim than the means divinely prearranged for meeting that evident need? The Day of Atonement was, as its name implies, that holy convocation in which the covenant people were cleansed from the sin contaminating their holiest service, "year by year continually," —the Fast of Absolution.

Hence follows the meaning of that festival which formed the climax of the festive seasons of the year, the Feast of Tabernacles. Naturally enough it was jubilant and exultant; dances and singing and mirth were its natural accompaniments. For a time, at least, there was a joyous sojourn in the courts of the Lord's house, and a kind of Paradise restored where man might hear the voice of God amidst the leaves of the trees in which the swallow had built a nest for herself. The season was a symbolic representation of the joy of the elect, who dwell in Jehovah's temple fearlessly and gleefully. The Feast of Tabernacles, religiously regarded, was the Feast of the Joy of the Reconciled.

Such, at any rate, were the religious truths these festivals were fitted to convey, and the types of religious life they were adapted to gratify, mould, and objectify. Doubtless the picture drawn is ideal, as has been the whole delineation of the significance of the Levitical sacrifices. Undoubtedly also the realization was but rarely attained, and that not in the entire nation, but in the sanctified heart of some solitary worshipper like David or Ezekiel. Nevertheless, these Divine object-lessons were not without their value. They were at once an exercise and an embodiment of an indispensable form of educational religion. They were admirably qualified for a paternal education of a religious childhood, if they fell short of a personal culture of a religious manhood. Add the further truth, so clearly taught in the old covenant, of the preparatory character of Judaism, and this divinely given cultus by presentation and atonement was blessed and stimulating indeed, "a schoolmaster to bring us to Christ."

C. The Application of the Principles deduced to the Entire Scheme of the Levitical Sacrifices.

There is, alas! no royal road to the comprehension of the Levitical sacrifices, and in the esteem of the present writer it is only after a laborious, observant, protracted, and possibly wearisome journey through a wide realm of detail, that anything like sure approach can be made to a mastery of the difficulties of the way. A few jottings only of that journey have been given, a few impressions recorded in transit, but even now some advance can be made to the promised land of intelligibility. To speak without figure, a complete synthesis of the facts and interpretations already obtained could only result upon a full and exhaustive survey by the light of the principles deduced of the entire Jewish calendar of sacrifice. Such a survey is precluded by our limits ; but some suggestive outlines thereof may now be drawn.

Let us suppose ourselves standing within the entrance of the court of the tabernacle or the temple as twilight is passing into dawn on the morning of the 1st of Abib, or, as it was afterwards called, the 1st of Nisan. For years the same round of ritual has been pursued, at once reminding the chosen people of their exceptional religious privileges and expressing with eloquent symbol the religious sentiments which so benevolent a religious system could evoke and educate, and once more the blank page of the new year is being presented for completion, and the services of the year are recommencing. Before our eyes the barefooted priests, who are to officiate in their course, are already preparing themselves for their solemn duties by ablution at the brazen laver, whilst, on the hearth of the altar of burnt offerings the remnants of the first evening sacrifice of the new year are still burning. The ceremonies of the day begin. First comes the continuous burnt offering. One of the elders of the people possibly presents himself in the people's name at the altar, bringing with him the appointed lamb for the sacrifice and the appointed meat and drink offerings. He is seen to lay his hand with some force upon the victim's head, thus dedicating it in the name of the entire people as a burnt offering in its behalf. He draws his knife and cuts its throat. The priest, who is ready with a basin, collects the streaming blood and dashes it as an atonement against the sides of the altar, then dissects and cleanses the carcase in the prescribed manner, and, laying the pieces in order upon the hearth, the morning oblation rises into the air, "a sweet savour unto Jehovah;" and once more the daily burnt sacrifice has been presented as an acceptable token and memorial of the nation's consecration to Jehovah.

But the day is a new moon, a more emphatic and memorable day of grace, and a more elaborate offering is added to the ordinary daily presentation. The task of the national representative, whoever he may be, is not yet complete, and he again presents himself in the same place with two young bullocks, a ram, and seven lambs for a burnt offering, together with the prescribed offerings of meat and wine, and also with a kid for a sin offering. Analogy would suggest that the sin offering is first made. Again the offering is formally made to the priests at the brazen altar, clad as before in their white robes and parti-coloured girdles, but increased in number; again the hand is impressed upon the head of the victim; again the animal is slain in the nation's behalf; again one of the priests, the accredited representatives of Jehovah, collects the blood of the slaughtered beast; but there the similarity of the ceremonial ends. According to the ritual ordained for the sin offering, some of the blood is more carefully smeared upon the horns of the altar, and is thus brought in more solemn memorial before the Lord, whilst the remainder is poured away, its end being achieved, at the base of the altar; some few portions of the fat are alone consumed by fire, the offering partaking more of the nature of an atonement than a gift, and for the same reason the rest of the carcase is not burnt within the sacred precincts of the holy place, but in some clean spot without the camp. Then follows the large monthly burnt offering before described, which puts the larger number of priests in requisition, the same form of ritual being gone through as in the case of the "continuous" sacrifice, and the same truth being signified with more display. Thus, at the opening year, the chosen nation is again reminded of its consecration, and reconsecrated to God in emphatic manner, the doctrine being simultaneously declared by the presentation of the sin offering as well as by the form of blood sacrifice, that even the best hours of religious acknowledgment in the most prominent days of a sanctified people are not untainted by sin, but call for humiliation and atonement.

The national offerings made, and the golden candlestick replenished in the holy place, the official offerings follow. The high priest, in his official robes of white and blue, "Holiness to the Lord" glistening in gold upon his mitre, his jewelled breastplate flashing and sparkling in the early sun, passes to the performance of his exalted functions, the bells and pomegranates at the fringe of his broidered tunic ringing as he goes to present his daily sacrifice. Now he burns his offering of meal at the altar of burnt offering, and, by a gift of his substance, consecrates himself anew to the Lord, no effusion of blood being in his case necessary, because of the peculiar holiness supposed to attach to his sublime office; now he advances to the holy place, and, drawing back the chequered curtain, "a thing of beauty and of glory," is hidden from view for a time, but within, we know, he is burning incense before the Lord on the golden altar, as a further testimony of priestly consecration—presenting solemnly this exceptional holocaust without blood.

The personal offerings now succeed. These, of course, vary from day to day according to the number of those who are religiously impressed with the necessity of sacrifice, and according to the mode of impression. For, legally compulsory as several of the varieties of individual sacrifices were, there was an element of freedom in some, and of limitation in all; and as manifestly as the burnt offerings and peace offerings were purely voluntary, it is equally evident that the sin offerings and trespass offerings were largely influenced by time and space.   A Jew who lived remote from Jerusalem, for example, might know the Law, but could not possibly fulfil it; thus there would be, even with the enthusiastically religious, a more probable remembrance and observance upon certain set occasions, such as the annual feasts.   Nor must the hardness of the human heart be forgotten, and the rare virtue of living up to spiritual privileges.   Still, the supposition is that we are standing in the court of the tabernacle on a New Year's Day.   Although not dignified with the importance of Pentecost or the great Day of Atonement, it is still a festal day, and offerings of many kinds will certainly be presented.   At one hour, full of gratitude to God, and anxious for service and self-abnegation, a man brings his bull, or his ram, or his goat, for a burnt offering, according to his means and inclination, whilst his poorer neighbour presents his pair of pigeons.   The customary ritual is gone through, each stage of which is symbolically expressive of the act and method of consecration, until the holocaust rises "as an offering of fire of a sweet savour unto Jehovah," and the deed of personal consecration is complete.   At another time it is an omission of some sacred duty which is to be remembered before the Lord, and in that obedience which is dearer even than sacrifice, an Israelite from the ranks is leading his spotless shaggy she-goat to the altar, when again the ceremonies of presentation, of imposition, and of slaughter are carefully gone through, each stage in the sanguinary proceeding having its own spiritual suggestiveness for the religiously minded, the blood is smeared upon the horns of the altar to bring the medium of atonement before the Lord, and, the expiation for the unwitting sin being ended, the offerer walks away, mentally at rest.   Or perhaps it is a trespass offering which is being brought in repentant recollection of some deed of fraud, a kind of conscience money; in acknowledgment of wrong done to God as well as man, the substitutionary ram is presented and slain, whilst the story of the fraud is told over the head of the slaughtered beast, the priest placing a judicial value upon the wrong done to Jehovah, and accepting the ram in lieu thereof, a monetary recompense being made to the injured neighbour. Or it may be a peace offering which is brought by a whole family in joyful recognition of the Divine goodness, the priest being welcomed to the hallowed society; the victim is slain, and the sin present even in such united religious joy atoned; and the feast follows within the sacred precincts of the holy place—a love feast indeed, a banquet where "the banner over them was love."   Or, descending to the less frequent instances of the Levitical ceremonial, "now a Hebrew woman, but recently a mother, is modestly presenting herself with her offering of pigeons; and now the high priest is passing through the gate of the court, attended by a Levite carrying birds and scarlet wool and hyssop—he has been summoned without the camp to examine a restored leper. Anon an application is made for the means of purifying some tent where the dead is lying.   At one hour a householder is compounding for the property which he has voluntarily vowed unto the Lord; the next, a Nazarite, with unshorn hair and beard is presenting the prescribed sacrifices for release from his vow."

Such might have been the sights afforded to the observer by a single day.   From early morning to the hour of the evening sacrifice there was oftentimes, we may assume, one long series of presentations by all grades of people and for all varieties of experience; and a similar course was pursued the whole year round, as we shall presently detail at more length after a brief digression which is rather a further explanation.

To test the usefulness and the sufficiency of the explanatory principles already deduced, let attention be concentrated upon two of those peculiar ceremonies which might be occasionally witnessed, namely, that of the purification of the dead and that of the consecration to the priesthood.

Analyze, for example, the rites ordained for the purification of the dead—interpret them by the light of the principles previously deduced—and the ceremony would suggest some such series of thoughts as the following. The rite was a purification, and as such pointed to the great doctrine of original sin. It was a purification of an exceptionally solemn kind, and it was a purification of a solemn kind from its singular blending of the atoning with the cleansing element of the Levitical worship. Such is an induction from the various features in which the ritual resembled, and differed from, the general course of procedure. According to the Law, a dead body contaminated all in its vicinity. "To be in a tent at the time of the death of an inmate, to enter a tent where a dead body lay, to touch a corpse, a grave, or a bone, was to contract uncleanness for seven days." The process of purification was very arresting, from its peculiarity. Like most processes of purification, it was a form of aqueous ablution; but the water employed had been specifically prepared. A red cow was brought to the son or heir of the high priest, by the popular representatives, for slaughter without the camp. Very little ceremonial was observed, but all was singularly expressive. The blood was sprinkled seven times towards the tabernacle, and then the whole of the carcase—not a part—together with the skin and the blood and dung, was burnt; a little cedar-wood, hyssop, and scarlet wool being thrown into the fire. From the ashes the water of purification was prepared. When occasion called, the ashes were mixed with spring water, and sprinkled, by means of a bunch of hyssop, on the third and seventh day after defilement, upon the tent and the vessels and persons it contained; after the customary ablution of the person, the unclean became pure in the evening. After ablution also, all those who had had any share in the ritual, and who were thus rendered unclean, were also purified. Now, the use of water associates this curious rite with the other rites of purification, and therefore shows that, according to the Levitical conception, contamination by the proximity of death was regarded as a form of involuntary sin, which, like parturition, proclaimed the natural depravity of man, to be obviated by special ceremonial. But the peculiarities of ritual imparted a specific character to this form of purification. Not simply was water to be used, but running or spring water—water at its greatest power of cleansing; *living* water, as the Hebrew expressively puts it. Further, this "water of iniquity" was a lye prepared by the admixture of these ashes of the red cow. What additional significance is thereby given? These ashes were loudly eloquent of atonement, and nothing but atonement. Let it be noted that this red cow was manifestly a kind of sin offering—indeed, it is actually so called: did not the blood manipulation point to the same conclusion?—but that it differs in many essential points from the sin offering proper. Like the latter, it was a national propitiation, and was therefore brought by the representatives of the tribes; but, unlike the latter, it consisted of a cow—most probably that it be not confounded with the bullock enjoined for the sin offering for the congregation, and that at the same time its inferior grade be denoted. Then let it also be observed that this cow was in no sense a presentation, like the sin offering proper. It was not offered at the altar of burnt offering, but without the camp; no portions were reserved for priestly use. It was not submitted to the customary rites of presentation; even the skin and fæces were burnt, and not separated. In fact, this red cow was an atonement by substitution—this, and nothing more. Its blood was sprinkled, like the blood of the sin offering, before the tabernacle seven times, thus bringing the appointed means of "covering" emphatically before Jehovah; scarlet wool—blood-coloured wool—was thrown into the flames when the carcase was burnt; nay, the very colour of the cow was selected as the colour of the blood which atoned; and so completely was the victim regarded as a substitute, that every ministrant at the ritual was rendered unclean thereby, and the high priest was precluded from officiating, lest he be incapacitated for his other exalted functions, and so his son, his nearest kinsman, and official representative took his place. Thus, in pictorial and impressive form, the momentous truths were inculcated of death as the punishment of sin ordained by the Divine anger, and of the counteraction of the influence of death by an appointed substitute. There is not a detail of the involved ritual which cannot be explained by the aid of such principles as we have deduced.

So, too, so elaborate a ceremonial as the consecration of a priest becomes at once lucid, brilliant, suggestive, and religious by the application of the principles in question. As we have seen, a bullock and two rams, unleavened bread and wheaten cakes, were brought to the door of the tabernacle, where the candidates to be initiated were washed with water, arrayed in official garments, anointed with the holy oil, atoned for by a sin offering, sanctified by a burnt offering, and admitted to fellowship by a peace offering. In one significant particular the ritual of this closing sacrifice differed from that customarily observed in sacrifices of the same class. After the habitual imposition of the hand, and slaughter, some of the collected blood was put upon the tip of the right ear, the thumb of the right hand, and the toe of the right foot, and was sprinkled upon the clothing of the newly ordained priest, in addition to the usual smearing of the horns of the altar. Now, as most investigators have pointed out, this consecration consisted of two sets of three acts. In the first place, there was a solemn purification, an express investiture, and a formal anointing; and in the second place, there followed a triple sacrifice in the noteworthy order of a sin offering, a burnt offering, and a peace offering. Every detail is luminous and has of itself a profound suggestiveness for the age contemporaneous, and although the minutiæ of the rite only receive their full illumination in Christianity, they nevertheless conveyed many a valuable lesson to the Jew. In fact, in its adaptation of the general ritual of Levitical sacrifice to the ordination of priests, the prescribed ceremonial is a simple and intelligible object-lesson in the requisites of acceptable religious service. In the set washing with water we have, as Oehler put it, " a symbol of the spiritual purification without which none can approach God, at least to atone." In the investiture there is the visible assumption of the priestly office. In the anointing, the Divine seal is attached to such acceptance of office ; whereas the sin inherent even in an accepted priest must be removed by a sin offering, upon which may follow the expressive sacrifices of consecration and fellowship. As for the varying features in the peace offering, where a different blood manipulation is gone through, what change could be more significant? Before admission to the communion of priests, and of the Deity whom the priests serve, there must be a specific atonement, and the atoning blood of the ram, " the ram of consecration," is placed not only in contact with the altar, but with the person and garments of the newly ordained priest, the very ceremonial signifying that the ear and hand and foot, which are to be swift to serve, must be atoned for before they are hallowed, and that the very garments of office must be cleansed before dedication to their sacred use.

With such daily observances, the Jewish year ran its course, the customary worship repeated evening and morning, in combination with the voluntary expression of religion by sacrifice, associating absolution, confession, and adoration with all the phases and grades of the national life. If the tribe of Levi sanctified itself by holy service in sacrifice, by the same means the farmer sanctified his toil, the mother her child, the father his skill, the prophet his calling, the singer his talent, the prince his government, and the elders their nation. Day by day these Levitical sacrifices were capable of proclaiming, in sanctuary, in palace, in market, in house, and in tent, religious truths of the highest importance. To this daily observance let the additional observances of the various festal seasons be added, and it will become yet more manifest how admirably this cultus of sacrifice at once educated and ministered to the Jewish phasis of religion.

From the 2nd of Abib to the 10th, the customary daily celebration of Divine service was observed, the interval being abnormally broken into solely by the increased consecration called for and symbolized by the double burnt offering of the sabbath. When God was especially remembered, man was to be especially consecrated. With the 10th of Abib came the Paschal feast, continued more or less till the Feast of Pentecost. And very full of spiritual suggestions was this opening festival of the year, every detail of the rites enjoined tending to deepen those suggestions. In its first institution, as we have seen, the Passover was a sacrificial admission to covenant rights, and every subsequent celebration thereof was at once a remembrance and a repetition of that initiatory ceremonial. From this fundamental significance all the peculiarities of this sacrifice follow. Thus the Paschal lamb was neither a sin offering pure and simple nor a peace offering; it did not in many important points come beneath the laws of the acknowledged sacrificial ritual. It was a kind of inclusive sacrifice, which conveyed the prominent teaching of several forms of sacrifice under one suggestive form. Thus first and foremost the Paschal lamb was an atonement of so potent a nature as to arrest the destroying arm of the angel of death, and of so emphatic a ritual as to be brought more into contact with the several households of the tribes than was the case in any other festal season. The time allowed to elapse between the selection of the victim and its slaughter, the minute injunctions for the sprinkling of the blood upon the lintel and doorposts, the command that no bone of the lamb was to be broken, the strict command that what remained was to be burnt by fire, the rapid manner of partaking,—all pointed to the offering as less intended for a feast than an atonement, and laid very exceptional stress upon the neutralizing power of the effused blood. Certain features of the feast were undoubtedly ordained because of the peculiar position of the Israelites in Egypt, and if that position be borne in mind, and the fundamental significance of the Passover as the great initiatory rite, all the superficial difficulties of the narrative are removed. It is, of course, not denied, but strongly believed, that there are features in this institution which nothing but the fulfilment of the type could perfectly explain, and which are the outcome of distinct Divine prevision; at the same time, it is contended that even so extraordinary a command as that of keeping the skeleton intact was intelligible to the Jew as a natural consequence of what he was able to apprehend of the meaning of the Passover. Possibly even this nineteenth century is a record of many facts likewise which seem to us to be of a present import only, which will only receive an adequate explanation in the light of a coming dispensation. Similarly with the following days of the Paschal feast and with the day of Pentecost, all the details of the injunctions relative thereto are nothing but exemplifications divinely prearranged of the leading fact taught thereby of the Feast of Consecration. Therefore, for example, was the pleasure of leavened bread eschewed; therefore were the firstfruits presented.

Nor need we go outside the principles already deduced for explanation of the remaining feasts and their observances. Pentecost past, the year rolled upon its course for a time, it is true, in a more level manner, the regularity of the daily celebration being only interrupted by the sabbatic and lunar formalities, every day, therefore, a kind of gospel being proclaimed of Divine mercy and forgiveness and reconciliation, with its invariable postulates of human sin and decadence, death and guilt. At length came the high season of the seventh month, heralded by the rousing blasts of the Feast of Trumpets.

The seventh month affords two very excellent tests of the adequacy of these principles of interpretation, namely, in their application to the elucidation of the great Day of Atonement and the Feast of Tabernacles. The ritual of the former need not be repeated ; it was undoubtedly exceptional ; it was as undoubtedly instructive ; indeed, the more minute and accurate the investigation bestowed even upon the more trivial points of observance, the more harmonious does it appear, and the more didactic. At first sight, it may be allowed, the ceremonial shows a laboured and officialistic respect to a mass of legal detail, valuable as a testimony to ecclesiastical thoroughness in routine, and to little else. Viewed more closely, the ceremonial is a complete and balanced whole, exact and even concise, forcible as well as clear in the religious lesson it has to convey. That lesson, as we have seen, is the atonement possible for the sins of the redeemed, for, be it observed, the stranger and the foreigner had no part in the worship of this day of national humiliation. Carrying this principle in the mind, the entire series of acts yields up its meaning. Not a soul in the priestly tribe, however holy and exalted his function, not a utensil in the consecrated place, however sacred and sublime its use, but must be atoned for. Hence the mediators and the instruments of mediation must be first removed from beneath the ban of uncleanness and sin. The solemn proceedings are therefore commenced by the offering of the bullock in expiation of the holy places and ministrants. The high priest, who leads in officiating, may not even wear his official robes till the ceremonial of expiation is completed, but stands at the altar clothed in white ; and, on the slaughter of the bullock, sprinkles the mercy-seat and the floors and the altars with the blood of atonement, and presents the blood before the Lord in atonement for his own sin and the sins of his kindred and tribe. The whole ritual is an emphatic act of atonement, as every detail shows. Atonement is likewise solemnly made by the blood of the ram in behalf of the nation. The remaining rite was an exquisitely symbolic act, declarative of forgiveness. Confessing over the head of the live goat the sins and iniquities of the entire nation, the high priest seemed to transfer those sins to the head of the animal, who bore them away from the dwelling-place of Jehovah, and carried them into the abode of Azazel. The sins were removed as well as covered. Now the priest may assume his golden garments ; now the people may present acceptable sacrifice ; now burnt offerings may typify the national consecration.

The ritual of the Feast of Tabernacles is somewhat less intelligible ; nevertheless, its secret was also largely open to the thoughtful and devout Jew. It very expressively followed the more serious service of the Day of Atonement, and gave visible and pleasant expression to the joy of the elect, who have been redeemed at the Passover, consecrated at Pentecost, and absolved at the great day of national expiation. This feast ended, the climax of the doctrinal teaching by symbol had been reached, and the year was brought to a close by the common series of daily, weekly, and monthly sacrificings.

Now, in view of this didactic sacrificial cultus, at once so eloquent and so disciplinary, it would certainly be interesting to inquire what contributions were thereby made towards a system of revealed religion. It would also be interesting to ask with what arguments the pious Jew would combat the assaults of disbelievers in what he regarded the Divine origin of his sacrificial creed. Nor could it be by any means impracticable, whilst it certainly would be of value, to frame both a systematic and apologetic theology of Judaism, in which such notes as the laws of purification and the injunctions for blood sacrifice, the significance of the priesthood and the explanation expressly assigned to the tabernacle, might, by an intellectual effort of no severe kind, be made to disclose the inmost messages of their symbolism, and become part of a concatenated doctrine of Old Testament theology, of its doctrine of sin and of salvation, of its doctrine of God and of man.   But after all, it is the practical aspect of this Old Testament faith which most calls for admiring regard. Its theological implications are of interest to the theologian, its practical implications are of human interest. And practically regarded, these Levitical sacrifices are noteworthy, first, as a means of religious education, and next as a means of religious satisfaction. They evolved religious sentiment, and they appeased it. However superficially this sacrificial cultus be regarded, it assuredly proclaimed such truths as these : the sinfulness of man (extending too beyond the bounds of volition, and affecting the race), the Divine alienation consequent thereupon, the need of atonement, its possibility, its method, the acceptability of the service of the reconciled. All these truths—which, to judge from Christianity, constitute the essentials of a religion adapted to man—were taught by arresting symbolism and an imposing ceremonial. They were equally capable of educating up to a high degree of religiousness and of ministering to the religious needs so matured. They affected too the whole range of life, training the Church, sanctifying the State, penetrating the home, and affecting the individual. They interwove the essentials of religion with all the relationships, duties, sorrows, and pleasures of life. According to its own ideal, the Jewish nation was a theocracy where reconciled rebels gave their every allegiance to the King of kings acceptably.

Thus, historically regarded, and without trespassing upon or forestalling the later revelations made by Christ and his apostles, the Levitical sacrifices are seen to be a profound recognition of the wants of man, and a response to his deepest needs. The Levitical sacrifices declared unmistakably, from the hour of their first promulgation, the necessity there was for atonement, and the Divine provision for that necessity. Indeed, it is simple truth to say that there is not a feature of the Levitical sacrifices which does not accentuate in some way, either the fact of estrangement from God with its large disabilities, or the fact of reconciliation to God with its large privileges. To how enormous an extent their teaching relied for confirmation and potency upon Christianity, we shall presently see ; just now the point upon which it is necessary to insist is the value of Judaism as a religious system apart from Christianity. The system was, alas ! ideal. The Jew seldom realized and never exhausted its magnificent possibilities. Nevertheless, how immense was its practical value, let the hundred and nineteenth psalm testify, with its hundred and seventy-six verses in praise of this very Levitical system, which the Psalmist is glad to recall, and which he feels it no exaggeration to describe—mass of commandments, laws, testimonies, statutes, though it be—as a fitting guide of youth, an object of great delight, a mine of wonders ; as the rule of the free and the song of the exile ; as sweeter than honey and more valuable than riches ; as life, light, and health ; a pleasant subject of meditation in this world and also in the eternity of Jehovah.

D. Relation of the Levitical Sacrifices to the Sacrifices of the Patriarchal Age.

Contrasting this detailed and expressive system of Levitical sacrifice with the brief records of the pre-Mosaic age, it would appear that the later cultus differed from the earlier in *authority*, in *complexity*, in *centralization*, in *doctrine*, and in *practical value*.

As regards the *authority* of the Levitical sacrifices, they are expressly ascribed to a Divine origin. " And Jehovah said unto Moses " is the almost invariable formula with which the several legal sections begin. In this there is a marked distinction from the days of the great fathers of the Hebrew nation. Whatever Divine influences were brought to bear upon Abel in the first recorded sacrifice—and it is easy to exaggerate those influences to the detriment of the inspiriting teaching of the narrative—it is manifest that from that time onwards the ever-growing system of worship by sacrifice was almost wholly a human development. "Almost wholly," we say, for sacrificial revelations were given to Noah and Abraham, but the one was simply an exhortation to sacrifice, and the other a correction of an erroneous inference. In fact, the patriarchal sacrifices are apparently representative of pure ethnic sacrifices, whereas the Divine acknowledgment and improvement of human religious ideas testify at once to the hardness of the human heart and to the gracious condescension of Jehovah.

So it is likewise evident that the Levitical sacrifices were an advance upon the patriarchal in *complexity*. Hereditary priests have taken the place of the father of the family, and all the various ceremonial of the court, the holy place, and the holiest, in all the mutations of the Jewish year, have superseded those two simple varieties mentioned in earlier times, the burnt offering and the festal offering—which were adapted on occasion, as best they could be, to all the changing and contrasted emotion of the religious life.

A third difference between the two dispensations is seen in the later *localization*. Abraham, Isaac, and Jacob, wherever God had revealed himself and made his presence known, could present their offerings of praise, and erect their holy places. The Levitical sacrifices are legitimate, so testifies the whole Pentateuch, at one sanctuary alone. There being a localization of Deity, or rather of his gracious presence, acceptable sacrifice must be offered in the neighbourhood of the mercy-seat.

There is a clearness too in the *doctrinal* implications of the Levitical rites, which is conspicuously absent from the earlier forms of worship. No such array of parallel principles can be inferred from the Genesis as has been deduced from the Exodus and the Leviticus. The acceptability of sacrifice, as a testimony to self-sacrifice even, has very much less evident sanction for Abraham than for Moses. The point is so certain that attention needs simply be drawn thereto. To an additional point, however, it is necessary to refer with some distinctness; the patriarchal cultus was a worship *by presentation*, the Levitical cultus was a worship by *atonement* as well. No reference is made in the Genesis, whether direct or indirect, by express statement, by ritual, or by any mention of a special manipulation of the blood of the victims offered, to the Levitical doctrine of expiation by blood. Animal sacrifices were made, it is true, but only because stock-farming as well as agriculture formed part of the staple labour of the ancestors of the Jewish nations, and gifts might be therefore made from the former as well as the latter, or because animal food was eaten by them as well as vegetable. The evidence would seem to be conclusive that not only did the Almighty, according to the testimony of the Pentateuch, adopt the results of human religious thought and practice, giving them at the same time a wider bearing and a more assured interpretation, but that he added to that interpretation the very significant doctrine peculiar to Judaism of the atonement for sin by the blood of a substituted victim.

And of course all these differences culminated in a difference of *practice*. The educational value of the religion of Moses was higher than that of the pre-Mosaic age, because more accurate and minute in doctrinal significance, just as, for the same reason, its value was increased as a discipline. A more developed and sound theology is always the cause of a profounder and more useful religious education, and a purer and more satisfying religious worship.

E. Relation of the Levitical Sacrifices to the Christian Sacrifices.

The religions of Moses and Jesus Christ both agree and differ in their sacrificial teaching.

They agree in dividing their doctrine of sacrifice into two parts; their doctrine of presentation and their doctrine of ¡atonement, according to both presentation being possible and atonement necessary. They also agree in asserting that atonement must precede sacrifice.

They differ in the material, directness, and timeliness of presentation, and in the method and frequency of atonement. To take the latter points first. The New Testament teaches that atonement is made for human sin by the substitution of the life of Jesus for that of the sinner. As Peter expresses it, "Christ, who his own self carried up our sins in his own body to the tree, that we, having died to sins, might live unto righteousness." Or, as Paul put it, adopting the Jewish synonym of blood for life, "Christ Jesus, . . . whom God set forth to be a propitiation, through faith, by his blood;" and according to the nature of the case this atonement or propitiation is made once for all. The Old Testament teaches that the Jew is atoned for by the blood, or life, of an animal substitute, which is so far from being presented once for all, that life must be effused on every occasion of worship. Similarly as regards the doctrine of presentation, there is a change of teaching: in the Old Testament, certain prescribed forms of offering are alone allowed, and the man is accepted because of the offering of his substance; in the New, self is more important, and the offering is accepted because of the man. There is an alteration in another respect: the New Testament demands no priestly mediation like that of the tribe of Levi in approaching the Majesty on high. And in yet a third respect there is a change: the offering of a reconciled heart may be made at any time and in any place at the free suggestion of the worshipper, and without legal restriction.

Without entering, therefore, upon abstract doctrinal discussion, and judging solely by the facts presented by the sacrificial conceptions of the two dispensations, they are manifestly connected, and that as the higher and the lower in a prearranged system of development. There is in Christianity an evident growth in reasonableness and freedom. In Christianity the fetters of Judaism are snapped, and its unintelligible features are explained. As Augustine said, "In the epoch of the old covenant the new lay latent, as a fruit does in a root," or, in the language of more modern times, we may say, the New Testament sacrifices are antitypes of those of the Old. In a word, judged by the definition of final cause, Christianity is the final cause of Judaism.

F. The Literature of the Levitical Sacrifices.

From the voluminous literature upon the Levitical sacrifices the following treatises are selected as of especial importance :—

I. Biblical Dictionaries and Cyclopædias. See the relative articles in Herzog, 'Realencyklopädie;' Riehm, 'Handwörterbuch des Biblischen Alterthums;' Smith, 'Dictionary of the Bible;' Winer, 'Biblisches Real-Wörterbuch.'

II. Commentaries. Baumgarten, 'Theologischer Commentar zum Pentateuch,' two vols., Kiel, 1843, 1844; Hirsch, 'Der Pentateuch Uebersetzt und Erklart,' Frankfort, 1878, five vols. (valuable for its rabbinic lore); Joule, 'Notes on Leviticus,' London, 1879; Kalisch, 'Leviticus,' especially Essay A, London, 1867; Knobel, 'Exodus und Leviticus,' 1857 (a second edition, edited by Dillmann, which is almost a new work, was issued last year).

III. Biblical Archæology and Theology. De Wette, 'Lehrbuch der Hebr-

Jüdischen Archäologie,' 4th edit., Leipsig, 1864; Ewald, 'Die Alterthümer des Volkes Israel,' 3rd edit., Göttingen, 1866 (English translation, 1876); 'Die Lehre der Bibel von Gott, oder Theologie des Alten und Neuen Bundes,' four vols., Leipsig, 1871—1875; Fairbairn, 'The Typology of Scripture,' two vols., 5th edit., 1870; Hofmann, 'Der Schriftbeweis,' 2nd edit., three vols., Nördlingen, 1857; Hoffmann, 'Abhandlungen über die Pentateuch-Gesetze,' Berlin, 1878 (valuable for its acquaintance with the synagogal literature); Jatho, 'Blicke in die Bedeutung des Mosaischen Cultus,' Hildesheim, 1876; Keil, 'Handbuch der Biblischen Archäologie,' 1st half, 1st edit., 1858, 2nd edit., 1875; Kliefoth, 'Liturgische Abhandlungen,' vol. iv., 2nd edit., 1858; Litton, 'The Mosaic Dispensation,' the Bampton Lecture for 1856; Lowman, 'Rationale of the Ritual of the Hebrew Worship,' London, 1748; Maurice, 'The Doctrine of Sacrifice,' new edit., London, 1879; Oehler, 'Theologie des Alten Testament,' vol. i., Tübingen, 1873 (translated into English, 1875); Saalschütz, 'Archäologie der Hebräer,' two vols., 1855, 1856; Salvador, 'Histoire des Institutions de Möise et du Peuple Hébreu,' two vols., 3rd edit., Paris, 1862; Schäfer, 'Die Religiösen Alterthümer der Bibel,' Münster, 1878; Schultz, 'Alttestamentliche Theologie,' vol. i., Frankfürt, 1869 (2nd edit., adapting results to the hypothesis of Graf and Kuenen, 1878); Steudel, 'Vorlesungen über die Theologie des Alten Testament,' Berlin, 1840; Spencer, 'De Legibus Hebræorum et earum Rationibus,' 1st edit., 1685; Tholuck, 'Das Alte Testament im Neuen Testament,' Gotha, 6th edit., 1868; Umbreit, 'Die Sünde, Beitrag zur Theologie des Alten Testament,' Gotha, 1853.

IV. Monographs on the Levitical Sacrifices. Bähr, 'Symbolik des Mosaischen Cultus,' in two vols., Heidelberg, 1837 (the first volume of a second and largely altered edition was issued at the close of 1875, but upon the doctrine of sacrifice all that has appeared is in the first edition); Hengstenberg, 'Die Opfer der Heiligen Schrift,' Berlin, 1859 (translated as an Appendix to his 'Commentary on Ecclesiastes,' in the Foreign Theological Library); Kurtz, 'Der Alttestamentliche Opfercultus,' Mittau, 1862 (translated in Foreign Theological Library); Outram, 'De Sacrificiis,' 1st edit., London, 1677 (translated into English, 1817); Stöckl, 'Liturgie und Dogmatische Bedeutung der Alttest. Opfer, Insbesondere in ihren Verhaltnisse zur Neutest. Opfertheorie,' 1848; Wangemann, 'Das Opfer nach Lehre des Heiligen Schrift,' two vols., Berlin, 1866.

V. Review Articles on the Levitical Sacrifices. De Chareney, 'Fragments sur la Symbolique Hébraique,' in the *Revue de Linguistique*, April, 1879; Listov, 'Was Bedeutet im Mos. Cultus das Versöhnen,' in the *Theological Tidskrift*, 1878; Mannheimer, 'Der Mosaismus im Gegensatz zum Œgyptenthum,' *Jüdisches Literaturblatt*, 1878; Marbach, 'Das Blut, eine Theologische Studie,' in *Hilgenfeld's Zeitschrift für Wissenschaftliche Theologie*, 1866; Neumann, 'Die Opfer des Alten Bundes,' in the *Deutsche Zeitschrift für Christl. Wissenschaft*, 1852, 1853, and 1857; Park, 'The Divine Institution of Sacrifice,' in the *Bibliotheca Sacra*, January, 1876; Riehm, 'Der Begriff der Sühne im Alten Testament,' in the *Studien und Kritiken*, 1877.

VI. Monographs on Related Themes. Auber, 'Histoire et Théorie du Symbolisme Réligieuse,' four vols., Paris, 1872; Ebrard, 'Die Lehre von der Stellvertretenden Genugthuung in der Heiligen Schrift Begründet,' Königsberg, 1856; Klaiber, 'Die Neutest. Lehre von der Sünde und Erlösung,' Stuttgart, 1836; Küper, 'Das Priesterthum des Alten Bundes,' Berlin, 1866.

VII. Jewish and Talmudic Literature. The tractates 'Sebachim' and 'Menachoth;' Ugolino, 'Thesaurus Antiquitatum Sacrarum.' The writings of Philo, especially the 'De Victimis' and the 'De Victimas Offerentibus.' Numerous extracts in Buxtorf, 'Lexicon Chaldaicum et Talmudicum;' Godwyn, 'Moses and Aaron;' Carpzov, 'Apparatus Criticus;' the works of Lightfoot, especially his 'Temple Service in the Days of our Saviour;' and Reland, 'Antiquitates Sacræ.' The commentary upon Leviticus of Raschi, edited by Berliner, 1866, and Schlossberg's 'Sifra,' 1862.

For a brief statement and criticism of the several schools of interpretation, the reader is referred to the chapter upon the Theories of the Old Testament Sacrifices reviewed in my work on Sacrifice.

THE BOOK OF LEVITICUS

INTRODUCTION

1. SUBJECT OF THE BOOK

LEVITICUS forms the centre and nucleus of the five books of Moses. Closely attached to it are the two Books of Exodus and Numbers, and outside of them, on either side, stand Genesis and Deuteronomy. The subject of the Book of Leviticus is the Sinaitic legislation, from the time that the tabernacle was erected. It does not, however, comprise the whole of that legislation. There is an overflow of it into the Book of Numbers, which thus contains the laws on the Levites and their service (Numb. i. 49—53; iii. 5—15, 40—48; iv. 1—33; viii. 5—26); on the order in which the tribes were to encamp (Numb. ii. 1—31); on the removal of the unclean from the camp (Numb. v. 2—4); on the trial of jealousy (Numb. v. 11—31); on the Nazarites (Numb. vi. 1—21); on the form of blessing the people (Numb. vi. 23—27); on the second month's Passover (Numb. ix. 6—12); on the silver trumpets (Numb. x. 1—10); besides a repetition of the laws on restitution (Numb. v. 6—10); on the lighting of the lamps (Numb. viii. 2—4); on the Passover (Numb. ix. 1—5). With these exceptions, the Book of Leviticus contains the whole of the legislation delivered in the district of Mount Sinai, during the month and twenty days which elapsed between the setting up of the tabernacle on the first day of the second year after quitting Egypt, and the commencement of the march from Sinai on the twentieth day of the second month of the same year. But while this was the whole of the Sinaitic legislation " out of the tabernacle," there were also laws given on Mount Sinai itself during the last nine months of the first year of the march from Egypt, which are recounted in Exod. xix.—xl. While, therefore, Leviticus is very closely connected with the early part of Numbers on one side, it is very closely connected with the latter part of Exodus on the other.

ANALYSIS OF ITS CONTENTS.

The book naturally falls into five divisions. The first part is on sacrifice; the second part records the establishment of an hereditary priesthood; the third deals with the question of uncleanness, ceremonial and moral; the fourth enumerates the holy days and seasons. The book ends with a fifth part, consisting of an exhortation to obedience, and there is attached to it an appendix on vows. The following is a more detailed sketch of the contents.

§ 1. *Sacrifice.*

A question is often asked whether the idea underlying Jewish sacrifice is (1) that of a gift to God, the Giver of all good things, by man, the grateful receiver of his gifts; or (2) that of appeasing and satisfying the justice of an averted Deity; or (3) that of symbolically manifesting full submission to his will; or (4) that of exhibiting a sense of union between God and his people. And this question cannot be answered until the different sacrifices have been distinguished from one another. For each of these ideas is represented by one or other of the sacrifices—the first by the meat offering, the second by the sin offering and trespass offering, the third by the burnt offering, the fourth by the peace offering. If the question be, Which of these was the primary idea of Hebrew sacrifice? we may probably say that it was that of symbolical self-surrender or submission in token of perfect loyalty of heart; for the burnt sacrifice, with which the meat offering is essentially allied appears to have been the most ancient of the sacrifices; and this is the thought embodied in the combined burnt and meat offering. But while this is the special idea of the burnt sacrifice, it is not the only idea of it. It contains within itself in a minor degree the ideas of atonement (ch. i. 4) and of peace (ch. i. 9, 13, 17). Thus it is the most complex as well as the oldest form of sacrifice. If we had no historical information to guide us (as we have Gen. iv. 4), we might reasonably argue from this very complexity to the greater antiquity of the burnt and meat offerings. Symbolism first embodies a large idea in an institution, and it then distinguishes the institution into different species or parts in order to represent as a primary notion one or other of the ideas only secondarily expressed or suggested in the original institution. The sin and trespass offerings, therefore, would naturally spring, or, we may say, be divided off, from the burnt and meat offerings, when men wanted to accentuate the idea of the necessity of reconciliation and atonement; and the peace offering, when they wished to express the joy felt by those who were conscious that their reconciliation had been effected.

The sacrifice of Cain and Abel appears to have been a thanksgiving offering of the firstfruits of the produce of the land and of the cattle, presented to the Lord as a token of recognition of him as the Lord and Giver of all. It is called by the name of *minchah*—a word afterwards confined in its signification to the meat offering—and it partook of the character of the meat offering, the burnt offering, and the peace offering (Gen. iv. 3, 4). Noah's sacrifices were burnt offerings (Gen. viii. 20); and this was the general character of subsequent offerings, though something of the nature of peace offerings is indicated by Moses when he distinguishes "sacrifices" from "burnt offerings," in addressing Pharaoh before the departure of the Israelites from Egypt (Exod. x. 25). The full idea of sacrifice, contained implicitly in the previous sacrifices, was first developed and exhibited in an explicit form by the Levitical regulations and institutions, which distinguish burnt offerings, meat offerings, peace offerings, sin offerings, and trespass offerings; and the special significations of these several sacrifices have to be combined once more, in order to arrive at the original, but at first less clearly defined, notion of the institution, and to constitute an adequate type of that which was the one Antitype of them all.

The typical character of sacrifices must not be confounded with their symbolical character. While they symbolize the need of reconciliation (sin and trespass offerings), of loyal submission (burnt and meat offerings), and of peace (peace offering), they are the type of the one Sacrifice of Christ, in which perfect submission was yielded (burnt offering) and exhibited (meat offering) by man to God; by which reconciliation between God and man were wrought by means of atonement (sin offering) and satisfaction (trespass offering); and through which the peace effected between God and man was set forth (peace offering). (See Notes and Homiletics on chs. i.—vii.)

The Section, or Part, on sacrifice, consists of chs. i.—vii.

Ch. i. contains the law of the burnt offering.
Ch. ii.   ,,   ,,   meat offering.
Ch. iii.   ,,   ,,   peace offering.
Chs. iv., v. 1—13   ,,   sin offering.
Chs. v. 14—35; vi. 1—7 ,,   trespass offering.

The following chapter and a half contain more definite instructions as to the ritual of the sacrifices, addressed particularly to the priests, namely—

Ch. vi. 8—13. The ritual of the burnt offering.
  ,,   14—23.   ,,   ,,   meat offering, and in particular of the priests' meat offering at their consecration.
  ,,   24—30. The ritual of the sin offering.
Ch. vii. 1—10.   ,,   ,,   trespass offering.
  ,,   11—21; 28—34   ,,   peace offering.
  ,,   22—27 contain a prohibition of eating the fat and the blood.
  ,,   35—38 form the conclusion of Part I.

§ 2. *Priesthood.*

The primary idea of a priest is that of a man who performs some function in behalf of men towards God which would not be equally acceptable by God if performed by themselves, and through whom God bestows graces upon men. The first priests were the heads of a family, as Noah; then the heads of a tribe, as Abraham; then the heads of a combination of tribes or of a nation, such as Jethro (Exod. ii. 16), Melchizedek (Gen. xiv. 18), Balak (Numb. xxii. 40). In many countries this combination of the highest secular and ecclesiastical office continued to be maintained—for example, in Egypt; but among the Israelites a sharp line of separation between them was drawn by the appointment of Aaron and his sons to the priesthood.

Priesthood and sacrifice are not originally correlative. A man who acts in behalf of others towards God, whether by making known to him their wants or interceding for them, is thereby a priest; and again, a man who acts in behalf of God towards man, by declaring to them his will and conveying to them his blessing, is thereby a priest. Sacrifice being one means, and at a particular time the chief means, of "calling upon" or approaching God and of receiving graces at his hands, it naturally fell to the priest to perform it as one of his functions, and by degrees it came to be regarded as his special function, and yet never in so exclusive a manner as to shut out the functions of benediction and intercession. The man through whose action, sacramental or otherwise, God's graces are derived to man, and man's needs are presented to God, is, by that action, a priest of God. To suppose that sacrifice, and in particular the sacrifice of animals, is necessary for either one or the other of the priestly functions, is to narrow the idea of priesthood in an unjustifiable manner.

When so complex a system as that of the Levitical sacrifices had been instituted, the appointment of an hereditary priesthood became necessary. And this appointment took away from the heads of families and the tribe leaders the old priestly rights which up to that time they had maintained, and which we see to have been exercised by Moses. We cannot doubt that this abolition of their ancient privileges must have been resented by many of the elder generation, and we find that it was necessary to enforce the new discipline by a strict injunction, forbidding sacrifices to be offered elsewhere than in the court of the tabernacle, and by other hands than those of the hereditary priesthood (see Notes and Homiletics on chs. viii.—x. and xviii.).

The Section, or Part, on the priesthood consists of chs. viii.—x.

Ch. viii. contains the ceremonies of the consecration of Aaron and his sons.
Ch. ix. recounts their first priestly offerings and benediction.
Ch. x. contains the account of the death of Nadab and Abihu, and the law against drinking wine while ministering to the Lord.

These three chapters constitute Part II.

§ 3. *Uncleanness and its Removal.*

Offences are of two kinds, ceremonial and moral; the former must be purged by purifying rites, the latter by punishment. A ceremonial offence is committed by incurring legal uncleanness, and this is done (1) by eating unclean food or touching unclean bodies (ch. xi.), (2) by childbirth (ch. xii.), (3) by leprosy (chs. xiii., xiv.), (4) by issues (ch. xv.); whoever offended in any of these ways had to purge his offence—in light cases by washing, in grave cases by sacrifice.

Moral offences are committed by transgressing God's moral law, whether written on the human heart or in his Law. The list of these offences commences with an enumeration of unlawful marriages and lusts (ch. xviii.), to which are added other sins and crimes (ch. xix.). They must not be allowed to go unpunished; else they bring the wrath of God upon the nation. The penalties differ according to the heinousness of the offence, but if they are not exacted, the guilt passes to the community. Yet a certain concession to human frailty is allowed. Moral offences differ in their character, according as they are committed with a determinate resolution to offend, or have arisen from inadvertence or moral weakness. It is for the former class that punishment, either at the hands of man or of God, is a necessity. The latter are regarded more leniently, and may be atoned for by a trespass offering, after the wrong inflicted by them on others has been compensated.

But after every purification for ceremonial and inadvertent moral faults has been made, and all penalties for presumptuous sins and crimes have been duly exacted, there will remain a residue of unatoned-for evil, and for the removal of this the ceremonial of the great Day of Atonement is instituted (see Notes and Homiletics on chs. xi.—xxii.).

The Section, or Part, on uncleanness and its " putting away," contained in chs. xi.—xxii., consists of four divisions: chs. xi.—xv.; chs. xvi., xvii.; chs. xviii.—xx.; and chs. xxi., xxii. The first division has to do with ceremonial uncleanness, arising from four specified causes, and its purification; the second with general uncleanness and its purification on the Day of Atonement; the third with moral uncleanness and its punishment; the fourth with the ceremonial and moral uncleanness of priests, and their physical disqualifications.

First division: Ch. xi. Uncleanness derived from eating or touching unclean flesh, whether of beasts, fishes, birds, insects, or vermin.

Ch. xii. Uncleanness derived from the concomitants of childbirth, and its purification.

Chs. xiii., xiv. Uncleanness accruing from leprosy to men, clothes, and houses, and its purification.

Ch. xv. Uncleanness derived from various issues of the body, and its purification.

Second division: Ch. xvi. General uncleanness of the congregation and of the tabernacle, and its purification by the ceremonies of the Day of Atonement.

Ch. xvii. Corollary to all the preceding part of the book. That sacrifices (chs. i.—viii.), which are the means of purification (chs. xi.—xvi.), are, since the institution of the hereditary priesthood (chs. viii.—x.), to be only offered at the door of the tabernacle.

Third division: Ch. xviii. Moral uncleanness connected with marriage forbidden.

Ch. xix. Other moral uncleanness forbidden.

Ch. xx. Penalties for moral uncleanness, and exhortation to holiness.

Fourth division: Chs. xxi., xxii. 1—16. Ceremonial and moral cleanness required in an extra degree in priests, and freedom from physical blemish.

Ch. xxii. 17—33. Freedom from blemish and from imperfection required in sacrifices.

These chapters constitute Part III.

§ 4. *Holy Days and Seasons.*

The weekly holy day was the sabbath. The injunction to observe it was coeval with the origin of mankind. It kept in mind the rest of God after his creative work, and foreshadowed the rest of Christ after his redeeming work. It anticipated the rest of his people in Canaan, and the further rest of the Christian dispensation, and the still further rest of paradise.

The monthly holy days were the new moons on the first day of each month; among which the new moon of the seventh month held a sevenfold sanctity, and was also observed as the New Year's Day of the civil year, being sometimes inexactly called the Feast of Trumpets.

The yearly holy days began in the first month with the festival of the Passover, to which was closely attached that of Unleavened Bread. These two festivals, united into one, represented historically the fact of Israel's deliverance from the bondage of Egypt, and typically they represented the future deliverance of the spiritual Israel from the bondage of sin, both at the first and at the second coming of Christ. The lamb, the exhibition of whose blood delivered from destruction, was a type of Christ. The festival served also as the spring harvest feast of the year.

The Feast of Pentecost, or the Feast of Weeks, observed seven weeks after the Passover, was the second or summer harvest festival. It might possibly have commemorated the gift of the Law at Sinai: it certainly was the day on which was instituted the new Law in Jerusalem (Acts ii.).

The fast of the Day of Atonement, observed on the tenth day of the seventh month, symbolically represented the removal of the sins of the world by Christ, at once the Sacrifice for sin offered on the cross (the sacrificed goat), and the Deliverer from the consciousness of the power of sin (the scapegoat). It also typified the entry of Christ into heaven in the character of our Great High Priest, with the virtue of his blood of Atonement, there to abide as the prevailing Mediator and Intercessor for his people.

The Feast of Tabernacles, celebrated for a week beginning on the fifteenth day of the seventh month, was the last and most joyous harvest-home festival of the year. Historically, it looked back to the day of joy when, safe in their booths at Succoth, the children of Israel felt the happiness of the freedom from Egyptian bondage which they had at last attained (Exod. xii. 37); and it looked forward to the period of peaceful enjoyment which was to come with the institution of Christ's kingdom on earth, and beyond that time, to the glories of the Church triumphant in heaven.

The sabbatical year, which required that every seventh year should be a year free from agricultural toil, enforced on a large scale the teaching of the sabbath, and it taught the lesson afterwards illustrated in the contrast of the lives of Mary and Martha (Luke x. 38—42), and the duty of trusting to the providence of God.

The jubilee, which restored all things that had been changed or depraved to their original state every fifty years, while it served as a means of preserving the commonwealth from confusion and revolution, foreshadowed the Christian dispensation, and after that the final restitution of all things (see Notes and Homiletics on chs. xxiii.—xxv.).

The Section, or Part, on holy days and seasons comprises chs. xxiii.—xxv.

Ch. xxiii.   The sacred days on which holy convocations are to be held.

Ch. xxiv.   Parenthetical. On the oil for the lamps, and the shewbread, and on blasphemy.

Ch. xxv.   The sabbatical year and the jubilee.

§ 5. *Final Exhortation.*

Many of the laws in the Book of Leviticus are without the sanction of any penalty. They are commanded, and therefore they ought to be obeyed. In place of a regular code of penalties for individual transgressions, and in addition to the penalties already declared, Moses pronounces blessing and cursing on the nation at large, according as it obeys or disobeys the Law. The rewards and punishments of a future life have no place here, as nations have no future existence. Twice in the Book of Deuteronomy Moses introduces similar exhortations (chs. xi., xxviii.). As a matter of history, we find that as long as the nation was, as such, loyal to Jehovah, it prospered, and that when it fell away from him the evils here denounced overtook it.

The exhortation is contained in ch. xxvi.

§ 6. *Appendix—Vows.*

The subject of vows is not introduced into the body of the book, because it was not the purpose of the legislation to institute them or to encourage them. At the conclusion a short treatise is added, giving no special approbation of them, but regulating them, if made, and appointing a scale of redemption or commutation.

This appendix occupies the last chapter—ch. xxvii.—being attached to the rest by a final declaration that it belongs to the Sinaitic legislation.

2. AUTHORSHIP AND DATE.

The question of authorship does not properly arise on this book. Whatever may be said of Genesis and Deuteronomy, the second, third, and fourth of the books of Moses stand or fall together, nor is there anything in the Book of Leviticus to separate it in respect to authenticity from Exodus which precedes, and Numbers which follows it. There is only one passage in it which can be regarded as seeming to indicate an author of later date than Moses. This is the following passage: "That the land spue not you out also, when ye defile it, as it spued out the nations that were before you" (ch. xviii. 28). It has been argued with some plausibility that, as Canaan had not spued out its inhabitants till after the death of Moses, these words must have been written by some one who lived later than Moses. But an examination of the context takes away all the force of this argument. The eighteenth chapter is directed against incestuous marriages and lusts; and, after the lawgiver has ended his prohibitions, he proceeds: "Defile not ye yourselves in any of these things: for in all these the nations are defiled which I cast out before you: and the land is defiled: therefore I do visit the iniquity thereof upon it, and the

land itself vomiteth out her inhabitants. Ye shall therefore keep my
statutes and my judgments, and shall not commit any of these abominations; neither any of your own nation, nor any stranger that sojourneth
among you: (for all these abominations have the men of the land done
which were before you, and the land is defiled;) that the land spue not you
out also, when ye defile it, as it spued out the nations that were before
you." In this passage, the words translated "vomiteth" and "spued" are
in the same tense. It is that tense which is ordinarily called a perfect.
But this so-called perfect does not necessarily indicate a past time. Indeed,
the Hebrew tenses do not, as such, express time, but only (when in the
active voice) action. We must look to the context in order to discover
the time in which the act takes place, took place, or will take place. In
the passage before us the words, "I cast out," in ver. 24 are expressed by a
participle, "used of that which is certainly and speedily coming to pass"
(Keil), meaning, "I am casting out;" and by a law of the Hebrew
language, as this participle and the rest of the context indicate present
time, the two verbs under consideration must indicate present time also.
Even if we were compelled to translate the two words as perfects, there
would be nothing impossible or unnatural in God's saying to Moses, and to
the children of Israel through him, that the land "has vomited," or "has
spued out," the nations of Canaan, the act being regarded as in the Divine
mind done, because determined on and in the course of immediate accomplishment. Or, still again, the land might be said to "have spued out"
the nations of Canaan in relation to the time when it should spue out the
degenerate Israelites.

Putting aside this passage, so easily explained, there is nothing in the
whole book which is incompatible with the authorship and the date of
Moses. This being so, the fact that it has come down to us as the work
of Moses, and that it by implication professes itself to be the work of
Moses, and that its character and language are, so far as we can judge,
such as would be in accordance with a work of Moses, leave the hypothesis
of the authorship of Moses as certain, on the score of internal evidence, as
any such hypothesis can be. Nor is there wanting any external evidence
which could be expected to exist. The Book of Joshua recognizes the
existence of "the Book of the Law of Moses" (Josh. xxii. 6; cf. i. 8; viii.
31—35). In the Book of Judges there is an apparent reference to Lev.
xxvi. 16, 17, in ch. ii. 15 ("Whithersoever they went out, the hand of the
Lord was against them for evil, as the Lord had said, and as the Lord had
sworn unto them"); and in ch. iii. 4 we find mention of "the commandments of the Lord, which he commanded their fathers by the hand of
Moses." In the Book of Judges, "the sacred character of the Levites,
their dispersion among the several tribes, the settlement of the high
priesthood in the family of Aaron, the existence of the ark of the covenant,
the power of inquiring of God and obtaining answers, the irrevocability of
a vow, the distinguishing mark of circumcision, the distinction between

clean and unclean meats, the law of the Nazarites, the use of burnt offerings and peace offerings, the employment of trumpets as a means of obtaining Divine aid in war, the impiety of setting up a king," are enumerated by Canon Rawlinson as "severally acknowledged, and constituting together very good evidence that the Mosaic ceremonial law was already in force" ('Aids to Faith: The Pentateuch,' London, 1862). In the Book of Samuel, "we meet at once with Eli, the high priest of the house of Aaron, . . . the lamp burns in the tabernacle, . . . the ark of the covenant is in the sanctuary, and is esteemed the sacred symbol of the presence of God (1 Sam. iv. 3, 4, 18, 21, 22; v. 3, 4, 6, 7; vi. 19) . . . there is the altar and the incense and the ephod worn by the high priest (1 Sam. ii. 28). The various kinds of Mosaic sacrifices are referred to : the burnt offering (*olah*, 1 Sam. x. 8; xiii. 9; xv. 22), the peace offerings (*shelamim*, 1 Sam. x. 8; xi. 15; xiii. 9), the bloody sacrifice (*zebach*, 1 Sam. ii. 19), and the unbloody offering (*minchah*, 1 Sam. ii. 19; iii. 14; xxvi. 19). The animals offered in sacrifice—the bullock (1 Sam. xxiv. 25), the lamb (1 Sam. xvi. 2), and the ram (1 Sam. xv. 22)—are those prescribed in the Levitical code. The especial customs of the sacrifices alluded to in 1 Sam. ii. 13 were those prescribed in Lev. vi. 6, 7; Numb. xviii. 8—xix. 25, 32; Deut. xviii. 1, *sqq*." (Bishop Harold Browne, 'Introduction to the Pentateuch,' in 'The Speaker's Commentary'). In the Books of Kings and Chronicles there are frequent allusions or references to the "Law of Moses" and its enactments (see 1 Kings ii. 3; viii. 9, 53; 2 Kings vii. 3; xi. 12; xxii. 8; xxiii. 3, 25; 1 Chron. xvi. 40; xxii. 12, 13; 2 Chron. xxv. 4; xxxiii. 8; xxxiv. 14). So too in Ezra and Nehemiah (see Ezra iii. 2—6; vi. 18; vii. 6; Neh. i. 7—9; vii. 1—18; ix. 14); and in Daniel (see Dan. ix. 11—13). Amos (ii. 7) apparently quotes Lev. xx. 3; Hosea (iv. 10) seems to quote Lev. xxvi. 26. Joel, the earliest of the prophets of the southern kingdom, implies throughout his prophecy the existence of the Levitical system, and he and Ezekiel appear to have undoubtedly had before them the twenty-sixth chapter of Leviticus (Joel i. 13, 14, 16; ii. 1, 14—27; Ezek. xxxiv. 25—31). The New Testament assumes throughout the Mosaic original of the whole Pentateuch.

Taking the authorship of Moses as proved, we have further to inquire as to the date of his composition of the book. On this point we cannot speak with certainty, but we may regard it as in the highest degree probable that the laws were written down as they were delivered to and by Moses during the fifty days previous to the departure of the children of Israel from Sinai, and that they were subsequently put together during one of the encampments in the wilderness.

3. LITERATURE.

The literature on Leviticus is very extensive, and belongs for the most part to two classes—commentaries on the Pentateuch with their introductions, and special dissertations on one or other of the subjects with which the Book of Leviticus deals. We make a selection of works under both headings.

To the first class belong Origen, 'Selecta in Levit.,' 'Hom. in Levit.' (Op., tom. ii.

p. 180, edit. Delarue); St. Augustine, 'Quæstiones in Heptateuchum,' Liber Tertius (Op., tom. iii. p. 674, edit. Migne); Theodoret, 'Quæstiones in Levit.' (Op., tom. i. p. 114, edit. Sirmond); Cyril of Alexandria, 'Glaphyra in Libros Mosis;' Bede, 'In Pentateuchum Commentarii—Leviticus' (Op., tom. ii. p. 334, edit. Migne); Calvin, 'Commentarii in Quatuor Mosis Libros' (Op., tom. i. p. 248, Amsterdam, 1671); 'Poli Synopsis Criticorum' (tom. i. p. 510, London, 1669); 'Critici Sacri' (vol. ii., Amsterdam, 1698); Clericus (Le Clerc), 'Mosis Prophetæ, Lib. IV.' (vol. i. p. 207, Amsterdam, 1710); Carpzov, 'Introductio ad Libros Veteris Testamenti: De Levitico' (p. 100, Leipsig, 1727); Matthew Henry, 'Commentary' (vol. i., 1737); Rosenmüller, 'Scholia' (Leipsig, 1824); Hävernick, 'Handbuch der Historisch-Kritischen Einleitung in das Alte Testament: Leviticus,' §§ 117—130 (Erlangen, 1836), and (a part of the above) his 'Introduction to the Pentateuch' (published by T. and T. Clark, Edinburgh, 1850); Hengstenberg, 'On the Pentateuch' (translated by Ryland, Edinburgh, 1847); Keil and Delitzsch, 'On the Pentateuch' (translated by Martin, vol. ii., T. and T. Clark, Edinburgh, 1878); Stuart, 'Introduction to the Old Testament;' Bush, 'Commentaries on the Five Books of Moses;' Baylee, 'Course of Biblical Instruction' (vol. i., St. Aidan's, 1865); Wordsworth, 'Commentary' (part ii., London, 1865); Harold Browne, 'Introduction to the Pentateuch' (in the 'Speaker's Commentary,' vol. i., London, 1871); Clark, 'Introduction to and Notes on Leviticus' (ibid.); Bonar, 'Commentary on Leviticus' (London, 1875); Lange, 'Commentary' (vol. ii., edit. Schaff, published by T. and T. Clark, Edinburgh); Blunt, 'Annotated Bible' (vol. i., London, 1878).

Under the second heading come Mede, 'The Christian Sacrifice, Book 2' (vol. i., London, 1664); Outram, 'De Sacrificiis' (London, 1677: English translation, London, 1817); Lightfoot, 'The Temple Service as in the Days of Our Saviour' (vol. i., London, 1684); Spencer, 'De Legibus Hebræorum' (Cambridge, 1727); J. Mayer, 'De Temporibus Sanctis et Festis Diebus Hebræorum' (Amsterdam, 1724); Deyling, 'Observationes Sacræ' (Leipsig, 1735); Bähr, 'Die Symbolik des Mosaischen Cultus' (Heidelberg, 1837); Davison, 'Inquiry into Primitive Sacrifice' (in his 'Remains,' Oxford, 1840); Tholuck, 'Das Alte Testament im Neuen Testament (Hamburg, 1849); Johnstone, 'Israel after the Flesh' (London, 1850); Maurice, 'The Doctrine of Sacrifice deduced from Scripture' (Cambridge, 1854); Fairbairn, 'The Typology of Scripture' (Edinburgh, 1854); Freeman, 'Principles of Divine Service' (London, 1855); Hengstenberg, 'Die Opfer der Heiligen Schrift' (Berlin, 1859); Kurtz, 'Der Alttestamentliche Opfercultus' (Mittau, 1864); Barry, Articles on 'Sacrifice' (in Smith's 'Dictionary of the Bible,' London, 1860); Rawlinson, Essay on 'The Pentateuch' (in 'Aids to Faith,' London, 1862); Kuepfer, 'Das Priestenthum des Alten Bundes,' 1865; Ebers, 'Egypten und die Bücher Moses' (Leipsig, 1868); Jukes, 'Law of Offerings;' Marriott, 'On Terms of Gift and Offering' (in his 'Memorials,' London, 1872); Edersheim, 'The Temple Service;' Willis, 'The Worship of the Old Covenant' (Oxford, 1880).

Philo Judæus (Op., Frankfort, 1691), and the Mishna (Surenhus. Amsterdam, 1688), should also be consulted.

THE
BOOK OF LEVITICUS

—◆—

PART I

THE LAWS AND REGULATIONS RESPECTING SACRIFICES

EXPOSITION

CHAPTER I.

THE SACRIFICES (chs. i.—vii.). There are five classes of sacrifices instituted or regulated in the first seven chapters of Leviticus, each of which has its special signification—the burnt offering, the meat offering, the sin offering, the trespass offering, and the peace offering. The burnt offering, in which the whole of the victim was consumed in the fire on God's altar, signifies entire self-surrender on the part of the offerer; the meat offering, a loyal acknowledgment of God's sovereignty; the sin offering, propitiation of wrath in him to whom the offering is made, and expiation of sin in the offerer; the trespass offering, satisfaction for sin; the peace offering, union and communion between the offerer and him to whom the offering is made.

The burnt offering (ch. i.) typifies the perfect surrender of himself, made by the Lord Jesus Christ, and exhibited by his life and death on earth; and it teaches the duty of self-sacrifice on the part of man.

Ver. 1.—**And the LORD called unto Moses.** The first word of the verse, in the original *Vayikra*, meaning "and called," has been taken as the designation of the book in the Hebrew Bible. The title Leviticon, or Leviticus, was first adopted by the LXX., to indicate that it had for its main subject the duties and functions appertaining to the chief house of the priestly tribe of Levi. The word "and" connects the third with the second book of the Pentateuch. God is spoken of in this and in the next book almost exclusively under the appellation of "the LORD" or "Jehovah," the word "Elohim" being, however, used sufficiently often to identify the two names. Cf. ch. ii. 13, xix. 12. **And spake unto him.** The manner in which God ordinarily communicated with a prophet was by "a vision" or "in a dream;" but this was not the case with Moses; "My servant Moses is not so, who is faithful in all mine house; with him will I speak mouth to mouth, even apparently" (Numb. xii. 8). The Levitical code of laws, therefore, was delivered to Moses in his ordinary mental state, not in trance, or dream, or ecstasy. **Out of the tabernacle of the congregation.** The tabernacle had just been set up by Moses (Exod. xl. 16). It derives its name *of the congregation*, or rather *of meeting*, from being the place where God met the representatives of his people (see Numb. xvi. 42). Hitherto God had spoken from the mount, now he speaks from the mercy-seat of the ark in the tabernacle. He had symbolically drawn near to his people, and the sacrificial system is now instituted as the means by which they should draw nigh to him. All the laws in the Book of Leviticus, and in the first ten chapters of the Book of

Numbers, were given during the fifty days which intervened between the setting up of the tabernacle (Exod. xl. 17) and the departure of the children of Israel from the neighbourhood of Mount Sinai (Numb. x. 11).

Ver 2.—**If any man of you bring.** Sacrifices are not now being instituted for the first time. Burnt offerings at least, if not peace offerings, had existed since the time of the Fall. The Levitical law lays down regulations adapting an already existing practice for the use of the Israelitish nation; it begins, therefore, not with a command, "Thou shalt bring," but, *if any man of you* (according to custom) *bring.* Any member of the congregation might bring his voluntary offering when he would. The times at which the public offerings were to be made, and their number, are afterwards designated. **An offering.** This verse is introductory to the ensuing chapters, and speaks of "offerings" in general. "Korban," which is the word here used for "offering," derived from *karab*, meaning "to draw near for the sake of presentation," is the generic name including all offerings and sacrifices. It is used in speaking of animal sacrifices of various kinds, including peace offerings and sin offerings (ch. iii. 1; iv. 23) and it is applied to vegetable offerings (ch. ii. 1, 13), and to miscellaneous offerings for the service of the tabernacle, such as wagons and oxen, silver vessels for the altar, gold, jewels, etc. (Numb. vii. 3, 10; xxxi. 50). It is translated by the LXX. into Greek by the word δῶρον, equivalent to the Latin *donum*, and our "gift." These offerings are now distinguished into their different kinds.

Ver. 3.—**If his offering be a burnt sacrifice.** The Hebrew term for "burnt sacrifice" is *olah*, meaning "that which ascends;" sometimes *kaleel*, "whole offering," is found (Deut. xxxiii. 10); the LXX. use the word ὁλοκαύτωμα, "whole burnt offering." The conditions to be fulfilled by an Israelite who offered a burnt sacrifice were the following: —1. He must offer either (1) a young bull without blemish, or (2) a young ram, or (3) a young he-goat, or (4) a turtle-dove, or (5) a young pigeon. 2. In case it were a bull, ram, or goat, he must bring it to the door of the tabernacle, that is, the entrance of the court in front of the brazen altar and of the door of the holy place, and there offer or present it. 3. In offering it he must place his hand firmly on its head, as a ceremonial act. 4. He must kill it, either himself or by the agency of a Levite. 5. He must flay it. 6. He must divide it into separate portions. 7. He must wash the intestines and legs. Meantime the priests had their parts to do; they had 1. To catch the blood, to carry it

to the altar, and to strike the inner sides of the altar with it. 2. To arrange the fire on the altar. 3. To place upon the altar the head, and the fat, and the remainder of the animal, for consumption by the fire. 4. To sprinkle or place a meat offering upon them. 5. The next morning, still dressed in their priestly garments, to take the ashes off the altar, and to place them at the east of the altar (ch. vi. 10). 6. To carry them outside the camp to a clean place, the bearer being dressed in his ordinary costume (ch. vi. 11). There were, therefore, four essential parts in the ritual of the burnt offering—the oblation of the victim (vers. 3, 4), the immolation (ver. 5), the oblation of the blood, representing the life (*ibid.*), and the consumption (ver. 9)—the first two to be performed by the offerer, the third by the priest, the fourth by the fire representing the action of God. The moral lesson taught by the burnt offering was the necessity of self-surrender and of devotion to God, even to the extent of yielding up life and the very tenement of life. As the offerer could not give up his own life and body and still live, the life of an animal belonging to him, and valued by him, was substituted for his own; but he knew, and by laying his hand on its head showed that he knew, that it was his own life and his very self that was represented by the animal. The mystical lessons taught to those who could grasp them were —1. The doctrine of substitution or vicarious suffering. 2. The fact that without the shedding of blood there was no acceptance. 3. The need of One who, being very man, should be able to perform an action of perfect surrender of his will and of his life. The fulfilment of the type is found in the perfect submission of Christ as man, throughout his ministry, and especially in the Garden of Gethsemane, and in the offering made by him, as Priest and willing Victim, of his life upon the altar of the cross. The burnt offering is to be **without blemish,** for had not the animal been perfect in its kind, it would not have served its moral, its mystical, or its typical purpose. The word ἄμωμος, used by the LXX. as equivalent to the Hebrew term, is applied to Christ in Heb. ix. 14 and 1 Pet. i. 19; and St. Paul teaches that it is the purpose of God that those who are adopted in Christ should also be "holy and without blemish" (Eph. i. 4). A priest had to certify that the victim was free from all defects. **He shall offer it of his own voluntary will** should rather be translated, *He shall offer it for his own acceptance.* The animal, representing the offerer, was presented by the latter in order that he might be himself accepted by the Lord. This aspect of the offering is brought out more clearly by the *minchah*, or meat offering, which always accompanied the burnt offering. The place where the presentation took place was **the door of the tabernacle,** that is, the space immediately within the eastern entrance into the court of the tabernacle, immediately facing the brazen altar, which stood before the east end of the tabernacle, where was the door or entrance which led into the holy place. "The presenting of the victim at the entrance of the tabernacle was a symbol of the free will submitting itself to the Law of the Lord" (Clarke). Cf. Rom. xii. 1: "I beseech you that ye present your bodies a living sacrifice, holy, acceptable unto God, which is your reasonable service."

Ver. 4.—**And he shall put his hand upon the head of the burnt offering.** This putting, or forcibly leaning, the hand on the victim's head, which is the most essential part of the oblation of the victim, was a symbolical act implying "This animal is now for present purposes myself, and its life is my life." It was this act of identification with the offerer which made it **be accepted for him to make atonement** (literally, *covering*) **for him.** The sin offering is the sacrifice which especially symbolizes and ceremonially effects atonement, but the idea of atonement is not absent from the burnt sacrifice. The aspect under which atonement is presented here and elsewhere in the Old Testament is that of covering. But it is not the sin that is covered, but the sinner. Owing to his sin, the latter is exposed to the wrath of a just God, but something intervenes whereby he is covered, and he ceases, therefore, to attract the Divine anger and punishment. No longer being an object of wrath, he becomes at once an object of benevolence and mercy. The covering provided by a sacrifice is the blood or life of an animal, symbolically representing the offerer's own life freely surrendered by him *for his acceptance,* and typically foreshadowing the blood of Christ.

Ver. 5.—**And he shall kill the bullock.** After having made the presentation, the offerer proceeds to the second part of the sacrifice, the immolation or slaying, which was to be performed **before the Lord,** that is, in front of the tabernacle, on the north side of the brazen altar. Then follows the third part of the sacrifice: **the priests, Aaron's sons, shall bring the blood, and sprinkle the blood round about upon the altar.** The priests caught the blood (sometimes the Levites were allowed to do this, 2 Chron. xxx. 16), and *sprinkled* or rather *threw it round about on the altar,* that is, so as to touch all the inner sides of the altar. "A red line all round the middle of the altar marked that *above* it the blood of sacrifices intended to be eaten, *below* it

that of sacrifices wholly consumed, was to be sprinkled" (Edersheim, 'The Temple'). This was in some respects the most essential part of the ceremony, the blood representing the life (ch. xvii. 11), which was symbolically received at the hands of the offerer, and presented by the priests to God. In the antitype our Lord exercised the function of the sacrificing priest when he presented his own life to the Father, as he hung upon the altar of the cross.

Ver. 6.—**He shall flay the burnt offering.** The hide was given to the priest (ch. vii. 8). The whole of the remainder of the animal was consumed by the fire of the altar; none of it was eaten by the offerer and his friends as in the peace offerings, or even by the ministers of God as in the sin offerings; it was a whole burnt offering. **His pieces,** into which it was to be cut, means the customary pieces.

Ver. 7.—**The priest shall put fire upon the altar.** The fire once kindled was never to be allowed to go out (ch. vi. 13). Unless, therefore, these words refer to the first occasion only on which a burnt sacrifice was offered, they must mean "make up the fire on the altar," or it might possibly have been the practice, as Bishop Wordsworth (after Maimonides) supposes, that fresh fire was added to the altar fire before each sacrifice.

Ver. 8.—**And the priests shall lay the parts, the head, and the fat, in order.** The head and the fat are designated by name, because, with the "pieces," they complete the whole of the animal with the exception of the hide. The *order* in which they were laid is said to have been the same approximately as that which the members held in the living creature.

Ver. 9.—**The priest shall burn all on the altar,** etc. The fourth and last part of the sacrifice. The word employed is not the common term used for destroying by fire, but means "make to ascend." The life of the animal has already been offered in the blood; now the whole of its substance is "made to ascend" to the Lord. Modern science, by showing that the effect of fire upon the substance of a body is to resolve it into gases which rise from it, contributes a new illustration to the verse. The vapour that ascends is not something different from that which is burnt, but the very thing itself, its essence; which, having ascended, is **of a sweet savour unto the Lord,** that is, acceptable and well-pleasing to him. The burnt offering, the meat offering, and the peace offering, are sacrifices of sweet savour (ch. ii. 2; iii. 5); the expression is not used with regard to the sin offering and trespass offering. St. Paul applies it to the sacrifice of Christ, in Eph. v. 2, "As Christ also loved us, and gave himself for us an offering and a sacrifice to

God for a sweet-smelling savour;" thus indicating, in an incidental manner, the connection between the Jewish sacrifices and the sacrifice of Christ, as type and antitype.

Ver. 10.—**If his offering be of the flocks.** The ritual of the burnt offering was the same, whether the victim was a bull, sheep, or goat.

Ver. 11.—**He shall kill it on the side of the altar, northward before the Lord.** In the sacrifice of the bullock it is only "before the Lord" (ver. 5). No doubt the same place is meant in both cases, but it is specified with more exactness here. On the western side of the altar was the tabernacle, on the east side the heap of ashes (ch. i. 16), on the south side probably the ascent to the altar (see Josephus, 'De Bell. Jud.,' v. 5, 6); on the north side, therefore, was the most convenient slaughtering place, and this is probably the reason for the injunction.

Ver. 14.—**If the burnt sacrifice for his offering to the Lord be of fowls.** A comparison of ch. xii. 8 leads us to infer that the permission to offer a bird was a concession to poverty. The pigeon and the turtle-dove were the most easy to procure, as the domestic fowl was at this time unknown to the Hebrews. The first and only allusion in the Bible to the hen occurs in the New Testament (Matt. xxiii. 37; Luke xiii. 34), nor is there any representation of the domestic fowl in ancient Egyptian paintings. The domicile of the bird was still confined to India. A single pigeon or turtle-dove formed a sacrifice, and there was no rule in respect to sex, as there was in the case of the quadrupeds.

Ver. 15.—**The priest shall bring it unto the altar.** The difference in the ritual for the burnt sacrifice of fowls is: 1. That the offerer is not commanded to lay his hand on the bird. 2. That the altar is the place of mactation, instead of the space on the north side of the altar. 3. That the priest slays it instead of the offerer. 4. That the blood (owing to its smaller quantity) is pressed out against the side of the altar instead of being caught in a vessel and thrown on it. There is no essential variation here; the analogy of the sacrifice of the animal is followed so far as circumstances permit. It is not certain that the word *malak*, translated *wring off his head*, means more than "make an incision with the nail;" but in all probability the head was to be severed and laid on the fire separately, after the manner of the other sacrifices.

Ver. 16.—**With his feathers**, rather *the contents of the crop*. This and the ashes are to be placed **beside the altar on the east part**, as being furthest from the tabernacle and nearest to the entrance of the court, so that they might be readily removed.

HOMILETICS.

Vers. 1, 2.—*The sacrificial system.* The religion of Israel, as exhibited to us in the Law, bears at first sight a strange appearance, unlike what we should have expected. We read in it very little about a future life, and not much about repentance, faith, and prayer, but we find commanded an elaborate system of sacrifices, based upon a practice almost coeval with the Fall.

I. SACRIFICE WAS USED IN ANTE-MOSAIC DAYS AS A MEANS OF APPROACH TO GOD. "In process of time it came to pass that Cain brought of the fruit of the ground an offering unto the Lord. And Abel, he also brought of the firstlings of his flock and of the fat thereof" (Gen. iv. 4). The covenant with Noah was made by sacrifice: "And Noah builded an altar unto the Lord, and took of every clean beast and of every clean fowl, and offered burnt offerings on the altar. And the Lord smelled a sweet savour. . . . And God spake unto Noah, and to his sons with him, saying, And I, behold, I establish my covenant with you, and with your seed after you" (Gen. viii. 20, 21; ix. 8, 9). When Abraham first entered Canaan, he "builded an altar unto the Lord who appeared unto him" (Gen. xii. 7), as the means of communicating with him. At his next halting-place, "he builded an altar unto the Lord," as the means of "calling upon the name of the Lord" (Gen. xii. 8; xiii. 4). On removing to Hebron, again he "built there an altar unto the Lord" (Gen. xiii. 18). The covenant with Abraham was made by sacrifice (Gen. xv. 9); and at Jehovah-jireh, Abraham "offered a ram for a burnt offering in the stead of his son" (Gen. xxii. 13). At Beer-sheba Isaac "builded an altar and called upon the name of the Lord" (Gen. xxvi. 25). At Shalem Jacob "erected an altar and called it El-elohe-Israel" (Gen. xxxiii. 20). At Beth-el he "built an altar and called the place El-beth-el" (Gen. xxxv. 7). At Beer-sheba he "offered sacrifices unto the God of his father Isaac" (Gen. xlvi. 1). During the sojourn in Egypt it is probable that the practice of sacrifice was discontinued through fear of giving offence to the religious feelings of the Egyptians (Exod. viii. 26) ; but the idea of sacrifice being the appointed means of serving God was preserved (Exod. v. 3 ; viii. 27). Moses, Aaron, and the elders of Israel took part in a sacrificial meal with Jethro in the wilderness (Exod. xviii. 12). And the covenant made at Sinai was ratified by burnt offerings and peace offerings (Exod. xxiv. 5). Indeed, the Book of Psalms declares the method of entering into covenant with God to be " by sacrifice." " Gather my saints together unto me ; those that have made a covenant with me by sacrifice " (Ps. l. 5). The Christian covenant was thus ratified (Heb. ix. 15), as well as the covenants of Noah, Abraham, and Moses.

II. THERE ARE THREE CLASSES OF SACRIFICES UNDER THE MOSAIC DISPENSATION, ESSENTIALLY DIFFERING IN CHARACTER—

Burnt offerings ;
Peace offerings ;
Sin offerings ;

beside Meat offerings, ordinarily attached to the burnt offerings, and

Trespass offerings, a species of sin offering.

III. WHAT WAS THEIR MEANING. 1. In general, they served, as before, as a means of reconciliation between God and man, as a means of access for man to God. This purpose they fulfilled to all humble-minded men, whether their full meaning was understood or no. To the more spiritually minded they were also a means of instruction in sacred mysteries to be revealed hereafter.

2. Specifically, they each taught their own lesson and brought about, symbolically and ceremonially, each their own effect.

The sin offering taught the need of, and symbolically effected, the propitiation of God's anger and the expiation of man's sin.

The burnt offering taught the lesson of self-surrender, and symbolically effected the surrender of the offerer to God.

The peace offering taught the lesson of the necessity and joyousness of communion between God and man, and symbolically represented that communion as existing between the offerer and God.

IV. WHENCE THEY DERIVED THEIR EFFICACY. Their efficacy was derived from representing and foreshadowing the sacrifice of Christ on the cross, the sin offering typifying the propitiation and expiation once for all there wrought, the burnt offering the perfect self-surrender of the sinless sufferer, the peace offering the reconciliation thereby effected and continued between God and his people.

Vers. 3—17.—*The burnt offering.* It was wholly consumed by the fire of God's altar; nothing was left for the after consumption either of the offerer or even of God's ministers, as in the other sacrifices.

I. IT TYPIFIES THE ENTIRE SELF-SURRENDER OF CHRIST TO GOD.

1. In his eternal resolve to redeem by becoming man.
2. In the humility of his birth on earth.
3. In the silence in which his youth was spent.
4. In the narrow limits within which he confined his ministry.
5. In the victory won over his human will in the Garden of Gethsemane.
6. In his yielding his life to his Father on the cross.

II. EXAMPLE HEREIN TO US.

1. We must surrender what is evil—
Bad habits, *e.g.* sloth, drunkenness.
Bad affections, *e.g.* love of money, bodily indulgence.
Bad passions, *e.g.* ill temper, pride.

2. We must surrender what God does not think fit to give us, though not in itself evil, such as—
Health;
Domestic happiness,
Worldly success.

III. THE CHRISTIAN TEMPER RESULTING FROM SELF-SURRENDER.

1. Acquiescence in God's will.
2. Cheerfulness in rendering that acquiescence.

3. Spiritual peace and happiness arising from the consciousness of having yielded our will to our Father's will.

4. Love to the brethren. Cf. Eph. v. 2: "Walk in love, as Christ also loved us, and gave himself for us an offering and a sacrifice to God for a sweet-smelling savour."

Vers. 5—9.—*Mediation.* The sacrificial act cannot be completed, though it can be begun, by the offerer alone. The intervention of God's priest is requisite, and it is his hand which performs the most solemn portion of the rite. Thus there is taught the need of mediation and of a mediator when a work of atonement is to be accomplished. "The expiation was always made or completed by the priest, as the sanctified mediator between Jehovah and the people, or, previous to the institution of the Aaronic priesthood, by Moses, the chosen mediator of the covenant. . . . It is not Jehovah who makes the expiation, but this is invariably the office or work of a mediator, who intervenes between the holy God and sinful man, and by means of expiation averts the wrath of God from the sinner, and brings the grace of God to bear upon him" (Keil). Hence, the great work of atonement, of which all other atonements are but shadows, was performed by the One Mediator between God and man, the man Jesus Christ.

HOMILIES BY VARIOUS AUTHORS.

Entire consecration, as illustrated in the burnt offering. Ch. i.; cf. Rom. xii. 1.— We start with the assumption that the Book of *Exodus* presents "the history of redemption." It is an account of how the Lord delivered the people he had chosen out of bondage, and brought them to himself (Exod. xix. 4). It contains, moreover, an account of the erection of the tabernacle, or "tent of meeting," where God proposed to dwell as a Pilgrim in the midst of a pilgrim people, and out of which would issue his commands as their Guide and Leader. In this Book of *Leviticus*, then, we have the Lord speaking "out of the tent of meeting" (ver. 1), that is, to a people in *covenant relations* with himself.

This helps us to understand why the "burnt offering" is treated first. Not only was it the very oldest offering, but it was to be the daily offering (Numb. xxix. 6); morning and evening was a holocaust to be presented to the Lord. It was, therefore, manifestly meant to express the proper state or condition of those professing to be God's covenant people. It is on this account that we entitle this a homily on *Entire Consecration.*

I. This IDEA OF ENTIRE CONSECRATION IS ONE WHICH ALL CLASSES OF GOD'S PEOPLE ARE EXPECTED TO EXPRESS. The poor, who could only bring "turtle-doves" or "young pigeons," the representatives of domestic fowls at that time, were just as welcome at the tabernacle as those who could bring lambs or bullocks. Consecration is an idea which can be carried out in any worldly condition. The poor widow with her two mites carried it out more gloriously than her neighbours in the midst of their abundance. Complete self-surrender is not the prerogative of a class, but the possibility and ideal of all.

II. CONFESSION OF SIN IS AN EXPECTED PRELIMINARY TO CONSECRATION. The Jew, whatever was his grade in society, was directed either expressly to "lean " (סָמַךְ) his hand upon the head of his offering, or, as in the case of the fowls where it was physically impossible, to do so by implication; and this was understood to represent, and some believe it to have been regularly accompanied by, confession of sin. Of course, confession of sin is not of the *essence* of consecration; we have in the case of our blessed Lord, and of the unfallen angels, similar consecration, where no sense of sin is possible. And we are on the way to consecration in the other life, divorced from the sense of sin. Meanwhile, however, confession is only just, since sin remains with us. Indeed, the consecration of redeemed sinners will not prove very deep or thorough where confession of sin is omitted.

III. The SPECTACLE OF A SUBSTITUTE DYING IN OUR ROOM AND STEAD IS WELL FITTED TO DEEPEN OUR SENSE OF CONSECRATION. The slaughter of the animal, upon whose head the sins have by confession been laid, must have exercised upon the offerer a very solemnizing influence. There is nothing in like manner so fitted to hallow us as the spectacle of Jesus, to whom these sacrifices pointed, dying on the cross in our stead. The love he manifested in that death for us constrains us to live, not unto ourselves, but unto him who died for us and rose again (2 Cor. v. 14, 15). The moral power of *substitution* cannot be dispensed with in a sinful world like this.

IV. THE ACCEPTANCE OF THE BLOOD UPON THE ALTAR, THAT IS, OF LIFE AFTER THE DEATH-PENALTY HAS BEEN PAID, ALSO HELPS TO DEEPEN THE SENSE OF CONSECRATION. For when the priest by Divine direction, sprinkled the blood of the sacrifice all round about upon the altar, it was to indicate the acceptance on God's part of the life *beyond death*. It indicated that God was satisfied with the substitution, that the penalty had been paid by the death of the victim, and that in consequence the blood, that is, the life—for the life was in the blood (ch. xvii. 11)—could be accepted. Acceptance in and through another was what this portion of the ritual implied, and this is well calculated to deepen the sense of consecration. For, according to the typology, the Person in whom we are accepted is he to whom we ought to be consecrated. It is when we realize that we are accepted in Christ that we feel constrained to dedicate ourselves unto him. The one good turn deserves another, and we are held under a sense of sweetest obligation.

V. THE CONSECRATION OF THE CHILD OF GOD IS THE COMPLETE SURRENDER OF SELF TO THE OPERATION OF THE HOLY GHOST. Ewald has most pertinently remarked that among the Greeks and other nations such holocausts as were daily presented by the Jews were rarities. The idea of entire consecration is too broad for a heathen mind. Partial consecration was comparatively easy in idea, but a "surrender without reserve" is the fruit of Divine teaching. Now this is what the burning of the holocaust in the sacred fire of the altar signified. For, since all sensation had ceased before the sacrifice was laid upon the altar, the burning could not suggest the idea to the worshipper of pain or penalty. The fire had come out from God as the token of acceptance (ch. ix. 24). It is, moreover, one of the recognized symbols of the Holy Ghost. Consequently, the exposure of every portion of the sacrifice to the altar fire represented the yielding of the grateful worshipper in his entirety to the operation of God the Holy Ghost. This, after all, is the essence of sanctification. It is the surrender of our whole nature, body, soul, and spirit, to the disposal of the Holy Ghost. This is devotedness indeed. Nowhere has the idea been more felicitously wrought out than in a little posthumous volume of F. R. Havergal's, entitled 'Kept for the Master's Use.' We cannot better convey the idea of the burnt offering than by copying her simple foundation lines upon which she has built her chapters.

"Take my life, and let it be
Consecrated, Lord, to Thee.

Take my moments and my days;
Let them flow in ceaseless praise.

Take my hands, and let them move
At the impulse of Thy love.

Take my feet, and let them be
Swift, and 'beautiful' for Thee.

Take my voice, and let me sing
Always, only, for my king.

Take my lips, and let them be
Filled with messages from Thee.

Take my silver and my gold:
Not a mite would I withhold.

Take my intellect, and use
Every power as Thou shalt choose.

Take my will and make it Thine:
It shall be no longer mine.

Take my heart; it *is* Thine own:
It shall be Thy royal throne.

Take my love: My Lord, I pour
At Thy feet its treasure-store.

Take myself, and I will be
Ever, *only*, ALL for Thee."

R. M. E.

Vers. 1—14.—*The weakness of man and the grace of God.* Measureless is the distance between man and his Maker. And it is sometimes emphasized in such a way as to repress thought and stifle the aspirations of the human breast. In Scripture it is not brought forward as a rayless truth, but is shown to be replete with profit and joy. To consider it increases humility, indeed, but also intensifies gratitude and love. For the less has been blessed by the Greater, and we are permitted to say, looking upon the attributes of the Eternal as exercised towards us in mercy and favour, "This God is our God: we will rejoice in his salvation."

I. MAN IS IGNORANT: THE GRACE OF GOD IS SEEN IN THE DISTINCT ENUNCIATION OF HIS WILL. The light of reason, the voice of conscience, the promptings of emotion,— these can inform us only to a slight extent of the worship and service likely to be acceptable to God. Hence the surpassing worth of the full, clear-toned, authoritative utterances of Scripture. That God is Spirit, Light, and Love, that he is holy and almighty, are declarations for which we must be devoutly thankful. The Epicureans pictured the happy gods as dwelling in unruffled serenity far from all cognizance of or interference with the concerns of men. Inspiration removes our suspicions, reassures us with the words, "The eyes of the Lord are over the righteous, and his ears are open unto their prayers." *Errors in the manner of our approach are prevented.* Some would have presumptuously drawn near without the accustomed offering; others might bring unsuitable gifts—human sacrifices, unclean animals, etc. A God less kind might suffer the people to incur the terrible consequences of ignorance, but no! if Nadab and Abihu perish it shall not be for lack of instruction. "Go ye into all the world, teaching them to observe whatsoever things I have commanded you."

II. MAN IS FEARFUL AND PERTURBED IN THE PRESENCE OF GOD: IT IS GRACIOUSLY ORDAINED THAT SPECIAL MESSENGERS SHALL BE THE APPOINTED CHANNELS OF COMMU- NICATION. "The Lord called unto Moses, saying, Speak unto the children of Israel." When God appeared on Sinai and thundered out His Law, the terrified people implored that God might not Himself speak again lest they should die. Their entreaty was regarded, and Moses became the medium of conveying the mind of God. Should Jehovah be for ever appearing in person, his visits would be attended with such over- whelming awe that the purport of his words might be in danger of being lost or mis- taken. When embarrassed, man's thoughts are dispersed, and memory fails. It was better, therefore, that holy men should speak unto men as moved by the Holy Ghost. The striking instance is the assumption of our nature by the Son of God, putting a veil over the features of Deity that weak sinful mortals might draw near without trembling and admire the gracious words proceeding out of his mouth. Even children hear and understand the words of Jesus. And here we may remark that *the utterances of the messengers must be received as coming from the Most High.* In the appointed place God talked with Moses, and on his repeating the instructions to the Israelites they were bound to attend to them. It is equally incumbent upon us to respect the decrees of God delivered through prophets and apostles, and above all to honour the Father by honouring the Son, believing his words, trusting him as the Teacher sent from God. Preachers are "ambassadors for Christ." We would give thanks without ceas- ing when hearers receive the truth from our lips, not as the word of men, but the word of God (1 Thess. ii. 13).

III. MAN IS SINFUL: THE GRACE OF GOD PROVIDES MEDIATORIAL ACCESS TO THE HOLY ONE. 1. *Sacrifices appointed.* "Bring an offering" without blemish, and place your hand upon its head, to show that it is willingly offered and stands instead of the offerer. And "it shall be accepted to make atonement" for you, to cover your person and works with the robe of mercy and righteousness, so that the Divine gaze may be fastened upon you without displeasure. By the grace of God it was arranged that Jesus Christ should taste death for every man. His was the one offering that, through accomplishing the will of God, sanctifies all who make mention of his name. Who will hesitate to appear before the Most High? Let faith lay her hand upon the Saviour, rejoicing in the conviction that "while we were yet sinners Christ died for us." 2. *A priesthood.* The Levites were set apart for the service of Jehovah, instead of all the firstborn of Israel. And of the Levites, the sons of Aaron were to minister continually before the Lord, observing all his regulations and maintaining constant purification of themselves, so that without insulting the holiness of God they might interpose between him and his people. Priesthood bridged the chasm between sinful creatures and a pure Creator. The priesthood sanctified the entire nation, which was theoretically a "kingdom of priests." Jesus Christ has concentred the priestly functions in himself. He has entered into the heaven as our Forerunner, to sprinkle the atoning blood on the altar. And now with true heart in full assurance of faith we may draw nigh to God.

IV. MAN'S CONDITION VARIES: THE GRACE OF GOD PROVIDES FOR ITS INEQUALITIES. 1. *Notice is taken of the poor, and appropriate offerings permitted.* Oriental monarchs often despised and rejected the subjects who were unable to enrich their royal coffers. But God is no respecter of persons. It is one of the glories of the gospel that it has been preached to the poor, and is adapted to their needs. God expects every man to come and testify his respect and affection. The poor may bring "turtle-doves or young pigeons." The way was thus opened for the parents of him who "became poor for our sakes." It is to be feared that many withhold a contribution because it seems so insignificant. But the Lord is as sorry to see the mite retained in the pocket as the gold which the wealthy refuse to part with. "If there be first a willing mind it is accepted according to that a man hath." Do not decline to engage in Christian work on the plea of defective ability! Surely some fitting department of service can be found. It is often the one talent that is hid in a napkin. 2. *The offering of the poor is pronounced equally acceptable.* Note the repetition of "it is a sacrifice, of a sweet savour unto the Lord" after the 17th verse. It is rather the spirit than the action itself which God regards. Not the results of labour so much as its motives and the proportion of ability to accomplishment.—S. R. A.

Vers. 1—9.—*The greatness of God.* Too wide a field lessens the thoroughness of observation. Hence it is allowable and advantageous to distinguish in thought what is in reality inseparable, in order, by fixing the attention upon certain parts, to acquire a better knowledge of the whole. Such a method recommends itself in dealing with the attributes of God. To attempt to comprehend them all in one glance is, if not impossible, at least of little result in increasing our acquaintance with His character. Let us observe how the hints in this chapter present us with the greatness of God in varied aspects.

I. THE HOLINESS OF GOD DEMANDS A SACRIFICIAL OFFERING FROM ALL WHO WOULD SEEK HIS FAVOUR. The offerings here spoken of were spontaneous free-will offerings. They indicated a desire on the part of man to draw nigh to Jehovah, and they also manifested a sense of disturbance wrought by sin in man's relations with his Maker. Once man walked with God in uninterrupted harmony. Then transgression chased innocence away, and shame drove man to hide himself from the presence of God among the trees of the garden. The consciousness of sin renders an offering necessary, under cover of which ("to make atonement for him") we may venture to an audience with the Holy One. Thus can fellowship be resumed. The Antitype of these sacrifices, Jesus Christ, is now our peace. He was "once offered to bear the sins of many." "By one offering he hath for ever perfected them that are sanctified." The old cry, "How shall man be just with God?" is still uttered, and the response comes, "Being justified freely by his grace through the redemption that is in Christ Jesus."

II. THE MAJESTY OF GOD REQUIRES THAT THE REGULATIONS FOR APPROACH WHICH HE HAS APPOINTED BE STRICTLY OBSERVED. The condescension of God in manifesting himself to the Israelites might be fraught with danger if it led to presumption and to holding in light esteem his awe-inspiring attributes. Instructions are consequently given relating to the minutest details; everything is prescribed. God is pleased with the free-will offering, and it will be accepted if the precepts are adhered to; but it must in no wise be supposed that the sincere expression of affection can excuse wilful neglect of appointed rules. The love of an inferior for his superior must not prevent the exhibition of due respect. God will be had in reverence by all that are about him. Nor is it open to man arrogantly to pronounce that a consecrated way of access through Jesus Christ may be set aside as unnecessary. Christianity may have broadened the road of approach, but it remains true that there is still an appointed road. To refuse honour to Christ is to treat God with disrespect. "Now is the Son of man glorified, and God is glorified in him." Christless worship, thanksgiving, and prayer, must be shunned.

III. THE HONOUR OF GOD EXPECTS AN OFFERING TO CONSIST OF THE BEST THAT MAN POSSESSES. If poor, a turtle-dove would not be rejected, but for a rich man to offer the same would be treated as an insult to God. And the offering from the herd or flock must be "a male without blemish." Strength and beauty combined are requisite to satisfy the searching eye of the High and Lofty One. We see these requisites embodied in the Lamb of God, the perfect Sacrifice, "holy, harmless, undefiled." He knows little of God who imagines that he will be put off with scanty service, mean oblations. We ought to ask, not what is there can be easily spared, but how much can possibly be laid upon the altar. Let us not mock him by indulging in our own pleasures, and then giving to him the petty remnants of our poverty! Let us strive so to act that the firstfruits of our toil, the chiefest of our possessions, the prime of our life, the best of our days, shall be devoted to purposes of religion! Bestow upon God the deepest thoughts of the mind, the strongest resolutions of the will, the choicest affections of the heart.

IV. THE PERFECTION OF GOD NECESSITATES ORDERLY ARRANGEMENT IN ALL THAT CONCERNS HIS WORSHIP AND SERVICE. There is an appointed place for the offering, "the tabernacle of the congregation." The wood must be laid "in order upon the fire" (ver. 7), and the different parts of the victim must likewise be placed "in order upon the wood" (ver. 8).

To constitute a chaos round about the throne is to derogate from the homage a king inspires. It intimates his powerlessness, his want of intelligent forethought and present control. Law reigns everywhere throughout the dominions of Jehovah. The heavenly bodies speak of the symmetry he loves, and plants, animals, and minerals teach the same grand truth. "Order is Heaven's first law." "God is not the author of confusion, but of peace." In the worship of the sanctuary order and decency are of pre-eminent importance. Whatever shocks a devout mind is likely to be offensive to him all whose ways are perfect. Arrangement need not degenerate into formality. The Sunday dress, the preparation for God's house, and the quiet attitude therein, are all important adjuncts to the spiritual education of the young.

Be it observed further that order means *economy of space and time.* Those who have no room nor leisure to be orderly do least and retain least. The laws of God are ever synonymous with the true interests of man.

V. THE PURITY OF GOD OBLIGES THAT THE OFFERING BE CLEANSED FROM DEFILE- MENT. Those parts of the victim naturally subject to defilement are to be washed in water, "the inwards and the legs." One might deem this a superfluous proceeding, since they were to be so soon burnt upon the altar. But this would mean an extremely erroneous view of the solemnity of a sacrifice. Those who have not time to serve God properly had better not try it at all. He who counts it a trouble to read and pray has little conception of the insult he offers to God. Before we bow before the Lord to render our tribute of adoration and praise, it were well to purify our hearts, to hallow the desires that may have become impure, to call home our wandering thoughts, and to loose the dusty sandals from the feet which have been treading in the ways of the world. The Almighty desires no part to be absent from the offering. The affections, the strength, the time, the money, that have been lavished on unworthy objects are not in themselves sinful, they are unclean and require the sanctifying influence of the blood of Christ, and the water of the Word, and then they are fit to be rendered unto God and consumed in the fire that testifies his acceptance of the worshipper.—S. R. A.

Ver. 9.—*Our reasonable service.* The burnt offering appears to have been the most general of the sacrifices presented to Jehovah, and to have had the widest significance. Its spiritual counterpart is furnished in Rom. xii. 1. Meditation upon the prophetic symbol will shed light upon the "living sacrifice" of the gospel dispensation.

I. The nature of the Christian offering as thus symbolized. 1. *It is a surrender to God of something that belongs to us.* Property inherited and acquired is the material of the sacrifice. Not only what has come to us by natural endowment, but that which is the result of toil—the cattle that were given to us, and the produce we have reared. God demands our hearts, our minds, our talents; and he looks for the devotion to him of any increment that effort may secure. Just as Barnabas sold his land and laid the price at the apostles' feet, and the Apostle Paul commanded that each Corinthian should "lay by him in store as God hath prospered him." 2. *It is a voluntary surrender.* The man "shall put his hand upon the head of the burnt offering," to evince his willingness to part with the animal. All "the cattle on a thousand hills" are really owned by Jehovah, yet does he treat man as proprietor, and does not take by violence the necessary sacrifices for his glory, but leaves it to man freely to recognize his God, and to pay his just dues. "Voluntary" in no wise excludes the force of motives, since every decision has motives, as an antecedent if not as an efficient cause. Freedom implies absence, not of inducements, but of constraint. Man has the power to withhold from the service of God his faculties and possessions. He is ever appealed to in Scripture as a reasonable individual, capable of deciding to what purposes his abilities shall be devoted. "Yield yourselves unto God." 3. *The surrender must be complete.* It was not possible to offer part of a goat or lamb, the victim must be given in its entirety. The blood is sprinkled round about, and "all" the parts are burnt upon the altar. The disciple must follow the Lord fully. No putting of the hand to the plough and looking back. No keeping back part of the price. The believer is bought by Christ, body and soul. The reason why many seem to have offered themselves to God in vain, is because they have done it in a half-hearted way, they have not "sought him with their whole desire."

II. The manner in which the offering is devoted to God. 1. *By the death of the victim.* Death is the total renunciation of present enjoyment—the extremest proof of an intention to set one's self apart for a certain object. If it does not suffice to prove sincerity and entire consecration, then proof is impossible. "All that a man hath will he give for his life." Like the apostle, it behoves Christians to "die daily." At baptism there was the emblem of death to the world. "Old things have passed away." Our death to sin, however, resembles the crucifixion of our Lord, a lingering painful death. We mortify the deeds of the body, crucify the flesh, deny ourselves. "If any man will lose his life he shall save it." 2. *By cleansing water and purifying fire.* "Sanctify them through thy truth: thy word is truth." "Having these promises, let us cleanse ourselves from all filthiness of the flesh and spirit." "Every one shall be salted with fire." "The trial of your faith which is much more precious than of gold that perisheth, though it be tried with fire." All that is earthly is consumed. The smoke, rising from the material sacrifice, reminds us of the pure metal that is free from dross, and remains to "praise, honour, and glory." Learn to welcome the tribulations of your lot as being the discipline that makes the surrender of yourselves complete. Martyrs have experienced actual flames, the fire may assume another shape to you. Perhaps temptations assail you, and difficulties wear away your strength. Glorify God in the fires. Fire is an emblem of the Holy Spirit, and as Christ offered himself through the Eternal Spirit, so does his Spirit abide with his people, to hallow them, to put away sin, to make them pleasing unto God. 3. *By means of the ordained mediator.* The priest must take the slain animal to perform the necessary rites. Otherwise, however free from fault, the offering will bring loss, not gain, to the offerer. If all believers are now "a holy priesthood, to offer up spiritual sacrifices," they are only "acceptable to God by Jesus Christ." Our Saviour must be our "Daysman," to come between us and God, and present us to his Father. His life, death, and intercession must be the inspiration of our lives, the spring of our hopes, the constraining influence that shall make us dedicate all we have and are to God. "No man cometh unto the Father but by me." We determine to know nothing save Christ and him crucified. "In Christ Jesus" we "are made nigh."

III. The effect of the offering. 1. *It pleases God.* Anthropomorphic expressions are employed, not to degrade the Almighty, but to clarify our conceptions, and to make the truth plain to the dullest eyed. "It is a sweet savour unto the Lord." The smell is repulsive, and cannot be supposed to be grateful in itself to him who is a Spirit.

But it is the disposition to honour and please God that he delights to observe in his children. A parent may admire the rudest sketch if his little one brings it as a token of love, and may esteem the commonest fare a banquet, and ill-dressed food a feast, if regard and affection have contributed to its preparation. The agony and wounds of the Redeemer were not watched by the Father with unmingled delight. As we shudder at the spectacle of the Holy One made a curse for us, and yet rejoice in the all-sufficiency of his burden-bearing ; so the Father felt the keenest pangs that rent the breast of his beloved Son, and only joyed in the sublime manifestation of filial devotion, content to endure torture and insult that the blot on his Father's world through the presence of sin might be erased even at such infinite cost. Wherein we are partakers if the sufferings of Christ our Sacrifice is fragrant to the Father. The apostles, in preaching the gospel, became " unto God a sweet savour of Christ." If we walk in love, we cause the incense of love to ascend with sweet odour to heaven (Eph. v. 2). Jesus ministered to the wants of many, and the Philippians, in supplying the necessities of Paul, Christ's servant, were an " odour of a sweet smell, a sacrifice well-pleasing unto God." 2. *It procures for the offerer satisfaction of conscience and the favour of God.* The sacrifice is accepted, communion is re-established, sin is covered. There is an inward contentment in all religious acts that is of itself evidence of the reality of religion, and its adaptation to our circumstances. Never did any man abstain from selfish, sinful gratification, or pursue the rugged path of holiness and virtue, without being solaced by the consciousness of having done what was right, what was in harmony with the noblest dictates of his nature. The self-denying, God-serving life is the happiest and most blessed life. Then do we walk in the light of God's countenance, and drink of the river of his pleasures.—S. R. A.

Vers. 1, 2.—*Sacrificature.* The Book of Exodus closes with an account of the entrance of the Shechinah into the tabernacle ; with the manner in which that sacred structure was enveloped by the cloud of the Divine presence ; also that in which, by rising from the tabernacle, God gave his order for his people to march, and, by resting upon it, to halt and encamp. The Book of Leviticus is concerned with the revelations which God gave to Israel from this habitation of his holiness, in which the laws published from Sinai were amplified (comp. ch. vii. 37, 38). The text lays down broad principles upon the subject of sacrificature, which is considered first in order, because of its great importance to the Levitical system, and to that more glorious system of the gospel which it shadowed forth. We learn that—

I. SACRIFICATURE HAS GOD FOR ITS AUTHOR. 1. *It existed before the time of Moses.* (1) Its prevalence amongst the nations argues its origin to be prior to the dispersion (Gen. xi. 9). How else can this fact be explained ? (2) We read of it in patriarchal times. The Hebrew patriarchs offered sacrifices (Gen. xii. 7, *et al. freq.*). So did Job, who lived in the land of Uz, on the border-land between Idumea and Arabia, probably about the time of Joseph (Job i. 5 ; see also Exod. xviii. 12). So did Noah (Gen. viii. 20). (3) The first family had sacrifices which they presented when they appeared before the Shechinah, which flamed between the cherubic emblems set up eastward of Eden (Gen. iv. 3, 4). 2. *It could not have been invented by man.* (1) It was, in the nature of the thing, most unlikely to have occurred to any finite mind. (2) If it did so occur, would God have accepted it ? Does he approve will-worship ? (see ch. x. 1, 2). What right has a sinner to propose terms of reconciliation to his Maker ? His place is to throw himself absolutely upon the Divine mercy, and wait to " hear what God the Lord may speak " (Ps. lxxxv. 7, 8). 3. *Here we have it authorized by God.* (1) " And the Lord called unto Moses," etc. (2) So we find God directing Abraham respecting the manner in which sacrifices should be ordered in his worship (Gen. xv. 9 ; see also xxii. 2). (3) The " coats of skins " in which our first parents were clothed were presumably from animals offered in sacrifice. Animals were not in those days killed for food (Gen. i. 29 ; comp. with ix. 3). Since it was " the Lord God " who clothed them, the institution of sacrificature would date from that time, and be a revelation of mercy immediately from him. God is the Author of reconciliation (John iii. 16 ; Rom. v. 8 ; 1 John iv. 9).

II. IT WAS PUBLISHED FROM HIS SANCTUARY. 1. *There are revelations of God in nature.* (1) These are exhibited in our treatises on Natural Theology. Who can fail to see the Designer in the works of design? (2) The Scriptures recognize this voice (Ps. ix. 1; xix. 1, etc.; Acts xiv. 17; xvii. 27; Rom. i. 20). 2. *But these are evident only after the hint of them is given.* (1) We have no innate ideas. The Namaquans and other African tribes were found by Moffat, Ridsdale, and other missionaries, without a glimmer of an idea of God or of immortality. (2) The traditions of the Gentiles were originally from a pure source, but became corrupted in transmission. (3) There are no "deists," *i.e.* natural theologians, where the Bible has not been before them. They do not own the source from whence they derive the hints which guide them in their reasonings. 3. *Sacrificature is not taught in nature.* (1) The book of nature was written too soon. The Creation preceded the Fall. (2) That it is, is not presumed. Sacrificature is excluded from the creed of the deist. (3) This subject belongs to the sanctuary. "And the Lord called Moses and spake *out of the tabernacle* of the congregation," etc. Even the Garden of Eden, where, we presume, it was first instituted, was "planted," and planted to be a temple for Divine worship. (4) Yet without sacrificature there can be no acceptable worship. Cain, the deist, was rejected because he came before God without blood-shedding (see ch. xvii. 11; Heb. ix. 22). Let no man think he acceptably serves God when he neglects the services of the sanctuary under the pretext of "worshipping the God of nature in the fields."

III. The sacrifices approved are "from the herd and from the flock." 1. *They are selected from the animals that are clean.* (1) They have the marks of cleanness, viz. parting the hoof and chewing the cud (ch. xi. 3). But all clean creatures were not proper for purposes of sacrifice. Those of the "herd" (בקר, *baker*) are distinguished as the bull, heifer, bullock, and calf. Those of the "flock" (צאן, *tson*) as sheep and goats; for this word is used to describe these animals promiscuously (see ver. 10). (2) This reminds us of the purity of God, who can accept nothing that is polluted—"who will in no wise clear the guilty"—who requires purity in his worshippers (Ps. xxiv. 3, 4). (3) It points to the purity of the Great One sacrificed for us, covered in whose righteousness we are justified or accounted as just persons, and in whose atoning blood we are washed and made clean. 2. *They are gregarious creatures.* (1) This feature is prominently noticed here—"herd," "flock." Man is a social being. He is set in families, tribes, nations, and even internationally united. Solitary confinement is amongst the most horrible of punishments. (2) Hence guilt and depravity become hereditary. And as we have been represented to our ruin by our common progenitor, so by the representation of the second Adam we have salvation. (3) Sin is dissocializing. Consider its fruits—Hatred—variance—strifes—murders. (4) True religion perfects the social principle, centres all union in God. A universe can meet in him. A universe can hold communion in him. The genius of religion is love. The heaven of heavens is love.—J. A. M.

Vers. 3—9.—*The burnt sacrifice of the herd.* Having given general instructions concerning the great business of sacrifice, the Most High descends to particulars, and here describes the burnt sacrifice of the herd. These particulars contain specific directions—
I. As to the quality of the victim. 1. *It must be a male.* (1) Females were not only admitted for burnt offerings under the patriarchal dispensation, but upon one memorable occasion even prescribed (see Gen. xv. 9). The ceremonial distinction between male and female was not then, probably, so strongly defined as afterwards it became under the Law. Under the gospel it is abolished (Gal. iii. 28). (2) The male is the stronger animal; and the horns, in the ox, which are symbols of power, are more developed in the male. The male, therefore, would represent the excellence of strength. (3) Thus Christ, as the "Power of God," would be preindicated (1 Cor. i. 24). By his sacrifice of himself he destroyed him that had the power of death, and became the "power of God unto salvation" to every believer (Rom. i. 16; 1 Cor. i. 18). 2. *It must be without blemish.* (1) The rabbins reckon no less than fifty things, any one of which would, in their judgment, render an animal unfit for sacrifice; five in the ear, three in the eyelid, eight in the eye, etc.; but they trifle outrageously. Any obvious defect or redundancy of parts would mar it for sacrifice, and so would any disease by which it might be afflicted. (2) This reminds us that Christ, who is accepted of God as our Sacrifice, is without deficiency or redundancy, weakness or malady (1 Pet. i. 19).

In everything perfect. (3) We are further taught that the best should be given to God. The best thoughts; the best affections; the best gifts; the best service.

II. AS TO THE DUTY OF THE OFFERER. 1. *With a view to procuring the acceptance of his offering.* (1) His gift must be offered freely. "He shall offer it of his own voluntary will." The sacrifice of himself, which Christ offered for us, was voluntary (Gal. i. 4; ii. 20; Eph. v. 25; Titus ii. 6, 14). God expects the homage of the heart (John iv. 23, 24). (2) It must be offered at the *door* of the tabernacle. The altar was at the door. We enter the heavens through the *blood* of Jesus (Heb. x. 19—21). The Jewish sacrifices were never resumed after the destruction of their city and temple, for they hold it unlawful to sacrifice anywhere out of Jerusalem. Yet they will not see that the antitypes have come, and that the types are therefore no longer necessary. (3) He must lay his hand upon its head. This action expressed, (*a*) That the offerer confessed himself a sinner deserving to be sacrificed. (*b*) That he ceremonially transferred his guilt to a substitute in anticipation of the Great Substitute promised who should truly bear the punishment of sin (1 Pet. ii. 24). (*c*) That he trusted in the mercy of God through the vicarious sufferings of Messiah (Dan. ix. 26). 2. *With a view to the making an atonement for his sin.* The direction is (1) That he should kill the bullock "before the Lord." The Shechinah was there in the most holy place. The transaction is between the Lord and the soul of the sinner. In all worship we should realize the presence of the Lord. (2) "He shall flay the burnt offering and cut it into his pieces." This operation was here performed, not by the priest, but by the offerer. In the time of the temple this was done by the priests, who were then -more numerous and better skilled in the proper mode of doing it. For this service they claimed the skin (ch. vii. 8; 2 Chron. xxix. 34). (3) People and priests alike were concerned in the Great Sacrifice on Calvary. It was done with "wicked hands" (Acts ii. 23).

III. AS TO THE DUTY OF THE PRIESTS. 1. *With respect to the blood.* (1) They were to sprinkle with it round about the altar. The altar upon which Jesus was offered was, in its more restricted sense, the hill of Calvary. On that hill his precious blood was literally sprinkled. (2) The position of the altar is noted, viz. " by the door of the tabernacle of the congregation." In the wider sense the altar on which Jesus suffered was this planet, which is, as it were, the entrance or vestibule of the great temple of the universe, of which the heavens are the holy places (see Heb. iv. 14). 2. *With respect to the water.* (1) Water is one of the great purifiers in the kingdom of nature, and is therefore used as an emblem of the Holy Spirit, the Great Purifier in the kingdom of grace (John vii. 38, 39). So a controversy about baptism with water is described as a "question about purifying" (John iii. 25). (2) With water the priest was to wash the inwards and the legs. The inwards were a type of the soul; and God requires "truth in the inward parts," in the "thoughts and intents of the heart." Every pollution, also, connected with our "walk and conversation" must be laved away. To express this truth Jesus washed his disciples' *feet.* 3. *With respect to the fire.* (1) It was "put" upon the altar. This does not say that it was kindled by the priest. The fire was of God's own kindling (see ch. ix. 24; x. 1, 2). (2) It was, however, fed with fuel by the priests. Human agency co-operates with Divine even in the most sacred things (Phil. ii. 12, 13). (3) The parts of the sacrifice were laid in order on the wood. The quarters were laid together in their relative positions. So with the head, the fat, and the inwards. Thus the whole animal was consumed. Our whole being should be offered to God in the flames of love (Deut. vi. 5).—J. A. M.

Vers. 10—17.— *The burnt offering of the flock and of the fowls.* The ceremony of the offering of the flock is almost identical with that of the herd described in the verses preceding. In that of the fowls there is a wider dissimilarity.

I. THE VARIETY OF THE VICTIMS CLAIMS ATTENTION. 1. *Five or six kinds of victims were accepted.* (1) These were beeves, sheep, goats, turtle-doves, pigeons. To these may be added the clean birds, supposed to have been sparrows, which were required in the particular ceremony of the cleansing of the leper. (2) All these, excepting the last, were proper for burnt offerings. They are notable as mild, gentle, inoffensive, and useful creatures. They are therefore fittingly used as types to describe the innocence and meekness of Jesus (John i. 36; Isa. liii. 7). (3) As Christians we have nothing to do with the ferocity of the tiger or the rapacity of the wolf. If we have the wisdom of the serpent, it must be associated with the harmlessness of the dove (see Matt. x. 16). 2. *But what are the lessons conveyed in this variety?* (1) It evinces the insufficiency of the sacrifices of the Law. If one sacrifice or one kind of sacrifice could really take away sin, why repeat it or have recourse to others? Their usefulness therefore was in the manner in which they foreshadowed the better Sacrifice. (2) By contrast it evinces the sufficiency of the Great Sacrifice of the New Testament. No single sacrifice or kind of sacrifice could body forth all that was required in a sufficient Saviour; therefore the number and variety of the types. But Jesus offered himself alone and once, because everything centred in him. Supplementary sacrifices such as that of the Mass, are blasphemous impertinences. (3) It further evinces the mercifulness of Divine justice. Here was the bullock for the rich man. Here was the sheep or goat for the man in moderate circumstances. Here were the turtle-doves or pigeons for the poor (2 Cor. viii. 12). Here is Christ without money and without price for all.

II. THERE ARE NOTABLE OMISSIONS. 1. *The placing of the offerer's hand upon the head of the victim.* (1) This is mentioned in connection with the offering from the herd (ver. 4). Omitted in the description of the offering from the flock. Also from the offering from the fowls. It may have been done nevertheless. (2) It was very expressive of the transfer of sin to the victim. Possibly Paul refers to this custom—of course, taking it in its application to the gospel—when he speaks of the "laying on of hands" as amongst the "first principles of the doctrine of Christ" (Heb. vi. 2). (3) If in any case it was omitted, it would then suggest the important truth that the *hand of God* laid upon Christ the iniquity of us all (Isa. liii. 6, 10). 2. *The flaying of the skin.* (1) This is described in the account of the herd, but omitted in that of the flock (ver. 6). It appears, nevertheless, to have been done also in the latter case. (2) The skin is the natural clothing or covering of the animal. If the coats of skins with which God clothed Adam and Eve in substitution for their covering of fig leaves by which they expressed their sense of shame for their sin, were those of sacrificed animals, then it vigorously sets forth the manner in which we receive "beauty for ashes" when invested with the righteousness of Christ. 3. *Instead of the "door of the tabernacle of the congregation" which is mentioned in connection with the herd, "northward" is the term used in connection with the flock* (comp. vers. 5, 11). These expressions are generally synonymous (ch. vii. 2). Standing at the door of the tabernacle of the congregation, the worshipper held communion with God and with the whole congregation. He stood at the north side of the altar, because that was the place of rings to which the victims were fastened in order to be slain. The hill of Calvary also was situate north-west of Jerusalem. How humiliating that our communion with God and his Church must be through *suffering* and *blood!*

III. DIFFERENCES ARE NOTICEABLE IN THE BURNT SACRIFICE OF FOWLS. 1. *In this case two birds were brought.* (1) One, however, only is offered as a burnt sacrifice. The singular is used in this description. (2) The other was to be used as a sin offering (see ch. v. 7; xii. 8; xiv. 22). 2. *They were cloven but not divided.* (1) This was in accordance with the directions given to Abraham (Gen. xv. 10). (2) The cleaving was required for the removal of the intestines, but the wings must not be divided, for the power for flight of Christ to heaven cannot be impaired (Acts ii. 24). (3) The head was wrung off, and the blood wrung out by the side of the altar. 3. *The crop and feathers were cast into the place of ashes.* (1) This was during the tabernacle "by the side of the altar on the east part." All the ashes went there (see ch. vi. 10). (2) In the temple the place of ashes was a closet under the altar. In allusion to this the souls, that is to say, the bodies, of the martyrs are represented as under the altar, crying for vengeance upon their persecutors (Rev. vi. 9—11). Reflect: The poor man's pigeons as truly as the rich man's bullock was "of a sweet savour unto the Lord" (see Eph. v. 2; also 1 Pet. ii. 5).—J. A. M.

Vers. 1, 2.—*God in special manifestation.* Always and everywhere God has been revealing himself. There is no time when, no place where, men might not have "seen him who is invisible." Nowhere has he left himself without witness (Acts xiv. 17). Always might "his eternal power and Godhead have been understood" (Rom. i. 20). But the eyes of man were blinded, and his "foolish heart was darkened," so that by his own wisdom he knew not God. It is certain that he would have remained in ignorance but for those *special manifestations* of which the sacred Scriptures are the record. The text reminds us that these include—

I. HIS PECULIAR PEOPLE. Out of the human race God chose one people, "the congregation," "the children of Israel," to whom he would appear, by whom the knowledge of his nature and will should be retained, and through whom he should be made known to others. To this congregation "were committed the oracles of God;" and while surrounding nations were stumbling in the darkness, Israel was walking in the light of the Lord.

II. HIS OWN HOUSE. "God spake out of the tabernacle," etc. This his dwelling-place in Israel had just been constructed, and there, in the most holy place, he had signified his presence by the glory-cloud. That was none other than the house of God, his abode in the midst of the congregation.

III. HIS CHOSEN MINISTER. "The Lord called unto Moses." The experiences of Sinai had shown that there was need of mediation between the Majesty of heaven and the children of earth. God, therefore, chose to reveal his mind through the one man who was fittest for close access, and who would calmly receive and faithfully announce his will—the courageous, devoted, magnanimous Moses.

IV. HIS PARTICULAR DIRECTIONS. "Speak . . . and say . . ." Then follow the instructions of this book of the Law: particular and precise regulations, by attention to which the congregation might worship with acceptance and "live in holiness and righteousness before God."

In the dispensation in which we now stand we have analogous special manifestations. 1. *The Church of Christ* is now the congregation of the Lord, the "Israel of God;" not the members of any visible organization, but all those of every society who love and honour Christ, "both theirs and ours." To such "he manifests himself as he does not unto the world;" in them his Holy Spirit dwells; through them he works on the world without. 2. *The Christian sanctuary* is now the house of the Lord, the "place of his abode." There he makes his presence felt; there he causes us to behold his glory, the beauties of his character, the glories of his grace. At the table of the Lord, more especially, the risen Master meets with his true disciples, the Divine Host with his human friends and guests, to receive and return their love, to accept their vows, to impart his benediction and his blessing. 3. *The Christian ministry* is now the chosen channel of his communications. Not necessarily those ordained with human hands; these if sent by God, but only if sent of him; and beside these, all whose hearts he has touched (1 Sam. x. 26), whose minds he has filled with spiritual understanding (Col. i. 9), and whose lips he has opened (Ps. li. 15); all those on whose soul there really rests the "burden of the Lord." 4. *The New Testament* now contains the Divine instructions. These are (1) few in number; (2) moral and spiritual rather than formal and mechanical in their nature; (3) adequate to penetrate to the deepest springs of the soul, and to cover the widest particulars of the life.

It becomes us, in view of these special manifestations of God in Christ, (*a*) to associate ourselves immediately with the recognized people of God; (*b*) to seek, constantly and sedulously, his face and favour and the knowledge of his will, in his house; (*c*) to hold ourselves ready to speak for him to others or to receive his message from others, as his Spirit shall prompt us or them; (*d*) to master and foster those principles of righteousness which Christ has taught us, that we may cultivate our character and regulate our lives according to his holy will.—C.

Vers. 2—17.—*The true end of sacrifice,—entire consecration to God.* We shall reach the end for which God introduced all that apparatus of Divine worship so elaborately described in this book if we take the following steps:—

I. THE SEPARATING PRESENCE OF SIN IN THE HEART AND LIFE OF MAN. But for the sin which "separates between us and our God" there would have been unrestrained communion between man and his Maker in every age and land: no need of mediation, of special arrangements, of careful limitations, of means and media of approach. Every line of this chapter, as also of this book, speaks of sin—sin in the soul, sin in the life, sin on the conscience, sin as a hindrance in the way of man.

II. THE EFFORT OF MAN TO FIND A WAY BACK TO GOD. It is impossible to forget that while Israel was offering its sacrifices as God directed, other nations were bringing their victims in such ways as they deemed best. The commonness of sacrifice, its prevalence outside the holy nation, speaks eloquently enough of man's conscious distance from God, and of his desire and endeavour to find a way back to his favour. "Wherewith shall I come before the Lord?" This is the anxious question of sin-stricken, unenlightened man. "Shall I come with burnt offerings . . . will the Lord be pleased with thousands of rams?" This is his suggestion in reply. It is affecting to think of the multitudes of sacrifices under every sky, as instances of men "feeling after" the mercy of an offended God, groping in the dimness or the darkness towards reconciliation and peace.

III. THE DIVINE PROVISION FOR MAN'S RETURN AND ACCESS TO HIMSELF. 1. *Under the old dispensation.* Man was to bring to the altar of God suitable offerings; such as were within his reach; the best of the kind; an unblemished male. It might be from his herd (ver. 2), or from his flock (ver. 10), or it might be a fowl of the air (ver. 14). The priest was to pour the blood round about the altar (vers. 5, 11), and the carcase was to be consumed upon the altar,—a whole burnt offering unto the Lord. 2. *Under the new dispensation.* Instead of "the blood of bulls and goats," God has provided one offering which suffices for all souls of every land and age, even his own beloved Son. This was the "Lamb of God" (1), absolutely perfect, "without blemish and without spot" (1 Pet. i. 19; Heb. ix. 14); (2) shedding his own blood (Heb. ix. 12), giving "his soul (his life) an offering for sin" (Isa. liii. 10); "putting away sin by the sacrifice of himself" (Heb. ix. 26); (3) accepted of God; "an offering . . . of a sweet savour unto the Lord" (ver. 17; Eph. v. 2). Through that shed blood of "the Lamb that was slain" for us we have access at all times, forgiveness of sin, reconciliation to God. But not without

IV. PERSONAL SPIRITUAL PARTICIPATION. The offerer under the Law took personal part in the offering: he brought his victim to the tabernacle (ver. 10); he killed it with his own hands (vers. 5, 11); he also "put his hands upon the head" of the animal (ver. 4). The sinner, under the gospel, does not provide the sacrifice: "Christ our passover *is* slain for us." But he does take a personal participation: "by faith he lays his hand on that dear head of his;" he acknowledges that he himself is worthy of death; believes and appropriates to his own need the fact that Jesus died for his sin; earnestly desires that his guilt may be transferred to the Lamb of God; entreats that that shed blood of his may atone for and cover his iniquity.

V. THE END OF SACRIFICE,—ENTIRE PERSONAL CONSECRATION. The consumption of the whole animal in the fire pictures the complete dedication of the Saviour, his absolute and entire consecration to the work which the Father gave him to do. It symbolizes ours also. Accepted by God through the atoning blood of the Lamb, we are to dedicate ourselves to him. Our personal consecration 1. Should follow upon and grow out of our acceptance through a crucified Saviour. 2. Should be thorough and complete: including heart and life, body and spirit, things sacred and things secular. 3. Will then be well pleasing to God, "an offering of a sweet savour unto the Lord" (ver. 17).—C.

Vers. 2—17.—*Principles of spiritual sacrifice.* All who know God are engaged, frequently, if not continually, in sacrificing unto him. Here are principles of sacrifice by which we may be guided.

I. THAT GOD DESIRES AND DEMANDS THE BEST WE CAN BRING. If the offering were of the herd, it was to be a "male without blemish" (ver. 3); so also if of the flock (ver. 10). Not that which was of small account and could be well spared, but the worthiest and best. *The best for the Highest.* Not "that which costs us nothing" (2 Sam. xxiv. 24) for him who has given us everything; rather the costliest of our treasures for him who, "though he was rich, for our sakes became poor." We may well break the rarest alabaster for him whose "body was broken" for our sin; may well pour out the most precious spikenard for him who poured out his life-blood for our redemption. "Worthy is the Lamb to receive *riches*" (Rev. v. 12). When we worship him, or work for him, or give to his cause, we should bring, not our exhaustion, but our vigour; not our languor, but our energy; not costless effort, but that which has taken time and trouble to produce—the gold rather than the silver, the silver rather than the pence; not anything that will pass in the sight of man, but the very best we can bring to his presence.

II. THAT GOD ACCEPTS THE BEST WE ARE ABLE TO BRING. If he could not afford a bullock, the Hebrew worshipper might bring a sheep; or if that were beyond his means, a turtle-dove or pigeon (vers. 2, 10, 14). God accepts gifts "according to that a man hath," etc. (2 Cor. viii. 12). He who approved the widow's mites more than the rich men's gold still "sits over against the treasury," and accepts what we can bring, however humble it be, if we bring with it "the willing mind." In the balances of heaven a conversation in a garret by the bedside of a pauper may weigh more than the greatest sermon before the noblest audience.

III. THAT GOD REQUIRES THE FULL CONSENT OF OUR OWN MIND. "He shall offer it of his own voluntary will" (ver. 3). The excellency, the beauty, the acceptableness of our offering lies largely in the hearty good will with which we bring it. "The Lord loveth a cheerful giver" (2 Cor. ix. 7). (See 1 Chron. xxix. 6, 9.)

IV. THAT OUR OFFERING MUST BE MADE CONSCIOUSLY UNTO THE LORD. He shall offer it "before the Lord" (ver. 3); he shall kill it "before the Lord" (ver. 11). When the victim was slain the offerer was to have in his mind the presence of God, and was to present it consciously to him. Whatever form our sacrifice may take—prayer, praise, inquiry of the Lord, contribution, exhortation—it must be not mechanical, but spiritual; it must be religious; it must be rendered "as to the Lord, and not unto men."

V. THAT GOD DESIRES OBEDIENCE IN THINGS BEYOND OUR UNDERSTANDING. Doubtless the priests of the tabernacle failed to see the import of many of the Divine directions. The people also must have been at a loss to understand the reason of many details of the service (vers. 6, 8, 11, 15, 17). But both priests and people were required to conform under penalty of severe displeasure. In many things unintelligible to them do our children and the uninstructed conform, because they rightly trust to those who are older and wiser. There are many things concerning which we have all to feel ourselves to be the little children we really are in the presence of the heavenly Father, and we must do unquestioningly what he bids us. Let us try strenuously to understand, and when we fail to reach the Divine meaning, trustfully conform.

VI. THAT THERE CAN BE NO WASTE IN THE FULLEST SACRIFICE WE LAY ON HIS ALTAR. In the burnt offering the whole victim was consumed; no part was saved for food. "To what purpose is this waste?" is it asked? We reply: 1. That the God in whom we live and whose we are is worthy of everything we can offer him. 2. That we never so truly realize the end and reach the height of our manhood as when we are devoting ourselves to God. 3. That we may count on a large and generous response at his liberal hand. 4. That we gain in spiritual profit far more than we lose in material reduction.—C.

Ver. 17 (latter part).—*God's pleasure in man.* We believe—

I. THAT GOD IS A BEING OF SUPREME BLESSEDNESS. He is the ever-blessed God, the source and fountain of all joy. He who gives such boundless bliss to his creation must be divinely blessed. He could not give what he has not in himself.

II. THAT SOME PART OF HIS JOY HE FINDS IN MAN. What constitutes the happiness of the Supreme? "The Lord will rejoice in his works;" but it is a larger truth that "the Lord taketh pleasure in his people" (Ps. cxlix. 4); that "the Lord's portion is his people" (Deut. xxxii. 9).

III. THAT HIS GOOD PLEASURE IN US IS IN—

1. Our complete but conscious consecration of ourselves. The "offering made by fire" was "of a sweet savour unto the Lord," not as typifying the annihilation of our self, absolute absorption of self in God (the Hindoo theory), but as expressing the offerer's desire to dedicate himself and all that he had to God,—voluntary, conscious devotion.

2. Our self-surrender to his Son our Saviour. That which, above all else, God says to us now is, "This is my beloved Son: hear ye him;" and the initial, essential, decisive step for us to take, in order to give him pleasure, is to "receive," to "believe in," to accept Jesus Christ as Teacher, Saviour, Lord, and Friend.

3. Our conformity to his revealed will, by (1) reverence (Ps. cxlvii. 11); (2) holy confidence in his pardoning love (Ps. cxlvii. 11); (3) patient endurance of wrong (1 Pet. ii. 20); (4) generous service of others (Phil. iv. 18; Heb. xiii. 16).—C.

The first part of this book, which may be called the spiritual statute-book of Israel as the congregation of the Lord, is occupied with *the laws of sacrifice,* chs. i.—vii. The underlying fact is that of sin as separation from God; but the book, as regulating the intercourse between the sinful people and the holy object of their worship, is itself a constituent part of the gracious covenant made with Israel. While it deepens the sense of sin, it provides the means of reconciliation and sanctification, and therefore the laws prescribed, while, as laws, restraining liberty and giving form to religious acts, at the same time embody in themselves the grace of God in the covenant relation between Jehovah and his people.

Vers. 1—17.—*Law of the burnt offerings.* The object of worship, place, worshipper, offering, are all clearly set forth. The way of obedience made plain.

Ver. 1.—"*And the Lord called unto Moses, and spake unto him out of the tabernacle of the congregation.*" This is the foundation on which the whole of positive religion is built up, the *Divine voice* speaking through a *mediator,* at an *appointed place,* and in a distinct, *authoritative manner.* Notice—

I. THE DIVINE VOICE. "The Lord," Jehovah, that is, the God of *revelation* and *covenant.* 1. The beginning of all true religion is the *gracious manifestation of God.* It is a very different spiritual structure which is built upon this foundation from that which is raised on men's own thoughts. Compare the corruptions of traditional religions, heathenism, with the Old Testament revelation; the vague and doubtful attempts of religious philosophy to provide an object of supreme reverence. The name *Jehovah* betokened a progress in special revelation. The *Elohistic* worship of the earliest ages, while resting, no doubt, on direct communications of God's Spirit, without which there can be no living intercourse between the creature and the Creator, was elementary in its character, suited to the childhood of the world—God revealed first as the God of creation, the object of reverential obedience in the sphere of natural life and the simplest laws of righteousness. As the relations of mankind to one another grew more numerous and complicated, the idea of religion enlarged; the object of worship was the God of a people, the God of families, the God whose name was distinctly named, as distinctly as the people's, between whom and a certain portion of mankind there was a direct covenant, involving gracious vouchsafements on one side, and faithful service on the other. This is the connection between the Book of Exodus and that of Leviticus, which the very opening words remind us is very close. In the former book we are in the presence of Jehovah. In this we are listening to his voice, a voice which speaks clearly and fully what are the ordinances of his will. 2. *The invitation and summons.* "*The Lord called* unto Moses." We must notice here the two elements of law and grace combined, which is the very essence of the book. All the regulations of the Mosaic economy were based upon the fact that Jehovah was in close fellowship with his people. Just as a made road brings the points between which it lies nearer, by opening the means of intercourse, so sacrifices were a token of covenant relation, and a perpetual *call* of Jehovah to his people to approach him. *The Lord called* that he might bestow his special grace on those who obeyed his call. He called with the voice of command and authority, that his people might henceforth know fully and without possibility of mistake what they had to do. So still there is a gracious call of the gospel, which invites freely and universally, but it is at the same time the proclamation of a new law of righteousness, as in the Sermon on the Mount, and in the whole revelation of duty in the Christian Church. Notice—

II. THE FACT OF MEDIATION. "*The Lord called unto Moses, and spake unto him.*" "The Law was given by Moses." "It was ordained by angels in the hand of a mediator," through the instrumentality of an appointed servant, who should be between Jehovah and his people. Moses united in himself remarkably the three elements of the office— the *prophetic,* as echoing the voice of God; the *priestly,* as the medium of offered service; the *kingly,* as the legislator and ruler, both proclaiming and administrating the Divine Law. We see also represented in the case of Moses the union of the two qualifications for the fulfilment of the office of mediator—the *personal merit* and the *Divine appointment.* Moses stood apart from the people in his character and personal eminence. He was anointed to his office, and manifestly favoured of God with special communications. In all these respects he is the type of the perfect Mediator. Jesus Christ was *in himself* able to be between God and man. His mediation is fact, history.

III. THE FACT OF MEDIATION WAS BASED UPON THE FACT OF COVENANT, THE

RELATION BETWEEN THE PEOPLE AND JEHOVAH, THE GOD OF REVELATION, MUTUAL PLEDGE, AND PROMISE. The whole structure of the ceremonial law was built up on reciprocal obligation. Living intercourse between God and man is the spiritual reality which binds together all the details of this book of the Law. A development, therefore, of the first and greatest commandment, "Thou shalt love the Lord thy God," etc. The acceptableness of religious worship lies in the fellowship of love.

IV. THE PLACE OF MEETING BETWEEN GOD AND MAN. "*Out of the tabernacle of the congregation,*" or "the tent of meeting." A temporary provision, afterwards superseded by a more permanent and elaborate structure, but in its external features betokening the dispensational character of the Law. The central fact was a gracious manifestation of God, a meeting-place inviting to intercourse, an appointed form of worship, the stepping-stone to a higher communion. "God dwelleth not in temples made with hands." The tabernacle was subsequent to the covenant. The life of fellowship preceded the act of fellowship. The people are God's before they receive the Law. There are three elements in the *tabernacle*, representative of universal and abiding truth. 1. *The Lord speaks out of it.* Positive revelation the foundation of positive religion. The soul waits upon God. Gracious messages the beginning of Divine work in and for man. There were gropings of natural religion worth nothing in themselves. The Spirit of God calls the spirit of man to a higher life. The true faith rests on the Word, honours the ordinances, seeks the place where God speaks in the most distinct and emphatic manner. This finds illustration both individually and in the history of God's people. 2. *Tabernacle of the congregation.* Fellowship an essential fact of the religious life. Man a moral being, only as he is in society. As it is the *fruit* of religion, so it is the *seed* from which springs the true life, both of nations and individuals. The tabernacle or temple the centre of the Hebrew national existence. The tent of meeting also the palace-chamber of the Great King. Jehovah's throne amongst his people the true source of all power and centre of all authority. All places of worship, as meeting-places of the congregation or Church, witness to the presence of Jehovah, of Jesus Christ, the Lord, in the midst of his people, and to the kingdom of God in the world. No doctrine of the Church consistent with this fact of Jehovah speaking out of the tabernacle of the congregation but that which recognizes the position of all believers as the same. "Where two or three are gathered together," etc. 3. *The place of meeting was both the centre to which offerings were brought and from which blessings were taken.* A true religion must embrace both the passive and the active elements—*Mind, heart, will.* Christianity did not abolish sacrifice and offerings, lifted up the lower into the higher, the local and temporary into the universal and perpetual. No material edifice, no priestly caste, no mere prescription of rites, can limit religious service. The temple of the Jews was destroyed, but in place of it we possess the risen glory of Christ, the spiritual presence of the Living One, the communion of saints, the ceaseless offering up of spiritual sacrifices acceptable to God through Jesus Christ. The Law which was given on the mount from the lips of Jesus requires a higher righteousness than the righteousness of legalists.—R.

Ver. 2.—"*Speak unto the children of Israel, and say unto them, If any man of you bring an offering unto the Lord, ye shall bring your offering of the cattle, even of the herd, and of the flock.*" Here is the great fundamental principle, as it were the *preamble* of the law of offerings. Notice—

I. THE DIVINE LAW IS UNIVERSAL. "*Any man of you.*" No respect of persons with God. Same law to rich and poor, wise and unwise, as to its essential requirements. These *private offerings* represented personal religion. There may be differences of official duty, but what we bring to God for ourselves must be without respect to anything but the real relation between our soul and God.

II. ALL OFFERINGS MUST BE VOLUNTARY. No compulsion with God but the compulsion of heart and conscience. True worship is not a mere objective obedience. "If any man *bring* an offering." It is brought by a willing mind, not out of caprice, not to any place or to any God, but with intelligent acceptance of the will of God as coincident with our own will. When we bring offerings we should know what it is in our hearts to bring, not trust to the impulse of the moment or the variations of fluctuating feelings.

III. The essential characteristic of the offering is surrender, ackowledg-ment of the Lord's claim over us. "*Out of the herd or flock.*" That is, out of our own possessions, valued, known, intimately associated with ourselves. A religion which costs us nothing cannot be real. The more of one's self there is in it, the more really offered it is. The mistake of all ritualism is that it leads us to offer up another's offering instead of our own. We observe the rite, we repeat by rote the words, we listen to the music, but is the offering out of our own herd or flock? Jesus will have no disciple who does not first count the cost.

IV. While the offering is voluntary, it is still prescribed. "*Ye shall bring your offering of the cattle.*" An enlightened recognition of Divine commandments is necessary to acceptable worship. "Faith cometh by hearing, hearing by the Word of God." "Not every man that saith, Lord, Lord; . . . but he that doeth the will of my Father which is in heaven"—"the things that I say." The liberty of the gospel is not licence. The doctrines, rules, and practical teachings found generally in the New Testament, though not systematized there, are yet positively given. While we are delivered from the bondage of a legal dispensation, we are yet under law to Christ. Will-worship is unchristian. Tendency of our time is to an individualism which is dangerous. The study of the Old Testament in the light of the New a wholesome antidote. Yet our faith must always work by love (*vide* Gal. v.).—R.

Ver. 3.—*The burnt sacrifice.* The most ancient, that which represents all others. Notice—

I. The main principle represented—Self-surrender in order to self-pre-servation through the covenanted mercy of Jehovah. In this principle there are included these points: 1. Recognition of the *supreme claim of God.* 2. *Substitu-tionary surrender*, a life for a life, the victim for the offerer. 3. *Expiation of sin and acceptance*, by the restoration of the covenant relations between God and man, proceed-ing from Divine love, but resting on the offering as representing a fulfilment on both sides of the contract—God forgiving, man obeying. 4. The union of the two elements of blood and fire, *i.e.* of atonement and purification, the negative holiness and the positive holiness, justification and sanctification, fulness of grace.

II. Details of the sacrifice. Ver. 3.—"*Of the herd, . . . a male without blemish.*" God must have our best. We must make our religious service a reality, putting into it our strongest faculties, best opportunities, counting all things but loss for Christ. Examples in the offerings of great faith. Nothing should be blemished in the house of God, in private religion, in acts of charity. "*Thou God seest me.*" "*Of his own voluntary will.*" Although a law, it is of no validity but as an appeal to the free heart of man. Anticipation of the gospel, the Law a schoolmaster to bring us to Christ. The highest state of life is when law is absorbed in the activity of the nature; we are likest God when we are by grace a law unto ourselves, "*willing to do his will.*" "*At the door of the tabernacle of the congregation before the Lord.*" Here are the three elements of religion recognized: 1. *Publicity.* 2. *Fellowship.* 3. *Divine order.* Secret religion is a contradiction. The profession is part of the sacrifice. "*Thy vows are upon me, O Lord.*" The congregation is a cloud of witnesses, both sustaining personal religion and supplying a constant test of sincerity. And whatever we do, we do before the Lord. His face we desire to seek, and in the light of his manifested favour we rejoice. There are special appointments which all true worshippers will honour: the sabbath, the Word, the congregation, the ordered life of the Christian Church.—R.

Ver. 4.—"*And he shall put his hand upon the head of the burnt offering; and it shall be accepted for him to make atonement for him.*" A most significant commandment, full of gracious meaning for those who observed it.

I. All atonement rests upon free grace. "*Accepted for him to make atone-ment.*" God *sets forth* the propitiation, declares *his* righteousness for the remission of sins. It shall be accepted, not because it is in itself an equivalent, but because a merciful Father accepts it.

II. The victim accepted proclaims the conditional nature of the grace. It is free as being unmerited, and yet it is the expression of a loving will, and comes forth from an infinite nature. God forgives because he chooses to forgive, yet he for-gives by the method which he proclaims. The lower sacrifice points to the higher.

III. The offerer's faith is as truly needful as the victim he brings. "Without faith it is impossible to please God." The hand put upon the head of the victim signified the identification of the offerer and offered. Whether the confession of sins was included or not is of little importance. Faith is self-surrender. In all atonement there are three parties represented—the offender, the offended, the mediator. The hand of the offender sets forth his whole activity and conscious self. His connection with the victim is itself confession of sin and acceptance of the covenanted mercy of Jehovah. We lay our hand on the head of Jesus by the spiritual identification which includes the application of the mind to his truth, the yielding of the heart to his love, and the consecration of the life to his service.—R.

Vers. 5—9.—*The killing, flaying, and consuming of the victim.* Full, throughout, of the idea of *atonement.* The three main elements are—I. The *blood.* II. The *fire.* III. The *sweet savour* unto the Lord. Consider—

I. The sprinkled blood. The *offerer* killed the victim. The *priests* received the blood and sprinkled it upon the altar. The two chief elements of atonement were thus united—the human and the Divine. Atonement is reconciliation on the ground of a restored covenant through sacrifice. The blood *shed* represented the fact of life for life offered by faith. The blood *sprinkled* by priests, represented the Divine offer of mercy through an appointed mediation, at the place and time prescribed by God's gracious will. His will is our sanctification. The sacrifice of Christ is an outcome of Divine love received on behalf of the sinner as being offered by him in believing surrender to God and renewal of the covenant.

II. The fire. The offering flayed and cut in pieces. Fire and wood placed by the priests on the altar, etc. All these details belong to the one fact that the offering is not only presented, but consumed, and consumed in pieces. The idea is that of the mingling together of the will of Jehovah with the offered obedience of his creature. A representation of the promised sanctifying grace which renews the whole man, gradually, but with comprehensive application of the Spirit of God to every part of the being and character. The ablution would convey the idea of the washing of regeneration. All which is specially significant of life and activity, " *the inwards and the legs,*" is washed in water before placed on the altar. The whole is then termed, " *a burnt sacrifice,* an *offering made by fire.*" The fire represented at the same time purification and destruction. As applied in the name of God, it promised his bestowment of the supernatural power which should at once destroy the evil and renew the good. Hence the gift of the Holy Spirit was symbolized by fire. We must be wholly offered, we must be penetrated and pervaded by the Spirit. The application of the *fire* is not only in a *first* baptism of the Spirit, but in the sanctifying work of *life,* in which oftentimes consuming dispensations are required, which, while they burn up, do also renew and recreate. Are we yielding up *all* to this gracious process on God's altar?

III. The sweet savour unto the Lord. Fragrant ascent of man's offering. Nothing is said of the addition of incense, therefore the mere smoke and steam of the offering itself is described as "sweet savour." The obedience of faith is acceptable to the Lord. Nothing can more decidedly set forth the freeness and fulness of pardon and reconciliation. The Divine will is entirely reunited with the human will. Thus every sacrifice pointed to the end of sacrifices. When it is offered, when the fire has done its work, there is peace with God. So the Lord Jesus, anticipating the conclusion of his sufferings and his return to heaven, exclaimed, "The hour is come, glorify thy Son." "I have glorified thee on the earth. I have finished the work which thou gavest me to do." Resting on that finished sacrifice, we can rejoice in our obedience as a sweet savour to the Lord, notwithstanding that in itself it is necessarily consumed by the perfect righteousness of the Divine Law. The blood and fire of the cross of Calvary are already upon the altar. We are able in the resurrection and ascension to behold the manifest tokens of acceptance. The fragrance of the Saviour's risen glory and eternal righteousness are not only before God, well pleasing to him, but are also ours by faith, mingling with the imperfection of a fallen humanity, and lifting it up to angelic life and spotless purity and joy in the presence of God.—R.

Vers. 10—13.—*The offering from the flocks.* Sheep or goat. This is a repetition of the same law as applied to the offering of lower value. The great spiritual fact is thus set forth that God is no respecter of persons. His Law applies to all sorts and conditions of men, and his grace is coextensive with his Law. The rich man's offering and the poor man's substantially the same. The only unchangeable condition is the relation of the offering to the offerer. It must represent sincere, heartfelt surrender to God. It must not be a wild animal caught for the purpose, but that which, having been associated with the personality and life, represents both the man himself and his house and family. Hence in the early Church, baptism was a consecration both of the individual and of his household, an offering of all to the Lord. Many applications of this idea. All can give something. Religion sanctifies the world through the sanctification of souls. The Spirit creates afresh the inner man, then all follows.—R.

Vers. 14—17.—*The offering of fowls—turtle-doves or young pigeons.* The great abundance of these birds in the East would make the provision one which was easy even for the poorest to fulfil. How gracious this appointment! God is no "hard master." He delights not in mere burdensome sacrifice—no costliness, suffering, or privation has merit with him. He demands the willing obedience of the heart. He asks for that which really represents a surrender of self. All these minute regulations were simply intended to develop the principle of voluntary obedience. There was the same subdivision in the case of the bird as in the case of the quadruped, to remind the very poorest and humblest offerer that he must not shelter himself in the insignificance of his offering from the obligations which it represented. The application of fire to the second bird denoted the application of the righteousness of God to the life of the offerer, and while it was as a prescribed offering a promise of acceptance, and therefore of renewing grace and spiritual restoration, it was on the part of the offerer the pledge and promise of an entire obedience in which body, soul, and spirit, all the life and all the possessions, should be consecrated to God.—R.

EXPOSITION.

CHAPTER II.

THE MEAT OFFERING. The regulation of the burnt offering as a Levitical institution is immediately followed by a similar regulation of the meat offering, consisting of flour and oil, with salt and frankincense, and usually accompanied by the drink offering of wine. The sacrifice of the animal in the burnt offering had represented the entire surrender of the offerer's will and life to God; the presentation of the fruits and products of the earth in the meat offering represents man's gift of homage, whereby he acknowledges God's sovereignty over all things and over himself, by offering to him a portion of that which he had graciously bestowed in abundance. David's words, "All things come of thee, and of thine own have we given thee . . . all this store cometh of thine hand, and is all thine own" (1 Chron. xxix. 14, 16), express the idea underlying the meat offering. In the acted language of symbolism, it not only recognized the supremacy of God, but made a tender of loyal submission on the part of the offerer; as gifts of homage did in the case of Jacob and Esau (Gen. xxxii. 20), and as they do to this day throughout our Indian empire, and generally in the East.

Ver. 1.—**And when any will offer a meat offering unto the Lord.** The word used in the original for "meat offering" (*minchah*), means, like its Greek equivalent, δῶρον, a gift made by an inferior to a superior. Thus the sacrifices of Cain and Abel were their "minchah" to God (Gen. iv. 3, 4), the present sent to Esau by Jacob was his "minchah" (Gen. xxxii. 13), and the present to Joseph was his brethren's "minchah" (Gen. xliii. 11). It is therefore equivalent to a gift of homage, which recognizes the superiority of him to whom it is offered, and ceremonially promises loyal obedience to him. Owing to its use in this passage, it came gradually to be confined in its signification to vegetable gifts,—unbloody sacrifices, as they are called sometimes, in contrast to animal sacrifices—while the word "corban" came to be used in the wider acceptation which once belonged to "minchah." The conditions to be fulfilled by the Israelite who offered a meat offering were the following. 1. He must offer either (1) uncooked flour, with oil, salt, and frankincense, or (2) flour made into an unleavened cake (whether of the nature of biscuit or pancake), with oil, salt, and frankincense; or (3) roasted grains, with oil, salt, and frankincense. 2. He must bring his offering to the court of the tabernacle, and give to the priests at least as much as one omer (that is, nearly a gallon), and not more than sixty-one omers. The priest receiving it from him must: 1. Take a handful of the flour, oil, and salt, or a proportionate part of the cake (each omer generally made ten cakes) in place of the flour, and burn it with all the frankincense as a *memorial* upon the altar of burnt offering. 2. With his brother priests he must eat the remainder within the precincts of the tabernacle. Here the essentials of the sacrifice are the presentation made by the offerer, and the burning of *the memorial* on the altar, followed by the consumption of the remainder by the priests. The moral lesson taught to the Israelite completed that of the burnt offering. As the burnt offering taught self-surrender, so the meat offering taught recognition of God's supremacy and submission to it, the first by the surrender of a living creature substituted for the offerer, the second by the gift of a part of the good things bestowed by God on man for the preservation of life which, being given back to God, serve as a recognition of his supremacy. Spiritually the lesson taught the Jew was that of the necessity of a loyal service to God; and mystically he may have learnt a lesson (1) as to the force of prayer rising up to heaven as the incense which had to be offered with each form of the meat offering; (2) as to the need of purity and incorruption, symbolized by the prohibition of leaven and honey, and the command to use salt. The supplemental character of the meat offering accounts for the order in which it here stands, not arbitrarily interposed between two animal sacrifices, but naturally following on the burnt offering, as an adjunct to it and the complement of its teaching. So close was the union between the two sacrifices, that the burnt offering was never offered without the accompaniment of the meat offering (Numb. xv. 4). It has been also maintained that the meat offering, like the drink offering, was never made independently of the animal sacrifice; but this cannot be proved. On the contrary, the manner in which laws regulating it are here laid down, lead to the inference that it might be offered, when any willed it, by itself. The close connection between the sacrifice of an animal and the offering of cakes of flour, and of wine, is noticeable in heathen sacrifices likewise. The very word, *immolare*, translated "to sacrifice," is derived from the *mola* or salt-cake offered with the animal; and the other word ordinarily used in Latin for "sacrifice," that is, *mactare*, is

derived from the victim being enriched (*magis auctus*) with the libation of wine. Thus we see that the offering of the fruits of the earth was regarded, elsewhere as well as in Judæa, as the natural concomitant of an animal sacrifice, and not only that, but as so essential a part of the latter as to have given a name to the whole ceremony, and not only to the whole ceremony, but to the specific act of the slaughter of the victim. The thought of the heathen in offering the fruits of the earth was probably not much different from that of the Israelites. It was his gift to the superhuman power, to which he thus acknowledged that he owed submission. We may further notice that salt was enjoined in the heathen as in the Jewish sacrifices as indispensable. Pliny says that the importance of salt is seen especially in sacrifices, none of which are completed without the salt-cake ('Hist. Nat.,' 31, 7) The now obsolete use of the word "meat" in the sense of "food," in contrast to "flesh," creates some confusion of thought. "Fruit offering" would be a better title, were it not that the signification of "fruit" is going through a similar change to that which "meat" has undergone. "Flour offering" might be used, but an alteration in the rendering is not imperative.

Ver. 2.—**He shall take thereout his handful.** This was the task of the priest. The handful that he took and burnt upon the altar has the technical and significative name of **the memorial**. It acted as a memorial before God, in the same way as Cornelius's prayers and alms—"Thy prayers and thine alms are come up for a memorial before God" (Acts x. 4)—being something which should cause God to think graciously of the offerer. The **frankincense** is not mixed with the flour and the oil and the salt, as a constituent element of the offering, but is placed upon them, and is all of it burnt in "the memorial," symbolizing the need of adding prayer to sacrifice, that the latter may be acceptable to God.

Ver. 3.—**The remnant of the meat offering shall be Aaron's and his sons'.** The meat offerings must have gone far to supply the priests with farinaceous food, as, for every handful of flour burnt on the altar, nearly a gallon went to the priests. They had to eat it within the precincts of the tabernacle, as was the case with all meats that were *most holy*, viz. the minchahs, the shewbread, and the flesh of the sin offering and of the trespass offering (ch. x. 12). Other meats assigned to the priests might be eaten in any clean place (ch. x. 14). The priests' own meat offerings were wholly burnt (ch. vi. 23).

Vers. 4—11.—The second form of meat offering, when the flour and oil were made up into four varieties of cakes. The ritual of offering is not different from that of the first form. The frankincense is not mentioned, but doubtless is understood. The rabbinical rule, that meat offerings, when following upon burnt offerings or peace offerings, had no frankincense burnt with them, rests on no solid foundation.

Vers. 11, 12.—**Ye shall burn no leaven nor any honey, in any offering of the Lord made by fire.** Leaven and honey are not forbidden to be offered to the Lord; on the contrary, in the next verse they are commanded to be offered. The prohibition only extends to their being burnt on the altar, owing, no doubt, to the effect of fire upon them in making them swell and froth, thus creating a repulsive appearance which, as we shall see, throughout the Mosaic legislation, represents moral evil. The firstfruits of honey are to be offered (cf. Exod. xxii. 29), and leaven is to be used in the two wave loaves offered at the Feast of Pentecost as firstfruits (ch. xxiii. 17). The words translated **As for the oblation of the firstfruits, ye shall offer them unto the Lord,** should be rendered *As an oblation of firstfruits ye shall offer them* (that is, leaven and honey),

but they shall not be burnt on the altar. The mark in A. V. denoting a new paragraph at the beginning of ver. 12, should be removed.

Ver. 13.—**Every oblation of thy meat offering shalt thou season with salt.** Salt is commanded as symbolizing in things spiritual, because preserving in things physical, incorruption (cf. Matt. v. 13; Mark ix. 49; Luke xiv. 34; Col. iv. 6). It is an emblem of an established and enduring covenant, such as God's covenant with his people, which is never to wax old and be destroyed, and it is therefore termed **the salt of the covenant of thy God.** Hence "a covenant of salt" came to mean a covenant that should not be broken (Numb. xviii. 19; 2 Chron. xiii. 5). The use of salt is not confined to the meat offering. **With all thine offerings thou shalt offer salt.** Accordingly we find in Ezek. xliii. 24, "The priest shall cast salt upon them, and they shall offer them up for a burnt offering."

Vers. 14—16.—The third form of meat offering, parched grains of corn, with oil, salt, and frankincense. The mark of a new paragraph should be transferred from ver. 12 to the beginning of ver. 14.

HOMILETICS.

Vers. 1—16.—*The meat offering.* It consisted of a gift to God of the products of the earth most needed for the support of life—flour and oil, to which were added salt and frankincense, and it was generally accompanied by the drink offering of wine. It was offered to God in token of the recognition of his almighty power which gave the corn, the olive, and the vine, and of the submission of the creature to him, the merciful Creator.

I. IT WAS A GIFT OF HOMAGE. As such, it had a meaning well defined and well understood in the East, that meaning being an acknowledgment of the sovereignty of God, and a promise of loyal obedience on the part of the offerer.

II. SCRIPTURAL EXAMPLES OF THE GIFT OF HOMAGE. 1. The sacrifices of Cain and Abel. Whether the sacrifice was of the fruits of the ground or of the flock made no difference. Each was the "minchah," or "gift," of the offerer, acknowledging God as his God—one, however, offered loyally, the other hypocritically (Gen. iv. 3, 4). 2. The present sent to Esau by Jacob (Gen. xxxii.; xxxiii.). Jacob had sent a humble message to his brother (Gen. xxxii. 3), but this was not enough, "The messengers returned to Jacob, saying, We came to thy brother Esau, and also he cometh to meet thee, and four hundred men with him" (Gen. xxxii. 6). Then Jacob, terror-stricken, sent his gift of homage (Gen. xxxii. 13), which symbolically acknowledged Esau as his suzerain lord. Esau, by accepting it (Jacob "urged him and he took it"), bound himself to give protection to his brother as to an inferior, and offered to leave some of his soldiers with him for the purpose (Gen. xxxiii. 15). 3. The present carried by Jacob's sons to Joseph when they went down into Egypt (Gen. xliii. 11). 4. The present without which Saul felt that he could not appear before Samuel (1 Sam. ix. 7). 5. The gifts presented to the young Child by the Wise Men of the East (Matt. ii. 11).

III. EXAMPLES OF THE GIFT OF HOMAGE IN THE PRESENT DAY. 1. At an Indian durbar, every one of the dependent princes brings his present, and offers it to the representative of the Empress of India. 2. Presents are always brought by natives of India to British officials set over them, when they have a request to make, and ceremonially accepted by the latter by a touch of the hand. 3. In the Abyssinian war a present of a thousand oxen and five hundred sheep was sent by King Theodore of Abyssinia to Lord Napier of Magdala, in token of submission at the last moment, and rejected by the English general. Had he accepted it, he would have been bound to give the king protection.

IV. LESSONS TO US FROM THE MEAT OFFERING. 1. To give to God of the worldly goods which God has given to us (1) freely, (2) cheerfully, (3) loyally. Our motive must not be self-ostentation, nor the praise of men, nor our own gratification. By our offering to God we must recognize God's claims over us, and openly profess our loving submission to them. This throws a new light on the practice of almsgiving in the weekly offertory of the Church. 2. To give a hearty and loyal service to God in other respects besides almsgiving, such as obedience to his commandments, doing his will on earth.

V. THE GIFT OF HOMAGE CALLS FORTH A REQUITING GIFT. Esau gave protection in return for cattle. Joseph gave sacks of corn in return for "a little balm and a little honey, spices and myrrh, nuts and almonds." The representative of the Crown of England gives back to each prince at a durbar a present greater than he has received. So we give to God repentance, and receive back from him forgiveness; we give faith, and receive grace; we give obedience, and receive righteousness; we give thanksgiving, and receive enduring favour; we give, in the sacrament of the Lord's Supper, the "creatures of bread and wine," and we receive back "the strengthening and refreshing of our souls by the Body and Blood of Christ."

Ver. 13.—*Salt* was to be used with all the sacrifices. Cf. Ezek. xliii. 24; Mark ix. 49.

I. WHAT IT RECALLED TO THE MIND OF THE OFFERER. The eating of bread and salt together being the ceremony which finally ratified an agreement or covenant (as it still is in Arabia), salt was associated in the mind of the Israelite with the thought of a firmly established covenant. Each time, therefore, that the priest strewed the salt on the offering there would have been a reminder to all concerned of the peculiar blessing enjoyed by the nation and all members of it, of being in covenant with God, without which they would not have been in a state to offer acceptable sacrifices at all.

II. WHAT IT SYMBOLIZED. The effect of salt being to preserve from corruption, its being sprinkled on the sacrifice taught the offerer the necessity of purity and constancy in his devotion of himself to God.

III. THE SYMBOL TAKEN UP AND APPLIED IN THE NEW TESTAMENT. 1. The Christian's speech is not to be corrupting, but edifying. "Let your speech be always seasoned with salt, that ye may know how ye ought to answer every man" (Col. iv. 6). "Let no corrupt communication proceed out of your mouth, but that which is good for the use of edifying, that it may minister grace unto the hearers" (Eph. iv. 29). 2. Christian men are to be salted with fire, as the sacrifices are salted with salt (Mark ix. 49), and the life of the collective body of Christians, the Church, is to be, in its effects upon the world, as salt. "Ye are the salt of the earth" (Matt. v. 13). "Have salt in yourselves" (Mark ix. 50). Men influenced by the Spirit of Christ, having been themselves salted with fire, have now become the salt which saves the world from perishing in its own corruption.

IV. THE SALT MAY LOSE ITS SAVOUR (Matt. v. 13; Mark ix. 50; Luke xiv. 34). This is the case when "doctrine" being no longer characterized by "uncorruptness, gravity, sincerity" (Titus ii. 7), religion becomes changed into superstition, thenceforward debasing instead of elevating mankind; or when it stirs men to acts of fanaticism, or rebellion, or cruelty; or when the spiritual life becomes so dead within it that it abets instead of counteracting the wickedness of the world.

V. SALT SYMBOLIZES PERMANENCY AS WELL AS PURITY. Our love for Christ must be, St. Paul teaches us (Eph. vi. 24), a love "in sincerity," or rather, as the word should be translated, "in incorruption," that is, an abiding love, without human caprice or changeableness; and our obedience to God must be constant, without breaks in its even course, and lasting to the end of life. "Because iniquity shall abound, the love of many shall wax cold. But he that shall endure unto the end, the same shall be saved" (Matt. xxiv. 12, 13). "Be thou faithful unto death, and I will give thee a crown of life" (Rev. ii. 10).

HOMILIES BY VARIOUS AUTHORS.

Consecrated life-work, as brought out in the meat offering. Ch. ii. 1—11; cf. John iv. 34; Acts x. 4; Phil. iv. 18; John vi. 27. The idea prominently presented in the burnt offering is, we have seen, *personal consecration,* on the ground of *expiation* and *acceptance* through a substitute. In the meat offering, to which we now address ourselves, we find the further and supplementary idea of *consecrated life-work.* For the fine flour presented was the product of labour, the actual outcome of the consecrated person, and consequently a beautiful representative of that whole life-work which results from a person consciously consecrated. Moreover, as in the case of the burnt offering there was a daily celebration, so in the case of this meat offering there was a perpetual dedication in the *shew-bread.* What we have in this chapter, therefore, is a voluntary dedication on the part of an individual, corresponding to the perpetual dedication on the part of the people. The covenant people are to realize the idea of consecration in their whole life-work. Lange has noticed that here it is the soul (נֶפֶשׁ) which is said to present the meat offering, something more spiritual, as an act, than the presentation of the burnt offering by the man (אָדָם). We assume, then, that the leading thought of this meat offering is *consecrated life-work,* such as was brought out in all its perfection when our Lord declared, "My meat is to do the will of him that sent me, and to finish his work" (John iv. 34).

I. WORK DONE FOR GOD SHOULD BE THE BEST OF ITS KIND. The meat offering, whether prepared in a sumptuous oven (תַּנּוּר) such as would be found with the wealthy, or baken in a pan (מַחֲבַת) such as middle-class people would employ, or seethed in a common dish (מַרְחֶשֶׁת) the utensil of the poor,—was always to be of fine flour (סֹלֶת), that is, flour separated from the bran. It matters not what our station in life may be, we may still present to God a *thorough* piece of work. "Whatsoever thy hand findeth to do, do it with thy might" (Eccles. ix. 10) is an exhortation applicable to all. The microscopic thoroughness of God's work in nature, which leads him to clothe even the grass, which is to-morrow to be cast into the oven, with more glory than Solomon (Matt. vi. 28—30), is surely fitted to stimulate every consecrated person to the most painstaking work.

And here we are led of necessity to the life-work of Jesus Christ, as embodying this idea perfectly. How thoroughly he did everything! His life was an exquisite piece of moral mosaic. Every detail may be subjected to the most microscopic criticism, only to reveal its marvellous and matchless beauty.

II. WORK DONE FOR GOD SHOULD BE PERMEATED BY HIS SPIRIT AND GRACE. The fine flour, be it ever so pure, would not be accepted dry; it required *oil* to make it *bakeable.* Oil has been from time immemorial the symbol of Divine *unction,* in other words, of the Holy Spirit's gracious operation. Hence we infer that work done for God must be done in co-operation with the Spirit. It is when we realize that we are fellow-workers with God, that he is our Partner, that he is working in us and by us, and when, in consequence, we become spiritually minded, walking in the Spirit, living in the Spirit,—it is then that our work becomes a spiritual thing.

And here, again, would we direct attention to the life-work of Christ, as spiritually perfect. The gift of the Spirit at his baptism, the descending dove, an organic whole (Luke iii. 22), signalizes the complete spirituality of Jesus. He was "filled with the Spirit," it was "in the power of the Spirit" he did all his work. Herein he is our perfect Example.

III. WORK CAN ONLY BE DONE FOR GOD IN A PRAYERFUL SPIRIT. This follows naturally from what has been already stated, but it requires to be emphasized in view of the *frankincense* which had in every case to accompany the meat offering. This is admittedly the symbol of devotion (cf. Kalisch, *in loco*). A life-work, to be consecrated, must be steeped in prayer; its Godward object must be kept constantly in view, and stated and ejaculatory prayer must envelop it like a cloud of incense.

It is, again, worth while to notice how the perfect life-work of Christ was pervaded by prayer. If any one since the world began had a right to excuse himself from the formality of prayer in consequence of his internal state of illumination, it was Jesus

Christ. And yet we may safely say that his was the most prayerful life ever spent on earth. As Dr. Guthrie once said, "The sun as it sank in the western sea often left him, and as it rose behind the hills of Moab returned to find him, on his knees." We need not wonder why he spent whole nights in supplication, for he was bringing every detail of his work into Divine review in the exercise of prayer. There is consequently a most significant appeal issuing out of his holy life, to work prayerfully at all times if we would work for God.

IV. WORK FOR GOD MUST BE DIVORCED FROM MALICE AND FROM PASSION, AND DONE IN CALM PURITY AND STRENGTH. Much of the world's work has malice and passion for its sources. These motives seem to be symbolized by the *leaven* and *honey*, which were forbidden as elements in the meat offering. Care should be taken in work for God that we do not impart into it worldly and selfish motives. Such are sure to vitiate the whole effort. The Lord with whom we have to do looks upon the heart, and weighs the motives along with the work.

What a commentary, again, was the perfect life of Jesus upon this! Malice and passion never mixed with his pure motives. He sought not his own will, nor did he speak his own words, but calmly kept the Father's will and glory before him, all through.

V. WORK FOR GOD SHOULD BE COMMITTED TO HIS PRESERVING CARE. For it is to be feared we often forget to season our sacrifices with *salt*. We work for God in a consecrated spirit, but we do not universally commit our work to his preserving grace, and expect its permanency and purity. Work for God *should* endure. It is our own fault if it do not.

Our blessed Lord committed his work to the preserving care of the Father. He was, if we may judge from Isa. xlix. 4, as well as from the Gospel, sometimes discouraged, yet when constrained to say, " I have laboured in vain, I have spent my strength for nought, and in vain," he could add, " Yet surely my judgment is with the Lord, and my work with my God."

VI. WORK DONE FOR GOD IS SURE TO BENEFIT OUR FELLOW-MEN. The meat offering was only partially burnt on the altar—a handful, containing, however, all the frankincense, was placed in the sacred fire, and thus accepted; the rest became the property of the priest. How beautifully this indicated the truth that when one tries to please God, his fellow-men, and especially those of the household of faith, are sure to participate in the blessing! The monastic idea was an imperfect one, suggesting the possibility of devotion to God and indifference to man coexisting in the same breast. We deceive ourselves so long as we suppose so.

Our Master went about doing good; he was useful as well as holy; and so shall all his followers find themselves, if their consecrated life-work is moulded according to the pattern he has shown us. Faithfulness in the first table of the Law secures faithfulness in the second.—R. M. E.

About honouring God with our firstfruits. Ch. ii. 12—16; cf. Prov. iii. 9; 1 Cor. xv. 23; Jas. i. 18. This arrangement about the firstfruits, though appended to the meat offering, demands a special notice. The meat offering, we have seen, affirms the general principle that our life-work should be dedicated to God. But here in the firstfruits we have a special portion which is to be regarded as too sacred for any but Divine use. This leads us directly to affirm—

I. WHILE GOD HAS A RIGHT TO ALL, HE CLAIMS A SPECIAL RIGHT TO THE FIRST-FRUITS OF ALL OUR INCREASE. The danger is in losing sight of the special claim in asserting the general principle. For instance, we must not deny God a special claim upon the first day of the week, because we acquiesce in the general principle that he has a right to all our time. Again, we must not withhold our tithes, a certain proportion of our substance, through an easy-going statement that he has a right to all our substance. We must condescend to particulars.

II. THE DEDICATION OF THE FIRSTFRUITS EXTENDED TO ANIMALS AS WELL AS TO THE VEGETABLE KINGDOM. The dedication of the firstborn of man and beast is manifestly part and parcel of the same principle (Exod. xiii. 1—16). This leads up to God's right to the Firstborn of the human race, to him of whom the Father said, " I will make him my firstborn, higher than the kings of the earth" (Ps. lxxxix. 27). Jesus is the Firstborn of humanity, the flower and firstfruits of the race. Hence we find the expression used regarding the risen Saviour, "But now is Christ risen from the dead, and become the firstfruits of them that slept" (1 Cor. xv. 23). He is also called "the firstborn from the dead" (Col. i. 18). Of him, therefore, pre-eminently was the dedication of the firstfruits typical.

If God has a right to the firstfruits of the life-work of the human race, he receives them in the perfectly holy life of Jesus Christ. So that, as we found the meat offering pointing to this, so do we find this arrangement about the firstfruits.

III. GOD HAS ALSO A RIGHT TO SERVICE, EVEN THOUGH IT MAY NOT BE PERFECT. This seems to be the principle underlying the "oblation of the firstfruits." This, as we learn from ch. xxiii. 15—21, was presented at Pentecost, and consisted of two tenth-deals of flour baked with leaven. Such an arrangement points to the possibility of imperfection in serving God, which was met by the *sin offering* accompanying it. If, then, the firstfruits at the Passover, presented with oil and frankincense, typified Christ the Firstfruits in all his perfection; the oblation at Pentecost typified believers, Gentiles and Jews, who are trying, though imperfectly, to realize a consecrated life-work. God does not reject the labours of his people, even though they are very far from perfect. He has provided a sin offering to meet the imperfections of the case and render all acceptable to him.[1]

IV. THE DEDICATION OF THE FIRSTFRUITS WAS THE EXPRESSION NOT ONLY OF THANKSGIVING BUT ALSO OF FAITH. God's rights first, even before man's need has been met. It was seeking God's kingdom first, in the assurance that all the needful things shall be added (Matt. vi. 33). It is most important that we should always act in this trustful spirit. This faith is, in fact, a kind of firstfruits of the spiritual life which the Lord expects, and in rendering it to him we experience wondrous comfort and blessing.—R. M. E.

Vers. 1—3.—*Mediate and immediate presentation.* The abrogation by Christianity of the rites and ceremonies of Judaism does not prevent the necessity nor dispel the advantages of becoming acquainted with the laws by which the ancient sacrifices were regulated. The mind of God may be ascertained in the precepts delivered in olden days, and underlying principles recognized that hold good in every age. The very fact that truth has thus to be searched for, and by patient induction applied to present conditions, should prove an incitement rather than a hindrance to investigation. Freeing the kernel from its husk, grasping the essence and neglecting the accidents, preferring the matter to the form, we shall behold in the Law prophecies of the gospel, and admit the likeness that proclaims both to have proceeded from the same God.

I. A DISTINCTION IS MADE BETWEEN OFFERINGS ACCEPTED BY GOD DIRECTLY, AND THOSE PRESENTED TO HIM INDIRECTLY FOR THE USE OF HIS APPOINTED SERVANTS. The flour being brought to the priests, a handful was taken, and with frankincense was burnt upon the altar, rising to heaven in the form of smoke and perfume. The remainder of the flour was for the consumption of the priests. This distinction is applicable to many Christian offerings. The money given for the erection or support of a place of prayer, the surrender of time and thought for public worship, or for evangelistic work, the acknowledgment of Jesus Christ by baptism and by partaking of the Lord's Supper, the devotion of our strength and influence to God's service,—these may be considered as gifts presented straight to God himself. They are laid upon the altar, enwrapped in the fire of holy love, perfumed with prayer, and are consumed with the zeal of God's house. But there are other oblations which must be regarded in the light of mediate presentations to God, such as, supporting the ministry at home and missionaries abroad, ministering to the need of the aged and feeble, and giving the cup of water to the disciples of Christ. This distinction is not meant to glorify the one class in comparison with the other, but to clarify our views, and to lead to the inquiry whether we are doing all we can in both directions. There is an idea in many minds that if the works of benevolence and charity be performed, the other duties of gathering together in the solemn assembly and of avowal of attach-

[1] Cf. Lowe's 'Annual Feasts of the Jews,' pp. 22—45.

ment to Christ are of little importance. The burning of a portion of the offering upon the altar rebukes such a conception. And similarly we learn that the punctual attendance upon the means of grace, and the regular offering of praise and prayer, must not exclude the exercise of hospitality and sympathy.

II. Looking at these two classes separately, we remark, respecting the bestowment of the "remnant" upon the priests, that OFFERINGS TO GOD MUST BE PRESENTED IN THEIR ENTIRETY. All the flour brought was considered "most holy," and could not be employed thereafter except for the benefit of "sacred" persons. A man was at liberty to offer or withhold, but once having vowed, he could not withdraw even a portion of his present. God will not be satisfied with a share of a man's heart. If it be given at all, it must be the whole heart. And once having engaged ourselves to be his, there can be no revocation of faculty, affection or time. To look back after taking hold of the plough is to mar religious dedication. The mistake of Ananias was in pretending to give the full price, and attempting to conceal a portion of it. Oh that we could make religion permeate our lives, hallowing even our secular employments by doing all to the glory of God!

III. With respect to the portion burnt for a "memorial," observe that AN OFFERING HAS A DOUBLE INTENT; IT EVINCES A GRATEFUL REMEMBRANCE BY THE WORSHIPPER OF GOD'S BOUNTY AND REQUIREMENTS, AND IT ENSURES A GRACIOUS REMEMBRANCE OF THE WORSHIPPER ON THE PART OF GOD. The special significance of the "minchah" lay in its expression of thankfulness, and of desire by that expression to secure the favour of the God by whom our needs are supplied. To appreciate past kindness is to show a fitness to receive additional mercies in the future. To remember God is to be remembered in turn by God. At the Communion we take the bread and wine as Christ's memorial, and he, the Master of the feast, approves the spirit and the act, and thinks upon us for good. Self-interest recommends us to honour the Lord. To save a handful of meal would be to lose a coming harvest, and to save ourselves temporally is to lose eternally.

IV. ALL OFFERINGS MADE IN THE APPOINTED WAY ARE WELL PLEASING UNTO GOD. The meal oblation differed from the sacrifice of a lamb or bullock, perhaps was not so expensive, and all of it was not consumed by fire; yet it was also declared to be "of a sweet savour unto the Lord." We should not trouble ourselves because our kind of service is distinct from that which our fellows render, or is treated by the world as less important. The mites of the widow lie side by side in the treasury with the shekels of the wealthy, and will receive quite as much notice from the Lord of the sanctuary. If a niche in the temple of heroes is denied to us, or if the eloquence that sways the wills of men belongs not to our tongue, yet may we with kindly words and manly actions and loving tones do our little part in Christianizing the world, and our efforts will win the commendation of him who "seeth not as man seeth." And further, let us not be sad because at different periods we do not find ourselves able to render the same service. In the winter we may sacrifice from our herds and flocks, but must wait till the summer for the firstfruits of the field. Youth, manhood, and age have their appropriate labours. Leisure and business, health and sickness, prosperity and adversity, may present to the Lord equally acceptable offerings.—S. R. A.

Ver. 13.—*The salt of the covenant.* It has been thought by some unworthy of the notion of an Infinite Being to consider him as concerned about such petty details as those here laid down for observance. But since the Deity had to deal with uninstructed creatures, with men whose ideas of his greatness and holiness were obscure and imperfect, it was surely wise to act according to the analogy furnished by the customs of earthly monarchs, whose courts require attention to be paid to numberless points of behaviour. Only thus could the august nature of Jehovah, the majesty of his attributes, and the solemnity of religious worship be duly impressed upon the minds of the Israelites. Every rite had a meaning, and to add salt to every offering was a command we shall find it interesting to study.

I. OBEDIENCE TO THIS COMMAND CONSTITUTES EVERY OFFERING A PART OF THE COVENANT BETWEEN GOD AND HIS PEOPLE. It was by virtue of a special covenant that the nation had been selected as the vehicle of Divine revelation and the repository of Divine favours. The relation of superiority in which God stands to man, places in a strong light his condescension in making an agreement by which he binds himself as well as the people. Every covenant implies mutual obligations. God promised to guide and bless the Israelites if they, in their turn, kept his commandments and held him in proper esteem. To put salt, therefore, in compliance with his behest, was to acknowledge that the covenant remained in force, and the act became a present instance of the existence of the covenant. It was as much as to say, "I present this gift because of the covenanted relationship in which I stand to Jehovah." The covenant of the gospel is ratified in Christ for all his faithful seed, who are made partakers of the blessing promised to Abraham (Gal. iii. 16). Hence whatever we do is in the name of Christ, recognizing our sonship, heirship, and co-heirship. The covenant influences, embraces all thoughts and deeds.

II. SALT, AS THE EMBLEM OF HOSPITALITY, SHOWS THAT SERVICE TO GOD IS A FEAST OF FRIENDSHIP. The offering of flour on which oil was poured was itself indicative of a friendly meal, and this view was strengthened by adding salt to the sacrifice. So surprising is the intimacy to which the Most High admits his people, that they may be said to feed daily at his table; all the fruits of the earth are the product of his bounty, which honours men as his guests. We do but render to God what he first bestowed, and in thus approaching we enjoy his presence and favour. It is permitted us to make ready for the Passover, whereat the Lord shall sit down with his disciples.

III. SALT, AS A PRESERVATIVE, REMINDS US OF THE PURITY WHICH SHOULD CHARACTERIZE OUR LIVES. Nothing that partakes of corruption is fit to be brought unto the ever-living God. "Let us cleanse ourselves from all filthiness of the flesh and spirit." "Flesh and blood" tend to impurity and death, and "cannot inherit the kingdom of God." Our speech must be with grace, seasoned with salt, lest anything destructive of peace or edification should issue from our lips. Apart from the life that is instilled through faith in Christ, man is dead, and decay is loathsome. Without faith our walk and conversation cannot please God, nor are we "the salt of the earth." Christians are salted with the purifying fire of trial (Mark ix. 49).

IV. SALT TEACHES US THE PERPETUITY OF OUR FRIENDSHIP WITH GOD. A covenant of salt is for ever. (See Numb. xviii. 19 and 2 Chron. xiii. 5.) It lasts as long as the conditions are observed by us, for God will never change, nor desire on his part to revoke his blessing. Let us rejoice in the truth that he abideth faithful, and in the thought of the indissoluble alliance thereby created. He does not wish to treat us as playthings, invented to amuse him temporarily, and then to be tossed aside. We are put in possession by the great Healer and Life-restorer of imperishable principles, seeds of righteousness, that avert corruption and defy decay. Our devotion is not a hireling service that may soon terminate, but a consecration for the everlasting ages.—S. R. A.

Vers. 7—13.—*The offering of daily life.* It is interesting to perceive how the instructions here recorded made it possible for all classes of the people to bring sacrifices to Jehovah. None could complain of want of sufficient means or of the necessary cooking utensils. All such objections are forestalled by these inclusive arrangements. Whether consisting of "cakes" or "wafers," whether baked on a flat iron plate or boiled in a pot, the offering was lawful and acceptable. How, then, can we imagine that Christian work and gifts are so restricted in their nature as to be procurable only by a few?

I. THE MATERIAL OF WHICH THIS OFFERING WAS COMPOSED. "His offering shall be of fine flour." The sacrifice God desires is of what man deems most precious, viz. life. As the animal was killed, giving up its life to God, so now there is presented in this oblation: 1. Something that belongs to *daily* life. 2. Contributing to its *support;* 3. and *enjoyment.* By bestowing of our substance upon God, all our property is sanctified. To set apart specifically a portion of time in which to worship God, hallows the remainder of the week. See in Jesus the true Meal Oblation, the Bread of Life. We ask the Father to accept his offering on our behalf, and we also live on him as our spiritual food. 4. The sample presented must be of *the best of its kind.* God will not be slighted with scanty adoration and inferior exercise of our powers. Only wheaten flour is permitted.

II. ACCOMPANIMENTS OF THE OFFERING. Allusions to the Jewish sacrifices are frequent in the New Testament, and we cannot be wrong in guiding ourselves by such an interpretation of these figurative regulations. 1. Oil must be added. It was the element of consecration, and reminds us of the needful anointing of the Spirit to qualify us for our duties. "Ye have an unction from the Holy One." As used, like butter, to impart a relish to food, it became a symbol of gladness. So the Christian motto is, "Rejoice in the Lord alway." 2. Frankincense is required that a pleasant odour may ascend to the skies. So may our service be redolent to earth and heaven of a fragrant savour. In Rev. viii. 3, incense is offered with the prayers of the saints, and speaks to us of the intercession of Christ, by which our pleadings are made effectual. Let prayer be the constant attitude of our souls, and let us connect the Saviour with all we do and say. 3. It must be seasoned with salt, a remembrance and an emblem of God's covenant, by which his people are admitted to intimacy and friendship with him. The status of the believer is an indissoluble alliance with the Almighty on the ground of promise and oath. This is his privilege and motive power. Every sacrifice must be salted with the salt of holy obedience, producing peace and purity, and preserving it from corruption.

III. THINGS PROHIBITED. 1. Leaven, the emblem of wickedness, of hypocrisy, of fermenting putridity. 2. Honey, which, though sweet and increasing the delight with which food is partaken of, quickly turns to bitterness and corruption. It is regarded as typical of fleshly lusts which war against the soul, that love of the world which mars Christian character. The warning conveyed by these prohibitions is worthy of being sharply outlined in modern days, when the tendency waxes stronger to obliterate the dividing line between the Church and the world, and attempts are made to purify the impure, or to whiten the outside of sepulchres, and to seduce Christians into the belief that all the pursuits and pleasures of life may be harmlessly indulged in, and even sanctified to the glory of God. The first intention may be good, but the ultimate issue is unbounded licence. Christ and Belial, light and darkness, can have no lasting concord. We may, however, take the leaven and honey as indicating the truth that some things lawful in themselves and at certain seasons, are at other times displeasing to God. The mirth and music and demeanour that are innocent as such, may not befit us in the solemnity of special circumstances, for example, the worship of the sanctuary. "To everything there is a season."

CONCLUSION. The perfect realization of every offering is seen in the Lord our Saviour. What a matchless life was his! No stain of malice or lust; grace, beauty, purity, all exemplified in fullest degree; on him the Spirit ever rested; his words and works a continual sacrifice to his Father, evoking the exclamation, "This is my beloved Son: hear him." As the heavenly Manna, he satisfies the wants of his kingdom of priests, and his Body was consumed in the flames of Calvary as our memento before God.— S. R. A.

Vers. 1, 2.—*The minchah, a type of Christ.* Because the minchah was an offering without blood, and therefore was not intended as a sacrifice for sin (Heb. ix. 22), some have supposed that it was in use before the Fall. This opinion, however, has but little to sustain it. We certainly read of the minchah as having been offered by Cain (Gen. iv. 3); but then Abel, at the same time, offered the holocaust, or sin offering, which no one dreams of having formed any part of the original worship in Eden. Cain's fault was not in having offered the minchah, but in not associating with it some sin sacrifice. It is questionable whether the minchah, under the Law, was ever offered without such an accompaniment. Yet we may view the minchah as a type of Christ. For—

I. ALL THE HOLY BREAD TYPIFIED CHRIST. 1. *The manna was of this class.* (1) It is called "*bread* from heaven" (see Neh. ix. 15). (2) Compare John vi. 31—35, 41, 48—51. 2. *The shew-bread also was of this class.* (1) It was the bread of heaven, for it rested in the sanctuary, which was one of the typical "heavenly places." (2) It rested under the splendours of the Shechinah, and therefore took its name, "Bread of Faces," viz. of God. The Bread of the Sacred Presence. 3. *So was this bread of the minchah.* (1) This, indeed, was offered in the outer court; for there the altar stood. But so was Christ offered "outside the gate" of Jerusalem, and outside the courts of heaven. (2) But it was, like the shew-bread, destined to be eaten in the sanctuary. So is Christ eaten by his spiritual priesthood in his kingdom of heaven upon earth.

So is he destined to nourish the joys of the glorified in the heaven of heavens (Luke xxii. 30). (3) This was a *Eucharistic* offering, and equivalent to the bread of the Christian Eucharist (Matt. xxvi. 26 ; 1 Cor. x. 16).

II. THIS BREAD HAD THE QUALITY OF EXCELLENCE. 1. *As bread it was the staple of food.* (1) We can dispense with luxuries, but bread is necessary. It is "the staff of life." So is Christ. (2) Bread is, by a figure of speech, put for everything needful for the body (Matt. vi. 12). Christ is, by no figure of speech, everything needful to the soul. 2. *This bread was of "fine flour."* (1) It may have been of barley as well as of wheat (see Numb. v. 15). Every variety of spiritual nourishment may be found in Christ. (2) But the flour must be "fine." The nourishment we find in Christ is of the finest order. Christ is God's best Gift to us. So is Christ our best Gift to God. All secondary gifts are valuable as they are offered in his Name (2 Cor. ix. 15).

III. IT HAD NOTICEABLE ADJUNCTS. 1. *Oil was poured upon it.* (1) The oil was from the olive, a tree full of fatness (Judg. ix. 9). It is a symbol of the Holy Spirit's grace (Matt. xxv. 4). (2) The fine flour was anointed with it. Messiah is so named because anointed with the Holy Ghost without measure. The Greek synonym of the Hebrew Messiah is *Christ* (Isa. lxi. 1; Acts iv. 27; x. 38; Heb. i. 9). (3) We are called *Christians* because anointed by the Spirit of Christ (see 2 Cor. i. 21; 1 John ii. 20, 27). 2. *It was offered with frankincense.* (1) This was a favourite spice, which appears not to have been yielded by one tree alone, but probably was compounded from several. We read of "spikenard and saffron; calamus and cinnamon, *with all trees of frankincense*" (Cant. iv. 14). (2) It is associated with the Bridegroom in the Song of Songs, to express the perfections of his holy character, by which he is infinitely attractive to his Spouse, the Church. He is there described as coming up out of the wilderness "like pillars of smoke," probably alluding to the Shechinah, and "perfumed with myrrh and *frankincense,* with all the powders of the merchant" (Cant. iii. 6). (3) In these perfections he is no less grateful to God when offered up to him (Matt. iii. 17; xvii. 5; 2 Pet. i. 17). As we become Christ-like, we are also well pleasing in his sight. The faithful minister of the Word is "unto God a sweet savour of Christ" (2 Cor. ii. 15).— J. A. M.

Vers. 1—10.—*The feast upon the minchah.* In our remarks upon the two first of these verses, we viewed the minchah, or meat offering, as a type of Christ. Upon this point additional light may be incidentally thrown as we now proceed to consider the feast upon the minchah. For this we hold to be designed to represent our fellowship with God in Christ.

I. FEASTS HAVE EVER BEEN REGARDED AS TOKENS OF FRIENDSHIP. 1. *Secular history abounds in examples.* (1) These date back to very ancient times. The ancient Egyptians, Thracians, and Libyans made contracts of friendship by presenting a cup of wine to each other. Covenants were made by the ancient Persians and Germans at feasts. The Pythagoreans had a symbol, "Break no bread," which Erasmus interprets to mean "Break no friendship." (2) Similar usages still obtain. It would be considered amongst us a most incongruous thing for persons at enmity deliberately to sit down at the same table. So according to our laws, if a person drinks to another against whom he has an accusation of slander, he loses his suit, because this supposes that they are reconciled. 2. *Sacred history also furnishes examples.* (1) Isaac and Abimelech made a covenant with a feast (Gen. xxvi. 30, 31); so did Jacob and Laban (Gen. xxxi. 54); so did David and Abner (2 Sam. iii. 20). (2) The verb (ברה, *bera*) to eat, in the Hebrew, if not the root of the word (ברית, *berith*), covenant, is at least a kindred word. (3) Hence in apostolic times, Christians were forbidden to eat with wicked persons (1 Cor. v. 11; see also Gal. ii. 12). It must never be forgotten that the "friendship of the world is enmity against God."

II. THE FEAST OF THE MEAT OFFERING WAS A SYMBOL OF FELLOWSHIP WITH GOD. 1. *The "memorial" of the minchah was God's meat.* (1) The offerer separated a portion of the mass, which was called the memorial, or representation of the whole. Thus he took from the bulk of the fine flour a handful. To this he added a suitable proportion of oil. The whole of the frankincense was devoted. (2) The priest then burnt the complete memorial upon the altar of burnt offerings. (3) God signified his acceptance of it by consuming it in fire, which was not of human kindling, but had issued from his Shechinah. The portion thus consumed was regarded as " God's food," or " meat," of the offering which he was pleased to accept. This was one part of the feast. 2. *The remnant was then eaten by the priests.* (1) The priests here are not to be viewed as types of Christ. The high priest alone seems to have represented him (Heb. iii. 1 ; viii. 1 ; ix. 11). (2) The common priests were representatives rather of the holy people. Hence the whole nation of Israel were regarded as a " kingdom of priests " (Exod. xix. 6). The people, therefore, and in particular the offerer, representatively, feasted with God. (3) Under the gospel even this official representation is changed. The people of God are now an holy priesthood, not by representation, but in right of their spiritual birth (1 Pet. ii. 9). They draw nigh unto God (Heb. x. 19—22). They feast with him at his table and in his very Presence. (4) All this, amongst many other blessed things, is set forth in the Christian Eucharist, or Supper of the Lord.

III. CHRIST IS THE MEDIUM OF THIS FELLOWSHIP. 1. *Obviously so since the minchah was a type of Christ.* (1) This has been sufficiently shown (see Homily on vers. 1, 2). (2) We may add that the argument is sustained by the use of the term "memorial." When the firstling of the cattle was taken instead of the rest, it is called making a memorial to God (Exod. xxxiv. 19 ; see Hebrew text). This represented the taking of the Great Firstborn instead of all men, and the firstling of the cattle was only a *memorial*, not the real sacrifice. (3) It is a great truth that Christ is our one way of access to God (John xiv. 6). ".He is our peace ; " and it is through the frankincense of his presence that our offering becomes a " sweet savour "—a savour of rest, " unto the Lord " (vers. 2, 9). 2. *Christ is delectable food to faith.* (1) Sometimes in the minchah the flour was unbaked (ver. 2). In this case the oil accompanying it was unmingled. The portion reserved for the priests might, therefore, be mingled by them in any way they pleased to render it most palatable. (2) In other cases the bread was prepared to their hands. Sometimes baken in the oven in cakes, mingled with oil, or in unleavened wafers, with oil poured upon them (ver. 4). Sometimes in a pan or flat plate, mingled with oil or oil poured over it (vers. 5, 6). Sometimes in the frying-pan or gridiron, with oil (ver. 7). (3) The bread of life is essentially good and nourishing. It is at the same time capable of being served up in such variety as to suit every taste that is not vicious. It is the privilege of the scribe instructed in the kingdom to bring out " things new and old," to set old things in new lights, and to show that there is " nothing new under the sun ; " for all things are as old as the councils of eternity.— J. A. M.

Vers. 11—13.—*Notable things.* After describing the minchah under sundry forms, and before proceeding to the meat offering of the firstfruits, certain notable things are mentioned which the minchah has in common with sacrifices in general. These now claim attention, viz.—

I. THE PROHIBITION OF LEAVEN (ver. 11). The reasons of this appear to be : 1. *Because of its fermenting properties.* (1) These, which, under the action of heat, throw the lump into commotion, represent the evil passions of the heart (see 1 Cor. v. 6—8). But since the meat offering is taken as a type of Christ, it was most fitting that everything suggestive of these should be excluded. In him was no ferment of anger or discontent when he was subjected to the fiercest fires of the wrath of God (Isa. liii. 7). What an example has he left to us! (2) By its fermenting properties, leaven tended to reduce substances to corruption. But since our " Bread of Life," our " Firstfruit " of the resurrection, could not " see corruption," because he was the " Holy One," it was most proper that leaven should be absent from his type (Ps. xvi. 10; Acts ii. 31). 2. *That the Hebrews might be reminded of their deliverance from Egypt.* (1) For they were, at the time of the Exodus, so hurried that they had to take their dough as it was without being leavened (Exod. xii. 39). It was most salutary to keep alive the remembrance of such mercies as they then experienced, and of the stupendous works with which they were associated. (2) But since those things were all typical of gospel blessings, so must it be most edifying to us to remember the spiritual bondage and darkness from which we have been emancipated by the hand of that great Prophet "like unto Moses," to whom it is our duty to hearken in preference to him.

II. THE PROHIBITION OF HONEY (ver. 11). The reasons of this appear to be : 1. *Because honey was a symbol of carnal pleasures.* (1) It was in this light viewed by Philo and by Jerome: and certainly the similitude is apt. Though luscious to the palate, it is bitter to the stomach. So evermore is sensual gratification (see Prov. xxv. 16, 27). (2) The exclusion of honey from the sacrifices and offerings of the altar will, therefore, convey important morals, viz. (a) considering these as types of Christ, (b) considering them also as types of such spiritual sacrifices as we can present acceptably to God through Christ. Another reason may be: 2. *Because honey was offered with the abominations of the heathen.* (1) Honey was offered to Bacchus and to the *dii superi*, the *dii inferi*, and departed heroes. Hence Orpheus, in beginning his hymns, calls the infernal gods μειλίχιοι θεοί, and the souls of the dead, μέλισσαι. The origin of which custom is thus explained by Porphyry, "They made honey a symbol of death; and therefore poured out a libation of honey to the terrestrial gods" (see Brown's 'Antiquities,' vol. i. p. 331). (2) The Hebrews were instructed scrupulously to avoid the customs of the pagans (see Deut. xii. 29—31). Let Protestants studiously avoid the abominations of the Romish Antichrist (Rev. xviii. 4). (3) Leaven and honey might be offered with the oblation of the firstfruits; but they must not come upon God's altar. This is the teaching of ver. 12. The loaves of the firstfruits, which were perquisites of the priests, were even ordered to be baken with leaven (ch. xxiii. 17). So in like manner honey was to be offered to them (2 Chron. xxxi. 5). There are things which may be lawfully offered to man that may not be offered to God. As leaven and honey minlged with the bread, even of the priests, so human conversation, at its best, is but imperfect.

III. THE REQUISITION OF SALT (ver. 13). The reason of this appears in the many excellent things of which salt was the symbol. 1. *It was a symbol of purity.* (1) Hence it is described as "the salt of the covenant of God." The Hebrew term for covenant (ברית, *berith*) literally signifies *purification ;* and the covenant of God is the gospel which is instituted of God for our purification from sin. (2) Perhaps it was religiously, viz. in relation to the covenant, rather than for hygienic purposes, that infants were rubbed with salt (see Ezek. xvi. 4). 2. *It was a symbol of friendship.* (1) The effect of a covenant to the faithful is friendship. So, in token of friendship, the ancient Greeks ate bread and salt together. And the Russian emperors had a custom, derived to them from antiquity, of sending bread and salt from their tables to persons they intended to honour. (2) The delights of friendship are also set forth in this symbol. The following is rendered by Dr. A. Clarke from Pliny :—" So essentially necessary is salt that without it human life cannot be preserved : and even the pleasures and endowments of the mind are expressed by it ; the delights of life, repose, and the highest mental serenity are expressed by no other term than *sales* among the Latins. It has also been applied to designate the honourable rewards given to soldiers, which are called *salarii* or *salaries.* But its importance may be further understood by its use in sacred things, as no sacrifice was offered to the gods without the *salt-cake.*" (3) But that "conversation" of Christians is best "seasoned" that has the "salt of the covenant" (see Job vi. 6 ; Col. iv. 5, 6). 3. *It was a symbol of perpetuity.* (1) This is suggested by its preserving properties. It is used to preserve meat and other things from decomposing. It is in this the very opposite of leaven ; so, the reason which includes the one excludes the other. (2) Hence by the symbol of salt the perpetuity of God's covenant is expressed. Thus, " It is a covenant of salt *for ever* before the Lord" (Numb. xviii. 19 ; see also 2 Chron. xiii. 5). (3) Christians, who are the people of the covenant, are the preservers of the earth (see Matt. v. 13). Take the Christians out of the world, and it will rot. 4. *The qualities of salt should distinguish all sacrifices.* (1) They do distinguish the Great Sacrifice of Calvary. (2) All Christian offerings should resemble that. In allusion to the salting of sacrifices preparatory to their being offered up in the flames of the altar, our Lord says, " Every one shall be salted with fire," or rather, "salted *for the* fire," viz. of the altar, " and," or rather, " *as* every sacrifice is salted with salt " (Mark ix. 49, 50). " We may reasonably infer, that as salt has two qualities—the one to season meat, the other to preserve it from corruption ; so it fitly denotes that integrity and incorruptness which season every sacrifice, and render men's persons and services grateful to God " (Old Bible).—J. A. M.

Vers. 14—16.—*The minchah of the firstfruits.* Having viewed the minchah as a type of Christ, and having considered the feast upon it as expressing fellowship with God in him, we proceed to consider the offering of the firstfruits, which is still the minchah under yet another form. The text brings before us—

I. THINGS PECULIAR TO THE OFFERING OF THE FIRSTFRUITS. These are: 1. *The matter of the offering.* (1) It is specified as "green ears of corn." Still, observe, it is of the nature of bread, and so still typifies Christ, the Bread of Life. (2) But in this case the life is in the grain. In this view Christ compares himself to a corn of wheat (John xii. 24). In this passage there is also a reference to Ps. lxxii. 16, which is construed by learned Jews thus: "*He* shall be a *corn of wheat* in the earth on the top of the mountains." (3) It is specified as "firstfruits." As the firstborn of every animal was the Lord's (Exod. xii. 29; xiii. 12, 13; Numb. xviii. 16), so did he claim the vegetable firstfruits. And as Christ is "the Firstborn of every creature" (Col. i. 15), the Antitype of every firstborn,—so is he the Firstfruits of everything in the creation. Through him all things are blessed to our use and benefit. (4) In this character Jesus will come out in full form in the resurrection. He is the "First-begotten from the dead" (Rev. i. 5). The "Firstfruits of them that slept" and still sleep (1 Cor. xv. 20, 23; 1 Thess. iv. 14). Thus is he "the Beginning [or Chief] of the [new] creation of God" (Rev. iii. 14). 2. *The treatment it received.* (1) The corn was dried by the fire. It was not allowed to dry gradually and gently in the air, but was violently scorched. Here was set forth expressively that fire of grief and sorrow which parched the soul of Jesus. The fires of his zeal for the glory of God, which was outraged by the sinfulness of men, entered into his very soul (Ps. cxix. 139). So did the corresponding flames of sympathy for that humanity which he had so wondrously assumed; consuming, because of its sinfulness, under the fires of God's anger. (2) It was beaten. This threshing of the wheat represented the severity with which Jesus was treated, (*a*) in the court of Caiaphas; (*b*) in the hall of Pilate; (*c*) at the place called Calvary (Isa. liii. 5, 8).

II. THINGS COMMON TO THE FIRSTFRUITS AND OTHER FORMS OF THE MINCHAH. 1. *It was offered upon the altar of burnt offerings.* (1) Touching the altar, it became a sacrifice to God. (2) Consumed in the fire, it was accepted by God. 2. *It was offered with oil.* (1) The natural use of this was that the offering thereby became more readily consumed. The flame of oil is bright and fervent. (2) This was a symbol of the Holy Spirit's grace, which without measure rested upon Christ (see Ps. lxix. 9; John ii. 17). 3. *It was offered with frankincense.* (1) The physical use of this would be to take away from the tabernacle the smell of a slaughter-house, and to fill the courts with a grateful odour. (2) The spiritual use was to prefigure the fragrance of the merits of Jesus, (*a*) in his sacrifice (Eph. v. 2); (*b*) in his intercession (Rev. viii. 3, 4). Thus the offensiveness of the flesh in us is destroyed, and the living sacrifice becomes acceptable (Rom. xii. 1).—J. A. M.

Vers. 1—16.—*Our recognition of the hand of God in the blessings of life.* The fact that the law of the meat offering follows that of the burnt offering is itself significant. It suggests—

I. THE TRUE ORDER OF THE DIVINE LIFE IN MAN. It is, indeed, a mistake for the human teacher to attempt to lay down precise lines of thought and feeling along which souls must move. "The progress of religion in the soul" varies with individual experience. The action of God's Spirit is not limited, and while we should seek to lead all souls to walk in the road by which we are travelling, we should not be anxious that they should tread in our own steps. On the other hand, there is an order of thought and experience which may not be inverted. First the burnt offering, then the meat offering; first the soul's presentation of itself as a sinner to ask forgiveness and to offer itself to God, *then* the service of recognition of him and gratitude for his gifts. It is a serious, and may be a fatal, spiritual error to attempt to gain God's favour by doing those things which are appropriate to his children, without having first sought and found reconciliation through a crucified Saviour. Start at the starting-point of the Christian course, lest, when the goal is reached, the crown be not placed upon the brow.

II. OUR GRATEFUL RECOGNITION OF GOD'S CONSTANT GOODNESS TO US. The meat offering was a sacrifice in which the worshipper acknowledged that the various blessings of his life came from God and belonged to him. He brought fine flour (ver. 1), and oil (ver. 1), also wine as the accompanying drink offering (ch. xxiii. 13). The chief produce of the land, the principal elements of food were, in a sacred hour, at the holy place, and, by a pious action, solemnly recognized as gifts of God, to be gratefully accepted from his hand, to be reverently laid on his altar. We are thankfully to acknowledge: 1. *God's kindness in supplying us with that which we need.* Bread (corn) will stand for that food which is requisite, and when we consider the goodness of our Creator, (1) in originally providing that which is so wholesome and nourishing to all men; (2) in multiplying it so freely that there is abundance for all; (3) in causing it to be multiplied in such a way as ministers to our moral and spiritual health (through our intelligence, activity, co-operation, etc.); (4) in making palatable and pleasurable the daily meals which would otherwise be (as sickness occasionally proves) intolerably burdensome;—we have abundant reason for blessing God for his kindness in respect of the necessaries of life. 2. *His goodness in providing us with that which is superfluous.* A very large part of the enjoyment of our life is in the use of that which is not necessary but agreeable; in the appropriation of that which is pleasant,—the exquisite, the harmonious, the fragrant, the delicately beautiful, etc. This also is of God. *He* "makes our cup to run over;" from him come the fruits and the flowers, as well as the corn and the grass. Nay, he has closely associated the superfluous with the necessary in nature as in human life. The common potato does not grow without bearing a beautiful flower, nor the humble bean without yielding a fragrant odour. As the Hebrew brought his oil and his wine to the altar of gratitude, so should we bring our thanksgiving for the delicacies, adornments, and sweetnesses which come from the bountiful hand of Heaven.

III. THE NECESSITY FOR PURITY IN OUR SERVICE. There might not be leaven nor honey (ver. 11); there must be salt (ver. 13). Everything associated with corruption must be avoided; that which was antiseptic in its nature should be introduced; "nothing which defileth" before him; the "clean hands and the pure heart" in "the holy place" (Ps. xxiv. 3, 4). (See "Purity in worship," *infra*.)

IV. THE ACCEPTABLENESS OF OUR GRATITUDE TO GOD. All the frankincense was to be consumed on the altar, and the burning of the other offerings with this fragrant incense accompanying it betokened that it was, as stated, a "sweet savour unto the Lord" (vers. 2, 12). God is not to be worshipped with men's hands, as though "he needed anything" (Acts xvii. 25); but he takes delight in his children: 1. Realizing his presence. 2. Recognizing his hand in their comforts and their joy. 3. Responding to his fatherly love with their filial gratitude and praise.

V. THE WHOLESOME INFLUENCE OF GRATEFUL SERVICE ON OUR OWN HEARTS. He who "knows what is in man," warned his people against saying in their heart, "My power and the might of my hand hath gotten me this wealth" (Deut. viii. 17). Such a sacrifice as that of the meat offering—a service of grateful acknowledgment of God's hand—is fitted to render us the greatest spiritual benefit, by: 1. Helping us to keep a humble heart before God. 2. Causing us to be filled with the pure joy of gratitude instead of being puffed up with the mischievous complacency of pride.—C.

Vers. 11—13.—*Purity in worship.* When the Hebrew worshipper had presented his burnt offering, had sought forgiveness of sin, and had dedicated himself to God in sacred symbolism, he then brought of the produce of the land, of that which constituted his food; and by presenting flour, oil, and wine, with frankincense, he owned his indebtedness to Jehovah. In engaging in this last act of worship, he was to do that which spoke emphatically of purity in approaching the Holy One of Israel. By Divine direction he was—

I. CAREFULLY TO EXCLUDE THAT IN WHICH THERE WAS ANY ELEMENT OF IMPURITY. Leaven is "a substance in a state of putrefaction;" honey "soon turns sour, and even forms vinegar." These were, therefore, expressly interdicted; they might not be laid on the altar of God. But so important was this feature that positive as well as negative rules were laid down. The offerer was—

II. CONSTANTLY TO INTRODUCE THE CORRECTIVE OF IMPURITY. "Neither shalt thou suffer the salt . . . to be lacking;" "with all thine offerings thou shalt offer salt." Salt is the great preservative from putrefaction, fitting type of all that makes pure in symbolic worship.

When we come up to the house of the Lord to "offer the sacrifice of praise" or to engage in any act of devotion, we must remember that—

I. GOD LAYS GREAT STRESS ON THE PURITY OF OUR HEART IN WORSHIP. Only the pure in heart can see God (Matt. v. 8). Without holiness no man shall see him (Heb. xii. 14). They must be clean who bear the vessels of the Lord (Isa. lii. 11). None may ascend his holy hill but " he that hath clean hands and a pure heart." "If we regard iniquity in our heart, the Lord will not hear us " (Ps. lxvi. 18). We have not now laid down for us any precise directions as to what words we shall use, what forms we shall adopt, what gifts we shall devote, but we know that the chief thing to bring, that without which all is vain, is a right spirit, a pure heart, a soul that is seeking God and longing for his likeness. The interdiction of the leaven and honey, and the requirement of salt, suggest that—

II. GOD DESIRES A VIGILANT EXCLUSION OF EVERY UNHOLY THOUGHT WHEN WE DRAW NIGH TO HIM. We may be tempted to allow corruption to enter into and mar our worship or our Christian work, in the form of: 1. An unworthy spirit of rivalry. 2. An ostentation of piety. 3. Self-seeking by securing the favour of man. 4. Sensuous enjoyment (mere artistic appreciation, etc.). 5. A spirit of dislike or resentment towards fellow-worshippers or fellow-workers. Such spiritual "leaven" must not be brought to the altar; such sentiments must be shut out from the soul. We must strenuously resist when these evil thoughts would enter. We must vigorously and energetically expel them if they find their way within the heart (Prov. iv. 23).

III. GOD DESIRES THE PRESENCE OF THE PURIFYING THOUGHT IN DEVOTION. There must not only be the absence of leaven, but the presence of salt; not only the absence of that which corrupts and spoils, but the presence of that which purifies. There must be the active presence of sanctifying thoughts. Such are: 1. A profound sense of the nearness of God to us. 2. A lively sense of our deep indebtedness to Jesus Christ. Let these convictions fill the soul, and the lower and ignobler sentiments will fail to enter or will quickly leave. If we feel our own feebleness and incapacity, we may fall back on the truth that—

IV. GOD HAS PROMISED THE AID OF HIS CLEANSING SPIRIT. We must pray for "the renewing of the Holy Ghost" (Titus iii. 5); that he will "cleanse us from our sin;" will give us " truth in the inward parts;" will make us "clean," "whiter than snow ;" will "create in us a clean heart, and renew a right spirit within us" (Ps. li.; and see Ps. xix. 12—14; cxxxix. 23, 24).—C.

Vers. 3—10.—*Priest and people: reciprocal services.* Two things are stated in the Law concerning the priesthood.

I. THAT EVERY POSSIBLE THING WAS DONE TO IMPART TO THEM PECULIAR SANCTITY. They were separated and sanctified by various ceremonies and services.

II. THAT SPECIAL SANCTITY WAS ASSOCIATED IN THE MINDS OF THE PEOPLE WITH THEIR PERSON AND OFFICE. So much so that offerings given to them were lawfully regarded as presented to Jehovah. In the meat offering " the remnant" (the greater part) was to be "Aaron's and his sons'," and this is declared to be "a thing most holy." To these statements we may add—

III. THAT WHILE THEIR NEARNESS TO GOD CONFERRED SPECIAL PRIVILEGE, IT DID NOT ENSURE PERSONAL HOLINESS (ch. x. 1; 1 Sam. ii. 17, 23; Mal. i. 6—10; ii. 1—9).

IV. THAT IN PROPORTION TO THEIR PERSONAL EXCELLENCE WOULD BE THE OFFERINGS OF THE PEOPLE. Few meat offerings would be brought whereby a rapacious, or arrogant, or impure, or unsocial, or irreverent priesthood would be benefited; but free and full offerings would come to the altar where blameless, beloved, and honoured men were ministering.

The Christian ministry is unlike the Jewish priesthood in that: 1. It is not hereditary; it is (or should be) only entered upon where there is individual fitness for the office. 2. It offers no sacrifices (Heb. x. 11, 12). 3. It approaches God *with* men rather than *for* them. Yet it is like that ancient priesthood, in that it is a section of God's people set apart for conducting Divine worship and for the service of society in all sacred things. We are reminded—

I. THAT IT IS THE WILL OF CHRIST THAT CHRISTIAN MINISTERS SHOULD BE SUSTAINED BY THE PEOPLE'S OFFERINGS (1 Cor. ix. 11, 13, 14).

II. THAT WHAT IS PRESENTED TO THEM FOR THEIR WORK'S SAKE, CHRIST COUNTS AS OFFERED TO HIMSELF (Matt. x. 40, 41; Phil. iv. 18).

III. That in the relations of minister and people there should be recipro-cal generosity. On the part of the latter let there be: 1. Full appreciation of the high nature and the large number of their services. 2. Generous overlooking of lesser faults, remembering human frailty. 3. Constant credit for purity of motive. 4. Active sympathy and co-operation; and 5. Substantial practical support. He who has "the burden of the Lord" upon his heart should not be weighed down with tem-poral anxieties. On the part of the former, let there be: 1. Complete subordination of temporal to spiritual solicitudes. 2. Free and generous expenditure of love and strength, both on individual souls in special need, and on the Church and the world. Reciprocal indifference and closeness will end in leanness of soul; reciprocal love and generosity in largeness of heart and nobility of life (Luke vi. 38).—C.

Vers. 1—3.—*The meat offering.* The offering of meat or food, consisting of fine flour, with frankincense, cakes and wafers, parched grain, suited to all classes. The general meaning was probably *eucharistic.* A portion of bread, firstfruits, offered in the fire as a memorial of Divine goodness and pledge of the future life. Several parti-culars noticeable. 1. It was what made part of the daily meal of the house. 2. Frank-incense mingled with it, and oil poured upon it; the prayers and thankful worship of the offerer, which were the work of God's Spirit, returned to him. 3. It was partly consumed by fire, and partly "a thing most holy," or set apart to the Lord, eaten by the priests, supporting the temple worship. 4. If baked, no leaven in it nor honey, no corruption, a pure sacrifice. 5. Every offering seasoned with salt, "the salt of the covenant of thy God," *i.e.* the emblem of Divine grace, which, while it accepts man's obedience, overlooks and pardons its imperfection.—R.

Vers. 4—16.—*The various kinds of meat offerings.* Without dwelling on every minute regulation, the following main points may be distinguished as representative.

I. Offered food. Acknowledgment of dependence. Praise for life and its gifts. Joys and pleasures should be consecrated. The will of God in them and over them. Family worship a duty. Recognition of God in common life. Firstfruits are God's, not the remnant or gleanings of our faculties and opportunities, but all.

II. Offering divided between offerer and priests. Connection of daily labour and its results with the sanctuary and religious duties. The secular and sacred only nominally distinct. The house of God and the house of man should open into one another. Nothing should be allowed to interfere with the holiness of that which is assigned to God's service in the sanctuary. "*It is most holy.*" Too often Christians fall into a carelessness with respect to sacred appointments which reacts on the spirit and life. Our partnership with God involves responsibility.

III. No leaven, no honey. In all things purity and humility. There must be no corrupt principle admitted into our service of God. The doctrine must be purified of leaven. The motives must be examined. We ought not to serve God for the sake of filthy lucre, under the influence of mere sensational excitement. Truth and sobriety in worship.

IV. Salt with every sacrifice. All must be brought to God in the spirit of penitent faith. Salt preserves life, sets forth the dependence of man upon God. The gracious covenant is the source of all. He who commands is himself the giver of all power to fulfil his word. He is the Alpha and the Omega of the spiritual life.

V. Frankincense and oil. Fragrance and brightness. Heaven and earth mingled together. Reconciliation of God and man. The outpoured spirit of light and life. Joy in God and in his gifts. The anointing oil mingled in the fire and increased the flame. The Messiah is the true Anointed One. Every Israelite, in a lower degree, was himself a Messiah, an anointed one, taken up into the Son of God and blessed. The people are a holy, consecrated people, separated unto Jehovah. Every individual act of religion is acceptable as the oil of the Spirit is poured upon it. What a new view of life can thus be obtained! Make all a meat offering to the Lord.—R.

EXPOSITION.

CHAPTER III.

THE PEACE OFFERING. The peace offering, though the instructions here given respecting it precede those relating to the sin offering (for a reason to be stated hereafter), is the last in order of the sacrifices when they were all presented together. First, the sin offering taught the need of, and symbolically wrought, propitiation and atonement; next the burnt offering represented the absolute surrender of man's will to God's will; then the meat offering, by its gift of homage, declared the loyal submission of the offerer; and then followed the peace offering, symbolizing the festive joy which pervades the souls of those who are in communion with God. The essential characteristic of the peace offering is the feast upon the sacrifice, participated in symbolically by God (by means of the part consumed on the altar, and the part eaten by his ministers) and actually by the offerer and his companions. It served as a memorial to the Israelites of the institution of the covenant between God and themselves (a covenant in the East being ordinarily ratified by the parties to it eating together), and reminded them of the blessings thence derived, which naturally called forth feelings of joyous thankfulness; while it prefigured the peace wrought for man by the adoption in Christ, through which he has communion with God.

Ver. 1.—**Peace offering**, *Zebach shelamim*, "sacrifice of peace offerings." The singular, *shelem*, occurs once (Amos v. 22). The conditions to be fulfilled by a Jew who offered a peace offering were the following:—1. He must bring either (1) a young bull or cow, or (2) a young sheep of either sex, or (3) a young he-goat or she-goat. 2. He must offer it in the court of the tabernacle. 3. In offering it he must place, or lean, his hand upon its head. 4. He must kill it at the door of the tabernacle. 5. He must provide three kinds of cakes similar to those offered in the meat offering, and leavened bread (ch. vii. 11—13). The priest had: 1. To catch the blood, and strike the sides of the altar with it, as in the burnt sacrifices. 2. To place upon the burnt offering, smouldering upon the altar, all the internal fat of the animal's body, together with the kidneys enveloped in it, and, in the case of the sheep, the fat tails, for consumption by the fire. 3. To offer one of each of the three different kinds of unleavened cakes, and one loaf of the leavened bread, as a heave offering. 4. To wave the breast of the animal backwards and forwards, and to heave the leg or haunch upwards and downwards, in token of consecration (see notes on ch. vii. 14, 30, 31). 5. To take for his own eating, and that of his brethren the priests, the three cakes and loaf and haunch that had been heaved and waved. 6. To return the rest of the animal, and the remaining cakes and loaves, to the offerer, to serve as a feast for him and his, to be eaten the same or the next day, in the court of the tabernacle. The lesson taught by the peace offering was the blessedness of being in union with God as his covenant people, and the duty and happiness of exhibiting a joyous sense of this relation by celebrating a festival meal, eaten reverently and thankfully in the house of God, a part of which was given to God's priests, and a part consumed symbolically by God himself. The burnt offering had typified self-surrender; the meat offering, loyal submission; the peace offering typified the joyous cheerfulness of those who, having in a spirit of perfect loyalty surrendered themselves to God, had become his children, and were fed at the very board at which he deigned symbolically to partake. The most essential part of the meat offering was the presentation; of the burnt offering, the consumption of the victim on the altar; of the peace offering, the festive meal upon the sacrifice. The combined burnt and meat offering was the sacrifice of one giving himself up to God; the peace offering, that of one who, having given himself up to God, is realizing his communion with him. In this respect the peace offering of the old dispensation foreshadows the Lord's Supper in the new dispensation. Several other names have been proposed for the peace offering, such as thank offering, salvation offering, etc. No name is more suitable than peace offering, but the word must be understood not in the sense of an offering to bring about peace, but an offering of those who are in a state of peace, answering to the Greek word εἰρηνική, rather than to the Latin word *pacifica*. "A state of peace and friendship with God was the basis and *sine quâ non* to the presentation of a *shelem*, and the design of that presentation, from which its name was derived, was the realization, establishment, verification, and enjoyment of the existing relations of peace, friendship, fellowship, and blessedness" (Kurtz, 'Sacrificial Worship').

Vers. 3, 4.—" There were four parts to be burned upon the altar : (1) **the fat that covereth the inwards,** *i.e.* the large net, *omentum,* ἐπίπλους, caul, or adipose membrane found in mammals, attached to the stomach and spreading over the bowels, and which in the ruminants abounds with fat; (2) **all the fat which is upon the inwards,** *i.e.* the fat attached to the intestines, and which could be peeled off; (3) **the two kidneys, and the fat that is on them, which is by the flanks,** or loins, *i.e.* the kidneys and all the fat connected with them ; the kidneys are the only thing to be burnt except the fat; (4) the smaller net, *omentum minus,* or **caul above the liver,** which stretches on one side to the region of the kidneys, hence **on the kidneys** ; עַל = by them, not *with* them " (Gardiner).

Ver. 5.—**Upon the burnt sacrifice.** The peace offering is to be placed upon the burnt offering previously laid upon the fire. Symbolically and actually the burnt offering serves as the foundation of the peace offering. Self-surrender leads to peace ; and the self-sacrifice of Christ is the cause of the peace subsisting between God and man.

Ver. 9.—**The whole rump** should no doubt be *the whole tail,* consisting chiefly of fat,

and always regarded as a great delicacy in the East (see Herod., iii. 113 ; Thompson, 'Land and the Book,' p. 97). The burning of the fat tail upon the altar, together with the internal fat, is the only point in which the ritual to be used when offering a sheep (vers. 6—11) differs from that used in offering a bull or cow (vers. 1—5), or a goat (vers. 12—16).

Ver. 11.—**It is the food of the offering made by fire unto the Lord** ; literally, *It is the bread of the offering by fire to the Lord.* The idea of the peace offering being that of a meal at God's board, the part of the animal presented to God upon the altar is regarded as his share of the feast, and is called his food or bread. Cf. Rev. iii. 20, " I will come in to him, and will sup with him, and he with me."

Ver. 17.—**Eat neither fat nor blood.** These are forbidden to be eaten, as belonging to God. The fat, that is, the internal fat, is his portion in the common feast of the peace offering, and the blood is presented to him in all the animal sacrifices, as the material vehicle of life (see ch. vii. 22—27). The remaining regulations as to the various sorts of the peace offerings, the priests' portions of them, and the festive meal on the sacrifices, are given in ch. vii. 11—34.

HOMILETICS.

Vers. 1—17.—*The peace offering* was not a sacrifice denoting self-devotion like the burnt-offering, nor a tender of homage like the meat offering, but a feast upon a sacrifice, which God and man symbolically joined in partaking of. The offering consisted of an animal and unleavened cakes and (generally) leavened bread, of which a share was given to God's altar and priests on the one hand, and to the offerer and his friends on the other. It represented the blessedness and joyousness of communion between God and man. "The character of these feasts cannot be mistaken. It was that of joyfulness tempered by solemnity, of solemnity tempered by joyfulness. The worshipper had submitted to God an offering from his property ; he now received back from him a part of the dedicated gift, and thus experienced anew the same gracious beneficence which had enabled him to appear with his wealth before the altar. He therefore consumed that portion with feelings of humility and thankfulness; but he was bidden at once to manifest those blissful sentiments by sharing the meat, not only with his household, which thereby was reminded of the Divine protection and mercy, but also with his needy fellow-beings, whether laymen or servants of the temple. Thus these beautiful repasts were stamped both with religious emotion and human virtue. The relation of friendship between God and the offerer which the sacrifice exhibited, was expressed and sealed by the feast, which intensified that relation into one of an actual covenant; the momentary harmony was extended to a permanent union. And these notions could not be expressed more intelligibly, at least to an Eastern people, than by a common meal, which to them is the familiar image of friendship and communion, of cheerfulness and joy " (Kalisch).

I. IT WAS A FEDERAL FEAST, REMINDING THE ISRAELITES OF THE INSTITUTION OF THE COVENANT. In early times the method of making a covenant was dividing animals in halves and passing between them (see Gen. xv. 9, 10 ; Jer. xxxiv. 18, 19), or otherwise offering them in sacrifice (Gen. viii. 20 ; xv. 9 ; Ps. l. 5), and then feasting together.

When Abraham's servant asked for Rebekah for his master, he refused to eat and drink until he had made his agreement (Gen. xxiv. 33); but after it was completed, "they did eat and drink, he and the men that were with him" (Gen. xxiv. 54). Jacob held a solemn feast after he and Laban had made a covenant together (Gen. xxxi. 54). The feast upon the peace offerings, whether offered by the whole congregation or by individuals, served as a memorial of the covenant made between God and their fathers (see Exod. xxiv. 5, where the name peace offering is first used), and it made them rejoice in being God's peculiar people in union and communion with him.

II. IT LOOKED FORWARD AS WELL AS BACKWARDS. Like the Passover, it at once commemorated an historical event and prefigured a blessing to come. The Passover looked backwards to the deliverance from Egypt, and forward to "Christ our passover sacrificed for us;" and in like manner the peace offering feast commemorated the making of the covenant, and prefigured the blessed state of communion to be brought about by the sacrifice of the cross. Communion is typified and proved in the New Testament as well as the Old by eating and drinking together (Luke xiv. 15; Acts x. 41; Rev. xix. 9).

III. SACRIFICE IN RELATION TO CHRISTIANS. We have no sin offering to offer. The full, perfect, and sufficient Sacrifice for sins was made once for all upon the cross; we have only to appropriate the merits of that one offering by faith. Nor have we a burnt offering to offer. The full surrender of himself by a perfect Man was once for all made in the Garden of Gethsemane and on Calvary; we can but follow the great Example. But we may still offer the meat offering, in a spiritual sense, by giving the service which declares us to be faithful subjects of God; and we may spiritually offer the peace offering, whenever with grateful hearts we offer praise and thanksgiving to God for having brought us into union and communion with himself.

IV. THE HOLY COMMUNION IS THE SPECIAL MEANS OF OUR EXHIBITING THE JOYOUS SENSE OF BEING THE CHILDREN OF GOD. It is not a sin offering, being neither a repetition nor a continuation, but a commemoration, of the great Sin Offering of the cross; it is not, therefore, propitiatory. Neither is it a burnt offering, for Christ's self-surrender cannot be reiterated or renewed, but only commemorated. But it answers to the meat offering, inasmuch as in it we offer our alms and "the creatures of bread and wine" as tokens of our loyalty, and receive back in requital "the strengthening and refreshing of our souls by the Body and Blood of Christ." And it is a peace offering, for therein we feast at God's board, exhibiting our joyful thankfulness for having been admitted into covenant with him, offering "our sacrifice of praise and thanksgiving," and rejoicing in the assurance thus given us "that we are very members incorporate in the mystical body of" Christ our Lord.

V. THE BLESSEDNESS OF A SENSE OF PEACE WITH GOD. First, we must feel the need of reconciliation, and a desire to rid ourselves of the obstacles in the way of it. Then we must go to Christ to have our sins nailed to his cross; and thus, "being justified by faith, we have peace with God through our Lord Jesus Christ" (Rom. v. 1), "and the peace of God, which passeth all understanding, shall keep our hearts and minds through Christ Jesus" (Phil. iv. 7), "and the God of peace shall be with us" (Phil. iv. 9).

HOMILIES BY VARIOUS AUTHORS.

Fellowship with God and man as illustrated in the peace offering. Ch. iii.; also vii. 11—21, 28—34; xix. 6—8; xxii. 29, 30; cf. 1 John i. 6, 7; John vi. 33. We have found in the burnt offering the principle of entire *personal consecration*, and in the meat offering that of *consecrated life-work*. We have seen how these have their perfect fulfilment only in the case of Jesus Christ, while in other cases they are preceded by an acknowledgment of sin and shortcoming, and of acceptance as coming through another. In the peace offering we have a further stage of religious experience. Part of the sacrifice, whatever it may be, is burned on the altar, part is assigned to the priests, and part is returned to the offerer, to constitute the staple of a social feast. Moreover, the portion laid upon the altar is expressly called "the bread of God" (לֶחֶם אִשֶּׁה לַיהוָה), ver. 11. Hence the idea of the offering is that God and his mediating priests and his sacrificing servants are all partaking of the one animal, the one food; that is to say, are all *in fellowship*. This is the crown of religious experience—conscious fellowship with God and with one another. It is what John refers to when he says, "If we say that we have fellowship with him, and walk in darkness, we lie, and do not the truth: but if we walk in the light, as he is in the light, we have fellowship one with another, and the blood of Jesus Christ his Son cleanseth us from all sin" (1 John i. 6, 7).

I. IN HOLDING FELLOWSHIP WITH GOD AND MAN LARGE LIBERTY OF SELECTION IS ALLOWED. The animal presented might be a female or a male, and even, in the case of a free-will offering, an animal might be presented which had something superfluous (ch. xxii. 23). For, if fellowship is to be expressed, then, provided God is presented with what is perfect, what remains to represent man's share in the fellowship might fairly enough be imperfect. This wider range of selection emphasizes surely the fact that we may hold fellowship with God through any legitimate thing. We shall presently indicate the subject-matter of fellowship with God; meanwhile it is well to notice the large selection allowed.

II. IT IS A PRELIMINARY OF FELLOWSHIP WITH GOD TO ACKNOWLEDGE SIN AND RECEIVE ACCEPTANCE THROUGH A SUBSTITUTE. God's rights are thus respected and acknowledged as our Moral Governor. To venture into the charmed circle of fellowship without the benefit of the bloodshedding is to presume before God. Hence the peace offering was done to death, and its blood sprinkled on the altar before the feast began. The fellowship with God, which has not been preceded on the part of sinners like ourselves by confession of sin and acceptance, is sure to be hollow at the best.

III. IN ANY FELLOWSHIP WITH GOD WE MUST RECOGNIZE HIS RIGHT TO THE BEST PORTION OF THE FEAST. The priest was directed to take the fat that covereth the inwards, and all the fat that is upon the inwards, with the kidneys and the lobe of the liver, and, in case of a sheep, the tail of fat, and he was to burn all these upon the altar of burnt offering, in the ashes of the burnt offering. This was recognizing God's right to the best portion—to the *flos carnis*, the "tit-bits," as we would call them. Now, it is only natural to suppose that, whatever be the subject-matter of our fellowship with God he will enter more fully into the fellowship and make more of it than we can do. This will be more apparent when we notice in the sequel the different legitimate subjects of fellowship.

IV. IN FELLOWSHIP WITH ONE ANOTHER, MOREOVER, WE MUST RECOGNIZE THE POSSIBILITY OF OTHERS ENTERING INTO THE SUBJECT MORE FULLY THAN OURSELVES. The priestly class had the wave breast and heave leg assigned to them as their share. Next to God's portion, these were the best portions of the beast. It indicated plainly the liberal scale of "ministerial support" which God would foster, and it prompted the self-denial of true fellowship. For a feast is a poor thing in which the host retains the best things for himself. His pleasure should be to confer the best on others. For the time being he literally "esteems others better than himself."

V. LET US NOW INDICATE THE LEGITIMATE SUBJECT-MATTERS FOR FELLOWSHIP WHICH ARE TYPIFIED IN THE PEACE OFFERINGS. Here, then, we have three sets of individuals partaking of the one organic whole—God on his altar, his mediating priests at the tabernacle, and the offerer and his friends. What does the organic whole represent? And the only answer is, what God and man *can have fellowship about*. This evidently includes a very wide range indeed.

1. *Jesus Christ.* He is the great subject-matter of fellowship as between God and man, and between man and man. Hence he is called "the bread of God" which came down from heaven, the bread on which, so to speak, God feeds, as well as the bread he gives to nourish the world. If we think for a moment of the supreme delight which God the Father takes in his well-beloved Son, it is only faintly imaged by the portions placed upon the altar. What fellowship must God have in looking down upon his Son dedicated to life and death to redeem and sustain a sinful race! Indeed, we cannot enter into such an unparalleled experience; no wonder it should be said, "All the fat is the Lord's." Yet this does not prevent us on our part from feasting joyfully and by faith upon Jesus. He becomes the subject-matter of our fellowship and joy.

2. *God's Word.* This is another subject-matter of fellowship. How often does God use it in communicating with our souls! and is it not the choicest phraseology we can

find in returning his fellowship through prayer? How much more, besides, does God see in the Word, and get out of it, than we do! If the crucible of criticism is only revealing the splendours of the Word, how much more must God see in it! "Thy word is very pure, therefore thy servants love it."

3. *Ourselves.* For fellowship is having something in common with another. If, then, we are altogether consecrated to God, if we say from the heart, "Lord, we are thine; undertake for us," we become, so to speak, the medium of fellowship as between God and us. God's delight in us is beyond conception. "The Lord taketh pleasure in them that fear him, in them that hope in his mercy." And, as we realize God's right and delight in us, life becomes a joyful feast to us. The exercise of all our powers becomes a conscious joy, a feast of love, and all around us are the better for our being.

4. *Every legitimate subject or engagement.* For all may be made subject-matter of fellowship with God. Nothing worth living for but may be made the medium of communion with him. All learning will prove more delightful if undertaken with God. All social engagements will prove more enjoyable if spent with God. Every occupation, in fact, becomes increasingly blissful in proportion to our fellowship with God in it. It is the feast of life: he sups with us, and enables us to sup with him (Rev. iii. 20).

5. *Every blessing received and vow registered.* For this peace offering was either the expression of praise for some mercy received or the covenant-sign of some fresh resolution. It corresponded very largely to our Eucharistic celebrations. Just as in feasting upon the symbols of our Saviour's dying love we hold fellowship with God and with each other in thinking of all we have received and all we now resolve, so was it in the older feast. The offerer, as he entertained his friends, rejoiced in the goodness he had got from God, and pledged himself in gratitude. The peace offering thus expresses the truth regarding the fellowship possible between God and man, and between the brotherhood.—R. M. E.

Vers. 1—5.—*A general view of offerings.* A supplementary account of the manner in which the peace offerings are to be presented unto the Lord is contained in ch. vii. Reserving fuller distinct consideration of them till our arrival there, it may be instructive now to derive some general lessons from a comparison between this present chapter and the preceding chapters, which tell us of the burnt and meat offerings.

I. EACH SEASON AND CIRCUMSTANCE HAS ITS APPROPRIATE OFFERING. Different names are bestowed upon the offerings. A general name for all is *corban*, a gift, a means of approach. It may be "a burnt offering" (ch. i. 3), significant of entire dedication; or "an offering of an oblation" (ch. ii. 1), a present of flour or grains, an acknowledgment of God's goodness, and an expression of desire to obtain his good will; or "a sacrifice of peace" (ch. iii. 1), denoting a wish to live in concord with Jehovah, recognizing his will and enjoying his favour. Thus the devout Israelite could never be without a fitting means of approach, whatever his state of mind or whatever the crisis in his life. So we may always have something to offer our heavenly Father, whether in suffering or health, in adversity or prosperity, in age or youth, desiring increased sanctification, or blessing, or usefulness, whether thankful for the past or requesting grace for the future. Even the one atonement of Jesus Christ, like a prism that exhibits different colours according to our position, may appear a diversified offering, according as the pressing need of the moment may seem to be deliverance from wrath, peace, happiness, self-dedication, temporal prosperity, or the light of God's countenance.

II. BY THE DIFFERENCE IN OFFERINGS GOD SEEMS TO DESIRE TO AWAKEN AND DEVELOP DIFFERENT MORAL SENTIMENTS. Our chequered experience has its part to fulfil in calling into play every faculty of the mind and spirit. God likes a good "all-round" character, strong at all points, and only exercise can secure this. He would have his people attend to all the requirements of the Christian life, to manifest all the virtues, knowledge and faith, gratitude and hope, patience and vigour. We must not deem any voyage or journey superfluous; no accident but may benefit us; the holiness meeting, the evangelistic service, the workers' conference,—each may be profitable in turn.

III. ONE OFFERING DOES NOT INTERFERE WITH THE PRESENTATION OF ANOTHER OF A DIFFERENT KIND. In ver. 5 we read that the fat of the peace offering is placed upon the burnt offering, probably upon the remains of the morning sacrifice. So that the one becomes a foundation for the other, and clashing is obviated. The sacrifice of the congregation does not prevent the sacrifice of the individual, nor does the general offering prove a hindrance to the special. Family prayer is no obstacle to private supplication, nor does the stated worship of the sanctuary exclude extraordinary gatherings. The fear of some good people lest regular meditation and service should grow formal and check any outburst of enthusiasm, or any sudden prompting to special effort, is seen to be groundless.

IV. CERTAIN REGULATIONS ARE COMMON TO ALL OFFERINGS. *Burning on the altar* belongs to bloody and unbloody sacrifices, death and sprinkling of blood of necessity only to the former. In every case the offering must be of *the best of its kind,* if an animal "without blemish," if of grain "fine flour." What we say or do for God should be with our might; in whatever service for him we engage, it must be with full affection and earnest zeal. And every sacrifice required *the mediation of a priest.* Christ must be the inspiration of our acts, the way of acceptance consecrating all our gifts of money, strength, and time. By him we die (as did the sentient victim) to the world, by him we live to the glory of God.—S. R. A.

Vers. 16, 17.—*Jehovah's portion.* As the Author of life and the Giver of all bounty, God might have claimed the whole of every sacrifice. But he discriminated between the parts of the victim, sometimes reserving for himself the greater share, at other times only a small proportion of that presented to him. In the peace offering there was selected for the altar, as God's perquisite, the "fat" of the animal, and the remainder went to the priests and the offerer.

I. LEARN THAT NOT THE MEANEST BUT THE CHOICEST PORTIONS MUST BE RESERVED FOR GOD'S SERVICE. Low conceptions of his majesty and perfection lead to such religious observance as is an insult rather than an honour. To defer reading the Scriptures or prayer till the mind and body are fatigued, is an infraction of this rule. Let our freshest moments, our sweetest morsels of thought and power, be set apart for the Lord! And similarly, ask not, How near can I walk to the dividing line between the Church and the world? or, Which of my amusements can I with least self-denial renounce in order to do his will? May we not behold the same lesson inculcated in the distinction indicated in this chapter, between a peace and a burnt offering? The latter, being wholly devoted to the Lord, must consist of a male victim; the former, intended principally for the participation of the offerers, may be male or female (ver. 1). It cannot be right, then, to imagine that any qualifications will suffice for entire consecration to God's work. Ministers and missionaries should be numbered amongst men of highest intellect and intensest spirituality.

II. SEE HOW GOD ACCEPTS THE OFFERINGS OF HIS CREATURES AS THE MATERIALS FOR HIS DELIGHT AND GLORY. The burnt fat is "food" for the fire offering, and is termed in another place, the "bread of God." It becomes "a sweet savour" that is, eminently pleasing to the Holy One. In the word "food" we discern the purport of the peace offering as a sacrificial meal, in which, by returning to God what he had previously bestowed, the worshipper: 1. *Acknowledged his indebtedness and thanks.* 2. *Was made a guest at the table of the Lord,* inasmuch as he ate part of the animal that was "food for the fire offering;" and 3. *Had all his other provisions sanctified* for the sustenance of life, being allowed to consume the entire portions of animals not fit for sacrifice.

III. RECOLLECT THE OBLIGATORINESS OF DIVINE STATUTES. 1. *They prohibit as well as command.* "Thou shalt not" occupies as prominent a position in the Decalogue as "Thou shalt." Not only does man need both to try him (as with our first parents) and direct him, but one really involves the other. Observe that what man might not consume himself might be properly consumed on the altar; so the adoration and unquestioning fidelity that are out of place in reference to any finite beings, are becoming in relation to God. 2. *They are equally binding on all generations.* They respect us as well as our fathers, and herein the laws of God differ from the mutable proclamations of human lawgivers. The precepts of God only change with a new dispensation. This is the meaning of the word "perpetual." There is a sense, indeed, in which no Divine statute alters, being continued in spirit though the letter may have varied. 3. *They enter into all phases of life.* The prohibition was to be acted upon in "the dwellings" as well as at the tabernacle. Let us not make too great a distinction between the homage of the house of God and the home or the workshop and the factory! It is the characteristic of the gospel times to have the Law written on the heart, so that we carry it with us wherever we go. Thus are we prevented from sinning against God.—S. R. A.

Vers. 1—5.—*The peace offering.* We may get a clear conception of the peace offering by noticing the points of difference between it and the burnt offering described in the first chapter of this book.

I. It DIFFERS IN ITS TITLE. 1. *The burnt offering is in the Hebrew called* (עולה) *olah.* (1) This term comes from (עלה) *alah*, to ascend. The reason is that the whole animal was converted, by the action of the fire of the altar, into flame and sparks, vapour and smoke, in which forms it rose from the altar, and as it were *ascended* to God. (2) It described the completeness in which Christ offered himself to God in the flames of the "spirit of burning" (Heb. ix. 14). (3) It also sets forth how completely we should devote ourselves as living sacrifices to God (Rom. xii. 1), and how constantly our thoughts and affections should rise into the heavens (Phil. iii. 20; Col. iii. 1—3). 2. *This is called* (שלמים) *shelamim.* (1) The verb from which this noun is derived is (שלם) *shalem*, to complete or make whole; and the noun is well rendered *peace offering.* (2) It was, therefore, considered as making up that which was lacking in the sinner, in order to reconcile him to God. In cases of distress, peace offerings as well as burnt offerings were offered up (Judg. xx. 26). So are we "reconciled to God by the death of his Son." (3) In making covenants, or entering into the covenant, peace offerings were associated with burnt offerings in like manner (Exod. xxiv. 5). Paul manifestly alludes to the peace offering in Eph. ii. 14—19. "He is our peace" is equivalent to saying, "He is our peace offering."

II. It DIFFERS IN ITS VICTIMS. 1. *In respect to the kinds.* (1) Three classes of animal were specified as proper for the holocaust: there were those of the herd; there were those of the flock; and there were those of the fowls. (2) In the peace offering there are only two. Animals from the herd and from the flock are specified, but there is no mention of turtle-doves or young pigeons here. The reason of this is that it would be difficult to treat fowls as peace offerings were treated in relation to the fat; and the animals are so small that if divided as peace offerings the portions would be small. There is thoughtful consideration for the welfare of his people in all the laws of God. 2. *In respect to the sexes.* (1) The animals devoted as burnt offerings were males. This is specified in relation to the burnt offering of the herd. Also to that of the flock. Masculine pronouns are used in relation to that of the fowls. The neuter, "it," ver. 15, should have been rendered "him" (see Hebrew text). (2) In respect to the peace offering, the matter of sex is optional. (3) The reason may be this. The burnt offering appears to have been partly an expression of adoration, in which it is proper to give to God all our strength and excellence. The peace offering was divided between God, the priests, and the offerer. Here, then, was a feast of *friendship*, and the sexes are helpful to our friendships.

III. It DIFFERS IN THE TREATMENT OF ITS VICTIMS. 1. *There were points of agreement here.* (1) The offering must be without blemish. Acceptable service must be without blemish, and this can only be rendered to God through Christ (Jude 24, 25). (2) The hand of the offerer must be laid on the head of the offering. This was intended as a solemn transfer of sin, and acknowledgment that the suffering is vicarious. How graphically expressive of the faith of the sinner in the great Saviour! (3) The sacrifice must be killed at the door of the tabernacle. Christ is the door. There is no other entrance into the holy place of his Church on earth but by him. The holy led to the holiest. If we do not belong to his spiritual Church on earth, we cannot belong to his glorious Church in heaven. There was a visible Church near, but still, in the bulk of its members, *outside* the door! Still there are multitudes only in the outer courts. (4) The blood must be sprinkled upon the altar round about. It is by the *blood* of Jesus that we enter the "new and living way." 2. *But there were points of difference.* (1) Instead of the holocaust the fat only was offered here (vers. 3—5). The fat in the peace offering appears to correspond to the oil in the meat offering. (2) In this view it will represent those graces of the mind which are the fruits of the Spirit. (3) Burnt offerings and peace offerings were consumed together (ver. 5). The great sacrifice of Christ prepares the altar for sacrifices of praise. These were not accepted till we were reconciled through him.—J. A. M.

Vers. 6—17.—*The peace offering of the flock.* The ceremony in relation to this is almost identical with that of the herd already described. Nevertheless, there are a few expressions in the course of the description which are not found in the former paragraph. We call attention to—

I. THE DESCRIPTION OF THE FAT OF THE LAMB. Vers. 8—10. 1. Note the expression, "*The fat thereof, and the whole rump.*" The "and" here is expletive rather than copulative, thus, "The fat thereof, *even* the whole rump." But the "rump," as vulgarly understood among us, is muscle, not fat. The part here indicated is the *tail.* This is evident from what follows, viz. "It shall be taken off hard by the back-bone." The tail of the sheep even in our climate is fat, but in the East it is remarkably so, some of them weighing from twelve to forty pounds. 2. The portions burnt were *very inflammable.* (1) Here, in addition to the fat of the tail, was all the fat of the inwards, which in a sheep might weigh eight or ten pounds. This, when ignited, would be consumed, whatever else may have been laid upon the altar. (2) These parts were considered to be the seat of the animal passions. In this view the lesson of their consumption upon the altar would be that our passions should be in complete subjection to God. Also to impress upon us that, if not consumed in the milder fires of his love, how obnoxious they are to the fierce fires of his wrath! (3) The rapid consumption of the fat of lambs upon the altar is therefore appropriately used to describe the extermination of the wicked. "But the wicked shall perish, and the enemies of the Lord shall be as the fat of lambs: they shall consume; into smoke shall they consume away" (Ps. xxxvii. 20). Fire, it would seem, will be the chief instrument which Providence will summon for the destruction of the forces of Antichrist (Rev. xvii. 16; xviii. 9; xix. 3, 20; xx. 9, 14).

II. THE EXPRESSION, "FOOD OF THE OFFERING MADE BY FIRE UNTO THE LORD" (ver. 11). 1. Thus, what was consumed by fire is called *God's food.* (1) Some construe this to mean that what is consumed is food for the fire. But this is to give no information. Nor would this be a sufficient reason for the prohibition of the fat as food for an Israelite (see vers. 16, 17). Note, the fat intermingled with the flesh was not forbidden, but those portions only which were prescribed to be offered upon the altar (see Neh. viii. 10). (2) But how could God be said to feast upon such food? Not literally, certainly (see Ps. l. 13). But figuratively. Thus his attributes of justice and mercy are, so to speak, hungry for satisfaction; and this satisfaction they find in that sacrifice of Christ, in virtue of which he is not only merciful, but just in justifying the ungodly (Rom. iii. 24—26). (3) To avail ourselves of this mercy of God, we must justify him, viz. by hearty repentance and true faith. While God magnifies his justice in his mercy, we, too, must magnify his justice in his mercy. 2. The portions of the peace offering not consumed upon the altar were *eaten by men.* (1) Here, then, was the expression of a fellowship between God and men, which is established through sacrifice. This glorious privilege is set forth also in the Christian Eucharist. We feast with the Lord at his table (1 Cor. x. 21). (2) Here also was fellowship between religious men. The priest had his portion, and the offerer his. That the offerer should feast with a Gentile would have been profanity. So the fellowship of Christians is with the holy universe (Heb. xii. 22—24).

III. THE NOTE PROHIBITING THE EATING OF BLOOD. Ver. 17. 1. What are the reasons for this? (1) The first is that the blood is the life of the flesh. The prohibition of blood as food is a Noachian precept, and this reason is given there. The object is to set a store upon life (see Gen. ix. 4—6). (2) The second is that blood is given upon the altar to make atonement for the soul, viz. life for the life (Lev. xvii. 10—14). The atoning blood of Christ must not be treated as a common thing (Heb. x. 29). 2. We may here refer to a circumstance in connection with the bleeding of the sacrifice. (1) The Jews tell us that the animal, after the slaughtering, was suspended on hooks near the place of rings for the removing of the skin. How suggestive of the hanging of Jesus upon the tree of his cross! (2) The next thing was the opening of the heart, to let the remaining blood escape. That this should happen to Christ was a special subject of prophecy (Zech. xii. 10; John xix. 34). (3) To human appearance this prophecy seems to have been fulfilled as by accident. The same remark may be applied to the fulfilment of many prophecies. There are no mere accidents. The careful hand of an allwise Providence is in everything.—J. A. M.

Vers. 1—16.—*The foundation of fellowship with God.* The "sacrifice of peace offering" was one of fellowship. Its distinctive features are brought out in ch. vii. (see Homily there). The sacrifice enjoined in this (third) chapter is preliminary to the sacred feast which was to follow. Its significance is found in the fact that the act of communion with God could only come after the oblation had been presented. We learn, therefore—

I. THAT SACRED JOY BEFORE GOD CAN ONLY FOLLOW RECONCILIATION WITH HIM. The Hebrew people might not come to the tabernacle and have a solemn feast near the sacred Presence until the animal had been slain and its blood sprinkled on the altar (vers. 1, 2, 8, 13). Conscious unworthiness must first be taken away by the shed blood of bull or lamb, and then priest and people might rejoice together before the Lord. First purity, then peace (Jas. iii. 17). We may aspire (1) to sit down with the people of God at the table here, or (2) to mingle with those who shall partake of the marriage supper of the Lamb hereafter; but there is no welcome from lips Divine until sin has been confessed and forgiven. First, penitence at the cross of the Redeemer and trust in his atoning sacrifice; then fellowship with God and his people.

II. THAT A FULL SELF-SURRENDER MUST PRECEDE THE ACT OF COMMUNION. When the animal had been slain, the priest was to present to God the fat, the kidneys, etc. (vers. 3, 4, 9, 10, 14, 15), special stress being laid on "the inwards;" the best and richest parts, those which had been the life of the animal, were offered to the Lord, as representing the animal itself, and so the offerer himself. He symbolically offered himself to God through these vital parts of the victim. When we draw near to a service of sacred fellowship and joy, or when we anticipate the communion of the skies, we should act on the truth that "our God has commanded our strength" (Ps. lxviii. 28), that the appeal for his mercy through Christ should be accompanied with a free, full surrender of our whole selves, the consecration of our very best, the "inward parts"—the understanding, the affections, the will—to him and his service.

III. THAT FAITH IN CHRIST AND THE CONSECRATION OF OURSELVES RESULT IN HIS PERFECT PLEASURE WITH US: "It is an offering . . . of a sweet savour unto the Lord" (vers. 5, 16). When the oblation was complete, then the offerer stood in the position of one who might rejoice in the Divine Presence and feast with the holy people and with God. Accepted in Christ, and having "yielded ourselves unto God" in unreserved consecration, we may feel that God's good pleasure, his full Divine complacency, rests upon us; we may walk in the light of his reconciled countenance all the day long. Two supplementary truths offer themselves to our thought in these verses. 1. *That every soul must personally and spiritually engage in acceptable service.* The offerer was "to lay his hand on the head of the offering,"—striking and significant act, by which he clearly intimated his consciousness of sin, and his desire that the victim might represent him in the sight of God—*its* blood *his* life, *its* organs *his* capacities. We may not trust to our mere bodily presence while God is being approached and besought, or while Christ's redeeming work is being pleaded, or while words of dedication are being uttered in prayer. There must be the positive, sympathetic, personal participation, or we stand outside the service and the blessing. 2. *That we must intelligently discriminate between the obligatory and the optional in the service of God.* Certain things were imperative in the act of worship, other things were left to the choice of the individual. In the gospel of Christ and the worship of God there are things essential that none may depart from, *e.g.* the humble heart, the act of faith and self-surrender, the spirit of obedience toward God and of love toward man; there are other things which are left to personal discretion, *e.g.* times and methods of devotion, scale of contribution, sphere of usefulness. Yet in these optional matters we are not to act inconsiderately or irrationally, but according to the direction of wisdom and the teachings of experience.—C.

Ver. 17.—*The guarding of sacred feeling.* No little stress is laid on the prohibition of two things—the fat and the blood of slain animals: it was to be "a perpetual statute for your generations throughout all your dwellings." The fat thus interdicted was that which was offered in sacrifice (vers. 3, 4, 9, 10), not that which was interlined with the lean (Neh. viii. 10). We may look at—

I. THE MEANING OF THIS PROHIBITION IN THEIR CASE. Evidently both the fat and the blood were disallowed as food because they were offered in sacrifice to Jehovah. On this account they were to be preserved sacred. They were not to be treated as ordinary things, vulgarized, lowered in public estimation; a feeling of their sacredness was to be cherished and carefully preserved by daily habit. To be continually using these parts as meat and drink at table would have the effect which was to be deprecated. It was, therefore, an act of religious duty to abstain from them. By such abstinence their feelings of reverence and piety would be guarded and preserved. Was it not for a similar reason, viz. that no violation should be done to the sacred sentiment of maternity, that the law was thrice repeated, "Thou shalt not seethe a kid in his mother's milk" (Exod. xxiii. 19, etc.)? The influence of daily habit on the finer sentiments of the soul is very gradual and imperceptible, but in the end it is very great: it is often decisive for good or evil.

II. ITS BEARING ON OUR OWN RELIGIOUS LIFE. We are to guard most sedulously our sacred feelings; to "keep our heart above all keeping" (Prov. iv. 23). Among other perils to be avoided is that of allowing sacred things to be vulgarized by too frequent use, to lose their force and virtue by reason of over-familiarity. With this end in view, there will be, on the part of the prudent, a certain measure of: 1. *Wise limitation.* This will apply to (1) the use of the Divine name (the avoidance of profanity); (2) the employment of pious phraseology in ordinary speech (the avoidance of offensive and injurious cant); (3) the repetition of sacred formulæ (the avoidance of a Pharisaic formalism); (4) the multiplication of holy days (Rom. xiv. 6). (5) These matters, and such as these, are questions of expediency, to be determined by practical Christian wisdom. Both extremes are to be avoided—the *neglect* of good things and so the loss of spiritual help, and their *excessive use* resulting in the loss of the sense of sacredness. The latter is a subtle and strong evil, for when sacred things have lost their sanctity to us, there is little left to elevate and restore. "If the salt have lost *its* savour," etc. But beside wise limitation, there must be: 2. *Positive spiritual endeavour.* It will by no means suffice to conform to good rules of speech and behaviour: such abstinences will not preserve a reverent and loving spirit; we must *think seriously* and *pray earnestly.* (1) By serious thought we must be frequently realizing how great is our indebtedness to the heavenly Father; how real is our need, as sinners, of the Divine Saviour; how urgent is our want, as weak and struggling souls, of the influence of the Holy Spirit! (2) By earnest prayer we must be drawing down from on high that spiritual replenishment which God is willing to bestow on all seeking souls, and without which all life will languish, all means and methods prove fruitless and vain.—C.

Vers. 1—17.—*The peace offerings,* also called *thank offerings* or *salvation offerings.* The twofold object—to acknowledge salvation received, to supplicate salvation desired. Three kinds—praise offerings, vow offerings, free-will offerings. Considerable freedom permitted in them, though still restrictions observed. Male and female victims, of the herd and flock, but only those without blemish. No pigeons permitted, because a pair of pigeons insufficient for the sacrificial meal, which was so important a constituent of the service. Combination of the burnt sacrifice with the peace offering in the consumption by fire of the suet or fat of the internal organs, and of the fat tail of the sheep. The fat and the blood offered to the Lord in a special manner, by fire and sprinkling "on the altar round about."

Ver. 1.—*The offering distinguished. Oblation* denotes its voluntary character; *sacrifice* its intimate connection with the altar, that is, its participation in the atoning significance of all the bloody sacrifices which carried in them the idea of reconciliation with God through the blood of the covenant. *Peace offering,* the specific distinction, recognizing the fact that, whether the prominent feeling expressed was praise or prayer, still the offerer was standing on the ground of covenant fellowship with God. We may take these offerings generally to symbolize *salvation as a realized fact.* We find under this general fact these *three constituent spiritual realities included:* I.

Intercourse re-established between God and man, and expressed in grateful praise and willing dependence. II. *Salvation as a fact resting on continued faith;* the three parts of the sacrifice being the offerer's part, the priest's part, and Jehovah's part,—all essential and harmonized in one offering. III. *Joy of salvation,* both individual and social, typified in the sacrificial meal, God, as it were, giving back the victim to be the source of delight both to the priest and the offerer. On each of these points the details of the sacrifice have their significance.

I. RECONCILIATION. Re-established intercourse between God and man, grateful praise, willing dependence. Here we may notice the two sides of the sacrifice: that turned *towards man*—it is *willingly* brought, it is a *valuable* gift, it is brought as a *peace offering* to give praise or to accompany vows and prayers; that turned *towards God,* it is a confession of sin, an obedience rendered to the Law, a renewal of the covenant, a confirmation of the promises, a seal of grace. *Intercourse between man and God.* 1. Distinguish between the truth as set forth in Scripture, and man's self-derived ideas. (1) Consider the non-scriptural views: the notions of the mystic or of the transcendentalist—man's lifting himself to God, or being lifted up by ecstasy; the rationalistic conception that God and man meet in nature, or in human consciousness, and that such intercourse in the mere laws of fact or thought is sufficient. All *such* reconciliation ignores the fallen state of man, can supply no gospel of peace, is contradicted by the plain development of righteousness in the course of the world; and therefore the necessity made evident that man, as going on to meet the future, should be prepared to meet his God in judgment, in the great adjustment of right and wrong. The mere moralist falls into a similar error when he teaches that the partial obedience of human life to Divine Law, the recognition practically of an ideal moral standard, is a reconciliation between the highest moral Being and his creature. (2) Place opposite to these defective and erroneous views the teaching of Scripture. Out of the original source of all, *the will of God,* that is, his infinite nature or character, in actual relation to his universe, comes forth the reconciliation. Revelation from the beginning an invitation of God to man to intercourse. The Mosaic Law was the development of the preceding covenant, which, under patriarchal ministry, was a gospel of peace. The reconciliation was placed on the foundation of sacrifice, that is, man's surrender, blending with God's promise of forgiveness and life, the preservation of righteousness in the acceptance of man's homage to the Divine character, the assurance of peace in a covenant of friendship and interchange of love. 2. This intercourse between God and man being thus established, it is expressed in *grateful praise and willing dependence* on man's part, in the bestowment of *peace and sanctification* on God's part. The *peace offering* typified the life of man as a continual reciprocation of covenant intercourse: the presentation of gifts to God, the acceptance in return of Divine grace. Thus was religion set forth. It is not separated from the earthly life, but it is its consecration. It is not a meritorious purchase of Divine favour, or turning away of wrath, or covering of the reality of transgression with sacrifice, but a thankful dedication of saved life, a subjection of all to the will of the Father, an appropriation of heavenly gifts. Perhaps the fact that no poor man's offering is prescribed may indicate that the truth was already implied, though not so distinctly expressed as afterwards in the Psalms and Prophets, that God would have mercy and not sacrifice, that he laid no stress upon the actual presentation of a peace offering so long as the man himself and his life were offered in devout obedience and thankful spirit. "Whoso offereth praise glorifieth me: and to him that ordereth his conversation aright will I show the salvation of God" (Ps. l. 23).

II. SALVATION AS A FACT RESTS ON CONTINUED FAITH. In every peace offering there were three parts—the offerer's, the priest's, Jehovah's. On each occasion, therefore, the main elements of salvation were recognized, which were these: 1. *Free grace.* 2. *Mediation.* 3. *Self-surrender.* In each the offerer's faith makes salvation a fact. 1. In bringing a peace offering to Jehovah, the worshipper cast himself by faith on the free grace which opened the way for him to reconciliation and peace. "We love him because he first loved us." The Jew failed to see this freedom of Divine love, and hence became a bond slave under the power of his ritual. The gospel has exalted the Divine element so high above the human in the advent of the Son of God, that it is no longer possible to hide it. "God was in Christ reconciling the world unto himself." "The Lord hath visited his people." We build all on the foundation stone which God himself hath laid. We begin with the person of Christ, divinely glorious. Our faith lays hold of eternal life in him who was the Life and the Light of men. 2. The offerer brought the victim, but the priestly *mediation* was a necessary part of the ceremony. Salvation as a fact rests not only upon the free and infinite love of God, but upon the manifested righteousness and ceaseless intercession of the Saviour. "Aaron's sons sprinkle the blood; Aaron's sons burn the fat on the altar on the burnt sacrifice; a sweet savour unto the Lord." Our life as a saved life is a continual application to ourselves by faith of the merit and efficacy of the Saviour's atonement and ministry as our great High Priest. The "truth as it is in Jesus" is the food of our thoughts, the joy of our hearts, the strength of our obedience. Salvation as a fact is realized forgiveness, progressive holiness in communion with Christ, victory through his grace over the world and all enemies, and at last participation in the glorification of the Divine Man, and admission into his eternal kingdom. 3. *Self-surrender* was both in the presentation of the offering and in the position of the offerer, laying his hand on the head of the victim, killing it, and giving up the assigned portions to the altar and fire; all was confession, consecration, obedience. Our faith is essentially a yielding of ourselves to God. We find our salvation a fact, just as we "put off the old man and put on the new man;" just as we "count all things loss for the excellency of the knowledge of Christ Jesus our Lord." Our offering is a peace offering, both of the past and for the future. We are no longer our own. Christ is all to us, and so we are Christ's, and Christ is God's.

III. JOY OF SALVATION, typified in the sacrificial meal, in which the representatives of God and man, in the priests and offerer, met together in social festivity. This was anticipation of the sacred meal, the Supper of the Lord, in which sacrificial joy was celebrated in the new society, in the kingdom of God. The Christian's joy is pre-eminently joy of salvation. He builds all happiness on the fact of reconciliation with God. He lives his new life not unto himself, but unto Christ and to Christ's people. The social gladness, which was an element in the peace offering, points to the fact that the redemption of Christ effects a deliverance of society from its bondage and misery, as well as the individual soul from its sin and ruin. Such a message is specially wanted in these times, when the world groans under its burdens, and strives in vain after a true liberty and peace. What offerings are laid on the altar of war! Yet they are consumed in vain. There is no happy banquet of fellowship and brotherhood coming out of such sacrifices. God invites us to the joy of a new-made world. He bids us proclaim the way of peace to be through the obedience of Christ. How sweet the savour to the Lord when the whole human family shall offer up its peace offering, acceptable, because identified with the offering of Calvary, uniting all together in a sacred festivity of gladness!—R.

Vers. 3, 4.—" The fat that covereth the inwards;" " the caul above the liver, with the kidneys;" " *all the fat is the Lord's*" (ver. 16). The sweet fat, or suet, was burned as a sweet savour to the Lord. This might be either because fat of this kind was a sign of perfection in the animal life, or because the offering in the fire would be increased by the oily matter, and would make the burnt offering more imposing. Any way the dedication to the Lord is the main idea.

I. RELIGIOUS SERVICE SHOULD TAKE UP INTO ITSELF THE HIGHEST FACULTIES AND NOBLEST AFFECTIONS. The worship of the sanctuary; the active efforts of Christians in the spread of the gospel; charity;—in all such sacrifices let " *the fat be the Lord's.*"

II. THE PROSPERITY OF HUMAN LIFE IS ONLY SAFE AND BLESSED WHEN THE SUBSTANCE OF IT IS CONSECRATED ON THE ALTAR. Men become victims of their own success because they withhold the fat from the Lord, and it becomes a curse to them.—R.

Ver. 5.—" And Aaron's sons shall burn it on the altar *upon* the burnt sacrifice, which is upon the wood that is on the fire: it is an offering made by fire, of a sweet savour unto the Lord." Notice the preparation thus made for the acceptance of man's offering. There is the *altar*, the *fire*, the *wood*, the *burnt sacrifice*, the offering of the *consecrated fat*. Thus ch. vi. 12, it is said, " the priest shall burn wood every morning at the altar, and lay the burnt offering in order upon it; and he shall burn thereon the fat of the peace offerings." The abiding sacrifice, on the abiding altar, with the abiding fire, receives the occasional offering of the individual worshipper. Here is the great truth of an abiding merit, an ever-living intercession set forth.

I. God, by his grace, has provided for us THE TRUE METHOD OF RIGHTEOUSNESS AND ACCEPTANCE. 1. The superiority of Christ's sacrifice to all other—because of his person, his active and passive obedience, his declared acceptance by his baptism, transfiguration, resurrection, ascension. 2. The simple work of faith, in laying the offering on the ashes of the burnt sacrifice, in attaching the imperfect obedience of man to the infinite merit of Christ. A peace offering in the highest sense when we thus lay all upon the altar of the true mediation. The fire consuming denoted acceptance. God, in Christ, declares himself not only well pleased in his beloved Son, but in all who spiritually are identified with him. The lesser burnt offering is absorbed into the greater and abiding burnt offering, our obedience in Christ's.

II. Thus is set forth THE TRUE ORDER OF THE ETHICAL LIFE. The lesser sacrifice *upon* the greater. The peace offering on the burnt offering. 1. Common mistake to attempt to reverse this order. Man supposes himself capable of building up merit by moral acts. God teaches him that all ethical worth must rest upon religious completeness. The relation between God and man must be true and perfect, otherwise morality is not real, but only disguised selfishness. 2. The offering up of human life in activity, in suffering, cannot be *peace* offering unless it be religious. We want the greatest motive to actuate and sustain. We seem to waste our offering unless we can see it in its relation with God's work, with a redeemed and renewed world. 3. The sweetness of life is a return into our own hearts of what the Lord hath found delightful. The "*sweet savour*" of a consecrated obedience pervades the whole existence, and makes it fragrant both to ourselves and others. Wonderful transmuting power of religion in giving value to the apparently worthless in human character, and beauty to the commonest, and nobleness to the humblest; the whole garment of sanctity covering the native imperfections. Yet no sweet savour without fire. There must be the reality of a spiritual life—the power of God, not the mere form and appearance of the offering.—R.

Vers. 6—16.—*Varieties in the offerings—unity in the sacrifice.* Whether from the herd or from the flock, an offering of larger or smaller value, the same principle applies —the unblemished gift, the separation of the fat and of the blood, the observance of all prescribed order and detail.

I. Here is the TRUE RELIGIOUS LIBERTY. Obedience according to ability, "doing the will of God from the heart." The variety which is necessitated in God's children by their different capabilities and circumstances is not displeasing to him. If we cannot bring an offering from the herd, then from the flock; if not a sheep, then a lamb; if neither, then the will for the deed. Yet all can do something. "Unto every one of us is given grace according to the measure of the gift of Christ" (Eph. iv. and 1 Cor. xii.).

II. Here is the secret of SOCIAL PEACE AND STRENGTH—the only true equality ; God's altar bringing together rich and poor, high and low. All, offering what they can to him, find out each other's nearness and worth. In the house of God the poor man may be a higher servant of the sanctuary than the rich. Society rests on religion as its basis. Mistake of philosophy, which gives us not brotherhood but altruism—not family life but mere expediency. The true conception of a State is every one having a place, and every one in his place. None but the religious view, which makes the altar of God the centre, really effects this union of the individual interest with that of the community. The true mother does not despise the sickly child. Philosophy exalts the great and depresses the little. Religion humbles the great and exalts the low. The revelation is to babes. The offering is accepted from the weakest hands. All are one in Christ. The perfect Sacrifice blends all together.—R.

EXPOSITION.

CHAPTER IV.

THE SIN OFFERING (chs. iv., v. 1—13). At the time of the Mosaic legislation, burnt offerings and meat offerings were already in existence, and had existed from the time of the Fall. A beginning, therefore, is made with them, and the regulations of the peace offerings naturally follow, because these sacrifices succeed in order to the burnt and meat offerings, and because sacrifices in some respects of the same nature as peace offerings had previously existed under a different name (cf. Exod. x. 25 with Exod. xxiv. 5, and see above notes on ch. iii.). The sin and trespass offerings, therefore, are left to the last, though, owing to their meaning, they were always offered first of all, when sacrifices of all three kinds were made together. They are the means of ceremonially propitiating God when alienated from his people, or from any individual member of it, by sin, which they legally atone for. The need of expiation is implied and suggested by the offering of the blood, both in the burnt sacrifice and the peace offering (cf. Job i. 5). But this was not sufficient; there must be a special sacrifice to teach this great truth as its primary lesson. The sin offering typifies the sacrifice of our Lord JESUS CHRIST upon the cross, as the great Sin Offering for mankind, whereby the wrath of God was propitiated, and an expiation for the sins of man was wrought, bringing about reconciliation between God and man.

Ver. 2.—**If a soul shall sin.** The conditions to be fulfilled in presenting a sin offering differed according to the position held by the offerer in the state. If it were the high priest, he had (1) to offer a young bull in the court of the tabernacle; (2) to place his hand upon it; (3) to kill it; (4) to take the blood into the holy place of the tabernacle, and there sprinkle some of it seven times in the direction of the vail that divided off the holy of holies within which the ark was placed, and to smear some of it on the horns of the golden altar of incense; (5) to pour out the rest of the blood at the foot of the altar of burnt offering in the court of the tabernacle; (6) to burn all the internal fat upon the altar of burnt offering; (7) to carry the whole of the remainder of the animal outside the camp, and there to burn it. If it were the congregation that made the offering, the same conditions had to be fulfilled, except that the elders of the congregation had to lay their hands on the animal. If it were a ruler, the animal offered was to be a male kid, and the priest, instead of taking the blood into the sanctuary, was to smear it on the horns of the altar of burnt sacrifice in the court. If it were an ordinary member of the congregation, the animal was to be a female kid, or ewe lamb, which was to be dealt with in the same manner; or in some cases two turtledoves or two young pigeons, one for a sin offering (whose blood was all sprinkled round the inner side of the altar), the other for a burnt offering (which was to be treated according to the ritual of the burnt offering), or even the tenth part of an ephah of flour (without oil or frankincense), a handful of which was to be burnt, and the remainder delivered to the priest for his consumption. The moral lesson taught to the Jew by the sin offering was of the terrible nature of sin, and of the necessity for an expiation for it in addition to penitence. Mystically he might see that, as the blood of bulls and goats could not of its own virtue take away sin, there must be an offering, foreshadowed by the sacrifice of the animals, which should be effectual as these were symbolical. The type is fulfilled by the atonement wrought by Christ's blood shed on the cross (see Heb. x. 1—21). Further, the ceremonial cleansing of the sinful Israelite by the sin offering in the old dispensation foreshadows the effect of baptism in the new dispensation, for, as Calvin has noted in his Commentary, "As sins are now sacramentally washed away by baptism, so under the Law also sacrifices were expiations, although in a different way."

If a soul shall sin through ignorance. The expression, "through ignorance" (*bishgagah*), is intended to cover all sins except those committed "with a high hand," or defiantly, whether the agent was ignorant that they were sins or was led into them by inconsiderateness or infirmity (cf. Ps. xix. 12, 13, "Who can understand his errors? Cleanse thou me from secret faults. Keep back thy servant also from presumptuous sins"). A better translation of *bishgagah* would be *by want of consideration*, or *by inadvertence*. Our Lord could say, even of those who crucified him, "Father, forgive them; for they know not what they do;" and therefore even for them a sin offering might be made and be accepted. But for deliberate and determined sin the Law has no atonement, no remedy. The words, shall do against any of them, *i.e.* against the commandments, would be better rendered *shall do any of them,* i.e. the things which ought not to be done. There is no exact apodosis to this verse; it is a general heading to the chapter.

Vers. 3—12.—The case of the high priest. He is designated **the priest that is anointed,** in respect to which title, see notes on ch. viii. In case he sins in his representative character, his sin is such as *to bring guilt on the people* (this is the meaning of the words translated **according to the sin of the people**), and a special sin offering must therefore be made. He is to **take of the blood of the animal sacrificed, and bring it to the tabernacle of the congregation: . . . and sprinkle of the blood seven times before the Lord, before the vail of the sanctuary. And put** some of the blood on the horns of the altar of sweet incense. This was a more solemn method of presenting the blood to the Lord than that used in the burnt offering; the offering of the blood, which was the vehicle of life, being the chief feature in the sin offering, as the consumption of the whole animal by the altar fire was in the burnt offering. In the burnt offerings and peace offerings the blood was thrown once on the altar of burnt sacrifice (see ch. i. 5); now it is sprinkled, in a smaller quantity each time, but as often as seven times (the number seven symbolically representing completeness), before the vail which shrouded the ark. *The altar of sweet incense* is the golden altar, which stood within the tabernacle, in front of the vail. Perhaps the reason why *the horns of the altar* are specially appointed to have the blood placed on them is that they were regarded as the most sacred part of the altar, because they were its highest points, in which its elevation towards heaven culminated. The remainder of the victim's blood is to be poured **at the bottom of the altar of the burnt offering,** in the court of the tabernacle, to sink into the ground, because no more of it was wanted for ceremonial use. The internal fat is to be burnt **upon the altar of the burnt offering,** but not actually upon the smouldering burnt sacrifice, as in the case of the peace offerings; the sin offering preceding the burnt offering in order of time, while the peace offering followed it. The remainder of the animal is **to be carried without the camp . . . and be burnt,** because its flesh was at once accursed and most holy. It was accursed, as having been symbolically the vehicle of the sins laid upon it by the offerer; therefore it must not be consumed upon the altar of God, but be destroyed with fire outside the camp, typifying the removal from God's kingdom, and the final destruction of all that is sinful. But yet it was most holy, as its blood had been taken into the tabernacle, and had served as a propitiation; therefore, if it had to be burnt, it yet had to be burnt solemnly, reverently, and as a ceremonial act, in a place appointed for the purpose. The writer of the Epistle to the Hebrews notices that one of the points in which our Lord was the antitype of the sin offering was that he "suffered without the gate," "that he might sanctify the people with his own blood" (Heb. xiii. 12), which was thus indicated to have been carried within the sanctuary, that is, into heaven.

Vers. 13—21.—The case of the whole congregation. A nation may become guilty of national sin in different ways, according to its political constitution: most directly, by the action of a popular Legislature passing a decree such as that of the Athenian assembly, condemning the whole of the Mitylenean people to death (Thucyd., iii. 36), or by approving an act of sacrilege (Mal. iii. 9); indirectly, by any complicity in or condoning of a sin done in its name by its rulers. The ritual of the sin offering is the same as in the case of the high priest. **The elders of the congregation** (according to the Targum of Jonathan, twelve in number), acting for the nation, lay their hands on the victim's head, and the high priest, as before, presents the blood, **by sprinkling it seven times before the Lord, even before the vail; and putting some of the blood upon the horns of the altar which is before the Lord, that is in the tabernacle of the congregation.** It is added that he shall thus **make an atonement,** or covering of sin, **for them, and it shall be forgiven them.**

Vers. 22—26.—The case of a ruler or nobleman. The clause, **Or if his sin . . . come to his knowledge,** should be rather translated, *If perhaps his sin come to his knowledge.* He is to offer **a kid of the goats,** or rather *a he-goat.* The blood is not to be carried into the tabernacle, as in the two previous cases, but **put upon the horns of the altar of burnt offering,** which stood outside in the court, and, as a consequence of the blood not having been taken into the tabernacle, the flesh is not to be burnt outside the camp, but to be eaten by the priests in the court of the tabernacle (see ch. vi. 26).

Vers. 27—35.—The case of a common man. He is to offer **a kid of the goats,** or rather *a she-goat.* The ritual is to be the same as in the previous case.

HOMILETICS.

Vers. 1—35.—*The sin offering* signifies and ceremonially effects propitiation and expiation. Its characteristic feature, therefore, is the presentation of the blood of the victim, which in this sacrifice alone (when it was offered for the high priest or the whole congregation) was carried into the tabernacle and solemnly sprinkled before the vail which covered God's presence.

I. WHEN IT WAS TO BE OFFERED. On certain solemn public occasions, and whenever the conscience of an individual was awakened to being out of communion with God. The contraction of certain defilements and the commission of certain sins excluded the delinquent from God's people, and when this had occurred, he might not be readmitted until he had brought a sin offering to be offered in his behalf.

II. HOW IT WAS EFFECTIVE. The fact of God's appointing it for a certain end made it effective for that end; but we are allowed to see why God appointed it, and this was because it was a shadow of the Great Atonement to be wrought for all mankind by the Christian Sin Offering of the cross. For the result of original sin and the consequent growth and spread of wickedness upon the earth had separated between God and man. How were they to be reconciled? Christ became the representative of sinful man, and the substitute for him, and in this capacity he bore the penalty of sins, (1) in the Garden of Gethsemane, (2) on the cross—thus restoring man to communion with God.

III. THINGS TO BE NOTED—
1. The wrath of God against sin.
2. The love of God towards sinners.
3. The justice of God.
4. The love of Christ in his incarnation.
5. The obedience of Christ in his death.
6. The blessed result to man, namely, union and communion with God, through Christ the Peace-maker.

IV. THE OFFERING MADE ONCE FOR ALL. The Jewish offerings could be brought again and again; the Christian Sin Offering could be made but once. There can be no repetition of it, no continuation of it; but its effects are always continuing, and applicable to all Christ's people. Its benefits are to be grasped and appropriated, each time that they are needed, by faith. As the Israelite laid his hand on the sin offering, so we lean by faith on Christ, and may constantly plead the merits of the offering which cannot be renewed. In case we have fallen into sin, we may not, like the Israelite, bring our bullock for sacrifice; we cannot renew the Great Sacrifice typified by the bullock's sacrifice; but, by repentance and by faith in the atonement wrought by the sacrifice of Christ's death, we can be restored.

V. FEELINGS AWAKENED—
Thankfulness for God's mercy in finding a way of escape;
Thankfulness for Christ's love in working out man's salvation;
A blessed sense of peace resulting from the consciousness that the Great Atoning Sacrifice has been offered.

HOMILIES BY VARIOUS AUTHORS.

Atonement for the penitent, as illustrated in the sin offering. Ch. iv.; v. 1—13; cf. Ps. xix. 12; Gal. vi. 1; 1 Tim. i. 13, etc. The offerings already considered, viz. the burnt offering, the meat offering, and the peace offering, have respectively emphasized the ideas of *personal consecration, consecrated life-work,* and *fellowship.* Moreover, they are to be regarded as voluntary offerings, depending upon the impulse of the heart for their celebration. Special experience might impel an Israelite to express his consecration or his fellowship, and he would then bring the appointed sacrifice.

But here we come across an offering which is *imperative.* The moment an Israelite became convinced of sin, then he was bound to bring the offering prescribed. Besides, the sin offering is Mosaic in its origin; it had no existence, as such, before the promulgation of the covenant at Sinai; and consequently it is to be taken as the rule for *penitents*, whose consciences have been educated in a more thorough detection of sin through the Law. "By the law is the knowledge of sin." We have at this stage, consequently, a perceptible elevation of the moral standard.

I. THE FIRST LESSON OF THE SIN OFFERING IS THAT SIN IS A NATURE. The superficial treatment of sin deals with outward and conscious acts, such as trespasses; what God declares by his Law is that, behind all conscious acts of the will, there are *natural* movements of which we are not conscious, and for which, nevertheless, we are responsible. This important principle is affirmed by all these minute regulations about sins of ignorance. The thoughtful Israelite would see from this that sin is a much wider and deeper thing than he at first suspected; that the motions of his personal being are more numerous and varied than he supposed; that deliberation, in fact, is not essential to every sin, and does not cover responsibility. In other words, he would look within and realize that sin is a nature, working on, sometimes consciously and sometimes unconsciously, and that for all its workings he will be held accountable.

No more important principle lies in the field of self-examination. Without it there can be no thorough treatment of sin. With it we stand abashed and humbled under a sense of the unknown sin as well as of the known. We cry with David, "Who can understand his errors? cleanse thou me from secret faults. Keep back thy servant also from presumptuous sins; let them not have dominion over me: then shall I be upright, and I shall be innocent from the great transgression" (Ps. xix. 12, 13; cf. also Shedd's 'Discourses and Essays,' No. VI.).

II. SIN VARIES IN ITS HEINOUSNESS. The Israelite not only recognized this whole category of sins of ignorance marshalled in the Law before him; he also saw a difference of treatment in the cases under review. A sin of ignorance on the part of the high priest was made more emphatic than one on the part of a prince or a private person. The high priest's representative position and character modified the whole case. His sin of omission or neglect became much more serious than a private individual's could be. He was consequently directed to bring a bullock, the same offering as for a sin on the part of the collective people; for his representative character made him, so to speak, a *moral equivalent* to them. While, therefore, it is well to recognize sin as a nature, we must also remember that God does not treat sin in the mass, but discriminates between the more or less guilty. In his morality there are the most delicate appreciations and adjustments. Penitence must likewise be discriminating as well as profound. Self-examination may be a most humiliating and disappointing process, but we should weigh the relations of our faults and sins when we discover them and deal faithfully with ourselves.

III. YET ALL SINNERS ARE PLACED WITHIN REACH OF AN APPROPRIATE ATONEMENT. The high priest and the collective people, the prince and one of the common people, each and all had their prescribed offering and guaranteed atonement. And when people proved so poor that they could not offer turtle-doves or young pigeons, they were directed to bring an ephah of fine flour, with which the priest would make atonement. And as for this atonement, it is in all cases secured by the *surrender of life*. Even the ephah of flour conveyed this idea, for the germ is hopelessly sacrificed in its manufacture. The one idea binding the various sacrifices together is the surrender of life. That this idea is to be attributed to substances in the vegetable kingdom as well as the animal, is evident from John xii. 24, "Verily, verily, I say unto you, Except a corn of wheat fall into the ground and die, it abideth alone: but if it die, it bringeth forth much fruit."

And it need scarcely be added that the atonement of which these sin offerings were types is that of the Lord Jesus, who "was once offered to bear the sins of many" (Heb. ix. 28; also vers. 11—14). In the proclamation of the gospel, this most appropriate atonement is put within the reach of all. No sinner is excluded from the possibility of atonement except through his own self-will.

IV. THE RECONCILIATION WITH THE PENITENT, WHICH ATONEMENT SECURES, IS A MATTER OF DEEP DELIGHT TO GOD. For not only is the blood of the sacrifice accepted at the appropriate spot, whether vail and altar of incense, or the brazen altar only, according to the *status* of the penitent; but there is besides an acceptance of the best portions of the animal upon the altar, indicating that God is delighted with the accomplished atonement. It was, so far as God was concerned, as much a feast as the peace offering. It expressed, consequently, that God was delighted beyond all our conception with the reconciliation.

It is well to make this idea always emphatic. Our blinded souls are ready to imagine that we are more anxious for reconciliation, and would be more delighted with it when it came, than God can be. The truth, however, is all the other way. The reconciliation begins with God, the atonement is due to his wisdom and mercy, and over the actual consummation he rejoices with "joy unspeakable and full of glory."

V. THE RECONCILIATION IS ALSO MEANT TO BE A FEAST OF DELIGHT TO ALL GOD'S SERVANTS WHO ARE INSTRUMENTAL IN BRINGING IT ABOUT. For we must notice that, in the cases where the priests are not penitents themselves, but mediators, they are allowed to make a feast of what is left after the best portions are dedicated to God. Of course, when they are penitents, as in the case of a personal or a congregational sin, the carcase is to be considered *too holy* for the priests to partake of it; hence it is disposed of in its entirety in a *clean* place beyond the camp. This was the solemn way of disposing of the whole carcase. But in the other cases the priests were directed to feast upon the remainder of the offering, as those bearing atonement. So far they enjoyed what was their lot in the peace offering. As a feast, and not a lugubrious fast, it surely was intended to indicate their personal joy and satisfaction in the reconciliation they were instrumental in bringing about.

Luke xv. presents the joy of the Godhead and of the angels over returning penitents. It is this spirit we should cultivate. It will require, of course, much personal dealing with souls, but it is worth all the trouble to be instrumental in leading them to peace with God, and to the joy that results therefrom.—R. M. E.

Vers. 1, 9.—*Unintentional transgression.* God is the source of authority and law. From him instructions emanate. His words are to be communicated to the people. Like unto Moses, ministers and teachers receive truth not to secrete it in their own breasts, but to impart it for the guidance of those under their charge. "The Lord spake, . . . saying, Speak unto the children of Israel." May we listen carefully, lest the utterances of the "still small voice" should be misheard, and the counsels intended for comfort and direction prove a false light, speeding the unconscious traveller to the very pitfalls he was to avoid.

I. THE UNIVERSALITY OF TRANSGRESSION. Provision is announced for cases of sin, and the possibility of its commission by all classes is thus shown. 1. *The ordinary citizen* may err; one of "the people of the land" (see ver. 27). Poverty and obscurity are not safeguards against unrighteous acts. 2. *The man of rank,* the "ruler" (ver. 22) or prince, is liable to sin. Honour and responsibility do not guarantee or produce immunity from transgression. 3. *The whole congregation* (ver. 13) is not exempt, for collective wisdom and might are not effectual barriers against the encroachments of unlawful desire and action. In the multitude of counsellors safety is often thought to lie, but the "people" may do wickedly as well as an individual. This was exemplified at Mount Sinai and Baal-peor, and modern instances abound. Even—4. *The man specially consecrated to holy service,* the "anointed priest" (ver. 3), may incur guilt and bring punishment upon the people. How cautious we should be! What searching of ourselves with the candle of the Lord; what prayer for knowledge and strength should distinguish us all!

II. THE POSSIBILITY OF UNINTENTIONAL TRANSGRESSION. A distinction is intimated between sin that arises from mistake ("ignorance," ver. 2), that is at first "hid" from perception and afterwards becomes known (vers. 13, 14), awaking penitence and a desire to undo the wrong perpetrated, and sin that is wilful, committed with a high hand, with an attitude of defiance, a sin against light and knowledge. Inadvertent sinning is possible through (1) carelessness of behaviour, heedless conduct, acting without previous deliberation; or (2) a misunderstanding of the Law, failure in correct interpretation, or in remembering the precise precept at the moment; or (3) a sudden outburst of passion, blinding the judgment and hurrying the will to words and deeds afterwards repented of.

III. THE GUILT OF SUCH TRANSGRESSION. This is assumed by the atonement necessary to shield the doer from penalty, and by the expressions employed in vers. 13, 22, and 27. "Guilty" refers to the consequences of sinning, the state of wrath into which the sinner enters, and the moral devastation to which he is liable, and from which preservation is possible only through an offering. Learn, then, that ignorance does not of itself excuse violation of God's commands, but it permits resort to such an atonement as will procure God's forgiveness. Paul said, "I obtained mercy because I did it ignorantly and in unbelief." Whereas if we sin wilfully, there is no more sacrifice for sins. The soul that doeth presumptuously shall be cut off from among the people.—S. R. A.

Ver. 3.—"Let him bring for his sin, which he hath sinned." *The atonement for involuntary transgression.* The Book of Leviticus well repays careful perusal in days when there are many attempts made to lessen men's sense of the enormity of sin and of the necessity of a propitiatory offering. Its teachings are impressive, its pictures vivid.

I. Sin inflicts an injury upon the holiness of God, and exposes man to penal consequences. The words used to denote sin imply a turning aside from the path marked out, a deviation from rectitude. Man misses his way, goes astray like a lost sheep. He does what he ought not to do (ver. 2), and thereby the precepts of God are slighted and God's honour is wounded. This cannot be permitted with impunity. The wrath of God, not a base but holy passion, is aroused, and vengeance or holy indignation threatens to visit the transgressor. We think wrongly of our sinful acts if we minimize their awful importance, or pay regard simply to the injury done to ourselves. This is the least part. The Supreme Being is concerned, and it is his displeasure we have to fear. Sin cuts at the root of government, assails the foundations of the eternal throne.

II. Every transgression is recognized as sinful, whether arising from ignorance or wilfulness, whether an act of omission or commission. An atonement is insisted on even for what we deem the least flagrant derelictions. Man is so ready to extenuate his crimes, that God strips off the veil, and exposes sin in all its guiltiness, a thing to be loathed and shunned wherever met, requiring purification on our part, however accidentally we may have come in contact with it. That without intention we trod upon a venomous serpent, does not protect us from its fangs. We shall need the remedy, however the poison may have been injected.

III. Penitence and confession are insufficient to obliterate the memory of the sin. To regret the act and to express sorrow and to determine not to offend again, are good as far as they go, but, to wipe out the stain, blood must be shed. This only can whiten the defiled robes. Sinner, behold the Lamb of God, which taketh away the sin of the world! To have the sin brought to your knowledge, so that you take a more adequate view of its sinfulness, to pour forth agonizing cries and floods of tears, will not obtain forgiveness, unless accompanied with the presentation to the Father of the righteousness of his Son.

IV. Sin becomes more conspicuous and far-reaching when committed by the occupants of a lofty position. The high priest was the representative of the nation, and hence his offering must equal in value that presented by the whole congregation. So likewise the sin of a ruler was more visible than that of a subject, and wronged God the more, and whilst a she-goat sufficed for one of the people, for him only a he-goat was allowed. Not without reason did the apostle exhort that intercession be made "for kings, and all that are in authority." Iniquity in high places in the Church and in society causes the greatest scandal, becomes most hurtful in its effects, and is most offensive to God. Both the animal offered and the ritual observed testified to the relative enormity of transgressions by different classes. Between the sins of each order in themselves no distinction was made.

V. By the appointed victim reconciliation is possible to all inadvertent offenders. We reserve this to the last, in order that the cheeriest aspect may be uppermost. Divest honour of its consequent responsibility we cannot, but we point to the ample provision for forgiveness afforded to comfort the prince and the peasant, the priest and the layman, the individual and the nation. Our Redeemer, Jesus Christ, has given his life a ransom for the many. He satisfies all claims, reconciles us unto God, so that our trespasses are not imputed unto us.—S. R. A.

Vers. 3—12.—*Rites essential to an atonement.* Who could stand in the tabernacle court without having imprinted on his mind the view God takes of the guilt of sin, and the necessity for the sinner's deliverance from its results? The victims brought for sacrifice, the priests devoted to the sacrificial work, the altars of burnt offering and incense, the vail that separated the holy from the holiest place—all these were eminently calculated to deepen the Israelites' conviction of the holiness of the Almighty, and the awfulness of violating his injunctions. Neglecting the distinctions enumerated in this chapter according to the rank occupied by the transgressor, let us take a general survey of the conditions enforced in a proper offering for sin.

I. THE DEATH OF AN APPOINTED VICTIM. The hand of the offerer is placed on the animal's head, and the animal's life is surrendered to the will of God. "Without shedding of blood is no remission." This tragic spectacle attests forcibly the rigour of God's requirements. Christ died as our representative, so that in him we all died (2 Cor. v.), and those who rejoice in the thought of his salvation place their hands by faith upon him, believing that he was "made a curse" for them. Holiness demands an unblemished victim in each case. Hence the impossibility of man becoming his own atonement. Sin cannot expiate sin.

II. THE SPRINKLING OF THE BLOOD BY THE HIGH PRIEST UPON THE HORNS OF THE ALTAR. "The blood is the life," and is in this manner brought into the immediate presence of God, symbolized by the altar of burnt offering in the court or incense in the sanctuary. The horns represent the might of the altar, so that to smear them with blood was to carry the offering to the place where the acceptance by God of offerings or praise culminated. Sin dishonours God, and therefore the significance of the offering for sin depends chiefly upon its presentation where God was pleased to vouchsafe his favour to man. Where sin was most dishonouring, as in the event of transgression by the anointed priest, the blood had to be sprinkled before the vail that covered the Shechinah. By his death Christ entered into heaven, presenting his own precious blood to the Father, and now makes intercession as the appointed Mediator.

III. THE POURING OUT OF THE BLOOD AT THE FOOT OF THE ALTAR OF BURNT OFFERING. It is said that, at the building of the temple, conduits were constructed to drain the blood into the valley of Kedron; in the wilderness it sufficed to let it flow into the earth. The life of the animal was thus completely surrendered to God. Jesus gave himself up to do the will of God. His self-sacrifice is the basis of ours. We must live, not to ourselves, but to him. He considered not his time, words, works, as his own, and we must regard ourselves as devoted to the Father.

IV. THE BURNING OF THE FAT. Thus God would be glorified by the choicest portions, analogous to the ceremony enacted in connection with peace offerings. This resemblance seems designed to teach: 1. That by this sin offering agreement was re-established between God and man. 2. And that God's portion of the victim might be treated in the usual way, the transgression not being on God's side, but on that of man, who therefore is not permitted, as in the peace offering, to eat his part in the enjoyment of a feast. There is thus: 3. A reminder that but for sin man too might have shared in the sacrificial meal with God, but transgression had interrupted the communion, and deprived him of his former privilege. By the obedience unto death of Jesus Christ, God was glorified, and Christ became the "propitiation for our sins."

V. THE CONSUMPTION OF THE CARCASE BY FIRE OUTSIDE THE CAMP. No part of the animal was food for man, but the remainder was to be carried to a clean place, and there burnt. Every detail of the ceremony speaks of God's hatred of sin, and the blessings which man thereby loses, and the need for entire devotion of the victim that is to atone for sin. Nothing must be left, lest it should defile. The Epistle to the Hebrews alludes to the fact that Christ suffered without the gates of the holy city; to such a death of shame was he exposed in order to bear our sins.

CONCLUSION. Beware of transgression! Behold the sternness of God in dealing with it. Admire his grace in furnishing an expiation, and with grateful love avail yourselves of the sacrifice of the Saviour.—S. R. A.

Vers. 1—3.—*The sin offering for the priest.* The revelations contained in the preceding chapters, and commencing with the words, "And the Lord called unto Moses," etc., appear to have been given at one diet, and now we are introduced to a new series by similar words, "And the Lord spake unto Moses," etc. The offerings described in the earlier series, viz. the burnt offering, the meat offering, and the peace offering, were similar to those offered by the patriarchs; but these now to be described seem to be characteristic of the Levitical dispensation. In the verses more immediately before us we have to contemplate—

I. THE PRIEST AS A SINNER. 1. *May he be viewed in this character as a type of Christ?* (1) He is distinguished as "the priest that is anointed." Some suppose this determines him to be the high priest. That the high priest was a remarkable type of Christ there can be no question (Heb. iii. 1). (2) But Christ was sinless. By the miracle in his birth he avoided original sin (Luke i. 35). In his life he "fulfilled all righteousness" (Matt. iii. 15; Heb. iv. 15; vii. 26). (3) Yet so was our sin laid to his account that he vicariously stood forth as the universal sinner. "The Lord made to meet upon him the iniquity of us all" (Isa. liii. 6, margin). 2. *He may be viewed as a type of the Christian.* (1) He was not necessarily the high priest because "anointed." Aaron's sons were consecrated with Aaron (ch. viii. 2). This expression may, therefore, simply import that he was a priest who had come to official years, and therefore had received consecration (see ch. vii. 6, where minors and females are reputed to be "among the priests"). (2) The priests in general were representatives of the nation of Israel, who were, in consequence, viewed as a "kingdom of priests" (Exod. xix. 6). (3) And they typified the Christians (1 Pet. ii. 9). We do not exercise our priesthood by proxy, but ourselves "draw nigh unto God." This supplies a good reason for their being "anointed," for "Christians," as their name imports, are *anointed ones* (see 2 Cor. i. 21; Heb. i. 9; 1 John ii. 20, 27).

II. THE PRIEST AS NEEDING A SIN OFFERING. 1. *His sin is that of ignorance.* (1) The case of Eli could not be brought within this statute (see 1 Sam. iii. 14). For obstinate sin there is no mercy (see Numb. xv. 30, 31; Heb. x. 26—29). True Christians do not wilfully sin (see Matt. xiii. 38; John viii. 44; 1 John iii. 6—10). Not all who profess the Christian name have a right to the title. (2) There are sins that are not wilful: sins of surprise; sins of inattention; sins of neglect in consequence (Gal. vi. 1; Jas. v. 19, 20). But these *are* sins. (3) The sin offering is the only remedy for these. Though ignorance may be pleaded in extenuation, it cannot be pleaded in exculpation (see 1 John i. 7—9). 2. *The priest must bring a bullock.* (1) The common people may bring a kid (ver. 28). Even a ruler may bring a kid (ver. 23). But the priest must bring the larger animal. He has to bring the same which is offered for the whole congregation. (2) Much is expected of professors of religion; and more especially so of office-bearers and ministers. They should have more perfect knowledge in that which is the principal business of their life. They may, from their position, more easily misguide the people. The words in the text rendered "If the priest that is anointed do sin according to the sin of the people," some construe "If the anointed priest shall lead the people to sin." It is a fearful thing to be a "blind leader of the blind" (see Rom. ii. 21). (3) Conspicuous men should consider this. Churchwardens in Episcopal Churches; deacons in Congregationalist Churches; leaders in Methodist Churches; ministers in all; they should watch; they should pray; they should seek the prayers of their Churches (Eph. vi. 19; Col. iv. 3; 1 Thess. v. 25; 2 Thess. iii. 1).— J. A. M.

Vers. 1—12.—*The sin offering viewed as typical of the Sacrifice of Calvary.* This subject will be best considered by citing some of the more notable references to it contained in the Scriptures of the New Testament.

I. IT IS EVINCED FROM ROM. VIII. 3: "For what the Law could not do, in that it was weak through the flesh, God sending his own Son in the likeness of sinful flesh, and for sin," *i.e.* by a sin offering (the Greek term here used is that by which the LXX. commonly translate the Hebrew for "sin offering"), "condemned sin in the flesh," etc. The "flesh" that was "weak" here, we take to be: 1. *Not our fallen nature.* (1) The word "flesh" is used for this. It is so used in the connection of this very passage (vers. 4—8; see also Gal. v. 16, 17). This circumstance has led expositors to accept the term here in that sense. (2) But as a matter of fact, is the Law of God weak through our fallen nature? Certainly not. The Law answers all God ever intended it to answer. His purposes cannot be frustrated. 2. *But the flesh of the sin offerings.* (1) These were constitutionally weak for the purpose of condemning sin. The flesh of bulls and goats is not "sinful flesh." Therefore sin could not be condemned in it. (2) This weakness was no frustration of God's purposes, for he never intended that sin should be condemned in such flesh as theirs (Ps. lxix. 30, 31 ; li. 16 ; Heb. x. 4). He intended these to foreshadow something better, viz. : 3. *The Sin Offering of Calvary.* (1) This was made in a *human* body. Being in the " likeness of sinful flesh ; " there was no constitutional weakness here (Heb. x. 5—10). (2) The glorious Person who assumed the " likeness of sinful flesh " was God's " own Son." Thus by virtue of his Divinity not only has he condemned sin in the flesh, but he enables us to fulfil the righteousness of the Law in the spirit of the gospel.

II. IT IS EVINCED IN 2 COR. v. 21 : " He was made sin," *i.e.* a sin offering, " for us, who knew no sin ; that we might be made the righteousness of God in him." 1. *His righteousness is the righteousness of God.* (1) Because he is God himself. The Father was in him. Whoever failed to discern the Father in him did not comprehend him, did not know him (John xiv. 7—11). (2) He was approved of God (Matt. iii. 17 ; xvii. 5). His resurrection placed this beyond question (Acts ii. 22—24). 2. *This we receive, by imputation, in exchange for our sin.* (1) The transfer of the sin was set forth in the laying on of the hand of the offerer upon the bullock at the altar, while it was yet alive. The Jews give us these as the words uttered by the offerer, " I have sinned ; I have done perversely ; I have rebelled, and done (here specifying mentally or audibly the cause of his offering). But I return by repentance before thee, and let this be my expiation." (2) The substitute is then condemned while the offerer is justified. Not only is he released from the obligation to die, but is taken into fellowship with God, and feasts with him upon the meat and drink offerings accompanying (Numb. xv. 24).

III. IT IS EVINCED IN HEB. IX. 28 : " Christ was once offered to bear the sins of many ; and unto them that look for him shall he appear the second time without sin," *i.e.* without a sin offering, " unto salvation." The allusions here are to the sin offering of the Law. The teaching is that, whereas at his first advent he appeared in the similitude of sinful flesh for the purposes foreshadowed in the sin offering, when he comes the second time it will be in the glorious similitude of humanity, in innocence and holiness, to effect in us all the glories destined to follow upon his former meritorious sufferings (1 Pet. i. 11).

IV. IT IS EVINCED IN HEB. XIII. 10—13 : " We have an altar, whereof they have no right to eat which serve the tabernacle. For the bodies of those beasts, whose blood is brought into the sanctuary by the high priest for sin, are burned without the camp. Wherefore Jesus also, that he might sanctify the people with his own blood, suffered without the gate. Let us go forth, therefore, unto him without the camp, bearing his reproach." 1. This passage, like those already cited, asserts generally the fact that the sin offering was a type of the sacrifice of Christ. 2. But it also points out the typical import of the burning of the body in the place of ashes without the camp. What is this place of ashes but Calvary, Golgotha, the place of a skull, which was outside the gate of Jerusalem ? 3. It furthermore proves that the consumption of the body of the beasts in the fire, viz. after they had been bled at the side of the altar, foreshadowed the " suffering " of Christ. " He *suffered* without the camp." This suffering then being distinguished from that represented by the bleeding, it must refer to that agony of soul which Jesus suffered from the fire of God's wrath against sin. 4. Since the altar which supplies our Eucharistic feast is that of Calvary ; and since the priests under the Law did not eat of the bodies of those beasts which were burnt without the camp, which were types of Christ, those who serve the tabernacle have no right to eat of our altar. Therefore those who embrace Christ and rejoice in his fellowship must, in the first place, renounce the ceremonial law of Moses (Gal. ii. 19—21 ; iii. 1—3).—J. A. M.

Vers. 13—21.—*Sin offering for the congregation.* The congregation of Israel sustained a twofold character, viz. a political and an ecclesiastical ; for it was at once a Nation and a Church. Here we have—

I. THE SIN OF A NATION. Ver. 13. 1. *The commandments of the Lord concern nations.* (1) Nations are constituted under the control of his providence. We see this in the account of their origin at Babel (Gen. xi. 6—8). In the teaching of prophecy (Gen. ix. 25—27 ; xvii. 4, 6, 16). In the inspired review of their history (Acts xvii.

26). (2) God has ever held nations responsible to him (Job xii. 18; Jer. xxvii. 6; Dan. ii. 21; iv. 32). (3) The Hebrew nation more especially so. He raised them up in pursuance of his promise to their fathers. He preserved them in Egypt. He brought them forth with an outstretched arm. He gave them a code of laws at Sinai. He gave them possession of the land of Canaan. In visible symbol he guided their government. (Ps. cxlvii. 19, 20; Rom. ix. 4, 5). 2. *Therefore nations may sin against him.* (1) Where a law is there may be transgression (1 John iii. 4). God has not left himself without witness (Acts xiv. 17). (2) The Gentile nations sinned in throwing off their allegiance to the true God and joining themselves to idols. They have in consequence sunk into the most abominable immoralities (Rom. i. 21—32). (3) The Hebrews followed the bad example of their neighbours. (*a*) In asking a king to be like them (1 Sam. viii. 7, 8). (*b*) In their idolatries (1 Kings xii. 26—30; 2 Kings xxi. 11). They became demoralized by licentiousness and violence (Isa. i. 4).

II. THE SIN OF A CHURCH. 1. *The commandments of the Lord concern Churches.* (1) The Church of God in the noblest sense is a grand unity existing throughout the universe and throughout the ages. This is the corporation against which the gates of hell cannot prevail (Matt. xvi. 18). (2) This invisible Church has visible representatives on this earth. The congregation of Israel was such a representative (Acts vii. 38; collate Ps. xxii. 22 with Heb. ii. 12). Now under the gospel these representatives are many. There is a Church where two or three are met together in the name of Jesus. 2. *These Churches are responsible to God.* (1) They have to maintain the purity of faith (Titus iii. 10; 2 John 10; Jude 3; Rev. ii. 13). (2) They have to maintain purity of discipline, viz. by persuasion, by admonition, and by expulsion of incorrigible offenders. Excision in the Jewish Church was accompanied by the infliction of death; for the laws of the nation and those of the Church were one (Exod. xxxi. 14; Numb. xv. 34, 35). Now it means withdrawment from the companionship of the offender (Matt. xviii. 17; Rom. xvi. 17; 1 Cor. v.; 2 Thess. iii. 6, 14; 2 Tim. iii. 5).

III. THE OFFERING FOR SIN. 1. *Communities are punished in this world.* (1) This is evident from the nature of the case. There is no future resurrection of communities. Disintegration to a community is its utter extinction. (2) Nations meet their punishment in adversities which are ordered by Providence. These are the sword (1 Sam. xii. 9—15); the pestilence (Deut. xxviii. 21); the consequence is famine, and wasting, possibly, unto extinction. God stirs up one nation against another to punish its pride (Isa. xli. 2, 25; xlv. 1—4; xlvi. 10; Jer. l. 21—32). (3) Churches have their punishment in this world. It may come in the form of spiritual leanness. In abandonment to apostasy (Isa. lxvi. 3, 4; 2 Thess. ii. 11). The candlestick may be taken out of its place (Matt. xxi. 41—43; Rev. ii. 5). 2. *Punishment may be averted by sacrifice.* (1) Sacrifices of the Law were concerned with communities. The text furnishes an example. The community may be civil. It may be ecclesiastical. When sacrifice is accepted, no punishment is inflicted. This is the import of the assurance, " It shall be forgiven them." (2) The sacrifice of Calvary is no less concerned with communities. Churches feel it as well as individuals. Nations feel it as well as Churches. Churches and nations also should plead it far more than they do. 3. *There is no mercy for wilful sin.* (1) To avail ourselves of the benefits of atonement, there must be repentance. This was expressed when the elders of the congregation, on behalf of their constituents, laid their hands upon the bullock (see ver. 15). The gospel of this is obvious. (2) There must also be faith. The faith expressed in the laying on of hands was carried further in the sprinkling of blood (see vers. 16, 18). The vail was a type of Christ, who is our " Way " to God, the " Door " to us into the temple of the Divine Presence (Heb. x. 19, 20). The blood sprinkled upon the vail set forth the laying of our sin upon him who thereby consecrates for us the way. He also is our altar of incense upon whom the blood of our guilt is laid, and by whose intercession we are rendered acceptable to God (1 Pet. ii. 5). (3) Judgment is reserved for the obstinate. When a Church becomes apostate and will not repent, it must be destroyed. Such was the case with Judaism, which was removed amidst the slaughter of the destruction of Jerusalem. Such will be the doom of the Babylonish harlot (Rev. xviii. 4—8). And what hope is there for nations when they become infidel? If sins of ignorance cannot be forgiven without a sin offering, what must be the fate of communities guilty of presumptuous sins!—J. A. M.

Vers. 22—35.—*The sin offering of the ruler and of any of the people.* As in the preceding paragraph we have lessons from the relation of sin offering to communities, here we are reminded—

I. THAT INDIVIDUALS ARE RESPONSIBLE TO GOD. We have: 1. *The responsibility of the ruler.* (1) Rulers stand related to subjects. Their influence is extensive in proportion to the elevation of their rank. The Jews construe this law to relate to the king; but the term for ruler (נשיא, *nasi*) is not so restricted in Scripture (see Numb. x. 4). This law was in force 400 years before there existed a king in Israel. (2) As rulers of subjects they stand related to God (Prov. viii. 15, 16; 2 Sam. xxiii. 3). Note: here only, the commandment transgressed is said to be the "commandment of the Lord his God" (ver. 22). This is to remind him that if he rules others, God rules him, and will call him to account for the manner in which he uses his authority. (3) The individual is not sunk in the office. Men are too apt to forget this, particularly so when they sit in conclave. So far from neutralizing, it makes individuality more conspicuous, and should render it more intense. 2. *The responsibility of the private person.* (1) Subjects stand related to rulers. They have relative as well as personal duties. They have public as well as private interests and obligations. (2) They stand as subjects to rulers in relation to God. This is recognized in his laws. (See Exod. xxii. 28; the margin construes the term אלהים, rendered "gods," by "judges." Magistrates are here presented as representatives of the Elohim.) They are to respect and sustain authority in righteousness (1 Tim. vi. 1). To pray for those in authority (1 Tim. ii. 1, 2). (3) The individual is not sunk in the subject. None are too obscure to be noticed by God; too insignificant to escape his inquisition.

II. THAT SIN OFFERING IS PROVIDED FOR INDIVIDUALS. 1. *It is appointed for the ruler* (vers. 22—26). (1) He has to bring a "kid of the goats," not a bullock, which was required from the priest and from the congregation. The blood of the kid was to be sprinkled simply upon the horns of the altar of burnt offering, whereas the blood of the bullock was also sprinkled upon the altar of incense and the vail. A further difference was that whereas the bodies of the beasts offered for the priest and for the congregation were burnt without the camp, the kid of the ruler was treated as the peace offering. (2) These differences show that the sin of the ruler, though so heinous as not to be forgiven without sacrifice, was yet not so heinous as that of the priest. More is expected from men of religious profession. Nor was the sin of the ruler regarded as so heinous as that of the congregation. "It is bad when great men give ill examples, but worse when all men follow them" (Matthew Henry). 2. *It is appointed for the common person* (vers. 27—35). (1) Whereas the offering of the ruler is defined to be "a kid of the goats," that of the private individual may be either a kid or a lamb. As he has more liberty in his sacrifice, so has he in his conduct. Freedom is limited in the ratio of elevation. The humble should not be envious of the great. (2) The offering of the private person was to be a *female*, which was proper to one having no authority; whereas, and for the opposite reason, the ruler had to bring a *male*. (3) These differences go to show that the sin of a ruler is more serious than that of a common person. If his privileges are greater, so are his responsibilities. If his position is elevated, his influence, for good or evil, is proportionately great.

III. THAT SIN OFFERING IS DISCRIMINATIVE. 1. *As to the nature of the sin.* (1) It is for sin *against God.* It seems to have nothing to do immediately with sins against our fellows or against society. These, of course, may be constructively viewed as offences also against God. If this were more considered, men would be more respectful to their fellows, who are "made after the image of God" (see Jas. iii. 9). (2) It is for sin against his negative commandments. This is the teaching of vers. 2, 15, 22, 27. (3) It is for sin *ignorantly* committed against them (see John xvi. 2, 3; Acts iii. 17; 1 Cor. ii. 8). Ignorance is no plea for mercy without sacrifice. It *is* a plea for mercy *with* a sacrifice (see Luke xxiii. 34; 1 Tim. i. 13). 2. *As to the time of the offering.* (1) "And is guilty," viz. before the punishment of his sin has come upon him. If he discover his sin in time and bring his sin offering, it may avert that punishment. Men should never try to hide their sins from their own souls. On the contrary, they should diligently seek to discover them. We should plead the sin sacrifice for those we have not discovered (see Ps. xix. 12; cxxxix. 23, 24; 1 John i. 7). (2) "Or if his sin, wherein he hath sinned, come to his knowledge," viz. by the punishment of it overtaking him (see 2 Sam. xxxi. 1). When calamity comes we must not too readily relegate it to the category of mere physical sequence, but confess the hand of God. Timely sacrifice may stay a plague (see 2 Sam. xxiv. 25). 3. *For obstinate infidelity there is no mercy.* (1) This is what Paul, alluding to the sin offering, calls *wilful* sin (Heb. x. 26). His argument goes to show that the Great Sacrifice of Calvary is the anti-type of that offering. (2) The Law had no provision of mercy for presumptuous sins, whether the precept outraged were negative or positive (see Numb. xv. 27—31). An awful instance of the severity of the Law is described in Numb. xv. 32—36. This instance is referred to by Paul, who goes on to state that the gospel has its correspond-ing law of extremity, but with a " much sorer punishment " (Heb. x. 28, 29). If the extreme penalty of the Mosaic Law was the infliction of death upon the body, what punishment can be " much sorer " but the " destruction of both body and soul in hell " (Matt. x. 28)?—J. A. M.

Ver. 2.—*The mind of God respecting the sin of man.* "If a soul shall sin." This chapter which treats of this sin offering, and more especially these words of the second verse, may remind us—

I. THAT ALL MEN HAVE SINNED, AND ARE GUILTY BEFORE GOD. The stern facts of the case make the words, " If a soul shall sin," equivalent to " When a soul sins." The succeeding chapters provide for all possible cases, as if it were only too certain that men in every station and in every position would sin. So in John we have, " If any man sin," accompanied by the plain utterance, " If we say that we have no sin, we deceive ourselves," etc. (1 John i. 8; ii. 1). It is a significant fact that, in providing for the people of God, the Divine Legislator had to contemplate the moral certainty that all, even those standing in his immediate presence and engaged in his worship, would fall into sin and condemnation. This significant provision is only too well confirmed by : 1. The record of Hebrew history. 2. Other statements of Scripture (Ps. xiv. 2, 3; Rom. iii. 10, 23 ; Gal. iii. 22; 1 John i. 10). 3. Our observation and knowledge of man-kind. 4. Our own conscience : every soul does sin in thought, in word, in deed ; doing those " things which ought not to be done " (ver. 2), and leaving undone (not thought, not spoken, not fulfilled) those things God righteously requires. " The God in whose hand our breath is, and whose are all our ways, have *we* not glorified " (Dan. v. 23).

II. THAT SIN WAS (AND STILL MAY BE) DIVIDED INTO THE PARDONABLE AND UN-PARDONABLE. The words, " If a soul shall sin," are preparatory to the announcement of Divine provision for pardon. But there is a line drawn between sin and sin. Refer-ence is frequently made to sinning " through ignorance " (vers. 2, 13, 22, 27). This is distinguished from " presumptuous sin " (Numb. xv. 30, 31 ; Deut. xvii. 12). For the one there was pardon ; for the other, instant execution. The word " ignorance " was not confined to mere inadvertence ; it extended to sins of unpremeditated folly and passion ; probably to all sins but deliberate, high-handed rebellion against God and his Law (ch. xvi. 21 ; comp. Acts iii. 17 ; 1 Tim. i. 13). Pardon was provided, but there was a limit to the Divine mercy ; there *was* iniquity for which no sacrifice availed (1 Sam. iii. 14). Under the gospel there is one " unpardonable sin," the sin " against the Holy Ghost " (Matt. xii. 31, 32). In the time of our Lord, this sin took the special form of blasphemy against the Spirit of God. In our time it resolves itself into a persistent and obdurate resistance of his Divine influence. This necessarily ends in final impenitence and ultimate condemnation. This one sin excepted, the mercy of God in Christ Jesus extends (1) to the blackest crimes ; (2) to the longest career in wrong-doing ; (3) to the guiltiest disregard of privilege and opportunity.

III. THAT GOD HAS PROVIDED FOR THE PARDON OF SIN BY SACRIFICE. It is a striking fact that the same word in Hebrew which signifies sin is also used for " sin offering." So closely, so intimately in the will of God, and hence in the mind of man, were the two things connected—sin and sacrifice. All unpresumptuous sins might be forgiven, but not without shedding of blood. Sin, in God's thought, means death, and the sinner must be made to feel that, as such, he is worthy of death. Hence he must bring the animal from his herd or flock, and it must be slain, the guilt of the offerer having been solemnly confessed over, and (by imputation) formally conveyed to the victim's head. The life of the one for the life of the other. Doubtless it sufficed for the time and for the purpose, but it was not the redemption which a guilty race needed, and which a God of boundless peace was intending and was thus preparing to supply. The sin offering was prophetic, symbolical. The blood of bulls could not take away the sin of the world; only the slain Lamb of God would avail for that (Heb. x. 4; John i. 29). But "the blood of Jesus Christ his Son cleanseth us from *all* sin;" "If *any* man sin, . . . he is the propitiation for our sins . . . for the sins of the whole world" (1 John i. 7; ii. 1, 2). "He hath made him to be sin (a sin offering) for us, who knew no sin; that we might be made," etc. (2 Cor. v. 21). We learn from the foregoing: 1. The one great and deep want of the world. We *have* bodies that need to be clothed, fed, etc., but this is nothing to the fact that we *are* souls that have sinned, needing to be forgiven and accepted of God. 2. The inestimable advantages we now enjoy. If the Jew had great advantages over the Gentile, we are far more privileged than he. There has been offered for us "one sacrifice for sins for ever" (Heb. x. 12), available for all souls, under the heaviest condemnation, for all time. 3. Our proportionate guilt if we are negligent (Heb. x. 29).—C.

Vers. 3, 13, 22, 27.—*Gradations in guilt.* In Israel, as we have seen, sin was divided into the pardonable and the unpardonable—into "sins through ignorance" and sins of presumption. But this was not the only distinction. Of those which might be forgiven there were some more serious than others, demanding variety in expiation. Special regulations were given as to the sin of the "priest that is anointed" (ver. 3), the "whole congregation of Israel" (ver. 13), the ruler (ver. 22), etc. These distinctions teach us—

I. That special privilege carries with it peculiar responsibility. The high priest, if he sinned, was to bring a bullock without blemish (ver. 3), and every detail of the sin offering was to be carefully observed in his case (vers. 4, 5, etc.). His transgression was accounted one of greater guilt, needing a more considerable sacrifice. His nearer access to God, his larger share of sacred privilege, made his accountability and his guilt the greater. The children of privilege are the heirs of responsibility; the more we have from God, the closer we are admitted to his presence, the clearer vision we have of his truth and will,—the more he expects from us, and the more heinous will be our guilt in his sight if we depart from his ways.

II. That the profession of piety carries with it increase of obligation. The high priest's enlarged accountability was partly due to the fact that, as high priest, he professed to stand in very close relation to God; he was, in public estimation, the first minister of Jehovah; he was regarded as the holiest man in the whole congregation. Special obligation, therefore, rested on him, and any slight irregularity on his part was most serious. Profession of godliness is a good and desirable thing. 1. It is the *right* thing: it places us in the position in which we ought to stand; it is being true to ourselves. 2. It is the will of Christ as revealed in his Word (Matt. x. 32). 3. It adds to our influence on behalf of righteousness and wisdom. 4. It is an additional security against the power of temptation. But it enhances responsibility; it increases obligation. For if, professing to love and honour Christ, we do that which he has expressly forbidden, we bring his sacred cause into contempt, and "make the enemy to blaspheme." Rise to the full height of duty, influence, privilege, but remember that on that height are some special dangers, and that a fall therefrom is to be dreaded with holy fear, to be shunned with devoutest vigilance.

III. That influence confers added responsibility on those who wield it. Special provision is made for the sin of the ruler, "When a ruler hath sinned," etc. (vers. 22, 23, etc.). A ruler enjoys a position of prominence and power; his influence is felt afar. What he does will decide, to some considerable extent, what others will do. He has the peculiar joy of power; let him remember that power and responsibility are inseparably united. Let all those who hold positions of influence, all whose judgment and behaviour are importantly affecting the convictions and character of their fellows, realize that if they sin, and thus encourage others in error and transgression, they are specially guilty in the sight of God.

IV. That communities of men, as such, may fall into serious condemnation. "The whole congregation of Israel" might "sin through ignorance;" it might be led, unwittingly, into practices that were forbidden. In that case, though men have great confidence when they err in large companies, it would be guilty before God; and though it might be inadvertently betrayed into folly, it would be condemned of him, and must bring its oblation to his altar (see Homily on "Collective," etc., *infra*).

V. THAT NO MEASURE OF OBSCURITY WILL CLOAK SIN FROM THE SIGHT OF GOD. "If any one of the common people sin through ignorance," etc. (ver 27, etc.), he must bring his kid (ver. 28) or his lamb (ver. 32), and the atoning blood must be shed. We shall not escape in the throng. In the hundreds of millions of fellow-travellers along the path of life, God singles each of us out, and marks our course, and searches our soul. He esteems every human child, however disregarded of men, to be worthy of his watchful glance; is displeased with each sinful deed or word, but is ready to forgive when the penitent seeks mercy in the appointed way (vers. 31, 35).—C.

Vers. 13, 14.—*Collective guilt unconsciously incurred.* We learn from the special provision made for the "sin in ignorance" of "the whole congregation of Israel"—

I. THAT, THOUGH GOD DEALS PRIMARILY WITH INDIVIDUAL SOULS, HE HAS DIRECT RELATIONS WITH COMMUNITIES. Ordinarily, constantly, God comes to the individual soul, and says, "*Thou* shalt" or "Thou shalt not;" "My Son," do this and live, etc. But he has his Divine dealings with societies, with secular and sacred communities also; with (1) nations, (2) Churches, (3) families.

II. THAT COMMUNITIES, AS SUCH, MAY INCUR HIS CONDEMNATION. A "whole congregation," an entire people, may sin (ver. 13). 1. The nation: witness the Jewish people, again and again denounced and punished. 2. The Church: witness the Churches of Galatia (Epist. to Gal.), the Churches of Asia Minor (Rev. ii., iii.). 3. The family.

III. THAT THIS GUILT MAY BE CONTRACTED UNCONSCIOUSLY. "The thing be hid from the eyes of the assembly" (ver. 13). 1. *The Jewish nation,* "through ignorance, killed the Prince of Life" (Acts iii. 15, 17). Under some of the better and worthier emperors as well as under the viler, Rome martyred the Christians, thinking them injurious to that human race which they were regenerating. 2. *The Church of Christ* has unconsciously fallen, at different times and places into (1) error, (2) laxity of conduct, (3) unspirituality in worship and life, (4) inactivity. 3. *Families* fall into (1) undevoutness of habit; (2) unneighbourliness and inconsiderateness; (3) ungraciousness of tone, and unkindness of behaviour in the home circle.

IV. THAT RECOGNITION OF WRONG MUST BE IMMEDIATELY FOLLOWED BY PENITENCE AND FAITH. When "the sin was known," the congregation was to "offer a young bullock," etc. (ver. 14). Let every nation, Church, society, family: 1. Remember that it is fallible, and may fall unconsciously into sin. 2. Readily, and with open mind, receive expostulation and warning from others. 3. Upon conviction of wrong, resort in penitence and faith to the all-sufficient Sacrifice of which the sin offering was the type.—C.

Vers. 11, 12.—*Full acceptance with God.* The carrying away of all the offered animal (save that part which had been presented to God in sacrifice) and the burning of it in "a clean place" (ver. 12), was probably meant to represent the full and perfect acceptance of the offerer by the Holy One of Israel. When the victim had been slain and its blood outpoured on the altar and its richest part accepted in sacrifice, there might seem to have been sufficient indication of Divine mercy. But one sign more was added: the animal which represented the worshipper having shed its blood, and that shed blood having been received as an expiation, it became holy; when, therefore, its flesh was not eaten by the priest (ch. vi. 26) in token of its sanctity, every part of the animal was solemnly and reverently consumed, in "a clean place." Nothing pertaining to that which had become holy through the shed blood should be treated as an unholy thing. Looked at in this light, we gain the valuable thought that when sin has been forgiven through faith in the shed blood of the Redeemer, the sinner is regarded as holy in the sight of God. As everything was thus done by pictorial representation to express the thought of the fulness of Divine forgiveness, so everything was stated in explicit language through the psalmists and prophets to the same effect (Exod. xxxiv. 6, 7; Ps. lxxxvi. 5, 15; ciii. 8; cxlv. 8; Isa. i. 18; lv. 7). So, also, our Lord, in the "prince of parables," included everything that could be introduced—the robe, the ring, the shoes, the fatted calf—to present in the strongest colouring the precious truth that

God does not grudgingly or imperfectly forgive, but that he "*abundantly* pardons." The subject demands our consideration of two things—

I. THE FULNESS OF GOD'S ACCEPTANCE. God's mercy in Christ Jesus embraces: 1. The entire forgiveness of all past sins, so that all our numerous transgressions of his Law, both the more heinous and the less guilty, are "blotted out" of his "book of remembrance," and no more regarded by him; and so that all our more numerous shortcomings, our failure to be and to do that which the heavenly Father looked for from his children, are entirely forgiven. 2. The overlooking of our present unworthiness; so that the scantiness of our knowledge, the imperfection of our penitence, the feebleness of our faith, the poverty of our resolutions, and our general unworthiness do not stand in the way of his "benign regard." 3. The bestowment of his Divine complacency; so that he not only "receives us graciously," but "loves us freely" (Hos. xiv. 2, 4). He feels toward us the love and the delight which a father feels toward the children of his heart and his home. But to gain this inestimable blessing, let us be sure that we have fulfilled—

II. THE CONDITIONS ON WHICH IT IS BESTOWED. These are twofold. Paul has expressed them thus: (1) repentance toward God; and (2) faith toward our Lord Jesus Christ (Acts xx. 21). He who inspired Paul has taught us the same truth in his own words (Luke xxiv. 47; Acts xxvi. 18). There must be the turning of the heart, in shame and sorrow, from sin unto God, and the cordial acceptance of the Lord Jesus Christ as the Divine Teacher, the all-sufficient Saviour, the rightful Lord of heart and life, which he claims to be.—C.

Vers. 3, 13, 22, 27.—*Access for all: comparison and contrast.* In the statutes of the Law given in this chapter we are reminded, by comparison and by contrast, of two of the main features of the gospel of Christ. We are reminded by comparison of—

I. THE ACCESS THAT WAS PERMITTED TO EVERY ISRAELITE, AND IS NOW GRANTED TO US. No single individual in the whole congregation of Israel could feel that he was forbidden to go with his offering "before the Lord," to seek forgiveness of his sin. The priest could not think his office stood in his way (ver. 3); nor the ruler his function (ver. 22); nor could any humble son of Abraham suppose himself too obscure to find attention at the door of the tabernacle (ver. 27). Special and explicit legislation provided for each case, and there could not have been one Hebrew family which did not know that the tabernacle of the Lord was open to all, and that on the altar of sacrifice every offender might have his offering presented and come "down to his house justified." Thus broad, and indeed broader still, is the permission to approach which is granted in the gospel. For not only is the Christian sanctuary open to prince and people, to minister and member, to every class and rank, but in Christ Jesus there is neither circumcision nor uncircumcision, neither Greek nor Jew, neither male nor female; every distinction of every kind has disappeared, and is utterly unknown. We are reminded by contrast of—

II. THAT ACCESS WHICH WAS DENIED TO THEM, BUT WHICH IS OFFERED TO US. The ordinary Jew, one of the "common people," could go no further than the "door of the tabernacle:" there his entrance was barred. At that point he had to leave everything to the officiating priest; it was not permitted to him to enter the holy place, to sprinkle the blood upon the altar, to present any part of the victim in sacrifice;—another must do that in his stead. But in Christ Jesus we have: 1. Access to God our Father in every place (Eph. ii. 18; iii. 12; Heb. xiii. 15). 2. Right to plead, ourselves, the one Great Propitiation for sin. 3. Right to present ourselves and our gifts on his altar to God and his service (Rom. xii. 1; Heb. xiii. 16). 4. Access to the table of the Lord (1 Cor. xi. 28). Let us try to realize (1) the height of our Christian privilege, and (2) the corresponding weight of the responsibility we bear. From us to whom such full and close access is given will much fruit be required to the glory of his Name, in the growth of our own souls and the salvation of others.—C.

Vers. 1, 2.—*The sin offering.* The main points in this offering were these: I. The Law of God is made the standard of righteousness. II. Sin is offence against the Law. III. Offences of ignorance or error involve guilt; that is, require that the Law shall be honoured in view of them. IV. There is forgiveness with God for all sin. V. Those who are in the most responsible position are the most called to offer sacrifice for their sin. VI. The forgiveness of sin is only through expiation, in recognition of an atonement. These points embrace much of the teaching of the Mosaic economy. Consider—

I. THE LAW OF GOD THE STANDARD OF RIGHTEOUSNESS. The sin which has to be expiated is "*sin against any of the commandments of the Lord.*" While distinction was plainly made from the first between the fundamental moral law, as in the ten commandments, and the ceremonial law—still all that was "*commanded of the Lord*" was law to Israel—was to be strictly observed, involved the covenant relation between God and man, to violate which was to be estranged from the peace of God. The ceremonial law, taken in connection with the Decalogue and the whole of the Mosaic appointments, set forth this great truth, that the existence of man in all its extent was subject to the will of God, and that that will as declared was law, which must be obeyed at peril of Divine displeasure. So there is still the same subjection of man to *law*, which is: 1. The *law of the heart* or of the inward man. 2. The *law of ethics*, of man's relations to his fellow-man. 3. The law of *the religious life*, of man's worship of God. The *standard of righteousness* must be applied in each of these spheres of Law, which our Lord shows by his Sermon on the Mount, when he proclaims the will of God to be holiness in all these respects—*poverty and purity of heart, love to neighbours, sincerity and devotion in the worship of God*. Against the Law any offence is sin. Therefore, as the gospel was a new proclamation of the Law, so was it a new revelation of sin; for Christ, by the Spirit, came to "convince the world of sin," by revealing the law of righteousness.

II. SIN IS OFFENCE AGAINST THE LAW. The fundamental conception of the Mosaic economy was the fellowship of God and man—the true blessedness of human existence. The Law was a setting out of the boundaries of that ground of fellowship where alone God and man could meet together. Whether it was civil law, or moral law, or ceremonial law, the same twofold reference was in each to the will of God as Creator, King, Redeemer, to the trustful subjection of man to Divine authority. An offence against Law in this wide sense of the word must include not only a deliberate setting up of the will of the creature against the Creator as in immorality or intentional disobedience of any kind, but anything in the conduct which hinders the fulfilment of the Divine purposes, anything which opposes the Law as an active principle. We recognize the same universality of sanction to law in that inevitableness which we attach to the laws of nature, whether physical or social. They work out their results both in the individual and in society, apart from all respect of persons. The good man violating a law of nature must suffer the consequences. Not because he is punished by the God of providence, but because he has put himself in the way of the great chariot of the world's onward progress, and has become so far an offence and a stumbling-block, which must be treated as such. It was a grand advance in revelation that all human life was regarded as based upon law, and all law was declared to be God's Law. Therefore, all rightness, all happiness, both positive and negative, must be from God, the fruit of a living fellowship between the creature and the Creator.

III. EXTENSION OF GUILT TO OFFENCES OF IGNORANCE AND ERROR. The word rendered *ignorance* signifies wandering from the way. Therefore the idea of the offence is not that of absolute ignorance of the Law itself, which would exclude the idea of guilt altogether, but rather that of inadvertence, through carelessness, through human infirmity of any kind, or through the connection of our own life with the life of others. "There are many things which man's conscience would pass over, many things which might escape man's cognizance, many things which his heart might deem all right, which God could not tolerate; and which, as a consequence, would interfere with man's approach to, his worship of, and his relationship with God" (Macintosh). Hence the need of a Divine atonement—for as David prays we must all pray, "Cleanse *thou* me from secret faults" (Ps. xix. 12). Now, the sin offering pointed to the fact that such secret faults, unintentional violations of the Law, involved guilt, inasmuch as they were occasions demanding that the Law should be vindicated and honoured as truly as the greatest offences. This has been universally recognized in the law of nations as a natural principle of justice. The overt act is alone before the eye of the law, not the secret intention except as it changes the character of the overt act. The offence of man-slaughter embraces a large number of cases where ignorance and error might be pleaded, but are not sufficient to remove the liability of the offender. Guilt is not merely conscious or subjective liability to punishment, but objective liability as well. Thus is the conscience of man enlightened and its power enlarged by the revelation of God. As Adam knew his sin much more clearly when God had called him into colloquy, so the Law of Moses was an appeal to the conscience, a quickening of it, a setting up of the Divine mirror before man, that he might know himself. See this whole doctrine of guilt treated by St. Paul in Rom. vii., "Sin by the commandment became exceeding sinful." "I was alive without the Law once, but when the commandment came, sin revived, and I died."

IV. The offering for sin is the pledge of Divine forgiveness. The sin of ignorance represented God's view of sin as contrasted with man's view. Therefore, as it was an atoning offering, it proclaimed both the righteousness of God as condemning *all* sin, and the covenant mercy of God as forgiving *all* sin. Man would naturally take account only of known sins, but the true peace is that which proceeds from the assurance of entire and infinite atonement. How different is such a revelation of mercy from any of the heathen satisfactions which were mere attempts to appease the Divine wrath as a recognized danger! But dangers are not only seen, but unseen. In the case of natural laws, how often we find that we have broken them when we knew not! The true safety is that which we know is not only partial and probable, but absolutely secured against all possible contingencies. God's thoughts are not as our thoughts. He invites us to hide under the shadow of his wings.

V. Responsibility in proportion to privilege. The priest represented the people. The congregation was the nation in its collective capacity, therefore it represented not only the individuals as sinners, but the special relation of the community to Jehovah as the body to the head. The official position of the high priest was one of peculiar dignity and solemnity, therefore the sin of the individual in his case was more than his own sin—it was the violation of that larger relation in which the people as a whole stood to their God. All superior knowledge, all elevation of office and vocation, all representation, carries with it special responsibility. Those who are ministers of God must feel their sins as heavier burdens, requiring to be put away by special acknowledgment, by extraordinary effort. There are sins which none but the high priest and the congregation could commit. So there are sins of official life and sins of Church life, which we are apt to overlook because they are less upon the individual conscience than our own personal sins; but God shows us by the regulations of his Law, that we must hate them and avoid them and seek their forgiveness, even as though they were deliberate and individual offences. How often men have done, in the name of their religious system or in their official capacity, what, if it had been ascribed to themselves in their private life, they would have immediately condemned! The purity of Church officers and of Church life in general has much to do with the growth of Christianity. The history of ecclesiastical errors is a very sad one. It was the absolute purity of Christ which so severely condemned the religious leaders of his time. They suffered their consciences to be blinded by the corruption of the system under which they lived. They did evil, thinking often that they did God service. Yet the Church and its rulers will be judged, not by the standard of its own degeneracy, but by the Law of God. Judgment begins at the house of God. *There* are the most responsible men, *there* are the greatest offences, and *there* must be the most exemplary manifestation of Divine righteousness. The clearing away of sin from the Church is the preparation for the pure worship of God, for the re-established relation between the covenant king and his people, for the outpoured blessings of the throne of grace.

VI. The forgiveness of sin, only by expiation, through atonement. This is especially set forth by the sin offering, for it represented the Divine demand of expiation in cases where human ignorance or error might be pleaded in excuse on man's side. What we require is not mere proclamation of pardon, but a peace which is settled on eternal foundations. So long as there remains in the mind of the sinner the thought that God is not satisfied, there must be a barrier to fellowship. The setting forth of the sin offering was a provision of Divine righteousness as the condition of peace. God does not overlook sin as that which has excuse made for it; he puts it away as that which is atoned for.   All the details of the ceremony, especially the connection of the blood of the sin offering with the two altars—that of incense and that of burnt offering— pointed to the completeness of the atonement which God provided.   In the antitype, the great sacrifice offered by our Lord Jesus Christ, whose soul was made an offering for sin, we must lay great stress on the Divine perfection of the Victim offered, his coming forth from God, his representation in himself of Divine righteousness; for Christ is not a Saviour merely from individual transgressions, but from sin itself as an evil principle at work in the nature of man.   Unless we hold firmly to this atoning per- fection of Christ, we cannot proclaim the regenerating gift of the Holy Spirit, for the new life must be founded in a perfect justification; the same faith which admits us into the forgiveness of sins through the blood of Christ, also admits us into that fellowship and vital union with the living Redeemer, which is the commencement of a new life in the Spirit.   The Apostle Peter (1 Pet. i. 2) puts the sanctification of the Spirit and the sprinkling of the blood of Jesus Christ in juxtaposition.   They are included in the one Sacrifice of Calvary, whereby atonement is made, and the power of an endless life is revealed in him who, having offered himself through the Spirit without spot, rose again from the dead to become the Captain of salvation, the Firstborn among many brethren, the second Adam, the man who is made, by his Divine work, a quickening spirit. " Christ is God's," and " ye are Christ's."—R.

Vers. 3—12.—*The high priest's burnt offering.*   The difference between the high priest's offering and that for the whole congregation on the one hand, and the offering for an offending ruler or any of the common people on the other, lay in the sprinkling of the blood of the victim seven times before the Lord, before the vail of the sanctuary. This betokened the purifying by this sacrifice of the public worship of the people as distinguished from their private and individual life.   The different modes of sprinkling the blood marked successive degrees of consecration, from the altar of burnt offering without to the vail in the sanctuary, which especially represented Jehovah's presence. The high priest was an embodiment of the people's sanctity as a worshipping people. The great truth taught is the necessity of connecting together worship with the revela- tion of Divine righteousness and grace.   The only true religion is that which rests on the twofold basis—God's provided atonement for sin; man's faith and obedience towards God.

SHOW THAT THERE IS "INIQUITY IN OUR HOLY THINGS."   This was recognized by the Apostle Paul at Athens.   " Whom therefore ye ignorantly worship, him declare I unto you."   The want of true knowledge renders the worship unacceptable.   But not ignorance only; indifference, heedlessness, the superstition which proceeds from a corrupt heart, the falsehood which has grown up from the root of sin in human nature and which the individual man may adopt from tradition without perceiving its falsity.   The religious leaders of a people may be especially guilty of defiling the popular worship. The priest, by his false theology, or his corrupt ritual, or his lack of spirituality, may involve the congregation in sin.   In the house of God itself there may be sinful defect of reverence, sinful disorder, sinful coldness and dulness, sinful pride and worldliness, sinful wanderings of thought and self-assertion.   Our worship needs to be sprinkled with the blood of our Great Sacrifice before it can be accepted.   It is especially incumbent on the religious teachers and ministers of the sanctuary that they be prominent in confessing sin, in urging the necessity of more sanctification, in exalting the merit of Christ that worship be presented through him.—R.

Vers. 13—21.—*The whole congregation sinners through ignorance.*   The sacrifice is very similar to the high priest's.   The ruling thought in both cases is that of sin attaching to those who represent the covenant of God.   The people, whether as a nation or assembly, or as a house of God, a worshipping congregation, whether in its elders or rulers, or in its high priest, were in a covenant relation to Jehovah; therefore might offend against that relation, and required atonement to be made.   Take up the subject of *national sins.*

I. A NATION MAY BE GUILTY.   1. *Negatively*, violating the commandments of God. Political unwisdom, producing national disorder, ignorance, division of classes from one another, decay of commerce, and distress.   International confusion and war.   2.

Positively irreligious. Growth of vices till they become national. Combinations of great masses of people to uphold wrong and protect interests which impede the advance of morality. Sins of rulers in dishonest legislation. State interference with religious liberty. Spread of superstition, for which the nation as a whole is accountable. Indifference of the more privileged classes to the moral and religious condition of the multitudes. Guilty leaders followed.

II. NATIONAL SINS SHOULD BE NATIONALLY CONFESSED AND PUT AWAY. While there are prominent members of the nation who should set an example of penitence and sacrifice, the whole people should be summoned to a united acknowledgment of their position before God. The national fast, if rightly conducted, and emanating from a widespread sense of sin, and not from a mere royal command, must be pleasing to God. At such times the chief stress should be laid not upon the performance of external rites, but upon the facts of the moral state of the people and the gospel call to repentance and faith.

III. THERE IS A FORGIVENESS OF NATIONS AS WELL AS OF INDIVIDUALS. "And the priest shall make an atonement for them, and it shall be forgiven them." We cannot doubt that God, as a Moral Governor, punishes nations. History proves that there is not a mere natural rise and fall of great powers by the working of ordinary physical, social, and economical laws; but there is an ordering of events, so as to visit national sins upon nations. Great illustrations : in France ; in United States for slavery ; in our own history, Spanish Armada—" Afflavit Deus, et dissipantur." Many instances of change for the better in affairs of nations: France, Italy, America, England at the Commonwealth. Preservation from impending evils. Special help in internal troubles and international relations. We must watch the will of Providence over long periods, and adapt facts and principles to one another. Testimony in the Old Testament, and especially in the Psalms, to the government of God in nations.—R.

Vers. 22 — 26. — *A ruler can sin through ignorance, and requires atonement.*
I. OFFICIAL POSITION IS MORAL RESPONSIBILITY. Whether the office be inherited or appointed, the ruler is in a special relation to God and to the people. He must jealously guard his office, and the more exalted he is, the more he should preserve a conscience void of offence towards God and towards man.

II. THE RULER SHOULD SET THE EXAMPLE of respecting the requirements of God's Law. If the people see their natural leaders and official superiors confessing sin and seeking atonement, religious reverence and obedience will spread through all classes. Fearful curse of wicked rulers. Those in high positions should search their lives and hearts, lest, by their neglect, or ignorance, or sin of any kind, they bring Divine displeasure on the people.

III. The sacrifice is not the same for the ruler as for the man. An OFFICIAL POSITION IS NOT TO HIDE AN INDIVIDUAL AND PERSONAL ACCOUNTABILITY. Too often sins are committed in office, of which men would be ashamed if their own names were connected with them. We may distinguish the official from the personal, but we must remember that God requires both to be pure and holy.—R.

Vers. 27—35.—*The sins of the common people.* The idea of the distinction is that those who, by their distance from the sanctuary and their lack of education, are more exposed to the possibility of offence, are less guilty, and therefore require a somewhat lower sacrifice. A female kid or a lamb would suffice ; but the same ceremonies were indispensable—the laying on of hands, the touching of the horns of the altar of burnt offering with blood, the pouring out of the blood at the bottom of the altar, the fire offering of sweet savour to the Lord. Thus the least sins, the sins of the least responsible people, the sins of ignorance and mere ceremonial uncleanness, were connected with the greatest, and the people were reminded that all sin, as transgression of the Law, must be atoned for, and without atonement there is no forgiveness. Subject—*Sins of the common people.*

I. We are taught to DEAL WITH THEM PITIFULLY, with consideration of circumstances, with remembrance of their comparative lesser guilt. Mere denunciations, unqualified condemnation, injurious. We should teach people the Law that they may see the sinfulness of sin, but in the spirit of love, lest they be blinded and hardened by a bewildering confusion of conscience and despondency. The traditional condemnation attached to those sins to which the masses are especially tempted might mislead, if not modified by the respect to antecedents.

II. We must hold fast to the Scripture representation—ALL SIN IS GUILT. The attempt to uplift the lower classes, without the power of atonement, by means of mere moral or intellectual appliances or social influences, must be a failure in the long run. Those who make it injure themselves. Nothing delivers them from sin but the power of Christ. Nor will it avail to imitate the folly which "*makes light of sin.*" Cf. the Saviour's instructions in Sermon on the Mount (Matt. vii.). While we avoid censoriousness and uncharitable judgment, we must cultivate a wise caution, lest we cast our pearls before swine. The Spirit of Christ is our only guide and strength.

III. The prescriptions of the Law varied according to the opportunity of the offender. We must SMOOTH THE WAY FOR RETURN TO GOD. By adapting the commandments to the capacity and opportunity of men. By teaching them the spirituality of the gospel method, which lays the chief stress on motive and affection, not on mere external value in the gift. By sympathy and co-operation helping them to find the way, holding them up in it for a time, surrounding them with cheerful companionship and encouraging words.

IV. The common people being thus marked out, reminds us that there is a special urgency upon the Christian Church in THE MISSION OF THE GOSPEL TO THOSE THAT ARE AFAR OFF. We are apt to think it enough to care for those in and about the temple. The common people heard Jesus gladly. To the poor his gospel is especially preached. If all the sacrifices typify the Great Sacrifice of Calvary, and the sin offering more particularly, the adaptation of the doctrine of Christ to the masses is thus set forth ; we must present the sin offering, if we would redeem society from its teeming miseries.

EXPOSITION.

CHAPTER V.

THE SIN OFFERING—*continued* (vers. 1—13). The subject of the next thirteen verses is still the sin offering, not the trespass offering, as has been supposed by some. The first six verses state three specific cases for which sin offerings are required, and the remaining seven verses detail the concessions made to poverty in respect to the offerings required. The cases are those of a witness, of one ceremonially defiled, and of one who had sworn thoughtlessly. The concessions granted are two: two turtle-doves or young pigeons are allowed instead of a lamb, and the tenth part of an ephah of fine flour, without oil or frankincense, is allowed instead of the two turtle-doves or young pigeons. The latter concession is the more remarkable as the sacrifice by its means changes its character from a bloody to an unbloody offering.

Ver. 1.—The case of a witness on oath. If a man hear the voice of swearing, that is, if he was one of a number of persons adjured to speak according to the manner in which oaths were administered in Jewish courts of justice (see Matt. xxvi. 63; 2 Chron. xviii. 15),

and he did not give evidence of what he had seen or heard, he had to bear his iniquity, that is, he was regarded as guilty; and as this was an offence which could be atoned for by a sacrifice, he was to offer as a sin offering a ewe lamb, or a female kid, or two turtle-doves, or two pigeons, or the tenth part of an ephah of flour. This injunction is a direct condemnation of the approved teaching of Italian moral theologians of paramount authority throughout the Roman Church, who maintain that, in case a crime is not known to others, a witness in a court of justice "may, nay, he is bound to, say that the accused has not committed it" (St. Alfonso de' Liguori, 'Theol. Mor.,' iv. 154).

Vers. 2, 3.—Two cases of a man ceremonially defiled. If he had touched a dead body or any other substance conveying uncleanness, and it were hidden from him, that is, if he had done it unwittingly, or from forgetfulness or neglect, had failed to purify himself immediately, he must offer his sin offering, as above.

Ver. 4.—The case of a man who had neglected to fulfil a thoughtless oath. If he sware to do evil, or to do good, that is, to do anything whatever, good or bad (see Numb. xxiv. 13), and failed to fulfil his oath from carelessness or negligence, he too must bring his offering, as above.

Vers. 5, 6.—In the four cases last mentioned there is first to be an acknowledgment of guilt, **he shall confess that he hath sinned in that thing**, and then the sin offering is to be made. Confession of sin probably preceded or accompanied all sin offerings. The use of the word *asham*, translated **trespass offering** in ver. 6, and the character of the four cases have led many commentators to regard vers. 1—13 as dealing with the trespass offering rather than the sin offering. But if this were so, the words *trespass offering* and *sin offering* would be used synonymously in this verse, which is very unlikely, when they are immediately afterwards carefully distinguished. It is best to render *asham* "for his trespass," that is, in expiation of his guilt, as in the next verse, in place of a *trespass offering*.

Vers. 7—13.—**If he be not able to bring a lamb.** Sin offerings being not voluntary sacrifices but required of all that were guilty, and the four last-named cases being of common occurrence amongst the poor and ignorant, two concessions are made to poverty: two birds (one to be offered with the ritual of the sin offering, the other with that of the burnt offering), or even some flour (either three pints and a half or three quarts and a half, according as we adopt the larger or smaller estimate of the amount of the ephah), are allowed when the offerer cannot provide a lamb or a kid. There is thus typically set forth the freedom with which acceptance through the great propitiation is offered to all without respect of persons. The non-bloody substitute, being permitted only as an exception for the benefit of the very poor and only in the four cases above specified, does not invalidate the general rule that without the shedding of blood there is no remission of sin.

HOMILETICS.

Ver. 5.—*Confession of the sin committed* is required of the man who is allowed to offer a sin offering. It is likewise required before a trespass offering is accepted, as appears from Numb. v. 6, 7. "When a man or woman shall commit any sin that men commit, to do a trespass against the Lord, and that person be guilty, then they shall confess their sin that they have done."

I. TRADITIONAL FORM OF CONFESSION. "The sacrifice was so set, as that the offerer, standing with his face towards the west, laid his two hands between his horns and confessed his sin over a sin offering and his trespass over a trespass offering; and his confession was on this wise: 'I have sinned, I have done grievously, I have rebelled and done thus and thus; but I return by repentance before thee, and let this be my expiation'" (Lightfoot, 'Temple Service,' ch. viii.). "I beseech thee, O Lord; I have sinned, I have transgressed, I have rebelled, I have (here the person specified the particular sin which he had committed, and for which he wanted expiation); but now I repent, and let this be my expiation" (Outram, 'De Sacrificiis,' I. xv. 9). That some such form as this was used, according to the universal tradition of the Jews, we may conclude with tolerable certainty from the present passage in Leviticus and that in Numb. v. 6, 7.

II. THIS CONFESSION WAS INTENDED TO SPRING FROM FEELINGS OF REPENTANCE. All that could be enforced as a common and public discipline was the open confession of the sin. But no Israelite could have believed that the confession would be acceptable unless it proceeded from a penitent heart. This was left, as it must be left, to the individual conscience, but it was suggested and morally demanded by the injunction to confess.

III. THE OFFERING OF THE SIN OFFERING AND TRESPASS OFFERING WAS NOT THEREFORE AN EXTERNAL CEREMONY ONLY, BUT A SPIRITUAL PENITENTIAL ACT. As the offering of the burnt offering implied the spiritual act of self-surrender, and of the meat offering the spiritual act of submission, and of the peace offering the spiritual act of holy joy, so the offering of the sin and trespass offering implies the spiritual act of repentance. None of these sacrifices perform their work as *opera operata*, without reference to the religious state of the offerer's mind and soul.

Vers. 7—13.—The sacrifices to be offered as sin offerings are specified, nor may they be multiplied. They do not differ according to the heinousness of the offence which they are to atone for, but according to the means of the offerer. The moral reason of this was probably to prevent the idea arising that the costliness of the sacrifice might compensate for the greater sin, and that men might sin the more if they were willing to pay for it by more sacrifices. The difference in the sacrifice appointed for each class might serve to point out that a sin is greater in a man of prominent position than in a man of less influence, owing to its effects upon a larger circle. The concession made to the poor shows that none are to be shut out from communion with God for their want of worldly means. The expiation must be made, that the sinner may recover his covenant relations with God; but it shall be of such a nature that none shall be prevented from making it by their poverty. Here then is a foreshadowing of the free grace of God in the gospel dispensation. "Ho, every one that thirsteth, come ye to the waters, and he that hath no money; come ye, buy and eat; yea, come, buy wine and milk without money and without price" (Isa. lv. i.). "Let him that is athirst come. And whosoever will, let him take the water of life freely" (Rev. xxii. 17).

HOMILIES BY VARIOUS AUTHORS.

Vers. 1—13.—*Guilt removed.* The Psalmist cried out, "Who can understand his errors? cleanse thou me from secret faults." To dwell upon the manner in which sin may be committed, and to try to deepen our sense of its flagrancy, is not a pleasant employment, but it is highly necessary. And, blessed be God! a rainbow of cheerful hope spans the dark cloud of transgression; the same page that speaks of sin tells also of forgiveness.

I. This chapter reminds the Israelites of several ways in which, without having been resolutely determined upon, sin might result. Through silence and concealment of knowledge (ver. 1), through defilement by contact with uncleanness of man or beast (ver. 2), or through rash declarations (ver. 4), it was possible inadvertently to transgress the laws of God. SIN ASSUMES MANY FORMS. It may be of the voice or the finger, by word or deed. It may be by forcible repression of the truth or by careless voluble utterance. It may be incurred in connection with the noblest or the lowest parts of God's creation. *This thought should beget constant watchfulness* in speaking and acting. We can never be sure of preserving ourselves from contamination with evil. "Let him that thinketh he standeth take heed lest he fall." The abolition by the gospel of ceremonial restrictions has rather increased than diminished the strictness of the universally obligatory precepts, making them more searching in character. Our Lord taught that there may be adultery in a look, murder in a thought.

II. We find one law applicable to these different cases, one sentence pronounced, one ordinance appointed. THE IMPORTANT FACT COMMON TO ALL FORMS OF SIN IS THAT THEY INVOLVE THE OFFENDER IN GUILT. About the particular sin we need not trouble so much as about the fact of transgression and consequent demerit. "He shall bear his iniquity" (ver. 1). "He shall be unclean and guilty" (ver. 2). Jehovah can no longer look upon his subject with favour; sin places him under a cloud, mars him in the sight of God. *Only ignorance can keep a man at ease* under such circumstances. The awakened soul exclaims, "I have sinned: for I have transgressed the commandment of the Lord." The peace of the wicked is like the calm that often precedes the tempest. It is the office of the Word of God to convince the ungodly of their hard speeches and ungodly deeds, and the question the preacher loves to hear is that which shows that the arrow has reached its mark, when the agonized sinner inquires, "What must I do to be saved?"

III. "By the Law is the knowledge of sin," but to leave the matter here would be to subject the transgressor to intolerable anguish. THERE IS A TWOFOLD METHOD OF EXPIATION, to restore communion with God. There must be *confession of blameworthiness.* "I have sinned against heaven and before thee." "He shall confess that he hath sinned in that thing" (ver. 5). This acknowledgment by the individual is due to the majesty of God, and is the first step towards obliterating the injury caused by sin. The forces of government have not henceforth to fear assault by the criminal; once arrayed against him in hostile phalanx, they now wear a milder look. The rebel has voluntarily put the yoke of submission upon his neck, and this public token goes far to countervail the damage suffered by the king's honour. And, secondly, there must be *the presentation of an atonement* by the priest. The transgressor is not holy enough to appease offended Deity himself; an unblemished offering is demanded, which must be slaughtered by God's servant and its blood sprinkled upon the altar, and the other rites of a sin offering duly performed. It is not sufficient to acknowledge and repent of our misdeeds; we want a sin offering, the Lamb of God, so that we can make mention of his righteousness and enjoy the atoning virtue of his precious blood. It is not the offender but the priest who makes atonement (ver. 6). Apart from our great High Priest, our prayers, confessions, vows, and gifts are of no avail. "No man cometh unto the Father but by me."

IV. Either a lamb or a kid, two turtle-doves or pigeons, or a homer of fine flour would be accepted as a 'propitiatory offering. NO CLASS OF THE COMMUNITY IS DE-BARRED FROM AN ATONEMENT BY LACK OF MEANS. Regard is here paid to the resources of the humblest ranks. The same end is attained under the gospel by providing a way of salvation accessible to all, suited to the illiterate and the learned, the men of substance and the poor. And *in each case the forgiveness is complete.* "It shall be forgiven him." The deed done cannot be undone, but its consequences may be averted. God treats the believer as if he had never sinned; his iniquities are cast behind the back of Deity and remembered no more. Fears are banished, fellowship is resumed. With every subsequent transgression the same course must be adopted. Whilst in the world stains are frequent, and frequent must be our resort to the crimson tide that flows from the cross of Christ. What unity of plan and procedure is visible in the Law and the gospel!—S. R. A.

Vers. 1—13.—*The trespass offering.* This was very much of the nature of the sin offering. Julius Bate translates the word (אשם, *asham*) "guilt offering."* Possibly the "sin offering" and the "burnt offering" may be here comprehended under the general expression, "trespass offering" (see ver. 7). We have here brought under our notice—

I. EXAMPLES OF THE TRESPASS. Vers. 1—4. Taken in order these are: 1. *Conceal-ing the truth when adjured.* (1) The Hebrew law recognized a power of adjuration. This is assumed in the words "And if a soul sin," etc. (ver. 1). The adjuration in such a case is called the "oath of the Lord" (see Exod. xxii. 11). Paul refers to this law when he says, "An oath for confirmation is the end of all strife" (Heb. vi. 16). (2) The Hebrew history furnishes notable examples of adjuration. Saul, pursuing the Philistines, "adjured the people, saying, Cursed be the man that eateth food until the evening, that I may be avenged on mine enemies" (1 Sam. xiv. 24). Caiaphas said to Jesus, "I adjure thee by the living God, that thou tell me whether thou be the Christ, the Son of God" (Matt. xxvi. 63). (3) To conceal the truth when adjured was a crime meriting death. Achan and his family perished in the valley of Achor for his crime in concealing the "accursed thing" (see Josh. vi. 17—19; vii. 11, 23—26). Jonathan, in unwittingly trespassing in the adjuration of Saul, was in danger of losing his life (1 Sam. xiv. 43). 2. *Touching an unclean thing.* (1) The law of the case was that whoever touched any unclean thing, the carcase of an unclean animal, a living person who was leprous or otherwise unclean, or the corpse of a man, became unclean. The purpose was to show how scrupulously we should avoid social contact with those whose influence would be demoralizing (see Jas. iv. 4). (2) Being thus unclean, before he can appear in the sanctuary, he must "wash his clothes, and be unclean until the even," viz. when the daily sacrifice was offered. This shows how we must be purified by the washing of regeneration before we can mingle in the congregation of the heavenly temple. (3) But if a person had inconsiderately entered the sanctuary unclean, not knowing that he was polluted, he has trespassed against the Law, and is guilty. As soon as he becomes aware of his guilt he must bring a trespass offering or bear his sin. 3. *Swearing rashly.* (1) Ver. 4 is somewhat obscure, but this appears to be the mean-ing: If a man swear to do something without knowing whether it be good or evil, but afterwards it becomes evident that to carry out his oath would be evil; now he is in a dilemma: If he perform his oath he is guilty of doing evil; if he refrain he is guilty of violating his oath. (2) In either case, then, he has to bring a trespass offering with an humble confession of his sin. If he fail in this then his guilt is upon him. The lesson is that we should be slow to swear, lest our oaths should prove rash and involve us in humiliation or ruin.

II. PROVISIONS OF MERCY. 1. *Confession must be made.* (1) Not of sin in general. There is comparatively little humiliation in general confession. Individuality loses itself in the multitude. (2) But in particular, "that he hath sinned *in this thing.*" Sin thus carried home humbles us into the dust. Such was the confession of Achan (Josh. vii. 20), who, though his sin was "unto death," may yet have found the mercy of God to his soul. Such was the confession of David (Ps. li. 4). 2. *It must be accompanied with sacrifice.* (1) "And he shall bring," etc. (ver. 6). Here the "trespass offering" is also called a "sin offering." It is in this case specified to be "a *female* from the flock, a *lamb* or *kid* of the goats." This was the sin offering for any of the common people. The presumption therefore is that for a ruler a *male* kid should be brought for a trespass as for a sin offering; and for a priest, a *bullock* (comp. iv. 4, 23, 28). (2) Confession without atonement will not be accepted. If Achan found acceptance with God in the spirit it must have been immediately through the atonement of Calvary. Atonement without confession will not avail. We have to "work out our own salvation;" meanwhile "God worketh in us both to will and to do." 3. *The poor have special consideration.* (1) Those who may not be able to furnish a lamb may bring either a pair of turtle-doves or a brace of young pigeons. The alternative here appears to be because in certain seasons pigeons in the East are hard and unfit for eating. Turtle-doves are then very good. That must not be given to God which would not be acceptable to man. (2) Two are specified, which are to be thus disposed of: one is offered for a sin offering, the other for a burnt offering; and they are offered in this order. The sin offering goes first to make an atonement; then follows the burnt offering, which is a sacrifice of adoration. Before we can properly praise God we must be at peace with him. (3) Those so very poor as not to be able to bring a brace of pigeons may bring a tenth part of an ephah (about three quarts) of flour. A memorial of this is burnt upon the altar. There must be no oil in the flour to render it tasteful; no frankincense with it to give it fragrance: "it is a sin offering," and sin is distasteful and odious. The remnant is the priest's as a "meat offering."

The interchanging of these offerings, sin and trespass, sin and burnt, sin and meat, shows how they are intended to represent the same great subject under its various aspects. No one typical sacrifice could sufficiently body forth all the merits of that blessed Person who "made his soul a (אשם, *asham*) *trespass offering*" (Isa. liii. 10).— J. A. M.

Ver. 1.—*Fidelity in bearing witness.* The sinfulness of withholding evidence in a court of law is here formally and solemnly incorporated in the divine statutes. We may remind ourselves—

I. THAT WE SPEND OUR LIFE IN THE SIGHT OF MAN AS WELL AS UNDER THE EYE OF GOD. That we do everything in God's view is a truth the fulness and the greatness of which we cannot exaggerate. "Thou God seest me" should be as a frontlet for every man to wear between the eyes of his soul. But not unimportant is the truth that we act daily and hourly in the sight of man. 1. A very large proportion of our deeds is done obviously and consciously before man. 2. Many that we think are wrought in secret are seen by some unknown witness. 3. Many leave traces which point unmistakably to our agency. "Be sure your sin will find you out." Sooner or later, in unsuspected ways, our evil doings come under the eye of human observation, and under the ban of human condemnation.

II. THAT IT IS OFTEN OUR DUTY TO SCREEN AN OFFENDER FROM PUBLIC NOTICE. This is not in the text, but it belongs to the subject. He who would "do what wrong and sorrow claim" must sometimes "conquer sin and *cover shame*." There are many cases in which public justice does not demand inquiry and reprobation, but private consideration does call for tenderness and mercy (John viii. 7). "Of some have compassion, making a difference" (Jude 22).

III. THAT IT IS OFTEN OUR DUTY TO BEAR WITNESS AGAINST A WRONG-DOER. 1. It is our duty to God, for he has ordained human justice. "The powers that be are ordained of God" (Rom. xiii. 1—4). The Jewish judges had the right to adjure a witness to speak the truth in the name of the Supreme Judge ("hear the voice of swearing:" see 1 Kings viii. 31; Matt. xxvi. 63, 64). If, therefore, under an oath we withhold what we know, we are disregarding a demand that comes indirectly and ultimately from God himself. 2. It is also our duty to society. The commonwealth of which we are members has a right to expect that we shall take our share in the necessary conviction and punishment of crime. When solemnly summoned to state what we know, and especially when an oath of the Lord is upon us, we are not free to keep back evidence, but are bound to disclose it. 3. It may be our duty to the offender himself. For it is better for him that he should bear the penalty due to his crime than that he should elude justice and be encouraged in transgression. 4. It is further our duty to ourselves, for if we are called on to bear witness, and if we undertake, or are even supposed to undertake, to speak all we know, and if then we suppress important testimony, we are consciously misleading those who hear; we are not "doing the truth," but are acting falsely, and are injuring our own soul thereby.

IV. That negligence in such social obligations is a serious offence in the sight of God. *It is sin.* It is a thing to be repented of and to be forgiven.—C.

Vers. 2, 3.—*Shunning the impure.* We naturally ask, Why such stringent regulations as to everything of man or beast that was "unclean"? We may understand—
I. The explanation (the ʿrationale) of these requirements. 1. The two main truths God was teaching his people were the divine unity, and purity of heart and life. The state of surrounding heathendom made these two lessons emphatically and particularly necessary. 2. God's method of teaching was pictorial: it was by rite, symbol, illustration. The world was in its religious childhood. 3. Under this method bodily ills naturally stood for spiritual evils; as wholeness of the body stood for health of the soul, so the sickness of the body answered to the malady of the soul, and the uncleanness of the one to the impurity of the other. 4. Hence would result the fact that the careful avoidance of the one would be an instructive lesson in the shunning of the other. Associating the two things so closely in their minds, commanded to shun most scrupulously all bodily uncleanness, taught to look at the least defilement as a transgression of the law, they would necessarily feel, with all desirable intensity, that every moral and spiritual impurity must be most sensitively avoided. Therefore such enactments as those of the text.
II. Their moral significance. They say to us: 1. That we should avoid all that is *suggestive* of impurity. 2. That we should shun everything which can, in any way or in the least degree, be communicative of spiritual evil. 3. That a stain upon the soul may be contracted without our own knowledge; "if it be hidden from him." This may be through books, friends, habits of speech. 4. That we should point out to the unwary their danger or their error. 5. That on the first intimation of error we should penitently return on our way.—C.

Ver. 4.—*Redeeming promises.* The reference in the text is to inconsiderate oaths: the hasty undertaking, before God, to do some act of piety or kindness on the one hand (swearing "to do good"), or of retribution and permissible punishment on the other (swearing "to do evil"). It is contemplated that such pledges into which the Divine Being is introduced, rashly and thoughtlessly taken, may be overlooked and remain unfulfilled. We learn—
I. That the formal association of the Divine Being with any act lends to it an inviolable sacredness. That which is done before God, or with which his holy name is intentionally associated, must be regarded as peculiarly sacred: even if done impulsively and without due deliberation, an obligation is thereby incurred: "God's vows are upon us."
II. That it is wise on ordinary occasions not to incur such multiplied responsibility. Better to use the yea, yea, or nay, nay; the simple affirmation or denial with the lesser obligation than to strengthen our utterance with an oath, and so run the risk of more serious sin in non-fulfilment. Calm, quiet, unimpassioned words are best for daily use. Reserve oaths for large occasions.
III. That such responsibility as we do incur we must religiously discharge. If we only affirm in our own name, but far more if we introduce the Divine name, we must see to it that we redeem our word. Negligence, on whatever grounds, though it be through sheer inadvertence—if "it be hid" from us—is culpable in the sight of God. Wherefore: 1. Study to avoid promising without a due sense of the bond that is entered into. 2. Take the earliest opportunity of redeeming your word, for good or evil. 3. *Make* an opportunity, if one does not soon offer. 4. Take necessary means of

keeping the promise in remembrance; by natural, or (if necessary) by artificial means. We may infer—

IV. THAT IF SPECIAL RESPONSIBILITY ATTACHES TO A PROMISE WITH WHICH GOD'S NAME IS ASSOCIATED, SO DOES IT TO ONE IN CONNECTION WITH HIS CAUSE. If we cannot vow, before him, to do any humblest thing without incurring added liability, neither can we undertake to serve in the affairs of his kingdom without similar obligation. A promise made to take any post or fill any office in the Church of Christ should be regarded as exceptionally sacred and binding; neglect by inadvertence is wrong, *sinful.* We are bound to keep before our mind and on our heart anything with which God's name and cause are immediately connected.—C.

Vers. 5—13.—*Pardon possible to all.* The requirements of the Law, as stated in these verses, speak of the possibility of pardon for every offender, if he be willing to submit himself to the will of God. We have—

I. CONFESSION OF SIN. "He shall confess that he hath sinned" (ver. 5). It is believed that confession was always required from the offerer when he laid his hand on the victim's head. It was a marked feature in the ceremonies of the Day of Atonement; it is expressly enjoined here. This was not only necessary from all, but possible to all; within every one's power: none would be unable, and none would be unwilling, but the impenitent who were unprepared for pardon.

II. AN OFFERING WHICH EVERY ONE COULD PRESENT. He that could do so was to bring a lamb or kid (ver. 6); he that could not might bring "two turtle-doves, or two young pigeons" (ver. 7); if this were beyond his means, he might bring a portion of "fine flour" (ver. 11). The costliness of the offering was thus graciously graduated to the circumstances of the offerer. And of so much importance did it appear to the Divine Legislator that the sacrifice should be within the reach of all, that he allowed a deviation from the otherwise unalterable rule that there must be the shedding of blood for the remission of sins (ch. xvii. 11; Heb. ix. 22). The very poor might bring flour (ver. 11), though, in order that there might be no mistake as to the import of it, it was specially prohibited to mix oil or frankincense with it (ver. 11).

III. A PLACE OF APPROACH OPEN TO ALL. The transgressor, convinced of his error, was to take his offering "unto the Lord," by taking it "to the priest." The priest at the door of the tabernacle was always approachable; never a day when he might not be found.

IV. INSTRUCTIONS THAT ALL COULD UNDERSTAND. There could be no doubt or difficulty as to what precise things were to be done. What offering should be presented, whither it should be taken, what should be done with it,—all this was so explicitly and clearly laid down in the Law (vers. 6—12), that every Israelite who had the burden of conscious sin upon his soul, knew what he should do that the guilt might be removed, and that he himself might stand clear and pure in the sight of God.

In the gospel of Christ we have analogous but fuller advantages. We have—

1. *Confession of sin.* We must all say, as we all can say, "Father, I have sinned" (Luke xv. 21). (See Rom. x. 10; John i. 9.)

2. *One Offering that all can plead.* No need of lamb, or goat, or turtle-dove, or even the humble measure of flour. The rich and the poor of the land may say, "Nothing in my hand I bring;" for they have but to plead the one Great and All-sufficient Sacrifice that has been presented, once for all (Rom. vi. 10; Heb. ix. 28; 1 Pet. iii. 18), and they will find mercy of the Lord. The richest can do no more; the poorest need do no less.

3. *An open throne of grace.* "In Christ Jesus our Lord we have boldness and access with confidence" (Eph. iii. 11, 12). No day nor hour when the way to the mercy-seat is barred; from every home and chamber the sin-laden, struggling soul finds its way thither: one earnest thought, and it is there!

4. *Familiar knowledge of the will of God.* Every unlettered man and untutored child may know what is "the will of God in Christ Jesus concerning us." Our statute-book, our New Testament, makes it clear as the day that, if we would find forgiveness of our sin, we must not only confess our transgression, but have faith in the Lord Jesus Christ, and by faith we shall be saved.—C.

Vers. 1—13.—*Cases of concealment of knowledge and ceremonial uncleanness.* They are in some sense trespasses, although not properly under the head of trespass offerings. The ground of guilt is *covenant relation violated.* We may take this in its twofold aspect—

I. As revealing THE POSITIVE VALUE OF THAT COVENANT RELATION. 1. It separated from the unclean, and therefore enforced holiness. 2. It maintained society. Man's duty to his fellows was exalted. He must speak the truth, the whole truth, nothing but the truth; for we are members one of another. 3. It promoted vigilance and circumspection in conduct, both personal and relative. See that you are pure both in your intentional acts and in your circumstances; walk in wisdom towards them that are without.

II. The offering provided and the atonement possible in all cases, even the most minute, plainly said, GOD WILL ABUNDANTLY PARDON; HIS LAW IS LIBERTY." The covenant was not intended to be bondage; it was salvation, not destruction. If any man sin, there is forgiveness. But this waited to be gloriously illustrated when the perfect fulfilment of the Law was set forth in him who offered himself without spot, " able to save unto the uttermost all who come unto God through him."—R.

EXPOSITION.

THE TRESPASS OFFERING (ch. v. 14—19, vi. 1—7). The new heading with which ver. 14 begins indicates that it is here and not at ver. 1 that the section on trespass offerings commences. Sin offerings and trespass offerings are not distinguished from each other in Ps. xl. 6; Heb. x. 8; and the classification of the sins which require one or the other offering has caused great perplexity to commentators. It would appear that, primarily, the trespass offering was reserved for those cases in which reparation had to be made. Thus, if a man failed to pay his tithes and offerings to the Lord (ver. 14), he must bring his trespass offering; or if he refused to restore a deposit to his neighbours (ch. vi. 2), he must bring his trespass offering; and his trespass offering is not received until he has made satisfaction to the party wronged, and paid, as a fine, one-fifth of the value of the thing that he had appropriated. But the class of crimes for which the trespass offering was required came to be enlarged by the addition of other cases, similar in character to the first, but not identical, whereby wrong was done to the Lord (as by transgressing his commands otherwise than by withholding tithes and offerings, ver. 17), or to man (as by wronging a female slave, ch. xix. 20, where the wrong is not estimated by money). These cases are distinguished with difficulty from those for which a sin offering is required. The same act might render it incumbent on a man to offer either a sin offering or a trespass offering, or both: the sin offering would teach the need of, and would symbolically effect, expiation for sin; the trespass offering would teach the necessity of, and would require at the offerer's hands, reparation for wrong. While the sin offering typified the expiation wrought upon the cross, the trespass offering typified the satisfaction for sin effected by the perfect life and voluntary death of the Saviour.

Vers. 14, 15.—**If a soul commit a trespass.** Two previous conditions were required of the Israelite before he might offer his trespass offering. 1. He must make compensation for any harm or injury that he had done. 2. He must give to the injured party a fine equal to one-fifth (*i.e.* two-tenths) of the value of the thing of which he had deprived him, if the wrong was capable of being so estimated. In performing his sacrifice, he had (1) to bring a ram to the court of the tabernacle; (2) to present and to kill it: while the priest (1) cast the blood on the inner sides of the altar; (2) burnt the internal fat and the tail; (3) took the remainder to be eaten by himself and his brother priests and their sons in the court of the tabernacle (ch. vii. 2—7). The special lesson of the trespass offering is the need of satisfaction as well as of oblation, and thus it supplies a representation of one feature in the great Antitype, who was the " full, perfect and sufficient sacrifice, oblation, and satisfaction for the sins of the whole world." **Through ignorance** (see note on ch. iv. 2).

Vers. 15, 16 refer to sins of omission,

offences **in the holy things of the Lord**; that is, withholding tithes and offerings. The non-payment of tithes and offerings was looked upon as robbing Jehovah (Mal. iii. 8), and therefore it is that a trespass offering, involving compensation, and not only a sin offering, is required to atone for the offence. The ram that is to be offered is to be of a value fixed by the priest (**with thy estimation,** *i.e.* according to the estimation of the priest), and the priest is to estimate it **by shekels of silver;** implying that its value must amount at least to *shekels* (in the plural), meaning two shekels (see Ezek. xlvii. 13, where "portions" means "more than one portion," *i.e.* "two portions"). The shekel is considered to be equal to 2*s.* 7*d.* The **shekel of the sanctuary** means the shekel according to its exact weight and value,

while still unworn by traffic and daily use. Beside offering the ram, he **is to make amends for the harm** (or rather *sin*) **that he hath done in the holy thing, and . . . add the fifth part.** The fifth part is probably appointed as being the same as two-tenths of the principal sum. Full satisfaction is the marked feature of the trespass offering. In Luke xix. 8, "Zacchæus stood, and said, . . . Behold, Lord, . . . if I have taken anything from any man by false accusation, I restore fourfold." He went far beyond his legal obligation in respect to compensation. (Cf. 2 Sam. xii. 6, "He shall restore the lamb fourfold.")

Vers. 17—19. Sins of commission may be atoned for by the trespass offering as well as sins of omission.

HOMILETICS.

Vers. 14—19.—*The trespass offering* differs from the sin offering in that it was not allowed to be presented until reparation had been made for the evil done by him who desired to offer it. Its special lesson to the Israelite was that satisfaction for sin is necessary for restoration to communion as well as sacrifice.

ITS TYPICAL LESSON. Satisfaction implies that there is a debt due which must be paid. The debt is due to God; the debtor is man. Christ took upon himself the payment of the debt, which man could not pay. He paid it in two ways: 1. By bearing the punishment due for its non-payment by man. 2. By rendering in his own person that perfect obedience which man had failed to render, and by that failure had become a helpless debtor. Having compensated for man's disobedience by the perfect obedience of his life, he bore the punishment still due for that previous disobedience by the sacrifice of his death. Thus man's forgiveness became not only a matter of mercy on God's part, but of his justice. (See St. Anselm's 'Cur Deus Homo?' and Archbishop Thomson's 'Essay on the Death of Christ' in 'Aids to Faith.')

HOMILIES BY VARIOUS AUTHORS.

Restitution as inculcated in the trespass offering. Ch. v. 14—vi. 7; comp. Phil. iv. 8, 9; Luke xix. 8; Matt. v. 23, 24. The trespass offering, in emphasizing the idea of *restitution*, is needful to complete the list of sacrifices. Without the just dealing this sacrifice demands, the personal consecration, fellowship, and atonement would savour of what was unreal and vain. God's mercy secures morality, and his Word condemns every desire to enjoy his grace and the fruits of injustice at the same time. Let us, then, notice—

I. THE POSSIBILITY OF WRONGING BOTH GOD AND MAN UNINTENTIONALLY. This passage presents this possibility. An Israelite might miscalculate the amount of his offerings, and find, on examination, that he has defrauded his God. This omission must be made good. Or again, he might commit, through want of thought, something God had forbidden, and for this sin of commission he must make restitution according to the estimation of the priest. The possibility of wronging a fellow-man unintentionally is too obvious to require illustration.

Of the first wrong we have, in these gospel times, an instance in *defective liberality* on the part of Christians. How many fail to calculate how much they owe to God! *Systematic beneficence* is a general principle, but it is applied only in the rough, and a faithful analysis will generally prove that God has been defrauded. We defraud God also in the matter of *time* and of *work*. We grudge him his own day; we give him stinted service. A quite appreciable defalcation under such heads as these might be made out against most of us.

Again, unintentional wrong is often done a neighbour in, for example, an *unexpected failure* in business. There are many, let us believe, who reach bankruptcy without intending it. They erred with the very best intentions, and through faulty management allowed their affairs to become hopelessly involved. But the loss suffered by a man's neighbours is not the less real because of his good intentions. Nor will these good intentions pass as good bills with the wronged neighbour's creditors.

II. LET US NOTICE THE POSSIBILITY OF DELIBERATELY WRONGING OUR NEIGHBOUR. We have intentional trespass against man brought out in the opening verses of the sixth chapter. We have here such sins contemplated as falsity in trust, robbery, oppression, and tergiversation about property which has been found. Here the intention as well as the act is at fault.

Our present *mercantile immoralities* afford ample illustrations. In fact, business qualities are regarded by many as consisting in the advantage which a man is able, legally, to take of his neighbour. Men, without sufficient courage to become highway robbers, can take advantage of a neighbour behind the hedge of some blundering act of parliament.

III. THE LAW OF MOSES DEMANDED RESTITUTION IN ALL THESE CASES AS A CONDITION OF PARDON. Unless the trespassers brought the amount of the defalcation, with a double tithe in addition, and the prescribed ram for a trespass offering, God refused them pardon and fellowship.

The case of Zacchæus is in point. His interview with Jesus led to the desire of restitution arising naturally in his heart. "If I have taken anything from any man by false accusation, I restore him fourfold" (Luke xix. 8). God's forgiveness is not independent of moral feeling. God will not forgive trespass so as to encourage the continuance of injustice. There must be restitution and compensation, or he will not grant pardon.

IV. AT THE SAME TIME, THAT RESTITUTION SHOULD NOT BE REGARDED AS MERITORIOUS, THE LAW REQUIRED A TRESPASS OFFERING IN ADDITION. There have been cases of restitution by bankrupts and other trespassers, but they are so blazed abroad in the newspapers, that the public is ready to set them down as meritorious, and almost supererogations. But the Divine Law excluded all possibility of boasting, by attaching a trespass offering to the restitution. A ram must be brought; confession of sin must be made over it in the usual fashion; it must be slain; its blood must be sprinkled as in the former cases; the choice portions are dedicated to God on his altar; and the remainder eaten by the priests.

All this was to show that, even for such an act as restitution, atonement was needful. It could not stand alone; it had no inherent merit; it was only tardy justice; and for the wrong there is need of atonement as well as reparation. And surely the same great truth meets us in the Christian life. Jesus as the Trespass Offering—and this is the phraseology employed in Isa. liii. 10 regarding him—must encircle us with his merits, even when we are conscientiously making restitution. It is as *penitents* we should do this. Even though the world glories in the reparation of wrong as something in its view most meritorious, the persons making reparation should do so in a penitent spirit, having regard always to the atoning merits of the Saviour.

V. THE COURAGE NECESSARY TO MAKE RESTITUTION MUST BE SUSTAINED BY THE FEARLESS PROCLAMATION OF GOD'S LAW. A certain *antinomianism* is encouraged, if not proclaimed, by a loose presentation of God's gospel. Immoralities are tolerated in commerce on the part of professing Christians, that go far to defeat the mission of Christianity. It is essential, in these circumstances, that we should cultivate the courage of men, and sustain their resolutions to be honest and just in making all possible restitution. God requires no less honesty in his gospel than he did in his Law. He never meant his pardon to be enjoyed along with the fruits of wrong-doing. These must be surrendered if it is to be enjoyed. "If it is absolutely impossible to be saved by the works of the Law, it is not less impossible to be saved without the works of *faith*, for faith without works is no faith at all." We must consequently think on "whatsoever things are honest" (Phil. iv. 8), and remember our Saviour's words, "If thou bring thy gift to the altar, and there rememberest that thy brother hath ought against thee; leave there thy gift before the altar, and go thy way; first be reconciled to thy brother, and then come and offer thy gift" (Matt. v. 23, 24).—R. M. E.

Vers. 14—16.—*Trespass amended.* I. To WITHHOLD FROM GOD HIS DUES IS SINFUL. The rigour of Leviticus may well sharpen that perception of sin which is so apt to become dim. God is wealthy, and yet will not submit tamely to robbery. Minute instructions were given concerning the offering of tithes, etc., for the use of his servants at the tabernacle, and for his glory ; and to omit such offerings and to employ them in profane uses is here counted as acting covertly, as faithless dealing. For it was a condition of the covenant that the people should purchase their exemption from entire devotedness, by recognizing that it was incumbent on them to support those engaged wholly in God's service ; and to neglect this condition was, in truth, a breach of trust. It is not less needful to-day that Christians should contribute of their substance to the carrying on of the work of the Church. Nor is it less important to call attention to the trespass committed by failing to present to God the emotion he claims. Many imagine that they are comparatively faultless if they abstain from open notorious wickedness, and they overlook their fatal omissions in the matter of religious service, affection, and faith. " Thou shalt love the Lord thy God with all thine heart," etc. " Trust ye in the Lord for ever." Not to confess Christ is considered as denying him. Besides, it is in the passage before us assumed that the property which ought to have been devoted to the Lord has been consumed for personal enjoyment. And similarly, we may argue that the love and time and strength not used as required for God, are lavished upon other objects, and a wrong is done to our Father in heaven.

II. To COMMIT A TRESPASS UNINTENTIONALLY DOES NOT PREVENT THE NECESSITY OF AN ATONEMENT. This is a lesson frequently enforced in the Law. " Though he wist it not, yet is he guilty, and shall bear his iniquity " (ver. 17). Evidences of the same Divine Law are visible in the consequences that follow mistakes in life, where accidental errors, wrong judgments, hasty steps, are productive of as injurious effects as if the word or action had been planned with utmost deliberation, and its result foreseen. Any other arrangement might augment men's carelessness, and prove in the end more harmful than the apparently inequitable law. We are taught the infinite importance that attaches to our actions, linked on as they are with a chain of invariable results. To sin is to run counter to widespreading principles ; it is not a little matter that may be contemned ; it makes a breach in the fortress of right and justice, and this breach must be repaired ere the offender can be regarded as on the side of the eternal verities. " The soul that sinneth, it shall die." If not the transgressor, then an unblemished ram must be slaughtered as his substitute, that blood may cleanse the stain, and cover the transgressor from wrath. How easy is the way made under the gospel, whereby, after the sin offering of Christ, all our sins are forgiven us for his name's sake !

III. ACQUAINTANCE WITH THE WRONG DONE MUST BE FOLLOWED BY AN ENDEAVOUR TO AMEND IT. The high priest is to value the " harm," and a fifth being added to the amount, the priest receives it as compensation. The offender has gained nothing by his sin. Sin never profits in the end. The restitution is thorough. We may reasonably distrust the sincerity of a repentance that is unaccompanied by reformation. When conscience money is brought, then the confession and desire of the offender to undo the evil wrought, as far as possible, are patent. The atonement and the restitution together procure the forgiveness of the supplicant. What avails it that men have learnt their " trespass," unless it lead to amendment ? Knowledge is designed to be the forerunner of action. Like electricity, it furnishes light and moving power.— S. R. A.

Vers. 14—19.—*Trespass in sacrilege.* The verses now under consideration form a distinct matter of revelation, or were communicated to Moses at a separate time. This we infer from the opening words, " And the Lord spake unto Moses," comparing them with like expressions twice used already (see ch. i. 1 ; iv. 1).

I. WILFUL SACRILEGE WAS PUNISHABLE WITH DEATH. 1. *It is fraud " in the holy things of the Lord."* (1) These are such things as belong to him by requirement of his Law or by solemn dedication. Thus he claims half a shekel per head ransom money when the people are numbered (Exod. xxx. 11—16). He claims the firstborn or a redemption for it (Exod. xxxiv. 11, 20 ; Numb. xviii. 16). He claims the firstfruits of the harvest (ch. xxiii. 10—14 ; Prov. iii. 9). He claims tithes (ch. xxvii. 30—32).

The treasures of the temple of whatever kind were also holy things. (2) To withhold any of these dues, or to profane by eating that which belonged to the priests, was a sacrilege, and, if wittingly done, exposed the criminal to death (see Lev. xxii. 14—16; comp. ver. 9). 2. *This was the crime of Achan.* (1) Joshua's adjuration devoted all the spoils taken at Jericho to the Lord (Josh. vi. 17—19). Achan, therefore, not only incurred the curse of the adjuration, but was also guilty of sacrilege. He is, therefore, said to have "transgressed the covenant of the Lord" (Josh. vii. 11, 15). (2) His punishment was consequently signal. For his sake the children of Israel were smitten before the men of Ai, and the anger of the Lord was only averted from the nation by their stoning and burning Achan, his family, and all pertaining to him (Josh. vii. 24—26). 3. *This also was the crime of Ananias and Sapphira.* (1) Under the glorious influences of the Holy Spirit at the Pentecost, the Church agreed to have all things in common, to which Ananias and Sapphira were consenting parties. They accordingly sold a possession which had been thus devoted to God, but secretly reserved part of the price, placing the balance only at the apostles' feet. (2) This crime was miraculously punished with death. The punishment evinced that the spirit of the Law is still in the gospel. Query: How does this bear upon those who have vowed that a proportion of their revenue should be sacred to God, but with increasing prosperity have become worldly, and withdrew the hand (see Mal. iii. 8—12)?

II. SACRILEGE THROUGH INADVERTENCY ADMITS OF REPARATION. 1. *In cases that are undoubted.* (1) This class of cases is described ver. 15: "If a soul commit a trespass, and sin through ignorance, in the holy things of the Lord," etc. He knows what he did, though ignorant that it was sacrilege, but is now better informed. (2) His duty now is clear: "He shall bring for his trespass unto the Lord a ram without blemish out of the flocks." He brings a *male*, probably in recognition that his sin was an interference with things concerning *rulers* ecclesiastical. "With thy estimation by shekels of silver, after the shekel of the sanctuary, for a trespass offering." (3) But how are we to understand this? It may mean that payment may be made in money or silver, according to the estimated value of the harm sustained by the trespass. Some read, "by thy estimation *two* shekels of silver," etc., which would be a restoring fourfold, half a shekel being the atonement money. This is given to the temple (see Exod. xxx. 13). "And he shall add to it a fifth, and give it to the priest." With this he is accepted. 2. *In cases that are doubtful.* (1) These are described ver. 17: "And if a soul sin, and commit any of these things which are forbidden to be done by the commandments of the Lord; *though he wist it not*, yet," etc. He suspects that he may have trespassed in sacrilege, but is not sure; "Yet is he guilty." The very doubt makes him guilty. (2) This principle is recognized in the precepts of the New Testament. Paul doubtless deduced from this Law his declarations, that "Whatsoever is not of faith is sin," and that "He that doubts is damned," or condemned. (3) This person also must bring a ram with his estimation for the hypothetical harm; but in this case there is no addition of the fifth. Learn that ignorance is a crime, as it leads to transgression: therefore study God's Law. Cultivate a tender conscience.—J. A. M.

Vers. 15, 16.—*Restitution to God.* The trespass for which "God spake unto Moses" that the children of Israel should make atonement, was an offence in which there was present the element of reparable wrong-doing. Something, it was contemplated, would be done which could be in some respects made good, and where this was possible it was to be done. In most cases this would refer to wrong done to man; but here we have the truth that God may be wronged, and that he condescends to receive restitution at our hands. We may look at—

I. SIN REGARDED AS A DEBT WHICH IS DUE TO GOD. Jehovah was sovereign Lord of the Hebrew commonwealth, and actual proprietor of all; anything withheld from those who were his ministers was a sacred due withheld, a debt undischarged. Our God is he: 1. Who has placed us under immeasurable obligation—by creation, preservation, benefaction, fatherly love, Divine interposition. 2. To whom we owe everything we are and have—our hearts and lives. 3. From whom we have withheld that which we shall never be able to pay: our reverence, gratitude, obedience, submission; "ten thousand talents" (Matt. xviii. 24). But there are some special defaults:—

II. ARREARS IN HOLY THINGS. "If a soul commit a trespass . . . in the holy things of the Lord" (ver. 15). The Israelites were under many injunctions; they probably received professional instruction from the Levites, as well as religious teaching at home (Deut. vi. 7). But they might be betrayed into ignorance or fall into forgetfulness, and they might come short of their duty (1) in the offerings they were to bring to the altar, (2) in the contributions they were to make to the ministers of God. They might ignorantly rob God in offerings and in tithes, as they even did *intentionally* (Mal. iii. 8). We also may fall far short of what we should bring to God; we may take a totally inadequate view (1) of the nature of the worship we should render, (2) of the frequency of our devotional engagements, (3) of the contribution we should give to the support of the Christian ministry, (4) of our due share in the maintenance of the cause and the extension of the kingdom of Christ. Thus we may ignorantly but guiltily (ver. 17) fall short of our sacred obligations.

III. THE ATONEMENT WHICH MUST BE FIRST PRESENTED. First of all, there was the offering "not without blood" to be made: the ram must be brought by the offender, and "the priest shall make an atonement for him with the ram, . . . and it shall be forgiven him." First, we must plead the atoning blood of the slain lamb, seeking and finding forgiveness through the Saviour's sacrifice. But this is not all; there is—

IV. THE RESTITUTION WHICH SHOULD SUBSEQUENTLY BE MADE. The Jew was required to "make amends for the harm he had done in the holy things," and not only to give an equivalent to that which he had withheld, but to "add the fifth part thereto;" he was not only to make up, but do more than make up for his default. We cannot and we need not attempt to act according to the letter of this injunction, but we may and should act in the spirit of it, by *letting our consciousness of past deficiency in the worship and the service of Christ incite us to multiplied endeavours in the future.* In looking back we recall negligences to attend the sanctuary, to come to the table of the Lord, to worship God in the secret chamber of devotion; therefore let us seek his face and his favour with constancy and earnestness in the days to come. We have not served his cause and our generation according to the measure of his bountiful dealings with us; therefore let us open our hand freely, and give far more generously than we should otherwise have done to those various agencies of beneficence which are turning the wilderness of wrong into the garden of the Lord.—C.

Ver. 17.—*Unconscious sin.* Is there not something here contrary to our generally received ideas respecting sin? *Can* a man sin "though he wist it not"? The text suggests—

I. THAT WE COMMONLY CONNECT WITH OUR IDEA OF SIN THE CONSCIOUSNESS OF GUILT AT THE TIME OF TRANSGRESSION. Sin is only possible to intelligent, responsible beings; it implies the power of discernment; it is usually followed by self-reproach; it seems, at first sight, to involve a consciousness in the soul of error and wrong-doing at the moment of commission. Hence men expect to be excused if they can say they did not know it was wrong at the time, etc.

II. THAT THIS THOUGHT ABOUT SIN IS BASED ON TRUTH. It is true: 1. That sin is a wilful departure from rectitude: it is the soul consenting to commit some one of "those things which are forbidden to be done by the commandments of the Lord." Where the will does not consent, there is no moral character in the act at all. 2. That the less there is of knowledge, the less there is of guilt (Luke xii. 48). 3. That in the absence of all possible knowledge, there is entire freedom from guilt. "Where no law is, there is no transgression" (Rom. iv. 15). Scripture confirms what our reason declares, that there can be no condemnation where there are no means of knowing "the commandments of the Lord." But we are bound to remember for ourselves, and to impress on others, the opposite aspect, viz.—

III. THAT THIS TRUTH IS SUBJECT TO VERY GRAVE QUALIFICATIONS. 1. Attainable knowledge not gained involves sin. The Jews ought to have known that it was obligatory on them, and highly beneficial to them, to be loyal to Jehovah, to be obedient to his servant Moses, to receive the exhortations of the prophets; their ignorance was culpable, and therefore their errors were sinful. So with their non-recognition of Jesus Christ. So with our ignorance of that which is most binding on us and most beneficial to us. We ought to know that the service of Christ is the chief duty and the supreme blessing; in our ignorance is our guilt. 2. Needless forgetfulness is sin. It was criminal on the part of the Jews of the prophetic age to forget the merciful and mighty interpositions of God in earlier days; on the part of those of our Lord's day to forget the mighty works by which he proved himself to be the very Son of God. It is criminal on our part to forget those vital truths of which God's Word reminds us. 3. The blunting of our spiritual perceptions is sin. When we are blind to the truth which is before us, because our prejudice, or our pride, or our passion, or our worldly interests distort our vision, or because long continuance in folly has blunted our spiritual powers, we are guilty; we "know not what we do," even when we are crucifying a Messiah; but the guilt in the action lies chiefly in the existence of these enfeebled or perverted faculties, and, though we "wist not," yet we "are guilty" in the sight of God.

IV. THAT UNCONSCIOUS SIN CARRIES ITS PENALTY WITH IT. "He shall bear his iniquity." The penalty is threefold: 1. The displeasure of God—his condemnation. 2. Serious harm done to our own soul. 3. Awaking, soon, to the conviction that we have done grievous wrong to others,—it may be a reparable, but it may be an irreparable, wrong.—C.

Vers. 14—ch. vi. 7.—*The trespass offerings.* Distinguished as: 1. Being violations of *rights of property*, either religious or non-religious property. 2. Including a *fine*, *apportioned by the priest, for restoration.* 3. *Without distinction of persons or circumstances.* 4. The victim, *a ram without blemish* from the flocks, and the *atonement* both *sacred* as producing *Divine forgiveness*, and *secular* as including *pecuniary indemnity* ; the blood being in this case merely swung against the side of the altar, not smeared on the horns.

Ver. 17.—*The unwitting trespass.* "Though he wist it not, yet is he guilty, and shall bear his iniquity."

I. THE ABSOLUTE PERFECTION OF THE DIVINE LAW. It must be maintained: 1. As a revelation of the character of God. 2. As a basis on which the moral law is placed. 3. As a means of convincing man of sin, separating the idea of guilt from arbitrary, capricious, local, individual, emotional respects.

II. THE INFINITE FULNESS OF THE DIVINE COMPASSION. 1. *Atonement is provided* not only for sins repented of and confessed, but for offences unwittingly committed. God is thus represented as the shield of his creature, amid the working out of his inscrutable will in the universe. 2. The mind obtains *wonderful peace* when it is assured that all possible liabilities are foreseen and averted. 3. *Forgiveness* is not a mere doing away of sin in the conscience, but a removal of the burden from the life. The Law has nothing more against us.—R.

EXPOSITION.

CHAPTER VI.

THE TRESPASS OFFERING—*continued* (vers. 1—7). The next seven verses, which in the Hebrew arrangement form the conclusion of the previous chapter, enumerate cases of fraud and wrong, for which a trespass offering is required. They are moral, not ceremonial offences. Reparation and the payment of a fine are demanded before the offering is made.

Ver. 1.—**And the Lord spake.** The six following verses contain a separate communication from the Lord to Moses, but in continuance of the subject which began at ch. v. 14.

Ver. 2.—This verse would be better translated as follows:—**If a soul sin, and commit a** trespass against the Lord, and falsely deny to his neighbour something that was delivered to him to keep, or something that he had received in pawn, or something that he had taken away by violence, or hath got something by oppression from his neighbour. Cf. the injunction in ch. xix. 11: "Ye shall not steal, neither deal falsely, neither lie one to another." Exod. xxii. 7—13 contains earlier legislation on the subject of things taken in trust.

Ver. 3.—**Or have found that which was lost.** Cf. Deut. xxii. 2, 3, "Thou shalt bring it unto thine own house, and it shall be with thee until thy brother seek after it, and thou shalt restore it to him again. In like manner shalt thou do with his ass; and so shalt thou do with his raiment; and with all lost thing of thy brother's, which he hath lost, and thou hast found, shalt thou do likewise." **And sweareth falsely.** By previous legislation it had been appointed that, in case of a doubt arising as to what had become of property delivered to another to keep, there should be " an oath of the Lord between them both, that" the latter " hath not put his hand unto his neighbour's goods ; and the owner of it shall accept thereof, and he shall not make it good" (Exod. xxii. 11). This opened the way to false swearing where men were dishonest. **Sinning therein.** Wrong to man is sin against God in every case, but a special sin against

God is committed when an appeal has been made to him by oath, and the oath has been false.

Ver. 4.—As before, the profit gained by fraud or violence is to be given up, and with it a fine is to be paid, amounting to one-fifth of the value of the thing appropriated.

Ver. 5.—**In the day of his trespass offering** is a better rendering than that of the margin, "in the day of his being found guilty," or "in the day of his trespass." The reparation is to take place, and immediately afterwards the offering is accepted.

HOMILETICS.

Ver. 3.—*Swearing falsely* is in an especial manner a sin against God, because in an oath an appeal is directly made to God, and if the thing sworn to is false, God is called to witness to a thing as true which the swearer knows to be false. It is also in an especial manner a sin against society, as mutual truth-telling is the very bond of social trust. When the moral and religious tone of a nation stands high, "an oath for confirmation is the end of all strife" (Heb. vi. 16), and on the other hand, when either a disbelief in God's providence or a casuistical theology saps the confidence placed in promises confirmed by oaths, society is perilously near its dissolution (see Bishop Sanderson's 'Obligation of Oaths'). The sanctity of an oath is guarded by a special commandment in the Decalogue.

Ver. 5.—*Repentance, confession, satisfaction, absolution,* follow each other in order. Without repentance confession is vain ; without confession satisfaction is impracticable ; without satisfaction there is no absolution. In the present case, the sense of absolution was conveyed to the soul of the sinner by the acceptance of his offering for trespass, after which he ceased to be, what he was before, virtually excommunicate from God's people. The greater moral offences were punished either by death (Exod. xxi. 12—17 ; xxxi. 15 ; xxxii. 27 ; ch. xx. 9—16 ; xxiv. 23 ; Numb. xxv. 5 ; Deut. xiii. 9 ; xix. 11 ; Josh. vii. 25), or by formal excommunication, when the offenders were cut off from the people of the Lord, though their lives were spared (ch. vii. 20, 21 ; Gen. xvii. 14). But there was, and there is, an excommunication, not formally pronounced, when a man feels that his sin has separated between him and his God. In these cases the sin offering or the trespass offering restored to communion, but they might not be offered, that is, absolution might not be effected by them, unless preceded by repentance and confession, and, where the nature of the case admitted of it, by satisfaction for the wrong done.

HOMILIES BY VARIOUS AUTHORS.

Vers. 1—7.—*Dishonesty atoned for.* The rebukes tacitly administered by the Law in cases of unjust dealing are neither effete nor unnecessary in modern days. The practices here reprehended still survive, commercial immorality is even yet a fruitful topic of remark. Temptations to dishonesty abound, and are as potent as of yore, for the springs of evil in the human breast remain unaltered, pouring forth their dark and bitter waters. And whilst it is not by works that the children of God expect to be justified, yet may their good works glorify God ; and to guard against the deeds of injustice to which men are prone is to adorn the doctrine of God our Saviour. Happy the congregation of Christians none of whose members has ever been convicted of the transgressions mentioned in these verses!

I. THE SIN DESCRIBED. 1. *Its main feature is the unlawful possession of another's property,* through wrongful acquisition or detention. Force or deceit has been employed in procuring or retaining the goods. This sin may be committed in little things or great, and by communities as well as individuals. 2. *Its source is avarice.* The eye beholds, the heart covets, the will consents, and the hand grasps, as in the history of

Achan, who robbed God (Josh. vii. 21). There is thus the evil co-operation of the senses and faculties, sin in inward thought and outward act. The temporary gratification of the flesh is preferred to the durable contentment of the spirit; self is brought into hideous prominence, as if it could never be coincident with the interest of others and of God. It is classed with sins of ignorance because, though wittingly done, the covetous desire seems to blind the moral sight, and man acts as if under the constraint of a foreign power. Beware of greed! it is insidious in its approaches, and awful in its effects. 3. *It is aggravated by falsehood.* One sin drags another in its wake; avarice prepares the way for lying, even demands it that its designs may be achieved. What has been taken by force is often defended by perjury. The pillars of wickedness are unstable; they need each other's support, for they cannot stand alone in their own native strength. A covetous heart calls for a deceitful tongue.

II. THE REPARATION. Real happiness does not accompany sin; it is a thorny rose, a cup with nauseous elements, a nightmare sleep. Though no human eye detect the wrong, the sinner is guilty, and knows that One above will not recognize the right of might and violence, nor allow his name to be used with impunity as a shield to vice. Remorse tortures the transgressor, until he is driven to confess his crime and to make amends for it. The Law mercifully appoints a salve for the bleeding conscience. 1. *Full restitution to the rightful owner.* The property stolen or retained, together with an added fifth, is returned as compensation for the injury suffered. Sin is shown to be unprofitable, and no length of possession is allowed to supply a reason for inequitable retention. Lapse of time must never be supposed to bar recovery of rights. Are there no persons in our assemblies to whom this law is applicable? 2. *Acknowledgment of an offence committed against God.* It was "a trespass against the Lord" (ver 2), and in several respects. His commandments were broken, notably the second, third, eighth, and tenth (Exod. xx.). An atonement is required, the sacrifice of a ram, the fat parts of which are burnt on the altar, and the rest eaten by the priests. The two branches of the moral law are closely connected. To violate the one is to dishonour the other. Experience attests their contiguity. Those who best regard the interests of their neighbours are the men that are jealous for the honour of God. Forget not to impress upon children the importance of asking, not only their parents' pardon, but the forgiveness of their heavenly Father when they have acted dishonestly or unkindly. Frequently the newspapers record the receipt by the Chancellor of the Exchequer of money sent because of unpaid taxes. Do the senders always remember that they have sinned against God as well as man; and implore forgiveness in the name of Jesus Christ?—S. R. A.

Vers. 1—7.—*Restitution.* This paragraph ought to have been included in the preceding chapter, as it is the conclusion of the subject there considered. The last paragraphs treated of sacrilege, or trespass in the holy things of God; this has reference to trespass between man and man. We have here—

I. AN ENUMERATION OF WRONGS. These may be distributed into two classes, viz.: 1. *In matters of fraud.* These may be (1) in respect to things in custody, "that which was delivered him to keep." Under this heading may be ranged things left in pledge, the possession of which is afterwards denied. Also things borrowed and fraudulently retained. (2) In respect to "fellowship." This may refer, in matters of partnership, to claiming for sole interest profits that should be divided, or shifting liabilities which should be jointly borne wholly to the partner's account. The Hebrew here is "putting of the hand," which the margin interprets "in dealing." Any fraud in trade would, therefore, come under this head, viz. by light weight, short measure, false balances, false samples, adulterations, misrepresentation of values, or saunterings by which an employer is robbed of his time. (3) In respect to trusts. Executors so managing estates as to enrich themselves at the expense of their wards. Public servants manipulating accounts to pocket balances, or taking bribes to favour particular contractors to the prejudice of competitors or of the public. (4) In respect to "the lost thing which he found." Solon's law was, "Take not up that which you laid not down." Historians relate that in England, in the days of Alfred the Great, golden bracelets might be safely hung up in the road. Whoever retains what he found when he knows who the owner is, or without using diligence to discover him, is a thief.

2. *In matters of violence.* Such as (1) "A thing taken away by violence." A horrible example is furnished in the case of the vineyard of Naboth (1 Kings xxi. 15, 16). (2) Any kind of oppression. Exactions under pressure of necessity. Exactions under threats. Withholding adequate remuneration for service (see Jas. ii. 6 ; v. 4—6).

II. AGGRAVATIONS OF THE WRONGS. These are : 1. *When lies are told to cover them.* (1) Some may have the hardihood stoutly to deny, in the face of witnesses to the contrary, that they came into fraudulent possession of property. (2) It is more easily denied when there are no witnesses to attest delivery, or prove custody or trust against the holder. (3) Lies are told in the forms of evasion, shuffling, and false colouring. 2. *When oaths are taken to give countenance to the lies.* (1) God is a *witness* of everything (2 Chron. xvi. 9 ; Ps. xxxiv. 15 ; Prov. xv. 3). He is often a silent observer. It is an awful aggravation of a wrong to think that it is done under the eye of God. (2) But when an oath is taken to cover a wrong, God is *appealed* to. What a fearful outrage against the God of truth, to be thus called in to attest a lie ! (3) Whether a wrong be done before God as a " witness," which it must be if it is done at all ; or whether he be " appealed " to by an oath, every trespass against man is also " a trespass against Jehovah " (see Jas. v. 4). Trespasses cannot, therefore, be treated lightly because of the insignificance of the person wronged, when the Almighty also is concerned. In all the interest which God takes in the justice of human actions, he has the good of man at heart.

III. THE LAW OF REPARATION. 1. *He shall make up the wrong to the person injured.* (1) " He shall restore it in the principal." If this cannot be done in the identical thing, then an " estimation " of its value must be taken, and payment made, viz. " in shekels of silver, after the shekel of the sanctuary " (comp. ch. v. 15). (2) " He shall add the fifth part more thereto." This is a proper consideration for the inconvenience the owner may have suffered through the fraud. But if the " estimation " be, as some read it in ch. v. 15, " two shekels," then the restoration would be " fourfold," since the atonement money was " half a shekel." This would agree with Exod. xxii. 1 (comp. also 2 Sam. xii. 6 ; Luke xix. 8). (3) And he shall " give it unto him to whom it appertaineth, in the day of his trespass offering." The trespass offering will not be accepted else. Job's friends had to make peace with him before their sacrifices would be accepted (Job xlii. 8 ; see also Matt. v. 23, 24). 2. *He shall then " bring his trespass offering unto the Lord."* (1) " A ram that is perfect." God will accept nothing that is imperfect. Therefore we must come to him through Christ, who can invest us with his righteousness. (2) " With thy estimation, for a trespass offering, unto the priest." This, according to ch. v. 15, would be of the value of two shekels. (3) " And the priest shall make an atonement for him," etc. Reflect : What a power there is in conscience ! What a costly thing is sin ! How carefully should it be avoided ! Let us avail ourselves of the benefits of redemption.—J. A. M.

Vers. 1—7.—*Human ownership and dishonesty.* From the Divine directions here given as to the trespass offering, in the case of wrong between man and man, we gather—

I. THAT GOD ALLOWS US TO CONSIDER HIS GIFTS AS BELONGING TO OURSELVES. By inheritance or by labour we acquire property ; a man has a right to say, concerning an object thus legally acquired, "This is mine." The possession of property is carefully guarded by the declarations of God's Word ; " the commandments of the Lord " make the violation of this right a very serious sin (see text). It is well, however, to remember that human ownership is never absolute ; it is subject to : 1. God's prior and supreme claim (Ps. xxiv. 1 ; 1 Chron. xxix. 11 ; Hag. ii. 8). 2. Our duty, in holding it, to keep in view the general good ; *e.g.* large landowner has no right to let ground lie waste, and be covered with seed-sowing weeds. 3. Our liability, at any hour, to lay it down at God's will.

II. THAT MEN FIND VARIOUS WAYS OF DISREGARDING THIS RIGHT. Many forms of dishonesty prevail in every land ; it is an inevitable excrescence of sin. Five special cases are here provided against : 1. Breach of trust, or failure to return anything borrowed ; lying in " that which was delivered him to keep " (ver. 2). 2. Unfairness in partnership or co-operation ; " in fellowship." 3. Violent appropriation or hardship (oppression),—" a thing taken away by violence " (ver. 2).   4. Fraud in trading,—" hath deceived his neighbour " (ver. 2).   5. Illegal retention of something accidently acquired, —" have found that which was lost," etc. (ver. 3).

III. THAT DISHONESTY IN ANY FORM IS A SERIOUS SIN AGAINST GOD, as well as a wrong done to our neighbour.   By committing any one of these offences a soul is said to " sin, and commit a trespass against the Lord " (ver. 2) ; " he sins therein " (ver. 3); " he hath sinned, and is guilty."   Evidently the taking from our neighbour " that which is his " is a high misdemeanour in the sight of God.   Two of the " ten commandments " (Exod. xx.) are directed against it: " Thou shalt not steal ;" "Thou shalt not covet," etc.   Theft, dishonesty, is a treble sin : it is a wrong to our fellow; it is an injury to ourself (spiritual demoralization) ; it is an offence against God.

IV. THAT IT CALLS FOR RESTITUTION AS WELL AS SACRIFICE.   1. We must, indeed, bring our sacrifice to God.   The Jew was to bring his " ram without blemish " (ver. 6), and an atonement was to be made before the Lord, and his trespass was forgiven him (ver. 7).   We must bring the sacrifice of a contrite spirit, and plead the One Sacrifice for all sin, and we shall be forgiven.   2. But we are also bound to make restitution where that is possible.   The Jew was to " restore it in the principal, and ... add the fifth part more thereto " (ver. 5); he was to more than make up for the injury he had done. And (1) in order that the will of Christ concerning us in such case may be fully done (see Matt. v. 24), (2) that our own conscience may be perfectly clear and unstained, and (3) that our brother may have reason to be entirely satisfied with us,—let us make *not only adequate but ample* or even overflowing compensation for the wrong which we have done.—C.

Ver. 3.—*Sin a germ as well as a fruit.*   It is contemplated by the Supreme Legislator, that if a man once cherish a dishonest thought, he will probably go beyond fraud to falsehood (" and lieth "), and, when necessary, from falsehood to perjury (" and sweareth falsely ").   This is true to life.   Sin is not only the consequence of the evil that came before it, but it is the cause of more sin which is to follow ; it is not only the child but the parent of wrong.   Learn that—

I. NO MAN WHO SINS CAN TELL HOW FAR HIS SIN WILL TAKE HIM.   Hazael, Gehazi, Ahab, Judas, etc.; " facilis descensus Averni."

II. IT IS IN THE NATURE OF SIN TO TEMPT TO FURTHER SIN.   The instances with which we are familiar are not remarkable exceptions; they are illustrations of a principle at work everywhere and always.   "There's not a crime but takes its change out still in crime, when once rung on the counter of this world ;" dishonesty naturally, if not necessarily, leads to lying, and lying to perjury.   One sin is the germ of another, and is sure to bear fruit.

III. IT IS A PART OF THE PENALTY OF SIN THAT IT SHOULD DO SO.   We sometimes think that sin carries no penalty ; so it seemed to the Psalmist (Ps. lxxiii.), but he was wrong, as he owned (ver. 15).   It not only ends disastrously (" then understood I their *end* "), but it results in certain, immediate, spiritual injury.   On the day in which the forbidden fruit is eaten, we *do* die,—in the soul.

IV. THIS FACT OF THE DIFFUSIVENESS OF SIN HELPS TO EXPLAIN THE EXCEEDING EVIL OF IT IN THE SIGHT OF GOD.   It may well be accounted " an evil and bitter thing," a thing which he " hates," which he " abhors," etc.

These considerations furnish (1) a very strong reason for repentance, etc ; and (2) an equally strong inducement for the cultivation of holiness in the heart and life of the good.—C.

Vers. 1—7.—*Trespasses done wittingly.*   These were acts of lying, fraud, deceit, violence, or any social wrong involving conscious trespass on the rights of our neighbour.

I. SOCIAL MORALITY RESTS UPON RELIGION.   Offences against neighbours, offences against God.   No true support of society apart from faith.   Follies of the modern sceptical school.   Enthusiasm of humanity, atheism, development of morality out of a physical basis,—mere dreams of the intellect.   Facts of history show that corrupt religion is corrupt morals ; that an atheistic society is mere organized selfishness.

II. THE TRUE HEALING PRINCIPLE OF SOCIETY.   The preservation of individual rights in the spirit of a common allegiance to God.   We are all brethren.   If one offend, let his offence be both readily acknowledged and atoned for, and readily forgiven. So long as we simply pay back, we do not heal the hurt; we must more than pay back. His restitution was of the principal and the fifth part more thereto. Such a regulation was founded on the Divine love, as the essence of the Divine Law. We must remedy wrongs in the spirit of benevolence.

II. As TYPICAL OF THE CROSS OF CHRIST, THE DIVINE FULNESS OF REDEMPTION is set forth. The offences of men are more than made up for. Their redeemed state is an advance upon their state of innocence. The new Law is better than the old. Christ in us is not only the crucifixion of sin and the world, but "the hope of glory." The believer will find in the blood of the atonement both a cleansing away of guilt, and a washing of regeneration and renewing of the Holy Ghost.—R.

EXPOSITION.

The following section (ch. vi. 8—vii. 38) is a supplement to ch. i.—vi. 7, containing the regulations addressed to the priests relating to the ritual of the several sacrifices. Vers. 8—13 of ch. vi. contain the further ritual of the burnt sacrifice; vers. 14—23, that of the meat offering; vers. 24—30, that of the sin offerings; vers. 1—6 of ch. vii., that of the trespass offering; vers. 11—36, that of the peace offering; vers. 7—10 declare the portion of the priests in all the offerings; vers. 37, 38 conclude the section.

Vers. 8—13.—(See note on ch. i. 3.) The further ritual of the burnt offering is exhibited in the particular instance of the lamb sacrificed every evening (Exod. xxix. 38). In other cases the ritual was to be the same. Instead of **It is the burnt offering, because of the burning upon the altar all night unto the morning**, the reading should be, *It, the burnt offering* (viz. the evening sacrifice), *shall burn upon the hearth upon the altar all night unto the morning.* The priest is to wear his priestly dress already appointed (Exod. xxviii. 40)—which was a white linen garment, covering the whole person like a close-fitting English surplice, fastened by a sash—while he is actually officiating at the altar; and thus vested, he is to remove from the altar **the ashes which the fire hath consumed with the burnt offer-ing**, or rather, as it would be better translated, *the ashes to which the fire hath reduced the burnt offering*, and **put them beside the altar**, that is, on the ash-heap to the east of the altar. On leaving the court of the tabernacle, he is to change his dress, and to carry the ashes of the sacrifice **without the camp unto a clean place.** The priest is also instructed to lay fresh wood on the altar fire **every morning**, in preparation for the morning sacrifice of the lamb (Exod. xxix. 38). **The fat of the peace offerings**, that is, the parts of the peace offerings that were burnt on the altar, were laid on the burnt offering. The altar fire was **never** to go out, because the daily sacrifices constantly burn-ing on the altar symbolized the unceasing worship of God by Israel, and the gracious acceptance of Israel by God. The ever-burning sacrifice was the token of the people being in communion with God.

Vers. 14—18.—The further ritual of the meat offering (see note on ch. ii. 1). The greater part of it is to be given to the priests, and they and the males of their families are to eat it without adding leaven to it. **With unleavened bread shall it be eaten** (ver. 16) should rather be rendered, *Unleavened shall it be eaten.* Not only is it most holy itself, but **every one** (or rather *everything*) **that** toucheth the offerings shall be holy. The touch of the offering conveys the character of holiness to the thing touched, which must, therefore, itself be treated as holy.

Vers. 19—23.—The meat offering of the high priest at his institution. This was to be not of uncooked flour, but in the form of a pancake, made out of one-tenth of an ephah of flour. It, of course, accompanied the burnt offering appointed for the occasion. **Half of it** was burnt **in the morning**, that is, at the morning sacrifice, **and half thereof at night**, that is, the other half at the evening sacrifice, none being reserved for consump-tion by the priests. This meat offering, having first been offered at the consecration of Aaron, was afterwards to be offered at the consecration of each succeeding high priest, the expression **Aaron and his sons** meaning here the successive high priests. The state-ment that the offering is to be **perpetual**, has led to the belief that it was made every day by the high priest, from the time of his con-secration onwards, and there is thought to be an allusion to this sacrifice in Ecclus. xlv. 14; but the more probable opinion is that it was only made on the day of consecration, that is, on the first day that he was qualified to act as high priest.

Vers. 24—30.—Further ritual of the sin offering (see note on ch. iv. 2). The flesh of the sin offerings is to be eaten by the priests and the males of their families **in the holy place**, that is, within the precincts of the sanctuary, with the exception of the sin offerings of the high priest and of the congregation, **whereof . . . the blood is brought into the tabernacle of the congregation to reconcile** withal **in the holy** place, which was to be **burnt in the fire** without the camp. The holiness of the offering is manifested: 1.

By the command that no drop of the blood which might have been accidentally spilt upon the offerer's dress should be taken out of the tabernacle court. 2. By the order to break or scour the pot in which it was boiled for the priests' eating.

HOMILETICS.

Vers. 8—30.—*The priests' ritual.* Hitherto the command had been, "Speak unto the children of Israel, and say unto them" (ch. i. 2; iv. 2);   Command Aaron and his sons;" the reason being that the injunctions which follow are specially addressed to the future priesthood.

I. PRECISION OF THE POSITIVE RULES AND REGULATIONS GIVEN TO THE AARONIC PRIESTHOOD. Nothing is left to the individual's origination, all is ruled for him—every act that he performs, and each word that he speaks; and any failure in the ritual vitiates the whole ceremony.

II. CONTRAST IN THIS RESPECT WITH THE RITUAL OF THE CHRISTIAN CHURCH. In the New Testament there are no such minute ritual regulations as in the Book of Leviticus. Search through the Gospels, and we find the principles of worship established. Search the Epistles, and we find order and uniformity in religious ministrations commanded, but no such specifications of manual acts as those given in the earlier dispensation.

III. THE REASON OF THE DIFFERENCE. It is a higher and a nobler state to be allowed freely to apply a principle than to be bound down to a certain course by a definite and unchanging rule. The former is the conditions of sons, the latter of servants. "The servant knoweth not what his lord doeth." The Jew was in this position. He did not know what it was that he was representing and rehearsing in type. He must, therefore, be hedged about with rules, lest, in his darkness and ignorance, he should go astray and mar the lesson that he had unwittingly to teach. But "henceforth," says our Lord, "I call you not servants, for the servant knoweth not what his lord doeth, but I have called you friends." Accordingly, just as in matters of morals the principles contained in the Sermon on the Mount are given to Christians instead of bare negative or positive rules of conduct; so in matters of worship, certain principles are laid down as to the nature of true worship and how it is to be offered (John iv. 21—24), and a few general rules commending uniformity and order in public worship (1 Cor. iv. 17; xi. 16; xiv. 33, 40), and declaring its ends to be the edification of the people (1 Cor. xiv. 26); and then the work of composing its Liturgy and common prayers is delivered to the Church without any other restraint than that of embodying in them settled forms of administration of the two sacraments of Baptism (Matt. xxviii. 19) and of the Lord's Supper (Matt. xxvi. 26; Mark xiv. 22; Luke xxii. 19; 1 Cor. xi. 26), using the Lord's Prayer (Luke xi. 2), and of "asking" in the name of Jesus Christ (John xvi. 24). Therefore, "it is not necessary" in the Christian Church, as it was in the Jewish Church, that "ceremonies be in all places one, and utterly like: for at all times they have been divers, and may be changed according to the diversities of countries, times, and men's manners, so that nothing be ordained against God's Word. . . . Every particular or national Church hath authority to ordain, change, and abolish, ceremonies or rites of the Church ordained only by man's authority, so that all things be done to edifying" (Art. XXXIV.).

IV. A PRECOMPOSED LITURGY IS NOT DISPLEASING TO GOD. However much the liberty of the Christian Church may in this respect be superior to Jewish bondage, yet it is evident from the Levitical laws and regulations that a prearranged and formal method of approaching God is in accordance with his will, as recorded in his holy Word.

HOMILIES BY VARIOUS AUTHORS.

Quench not the Spirit. Ch. vi. 8—30. Cf. Eph. iv. 30; 1 Thess. v. 19. We have here sundry sacrificial laws enabling us the better to understand the details of the preceding sacrifices; but the cardinal idea in them all, as we shall now see, is that which heads this homily, "Quench not the Spirit." And—

I. THE FIRE OF THE BURNT OFFERING WAS TO BE CAREFULLY PRESERVED, SO THAT IT SHOULD NEVER GO OUT. This necessitated a regular removal of the ashes to the clean place selected for their reception without the camp. These ashes represented what would not ascend in the fire, and were a fitting symbol of the dross and corruption which attaches to all human services. Everything which would prevent the fire from burning was to be removed. Now, we have already seen that the fire of the altar symbolizes the Holy Spirit. It is what came from God in the first instance, and what renders the sacrifice acceptable. Hence the lesson about the perpetuation of the altar-fire is to remove everything which would hinder or would quench the free action of the Spirit within us. The purer we try to be, the freer will the movements of the Holy Ghost be within us. On the other hand, negligence in life must interrupt the spiritual action. Let us diligently use every means, like the priest laying on the wood and clearing away the ashes from the altar, and the Holy Spirit as a fire within us will make us ardent and enthusiastic in the Divine life.

II. NEW OBEDIENCE OUGHT TO BE AS HOLY IN OUR EYES AS ATONEMENT. This principle is symbolized for us in the details about the meat offering (vers. 14—18). For the priests are not only to burn carefully the due proportion upon the altar, but also to prepare the remainder for themselves without leaven, and to regard it as a "holy of holies" (קֹדֶשׁ קָדָשִׁים), like the sin offering and the trespass offering. If, then, we saw reason to regard the meat offering as emphasizing the idea of *consecrated life-work*, this direction to the priests about regarding the meat offering as just as holy as the sin offering or trespass offering, embodies the idea that "new obedience" should be as holy in our eyes as "atonement." Now, there is no principle more likely to please the Holy Spirit, to foster his indwelling, and to maintain his reign. The whole Christian life is elevated in tone when this ideal is comprehended. The perfection of our Saviour's atonement and righteousness is to be the model of our lives.

III. A CLASS IS NEEDFUL WHOSE SELF-DENYING LIVES ARE ABOVE SUSPICION. This seems taught by the arrangement that the meat offering of the priests must be wholly burnt (vers. 19—23). The life-work is to be all consecrated, all a dedicated thing. Never are the officers of God to be " off duty," "out of season" as well as "in season" should they serve God.

Now, the self-denial of a class of men, if realized, goes far to secure the continuance and blessing of the Spirit. The Holy Spirit is the Spirit of self-denial—this is the most important evidence of his work—and the demonstration of this to men is a concomitant of his abiding.

It need hardly be observed—it is so evident—that Jesus, our Great High Priest, realized self-denial in all its fulness. He could say, as none other can, "My meat is to do the will of him that sent me, and to finish his work" (John iv. 34). Every portion of our Lord's life-work was laid upon the altar, permeated with the oil of the Spirit, and enveloped in the incense of prayer. It is for priestly believers to follow in his steps.

IV. THE CONSECRATING POWER OF THE ATONING SACRIFICE SHOULD BE KEPT CONSTANTLY IN VIEW. In the remaining verses (vers. 24—30), we have brought before us the intense holiness of the sin offering. It is to be regarded as a "holy of holies" (קֹדֶשׁ קָדָשִׁים). In ordinary cases the priest is to eat that which remains after God's share has been offered on the altar, to sustain him in his atoning duties, and to sustain also his sense of consecration. In the more important cases, such as are referred to in ch. iv. 1—21, the remainder of the animal was to be carried out to the clean place outside the camp, and burned there in the place of the ashes. Moreover, every person and thing which touched the flesh was thereby consecrated. So intensely holy was the atoning sacrifice, that it pervaded with its sanctifying power everything in contact with it.

That this is typical is clear. A similar but much more real consecration attaches to the atoning sacrifice of Christ. And this great truth must be kept in view if we would preserve the Spirit within us. To separate consecration from the atoning work of Jesus must ever be grieving to the Spirit, whose chief mission is to take of the things of Christ and show them unto men (John xvi. 14, 15).

We have thus discovered in these miscellaneous laws what course we should follow, if the Spirit is not to be quenched within us but is to abide. We must diligently use the appointed means, we must have the highest possible ideal of a consecrated life, and we must give all honour to the atoning sacrifice of Jesus. In such circumstances we shall retain, in large and abiding measure, the Holy Spirit within us.—R. M. E.

Ver. 13.—*The ever-burning fire.* The special directions for the benefit of the priests are fittingly separated from the instructions common to all the people. In front of the tabernacle stood the altar of burnt offering, and on this a fire was kept constantly burning, in obedience to the injunction of the text. For a description of the altar, see Exod. xxvii. 1—8. Let us advance in thought, and behold the flames and curling smoke, and hear the lessons the fire preaches.

I. Consider it as THE FULFILMENT OF AN ORDINANCE. From his relationship to God, man is bound to obey him, and this same relationship causes that the majority of God's utterances to man are in the nature of commands, such commands, however, containing virtual promises. And *those are most honoured who have most commands.* The priests occupied the highest posts in the estimation of the people, simply because they were entirely devoted to the behests of the Almighty. To lay sticks in order upon the altar and set fire to them, was in itself a humble occupation, but the fact that it was performed for the glory of God elevated its character in the eyes of all. *Menial duties are ennobled when discharged as unto the Lord.* The fire was an emblem of worship, of praise, and supplication, ascending to the Most High from his faithful people. *That it was perpetual indicated God's desire to be worshipped, not with fitful enthusiasm, but with steady regularity.* There were times when the fuel was renewed, just as men may have their seasons of devotion at morning and at night, on the Lord's day and on a certain week-day, but there must be always a flame of service to testify to the obedience and affection of the people. The fire was kept alight by successive generations in their turn. *To no one age is it exclusively given to sound the praises and do the will of the Eternal.* When one servant falls asleep, having done the will of God, his younger comrade must step into his place and continue the work. Even the materials so soon to be consumed must be deposited upon the altar in an orderly manner. It is said by the rabbins that care was taken in selecting the sticks, no rotten ones being allowed. *Whatever is done for God must be done to the best of our ability.*

II. Consider it as THE ENJOYMENT OF A PRIVILEGE. Once the fire was consecrated by the approach thereto of the glorious fire from God's presence instantly consuming the sacrifice (ch. ix. 24). The flames became henceforth *a token of God's acceptance of the offerings of his servants, and his consequent reconciliation and favour.* If any Israelite doubted the reality of Jehovah's existence or his willingness to bless the nation, a glance at the fire was sufficient to dismiss all doubt, and to inspire his breast with a consciousness of blessing.

The perpetual fire symbolized *God's unchangeable protection of his people.* Through the hours of daylight and through the watches of the night the flames ascended on high; they knew no cessation; they spoke of him who "never slumbers nor sleeps," upon whose brightness no darkening shadow ever rests. This altar-fire consumed the various offerings presented. *It kindled other fires*—from it the burning coals for the golden altar of incense were taken; it was the fire-foundation on which the sacrifices were laid, and by which they were consecrated. It is the loving sacrifice of Christ that generates holy lives in his followers. By his ascension the fire of the Holy Spirit descended upon the Church, kindling sparks of hallowed emotion, and making the thoughts and words and acts of Christians an ever-brightening **blaze** of sacred service.—S. R. A.

Vers. 25.—29.—*The holiness of the sin offering.* This offering was to expiate offences committed directly against God, and which involved, therefore, the deeper wrong. A peculiar sacredness attached to the sacrifice. Only the priests might partake of it, for it was "most holy." As all Christians are made "priests unto God," it is permitted them to feed upon him who died to save them from sin. They live by faith in the Son of God. Union with their Divine Lord consecrates them, imperishable principles sustain them.

I. WHAT IS OFFERED UNTO GOD ACQUIRES THEREBY A SACRED CHARACTER. It is set apart, belongs to him henceforth. He accepts the gift, and his holiness is imparted to all his possessions. His people are holy, and so are his house and his statutes.

Christ, having dedicated himself to the Father, could declare "I sanctify myself." It is no light matter for a man to take upon himself allegiance to a holy God, to "vow to be his, yea, his alone." God himself must sanctify us wholly, that body, soul, and spirit may be preserved blameless. Some article of furniture that is owned by a celebrated monarch is invested with importance by that fact, and numbers view it with eager interest. The servant wearing his famous master's livery is regarded with attention. Surely, then, those are worth our notice who are consecrated to the service of the King of kings, vessels meet for his use.

II. HOLINESS TENDS TO COMMUNICATE ITSELF TO ALL THAT IS BROUGHT INTO CONTACT WITH IT. Whoever touches the sin offering shall be holy. Like leaven, the sacredness spreads. The prospect of the world's improvement lies in the hope of its permeation by Christian principle. By touching the Saviour, the sick were healed, and by placing the hand of faith now upon Christ's bleeding body, the sinner is sanctified in the sight of God. That holiness extends is recognized in the apostle's declaration, that "the unbelieving husband is sanctified by the wife." Continual contact with sacred rites and offerings renewed the holiness of the priests. So let us seek to draw near unto our God by the Living Way, having our hearts sprinkled and bodies washed.

III. In spite of this consecrating power, WHAT IS HOLY MUST NOT BE THOUGHTLESSLY PLACED IN PROPINQUITY WITH WHAT IS DEFILING. Let blood from the offering stain the garment, and it must be cleansed "in the holy place," not carried without into the region of things common and unclean. If the flesh was boiled in an earthen vessel, the fat might penetrate through the porous surface, so that no after rinsing or scouring would remove it, as in the case of copper ("brazen") vessels. The earthen pot must consequently be broken, to prevent all risk of any portion of a sin offering being contaminated by touching subsequent food. Learn from this not to profane what is dedicated to God. Our Lord's words to Mary after his resurrection are significant: "Touch me not." The precept of Paul was, "Be ye not unequally yoked together with unbelievers: for what fellowship hath righteousness with unrighteousness?" We must not cast pearls before swine. Let us not commingle sordid motives and methods with the worship of the sanctuary. Jests founded upon the Word of God are to be shunned. Previous prayer will not sanction worldly entertainments and amusements. In many directions the regulations of Leviticus may be remembered with advantage to-day.—S. R. A.

Vers. 8—13.—*The law of the burnt offering.* With this paragraph the Jews begin the twenty-fifth section of the Law; and, as a new subject is here introduced, this ought to have been the commencement of the chapter. In some of the best editions of the Hebrew Bible, the paragraph preceding this is properly made the sequel of the fifth chapter, and the sixth commences with this. The burnt offering was treated of before, viz. in the first chapter, with more particular reference to ceremonies relating to those who brought it; here it is considered in relation to the priests who offered it. We have now to consider—

I. THE LAW OF THE BURNT OFFERING AS TO THE SACRIFICE. And we observe: 1. *That the offering was ever upon the altar.* (1) The evening sacrifice was "burning upon the altar all night unto the morning." For the particular reference here is to the daily sacrifice of a lamb for the whole congregation. (2) This was then followed by the corresponding morning sacrifice. This, together with the occasional sacrifices which were offered throughout the day, would keep the altar fully occupied until the evening. (3) Thus there was kept up a constant "remembrance of sins" day by day, the year round, and "year by year continually." For the repetition of the sacrifices showed that "they could never take away sins." These could only be removed "through the offering of the body of Jesus Christ once" (see Heb. x. 1—10). 2. *That the fire was kept ever burning.* (1) This was not common fire, but came forth from God (see ch. ix. 23, 24). It was an emblem of the Holy Spirit; and sometimes represented his wrath, sometimes his love (Isa. iv. 4; Mal. iii. 2, 3; Matt. iii. 11; Acts ii. 3, 4; Heb. x. 26, 27; xii. 29). (2) God commanded that it should "not be put out." He will consume with the fire of his wrath those who quench the fire of his love. Even if we be not always offering sacrifices, love must be kept always burning in the heart (1 Thess. v. 19; 2 Tim. i. 6). (3) The priests were instructed how they should keep it alive. They were to put on wood. On this to lay the burnt offering. So the Great Sacrifice was laid on the wood of the cross, when the fires of God's wrath entered into his very soul. The fat of the peace offerings was placed on the burnt offering. So the fire was maintained (see Isa. xxxi. 9). The fire was kept ever burning, to show that God's wrath could never be quenched until the blood of Christ should quench it.

II. THE LAW OF THE BURNT OFFERING AS TO THE PRIEST. 1. "*Aaron and his sons* " *together are addressed*. Ver. 9. (1) The high priest of the Law was undoubtedly a type of the "Great High Priest of our profession." When Aaron, the high priest, is here mentioned with his sons, the priests, the suggestion is that in his absence they acted as his representatives in connection with the burnt offering. So here they also may be viewed as types of Christ. (2) The sons of Aaron, in their character of ordinary priests, represent Christians. In what they did, therefore, there may have been a twofold typical meaning. 2. *They attended the altar in their holy garments*. (1) These were composed of white linen. "His linen garment, and his linen breeches" (Exod. xxviii. 40—43). They symbolized purity and righteousness (Ps. cxxxii. 9; Rev. iii. 4; vii. 13, 14; xix. 8). (2) As types of Christ in offering up his own sacrifice of himself to God, they would shadow forth his righteousness. As typifying Christians, they would foreshow how we must be clothed with the "robe of righteousness and garment of salvation" through Christ's merits, before our spiritual sacrifices can be accepted. (3) Even when the priest took up the ashes from the consuming burnt offering to put them beside the altar, he wore his holy garments. This was proper, for the fire was still consuming the sacrifice. But, 3. *He changed his garments to carry the ashes outside*. (1) He had to carry them forth without the camp. Was not Calvary this place of ashes (comp. ch. iv. 12; Heb. xiii. 11, 12)? (2) But they were to be laid in a "clean place." The tomb of Joseph was such a place. It had not been polluted by the touch of a dead body (see John xix. 41, 42). Nor did the ashes of the world's Great Burnt Offering pollute it. They were holy. Because he was the "Holy One" of God, his body "could not see corruption" (Acts ii. 31). (3) The holy raiment was laid aside when this service was performed, to show that now, as far as the work of sacrifice was concerned, that was "finished" when Jesus expired upon the cross. Let us rejoice in an "eternal redemption," in an "everlasting salvation."—J. A. M.

Vers. 14—23.—*The law of the meat offering*. As the law of the burnt offering, laid down in the preceding paragraph, viz. in relation to the service of the priest, was before mentioned, more particularly in respect to the offerer, so is the law of the meat, or more properly the bread, offering, here introduced for a similar reason, after being formerly mentioned likewise (see ch. ii.). The subject is presented in two aspects, and we have to consider—

I. THE LAW OF THE BREAD OFFERING OF THE PEOPLE. In this case: 1. *A memorial of it was burnt upon the altar*. (1) The memorial represented the whole. The bulk consisted of at least an omer, or about three of our quarts, of fine flour, of which a handful was taken for the memorial. There was with the omer of flour, a log, or little more than a half pint, of oil, of which a fitting quantity was added to the handful of flour. The memorial was completed by the addition of all the frankincense. As the name of a thing stands for the thing, so did the memorial stand for the whole offering; it was like a *quit rent*, a discharge for all demands on the estate. (2) It was burnt upon the altar for a sweet savour unto the Lord. It could not be *that* to him in a physical sense; this expression must be *morally* interpreted. (*a*) It was a thank offering, and gratitude from his intelligent offspring is ever pleasing to his goodness (Ps. xxvii. 6; l. 23; Rom. xii. 1; 1 Thess. v. 18). (*b*) It was placed on the altar of burnt offerings, and mingled among the sacrifices offered, to make atonement for sin, and so, coming up as it were "through Jesus Christ" in whom the Father is ever well pleased, it becomes "acceptable" (1 Pet. ii. 5). 2. *The remainder was eaten by Aaron and his sons*. (1) Aaron ate of it, who was the type of Christ; and his sons also, who were types of Christians. So Jesus and his disciples together ate the Passover (Luke xxii. 15). And he gave to his disciples the bread and wine of his Eucharist. (2) The bread offering was to be eaten without leaven. This substance was regarded as an emblem of evil dispositions, malice, wickedness, insincerity (1 Cor. v. 6—8). These must be absent from those who feast with Jesus. (3) It was to be eaten in the holy place. This holy place was not the innermost court, which was a type of "heaven itself" (Heb. ix. 24). It is explained to be the "court of the tabernacle of the congregation," which was a figure of the Church in its earthly aspect—the kingdom of heaven upon earth. Those who elect to worship God outside his Church, are not following out his instructions. (4) The males only must eat of it. The daughters of the priests were permitted to eat of the "holy things," such as might be carried out of the court, such as the tithes and firstfruits, and the shoulder and breast of the peace offerings. But of the "most holy things" eaten in the sanctuary they may not eat. It was the Seed of the woman who is most holy, not the woman herself; the son, not the daughter, therefore, was holy unto God. Now that most holy Seed has come, the distinction between male and female is abolished (Gal. iii. 28). (5) The priest must not eat it unless he be clean. "Every one that toucheth it shall be holy" (ver. 18). To eat and drink unworthily of the Christian Eucharist is a serious thing (see 1 Cor. xi. 27—34).

II. THE LAW OF THE BREAD OFFERING OF THE PRIESTS. In this case: 1. *The whole was offered upon the altar.* (1) Here was no "memorial," as in the offering of the people. The omer of fine flour was all burnt upon the altar (ver. 23). "Had the priests been permitted to live on their own offerings, as they did on those of the people, it would have been as if they had offered *nothing,* as they would have taken again to themselves what they appeared to give unto the Lord" (A. Clarke). (2) It was offered in two portions: half in the morning, and the complement at night (ver. 20). And as it is called a "meat offering perpetual," it is generally understood that the high priest repeated this offering daily throughout his pontificate. (3) This he appears to have done not for himself only, but on behalf of the priesthood in general. This seems expressed in the words, "This is the offering of Aaron and of his sons, which *they* shall offer unto the Lord in the day when *he* is anointed," etc. (ver. 20). Here "they" offer it; but afterwards we read, "And the priest of his sons that is anointed in his stead," viz. as high priest at his demise, "shall offer it" (ver. 22). Taken together, these passages show that the high priest offered it for the priesthood in general. 2. *None of it was to be eaten by the priests.* (1) It appears to have been of the nature of the sin offering; for there is no frankincense offered with it. This was the case with the poor man's sin offering (see ch. v. 11). In sin there is nothing grateful to God. (2) By his eating of the sin offerings, the typical transfer of the sins of the people to the priest was signified (see ch. x. 17). It would not be proper, therefore, for him to eat the sin offering in which he was personally concerned. He must rather see his sin transferred to the altar, and there consumed along with the lamb of the daily sacrifice. So may we see our sins consumed.—J. A. M.

Vers. 24—30.—*The law of the sin offering.* This law comprehends a variety of particulars, which may be ranged under two heads—

I. AS IT RESPECTS THE BLEEDING. The particulars under this head are: 1. *The place:* "Where the burnt offering is killed shall the sin offering be killed." (1) In the account of the sin offering (ch. iv.), the place is implied rather than specified; but the position of the altar is described in the account of the burnt offering. It stood "at the door of the tabernacle of the congregation," and the burnt offering was killed "on the side of the altar northward" (ch. i. 3, 5, 11). Accordingly, Jesus "suffered without the gate," and Calvary was northward of Jerusalem. The evangelical teaching is that a sinner has access to God only through Christ, who declares himself to be the "Door" and the "Way" (John x. 9; xiv. 6). (2) The association here of the sin offering with the burnt offering is significant. The burnt offering expressed adoration, and was offered for sin generally. The sin offering was more specific. Confession of sin should be particular, and faith individual, fully to realize the benefits of the common salvation (1 Tim. iv. 10). Let no man trust vaguely to the provisions of mercy. Let the sinner see in the death of Christ the very image of himself, with all his iniquities and abominations, suffering and satisfying the claims of Divine justice. 2. *The presence:* "Before the Lord" (ver. 25). (1) This means more than being in the presence of One who is omnipresent. There was a manifestation of a special presence of Jehovah in the glory behind the vail. In a special sense Jesus promises to be present where two or three are met in his name. (2) This presence of God was at once judicial and merciful. The throne of his glory was a propitiatory, but he was there armed with fire to smite with destruction any who dared to set him at defiance (Ps. xcvii. 2, 3; lxxxix. 14).   3. *The reason :* "It is most holy"(ver. 25). What? (1) Not the sin laid on the sacrifice. Sin seen in the sacrifice is exceeding sinful. That which could cause the Son of God his agonies is horrible and abominable in the extreme. (2) Not the sin, but its condemnation in the sacrifice. The sacrifice of Christ, by which sin is removed out of the sight of God, is indeed "most holy." Had Jesus not been "most holy," he could never have accomplished this miracle of grace and mercy. (3) The blood of the sin offering, if sprinkled upon any garment, must be washed out within the sanctuary. And if the blood of the type must not be treated as a common thing, much more must we reverence that blood which cleanseth from all sin.

II. As it respects the eating. 1. *It was to be eaten by the priest.* "The priest that offereth it for sin shall eat it." (1) By this ceremony the "sin" (חטאת, *chattath*) became, in a sense, assimilated in the body of the priest (see ch. x. 17; Hos. iv. 8). This represented the manner in which Christ, becoming incarnate among us, appeared "in the likeness of men," and "in the likeness of sinful flesh" (Rom. viii. 3; 2 Cor. v. 21; Phil. ii. 6—8). (2) The converse of this is in the Eucharist, in which we symbolically partake of the pure body of Christ. As he became assimilated to our likeness that he might expiate sin by the sacrifice of himself, so we now become assimilated to his pure nature that we may inherit the rewards of his righteousness. There is a mystical incarnation of Christ in his believing people (Eph. iii. 16—19). 2. *It was to be eaten in the holy place* (ver. 26). (1) Observe, not in the most holy place; that place within the vail in which the Shechinah abode between the cherubim. That was the type of the heaven of heavens, where the "angels do always behold the face of God" (Matt. xviii. 10). No sin could enter there (Isa. xxxv. 8—10; lx. 20—22; Rev. xxi. 27; xxii. 14, 15). (2) But "in the court of the tabernacle of the congregation," the type of the Church in its earthly aspect, which is entered by way of the laver of washing and the altar of sacrifice. It is while we remain in this world that we can avail ourselves of the provisions of mercy. 3. *But certain sin offerings must not be eaten.* (1) The priests were forbidden to eat of those whose blood was brought into the tabernacle to reconcile withal (ver. 30; see also ch. iv. 5, 6, 16, 17). (2) In this the gospel is superior to the Law. Jesus has carried his blood into the holy place of the true temple, to reconcile withal (Heb. ix. 11, 12). Yet we may eat of his altar (Heb. xiii. 10—12). (3) Those who serve the tabernacle have no right to eat of our altar, because the tabernacle law forbids them; therefore to avail themselves of the gospel they must renounce the Law (see Gal. v. 3, 4). And their case is fearful who now attempt to make atonement for themselves, for they "shall be burnt in the fire" (ver. 30). Such is the peril of those who trust to works of supererogation or to anything but Christ.— J. A. M.

Vers. 8—13.—*Three principles of piety.* We gather from this clause— I. That holiness becomes the house of God. It seems generally agreed that the linen garments, in which the priests were to be robed when engaged in sacrificial acts (ver. 10), signified the purity of heart which should characterize the worshipper of God (see Exod. xxviii. 42; Ezek. xliv. 19). Certainly it is only the "pure in heart" who can hope to "see God," either by faith here or in beatific vision hereafter (see Ps. xciii. 5).

II. That there is no drudgery in the service of God. Very homely and humble details of sacred work were to be done by the officiating priest. He was to be very careful as to the clothes he wore, changing them at regulated times (vers. 10, 11); he was .to "take up the ashes . . . and put them beside the altar" (ver. 10), and to "carry forth the ashes without the camp," etc. (ver. 11). These acts were mean enough in themselves. Elsewhere they would have been accounted menial, but in so sacred a service as the direct worship of Jehovah they acquired sanctity, and even dignity. They were solemn ceremonies, reverently performed. The slightest engagement in the worship of God deserves to be esteemed sacred (Ps. lxxxiv. 10). Any humble deed done or simple word spoken, (1) as in the presence of the observing and approving Master, or (2) consciously and designedly for the glory of his name, or (3) as unto one for whom he died and whom he loves (Matt. x. 40—42), rises to high rank in the esteem of Heaven. The cheerful, loving service of a Divine Redeemer does not contain one act of drudgery; it is all upon the high level of holy, happy, elevating service.

III. THAT THERE MUST BE CONSTANCY IN OUR CONSECRATION TO GOD. "The fire shall ever be burning upon the altar; it shall never go out" (ver. 13). As soon as the victim was slain and his shed blood was sprinkled on the altar, there was forgiveness and acceptance, and the burning of the whole animal by the heaven-kindled fire indicated the accepted consecration of the offerer. When, therefore, the priest was instructed to keep the fire perpetually burning on the altar, it signified God's readiness to receive the perpetual devotion of the Israelites themselves to him and to his service. To us the most instructive lesson it conveys is that we must keep steadily and unfailingly burning the fire of consecration in our hearts;—*that* must "never go out." 1. The passions of youth must not be permitted to extinguish it. 2. Nor the toils and anxieties of our prime. 3. Nor the mysterious and perplexing troubles that, like whelming billows (Ps. xlii. 7), go over us. 4. Nor the distressing doubts which the enemies of the faith raise within us. 5. Nor the comforts and indulgences of prosperous periods in our life. It must be diligently and devoutly fed by (1) earnest thought—meditation; (2) regular worship with the people of God; (3) steadfast Christian work; and (4) the private believing prayer which finds such utterance as this, "O thou who camest from above!" etc.—C.

Vers. 14—18.—"*Fellowship with the Father.*" In these renewed directions (see ch. ii.) concerning the meat offering, we have the striking expression, "I have given it unto them for their portion of my offerings" (ver. 17). So that this sacrifice, beside furnishing an opportunity to the people of acknowledging their indebtedness to God as the generous Giver of all blessings, provided an opportunity to the priests of fellowship with God. He shared these "his offerings" with his ministers, and they ate with him "in the holy place" (ver. 16), within the precincts of his house. "And truly *our* fellowship is with the Father, and with his Son Jesus Christ" (1 John i. 3). In Divine and human fellowship under the gospel, there is—

I. FEASTING TOGETHER. The truest Christian counterpart of the sacred service described in the text is found in the Lord's Supper. There we, who are all "priests unto God" (Rev. i. 6; 1 Pet. ii. 5, 9), meet at the table of the Lord (1 Cor. x. 21), and eat and drink in his presence, rejoicing in his redeeming love, renewing before him our vows.

II. SPEAKING ONE TO ANOTHER. 1. *God to man* in (1) the pages of revelation; (2) the words of those whom his Spirit prompts to remind us of his will or to explain it; (3) the direct communications of his Spirit. 2. *Man to God* in (1) the accents of praise; (2) the breath of supplication.

III. REJOICING IN ONE ANOTHER. 1. *God in man* (Deut. xxxii. 9; Ps. xxxv. 27; cxlvii. 11; Hab. iii. 18; Eph. v. 27; Rev. xxi. 2). 2. *Man in God* (Ps. xvi. 5; lxxxix. 16; cxlix. 2; Phil. iii. 3; iv. 4).

IV. WORKING TOGETHER. We are "workers together with him" (2 Cor. vi. 1); "labourers together with God" (1 Cor. iii. 9). While God is working in us and through us, he is also working *with* us; united with us in working out the reconciliation and regeneration of the world.—C.

Vers. 27—29.—*Communicated sanctity.* When any victim had been presented in sacrifice to God, and had been slain, its blood (the "blood of atonement"), and also its flesh, became "most holy" (ver. 29). And whatsoever was touched by the one or the other received, in virtue of such contact, a communicated sanctity (vers. 27, 28). The lesson here conveyed is that whatsoever comes into close association with a holy one or a holy thing does thereby acquire a measure of sacredness, and should be treated accordingly by us. This imparted sanctity gives back again to that which acts upon it some additional importance; it reflects that which it receives on the object from which it comes. We have abundant illustration of this truth; sanctity is communicated—

I. FROM THE GOD-MAN TO HUMAN NATURE. Man is far more to God and to the spiritual universe now that the "Word was made flesh," that "himself" was "partaker of flesh and blood." In Jesus Christ the Divine touched the human, and henceforth the human is holy.

II. From the life and death of Jesus Christ to the life and death of men. Poverty, shame, sorrow, tears, the grave,—are not these other than they were, sacred things, since he "had not where to lay his head;" since the crown of thorns rested on that sacred head; since the Man of sorrows bore his burden; since "Jesus wept;" since they "laid him in a sepulchre"?

III. From the service to the sanctuary. "This is none other than the house of God."

IV. From the function to the minister. "Esteem them very highly in love for their work's sake."

V. From the spirit to the body. The exceeding preciousness of the human spirit imparts a sanctity to the body which is its residence and organ.

VI. From the truth to the Word. We must deal reverently with the words in which the eternal truth of God is uttered.—C.

Vers. 19—23.—*Ministerial function and obligation.* This instruction is supplementary to that given in Exod. xxix. We may gather from it—

I. That entrance on sacred work should be accompanied with special solemnities. The commencement of any ministry may well be attended with such observances as shall impress upon the mind the sanctity and weight of the obligations which are incurred.

II. That the acceptance of sacred obligations should be regarded as a time for thankfulness as well as seriousness of spirit. The priest was to bring a "meat offering"—fine flour and oil (vers. 20, 21)—the token of gratitude for God's bountiful provision. There are, in truth, few things for which we have such reason to be thankful to God as for his providential guidance to that post for which we are fitted, at which we can usefully expend our powers; more particularly if this be one in close connection with his service.

III. That those who hold sacred offices are, with all the people of God, stewards of their secular possessions. The priest, as well as the layman in Israel, was to bring his meat offering. He, too, was indebted to the Divine Sovereign for all temporal blessings, and should make suitable acknowledgment of his debt. Those who now serve in sacred things, in the gospel of the Saviour, are men who receive and hold secular as well as spiritual treasures, and they, too, have their obligations, which they must not disregard.

IV. That what we give to God and his cause should be given absolutely, without thought of return. The people gave their offerings, part being burnt and the rest being the portion of the priests; but every "meat offering for the priest was to be wholly burnt: it was not to be eaten" (ver. 23). The priests were not to *take back again* for their own use that which they had presented to God. What they offered was to be given wholly, utterly, with no thought of receiving it again. When we give to our brother, we do best when we are "hoping for nothing again" (Luke vi. 35). When we give to God, either in worship or in contribution to his cause and kingdom, we do best when we are filled with a sense of his immeasurable goodness to us, and with a desire to do something to his praise. We should feel that (1) it is a high honour to be allowed to give anything to him, and that (2) the utmost we can give is a poor tribute indeed when presented to him who gave himself for us.—C.

Vers. 8—30.—*Instructions on the offerings for the priests.* Ver. 13, "The fire shall ever be burning upon the altar; it shall never go out."

I. The perpetuity of religious obligation. 1. As springing out of the *relation between man and God,* as underlying the whole of human existence. "*In him we live, and move, and have our being.*" 2. *The all-embracing love of God.* The fire came originally from him, and must be kept up to betoken his ceaseless care of his creatures. 3. *The positive expression of religious feeling* can never be dispensed with, should be maintained in uninterrupted order.

II. The maintenance of worship is a duty which is devolved upon consecrated persons, and their official position, in an especial manner. Vain to expect that the fire will not go out, unless appointed persons attend to it. Mere individualism is abuse of liberty, and ends in irreligious disorder and extinction of the fire of God's house.

Priestcraft is no argument against a special ministry in the Church. All must help to maintain the fire, but some must take the command as addressed to them in a special manner. They must separate themselves to the work, both by appropriate manner of life and recognition of special duties. Religion is not only in temples, but if the fire goes out there, it will go out everywhere.—R.

Vers. 14—18.—*Meat offering.* " All the males of the sons of Aaron shall eat of it," with unleavened bread, in the court of the tabernacle of the congregation. " It is most holy, as is the sin offering, and as the trespass offering." " Every one that toucheth them shall be holy."

I. The ministry of religion should be fulfilled in the spirit of thankful devotion. 1. The best of the Church should be consecrated to its highest positions. 2. Their service should be rendered as a delight. 3. Their religious earnestness and cheerfulness should be cultivated by fellowship and brotherhood. 4. They should be closely united with the people, not separated from them by spiritual pride and a misanthropic asceticism.

II. Holiness the imperative requirement of God's ministers. Not mere ceremonial holiness. 1. Holiness of character and life. 2. Holiness in the service of the sanctuary—purity of worship, singleness of heart, orderliness and decency, with simplicity and manifest sincerity.

III. The sanctifying influence of a true and pure worship extends through society. Every one holy by contact with the holy. 1. *The persuasive effect* of a real and well-sustained religious service. The common mistake is to suppose that morality leads of itself to religion or may be substituted for it. 2. *The true order of life* is set before us here in the Law of Moses : the nearer to God, the holier; the more closely connected with the worship of God, the more separated from and defended against the impurities of the world. 3. *The reaction of the holy life on the sanctuary.* The revival of religion must be a reciprocal action of the Church on the ministry, and of the ministry on the Church.—R.

Vers. 19—23.—The high priest's offering in the day when he is anointed—a perpetual meat offering ; offered not during the days of the anointing, but when it was completed, and it was *wholly burnt.* Fine flour baked as an oil-cake ; not a bleeding sacrifice, therefore, but only a thank offering, to denote that expiation was always made, and the high priest offered the fruits of sanctification. This may be viewed—

I. In its typical application to the Lord Jesus Christ. 1. His *entire consecration* to his mediatorial office. 2. His *personal perfection* as needing no expiation, offering only the fine flour of his unspotted humanity, mingled with the oil of the Spirit of God, and with the fire of actual human experience applied to it. 3. His *acceptance by the Father* on our behalf; " wholly burnt."

II. In its lesser application to the ministry of the sanctuary. 1. The *true ordination* not a mere human rite, but a Divine acceptance of personal consecration. " I have chosen you," said Jesus, " and ordained you." 2. The minister of God should offer his *fine flour,* his highest gifts—his intellect, culture, sifted knowledge, prepared thought. He should put nothing which he himself has not toiled to make worthy on the altar. 3. With all we present, *the oil of grace* must be mingled, and it must be prepared by *actual fire of experience.* No man can teach and minister spiritual blessings to others who is not himself practically acquainted with the truth. 4. " Every meat offering for the priest shall be wholly burnt : it shall not be eaten." No ministry can be divinely blessed which is not fulfilled in the spirit of single-hearted, self-consuming devotion. We must hate our life for Christ's sake, and take up his cross, if we are to follow him.—R.

Vers. 24—30.—*Special regulations as to the sin offering.* Peculiar sanctity of the flesh and blood of the sin offering, pointing to the atonement. In all cases, whether the sin offering of the people, or of the priest, or of the great day of atonement, the same holiness of the victim and of the blood is insisted upon. Here there is—

I. The necessity of atonement. 1. As prescribed by God, coming forth from his infinite holiness. 2. As connected with mediation, not in atonement dependent upon the chance merit of man, but the gracious promise of God's free and sovereign mercy. 3. As set forth in the flesh and blood of the victim, clearly indicating a substitutionary merit.

II. THE TYPICAL FULFILMENT OF THE SIN OFFERING IN JESUS CHRIST, at once the High Priest and the Victim. 1. Most holy in his person and his blood. 2. Connected with the burnt offering, as presented in the same place. The cross was a whole offering in the fire of suffering, in the consuming righteousness of the Divine Law. 3. Imparting the holiness to him who shall touch it. Healing virtue from Christ; sanctification from the cross. 4. The very vessels are sanctified. So the Spirit of Christ cleanses the world. The diffusion of the Christian doctrine and life lifts up all that belongs to human existence into a higher sphere.—R.

EXPOSITION.

CHAPTER VII.

CONTINUATION OF THE SUPPLEMENTAL REGULATIONS ADDRESSED TO THE PRIESTS, RESPECTING THE RITUAL OF THE SACRIFICES. This chapter treats of the ritual of the trespass offering and the peace offerings, as the last chapter treated of that of the burnt offering, the meat offering, and the sin offering. The LXX. version attaches the first ten verses of this chapter to ch. vi., beginning ch. vii. with our ver. 11.

Vers. 1—6.—Further ritual of the trespass offering (see note on ch. v. 14). It is to be noted that the blood of the trespass offering is not to be placed on the horns of the altar, as was the rule in the ordinary sin offering, but cast against the inner side of the altar, as in the burnt offering and peace offering. The rump in ver. 3 should be translated *tail*, as in ch. iii. 9.

Vers. 7—10 contain a general precept or note as to the priests' portion in the sin offering, trespass offering, burnt offering, and meat offering. The officiating priest was to have the flesh of the trespass offering and of the sin offering (except the fat burnt on the altar), and the skin of the burnt offering and the cooked meat offerings (except *the memorial* burnt on the altar), while the meat offerings of flour and of parched grains, which could be kept longer, were to be the property of the priestly body in general, all the sons of Aaron, . . . one as much as another. The skins of the peace offerings were retained by the offerer ('Mishna, Sebach,' 12, 3).

Vers. 11—21.—Further ritual of the peace offering (see note on ch. iii. 1). There are three sorts of peace offerings—thank offerings (vers. 12—15), votive offerings, and voluntary offerings (vers. 16—18). Of these, the thank offerings were made in thankful memorial for past mercies; votive offerings were made in fulfilment of a vow previously taken, that

such offering should be presented if a certain condition were fulfilled. Voluntary offerings differ from votive offerings by not having been previously vowed, and from thank offerings by not having reference to any special mercy received. The thank offering must be eaten by the offerer and his friends, on the same day that it was offered ; the votive and the voluntary offerings, which were inferior to the thank offering in sanctity, on the same day or the next. The reason why a longer time was not given probably was that the more the meal was delayed, the less would a religious character be attached to it. The necessity of a quick consumption also took away the temptation of acting grudgingly towards those with whom the feast might be shared, and it likewise precluded the danger of the flesh becoming corrupted. If any of the flesh remained till the third day, it was to be burnt with fire; if eaten on that day, it should not be accepted or imputed unto him that offered, that is, it should not be regarded as a sacrifice of sweet savour to God, but an abomination (literally, *a stench*), and whoever ate it should bear his iniquity, that is, should be guilty of an offence, requiring, probably, a sin offering to atone for it. The bread gift accompanying the animal sacrifice was to consist of three kinds of unleavened cakes, and one cake of leavened bread, and one out of the whole oblation, that is, one cake of each kind, was to be offered by heaving and then given to the officiating priest, the remaining cakes forming a part of the offerer's festive meal. If any one took part of a feast on a peace offering while in a state of Levitical uncleanness, he was to be cut off from his people, that is, excommunicated, without permission to recover immediate communion by offering a sin offering. St. Paul joined in a votive offering (Acts xxi. 26).

Vers. 22—27.—Repetition of the prohibition of eating the fat and the blood, addressed to the people in the midst of the instructions to the priests. **Ye shall eat no manner of fat** must be taken to mean none of the fat already specified, that is, the internal fat, and, in the case of the sheep, the tail. It is uncertain whether the law as to fat was regarded as binding upon the Israelites after they had settled in Palestine. Probably it was silently abrogated; but the prohibition of blood was undoubtedly perpetual (Deut. xii. 16), and it is based on a principle which does not apply to the fat (ch. xvii. 11).

Vers. 28—34.—Continuation of the ritual of the peace offerings (see note on ch. iii. 1). The equal dignity of the peace offerings with the other offerings is vindicated by the command that the offerer **shall bring it** with **his own hands,** whereas it might have been regarded as merely the constituent part of a feast, and so sent by the hand of a servant. **The breast and the right shoulder** were to be waved and heaved (for "heaved" does not merely mean "taken off," as some have said). The waving consisted of the priest placing his hands beneath those of the offerer who held the piece to be waved, and moving them slowly backwards and forwards before the Lord, to and from the altar; the heaving was performed by slowly lifting the pieces heaved upwards and downwards. The movements were made to show that the pieces, though not burnt on the altar, were yet in a special manner conse-

crated to God's service. *The right shoulder* was most probably the hind leg, perhaps the haunch. The Hebrew word is generally translated "leg" (Deut. xxviii. 35; Ps. cxlvii. 10). This part was the perquisite of the officiating priest; the waved breast was given to the priests' common stock. Afterwards an addition was made to the priests' portion (Deut. xviii. 3; see 1 Cor. ix. 13).

Vers. 35, 36.—Conclusion of the section. This is the portion **of the anointing of Aaron, and of the anointing of his sons,** may be translated simply, *This is the portion of Aaron, and the portion of his sons,* as the word "*mischah*" will bear the meaning of portion as well as of anointing. This rendering, however, is not necessary, as it was the anointing of Aaron and his sons that entitled them to these portions.

Vers. 37, 38.—Conclusion of Part I. **The law of the burnt offering** is contained in ch. i. 1—17; vi. 8—13: **of the meat offering,** in ch. ii. 1—16; vi. 14—23: **of the sin offering,** in ch. iv. 1—35; v. 1—13; vi. 24—30: **of the trespass offering,** in ch. v. 14—19; vi. 1—7; vii. 1—6: **of the consecrations,** in ch. vi. 19—23, supplementing Exod. xxix. 1—37: **of the sacrifice of the peace offerings,** in ch. iii. 1—17; vii. 11—21; 28—34. Together, the sacrifices teach the lessons of self-surrender, loyalty, atonement, satisfaction, dedication, peace.

HOMILETICS.

Ver. 13.—Leavened bread was not to be offered on the altar, for a reason before assigned; but, though not offered on the altar, it may yet be consecrated to God, not by burning, but by heaving. Thus there are lives which cannot be wholly devoted to God and his active service, and yet can be consecrated to him. Leavened bread was the bread commonly used, and the secular life of a man engaged daily in the occupations of politics, or of business, or of labour, may be sanctified, and, being sanctified, may be accepted by God as freely and fully as are those directly given up to his especial service.

Ver. 19.—*That which is itself unclean makes whatever it touches unclean also.* So in the moral sphere, "evil communications corrupt good manners" (1 Cor. xv. 33), and "a little leaven leaveneth the whole lump" (1 Cor. v. 6), and so with respect to the spread of heresy, "Their word will eat as doth a canker (or gangrene)" (2 Tim. ii. 17).

On the other hand, that which is itself holy makes that which it touches to be holy (ch. vi. 18). Therefore, when the Holy One was on the earth, "the whole multitude sought to touch him: for there went virtue out of him, and healed them" (Luke vi. 19); and they "brought unto him all that were diseased; and besought him that they might only touch the hem of his garment: and as many as touched were made perfectly whole" (Matt. xiv. 35, 36). Thus the woman with an issue of blood "came behind him, and touched the border of his garment: and immediately her issue of blood stanched. . . . And when the woman saw that she was not hid, she came trembling, and falling down before him, she declared unto him before all the people for what cause she had touched him, and how she was healed immediately" (Luke viii. 44—47).

Hence, when mankind had fallen in Adam, for the restoration of the race a new Head was found in Christ Jesus, into whom each person is baptized, and by a mystical contact with whom he may be sanctified.

Ver. 25.—To eat of the fat *of which men offer an offering made with fire unto the Lord*, is to rob God of his chosen offering. The injunction condemns sacrilege in all its forms. Whoever takes to his own use things dedicated to God, " eats the fat ; " and " the soul that eateth it shall be cut off from his people."

Ver. 34.—The wave breast and the heave shoulder were to be the priests', as well as the meat offering (ver. 10) and other portions. Thus is taught the lesson enforced by St. Paul (1 Cor. ix. 13, 14), " Do ye not know that they which minister about holy things live of the things of the temple ? and they which wait at the altar are partakers with the altar ? Even so hath the Lord ordained that they which preach the gospel should live of the gospel." The adequate maintenance of the Levitical priesthood was carefully provided for under the old dispensation by means of offerings and of tithes ; and " the labourer is worthy of his hire " (Luke x. 7), and " let him that is taught in the Word communicate unto him that teacheth in all good things " (Gal. vi. 6), are principles of the new dispensation likewise.

HOMILIES BY VARIOUS AUTHORS.

Ministerial support. Ch. vii. ; cf. 1 Cor. ix. 13 ; x. 18. We have in this chapter a detailed account of the disposal of the offerings already referred to. The leading idea of the passage is the perquisites of the priests, and the Christian counterpart of this is *ministerial support.* And in this connection let us observe—

I. IN ALL THE OFFERINGS THE FIRST CONCERN WAS TO ALLOCATE TO GOD HIMSELF HIS DUE. In particular he had appropriated to his own use, that is, to manifest atonement, the *blood* of all the sacrifices ; and consequently it was never to be eaten, for this would be a profane use of such a sacred thing (vers. 26, 27). It is only when we come to the realities out of the types and shadows, that we find Jesus declaring, " Whoso eateth my flesh, and *drinketh my blood*, hath eternal life ; and I will raise him up at the last day. For my flesh is meat indeed, and my blood is drink indeed " (John vi. 54, 55). Atoning blood can only be partaken of *by faith.* Moreover, the Lord appropriated the fat—the large amount of suet about the animal—which was absolutely necessary to feed the fire. This was to be devoted, therefore, to this sacred use and withdrawn from all profane use. There were other portions, such as the sheep's tail, the kidneys, and the caul above the liver, which were burned always on the altar as God's portion. The general principle, therefore, is plain of first giving unto God his due.

Now, in this particular question of ministerial support, it is with this idea of *stewardship unto God* that we must begin. Men must first realize their obligation to God above before they will do justly by his ministers. The human obligation is best enforced by emphasizing the Divine. If men give God his due, if they are faithful stewards unto him, if they keep zealously the first table of the Law, they will not wrong their neighbours by disregarding the second table ; above all, they will not wrong God's ministers.

II. AFTER GOD'S PORTIONS WERE DEDICATED, THE BEST OF THE RESIDUE BECAME THE PRIESTS'. In some cases the priest got the whole ; for example, in a private sin offering or trespass offering, and when, as in the peace offerings, the remainder was shared with the person presenting the sacrifice, the priest's portion was always the best. The wave breast and the heave leg, the " choice cuts," as we would now call them, of the carcase, were assigned to the priests. In fact, there is peculiar generosity enjoined in supporting the officers of God.

There is a fashion in a business age of regarding the minister very much as an ecclesiastical tradesman, who is to be dealt with on business principles ; that is, as much work is to be got out of him as possible for the minimum of pay. The sooner such poor notions cease, the better for the cause of God. " And we beseech you, brethren," says the apostle, "to know them which labour among you, and are over you in the Lord, and admonish you; and to esteem them very highly in love for their work's sake" (1 Thess. v. 12, 13). If ministers are rightly regarded, the people will feel it to be their duty, as Israel was instructed to do, to give them the best support they can.

III. A PROPERLY SUSTAINED PRIESTHOOD WAS IN A POSITION TO EXERCISE FAITHFUL DISCIPLINE IN THE CHURCH. This ministerial support chapter, as we may properly regard ch. vii., is most particular in debarring the unclean from Church privileges. Whether we are to understand the "cutting off from the people" as death, as the Vulgate appears to do, or as only excommunication, one thing is certain, that the priesthood, assigned its true dignity and supported accordingly, were thereby encouraged to be faithful in the exercise of discipline.

And this relation of proper ministerial support to Church discipline is most important. It is when the office is degraded in men's minds to a mere profession, and they consequently refuse it adequate support, that they are unwilling to submit to the discipline God's ministry should wield. To the elevation of the office in the eyes of men, and to the consequent increase of its support, all wise members of the Church of Christ should devote their attention.—R. M. E.

Vers. 15—18.—*Fidelity to precept enforced.* The peace offering was essentially a tribute of gratitude and praise. It was especially suited to national festivities and family rejoicings. Cakes and bread accompanied the flesh of the sacrificial animal. Three classes of peace offering are spoken of, viz. for thanksgiving, or for a vow, or as a free-will offering. The flesh must be partaken of by the offerers (the priests having received their portion) and consumed on the first day in the case of the first-mentioned class, and by the close of the second day in the case of the others. The stress laid upon this command may set in clear light the obligatoriness of Divine instructions.

I. STRICT OBSERVANCE IS DEMANDED, EVEN THOUGH THE SIGNIFICANCE OF THE PRECEPT BE NOT PERCEIVED. Little explanation is afforded in the Law of the many ceremonies instituted. The Israelites were treated as children, whose chief virtue is unquestioning obedience. Why should the flesh be so quickly consumed? The devout Israelite might not know, yet must he rigidly conform to the order. He is not to reason, but to do. This course may be recommended to the many who wish a full explanation of the reasons for the institution of the ordinances connected with the Christian Church. Reliance may be placed upon the wisdom of the Divine Legislator, and faith rather than knowledge may glorify God. "The secret things" (the explanations, the reasons) "belong unto the Lord our God; but those things which are revealed" (the facts, the commands) "belong unto us for ever, that we may do all the words of the Law." That Jesus Christ has ordained Baptism and the Lord's Supper is sufficient to lead us to practise them, however confused may be our apprehension of the mysteries and principles involved. And in relation to the counsels addressed to us for the guidance of our lives, and the events that are seen to necessitate certain action upon our parts, it may still be said, "What I do thou knowest not now, but thou shalt know hereafter."

II. MORE LIGHT MAY BE EXPECTED TO DAWN UPON US CONTINUALLY AS TO THE MEANING OF DIVINE ORDINANCES. Faith is not intended to exclude or supersede knowledge, but to form a basis for it, an avenue through which it may pass to the mind, an appendix by which its volume may be supplemented. Patient and prayerful study is ever rewarded with keener appreciation of the will of God. If the Israelites reflected for a moment, they would call to mind warnings against desecrating holy things, and against treating what was offered to God as if it were a portion of common food. Surely God would distinguish thus between ordinary slaughter and sacrificial victims, and would guard against that additional risk of putrefaction to which flesh is liable in a hot climate, and which, if it occurred, would be an insult to his majesty. For us at any rate the types and ceremonies of Judaism have been interpreted by Christianity. The Great Prophet has revealed the obscure, and, endowed with his Spirit, apostles have been inspired to comment authoritatively upon the preceding dispensation. And we need not limit our aspirations after an intelligent perception of the meaning of Christian laws. Events as they occur, and reverent, persevering investigation, may unfold to us with increasing clearness the ways of God. But we ought not to delay observance of his precepts until their design is fully manifest. That servant is slothful who refuses to work by candle-light, and waits for the brightness of the sun.

III. PARTIAL DISOBEDIENCE NEUTRALIZES THE EFFECT OF A RELIGIOUS OBSERVANCE, AND MAY APPEAR MORE OFFENSIVE THAN TOTAL NEGLECT OF THE DIVINE COMMANDS. Let the worshipper trifle with the Law and venture to eat the flesh on the third day, and he shall find to his cost that the whole of his offering is rejected; it is not pleasing to God, and will not procure him favour. His effort proves useless, it shall not be reckoned to his credit. Worse still, his offering "shall be an abomination" in the eyes of God ; there shall be no grateful odour exhaled, but it shall be a stench in his nostrils. Sin has not been obliterated but augmented by the sacrifice. When the Earl of Oxford would honour King Henry VII. by the presence of a large body of retainers, the king only saw in the men an infraction of the law, and could not consent to have his laws broken in his sight. Honour and dishonour are an ill-assorted pair. The partially obedient worshipper shows himself as knowing God's will and doing it not. Total abstinence might have proclaimed him sinful through ignorance. Half-heartedness is often as productive of evil effects as flat rebellion. It is not for us to presume to say what may be disregarded and what not. To follow the Lord fully is the path of duty and of safety.—S. R. A.

Vers. 29—34.—*The threefold participation.* In the case of the peace offerings, there was a recognition of rights due to God, to his priests, and to the people presenting the victims.

I. THE PORTION RESERVED FOR GOD. The fat parts and the blood were not to be eaten by man ; the former must be burnt upon the altar, the latter poured out at its foot. *There are claims God will not waive.* The homage man owes to his Maker can never be remitted. Full trust and unfaltering obedience can be demanded only by an Infinite Being. *Life must be acknowledged as dependent upon him.* "The blood is the life," and for the Israelite to drink it is to be cut off from the congregation. *The choicest portions belong to God.* He will not put up with inferior parts. They mock him who fancy that a remnant of time and money and strength will suffice for his service.

II. THE SHARE ALLOTTED TO THE PRIESTS. *God takes care of his chosen servants,* provides amply for their wants. The priests devoted wholly to the work of the tabernacle shall not be forgotten, but considered as one with their Master, so that whenever he is honoured they shall be likewise thought of. To wear God's uniform is to be well cared for, to receive good wages, to be sure of a pension. Once taken into his employ, our future comfort is assured. And those who preach the gospel may claim to live by it. See this principle enunciated and inculcated in 1 Cor. ix. 7—14. *Variety is secured.* Food to eat, skins to wear. The atonement of the priest "covered" the sinner, and the covering of the animal was naturally appropriated to the use of the officiating priest. Both flour and flesh fell to the lot of the priests. *The quality shall not be inferior.* Portions are selected, the breast and the shoulder, which were counted as most delicate in flavour and nutritious in substance. Why should God's messengers yield to fear lest they should be neglected? He feedeth the ravens, clothes the lilies in splendour, and will not forsake those whom he has called to do his work in the world.

III. THE REMAINDER HANDED BACK TO THE PEOPLE. *We have not to do with an avaricious, unreasonable God.* He might justly have claimed the absolute disposal of all brought to his shrine as an offering, but he graciously received a "memorial" for himself and a portion for his ministers, and the rest was returned to the worshippers, consecrated, and for their festal enjoyment. Let us but acknowledge God's require-ments, and we shall find that we are not debarred from the innocent pleasures of life, but can enter upon them with sacred enhancing zest. By spending money in the purchase of ointment for the Saviour, Mary did not deprive herself of all her store, but rather increased the satisfaction with which she indulged in the customary household expenses. We are sure that the widow who cast her all into the treasury was not allowed to remain utterly destitute. She had really made a profitable investment of her little capital. Emptying her hands was only preparatory to having them filled.

How ennobling the thought of being sharers with God and his servants! We all partake of the same food, and are made "one bread and one body" (1 Cor. x. 17). There is a better sauce than hunger! It consists in previous dedication to God. Selfish exclusion of the rights of God diminishes the intensity and narrows the sphere of our delights. Not the miser, but the Christian donor, knows the joys of property.—S. R. A.

Vers. 1—8.—*The law of the trespass offering.* This, like the other offerings, was generally considered before (see chs. v. and vi. 1—7). The repetition here, according to Hebrew usage, gives emphasis and solemnity to the injunctions. The subject is reopened to show more particularly the duties and privileges of the priesthood concerning it. And we notice—

I. THAT THE TRESPASS OFFERING IS DESCRIBED AS MOST HOLY. 1. *It was most holy as typifying Christ.* (1) Intrinsically there could be neither sin nor holiness in the animal that was offered up. It was not a moral being. Nor could it be most holy in the sense of removing moral guilt; for it could not do this. For this purpose God never "required" it; never "desired" it (1 Sam. xv. 22; Ps. xl. 6; li. 16; Isa. i. 11; Hos. vi. 6; Heb. x. 1—4). (2) But the guilt offering of Calvary can literally "take sin away," and so accomplish the *will*, the *desire*, and the *requirement* of a just and merciful God (Ps. xl. 6—8; Heb. x. 4—10). Christ is therefore indeed "Most Holy;" and the guilt offering of the Law was so called putatively as typifying him. Accordingly, 2. *It was killed at the north side of the altar.* (1) "It is most holy. In the place where they kill the burnt offering shall they kill the trespass offering" (vers. 1, 2). But the burnt offering was killed at the north side of the altar (ch. i. 11). So was Calvary at the north side of Jerusalem. (2) Because this is given as a reason why the trespass offering was to be accounted "most holy," the Jews have countenance here for their tradition that the less holy sacrifices were slain at the south-west corner of the altar. 3. *It was eaten in the holy place.* (1) "Every male among the priests shall eat thereof: it shall be eaten in the holy place: it is most holy" (ver. 6). This was what the Jews distinguished as "the eating within the curtains," in allusion to the court of the tabernacle, which was enclosed with curtains. (2) In these feastings the priests cultivated fellowship; and the fellowship was religious in proportion as they had the vision of their faith clear to look to the end of the things to be abolished. Faith is the true principle of religious fellowship. (3) The females "among the priests" might eat of the "holy things;" but of the things distinguished as "most holy" they had no right to eat. Since the Fall down to the coming of the "Seed of the woman," a distinction between male and female was maintained, but now it is abolished. God's curse upon the woman has strangely been converted into the greatest blessing to mankind. Even in anger God is love.

II. SUNDRY DIRECTIONS GIVEN TO THE PRIESTS. 1, *With the blood of the guilt offering they were to sprinkle the altar.* (1) The altar was the raised platform upon which the sacrifices were offered up to God. The eminence of Calvary was, more particularly considered, the altar upon which the Great Sacrifice was offered. But in the grander sense, when the great universe is viewed, as Paul views it, as the true temple of God, the earth itself was the altar. The welfare of the universe is concerned in the death of Christ (Eph. i. 10; Phil. ii. 9, 10; Col. i. 20). (2) The sprinkling of the altar with the blood, in this view, would show that the earth, the common inheritance of man, which was cursed for his sake, is redeemed with the price of the precious blood of Jesus, And being redeemed by the *price* of his blood, it is destined also to be redeemed by the *power* of his arm (see Eph. i. 14; iv. 30). What glorious things are in reversion! (3) The Mishna records a tradition thus rendered by Bishop Patrick: "That there was a scarlet line which went round about the altar exactly in the middle, and the blood of the burnt offerings was sprinkled round about *above* the line, but that of the trespass offerings and peace offerings round about *below* it." But these traditions are generally refinements without authority. Let us be thankful for the "sure word of prophecy." 2. *They were to burn the fat upon the altar.* (1) Not the fat intermingled with the flesh. This was not offered upon the altar, except, of course, in the holocaust; nor was it forbidden as food. Had it been so, what embarrassments must tender consciences have suffered! There is nothing unreasonable in the service of God. (2) The fat burnt was chiefly that found in a detached state, viz.

the *omentum*, or *caul*, the fat of the *mesentery* and that about the *kidneys*, with the *rump* or *tail* of the sheep. This last was in the East so enormous that it had in some cases to be supported by a little cart fastened behind the animal (see Ludolf's 'History of Ethiopia,' p. 53). 3. *They had the privilege of claiming the skin* (vers. 7, 8). (1) This privilege probably dates from the days of Eden. Immediately after the Fall, our first parents covered themselves with the leaves of the fig, symbolically to express their sense of shame on account of their sin. In exchange for these, God graciously clothed them with skins, which we may presume were those of animals offered in sacrifice. Here, then, was the robe of an imputed righteousness to cover their sin and shame. (2) If these skins were those of animals offered in sacrifice, then Adam must have acted as a priest, and of course by Divine appointment. As a priest, then he would receive the skins. To this hour those descendants of Adam who act as spiritual priests are those who are invested with the robe of the righteousness of Christ.—J. A. M.

Vers. 9—15.—*The peace offering of thanksgiving.* At the conclusion of the instructions concerning the trespass offering, we have a few directions concerning the meat offering (vers. 9, 10). Whatever of it was dressed was to be given to the priest that offered it, to be consumed by himself and his family. But that "mingled with oil, and dry" was to be divided amongst the sons of Aaron. The reason appears to be economical. What was prepared would not keep, and was therefore to be consumed at once; that which would keep was to be divided, to be used according to convenience. The God of grace is also the God of providence. And his providence is especially concerned for those who seek his grace. After these notes, the law of the sacrifice of the peace offering is formally considered.

I. THE PEACE OFFERING OF THANKSGIVING. 1. *There is fitness in this association.* (1) The peace offering has its name, שלמים (*shelamim*), from שלם (*shalem*), to complete or make whole. It was instituted to express the manner in which our breaches of the covenant are made up by Christ. How the variance between God and man is composed through his atoning sacrifice! (2) What, then, more fitting than that we should express our thankfulness to God in connection with the peace offering? Praise breaks spontaneously from the heart that is "reconciled to God through the death of his Son" (see Isa. xii. 1). 2. *A bread offering accompanied this.* (1) One portion of this bread offering was unleavened (ver. 12). This portion was presented upon the altar. As leaven symbolized evil dispositions, no trace of it should be found in anything that touched God's altar (ch. ii. 11). (2) But the other portion was leavened (ver. 13). This portion was eaten by the worshipper, and expressed that he had evil dispositions that needed purging out. What a difference there is between the holy God and sinful man! What a merciful provision is that of the gospel of peace, that reconciles sinners to God!

II. THE THANKSGIVING IN THE HEAVE OFFERING. (Vers. 14, 15.) 1. *This was taken from the whole oblation.* (1) The word for *oblation*, משאת (*masseath*), denotes that which is borne or carried, from נשא (*nasa*), to bear or carry. It generally describes anything which was carried to the temple to be offered to God. It also expresses the design of all sacrifices to be the *carrying* or *bearing* of sin (see Exod. xxviii. 38; also ch. x. 17; xvi. 21). (2) In the offerings of the Law this was *typical*; but in the offering of Christ *real* (see Isa. liii. 4, 12; John i. 29, margin; 1 Pet. ii. 24). (3) From the number of these typical sin-bearers borne to the temple, the heave offering was to be taken. It was a representative of the whole of them, and suggested that what was specifically expressed in it might be predicated of any of them. 2. *It was lifted up in faith and gratitude to God.* (1) The heave offering had its name, תרומה (*terumah*), from רם (*rum*, to lift up), because it was *lifted up*, viz. toward heaven, by the priest. (2) This action expressed thankfulness to the source whence all blessings come to us, and especially those of redemption. Christ is the "Lord from heaven," the "heavenly gift" of a gracious Father (see John iii. 13, 16, 31; iv. 10; vi. 32, 33; 1 Cor. xv. 47; Heb. vi. 4). 3. *It became the priest's who sprinkled the blood of the peace offering.* (1) Those who make their peace with God through the blood of the cross not only offer thanks, but enjoy the blessings of thanksgiving. Thus a grateful heart is a "continual feast." (2) It was eaten the same day that it was offered. In the very act of thanksgiving to God for his blessings we are blessed. Those who in everything "give thanks" can "rejoice evermore" (1 Thess. v. 16—18). (3) It was shared by the priest in his own community (see Numb. xviii. 8, 11, 18, 19). Shared domestically. Shared religiously. The stranger had no part nor lot in the matter.—J. A. M.

Vers. 16—27.—*The sanctity of the service of God.* The peace offering may be offered for thanksgiving, in which case it has appropriate ceremonies (vers. 12—15). There is also the peace offering of a vow, the ceremonies of which are the same as those of the voluntary offering (ver. 16; also ch. xix. 5—8). In connection with this subject, we are admonished of the sanctity of the service of God; and similar admonitions are given in what follows.

I. WE SEE THIS SANCTITY IN THE SANCTIONS OF THE LAW OF THE PEACE OFFERING. 1. *Consider the precept.* (1) Look at it in the *letter.* "It shall be eaten the same day that he offereth his sacrifice." The same day in which the fat is burnt on the altar, the flesh is consumed by the worshipper and his friends. What remains must be eaten on the morrow. If any remain over to the third day, it must not then be eaten, but burnt with fire. (2) The first reason for this is *hygienic.* The flesh would, of course, be wholesome on the day it was killed, and so it would continue to be on the day following. But on the third day, in a hot climate, it would tend to corruption. The laws of health are well considered in the Levitical system, upon which account the study of that system may be commended to the votaries of social science. (3) But there must be a deeper reason still, else the penalties would not be so formidable as they are. The peace offering was undoubtedly a *type of Christ* in his passion (Eph. ii. 13—18). Our Lord was *two days* in the tomb after his death without seeing corruption. Then rising from the dead on the third day, the typical sacrifices of the Law, having answered their end, were abolished. This abolition was foreshadowed in the burning of what remained of the peace offering on the third day (1 Cor. xv. 3). To eat of the typical peace offering on the third day would be therefore highly improper, as it would suggest return to the "beggarly elements" *after* the "bringing in of the better hope" (Gal. iii. 3; iv. 9—11, 30, 31; v. 1—4). (4) If the "third day" represent the Christian dispensation in which typical sacrifices are done away, how are we to view the "two days" during which they were serviceable? There were exactly two great dispensations before the Christian, in which typical sacrifices were ordained, viz. first, the Patriarchal, from Adam to Moses; and secondly, the Levitical, from Moses to Christ. 2. *Consider the penalties.* (1) If the flesh of the peace offering be eaten on the third day, the sacrifice "shall not be accepted." The reason will now be obvious. In the third, or gospel, dispensation, there is a better Sacrifice. Typical sacrifices are now out of place and worthless, since the Antitype is come. (2) "It shall not be imputed to him that offereth it." The typical sacrifices were useful in procuring the "forbearance of God" until the true atonement should be made; but now it is made, Christ will profit *them* nothing who return to the Law. (3) "He shall bear his sin." He shall be treated as the sacrifice was treated. He shall himself be sacrificed for his own sin.

II. THIS SANCTITY IS FURTHER SEEN IN THE PENALTIES IMPOSED IN OTHER CASES. Thus: 1. *When the flesh of sacrifice is unlawfully eaten.* (1) This would happen if it had touched "any unclean thing" (ver. 19). Instead of being eaten, it should then be "burnt with fire." The teaching is that an unclean thing is of no use for purposes of atonement. The sacrifice of Christ could not be accepted were he not immaculate. (2) It would happen if the eater were unclean. "As for the flesh, all that be clean shall eat thereof" (Hebrew, "The flesh of all that is clean shall eat the flesh"), *i.e.* every clean person shall eat the flesh of his peace offering. As Christ is without spot of sin, so is his flesh meat only to the holy. "But the soul" etc. (vers. 20, 21). To the wicked, the very gospel becomes the savour of death (1 Cor. xi. 29; 2 Cor. ii. 15, 16). 2. *When holy things are profaned.* (1) When the fat is eaten (ver. 23)—the fat of such animals as were offered in sacrifice. There is no law against the eating of the fat of the roebuck or the hart. And that portion of the fat which was offered in sacrifice. The fat mingled with the flesh, which was not burnt on the altar, was not forbidden. There must be the most careful avoidance of whatever would profane the sacrifice of Christ. The fat even of an animal of the sacrificial kind, which by any accident might be rendered unfit for sacrifice, must not be eaten (ver. 24). The moral here is that the very appearance of evil must be avoided. (2) When the blood is eaten. This law is universal. Blood, viz. of every description of animal, is forbidden. The Jews properly expound this law as forbidding the *blood of the life* as distinguished from the *gravy*. And the reason given for the prohibition is that the life maketh atonement for the life. Our life, which is redeemed by the life of Jesus sacrificed for us, must be *wholly* given to God. The highest sanctity is associated with the blood of Christ. (3) "That soul shall be cut off from his people" (vers. 20, 21, 25, 27). The penalty in all these cases is extreme. It means separation from religious and civil privileges, if not also death. The penalties of the Mosaic Law terminated in the death of the body; but "a much sorer punishment" is reserved for those who despise and desecrate the blood of Christ (Heb. x. 28, 29).—J. A. M.

Vers. 28—38.—*The service of the oblation.* In the service of the oblation of the peace offering there are two actors, viz. the offerer and the priest. These had their respective duties, which are severally brought under our notice in the text. We have—

I. THE DUTY OF THE OFFERER. 1. *He had to bring his oblation unto the Lord.* (1) The "oblation" here is not the "sacrifice," but "*of the* sacrifice" (vers. 28—30). It was that portion of the sacrifice which, more especially, was claimed by God, viz. the fat prescribed to be burnt upon the altar. It included also the breast and right shoulder. (2) This he was to bring in person. "His own hands shall bring the offerings of the Lord made by fire," etc. This requisition is so express that even women, who under other circumstances never entered the court of the priests, did so when they had offerings to bring. The Hebrew name for oblation (קָרְבָּן, *korban*) is derived from a root (קָרַב, *koreb*) which signifies to approach or draw near. By the introduction of our Great High Priest, we personally, under the gospel, "approach" or "draw nigh" unto God (see Heb. vii. 19; x. 21, 22). We cannot save our souls by proxy. We cannot acceptably serve God by proxy. 2. *He had to bring the fat laid upon the breast.* (1) What our version construes "the fat *with* the breast" (ver. 30), may be better rendered, as it is by the learned Julius Bate, "the fat *upon* the breast," *i.e.* laid upon the breast (comp. ch. viii. 26, 27). The breast was that appointed to be waved before the Lord; and it would appear that it was waved with the fat laid upon it. The breast was the natural symbol of *heartiness* and *willingness*. This action would, therefore, express the cheerful and grateful willingness of the offerer, and his earnest desire that his offering might be graciously accepted. What we devote to God should be heartily given (2 Cor. ix. 7). (2) The "heave shoulder" was also brought. This was the right shoulder. It had its name from the ceremony in which it was moved up and down before the Lord. As the "breast" symbolized *affection*, so the "shoulder" expressed *action*, and the "right" shoulder, action of the most *efficient* kind. Love expresses itself in deeds (Matt. xxii. 37—40; Luke vi. 46; Rom. xiii. 9; Gal. v. 14; Jas. ii. 8).

II. THE DUTY OF THE PRIEST. 1. *He had to offer up the oblation.* (1) The Mishna says this was done by the priest placing his hands under those of the offerer, upon which the wave breast was laid, and then moving them to and fro. The priest certainly had a hand in the ceremony of waving the breast (see Numb. vi. 20). And if we regard him as a type of Christ in this, then the teaching appears to be that we should look to Jesus to sustain the fervency of our love in the offering of our oblations of prayer and praise and service. (2) The priest in the next place, it appears, offered up the fat in the fire of the altar (ver. 31). Then the right shoulder was "given to the priest for an heave offering" (ver. 32). This, we are told, was moved up and down. Thus these motions of the wave breast and heave shoulder were at right angles, and so they formed the figure of a cross. Houbigant thinks that by this "was adumbrated the cross upon which that Peace Offering of the human race was lifted up, which was prefigured by all the ancient victims" (comp. John xxi. 18, 19; 2 Pet. i. 14; together with the historical tradition concerning the crucifixion of Peter). 2. *The breast and shoulder were then claimed by the priest.* (1) They had these by a Divine ordinance (vers. 31—34). They were first given to God, and now became God's gift to his ministers. What is given to sustain the ministry should not be regarded by the giver as a gratuity, but as a service loyally and faithfully rendered to God (see Numb. xviii. 20—24). Ministers should receive their support as from the hand of God (see 2 Cor. ix. 11; Phil. iv. 18). (2) They had it by a birthright. It was given to "Aaron and his sons." Those who were not sons of Aaron had no part nor lot in the matter. And true ministers of the gospel must be sons of Jesus; they must be spiritually born, or they are intruders into sacred functions (see Ps. l. 16; Acts i. 25; Rom. i. 5; 1 Tim. i. 12; 2 Tim. iv. 5). (3) They had it also by consecration. The sons of Aaron, though as their birthright were served from the altar, had no title to serve the altar until anointed for that service. So the birth of the Spirit, by which we become sons of Jesus, does not alone constitute ministers. For the ministry they must have a special vocation. Note: "Aaron presented his sons to minister unto the Lord," in which he acted as the type of Christ, who calls and qualifies those he sends. If the harvest be plenteous and the labourers few, the more urgently should we "pray the Lord of the harvest that *he* would send forth labourers."—J. A. M.

Vers. 1—10.—*Emphatic truths* or *things God lays stress upon.* The great particularity and the occasional repetition shown in these ordinances point to the truth that God desired his people to attach very great weight to them. His servants were to understand that he laid great stress upon—

I. THE WAY IN WHICH HE WAS APPROACHED IN WORSHIP. Distinctions were drawn beween different offerings, the import of which we now find it hard to trace. Though, indeed, it is stated that "as the sin offering so the trespass offering; there is one law for them" (ver. 7), yet there were differences in the way in which the blood was disposed of by the priests, etc. (cf. ver. 2 and ch. iv. 6, 7). Minute details were entered into respecting the disposal of the various parts of the animal (vers. 3, 4, 8). Precise directions were given regarding the eating of the offerings by the priests (vers. 5, 9, 10). It appears to us that there must have been but very faint moral significance in these arrangements to the mind of the Hebrew worshipper. But if this were so, the very particularity of the precepts indicated God's determination that his people should show the utmost vigilance and attention in their approaches to himself. We may wisely learn therefrom that, though our Divine Master has left all details in worship to our spiritual discernment, he is far from indifferent to the way in which we approach him. We should show the utmost care: 1. *To draw nigh to his throne of grace in a right spirit*—a spirit of reverence, trust, expectation, holy joy. 2. *To use those methods of approach which are most likely to foster the true spirit of worship*—having enough of simplicity to favour spirituality of mind; having, at the same time, enough of art and effort to meet the cultivated tastes of all who take part in devotion.

II. THE FACT THAT SIN MEANS DEATH IN HIS SIGHT. The first "law of the trespass offering" (ver. 1) relates to the killing of the animal and the sprinkling of its blood "round about the altar" (ver. 2). *The* thing in these sacrifices is the application of the blood for atonement : no offering on the altar, no eating of the flesh, until life had been taken, until blood had been shed and sprinkled. The sinner must own his worthiness of death for his trespass, and, if he is to find acceptance, must bring a victim, whose life shall be forfeited instead of his own, whose atoning blood shall make peace with God. This is the foundation truth of Old Testament sacrifices; it is the ground truth of the sacrifice on Calvary.

III. THE TRUTH THAT OUR VERY BEST, OUR OWN SELF, IS TO BE CONSECRATED TO GOD. The best of the slain animals, the vital parts, had to be presented in holy sacrifice on the altar (vers. 3—5). When the atoning blood has brought reconciliation, we are to present our best, our very selves, in acceptable sacrifice to our Saviour.

IV. THE TRUTH THAT ALL WHICH IS PRESENTED TO GOD IS TO BE REGARDED AS HOLY IN HIS SIGHT. Only the priests might eat of the flesh of the offered animal, and they only "in the holy place," for "it is most holy" (ver. 6). Everything became holy when brought to "the door of the tabernacle" and presented to Jehovah. When we dedicate ourselves to his service in the act of self-surrender, we yield everything to him. And then: 1. *Our bodies* become a living sacrifice (Rom. xii. 1; 1 Cor. vi. 13, 20). 2. *Our whole lives* are to be lived and spent before him as holy (1 Cor. x. 31).—C.

Vers. 14, 28—34.—*The kingdom of God: lessons from the heave offering.* The ceremony of the heave offering and wave offering was a striking incident in the rite of the peace offering. "According to Jewish tradition it was performed by laying the parts on the hands of the offerer, and the priest, putting his hands again underneath, then moving them in a horizontal direction for the waving and in a vertical one for the heaving . . . the waving was peculiarly connected with the breast, which is thence called the wave breast (ver. 31), and the heaving with the shoulder, for this reason called the heave shoulder" (ver. 34). The main truth to which this symbolic act pointed was probably—

I. GOD'S UNIVERSAL SOVEREIGNTY. As these parts of the animal were solemnly directed upwards and downwards and laterally, in all directions, the offerer intimated his belief that the realm of Jehovah was a boundless kingdom, reaching to the heavens above, to the dark regions below, to every corner and quarter of the earth. We do well to meditate on the truth thus pictorially presented; but in so doing we are necessarily reminded how much more we have learned both from revelation and human science of the wide reach of his reign. We may think of his Divine kingdom as including: 1. Heaven and all its worlds and inhabitants. 2. Hades—the grave and those who have "gone to the grave." 3. The earth and all that is thereon: (1) all human beings; (2) all unintelligent creatures; (3) all vegetable life; (4) all inanimate treasure—gold, silver, etc. We are reminded of the propriety of—

II. OUR FORMAL RECOGNITION OF THIS FACT. The Hebrew worshipper was encouraged to bring his peace offering to the altar, and then to go through this simple but suggestive ceremony, thus formally acknowledging the truth. No similar provision is made for our utterance of it; but it is open to us to declare it in sacred words and in most solemn forms: 1. *In adoration.* "Thine, O Lord, is the greatness and the power . . . for all that is in the heaven and in the earth is thine," etc. (1 Chron. xxix. 10, 11; 1 Tim. i. 17; Deut. x. 14; Ps. xxiv. 1). 2. *In praise.* When we "sing unto the Lord," there should be full and frequent ascription of everything "in the heavens above and the earth beneath" to him as the Author and Owner and Ruler of all. We also see—

III. OUR APPROPRIATE ACTION THEREUPON. The Jewish worshipper was directed to "wave" and "heave" the breast and shoulder; these joints in particular and in preference to any other, "probably from their being considered the more excellent parts." When the fat had been burned upon the altar (ver. 31), these joints were reserved "unto Aaron the priest and unto his sons for ever" (ver. 34). We gather therefrom that we are to make practical recognition of the truth that God's kingdom extends everywhere, and includes every one, by: 1. Dedicating our best to his service: *our affections* (suggested by the breast); *our strength* (suggested by the shoulder). 2. Bringing our offerings to his cause—for the support of those who minister in holy things, and for the maintenance of those various agencies which are working for the glory of his Name.—C.

Vers. 11—18, 30.—*Four thoughts on sacred service.* We gather from these words—

I. THAT THERE IS A JOYOUS AND SOCIAL ELEMENT IN SACRED SERVICE. There were not only sin and burnt offerings, but also meat and peace offerings, in the Hebrew ritual. Those who were reconciled unto God might rejoice, and might rejoice *together*, before him. They might hold festive gatherings as his servants and as his worshippers; they might eat flesh which had been dedicated to him, and bread, even *leavened* bread (ver. 13), and they were to "rejoice in their feast" (Deut. xvi. 14). The prevailing tone of the true Christian life is that of sacred joy. Even at the remembrance of the Saviour's death humility and faith are to rise into holy joy.

> "Around a *table*, not a *tomb*,
>   He willed our gathering-place should be.
> When going to prepare our home,
>   Our Saviour said, 'Remember me.' "

Whether in ordinary worship, or at "the table of the Lord," or in any other Christian festival, we are to "rejoice before the Lord" together.

II. THAT THERE IS A SPONTANEOUS AS WELL AS A STATUTORY element in sacred service. "*If* he offer it for a thanksgiving then *he shall* offer," etc. (ver. 12). "*If* the sacrifice . . . be a vow, or a voluntary offering, it *shall* be eaten," etc. (ver 16). God's Law says, "*thou shalt*," but it finds room for "*if thou shalt*." There are many things compulsory, and we have nothing to do but cheerfully and unquestioningly obey. There are also many things optional, and we may allow ourselves to act as devotional and generous impulses may move us. The mind which is constitutionally legal should cultivate the spontaneous in worship and benefaction; the impulsive must remember that there are statutes as well as suggestions in the Word of God.

III. THAT THERE MAY BE NOT ONLY FUTILITY BUT EVEN GUILT in connection with sacred service. Disregard of the prohibition to eat on the third day entirely vitiated the worthiness of the offering: in such case it would "not be accepted," neither "imputed unto him that offered it;" it would be counted "an abomination," and the soul that so acted was to "bear his iniquity" (ver. 18). The service we seek to render God may be: 1. Wholly vitiated so as to be entirely unacceptable, and draw down no blessing from above; or may even be: 2. Positively offensive in the sight of God, and add to our guilt, if it be (1) unwilling, grudging; (2) unspiritual, soulless; (3) slovenly, careless, the offering of our exhaustion instead of our energy; (4) ostentatious or (still worse) hypocritical; (5) much mixed with worldly, or vindictive, or base thoughts.

IV. THAT PERSONAL SPIRITUAL PARTICIPATION IS NECESSARY in sacred service. "His own hands shall bring the offerings" (ver. 30). God would be approached by His people themselves, and though he had graciously granted human mediation in the form of a sacrificing priesthood, yet he desired that every Israelite who had an offering to present should bring it with his own hand to the door of the tabernacle. Religion is a personal thing. We may accept human ministry, but we must come ourselves to God in direct, immediate devotion and dedication. Every man here must bear his own burden (Gal. vi. 5). There is a point beyond which the most ardent affection, the most earnest solicitude, the most burning zeal cannot go—for others. They must, themselves, approach in reverence, bow in penitence, look up in faith, yield in self-surrender, present daily sacrifices of gratitude, obedience, submission.—C.

Vers. 20, 21.—*Divine and human severity.* There is something almost startling in the closing words, "That soul shall be cut off from his people." It suggests thoughts of—

I. APPARENT DIVINE SEVERITY. 1. *That God sometimes seems to be severe in his dealings with men.* These particular injunctions must have had to the Jews an aspect of rigour. An Israelite excommunicated for one of these offences probably felt that he had been hardly dealt with. God's dealings have an occasional aspect of severity (see Rom. xi. 22). So with us. In his providence comparatively slight faults, errors, transgressions, are sometimes followed by most serious evils—disgrace, sorrow, loss, death. 2. *That the light of after-days often explains his dealing with us.* We can see now that the paramount and supreme importance of maintaining the purity of Israel, its separateness from all the abominations of surrounding heathendom, made the most stringent regulations on that subject necessary and wise, and therefore kind. So with us. Looking back on the way by which we have been led, we frequently see that that very thing which at the time was not only distressing but perplexing, was the most signal act of the Divine wisdom and goodness, the providential ordering for which, above every other thing, we now give thanks. 3. *That present faith should rise to the realization that, somewhere in the future, apparent severity will bear the aspect of wise and holy love.* "What we know not now we shall know hereafter." "Then shall we know," etc. (1 Cor. xiii. 12).

II. OCCASIONAL HUMAN SEVERITY. 1. *That we are sometimes obliged to seem severe* towards those for whom we are responsible. (1) The statesman is obliged to introduce a severe measure; (2) a father to take a strong and energetic course; (3) a Church to excommunicate a member. 2. *That apparent severity is sometimes the only rightful course* which wise and holy love can take. It is the action which is (1) due to itself (Jas. iii. 17); (2) due to the object of its affection (1 Tim. i. 20).—C.

Vers. 15—17.—*Three features of acceptable service.* We have commanded or suggested here—

I. CAREFUL PRESERVATION OF PURITY. The "flesh of the sacrifice of his peace offering" was to be eaten on the very day of its presentation (ver. 15); that of another kind of offering might be eaten partly on the day following (ver. 16), but on no account might anything offered in sacrifice be partaken of on the third day (vers. 17, 18). It was one of the objects, probably the primary intention, of this restriction, that nothing offered to God should be allowed to become unsound. No danger was to be incurred in the way of putrefaction. Another statute in defence of purity in worship! In the service of the Holy One of Israel we must be pure in thought, in word, in act. He is "of purer eyes than to behold evil," etc. (Hab. i. 13), and can find no pleasure in any service tainted with iniquity. The connection in which this restriction occurs suggests that, especially in those religious engagements in which we find social pleasure, we should be careful to maintain purity of spirit, integrity of heart.

II. CAREFUL RETENTION OF SACREDNESS OF THOUGHT. The partaking of the flesh and the bread which had been presented to God, though these were eaten at home, was to be regarded as a sacred act. It was sacramental. Therefore it was fitting that no great interval of time should come between the act of presentation and the consumption. For the consequence would inevitably be that the sacred festival would tend to sink to the level of an ordinary meal. Sacred thoughts would be less vivid and less frequent; the engagement would become more secular and more simply social as more time intervened. We learn that we should take the greatest care to retain in our mind the sense of the sacredness of religious acts during their performance. When they become mechanical, or wholly bodily, or simply social; when the realization of the religious and the Divine element falls out, then their virtue is gone; they are no longer "an acceptable offering unto the Lord." We must accomplish this end by: 1. Studious spiritual endeavour to realize what we are doing. 2. By wise precautions, judicious measures, which will tend to preserve sanctity and to guard against secularity of thought.

III. UNSELFISHNESS IN RELIGIOUS SERVICE. The commandment to consume everything within one or two days pointed to an increase in the number of partakers; it suggested the calling together friends and dependents; also the invitation of the poor and needy. This was not only the design but the effect of the injunction (see Deut. xii. 18; xvi. 11). The Israelites, in "eating before the Lord," showed a generous hospitality while they were engaged in an act of piety and of sacred joy. Let unselfishness be a prominent feature in our religious institutions. It is well to remember: 1. That selfishness is apt to show itself here as elsewhere. 2. That it is never so inconsistent and unsightly as in connection with the service of God. 3. That it is a painful exhibition to the Lord of love. 4. That the more generous and self-forgetting we are in sacred things, the more we approach the spirit and life of our Divine Exemplar (Phil. ii. 4—8).—C.

Vers. 1—10.—The trespass offering, burnt offering, and meat offering, affording *support to the minister of the sanctuary and occasion for feasting.*

I. It is the intent of true religion that those consecrated to its service should be provided for liberally.

II. Acknowledgment of sin and atonement made lead to rejoicing, and the festival life of man grows out of reconciliation with God.

III. TYPICALLY; Christ the High Priest is rewarded in the sanctification of his people. " He shall see of the travail of his soul, and be satisfied."—R.

Vers. 11—21.—The peace offerings and thank offerings. The unleavened bread and the leavened bread, both offered. The offerings must be quickly eaten, and all uncleanness must be avoided as iniquity. Thus are taught—

I. THE DUTY OF THANKFULNESS. 1. It should be *cheerful*, glad, pure, speedy. 2. It should be *religious*, expressed towards God as the Author and Giver of every good gift. 3. It should be *social*, recognizing both the house of God and family life.

II. THE NECESSITY OF HOLINESS in all things and at all times. Thanks—vows—voluntary offerings;—in all there must be separation to God, and from the corrupt and unclean. 1. In nothing more need of *vigilance* than in expressing the heart's more joyful feelings. Possibility of prolonging the joy till it becomes corrupt. Hilarity overbalancing the soul. Intemperance in enjoyments. 2. *The uncleanness of the world is apt to cling to us.* We should especially watch against carrying the impure spirit into the sanctuary. The mind should be free, the heart calm, the soul hungering and thirsting after spiritual delights, when, on the Lord's day, we enter the courts of his house to offer sacrifice. 3. Fellowship with God's ministers and his services. One voice, but many hearts. True mediation when all alike by faith depending on Christ.—R.

Vers. 22—27.—*Instructions for the people on the fat and on the blood.* The prohibition of fat was to secure *the rights of Jehovah* from invasion. The fat was a gift sanctified to God. The prohibition of the blood was to keep up the idea of *atonement*, the blood being regarded as the soul of the animal which God had appointed as the medium of atonement for the soul of man. Here is—

I. THE SUPREMACY OF THE DIVINE CLAIMS. 1. The recognition by the conscience in *doctrine*, in the place religion holds in the *life*. 2. *The social state* should be regulated on this principle. Man must not invade God's rights if he would retain God's blessing. Observance of the sabbath. The law of nations rests on the Law of God. 3. The *individual believer* will take care that he robs God of nothing. His service demands the fat, the choicest faculties, the deepest feelings, the largest gifts.

II. THE RIGHTEOUSNESS OF GOD MADE THE RIGHTEOUSNESS OF MAN. Life for life. The blood sanctified, the blood saved. On the foundation of a perfect reconciliation alone can a true humanity be preserved and developed. Mistake of the ancient Greeks in worshipping *humanity unredeemed*, leading to animalism, and eventually to the substitution of mere art for morality, therefore the degradation of humanity. The elevation of the soul is the elevation of the whole man; " Im ganzen, guten, schoenen resolut zu leben," is a motto only to be adopted in the Christian sense. " He that saveth his life shall lose it ; " he that offers it up to God shall redeem it.—R.

Vers. 28—38.—The *wave breast* and the *heave shoulder* given to the priests. God's share and his ministers' share must be both *fully given* and *carefully set aside* and *publicly offered up. Generous support of the sanctuary.*

I. SERVICE OF GOD'S HOUSE REQUIRES SPECIAL OFFERINGS; which should be: 1. Large and freely bestowed. Reciprocal blessings; those that give receive, and as they give, they receive. 2. The ministry should be so provided for that the service rendered be joyful and unrestrained. 3. The subordinate arrangements of the sanctuary should partake of the cheerfulness which flows from abundance. A festival of worship.

II. SANCTIFICATION OF GIFTS. Both by personal preparation and by systematic beneficence. Lay aside for God as we are prospered. God's claims should precede all others. The blessing of the sanctuary overflows into common life.

III. PUBLICITY A POWERFUL STIMULUS AND A BINDING PLEDGE. *Waving* and *heaving* represented extent and elevation. Much in example. Our gifts should not be ostentatiously published, but yet, if held up to God, and so presented as to set forth the universality of our consecration to him, they will both glorify his Name and incite others to his service.—R.

PART II.

THE INSTITUTION OF AN HEREDITARY PRIESTHOOD

EXPOSITION.

CHAPTER VIII.

THE CONSECRATION OF AARON AND HIS SONS is the natural sequel of the foregoing division of the book. The sacrificial system, which had now been instituted in its completeness, required a priesthood to administer it. Originally the head of each Hebrew family was priest to his own household, to offer gifts betokening self-surrender and communion with God—burnt sacrifices and sacrifices similar in character to the peace offerings. The first step from hence to the hereditary priesthood was the hallowing the firstborn of the Israelites to God's service, after the Israelitish firstborn had been delivered from the destruction which fell upon the firstborn of Egypt (Numb. iii. 13). The second was the substitution of the tribe of Levi for the firstborn (Numb. iii. 41—45), on account of the zeal which the Levites exhibited above the other tribes at the time of the idolatry of the golden calf (Exod. xxxii. 26). Now, out of the tribe of Levi is chosen the one family of Aaron, to form an hereditary priesthood, consisting at first of five persons, quickly reduced to three by the death of Nadab and Abihu. This small body would have been sufficient for the needs of the people while they were still in the wilderness, and leading the life of the camp. With the increase of the nation the family of Aaron and his sons increased likewise, until, in the time of David, it was necessary to subdivide it into twenty-four courses for the orderly fulfilment of the functions of the priesthood. As the institution of the priesthood was necessary for carrying out the sacrificial system, so the sacrifices were necessary for the consecration of the priests. By means of the sacrifices the priests are consecrated, Moses performing on the occasion, and for the last time, the priestly functions. Appended to the record of their consecration is an account of the first acts of the newly created priests (ch. ix.), and of the death of two of them (ch. x.). This is the only historical section in the book; and the death of the blasphemer (ch. xxiv.) is the only other historical event recorded in it, if at least we except such passages as, " And he did as the Lord commanded Moses " (ch. xvi. 34; xxi. 24; xxiii. 44).

Vers. 1—5.—These verses contain the preliminaries of the ceremony of consecration. Aaron and his sons are to be brought to the door of the tabernacle, together with all that is necessary for the performance of the rite that is about to take place. The words in the second verse, **a bullock for the sin offering, and two rams, and a basket of unleavened bread,** should be translated, *the bullock for the sin offering and the two rams and the basket.* **The garments, the** anointing oil, *the bullock, the two rams,* and *the basket of unleavened bread* and cakes, had all been previously enjoined, when Moses was on the mount (Exod. xxviii., xxix., xxx.). These previous injunctions are referred to in the words, **This is the thing which the Lord commanded to be done** (ver. 5).

Ver. 6.—Washing, robing, anointing, sacrificing, are the four means by the joint operation of which the consecration is effected. The washing, or bathing, took place in the sight of the people. The whole of the person, except so much as was covered by the linen drawers (Exod. xxviii. 42), **was washed.** The symbolical significance is clear. Cleansing from sin precedes clothing in righteousness and spiritual unction.

Vers. 7—9.—The robing. The various articles of the priestly dress had been appointed and described before (Exod. xxviii., xxix.). In these verses we see the order in which they were put on. After the priests had, no doubt, changed their linen drawers, there came, first, **the coat,** that is, a close-fitting tunic of white linen, made with sleeves and covering the whole body; next **the girdle of the tunic,** that is, a linen sash for tying the tunic round the body, with variegated ends hanging on each side to the ankles; thirdly, **the robe**, that is, a blue vesture, woven of one piece, with holes for the head and arms to pass through, reaching from the neck to below the knee, the bottom being ornamented with blue, purple, and scarlet pomegranates, alternating with golden bells; fourthly, **the ephod**, which consisted of two shoulder-pieces, or epaulettes, made of variegated linen and gold thread, fastened together in front and at the back by a narrow strap or band, from which hung, before and behind the wearer, two pieces of cloth confined below by **the curious girdle of the ephod**, that is, by a sash made of the same material as the ephod itself. Into the ephod were sewn two onyxes, one on each shoulder, in gold filigree settings, one of them engraven with the names of half of the tribes, and the other with the remaining half; and from two rosettes or buttons by the side of these stones depended twisted gold chains for the support of the breastplate. Fifth came **the breastplate**, which was a square pocket, made of embroidered linen, a span long and a span broad, worn upon the breast and hanging from the gold chains above mentioned, the lower ends of the gold chain being tied to two rings at the upper and outer corner of the breastplate, while the upper and inner corner of the same was attached to the ephod by blue thread running through two sets of rings in the breastplate and ephod respectively. The outer side of the breastplate was stiffened and adorned by twelve precious stones, set in four rows of three, each stone having on it the name of one of the tribes of Israel. The breastplate being double and the two sides and the bottom being sewn up, the pocket formed by it had its opening at the top. Into this pocket were placed **the Urim and the Thummim**, which were probably two balls of different colours, one of which on being drawn out indicated the approval of God, and the other his disapproval, as to any point on which the high priest consulted him. (The Jewish tradition, that the Divine answer by the Urim and the Thummim came by a supernatural light thrown on certain letters in the names of the tribes, has no foundation.) The last part of the dress to be put on was **the mitre**, or head-dress of linen, probably of the nature of a turban; to which, by a blue string, was attached **the golden plate**, in such a way that it rested lengthwise on the forehead, and on this plate or **holy crown** were inscribed the words, " Holiness to the Lord." The investiture took place **as the Lord commanded Moses**, that is, in accordance with the instructions given in Exod. xxviii.

Its purpose and its meaning in the eyes of the people would have been twofold: first, after the manner of the king's crown and the judge's robe, it served to manifest the fact that the function of priest was committed to the wearer; and next, it symbolized the necessity of being clothed upon with the righteousness of God, in order to be able to act as interpreter and mediator between God and man, thus foreshadowing the Divine Nature of him who should be the Mediator in antitype.

Vers. 10, 11.—The anointing is still more specifically the means of consecration than the investing or the washing. (For **the anointing oil**, which is here referred to as a thing well known, see Exod. xxx, 22—25, where its component parts are designated.) The consecration of things as well as of persons is sanctioned by the action of Moses, who **anointed the tabernacle and all that was therein, and sanctified them.** They were thus set apart for holy purposes. By *all that was therein* would be meant the ark, the vail, the altar of incense, the candlesticks, the table of shew-bread. After the tabernacle and its furniture had been anointed, **the altar**—that is, the brazen altar—**and all his vessels, both the laver and his foot, sprinkled**; not once only, as the things within the tabernacle, but **seven times**, to show that it was specially holy, although situated only in the court. *The laver*, for the priests' use, was between the door of the tabernacle and the brazen altar of burnt offering. Its *foot*, or base, is described in Exod. xxxviii, 8, as made, according to the translation of the Authorized Version, " of brass, of the looking-glasses of the women assembling, which assembled at the door of the tabernacle."

Ver. 12.—**He poured of the anointing oil upon Aaron's head.** The change of the verb *poured* for *sprinkled*, indicates that the amount of " the precious ointment" poured " upon the head, that ran down unto the beard, and went down to the skirts of his garments " (Ps. cxxxiii. 2), was far greater than that with which the furniture of the tabernacle had been anointed. The oil sprinkled on the holy things sanctified them as means of grace. The oil poured upon Aaron represents the grace of the Holy Spirit, coming from without, but diffusing itself over and throughout the whole consecrated man.

Ver. 13.—The investiture of **Aaron's sons** —Nadab, Abihu, Eleazar, Ithamar—follows the consecration of their father. They are robed, according **as the Lord commanded Moses** in Exod. xxviii. 40, in the white tunic, the sash, and the cap. But there is no statement here of their being anointed, although their anointing is ordered in Exod.

xxviii. 41, and still more imperatively in Exod. xl. 15. They are spoken of as "anointed" in ch. vii. 36, and as having "the anointing oil of the Lord upon them" in ch. x. 7. On the other hand, the high priest is specially designated as "the priest that is anointed" (ch. iv. 3). It is probable that the personal anointing of the ordinary priests was confined to their being sprinkled with oil, as described below in ver. 30; but that they were regarded as virtually anointed in Aaron's anointing. The Levites had no special dress until they obtained permission from Herod Agrippa II. to wear the priestly robes (Joseph., 'Ant.,' xx. 9, 6).

Vers. 14—32.—After the bathing, the robing, and the anointing, follow the sacrifices of consecration—the sin offering (vers. 14—17), the burnt offering (vers. 18—21), the peace offering (vers. 22—32).

Ver. 14.—**The sin offering.** This was the first sin offering ever offered. There had been burnt offerings and sacrifices akin to peace offerings before, but no sin offerings. At once the sin offering takes its place as the first of the three sacrifices before the burnt offerings and peace offerings. Justification comes first, then sanctification, and, following upon them, communion with God. The victim offered by and for Aaron and his sons is a bullock, the same animal that is appointed for the offering of the high priest (ch. iv. 3).

Vers. 15—17.—**And Moses took the blood.** Moses continues still to act as priest, and the new sacrifice is once offered by him. He performs the priestly act of presenting the blood; but on this occasion, which is special, the blood is not dealt with in the manner prescribed for the high priest's offerings (ch. iv. 6). The reason of this is that Aaron was not yet high priest, and also that the offering was made not only for Aaron, but also for his sons; and further, the blood as well as the anointing oil was required to purify the altar, and sanctify it (see Heb. ix. 21). Although the blood was not "brought into the tabernacle," yet the bullock was burnt with fire without the camp, not eaten according to the rule of ch. vii. 26, 30. This was necessary, as there were as yet no priests to eat it.

Vers. 18—21.—There is no deviation on the present occasion from the ritual appointed for the burnt offering. After the sin offering, righteousness is symbolically imputed to Aaron; after the burnt offering, holiness; then follows the peace offering of the ram, which completes and sacrificially effects the consecration.

Vers. 22—29.—The ram offered as a peace offering is called **the ram of consecration,** or literally, *of filling,* because one of the means by which the consecration was effected and exhibited was the filling the hands of those presented for consecration with the portion of the sacrifice destined for the altar, which they **waved for a wave offering before the Lord,** previous to its consumption by the fire. This portion consisted of the internal fat and tail, which was usually burnt (ch. vii. 31), and the heave offering of **the right shoulder,** or hind leg, which generally went to the officiating priest (ch. vii. 32), and one of each of the unleavened cakes. After this special ceremony of waving, peculiar to the rite of consecration, the usual wave offering (the breast) was waved by Moses and consumed by himself. Ordinarily it was for the priests in general (ch. vii. 31). The blood was poured on the side of the altar, as was done in all peace offerings, but in addition, on the present occasion, it was put upon the tip of the **right ear, and upon the thumb of the right hand, and upon the great toe of the right foot** of the priests who were being consecrated, symbolizing that their senses and active powers were being devoted to God's service. The same ceremony is to be used in the restoration of the leper (see ch. xiv. 14).

Ver. 30.—The sprinkling with oil and blood completes the ceremony of anointing, and suffices of itself for the sons of Aaron, in addition to their virtual participation in the anointing of their father (ver. 12). "In the mingling of the blood and oil for the anointing seems to be taught that not sacrifice for sin alone suffices; but that with this must be joined the unction of the Holy Spirit" (Gardiner).

Vers. 31, 32.—The flesh of the peace offering is given to Aaron and his sons to eat, not in the capacity of priests (for the peace offerings were not eaten by the priests), but as the offerers of the sacrifice.

Vers. 33—36.—The sacrificial ceremonies were repeated for **seven days,** during which Aaron and his sons remained in the court of the tabernacle, but did not enter the holy place, abstaining throughout that time from ministering, as the apostles did during the interval between the Ascension and the day of Pentecost. The words, **Ye shall not go out of the door of the tabernacle,** should rather be, *Ye shall not go away from the entrance of the tabernacle,* and **for seven days shall he consecrate you,** should rather be, *during seven days ye shall be consecrated*

HOMILETICS.

Vers. 1—36.—*Priesthood*, which had existed from the beginning of the world, is now for the first time made the exclusive and hereditary function of one family so far as the Israelitish nation is concerned.

I. AARON AND HIS SONS ARE APPOINTED, NOT BY THE NATION, BUT BY GOD. In Exod. xxviii. 1, we read, "And take thou unto thee Aaron thy brother, and his sons with him, from among the children of Israel, that he may minister unto me in the priest's office." In ch. viii. 2—5, "Take Aaron and his sons with him. . . . And Moses said unto the congregation, This is the thing which the Lord commanded to be done." In Numb. xviii. 7, "I have given your priest's office unto you as a service of gift." In 1 Sam. ii. 28, "Did I choose him out of all the tribes of Israel to be my priest, to offer upon mine altar, to burn incense, to wear an ephod before me? and did I give unto the house of thy father all the offerings made by fire of the children of Israel?" These texts and the whole tenor of Holy Scripture clearly declare that the appointment of Aaron and his sons to the priesthood was the act of God. On the other side, there is no statement whatever to prove or to indicate that they were, as has been affirmed, merely the delegates of the people, so far as the priestly capacity of the latter is concerned. The only passage alleged to have a bearing in that direction is the following :—"Take the Levites from among the children of Israel, and cleanse them. . . . And thou shalt bring the Levites before the Lord: and the children of Israel shall put their hands upon the Levites" (Numb. viii. 6—10). It is argued that the laying on of hands upon the Levites by the congregation was a delegation of power already existing in the congregation to them. If this were so, still the Levites were not the priests; the act would have been a delegation of the right and function only which the Levites possessed—and these were not priestly functions, but the office of waiting upon the service of the tabernacle. But the laying on of hands, in itself, means no more than setting apart, and, in the case of the Levite, we are told that its special meaning was setting apart as an offering or sacrifice. "And Aaron shall offer the Levites before the Lord for an offering of the children of Israel, that they may execute the service of the Lord. . . . And Aaron offered them as an offering before the Lord; and Aaron made an atonement for them to cleanse them. And after that went the Levites in to do their service in the tabernacle of the congregation before Aaron, and before his sons: as the Lord had commanded Moses concerning the Levites, so did they unto them" (Numb. viii. 11—22). The consecration of the priests was entirely distinct from the dedication of the Levites, and had taken place previously to it. The priest was the minister of God ; the Levite was the minister of the priest. None can make a priest of God but God himself.

II. QUALIFICATIONS FOR THE PRIESTHOOD. 1. Aaronic descent (see Exod. xxviii.; ch. viii.; 2 Chron. xxxi. 17—19; Ezra ii. 62; Neh. vii. 64). 2. Physical integrity and freedom from blemish. "No man that hath a blemish of the seed of Aaron the priest shall come nigh to offer the offerings of the Lord made by fire : he hath a blemish ; he shall not come nigh to offer the bread of his God. He shall eat the bread of his God, both of the most holy, and of the holy. Only he shall not go in unto the vail, nor come nigh unto the altar, because he hath a blemish ; that he profane not my sanctuaries" (ch. xxi. 21—23). 3. Respectable marriage (ch. xxi. 7); in the case of the high priest, marriage with one previously unmarried, "in her virginity" (ch. xxi. 13). The two last qualifications symbolize the integrity of heart and purity of life and surroundings which are requisite in the minister of God. Further, at the time of his ministrations, the priest must be free from any ceremonial uncleanness (ch. xxii. 3, 4), and must abstain from wine (ch. x. 8, 10), the purity and collectedness demanded of God's minister at all times being specially required while he is officiating.

III. WHEREIN THE PRIEST'S OFFICE CONSISTED. 1. It consisted in "offering gifts and sacrifices for sins" (Heb. v. 1), this expression including all kinds of offerings and sacrifices by which men drew near to God, together with the burning of incense symbolical of prayer. The priest's action was necessary for the offering of the sacrificial blood and burning the flesh upon the altar, and in some cases for consuming a portion of the victims themselves. 2. It consisted in bestowing benedictions (see Numb. vi. 23—27, "Speak unto Aaron and unto his sons, saying, On this wise ye shall bless the children of Israel. . . . And they shall put my Name upon the children of Israel; and I will bless them "). 3. It consisted in mediating between God and man, as in the rebellion of Korah, Dathan, and Abiram, when "Moses said unto Aaron, Take a censer, and put fire therein from off the altar, and put on incense, and go quickly unto the congregation, and make an atonement for them : for there is wrath gone out from the Lord; the plague is begun. And Aaron took as Moses commanded, and ran into the midst of the congregation ; and, behold, the plague was begun among the people : and he put on incense, and made an atonement for the people. And he stood between the dead and the living; and the plague was stayed " (Numb. xvi. 46—48). 4. It consisted in their being the teachers of the people, " That ye may teach the children of Israel all the statutes which the Lord hath spoken unto them by the hand of Moses " (ch. x. 11). " They shall teach Jacob thy judgments, and Israel thy Law " (Deut. xxxiii. 10). " For the priest's lips should keep knowledge, and they should seek the Law at his mouth " (Mal. ii. 7). Besides being teachers, they were judges of differences, " By their word shall every controversy and every stroke be tried " (Deut. xxi. 5; see Deut. xvii. 8—12 ; 2 Chron. xix. 8—10). They were also leaders of the people's devotions : " Let the priests, the ministers of the Lord, weep between the porch and the altar, and let them say, Spare thy people, O Lord, and give not thine heritage to reproach, that the heathen should rule over them : wherefore should they say among the people, Where is their God ? " (Joel ii. 17). 5. In addition, " to the priests belonged the care of the sanctuary and sacred utensils, the preservation of the fire on the brazen altar, the burning of incense on the golden altar, the dressing and lighting of the lamps of the golden candlestick, the charge of the shew-bread and other like duties. They were necessarily concerned in all those multitudinous acts of the Israelites which were connected with sacrifices, such as the accomplishment of the Nazarite vow, the ordeal of jealousy, the expiation of an unknown murder, the determination of the unclean and of the cleansed leprous persons, garments, and houses; the regulation of the calendar, the valuation of devoted property which was to be redeemed ; —these and a multitude of other duties followed naturally from their priestly office. They were also to blow the silver trumpets on various occasions of their use, and, in connection with this, to exhort the soldiers about to engage in battle to boldness, because they went to fight under the Lord " (Gardiner).

IV. THE EXERCISE OF THE PRIEST'S ESSENTIAL FUNCTIONS WAS CONFINED EXCLUSIVELY TO THEIR ORDER. It has been argued that the office of performing sacrifice was shared by (1) the Jewish monarchs, (2) the rulers, (3) the Levites, (4) the people in general. 1. The first hypothesis has been supported by an appeal to the following passages :— Solomon "came to Jerusalem, and stood before the ark of the covenant of the Lord, and offered up burnt offerings, and offered peace offerings, and made a feast to all his servants" (1 Kings iii. 15); " And the king, and all Israel with him, offered sacrifice before the Lord. And Solomon offered a sacrifice of peace offerings, which he offered unto the Lord" (1 Kings viii. 62, 63). They do not, however, mean more than that Solomon presented the offerings for sacrifice, the essential part of which ceremony was no doubt performed, as always, by priests. Saul, indeed, sacrificed at Gilgal, on plea of necessity, but, in spite of even that plea, was reproved by Samuel as having " done foolishly " (1 Sam. xiii. 13); and Uzziah "went into the temple of the Lord to burn incense upon the altar of incense; " but Azariah the priest " withstood Uzziah the king, and said unto him, It appertaineth not unto thee, Uzziah, to burn incense unto the Lord, but to the priests the sons of Aaron, that are consecrated to burn incense: go out of the sanctuary; for thou hast trespassed ; neither shall it be for thine honour from the Lord God. . . . And the leprosy even rose up in his forehead before the priests in the house of the Lord " (2 Chron. xxvi. 16—20). These cases disprove the priestly power of the monarch. 2. The supposition that the nobles could perform priestly acts rests upon the fact that the name *cohen* is sometimes applied to them (2 Sam. viii. 18; 1 Kings iv. 2, 5); but the word (the derivation of which is doubtful) appears to have a wider usage than that of " priest," and to mean also "officers" (cf. 1 Chron. xviii. 17). 3. The destruction of the company of Korah, because, being Levites, they "sought the priesthood also " (Numb. xvi. 10), disposes of the priestly rights of the tribe of Levi. 4. And the swallowing up of Dathan and Abiram, whose sin was that of desiring to equalize themselves with the family of Aaron, on the plea that the latter " took too much upon them, seeing that all the congregation were holy, every one of them" (Numb. xvi. 3), disproves the right of all the congregation to exercise priestly function, however much they might be, in a sense, a nation of priests. According to the Mosaic legislation, the spiritualty and temporalty were kept apart, nor were they united, except when royal powers came, in the later days of the nation's history, to be attached to the office of high priest—a course which a considerable section of the Christian Church attempted, with less excuse, to follow in mediæval and subsequent times, when the principle, " My kingdom is not of this world" (John xix. 36) became obscured or forgotten.

V. THE CEREMONIES OF THE CONSECRATION. 1. Bathing, robing, anointing, signifying cleansing, justifying, sanctifying. 2. Sacrifices in their behalf—sin offerings, burnt offerings, peace offerings, symbolizing their reconciliation with God, the surrender of themselves to him, and their peace with him. 3. Watching for seven days in the tabernacle court, each day renewing the sacrifices; giving opportunity for self-recollection, and for devoting themselves heart and soul to him whose special servants they were to be.

VI. THE AARONIC PRIESTHOOD WAS A TYPE OF THE PRIESTHOOD OF CHRIST. The type was accomplished in the Antitype, and the Levitical priesthood is now wholly abolished (see Heb. vii. and viii.).

VII. LIKENESS YET CONTRAST OF THE CHRISTIAN MINISTRY. We learn from Eph. iv. 8, 11, 12, that on Christ's ascension into heaven, he received of his Father the gifts of the holy Ghost, which he then bestowed upon his Church, to be administered and dispensed by apostles, prophets, evangelists, pastors, and teachers; the grace of government being ministered by apostles, and, after they had died out, by bishops; the grace of exposition by prophets; the grace of conversion by evangelists; the grace of edification by pastors and teachers, or presbyters. We should note here the superiority of the Christian to the Jewish ministry, the functions of offering sacrifice and of mediating between God and man being far inferior to that of being the dispensers to man of the gifts of the Holy Ghost himself; and the error of any who think to dignify and elevate the character of the Christian ministry by assimilating it to the Jewish.

VIII. THE NEED OF AN OUTWARD CALL IN BOTH CASES. " No man taketh this honour unto himself, but he that is called of God, as was Aaron" (Heb. v. 4); so that even Christ waited to be " called of God" before commencing his ministry. The outward sign of Aaron's having been called of God was his anointing, and the other ceremonies of initiation; and every subsequent high priest had to be anointed and initiated in the same manner as Aaron, and by the same forms, before he was regarded, and before he could become, high priest. The outward sign of the call in the Christian ministry is the laying on of hands. So it was in the case of the seven deacons (Acts vi. 6), and in St. Paul's case (Acts xiii. 3), and in that of Timothy (1 Tim. iv. 14). And all subsequent ministers of Christ have to be appointed in like manner by those " who have publick authority given unto them in the Congregation, to call and send Ministers into the Lord's vineyard" (Art. XXIII.).

IX. ALL CHRISTIANS ARE A ROYAL PRIESTHOOD (1 Pet. ii. 9). As the Israelites were a kingdom of priests (Exod. xix. 5), so too are Christians consecrated to God in baptism, channels of grace to each other, and therefore each in a special manner his brother's keeper. Practical duties thence flowing—brotherly affection, loving-kindness, care for the souls of others, tenderness to the weak.

HOMILIES BY VARIOUS AUTHORS.

Priestly consecration. Ch. viii.; cf. Luke iii. 21, 22; Heb. iv. 14—16; v.; vii.; viii.; ix.; 1 Pet. ii. 4, 5, 9. In this chapter we have the history of the consecration of the Aaronic priesthood. The stages were briefly these :—Lustration, or, as we would now say, *baptism;* investiture; anointing; atonement; dedication; consecration; and, finally, communion. The mediation and ministry of this priesthood were essentially *dramatic* in character, hence it took a long time to present, in the dramatic form, the various ideas which have been just set down as the stages of consecration. Not only so, but they were emphasized by a sevenfold repetition; for seven days the process was to be repeated, at the end of which time Aaron and his sons were regarded as duly set apart for their work. Let us, then, compare the consecration of the high priests with the consecration of the immortal High Priest, Jesus Christ; and, secondly, the consecration of the minor priests with the consecration of believers, who are, as the passage cited from 1 Peter shows, "priests unto God."

I. The consecration of Aaron compared with the consecration of Christ. Now we have in this comparison, first a *contrast*, and then a *parallel*. It will be useful to take these up in this order—

1. *The elements of contrast in the consecrations.* And here we notice: (1) That Aaron's consecration implies his *infirmity and sinfulness*, whereas *Christ never assumed the penitential position.* The baptism of Jesus Christ (Luke iii. 21, 22) is the historical counterpart of Aaron's consecration. And although John's baptism was unto repentance, we know our Lord took up the sinless position even unto the end, challenging all comers to convince him of sin (John viii. 46). We shall see presently what his acceptance of John's baptism signified. One thing meanwhile is clear, that he professed to be "holy, harmless, undefiled, and separate from sinners." Now, in this respect he was a complete contrast to Aaron. Aaron, in the consecration, takes up the penitential position. He has to be typically washed and sprinkled with blood. (2) Aaron's consecration implied a *temporary high priesthood, while Jesus is set apart to an everlasting priesthood.* The association of Aaron's sons with him in the priesthood indicated plainly that death would sooner or later necessitate a successor. Moreover, there are sundry indications in the regulations about the successors. It was, therefore, only a temporary office. "They were not suffered to continue by reason of death." But Jesus was set apart to an everlasting office. "This man, because he continueth ever, hath an unchangeable priesthood" (Heb. vii. 24—28). So much briefly about the contrast.

2. *The parallel in the consecrations.* And here we have to notice: (1) *Both Aaron and Christ are formally set apart.* What Moses did for Aaron, John the Baptist did for Christ. Not, of course, that our Lord's priesthood had an existence only after his baptism; we merely mean that the baptism in the Jordan was the formality with which his ministry began, and corresponded to the consecration of Aaron by Moses. The crowd at the tabernacle door to witness Aaron's consecration corresponded to the crowd of candidates at the Jordan who witnessed the baptism of Jesus, though its significance and singularity they did not appreciate. (2) *Both Aaron and Christ willingly dedicated themselves to their work.* We have already noticed how Aaron needed a cleansing by water and blood, which Jesus did not. The sin offering is what Jesus provided for others, not what he requires for himself. But when we enter this caveat about the different relations of the two persons towards *atonement*, we are in a position to appreciate the parallel between them in personal dedication. This was what Aaron's *burnt offering* implied. He offered himself willingly for the priestly work. And the same dedication of self we find in the baptism of Jesus. He claimed baptism after all the people (ἅπαντα τὸν λαόν) were baptized (Luke iii. 21), in other words, after the movement inaugurated by John had become *national*. John did not at first understand why a sinless One like Jesus should demand baptism from one who was sinful. But Jesus quieted his fears by the assurance, "Thus it becometh us to fulfil all righteousness" (Matt. iii. 15). The meaning of the act on Christ's part can only have been that he dedicated himself to the fulfilment of all that was needed to realize the national hope. Now, the national repentance was in hope of *pardon*, and so Jesus' dedication at the Jordan was to death and to all that his priesthood implies, that the people may have their place as pardoned and accepted ones in the kingdom of God (cf. Godet upon Luke iii. 21, 22; also his 'Etudes Bibliques,' tom. ii. p. 105). This dedication of Jesus at the Jordan was the spirit of his ministry, and above all of his death. It is this he refers to in the momentous words, "For their sakes I sanctify (ἁγιάζω) myself, that they also may be sanctified through the truth" (John xvii. 19). (3) *Both Aaron and Jesus received certain blessings from God in response to their self-dedication.* The gracious gifts of God to his high priests may for brevity's sake be summed up into *three.* (a) The gift of revelation, to enable them to understand their office, and faithfully to fulfil it. This is presented in the *investiture* of Aaron,

especially in the arrangement about the *Urim and Thummim.* The beautiful garments and this mysterious portion which lay upon the high priest's bosom were to convey certain ideas about the office, and to secure in him the *oracular* man (cf. Ewald's 'Antiquities of Israel,' pp. 288—98). Now, in the baptism of Christ, as he was praying with uplifted eye, he saw "heaven opened;" that is, the source of light, the fountain of all knowledge, was opened to him. In other words, he obtained and had continued to him a full revelation of all which he needed for his work. (*b*) The gift of UNCTION OR INSPIRATION, to enable them to interpret the revelation already guaranteed. This was indicated by the anointing of Aaron, not only on the head, but on the ear, hand, and foot. In this way the needful inspiration was symbolized, and the ritual of the ram of consecration coincided therewith. In Christ's case the perfect inspiration was symbolized by the *descent of the dove.* The dove being an organic whole, a totality, indicates that to Jesus there was communicated the entirety of the Holy Spirit, for the purposes of his priesthood. "The Holy Spirit was not given by measure unto him," and "out of his fulness do all we receive, and grace for grace" (John iii. 34; i. 16). (*c*) The gift of COMMUNION AND ABIDING. Aaron, after the ritual of the sin offering, burnt offering, and consecration offering was over, and the best portions had been laid upon God's altar, was called to communion in the feast at the door of the tabernacle. There he was to abide in the enjoyment of fellowship with God, and in this spirit was to do all his work. And the assurance of sonship which Christ received in baptism corresponded to this. The words of the Father, "This is my beloved Son, in whom I am well pleased;" and "Thou art my beloved Son; in thee I am well pleased" (Matt. iii. 17; Luke iii. 22), spoken respectively to John and to Jesus, convey the state of sweet assurance of sonship in which our Lord lived all his life. It was this supported him when he foresaw the dispersion of the disciples, "Behold, the hour cometh, yea, is now come, that ye shall be scattered, every man to his own, and shall leave me alone: and yet I am not alone, because the Father is with me" (John xvi. 32). The Great High Priest performed his mediatorial work in an assurance of sonship and in the enjoyment of fellowship. It was only in the climax of his sufferings on the cross, when the desolation came upon him, that for a season he seemed to lose sight of his sonship, and was constrained to cry, "My God, my God, why hast thou forsaken me?"

II. THE CONSECRATION OF THE MINOR PRIESTS COMPARED WITH THE CONSECRATION OF BELIEVERS. Now here we have to notice—

1. *That the sons of Aaron were consecrated along with Aaron.* It was one consecration. Although the high priest received special anointing, and was chief of the group, the others shared his consecration. The one oil and the one consecrating blood went upon all. The one burnt offering was presented on behalf of all, and they all partook of the one feast and fellowship at last. And is this not to indicate that all believers share in the consecration of Jesus, their Great High Priest? It is the Spirit of Christ and the mind of Christ which is made over to them. He is the reservoir, and out of his fulness all the minor receptacles receive.

2. *This fellowship in consecration was with a view to fellowship in service.* The priestly service was so arranged that all had a share in it. There were, of course, services in connection with atonement which only the high priest could perform, but there was ample work about the tabernacle for all the minor priests. In the same way the life of believers is to be a consecrated fellowship with Christ in work. "Fellow-workers with God" is the great honour of the religious life. A Divine partnership is what we are asked to enter upon. And this is the greatest honour within the reach of man.—R. M. E.

Vers. 4, 5.—*The installation of Aaron.* The origin of any order of men is traced with interest, and the account given of the appointment of a special class to wait upon the Lord in the service of his sanctuary cannot be read without profit.

I. THE ASSEMBLING OF THE PEOPLE TO WITNESS THE INSTALLATION. 1. *It deeply concerned them; the office was created for their benefit.* We may witness the investiture of a knight of the Garter, and deem it a gorgeous scene, but one bearing no practical relationship to us. Not so with the coronation of our prince or the ordination of our pastor. By the mediation of the priests the Israelites were to find acceptance with God. And Jesus Christ has been inducted into his lofty position for the advantage of his people. Why, then, turn away and refuse to enjoy this best of privileges? He waits to intercede on our behalf. It is no idle ceremony that the Word of God records, but one having to do with our daily sins, fears, trials, troubles, joys, and blessings. The titles and qualifications of Jesus Christ are of vital moment to our welfare. 2. *It was designed to impress them with a sense of the dignity and authority of the priesthood, and of the need of holiness in order to have access unto God.* How important the functions to be fulfilled by men who are thus solemnly prepared for their efficient discharge! And how august the Being who could demand such qualifications in those devoted to his service! No careful student of the Gospel narratives but must be struck with the manner in which Jesus Christ was fitted for his office, "perfected" by his obedience, made a "a merciful and faithful High Priest" by his humiliation, and with "the blood of his cross" making reconciliation with God. 3. *The presence and tacit concurrence of the people signified a willingness to obey the priests, to honour and support them.* They were made parties to the transaction, and acquiesced in its significance. It were well that the meaning of our presence at various meetings were better realized, and that we did more fully redeem the pledges thus implicitly given. God would have all his people enter into contracts with a clear understanding. To secure a compact by concealment of the obligations imposed is no part of his plan of procedure.

II. THE DECLARATION OF MOSES: "This is the thing which the Lord commanded to be done:" 1. *Reminds us of the caution to be exercised lest human devices should be thrust forward in religious notions or practices.* Men are ready to formulate their own ideas, and to make them ordinances of God's house or kingdom. Ready, too, to renounce what has been instituted, to abolish observances as unnecessary, or to relegate certain attitudes of the Spirit to heathenism and infancy, to make light of sin and of the need of a high priest or a sacrifice. 2. *A Divine call is requisite to the undertaking of religious functions.* Moses acted as the representative of Jehovah, empowered to consecrate Aaron and his sons. "So also Christ glorified not himself to be made a high priest, but he that said unto him," etc. 3. *Contained an intimation that he who appointed could also dismiss the Aaronic priesthood.* The legislator has power to revoke his edicts. It was God who caused the order of Aaron to be succeeded by the order of Melchizedek. 4. *Indicates the intrinsic superiority of the prophetic to the priestly office.* Moses institutes Aaron, the prophet consecrates the priest. Priesthood is remedial, adapted to a peculiar constitution of things. It is a sort of interregnum that is finally to pass away when "the Son shall have delivered up the kingdom to God the Father." It is connected with sin, and sin is being destroyed. Before Adam fell, he received communications from God; the prophetic revelation preceded the priestly sacrifices. The subordination of the priests is often evinced in the Hebrew records, where the denunciations of the prophets show that the priestly ceremonies were intended to be subservient to, not exclusive of, moral sentiments and duties.—S. R. A.

Vers. 6—12.—*The High Priesthood of Christ.* To direct the thoughts of a congregation to Jesus Christ is never unseasonable. The Epistle to the Hebrews warrants the assumption that in the rites here described are symbolized the characteristics of our Great High Priest. The consecration consists of two parts—the anointing and clothing of the person of Aaron, and his offering of sacrifices; and it is on the former we are now to dwell, reminding us of that Person in whom "all beauties shine, all wonders meet, all glories dwell."

I. See typified THE PURITY OF CHRIST in the washing of the priest from head to foot. As an Eastern climate demands thorough ablution for cleanliness, so was this a lesson man needed to learn, that only purity is fit to come into contact with God. Priesthood bridged the gulf between sinful man and a Being unsullied by admixture of evil. Like all God's dealings, it humbled and exalted man. Taught plainly that he was too polluted to approach his Maker, with equal distinctness he was shown a way in which he might draw near with clean hands and a pure heart. The material and ceremonial purity of Aaron was eclipsed by the total freedom from taint of Christ. He bathed, indeed, in the crystal waters of Jordan at his entrance upon his public ministry, but those waters were stained compared with the purity of his soul.

II. Observe THE SPLENDOUR OF HIS ENDOWMENTS. For every post a certain character is requisite. The putting on of garments represented the bestowment upon Aaron of the qualities essential to the proper discharge of his duties. This was the apparel respecting which the Lord said unto Moses, "Thou shalt make holy garments for Aaron thy brother, for glory and for beauty." Looking at the high priest thus arrayed, we see symbols of the ornaments and graces of Jesus Christ. Note the choice quality of the attire. Everything of the best, fine linen, gold unalloyed, stones precious and rare. The oil is "costly ointment." Search out all that is best in human nature, all that challenges admiration and excites esteem, and an example of all is found in Jesus Christ. Possessed of every gift, power, and skill, loveliness and majesty, perfect in intellect, emotion, and will, he was victorious over every temptation, and unscathed by every trial. This dress of Aaron emblematized positive virtue; so Christ was upright, not only like Adam as he left the hands of God, but as acquiring and exhibiting every grace that can adorn humanity. There was virtue in exercise, virtue visible and potent. The tree put forth its leaves, its blossoms, and its fruit.

III. The high priest maintained A CONSTANT REMEMBRANCE OF THE PEOPLE. Hence the breast-plate bearing the names of the twelve tribes, which were also inscribed upon the onyx stones of the shoulder. The people were borne in the positions that indicated power and sympathy. What the bosom desires the arms accomplish. Let others write their names upon lofty pillars or granite rocks; let statesmen, warriors, nobles, inscribe themselves upon the roll of fame; "Give me," says the Christian, "a place upon the Saviour's breast; for there on the heart of Christ, under the glance of infinite mercy, where the love of God delights to rest, are the names of all his followers graven for ever."

IV. In the breast-plate were put the Urim and Thummim, by means of which was ascertained and made known the will of God. REVELATION OF GOD was thus part of the high priest's functions. The priestly and prophetic offices were intertwined. Though we may single out an office of Christ for distinct consideration, as we may distinguish one of the hues of the rainbow, yet let us not forget that it is the combination which is of such surpassing excellence and glory. It has been well said that Christ is called the Wisdom of God in the Old Testament, and the Word in the New. Full vocal expression was reserved for the time when he could joy to say, "I have declared unto them thy Name, and will declare it." It is by the priesthood of Christ that we learn in particular the grace of God. It is written on all creation, but to our blurred vision the letters are oft obscure. On the cross of Christ, where he becomes at once the Offerer and Victim, these words glisten with heavenly radiance, luminous not only in noontide prosperity, but in the dark midnight of affliction, "God is love."

V. The high priesthood is AN OFFICE OF AUTHORITY, and this authority is THE SUPREMACY OF HOLINESS. Upon the head is placed the mitre, a cap or turban, and upon the mitre is fastened a golden plate or diadem, inscribed "Holiness unto the Lord." Christ's is a royal priesthood, and his sway is the result of his consecration to God. He rules by right of character, by right of rank, by right of work. The "holy crown" is the guarantee for the acknowledgment of his claims to hearty, unreserved obedience. If to-day men demand authority as priests, at least let the holiness of their lives support their pretensions.

VI. By the pouring of the oil upon Aaron's head we see intimated ENTIRE DEDICATION TO GOD'S SERVICE. This holy unction set apart the high priest for hallowed toil, and became an emblem of the fortifying, sustaining, vitalizing presence of the Spirit of God. "The Spirit of the Lord God is upon me, because he hath anointed me." It is the oil of gladness, the dew of the blessing of the Lord. It is a token of perpetuity. The brightest pageant fades, the show of to-day is forgotten ere the morrow dawns, but the priesthood of Christ knows neither ebb nor flow.—S. R. A.

Vers. 14—30.—*The triple offering.* Under the Christian dispensation only two classes of priests remain—the real High Priest, Jesus Christ, and his people who are figurative priests offering up spiritual sacrifices. The ceremonies described in this chapter may throw light upon our position and duties as the followers of Christ, and remind us of the superiority of Christ to Aaron.

I. OUR RESEMBLANCE TO AARON IN THE TRIPLE OFFERING WE ARE REQUIRED TO

MAKE. 1. The sin offering. Priesthood commences by *self-abnegation,* the confession of sin and renunciation of personal merit. By this offering the altar is sanctified (ver. 15), on which afterwards all other gifts will in due course be laid. Until the Saviour has been recognized as made a curse for us, there is no foundation for the life that will please God. The house must be cleansed ere its worthiest inhabitant will condescend to enter. 2. The burnt offering. Here the positive side begins, of *devotion to God.* The parts of the ram are placed upon the purified altar, and the flames emit an odour fragrant to God. The man who has confessed his unworthiness and pleaded the merits of Jesus Christ, dedicates himself to him who died for him. He is not his own, and must henceforth glorify God. "Lord, what wilt thou have me to do?" is his cry. 3. The consecration offering. This results from the others, and is their natural completion by bringing full hands (consecration equals "fulnesses" in original) to God. *Entire dedication and consequent communion with God* its signification. The blood of the ram is sprinkled upon the ear, that it may hearken to the commands of God, and, whilst attentive unto him, disregard the whispers of evil. Also upon the right hand, that all its acts may be in conformity with righteousness, the might of the man going forth in holy deeds. And upon the right foot, that its steps may be ordered by the Lord and its owner may ever tread the ways of obedience and sanctification. Every faculty is enlisted in the service of God. By the wave and heave offerings and the presentation of cakes we learn the necessity of looking upon all our property and all that supports life as belonging to God, who must have his special share and be glorified thereby as well as by our joyful use of the remainder. To fill the hands for God is to complete our consecration, and to live upon heavenly food in the enjoyment of his blessing. By giving to him we get for ourselves.

II. The superiority of Christ to Aaron. 1. *His consecration was total, whilst Aaron's was but partial.* There were many periods when the high priest was seeing to his own peculiar wants and offering for his own especial infirmities. The whole career of Jesus Christ was an offering for others, originated and executed for the good of man and the glory of his Father. He "came not to do his own will." Aaron might lay aside his robes of office and take his repose, but the Son of man was ever clothed with his official character. And this is still clearer when we remember the present position of our High Priest and his unceasing, unintermitted intercession. 2. *The holiness of Aaron was ceremonial and symbolical, that of Christ is literal and real.* Jesus was on earth holy, harmless, undefiled. The searching eye of God can discern in his righteousness no stain nor flaw. So far was Aaron from reaching perfection that, because of rebellion at Meribah (Numb. xx. 24), he was not permitted to enter the land of promise. 3. *The atonement of Jesus Christ is actual, that of Aaron was only typical.* After these rites of consecration were observed, the priests were qualified to present the offerings and sacrifices of the people unto God, and to make reconciliation for them. But there was no inherent virtue in those sacrifices to remove the guilt of sin; it is the blood of Christ that has power to cleanse the conscience from dead works. He bore our sins in his own body on the tree, and brought in everlasting righteousness. 4. *The priesthood of Christ is perpetual, that of Aaron only survived by successors.* The high priests died and passed away, their places occupied by others. Jesus abides for ever; he hath an unchangeable priesthood, after the order of Melchizedek. If, then, the Israelites found satisfaction in contemplating the functions of dying men, with what profound delight should we avail ourselves of the intercession of him who ever lives to save!—S. R. A.

Vers. 1—6.—*The baptism of Aaron and his sons.* Hitherto this book consists of precepts and directions concerning the sacrifices and services of the tabernacle; but here a new section commences, in which the directions are described as carried into effect. This section appropriately commences with the history of the consecration of Aaron and his sons, with whom principally was to rest the carrying out of the laws. The verses before us describe—

I. The preparations for the ceremony. 1. *These were directed by the Lord.* (1) He had formerly given very particular directions from the summit of Mount Sinai (Exod. xxviii., xxix.). In pursuance of these instructions, the holy garments were made and other preparations completed. Note: The leadings of providence should be closely followed. (2) Now the time has come for carrying the directions of Deity into fuller accomplishment. The tabernacle has been finished and occupied by the presence of God; the laws have been published; and the next thing in order is the consecration of the priests to serve the tabernacle. The Lord is a God of order. In his service "all things" should be done "decently and in order." 2. *His directions were given by the hand of Moses.* (1) Moses was instructed to "take Aaron and his sons," etc. (vers. 2, 3). These instructions he punctually obeyed (ver. 4). In this fidelity Moses was a type of Christ, with these differences: (*a*) Moses was faithful "as a servant," Christ "as a Son." (*b*) The house of Moses was ceremonial and typical, that of Christ spiritual and living (see Heb. iii. 1—6). (2) Moses, who was instructed to consecrate Aaron and his sons, had himself no human consecration. He was an extraordinary servant of God. We do not read of the apostles of Christ receiving any baptism of water or ordination by imposition of hands. God can send by whom he pleases and when he pleases, without any human sanction (see Gal. i. 15—19). 3. *The congregation was assembled to witness the ceremony.* (1) This was a wise arrangement, to inspire them with proper respect for the servants of God. They were prone enough to say, "Ye take too much upon you, ye sons of Levi." Ministers were publicly ordained in the primitive Church. (2) The address of Moses to the congregation was brief and to the point: "This is the thing which the Lord commanded to be done" (ver. 5). The command, which was given from Sinai, the congregation were acquainted with. The time to carry it out was now given from the sanctuary (ch. i. 1). We should look to God for guidance in reference to times and seasons, as well as to the services to be rendered for him.

II. THE BAPTISM OF AARON AND HIS SONS. 1. *This was the initiatory rite of the consecration.* (1) It was the first act (ver. 6). And as Moses washed Aaron at the door of the tabernacle of the congregation, so was Jesus washed by John at his entrance upon his public ministry (see Matt. iii. 16; iv. 1, 17). Like Moses, John also was a Levite. (2) The sons of Aaron were baptized with him. To them also it was the rite of initiation. So are the sons of Jesus initiated into his discipleship by baptism (see Matt. xxviii. 18—20, margin; Acts ii. 41; x. 48). The initiatory office of baptism is also expressed in the phrase "born of water" (John iii. 5). 2. *It set forth the necessity of purity in the servants of God.* (1) Water, being one of the great purifiers in the kingdom of nature, is used in Scripture as an emblem of the Holy Spirit, the Great Purifier in the kingdom of grace (Isa. xliv. 3; John vii. 38, 39). Hence a dispute about "baptism" is called a "question about purifying" (John iii. 25, 26). (2) The requisition of baptism declared the necessity of the baptism of the Holy Ghost. This is the source of the spiritual birth in which commences the spiritual life which is the life of heaven. 3. *As to the form of this baptism.* (1) The record here is simply that "Moses brought Aaron and his sons and washed them with water" (ver. 6). But by reference to Exod. xxx., we learn that this washing was done at the laver. In allusion to the ceremonial baptisms of the Law, the baptism of the Spirit under the gospel is described as the "laver of regeneration" (Titus iii. 5, 6). (2) From the same reference in Exodus we learn, further, that the washing of Aaron and his sons extended to their "hands and feet." There is no proof that they were bodily plunged in the laver. We are reminded how Jesus washed his disciples' feet (see John xiii. 8—10). The Jews have a tradition that a tap was turned on, from which, by the flowing of the water over their hands and feet, the washing was accomplished (see Brown's 'Antiquities,' vol. i. p. 148). In baptism, the element should be active and the subject passive, for the thing signified, the Holy Ghost, certainly is not passive (see Acts ii. 16—18, 33; x. 44—48).—J. A. M.

Vers. 7—9.—*The holy garments of Aaron.* The high priest of the Levitical dispensation is allowed to be an eminent type of the "Great High Priest of our profession." His attire was intended to foreshow the qualities by which the Redeemer is distinguished. Else it would be difficult to account for the minute care with which they were designed, and the manner in which the workmen were inspired to make them (see Exod. xxviii. 2—4; xxxi. 3—6). Let us attend to—

I. THE COAT WITH ITS GIRDLE. 1. *The coat.* (1) According to Josephus, "it was a tunic circumscribing the body, with light sleeves for the arms, and reaching to the heels" ('Ant.,' iii. 7). It was white, to denote purity. (2) It was bound with the girdle about the loins. This also was white, and denoted truth, which is another expression for purity (see Eph. vi. 14). (3) The coat was an inner garment, and bound close to the body with the girdle, to suggest that purity and truth should be found "in the inner parts" (Ps. li. 6; Jer. xxxi. 33; Rom. ii. 29). 2. *There were also breeches.* (1) These are not mentioned here, but they are described in Exod. xxviii. 42, "And thou shalt make them linen breeches to cover their nakedness" (Hebrew, "the flesh," etc.); "from the loins even unto the thighs they shall reach." (2) These also were white, expressive of purity, and without these the priest may not appear in the presence of God. They imported that "flesh and blood cannot enter into the kingdom of heaven" until "clothed upon" (see Ezek. xliv. 17, 18; 2 Cor. v. 2, 3; Rev. iii. 18).

II. THE EPHOD WITH ITS ROBE. 1. *The ephod.* (1) It was a short tunic, according to Josephus, reaching to the loins. It consisted of a rich cloth composed of blue, purple, scarlet, and fine twined linen, interwoven with threads of gold, and wrought, some think, into figures of cherubim and palm trees. It was without sleeves, but resting upon the shoulders. (2) It was an emblem of redemption. Ephod (אפוד) comes from the verb (פד or פדה), *to redeem.* This is the derivation given by Alexander Pirie, the author of a learned 'Dissertation on Hebrew Roots.' 2. *The robe of the ephod.* (1) This, and the holy garments in general which were associated with the ephod, from it derive the name of the "robe of righteousness" and "garments of salvation" (see Isa. lxi. 10, margin). They were the garments in which the typical high priest carried out the business of redemption. (2) The colour of the robe was blue—the dye of heaven, which was with the ancients the symbol of divinity. This over the coat, the emblem of purity, would mark the purity of Messiah to be Divine; so, not derived, but essential and absolute. (3) Upon the hem of the robe round about were "golden bells," which, when they sounded, indicated the sound of salvation. And they were on the "hem" of the robe when the high priest went up into the holy place, that the sound might be heard below. The sound of the gospel accordingly was heard below, as a "sound from heaven," when Jesus went up into the heavens. (4) The pomegranates alternating with the bells suggested the fruit which follows the preaching of the gospel.

III. THE BREASTPLATE WITH THE URIM AND THUMMIM. 1. *The Urim and Thummim were the stones set in the breastplate.* (1) In the text we read of the Urim and Thummim, but here is no mention of the stones. In the parallel place (Exod. xxix. 8—12) the stones are mentioned, but we read there nothing of the Urim and Thummim. This is intelligible if they be the same; but if not, the double omission in things so important is inexplicable. (2) An attentive consideration of Exod. xxviii. 29, 30 will show that the Urim and Thummim are the substance upon which the names of the tribes were engraven. The use ascribed to the stones in one verse is in the next ascribed to the Urim and Thummim. 2. *They represented the saints as cherished in the heart of Christ.* (1) The names of the tribes of Israel were there; and the spiritual Israel are upon the heart of Jesus. These names were *engraven* to show how deeply and permanently our interests have entered into his sympathies. They are engraven in *gems* to show how precious to him are his saints (Mal. iii. 17). The gems were various, and yet all were united in the breastplate of the high priest, to show how individuality can be preserved in those who are united in the love of Jesus. (2) These were called the Urim and Thummim, lights and perfections, or lights and perfect ones. So are Christians called the lights of the world, because they reflect the splendours of the Light of the world. They are perfect ones also, viz. in the loveliness of Jesus (Matt. v. 15, 16; Jude 24). (3) The breastplate was fastened to the ephod with golden chains, which were also connected with rings in the curious girdle of the ephod, from which it was forbidden to separate it (Exod. xxviii. 28). So are we with precious bonds girded to the Redeemer, from which blessed union it would be sinful and disastrous to become dislinked. (4) There were also connected with this robe of redemption on the shoulders of the high priest onyx stones, set in sockets of gold, upon which the names of the tribes of Israel were again engraven. So does Jesus bear his saints upon his shoulder as well as upon his heart. They have his sustaining power as well as the animation of his love.

IV. THE MITRE WITH ITS GOLDEN PLATE. 1. *The mitre.* (1) This was like a turban bound round the head. (2) It was an ornament of honourable distinction. The term here used is rendered "diadem" in Job xxix. 14. 2. *The golden plate.* (1) This was upon the front of the mitre. It appears to have been ornamented with flowers and leaves. Possibly there is an allusion to this when the Psalmist, speaking of Messiah, says, "but upon himself shall his crown flourish." This plate is called the "holy crown" in the text. (2) The inscription upon it characterized Christ. The words were "Holiness unto the Lord," or "The Holy One of Jehovah." If these holy garments were intended to create respect for the priesthood among the people of Israel, how we should reverence the glorious Antitype!—J. A. M.

Vers. 10—12.—*Levitical anointings.* The subjects of these anointings, as brought under our notice in the text, are, generally, "the tabernacle and all that was therein." From amongst these included things we have afterwards particularly specified, "the altar and all his vessels," and "the laver and his foot." The anointing of Aaron also is distinctly mentioned. We shall review these in order.

I. THE TABERNACLE. 1. *This was an emblem of the moral universe.* The holy places represented the heavens (Heb. viii. 1, 2). Thus (1) the most holy place, where the shechinah was, represented the "heaven of heavens," the "third heaven," or that which, by way of distinction and excellence, is called "heaven itself" (Heb. ix. 24). (2) The holy place, which must be passed through in order to reach the most holy, represented those regions of the moral universe through which Jesus passed on his way from his cross to the throne of his majesty (Heb. iv. 14; vii. 26). In that passage he was "in paradise," and sometimes manifesting himself to his disciples (see Ps. xvi. 10; Acts ii. 23—32; Luke xxiii. 43; xxiv. 15, 16, 31, 36, 51). The spiritual world is not far from us. (3) If the most holy place represented the "*third*" heaven," and the holy place leading to it the *second*, then the court of the priests will stand for the *first*. It describes the "kingdom of heaven" on earth, in other words, the spiritual Church of God. In this we are already "come," in faith and hope and joy, "unto Mount Sion, and unto the city of the living God, the heavenly Jerusalem," etc., and hear the very voice of Jesus from the heavens above us (see Heb. xii. 22—25). (4) The courts outside represented the Church in its visible part, viz. the court of Israel, the court of the women, and the court of the Gentiles. The distinctions which formerly existed here are now done away, so that instead of three, the courts are one (see Gal. iii. 25—28; Eph. ii. 11—19). It is well to be found in these courts, for all outside are in alienation. But we should not rest satisfied with the profession of the outer court. Without the spiritual experience of the court of the priests we can never pass into the heavens "whither the Forerunner is for us entered" (Heb. vi. 19, 20). 2. *It was sanctified with the holy anointing oil* (ver. 10). (1) This oil represented the Holy Spirit in his gifts and graces (comp. Acts i. 5 with x. 38; see also 2 Cor. i. 21; 1 John ii. 20, 27). It was of peculiar composition. The formula is given in Exod. xxx. 23—25; but on pain of excommunication it must not be put to common use (Exod. xxx. 31—33). The person and offices of the Holy Ghost must be held in the greatest reverence; to profane these is fatal wickedness (Matt. xii. 31, 32). (2) With this oil the tabernacle was "sanctified," that is, separated to God. It was so separated to him for services of worship. Also to be a shadow of heavenly things. So the moral universe is claimed by God. The gifts and graces of the Holy Spirit are the principles of universal sanctification.

II. THE ALTAR AND THE LAVER. 1. *The altar and all his vessels.* (1) This is obviously the altar of burnt offerings which stood in the court of the priests. The "vessels" were those for receiving the blood of the sacrifices, and all the implements used in connection with the service of the altar. (2) It typified Calvary, the altar upon which the Great Sacrifice of the gospel was offered. And taken in a grander sense, in consistency with the magnificence of the figure in which the tabernacle represents the great universe of God, this earth was the altar upon which our Lord was offered. (3) The altar was sprinkled with the oil "to sanctify it." The earth is thereby marked out as destined to be sanctified to God, and sanctified too by the gifts and graces of the Holy Spirit. It was sprinkled "seven times," to show the perfectness of that sanctification. And is not this the burden of prophetic hope (Ps. xxxvii. 10, 11, 34; Isa. xi. 6—9)? 2. *The laver and his foot.* (1) This also was located in the court of the priests. In it they washed their hands and feet, and also the parts of the sacrifices requiring washing according to the Law. (2) The anointing of this was "to sanctify it," or separate it to God. It was separated to him for the purposes of the ceremonial service. It was also separated, to represent the "laver of regeneration" under the gospel, or the "renewing of the Holy Ghost" (Titus iii. 5). Those who are spiritually baptized into Christ are anointed with the gifts and graces of his Holy Spirit.

III. AARON. 1. *The oil was poured upon Aaron's head.* (1) This anointing was profuse. "Poured" (see Ps. cxxxiii. 2). (2) It was "to sanctify him." He was thus separated to accomplish the service of God in the tabernacle. He was also separated to typify the Great High Priest of the gospel. 2. *But when was the true oil poured upon Jesus?* (1) We have seen that, as Aaron was washed with water, so was Jesus, viz. at the Jordan (notes on vers. 1—6). But the baptism of Jesus there was not so truly that conferred by John as that which came upon him from heaven (Matt. iii. 16). (2) The second act in the consecration of Christ appears to have been in the mount of transfiguration. There he had the "oil that maketh the face to shine," and was "anointed with the oil of gladness above his fellows" (Ps. xlv. 7). This dazzling lustre of the Holy Spirit was so profuse as to stream not only out of the pores of his skin, but to brighten all his raiment (comp. Ps. cxxxiii. 2; Matt. xvii. 2). (3) As at the Jordan the voice of the Father was heard from the excellent glory approving, so on Tabor the same voice is heard again (comp. Matt. iii. 17; xvii. 5). He that received the Spirit "not by measure" is emphatically THE *Messiah,* THE *Anointed One.*—J. A. M.

Vers. 13—21.—*The vesting of the priests and the offerings for them.* In the order of the ceremonies at the consecration of the priests, after the anointing of Aaron, we have—
I. THE CLOTHING OF AARON'S SONS. (Ver. 13.) 1. *They were types of Christians.* (1) The high priest, as we have seen, was a type of Christ. So were the priests in general types also of him, viz. in everything in which they acted as representatives of the high priest. (2) But under usual conditions they should be viewed as emblems of Christians. This is evidently taught in such references as Exod. xix. 6; Heb. x. 9—22; 1 Pet. ii. 9; Rev. i. 6; v. 10. 2. *Their holy garments resembled some of Aaron's.* (1) Aaron had some by which he was distinguished from his sons, and so has Christ unique qualities. In everything pertaining to his Divinity he stands alone. He claims the deepest reverence. (2) The coats and girdles which Moses put upon the sons of Aaron were similar to those articles bearing the same name in which Aaron was clothed. In Aaron's case, as we have seen, they denoted purity and truth; and so do they denote these qualities in relation to his sons (see Eph. vi. 14; Rev. xix. 8). (3) This identity suggests that Christians have their righteousness in virtue of their association with Christ (see Jer. xxiii. 6; Rom. iii. 22; 1 Cor. i. 30; Phil. iii. 9). This is otherwise shown in the fact that the claim of the Levitical priests to those holy garments was in virtue of their being sons of Aaron. Only the "seed" of Messiah (Isa. liii. 10, 11), are clothed in the "white linen which is the righteousness of the saints." 3. *Moses also "put bonnets upon them."* (1) These, like the coats, were made of white linen, and so, likewise, expressed purity. They were similar to the turban of Aaron, minus the "plate of the holy crown of pure gold," and its fastenings of lace-work of blue (Exod. xxxix. 30, 31). (2) These bonnets were "for glory and for beauty" (Exod. xxviii. 40). For "glory," *i.e.* honour, viz. as they served to distinguish the priests as the ministers of God. If a messenger be despised, his message may be brought into contempt. And for "beauty," viz. as they represented the "beauty of holiness." True Christian honour is evermore the associate of holiness.
II. THE OFFERINGS FOR THE PRIESTS. In respect to these we observe: 1. *The priests laid their hands upon the heads of the animals* (vers. 14, 18). (1) This was the sign of the confession of sin. It was also the sign of the transfer of sin, so constituting the animal (in type) vicariously a sinner or sin-bearer, liable to suffer its penalty. (2) The next thing in order, therefore, was the bleeding of the animal, in consideration of which the offerer stands justified or released from the obligation to suffer. (3) The reference in all this to the vicarious sacrifice of Christ and our justification through faith in him cannot be mistaken. (4) But why did Aaron, the type of Christ, act thus? Christ had no sin of his own to confess, and needed no sacrifice for himself. The answer is that Aaron, in this, acted not as a type of Christ, but for himself as a sinful man, and representatively for the people (see Heb. v. 1—3). In this Aaron is *contrasted*

with Jesus (see Heb. vii. 26—28).   2. *The altar was purified with the blood* (vers. 15, 19).   (1) The earth, as the altar upon which the great Antitype was offered, is purified by his blood.   (*a*) As respects its inhabitants.   (*b*) As respects itself.   The inheritance of man is also redeemed by Christ from the curse of sin.   (*c*) The full effects of this will be seen "in the regeneration" or renewed state of the earth indicated in prophecy. (2) The altar was purified with the typical blood "to make reconciliation upon it."   So is this earth for the same purpose sanctified by the blood of Jesus.   There is no other planet, at least so far as we are concerned, thus sanctified.   Therefore if we be not *here* "reconciled to God through the death of his Son," there is no hope for reconciliation hereafter or elsewhere (see Heb. x. 26, 27).   3. *The offerings were presented upon the altar.*   (1) In the case of the sin offering, the fat was burnt upon the altar, while the body of the beast was burnt without the camp (ver. 16, 17).   Not only was Christ offered up as a sacrifice for sin generally upon this earth, but more particularly "without the gate," viz. of Jerusalem (comp. Heb. xiii. 11, 12).   (2) In the case of the burnt offering, the whole ram was burnt upon the altar.   This holocaust showed how absolutely God claims us, and therefore how completely we should be devoted, and, so to speak, consumed, in his worship and service (Ps. lxix. 9; John ii. 13—17).— J. A. M.

Vers. 22—36.—*The ram of consecration.*   This and the ceremonies connected form the principal subject of the verses now recited.   We notice—

I. THAT IT WAS A PEACE OFFERING.   1. *The first ram was a burnt offering.*   (1) It was wholly consumed upon the altar.   It was regarded wholly as the "food of God" (ch. iii. 11; xxi. 6; Ezek. xliv. 7; Mal. i. 7, 12).   (2) In this sacrifice God is contemplated as a righteous Judge, whose justice claims everything we are and have, and who, until that justice is satisfied, can have no fellowship with man.   2. *Burnt offerings were usually accompanied by peace offerings.*   (1) Of these a portion was eaten by the worshipper.   This was the expression of peace, reconciliation, fellowship. Constantly associated with the holocaust, the opportunity of ceremonially feasting with God was never wanting.   In the peace offering faith discerns the sacrifice of Christ to have so completely met the claims of infinite justice, that we are now accepted into favour.   (2) As in the other sacrifices, the hands of Aaron and his sons were laid upon it to confess their sinfulness, their need of a Saviour, and their faith in the Redeemer of promise.   It was slain accordingly, to foreshadow the death of Messiah.   The fat and gall were burnt, to show how our evil passions, the old man, must be crucified with him, that the body of sin may be destroyed.

II. THAT ITS BLOOD WAS USED IN A REMARKABLE WAY.   1. *It was sprinkled upon Aaron.*   (1) Upon his person.   (*a*) On the tip of his right ear, to express *obedience* (Exod. xxi. 6).   And our Lord's obedience was unto death (Phil. ii. 8).   (*b*) On the thumb of the right hand, to express the service of *doing*.   Christ fulfilled all righteousness, and finished the work that was given him to do (John iv. 34; v. 17; ix. 4; xvii. 4; Heb. x. 5—7).   (*c*) On the great toe of the right foot, to express the *ways*.   All the ways of Jesus were infinitely pleasing to God (Ps. i. 6; xviii. 20, 21; Acts x. 38).   (*d*) The comprehensive teaching here is the complete consecration of all faculties and energies (see 1 Pet. i. 15).   (2) Upon his garments.   In this baptism oil also was used (ver. 30).   While in detail these garments represented moral qualities, collectively taken they expressed *office*.   Hence from the earliest times a person introduced into office is said to be invested in it, from *in*, used intensively, and *vestio*, I clothe. The office of the high priest was to minister in the very presence of God (see Heb. viii. 1, 2).   (3) Jesus, who was washed with water at the Jordan, and anointed with oil on the mount of transfiguration, received the final baptism of his consecration, that of his own blood, in Gethsemane and Calvary.   As the voice of God accredited him in each of the earlier baptisms, so it accredited him again as he was about to enter into this (comp. Matt. iii. 17; xvii. 5; John xii. 27—33).   2. *It was sprinkled upon Aaron's sons.*   (1) Upon their persons (ver 24).   The sons of Aaron were here treated in like manner as Aaron was, to show how in all these things Christians are called to be like Christ (see Matt. xx. 22, 23).   This remark will be especially applicable to ministers, who should be "examples to the flock" (see Isa. lxvi. 21; 1 Cor. ix. 13). (2) Upon their garments (ver. 30).   The office of the priesthood was to minister in the presence of God in his tabernacle. So the spiritual priesthood have access to God in heaven. We must be anointed with the unction of the Holy One, and sprinkled with the blood of Christ, that we may enter into that most holy place (Heb. x. 19—22; 1 John ii. 20, 27).

III. THAT IT FILLED THE HANDS OF AARON AND HIS SONS. 1. *It was treated as a wave offering.* (1) The breast had the fat laid upon it. A bread offering also was laid upon it. The whole was then waved before the Lord. The shoulder also was heaved (see Exod. xxix. 27). Thus God was praised as the Creator and Dispenser of every good and perfect gift. (2) Moses acted as priest in all this ceremony. He put these things upon the hands of Aaron and his sons, and waved and heaved them. From this action the ram of consecration took its name (איל מלאים, *eil milluim*), the *ram* of *filling up.* Thus the essence of the consecration was the filling the hand with the oblation, or conferring the right to offer sacrifices to God (see Ezek. xliii. 26, margin). (3) The wave breast then came to the lot of Moses, and Aaron and his sons appear to have shared it with him as the feast upon the sacred food (see ver. 31). 2. *The ceremonies of the consecration lasted seven days.* (1) Seven is the numeral of perfection, so at the close of the seven days this was a perfect consecration, intimating that all the powers of the consecrated ones should be wholly given to God. (2) They "kept the charge of the Lord," during these seven days, "at the door of the tabernacle." They were not as yet qualified to enter the holy place, and they must not leave the court of the priests on pain of death (see 1 Kings xix. 19—21; Matt. viii. 21, 22; Luke ix. 61, 62). (3) "Aaron and his sons did all things which the Lord commanded by the hand of Moses." Had Jesus failed in any point, his consecration would be imperfect; he could not have become our Saviour.—J. A. M.

Vers. 3—5.—*A time for publicity.* The solemn inauguration of Aaron and his sons into their sacred office was to have the utmost possible publicity. This was—

I. A DIVINE INSTRUCTION. The Lord said, "Take Aaron . . . and gather thou all the congregation together," etc. (vers. 1—3). "This is the thing which the Lord commanded to be done " (ver. 5).

II. A PROVISION AGAINST POPULAR JEALOUSY. The scene described in Numb. xvi. shows only too well how necessary it was to convey to "all the congregation " the truth that Aaron and his sons were divinely appointed to their office. This the more because of the near relationship between Moses and Aaron.

III. A PROVISION FOR POPULAR ESTEEM. It was in the last degree desirable that the people should have an exalted idea of the priesthood, and, more especially, of the high priesthood. Everything which would contribute to this would be of real religious service. It was, therefore, fitting that " all the congregation " should be spectators of the impressive solemnities of the inaugural scene.

IV. A HELPFUL INFLUENCE ON THEIR OWN MINDS. It was of equal importance to the Hebrew commonwealth that the priests themselves should cherish a profound sense of the sacred and elevated character of their work. For any irreverence or neglect of theirs was calculated to involve the community in sin and in disaster (see 1 Sam. i. 17; Mal. ii. 8). So solemn and impressive a ceremony as this, in the sight of all the people, would exert a salutary influence on the mind both of father and sons.

In ordinary life, piety and publicity are strangers. Devotion shuts itself in the inner chamber (Matt. vi. 6), or climbs up into the fold of the mountain (Matt. xiv. 23). We nourish our holiest thoughts, and form our best resolves, not in the glare of the public gathering, but in the secret place, when alone with God. Nevertheless, there are occasions when we should not shun publicity; when it is not modesty but weakness to do so. When we avow our attachment to our Saviour, and thus "confess him before men " (Matt. x. 32); still more, when we enter upon any responsible office in connection with his Church (*e.g.* the Christian ministry); and yet more, if we are summoned, as Aaron was, to any post of unusual eminence and responsibility, we do well to take the vows of God upon us before " all the congregation." If not " a thing which the Lord commanded to be done," it is (1) a Divine suggestion (Acts vi. 7; xiii. 3; 1 Tim. vi. 12); (2) instructive to the people; (3) helpful to ourselves. We need all the influences we can gain from every source to incite us to zealous labour, and to strengthen us against temptation. It is right and wise to avail ourselves of all the help we gain from the remembrance that we have confessed Christ our Lord, and pledged ourselves to do his work before "all the congregation," "before many witnesses."—C.

Vers. 6—9, 14.—*The human and Divine priesthood—contrast.* The setting apart of Aaron for his life-work, the high priesthood of Israel, naturally suggests to us the entrance of our Great High Priest on the work which his Father gave him to do. Between Aaron and Christ there are many points of resemblance (see below); there are also significant contrasts. Respecting "the High Priest of our profession" (Heb. iii. 2), it is *not* the case that there was—

I. APPOINTMENT TO OFFICE IN VIRTUE OF HUMAN BIRTH. Aaron was chosen to the office of high priest, partly in virtue of his descent from Levi (perhaps partly in virtue of his brotherhood to Moses). His personal qualities were not such as to make him the most suitable man for the office, independently of considerations of lineal descent and human relationship. Jesus Christ did not owe his position as our High Priest to his human birth. He was not, indeed, of the tribe of Levi, but of Judah, "after the flesh." And though, through his mother, he was a son of David, in the matter of human descent, this was not in any way material to his ascent to royal power. His right of office came not thence.

II. IMPOSING INAUGURAL CEREMONY. The scene described in this chapter was striking, imposing, memorable; it would long be borne in mind, never, indeed, forgotten by those who witnessed it. It formed part of the national history. Imagination on our part readily places before us the solemn and suggestive ceremonies which riveted the eyes of the congregation of Israel. Through no such solemnities did One greater than Aaron think well to pass as he entered on his work. It is said that his contemporaries expected the Messiah to descend amongst them from the heavens while they were worshipping in the temple. This he distinctly refused to do (Matt. iv. 5—7). The ceremony of the baptism by John was simple in the extreme. Long chapters of Old Testament Scripture (Exodus and Leviticus) are occupied in narrating the inaugural ceremonies of the human priesthood; five verses suffice to chronicle those of the Divine (Matt. iii. 13—17). The profounder work of the Lord from heaven was more fittingly commenced by that quiet scene on the banks of Jordan.

III. OUTWARD AND VISIBLE DISTINCTION. (Vers. 7—9.) The appearance of Aaron and of his successors in their pontifical attire, as described in this chapter, with rich and coloured garments about them, and the mitre on their head glittering with golden diadem, must have been impressive and imposing enough in the eyes of the people. How striking the contrast with him who was the carpenter's Son of Nazareth, who shunned all ostentation and parade (Matt. xii. 19), who had "no beauty" (of outward appearance) "that we should desire him" (Isa. liii. 2), who attracted disciples to his feet, and sinners to his side, only by the wisdom of his words, and the grace of his spirit and the beauty of his life!

IV. NEED OF PURIFICATION. "Moses brought Aaron and his sons, and washed them with water" (ver. 6). It was needful that they should go through a ceremony which signified the putting away of "all filthiness of the flesh and spirit" (2 Cor. vii. 1). No need of this in the case of the holy Saviour. Whatever his baptism signified, it did not mean this. He was "a High Priest, holy, harmless, undefiled," requiring no cleansing streams whatever (Heb. vii. 26 ; see John xiv. 30).

V. NEED OF PARDON. "And he brought the bullock for the sin offering : and Aaron," etc. (ver. 14). Before the human high priest could be admitted to the altar, his own sin must be forgiven. Christ entered on his work, not needing to present any oblation. With him, as he was, the Divine Father was "well pleased" (Matt. iii. 17).

In entering on any work to which we may be called of God, we must remember that (1) we have need to purify ourselves of the sin-stains that are left on the soul; (2) we have need to seek for pardon for a faulty past before we go forth to a new future; (3) we may be careless of outward distinctions, considering the lowliness of our Lord.—C.

Vers. 7—9.—*The human and Divine priesthood—comparison.* Between the priesthood of Aaron and that of the Lord Jesus Christ there are not only points of contrast (see above) but also of resemblance. The "holy garments" in which the human priest was attired supplied marked and intentional suggestions of the attributes and the work of the Divine. Thus we are reminded by Aaron's appearance of—

I. HIS PERSONAL HOLINESS. "The stuff of all of them was linen, and . . . must be understood to have been white." This was associated with the idea of bodily cleanness, and hence with righteousness of soul (see Rev. xix. 8). The High Priest of our profession was he "that loved righteousness," of whom it was true that "the sceptre of righteousness was the sceptre of his kingdom" (Heb. i. 8, 9).

II. HIS ALL-SUFFICIENT STRENGTH. The girdle with which Aaron was girded (ver. 7) was suggestive of strength, activity, readiness for the appointed work. To "gird up the loins" was to be prepared for immediate and effective action. Christ is he who always stands ready and mighty to save; prepared at the moment of *our* readiness to put forth his arm of power, and to redeem us with the "saving strength of his right hand."

III. HIS REPRESENTATIVE CHARACTER. On the breastplate of the ephod (ver. 8) were the names of the twelve tribes of Israel. With these on his person he appeared before God in the holy place; evidently representing them and appearing on their behalf. Our Divine Redeemer, assuming our human nature, suffered and died in our stead, and now "appears in the presence of God *for us*" (Heb. ix. 24).

IV. HIS SPIRITUAL FITNESS FOR HIS GREAT WORK. The "Urim and Thummim" (ver. 8) signified "lights" and "perfections;" they were the means by which Aaron received inspiration from Jehovah. Our Lord was one "in whom dwelleth all the fulness of the godhead bodily" (Col. i. 9), particularly (see context) Divine wisdom. He is—not merely *has*, but *is*—"the truth" (John xiv. 6), and He *is* "the wisdom of God" (1 Cor. i. 24, 30; Col. ii. 3). He who, in the exercise of absolute wisdom, knows the mind of the Father, and "knows what is in man" also, is that omniscient One who is perfectly equipped for the wondrous problem he has undertaken to work out.

V. THE FINAL TRIUMPH OF HIS CAUSE. "He put the mitre upon his head" (ver. 9). The high priest of Israel had a touch of royalty—he wore a crown upon his head. The High Priest of man is royal also. "Upon *his* head are many crowns." He is "exalted to be a prince" as well as a Saviour. And he is "able even to subdue all things unto himself" (Phil. iii. 21; see Phil. ii. 9, 10).

VI. HIS ULTIMATE DESIGN. "Upon the mitre, even upon his forefront, did he put the golden plate" (ver. 9), and on this golden diadem were inscribed the sacred, significant words, "Holiness to the Lord" (Exod. xxviii. 36). Did not this sentence, placed in the forefront of the high priest's mitre, signify that the great end of his ministrations was the establishment among all the tribes of Israel of "Holiness to the Lord"? The purpose for which he was appointed would not be attained until that great and noble aim was reached. For that he lived and wrought. That, too, is the end of the Divine priesthood. Christ came to "put away sin by the sacrifice of himself" (Heb. ix. 26), to establish on the earth that kingdom of God which is "righteousness, peace, and joy in the Holy Ghost."

Let us learn—1. The exceeding greatness of our privilege. *In* Jesus Christ himself (and in his salvation) are these great excellencies; they were only *upon* and *outside* the Hebrew priest. 2. The corresponding guilt of (1) defiant rejection, (2) frivolous disregard, (3) continued indecision (Heb. ii. 3).—C.

Ver. 2.—*Spiritual apparel.* "Take Aaron and his sons with him and the garments." Aaron and his sons were about to be *invested*. Their formal investiture of the priestly office was to be signified and symbolized by their putting on the sacerdotal garments. The robes of office are fully described (vers. 7—9). These "holy garments" (Exod. xxviii. 2) not only gave an imposing and inspiring appearance to the officiating priests, but they severally and separately suggested certain spiritual qualities. The white linen spoke of righteousness, the girdle of activity or strength, etc. (see above).

We who are servants of Jesus Christ are also priests (1 Pet. ii. 5; Rev. i. 6). There are certain things in which we are to be robed. We are, speaking generally, to "put on the Lord Jesus Christ" (Rom. xiii. 14); to put on "the new man," etc. (Eph. iv. 24). But there are certain graces which we are more particularly to wear.

I. THE ROBE OF HUMILITY. This is the beginning and the end, the first and the last grace, the foundation and the topstone of Christian character: we may call it an under-garment and an overcoat of the Christian wardrobe. "Be clothed with humility" (1 Pet. v. 5).

II. THE GARMENT OF FAITH. This is that clothing without which we cannot be justified before God now, nor permitted to sit down to the heavenly banquet hereafter (Matt. xxii. 11, 12).

III. THE GIRDLE OF TRUTH. (Eph. vi. 14.) It is truth, heavenly wisdom, which knits all other things together, and gives play and power to the spiritual faculties.

IV. THE SANDALS OF PEACE. (Rom. x. 15; Eph. vi. 15.)

V. THE CROWN OF RIGHTEOUSNESS. (2 Tim. iv. 8.) Righteousness is the regal thing; when that is gone the crown is fallen from our head (Lam. v. 16).

To those who "overcome" (Rev. iii. 5), who are "faithful unto death" (Rev. ii. 10), who "keep the faith" (2 Tim. iv. 7), it shall be given to: 1. Be clothed in white raiment" (spotless purity). 2. To receive "the crown of life" (life in all its celestial fulness and blessedness). 3. To wear "the crown of righteousness"—"a crown of glory that fadeth not away" (1 Pet. v. 4).—C.

Vers. 6, 8, 23, 24, 30.—*Equipment for special work.* There was a sense in which the whole congregation of Israel constituted a priesthood. It was an early promise that they should be a "kingdom of priests and a holy nation" (Exod. xix. 6). And such, indeed, they were, so far as they entered into and fulfilled the purposes of God. They were: 1. Separate from surrounding people (holy unto the Lord). 2. Permitted to draw near to God. 3. Allowed to bring the sacrificial victim to the holy place and slay it; indeed, in the case of the paschal lamb, they acted as priests without aid from any other hand.

But there were those who were: 1. Separated from them, and were thus holier than they. 2. Allowed to draw nearer to the Divine presence. 3. Designated to be continually offering up sacrifices to Jehovah. These were the priests and the high priests of the Lord in an especial sense, and they needed special equipment for their special work. From this chapter we select four principal points—

I. SPECIAL CLEANSING OF SOUL. (Ver. 6.)

II. SPECIAL CONSECRATION OF SPIRIT. (Vers. 23, 24.) One of the most significant rites in the entire ceremony of consecration was the taking by Moses of the blood of the "ram of consecration" (ver. 22), and putting it "upon the tip of Aaron's right ear, and upon the thumb of his right hand, and upon the great toe of his right foot." The interpretation of this symbolism hardly admits of error. What other truth could it import but that Aaron was thus set apart, not only generally for the service of the Lord, but specially in every member of his frame, in every faculty of his mind? He was to have: 1. *An open ear*, to welcome every word of the Lord. 2. *A ready hand*, to discharge diligently and conscientiously his daily duties. 3. *A quick foot*, to run in the way of God's commandments.

III. SPECIAL SYMPATHY WITH MEN. (Ver. 8.) The plate on which were inscribed the names of the twelve tribes was, as the word indicates, a *breast*-plate: so that the high priest symbolically bore the children of Israel on his heart. He carried their burden into the presence of God.

IV. SPECIAL ENDOWMENT. (Ver. 30.) The precious ointment, the anointing oil, upon the head that ran down upon Aaron's beard, that went down to the skirts of his garments (Ps. cxxxiii. 2), probably symbolized the grace of the Spirit of God outpoured upon the heart, affecting the whole nature, diffusing the delightful fragrance of piety and virtue.

We learn from these particulars—1. That we must not covet posts of special difficulty except we are equipped with peculiar qualifications. Not every good or every earnest Christian man is fitted to take high office in the kingdom of God. 2. That if we feel ourselves summoned to special work, we must seek all possible spiritual equipment. The conditions of successful service are those indicated above: (1) The full cleansing of our souls and lives from impurity (Ps. li. 7, 10, 11, 13; Isa. lii. 11; 1 John iii. 3). (2) The dedication of our whole selves to the service of Christ; heart and life; soul and body; having every faculty of the mind, every organ of our frame (ear, hand, foot), ready for sacred work. (3) Tender sympathy with men; "a heart at leisure from itself to soothe and sympathize." We shall *do* but little *for* men except we acquire the blessed art of *sympathizing with* them. A sympathetic spirit is a helpful, influential, winning spirit. (4) Endowment of all needful grace from on high. This must be gained from God, who, in answer to believing prayer, "giveth liberally." Purity, consecration, sympathy, grace,—these are the qualifications for high office, the sources of power, the assurance of success.—C.

Vers. 33—36.—*The burden of the Lord.* It is in our nature to love distinction, office, power. The instincts and impulses of our humanity enter with us into the service of the Lord; they belong to us as subjects of the kingdom of Christ (see Mark x. 28, 35, etc.). But here, as elsewhere, distinctions and duties, prizes and perils, honours and anxieties go together. We are reminded—

I. THAT PROTRACTED PREPARATION MAY BE NECESSARY for high office in the Church (ver. 33). Aaron and his sons were required to go through consecration services for seven days. It seems to us as if they must have become wearisome by exceeding length. But for such services as he and they were to render, such preparation was none too long. Consider how Moses was long in Midian, and Paul in Arabia, preparing for after-work. Our Lord himself went "into the wilderness" and into "desert places," preparing himself for his Divine ministry. In proportion to the seriousness, the greatness of the work we have to do, we may expect to find the extent and severity of the preparatory work.

II. THAT UNPALATABLE COMMUNICATIONS MAY HAVE TO BE MADE, in conformity with God's will. Moses might have shrunk (probably would have done so) from voluntarily imposing such protracted services on Aaron; but he had no option. God's will was clear, and he had no course but to obey; "so I am commanded," said he (ver. 35). Again and again the minister of Christ has to say or do things he would gladly leave unsaid or undone. But in such cases he must "not confer with flesh and blood" (Gal. i. 16), but do the will of the Master he serves (see 1 Sam. iii.).

III. THAT DISOBEDIENCE TO THE CLEAR WILL OF GOD INVOLVES great danger: "Keep the charge of the Lord, that ye die not" (ver. 35). We cannot undertake great duties without incurring the most serious responsibilities and running grave risks. If we take the post of "watchman unto the house of Israel," we must speak the true and faithful word, or the blood of souls will be required at our hand (Ezek. xxxiii. 7, 8). They who stand in God's house and speak in his Name, but who depart from his Word, grievously mislead their brethren, and must be answerable to the Lord their Judge at the day of account.

IV. THAT AN OBEDIENT HEART NEED NOT, AND WILL NOT, SHRINK FROM THE COMMANDMENTS OF THE LORD. (Ver. 36.) Aaron and his sons did not question or hesitate; they obeyed. Doubtless they found, as we shall find, that: 1. What seems formidable in prospect becomes simple and manageable in actual engagement. 2. God helps with his inspiring Spirit those who go with alacrity to their work. 3. There are unsuspected pleasures in sacred service. "His commandments are not grievous;" his "yoke is easy, his burden light;" his statutes are not our complaints but our songs in the house of our pilgrimage (Ps. cxix. 54).—C.

Vers. 1—5.—*Public inauguration of Divine service.* I. ALL THE PEOPLE GATHERED TOGETHER. 1. *Religion is universal,* as human necessity and sin. God and man reconciled and united in fellowship. No human condition dispenses with worship. We should labour to get *all the people* to the tabernacle. God invites them. His ministers should summon them. No excuse can be suffered either for their absence or for the lack of success in gathering them together. We shall succeed best when we speak to them in the Name of God and with his own Word. Lower means and motives, if employed at all, must be kept in subordinate places. 2. There are *no secrets in religion;* no esoteric doctrine; no rites or privileges which are not for the people. If the priests are set apart, the people witness their consecration, and sanction it and take part in it. The priests are for the people. A Church which withholds a part of the Lord's Supper from the congregation cannot be a true Church. In the commandment to gather the people was the implicit doctrine of universal priesthood, afterwards (as in 1 Pet.) more perfectly expressed when the great High Priest had come.

II. THE FOUNDATION ON WHICH ALL RELIGION STANDS IS THE REVEALED WORD AND

WILL OF GOD. The Lord spake to Moses. Moses did as the Lord commanded him. Moses said to the congregation, "This is the thing which the Lord commanded to be done." Mere will-worship is unacceptable to God. We must beware of *two errors*. 1. Dependence on mere *tradition* in contrast with the Word. No need of a supplementary revelation, for it implies that the Word was not sufficient—no authority in it, for the fathers and those who handed on the tradition were liable to err and falsify. 2. Expediency may mislead us into disobedience; fashion in worship; convenience consulted; pure truth hidden; man usurping God's place.

III. PUBLIC CONSECRATION OF PRIESTHOOD. The people saw the men, their garments, the consecrating oil, the atoning sacrifices, the basket of unleavened bread. 1. Spiritual leaders should be distinguishable, both personally and officially. 2. We should remember they are men, and liable to sin, and needing the same sacrifices as all others. 3. The unleavened bread of sincerity and truth is their main qualification. 4. They are nothing unless anointed, *i.e.* they are wholly dependent on the Spirit of God—not a line of succession, but a personal inspiration. 5. Their ministry being for the people, among the people, and with the help of the people, let the people by their assembly sanction their election and approve their consecration. A God-given ministry is not imposed upon congregations, but welcomed by their free choice.—R.

Ver. 6.—"*And Moses brought Aaron and his sons, and washed them with water.*" Not hands and feet only, as in daily ministrations, but the whole body, symbolizing entire spiritual cleansing.

I. Take this cleansing as MAN'S OBEDIENCE. It set forth: 1. Confession of sin and dependence on Divine grace. 2. Personal consecration—entire devotion to the service of God. 3. As performed by priests, the acceptance of a place in the priestly office and before the altar demanded conspicuous holiness and purity.

II. Thus was typified THE DIVINE PROMISE. 1. That man should be cleansed really by the Spirit. 2. That a perfect high priesthood should be provided. 3. That the necessary imperfection and impurity of an earthly service should be swallowed up hereafter in the holy perfection of the heavenly service, when all that approach God shall be like him.—R.

Vers. 7—9.—*Aaron's dress.* Coat, girdle, robe, ephod, breastplate, Urim and Thummim, mitre, golden plate, and crown,—all significant, and fulfilled in Christ. The two main ideas are *mediation* and *government*.

I. The high priest is clothed as MEDIATOR. 1. To offer sacrifice for sins. 2. To enter into the presence of Jehovah as intercessor. 3. To obtain and pronounce, as representative, the Divine benediction.

II. The high priest is clothed as KING. 1. With power to guide, counsel, command as an oracle. 2. With exalted personality to receive homage as the king of righteousness, the glory of God revealed. 3. As crowned, to establish and maintain his kingdom among men—ruling their hearts and lives, not by the power of this world, but by the priestly power of fellowship with God, for man is himself made kingly as he is admitted into the innermost chamber of God's presence.—R.

Vers. 10—12.—*Anointing.* The tabernacle, the altar, the vessels, the laver and its foot, Aaron the high priest. The main intention to lift up the thoughts of all, both priests and people, to Jehovah as the Source of all good gifts. The sprinkling was seven times, to denote the covenant relation between God and Israel.

I. The service of God requires SPECIAL CONSECRATION—both of persons and places and instrumentalities. 1. To keep the world's corruption away. 2. To exalt the faculties and feelings. 3. To help us to maintain the remembrance of the Divine covenant, and therefore to lay hold by special intercourse with God of his gifts. 4. To enable us, by concentration of efforts, to make the influence of religion more powerful in the world. Great mistake to suppose that, by breaking down distinctions between the believing and the unbelieving, the multitudes are brought nearer to God; on the contrary, the effect is to lessen the spiritual efficacy of religious ordinances, and to postpone the triumph of God's people.

II. The TRUE ANOINTING OF THE SPIRIT, THE TRUE DISTINCTION OF THE MINISTRY AND

OF THE MEANS EMPLOYED. 1. Distinguish between the rite itself and its fulfilment. Man anoints with oil, God with the Spirit. The two baptisms with water and with the Holy Ghost. 2. Special responsibility of those in office for the possession of spiritual power. We must not worship our own nets. They are nothing if not successful. By their fruits the living trees will be known. 3. God will be inquired of to bestow his grace; the anointing by his commandment was a renewal of his promise to bestow his gifts when they are asked. It was a covenant ceremony, and represented a covenant life. 4. Spiritual men engaged in the fulfilment of spiritual duties will, as much as possible, separate themselves from all earthly entanglements and incumbrances. The oil was poured on the head of the priest, and flowed downwards to the skirts of his garments, to signify that he must be totally possessed by the claims of his office, and endowed in every energy and act by the bestowment of the Spirit. What an encouragement to holiness, and at the same time what an incentive to prayer! We are kings and priests. If we forget our anointing, we not only lose our priestly purity, but our princely power over the world. A degraded priesthood the curse of the Church and the plague of mankind. A revived ministry the hope of the future. " Brethren, pray for us." " Ye have an unction from the Holy One."—R.

Vers. 13—36.—*The sacrifices of consecration.* Aaron and his sons. Holy week of separation. "So Aaron and his sons did all things which the Lord commanded by the hand of Moses." Moses, the mediator of the covenant, consecrated those who should afterwards fulfil the functions of the sanctuary. The order of the sacrifices was: 1. The sin offering. 2. The burnt offering. 3. The peace offering. Or (1) *expiation*, (2) *obedience*, (3) *acceptance*—the three great facts of the covenant life of God's people. That all these should be included in the consecration of the priesthood betokened the entire subordination of that mere temporary mediation to the fundamental relation between God and man. No priest was between the holiness of God and the sinfulness of men in any other sense than as a servant of that covenant which came out of the free grace of God. Here there is—

I. THE TRUE BASIS OF RELIGION set forth. It rests on (1) *the universal necessity of man*, and (2) *the universality of Divine grace.* Illustrate from history of man's religions how this basis has been ignored. Priesthood raised above people as though holy in themselves. Favouritism in heaven the exciting motive to sacrifices. Merit in man the measure of peace.

II. The typical significance of the Mosaic economy pointing to the PERFECTION OF THE DIVINE PROVISION FOR HUMAN SALVATION. All the priests, Aaron and his sons, are sinful, and require sacrifices of atonement. Their confession of imperfection was itself an appeal to God to supply the sinless priest, the perfect service, the everlasting mediation. Jesus Christ the High Priest. 1. His *official perfection*, arising out of his personal dignity as Son of God, and yet able to sympathize with those for whom he intercedes as Son of man. Spotless purity and perfect obedience could alone satisfy the requirements of a perfect Law. 2. Our faith in Christ sees in him not only a priestly Person, but *a Sacrifice actually offered.* The true sacrificial work of Christ was not merely his humiliation in living a human life, but his death on the cross, which was supremely the offering up of his blood, his life, as a true substitution for man. The death of the victim was a necessary part of the ceremony. Thus our High Priest must enter the holiest with blood, and no blood but his own could represent the whole humanity of man offered up—no sufferings but his could express perfect fulfilment of the Father's will. 3. The priesthood of Christ *secures our acceptance, and makes our religious life liberty*, not bondage.—R.

EXPOSITION.

CHAPTER IX.

THE FIRST PRIESTLY ACTS OF AARON AND HIS SONS are recounted in the chapter following that which narrates their consecration.

Vers. 1—6.—On the eighth day. The

seven days of consecration being now over, Aaron for the first time offers a sin offering and burnt offering for himself, and a sin offering, a burnt offering, a peace offering, and a meat offering for the congregation. He is still instructed by Moses as to what he is to do, but it is through him that the command is given to the people to present their offerings, and it is he that slays the victims and offers their blood. His own sin offering is a young calf, or young bull calf, whereas the sin offering commanded for the high priest on ordinary occasions was a young bull, further advanced in age (ch. iv. 3); and in presenting the blood he does not take it into the sanctuary according to the regulations in ch. iv. 6, but uses it as Moses had done in the sin offerings of the previous week, the purpose of the difference being to show that Aaron's full dignity had not yet devolved upon him. This did not take place until he had gone into the tabernacle with Moses (ver. 23). A ram is again taken for the burnt offering, as had been the case in Moses' sacrifice of the previous week. The children of Israel now present a kid, the offering generally made by a prince, that for the congregation being a young bull. In the words for to day the Lord will appear unto you, Moses promises the Divine appearance afterwards vouchsafed (ver. 23).

Ver. 7.—**Make an atonement for thyself, and for the people.** By means of the sin offering for the high priest, whose sin brought guilt both on himself and upon the people (ch. iv. 3). After he had (symbolically) purified himself and them of *this* guilt, he was to offer the offering of the people, which should purify them from the guilt contracted by their own sins, and make an atonement for them.

Vers. 8—14. — The high priest's sin offering and burnt offering for himself. The meat offering does not appear to have accompanied the burnt offering—the law having not yet been promulgated which ordered that the two sacrifices should always be presented together (Numb. xv. 4). **The burnt offering, with the pieces thereof,** in ver. 13, should rather be *the burnt offering in its several pieces.* The sinfulness of the Aaronic priesthood and the need of a perfect priest is indicated by this sacrifice (see Heb. vii. 24—27).

Vers. 15—21.— The people's sin offering, burnt offering, meat offering, and peace offerings follow. The meat offering is said to have been burnt upon the altar, beside the burnt sacrifice of the morning. It is probable that, on this occasion, the people's burnt offering, which consisted of a calf and a lamb, took the place of the ordinary morning sacrifice of a lamb (Exod. xxix. 38). Aaron is said to have offered the burnt offering according to the manner, or, as it is given in the margin, *ordinance*, that is, he burnt the flesh on the altar (ch. i. 7—9); he also burnt the handful of the meat offering, and he burnt the fat of the peace offering, upon the altar. He had previously

burnt the fat of his own sin offering, and the flesh of his burnt offering. Fire, therefore, was present upon the altar, and was used by Aaron, as by Moses, for sacrificial purposes *before* the fire came out from the Lord as described in ver. 24.

Ver. 22.—**And Aaron lifted up his hand** or (according to the more probable reading) *hands.* This was the first priestly benediction by Aaron, given from the elevated standing-place which he occupied by the side of the altar.

Ver. 23.—**Moses** (for the last time) **and Aaron** (for the first time) **went into the taber**nacle in the character of priest. During this visit Moses committed to Aaron the care of the things within the tabernacle, as he had already given him the charge of all connected with the sacrifices of the court. Not till after this is Aaron fully initiated into his office. "No man taketh this honour unto himself, but he that is called of God, as was Aaron" (Heb. v. 4). On coming out from the tabernacle, Moses and Aaron, standing near the door, unite in blessing the congregation, in order to show the harmony between them and the capacity of blessing in the Name of the Lord enjoyed by Aaron as by Moses. The latter has now divested himself of that part of his office which made him the one mediator between God and his people. Aaron is henceforth a type of Christ as well as Moses. While giving the joint blessing, the glory of the Lord appeared unto all the people, proceeding from the ark, and enveloping the lawgiver and the priest as they stood together.

Ver. 24.—**And there came a fire out from before the Lord.** The sacrifices were already smouldering on the altar, a ram, a calf, and a lamb, besides the internal fat of a young bull, a kid, a bullock, and a ram, and a handful of flour. They would have continued smouldering all the day and the night, but a miraculous fire issued from the tabernacle, and consumed the whole in the sight of the people. So fire fell and consumed Solomon's sacrifice at the dedication of the temple. Jewish tradition reports that the fire was always kept alive until the reign of Manasseh, when it became extinguished. When the people saw this sight, they shouted, and fell on their faces. They had been standing in a state of intense expectation, awaiting the fulfilment of the promise that the Lord would appear unto them to-day, and watching the acts of the two brothers; and their feelings are now raised to the utmost enthusiasm and awe by the appearance of the glory of the Lord and the action of the Divine fire. See 2 Chron. vii. 3.

HOMILETICS.

Vers. 8—23.—The first act of the new priesthood is sacrifice, by which reconciliation was ceremonially effected; the second (vers. 22, 23), a double benediction. As soon as the people are reconciled to him, God's blessing abundantly pours itself on them. The sacrifice is: 1. For themselves, showing the weakness of the Aaronic priesthood. 2. For the people, showing its power.

Ver. 24.—*Miraculous confirmation of the new polity* is given by a fire issuing from the presence of God.

I. INSTANCES OF A LIKE KIND OF DIVINE AGENCY BY FIRE. 1. The case of Gideon. "And the angel of God said unto him, Take the flesh and the unleavened cakes, and lay them upon this rock, and pour out the broth. And he did so. Then the angel of the Lord put forth the end of the staff that was in his hand, and touched the flesh and the unleavened cakes; and there rose up fire out of the rock, and consumed the flesh and the unleavened cakes" (Judg. vi. 20, 21). 2. The case of Elijah. "Call ye on the name of your gods, and I will call on the Name of the Lord: and the God that answereth by fire, let him be God. And all the people answered and said, It is well spoken. . . . Then the fire of the Lord fell, and consumed the burnt sacrifice and the wood, and the stones, and the dust, and licked up the water that was in the trench" (1 Kings xviii. 24—38). 3. The case of Solomon. "Now when Solomon had made an end of praying, the fire came down from heaven, and consumed the burnt offering and the sacrifices; and the glory of the Lord filled the house. And the priests could not enter into the house of the Lord, because the glory of the Lord had filled the Lord's house" (2 Chron. vii. 1, 2).

II. THE RESULT IN EACH CASE IS AWE. 1. "Gideon said, Alas, O Lord God! for because I have seen an angel of the Lord face to face. And the Lord said unto him, Peace be unto thee; fear not: thou shalt not die" (Judg. vi. 22, 23). 2. "And when all the people saw it, they fell on their faces: and they said, The Lord, he is the God; the Lord, he is the God" (1 Kings xviii. 39). 3. "And when all the children of Israel saw how the fire came down, and the glory of the Lord upon the house, they bowed themselves with their faces to the ground upon the pavement, and worshipped, and praised the Lord, saying, For he is good; for his mercy endureth for ever" (2 Chron. vii. 3).

III. THE PRESENT A FITTING OCCASION FOR A MIRACULOUS INTERVENTION. A miracle is to be expected at the introduction of any new system which emanates from God, because it is a means of showing Divine approval which cannot be gainsaid; but it is not to be expected frequently afterwards, or it would lose its special effect of impressing by its strangeness. The institution of the Law is such an occasion, and accordingly fire and smoke and earthquake showed the presence of God on Sinai. The institution of an hereditary priesthood was a part of the legislation which, being a vast change on the previously existing system, specially required a sign of God's approval which all might see. The erection of Solomon's temple was a like occasion. So at the institution of the Christian dispensation, miraculous gifts were vouchsafed to the apostles—speaking with tongues, prophecy, gifts of healing, and the rest—which were not intended to continue, and died out as soon as the Church was regarded as no longer coming into being, but fully formed. No new doctrine must be accepted except upon the testimony of miracle, but a succession of miracles is not required to certify doctrine which has been once confirmed by miraculous means.

IV. SIMILARITY YET DIFFERENCE OF THE PENTECOSTAL FIRE. It was given at the institution of the new apostolic ministry. It was a confirmation of its authority to the minds of the recipients as well as others. But it indicated more than a mere Divine approval of a new system. It symbolized the gift of the Holy Ghost, and therefore it did not consume a sacrifice, but "it sat upon each" of those who were to be the instruments of the Holy Ghost in converting the world, and the ministers of the new dispensation. The fire of jealousy, which struck to the earth those who approached the Divine presence unbidden, has become the fire of love.

HOMILIES BY VARIOUS AUTHORS.

A sign expected and received. Ch. ix.; cf. 2 Chron. v. 13, 14; Ezra vi. 16—22; Acts i.; ii. We have now before us the hopeful fashion in which Aaron and his sons entered upon their work. The consecration being completed on the eighth day, Moses directed them to take for themselves a sin offering and a burnt offering, and to receive at the hands of the people similar offerings, and, in addition, a bullock and a ram for peace offerings, with the usual accompaniment of a meat offering, and to expect a sign from the Lord at the conclusion of the service. "To-day," said he, "the Lord will appear unto you." A penitent yet consecrated priesthood, acting on behalf of a penitent and consecrated people, are warranted in expecting a sign from God himself. The first priestly service is thus filled with hope, and the hope was realized at the end of it. The following lessons are plainly taught by this passage—

I. THE ONE INDISPENSABLE PRELIMINARY TO EXALTATION FROM GOD IS HUMILIATION BEFORE HIM. Both priests and people must bring their sin offering and appear in penitential mood. Unless we humble ourselves under the mighty hand of God, we need not expect to be exalted (Matt. xxiii. 12; 1 Pet. v. 6). Hence the Law of the Divine dealings has been to "hide pride from man" (Job xxxiii. 17). It is only when we have pride eliminated that we have room for blessing.

II. CONSCIOUS DEDICATION TO GOD IS AN EARNEST OF BLESSING ON ITS WAY. The priests and people both bring their burnt offerings as well as their sin offerings. They realize how reasonable it is to dedicate themselves to the Lord, who has been so merciful in his dealings with them. It was the same with Solomon and his associates at the dedication of the temple. It was the same with the disciples previous to the Pentecostal baptism. It was consecrated men and women who expected special blessing. And it is the same still; self-emptied, self-dedicated sinners are being qualified for special blessing.

III. THE UNION OF NUMBERS IN DESIRE AND IN HOPE IS ALSO A SIGN OF A COMING BLESSING. The people assembled in their thousands before the tabernacle, and the priests co-operated with them in their offices. One heart and hope animated the host. We see the same unity at the dedication of Solomon's temple. "It came even to pass, as the trumpeters and singers were *as one*, to make *one sound*," etc. (2 Chron. v. 13). We see the same unity before Pentecost. "These all continued with one accord in prayer and supplication, with the women, and Mary the mother of Jesus, and with his brethren" (Acts i. 14). Such a union of numbers in desire and in hope should be encouraged continually. It need not be disregarded. It is a sign surely that blessing is on its way when such happy union of heart and hope takes place.

IV. GOD'S RIGHTS MUST BE CAREFULLY REGARDED IF HIS SPECIAL BLESSING IS TO BE OBTAINED. The priests were directed to lay the best portions on the altar, to pay thus their due to God, before the blessing is vouchsafed. This element is sometimes overlooked. People make "systematic beneficence" depend upon special blessing, instead of *preceding* it. But it is manifest, from Mal. iii. 10, that God asks for proof, in the payment of Divine dues, of people's desire for special blessing. It is idle to expect great blessing from above if men wrong God as they do. His proportion of our substance can be calculated in cool blood and paid conscientiously, without waiting for a baptism in order to do so, and if we are prepared to exhibit our sense of obligation to God in this real way, we may hope for a very special baptism.

V. BENEDICTION MAY BE PRONOUNCED WITH CONFIDENCE IN THE LIGHT OF PROMISED BLESSING. At the conclusion of the ritual, Aaron proceeded to bless the people. His benediction preceded the Divine manifestation. It was pronounced in full view of the promise. It was, as we shall soon see, amply redeemed. And does not this fact throw light upon all benedictions? They are not blessings conveyed through the person pronouncing them, but blessings guaranteed, so to speak, to proceed from God himself on the ground of his own promise. It is the faithful Promiser the people are to look to, not his officer in pronouncing the benediction.

VI. GOD WAS PLEASED TO MANIFEST HIMSELF AS CONSUMING FIRE UPON HIS ALTAR. What God gave was additional fire to the sacred deposit already so carefully preserved.

An intense flame rose up from the altar, having first issued from the tabernacle; and all the people rejoiced because of it. "When all the people saw it, they shouted, and fell on their faces." God is a consuming fire in the way of acceptance, just as well as in the way of wrath. The psalmist gives us clear evidence of this in his prayer, "Remember all thy offerings, and accept ('reduce to ashes,' יְדַשְּׁנֶה) thy burnt sacrifice" (Ps. xx. 3). The case of Elijah at Carmel goes to demonstrate the same thing (1 Kings xviii. 24, 36). And when we reach the history of Pentecost, with the Spirit as "tongues of fire" settling down on the disciples, we can have no doubt as to the significance of the manifestation (Acts ii.). "God is light," and along with light there is heat and sublimation. He interposes no screen to prevent the heat-rays from reaching men's hearts. They become fervent in spirit, and thus serve the Lord (Rom. xii. 11). It is this visitation we all need—God accepting us as "living sacrifices," and enabling us most ardently to serve him. May none of us experience the consuming fire of the Divine wrath, but that of the Divine love and mercy!—R. M. E.

Vers. 23, 24.—*The glory of the Lord.* The petition of Moses was, "Show me thy glory." The wisdom, power, and goodness of the Almighty are visible in all his works, and "the heavens declare his glory," but man longs for a fuller display of the matchless perfections of Deity. The artist is superior to his handiwork, and to view God is a greater satisfaction than to contemplate the evidences of his existence and skill that lie around us. To behold him as he is, to "see his face" in its undimmed lustre,—this is reserved as the special joy of heaven. In the mean time, it was permitted the Israelites to gaze upon material manifestations of his presence, and it is the delight of Christians to catch spiritual glimpses of his glory, by faith seeing him who is invisible.

I. THE FORM ASSUMED BY THE GLORY OF THE LORD. 1. *A brightness manifest to all the people.* Compare this passage with Numb. xvi. 42, and the conclusion is natural that there was a brilliant illumination of the cloud that ordinarily rested upon the tabernacle. Therein Jehovah was ever visible, but now revealed in such wondrous guise that his glory was patent to the dullest eye. Deity no longer concealed but expressed. When Jesus Christ came as the Word, the evangelist declares, "We beheld his glory, as of the only begotten of the Father." The face is the noblest part of the body, the dial-plate of character, the index of the soul; hence in the face of Jesus Christ we behold the light of the knowledge of the glory of God. The gospel dispensation "exceeds in glory" (2 Cor. iii. 9), for it is the "ministration of the Spirit," the "ministration of the righteousness" of God. The answer to the request of Moses was contained in the assurance that all the goodness of God should pass before him; and when there is an outpouring of the Spirit, so that many turn to the Saviour and rejoice in the mercy and loving-kindness of God who will have all men to be saved, then is the glory of the Lord revealed and all flesh see it together. 2. *A mighty energy,* as flaming fire, attesting the acceptance of the sacrifices. These were suddenly consumed, showing that the power of God can accomplish at once what at other times requires a long period under the operation of customary laws. There is not merely attractive brilliancy in God, there is majestic might which may be used for or against us, according to our obedience or disobedience. When tongues of fire sat upon the disciples at Pentecost, their whole being—body, soul, and spirit, mind, affection, and will—seemed immediately permeated with the Spirit of Christ, and they spoke with boldness and witnessed with great power, so that thousands were added to the Church. Let God appear, and men shall be saved, not in units, but in multitudes. Who can tell what shall be the result of Christ's appearing in glory? This we know, that the offerings upon the altar, the Christians dedicated to his service, shall be transformed into his likeness, the imitation not gradual as in ordinary seasons, but instantaneous. 3. *The unusual glory proceeding from the ordinary manifestation.* The fire "came out from before the Lord." It was not a different power, therefore, but the usual Shechinah fire exhibited to all in wondrous operation. The truths that evoke such feeling and lead to such holy action in times of refreshing and revival, are those which have been previously insisted on, only now accompanied with potency, the breath of the Spirit kindling the embers into a glow, and causing the heat so to radiate as to affect large circles of humanity. The arm of the Lord, alway present, is revealed; its might, perceived by the few, is shown to the many.

II. THE TIME AT WHICH THE GLORY OF GOD APPEARS. 1. We may expect it *at eventful stages in the history of his Church.* Here at the establishment of the order of priesthood, to sanction it, to express approval of the men appointed, and to complete their consecration. The altar fire and all its future offerings were thus hallowed. When some principle of the Divine government is to be vindicated, or some messenger honoured in the sight of the people, or a new departure made in the accomplishment of his purposes, then may we anticipate displays of supernatural beauty and force. 2. *When his instructions have been respected, his commands faithfully observed.* There had been seven days of watching, and the eighth day was marked by confession of sin and dedicatory sacrifices. God was honoured, and evinced his delight thereat. Sanctification precedes the manifestation of Divine power (Josh. iii. 5; ch. ix. 4). 3. *When it has been prophesied by his servants.* This was a fulfilment of Moses' prediction, and may incite us to study Scripture and value its prophetic statements. It is remarkable how the way has been ever prepared for "mighty works" by previous announcement, as if to fit men to appreciate the miracles and to recognize them as coming from God. The herald proclaims the advent of the king. 4. *When his servants have drawn nigh to his presence, and invoked a blessing upon the people.* Prayer is the fleeting breath that proves of such marvellous efficacy in securing tokens of God's favour. Would we see the glory of God in the sanctuary? then let us try to approach the very throne of Deity. To be led in supplication into the holiest of all is to "bring all heaven before our eyes." Jesus, our Prophet-Priest, ascended as he was blessing the disciples; the fruits of his invocation were quickly seen at Pentecost, and they continue to enrich and gladden the Church.

III. THE EFFECT IT PRODUCES. 1. *Enthusiasm.* The people "shouted" for joy and thanksgiving, they gave utterance to their admiration and excitement. That Jehovah should condescend thus to visit his children, that the Infinite One should so openly reveal himself! The coldest are warmed into emotion, the hardest surfaces yield, the sternest natures cannot repress exclamations of astonishment when they perceive the signs of a presence more than mortal. 2. *Reverence.* "They fell on their faces," to worship. Awe filled their minds and prostrated their bodies. Never should excitement lead to forgetfulness of the respect due to God. And if it be otherwise, there is reason to suspect the genuineness of the professedly Divine exhibition of approval. We may fear lest the fire has been begotten not of heaven but of earth.

CONCLUSION. Will any refuse to behold in Christ "the brightness of the Father's glory"? Here "all" the people saw the glory. Age, sex, or rank no hindrance. There may be a difference in the apprehension of the significance of the spectacle, but it should awaken gratitude and veneration in every breast.—S. R. A.

Vers. 1—7.—*The eighth day.* There is sacred mystery in the numbers of Holy Scripture well worthy of attention. We have an example before us.

I. ON THIS DAY THE CONSECRATIONS WERE COMPLETED. 1. *The eighth is a day signalized by sanctity.* (1) All children were, according to the Law, in the uncleanness of their birth until the eighth day. Then they received circumcision, and thenceforward were recognized as holy, having the seal of the covenant or purification of God upon them (ch. xii. 2, 3). (2) The young of beasts, in like manner, were ceremonially unclean before their eighth day. They were therefore unfit to be offered as sacrifices. But on the eighth day and thenceforward that unfitness ceased; they were accounted clean (ch. xxii. 27). (3) Persons unclean through leprosy, or through any issue, or a Nazarite in case of accidental defilement by the dead, all had to abide seven days in uncleanness. The eighth day, in all such cases, was memorable as that upon which they were accounted clean (ch. xiv. 8—10; xv. 13, 14; Numb. vi. 9, 10). (4) So here, the tabernacle, the altar, all the vessels of the ministry, together with the priests, were seven days in the process of purification, and on the eighth day the purity of all became established (comp. Ezek. xliii. 26, 27). 2. *These things point to gospel times.* (1) The pollutions of the birth refer to original sin. This, in the case of the children, is so obvious as to need no comment. The reason of the law of uncleanness in relation to the young of animals is that in the Levitical system they were made representatives of human beings. (2) The pollutions of adults would stand for sins committed "after the similitude of Adam's transgression." (3) All were "purged with blood," the blood of circumcision or that of animal sacrifices, which anticipated that precious blood of Christ by which we are redeemed from " all sin." 3. *But what has this to do with the " eighth day " ?* (1) The eighth day remarkably characterizes the gospel. Since in the week there are seven days, the "eighth" day and the "first" are obviously the same. Now, it was on the "first day of the week" that Jesus rose from the dead (Matt. xxviii. 1). On the first day he seems to have several times appeared to his disciples during the forty days of his sojourn on the earth after his resurrection. On the first day he ascended into heaven, if we take the " forty days " to be clear days. The memorable day of Pentecost is calculated to have fallen upon the first day of the week. The early Christians kept the first day sacredly, as the seventh had been by the Jews (see Acts xx. 7 ; 1 Cor. xvi. 2). This was called " the Lord's day " (Rev. i. 10), just as our Eucharist is called " the Lord's Supper," because he instituted it. (2) But why should the eighth day have been chosen thus to characterize the gospel? This question may be better answered as we proceed to notice—

II. That on this day the Lord was to appear. (Ver. 4.) 1. *This promise had an immediate fulfilment.* The Shechinah that had been in the thick darkness of the most holy place, shined forth in brightness upon the people (ver. 23). 2. *It had a fuller accomplishment in the gospel.* (1) Christ is the true Shechinah (comp. Isa. xl. 5 with Matt. iii. 3; see also Matt. xvii. 2; John i. 14; ii. 11; xi. 40; xiv. 9; 2 Cor. iv. 4; Col. i. 15; Heb. i. 3). (2) The Shechinah also appeared after our Lord's ascension, viz. in the wonders of the memorable day of Pentecost. 3. *The crowning manifestation is reserved to the great day.* (1) Then Jesus will be revealed "without sin." He will not then appear amid circumstances of humiliation, as in his first advent. (2) He will be revealed "in all his glory." (*a*) "His own," Messiah's, glory. (*b*) That of "his Father," as "the God of glory." (*c*) "With the glory of his holy angels," who attend the "King of glory" as his retinue. 4. *This will be the glory of the eighth day.* (1) The six days of the creation week are supposed by Barnabas to represent six chiliads, or periods of a thousand years, during which the world is to be in toil and sorrow. The sabbath at the end of these represents the thousand years of John (Rev. xx. 6), distinguished as " *the* Millennium." The Rabbi Elias and other authorities are cited in favour of this view; and it is countenanced by the course of the fulfilment of prophecy. (2) At the close of this age is the final judgment, which introduces a still more glorious state, described as "a new heaven and a new earth" (see Rev. xxi. and xxii.). This, then, is the eighth day. As the Millennium (Rev. xx.) is the fulfilment of the Jewish sabbath, so is the superior blessedness to follow the fulfilment of the Christian (Heb. iv. 6—9, margin). Then will everything in earth and heaven be consecrated.

III. Then will the value of the Great Sacrifice appear. 1. *As averting the evils of sin.* (1) Who, without the purification of the gospel, can encounter the brightness of that Epiphany (Mal. iii. 2) ? (2) But those who possess this purity need have no fear of the horrors of the "outer darkness" (Rev. xxi. 7, 8; xxii. 14, 15). 2. *As procuring ineffable bliss.* (1) The consecration of the eighth day resulted from the ceremonies of the days preceding. So will the purity of the heavenly state rise out of the tragedies and horrors of Calvary. (2) The summoning of the sacrifices on the eighth day was, amongst other things, to witness this. All were summoned, viz. sin, burnt, peace, and bread offerings. In the blessings of the gospel we have all that was foreshadowed by Levitical oblations of every kind. (3) The song of Moses and of the Lamb will swell the rapture of heaven.—J. A. M.

Vers. 8—24.—*Aaron's first priestly services.* Moses officiated as the priest of the Lord until the consecration of Aaron and his sons was completed. Now they enter upon their functions, and the verses recited furnish us with an account of their first services. In reviewing these we notice—

I. The offerings. 1. *Aaron's offering for himself.* (1) The Jews say this was intended to make atonement for his sin in connection with the golden calf. Possibly this may have been so ; for we have no record elsewhere of any formal atonement for that offence. Aaron, doubtless, had many offences to atone for. The sacrifice of Christ is not only for sins, but also for sin. (2) Aaron's own hands slew this victim. What a graphic confession of sin was this! What an unequivocal acknowledgment of his deserving to die! Our confession of sin before God should be with deep conviction and reality. (3) He put the blood upon the horns of the altar. These were fronting the vail, behind which was the ark of the covenant and the glory of the Lord. This putting of the blood with the finger before the face of God was, as it were, pointing it out to him, calling his attention to it. So should the faith of the sinner point out to God's mercy the blood of the cross which satisfies his justice. (4) Aaron's sons served with him at the altar. They brought the blood to have it sprinkled. This was the confession of their part in the guilt of their father. Guilt is hereditary and relatively distributive (see Numb. xvi. 32, 33; Josh. vii. 24, 25). It was also an expression of their faith in the blood of the common Redeemer. (5) This offering of Aaron for his own sin before he could offer for the people suggests the imperfection of the Levitical priesthood, and therefore the necessity of the priesthood of the gospel (see Heb. v. 3; vii. 26—28; ix. 7—14). 2. *The offerings for the people.* (1) Aaron himself slew also these victims (vers. 15, 16). This he did as the representative of the people. Individuals were directed to slay their own victims (comp. ch. i. 5, 11; iii. 4, 8, 13). But these were for the congregation. (2) The sons of Aaron helped him here also. They " presented unto him the blood, which he sprinkled upon the altar round about." They also brought the fat of the inwards to him (vers. 18—20). This was suggestive of the nature of the Levitical priesthood, which was destined to pass from hand to hand. The comparison here is favourable to the priesthood of Christ, which is " unchangeable " (Heb. vii. 23—25). (3) The breast and shoulder were waved and heaved, and afterwards came to the lot of Aaron and his sons. Here we are taught that it is God's order that " they which preach the gospel should live of the gospel " (see 1 Cor. ix. 13, 14; Matt. x. 10).

II. The blessing. 1. *The blessing from the altar* (ver. 22). (1) As Aaron, standing upon the altar, pronounced his first blessing upon the people, this shows the Source from whence all blessing springs. Even in heaven, the Great Sacrifice of the altar of Calvary will be the burden of the song of the redeemed (Rev. v. 9—14). (2) In blessing, Aaron acted as the type of Christ, who, while he moved about upon this earth, which was the altar of his sacrifice, dispensed blessings in a thousand forms. Witness (*a*) the beatitudes in the Sermon on the Mount. (*b*) The miracles of beneficence. (*c*) His official benedictions. (3) As Aaron, standing upon the altar, lifted up his hands, blessed the people, and then went into the holy place, so Jesus, standing on the Mount of Olives, after lifting up his hands and blessing his disciples, ascended into the holy place of the heavens (comp. Luke xxiv. 50, 51). 2. *The blessing from the holy place.* (1) Coming forth from the holy place, Aaron again blessed the people. The words of the benediction are given in Numb. vi. 23—27. Between these and those of the apostolic benediction, which sets forth the genius of the gospel, there is remarkable correspondence (see 2 Cor. xiii. 14). (2) In response to this second benediction, " the glory of the Lord appeared unto all the people." We are here reminded how Jesus, before ascending into heaven, encouraged his disciples " not to depart from Jerusalem, but wait for the promise of the Father," and how, " when the day of Pentecost was fully come," that promise was verified. (3) " And there came a fire out from before the Lord," etc. (ver. 24). This was the emblem of the Holy Spirit, whose baptism, like fire, searches into substances, while water can only wash the surfaces (Matt. iii. 11, 12). So in the baptism on the day of Pentecost, tongues of flame sat on the disciples (Acts ii. 3). (4) The consuming of the fat of the inwards on the altar by the sacred fire foreshowed how the body of our sins is destroyed in the sacrifice of Christ, who, " through the Eternal Spirit, offered himself without spot to God " (Heb. ix. 14). It also describes the manner in which the wicked will be treated who persist in their rebellion against God (Ps. xxxvii. 20). Those whose sins are not consumed in the fires of love will themselves be consumed in the fires of wrath.—J. A. M.

Vers. 1—6.—*Appearing together before God.* It is true that we are always " in the presence of the Lord." " He is not far from any one of us." " He compasses our path and our lying down: he besets us behind and before." There is no man who at any moment may not use the prophet's words, " The Lord, *before whom I stand*." But it is also true that God would have us place ourselves consciously and in company before him; that we should gather together at his house and worship in " his holy temple." We gain thoughts on this subject from our text, viz.—

I. God's call to his own presence. (Vers. 5, 6.) It was at the Lord's own command that "all the congregation drew near and stood before" him. The entire scene was due to explicit Divine direction. It is God himself who calls us to his presence. We may venture to ask why he does so, and to answer by suggesting: 1. That it is a part of his Divine satisfaction in us to receive our united homage and thanksgiving; and 2. That he knows that public worship is best suited to impress our minds and strengthen our souls in heavenly wisdom. But we are certain that *it is his will*, for whatever reasons. "Not forsaking the assembling of ourselves together," etc. (Heb. x. 25; see Acts ii. 42). The presentation of ourselves before God should be measured thus: (1) multiplied by (*a*) our sense of God's pleasure with our worship; (*b*) our need of spiritual refreshment and elevation; (*c*) usefulness to others by way of encouragement in piety. (2) Limited by home duties and the other claims of our outer life.

II. The human instrument in this sacred summons. (Vers. 1, 3.) Here we have a double human instrumentality: Moses called Aaron, etc. (ver. 1), and Aaron was instructed to take on himself the duty of summoning the children of Israel to bring their sacrifices before the Lord (ver. 3). God continually speaks to us through man. Some men are his spokesmen in an especial sense and in a large degree; all of us are to be listeners to those who speak in his name. Those who speak for him are to be faithful and earnest in summoning his people to "stand before the Lord." Does the prophet ask, "What shall I cry?" Surely, one answer of the heavenly voice is, "O come, let us worship and bow down: let us kneel before the Lord our Maker" (Isa. xl. 6; Ps. xcv. 6; see Ps. c. 2, 3, 4).

III. The spirit in which we should respond. We should come before the Lord: 1. In a spirit of *humility*. Aaron himself was to take a sin offering (ver. 2), and this after all the sacrifices described in the preceding chapter. The people also were to present a sin offering (ver. 3). Though we may be in a state of reconciliation with God, we have need of the spirit of penitence at all times, and, when we draw near to the throne of grace, should ask that the mercy of God in Jesus Christ may cover our offences and shortcomings. 2. In a spirit of *consecration*. Aaron was to take a ram for a burnt offering (ver. 2); the people a calf and a lamb for the same kind of sacrifice (ver. 3). They were—as we are—to be ready to consecrate themselves unto the Lord, to offer themselves in spiritual sacrifice on his altar. We are to go up to God's house ready to renew our vows unto him. 3. In a spirit of *gratitude and joy*. The children of Israel were not to omit the meat offering or the peace offering (ver. 4). We are to take with us before God a heart full of thanksgiving for his bounty; also of social, sacred joy. We are to rejoice together before him. 4. In a spirit of *devout expectation*. The Hebrew worshippers were to look for the manifestation of Jehovah: "To-day the Lord will appear unto you" (ver. 4). We, too, are to expect that God will be with us; that he will draw nigh unto us when we draw nigh unto him (Jas. iv. 8); that Christ our Lord will "manifest himself unto us," will "come unto us, and make his abode with us" (John xiv. 21—23).—C.

Ver. 7.—*Sacrifice for sin*. We may look first at our subject simply as an incident in human history, apart from the consideration of its place in the inspired record. Then we have—

I. A representative scene in the history of man. The most eminent civilian in the nation says to the most eminent ecclesiastic, "Go unto the altar, and offer thy sin offering, . . . and make an atonement for thyself, and for thy people." Under every sky, in every age, we have the sad, solemn facts of which these words are the expression. 1. Man conscious of sin, saying, "I ought" and "I ought not," knowing in his heart that he has done that which should have been left undone, and has omitted to do that which he should have done; with the language of conscious guilt upon his lips. 2. Man seeking reconciliation with an offended God, feeling and owning that, in addition to other duties, and even above all other considerations, he must seek and find a way by which God, by which the Supreme Power, may be conciliated. 3. Man seeking restoration by sacrifice; practically acknowledging that death is due to sin, dramatically appealing to the offended Power to accept the life of the slain animal instead of his own; "making atonement" for sin. The priest at the altar is a picture which all nations have presented—a picture of humanity conscious of its guilt seeking mercy and restoration, hoping to attain it by a substitutionary sacrifice. The want is deep and wide; how shall it be met? It was met, in the first instance, by the ritual under the Law, by—

II. GOD'S TEMPORARY PROVISION. "The Lord commanded" Moses to say to Aaron, "Go unto the altar," etc. This act of religious service was done by Divine direction. Elsewhere men were blindly groping after him, and endeavouring to find a way of approach and reconciliation. Here, in the wilderness of Sinai, was a people, the nucleus of a nation, which "knew what it worshipped" (John iv. 22), which was taught of God himself. The Hebrew nation had been divinely instructed, and by its sacrifices declared : 1. That God had included all under sin, both priest and people, "for thyself and for the people." 2. That sin was deserving of death. 3. That a sin offering would be accepted by the merciful and righteous One. 4. That only a separated and holy man might approach the altar in sacrifice. 5. That the sin offering, having been presented and accepted, by the Holy One, all who would might, in sacred symbolism (the burnt offering), consecrate themselves to the service of a gracious God. But we must look further to—

III. THE DIVINE INTENTION WHICH LAY BEHIND. "This commandment of the Lord" was not *final*. It was adequate for the purpose. It was good for a time, for a dispensation; but it did not meet the wants of the race. Nor did it realize "the eternal purpose which he purposed" (Eph. iii. 11), nor exhaust the possibilities of the Divine wisdom and grace. "It is not possible that the blood of bulls and of goats should take away sins" (Heb. x. 4). God would manifest his power and love in a far mightier way than this. 1. The altar should give place to the cross. 2. The victim from the herd and flock to the Lamb of God himself. 3. The fallible, changing priesthood to the holy, ever-living Saviour. 4. The many offerings continually repeated to the "one Sacrifice for sins for ever" (Heb. x. 12).

1. With the pagan and the Jew, we share the common human consciousness of sin and need. 2. With the Jew, in distinction from the pagan, we have a divinely sanctioned method of approach and reconciliation. 3. With immeasurable advantage over Jew and pagan, we all have access at all times through the one Mediator, and can plead at every hour the one all-sufficient Sacrifice for sin. How great and high the privilege! How serious and solemn the responsibility!—C.

Vers. 8—21.—*The priest at the altar.* Aaron now enters on the great and high work to which he is appointed—that of God's chosen high priest. He "went unto the altar." As we follow him in that first official act (ver. 8) and see him, with the help of his sons (ver. 9), slaying the calf or the goat (vers. 8, 15), putting the blood on the horns, or pouring it at the bottom of the altar (ver. 9), we are reminded of fundamental truth which does not belong to one dispensation or one race, but to man everywhere and always.

1. THE SAD ASSUMPTION—UNIVERSAL GUILT. Some truths are rather assumed than enunciated in Scripture: this is one. Not that it is not stated (Rom. iii. 9, 23; Gal. iii. 22, etc.). But it is more often taken for granted. Thus in this scene. Aaron and his sons present sin offerings for themselves. It is assumed that there are not only "sinners of the Gentiles" needing mercy, but that the "holy nation" itself, the priestly family itself, nay, the high priest himself, is numbered among the sinful. This accords with our experience. 1. A large proportion of men are *notoriously*, presumptuously guilty; their lives proclaim aloud that they are transgressors against God. 2. Of the rest, a very large proportion are *confessedly* guilty; they allow freely that they have sinned by omission and commission. 3. The rest are *evidently mistaken* concerning themselves. If not apparent to human eye, it is obvious to the Divine that their lives are faulty and their souls stained. There is not one exception in the whole camp, in the entire congregation, in the nation, in the race. *All* have sinned, and need atonement.

II. THE FIRST DEEP NEED OF THE SOUL—DIVINE MERCY. The first sacrifice presented by Aaron for himself was "the calf of the sin offering" (ver. 8); the first for the people was "the goat which was the sin offering" (ver. 15). Man can do nothing in God's service till he is pardoned and accepted. "Forgiveness of sins" is the first great need of the soul, as it is the first great gift of the gospel (Luke xxiv. 47; Acts ii. 38;

xxvi. 18, etc.). "There is forgiveness with God, that he may be feared" (Ps. cxxx. 4). There would be no "fear," no reverence, no worship, no service of the Holy One, if forgiveness of sin were not attainable at once. That is the starting-point and condition of human devotion.

III. THE ATTENDANT SPIRITUAL STEP—SELF-SURRENDER. When Aaron had presented the sin offering for himself, he had not concluded his oblation; "he slew the burnt offering" also (ver. 12). So with "the people's offering" (vers. 15, 16). The significance of this second sacrifice was that the worshipper consecrated himself on the altar (to the service) of Jehovah. A perfect picture of sacred and abiding truth. We cannot go in humility and penitence, seeking mercy through Christ Jesus, without offering ourselves to him who has bought us with the price of his own blood. The soul longing for reconciliation with God offers itself freely in holy service unto him, lays itself on his altar, a "whole burnt offering unto the Lord." A living faith in Christ implies the eager taking of everything from him, and the cheerful giving of everything to him.

IV. THE CERTAIN ISSUE—A BLESSED SPIRITUAL ESTATE. A "meat offering" and "peace offerings" (vers. 17, 18) came after the other two. Sin forgiven, self surrendered, —then comes a sense of reconciliation, grateful acknowledgment of God's kindness, a holy joy in him (Rom. v. 1, 11). The assurance in the heart of Divine forgiveness, and the consequent surpassing peace and elevated joy, may not immediately follow. In the Divine life, the peace offering does not always come directly after the burnt offering. But it *will* come; it *does* come; and then, "oh, the blessedness of the man whose transgression is forgiven!" etc. (literal translation, Ps. xxxii. 1). "Seek, and ye shall find" (Matt. vii. 7).—C.

Ver. 22.—*Holy invocation.* This was an *imposing* act of piety, one which our imagination easily presents to our minds, and which affects us as profoundly interesting. The high priest, after solemnly and with holy awe offering the sacrifices of himself and the people, comes forth from the Divine presence, and with hands lifted up to heaven, utters, amid intense silence, the sacred words, "The Lord bless thee and keep thee," etc. (Numb. vi. 23—26). It was a scene fitted to subdue and sanctify the heart. It was also a *beautiful* act of piety. There is an admirable conformity to what is fitting and excellent in the nature of things, that the man who had gone with the people's burden of sin into the presence of God, and who had there sought and found for the people the Divine mercy, should, as he came from the holy place, bring to the people the blessing of the Most High. It was also an *instinctive* act of piety. It teaches us—

I. THAT HE WHO WOULD BLESS HIS RACE MUST FIRST BE RIGHT WITH GOD. Aaron could not have ventured on the holy invocation, if he himself had not been in the conscious enjoyment of the Divine favour. We must not expect to render any substantial religious service to our generation, if we have not ourselves returned unto our Father, and been reconciled unto him through Christ. Without all contradiction, the less is blessed of the better, and "he that is least in the kingdom of heaven is greater than" any one who stands without.

II. THAT THE NEARER A MAN IS TO GOD THE MORE EFFECTUAL IS HIS HOLY INVOCATION. It was directly after offering sacrifice, and in close connection with that act, immediately after standing at the altar of Jehovah, that Aaron "lifted up his hand and blessed the people." It is not the official in the kingdom of Christ—all we are brethren —but it *is* the man who "walks with God," who "stands before God" continually, who "abides in Christ," who is "beloved of the Lord,"—it is he whose word of holy, earnest invocation will most avail to bless.

III. THAT THERE ARE MANY UNKNOWN BENEFACTORS OF OUR RACE WHO BRING DOWN THE BLESSING OF GOD UPON US. "More things are wrought by prayer than this world dreams of"—by *interceding* prayer, by the earnest, believing invocation of the holy. Who shall say what essential service some have rendered who have quietly and secretly brought down the blessing from on high? Perhaps the uplifting of holy hands in the silent chamber may have done more to end the great campaign which is lasting through the centuries, than some notable and noisy lives men talk much of.

IV. THAT THOSE WHO HAVE INTERCEDING KINDRED SHOULD REALIZE THEIR SPECIAL RESPONSIBILITY. They are the subjects not only of direct human influence, but of those Divine influences which are thus drawn down from above.

V. THAT CHRIST ALONE CAN CONFER THE PEACE WE NEED. "The Lord . . . give thee peace," uttered the Hebrew priest (Numb. vi. 26). "Peace I leave with you, my peace I give unto you," said the Lord from heaven (John xiv. 27). Aaron's was a *human invocation*; Christ's was a *Divine bestowal*. Aaron might hopefully invoke; Christ positively confers. "In him is life," and all that makes life precious in the sight of God; it is in his right hand to bestow fulness of life on us. Let us be attracted to him, be attached to his service, abide in him, walk with him, and he will "*lay his hand upon us*," and bless us with all those heavenly blessings which reside in him and are in his power to impart.—C.

Vers. 23, 24.—*The manifested presence.* The fulfilment of the Divine promise (ver. 6) by the manifested presence of Jehovah suggests—

I. ITS CONSISTENCY WITH OTHER DIVINE MANIFESTATIONS. God so revealed his presence when he did visibly appear to man, that there should be no delusion in the matter. None could, none did, mistake the "glory of the Lord" for the Lord himself (Exod. iii. 2; xxiv. 16, 17; xxxiii. 9; 2 Chron. vii. 1; 1 Kings xviii. 38; Isa. vi. 1).

II. ITS THREEFOLD SIGNIFICANCE. It plainly intimated: 1. God's presence in the midst of the camp. 2. His acceptance of their sacrifice and his pleasure in his people. 3. His approval of the Aaronic appointment, and of the way in which his service had been conducted. This emphatically, for the time chosen was the first day on which the high priest had served at his altar.

III. ITS IMMEDIATE EFFECT ON THE MIND OF THE MULTITUDE. When "all the people saw," they were incited to (1) rapturous delight: "they shouted;" and (2) reverential prostration: they "fell on their faces." At such a vision reverence and joy mingled within them, and stirred their souls to intense spiritual emotion. A visible appearance, acting strongly on the soul through the senses, produces an immediate and powerful *present* effect. How deep it will descend, and how long it will last, depends on the sincerity, spirituality, fulness of the meditation, prayer, resolution, which follows the awe-inspiring spectacle. Far more depends on the wisdom with which the next hour (day) is spent, than on the excitements of the moment.

IV. ITS CHRISTIAN COUNTERPART. There is in the Christian dispensation: 1. The temporary miraculous element. Here we have, as the counterpart, the "cloven tongues like as of fire" (Acts ii. 3). 2. That that which is more important is the permanent supernatural element. Here we have the Divine illumination, the baptism of the Holy Ghost. Not the "glory of the Lord" visible to the eye, but the grace of God apprehended by the understanding mind; not the outward appearance, but the inward influence and indwelling; not the symbol of the Divine presence outside the tabernacle, but the very Spirit of the living God within the temple of the human body (1 Cor. iii. 16; vi. 19). When we go up to the house of the Lord to "behold the beauty of the Lord," to "see his glory . . . in the sanctuary" (Ps. xxvii. and lxiii), we go up to behold no visible grandeurs, but to do that which is better far for all spiritual well-being: (1) to realize his nearness to us; (2) to learn and welcome his truth; (3) to pour out our hearts before him in adoration, praise, and prayer; (4) to open our souls to receive his indwelling, sanctifying Spirit.—C.

Vers. 1—24.—*Subject: God's glory manifested in the blessedness of his people.* The priests enter upon their office, offer sacrifices for themselves and the people, and receive tokens of Jehovah's presence and blessing. "*And Aaron lifted up his hand towards the people*," etc. (vers. 22—24). The main facts described are: 1. The *joint blessing* of the mediator of the Law and the high priest on the people, the solemn conclusion of the consecration and inauguration. 2. The *glory of the Lord appearing* unto all the people. 3. *The fire* from before the Lord *consuming* the burnt offering and the fat. 4. *The whole people beholding the sign,* accepting it as from God, and rejoicing in it with adoring homage.

I. MAN BLESSED IN GOD. 1. *Religion as revealed and set forth* in the mediation of law and sacrifice, the only true *element of fellowship* between the creature and Creator. Natural religion a spurious substitute and insufficient. Moses and Aaron both typical of him in whom God invites us to receive the fulness of grace. 2. The blessings *pronounced and published.* In the promises of Scripture, in the history of redemption, in the individual experience of believers. Godliness hath the promise of both worlds in the best sense. Old and new covenants really one.

II. DIVINE GLORY MANIFESTED in response to man's faithfulness. 1. Look for it especially *in connection with the sanctuary.* After great confession and universal seeking of God's favour. An outpoured grace in revived religion, in manifest success in spiritual service, in the fellowship of priests and people with one another, in the providential signs of Divine interposition for the Church's extension. 2. *Unto all the people.* The blessing of religion is for the multitude, for the nation, for the world. Yet those who would see the glory must come around the centre of its manifestation in the holy place. We can see the glory of the Lord in creation, in providence, in the written Word, only as we are taught by the Spirit and recognize the true order of the Divine kingdom, which places the throne of righteousness, the mercy-seat, in the midst, and makes the glory to radiate from that.

III. RELIGIOUS JOY AND PRAISE stirred up by signs of grace. 1. Heartfelt and outspoken. 2. Uniting all in common exaltation. 3. Deeply humble and adoring. 4. Not dependent on external miracle, but finding occasion in every proof of fire from heaven, in the Church and in the world.—R.

EXPOSITION.

CHAPTER X.

THE DEATH OF NADAB AND ABIHU, THE SONS OF AARON (vers. 1—7). The first day of Aaron's ministry had not yet closed. He had offered the sacrifices, and had entered into the holy place with Moses, and had returned to the court of the tabernacle, where the people had been standing in mute expectation, and God had shown his approval and his confirmation of him in his priestly acts by consuming the sacrifices, as they lay on the altar, with a miraculous fire emblematic of himself, when a rash act on the part of his two eldest children changed the day from one of rejoicing to one of mourning. It would seem that Nadab and Abihu, being already in a state of exaltation from the events of the day, in which they had taken so prominent a part, felt bound, when the fire came forth from God, and the people shouted and fell on their faces, to take some step whereby to acknowledge on the part of the people the graciousness displayed so visibly by the Lord. Moses and Aaron had been parted from them when they went into the tabernacle, and were now facing the congregation, the ministers rather of God to man than of man to God, and Nadab and Abihu appear to have regarded themselves as the representatives of the people. Without waiting for instructions, they rose from their prostration, and, preparing to make a return to God for his gift of fire by the offering of incense sym-

bolical of prayer, they lit their censers from one of the fires which had been made for boiling the sacrificial flesh, and, putting incense upon them, started forward, with the intention of carrying the burning incense to the golden altar of prayer in the holy place. They reached the door of the tabernacle, where Moses and Aaron were standing, when they were met by a blast of the same fire which had already swept to the brazen altar, and they fell dead. They had acted presumptuously. They had not, like Eleazar and Ithamar, waited for the Divine command, but, in their haste, they had irreverently broken the custom, which rested upon a Divine command, of taking the fire for the altar of incense from the altar of burnt sacrifice alone. The fact that this offence was the transgression of a positive rather than of a moral precept, would have made the lesson the more complete and emphatic. They—the newly ordained priests—had, with whatever good intentions, done what God had not commanded, and in doing it had done what he had forbidden. Like Uzzah afterwards (2 Sam. vi. 7), they died for it, that others might fear to do the same. Will-worship (Col. ii. 23) received thereby an emphatic condemnation, and priests and people were taught, in a manner not to be forgotten, that "to obey is better than sacrifice" (1 Sam. xv. 22).

Ver. 1.—Nadab and Ahibu are said to have each taken his censer. This is the first time that the word used in the original is translated "censer." It means any vessel or pan that will hold embers or tinder (see Exod. xxv. 38; xxvii. 3, 23; xxviii. 3). They put fire therein, and put incense thereon. No doubt they used the incense ordered in Exod. xxx. 34. They are not found fault with for the incense, but for the fire that they used. They offered strange fire, that is, fire not taken from the altar of burnt offering, which they might have feared to approach after the miracle that had occurred. In ch. xvi. 12 it is ordered that, on the Day of Atonement, the incense fire should be taken from the brazen altar, and this was no doubt the rule on all occasions, though the law has not been recorded.

Ver. 2.—And there went out fire from the Lord, and devoured. These are the exact words used in ch. ix. 24 of the fire that consumed the sacrifices. The fire was the same; its source was the same; its effect was the same, and yet how different! They died before the Lord; that is, they were struck dead at the door of the tabernacle.

Ver. 3.—This is that the Lord spake (see Exod. xix. 22; xxviii. 41; xxix. 44; ch. viii. 33). God will be sanctified either by the obedience or by the punishment of those that come nigh him, that is, his priests. If they have greater privileges, they have greater perils (cf. Matt. xi. 21). Aaron held his peace—in submission (see Ps. xxxix. 9; Job i. 22), acknowledging that Moses had justified the act of God in executing so terrible a judgment.

Ver. 4.—Uzziel was the youngest brother of Amram (see Exod. vi. 18—22). His sons, Mishael and Elzaphan, were therefore second cousins of Nadab and Abihu, who are here called their brethren. (Cf. the use of the term "brothers of the Lord," applied probably to his first cousins in the New Testament.)

Ver. 5.—They went near, and carried them in their coats out of the camp. Their *coats* were the tunics which they had put on as their priestly attire (ch. viii. 13). The lightning flash which had struck them down had not injured their clothes. As Mishael and Elzaphan became ceremonially defiled by contact with the corpses, and as the Passover was now at hand, it has been thought that it was in reference to their case that the concession was made, that those defiled by a dead body might keep the Passover on the fourteenth day of the second instead of the first month (Numb. ix. 6—11). The defilement caused by death ceased when Christ had died.

Ver. 6.—Uncover not your heads. They are to abstain from all the conventional signs of mourning, in order to show that they acknowledged the justice of the punishment. The whole house of Israel, that is, the people in general, might mourn the death of their priests, but the high priest and his remaining sons must prove their submission to the Divine chastisement by crushing their individual feelings of sorrow. A murmur on their part would have brought God's wrath on themselves and on the whole congregation, which they represented (ch. iv. 3). *Uncover not your heads* may be otherwise translated, *Let not your hair fall dishevelled* (see ch. xxi. 10).

Ver. 7.—The priests are not to be taken away from their duties at the door of the tabernacle, that is, the court in front of the tabernacle, even for the sake of burying their dead. They had now been in the court for eight days continuously, and they had to remain there until, in the fulfilment of their public function, they had eaten the sacrificial meal. Cf. Matt. viii. 21, 22, "Lord, suffer me first to go and bury my father. But Jesus said unto him, Follow me." God's service comes before all things.

HOMILETICS.

Vers. 1, 2.—*The sinfulness of man mars the full effect of the good purposes of God* on the very day of the consecration of the priests.

I. THE SIN OF NADAB AND ABIHU. Presumption. They chose their own method of returning thanks and giving praise to God, a method unsanctioned by God's command, unauthorized by their official superiors.

II. THEIR PUNISHMENT. Death. We might have thought that a lesser penalty would have sufficed for such a sin, if we had not had their example before us.

III. ITS LESSONS. 1. *The necessity of obedience to positive precepts as well as moral commands.* Moral commands, which rest for their basis on some reason which we can apprehend, being in their nature of far greater importance than positive precepts, which are binding simply because they have been ordered, we are tempted to undervalue the latter. We say, "I know God's purpose, and will carry it out; it is slavish to be bound by the letter. He will prefer the course which has now become the best to that which he commanded under perhaps altered circumstances." This arises from pride. We make ourselves judges of God's purposes, in respect to which we are in truth ignorant or can at best guess blindly. There may be a thousand other objects of the Divine counsels beside that which we think that we see, which we regard as the only one. The questions which alone we must ask are, "Does this injunction come from God? and does it affect me?" If so, we must obey it without respect to consequences, and we may not substitute for it a course of action which appears to ourselves better adapted to effect the end which we suppose to be in view. 2. *The special necessity of this obedience in Divine worship.* God knows how he wills to be worshipped, and why he should be so worshipped. Man does not. Under the old dispensation, the forms of worship appointed by him were typical. What they were typical of he knew, but man did not; therefore man could not judge of their propriety. Under the new dispensation, he has by positive injunction appointed two rites —the sacrament of Baptism and the sacrament of the Lord's Supper. To dispense with either of them would be an act of the highest presumption. He appointed certain forms by which they were to be administered. Human authority may not in baptism change water for any other element, or substitute other words than those appointed, nor may it alter the form of the consecration in the administration of the Holy Communion; nor when Christ has said, "Drink ye all of this," may it, without sin, enjoin, "Ye shall not all drink of it." 3. *Human authority to be obeyed where God has not spoken.* There must be regulations of some kind for Divine worship, and these it is the office of the Church to supply, ordaining, abolishing, and changing, as it seems good from time to time. "Every particular or national Church hath authority to ordain . . . ceremonies or rites of the Church;" and also "to change and abolish" them when "ordained by man's authority, so that all things be done to edifying" (Art. XXXIV.). When once ordained, they have a binding force over the conscience until abolished by the same authority. "Whosoever through his private judgment, willingly and purposely, doth openly break the tradition and ceremonies of the Church, which be not repugnant to the Word of God, and be ordained and approved by common authority, ought to be rebuked openly (that others may fear to do the like), as he that offendeth against the common order of the Church, and hurteth the authority of the Magistrate, and woundeth the consciences of the weak brethren" (Ibid.). Although the intention be good, though the purpose be to improve the worship of God, and, as in the case of Nadab and Abihu, to light up in the sanctuary the golden altar of incense and prayer, yet, if a man act without the authority of his Church, he is guilty of presumption, and will have to bear his iniquity.

Ver. 2.—*Fire* was the instrument of the destruction of Nadab and Abihu, whilst just before it had been the means of consuming the sacrifice, and in passing to the altar it had probably bathed Moses and Aaron in its harmless flames as they stood at the door of the tabernacle. Thus it is that the same thing serves as a means of glorification or of destruction, according to the qualities of that with which it comes in contact. The discipline of daily life makes one a saint, another a more determined sinner. The discipline of suffering softens one heart, hardens another. The difficulties of religious belief make one the more submissive, another an unbeliever. God is the joy of the believer and the misery of the infidel. And so we may suppose that it will be hereafter. The presence of God will be the exceeding great reward of those who have sought him, and that same presence would be the torture of those who have not submitted their wills to his. It may be that this in itself will be sufficient to constitute the punishment of the unrighteous in the world to come.

Ver. 3.—*Increase of privilege involves increase of danger.* The nearer men are brought to God, the more liable they are to chastening at his hands. This is more particularly the case with those who are made his ministers. What might pass unpunished in others will be punished in them. What would be allowed in others will not be allowed in them (ver. 6). Had Nadab and Abihu not been called to be priests, they would not have met their untimely fate; and had Aaron, Eleazar, and Ithamar been laymen, they would have been permitted to make use of the ordinary signs of mourning for their dead. But God's work must come before any other duty, and if it be not done as God has willed it to be done, a sorer punishment will fall upon those who have specially devoted themselves to the immediate service of God than on others. This is a solemn thought for those who are ordained to be the ministers of God.

HOMILIES BY VARIOUS AUTHORS.

Counterfeit fire. Ch. x, 1—11; cf. Acts v. We have considered the consecration both of the high priest and of the minor priests, and how, entering upon their office in expectation of a sign, they got it in the outflash of the "consuming fire." But sad to say, two of the minor priests so provoke the Lord by their presumption that they are instantly consumed. Having already contrasted the high priest's consecration with Christ's baptism, and the descent of the fire with the effusion of the Spirit at Pentecost, we cannot resist the parallel presented by the case of Ananias and Sapphira to this case of Nadab and Abihu. If believers are rightly regarded as "priests unto God," then the case of Ananias and Sapphira is one of presumption in an assumed priesthood. The parallel will help us to definite ideas about the sin.

I. HONOUR IS OFTENTIMES TOO MUCH FOR SOME MINDS. And it is generally a minor class of mind that gets intoxicated with position and success. Nadab and Abihu, elevated to the priesthood, are so elated as to suppose that everything becomes them. Moreover, allied with this mental intoxication and excitement there often is physical intoxication. Indulgence is thought a proper thing for the upstart, and so he feeds his presumption by excess. The probabilities are in favour of supposing that Nadab and Abihu had indulged in wine or strong drink immediately on their elevation to the priesthood (cf. vers. 9, 10), and, in consequence, were incapacitated for distinguishing between the holy fire and its unholy counterfeit. It is not every one who can stand a "full cup," or walk with it steadily. If with honour there comes not a quiet spirit, it becomes a curse rather than a blessing.

II. SELF-CONFIDENCE IS THE NATURAL RESULT OF THE INTOXICATION OF SUCCESS. Nadab and Abihu, in their folly, think that they can guide themselves in priestly duty. Their venerable uncle, Moses, is not to be consulted by such dignitaries as they are. They can approach the Divine presence in a perfectly new and original way. The fire which came originally from heaven, and which has been most carefully preserved as a sacred deposit, is not, they believe, a bit better than fire they themselves can kindle. They will not depend upon it, but furnish a good fire themselves. Their spirit is self-confidence all through. The licence of innovation was most uncalled for at such a time, seeing that the ritual was only in process of reception from heaven. There was no excuse for their course at all.

III. GOD NEVER GRANTS A MANIFESTATION, BUT SATAN GETS UP THROUGH SELF-CONFIDENT MEN A COUNTERFEIT. Nadab and Abihu believed they could produce as good a fire as God. Ananias and Sapphira believed that hypocrisy could conduct itself as creditably as Pentecostal devotion. To every suggestion of a "year of grace," there comes the counter-suggestion of a "year of delusion." All fire is equally common, or, for that matter, equally sacred, to the self-confident mind. Special inspirations are incredible. Censers can be filled on the most rational principles, and God does not refuse any man's person.

Paul, in 1 Cor. xiii., conveys the idea of counterfeit eloquence, a loveless exhibition of oratory that casual observers might pronounce angelic; of counterfeit enthusiasm, and even faith, so that neither mysteries nor mountains can retard the loveless spirit's prayers; of counterfeit martyrdoms, giving up the body to be burned after giving up fortune to the poor; and yet, because love is wanting in such cases, they constitute an unacceptable and profitless service.

IV. THOSE WHO PRESUME WITH THEIR COUNTERFEITS MUST ACCEPT OF THE JUDGMENT THEY DESERVE. Nadab and Abihu, despising the Divine fire, and coming into competition with their own, are consumed by it. In a moment they experience how God is a "consuming fire" to all presumption. Ananias and Sapphira feel the same. They fall before the deserved vengeance of the Most High. God offers us the great alternative—either sanctification through the fire of the Holy Ghost, or destruction from the presence of the Lord and the glory of his power. God will be sanctified in some way:

if the wrath of man does not turn to praise, it will glorify God in being restrained (Ps. lxxvi. 10).

V. IT IS CLEAR THAT GOD ONLY ACCEPTS WHAT HE HIMSELF INSPIRES. This is the lesson of this sad providence. We must bring back to God what he has given. Independent offerings are not acceptable. To come to him in a way of our own devising, instead of by Jesus Christ; to come to him in a self-confident spirit, instead of in the humility inspired by the Holy Ghost; to come to him with proud, cold hearts, instead of with warm and ardent ones, is to be sent empty away. He refuses all such counterfeit offerings; he must have Divine fire or none.—R. M. E.

Submission in bereavement. Ch. x. 3—7; 12—20; cf. 2 Sam. xii. 15—23; Job i. 18—21; John xi.; 1 Thess. iv. 13—18. The conduct of Aaron under the bereavement is most instructive. He holds his peace and is prepared to do whatever Moses commands. And here we have to notice—

I. GOD'S SERVICE AND GLORY MUST TAKE PRECEDENCE OF EVERY OTHER CONSIDERATION. The surviving priests were to leave the mourning and the funeral arrangements to their brethren. The bereavement is not to interfere with their priestly service and consecration. God asserts his claims as paramount. "He that loveth father or mother more than me," said God incarnate, "is not worthy of me: and he that loveth son or daughter more than me is not worthy of me" (Matt. x. 37). It is ideally possible, therefore, to be so filled with a sense of consecration to God that every other consideration is made to dwindle into insignificance. Is not this what we shall realize in heaven?

II. SUBMISSION TO GOD'S CLEARLY EXPRESSED WILL IS A RELIEF TO THE SOUL WHICH HAS BEEN UNCERTAIN BEFORE IT. The thought that God willed the death of those dear to us, has a wonderfully calming influence upon us. We may see no reason for the stroke, and God may not for a long season show us his reason, but we can believe he has one and a good one, and that "he doeth all things well." The death of Nadab and Abihu was as clearly a token from God as the previous manifestation. Job, again, shows the same submissive spirit under a still greater bereavement (Job i. 18—21). So did David on the death of his child (2 Sam. xii. 15—23). So did Mary and Martha on the death of Lazarus (John xi.). All these worthies rested, as we all may rest, and there is no other rest but in the will of an all-wise God. Uncertainty is trying, but even the certainty of bereavement and of sorrow has an element of rest in it.

III. AARON IS CAUTIONED AGAINST ANY USE OF WINE OR STRONG DRINK WHEN ENGAGED IN PRIESTLY SERVICE. Doubtless the primary significance of this injunction was, as already noticed, that Nadab and Abihu had erred therein. But it seems to carry also a beneficial caution. For at no time are people more tempted to resort to wine and strong drink than when in bereavement. A little stimulus, they fancy, will sustain them. So they take to "the bottle" to replenish their courage. The result is that they fall into deeper troubles than ever. Aaron is the better of this injunction to abstain at this time when his sorrow is so keen.

IV. SORROW NECESSITATED FASTING INSTEAD OF FEASTING. After the terrible trial, Aaron and his surviving sons had no appetite for the feasting to which they were entitled; and so they seem to have burned the sin offering in its entirety instead of eating of it. Moses, in directing the sorrowing priests to proceed to the feast of fellowship, made no due allowance for their condition. Aaron instinctively saw the incongruity of feasting when his heart was so sore, and therefore he acted in the *spirit* of the Law, which disposed of what could not be used in the fire of the altar.

And might not those who turn a house of mourning into a house of feasting learn a lesson of propriety here? Eating and drinking in connection with wakes and funerals have been carried oftentimes to most unseemly excess. The whole spirit of sorrow evaporates before the copious offerings to the "belly-god," and instead of spiritual profit there is spiritual deterioration.

Fasting is an effort of nature to say a word for the spirit within. Sorrow takes the edge off appetite, and rebukes feasting that the soul may have a season of repair. If the sad heart gets fair play, it will emerge from its sorrows purified and elevated.

V. THE SPIRIT MAY SOMETIMES MOST PROPERLY SUPERSEDE THE LETTER. We have seen how fatal was the innovation of the presumptuous priests. But in this same chapter we come across an innovation on the part of Aaron, at which Moses and God were content. There is all the difference between rigidity which must not be broken, and a law whose spirit can move freely amid its forms. It was the latter which God gave. There are necessities which arise from time to time and are themselves laws to the spiritual mind. We should be jealous of ourselves in the exercise of our liberty, but, at the same time, we ought to realize our freedom as God gives it to us in his Law. —R. M. E.

Vers. 1, 2.—*Disobedience swiftly punished.* What a contrast between the two scenes! Aaron and Moses entering the tabernacle and returning to bless the people and to participate in the rejoicing caused by the appearance of God's glory, and Nadab and Abihu approaching the same sacred place only to be consumed by the fire of judgment, their offerings rejected, themselves destroyed! The judgments of God are not pleasing to contemplate, but they are necessary to completeness of view, and to the begetting in us of due caution when we venture into his presence, lest our holy boldness degenerate into a presumptuous disregard of his regulations.

I. THE ACT OF RASH DISOBEDIENCE. 1. We see *two brothers sinning against God.* Brothers may be mutually helpful or injurious. To witness the union of members of a family in pious zeal is delightful, but too often relationship is provocative of harm rather than of blessing. Elder brothers, beware of leading your younger relations into sin! 2. *Two that were intimately related to holy men* were not thereby shielded from thoughtless action and severe judgment. Alas! that the children of godly parents should ever belie their ancestry. Here the sons of Aaron and nephews of Moses dishonoured their relationship. 3. *Two young men* brought destruction upon themselves and grief upon their friends. They died childless, and, if more than youths, could yet hardly have attained to any great age. Eleazar, the next brother, was perhaps not twenty at this time, for he was not included in the list of the men forbidden to see or enter the land of promise. We are apt to censure the evil deeds of young men too gently, and to look upon youth as more of an excuse than God seems here to regard it. Experience proves that if youth naturally inclines to sin, so also is it, equally with age, visited with righteous retribution. 4. *Two that had been openly dedicated to the service of God* were unmindful of his precepts. They had just been consecrated as priests. This did not prevent them from violating the Law, nor protect them from the consequences of their behaviour. There is danger as well as honour involved in waiting upon God. If Peter had not been called to the lofty position of discipleship, he had not denied his Master. By smiting these two priests, sons of the high priest, Jehovah taught the people that sin could be committed by, and would not be pardoned in, the most exalted of the nation. It was a conspicuous, forcible demonstration of the majesty and holiness of God. 5. *Two that had recently beheld the glory of the Lord* forgot the obedience their position demanded. Perhaps it was the very excitement consequent on such a scene that unduly elevated them, so that, becoming giddy, they reeled into the abyss of impetuous self-will and awful penalty. We must guard against imprudent familiar handling of Divine things after the grace of God has visited us with wondrous revelations of his mercy and favour. It is evident that even if displays of supernatural power were frequent, they would not prove a security against transgression. Some have turned the grace of God manifested in full and free salvation through Christ into a covering for licentiousnes and irreverence.

II. THE GLOOMY CHANGE EFFECTED BY SIN. 1. *A day of hallowed joy becomes a day of mourning.* This is the bitter chequered experience of life. The sunny skies soon grow dark with clouds, the quiet waters are lashed into tempestuous fury. Men are almost afraid of seasons of ecstatic rejoicing, as if a reaction must quickly ensue; the gladness seems itself a presentiment of coming trouble. Sorrow treads close upon the heels of mirth. Sin may well excite in us sentiments of aversion when we see how it has disfigured the fair features of creation's landscape, changing songs into sighs and smiles into tears. Many a day that began with singing and prayer has ended with wailing and remorse. 2. *The fire of Divine approval is changed into the fire of Divine wrath.* The men became a sacrifice to God's glory indeed, but were not an offering voluntarily laid upon his altar. It seemed fitting that the punishment should bear an analogy to the sin. Strange fire was punished with hallowed fire. The conception of a mild Deity unmoved to indignation at acts unaccordant with his will is not justified by Scripture, nor is it in harmony with the utterances of conscience or the testimony borne by the existent laws of his moral government of the world. 3. *Not even the profession of desire to honour God excuses the wilful neglect of his injunctions.* To substitute human inventions for scriptural institutions is a dangerous practice. Reason may discern little difference of moment, but it is not safe to argue that therefore the particular observance is immaterial, and rests on no rational ground of distinction. The loyalty that will presume to alter the king's ordinances is of doubtful character and certain of rejection.—S. R. A.

Ver. 3.—*A bereaved parent.* Who can stand in the presence of death unmoved? A gulf separates us from the departed friend; the past is like a dream. The partnership between soul and body has been dissolved, and already the clay tabernacle, deprived of its tenant, shows signs of crumbling into decay. The form is the same, but the animating principle has fled. The casket has been rifled of its jewel; we survey the husk, but the kernel has vanished.

I. HERE WAS AN INSTANCE OF SUDDEN DEATH. This is the more startling. The festival is changed into a funeral. The active frame is motionless, the busy brain that teemed with thought is still; we call aloud, but there is no reply; we bend down to touch the lips, but we receive no responsive kiss. How weak is man, when a stroke deprives him of all his faculties, removes him from earthly ken, and his place knows him no more!

II. IT IS SAD WHEN CHILDREN DIE BEFORE THEIR PARENTS. Then the cup of bereavement contains an added element of bitterness. The natural order is inverted. Pathetic was the expression of Burke's grief at the loss of his only son. "I am stripped of all my honours; I am torn up by the roots, and lie prostrate on the earth. I have none to meet my enemies in the gate. They who ought to have succeeded me have gone before me. They who should have been to me a posterity are in the place of ancestors." To see the budding rose suddenly blighted, all the promise of life unrealized, is enough to rend a parent's heart with disappointment.

III. IT IS SADDER STILL WHEN DEATH IS THE DIRECT RESULT OF THOUGHTLESS, SINFUL CONDUCT. Then no gleam of light tempers the darkness. If the flower be transplanted to adorn the heavenly garden, there will be joy at the thought to alleviate the sorrow. But when the removal appears like that of tares to be burned, who shall assuage the pangs of bereavement? Children! strive so to live that if Providence call you away in early life, the memory left behind may be sweet and fragrant, pleasant and reassuring. *Let us not too hastily assume the death of the youthful to be a judgment.* We may have no Moses at our side, as here, to interpret the harrowing scene. We would not rush instantly to adverse conclusions, nor misconceive the dispensation. Even in the case before us we are not warranted in deciding upon the ultimate fate of Nadab and Abihu. Death is truly in every case *a particular instance of a general law.* "This is it that the Lord spake, saying, I will be sanctified," etc. It ever reminds us of its connection with sin, and every time we are called to stand by the grave we should be impressed with a deeper sense of the enormity and awfulness of sin in God's sight. Beholding the effect, let us hate the cause.

IV. Aaron furnishes AN EXAMPLE OF FITTING BEHAVIOUR UNDER TRIAL. He could not rejoice to see the withering of his cherished hopes; God expects no such unnatural triumphing over the instincts of affection. But he refrained from murmuring, he "held his peace." "I was dumb, I opened not my mouth, because thou didst it." Open the quivering lips, and the pent-up agony of the spirit may find vent in the utterance of expostulations and reproaches unworthy of a child of God. Job's wife tempted him to "curse God and die," but he "sinned not with his lips." He was, indeed, able to say, "Shall we receive good at the hands of God, and shall we not receive evil?" "The Lord gave, and the Lord hath taken away; blessed be the Name of the Lord." It was after this that he "uttered that he understood not."

V. TO REPRESS REPINING IS ACCEPTED AS TACIT ACQUIESCENCE IN THE EQUITY OF DIVINE JUDGMENTS. His ways are often mysterious, but his wisdom cannot err nor his love prove unkind. The greatest degree of affection for our fellow-creatures must never be allowed to lessen our supreme regard for the glory of the Creator. "It is the Lord: let him do what seemeth him good." Listen to the voice from under the trees of the Garden of Gethsemane: "Father, not my will, but thine be done." Fond parents have sacrificed their children for the good of the commonwealth, how much more shall they be content to leave them in the hands of God, to be dealt with according to his infinite justice and mercy! It was the glory of the Father that necessitated the surrender of his beloved Son to death for the redemption of the world.—S. R. A.

Vers. 6, 7.—*Restrictions and infirmities of religious service.* That honour involves responsibility is implied in many of these ordinances, and is recognized in the judgment passed on the conduct of men occupying conspicuous positions in society and in the Church. To be dedicated to God's service was an inestimable privilege conferred on Aaron and his family. Their time and labour were bestowed upon high and holy employments. The seal of God was stamped upon their brow, the people regarded them with respect and provided for their maintenance. Compare the honourable position of ministers, missionaries, yea, all the followers of Christ now, and note that there are special restrictions consequent upon their consecration, and common infirmities to which they are subject equally with others.

I. The restrictions. 1. *Forbidden to mingle with the world in its engagements.* "Not go out of the sanctuary," at least for a season, they are deprived of the liberty others enjoy. Pursuits which may be harmlessly indulged in by others are unbecoming to them. 2. *Prohibited from contact with all that is defiling.* They must not touch the dead bodies of their relations; the cousins of Aaron shall perform the last offices for their brethren. What concord hath the Spirit of life with death? To profane the holy unction is to incur the Divine displeasure. "Neither filthiness, nor foolish talking, nor jesting, which are not convenient." " Have no fellowship with the unfruitful works of darkness." 3. *Free manifestation of grief at God's visitations not permitted.* The usual relief found in expression is excluded; there must be no signs of mourning upon the priests. Let it suffice for the nation to "bewail the burning." How shall the oil of gladness consort with mourning? The people of God are not to be demonstrative in their sorrow at his chastisements, lest it be misconstrued, and others, taking occasion from their example, go further and even denounce the ways of God, and so " wrath come upon" them. We must remember the wisdom of the Almighty and the glory due unto his Name. Will not the world entertain hard thoughts concerning him if we his servants are over-loud in lamentation?

II. The infirmities which are not prevented. 1. *They are subject to the common losses and bereavements.* There is no special providence in this respect. Even Aaron and his sons have to bow before afflicting dispensations. If it were otherwise great part of the discipline of life would be omitted from the training of God's chiefest scholars. 2. *They also feel the natural pangs of sorrow.* It is evidently so in the present case, or the command to refrain from the usual manifestations of grief would not have been issued. God's ministers are not expected to become hard-hearted and callous, but they are not to give way to outbursts of anguish. 3. *They are liable to commit acts displeasing to God.* Nadab and Abihu are a solemn warning of the possibility of transgression. Even Christians of repute fall into grievous sin. They get hurried away by worldly passion, and offer unacceptable worship.

Conclusion. Observe the influence of our behaviour upon (1) the honour of God, and (2) the welfare of our fellows. He who expects great things of us will also, if we ask him, accord us the necessary strength to enable us to comply with his demands. Whilst conscious of the importance attaching to all our actions, we need not be depressed with a load of anxiety. We may " rejoice in the Lord alway."—S. R. A.

Vers. 1—7.—*Nadab and Abihu.* When the fire of God came upon the sacrifices, " the people shouted, and fell on their faces." While thus in an attitude of prayer, Nadab and Abihu snatched their censers, put fire into them, and put incense upon the fire, as though to send up the prayers of the people to God. In this they sinned, and in consequence paid a fearful penalty. Let us consider—

I. The nature of their sin. We are told: 1. *That they offered strange fire to God.* (1) The censers were right. They were doubtless those made under the direction of Bezaleel and Aholiab according to patterns shown in the mount (Exod. xxv.

40). (2) The composition of the incense also was right; we have no intimation to the contrary. Under proper conditions, therefore, the incense might appropriately ascend with the "prayers of the saints" (see Luke i. 9, 10; Rev. viii. 3, 4). (3) But the fire was wrong. It was a fire of their own kindling: not that which came forth from the Lord. It therefore represented their own spirit rather than the Spirit of God. No prayer can be acceptable that is not divinely inspired (see Isa. l. 10, 11; Rom. viii. 26, 27; Jas. iv. 3). It matters not how correct the form of words: the censer is nothing; or how orthodox the sentiment: the composition of the incense is nothing, without the sacred fire (1 Cor. xiii. 1, 2). 2. *That they acted without direction.* (1) This is the force of the words, "which he commanded them not." Their crime was not in doing what was forbidden, but in doing what was not enjoined. Will-worship is offensive to God. No body of uninspired men has any business to "decree rites and ceremonies." We should study the written Word to "prove what is that good and acceptable and perfect will of God" (see Deut. iv. 2; Prov. xxx. 6; Rom. xii. 2; Rev. xxii. 18, 19). (2) These transgressors were moved by a criminal pride. What had been done hitherto was done by Aaron, his sons only helping him; and done under the direction of Moses. They set divinely constituted authority at naught, which amounted to the despising of the authority of God. It was the very sin of Korah and his company (see Numb. xvi.). (3) They introduced confusion. One priest at a time should offer incense in order to foreshadow that One true Priest whose merits, as incense, invests with acceptable fragrance and gives direction to the prayers of the saints (see Psa. cxli. 2, margin; Rom. viii. 34; Heb. ix. 24; Rev. viii. 3, 4). Here two at once rush in. These foreshadow the confusion of that antichrist which would make "priests" and "saints" and "angels" rivals of the one only Mediator (1 Tim. ii. 5, 6).

II. THE LESSONS OF THE PUNISHMENT. 1. *God is not to be trifled with.* (1) He "will be sanctified in them that come nigh" to him (see Exod. xix. 22; Deut. xxxii. 48—51; Isa. v. 16; Ezek. xx. 41). (2) He is "a consuming fire." He will consume our sins in the sacrifice of Christ in his mercy, or he will make us a sacrifice and consume us in his anger. "He that believeth not shall be damned." 2. *His vengeance is often retributive.* (1) They sinned by fire; they suffered by fire (see Prov. i. 31; Isa. iii. 10, 11; Hos. viii. 11). (2) They preferred a fire of their own kindling to the fire of God; God's fire put their censers out, together with the light of their life. Twice we are reminded that they had no children, viz. Numb. iii. 4; 1 Chron. xxiv. 2. So completely was their light extinguished! "Quench not the Spirit." 3. *His retributions are sometimes summary.* (1) Their presumption was hasty and their destruction was swift (see 2 Pet. ii. 1). (2) They found "no space for repentance." They "died before the Lord," in presence of the mercy-seat, but finding no mercy. No wrath is more terrible than "the wrath of the Lamb." (3) As their sin foreshadowed that of the Babylonish antichrist, so did their punishment betoken his (see 2 Thess. ii. 3—8; Rev. xviii. 8). That judgment will be "before all the people." In it God will be signally "glorified." 4. *Mourning for the dead has its laws and limitations.* (1) It must not interrupt the service of God (vers. 6, 7; see Neh. vi. 3; Matt. viii. 21, 22; xii. 47—49). (2) "Aaron held his peace." Did not murmur against God. Moses soothed him by showing that it was a necessary act of justice. Wherein God is glorified we should be content. (3) It must not have expression in the holy place, which is a type of heaven. There the wisdom and justice of the judgments of God will be so manifest that the punishment of the wicked cannot be mourned. (4) But mourning is proper in the camp (vers. 4—6). The funeral procession through the camp of those corpses, wrapped in the very vestments in which the deceased too vainly gloried, would be an affecting sight. Nadab and Abihu, who had been in the mount, beholding the glory of the Lord (Exod. xxiv. 1), are now by wrath issuing from that same glory brought very low. When a king falls he often finds a scaffold at the foot of his throne. "Be not high-minded, but fear."— J. A. M.

Vers. 1—3.—*Sin and penalty in sacred things.* The story of the guilt and doom of the sons of Aaron constitutes a sad episode in the recital of the sacred precepts of the Law. We look at—

I. THE CHARACTER OF THE TRANSGRESSION. It appears (from ver. 16, compared with ch. ix. 15) that this forbidden act was done very soon indeed after the solemnities described in the preceding chapter (ix.). Otherwise we should have inferred that it was familiarity with sacred rites which had bred irreverent unconcern, and issued in disobedience. We seem shut up to the conclusion that these young men, even when the solemn inaugural scenes were fresh in their memories, and the commandments of the Lord clearly before their minds, deliberately and wantonly took fire from another source than the heaven-kindled flame on the brazen altar (ch. ix. 24). Their action was, therefore, not only a defiant violation of the Law they had received from Moses, the servant of Jehovah, but it was a perverse disregard of the manifest will of God, made known in special supernatural disclosure.

II. THE EXPLANATION OF THE PUNISHMENT. (Ver. 2.) This may seem severe, has seemed so to some. Why not exclusion from office or excommunication from the congregation of the Lord? Why the extreme penalty for one act of error in worship? The answer is manifold. 1. Their deed was (as has been said) an act of wilful and wanton disobedience. 2. It was committed by those who were in high position. 3. It was a sin on the part of men in the enjoyment of high privilege, and in the exercise of no slight influence. 4. It was an evil thing done in the holy place and before the very face of God; it was disobedience in connection with the public worship of Jehovah— the supreme sphere of activity, in regard to which it was of vital consequence to the nation that everything should be done aright. 5. One signal mark of high displeasure might be mercy as well as justice—inspiring holy awe and saving many others from similar transgressions.

III. THE LESSONS WHICH THE SIN AND THE PENALTY LEAVE BEHIND THEM. We learn from this solemn and painful scene: 1. That God's will must be sedulously regarded in our approaches to himself: "I will be sanctified in them that come nigh me" (ver. 3). 2. That God will vindicate his Law in unmistakable ways: "before all the people I will be glorified" (ver. 3). 3. That there is no exemption from exposure to temptation: not (1) sonship of the holy; (2) being in a holy place; (3) engagement in holy things; (4) recency of special privilege. 4. That the heinousness of sin depends on many things beside the nature of the overt act. 5. That between sin and suffering there will be found a striking correspondence. With fire they sinned, and by fire they were consumed. God makes meet penalty to overtake transgression: whatsoever a man sows, *that* he reaps (Gal. vi. 7). Sins against the soul lead to spiritual injury; against the body, to weakness, disease, and death; against society, to social dishonour and shame, etc.—C.

Vers. 1, 3.—"Strange fire." "I will be sanctified in them that come nigh me." *Great and small things in the worship of God.* Doubtless it seemed to Nadab and Abihu a matter of no consequence at all that they should take fire from one altar rather than from another. To us it may seem a comparatively *small* thing, when viewed in connection with the terrible doom that immediately ensued. Obviously, however, it was a *great* thing in the sight of God. The act of punishment by which he showed his high displeasure, and the words of the text, sufficiently prove this. The seriousness of this particular transgression on the part of the sons of Aaron arose from several attendant considerations (see Homily on "Sin and penalty," etc.): its seriousness to us, in the fact that we may be disregarding as small and insignificant that which, in God's sight, is great and even vital; that we may be approaching him with what we think acceptable service, when he is prepared to reject it as "strange fire," and condemn us severely for our disregard of his revealed will. In connection with the worship of God, there is—

I. THE APPARENTLY AND INTRINSICALLY SMALL. So far as the things themselves are concerned, it is of no consequence to that most High God "who dwelleth not in temples made with hands," what is (1) the style of architecture of our sanctuaries, (2) the character of their furniture, (3) the order of the services, (4) the number of ministrants who serve at pulpit or desk, (5) the particular text chosen for the day, etc. The judgment of good and faithful men may differ on these things, and their differences may be of no moment in the sight of God; in no way invalidating the service rendered, or lessening or lowering the blessing gained. But even in connection with the smaller matters, as also apart from that connection, there is—

II. THE ACTUALLY AND INTRINSICALLY GREAT. It is of the most serious importance that: 1. In all things, weightier and lighter, we should study to follow the will of Christ. His will is revealed in his own words, and in the acts and words of his apostles. Thence we must studiously deduce his desire concerning us. 2. We should make all things conduce to a reverential spirit. "God will be sanctified," etc. The service which does not tend to impress the worshipper with the greatness, majesty, holiness, wisdom, faithfulness of God, is fatally defective, is essentially faulty. 3. We should exalt Jesus Christ as a Saviour from sin. The prominence and priority given to the sin offering in this book point clearly to the truth that "the Lamb of God that taketh away the sin of the world" should have the principal place in Christian worship. He, the Divine Son, is also to be "sanctified in them that come nigh." 4. We should present the entire truth of revelation; not that part which we prefer, which falls in with our tastes or acquirements, but the "whole counsel of God." Guiltily disregarding these imperative matters, we (1) not only do not offer acceptable sacrifice, but (2) render ourselves obnoxious to our Master's Divine dissatisfaction, to his displacement of us from his service, to his severe rebukes (Rev. ii., iii.). The slightest deviation from the will of Christ, if caused by faulty negligence, and still more if due to wilful disobedience, is a serious transgression; on the other hand, faithfulness in small things, rendered cheerfully and in a loving spirit, is certain of Divine acceptance and approval.—C.

Vers. 3—7.—*Self-restraint and utterance.* "And Aaron held his peace," etc. The sequel to the sad story of the sin and death of Nadab and Abihu carries with it three lessons we shall do well to learn.

I. THAT A MAN IS LESS HONOURED BY EXALTED OFFICE THAN BY LOFTY ACTION. We pay a certain respect to Aaron as the first high priest of the ancient Law, type of the "High Priest of our profession." But we pay a higher honour to him and feel a deeper regard for him, as one who acted nobly at a most trying time. Such a scene might well have unmanned him. We could not have blamed him had he given way to violent agitation, even in the house of the Lord. There is, in sorrow, a descending scale, and his was at the very bottom of its dark depths. Bereavement, the saddest of all losses; the death of a child, the saddest of all bereavements; the death of two sons in their manhood, the saddest form which the loss of children can assume; its startling, awful suddenness; its occurrence under the aggravating conditions of guilt and dishonour;— such was the staggering blow that fell on Aaron then! There is a nobleness of self-restraint which is truly touching, which excites our hearty admiration, in the fact that "Aaron held his peace." He did not give way to tempestuous emotion or to querulous complaint; he acted as became him: standing where he stood in the near presence of God, he bore the blow in sacred silence, he opened not his mouth, he was dumb, because he felt the Lord had done it (Ps. xxxix. 9). There is nothing manlier, nobler, more admirable than calmness in the overwhelming hour. It is born of (1) devoutness, a profound sense of the presence and sovereignty of God; and of (2) self-culture, the training of our own spirit, the "keeping of our heart" (Prov. iv. 23).

II. THAT THE DEVOUT HEART WILL RECOGNIZE THE RIGHTNESS OF SUBORDINATING PERSONAL SENTIMENT TO THE SERVICE OF GOD. (Ver. 6.) This melancholy occurrence had taken place in vindication of the honour of God (ver. 3). The one feeling which was to fill the hearts of those who stood before God was an unquestioning acceptance of the severe and afflictive decree of the Holy One. To show the ordinary signs of sorrow might be open to misconstruction; might appear as a protest against the death-penalty. In the cause of righteousness the natural feeling of father and sons must be energetically suppressed. And it was done. There come times in our history when, in the highest interests of all, in the service of God and of our kind, we are called upon to make parental, conjugal, fraternal, friendly emotions give place to calmness of spirit. When that hour comes, we, if we have Aaron's spirit, shall obey as he obeyed.

III. THAT GOD DESIRES US TO GIVE PLAY TO HUMAN FEELING WHEN HIS LAW IS NOT BROKEN OR HIS SERVICE HINDERED THEREBY. 1. The relatives of the dead were to carry their bodies decently and reverently "from before the sanctuary" (ver. 4). 2. The whole house of Israel were to "bewail the burning which the Lord had kindled" (ver. 6). Where the lamentation was natural, and where there was no peril of its being misinterpreted, it was not only allowed but encouraged of God. Stoicism is no part of Christianity. We are to be natural and sympathetic. Jesus "rejoiced in spirit" and "wept" himself. He intimated his wish that we should act naturally, in accordance with our surrounding circumstances and inward spirit (Matt. ix. 15—17; John xvi. 20—22; Jas. v. 13). *Sympathetic* as well as natural: "rejoice with them that do rejoice, and weep," etc. (Rom. xii. 15).—C.

Vers. 1—7.—*Strange fire; and Jehovah's judgment upon it.* Ver. 3, "Then Moses said unto Aaron, This is that the Lord spake, saying, I will be sanctified in them that come nigh me, and before all the people I will be glorified. And Aaron held his peace."

I. A GREAT OFFENCE against the holiness of God. 1. *Defilement of his worship.* Violation of his written Word. Introduction of self-will and mere human device. Abuse of the joyful spirit of praise to insolent self-assertion and disregard of decencies and reverence. 2. Special profanation of the sanctuary by *disobedience of priests.* Holy offices dishonoured is a fearful evil. 3. *Hiding of God's glory* with false glory. Ritualism. Mere show of human talent. Abuse of music. Forgetfulness of God in his service. Temptation to vain-glory.

II. A SOLEMN VINDICATION of the sanctity of God's house and Law. Strange fire offended, true fire punished. 1. Profitableness of the study of providence, especially ecclesiastical history, as revealing the "consuming fire" of righteousness in the Church. 2. Representative character of all God's people, and especially those in prominent position. God glorified *in us*, whether by life or by death. 3. Double aspect of all Divine visitations of judgment, as confirming at once the strength of the Law and the faithfulness of the covenant, therefore both warning and encouragement. "Aaron held his peace," for he could only acknowledge the righteousness of God. Grace is above nature, and controls and exalts it.

III. A GREAT LESSON on the infirmity of man and the necessity of redemption. Immediately that the temple service was inaugurated, man spoiled it, as it were, by his sin. Compare the inauguration of earthly life spoiled by the sin of Adam and Eve; the new world after the Flood by Noah's sin (Gen. ix.); defection in the new land of Canaan (Judg. ii. 13); Solomon (1 Kings xi.); the corruption of the early Church (Acts xx. 29, etc.); the final apostacy (Rev. xx. 7—10). On what can we depend but the preserving mercy, the rescuing grace of him who has redeemed us? The "strange fire" was thus solemnly condemned only for the sake of calling out faith and attaching the people of God the more firmly to that fire of his love which, while it consumed the Sacrifice on the cross, did also prepare the way for all into the holiest, that all might be kings and priests unto God through Christ.—R.

EXPOSITION.

THE COMMAND TO ABSTAIN FROM WINE (vers. 8—11). The law given to Aaron (some manuscripts read Moses) against the use of wine by the priests during their ministrations, by its juxtaposition with what has gone before, has led to the probable supposition that Nadab and Abihu had acted under the excitement of intoxicating drink. It is possible that the sacrificial meals on the peace offerings had begun, and that at the same time that the congregation was feasting, the two priests had refreshed themselves with wine after their long service. The special ceremonial meal of the priests had not yet been eaten.

Ver. 10.—Wine and other intoxicating liquors (שֵׁכָר, whence the Greek word σίκερα, Luke i. 13, was made from dates, or barley, or honey) are forbidden to the priests during their ministrations, that they may put a difference between holy and unholy; that is, that their minds may not be confused, but be capable of distinguishing between right and wrong, what ought and what ought not to be done. Nadab and Abihu, on the contrary, had not distinguished between the sacred and profane fire, or between God's commands and their own unregulated impulses. If they had partaken too freely of the wine provided for the drink offerings, their sin would be similar to that of the Corinthians in their abuse of the Lord's Supper. As to the use of wine by the

minister of God under the New Testament,
see 1 Tim. iii. 2, 8; v. 23. The spiritual
emotion, which, in the service of God, shows
itself in pouring out the feelings in "psalms
and hymns and spiritual songs," is contrasted, in Eph. v. 18, 19, with the physical
excitement caused by wine, the former being
commended and the latter forbidden.

Ver. 11.—**That ye may teach the children
of Israel.** This shows that one part of the
priest's office was teaching the Law (cf.
Deut. xxiv. 8; Mal. ii. 7).

Vers. 12—20.—Moses takes care that the
remaining part of the ritual of the day
shall be carried out in spite of the terrible
interruption that has occurred. Under his
instructions, Aaron and Eleazar and Ithamar
eat the remainder of **the meat offering** (ch.
ix. 17), in the court of the tabernacle, and
reserve **the wave breast and heave shoulder
to eat in a clean place,** that is, not necessarily within the court; but he finds that the
sin offerings (ch. ix. 15), which ought to be
eaten by the priests, had been burnt. The
rule was that, when the blood was presented
in the tabernacle, the flesh was burned;
when it was not, the flesh was eaten by the
priests. In the present case, the blood had
not been brought within the holy place, and
yet the flesh had been burned instead of
being eaten. Moses **was angry with Eleazar
and Ithamar,** and demanded an explanation.
Aaron's plea of defence was twofold. 1. His
sons had fulfilled aright the ritual of their
own sin offering and burnt offering, that
is, the offerings made for the priests, and it
had been rather his duty than theirs to see
that the ritual of the sin offering of the
congregation had been properly carried out.
2. The state of distress in which he was,
and the near escape that he had had from
ceremonial defilement, and the sense of
sin brought home to him by his children's
death, had made him unfit and unable to
eat the sin offering of the people, as he
should have done under other circumstances.
With this plea Moses **was content.** It was
true that the letter of the Law had been
broken, but there was a sufficient cause for
it (see Hos. vi. 6; Matt. xii. 7). It appears
from hence that the expiation wrought by
the sin offering was not complete until the
whole ceremony was accomplished, the last
act of which was the eating of the flesh by
the priests in one class of sin offering,
and the burning the flesh outside the camp
in the other. It has been questioned, what
is the full meaning of the expression,
God **hath given it you**—the flesh of the sin
offering—**to bear the iniquity of the congregation, to make atonement for them
before the Lord.** Archdeacon Freeman expresses the view of A Lapide, Keil, and

many others when he says that, by eating
the flesh of the offering, the priests "in a
deep mystery neutralized, through the holiness vested in them by their consecration,
the sin which the offerer had laid upon the
victim and upon them" ('Principles of
Divine Service,' pt. ii.). Oehler, on the
other hand (Herzog's 'Cyclop.,' x.), maintains that the priests did no more by this
act than *declare* the removal of the sin
already taken away; with which accords
Philo's explanation ('De Vict.,' 13, quoted
by Edersheim, 'Temple Service,' ch. vi.)
that the object of the sacrificial meal
was to carry assurance of acceptance
to the offerer, "since God would never
have allowed his servants to partake of
it had there not been a complete removal
and forgetting of the sin atoned for."
Neither of these explanations seems to
be altogether satisfactory. The former attributes more meaning to the expression
bear the iniquity than it appears to have
elsewhere; *e.g.* Exod. xxviii. 38 and Numb.
xviii. 1, where Aaron is said to *bear the iniquity of the holy things* and *of the sanctuary ;*
and Ezek. iv. 4—6, where the prophet
is said to *bear the iniquity* of Israel and
Judah. The latter interpretation appears
too much to evacuate the meaning of the
words. It is quite certain that the part
of the ceremony by which the atonement
was wrought (if it was wrought by any
one part) was the offering of the blood
for the covering of the offerer's sins, but
yet this action of the priests in eating the
flesh of the victim was in some way also
connected with the atonement, not only with
the assurance of its having been wrought;
but in what way this was effected we are
not told, and cannot pronounce. The words
bear the iniquity are equivalent to making
atonement for by taking the sin in some
sense upon themselves (cf. Isa. liii. 11, "He
shall bear their iniquities," and John i. 29,
"Behold the Lamb of God, that taketh away
[or beareth] the sin of the world"). Accordingly, Bishop Patrick comments: "The very
eating of the people's sin offering argued
the sins of the people were, *in some sort*,
laid upon the priests, to be taken away by
them. From whence the sacrifice of Christ
may be explained, who is said to *bear our
iniquity* (as the priest is here said to do), all
our sins being laid on him, who took upon
him to make an expiation for them by the
sacrifice of himself. For the priest, hereby
eating of the sin offering, receiving the
guilt upon himself, may well be thought to
prefigure One who should be both Priest and
Sacrifice for sin; which was accomplished
in Christ" (on Lev. x. 17).

HOMILETICS.

Ver. 11.—*That priests are teachers* is assumed all through the Old Testament. The contrast in this respect which has been found by some between the prophets and the priests, the former being the spiritual guides of the people, and the latter the organs of a dull ceremonial routine or even rude slayers of beasts, has no foundation in fact. It is true that the primary work of the priest was to teach by type and rite, and the primary work of the prophet to declare God's will by word of mouth; but they were co-ordinate, not hostile, influences and powers, having the same end in view, which they carried out, partly by the same, partly by different means. If the prophet sharply reproves the priests, it is because they are bad priests, not because they are priests (Mal. ii. 1); and when he strikes at the priest, he sometimes strikes at the prophet in the same breath (Jer. v. 30, 31).

THE MINISTER OF THE GOSPEL IS THE SUCCESSOR AND REPRESENTATIVE OF BOTH PRIEST AND PROPHET. He has to conduct the public worship of God, which must always be a solemn occupation, though now disembarrassed of the minute regulations of the Judaic Law, and he is a channel through whom the Divine blessing flows; in this he represents the priest. He is the expounder and preacher of God's Word; herein he represents the prophet. He teaches God's commandments and applies them to the consciences of individuals; herein he does the work of both priest and prophet. But he holds a higher office than either one or the other, inasmuch as he is the dispenser of the gifts of the Holy Ghost for the good of man, which were purchased for man by Christ's death, received by him of his Father at his ascension, and shed forth upon his Church in the form of graces dispensed by the apostolic ministry (see Eph. iv. 7—11).

HOMILIES BY VARIOUS AUTHORS.

Vers. 8—11.—*Abstinence enjoined.* Without asserting positively that inflammatory drink was the cause of the unhallowed presentation made by the sons of Aaron, we may believe that it was the wise and merciful intention of the prohibition herein contained to guard against a possible source of similar heedless attendance upon God in his sanctuary.

I. THE FUNCTIONS OF THE PRIESTS. 1. To observe the various rites connected with the worship of God. 2. To see that nothing unholy entered the precincts of the tabernacle. The incense, which might suffice without, would be an insult to Jehovah within. The fire, useful for common cooking purposes, would be counted "strange fire" if presented to the Lord. 3. To advise the people concerning the distinction made by the Law between things clean and unclean. There was the food permissible to be eaten, the diseases requiring separation, the times in which ceremonial uncleanness was contracted, etc. All these matters were under the supervision of the priests. 4. To instruct the people generally in the statutes of the Lord. In the absence of written documents, this was a very important part of the duties of the priests, and furnished one of the reasons for afterwards locating their cities amongst the different tribes of Israel. This teaching was the origin of the present exposition of Scripture by the preacher, being now the chief feature of the minister's office. Is the acquaintance of the people with the Bible at all commensurate with the many advantages they enjoy? The Israelites may rise up in the day of judgment to condemn the ignorance of modern civilization.

II. THE IMPORTANCE OF RIGHTLY DISCHARGING THESE FUNCTIONS. Consider the happy results that would flow from a proper fulfilment of their obligations, and the dire effects of lax observance of the regulations of the priesthood. In this latter event God would be insulted and profaned, his indignation would destroy the slothful servants, and the nation of Israel would relapse into a state of idolatry and disgrace. No priest lived or died unto himself. The progress and comfort of others were inseparably bound up with his due attendance at the altar.

III. THE NECESSITY OF ABSTAINING FROM WHATEVER IMPAIRS CLEARNESS OF

THOUGHT AND STEADINESS OF CONDUCT. The effects of "wine" or "strong drink" are various in different men and at different stages. Carelessness, excitement, stupefaction,—either might ensue, and bring upon the offender the wrath of God. The principle is obvious that *the service of God may require abstention from enjoyments otherwise permissible.* As the number of priests was at this time so limited, the injunction of the text practically enforced almost continuous abstinence upon them. Enthusiasm stimulated by unworthy means, boldness engendered by false heat, an inability to declare the whole counsel of God, imagination running riot among his precepts,—these are offensive to God in his servants, and expose the possessors to his judgments. To walk not in the path of danger is better than to calculate upon successfully encountering its risks. The householder who cuts off the supply of gas is in no fear of an explosion, nor needs continually to examine the pipes. This prudent method is to be commended where the light furnished is unsteady, or superfluous because of the shining of the purer light. Drink not at the ruddy stream, and you will not dread its poison.—S. R. A.

Vers. 8—11.—*Sobriety in the priesthood.* The Jews say that Nadab and Abihu were inebriated when they sinned in offering strange fire, and that this law, forbidding intoxicants to the priests while serving in the holy place, was given in consequence. It is remarkable that, whereas both before and after this God spake " by the hand of Moses," the instruction before us was given, immediately, "to Aaron." The reasons for the prohibition are—

I. THAT MINISTERS SHOULD BE RECOLLECTED IN THE PRESENCE OF GOD. 1. *He was present in the tabernacle.* (1) In the text, as in many places, it is distinguished as the "tabernacle of the congregation." The original (אהל מועד, *ohel mohghed*) might perhaps be better rendered, "tabernacle of *meeting.*" This would not exclude the idea of the congregation or meeting of the people, while it recognizes another more important truth, viz. that the tabernacle was the place appointed for *God* to *meet* with his people (comp. Exod. xxv. 22; xxix. 42, 43; xxx. 6, 36). (2) Apart from this criticism, the fact is patent that the symbol of the Divine presence was there. Where the Shechinah is, the ground is holy; and it behoves the worshipper to put away irreverence, and, with clearness of intellect as well as fervour of holy zeal, to wait upon the Lord (see Exod. iii. 5; xix. 12; Josh. v. 15). (3) We should never forget that in our Christian assemblies God is no less certainly present (see Matt. xviii. 20; Luke xxiv. 36; Rev. i. 13). 2. *And God is jealous of his honour.* (1) This important truth is here intimated in the caution, "lest ye die." Confused by inebriation, some error might be committed which would involve fatal consequences (see context). (2) Now, since this enactment, to taste the cup whose effects may expose to the liability of committing such an error, is itself a crime to be visited with death. The spirit of this instruction is that we must not tempt Satan to tempt us; that we are only safe when at the utmost distance from sin. (3) Abstinence at other times was not obligatory upon the priests, but they might become Nazarites if they pleased. Gospel ministers should be sober men (1 Tim. iii. 3).

II. THAT THEY NEED THEIR FACULTIES TO KEEP THEIR CHARGE. 1. *They have to judge in holy things.* (1) In the service of the tabernacle some food was "most holy," and had to be eaten beside the altar (ver. 12). This must not be eaten by "females among the priests." Yet a son of Aaron who had such a blemish as would preclude his attendance at the altar may eat of it (ch. xxi. 22). In some cases "holy" meats might be eaten by the priests and their families, but not by ordinary Israelites (ver. 14); while in others the offerer had his share of the offering. (2) Holy things might be polluted by accident. Thus a defiled person touching them would profane them (ch. vii. 19); or the flesh of the peace offering eaten on the third day, even by a priest, is profaned, and the priest punishable (ch. vii. 18; xix. 7, 8). Unclean persons must not eat of the holy things on pain of excommunication (ch. vii. 20, 21). (3) For the carrying out of all these laws, together with those of the distinction between persons, animals, and things. clean and unclean, the priest needed a clear head, (*a*) that he might save his soul alive, (*b*) and that he might fittingly typify Christ, whose judgment in moral and spiritual causes is true. (4) Therefore he must abstain from wine and strong drinks (see Isa. xxviii. 7). And ministers of the gospel must be sober. If not types, they are "ambassadors," of Christ. They need a sound judgment to pronounce clearly and firmly against the efforts of antichrist to profane the laver and the altar in the sanctuary. 2. *They have to teach the statutes of the Lord*. (1) The Law is the standard of appeal. It was spoken by the Lord from Sinai. It was "given by the hand of Moses," who authenticated it to be the Word of God by many miracles. The gospel is the "engrafted Word" (Jas. i. 21), "spoken to us by the Son of God, confirmed by them that heard him, and authenticated by signs and wonders and divers miracles and distributions of the Holy Ghost (Heb. i. 1, 2; ii. 3, 4). (2) The duty of teaching the laws of the Old Testament devolved upon the priests (Deut. xxiv. 8; Neh. viii. 2, 8; Jer. xviii. 18; Mal. ii. 7). Christian ministers now stand in a similar relation to the Church under the New Testament. (3) If sobriety was necessary in the teachers of the Law, it is surely no less necessary in those who teach the vital truths of the gospel (2 Tim. ii. 15; Titus i. 7—9). Ministers of the New Testament may become Nazarites if they please; they should at least be Nazarites when "holding forth the Word of life."—J. A. M.

Vers. 12—15.—*The eating of the holy things*. In the words of the last paragraph God speaks immediately to Aaron; here Moses resumes, addressing now "Aaron and his sons *that were left*," or who had escaped the terrible judgment in which Nadab and Abihu were involved. He repeats his instructions concerning—

I. THE MEAT OFFERING REMAINING OF THE OFFERINGS MADE BY FIRE. 1. *This was accounted "most holy."* (1) This is equivalent to calling it the "bread of God" (comp. xxi. 6, 22). It was therefore "most holy," as typifying Christ (John vi. 33). He is "most holy" in the mystery of his birth, as "coming down from heaven" (Luke i. 35). Also in his death, by which he was able to "give his life unto the world." (2) It was the priests' due, or appointment, viz. from God. For it was first given to God, and now came from him. So Jesus, whom we bring to God as the Atoning Sacrifice for our sin, God gives to us for the nourishment of our souls. To the spiritual priesthood he is still the "Bread of God that cometh down from heaven." 2. *It was to be eaten*, viz. (1) "Beside the altar." Jesus becomes the food of his people *after his passion*. The bread of the Eucharist was "broken" before it was "given" to the disciples to eat (Matt. xxvi. 26; John xii. 24; 1 Cor. xi. 23—26). The Lord's table is furnished from the altar that was without the camp (Heb. xiii. 10—12). (2) It was to be eaten "without leaven." There was neither "malice" nor "wickedness" in Jesus, nor should there be in those who seek his fellowship (1 Cor. v. 6—8). He is the Truth—Truth itself—Truth essential; fellowship with him, therefore, must be in "sincerity and truth." (3) It was to be eaten "in the holy place." The joys of the Christian profession should be sought in the fellowship of the saints. Odd persons, who stand aloof from Church communion, are not serving God according to his order.

II. THE WAVE BREAST AND HEAVE SHOULDER. 1. *These were accounted "holy."* (1) They were so because they had been offered to God. Julius Bate construes the words rendered "wave breast and heave shoulder" (ver. 14), "the breast that is *presented*, and the shoulder that is *lifted up*." This at least expresses the spirit of the original. (2) The "holy" as well as "most holy" bread is the same as the bread of God (see ch. xxi. 22), and equally points to Christ. Both were alike the priests' due or appointment (Exod. xxix. 24). 2. *The holy things were to be eaten in a clean place*. (1) This marks the difference between the "holy" and the "most holy." The "most holy" must be eaten in the holy place, in the court of the priests, and therefore by the priests alone, but the "holy" may be eaten in the houses, and therefore by the daughters of the priests. (2) The moral teaching is that while the "most holy" communion with Christ is by the altar-side in his Church, we may have "holy" communion with him in our families. The ordinary meals of godly persons will be received as from God with thanksgiving, and thereby become in a sense sacramental (see 1 Cor. x. 18—31). (3) The one limitation is that the holy things of the peace offerings must be eaten "in a clean place." Viewed in the letter, this means that the house must not be polluted by the dead, or by a leper, or anything for which the purifications of the Law may be required. Viewed in the spirit, the teaching is that if we would have communion with Christ in our families, vicious dispositions and ungodly strangers must be excluded. "The friendship of the world is enmity against God" (see 2 Cor. vi. 14—18; Jas. iv. 4; 1 John ii. 15).—J. A. M.

Vers. 16—20.—*Moses and Aaron an allegory.* Moses may be taken as the impersonation of the Law which was given by his hand (see Luke xvi. 29; Acts xv. 21). Hence the "body of Moses," about which Michael disputed with Satan, is by some supposed to denote the substance of the Law (Jude 9). In this view he appeared upon the mount of transfiguration, surrendering to Christ, who, in like manner, impersonated his gospel (Matt. xvii. 3—5). So the vail over Moses' face represented the shadows in which the Law invested the glory of the Lord until the death of Christ, when the darkness passed away and the true light shined forth. Hence, when the vail, that is to say, the flesh of Christ, was torn in death, the vail of the temple was rent from the top throughout (Matt. xxvii. 50, 51; 2 Cor. iii. 7; Heb. ix. 3, 8; x. 19, 20). Aaron's function was to bring out the spiritual meaning of the Law; and so he was a type of Christ, who came not to destroy but to fulfil it. Bearing these things in mind, light may be let in upon the remarkable passage before us. We have here—

I. THE ANGER OF MOSES. 1. *Look at the history in the letter.* (1) Moses had given instructions to Aaron and his sons respecting the goat which was to be offered for the sin of the people (see ch. ix. 15, 16). (2) These instructions were not fully carried out. The goat was killed and its fat burnt upon the altar; but the flesh was not eaten in the holy place. (3) Moses made search, and behold the goat was burnt, probably without the camp (ch. iv. 12; vi. 11). This angered him, and led him to question the "sons of Aaron *who were left,*" or had escaped the fire that consumed their brethren, as to why they had deviated from his directions. 2. *Now look at the moral.* (1) It should have been eaten in the holy place, because it was "most holy," that is to say, the "bread of God" (ch. vi. 16, 17; xxi. 22); that which wrath was to feed upon. This significantly pointed to Christ. After declaring himself to be the "bread of God which cometh down from heaven," he explains, "the bread that I will give is my flesh, which I will give for the life of the world" (John vi. 51). How remarkably the mysteries of the bread offering and the "flesh" of the sin offering, associated on the Levitical altar, are again associated in this gospel explanation! (2) By the fire of God feeding upon the sin offering, it bore "the iniquity of the congregation, to make atonement for them before the Lord" (ver. 17). But this is said of the eating of the flesh by Aaron and his sons. By eating the flesh of the sin offering, then, Aaron was to appear as in the place of it (comp. 1 Cor. x. 7). This significantly indicated that the true sin offering was not to be an animal, but a *man.* (3) The rule is laid down that if the blood was not brought in within the holy place, the flesh should be eaten in the holy place (ver. 18). That rule showed that the Law priests were typically to bear the iniquity of the people, until that High Priest should come who would carry his own blood into the holy place not made with hands. In that event their functions were destined to cease.

II. THE EXPLANATION OF AARON. 1. *The anger of Moses was with the sons of Aaron.* (1) We are not told that he felt any anger towards Aaron. We see a propriety in this when we consider that Aaron was a type of Christ. Moses directed Aaron all through the ceremonials of his consecration, and so Christ in this world, in which he was consecrated to his priesthood, was "made under the Law." But the Law could have no anger against Christ, "who fulfilled all its righteousness," and in every way "magnified and made it honourable." (2) But against the sons of Jesus, who are far from being as perfect as their Head, the Law may have occasion for anger. 2. *But Aaron speaks in his own person for his sons.* (1) (See ver. 19.) So Jesus takes the faults of his children upon himself (see Matt. viii. 16, 17; 1 Pet. ii. 24). (2) And speaking for them thus, Aaron was able to appease Moses. Not only was Moses "satisfied," as in the text, but what Aaron urged was "well pleasing in his eyes," as in the Hebrew. So triumphantly is Jesus able to deliver us from the anger of the Law (Rom. v. 9, 20, 21). 3. *But what is the import of Aaron's words* (ver. 19)? (1) Here he concedes that the sin offering had been offered, and that, under usual conditions, to have complied with all the directions of Moses would have been proper. But he explains, "such things have befallen me," referring to his parental sorrow in the loss of his sons under most distressing circumstances. He was, therefore, a mourner, not outwardly (see vers. 4—7), but in spirit, so, had he eaten the sin offering, would it have been accepted by the Lord, viz. who *looketh upon the heart?* Moses had nothing to reply to this (comp. Deut. xii. 7; 1 Sam. i. 7, 8; Hos. ix. 4). (2) But was there not a prophetic meaning in these words of Aaron? As Caiaphas "spake not of himself, but being high priest that year, he prophesied that Jesus should die for that nation" (John x. 50, 51), does not Aaron as truly in the spirit of prophecy here say that the death of the priest sets aside the type (see Col. ii. 14)? (3) The consent of Moses shows how the Law bears testimony to Christ, and is itself to vanish as a shadow when the substance takes its place. (4) It also shows that it is proper to break the Law in the letter, when to do so is necessary to its observance in the spirit. The spirit of the Law is the gospel.—J. A. M.

Vers. 8—10.—*Wine and worship.* The prohibition of the text only extends to the priest about to officiate in the worship of God; "when ye go into the tabernacle." It had no reference to the domestic use of wine; nor did it separate "strong wine" from sacred service altogether (Exod. xxix. 42; Numb. xxviii. 7). Perhaps, as some think, it was consequent upon the foregoing scene. But if not so closely connected with it as to be occasioned by it, the fact that its announcement followed that scene in order of time suggests the truth—

I. THAT FROM THE WORSHIP OF GOD EVERY TEMPTATION SHOULD BE RELIGIOUSLY EXCLUDED. If intoxicants would have even the slightest effect on the understanding so that error might be committed, they should be scrupulously avoided: and so with any and every source of peril, whatever it may be. Whatsoever would lead the mind away from God and his truth; whatsoever would interfere with the purity, sincerity, spirituality of public worship, should be shunned. It may be beautiful attire, ornamentation, music, rhetoric, philosophizing, etc. Every man must judge for himself; "happy is he who condemneth not himself in that thing which he alloweth" (Rom. xiv. 22).

II. THAT IN THE WORSHIP OF GOD EVERY FACULTY SHOULD BE IN FULLEST EXERCISE. If intoxicants are anywise injurious, they enfeeble, they make the body drowsy, the intellect clouded, the spirit heavy and unaspiring. To the worship of God we should bring our best; not by any means the lame and the blind, etc. (Mal. i. 8), nor the second best, but the very best we can bring—the flower in the bud, the fruit adorned with its bloom; not the wearied bodily frame that sinks to sleep while God is being approached; not the mind that has lost its elasticity and strength, but our most viligant and wakeful, our most vigorous and energetic self. We should bring to his altar the power that can discern between the evil and the good, between the acceptable and the offensive (ver. 10); and the power that can rise on fleetest and most enduring wing into the heavens of joyful praise and earnest prayer and saving truth.

III. THAT FOR THE WORSHIP OF GOD THERE SHOULD BE CAREFUL PREPARATION. The priests were, in virtue of this and other precepts, to consider carefully beforehand what they should do and what they should avoid, that they might be ready to minister unto the Lord. Whether our offering of spiritual sacrifices unto God in his sanctuary (1 Pet. ii. 5) be acceptable or not, depends not more on the provision which is prepared *in* the house for us than on the conscientious preparing of our heart before we go up *unto* it.—C.

Ver. 11.—*Instruction as well as sacrifice.* These words point to—

I. A SECONDARY DUTY OF THE PRIESTHOOD—INSTRUCTION. No doubt the primary object of their appointment was sacrifice. Their function was, first of all, to mediate between God and the people, to stand at his altar and present sacrifices unto him. But this did not constitute their whole duty; they were to "teach the children of Israel all the statutes which the Lord had spoken." No doubt the whole tribe of Levi was associated with the priesthood in "teaching Jacob the judgments and Israel the Law" of the Lord (see Deut. xxxiii. 8—11; Mal. ii. 7; Hos. iv. 6).

II. THE TWOFOLD TASK THIS INSTRUCTION INVOLVED. The priests and Levites would have: 1. To make known the particular precepts of the Law, so that the people might bring their proper sacrifices, come at the appointed seasons to the sacred festivals, shun all those things which were prohibited, act rightly in their various domestic and social relations, etc. 2. To explain the spirit and significance of the ritual, so that when the worshippers came to the tabernacle they might not only go through the right forms, but also enter into the spirit of them; so that they should be affected by a sense of sin, by a hope of forgiveness, by a desire to dedicate themselves unto God, by a spirit of holy joy in God and of brotherly love toward their fellows. To communicate all the particulars of the Law, and leave uninterpreted their spiritual significance, would have been to omit an essential part of their sacred duty as religious instructors of the nation. We may be reminded of—

III. THE OBLIGATIONS OF THE CHRISTIAN MINISTRY. The privilege of those who minister for Christ is also twofold: 1. To lead souls with them to God; to suggest those thoughts and words through which the worshippers may address themselves to him and make their own personal, direct appeal to him. 2. To instruct in Christian truth. And this instruction is to combine two things: it is (1) to make known the will of God as stated in the sacred Scriptures; (2) to impress that will on the conscience of the congregation. The Christian minister seeks to *enlighten* and to *enforce*. Then he must leave those whom he serves, to act; they must then "bear their own burden." Thus we come to—

IV. THE DUTY OF THE CHRISTIAN CONGREGATION. That is, to avail themselves of the work of the minister. 1. To follow him spiritually and sympathetically to the throne of grace and, with him, draw nigh to God in prayer. 2. To seek to understand the mind of God as it is stated and explained. 3. To apply to themselves and their own need the exhortations which are given.—C.

Vers. 12—20.—*The spirit of obedience.* The words of Moses appear to have followed closely upon the incidents described in the opening verses of the chapter. Thus viewed, they show—

I. THAT THE SIN OF SOME MUST NOT INTERFERE WITH THE SERVICE OF OTHERS. (Ver. 12.) Consternation or resentment might have led Aaron and "his sons that were left" to leave the remainder of their sacred duties undischarged. This must not be. The sin of the two sons must not interrupt the service of the Most High. His worship must not cease because two men have erred. Men often plead the inconsistencies and transgressions of others as an excuse for their own shortcoming. They decline to worship God, or to sit down to the table of the Lord, or to work in the vineyard of the Great Husbandman because of their resentment against the wrong-doing of their fellows. This may satisfy themselves, but it will have no weight at all in the balances of the Divine Judge.

II. THAT THE SIN OF SOME NEED NOT INTERFERE WITH THE PRIVILEGE OF OTHERS. (Ver. 14.) The whole congregation were to "bewail the burning which the Lord had kindled" (ver. 6). But they were, nevertheless, to "eat in a clean place of the sacrifices of peace offerings." The saddest things need not interpose to prevent our enjoyment of the sacred privileges with which God has provided us.

III. THAT RESPONSIBLE MEN MAY WELL BE VIGILANT IN ALL MATTERS PERTAINING TO THE SERVICE OF GOD. (Vers. 16—18.) Moses "diligently sought" the goat which should not have been burnt, but eaten. He showed a holy solicitude to conform to the exact requirements of "the Law of the Lord," and a commendable concern when he thought he discovered a slight departure therefrom. In Christ Jesus we are not bound by any minute commandments like those which regulated the temple service of the Jews. But there is room enough in the Church of Christ for holy vigilance on the part of those who are "over others in the Lord." They should watch keenly to observe and to correct the slightest departure from the spirit of the Master; from the spirit (1) of reverence, or (2) of earnestness, or (3) of humility, or (4) of charity.

IV. THAT THE SPIRIT OF OBEDIENCE IS EVERYTHING IN THE SIGHT OF GOD. There is something profoundly touching in the excuse (ver. 19) which Aaron urged. His sons who "were left" had, spite of their bereavement and their fraternal sorrow, "offered their sin offering and their burnt offering before the Lord;" they had laid great restraint upon their feelings; they had striven to render the service required of them. And when "such things had befallen him;" when Aaron "held his peace," indeed, but "his sorrow was stirred;" when his parental heart was bleeding,—would the eating of the flesh of the goat in such a "day of desperate grief" have been an acceptable service in the sight of the Lord? Would an act in which there must have been so large a measure of constraint have been in accordance with the will of God? Moses was content with Aaron's plea; he felt that it was sound. We may infer that he was right in accepting it. Had

Aaron repined, or had he resented the retributive act of God, he would certainly have sinned. But this he did not. He summoned himself and his sons to continue in the service of the Lord, and only stopped at the point where overcoming sorrow laid its arresting hand upon him. God desires of us (1) the will to serve him, (2) the faith in him which uncomplainingly accepts his decisions when these are painful and perplexing, and (3) the endeavour, to the height of our power, to continue at our post. When the spirit of obedience is thus in our hearts, he does not exact a strict measure of work to be accomplished by our hands.—C.

Ver. 12.—*That which is left to us.* "His sons that were left." Happily and mercifully, it is not often that we suffer such a breach in our life or in our home as that which Aaron was called upon this day to endure; but inroads are made, suddenly or gradually, upon our sources of joy. Accident (as we call it), disease, treachery, misfortune, the hand of time,—these take away our treasures; they strip the goodly tree of its branches, as well as of its leaves. But "though much is taken, much abides." The good man has always consolation in that which is left to him. There is left to us—

I. SOME HUMAN AFFECTION. If not "sons that are left," or daughters, yet friends whose attachment has grown with the growing years.

II. SOME HUMAN ESTEEM. There are those—it may be many, at any rate a few—who hold us in genuine regard; who honour us, and pour on our wounded spirit the precious ointment of their esteem.

III. Solacing memories of faithful work.

IV. The consciousness of our own integrity (Ps. xli. 12).

V. The abiding favour and friendship of the Lord (Ps. cxxv. 2).

VI. The hope of eternal life in the presence of God (2 Tim. iv. 6).—C.

Vers. 8—20.—The ministers of God's house must be examples of purity and obedience.

I. The influence of PERSONAL CHARACTER on the work of the teacher, "that ye may teach the children of Israel all the statutes," etc. (ver. 11). 1. Self-control and temperance necessary to a wise judgment and a correct life. Possibly the offence of Nadab and Abihu owing to intemperance. 2. The teacher needs the respect of the taught to uphold him in his work. 3. The difference between the holy and the unholy, the clean and the unclean, should be *seen* as well as *heard* described.

II. The SUPPORT OF THE MINISTRY may be safely left to come out of the faithful discharge of duty. If the priests are at their post, they will get their portion (vers. 12—15). "It shall be thine by a statute for ever."

III. The ERRORS AND OMISSIONS, as well as sins of the ministry, should be "diligently sought after." But in the spirit of charity, not with harsh and censorious judgment. Aaron's excuse was the overwhelming stress of natural feeling. Ministers are but men. Domestic affliction often clouds their mind and burdens their spirit. Moses was content when he understood that the law of nature was honoured; and there is no true sanctity in observances which violate the first principles of humanity, and subvert the natural feelings of the human heart. The slavish system of Rome exalts religious law at the expense of natural justice, and destroys man while it professes to save him. No true religion is cruel. The Spirit of Christ is the spirit of mercy.—R.

PART III

UNCLEANNESS, CEREMONIAL AND MORAL: ITS REMOVAL OR ITS PUNISHMENT

SECTION I

EXPOSITION

CHAPTER XI.

THE two preceding parts having made manifest the way of approach to God by means of sacrifice and the appointed priesthood of mediation, there follows a part having for its subject that which keeps man apart from God, namely, uncleanness, whether ceremonial uncleanness, which may be removed by ceremonial observances, or moral uncleanness, that is, unrighteousness, which, so far as it is a ceremonial offence, may be also dealt with ceremonially, but in respect to its moral character demands punishment. This part consists of four sections. The first section, comprising chs. xi.—xv., treats of ceremonial uncleanness, caused (1) by unclean food (ch. xi.); (2) by childbirth (ch. xii.); (3) by the leprosy of man and of garments and of houses (chs. xiii., xiv.); (4) by issues (ch. xv.). The second section deals with the uncleanness contracted every year by the whole congregation, to be annually atoned for on the great Day of Atonement (ch. xvi.), followed by a parenthetical chapter as to the place in which sacrifice is to be offered—sacrifice being the means by which purification from uncleanness is to be effected (ch. xvii.). The third section is on moral uncleanness, or sin (chs. xviii., xix.), and its punishment (ch. xx.). The fourth relates to the ceremonial and moral uncleanness of priests (chs. xxi., xxii.).

The idea underlying ceremonial uncleanness is not peculiar to the Jews. With the Greeks the idea of moral beauty was borrowed from physical beauty, and the standard of moral excellence was the beautiful. With the Hebrews physical ugliness is taken as the symbol of moral ugliness or deformity: whatever is foul is the type of what is evil. That which we have a natural admiration for is good, said the Greek; that which we have a natural repugnance for represents to us what is evil, said the Hebrew. In either case, taste appears to take the place of moral judgment; but in Greek philosophy, moral taste and moral judgment had come to be identical, while the Hebrew knew that what taste condemned was not therefore of itself evil, but only symbolical and representative of evil.

Another principle underlies the Hebrew theory of uncleanness. It is that whatever is itself foul, and therefore symbolical of sin, conveys the quality of foulness, and therefore of ceremonial uncleanness to any one it comes in contact with, and often to anything which it touches. Thus a dead body, quickly assuming a loathsome appearance in the East, where the setting in of corruption is very rapid, is unclean itself, and conveys uncleanness to those who touch it. The leper is unclean, and transmits uncleanness by his touch; and certain foul diseases and fluxes from the human body have the same effect. These and such like things, being always repulsive, always cause uncleanness; but there are others which, while in some associations they are utterly repellent, in others are not so. For example, there are some vermin and insects which are pretty to the eye, but the thought of eating them creates a natural feeling of disgust. These, in so far as they are not repulsive, that is, as creeping or flying creatures, are not unclean, nor does their touch produce uncleanness, but as objects of food they are "an abomination."

Hence we are able to explain the distinction of clean and unclean animals. It does not rest upon a sanitary basis, though the prohibition to eat carnivorous and other animals repulsive to the taste is probably in accordance with the rules of health. Nor is it based on political reasons, though it is probable that the distinction kept the Jews apart from other nations, and so served an important political purpose. Nor is the injunction in the main theological, though we know that in later times the favourite interpretation was that the clean animals represented the Jews, and the unclean animals the Gentiles (Acts x. 28). Rather it was that certain creatures were forbidden because they were offensive to the taste, and, being so offensive, they were symbolical of vicious things, which must be avoided, lest they make those that partake of them or touch them to become vicious like themselves.

Vers. 2—8 contain the regulations relating to the eating of quadrupeds; vers. 9—12, those relating to fish; vers. 13—19, those relating to birds; vers. 20—23, those relating to flying insects; vers. 29, 30, those relating to unwinged creeping things; vers. 41—44, those relating to vermin. Vers. 23 —28 and 31—40 extend the defiling effect to the simple touch of the dead carcases of animals, whether edible or not.

Ver. 1.—The Lord spake unto Moses and to Aaron. Aaron, having now been consecrated high priest, is joined with Moses as the recipient of the laws on cleanness and uncleanness in ch. xi. 1; xiii. 1; xiv. 33; xv. 1. His name is not mentioned in ch. xii. 1; xiv. 1; xvii. 1; xviii. 1; xix. 1; xx. 1; xxi. 1, 16; xxii. 1, 17, 26. Probably there is no signification in these omissions.

Ver. 2.—These are the beasts that ye shall eat. In order that the Israelites might know how to avoid the uncleanness arising from the consumption of unclean flesh, plain rules are given them by which they may distinguish what flesh is clean and what is unclean. The first rule is that anything that dies of itself is unclean, whether it be beast, bird, or fish. The reasons of this are plain: for (1) the flesh still retains the blood, which no Israelite might eat; and (2) there is something loathsome in the idea of eating such flesh. Next, as to beasts, a class is marked off as edible by two plainly discernible characteristics, and instances are given to show that where there is any doubt owing to the animals possessing one

of the characteristic marks only, the rule is to be construed strictly. As to fish and insects, equally plain rules, one in each case, are laid down; but as birds are not readily distinguished into large classes, the names of those that are unclean are given one by one, the remainder being all of them permissible. Thus the simple Israelite would run no risk of incurring uncleanness by inadvertently eating unclean food, whether of beast, bird, fish, or insect. The object of the regulations being to exclude all meats naturally offensive to the human taste, all carnivorous quadrupeds are shut out by the rule of chewing the cud (ver. 3), with the same purpose, birds of prey and birds that eat offal are prohibited (vers. 13—19), and scaleless fish on account of their repulsive appearance (vers. 9—12), as well as beetles, maggots, and vermin of all sorts. In the case of beasts and fish, the rules laid down to mark off those things that are offensive, being general in their application, are such as to include in the forbidden class some few which do not appear naturally loathsome. This is owing partly to the difficulty of classification, partly to a change of feeling which experience has wrought in the sentiments of mankind with regard to such edibles as swine's flesh and shell-fish.

Vers. 3, 4.—Whatsoever parteth the hoof, and is clovenfooted, should rather be translated, *Whatsoever parteth the hoof, and completely divides it.* The camel parts but does not wholly divide the hoof, as there is a ball at the back of the foot, of the nature of a heel.

Ver. 5.—The coney, Hebrew, *shaphan;* the *Hyrax Syriacus,* or *wabr,* still called in Southern Arabia *tsofun,* a little animal similar to but not identical with the rabbit. "They live in the natural caves and clefts of the rocks (Ps. civ. 18), are very gregarious, being often seen seated in troops before the openings of their caves, and extremely timid, as they are quite defenceless (Prov. xxx. 26). They are about the size of rabbits, of a brownish-grey or brownish-yellow colour, but white under the belly; they have bright eyes, round ears, and no tail. The Arabs eat them, but do not place them before their guests" (Keil).

Ver. 6.—The hare, because he cheweth the cud, but divideth not the hoof. There is little doubt that the same animal as our hare is meant. Neither the hare, however, nor the hyrax chews the cud in the strict sense of the words. But they have the appearance of doing so. The rule respecting chewing the cud was given to and by Moses as a legislator, not as an anatomist, to serve as a sign by which animals might be known to be clean for food. Phenomenal not scientific language is used here, as in Josh. x. 12, " as we might speak of whales and their congeners as fish, when there is no need of scientific accuracy " (Clark). " All these marks of distinction in the Levitical law are wisely and even necessarily made on the basis of popular observation and belief, not on that of anatomical exactness. Otherwise the people would have been continually liable to error. Scientifically, the camel would be said to divide the hoof, and the hare does not chew the cud. But laws for popular use must necessarily employ terms as they are popularly understood. These matters are often referred to as scientific errors; whereas they were simply descriptions, necessarily popular, for the understanding and enforcement of the law " (Gardiner).

Ver. 7.—**The swine, though he divide the hoof, and be clovenfooted.** Here, again, the description is not according to anatomical analysis, but to ordinary appearance. The pig appears to be cloven-footed, and it would be misleading to give any other account of his foot in ordinary speech, but scientifically speaking, he has four toes. The prohibition of the use of swine's flesh does not arise from the fear of trichinosis or other disease, but from the disgust caused by the carnivorous and filthy habits of the Eastern pig. The repulsion originally felt for swine's flesh was natural, and, where the animal is carnivorous, is still natural, but where its habits are changed, and it has become simply graminivorous, the feeling has ceased to exist.

Ver. 8.—**Of their carcase shall ye not touch.** This prohibition is founded upon the same feeling of disgust as the prohibition of eating their flesh. Whatever is foul must be avoided.

Vers. 9—12.—**Whatsoever hath fins and scales.** The absence of fins and scales, or their apparent absence—for phenomenal language is used, as before—gives to fish a repulsive look, on which is grounded the prohibition to eat them. Eels and shell-fish are thus forbidden, though a long course of experience has now taken away the feeling of repulsion with which they were once looked upon. The flesh of the beasts forbidden to be eaten is only described as unclean, but that of the prohibited fish, birds, insects, and vermin, is designated as **an abomination unto you.**

Vers. 13—19.—The unclean birds are those which are gross feeders, devourers of flesh or offal, and therefore offensive to the taste, beginning with the eagle and vulture tribe. It is probable that the words translated **owl** (ver. 16), **night hawk** (ver. 16), **cuckow** (ver. 16) should be rendered, *ostrich, owl, gull,* and perhaps for **swan** (ver. 18), **heron** (ver.

19), **lapwing** (ver. 19), should be substituted *ibis, great plover, hoopoe.* In the case of the **bat,** we have again phenomenal language used. Being generally regarded as a bird, it is classed with birds.

Vers. 20—23.—**All fowls that creep** should rather be rendered *all winged creeping things,* that is, all flying insects. None are allowed except the *Saltatoria,* or locust family. The word translated **beetle** signifies a sort of locust, like the other three words. That the locust was a regular article of food in Palestine is amply proved. " It is well known that locusts were eaten by many of the nations of antiquity, both in Asia and Africa, and even the ancient Greek thought the *cicadas* very agreeable in flavour (Arist.'Hist. An.,' 5, 30). In Arabia they are sold in the market, sometimes strung upon cords, sometimes by measure, and they are also dried and kept in bags for winter use. . . . They are generally cooked over hot coals, or on a plate, or in an oven, or stewed in butter, and eaten either with salt or with spice and vinegar, the head, wings, and feet being thrown away. They are also boiled in salt and water, and eaten with salt or butter. Another process is to dry them thoroughly, and then grind them into meal, and make cakes of them" (Keil). (Cf. Matt. iii. 4.) The expression **goeth upon** all **four,** means grovelling or going in a horizontal position, in contrast with two-legged birds, just spoken of.

Vers. 24—28.—These verses contain an expansion of the warning contained in ver. 8, to the effect that the touch of the dead bodies of the forbidden animals was defiling, as well as the consumption of their flesh. A further mark of an unclean animal is added in ver. 27 : **Whatsoever goeth upon his paws;** that is, whatever has not hoofs, but goes stealthily, like beasts of prey of the cat kind. It includes also dogs.

Vers. 29, 30.—**The creeping things that creep upon the earth.** This class contains things that go on their belly, but have not wings, like the previous class of creeping things (vers. 20—23). By the words translated **tortoise, ferret, chameleon, lizard, snail, mole,** different varieties of the lizard are probably meant. The **mouse** is joined by Isaiah with " eating swine's flesh and the abomination " (Isa. lxvi. 17).

Vers. 31—38.—As the little animals just mentioned—weasels, mice, and lizards—are more likely than those of a larger size to be found dead in domestic utensils and clothes, a further warning as to their defiling character is added, with rules for daily use. The words translated **ranges for pots** (ver. 35) should rather be rendered *covered pots,* that is, pots or kettles with lids to them. **Seed which is to be sown,** that is, seed corn, is not defiled by contact with these dead animals, unless it has been wetted by **water being put on it**, in which case the moisture would convey the corruption into the seeds.

Vers. 39, 40.—The loathsomeness of the bodies of even clean animals that have died a natural death, makes them also the means of conveying defilement **to any one who** touches them.

Vers. 41—43.—The last class is that of vermin, which constitute a part of the unwinged creeping class already spoken of (vers. 29, 30). **Whatsoever goeth upon the belly** indicates snakes, worms, maggots; **whatsoever goeth upon all four**, things that grovel, as moles, rats, hedgehogs; **whatsoever hath more feet, or** *doth multiply feet*, centipedes, caterpillars, spiders.

Vers. 44—47.—These concluding verses give a religious sanction to the previous regulations, and make them matters of sacred, not merely sanitary or political, obligation. They were to **sanctify themselves, that is,** to avoid uncleanness, because God is holy, and they were God's. They were thus taught that ceremonial cleanness of the body was a symbol of holiness of heart, and a means of attaining to the latter. **For I am the Lord that bringeth you up out of the land of Egypt.** It is possible that Egypt may be named as being the land of animal-worship. **To be your God; ye shall therefore be holy, for I am holy.** The only way by which there can be communion between God and man_is the way of holiness.

Jewish industry and care has counted the number of letters in the Pentateuch, and marked by the use of the letter ו in larger type, in the word גחון, which occurs in ver. 42, that that letter is the middle letter of the whole work, from the beginning of Genesis to the end of Deuteronomy. It is easy to see what a protection to the text such minute and scrupulous care must be.

HOMILETICS.

Meats distinguished into clean and unclean now for the first time.

I. ORIGINALLY MAN'S LIBERTY WITH RESPECT TO EATING FLESH WAS UNRESTRICTED. Such is St. Paul's teaching: "Meats, which God hath created to be received with thanksgiving of them which believe and know the truth. For every creature of God is good, and nothing to be refused, if it be received with thanksgiving" (1 Tim. iv. 3, 4). "Unto the pure all things are pure" (Titus i. 15). "The earth is the Lord's, and the fulness thereof" (1 Cor. x. 26). "I know, and am persuaded by the Lord Jesus, that there is nothing unclean of itself" (Rom. xiv. 14). And our Lord has taught, that "there is nothing from without a man, that entering into him can defile him" (Mark vii. 15).

II. THE RESTRAINTS NOW INTRODUCED WERE ONLY TEMPORARY. They were only intended to serve a purpose for a time, while the principle underlying them is of permanent application. So the sabbatical law is of permanent obligation, but the form which that law took in the Mosaic dispensation was temporary, and has been abrogated without injury to the binding force of the sabbatical law, that one seventh of our time should be given to God.

III. THE PURPOSE OF THESE RESTRAINTS. Their object was educational. They were intended to teach, in a manner that the Israelites were capable of apprehending, and that was consonant with the rest of the Mosaic legislation, an abhorrence of spiritual evil, by fostering an abhorrence of physical foulness which was taken as the representative of moral evil.

IV. THEIR LESSON WAS TAUGHT. When the time of the institution of the new dispensation had arrived, the distinction between good and evil had been taught by the difference between fair and foul, or if not taught, it could be now taught in a better way than by sensible types and figures. Teaching by word had taken the place of teaching by images.

V. THEIR INTENTION WAS PERVERTED. The more carnal minded among the Jews rested in the letter of the command, and added other material injunctions to it, "in the washing of cups, and pots, brasen vessels, and tables" (Mark vii. 4). With them the command had failed in its purpose, and they satisfied themselves with a mere external observance of the letter. This our Lord sharply reproved: "There is nothing from without a man, that entering into him can defile him: but the things which come out of him, those are they that defile the man. . . . Do ye not perceive, that whatsoever thing from without entereth into the man, it cannot defile him; because it entereth not into his heart, but into the belly, and goeth out into the draught, purging all meats?[1] And he said, That which cometh out of the man, that defileth the man. For from within, out of the heart of men, proceed evil thoughts, adulteries, fornications, murders, thefts, covetousness, wickedness, deceit, lasciviousness, an evil eye, blasphemy, pride, foolishness: all these evil things come from within, and defile the man" (Mark vii. 15—23). This teaching prepared the way for the abolition of the restriction.

VI. RESTORATION OF THE ORIGINAL LIBERTY. First taught by the vision of St. Peter. "Peter went up upon the housetop to pray about the sixth hour: and he became very hungry, and would have eaten: but while they made ready, he fell into a trance, and saw heaven opened, and a certain vessel descending unto him, as it had been a great sheet knit at the four corners, and let down to the earth : wherein were all manner of fourfooted beasts of the earth, and wild beasts, and creeping things, and fowls of the air. And there came a voice to him, Rise, Peter; kill, and eat. But Peter said, Not so, Lord; for I have never eaten anything that is common or unclean. And the voice spake unto him again the second time, What God hath cleansed, that call not thou common. This was done thrice: and the vessel was received up again into heaven " (Acts x. 9—16). The first purpose of this vision was to show the acceptance of the Gentiles, who, according to the now received Jewish interpretation, were represented by the unclean beasts; but that was not the only lesson taught; there was also involved the conception that the whole system of clean and unclean meats was abolished. This doctrine, as we have seen, was adopted and enforced by St. Paul, and he says that it is as a Christian that he has learnt this lesson, " I know, and am persuaded by (in) the Lord Jesus, that there is nothing unclean of itself. . . . All things indeed are pure" (Rom. xiv. 14—20). "Meat commendeth us not to God" (1 Cor. vii. 8). "For the kingdom of God is not meat and drink; but righteousness, and peace, and joy in the Holy Ghost " (Rom. xiv. 17).

VII. PROHIBITION OF BLOOD, AND THINGS STRANGLED, CONTINUED BY THE COUNCIL OF JERUSALEM. The Council of Jerusalem, in deciding the terms on which the Gentiles should be admitted to the Christian Church, forbade the eating of things offered to idols, and blood, and things strangled. The first of these restrictions rested on a different principle; the second and third are a continuation of the Mosaic regulations, and the reason why they are retained is given. "For Moses of old time hath in every city them that preach him, being read in the synagogue every sabbath day " (Acts xv. 21). Inasmuch as the Christian Church consisted of Jews and Gentiles, and the former of these regarded themselves as bound by the Mosaic legislation, the Synod of Jerusalem desired that the Gentiles should concede to their brethren so far as not to partake of those things which Jewish Christians thought themselves bound to abstain from, lest there should be a schism between the two divisions of the Church. This law had become one of charity solely, and would naturally be abrogated, or rather cease to bind, when the occasion for it ceased. As in the parallel case of meats offered to idols, " no man " was to " put a stumbling-block or an occasion to fall in his brother's way " (Rom. xiv. 13). " It is good neither to eat flesh, nor to drink wine, nor anything whereby thy brother stumbleth, or is offended, or is made weak " (Rom. xiv. 21). " If meat make my brother to offend, I will eat no flesh while the world standeth, lest I make my brother to offend " (1 Cor. viii. 13). But no flesh was now forbidden by a positive regulation of God. The rule had become one of charity, and when the number of Jewish Christians ceased to be considerable in relation to Gentiles, it naturally came to an end.

Ver. 44.—" Ye shall be holy; for I am holy." This is the pervading principle of both dispensations.

I. ORIGINALLY MAN WAS CREATED IN THE IMAGE OF GOD. (Gen. i. 27.) St. Paul tells us that the likeness consisted " in righteousness and true holiness " (Eph. iv. 24). The likeness continued until man fell. After the Fall, God's image, though not obliterated, was no longer reflected in man, except in a blurred and perverted manner, as in a cracked mirror. Man ceased to be holy, and his communion with God was lost.

II. THE DESIRED EFFECT OF REVEALED RELIGION IS TO RECOVER THE LOST IMAGE AND SO TO RESTORE COMMUNION BETWEEN GOD AND MAN. Under the old dispensa-

---

[1] Or, " This he said, making all meats clean" (Revised Version).

tion, a legal and conventional holiness was brought about by means of the sacrifices and purifications. Man was replaced in a state of symbolical, though not real holiness, and so far and so long as that state was maintained by ceremonial rites and cleansings, the relation of communion with God was symbolically restored and preserved. In the new dispensation, that which was symbolized only before, became really effected in the case of those who, having been adopted in Christ, were sanctified by the operation of the Holy Spirit in their heart, and thus "put on the new man, which, after God, is created in righteousness and true holiness" (Eph. iv. 24).

III. HIGHER CONCEPTION OF HOLINESS UNDER THE GOSPEL THAN THE LAW. Under the Law, on the principle, "Ye shall be holy," is founded the command to abstain from ceremonial uncleanness or defilement; "Ye shall therefore sanctify yourselves, . . . neither shall ye defile yourselves with any manner of creeping thing that creepeth on the earth" (ch. xi. 44). In the New Testament, the same principle is invoked as the ground of avoiding moral, not physical, uncleanness, "For this is the will of God, even your sanctification, that ye should abstain from fornication . . . for God hath not called us unto uncleanness, but unto holiness" (1 Thess. iv. 3—7). And the very text before us is quoted for the purpose of urging upon the Christians no mere ritual purification, but the highest spirituality of life. "As he which hath called you is holy, so be ye holy in all manner of conversation; because it is written, Be ye holy; for I am holy" (1 Pet. i. 15, 16).

IV. PRACTICAL CONCLUSION. "Having therefore these promises, dearly beloved, let us cleanse ourselves from all filthiness of the flesh and spirit, perfecting holiness in the fear of God" (2 Cor. vii. 1). "What manner of persons ought ye to be in all holy conversation and godliness?" (2 Pet. iii. 11). Carnal cleanness is not sufficient; moral uprightness is not sufficient; our aim must be holiness, as God is holy, and as this holiness was manifested in Christ.

HOMILIES BY VARIOUS AUTHORS.

The religious use of nature. Ch. xi.; cf. Ps. civ., cvii.; Job xxxviii.—xli.; Matt. xiii.; 2 Sam. xxii. 34. We pass now to the relation in which the Lord's people are to stand to animated nature. So far from treating it with indifference, they were bound to regard certain animals as clean and certain others as unclean, and to regard their use of and contact with them as of religious importance. The temptation to use nature as something outside religious considerations was hereby avoided, and the Jew was led to regard every animal as having some religious significance to him. A literal watchfulness was thus inculcated of the most painstaking character. The Jew, wherever he went, was on his guard against the unclean, and was providing for his use only what was legally clean and pure.

I. NATURE IS A REVELATION OF GOD IF WE ONLY HAD ITS KEY. It is too often forgotten that nature was the first revelation of God to his creatures. The Bible is the supplementary revelation necessitated by sin. To our first parents before the Fall, nature had a deeper meaning, most probably, than it has yet had to us. The interpretation of nature is most important, and there is no need that it should be "agnostic" or irreligious. Provided scientific fact be welcomed, there is no detriment, but rather there is gain, in looking at our surroundings in a religious spirit. Science is not bound to become a department of theology, and to be running up into theological statements; neither, on the other hand, is it bound to indulge in atheistic ones. The "argument of design" may not be a part of science, but it is just as true that the argument of *chance*, which is the only alternative, is no part of true science either. But while science is under no obligation to become theological, it is right that nature should be regarded religiously. Natural religion has its sphere just as well as supernatural religion.

II. WE INSTINCTIVELY USE ANIMATED NATURE TO ILLUSTRATE THE CHARACTERISTICS OF MANKIND. The animals become our picture alphabet, by whose help we spell out character. Indeed, so close are the affinities beween the lower animals and the successive stages of human character, that one ingenious foreign writer points out an analogy between the development in nature and the development in individual human nature

"Man passes still to-day," says M. Secretan,[1] "through the form of the ape, and he passes through it visibly; the embryonic evolution continues itself in the transformations of the first age, the spiritual development allies itself to the corporeal evolution, it is regulated by the same laws. Just as the human body reproduces in summary form the whole history of organized nature, the spirit of a civilized person reproduces in abridgment the whole history of the human spirit, and the two histories are inseparable. The characteristic of the ape, imitation without intelligence, is also the characteristic of the child when he is put in possession of his organs. This phase is essential; the child would not learn to eat, he would not learn to walk, he would not learn especially to speak, and by consequence to think, were he not, during some period and in certain respects, a little parrot and a little ape. Simian imitation is the process by which the acquisitions of the species are appropriated by the individual. Simian imitation, by which I mean the reproduction of movements of which the intention is not comprehended, is the normal and desired transition between instinct and the reflective intelligence, which is the properly human condition." There seems, therefore, to be a reason in the very nature of things for the illustration of moral or immoral qualities from the animals. Amid other uses served by the lower creation, there is certainly this one of furnishing illustrations of character. Our Lord's parables embody the principle of the spiritual significance of nature in its broadest applications.

III. BY THE DIVISION OF THE ANIMALS HERE PROPOSED IMPORTANT MORAL QUALITIES ARE COMMENDED AND IMMORAL ONES CONDEMNED. A scientific division was not needed for a religious purpose. A popular division, easily apprehended, would serve infinitely better. The distinctions drawn are such as may be seen at a glance.

1. *Quadrupeds.* The clean are those who divide the hoof and chew the cud. In other words, the ruminants are to be regarded as the clean. All other quadrupeds are to be accounted unclean. That there may be no mistake, the camel, coney, hare, and swine are emphasized as unclean, because possessing only one of the required characteristics. The flesh of the ruminants is generally considered as more wholesome than that of the other quadrupeds; but this would scarcely determine the division. Let the fact, however, be noted that *reflection* finds its fitting illustration in the rumination of these animals, and that they are justly regarded as both *sure-footed* and *cleanly*; then we see a moral purpose in the distinction. If the Lord's people were to associate with these animals and use them for food, while the other quadrupeds were to be avoided, it was to teach them to *reflect* faithfully upon what God gave them, to be *steadfast* in running the race he sets before them, and to be *pure* in their walk and conversation. That such moral ideas were associated with the clean animals is corroborated by such passages as 2 Sam. xxii. 34; Ps. xviii. 33; Hab. iii. 19; with which may be compared 1 Sam. ii. 9.

2. *Fishes.* Here, again, the clean ones are those which have both fins and scales. All that have not these two characteristics are to be deemed an abomination, such as sharks, eels, and the swarmers generally (שֶׁרֶץ). That moral characteristics are illustrated in fish as well as in quadrupeds is acknowledged by the common usage of language. Do we not call men of a rapacious disposition "sharks;" and say of men of uncertain and cunning ways that they "wriggle like eels"? It seems certain, therefore, that the distinction here made, while perhaps having some foundation in the quality of the flesh, is primarily to illustrate disposition, and to guard the Jews against the selfishness and rapacity associated with the unclean fishes.

It could hardly be *locomotion* which is referred to in this animal kingdom, since some of the unclean fishes, for example, the sharks, are remarkable for their speed. Moreover, the fact of sharks and some other fishes having scales, though of almost microscopic character, is no argument against the fidelity of the record. The Law was given primarily to a people of simple and not scientific habits—not to microscopists. Its popular style and adaptation to common life are among its highest recommendations.

3. *Birds.* Here, again, when the words are looked carefully into, the distinction seems to be that clean birds are such as feed on grain and grasses, while the carnivorous birds are excluded as unclean. In no more striking way could *unholy appetites* be illustrated and condemned. Restraint and purity were thus inculcated.

4. *Reptiles.* Of these permission is given to eat four kinds of locust, all of which

[1] 'Discours Laïques,' p. 72.

are distinguished as *leapers*, and not *runners*. Locomotion in this case, rather than food, is the ground of the distinction. When besides, we remember the migratory character of these insects, there is conveyed an excellent illustration of the *stranger spirit*, which alights on earth only so far as is needful, and takes more kindly to the air. If God's people should be "strangers and pilgrims upon earth," if they should be setting their affections on things above, the locust tribes, which the Jews were allowed to eat, most admirably illustrated the required spirit.

On the other hand, the mole, the mouse, the lizard (צָב, not "tortoise," as in English Version), gecko (אֲנָקָה, not "the ferret," as in English Version), monitor (כֹּחַ, from its great strength—not "the chameleon"), lizard and sand-lizard (חֹמֶט, from lying on the ground—not "snail," for they are eaten by Jews and Orientals, as not unclean), and chameleon are to be regarded as unclean. Earthliness and ugliness—in one word, the repulsiveness of sin—seem indicated by this distinction.

We have thus inculcated, by this easy, popular division of the animals, important moral qualities to be cultivated and immoral qualities to be avoided. Animated nature became thus a mirror for human nature. The living world around man was thus made to take up a parabolic language and promote his sanctification.

IV. The defiling character of death through natural causes was to be constantly recognized. Even a clean animal which had died of itself was not to be eaten or touched with impunity. Defilement was the result of such contact. The lesson of mortality as the penalty of sin was thus illustrated. Men might devote an animal to death for sacrificial purposes or for their own use, but when death came as the debt of nature, at once its defiling character must be realized, and purification sought accordingly.

The laws of this chapter entailed constant watchfulness. No careless living was possible under the Jewish *régime*. In the same spirit surely should we "watch and pray, lest we enter into temptation." In the same spirit should we ask ourselves, What spiritual lessons is surrounding nature communicating to our spirits? Not in vain, and not for mere utility, has such an environment been thrown around us.—R. M. E.

Vers. 1—8.—*Clean and unclean.* As man is made after the image of God, so is the outward and sensible world constituted as a kind of apographa to represent the spiritual world which is the subject of faith (Rom. i. 20). The key to unlock the mysteries of this system is to be found in the Scriptures of truth; and animals, according to it, are to be viewed as representing men.

I. The Law distributes them into two classes. 1. *The clean.* The marks of cleanness are: (1) That they "divide the hoof." By the division of the hoof, as in the ox and sheep, the animal is able so to order its steps as not to throw up the mud upon itself, as the horse does whose hoof is not cloven. (2) They "chew the cud." So their food is more perfectly prepared for digestion. The manner in which this is done, while the creature rests, is so suggestive of thoughtfulness and meditation that it is described as *ruminating*. (3) The clean animals were therefore chosen to represent the Israelites, who were a holy nation. They were ceremonially holy: (*a*) So *walking* in the ways of God's commandments as not to be polluted with the abominations of idolatry. (*b*) So *meditating* upon the Law as inwardly to digest it to their nourishment (see Ps. i. 2; 1 Tim. iv. 13—15). (*c*) Thus also they became morally greatly superior to the nations around them. 2. *The unclean.* (1) The Gentiles in contrast to the Jews were so, ceremonially, and were therefore shut out from communion with the Jews. But it was competent to them to be made holy by becoming proselytes. (2) They were in general idolaters, and so morally abominable. It was mainly to keep the Israelites from being contaminated with the idolatries of their neighbours, that these laws were instituted (see ver. 45; xx. 23—25; Deut. xiv. 1—3). 3. *There are but two classes of men.* (1) Though some animals divide the hoof, they are not clean unless they also chew the cud. The hog is of this order, and is filthy to a proverb (2 Pet. i. 22). So it does not make men clean to have the faculty for walking cleanly when their disposition otherwise leads them to wallow in the mire of sin. (2) Though some chew the cud, yet if they divide not the hoof they are unclean. The "camel," the "coney," and the "hare," or whatever creature, the word ארנבת may describe, are of this order. For what good is the semblance of meditation and repentance, if the walk of the life be not clean (Jas. i. 20)?

(3) As there are varieties of clean and also of unclean animals, so are there varieties and degrees of goodness, on the one hand, and of wickedness on the other, amongst men. Still the classes are but two. The one is led by Christ, the other by Satan (Matt. xii. 30 ; xxv. 2, 32, 33). To which class do you belong ?

II. THE LAW IN THE LETTER IS NOW CHANGED.   1. *The gospel is freely preached to the Gentiles.* (1) They are not now under obligation to be proselyted to Judaism. This subject was debated in the early Church, and settled at the Council of Jerusalem. (2) The same decision, which was at the instance of Peter to whom the Lord had assigned that distinction (see Matt. xvi. 19), released the Jews also from the yoke of the Law (see Acts xv.). 2. *This was according to prophetic indication.* (1) Under the figure of the unclean wolf dwelling with the lamb, etc., Isaiah (xi.) describes the Gentile and Jew as to be wonderfully reconciled in the days of Messiah. (2) To show that the Jew must have no fellowship with the Gentile, the Law forbade the yoking together of the clean ox with the unclean ass (Deut. xxii. 10). But prophecy anticipates the blessedness of the time when the seed, viz. of the gospel, should be sown beside all waters—not those of Judæa only, but of the wide world ; and that in this business the ox and the ass—the Jew and the Gentile—should become fellow-workers (see Isa. xxxii. 20 ; comp. also Deut. xxv. 4 ; 1 Cor. ix. 9—11 ; 1 Tim. v. 18). 3. *Peter's vision instructed him that this time was come.* (1) The animals contained in the sheet were those described as *unclean* in the Law, and represented the Gentiles. Peter, therefore, when commanded to kill and eat, hesitated, for that he " had never eaten anything that was common or unclean." He therefore held that " it was an unlawful thing for a man that is a Jew to keep company or come unto one of another nation." (2) But the linen sheet which enclosed the animals was the emblem of purity ; and they were thrice lifted into the heavens. To these symbols agreed also the voice which said, " What God hath cleansed that call not thou common." (3) When therefore Peter had all this corroborated by the counter-vision of Cornelius, he was convinced that henceforth he "should not call any man common or unclean." For the universality of the mercy of the gospel had been testified in that the sheet was knit at the four corners, showing that the Gentiles were to be gathered together from the four quarters of the world.

III. THE LAW IN ITS SPIRIT STILL ABIDES.   1. *For the gospel is that spirit.* (1) The glory on the face of Moses was veiled to the Jews. So concerned were they with the letter that they could not steadfastly look upon the true glory of their own Law. Moses therefore put a vail upon his face, viz. the vail of the letter. This vail is still upon their hearts, and must so remain until they turn to the Lord, or become converted to Christ. (2) When Moses turned to the Lord, from whom he derived his glory, he took off the vail ; and it is the same glory which falls upon us. The only difference is that in the spirit of the Law we see the glory of the Lord reflected from the face of Moses ; but in the spirit of the gospel we see the same glory as Moses himself saw it, immediately, in the face of Jesus. (3) Thus passing from the Law to the gospel, a spiritual person is changed from glory to glory. This brightening transfiguration is effected " by the Spirit of the Lord," or, as the margin construes it, " by the Lord who is the Spirit," viz. of the Law. The Spirit of the Lord is the Spirit of the Law. 2. *The gospel insists upon moral purity.* (1) We have seen that the law of yoking together the ox and the ass is repealed under the gospel. This was as to the letter. But we shall find it still insisted upon, viz. as to the spirit. For Paul clearly refers to it (2 Cor. vi. 14) when he forbids the unequal yoking together of Christians and infidels. (2) In the spirit of it Christ came not to destroy, but to fulfil, the Law, and that to the jot and tittle (Matt. v. 17—20). What a rebuke is here to the antinomian ! What a stumbling-block to the Jew is the antinomianism in false theories of Christianity ! Christians who neglect the study of the Law miss the benefit of many glorious views of precious gospel truth. How just is the remark of Augustine, that " the Old Testament, when rightly understood, is one great prophecy of the New"!—J. A. M.

Vers. 9—12.—*The waters and their inhabitants.* " Here," says Maimonides, " the exposition of this sentence, ' A word spoken according to his two faces is as apples of gold in (מֹשְׂכִּיּוֹת) *maschyoth* of silver ' (Prov. xxv. 11). *Maschyoth* are a kind of *lattice* or *network* having very small interstices. Therefore ' when a word spoken according to both its faces ' (that is, according to its exterior and interior signification) is likened to 'apples of gold in network of silver,' the meaning is that the exterior sense is good and precious as silver, but the interior is much more excellent as gold. An apple of gold covered with a silver network, viewed at a distance, seems to be all silver; but if by the worth and beauty of the silver you be attracted to view it more narrowly, you may discover the apple of gold that is vailed within. So are the words of the Law in the letter useful and excellent for direction in morals, or for the outward government of the Church, while the interior part or spirit is of superior excellence to build up the believer in the sublime mysteries of faith." According to this principle, let us consider here—

I. THE MYSTERY OF THE WATERS. 1. *They denote multitudes of peoples.* (1) This is expressed in such passages as Isa. lv. 5 and Rev. xvii. 15. (2) The reason, perhaps, is that they lave the shores of the earth and are the highway of commerce. At all times they sustain a multitude of navigators; and at one time, in the ark of Noah, the entire population of the world was afloat. (3) In the text the waters are distributed into "seas" and "rivers." 2. *The sea may be diversely considered.* (1) Before the formation of light, when its consistency was muddy, it was called the *deep*, or the *abyss*, and was the symbol of *hell* (Gen. i. 2; Luke viii. 31; Rom. x. 7; Rev. xx. 3). (2) Under the action of light, the earthy particles precipitated, and the upper portion became gradually clearer and more liquid. Then the mass received the name of "seas" (Gen. i. 10). In this condition the waters became stocked with living creatures and capable of supporting fleets, when it became a figure of the peoples of the world. (3) When disturbed by fierce winds, and the sediment from the bottom worked up, as if the abyss of hell had been moved, the state of the wicked is described (see Isa. lvii. 20). The winds by which the wicked are stirred are their passions, and the effects are turbulence and insurrection (see Ps. lxv. 7; cvii. 26; Jude 13). (4) We carry waves and storms within us; they threaten to drown us (Jas. i. 6); none can save us from ourselves but that Jesus who miraculously stilled the tempest (Matt. viii. 26). 3. *Rivers also may be variously considered.* (1) They are taken in a good sense when they keep their channels, for then they are sources of blessing. The river of Eden represented the *covenant* of God, which, branching into "four heads," showed how the blessings of the gospel were to be carried to the four quarters of the world (Gen. ii. 10; Psa. xxxvi. 8; xlvi. 4; lxv. 9; Rev. xxii. 1). The peaceful *people of the covenant* would also be represented. (2) Rivers are taken in a bad sense when they overflow their banks, in which case they become muddy, and carry desolation where they rush. Hence they are compared to invading armies and to ungodly men moved to violence (Judg. v. 21; Ps. lxix. 15; Isa. viii. 7, 8; xviii. 2; lix. 19; Rev. xii. 15).

II. THE INHABITANTS OF THE WATERS. 1. *The clean are distinguished by fins and scales.* (1) The fins are their instruments of locomotion. By means of these they rise to the surface and swim in purer water under the clearer light of the heavens. Thus they teach us that a holy people should be active, not in the darkness of sin and ignorance, but in the day of goodness and truth (John iii. 21; viii. 12; ix. 4, 5). (2) The scales, which have a beautiful metallic lustre, suggest the idea of armour; and, when the creature swims near the surface, these brilliantly reflect the glories of the sun. They teach us to "put on the armour of light" (Rom. xiii. 12; Eph. vi. 7). 2. *The unclean are those without fins and scales.* (1) Those destitute of both, like the eel, shun the light, and bury themselves in the mud at the bottom. They teach us to avoid the corresponding habits of the wicked, who rush into sin and ignorance and wallow in moral filth (Job xxiv. 13—17; John iii. 19, 20; Eph. v. 13). (2) Those who have fins but no scales are covered with a thick glutinous matter, which in appearance contrasts unfavourably with the silver and golden armour in which the clean creatures are clad. If they use their fins to rise out of their depths, it is to make havoc upon shoals of brighter creatures. So are the wicked bloodthirsty and voracious, who therefore should be shunned. (3) In the imagery of the prophets, anti-Christian kingdoms are sometimes described as great sea-monsters (see Dan. vii. 2, 3; Rev. xiii. 1). Such kingdoms must be held in abomination by the thoughtful student of the Law, and the time, earnestly longed for, when the Lamb will appear on Mount Sion.— J. A. M.

Vers. 13—25.—*Flying creatures.* So conflicting are the opinions of the learned as to many of the animals indicated in the Hebrew names in the verses before us, that it appears hopeless to expect certainly to identify them.   This fact in itself ought to convince the Jew that the Law, in the letter, is abolished; for he cannot tell whether he has not repeatedly eaten abominable things, or that contact with the carcases of such has not made him unclean.   As to the spirit of the Law, there are broad indications of cleanness and uncleanness to which we may profitably attend.

I. THE UNCLEAN ARE IN GENERAL BIRDS OF PREY.   1. *Conspicuous amongst these are the eagles.*   (1) There is little doubt that first name (נשר) is truly rendered "eagle." The term expresses the propensity of that creature for *lacerating* and *tearing in pieces* the flesh of its prey.   (2) Its associates in the group (vers. 13, 14) are similar in nature. The "ossifrage," or *bone-breaker*, is probably the sea-eagle, whose habit is to break bones to get at the marrow.   The "ospray" has its name in the Hebrew from its *strength*, and is generally understood to be the *black eagle*.   The "vulture"—if that truly renders the original—is one of the largest and most formidable of the eagle kind. And what is construed the "kite," being in the same group, is probably some other description of eagle.   2. *These are emblems of evil spirits.*   (1) This, indeed, is true of all unclean birds, in proof of which see Matt. xiii. 4, compared with 19, and Rev. xviii. 2.   They are so: (2) From their traversing the air (see Eph. ii. 2).   This is eminently the case with eagles, whose flight is towering, and whose nests even are in inaccessible mountain heights.   (3) From the formidableness of their attacks.   From dizzy heights they swoop down upon their prey.   They are armed with powerful talons, and strong, sharp, hooked beaks fitted to inflict dreadful wounds, tearing as they grip the flesh of their quivering victims (Job xxxix. 30).   3. *They also represent wicked men.*   (1) Wicked men are the "children of Satan," and naturally exhibit the family likeness. The kings of Babylon and Tyre are compared to the eagle (Ezek. xvii. 3, 7).   The persecutors of the people of God are likewise so compared (Lam. iv. 19).   The Roman armies, whose standards were eagles, are called eagles by our Lord (Matt. xxiv. 28). (2) The lesson for us is to avoid the disposition of the wicked, and to beware of their relentless voracity and diabolical cruelty.   God is stronger than the "powers of the air."

II. SOME UNCLEAN BIRDS ARE PROWLERS OF THE NIGHT.   1. *This characterizes the next group* (vers. 15—19).   (1) The Hebrew name for the "raven" (ערב) is that commonly used for *evening*.   Our name "raven" probably comes from their *ravening*. The raven Noah sent forth from the ark, which wandered to and fro, and resting upon floating carcases or what dry thing it could find, was an emblem of an unclean dark spirit, which is cast out from the Church of God, and from the hearts of his people, and wanders among the moral carcases, the dead in trespasses and sins (comp. Zech. xiii. 2; Matt. xii. 43).   (2) Keep close to Jesus, lest, departing from him, we may invite this unclean spirit to return with seven others more wicked than himself. 2. *With the raven owls are associated* (vers. 16—19).   (1) These are creatures whose vision will not endure the blaze of day, but who have wonderful sight in the dark. That rendered "hawk" has its name here (ראה) from the *swiftness* of its flight; but in Dan. xiv. 13 (ראה) from the sharpness of its *sight*.   (2) They are distinguished from each other by particular habits.   That in our version called the "night hawk" (תחמס) is the screech-owl.   Its screams are violent; and these birds in general make fearful and doleful sounds in the night.   This does not argue favourably for the happiness of evil spirits.   (3) Wicked men also, like owls, hate the light.   When honest people of the day are sleeping, these prowlers are plotting mischief.   Witness the burglaries, the murders, the prostitutions, the debaucheries, practised by them under the cover of darkness.

III. UNCLEAN BIRDS ARE GROVELLING IN THEIR HABITS.   1. *Such are the "fowls that creep going upon all four."*   (1) The bat is a creature of this class.   It has claws attached to its leathern wings, which serve it instead of feet to crawl by.   (2) This description includes also insects from which exceptions are taken in the verse following. 2. *They are types of wicked intelligences.*   (1) Some devils have a passion for enshrining themselves in organic bodies.   The incarnation of Satan in the serpent was not the last attempt.   There were demoniacal possessions in our Lord's day; and when expelled from human beings, they preferred the bodies of swine to having no organic habitation.   (2) Wicked men grovel in the most revolting moral filth.   3. *In what contrast to these are the good!*   (1) The dove sent forth by Noah is a figure of the Spirit of God, the gracious

Messenger and Dispenser of peace to the Church; but who is often grieved by the impurities of men (Matt. iii. 16). The fruit of the Spirit, is peace; and those who exemplify it are called doves (Matt. x. 16). (2) The lark also is a clean creature, who soars high and sings gloriously in the light of the morning. How angelical! how saintly! (3) While winged insects that could not leap from the ground were unclean, to show that those men are morally so who are wholly given to the cares of this world; those with *benders* above their feet, in our version called "legs," those with crouching joints to stoop and spring with, as locusts and grasshoppers, for the opposite reason are clean. The Baptist lived principally upon locusts in the wilderness.—J. A. M.

Vers. 26—47.—*Unclean, creeping, and dead things.* It is evident, from the concluding verses of this chapter (see vers. 43, 44), that these laws were designed to teach the nature of the holiness of God. It therefore follows, unless that holiness consist in not eating the flesh or touching the carcases of certain creatures, which it would be absurd to suppose, these creatures must in their habits represent evils which men should abominate, and clean creatures, on the contrary, virtues which they should cultivate. Let us therefore seek the spiritual lessons from—

I. THE UNCLEAN CREEPING THINGS THAT CREEP. These are opposed to creeping things that leap, some of which are clean (see vers. 21, 22). Their steady attachment to the earth, never rising above it, represents an inveterate worldliness which a holy people must hold in abhorrence. Samples are given under the following groupings (see ver. 42), viz.: 1. *Those that have no feet*, "Whatsoever goeth upon the belly." (1) Serpents, snakes, vipers, and worms of all kinds are included under this description. The serpent has given its name to Satan ever since he enshrined himself in a creature of that kind (see Gen. iii. 1; 2 Cor. xi. 3; Rev. xii. 9; xx. 2). And wicked men are the "children of the devil," and so are described as the "seed of the serpent," and a "generation of vipers" (Gen. iii. 15; Matt. iii. 7). (2) Serpents are abominable for their unclean habits, lurking in the dust or mire, and eating their meat from the dust (Gen. iii. 14; Isa. lxv. 25; Micah vii. 17). Worms are bred in corruption and feast upon carrion (Exod. xvi. 20; Job vii. 5; xix. 24; Acts xii. 23). What a picture of those who wallow in sin! Serpents are double-tongued (Ps. cxl. 3), teaching us to abhor deception. They nourish poison, which is deadly (Numb. xxi. 9), teaching us to detest malignity (see Isa. xli. 24, margin; Rom. iii. 13). The worm of the damned dieth not (Isa. lxvi. 24; Mark ix. 44). 2. *Those that have four feet*, "Whatsoever goeth upon all four." (1) The weasel and the ferret are remarkable for their stealthy sliding motion in closing upon their prey. They teach us that slyness and treachery are an aggravation of violence, which should be held in abomination. The "mouse" (ver. 29) is to be taken as the representative of everything of the *mus* kind; but it is difficult to say what animal is meant by the word (צב) rendered "tortoise." By some it is thought to be the *crocodile*; by others the *toad*. Its name indicates some habit of *swelling*, and may teach us to abominate all impudence, ostentation, and vanity. (2) The animal called "chameleon" (ver. 30) is by some thought to be the *mongoose*, a creature which eats snakes, rats, mice, and other vermin; while Bochart concludes that the *chameleon* is intended by the word we translate "mole." Creatures of the lizard kind, excepting the aquatic sort, such as the crocodile, live on flies. God makes some unclean creatures useful in exterminating others; so he deals amongst wicked nations, punishing them by one another in their turn. 3. *Those that have more feet.* (1) Under this description we have centipedes, caterpillars, perhaps, and innumerable creatures, with legs more in number than four. Amongst these there is scope for naturalists to describe qualities all which will convey moral lessons. (2) The one thing we mark in creatures that "multiply feet," as the Hebrew expresses it, is the slowness yet steadiness and stillness of their progress. The stealthy, insinuating false teachers who troubled the early Churches, and who have their representatives in modern times, are compared to these creeping things (see 2 Tim. iii. 6; Jude 4).

II. THE LAWS OF CONTAMINATION. These are ranged under two heads: 1. *The polluting of persons.* (1) This is done by their touching the carcase of an unclean creature. Whatsoever is unfit for food must not be touched (see Gen. iii. 3). Whom we cannot commune with we must avoid. (2) It may be done by their touching the carcase of a creature originally clean that has died of itself. Because in this case it could not be a type of Christ, who died voluntarily, for he had no sin of his own to doom him to die. All intercourse of Christians should be in Christ, who is our life. 2. *The polluting of things.* (1) Vessels of any sort are rendered unclean by contact with the carcase of an unclean thing. These represent human beings in the capacity of servants, whether to God or man (Rom. ix. 21 ; 2 Tim. ii. 20, 21). Some being polluted are to be broken, to show that sin leads to destruction (Rom. ix. 22). Others may be purified by water, to show that sin may be removed by the sanctifying grace of the Spirit of God. There is a happy time coming (see Zech. xiv. 20, 21). (2) Clean meat may become polluted by contact with anything unclean. This law teaches that " evil communications corrupt good manners." (3) If an unclean thing fall into a fountain or well in which there is plenty of water, it does not render the water unclean (ver. 36). The living water is an emblem of the Holy Spirit, who cannot be rendered unholy by anything that sinners may do. For a like reason, perhaps, seed that is to be sown, which is a figure of Christ, cannot be rendered impure (ver. 37). But if water be put upon the seed for any other purpose, the figure is changed and the case is altered (ver. 38).—J. A. M.

Vers. 11—13.—*The abominable thing.* All the " unclean " animals were spoken of as " abominable." The Israelites were to learn to regard all creatures which were forbidden for food as offensive in their sight. Many of those prohibited were, for one reason or another, objects of natural aversion ; fitting, therefore, to be types and pictures of " that abominable thing which God hates " (Jer. xliv. 4). Probably nothing in nature affords such a vivid conception of that which is loathsome and disgusting as certain members of the animal world. " The ugliness and spitefulness of the camel, . . . the filthy sensuality of the hog, the voracious appetency of the dog, the wolf, and the hyena, the savage ferocity of the tiger, the sluggishness of the sloth, the eagle clutching innocence in its talons, the vulture gorging on putrescence, the slimy fish that creeps among the mud, the snake watching in the grass, the scaly thing that crawls on all the land and in all the sea;"—here we have a striking and almost terrible picture of the repulsiveness of sin. The training of the Hebrew mind to look on " unclean " animals with greatest aversion helped them to view sin in the light in which God would have us regard it, viz.—

I. AS A THING WHICH HE HATES UTTERLY. " It is even an abomination unto him," it is " that abominable thing which he hates." He is " of purer eyes than to behold evil, and cannot look on iniquity." The falseness, the impurity, the grossness, the oppression, the selfishness, the profanity, the ingratitude of human nature, are as unendurable in God's sight—things from which he turns with as pained and troubled an eye— as are the most revolting actions of the unclean among the beasts of the field or the reptiles that crawl on the earth, in our esteem. Language fails to express the idea ; the vilest habits of the lowest creatures will alone convey the thought of the repulsiveness of sin in the sight of God.

II. AS A THING WHICH THE HOLY HATE. Holy angels, the " spirits of just men made perfect," holy men on earth,—all holy spirits, like the Holy One himself, hate sin, shrink from the sight of it, regard it " even as an abomination." David records for us his intolerance of iniquity (Ps. ci.). Peter tells us of the vexation of Lot's righteous soul with the unlawful deeds and filthy conversation of the wicked (2 Pet. ii. 7, 8). The message that comes from the attitude of the holy is, " Ye that love the Lord, *hate evil* " (Ps. xcvii. 10).

III. AS A THING WHICH WE MUST LEARN TO HATE. 1. If we are numbered among the holy, we are hating sin ; as far as our spirit is sanctified by the truth and by the Spirit of God, so far sin is to us " that abominable thing." 2. But we need to learn more of its hideousness, and to shrink from it with more of Divine repugnance. 3. And if we are practising any evil habit, and therefore cherishing it, and not only enduring but even loving it, there must come a time of disenchantment when the evil thing will assume to our eye its own hateful aspect. It is (1) a *painful* thing to consider that we may be, with so many others, liking that which we should be loathing ; choosing and cherishing that which we should be indignantly repelling or expelling. (2) A *needful* thing to keep an open eye to see that to which we may now be blind ; to be willing to learn that which our true friends may have to teach us ; to be ready and eager to receive enlightenment from God (Ps. cxxxix. 23). (3) A *fearful* thing to think how many live and die in the love of that which is loathsome, and will only learn in retributive scenes what an abominable thing is sin.—C.

Ver. 3.—*Health a duty as well as a blessing.* Undoubtedly there were moral and religious grounds for the legislation of this chapter (see subsequent Homilies). It was designed to express and convey religious truth. But we may well believe that the Divine purpose therein was, in part, sanitary. It was chiefly as the Father of their spirits and Sovereign of their souls that God thus spoke on the "clean and the unclean;" but it was also as the Author of their bodily frames. He desired that those who were to be known for ever as his people should be healthy in frame as well as pure in heart. The injunctions given in this chapter tended to that result. Those animals there allowed are the best fitted for food. Human science confirms, here as elsewhere, Divine instruction. "The grain-eating and ruminative animals, which divide the hoof and chew the cud, are altogether the most healthful and delightful for the table." The flesh of swine, interdicted by sacred Law, has been proved to be the source of hurtful and repulsive maladies. No nation on earth has been healthier than the Hebrew. While providing for the religious education and moral security of his people, God was concerning himself for their bodily well being.

Health is the greatest of earthly blessings. Without it we can do little and enjoy nothing. With it we can accomplish much and triumph over almost every obstacle in our way. A sound constitution is a thing to be profoundly thankful for. But it is for us not only to accept this great gift thankfully, but also to guard it diligently and religiously. There are four reasons why we should regard it as a sacred duty to preserve the health of our body by those obvious means which are within our reach (activity, moderation, cleanliness, contentedness, etc.).

I. BECAUSE THE HUMAN BODY IS THE FAIR WORKMANSHIP OF GOD. That which our heavenly Father has made so exquisitely (Ps. cxxxix. 14) we should treat as a thing to be protected, to be preserved in its excellency. "Everything is beautiful in its season;" every period and phase of our humanity—smiling infancy, blithe childhood, sunny youth, vigorous young manhood, grave prime, grey-headed age, etc.

II. BECAUSE THE HUMAN BODY IS THE HOME AND ORGAN OF THE HUMAN SPIRIT. In our bodies we ourselves dwell—our thinking, reasoning, loving, hoping, striving selves. Our bodily faculties are the organs of our spiritual activities; therefore they are sacred.

III. BECAUSE THE HUMAN BODY IS THE DWELLING-PLACE OF THE HOLY GHOST. (1 Cor. iii. 16, 17; vi. 19, 20; 2 Cor. vi. 16).

IV. BECAUSE HEALTH IS A CONDITION OF USEFULNESS. It is true that men have been found (like Richard Baxter) to work for years in sickness and pain, but it is only a few rare spirits that can triumph thus over bodily infirmity. If we desire to bear the fullest possible witness and to do the noblest possible work for our God and our generation, we must not be indifferent to the state of our body. The stronger and healthier we are in our physical frame the more cheerful will be the tone of our spirit, the more attractive will be the aspect of our life, the more strenuous and the longer continued will be the labours of our hand.—C.

Vers. 4—47.—*Clean and unclean—a lesson on sin.* Why all these minute distinctions? Why disallow many creatures for food, the flesh of which is not unwholesome? What means all this elaborate system of the clean and the unclean, of that which may be taken and that which must be strictly and piously shunned? It was—

I. AN EARLY LESSON IN A RELIGIOUS SCHOOL. The people of God were in process of spiritual cultivation; they were being thus trained for our benefit, that they might give to all lands and times a body of sacred truth which it took them long to learn. God would, with this end in view, implant within them, deeply rooted, the idea of holiness. This distinction of clean from unclean was a daily lesson in sanctity, in the conception of separateness of the pure from the impure, of that which might be partaken of from that which might not be touched, of that which could be liked and chosen from that which was to be detested and avoided. They could not fail to understand, they could not fail to be profoundly impressed with the thought, that all around them were things which, for God's sake, in obedience to his plain commandment, they must shrink from and shun. So the idea of holiness, of sacred separation, of freedom from that which defiles (ver. 44), was planted within the soul, and grew in the nation; and it was ready when the time came for the great redeeming purpose of God to be revealed. There was a people well schooled in the essential idea of holiness.

II. A REMINDER OF THE PREVALENCE OF SIN. Connecting uncleanness, defilement, with so many living creatures, there would be before their eyes continual reminders of that which was evil; they would be constantly or frequently put in remembrance that they lived in a world of sin and danger. "All living nature . . . transmuted into a thousand tongues to remind and warn of sin and uncleanness. The living monitor would meet the devout Jew at every point, and call to him in words of sacred admonition from every direction. Looking out at his door, the passing of a camel or a bird of prey would be a memorial to him . . . to guard the approaches of uncleanness. Sitting down under his vine or fig tree, or going forth to gather flowers, the insects crawling on the leaves would be monitors of the presence of evil," etc. (Seiss).

III. A PICTURE OF THE MANY-SIDED NATURE OF SIN. The unclean animals being associated in his mind with sin, the Jew would naturally connect particular sins with those animals whose habits suggested the thought: the fox would remind him of the evil of treachery and low cunning; the tiger, of ferocity; the hog, of sensuality; the vulture, of gluttony, etc.; he would see before him living pictures of various forms of sin, and would be reminded that evil in every form, temptation in every phase, were about him, and that vigilance was needful at every hour of his life, at every step of his course.

We may learn from these thoughts: 1. That holiness includes, if it is not contained in, separateness of soul and life from that which is evil. Though not minute legal precepts, yet other voices say clearly, forcibly, imperatively to us, "Be ye separate; touch not the unclean thing." 2. That sin, with its taint and temptation, is on every hand; and not only all around us but, what is more and worse, within us. "Watch and pray," say the heavenly voices. 3. That sin is multiform in our day and land as it was in theirs. It approaches by every avenue, drapes itself in every costume, assumes every air and attitude, must be promptly recognized, wisely parried, stoutly fought, patiently and repeatedly subdued.—C.

Vers. 4—47.—*Clean and unclean—three side truths.* I. THAT GOD DOES SOME THINGS TO PROVE US. There were plain, palpable reasons of a sanitary or moral nature for many of these prohibitions; for many others there were, doubtless, valid reasons which escape our view. Probably some remain for which there was no reason in the nature of the case, but it seemed good to the Divine Ruler of Israel to issue them as tests of obedience. Such was the prohibition of the forbidden fruit in Eden. Such were certain statutes on other subjects. Occasionally these laws regulating the dietary must have been severely testing. The fisherman, *e.g.*, must have been sometimes tried when he landed fine palatable fish which were forbidden, and which had to be cast again into the sea. God's dealing may seem arbitrary to us. Enough that he, our Father, who has given us so much, who has indeed given us everything we are and have, and to whom we are looking for everything we shall be and shall enjoy in the furthest future, holds out of reach or takes back again that which we would fain have or keep. God tries us, and we must submit with filial trustfulness and cheerfulness.

II. THAT IN DOUBTFUL CASES WE DO WELL TO ABSTAIN. "There was a difficulty in determining the case of the camel whether or not it really divides the hoof wholly, and the case of the hare whether it really chews the cud." These, however, are prohibited. We are often placed in circumstances in which we are doubtful as to the legality of pleasures to be enjoyed or profits to be realized. In such cases it is well to keep our "hands off." Abstinence will result in an infinitesimal loss; indulgence might end in serious mischief (see 1 Thess. v. 22).

III. THAT WE ARE MOST IMPORTANTLY AFFECTED BY THE THINGS WHICH WE APPROPRIATE. Stringent and detailed dietary laws may seem to us to be a redundant part of revelation. They would not have been added, probably, but for the direct religious aspect they wore. But, apart from their primary object, they teach us the valuable lesson that it is a matter of serious if not supreme importance to be appropriating right things every day. 1. *Right food for the body.* Many men are less devout, less useful, less excellent and admirable in heart and life, because of the unguarded and intemperate way in which they eat and drink. We may be neither gluttons nor drunkards; yet we may lower our character and lessen our influence by ill-regulated appetite in eating and drinking. Profoundly true and urgently demanded as were the words of our Lord (Matt. xv. 11), "not that which goeth into the mouth defileth a man," we may be sure that Jesus Christ would have us exercise such self-restraint, and, if need be, such self-denial as will keep us from all grossness of thought and habit, from all degeneracy of spirit (Matt. xvi. 24; see 1 Cor. x. 31). 2. *Right thoughts for the mind.* That which the mind is appropriating, day by day, is determining its nature. It makes all the difference whether, mentally, we are eating and drinking that which is pure, wholesome, clean, refining, or that which is gross, noxious, unclean, deteriorating. How immeasurably important the companions we choose, the books we read, the conversations in which we indulge! 3. *Right resolutions for the soul.* The soul is entertaining desires and coming to conclusions, on larger and lesser things, every day. If these be unworthy, it is growing in evil; if these be honourable and excellent, it is growing in rectitude, in spiritual beauty, in usefulness, as the days and months go by.—C.

Vers. 46, 47.—*Clean and unclean—the abolition of the law.* "This is the law" (ver. 46). But "it is the law" no longer; consider—

I. THE FACT THAT THIS LEVITICAL LAW HAS BEEN SET ASIDE. 1. Perhaps by the word of our Lord in Mark vii. 15, especially taking the translation of ver. 19, "This he said, making all meats pure" (Farrar, 'Life of Paul,' vol. i. p. 276). 2. Certainly by the heavenly voice and the apostolic conduct (Acts x. 14, 48). 3. By united apostolic agreement (Acts xv. 22—29). 4. By inspired Epistles (1 Cor. viii. 8; Rom. xiv. 4; 1 Tim. iv. 3, 4). Clearly we are not under any obligation to observe these statutes. We learn from this our immunity—

II. THAT SUCH PICTORIAL TEACHING IS NOT NOW NEEDED. What moral and spiritual lessons were to be conveyed by these injunctions and by the habits of thought and deed they created, have been learnt; the rudimentary lesson is no longer needed. We are supposed to understand or to be able to learn in other ways what God means by holiness, how hateful sin is in his sight, how prevalent it is, how manifold in its shapes and colours, how sedulously it is to be avoided.

III. THAT GOD TRUSTS US TO ACT ARIGHT IN THIS MATTER OF BODILY NOURISH-MENT. The Law treated the race as if it were in its religious childhood; the gospel as if it had attained to manhood (Gal. iv. 1, 23). Christ our Lord trusts us to act wisely and faithfully. We must honour his Divine confidence in us. We shall do so by: 1. Intelligent study of what is really wholesome and health-giving. 2. Moderation in the use of that which is "good for food." 3. Endeavour to make the body the active servant of the soul.—C.

Vers. 24—28, 39, 40.—*The significance of death.* "Whosoever toucheth the carcase shall be unclean." What is the meaning of these minute and stringent regulations touching the dead bodies of animals, both clean (vers. 39, 40) and unclean (vers. 24—28)? The answer to this question is in the fourfold consideration—

I. HOW MUCH GOD MAKES OF DEATH. Death is the key-note of very much of sacred Scripture. "Thou shalt die" is a constantly recurring refrain. "And he died" is a continually repeated statement. It was the death of the slain victim at the altar that made expiation for the sinner. It is the death upon the cross which constitutes the sacrifice for the world's sin. The death of the soul is the awful punishment of guilt hereafter as it is on earth. It was the death of these animals that made their carcases unclean. In the Old Testament and New, God makes much of death.

II. THE SIGNIFICANCE OF DEATH. Death is odious and intolerable in God's sight: it must be made to seem so in man's; for: 1. It is the *consequence of sin* in man. 2. It is the *picture of sin* in man. 3. It is a *reminder of the painful and hateful presence* of sin in man.

III. THE AVOIDABLENESS OF SIN. The fact that the dead carcase could be and must be avoided, and that contraction of ceremonial defilement could be prevented, indicated to the Jew and now intimates to us that sin may be and must be shunned. Two things were and are necessary: 1. *Carefulness*: scrupulous regard to the known laws (vers. 32, 34, 38). 2. *Self-sacrifice*: things made unclean must be broken up, disused, cast away, at whatever cost (vers. 33, 35).

IV. THE REMOVAL OF THE STAIN OF SIN. "It must be put into water; . . . so it shall be cleansed" (ver. 32). "There is a fountain filled with blood," etc.—C.

Ver. 44.—*Sacred separation.* "Ye shall therefore sanctify yourselves." The root-thought of sanctity is separateness. A man sanctifies himself when he separates himself from that which is evil and impure; so with a nation or a family. These strict laws concerning the clean and the unclean had important reference to—

I. NATIONAL SEPARATION. 1. God purposed to establish a holy nation. He designed, by various methods, to separate for himself a people free from the idolatry and the immorality of the race. 2. He therefore determined to separate Israel from international intercourse. The people of God were not to have any outside social relations, were not to intermarry with neighbouring nations. 3. Therefore, beside geographical obstacles and positive prohibitions, God interposed a precise and separating dietary. This created a strong barrier between his people and all others. The laws of food affect us powerfully in our social relations. Free intercourse is impossible without hospitality, and hospitality is impossible where distinctions as to eating and drinking are not only numerous but sacred and binding. A Hebrew could not sit down to the table of an Egyptian or an Arab without offending his host and sinning against his God. Moreover, such distinctions would generate and foster feelings of moral aversion toward those who did not observe them, and this would be another strong fence, helping to maintain separateness. The Jews may have carried this far beyond the original intention of the Divine Legislator; but at that point in the religious history of the world, all considerations were second, *longo intervallo*, to the one supreme end of keeping Israel separate and pure. God has, in his providence, divided the human race into nations by separating seas and mountains; there are many obvious advantages in this: it makes government, and therefore order and security, a possible thing. It makes possible national influence for good. How much of benefit and blessing to Europe and the world has arisen and will arise from the fact that he who is Lord of the sea and the rock has cut a channel and filled it with the dividing waters between the continent and this Heaven-taught land of ours (Ps. cxlvii. 20)!

II. FAMILY SEPARATION. "God setteth the solitary in families" (Ps. lxviii. 6). But he thereby not only makes the lonely to be social and joyous; he separates one small group of souls from all others. The family unites its members into one fellowship; it also divides the nation into separate circles. It is a fence which shuts out as well as it shuts in. It is one of the most imperative and sacred duties which God lays upon us who are parents to see that no injurious, no poisonous, no ruinous element, in the shape of a contaminating human soul, is admitted within the gates of family life.

III. INDIVIDUAL SEPARATION. With us (speaking generally) God wills how separate the nation shall be; the human parent determines how separate the family shall be; each individual soul must decide how separate he and his life shall be. There is a sin-stained, corrupted world encompassing us; we must choose, for ourselves, how far we will enter it, how free our intercourse with it shall be. There are, however, some general principles. 1. We must have something to do with it (John xvii. 15; 1 Cor. v. 9). 2. We must impose some restraints on ourselves; we must draw some lines of limitation; we must "sanctify (separate) ourselves." 3. We should refrain from familiar association with the openly ungodly; for by such familiarity we should identify ourselves with their principles and countenance their evil ways. 4. We should avoid intimacy with the irreligious and undecided; for if we mingle continually with those who walk on lower spiritual ground, we shall surely fall to their level (Prov. xiii. 20).—C.

Ver. 45.—*High reasons for holiness.* The height of human character depends on the nature of the motives by which men allow themselves to be governed. It is certain (1) that we are all actuated by a great variety of motives; (2) that we are affected by many considerations in our choice of the better path; (3) that of the right motives which actuate us some are much higher than others; (4) that while it is well to be moved by every honourable impulse, we should seek to be mainly moved by the highest and best of all.

Here we have three of the highest possible motives for the best possible estate, three high reasons for holiness.

I. GOD, IN HIS SOVEREIGNTY, COMMANDS IT, AND IT IS OUR HIGHEST DUTY TO OBEY HIM. "I am . . . *your God: ye shall.*" Duty is one of the highest of all considerations, if not positively the very highest. Our duty to obey God when he says "ye shall" is clearly the highest of all duties.

II. GOD HIMSELF IS THE HOLY ONE, AND IT IS OUR HIGHEST HONOUR TO BE LIKE HIM. "Ye shall be holy; for I am holy." He is the "Holy One of Israel," the "holy, holy, holy Lord God of hosts." "He is light, and in him is no darkness at all." There is no conceivable ambition man can cherish that is so high as the aspiration to be like God, the righteous Father of souls (see Matt. v. 48).

III. GOD, OUR REDEEMER, DESIRES IT, AND IT IS OUR HIGHEST SATISFACTION TO PLEASE HIM. "I am the Lord that bringeth you up out of the land of Egypt." If there were anything we desired to withhold from him who is "our God," the God from whom we came, to whom we belong, and before whom we stand, still there can be nothing we will keep back from *him who is our Redeemer*, who has "brought us out of the land of Egypt, out of the house of bondage." "To Jesus, our Atoning Priest," we bring (1) our promptest and devoutest attention, (2) our unquestioning faith, (3) our most cheerful obedience. We *run* to keep *his* commandments.—C.

Ver. 45.—*Holiness and its requirements.* When a man has purified himself and taken upon himself vows of devotedness to God, then is he prepared to be the recipient of Divine communications. After Aaron's consecration, he is instructed both separately, and conjointly with Moses (ch. x. 8; xi. 1). The legislator and the priest act in harmony under a theocracy; the laws of God are the statutes of the nation.

I. THE SANCTIFICATION REQUIRED OF THE PEOPLE OF GOD. 1. *It is a necessary consequence of his character and of the relationship they sustain to him.* What the Master loves, the servant must love; what the King is, that his subjects become. Sanctity is the glory of God. To be untarnished, free from taint, this is his prerogative and separates him from all idol gods. Holiness is not so much one special attribute as the all-embracing purity, the bright cloud that invests his excellences with spotless splendour. Evil flies from his presence. Unless, therefore, his people manifest this separation from impurity, how can he take delight in them and bless them? Unless they reflect something of his image, how can he acknowledge them as his children? He says, "Be ye holy; for I am holy." 2. *The intention of God has been signified in delivering his people from bondage.* He declares himself Jehovah, the bringer-up of the Israelites from the land of Egypt, in order to be to them for a God (Elohim). This same design is expressed in ch. xx. 26, "I the Lord am holy, and have severed you from other people, that ye should be mine." To what purpose was the yoke of idolatrous sinful Egypt broken, if Israel remained impure and unholy? The intent of Jehovah would be frustrated. A similar line of argument is pursued in 1 Pet. i. 15—19, where the precept of the text is enforced by reference to the cost of redemption—not corruptible things, but the precious blood of Christ being the price of our ransom. We make the grace of God and the gift of his Son of none effect if we continue in the former sins. 3. *This same deliverance is appealed to as a claim upon his people's gratitude and obedience.* The very kindness of Jehovah in emancipating the nation and guiding them through the wilderness constituted a valid reason for abstaining from all that God forbade. Unworthy are they of being the recipients of mercy who do not feel themselves bound thereby to please this merciful Lord. Shall not the love of Christ constrain us to live unto him, acknowledging that we are henceforth not our own? Conduct actuated by such motives is not servitude. It accords with the dictates of reason, conscience, and emotion. Compared with the bondage from which Christ releases us his yoke is easy, and his burden light indeed.

II. WHAT THIS SANCTIFICATION INVOLVES. 1. *Adherence to distinctions unknown to the world in general.* Some animals were to be regarded as totally unfit for food, others unclean under certain conditions. It was not the business of these teachers to make the distinctions, but to explain and enforce them. The popular classification was adopted—it would be the only one intelligible. *Even in trivial matters God's people are to be distinguished from the heathen.* These distinctions were not simply arbitrary; they depended on considerations sanitary, ethical, and instinctive. Thankful for the relief the gospel affords us from the burdensome ceremonies of the Law, knowing that " every creature of God is good," we have yet to do all, whether we eat or drink, to the glory of God. His gifts are to be received with thanksgiving, sanctified by the Word of God and prayer. We are not " subject to ordinances that perish with the using," yet are we to set our affection on things above, and to mortify our members which are upon the earth; observances which the majority of mankind practise not. The line of division between things pure and defiling is plainly marked if we apply our eyes to survey it. Others may call us bigoted, narrow-minded, straight-laced, but we prefer the commendation of our Master to the good-will of men. 2. *Possible loss of property.* How vexatious to an Israelite to be obliged to destroy a vessel because it was polluted (ver. 33), or a cooking-range (ver. 35), or some moistened seed (ver. 38)! Many like a religion that costs them nothing, that is not particular about trifles. Very real is that man's religion who refuses to employ ill-gotten gain or dishonest measures, and who would renounce connection with a firm rather than be a party to unjust proceedings. Pity that so much evil should be condoned and defiling association suffered for sake of the profit it brings! If thy hand or thy foot cause thee to stumble, cast it off. 3. *Continual care and trouble.* To touch a dead animal necessitated ablution of the clothes, and the vessel which should be accidentally made "unclean" must be thoroughly washed, and both man and utensil remained ceremonially unclean till the evening. At any moment an Israelite might be compelled to repair the inroads of pollution, and constant caution was requisite to abstain from needlessly incurring stain. The sanctity God desires is a life-long work, and lovers of ease had better not undertake it. To be like him who was " holy, undefiled, separate from sinners," is to take up the cross and deny one's self. " Watch and pray unceasingly " must be our motto. Thanks be to him who hath opened a "fountain for sin and uncleanness," wherein at all seasons we may bathe and come forth white as snow! Thus shall we show forth the praises of him who hath called us. Let us learn to welcome the opportunity of testifying our love to him who gave himself for us.—S. R. A.

Vers. 1—47.—*Holiness.* Ver. 45, " For I am the Lord that bringeth you up out of the land of Egypt, to be your God: ye shall therefore be holy, for I am holy."

I. THE BASIS ON WHICH HOLINESS RESTS. The Divine call. 1. All religion must find its real strength as well as its root in Divine love. " We love him because he first loved us." A redeemed life must be holy. " He that hath this hope in him purifieth himself, even as he is pure." We begin our holiness with the cross of Christ. He has cleansed us with his blood, therefore we must be clean. 2. The deliverance effected by God for his people is made the pledge of an eternal life by *the special covenant,* which separated them from all others. We must have fact and positive revelation and direct promise to fall back upon. He also calls us to himself, declares himself our God. He says, " Be ye holy; for I am holy." Likeness to God is our rule; fellowship with God is our strength and joy.

II. THE NATURE AND METHOD OF HOLINESS. 1. The holiness which God requires is *personal holiness*—holiness in life, manners, habits, food, everything which concerns the man himself. The distinctions of clean and unclean animals, etc., refer to natural laws of health and life. 2. Holiness must be the characteristic of *God's people as a community.* The laws of cleanliness separated the nation as a whole from other nations. They applied to all classes, and to every individual. The Church must be a holy Church. The lack of discipline is a terrible hindrance to the advance of religion. We must keep off the unclean. The covenant blessing will not be given unless the covenant law be observed. "Let a man examine himself." Defilement of sacred things is judgment to ourselves. 3. The holiness of this world's life is a promise and prediction of *the higher holiness* of the everlasting life. The clean and unclean animals were distinguished that the taint of death might be removed in the case of those fit for food. The distinction itself seemed to say all would be clean to you if it were not for death. When we are above the conditions of earthly life, then to be holy will be to be really like God—not in a mere negative purity of not being contaminated, not sinning; but being spiritually created afresh, with immortal natures, with perfect hearts to serve God, with life interpenetrated by his Divine glory. The holiness of the best Christian on earth is but an imperfect thing, largely a holiness of external regulation and separation from the unclean; but the holiness of the angelic nature will be a real and positive participation of the Divine.—R.

EXPOSITION

CHAPTER XII.

UNCLEANNESS DERIVED FROM CHILDBIRTH. As there is a natural disgust felt for some kinds of food, which serves as a foundation for the precepts of the last chapter, so there is an instinct which regards some of the concomitants of childbirth, and some diseases, as foul and defiling. In accordance with these instincts, purifying rites are commanded for the restoration of those affected to ceremonial cleanness. These instincts and consequent regulations respecting women in childbirth are found in very many different nations. "The Hindoo law pronounced the mother of a new-born child to be impure for forty days, required the father to bathe as soon as the birth had taken place, and debarred the whole family for a period from religious rites, while they were 'to confine themselves to an inward remembrance of the Deity;' in a Brahmin family this rule extended to all relations within the fourth degree, for ten days, at the end of which they had to bathe. According to the Parsee law, the mother and child were bathed, and the mother had to live in seclusion for forty days, after which she had to undergo other purifying rites. The Arabs are said by Burckhardt to regard the mother as unclean for forty days. The ancient Greeks suffered neither childbirth nor death to take place within consecrated places; both mother and child were bathed, and the mother was not allowed to approach an altar for forty days. The term of forty days, it is evident, was generally regarded as a critical one for both the mother and the child. The day on which the Romans gave the name to the child—the eighth day for a girl, and the ninth for a boy—was called *lustricus dies*, 'the day of purification,' because certain lustral rites in behalf of the child were performed on the occasion,

and some sort of offering was made. The *amphidromia* of the Greeks was a similar lustration for the child, when the name was given, probably between the seventh and tenth days" (Clark).

Vers. 2—4.—**She shall be unclean seven days.** The mother is to be *unclean seven days*, and after that to be **in the blood of her purifying three and thirty days** (ver. 4). The difference between these two states may be seen by looking on to ch. xv. 19—28, and comparing that passage with ver. 4 of this chapter. In the first stage, during the seven days, she made all that she touched unclean; in the second stage, during the thirty-three days, she was only required to **touch no hallowed thing, nor come into the sanctuary**, as she was progressing towards cleanness. The number of days during which she is to be altogether unclean is to be **according to the days of the separation for her infirmity**, that is, seven days, as in the case of her monthly courses (see ch. xv. 19). **In the eighth day the flesh of his foreskin shall be circumcised.** The Levitical legislation recognizes the regulation as to the day of the circumcision made at the time of the covenant with Abraham. "And he that is eight days old (or a son of eight days) shall be circumcised among you, every man child in your generations" (Gen. xvii. 12). **Until the days of her purifying be fulfilled.** "When in a state of impurity, the Hebrews were forbidden to enter the sanctuary, to keep the Passover, and to partake of holy food, whether of sacrificial meat, of sacred offerings and gifts, or of shew-bread, because the clean only were fit to approach the holy God and all that appertains to him (Lev. vii. 19—21; xxii. 3; Numb. ix. 6; xviii. 11; 1 Sam. xxi. 5)" (Kalisch).

Ver. 5.—**If she bear a maid child, then she shall be unclean two weeks; . . . and she shall continue in the blood of her purifying threescore and six days.** The reason why the duration of the mother's uncleanness is twice as long at a girl's birth as at a boy's, would appear to be that the uncleanness attached to the child as well as to the mother, but as the boy was placed in a state of ceremonial purity at once by the act of circumcision, which took place on the eighth day, he thereupon ceased to be unclean, and the mother's uncleanness alone remained; whereas in the case of a girl, both mother and child were unclean during the period that the former was "in the blood of her purifying," and therefore that period had to be doubly long. See Luke ii. 20, where the right reading is, "When the days of *their* purification, according to the Law of Moses, were accomplished." For eight days the infant Saviour submitted to legal uncleanness in "fulfilling all righteousness" (Matt. iii. 15), and therefore the whole forty days were spoken of as "the days of *their* purification."

Vers. 6, 7.—The previous verses having stated the conditions and the term of continuance of the uncleanness arising from childbirth, the three final verses describe the offerings to be made by the woman for her purification. **She shall bring a lamb of the first year for a burnt offering, and a young pigeon, or a turtledove, for a sin offering.** Two things are noticeable here: first, that the burnt offering, symbolizing self-devotion, is far more costly and important than the sin offering, which had not to be offered for any individual personal sin, but only for human sin, "which had been indirectly manifested in her bodily condition" (Keil); and secondly, that in this one case the sin offering appears to succeed the burnt offering instead of preceding it. No doubt the changed order is owing to the cause just mentioned; the idea of sin, though it may not be altogether put aside (Gen. iii. 16), is not to be prominent, as though it were peculiar to the special woman who was purified.

Ver. 8.—**If she be not able to bring a lamb.** A concession is made to poverty, which in later times appears to have been largely acted on. It was, as we know, taken advantage of by the mother of our Lord (Luke ii. 21).

HOMILETICS.

Ver. 6.—Generation, conception, and birth, not having anything sinful necessarily connected with them, the sin offering in this case is rather an intimation of original sin than an atonement for actual sin; the "sorrow" attached to childbirth being especially connected with the fall of man as a result of Eve's share in bringing it about (Gen. iii. 16). There is nothing in the Bible to countenance ascetic or Manichæan views of marriage intercourse. Where any prohibitory injunctions are given on the subject, the purpose is to avoid ceremonial, not moral, uncleanness (Exod. xix. 15; 1 Sam. xxi. 4; cf. ch. xv. 18).

Ver. 8.—Some fifteen hundred years after this law of purification after childbirth had been given to and by Moses, a man child was born in a country which did not at the time of the legislation of Moses belong to the Israelites, and which those whom Moses addressed had never seen. The country was Palestine, the city Bethlehem. The birth took place in a stable, for the mother was poor. For eight days she remained unclean, and on the eighth day the child was circumcised, and "his name was called Jesus" (Luke ii. 21). For thirty-three days longer she continued "in the blood of her purifying" (ch. xii. 4), and then "when the days of their purification according to the Law of Moses were accomplished, they brought him to Jerusalem, to present him to the Lord, and to offer a sacrifice, according to that which is said in the Law of the Lord" (Luke ii. 22, 24). Had the mother been wealthy, she would have offered a lamb for a burnt offering, and a young pigeon, or turtle-dove, for a sin offering, but though of the house and lineage of David, she was poor, and her sacrifice was therefore "a pair of turtledoves, or two young pigeons"—one of the birds being for a burnt offering, betokening the devotion of her life afresh to God after the peril that she had gone through; the other for a sin offering, recognizing her share in the penalty of Eve as partaker in original sin. "On bringing her offering, she would enter the temple through 'the gate of the firstborn,' and stand in waiting at the gate of Nicanor, from the time that the incense was kindled on the golden altar. Behind her, in the court of the women, was the crowd of worshippers, while she herself, at the top of the Levites' steps, which led up to the great court, would witness all that passed in the sanctuary. At last one of the officiating priests would come to her at the gate of Nicanor, and take from her hand the poor's offering, which she had brought. The morning sacrifice was ended, and but few would linger behind while the offering for her purification was actually made. She who brought it mingled prayer and thanksgiving with the service. And now the priest once more approached her, and, sprinkling her with the sacrificial blood, declared her cleansed. Her 'firstborn' was next redeemed at the hand of the priest with five shekels of silver; two benedictions being at the same time pronounced—one for the happy event which had enriched the family with a firstborn, the other for the law of redemption ".(Edersheim, 'Temple Service'). It was probably as she descended the steps that Simeon took the babe from her arms, and blessed God and them, and that Anna " gave thanks likewise unto the Lord, and spake of him to all them that looked for redemption in Jerusalem " (Luke ii. 38). " And when they had performed all things according to the Law of the Lord, they returned into Galilee, to their own city Nazareth " (Luke ii. 39). Thus obediently did the virgin mother of the Lord submit herself to the regulations of the Levitical Law, and thus humbly and graciously did the infant Saviour begin from the day of his birth to " fulfil all righteousness" (Matt. iii. 15) in his own person, though by the hands of others.

Lessons—1. To obey the positive laws and to submit to the positive institutions of the religious community to which we belong. 2. To take measures, when we have even involuntarily and without sin on our part ceased to be in open communion with God and God's people, to recover that communion. 3. To see that the measures which we take with this end are appointed by God or by his authority, and are in accordance with his will. 4. To be sure that such steps as we take be accompanied by an acknowledgment of sin and a throwing ourselves for acceptance on the merits of the sacrifice of the cross (which is our sin offering), and a consecration of ourselves to God's service (which is our burnt offering).

HOMILIES BY VARIOUS AUTHORS.

Vers. 1—8.—*The purification of the Church.* At the commencement of his treatise on this Book of Leviticus, Cyril of Alexandria truly says, that as the Word of God came into the world arrayed in flesh, in which bodily appearance he was seen of all, while his divinity was seen only by the elect; so has the written Word a letter, or outward sense, which is obvious to ordinary perception, and an inward meaning which must be spiritually discerned. According to this rule, the purification of the Church is the subject of the text, which is presented under two aspects. It is—

I. DISTRIBUTIVELY CONSIDERED. The necessity of the spiritual birth may be collected : 1. *From the impurity of the natural.* (1) This is expressed in the ceremonial uncleanness of the mother. In case of the birth of a son, she had to remain forty days in a state of impurity. During this period she must not touch any hallowed thing, else it became polluted; and she must not enter the holy place of the temple. In case her child were a daughter, the term of this uncleanness was doubled. " Who can bring a clean thing out of an unclean?" (2) Her uncleanness is in her *blood*, which is the same as saying it is in her *nature*. To be " born of blood " is therefore a periphrasis for a natural birth in depravity, and it is consequently opposed to the spiritual birth (see John i. 13). (3) This maternal uncleanness is also described as her " infirmity," in allusion to the pain, sorrow, and weakness through which she passes; and calls to remembrance the curse upon the original offence (Gen. iii. 16). The birth amidst this " infirmity " shows the utter helplessness and sorrowfulness of our moral state by nature. (4) No wonder, then, that the child also should be accounted unclean. Until the eighth day he had no sign of the covenant upon him. But an infant could not have " sinned after the similitude of Adam's transgression; " therefore this exclusion from the covenant from the birth evinces hereditary depravity and guilt (Ps. li. 5; Eph. ii. 3). 2. *From the rite of circumcision.* (1) It was the sign of introduction into the covenant of God (Gen. xvii. 9—14). This supposes a spiritual birth, since the pollutions of the natural birth excluded the child from the favour of God. (2) The sign expressed this moral change to be the cutting off all that was forward in fleshly desires (see Deut. x. 16; Rom. ii. 28, 29; Phil. iii. 3). These, however necessary to the natural man, must not rule us here; for when the seven days of the world are over, they will be no more (see Matt. xxii. 30 ; 1 Cor. xv. 50 ; 2 Cor. v. 2—4 ; see also Homiletic notes on ch. ix. 1—7). (3) Hence, the "baptism of the Holy Spirit" is another way for expressing the "circumcision of the heart," and therefore it is called the "circumcision of Christ," or of Christianity (Col. ii. 11, 12). By parity of reason, the "baptism of water" corresponds to the "circumcision which is outward in the flesh." (4) Circumcision was proper to express the necessity of a spiritual birth in the dispensation of the covenant before Christ came, as it figured his sacrificial death (the "cutting off" of the "Holy Seed"), through which we claim the blessings of salvation. Now he has come, the type is fittingly abolished, and the baptismal water introduced, which is the emblem of the purifying spirit of the gospel.

II. COLLECTIVELY CONSIDERED. 1. *The Church is the mother of the children of God.* (1) Every man was intended to be a figure of Christ. The first man was such (Rom. v. 14). This privilege is shared by his male descendants (Gen. i. 26, 27 ; 1 Cor. xi. 7). So every woman was intended to be a figure of the Church of God (1 Cor. xi. 7—9). The marriage union, therefore, represents the union between Christ and his Church (Eph. v. 22—32). And the fruit of marriage should represent the children of God (see Isa. liv. 1—8 ; xlix. 20—23 ; Gal. iv. 25—31). (2) But all this may be reversed. Men, through perversity, may come to represent Belial rather than Christ. Women may become idolatrous, and represent an anti-Christian rather than a Christian Church. Thus Jezebel, who demoralized Ahab, became a type of those anti-Christian State Churches which demoralize the kings of the nations (see Rev. ii. 20—23 ; xvii.). 2. *In her present state she is impure.* (1) Under the Law she was far from perfect. The elaborate system of ceremonial purifications imposed upon her evinced this. Her history and the judgments she suffered go to the same conclusion. The uncleanness of the mother in the text is not an exaggerated picture. (2) Nor is she perfect under the gospel. The saints are in her. Many of her children have experienced the circumcision of the heart. But many more have only had that which is outward in the flesh. The "tares"—hypocrites and unbelievers—are mingled with the "wheat," a state of things which is destined to continue "until the harvest" (Matt. xiii. 30, 39). 3. *But she is in the process of her purification.* (1) The first stage in this process was marked by the rite of circumcision. During the time prior to that event, she was in her "separation," viz. from her husband and friends, and those in necessary attendance upon her were unclean. This indicates the great difference which the cutting off of the Great Purifier of his people makes to the spiritual liberty of the Church (Rom. vii. 1—4). (2) Still the period of her uncleanness was extended to forty days from the beginning. Her "separation" terminated on the eighth day, but during the whole period she must not eat the Passover, nor the peace offerings, nor come into the sanctuary (ver. 4). These forty days may be presumed to be similar in typical expression to the forty years of the Church in the wilderness before it was fit to enter Canaan (see Deut. viii. 2, 16). (3) In the case of the birth of a female this period of forty days was doubled. This may be designed to show that under the gospel, where the distinction of male and female is abolished (Gal. iii. 28 ; Col. iii. 11), still the wilderness state of the Church is continued. Our Lord was forty days upon earth before he entered into his glory, and in that state represented the state of the Church that is spiritually risen with him, but not yet glorified. (4) The entrance of the mother into the temple when her purification was perfected represented the state of the Church in heaven (see Eph. v. 27). The offerings with which she entered showed that her happiness is the purchase of the Redeemer's passion. Her feasting upon the holy things expressed those joys of the heavenly state elsewhere described as "the marriage supper of the Lamb" (Rev. xix. 7—9).—J. A. M.

Born in sin. Ch. xii. ; cf. Gen. iii. 16 ; Ps. li. 5 ; Luke ii. 21—24 ; 1 Tim. ii. 15. From the division of the animals into clean and unclean, and the sanctity thereby inculcated, we are invited to proceed to those personal liabilities to uncleanness for which due rites were provided. The first of these takes life at its fountain-head, and refers to the uncleanness connected with birth. Motherhood involved a longer or shorter period of ceremonial separation—forty days in the case of a son, seventy days in the case of a daughter, after which a burnt offering and a sin offering are to be presented to the Lord, and atonement made for her that she may be clean.

I. LET US START WITH THE PHYSICAL FACT THAT NATURE HAS ASSOCIATED WITH CHILDBIRTH A SENSE ON THE MOTHER'S PART OF PERSONAL UNCLEANNESS. The "issue of her blood" (ver. 7) stamps the physical process with defilement. No mother can avoid this sense of personal uncleanness, not even the blessed Virgin (Luke iii. 22—24). Upon the fact it is needless to dwell.

II. THE MORAL COUNTERPART TO THIS IS THE FACT THAT SIN IS TRANSMITTED BY ORDINARY GENERATION. As David puts it in Ps. li. 5, "Behold, I was shapen in iniquity; and in sin did my mother conceive me." From generation to generation is the legacy of evil transmitted. Hereditary *sin* must be recognized as a much wider phenomenon than "hereditary genius." The law of heredity must be accepted as at the bottom of human experience. If the mother, in spite of all her fondness for her babe, finds that she has transmitted sinful qualities; if this is the universal experience in ordinary generation, then the sense of uncleanness, physically induced, contracts a moral significance.

III. THERE IS AT THE SAME TIME A SENSE OF JOY AND TRIUMPH ASSOCIATED WITH THE BIRTH OF CHILDREN. If there is an element of sorrow and of judgment, as God indicates by his utterance at the Fall (Gen. iii. 16), there is also an element of triumph, caught from the "protevangelium," which speaks of victory through the woman's seed (Gen. iii. 15). Our Lord even speaks of it as an appropriate figure of the coming apostolic joy: "A woman when she is in travail hath sorrow, because her hour is come: but as soon as she is delivered of the child, she remembereth no more the anguish, for joy that a man is born into the world" (John xvi. 21). The sorrow is the preliminary of joy, the joy is its crown.

IV. THE TWO ELEMENTS OF JOY AND JUDGMENT HAD THEIR EXPRESSION IN THE BURNT AND SIN OFFERING THE MOTHER WAS DIRECTED TO PRESENT TO THE LORD. The ritual is the same whether it be a son or a daughter. The difference in the time of separation was due to a supposed physical fact that "a female child causes the mother more labour and a longer illness. This belief," continues Ewald, "(even though it may have little ground in fact), was itself caused by the well-known primitive disfavour with which the birth of a girl was regarded."[1] No moral significance is to be attached, therefore, to the difference in the duration of the mother's separation. But at the end of either period there is to be brought a burnt offering and a sin offering. The burnt offering is to be, if the mother can afford it, "a lamb of the first year," while the sin offering is only to be "a young pigeon" or a "turtledove." It is evident, therefore, that, while a poor mother might bring as her burnt offering a "turtledove" or "young pigeon," the ritual attaches emphasis to the burnt offering rather than to the sin offering. It has even been supposed that the burnt offering took precedence in the order of time in this particular instance. At all events, the *joy of consecration*, which the burnt offering expresses, is more emphatic in this ritual than the *atonement* for unavoidable defilement, which is expressed by the sin offering. The undertone of judgment is certainly discernible, but high above it sound the notes of grateful, holy joy. The mother rejoiced that, though unavoidably unclean in her child-bearing, the Lord had put away her uncleanness, and she was ready to dedicate herself and her child unto the Lord in the rite of the burnt offering.

V. THIS RITUAL RECEIVES PECULIAR EMPHASIS FROM ITS CELEBRATION BY THE VIRGIN MOTHER. Mary had the usual physical concomitants in the birth of Jesus, we have every reason to believe, the termination of which this ritual of purification was intended to celebrate. The sense of uncleanness was manifestly hers, since she enters upon the ritual as no exception to the general rule and law. Not only so, but Luke boldly states, "when the days of *their* purification, according to the Law of Moses, were fulfilled" (τοῦ καθαρισμοῦ αὐτῶν, not αὐτῆς), including Jesus along with Mary, for Oosterzee's notion that it is *Joseph* and Mary, not Jesus and Mary, will not satisfy the case. In what sense, then, was Jesus associated with his mother in a ritual of purification? It is certain that there was not transmitted to Jesus any sinful disposition or qualities, as in ordinary generation. His whole life belied this idea. He was "holy, harmless, undefiled, and separate from sinners." But this does not prevent the idea being accepted that there was transmitted in his extraordinary generation *responsibility*

[1] Ewald's 'Antiquities of Israel,' p. 156; cf. also Wcemse on 'The Ceremonial Law,' p. 5

for human sin. In other words, Jesus Christ was born with a liability on account of the sins of others. Having entered into the human family, having condescended to be born, he became liable for the responsibilities and debts of the human family, and the ritual so regarded him. Not only so, but our Lord had entered upon his "bloody passion" when at eight days old he had passed through the painful operation of circumcision. The rites in the temple thirty-three days after only expressed in legal form the liability on account of human sin upon which he had already entered. But if the atonement of the sin offering has thus a distinctive meaning in this exceptional case, the burnt offering had also its fulfilment. Mary dedicated, not only herself, but her Son, according to the Law of the Lord, "Every male that openeth the womb shall be called holy to the Lord." Simeon and Anna recognized in the infant the dedicated Messiah. Thus did Mary, as mother of Jesus, fulfil all righteousness.

VI. WE ARE SURELY TAUGHT HERE THE GENERAL PRINCIPLE THAT IT IS THROUGH SORROW AND HUMILIATION THAT TRIUMPH IS REACHED. The hope of a triumphant woman's seed sustained Jewish mothers in their sorrow. They looked for salvation through child-bearing, according to the idea of the apostle (1 Tim. ii. 15). God's meaning was through *the* child-bearing (διὰ τῆς τεκνογονίας), that is, the motherhood of the Virgin. Yet the hope sustained multitudes of mothers in their agonies. At length the Conqueror of the devil appeared. He came as an infant, and braved the dangers of development, and became "the Man of sorrows," and passed through death to victory. To the same law we must constantly conform. Humiliation is the price of exaltation in the case of Jesus and of all his people. The apostles had their season of sorrow in connection with Christ's crucifixion, and so sore it was that our Lord does not hesitate to compare it to a woman's travail; but at Pentecost they got the joy and exhilaration which compensated for all. The law of the kingdom is that we enter it through much tribulation. "He that humbleth himself shall be exalted" (Luke xiv. 11). When we humble ourselves under a sense of sin, when we humble ourselves under a sense of unprofitableness, then are we treading the path which leads to power and triumph.—R. M. E.

Vers. 1—8.—*The statutes on maternity.* We may seek—

I. THE EXPLANATION OF THIS STATUTE. And we shall find the explanation (1) not in the notion that any actual sin is involved in it; (2) but in the fact that there is connected with it that which is painfully suggestive of sin. (There was nothing actually "unclean" in the camel or hare, but it was constituted so because it was fairly suggestive of it.) 1. The sorrow of maternity (John xvi. 21) points clearly to the primeval curse, and therefore to the primeval sin (Gen. iii. 16). 2. The birth of a human child means the entrance into the world of one in whom are the germs of sin (Ps. li. 5; lviii. 3; Eph. ii. 3). 3. Maternity suggests the sexual relation, and that suggests the abounding and baneful sin of impurity. Hence sin is associated with the birth of the human infant, and the physical condition (ver. 7) attending it is typical of sin, constitutes "uncleanness," and necessitates purification.

II. THE THOUGHTS WE GAIN FROM THIS STATUTE. We learn: 1. *The communicativeness of sin.* We transmit our follies, our errors, our iniquities, by ordinary generation. Our children, because they *are* our children, will go astray, and will be in danger of those very errors into which we ourselves have fallen. Those who become parents must take the responsibility of bringing into the world children like themselves, who will inherit their dispositions, their habits of thought, their character. Sin is communicated from generation to generation through heredity, and also through the contagiousness of evil example. There is nothing more diffusive. 2. *The extension of the consequences of sin.* How sin sends forth its stream of sorrow! The pangs of maternity, answered by the opening cry of the infant as it enters the world—do these not speak the truth, that a world of sin is a world of sorrow, that succeeding generations of sinners are succeeding generations of sufferers, and that this will be so to the end of the world? 3. *The removableness of guilt from the sight of God.* The "uncleanness" of the mother was not irremovable. It did temporarily but did not permanently separate her from the sanctuary (ver. 4). After a limited retirement she might come with her sin offering and her burnt offering to "the door of the tabernacle" (ver. 6). If she were poor she might bring an offering within the reach of the poorest.

(ver. 8), and the priest would "make atonement," and she would "be clean" (ver. 8). Whatever guilt we contract, whether in communicating evil to others or as the indirect consequence of the sin of others, by whatsoever our souls have been defiled, our lives stained and corrupted, we may all come to the cross of the Redeemer, and through his atoning sacrifice be made clean in the sight of God. And thus coming, our sin offering will not be unaccompanied by a burnt offering; the forgiveness of our sin will be followed by the dedication of our whole selves to the service of the Lord.—C.

Vers. 2—7.—*Woman under the Law and under the gospel.* Every childbirth re-echoes in the ears of woman the sentence passed upon her ancestress Eve. That such a season of rejoicing should be attended with such throes of agony speaks loudly of the curse entailed by sin. There is no earthly pleasure entirely free from its shadow, pain. Great movements of society, deep thoughts, even inspiring melodies, are not ushered into the world without the pangs of travail.

I. THE LAW REMINDS US HERE OF WOMAN'S CONNECTION WITH THE PRIMAL SIN. 1. She is to be considered "unclean" for a fixed period after bringing forth a child. In the first part of "separation for her infirmity," she communicates defilement to whatever she touches, and must therefore, as far as possible, remain apart. But in the succeeding thirty-three or sixty-six "days of her purifying," she may fulfil her domestic duties, only she must not come into contact with hallowed things, not partake of sacrificial meals, nor enter the sanctuary. Thus the fulfilment of her maternal hopes renders her unfit for a season to join in the worship of the holy God. She is led to rejoice with trembling; she is at once exalted and depressed. She sees that the new life is not separate from corruption, is allied to uncleanness and death, and in order to be redeemed requires hallowing by obedience to God's ordinances. 2. To cleanse the mother from the stains of childbirth and to allow of restored fellowship with God, atonement is requisite. First a burnt offering, that the life spared and secluded temporarily may be wholly surrendered in spirit to the Author and Sustainer of life. Then a sin offering to expiate all ceremonial offences connected with the begetting of children. If these rites appertain simply to the parent, yet must the knowledge of them afterwards acquaint the child with the state of separation from God into which it was the unwitting instrument of introducing the parent, and there is at least a hint that the origin of life is not free from taint.

II. THE LAW INDICATES THE INFERIOR ESTEEM IN WHICH WOMAN WAS ANCIENTLY HELD. 1. The uncleanness contracted by bearing a female child lasted twice as long as when a boy was born. This has indeed been explained on physiological grounds, as formerly maintained. But there is ample warrant for the other view (see 1 Sam. i. 11; Jer. xx. 15, and John xvi. 21, for the joy caused by the birth of a male child). In ch. xxvii. 5, the female is esteemed at half the price of the male. Each mother of a male might cherish the hope that to her was granted the promised seed—the Messiah. 2. No rite of initiation into the covenant for the female. The Jews regarded circumcision as the badge of honour, the mark of privilege and blessing. Woman entered the nation without special recognition. She was not capable of becoming the head of a family, on whose proved nationality so much depended, for if she married she became a member of her husband's family.

III. THE GOSPEL DIGNIFIES THE POSITION OF WOMAN. 1. It abolishes before the Lord distinctions of sex. "There is neither male nor female; ye are all one in Christ Jesus." "There is neither circumcision nor uncircumcision." Woman has equal rights with man, saving only what natural modesty forbids her claiming, and what is the general law promulgated from the first (Gen. iii. 16), that the husband shall rule over her. Both men and women are baptized (Acts viii. 12) and endowed with the Spirit. 2. It is the glory of woman to have been the medium of the incarnation of the Son of God. Her shame is removed. Even the poverty of woman is ennobled by the example of the Virgin Mary bringing her "pair of turtledoves or two young pigeons." 3. Woman's quick appreciation of truth and steadfast fidelity are specially notable under the preaching of Christ and the apostles. Ready to adore the Lord as an infant, to supply his wants during his ministry, to bathe his feet with repentant, grateful tears, to anoint him before his burial, to follow him on the road to Calvary, to be nearest to him at the cross, and the first at his grave on the Resurrection morn, woman occupies a place in the gospel records alike conspicuous and honourable.   Nor are the faith and love and devotion of woman less marked in the Acts and the Epistles.   Well has woman striven to erase the stigma of the first transgression.   Eighteen centuries of the continually progressive elevation of woman in the social and mental scale have only attested the cardinal principles of Christianity.   The position of woman in any nation now serves as an index to the stage of civilization which it has reached.—S. R. A.

Chs. xii.—xv.—*Ceremonial purifications.*   For defilement from secretions and from leprosy.   The double object—to exalt the sacred laws, to honour the natural laws of health and cleanliness.   Thus we are taught—

I. RELIGION PRESERVES, PURIFIES, EXALTS HUMAN NATURE.   The facts of family life are to be connected with the sanctuary.   The more we think of both the joyful and the sorrowful events of our individual and social life as intimately bound up with our religion, the better we shall be prepared to find God's blessing always both preserving and sanctifying.

II. ALL REGULATIONS WHICH CONCERN THE BODILY LIFE AND THE TEMPORAL HAPPINESS OF MEN SHOULD BE SURROUNDED WITH RELIGIOUS REVERENCE.   Science is a curse to the world unless it is the handmaid to religion.   Our bodies are the temples of the Holy Ghost.   Our earthly life is the threshold of eternity.

III. TYPICALLY.   Leprosy represents human depravity and misery.   We see it brought into relation to the cleansing blood of atonement.   The sin which works death both by the individual acts and by contact with others, both in person and in condition, is cleansed away both in guilt and in power.   The leper is not excluded from mercy, but is dealt with by the priest as having his place in the covenant.   Our vileness does not shut us out from the love of God, but his love is revealed as an atoning love. "He is able to save unto the uttermost," but it is "those who come unto God by him."—R.

EXPOSITION.

CHAPTER XIII.

UNCLEANNESS DERIVED FROM LEPROSY OR CONTACT WITH LEPERS AND LEPROUS THINGS (chs. xiii., xiv.).   A third cause of uncleanness is found in a third class of offensive or repulsive objects.   There is no disease which produces so foul an appearance in the human form as leprosy.   There was, therefore, no disease so suitable for creating ceremonial, because representing spiritual, uncleanness.

The name leprosy has been made to cover a number of diseases similar but not identical in character.   There are many spurious forms of leprosy, and many diseases akin to leprosy which do not now come under discussion.   The disease here dealt with is elephantiasis, especially in its anæsthetic form, which is otherwise called white leprosy. The two varieties of elephantiasis—the tuberculated and the anæsthetic—are, however, so closely connected together that they cannot be separated, the one often running into the other.   The first symptom of the

malady is a painless spot, which covers an indolent ulcer.   This ulcer may continue unprogressive for months or for years, during which the person affected is able to do his ordinary business; but at the end of these periods, whether longer or shorter, it produces a more repulsive and foul disfigurement of the human face and frame than any known disease, the features of the face changing their character, and part of the body occasionally mortifying and dropping off.   Death at last comes suddenly, when a vital part of the body has been affected.

The home of leprosy has in all ages been Syria and Egypt and the countries adjacent to them, but Europe has not escaped the scourge.   In the Middle Ages, no European country was free from it; London had at one time six leper houses; cases were found not unfrequently in Scotland till the middle of the last century; and there was a death certified by medical science to have resulted from leprosy in the city of Norwich in the year 1880.[1] The object of the regulations relating to leprosy is no more sanitary than of those relating to unclean meats. Like the latter, they may have served a sanitary purpose, for leprosy is, according to the prevailing medical opinion, slightly, though only slightly, contagious. Because leprosy was hideous and foul, it therefore made the man affected by it unclean, and before he could be restored to communion with God and his people, he must be certified by God's priest to be delivered from the disease. As in the previous cases, physical ugliness and defilement represent spiritual depravity and viciousness. "The Levitical law concerning leprosy reveals to us the true nature of sin. It shows its hideousness and its foulness, and fills us with shame, hatred, and loathing for it. And it reveals to us the inestimable benefit which we have received from the incarnation of the Son of God, 'the Sun of Righteousness, with healing in his wings' (Mal. iv. 2); and fills us with joy, thankfulness, and love to him for his infinite goodness to us" (Wordsworth). Leprosy, the most loathsome of all common diseases, is the type and symbol of sin, and the ceremonial uncleanness attaching to it is a parable of the moral foulness of sin.

Ver. 2.—The word translated **plague** of leprosy literally means *stroke*. It seems to be used in the sense of *spot*. **Then shall he be brought unto Aaron the priest.** That the regulations respecting leprosy were not sanitary arrangements, as has been sometimes represented, is indicated by the authority over the leper being vested in the priest rather than in the physician, and the question of whether a man was a leper or no being decided by the former rather than the latter. It is to be noted also that the priest is not made unclean by his contact with the leper, because he is in the performance of his duty. The supposed leper may be brought either to Aaron **or unto one of his sons the priests;** that is, to the high priest or to the ordinary priest, and those descendants of Aaron who were disqualified by physical infirmities from officiating at the altar were permitted to act as examiners in leprosy.

Ver. 3.—**When the hair in the plague is turned white.** This is the first symptom, and the most noticeable as the commencement of the disease. The hair around the spot loses its colour and becomes thin and weak, the separate hairs being hardly stronger or individually thicker than down. The second symptom is when **the plague in sight be deeper than the skin of his flesh;** that is, below the upper skin, or cuticle, and in the real cutis. These two symptoms distinguish real leprosy from other affections which at first bear a similar appearance.

Vers. 4—8.—In case the symptoms are not decisive, **then the priest shall shut up** him that hath **the plague seven days.** The words thus translated would perhaps be better rendered, *then the priest shall bind up the part affected for seven days.* The priest is to delay his judgment for a week, and, if necessary, for a second week, during which period the patient is, according to the rendering, either to be confined to his house or, more probably, to have the spot bandaged. Whether the disease be or be not leprosy will probably have declared itself by the end of that time; and if **the plague be somewhat dark** on the fourteenth day, that is, if it has begun to lose its colour and to fade away, and has **not spread in the skin,** the priest is to decide that it is not real leprosy, and **pronounce** the man **clean.** He is still, however, to be kept under supervision, and if the spot is found to spread, he is to be pronounced **unclean,** as it is proved to be a leprosy.

Vers. 9—11.—The method of procedure in the case of a doubtful leprosy having been laid down in the previous verses, the rule for dealing with an unmistakable case is here given. When the characteristic white spot and white hair are present (if **the rising be white in the skin, and it have turned the hair white**), and if a third symptom be present—if there be **quick raw flesh in the rising,** that is, if there be an

---

[1] The following description is given by the physician who attended the sufferer:—"The case of leprosy occurred in a man aged fifty-eight. He had suffered for many years from a severe scaly disease of his skin; the last two or three years of his life it assumed the form of true leprosy, such as one reads of as having occurred in former times. His skin became thick, hard, and hypertrophical, and formed one mass of large scales, covering the whole of his body, including his face and head, both of which were greatly swollen; indeed, he seemed as if he were encased in a large scaly envelope. The movement of his joints produced deep, painful, and bleeding fissures. The nails also became misshapen, rough, and ragged, and were replaced by scaly incrustations. After lingering for some months in this condition, he died in November, 1880. I believe the case was a typical case of leprosy, or as nearly allied to it as possible."

ulcer underneath the white scab, there is to be no delay, as in the previous case, but judgment is to be passed at once. **The priest shall pronounce him unclean, and shall not shut him up: for he is manifestly unclean.**

Vers. 12—17.—**If a leprosy break out abroad . . . and cover all the skin.** There was a form of disease similar to true leprosy, and bearing the name of leprosy, and by some thought to be the final phase of true leprosy, which was yet not to cause legal uncleanness. It was distinguishable from the leprosy which caused uncleanness by a diffusion of the white flakes over the whole body, and by the absence of any patches bearing the appearance of raw flesh (vers. 12, 13). Real leprosy might pass into this harmless kind or phase, and it was known to have done so as soon as the raw patches of flesh had disappeared (vers. 16, 17). When this had taken place, **the priest pronounced** him **clean.**

Vers. 18—23.—The method of discriminating between a leprous spot and the reappearing scar of an old ulcer. A reappearing ulcer is to be regarded as leprous if it have the characteristic marks of leprosy; that is, if it be below the cuticle, and the hairs round it are turned white. If it has not these marks, it has to be watched for seven days, and if in that time it does not spread, it is to be declared a burning boil, or rather *an ulcerous scar,* in which case **the priest shall pronounce him clean.**

Vers. 24—28.—The method of discriminating between a leprous spot and the scar of a burn. **If there be any flesh, in the skin whereof** there is **a hot burning.** This rendering indicates that the authors of the Authorized Version thought a disease of the nature of a carbuncle to be meant; but it is better to take the words literally as they are translated in the margin, *If there be any flesh, in the skin whereof there is a burning of fire;* that is, a scar from a burn. The leprous spot and the scar are to be distinguished as in the previous case. An old ulcer or burn is a more likely place for a leprous spot to appear than any part of the body which is sound, just as in the moral sphere sin fixes on some old wound of the soul to burst out in.

Vers. 29—37.—The method of discriminating between a leprous spot on the head or beard and an ulcer in the same place. The symptoms of leprosy are the same as before, except that the hairs in this case are of a reddish-yellow colour instead of white. The treatment is also the same, with the addition of shaving the head or beard except at the place where the suspicious spot has appeared. In ver. 31 the priest is ordered to shut up (or bandage) the patient, if (1)

the spot be only in the upper cuticle, and (2) there is **no black hair in it.** We should have expected rather from the second condition *if there be black hair in it,* or *if there be no yellow hair in it;* and Keil accordingly proposes to omit the negative or to change the word "black" for "yellow," the two words in the original being easily interchangeable. The present reading is, however, defensible. The fact of the spot being not below the cuticle was a very favourable symptom; there being no black hair was a very unfavourable symptom. Under these circumstances, the priest delays his judgment in the ordinary way.

Vers. 38, 39.—The method of discriminating between leprous spots and freckled spots. In case the **spots in the skin of their flesh** be **darkish white**; that is, of a dull or pale white, then it is only a **freckled spot that groweth in the skin.** This is "the harmless *bohak* (ἀλφός, LXX.), which did not defile, and which even the Arabs, who still call it *bahak,* consider harmless. It is an eruption upon the skin, appearing in somewhat elevated spots or rings of unequal sizes and a pale white colour, which do not change the hair; it causes no inconvenience, and lasts from two months to two years" (Keil). The man or woman who has this is clean.

Vers. 40—44.—Leprosy appearing on the bald head. Though leprosy makes the hair drop off around the leprous spot, baldness is in itself no sign of leprosy, whether at the back or front of the head (vers. 40, 41); but as the bald head is a not unusual place for the leprous spot to appear, any eruption upon it is therefore to be watched and tested as before.

Vers. 45, 46.—The cases for examination having been discussed, the law for the treatment of the man in whom leprosy has been proved to exist is pronounced. **The leper in whom the plague** is is to be excluded from the camp, lest others should contract defilement from him. He is for the same reason to **cry, Unclean, unclean,** lest any wayfarer should unwittingly come in contact with him; and **his clothes shall be rent, and his head bare, and he shall put a covering upon his upper lip,** these being the signs of mourning for the dead. The bared or dishevelled head (see ch. x. 6) and the covered lip are incidentally mentioned as signs of mourning in Ezek. xxiv. 17, and the covered upper lip as a mark of shame in Micah iii. 7. By the expression, **He shall dwell alone,** is meant he shall dwell apart from those who were clean. Of course, lepers would naturally associate with each other, and so we find that they actually did (Luke xvii. 12). As their presence was supposed to defile any place that they entered, they were punished in later times with forty stripes if they did not observe the restraints laid down for them. "They were, however, admitted to the synagogue, where a place was railed off for them, ten handbreadths high and four cubits wide, on condition of their entering the house of worship before the rest of the congregation and leaving it after them" (Edersheim, 'Temple Service'). The exclu-sion of the leper was not for the purpose of avoiding contagion, nor to serve as a penalty for having contracted so loathsome a disease, but primarily to prevent the spread of cere-monial uncleanness communicated by his touch, and typically and mystically to teach that the fate brought upon a man by unre-moved sin is separation from the people of God here and hereafter.

HOMILETICS

Vers. 1—44.—*Leprosy is regarded as the type of sin* in a more especial way than other foul and ugly things. Affections of the body often serve as means of representing to ourselves the affections of the mind. This is witnessed to by ordinary language. The words, "see," "perceive," "feel," originally expressive of bodily acts, have come to signify mental acts, and so in other cases, "healthy," "diseased," "upright," "debased," are words which we apply to men in their moral even more than in their physical capacity (cf. Isa. i. 5, 6, "The whole head is sick, and the whole heart faint. From the sole of the foot even unto the head there is no soundness in it; but wounds, and bruises, and putrifying sores: they have not been closed, neither bound up, neither mollified with ointment"). Points of similarity between leprosy as it affects the body and sin as it affects the soul are—

I. ITS MYSTERIOUS ORIGIN. Whether by hereditary transmission or for other untraceable causes, it makes its appearance in the flesh of those whom it attacks without any special personal act of theirs to have brought it on.

II. ITS SLIGHT BEGINNING. It appears to be as nothing—as a mere spot in the skin, such as often comes and goes without injury.

III. ITS PAINLESSNESS IN ITS FIRST STAGES. It does not interfere with the common pleasures or occupations of life. There is a spot which a keen eye may observe, but it causes no trouble, and men go on anticipating no evil from it.

IV. THE SLOWNESS OF ITS GROWTH. "Sometimes months, sometimes years, even to the extent of twenty or thirty years, intervene between the first appearance of the spots and their development" (Gardiner). "Very frequently, even for years, before the actual outbreak of the disease itself, white yellowish spots are seen lying deep in the skin" (Trusen, 'Krankheiten der Alten Hebr.'). In other cases it develops more rapidly, according to the part of the body in which it has fixed itself, and the general health of the patient.

V. ITS INSIDIOUSNESS. After it has long continued without producing mischief, the person affected recovers hope, and thinks that no harm will come of it, but the evil remains, and waits its time for exhibiting itself, hiding itself meantime and lingering in the system.

VI. ITS RESISTLESS PROGRESS IF NOT ERADICATED IMMEDIATELY THAT IT APPEARS. "It is asserted that it yields to medical treatment in its earliest stages, when the spots first appear, and a number of distinct cases of cure are recorded. After the leprosy has once acquired a certain degree of development, there is no known means of cure. Everything hitherto attempted has been found to rather aggravate than mitigate the disorder. It is certain that, after it has once become developed to any considerable extent, it is incurable by any remedies at present known, although spontaneous cures do sometimes occur" (Gardiner).

VII. ITS FINAL HIDEOUSNESS. First it affects the hair around the spot, and changes its colour and its character till at last it falls off. "The spots afterwards pierce through the cellular tissues and reach the muscles and bone. Hard gelatinous swellings are formed in the cellular tissue; the skin gets hard, rough, and seamy, lymph exudes from it, and forms large scabs, which fall off from time to time, and under these there are often offensive running sores. The nails then swell, curl up, and fall off, *entropium* is formed, with bleeding gums, the nose stopped up, and a considerable flow of saliva" (Trusen). "A characteristic of the disease is the horribly repulsive features of its later stages, when the face becomes shockingly disfigured, and often the separate joints of the body become mortified and drop off one by one" (Gardiner).

VIII. THE SUFFERING ENTAILED BY IT AT LAST. As if to make up for the painlessness of its earlier stages, it not only causes in its final stage a constant pain of body, but a distress of mind and horror on the part of the sufferer at having become so loathsome and offensive an object to himself and to others.

IX. ITS UNEXPECTED ENDING. "A characteristic of the disease is its usually sudden and unexpected termination at the last, when the leprosy reaches some vital organ, and gives rise to secondary disease, often dysentery, by which life is ended" (Gardiner). "The patient gets thin and weak, diarrhœa sets in, and incessant thirst and burning fever terminate his sufferings" (Trusen).

X. ITS LIKENESS TO A LIVING DEATH. "Leprosy was not merely the emblem of sin, but of death, to which, so to speak, it stood related, as does our actual sinfulness to our state of sin and death before God. A rabbinical saying ranks lepers with those who may be regarded as dead" (Edersheim).

In all these respects, by the bodily state of the leper was manifested and parabolically set forth the state of the soul given up to the dominion of sin. Like leprosy, sin springs up mysteriously in the heart, owing to some previously existing corruption; at first it does not cause pain, but it promises pleasure, and gives some enjoyment to the senses; its true character is often not developed for years, but it gradually takes more and more possession of the soul, till it becomes unconquerable by any internal or human power; then it shows itself in its true form, repulsive instead of attractive, full of pain instead of pleasure, ending in a sudden destruction and a death of the soul.

CONCLUSION. 1. Negative. Avoid those things which will bring the soul into a state analogous to the leprous body. "Enter not into the path of the wicked, and go not in the way of evil men. Avoid it, pass not by it, turn from it and pass away." "For the lips of a strange woman drop as an honeycomb, and her mouth is smoother than oil: but her end is bitter as wormwood, sharp as a two-edged sword. Her feet go down to death; her steps take hold on hell. . . . Remove thy way far from her, and come not nigh the door of her house: lest thou give thine honour unto others, and thy years unto the cruel: lest strangers be filled with thy wealth; and thy labours be in the house of a stranger; and thou mourn at the last, when thy flesh and thy body are consumed, and say, How have I hated instruction, and my heart despised reproof; and have not obeyed the voice of my teachers, nor inclined mine ear to them that instructed me!" "Let not thine heart decline to her ways, go not astray in her paths. For she hath cast down many wounded: yea, many strong men have been slain by her. Her house is the way to hell, going down to the chambers of death" (Prov. iv. 14, 15; v. 3—13; vii. 25—27). 2. Positive. Seek those things which will give health and strength to the soul. "Happy is the man that findeth wisdom, and the man that getteth understanding. For the merchandise of it is better than the merchandise of silver, and the gain thereof than fine gold. She is more precious than rubies: and all the things thou canst desire are not to be compared unto her. Length of days is in her right hand; and in her left hand riches and honour. Her ways are ways of pleasantness, and all her paths are peace. She is a tree of life to them that lay hold upon her: and happy is every one that retaineth her" (Prov. iii. 13—18).

Vers. 45, 46.—*The extrusion of the leper from the camp is a type of excommunication from the Christian Church.* The right of separating from the community such as will not submit to discipline belongs to all bodies secular and ecclesiastical. Civil societies exercise this right by inflicting the penalties of death, imprisonment, or exile; the Church's penalty is suspension of communion, or excommunication. (For an account of Jewish and Christian excommunication, as founded on scriptural authority, see article in Smith's 'Dictionary of the Bible,' vol. iii. appendix.)

The purpose of the exclusion of the leper was to prevent legal uncleanness being spread by his means: the purpose of the excommunication of the sinner is twofold— partly for his own benefit, partly for that of the community. The power of admitting into the Church and excluding from it by the use of the proper means was promised to St. Peter (Matt. xvi. 19), and given to all the apostles (Matt. xviii. 15—18; John xx. 23). The power of admission was exercised every time that baptism was administered, that of exclusion was exercised by St. Paul in the case of the incestuous Corinthian (1 Cor. v. 3—5), and in the case of Hymenæus and Alexander (1 Tim. i. 20). St. Paul incidentally states that the purpose of their excommunication was (1) "to deliver such an one unto Satan, for the destruction of the flesh, that the spirit may be saved in the day of the Lord Jesus;" and (2) "to purge out the old leaven, that ye may be a new lump" (1 Cor. v. 5, 6). So far as the effect on others is concerned, the severance of the leper has an analogous object with that of the severance of the sinner; but the effect of the Church's discipline on the soul of the sinner ought to have a result which the penalty inflicted on the leper could not bring about. What this result should be is shown in the case of the incestuous Corinthian. The reproof was stern and the punishment sharp, but it produced repentance, and then the continuance of the infliction of the penalty ceased. "Sufficient to such a man is this punishment, which was inflicted of many. So that contrariwise ye ought rather to forgive him, and comfort him, lest perhaps such a one should be swallowed up with overmuch sorrow. Wherefore I beseech you that ye would confirm your love toward him" (2 Cor. ii. 6—8). Church discipline is a condition of the well-being of the Church, and it must be put in practice in the case of both immorality (1 Cor. v.) and heresy (1 Tim. i. 20), but no Church discipline can have good results which has not for its first object the good of the sinner, and which is not exercised in the spirit of love. There have been periods in the history of the Church when a sincere desire to prevent contamination by supposed heterodox teaching has wrought far more harm than could have been produced by any amount of liberty or licence, whether of thought, or speech, or act.

HOMILIES BY VARIOUS AUTHORS.

The diagnosis of sin as illustrated in the leprosy. Ch. xiii.; cf. 2 Kings v.; Ps. lxxxviii.; Matt. viii. 1—4; Luke v. 12—15. The preceding chapter brings forward sin as an inheritance through ordinary generation. No thorough sense or treatment of sin can be reached unless it is recognized as a *nature*. But God went further in his education of his people. He took one disease with unmistakable characteristics; he legislated about it, doomed the possessor of it to a certain treatment, and so made plain to all his attitude towards sin.

The case of Naaman (2 Kings v.) demonstrates that leprosy was not treated in Syria as it was among the Jews. Though a leper, he could enjoy the society of his family, wait upon his king, and command the army. The disease entailed no penalties at Damascus such as existed in Samaria. No sanitary solution, therefore, of this Mosaic law will satisfy the conditions; we must look to moral and spiritual considerations for the solution.[1] Hence we are constrained to start with the canon of interpretation that leprosy was a disease selected for treatment among the Jews to illustrate the treatment of sin.

I. As soon as the disease is suspected, the person is to go, or be brought, not to a physician, but to one of the priests. This took it out of the category of diseases curable by ordinary means. Hence the term for "leprosy" (צָרַעַת, from צָרַע, to strike down) signifies "the stroke of God." It was deemed a Divine infliction, which, if not divinely cured, would terminate fatally, and, though not disseminated by contact, was transmissible from parent to child. In handing it over in such circumstances for religious treatment, there was afforded one of the most striking illustrations of the nature of sin. Sin is a disease which none but the Divine Physician can cure. All effort at self-cure, all effort after merely human cure, is unavailing. Of course, sinners are induced to believe in the curability of the incurable, else there would be no sale for many a "patent medicine," and no opening for many a spiritual imposture. But God has made it sufficiently plain, by statement and illustration, that sin is a

[1] Cf. Trench 'On the Miracles,' the chapter on 'The Cleansing of the Leper.'

disease with which only he himself can deal. Hence he handed its symbol, the leprosy, to a priest, and not to a physician.

II. THE PRIEST, IN INVESTIGATING THE DISEASE, IS TO ASCERTAIN WHETHER IT IS SUPERFICIAL OR VITAL. It may be only a "scab" or a "burning boil," a mere superficial eruption, in which case the priest is to comfort the patient with the assurance that he is clean. But if the disease is seen to go down into the vitals of the patient, to be deep and hidden, then the priest is to pronounce him unclean.

For sin is no superficial matter, but a vital and fatal evil. It eats below the appearances into the very vitals of the being, and, unless divinely checked, must run its fatal course.

III. THE PENALTY OF PRONOUNCED LEPROSY IS A LIVING DEATH, AND A CONSEQUENT EXCLUSION FROM THE CAMP OF GOD. "The leper in whom the plague is, his clothes shall be rent, and his head bare, and he shall put a covering upon his upper lip, and shall cry, Unclean, unclean. All the days wherein the plague shall be in him he shall be defiled; he is unclean: he shall dwell alone; without the camp shall his habitation be" (vers. 45, 46). It is instructive to analyze this sentence. And—

1. *The leper was to regard himself as virtually a dead man.* This is implied by the rent clothes and the bare head, the signs of Oriental mourning, He was to be his own chief mourner. The same idea was carried out in the Middle Ages, when the mass for the dead was said over the leper. Longfellow refers to this in his 'Golden Legend,' when he says of Prince Henry—

> " Why, in Saint Rochus
> They made him stand, and wait his doom :
> And, as if he were condemned to the tomb,
> Began to mutter their hocus-pocus.
> First, the mass for the dead they chaunted,
> Then three times laid upon his head
> A shovelful of churchyard clay,
> Saying to him, as he stood undaunted,
> ' This is a sign that thou art dead;
> So in thy heart be penitent!'
> And forth from the chapel door he went
> Into disgrace and banishment,
> Clothed in a cloak of hodden gray,
> And bearing a wallet, and a bell,
> Whose sound should be a perpetual knell
> To keep all travellers away."

In the leper we have, therefore, the finest possible illustration of what spiritual death is. It is not a state of unconsciousness, but a state of consciousness. A sense of hopeless doom goes to make up this living death. Here have we vividly presented what "dead in trespasses and sins" must mean. 2. *The leper was to cry out as he met a passenger, " Unclean, unclean !"* That is, he was to encourage the consciousness of personal uncleanness. In no way could a penitent spirit be more powerfully illustrated. A perpetual humiliation was thus kept up, a sense of vileness and uncleanness, which is wholesome for the soul. Doubtless the sense of uncleanness might be impenitent; the poor leper might regard himself as a victim of providence instead of one deserving the stroke. But his cry is a very vivid representation of what humiliation for sin should be. 3. *The leper must isolate himself from the society of the pure, and dwell without the camp.* Isolation is what the leper is required to enter, and what we may be sure he does enter willingly. To a doomed man like him, contact with the clean and pure would be painful. Isolation would be easier to bear than society. So is it with sin. It is an isolating, repellent power. The sinner would not choose the society of the holy. Heaven would be a more painful place for a sinful soul than Gehenna itself. Hence we find in Rev. xxi. that while the new Jerusalem is to have nothing that defileth within it, no precaution to ensure this is needed; the gates remain open, for sinners would not, even if they could, court the society of the holy.

The isolating power of sin may be illustrated from the case of Byron. Two quotations are worth giving in this connection.

" I loved—but those I loved are gone;
  Had friends—my early friends are fled.
How cheerless feels the heart alone,
  When all its former hopes are dead!
Though gay companions o'er the bowl
  Dispel awhile the sense of ill;
Though pleasure stirs the maddening soul,
  The heart—the heart—is lonely still."

And again in the stanzas written at Missolonghi, when he was thirty-six—

"My days are in the yellow leaf;
  The flowers and fruits of love are gone:
The worm, the canker, and the grief
  Are mine alone!

"The fire that on my bosom preys
  Is lone as some volcanic isle;
No torch is kindled at its blaze—
  A funeral pile."

Was it not to taste the full consequences of human sin that our Lord had to enter the desolation which constrained the cry on the cross, "My God, my God, why hast thou forsaken me?"

IV. ON THE OTHER HAND, THE PRIEST IS DIRECTED HOW HE MAY ASCERTAIN WHEN THE LEPROSY HAS BEEN CURED. For this direction contemplates cases of cure, where "the stroke of God" in the leprosy has been followed up by the mercy of God in removing it. Now, one general principle runs through the cases of cure. If the priest has evidence that the disease has *all come to the surface*, then he is to pronounce the leper clean. The spiritual counterpart of this is not far to seek. If sin be hidden, if the sinner, like the Psalmist, keep silence about it, then his bones wax old through his roaring all the day long, and his moisture is turned into the drought of summer (Ps. xxxii. 3, 4). But if the sinner confesses his sin, acknowledges all he knows, and that there is much besides known only to the Lord—in a word, if the sinner makes "a clean breast" of everything, then is the cure of God in process of accomplishment. The lesson here is consequently the great desirability of a full and heartfelt confession of sin. There is hope of a man when he hides nothing from the Lord.

V. MAN SHOULD BE AS CAREFUL ABOUT HIS ENVIRONMENT AS ABOUT HIMSELF. It is evident from the possibility of leprosy infecting garments, and even houses, that the disease was contemplated as having a much wider range than the person of the leper. The directions given to the priest, moreover, contemplate the purification of man's surroundings. Every effort is to be made to stamp out the plague. The pure or purified are to be surrounded by the pure.

Now, this conveys the spiritual lesson surely of man taking the utmost pains to have a pure atmosphere, so to speak, in which to cultivate purity of life. Wherever sin is allowed free play, it will extend its ravages to man's environment. The world itself is a different world through man's sin. The duty of God's people in this case is plain. "The very appearance of evil" must be avoided (1 Thess. v. 22). We must carefully keep ourselves unspotted from the world (Jas. i. 27). Whenever we find sin tempting us, we must, if possible, have it removed and consumed. Does it meet us in literature? let us avoid it, and, if possible, destroy it. And even the ravages of sin in the world itself must be contemplated in the hope of having them one day completely removed. Let sin be slain in the light of day is the great practical lesson of this chapter.—R. M. E.

Vers. 1—59.—*Leprosy*. That leprosy is a type of sin is evident from David's allusion in confessing his own horrible offences (see Ps. li. 7). This also appears from the words of Jesus to the only leper, out of the ten cleansed by him, who returned to give glory to God: "Thy faith hath saved *thee*" (see Luke xvii. 11—19). The others had faith which availed them to remove the leprosy of the body; but this man's faith availed to remove the leprosy of the soul. Hence this plague often came as a judgment from Heaven upon sin (see Numb. xii. 10; 2 Kings v. 27; 2 Chron. xxvi. 19), from which circumstance, perhaps, it had its name (צרעת), tsaraath, from (צרע), tsaro, to smite. As there is no disease whose description engages so much space in Scripture, leprosy must be regarded as a very special type of sin.

I. IT IS A PLAGUE MOST LOATHSOME. 1. *So it is described.* (1) According to Scripture it appeared in a "rising," or "scab," or "bright spot" (ver. 2). From one or more of these centres it "spread" (vers. 8, 12, 22, 36), exhibiting "quick raw flesh" (vers. 10, 15), and this as it dried turned to a white scurf (ver. 13). Job is, by some, supposed to have been afflicted with leprosy (see Job vii. 5). (2) Travellers give frightful accounts of it. Maundrell describes it as he witnessed it in Palestine, and states it to be "the utmost corruption of the human body at this side the grave." 2. *Is not this a true picture of sin?* (1) View it in the haunts of the "criminal classes." What spectacles are witnessed in police courts! what distortion of features, what mutilations, the humanity almost battered out of them through the violences of dissipation! (2) No less loathsome to the eye of God are the hearts of many who outwardly seem respectable (Jer. xvii. 9). Sin is called "corruption," and seducers to sin "corrupters" (Eph. iv. 22; 2 Pet. ii. 19). Learn to loathe sin.

II. IT IS A DISEASE DEEPLY SEATED. 1. *Surface evils may be mistaken for sin.* (1) When symptoms go no deeper than the skin, they are no proof of leprosy (vers. 4, 34). Errors of judgment sometimes are mistaken for sins. Sincere Christians should be careful not to condemn themselves when God does not condemn them. (2) Surface evils may be very painful. There were "burning boils," which did not compromise the cleanness of the sufferer (vers. 23, 28). So may we smart under reproaches and scandals raised by the malignity of enemies, and perhaps sometimes through our own unwisdom, which God will not impute to us for sin. 2. *When the evil is in the flesh there is uncleanness.* (1) This was a capital test of leprosy (vers. 3, 20, 30). This disease may be handed down from father to son (see 2 Kings v. 27). So sin is "that which cometh out of the heart" (Matt. xv. 18—20; 1 Cor. viii. 7; Titus i. 15; Heb. xii. 15, 16). Like its type, sin also is hereditary (Rom. v. 12). (2) Mental rebellion against God is of the worst kind. Hence the emphasis with which the uncleanness of the leper is pronounced whose leprosy is in his *head* (see vers. 43, 44). Satan is intellect without God. Keep a pure faith and it will keep you.

III. IT IS A MALADY FEARFULLY CONTAGIOUS. 1. *Such was the figure.* (1) Leprosy works secretly at first, and for years may be concealed. Its early appearance may be limited to a pimple; but so rapidly does it spread that "seven days" may be sufficient for it to become pronounced (vers. 22, 27, 36). (2) It may pass from the leper to his neighbour. Robinson says, "That it was contagious, all histories, sacred and profane, agree" ('Theological Dictionary'). It was therefore necessary to provide that lepers should dwell apart (ver. 46; Numb. xii. 15; 2 Chron. xxvii. 21). (3) Property as well as persons caught the plague. Garments had to be destroyed for it (ver. 52). Houses also (ch. xiv. 45). 2. *The reality answers to the figure.* (1) Sin in the individual gathers strength by habit, and infects the faculties until the heart is sick, the head faint, and the whole man is a mass of moral putrescence (Isa. i. 6). (2) By precept and example he demoralizes his neighbours, and brings down the judgments of Heaven upon them (Josh. vii. 1, 11, 12; Eccles. ix. 18). (3) The plague of sin affects the material prosperity of individuals and of nations. No wonder the leper should be accounted ceremonially unclean, and the sinner avoided by the holy universe.—J. A. M.

Vers. 1—59.—*The priest's adjudication.* We have considered the plague of leprosy as an emblem of sin; the adjudication upon it will suggest thoughts concerning the treatment of sin. In this business the principal actor was the priest, who must be viewed as the type of Christ. The judgment in this case will be disciplinary rather than final; for when Messiah will come to judge the world at the last day, he will appear not as a priest but as a king. We are now concerned with the functions of the priest.

I. HE HAD TO EXAMINE THE SUSPECTED PERSON. 1. *In this he proceeded according to the Law.* (1) He had his rules for determining the presence of the plague. (2) So by the Word of God is our moral cleanness or uncleanness to be determined (Rom. ii. 13; iii. 20; 1 Cor. xiv. 24, 25; Jas. i. 22—25; ii. 9). (3) Conviction is carried

home by the Spirit of Christ. 2. *When the case was dubious judgment was deferred.*
(1) Meanwhile the suspected person was "shut up" (vers. 4, 21, 31) that opportunity
might be given for the manifestation of the symptoms. So are sinners "shut up" by
the Law to the faith of the gospel (see Rom. xi. 32, margin; Gal. iii. 23). (2) At the
end of "seven days" judgment was given; or, if the symptoms were not then sufficiently
manifest, a second period of seven days was allowed, which was the final term. Could
these periods refer to the dispensations of our probation? In this case the leper must
be taken to personate a class of sinner according to the type of his disease, whether
proceeding from the "rising," or the "boil," or the "scab." In any case, a sufficient
probation is given us in this world for the manifestation of our real character, which
probation we should be careful to improve. 3. *A leprous garment was treated as representing its owner.* (1) It had to be inspected by the priest for his judgment and
sentence, as though it had been a person. In case the plague in it were not pronounced,
it had to be "shut up" and examined again after the same intervals of "seven days"
(vers. 50, 54). The expense and trouble of this, particularly if it had to be brought
from a distance, would be as much as the garment was worth, so that the Law is unaccountable unless it was intended to serve a typical purpose. (2) Agabus the prophet
made Paul's girdle emblematically to represent that apostle (Acts xxi. 11). The
"owner" of a leprous house, obviously for the same reason, had to "come and tell
the priest" (ch. xiv. 35). (3) The washing of the garment in this case suggests the
washing of regeneration.

II. HE HAD TO PRONOUNCE UPON HIM. 1. *In some cases the verdict was an acquittal.*
(1) If the suspected leprosy proved to be but a surface evil, the subject was pronounced
clean (ver. 6). Jesus does not mark as sins infirmities which spring not from an evil
nature. The person acquitted, however, had to wash his clothes (ver. 34). There is
no person so faultless as not to need the laver of regeneration. (2) If a leper be "white
all over," no proud flesh, no ichor, being visible, he is pronounced clean (ver. 13). The
virulence of the disease is over; God's mercy has reached him; the sinner is forgiven.
But the marks of an old dissipation often remain after forgiveness. Though now clean,
there can be no question that he had been a leper. (3) Another case is given. A leper,
supposing his disease gone, presents himself to the priest for his cleansing; but the
priest, discovering "raw flesh," sends him away unclean; in time, however, he becomes
cured, returns to the priest, and on the second application is pronounced clean (ver.
17). This case is like that of the sinner whose repentance is not perfect, and at the
altar he discovers that until he is reconciled to a brother whom he had wronged his
gift cannot be accepted; the reconciliation made, he returns and finds the favour of
God (Matt. v. 23, 24). 2. *In other cases the judgment was "Unclean."* (1) When
the plague is pronounced, as in cases of "old leprosy," deliberation was unnecessary;
judgment came speedily (vers. 10, 11). So with the openly wicked (Ps. ix. 16; Prov.
v. 22; xi. 5). (2) In all cases evidence must be clear. Time, therefore, was given for
the plague to pronounce itself. So, before judgment could overtake the Amorites, their
iniquity must be full (Gen. xv. 16; see also Dan. viii. 23; Matt. xxiii. 32, 33; 1 Thess.
ii. 16). (3) Jesus is unerring in his judgments. He is the faithful as well as merciful
High Priest. 3. *The sentence.* (1) The leper has to dwell without the camp (ver. 46).
So must the open sinner be put out of the Church (see 1 Cor. v. 11—13). Hypocrites
and unbelievers, though in the Church in the visible part, are not recognized by God
as members of the Church in the spiritual part. (2) The leper has to behave as an
excommunicate seeking for the mercy of God. His clothes are rent to express extreme
grief and sorrow. His head is bare, turbanless, to express deep humiliation. He put
a covering upon his upper lip; had his jaw tied up with a linen cloth as a corpse, to
express his state as that of a living death (see 2 Kings v. 7; Ezek. xxiv. 17), and he
was to cry "Unclean!" (ver. 45). When we confess that we are dead in trespasses and
sins, and sorrow to repentance, there is hope for us in God. (3) But as the garment
that remains unclean after two washings, to save it from destruction must have the
leprous piece rent from it; so if a "right hand" or "right eye" prevent us from realizing
the benefits of redemption, they must be separated (ver. 56). But if all efforts to save
the garment fail, then its doom is to be burnt (see Matt. v. 29, 30; xviii. 8, 9).—J. A. M.

Vers. 45, 46.—*A picture of sin.* The stringent rules for the treatment of the leper are not sufficiently explained by sanitary considerations. The Jews saw in the leper a symbol of the sinner visited with the displeasure of God. His was a stroke of smiting (" plague of leprosy ") from the hand of Jehovah, which made him "utterly unclean" (ver. 44). The instructions of this chapter may convey to us important truth respecting the sinner's condition. To behold it thus forcibly depicted may administer a wholesome warning.

I. THE CORRUPTION EFFECTED BY SIN. Cannot but shudder at : 1. Its *loathsomeness*, destroying man's appearance, making him offensive to the sight. How abominable is wickedness to the pure eyes of God, and if our moral sense were keener, what constant shocks should we receive from the wicked conduct of men! What want of taste to indulge in sin! what disharmony of relationship it introduces! 2. Note its *tendency to spread* until it becomes total. The commission of one crime often leads to another which still more impairs the soul; the inordinate gratification of appetite in one direction is provocative of intemperance in another; to lose modesty is often to lose natural affection. At last the whole constitution betrays the effects of sin, body, mind, and spirit are alike unpleasant to contemplate. 3. Its *destruction of vital power*. It was termed by the Jews a "living death." Of its worst form, where the limbs mortify and drop off, no special mention is made in the Law; indeed, the supposition is that, after the expiration of a certain time, the disease will have so spread as to become harmless, and the man may be termed "clean" (ver. 17). The disease appears to have become more malignant in subsequent ages, and thus to typify even more accurately the waste of strength produced by evil habits. The mental and moral faculties are enervated by sin, the sinner is led captive by the devil at his will. To understand a principle we must push its application to extreme consequences, and if we would entertain fitting conceptions of sin we must regard it not when most refined, not when in its commencement, but in its gross final results. To dread fire, think of the conflagration that visits a town with disorder and ruin!

II. THE EXCLUSION IT ENTAILS FROM HOLY PRIVILEGES. The leper was separate from the people and the sanctuary. 1. *Contact with the sinner defiles*, except in appointed cases, where the servant of God in fulfilment of duty (as the priest in examination) seeks out the moral leper. If men mingle with sinners, having Christ's end in view, to do them good, the association is pardoned. Otherwise "one sinner destroyeth much good," "evil communications corrupt good manners." Men should naturally shun the company of the debased as they would the presence of those afflicted with an infectious disease. 2. *The semblance of sin must be guarded against*. All that appears like it (vers. 5, 6) needs suspicious treatment. Better to err on the safe side, not pronouncing at first decidedly, but watching the operation of a plan, or society, or principle, and ere long its true character will be manifested by development. 3. *Continuance in sin means separation from the Church and the fellowship of right-minded people*. The leper must "dwell alone, without the camp." Our Lord and his apostles insisted on the maintenance of discipline in Christian bodies. The persistent sinner will find himself eventually cut off from intercourse with his former friends, for ungodliness is an effectual barrier, creating uncongeniality of sentiment and behaviour. 4. *Dismission from the presence of God is the worst penalty of sin*. The Psalmist might lament his enforced absence from the tabernacle where he had seen the power and glory of God; but how much more the man who was so near the hill of Zion, and yet so far off by reason of symbolical impurity! Sin kept God and man asunder, and to remove it came the Lord Jesus Christ. The awful sentence finally pronounced upon the unrighteous is "Depart from me!" What absence of joy and peace and love is contained in the words, "the outer darkness"!

III. THE EXPRESSIONS OF FEELING THAT BEFIT THE SINNER'S STATE. 1. *Grief*. The leper wore the garb of mourning. There needs the godly sorrow that worketh repentance. Reflect not simply upon the sad consequences of sin, estrangement from God, deprivation of his favour, but upon their source, and learn to hate sin as an abomination. 2. *Humiliation*. The uncovered head attested the leper's shame. "I abhor myself" is fitting language for polluted lips. 3. *Acknowledgment of guilt*. Listen to the cry, "Unclean!" The upper lip was shrouded in a covering that enjoined general silence, except on the approach of a stranger, who might be thereby defiled. "We are all as an unclean thing." When sin lies heavily upon the conscience, it is felt to be no time for ordinary conversation, much less for frivolous gossip, though under such a veil anxiety is often hid.

CONCLUSION. By the Law was the knowledge of sin, but by the gospel is proclaimed its remedy, forgiveness and sanctification through Christ. The priest was not dependent upon his own judgment, but was guided by fixed rules in deciding upon leprous cases. Yet he did not heal; the sufferer was left to nature's care, and to indulge the vague hope of recovery. The gospel bids all sinners lay aside their fears and rejoice in a panacea that never fails. The interposition of God by prophets which resulted in miraculous cures of leprosy prepared the way for the marvellous works of the Redeemer, who evinced by his restoring the body to health his power also to heal the soul. Thus what was faintly foreshadowed under the old dispensation has been brightly revealed in the new. The enumeration of the feelings appropriate to the sinner is incomplete, therefore, without adding to them hope, in the sense not of wishful longing, but of certain anticipation of salvation.—S. R. A.

Ver. 3.—"It is a plague of leprosy." *The chosen type of sin—its individual aspect.* The conjecture that leprosy was contracted by the children of Israel in the hot and dusty brick-fields of Egypt is probable enough. The definition that it was "any severe disease spreading on the surface of the body in the way described in the chapter, and so shocking of aspect . . . that public feeling called for separation," is near enough for our purpose. There can be no question that it was the divinely chosen type of sin.

All disease is pictorial of sin. It is to our bodily frame the very thing that sin is to our soul. Sin is the *derangement or disorder of the soul,* as sickness is of the body. It is an inward disorder, showing itself in some outward manifestation of a displeasing or painful character. It is something wrong within—some faculty (organ) not doing what it was made to do, or doing what it was not meant to do, causing disturbance and distress. But leprosy was selected by the Divine Ruler of Israel as a disease which should be regarded by his people as specially typical and suggestive of sin. It was admirably fitted so to be, whether looked at in its individual or in its social aspect. We will take the former first.

I. THE OBSCURITY OF ITS ORIGIN. By what sad and strange process came it to pass that man's bodily frame—fashioned by the Divine Creator, made clean and pure, wholesome and fair—has become the seat of such a foul disorder? How can it be that the little child whose flesh is beautiful and spotless, the very picture of all that is clean and sweet, grows up into a man who is "full of leprosy," covered from head to foot with revolting sores? And whence came sin into the soul and life of man? How came it here to blot and mar God's fair creation? How comes it to pass that into the heart of the innocent and lovely child there enters the very vilest spirit, showing itself in the most shocking words and the most revolting deeds, in later life?

II. ITS STUBBORNNESS. When, after seven days, the Hebrew priest could see no signs of true leprosy, he did not pronounce the patient clean: he shut him up other seven days (ver. 5), and examined him again. Leprosy was a tenacious and stubborn disease, disappearing and reappearing. After a long interval it might, under exciting cause, come once again to the surface. How like the affliction of the soul—sin! How tenacious is its hold on the human heart! It disappears and we are grateful, congratulatory, triumphant. But the inducing circumstances, the favourable conditions arise and conspire, and behold there is its hateful face again. We "would do good," we resolve to do good, but, alas! "evil is present with us" once more (Rom. vii. 21).

III. ITS DEATHFULNESS. The outward appearance was due to inward derangement; the springs of health were poisoned; the internal processes necessary to health were stayed; and the consequence was that feature after feature, limb after limb, decayed and fell away. The man was in a constant process of dissolution. It was death above the ground—death in a living form! Sin is death. The soul that lives in sin is "dead while it lives." It *is* not that which it was created to be, *does* not that which it was created to do. Its spiritual faculties (the organs and members of the soul) are in a state of continual dissolution, becoming feebler and feebler, till they are wholly lost. It is a living death.

IV. ITS INCURABLENESS BY MAN. The Jews did not bring the physician to the leper;

they regarded leprosy as a visitation from God, and considered it incurable by human art. Sin is incurable by mere human methods. Rules for the regulation of human conduct; pledges or vows of abstinence from particular temptations; parental, magisterial, social vigilance; penalties inflicted by ourself or by others for disobedience;— these are well enough in their way. They are sometimes desirable, sometimes necessary; *but they do not cure.* Nothing human will cure the soul's disorder; only the Almighty Hand can minister to the "mind diseased."

When Jesus Christ would prove to John that he was indeed the "One that should come," and that there was no need to "look for another," he added to the recital of his benefactions, "the lepers are cleansed" (Matt. xi. 5). It was a true mark of the Messiah. The coming Saviour was he who had power to cure the incurable, to touch the foulest of the foul with the finger of the Divine mercy and sovereign power, and to make even him whole and pure. To that Divine Physician the man fullest of the leprosy of sin may go and say, "Lord, if thou wilt thou canst make me clean" (Luke v. 12).—C.

Ver. 5.—*The chosen type of sin—its social aspect.* We have seen (*vide* previous Homily) how true a picture is leprosy of sin in its individual aspect; we now regard the subject in its more social aspect. What this terrible disease was to a man as a member of the Hebrew commonwealth, that is sin to a man as a member of society to-day.

I. ITS LOATHSOMENESS. It is quite possible that the leprosy from which the Israelites suffered was a contagious disorder. It is also possible that the dread of contagion, though there was no actual danger (as in cholera), may have had its influence in the matter. But there is no convincing evidence that it was contagious. There are indications that it was not (action of the priests, etc.); and the exclusion of the leper from the camp is fully accounted for in another way. The loathsomeness of the disease is a sufficient explanation. Whoever has seen any one suffering acutely from a kindred malady will perfectly understand and appreciate this legislation on that ground alone. It is difficult, if not impossible, to recover altogether from the mental effect of so shocking and so repulsive a spectacle. The vision haunts the memory for years. In this aspect leprosy is a striking picture of sin; for that is a thing odious and abominable in the last degree—loathsome to the Holy One of Israel, hateful to all holy souls. In its viler forms it is a thing which we—even with our imperfect purity—cannot "look upon" (Hab. i. 13); how much more horrible and hateful must it be in his sight whose thoughts of holiness as well as of mercy are as much higher than ours as the heavens are higher than the earth (Isa. lv. 9)!

II. ITS DIFFUSIVENESS. Though not, probably, contagious, leprosy was diffusive and communicable from parent to child. It was one of the crucial tests in the case that *it spread* over the skin (vers. 7, 8), that it "spread much abroad" (vers. 22, 27). As this typical disease spread from one part of the body to another, from one limb and organ to another, until it sometimes covered the entire frame, so sin, of which it was the divinely chosen type, is *a thing that spreads.* It is an emphatically diffusive, a communicable thing. It spreads: 1. From faculty to faculty of the same human spirit; one sin leads on to another, as theft to violence, or drunkenness to falsehood, or impurity to deception. 2. From parent to child. 3. From man to man, through the whole "body politic." It spreads much abroad through any and every body, civil or ecclesiastical, into which it enters.

III. ITS SEPARATING EFFECT. "He shall dwell alone: without the camp shall his habitation be" (ver. 46). Leprosy separated between husband and wife, parent and children, friend and friend; it sundered one human life from that of the commonwealth, and was a source of sad and, so far as the preciousness of life was concerned, a fatal loneliness. Sin is *the* separating power. 1. It comes between man and God (Isa. lix. 2). It places him outside the gates of the spiritual kingdom; it deprives a man of all fellowship with the heavenly Father; it leads him out into a "far country" of alienation, of dread, of dissimilarity. 2. It comes between man and man. It is the endless and bitter source of estrangement, animosity, war; it makes lonely the life that should be full of sweet and elevating fellowship.

IV. ITS PITIFULNESS. Who could see the poor leper, with rent clothes, with bare head, with covered lip, passing through the camp, crying, "Unclean, unclean!" on his way to a dreary and, it might be, life-long solitude and not be affected with a tender pity? He might be "unclean," but he was miserable, he was lost; the light of his life had gone out. Sin is not more condemnable than it is pitiable. Blame the erring, reproach the faulty, remonstrate with the foolish and the mischievous (1 Tim. v. 20), but pity those whom sin is shutting out from all that is best below, and will exclude from all that is bright and blessed above. Remember the "great love (of pity) wherewith he loved us, even when we were dead in sins" (Eph. ii. 4, 5), and pity with a profound compassion and help with an uplifting hand those who are still down in the mire of sin, still far from the kingdom of God.—C.

Ver. 3.—*Conviction of sin.* "And the priest shall look on him, and pronounce him unclean." In the Hebrew commonwealth: 1. There were those who were reasonably suspected of leprosy, *i.e.* of "uncleanness." 2. It was a matter of the gravest consequence to know whether these suspicions were well founded or not. For ascertained leprosy meant unfitness to approach God in worship, exclusion from the fellowship of his people, etc. 3. It was the function of the priest to decide positively in the matter. The priest was to "look on him, and pronounce him unclean," or, on the other hand, to rule that he was clean (ver. 6).

In every commonwealth to-day, in the whole human world—

I. THERE ARE THOSE REASONABLY SUSPECTED OF SIN. These are not the few exceptions; they are the multitude without exception (Ps. xiv. 23).

II. IT IS A MATTER OF THE GRAVEST CONSEQUENCE TO KNOW WHETHER WE ARE SINFUL OR NOT. For sin means (1) unlikeness to God; (2) separation from God; (3) condemnation by God, both here and hereafter; (4) exclusion from the home of the holy. Hence we must ask—

III. WHO ARE THEY ON WHOM THIS GREAT DECISION IS DEVOLVED. It rests with no human priest to decide on our state before God. Our own heart must condemn us if we are to have that *conviction of* sin which leads to *contrition for sin* and to "repentance and *remission* of sin." 1. God will be our Divine Helper. He helps us to a right conclusion by his informing Word and by his illuminating Spirit. 2. Our fellow-men will be human helpers; they will guide us to an understanding of the Word of the Lord, and, directed by their own experience, will lead us to judge truly concerning our spiritual condition. Their aid will be ministerial, not authoritative. 3. We ourselves must decide in the last resort. This is one of those grave matters in which "every man must bear his own burden." We must recognize, with the eyes of our own soul, the signs and tokens of guilt in our heart and life. It must be the deliberate utterance of our own judgment, as well as the sigh of our own spirit, and the cry of our own lips, "I have sinned against the Lord;" "Unclean, unclean!" When we look at our inner selves as well as outer life; when we consider what we have left undone of all our obligations, as well as what we have done that has been forbidden; when we contrast our hearts and lives with the precepts of God's holy Law and the ideal of human perfection in the example of our sinless Saviour; we shall have no hesitation in concluding that we are "utterly unclean," that we deserve exclusion from the friendship of God and the fellowship of the holy, and that it is our heavenly wisdom to seek at once his blessed presence who will say to us, "Wilt thou be made whole?" and to gain at once the touch of his mighty hand who, in answer to our earnest prayer, will respond by saying, I will; be thou clean."—C.

Vers. 40—44.—*Affections of the mind.* We learn lessons concerning—
I. THE BLEMISH OF MENTAL PECULIARITY. (Ver. 40.) Evidently baldness was an unusual and an unsightly thing among the Israelites. Otherwise it would not have excited notice and could not have created derision (2 Kings ii. 23; Isa. iii. 24; Ezek. vii. 18). It was regarded as an unbecoming peculiarity. Affecting the head, we may regard it as a type of mental peculiarity which does not amount to a serious sin, but is yet unusual and unbecoming. Many men who are substantially sound in heart and life, loving that which is highest and doing that which is just and right, are yet affected and afflicted by mental peculiarities—oddities, crotchets, fancies, awkwardness or crookedness of mental habit; things which are not formidably bad, but which,

because they are superficial, strike the eye, provoke general remark, and stand in the way of effective service. 1. It is right that those who observe them in others should remember that they are *only* blemishes, and nothing more; detracting in some degree from "the beauty of holiness," but not inconsistent with real and even admirable excellence. "He is bald, yet he is clean" (ver. 40). 2. It is right that those who possess them should reflect, and act on the reflection, that these things, though only blemishes, may importantly diminish the power of the possessor to influence, guide, and win other people. The candle (character) is of much more importance than the candlestick (mental habit), but if character be obscured by some darkening "bushel," and not put on the candlestick of pleasant and agreeable habits, it will not "give light to all that are in the house" (Matt. v. 15).

II. THE EVIL OF ERROR. There might come on the bald head a spot, a sore; this might be a "white reddish sore"—leprous (vers. 42, 43). But it might not; it might be nothing but a boil or some cutaneous disorder, which was not leprosy. In that case the patient would be treated as described in vers. 2—6. There would be something wrong, but it was not the unclean thing, leprosy. There is a mental disease which is something more serious than peculiarity and something less serious than guilty perversity. It is error; the arrival at wrong conclusions. There may be but small faultiness in coming to convictions which are not correct, but there may be positive disaster resulting therefrom. A man may innocently take the wrong road, but his innocency will not save him from walking into the bog or over the precipice to which it leads. Error is not the worst thing in the world, but it is a seriously bad and dangerous thing. When we are earnestly warned, by obviously thoughtful and godly men, that we are wrong in our judgments, it becomes us to listen patiently and consider well whether we are in the right track, or whether we have mistaken a false path for the "path of life."

III. THE SIN OF MENTAL PERVERSITY. (Vers. 43, 44.) There is great significance in the sentence "the priest shall pronounce him utterly unclean." The man who had leprosy in the head was accounted unclean in an especial degree: he was *utterly* unclean. Sin, of which this malady was so striking a type, never assumes so dangerous a phase as when it appears in the form of a perverted judgment or a darkened conscience. When, by sinning, a man has blunted his spiritual perceptions so that he "calls evil good, and good evil," he is in the last stage of moral decline; death is near at hand. If "our eye be evil" (if our judgment be perverted, our faculty of spiritual perception be diseased), our "whole body is full of darkness;" if "the light that is in us" (our own mental and spiritual faculty) be darkness, how great is that darkness!" (Matt. v. 23). Witness the Pharisees in their treatment of our Lord. We may well be actively on our guard against, and may well be earnest in prayer that God will deliver us from, that of which leprosy in the head is the painful picture,—a guilty, blinding, ruinous perversity of mind.—C.

Ver. 46.—*The right and duty of excommunication.* "He shall dwell alone; without the camp shall his habitation be." The right of expulsion from the Jewish camp would be founded, in the mind of Moses, on the Divine commandment (text; Numb. v. 2, etc.). That was all-sufficient for the great legislator. We may, however, "justify the ways of God to men" to our mind by the considerations: 1. That if the disease were not positively contagious, the dread of contagion would be most harmful to the community. 2. That the exceeding repulsiveness of the leper was ample reason for his being kept from the sight of men, women, and children. 3. That the most important and salutary lesson concerning sin was thereby vividly enforced, viz. that the sinner is, through his iniquity, separated from all that is purest and best. Unquestionably, with this and other clear commandments from Jehovah, it was both the right and the duty of the Hebrew commonwealth to expel the leper from the camp. Excommunication from human society is a sad and severe measure; but it is, in many cases, lawful and even obligatory. The foul and the "unclean" must be separated sometimes, even now and here, from the holy and the pure. Excommunication may be—

I. THE RIGHT AND DUTY OF THE NATION. 1. The nation has a right to transport or imprison those of its members who have committed crime, and who have shown that their presence "in the camp" is noxious and dangerous to the rest. 2. The nation is bound to exclude from town and city those who endanger its morals. The opium-seller, *as such*, is righteously excluded; the man who would sell poisons without restriction is disallowed; and an unlimited number of dramshops, with their terrible enticements, is (or, surely, should be) prohibited. A community has the right to say, "We will not allow any man, for the sake of gain, seriously to imperil the morals, the health, and the lives of the people; if you want to practise these things, you must go 'without the camp.'"

II. THE RIGHT AND DUTY OF THE SOCIAL AND THE FAMILY CIRCLE. 1. We ought not to admit to our intimacy any "unclean" human spirit. We should fence our social circles so that no man sits down to our table or our hearth to infect and poison our own minds. 2. But it is, in an especial degree, both our right and our duty, as parents, to guard the *family circle* from the intrusion of "the unclean." What untold evils, what unimaginable sorrows, have befallen family life, because parents have not, with holy vigilance, saved their sons and daughters from the companionship of the corrupt! Of every "unclean" soul let the human father say, with sternest inflexibility, "Without the camp shall *his* habitation be."

III. THE RIGHT AND DUTY OF THE CHURCH. There can be no doubt of this. 1. *It is the divinely appointed way.* It was instituted by our Lord himself (Matt. xviii. 17, 18). It was enjoined by the Apostle Paul (1 Cor. v. 2, 5, 11; Titus iii. 10); it was also practised by him (1 Tim. i. 20). 2. *It is the legitimate and becoming method.* Any interference by a Christian Church with civil rights goes beyond the Word of the Lord, brings the Church into conflict with the secular power, and is likely to lead to confusion and trouble. Exclusion from its own fellowship is a natural and incontestable right. 3. *It is sometimes the only course that is open.* It is needful for the purity of the Church itself; the leaven must not injure the whole lump. It is needful also for the offender. And it is well to remember these two things in such a sad necessity: viz. (1) that excommunication was resorted to in apostolic times with a distinct view to the benefit of the offender (1 Cor. v. 5; 1 Tim. i. 20); and (2) that of two cases reported in Scripture, one relates the restoration of the excommunicated member (2 Cor. ii. 6—8). Let the Church make paramount the preservation of its own purity, but let it encourage, expect, and welcome penitence.—C.

EXPOSITION.

LEPROSY IN CLOTHES (vers. 47—59). To account for the use of the name leprosy in this connection, an ingenious theory has been propounded that the same cause produced a like effect in the human frame in clothes and in houses. "There is here described a disease whose cause must have been of organic growth, capable of living in the human being and of creating there a foul and painful disease of contagious character, while it could also live and reproduce itself in garments of wool, linen, or skin; nay, more, it could attach itself to the walls of a house and there also effect its own reproduction. Animalcules, always capable of choice, would scarcely be found so transferable, and we are therefore justified in supposing that green or red fungi, so often seen in epidemic periods, were the protean disease of man and his garment and his house" (Dr. Mitchell, 'Five Essays'). It is not necessary to have recourse to this tempting but unproved hypothesis, inasmuch as the similarity of appearance presented by the two affections is enough to account for their going by the same name. Leprosy in garments and in leather is a mildew which cannot be got rid of, called leprosy by analogy. Like other causes of uncleanness, it makes the material unclean, because it gives a repulsive appearance to it, reminding the beholder of the disease which it resembles. "Leprosy in linen and woollen fabrics or clothes consisted in all probability in nothing but so-called mildew, which commonly arises from damp and want of air, and consists, in the case of linen, of round, partially coloured spots, which spread and gradually eat up the fabric, until it falls to pieces like mould. In leather, the mildew consists more strictly of 'holes eaten in,' and is of a greenish, reddish, or whitish colour, according to the species of the delicate cryptogami by which it has been formed" (Keil).

Ver. 47.—Whether it be a woollen garment, or a linen garment. Wool and flax are the two materials for clothes mentioned in Deut. xxii. 11; Prov. xxxi. 13; Hos. ii. 7.

Ver. 48.—Whether it be in the warp, or woof. It is hardly possible that such a fault as leprosy or mildew could appear in one set of the threads without affecting the others, provided that both were equally good when they were made up into the cloth; but it is quite possible that a heap of yarn, used either for the warp or for the woof, might have been injuriously affected before it was woven, and then the fault would naturally make its appearance where the mischief had been originally done. Whether in a skin, or in anything made of skin. An example of the first would be a sheepskin cloak; the second would designate anything made of leather.

Vers. 49—59.—The priest is to deal with the texture as nearly as may be in the same way that he dealt with the human subject, in order to discriminate between a temporary discolouration and a real leprosy. He shall shut up it that hath the plague seven days (ver. 50), may, as before, mean, He shall bind up the place affected seven days. If the priest judges that it is leprosy, he is to burn the garment, if not, to tear out the piece affected, whether it be in the warp, or in the woof, that is, in whatever part it appears, and to wash the remainder twice. The expression, whether it be bare within or without, literally, whether it be bald in the head thereof or in the forehead thereof, means, "whether the fault appear in the front or in the back of the texture."

HOMILETICS.

Vers. 47—59.—On purity of garments. There are passages in different parts of Holy Scripture which it is necessary to put together in order to get a comprehensive view of what only at first sight appears to be a slight subject.

I. The first result of the Fall was a consciousness of sin on the part of Adam and Eve, which caused a sense of their nakedness. This nakedness they in vain attempted to cover by aprons of fig leaves (Gen. iii. 7). But their self-made covering was not sufficient; they "were afraid because they were naked, and they hid themselves from the presence of the Lord God amongst the trees of the garden" (Gen. iii. 8, 10). God's first gift to man after sentence had been passed upon him was that of clothes: "Unto Adam also and to his wife did the Lord God make coats of skins, and clothed them" (Gen. iii. 21). This gift is the more significant in that the Hebrew word used for "atonement" is "covering." Here, then, in God's first gift to man was foreshadowed his future gift of an atonement. "The outward and corporeal here manifestly had respect to the inward and spiritual. The covering of the nakedness was a gracious token from the hand of God that the sin which had alienated them from him and made them conscious of uneasiness was henceforth to be in his sight as if it were not; so that in covering their flesh, he at the same time covered their consciences. . . . It was done purposely to denote the covering of guilt from the eye of Heaven—an act which God alone could have done" (Fairbairn, 'Typology of Scripture'). The more that we consider the force of the Hebrew term for "atonement," the more significance shall we attach to the first gift of coats. "To expiate, literally, to cover up, does not mean to cause a sin not to have been committed, for that is impossible; nor to represent it as having no existence, for that would be opposed to the earnestness of the Law; nor to pay or compensate it by any performance; but to cover it before God, i.e. to deprive it of its power to come between us and God" (Kahnis).

II. We have seen with what care God appointed "holy garments" for the Jewish priesthood, "for glory and for beauty" (Exod. xxviii. 2, 40; xxxix. 1—43; ch. viii. 7—9), and special instructions are afterwards given as to the dress to be worn by the high priest when he entered the holy of holies (ch. xvi.; cf. Ps. cxxxii. 9).

III. Uncleanness derived from the touch of unclean things entailed washing the clothes worn at the time (ch. xi. 28, 40; xvi. 26).

IV. In Zech. iii. 3—5 we read, "Now Joshua was clothed with filthy garments, and stood before the angel. And he answered and spake unto those that stood before him, saying, Take away the filthy garments from him. And unto him he said, Behold, I have caused thine iniquity to pass from thee, and I will clothe thee with change of raiment. And I said, Let them set a fair mitre upon his head. So they set a fair mitre upon his head, and clothed him with garments. And the angel of the Lord stood by." Here we are directly taught that filthy garments typify iniquity, and that the removal of filthy garments typifies the passing away of iniquity. Isaiah explains the meaning of the putting on of new garments: "He hath clothed me with the garments of salvation, he hath covered me with the robe of righteousness, as a bridegroom decketh himself with ornaments, and as a bride adorneth herself with her jewels" (Isa. lxi. 10).

From these passages of the Old Testament we find that clothing is connected with the idea of atonement, that God will not be approached except in holy garments, that foul garments typify iniquity, that garments which have contracted ceremonial uncleanness must be washed, that clean garments typify salvation and righteousness.

From the New Testament we learn what are the materials of the robe of salvation. They are the righteousness of Christ imputed to man—such is the argument of the Epistle to the Romans and the Epistle to the Galatians—and the righteousness inwrought in man by the indwelling of the Holy Ghost—"for the fine linen is the righteousness of saints" (Rev. xix. 8). If these form the materials of the Christian's spiritual raiment, there will appear no leprosy or mildew either in warp or woof. But if in place of one of these there be employed human merit or sanctity or other material, the plague will appear in the garment. "*And the priest shall rend it out of the garment, or out of the skin, or out of the warp, or out of the woof: and if it appear still in the garment, either in the warp, or in the woof, or in anything of skin; it is a spreading plague; thou shalt burn that wherein the plague is with fire.*" But there is this difference between leprosy in the garment and leprosy in the flesh, that in the former case the man may still be saved: "It shall be revealed by fire; and the fire shall try every man's work of what sort it is. . . . If any man's work shall be burned, he shall suffer loss: but he himself shall be saved; yet so as by fire" (1 Cor. iii. 13—15). And therefore St. Jude, in special reference to this passage, writes, "And of some have compassion, making a difference: and others save with fear, pulling them out of the fire; hating even the garment spotted by the flesh" (Jude 22, 23). The Christian is to hold in abhorrence "the garment" defiled with a like disease to that which attacks "the flesh," and is to cast it into the fire, but at the same time he is to "pull" the wearer himself "out of the fire," "saving" him "with fear." If the disease be true leprosy, but has not penetrated deeper than the garment, the garment must be burnt, but the wearer may still be "saved; yet so as by fire;" it will be a work of "fear" and anxiety. If it be not true leprosy, and even if it be—for here the antitype transcends the type—it will be possible to "wash his robes and make them white in the blood of the Lamb" (Rev. vii. 14).

Warning—"I counsel thee to buy of me gold tried in the fire, that thou mayest be rich; and white raiment, that thou mayest be clothed, and that the shame of thy nakedness do not appear" (Rev. iii. 18). "Blessed is he that watcheth, and keepeth his garments, lest he walk naked, and they see his shame" (Rev. xvi. 15). "Friend, how camest thou in hither not having a wedding garment? And he was speechless" (Matt. xxii. 12).

HOMILIES BY VARIOUS AUTHORS.

Vers. 47—59.—*Impure surroundings.* Our garments are our immediate surroundings, and there may be in them as well as in ourselves that which is offensive and "unclean." There was an impurity in the garment as well as in the human body against which the Law provided. The classing of clothes and houses with the human skin as leprous, "has moved the mirth of some and the wonder of others . . . but the analogy between the insect which frets the human skin and that which frets the garment that covers it, between the fungous growth that lines the crevices of the epidermis and that which creeps in the interstices of masonry, is close enough for the purposes of ceremonial law." The legal provision here made for the leprous garment suggests to us—

I. THE IMPURE SURROUNDINGS BY WHICH WE MAY BE ENVIRONED. These are many: 1. Depraved tastes and cravings in our body (for the body is the *immediate* clothing of the spirit). 2. Unholy companionships. 3. Corrupt political associations. 4. Impure, demoralizing books (or any form of hurtful literature). 5. *Injurious occupation*—that which wounds the conscience or enfeebles the inner life. 6. *A deadening Church*—a religious society where the form without the power of godliness is left.

II. THE DIVINELY SUGGESTED TREATMENT OF THEM. We gather from these verses that we should: 1. *Exercise vigilance in detecting.* With the same carefulness with which the priest made himself sure in the matter of the leprous garment (vers. 50—57), we must make certain whether there be in any of our surroundings—or of those for whom we are responsible—the plague which will work spiritual mischief in the heart and ultimate ruin to the character. 2. *Make serious effort to cleanse.* If, after seven days, there had been no spreading of the plague, the priest was to *wash* the garment (ver. 54), and if the plague departed, it was to be washed a second time, and then it was clean (ver. 58). All that was salvable was to be saved. If by vigorous and repeated washing any spotted garment could be preserved, it was not to be destroyed. All that is reformable in our institutions and surroundings must be reformed. We must cleanse where we can make pure and where it is unnecessary to destroy. But sometimes we must: 3. *Unscrupulously destroy.* When unmistakable signs of leprosy appeared, the priest was to " burn that garment ; " it was to " be burnt in the fire " (ver. 52). When we find in anything that surrounds us and that is exerting an influence upon us, that which is really hurtful to us—that which would lead us astray from God, we must sacrifice it altogether, at whatever cost (see Mark ix. 43—47). Our belongings must be put into the fire rather than be permitted to stain our soul.—C.

EXPOSITION.

CHAPTER XIV.

THE FORM OF PURIFICATION OF THE LEPER (ch. xiv. 1—32). This is the most minute of all the forms of purification, those for purification from contact with a dead body (Numb. xix.) and for the cleansing of a defiled Nazarite (Numb. vi.) being alone to be compared with it in this respect. Some purifications were accomplished, as we have seen, in a very summary manner : one who touched the carcase of a beast that had died a natural death had only to wash his clothes (ch. xi. 40). The greater and more significative the defilement, the more careful and the more significative must be the cleansing. Leprous uncleanness excluded the leper both from the camp and from the sanctuary, from the rights both of citizenship and of Church-membership, with which the rights of the family were also associated ; consequently there had to be a double form of restoration, each with its special ceremonies. The manner of the first reconciliation is detailed in vers. 1—8, of the second in vers. 9—32.

Ver. 2.—**This shall be the law of the leper in the day of his cleansing.** The ceremonies in the first stage of cleansing, which restored the outcast to the common life of his fellows, were the following : 1. The priest formally examined the leper outside the camp, and

made up his mind that he was clean. 2. An earthen vessel was brought with fresh water, and one of two birds was killed, and its blood was allowed to run into this water. 3. The other bird was taken and dipped in the vessel, with a piece of cedar wood and hyssop, which had first been tied together by a band of scarlet wool ; and the leper was sprinkled seven times with the blood and water dripping from the feathers of the living bird. 4. The priest pronounced the man clean. 5. The bird was let fly into the open field. 6. The man washed his clothes, shaved his whole body, and bathed. 7. He returned within the camp, but not yet to his tent.

Ver. 3.—**The priest.** The agent is still the priest, not the physician. **The priest shall go forth out of the camp.** " May we not (as Hesychius suggests) see a figure here of the compassion of our Great High Priest, who has *gone forth out of* heaven itself, the camp of angel hosts, and has come down to earth, not only to examine but to heal the moral leprosy of sin, ' to seek and to save the lost ' (Luke xix. 10), and who carefully examines and scrutinizes all the secrets of all hearts (Heb. iv. 12) ? And he was exempt from all contagion of sin while he lived and moved among sinners (Matt. ix. 11 ; Luke xv. 1), and was ' holy, harmless, and undefiled ' (Heb. vii. 26) " (Wordsworth). **And the priest shall look.** In later times it was ordered that the examination was not to take place on the sabbath, nor in the early morning, nor in the late afternoon, nor inside a house, nor on a cloudy day, nor in the glare of midday, and that the priest must have good eyesight, and only determine one case at a time; nor was he allowed to pronounce judgment on his own kindred. **And, behold, if the plague of leprosy be healed in the leper.** The plague of leprosy is healed before the ceremony of purification begins, but the leper is not *pronounced clean* until he has been sprinkled with the blood and water (ver. 7).

Ver. 4.—Cedar wood, and scarlet, and hyssop. " Cedar wood, and hyssop, and scarlet " are also to be burnt with the red heifer for the ashes for the water of separation (Numb. xix. 6), and they appear to have been commonly employed in purifications (Heb. ix. 19). The antiseptic properties of cedar made it peculiarly suitable for such occasions. The hyssop " was probably not the plant which we call hyssop, the *Hyssopus officinalis,* for it is uncertain whether this is to be found in Syria and Arabia, but a species of *origanum* resembling hyssop, the Arabian *zâter,* either wild marjoram, or a kind of thyme" (Keil on Exod. xii. 21). The Psalmist's cry, " Purge me with hyssop, and I shall be clean" (Ps. li. 7), shows the common use to which it was put. In the present case, the sweet smell both of the wood (one cubit's length of which was used) and of the herb would have still further adapted them for symbolizing the redemption of the leper's flesh from corruption and putrefaction. The *scarlet* was probably a band of scarlet wool with which the cedar and the hyssop were tied—not to the bird (for we have no account of their being afterwards removed), but (as in the burning of the red heifer) one to the other. The colour of the wool was appropriate, not only because it was about to be dipped in the blood and water, but also because it symbolized the purified and now healthy blood.

Ver. 5.—One of the birds be killed in an earthen vessel over running water. A small quantity of water was placed in an earthenware dish, and one of the birds was killed over the dish in such a way that the blood dripped into the water. The water was needed, as there would not have been sufficient blood in the bird for the seven sprinklings which were to be made. It was to be *running,* literally, *living,* water; that is, fresh water taken from a fountain or a running stream, in order that it might be as pure as possible. Symbolically, the cleansing power of water as well as of blood is indicated.

Ver. 6.— As for the living bird, he shall take it. The wings and tail of the bird were extended, and in this position it was dipped into the blood and water in the earthenware dish, and with it, the bunch made up of cedar, hyssop, and scarlet wool.

Ver. 7.—And he shall sprinkle upon him that is to be cleansed from the leprosy seven times. It is not certain whether the seven sprinklings were made upon the forehead of the person to be cleansed, or on the back of his hand. The feathers of the bird and the bunch of hyssop would be specially instrumental in the seven sprinklings. **And shall pronounce him clean.** Having assured himself that he was healed (ver. 3), the priest now pronounces him to be clean. He looses as well as binds. It had been his office to declare the man a leper, and thereby to shut him out from the people of the Lord (ch. xiii. 8, 15, 22, 25, 36, 44, 46). Now he pronounces him to be no leper, and therefore, after some further ceremonies, readmits him (vers. 8, 20, 31). **And shall let the living bird loose into the open field.** The symbolism of the two birds, which has been much misinterpreted, is essentially the same as that of the two goats on the day of atonement, though each ceremony has its distinctive features. The *killing* of the living bird was not a true sacrifice, as was the offering of the goat to Jehovah, but by its death it represented the state in which the leper had legally been, and to which he would have been physically reduced had not a remedy been found. The deathly and unclean state of the leper having been symbolically transferred from the dead bird to the living bird by the latter's being sprinkled in the former's blood, the living bird stands in the position of the scapegoat, on whom the sins of the people were laid. The bird is then *let loose into the open field;* literally, *upon the face of the field;* and it flies off, carrying with it the leper's uncleanness, and assuring him by every forward movement that it makes that the living death has passed from him, just as each step of the scapegoat appeared to the Israelites to remove their sins from them. A large number of commentators, on the other hand, consider the released bird to symbolize the health and freedom now given back to the leper, and they dwell on the rapid and uncontrolled movement of birds as being peculiarly suitable for representing this recovered liberty. But this interpretation, to which there are many objections, appears to be altogether incompatible with the fact that the same ceremony is used in the cleansing of the leprous house, whereas the house could certainly not be represented as " recovered to unrestrained liberty" (Lange). The common patristic view, that the two birds represent the two natures of the one Great Sacrifice offered to redeem man from sin, seems to be out of place here.

Ver. 8.—After the healed leper has washed his clothes, and shaved off all his hair, and washed himself with water, so as to leave no

remnant of his former defilement that can be removed, the first stage of his purification is over. He is restored to the camp, but not yet to the sanctuary, nor to his position as head or member of his family. He has still to undergo another week's purgation, and until that time has elapsed he may not live in his tent.

Vers. 9—32.—The ceremonies in the second stage of cleansing, which restored the late outcast to his home and to his covenant-right, were the following; 1. At the end of seven days he repeated the process of washing, shaving, and bathing. 2. On the eighth day he brought a lamb for a trespass offering, a log of oil, a meat offering, a sin offering, and a burnt offering. 3. The priest that officiated at the cleansing presented him and his offerings at the door of the tabernacle. 4. He offered the trespass offering and the log of oil for him. 5. He slew the trespass offering and put some of the blood of it on different parts of the man's body. 6. He poured some of the oil into his left hand, and having sprinkled some of it seven times before the Lord, he placed some of it on those parts of the man's body on which the blood had been placed, and poured the rest upon his head. 7. He offered the sin offering, the burnt offering, and the meat offering.

Ver. 9.—**But it shall be on the seventh day.** The pause for seven days, followed by placing the blood on the tip of the right ear, and on the thumb of the right hand, and on the great toe of the right foot, and the subsequent anointing with oil, irresistibly call to mind the ceremonies of the consecration of priests (ch. viii. 35, 23, 24, 12, 30), and no doubt they are intended to do so. The whole nation was in a sense a priestly nation, and the restoration of the lapsed member to his rights was therefore a quasi-consecration.

Ver. 10.—**On the eighth day he shall take two he lambs without blemish, and one ewe lamb of the first year without blemish, and three tenth deals of fine flour.** Every sacrifice is to be provided and offered by the restored leper, except the peace offering. It is certainly singular that the peace offering should be omitted, and that the trespass offering should be required. The former fact may be accounted for by the supposition that though the peace offering was not required, the late leper was, after his other sacrifices, put in a position where he might offer it when he would of his own free will. But the requirement of the trespass offering is more difficult to explain. What wrong had the leper done? and what satisfaction had he to make? The usual answer to this question is that he had wronged Jehovah in that, however involuntarily, he had failed

to bring him the offerings and service which he would have brought had he not been excluded from the camp. But this is a very forced explanation, and it is incompatible with other parts of the Law. For the leper was not the only unclean person who, owing to his uncleanness, was prevented from offering his gifts and worship at the tabernacle or temple. The woman who had an issue of blood for twelve years (Luke viii. 43) during that time would have been excluded from the sanctuary. But no trespass offering is required of those that have been unclean through issues. We must, therefore, look for some other explanation of the requirement in the case of the cleansed leper. And a simpler one is at hand. Leprosy was the type of sin—of all sin whatsoever. When, therefore, the expiatory sacrifices were demanded, both kinds—the trespass offering and the sin offering—had to be offered, because expiation had to be made for the uncleanness which represented all unrighteousness—trespasses as well as sins. It might be that the man had not committed a trespass; he might also not have committed sin; but he had been stricken with the foul disease which symbolized both one and the other, and therefore he had to offer on his cleansing the sacrifice appropriate to each. There is a difference in the ritual of the trespass offering in the present case, intended perhaps to distinguish it from those trespass offerings which were made when a man had in his mind a certain wrong or injury which he had committed, and for which he wished to make compensation. On this occasion (1) the animal presented was not required to be of a particular value, as in the ordinary trespass offerings; (2) it was waved, whereas the ordinary trespass offerings were not waved; (3) it was waved by the priest, whereas other wave offerings were waved not by the priest, but by the offerer, whose hands were guided by the priests. Nor (4) did the offering of oil accompany the presentation of other trespass offerings. For whatever reason it be, the most characteristic feature of the sacrificial cleansing of the leper is the trespass offering, and the way that it was dealt with.

Ver. 12.—**The log of oil,** amounting to something more than half a pint, is waved by the priest, together with the lamb for the trespass offering, as **a wave offering before the Lord,** in order that a special consecration may be given them. They thus become qualified for the purposes for which they are presently used.

Ver. 14.—**And the priest shall take** some **of the blood of the trespass offering, and the priest shall put it upon the tip of the right ear of him that is to be cleansed.** The

Mishna describes the ceremony as follows :— "The leper stands before the trespass offering, lays his hand upon it and kills it. Two priests catch up the blood one in a vessel, the other in his hand. He who catches it up in the vessel goes and throws it on the side of the altar, and he who catches it in his hand goes and stands before the leper. And the leper who had previously bathed in the court of the lepers, goes and stands in the gate of Nicanor. Rabbi Jehudah says he needs not bathe. He thrusts in his head (viz. into the great court, which he may not yet enter), and the priest puts of the blood upon the tip of his ear; he thrusts in his hand, and he puts it upon the thumb of his hand; he thrusts in his foot, and he puts it upon the great toe of his foot" ('Negaim,' xiv. 7, quoted by Edersheim, 'Temple Service,' ch. xviii.). No doubt, the ear, the thumb, and the great toe are selected for the purpose of showing, as in the case of the consecration of the priest, that the senses and the active powers of the restored Israelite must be dedicated henceforth to God.

Vers. 15—18.—**And the priest shall take some of the log of oil, and pour it into the palm of his own left hand.** This ceremony is altogether peculiar to this purification. The joint use of blood and oil is not singular (see ch. viii. 30), but elsewhere there is no **sprinkling of the oil . . . seven times before the Lord,** and in the consecration of priests there was no anointing of the different members with oil as well as with blood. The Mishna (as before cited) continues the description of the ceremony as follows:— "The priest now takes from the log of oil and pours it into the palm of his colleague, though if he poured it into his own it were valid. He dips his finger and sprinkles seven times towards the holy of holies,

dipping each time he sprinkles. He goes before the leper, and on the spot where he had put the blood he puts the oil, as it is written, 'Upon the blood of the trespass offering.' And the remnant of the oil that is in the priest's hand, he pours on the head of him that is cleansed, for an atonement; if he so puts it, he is atoned for, but if not, he is not atoned for. So Rabbi Akiba. Rabbi Jochanan, the son of Nuri, saith, This is only the remnant of the ordinance, whether it be done or not, the atonement is made; but they impute it to him (the priest), as if he had not made atonement." The double sprinkling with blood and oil betokened dedication as in the case of the priests, the blood specially denoting reconciliation, and the oil the strengthening power of God by which the new life was to be led.

Vers. 19, 20.—**The priest shall offer the sin offering.** The sin offering is due, according to the regulation given in ch. v. 3, in consequence of the man having been in a state of uncleanness. It is followed by the burnt offering and the meat offering, and then the man is restored to his state of legal cleanness, and of communion with God as well as with his fellows.

Vers. 21—32.—**And if he be poor, and cannot get so much.** The concession to poverty consists in the substitution of two turtledoves, or two young pigeons, for the two lambs required for the sin offering and the burnt offering, and one tenth-deal of flour for three tenth-deals of flour in the meat offering. But no difference is made as to the lamb required for the trespass offering, or the log of oil. These must be provided by the poor as well as by the rich, and the ceremonies used at their offering must be the same for poor and rich, as they are essential to the rite.

HOMILETICS.

Vers. 1—32.—*The cleansing of the leper represents the absolution of the sinner,* as his exclusion from the camp represented spiritual excommunication.

I. THE LAW OF CHRISTIAN EXCOMMUNICATION AND ABSOLUTION. "I will give unto thee the keys of the kingdom of heaven: and whatsoever thou shalt bind on earth shall be bound in heaven: and whatsoever thou shalt loose on earth shall be loosed in heaven" (Matt. xvi. 19). "Whatsoever ye shall bind on earth shall be bound in heaven: and whatsoever ye shall loose on earth shall be loosed in heaven" (Matt. xviii. 18). "Whose soever sins ye remit, they are remitted; and whose soever sins ye retain, they are retained" (John xx. 23).

II. THE USE OF KEYS. 1. To admit. 2. To shut out. 3. To readmit. 1. The spiritual keys are used by God's ministers for the purpose of admission, whenever they introduce into Christ's kingdom, the Church, a new member by the use of the initiatory rite of baptism, which they are commissioned to employ for that end. 2. They are used for the purpose of exclusion, whenever the Church, or any duly constituted section of the Church, following the example of the Corinthian Church, as instructed and guided by St. Paul, shuts out from its fold one who has been guilty of gross immorality (1 Cor. v.) or of depraving the faith (1 Tim. i. 20), and continues obstinate in his sin. 3. They are used for the purpose of readmission, when the Church has become satisfied that the sinner whom she had excluded from her fold has ceased to be a sinner, and thereupon, like the Corinthian Church, once more under the direction of St. Paul, "forgives him and comforts him, lest such an one should be swallowed up with overmuch sorrow," and confirms its love towards him (2 Cor. ii. 7, 8).

III. THE FORMS FOR ADMISSION, EXCLUSION, AND READMISSION IN THE OLD AND NEW DISPENSATIONS. The form of admission into covenant with himself is, as we should expect, fixed by Divine authority in both dispensations. In the old dispensation it was circumcision. " Every man child among you shall be circumcised. And ye shall circumcise the flesh of your foreskin; and it shall be a token of the covenant betwixt me and you. And he that is eight days old shall be circumcised among you, every man child in your generations, . . . and my covenant shall be in your flesh for an everlasting covenant " (Gen. xvii. 10—13). In the New Testament it is baptism in the Name of the Father, and of the Son, and of the Holy Ghost. "Go ye therefore, and teach (make disciples of) all nations, baptizing them in the Name of the Father, and of the Son, and of the Holy Ghost " (Matt. xxviii. 19). " Ye are all the children of God by faith in Christ Jesus. For as many of you as have been baptized into Christ have put on Christ " (Gal. iii. 26, 27). These forms are unchangeable by any human authority.

The form of exclusion from the covenant people was not so definitely fixed under the old as the new dispensation. In the former it is ordained that for various transgressions a soul shall be cut off. " The uncircumcised man child whose flesh of his foreskin is not circumcised, that soul shall be cut off from his people; he hath broken my covenant" (Gen. xvii. 14). " If a man shall lie with a woman having her sickness, . . . both of them shall be cut off from among their people " (ch. xx. 18). But it is only in the case of leprosy that the method of exclusion is given in detail. There we have seen that it is to consist of a careful examination on the part of God's priest, and a pronunciation by him of the undoubted existence of the uncleanness in the person suspected, after which the latter is to exhibit all the signs of one mourning for himself as dead, to dwell alone, and " without the camp shall his habitation be " (ch. xiii. 45, 46). So in the New Testament the power of " binding" as well as of " loosing," and of " retaining" bound as well as of " forgiving," is granted, and the obligation of exerting this power is involved in its grant; but no especial form by which it is to be done is given. It is only in the case of the incestuous Corinthian that we have an example of the way in which St. Paul judges that it shall be done. From thence it appears that the decision is to be passed by the chief Church officer, in the name of Jesus Christ, and promulgated by the assembled Church, the result being that the offender is translated from the kingdom of Christ to the outer world, the kingdom of Satan, " for the destruction of the flesh, that the spirit may be saved in the day of the Lord Jesus " (1 Cor. v. 3—5).

Nor is there any form definitely appointed either in the old or in the new dispensation for the readmission of those that had been cast out. No doubt in the old dispensation, it was always effected by the means of sacrifice, but we have a definite statement of the form adopted only in the case of reconciliation after leprosy. This form we have seen to be very elaborate and significative. Similarly in the new dispensation, we find no form authoritatively given for the restoration of the penitent; only we have, as before, the instance of the incestuous Corinthian, from which we learn that after sufficient punishment such a one is to be forgiven and taken back to the love of the brethren; and we have the general principle laid down elsewhere, " If a man be overtaken in a fault, ye which are spiritual, restore such an one in the spirit of meekness; considering thyself, lest thou also be tempted " (Gal. vi. 1).

The fact of a divinely authorized form being given for admission into covenant with God, but none for exclusion from it by excommunication or readmission to it by absolution, is significant. The first is under the new dispensation a sacrament ordained of Christ; the others are ecclesiastical rites, valuable for the well-being of the Church, but not appointed by its Founder as a necessary condition of its existence.

IV. THE OFFICE OF THE PRIEST IN CLEANSING. 1. He did not cure the leprosy.

"If the plague of leprosy be healed in the leper" (ver. 3), then the priest shall begin the cleansing ceremonies. The healing of the disease was the work of God. 2. The action of the priest is necessary for the cleansing. If the *healing* is the work of God, the *cleansing* is the work of the priest. It is a complex ceremonial act, the result of which is not to deliver from the leprosy, but to serve as an assurance to the man himself and to the whole community that he is delivered from it, and therefore fit to be reinstated, and by that act reinstated, in the position of full communion which he had lost. So with absolution; it is God alone that forgives and heals sin. But after this has been accomplished, still it is necessary that a solemn ecclesiastical ceremony should reinstate in the communion of the faithful one who has been formally severed from it. And where the formal act of severance has not taken place, but a man's distressed conscience tells him that he has separated himself from God, and can hardly allow him to believe in his forgiveness, the solemn declaration of that forgiveness by God's minister serves as an assurance to the trembling soul, and restores to him the sense of peace which was lost.

HOMILIES BY VARIOUS AUTHORS.

The cleansing of sin as illustrated in the cleansing of the leper. Ch. xiv.; cf. 2 Kings v.; Matt. viii. 1—4; Luke v. 12—15. We have seen the possibility of a cure of leprosy in the directions for its diagnosis given to the priests. The cured leper had also to be cleansed before admitted to the society of the faithful. In this chapter we have the cleansing of the leper detailed. In this we are to discern the cleansing of sin.

Naaman's case is instructive upon this point. He was cured by Divine power. But he was not ceremonially cleansed or received into the fellowship of the Church of God. In his case the two elements of cure and cleansing were separated. But when our Lord directed the cured leper to go and offer for his cleansing the gift that Moses commanded for a testimony unto them, the elements were united. In the case of the cure of the leprosy of sin and its concomitant, the cleansing, the Great Physician who cures and the Priest who cleanses are one. It is our Divine Saviour who accomplishes both.

I. WE MUST NOT CONFOUND THE CURE WITH THE CLEANSING OF SIN. The cure of sin is the sanctification of the inward nature, the imparting of the principle of righteousness, the regeneration of the once unholy nature. This is quite distinct from the cleansing which proceeds from the blood of Jesus Christ. In the latter case there is a justification through faith in his blood, so that we are accepted as well as pardoned on the ground of his merits. The one is a work of God *in* us, the other is a work of God *on* us. We are not accepted because we are regenerated; we are accepted "in the Beloved." The leper was not accepted on the ground of his cure, but on the ground of his sacrifice. The ritual of the leper is, therefore, admirably adapted to keep the two ideas distinct of justification and sanctification.

II. THE RESTORATION OF THE LEPER EMBRACED TWO STAGES, WHICH HAVE THEIR COUNTERPART IN THE EXPERIENCE OF THE SINNER. These stages are, first, the restoration of the leper to the society of the living, and, secondly, his restoration to the society of the saints.

1. *Restoration to the society of the living.* The priest was directed to go to the leper outside the camp, and if he was satisfied about his cure, then he was to receive on the leper's behalf "two live birds, and cedar wood, and scarlet, and hyssop." One of these is to be killed in an earthen vessel over running water, and its blood mingled with the water in the vessel. Of the cedar wood, scarlet wool, and hyssop the priest is to make a brush, in which he is temporarily to tie the remaining live bird, and having dipped them in the blood and water, he is to sprinkle therewith the leper seven times, pronouncing him clean, and then let the live bird free. The leper is then to wash his clothes, shave off all his hair, wash himself carefully, and come into the camp, waiting, however, a week before taking up his permanent abode in his own tent.

Now, it seems clear that in this first stage of the leper's restoration the live bird, baptized with water and blood, and then let loose to join its mates in the open fields, was a symbol of the healed leper, now to be restored to the fellowship of men. It has been, indeed, said that the live bird here is parallel to the live goat on the Day of Atonement, and should rather be supposed to carry the leper's sin away. But, inasmuch as the live bird here receives a similar baptism to the leper himself, the first interpretation is preferable. Living water and blood, therefore, are the elements of the leper's purification—symbols of the Spirit and the blood of Jesus Christ. The brush of hyssop was the means by which these were applied to the leper, and might fittingly represent the Word of God, immortal like the cedar, humiliating like the hyssop, and invigorating like the "coccus-wool," by which the atonement and Spirit of Christ are applied to the sinful soul. It is thus by the blood of Jesus and the Spirit of Jesus that the soul, dead through the leprosy of sin, is restored to the society of the living. "And you hath he quickened, who were dead in trespasses and sins" (Eph. ii. 1).

2. *Restoration to the society of the saints.* After seven days' sojourn in the camp, but not in his own tent, the leper was allowed to approach the tabernacle with two he-lambs without blemish, one ewe-lamb without blemish of the first year, and three tenth-deals of fine flour for a meat offering, mingled with oil, and one log of oil. These were to be used as a trespass offering, a sin offering, and a burnt offering. These suggest respectively a sense of *unprofitableness* or shortcoming, *atonement,* and *personal consecration.* The blood of the trespass offering is to be applied to the right ear, thumb of right hand, and great toe of the right foot, and the oil of consecration to be added thereto. This corresponds exactly to the consecration of the priests (ch. viii.). It suggests that it is *out of a sense of past unprofitableness that future consecration comes* (cf. Luke xvii. 5—10). It is when we realize how we have wronged our Lord that we are prepared to live, not unto ourselves, but unto him who died for us, as our atoning Sacrifice, and rose again (2 Cor. v. 14, 15). In case of the poverty of the leper, he is instructed to bring one lamb for the trespass offering, with turtle-doves or young pigeons, in place of two additional lambs, for the sin offering and burnt offering, and a smaller meat offering. But the emphasis being laid on the trespass offering is surely to show that a sinner, when quickened by the Lord, is to sincerely lament the profitless, isolated life he lived, and to resolve to dedicate himself with full purpose of heart to the service of the Saviour whose blood has taken away his sin. The saints are those who begin in a sense of trespass a life of grateful devotion.

III. MAN'S HOME IS TO BE CLEANSED AND RESTORED IN THE SAME SPIRIT AS HIMSELF. The priest is directed to investigate a plagued house, and if by the use of prompt measures the plague is stayed and extirpated, then the first part of the ritual is to be carried out. One live bird is to be killed over the running water, and the house sprinkled with the blood and water as before, and then the other live bird liberated. Thus was the restoration of the house to the society of its mates, so to speak, symbolized. We have already taken this to indicate the careful purification of our environment, and there is no more important duty attaching to the religious man. Atonement is due, not only for the sin as it affects the person, but for sin in its ravages in the world. This blighted world of ours has need of atoning blood, and purification even by fire, before it can be restored to the favour of God. Christ has consecrated it through his blood, and his providence and Spirit will yet make the requisite arrangement for its complete purification and restoration to the holy. —R. M. E.

Vers. 1—20.—*Restoration suggestions.* The ceremonies here enjoined in the event of leprosy being healed suggest four things.

I. AN INTERESTING PASSAGE IN THE LIFE OF OUR LORD. Our Saviour's experiences may be divided into: (1) his sufferings and death; (2) his life (and example); (3) his works. Of these the last may be the least important, but they will never be *unimportant.* They will always remain one strong, convincing proof of his Godhead. And of these works the healing of leprosy—incurable by human art—was one of the most decisive. In this work of mercy, more vividly than in any other, we see him before us as the Divine Healer of the sin-smitten heart of man. Great interest belongs, therefore, to the incident related in Luke v. 12—15. And in the instruction given in ver. 14 we see our Divine Lord: (1) mindful of the Law of Moses, which he ever honoured (Matt. iii. 15; v. 17); (2) while desirous of avoiding a noisy and hurtful notoriety, taking due measures to establish the reality of his work.

II. THE CONSIDERATION WE OWE TO OUR FELLOW-MEN. In virtue of the Divine precept the leper might not enter human society. But this was not the only ground of exclusion; by reason of the character of his malady he was wholly unfit to enter. Once exiled, therefore, he might not return until every guarantee had been given that he was "whole," until numerous and prolonged ceremonies of cleansing had removed all stigma from him, and made him likely to receive a cordial welcome back. Hence the elaborate ceremonial of the text: (1) priestly examination (vers. 2, 3); (2) the ceremony of the two birds (vers. 4—7); (3) personal ablution (ver. 8); (4) further exclusion for a week (ver. 8); (5) additional ablution, etc. (ver. 9); (6) offerings at the altar, attended with peculiar rites with the blood and oil (vers. 10—20). When by any folly or guilt of ours we have incurred the distrust or dislike of our brethren, it is due to them that we should give them every possible guarantee of our "cleanness," our integrity of heart and life, before they abandon their suspicion and give us again their cordial confidence. Society has a right to require that the man whom it has necessarily shunned is pure of his moral and spiritual malady. We may be unable to gain any certificate of character, but we may, to regain confidence and readmission to human fellowship, (1) show ourselves as humble, earnest worshippers in the house of the Lord; (2) seek the open confidence of the acknowledged servants of Christ; (3) give the pledge of a scrupulously virtuous life, that we are really "washed and sanctified . . . by the Spirit of our God" (1 Cor. vi. 11).

III. THE OBLIGATIONS OF OFFICE. Those who hold high office have sometimes uninviting duties to discharge. The priests of Israel held honourable rank in the nation; doubtless they received a large share of public deference, and were regarded as those who occupied an enviable position. But their duties embraced some offices from which the humblest in the land might shrink. They had to make a most careful examination of the man who believed himself healed of leprosy. Probably, in their eagerness to return to the camp, these afflicted ones often sought readmission when the disease was still upon them. But the priest must examine all who came, clean or unclean. Those who now hold honourable positions in society (the minister, the medical man, etc.) must hold themselves ready, not only to do those duties which are inviting and congenial, but those also which are unpleasant and even painful, whether to the flesh or to the spirit.

IV. THE OUTLOOK OF HUMAN MISERY. What was the prospect of the exiled leper? Human art had given him up as incurable, and human fellowship had cast him out as unworthy. What could he hope for? There were only two possible remedies—a Divine cure or the grave; the one blessed enough but sadly improbable, the other sad enough but a welcome certainty. If for a while we look at leprosy as the picture, not of human sin, but of human misery, we may be reminded that, for a Christian man, there are two remedies: (1) deliverance in time from affliction (Ps. xxx. 11); (2) comfort in affliction during life, and then "the glory which shall be revealed" (Rom. viii. 18). Though the night of weeping be life-long, "yet joy cometh in the morning" of the everlasting day.—C.

Vers. 4—9.—*Admission (or readmission)*. When leprosy had departed from the flesh, he who had been, but no longer remained, a leper was, in the sight of Jehovah and of his people, still ceremonially unclean. He was in a bodily condition which made him *readmissible* to Divine and human fellowship, but he must first "be cleansed" (ver. 4) before he would be *readmitted*. The ceremonies here prescribed give a picture of our readmission to the favour of God and the fellowship of his people.

I. SACRIFICE OF ANOTHER'S LIFE. As a "clean bird" (ver. 4) was taken and its blood was shed (ver. 5), as the life-blood of the pure and innocent creature was poured out that the leper might be clean and pure in the sight of God, so is the life-blood of the spotless Lamb shed for us. There must be for our acceptance and admission, or readmission after backsliding, a "sacrifice for sin."

II. PERSONAL APPLICATION OF THAT SACRIFICE. "He shall sprinkle upon him that is to be cleansed . . . seven times" (ver. 7). "The living bird" was to be "dipped in the blood of the bird that was killed." Here is the truth that if the "blood of Christ" is to be effectual for our salvation, it *must be applied* to our individual conscience. We who seek to be cleansed from all iniquity and condemnation, must ourselves personally apply for mercy through the shed blood of the Redeemer. By an act of living faith we must bathe in the " fountain opened for sin and for uncleanness."

III. PERSONAL PUTTING AWAY OF DEFILEMENT. The leper was to "wash his clothes, and shave off all his hair, and wash himself in water, that he may be clean." And again, after a week's interval, was to shave and to wash, removing all his hair, even to the eyebrows (ver. 9); everything about him that could in any possible way be defiled by the plague was to be carefully removed. So, if we are to be admitted (or readmitted) to God's favour and man's communion, we must deliberately put away from ourselves, from heart and life, every evil way, everything which is, or may be, tainted with iniquity (2 Tim. ii. 19).

IV. DIVINE ACKNOWLEDGMENT OF OUR INTEGRITY. Everything here pointed to the fact that the Divine Ruler of Israel was prepared to acknowledge the cleanness of the leper. The water was to be " running water " (ver. 5)—pure, as opposed to that which was stagnant and foul; "cedar wood " was to be used (ver. 6), type of that which is fragrant and healthful; the " scarlet" wool (ver. 6) hinted the red and healthy blood, which had been impure but was so no longer; "hyssop" (ver. 6) was suggestive of fragrance; but that which, above all, was indicative of God's acknowledgment of the wholeness of the leper was the action respecting the living bird: that was released, let "loose into the open field " (ver. 7). This either signified that the uncleanness of the leper was borne away on the wings of the bird, where it should never be found again (a similar institution to the scapegoat, ch. xvi. 22, 23), or that the leper was thenceforth free to go whithersoever he pleased. Either way, it expressed symbolically the truth that there was reinstatement for the man who had been healed in the privileges he had forfeited. We have in the Scriptures every possible assurance that "repentance toward God, and faith toward our Lord Jesus Christ," are followed by fulness of Divine favour. The returned prodigal has the kiss of reconciliation, the ring and robe of honour, and the feast of joy. " Being justified by faith, we have peace with God . . . and rejoice in hope of the glory of God " (Rom. v. 1, 2). The soul that is healed of its sore disease is pronounced clean in the sight of God, and is free of its Father's house, to enter its many rooms and partake of its many joys.—C.

Vers. 10—20.—*Final rites of readmission.* By the series of final rites of restoration recorded in these verses, the leper once more took his place as one of a holy nation admitted to the presence of God: he was "presented before the Lord at the door of the tabernacle," etc. (ver. 10). His formal acceptance at the house of the Lord, and entrance again on the privileges of the peculiar people, reminds us that our entrance, whether in the first instance or after backsliding and return, upon the fulness of sacred privilege must be—

I. ATTENDED WITH HUMILITY. The leper was to bring his sin offering, which must be slain in the holy place (vers. 13, 19). Over the head of the animal he was to confess his sin, and then, with his guilt thus transferred, the blood of the sin offering atoned for past wrong. All approaches to God by the human spirit should be accompanied with a sense of unworthiness. " Blessed are the poor in spirit: for theirs is the kingdom of heaven " (Matt. v. 3).

II. IN THE SPIRIT OF CONSECRATION. The leper was to bring his burnt offering as well as his sin offering (vers. 13, 19, 20). By this he symbolically presented himself wholly unto the Lord, laid himself on the altar of sacred service. When we turn, or return, unto God it must be in the spirit of full, unreserved dedication. We are to " present our bodies a living sacrifice, holy, acceptable unto God, our reasonable (*i.e.* rational, spiritual) service " (Rom. xii. 1).

III. IN THE SPIRIT OF THANKFUL JOY. The leper was to bring "three tenth deals of fine flour for a meat offering, mingled with oil " (vers. 10, 20). This was a sacrifice of praise and thanksgiving, rendered under a sense of deep indebtedness for Divine bounty. It was certainly suitable enough in the case of the leper, whose malady had been removed by the healing hand of God. Nor is the consciousness of our deep indebtedness, the presentation of our utmost thanks, one whit less becoming, less demanded and required of God, when we come to his house, or to the table of the Lord, after months or years, or (it may be) a life of absence, negligence, estrangement. It should be with hearts overflowing with holy gratitude and sacred joy that we present ourselves before him.

IV. WITH A SENSE OF GOD'S FULL ACCEPTANCE OF OUR WHOLE HEART AND LIFE. There was one very significant ceremony through which the leper who was being 'eansed had to pass: the priest was to put some of the blood of the trespass offering upon the tip of the right ear, and the thumb of the right hand, and the great toe of the right foot (ver. 14). Afterwards the priest did the same thing with the oil, pouring the remnant of the oil upon the leper's head (vers. 17, 18). The application of the blood of atonement to these bodily extremities indicated God's acceptance of the leper throughout the entire man; every part of him was now holy unto the Lord; even every part of that bodily frame which had been the very picture and type of all uncleanness. The application of the oil denoted that the leper was thenceforth to regard himself as God's accepted servant in every sphere of human action; he was to be: 1. A reverent waiter and watcher before God, eagerly learning his will. 2. An active, industrious minister, doing his work in every way open to him. 3. A conscientious exemplar, walking in the ways of the Lord blameless. We, too, returning unto God, pleading the blood of the Lamb, offering ourselves unto him, reverently rejoicing in his mercy, are to understand and realize that (1) God accepts us unreservedly as his own, and (2) expects us to be eager to serve him in every open way—*learning, labouring, living* to his praise.—C.

Vers. 21—32.—*Divine considerateness.* If there had been one parenthetical verse introduced or added intimating that Divine allowance would be made for the poor, we should have thought that sufficient for the purpose. But we have more than that here. We have legislation for the poor fully stated, and the whole body of injunctions restated for their especial benefit (vers. 21—32). This brings out into bold relief God's mindfulness of the peculiar necessities of men—his Divine considerateness. We see illustrations of this in—

I. SACRIFICES BROUGHT TO HIS ALTAR. Notably this kindly provision for the poor in the case of the healed leper; but not this alone (see ch. v. 7; xii. 8).

II. GIFTS BROUGHT TO HIS TREASURY. The widow with her two mites cast in more, weighed in the balances of heaven, than did the rich with their abundance (Mark vii. 41—44; see 2 Cor. viii. 12).

III. OUR POWERS IN CHRIST'S SERVICE. To him who having received two talents gained two others beside them, was accorded by the Lord, when he returned and reckoned with his servants, approval quite as cordial as that rendered to him who having received five talents gained five talents more (Matt. xxv. 19—23). Equally cordial would have been the welcome to him who had been entrusted with only one, if he had gained one talent beside that.

IV. OUR STRUGGLE WITH TEMPTATION. When the agonizing Master returned and found those he left to watch and pray "asleep, for their eyes were heavy," he gently rebuked them; but he considerately extenuated their fault by saying, "The spirit indeed is willing, but the flesh is weak" (Matt. xxvi. 40, 41). "He knoweth our frame; he remembereth that we are dust."

V. OUR ENDURANCE OF EVIL. God sends us privation, sickness, disappointment, perplexity, loss, bereavement, exceeding great sorrows, burdens grievous to be borne; he calls upon us to "endure as seeing him who is invisible," to be "in subjection to the Father of spirits." He expects that we shall not repine and rebel, but submit and serve. Yet he who knows all men, and who knows "what is in man" (John ii. 25), who created us and made us what we are, understands and weighs our peculiar personal difficulties, temperaments, dispositions; he knows how much we strive to yield and acquiesce, and "judges righteous judgment." He is *just, yet merciful,* we say. We may also say, He is just, *and therefore* merciful. He has the requisite justice of Divine considerateness.

Let us—1. Take heart to serve so gracious and considerate a Lord. 2. Feel impelled to serve him all the more faithfully and devotedly because he is so worthy and righteous a Master. 3. Try to copy his grace and his righteousness in our dealings with our fellows (Luke vi. 36).—C.

Vers. 1—20.—*Thorough purification.* Spiritual disease is often neglected by persons who are extremely anxious respecting some disease of the physical frame. For the former they seek no remedy, and display no concern as to its ultimate issue, whereas the latter is viewed with unceasing distress. Would that every spiritual leper entertained just conceptions regarding his state! The ceremonies of this chapter are pregnant with interest for us to-day. Two stages in the leper's cleansing are set before us.

I. THE RETURN TO THE CAMP. 1. The supposition that the leper might recover from his leprosy and be clean shows man's superiority to inanimate nature. When endeavours are being made to confound matter and mind, and to reduce man to a level with the earth on which he lives, it is not unworthy of notice that the legislator here marks a vital distinction between a man and a dwelling. The latter, if on investigation pronounced utterly unclean, was destroyed (ver. 45), and so with garments (ch. xiii. 52), but the leprous man ever contained possibilities of recovery. Let us hold fast to the truth here imaged, and delight in the thought that no sinner is beyond hope of amendment. 2. As the priest journeyed outside the camp to the leper (ver. 3), we are reminded of him who "suffered without the camp," who in his condescending love left his Father's throne to dwell with the outcasts of earth, and who in his abode with men selected not the richest and purest, but the poor and the sinful, as the recipients of his intimacy and favour. 3. The death of the one bird showed forth the condition from which, by God's grace, the leper had been rescued; the flight of the other bird, previously dipped in the blood, symbolized the enjoyment of life granted through the death of the appointed victim. How aptly does this apply to our deliverance through Jesus Christ, so that "we have passed from death unto life"! Delight in our present position should be combined with thankful remembrance of the means by which it has been secured to us. 4. The concomitants indicated the completeness of the new life received. There is no reason to reject the general interpretation that the cedar wood was an emblem of uncorruptness, the scarlet wool or braid of freshness and fulness of life, and the hyssop with its detergent properties of cleanness. These were employed in the preparation of the "water for separation" (Numb. xix.). Jesus Christ came that we might "have life, and have it more abundantly." He brought "life and incorruption to light through the gospel." He quickens those "dead through trespasses and sins." Life that invigorates the entire spirit is his "free gift." 5. What trouble was necessary, and would be willingly incurred, in order to regain temporal advantages! Unless cleansed by ablution of himself and clothes, and the removal of hair from the head, no entrance into the assembly of his brethren was permissible. Yet how readily would all be performed, just as to-day no efforts are deemed too great to allow of participation in valued social or political movements! But for the cleansing from sin any commandment is accounted vexatious! Few care to sacrifice time or labour to become citizens of the heavenly commonwealth.

II. THE RETURN TO THE TENT. 1. The provision for restoring the leper proves that God has no desire to exclude men unnecessarily from religious privileges. The seven days' interval served to guard against a possible error on the part of the priest, and impressed the leper with a deeper conviction of the holiness of God. It is only sin that bars men from the light of God's presence, and only obstinate persistence in sin that need cause despair of forgiveness. "Ye will not come unto me that ye might have life" was our Lord's indictment of men's impenitent folly. 2. See, once more, the function of the priest to appear between man and God. "The priest that maketh him clean shall present the man before the Lord," and "the priest shall make an atonement for him before the Lord." We have our Advocate with the Father, in whose name, and sheltered by whose intercession, we may approach boldly the throne of grace. Hereafter he shall present us holy and without blemish, and unreprovable before him (Col. i. 22; Jude 24). Having Christ to introduce us, who can be afraid? 3. The cleansing not complete without an atonement. All marks of disease may have disappeared, or at least the fear of infection may have vanished, and yet to enter upon the fresh period of existence is not sufficient unless the past transgressions be remembered and atoned for. To forsake sin is well, but, in addition, the sin of the past must be confessed and pardoned. The sacrifice of Jesus Christ enables the sinner to start upon his pilgrimage with shoulders eased from the burden of guilt. A gulf separates him from the land of iniquity and stumbling; he is free to commence again under happier auspices. The old score is wiped out; a clean tablet marks the returned prodigal's position. 4. The purification must be coextensive with the disease. Leprosy affected the whole man; hence the tips of the ear, the hand, and the foot must be touched with the atoning blood, that all parts may be redeemed from corruption. All spheres of activity must be brought under the power of the cross of Christ. 5. The cleansing becomes a consecration of the entire man. The resemblance of this rite to that enjoined at the setting apart of the priests to their holy office cannot fail to be observed. The leper offered a trespass offering to compensate for breaches of the commandment committed by reason of his absence through sin from the sanctuary, a sin offering because of transgressions inadvertently committed, a burnt offering as an act of individual worship in which there was self-surrender to the Lord, and a meat offering, the natural accompaniment testifying grateful homage. And, besides blood, oil also was sprinkled upon the leper, and poured upon his head, and sprinkled seven times (the covenant number) before the Lord, so that we have here a recognition of the truth that Israel was intended to be a "kingdom of priests." Typical of the sanctification required in the people of God, reaching to every part of their character, until all is brought into captivity to the obedience of Christ. "As ye presented your members servants to uncleanness and to iniquity unto iniquity, even so now present your members servants to righteousness unto sanctification." 6. The consecrated man is fit for the discharge of ordinary duties and the enjoyment of lawful pleasures. After the sacrifices, the man could once more enter his tent and mingle with his family, and pursue his wonted avocation. Jehovah proved himself in these regulations the God of the families of Israel. He protected their relationships and imparted to them his blessing. It is a mistaken idea to place affection for our kindred before love to God. Regard for God is the surest guarantee for the performance of human obligations. Well for the land if this were oftener remembered in the establishment of households and in the contracting of domestic ties!

Conclusion. Only when "clean" could the leper send for the priest. We go to Jesus Christ with all our guilt; he looks upon us and pronounces us clean, he touches us, and lo! we are healed; for there is sanatory power in his look and touch. What the Saviour exemplified when on earth, he is constantly effecting now from heaven.—S. R. A.

Vers. 1—9.—*The cleansing of the leper—ceremonies outside the camp.* As leprosy is evidently a remarkable emblem of sin, so must the cleansing of the leper represent the purification of the sinner, and the laws of the cleansing, the provisions of the gospel. The text brings under our notice—

I. THE CONDITIONS REQUIRED. These were: 1. *That the leprosy be healed.* (1) Healing and cleansing are distinct things. The priest did not heal. Before proceeding to cleanse he had to see that the leprosy was healed (ver. 3). Our Lord healed lepers, and then sent them to the priest to be cleansed (see Matt. viii. 2—4; Mark i. 40—44; Luke v. 12—14; xvii. 14). (2) The gospel of this is that repentance is not salvation. The body may be healed, outward reformation may be considerable, while the heart is morally putrescent (see Matt. xxiii. 25—28). The leper, though healed, unless also cleansed, must not enter the holy place or eat of the holy things. A genuine change of heart will manifest itself in a pure life. When these exist together, fellowship with God is established. 2. *That the priest certify the fact.* (1) "He shall be brought unto the priest," viz. for this purpose. He is brought by his friends, or they apprise the priest of his condition. Those are the true friends of sinners who bring them to Jesus in person or in prayer. (2) "The priest shall go forth out of the camp." This did Jesus, who came to seek and save the lost. The Pharisees found fault with him for mingling with "publicans and sinners" when he acted as the priest among the lepers. (3) The repentance that satisfies Jesus is genuine (see Luke xviii. 10—14). And this he certifies in his offices of cleansing.

II. THE OFFERING MADE. 1. *The sacrifice.* (1) This consisted of two birds. We say "this" in the singular, for the birds must be together viewed as one sacrifice. Unitedly they were intended to prefigure the one true Sacrifice for sins. (2) The birds were "alive," to represent him that "hath life in himself." (3) They were "clean." They might be sparrows or quails—any wild birds of the clean kinds. Cleanness was requisite to foreshadow One whose birth and life were spotlessly pure. 2. *Its treatment.* (1) One bird was killed over running or "living" water, which was the emblem of the living, purifying Spirit of God. Blood and water together flowed from the opened side of Jesus (see John xix. 34, 35; 1 John v. 6, 8). The infinitely superior virtue of the blood of Christ lay in that, being God as well as man, he was able to offer himself *through the eternal Spirit* without spot (Heb. ix. 13, 14). (2) The "living bird" was dipped "in the blood of the bird that was killed," to show that our guilt was laid upon the *soul* of Jesus as well as upon his body. This truth is indeed expressed in the *blood* shed; for the "blood is the life of the flesh." But to impress it upon us it is here presented under another figure (see Isa. liii. 10—12).

III. ITS APPROPRIATION. This was: 1. *Through the sprinkling of blood.* (1) The atonement availed the leper nothing without the application of the blood to his person. So the blood of Christ avails only to those who appropriate its benefits by faith. (2) The blood was sprinkled upon the leper "seven times" to express perfection and sufficiency, and to point to the seventh period or rest of the gospel (Heb. iv. 10), in which the atonement by Christ satisfies all the promises of the types. Then he was pronounced "clean." (3) The next thing was to let the living bird, stained with the blood of that killed in sacrifice, loose in the open field. What a lively picture! As the leper is assured that he is clean, he sees his guilt carried away, and loses sight of it as the bird disappears in the wood. So does Christ bear our sins into oblivion. 2. *Through the washing of water.* (1) The leper was to wash his clothes and appear in clean white linen, the emblem of the "righteousness of the saints." (2) He had also to shave off all his hair, which had been dishonoured by the plague, that a new growth might crown him in purity. (3) He had likewise to wash his flesh; and that too "seven times," to express the thoroughness of his purification (comp. 2 Kings v. 10; also Ps. li. 2). But the true purifier is that sevenfold Spirit of the gospel, issuing as the river of life, from the throne of God and of the Lamb (Rev. v. 6; xxii. 1). 3. *By the ministry of the word.* (1) The blood was sprinkled upon the leper by means of a whisk composed of "cedar wood, and scarlet, and hyssop." A branch of hyssop seems to have been tied to a handle of cedar by a thread of scarlet wool. But the materials used were evidently intended as emblems, else they would not have been so carefully specified. And we find these very materials on another occasion, thrown into the fire of the altar, to be consumed with the red heifer (see Numb. xix. 6). (2) As to the hyssop and cedar, they seem to be, as it were, at the extremes in the kingdom of trees, and so generally represent that kingdom. For Solomon in his wisdom "spake of trees, from the cedar tree that is in Lebanon even unto the hyssop that springeth out of the wall" (1 Kings iv. 33). We know that the servants of God are compared to trees (Ps. i. 3; xcii. 12; Isa. lxi. 3). They are various in their abilities, yet all serviceable as ministers and instruments of the gospel (1 Cor. xii. 21). (3) As to the wool; it is from the fleece of an animal proper for sacrifice, and its colour is that of blood. A cord of the same colour was hung from her window by Rahab, to express faith in the blood of the Passover to protect her and her house from destruction. It would not be lawful in her to sacrifice a lamb and sprinkle its blood; but she did what she might, and expressed her faith by this sign (Josh. iii. 18, 19). The scarlet cord of a common faith in the blood of Christ binds his servants together, and in their unity makes them efficient instruments in carrying his gospel to mankind. (4) If it be asked why should the cedar and scarlet and hyssop be burnt with the red heifer, the answer is that there is a sense in which faithful ministers may be "offered upon the sacrifice and service" of the faith of those they benefit (see Acts ix. 4; 2 Cor. i. 5, 6; iv. 10; Phil. ii. 17; iii. 10; Col. i. 24; 2 Tim. i. 8; ii. 10).—J. A. M.

Vers. 10—32.—*The cleansing of the leper—ceremony in the tabernacle.* The ceremonies for the cleansing of the leper were distributed into two series. The first were conducted "outside the camp." This suggests that the leper must be taken not only as a type of sinners in general, but of the "sinners of the Gentiles" in particular (comp. Heb. xiii. 10—12). The ceremony in the tabernacle, therefore, must refer to the reception of the Gentiles by the gospel into the fellowship of the saints. We notice—

I. THE PRESENTATION. 1. *This took place on the eighth day.* (1) The ceremonies in the camp extended over seven days, on the last of which the leper was then pronounced clean. He was now, therefore, eligible to leave his alienation, and mingle

with the children of Israel as a fellow-citizen. (2) Entering the sanctuary, he came
into Church recognition. For the court of the priests represented the Church in the
visible part (see on ch. viii. 10—12). This was on the eighth day, which, in the
week, corresponds with the first day, a day so memorable for great events of the gospel
that, as the "Lord's day," it came to replace the Jewish "sabbath" (see on ch. ix.
1—7). The Hebrew term for eight (שמנה), *shemenah*, is derived from (שמן) *shemen*, fat
or oil; and the oil and fat so extensively used in connection with the offerings and
baptisms of the Law represented the Spirit of God in his illuminations and joy-
inspiring graces. The *eighth* day, or *day of oil*, was, therefore, appropriately the
emblem of the "days of the Son of man," the dispensations of the Spirit. 2. *He was
introduced by the priest.* (1) He was presented "before the Lord" (ver. 11). As a
commoner might be presented by a peer to a monarch at a *levée*, so was the leper presented by the priest to the Lord, who, in his Shechinah, was enthroned upon the
mercy-seat. So are the spiritual priests of the gospel introduced by the Great High
Priest of our profession (see Heb. x. 21, 22). (2) Being recognized by the King of
glory, he became fit for the best society, and could freely mingle with the congregation
of Israel, or princes of God. So when God accepts the sinner, though he had been a
sinner of the Gentiles, that becomes his passport to the Church (see Acts x. 47).
3. *The leper did not appear empty.* (1) It would have been a departure from all
precedent in the East to be presented to a monarch without bringing gifts. When the
Queen of Sheba came to Solomon, she was laden with rich presents (1 Kings x. 10).
(2) But when we come into the presence of God, what have we to bring? The leper
brought three blemishless lambs; one for a trespass offering, another for a sin offering,
and the third for a burnt offering. He brought also three tenth-deals of fine flour
mingled with oil, for a bread offering, together with a log of oil. And we can bring
Christ, with the Spirit of his grace, the antitypes. (3) But "shall we offer unto the
Lord that which cost us nothing?" There was a commercial value in the gifts of the
leper; but our "Gift" is "unspeakab'e," infinitely above all merchandise, such as we
could never procure for ourselves. With him we must consecrate *ourselves*, and our
property "as God may prosper us" (Rom. xii. 1; 1 Cor. xvi. 2).

II. THE CEREMONIES OF THE PRESENTATION. 1. *The sacrifices were of all the kinds.*
(1) The lamb for the trespass offering. This was to make atonement for *transgression*,
in order to *justification*. (2) The ewe-lamb for a sin offering. This was to make
atonement for *impurity*, in order to *sanctification*. (3) The burnt offering, to make
atonement for *irreverences* and *imperfections* in *adoration*. And with this was associated the bread offering, to express *gratitude* and *communion*. (4) The order is
admirable. When our trespasses are *forgiven*, and our hearts *cleansed* from sin, then
are we in the moral state to *adore* with *gratitude*. 2. *The baptisms were ample.*
(1) The washings at the laver in the tabernacle appear to have been exclusively those
of the sacrifices and priests. The baptisms of the Israelites were in their dwellings
(Luke xi. 38). The leper was washed with water outside the camp. Cornelius and
his company, in whom the kingdom of heaven was opened to the Gentiles by Peter's
key, received the baptism of the Holy Ghost *before* they had any *visible* Church
recognition (Acts x. 44—48). (2) The leper's baptisms of blood began outside the
camp. The blood of the bird was there seven times sprinkled upon the leper. But
now, in the tabernacle, he is again sprinkled with the blood of the trespass offering.
It was put on the tip of his right ear, to engage him in future to hear the Law of God;
on the thumb of his right hand, to engage him to do the will of God; and on the great
toe of his right foot, to engage him to walk in his holy ways. (3) As there was no
baptism of water ministered to the leper in the tabernacle, so was there no baptism of
oil ministered to him outside the camp. Coming into the sanctuary, he sees the oil
first "sprinkled seven times before the Lord" (ver. 16). Then oil was put upon him
over the blood on the tip of his right ear, the thumb of his right hand, and the great
toe of his right foot (ver. 17). The remnant of the oil was then poured upon his head.
In this an "atonement was made for him before the Lord" (ver. 18). Bishop Patrick
says, "The blood seems to have been a token of *forgiveness;* the oil of *healing*."
Together they show the intimate connection between the Son of God and the Spirit of
God in the work of redemption and salvation. 3. *The circumstances of the poor are
considered.* (1) He may substitute doves for the lambs of the burnt offering and sin

offering, and one tenth-deal of flour for three. "My son, give me thine heart;" and with that the *calves of thy lips* shall be accepted instead of the *calves of the stall*. (2) But the lamb of the trespass offering he must bring. "This may well be looked upon as a figure of the Lamb of God, who alone taketh away the sins of the whole world" (Old Bible).—J. A. M.

EXPOSITION.

THE LEPROSY OF A HOUSE, AND ITS CLEANSING (vers. 33—53). The subject of leprosy in houses must be regarded from the same point of view as that of leprosy in clothes. The regulations respecting it are not sanitary laws, as Lange represents them, but rest, as Keil argues, upon an ideal or symbolical basis. The same thought is attached to all species of uncleanness. Something—it matters not what—produces a foul and repulsive appearance in the walls of a house. That is in itself sufficient to make that house unclean; for whatever is foul and repulsive is representative of moral and spiritual defilement, and therefore is itself symbolically defiling and defiled. It has been suggested that the special cause of the affection of the houses in Canaan was saltpetre exuding from the materials employed in their building, or iron pyrites in the stone used. This may have been so, or more probably it was the growth of some fungus. Whatever it was, the appearance created by it was so similar to that of leprosy in the human body, as to derive its name from the latter by analogy.

Ver. 34.—**When ye be come into the land of Canaan, which I give to you for a possession.** This is the first instance of a law being given which has no bearing on the present condition of the Israelites, but is to regulate their conduct when they had come into the promised land. From the time of Abraham downwards, the assurance of their entrance into that land had been possessed by the people of Israel (Gen. xvii. 8), and the expectation of the speedy fulfilment of that promise had been quickened by their exodus from Egypt, and the preparations made to march through the wilderness. There would, therefore, be nothing surprising to them in receiving instructions to guide their conduct when the entrance should have been effected. As the question is one of leprosy, it is natural that it should be treated of with the leprosy of the human subject and the leprosy of garments; but as it is not of immediate application, it is placed at the end, and dealt with after the rest of the subject has been discussed, being appended to the law of cleansing the leper, instead of preceding it. **And I put the plague of leprosy in a house of the land of your possession.** This expression has led to the idea that the leprosy of houses was a special infliction at God's hand in a manner different from other inflictions or diseases; but the words do not mean that. All that is done is in a sense done by God, inasmuch as his providence rules over all; and, therefore, by whatever secondary cause a thing may be brought about, it is he that does it. It is God that feeds the birds (Luke xii. 24), God that clothes the grass (Luke xii. 28), nor does one sparrow fall to the ground without him (Matt. x. 29). It is he, therefore, that *puts the plague in a house*, as the Lord of all things (cf. Isa. xlv. 6, 7, "I am the Lord, and there is none else. I form the light, and create darkness: I make peace, and create evil: I the Lord do all these things"). The expression militates, though not strongly, against the notion that the house caught the leprosy from the leper that lived in it.

Vers. 35—44.—The examination of the suspected house by the priest. First, the house is to be **emptied** of its furniture, lest the latter should contract a ceremonial uncleanness in case the house were found to be leprous, but not, it will be noted, lest it should convey contagion or infection. Then the priest is to examine the discolouration, and if it bear a suspicious appearance, the house is to be shut up for seven days. It at the end of that time the spot has spread, he is to have the part of the wall in which it shows itself taken down and carried away, and built up again with new stones and mortar and plaster, the parts adjoining to the infected place having been first well scraped. If this treatment does not succeed in getting rid of the mischief, the priest is to determine that it is a **fretting leprosy in the house: it is unclean.**

Ver. 45.—As the leper was removed from the camp, so the leprous house is to be utterly pulled down; the house, the stones of it, and the timber thereof, and all the morter of the house; and all its materials carried forth out of the city into an unclean place.

Vers. 46, 47.—The leprous house conveys uncleanness to those that enter it, but of so slight a nature that it ceases with the evening, and requires only that the clothes of the wearer be washed. Such a regulation would have been ineffectual for preventing the spread of infection, if that had been its purpose.

Vers. 48—53.—The ceremony of cleansing the house is as similar to that of cleansing the leper as circumstances will permit. In case there is no reappearance of the mischief after the new stones and plastering have been put in, the priest shall pronounce the house clean, because the plague is healed. First, the priest assures himself that *the plague is healed,* then he *pronounces the house clean,* and still after that the *cleansing* is to take place (cf. vers. 3, 7, 8). The

cleansing is effected by the same ceremony as that of the leper himself, by the two birds, and cedar wood, and scarlet, and hyssop. The use of this ceremony in the cleansing of a house shows that, in the case of the leper, the symbolical meaning of letting go the living bird out of the city into the open fields cannot be, as has been maintained, the restoration of the cleansed man to his natural movements of liberty in the camp. If a bird's flight represents the freedom of a man going hither and thither as he will, it certainly does not represent any action that a house could take.

Vers. 54—57.—These verses contain the concluding formula for chs. xiii., xiv. The various names of leprosy and its kindred diseases are resumed from ch. xiii. 2.

HOMILETICS.

Vers. 33—53.—*On uncleanness in houses.* There are two metaphors commonly used in Holy Scripture for designating God's covenant people. They are (1) God's household; (2) God's house.

I. GOD'S HOUSEHOLD. As the household of God the Father, "of whom the whole family in heaven and earth is named" (Eph. iii. 15), they are the members of that august brotherhood gathered together in Christ, of which God himself is the spiritual Father, into which all that are adopted in Christ are incorporated, ceasing to be "strangers and foreigners," and becoming "fellow-citizens with the saints and of the household of God" (Eph. ii. 19).

II. GOD'S HOUSE. The representation that God's people form his house is of a more singular character, and less capable of bring immediately grasped. It is even more commonly employed than the other. In the Epistle to the Corinthians, we read of Christians, that is, the collective body of Christians, being "God's temple" (1 Cor. iii. 16); "for ye are the temple of the living God; as God hath said, I will dwell in them, and walk in them; and I will be their God, and they shall be my people" (2 Cor. vi. 16). In the Epistle to the Ephesians, St. Paul dwells at length on the idea of the Christian Church being built up of living stones into a temple for God's Spirit: "Ye are built upon the foundation of the apostles and prophets, Jesus Christ being himself the chief corner stone; in whom all the building fitly framed together groweth unto an holy temple in the Lord: in whom ye also are builded together for an habitation of God through the Spirit" (Eph. ii. 20—22). And in the Epistle to Timothy, he speaks of "the house of God, which is the Church of the living God, the pillar and ground of the truth" (1 Tim. iii. 15). Similarly, the writer of the Epistle to the Hebrews, having described Christ "as a Son over his own house," continues, "whose house are we" (Heb. iii. 6); and St. Peter writes, "Ye also, as lively stones, are built up a spiritual house" (1 Pet. ii. 3). Just as God's Spirit dwells within the heart of each individual Christian, so, and in a more special manner, he dwells within the Church, his house not being made by hands, or constituted of wood and stone, but of the spirits of those who form the Church.

III. GOD'S HOUSE MAY NEVER BE DESTROYED, BUT IT MAY BE DEFILED. "Upon this rock" (that is, upon himself as confessed by St. Peter), "I will build my Church, and the gates of hell shall not prevail against it" (Matt. xvi. 18). But though not destructible by the power of evil, it may yet be defiled. "If any man defile the temple of God, him shall God destroy; for the temple of God is holy, which temple ye are" (1 Cor. iii. 17). That which defiles God's house is unrighteousness and falsehood, just as physical and ceremonial uncleanness defiles the camp (Deut. xxiii. 12). If the latter be allowed to continue in the camp, God will symbolically "turn away" from it ; "for the Lord thy God walketh in the midst of the camp, to deliver thee, and to give up thine enemies before thee ; therefore shall thy camp be holy : that he see no unclean thing in thee, and turn away from thee" (Deut. xxiii. 14). If the former be found, "the Holy Spirit of God" will be "grieved" (Eph. iv. 30), and "vexed," so that God is turned into an "enemy" (Isa. lxiii. 10).

IV. THE CLEANSING OF GOD'S HOUSE. As soon as there is a *primâ facie* appearance of immorality, or irreligiousness, or superstition in a National Church, a diligent examination should be made by those placed in authority by God. Perhaps it is only an appearance, which will die away of itself. If it does so, no further measures are needed. But "*if the plague spread in the walls of the house ; then the priest shall command that they take away the stones in which the plague is, and they shall cast them into an unclean place without the city : and he shall cause the house to be scraped within round about, and they shall pour out the dust that they scrape off without the city into an unclean place.*" Those whose office it is, must not shrink from removing the stones in which the mischief is found, that is, of casting out those who are incurably affected with irreligion, immorality, or superstition. "*And they shall take other stones, and put them in the place of those stones ; and he shall take other morter, and shall plaister the house.*" Discipline must be exercised by substituting sound teachers and members of the flock for those that have become unsound. This is the work of reformation. This is what was done for the Jewish Church by Joash, when he "was minded to repair the house of the Lord. . . . So the workmen wrought, and the work was perfected by them, and they set the house of God in his state, and strengthened it" (2 Chron. xxiv. 4—13) ; and by Hezekiah, when he said unto the Levites, "Sanctify now yourselves, and sanctify the house of the Lord God of your fathers, and carry forth the filthiness out of the holy place. For our fathers have trespassed, and done that which was evil in the eyes of the Lord our God, and have forsaken him. . . . And the priests went into the inner part of the house of the Lord, to cleanse it, and brought out all the uncleanness that they found in the temple of the Lord into the court of the house of the Lord. And the Levites took it, to carry it out abroad into the brook Kidron" (2 Chron. xxix. 5—16) ; and by Josiah, when "he began to purge Judah and Jerusalem . . . when he had purged the land and the house he sent . . . to repair the house of the Lord his God . . . and they gave the money to the workmen that wrought in the house of the Lord, to repair and amend the house: even to the artificers and builders gave they it, to buy hewn stone, and timber for couplings, and to floor the houses which the kings of Judah had destroyed" (2 Chron. xxxiv. 3—11). And this is what was done for the greater part of the Christian Church in the West in the sixteenth century. But if these measures prove ineffective, "*if the plague come again, and break out in the house, after that he hath taken away the stones, and after he hath scraped the house and after it is plaistered ; then the priest shall come and look, and, behold, if the plague be spread in the house, it is a fretting leprosy in the house : it is unclean. And he shall break down the house, the stones of it, and the timber thereof, and all the morter of the house ; and he shall carry them forth out of the city into an unclean place.*" So it was with the Jewish Church. The reformations of Joash, of Hezekiah, of Josiah, were ineffectual, and the Babylonian captivity followed. And so it will be with the various National Churches of Christendom : any one of them to which the taint of impurity in life or doctrine obstinately adheres, will be destroyed utterly when God's forbearance shall have at length come to an end.

V. WARNING. "Remember therefore from whence thou art fallen, and repent, and do the first works; or else I will come unto thee quickly, and will remove thy candlestick out of his place, except thou repent" (Rev. ii. 5). "Repent ; or else I will come unto thee quickly, and will fight against them with the sword of my mouth" (Rev. ii. 16). "Remember therefore how thou hast received and heard, and hold fast, and repent. If therefore thou shalt not watch, I will come on thee as a thief, and thou shalt not know what hour I will come upon thee" (Rev. iii. 3). "As many as I love, I rebuke and chasten : be zealous therefore, and repent. Behold, I stand at the door, and knock : if any man hear my voice, and open the door, I will come in to him, and will sup with him, and he with me" (Rev. iii. 19, 20).

HOMILIES BY VARIOUS AUTHORS.

Vers. 33—53.—*Cleansing the corrupt house.* That the Divine Lawgiver should, in this tabernacle period of Israel's history, anticipate a time when their future houses would be affected by some disorder similar to leprosy in the human skin, and that he should direct a treatment of such houses closely corresponding with that of the human leper, is exceedingly remarkable. Nothing could possibly impress the Hebrew mind more powerfully with the idea that "the face of the Lord was against" that spiritual evil of which leprosy was the chosen type. How direct the argument and forcible the conclusion that, if not only every remotest particle of leprosy itself was to be ruthlessly put away but also anything which to the bodily eye had even a near resemblance to it, and was thus suggestive of it,—how offensive, how intolerable, in the sight of God must that evil thing itself be held! Here are—

I. THREE MAIN PRINCIPLES ON THE SUBJECT OF CORRUPTION. In God's view, as we gain it from his Word, 1. Corruption (impurity) may attach to the "house" or community as well as to the individual. We read of "the iniquity of the house of Israel," and of "the iniquity of the house of Judah" (Ezek. iv. 5, 6); of "the house of Israel dealing treacherously with God" (Jer. iii. 20), etc. 2. That earnest effort should be made to cleanse it from corruption. The leprous house of stone was to be cleansed: the stones in which the plague was were to be taken away (ver. 40); the house was to be scraped round about, and its unclean dust cast out of the camp (ver. 41); other stones were to be placed and other mortar used instead (ver. 42); the leprous part was to be removed and the house renovated. So must the contaminated community purify itself, removing that from it which is evil and corrupting—its Achan, its Ananias and Sapphira, its Simon the sorcerer, its guilty member (1 Cor. v.), etc. 3. That, all efforts failing, the house will be destroyed. "He shall break down the house, the stones of it," etc. (ver. 45). A community of any kind that is incurably corrupt (1) had better be broken up deliberately by the hand of man; but if not (2), will certainly be dissolved in time by the hand of God. The history of the world abounds in proofs that moral and spiritual corruption lead on to feebleness, decay, dissolution.

II. THREE MAIN APPLICATIONS OF THE PRINCIPLES. To any leprous "house," to any community into which seeds of corruption have been introduced, these principles will apply. They may with peculiar appropriateness be referred to: 1. *The nation.* The "house of Judah" and the "house of Israel" were continually warned that they had erred from the ways of the Lord and become corrupt, that they must cleanse themselves from their impurities, or that they would be abandoned by God to their doom. Assyria, Judæa, Egypt, Greece, Rome, the Ottoman Empire, provide striking and eloquent illustrations. 2. *The family.* The "house of Eli" and the "house of Saul" illustrate the principles of the text; so also many a "house" in Christian times that has risen to honour and influence, that has grown leprous (corrupt), that has not heeded the warnings of the Word of God to put away the evil of its doings, and that has fallen into decay and has disappeared. 3. *The Church.* This is the "house of God" on earth (1 Tim. iii. 15; 2 Tim. ii. 20; Eph. ii. 19; Heb. iii. 6). This house may show signs of leprosy; and in individual Churches corruption may break out—in *doctrine* (Galatia), in *public worship* (Corinth), in *morals* (Pergamos, Thyatira), in *spiritual life* (Ephesus, Sardis, Laodicea). The corrupt Church must be cleansed, or it will be disowned of the Divine Lord, and it will perish in his high displeasure (Rev. ii. 5, 16, 23, 27; iii. 3, 17—19).—C.

Vers. 33—57.—*Leprosy in a house.* From the first of these verses it is concluded that leprosy was not an ordinary disease, but a plague inflicted immediately by a judgment from God. That it was so inflicted in some instances upon persons cannot be disputed (see Numb. xii. 10; 2 Kings v. 27; xv. 5), and God threatens to curse the house of the wicked with such a plague (Zech. v. 4). The Jews view it in this light, and consequently regard leprosy as incurable except by the hand of God. But in

Scripture, what God *permits* is often represented as his *doing*; and evils that Satan inflicts may require the power of God to remove.

I. WHAT ARE WE TO UNDERSTAND BY THE HOUSE? 1. *There is the obvious literal meaning.* It is an ordinary habitation (differing, indeed, from the tents in which the Israelites sojourned in the wilderness), composed of stones, and mortar, and wood, and plaster. 2. *It must also have a moral interpretation.* (1) If in the person leprosy has a twofold meaning, viz. a literal and moral; and if the garment plagued with leprosy has a moral as well as a literal meaning, so, by parity of reason, must the house. (2) It cannot be supposed that for sanitary reasons simply the leprosy in the house should occupy the space it takes in the Scriptures. (3) Over and above the sanitary regulations, we find regulations for the ceremonial cleansing, in which are sacrifices and sprinklings, "to make an atonement for the house" (vers. 48—53). These in other cases are admitted to have reference to the provisions of the gospel for moral purposes, and therefore should be so considered here. 3. *It should be taken to represent a community.* (1) It is used sometimes to describe a *family.* Thus we read of the "house of Cornelius," and of Noah saving "his house" (Acts x. 2; Heb. xi. 7). (2) It is also used to express a *lineage.* Thus we read of a long war raging between the "house of Saul" and the "house of David" (2 Sam. iii. 1). (3) The larger community of a *nation* is called a "house." Thus we read repeatedly of the "house of Israel," the "house of Judah," and Egypt is spoken of as the "house of bondage" (Deut. viii. 14). (4) An ecclesiastical community is in like manner described as a house. Paul speaks of the "house of God, which is the Church of the living God" (1 Tim. iii. 15; see also Heb. iii. 2—6; x. 21; 1 Pet. iv. 17). 4. *A leprous house is a demoralized community.* (1) Thus a family of wicked persons, or in which are members scandalous for irreligion and vice, is morally a leprous house. Such was the house of Eli. (2) A lineage of wickedness also is a leprous house. Such was the house of "Jeroboam, the son of Nebat, who made Israel to sin." Such that of Omri. (3) A nation given to idolatry such as Israel became before the Assyrian captivity, and Judah before the Babylonish, may be regarded as a leprous house. So are modern nations demoralized by atheism, infidelity, sabbath desecration, drunkenness, and dissipation, leprous houses. (4) A Church holding out the poison cup of "damnable heresy" to intoxicate nations, encouraging vice by "indulgences," and "red" with the "blood of the saints and martyrs of Jesus," is a house fearfully smitten with the plague of leprosy.

II. WHAT TREATMENT SHOULD IT RECEIVE? 1. *The leprosy should be reported to the priest* (vers. 34, 35). (1) The Priest is Christ, to whom we must carry all our concerns in prayer—domestic, political, ecclesiastical. The voice of suffering cries to him for judgment upon oppressors (Jas. v. 4), and the voice from the ashes of the martyrs loudly imprecates judgment upon their persecutors (Rev. vi. 9—11). (2) Faithful ministers of Christ should be apprised of the symptoms of the plague of heresy or immorality, that they might use their good offices and influence to stop the mischief. (3) Any of the spiritual priesthood, persons of recognized sanctity and probity, might be informed of the spreading of moral leprosy, whether it be in the family, or State, or Church. 2. *Warning should be given to those concerned.* (1) The priest himself gives the warning. The premonitions of Jesus are written in his Word. It tells us of days of judgment upon nations, upon Churches, upon individuals. (2) Faithful ministers of Christ will utter his words. No false notions of "charity" will prevent them from sounding the alarm. (3) The use of the warning is to have everything removed from the leprous house before the priest's inquisition for judgment; for whatever he finds in the unclean house will be concluded to be unclean (see Rev. xviii. 4). 3. *It will be duly inspected.* (1) Christ moves in all communities, though unseen, and more particularly amongst the candlesticks, or Churches. His eyes are as flames of fire, searching into all secrets of the "reins and hearts" (Rev. i. 12—16, 23). (2) The light of God's Word should be let in to discover the heresy that may plague any Church, and to rebuke the laxity of discipline which may connive at licentiousness (Rev. ii. 14—16, 20—23). 4. *It will be shut up for seven days.* (1) The priest himself withdraws. Jesus cannot abide in a foul community. (2) Whoever enters it during this interval becomes unclean (ver. 46). Where Jesus cannot abide, his people should not go. (3) He that lieth in the house or eateth in it shall wash his clothes (ver. 47). Fellowship in such a community compromises righteousness. What is the condition of those who are perverted to heresy! 5. *Efforts towards a reformation should be made.* (1) Where the plague may appear superficial, the place must be scraped; where it has eaten deeply, the stones affected must be removed and new ones substituted, and the whole plastered afresh. (2) However painful the process, the scraping of discipline must be endured (Job xxii. 23). There must be an excision of scandalous offenders (1 Cor. v. 13). 6. *The sequel.* (1) If the plague remain through the days of trial, breaking out afresh, notwithstanding the efforts for reformation, when the case is hopeless, then comes the visitation of judgment. The house is demolished and the wreck carried outside the city to an unclean place (see Rev. xxii. 15). (2) If the reformation has proved successful, the house abides. The ceremonies of the shedding and sprinkling the sacrificial blood (vers. 48—53) show that salvation is through faith in the merits of Christ. To those merits we are indebted for a present and an everlasting salvation.—J. A. M.

EXPOSITION.

CHAPTER XV.

RUNNING ISSUES FROM THE HUMAN BODY. These are the fourth cause of ceremonial uncleanness. We are not to look for a moral basis for the regulation on account of any vicious habit connected with such issues. They are foul and repulsive, and simply for that reason they are causes of ceremonial uncleanness to those who suffer from them, and to those who come in contact with persons suffering from them.

Vers. 2—15.—The first case of an issue. It appears to be identical with the disease called by physicians gonorrhea, or, perhaps, blenorrhea (cf. ch. xxii. 4; Numb. v. 2).

Vers. 16, 17.—The second case of an issue (cf. ch. xxii. 4; Deut. xxiii. 10; Gen. xxxviii. 9, 10).

Ver. 18.—The third case of an issue (cf. Exod. xix. 15; 1 Sam. xxi. 5; 1 Cor. vii. 5).

Vers. 19—24.—The fourth case of an issue—that of ordinary menstruation (cf. chs. xii. 2; xx. 18).

Vers. 25—30.—The fifth case of an issue —that of excessive menstruation, or menstruation occurring at the wrong time. This was probably the disease of the woman "who had an issue of blood" (Matt. ix. 20; Mark v. 25; Luke viii. 43).

Ver. 28.—**If she be cleansed of her issue.** In the first and the fifth cases, the presentation of two turtle-doves or two young pigeons as a sin offering and a burnt offering is enjoined as the ceremonial cleansing required. In the other cases a sacrifice is not demanded.

Ver. 31.—**That they die not in their uncleanness, when they defile my tabernacle that is among them.** The main purpose in the laws of uncleanness is to keep first God's house and then God's people free from the danger of defilement by foul things presenting themselves freely before him and among them. These foul things, symbolizing sinful things, create a ceremonial defilement symbolizing moral defilement.

HOMILETICS.

Ver. 25.—*The figure of the "woman which was diseased with an issue of blood twelve years"* seems to rise up before us as we read this verse. Jesus was going on an errand of mercy to heal the daughter of Jairus, and as he went the people thronged him. "And a certain woman, which had an issue of blood twelve years, and had suffered many things of many physicians, and had spent all that she had, and was nothing bettered, but rather grew worse, when she had heard of Jesus, came in the press behind, and touched his garment" (Mark v. 25—27).

I. THE WOMAN'S STATE OF CEREMONIAL UNCLEANNESS. For twelve years she had not been allowed within the precincts of the temple, and had been unable, therefore, to take part in the public worship of God as appointed in the books of Moses. And during the whole of the same long period she had been in a state of separation from all about her: whoever touched her became unclean; the bed she lay upon was unclean; the seats that she sat upon were unclean; whoever touched the bed that she lay upon or the seat that she sat upon was unclean. No wonder if for this reason alone "she had spent all her living upon physicians" (Luke viii. 43).

II. HER STATE OF PHYSICAL SUFFERING. She was afflicted with an exhausting disease, wasting her vital powers, and she suffered not only from that cause, but also from the vain attempts made by many physicians to relieve her, as well as from the anxiety of mind inseparable from her state of ceremonial impurity.

III. WHAT SHE SOUGHT. Not to be cleansed as by a priest—this could not be until she had been cured—but to be healed as by a physician. "For she said, If I may touch but his clothes, I shall be whole" (Mark v. 28). The Great Physician accepts her, and fulfils her desire; for however imperfect her faith might be, and however uninstructed she might herself be, yet there was faith in her sufficient "to make her whole" (Matt. ix. 22).

IV. HOW THE HEALING WAS WROUGHT. The cure was effected by the power of Christ conveyed through the touch of his garment, on the condition of the woman's faith. In each of the miracles he uses such means as he thinks fit, and often different means, probably with the purpose in each case of awaking the spirit of the person to be healed so as to become capable of receiving the spiritual gift. As in the case of the lepers on whom he laid his hand, instead of becoming himself unclean, he becomes the channel of renewed life and health to those whom he touches.

V. THE CEREMONIAL CLEANSING STILL TO BE EFFECTED. As the leper, after he had been healed by our Lord, had to "go and show himself to the priest, and offer the gift that Moses commanded" (Matt. viii. 4), so no doubt the woman cured of the issue of blood had to fulfil the legal requirement for her cleansing, by offering her sin offering and her burnt offering on the eighth day after her healing.

VI. SPIRITUAL APPLICATION OF THE MIRACLE. Sin can only be healed by the power of God through Christ brought into spiritual contact with the soul of the sinner, and there must be something of faith and love in the heart of the sinner, however imperfect its manifestation may be, in order that spiritual contact between God's Spirit and his spirit may take place.

HOMILIES BY VARIOUS AUTHORS.

Secret sins. Ch. xv.; cf. Ps. xix. 12; 1 Tim. i. 13. We have already had occasion to discern as a clear lesson of the old ritual that *sin is a nature.* The old law did not confine itself to overt acts, but insisted on "sins of ignorance" being regarded as elements of guilt (cf. ch. iv.). Then again we have sin shown to originate in birth (ch. xii.); we have its tangible effects strikingly illustrated in the law of the leprosy (chs. xiii., xiv.); and now we have the analysis of sin completed in these laws about issues.

I. IT IS A PHYSICAL FACT THAT MEN AND WOMEN MAY BECOME UNCLEAN WITHOUT ANY ACT OF VOLITION ON THEIR PART. Into the particulars of menstruation and of *gonorrhea benigna* it is unnecessary to enter. The chapter before us states the fact, and asserts the legal uncleanness which is thereby entailed. If involuntary results entail uncleanness, it is clear that voluntary elements entering in (ver. 18) must increase the sense of uncleanness. Experience confirms the Divine decision. There is a sense of uncleanness which arises as soon as the man or woman becomes conscious of the issue.

II. IT IS EVIDENT FROM THIS THAT SIN HAS A SPHERE OF OPERATION BEYOND CONSCIOUS VOLITION. Just as physically a man or woman contracts uncleanness during the unconsciousness of sleep, so morally we find sinful issues coming forth from the evil heart and nature ere ever we are aware. In strict conformity with this fact, Jonathan Edwards was accustomed to analyze his dreams, believing that, in these involuntary movements of the mind, the moral tendencies of the indwelling spirit may often be detected, and by greater watchfulness subdued. "No mind," says Dr. Shedd, "that thinks at all upon sin can possibly stop with the outward act. Its own rational reflection hurries it away, almost instantaneously, from the blow of the murderer—from the momentary gleam of the knife—to the *volition* within that strung the muscle and nerved the blow. But the mind cannot stop here in its search for the essential reality of sin. When we have reached the sphere—the *inward* sphere—of volitions, we have by no means reached the ultimate ground and form of sin. We may suppose that because we have gone beyond the outward act—because we are now *within* the man—we have found sin in its last form. But we are mistaken. Closer thinking, and what is still better, a deeper experience, will disclose to us a depth in our souls lower than that in which volitions occur, and a form of sin in that depth, and to the bottom of it, very different from the sin of single volitions. The thinking mind which cannot stop with mere effects, but seeks for first causes, and especially the heart that knows its own plague, cannot stop with that quite superficial action of the will which manifests itself in a volition. The action is too isolated—too intermittent—and, in reality, too feeble, to account for so steady and uniform a state of character as human sinfulness. For these particular volitions, ending in particular outward actions, the mind instinctively seeks a common ground. For these innumerable volitions, occurring each by itself and separately, the mind instinctively seeks *one single indivisible nature* from which they spring. When the mind has got back to this point, it stops content, because it has reached a central point." This most important truth, then, is most powerfully presented by this law regarding issues. We are held responsible for much more than the voluntary element in life.

III. THE FRUITLESSNESS OF THESE OUTCOMES OF NATURE SHOULD ALSO RECEIVE A PASSING NOTICE. The issues spoken of in this chapter are, with one exception, fruitless issues. In no plainer way could the fruitless issues of man's evil nature be illustrated. If " out of the heart are the issues of life," out of man's evil heart of unbelief are issues of fruitlessness and death.

IV. FOR THESE UNCLEANNESSES, INVOLUNTARY AND SECRET, GOD PROVIDED A FITTING ATONEMENT. It is very noticeable that, while the reality of the guilt in these cases is made manifest, it is the smallest sacrifice, two turtle-doves, or two young pigeons, which God requires. There is no exaggeration in dealing with the secret sins. Done in ignorance, they are not placed upon the same level with voluntary transgressions. At the same time, they are not winked at.

The sin offering is, of course, a type of Christ, our Atoning Sacrifice. It is on the ground of his atonement that we ask cleansing from secret faults (Ps. xix. 12) as well as from conscious transgressions. In truth, we are encouraged to come and to acknowledge that sin is a much larger matter than we are conscious of, that, in fact, it goes beyond all our conceptions, but at the same time is within the reach and grasp of our Lord's atoning power. If he thus sets our secret sins in the light of his countenance, it is that he may have them entirely removed. Saul may have committed his sins of persecution ignorantly in unbelief, but he needs to obtain mercy on account of them (1 Tim. ii. 13). Superficial views of sin would lead men to imagine that a sin done in ignorance is not a guilty thing. God thinks differently, because he looks into the heart and discerns the deep-seated source.

The burnt offering was to express the renewed sense of consecration which the cleansing brings. Out of defilement the soul passes, by Divine grace, into devotion.

The whole analysis of sin in these chapters (xiii.—xv.) is profound and philosophical. In fact, portions of Scripture apparently repulsive become replete with wholesome truth when handled humbly and reverently.—R. M. E.

Vers. 1—33.—*Uncleanness.* Had sin never entered, there had been no disease. Diseases are consequences of sin; their symptoms are therefore taken as emblems of it. So when our Lord miraculously " healed all manner of sickness, and all manner of disease," he evinced ability to remove all corresponding moral evil. The examples specified in the Law are typical or representative, and are such as have symptoms pronounced and visible.

I. THOSE WHO HAD ISSUES IN THE FLESH WERE UNCLEAN. 1. *Out of a pure heart are the issues of life* (see Prov. iv. 23). (1) The blood, which is the life of the flesh, issuing from the heart, passes along the arteries to the extremities of the body, and carries nourishment to every part. (2) This is a fine emblem of the heart of the " good treasure," whose influence upon any corporation, whether domestic, civic, or ecclesiastic, is life-giving (Luke vi. 45). But: 2. *Out of a foul heart are the issues of death.* (1) If the blood is poisoned at its source, the poison is carried to the extremities, and will break out in ulcers and purulent issues. (2) As these symptoms declare the badness of the blood at the heart, which, if not purified, must terminate in mortification and death, so are they appropriate emblems of moral impurity (see Matt. xii. 34, 35;

Mark. vii. 20—23; Jas. i. 21). (3) Or if the blood, which is the life, flow away from the body, that also is a fitting emblem of sin which is spiritual death. Therefore the woman who has an issue of blood is accounted unclean, as being in that condition in which the streams of the fountain of life are diverted from their uses of health and nourishment. Those who reject the life-giving efficacy of the gospel are morally dead, and must, if they remain so, rot in their iniquities (see Lam. i. 9, 17; Ezek. xxxvi. 17). 3. *The Law enjoined the separation of the unclean.* (1) They must not come into the tabernacle. They are unfit to stand in God's presence or to mingle with his people. They must not eat of the holy things. They are in no moral condition to hold fellowship with God and his Church (see Ps. xxiv. 4; Matt. v. 8). (2) They have to remove outside the camp, like the leper (see Numb. v. 2, 3). There they must remain until they are healed and cleansed. (3) They transgress these bounds at their peril. They may be stoned to death by the people, or God himself may deal with them (ver. 31; Exod. xix. 12, 13). The profane under the gospel have a "much sorer punishment" (see Heb. x. 26—31).

II. THEY RENDERED UNCLEAN WHATEVER THEY TOUCHED. 1. *This signified the contagion of sin.* (1) *Persons* were rendered unclean by contact with them (vers. 7, 19, 26). We cannot have fellowship with sin and with God (1 Cor. v. 11; xv. 33; 2 Cor. vi. 15—18; Eph. iv. 29; Jas. iv. 4). (2) *Things* touched by them were also rendered unclean. The bed, the chair, the saddle, etc. (vers. 4, 12, 20). These things may represent men in their properties or attributes, or in their usages, which are all damaged by the influence of sin (1 Thess. iv. 4). (3) Those who touched things rendered unclean by contact, also became unclean (vers. 5, 6, 21—23). What a picture of the spreading power of evil example! How careful should we be to save ourselves from the untoward generation! 2. *Even when cured they must be cleansed.* (1) Genuine repentance may cure sinful habits, but does not cancel guilt nor purify from sin. The utmost it could do is to prevent accumulations of guilt; the old score remains to be dealt with. It does not touch the depravity of the heart (see Matt. xxiii. 25). (2) Time is given to test the cure. Where the disease was rooted, "seven days" of quarantine were required (see vers. 13, 24, 28). The repentance of a moment after a life of evil habits may prove illusive. (3) Where no disease existed, but uncleanness was contracted by contact, the quarantine was "until the even." The time here indicated was that of the evening sacrifice, which pointed significantly to the evening of the Jewish day, otherwise called the "end of the world" or age, viz. when Jesus "appeared to put away sin [sacrifices] by the sacrifice of himself," and remove ritual obligations. 3. *Observe the ceremonies of cleansing.* (1) Some who were made clean by contact had to wash their hands (ver. 11; comp. Luke xi. 38—41). This was when they were *passive* when the contact was inflicted. But if *they* neglected to rinse their hands, then they were as though they were *active*, so they had to wash their flesh and their clothes, and be unclean until the even. No special sacrifices were prescribed. They availed themselves of the daily sacrifice ever on the altar. So in our contact with the moral filth of this world, which is often unavoidable, we have the fountain of the house of David ever flowing, to enable us, almost without an interruption, to walk in the light (see 2 Cor. vii. 1; 1 John i. 7; comp. John xiii. 10). (2) The person healed of an issue had to bathe his flesh and wash his clothes on the seventh day, when he became "clean." So far he cleansed *himself*. The spirit of the Law was fulfilled thus far if he put away all his evil ways (see Isa. i. 16; Matt. xv. 20; Jas. iv. 8). He was clean so far as repentance could make him so, which was *externally* only, or before his fellow-men. (3) He still needed the removal of sin from his *soul*. He had, therefore, now on the eighth day, to bring his sin offering and burnt offering, that with these the priest should "make an atonement for him before the Lord for his issue" (vers. 14, 15, 29, 30). Christ is the Healer and Cleanser (comp. Matt. viii. 16, 17, with Isa. liii. 4, 5).—J. A. M.

Vers. 1—33.—*Personal purity.* It is not permissible to treat this chapter in any detail; to do so would be to act inconsistently with the very object of the legislation, viz., the encouragement of all delicacy of thought as well as propriety of conduct. But the fact that such a chapter as this (with others like it) is found in Scripture is suggestive and instructive. We gather—

I. THAT PERSONAL PURITY WAS AND IS A MATTER OF THE VERY GREATEST CONSEQUENCE IN THE SIGHT OF GOD. Into the relation of the sexes, and into the thoughts, words, and actions which belong to that relation, sin has introduced confusion and degradation. That which should have been the source of nothing but pure and holy joy has become the ground on which the very worst and most debasing consequences of sin are exhibited. Save, perhaps, in some phases of heathen idolatry, there is nothing in which man has shown so grievous a departure from the will of God, and so pitiful a spectacle of uttermost degradation, as in the realm of the sexual relations. It was the design of the Holy One of Israel to train for himself a people which should be free from the flagitious and abominable corruption into which the heathen nations had sunk. But he desired to go further than this: to promote and foster, by careful legislation, not only (1) morality in its more general sense, but also (2) decency of behaviour, and even (3) delicacy of thought. The Jews were taught and trained to put far away from them everything that was unclean. With this view it was made unlawful not only for those who had knowingly violated moral laws, but for those who had unwittingly offended the laws of ceremonial cleanliness, to draw near to their God or to their fellows.

II. THAT SPECIFIC INSTRUCTIONS THEREON ARE A MATTER OF HOLY EXPEDIENCY. It was needful that the children of Israel should receive particular and precise instructions, for they were to be separated from all surrounding nations in their customs, and so in their character—notably in this matter of purity. Moreover, they were admitted to the near presence of God, and must therefore be clear of all impurity; death would be the penalty of defiling the tabernacle of God (ver. 31). Special admonitions and special care are needed: 1. In the case of those who are placed in circumstances of peculiar delicacy. 2. In the case of those who are bound to be above all suspicion of any kind of indelicacy. 3. In the case of the young, who may be led into evil, the magnitude and consequences of which they cannot know. Parental warning, wisely and timely given, may save sons and daughters from much bodily mischief and spiritual suffering.

III. THAT, IN THIS MATTER, WE MUST CONSIDER WHAT IS DUE, NOT ONLY TO OURSELVES, BUT TO OTHERS ALSO. All those details of Divine precept, by which every person and article anywise brought into contact with the unclean man or woman (vers. 4—12, 20—24, 26—27) became unclean, bring out the important truth that impurity is an essentially communicable evil. It is so physically; "let sinners look to it." It is so spiritually. How guilty in the very last degree are those who drive a nefarious trade in corrupt literature! How shameful to put indecent thought into print to pollute the young! How demoralizing to the soul, how displeasing to God, how scrupulously to be avoided, the questionable conversation that borders on the indelicate and impure (Eph. v. 3, 4, 12; Col. iii. 8)!—C.

PART III.

SECTION II.

EXPOSITION.

CHAPTER XVI.

THE CEREMONIAL PURIFICATION OF THE WHOLE CONGREGATION ON THE GREAT DAY OF ATONEMENT. This chapter, containing the account of the institution of the ceremonial to be used on the Day of Atonement, would take its place chronologically immediately after the tenth chapter, for the instructions conveyed in it were delivered to Moses "*after the death of the two sons of Aaron, when they offered before*

the Lord and died" (ver. 1), when the fate of Nadab and Abihu would naturally have led Aaron to desire a more perfect knowledge than had as yet been imparted to him as to the manner in which he was to present himself before the Lord. Logically it might either occupy its present position, as being the great and culminating atoning and cleansing ceremony, or it might be relegated to a place among the holy days in ch. xxiii., where it is, in fact, shortly noticed. That it is placed here shows that the most essential characteristic of the Day in the judgment of the legislator is that of its serving as the occasion and the means of "*making an atonement for the holy sanctuary, and making an atonement for the tabernacle of the congregation, and for the altar, and for making an atonement for the priests, and for all the people of the congregation*" (ver. 33).

Annually there gathered over the camp, and over the sanctuary as situated in the midst of the camp, a mass of defilement, arising in part from sins whose guilt had not been removed by the punishment of the offenders, and in part from uncleannesses which had not been cleansed by sacrifices and the prescribed ceremonial rites. Annually this defilement had to be atoned for or covered away from the sight of God. This was done by the solemn observance of the great Day of Atonement, and specially by the high priest's carrying the blood of the sacrifices into the holy of holies, into which he might enter on no other day of the year; while the consciousness of deliverance from the guilt of sin was quickened on the part of the people by their seeing the scapegoat "*bear away upon him all their iniquities unto a land not inhabited*" (ver. 22).

Ver. 2.—**Speak unto Aaron thy brother, that he come not at all times into the holy place within the vail before the mercy seat, which is upon the ark; that he die not.** Nadab and Abihu having died for their rash presumption in venturing unbidden into the tabernacle, it was natural that Aaron, who had as yet but once penetrated into the holy of holies, should be struck with fear, and that he should desire Divine instruction as to the times and manner in which he was to appear before the Lord, lest he should be struck dead like his sons. If the attempt to enter the outer chamber of the tabernacle had been so fatal to them, what might not be the result to him of entering *within the vail* which hung *before the mercy-seat which is upon the ark*? The mercy-seat —*capporeth*, ἱλαστήριον, *propitiatorium*— formed the top of the ark, and was the place where God specially exhibited his Presence, on the occasions of his manifestation, by the bright *cloud* which then rested upon it between the cherubim. It was this Presence which made it perilous for Aaron to appear within the vail unbidden or without the becoming ritual; for man might not meet God unless he were sanctified for the purpose (Exod. xix. 14, 21—24; 1 Sam. vi. 19). The words, **for I will appear in the cloud upon the mercy seat**, refer to the Divine Presence

thus visibly manifested (see 1 Kings viii. 10—12), and not, as they have strangely been misinterpreted, to the cloud of smoke raised by the incense burnt by the high priest on his entrance. They do not, however, prove that the manifestation was constantly there, still less that it was continued, according to Jewish tradition, in later times. "The reason for the prohibition of Aaron's entrance at his own pleasure, or without the expiatory blood of sacrifice, is to be found in the fact that the holiness communicated to the priest did not cancel the sin of his nature, but only covered it over for the performance of his official duties; and so long as the Law, which produced only the knowledge of sin, and not its forgiveness and removal, was not abolished by the complete atonement, the holy God was and remained to mortal and sinful man a consuming fire, before which no one could stand" (Keil).

Ver. 3.—**Thus shall Aaron come into the holy place.** "Thus" would be translated more literally by *With this.* He must come supplied with the specified offerings, dressed in the appointed manner and using the ceremonial here designated. The efficacy of the acts of the high priest on this day and throughout his ministrations depended not upon his individual but on his official character, and on his obedience to the various commandments positively enjoined. Personal worthiness would not qualify him for his service, nor personal unworthiness hinder the effect of his liturgical acts (cf. Art. XXVI., 'Of the Unworthiness of the Ministers, which hinders not the effect of the Sacrament'). Aaron's special offerings for himself on this great day are to be **a young bullock for a sin offering, and a ram for a burnt offering.**

Ver. 4.—His special garments for the occasion are the **holy linen coat, . . . the linen breeches, . . . a linen girdle, . . . and the linen mitre.** In the original the definite article is not expressed. The reading should therefore be, *He shall put on a holy linen coat, and he shall have linen breeches upon his flesh, and shall be girded with a linen girdle, and with a linen mitre shall be attired.* The clothing was white from head to foot, differing therein from the dress of the ordinary priest, inasmuch as the sash or girdle of the latter was of variegated materials, and differing also in the shape of the mitre. The white clothing was not intended to symbolize humility and penitence, as some have thought, for white is not the colour in which penitents are naturally dressed. Rather it was symbolical of the purity and holiness which the ceremonies of the day symbolically effected, and which was specially needed to be exhibited in the person of the high priest. In the visions of Ezekiel and

Daniel, the angel of God is clothed in *linen* (Ezek. ix. 2, 3, 11; x. 2, 6, 7; Dan. x. 5; xii. 6, 7). And the colour of the angelic raiment is described in the Gospels as *white* : "his countenance was like lightning, and his raiment white as snow" (Matt. xxviii. 3); "they saw a young man sitting on the right side, clothed in a long white garment" (Mark xvi. 5); "two men stood by them in shining garments" (Luke xxiv. 4); she "seeth two angels in white sitting" (John xx. 12). So, too, the wife of the Lamb, in the Book of the Revelation, has it "granted to her that she should be arrayed in fine linen clean and white: for the fine linen is the righteousness of saints" (Rev. xix. 7, 8). The white linen dress of the high priest, therefore (which must have given the appearance of the English surplice tied in at the waist), was intended to symbolize the purity and brightness which forms the characteristic of angels and saints, and, above all, of the King of saints. "The white material of the dress which Aaron wore when performing the highest act of expiation under the Old Testament was a symbolical shadowing forth of the holiness and glory of the one perfect Mediator between God and man, who, being the radiation of the glory of God and the image of his nature, effected by himself the perfect cleansing away of our sin, and who, as the true High Priest, being holy, innocent, unspotted, and separate from sinners, entered once by his own blood into the holy place not made with hands, namely, into heaven itself, to appear before the face of God for us and obtain everlasting redemption (Heb. i. 3; vii. 26; ix. 12, 24)" (Keil). The symbolism of the *holy garments* as indicating holiness and purity, is strengthened by the command that Aaron is to **wash his flesh in water, and so put them on.**

The high priest's acts on this day, so far as they are recounted in this chapter, were the following. 1. He bathed. 2. He dressed himself in his white holy garments. 3. He offered or presented at the door of the tabernacle a bullock for a sin offering for himself and his house. 4. He presented at the same place two goats for a sin offering for the congregation. 5. He cast lots on the two goats, one of which was to be sacrificed, the other to be let go into the wilderness. 6. He sacrificed the bullock. 7. He passed from the court through the holy place into the holy of holies with a censer and incense, and filled the space beyond the vail with a cloud of smoke from the incense. 8. He returned to the court, and, taking some of the blood of the bullock, passed again within the vail, and there sprinkled the blood once on the front of the

mercy-seat and seven times before it. 9. He came out again into the court, and killed the goat on which the lot for sacrifice had fallen. 10. For the third time he entered the holy of holies, and went through the same process with the goat's blood as with the bullock's blood. 11. He purified the other part of the tabernacle, as he had purified the holy of holies, by sprinkling with the atoning blood, as before, and placing some of it on the horns of the altar of incense (Exod. xxx. 10). 12. He returned to the court, and placed the blood of the bullock and goat upon the horns of the altar of burnt sacrifice, and sprinkled it seven times. 13. He offered to God the remaining goat, laying his hands upon it, confessing and laying the sins of the people upon its head. 14. He consigned the goat to a man, whose business it was to conduct it to the border of the wilderness, and there release it. 15. He bathed and changed his linen vestments for his commonly worn high priest's dress. 16. He sacrificed, one after the other, the two rams as burnt offerings for himself and for the people. 17. He burnt the fat of the sin offerings upon the altar. 18. He took measures that the remainder of the sin offerings should be burnt without the camp. In Numb. xxix. 7—11, twelve sacrifices are commanded to be offered by the high priest on this day, namely, the morning and evening sacrifice; a burnt offering for the people, consisting of one young bullock, one ram (as already stated), and seven lambs; and one goat for a sin offering; so that in all there were fifteen sacrifices offered, besides the meat and drink offerings. The punctiliousness of the Jews in later times was not content that the ceremonies should begin on the day itself. Preparations commenced a full week previously. On the third day of the seventh month, the high priest moved from his house in the city into the temple, and he was twice sprinkled with the ashes of the red heifer, by way of precaution against defilement. He spent the week in practising and rehearsing, under the eye of some of the elders of the Sanhedrim, the various acts that he would have to perform on the great day, and on the night immediately preceding it he was not allowed to sleep. In case of his sudden death or disqualification, a substitute was appointed to fulfil his function.

Ver. 5.—**And he shall take of the congregation of the children of Israel two kids of the goats.** It was necessary that the sacrifice offered for a person or class of persons should be provided by the offerer or offerers. The *two kids of the goats*, or rather the *two he-goats*, constituted together but one **sin offering.** This is important for the understanding of the sequel.

Ver. 6.—**And Aaron shall offer his bullock**

... and make an atonement for himself, and for his house. The first step is an expiatory offering to reconcile the officiating priest and the remainder of the priestly house to God. This was necessary before his offerings for the people could be accepted. It indicates the defects inherent in a priest whose nature was only that of man, which is compassed about with infirmities. The *offering* here commanded is not the slaying, but the solemn presentation, of the bullock to the Lord. In after times the following form of confession was used by the high priest when he laid his hand upon the bullock:—" O Lord, I have committed iniquity; I have transgressed; I have sinned, I and my house. O Lord, I entreat thee, cover over the iniquities, the transgressions, and the sins which I have committed, transgressed, and sinned before thee, I and my house; even as it is written in the Law of Moses thy servant, ' For on that day will he cover over for you, to make you clean; from all your transgressions before the Lord ye shall be cleansed " (Edersheim, ' Temple Service ').

Vers. 7, 8.—It must be carefully noted that, as the two goats made one sin offering (ver. 5), so they are both **presented before the Lord at the door of the tabernacle of the congregation.** By this solemn presentation they became the Lord's, one as much as the other. After this, Aaron is to cast lots **upon the two goats.** The two goats, of the same size and appearance as far as possible, stood together near the entrance of the court. And by them was an urn containing two lots. These the high priest drew out at the same moment, placing one on the head of one goat, the other on the head of the other goat. According as the lot fell, one of the goats was taken and at once offered to the Lord, with a view to being shortly sacrificed; the other was appointed for a scapegoat, and reserved till the expiatory sacrifices had been made, when it too was offered to the Lord, and then sent away into the wilderness. After the lot had been chosen, the two goats were distinguished from each other by having a piece of scarlet cloth tied, the first round its neck, the second round its horn. **One lot for the Lord, and the other lot for the scapegoat.** The last word is in the original *la-azāzel*, and being found only in this chapter, it has caused a great discrepancy of opinion among interpreters as to its meaning. It has been diversely regarded as a place, a person, a thing, and an abstraction. The first class of interpreters explain it as some district of the wilderness; the second understand by it an evil spirit; the third take it as a designation of the goat; the fourth translate it, "for removal." The first interpretation may be

summarily rejected. If a localized spot were meant, that spot would have been left behind by a people constantly on the move. The second hypothesis—that *azāzel* was an evil spirit, or the evil spirit—has been embraced by so considerable a number of modern expositors, that it is necessary to dwell upon it at some length. But, indeed, it has little to recommend it. It has been argued that *azāzel* must be a proper name, because it has no article prefixed to it, *la-azāzel*. This is a grammatical error. When a noun expresses an office or a function, and has the preposition *le* or *la* prefixed to it, it does not take an article in Hebrew any more than in French; *e.g.* in the verse, " Jehu ... shalt thou anoint to be king (or for king) over Israel; and Elisha ... shalt thou appoint to be prophet (or for prophet) in thy room " (1 Kings xix. 16), the Hebrew is *le-melek* and *le-navi*, without the article. The same idiom will be found in 1 Sam. xxv. 30; 2 Sam. vii. 14. With greater plausibility it is argued that ver. 8 contrasts Jehovah and Azazel, and that if *la-Yehovah* be translated " for Jehovah," or " for the Lord," *la-azāzel* must be translated " for Azazel." It may be allowed that there is a *primâ facie* likelihood that, where words are thus contrasted, if one designates a person, the other would designate a person. But it is an incredibly rash assertion that this is always the case. All depends upon the idea which the speaker or writer has in his mind and desires to express. As part of the same argument, it is urged that the preposition, being the same in both clauses of the sentence, must be translated by the same word. This is certainly not the case. The natural meaning of *le* with a proper name is " for," and with a word expressing the performance of some function (technically called *nomen agentis*) it means " to be " (see the passage quoted above from 1 Kings xix. 16). Unless, therefore, *azāzel* be a proper name (which has to be proved, not assumed) the preposition need not and ought not to be translated by " for " but by " to be." The word *le* is used with great latitude, and often in a different sense in the same sentence; *e.g.* Exod. xii. 24; ch. xxvi. 12. The objections to the theory that *azāzel* means an evil spirit are of overwhelming force. It will be enough to name the following. 1. The name *azāzel* is nowhere else mentioned. This could not be, if he were so important a being as to divide with Jehovah the sin offering of the congregation of Israel on the great Day of Atonement. 2. No suitable etymology can be discerned. The nearest approach to it is very forced—" the separated one." 3. The notion of appeasing, or bribing, or mocking the evil spirit by presenting to him a goat, is altogether alien from the spirit of the rest of the Mosaic institutions. Where else is there anything like it? 4. The goat is presented and offered to Jehovah equally with the goat which is slain. To take that which has been offered (and therefore half sacrificed) to God and give it to Satan, would be a daring impiety, which is inconceivable. That *la-azāzel* means "for removal" is the opinion of Bähr, Tholuck, Winer, and others. There is nothing objectionable in this interpretation, but the form of the word *azāzel* points rather to an agent than to an abstract act. *Azāzel* is a word softened (according to a not unusual custom) from *azalzel*, just as *kokav* is a softened form of *kav-kav*, and as Babel is derived from Balbel (Gen. xi. 9). *Azalzel* is an active participle or participial noun, derived ultimately from *azal* (connected with the Arabic word *azala*, and meaning removed), but immediately from the reduplicate form of that verb, *azazal*. The reduplication of the consonants of the root in Hebrew and Arabic gives the force of repetition, so that while *azal* means removed, *azalzal* means removed by a repetition of acts. *Azalzel*, or *azāzel*, therefore, means one who removes by a series of acts. "In this sense the word *azāzel* is strictly expressive of the function which is ascribed to the scapegoat in vers. 21, 22; namely, that he '*be sent away, bearing upon him all the iniquities of the children of Israel into the wilderness.*' It properly denotes one that removes or separates; yet a remover in such sort that the removal is not effected by a single act or at one moment, but by a series of minor acts tending to and issuing in a complete removal. No word could better express the movement of the goat before the eyes of the people, as it passed on, removing at each step, in a visible symbol, their sins further and further from them, until, by continued repetition of the movement, they were carried far away and removed utterly" (Sir W. Martin, 'Semitic Languages'). That it is the goat that is designated by the word *azāzel* is the exposition of the LXX., Josephus, Symmachus, Aquila, Theodotion, the Vulgate, the Authorized English Version, and Luther's Version. The interpretation is founded on sound etymological grounds, it suits the context wherever the word occurs, it is consistent with the remaining ceremonial of the Day of Atonement, and it accords with the otherwise known religious beliefs and symbolical practices of the Israelites. The two goats were the single sin offering for the people; the one that was offered in sacrifice symbolized atonement or covering made by shedding of blood, the other symbolized the utter removal of the sins of the people,

which were conveyed away and lost in the depths of the wilderness, whence there was no return. Cf. Ps. ciii. 12, "As far as the east is from the west, so far hath he removed our transgressions from us;" and Micah vii. 19, "He will turn again, he will have compassion upon us; he will subdue our iniquities; and thou wilt cast all their sins into the depths of the sea." The eighth verse should be translated as it stands in the Authorized Version, or, if we ask for still greater exactness, *And Aaron shall cast lots upon the two goats; one lot for the Lord, and one lot for a remover of sins.*

Vers. 9, 10.—These verses might be translated as follows:—*And Aaron shall bring in the goat upon which the lot for the Lord fell, and shall offer him for a sin offering. But the goat, upon which fell the lot for a remover of sins, shall be presented alive before the Lord, to make an atonement with him, and to send him away for a remover of sins into the wilderness.* We are justified in inserting the words, "of sins," after "a remover," because "the use of the word *azal*, from which the word rendered by 'remover' is derived, is confined in the Hebrew dialect to the single purpose or institution which is here under consideration; so that this particular word must have conveyed to the mind of a Hebrew hearer or reader this notion of a removal of *sins*, and none other" (Sir W. Martin, 'Semitic Languages'). The goat is both **presented before the Lord**, and subsequently (ver. 20) offered to him, the priest laying his hands upon him and making a confession of the sins of the people. After he has thus become the Lord's, how could he be given up to Satan? The purpose of his being set apart is **to make an atonement with him** (not *for him*, as some commentators explain it wrongly). As atonement was made by the blood of the sacrificed goat ceremonially covering sin, so it was also made by the live goat symbolically removing sin. But the atonement in both cases has reference to God. How could an atonement be made by an offering to Satan, unless Satan, not God, was the being whose wrath was to be propitiated, and with whom reconciliation was sought?

Ver. 11.—After having *offered* the bullock for his own sin offering, and *presented* the two goats, which constituted the sin offering of the people, and *offered* one of them, Aaron **kills the bullock for the sin offering.** A considerable interval had to elapse before he could make use of the bullock's blood for purposes of propitiation, and during this interval, occupied by his entrance into the holy of holies with the incense, the blood was held by an attendant, probably by one of his sons, and prevented from coagulating by being kept in motion.

Vers. 12, 13.—This is the first entry of the high priest into the holy of holies. He takes with him a censer—literally, *the censer*, that is, the censer that he was to use on the occasion—full of burning coals of fire from off the altar; and his hands are full of sweet incense beaten small; his object being to fill the holy of holies with the smoke of the incense which may serve as at least a thin vail between himself and the Presence of the Lord, that he die not (cf. Exod. xxxiii. 20, "Thou canst not see my face: for there shall no man see me, and live;" cf. also Gen. xxxii. 30; Deut. v. 24; Judg. vi. 22; xiii. 22). Here we see taught the lesson of the vision of God, as he is, being impossible to the human faculties. He must be vailed in one way or another. After passing through the outer chamber of the tabernacle, the high priest found himself in the smaller chamber where stood the ark. Immediately he threw the incense on the coals of the censer, until the holy of holies was filled with the smoke, after which, according to later practice, he offered a prayer outside the vail. The following form of prayer, breathing, however, the spirit of ages long subsequent to the tabernacle, or even the first temple, is found in the Talmud : — "May it please thee, O Lord our God, the God of our fathers, that neither this day nor this year any captivity come upon us. Yet if captivity befall us this day or this year, let it be to a place where the Law is cultivated. May it please thee, O Lord our God, the God of our fathers, that want come not upon us this day or this year. But if want visit us this day or this year, let it be due to the liberality of our charitable deeds. May it please thee, O Lord, the God of our fathers, that this year may be a year of cheapness, of fulness, of intercourse and trade; a year with abundance of rain, of sunshine, and of dew; one in which thy people Israel shall not require assistance one from another. And listen not to the prayers of those who are about to set out on a journey (against rain). And as to thy people Israel, may no enemy exalt himself against them. May it please thee, O Lord our God, the God of our fathers, that the houses of the men of Saron (exposed to floods) may not become their graves" (Edersheim, 'Temple Service').

Ver. 14.—The second entry of the high priest into the holy of holies took place very soon after the first entry. Immediately that he had returned after lighting the incense, and perhaps offering a prayer, he took of the blood of the bullock, which he had previously killed, went back without delay, and sprinkled it with his finger upon the mercy seat eastward, that is, on the front of the ark beneath the Presence enthroned upon the mercy seat, and shrouded by the smoke of the incense; and before the mercy seat, that is, on the ground in front of it, he sprinkled of the blood with his finger seven times. In after times, when the ark was gone, the high priest sprinkled upwards once and downwards seven times.

Ver. 15.—The third entry was made as soon as he had killed the goat which formed a moiety of the sin offering of the congregation, when he brought his blood likewise within the vail, and did with that blood as he did with the blood of the bullock, sprinkling it the same number of times as before. "By the entrance of the high priest into the holy of holies is set forth that atonement could only be effected before the throne of Jehovah" (Clark).

Ver. 16.—The two sprinklings, first with the bullock's blood, then with the goat's blood, on the front of the ark and on the ground before it, effected the symbolical atonement which was required annually even for the holy of holies because it was pitched in the midst of sinful men. There remained the outer chamber of the tabernacle and the altar of burnt sacrifice to be atoned for. Accordingly, the high priest proceeds to do so for the tabernacle of the congregation, that is, to make a similar atonement by similar means outside the vail as he had made inside it. He would therefore have made one sprinkling with the blood upon the vail, and seven sprinklings before it, after which he placed the blood upon the horns of the altar of incense, according to the command given in Exod. xxx. 10. In later times it became customary also to sprinkle the top of the altar of incense seven times.

Ver. 17.—There shall be no man in the tabernacle of the congregation. From the first entry until the work of atonement was completed, both for the holy of holies and for the tabernacle, no one but the high priest was to be allowed within the door of the tabernacle, not only that there might be no witness of the withdrawal of the awful vail, but also that the rite of purification might not be interfered with by an impure presence. Even on the Day of Atonement the dwelling-place of God, typical of heaven, was closed to the eye and foot of man, "the way into the holiest of all being not yet made manifest" (Heb. ix. 8), until the Divine High Priest opened the way for his people by his own entrance.

Vers. 18, 19.—The holy of holies and the outer chamber of the tabernacle having been reconciled, the high priest shall go out unto the altar that is before the Lord—that is, the altar of burnt sacrifice in the court, standing in front of the tabernacle, not the altar of incense, as has been supposed by some —and shall take of the blood of the bullock, and of the blood of the goat, and put it upon the horns of the altar round about. And he shall sprinkle of the blood upon it with his finger seven times. This completes the ceremony of "*making an atonement for the holy sanctuary, and making an atonement for the tabernacle of the congregation, and for the altar*" (ver. 33.)

Vers. 20, 21.—The second part of the ceremonies of the day now commences. It was not enough that the defilement of the sanctuary should be covered, and the sins of the priests and people atoned for by the blood of the sacrifices. There remained a consciousness of sin. How was this to be taken away? To effect this, Aaron proceeds to the unique ceremony of the day by which the utter removal of sin from the reconciled people is typified. He shall bring the live goat; this should be translated *offer the live goat*. It is the word used above for the *offering* of the goat that was slain, and it is the word always used for offering sacrifices to the Lord. The first goat had been offered in the usual manner, the offerer laying his hand on his head and perhaps praying over him. Now the second goat is offered, the high priest having to lay both his hands upon the head of the live goat, and confess over him all the iniquities of the children of Israel, . . . putting them upon the head of the goat. The confession of sins, at first extempore, would naturally, as time progressed, become stereotyped into a liturgical form, as it is found in the Mishna: " O Lord, they have committed iniquity; they have transgressed; they have sinned,—thy people, the house of Israel. O Lord, cover over, I entreat thee, their iniquities, their transgressions, and their sins, which they have wickedly committed, transgressed, and sinned before thee, —thy people, the house of Israel. As it is written in the Law of Moses thy servant, saying, ' For on that day shall it be covered over for you, to make you clean; from all your sins before the Lord ye shall be cleansed ' " (Edersheim, ' Temple Service '). During this confession of sins the people remained prostrate in humiliation and prayer in the court of the tabernacle, and it was the custom of the high priest to turn towards them as he pronounced the last words, " Ye shall be cleansed." At the conclusion of the confession, the high priest handed over the goat to a fit man, that is, to a man who was standing ready to take charge of him, and sent him away by his hand into the wilderness.

Ver. 22.—Then the goat went forth, bearing upon him all their iniquities. The slain goat had symbolized and ceremonially

wrought full atonement or covering of sins; but in order to impress upon the mind of the nation a joyful sense of entire liberation from the burden of sin, the second symbol of the disappearing goat is used; so that not only sin, but the consciousness and the fear of the taint and presence of sin, might be taken away from the cleansed and delivered people. The goat is to bear the iniquities of the people unto a land not inhabited. The latter words—in the original, *eretz gezerah*—would be more correctly translated, *a land cut off*, that is, completely isolated from the surrounding country by some barrier of rock or torrent, which would make it impossible for the goat to come back again. Thus the sins were utterly lost, as though they had never been, and they could not return to the sanctified people. The Hebrew word *gazar*, to cut (1 Kings iii. 25; Ps. cxxxvi. 13), is represented in Arabic by *jazara*, and the substantive *gezerah* by *jazirah*, which means an island, or an area surrounded by rivers. The word is still in use in countries where Arabic is spoken, as the designation of a district divided from the neighbouring territories by rivers cutting it off, and making it a sort of island or peninsula. Into such a district as this, the man who led the goat was to let him go. In later times, contrary to the spirit of the Mosaic appointment, the goat was pushed over a projecting ledge of rock, and so killed, a device of man clumsily introduced for the purpose of perfecting a symbolism of Divine appointment. It was more in accordance with the original institution that " the arrival of the goat in the wilderness was immediately telegraphed by the waving of flags, from station to station, till a few minutes after its occurrence it was known in the temple, and whispered from ear to ear, that the goat had borne upon him all their iniquities into a land not inhabited " (Edersheim, ' Temple Service '). Both the goat that was sacrificed and the goat that served as remover of sins typified Christ. The first presents him to our faith as the Victim on the cross, the other as the Sin-bearer on whom the Lord laid " the iniquity of us all " (Isa. liii. 4; cf. 2 Cor. v. 21; Gal. iii. 13). " The reason for making use of two animals is to be found purely in the physical impossibility of combining all features that had to be set forth in the sin offering in one animal " (Keil).

Vers. 23, 24.—In later times another scene was interposed at this point. The high priest, having sent away the man with the goat, recited the passages of Scripture which commanded the observance of the Day of Atonement (chs. xvi.; xxiii. 27—32; Numb. xxix. 7—11), and offered prayers in which the people might mentally join.

Then he went back into the tabernacle of the congregation (not into the holy of holies), and, as all the special atoning and purifying services of the day were now over, he there took off his linen dress, and put it away; and after bathing in the holy place, that is, in that part of the sanctuary set apart for that purpose, he put on his ordinary high-priestly garments, and sacrificed first a goat for a sin offering (Numb. xxix. 16), next his own burnt offering of a ram, and then the burnt offering of the people, which was also a ram and other victims (Ibid.).

Ver. 25.—After the flesh of the burnt sacrifice had been placed in order on the altar, the fat of the sin offering, that is, of the bullock (ver. 6) and of the goat (ver. 15) and of the other goat (Numb. xxix. 16), is placed upon it, and burnt upon the altar, according to the regular practice.

Ver. 26.—The man that let go the goat which served for a remover of sins is to wash his clothes, and bathe his flesh before he comes into the camp. This is not ordered on account of any special defilement attaching to the scapegoat, but only because it had been the symbolical sin-bearer, and therefore conveyed legal uncleanness by its touch. The man who bore the flesh of the other goat to be burnt had to do exactly the same thing (ver. 28).

Vers. 27, 28.—As the blood of the bullock and the goat which had been offered in the special expiatory sacrifices of the day had been carried within the sanctuary (vers. 14, 15), their bodies had to be burnt without the camp (ch. iv. 12). Our Lord being the antitype, not only of Aaron as the Great High Priest, but also of the expiatory sacrifices as the Great Sin Offering, the author of the Epistle to the Hebrews notices that the fact of Christ's having "suffered without the camp" serves as an indication that his blood had in its atoning effects been carried by him into heaven, the antitype of the holy of holies (Heb. xiii. 12). The flesh of the other goat, offered as a sin offering, would have been eaten by the priests in the evening, at a sacrificial meal (ch. x. 17, 18).

Vers. 29—31.—The ceremonies of the Day of Atonement are not appointed for once only, but they are to be of annual observance. This shall be a statute for ever unto you, as long as the nation should exist, that in the seventh month, on the tenth day of the month, ye shall afflict your souls, and do no work at all. The seventh is the sacred month, in which the first, the tenth, the fifteenth, and following days are appointed as holy seasons. The Day of Atonement is the single fast of the Jewish Church occurring once a year only. On it all the members of that Church were to *afflict their souls*, on pain of death (ch. xxiii. 29). The

fast began on the evening of the ninth day, and ended on the evening of the tenth, when it was succeeded by general feasting. During the whole of the twenty-four hours *no work at all* was to be done. In this respect the Day of Atonement was put on a level with the sabbath, whereas on the annual festivals only "servile work" was forbidden (see ch. xxiii. 7, 21, 25, 35). On this day, therefore, as on the weekly sabbath, it was not permitted to collect manna (Exod. xvi. 26), or to plough or reap (Exod. xxxiv. 21), or to light a fire (Exod. xxxv. 3), or to gather wood (Numb. xv. 32—36), or to carry corn or fruit (Neh. xiii. 15), or to sell food or other goods (Neh. xiii. 16), or to bear burdens (Jer. xvii. 22, 23), or to set out grain for sale (Amos viii. 5). And these regulations applied to strangers that sojourned among them as well as to themselves. It was a sabbath of rest; literally, *a sabbath of sabbatism*. The purpose of the abstinence from food and labour was to bring the soul of each individual into harmony with the solemn rites of purification publicly performed not by themselves, but by the high priest.

Vers. 32, 33.—That there may be no mistake, it is specifically enjoined that not only Aaron, but the priest, whom he shall anoint, and whom he shall consecrate—meaning, *the high priest that shall be anointed, and shall be consecrated*—to minister in the priest's office in his father's stead—that is, to succeed from time to time to the high priesthood—shall make the atonement, and shall put on the linen clothes, even the holy garments. Again it may be noticed that the white robes are termed, not the penitential, but the holy, garments.

Ver. 34.—This shall be an everlasting statute unto you. It lasted as long as the earthly Jerusalem lasted, and until the heavenly Jerusalem was instituted, when it had a spiritual fulfilment once for all. "Of old there was an high priest that cleansed the people with the blood of bulls and goats, but now that the true High Priest is come, the former priesthood is no more. It is a providential dispensation of God that the city and temple of Jerusalem have been destroyed; for if they were still standing, some who are weak in faith might be dazzled by the outward splendour of the literal types, and not drawn by faith to the spiritual antitypes. If there are any, therefore, who, in considering the Levitical ritual of the great Day of Atonement, and in looking at the two he-goats—the one sacrificed, the other let go, charged with sins, into the wilderness—do not recognize the one Christ who died for our sins and took away our sins, and do not see there the 'everlasting statute' of which God here speaks by

Moses, let him go up thrice a year to Jerusalem, and there search for the altar which has crumbled in the dust, and offer up his victims there without a priest. But no; thanks be to God, the earthly priesthood and temple are abolished, that we may raise our heart to the heavenly, and look up with faith and love and joy to him who offered himself once for all, and who ever liveth to make intercession for us " (Origen, ' Hom.' x., as quoted by Wordsworth). **And he did as the Lord commanded Moses; that is.** Moses announced to Aaron the Law which was to be carried out about five months later.

HOMILETICS.

Vers. 1—28.—*Union and communion with God* is that which the undepraved heart of man most longs for, and which religion is especially intended to bring about. That this may be effected, the barrier of sin, and of that which represents sin—ceremonial uncleanness—must be broken down. If sin and uncleanness cannot be taken away so as to be as though they had not been, they must, according to their nature, be either punished as justice demands, or be so covered over as to be withdrawn from the sight of the Divine eye. This covering or atonement is wrought by sacrifices for sin, and ceremonial purifications. Hence the public and private sin offerings, and the various forms of cleansing. But in spite of penalties inflicted and sacrifices offered, a mass of crime and sin and uncleanness accumulates year by year, which has not been avenged or cleansed, and this defilement affects the very tabernacle of God and his holy things, as well as the congregation of living men. Therefore an annual atonement and reconciliation were required, which were effected each year on the great Day of Atonement.

I. THE CEREMONIES.

1. Bathing.

2. Robing in white garments.

3. The sin offerings.

4. The entry into the holy of holies.

5. The sprinkling of the blood of the sin offerings on the ark and before the mercy-seat.

6. The scapegoat.

II. THEIR MEANING. All is typical of Christ.

1. Washing with his blood and in the waters of baptism.

2. Clothing with his righteousness.

3. Christ the Sin Offering on the cross.

4. Christ's ascension and entry into heaven (Heb. ix., x.).

5. Christ's life-blood offered on the cross, and carried by him into heaven.

6. Christ the Sin-bearer and the Remover of sins.

III. THE LESSONS. 1. *Reconciliation between God and man has been effected.* For Christ has come and has offered himself as a sin offering. The mass of sins which gathered over mankind age after age, has been covered or atoned for by the blood of Christ, shed by him upon the cross; and those who were alienated are now reconciled. Christ is the all-prevailing Peacemaker, who has united man with man, and man with God. " He is our peace, who hath made both (Gentile and Jew) one, and hath broken down the middle wall of partition between us; . . . for to make in himself of twain one new man, so making peace; and that he might reconcile both unto God in one body by the cross, having slain the enmity thereby. . . . For through him we both have access by one Spirit unto the Father. Now therefore ye are no more strangers and foreigners, but fellow-citizens with the saints, and of the household of God " (Eph. ii. 14—19). And this reconciliation was wrought by one offering, once for all offered. The high priest's atonement was made annually, for the blood of bulls and goats could not, effectually and permanently, but only symbolically and temporarily, take away sins (Heb. x. 4). " But this man, after he had offered one sacrifice for sins for ever, sat down on the right hand of God. . . . For by one offering he hath perfected for ever them that are sanctified " (Heb. x. 12—14). And it was wrought for all mankind. How, then, are all to share in it? By realizing their adoption in Christ, which has been potentially bestowed upon the whole family of man, and is made effective to each individual by his " belief " " in the Word of truth," and his being " sealed " in baptism " with the Holy Spirit of promise " (Eph. i. 13). The spiritual bathing, and clothing in white garments, which are now the privileges of every Christian, derive their sacramental force solely from the Sacrifice of the cross.

2. *Christ has opened for us the way to heaven.* Christ is not only the antitype of the sin offering made for the congregation, but also of the high priest who sacrificed the offering ; for he, the Priest, offered himself, the Victim. The holy of holies, wherein the presence of God exhibited itself, was the type of heaven. Into this place " went the high priest alone once every year, not without blood, which he offered for himself, and for the errors of the people : the Holy Ghost this signifying, that the way into the holiest of all was not yet made manifest " (Heb. ix. 7, 8). Alone, the high priest entered beyond the mysterious vail, and no one might be present, even in the outer chamber of the tabernacle, at the time of his entrance, nor while he was fulfilling his functions before the ark. He could not take any one with him. Not even after the atonement had been made, could those who had been reconciled, whether priests or people, enter there. The vail was drawn again, and all was shrouded in silence and mystery as before. But " Christ is not entered into the holy places made with hands, which are the figures of the true ; but into heaven itself, now to appear in the presence of God for us " (Heb. ix. 24). At his ascension he entered heaven, and (unlike the high priest) there he remained at the right hand of God (Heb. x. 13), having received gifts for men from his Father, and having bestowed them upon his Church by the operation of his Spirit (Eph. iv. 8—11). And not only so, but he opened the way to all his followers. He was the mystical Head, and where the Head was, there the Body would be likewise. By his death he purchased for man an entrance into the presence of God, and an eternal continuance before the throne. " Having therefore boldness to enter into the holiest by the blood of Jesus, by a new and living way, which he hath consecrated for us through the vail, that is to say, his flesh ; and having an high priest over the house of God ; let us draw near with a true heart in full assurance of faith, having our hearts sprinkled from an evil conscience, and our bodies washed with pure water " (Heb. x. 19—22).

3. *Christ has borne, and borne away, our sins.* " Surely he hath borne our griefs, and carried our sorrows : yet we did esteem him stricken, smitten of God, and afflicted. But he was wounded for our transgressions, he was bruised for our iniquities : the chastisement of our peace was upon him, and with his stripes we are healed. All we like sheep have gone astray ; we have turned every one to his own way ; and the Lord hath laid on him the iniquity of us all " (Isa. liii. 4—6). " Christ was once offered to bear the sins of many " (Heb. ix. 28). " Who his own self bare our sins in his own body on the tree, that we, being dead to sins, should live unto righteousness : by whose stripes ye were healed " (1 Pet. ii. 24). Christ, by his sacrifice, not only earns for us forgiveness of sin, but also gives us a consciousness of their forgiveness. Those who, in self-abasement and self-abandonment, have thrown themselves at the foot of the cross, have arisen assured of the pardon of their sins, as though they had seen and felt the burden of them taken off from their necks, and carried step by step into a land cut off, from whence no return for them is possible. If there are any who feel overcome by the weight of their sins, they are taught here that, if they cannot bear them, there is One who can bear them, and that, though they cannot free themselves from them, yet they can be freed. " Behold the Lamb of God, which taketh away the sin of the world ! " (John i. 29).

IV. WARNING. Washed, robed, reconciled, and delivered from sin, and from the consciousness of sin,—what more could have been done for us that God has not done ? What return are we to make ? We are to live as children of God. " Let us hold fast the profession of our faith without wavering ; (for he is faithful that promised ;) and let us consider one another to provoke unto love and to good works " (Heb. x. 23, 24). *Further warning.* The danger of falling away after having been forgiven and admitted to the privileges of sonship. " For if we sin wilfully after that we have received the knowledge of the truth, there remaineth no more sacrifice for sins, but a certain fearful looking for of judgment and fiery indignation, which shall devour the adversaries " Heb. x. 26, 27). One unclean spirit may be exchanged for seven (Matt. xiii. 43—45).

"See that ye refuse not him that speaketh. . . . For our God is a consuming fire" (Heb. xii. 25, 29).

Vers. 29—34.—*The annual reiteration of the purification made on the Day of Atonement* testifies to the imperfections of the Law. "For the Law can never with those sacrifices which they offered year by year continually make the comers thereunto perfect. For then would they not have ceased to be offered?" (Heb. x. 1, 2). Had they done their work perfectly, a repetition of them would not have been required, "because that the worshippers once purged should have had no more conscience of sins" (Heb. x. 2). There was a triple imperfection—in the priest, in the victim, in the effect of the sacrifices. The Levitical priesthood was formed of sinful men, as was testified by the sin offering which the high priest had first to offer for himself before he could offer one for the people: here there was no perfect mediator. The victims were a bullock and a goat; but "it is not possible that the blood of bulls and of goats should take away sins" (Heb. x. 4): here there was no perfect sacrifice. The atonement had to be repeated annually: here there was no perfect result from the offering made. By its very imperfection the Law points forward to and awakens the desire for a better covenant, with a priest after the order of Melchisedec, "holy, harmless, undefiled, separate from sinners" (Heb. vii. 26), with a sacrifice which could sanctify (Heb. x. 10), and which is and can be only "once offered," because it is "a full, perfect, and sufficient Sacrifice, Oblation, and Satisfaction for the sins of the whole world" (Service for Holy Communion).

HOMILIES BY VARIOUS AUTHORS.

Vers. 1—34.—*The great Day of Atonement* (vers. 29—34). One day in the year set apart to the most solemn representation possible of the two facts—the sinfulness of man, the righteous love of God. Atonement underlying the whole of the ceremonial Law, but the insufficiency of the daily sacrifices, set forth by the separation of one day for the special sacrifice, thus pointing to *one* atonement in which all other atonements should be perfected. Solemn warning in the death of the two sons of Aaron, proclaiming the unchangeableness of Divine Law, and unapproachableness of God in his infinite righteousness. Necessity that, while the cloud upon the mercy-seat spoke of holiness and majesty, there should be a more emphatic testimony to love and mercy. Yet that testimony must be in the way of Law and ordinance, therefore itself maintaining that God is just while he is merciful. These preliminary considerations prepare us to take the "great Day of Atonement" as a typical prophecy fulfilled in the revelation of Christ. Notice—

I. THE MEDIATION BETWEEN GOD AND MAN MUST BE A PERFECT MEDIATION. 1. *Personal perfection.* For ordinary ministration, washing feet and hands sufficient. For the great day, entire cleansing. This must be. A fellow-creature, imperfect and sinful, may be employed as a channel of communication between God and us, but not as the efficient Mediator undertaking for both. The spotlessness of Jesus must be more than relative, more than character; it must be absolute, therefore, only as we see it in the Incarnation. Nor can we find satisfaction in the humanity of Christ unless we believe that it was capable of rendering to God an infinitely acceptable sacrifice; therefore, while it was flesh, it must have been free from all taint of sin. We lay our sins on him; then he must be himself absolutely sinless, or else our sins will be increased by his. Only in the pre-existence of the Second Person in the Trinity can we find a support for this doctrine of personal perfection in the man Christ Jesus.

2. *Official perfection.* The high priest must be clothed in spotless garments. "*Holy garments.*" He put off his "golden garments," and put on the white linen, emblematical of official perfection. The continual repetition of the sacrifices and the priestly ablutions, together with the special priestly offerings, represented the necessary imperfection of the ceremonial atonement. The priest's office was seen in its height of dignity in the high priest's office; the high priest's office in its most solemn duty, to enter the holiest once a year and make atonement for all. But the true High Priest

and the true mediation were yet to come. The ministry of Christ was a *perfect offering of man to God,* in his active and passive obedience, and a *perfect revelation and assurance of Divine favour to man ;* in the *facts of his earthly life,* promising healing and restoration for human woes, and life from the dead ; in the development of a perfect humanity by example ; in the unfolding and proclamation of the heavenly kingdom, which actually commenced in his person, and proceeded in ever-widening spheres of spiritual life in his Church ; in his *risen glory and the bestowment of the Holy Spirit,* which were the completion of his official work as Mediator, for he said that if he went to the Father (that is, as Mediator), he would send the Comforter. Thus the vail was taken away, and the way into the holiest made manifest (Heb. ix. 8 ; x. 19—23). Our High Priest is not one of an imperfect succession of Aaron's sons, but after the order of Melchisedec, coming forth directly from God, and standing in unique perfection ; the pledge at once of Divine acceptance and the spiritual liberty of the gospel.

II. VICARIOUS ATONEMENT. The three facts of the day were : 1. The blood of the victims shed and sprinkled. 2. The living way opened between the throne of God and his people. 3. The public, solemn putting away of sins and their loss, as guilt, in the wilderness. In the true atonement, thus represented, these are the essential factors— *expiation, reconciliation, restoration.*

1. *Expiation.* The blood of the bullock, the blood of the goat, brought in before the mercy-seat, sprinkled seven times, etc. No remission of sins without blood. A tribute to the holiness of God, therefore to the perfection of the Divine government. No peace can be true and abiding which has not its roots in the unchangeableness of God. Notice how the modern feeling of the steadfastness and uniformity of nature vindicates the necessity of a forgiveness of sin which is a maintenance of Law. The sufferings of Christ must be viewed, not as the arbitrary assignment of a penalty, but as the sufferings of the sacrificial Victim, *i.e.* of him whose blood, that is, his life, was freely offered to seal the covenant, and who, being in the form of a servant, obeyed even unto death ; made of a woman, made under the Law, therefore both having a fleshly, mortal nature, and being in a position of obedience, wherein he must, as a true Son, " fulfil all righteousness." The cross was an open conflict between righteousness and unrighteousness, in which the true representative Seed of the woman, the true Humanity, was bruised, and, as a Victim, laid bleeding and dying on the altar ; but in which, at the same time, the acceptance of the offering, as proved by the Resurrection and Ascension, was a manifestation of the victory of righteousness and the putting away of sin. The universality of the expiation was represented by the offering for priests and people alike, for the holy place, for the very mercy-seat, for all the worship and religious life of the congregation. Apart from the merit of the Saviour's blood, there is no acceptance of anything which we offer to God. The attempt to eliminate all distinctive recognition of expiation from religious worship, is the folly of our times in many who reject the teaching of Christianity. A temple without a sacrifice, without the blood which is the remission of sins, is a contradiction of the first truth of Scripture, that man is a fallen being, and can therefore be acceptable to God only on God's own revealed terms of atonement.

2. *Reconciliation* (vers. 11—14). The true conception of salvation is not a mere deliverance from the punishment of sin, but living fellowship between God and his creature. The life of man is the outcome of God's wisdom, power, goodness, unchangeable and everlasting. He carries eternity and divinity in his very nature and existence. His future blessedness, yea, his very being, must be secured in God's favour. The burning coals of fire from off the altar, and the sweet incense beaten small, rising up as a cloud before the mercy-seat, betoken the intermingling of the Divine and human in the life of God's reconciled children. This is maintained by the offerings of faith and prayer : the light of Divine truth penetrating the mind and life of man, the heart rejoicing in God and seeking him by a constant reference of all things to him, and dependence of daily life on his mercy. When thus the will and love of God underlie all our existence and pervade it, there is an open way between this world and heaven ; the two are intermingled. Man becomes what he was made to be—a reflection of his Maker's image. " I will say, It is my people, and they shall say, The Lord is our God." Christianity has the only true message of hope for the world, because it proclaims reconciliation between the infinite perfection of God and the polluted and imperfect humanity which he has redeemed.

3. *Restoration* (vers. 20—28). *The scapegoat*—an emblem of the entire deliverance of man from the guilt and misery of sin. The necessity of this proclamation of a new world. Heathen minds recognized the evil of sin, but lay under the spell of fatalistic despair. " No symbol could so plainly set forth the completeness of Jehovah's acceptance of the penitent, as a sin offering in which a life was given up for the altar, and yet a living being survived to carry away all sin and uncleanness." The commencement of all renovation of character and life is the sense of entire forgiveness, perfect peace with God. The sins are gone into the wilderness, they have not to be cleansed away by any efforts of ours. Spiritual restoration lies at the root of all other. " *The kingdom of God* " is *first* " *righteousness*," then " *peace*," and then " *joy in the Holy Ghost*." This is the Divine order of restoration. But as the priest put his hand upon the head of the goat, and confessed over him all the iniquities of the children of Israel, so in the Divine work of grace on behalf of man, there must be the living faith which blends the penitent submission of the human will with the infinite sufficiency of the Divine righteousness and power.—R.

Ver. 31.—"*A sabbath of rest*." " Ye shall afflict your souls." The true penitence is the true peace. The " sabbath " represents the joyful acceptance of the creature, and his entrance into the Divine satisfaction. The Lord rested, and he invites man to rest with him. Sin is the only obstacle to that reconciliation and fellowship which blends man's sabbath with God's sabbath. " Once a year " the Jews celebrated this restoration, to us a statute of daily life—every day a sabbath.—R.

The climax of sacrificial worship, the Day of Atonement. Ch. xvi. ; cf. John i. 29; 1 Cor. v. 7; Heb. ix. x. The sacrifices already considered all bring out with more or less emphasis the idea of atonement. But to render this cardinal idea of our religion still more emphatic, it was ordained that the tenth day of the seventh month in each year should be a day of special humiliation on the part of the people, and special ritual on the part of the priests. The directions about it were apparently given immediately after the presumption and death of Nadab and Abihu, the sons of Aaron. They must have ventured, we think, into the very " holiest of all," with their censers of unholy fire. The stages in atonement may be set forth in the following way :—

I. THERE IS THE VOLUNTARY HUMILIATION OF THE HIGH PRIEST. The Day of Atonement was the high priest's day; he undertook the atoning work, and no man was to venture near the tabernacle (ver. 17) while he was engaged in it. The first thing required of him was *humiliation*. He had to lay aside his glorious garments in which he usually ministered, and to assume plain white linen ones; he had to bring a sin offering for himself and household ; he had thus to humble himself under the mighty hand of God, before he could be exalted by admission to the Divine presence. Now, it requires the high priest with his sin offering to typify with any adequacy Jesus Christ. For he is both our High Priest and our Sin Offering. He humbles himself to die as a Sacrifice upon the cross; he is a voluntary Sacrifice—he offers himself (Heb. vii. 27). The humiliation of our High Priest can only be judged by our conception of the *glory* of Divinity which he temporarily resigned, added to the depth of ignominy into which in his crucifixion he came. All this was necessary that a way of reconciliation might be opened up for sinners.

II. THE HIGH PRIEST WAS REQUIRED NEXT TO PERFUME THE AUDIENCE CHAMBER WITH INCENSE. He proceeded with a censer of coals from off the altar, and a handful of incense, and was careful to fill the holy of holies with the fragrant cloud. Here again does it require the incense, in addition to the priest, to typify the relations of Jesus to our atonement. The work of atonement begins in his intercession. Think how he prayed during his life on earth—how earnest his prayer in Gethsemane was when he sweat as it were great drops of blood; think, further, how his intercession is continued in the heavenly places. Prayer is the beginning, middle, and end of the redemptive work. Without this incense, even the blood of the unblemished lamb would lose much of its effect.

It seems evident from this that we must put away those hard and business-like illustrations of atonement, as a hard bargain driven on the one side and paid literally and in full on the other. We must allow a sufficient sphere in our conceptions for the play of intercession and appeal, and remember that, while it is a God of justice who is satisfied, he proves himself in the transaction a God of grace.

III. AFTER THE INCENSE THERE IS BROUGHT IN THE BLOOD, FIRST OF HIS OWN SIN OFFERING, AND THEN OF THE PEOPLE'S. The blood of Jesus Christ is symbolized by both, and the act of sprinkling it before God is also to be attributed to our Great High Priest. "For Christ is not entered into the holy places made with hands, which are the figures of the true; but into heaven itself, now to appear in the presence of God for us." "Neither by the blood of goats and calves, but by his own blood he entered in once into the holy place, having obtained eternal redemption for us" (Heb. ix. 24, 12). Now, the presentation of blood unto God, and the sprinkling of it seven times in the appointed place, represented the appeal which the self-sacrifice of Jesus, his Son, is so well calculated to make to the Divine mercy in the interests of guilty men. The law of mediation is that self-sacrifice stimulates the element of mercy in the Judge.[1] And if it be objected that surely God does not require such an expensive stimulant, the reply is that the self-sacrificing Son and the stimulated Father and Judge are in essence one. The act is consequently a Divine self-sacrifice, to stimulate the element of mercy towards man, and make it harmonize with justice. Here then we have remission of sins secured through the shedding of the blood of Jesus. Pardon and reconciliation are thus put within the reach of the sinner.

IV. BUT THE HIGH PRIEST WAS EXPECTED NOT ONLY TO SECURE THE PARDON OF SINS, BUT ALSO TO PUT IT AWAY BY THE DISMISSAL OF THE SCAPEGOAT. For the pardon of sin is not all man needs. He requires sin to be put away from him. He needs to be enabled to sing, "As far as the east is from the west, so far hath he removed our transgressions from us" (Ps. ciii. 12). Now, this putting away of sin was beautifully represented in the dismissal of the scapegoat. This second sin offering, after having the sins of the people heaped upon its head by the priestly confession, is sent away in care of a faithful servant to the wilderness, there to be left in loneliness either to live or die. Here again we have a type of Jesus. He is our Scapegoat. He carried our sins on his devoted head into that wilderness of desolation and loneliness, which compelled from him the cry, "My God, my God, why hast thou forsaken me?" There did he fully atone for them, and secured their annihilation. As we meditate upon this portion of his mediation, we are enabled by the Spirit to realize that sin is put away through Christ's sacrifice of himself (Heb. ix. 26). That desolation of the Redeemer into which he entered for us interposes itself, so to speak, between us and our sins, and we feel a wholesome separation from them. How can we ever love sin when we realize that it led our Lord to this?

V. THE HIGH PRIEST, HAVING THUS DISPOSED OF SIN, RESUMED HIS GLORIOUS GARMENTS, AND OFFERED THE BURNT OFFERING FOR HIMSELF AND THE PEOPLE. The stages already noticed have been prayer, the remission of sins through the shedding of blood, and the putting away of sin through the dismissal of the victim. Now comes dedication as the crowning purpose of the atonement, and which the burnt offering all along has indicated. It is Christ who offers this burnt offering, and *is* the Burnt Offering. That is to say, he has offered for men a perfect righteousness, as well as afforded us a perfect example. Our consecration to God is ideally to be a perfect one—but really how imperfect! but Christ is made unto us sanctification; we are complete in him; we are accepted in the Beloved; and we learn and try to live as he lived, holy as he was holy.

Moreover, upon the burnt offering was presented the fat of the sin offering, the Lord thus emphasizing his satisfaction with the atonement, and his acceptance of it. The remainder of the sin offering, as a sacred thing, is carried to a clean place without the camp, and there burned. In no more beautiful way could God convey the assurance to his people that the ritual of atonement was complete and acceptable to him. It is when we gratefully dedicate ourselves to God, which is our reasonable service, that we receive the assurance of acceptance in the Beloved.

VI. THE WASHING OF THE THREE MEN OFFICIATING ON THE DAY OF ATONEMENT CONVEYS SURELY THE IDEA OF THE CONTAMINATING POWER OF SIN. For the high priest, before he puts on the glorious garments and presents the burnt offering, is

Cf. Mozley, *ut supra*, p. 169.

required to wash himself in water. The man who piloted the scapegoat to the wilderness has also to perform careful and complete ablutions. And so has the man who took the remains of the sin offering beyond the camp. For all three had to deal with sin, and are ceremonially affected by it. Most vivid must have been the impression thus produced upon the people. Sin would appear the abominable thing which God hates, when it is so defiling.

We have here the climax of the sacrificial worship. The Day of Atonement would be a rest indeed to the sin-burdened people. At the tabernacle they see in ritual how God could be reconciled to man, and how he could pardon and put away sin. As the smoke of the burnt offering passed up to heaven, many a soul felt that a burden was gone, and that the heavens were smiling once more. May the experience of the day of atonement abide in our hearts still, for we need it as much as the pilgrims long ago.—R. M. E.

Vers. 1—4.—*The high priest on the Day of Atonement.* The Jewish high priest was an eminent type of Christ. He was this on ordinary occasions of his ministry, in respect to which Jesus is called "the High Priest of our profession" (Heb. iii. 1). But he was especially so upon this great occasion of his entrance into the most holy place.

I. THE MOST HOLY PLACE OF THE TEMPLE WAS A TYPE OF HEAVEN. 1. *The tabernacle was a figure of the universe.* (1) It represented the *material* universe. In allusion to this, Paul speaks of the universe as the great house built by the hands of God (see Heb. iii. 3, 4). And our Lord, also, alluding to the temple with its many courts and offices, speaks of the universe as his Father's house (John xiv. 1). (2) It likewise represented the *moral* universe. In this light it is also viewed by Paul in the same connection as that in which he likens it to the material (see Heb. iii. 6). In many places of Scripture the people of God are described under the similitude of the temple (see 1 Cor. iii. 16; 2 Cor. vi. 16; Eph. ii. 21, 22; 1 Pet. ii. 5). 2. *The holy places signified the heavens.* (1) Amongst the coverings were what our version calls " badgers' skins," but the original word (תחש), *techesh*, in ancient versions is explained to denote a colour, viz. *blue.* The covering may have been composed of rams' skins dyed *blue*, as the other covering was of "rams' skins dyed *red.*" Blue was the proper colour to suggest the *air*, while the red would suggest the golden glow of the *light* in the ethereal heavens. (2) Josephus, speaking of the gate of the porch of the temple, which stood always open, styles it an "emblem of the heavens." And the vail leading from the porch to the holy place, made like Babylonish tapestry (Josh. vii. 21) of blue, purple, scarlet, and fine twined linen, he compares to the elements ('Wars,' v. 5). Josephus also describes the branched candlestick, with its seven lights, as emblems of the planets of the solar system. (3) But whatever may be said of details, the broad fact is not left to conjecture or even to tradition; for Paul tells us plainly that the holy places were patterns of the heavens (Heb. iv. 14; ix. 23). 3. *The most holy place figured the supreme heaven.* (1) This must be obvious from the fact that the Shechinah was there. God appeared then in regal state upon his throne of glory. The cherubim around him represented the powers of creation, physical and intellectual, which all wait upon him to fulfil his will everywhere in the great universe. Their faces were so placed that, while they all looked inward upon the propitiatory, they also looked outward in all directions upon the house. (2) This innermost sanctuary Paul accordingly describes as "heaven itself"—an expression synonymous to the "third heaven," and "heaven of heavens" (Heb. ix. 24; 2 Cor. xii. 2, Deut. x. 14; Ps. cxv. 16). It is the palace of God and of angels.

II. THE ENTRANCE OF THE HIGH PRIEST INTO THE MOST HOLY PLACE ADUMBRATED THAT OF JESUS INTO HEAVEN. (See Heb. viii. 1, 2; ix. 11, 12, 23, 24.) 1. *He entered in his white garments.* (1) Not in his "golden robes." These are vulgarly supposed to have been his nobler vestments, and it is thought that entering in his white garments he appeared in "mean" attire, to express "humiliation" and "mourning" (see Matthew Henry, *in loc.*). (2) But is this opinion just? Where are the white robes of the high priest so described in Scripture? Is it not rather the other way (see Ezek. xliv. 17)? Are the seven angels (Rev. xv. 6) described as in mean attire? As a matter of fact, did Jesus *meanly* or *mourningly* enter heaven? Was it not rather his entrance "into his glory" after his "sufferings" were "finished" (Luke xxiv. 26)? (3) The white robes represented the glorious body of his resurrection (see 1 Tim. vi. 14—16; Heb. ix. 24, 25). And a specimen of the quality of these garments was given on the mount of transfiguration, when the light of his glory was so white that no fuller on earth could make linen to compare with it (see Matt. xvii. 2; Mark ix. 3). 2. *Note now the allusion to Nadab and Abihu.* (1) (See ver. 1; refer also to ch. x. i, 2.) This terrible event occurred in the wilderness of Sinai (Numb. iii. 4), where the Law was given, and where these very men were called up with Aaron to witness the glory of the Lord (Exod. xxiv. 1). Whatever induced them to offer strange fire, they became, in the sequel, a figure of Jesus, who came not with legal righteousness, and whom the fire of God was to search to the utmost. (2) Aaron now became a similar type (see ver. 2). He was to die if he came near Jehovah, and so represented Jesus, who, in the union of his manhood with the Godhead, was to die. This issue was only averted from Aaron by the substitution of animal sacrifices, which were to procure the "forbearance of God," until Immanuel should put away typical sin sacrifices by the sacrifice of himself. (3) To avert death from Aaron, God appointed that incense also should be fumed before the mercy-seat, in the cloud of which he would appear (vers. 2, 12, 13). The cloud tempered the fierceness of the fire of the presence of God, and showed that, in virtue of the intercession of Christ, man may see God and live.—J. A. M.

Vers. 5—28.—*The sacrifices of the Day of Atonement.* Upon ordinary occasions sacrifices might be offered by common priests, who might act as representatives of the high priest or as representatives of the people, and so be types of Christ, or types of Christians. But upon this day the high priest must act in person, which leaves no doubt as to these transactions being eminently emblematical of Christ and of his great work. We notice—

I. THE OFFERINGS FOR AARON AND HIS HOUSE. (See ver. 6.) 1. *In these Christ is viewed in his relation to his Church.* (1) The Christian Church is the house or family of Jesus (Heb. iii. 6). (See Ps. cxxxv. 19, where the "house of Aaron," as opposed to the "house of Israel," may be spiritually construed to denote the *Christian* as opposed to the *Hebrew* Church.) (2) To his Church Jesus stands in the relations of (*a*) Priest, (*b*) Sacrifice, (*c*) Bondsman. He bears our sin in his own person, and dies for us, as Aaron would have died for his own sin and that of his house, had not the sin sacrifices been substituted to procure the forbearance of God until our competent Aaron should appear to satisfy all the claims of justice and mercy. (3) Aaron, in making atonement for himself and his house, evinced that Christ should be a priest having compassion (see Heb. v. 2, 3). For though Jesus had no sin of his own, yet did he take upon him our nature, with its curse, so as to be "touched with the feeling of our infirmities" (comp. Heb. vii. 28, margin; ii. 18; iv. 15). What a blessed assurance for us! 2. *But Christ cannot be of the family of Aaron.* (1) Aaron for himself and for all his house needed sacrifices to atone for their own sins; how then could they put away sin from others? This they could only do typically and ceremonially (see Heb. vii. 26, 27). (2) Provision was made in the family of Aaron for the transmission of the priesthood from hand to hand; it was therefore never contemplated that any member of that house should have the priesthood in perpetuity. But this we must have in the office of a perfect Priest. His intercession must have no interruption (see Heb. vii. 23—25). (3) To fulfil these conditions, Christ is come, a high priest after the order of Melchisedec (Ps. cx. 4; Heb. vii. 15—22). He sprang from Judah, of which tribe Moses spake nothing concerning priesthood (Heb. vii. 11—14). We may praise God for the perfection of the priesthood of Christ, which needs no supplement in the offices of mortals.

II. THE OFFERINGS FOR THE PEOPLE. 1. *There was the burnt offering.* (1) This, under ordinary circumstances, for the individual might be a bullock, or a ram, or a he-goat, or, in case of poverty, a pigeon; but in this case for the nation, as in the consecration of the priests, the ram is specified (ch. i. 3, 10, 14; viii. 18). It is suggested that this animal was chosen for the offensiveness of its smell, in order to represent the odiousness of sin. (2) In this case also the high priest in person, and alone, officiated. No one was to remain with him in the tabernacle of the congregation (ver. 17). What an expressive figure of Christ (see Isa. lxiii. 3, 5; Zech. xiii. 7; Matt. xxvi. 31,

56; John xvi. 32)! No one *could* help Jesus in his great work of atonement. 2. *The sacrifice of the two goats now claims attention.* (1) Two are brought, to foreshadow what one could not adequately, viz. that one part only of the compound person of Christ could die, while both parts were necessary for his making atonement. The animal on which the lot fell to be the scapegoat was to stand alive before the Lord, to make atonement with him (ver. 10; see Heb. viii. 3; 1 Pet. iii. 18). The "somewhat" which our high priest has to offer is his humanity, which his Godhead supported and rendered infinitely efficacious for the expiation of sin. (2) In casting lots upon the goats, one for the Lord, and the other for the scapegoat, we are taught that the sufferings of Christ were ordered by the providence of God (see Acts iv. 28). This is amply evinced in the wonderfully detailed anticipations of prophecy. (3) Aaron laid his two hands upon the head of the creature that was to be the scapegoat, and confessed the sins of the congregation. These were such as may not have been atoned for by the usual sacrifices. And they are summed up as "iniquities" and "transgressions" and "sins" (ver. 21). Laden with these, (4) he was sent away "by the hand of a man of opportunity" (ver. 21, margin). Such was Simon the Cyrenian, who bore the cross on which the atonement was to be made for sin (Matt. xxvii. 32; see Gal. vi. 14; Eph. ii. 16; Col. ii. 14). Jesus was hurried along to his execution by the rabble rather than by any officer appointed to lead him. And as the man of opportunity was to be unclean until he had bathed his flesh and washed his clothes, so will the blood of the murder of Jesus be upon the Jews until it is cleansed by their repentance and faith (comp. Matt. xxvii. 25 and Joel iii. 21). (5) The scapegoat was to go away with its burden into a "a land not inhabited," or "land of separation," a "wilderness," a place in which it might be lost sight of. This was designed to teach us how effectually our sins are borne away into oblivion by Christ (Ps. ciii. 12; Isa. xxxviii. 17; Micah vii. 19; John i. 29; Heb. viii. 12). To set forth this important truth, it was also ordered that the bodies of those beasts whose blood was brought into the sanctuary by the high priest for sin, were *burnt without the camp* (ver. 27; Heb. xiii. 11, 12). So, like the "man of opportunity," whoever burnt the sin offering became unclean, and so remained until he had washed (see Zech. xiii. 1). Have we been purified from all complicity in the guilt of the crucifixion of Jesus?—J. A. M.

Vers. 29—34.—*The Day of Atonement.* In this summary we have the design of the statute.

I. Atonement was made for the tabernacle. 1. *The work of Christ affects the material universe.* (1) The tabernacle, we have seen (see on vers. 1—4), was a type of the universe, material and moral; and that the holy places represented the heavens. The sprinkling of the tabernacle and its holy places, therefore, teaches that the universe is affected by the atonement of Christ (vers. 15—19, 33; Heb. ix. 12, 23, 24; Rev. v. 6). (2) Aaron, as the type of Christ, entered into the holiest place, but then only once in the year, nor could he without dying open an entrance into it even for his son, who, in his turn, could only enter there as the type of Christ. This showed that, while the tabernacle stood, the way into the holiest was not made manifest. But the vail was not only rent in the torn flesh of Jesus, so that he himself became the Way, but he entered heaven himself once for all (Heb. x. 19, 20). (3) Do we avail ourselves of the privileges of our spiritual priesthood (Heb. x. 21, 22)? 2. *The work of Christ influences the moral universe.* (1) Angels, therefore, manifested interest in the sufferings of Christ and the glories that should follow (Exod. xxv. 20; Dan. viii. 13; 1 Pet. i. 11—13). The sprinkling of the holy places teaches that, through the atonement of Christ, holy angels are reconciled to us. By the sanctifying power of his grace we are brought into sympathy with them. (2) They are now, therefore, interested in the welfare of the Church; and are themselves a part of the great family of Jesus (see Dan. xii. 5, 6; Eph. i. 10; iii. 10, 15; Phil. ii. 9—11).

II. Atonement was made for the people. 1. *None were exempted from the need of it.* (1) Aaron and his house were in the same category with the people in this respect. Though types, they were yet sinful men. (2) But through the bloodshedding of this day, all stood "clean from all sins before the Lord," *i.e.* he looked upon them and accepted them as clean. So in the great day of judgment will he look upon us and accept us as clean through the sprinkling of the blood of Jesus

Christ (Jude 24). 2. *It was a general expiation.* (1) It occurred but once in the year. It was to atone for iniquities, transgressions, and sins, which, through ignorance, inadvertency, or perhaps neglect, had not been atoned for by ordinary sacrifices. Christ not only atones for particular sins, but for sin itself. (2) It was repeated every year. The utmost the Jewish priest could do was to call sin to remembrance, and point to a greater than himself, who needed not to repeat his offering (see Heb. x. 1—3).

III. THE DAY OF ATONEMENT WAS TO BE KEPT AS A SABBATH. 1. *In it they were to afflict their souls.* (1) (See ver. 31; also Ps. xxxv. 13; Isa. lviii. 6, 7, 13; Dan. x. 3, 12.) (2) Resting from the toil of the world, with afflicted souls, while their sins were called to their remembrance, suggests that repentance towards God must accompany faith in the Lord Jesus Christ (Acts xx. 21). 2. *In it they were to rest.* (1) This suggested relief from the burden of sin. What a gracious sabbath in the soul is the sense of sins forgiven! (2) This would be all the more expressive upon the year of jubilee, which, every forty-ninth year, came in on the Day of Atonement (ch. xxv. 9). 3. *The time was the tenth day of the seventh month.* (1) Dr. Lightfoot computes that this was the anniversary of the day on which Moses came the last time down from the mount, bringing with him the renewed tables, and having the glory shining in his face. (2) Jesus appears literally to have ascended into the heavens, as his type passed behind the vail, on the tenth day of the seventh month (see reasoning conducting to this conclusion in the appendix of Mr. Guinness's work on 'The Approaching End of the Age'). It was the time of the vintage, and marks the fulness of the atonement (see Mark xii. 1—9; comp. Rev. xix. 15). (3) It may prove that, on some anniversary of this day, Jesus will come down from heaven, in a glory immeasurably brighter than that in which Moses descended from the mount, to set up his kingdom upon this earth (see Acts i. 11). The vintage of his wrath upon his enemies precedes the sabbath of his kingdom.—J. A. M.

Ver. 6.—*A solemn ceremony.* There was risk involved in drawing nigh to the manifested presence of the Deity. God desired not that the judgment upon Nadab and Abihu should be repeated; rather would he be "sanctified" by reverent approach at appointed seasons in appointed ways. The Almighty can cause the wrath of man to praise him, but he prefers to be honoured by the affection that seeks diligently to observe his precepts. Hence the directions issued concerning the great Day of Atonement, on which the high priest was to come into closest contact with Jehovah. Let us consider those directions so far as they related to the purging away of the uncleanness of the priests.

I. THE FACT THAT THE HIGH PRIEST WAS TO MAKE ATONEMENT FOR HIMSELF AND HIS HOUSE. 1. *It prevented pride, keeping alive in his breast a sense of infirmity.* The expression, "for his house," means his sons, and afterwards all who were of the priestly order. The pomp of office requires some guarantee against undue exaltation. A lofty position is apt to turn a weak man's head, and his fall becomes the more calamitous. It is certain that the highest in the Church of Christ cannot claim exemption from sin. 2. *It enkindled sympathy with those for whom he had to exercise his sacred functions* (see this beautifully insisted on in the Epistle to Heb. v. 2, 3). Note likewise the superiority of Christ's sympathy because of exquisite holy tenderness of spirit, unblunted by passion. Jesus Christ acquired a fellow-feeling by his humiliation in becoming man, and in being tempted in all points like as we are, whereas Aaron was exalted to be a high priest, and needed to remember his humanity. If Aaron forgot this, and treated the worshippers gruffly, not only would their feelings be wounded, but his intercession would be so much the less efficacious, for even under the Law sentiment was requisite as well as symbol. 3. Its priority to the atonement made for the people *emphasized the truth that only the cleansed can make others clean, only the sinless can rightly intercede for the sinful.* Because Jesus Christ is holy, he sanctifies his followers. He who was eminently forgiving could pray to his Father to forgive his murderers. None but believers saved through grace should preach the gospel. 4. *It prophesied the eventual supersession of Aaron's order by a perfect priesthood.* There was evidence of defect in its very face. Not always could God be satisfied with or man rejoice in imperfect mediation. An intercessor needing forgiveness for himself, a purifier who had constantly to cleanse himself, pointed to the advent of One who should have no need to offer up yearly sacrifice on his own account, whose purity should be real, not merely ceremonial and symbolical.

II. THE CEREMONY ENJOINED. 1. *The attire.* The gorgeous clothing of colour, gold, bells, and pomegranates, was laid aside, the whole body washed in water, and a garb of white linen donned. It was a day in which the fact of sin was prominent, and splendour ill befitted such an occasion. Besides, the high priest was not to look upon himself this day as representing God to the people, but as presenting the people to God, and a humble demeanour, indicated by plain attire, was appropriate to this function. Then, too, the white linen spoke of the holiness which the day's services were to secure. It was the garment of salvation, in which God manifested his willingness to be the Saviour of the people from their sins. 2. *The sacrifices,* a sin offering and a burnt offering. Leaving consideration for the present of what was peculiar to the day in the former, here note (1) that a harmony is observable in all God's laws. Whilst this sin offering had its special rites, in other respects it was to be treated according to the general rules—a portion consumed on the altar, and the carcase burnt outside the camp. A likeness is traceable in the dealings of God, whether ordinary or extraordinary. Underlying features are discerned similar to those ascertained in other departments. Miracles have their customary analogies and laws; the operations of the Spirit proceed on familiar lines and principles; the worship and service of heaven will present some of the aspects that have marked the gatherings in the sanctuaries of earth. (2) Again we observe how purification precedes consecration. The burnt offering followed the sin offering. After fresh ablution, the high priest arrayed himself in his usual vestments, and proceeded to place the holocaust upon the altar, to be the emblem of unreserved surrender to God's glory. Having been bought with the precious blood of Christ, and thus redeemed from sin, we are enabled to dedicate ourselves to the service of God. It is in vain that men attempt the latter without the former. 3. *The entrance into the holy of holies.* How solemn and full of awe the moment in which the priest drew aside the vail and came near to the Divine presence! He was alone with God! It was dark but for the mysterious light that appeared between the cherubim, and the glowing coals on which he put the incense. Not too clearly might man contemplate even "the cloud" that was the enwrapment of Jehovah; the cloud of incense must cast an additional covering over the mercy-seat. Not lingering to indulge profane curiosity, the high priest sprinkled the blood of the sin offering upon the front of the mercy-seat, and upon the floor of the holy place. What a view was thus obtained of the majesty of God! what thoughts of his condescension in permitting a sinful creature to have such access to him! May not we learn the impiety of seeking to pry too closely into the mysteries of the Divine existence? Prayer becomes us in appearing before him; then do we know most of God, and protect ourselves from death. And the prayer is made efficacious through the atoning blood. The ark containing the commandments which we have transgressed is covered by the golden plate of Divine mercy, and that mercy is everlastingly secured by the atonement wherewith it is honoured and appealed to.

CONCLUSION. The privilege of the high priest was nothing to what we enjoy. What boldness we may use in entering into the holiest by the blood of Jesus! What remission of sins, what freedom from guilt, what liberty and gladness are ours! *Our High Priest has entered as our Forerunner,* not for us merely, *into heaven itself* (Heb. ix. 8). As Aaron came forth from the sanctuary to the Israelites, so shall Christ appear, apart from sin, to them that wait for him unto salvation. He shall "receive us unto himself."—S. R. A.

Vers. 29—34.—*The Day of Atonement.* This was a day second to none in importance. The rites then celebrated were the most awe-inspiring of all, and concerned the whole nation, which stood watching outside the sacred enclosure of the tabernacle. Not the slightest deviation from the established ritual was allowable; it was too significant and solemn in character to permit of alteration.

I. It was A DAY OF UNIVERSAL ATONEMENT. The high priest made atonement for himself and the order of priests, for the people of the congregation, for the brazen altar, for the tabernacle, and for the sanctuary. Thus was taught the truth that sin mingles with the holiest of men and their deeds, with the holiest things and places. Defilement attaches to our highest acts of worship, to our best thoughts and prayers. The tabernacle needed cleansing because of the "uncleanness" of the people (ver. 16) among whom it was situated. The noblest men receive some degree of contamination from their surroundings, and the purest principles have some alloy adhering to them through use. Mere ignorance of specific transgressions was not sufficient to obviate the necessity of atonement. Sin was there, though they should discern it not. "I know nothing against myself, yet am I not hereby justified." Could any spectacle more vividly impress upon the mind the reality of sin and the need of its removal?

II. It was A DAY OF HUMILIATION. "Ye shall afflict your souls." The word implies self-denial and consequent fasting. Not lightly was sin to be regarded! We are ever ready to extenuate our guilt and to minimize its enormity. The transgressions in respect of which a sin offering was prescribed were not high-handed acts of rebellion, but such as resulted from man's frailty, from natural depravity. Yet this was not deemed an excuse of itself, it only showed the importance of providing for its atonement. No man with a perception of the magnitude of his iniquity can retain a heart at ease, a conscience at rest. If there be such quietude, it is an evidence of the deadening influence of sin. Though sin has been overruled to the glory of God, it is in itself abominable, and must be viewed with abhorrence. Well may we bow before God in deep abasement!

III. It was A DAY OF REST. No work of any kind was permitted—it was a "sabbath of sabbaths." All the attention of the people was concentrated upon the ceremony observed by the high priest. What a rebuke here to those who cannot spare time to think of their state before God! Surely the transcendent importance of religion justifies occasional abstention from ordinary labour. What shall it profit a man if he gain the whole world and forfeit eternal life? The constitution of our minds does not enable us to think seriously of many things at once. Let not the concerns of the soul be thereby shelved. If we will not afford the necessary period here, there will come a long season of forced meditation, when the subject of sin and its forgiveness shall pierce us through and through with unutterable remorse.

IV. It was A FIXED DAY. God, in his merciful forethought, set apart the tenth day of the seventh month, lest the Israelites should forget the duty incumbent upon them. There are many advantages in having a time determined upon for religious worship. It comes regularly, and even children look for it. It prevents excuses, ensures due remembrance, and leads to fitting preparation. What is to be done at any time is practically for no time. But the observance of such days needs to be guarded against degenerating into formalism and routine. And under the gospel no adventitious sacramentarian importance must be annexed to these seasons, otherwise we fall under the censure of the apostle, as observing "days, and months, and seasons, and years." Oh! for wisdom to distinguish between the true and the false in ordinances!

V. It was A DAY OF YEARLY OBSERVANCE. The imperfection of other sacrifices and purifications was thus clearly demonstrated, for however attended to they did not exclude the Day of Atonement. And the yearly repetition of the day itself told the same tale, pointed the same moral of the impotence of the sacrifices of the Law to "make the comers thereunto perfect" (see Heb. x. 1—4). The day served its purpose indeed, but only by shadow and prefiguration. Compared with the Crucifixion, it was but a "splendid failure" to pacify the conscience, cleanse the heart, and quicken the life of those who participated in its effects.

VI. It was A DAY OF HUMILIATION THAT PREPARED THE WAY FOR A JOYOUS FESTIVAL. After five days commenced the Feast of Tabernacles, distinguished for its rejoicing beyond all others. The ceremonies of the Day of Atonement closed with a burnt offering, in which the people symbolically renewed their self-dedication to the worship and service of God; and very appropriately the chief feature of the Feast of Tabernacles was the large number of burnt offerings presented, as if the people should testify their gladness at the thought of pardoned iniquity, and of belonging to a God who so graciously blessed them and granted the increase of their fields. The man whose sin is forgiven and put away is truly happy. He can devote himself to God with glad ardour. The cloud that brought the storm and darkness has passed to the far horizon, and now it is brightened with many hues from the dazzling sun. Grief on account of sin is not designed to mar permanently the pleasure of our days. The depression is succeeded by elevation of soul.

The surgeon's lance may have pained us, but now we are tranquil through the relief afforded.—S. R. A.

Vers. 1, 2.—*The peril of privilege.* Was it, then, necessary to contemplate the possibility of Aaron's dying at his post? Was he, the chosen servant of God, who had been so solemnly inducted into his office (chs. viii., ix.), in actual peril of death as he ministered unto the Lord? Could he draw too near to God, so as to endanger his very life? It was even so. His two sons, Nadab and Abihu, had paid the extreme penalty of their sin in the service of Jehovah; " they offered before the Lord, and died " at their post. And if Aaron had violated the precepts here given, it is certain that from "the cloud upon the mercy seat" would have flashed the fatal fire which would have destroyed the high priest himself. We are not afraid now (1) of such condign and signal punishment as befell the sons of Aaron: God does not visit us thus in these days; nor (2) of coming too often or drawing too near to God. The barriers which then stood between the manifested Deity and the common people are removed. We may "come at all times" to the mercy-seat, and are in much greater peril of God's displeasure for "restraining prayer," than for intruding into his presence without need. Nevertheless, privilege has its own peculiar peril, and the penalty is very serious: it is death; not physical, but spiritual, eternal death. There may be in our case—

I. PRESUMPTION FROM OFFICIAL POSITION. It is only too possible that those who " offer before the Lord " may come to regard their official duties as things which avail before him, independently of the spirit in which they are rendered. " Many will say, ... have we not prophesied in thy Name . . . and in thy Name done many wonderful works? And then will I profess unto them, I never knew you " (Matt. vii. 22, 23). Many may say, " Have we not preached thy gospel, taught thy truth, evangelized in thy Name?" etc., and—trusting in their official works instead of looking to their inner spirit, and instead of attaching themselves to Christ in penitence and faith—be condemned at his bar.

II. FORMALISM FROM FAMILIARITY. It is all too possible for those who " offer before the Lord " to die a spiritual death, because they lose all real and living appreciation of the things they say and do. There is a subtle but powerful tendency in the human mind to do mechanically and unintelligently that with which it is exceedingly familiar. Not even the most sacred words or solemn rites are proof against it. We may, at the desk, or pulpit, or even at the table of the Lord, take words upon our lips which find no answer in the soul. We may be obnoxious to our Lord's reproach (Matt. xv. 8). To use sacred language without sacred feeling is to move away from the fountain of life; to have entered the precincts of habitual formalism is to have passed the outer portals of the kingdom of death.

III. DISOBEDIENCE FROM DISREGARD TO THE WILL OF GOD. We are not bound to a rigid correspondence with every minute New Testament practice. There are some matters in which changed circumstances demand other methods. But we are bound to search the Scriptures to find the will of our Lord in the worship we render and the work we do for him. If we follow nothing better than " the traditions of men," or our own tastes and inclinations, we may find ourselves in the wilderness—a long way from the water of life.

Whatever position we occupy in the Church of Christ, however much of " the honour that cometh from man " we may enjoy, it is essential that we: 1. Cherish the spirit of humility, and exercise a living faith in Jesus Christ. 2. Realize the truth we speak, and spiritually participate in the services we conduct. 3. Have supreme regard to the will of our Master, seeking to learn that will as devoutly, patiently, studiously, as we can. These things must we do "that we die not" before the Lord.—C.

Vers. 2—17.—*Type and antitype—the priest.* The high priest offering sacrifices for the sin of the people was a clear type of " the High Priest of our profession," who offered the one sacrifice for sin, who became the Propitiation for our sin, even for the sins of the whole world (1 John ii. 2). We have—

I. FOUR FEATURES OF RESEMBLANCE. 1. Aaron acted under Divine direction. He was appointed by God to take the post he took, and was charged to do everything he did. He might not deviate in any particular from the instructions which came from heaven. "Aaron shall" is the continually recurring strain; almost every other verse contains this formula; departure from direction was utter failure in his work and death to himself (ver. 2). 2. Aaron divested himself of his rich attire—he wore not the ephod with precious stones, nor the mitre glittering with golden crown; this splendid attire he laid by on this occasion, and he put on the simple linen coat, and was girded with a linen girdle, and wore a linen mitre (ver. 4). 3. Aaron did his priestly work alone. "There shall be no man in the tabernacle when he goeth in . . . until he come out" (ver. 17). No other foot but his might enter within the vail; no other hand but his might sprinkle the blood on the mercy-seat. 4. Aaron bore a heavy burden for the people. "So laborious and trying was his work that, after it was over, the people gathered round him with sympathy and congratulation that he was brought through it in safety." So Christ, the great antitype, (1) was appointed of God (Heb. v. 4, 5); he was "the Anointed," the Sent One; he "came to do his Father's will," and though under no such minute commandments as those which regulated the actions of Aaron, he was ever consulting the will of the Father, doing "nothing of himself" (John v. 19—30; viii. 28; ix. 4). (2) Divested himself of the robe of his divinity, and put on the frail garment of our humanity (John i. 14; Heb. ii. 14; Phil. ii. 7). (3) "Trod the winepress alone." "Ye shall leave me alone," said he (John xvi. 32). and alone he agonized in the garden, and alone he suffered and died on the cross. His was a most lonely life, for not even his most loved disciple understood the meaning of his mission; and his was a lonely death, none of those who stood weeping by being able to take any part in the sacrificial work he then wrought out. (4) Bore so heavy a burden for us that his heart broke beneath it.

II. THREE POINTS OF CONTRAST. 1. Aaron was compelled to present offerings for himself (vers. 6, 11—14). 2. Had to present an offering that was provided for him; a bullock had to be brought from the herds of Israel (ver. 6), or he would have been a priest without an offering. 3. Could offer no availing sacrifice for deliberate transgressions: presumptuous sin had already paid the penalty of death. But Christ Jesus, our Great High Priest, (1) needed not to present any sacrifice for himself; the holy, harmless, undefiled One, separate from sinners, did not need to offer up sacrifices first for his own sins (Heb. vii. 26, 27). (2) Had no need to procure a victim, for himself

> " . . . came down to be
> The offering and the priest."

He appeared to put away sin by the sacrifice of himself (Heb. ix. 26). (3) Offered a sacrifice which avails for all sin. His blood "cleanseth us from all sin" (1 John i. 7; 1 Cor. vi. 11; Eph. i. 7; Heb. ix. 14; vii. 25, etc.).—C.

Vers. 7—10, 15, 21, 22.—*Type and antitype—the offering.* The most striking feature of the whole service on the great Day of Atonement was the action of the high priest in regard to the two goats brought to the tabernacle door (ver. 7). They clearly point to that "Lamb of God" who came to "take away the sin of the world" (John i. 29). That there were two goats rather than one presents no difficulty at all; there might well have been more than one to typify the Sacrifice which they foreshadowed. We learn—

I. THAT GOD ADMITS VICARIOUS SUFFERING INTO HIS RIGHTEOUS REALM. The innocent goat would shed its blood, would pour out its life, that the guilty human souls might not die, but live. It was a Divine appointment, and shows clearly that the propitiatory element was allowed by the Holy One of Israel. The vicarious principle has a large place in the kingdom of God on earth. Involuntarily and also voluntarily we suffer for others and others for us. Man bears the penal consequences of his brother's sin. He does so when he cannot avoid so doing; and he does so frequently with his own full consent; indeed, by going far out of his way on purpose to bear it. Vicarious suffering runs through the whole human economy. But there is only One who could possibly take on himself the penalty of the world's sin—only One on whom could possibly be "laid the iniquity of us all." That one is the spotless "Lamb of God," that Son of God who became sin for man; he, "for the suffering of death was made a little lower than the angels," and took on him a mortal form. "Surely *he* hath borne our griefs, and carried our sorrows; . . . he was wounded for our transgressions, he was bruised for our iniquities," etc. (Isa. liii. 4, 5; 1 Pet. ii. 24).

II. THAT THE SACRIFICE OF CHRIST AVAILS TO REMOVE COMPLETELY ALL CONDEMNATION. When the children of Israel saw the live goat, over whose head their sins had been confessed, being led away into the waste wilderness where it would never more be seen (ver. 22), they had a very vivid assurance made through their senses to their soul that "their transgressions were forgiven, and their sins covered." No such dramatic assurance have we now, but we may have the utmost confidence that our sins are forgiven us "for his Name's sake;" that "there is no condemnation to us who are in Christ Jesus," to us "who have redemption through his blood, even the forgiveness of sins" (Acts xiii. 39; Rom. v. 9). Trusting in the slain Lamb of God, we may see, by the eye of faith, all our guilt and all our condemnation borne away into the land of forgetfulness, where God will remember it no more for ever.

III. THAT NO SACRIFICE WILL AVAIL ANYTHING WITHOUT ACTIVE PARTICIPATION ON OUR PART. Useless and unavailing altogether the slaying of the one goat and the sending away of the other without the act of confession and the imposition of hands by the high priest (ver. 21); this part of the solemn ceremonial was essential; apart from that everything would have been vain. And without our personal spiritual participation the sacrifice of the Lamb of God will be all in vain. 1. There must be the confession of our sin; a confession of sin which springs from contrition for sin, and is attended by a determination to put all sin away (repentance). 2. Faith in the Divine Redeemer. "Our faith must lay its hand on that dear head of his." 3. And this must be the action of our own individual soul. Whatever guidance and encouragement we may gain from the ministers of Christ, *we ourselves* must repent and believe.—C.

Vers. 29—31.—*The great anniversary—sacred seasons.* The Jews had other special days beside the Day of Atonement. They had their weekly sabbath, the new moon sacrifices, their festivals or "holy convocations" (ch. xxiii.), etc. But this was the "grand climacteric;" there were "high days" during the year, but this was *the* day *of* the year to every devout Israelite. No other was comparable to it in solemnity and sacred importance. Several features of peculiar interest combined to raise it above all other occasions. 1. It was the one annual solemnity prescribed by the Law. 2. It was a day of perfect rest from labour (vers. 29, 31). 3. It was the one day of universal fasting enjoined or encouraged in the Law (vers. 29, 31). 4. It was a day of self-examination and spiritual humiliation (ver. 29). 5. On that day the high priest went perilously near to the manifested presence of God—then, and then only, entering within the vail, and standing in presence of the mercy-seat and the mysterious, awful Shechinah (ver. 12). 6. On that day unusual sacrifices were offered unto the Lord, and a striking spectacle witnessed by the whole camp, the live goat being led away into the wilderness (ver. 21). 7. Then, also, the people felt themselves in an unusually blessed relation to Jehovah—free, as at no other time, from all their sin; they were "clean from all their sins before the Lord" (ver. 30). We may, therefore, well pronounce this the great anniversary of the Hebrew Church. It must have had hallowing influences in both directions of time: it must have been anticipated with interest and awe; it must have left behind it sacred shadows of holy feeling—of unity, reverence, joy in God. The holding of this anniversary "by statute for ever" suggests to us—

I. THAT IN CHRIST JESUS THE OBSERVANCE OF DAYS IS AN OPTIONAL THING. There are valid grounds for believing that it is the will of Christ we should observe the Lord's day as the disciples of him who is "the Resurrection and the Life." But the enforcement of the observance of sacred days by statute binding on the Christian conscience is expressly disallowed (Gal. iv. 10, 11; Rom. xiv. 5, 6; Col. ii. 16).

II. THAT IT IS WISE, AS A MATTER OF CHRISTIAN LIBERTY, TO OBSERVE SOME ANNIVERSARIES. God has, in his providential arrangements, made certain points to be regularly recurring. Time is so measured that we must be periodically reminded of interesting events. God put the lights in the firmament in order that they might not only "give light upon the earth," but that they might be "for signs and for seasons, and for days and for years" (Gen. i. 14). 1. *A Church* should observe: (1) the day of its institution, or (2) the day on which it was conscious of revival, or (3) any particular day which is, to itself, fruitful of sacred suggestions. 2. Individual Christian men may observe (1) the last day of the old year, (2) the first day of the new year, (3) the anniversary of their birthday, or (4) the anniversary of the day which has the most hallowed associations to their mind,—the day of religious decision or that of reception into the visible Church of Christ.

III. THAT THERE IS A TWOFOLD USE WE MAY MAKE OF SUCH ANNIVERSARIES. 1. Solemn retrospect; with careful retreading of past experiences, free and full acknowledgment of God's goodness and our own manifold shortcomings, simple faith in the Divine promise of forgiveness through Christ. 2. Thoughtful forecast; with studious consideration of what may yet be done for the Master and mankind, devout reconsecration of self to the service of the Saviour, believing prayer for Divine guidance and guardianship through future years.—C.

Vers. 33, 34.—*The imperfect ritual and the All-sufficient Sacrifice.* If we place ourselves at the standpoint of a devout and inquiring Hebrew worshipper, we can suppose ourselves to ask, on the morning and evening of the Day of Atonement—

I. WHY THIS ANNUAL CEREMONY? Have not numerous sacrifices been presented all the year round without intermission? Have not daily offerings been laid on the altar, morning and evening? and double sacrifices every sabbath day? and special offerings every month? And have not the people been bringing their presentations, from flock and herd, as piety has dictated, or special circumstances have required, all through the seasons? Have not these "come up with acceptance" before the altar of Jehovah? Has not sin *been* atoned for? What need, then, of these annual solemnities, of this very special ceremony at the tabernacle?

And if to such reflecting worshipper it should occur that the blood of lambs and bullocks, of doves and pigeons, was no real substitute for the forfeited life of men, would he not take a further step in his inquiry, and ask—

II. CAN THIS SUFFICE, ALL OTHER FAILING? What is there in the ceremonies of this sacred day which will avail, if all the year's sacrifices are insufficient? Will the fact that one man will stand in the inner instead of the outer side of a separating vail, and sprinkle blood on one article of tabernacle furniture rather than another,—will this make the difference between the adequacy and the inadequacy of animal sacrifice for human sin? Will the ceremony of slaying one goat and leading the other out into the wilderness constitute the one needful thing that is wanted to remove the guilt of a nation? Surely something more and something greater is wanted still. To these suggested and probable inquiries of the Hebrew worshipper, we reply—

III. THESE TYPICAL SOLEMNITIES DID NOT SUFFICE. It was a striking mark of their insufficiency that the very altar and tabernacle of the congregation, even the "holy sanctuary" itself (ver. 33; see ver. 16 and Heb. iv. 21), had to be "atoned for." Even they became affected by the "uncleanness of the children of Israel." Here was imperfection legibly written on the holy things. And our instructed reason tells us that these things were inherently unsatisfactory. "It is not possible that the blood of bulls and of goats should take away sins" (Heb. x. 4). Such "gifts and sacrifices could not make him that did the service perfect" (Heb. ix. 9; vii. 18, 19). They only served for a time, and drew their temporary sufficiency from the fact that they were to be completed and fulfilled in one Divine Offering, which should be presented in "the fulness of time." And thus we come to—

IV. THE ONE ALL-AVAILING SACRIFICE. In the one Great Sacrifice at Calvary, the death of the Lord Jesus Christ, there is everything which a guilty race requires. 1. No need, now, for annual sacrifices; "in those sacrifices there is a remembrance again made of sins every year" (Heb. x. 3). "But this man, after he had offered one sacrifice for sins for ever," etc., "by one offering he hath perfected for ever them that are sanctified" (Heb. x. 14). Not "once a year," but once for all, once for ever! 2. No need for purifying the holy place. He hath passed into the heavens; has sat down at the right hand of God. The "uncleanness" of man cannot stain his throne of grace. 3. No question as to the efficacy of his atonement. "If the blood of bulls and of goats," etc. (Heb. ix. 13, 14). 4. No limit to the application of his atoning death. The cross of Christ is that on which not merely "all the people of the congregation" (ver. 33), but all human souls in every land and through every age may look, in which they may glory, at which they may leave their sin and fear, from which they may date their inextinguishable hope and their everlasting joy.—C.

EXPOSITION.

CHAPTER XVII.

This chapter finds its natural place here as the supplement of all that has gone before. The first part of the book contains the institution or regulation of the sacrificial system (chs. i.—vii.). This chapter, therefore, which gives injunctions as to the place where all sacrifices are to be offered, might well, as Knobel has remarked, have taken its place as ch. viii. The second part contains the institution of the hereditary priesthood (chs. viii.—x.). This chapter, therefore, which forbids for the future all offering of sacrifices in the open fields, and commands that they shall be brought "*unto the priest, unto the door of the tabernacle of the congregation,*" would still more fitly find its place after ch. x. But the first two sections of the third part (chs. xi.—xvi.) contain the laws and rules respecting cleansing from ceremonial defilement, and this cleansing is to be mainly effected by the means of sacrifice. Therefore the rule as to the place where sacrifice shall be offered is most naturally given here, where it is found (ch. xvii.), forming a close not only to Parts I. and II., but also to the two sections of Part III., which contain the regulations as to purification by sacrifice. It is altogether a mistake to make a Second Book begin with ch. xvii., as is done by Lange and Keil.

The first injunction contained in the chapter (vers. 2—7) is very generally understood to mean that while the Israelites lived in the wilderness, all animals fit for sacrifices which were slain for food should be so far regarded as sacrifices that they should be brought to the door of the tabernacle and slain in the court, an offering of the blood and fat being made to the Lord. Thus the ordinary slaughtering of domestic animals, it is said, became sanctified, and the dignity of life made clear: God is the Lord of life; he gave it, and it must not be taken away unless the blood, which is the vehicle of life, be offered to him by being presented sacrificially on his altar, or, where this is not possible, as in the case of wild animals, by being reverently covered with earth. Such a rule as this respecting the slaughter-

ing of domestic animals, difficult to carry out in any case, would become impossible to obey after the camp had been expanded into a nation, and it is therefore supposed that it is by anticipation repealed in Deut. xii. 15 ("Notwithstanding thou mayest kill and eat flesh in all thy gates, whatsoever thy soul lusteth after, according to the blessing of the Lord thy God which he hath given thee"), while the regulations as to restricting the offering of sacrifice to the court of the temple, and as to pouring blood on the earth, are there emphatically enforced. This view of the text is erroneous, and must be rejected. The injunction does not refer to the ordinary slaughter of domestic animals for food, but only to sacrifices. Hitherto it had been the right and the duty of the head of each family to offer sacrifice for his household, and this he did wherever he thought proper, according to the ancient patriarchal practice, and most naturally in the open fields. This duty and liberty is now abolished. The Aaronic priesthood has superseded the older priestly system, and henceforth every sacrifice is to be offered in the court of the tabernacle, and by the hand of Aaron's sons. The change was most momentous, but it could not but be made after the consecration of Aaron and his sons for an hereditary priesthood. A second reason for the change being made was the immediate danger to which a rude and superstitious people was exposed, of offering the parts which they were bound to set aside for the altar of God to some other deity, if God's priests and altar were not at hand. The imaginations of the Israelites, corrupted by their stay in Egypt, peopled the fields with beings answering to the Pan and the satyrs of the Greeks; and to these the sacred portions of the animals slaughtered elsewhere than at the tabernacle were offered.

Ver. 3.—**What man soever** there be **of the house of Israel, that killeth an ox, or lamb, or goat.** The use of the word *killeth*, instead of *sacrificeth*, is one of the chief causes of the error referred to above, which represents this command as applying to the slaughter of domestic animals. But it is always permissible to use a generic in place of a specific term, and its use proves nothing.

Probably the sacred writer uses it as a less sacred term, and therefore more suitable to sacrifices offered to the spirits of the fields and woods. If ordinary slaughtering were meant, there is no reason why pigeons and turtle-doves should not be added to the *ox, or lamb, or goat.* That every *ox, or lamb, or goat,* to be killed **in the camp, or . . . out of the camp,** for the food of more than 600,000 men, should be brought to so confined a space as the court of the tabernacle for slaughter, where the animals for the daily, weekly, annual, and innumerable private sacrifices were also killed, appears almost incredible in itself. How would the drivers have made their way into it? and what would have soon been the state of the court? It is true that animal food was not the staple sustenance of the Israelites in the wilderness; but not unfrequently, after a successful war or raid, there must have been a vast number of cattle killed for feasting or reserved for subsequent eating.

Ver. 4.—In case a man offers a sacrifice elsewhere than at **the door of the tabernacle of the congregation, . . . blood shall be imputed unto that man;** that is, it shall no longer be regarded as a sacrifice at all, but an unjustifiable shedding of blood, for which he is to **be cut off from among his people,** that is, excommunicated.

Ver. 5.—**To the end that the children of Israel may bring their sacrifices.** This passage tells us the purpose of the previous command: it is to prevent sacrifices being sacrificed (the word is twice used in the original) **in the open field,** or anywhere else than in the court of the tabernacle. It follows that the command refers to sacrifice, not to mere slaughtering. Clark, taking the opposite view of the command, is obliged to change the translation, *sacrifices which they offer in the open field,* into "beasts for slaughter which they now slaughter in the open field" ('Speaker's Commentary'); but he has no authority for doing so. *Zabach* means always, in the Pentateuch, to slay in sacrifice. These field sacrifices, when offered to the Lord in the proper place and with the proper ceremonies, would become **peace offerings unto the Lord.**

Ver. 6.—**The priest,** that is, the Levitical priest, is henceforth to **sprinkle the blood upon the altar of the Lord . . . and burn the fat for a sweet savour,** which were the two parts of the sacrifice which were essentially priestly in their character. The old priestly function of the head of the family is disallowed.

Ver. 7.—**And they shall no more offer their sacrifices unto devils, after whom they have gone a whoring.** The word rightly translated *devils* means, literally, shaggy goats

(see 2 Chron. xi. 15; Isa. xiii. 21; xxxiv. 14; where the word occurs). It is generally supposed that the Israelites borrowed their worship of the goat-like spirits of the woods and fields from Egypt. That goat-worship prevailed there in a very foul shape we know (Herod., ii. 42), but sacrifices in the open fields are rather a Persian habit (Herod., i. 132). Pan-worship, however, was common to most if not to all agricultural nations. The injunction which follows, **This shall be a statute for ever unto them throughout their generations,** which cannot be confined to the last few words or verses, shows that the command of ver. 3 refers to sacrifices, not to ordinary slaughtering. Had slaughtering been meant, the statute could not have been intended to be more than temporary in its obligation. The importance attributed to the regulation is further shown by the declaration previously made, that whoever transgressed it should be *cut off from among his people,* or excommunicated. In fact, it makes an era in the history of the chosen people. The old patriarchal priesthood having ceased, and the Aaronic priesthood substituted for it, the tabernacle is appointed to serve as a religious centre to the race. Whenever, from this time onwards, sacrifices were offered, without offence, elsewhere than in the court of the tabernacle or temple, as by Samuel (see 1 Sam. xiii. 8), and by Elijah (1 Kings xviii. 32), it was done by the direct order or dispensation of God.

Vers. 8, 9.—So essential is the regulation to the maintenance of the Israelitish polity, that it is extended to **the strangers which sojourn among them,** not confined to those who were **of the house of Israel;** and the penalty of excommunication is appointed for both classes alike in case of disobedience. It may be noticed that this verse assumes that burnt offerings and peace offerings are offered by the strangers that sojourn among them, as well as by the Israelites by race.

Vers. 10, 11.—The appointment made just above, that the blood of all animals slain in sacrifice should be offered to the Lord on his altar in the court of the tabernacle, leads naturally to a reiteration of the prohibition of the eating of blood, and a statement of the reason of that prohibition. "But flesh with the life thereof, which is the blood thereof, shall ye not eat," was given as a command to Noah (Gen. ix. 4). It has already been repeated twice in the Book of Leviticus (chs. iii. 17; vii. 26), and it is still again found in ch. xix. 26; Deut. xii. 16; xv. 23. The present is the *locus classicus* which explains the earnestness with which the rule is enforced. It begins with an extension of the obligation from the Israelites to the sojourners among them, and with a solemn declaration that, in case of transgression, God will take into his own hands the punishment of the offenders; not only is he to be cut off or excommunicated by political or ecclesiastical authority, but God himself will set his face against that soul that eateth blood, and will cut him off from among his people, by death, or such means as he chooses to adopt. Then follows the reason for the prohibition. For the life of the flesh is in the blood. The blood may not be eaten because it is the vehicle of life, literally, *the soul of the flesh*, that is, it is the seat of the animal life of the body. "It is the fountain of life," says Harvey; "the first to live, the last to die, and the primary seat of the animal soul; it lives and is nourished of itself, and by no other part of the human body." In consequence of possessing this character, it is to be reserved, to make an atonement for your souls upon the altar; for thus only blood became qualified for the purpose of atonement. The clause, for it is the blood that maketh an atonement for the soul, should be translated, *for the blood maketh atonement by means of the soul*, i.e. by means of the life which it contains. It is because the blood is the vehicle of the animal's life, and represents that life, that it serves to cover, or make atonement for, the soul of the offerer of the sacrifice, who presents it instead of his own life.

Ver. 12.—This verse emphatically restates that the atoning power of the blood, as being the seat of life, is the reason that the eating of it is forbidden, and the same statement is repeated in a different connexion in ver. 14.

Vers. 13, 14.—Negatively, it has been ordered that blood shall not be eaten; positively, that it is to be offered to God. But there may be cases where the latter command cannot be carried out, as when animals are killed in hunting. On such occasions the man who kills the animal, whether he be an Israelite or a sojourner, is to pour out the blood thereof, and cover it with dust, regarding it as a sacred thing.

Vers. 15, 16.—There is still another possible case. The blood of an animal may not have been shed, or not shed in such a way as to make it flow abundantly, as when the animal has died a natural death, or been killed by wild beasts. In this case, as the blood still remains in the body, the flesh may not be eaten without defilement. The defilement may be cleansed by the unclean man washing his clothes and bathing, but if he neglect to do this, he shall bear his iniquity, that is, undergo the consequence of his transgression, which he would not have undergone had he been ceremonially cleansed (cf. Exod. xxii. 30; ch. xi. 39; Deut. xiv. 21). The prohibition of the eating of blood was continued by the Council of Jerusalem, but the observance of the regulation was no longer commanded as a duty binding on all men, but as a concession to Jewish feelings, enabling Jewish and Gentile converts to live together in comfort (see 1 Sam. xiv. 32; Ezek. xxxiii. 35; Acts xv. 20).

HOMILETICS.

Vers. 1—9.—*Sacrifice is not in itself enough;* there must be uniformity in the manner in which it is offered, and identity of place in which it is made. The seven first chapters of the Book of Leviticus have given a minute statement of the ceremonies which are always to be unfailingly observed. Incidentally, it had been taught in these chapters that the place of sacrifice was the court of the tabernacle, but now every other place of sacrifice is stringently forbidden.

I. THE TABERNACLE AND AFTERWARDS THE TEMPLE WERE THE CENTRE OF THE JEWISH CHURCH, AND THEREFORE OF THE JEWISH STATE. Every community which is to be permanent must have a central idea, and that idea must be embodied in some formula, or still better in some institution. The tabernacle or the temple was such an institution to the Jew. It summed up in itself, and was the symbol to the Jew of all that he valued. It was the rallying point of the nation, the thing that each citizen was willing to live for and die for, whatever other differences might divide him from his fellows. This gave a strength and unity to the different tribes, which would otherwise have probably all fallen apart, and though it was not strong enough to prevent the great schism, Jeroboam's plan of supplying its place by an unreal substitute showed its force; it survived the destruction of the material temple by Nebuchadnezzar, preserved the exiled fragments of the nation during the Captivity, and inspired courage to return to Jerusalem and rebuild what they had lost. Nay, even now its memory keeps together the scattered members of a dispersed nation, and forms them into one people.

II. THE TABERNACLE OR TEMPLE WAS THE EFFECTIVE SIGN OF UNITY TO THE JEWS BECAUSE IT CONTAINED THE ARK. The ark was the visible symbol of the presence of God among his chosen people. Therefore the hearts of the people went out towards the sanctuary with adoration and love. Therefore all the sacrificial rites had to be performed before the door of the sanctuary, not only while they lived in the wilderness, but when they were settled in Canaan. The journeys up to Jerusalem at the three great festivals intensified their love for the temple, and made them feel their union and communion with one another and with God. Nor did the institution of synagogues throughout the land interfere with this feeling, as the worship conducted in them was recognized as being of an inferior description to that which could be celebrated at the temple alone. The temple was, in the estimation of the Jew, the local abiding-place of God upon earth. Even when the ark and the mercy-seat were gone, it retained this character above every other spot.

III. THE IDEA OF A LOCAL PRESENCE OF GOD IN ANY GIVEN PLACE ON EARTH IS ABOLISHED. "Believe me, the hour cometh, when ye shall neither in this mountain, nor yet at Jerusalem, worship the Father. . . . the hour cometh, and now is, when the true worshippers shall worship the Father in spirit and in truth: for the Father seeketh such to worship him. God is a Spirit: and they that worship him must worship him in spirit and in truth" (John iv. 21—24). "For from the rising of the sun even unto the going down of the same my Name shall be great among the Gentiles; and in every place incense shall be offered unto my Name, and a pure offering: for my Name shall be great among the heathen, saith the Lord of hosts" (Mal. i. 11). There is no local or material centre to the Christian Church; no one city holy because it contains the temple; no one temple holy because it contains the visible presence of God; no one high priest on earth holy because alone privileged to enter into that presence. The spiritual has superseded the material.

IV. THE UNITY OF THE CHRISTIAN BODY IS TO BE OTHERWISE MAINTAINED. Its unity is commanded and prayed for by Christ: "Holy Father, keep through thine own Name those whom thou hast given me, that they may be one, as we are." "Neither pray I for these alone, but for them also which shall believe on me through their word; that they all may be one; as thou, Father, art in me, and I in thee, that they also may be one in us: . . . that they may be one, even as we are one: I in them, and thou in me, that they may be made perfect in one" (John xvii. 11, 20—23). And it is enjoined by the apostle, "Endeavouring to keep the unity of the Spirit in the bond of peace" (Eph. iv. 3). So far and at such times as Judaical and materializing views have prevailed in the Church, attempts have been made to preserve this unity in the Jewish manner, by making an earthly head of the Church, round which the members might gather.

V. THE TRUE BONDS OF UNITY IN THE CHRISTIAN CHURCH. 1. The common possession of the "one Spirit" (Eph. iv. 4), who unites all the members by the internal cohesion of unanimity and love. 2. The common possession of the "one Lord" (Eph. iv. 5), the invisible Head of the body, from whom there flows down into the members a life shared by all alike. 3. The common possession of the "one God and Father of all" (Eph. iv. 6), whose Fatherhood makes us all brethren. 4. The common possession of "one faith" (Eph. iv. 5), "once (for all) delivered to the saints" (Jude 3). 5. The common possession of "one hope" (Eph. iv. 4) of eternal life. 6. The common possession of "one baptism" (Eph. iv. 5), by which we were made members of the "one body" (Eph. iv. 4). 7. The common possession of the other sacrament appointed to continue "till he come" (1 Cor. xi. 26). 8. The common possession of the ministry instituted "for the perfecting of the saints, for the work of the ministry, for the edifying of the body of Christ: . . . that we may grow up into him in all things, which is the head, even Christ" (Eph. iv. 12—15).

VI. THE NATIONALITY AND INDEPENDENCE OF CHURCHES NOT INCOMPATIBLE WITH CATHOLIC UNITY. If there were one visible head of the Church on earth, or one divinely constituted earthly centre of Christendom, there could be no such thing as an independent or a National Church. But this conception of the Church Catholic, partly Judaical, partly feudal, is wholly false. The possession of the above-named qualifications makes a particular Church partaker in Catholic unity, the ideal Christian Church consisting of a federal union of such Churches in union and communion one with another, agreeing in their belief, but not necessarily uniform in their ceremonies and rites (Art. XXXIV.).

Vers. 10—13.—*The eating of blood is strictly prohibited*; therefore our Lord's words must have sounded so much the more strange in the ears of the Jews, when he said, "Except ye eat the flesh of the Son of man, and drink his blood, ye have no life in you" (John vi. 53). The reason why blood may not be eaten is that the life of the flesh is its blood (ver. 11). Eating the blood was the same thing as eating the life of the animal. Therefore his Jewish auditors would understand our Lord to mean by the words, "Whoso eateth my flesh, and drinketh my blood, hath eternal life; and I will raise him up at the last day" (John vi. 54), that whoso became a partaker of his life, would thereby become a possessor of eternal life, and, possessing that, would share in its privileges—resurrection and immortality (see Wordsworth, *ad loc.*) There is an eating and drinking of Christ's flesh and blood, that is, a partaking of his life and Spirit, which may be accomplished without any outward act whatever; but no doubt a special method of performing this mysterious act was instituted when "Jesus took bread, and blessed it, and brake it, and gave it to the disciples, and said, Take, eat; this is my body. And he took the cup, and gave thanks, and gave it to them, saying, Drink ye all of it; for this is my blood of the new testament, which is shed for many for the remission of sins" (Matt. xxvi. 27, 28). It may well be questioned whether a Church which forbids its members to drink of that cup does not shut them out from a full partaking of the life of Christ, so far as that blessing is imparted by that ordinance.

HOMILIES BY VARIOUS AUTHORS.

Grace before meat. Ch. xvii.; cf. 1 Cor. x. 31. From the perfect atonement God provides, we are invited next to turn to the *morality* he requires. And no better beginning can be made than the acknowledgment of God in connection with our food. The beautiful way the Lord secured his own recognition as the bountiful Giver was by enacting that blood, since it is the means used in atonement, must be devoted to no meaner use. Hence it was to be carefully put away, either by the priest at the tabernacle, or by the huntsman in the dust of the wilderness, and the animal used as a peace offering before God (ver. 5). What we have consequently in this chapter is the *religious use of food*, or, as we have put it, "Grace before meat." In this connection let us observe—

I. THAT GOD HAS IMPLANTED SOME MEMENTO OF HIMSELF IN ALL OUR FOOD. Vegetable as well as animal life, of which we are reminded at every meal, is the sign manual of the living God. It is worse than stupidity not to recognize in the food we eat the gifts of his bounteous hand. "Every good gift and every perfect gift is from above, and cometh down from the Father of lights, with whom is no variableness, neither shadow of turning" (Jas. i. 17). Why personify nature into a giver as a mere subterfuge for gross ingratitude? The Divine hand is behind the whole, and an honest heart can see it and will bless it as the source of all!

II. GOD REMINDS US AT EVERY MEAL OF ATONEMENT AS THE PRELIMINARY TO PEACE AND FELLOWSHIP. For all our food once thrilled with organic life. There is literally the sacrifice of life, vegetable and animal, in every meal. Vegetarians sacrifice microscopic life, after all their efforts to sacrifice nothing but vegetable life. Thus our race is reminded of the first principle of atonement, every time we sit down at the table which a bounteous providence has spread. In fact, it is our own fault if every feast be not in a certain sense sacramental. The Supper of the New Testament, as well as the Passover of the Old, embodies the sacrifice of life in order to the support of man. It is on this principle that the world is constituted. If, then, we listened to the voice of Nature as we ought to do, we would hear her calling in every feast for the grateful recognition of that principle in atonement to which we have referred. Peace and communion are really based in the order of nature upon the sacrifice of life. "Vicarious sacrifice" is a principle of vast range, and the atonement of Jesus is but a single application of it.

III. THE RECOGNITION OF GOD IN EVERY PLEASURE WILL MAKE IT DOUBLY DELIGHTFUL. It is evident that God contemplated hunting as something which might be enjoyed religiously. The blood of the animal was to be carefully covered with dust in the hunting-field. Such a recognition of God may be carried into all legitimate enjoyment. As Charles Lamb suggests saying grace before entering upon new books, as something more fitting than a formal grace before gluttony, let us by all means carry the good custom into everything. We may develop our muscular powers in a religious spirit. Let us have religion in bodily exercise, religion in our social enjoyments, religion in business, religion in politics, religion in all things. "Whether ye eat or drink, or whatsoever ye do, do all to the glory of God." We should recognize a "muscular Christianity," and a mercantile Christianity, and a Christianity "which doth not behave itself unseemly" in society; in a word, the adaptability of the religious spirit to all lawful relations. The sooner we recognize and realize this, the better.—R. M. E.

Vers. 1—16.—*Statutes concerning blood.* The sacredness of blood is everywhere marked in Scripture. The chapter before us contains some of the more important statutes concerning it.

I. IN RESPECT TO THE BLOOD OF SACRIFICE. 1. *It must be brought to the door of the tabernacle.* (1) This requisition does not apply to animals ordinarily killed for food (comp. Deut. xii. 15, 21). (2) It applies to the blood of sacrifices. (*a*) To the blood of those offered at the door of the tabernacle. As a matter of course, the blood of such sacrifices would be sprinkled and poured out at the altar. (*b*) To the blood of those also offered outside the camp (vers. 3, 5). Sacrifices were formerly offered wherever the providence of God might indicate (Gen. xii. 8; Job i. 5). God still reserved to himself the right to sanction the offering of sacrifices where he pleased (see Judg. vi. 26; xiii. 19; 1 Sam. vii. 9; 2 Sam. xxiv. 18; 1 Kings xviii. 23). Without such sanction, the altar of the tabernacle is the one place appointed for the shedding of sacrificial blood. (3) Public worship is encouraged by this law (Heb. x. 25). 2. *The penalty of disobedience is excision.* (1) The statute was enacted to prevent idolatry. Sacrificing elsewhere, they might be tempted to sacrifice to devils (ver. 7). The heathen thought the spirit of their god resided in his idol; such spirits are here called "devils." All idolatry is from Satan, and is devilish (1 Cor. x. 20). The word (לשעירים) here translated "devils" is elsewhere rendered "goats." Perhaps the idols in which these spirits of devils were supposed to reside were of the goat-like form. Goats were worshipped in Egypt, and probably also in Canaan. (2) Blood is imputed to him that sheds blood in sacrifice elsewhere than at the altar of the tabernacle (ver. 4). To bring the blood to the door of the tabernacle taught the worshipper to discern Christ, through whose blood we enter heaven. To miss this lesson was to degenerate into abominable and fatal idolatry (see Isa. lxvi. 3). This law applied to proselytes as well as to native Israelites (vers. 8, 9). There is but one way to God for the Jew and Greek (Rom. iii. 30). "He that believeth not shall be damned" (see ver. 4).

II. IN RESPECT TO FOOD. 1. *Blood as food is absolutely forbidden.* (1) The prohibition is among the Noachian precepts. He who reserved the tree of knowledge of good and evil in his grant of vegetables to man for food, reserved blood in his grant of animals (Gen. ix. 4, 5). Being a Noachian precept, this law is obligatory upon the human family at large. (2) The prohibition of blood was formally incorporated into the Levitical code (see ver. 10; also chs. iii. 17; vii. 26; Deut. xii. 25). The abrogation of the Levitical Law, however, does not repeal the Noachian precept. Unless, therefore, it can be shown that the Noachian precept is abrogated, it is still unlawful both to Jew and Gentile to eat blood. (3) So far from being repealed, this precept is re-enforced under the gospel (Acts xv. 28, 29). This "burden" our Lord still lays upon the Churches, even after the destruction of Jerusalem (see Rev. ii. 14—24). The significance of this term "burden" must not be overlooked (comp. Acts xv. 28 with Rev. ii. 24). 2. *Two reasons for the prohibition are assigned.* These are: (1) That "the *life* of the flesh is in the blood." This is philosophically true. Cut a nerve, you paralyze a member, but it lives; cut off the blood, the member mortifies. Blood flows to a wound, becomes vascular there, knits the living parts, and it heals. The vitality of the blood is seen in its power of maintaining its temperature against the extremes of heat and cold. The lesson of this reason is to teach us the value of life. Hence in connection with the Noachian precept prohibiting the eating of blood, we have also the law guarding the life of man by the penalty of death to the murderer. (2) That "it is the blood that maketh an *atonement* for the soul" (ver. 11). That should not be treated as a common thing which is the principle of atonement, and the type of the precious blood of Christ. (3) For these reasons also things strangled are forbidden, things which died alone, or were torn; things not so killed as to let the blood properly flow from them. Thus the slaying of every animal used for food in the sacrificial way would remind the eater of the necessity of sacrifice for sin (see 1 Cor. x. 31). 3. *The penalty here also is excision* (1) If things strangled were eaten, the transgressor became unclean (see 1 Sam. xiv. 32, 33). He must wash his clothes, for his profession hath been polluted. He must wash his flesh, for his person is defiled. If he neglect this repentance and purification, he shall bear his iniquity; he is obnoxious to excision (ver. 16; ch. v. 17; Numb. ix. 13). (2) What, then, can be said for a Church which professes literally to drink the blood of Christ in the cup of the Mass? Is not that Church thereby guilty of outraging the law of all the dispensations? It would evade this impeachment by impudently authorizing the eating of blood. But no impudence can evade the penalty: "But flesh with the life thereof, which is the blood thereof, shall ye not eat. And surely your blood of your lives will I require." Does not this plainly say that God will require the blood of the life of the blood-eater? David abhors the practice of the Syrians, who made libations of blood to their gods, and prophetically denounces and rejects our antichristian idolaters (see Ps. xvi. 4). Drunk as she is with the blood of the saints and the martyrs of Jesus, God will give her blood to drink, for she is worthy. —J. A. M.

Vers. 1—7.—*One place of sacrifice.* It is of the essence of law to be impartial. Its precepts apply to all without distinction. "Aaron and his sons and all the children of Israel" are here included in the scope of the Divine commands. Let none deem himself too humble or too exalted to incur displeasure by infraction of the Law.

I. We see that A LAWFUL ACTION MAY BE UNLAWFULLY PERFORMED. A wrong time or place may vitiate a deed otherwise permissible. Animals were given to man as food, and to slaughter and eat them was not in itself sin, but after the issue of this prohibition it became sin to do so without presenting them at the tabernacle. "Blood shall be imputed unto that man; he hath shed blood." So the homicide justifiable in war becomes murder, and the intercourse of matrimony fornication, and the "word spoken in season" a casting of pearls before swine, by reason of impropriety of person or season.

II. THE PEOPLE OF GOD MUST EXPECT RESTRICTIONS TO BE PLACED UPON THEIR LIBERTY. The nations may follow their own devices and desires, the chosen people are under a covenant to obey the commands of the Legislator. They are assured that his wisdom and kindness will prevent the adoption of unnecessary and inequitable prohibitions. For all his precepts there are the best possible reasons, and therefore obedience is cheerfully rendered. Note the noble reply which Milton puts into the mouth of the seraph Abdiel, to the taunts of Satan ('Paradise Lost,' bk. vi. 170—181). Whilst the Israelites were in the wilderness, and the tabernacle abode in the midst of the camp, no hardship was involved in attending to this injunction, and it restrained them from evil practices, disciplining them against the time that they should enter the land of promise and have the injunction removed. Besides, animal food was scarce in the wilderness, as we learn from the complaints of the people.

III. To RECOGNIZE GOD IN OUR COMMON ACTIONS AND ENJOYMENTS HALLOWS LIFE —MAKES IT A RELIGIOUS SERVICE. The slain animal is consecrated as a peace offering, its blood being sprinkled on the altar, the fat burnt for a "sweet savour unto the Lord," and the remainder partaken of with gratitude and joy. God is honoured and man profited. Alas! that so many can continually receive God's mercies without acknowledgment, no blessing invoked, and no emotion of holy gladness sweetening the repast! The Christian ideal is to do all in the Name of Jesus and to the glory of God.

IV. To REFUSE TO GOD HIS RIGHTS IS TO COMMIT IDOLATRY. The Israelites were certain to turn the slaughter of an animal into a festival, and the question was, to whom should the feast be dedicated? Homage to the demons of the field could not be sanctioned, it was a breach at once of the first and seventh commandments. It is frequently forgotten that a neutral attitude in respect of God is impossible; we are either on his side or against him. Intellectualism, materialism, scientificism, agnosticism, it matters not by what name our rejection of the claims of religion is covered, it really designates the setting up of an idol upon the throne of the heart, and we adore the enemy of God.

V. THE PROBATIONARY CHARACTER OF MANY OF GOD'S REQUIREMENTS IS HERE MADE VISIBLE. In Deut. xii. the precept of the text is repealed as relating to the settled condition of life in Palestine, when it would manifestly be difficult to comply with the law. By that period the precept had served its purpose in training the Israelites to abstain from evil practices, and to honour Jehovah with all their substance. And we to-day have our wilderness system of probation and training, many rules designed to meeten us for the society of just men made perfect. The injunction of the text pointed to the transitory nature of the Law as a whole. It has been abrogated by the gospel, the dispensation of promise, the land of liberty and rest. Yet, as in their residence in Palestine, the Israelites continued to observe the spirit of the repealed Law, so do we, under the gospel, retain the principles that underlay the Mosaic legislation. To acknowledge God in every meal and mercy, to hallow the secular and to promote it to the sacred, this, as it is the object of Christian endeavour, is the spirit of the command we have been considering in Leviticus. And equally so, the principles and spirit of our Christian earthly life will be recognizable in the higher worship and service of heaven. The accident changes, the essence alters not.—S. R. A.

Vers. 1—7.—*Features of Christian service.* It is open to question whether the prohibition (vers. 3, 4) extends to all animals killed for food, or only to those slain in sacrifice. The former view is, in my judgment, the correct one; for (1) the instruction is explicit enough (vers. 3, 4), and without qualification; (2) the limitation is afterwards allowed in consideration of the change of circumstance (Deut. xii. 20, 21); and (3) the difficulty in the case is less on consideration than it at first appears. It is objected that this would be a burdensome prohibition; but (*a*) it only lasted (see above) while they were in the camp, near to one another, and all near to the tabernacle; and (*b*) much less flesh was eaten there and then than is eaten here and now. A more largely vegetable diet would probably be wholesome for us; it was undoubtedly so in the desert of Arabia. When we more carefully consider this precept, we see its beneficent character; we perceive—

I. A FATAL EVIL, FROM WHICH IT WAS DESIGNED TO SAVE THEM. The practices of Egypt clung to them; among these was demon-worship (ver. 7). They had gone after those demons, and offered sacrifices to them. If any animal might be killed anywhere for food, and the blood of it might not be eaten (chs. iii. 17; vii. 26), there would be a strong temptation to the superstitious to pour it out in sacrifice to those demons of whose malignant interposition they were afraid. This temptation must, at all cost, be guarded against. It would introduce or foster that idolatrous usage from which it was the supreme object of all these statutes to keep Israel free. And if no animal might be slain save at the tabernacle door, there would be no danger of this disastrous lapse into Egyptian superstition.

II. THE GOOD IT WAS DESIGNED TO DO THEM. It would confer a threefold boon upon them. 1. It would bring them often to the tabernacle, and so to the near presence and worship of God; it would multiply their sacrifices (vers. 5, 6). 2. It would lead them to associate their material blessings with the Divine hand; presenting them unto the Lord, they could not fail to be reminded that they were his gifts. 3. It would help them to look on Jehovah as their Divine Friend. These became peace offerings (ver. 5), and the essential thought of such offering was human fellowship with God.

We detect here some useful suggestions as to the true character of Christian service. 1. *We must not make our Christian worship too deprecatory in its character.* There is something painfully and dangerously like demon-worship in the devotion of some men; they seldom rise above the deprecatory in their thought, as if God were a being so stern and so reluctant to forgive that his people should spend all their devotional breath in deprecating his wrath. Surely to the God and Father of our Lord Jesus

Christ we should bring, beside this, our adoration, praise, gratitude, trust, love, consecration, etc. 2. *We must learn to connect daily blessings with the Divine hand.* We should, in thought though not in act, bring everything we have to "the door of the tabernacle," trace each good thing we enjoy to the generous Giver of all, to his heart of love as well as to his hand of bounty. 3. *We should bless God for revealing himself to us as our Divine Friend, in the person of Jesus Christ.* Jesus Christ has taught us to think and feel that we are the friends and guests of God (John xv. 14, 15; xiv. 23; Rev. iii. 20).—C.

Vers. 10—16.—*Atoning death.* We have here a repetition of a law which had already been twice delivered (chs. iii. 17; vii. 23—26). Its full and formal restatement is very significant, and this the more because of the emphatic utterance of Divine displeasure in the event of disobedience. "I will even set my face against that soul . . . and will cut him off," etc. (ver. 10). Obviously, the highest importance was attached by God to the observance of this injunction not to eat "any manner of blood." We regard—

I. THE PRIMARY SIGNIFICANCE OF THIS LAW. This is clearly indicated in vers. 11 and 12. We shall understand it if we consider the subject thus: 1. Happy and harmonious relations between Jehovah and his people were maintained by continual sacrifices at his altar. 2. In these sacrifices the life of the slain animal was accepted by God as an atonement for the forfeited life of the human transgressor. 3. But the blood of the animal was regarded as the seat and source of its life. When its blood was shed its life was taken, and the shed blood was sprinkled before the vail or poured on the altar (ch. ii. 6, 7), as standing for the life which had been offered by man, and been accepted by God. "The blood of bulls and of goats," therefore, however insufficient of itself for the high purpose of atonement for human sin, was yet the outward and visible means which the Holy One of Israel was pleased to appoint for reconciliation between himself and his people. Therefore it was to be held sacred; the idea of it must not be vulgarized, as it would inevitably be if blood were used as common food at ordinary meals. Its sanctity must be carefully fenced. Men must associate with it, in their minds, nothing but the forfeited life, the atonement, with which it was so closely connected. All their domestic and social customs (vers. 13, 15, 16) must be so ordered that the blood of animals, anywhere and anywise slain, should speak of those sacrifices at the altar in which the erring souls of men sought and found the mercy and the favour of their God.

II. ITS SIGNIFICANCE TO OURSELVES. It suggests to us the truth that, as the disciples of Jesus Christ, we also should count very sacred in our esteem the thought of atoning blood. 1. For we, too, are redeemed by "precious blood" (see 1 Pet. i. 18, 19; Eph. i. 7; Heb. ix. 12—14; Rev. v. 9). It may not have been needful that, in the literal sense, the blood of the Son of man should flow, but it was needful that his life, of which the blood is the source and the symbol, should be laid down. 2. Our Lord has given us a permanent institution, the object of which is to keep before our minds the shedding of his blood for our sins (Matt. xxvi. 28; 1 Cor. xi. 26). 3. By their words, he and his apostles laid the greatest stress on his atoning death as the source of our life and hope (John xii. 32; vi. 53; Luke xxiv. 46, 47; Heb. ix. 14; 1 John i. 7, etc.). 4. His atoning death was the object of our soul's trust when we entered our Christian course, and will be at the hour when we shall complete it. 5. It is the will of Christ that we should keep it continually in view throughout our life. It is our wisdom as well as our duty so to do, inasmuch as the contemplation of his death for our sins will minister (1) to our humility; (2) to our gratitude; (3) to a consecrated life of cheerful obedience and submission.—C.

Vers. 1—9.—*Sanctity of animal life.* All God's people commanded to observe restrictions as to the shedding of blood. Door of the tabernacle connected with the sphere of common life; thus religion and its duty threw sacredness over all things.

I. THE DOMINION OF MAN OVER THE LOWER CREATION. 1. *Appointed by God* (see Gen. i. 26 and Ps. viii.). 2. *Limited in its extent,* by necessity, humanity of feeling, provision for the higher purposes of human life. 3. *Capable of being blended with the Law of the sanctuary.* We should afford all creatures dependent on us, as much as possible our own sabbath of bodily rest. We should make it a religious duty to protect them from injury and suffering. In so far as we use them for food, an offering of them should not be to the god of sensuality, but to him whose Law requires temperance, self-restraint, and reverence for the lower nature, that it may support the higher. All with thanksgiving.

II. POWER OF LIFE AND DEATH IS IN AND FROM GOD. As entrusted to man, whether over the lower animals or over his fellows, it is a power to be exercised as in the sight of God and at the door of his house. 1. Shedding of blood *a solemn responsibility.* In common life, lest we be guilty of cruelty and destruction of a true and valuable element in the world's welfare. In execution of law, lest we give to that which represents the Divine will the appearance of injustice and wantonness. Even in healthy sport, care must be taken lest there be an overbalance of the mind towards shedding of blood or disregard of suffering. In all questions of difficulty, bring the matter to the door of the tabernacle. 2. The sacredness of blood points to atonement. The devoted and slaughtered animal was received back again as a Divine gift for the use of the offerer, thus lifting up death into life. Sacrifice is not God's delight in death, but his promise of salvation. The sanctity attached to the blood of victims prepared the way to the higher sanctity attached to the blood of Christ. The Old and New Testaments explain one another.

III. PRESERVATION FROM IDOLATRY AND FALSE WORSHIP IN THE POSITIVE REGULATIONS OF THE LAW. Mistake of supposing that mere negative religion will purify men from corruption. Against the worship of devils we are never safe except as we are engaged in the worship of the true God.—R.

Vers. 10—16.—Ver. 11, " The life of the flesh is in the blood : and I have given it to you upon the altar to make an atonement for your souls : for it is the blood that maketh an atonement for the soul."

I. THE NATURAL BASIS OF ATONEMENT. 1. The *preciousness* of life. The blood is the seat of life. 2. The exchange of the altar, blood for life, a lower for a higher, requires a *supplementary value*, which is represented by the altar itself. 3. *The law* proclaimed at the first against the shedding of blood taken up into the higher law of *redemption* ; righteousness becoming at the altar of God the refuge of man.

II. ATONEMENT FOR THE SOUL PROVIDED BY DIVINE LOVE. " I have given it you to make an atonement." 1. All atonement must proceed from Divine love, otherwise it will be heathenish as effecting a change in God. Christ is *set forth* a propitiation. 2. Atonement is *made*, i.e. by being offered, the blood shed at the tabernacle door, offered upon the altar. Thus the sacrifice is a revelation and consecration of the bond of union in the covenant relation between God and man. 3. The blood, while representing the life, also represents the obedience active and passive of Christ, which was both a rendering up to God of a perfect humanity, and an exaltation of the Law in the sufferings and death of Calvary ; the old man crucified, the new man glorified. 4. All human merit is excluded : " *I have given it you.*" No amount of sacrifice would be of any avail except it be according to the will of God. We give back to him of his own. Hence the difference between the Jewish sacrifices and those of pagan nations, and between the morality which is founded on the sacrifice of Christ, and that which proceeds from mere self-will or an unjustifiable and false exaltation of human nature as it is. He that is not clean as God makes him clean shall " bear his iniquity." Necessity of insisting on this doctrine of atonement in the present day. Falsehood as to humanity, in the way of all true progress. Those who boast are not those who make sacrifices to elevate man. " Survival of the fittest " a cruel remedy for the world's miseries. Christ's doctrine is elevation of the lowest. Atonement for your souls is the beginning of all true life.—R.

Ver. 11.— *The sanctity of the atoning blood.* No act was more strongly denounced than that of eating any manner of blood. The man guilty of that deed, whether an Israelite or a stranger sojourning in the land, was threatened with the displeasure of God and severest penalty. It seemed to partake of the nature of a ceremonial rather than a moral offence, yet it must be remembered that violations of ritual become moral transgressions when they are committed against the known will of the recognized

Legislator. This is especially the case when, as here, the Lawgiver condescends to explain the reason upon which the prohibition is founded. Such explanation ought to secure intelligent observance of the enactment. And that enactment was but the reissue of the former decree that gave animals to man for food, but annexed a prohibition against tasting the blood (Gen. ix. 4).

I. The fact stated, that THE SHEDDING OF BLOOD CONSTITUTES AN ATONEMENT. Illustrated by the numerous sacrifices of the patriarchs, and the provisions of the Law that sacrifices should form a part of all national and individual festivals, as well as of all offerings to wipe away inadvertent transgression. See it in the sprinkling of the book and vessels and people at the ratification of the covenant. It is confirmed by the wellnigh universal practice of heathen nations, and is proved by direct Scripture statements in the Old and New Testaments. "Without shedding of blood is no remission" (Heb. ix. 22). It typified, therefore, the offering of Jesus Christ, whose blood redeems us "from our vain manner of life" (1 Pet. i. 18). "The blood of Jesus Christ his Son cleanseth us from all sin." This Mosaic way of speaking is ingrained in the apostles, showing how they regarded the death of Jesus as the fulfilment of the types of the Law.

II. The truth implied that THE CHIEF VIRTUE OF BLOOD AS AN ATONEMENT IS DERIVED FROM GOD'S APPOINTMENT. "I have given it unto you" indicates that the blood of animals had no intrinsic efficacy to atone for sin. And the same truth is shadowed forth in the words, "upon the altar." There was no difference in itself between blood ordinarily spilt and that presented before God, but the presentation constituted the difference. To sprinkle the blood upon the altar was to bring it emblematically into the very presence of the Deity. "God set forth" Christ Jesus "to be a propitiation, through faith, by his blood."

III. The reason afforded for the selection of BLOOD, that it IS THE VEHICLE OF LIFE. Physiology, and especially recent investigations with the microscope, confirm the dictum of Scripture, that "the blood is the life." It nourishes and sustains the whole physical frame; if it deteriorate in quality the body weakens, if it diminish in quantity power is lessened. 1. By such an atonement *God is recognized as Lord of life* and of all its consequences. He gave and takes away, to him alone should life be offered. Thus the sanctity of life was enforced. Man was not to feast upon that which was God's prerogative; blood must be poured upon the ground like water, thus returning to the earth. 2. *The enormity of sin is represented*, as enacting the utmost for an atonement that can be rendered. "Life is the most cherished of possessions, since man is powerless to create or to restore it." The crowning proof of Christ's compassion was that he gave "his life" a ransom for the many, and the gift revealed the awfulness of sin to require such a redemption. 3. *It represents the substitution of one life for another*, death being the sentence pronounced upon the sinner. "When thou shalt make his soul an offering for sin" was Isaiah's prediction of the sacrifice of Christ. It may be observed that the word in the text translated "soul" and "life" is the same, corresponding to the use made of the equivalent Greek word in Matt. xvi. 25, 26. That but for the death of Jesus Christ we must have been subject to eternal death, is the plain import of many passages in the Word of God.

IV. THE FUTURE ADVENT TYPIFIED OF ONE WHO SHOULD BY HIS OFFERING FULFIL ALL THE CONDITIONS OF A PERFECT ATONEMENT. Every Israelite might not perceive in the insufficiency of his sacrifices a prediction of the Lamb of God, but there it was portrayed visibly enough. An innocent, holy, human victim, a voluntary offering, being himself the Lawgiver, and by incarnation subjecting himself to the Law, making adequate acknowledgment of the righteousness of God and of the ill deserts of God's rebellious sinful children, revealing to man at once the loving heart of God and the hatefulness of sin which had estranged man from his Father in heaven, by his death exhibiting the length to which sin will go, and the willingness of Divine holiness and love to submit to extreme degradation and anguish in order that the curse might be removed and man's heart won,—this is the atonement of truest efficacy, a mighty moral power with God and man. This is the death that gives life to the world, the blood that cries out, not for vengeance, but for mercy, that sanctifies not merely to the purifying of the flesh, but to the purging of the conscience from dead works to serve the living God. And the shedding of the blood of Christ was the signal for release from the ceremonies and restrictions imposed by the Mosaic **Law.** The prohibition of the text had served its purpose.

CONCLUSION. With what rejoicing should we approach our altar, the cross of Christ (Heb. xiii. 10)! And what guilt we incur if we slight the blood of Christ as little available for salvation, or, though professing to believe, yet by conduct show that we count the blood of the covenant an unholy thing!—S. R. A.

PART III.

SECTION III.

EXPOSITION.

CHAPTER XVIII.

MORAL UNCLEANNESS AND ITS PUNISHMENT. This being the subject of the three following chapters (chs. xviii.—xx.), they naturally form a sequence to chs. xi.—xvii., which have dealt with ceremonial uncleanness and its purification. It is a remarkable thing that, except by implication in connection with the sin offerings and the trespass offerings and the ceremonies of the Day of Atonement, there has not yet been a single moral precept, as such, in the Book of Leviticus, and there has been very little recognition of sin as distinct from pollution. All has been ceremonial. But the ceremonial is typical of the moral, and from the consideration of ceremonial uncleanness and its remedy, we now proceed to the consideration of moral uncleanness and its penalty. It is to be noticed too that, while the ensuing laws are commanded as the positive injunction of God (vers. 2, 30), which of itself is sufficient to give them their authority and force, they are still founded, like the ceremonial prohibitions, upon the feelings of repugnance implanted in the mind of man. To enter into the marriage relation with near relatives is abhorrent to a sentiment in mankind so widely spread that it may be deemed to have been originally universal, and the same abhorrence is entertained towards other foul sins of lust. Ugliness, which creates disgust by its ugliness, symbolizes sin; immorality, which inspires abhorrence by its immoral character, proves itself thereby to be sin. The section deals first with sin in the marriage relation, next with sexual impurities connected with marriage, then with other cases of immorality, and

lastly with the penalties inflicted on these sins in their character of crimes.

Vers. 1—5 form an introduction to the Hebrew code of prohibited degrees of marriage and of forbidden sins of lust. The formal and solemn declaration, I am the Lord your God, is made three times in these five verses. This places before the people the two thoughts: 1. That the Lord is holy, and they ought to be like him in holiness; 2. That the Lord has commanded holiness, and they ought to obey him by being holy. Because the Lord is their God, and they are his people, they are, negatively, to refrain from the vicious habits and lax customs prevalent in the land of Egypt wherein they dwelt, and in the land of Canaan whither they were going, the sensuality of which is indirectly condemned by the injunctions which command purity in contrast to their doings; and, positively, they are to keep God's statutes, and his judgments, as laid down in the following code, which if a man do, he shall live in them. The latter clause is of special importance, because it is repeated in the same connection by Ezekiel (Ezek. xx. 11, 13, 21), and in the Levitical confession in the Book of Nehemiah (Neh. ix. 29), and is quoted by St. Paul in a controversial sense (Rom. x. 5; Gal. iii. 12). Its full meaning is that by obedience to God's commands man attains to a state of existence which alone deserves to be called true life—"the life which connects him with Jehovah through his obedience" (Clark). And this involves the further truth that disobedience results in death. Accordingly, St. Paul uses the text as being the testimony of the Law with regard to itself, that salvation by it is of works in contrast with faith. (Cf. Luke x. 28.) We have no evidence to tell us what were *the doings of the land of Canaan* in respect to the marriage relation, but this chapter is enough to show that the utmost laxity prevailed in it, and we may be sure that their religious rites, like those of Midian (Numb. xxv.), were penetrated with the spirit of licentiousness. With regard to *the doings of the land of Egypt,* we have fuller information. We know that among the Egyptians marriage with sisters and half-sisters was not only permissible, but that its propriety was justified by their religious beliefs, and practised in the royal family (Diod. Sic., i. 27; Dio. Cass., xlii.). Other abominations condemned in this chapter (ver. 23) also, as we know, existed there (Herod., ii. 46), and if queens could be what in later times Cleopatra was, we may imagine the general dissoluteness of the people. Among Persians, Medes, Indians, Ethiopians and Assyrians, marriage with mothers and daughters was allowed, and from the time of Cambyses, marriage with a sister was regarded as lawful (Herod., iii. 31). The Athenians and Spartans permitted marriage with half-sisters. All these concessions to lust, and other unclean acts with which the heathen world was full (ver. 22; Rom. i. 27), were fallings away from the law of purity implanted in the heart of man and now renewed for the Hebrew people.

Ver. 6.—The next thirteen verses contain the law of incest, or the prohibited degrees of marriage. The positive law of marriage, as implanted in the human heart, would be simply that any man of full age might marry any woman of full age, provided that both parties were willing. But this liberty is at once controlled by a number of restrictions, the main purpose of which is to prevent incest, which, however much one nation may come to be indifferent to one form of it, and another to another, is yet abhorrent to the feelings and principles of mankind. The Hebrew restrictive law is contained in one verse. **None of you shall approach to any that is near of kin to him, to uncover their nakedness: I am the Lord.** All that follows (vers. 9—18) is simply an amplification and an explanation of the words, *near of kin to him.* These words would be literally rendered, *flesh of his flesh,* or less probably (as in the margin), *remainder of his flesh.* They certainly include within the compass of their meaning those that are near by affinity, as much as those that are near by consanguinity. This is proved by the instances given below, where no difference is drawn between blood relations and relations by marriage, the latter being supposed to become the former, in consequence of the marriage that has taken place. Nearness of kin is generally counted by "degrees;" but, unfortunately, this word is itself ambiguous, for it is used in different senses by canonists and by civilians. So far as the direct line is concerned, the same method of calculation is observed by the canon and by the civil law. There is one degree

from the son to the mother, two degrees to the grandmother; one degree from the father to the daughter, two degrees to the grand-daughter. But this is not so with the collateral lines. A brother and sister, for example, are regarded by the canon law as in the first degree of kinship, because there is only one step to the father, in whom their blood meets; but the civil lawyers consider them as being in the second degree, because, as they calculate, there is one step from the brother to the father, and a second from the father to the sister. An aunt is, according to the canonists, in the second degree of propinquity, because there are two steps from her nephew to his grandfather, who is likewise her father, in whom their blood unites; but, according to the civilian's calculation, there are three steps, namely, from her nephew to his grandfather, two steps, and a third from that grandfather to his daughter the aunt; and therefore the aunt and nephew are in the third degree of propinquity. The case of an uncle and niece is exactly the same as that of a nephew and aunt. On the same principle, according to the canonists, first cousins are in the second degree of kinship; according to the civilians, in the fourth. Propinquity by affinity is calculated in just the same way; so that the brother's wife is in the same degree of relationship as the brother, and wife's sister as the sister by blood. In the code before us, confirmed by that in Deuteronomy, marriage is forbidden with the following blood relations: mother (ver. 7), daughter (ver. 17), sister (ver. 9; ch. xx. 17; Deut. xxvii. 22), granddaughter (ver. 10), aunt (vers. 12, 13; ch. xx. 19); and with the following relations by affinity: mother-in-law (ver. 17; ch. xx. 14; Deut. xxvii. 23), daughter-in-law (ver. 15; ch. xx. 12), brother's wife (ver. 16; ch. xx. 21), stepmother (ver. 8; ch. xx. 11; Deut. xxii. 30; see Gen. xlix. 4; 1 Cor. v. 1), stepdaughter and step-granddaughter (ver. 17), uncle's wife, or aunt by marriage (ver. 14; ch. xx. 20); putting aside for the present the question of who is meant by *a wife to her sister,* in ver. 18. In these lists, according to the canonists' method of reckoning, the mother, the daughter, and the sister are related in the first degree of consanguinity; the wife's mother, the wife's daughter, the stepmother, the daughter-in-law, the brother's wife, are related in the first degree of affinity. The granddaughter and the aunt are in the second degree of consanguinity; the wife's granddaughter and the uncle's wife in the second degree of affinity. According to the civilians' reckoning, the following would be the degrees of propinquity:—The mother and the daughter would be in the first degree of consanguinity; the wife's mother, the wife's daughter, the stepmother, the daughter-in-law, would be in the first degree of affinity. The sister and the granddaughter would be in the second degree of consanguinity; the brother's wife and the wife's granddaughter would be in the second degree of affinity. The aunt by blood would be in the third degree of consanguinity, and the uncle's wife, or aunt by marriage, would be in the third degree of affinity. The wife's sister, with regard to whom it is questioned whether she is referred to or not in ver. 18, is in the first degree of affinity (a man's wife being regarded as himself) according to the canonists' reckoning, and in the second according to the civilians'. There is no mention made in the code of the grandmother, the niece, and the cousin-german. All of these are in the second degree of consanguinity according to the canon law; and according to the civil law, the grandmother would be in the second degree, the niece in the third, and the cousin-german in the fourth. It may reasonably be supposed that by the expression, *None of you shall approach to any that is near of kin to him, to uncover their nakedness*, intercourse is forbidden between all those who are related by consanguinity or affinity in the first and second degrees according to the canonists' reckoning (except cousins-german, whose case is considered below); in the first, second, and third degrees according to the civilians' method of calculating; whether they are mentioned by name in the list or not. It is only by implication, not by direct injunction, that marriage even with a daughter is forbidden (ver. 17).

Vers. 7, 8.—Incest with a stepmother is placed next after that with a mother. On account of the unity caused by marriage ("they shall be one flesh," Gen. ii. 24), the stepmother's nakedness is **the father's nakedness.** The tie of affinity is thus declared to be similar in its effects to the tie of consanguinity. Reuben's sin, by which he forfeited his birthright, is connected with this offence, but is of a more heinous character, as his father was alive at the time of his transgression (Gen. xlix. 4). It is one of the sins which Ezekiel enumerates as those which brought the judgment of God on Israel (Ezek. xxii. 10). "That one should have his father's wife" is declared by St. Paul to be "such fornication as is not named among the Gentiles," and to call for the excommunication of the offender (1 Cor. v. 1—5). Adonijah's marriage with Abishag, so strongly resented by Solomon on political grounds, is not denounced as morally reprehensible, probably because Abishag was not the wife of David in such a way as to cause the marriage with his son to be abominable in the eye of the law (cf. 1 Kings i. 4 with Amos ii. 7). Absalom's "going in unto his father's

concubines" was regarded as the final act which made reconciliation with his father impossible (2 Sam. xvi. 22; xx. 3). The history of the Church has shown that marriage with the stepmother has had to be again and again prohibited by Council after Council (see Smith and Cheetham's 'Dictionary of Antiquities,' *s.v.* 'Prohibited Degrees').

Ver. 9.—In the third place, incest with a sister is forbidden, and it is specifically stated that under the term "sister" is meant the half-sister, the **daughter of thy father, or . . . thy mother, . . . born at home,** as would naturally be the case if she were the father's daughter, **or born abroad,** that is, the daughter of the mother by a previous marriage, when she belonged to a different household. Tamar's appeal to Amnon, "I pray thee speak unto the king; for he will not withhold me from thee," exhibits to us the poor woman grasping at any argument which might save her from her half-brother's brutality, and does not indicate that such marriages were, in the time of David, permissible (2 Sam. xiii. 29). The exact degree of relationship which existed between Abraham and Sarah is not altogether certain (cf. Gen. xx. 12 with xi. 29). Ezekiel reckons this sin in the catalogue of the iniquities of Jerusalem (Ezek. xxii. 11).

Ver. 10.—The fourth case of incest which is prohibited is that with a granddaughter, whether the daughter of son or daughter, for, as they are descended from the grandfather, **their's is thine own nakedness.**

Ver. 11.—Incest with a half-sister on the father's side is again forbidden. Perhaps "the prohibition refers to the son by a first marriage, whereas ver. 9 treats of the son by a second marriage" (Keil).

Vers. 12—15.—Fifthly, incest with a paternal or maternal aunt is forbidden; sixthly, with an aunt by marriage; seventhly, with a daughter-in-law. The last of these finds its place in Ezekiel's catalogue of abominations (Ezek. xxii. 11; cf. Gen. xxviii. 18, 26).

Ver. 16.—The eighth case of incest is intercourse with a brother's wife. Yet this is commanded under certain circumstances in the Book of Deuteronomy, and was practised in patriarchal times (Gen. xxxviii. 8). The following are the circumstances under which it is commanded. "If brethren dwell together, and one of them die, and have no child, the wife of the dead shall not marry without unto a stranger: her husband's brother shall go in unto her, and take her to him to wife, and perform the duty of an husband's brother unto her" (Deut. xxv. 5). It has been asked, "How can the same thing be forbidden as immoral in Leviticus, and

commanded as a duty in Deuteronomy?"
Bishop Wordsworth replies, "In a special
case, for a special reason applicable only to
the Jews, God was pleased to dispense with
that law, and in the plenitude of his omnipotence to change the prohibition into a
command. . . . God cannot command anything that is sinful. For sin is 'transgression of the Law' (1 John iii. 4), and
whatever he commands is right. But it
would be presumptuous to say that *we* may
dispense with God's law concerning marriage, because he in one case dispensed with
it; as it would be impious to affirm that
murder is not immoral, and may be committed by us, because God, who is the sole
Arbiter of life and death, commanded Abraham to slay his son Isaac." The levirate
marriage was not a concession to the desires
of the second brother, but a duty enjoined
for a family or tribal purpose, and it was
plainly at all times most distasteful. Thus
Onan refused to perform his duty to Er's
wife (Gen. xxxviii. 9); the legislation in
Deuteronomy anticipates objection on the
part of the brother, and institutes an insulting ceremony to be gone through by
him if he declines to do his duty to his dead
brother (Deut. xxv. 9, 10), which we see
carried out in some of its details in the
case of Ruth's kinsman (Ruth iv. 7, 10).
Indeed, in such a marriage, the second husband seems rather to have been regarded as
the continuation of the first husband than
as having a substantive existence of his own
as a married man. He performed a function
in order "that the name of his brother
which is dead may not be put out of Israel"
(Deut. xxv. 6), "to raise up the name of
the dead upon his inheritance, that the
name of the dead be not cut off from among
his brethren" (Ruth iii. 10). The second
husband's position may be compared to that
of the concubine presented by Rachel to
her husband. "Behold my maid Bilhah,
go in unto her; and she shall bear upon my
knees, that I may also have children by
her" (Gen. xxx. 3). The whole object of
the rule was that, as the elder brother could
not keep up the family by begetting an
heir, the younger brother should do it for
him after his death.

Ver. 17.—The ninth form of incest prohibited is intercourse with a stepdaughter,
or step-granddaughter, or mother-in-law.
The expression made use of, **Thou shalt not
uncover the nakedness of a woman and her
daughter,** covers the case of a man's own
daughter, and it is singular that it is only
in this incidental manner that it is specifically named. But it has been already disposed of by the general command, *None of
you shall approach to any that is near of
kin to him, to uncover their nakedness.* The

daughter being nearest of kin, this command was sufficient without further specifi-
cation. The niece and probably the wife's
sister are forbidden by the same general
rule (see following note).

Ver. 18.—**Neither shalt thou take a wife
to her sister, to vex her, to uncover her
nakedness, beside the other in her life time.**
Do these words refer to the marriage of two
sisters or not? It has been passionately
affirmed that they do, by those who are
opposed to permission being granted for
marriage with a deceased wife's sister, and
by those who are in favour of that measure,
each party striving to derive from the text
an argument for the side which they are
maintaining. But Holy Scripture ought
not to be made a quarry whence partizans
hew arguments for views which they have
already adopted, nor is that the light in
which a commentator can allow himself to
regard it. A reverent and profound study
of the passage before us, with its context,
leads to the conclusion that the words have
no bearing at all on the question of marriage with a deceased wife's sister, and thus
it may be removed from the area and
atmosphere of angry polemics. It is certain that the words translated *a wife to her
sister* may be translated, in accordance with
the marginal rendering, *one wife to another*.
The objections made to such a version are
arbitrary and unconvincing. It is in accordance with the genius of the Hebrew
language to take "father," "son," "brother,"
"sister," in a much wider acceptation than
is the case in the Western tongues. Anything that produces or causes is metaphorically a "father;" anything produced or
caused is a "son;" any things akin to each
other in form, shape, character, or nature,
are "brothers" and "sisters." This is the
name given to the loops of the curtains of
the tabernacle (Exod. xxvi. 3, 5, 6), the
tenons of the boards (Exod. xxvi. 17), and
the wings of the cherubim (Ezek. i. 11, 23).
Indeed, wherever the expression, "a man to
his brother," or "a woman to her sister," is
used (and it is used very frequently) in
the Hebrew Scriptures, it means not two
brothers or two sisters, but two things or
persons similar in kind. This does more
than raise a presumption—it creates a high
probability—that the expression should be
understood in the same way here. But a
difficulty then arises. If the right reading
is, *Neither shalt thou take one wife to another*,
does not the verse forbid polygamy altogether, and is not polygamy permitted by
Exod. xxi. 7—11; Deut. xxi. 15—17; xvii.
17? Certainly, if so important a restriction
was to be made, we should expect it to be
made directly, and in a manner which could
not be disputed. Is there any way out of

the difficulty? Let us examine each word of the Law. *Neither shalt thou take one wife to another, to vex, to uncover her nakedness upon her in her life time.* The two words, *to vex*, have not been sufficiently dwelt on. The Hebrew, *tsarar*, means to distress by packing closely together, and so, to vex, or to annoy in any way. Here is to be found the ground of the prohibition contained in the law before us. A man is not to take for a second wife a woman who is likely, from spiteful temper or for other reasons, to vex the first wife. Rachel vexed Leah; Peninnah vexed Hannah; the first pair were blood relations, the second were not; but under the present law the second marriage would in both cases have been equally forbidden, if the probability of the provocation had been foreseen. It follows that polygamy is not prohibited by the text before us, but that the liberty of the polygamist is somewhat circumscribed by the application of the law of charity. It follows, too, that the law has no bearing on the question of marriage with a deceased wife's sister, which is neither forbidden nor allowed by it. Are we then to conclude that the Law of Moses leaves the case of the wife's sister untouched? Not so, for the general principle has been laid down, *None of you shall approach to any, that is near of kin to him, to uncover his nakedness,* and, as we have seen, the expression, *near of kin*, includes relations by affinity equally with blood relations; as therefore the wife's sister is in the canonists' first degree of affinity (and in the second according to the civilians), it is reasonably inferred that marriage with her is forbidden under the above law, and this inference is confirmed by marriage with the other sister-in-law—the brother's wife—being, as the rule, prohibited. It can hardly be doubted that marriage with the grandmother and with the niece—both in the second degree of consanguinity according to the canonists, and the third degree according to the civilians—and incest with a daughter are forbidden under the same clause.

The present verse completes the Levitical code of prohibited degrees. The Roman code of restrictions on marriage was almost identical with the Mosaic tables. It only differed from them by specifically naming the grandmother and the niece among the blood relations with whom a marriage might not be contracted, and omitting the brother's wife among relatives by affinity. In the time of Claudius, a change was introduced into it, for the purpose of gratifying the emperor's passion for Agrippina, which legalized marriage with a brother's daughter. This legalization continued in force until the time of Constantius, who made marriage with a niece a capital crime. The imperial code and the canon law were framed upon the Mosaic and the Roman tables, and under them no question arose, except as to the marriage of the niece, the deceased wife's sister, and the first cousin. Marriage with the niece was forbidden by Constantius, as we have said, in the year 355, on penalty of capital punishment for committing the offence, and marriage with a deceased wife's sister was declared by the same emperor to be null. The canons of Councils and the declarations of the chief Church teachers are in full accordance with the imperial legislation, condemning these marriages without a dissentient voice. The only case in which no consensus is found is that of the marriage of first cousins. By the earliest Roman law these marriages had been disallowed (Tacitus, 'Annal.,' xii. 6), but in the second century B.C. they had become common (Livy, xlii. 34), and they continued to be lawful till the year A.D. 384 or 385, when Theodosius condemned them, and made them punishable by the severest penalties possible. This enactment lasted only twenty years, when it was repealed by Arcadius, A.D. 404 or 405. No adverse judgment respecting the marriage of first cousins was pronounced by the Church until after the legislation of Theodosius, but it appears that that legislation was promoted at her instance, and from that time forward the tendency to condemn these marriages became more and more pronounced. See the canons of the Councils of Agde, Epaone, Auvergne, Orleans, Tours, Auxerre, in the sixth century, and of the Council in Trullo in the seventh century. The reformers of the sixteenth century in England, entrenching themselves, as usual, behind the letter of Scripture and the practice of the primitive Church, forbade marriages of consanguinity and affinity in the first, second, and third degrees according to the reckoning of the civil law, and in the first and second degrees according to the reckoning of the canon law, excepting those of first cousins, on which the early Christians pronounced no decisive judgment.

Ver. 19.—The marriage restrictions having been laid down, there follows in the five next verses the prohibition of five sexual impurities unconnected with marriage except by their subject-matter. The first is to **approach unto a woman to uncover her nakedness, as long as she is put apart for her uncleanness,** that is, either for seven days at the time of her ordinary illnesses (ch. xv. 19), or any longer time that her illness might last (ch. xv. 25), or for forty days after the birth of a man child (ch. xii. 2—4), or for eighty days after the birth of a girl (ch. xii. 5). The penalty for the offence within the seven days is death if committed wilfully (ch. xx. 18); if fallen into unknowingly, a ceremonial penalty of seven days' uncleanness is incurred (ch. xv. 24). It is twice referred to by Ezekiel as a gross sin (Ezek. xviii. 6; xxii. 10).

Ver. 20.—The second prohibition is, **Thou shalt not lie carnally with thy neighbour's wife**—a prohibition already made in other words in the ten commandments. The punishment for adultery is death by stoning (ch. xx. 10; Deut. xxii. 22; John ix. 5)— a more severe penalty than was usually inflicted in other nations.

Ver. 21.—The third prohibition is, **Thou shalt not let any of thy seed pass through the fire to Molech.** The words *the fire* are properly inserted, though not expressed in the original (cf. Deut. xviii. 10; 2 Kings xxii. 10). What was the nature and purpose of the idolatrous rite in question is, however, uncertain. It is generally assumed that reference is made to the practice of offering children in sacrifice to Molech, Deut. xii. 31, Ezek. xvi. 20, and Ps. cvi. 37 being quoted in support of that view. But it is by no means certain that this was the case. It might have been a rite by which children were dedicated to Molech— a baptism by fire, not resulting in the death of the child. Its mention here, in close connection with carnal sins, has led some to regard it as an impure rite; but this is a mistaken inference, for the prohibition of adultery naturally suggests the prohibition of a spiritual unfaithfulness. That it was some kind of idolatrous ceremony is shown by the addition of the words, **neither shalt thou profane the name of thy God.** But if the children were burnt to death in honour of the idol, from the beginning, we should expect to find a notice of the fact in less ambiguous language than the expression, *pass through the fire*, conveys, earlier than the days of Ahaz. It is easy to imagine that what began as a dedication ceremony may have become converted into an absolute sacrifice, retaining still its original designation. Molech was a Canaanitish and Phœnician deity, the name meaning King, just as Baal means Lord (see Selden, 'De Diis Syris,' i. 6). Jarchi, quoted by Wordsworth, describes the idol as "made of brass, having the face of an ox, with arms stretched out, in which the child was placed and burnt with fire, while the priests were beating drums, in order to drown the noise of its shrieks, lest the fathers might be moved with pity thereby." The place where the children were offered, in the later period of the Jewish history, was the valley of Hinnom (Jer. vii. 31; xxxii. 35; 2 Kings xxiii. 10).

Ver. 22.—The fourth prohibition forbids the sin of Sodom (see Gen. xix. 5; Judg. xi. 22; Rom. i. 27; 1 Cor. vi. 9; 1 Tim. i. 10). The penalty is death (ch. xx. 13).

Ver. 23.—The fifth prohibition (see Herod., ii. 16). The penalty is death (ch. xx. 15).

Vers. 24—30.—These verses contain a warning against the sins of incest and impurity already specified. The reason why the Canaanites were cast out before the Israelites was that **they were defiled in all these things, . . . and the land was defiled by** them. God **visited the iniquity** of these debased races, **and the land itself vomited out her inhabitants** on account of their **abominations.** The fate of the Canaanites was therefore a witness to them of what would be their fate if they did like them. **Defile not ye yourselves in any of these things. . . . Ye shall not commit** any **of these abominations, . . . that the land spue not you out also, when ye defile it.** Special penalties are appointed for particular sins further on. Here there are but two punishments denounced, one for individual sinners, the other national. The individual sinner is to be cut off from the nation by excommunication, **For whosoever shall commit any of these abominations, even the souls that commit them shall be cut off from among their people.** The nation, if it does not thus purify itself by cutting off from itself the authors of these corruptions, is to perish like the Canaanites. The words **vomiteth** (ver. 25) and **spued out** (ver. 28) are in that tense of the Hebrew verb which is generally called by grammarians a preterite, but this tense does not necessarily imply a past time; the time referred to depends on the context. The previous verbs, "I cast out," "I do visit," being present in sense, the two verbs, "vomiteth out (her inhabitants)," and "spued out (the nations that were before you)," are present also (see Introduction).

HOMILETICS.

Vers. 1—18.—*The restraints thrown about marriage by God's Law* are not meant to confine within the narrowest limits that which is a necessary evil, but to guard a holy institution, and prevent its being corrupted by abuse. Manichæanism and asceticism, which is essentially Manichæan in its character, denounce the body and the bodily affections as being in themselves bad; stoicism strives to crush out or eradicate natural feelings, to make place for a passionless calm. God's Law and the doctrine of the Church declare that it is the abuse, not the use, of the body that is wrong ; and, like the better forms of philosophy, occupy themselves with regulating, controlling, ruling man's passions, instead of vainly attempting to kill them. "Marriage *is* honourable in all, and the bed undefiled: but whoremongers and adulterers God will judge" (Heb. xiii. 4).[1]

I. MARRIAGE WAS INSTITUTED AS THE PRIMEVAL LAW AT THE CREATION OF WOMAN. "So God created man in his own image, in the image of God created he him; male and female created he them. And God blessed them, and God said unto them, Be fruitful, and multiply, and replenish the earth" (Gen. i. 27, 28). "And Adam said, This is now bone of my bones, and flesh of my flesh : she shall be called Woman, because she was taken out of Man. Therefore shall a man leave his father and his mother, and shall cleave unto his wife : and they shall be one flesh" (Gen. ii. 23, 24).

II. PARALLEL BETWEEN THE MARRIAGE LAW AND THE SABBATICAL LAW. 1. The sabbatical law, in like manner as the marriage law, was instituted at the creation (Gen. ii. 3). 2. Both laws took a special form for the patriarchal and Israelitish Churches. 3. In both cases an alteration was made by the authority of our Lord, the obligation of the laws still continuing as before. The form which the law of the sabbath took for the Jewish people may be seen in the seventh commandment and other Mosaic injunctions respecting the seventh day. The law of marriage likewise underwent a change from its original character, and instead of enjoining monogamy, it allowed polygamy ; and "because of the hardness of men's hearts," it permitted divorce for light causes (see Matt. xix. 3—12). The manner of observing the sabbatical law was changed for Christians by the authority which our Lord declared himself to possess for the purpose (Matt. xii. 8), and which the constant habit of the earliest Christians, of assembling on the first day of the week and regarding it as the commemoration of the Resurrection day, proves him to have exercised. In like manner, he restored the law of monogamy (Matt. xix. 8), and withdrew the licence for divorce, except in the one case of adultery on the part of the wife (Matt. xix. 9). In respect to the Levitical restraints on marriage he made no change, as is again proved to us by the universal recognition of these obligations on the part of the early Christians.

III. ADDITIONAL SANCTITY WAS ADDED TO MARRIAGE BY CHRISTIANITY. In the Epistle to the Ephesians, St. Paul points out the analogy which exists between the relation of husbands to wives, and of wives to husbands, and the relation of Christ to the Church, and of the Church to Christ. "The husband is the head of the wife, even as Christ is the head of the Church : and he is the saviour of the body. Therefore as the Church is subject unto Christ, so let the wives be to their own husbands in everything. Husbands, love your wives, even as Christ also loved the Church, and gave himself for it. . . . For no man ever yet hated his own flesh ; but nourisheth and cherisheth it, even as the Lord the Church : for we are members of his body, of his flesh, and of his bones. For this cause shall a man leave his father and mother, and shall be joined unto his wife, and they two shall be one flesh. This is a great mystery : but I speak concerning Christ and the Church" (Eph. v. 23—32). An inference has been drawn from these words that Christ instituted holy matrimony as a sacrament of the Christian Church. Such inference is altogether false. Marriage was not considered one of seven sacraments until the days of the Schoolmen ; but the passage exhibits the holiness of marriage in a new light, and gives a new reason for its being regarded as holy. The "mystery" is the analogy which exists between married persons and Christ and the Church. St. Paul quotes the words of institution from the Book of Genesis, showing what a high estate matrimony is, and gives this further reason for its holiness, which had not previously been known to exist. Such a thought as this takes marriage out of the sphere of carnal things, refining, purifying, and sanctifying it in a manner not yet appreciated wherever celibacy is regarded as a higher and holier condition.

IV. THE CAUSES FOR WHICH MATRIMONY WAS ORDAINED. "First, It was ordained for the procreation of children, to be brought up in the fear and nurture of the Lord, and to the praise of his holy Name. Secondly, It was ordained for a remedy against sin, and to avoid fornication. . . . Thirdly, It was ordained for the mutual society, help,

---

[1] "*Let* marriage *be* had in honour among all, and *let* the bed *be* undefiled : for fornicators and adulterers God will judge."—Revised Version.

and comfort, that the one ought to have of the other, both in prosperity and adversity " (Form of Solemnization of Matrimony). The third of these causes has been too often forgotten in the Christian Church, and the second has been too much dwelt upon; the consequence of which has been a low estimate of marriage, and therefore of woman. St. Paul's words ought to show us that it is this characteristic which gives its Christian aspect to marriage.

V. DUTIES OF HUSBANDS AND WIVES TOWARDS EACH OTHER. On the one side, love and protection (Eph. v. 25); on the other side, love and submission (Eph. v. 24, 33).

Vers. 19—23.—The preservation of the marriage relationship in its purity is the safeguard against sins of lust, which will be sure to invade a society wherever licentiousness or asceticism has dishonoured marriage.

Vers. 24—30.—Dissolute morals in respect to the relations of the sexes is always a symptom which precedes the ruin of an empire or the fall of a nation. It is both a sign and a cause—a sign of a general corruption, which will show itself elsewhere and under other forms; and a cause of the coming evils, as indulgence in bodily pleasures and Sybarite excesses takes away the firmness of will and readiness to endure hardness which are necessary conditions of both soldiers and citizens doing their duty to the State. When a country is sunk in dissoluteness there is, generally speaking, no renovation for it except by the irruption of a new race, as of the Israelites in Canaan, or of the barbarous nations on the breaking up of the old Roman Empire. The moral reason of the extermination of the Canaanites was the danger of their licentiousness spreading, as has often been the case, to the conquerors (cf. Numb. xxv. 17, 18).

HOMILIES BY VARIOUS AUTHORS.

Unworldliness. Ch. xviii.; cf. Rom. xii. 2. The next element in the morality required of the Lord's people is non-conformity to this world. We are such imitative creatures that we are prone to do as our neighbours do, without questioning the propriety of their conduct. Whenever we adopt the ordinary standard of life, without inquiring how it is related to the Divine standard, we are conforming to the worldly spirit. The worldly conduct may be much higher in one age than in another, and in one country than in another; but *the essence of worldliness is unquestioning conformity to the standard of our neighbours.*

In the present chapter we have a fearful picture of the morality, or rather immorality, of Canaan. It may be read in connection with Rom. i. 18—32, as showing the depth to which unrestrained desire may descend. Not only do the Canaanites appear to have indulged in the most reckless licentiousness with nearest relatives, but also to have indulged in sodomy, and even to have descended to carnal intercourse with beasts. That is to say, they gave up their high vantage-ground as intellectual and moral beings, and descended to the level of brute beasts (cf. 2 Pet. ii. 12). We would require to go to the dark places of heathenism, which are still " full of the habitations of cruelty " (Ps. lxxiv. 20), to find an exact parallel at present for Canaan. The progress of civilization has smoothed the surface of society, however little it may have touched its heart. But what we must notice is that the principle of worldly conformity may be just as active in our boasted civilization, as in the darkest haunts of heathenism.

I. THE HIGHEST CIVILIZATION IS NO SUFFICIENT REASON FOR A CERTAIN LINE OF CONDUCT. The Israelites had been developed in Egypt, which was then at the head of civilization. It would be a very great temptation, therefore, to these liberated bondmen to walk according to the customs and ordinances of Egypt. They would be tempted to do many things on no higher ground than that they had seen them done in Egypt. No wonder, therefore, that the Lord admonishes them in these terms : " After the doings of the land of Egypt, wherein ye dwelt, shall ye not do " (ver. 3).

And yet is not this exactly the position taken up by many at this hour? They do many things " on the very highest authority." The reason of the course, its moral value, is never thought of, but simply the precedent which can be produced for it. This spirit of "simian imitation" is worldliness pure and simple. The highest civilization is not necessarily moral, much less religious : why should I conform to the demands of a capricious code of laws, which may have no valid moral principle within them at all ? God surely has not given us reflection and conscience to be ignored in such a way as this.

II. PREVAILING CUSTOM IS NO SUFFICIENT REASON EITHER FOR A CERTAIN LINE OF CONDUCT. The Israelites, in coming into Canaan, would find the inhabitants the freest and easiest possible in the matter of morals. No restraint appears to have been put upon their passions. They did whatever was right in their own eyes. Their lusts were their law. Now, were the Israelites to go into the land in the "jolly-good-fellow" style, they would be popular at once. The entrance into Canaan would in such a case have been an easy and triumphal march. Conformity to prevailing custom would have made the immigration a God-send to the beastly inhabitants. It would have given novelty to their desires. Hence God warns his people in the words, "And after the doings of the land of Canaan, whither I bring you, shall ye not do : neither shall ye walk in their ordinances" (ver. 3).

The snare of popularity prevails at present as powerfully as it did when Israel was about to enter Canaan. There is a great disposition with professedly religious people, "when at Rome, not to quarrel with the pope." Conformity to prevailing custom is a popular *rôle* to play. It costs nothing, except indeed the sacrifice of principle, and it gains in the worldly sense much. But no thinking mind imagines it is a rule of human conduct which will stand a moment's consideration. Why should I yield to what may be a senseless and even an immoral custom, simply because it is a custom ? I have not been endowed with reason for such an irrational result as this.

III. WHEN MEN SACRIFICE THEIR MANHOOD TO WORLDLY CONFORMITY, THEY FIND EVENTUALLY THAT THEY HAVE TAKEN A SUICIDAL COURSE. The course of the Canaanites was a suicidal one. The land was spuing them out (ver. 28). The selfish, lustful lives they led, the brutalities they practised, became their scourge, and they were fading away. The same result is found among the heathen nations. The sacrifice of manhood to bestiality must pay the penalty of eventual extinction.

And though at first sight the operation of the principle may be retarded by the higher *morale* of civilization, there can be no doubt that the suicidal character of worldly conformity is a real experience. An individual loses mental as well as moral power, who conforms without question to the worldly customs of his time, and thus sacrifices his manhood. The easy-going, popular individual, who does this, that, and the other, for fear of being thought singular, is found to have very little strength of mind to begin with, and less every day he lives. In fact, nature is constructed upon the principle that the despised talent of manhood is forfeited when not employed, and there is a clear descent in the scale of being.

IV. GOD HAS GIVEN US SUFFICIENTLY PLAIN STATUTES AND LAWS TO RE-INFORCE US IN OUR COMBAT WITH THE WORLD. "Ye shall do my judgments, and keep mine ordinances, to walk therein : I am the Lord your God. Ye shall therefore keep my statutes, and my judgments ; which if a man do, he shall live in them : I am the Lord" (vers. 4, 5). "And be not conformed to this world : but be ye transformed by the renewing of your mind, that ye may prove what is that good, and acceptable, and perfect will of God" (Rom. xii. 2). Transformation, "transfiguration" ($\mu\epsilon\tau\alpha\mu\rho\rho\phi\sigma\tilde{v}\sigma\theta\epsilon$; cf. Matt. xvii. 2 ; Mark ix. 2) as we might call it, that is, a bringing of ourselves into conformity to a Divine ideal ; this is what unworldliness consists in. We do not cease to be worldly when we surrender half a dozen suspicious pleasures. We cease to be "worldly" only when we refuse to accept of the prevailing worldly standard as our law of life, and seek earnestly to know "what is that good, and acceptable, and perfect will of God."

And to help us to this God has not only given us a book so plain and practical upon matters of daily life that he that runs may read ; but he has also embodied his ideal in the perfect manhood of his Son. We have simply to ask the question, "What would Christ, were he in our circumstances, do?" and instantly we are enabled to decide on an appropriate and an unworldly course of action. It is this manly rule of life to which we are called. To bow down to the customs of even the best society or the highest civilization without inquiring how these customs stand towards the Divine

Law, is to sacrifice our birthright of manliness for a mess of the rudest pottage.—
R. M. E.

Vers. 1—30.—*Abominable doings.* This chapter contains laws against abominations
practised by the heathen, together with reasons why they must be avoided by the
people of God. Foremost amongst these reasons is—

I. THAT THEY ARE FORBIDDEN BY GOD. This is the highest reason, for: 1. *He is
the supreme Arbiter of men* (vers. 5, 6, 24): "I am the Lord." (1) He is our Creator.
His power over the work of his hands is absolute. It is our wisdom to confess this
without gainsaying. (2) He is our Governor. He has not abandoned his creation to
mechanical laws. The providence of his intelligence is everywhere and ever active.
This his people saw in the miracles of the Exodus. (3) Moral beings are morally
responsible to a God of holiness and truth. His will is law. It is truth. It is purity.
2. *He is the covenant Friend of his people* (vers. 1, 4, 30): "I am the Lord your God."
(1) The covenant relationship is set forth in this declaration. It therefore suggests all
the promises. Blessings pertaining to this life; also to that which is to come.
What glorious blessings! (2) Gratitude is appealed to here. Love should constrain
us. The obedience of love is the purest. It is most acceptable to God. It is most
perfect; for the whole being is in it.

II. THAT THE HEATHEN HAVE PRACTISED THEM. 1. *They were the doings of the
Egyptians* (ver. 3). (1) The corrupt state of heart which prompted them, and which
was aggravated by their repetition, was that from which the children of Israel suffered
cruel and relentless persecutions and oppressions. The bitter experience they had of
these abominations should lead them scrupulously to avoid them. (2) If they had
learnt to follow their vices, it is time to unlearn them, now that they have been
delivered from Egypt. Providence furnishes men with opportunities favourable to
repentance and reformation. We are answerable for these. 2. *They were the doings of
the Canaanites.* (1) Customs common to the heathen should be viewed with suspicion by the people of God. The practices of custom come to be called "ordinances"
(see ver. 3). Ordinances of man must not be confounded with ordinances of God. (2)
We need admonition here. It is easy to flow with the stream; difficult to stem the
torrent. We must brace ourselves to this. We should look to God to nerve our
resolution.

III. THAT THE MATTER IS VITAL. 1. *God leads his people into temptation.* (1) Thus
he led his people into Egypt. Now he conducts them in amongst the Canaanites. "Shall
there be evil in a city and the Lord hath not done it?" (see Isa. xlv. 7; Amos iii. 6).
(2) Yet is not God the Author of *moral* evil. Physical may exist apart from moral
evil. Witness the afflictions of Job (see also John ix. 1—3). (3) God leads men into
temptation, not that they may fall into it, but that they may learn to resist it, and so
form a strong moral character. 2. *There is life in the Law to those who can keep it.*
(1) In so far as it is fulfilled, it brings the benefits of a wise and good code (Deut. iv. 8;
Neh. ix. 13, 14; Ps. cxlvii. 19, 20). (2) But who can so fulfil it as to ensure eternal
life? Not one (see Luke x. 25—28; Rom. x. 5). (3) Therefore faith is declared to
be the principle of justification (Hab. ii. 14). Upon this Paul founds his reasoning
(Gal. iii. 10—14; Rom. i. 16, 17; Phil. iii. 9). 3. *Ruin is denounced upon the
transgressor.* (1) Faith is the principle of a true obedience. The transgressor of the
Law denies his faith and comes under the curse (Heb. x. 38; Deut. xxvii. 26; Jer. xi. 3)
(2) For his sake the land is cursed (ver. 25). So defiled may it become as to be unfit
for the tabernacle of God. The curse upon the ground for man's sake came in the form
of a deluge of water; it will yet come in a flood of fire (Gen. iii. 17; v. 29; 2 Pet. iii.
7). (3) The transgressor is cut off from among his people (ver. 29; comp. 1 Cor. iii.
17). The abomination in which he is held is vigorously set forth under the figure of
the land vomiting and spuing out its inhabitants (vers. 25, 28). So were the Egyptians
ejected. So were the ancient Canaanites (see Gen. xv. 16; Rev. iii. 16). So in turn
were the Israelites (Ezek. xx. 11, 13, 21). We should not be highminded, but fear
(Rom. xi. 19—21; Heb. iv. 11). "Lay the ear of your faith to the gates of the
bottomless pit, and hear the doleful shrieks and outcries of damned sinners, whom
earth hath spewed out, and hell has swallowed, and tremble lest this be your portion
at the last" (M. Henry).—J. A. M.

Vers. 1—4.—*Two aspects of sin.* There are many ways in which sin may be regarded. Directed by these words, we may look at it in—

I. ITS UGLY ASPECT AS SEEN IN HUMAN ILLUSTRATIONS. The children of Israel were warned to separate themselves in every way from "the doings of the land of Egypt" and from "the doings of the land of Canaan" (ver. 3). These were to be a beacon to them; they were things to be hated and shunned. To those who had not been brought down themselves to the same low moral level, these doings would appear the shameful things they were—base, corrupt, vile. It is well for us to glance at, though not to dwell upon, sin in its last and worst developments, in its final issues; to see and understand what it leads to and ends in. Look at intemperance, dishonesty, cruelty, cupidity, profanity, impurity, as these sins are seen in their full development and complete outworking; see how utterly vile and hideous they appear to those in whom any purity is left. You would not resemble these; you start and shrink at the very thought of it; then do not move one inch down the smooth decline, do not take one step along "the primrose path of dalliance" with temptation. If we would keep well away from the beginnings of evil, we shall find a strong inducement to purity and honour by one thought of "the doings of the land" of impurity and shame.

II. ITS EVIL ASPECT AS GATHERED FROM THE COMMANDMENTS OF GOD. "I am the Lord your God . . . Ye shall not do . . . Ye shall do my judgments, and keep mine ordinances, to walk therein: I am the Lord your God." These solemn and weighty words introduce the prohibition of various evil lusts; these unholy passions were not only to be loathed and shunned because of the shamefulness of them in themselves and because of the evil consequences they would entail, but also and chiefly because they were imperatively disallowed by God. "I am the Lord . . . ye shall not do these things," etc. God's decisive disapproval is enough for us; it is final; it should be all-prevailing. For: 1. *His sovereignty suffices,* without further thought. He is "the Lord our God." Surely our Divine Creator, he from whom we came, in whom we live, without the continual exercise of whose power we should cease to be, to whom we owe all that we are and have, has sovereign right to decide concerning us, what things we may do and what things we shall shun. It is enough, it is more than enough, that the Lord our God says, concerning anything, "Ye shall not do it." 2. Nevertheless, there is the further thought that *God knows best* what is good and evil. He who made us, who "knows what is in man," who sees the end from the beginning, and knows what are the tendencies and issues of all things, can surely decide better than we can what are the desirable relations we should hold with our fellows; how near we may approach them; what may be our alliances and intimacies with them, etc.; which is the right and true path in which to walk. 3. And there is this additional thought that *his Divine interest in us is equal to his Divine knowledge of us.* We are sure that God will not deny us any really desirable thing; that he seeks our happiness and well-being; that if he limits our liberty or narrows our delights, it is purely because he is working out our true and lasting good.

Therefore, if we would not "condemn ourselves in those things which we allow" (Rom. xiv. 22), we must not only shrink from those evils which show themselves in the "doings of the land" of ungodly men, but also consult the commandment of the Lord. We must ask ourselves what those actions and relations are which he has forbidden. We must remind ourselves of his sovereignty over us, his knowledge of us, and his good pleasure toward us; we must also sedulously banish from our mind as well as put away from our life the evil thing to which we may be tempted.—C.

Ver. 5.—*Life in obedience.* The Apostle Paul, both in his letter to the Romans (x. 5), and in that to the Churches of Galatia (iii. 12), brings this passage to prove that salvation under the Law was by obedience rather than by faith. We may approach the main thought of the text by two preliminary remarks on the relation of these two principles of life, showing the consistency of the Law and the gospel. We maintain—

I. THAT, UNDER THE LAW, MERE CONFORMITY OF CONDUCT WITHOUT FAITH WAS UNACCEPTABLE TO GOD. It is a mistake to suppose that God's requirements of his ancient people were satisfied with a purely mechanical obedience. They were not only to "walk in his ways," but they were also to "fear the Lord their God, and *to love him* and to serve him *with all their heart and with all their soul*" (Deut. x. 12; see also Deut. vi. 5; xi. 13; xxx. 16, 20). They were not only to act righteously toward their neighbour, but to love him (ch. xix. 18). They were to "afflict their souls" on the Day of Atonement and Reconciliation (ch. xvi. 29). There can be little doubt that it was the duty of the priests and Levites to instruct the Hebrew worshippers to present their sacrifice unto the Lord, believing and feeling that he was there to receive their offering and to accept their penitence and their faith.

II. THAT, UNDER THE GOSPEL, A LIVING FAITH IS CONSTANTLY ASSOCIATED WITH ACTIVE OBEDIENCE. We are not saved by works, but by faith in Jesus Christ (Rom. iii. 28; v. 1; Eph. ii. 8, etc.). Yet the faith which saves is a "faith which worketh by love" (Gal. v. 6; Jas. ii. 18, 20, 22, etc.).

But the primary truth which is taught in this passage is rather this—

III. THAT SPIRITUAL OBEDIENCE IS THE SECRET AND THE SOURCE OF TRUE HUMAN LIFE. 1. It is the secret of all real life. What *is* human life? In what does it actually consist? The life of the brute consists in the performance of its animal functions, in its outward, sensible existence. But the life of a man consists in something higher. *We* live when our souls live, when we live before God and unto him; if a man will do God's will and keep his statutes and his judgments, "*he shall live in them;*" he will find his true life in the doing and the keeping of these; "this *is* life eternal, to know thee," etc. (John xvii. 3). To know God, to know him as he is revealed to us in Christ Jesus, to worship him, to rejoice in him, to love and to please him, to be gratefully and cheerfully obedient to his will in all things,—this is human life; all else is immeasurably below it. There is nothing worth calling life apart from the holy and happy service of God; a spiritual not a servile obedience is the secret of life on earth. 2. It is also *the source of the higher human life which is beyond*. The Jew who kept God's statutes not only found a true life *in* his obedience, but he also gained a true life *through* his obedience. God bestowed on him his Divine favour, conferred on him all those outward blessings which were then regarded as the highest token of the favour of the Eternal; he lived in the smile and the benediction of Jehovah. Our hope is brighter and more far-reaching than his. He had some glimmering of the blessedness beyond, but it was faint and feeble. We know that if our faith in a Divine Redeemer is manifested in a lasting spiritual obedience, we "shall live" a life of which the Jew had little thought, and of which we ourselves can only form some struggling anticipation. We know that if "we are faithful unto death," we shall have "a crown of life." The obedience of faith, continued to the end, will introduce us to the life which is (1) one of celestial fulness; (2) free from present care, sorrow, sin; (3) everlasting.—C.

Vers. 6—23.—*Impurity—its extent and source.* There are times when and conditions under which it is both our right and our duty to speak on this subject. We may offend delicacy by speech, and must therefore be careful what we say. But we may neglect obligation and opportunity by silence, and must therefore use fitting occasion for speech. There is a time to warn the young against an evil which may slay them with a mortal wound. We may glance, and only glance, at—

I. THE FEARFUL LENGTH TO WHICH IMPURITY MAY PASS. God made man male and female that, related to one another thus, they might be happy in one another's fellowship; that husband, wife, and child might complete the harmony of human life. But for the confusing and disturbing element of sin, there would have been nothing but holy conjugal affection and happy human homes. How dark and sad a contrast to this does society present! How melancholy the thought that impurity should not only have tainted so many souls, but should have taken so may forms! that not only have the natural relations of the sexes been too unlimited, too unrestrained, but that sin of this description has taken unnatural, shocking, and abominable forms! that its dark and shameful manifestations are such as we hardly like to name, and do not dare to think of (vers. 22, 23)! Only a holy compulsion will induce us even to make passing reference to such things. So low, to such dark depths, into such a "far country" of vileness does the sin of impurity extend.

II. THAT GUILTY INDULGENCE IS THE ONLY EXPLANATION OF THIS EVIL PROGRESS. How can such things be? is the simple question of the pure heart. How by any possibility can human nature sink into such a gulf of depravity? How can we account for it that the soul which once knew the innocency of childhood finds an awful pleasure in such shameful deeds? The answer is undoubtedly here. The very possibility of it is a part of the penalty of the sins which have been committed. Sins of impurity leave a stain upon the soul; the seducer has not only to suffer the rebuke of God, the reproaches of the one he has wronged and ruined, and the stings of his own conscience—some day to be awakened, but he has to "bear his iniquity" in a depraved taste, in a stained and injured nature, in a lowered and baser appetite. In this, as in other matters, perhaps more fearfully than in most, "he that sinneth against God wrongeth his own soul" (Prov. viii. 36). Let the man who gives way to impurity remember that he is travelling on a downward course that ends in saddest depravation of soul, and that will leave him open to those more vile temptations which would disgrace and even disgust him now.

III. THE TRUE TREATMENT OF THIS DESTROYING SIN. Trace the evil back from its worst developments to its mildest form; from its fullest crime to its source in the soul. Incest, adultery, fornication, seduction, indecency, indelicate conversation, *the impure thought*. This last is the source of all. It is that which must be assailed, which must be expelled.

In this matter of the relation of the sexes, there are three main truths. 1. God gives to most of us the joy of conjugal love, and this is to be sanctified by being accepted as his gift (Jas. i. 17). Where it is denied we must be well satisfied with other mercies so freely given. 2. Its lasting happiness is only assured to the pure of heart. With all others its excellency will soon fade and die. 3. Therefore let us, by all possible means, guard our purity: (1) by avoidance of temptation (evil company, wrong literature); (2) by energetic expulsion of unworthy thoughts; (3) by realization of the presence of the heart-searching Holy One; (4) by earnest prayer; let us "keep our heart beyond all keeping," etc. (Prov. iv. 23).—C.

Vers. 24—30.—*The penalty of sin.* The disastrous consequences of iniquity are clearly and strongly expressed in these concluding words of the chapter. We have the truth brought out—

I. THAT BY SIN WE CORRUPT OURSELVES. "Defile not ye yourselves in any of these things" (ver. 24); "that ye defile not yourselves therein" (ver. 30). Our Lord tells us that "out of the heart proceed evil thoughts, murders, adulteries, fornications," etc., and that "these things defile a man" (Matt. vii. 19, 20). And Paul tells us that we "are the temple of God," and that "if any man defile the temple of God, him shall God destroy" (1 Cor. iii. 16, 17). Those sins which a man commits against his own spirit or his own body—those wrongs which a man does himself—end in positive and serious injury. They enfeeble, they degrade, they brutalize, they bring down a man's tastes and appetites to the meanest levels, they lay and leave his nature open to the worst temptations. In the practice of vice a man sinks down daily until he becomes thoroughly corrupt, averse to all that is holy, prone to everything impure.

II. THAT BY SIN WE CONTAMINATE SOCIETY. "In all these the nations are defiled" (ver. 24); "and the land is defiled" (vers. 25, 27). Societies as well as individuals become corrupt. Even one Achan defiled the whole camp of Israel and paralyzed its power. One incestuous member of the Corinthian Church infected and stained that Christian society. How much more will many evil-doers corrupt the community! It may not take a large number of unholy, impure, unrighteous souls to make a Church or society "defiled" in the sight of the Holy One, no longer a fit dwelling-place for his Holy Spirit, a community to be abandoned to itself.

III. THAT BY SIN WE INCUR THE HIGH DISPLEASURE OF ALMIGHTY GOD. "Ye shall not commit any of *these abominations*" (vers. 26, 27, 29), "of *these abominable customs*" (ver. 30). The Holy One, in his righteous indignation, threatens that "the land shall spue them out" if they indulge in such iniquities. No stronger language could be employed to indicate the uttermost conceivable detestation and abhorrence which God has of such sins as these described. "It is a fearful thing to fall into the hands of the living God" (Heb. x. 31); and it is a fearful thing to have done or to have become that which God regards with Divine abomination, to be the object of his awful resentment and indignation; to have to feel that he, the Divine Father and the righteous Judge, cannot look on us without terrible aversion.

IV. That by sin we are determining our doom. (Ver. 29.) Whether by being "cut off from among the people" we understand excommunication and exile or death, the penalty is severe. It is certain that ver. 28 points to stern rejection and utter destruction. 1. It is certain that by open sin we expose ourselves to exile from the Christian Church, and even to banishment from all decent and honourable society. The Church, the family, and the social circle must exclude the wanton offender for the sake of their pure and innocent members. 2. Also that by continuance in deliberate sin, whether open or secret, whether of the body or of the soul, we shall be rejected from the city of God. "There shall in no wise enter into it any thing that defileth, neither whatsoever worketh abomination" (Rev. xxi. 27).—C.

Vers. 1—30.—Ver. 5, "Ye shall therefore keep my statutes, and my judgments: which if a man do, he shall live in them: I am the Lord."

I. The true morality is based upon the true religion. 1. Special need of insisting on this in times when men seek to make light of religious obligation. 2. Historical confirmation: Egypt, Persia, Greece, Rome,—all corrupt because degenerate. No protection, as luxury increases, from relaxation of manners save in religious safeguards. 3. The life of faith is life in commandments. The Lord is both the Object of faith and the Ruler of life. The commandments do not give faith or dispense with it, but reveal, test, and approve it.

II. The world without God is a world of abominations and death. All God's laws contribute to health and happiness. His judgments on the nations were the clearing away of moral filth and disorder. The state of the heathen is an indisputable evidence of man's natural depravity and ruin. Intellect, physical prowess, wealth, learning,—all were rendered useless, and worse than useless, by moral weakness.

III. Judgment and mercy went hand in hand in the Divine dispensation. The offender was excommunicated that he might have opportunity for repentance—which made a warning to all. The land was to be kept from defilement that it might be the land of God's people. The sanctity of the bodily life, of personal purity, of domestic relationship, of the family, and so of the nation, are all made to depend on the sanctity of the first and deepest of all relations—that between man and God. "I am the Lord." The land is mine first, then yours. The Law is your safety and peace.—R.

Vers. 1—5.—*Obedience enjoined.* A nation's importance is not to be reckoned according to its size, but more according to the character of its people and of the great men who have belonged to it. That must ever be a distinguished nation which has had a Moses ruling over it, a man with whom God spoke face to face, instructing him by what rules to govern the people. Those rules form a code second to none in history for purity, justice, and completeness. At the head of a number of separate precepts stands the special injunction of the text, calling upon the Israelites to respect the entire Law.

I. A reminder that in every place there are evil practices to be shunned. The present position of every individual is an isthmus connecting the continent of the past and the future. Israel in the wilderness journeying from Egypt to Canaan was but like many between youth and manhood, school and business, activity and retirement. Such a transition state may be profitably used as a time of thought and resolution. In no position must we expect freedom from temptation. The conduct of the Egyptians and of the Canaanites must alike be avoided (ver. 3). And those who defer religious decision until a season of immunity from danger arrives, may tarry in vain. The wilderness has its lawless manners as well as the settled country. How necessary to be upon our guard lest we be corrupted by the customs of our neighbours! Happy the college, the mart, the home, that is less likely to contaminate than to purify!

II. Compliance with the laws of God is the best preservative against imitating sinful customs. He runs quickest away from evil who pursues the good in front of him. Simply to retreat from danger, backing from it, is a slow and insecure method. We want more than negative righteousness, we need positive fulfilment of holy commands to ensure us against adopting odious habits. *It is not safe to take men as our patterns of behaviour.* "Be ye imitators of God as beloved children."

Egyptians and Canaanites were equally unfit to be followed. The Apostle Paul did not set up his own life as a model except in so far as he also imitated Christ (1 Cor. xi. 1). *Obedience is here described in three ways,* as *doing* the judgments of God, *keeping* his ordinances, and *walking* therein (ver. 4). Great is the privilege that moderns enjoy in having so many copies of God's Word multiplied as to be easily accessible to all. Surely we ought to meditate therein day and night, that we may order our steps thereby.

III. Obedience may be stimulated by reflection. 1. *Upon the right of God to issue commands.* "I am Jehovah" is his claim to attention as the Fount of law, and a claim which no thoughtful mind should reject. The ever-living Almighty Holy One possesses in himself every attribute that demands our homage. To withhold it is to violate congruity, to act in a manner out of harmony with what fitness requires. 2. *Upon our acceptance of his lordship over us.* "I am the Lord your God." We have entered into covenant relationship with him, and we break the terms of agreement if we fail to keep his statutes. The plural form of "God" may, without forcing, be taken here to indicate that the Israelites had deliberately bound themselves to the one Jehovah as their "Gods," instead of the idols of the nations round. God is our Father, how shall we be disobedient children? our King, how can we act as rebellious subjects? our Lawgiver, how can we dare to transgress his commandments? 3. *Upon the blessedness attained by observance of God's statutes.* "Which if a man do, he shall live in them." Man thought to increase his power by tasting forbidden fruit, but he lost his life, and only regained it in proportion as he returned to obedience. It is true that the impossibility of perfectly keeping the Law foreshadowed the necessity of another way of salvation, but according as the Israelites adhered to the Law in letter and spirit, so they experienced happiness and the favour of God, which is life indeed. We rejoice in the gospel plan of faith in Christ, not as making the Law inoperative, but as enabling us to fulfil its aim, to accomplish its real design—sanctification of life; and therein delivered from thraldom, we enter upon the life eternal that comprehends all blessing. We listen to the Law now, not as if it were the stern prescription of a hard Taskmaster, but as the instruction of a loving, all-wise Friend, which the more closely we follow, the more prosperous our career will be. "Freely we serve, because we freely love."—S. R. A.

Vers. 24, 25.—*Abominations denounced.* Some chapters of law, as of history, are not pleasant reading. That they should have been found necessary is a proof of the fearful depravity into which man may fall, sinning against natural instincts, hurried away and blinded by passion so as to overstep the bounds of decency. The prohibitions of this chapter were designed to hallow marriage and the family relationship. Their observance would tend to benefit the entire nation, for the laws of God are framed with benevolent wisdom. To sin against them is to wrong one's own soul.

I. The denunciations and threatenings evince God's hatred of abominable conduct. "That the land spue not you out also." "The souls that commit them shall be cut off from among their people." Strong is the language applied to sinful practices—they are "wickedness" (ver. 17), "abomination" (ver. 22), "confusion" (ver. 23). The Law will have no compromise, admits of no alternative amongst God's people, the command is, "Thou shalt not." Wickedness is not to be tolerated even in the stranger (ver. 26); he is not obliged to conform to all the ceremonies, but he must rigidly abstain from every moral offence. The New Testament relaxes not one jot in condemnation of all that is impure and filthy in conduct and even language (see Rom. i. 18, 32; 1 Cor. vi. 9, 10; Eph. v. 3—5; Rev. xxi. 8).

II. The delay between sin and punishment is a mark of the kindness and long-suffering of God. (See Peter's argument in 2 Epist. iii. 9.) In Gen. xv. 16 it was expressly declared, "the iniquity of the Amorites is not yet full." They were allowed four hundred years to repent, or to fill up the cup of their iniquity, and they chose the latter. This is the clearest answer to any who would impugn the justice of God's dealing with the Canaanites in exterminating them with fire and sword. Oh, the folly of men who abuse precious time by laughing at solemn announcements of coming woe, instead of employing it in making their peace with God! By every moment that intervenes between the sinner and death God urges him to seek pardon and amendment.

III. The instances recorded show the certain visitation of sin with God's displeasure. Delay is no guarantee of final immunity from punishment. The heathen were at last driven out of the land, and likewise the Israelites who succeeded felt the wrath of God on account of the shameful customs in which they indulged. *God is impartial*, and does not spare sin in his people or his enemies. As the denunciation shows God in principle and language, so the fulfilment of his threat demonstrates him in act, and is a further vivid evidence of his dislike of all wickedness. Nathan was God's messenger to rebuke and threaten David, as afterwards John the Baptist denounced Herod for taking his brother's wife. Just retribution foretells a day of judgment, when inequalities of punishment shall be righted and God's equity triumphantly vindicated. Here we see sufficient to establish the fact of the existence of a moral government (Eccles. viii. 11—13).

IV. The climax of sin is reached when nature herself seems to abhor the sinner. Graphic is the picture of the land loathing its burden and vomiting forth its inhabitants. As a leprosy infected walls and garments, so the abominations of the heathen defiled the land itself that it stank. The results of immorality upon the state of society and of individuals have been appalling. Eventually everything has sunk into ruin, disintegration and corruption have prevailed. The population decreases by sickness and barrenness and murder. The arts and sciences decay, literature is blighted, philanthropy unknown. The text reminds us that a closer connection exists between man and inanimate nature than we sometimes think (see this also suggested in Rom. viii. 20 and Gen. iii. 17).

Conclusion. If the subject is painful, the lesson may be salutary. Sin is widespread. "Let him that thinketh he standeth take heed lest he fall." We may be glad of the healthful influence of Christianity, rightly directing public opinion, and erecting it into a safeguard against evil. "Having these promises, let us cleanse ourselves from all filthiness of the flesh and spirit, perfecting holiness in the fear of God."—S. R. A.

EXPOSITION.

CHAPTER XIX.

From the prohibition of moral uncleanness exhibiting itself in the form of incest and licentiousness, the legislator proceeds to a series of laws and commandments against other kinds of immorality, inculcating piety, righteousness, and kindness. Chapter xix. may be regarded as an extension of the previous chapter in this direction, after which the subject of ch. xviii. is again taken up in ch. xx. The precepts now given are not arranged systematically, though, as Keil has remarked, "while grouped together rather according to a loose association of ideas than according to any logical arrangement, they are all linked together by the common purpose expressed in the words, ' Ye shall be holy: for I the Lord your God am holy.'" They begin by inculcating (in vers. 3, 4) duties which fall under the heads of (1) the fifth commandment of the Decalogue, (2) the fourth, (3) the first,

(4) the second. These four laws are, in their positive aspects, (1) the religious law of social order, on which a commonwealth rests; (2) the law of positive obedience to God's command because it is his command; (3) the law of piety towards the invisible Lord; (4) the law of faith, which trusts him without requiring visible emblems or pictures of him. In vers. 11, 14, 16, 35, 36, obedience is inculcated to the eighth and the ninth commandments, which are the laws of honesty and of truthfulness; in ver. 12 to the third commandment, which is the law of reverence; in vers. 17, 18, 33, 34, to the sixth commandment, which is the law of love; in vers. 20, 29, to the seventh commandment, which is the law of purity; in vers. 9, 10, 13, the spirit of covetousness is prohibited, as forbidden in the tenth commandment, which is the law of charity. Thus this chapter may in a way be regarded as the Old Testament counterpart of the Sermon on the Mount, inasmuch as it lays down the laws of conduct, as the latter lays down the principles of action, in as com-

prehensive though not in so systematic a manner as the ten commandments.

Ver. 2.—**Ye shall be holy : for I the Lord your God am holy.** The religious motive is put forward here, as in the previous chapter, as the foundation of all morality. It is God's will that we should be holy, and by being holy we. are like God, who is to be our model so far as is possible to the creature. So in the new dispensation, "Be ye therefore perfect, even as your Father which is in heaven is perfect" (Matt. v. 48). " As he which hath called you is holy, so be ye holy in all manner of conversation " (1 Pet. i. 15).

Ver. 3.—**Ye shall fear every man his mother, and his father.** The words *fear* and *reverence* are in this connection interchangeable. So Eph. v. 33, " Let the wife see that she reverence her husband," where the word " reverence " would be more exactly translated by " fear." St. Paul points out that the importance of the fifth commandment is indicated in the Decalogue by its being " the first commandment with promise," that is, with a promise attached to it (Eph. vi. 2). The family life is built upon reverence to parents, and on the family is built society. Obedience to parents is a duty flowing out of one of the first two laws instituted by God—the law of marriage (Gen. ii. 24). The second law instituted at the same time was that of the sabbath (Gen. ii. 3), and in the verse before us observance of the sabbatical law is likewise inculcated, in the words that immediately follow—**ye shall keep my sabbaths.**

Ver. 4.—**Turn ye not unto idols.** The word used for idols, *elilim*, meaning nothings, is contrasted with *Elohim*, God. Ps. cxv. exhibits this contrast in several of its particulars. Cf. St. Paul's statement, " We know that an idol is nothing in the world, and that there is none other God but one " (1 Cor. viii. 4). " If the heart of man becomes benumbed to the use of images of false gods of any kind, he sinks down to the idols which are his ideals, and becomes as dumb and unspiritual as they are " (Lange). The remainder of the verse forbids the transgression of the second commandment, as the earlier part of the verse forbids the transgression of the first commandment; **nor make to yourselves molten gods,** as was done by Jeroboam when he set up the calves (1 Kings xii. 23).

Vers. 5—8.—The unsystematic character of this chapter is indicated by prohibitions under the fifth, fourth, first, and second commandments (vers. 3, 4) being succeeded by a ceremonial instruction respecting the peace offerings, repeated from ch. vii. 16—18. The words, **ye shall offer it at your own will,** should rather be, *for your acceptance,* as in ch. i. 3. In the seventh chapter a

distinction is drawn between the peace offerings that are thank offerings, which must be eaten on the first day, and the peace offerings which are vow or voluntary offerings, which may be eaten on the first or second day. In the present *résumé* this distinction is not noticed. Whoever transgresses this ceremonial command is to bear **his iniquity** and to be cut off from among **his people,** that is, to be excommunicated without any appointed form of reconciliation by means of sacrifice.

Vers. 9, 10.—The injunction contained in these verses, to not wholly reap the corners of thy field, neither ... gather the gleanings of thy harvest, is twice afterwards repeated (ch. xxiii. 22; Deut. xxiv. 19—22). In Deuteronomy, the oliveyard is specified together with the harvest-field and the vineyard, and it is added that, if a sheaf be by chance left behind, it is to remain for the benefit of the poor. The object of this law is to inculcate a general spirit of mercy, which is willing to give up its own exact rights in kindness to others suffering from want. The word here used for **vineyard** covers also the oliveyard. The expression, **neither shalt thou gather** every grape of thy **vineyard,** would be more literally rendered, *neither shalt thou gather the scattering of thy vineyard,* meaning the berries (grapes or olives) which had fallen or which were left singly on the boughs.

Ver. 11.—Stealing, cheating, and lying are classed together as kindred sins (see ch. vi. 2, where an example is given of theft performed by means of lying; cf. Eph. iv. 25 ; Col. iii. 9).

Ver. 12.—**And ye shall not swear by my name falsely.** These words contain a positive permission to swear, or take a solemn oath, by the Name of God, and a prohibition to swear falsely by it (see Matt. v. 33).

Ver. 13.—Cheating and stealing are again forbidden, and, together with these, other forms of oppression although legal. The command to pay labourers their hire promptly—which covers also the case of paying tradesmen promptly—is repeated in Deut. xxiv. 14 (cf. Jas. v. 4).

Ver. 14.—**Thou shalt not curse the deaf.** The sin of cursing another is in itself complete, whether the curse be heard by that other or not, because it is the outcome of sin in the speaker's heart. The suffering caused to one who hears the curse creates a further sin by adding an injury to the person addressed. Strangely in contrast with this is not only the practice of irreligious men, who care little how they curse a man in his absence, but the teaching which is regarded by a large body of Christians as incontrovertible. " No harm is done to reverence but by an open manifestation of insult. How, then, can a son sin gravely when he curses his father without the latter's knowing it, or mocks at him behind his back, inasmuch as in that case there is neither insult nor irreverence? And I think that the same is to be said, even though he does this before others. It must be altogether understood that he does not sin gravely if he curses his parents, whether they are alive or dead, unless the curses are uttered with malevolent meaning." This is the decision of one that is called not only a saint, but a " doctor of the Church" (Liguori, ' Theol. Moral.,' iv. 334). " Whoso curseth his father or his mother, his lamp shall be put out in obscure darkness," says the Word of God (Prov. xx. 20). **Nor put a stumblingblock before the blind, but shalt fear thy God.** By the last clause the eye is directed to God, who can see and punish, however little the blind man is able to help himself. (Cf. Job xxix. 15, " I was eyes to the blind, and feet was I to the lame.")

Ver. 15.—Justice is to be done to all. The less danger of **respecting the person of the poor** has to be guarded against, as well as the greater and more obvious peril of **honouring the person of the mighty.** The scales of Justice must be held even and her eyes bandaged, that she may not prefer one appellant to another on any ground except that of merit and demerit. " If ye have respect to persons, ye commit sin, and are convinced of the law as transgressors " (Jas. ii. 9).

Ver. 16.—**Thou shalt not go up and down as a talebearer among thy people.** For the evil done by mere idle talebearing, see Bishop Butler's sermon, ' Upon the Government of the Tongue,' and four sermons by Bishop Jeremy Taylor, on ' The Good and Evil Tongue; Slander and Flattery; the Duties of the Tongue.' **Neither shalt thou stand against the blood of thy neighbour**; that is, thou shalt not endanger his life, which is the result of the worst kind of talebearing, namely, bearing false witness against him. Thus the effect of the false witness of the two men of Belial against Naboth was that " they carried him forth out of the city, and stoned him with stones, that he died " (1 Kings xxi. 13; cf. Matt. xxvi. 60; xxvii. 4).

Ver. 17.—On the one side we are not **to hate our brother in our heart**, whatever wrongs he may commit; but on the other side, we are **in any wise to rebuke our neighbour** for his wrong doing. So our Lord teaches, " If thy brother trespass against thee, rebuke him " (Luke xvii. 3); and he appoints a solemn mode of procedure, by which this fraternal rebuke is to be conveyed in his Church : " If thy brother shall trespass against thee, go and tell him his fault between thee and him alone: if he shall hear thee, thou hast

gained thy brother. But if he will not hear thee, then take with thee one or two more, that in the mouth of two or three witnesses every word may be established. And if he shall neglect to hear them, tell it unto the Church; but if he neglect to hear the Church, let him be unto thee as an heathen man and a publican " (Matt. xviii. 15—17). Therefore St. Paul warns his delegates, Timothy and Titus, " Them that sin rebuke before all " (1 Tim. v. 20). " Reprove, rebuke " (2 Tim. iv. 2). " Rebuke them sharply " (Titus i. 13). " Rebuke with all authority " (Titus ii. 15). By withholding reproof in a bitter spirit, or from a feeling of cowardice, we may become partakers of other men's sins. Whoever fails to rebuke his neighbour when he ought to do so, *bears sin on his account* (the more correct and less ambiguous rendering of the words translated in the Authorized Version, **suffer sin upon him,** cf. Numb. xviii. 22, 32). God's people are their brothers' keepers (Gen. iv. 9).

Ver. 18.—Revenge and malice are forbidden as well as hatred, and the negative precepts culminate in the positive law, **Thou shalt love thy neighbour as thyself,** which sums up in itself one half of the Decalogue (Matt. xxii. 40). " For he that loveth another hath fulfilled the Law. For this, Thou shalt not commit adultery, Thou shalt not kill, Thou shalt not steal, Thou shalt not bear false witness, Thou shalt not covet; and if there be any other commandment, it is briefly comprehended in this saying, namely, Thou shalt love thy neighbour as thyself. Love worketh no ill to his neighbour : therefore love is the fulfilling of the Law " (Rom. xiii. 8—10).

Ver. 19.—**Ye shall keep my statutes.** Having arrived at the general conclusion, " Thou shalt love thy neighbour as thyself," in the previous verse, the legislator pauses, and then presents a collection of further laws, arranged as before in no special order. The first is a mystical injunction against the confusion of things which are best kept apart, illustrated in three subjects—diverse kinds of cattle in breeding, mingled seeds in sowing a field, and mixed materials in garments. In Deut. xxii. 10, a further illustration is added, " Thou shalt not plow with an ox and an ass together." The existence of mules, which we find frequently mentioned in the later history (2 Sam. xiii. 29; xviii. 9 ; 1 Kings i. 33), may be accounted for by supposing that the positive precept with regard to breeding cattle here laid down was transgressed, or that the mules were imported from abroad (see 1 Kings x. 25). The word used here and in Deut. xxii. 11 for a **garment mingled of linen and woollen,** is *shaatenez,* an Egyptian word, meaning probably mixed. The difficulty raised on this verse by the allegation that the high priest's dress was made of mixed materials, is met by the answer that, if it were of mixed materials (which is uncertain, for wool is not mentioned in Exod. xxviii., nor is it quite determined that *shesh* means linen), the mixture was not such as is here forbidden. The moral meaning of the whole of this injunction is exhibited in the following passages from the New Testament, "Ye cannot drink the cup of the Lord, and the cup of devils" (1 Cor. x. 21). "Be ye not unequally yoked together with unbelievers: for what fellowship hath righteousness with unrighteousness? and what communion hath light with darkness? and what concord hath Christ with Belial? or what part hath he that believeth with an infidel? and what agreement hath the temple of God with idols?" (2 Cor. vi. 14—16). "He cannot love the Lord Jesus with his heart," says Hooker, "who lendeth one ear to his apostles and another to false teachers, and who can brook to see a mingle-mangle of religion and superstition" ('Serm.' v. 7, quoted by Wordsworth).

Vers. 20—22.—A distinction is drawn between adultery with a free woman, or a betrothed free virgin, which was punishable with death (ch. xx. 20; Deut. xxii. 23), and with a slave betrothed to another man (probably a slave also). In the latter case a lesser punishment, no doubt that of scourging (according to the Mishna to the extent of forty stripes), was to be inflicted on one or both, according to the circumstances of the case. The words, **she shall be scourged,** should be translated, *there shall be investigation,* followed, presumably, by the punishment of scourging, for both parties if both were guilty, for one if the woman was unwilling. The man is afterwards to offer a trespass offering. As the offence has been a wrong as well as a sin, his offering is to be a trespass offering (see on ch. v. 14). In this case the fine of one-fifth could not be inflicted, as the wrong done could not be estimated by money, and the cost of the ram seems to be regarded as the required satisfaction. No mention is made of damages to be paid to the man to whom the slave-girl was betrothed, probably because he was himself a slave, and had not juridical rights against a freeman.

Vers. 23—25.—The eating of the fruit of young trees by their owners for five years is forbidden, on the principle that such fruit is unclean until it has been sanctified by the offering of a crop as firstfruits to the Lord for the use of the servants of the tabernacle, and a full crop is not to be expected until the fourth year from the time that the trees were planted. The fruit is at first to be counted as uncircumcised, being regarded in a position similar to that of the heathen, that is, unclean, from not having been yet sanctified by the offering of the firstfruits. This sanctification takes place in the fourth year.

Vers. 26—28.—After a repetition of the fundamental ceremonial law against eating things which have the blood in them (the LXX. rendering, ἐπὶ τῶν ὀρέων, "upon the mountains," arises from a mistaken reading), follow prohibitions (1) to **use enchantment,** literally, *to whisper or mutter after holding communication with serpents* (if the word *nichesh* be derived from *nachash,* a serpent); (2) to **observe times,** or rather, according to a more probable etymology, *exercise the evil eye;* (3) to **round the corners of your heads,** that is, use a sort of tonsure, as was done by some Arabian tribes (Herod., iii. 3) in honour of their god Orotal, and by the Israelites as a form of mourning (Deut. xiv. 1; Isa. xxii. 12); (4) to **mar the corners of thy beard,** a fashion of mourning which accompanied the tonsure of the head (see ch. xxi. 5; Isa. xv. 2; Jer. xlviii. 37); (5) to **make any cuttings in your flesh for the dead,** another form of mourning, associated with the two previously mentioned practices (see ch. xxi. 5; Deut. xiv. 1; Jer. xvi. 6; xli. 3; xlviii. 37); (6) to **print any marks upon you,** that is, tattoo themselves in memory of the dead. All these customs were unbecoming the dignity of God's people, and had been connected with idolatrous practices.

Ver. 29.—**Do not prostitute thy daughter.** This is a peremptory prohibition, applying to every Jewish maiden, introduced in this place with a primary relation to the sanctification of lust by the dedication of young girls at some heathen temples; but by no means confined in its application to such practices. All legal sanction of the sin of prostitution is forbidden, for whatever purpose it may be given; and the certain result of such sanction is indicated in the final words of the verse, **lest the land fall to whoredom, and the land become full of wickedness** (cf. Deut. xxiii. 17).

Ver. 30.—The command in this verse differs from that in ver. 3 by adding the injunction to **reverence my sanctuary** to that requiring the observance of the sabbath. It is a matter of experience that where the sabbath is not kept, God's sanctuary is not reverenced, and that that reverence increases or falls away according as the obligation of the sabbatical law, whether in its Jewish form or its Christian form, be more or less recognized. The sabbatical ordinance is necessary as a previous condition of religious worship. Without it, the business and pleasure of the world are too strong to give way to the demands upon time made by the stated service of

God. The verse is repeated in ch. xxvi. 2. "When the Lord's day is kept holy, and a holy reverence for the Lord's sanctuary lives in the heart, not only are many sins avoided, but social and domestic life is pervaded by the fear of God, and characterized by devoutness and propriety" (Keil).

Ver. 31.—This verse contains a prohibition of all dealings with those that have familiar spirits or are wizards. The punishment of such persons is appointed in the next chapter. Both in the Old and the New Testament, the real existence of evil spirits and their power of communicating with the human spirit is assumed.

Ver. 32.—Reverence for the old is inculcated as being a part, not merely of natural respect, but of the fear of God. In the East this virtue, implying deference on the part of the strong to the weak, and of the inexperienced to the wise, exists in larger influence for good than in the West, where, however, its place has been, but only partially, supplied by the greater deference paid by man to woman (cf. Prov. xvi. 31; xx. 29).

Vers. 33, 34.—The command already given "neither to vex a stranger, nor oppress him" (Exod. xxii. 21), on the pathetic ground that "ye know the heart of a stranger, seeing ye were strangers in the land of Egypt" (Exod. xxiii. 9), is broadened in these verses to the positive law, thou shalt love him as thyself. "The royal law of ver. 18 is expressly extended to the stranger, and notwithstanding the national narrowness necessary to preserve the true religion in the world, the general brotherhood of mankind is hereby taught as far as was possible under the circumstances" (Gardiner).

Vers. 35, 36.—These verses, beginning with the same words as ver. 15, Ye shall do no unrighteousness in judgment, contain another and wider application of that principle. Ver. 15 prohibited unrighteousness in the judge, or in one who was in the position of a judge; these verses forbid it in merchants and tradesmen. It is the more necessary to condemn dishonesty, in unmistakable terms, as men who make a profession of religion, and therefore would be shocked at stealing, have often less scruple in cheating. Here and in Deuteronomy, where the Law is repeated, a religious sanction is given to the command; "For all that do such things, and all that do unrighteously, are an abomination unto the Lord thy God" (Deut. xxv. 16). Cf. Prov. xi. 1, "A false balance is abomination to the Lord: but a just weight is his delight;" and xx. 10, "Divers weights, and divers measures, both of them are alike abomination to the Lord;" see also Micah vi. 10, 11 and Ezek. xlv. 10.

Ver. 37.—Moral precepts are rested on their right foundation—the command of God and the religious motive.

HOMILETICS.

Ver. 1.—*Morality has a basis of its own.* The moral philosopher, if asked, "Why should I act morally?" replies, "Because it is right for you to do so." If asked further, "Why is it right for me to do so?" he replies, "Because your conscience tells you that it is." If asked why conscience should be obeyed rather than passion, he replies, "Because it possesses greater authority, even if it has less power;" and in proof of this he points to the approval or disapproval which it stamps upon acts according to their character. Morality can be proved to be reasonable, apart from religion.

But it cannot be enforced. If a man denies that his conscience commands him to perform a moral action, the verdict of the general conscience of mankind may be quoted against him as contrary to that of his own, but he can repudiate the authority of that verdict so far as he is himself concerned. He can reasonably maintain that the general conscience may be misled by prejudice or superstition, and that his own conscience is more enlightened than that of the mass. In this manner the philosopher, or any one who regards himself as a philosopher, finds a way of evasion ready at hand.

With the masses, moral teaching, unaccompanied by religious sanction, is still less effectual. The general good of mankind, or the duty of obeying the highest principle of our nature, has never restrained, and never will restrain, the mass of mankind from yielding to the force of strong passion or desire.

In the present chapter we find the moral duties—those of the second table as much as the first—rested upon a religious basis. They are God's commands, whether that command be given by written precept or by an instinct engraven on man's heart. And because they are God's commands in both these ways, they are to be obeyed. Thus there is an appeal from man's mind to something higher than himself, to which man will submit.   The effort to preserve morality in a nation without religious sanction and religious motive is like the attempt to keep alive the flame of a fire, when the fuel from which the flame is derived has been withdrawn.   One generation may continue moral; the next will certainly be licentious.   "I am the Lord" is a basis of morality which never fails.

Ver. 3.—*The laws of submission* (1) *to human authority and* (2) *to sacred ordinances, for the Lord's sake,* are enjoined in this verse.

1. The family is an institution of God's appointment (Gen. i. 28; ii. 24).   The command to children to honour their father and mother is distinguished in the Decalogue by a blessing attached to it (Exod. xx. 12; Eph. vi. 2); and a special blessing is bestowed on the house of the Rechabites for obeying it (Jer. xxxv. 18).   St. Paul enjoins the observance of the duty, both as an act right in itself and as positively commanded in God's Law (Eph. vi. 1, 2).   The father's duty is "nurture and admonition of the Lord" (Eph. vi. 4), including guidance, remonstrance, reproof (1 Sam. ii. 23). By means of this institution the character of every member of the commonwealth is formed, at the moment when alone it is plastic, by the influence best adapted for turning it to good.   Contrast the system adopted by Rousseau for dealing with his children, and the probable results on parents, children, and the State.   Cf. the Form of Solemnization of Matrimony: "Marriage was ordained for the procreation of children, to be brought up in the fear and nurture of the Lord, and to the praise of his holy Name."

An analogous position to that of the parent is afterwards held by the civil magistrate in respect to the subject, and by the pastor in respect to a member of his flock.   Therefore, in order to carry out the commandment, a man has not only "to love, honour, and succour his father and mother," but also "to honour and obey the queen, and all that are put in authority under her: to submit himself to all his governors, teachers, spiritual pastors and masters: to order himself lowly and reverently to all his betters" (Church Catechism).   On the other hand, the authorities in the State and in the Church have their duties also, not now the same as those of the parent towards the child, on account of the changed position of him who was once a child, but nevertheless analogous to them.   So in other cases, wherever men stand in a relation to each other similar to that of parent and child, obligations similar to those which bind parents and children arise.

2. Sabbatical observance appears, at first sight, a small thing to place on a level, as here, with the fifth commandment, or, as in the Decalogue, with the first, second, and third commandments; but when we examine into it closely, we find that this disproportion does not exist.

I. ITS INSTITUTION.   It shares with the ordinance of marriage alone the characteristic of having been instituted at the creation of the world.   "And God blessed the seventh day, and sanctified it: because that in it he had rested from all his work which God created and made" (Gen. ii. 3).   Being coeval with creation, the sabbatical law, like the marriage law, is of universal obligation on all mankind.

II. ITS JEWISH FORM.   The sabbatical law was observed during the period preceding the Mosaic Law (Exod. xvi. 22—30).   For the Jews it took the form given it in the fourth commandment (Exod. xx. 8—11; Deut. v. 12—15) and other Mosaic injunctions (Exod. xxxi. 13, 14; xxxv. 2, 3; Numb. xv. 32—36).   To them it commemorated the rest after the Creation and the rest after the toils of Egypt, while it looked forward to the rest of Canaan while they wandered in the wilderness (Ps. xcv. 11), and, after they had entered Canaan, to the still further rest of the Messianic kingdom (Heb. iv. 8); and it was to be kept with such severity that no work at all was to be done upon it, even to the extent of gathering sticks or lighting a fire.

III. ENDS SERVED BY THE JEWISH FORM.   1. It formed a very noticeable distinction between the Jews and the neighbouring nations, and so it was a preservative from idolatry.   2. It served, like circumcision, as a symbol constantly reminding them that they were God's people, and should live in accordance with their profession.   "Moreover also I gave them my sabbaths, to be a sign between me and them, that they might know that I am the Lord that sanctify them" (Ezek. xx. 12).

IV. THE CHRISTIAN FORM.   Christ declared his lordship over the sabbath day (Matt.

xii. 8), but he did not exercise that lordship for the purpose of destroying it as an institution, but merely of adapting the primary law of the sabbath to altered circumstances. The Jewish sabbath, as such (that is, in its peculiarities), ceased to be binding, but the obligation of sabbatical law continued, and the ordinance took a changed form. By apostolic authority, as proved by apostolic practice, the Christian sabbath was kept on the first day of the week—the anniversary of Christ's resurrection—and the severity of its character was abrogated.   As God had rested on the seventh day after his labour of creation, so Christ had rested in the grave on the seventh day after his labour of redemption. Why should the seventh day be any longer kept? "The Jewish sabbath died out in the course of the first generation of Christians, as circumcision died out, as the temple, as the Law itself died out. . . . The Lord's day was a Divine and more immortal shoot from the same stock. It was rooted in the primitive law of the Creation. It recognized and adopted the old weekly division of time, that perpetual and ever-recurring acknowledgment, wherever it was celebrated in all the world, of the Divine blessing and promises. It had the Divine sanction of the tables of stone—those tables, written by God's own finger, and therefore greatly superior in sanctity and enduring weight to the temporary enactments of the ceremonial law. It took up the old series of commemorations and sacred anticipations. It bade the true Israel of God record with gratitude and keep in mind, by the weekly institution and its recurring festival of rest and praise, the creation of mankind, the deliverance from Egypt, the entrance of the people into the promised land, the return from captivity, the coming of the Messiah; and to look forward under the dispensation of the Holy Ghost to the crowning and final mercy of the long scheme of Providence, the eternal rest in heaven which yet remaineth for the people of God" (Bishop Moberly, 'The Law of the Love of God').

V. THE ENDS OF THE SABBATICAL INSTITUTION. 1. To reserve a certain sufficient part of time free for spiritual interests. 2. To teach the lesson of obedience to positive precept in religious things. The appointment of one-seventh of our time for this purpose is wholly arbitrary. There is no account to be given of it except that it is God's will. There is no other account to be given of weeks. Months and years have their reasons in physical nature; not so weeks. God has commanded, and because he has commanded, the weekly rest is observed by those who love God; and not only is the weekly rest observed, but a loving obedience is paid to all religious institutions and ordinances established by lawful authority.

VI. EFFECT ON THE INDIVIDUAL CHRISTIAN'S LIFE. "The Christian man, desirous of loving God with all the affection of his heart, with all the rational intelligence of his mind, with all the devotion of his life, with all the energy of his strength, in the love taught him under the fourth law, will yield himself up gratefully and religiously to obey all duly ordered positive laws of the Church of God. The Sunday and its sacred observance will be to him the centre, and furnish, so to speak, the form of his own way of life, and that of all his family and dependents. He will regard it every time it returns as God's holy day of rest, the weekly commemoration of the primeval rest of God and of all the signal mercies of the elder covenant. Knowing himself to be of the true Israel of God, he will not forget the blessings connected by God himself with the sabbatical institution, vouchsafed to his fathers in the faith. He will celebrate it weekly as the feast of the Lord's resurrection, and all the blessings of that resurrection; as the feast of the Holy Ghost the Giver of peace and rest in the Church, as the weekly antepast of that glorious and unending rest in the presence of God which still remaineth for the people of God. It will be to him a day of rest, peace, prayer, praise, and holy joy; no mournful and austere time, but on the contrary, a thankful happy time. He will remember his Lord's injunction not to forbid or refuse works of necessity or mercy on that day. He will gratefully shut up the records of the cares, the interests, and the occupations of the week, and give that holy day to God; not discharging himself of his duties of worship by an attendance in God's house or holding himself at liberty to make his own convenience or inclination the rule of obedience; but faithfully, dutifully, and completely sanctifying that day to rest, worship, and the thought of God and heaven. And the other days, the train of Sunday, will borrow of its light; each having its own sacred, special commemoration belonging to it, and each reflecting some of the brightness of the Sunday just preceding and catching more and more from that which follows" (Moberly, 'The Law of the Love of God').

VII. RESULTS OF ITS NEGLECT. 1. To the individual: (1) an unloving spirit arising from a consciousness of disobedience to a command; (2) a habit of refusing to submit to positive injunctions, and, growing out of that, a habit of choosing which of God's commandments he will obey; (3) a loss of religious opportunities, and consequently a gradual falling away from the habit of public worship, and therefore from the spiritual life; (4) a sense of being overwhelmed by the business and worries of life which continue without cessation, and thence a want of calm peacefulness and cheerfulness. 2. To a nation: (1) growth of ungodliness and irreligion; (2) increase of self-indulgence and mere amusement-seeking; (3) growing oppression of the poor, who are made to serve the amusements or requirements of the rich instead of enjoying their weekly rest and refreshment of body and mind and soul; (4) the displeasure of God, whose primeval law is disobeyed.

Ver. 4.—This verse contains the laws of piety and of faith. "*Turn ye not unto idols*" forbids the worship of false gods; "*nor make to yourselves molten gods*" forbids in addition the sin of worshipping the true God under the form of a molten shape.

I. The great temptation to the Jews down to the time of their captivity appears to have been that of taking the gods of the nations round about them as their gods; Baal, Ashtoreth, Molech, Chemosh, drew off their affections from Jehovah. They did not desire apparently to give up the worship of God altogether, but to combine the worship of false gods with it, that is, to transfer a part of the religious affections which were due to God to some other object. This is done in the present day, (1) by the Roman Catholic Church, which sanctions the transference of worship which ought to be confined to God, from him to St. Mary and other saints; and the moral and religious regard, which is due to God alone, not only to saints, but to a living man, who has been called the idol of the Vatican; (2) by worldly men, who occupy their thoughts and feeling to such an excessive degree with the things of sense as to shut out Divine and spiritual things; (3) by sophists, who, by the exercise of a subtle intellect in a presumptuous spirit, shut out God from their ken, and worship the universe, or humanity, or nothing.

II. The Jews were also guilty of the kindred sin of worshipping Jehovah under the form of an idol. This was the sin of Aaron's calf, which represented, not any strange god, but Jehovah himself (Exod. xxxii. 5), and this was the case with Jeroboam's two calves of gold (1 Kings xii. 26—33). This offence is committed by any Christians who adore a representation of the Deity, sculptured or painted, or any sign or symbol of him, of whatever material or appearance it may be. It is the sin of men or Churches which have faith to believe that there is a God, but so feeble a faith that they require visible symbols of his presence instead of bravely trusting in the Unseen. The Israelites said to Aaron, "Up, make us gods, which shall go before us; for as for this Moses, the man that brought us up out of the land of Egypt, we wot not what is become of him." When they could not see Moses, the servant of God, they required a visible image of God. They could not trust him unseen; they required proof of his nearness; and this craving of a feeble faith led them to prefer the symbol of "a calf that eateth hay" (Deut. iv. 15) to no similitude at all. "Other nations, surrounding the Jews on every side, had their visible objects of worship, making their task of Divine duty and faith more easy. But to acquiesce in their unseen God, *I am*; to obey without immediate continual consciousness of his nearness; to trust in his protection at times when they had no sensible aid to help them to realize to their imagination his power; to let loose, as it were, their prayers into the air, without having some representative figure, or emblem, at the least, at which to point them;—all this was too difficult a task for a feeble faith in things invisible and spiritual" (Moberly, 'The Law of the Love of God').

The same feebleness of faith has produced the worship of images in the Christian Church. It was not till the seventh century that they crept into use for aids in worship, and when they were approved in the eighth century by the second Council of Nicea, that Council was at once rejected, and its doctrine of images was repudiated by the Council of Frankfort and the bishops of Charlemagne's empire.

In like manner, a feeble faith craves for full light, for demonstration, for infallibility, where God has only given twilight moral certainty, and an authority which is not absolute. It craves for immediate resolution of spiritual difficulties where God demands a patient dealing with them ; it asks after a sign where no sign is to be given ; it seeks out for itself mediators instead of going straight to God.

Not only does the use of images in worship arise from a feeble faith, but it makes that faith feebler and feebler, and thus leads to materialism. After a while the symbol becomes substituted for the thing symbolized by it, and the affections which the emblem was intended to excite toward an unseen object, do not pass beyond the external sign. Materialism and weakness of faith are the spiritual effects of worshipping images and craving after visible symbols.

" A brave contentment with an invisible God, showing itself in faithful and strong-hearted maintenance of piety in the absence (if it should so please God) or the apparent scantiness of signs, tokens, miracles, and other visible indications of the presence and protection of the Omnipresent and Omnipotent, and a like courageous and faithful abstinence from making to themselves unauthorized images, symbols, and emblems of him who communicated with the people without similitude, must be the particular quality or part of Divine love enjoined under the second law. The peculiar affection enjoined is the brave, trusting, spiritual faith in God invisible, spiritual, absent to our sense, dim in his tokens, obscure sometimes in his providences, not demonstrable in his evidences, not invariable in his benefits. . . . Possessed of this spiritual faith in the Unseen, a man walks along his narrow path of life with a confidence, security, and cheerfulness which establish at once his comfort and his safety " (Moberly, ' The Law of the Love of God ').

Vers. 9, 10.—*The law of kindness is a necessary complement to the other laws,* to make up the perfect character. A stern, just man is not the Christian ideal. The mercy and loving-kindness of God must be our model, as well as his other qualities.

> " The quality of mercy . . . is twice blessed ;
> It blesseth him that gives, and him that takes."

The man who leaves something for others that he might have taken for himself, such as the gleanings of his field, rises from the level of justice to that of generosity, and is educated to understand the noble impulses of a liberal heart and the blessedness described in the one saying of our Lord that is not recounted in the Gospels, " It is more blessed to give than to receive."

Vers. 11, 13, 35, 36.—*Stealing is forbidden by the law of man, and by the Law of God.* It is forbidden by the law of man in order to prevent injury being done to a citizen, and its sanction is fear of punishment. Remove the fear of punishment, and the goods of another will no longer be respected. It is forbidden by the Law of God because it is displeasing to God ; because honesty and uprightness are in themselves right; because to defraud another is in itself wrong. Take away the fear of punishment, and there will remain as scrupulous a care not to trespass on the rights of another as before. The law of honesty, as inculcated by God, has a dominating power and influence in all conditions of life.

Cheating is to stealing as equivocation is to lying. Both are equally immoral. Cheating and equivocating only differ morally from stealing and lying by being more mean and cowardly. The law of man cannot prevent cheating. It can indeed send inspectors to see that there are *"just balances, just weights, a just ephah, and a just hin ;"* but that is not enough to prevent cheating. The only thing that will do this is the fear of the Lord and the consciousness that the unjust appropriation of anything, however small, is contrary to the will of God. Hence we may see the infinite importance for the well-being of a country that the moral teaching of children in public schools be rested upon a religious basis. The precept is reproduced in the New Testament: " Let him that stole steal no more : but rather let him labour, working with his hands the thing which is good, that he may have to give to him that needeth " (Eph. iv. 28).

Lying is joined with stealing and cheating, not only because it may be used as a means of cheating (ch. vi. 2), but because it is a fraud in itself and a sin against uprightness and honesty. The essence of the sin consists in deceiving our neighbours. " Men, as men," says Bishop Taylor, "have a right to truth;" "for there is in mankind a universal contract implied in all their intercourses, and words being instituted to declare the mind, and for no other end, he that hears me speak hath a right in justice to be done him that, as far as I can, what I speak be true; for else he by words does not know your mind, and then as good and better not speak at all" ('Ductor Dubitantium,' 3, 2, 5). There are certain classes of men who have not a right to truth, such as madmen, and sick persons under special circumstances; and in these cases it is justifiable to say to them what is best for them, whether true or not; and in case of declared war the right to truth ceases, and is known to cease, so that no immoral deception takes place when false news is spread or stratagems adopted. But in time of peace and in ordinary cases, "Thou shalt not deceive thy neighbour" is the rule of conduct. Whether this deception takes place by means of a lie, or of an equivocation, or of a mental reservation makes no difference in the morality of the act. The defence of equivocation rests upon a confusion of two things totally different—material truth and moral truthfulness. The statement that the sun rises or sinks is materially false, because it remains stationary. But the man who makes such a statement is morally truthful, if he makes it not intending to deceive his neighbour and knowing that he will not be deceived. A statement that the sun had not risen (in the morning) or gone down (in the evening), if made with the purpose of deceiving the person addressed, and with an ulterior object on the part of the speaker, although materially true, would imply moral untruthfulness on the part of the speaker, and therefore is a lie. Bishops Taylor and Sanderson were some of the first theologians who, recurring to the severer morality of Augustine and the early Fathers, cast away with scorn the puerile confusion between moral truthfulness and material truth on which the system of modern Roman casuistry in this department rests. "He that tells a lie," says Bishop Taylor, "and by his mental restriction says he tells a truth, tells two lies" ('Ductor Dubitantium,' iii. 28). On the other hand, the Church of Rome teaches that the person addressed may be deceived to any amount, provided that the deception is effected by a form of words which is true in some sense apprehended by the speaker, though untrue in the sense understood by the other party. Accordingly, it is taught by an authority that may not be gainsaid by any member of that communion, that if a man prefixes the words "I say that" to a sentence, he may with a good reason make any false statement that he pleases, because in his own mind he means only to declare that he is making use of the words following that prefix, not that he is asserting their truth, as the person that he addresses supposes him to be doing (S. Alfonso de' Liguori, 'Theol. Moral.,' iv. 451). Contrast with this the injunctions of the apostle, "Wherefore putting away lying, speak every man truth with his neighbour: for we are members one of another" (Eph. iv. 25); "Lie not one to another, seeing that ye have put off the old man with his deeds" (Col. iii. 9); and the command of the prophet, "Speak ye every man the truth to his neighbour; execute the judgment of truth and peace in your gates: and let none of you imagine evil in your hearts against his neighbour; and love no false oath: for all these are things that I hate, saith the Lord" (Zech. viii. 16, 17); and the teaching of the early Church, "A man lies when he thinks something to be false and says it as though true, whether it be true or false. Mark the addition that I have made. Whether it be really true or false, yet, if a man thinks it false and assert it as true, he lies, for he is aiming to deceive. . . . His heart is double, not single; he does but bring out what he has there" (St. Augustine, 'Serm.' 133); and the teaching of the reformed Church, "Our result is that the party swearing after this manner both sinneth in his equivocal oath, and is notwithstanding that tacit equivocation bound in conscience unto the performance of his promise in that sense which the words yield of themselves, and are, without constraint, apt to beget upon the minds of others. Unless he act accordingly, he is not guiltless of perjury" (Sanderson, 'Obligation of Oaths'). In the Book of the Revelation we read, "But the fearful, and unbelieving, and the abominable, and murderers, and whoremongers, and sorcerers, and idolaters, and all liars, shall have their part in the lake which burneth with fire and brimstone" (Rev. xxi. 8).

Ver. 12, "*Ye shall not swear by my Name falsely, neither shalt thou profane the Name of thy God*," contains three injunctions: First, a command that on due occasions we are to make appeal to God by solemn oath; secondly, a prohibition of perjury; thirdly, a command to reverence God's Name.

I. To SWEAR BY GOD'S NAME IS COMMANDED, AS BEING A RECOGNITION OF HIM AS SUPREME LORD. Thus in Deuteronomy we read, "Thou shalt fear the Lord thy God, and serve him, and shalt swear by his Name" (vi. 13); in the Psalms, "Every one that sweareth by him shall glory (or be commended)" (lxiii. 11); in Isaiah, "He that sweareth in the earth shall swear by the God of truth" (lxv. 16); in Jeremiah, "Thou shalt swear, The Lord liveth, in truth, in judgment, and in righteousness" (iv. 2); "Thy children have forsaken me, and sworn by them that are no gods" (v. 7); "And it shall come to pass, if they will diligently learn the ways of my people, to swear by my Name, The Lord liveth; as they taught my people to swear by Baal; then shall they be built in the midst of my people" (xii. 16).

II. GOD SWEARS BY HIMSELF. "By myself have I sworn, saith the Lord, for because thou hast done this thing, and hast not withheld thy son, thine only son: that in blessing I will bless thee" (Gen. xxii. 16, 17). "I have sworn by myself, the word is gone out of my mouth in righteousness, and shall not return, That unto me every knee shall bow, every tongue shall swear" (Isa. xlv. 23). "For when God made promise to Abraham, because he could swear by no greater, he sware by himself, saying, Surely blessing I will bless thee, and multiplying I will multiply thee. . . . Wherein God, willing more abundantly to show unto the heirs of promise the immutability of his counsel, confirmed it by an oath: that by two immutable things, in which it was impossible for God to lie, we might have a strong consolation" (Heb. vi. 13—18).

III. GOD'S COMMAND MADE OF NONE EFFECT BY JEWISH TRADITIONS. These are summed up in the following passage of Philo Judæus:—"Let the word of the good man be a firm oath, immovable trust, free from falsehood, based on truth. But if this be not sufficient, and necessity compel him to swear, he should swear by the health or sacred age of his father or mother if they are alive, or by their memory if they are dead. For they are images and representations of Divine power, inasmuch as they brought into being those that did not exist before. They too deserve praise who, when they are compelled to swear, suggest the thought of reverence both to the bystanders and to those who impose the oath by the limitation and unwillingness which they show. For, saying aloud, 'Yes, by ——,' and, 'No, by ——,' and adding nothing, under the appearance of sudden interruption, they show that they do not swear a complete oath. But let a man add thereto what he pleases, such as the earth, the sun, the stars, the heaven, the whole world, provided he does not add the highest and most awful Cause" ('De Special. Legibus').

IV. CHRIST FORBIDS SWEARING. "Ye have heard that it hath been said by them of old time, Thou shalt not forswear thyself, but shalt perform unto the Lord thine oaths: but I say unto you, Swear not at all; neither by heaven; for it is God's throne: nor by the earth; for it is his footstool: neither by Jerusalem; for it is the city of the great King. Neither shalt thou swear by thy head, because thou canst not make one hair white or black. But let your communication be, Yea, yea; Nay, nay: for whatsoever is more than these cometh of evil" (Matt. v. 33—37). Nearly the same words are repeated in Jas. v. 12.

V. CHRIST'S COMMAND LIMITED IN ITS EXTENT. His prohibition refers to ordinary swearing, not to solemn oaths taken in courts of justice or under similar circumstances. This is plain by the fact that at his own trial he replied to the adjuration of the high priest, which adjuration was the Jewish manner of taking an oath in a court of justice, "Jesus held his peace. And the high priest answered and said unto him, I adjure thee by the living God, that thou tell us whether thou be the Christ, the Son of God. Jesus said unto him, Thou hast said" (Matt. xxvi. 63, 64). Because the high priest's words were "the voice of swearing" (ch. v. 1), Jesus broke his silence and spoke in obedience to the adjuration; and oaths are spoken of with approval in the Epistle to the Hebrews (vi. 13—18).

VI. WHAT AN OATH IS. It is an appeal to the tribunal of God, the person swearing (or adjured) calling God to witness to the truth of his words. Its purpose is "an end of all strife" (Heb. vi. 16). When no circumstantial evidence is forthcoming, the only means of arriving at truth is the awe of God solemnly invoked by an oath, and the dread of offending him by perjury. Where either sophistical casuistry or a secret—still more an open—scepticism undermines or destroys the sense of the obligation of oaths in a nation, that nation is hurrying on its way to destruction.

VII. PERJURY. The more solemn an oath is, the greater is the sin of perjury. If to swear by God's Name is a method of arriving at truth appointed by God himself, to swear by his Name falsely subverts the purpose of the command and insults the majesty of God.

VIII. IRREVERENCE. Not only deliberate perjury but any kind of irreverence is forbidden by this injunction. "The Christian man . . . will endeavour to recognize with faithful respect that holy Name wherever it meets him in his walk of life. As it is an appellation of the most high God, he will never utter it hastily or thoughtlessly. He will surely not use it at all except he have occasion to speak of it seriously and carefully. It is needless to say how totally he will refrain from such wanton profanation as that of garnishing his common speech by using the Name or referring to the doings of the Most High; still less how impossible it would be for him to allege the sacred Name, literally or by implication, in support of falsehood; nay, how impossible it would be that he should assert what is false at all, seeing that the Name of God is all around him, and that the most secularly sounding asseverations are nothing else than allegations of that Name. He will be much on his guard in prayers, lest, while he utters the sacred Name and the words which belong to it, his mind should wander away from the thoughts which ought to accompany it, and he should break the commandment. He will not shrink from the seemly reverence which the Church orders to be paid to the Name of Christ" (Moberly, 'The Law of the Love of God').

Vers. 18, 34.—We have the testimony of our Lord (Matt. xxii. 9) and of the Apostle St. Paul (Rom. xiii. 9; Gal. v. 14) that to obey the injunction, "*Thou shalt love thy neighbour as thyself,*" is to fulfil all the commandments of the second table of the Law; and for that reason St. James calls it a royal law (Jas. ii. 8). Here, therefore, the Levitical Law culminates in its highest point, so far as our duties towards men are concerned. Lest the Jew should confine the idea of *thy neighbour* to his own kindred and race, an equal love is specifically commanded for *the stranger that dwelleth with you.* Not only, *Thou shalt love thy* Jewish *neighbour as thyself,* but also *Thou shalt love the stranger that dwelleth among you as thyself.* The force of the comparison, *as thyself,* may be studied in Bishop Butler's sermon 'Upon the Love of our Neighbour.'

But though the Law. culminates in the two kindred commands, "Thou shalt love the Lord thy God;" "Thou shalt love thy neighbour as thyself;" Christianity does not. Christianity goes beyond the highest point to which the Law soars. Not only does it name the neighbour and the stranger as those whom we are to love, but also the enemy. "Ye have heard that it hath been said, Thou shalt love thy neighbour, and hate thine enemy. But I say unto you, Love your enemies, bless them that curse you, do good to them that hate you, and pray for them which despitefully use you, and persecute you; that ye may be the children of your Father which is in heaven" (Matt. v. 43—45). The motive in the gospel is also higher than the Law. In the Law the motive in the case of the stranger is human sympathy arising from common suffering, "*for ye were strangers in the land of Egypt.*" In the gospel it is the desire to be like God in his dealings with men, "for he maketh his sun to rise on the evil and on the good, and sendeth rain on the just and on the unjust" (Matt. v. 45), "for he is kind unto the unthankful and to the evil. Be ye therefore merciful, as your Father also is merciful" (Luke vi. 35, 36).

Ver. 19.—The moral meaning of the command, "*Thou shalt not sow thy field with mingled seed,*" receives an illustration from the parable of the "man which sowed good seed in his field: but while men slept, his enemy came and sowed tares among the wheat, and went his way. But when the blade was sprung up, and brought forth fruit, then appeared the tares also" (Matt. xiii. 24—26). God's servant must sow of the best; if the tares are mixed with the good seed, it must be the enemy's doing, not his. One of the preparations made by the Jews for an approaching Passover was to go over the fields near Jerusalem, and root up plants that had grown from *mingled seeds.* But in the spiritual sphere this is not to be done. If the enemy has succeeded in introducing the tares, they are for the sake of the wheat to be let to grow together until the harvest (Matt. xiii. 30).

Ver. 32.—*Respect for old age* is not only inculcated as a preservative against the rule of brute force, but as a part of the fear of God, the parent's relation to the child representing that of God to his creature.

Ver. 37.—*Moral commandments have a double sanction.* They are to be obeyed (1) because they carry their own sanction with them, (2) because they are commanded. In the latter respect all Divine injunctions stand on a level. All transgressions of what is commanded are equally sin, but they are not equal sins. A man who steals is not guilty of an equally heinous sin with the man who commits murder, but he is equally guilty of sin, because both murder and theft are forbidden. *All* God's *statutes, and all* his *judgments* are to be observed without exception, in order to be righteous according to the righteousness of the Law. "For Moses describeth the righteousness which is of the Law, That the man which doeth those things shall live by them" (Rom. x. 5). "This do, and ye shall live" (Luke xi. 28).

HOMILIES BY VARIOUS AUTHORS.

Vers. 1, 2, 4, 5, 12, 26—28, 30—32, 36, 37.—*Religion and superstition.* It is not always easy or even possible to distinguish between religion and superstition. We may fall into the latter when we are seeking to practise the former; or we may, from undue fear of the latter, neglect the former. In this chapter the Jews were taught (and we are thereby encouraged) to avoid the one, and to perfect the other in the fear of God. I. The superstition which was to be shunned. 1. Clearly and decisively everything that was in any way *idolatrous* was condemned; "turn ye not unto idols" (ver. 4). 2. All that was distinctively or closely connected with heathen worship was also forbidden: the use of enchantments, the superstitious observance of lucky or unlucky times, also superstitious cutting of the hair or of the flesh (vers. 26—28); resorting to wizards, etc. (see 1 Chron. x. 13). There is amongst us much adoption of practices which are idle and vain, not warranted in Scripture nor founded on reason. Such things are to be deprecated and shunned. They are (1) useless; (2) harmful, as taking the place in our thought which belongs to something really good and wise; (3) displeasing to the God of truth. II. The religion which was to be cultivated and practised. The Jews were to cherish and cultivate, even as we are, (1) sanctity like that of God himself (ver. 2), entire separateness of spirit and so of conduct from every evil thing; (2) reverence for his holy Name (ver. 12), and consequent abstention from everything bordering on profanity; (3) regard for divinely appointed ordinances—the sabbath and the sanctuary (ver. 30); (4) gratitude for his redeeming mercy (ver. 36), "I am the Lord your God, which brought you out of the land of Egypt;" (5) spontaneous dedication to his service (ver. 5). "At our own will" we must bring ourselves and our offerings to his altar; (6) daily, hourly consultation of his holy will, "Therefore shall ye observe all my statutes, and all my judgments, and do them" (ver. 37).—C.

Vers. 3, 32.—"*Honour to whom honour.*" It is uncertain whether we shall receive the honour which is due to us. Possibly we may be denied some to which we are entitled; probably we have experienced this wrong already, in larger or smaller measure, and know the pain of heart which attends it. Let us, therefore, resolve that we will *give* that which is due to others. The two passages connected in the text remind us that we should pay deference to—
I. Those who carry the weight of years. "'Thou shalt rise up before the hoary head, and honour the face of the old man." "Respect the burden, madam," said Napoleon, inviting a lady to move out of the way of one who was carrying a heavy weight. Those who have travelled far on the rough road of life, and are worn with many and sad experiences, on whom the privations of age are resting,—these carry a heavy weight, a burden we should respect. They are as wounded soldiers on whom the battle of life has left its scars, and these are marks of honour that demand the tribute of youth.
II. Those who have attained to wisdom. The young are apt to think that they

can reach the heights of wisdom without laboriously climbing the steeps of experience. They find that they are wrong. Time proves to each generation of men that wisdom, whether it be that of earth or of heaven, is only gained by the discipline of life. There are men who pass through human life and learn nothing in the passage; the folly of youth cleaves to them still. Such men must be comparatively unhonoured, receiving only the respect which is due to old age as such. But when men have gathered the fruits of a long and large experience—and especially when men of intelligence and piety have stored up the truth which God has been teaching them as he has led them along all the path of life—they are worthy to receive our sincerest honour, and we must know how to "rise up before the hoary head" in their case. With all and more than all the respect we pay to the learned, we should receive men whom God has been long teaching in his school—those who have learnt much of Jesus Christ.

III. THOSE WHO HAVE LAID US UNDER SPECIAL OBLIGATION. 1. Aged men who have lived a faithful life have done this. For they have lived, not only for themselves, but for their kind. They have wrought, struggled, suffered in order that they might help us and others to walk in the light, to enter the kingdom, to enjoy the favour of God; and they have earned our gratitude by their faithful service. 2. Our parents have done this also. "Ye shall fear every man his mother, and his father." What benefits our parents have conferred on us, what kindnesses they have rendered us, what sacrifices they have made for us, what anxious thought and earnest prayer they have cherished and offered on our behalf,—who of us shall reckon? The debt we owe to them for all they have done for us is the heaviest of all, next to that supreme indebtedness under which we stand to God. But it is not only the obligation we have thus incurred which demands our filial reverence; it is the fact that our parents are—

IV. THOSE WHO STAND IN A SPECIAL RELATIONSHIP TO US. 1. We should remember that fatherhood is the human relationship which most closely resembles and most fully reveals that in which God himself stands to us all. Christ came to reveal the Father unto man as the Father of souls. Therefore it is to be highly honoured. 2. Fatherhood (parenthood, for the mother is not to be left out of our thought) in the best state of human society has received the largest share of honour. We may gather from this fact that it is a divinely implanted instinct, only absent when the race has miserably degenerated under sin. 3. Honour given to parents as such is imperatively required by God. It was a patriarchal and Jewish, as it is now a Christian, virtue. After the injunction stand these significant words, "I am the Lord." "Children, obey your parents in the Lord" (Eph. vi. 1). Filial disobedience and unkindness are grievous sins in his sight. Filial love, honour, and considerateness are well-pleasing unto the Lord.—C.

Vers. 9, 10, 13, 14, 33, 34.—*Considerateness.* We gather from these verses—

I. THAT THE FEAR OF GOD WILL SURELY LEAD TO THE LOVE OF MAN. That piety which begins and ends in acts of devotion is one that may be reasonably suspected: it is not of the scriptural order. True piety is in consulting the will of the heavenly Father (Matt. vii. 21), and his will is that we should love and be kind to one another (Eph. iv. 32). Philanthropy is a word which may not have its synonym in the Old Testament, but the Hebrew legislator was not ignorant of the idea, and the Hebrew people were not left without incitement to the thing itself. Hence these injunctions to leave some corn in the corners of their fields, and the scattered ears for the reaping and gleaning of the poor (ver. 9); to leave also some clusters of grapes which had been overlooked for needy hands to pluck (ver. 10); to take no advantage of the weaker members of their society, the deaf and the blind (ver. 14); and to show kindness to the stranger (ver. 34).

II. THAT CONSIDERATENESS IS A GRACE WHICH IS PECULIARLY PLEASING TO GOD. The Jews were expressly enjoined to (1) show kindness to the poor (ver. 10); (2) to be careful of those who suffered from bodily infirmity (ver. 14); (3) to interest themselves in the stranger (vers. 33, 34). There is something particularly striking in the commandment that they were to refrain from cursing the deaf. Even though there might be no danger of giving positive pain and exciting resentment, yet they were not to direct harsh words against any one of their more unfortunate brethren. This legislation for the weak and the necessitous presents a very pleasant aspect of the Law. It also reminds us of some truths which come home to ourselves. We may observe: 1. That power is apt to be tyrannical. The history of nations, tribes, individuals, is the history of assertion and assumption. The strong have ever shown themselves ready to take advantage of the weak. Hence the oppression and cruelty which darken the pages of human history. 2. That God would have us be just to one another. In most cases, if not in all, we can take no credit for our superior strength, and build no claim on it. In many cases, if not in most, we can impute no blame to others for their weakness: the unfortunate are not necessarily the undeserving, and we have no right to make them suffer. 3. But beyond this, God would have us be specially kind to the necessitous *because they are needy*. Here are these statutes in respect of the poor, the afflicted, and the stranger. The devotional Scriptures speak more fully of this sacred duty (Ps. xli. 1, 2; lxii. 13; cxii. 9, etc.). The prophets utter their voice still more forcibly (Isa. lviii. 6—8; Ezek. xviii. 7; Neh. v. 10—12; Jer. xxii. 16; Amos iv. 1, etc.). Our Lord has, with strongest emphasis, commended to us considerateness toward the weak and helpless (Matt. x. 42; xviii. 6, 10, 14; xxv. 34—40, etc.). His apostles spoke and wrote in the same strain (Rom. xii. 15; 1 Cor. xii. 26, etc.). But that which, above everything, should lead us to be considerate toward the poorer and weaker members of our community is the thought that to do so is *so truly and emphatically Divine*. God himself has ever been acting on this gracious principle. He interposed to save the children of Israel because they were weak and afflicted. Again and again he stretched out his arm of deliverance, saving them from the strong and the mighty of the earth. On this Divine principle he deals with us all. He "knows our frame, and remembers that we are dust." "Like as a father pities his children, so he pities them that fear him." Our Saviour dealt with exquisite considerateness in all his relations to his undiscerning and unappreciative disciples; and now he is dealing with gracious forbearance toward us in all the weakness, poverty, shortcoming of our service. We are never so much like our merciful Master as when we speak and act considerately toward those who are poorer, weaker, and more helpless than ourselves.—C.

Vers. 11, 13, 15, 16, 35, 36.—*Integrity.* The Jews have always been considered a cunning and crafty race; they have been credited with a willingness to overreach in business dealings. Men would rather have transactions with others than with them, lest they should find themselves worsted in the bargain. This suspicion may be well founded; but if it be so, it ought to be remembered that it is the consequence of the long and cruel disadvantages under which they have suffered, and is not due to anything in their own blood or to any defect in their venerable Law. From the beginning they have been as strictly charged to live honourable and upright lives before man as to engage regularly in the worship of God. They have been as much bound to integrity of conduct as to devoutness of spirit. In these few verses we find them called to—

I. INTEGRITY IN DAILY TRANSACTIONS—HONESTY. "Ye shall not steal, neither deal falsely" (ver. 11). "Thou shalt not defraud thy neighbour, neither rob him" (ver. 13; see vers. 35, 36). Nothing could be more explicit than this, nothing more comprehensive in suggestion. No member of the Hebrew commonwealth could (1) deliberately appropriate what he knew was not his own, or (2) rob his neighbour in the act of trading, or (3) deal falsely or unrighteously in any transaction or in any relation, without consciously breaking the Law and coming under the displeasure of Jehovah. The words of the Law are clear and strong, going straight to the understanding and to the conscience. Every man amongst them must have known, as every one amongst us knows well, that dishonesty is sin in the sight of God.

II. INTEGRITY IN OFFICIAL DUTY—JUSTICE. (Ver. 15.) It is a pitiful thought that, in every nation, justice has been open to corruption; that men placed in honourable posts in order to do justice between man and man have either sold it to the highest bidder or surrendered and betrayed it from craven fear. God's clear word condemns such rank injustice, and his high displeasure follows the perpetrator of it. He who undertakes to judge his fellows must do so in the fear of God, and if he swerves from his integrity in his public acts, he must lay his account with heaven if not with man.

III. INTEGRITY IN WORD—TRUTH. "Ye shall not lie one to another" (ver. 11).

This, too, is a universal sin. Some nations may be more prone to it than others. The weak and the oppressed are too ready to take refuge in it; it is the resort of the feeble and the fearful. But it is also used with shameful freedom and shocking unconcern, as an instrument of gain and power. God has revealed his holy hatred of it. " Ye shall not lie." " Lying lips are abomination to the Lord;" " the Lord hateth a lying tongue " (Prov. xii. 22; vi. 17). Under the gospel of Christ, we are earnestly warned against it (Eph. iv. 25 ; Col. iii. 9). We are reminded that it is (1) a wrong done to our fellow-men ("we are members," etc.), and (2) closely associated with heathen habits (the "old man," etc.); and we may remember that it is (3) a habit most demoralizing to ourselves, as well as (4) something which utterly separates us from our Lord, being so contrary to his Spirit and so grievous in his sight.—C.

Vers. 17, 18.—*Love—its root and its fruit.* Two things lend a special interest to this passage. 1. It was twice quoted by our Lord (Matt. xix. 19 and xxii. 39). 2. It shows us the Law as closer to the gospel than we are apt to think ; it proves that, under the old dispensation, God was not satisfied with a mere mechanical propriety of behaviour, that he demanded rightness of feeling as well as correctness of conduct. We have—

I. THE BROAD PRINCIPLE OF GOD'S REQUIREMENT. Man is to "love his neighbour as himself" (ver. 18). No man, indeed, can (1) give as much time and thought to each of his neighbours as he does to himself, and no man (2) is so responsible for the state of others' hearts and the rectitude of their lives as he is for his own. But every man can and should, by power of imagination and sympathy, put himself in his brother's place; be as anxious to avoid doing injury to another as he would be unwilling to receive injury from another; and be as desirous of doing good to his neighbour who is in need as he would be eager to receive help from him if he himself were in distress. This is the essence of the " golden rule " (Matt. vii. 12).

II. THE ROOT FROM WHICH THIS FEELING WILL SPRING. How can we do this? it will be asked. How can we be interested in the uninteresting; love the unamiable; go out in warm affection toward those who have in them so much that is repulsive? The answer is here, " I am the Lord." We must look at all men *in their relation to God*. 1. God is interested, Christ is interested in the worst of men, is seeking to save and raise them; do we not care for those for whom he cares so much? 2. They are all God's children; it may be his prodigal children, living in the far country, but still his sons and daughters, over whom he yearns. 3. The most unlovely of men are those for whom our Saviour bled, agonized, died. Can we be indifferent to them ? 4. They were once not far from the kingdom, and may yet be holy citizens of the kingdom of God. When we look at our fellow-men in the light of their relation to God, to Jesus Christ, we can see that in them which shines through all that is repelling, and which attracts us to their side that we may win and bless them.

III. THE FRUITS WHICH HOLY LOVE WILL BEAR. There are two suggested in the text. 1. *Forbearance;* " not hating our brother in our heart," " not avenging or bearing any grudge against" him. Without the restraints and impulses of piety we are under irresistible temptation to do this. Unreasonable dislike on our brother's part, injustice, ingratitude, unkindness, inconsiderateness, features of character which are antipathetic to our own,—these things and such things as these are provocative of ill will, dislike, enmity, resentment, even revenge on our part. But if we remember and realize our brother's relation to the common Father and Saviour, we shall rise to the noble height of forbearance; we shall have the love which "beareth all things, believeth all things, hopeth all things, endureth all things " (1 Cor. xiii. 7). 2. *Restoration by remonstrance;* "Thou shalt in any wise rebuke thy neighbour, and not suffer sin upon him." Instead of nursing and nourishing our indignation, allowing our brother to go on in the wrong, and permitting ourselves to become resentful as well as indignant, we shall offer the remonstrance of affection; we shall "reprove, rebuke, exhort with all longsuffering " (2 Tim. iv. 2). We shall try to win our brother back to that path of truth or righteousness which he has forsaken ; so shall we " gain our brother " (Matt. xviii. 15), instead of "suffering sin upon him." This is the conquest of love, the crown of charity.—C.

Ver. 19.—*Aids to purity.* We shall first consider—

I. WHAT WAS THE PRIMARY PURPORT OF THIS TRIPLE LAW. We need not be surprised if we find here another aid to purity of heart and life, another fence thrown up against immorality. Idolatry and immorality, both of the very worst description, had covered and dishonoured the land of Canaan. It was of the last importance that the people of God should be guarded in every possible way against infection and guilt. Therefore the wise and holy Lawgiver instituted various measures by which his people should be perpetually reminded that they must be absolutely free from these heinous crimes. And therefore precepts which intimated the will of Jehovah in this matter were bound up with their daily callings and their domestic life. Our text is an illustration. In the management of their cattle, in the cultivation of their fields, in the making and wearing of their clothes, God was whispering in their ear, "Be pure of heart and life." Everything impressed upon their minds—these precise injunctions among other statutes—that there must be no joining together of that which God had put asunder, no mingling of those who should keep apart, no "defilement" (see Deut. xxii. 9), no "confusion" (ch. xx. 12). By laws which had such continually recurring illustration they would have inwrought into the very texture of their minds the idea that, if they wished to retain their place as the people of God, they must be pure of heart and life.

II. SECONDARY TRUTHS WHICH THIS LAW SUGGESTS. 1. It suggests simplicity in worship; there may be such an admixture of the divinely appointed and the humanly imported, of the spiritual and the artistic, of the heavenly and the worldly, that the excellency and the acceptableness will be lost and gone. 2. It suggests sincerity in service; in the service of the sanctuary or the sabbath school, or in any sphere of sacred usefulness, there may be such a mingling of the higher and the lower motives, of the generous and the selfish, of the nobler and the meaner, that the "wood, hay, and stubble" weigh more than the "gold, silver, and precious stones" in the balances of heaven, and then the workman will "lose his reward." 3. It suggests also the wisdom of taking special securities against specially strong temptations. God gave his people very many and (what seem to us) even singular securities against the rampant and deadly evil which had ruined their predecessors and might reach and slay them also. The circumstances and conditions of the time demanded them. Exceptional and imperious necessity not only justifies but demands unusual securities. Let those who are tempted by powerful and masterful allurements to (1) intemperance, (2) avarice, (3) worldliness, (4) passion, take those special measures, lay upon themselves those exceptional restraints which others do not need, but without which they themselves would be in danger of transgression.—C.

Vers. 23—25.—*The range of sin and the rule of God.* There is much uncertainty as to the intention of the Lord in this prohibition. I regard it as a lesson concerning—

I. THE DEPTH AND BREADTH OF THE TAINT OF SIN. The Israelites were to regard the very soil of Canaan as so polluted by the sins of its former inhabitants that the fruit which came from it must be treated "as uncircumcised" (ver. 23). Idolatry and impurity—the two flagrant sins of the Canaanites—are evils which strike deep and last long in the taint which they confer. Their consequences are penetrating and far-spreading. So, in larger or lesser degree, is all sin. It leaves a taint behind; it pollutes the mind; it mars the life; it makes its fruit, its natural growth and outcome, to be "as uncircumcised," to be unholy and unclean. And this is to an extent beyond our human estimate. If the Israelites had concluded that the iniquities of the Canaanites were to be regarded as polluting the very soil, they would not have reckoned that three years would be required to free the land from the taint of evil. But God made the purifying process extend over this protracted time. He knows that the stain of sin goes deeper and lasts longer than we think it does. What an argument this for expelling the idolatrous and unclean from our heart and life, for cultivating and cherishing the holy and the pure!

II. THE RANGE OF GOD'S CLAIMS. (Ver. 24.) Jehovah claimed the firstfruits of the land when the soil was cleansed: "all the fruit thereof shall be holy to praise the Lord." It was to be given (probably) to the priests. Thus God reasserted and confirmed his claim to all the produce of the land. This law would remind them that the whole soil was his, and that he had sovereign right to dispose of it as he willed, everything being of him and belonging to him. God claims all as his; and his claim is righteous. For we *have* nothing but that which we have received from him; we *are* nothing but that which he has created and preserved. "All our springs are in him," and all that we hold and occupy is his property. When we forget our derivation from him and our dependence upon him, he reminds us, by some providential privation, that we are falling from the spirit of reverence, gratitude, and submission which is the very life of our soul. And it is well for us voluntarily to set aside to his service the firstfruits of our labour, that we may be thus powerfully and practically reminded that we owe our very being and our whole substance to his bounty and his grace.

III. THE BENEFICENCE OF THE DIVINE RULE. By this provision God sought, as he is ever seeking, (1) spiritual well-being and (2) temporal prosperity. By teaching them the truths which this abstinence suggested, and by requiring of them the patient waiting and the childlike obedience involved in the fulfilment of his will, he was disciplining and perfecting their spiritual nature. By giving them leave to pluck and partake for themselves after the fourth year, he provided for their bodily wants and appetites. These two ends God has continually in view in all his providential dealing with ourselves. He seeks our present satisfaction, and also—and far more—our spiritual well-being; our *pleasure* as children of time and sense, and our *perfection* as children of the Father of spirits, as followers of the righteous Leader, as temples of the Holy Ghost.—C.

Ver. 30.—*Three helps to spiritual progress.* "There are many adversaries," it is true; many drawbacks, hindrances, difficulties in the way of spiritual advancement. But there are these three powerful aids.

I. ONE SACRED DAY IN EVERY SEVEN. "Ye shall keep my sabbaths." God has wrested from an exacting, rapacious world one-seventh of human life, and given it to us for the culture of the soul, for spiritual growth, for sacred usefulness. The observance of the sabbath is an act of (1) filial obedience to God, and (2) wise regard for our own true welfare.

II. A PLACE FOR SOCIAL WORSHIP. "Ye shall reverence my sanctuary." We have all the advantage of social influences, the impulse which comes from association, to impress, to direct, to establish the soul in heavenly wisdom. We should worship regularly at the sanctuary, because (1) we should not draw so near to God elsewhere, or gain in any other place such spiritual nourishment; (2) worship there helps to devotion everywhere.

III. DEVOTEDNESS OF HEART TO A DIVINE BEING. "I am the Lord." Not the ineffectual endeavour to fill and feed, to nourish and strengthen the soul with admirable abstractions; but holy thought and sanctifying feeling gathered round a *Divine One*: directed toward him who says, "Trust *me*, love *me*, follow *me*, exalt *me*."—C.

Social morality. Ch. xix.; cf. Matt. xxii. 35—40; Rom. xii.; Jas., *passim.* From the primary principle of *unworldliness,* we now have to proceed to sundry details about social morality. Although these details are given indiscriminately, it is yet possible to discern certain great principles among them. And—

I. ALL SOCIAL MORALITY IS MADE TO REST ON OUR RELATION TO GOD HIMSELF. In the Decalogue we have social morality, that is, our duty to man, based upon our duty to God; the "second table" rests upon the first. It is the same here. God brooks no rival (ver. 4). He sets himself as our model of holiness (ver. 2). He calls man to fellowship through the peace offering (vers. 5—8). His Name must be subjected to no profanation (ver. 12), and the sabbaths are to be strictly kept (ver. 30). In other words, we have the four commandments of the first table strewn up and down these details, and exhibiting the fountain-head of social morality in faithfulness to God.

It is significant that all the efforts to make out an "independent morality" by the elimination or ignoring of God are proving failures. He is, after all, the *sine quâ non* of real morality as well as of salvation. It is when his Name is feared and reverenced as it ought to be that man acts aright in his various relations.

II. COMPASSION FOR THE POOR AND AFFLICTED RESULTS, OF NECESSITY, FROM A DUE REGARD FOR GOD. For God is compassionate, and so should his people be. Hence the exhortation of vers. 9, 10, about leaving in harvest-time what would be a help to the poor and the stranger. This is grounded upon the great fact, "I am the Lord your God." Hence also the warning not to curse the deaf, nor to put a stumbling-block in the way of the blind, but "thou shalt fear thy God" (ver. 14). This consideration for the afflicted and for the poor is a most important element in social morality. Our asylums for the deaf, the dumb, and the blind are embodiments of this great social duty. The poor-law system, if a little more Christian sympathy were engrafted upon it, is a noble tribute to a sense of national obligation towards the poor. Better organizations even than these will yet be the fruit of the religious spirit. How to apply the principle that "he that will not work shall not eat," and at the same time show the due measure of compassion, is a problem demanding most careful solution.

III. MERCANTILE MORALITY IS STRICTLY ENJOINED. All stealing, lying, and dishonest dealing is denounced (ver. 11). No advantage is to be taken of a neighbour or of a servant (ver. 13). All arbitration is to be without respect of persons (ver. 15). Weights, measures, and balances are all to be just and true (vers. 35, 36). This branch of social morality requires the strictest attention from the Lord's people. It is here that continual contact goes on between them and the world. If religion, therefore, do not produce a higher type of mercantile morality than the world, it will be discredited. Nothing injures religion so much as the mercantile immoralities of its professors. Fraudulent bankrupts, dishonest tradings, overreachings,—these are what go to lessen the influence of religion among men. It is just possible that we may, in our eagerness to be always presenting the truth of the gospel to our fellow-men, have failed to enforce sufficiently the morality which must be the great evidence of our religious life. At present, in this peculiarly mercantile age, this department of morality needs most earnest attention.

IV. PURITY IS TO BE CULTIVATED IN ALL SOCIAL RELATIONS. Not only was immorality discountenanced (ver. 29), and punishment and trespass offerings directed in cases where immorality had occurred (vers. 20—22), but the very cultivation of the land, the rearing of cattle, the making of garments, and, in a word, all their associations were to be pervaded by the principle of purity (vers. 19, 23—25). For the use made of cattle, and of seed, and of raw material, might be prejudicial to purity in idea. Thus carefully does the Lord fence round his people with precautions.

V. SUPERSTITION IS TO BE DISCOURAGED. No enchantment was to be used, nor were they to round the corners of their heads or beards; they were to make no cuttings in their flesh for the dead, or print marks upon themselves (vers. 26—28). Nor were they to have recourse to familiar spirits or wizards, to be defiled by them (ver. 31). God treats his people as intelligent, rational beings; and so he discourages all resort to unmeaning and pretended inspirations.

VI. IT IS CLEARLY SHOWN THAT LOVE IS THE ESSENCE OF ALL SOCIAL MORALITY. Vengeance is discouraged (ver. 18)—it is the outcome of hatred, which is unlawful when borne towards a brother (ver. 17). The form of blood-feud (ver. 16), which existed and exists among the Oriental and wandering tribes, is denounced. In fact, the Law is brought to this simple issue, "Thou shalt love thy neighbour as thyself" (ver. 18). It is upon this that our blessed Lord seizes as the essence of the Divine Law (Matt. xxii. 35—40). Paul also brings this out clearly and emphatically (Rom. xiii. 9, 10). And this suggests—

1. That there is a legitimate self-love. There is a "better self" which it is our duty to love and cherish, just as there is a "worse self" which it is our duty to detest and mortify. When we consider this "better self," we do not suffer sin upon it, we try to keep it pure and subject unto Christ. We try to be faithful with ourselves. We foster what is good and holy within us. All this is most distinct from selfishness. The selfish man is his own worst enemy; the man who cultivates proper self-love is his own best friend.

2. This self-love is to measure our love to our neighbour. Now, our Lord brought out, by the parable of the "Good Samaritan," who is our neighbour. Every one to whom our heart leads us to be neighbourly. Neighbourhood is a matter of the heart. We must cultivate it. We shall have no difficulty in discerning the objects of our love. Let us then love them as we do ourselves. The golden rule is the essence of the Divine Law. "Do unto others as ye would that they should do unto you."

It is evident from this that Judaism was not intended to be an exclusive and selfish system, so far as outsiders were concerned. Men did not work it out properly, and this was why it became so narrow and selfish.—R. M. E.

Vers. 1—8.—*Purity in worship.* The laws set out in this chapter were before communicated to Aaron and his sons; now they are given to the people (vers. 1, 2). It is the privilege and duty of God's people to acquaint themselves with his will. They should learn the Law from the lips of Moses. They should learn the gospel from the lips of Jesus. It is a maxim of antichrist that "Ignorance is the mother of devotion." The mother of devotion, viz. to superstition, it is (see 1 John ii. 20, 21).

I. THE PEOPLE OF THE HOLY GOD MUST BE HOLY. (Ver. 2.) 1. *They must be separate from sinners.* (1) The people of God are distinguished by purity of heart. Of this God alone can take full cognizance. (2) Also by purity of life (Titus ii. 14). This is witnessed both by God and man. 2. *They must be separated to God.* (1) This is implied in the reason, viz. "for I am holy" (see Pet. i. 15, 16). Our Lord puts it strongly : "Be ye perfect, *even as* your Father which is in heaven is perfect" (Matt. v. 48). This cannot be understood *absolutely.* It must be interpreted *relatively*, viz. that as in his relations to us God is perfect, so are we to be perfect in our corresponding relations to him. But what are these? (2) As his servants. (*a*) We have our work assigned by his appointment. (*b*) He pays us our wages. In this life. In that to come. (3) As his children. (*a*) We have assurance of our adoption (Rom. viii. 16 ; Gal. iv. 6). (*b*) Consequently also concerning our heirship (Rom. viii. 17 ; Gal. iv. 7). (*c*) We have also blissful fellowship (John xvii. 21; 1 Cor. i. 9; 1 John i. 3, 7). 3. *Grace makes us to differ.* (1) This was ceremonially described in the Law. In order to partake of the holy things, the people must be made ceremonially holy by ablutions. (2) The truth of this is seen in the promise of the gospel. Before we can have spiritual communion with God we must be sanctified at the laver of regeneration, viz. by the renewing of the Holy Ghost.

II. THEIR HOLINESS WILL BE EXPRESSED IN PURE WORSHIP. 1. *They keep the sabbaths of the Lord.* (1) They cease from the toil of the world. So far the observance is outward. They also rest from the labour of sorrow and sin. This is an inward and spiritual observance. (2) They appear in the convocations of God's people. This worship may be public without any corresponding beauties of spiritual holiness. But the true worshipper mingles with the spiritual and heavenly portions of the Church as well as with the visible congregation (see Eph. iii. 15 ; Heb. xii. 22—24). (3) Parents are held responsible for instructing their children in the due observance of the sabbath. So in the fourth commandment in the Decalogue, "Thou, and thy son, and thy daughter." (4) Hence in the text (ver. 3), the injunction to keep God's sabbaths is associated with another touching the respect due from children to parents (comp. Exod. xx. 8—12). Parents are God's representatives to their children. (*a*) In their paternity. (*b*) In the providence they exercise during the helplessness and dependence of infancy and youth. (*c*) In their authority. This is from God, and it should be religiously maintained. Those who are allowed to break God's sabbaths will disobey their parents. 2. *They keep themselves from idols.* (1) They will not "turn" to them. We are so surrounded by them, that we cannot turn from the true worship without encountering them. (2) They will not "make" to themselves "molten gods." The allusion here is to Aaron's calf, which he intended to represent Jehovah Elohim. But in our godly parents, the work of God's hands, we have truer representations of the living Father than can possibly proceed from our own hands. (3) Idolatry is folly. Idols are *nothings* (אלילם; comp. 1 Cor. viii. 4). 3. *They serve God with reverence.* (1) They fear God, but not as slaves. They offer peace offerings to him which are offerings of friendship. They offer these also "at their own free will" (ver. 5). A constrained is an imperfect service. "God loveth a cheerful giver." (2) They worship him in faith. They will eat the peace offering the same day on which it is offered. They recognize the privileges of an early communion. What remains over on the second day they will eat. The dispensations of the types are two, viz. the patriarchal and Mosaic. But if any remain to the third day, this they burn with fire. Thus they express their faith in the Christian dispensation which should abolish the types by fulfilling them, and which should bring in better hopes.

(3) To return to the legal dispensation is now to provoke the anger of the Lord. Cyril of Alexandria argues that those who fail to see any spiritual meaning in the Law are still bound to keep it in the letter. But even that could do them no good, for according to the text, "If it be eaten at all on the third day, it is abominable; it shall not be accepted. Therefore every one that eateth it shall bear his iniquity," etc. (vers. 7, 8). To rejecters of the gospel now there is nothing but hopeless excision.— J. A. M.

Vers. 9—14.—*Kindliness*. In the earlier portion of this chapter purity of worship, with its associated reverence for the authority of God, in his representatives, viz. natural parents, and his institutions, as the sabbath, are enjoined. In the verses following our duties towards our fellows come more prominently before us, and in the text that class of those duties whose spirit is kindliness. Charity is sister to piety. We have here enjoined—

I. A GENEROUS CONSIDERATION FOR THE POOR. 1. *The needs of the gleaner are to be respected*. (1) In reaping the harvest, owners are instructed to spare the corners of their crops for the poor. What falls from the hand of the reaper is not to be gathered up again, but left to the gleaner. So in gleaning the vintage, the loose branches must be left to the poor and the stranger. (2) We must not consider that to be wasted which goes to the poor. (3) The harvest and vintage are seasons of joy. Such seasons should be seasons also of charity. Kindliness purifies and so heightens joy. 2. *The authority of God must be remembered*. (1) "I am Jehovah thy Elohim." This gives the poor and the stranger a Divine right in the gleanings, which now to disregard becomes impiety and injustice. Those who refuse their rights to the poor will have to answer for it to God (Ps. ix. 18; xii. 5; lxxxii.; Isa. x. 1—4). (2) The Divine example should inspire and guide us. "He openeth his hand, and satisfieth every living thing." Man must not attempt to close the hand of God by refusing to the poor their due. (3) The blessing of God is promised to those who consider the poor (see Deut. xxiv. 19; Ps. xli. 1; Prov. xiv. 21).

II. A CAREFUL AVOIDANCE OF INJUSTICE. 1. *Wrong must not be practised stealthily*. (1) "Ye shall not steal"—ye shall not injure your neighbour in a concealed way. To reap the harvest too narrowly would be to filch from the poor his due. (2) "Neither shall ye deal falsely." Thus there must be no concealing of faults in articles offered for sale. There must be no false representation of values either in vending or purchasing. 2. *Lies must not be uttered*. (1) "Neither lie one to another." When a lie is *acted* in false dealing, the next thing is to *utter* a lie to cover the wrong. One falsehood calls up another to keep it in countenance. (2) "And ye shall not swear by my Name falsely." Upon the principle that lies are called in to countenance the concealment of a wrong, oaths are suborned to countenance lies. Thus sin begets sin; and sin, in its offspring, becomes increasingly degenerate. (3) This last is frightful wickedness. "Neither shalt thou profane the Name of thy God." It is appealing to the God of truth to confirm a lie! 3. *Nor must wrong be openly perpetrated*. (1) "Thou shalt not defraud thy neighbour, neither rob him." Power must not be abused in oppression. Many of the forms in which this was done are described by Job (ch. xxiv.). (2) "The wages of him that is hired shall not abide with thee all night until the morning." It is the means of his living; and once earned, no more belongs to the employer than does the property of any other person. Huge injustice is practised by those who take long credit from tradesmen, who thereby are put to the utmost straits to meet their business claims and those of their families.

III. A TENDER RESPECT FOR THE CONDITION OF THE AFFLICTED. 1. "*Thou shalt not curse the deaf*." (1) Thou shalt not be enraged should a deaf man be unable to render the service of one who has his hearing. So it is unreasonable to blame for not having rendered service those who were not informed that such service was expected. (2) Thou shalt not curse, in his presence, a man that is deaf, because he is deaf and cannot hear it. So neither in his absence must a man be cursed, who is in the same case with the deaf, and cannot defend himself. 2. "*Nor put a stumblingblock before the blind*." (1) To do this literally would be a wanton cruelty. (2) Traps must not be laid for the unwary to their hurt, viz. in things material or in things spiritual (see Rom. xiv. 13). 3. "*But thou shalt fear thy God*." (1) Afflictions do not spring from the dust. They come from God or are permitted by him. To take advantage of them or to trifle with them is therefore to tempt the Lord. (2) The fear of the retributive justice of Heaven should restrain (see Luke xvii. 1). Biblical history abundantly proves that the law of retaliation is a law of God.—J. A. M.

Vers. 15—18.—*Justice.* As charity is sister to piety, so is justice related to both. This virtue is enjoined upon us—

I. IN RESPECT TO CONDUCT. 1. *In judgment justice should be impartial.* (1) Pity for the poor is, in the abstract, good. Yet must it not lead us to favour them against the right (Exod. xxiii. 3). (2) Respect for those who enjoy rank and station is not only lawful but laudable. But this must not lead us to favour them in judgment (see Jas. ii. 1—4). (3) The balances of justice are those of the sanctuary. They are true. They must be held by an impartial hand. It must not tremble under the excitement of pity, or of hope, or fear. 2. *In dealings justice should be strict.* (1) " Thou shalt not go up and down as a talebearer among thy people." Pedlaring is the vice here interdicted. This is rather the meaning of the word (רכיל) rendered " talebearer." Tramps, who have no settled residence, are oftentimes dishonest, and otherwise so dangerous to society, that every nation has its vagrant acts to control them. (2) The Jews in their dispersion are much given to pedlaring. It has been to them a necessity owing to the unfriendly laws of the nations with respect to them. How dreadfully their sin has been visited upon their head when their necessities urge them to violate their law ! (3) Pedlars have, amongst other evils, been notorious *tale-bearers.* By the slanders they have circulated not only has the peace of families been invaded, but communities and nations have been embroiled. The Jews say, " One evil tongue hurts three persons—the speaker, the hearer, and the person spoken of " (see Prov. xi. 13 ; xx. 19). 3. *The evils of injustice are serious.* (1) " Neither shalt thou stand against the blood of thy neighbour." Some are wicked enough of purpose to compass the blood of the innocent by falsehood (Prov. ii. 11, 12 ; Ezek. xxii. 9). (2) Slander may have this result without the intention of the slanderer. Who can control a conflagration ? (see Jas. iii. 6)

II. IN RESPECT TO MOTIVE. 1. *" Thou shalt not hate thy brother in thine heart."* (1) He is thy brother. He has a common fatherhood with thee in God. He has a common nature with thee. (2) He is therefore amenable with thee to the same tribunal. God, the Judge of all, surveys not the conduct only, but also the motive. 2. *" Thou shalt in any wise rebuke thy neighbour."* (1) Not to reprove his sin is to hate him. This is eminently so when he hath trespassed against thee. To conceal it in such a case is to nurse wrath against the opportunity for revenge (2 Sam. xiii. 22). Such conduct is utterly at variance with the spirit of the gospel (see Matt. xviii. 15 ; Luke xvii. 3). (2) To " suffer sin upon him " is to be an accomplice in his sin. The words may be construed, " nor bear his sin." This suggests that the accomplice, with the guilt, is also obnoxious to the punishment of the sinner. Men wreak their vengeance upon themselves. (3) In rebuking we should remember that the sinner is our " neighbour." It should be done in a neighbourly way. Thus, as far as practicable, privately. " Charity covereth a multitude of sins," viz. from others, though not from the sinner. And kindly. It is thus more likely to be well received, as it ought to be (see Ps. cxli. 5 ; Prov. xxvii. 5, 6). 3. *The root of justice is love.* (1) " Thou shalt not avenge." This is another way of saying, " Thou shalt forgive." With the spirit of vengeance there can be no peace in the world. God says, " Vengeance is mine ; " he claims the right to avenge because he alone is superior to all retaliation. (2) " Nor bear any grudge." Thou shalt not *insidiously watch* the children of thy people. How the Jews violated this law in their malignity against Jesus ! (see Mark iii. 2 ; Luke vi. 7 ; xiv. 1 ; xx. 2). (3) Contrariwise, " Thou shalt love thy neighbour as thyself." This is the spirit of the Law as well as of the gospel. The same Holy Spirit of love is the author of both (see Matt. vii. 12 ; xxii. 39 ; Rom. xiii. 9, 10 ; 1 Cor. ix. 19 ; Gal. v. 14).—J. A. M.

Vers. 19—28.—*Fidelity to God.* In the verses before us we note the injunction—

I. THAT THE STATUTES OF THE LORD MUST BE KEPT. These require : 1. *That there be no unnatural mixtures.* (1) For the examples furnished, sound economic and hygienic reasons may be given (ver. 19). (*a*) Cattle which God ordered " after their kind " (Gen. i. 25), are not to be let to gender with diverse kinds. Hybrids are degenerated creatures; they are monsters; and they are withal unfruitful. (b) Mingled seed must not be sown in the field. The plants of both kinds in such a case are found to be inferior (Deut. xxii. 9). The land also is impoverished. (c) Garments of mingled flax and wool are not to be worn. The mixture would induce electrical disturbances impairing to health. (2) But the spirit of the law is *moral*. The people of God are taught by it to avoid everything that would compromise their simplicity and sincerity (2 Cor. vi. 14). They must avoid marriages with the ungodly. In business they must be careful not to join in ungodly partnerships. In friendships they must choose those who are of the household of faith (Jas. iv. 4). 2. *That atonement be made for sin.* (1) The case (ver. 20) is that of a slave dishonoured and still held in bondage, who, through a subsequent offence, which, if she were free, would merit death (see Deut. xxii. 24), is now punished with scourging. The degree of guilt is modified by circumstances; and punishment is moderated accordingly (Luke xii. 47, 48). (2) But before the man can be forgiven he must confess his sin over a guilt offering. He must bring a ram. This was a well-known type of Christ, without whose atonement, no matter what scourging our sin may have brought upon us, there can be no forgiveness. 3. *That the fruit of a tree uncircumcised must not be eaten.* (1) For this law there are good economic reasons. It hurts a young tree to let the fruit ripen upon it; and therefore to circumcise it, or pinch off the blossoms of the first three years, will improve the quality of its fruit. In the fourth year, then, the fruit will be in perfection. (2) But the spirit of this law also is *moral*. (a) Trees are taken as emblems of men (Ps. i. 3 ; Matt. iii. 10; Isa. lxi. 3; Jude 12). (b) First thoughts and *forward* desires are vanity, and must be rejected as coming from the flesh (see Col. ii. 11). To let them ripen is to injure the character. (c) In the fourth year, when the fruit is in perfection, it is consecrated to God as the " firstfruit," which therefore is *not* always that which comes *first* in order of time, but the *best*. The service we render to God after the removal of inordinate desire by converting grace, is our firstfruit, or best service. (d) As to the *fourth* year, Christ who is the " Firstfruit " and " Firstborn of every creature," or Antitype of the firstborn of every kind of creature, appeared amongst us in the *fourth* millennium of the world. And when he comes again it will be to introduce the *fourth* dispensation, viz. the millennial. The three dispensations preceding we need scarcely specify to be the Patriarchal, Levitical, and Christian. (e) In the fifth year and thenceforward, the fruit was sanctified to the use of the owner. The consummation of our felicity will be in that glorious state to succeed the millennium, the " new heavens and new earth wherein dwelleth righteousness." We note—

II. THAT THE CUSTOMS OF THE HEATHEN MUST NOT BE FOLLOWED. 1. *Nothing must be eaten with the blood.* (1) At the time when animal food was granted to man the blood was reserved. The reservation corresponded to that of the tree of knowledge of good and evil when vegetable food was granted. In each instance the prohibition was given to common progenitors of the race, and therefore universally obligatory. Noah stood to the " world that now is " in a similar relation to that in which Adam stood to mankind at large. (2) The Noachian precepts in general were violated by the heathen, and in particular this precept respecting blood. The psalmist refers to the custom amongst the Syrians when he says, " Their drink offerings of blood will I not offer " (Ps. xvi. 4). And in these words there is a prophetic abhorrence of antichrist, who not only sets aside the Law of God by authorizing the eating of blood, but professes to drink the very blood of Jesus in the cup of the Mass. (3) The penalties of this abomination are tremendous. As in Eden the eating of the forbidden fruit became death, so in the Noachian precept God requires the blood of the lives of those who will eat flesh with the life thereof which is the blood (Gen. ix. 4, 5). Babylon who is also " drunk with the blood of the saints and martyrs of Jesus," is therefore doomed to drink blood, for that she is worthy (Rev. xvii. 6; xvi. 3—6). 2. *Superstition must be shunned.* (1) Thus augury is to be discouraged (ver. 26). This (נחש) *nachash*, or divining, may have been by *fire* or *serpents*. " Nor observe times," nor consult the clouds. The heavens were their gods, and the clouds they naturally regarded as their aspects toward men, as indicating their intentions. The revealed word of the true God is sufficient for all lawful purposes of sacred knowledge. (2) Distractions for the dead are to be discouraged. The heathen customs of cutting the hair and the flesh evinced the insanity of idolatry. Where the faith of a true religion is we have no need to mourn for the dead as those who have no hope.—J. A. M.

Vers. 29—37.—*The fear of God.* Of this excellent things are spoken by Solomon. It is the "beginning of knowledge," "hatred to evil," "strong confidence," a "fountain of life," "prolongs days," and "gives riches and honour." So here—

I. IT IS A SOURCE OF PURITY. 1. *To the family.* (1) There is a connection between vers. 29 and 30. Those who keep God's sabbaths will not profane their daughters either to idolatry or for gain. The fear of God nourished by the one will prevent the other. (2) In keeping God's sabbaths his sanctuary is reverenced. This furnishes an additional motive to social purity. For the sanctuary, whether it be composed of canvas, or of stone, or of flesh and blood, is the temple of the Holy Ghost. Who then can properly reverence it under one form and desecrate it under another? (see 1 Cor. iii. 16, 17; vi. 18, 19; 2 Cor. vi. 16) 2. *To the nation.* "Lest the land," etc. (ver. 29). (1) The family is the root of the nation. All nations extant are sprung from the family of Noah. (2) Nations are blessed or cursed in their families. (3) God asserts himself here, "I am Jehovah" (ver 30). The character of God is seen in his laws. It is pledged to maintain them.

II. IT ARMS AGAINST THE POWER OF DEVILS. 1. *Familiar spirits are more than myths.* (1) Their existence is not here challenged, but admitted (ver. 31; see also Acts xvi. 16, where the fact is put beyond question). (2) Pretenders to the unenviable distinction, as well as persons actually possessed of such devils, are here held up to reprobation. 2. *The fear of the Lord will preserve us from them.* (1) Their power is greatest over the "children of disobedience." The desperately wicked are given over by God to Satan (Eph. ii. 2; 1 Tim. i. 20). Such persons may seek wizards, or wise ones. (2) But godly persons will avoid them. They could not so reflect upon the wisdom and goodness of God that he should leave anything for our advantage to be communicated by wicked spirits. Spiritualism is a devilish delusion. Pride and selfishness will lead men into the snare. (3) In this prohibition God asserts himself, "I am Jehovah thy Elohim." He is our covenant Friend, who will so fully satisfy our lawful desires that we shall not need recourse to wicked expedients. He will also be our defence against the devices of the devil.

III. IT INSPIRES COURTESY. 1. *Respect for age* (ver. 32). (1) With age there should be the wisdom of experience, and this should be honoured by youth. Caryl well says, "He that wears the *silver crown* should be honoured in his capacity as well as he that wears the *golden crown.*" (2) In respecting age we are to "fear Jehovah Elohim," our covenant God, whose blessings are from father to son and from generation to generation (Gen. xvii. 7; Isa. li. 8; Luke i. 50). In the aged man we should see the representative of the "Ancient of days" (Dan. vii. 22). (3) It is a sad sign of the degeneracy of a nation when the child behaves himself proudly against the ancient (Job xxx. 1, 12; Isa. iii. 4, 5). 2. *Civility to strangers.* (1) "Thou shalt not vex," or oppress, "him;" but treat him as though he were a native. "Thou shalt love him as thyself." How tradition obscured this law when the question was prompted, viz. "Who is my neighbour?" (2) The Hebrew is reminded, in connection with this injunction, how bitterly he suffered in the land of Egypt from the operation of the opposite principle. He is also reminded how odious to God was that cruel oppression from which he brought him out, and therefore how, if he would conciliate his favour, he must act from a different principle.

IV. IT PROMOTES JUSTICE. 1. *In judgment.* (1) In the administration of law. (2) In arbitration. 2. *In dealings.* (1) Measures and weights must be true to the standards. These were kept in the tabernacle, and afterwards in the temple (ch. xxvii. 25; 1 Chron. xxiii. 29). Religion and business must not be divorced. (2) To use false balances, or weights, or measures is worse than open robbery. It is abominable hypocrisy. It is robbing under the very colour of equity.

God claims the authorship of these laws (vers. 36, 37). 1. They are worthy of him. He must be infatuated with ignorance or wickedness who would laud the "Roman virtue" in opposition to the "narrow spirit" of the Mosaic code. 2. They were eminently calculated to secure the happiness of the nation at home, and to promote its credit abroad. 3. Let us "observe" the Law of God to understand it, and, understanding, "keep" it. Then happy shall we be.—J. A. M.

Vers. 1, 2.—"*Ye shall be holy: for I the Lord your God am holy.*" Holiness.

I. THE UNIVERSAL REQUIREMENT. "Speak unto all the congregation," etc. 1. No exception. "All have sinned." 2. The nature of man requires him to be holy. The relation between man and God. The laws of God not mere arbitrary decrees, but the expression, in positive relation to the freedom of man, of the Eternal Reality of the universe. 3. The universality of revelation is the universality of responsibility. "Their line is gone out in all the earth." "Having not *the* Law, they are *a* law unto themselves." What was said to the Jews was said to the world. The blessedness of humanity is the realization of the Divine image. A holy God, a holy universe.

II. THE UNIVERSAL MOTIVE. "*For I am holy.*" 1. *Dependence* upon God the root of religion, not as mere blind dependence, but that of the children on the Father. 2. *Gratitude* the constant appeal of the heart. The Lord your God, who has done so much for you, requires your holiness. 3. The Divine command is related to and blessed with the *Divine provision of grace* in a specific system of holiness, in which the people of God are held up. Be holy, for I have *prepared* for your holiness. We are "created in Christ Jesus unto good works, which God hath before ordained that we should walk in them" (Eph. ii. 10). Work out salvation, for God worketh in you.

III. THE MEDIATING MINISTRY. "The Lord spake unto Moses, saying, Speak unto all the congregation." 1. Here is the *gracious method* by which our holiness is made possible. The *holy God* speaks. The holy *men of God* speak as they are moved by the Holy Ghost. The *holy Word* speaks, everywhere and always. The *holy life* is maintained among the holy people. 2. The holiness of humanity will be achieved as a fact through *a holy ministry* of the people of God to the world at large; of the consecrated few to the many. The hope of a revived *Church*, in a revived *ministry*. The spiritual leaders should feel their responsibility, both in teaching and in example. 3. *Personal holiness* must underlie all other. The purification of temples and services is not the sanctification God requires. He says not, "Be ye punctilious in worship and profuse in ritual;" but "Be ye personally holy, let your holiness be a transcript of mine, which is the holiness of will, of work, of thought, of character.—R.

Vers. 3—37.—*The holy Law in the holy life.* I. REVERENCE FOR PARENTS. True religion is seen in common, everyday life. If we love God, we love man. Family peace and order is best preserved by appeal to deep, religious motives. Natural affection is not sufficient against fallen human nature. "*God says, Thou shalt,*" must be the support of natural feeling.

II. SABBATH KEEPING. Not as a Jewish regulation, but as both the demand of physical nature and the gracious provision of God for us. "The Son of man is Lord of the sabbath;" therefore, while preserving it from abuse to the oppression of human liberty, sanctifying it for the higher place it occupies in the Christian scheme.

III. ABSOLUTE SEPARATION FROM IDOLATRY and all heathenism. Holy religion.

IV. WILLINGHOOD IN RELIGION. Ver. 5, "At your own will," or "that you may be accepted," *i.e.* do it as unto God, by his Word, for his glory, in dependence on his grace, with hearty resignation of self to him.

V. PHILANTHROPY AND COMPASSION FOR THE POOR. The true charity is a practical remembrance of the needy and suffering, beginning at home, from our own personal possessions. God is the Lord of all. All are brethren.

VI. HONESTY OF DEALING is only to be maintained by religion. Mere social considerations and political economy will never purify trade and sanctify men's intercourse with one another. Truth is safe in no keeping but that of the sanctuary.

VII. PROFANITY in speech and in act is an evil to be cured by positive religion.

VIII. THE JUSTICE OF THE LIFE is the justice of the heart in expression. The law that is kept sacred within will be honoured without respect of persons, and not by mere negation, but in active benevolence.

IX. REAL NEIGHBOURLINESS IS LOVE OF MAN PROCEEDING FROM LOVE OF GOD. No injury must be done either by word or deed, either by neglect of another's interests or unholy wrath against another or encouraging him to sin by withholding due rebuke. All summed up in the positive precept, "Love thy neighbour as thyself." All the various prescriptions of the Jewish law, both negative and positive, regard the pure and holy development both of individual and national life. Religion is the root, social morality is the blossom or the plant, national prosperity is the precious fruit, of which, if we would preserve the seed and perpetuate the blessing, we must see to it that we find the very inmost centre and kernel, which is the love of God as the Father of all, and the love of men as the brethren of the same Divine family.—R.

EXPOSITION.

CHAPTER XX.

The subject of ch. xviii. is resumed in this chapter; but that which was before considered as sin only is now regarded as crime, and penalties are attached according to the heinousness of the offence. For example, the sin of "giving of his seed to Molech," or which is the same thing, "letting any of his seed pass through the fire to Molech," had been forbidden as a sin in ch. xviii. 21; now it is condemned as a crime. The various penalties assigned in this chapter are (1) *burning with fire* (ver. 14); (2) *stoning with stones* (vers. 2, 27); (3) *being put to death* in a manner not specified (vers. 9, 10, 11, 12, 13, 15, 16); (4) *being cut off from among his people*, either by God himself (vers. 4, 5, 6) or by an agency not specified (vers. 17, 18); (5) *bearing his iniquity* (vers. 17, 19, 20); (6) *childlessness* (vers. 20, 21). The first of these penalties, *burning with fire*, does not mean that those on whom it was inflicted were burnt alive, but that their dead bodies were burnt after they had been stoned to death, as in the case of Achan (Josh. vii. 25). It is the punishment for taking a mother and daughter together into the same harem (ver. 14). *Stoning with stones* is appointed for crimes which are at once offences against religion and morals, viz. giving of his seed to Molech (ver. 2), and witchcraft (ver. 27). The other form of *putting to death*, which no doubt was strangling, is the penalty assigned to cursing parents (ver. 9), adultery (ver. 10), marriage or intercourse with a stepmother (ver. 11) or stepdaughter (ver. 12), the sin of Sodom (ver. 13), and bestiality (vers. 15, 16). *Cutting off from his people* may be effected either by death (vers. 4, 5, and perhaps 6), which is the penalty for Molech-worship, connivance at Molech-worship, and dealing with witches; or by excommunication (vers. 17, 18), which was the punishment for intercourse with a sister, or with one who was unclean by reason of her monthly sickness (see Exod. xxxi. 14).

The phrase, *bearing his iniquity*, means that the man continues in the state of a criminal until he has been cleansed either by suffering the punishment of his offence or making atonement for it, which sometimes he might, sometimes he might not, do. The man who committed incest with a sister would "*bear his iniquity*" (ver. 17), because he would be put in a state of excommunication without permission of restoration by means of sacrificial offerings. And so with the man who took his aunt by blood (ver. 19) or by marriage (ver. 20) as his wife,—he would not be allowed to recover his status by offering sacrifice. *Childlessness*, the punishment for marrying an uncle's or brother's wife, probably means that in those cases the offender's children should not be counted as his own, but should be entered in the genealogical register as his uncle's or his brother's children. (Cf. Deut. xxv. 10, where it is noticeable that the penalty is retained, even though the marriage with the brother's wife, which had been prohibited in general, had in the particular case become a duty for family or tribal reasons.)

Vers. 2, 3.—The close connection between giving of his seed unto Molech and defiling my sanctuary, and profaning my holy name, is explained and illustrated by Ezekiel in the judgment on Aholah and Aholibah. "They have caused their sons, whom they bare unto me, to pass for them through the fire, to devour them. Moreover this they have done unto me: they have defiled my sanctuary in the same day, and have profaned my sabbaths. For when they had slain their children to their idols, then they came the same day into my sanctuary to profane it; and, lo, thus have they done in the midst of mine house" (Ezek. xxiii. 37—39). Not only was the juxtaposition and combination of the worship of Molech and Jehovah an offence to him whose name is Jealous, but at the time that Molech-worship was carried on in the valley of Hinnom, idols were set up in the court of the temple itself, as we learn from the Book of Kings and from Jeremiah. "But they set their abominations in the house, which is called by my Name, to defile it. And they built the high places of Baal, which are in the valley of the son of Hinnom, to cause their sons and their daughters to pass through the fire unto Molech; which I commanded them not, neither came it into my mind, that they should do this abomination, to cause Judah to sin" (Jer. xxxii. 34, 35). And of Manasseh it is related, "He built altars in the house of the Lord, of which the Lord said, In Jerusalem will I put my Name. And he built altars for all the host of heaven in the two courts of the house of the Lord. And he made his son pass through the fire" (2 Kings. xxi. 4—6).

Vers. 4, 5.—There is to be no connivance with Molech-worship. The penalty is death, and is to be carried out by the proper tribunals, whose business it was to see that the stoning took place. So in Deuteronomy the duty of killing those who entice to idolatry is laid down. "Thou shalt not consent unto him, nor hearken unto him; neither shall thine eye pity him, neither shalt thou spare, neither shalt thou conceal him: but thou shalt surely kill him; thine hand shall be first upon him to put him to death, and afterwards the hand of all the people" (Deut. xiii. 8, 9). In the case of Molech-worship God declares that, if the tribunals of the nation fail to adjudge the penalty of death to the offender, he will himself take the matter into his hands, and cut him off with his family and all that follow him in his sin of unfaithfulness.

Ver. 6.—God will also himself **cut off from among his people** any that, not content with lawful and godly knowledge, **turn after such as have familiar spirits, and after wizards, to go a whoring after them.**

Vers. 7, 8.—A positive command, **Sanctify yourselves therefore, and be ye holy: for I am the Lord your God,** is introduced early in the list of penalties to show what is the main purpose of the latter. The only way in which the nation can recover holiness lost by the sins of its members, is by the punishment of the latter, or by their purification by means of sacrifice, according to the nature of the offence.

Ver. 9.—See above, the note on ch. xix. 14, which shows how God's word is made of none effect by man's traditions. God says that a man who **curseth his father or his**

mother shall be surely put to death. Human authority, incontrovertible throughout a great part of Christendom, declares that in most cases it is no grave sin.

Ver. 10.—The Hebrew punishment for adultery is more severe than that of most other nations. Death is again pronounced as the penalty of both adulterer and adulteress in Deut. xxii. 22. The crime is that of a man with a married woman, whether the man be married or not; it is not that of a married man with an unmarried woman, which, in a country where polygamy was allowed, could not be regarded in the same light.

Vers. 11, 12.—It should be noted that intercourse with a stepmother or daughter-in-law are put, by the punishment inflicted upon them, on the same level with adultery and unnatural crimes (vers. 10, 13, 15, 16).

Vers. 13—19.—(See ch. xviii. 22, 17, 23, 9, 19, 12.)

Vers. 20, 21.—**They shall die childless; ... they shall be childless.** "It cannot be supposed that a perpetual miracle was to be maintained through all the ages of Israel's history; but the meaning evidently is that the children of such marriages should be reckoned, not to their actual father, but to the former husband of the woman. In the strong feeling of the Israelites in regard to posterity, this penalty seems to have been sufficient" (Gardiner).

Vers. 22, 23.—The fact of the nations of Canaan being **abhorred by God** because they **committed all these things** shows that the Levitical code forbidding *all these things* was no part of any special law for that nation alone, but a republication of that Law which is binding on all nations because written on the conscience. The prohibited degrees in the Book of Leviticus form a part of the moral, not of the ceremonial, law, and are, therefore, of permanent and universal, not only of temporary and national, obligation.

Vers. 24—26.—The Israelites are to avoid all defilement, moral and ceremonial, because they are God's own possession, **separated from other people,** and **holy unto** him.

Ver. 27.—Those that deal in witchcraft are to be stoned.

HOMILETICS.

Vers. 1, 21.—*The difference between the religious and the secular law* is more marked in modern nations than in the Hebrew commonwealth; the primary object of the first being to forbid and prevent sin; of the second, to protect life and property. The distinction is shown by the separation of the eighteenth and the twentieth chapters; but as in the Mosaic legislation both the law which denounces sin and the law which pronounces penalties for crime proceeded from God, it was not necessary that the boundaries between the two should be marked and defined with the same exactness as when man is legislator; for man cannot venture to gauge the relative enormities of sins, and assign to them their respective punishments, except so far as he is led by the hand by the revelation of God. He can only judge of wrongs and injuries to his fellow-men. In the present age of the world, when the State and the Church are no longer identical, as they were in the case of the Israelites, each law fulfils its function best by confining itself to its proper sphere. The religious law, basing itself on the Divine Law, prohibits and denounces sin; the secular law, being an elaboration by the human intellect of the idea of justice in its various applications to the events of human life, condemns and punishes crimes, by which wrong is done to others.

Vers. 6, 27.—*The pursuit of knowledge by right means* is one of the highest and noblest occupations of the intellect of man, but the seeking after knowledge by unlawful means is so criminal as to lead God to cut off the presumptuous seeker from among his people. It was grasping after a forbidden knowledge by unrighteous means that brought death into the world (Gen. iii. 6). All dealing in necromancy and witchcraft involves this sin on the part of the inquirer into futurity, whether those whom they consult be merely deceivers or not.

Ver. 9.—Just as the negative law, "Thou shalt do no murder," involves the positive law, "Thou shalt love thy neighbour," so the law forbidding to curse a father or a mother contains within it the law of reverential submission to parents and to all in authority.

Ver. 26.—The command, "*Ye shall be holy unto me: for I the Lord am holy,*" is binding upon Christians far more strongly than on the Israelites. For—

I. CHRISTIANS HAVE A POWER GIVEN THEM WHEREBY THEY CAN BE HOLY WHICH THE ISRAELITES HAD NOT. St. Paul, having declared that the final purpose of God's election and our adoption in Christ is "that we should be holy and without blame before him in love" (Eph. i. 4), goes on to say that to those who believed, on hearing the gospel of their salvation preached, there was given the earnest of the Holy Spirit, with which they were sealed unto the day of redemption (Eph. i. 13, 14). The Spirit of holiness is given to every baptized Christian soul, in a way in which he was not imparted to the Israelites, the dispensation of types and shadows having given place to that of spiritual realities, and the promised Comforter having been sent, not only to be with us, but to be in us (John xiv. 16, 17 ; xvi. 7—15).

II. CHRISTIANS HAVE IN CHRIST AN EXAMPLE OF DIVINE HOLINESS WHICH THE ISRAELITES HAD NOT. They are therefore able to realize more fully than the Israelites the manner in which they are to "*be holy, for the Lord your God is holy.*" They see before them the example of One who is God, and who emptied himself of his glory and power, and was made man, and lived a life of perfect holiness on earth. On this model they can, by the help of that Spirit vouchsafed to each Christian, form their own lives. It is an ideal never to be attained, but yet to have an ideal is an inexpressible help.

III. CHRISTIANS, BY THEIR UNION WITH CHRIST AS THEIR HEAD, RECEIVE FROM HIM OF HIS HOLINESS. God has given Christ "to be the Head over all things to the Church, which is his body" (Eph. i. 22, 23), and has gathered "together in one all things in Christ" (Eph. i. 10), that we "may grow up into him in all things, which is the Head, even Christ: from whom the whole body . . . maketh increase . . . unto the edifying of itself in love" (Eph. iv. 15, 16). "Christ is the Head of the Church, as the husband is head of the wife" (Eph. v. 23), and "we are members of his body, of his flesh, and of his bones" (Eph. v. 30). The Word is "full of grace and truth . . . and of his fulness have all we received, and grace for grace" (John i. 14—16). From the mystical union between Christ and his Church there flow down graces upon those who are the members of his Church.

IV. CHRISTIANS CAN BY FAITH APPROPRIATE TO THEMSELVES OF THE HOLINESS OF CHRIST. By faith the holiness, whereby satisfaction was made by Christ for the sinfulness of all mankind, may be so realized by the believing Christian as to be regarded as though it were his own in respect to his own sins.

HOMILIES BY VARIOUS AUTHORS.

Human sacrifices. Ch. xx. 1—5; cf. Gen. xxii. 1—19; Micah vi. 7. In this chapter we come to a catalogue of *capital crimes.* Upon the whole list of cases we need not dwell; but the first has some interest as raising the question of "human sacrifices." How early the terrible practice of offering "the fruit of the body" in atonement for "the sin of the soul" arose, we can scarcely say. It has been supposed to be as early, at all events, as the time of Abraham. Some entertain the notion that the sacrifice of Isaac was primarily a temptation to imitate the custom existing in the land. But if the horrible custom existed in Abraham's day, nothing could more clearly convey that the Divine pleasure rested in other sacrifices altogether than the details of the escape of Isaac. The custom of human sacrifices was widespread, as investigations show.[1] Here and elsewhere the Lord sets his face against them. Let us see if we can grasp the principle involved.

I. HUMAN SACRIFICE IS THE NATURAL CLIMAX OF THE SACRIFICIAL IDEA. "If no scruples," says Ewald, "held a man back from giving the dearest he had when a feeling in his heart drove him to sacrifice it to his God just as it was, then he would easily feel even the life of a beloved domestic animal not too dear to be given up at his heart's urgent demand. Nay, only in the offering up of life or soul, as the last that can be offered, did it seem to him that the highest was presented. But the logical consequence of such feelings was that human life must ultimately be looked upon as incomparably the highest and most wondrous offering, whether the life offered be that of a stranger or, as that which is dearest to one, that of one's own child, or even of one's self. Thus human sacrifice was everywhere the proper crown and completion of all these utterances of the fear of God." The case of Abraham is one in point. When God for wise purposes demanded the surrender of the only begotten and well-beloved son, Isaac, he asked the patriarch for the greatest conceivable sacrifice; and, so far as intention is concerned, Abraham made the surrender. It has been called on the patriarch's part a "magnificent and extraordinary act of romantic morals."[2] While, therefore, it was in reality, as we shall see, a condemnation of human sacrifices as such, it illustrates their real spirit.

II. HUMAN SACRIFICE IS AT THE SAME TIME SUCH A MONSTROUS AND EXTRAVAGANT EXPRESSION OF THE SACRIFICIAL IDEA THAT NOTHING BUT A DIVINE COMMAND WOULD WARRANT THE ENTERTAINMENT OF IT. What distinguishes Abraham's case in connection with the proposed sacrifice of Isaac from that of all other sacrifices of human life is that he had a command of God to go upon, while the others followed the devices of their own hearts. So sacred should human life appear to men, that the idea of taking it away should only be entertained under the most solemn sanctions. Besides, but for the sin-distorted mind of man, it would appear that the consecration of human beings as "living sacrifices," is in itself far higher and nobler than their death (Rom. xii. 1). To take innocent infants and place them in the flaming arms of Molech must appear a most monstrous and exaggerated expression of the sacrificial idea.

But would God, in any circumstances, command human sacrifices? As a matter of fact, men were sacrificed through capital punishment. The present chapter is full of capital crimes. Men died under the direction of God for their crimes. This, however, is not the sacrificial idea, which involves the sacrifice of the *innocent* in the room of the guilty. This was doubtless what led the infants to be favourite sacrifices with the heathen—the innocency of the sufferer constituted the greater appeal to the angry deity. We observe, then—

III. THAT GOD FORBADE, UNDER THE PENALTY OF DEATH, HUMAN SACRIFICES, AND IN THE ONLY CASE WHERE HE SEEMED TO DEMAND A HUMAN SACRIFICE HE HAD PROVIDED A SUBSTITUTE. He made the offering of children to Molech a capital crime. This was not aimed at the idolatry only, but at the unwarranted exaggeration of the sacrificial idea. Besides, in the case of Isaac, just when Abraham was about to slay

[1] Cf. Smith's 'Dictionary of the Bible,' *s.v.* 'Molech;' also Ewald's references, note p. 69, of his 'Antiquities of Israel.'

[2] Mozley's 'Ruling Ideas in Early Ages,' p. 62; see also the chapter on 'Human Sacrifices.'

him, God interposed with a provided substitute. All God required in Abraham's peculiar case was the *spirit* of surrender. He guards, therefore, his prerogative of dealing with life, and enjoins his people only to take human life away when he directs them. They are not to presume to offer such a sacred gift as human life upon his altar in the way of sacrifice. They may dedicate themselves and their children as living beings to his service, but their death he requires not in such a voluntary fashion at their hands.

IV. AT THE SAME TIME, WE FIND HUMAN LIFE REGULARLY SACRIFICED IN THE ORDER OF DIVINE PROVIDENCE AND AT THE CALL OF DUTY. That is to say, though we have not monstrous and unhallowed sacrifices required of God at his altars, he does make demands on men and women to surrender, like Abraham, their sons, or to surrender themselves at the call of duty. This is indeed as real a sacrifice as in the arms of Molech, and at the same time a far nobler one. In fact, *self-sacrifice* seems to be a law of providence in the case of all who would be truly noble in their careers. The voluntary element, coming in along with the sweet reasonableness of the sublime necessity, vindicates the morality of the whole transaction. Men and women cheerfully lay down their lives in gradual sacrifice to duty's call, or sometimes in sudden and immediate sacrifice. And the act is moral as well as heroic.

V. THIS LEADS TO A LAST OBSERVATION, THAT HUMAN SACRIFICE HAD ITS GREAT CULMINATION AND CLIMAX IN THAT OF JESUS CHRIST. For what God did not require from Abraham—the actual sacrifice of his son—he has required of himself. The demand for a human sacrifice made only apparently in the case of Isaac, was made really in the case of Christ. An innocent, sinless human being was once commanded by his God and Father to lay down his life and bear, in doing so, the sins of man. Hence we find him saying, "Therefore doth my Father love me, because I lay down my life, that I might take it again" (John x. 17). It would seem a harsh command, a cruel necessity, were it not that the Father and Son are essentially one, and the commandment that the Son should die was virtually Divine self-sacrifice. "He who is sent is one in being with him who sends." The atonement of Christ is really the *self-sacrifice of God*.

Hence the only human sacrifice demanded is God incarnate responding to himself. The necessity for thus atoning for human sin at the expense of self-sacrifice is in the main mysterious. But its very mystery makes it more deeply profitable to faith. How great must God's love be when it leads him to lay down his own life and die ignominiously in the interests of men! The ram which was offered in the stead of Isaac is the type of the self-sacrificing Jesus who was offered for us.—R. M. E.

Vers. 1—5.—*Sin at its worst.* There is, perhaps, no development of sin which is more shocking to the renewed mind of man, and more offensive to the pure and gracious heart of God, than that which is here condemned. The verses intimate—

I. THAT SIN SOMETIMES LEADS TO A SHOCKING DISTORTION OF THE HUMAN JUDGMENT. How, we naturally ask, could men ever come to believe in the desirableness of such inhuman rites as those here prohibited? That any Divine Being could possibly be conciliated by the infliction of a cruel death, by the offering up of little children to consuming fires, by this presentation on the part of their own parents! How revolting and incredible seem such ideas! There is no account to be given of it but that sin, as it goes on its maleficent path, not only disfigures the life and corrupts the heart, but also degrades and distorts the understanding of men. It ends in the "evil eye" and so in the "great darkness" of the soul (Matt. vi. 23).

II. THAT GOD CANNOT AND WILL NOT PERMIT THE GLORY WHICH IS DUE TO HIMSELF TO BE GIVEN TO ANOTHER. "I will set my face against that man" (ver. 3). God has emphatically said, "My glory will I not give to another" (Isa. xlii. 8). The "face of the Lord is against" them that withhold their homage from the Creator, and offer worship and tribute to false gods. This, (1) not on the selfish ground that he can claim and secure something for himself which he desires, after the manner of men, but (2) on the ground that it is in itself right and fit that men should worship the one true God, and (3) also because idolatry is not only a guilty but a mischievous principle working every imaginable harm to those who commit it. If we are keeping back from God and giving to another or to ourselves the thought, interest, affection, regard, which is due to him, we must remember that we make the Almighty our enemy; his "face is against us."

III. THAT DELIBERATE TRANSGRESSION MAKES ALL WORSHIP UNACCEPTABLE, IF NOT SINFUL. The man who, while flagrantly violating the Law of Jehovah by " giving his seed unto Molech," presented himself, at the same time, before the tabernacle, was only " defiling the sanctuary " of the Lord and " profaning his holy Name " (ver. 3) by such worthless devotion. God did not desire to see in his presence a man who was wilfully and wantonly committing such a heinous sin. No man is more welcome to the throne of grace than the penitent sinner who is burdened with a sense of guilt and who craves the mercy and help of the Divine Saviour. But let not that man who is cherishing sin in his soul think that his offering is accepted of the Lord. It is hypocrisy, profanation (see Ps. l. 16 ; Isa. i. 11, 12).

IV. THAT UNREPENTED SIN MUST BEAR ITS DOOM. "He shall surely be put to death," etc. (ver. 2) ; "I will cut him off from among his people" (ver. 3). There is no provision here stated of mercy for the penitent. Probably none was allowed ; the exigencies of the situation demanded death under any circumstances. Under the present dispensation there is an offer of Divine mercy to the penitent, whatever their sins may be, however many, however great. But the impenitent must lay their account with the fact that they have offended One who " will by no means clear the guilty," who will " surely " punish and destroy.

V. THAT CONNIVANCE AT DEADLY SIN IS A GUILTY PARTICIPATION IN WRONG, AND MUST SHARE ITS MISERABLE DOOM. (Vers. 4, 5.) There are evils at which no friendship however dear, no kinship however close, may dare to wink. We must unsparingly denounce and even determinedly expose.

VI. THAT THOSE WHO ARE RESPONSIBLE FOR THE CHURCH'S WELFARE MUST WARN REPEATEDLY AGAINST THE MOST DANGEROUS SINS. *Again,* "Thou shalt say," etc. (ver. 1).—C.

Ver. 6.—*Credulity and faith.* This, also, is an injunction which Moses had given before, and which he was instructed to repeat (see ch. xix. 31). Our thought may be directed to—

I. THE PREVALENCE OF IMPOSTURE. There has never been a time nor a land without its " familiar spirits," its " wizards," or impostors of some kind and name. Men have claimed the power of gaining extraordinary access to the spiritual world, or superhuman knowledge of the future, and they have imposed on the ungoverned curiosity of their simple neighbours. The presence of such workers in magic is almost universal. The love of power and the love of money will account for it. So must it be while there is—

II. THE CORRESPONDING PREVALENCE OF CREDULITY. The number of " the simple " is very large everywhere. Men and women are always to be found, in pitiful abundance, who will respond to any claim made upon their belief. There is hardly an absurdity too glaring, a falsehood too palpable to be discredited by all. Let the impostor only be confident and pretentious enough, and he will find a number who will listen with eagerness and believe without question or proof.

III. ITS UTTER DELUSIVENESS. The entire system is false and rotten throughout; it is a mass of trickery, delusion, and disappointment. 1. Those who practise it soon impose upon themselves; they come to believe that they are really admitted to the secrets of the other world, and they are the victims of their own roguery. Sin tests no one so hard as the sinner himself; its rebound is terrible and deadly. He who, with guilty selfishness, would deceive his fellows, will soon entangle his foot in his own net and perish in his own snare (Ps. vii. 15 ; ix. 15). 2. They also grossly deceive their neighbours. They who listen to their voice believe that they are holding intercourse with heaven, or are gaining instruction from those supernaturally endowed, when the truth is they are only dealing with men who are unusually wicked, and who should only be heard to be disregarded or denounced.

IV. ITS SINFULNESS IN THE SIGHT OF GOD. Resort to imposture is positively wrong. In this book God uttered and repeated his Divine prohibition, and he strengthened his law by attaching the heaviest penalties to disobedience : "I will even set my face against that soul, and will cut him off," etc. The heinousness of the practice probably lay in the fact that it was a deliberate departure from the Lord himself. There was his house, and there were his prophets to resort unto; to pass these by in order to consult pretenders and impostors was to forsake God and to go " a whoring " after other beings and other things. And thus our thought is directed to—

V. THE EXCELLENCY OF A REASONABLE FAITH. The children of Israel had such access to the spiritual world and such knowledge of the future as it was good for men to have. Was not God himself, in manifested presence and in revealing grace, in their camp? Was he not speaking to them as to the future that was before them? Was he not ready to give them prophets who would not impose on them with shameful lies, but guide them with the word of truth? We, too, have all we need without having recourse to subtle and spiritualistic arts. We have: 1. The Word of God upon our tables and in our minds. 2. The devout counsels of wise and holy men. 3. The promised guidance of the Spirit of God. Fictitious arts are sinful and delusive. The wisdom that is from God is not only sound but sufficient. That which is more than this "cometh of evil."—C.

Vers. 7, 8.—*Sanctity—demand, inducement, promise.* Once "again" (ver. 2) Moses utters the Divine will in this great matter of holiness (see chs. xi. 44; xix. 2). We have—

I. GOD'S IMPERATIVE DEMAND OF SANCTITY. "Sanctify yourselves." "Ye shall keep my statutes, and do them." The Creator of the universe, the Author of our being, the Father and Sustainer of our spirits, has sovereign right to speak to us in such decisive tones. He demands of us that we shall be "holy," *i.e.* (1) that we shall expel from heart and life all those sinful habits by which men have defiled themselves: thus shall we "be severed from other people" (ver. 26), whose spirit and life are hateful; and (2) that we shall approach him, honour him, and pay him the tribute he asks of us, and also act righteously and blamelessly toward our fellows, "keeping his statutes and doing them."

II. THE HIGH INDUCEMENT HE PRESENTS TO US. "Be ye holy: for I am the Lord your God." We may gird ourselves to good and great things, animated by different motives; of these some may be higher, others lower. God summons us to be holy for the highest reason of all, viz. because we shall thus resemble him. "Be ye holy; for I am holy" (1 Pet. i. 16). Other reasons abound: holiness (1) is the best thing in itself; (2) saves us from many and great spiritual evils; (3) delivers us from dark and awful penalties; (4) allies us to the noblest created beings, etc.; but the best and loftiest of all considerations is that (5) it makes us like God, the Holy One, himself. His spirit is our spirit; his principles, our principles; his life, our life. We are "the children of our Father who is in heaven."

III. HIS PROMISED HELP. "I am the Lord which sanctify you." The action of God upon our souls has been treated, both by the foolish and by the wicked, as a reason for human impassiveness. Foolish men have said, "God is working for us and in us, therefore it would be irreverent for us to attempt to do anything; we should only interfere." Wicked men have said, "God works for us, therefore we may safely live in comfortable unconcern and guilt while we wait his time of deliverance." The "children of wisdom" have said, "God is ready to work with us, therefore let us strive with all our energies, for, with his help, we shall not strive in vain." This is the apostle's argument: "Work out your own salvation, . . . for it is God which worketh in you," etc. (Phil. ii. 12, 13). All our endeavours might be unavailing; we might contend against the strong current of sin and be baffled and borne along its stream, but if God himself is sanctifying us, we shall prevail. Let us go forth unto the struggle, for we shall assuredly succeed. God sanctifies us in such wise that he acts *with* us while he acts *in* us and *for* us. He sanctifies us by (1) the truth of his Word (John. xvii. 17): this we are to consult; by (2) the privileges of the sanctuary (Ezek. xxxvii. 28): of these we are to avail ourselves; by (3) his providential discipline (Heb. xii. 10): to this we are to submit; by (4) the indwelling of his Holy Spirit (Rom. xv. 16): for this we are earnestly to pray and expectantly to wait.—C.

Ver. 9 (latter clause).—*The unforgiven.* "His blood shall be upon him;" "their blood shall be upon them" (vers. 13, 16, 27). These words have a deeper significance than a mere repetition of the sentence, "He shall be put to death." They signify this: *his sin cannot be forgiven him.* It was the blood of the animal that "made atonement for the soul" (ch. xvii. 11). It was the shed blood, therefore, that was associated, in thought, with the penalty due to sin. And when the legislator said,

"His blood shall be upon him," he meant his *penalty* shall rest upon him—it shall not be borne and taken away by the blood of the substituted victim. In other words, "He shall bear his iniquity," or the penalty of his iniquity, himself (see ch. vii. 18). There have always been, and there will always be, in the world "the unforgiven;" men, like Cain, who bear about them the brand of an unpardonable offence; sons and daughters who have erred and have not been taken back into parental love; criminals that have lost the place in society which they have no hope of regaining; forlorn wretches that have so sinned against their conscience that they cannot forgive themselves, and have abandoned themselves to a terrible despair. But what of the Divine forgiveness or refusal to forgive? We are taught—

I. THAT PROVISION WAS MADE IN THE LAW FOR THE PARDON OF MANY OFFENCES. This was the end of all the sin and trespass offerings, and on the Day of Atonement "all the iniquities of the children of Israel, and all their transgressions" were "borne away" into the uninhabited land, into the wilderness of oblivion (ch. xvi. 21, 22).

II. THAT UNDER THE LAW THERE WERE OFFENCES WHICH COULD NOT BE THUS ATONED, AND WERE NOT FORGIVEN. Those who wrought shameful acts of idolatry or immorality could bring no oblation to the altar; they could look for no mercy; no blood of atonement was availing; their "blood was upon them;" they died before the Lord.

III. THAT, UNDER THE GOSPEL, MERCY IS OFFERED FOR THE WORST TRANSGRESSORS IF THERE BE PENITENCE AND FAITH. The one "unpardonable sin" (Mark iii. 29) is either (1) a sin which was possible in the days of the Incarnation and is absolutely beyond commission now, or (2) consists in that hardening of the heart against the Spirit's influence which results in final impenitence. But where there is repentance toward God and faith in our Lord Jesus Christ, there is an open gate into the kingdom of God's mercy, into eternal life. No heinousness of offence, no multiplicity of transgressions, bars the way. "By him all that believe are justified from all things, from which they could not be justified by the Law of Moses" (Acts xiii. 39).

IV. THAT MANY SOULS, THOUGH WALKING IN THE LIGHT OF THE GOSPEL, ARE CONTENT TO RANK AMONG THE UNFORGIVEN. In the light, in the full sunshine of privilege and opportunity, there are thousands of men who do not find, because they will not seek, the mercy and the friendship of God. They live unforgiven; "their blood is upon them." They go through life (1) with an oppressive sense of condemnation upon them; (2) excluding themselves from purest spiritual blessedness (Ps. xxxii. 1, 2); (3) voluntarily unfitted for the highest service man can render his brother.

V. THAT THE IMPENITENT PASS INTO THE FUTURE WITH UNFORGIVEN SIN UPON THEIR SOUL. How terrible to pass beyond the line which bounds the period of probation with our "blood upon us;" to pass on (1) to condemnation and reproach at the bar of God, (2) to exile from the heavenly city, (3) to the retribution which the justice of God must inflict! Go, in the day of grace, to the "Lamb of God, which taketh away the sin of the world," through whom there is "remission of sins" (Luke xxiv. 47).—C.

Ver. 23 (latter part).—*God's displeasure with ourselves.* "They committed all these things, and therefore I abhorred them." This expression arrests us by—

I. ITS SOMEWHAT STARTLING STRENGTH. "I abhorred them." Does God positively *abhor* man? the Creator his creature? the Father his child? Are we to understand that the Lord, who is "gracious and full of compassion, slow to anger, and plenteous in mercy," feels an actual *abhorrence* of those beings to whom he is so nearly and intimately related, those human spirits he formed for himself, to reflect his own image and to enjoy his own immortal blessedness? The word startles us; it may well alarm us; it suggests the question, Is it possible that we also may become such that our God may be compelled to look on us with a displeasure which amounts to abhorrence? We look at—

II. THE SAD AND SOLID TRUTH WHICH IT CONTAINS. "God hates the sin and loves the sinner," we say, and truly. Yet this sentence does not cover the whole truth of the case. God does pity the sinner, and seeks to save him. But *he is displeased with him also.* Of anything like malignity or ill will we rejoice to know that the holy and gracious One is absolutely incapable; but we are bound to believe that he feels a sacred and holy resentment against those who violate the laws of righteousness. 1. Scripture plainly affirms that he does. "Therefore I abhorred them;" "God is angry with the wicked every day" (Ps. vii. 11); "the Lord hath been sore displeased with your fathers" (Zech. i. 2); "they vexed his Holy Spirit" (Isa. lxiii. 10); "he looked on them with anger" (Mark iii. 5); to "them that obey unrighteousness" God will render "indignation and wrath" (Rom. ii. 8). 2. It is impossible wholly to separate the act from the agent. An act has no moral qualities at all apart from the disposition and character of him who does it. If our indignation is aroused by any shameful deed, it is because some *one* has wrought that which is wrong, and our feeling *must* extend to the perpetrator as well as to the crime. In theory it must do so; in fact it does so. We cannot see our own children doing that which is guilty without being displeased with *them* as well as excited with indignation against the wrong they have done. Our feelings of holy anger, indignation, righteous grief, etc., may not be *precisely identical* with those which are in the heart of God when he looks down on the sins of his human children, but they *answer to them*; they correspond with them; they enable us to understand how he, our Divine Father, feels toward us when we do those things which are offensive and grievous in his sight. Let us lay it well to heart that by (1) our positive transgressions of his holy Law, (2) our keeping back from him the love and the service which are his due, (3) the continued rejection of his overtures of mercy and reconciliation in Christ Jesus, we are offending, displeasing, grieving God. These our sins are drawing down upon our own souls the awful anger, the high displeasure, of that Almighty God in whom we live, who has ourselves and our future in his right hand of power, whom it is our chief duty, and should be our first desire, to conciliate and please. We glance at—

III. THE WELCOME TRUTH WITH WHICH IT IS CONSISTENT. While God hates sin and is divinely displeased with the sinner, he yet pities the sinner and seeks to save him. He condemns, but he invites. "Is Ephraim my dear son? . . . since I spake against him, I do earnestly remember him still" (Jer. xxxi. 20). As a human father over his lost son or erring daughter, only with immeasurably deeper love, he yearns over his wayward children, and goes out to welcome them home, when, returning to themselves, they return unto him (Luke xv. 11—24).—C.

Ver. 24.—*Three aspects of human life.* The verse suggests three thoughts concerning our human life—

I. THE EXCELLENCY OF OUR ESTATE. "A land that floweth with milk and honey." God gave the Israelites an excellent inheritance when he led them into the land of promise. For beauty, variety of scenery, fertility, etc., it was all that could be desired. Our present estate as citizens of time is one rich and full, a "land flowing," etc. We have: 1. The beauty and grandeur of the world. 2. Human love in its manifold forms, conjugal, parental, filial, fraternal, etc. 3. Sufficiency of all kinds of palatable food. 4. Intellectual gratifications. 5. Spiritual relationships and the sacred, enduring joys which belong to these.

II. THE TENURE UNDER WHICH WE HOLD POSSESSION. "I will give it unto you to possess it." We reckon that we "possess" many things. We call them "ours." We endeavour to secure them to ourselves by carefully drawn documents and witnesses. But what, when all has been done that can be done, is the tenure under which we hold everything? It is not the consent of man, but the will of God. God said to Israel concerning the country of the Canaanites, "Ye shall inherit their land, and I will give it unto you to possess it." He thought well to take it away from its former occupants and give it to them. There were, no doubt, the best reasons for this exchange; but Jehovah evidently assumed his perfect right to dispose as seemed well to him of his own. God always has the best grounds on which to deal with us, raising up or laying low; he never acts capriciously; but he often acts without assigning reasons to us, and in such wise that we cannot make any conjecture thereupon that is even probably true. We must recognize the fact that we hold everything at his will, and be perfectly ready to lay it down or to hand it on to another at the bidding of the Supreme. This is true of (1) our property and position, (2) our mental powers, (3) our health, and (4) our life on earth.

III. THE PAINFUL NEED TO SEPARATE OURSELVES FROM OTHERS. "I am the Lord your God, which have separated you from other people." By their daily habits and social customs (ver. 25), the Jews were cut off from intercourse with other people:

intermarriages were strictly prohibited (Deut. vii. 3, 4); they were to maintain a studied separateness from all surrounding nations. The conscientious service of God our Saviour involves some separateness on our part. 1. We have to form ourselves into separate societies, Christian Churches. From these we are bound, in faithfulness, to exclude those who do not profess to love our Lord Jesus Christ. This will produce resentment on their part, and cause them to ascribe to pride that which is due to simple loyalty to the Master. 2. We have to separate ourselves from those persons and things whose association would be injurious to the cause of Christ; from (1) unholy friendships, (2) institutions and customs which have evil features or evil tendencies, (3) the abounding spirit of worldliness and selfishness. We are bound to make it clear and plain to all that we are " on the Lord's side," and on the side of all those righteous and holy principles which he commends to us.—C.

Vers. 1—27.—*Sin unto death.* The offences described in this chapter were mentioned before. Such is our obtuseness that we need "line upon line." Adorable is that goodness of God which takes such pains with us. We have here—

I. PRESUMPTUOUS SINS AND THEIR PENALTY. 1. *Parents giving their seed to Molech.* (1) This infernal god was the King of Tophet (Isa. xxx. 33), and, in malignity, not to be distinguished from Satan. The sacrifices he demanded were human. By a refinement of cruelty he required parents to immolate their own offspring. They were offered to him in the horrible torments of fire. Nothing could be more devilish. (2) In denouncing death as the penalty for this sin, the reason given is that it " defiled the sanctuary and profaned the holy Name" of God (ver. 3). The temple and the Shechinah were in the land, and to commit this wickedness there was consequently to commit the highest crime against the most awful sacredness. Also the body of man is the temple of God, and to give that temple to Molech was, in this sense, to defile the temple of God (see 1 Cor. vi. 15; x. 21). (3) The penalty is denounced in order upon the Hebrew first. Having more light, he is in a higher degree responsible, and therefore is the first named to suffer (comp. Rom. ii. 9). Let not Protestant Christians forget their great responsibility. (4) But the " strangers that sojourn in Israel " are amenable to the same punishment. They must not abuse their hospitality by showing an example of wickedness. This consideration should restrain the licentiousness in foreign countries of some of our travellers. 2. *Persons having dealings with necromancy.* (1) The *principals* in this. Those "who have familiar spirits," or demons attendant upon them and obedient to their calls. " Wizards," or wise ones, viz. to pry into the "depths of Satan " (ver. 27). Such persons are accounted guilty of the highest crime, and were doomed to suffer death by stoning, without mercy. (2) Their *customers.* Those who have recourse to such abandoned persons to discover things which it has not pleased God to reveal. Such pruriency into Divine mysteries is defiling (ver. 6; ch. xix. 31). (3) Those who would be sanctified by God must first sanctify themselves from these abominations. If they refuse to do this, God will sanctify himself of them by cutting them off (vers. 6, 8). 3. *Children who curse their parents.* (1) Those guilty of this irreverence must be woefully destitute of the fear of God (see ch. xix. 32). Our fathers according to the flesh are to us representatives of our Father in heaven. (2) So heinous is this crime that it must be punished with death. There is no atonement for it. "His blood shall be upon him." He must be made himself the sacrifice for his sin. What an admonition to the fast youth of modern times! 4. *Excesses in uncleanness.* (1) Death, in one form or another, is the penalty for the horrible crimes specified (vers. 10—21). " Their blood shall be upon them;" " they shall be cut off from among their people;" "they shall bear their iniquity;" "they shall be stoned;" "they shall be burnt;" "they shall die childless." (2) In this last the retribution must come speedily. Their cutting off out of the land of the living must be before any issue could come of their crime. It may also imply that any issue they may have already should be involved in the punishment of their sin (comp. Numb. xvi. 32; Josh. vii. 24).

II. THE RESPONSIBILITY OF WITNESSES. 1. *To withhold testimony against sin is to incur its guilt.* (1) It is here taken as complicity in the crime. He that " hides his eyes from the man," that giveth his seed to Molech, so as to let him escape the hands of justice, is said to "commit whoredom with Molech " (vers. 4, 5). What a lesson is here to "peaccable" Christians who let swearers and other public offenders go unreproved! (2) He that "hides his eyes," in this case, is visited with excommunication. For complicity in this gross idolatry, here described as "whoredom," God, as a jealous husband, gives his writing of divorcement. "I will set my face against that man, . . . and will cut him off from among his people." Not only is he expelled from the Church, but also from the nation, if not in addition doomed to suffer a violent death (comp. chs. xvii. 10; xxvi. 17; Jer. xliv. 11—14; Ezek. xiv. 7—9; xv. 7). (3) For this culpable want of zeal for the honour of God, the tacit accomplice in the abominations of Molech involves also his family in his punishment (ver. 5). How many illustrations of this principle have we in the history of the kings! (see Exod. xx. 7). Sin is a desperate evil, and requires a strong hand to deal with it. 2. *The testimony against sin is a sanctification to the witness* (vers. 7, 8). (1) The faithful witness thereby sanctifies himself. (*a*) He clears himself of all complicity. (*b*) He approves himself to God as zealous for his truth, purity, and honour. (*c*) He fulfils the part of a true patriot; for nations are exalted by righteousness and ruined by crime. Public duty may cost us inconvenience, but it must not be neglected. (2) He is sanctified by the Lord (ver. 8). God will honour them that honour him. (*a*) He will bring them to dwell in the land (ver. 22). This possession was the earnest of the better Canaan. It was a "land flowing with milk and honey." (*b*) He will watch over them as a proprietor over precious treasure. "They shall be mine" (ver. 26; Exod. xix. 5, 6; Deut. vii. 6; Ps. cxxxv. 4). "Blessed are the people whose God is the Lord."— J. A. M.

Vers. 1—27.—*Punishments assigned to presumptuous sins.* I. THE LAW OF SOCIETY RESTS ON THE HIGHER LAW OF GOD. All legislation should be thus divinely sanctioned. The Bible is not a statute-book for nations, but a book of principles—to give light to the mind and heart of man as man. We must not enforce human law on Divine grounds, but we can use Divine revelation to ascertain the most satisfactory laws.

II. PUNISHMENTS vary from age to age and country to country, but the reason of punishment remains. The honour of the Law satisfied is the way of life opened.

III. The comparison between the Law and the gospel suggested by this chapter reveals the grace of God, the progress of humanity, the ultimate destiny of the race. The gradual extinction of the sins is the extinction of the laws which provided against them. "If ye be led of the Spirit, ye are not under the Law" (see Gal. v., and comp. Jas. i., ii.). The perfect law of liberty is a fulfilment of the old law, and therefore a blotting out of the handwriting of ordinances and nailing of them to the cross of Christ.—R.

PART III.

SECTION IV.

THE UNCLEANNESS AND DISQUALIFICATION OF PRIESTS.

EXPOSITION.

CHAPTER XXI.

The two remaining chapters of this division of the book (chs. xxi., xxii.) deal with the case of defilements attaching to the priesthood, over and above those which affect other men, whether ceremonial (chs. xxi. 1—6, 10—12; xxii. 1—9) or moral (ch. xxi. 7—9, 13—15); with the physical defects disqualifying men of the priestly family from ministering at the altar (ch. xxi. 16—24); with the privilege of eating of the holy things (ch. xxii. 10—13); ending with the injunction that the sacrificial victims, no less than the priests who sacrificed them, should be unblemished and perfect of their kind.

Vers. 1—6.—The first paragraph refers to ceremonial uncleanness derived to the priest from his family relations. The priest may not take part in any funeral rites, the effect of which was legal defilement, except in the case of the death of his father, mother, son, daughter, brother, and unmarried sister. These are all that appear to be mentioned. But what, then, are we to understand regarding his wife? Was the priest allowed to take part in mourning ceremonies for her or not? It is thought by some that her case is met by ver. 4, But **he shall not defile himself, being a chief man among his people, to profane himself.** The literal translation of this verse is, *He shall not be defiled, a lord (baal) among his people.* The word *baal*, or *lord*, is commonly used in the sense of *husband*. The clause, therefore, may be understood to forbid the priest to mourn for his wife, being rendered, *He shall not defile himself as an husband* (i.e. *for his wife*) *among his people.* This, however, is something of a forced rendering. The words are better understood to mean, *He shall not defile himself as a master of a house among his people;* that is, he may not take part in the funeral rites of slaves or other members of the household, which ordinarily brought defilement on the master of a house. Then is the priest forbidden to mourn for his wife? This we can hardly believe, when he might mourn for father and mother, son and daughter, brother and sister. Nor is it necessary to take this view. For the case of the wife is covered by the words. **For his kin, that is near unto him, . . . he may be defiled.** The wife, being so closely attached to the husband, is not specifically named, because that was not necessary, but is included under the expression, *his kin, that is near unto him,* just as daughter, grandmother, niece, and wife's sister, are covered by the phrase, " near of kin," without being specifically named in ch. xviii. (see note on ch. xviii. 18). Even when mourning is permitted, the priest is to use no excessive forms of it, still less any that have been used by idolaters. **They shall not make baldness upon their head, neither shall they shave off the corner of their beard** (see ch. xix. 27), **nor make any cuttings in their flesh** (see ch. xix. 28). And the reason why they are to avoid ceremonial uncleanness in some cases, and to act with sobriety and gravity in all, is that they are dedicated to God, **to offer the offerings of the Lord made by fire, the bread of their God;** that is, the sacrifices which are consumed by the fire of the altar symbolizing the action of God (see note on ch. iii. 11).

Vers. 7—9.—Moral uncleanness or defilement passes to the husband and father from an immoral wife or daughter, and therefore the priest is to be specially careful in the selection of his wife; and his daughter, if she leads a licentious life, is to be stoned to death, and then **burnt with fire,** because **she profaneth her father** (cf. 1 Sam. ii. 17). In a similar spirit, St. Paul gives directions as to the families of those to whom the ministry of the Spirit is assigned (1 Tim. iii. 11; Titus i. 6). Keil would unite ver. 4 in sense with vers. 7—9, and argues

that *he shall not defile himself, being a chief man among his people, to profane himself,* refers to the kind of marriage which the priest is to make, but the interposition of vers. 5 and 6 forbid this explanation of ver. 4.

Vers. 10—15.—The high priest, **upon whose head the anointing oil was poured, and that is consecrated to put on the garments,** symbolizing in his person the Holy One in a more special manner than the other priests, has to aim so much the more at symbolical holiness. He may not, therefore. incur legal uncleanness by taking part in the funeral rites, even of his father or mother, not being permitted to absent himself from the sanctuary, which he would have to do if he had thus ceremonially defiled himself. Nor is it enough that he should abstain from taking an immoral or a divorced wife; he may only wed **a virgin and of his own people,** whereas the other priests might marry widows and the daughters of strangers dwelling among the Israelites. In the ordinances for priests given in Ezek. xliv., the ordinary priests, as well as the high priest, are forbidden to marry widows, unless they be the widows of priests (Ezek. xliv. 22).

Vers. 16—24.—Perfection of the body being typical of perfection of the mind and of the whole man, and symbolical perfection being required of the priest of God, none may be admitted to the priesthood with bodily defects, or excrescences, or grievous blemishes. The translation **dwarf,** in ver. 20, is better than the marginal rendering " too slender," or withered. Being the descendants of Aaron, these priests, blemished as they were, were to be supported as the other priests were supported. **He shall eat the bread of his God,** both **of the most holy, and of the holy;** that is, the priests' portions of the meat offerings (chs. ii. 3, 10; vi. 17), of the sin offerings (ch. vi. 29), of the trespass offerings (ch. vii. 1), of the shewbread (ch. xxiv. 9), which were most holy, and of the heave offerings, wave offerings, firstfruit offerings, firstlings, and things devoted (Numb. xi. 11—19), which were holy. They were also apparently employed in the less formal and conspicuous duties of the priests, such as examining lepers, and any other functions which did not bring them **nigh unto the altar.** But they were not to profane God's **sanctuaries,** by which is meant the holy of holies, the holy place, and the court in which the altar stood. To none of these is the blemished priest to be admitted for the purpose of officiating, though he might enter the court and probably the holy place for other purposes, and might eat the offerings of the priests in the accustomed place.

HOMILETICS.

Vers. 7—9.—*The marriage of the clergy*, according to the discipline of the reformed Churches, is one of the points on which the latter bear a marked superiority to the Latin Church, which forbids its bishops and priests to marry; and to the Greek Church, which expects its priests to be married before ordination, forbids them to marry a second time, and requires celibacy in its bishops.

I. IT IS MORE SCRIPTURAL. In the Old Testament, the priests had the liberty of marriage; in the New Testament, the bishops or presbyters had the liberty of marriage, and Timothy and Titus are instructed by St. Paul to select married men for the clerical office (1 Tim. iii. 2, 4; Titus i. 6).

II. IT IS MORE PRIMITIVE. The misinterpretation of St. Paul's words, "the husband of one wife" (which, rightly interpreted, mean "a man faithful to one woman"), led in early time to the Greek discipline; but the Latin practice, condemned by the Greeks in the Council in Trullo, was not enforced upon the whole of the Western Church until the eleventh century, nor is it universal in it now.

III. IT IS MORE HUMAN. The attempt to crush instead of regulate God-given instincts, whether by philosophical sects or religious bodies, has always led to unspeakable evils. In the present case it has led to (1) immorality, as testified by the history of every country in which the practice has existed; (2) inhumanity, as exhibited in the Inquisition and at the stake, such as a celibate priesthood could alone have been guilty of; (3) disloyalty, which is naturally felt by those who, having their natural ties to their country severed, become the spiritual police of a foreign power.

IV. DUTIES CONNECTED WITH IT. 1. For each individual clergyman—to determine whether marriage will or will not "serve better to godliness" (Art. XXXII.). 2. To select a wife who will be "a help meet for him" (Gen. ii. 20). 3. To be "a man of one woman" (1 Tim. iii. 2; Titus i. 6), that is, faithful to his wife. 4. To "rule well his own house, having his children in subjection with all gravity" (1 Tim. iii. 4); "having faithful children not accused of riot or unruly" (Titus i. 6). 5. "To be diligent to form and fashion himself and his family according to the doctrine of Christ, and to make both himself and it, as much as in him lieth, wholesome examples and patterns to the flock of Christ" (Ordering of Priests). 6. For the wife and family—to follow his godly monitions, and to abstain from amusements of doubtful character or tendency.

V. MINOR ADVANTAGES ATTACHED TO IT. It gives occasion for the growth in the clergy of those graces of character which come from the cultivation and exercise of the affections—love, cheerfulness, self-restraint for the sake of others, hopes and fears for others—all of which are a prevention of selfishness. It gives a willing and unpaid body of assistants in ministerial work which, though not purely spiritual, has yet to be done by the clergy. It forms a natural link between the clergyman and his parishioners. It ensures the education of a considerable class throughout the country in the principles of religion. It spreads the practices of a religious household to households beyond the clergyman's home, by the natural effects of intermarriage and friendly intercourse. It gives a safe home to many girls seeking domestic service. It dissipates the false idea that the state of celibacy is a purer and more chaste condition than that of matrimony. It gives an opportunity of learning by experience the working of young people's minds and hearts, and women's feelings, which is not, as a rule, to be otherwise safely attained by the clergy.

HOMILIES BY VARIOUS AUTHORS.

Priestly qualifications. Ch. xxi.; cf. Heb. vii. 26—28; 1 Tim. iii. 1—12. From the moralities of the common people we have now to pass to the morality of the priestly class. As special officers, they require special qualifications. Not that there are to be two moralities in the Church of God. This idea is most baneful. Rather do the Divine regulations contemplate the rise of the whole people eventually into an ideal, which both classes are only distantly striving after. The priests, by conforming to certain regulations, were really showing to the people what all should eventually be as the people of God. Keeping this in view, we may profitably notice three requisites of the priesthood.

I. PHYSICAL PERFECTION. God ordained that he should be served only by men physically perfect. A physical blemish disqualified a man from *office*, though not from *support*. This was surely to show that it is the perfect whom God purposes to gather around him. It is not descent nor connection, but personal perfection, which qualifies for Divine service.

Now, in this present life, the ideal was only once realized, viz. in the person of the Great High Priest, Jesus Christ. He was physically and he was spiritually perfect. He was "holy, harmless, undefiled, and separate from sinners." In him, therefore, God secured a perfect servant.

And although God's servants do not as yet realize this idea of personal perfection, they are on the way to realize it. This constitutes the kernel of our Christian hope. The will of God is our sanctification; that is, our perfect adaptation in body, soul, and spirit for his service. Through the grace of God we are "going on to perfection," and a time is coming when we shall be presented "without spot, or wrinkle, or any such thing" before God. Hence we take this physical perfection required of the priests as a promise of perfection through grace in God's own time, that we may all serve him as priests in the sanctuary on high.

II. DOMESTIC PURITY. The Jewish priesthood were educated in the family for their work in the Church of God. Celibacy and isolation were not deemed conducive to sanctity of service. The priest was to be the head of a household, particular in selecting a pure and suitable wife, and ruling his household well. It may be safely asserted that it is only in such circumstances that a full experience of human nature and society can ordinarily be secured. The family is the Divine unit, the training-school for the larger society, the Church. Unless the priests, therefore, had a proper position at home, and governed properly their own households, they were not likely to rule well in the Church of God. Eli's case is surely one in point. A slack hand at home, he showed similar slackness in his public administration, and the interests of religion suffered.

And just as in the former case physical perfection betokened the personal perfection of the future life which the Lord's servants are to secure, so the domestic purity of the priesthood betokens the *perfect society* into which the Lord's people are to come. We see a similar adumbration of this in the New Testament direction about bishops and deacons being the husbands of proper wives and ruling their households well. The government in families is the preparation for the government in the Church of God. The reason is that the Church is the larger family. And so is the completed Church above to be a perfect family. We are on the way to a family circle and a family life of which the home circle on earth is the shadow. God will give his people the opportunity of serving him amid perfect social conditions.

It is in following up this thought that the Church collectively is likened to a pure and perfect bride—the Lamb's wife. It is the same thought which likens heaven to an everlasting *home*. And, indeed, society, as thus constituted and secured, is but the outcome of that Divine nature which, as a Trinity in unity, secured for itself perfect society from everlasting, and creates the same in the glorious purposes of grace.[1]

III. PUBLIC SPIRIT. We mention this as a third characteristic of the priesthood. This was illustrated in perfection by the high priest, who was to allow no private sorrow to interfere with his public service. The other priests were allowed more liberty in this regard, although theirs also had very definite limits; but the one great principle reinforced by these regulations was public spirit. The priest was to feel that, as a public officer, a representative man, it was his duty to sacrifice the personal and private to the common weal.

Now, it is instructive to observe that it was this principle which Jesus carried out all through. His life and death were the sacrifice of the private and the personal to the public need. The same spirit is imparted by the grace of God, and is more or less

---

[1] Cf. Pressensé's admirable volume, 'La Famille Chrétienne,' *passim.*

faithfully carried out by the Lord's people.   Moreover, we are on the way to its perfect illustration in the felicities of the heavenly world.   There none shall be for self or for a party, but all for the common weal.   Lord Macaulay represents ancient Rome as the embodiment of public spirit.

> "Then none was for a party;
>   Then all were for the State;
> Then the great man helped the poor,
>   And the poor man loved the great;
> Then lands were fairly portioned;
>   Then spoils were fairly sold;
> The Romans were like brothers
>   In the brave days of old."

However faithfully this reflects the condition of things in the golden age of Rome, one thing is certain, that the public spirit it indicates shall have its perfect embodiment in the society above.   Public life, divested of all suspicion of selfishness, will characterize God's redeemed ones.   All personal and private interests shall then merge themselves in the common weal, and as his servants serve God, they shall see his face and live out his public spirit.—R. M. E.

Vers. 1—24.—*Law of holiness for the priests.*   In all circumstances and relations of life the priests must be an example of purity.   The higher the office, the more conspicuous the example, and therefore the more solemn the duty of preserving both body and soul from defilement.

I. The blamelessness of the ministry a necessity of the Church's life. 1. Spiritual leaders a natural requirement and a Divine appointment.   We want teachers both in word and act.   The priesthood of the old dispensation was abolished, but in the new there are those who, both by their superior knowledge and piety and by their consecration of life to the sanctuary, become the responsible leaders of the Church. 2. An impure priesthood the greatest calamity to the cause of religion.   Like priest, like people.   The corruptions of the Middle Ages mainly traceable to the defilement of those who should have been first and foremost in faithfulness to truth and duty.   The hindrance to the spread of Christianity now is largely the indifference and blindness and worldliness of those who serve the sanctuary.   The life of the public representative of religion should be above reproach in all things.

II. God's house and cause should have the choicest and best of human capacity and energy devoted to it. 1. That the Church itself may be edified and become a praise unto God.   Our religion demands and satisfies our highest efforts.   The truth of God's Word is inexhaustible food for the mind and delight to the heart.   Endless scope for the development of human powers in the service of God.   Worship should be spotlessly pure, a glorifying of humanity in the light of Divine favour. 2. The world is won to God, not by hiding the graces of God's people, but by making the light to shine before men.   No limit to the demand upon the talents and energies of the Church. We should urge those naturally gifted and superior to take their proper places.   Yet natural defects can be wonderfully supplied by special Divine gifts.   Much work has been done by the physically weak, and even by those whose characters were faulty.—R.

Vers. 1—15.—*Distinctions and degrees in obligation.*   In the kingdom of God there is, as a rule, but one law for all subjects.   What applies to one applies to another.   The same principles of righteousness are obligatory on both sexes, on all classes, conditions, nations, generations of men.   This is importantly true; but it is a truth subject to certain not unimportant qualifications.   Of this latter we have—

I. Illustrations in the Mosaic Law. 1. Respecting ceremonial defilement certain distinctions were drawn.   (1) The commonalty were bound to avoid all defilement (by touching the dead, etc.), whenever it was practicable to do so; but it was anticipated that they would be compelled, sometimes, to become unclean, and legal purifications were accordingly enjoined.   (2) But the priests were to take peculiar care not to incur this ceremonial defilement (vers. 1—4).   Allowance was made for natural human feeling (vers. 2, 3), but the occasions when they might permit themselves to become unclean were carefully prescribed. (3) And the high priest was not permitted to incur defilement by "going in to any dead body" under any circumstances whatever, not even "for his father, or for his mother" (ver. 11). 2. So, respecting marriage alliances: (1) the whole people were under certain severe prohibitions (Deut. vii. 3, 4); but (2) the priests were more circumscribed (ver. 7); and (3) the high priest was still more limited in his choice (vers. 13, 14). The Hebrew nation was holy unto the Lord, and was required to separate itself from the actions of surrounding peoples; the priests were peculiarly holy, and must, therefore, be especially careful to walk in purity; the high priest was, in position and function, the holiest of all, and on him it was most particularly incumbent to shun every possible defilement, and to do that which was purest and worthiest in the sight of God. We have to consider what are—

II. THE ILLUSTRATIONS OF THIS PRINCIPLE UNDER THE GOSPEL. 1. Respecting *the avoidance of evil*, we may say that (1) the members of the Church of Christ are bound to avoid all appearance of wrong. They who bear the Name of the holy Saviour, though humblest members of the smallest Church, are, as professed followers of his, bound to walk as becometh the gospel of Christ, in all purity of heart and blamelessness of life; but (2) ministers of his Church, and their sons and daughters (vers. 9, 15), are especially bound to shun everything which would bring discredit on the holy Name of the Divine Redeemer (see 1 Tim. iii. 2—7; Titus i. 6—9). 2. And respecting the *contraction of intimate alliances* (especially the life-long alliance, marriage), we may contend that (1) all who are the avowed followers of Christ are bound to be circumspect in this most important matter (see 1 Cor. vii. 39; 2 Cor. vi. 14). The subject of forming a life-long alliance, by which such serious spiritual consequences *must* inevitably follow to two human souls, and such great and immeasurable results *may* follow, affecting numbers of human hearts and lives, and reaching to the most distant time, is not to be dismissed to the region of harmless but helpless humour, nor is it to be left to the direction of careless fancy or of worldly policy; it is a matter for the exercise of the fullest, profoundest, heavenliest wisdom which man and woman can command. (2) Of those who minister in the Church of Christ, it is yet more urgently demanded that in the intimacies they form and the life-long friendships they contract, they shall have regard not to a transient whim, nor to worldly advantage, but, first and foremost, to the glory of Christ and the well-being of those whom they live to serve.—C.

Vers. 16—24.—*Unblemished service.* We gain three truths from these verses.

I. THE PRIMARY TRUTH, INTENDED FOR THE HEBREW NATION. The special instruction contained in this passage is that the altar of God was to be honoured in every possible way; therefore to be preserved from everything that would bring it into disregard; and therefore to be unapproached by any priest who had a bodily blemish. It was impossible for the people to dissociate the altar itself from those who ministered thereat; if, therefore, any physical disfigurement had been allowed, and those who were uncomely or misshapen had been permitted to officiate, the sacred ordinances of God would have suffered, in some degree, from the association in thought of the man with the thing. The priest with a blemish might not "come nigh unto the altar, . . . that he profane not my sanctuaries" (ver. 23). We may learn, in passing, that it is almost impossible to overestimate the influence for good or ill which is unconsciously exerted by those who minister, in any function, in the Church of Christ on the popular estimate of their office.

II. THE SECONDARY TRUTH, APPLICABLE TO US ALL. In a typical system it is necessary that the body should frequently represent the soul, the organs of the one picturing the faculties of the other. The requirement of a perfect bodily frame on the part of those who "approached to offer the bread of their God" (ver. 17), intimated to them, and now indicates to us, the essential and eternal truth that *the best is to be brought to the service of God :* not that with which we can most easily part, but the very best that we can bring. 1. Not the unattractive service ("flat nose," "scabbed," etc.), but that which is as beautiful and inviting in its form as we can make it. 2. Not unacquaintance with our subject ("a blind man"), but the fullest possible acquisition and understanding. 3. Not an example which is defective, a walking which is irregular (a "lame man," "crookbackt"), but an upright, honourable demeanour, "walking in the commandments of the Lord blameless." 4. Not a feeble and faltering delivery ("brokenhanded"), but a facile, skilful "handling of the Word of God." We may note, before we pass, that the God whom we serve is *expectant, but is not inconsiderate.* He who refuses to allow a priest with any blemish "to approach to offer the bread of his God," expressly desired that such priest should "eat the bread of his God, both of the most holy, and of the holy" (ver. 22); he might not serve, but he should not suffer, on account of a bodily misfortune. God requires of us that, in approaching him, we should bring not our exhaustion but our freshness, not our hurried but our patient preparation, not our remnants but our substance, not our worthless belongings but our worthiest self; at the same time, he makes every allowance for our weakness, our infirmity, our human feebleness and frailty: "he knoweth our frame; he remembereth that we are dust."

III. A FURTHER TRUTH, RELATING TO THE FUTURE LIFE. We dare not hope to render to God any absolutely unblemished service here. "If we say that we have no sin, we deceive ourselves" (1 John i. 8). Here our holiest services are marred by spiritual imperfection. It should be our aim, our prayer, our endeavour, to make our worship, our work, and our life as little blemished as may be; to make all our service as elevated in spirit and motive as may be; and doing this, we may look confidently and joyously onward to the time when "his servants shall serve him" in the very fulness of their strength and joy, and when their service shall be not only undimmed by any gathering tear, but unstained with any rising thought of sin.—C.

Vers. 1—24.—*The perfection of the priesthood.* The priests, when officiating, and eminently so the high priest, were types of Christ. It was, therefore, needful that they should be holy and without blemish. They were also types of Christians, in which capacity also they must be holy, for true Christians are so, though not always without blemish. In any case, then—

I. THE PRIESTS MUST BE HOLY. 1. *They must be holy, as types of Christ.* (1) They "offered the bread of their God." So the "offerings made by fire" are called (ver. 6). The fire of the altar of Calvary is the Godhead in which the body of Christ became a sacrifice upon which the justice and mercy of God can feast. Christ, as our Priest, thus offers himself unto God. (2) They are "crowned" with the "anointing oil of their God" (vers. 10, 12). The anointing represented the lustre of the Holy Spirit's grace. When Jesus was "anointed with the oil of gladness" on the holy mount, he was "crowned with glory and honour," and that too "for the suffering of death" (comp. Heb. ii. 9; 2 Pet. i. 17). Thus was he "consecrated to put on the garments" of his resurrection, to enter the holy places for us (ver. 10). 2. *They must not defile themselves by mourning for the dead.* (1) If not officiating, they might defile themselves for kindred of the first degree. For a mother, father, son, daughter, brother, and for a sister that is a virgin. But not for a sister that is married. She is "one flesh" with her husband, incorporated in another family. (2) For his wife he shall not mourn (see ver. 4, margin; also Ezek. xxiv. 16—18). The wife of the true Priest is his Church; and she can never die; the gates of Hades cannot prevail against her (Matt. xvi. 18). Even her members do not suffer through death; it is but the gate of their promotion (John xi. 25, 26). (3) He must not make marks of distraction—baldness, quarters in the beard, cuttings in the flesh (ver. 5). What has the type of Christ to do with the abominations of the heathen? In profaning themselves they profaned their God (see ver. 6; and comp. John i. 14). (4) The priest officiating must not mourn; nor shall he leave the sanctuary to defile it. Jehovah dwells in the sanctuary of Christ's Body. The priesthood can never leave that sanctuary (ver. 12; Heb. vii. 23—28). 3. *They must be holy in their marriage.* (1) No priest must marry a whore, or one deflowered or divorced (ver. 7). The Babylonish harlot, then, however impudent and specious her pretensions, cannot be the Bride of Christ. Those who would be joined to Christ must not seek membership with her (Rev. xvii. 1—5; xviii. 4). (2) The bride of the high priest must be a virgin of his own people (vers. 13, 14). The descriptions of the true Church of Christ are widely different from those of the woman of the seven-hilled city (see 2 Cor. xi. 2; Eph. v. 27; Rev. xii. and xxi.). (3) His children must be holy (ver. 14). They are the children of the truth; the seed of Abraham's faith. If his daughter play the whore, she defiles him; and to purify himself he must give her up to be burnt with fire (ver. 9; Gen. xxxviii. 24). Such, accordingly, is to be the fate of the scarlet lady (Rev. xvii. 16, 17; xviii. 9, 10; xix. 2, 3).

II. THE PRIESTS MUST BE WITHOUT BLEMISH. 1. *Those who typified Christ must be so.* (1) We have an enumeration of blemishes, any of which would disqualify for that sacred office (vers. 18—20). No doubt Jesus was physically, as well as mentally and spiritually, a perfect human being. Those expressions in Isaiah (lii. 14; liii. 2) obviously had reference to his sufferings and humiliations. (2) He that had a blemish among the sons of Aaron "must not come nigh to offer the bread of his God." Had not Christ been perfectly free from sin, he could not have atoned for us (ver. 17; 1 Pet. i. 19). (3) "He shall not go in unto the vail" (ver. 23). He shall not represent him that is the Way to heaven, who is qualified to sanctify the people with his own blood (Heb. vii. 26—28; xiii. 10). 2. *Blemished priests might represent Christians.* (1) "The bread of their God they may eat" (ver. 22). Men that have infirmities may live on Christ; but he that represents that Bread must be without blemish. (2) Blemished ones might eat of the holy things, but unclean ones must not. Between infirmities and sins there is a wide difference. Infirmities do not exclude men from fellowship with God, but sins do (Isa. lix. 1, 2; Rom. viii. 35—39). Those who eat the bread of the Eucharist should be holy in life, else they profane the Name they profess to revere. (3) Too frequently have blemished priests represented gospel ministers. The New Testament gives laws to ministers and their wives; and those who instruct others should do so by example as well as precept (1 Tim. iii. 11; iv. 12). They should not be "blind," viz. to the meaning of God's Word. They should not be "lame" in hand or foot, but able to show an example in working and walking. They must have nothing superfluous nor deficient. "They must not be wise *above*," or wise *without*, " that which is written." The priest who was " holy to his God " was, therefore, to be holy to his people (vers. 6—8); and so must the gospel minister be esteemed for his work's sake (1 Thess. v. 13).—J. A. M.

EXPOSITION.

CHAPTER XXII.

This chapter, which is a continuation of ch. xxi., (1) commands that the ceremonially defiled priest shall not officiate or partake of the sacrificial offerings; (2) declares who may and who may not partake of the priests' portions of the sacrifices; (3) orders that every sacrificial victim be unblemished.

Vers. 1—9.—In the previous chapter, the priests have been commanded to avoid occasions of ceremonial defilement, but there are times in which they must be unclean. At these times they are here instructed that they must abstain from their priestly functions, and not even eat of the priests' portions until they have been cleansed. The command to **Aaron and to his sons, that they separate themselves from the holy things of the children of Israel**, in ver. 2, must be read in the light of the following verses, and understood to mean that they are *to separate themselves from the holy things* when they are unclean. The different forms of uncleanness which are to produce this effect are enumerated in vers. 4—6. In most cases the uncleanness would not last

beyond sunset on the day on which it was incurred, but occasionally, as when a priest became a leper, a permanent disqualification would be caused, or one that lasted for a considerable length of time. The law with respect to abstaining from holy things while unclean is to be of permanent obligation. Whoever disobeys it is to be **cut off from God's presence**; that is, he is to be excluded from the sanctuary by being deprived of his priestly office. Ver. 8 repeats the prohibition of eating flesh containing blood.

Vers. 10—13.—The previous paragraph having forbidden the priests to eat of the holy things while in a state of ceremonial uncleanness, naturally leads to the question, Who has the right of eating them? The answer is, the priest's family. The members of the priest's family here specified are those only about whom any question might have arisen, namely, the slaves, who, as being incorporated into the priest's household, have a right of eating of the priestly food not enjoyed by lodgers in his house or by servants hired with his money; and married daughters who have returned to their father's roof in consequence of the death of their husband, or of being divorced, without any children of their own. Under these circumstances, it is ruled that they become once more a part of the priest's family, and able to exercise the privileges of that position. The priest's wife and sons and unmarried daughters are not here mentioned, as no question arose about them.

Ver. 14.—As the sacrificial meals made a part of the stipends of the priestly body, any one who inadvertently took a share in them by eating of the holy thing unwittingly, when he had no right to do so, had to refund the value of the meat, with one fifth, that is, twenty per cent., added to it. He thus acknowledged that he had "committed a trespass in the holy things of the Lord," the case falling under the rule given in ch. v. 15, 16, "And he shall make amends for the harm that he hath done in the holy thing, and shall add the fifth part thereto, and give it unto the priest." In the fifth chapter a trespass offering of a ram is also ordered, which, though not specified, is probably understood here also.

Vers. 15, 16.—These verses present some difficulties of construction. The rendering of the Authorized Version is as follows: And they shall not profane the holy things of the children of Israel, which they offer unto the Lord; or suffer them to bear the iniquity of trespass, when they eat their holy things: for I the Lord do sanctify them. If this rendering is accepted, it would mean that the priests are not to profane the holy things by any irregularity on their part as to the eating of them, nor to suffer laymen to incur the guilt of a trespass by eating them. The marginal rendering, which is to be preferred, gives the passage as follows: And they shall not profane the holy things of the children of Israel, which they offer unto the Lord; or lade themselves with the iniquity of trespass in their eating. According to this translation, the meaning would be that laymen (who had been spoken of in the previous verse) should not profane the holy things, or become guilty of a trespass (as defined in ver. 15) by eating them. Technically and literally, David was guilty of this trespass in an aggravated form, when he and his followers ate the shewbread at Nob (1 Sam. xxi. 6), for the shewbread was not only holy, but most holy. But his act is excused by our Lord, on the plea of necessity (Matt. xii. 3, 4), even though it was done on the sabbath day (1 Sam. xxi. 5, margin).

Vers. 17—25.—Just as the priests who offer to the Lord are to be ceremonially and morally holy, so the animals offered to him are to be physically perfect, in order (1) to be types of a future perfect Victim, (2) to symbolize the "perfect heart" which God requires to be given to him, and (3) to teach the duty of offering to him of our best. Whatsoever

hath a blemish, that shall ye not offer. The list of blemishes and malformations which exclude from the altar is given; they are such as deform the animal, and make it less valuable: blind, or broken, or maimed, or having a wen, or scurvy, or scabbed, ye shall not offer these unto the Lord, nor any animal that is bruised, or crushed, or broken, or cut, that is, castrated in any manner. The clause following the mention of castration—neither shall ye make any offering thereof in your land—literally translated, neither shall ye make in your land, probably forbids castration altogether, not merely the offering of castrated animals in sacrifice. The expression, Ye shall offer at your own will, should be understood, as before, for your acceptance (see note on ch. ii. 1). Only one exception is made as to blemished offerings; an animal that hath any thing superfluous or lacking in his parts may be offered for a freewill offering, but not for a vow (for the distinction of these offerings, see note on ch. vii. 16). These rules as to unblemished victims are to apply to the offerings of strangers as well as of Israelites.

Vers. 26, 27.—Extreme youth is to be regarded as a blemish in an animal in the same way as other defects. During the young creature's first week of existence it is not considered as having arrived at the perfection of its individual and separate life, and therefore only from the eighth day and thenceforth it shall be accepted for an offering made by fire unto the Lord. Up to what age an animal might be offered is not stated. Gideon is narrated as offering a bullock of seven years old (Judg. vi. 25).

Ver. 28.—A lesson of charity is added. A young animal and its mother are not to be killed (though reference is specially made to sacrifice, the general word, not the sacrificial term, for slaying is used) on the same day, just as the kid is not to be seethed in its mother's milk (Exod. xxiii. 19; Deut. xiv. 21), nor the mother bird be taken from the nest with the young (Deut. xxii. 6). Thus we see that the feelings of the human heart are not to be rudely shocked by an act of apparent cruelty, even when no harm is thereby done to the object of that act. Mercy is to be taught by forbidding anything which may blunt the sentiment of mercy in the human heart.

Vers. 29, 30.—Two forms of peace offerings, the vowed and the voluntary offerings, having been mentioned in ver. 21, the law as to the third form, thanksgiving offerings, is repeated from ch. vii. 15 (where see note).

Vers. 31—33.—These verses form the conclusion of the Section and of the Part, enjoining obedience to God's commandments, reverence for his Name, and consequent holiness.

HOMILETICS.

Vers. 17—25.—*The perfection demanded in the sacrificial victims* contains a typical, a symbolical, and a moral lesson.

I. THEY MUST BE PERFECT, THAT THEY MAY BE TYPES OF CHRIST. The perfect Victim must not be represented by anything imperfect. There are but few points in which the perfection of Christ, both absolute and in relation to the work which as the appointed Victim he was to fulfil, could be foreshadowed by the animals offered in sacrifice, but this was one—that they should be without blemish and perfect of their kind. "The blood of Christ who through the Eternal Spirit offered himself *without spot* to God," is the antitype, we are taught in the Epistle to the Hebrews, to "the blood of bulls, and of goats, and the ashes of an heifer, sprinkling the unclean," which "sanctifieth to the purifying of the flesh" (Heb. ix. 13, 14). For "ye know," says St. Peter, "that ye were redeemed . . . with the precious blood of Christ, as of a lamb *without blemish and without spot*" (1 Pet. i. 18, 19); "who did no sin" (1 Pet. ii. 22); who "gave himself for us an offering and a sacrifice to God for a sweetsmelling savour" (Eph. v. 2). The physical freedom from blemish on the part of the animal typifies the "spotlessness" of Christ.

II. THEY MUST BE PERFECT, THAT THEY MAY SYMBOLIZE THE PERFECT HEART WITH WHICH ALL SERVICE MUST BE DONE TO GOD. They symbolized the integrity of soul with which the offerer made his offering, and the purity of intention required of all who present themselves or anything that they do to God and his service. A gift to God is unacceptable, and not accepted, if there be in it *anything superfluous*, viz. self-display, or *anything lacking*, namely, the spirit of love. God chose those whom he afterwards called into his Church to "be holy and without blame (or blemish) before him in love" (Eph. i. 4), "that ye may stand perfect and complete in all the will of God" (Col. iv. 12), "that ye may be perfect and entire, wanting nothing" (Jas. i. 4). Imperfection must always mark man and his work, seeing that "the infection of nature doth remain, yea in them that are regenerated" (Art. IX.); but the Christian must not rest satisfied with aiming at anything but the highest. His purpose, however marred, must be to please God perfectly.

III. THEY MUST BE PERFECT, BECAUSE WHAT WE GIVE TO GOD MUST BE COSTLY TO US. "And the king said unto Araunah, Nay; but I will surely buy it of thee at a price: neither will I offer burnt offerings unto the Lord my God of that which doth cost me nothing. So David bought the threshingfloor and the oxen for fifty shekels of silver" (2 Sam. xxiv. 24). "And if ye offer the blind for sacrifice, is it not evil? and if ye offer the lame and sick, is it not evil? offer it now unto thy governor; will he be pleased with thee, or accept thy person? saith the Lord of hosts" (Mal. i. 8). "But cursed be the deceiver, which hath in his flock a male, and voweth, and sacrificeth unto the Lord a corrupt thing: for I am a great King, saith the Lord of hosts, and my Name is dreadful among the heathen" (Mal. i. 14). The cost of our gifts to God need not be absolutely great—the widow's two mites, which make a farthing, may be more than all that the rich cast into the treasury (Mark xii. 41—44). Whatever we give, it must be of our best, the best effort of our intellect, the best affections of our hearts. Whatever we are most attached to, that we must be prepared to give up, if God demands the sacrifice at our hands.

HOMILIES BY VARIOUS AUTHORS.

Vers. 1—33.—*Holiness of priests and sacrifices.* While much that appertained only to a temporary dispensation, still *great principles* included in the formal regulations, as—

I. RELIGION SANCTIFIES, preserves, and perfects the whole humanity of man. 1. It preserves the true order—God first, the creature subject to the Creator. 2. It utilizes the central power of human nature, the moral and spiritual. The mind is the man, and the mind is not mere intellect, but moral consciousness and aspiration after God.

3. It puts the individual and the social in their true relation to that which supports both—the positive and public worship of God. The temple at Jerusalem represented the centre of the nation, Jehovah's throne. Humanity can be, will be, developed into a true family of nations only round the house of God. All non-religious influences are disintegrating to the nation and the world.

II. THE LIFE OF MAN IS THE SANCTIFICATION OF ALL OTHER LIFE ON THE EARTH. The lower natures depend on the higher. God has taught us by his Law not only to use them, but to reverence them and to hallow their instincts and the laws of nature as exhibited in them. Science may discover secrets, but it will not protect the weak. The reverence for that which is below us is even more a yielding up of our nature to the Spirit of God than the mere bowing prostrate before that which is above us. The selfishness and tyranny of the stronger over the weaker can only be cast out by religion.

III. ALL LAW IS CONSISTENT WITH FREE AGENCY. " At your own will." The true service of God is that which the heart renders. We blend our will with God's will in the acceptable life. At your will, but by the regulations of the Law. The mere capricious individualism of the present day is no true liberty, but becomes the most degrading bondage. The covenant relation of Jehovah with his people lay at the foundation of their obedience: " I hallow you," therefore hallow my commandments and my Name. In that loving bond of sanctification all believers find their strength. They are not their own, they are bought with a price. Paul rejoiced to be a "slave of Jesus Christ." The Jews made their Law unto death, not life, because they departed from its simplicity and forgot its spirituality, and " made the Word of God of none effect by their traditions," forging their own fetters. The key-note of the Law is redemption. " I am the Lord which brought you out of Egypt," etc. The key-note of redemption is love.—R.

Priestly disqualifications. Ch. xxii. ; cf. Matt. xxv. 31—46. We saw that inherited infirmity, such as is mentioned in vers. 18—21 of last chapter, while it excludes from office, does not exclude from sustenance. We now come across a disqualification sufficient to exclude from both office and support, and this is *contracted defilement.* Any priest venturing before God with uncleanness upon him will be cut off from his presence. We are taught hereby—

I. THAT IT IS CONTRACTED, NOT TRANSMITTED, DEFILEMENT WHICH NECESSITATES COMPLETE EXILE FROM JEHOVAH. The priest's child providentially scarred or maimed, whose blemish has been from the womb, and in which he had no voluntary share, which excluded properly from *office,* is not excluded from sustenance from the altar ; while, on the other hand, he who has through negligence or waywardness contracted defilement is, while it lasts, excluded altogether from the privileges of the priesthood.

The bearing of such an arrangement upon the question of *original sin* is plain on the least thought. The fact of original sin will not be questioned by any one who studies intelligently the question of heredity. Moreover, "representative responsibility," as a principle of providence, shows how we are held responsible for acts of others in which we have had no conscious share. At the same time, it is consolatory to think that transmitted evil will not of itself condemn its possessor to perpetual exile from God. When an infant dies, who has never been sufficiently advanced to contract any conscious defilement, who has never added to original sin any actual transgression, it is comforting to think that the righteous Governor will not exclude any such from the privilege of approaching him, but will purge away their inheritance of evil, and fit them for his everlasting fellowship. We believe in the salvation of the great multitude who die before coming to the years of discretion.

II. CASUAL, AS DISTINGUISHED FROM PERMANENT, CONNECTION WITH THE PRIESTHOOD DISQUALIFIES A PERSON FROM PARTAKING OF THE THINGS OF THE ALTAR. No mere casual guest, or even a hired servant of a priest's, was to eat of the holy things. If a servant had been purchased, and so became personally incorporated with the priestly family, he might eat of them. There is a corresponding casual and a corresponding permanent association with the Lord's work. Only those who enter on it with whole hearts, who dedicate themselves to it, body, soul, and spirit, need expect to participate in its privileges; while the mere casual associate will find himself excluded in the end.

III. The sacrifices were to be as unblemished as the officiating priests; any physical defect disqualified them from acceptance. The unblemished character of the sacrifices teaches the same truth which we have already considered. As the sacrifices were practically substitutions, their perfection was to teach man not only that his Substitute must be perfect if God would accept him, but that he himself must be perfected, if he is to serve God in the great hereafter in a priestly spirit. At the same time, man is encouraged in the present state to offer what he can, even though it be not perfect. God does not insist on the absolute perfection of the work of his people. If it is willing (ver. 23)—if it is really a "freewill offering"—then God will accept it in the spirit in which it is given. The perfection is to be kept steadily in view as the ideal to which we must always be struggling; meanwhile, we are to be doing all we can with willing minds, even though our work is often poor at best.

IV. Inhuman acts disqualify sacrifices otherwise acceptable. Thus a bullock, sheep, or goat, would not be acceptable till after the eighth day. It would have been inhuman to have denied it its week with its dam. Moreover, may not the seven days with the dam, like the seven days before the man-child's circumcision, represent a perfect period spent under parental care, and thus become an emblem of the providential use of the family institution?

Again, the dam and the young were not to be put to death on the same day. It has an inhuman appearance about it, like the seething of a kid in its mother's milk; and God arranged that the terms of the fifth commandment should be illustrated by, and not transgressed, even among the lower animals.

While, therefore, sacrificial worship entailed much suffering on the part of the innocent victims, there was a humane element to run through the service of the priests, and inhumanity would disqualify them from sacrificially serving God.—R. M. E.

Ver. 3.—*The service of abstention.* There were certain bodily conditions which, under the Levitical institutions, were suggestive of spiritual impurity, and those who suffered from them were accounted ceremonially unclean. Priests thus affected were disqualified for the ministry of the tabernacle, and were deprived, for a time, of sacerdotal privileges: they might not "go unto the holy things." Any priest who was disobedient to this precept would be "cut off from the presence of the Lord." To those who were thus unfortunate there was one service left,—the service of obedient abstention. They would be disappointed; they might feel somewhat humiliated; but there was left to them the opportunity of fulfilling the acceptable service of *offering not* or *eating not* "unto the Lord" (see Rom. xiv. 6).

It often happens to us that by some misfortune—perhaps, as here, some bodily affliction—we are disabled and detained from active service: it may be from (1) Christian work, or (2) public worship, or (3) daily duty (business or household activities). That which is unavoidable and for which we are not responsible may shut us out from many valued privileges. In this case we must render the service of abstention. We can—

I. Submit in patience.

II. Believe with cheerful confidence: have faith to accept the truth that ".they also serve who only stand and wait;" that God is as well pleased with the passive service of those whom he desires to "be still," as with those who—

> "... at his bidding speed,
> And post o'er land and ocean without rest."

III. Wait in hope. The hour will come, here or hereafter, sooner or later, when all bodily disabilities will have disappeared, and fullest access be given to the presence of the Lord.—C.

Vers. 10—15.—*The guilt of profanation.* That which had been offered in sacrifice was "holy unto the Lord;" these were "holy things" (ver. 10); "I the Lord do sanctify them" (ver. 16). They might only be partaken of by the priests and their families. Hence we have here a precise limitation of membership of the family; it included the returned daughter and the permanent servant, but did not include the hireling or the visitor, etc. We may note, in passing, (1) the regard which God paid (and still pays) to the sanctity of family life, and our duty to guard it ; (2) the fact, on the other hand, that mere blood relationship does not suffice to secure the favour of God; witness Nadab and Abihu. The son of the holiest minister of Christ may be a servant of the evil one, and an enemy of God. But *the* lesson of the text is—

I. THAT GOD WOULD HAVE US SEPARATE SOME THINGS FROM OTHERS WHICH WE MUST TREAT AS SACRED. "I the Lord do sanctify them" (ver. 16). That which is closely connected with himself is particularly "holy,"—his Name, his truth, his worship; also our own spiritual and immortal nature; the world which is to come, etc.

II. THAT WE ARE UNDER SOME TEMPTATION TO DISREGARD HIS HOLY WILL. Forgetfulness, the spirit of levity and untimely humour, the contagiousness of human example, that tendency towards the formal and mechanical which belongs to our frail humanity,—these things will account for it. The forms which this irreverence or profanation takes are manifold: (1) taking in vain the holy Name of God, our Father, Saviour, Sanctifier; (2) misuse of scriptural words—those especially which are of peculiar sacredness; (3) irreverence in prayer or praise; (4) the utterance of Divine truth by unhallowed, unappreciative lips; (5) the partaking of the sacramental elements by those who are unreconciled to God; (6) misappropriation of substance which has been dedicated to the service of Christ.

III. THAT MINISTERS OF CHRIST SHOULD BE SPECIALLY ON THEIR GUARD AGAINST THIS COMMON AND OFFENSIVE SIN. There are two reasons why those who minister in holy things should "watch and pray" against the commission of this wrong-doing. 1. They are under special temptation to commit it. Their very professional familiarity with the truth and service of God is likely to beget irreverence, utterance without feeling, action without inspiration. 2. Their example is more influential. Irreverence on the part of the minister is certain, in time if not immediately, to tell on the people. It will be communicated to them; or, at the very least, it will seriously lessen and lower the impression which would otherwise be made on their hearts and lives.—C.

Vers. 17—30.—*Characteristics of acceptable service.* The very fact that all the points here referred to have been fully brought out before lends strong emphasis to them as matters of vital importance in the estimation of God. If our worship and service are to be acceptable, there must be—

I. SPONTANEITY OF SPIRIT. "Ye shall offer at your own will" (ver. 19); "when ye will offer . . . offer it at your own will" (ver. 29). There is a wilfulness in worship which is blamable (Col. ii. 23); but there is a willingness, a "cheerfulness in giving," which is peculiarly acceptable unto God. The service which is rendered of necessity, under strong constraint and against the inclination of the spirit, has the least virtue, if, indeed, it have any at all. That which proceeds from a heart in fullest sympathy with the act, delighting to do the will of God (Ps. xl. 8), is well pleasing unto him.

II. COMPARATIVE EXCELLENCY. "Ye shall offer . . . a male without blemish, . . . whatsoever hath a blemish, that shall ye not offer: for it shall not be acceptable for you," etc. (vers. 19—22). If the Hebrew worshipper brought that creature from flock or herd which, as being blemished, was least valuable, he did that which was offensive rather than acceptable. He put his Creator and Redeemer (ver. 33) in the second place, and his own material interests in the first place. He was to bring his best to the holiest. We, too, must avoid this fatal error—must rise to this spiritual height. We must not put off *our* Redeemer with that which we shall miss the least—in kind, in substance, in time; we must bring to his altar the sweetness, the strength, and the beauty of all that we have to bring ; we must reserve the choice treasures for his hand of love. So far as may be in a world of imperfection, our offering to a Divine Saviour "shall be perfect to be accepted" (ver. 21).

III. REGARD FOR A SOLEMN PLEDGE. Absolute perfection, the positively whole and unblemished animal, might be difficult, or in some cases impossible, to secure. Hence some relaxation from the rule was allowed in the case of the free-will offering. But in the redemption of a vow no such departure was permitted (ver. 23). Any vow which was made unto God was considered to be in the last degree obligatory (Deut. xxiii. 21, 22; Eccles. v. 4, 5; Ps. lxxvi. 11). When "God's vows are upon us," when we stand pledged before him (1) to discharge certain functions, or (2) to abstain from certain evils or perils, we should feel that we are bound with peculiarly strong bonds to make our sacrifice, of whatever kind it be, in its fulness and integrity.

IV. ABSENCE OF IMPURITY. (Ver. 20; see ch. vii. 15—18.)

V. PREFERENCE OF THE DIVINE WILL TO HUMAN GRATIFICATION. "Strangers" might bring their offerings to the house of the Lord. It was a pleasing and gratifying thing to witness the stranger bringing his bountiful tribute to the altar of Jehovah. It gratified the national feeling. But nothing might be accepted from the foreigner which was not worthy to be laid on the altar of the Holy One of Israel. His will to receive only unblemished offerings must outweigh their readiness or eagerness to receive outside testimony to the excellency of their institutions. We may be too eager to welcome the tribute of the stranger; we must require of him that he worship in sincerity and purity. The honour and the will of God should be more to us than the passing gratification we gain from any source whatever. Whatever we lose, he must be honoured and obeyed.—C.

Vers. 27, 28.—*The culture of kindness.* The words of the text remind us, by contrast, of two truths which are of value to us as disciples of Christ. 1. That the human spirit is never too young to be offered to God, whether (1) in parental devotion or (2) in self-dedication (ver. 27). 2. That two generations of the same family may offer themselves simultaneously to the service of God. Parent and child have not unfrequently made profession, in the same hour, of attachment to Christ, and have simultaneously "given themselves unto the Lord." But the main lesson to be learnt is *the culture of kindness.* This was the end of the Divine precept. There would be an apparent ruthlessness in taking away the young immediately from its dam, and also in slaying mother and offspring together on the same day. Therefore these acts must be avoided. Everything should be done to foster kindness of heart, considerateness of feeling, as well as justice, purity, righteousness of life. The culture of kindness is an act of piety. It is well to consider—

I. THE TWO SPHERES IN WHICH IT SHOULD BE EXHIBITED. 1. The human world: the home; the social circle; mankind at large. 2. The animal world. Everything that has life has feeling, and has a claim on our considerateness. We may add to its pleasure or may multiply its pain; may prolong or shorten life.

II. THE TWO MOTIVES BY WHICH WE SHOULD BE ACTUATED. 1. The inherent excellency of kindness. Unkindness is a shameful, shocking, deteriorating thing; kindness is intrinsically beautiful, admirable. 2. The will of God. These his laws (and see Deut. xxii. 6; xxv. 4) are an indication of his will; and we may be sure it is the will of him who creates and sustains sentient life that his human children should be kind to the dumb creatures of his thought and skill.

III. THE TWO SOURCES OF CULTIVATION. 1. That of our own minds. We must impress on ourselves that it is no less a tyrannical and cruel thing to use our great power to oppress the feeble creatures at our feet than it would be for others of vastly superior size and strength to our own to oppress and injure us. We must remind ourselves of those obvious considerations which will foster kind feelings and restrain from hurtful actions. 2. That of those who teach us. The parents and teachers of youth who do not inculcate kindness toward the feeble, whether of the animal or the human world, sadly neglect their duty to their charge. Young people may grow up ignorant of languages or sciences, and they may yet be admirable and useful men and women; but those who have not learnt to hate cruelty and to admire kindness will have a blot on their character which no attainments will hide.—C.

Vers. 1—16.—*The eating of the holy things.* We have seen, in the preceding chapter, that blemishes which precluded a priest from ministering at the altar did not hinder him from eating of the holy things. The ordinary Israelite, therefore, would not, by similar blemishes, be debarred from the privileges of his religion. There are, however, other things which would disqualify. These are now brought under our notice, together with the provisions by which they might be removed. Consider—

I. DISQUALIFICATIONS FOR EATING OF THE HOLY THINGS. 1. *With respect to priests.* (1) A priest would be disqualified by any uncleanness in his flesh; thus, if he were a leper. The reason is that leprosy was a notable emblem of sin. Or if he had any running issue. Such things are in themselves loathsome, and evince a corrupt state of the body, and therefore fittingly represent moral corruption. This, under every dispensation, excludes men from that fellowship with God which was shadowed in the eating of the holy things. (2) He would be disqualified by contact with a human corpse, or with the carcase of any unclean animal. The moral lesson here is that "evil communications corrupt good manners," that the "friendship of the world is enmity against God." 2. *With respect to the families of priests.* (1) The stranger that sojourneth in Israel must become regularly proselyted to entitle him to the privileges of the Law. So those who would enjoy the corresponding spiritual privileges of the gospel must first become disciples of Jesus. (2) The hired servant in the family of a priest is not sufficiently incorporated in the family to entitle him to eat of the holy things. And there are servants of the gospel—persons who take a commendable interest in its outward prosperity—who yet are not of the "household of faith," and have no experience of its spiritual mysteries. (3) The daughter of a priest, by marrying a stranger, forfeits her right to eat of the holy things. If now in her father's house, she is simply a visitor, and has to be provided with common food. By yoking with the ungodly, the children of God forfeit his favour, and are only tolerated in the Church as visitors. 3. *These laws may not be invaded with impunity.* (1) If by accident they were transgressed, there was mercy for the offender when he made reparation. This was the original value, with a fifth part added (ver. 14). Paul obtained mercy for his sin against the gospel of Christ, "because he did it ignorantly in unbelief." (2) For the wilful presumptuous transgression of the Law there was no mercy in its provisions. "That soul shall be cut off from my presence" (ver. 3). "They shall therefore keep mine ordinance, lest they bear sin for it, and die therefore, if they profane it" (ver. 9). There is a law of extremity also under the gospel (Matt. xii. 31, 32; Acts v. 1—11; Heb. vi. 4—6; x. 26—29; 1 John v. 16).

II. HOW THESE DISQUALIFICATIONS MAY BE REMOVED. 1. *In some cases by statute.* (1) Thus the servant of the high priest, bought with his money, though formerly an alien, is now so incorporated into his family that he may freely eat of the holy things. Being purchased, he is *permanently* under the power of the priest, and has no option to leave his service. So we, being redeemed by the blood of Christ and by a thorough repentance and conversion, renouncing all freedom to act against his will, may claim the privileges of his service. (2) Those born in the house of the priest, viz. to his slaves or permanent servants, are also reckoned as belonging to his family, and privileged to fare as his own children. This birth into the household expresses more than mere natural descent from a godly ancestry. The children of the covenant made with Abraham were not those naturally descended from him, but those who were also the children of his faith. Natural birth in a godly family now gives the initiation to goodness, but the privileges of the gospel can only be enjoyed by those who follow up their advantages. (3) The daughter of a priest, as we have seen, by marrying a stranger, forfeited her right to eat of the holy things. She was the figure of a backslider. But if there were no issue of the marriage, and her husband were dead, and she return to the house of her father as in her youth, she may again partake of the holy things. This teaches us God's mercy to the wanderer from Christ who returns to him with a true conversion (see Luke xv. 11). 2. *In some cases by ordinance.* (1) If a man contract pollution by contact, he "shall not eat of the holy things, unless he wash his flesh with water" (vers. 4—6). As the baptism of *water* was necessary to qualify the *ceremonially* impure to eat of the holy things which were typical, so is the baptism of the *Holy Ghost* required to remove moral impurity, and give us the privilege of real fellowship with God (Heb. x. 22). (2) After this washing, "and when the sun is down, he shall be clean, and shall afterward eat of the holy things" (ver. 7). The *natural* or civil day began at sunrise; the *holy* day at sunset, viz. when nature is involved in the shadow of death. So it is in the turning from nature to grace that we enter into the privileges of fellowship with God.—J. A. M.

Vers. 17—33.—*Laws of the oblations.* These naturally follow those concerning the priests, which form the subject of the earlier portion of this chapter. They may be considered—

I. WITH RESPECT TO THE SACRIFICES. 1. *These must be the animals prescribed.*

(1) Clean creatures. To offer swine upon God's altar would be an outrageous insult to his purity. It would be figuratively equivalent to asking his acceptance and approval of passions and conduct the most filthy and loathsome. To attempt to foreshadow in the sacrifice of a hog the sacrifice of Christ would be against the most sacred propriety a horrible blasphemy. (2) Clean creatures of kinds specially selected by God. These are "of the beeves, of the sheep, or of the goats" (ver. 19). The roebuck and the hart are clean creatures, but not of the kinds selected, so, however they may be fitted to represent saints, viewed under particular aspects, they were too wild and intractable to be made fit emblems of Christ. 2. *They must be individuals without blemish.* (1) They must be free from disease. Therefore, if they have "scurvy," or a "wen," or a "running scab," which are symptoms of a diseased state of the blood, they are pronounced unfit. For disease is generally taken as an emblem of sin, and in this sense the reason should be understood, " because their corruption is in them" (ver. 25). (2) There must be no *natural* deformity, such as having any part too much extended, or, on the other hand, too much contracted. "We are shapen in iniquity." From our birth we are marred with moral deformities. But not so Jesus. He was in his birth the "holy thing." (3) They must have no *acquired* blemish—no blindness, lameness, fracture, or mutilation of any kind. By actual transgression we have fallen upon moral disasters. But Christ "fulfilled all righteousness," and must not be foreshadowed by any imperfect creature. (4) The same perfection was required in the sacrifice that was required in the priests. The best service and the best sacrifice should be given to the best Being (see Mal. i. 8, 12—14). The priest and the sacrifice were alike types of the same Lord Jesus, our Priest and Sacrifice. (5) But who is to judge of the fitness of the victim? The Jews say the sagan, or suffragan high priest, had to determine this. Now, Annas sustained that office under Caiaphas, and he accordingly sent Jesus bound to Caiaphas, viz. as a Sacrifice fit to be offered (see John xviii. 12—14, 24). The offerer also had to pass his judgment upon the creature he selects from his herd or flock. If Pilate be viewed as a representative person in this capacity, we hear him say, "I find no fault in this man." But God himself is the ultimate Judge; and has he not emphatically approved of Christ? (See Matt. iii. 17; xvii. 5; John xii. 28.) 3. *Blemished creatures may be given as free-will offerings.* (1) These were not prescribed in the Law, though permitted. They were things which piety might add to what was essential. They were not types of Christ, so they might be imperfect. (2) Piety will give to God the most perfect thing she possesses when she would acknowledge his worthiness to be honoured. But she would also express with humility the imperfection of her best services, and this she might do most appropriately in the offering of a blemished oblation. (3) But when the free-will offering is for a vow, then an imperfect thing will not be accepted. In this case the offering is prescribed in the Law because it is beyond the power of the offerer to retract (see Acts v. 4). And the sacrifice for a vow was a figure of Christ, who is pledged in the covenant of our redemption (see Ps. xxii. 25; xl. 6, 7).

II. WITH RESPECT TO THEIR OFFERING. 1. *They may not be offered till after the eighth day.* (1) For this there was a reason of humanity. The creature must remain "seven days under the dam." The Laws of God are framed to inculcate kindliness and tenderness of heart. (2) It has also a reason of health. For the animal is scarcely formed in the first week of its life. Its hair and its hoofs are not grown. It is not wholesome food. (3) But the typical reasons are the more important. The "eighth day" was that upon which circumcision took place. The import of both rites, that of circumcision and that of sacrifice, is the same. Both represent the cutting off of the Holy Seed out of the land of the living, to secure the blessings of the covenant to men. The Jews say that the eighth day was specified so that a sabbath must be included, for that "the sabbath sanctifies all things." No doubt, when the great sabbath of the eighth day arrives, which is that of the new heavens and earth, all things in that state will be sanctified. That state will be the consummation of the blessings of the covenant. 2. *An animal and its young may not be killed the same day.* (1) This law respects fowls as well as larger creatures (see Deut. xxii. 6). It inculcates tenderness of heart. (2) But it has also a gospel import. It teaches that utter desolation is inconsistent with the idea of atonement. Life is spared because life is sacrificed. The death of Christ is vicarious; it is for the life of the world. 3. *It should be eaten the same day on which it is killed.* (1) The moral here is that we must not delay to avail ourselves of the benefits of redemption in Christ. On the morrow (ver. 30) it may be too late. (2) On the third day it will be certainly too late (see ch. vii. 15 ; xix. 6, 7). The third day, or age, is that of our resurrection (see Hos. vi. 2). If we neglect salvation until then, it cannot be realized. Let us improve the opportunities of our probation. 4. *They should be offered devoutly.* (1) The Name of God must not be profaned. God's Name is hallowed by keeping his commandments (vers. 31, 32). The Name of God will be hallowed when his kingdom is come, for then his will shall be done upon earth as it is in heaven (Matt. vi. 9, 10). (2) He is to be recognized as our Redeemer. " I am the Lord which hallow you, that brought you out of the land of Egypt, to be your God." That redemption was only a figure of the great redemption through which God hallows his people in truth, of which also the oblations of the Law were figures. This is never to be forgotten.—J. A. M.

PART IV.

HOLY DAYS AND SEASONS: WEEKLY, MONTHLY, ANNUAL, SEPTENNIAL, AND EVERY HALF-CENTURY.

EXPOSITION.

CHAPTER XXIII.

THis Part consists of chs. xxiii. and xxv., with ch. xxiv. parenthetically introduced.

Every religion must have its round of holy days and seasons: 1. To give occasion for manifesting joyous thankfulness to the Giver of all good things. 2. To keep alive the memory of past events around which religious associations cling. 3. To impress upon the hearts of the worshippers those sacred mysteries which are regarded as essential characteristics of the system.

1. The duty and happiness of rejoicing before the Lord find a prominent place under the Mosaic dispensation, as they must in any religion where man feels himself in a covenant relation with God, brought nigh to him by himself, and no longer estranged from him who is his only true life and happiness. Accordingly, the first thought of the annual Jewish festivals is that of joyous thankfulness, such as is becoming to reconciled children grateful to their Father for the many bounties that they receive at his hands. The first gift of God of which man becomes conscious is that of the daily sustenance provided for him, and therefore we should expect holy days to be appointed to commemorate the goodness of God in bestowing the gifts of the earth. The first aspect, therefore, in which to regard the three great annual festivals—the Passover, Pentecost, and the Feast of Tabernacles—is that they were days of thanksgiving for the fruits of the earth dispensed by God to man.

First, with regard to the Passover. We read at vers. 10, 11, "*When ye be come into the land which I give unto you, and shall reap the harvest thereof, then ye shall bring a sheaf* [or *an omer*] *of the firstfruits of your harvest unto the priest: and he shall wave the sheaf before the Lord, to be accepted for you: on the morrow after the sabbath the priest shall wave it.*" The words, " the morrow after the sabbath," mean, as we shall see, the day after the first day of Unleavened Bread, that is, the second day of the feast, Nisan 16, which fell early in April, when the first barley was ripening in Palestine. On the 14th day of Nisan (the day of the Paschal sacrifice) a certain quantity of standing barley was marked off, by men specially appointed for the purpose, in a field ploughed the previous autumn and sown at least ten weeks before the Passover, but not prepared artificially in such a way as to hasten the crop. On the following day, Nisan 15, at sunset, three men were sent to the selected field, and, in the presence of witnesses, cut the ears of corn before marked, and brought them into the temple. On the next day, Nisan 16, this corn, whether in the form of a sheaf or of flour, was offered to the Lord by being waved before him, and then consigned to the priest. Here, by the presentation of the firstfruits of the year, an acknowledgment is made that the products of the earth are by right God's. This is one of the objects of the Feast of the Passover.

Secondly, as to Pentecost. After the sheaf, or omer, had been offered on Nisan 16, it was allowable to make the new year's barley into bread, but the dedication of the grain crops was not complete until a portion of the wheat crop had also been offered. This was done a week of weeks later, at the Feast of Pentecost, forty-nine days after the presentation of the barley, and fifty days after the first day of Unleavened Bread. On this day, two leavened loaves, of the same size as the shewbread loaves, were waved before the Lord, and then delivered to the priest. These loaves were made out of ears of corn selected and reaped as the barley had been seven weeks before, and then threshed and ground in the temple. They were regarded as the firstfruits of the wheat harvest, though they were not made of the first cut wheat; and from their presentation the festival has the name of the Feast of Harvest (Exod. xxiii. 16); the Feast of the Firstfruits of the Wheat Harvest (Exod. xxiv. 22); the Day of the Firstfruits (Numb. xxviii. 26); while, from its date relatively to the Passover, it is called the Feast of Weeks (Exod. xxxiv. 22; Deut. xvi. 10). The name, Feast of Pentecost, is found only in the Apocrypha (Tobit ii. 1; 2 Macc. xii. 32), and in the New Testament (Acts ii. 1; xx. 16; 1 Cor. xvi. 8). The meat offerings might not be made of the new year's flour until these two loaves had been offered.

Thirdly, with regard to the Feast of Tabernacles. The festivals connected with the seasons of the year and the products of the soil were not ended until the Feast of Ingathering (Exod. xxiii. 16; xxxiv. 22), or Tabernacles (ver. 34; Deut. xvi. 13; Ezra iii. 4; Zech. xiv. 16; Jer. vii. 2), had been celebrated. This festival occurred about the beginning of October, and com-

memorated the final gathering in of all the fruits of the year, specially of the olives and the grapes. It was observed by a general dwelling in booths made of the branches of palms, willows, olives, pines, myrtles, and other close-growing trees (ver. 40; Neh. viii. 15), in which all the Israelite males, with the exception of the sick, lived for seven days, and kept harvest home.

2. The second aspect in which to regard the annual festivals is the historical one. The *Passover* is characterized by its historical associations to a greater degree than either of the other festivals. The whole national life of the Israelites received its character from the Egyptian Exodus, and accordingly the anniversaries of their religious year began with its commemoration. It was the events which had taken place in Egypt which gave to the Paschal sacrifice and the Paschal feast their primary signification; and while to us the Passover festival serves as a proof of the truth of those events, to the Jew it served as a memorial of them, preventing them from ever being forgotten or disregarded (cf. Exod. xiii. 3—16). The ancient Christian Fathers suggested that the *Feast of Pentecost* commemorated the institution of the old dispensation at Sinai, as, to Christians, it recalled the institution of the new Law by the gift of the fiery tongues at Jerusalem. This suggestion was adopted by Maimonides and the later school of Hebrew commentators, and it is a very probable conjecture; but as no appearance of it is found in the Old or New Testaments, nor even in early Hebrew writers, it cannot be regarded as a certainty. Historically, the *Feast of Tabernacles* is generally considered to commemorate the dwelling in tents throughout the forty years' wandering in the wilderness; but if this were so, it would have been called the Feast of Tents, for the words "tent" and "tabernacle" differ, and the Israelites did not dwell in tabernacles in the wilderness. Rather, it commemorates the first encampment of the Israelites after setting forth from Egypt, which took place at "Succoth," the meaning of which word is "tabernacle" (Exod. xii. 37). Thus, as the event historically associated with the first harvest festival, the Passover, was the setting forth from Egypt, that associated with the last, the Feast of

Tabernacles, was the resting at the end of the first day's journey at Succoth, where the people now felt that they were free, and began to rejoice in their freedom.

3. The typical character of the feasts, as well as their historical character, is more apparent in the *Passover* than in the other two feasts. St. Paul's testimony on this point is sufficient: "For even Christ our Passover is sacrificed for us : therefore let us keep the feast, not with old leaven, neither with the leaven of malice and wickedness, but with the unleavened bread of sincerity and truth " (1 Cor. v. 7). Here we have the typical character of the Paschal lamb, and of the Feast of Unleavened Bread, authoritatively declared to us. The blood of the lamb slain on the night before the Exodus, being the means whereby the Israelites were delivered from the destruction which fell on all the rest of the inhabitants of the land, typified the still more efficacious bloodshedding by which the redemption of Christ's people was wrought. The *Feast of Pentecost*, if it commemorated the gift of the Law at Mount Sinai, pointed thereby to the giving of the better Law on the day when the Holy Ghost descended upon the apostles in Jerusalem ; and in any case, as a Feast of Firstfruits, it was emblematic of those firstfruits of the Christian Church presented to God on that day (Acts ii. 41). The *Feast of Tabernacles*, in which God's people commemorated their rejoicing in their newly found liberty after the slavery of Egypt, awaits its full typical fulfilment in the spiritual joy of the redeemed after they have been delivered from the burden of the flesh and the sufferings of the world ; but its typical meaning is partially fulfilled in the blessed peace and joy spread abroad in the hearts of the children of God by reason of their adoption in Christ, whereby we have obtained an inheritance with the saints (Eph. i. 11, 18).

In the annual fast held on the 10th of Tisri, the great Day of Atonement, the typical element outweighs any other. The present and the past sink away in comparison with the future. The day suggests no thought of the seasons or of the products of the earth, and it recalls no event of past history. It teaches a lesson—the need of reconciliation ; and by the entrance of the high priest into the holy of holies with sacrificial blood, and by the ceremony of the scapegoat, it typically foreshadows how that reconciliation is to be effected.

The monthly festivals had a purpose different from the annual. They occurred on the new moon, or the first day of each month, and their intention was to dedicate each month to God. Only one of these monthly festivals is mentioned in this chapter—the Feast of Trumpets. It is the feast of the new moon of the sacred seventh month, with which the civil year began. Because it was New Year's Day, it had more ceremonies attached to it than the first days of the other months. Whereas the feasts of the new moons in other months only sanctified the special month which they began, the Feast of Trumpets sanctified also the whole year, and was therefore an annual as well as a monthly feast.

The weekly festival was the sabbath (see Exod. xx. 10 ; Deut. v. 15). This feast sanctified each week, as the monthly feasts sanctified each month ; and like the annual festivals, it looked both backwards and forwards : backwards, to the sanctification bestowed upon it " Because that in it he had rested from all his work which God created and made " (Gen. ii. 3) ; forwards, to the great sabbath in which Christ rested in the grave, and yet further onwards to another sabbath still to be enjoyed by the people of God.

The sabbatical year and the jubilee were extensions of the sabbatical principle— certain civil and religious institutions and regulations being attached to each of them.

Ver. 2.—Concerning **the feasts of the Lord, which ye shall proclaim** to be **holy convocations, even these are my feasts.** The translation should rather be, *The appointed times which ye shall proclaim to be holy convocations, these are my appointed times.* The appointed times (*mo'adim*) include the great fast as well as the festivals, and the weekly and monthly as well as the annual holy days. The primary purpose with which the following enumeration of holy days is introduced, is to give a list of the *holy convocations.* While the Israelites were still dwelling in the wilderness, a *holy convocation* appears to have been a religious assembly of all the males in the court of the tabernacle. After the settlement in Canaan, a religious gathering for prayer or festive rejoicing *in all their dwellings*, that is, wherever they lived, would have satisfied the command to hold a holy convocation, except on the three great festivals, when all who could, "kept the feast" at Jerusalem. There were in all seven *holy convocations* in the year, besides the sabbath, namely, the first and last days of Unleavened Bread, the Feast of Pentecost, the Day of Atonement, the Feast of Trumpets, the first and last days of the Feast of Tabernacles.

Ver. 3.—**The seventh day is the sabbath of rest.** This is a very strong expression, literally, *the sabbath of sabbatism*, which doubles the force of the single word. **Ye shall do no work** therein. The sabbath and the Day of Atonement were the only days in which no work might be done, whereas on the other festivals it was only no servile work that might be done. It is not to be observed solely where the tabernacle is pitched or the temple is built, but in every town and village of Canaan—**in all your dwellings.** In the sanctuary itself the peculiar characteristics of the sabbath were a holy convocation, the renewal of the shewbread, and the burnt offering of two lambs with their meat and drink offerings (Numb. xxviii. 9, 10); elsewhere it was observed only by the holy convocation and rest from all labour. It commenced at sunset on Friday evening, and continued till sunset on Saturday evening. In later days the hour at which it began was announced by three blasts of the priests' trumpets, immediately after which a new course of priests entered on their ministry.

Ver. 4.—This verse repeats the statement or heading contained in ver. 2, with reference to the annual holy day, the sabbath having been disposed of in ver. 3.

Ver. 5.—**In the fourteenth day of the first month at even is the Lord's passover.** The month of Nisan was made the first month of the religious year in consequence of the original Passover having taken place in it (Exod. xii. 2). On the occasion of the first, or Egyptian, Passover, all heads of a family, either singly or two or three heads of families in conjunction, provided themselves with a lamb or a kid on the 10th day of Nisan, killed it in the evening of the 14th, and, taking a bunch of hyssop, dipped it in the blood and struck the lintel and two side posts of the doors of their houses with the blood. They then roasted the animal whole for eating, added to it unleavened bread, and garnished it with bitter herbs. They made themselves ready to eat it by dressing themselves for a journey, "with their loins girded, their shoes on their feet, and their staff in their hands" (Exod. xii. 11), and thus they ate it in haste, in a standing position. The meaning of the ceremony is explained by what was taking place at the same time. On the same night, after the

blood had been sprinkled upon the lintel and side posts, God slew the firstborn of all who had not exhibited this symbol of their having been brought into covenant with himself, and the Israelites set off hurriedly on their departure from Egypt. It was commanded that the day should be kept hereafter in like manner as a memorial, and that the following seven days should be kept as a Feast of Unleavened Bread (Exod. xii. 14, 15). This command is here concisely repeated, as it is again repeated in Deut. xvi. 1—8. One very considerable change was, however, necessarily made in the method of its observance. Originally, each head of a household or combination of households sacrificed the lamb himself, and sprinkled the blood upon the doorposts and lintel. But after the establishment of the Aaronic priesthood and the withdrawal of the priestly authority previously vested in each head of a house (chs. viii., ix.), and after the stringent prohibition of sacrificing elsewhere than in the court of the tabernacle had been issued (ch. xvii.), this could not continue. Accordingly, we find in the Book of Deuteronomy the direct injunction, "Thou mayest not sacrifice the Passover within any of thy gates, which the Lord thy God giveth thee: but at the place which the Lord thy God shall choose to place his Name in, there thou shalt sacrifice the Passover at even, at the going down of the sun, at the' season that thou camest forth out of Egypt" (xvi. 5, 6). A result from this rule was that every male Israelite had to present himself at Jerusalem, and there slay his lamb on the day of the Passover, which in the time of Nero, brought between two and three million pilgrims to Jerusalem each year. The crowd of pilgrims took their way to the temple, and were admitted into the court in three divisions. There they slew each man his lamb, while the priests offered the blood on the altar, and the Levites sang the Hallel (Ps. cxiii.—cxviii.). Then they bore away the lambs, roasted them whole on a spit of pomegranate wood, taking care that no bone should be broken, and prepared the Paschal supper. At the supper, as well as at the sacrifice, a change of manner was introduced. "As the guests gathered round the Paschal table, they came no longer, as at the first celebration, with their loins girded, with shoes on their feet, and a staff in their hands; that is, as travellers waiting to take their departure. On the contrary, they were arrayed in their best festive garments, joyous and at rest, as became the children of a king. To express this idea, the rabbis also insisted that the Paschal supper, or at least part of it, must be eaten in that recumbent position with which we are familiar from the New

Testament. 'For,' say they, 'they use this leaning posture, as free men do, in memorial of their freedom.' And again, 'Because it is the manner of slaves to eat standing, therefore now they eat sitting and leaning, in order to show that they have been delivered from bondage into freedom.' And finally, 'No, not the poorest in Israel may eat till he has sat down, leaning.' But though it was deemed desirable to sit leaning during the whole Paschal supper, it was only absolutely enjoined while partaking of the bread and the wine" (Edersheim, 'Temple Service'). The essentials of the Paschal feast were the Paschal lamb, the unleavened bread, and the bitter herbs (Exod. xii. 8). To these were afterwards added a dish formed from an animal sacrificed on the Passover day, a composition of dates and other dried fruits, and four cups of red wine mixed with water, the last of which came to be regarded as essential as that which had been commanded in the Law. The Rabbi Gamaliel is reported by the Mishna to have said, "Whoever fails to explain three things in the Passover fails to fulfil his duty. These are the Paschal lamb, the unleavened bread, and the bitter herbs. The Paschal lamb means that God passed over the houses of our fathers in Egypt, which were sprinkled with blood; the unleavened bread, that our fathers were hurried out of Egypt; the bitter herbs, that the Egyptians made the lives of our fathers in Egypt bitter" (Pes. x. 15). The wine was regarded so necessary an adjunct, that it is ordered that every householder must provide himself with four cups, even if he had to sell or pawn his coat, or hire himself out for a servant, or receive money from the poor's box, in order to do so (Pes. i.). The supper began with drinking the first cup of wine, before which a grace, or thanksgiving, of the following character was said:—"Blessed art thou, Jehovah our God, who hast created the fruit of the vine! Blessed art thou, Jehovah our God, King of the universe, who hast chosen us from among all people, and exalted us from among all languages, and sanctified

us with thy commandments! And thou hast given us, in love, the solemn days for joy, and the festivals and appointed seasons for gladness, and this, the day of the Feast of Unleavened Bread, the season of our freedom, a holy convocation, the memorial of our departure from Egypt. For us hast thou chosen; and us hast thou sanctified from among all nations, and thy holy festivals with joy and with gladness hast thou caused us to inherit. Blessed art thou, O Lord, who sanctifiest Israel and the appointed seasons! Blessed art thou, Lord, King of the universe, who hast preserved us alive, and sustained us, and brought us to this season" (Edersheim, 'Temple Service'). After drinking the first cup, there followed a general washing of hands, after which the company ate some of the bitter herbs. Then the second cup was filled, and in order to carry out the injunction of Exod. xii. 26, 27, the youngest member of the company inquired, "What mean ye by this service?" And the president of the feast replied, "It is the sacrifice of the Lord's Passover, who passed over the houses of the children of Israel in Egypt, when he smote the Egyptians, and delivered our houses." At the same time, he explained the purport of the unleavened bread and the bitter herbs, and called upon the company to give thanks for what God had wrought for them and for their fathers, ending with Ps. cxiii., cxiv., sung by all present. The second cup was then drunk, and after a second washing of hands, the unleavened bread was broken, and thanks again given, after which the pieces of bread, the bitter herbs, the other sacrificial dish (if any), and the Paschal lamb were partaken of in turn. The third cup was then filled, thanks were again given, and the cup was drunk. This cup had the name of the "cup of blessing," owing to the blessing said over it, and it was succeeded after an interval by the fourth cup, when Ps. cxv.—cxviii. (which, with Ps. cxiii., cxiv., made up the Hallel) were sung, followed by a prayer of thanksgiving.

HOMILETICS.

Ver. 5.—*The Paschal supper was observed by our Lord* in obedience to the command in Exod. xii. 14; ch. xxiii. 5; Deut. xvi. 1—8, in the following manner, so far as we are able to gather from the narrative of the gospel.

I. He sent Peter and John beforehand to prepare the Passover. The first step in the preparation of the Passover was the purchase of the Paschal lamb. We may see the two disciples, after they had been led by the man bearing a pitcher of water to the house where the feast was to be held, providing themselves with a lamb, unleavened bread, the bitter herbs, and that other dish into which the sop was afterwards dipped; then carrying the lamb to the temple, to be sacrificed in the court. This was on the afternoon of Nisan 14. Admitted into the court of the temple, in one or other of the three divisions into which the mass of the pilgrims and residents were divided, they would have slain the lamb, and, after the blood had been thrown on the altar by the priests, they would have carried the body to the house in which the preparations for the Master's eating the Passover were being made.

II. HE SELECTED HIS PASCHAL COMPANY. The rule was that the company should not consist of less than ten persons. In the present case it amounted to thirteen. Around him were gathered his twelve disciples, with whom "he desired with desire to eat the Passover before he suffered" (Luke xxii. 15).

III. HE ENTERED INTO JERUSALEM IN ORDER THAT HE MIGHT EAT THE PASSOVER IN THE PLACE WHICH THE LORD HAD CHOSEN. (Deut. xvi. 7.) "It was probably as the sun was beginning to decline in the horizon that Jesus and the other ten disciples descended once more over the Mount of Olives into the holy city. Before them lay Jerusalem in her festive attire. All around pilgrims were hastening towards it. White tents dotted the sward, gay with the bright flowers of early spring, or poured out from the gardens and the darker foliage of the olive plantations. From the gorgeous temple buildings, dazzling in their snow-white marble and gold, on which the slanting rays of the sun were reflected, rose the smoke of the altar of burnt offering. These courts were now crowded with eager worshippers, offering for the last time, in a real sense, their Paschal lambs. The streets must have been thronged with strangers, and the flat roofs covered with eager gazers, who either feasted their eyes with a first sight of the sacred city for which they had so often longed, or else once more rejoiced in view of the well-remembered localities. It was the last day view which the Lord had of the holy city till his resurrection. Only once more in the approaching night of his betrayal was he to look upon it in the pale light of the full moon. He was going forward to 'accomplish his death' in Jerusalem; to fulfil type and prophecy, and to offer himself up as the true Passover Lamb—'the Lamb of God which taketh away the sin of the world.' They who followed him were busy with many thoughts. They knew that terrible events awaited them, and they had only a few days before been told that these glorious temple buildings, to which, with a national pride not unnatural, they had directed the attention of their Master, were to become desolate, not one stone being left upon the other. Among them, revolving his dark plans and goaded on by the great enemy, moved the betrayer. And now they were within the city. Its temple, its royal bridge, its splendid palaces, its busy marts, its streets filled with festive pilgrims, were well known to them as they made their way to the house where the guest-chamber had been prepared for them" (Edersheim, 'Temple Service').

IV. HE ATE THE PASSOVER MEAL IN THE CUSTOMARY MANNER, YET WITH SUCH ALTERATIONS AS MADE IT A NEW INSTITUTION. For example: 1. He began with the first cup, over which he gave thanks as usual, and then gave it to the company to drink. It is of this cup that we read in St. Luke, "And he took the cup, and gave thanks, and said, Take this, and divide it among yourselves" (xxii. 17). 2. Instead of the first washing of hands, he "began to wash the disciples' feet, and to wipe them with the towel wherewith he was girded" (John xiii. 5). 3. The feast then continued in its usual order. The second cup, the unleavened bread (part of which was "the sop" given to Judas), the bitter herbs, and the eating of the lamb followed in order. 4. The Lord then took some of the unleavened bread, and when he had given thanks over it, or blessed it, he brake it, and gave it to the disciples, and said, "Take, eat, this is my body" (Matt. xxvi. 26; Luke xxii. 19; 1 Cor. xi. 24). 5. He took the third cup, called "the cup of blessing" (cf. 1 Cor. x. 16), "and gave thanks, and gave it to them, saying, Drink ye all of it; for this is my blood of the new testament, which is shed for many for the remission of sins" (Matt. xxvi. 27, 28; Mark xiv. 23, 24; Luke xxii. 20; 1 Cor. xi. 25). 6. The fourth cup, accompanied by the "hymn," or Hallel (Matt. xxvi. 30; Mark xiv. 26), no doubt finished the supper in the usual manner.

V. THE PASCHAL SUPPER THUS CEASED FOR EVER, AND THE LORD'S SUPPER WAS INSTITUTED IN ITS PLACE. The blood of the original lambs slain in Egypt received its efficacy in covering the people of Israel and delivering them from the visitation of God's angel of wrath, by its anticipatory representation of the blood of the true Lamb of God, which was shed for the deliverance of God's redeemed upon the cross. The time had now come for that blood to be shed, and therefore the memorial and typical sacrifices offered year by year necessarily ceased, the shadow being swallowed up in the substance, the type in the antitype. In like manner, the feast on the body of the lamb, which represented the body of Christ, necessarily ceased when there was no longer a lamb to be sacrificed. The Paschal feast, if continued longer, would have been an unmeaning form, because its meaning had become exhausted.

Yet, just as Christianity grew by God's will out of Judaism, so a new memorial of Christ sprang out of the old type. He took the bread that was before him, an accessory of the old feast, and consecrated it, together with the third cup, to represent his body and blood in the future, for a memorial, just as the body of the lamb which was eaten and the blood of the lamb that was shed had typically and by anticipation represented them in the past. Thus the dead wood of the old form, at the moment of perishing blossomed into new life.

The Passover was to be kept as "a feast to the Lord throughout your generations; ye shall keep it a feast by an ordinance for ever" (Exod. xii. 14); and any one who did not keep the feast was to "be cut off from Israel" (Exod. xii. 15). In like manner, the Lord's Supper is to continue, the bread is to be eaten and the cup to be drunk, as the means of showing forth the Lord's death "till he come." The one ordinance is of as permanent a nature as the other, and the neglect of it may cause people to incur a no less penalty in the second case than in the first.

HOMILIES BY VARIOUS AUTHORS.

The offering of rest: the sabbath. Ch. xxiii. 1—3; cf. Gen. ii. 2, 3; Exod. xvi. 22; xx. 8—11; Mark ii. 23—28; Rev. i. 10. In the sacrificial worship we come across what is essentially different as an offering from the sacrifice of an animal or of any palpable possession, and yet is a real sacrifice all the while—we mean that of *time*. The sabbath, as an offering of rest, has consequently a very high place among the Jews. As Ewald has remarked, it is the only sacrifice which finds a place among the ten commandments. No wonder he regards it as "the greatest and most prolific thought" in the Jewish religion. And here let us notice—

I. THE HIGH VALUE MAN USUALLY SETS ON HIS TIME. It is indeed said to be money. Many will make almost any other sacrifice more willingly than that of their time. They will give money, valuables, almost anything you like to ask, except their precious time. What a fuss made about an evening devoted to you by a busy friend, or half an evening, or sometimes half an hour!

Hence, in demanding from man a proportion of his time, God asks for what man esteems highly and is loth to give. Time is regarded as so peculiarly man's own, to do what he likes in, that it becomes no light sacrifice, but rather the crown of all sacrifices, when a considerable portion of time is made over unto God.

II. THE DEMAND GOD MAKES IS IN MAN'S INTEREST, FOR IT IS FOR REST AFTER LABOUR. Six days of work, and then, saith God, one day of rest. The body needs it. Seven days' unceasing toil would soon take the heart out of all workers, and bring on premature decay. God himself has set the example. After the untold labours of the creation, after the hard work—if we may reverently use such terms of God—of the creative periods, he has entered into the long sabbath of human history. He is in the midst of it now. This is implied by the words of Jesus, "My Father worketh hitherto, and I work" (John v. 17), in their connection. And so a restful Father in heaven calls upon his toiling children upon earth to rest, as he has done, one day out of seven, and not sink through unceasing labour. So consonant is this weekly rest with the laws of our physical nature, that some, who do not see clearly the scriptural proof and obligation of a holy day, believe that it might safely be allowed to rest upon the foundation of physical need. But the needs of others, alas! constitute no sufficient sanction with selfish men. God must speak and make his demand, else men will run counter to their general welfare in their self-indulgence.

III. GOD'S REST IS TO BE CHARACTERIZED BY SOCIAL WORSHIP. Man is not to spend his seventh day in inactivity. He is not to loiter about his tent or gossip at its door all the day. There is to be "an holy convocation" (מִקְרָא־קֹדֶשׁ). The day is to be celebrated by social worship. The people were expected to gather in their thousands to praise the Lord. Were it not for such a regulation as the sabbath, with its public services, even Judaism could not have survived.

The same reason still holds for a holy sabbath. In the interests of religion it must be observed. What would become of our holy religion if a set time for its weekly observance were not generally kept? Men need these "trysting times" and "trysting places" (as מוֹעֲרֵי, in ver. 2, might very properly be translated), that religion may keep its position among us.

We may imagine what our land would be if no Lord's day were kept, if no sabbath bells summoned people to public prayer, and no preachers got their weekly opportunities. It would soon be an irreligious land, carelessness and indifference reigning throughout it in a measure infinitely greater than they do even now.

IV. THE DAY OF REST IS TO BE REGARDED AS THE LORD'S. "It is the sabbath of the Lord in all your dwellings." The Jew regarded the sabbath as "the Lord's day." It was the day of the week that God regulated, and all whose hours he claimed as his. We claim as much for "the first day of the week" under our dispensation. We ask men to lay the day as a hearty offering on God's altar. They are not doing so while they spend it as they like. It is to be a holy day, not a holiday; a holy day, and therefore to a holy soul a happy day, the day in which we can rejoice and be glad. When we can say with John, "I was in the Spirit on the Lord's day," we are sure to have most precious visions of the Lord's beauty and glory (cf. Rev. i. 10, etc.).

It is no contention, therefore, about something Jewish, but simply about something honestly dedicated as a day to God. Those who contend against the strict observance of the Lord's day either labour under a total misapprehension about the way some people spend it, or are really bent upon devoting the day to their own purposes instead of to God's. If we are commonly honest, we shall esteem it only right to surrender as the highest offering of our religious life the seventh of our time to him who deserves it all.

"Man, then," says Ewald, "shall release his soul and body from all their burdens, with all the professions and pursuits of ordinary life, only in order to gather himself together again in God with greater purity and fewer disturbing elements, and renew in him the might of his own better powers. If, then, the interchange of activity and rest is already founded in the nature of all creation, and is the more beneficial and health-bringing the more regular its recurrence, so should it be found here too; yet not as when, in the night and in sleep, the body is cared for, but as when, in a joyous day of unfettered meditation, the spiritual man always finds his true rest, and thereby is indeed renewed and strengthened."—R. M. E.

Vers. 1—3.—*The sabbath.* This is here classed amongst the "feasts of the Lord." The greater number of these were first observed after the settlement of the Israelites in Canaan; but the Passover was an exception, which was held at the time of the Exodus, forty years earlier. The sabbath also was an exception. We have to consider—

I. THE OBLIGATION OF THE SABBATH. 1. *It is not altogether a Mosaic institution.* (1) Its original enactment took place at the close of the creation week. The words are these (see Gen. ii. 1—3). (2) It was, therefore, an Adamic law, and was obligatory upon mankind at large more than twenty centuries before the Israelites had an existence. (3) It was by the Israelites themselves recognized as a patriarchal law. For, in the wilderness of Sin, probably three months before they were fully constituted into a nation by receiving their own Law at Sinai, the double portion of manna which they gathered on the sixth day had respect to the sabbath to follow on the seventh (see Exod. xvi. 22—30). 2. *It was incorporated in the Sinai code.* (1) It formed the fourth commandment of the Decalogue (Exod. xx. 8—11). But even here it is introduced with the word "Remember," as a law already known to exist. The reason for its observance also is that given at the original institution. (2) As a Levitical law, however, it has an additional reason, viz. the deliverance of the children of Israel from the cruel servitude in Egypt, where they could not enjoy the rest of the ancient institution (Deut. v. 15; see also Heb. iv. 8, margin). (3) In this relation also *death* was made the penalty of its transgression (see Exod. xxxi. 13—15; Numb. xv. 32—36). 3. *The Levitical law of the sabbath is repealed.* (1) The body is of Christ, who fulfilled the type of the deliverance from the bondage of Egypt in emancipating us from the bondage of sin. (2) The Levitical penalty of death for the transgression of the Law is, of course, removed with the obligation of the Law itself. 4. *But the Adamic law remains.* (1) As Gentiles, we were never under the Levitical Law. The institution of the Levitical sabbath, or the incorporation of the patriarchal sabbath in the Mosaic code, left us still where we were, under the Adamic law. (2) And as the enactment of the Mosaic Law, which mainly concerned the Hebrew people and their land, left us where we were, so do we remain there after the abrogation of the Mosaic Law. (3) But what effect has that abrogation upon the Hebrew? It leaves him where he was before the publication of his Law, viz. in common with mankind at large, still under obligation to observe and keep the sabbath of the Adamic law. (4) This reasoning is equally good, whether we identify the sabbatic law as set out in the Decalogue with the Adamic law on the one hand, or with the Levitical on the other.

II. How IT SHOULD BE KEPT. It should be kept: 1. *As a day of rest from business.* (1) The idea of rest is expressed in its name. It was the most obvious idea in the injunction from the beginning. God *hallowed* it, or separated it from the six days of the week, because on the seventh day he rested from the work of the creation. (2) The *rest* of God does not imply that he was weary from his work, but that he ceased from the action of creating. This is the import of the word (וישבת). The teaching is that God so constituted his creation that his active creatures need a hebdomadal pause or rest. (3) To ensure this to them he mercifully constituted it into a law. He foresaw that otherwise it would be refused under the influence of cupidity, avarice, tyranny, and stupidity. 2. *As a day of holy convocation.* (1) Rest being secured from the toil of business, the activities of the soul have now to be turned into another course. *Change* really constitutes the *rest* of an essentially active nature. So the *rest* of God from creation is his *work* in providence and redemption. This our Lord taught us when he said, "My Father worketh hitherto," or *until now* (ἕως ἄρτι) (John v. 16, 17; comp. Ps. xxxi. 19). (2) That change which is the greatest from the activities of business is communion with God in his worship and service. This seems to have constituted the *blessing* of the seventh day, for on that day God visited his children in Eden. Ever since it has been the season sacred to religious services. (3) Men must not be diverted from this noblest of pursuits by seeking their own pleasure on the sabbath day (Isa. lviii. 13). 3. *As a day of prophetic anticipation.* (1) Barnabas (in his Epistolæ, cap. xv.) puts this subject thus: "Attend, my children, to what he says, '*finished in six days*'—that is to say, in six thousand years the Lord God will consummate all things, for with him the day is a thousand years, as he himself testifies, saying, 'Behold, this day shall be as a thousand years.' Therefore, children, in six days—that is, in six thousand years—all things shall be consummated. *And he rested the seventh day*, that is, when his Son shall come and make an end of the time of the wicked one, and shall judge the ungodly, and shall change the sun, and moon, and stars; then shall he rest gloriously in the seventh day." (2) These views seem to be in harmony with the sacred calendar of prophecy. And Paul in particular refers to the "*sabbath-keeping* which remaineth for the people of God" (Heb. iv.).—J. A. M.

Ver. 3.—*Aspects of the sabbath.* We are reminded of—

I. ITS ORIGIN IN EARLIEST HUMAN HISTORY. "The seventh day is the sabbath of rest" (see Gen. ii. 2, 3).

II. THE SPECIAL OBLIGATION RESTING ON ISRAEL, AS A REDEEMED PEOPLE, TO OBSERVE IT. "The Lord thy God brought thee out thence . . . therefore the Lord thy God commanded thee to keep the sabbath day" (Deut. v. 15). We, also, as those redeemed at far greater cost, may feel ourselves on this ground constrained to observe it.

III. ITS PLACE IN THE PROPHETIC TESTIMONY. It is deeply significant that the prophets, who were the rebukers of mere ritualism and the advocates of the moral and spiritual elements in religion, should have given so high a place as they did to the observance of the sabbath (see Isa. i. 10—15, comp. with lvi. 2 and lviii. 13, 14).

IV. ITS CHRISTIAN ASPECT. 1. It commemorates the greatest fact in human history —the resurrection of our Lord. The crowning act of redemption is more to us than the crowning act of creation. 2. Its obligation rests not on any one positive precept, but on the known will of Christ. 3. It meets the two great wants of man—his bodily and his spiritual requirements.   4. It is to be observed : (1) in the Church,—it is to be " an holy convocation ; " (2) in the home,—" in all your dwellings."   As individual souls we shall seek to honour our Lord and gain access of spiritual strength in the sanctuary ; as parents we shall do our best to make the sabbath a holy, happy, welcome day to the children in our homes.—C.

EXPOSITION.

Ver. 8.—The Feast of Unleavened Bread was instituted at the same time with the Feast of the Passover (Exod. xii. 15—17), and from the beginning the two festivals were practically but one festival, never separated, though separable in idea.   The Passover, strictly so called, lasted but one day, Nisan 14 ; the Feast of Un-leavened Bread lasted seven days, Nisan 15—21.   The whole made a festival of eight days, called indifferently the Feast of the Passover, or the Feast of Unleavened Bread. The bread to be eaten throughout the festival was unleavened, in order to remind the Israelites of the historical fact that on account of the urgency of the Egyptians, " the people took their dough before it was leavened, their kneadingtroughs being bound up in their clothes upon their shoulders " (Exod. xii. 34), and quitted the land of their affliction in haste.   Accordingly, in the Book of Deuteronomy it is appointed, " Seven days shalt thou eat unleavened bread therewith, even the bread of affliction ; for thou camest forth out of the land of Egypt in haste : that thou mayest remember the day when thou camest forth out of the land of Egypt all the days of thy life" (Deut. xvi. 3).

Vers. 7, 8.—The first and the last day were to be days of holy convocation, on which no servile work might be done.   It was on the first day, Nisan 15, that our Lord was crucified.   The Pharisees found nothing in the holiness of the day to prevent their taking virtual part in his seizure and con-demnation and death ; but we are told by St. John that " they themselves went not into the judgment hall, lest they should be defiled, but that they might eat the Pass-over " (John xviii. 28).   What is meant in this passage by " the Passover" is not the Paschal lamb which had already been con-sumed, but probably the peace offering, or chagigah, which had to be offered and eaten on the first day of Unleavened Bread.   The public sacrifices on each of the seven days of the week were two young bullocks, one ram, and seven lambs for a burnt offering,

with the accompanying meat offerings, and one goat for a sin offering (Numb. xxviii. 19—24).   And these were followed by peace offerings made at the discretion of indi-viduals, " according to the blessing of the Lord which he had given them" (Deut. xvi. 17).

Vers. 9—14.—A second command is given on the subject of the Feast of Unleavened Bread respecting those ceremonies which were only to be made use of when the Israelites had reached Canaan.   It has reference to the second day of Unleavened Bread, which is called the morrow after the sabbath, the first day of the feast being meant by the sabbath, on whatever day of week it may have occurred.   It was on this second day that the presentation of the first or wave sheaf of barley took place, according to the command, Ye shall bring a sheaf of the firstfruits of your harvest unto the priest : and he shall wave the sheaf before the Lord, to be accepted for you : on the morrow after the sabbath the priest shall wave it.   Which command was fulfilled in the following manner.   " Already, on the 14th of Nisan, the spot whence the first sheaf was to be reaped had been marked out by delegates from the Sanhedrim, by tying together in bundles, while still standing, the barley that was to be cut down.   Though for obvious reasons it was customary to choose for the purpose the sheltered Ashes valley across Kedron, there was no restric-tion on that point, provided the barley had grown in an ordinary field—of course in Palestine itself — and not in garden or orchard land, and that the soil had not been manured nor yet artificially watered.   When the time for cutting the sheaf had arrived, that is, on the evening of the 15th of Nisan (even though it was a sabbath) just as the sun went down, three men, each with a sickle and basket, formally set to work. But in order clearly to bring out all that was distinctive in the ceremony, they first asked of the bystanders three times each of these questions : ' Has the sun gone down ?' ' With this sickle ?'   ' Into this basket ?' ' On this sabbath ?'   (or first Passover day) ; and lastly, ' Shall I reap ?'   Having been each time answered in the affirmative, they cut down barley to the amount of one ephah, or ten omers, or three seahs, which is equal to about three pecks and three pints of our English measure. The ears were brought into the court of the temple" (Edersheim, 'Temple Service'). The sheaf composed of these ears (for the Authorized Version is right in considering that it is the sheaf, and not the omer of flour made out of the ears of barley, that is meant by עֹמֶר, though Josephus and the Mishna take it the other way) was on the following day waved by the priests before the Lord, in token of its consecration, and through it, of the consecration of the whole barley crop to the Lord. With it was offered the burnt offering of a lamb, a meat offering double the usual quantity, and a drink offering. This passage and vers. 18 and 37, are the only places in the Book of Leviticus where the drink offering is mentioned. Until the waving of the sheaf, **neither bread nor parched corn, nor green ears,** that is, no grain in any form, might be eaten. We may imagine how delicacies made of the new flour would at once appear in the streets as soon as the sheaf had been waved.

Vers. 15—21.—The Feast of Pentecost lasted but one day. **From the morrow after the sabbath**—that is, from the second day of Unleavened Bread—**the day that ye brought the sheaf of the wave offering; seven sabbaths,** i.e. weeks, were to be counted, making forty-nine days, and on the day following the completion of **the seventh sabbath** (meaning here the seventh week), the festival was to be held, whence its later name of Pentecost, or Fiftieth-day Feast. It would have fallen about the beginning of June—a season of the year which would have made the journey to Jerusalem easy. The characteristic offering of the day was that of **two wave loaves of two tenth deals . . . of fine flour . . . baken with leaven.** These loaves were regarded as **the firstfruits unto the Lord** of the wheat harvest, although the greater part of the crop had now been reaped and housed. They were to be leavened and **brought out of your habitations;** that is, they were to consist of such bread as was ordinarily used in daily life. They were made out of ears of wheat selected and cut like the barley in the Feast of Unleavened Bread, and then threshed and ground in the temple court. Each loaf contained an omer of flour, amounting to about five pints, and would therefore have weighed about five pounds. With these were offered two lambs, which were waved before the Lord by being led backwards and forwards before the tabernacle or the temple, and then the loaves were waved also, but they were not placed upon the altar, as they were leavened. The twentieth verse, which is somewhat obscure in the

Authorized Version, should be punctuated as follows. **And the priest shall wave them** (the two lambs) **with the bread of the firstfruits** (the two loaves) **for a wave offering before the Lord; with the two lambs they** (the loaves) **shall be holy to the Lord for the priest.** The other sacrifices to be offered on this day are described in the text as **seven lambs, . . . one young bullock, and two rams . . . for a burnt offering unto the Lord, with their meat offering, and their drink offerings, . . . and one kid of the goats for a sin offering.** In the Book of Numbers (xxviii. 27) they are stated to be "seven lambs," "two young bullocks," "one ram," with meat and drink offerings, and "one kid of the goats." Seeing that in Leviticus *one young bullock and two rams* are commanded, and in Numbers "two young bullocks and one ram," it is reasonable to suppose that a copyist's error has found its way into one or the other text. The feast was to be kept as a day of holy convocation, and no servile work was to be done upon it. The number of sacrifices offered by individuals who had come to Jerusalem caused the festivity to be in practice continued for several days subsequent to the festival itself.

Ver. 22.—**When ye reap the harvest of your land.** The legislator pauses in his enunciation of the festivals to add the rule of charity, already laid down in the nineteenth chapter, as to leaving the gleanings **unto the poor, and to the stranger.**

Vers. 23—25.—**In the seventh month, in the first** day of the month. Only one of the monthly festivals is named in this chapter, because it is the only one on which a holy convocation was to be held. The first day of the seventh month we should expect to be holier than the first day of any other month, on account of the peculiar holiness of the seventh month, and because it was the beginning of the civil year. It is to be a **sabbath;** that is, a festival observed by rest, and **a memorial of blowing of trumpets.** The latter words should be rather rendered *a memorial of a joyful noise.* That these joyful sounds were made by blowing the cornet, we may well believe from the testimony of tradition, but the text of Holy Scripture does not state the fact, and the use of the word *trumpets* in place of "cornets" leads to a confusion. Every new moon, and among them that of the seventh month, was observed by the blowing of trumpets (Numb. x. 10), but the trumpets then blown differed in their use and shape from the cornet. The trumpet was a long-shaped, metal instrument, at first used to give the signal for marching, afterwards to serve as the sign of the arrival of the monthly festival; the cornet was an animal's horn, or, if not a real horn, an instrument formed in the shape of a horn, and it was used to express joyful emotions, answering somewhat to our modern bell-ringing in the West, or firing unloaded guns in the East. Besides the blowing of trumpets, special sacrifices were appointed for the first of each month, "two young bullocks, and one ram, seven lambs," with their meat and drink offerings, for a burnt offering, and "one kid of the goats" for a sin offering (Numb. xxviii. 11—15). On New Year's Day, which, from its difference from the other new moons, was an annual as well as a monthly feast, the special offerings were "one young bullock, one ram, and seven lambs," with their meat and drink offerings for a burnt offering, and "one kid of the goats" for a sin offering; and these were to be in addition to the offerings made on the first day of each month (Numb. xxix. 2—6). It became a custom for the Levites to chant at the morning sacrifice Ps. lxxxi., and at the evening sacrifice Ps. xxix. The great joyfulness of the day is shown by the account given of its observance in the Book of Nehemiah. It was on the first day of the seventh month that Ezra read the Book of the Law publicly to the people, and when "the people wept, when they heard the words of the Law," Nehemiah and Ezra and the Levites said, "This day is holy unto the Lord your God; mourn not, nor weep. . . . Go your way, eat the fat, and drink the sweet, and send portions unto them for whom nothing is prepared: for this day is holy unto our Lord: neither be ye sorry; for the joy of the Lord is your strength. So the Levites stilled all the people, saying, Hold your peace, for the day is holy; neither be ye grieved. And all the people went their way to eat, and to drink, and to send portions, and to make great mirth, because they had understood the words that were declared unto them" (Neh. viii. 9—12).

Ver. 26—32.—The ceremonies to be observed on the **day of atonement** have been already described in ch. xvi., where it found its place as the great purification of the people and of the sanctuary. Here it is reintroduced as one of the holy days. It is the one Jewish fast; to be observed as a day of holy convocation, a day in which to **afflict your souls** and to **offer an offering made by fire unto the Lord**, and in which **no manner of work** was to be done; inasmuch as, like the weekly sabbath, it was **a sabbath of rest** from **the ninth day of the month at even, from even unto even**. The time of year at which it was appointed shows that one purpose of its institution was to make solemn preparation for the joyous festival of Tabernacles, which was to follow in five days' time, when the people ought to be in a state of reconciliation with God.

Vers. 33—36.—The third of the great festivals, the Feast of Tabernacles—beginning on the 15th of Tisri, as the Feast of Unleavened Bread began on the 15th of Nisan—lasted seven days, and was followed by an octave; on two days, the first day and its octave, there is to be **an holy convocation**, and on these **no servile work** is to be done. The eighth day is also **a solemn assembly**. The meaning of the word *atzereth*, translated *a solemn assembly*, is doubtful. It occurs ten times in the Hebrew Scriptures, and appears to signify (1) the last day of a feast (see John vii. 37, where mention is made of "the last day, that great day of the feast"); (2) a solemn assembly held on the last day of a feast; whence it comes to mean (3) a solemn assembly. The Jews gave the name to the Feast of Pentecost, as being the close of the Feast of Unleavened Bread. On each of the seven days of the Feast of Tabernacles was to be offered **an offering made by fire unto the Lord**. The sacrifices to be offered are enumerated in Numb. xxix. 12—38. There were to be sacrificed two rams, and fourteen lambs, and bullocks diminishing by one a day from thirteen on the first day to seven on the last. These formed the burnt sacrifices. The sin offering on each day was one kid of the goats. On the eighth day the burnt offering consisted of one bullock, one ram, seven lambs, and the sin offering, as before, of one kid of the goats. Thus there were offered in all, in the eight days, seventy-one bullocks, fifteen rams, one hundred and five lambs, and eight kids, beside meat and drink offerings.

Vers. 37, 38.—These verses form the conclusion of the immediate subject. The feasts have been enumerated in which holy convocations are to be held and public sacrifices offered; these sacrifices, it is explained, not including those of the sabbath or of individual offerers.

Vers. 39—44.—A further instruction respecting the Feast of Tabernacles is appended. **When ye have gathered in the fruit of the land**, not necessarily at the completion of the ingathering, but at the time at which the festival is held, **ye shall take you on the first day the boughs of goodly trees**. The word in the Hebrew, in its literal acceptation, means fruits of goodly trees, and hence in later times a misunderstanding arose (see 2 Macc. x. 6, 7), which led to the graceful practice of carrying in the left hand citrons (the fruit of goodly trees), and in the right hand myrtles, palms, and willows. It appears, however, that the word signifies in this place rather products than fruits, namely, leaves and branches. The command, therefore, would be, **ye shall take you . . . *products* of goodly trees, branches** of palm trees, and the boughs of thick trees, and willows of the brooks. Originally, the purpose of these boughs was to make booths, as is shown by Neh. viii. 15, 16, "Go forth unto the mount, and fetch olive branches, and pine branches, and myrtle branches, and palm branches, and branches of thick trees, to make booths, as it is written. So the people went forth, and brought them, and made themselves booths." And ye shall rejoice before the Lord your God seven days. Accordingly we find when the feast was observed by Ezra, after the long interval from the days of Joshua, "there was very great gladness" (Neh. viii. 17). The reason of the injunction to dwell in booths is that your generations may know that I made the children of Israel to dwell in booths, when I brought them out of the land of Egypt; that is, on the first night after they had been delivered from Egypt, and encamped at Succoth (Exod. xii. 37).

HOMILETICS.

Vers. 9—21; 39—43.—*The harvest festivals* among ourselves receive a sanction from the divinely appointed harvest festivals of the Jews, which were three in number.

I. THE PASSOVER HARVEST FESTIVAL. 1. On Nisan 14, the selection of the field and the ears of barley which were to be cut. 2. On Nisan 15, the progress of three appointed delegates to the spot, as the sun went down, with sickles and baskets; the reaping of the barley that had been marked to be cut, and its conveyance to the court of the temple. 3. On Nisan 16, the waving of one sheaf of the barley before the Lord, in token that the whole crop, of which it was the firstfruits, was offered to the Lord in gratitude for his having given it to man for his food. Not until the firstfruits had been presented to God might the new year's barley be used. The firstfruits having been made holy, the whole lump was holy.

II. THE PENTECOST HARVEST FESTIVAL. 1. At the beginning of the wheat harvest, the reservation of the field from which the ears of wheat were to be cut. 2. On the forty-ninth day from Nisan 15, the progress, as before, of three appointed delegates to the spot, with sickles and baskets; the reaping of the wheat that had been marked; its conveyance to the court of the temple; its threshing, winnowing, and grinding, and the formation out of it of two loaves made with leaven. 3. On the fiftieth day from Nisan 15, the waving of the two loaves before the Lord, in token that the whole wheat crop, like the barley crop before, was sanctified for the use of man by a sample portion of it having been given to God. Not till after this might the meat offering be made of the new flour. 4. On the same day and subsequent days, the private offering of first-fruits, which might not be brought until the national offering of the firstfruits of the wheat harvest had been made, but kept up the harvest joyousness from that time to the end of the year. From each of the twenty-four districts into which Palestine was divided came a company. Each morning, while they were on the road to Jerusalem, their leader summoned them with the words, "Come ye, and let us go up to Zion, and unto Jehovah our God" (Jer. xxxi. 6), and they answered, "I was glad when they said unto me, Let us go into the house of the Lord" (Ps. cxxii. 1). "First went one who played the pipe; then followed a sacrificial bullock, destined for a peace offering, his horns gilt and garlanded with olive branches; next came the multitude, some carrying the baskets with firstfruits, others singing the psalms which many writers suppose to have been specially destined for that service, and hence to have been called 'The Songs of Ascent,' in our Authorized Version 'The Psalms of Degrees.' The poorer brought their gifts in wicker baskets, which afterwards belonged to the officiating priests; the richer theirs in baskets of silver or of gold, which were given to the temple treasury. . . . And so they passed through the length and breadth of the land, everywhere waking the echoes of praise. As they entered the city, they sang Ps. cxxii. 2, 'Our feet shall stand in thy gates, O Jerusalem.' . . . As they reached the temple mount, each one, whatever his rank or condition, took one of the baskets on his shoulder, and they ascended singing that appropriate hymn, 'Praise ye the Lord. Praise God in his sanctuary; praise him in the firmament of his power' (Ps. cl.). As they entered the temple itself, the Levites intoned Ps. xxx., 'I will extol thee, O Lord; for thou hast lifted me up, and hast not made my foes to rejoice over me'" (Edersheim, 'Temple Service'). The ceremonies of the actual presentation are detailed in Deut.

xxvi., "Thou shalt go unto the priest that shall be in those days, and say unto him, I profess this day unto the Lord thy God, that I am come unto the country which the Lord sware unto our fathers for to give us. And the priest shall take the basket out of thine hand, and set it down before the altar of the Lord thy God. And thou shalt speak and say before the Lord thy God, A Syrian ready to perish was my father, and he went down into Egypt, and sojourned there with a few, and became there a nation, great, mighty, and populous: and the Egyptians evil entreated us, and afflicted us, and laid upon us hard bondage: and when we cried unto the Lord God of our fathers, the Lord heard our voice, and looked on our affliction, and our labour, and our oppression: and the Lord brought us forth out of Egypt with a mighty hand, and with an outstretched arm, and with great terribleness, and with signs, and with wonders: and he hath brought us into this place, and hath given us this land, even a land which floweth with milk and honey. And now, behold, I have brought the firstfruits of the land, which thou, O Lord, hast given me. And thou shalt set it before the Lord thy God, and worship before the Lord thy God: and thou shalt rejoice in every good thing which the Lord thy God hath given unto thee, and unto thine house, thou, and the Levite, and the stranger that is among you" (Deut. xxvi. 3—11).

III. THE INGATHERING HARVEST FESTIVAL. 1. The dwelling in booths for a week in memorial of the encampment at Succoth, when the Israelites for the first time felt themselves to be free men. 2. The rejoicing for the final ingathering of the olives and grapes and the other fruits of the earth. "Thou shalt keep the Feast of Ingathering, which is in the end of the year, when thou hast gathered in thy labours out of the field" (Exod. xxiii. 16). "Thou shalt observe the Feast of Tabernacles seven days, after that thou hast gathered in thy corn and thy wine: and thou shalt rejoice in thy feast, thou, and thy son, and thy daughter, and thy manservant, and thy maidservant, and the Levite, the stranger, and the fatherless, and the widow, that are within thy gates" (Deut. xvi. 13, 14). 3. The carrying of the *œthrog*, or citron, and of the *lulav*, or palm, together with a myrtle and willow branch. 4. On the last day of the feast, the drawing water from the pool of Siloam (a ceremony of a post-Mosaic date). "While the morning sacrifice was being prepared, a priest, accompanied by a joyous procession, with music, went down to the pool of Siloam, whence he drew water into a golden pitcher capable of holding three logs (rather more than two pints). . . . The priest then went up the rise of the altar and turned to the left, where there were two silver basins with narrow holes—the eastern a little wider for the wine, and the western somewhat narrower for the water. Into these the wine of the drink offering was poured, and at the same time the water from Siloam" (Edersheim, 'Temple Service'). Our Lord shows the true symbolism of this ceremony to be the gift of the Spirit. 5. The further post-Mosaic ceremony of lighting four golden candelabra in the court of the women on the night of the first day of the feast, the wicks in the candelabra having been made of the robes of the priests worn out during the past year. This ceremony probably symbolized illumination by the Spirit.

IV. MORAL LESSON. The duty of thankfulness. It is a rabbinical saying that the Holy Spirit dwells in man only through joy. This is an exaggeration, but it teaches a truth which is forgotten wherever asceticism comes to be a subject of admiration. The service of God is a joyous service. "Thou shalt rejoice before the Lord" (Deut. xvi. 11) is the injunction of the Old Testament; "Rejoice in the Lord alway; and again I say, Rejoice" (Phil. iv. 4), is that of the New Testament. It is right that there should be special occasions on which this joy may be exhibited and encouraged. Hence the reasonableness of festivals and holy days.

HOMILIES BY VARIOUS AUTHORS.

The Passover. Ch. xxiii. 4—8; cf. Exod. xii.; also 1 Cor. v. 7, 8. In addition to the weekly "offering of rest," there were emphasized offerings of a similar character at select seasons throughout the Jewish year. These were to bring to remembrance great national deliverances, or to celebrate the blessings with which Jehovah crowned the year. The first of these feasts was the Passover. It was to celebrate the deliverance preceding the Exodus. It began with a holy convocation; there was then a week of complete freedom from leaven; and then a holy convocation completed the special observances. Burnt offerings were also presented of a special character every day of the holy week. The following line of thought is suggested by this feast.

I. THE WHOLE POPULATION IN EGYPT WAS EXPOSED TO A COMMON DANGER. It is evident from the narrative that the destroying angel might justly have carried death into every house, and that it was only the special arrangement which prevented his doing so. For though a difference was made between the Egyptians and the Israelites, it had its reason and its root in God's sovereign grace. The Israelites may not have carried their enmity to God with so high a hand as the Egyptians, yet their pilgrimage demonstrated that the hostility was there. The judgment on the firstborn was consequently only a sample of what all deserved.

Unless we begin with the truth that "there is no difference," for "all have sinned and come short of God's glory," we are likely to underestimate the grace which maketh us afterwards to differ. We are not, properly speaking, in a state of probation, but in a state either of condemnation or of salvation. "He that believeth not is condemned already" (John iii. 18); "he that believeth is not condemned." When we start with the idea that we are really culprits and condemned already, we are stirred up to lay hold by faith of the deliverance. How we reach the blessed condition, "There is therefore now no condemnation," is beautifully symbolized by the Passover. For—

II. GOD'S PLAN OF DELIVERANCE WAS THROUGH THE SPRINKLING OF BLOOD. Each Israelite was directed to take a lamb and slay it, and sprinkle on the doorpost and lintel, with a hyssop branch, its blood. The destroying angel respected the sprinkled blood, and passed over the houses on which it appeared. Here was God's plan, by the sacrifice of the life of an innocent substitute to secure the remission of the sins of his people.

And need I say that the Paschal lamb was one of the most beautiful types of Jesus? He, as our Passover, was "sacrificed for us" (1 Cor. v. 7). It is through his blood we have remission. His life, laid down in payment of the penalty, secures our just release. The destroying angel passes over all who are under the shelter of Christ's blood.

III. THE PASCHAL LAMB WAS TO AFFORD LIFE AS WELL AS SECURE DELIVERANCE. Roasted with fire, with bitter herbs and unleavened bread, it was to be eaten by all the delivered ones. Within the blood-protected houses they stood and partook of a wholesome meal. It entered into their physical constitution, and strengthened them to begin their journey.

In the same way does Jesus Christ sustain all who trust in him. He becomes our Life. He strengthens us for our wilderness journey. The Exodus from Egypt becomes easy through his imputed strength. And so our Lord spoke not only of eating his flesh, but even of drinking his blood (John vi. 54), and so receiving his eternal life. Not more surely does vital power come to the body through the digestion of food than does spiritual power come to the soul through partaking by faith of Jesus Christ. We are not only saved from wrath through him, but sustained by his life.

IV. THE PASSOVER WAS THE DATE OF A NEW LIFE. An Exodus began with the first Passover, succeeded by a wilderness journey; and every succeeding Passover preceded a week of feasting on unleavened bread. Thus was a new and heroic life regarded as dating from the Passover. Hence the Lord changed the year at its institution, and made it the beginning of months with his people.

The same is experienced by believers. Unless our salvation by Christ's blood is succeeded by pure living and the putting away of "the leaven of malice and wickedness" (1 Cor. v. 8), we are only deceiving ourselves by supposing we are saved. Our salvation is with a view to our pilgrimage and purity. Therefore we must keep the Feast of Unleavened Bread as well as celebrate the Passover. It will not do to accept of salvation as an "indulgence." God makes no arrangement for impunity in sin. The death of the Lamb shows plainly that under God's government no sin will go unpunished. To purity we are consequently called as part and parcel of a Divine salvation.—R. M. E.

The Feast of the Firstfruits. Ch. xxiii. 9—14; cf. Prov. iii. 9; 1 Cor. xv. 20. The Feast of the Firstfruits began on the second day of the Feast of Unleavened Bread, as the fifteenth and sixteenth verses about Pentecost imply. And curiously enough, the sheaf of the firstfruits was to be waved "on the morrow after the sabbath," that is, on what corresponds to our present "Lord's day." Such a coincidence should not be overlooked, and was manifestly designed. If the Passover speaks of the death of Jesus, the firstfruits are surely intended to speak of his resurrection. The death of the Paschal lamb and the presentation of the firstfruits occupy the same temporal relation as the death of Jesus and his resurrection. Hence we find in this arrangement the following lessons:—

I. THE FIRSTFRUITS HALLOWED THE SUBSEQUENT HARVEST. They were a grateful acknowledgment of God's hand in the harvest, and at the same time the condition of its being properly gathered. As one writer has very properly said, "It removed the impediment which stood opposed to its being gathered, *the ceremonial impurity*, if I may so say, which was attached to it previous to the waving of the sheaf before the Lord, until which time it was unlawful to make use of it. The prohibition on this head was express. 'And ye shall eat neither bread, nor parched corn, nor green ears, until the selfsame day that ye have brought an offering unto your God: it shall be a statute for ever throughout your generations in all your dwellings' (ver. 14). There was, then, you perceive, an *imputed uncleanness* attached to the harvest before the offering of the firstfruits, but which, when the sheaf was presented, was done away; and thus it is written, 'he (the priest) shall wave the sheaf before the Lord *to be accepted for you*.'"[1] Now, it is very plain from this that Christ, the Firstfruits, hallows the subsequent human harvest. The great ingathering of souls depends on the preceding Firstfruits for consecration and acceptance. Thus do we see in symbol that he was "raised for our justification" (Rom. iv. 25).

II. THE FIRSTFRUITS WERE THE EARNEST OF THE COMING HARVEST. Here was a sample of what was coming and was at hand. It was first ripe, but the rest was on its way. In the very same way, the resurrection of the Saviour is the earnest and pledge of that of his people. Hence Paul says, "But now is Christ risen from the dead, and become the Firstfruits of them that slept. For since by man came death, by man came also the resurrection of the dead. For as in Adam all die, even so in Christ shall all be made alive. But every man in his own order: Christ the Firstfruits; afterward they that are Christ's at his coming" (Cor. xv. 20—23). Hence we take the risen Saviour as at once the *pledge* of the resurrection of his people, and the *sample* of what our resurrection is to be. On the *pledge* implied by his resurrection we need not dwell. It is clear from 1 Cor. xv. and from other Scriptures that his resurrection is the sure guarantee of ours.

The other thought involved is quite as precious. "Our citizenship is in heaven; from whence also we look for the Saviour, the Lord Jesus Christ: who shall change our body of humiliation, that it may be fashioned like unto his glorious body, according to the working whereby he is able even to subdue all things unto himself" (Phil. iii. 20, 21). Just as Jesus in his post-resurrection life of forty days on earth showed marvellous superiority to the laws of nature by which these bodies of humiliation are bound, just as he was able on ministries of mercy to pass with the speed of thought from place to place, to enter through barred doors, and vanish like a vapour when he had dispensed his peace,—so do we hope to be possessed of an organ more consonant to the aspirations of our spirits, and better adapted than our present bodies can be to fulfil the purposes of God. The forty days before the ascension of our Saviour afford the insight now needed into the conditions of our future life, when we too are gathered as sheafs that are ripe into the garner above. "We know that, when he shall appear, we shall be *like* him." —R. M. E.

The Pentecost. Ch. xxiii. 15—21; cf. Acts ii.; also Jer. ii. 3; Rom. xi. 16; and Jas. i. 18. Having found in the firstfruits a typical reference to the resurrection of Christ, we have no difficulty on the same line in finding in the harvest festival seven weeks thereafter typical reference to the harvest of the Church of God. Primarily it was eucharistic in character, but this does not exhaust its meaning. It was exactly fifty days after the Exodus that the Law was given on Sinai, and so Pentecost was associated from the outset with the "revival of the Church of God." What happened in the Pentecost after our Lord's last Passover was the baptism of the Holy Ghost and a revived interest in God's holy Law.

---

[1] Lowe, on 'The Annual Feasts of the Jews,' pp. 27, 28.

Now, on turning to the directions about Pentecost, we find that "firstfruits" were again to be presented to the Lord, but, unlike the earlier firstfruits during the week of unleavened bread, these were to be prepared with leaven, and they were to be accompanied by a sin offering as well as burnt offerings and peace offerings. It is evident, therefore, that there is an element in the Pentecostal ritual which is not to be found in the previous ritual at all.

If Christ is typified by the first of the firstfruits presented without leaven, his people gathered out of the nations may well be typified by the second firstfruits, the accompanying leaven indicating their sinful character, notwithstanding that they are his, and the sin offering most appropriately accompanying their typical dedication.

I. LET US OBSERVE THAT THE IDEA OF THE FIRSTFRUITS IS APPLIED TO THE LORD'S PEOPLE SEVERAL TIMES IN SCRIPTURE. Thus Jeremiah calls Israel "holiness unto the Lord, and the firstfruits of his increase" (ii. 3). The same thought reappears in Paul's Epistle to the Romans, "If the firstfruits be holy, the lump is also holy" (xi. 16). James also speaks of the Lord's children in such terms as these: "Of his own will begat he us with the word of truth, that we should be a kind of firstfruits of his creatures" (i. 18). The harvest-field of God is the world, and those who are already gathered are the firstfruits. They are so far the consecrated element in the mighty population, and in spirit are laid upon God's altar.

II. THERE SEEMS A SIGNIFICANCE IN THE TWO LOAVES. "Why," it has been said, "should the lump be divided into two parts, and not be presented whole? In order, I would venture to suggest, to set forth the *two component parts* of the Christian Church —the Jews and Gentiles, *both made one* in Christ."[1] Out of the harvest-field of the world the Lord requires two loaves to be presented, the Jews and the Gentiles, laid in their unity on his altar. Paul brings out this with great beauty in Eph. ii. 14—18, where the unity of Jews and Gentiles in Jesus Christ is pointed out.

III. AFTER ALL, THE CONSECRATION OF THE LORD'S PEOPLE IS AN IMPERFECT THING. Christ's consecration was perfect because sinless. Ours is imperfect and "mired with the trails of sin." Well may the firstfruits be baked with *leaven;* well may a sin offering be presented along with them. Our holiest acts could not stand alone, but need to be repented of. Atonement has to cover the holiest efforts of the Lord's people.

Thus is all spiritual pride kept under, since at our very best we are "unprofitable servants."

IV. THE PENTECOSTAL OUTPOURING AFTER OUR LORD'S ASCENSION PRESENTS THE REALITY OF WHICH THE RITUAL WAS THE TYPE. In this glorious ingathering there was: 1. A penitential spirit. It was for this Peter called (Acts ii. 38). 2. A worldwide imitation (Acts ii. 39). The promise was to those "that are afar off, even as many as the Lord our God shall call." 3. A separation of many from the world, that they might consecrate themselves to God (Acts ii. 41). 4. A great unity of spirit (Acts ii. 44—47). It is this vivifying inspiration we all need; and may God send it soon!—R. M. E.

The Feast of Trumpets. Ch. xxiii. 23—25; cf. Numb. x. 1—10; Exod. xix. 19; Ps. lxxxix. 15. The first mention of the trumpet is in Exod. xix. 13, 19, in connection with the giving of the Law. "When the trumpet soundeth long, they shall come up to the mount" (Exod. xix. 13). It was God's method of summoning the people to covenant privileges. It was further used for the calling of assemblies, for the beginning of journeys, for alarms, and at the new moons and festal seasons, when it was blown *over the sacrifices.* Those who knew the significance of the sacrifices could rejoice in the trumpet-sound which proclaimed them complete. No wonder it is said, "Blessed is the people that know the joyful sound" (תְּרוּעָה; literally, "sound of a trumpet"): "they shall walk, O Lord, in the light of thy countenance" (Ps. lxxxix. 15).

The analogy of faith, therefore, warrants us in taking the Feast of Trumpets as symbolical of God's message of mercy to man. The gospel preached is God's trumpet, summoning men to the privileges and duties of the Christian life. This suggests—

I. THE GOOD TIDINGS ARE OF A FINISHED SACRIFICE. It is only when the sacrifice of Jesus is the foundation of the appeal that man is arrested, trumpet-like, by the

[1] Lowe, *ut supra*, p. 50.

gospel. The Lamb has been slain, the atonement complete, and, consequently, poor sinners are summoned to joy.

It would be no such joyful message if we were summoned to establish our own righteousness instead of submitting, as now, to the righteousness of God. It is a present salvation, on the ground of the finished sacrifice of Jesus, which constitutes the fountain of the purest joy. No such joyful trumpet-tones were ever heard by human ears in other religions as God gives when he says, "I have heard thee in a time accepted, and in the day of salvation have I succoured thee: behold, now is the accepted time; behold, now is the day of salvation" (2 Cor. vi. 2).

II. THE GOSPEL TRUMPET SUMMONS US TO REST. On the Feast of Trumpets "ye shall do no servile work therein." It was a summons to sabbatic rest. And truly the gospel is a call to put off the servile spirit, the obedience which comes through fear, and to enter into God's rest. "We who believe do enter into rest." Christian experience is sabbath rest after the worry of worldly experience. We lay down our burden, and pass into Divine peace. The Saturday evening of experience is when, through grace, we put away our worldliness, our feverish anxieties, our low and selfish ideals, and the sabbath morning experience is rest in God's love and bounty.

III. THE GOSPEL TRUMPET SUMMONS US TO PERSONAL SACRIFICE. If the servile work is to be surrendered for sabbath rest, we must go forward to the duty indicated. "But ye shall offer an offering made by fire unto the Lord." For this is the gospel plan— acceptance and rest on the ground of a completed sacrifice, and the personal dedication as a living sacrifice in gratitude for such unmerited favour. From the one Great Sacrifice for us we proceed gratefully to such personal sacrifice as God's honour and glory require. The love manifested in the sacrifice of Christ "constrains us to live not unto ourselves, but unto him who died for us and rose again" (2 Cor. v. 14, 15). Self-righteousness is not self-sacrifice; rather is it proud bargaining for that which God offers as a gift. But, when the gift is accepted, self is in the acceptance crucified, and a life of devotion becomes self-sacrificing indeed.

IV. THE GOSPEL TRUMPET IS TO BE SUCCEEDED BY THE TRUMP OF THE RESURRECTION. All who in their graves of sin hear the voice of the Son of God, and who, through hearing, live (John v. 25), are destined to hear another joyful note from the same trumpet: "For the hour is coming, in the which all that are in the graves shall hear his voice, and shall come forth; they that have done good, unto the resurrection of life" (John v. 28, 29). This is "the voice of the archangel and the trump of God" through which the dead in Christ shall rise (1 Thess. iv. 16). "We shall not all sleep, but we shall all be changed, in a moment, in the twinkling of an eye, at the last trump: (for the trumpet shall sound,) and the dead shall be raised incorruptible, and we shall be changed" (1 Cor. xv. 51, 52).

Such are the summonses which God gives to men to privilege, to peace, and at the last to everlasting felicity. The preachers who give no uncertain sound, but proclaim with trumpet-tongue the gospel, are the heralds who are preparing for the day of the Lord, with its everlasting rest and light and love!—R. M. E.

The annual repentance—the Day of Atonement. Ch. xxiii. 26—32; cf. ch. xvi.; Heb. ix. 12. Into the ritual of the Day of Atonement we need not here enter, after what has been said on the subject under ch. xvi. But the reference here is to the spirit of repentance which was to characterize the people on that day. It was, in fact, a call to the whole congregation to repent and be reconciled to God. As the Day of Atonement is in all respects the climax of the sacrificial worship, it may be useful here to notice the spirit which belonged to that worship and the corresponding spirit in man which it demanded.

I. THE SPIRIT OF JUDAISM IS THAT OF EXCLUSION FROM THE DIVINE PRESENCE. Ever since man's fall until the vail was rent at the death of Jesus, man was deservedly kept at a distance from God. Sin is a separating power; as long as it is harboured it prevents near access to him. And even when, in the Exodus, God delivered a chosen people to bring them to himself (Exod. xix. 4), they were only permitted to come up to certain barriers round about the holy mount. When, moreover, the Lord transferred his dwelling-place from the top of Sinai to the tent or tabernacle provided by his pilgrim people, he insisted on having a private apartment, railed off from vulgar gaze, and only allowed one representative man, the high priest, to draw nigh unto him once a year. He certainly sent this honoured individual forth with his blessing, to encourage the people waiting without. But the whole arrangement of the Day of Atonement was on the principle of excluding the people until such times as they might profitably have closer access. "God sent his people," says an able writer, "his blessing, to show them that he had not forgotten them. But he would not see them. Even the high priest saw but a very little of him at this annual solemn time. The cloud of fragrant incense filled the most holy place, and barred the view." [1]

II. There is nothing so humiliating as this denial of access. On the Day of Atonement the people came to the tabernacle, and saw their select representative enjoy the privilege of drawing nigh to God all alone. Not a man of them dare venture beyond the vail. Nadab and Abihu, who seem to have done so, intoxicated by their elevation to the priesthood and perhaps also by wine, perished before the Lord. The Israelites felt at the tabernacle that they were an *excluded* people. This would lead to self-examination, and to repentance for the sin which excluded them. Doubtless the ritual of the great Day of Atonement would have a soothing effect upon their spirits. The blessing would fall upon their souls like balm. At the same time, they could not but feel that access to God was for them through a mediator, and that they were kept at a very humiliating distance.

III. Our Great High Priest has given us the reality of access in that he has become our Forerunner. This is the beautiful idea suggested by the apostle in the Hebrews (vi. 20). Christ has not entered the holiest to enjoy a privilege in solitude. He has entered it as our Forerunner, to announce our approach. This applies, not only to the everlasting felicity of heaven, but also to present devotional access to God. Through him we are permitted to draw nigh. The vail is rent; therefore we draw near with holy boldness. We are no longer an excluded people, but in the enjoyment of close communion. When the vail was rent at the death of Jesus, the ordinary priests were thereby raised to the privilege of the high priest. All had alike access to God. Hence we are to live up to our privilege as believers; for we are priests unto God, and access is our right through the rending of the vail of our Redeemer's flesh.

Thus do we see the secret of penitence on the Day of Atonement, and how it is the preliminary arranged by the All-wise to communion with himself close and eternal.— R. M. E.

The pilgrim spirit as illustrated in the Feast of Tabernacles. Ch. xxiii. 33—43; cf. Ps. xxxix. 12; Heb. xi. 13; 1 Pet. ii. 11. The seventh month was a very celebrated one in the Jewish year. It was the sabbatic month, so to speak, when religious services of the most important character took place. The Feast of Trumpets introduced the month, and joyful were the anticipations of blessing. Then on the tenth day, came the great ritual of atonement, with its penitential sadness. Then came, on the fifteenth day, the beginning of the Feast of Tabernacles. In the rainless harvest-time the people were expected, even after their settlement in Canaan, to spend a week in booths or tents, and with boughs of goodly trees, with palm branches, and with willows of the brook to rejoice before God. Now this feast was—

I. A celebration of the pilgrimage of the wilderness. It was "that your generations may know that I made the children of Israel to dwell in booths, when I brought them out of the land of Egypt" (ver. 43). It is most important to keep a great deliverance in mind. Hence the people were enjoined once a year to become pilgrims again, as their fathers had been. We should never forget how the Lord has led his people in every age out of bondage into pilgrimage and freedom as the avenue to rest.

II. It was a celebration of the Divine provision in the wilderness. For it was a harvest festival, and the fruits of the earth had been gathered in before the feast began. Before them lay, so to speak, the bounties of God's providence, just as the manna lay morning by morning before their fathers. God was praised, therefore, for crowning the *year* with his goodness, as their fathers praised him for crowning with his goodness each *day*. It was consequently a eucharistic service in the highest degree.

III. It was a celebration of the stranger and pilgrim spirit which God

---

[1] Tait's 'Thoughts for the Thoughtful,' p. 160.

FOSTERS IN ALL HIS PEOPLE. The voluntary leaving of their homes for a season to live in a " tented state " was a beautiful embodiment of the stranger and pilgrim spirit to which we are called. God in the wilderness dwelt as the Great Pilgrim in a tent with his pilgrim people; and year by year he enjoined his people in their generations to become literally "strangers with him" (Ps. xxxix. 12), as their fathers had been. And the same danger threatens us, to feel at home in this world and to give up the pilgrimage. Hence the apostle's warning is ever needful: "Dearly beloved, I beseech you as strangers and pilgrims, abstain from fleshly lusts, which war against the soul" (1 Pet. ii. 11). If the world does not seem strange to us, it is because we are not living as near as we ought to God. The more access we have to him, the greater will be our moral distance from the world.

IV. THE JOY OF THE FEAST OF TABERNACLES WAS ENHANCED BY THE HOME-GOING WHICH LAY BEYOND IT. The " tented state " is not intended to be permanent. Its value lies in its temporary nature. Canaan lay in sunlight beyond the wilderness, and the thought of " home " there encouraged them in their pilgrimage. The week's camping out after Canaan had been reached made them enjoy their home life all the more. In the same way, while we confess like the patriarchs to be " strangers and pilgrims upon the earth," we are seeking, and rejoicing in the prospect of yet reaching, a better country, with a city of God and permanent abodes (Heb. xi. 13—16). The pilgrimage is joyful because it is destined to end in the everlasting home. Perpetual pilgrimage no man could desire, for this would be perpetual exile from legitimate home joys. A long pilgrimage can be welcomed if it lead towards everlasting joy in the Father's house.

And is there not an element of triumph associated with such a celebration as this Feast of Tabernacles? It indicates victory over worldly feeling through faith in God. No wonder, then, that palm branches and goodly boughs were waved by joyous ones before the Lord. It is into victorious joy he summons all his people as the earnest of the everlasting joy with which he is yet to crown them.—R. M. E.

Vers. 4—14.—*The Passover*. Under this general title we include the Feast of Unleavened Bread, and the offering of the firstfruits which was connected with it. The history of the institution is given in Exod. xii. That the Passover was a type of Christ is evident (see 1 Cor. v. 6—8).

I. THE LAMB TYPIFIED HIS PERSON. (John i. 36.) 1. *It was taken from the flock* (Exod. xii. 9). (1) As it had been one with the flock, so was Jesus one with us. His humanity was no phantom, but a reality. (2) What an honour is conferred upon us, that the God of glory should stoop to assume our nature, to become " bone of our bone "! Let us not dishonour ourselves by sinning against such grace. 2. *It was a male of the first year.* (1) This was ordered because the male is the stronger animal, and was viewed as an emblem of excellence. Christ amongst men is the most excellent ; "the fairest amongst ten thousand." (2) Hence he is distinguished as " The Son of David," as "The Seed of Abraham," as " The Son of man." David had many sons, but in comparison with him they were nowhere; so he is *the* Son of David, the one glorious descendant who throws all others into the shade. So with the seed of Abraham. So with the sons of Adam. In the whole race there is no one to compare with him. 3. *It was without blemish.* (1) The blemishes that would disqualify a Paschal lamb were physical, and so, abstractedly considered, of little account. But these blemishes were typical of moral evils, and in this view were very important. (2) But Christ was, in the moral sense, absolutely blemishless. He was unique. Singular, however, not in eccentricity but in transcendent goodness. As under the microscope the works of God are seen to differ essentially from those of men, appearing more variously and wonderfully beautiful as they are more nearly examined under higher powers, so the more minutely Christ is considered the more wonderful and beautiful is he seen to be.

II. ITS SACRIFICE FORESHADOWED HIS PASSION. 1. *The lamb suffered vicariously.* (1) When taken from the flock the rest of the flock was spared. So was Jesus chosen that by his suffering his nation and his race might not perish (see John xi. 49—53). (2) The blood of the lamb was sprinkled on the doorposts of the houses to avert the wrath of the destroying angel. The firstborn in every house was sacrificed where no vicarious blood appeared. So are we saved from wrath by the sprinkling of the blood of Jesus Christ through faith. (3) Those saved from destruction through the blood of the lamb were immediately led out of Egypt, and set on their way to Canaan. So those justified through the blood of Christ are delivered also from the bondage of corruption, and set on their way to heaven. 2. *Remarkable circumstances claim attention.* (1) The lamb was to be "of the first year," *i.e.* in its prime. So was Christ in the prime of his manhood when he was offered. (2) It was to be offered "in the place which the Lord should choose" (Deut. xvi. 5—7). That place was Jerusalem (2 Kings xxi. 7; Ps. cxxxii. 13, 14). There also "our Passover was sacrificed for us." (3) "In the fourteenth day of the first month at even is the Lord's Passover" (ver. 5). Some think that our Lord, in accordance with the usage of the Karaites, or Scriptiarii, killed and ate the Passover a day earlier than the Pharisees, and that he expired on the cross at the time when the Traditionarii were employed in killing their Paschal lambs (see Ikenii, 'Dissert. Theolog.,' tom. ii. chs. ix., x., xi.). Be this as it may, the word in the text translated "at even" is literally *between the evenings*; that is, between the chronological and ecclesiastical, which would be at the "ninth hour," or three p.m. This was the very hour at which Jesus expired (Luke xxiii. 44—46). (4) It was ordered that no bone of the Paschal lamb should be broken. And whereas the legs of the malefactors were broken, the soldiers, seeing that Jesus was dead already, brake not his legs (see John xix. 31—36). Such things could not have been ordered by chance.

III. THE FEAST CORRESPONDED TO THE CHRISTIAN EUCHARIST. 1. *The latter was accommodated to the former.* (1) This is evident from the history of the institution. For the cup of the Eucharist Christ used that cup of the Passover, which was called by the Jews the "cup of blessing," and which description Paul applies to the Christian cup (1 Cor. x. 16). For the bread of the Supper he used that of the Passover (Luke xxii. 15—20). (2) So when Paul speaks of Christ as "our Passover sacrificed for us," he adds, "let us keep the feast," meaning, *allusively*, the Feast of Unleavened Bread, and *really* that which replaces it in the Church. 2. *Both are retrospective and anticipative.* (1) The Hebrews commemorated the type, viz. the deliverance from the destroying angel and from Egypt. The Christians commemorate the antitype, viz. the deliverance of souls from the anger of God and from the tyranny of sin. (2) The Hebrews anticipated their entrance into Canaan. The Christians anticipate the joys of heaven; the new wine of the kingdom. 3. *Both are tokens of Church communion.* (1) The Passover was not the rite *initiatory* into the Church of Israel. Circumcision was that rite. To this, baptism, under the gospel, corresponds, and is therefore called the circumcision of Christianity (Col. ii. 11, 12). (2) But it was the rite *continuative* of such communion. Exclusion from the Passover was excommunication under the Law. So is the Eucharist the sign amongst Christians of a continued Church communion.

"On the morrow after the sabbath," viz. of the Paschal week, the sheaf of the first-fruits was waved before the Lord (vers. 10, 11). This was a type of Christ in his resurrection as the Firstfruits of the great harvest (see 1 Cor. xv. 20—23). But when Christ died, the sabbath of the Paschal week happened upon the day in which he lay in the tomb (comp. John xix. 31; Luke vi. 1). Thus the morrow after this sabbath was precisely that first day of the week on which our Lord arose (Mark xvi. 9). How strengthening to faith are all these correspondences!—J. A. M.

Vers. 15—22.—*The Feast of Harvest.* This was the second of the three great festivals upon which all the males of Israel were required to assemble at Jerusalem (see Exod. xxiii. 14—17; Deut. xvi. 16). Let us consider—

I. THE DUTIES THEN ENJOINED UPON THE WORSHIPPERS. 1. *They were to meet in holy convocation.* (1) This was intended to keep alive their interest in the service of God. Were sabbaths and public services of religion to cease, men would soon forget God. (2) All Israel looked each other in the face. Religion is eminently social. And as these convocations were types of heavenly things, this suggested the recognitions and greetings of the future (see Heb. xii. 22, 23). (3) On this day servile work was to cease. The teaching here is that when we congregate in heaven we shall be emancipated from the curse of toil (comp. Gen. iii. 17; Rev. xxii. 3). 2. *They were to present two wave loaves.* (1) These were composed of two tenth-deals of fine flour. They were to sanctify the wheat-harvest as the sheaf of the firstfruits sanctified the barley harvest. Hence these also are called "firstfruits" (vers. 17, 20; Exod. xxxiv. 22). (2) They were to be baken *with leaven.* As the *unleavened* bread of the Passover was a memorial of the haste with which they departed from Egypt, this was to express thankfulness to God for the blessings of ordinary food, together with their rest in Canaan. (3) One loaf was to be eaten by the worshipper, while the other was God's. That more completely given to God was divided. One portion was burnt on the altar, while the priests took the remainder (Numb. xviii. 9—11). This explains the injunction that they should be waved along with the peace offerings. We learn here that our ordinary bread should be religiously eaten (see 1 Cor. x. 31). (4) These wave loaves constituted one of three meat offerings of the whole congregation. The first was the sheaf, or omer, of the firstfruits of the barley harvest (vers. 9—14). This was the second. And the third was the twelve loaves of the shewbread (Exod. xxv. 30; ch. xxiv. 5—9). Could there be here a prophetic anticipation of the order of the resurrection, viz. "Christ the Firstfruits; afterwards they that are Christ's at his coming;" and, finally, the "rest of the dead," destined to live again at the end of the millennial reign, when death shall be abolished? (comp. 1 Cor. xv. 23—26; Rev. xx.). (5) Beside the firstfruits, which were strictly national, each person had to bring his own firstfruits to the temple (see Deut. xxvi. 1—10). God would have us ever to remember that religion is personal as well as public. 3. *They were to offer sacrifices.* (1) The burnt offerings appointed were seven lambs of the first year without blemish, one young bullock, and two rams, or, as elsewhere expressed, two young bullocks and one ram (comp. ver. 18; Numb. xxviii. 27). As burnt offerings were intended to expiate sins against affirmative precepts, the godly worshipper would pray during the burning, as David prayed (Ps. xix. 13). The meat and drink offerings proper to burnt offerings accompanied (ver. 18). These were distinct from the two tenth-deals waved to sanctify the harvest. (2) A kid of the goats was appointed for a sin offering (ver. 19). As sin offerings were to expiate sins committed in ignorance, the thoughts of the worshipper were carried forward to the Great Sin Sacrifice of Calvary. (3) Two lambs of the first year were appointed for the peace offering. These were distinguished from those usually offered as "holy to the Lord for the priest." They were to be eaten by him before the Lord. For the meat offering which ordinarily accompanied the peace offerings, in this case the two loaves of the firstfruits were substituted (vers. 19, 20).

II. THE NOTES OF TIME, WITH THEIR REASONS. 1. *They counted from the putting in of the sickle.* (1) This, however, was not left to private option. That would have worked endless confusion; for it was a public, national, act. The Lord is a God of order (1 Cor. xiv. 40). It would have tended to will-worship. The evils of this are seen in the Romish Church. We cannot too literally abide by the letter of Divine precept. (2) It was limited to the second day of the Passover week (vers. 15, 16). From this reckoning the Jews call this Feast of Harvest (חמשים יום) *the fiftieth day.* For the same reason, it is in the New Testament called the *Pentecost* (Acts ii. 1; xx. 16; 1 Cor. xvi. 8). 2. *They commemorated the giving of the Law.* (1) The observance of the Passover was on the fourteenth of the first month (Exod. xii. 18), leaving seventeen days of that month to run. To these add thirty days of the second month, and we have forty-seven days. But the Law was given on the third day after Moses came into the wilderness of Sinai, which was in the beginning of the third month (Exod. xix. 1, 10, 11). These three days added bring the number up to fifty. (2) Well might the Israelites have a festival of thanksgiving for the giving of the Law; for thereby they were honoured and blessed as no other nation had ever been (Deut. iv. 8). 3. *They anticipated the publication of the gospel.* (1) The gospel is the Law of God, published from Zion, in contradistinction to that published from Sinai (see Isa. ii. 3). That publication took place "when the day of Pentecost was fully come." (2) The fifty days were counted from the second day of the Passover week, on which the firstfruits of the barley harvest were presented (vers. 15, 16). That "firstfruits" were a type of Christ in his resurrection. After that event he was seen of his disciples during forty days. The Pentecost followed exactly ten days after the Ascension (see Luke xxiv. 49; Acts ii. 1). (3) Note, further, that the Holy Ghost was given on the first day of the week. The Paschal lamb was eaten on Thursday. The Friday on which our Lord was crucified was the first day of the Passover week. On the Saturday the firstfruits were offered up. Consequently, the Pentecost, which was the fiftieth day after, would fall upon the Sunday. Thenceforth this became "the Lord's day," or the Christian sabbath (see Lightfoot on Acts ii.).

Where gratitude is there will be goodness. Hence the injunction to care for the poor and the stranger (ver. 22). This spirit of the Law is also the genius of the gospel.—J. A. M.

Vers. 23—44.—*The hebdomad.* Seven in Scripture is a very remarkable number. In the text it is repeated in so many forms that it forces itself upon our attention.

I. HEBDOMADS ARE CONSPICUOUS IN THE CHRONOLOGY OF THE LAW. 1. *They appear in the week of days.* (1) The foundation of this is the Creation week. The patriarchal sabbath became incorporated into the Mosaic Law. There were other weeks of days and sabbaths. In the text there are three of these, with a sabbath on the first and another on the eighth day. (2) Could there be in these an anticipation of the change of the sabbath from the seventh day to the first or eighth under the Christian dispensation? The sabbaths of the seventh and eighth days may point to the rest of the millennium in the first instance, and to that of the new heavens and earth in the second. In observing the Lord's day, it would be highly edifying to have these anticipations in mind. 2. *They appear again in the week of months.* (1) The entire cycle of the feasts of the Lord was comprised in such a week. It commenced on the 14th day of Abib, with the Passover, instituted in commemoration of the Exodus. Then followed, in their appointed seasons, the Feast of Unleavened Bread; that of the Firstfruits; the Feast of Harvest, which is also called the Feast of *Weeks* (Exod. xxxiv. 22; Deut. xvi. 10, 16; 2 Chron. viii. 13). The series ended with the festivals of the seventh month. (2) During the five months remaining there was no annual feast. The daily sacrifices and those of the sabbaths and moons were of course continued. (3) The moon was a symbol of the Church, and its changes represented the mutations through which it passes in this world, but when it has fulfilled its great week of changes it will be perfected for ever in heaven. 3. *They appear again in the week of years.* (1) The Law had its septenary division of years, with a continually repeated seventh year of rest for the land (chs. xxv. 3—7; xxvi. 34, 35; 2 Chron. xxxvi. 21). (2) Founded upon this also was a greater period of a week of weeks of years, with its year of jubilee (ch. xxv. 8—17). The lessons of the sabbatic and jubilee years will come under consideration in their proper places.

II. HEBDOMADS ARE CONSPICUOUS IN THE CHRONOLOGY OF PROPHECY. 1. *The days of the week are taken as prophetic.* (1) David, and Peter from him, notes that one day is with the Lord as a thousand years (Ps. xc. 4; 2 Pet. iii. 8). Paul also mentions the sabbath-keeping of the future "which remaineth to the people of God" (Heb. iv. 9). And John describes that rest as extending over a thousand years (Rev. xx. 4). (2) To this agrees the tradition in the house of Elias, a teacher who lived about two hundred years before our Lord, and which is thought to have been derived from Elijah the Tishbite. It purports that this world is to endure in its imperfect state six thousand years: two thousand before the Law; two thousand under the Law; two thousand under Messiah; and then a thousand years in a state of renovation (see Mede, 536, 776, 894; also Bishop Newton's ' Disser.,' vol. iii. 335). (3) The same view is no less definitely put forth by Barnabas. He makes each day of the Creation week represent a thousand years of the subsequent history of the world, and the sabbath he makes to stand for the reign of peace, or millennium of John. 2. *Dispensations are measured by weeks of times.* (1) The "times of the Gentiles" are accepted to be the same as the "seven times," during which Israel was destined to be trodden down of them. Upon the year-day principle these are the double of the "time, time, and dividing of a time" of Daniel and John, during which the little horn was to wear out the saints, and represent 2520 years. The larger period commences with the literal Babylon, and the smaller with the mystical. (2) But how can the Patriarchal, Levitical, and Christian dispensations be limited to six thousand years, if each is to extend over 2520? They do so by overlapping each other. Thus the patriarchal extends "from Adam to Moses" (Rom. v. 13, 14), which space comprises "seven times." The Jewish then reckons from Shem the patriarch, selected as the depositary of the covenant, to Jesus. The interval from Shem to Jesus measures "seven times." The dispensation of the Gentiles, already described as the "times of the Gentiles," forms the third. It began with the rise of the ancient Babylonish power, and will end with the overthrow of the mystical Babylon.

III. HEBDOMADS ARE NOT WITHOUT FOUNDATION IN NATURE. 1. *They are not very obviously marked in the heavens.* (1) The day is measured by the revolution of the earth upon its axis. The month is measured by the revolution of the moon in her orbit. The year is determined by the revolution of the earth about the sun. (2) But where are we to find the measure of the week? The quarters of the moon do not measure it, for the month is more than four times seven days. 2. *Yet they have a foundation in nature.* (1) It is now well known that changes in animals are regulated by weeks. Dr. Laycock, summing up what he had advanced on this subject in a series of remarkable papers, says, "The facts I have briefly glanced at are general facts, and cannot happen day after day in so many millions of animals of every kind from larva or ovum of a minute insect up to man at definite periods, from a mere chance or coincidence; and although temperature, food, domestication, and other modifying circumstances may and do interrupt the regularity with which the various processes I have alluded to are conducted, yet upon the whole it is, I think, impossible to come to any less general conclusion than this. That in animals changes occur every three and a half, seven, fourteen, twenty-one, or twenty-eight days, or at some definite number of weeks" (see *Lancet*, 1842—43). (2) The words recorded by Moses (Gen. i. 14) guide us to the consideration of the revolution of the *epacts*, or differences in solar and lunar measures of time. And it is most admirable that the epacts of the times of prophetic chronology as measured by true solar and lunar years come out in *weeks* (see Guinness's 'Approaching End of the Age').

From this interesting subject we learn: 1. That prophecy is from God. 2. That the God of nature is the God of providence. 3. That religion should be interwoven with secular concerns.—J. A. M.

Vers. 23—25.—*The Feast of Trumpets.* "The Old Testament," says Augustine, "when rightly understood, is one grand prophecy of the New." The New Testament is the key to the Old.

I. THE MOON WAS A SYMBOL OF THE CHURCH. 1. *Its lustre sets forth her beauty.* (1) Even in our Northern climate the moon is a beautiful object; but in Oriental skies she is remarkably so. Solomon compares the beauty of the bride to that of the moon (Song vi. 10). (2) She shines in a light borrowed from the sun. So is the lustre of Jesus the loveliness of his Church (see Isa. xxx. 26; comp. Matt. v. 14 with John viii. 12; Rev. xii. 1; xxi. 23). (3) As the moon enlightens the darkness in the absence of the sun, so is the Church the light of the world in the absence of her Lord (see Matt. v. 14; John i. 4; ix. 5; Phil. ii. 15). All men should be attracted to the communion of the Church by the charms of her beauty. Professors should beware how they may hinder this issue by their inconsistencies. 2. *Its changes set forth her vicissitudes.* (1) The renewals of the moon will represent the dispensations through which she passes. Thus the patriarchal, which is divided into two ages, viz. that before the Flood, and that which followed. The Mosaic, which also is divided into two ages, viz. that of the tabernacle and that of the temple, the latter being more eminently the age of prophecy. The Christian dispensation likewise is distributed into two ages, viz. the present militant and suffering age, and the triumphant age of the millennium to come. Perhaps the seventh moon may then anticipate the celestial state to follow (see Isa. lx. 19, 20). (2) The phases through which each moon passes will represent corresponding minor changes in the Church. She too has her waxings and wanings. Sometimes she is brightened by revivals of purity and zeal, which are followed by seasons of apostacy and degeneration. Sometimes she rejoices in seasons of peace and prosperity; then suffers persecutions and reverses.

II. THE SEVENTH WAS DISTINGUISHED AMONG THE MOONS. 1. *It was a high sabbath.* (1) The new moons were all observed as sabbaths. No servile work was done in any of them (see Amos viii. 5). They were memorials of the believers' rest from servility to Satan. (2) But this moon was the beginning of the civil year, and is believed to be the time of the Creation, when vegetable nature was in perfection. It gratefully commemorated the old Creation. It joyfully anticipated the new. 2. *It was a holy convocation.* (1) The people assembled for worship. This is God's order. Those who neglect public worship under the pretext of "worshipping the God of nature in the fields," follow their own order. (2) In company, they heard the Word of God (see

2 Kings iv. 23 ; Isa. lxvi. 23 ; Ezek. xlvi. 1 ; Amos viii. 5). (3) They feasted together upon the sacrifices (Numb. xxviii. 11—15). Thus they anticipated the spiritual festivities of the gospel, and the glorious festivities of heaven. (4) They rejoiced in the light of the moon (Ps. lxxxi. 3 ; lxxxix. 15, 16). If the Psalmist rejoiced in the anticipation of the light of the gospel moon, how much more should we rejoice under that light ? 3. *It was a memorial of blowing of trumpets.* (1) The trumpets were blown upon every moon, but on the seventh so signally that it thence became distinguished as the Feast of Trumpets. The trumpeting began at sunrise and continued till sundown. This moon not only ushered in the new month, as the others did, but also the new (civil) year. (2) The trumpets were sounded over the sacrifices. These were in greater number. There were not only the daily sacrifices, which were never superseded, and the ordinary sacrifices of the moons, but burnt offerings, meat and drink offerings, and a sin offering, proper to this feast (Numb. xxix. 2—6). The sounding of the trumpets over these indicated the preaching of the gospel to be the preaching of the *cross* of Christ (see Isa. xxvii. 13). (3) The trumpeting was in *memorial.* If it referred to the giving of the Law, we are reminded of the trumpet that then sounded from Sinai ; and the gospel law was sounded out from Sion. If the memorial referred to the Creation, then we are reminded that the Psalmist calls the word by which God made the world, " the voice of his thunder " (Ps. civ. 7). We are also reminded of the singing of the morning stars and shouting of the sons of God (Job xxxviii. 6, 7). The shouting and thundering at the Creation and at the giving of the Law and the preaching of the gospel are but the echoes of the voices and trumpeting of the Judgment of the great day. " He that hath ears to hear, let him hear." When the last trumpet is sounded, it will be, as on the Feast of Trumpets, at the finishing of the gathering of all the fruits of the earth.—J. A. M.

Vers. 26—32.—*The Feast of Expiation.* This great occasion, the ceremonies of which are more particularly described in ch. xvi., was to be—

I. A HOLY CONVOCATION, IN WHICH THE PEOPLE WERE TO AFFLICT THEIR SOULS.   Learn hence : 1. *That sin must be mourned.* (1) It should be mourned in *secret.* There are matters which it may be proper to confess to God alone. The confession of these to others would serve no useful purpose. It might even be productive of harm. (2) It should be *publicly* mourned. Where there are national sins they should be openly confessed. Sins against society should be publicly owned. The general public confession of sin is useful in calling individual sin to remembrance. (3) Contrition for sin is indispensable. To neglect it is to incur excision (ver. 29). 2. *The mourning must be thorough.* (1) No secular work must be done on this day in which men were to afflict their souls. Not only were they on this day to rest from " servile work," as on the other annual feasts ; the rest must be as strict as upon the weekly sabbaths. If we would have salvation, we must be in earnest. We must not suffer the claims of the world to divert us from this great business. (2) The soul must be afflicted with *fasting.* The *animal soul* is here referred to (see ch. xvi. 31 ; Numb. xxix. 7 ; Isa. lviii. 5, 6). The spirit of a religious fast is abstinence from all kinds of sin. 3. *The soul is to be afflicted because of the atonement.* (1) They were to bring an " offering by fire unto the Lord " on this day. The sin and trespass offering had respect to particular sins, but the burnt offering was for sin in the abstract. The sacrifices of this day were of the greatest importance, and eminently typified the Great Atonement of the gospel. (2) Penitence is never perfect till we get a view of Calvary. Because he is merciful we fear God with a gracious fear. With such a fear is holiness perfected (2 Cor. vii. 1).

II. THIS HOLY CONVOCATION WAS ON THE TENTH DAY OF THE SEVENTH MONTH. 1. *This was to suggest the riches of redemption.* (1) For the mystery of the number ten is *wealth.* So the Hebrew word for *ten* (עשר) is also the word for *riches.* (2) Hence because of his riches of merit and wealth of blessings, viz. as the Depository of all the promises, Christ is called a *Tenth* (see Isa. vi. 13). (3) When Isaiah calls Christ the Tenth, he describes the Tenth as of the nature of bread. Bread is the " staff of life," and Christ is the " Tree of life "—the Bread of immortality. Hence all the holy bread, as prefiguring Christ, was composed of *tenth*-deals of flour. So the meat, or bread, offering ; so the firstfruits ; so the shewbread ; even the manna was gathered in omers, or tenths (see Exod. xvi. 36 ; see also Mal. iii. 10). 2. *The association of the tenth day with the seventh month also is suggestive.* (1) It suggests the perfection of riches to be associated with the mysteries of the day. This we find only in connection with the great atonement of Christ. Other wealth is poverty compared with the "riches of Christ." (2) Note elsewhere the association of seven and ten in weeks of decades. Thus the term of human life is a week of decades, at the close of which the rich rewards of a faithful life are reaped (Ps. xc. 10). But "the wicked do not live out half their days." They come short of the "durable riches." The week of decades was the term of the Babylonish captivity (Jer. xxiv. 11; xxix. 10). And towards the close of that period the week of weeks of decades was revealed to Daniel as destined to mark the crisis of the great atonement (see Dan. ix. 24). (3) Dr. Lightfoot computes that the Feast of Expiation was the anniversary of that on which Moses came the last time down from the mount, bringing with him the unbroken tables and the assurance of God's reconciliation to Israel, the very glory of the gospel beaming in his face. Moses in this was a similar type to the high priest on the Day of Atonement (see 2 Cor. iii. 12—18). (4) It is still more remarkable that Jesus, on the anniversary of these events, actually entered the cloud of the Shechinah, and passed within the vail into the heaven of heavens (see reasoning to this conclusion in the appendix of Guinness's 'Approaching End of the Age'). These coincidences are not accidental. They are "the Lord's doing, and marvellous in our eyes." Such things as these, and in such the Holy Scriptures abound, prove them to be from God, and should encourage our faith and obedience.—J. A. M.

Vers. 33—44.—*The Feast of Tabernacles.* This was the last of the great annual festivals of the Hebrews. It was a season of great joyfulness. Let us notice—

I. THE REASONS OF ITS APPOINTMENT. 1. *It was to assure them of God's return to dwell with them.* (1) This reason is not given in the text, but may be gathered from the history. The commission to build the tabernacle of witness, which had been suspended in consequence of their rebellion, was renewed to Moses in the mount. When he brought them these good tidings, he directed them to construct booths, for they were to abide in their present encampment until the work should be accomplished. (2) In due time the Shechinah possessed the tabernacle. This glorious event foreshadowed the sublime mystery of the incarnation (comp. John i. 14). How wonderful is that grace of the gospel according to which believers become the shrines of Deity! (1 Cor. iii. 16; vi. 19; 2 Cor. vi. 16). 2. *It was to remind their children that their fathers camped in the desert.* (1) The condition of Israel in the wilderness described the Christian in his journey through the world in quest of the heavenly Canaan. (2) The dwelling in booths exhibited the changeful and unsettled nature of earthly things (see Heb. xi. 9). This fact is obvious; yet we need to be reminded of it. (3) The Hebrews dwelling happily in Canaan were not to forget the humble state of their fathers. Prosperity leads us to forget the day of humility; therefore this Divine institution recurring annually to counteract that tendency. In the review of the barbarity of our ancestors, we may feel more grateful to God for the blessings of civilization. 3. *It was to be a yearly national harvest thanksgiving.* (1) This is here specified in the note of time, viz. "when ye have gathered in the fruit of the land" (ver. 39). The vintage as well as the harvest was then gathered in (see Exod. xxxiv. 22; Deut. xvi. 13). The goodness with which God crowns the year should ever be celebrated by us with grateful hearts. (2) In Exodus the Feast of Tabernacles is called the Feast of Ingathering (xxiii. 16; xxxiv. 22). Thus viewed, it was an anticipation of the Resurrection. The general resurrection is that final ingathering at the end of the world's great year, of which the resurrection of Christ was the firstfruit (1 Cor. xv. 20). (3) This thanksgiving was on the fifteenth day of the seventh month, five days after the Day of Atonement, on which the people had afflicted their souls. The joys of salvation follow upon the sorrows of repentance. The joys of the Resurrection rise out of the horrors of Calvary.

II. THE MODE OF ITS CELEBRATION. 1. *It began and ended with a holy convocation.* (1) The first day, perhaps the fourteenth day of the seventh month, the eve of the feast, was kept as a sabbath from servile work. God should be served in our everyday employments; yet must there be cessation from those employments for his more especial service. Great importance is attached to social worship in Holy Scripture. (2) The eighth day also was a sabbath. This was distinguished as "that great day of the feast" (see John vii. 37). Upon it the full round of sacrifices were offered (ver. 37). On this day also the people of God returned to their houses, and so celebrated their entrance into Canaan after the toils of the wilderness, and anticipated the rest of heaven. The freedom from servile work on this day showed that at the last day all toil will terminate in the glorious rest of eternity. (3) This was the day on which "Jesus stood and cried, saying, If any man thirst," etc. (John vii. 37, 38). The occasion appears to have been that of the priest's pouring out as a libation water which he had drawn from the pool of Siloam in a golden flagon. This ceremony was not prescribed in the Law. Jesus calls off attention from human ceremonies to himself. 2. *On the fifteenth day they gathered the boughs for their booths* (ver. 40). (1) This employment had its obvious economic use. They needed the shelter which their tabernacles afforded. (2) But there was a religious import in what they did; and the trees were emblematical. The thick shady trees, such as the oak or beech, afforded shelter and protection, and suggested the protection and shelter of the covenant of God. The "palm" was an emblem of victory (Rev. vii. 9). The "willows of the brook" represented the thriving condition of the happy (Isa. xliv. 4). The olive was a symbol of peace (see Neh. viii. 15). When Jesus proved himself to be "the Resurrection and the Life" by his miracle upon Lazarus, the people acknowledged it by the boughs of trees (John xii. 13). 3. *Sacrifices were offered which were reduced in number each succeeding day.* (1) (For the account of the sacrifices, see Numb. xxix. 12—38.) (2) Could the reduction in the number be intended to foreshow that the typical sacrifices were destined to vanish away?

Jacob seems to have anticipated this feast on his entering into Canaan (see Gen. xxxiii. 17). Anticipations of the Law, as well as of the gospel, are often seen in the history of the patriarchs.

After the plague upon the enemies of Jerusalem in the last days of the Gentiles, the remnant will turn to the Lord, and keep the Feast of Tabernacles (see Zech. xiv. 16). The gospel teaches us now to go out to Christ without the camp.—J. A. M.

Vers. 4—8.—*The influence of sacred recollections.* The great festival of the Passover derived all its meaning from one memorable historic scene. It annually recalled one event of surpassing interest, and, by so doing, it impressed all susceptible souls with those leading truths to which God called Israel to bear its living testimony. We look at—

I. THE SPECIAL SCENE WHICH THIS FEAST COMMEMORATED, AND THE INFLUENCE IT WAS FITTED TO EXERT. What a night in Hebrew history that night of the Lord's Passover! What false confidence in every Egyptian, what agitated hearts and trembling hopes in every Hebrew, home! With what solemn awe, and yet with what thrilling expectation, did their forefathers in the land of bondage partake of that strange meal! With what eager carefulness did they see that the saving blood-stream marked the lintels of the door which would shut in their dear ones! And what a morning on the morrow! What joyous congratulations in each Hebrew home when they *all* met, in life and health, on that memorable march! And what terrible consternation, what wild cries of anguish and remorse in those Egyptian houses where the angel of death had *not* passed by, but had struck his fearful stroke! It was the hour of Jehovah's most signal interposition; it was the hour of national redemption. They might well remember it "in all their dwellings through all their generations." This festival recalled the scene and also the deliverance to which it immediately led. And the influence on the minds of all who observed it, both parents and children, was, or surely should have been: 1. To strengthen their attachment to one another. There was danger, with the distribution into tribes, and with the Jordan cutting off two tribes and a half from the rest, that their national unity might be lost, and thus the distinctiveness for which they were called into being disappear. These common, sacred memories would help to bind them together and to keep them one. 2. To preserve their allegiance to their Divine Deliverer. These sacred recollections must excite (1) a sense of deepest obligation; (2) a corresponding feeling of profound gratitude for such signal mercy; (3) a consequent renewal of their consecration of themselves to Jehovah's service; and especially (4) a determination to live that life of purity and separateness from heathen iniquity of which the "unleavened bread" spoke daily to their minds.

II. NATIONAL MERCIES WHICH WE HAVE RECEIVED FROM GOD AND THE INFLUENCE

THESE SHOULD EXERT ON US. We are apt to celebrate the greatness of our country with too little reference in our minds to the special favours we have received from God. The separation, through geological processes, of our land from the continent; the store of treasure laid up for our use beneath the surface; the mingling of races resulting in our strong English character; the upraising of mighty and godly men (Alfred, Wickliffe, Tindale, Wesley, etc.), who have wrought great things for us; the effectual and lasting deliverance of our land from the bonds and corruptions of Rome; the security of religious freedom; the rise and growth of the missionary and, subsequently, the evangelistic spirit, etc. These things and such things as these are national mercies, which we should frequently recall, and, remembering them, we should (1) guard against national boastfulness, as if our "right hand" had done everything; (2) cultivate a sense of national obligation, with its accompaniment of reverent gratitude; and especially (3) realize that we are what we are in order that we may bear witness to God's truth, and extend the kingdom of Jesus Christ.

III. SPECIAL INDIVIDUAL MERCIES WE HAVE RECEIVED AND THE INFLUENCE WE SHOULD GAIN FROM THEIR REMEMBRANCE. Every human life, when it has reached maturity, contains instances of special as well as ordinary loving-kindness from the hand of God. These may be (1) recovery from dangerous illness; or (2) extrication from financial embarrassment; or (3) preservation of some precious life; or (4) deliverance from forming a foolish and fatal friendship, or from the perils attending compulsory association with the wicked; or (5) sense, suddenly or gradually imparted, of the supremacy of sacred things resulting in the acceptance of Christ as Lord and Saviour; or (6) revival from spiritual sloth and backsliding. The remembrance of these calls for (1) humility, (2) gratitude, (3) consecration.—C.

Vers. 9—14.—*Provision and piety.* We have here—

I. THE DIVINE FORETHOUGHT. Jehovah (1) anticipated the religious wants of his people, and made due provision for them. "When ye be come into the land . . . and shall reap the harvest thereof, then ye shall bring," etc. (ver. 10). God has anticipated our spiritual necessities with every provision in the gospel; there will never arise any necessity for which there is not, in Christ Jesus and his salvation, an adequate supply. (2) Anticipated their bodily necessities. He was preparing for them corn and wine and oil in the land whither they went. So God is, through all the months between seed-sowing and harvest, "preparing us corn," providing for our nourishment, and also for our enjoyment. His hand of power is ever working (John v. 17) in anticipation of our wants and wishes.

II. HUMAN PIETY IN RESPONSE. The goodness of God, shown to us through all generations, demands intelligent and devout response. We are reminded by the beautiful act of symbolism here enjoined—the presentation of the first sheaf of the harvest unto the Lord (vers. 10, 11)—that our responsive piety should show itself in: 1. Conscious dependence on God, the Source of all life and strength; the waving of the firstfruits was a clear acknowledgment that the whole came from him and belonged to him. 2. Gratitude to God, the bountiful Benefactor. Undoubtedly this was to be a principal element in the institution; their hearts were to be filled with thankfulness for the harvest then about to be gathered in. There is not *less* gratitude due to our gracious God for giving us food as the result, in part, of our own labour, skill, intelligence, and patience; there is, in truth, *immeasurably more,* for it is the kindest way of doing the kindest thing; it is a way in which he has regard not only to our physical requirements, but also to our moral and spiritual well-being. 3. Fellowship with God. The meat and drink offerings (ver. 13) spoke of the fellowship of the worshipper with Jehovah himself. We are, as reconciled children, to have communion with the God whom we love, to rejoice in his presence, to sit down at his table. 4. Consecration to God. (1) The burnt offering (ver. 12) pointed to the dedication of themselves to the Lord; and (2) the strict injunction of ver. 14 intimated that they were to bring to the service of Jehovah the first produce of the fertile land he had given them. This is the culmination of true piety, the (1) presentation of ourselves to him as to the One whose we are (Rom. xii. 1; 1 Cor. vi. 19, 20), and (2) bringing the first and the best we have to his holy service (Prov. iii. 9); laying ourselves and our substance on the altar of our Lord.—C.

Vers. 15—22.—*Piety in prosperity.* We often speak of our duty in the day of adversity, of the spirit which true piety will then manifest. It is of equal consequence that we should consider what is its rightful attitude in the hour of prosperity. When the harvest is gathered, the nation is rich; when the fruits of the field are in the garner, the husbandman is safe for another year. The time of harvest may, therefore, stand for the position of prosperity. And these verses may suggest to us that when it is well with us in our outward circumstances there should be—

I. GRATEFUL ACKNOWLEDGMENT OF THE HAND OF GOD. At the Feast of Pentecost two loaves, leavened, of the finest flour, the firstfruits of the wheat harvest, were waved by the priest "for a wave offering unto the Lord." The successful agriculturist is apt to say to himself, if not to others, "This is the harvest I have grown;" is disposed to congratulate himself on the excellency of his own farming. By this act of waving the presentation loaves, the Hebrew husbandman said, "I have ploughed, and sown, and weeded, and reaped, and ground, and baked, but thou, Lord, hast given the increase; thine was the sun that shone, thine the rains that fell, thine the airs that blew, thine the wondrous power that made the elements of nature work out the germination and growth and ripening of the corn: unto thy Name be the honour and the praise." Whatever may be the sphere of our activity, the character of our success, this is to be "the spirit of our mind;" we are to be ready to make grateful acknowledgment of the hand of God in all satisfying results.

II. HUMILITY. "Ye shall sacrifice one kid of the goats for a sin offering" (ver. 19). The people of God were, on all occasions, even the most joyful, to own their unworthiness, and to seek the forgiving favour of God. The sin offering must find a place even at the Pentecostal feast. When we are most "glad in the Lord," we do well to make mention of our frailty, our folly, our imperfection, and to ask that, for our Saviour's sake, it may be forgiven, and we ourselves be accepted of God.

III. SACRED JOY. With the burnt offering there was to be the accompanying "meat offering, and their drink offerings" (ver. 18). And with the sin offering there were to be offered, "two lambs of the first year for a sacrifice of peace offerings" (ver. 19). Here was a very distinct note of sacred joy. When there is harmony without, there must be songs in the soul, but these should not be without strains of sacred music which will be acceptable in the ear of God. Let the voice of joy be heard in our halls, but let us be glad "before the Lord," remembering the goodness and realizing the presence of him whose we are and whom we serve.

IV. CONSECRATION. "They shall be for a burnt offering unto the Lord" (ver. 18). There is no time more appropriate than the hour of increase and prosperity to renew our vows unto our God, and rededicate our whole lives to his service.

V. CHARITY. (Ver. 22.) We must remember "the poor and the stranger." That is an evil and miserable prosperity, unsightly in the esteem of man and hateful in the sight of God, which seeks to wrap itself up in silken folds of selfish enjoyment; that is an honourable and admirable prosperity, blessed of God and man, which has a kindly heart and an open hand for those who are beaten in the battle, for those who are left behind in the race of life.—C.

Vers. 23, 24.—*The summons of God.* The trumpet utters a sound that summons attention from every ear. It is distinct from every other note; it is clear, startling, strong. When God bade his prophets declare his mind to the people he desired them to "blow a trumpet in Zion." The feast which was distinguished by the blowing of trumpets may have been intended to remind Israel, or may remind us of—

I. THEIR RESPONSIBILITIES UNDER THE LAW. When the sacred music was heard at this festival, the Jews could hardly fail to think of that august occasion, when "there were thunders and lightnings, and a thick cloud upon the mount, and the voice of the trumpet exceeding loud," etc. (Exod. xix. 16). They would thus realize that they were children of the Law, that they existed as a nation for the very purpose of receiving, preserving, and revealing the Law of the Lord, that they had entered into sacred covenant with Jehovah, that they had a great mission to fulfil. The trumpet was the voice of the Lord, saying to them, "Realize what you are."

II. THE PRIVILEGES WHICH WERE IMMEDIATELY BEFORE THEM. This was "New Year's Day" to them: the year was before them; it would be a year during which God would be speaking to them and they to him. Daily sacrifices would be laid on his altar. Special rites would demand peculiar devotion; one of these—the most sacred of all—was close at hand; privilege and opportunity were awaiting them, would meet them with the advancing seasons of the new year on which they had entered; the trumpet of the Lord said, "Listen and obey, for God is with you." The Feast of Trumpets reminds us of—

III. THE MORE GRACIOUS ERA TO WHICH WE BELONG. There was no such overwhelming scene at the inauguration of the gospel as that at the giving of the Law. No " voice of the trumpet sounding long, and waxing louder and louder," no " thunders and lightnings." The kingdom of God " came not with observation;" " he did not strive nor cry, nor cause his voice to be heard in the streets." Yet he " spake as never man spake " before, and as man will never speak again, and at the beginning of every year we may, without any trumpets sounding, hear a voice from heaven saying to us, " This is my beloved Son ; hear ye him." God summons us to learn of him, and know from him (1) how to be related to himself, (2) the spirit in which we should act to our fellows, and (3) the way to rule our own spirit and regulate our own life. We may also be reminded of—

IV. THE LAST DAY OF THIS DISPENSATION. The day draws on when the " trump of God " shall sound, summoning the dead to life, calling the living and the dead to judgment and award (see 1 Cor. xv. 52; 1 Thess. iv. 16). At any hour of our life, but especially on any anniversary, when we are reminded of the passage of our probationary life and the oncoming of the day of his appearing, we may well hear the summons of God to prepare for that great day.

> "Great God, what do I see and hear?
>
> *   *   *   *   *
>
> The trumpet sounds, the graves restore
> The dead which they contained before.
> Prepare, my soul, to meet him."
>
> C.

Vers. 33—43.—*Joy before the Lord.* The idea that, under the ancient Law, Israel was a peculiarly severe and gloomy nation, is essentially false. Gravity rather than light-heartedness may indeed have characterized them: they may have had much " seriousness of soul ; " but they were familiar with joy, and sometimes gave themselves up to great and continued gladness of heart. It was radiant sunshine in Israel during the Feast of Tabernacles. The whole engagements of the sacred festival suggest to us—

I. THAT SORROW IS OFTEN FOLLOWED BY JOY, AND THAT SACRED SORROW IS THE SOURCE OF PUREST JOY. It is significant that this Feast of Tabernacles came only five days after the Day of Atonement, the day on which they were commanded to " afflict their souls " (see vers. 27, 34). How often does a very small interval divide joy and sorrow ! so checkered are the scenes of our mortal life, that no man in brightest circumstances can ensure to himself five days' prosperity, and that no man under the darkest cloud need despair of seeing the sun break speedily and shine serenely on his path. And when sorrow is hallowed by reflection, submission, prayer, there is laid the foundation of purest joy. The happiness which is born of submission to the will of God is something which " satisfies and sanctifies the mind." It is a joy that lasts.

II. THAT PROSPERITY DOES WELL SOMETIMES TO TURN A BACKWARD LOOK ON THE ADVERSITY IT HAS LEFT BEHIND. (Vers. 40, 42, 43.) It was well for Israel, dwelling in strong and comfortable houses, to spend one week in the year in the " booths," which took them back in thought to the tents of the wilderness. When God gives either to a man or to a nation to rise out of obscurity and hardship into prominence and comfort, to pass from spiritual destitution to a state of abounding privilege and opportunity, nothing is more desirable than that he (or it) should occasionally revert to the old days of toil or want, and have his (its) heart filled with thankfulness to him who plants our feet upon the rock, who lifts us up to the high place of prosperity and power.

III. THAT HAPPINESS IS SAFE ONLY WHEN IT IS SANCTIFIED. The Hebrew nation was to " rejoice before the Lord seven days " (ver. 40). The heart of the people was to be filled with overflowing gladness, but it was to be poured out " before the Lord : " so it was safe and salutary. Happiness, success, attaining the height of our hopes,—this is very apt to run into (1) unrestrained mirth, or (2) proud complacency of spirit, or (3) unchristian selfishness. So it becomes a curse to him who should be blessed. Let us take care to " rejoice before the Lord," to turn joy into gratitude, to go with our gladness into the sanctuary of the Lord, to consecrate our substance to his service, to consult his will in the way in which we shall use our power or our opportunity ; then will our increase and elevation, of whatever kind it be, prove a blessing, and not a bane to ourselves and to our neighbours.

IV. THAT EARTHLY JOY IS THE JOY OF HAPPY PILGRIMAGE. Our earthly house is but a tabernacle (2 Cor. v. 1) ; it is to be soon taken down and to give place to a " house in the heavens." We are, as the Hebrew nation, dwelling in booths. This is but a transitory condition ; we must not think and act as if it were our " continuing city." Such joy as pilgrims have, who are ever looking forward to a blessedness to come, we may permit ourselves. But alas ! for him who " has his reward " here, and looks for none hereafter, whose only heritage is in the " world that passeth away." Well is it for him whose holy happiness is a preparation for, and an anticipation of, the blessedness which is beyond, which abides and abounds for ever.—C.

Vers. 1—44.—*The festivals.* Vers. 1—3, *the sabbath.* The three features of it are: the *convocation* ; *the rest* from all work ; the sabbath of the Lord *in their dwellings.*

I. The PUBLIC WORSHIP of God is the main reason for the sabbath. "Holy convocation." Necessity that one day should be appointed. Importance of preserving that day of worship from distraction and disturbance. Influence of public worship on the general interests of religion, and therefore on the individual, community, and the world at large.

II. REST. "Ye shall do no work." The physical necessity of an interval of rest. The moral importance of giving opportunity to the higher powers of the nation for free development. The reaction of the sabbath on the working capacity, both by physical recuperation and moral strength. The difference between God's Law and the " gospel of work" preached by many. The secularist empties life of its dignity and glory, and at last sacrifices it to the Molech of this world's necessities and pleasures.

III. The sabbath of God is a SABBATH IN OUR DWELLINGS. Religion sanctifies home life and family affection. Rest in the house of God is rest in the house of man. The law of religion shields all life from injury, and cherishes the glad and happy in the midst of the laborious and troublesome. We should take care that the sabbath at home is both rest and worship, that it is not spent in idleness or even self-gratification, but, being given to God, becomes the more really our own—not by slavish regulation of the hours, but by the spirit of worship pervading all our surroundings and employments. The sanctuary and the home open into one another.—R.

Vers. 4—8.—*The Passover and the Feast of Unleavened Bread.* This may be regarded as the opening festival of the year, and the closing one was the Feast of Tabernacles ; typically representing the life of God's people passing from redemption to restitution. The Jewish sacred year may be taken to represent the progress of Divine grace. The foundation of all is the Passover—redemption, the death of Christ the Paschal Lamb. The main ideas are—

I. All true life resting on the true beginning of peace and rest in the offering up of the Lamb of God for the sins of the world.

II. All true holiness, bread without leaven, pure fruits of man's labour, offered to God, springs out of faith. Morality is an outcome of religion. Reconciliation with God is the beginning of the consecrated life.

III. The Passover, a national celebration, set forth the true strength of the national life, as the life of God in the nation. The world can be renovated only as it is regarded as a world redeemed. Christianity is the only religion adapted to be a universal message to mankind. Hence its catholicity.—R.

Vers. 9—14.—*The first sheaf a wave offering of the harvest.* Festival of firstfruits. May be viewed (1) *naturally* ; (2) *typically.*

I. The consecration of human life and its results to God. 1. As an expression of thankfulness and praise. 2. As an act of faith and hope.

II. TYPICAL view of the firstfruits. 1. Christ the Firstfruits. In the Resurrection (1 Cor. xv. 20). Of humanity as renewed and restored to perfection. 2. The true doctrine of election, the firstfruits the pledge of the harvest. Israel separated from the world for the hope of the world. 3. Individually. Our present life consecrated is a pledge of future glory. We shall reap hereafter the full harvest of redemption. Profession and dedication. The wave offering, "before the Lord" and before his people, in the sanctuary; as a sacrifice; in the covenant.—R.

Vers. 15—22.—*Day of Pentecost* (cf. Acts ii.).

I. THE BLENDING TOGETHER OF THE NATURAL AND SPIRITUAL LIVES. The harvest of the earthly labour, the harvest of grace.

II. INTIMATE CONNECTION BETWEEN THE TWO FESTIVALS OF PASSOVER AND PENTECOST. The seven weeks', that is, week of weeks', interval, pointing to sacred bond between them. The fruits of righteousness are by Jesus Christ. Pentecostal grace flows from redemption as a fountain, as summer from spring, as harvest from seed-time.

III. HISTORICAL FULFILMENT of the idea of Pentecost in the outpouring of the Spirit, the ingathering of the firstfruits of the Christian Church, the beginning of the new life and new joy of the world. Christ arising and bringing forth fruit. Mingling together of the wave loaves and the bloody sacrifices, typical of the union of the work of Christ and the work of the Spirit. The sabbath in the harvest, the rest in the work, the true reward of life in the enjoyment of God. The mission of Christianity to the poor and the stranger. Universal joy. All the field brings forth blessed results for all the world.—R.

Vers. 23—25.—*The Feast of Trumpets.* "A sabbath, a memorial, a holy convocation." Probably recalling the giving of the Law from Mount Sinai. Therefore typical of the *proclamation of the gospel*, which is the new law of love.

I. The people of God unite together to spread the sound of the gospel in the world.

II. They rejoice in it. It is a festival—a work which is sabbatical.

III. It is immediately connected with the great Day of Atonement, and the proclamation will be no uncertain sound, but a distinct announcement of the saving truth set forth in the sacrificial death of Christ.—R.

Vers. 26—32.—*The great Day of Atonement* (see on ch. xvi. 29—34).—R.

Vers. 33—44.—*The Feast of Tabernacles* (cf. Neh. viii. 17; Zech. xiv. 16).

I. PRAISE FOR ACCOMPLISHED REDEMPTION AND THE BOUNTEOUS GIFTS OF PROVIDENCE. Reminiscences of the wilderness life. Fact that Israel neglected the feast from Joshua to Nehemiah, even in the time of great national prosperity in Solomon's reign, very instructive, pointing to ingratitude and unbelief. The religious life and the natural life blended. The joy of praise binding families together, and so nations and the world.

II. The symbolical meaning of the feast—THE GLORY OF ISRAEL AND THE ULTIMATE RESTITUTION OF ALL THINGS. The prophecy of Zechariah (xiv. 16) not to be taken literally, otherwise its significance is narrowed; but as a spiritual anticipation of the enlargement of the true Church until it shall embrace the world. The gospel invites men to rejoice in the Lord.

III. The feast on earth—A FORETASTE OF THE HIGHER LIFE OF HEAVEN. Dwelling in booths—temporary, frail, withering, yet by their nature, as pleasant places of shadow, pointing to the rest that remains for the people of God. The wilderness life leads on to the life of Canaan; the earthly festival to the heavenly; the frail tabernacle to the "city of habitations," "having foundations," etc.—R.

Ver. 4.—*Religious festivals.* This chapter has been termed, from its contents, the Calendar of Feasts. Underneath much that has been abolished by the gospel, we can trace principles and truths of permanent application, invested with interest for the Christian as well as the Jewish Church. Surface views are of little worth; if not misleading, they are at best transitory in nature.

I. TRUE RELIGION HAS ITS FESTIVALS. The word rendered "feasts" in the text means

" fixed times ; " but in ver. 6 " feast " is the translation of a word that signifies rejoicing, whose expression is dancing or processions. By their devotion to Jehovah, the Israelites were not to be continually shadowed in gloom, nor deprived of the legitimate mirth that attached even to heathen celebrations. Only they were to be the "feasts of the Lord," in his honour—not to the deification of Baalim or Ashtaroth. " Rejoice in the Lord " is our privilege as Christians, and to realize every privilege is also a duty. It is time that the popular idea were corrected which dissociates a profession of religion from all that savours of high enjoyment.

II. THE CHARACTERISTIC OF A FESTIVAL IS THE GATHERING TOGETHER OF GOD'S PEOPLE. "Convocation" gives the force of the original—it is "a place of calling." Solitary joy does not constitute a feast of Jehovah. Just as some are prone to neglect private meditation, so do others slight the public communion of saints. The chief promise of the Lord's presence is granted to those "assembling" in his name. We ought to make an effort to attend all the festivals of the Church; we are called to them, and are guilty of disobedience if, without reasonable excuse, we do not respond. Numbers exert an exhilarating influence upon the mind; a large meeting is generally inspiriting to all concerned. The gatherings, sometimes held apart from the tabernacle in accordance with the injunctions of this chapter, developed into the worship of the synagogue, the model of our services upon the Lord's day.

III. HOLINESS IS THE PURPOSE, AND SHOULD BE THE RULING FEATURE, OF THESE GATHERINGS. They are termed "holy" convocations, and are thus distinguished from the wild orgies of heathendom. Neither Roundhead austereness nor Cavalier licentiousness is here designed. Especially should we aim in our modern religious meetings at edification; not indulging to excess in humour and levity, but preserving decorum whilst rising to intelligent, godly enthusiasm. By such a time of sacred gladness we shall prove the truth of the utterance, " The joy of the Lord is your strength." The apostle intimates (1 Cor. xi. 10) that our behaviour in Church assemblies should be governed by a knowledge of the fact that the angels are spectators. Let our august visitors be treated with respect. So shall these meetings prove preparations for above, for the general assembly and Church of the Firstborn, and the innumerable hosts of angels.

IV. THE FESTIVAL INVOLVES ABSTINENCE FROM SERVILE WORK. (See ver. 7.) The usual occupations are renounced, and rest, not of indolence, but of spiritual activity, is enjoyed. The good that thereby results to the physical and spiritual frame can hardly be overestimated. Energy and time are not wasted, but improved. It is well that a man should not be always trammelled by the claims of business, but discern that there are other obligations it is incumbent on him to discharge. The chain that never leaves the neck will eat itself into the flesh, and liberty become impossible. If the head be continually bent towards the earth, it will become a matter of utmost difficulty to raise it to behold the heavens. To work at our worldly calling, to minister to the wants of the body, is not the only or the noblest task we are expected to perform; the soul has its rights and needs, and Jehovah his prerogatives.

V. FESTIVAL GATHERINGS ARE OF REGULAR RECURRENCE. " Which ye shall proclaim in their seasons." What is irregularly attended to is liable to be overlooked; what is anticipated can be prepared for. The weekly observance of a day of holy convocation prevents every pretext of forgetfulness and insufficient notice, and reminds us, in addition, of the flight of time. The methodical man parcels out his days; and a regard for order is evident in all the precepts of Scripture.—S. R. A.

Vers. 10, 11.—*The beginning of harvest.* Advantage was taken of the long sojourn in the wilderness to promulgate and instruct the people in the Law, that they might be ready to execute its commandments as soon as full opportunity was afforded by a residence in a settled country. To dwell upon such future observances could not but strengthen the faith of the people in God's intention to bring them eventually into the promised land. Of all the anticipations connected with that land, the most pleasing was the prospect of seeing the golden grain standing in the fields inviting the reaper's sickle.

I. THE RECOGNITION OF GOD AS THE GIVER OF ALL GOOD GIFTS. 1. *Here he is recognized as the God of providence,* whose kind hand enriches man with the fruits of earth, causing the seed to germinate, and perfecting and ripening it with sun, air, and rain. Israel thus rebuked the folly of surrounding nations, who deified the earth as a personal goddess; and the conceptions of the modern materialist who refuses to see in nature any trace of an overruling Deity, and of the pantheist who identifies God with his works, may be similarly reproved. And if the blessings received from Providence are to be acknowledged, surely the same argument will apply to all the many favours, temporal and spiritual, that stream upon us as the children of God. In fact, what have we of intellectual, physical, or propertied endowment that did not proceed from him? 2. *Recognized by the congregation as a whole.* Family, corporate, national religion is distinct in a sense from individual worship, and God may honour the one as such apart from the particular merits of the other. The entire body ought, however, to resemble the component units; otherwise there is felt to be an incongruity that mocks the Being whom we intend to magnify. The Americans have shown that, apart from what is called State religion, there may be hearty national recognition of God. 3. *The general does not exclude the personal acknowledgment of God's goodness.* In ch. ii. 14 are found regulations respecting the presentation of free-will individual firstfruit offerings. The service of the sanctuary should stimulate and not serve as a substitute for private prayer and praise. Let the congregational dedication be seconded by a personal self-surrender to the glory of God.

II. THE METHOD OF ACKNOWLEDGMENT. 1. *An offering brought to the Lord,* viz. a sheaf of barley, which is "waved" by the priest, the symbolical act indicative of surrender of property to God. By returning a portion of what was originally bestowed, God's proprietorship and man's stewardship are signified in fitting manner. Each Church and family should pay its tithe to the Lord, separating some of its members to religious work. 2. *Such an offering may provide for the support of God's appointed servants.* This sheaf was not consumed upon the altar, but was for the benefit of the priests. Those who by reason of exclusive devotion to the altar cannot find leisure to sow and reap, must be remembered by the people in whose behalf they labour. To assist the servants of Christ is to render help to the Master himself. Let the wealthy in the receipt of their dividends think upon the men who are their representatives in Christian effort. The division of labour must not allow one field of industry to be entirely isolated from the rest. 3. *Other offerings naturally accompany the particular presentation.* The one food reminds of other blessings, and so, besides the firstfruit sheaf, there are brought a burnt offering, a meat offering, and a drink offering, constituting a festal sacrifice. One gift prepares the way for another, opens the door so that a presentation of a different kind may follow. He who sets apart a portion of time for God is not likely to stop there, but will contribute money and influence likewise.

III. THE PRIORITY OF GOD'S CLAIM TO HONOUR. 1. *It precedes our own enjoyment.* No bread, nor parched corn, nor green ears must be tasted till Jehovah has been duly acknowledged as the bountiful Giver. The rent must be paid ere we can settle down to comfortable possession of the house. Men think they can without impropriety reverse this order, attending first to their own needs and pleasures, and then to God's requirements. In two ways they err—they dishonour their Maker, and they fail to hallow the enjoyment of their daily food and privileges by the happy consciousness that a portion has been previously dedicated to God. To acknowledge our indebtedness is to send us back rejoicing to our dwellings. 2. *It is not right to wait until the whole amount of blessing has been reaped.* At the very beginning of harvest this ceremony occurs, consecrating the harvest toil, ensuring the favour of God upon the remainder. Men who delay an offering until they know the exact amount of their savings, are likely to find the total less than they hoped. It is well to give in faith, seeing quite sufficient reason already to evoke a testimony of gratitude. "Honour the Lord with thy substance, and with the firstfruits of all thine increase: so shall thy barns be filled with plenty, and thy presses shall burst out with new wine." For the first convert in a place that seems teeming with promise of fruitfulness, we would at once give thanks. Ere the multitudes of happy dead can be raised and gathered into the heavenly garner, Jesus Christ is risen and become the Firstfruits of them that sleep. His appearance before God as the Perfect Offering guarantees an ample blessed harvest.—S. R. A.

Vers. 40—43.—*The Feast of Tabernacles.* There were three great festivals for the Israelites, the dates for which were plainly marked, and at which times it behoved the males of the nation as far as possible to be present at the sanctuary. It is the last of these we are about to consider. The regulations for its observance were enunciated in fullest detail. Were not the people thus reminded that they assisted in the celebration of the ceremonies of a royal court? The Christian Church has its festivals, prominent among which are its gatherings on the Lord's day, and the observance of the Lord's Supper. Much of what can be said with reference to the Israelitish feasts is applicable also to the latter.

I. THIS WAS THE MOST JOYOUS OF THE FESTIVALS. "Ye shall rejoice before the Lord your God." 1. See *God's delight in the happiness of his people.* He loves to witness their rejoicing. Religion was never intended to be synonymous with gloom or moroseness. 2. *This was the crowning festival of the year,* and therefore ought to be its climax of joy. For the child of God better days are ever in store; he need never pine for the past to return; each festival shall surpass the preceding. Jesus keeps the best wine till the last; not so with the world's pleasures. 3. It took place five days after the solemn Day of Atonement, when the national sin was purged, and Israel's communion with its God re-established. *To confess sin and obtain pardon is the fitting preparation for gladness of heart.* No man who has not experienced the feeling of relief from the burden of guilt and the emotion caused by restoration to his heavenly Father's favour, knows the meaning of real joy. Compared with this the delights of sense and intellect are flavourless. 4. *Joy reaches its highest expression in the presence of God.* "Rejoice *before the Lord,*" even the holy righteous God who searches the heart and tries the reins. We may without pride know that we have done what was right, and that the Being of beings approves our conduct and graces the festival with the light of his countenance. There is none of the secret misgiving that attends sinful banquets, where the laugh is hollow and the gaiety forced, from a conviction that conscience is being silenced and moral law violated. Cf. the rejoicing of the people, and the terror of Adonijah and his guests (1 Kings i. 40, 49). David danced for glee before the Lord when the sacred ark was brought into the city of David. "Rejoice, O daughter of Zion, for thy king cometh unto thee." We would fain have the children glad when it is said, "Let us go unto the house of the Lord."

II. THIS WAS A FESTIVAL OF GRATITUDE FOR RECENT BLESSINGS. 1. Another name for it was *the Feast of Ingathering.* All the produce of the ground had been garnered, the Lord had blessed them in all their increase—corn, oil, and wine; daily food and luxuries abounded; the booths were constructed of fruit trees and leafy palms. God's bounteous bestowment was acknowledged. Spiritual and temporal mercies had enriched the people and evoked manifestations of thanksgiving. So visibly dependent is man upon God for the germinating and maturing of the grain and fruit, that a harvest thanksgiving seems peculiarly appropriate, and again at the storing of the harvest, when the work for the year is practically ended, a festival is of evident fitness. The compassions of the Lord, "new every morning," furnish ample matter for devout meditation and praise. 2. *This feature of the festival was a reason why all should share in it,* not only the wealthy, high-born Israelites, but the strangers, the fatherless, the widow, and the poor (Deut. xvi. 14). God allows his sun to shine and rain to descend upon all, and he expects those who receive his lavish gifts to invite others to participate in the enjoyment thereof. Anticipating our Lord's directions to summon to a feast the poor and maimed and blind, the Israelites were accustomed to "send portions to them for whom nothing is prepared." Selfish exclusion was thus prevented, and universal rejoicing made possible. 3. *An offering to God from each was essential.* "They shall not appear before the Lord empty; every man shall give as he is able" (Deut. xvi. 17). Speech and sentiment without deeds are rightly deemed insincere. It is true of all converts from heathendom that when they give of their substance to God we may infer that they have first given him their hearts. The priests and Levites were in part supported by these national free-will presentations. If we esteem the Master, we shall treat his servants well for his sake.

III. THIS WAS A COMMEMORATION OF FORMER BLESSINGS. During seven days the Israelites dwelt in booths made of green boughs to remind them of the days when they sojourned in the wilderness (ver. 43). 1. *Previous experience may well be remembered.*

If it pass into oblivion, its lessons have not been graven on the mind, and our state has not proved the discipline it was designed to be. Stand, O believer, upon the mount of present station, and survey the path with all its windings by which you have ascended to this lofty summit. Such a review will be profitable in the extreme, it will produce deepened humility and thankfulness. Keil says, "the recollection of privation and want can never be an occasion of joy." Surely he forgets the Latin line, "hæc olim meminisse juvabit." Contrast ever heightens joy, a danger successfully surmounted is one of the most pleasing of memories. 2. *The exhibition of God's protecting grace and love demands particular recollection.* Not the might and resources of the Israelites, but the watchful, provident care of Jehovah, had led them safely through the desert. He had been to them "a booth for a shadow in the daytime from the heat, and for a place of refuge, and for a covert from storm and from rain" (Isa. iv. 6). The honour of God was concerned in having a permanent memorial of Israel's stay in the wilderness, and this institution was adapted to preserve the continued confidence of the people in him and consequent freedom from boastful self-assertion. In many ways, "the joy of the Lord is our strength." 3. *The deliverances wrought for our forefathers in olden days should excite gratitude to God in our breasts.* Can we recall unmoved the triumphs of the early Christians, or the heroism which God's Spirit enabled martyred Protestants to evince? The wonders of our age become the heirlooms of the ages that follow.

CONCLUSION. The sacrifice of Jesus Christ commemorated in the Lord's Supper was the Passover of the Church; the descent of the Spirit at Pentecost marked the era of the Church's Feast of Weeks; the Feast of Tabernacles yet waits its due counterpart, when the elect shall be gathered into the kingdom from every land, to celebrate the cessation of earthly toil, to exult in the complete removal of sinful stain, and to enter upon the undimmed, undying gladness of the eternal sabbath. Not one of God's people shall be missing through illness or distance of abode, and a retrospect of the pilgrimage of earth shall enhance the bliss of heaven.—S. R. A.

EXPOSITION.

CHAPTER XXIV.

A connection between ch. xxiii. and ch. xxiv. 1—9 is found by Keil in the fact that the oil for the holy lamps and the shewbread were offerings of the people, a sacrificial gift with which Israel was to serve the Lord continually. "The offering of oil, therefore, for the preparation of the candlestick, and that of fine flour for making the loaves to be placed before Jehovah, formed part of the service in which Israel sanctified its life and labour to the Lord its God, not only at the appointed festal periods, but every day; and the law is very appropriately appended to the sanctification of the sabbaths and feast days prescribed in ch. xxiii." But it is better to consider the whole chapter parenthetical between chs. xxiii. and xxv., the first part having been suggested by the list of days on which holy convocations were to be held, because it is connected with the temple or tabernacle service; the second part (the blasphemer's death) being inserted because it chronologically happened shortly

after the law as to holy convocations and festivals had been pronounced.

Vers. 1—4.—The ordinance on the lamps contained in the first three verses is repeated from Exod. xxvii. 20. The oil to be used for the lamps was to be **pure oil olive**, that is, oil made of picked berries, without any intermixture of dust or twigs; and it was to be **beaten** instead of "pressed," because when the berries were crushed in the olive-press, small portions of them became mixed with and discoloured the oil, which was, therefore, less pure than when the fruit was simply beaten and then left to drain. The lamps were **to burn continually**; that is, from evening to morning every night. **Without the vail of the testimony, in the tabernacle of the congregation**; that is, in the holy place, as distinct from the holy of holies. **Aaron**, either personally or by his sons (see Exod. xxvii. 21), was to dress the lamps every morning, and light them every evening (Exod. xxx. 7). The lamps were upon the seven-branched candlestick, which is called **the pure candlestick**, because made of gold. The light of the seven-branched candlestick symbolized the enlightening power of the Holy Spirit, which should illumine God's Church (Zech. iv. 2—6; Rev. 1, 12, 20).

Vers. 5—9.—The shewbread, or bread of

the face, that is, of the presence, was to be made of fine flour, that is, of wheat, and to consist of twelve cakes or loaves, to represent the twelve tribes of Israel, each loaf containing upward of six pounds of flour. The loaves were placed upon the pure table before the Lord; that is, on the golden table of shewbread within the sanctuary—which stood not far from the vail which partitioned off the holy of holies—toward the north, as the candlestick was toward the south. The loaves were set, not, probably, in two rows, six on a row, as they could have hardly stood in that position on so small a table as the table of shewbread (which was only three feet by one foot and a half), but *in piles, six in a pile.* Upon them, or more probably between the two piles, were placed two vials or cups filled with frankincense (Josephus, 'Ant.,' iii. 7, 6). The shewbread was renewed every sabbath day, with much ceremony. "Four priests," says the Mishna, "enter, two of them carrying the piles of bread, and two of them the cups of incense. Four priests had gone in before them, two to take off the two old piles of shrewbread, and two to take off the cups of incense. Those who brought in the new stood at the north side facing southwards; those who took away the old, at the south side, facing northwards. One party lifted off and the other put on, the hands of one being over against the hands of the other, as it is written, Thou shalt set upon the table bread of the Passover always before me" ('Men.,' xi. 7). The loaves that were removed were delivered to the priests for their consumption within the tabernacle, the whole quantity amounting to seventy-five pounds of bread per week. It was this bread which, in the pressure of necessity, Ahimelech gave to David and his men (1 Sam. xxi. 4—6). At the same time that the old loaves were changed, the frankincense was burned on the golden altar of incense for a memorial, even an offering made by fire unto the Lord. There is nothing in Scripture to prove whether the loaves were leavened or unleavened. As being the meat offering of the tabernacle, we should expect them to be unleavened, like the meat offering of the court, but there was a reason why the meat offering of the court should be unleavened, which did not operate in the case of the shewbread. A part of the ordinary meat offering had to be burnt on the altar of burnt sacrifice; therefore it could not be leavened, because no leaven might be burned on the altar; but the shewbread was not burnt on any altar, and consequently it need not for that reason be unleavened. The two Pentecostal loaves, which were offered to the Lord by waving instead of burning, were leavened. The probabilities derived from Scripture appear to be equally strong on either side. Josephus states that they were unleavened ('Ant.,' iii. 6, 6; 10, 7).

HOMILETICS.

Vers. 1—9.—The lamps of the seven-branched candlestick burnt throughout the whole night in the tabernacle; and the shewbread was constantly set forth upon the golden table. They may be taken to symbolize: 1. The constant illumination vouchsafed by God to his Church through the indwelling of the Holy Spirit. 2. The spiritual food constantly supplied by him in his Church to those who come in faith to have their wants supplied.

1. I. ILLUMINATION BY THE SPIRIT WAS PROMISED BY CHRIST. "The Comforter, which is the Holy Ghost, whom the Father will send in my name, he shall teach you all things, and bring all things to your remembrance, whatsoever I have said unto you" (John xiv. 26). "It is expedient for you that I go away: for if I go not away, the Comforter will not come unto you; but if I depart, I will send him unto you. . . . When he, the Spirit of truth, is come, he will guide you into all truth" (John xvi. 7—13).

II. THE FULFILMENT OF THE PROMISE COMMENCED ON THE DAY OF PENTECOST. "Therefore being by the right hand of God exalted, and having received of the Father the promise of the Holy Ghost, he hath shed forth this, which ye now see and hear" (Acts ii. 33).

III. THE ILLUMINATION IS PERMANENT THROUGH THE INSTRUMENTALITY OF A PERMANENT MINISTRY. "When he ascended up on high, he led captivity captive, and gave gifts unto men. . . . And he gave some, apostles; and some, prophets; and some, evangelists; and some, pastors and teachers; for the perfecting of the saints, for the work of the ministry, for the edifying of the Body of Christ" (Eph. iv. 8—12).

IV. CHRIST ABIDES BY HIS SPIRIT IN THE MIDST OF THE SEVEN GOLDEN CANDLESTICKS. "I saw seven golden candlesticks; and in the midst of the seven candlesticks one like unto the Son of man " (Rev. i. 12, 13). "These things saith he that holdeth the seven stars in his right hand, who walketh in the midst of the seven golden candlesticks" (Rev. ii. 1).

V. ANY BRANCH OF THE CANDLESTICK WHOSE LIGHT IS EXTINGUISHED WILL BE REMOVED. "Remember therefore from whence thou art fallen, and repent, and do the first works; or else I will come unto thee quickly, and will remove thy candlestick out of his place, except thou repent" (Rev. ii. 5).

2. I. CHRIST IS THE SPIRITUAL FOOD OF HIS CHURCH. "Then Jesus said unto them, Verily, verily, I say unto you, Moses gave you not that bread from heaven; but my Father giveth you the true Bread from heaven. For the bread of God is he which cometh down from heaven, and giveth life unto the world. Then said they unto him, Lord, evermore give us this bread. And Jesus said unto them, I am the Bread of Life: he that cometh to me shall never hunger; and he that believeth on me shall never thirst. . . . The Jews then murmured at him, because he said, I am the Bread which came down from heaven. . . . Jesus therefore answered and said unto them, Murmur not among yourselves. . . . I am the living Bread which came down from heaven: if any man eat of this bread, he shall live for ever: and the bread that I will give is my flesh, which I will give for the life of the world" (John vi. 32—51).

II. CHRIST'S SACRIFICE UPON THE CROSS SUPPLIES THE FOOD ON WHICH BY FAITH WE ARE TO FEED. "We have an altar, whereof they have no right to eat which serve the tabernacle" (Heb. xiii. 10).

III. ONE MEANS OF OUR THUS FEEDING UPON HIM IS THE SACRAMENT OF THE LORD'S SUPPER. "And as they were eating, Jesus took bread, and blessed it, and brake it, and gave it to the disciples, and said, Take, eat; this is my body. And he took the cup, and gave thanks, and gave it to them, saying, Drink ye all of it; for this is my blood of the new testament, which is shed for many for the remission of sins" (Matt. xxvi. 26—28).

IV. HE SUPPLIES THE NEEDS OF THOSE THAT THIRST AS WELL AS OF THOSE THAT HUNGER. "I will give unto him that is athirst of the fountain of the water of life freely" (Rev. xxi. 6). "Let him that is athirst come. And whosoever will, let him take the water of life freely" (Rev. xxii. 17).

V. HE FEEDS HIS PEOPLE NOT ONLY BY SACRAMENTS BUT BY THE WORD OF GOD PREACHED BY HIS MINISTERS. "Man shall not live by bread alone, but by every word that proceedeth out of the mouth of God" (Matt. iv. 4). "Take heed therefore unto yourselves" (the Ephesian elders), "and to all the flock, over the which the Holy Ghost hath made you overseers, to feed the Church of God" (Acts xx. 28). "He gave some, pastors and teachers" (Eph. iv. 11). "He saith unto him, Feed my lambs. . . . He saith unto him, Feed my sheep. . . . Jesus saith unto him, Feed my sheep" (John xxi. 15 —17). "The elders which are among you I exhort. . . . Feed the flock of God which is among you" (1 Pet. v. 1, 2).

HOMILIES BY VARIOUS AUTHORS.

Everlasting light. Ch. xxiv. 1—4; cf. Rev. i. 12—20; also Ps. xliii. 3. The holy place, like the most holy, had no windows, and consequently required illumination. This was secured by the golden candlestick, with its seven lamps. These were to be always emitting some light. If all the seven lamps were not lit during the daytime, one or two of them were. The idea carried out was that there should be in God's sanctuary *everlasting light*.

That the candlestick was taken as the symbol of God's *truth* is evident from Ps. xliii. 3, "Oh send out thy light, *even* thy truth : let them lead me ; let them bring me unto thy holy hill, and to thy tabernacles." In fact, God's essential nature as light was exhibited by the Shechinah in the holy of holies; then in the golden candlestick, we have the light *mediated* in the holy place in such a way as would suffice for the illumination of the ordinary priests at their sacred ministries. God's arrangement, therefore, for the dissemination of truth in this dark world of ours is what the golden candlestick is intended to convey. Rev. i. 12—20 throws clear light on the symbol. The Churches established in the world by God are the lamps (λυχνίαι) which he intends to shine till the dawn of the eternal day.

I. NOTICE THE UNITY OF ALL TRUE CHURCHES. For the seven lamps were united in the one candlestick, just as all true Churches are one in Christ. There is no incorporation necessarily implied, but this is also to be encouraged by every legitimate means. If unity in Christ be a real thing, it will show itself in some way or another before men.

II. THE OIL FOR THE LIGHT WAS TO BE BEATEN. The olives were to be placed in a mortar and beaten, and then the oil which flowed off without further pressure, the purest possible, was to be used for the light. God's truth is communicated to men in such a form that they must diligently co-operate with God before the benefit is obtained. No careless handling of truth will suffice. We must beat the olives well before we get the needful oil. Ministers must be diligent in their preparations, Christians of all classes must " search the Scriptures," if the requisite oil for the light is to be obtained. God might rain down oil from heaven, and save us a heap of trouble, but he would rather put it into the olive berries, and ask us to pound it out from these. Similarly, he has put in his Word " things hard to be understood," as well as things that are simple, to the end that we should diligently study it and get the sacred oil.

III. THE WICK HAD TO BE CAREFULLY TRIMMED, AND WHEN NEEDFUL SNUFFED. It was the high priest's special duty, in which, however, the other priests assisted. And is this not to indicate the work undertaken by Jesus Christ, who as High Priest walked among the golden lamps? (Rev. i. 12). A beautiful parallel passage is presented in Matt. xii. 20, where it is said, "smoking flax [i.e. ' a wick,'—λίνον] shall he not quench, till he send forth judgment unto victory." There may be pain in the process often by which our High Priest gets his wicks trimmed and luminous, but there is also mercy and tenderness ineffable. How often does he hold his hands around the expiring wick, and blow it gently into a flame again! Blessed are his dealings, when as the result his people, and especially his ministers, are made to shine as " lights in the world." Regarding the snuffers in this connection, we may quote an old and quaint writer. " The Lord," says Weemse, " commanded to make snuffers of pure gold for the snuffing of the lamps, and snuff-dishes to receive the snuff; he would have the snuff taken from the light, to signify that he would have the Word kept in sincerity and purity; and he would have the snuffers of gold, to teach them to be blameless and holy, who are censurers and correctors of others; and he would have the snuff-dishes of gold, to teach them that the covering of the offences of their brethren was a most excellent thing."

IV. THE LAMPS WERE LIT FROM THE ALTAR. That is to say, it was *Divine* fire which made the oil luminous. God is light, from him cometh all real illumination. So it is only when the Saviour baptizes men with fire, it is only when the Holy Ghost lights up the sacred page, it is only when the Spirit co-operates with the Word, that the truth appears in its brightness unto men. An earnest ministry is that which gives itself to prayer and to the ministry of the Word, prayer calling down the Divine fire which makes the entrance of the Word give light. Then may the lamps be expected to burn brightly and to light up the night of the world till the day dawns.—R. M. E.

The weekly offering. Ch. xxiv. 5—9; cf. 1 Cor. xvi. 2; 1 Tim. v. 17, 18. Along with the everlasting light from the golden candlestick, there was to be in the holy place a presentation of bread, which was made on the sabbath and lay before the Lord on the prescribed table all the week, becoming the property and support of the priests when they brought the fresh loaves on the succeeding sabbath. The loaves were to be twelve in number, to correspond to the tribes of Israel; they were arranged in two piles, upon the top of which there was placed a little incense, which was duly fired and thus ascended to heaven. The incense sanctified the offering. Now this " bread of the face," as it was called, bread intended for the Divine presence, was the dedication on the part of the people of the staple of life, first to God, and secondly to the support of his priests. As previously observed, it was the perpetual meat offering. Here it is interesting to notice it as a " weekly offering" prescribed in the Old Testament economy. What Paul urges on the Corinthians (1 Cor. xvi. 2), " Upon the first day of the week let every one of you lay by him in store, as God hath prospered him, that there be no gatherings when I come," is the exact counterpart of the shewbread. The Lord's day is to be the time for a weekly offering for the support of his cause.

I. WE ARE SURELY TAUGHT HERE HOW SYSTEMATIC OUR OFFERINGS SHOULD BE. There should be a regularity about them like the return of the holy day. It is only when this periodicity characterizes them that the Lord's cause is likely to be properly supported. A weekly offering is much more likely to be successful than a monthly, or quarterly, or annual offering. Liberality is to be a weekly exercise, like the ordinances of our holy religion.

II. OUR OFFERINGS SHOULD BE SANCTIFIED BY THE INCENSE OF PRAYER. This is only to say that liberality should be a religious act, part of our religious service. Then are we likely to be conscientious in discharging our obligations, when we carry our gifts into the presence of God. As Jesus stood over against the treasury in the temple, and saw the extraordinary liberality connected with the widow's two mites, so is he watching our offerings at his shrine, noticing whether they are generous and cheerful or given with a grudge, observing whether they are perfumed with incense or rendered obnoxious by worldliness and ostentation. It will tend to purify our liberality to envelop it in prayer.

III. GOD'S OFFICERS SHOULD BE REGARDED AS RECEIVING THEIR SUPPORT FROM HIS TABLE. That is to say, they are to be regarded as receiving their support from God, not directly from the people. It is this element of sanctity in the service of liberality which saves the dignity of the Lord's officers, and prevents them from being beggarly dependents upon the people. Conscientious people lay their offerings before God, and then God's officers receive their portion as from their Master in heaven. "And it shall be Aaron's and his sons';" and they shall eat it in the holy place.

IV. THE WEEKLY OFFERING SHOULD BE THE OUTCOME OF AN EVERLASTING ENGAGEMENT WITH GOD. "Every sabbath (the priest) shall set it in order before the Lord continually, being taken from the children of Israel by an everlasting covenant." That is, liberality is to be no spasmodic outburst, but a steady outcome of an engagement that is perpetual. God has laid his people under such obligation by his rich provision in the gospel, that we feel we can never adequately discharge it. Hence week by week our offerings are laid upon his altar, and we recognize the arrangement as a lasting one.

Amid all the changes of times and of Churches, here have we sound principles of Church finance. It is to the religious spirit of the people we must ultimately commit the interests of God's cause. When they bring regularly, prayerfully, perpetually, and at the same time realize that the Church officers are God's servants and depend upon God's altar, then is there no fear of any failure. God will stand between his servants and his people, and secure the interests of both.—R. M. E.

Vers. 1—4.—*The lighting of the sanctuary.* The face of Moses is glorious in the light of the gospel.

I. THE CANDLESTICK WAS AN EMBLEM OF THE CHURCH OF GOD. (See Rev. i. 20.) 1. *The candlestick in the holy place was one.* (1) So is the Church of God a unity. Christ has not two mystical bodies (Col. i. 18). He has not two brides (Eph. v. 23). It comprehends the whole body of the faithful. (2) It is unscriptural as well as invidious for any denomination to style itself " *The* Church." Denominations are not even "Churches," though often so misnamed; they are, at best, but divisions of the grand army of the saints. 2. *It carried seven lamps.* (1) These are called "candlesticks" (Rev. i. 20). The reason is that visible Christian corporations, which are called " Churches " in the plural (see Acts ix. 31; xv. 41; xvi. 5), are *types* of the more perfect unity. (2) "Seven" is a definite, put for an indefinite, number. It is the numeral for *perfection*, and likewise stands for *many* (see 1 Sam. ii. 5). So the seven Churches of Asia, to which the candlestick is compared, are to be taken as representing the multitude of the Churches of Christendom. These are, indeed, countless, if, as Chrysostom says, "where two or three are gathered together in the name of Jesus *there* is a Church." 3. *The candlestick was of pure gold.* This was to express the preciousness of the saints. (1) They are precious to God. He has redeemed them with the blood of Christ. He has prepared for them a heaven of inconceivable magnificence. (2) They are precious to the world. They are its light. They are its salt. The light in them, like salt, is purifying and preserving, as well as illuminating (Matt. v. 13—16.)

II. THE LIGHT IN THE CHURCHES IS THE WORD OF GOD. This may be taken in kindred senses. 1. *God's Word written.* (1) This is no uncertain light, as that of mere reason is. (2) It is no false light, as that of tradition often is. For, however pure it may have been at its source, it soon becomes corrupted in transmission. 2. *The personal Word of God.* (1) The presence of a personal Teacher in the living Spirit of Christ is a priceless blessing. (2) Such an Interpreter is infinitely better than popes or Councils. (3) Christians are still the disciples of the personal Jesus. They should cultivate in prayerfulness the simplicity and docility becoming such (see John vii. 17).

III. The oil that sustains the light is the Holy Spirit's grace. No wonder it must be "pure oil olive beaten for the light." 1. *Jesus had the Spirit without measure.* (1) The fulness of the Godhead bodily was in him. So was he anointed with the oil of gladness immeasurably above his fellows. (2) Thus was he constituted the Christ, or Anointed One. 2. *Of his fulness we receive grace.* (1) Christians, therefore, with propriety have their name from Christ. Those who first gave that name in derision little knew its propriety (see 2 Cor. i. 21; 1 John ii. 20, 27). (2) This anointing is illuminating. So we learn in these references from John. It enlightens the Christian himself. It enables him to illumine others.

IV. The oil was furnished by the worshippers. 1. *There is a sense in which believers bring the Holy Ghost.* (1) They do this by their faith. When the faith of the people is constant, the lamps of the Churches "burn continually." What an honour to the faithful! (2) Through unfaithfulness the candlestick (or lamp) may be removed (see Rev. ii. 5; also Matt. xxi. 43). How great is the responsibility of professors! 2. *The Holy Ghost is nevertheless the Gift of God.* (1) This is true of his type. Who but God could put oil into the olive? (2) So of the Antitype. Accordingly, in Zech. iv. 2, 3, the oil is represented as feeding the candlestick immediately from the olive. The figure is explained thus, "Not by might, nor by power, but by my Spirit, saith the Lord of hosts" (Zech. iv. 6).

V. Aaron among the lights represented Christ among his Churches. 1. *This we have from the nature of the case.* The high priest was, generally, a type of Christ. So in this particular. 2. *We have it also by special revelation* (see Rev. i. 13).

VI. The candlestick was without the vail. 1. *The Churches shine in this world.* (1) The sanctuary was the type of the kingdom of the heavens upon the earth. Here the candlestick was placed. (2) Every Church member should realize that he has his light from God that he may diffuse it (Matt. v. 14—16). 2. *The Shechinah was within the vail.* (1) There is no need of a candle in that bright Presence (see Isa. lx. 19, 20; Rev. xxi. 10, 23; xxii. 5). (2) The seven Churches are there lost in the one Church, which flames with the glory of God. If there are before the throne "seven lamps of fire," they are explained to be the "seven Spirits of God," or Holy Spirit, whose light is "sevenfold" or perfect (Rev. iv. 5; Isa. xxx. 26).—J. A. M.

Vers. 5—9.—*The bread of the presence.* As there was light on the candlestick in God's house, so was there bread on his table. It was called the "shewbread," literally, "bread of faces," or of the presence, viz. of Jehovah. Let us consider—

I. Its description. 1. *It was composed of fine flour.* (1) Christ is compared to a corn of wheat, viz. before it is ground, and while the life is whole in it (see Ps. lxxii. 16, where the "handful of corn" may be more literally construed a *corn of wheat*; and comp. John xii. 24, where Jesus evidently cites this passage and applies it to himself). (2) So is he compared to bread. This is corn whose life is sacrificed in the treatment to which it is subjected. Jesus calls himself the Bread who gives his life unto the world (John vi. 33). (3) The very manner in which corn loses its life to become nourishment, it being bruised and burnt, describes the sufferings of Christ in body and spirit from the hands of man and of God. (4) Bread is the staple in food. As without it there is no feast, so without Christ there is no true joy. As with it there is no hunger, so have we in him a satisfying portion. 2. *It was measured in tenths.* (1) Ten is the number for *riches*; and Christ, as the Rich One, is called a Tenth (see Isa. vi. 13). All the holy bread was measured in tenth-deals, to point to the "measure of the fulness of Christ" (Eph. iv. 7, 13). The riches of eternity are ours in him (see Homily on the Feast of Expiation). (2) But why *two* tenth-deals to each cake? Perhaps light may be let in upon this by noting that, on the sixth day, two omers, or tenths, of manna were gathered to prepare for the sabbath (Exod. xvi. 22). It was on the sabbath that the bread of the presence was replaced. (3) This correspondence further identifies the typical import of the presence-bread with that of the manna. Note in addition that, as the manna came from God out of heaven, this bread is distinguished as that which comes from the Divine presence; and the true Bread of Life came from heaven (John vi. 33, 38, 40, 50, 51, 58). 3. *The number of the loaves was twelve.* (1) Here was a loaf for every son of Israel. "There is bread enough in our Father's house." (2) This number was continued after the revolt of the ten tribes (2 Chron. xiii. 11). This fact suggests that the number is also typical in relation to the spiritual Israel; a view confirmed by the application of the number twelve to the New Testament Church. Thus upon the head of the sun-clothed woman is a coronet of twelve stars, obviously in allusion to the twelve apostles of the Lamb, who are described as twelve angels at the twelve gates of the mystical city, and whose names are inscribed upon its twelve foundations (Rev. xii. 1; xxi. 12, 14, 21). (3) Twelve also is the number of the Lamb himself. He is the true Tree of Life, having twelve manner of fruits, corresponding to the twelve months in the year (Rev. xxii. 2). So the one Bread of the Presence is distributed into twelve loaves. And "we being many are one bread" in him (see 1 Cor. x. 17). (4) This association of the months with the loaves opens a very interesting field of investigation. Is there not a great year of the world to be measured by soli-lunar time (see Gen. i. 14)? King, in his 'Morsels of Criticism,' has a dissertation concerning the sabbath and a sabbatical era, in which he unfolds from the sabbatical intercalation of the Levitical system a more perfect adjustment of lunar to solar time than the Gregorian. Intercalations on the principle of the Jewish sabbatic period will in 400 years adjust the solar and lunar time within one hour and forty minutes. In fifteen such periods, or 6000 years, the adjustment will leave only one hour to be accounted for. But every 144,000 years, which is the square of 12 in thousands, and a number very remarkable in the measures of the New Jerusalem, things are brought right to a second (see Rev. vii.; xiv. 3, 4; xxi. 17).

II. WHAT WAS DONE WITH IT. 1. *It was placed upon the table before the Lord.* (1) It was "before the Lord," for the Shechinah was separated from it only by the vail. The glory sometimes streamed out through the vail, as it did through the flesh of Christ on the mount of transfiguration. (2) It was then set in two rows of six over against each other. The purpose seems to have been to show how the tribes of the spiritual Israel will feast together in the fellowship of heaven. (3) It was in a sense there "continually," for it was replaced with new every sabbath. The Jews say, "The hands of those priests that put on were mixed with those that took off, that the table might be never empty." 2. *A memorial of it was burnt.* (1) It was "an offering made by fire unto the Lord." But how? Was it not eaten by the priests? When the cakes were removed the frankincense was burnt. This was the memorial of the whole; in this the whole was accepted as a burnt offering (comp. ch. ii. 2). This will explain the expression in the words of the angel to Cornelius, "Thy prayers and thine alms are come up for a memorial before God" (Acts x. 4). (2) But was this memorial burnt upon the table? We have no reason to think so. It was probably burnt upon the golden altar, which was the altar of incense. Note: the communion table ought never to be spoken of as an altar. It was from the table, not from the altar, that the priests ate the bread of the presence. (3) The spiritual priesthood alone have a right to partake of the true Bread of the Presence, and feast in fellowship with God.— J. A. M.

Vers. 1—4.—*Ourselves as lights.* There can be no doubt that the seven-branched candlestick in the holy place was typical of the Hebrew Church as the source of heavenly light. We therefore reach the subject of—

I. LIGHT DIVINELY KINDLED. All light must be of God, who himself is light (1 John i. 5). He has sought to illumine the human world in more ways than one. 1. He has given us the light of our spiritual nature—our reason, our conscience; "the spirit of man is the candle (lamp) of the Lord" (Prov. xx. 27). 2. This should have sufficed to us, but it did not; and God gave the revelation of himself in his Law. Amid the surrounding darkness there was light in Israel. The brightly burning lamp in the holy place represented the holy nation, the instructed people, with whom were the oracles of God, into whose minds the truth of heaven was shining. 3. Yet *this* did not suffice, and God gave the Light of the world, his only begotten Son. "That was the true light which, coming into the world, enlighteneth every one." 4. And he came that he might leave in the world the light of the Christian Church; those to whom and of whom he could say, "Ye are the light of the world." "As he was, so are we in this world," sources of heavenly illumination, of inward purity, of Divine wisdom.

II. Its TRUE CHARACTERISTICS. These are: 1. Purity: they were to bring "pure oil olive beaten." The light which is to shine in our words and from our character is to be such that there shall be the least possible admixture of error and corruption. 2. Fulness: we read of "the lamps" (plural), and we know that there were seven of these (Exod. xxv. 31, 32)—a complete, perfect number. The truth we are to make manifest is not only to be pure, but full. We must declare the "whole counsel of God;" the severe as well as the gracious, the less pleasant as well as the more acceptable, the deeper as well as the more superficial, the ethical as well as the doctrinal, aspects of the truth of God. 3. Constancy: they were "to cause the lamps to burn continually" (ver. 2), "from the evening unto the morning before the Lord continually" (ver. 3). Whether all day and all night long, or only (as seems more probable) through the night, the lamps were to burn all the appointed time without ceasing to shine; there was to be no fitfulness or unsteadiness about the light which shone "before the Lord." So our words and our deeds are to be *continually* reflecting the light of heavenly truth. In our work and in our play, in things sacred and in things secular, at home and from home, consciously and unconsciously, we are to be "bearing witness unto the truth," we are to be "shining as lights in the world."

III. Its MAINTENANCE. "Aaron shall order it." "He shall order the lamps." The Jewish priest was to take every care that the lamps burnt brightly and continually. 1. The Christian minister has to see that he does his part in "ordering the lamps." He must preach such truth and give such counsel as shall feed the fires of the soul most effectively. 2. Each Christian man must do his part also. Every one of us must (1) watch to see when the light is low; (2) replenish the spirit with sacred truth, that truth which nourishes and sustains the soul in the life of God; (3) seek from heaven those Divine influences which shall be as oil to the flame and make it

"... to his glory burn
With inextinguishable blaze."

C.

Vers. 5—9.—*The lesson of the loaves.* In this act of worship the Jews made weekly acknowledgment of the goodness of God to them and of their dependence on him; they presented to him a suitable offering of those things he had given them; and they silently pleaded for God's continued remembrance of them and their necessities. The lesson of these loaves, of this "bread of presence," is therefore—

I. THAT GOD'S GIFTS TO US ARE SUCH AS TO DEMAND OUR CONTINUAL ACKNOWLEDGMENT. The Hebrew priest was to place before the Lord bread, the source of strength (Ps. civ. 15); wine, the source of gladness (Ps. civ. 15); and frankincense (ver. 7), the source of sweetness. He was to renew these presentations every sabbath day "continually" (ver. 8), and the table was never to be without them. This was a constant acknowledgment by the nation, through the act of the priesthood, of its dependence on God for all the good gifts received at his hand. We also, in our way, are to make *continual* acknowledgment every sabbath day in the sanctuary, every day at the family altar, and in the chamber of devotion, of our absolute dependence on God, for (1) our *strength*,—all things that minister to our health and vigour of body, mind, spirit, being due to his providing love; for (2) our *gladness*,—all those comforts and enjoyments, all those happy memories and inspiring hopes which make the music of our life, which infuse joyousness and elasticity into our nature, coming from his bountiful hand; and for (3) the *sweetness* of our life,—all the tender affections, the delicate delights which belong to pure and holy love, being the gift of his kindness also.

II. THAT WITH OUR SENSE OF WHAT WE OWE TO GOD IT IS SUITABLE THAT WE PRESENT SOME OFFERING TO HIM. Of that which made Israel strong, the priest presented bread; of that which made it glad, wine; of that which was sweet, frankincense. 1. Our strength is in mental power, knowledge, gift of speech, bodily vigour, wealth; of these we should give a goodly share to the cause and kingdom of Jesus Christ. 2. Of our joy and gladness we should give to God our offering in gratitude, in thankful thoughts and in the voice of praise. 3. Of the affection which constitutes the sweetness of our life we are to give a large measure of love to him whom we have not seen, but whom we know as our Divine Redeemer and unchanging Friend.

III. THAT, SO DOING, WE MAY EXPECT RESPONSIVE BLESSINGS FROM HIM. This was to be done "for a memorial" (ver. 7), *i.e.* a "bringing to remembrance of the worshipper for his good." Jehovah was "continually" reminded of the devoutness of his people by the "bread of presence." He was thus continually appealed to, by that silent prayer, to "remember them for good." And as long as that act of worship in the holy place truly represented the spirit of the people, as long as it was *their* act, through the priests, of acknowledgment and consecration; so long was the Divine Sovereign well pleased with his subjects, so long was he ready to enrich and bless them. As long as we, instead of ascribing to ourselves the strength, joy, and sweetness of our lives, are honouring our God and Saviour for his goodness and grace therein, as long as we are cheerfully and generously giving to him and to his cause of that which he has given us; so long may we reckon on his gracious smile and look for his abundant blessing.—C.

Vers. 1—4.—*The lights in the sanctuary.* Pure oil furnished by the people. The high priest responsible for the maintenance of the lamps. Pure oil, pure lamps, pure candlestick, before the Lord continually. The main lessons are these—

I. PROGRESSIVE, CONTINUAL SANCTIFICATION of God's people provided for by his grace. 1. By the supply of the Spirit, the pure oil. 2. In and through the lamps; that is, the individual and positive manifestation of the spiritual life. 3. In connection with the golden candlestick, and in dependence on the ministry of the high priest; that is, by means of the Church and its ordinances, in so far as the manifestation and public maintenance of the light of life are concerned. Yet, as the people themselves provided the pure oil, we are reminded that personal sanctification is not dependent solely on public ordinances; but the Spirit worketh as he will (John iii. 8).

II. DIVINE FAITHFULNESS AND LONG-SUFFERING in the midst of the true Church. While the night is over them, the light still burns. While outside the temple there is gloom, within the sanctuary there is hope and promise.

III. TYPICALLY, THE PRESSED OIL AND BEATEN GOLD of the candlestick point to the connection of the work of the Spirit with the sacrificial work of Christ. The light of sanctification proceeds from the death of Christ, and is maintained by the priesthood of Christ.—R.

Vers. 5—9.—*The shewbread, or bread of the Presence.* Corresponding with the number of the tribes, and representing them; a national offering; a meat offering, with frankincense, drink offering, and salt. Taken from the people, eaten by the priests, every sabbath, for a memorial, by an everlasting covenant; "furnishing a striking figure of Israel's condition in the view of Jehovah, whatever might be their outward aspect. The twelve tribes are ever before him. Their memorial can never perish. They are ranged in Divine order in the sanctuary, covered with the fragrant incense of Christ, and reflected from the pure table whereon they rest beneath the bright beams of that golden lamp which shines, with undimmed lustre, through the darkest hour of the nation's moral night."

I. The perfect UNITY and completeness of the Church as before God. 1. As compared with the broken, external, visible unity. 2. As maintained by the Spirit and merit of Christ. 3. As hereafter to be manifested when there shall be no more temple, but the glory of God and of the Lamb are the temple of the heavenly Jerusalem.

II. The SAFETY and blessedness of God's people. Their memorial is before him. 1. Proceeding from the sanctuary, *i.e.* all blessedness the outcome of spiritual blessedness. 2. Committed to the Lord Jesus Christ as the Head of the true Israel, the Lord of the temple, in whom "all the promises are Yea and Amen." 3. Appealing to faith. The loaves were there to represent the continued life of the people; faith alone saw the reality.—R.

Vers. 2—4.—*The candlestick.* To many the regulations of Leviticus seem a cryptograph to which they have no key. To others, an inscription of old date with no reference to present concerns. Yet, dull-eyed must we be if we can discern no lessons for ourselves in the construction of the tabernacle and its furniture. The Hebrew can be translated into modern English, the Law stated in terms of the gospel. The tabernacle was the meeting-place of God with his people. It was his house, where his servants ministered and his guests were entertained. Light was needful therein,—the great requisite of life, without which men grow pale and plants sickly, work ceases, and festivity is impossible. Let us consider the candlestick with its light.

I. As SETTING FORTH THE CHARACTER AND ATTRIBUTES OF GOD. 1. *The characteristics of light.* (1) Its beauty. Naught excels it; it is splendour itself, and invests other objects with radiance. "God is light." What a combination of hues constitutes the pure white ray! (2) An emblem of knowledge. "Thy Word is a light unto my path." "To the Law and to the testimony: if they . . . no light in them." Light is the revealer—indicates our position and prospects. The wisdom of God is infinite; an inscrutable blaze that baffles the strongest vision. He devises plans for every emergency. Whilst men argue concerning the possibility of some works, he calmly does them; yea, whilst they prove (!) that no God exists, he is occupied in balancing the worlds, directing the course of the ages, hastening the day when all shall perforce know him. (3) Typical of joy. "Light is sown for the righteous, and gladness for the upright in heart." Illuminations are a worldwide method of rejoicing. The notions some hold concerning God as a hard Taskmaster, a Judge of severe countenance, a Father who never smiles, are not Biblical representations. We read of "the glorious gospel of the blessed (happy) God." Joy is an emotion that loves to communicate itself to others, and from the throne of God issues a stream of untainted happiness to enrich the lives of his children. 2. The burning lamps showed *the constant wakefulness of God.* The people retired to their couches for repose, darkness brooded over the camp, but the holy place was unaffected by the shadows of the night. God never slumbers nor sleeps. It may not have occurred to the Israelites that God heard prayer from o'er the compass of the globe; but, in order to be the God of the whole earth and to listen to the petitions of all its inhabitants, it follows of necessity that God has no couch in his sanctuary, for he resteth not. Whilst the day is closing in the one hemisphere it is beginning to dawn in the other. "In him is no darkness at all." 3. The candlestick indicated *perpetual existence.* "A statue for ever in your generations." Aaron might pass away, but the candlestick continued to give light in the tabernacle. Men die, God survives. As we behold the same sun and moon that gladdened the eyes of our forefathers, so it is the same God that hears our prayers and blesses us with the light of his countenance.

II. As SETTING FORTH THE RELATIONSHIP AND FUNCTIONS OF THE PEOPLE. 1. *Their privileged condition as favoured with a special revelation of the being and character of God.* They were the only nation to possess such a candlestick made "after the pattern showed in the mount." All the heathen constructed deities and images of Deity according to their own judgment, taste, and caprice. The night during which the lamp burned was a fit emblem of the moral state of the world lying outside Israel. The Israelites were blessed with the light of the Law; "to them were committed the oracles of God." In the symbols of the Law was taught the way of salvation, to be completed by a coming Mediator. So in Jesus Christ we have "the light of the knowledge of the glory of God." At the Feast of Tabernacles, when according to custom large golden lamps were lit at dark in the temple court, our Lord termed himself "the Light of the world." We have the Spirit of God to illumine our consciences, to show unto us the things of Christ. We read in the Revelation of the seven burning lamps before the throne, which are the sevenfold Spirit of God. In Zechariah's vision of the candlestick he saw the bowls supplied with oil from two olive trees, representing the continued grace furnished by the Spirit of God, keeping alight the knowledge of God in days of the Church's decline. And we have the Word of God, "a light shining in a dark place." Let not this light condemn us as did the sacred candlestick removed to Belshazzar's palace, where its rays revealed the fingers of a man's hand writing the monarch's doom. "The word that I have spoken, the same shall judge him in the last day." 2. *Their duty to minister to the glory of God.* The people were permitted, yea, expected, to bring the oil for the lamps, as they had previously offered the gold for the candlestick itself. They were to keep the light of God burning in the world. It is incumbent on Christians to support the ministry and the operations of the Church, that there may be a continual testimony to the existence and majesty of the Eternal. *God requires us to render the best service at our command.* It must be pure. The candlestick was of gold, as were the tongs and snuff-dishes, and the oil was of finest quality, free from dust, not crushed, but beaten. If preparing a meal for one we lightly esteem, little trouble is taken, but where we delight to honour our guest, what anxiety is displayed in all that concerns the banquet! *Our devotion must be regular.* The lamps were lit each evening, trimmed and dressed every morning. That the full light did not shine during the day is evident from 1 Sam. iii. 3. Josephus, however, says that three of the lamps burnt all day long. The lamp is said to "ascend," it rises to heaven as a tribute of adoration to God. We may think of him as viewing his world, and expecting light to arise from different quarters where his children dwell. But how often must disappointment accrue! No morning perusal of his Word, no evening worship. A mother on her birthday delights to turn over the letters from her children, that greet her upon her plate, but if one familiar handwriting be missed, what a shadow darkens her joy! The chill that creeps over her heart seems to nullify the gladness which the tokens of remembrance cause. Let not God have to sigh over our neglect. *All is accepted through the priesthood.* No Levite or layman must enter the holy precincts, the priests represent and are supported by the people. Jesus Christ is our means of access to the Father; through him our service is acceptable. To venture to draw nigh in our name is presumption; it sets at naught the solemn regulations of the Most High, and it will receive the rebuke it merits. The Son of man must walk in the midst of our golden candlesticks, or else we know not that they are in accordance with the Divine mind; and only thus can we hear the exhortations that shall prevent the candlestick from being removed out of its place because of failure to discharge its proper functions. —S. R. A.

Vers. 5—9.—*The shewbread.* The furniture and ministry of the tabernacle are most clearly understood in import, if it be remembered that they have a double reference. Like the clouds of the sky, one aspect is towards heaven, the other towards earth. In the ordinance of the shewbread, we may see imaged truths relating to God, and truths with more immediate reference to the position and duties of his people.

I. GOD AS THE PRESERVER OF LIFE. Food was essential to the conception of the tabernacle as the house of God. Unless he minister to the needs of his servants, they perish for lack of sustenance. "My Father giveth you the true Bread from heaven." The shewbread is literally the "bread of my face," or presence. Jesus Christ, the Bread of Life, appears continually before the presence of God. *God is never unprovided* with entertainment for his guests. He is *able also to supply the wants of all his people.* Twelve loaves indicate that every tribe is remembered. As we think of the shewbread, let it point us to him who pointed to the Bread upon the table of the last Supper and said, "This is my body." He was truly of the finest of the wheat, no corruption marred his perfection. He was prepared to be the Bread of the world by many sufferings, just as the flour of the shewbread underwent numerous poundings and bruisings.

II. THE PEOPLE CONTRIBUTING THE BREAD OF GOD. A parent bestows an allowance upon his children, and is none the less pleased when they devote a portion of it to purchasing some offering of regard to present to him. So from God do we derive all we possess; it is really his, and yet he graciously accepts as our gift to him what we consecrate to his service. This shewbread represented the result of toil in tilling, sowing, and reaping. The Israelites were expected *to offer of the best of their property.* Only fine wheaten flour is accepted to be placed upon the table. Love should secure this attention if naught else suffices. *All the people are bound to be represented before God.* The twelve cakes testified that God was reverenced and served by all the tribes. *The duty one of perpetual and unceasing obligation.* It recurred every week, and devolved on each succeeding generation. The continual observance of God's statutes is the token of the covenant. *The shewbread perfumed with incense.* The loaves were accepted indirectly by God, being consumed by his consecrated servants, but the incense was burned as God's special memorial. Prayer hallows every offering, without it our deeds and gifts lack the religious spirit that is the real honouring of God. And prayer should ever be in the Name of Christ, whose merits impart fragrance to our unworthy presentations. *We must not rest satisfied with our former religious deeds.* The offering of last week needs to be repeated, else it will grow stale and be offensive to God. With every day, in fact, should come a rededication. As our physical frame is in constant flux, so is it with our thoughts and emotions; they are really new, and must in their turn be laid before God.—S. R. A.

EXPOSITION.

The reason why the narrative of the blasphemer's death (vers. 10—23) is introduced in its present connection, is simply that it took place at the point of time which followed the promulgation of the last law. It serves, however, to vindicate by a memorable example the principle which is at the foundation of every Mosaic law. "I am the Lord" is the often-repeated sanction, whether of a moral law or of a ceremonial regulation. But this bastard Israelite, one of the mixed multitude that had followed in the flight from Egypt (Exod. xii. 38), blasphemed the Name of the Lord. If such blasphemy were to go unpunished, the obligation of law was dissolved. For, as Lange has said, " A community which suffers the reviling of the principle of their community without reaction, is morally fallen to pieces." He was brought, therefore, to Moses, and so solemn was the occasion, that Moses reserved the case, for which no provision had yet been made, for the special decision of God. The specific judgment on the man is that he shall die by stoning at the hands of the congregation, after the witnesses of his sin had laid their hands upon his head ; and a general law is founded on the special case.

Ver. 10.—**The son of an Israelitish woman.** This is the only place where the adjective *Israelitish* is found ; and the word "Israelite" only occurs in 2 Sam. xvii. 25. **Whose father was an Egyptian.** The man could not, therefore, be a member of the congregation, as, according to the subsequently promulgated law (Deut. xxiii. 8), the descendant of an Egyptian could not be admitted till the third generation. He seems to have committed two offences which led up to his great crime. First, he **went out among the children of Israel,** that is, he did not confine himself to his own part of the encampment, where the mixed multitude lived, but he intruded into the part set aside for pure Israelites ; and next, having thus put himself already in the wrong, **this son of the Israelitish woman and a man of Israel strove together in the camp.** According to Jewish tradition, the cause of quarrel was a claim set up by the Egypto-Israelite to encamp in the Danite quarters, on the ground that his mother was a Danite—a claim which he insisted on enforcing, although the judges gave a decision against him.

Ver. 11.—In the course of the struggle **the Israelitish woman's son blasphemed the name** of the Lord, **and cursed.** The word *nakav* is here rightly translated *blasphemeth* (cf. vers. 14, 16, 23), but the words *of the Lord* should be omitted, as they are not found in the original, and are not required. The LXX. have rendered *nakav* by a word meaning *pronounced,* and on this misunderstanding, adopted by the Jews, has been founded the Jewish precept forbidding the utterance of the Divine Name. Owing to that prohibition, the true pronunciation of the word written and called " Jehovah " has been lost. Wherever the Name occurred in Scripture, that of *Adonai,* meaning *Lord,* was substituted for it in public reading, the consonants only of the original name, Y H V H, being preserved in the written text, and the vowels of *Adonai,* namely *a o a,* being written underneath them in lieu of the original vowels. From the consonants Y H V H and the vowels *a o a* would be formed Yahovah or Jahovah, but the laws of the Hebrew language required the first *a* to be changed into *e,* and hence the name Jehovah. It is almost certain that the original vowels were *a* and *e,* which would form the name Yahveh, the Samaritans having always so pronounced it, according to the testimony of Theodoret. It is said that the high priest continued to utter the very name Yahveh on the Day of Atonement long after it had ceased to be used in the reading of the Scriptures, and that when he did so, those who heard it prostrated themselves, saying, " Blessed be the Name ! " After a time, however, he ceased to pronounce it aloud on that day also, lest it should be learnt and used for magical purposes. In consequence, perhaps, of the substitution of *Adonai* for *Yahveh,* the Septuagint version always reads for Yahveh, Κύριος: and the English version *the* LORD. In French and other versions the name is represented by *the Eternal*, and it has been proposed to substitute the latter rendering for *the* LORD in our own version. But it is more than doubtful whether we should then come nearer to the true sense of the original Yahveh, although at first sight it appears that this would be the case. For the word Yahveh is part of the causative form of the verb *havah*, or *hayah*, to be; but this verb is not used to express unchangeable or absolute existence, but rather an occurrence: its causative form, therefore, would signify that which brings about events; and the substantive derived from that causative form would signify, not one that eternally exists, but one that providentially governs. For an induction of instances for the further proof of the above meaning of the word Yahveh, we refer the reader to Sir William Martin's essay 'On the Divine Name' ('Semitic Languages,' pt. ii.), from which we transcribe the concluding paragraph. "This view of the Divine Name, to which we are led by the evidence of the Hebrew language itself, is in full conformity with the general religious teaching of the Old Testament, which is practical and moral; setting forth in form readily intelligible, the character of God in his relations to man. It does not concern itself with those problems which philosophy has ever been seeking to solve. It addresses itself to human needs and human duties, and not to abstract inquiries. Not that the highest abstract truths were unknown or untaught. Lawgiver and prophet and psalmist set before the people the greatness and the eternity of God in language most clear and impressive. Yet the Name whereby he was put before them as the object of their daily worship, was not one which would exalt him to the utmost above the frail and changeful and transitory lives of his worshippers, and thereby remove him far away from them into the height of a Being beyond man's search or comprehension; but rather a Name which should bring him nigh to them, as One ever mindful of them, ever carrying forward his great purpose for their good, working for their deliverance in every time of need; as One 'whose providence ordereth all things in heaven and on earth.' If this Name did convey to the mind of a Hebrew hearer the thought above expressed, it follows that the old rendering *Adonai*, Κύριος, or *Lord*, is to be preferred to that which has of late been substituted for it." **And they brought the blasphemer unto Moses.** This was in accordance with the counsel of Jethro, accepted by Moses (Exod. xviii. 13—26): "Moreover thou shalt provide out of all the people able men, such as fear God, men of truth, hating covetous-

ness; and place such over them, to be rulers of thousands, and rulers of hundreds, rulers of fifties, and rulers of tens: and let them judge the people at all seasons: and it shall be, that every great matter they shall bring unto thee, but every small matter they shall judge: . . . and they judged the people at all seasons: the hard causes they brought unto Moses, but every small matter they judged themselves."

Ver. 12.—**And they put him in ward.** The same course was followed in the case of the man found gathering sticks upon the sabbath day: "And they put him in ward, because it was not declared what should be done to him" (Numb. xv. 34). The same penalty was awarded in both cases.

Vers. 13, 14.—**Bring forth him that hath cursed without the camp;**—lest the camp should become polluted by his death—**and let all that heard** him **lay their hands upon his head.** The ceremony of laying on of hands in all cases set apart the person or thing on whom or on which they were laid for some special purpose. Its further signification was determined by the particular circumstances of the case. Here it probably returned back on the head of the blasphemer the guilt which otherwise would have adhered to the witnesses from the fact of their hearing his blasphemy, and appearing to acquiesce in it.

Vers. 15, 16.—In accordance with the judicial decision on the man is framed the general law against blasphemy and its penalty. It runs as follows: **Whosoever curseth his God shall bear his sin. And he that blasphemeth the name of the Lord, he shall surely be put to death, and all the congregation shall certainly stone him.** It has been questioned whether two offences or one are here contemplated, whether *cursing his God* is one offence, *bearing his sin* being its punishment, and *blaspheming the Name of the Lord* another and greater offence, for which the punishment is *stoning*; or whether the latter offence and punishment are a more specific statement of the offence and punishment which had only generally been described before. Those who take the first view point out that the present offender was an Egyptian, and urge that had he cursed *his God*, that is, the Egyptian god or gods, he would only have had to bear his sin; but that as he had blasphemed the Name of Israel's God, Jehovah, he was to be stoned. The second explanation, however, is the truer one. The Scriptures recognize but one God, and he is the Lord Jehovah. Whoever curses him *shall bear his sin*, that is, shall be guilty in such a way that his sin must be purged either by punishment or by sacrifice, and it is then further declared that this particular sin can be purged only by the death of the offender at the hand of the congregation.

Ver. 17.—In close connection with the command to slay the blasphemer is repeated the prohibition of murder, and the injunction that the murderer **shall surely be put to death.** Thus a distinction is sharply drawn between the judicial sentence carried out by the congregation, and the unsanctioned smiting the life of a man by another, and a warning is given against any man fanatically taking the law into his own hands, even in the case of a blasphemer.

Vers. 18—21.—A summary of the law respecting minor injuries is added to that respecting murder. **He that killeth a man, he shall be put to death, but he that killeth a beast shall make it good;** and this *lex talionis* shall apply to all damage done to another, **breach for breach, eye for eye, tooth for tooth** (see Matt. v. 38).

Ver. 22.—As it had been a stranger who had on this occasion been the offender, the law, **Ye shall have one manner of law, as well for the stranger, as for one of your own country,** with the sanction, **I am the Lord your God,** is emphatically repeated (see ch. xix. 34).

Ver. 23.—The penalty is inflicted on the offender solemnly as an act of the Law, not of mob fury. So it was by a judicial or semi-judicial proceeding that St. Stephen was stoned : " They brought him to the council, and set up false witnesses, which said, This man ceaseth not to speak blasphemous words against this holy place, and the Law " (Acts vi. 12, 13). And in spite of the violence exhibited, there was still some form of law, according to Jewish practice, observed in his stoning (Acts vii. 58). In the case of our Lord, on the other hand, when they regarded him as guilty of blasphemy on his saying, " Before Abraham was, I am" (John viii. 58), and " I and my Father are one" (John x. 30), the Jews "took up stones to cast at him," not waiting for a judicial condemnation, but, as they supposed, taking the law into their own hands. Had his death been by Jewish hands, it would at the last have been by stoning under this law. But the power of life and death had been taken away from the Jews by the Romans, " that the saying of Jesus might be fulfilled, which he spake, signifying what death he should die " (John xviii. 32).

HOMILETICS.

Vers. 11—16.—The Name of the Lord is a revelation of his nature. Names given or taken by man may be imposed from accidental circumstances. A name given by God denotes an essential quality of the thing named. Hence if we can arrive at the true meaning of God's Name, as revealed by himself, we shall have a manifestation of himself as he chose to reveal his nature to man.

I. After the primary Name of Elohim, where we mark the plural form of the noun, the Name by which he revealed himself to the patriarchs was that of *El Shaddai*, GOD ALMIGHTY. His omnipotence was the part of his nature which he specially manifested to them (Exod. vi. 3).

II. To Moses he revealed himself under the name of EHYEH, ASHER EHYEH, or I AM THAT I AM. The word *Ehyeh* is not used for absolute existence in any place where it is found in the Scriptures, but rather for condition or relation. " The meaning to be given to the words, if we guide ourselves by the evidence furnished by the Hebrew books, may be paraphrased in this way, '*I show myself from time to time, even as I show myself.* I stand from time to time in varying relation to men. This is my *Name*. Only from my dealings with men is my character to be apprehended by men '" (Sir W. Martin, 'Semitic Languages').

III. He also revealed himself to Moses as YAHVEH. Neither is this word used for absolute existence. It means the One who causes things to happen as they do.

IV. IN THESE THREE NAMES, THEN, WE FIND THE REVELATION THAT GOD THOUGHT PROPER THEREBY TO GIVE TO HIS ANCIENT PEOPLE. He is the Almighty Spiritual Being, who manifests himself as he wills to his creatures, and governs by his providence the universe and all the events of human life. This is the *proclamation* of his Name by God himself. " And Yahveh descended in the cloud, and stood with Moses there, and proclaimed the name of Yahveh. And Yahveh passed by before him, and proclaimed, Yahveh, Yahveh Elohim, merciful and gracious, longsuffering, and abundant in goodness and truth, keeping mercy for thousands, forgiving iniquity and transgression and sin, and that will by no means clear the guilty ; visiting the iniquity of the fathers upon the children, and upon the children's children, unto the third and to the fourth generation" (Exod. xxxiv. 5—7). In the Old Testament, then, God does not, by his Name, reveal his absolute nature, but his relation to man as the Supreme Moral Governor of the world, whose characteristic in that government was omnipotence, uncontrolled by anything but his own will, but guided by mercy and justice.

V. IN THE NEW TESTAMENT, NOT ONLY GOD'S RELATION TO MAN, BUT ALSO HIS OWN NATURE, IS REVEALED BY THE NAME OF FATHER, SON, AND HOLY GHOST. These names exhibit to us, so far as human faculties can apprehend them, the very Godhead, not merely as governing man, but in its essential character. "The revealed Name of God, given to the apostles in the tradition of holy baptism, is a revelation of truth. The entire Christian revelation is in the way of a summary contained in it. It is itself a doctrine and the sum of all doctrine. It was originally given in order that the world might be taught it ('make disciples of all nations'), and it contains all that the world, in the way of religion, needs to be taught. The apostles, indeed, by Divine inspiration, developed it into its essential and necessary details, summed into the Apostles' Creed; but in itself, that is, in the doctrine of the Holy Trinity, all was shortly comprised. In like manner, it is a creed and the sum of all creeds; for while we read that it was often used as a creed in early times, the structure of the subsequent authoritative creeds of the Church has been so framed upon it, and their contents so confined to it, that what we chiefly learn in all the articles of our belief, whether contained in the Apostles', the Nicene, or the Athanasian formula, is first, to believe in God the Father, who hath made all the world; secondly, in God the Son, who hath redeemed all mankind; and thirdly, in God the Holy Ghost, who sanctifieth all the elect people of God. . . . All the great elements and outlines of inspired teaching, as they are gathered into the Apostles' Creed, and all the minute expressions and articulations of truth as given to the Church in writing by the apostles, are to be regarded with deep, true, and habitual reverence for the sake of the Name of God" (Moberly, 'The Law of the Love of God').

VI. THE NAME JESUS CHRIST INDICATES THE WORK AND THE RELATION TO OURSELVES OF HIM WHO BEING MAN WAS ALSO GOD. 1. Christ is the Anointed One. "God anointed Jesus . . . with the Holy Ghost and with power" (Acts x. 38). "The Word was made flesh, and dwelt among us, . . . full of grace and truth" (John i. 14); "for God giveth not the Spirit by measure unto him" (John iii. 34); "for it pleased the Father that in him should all fulness dwell" (Col. i. 19). 2. Jesus is the Saviour. "Thou shalt call his name Jesus: for he shall save his people from their sins" (Matt. i. 21). "Neither is there salvation in any other: for there is none other name under heaven given among men, whereby we must be saved" (Acts iv. 12); "a Prince and a Saviour" (Acts v. 31); "a Saviour, Jesus" (Acts xiii. 23). "He was wounded for our transgressions, he was bruised for our iniquities: the chastisement of our peace was upon him; and with his stripes we are healed. . . . The Lord hath laid on him the iniquity of us all. . . . For the transgression of my people was he stricken" (Isa. liii. 5—8). The Name Jesus Christ, therefore, indicates that he who bore it was the promised Messiah (Dan. ix. 25; John i. 41), filled to the full with the grace of the Holy Spirit, and the Saviour of those that put their trust in him.

HOMILIES BY VARIOUS AUTHORS.

The crime of blasphemy. Ch. xxiv. 10—16; cf. 2 Chron. xxvi. 16—23; Dan. v. 1—4, 30. The sanctity of the Name of God is distinctly declared in the third commandment. There the Lord declared that he would not hold the blasphemer "guiltless." But it was not till the incident now before us that God showed his sense of the enormity of the crime. He here puts it into the category of capital crimes, and decrees the death of every blasphemer, whether he be a stranger or one born in the land.

Now, when we inquire, we find that he calls it "this glorious and fearful name, THE LORD THY GOD" (Deut. xxviii. 58). So glorious is it that inanimate things, when his Name is put upon them, cannot be desecrated with impunity. Thus his tabernacle could not be treated even by a king according to his capricious pleasure, but Uzziah, for presuming to burn incense within it, is doomed to leprosy and exile all his life (2 Chron. xxvi. 16—23). Belshazzar too paid the penalty of his life for desecrating the vessels belonging to the tabernacle (Dan. v. 1—4, 30).

The case before us was one of pure blasphemy. This reckless youth, the son of an Egyptian father, had blasphemed "the Name," and for this he was stoned to death after those who heard the blasphemy had laid their hands on his head.

I. LET US START WITH THE FUNDAMENTAL TRUTH THAT THE NAME OF GOD IS THE REVELATION OF HIS CHARACTER IN WORD. Hence to take up the Name of God lightly is to treat his character lightly. It is, in fact, to despise the Person, and is nothing less than treason against the Supreme King. The individual who blasphemes "the Name" would take up arms against the Person, and so must be treated as a rebel. When, therefore, we bear in mind that God makes known his Name that men may trust in him (cf. Ps. ix. 10), the blaspheming of his holy Name is really the rejection of his appeal for trust, the rejection of his merciful manifestation, and deserves the penalty attached to it.

II. MAN'S ATTITUDE TOWARDS GOD'S NAME DETERMINES HIS CHARACTER. In other words, the Name of God is the touchstone of human character. The person who curseth the holy Name, as this reckless youth did, is thereby judged. He has voluntarily set himself against the Almighty, he has become a rebel not in heart only but openly, and if the Most High is to exercise his authority, the blasphemer should die. It is, moreover, a mistake to imagine, because sentence is not now executed so speedily against blasphemers, that their awful sin has become less heinous in the lapse of ages. The shortsighted individual who defies the Almighty will find eventually how hard are the bosses of his buckler.

III. THE PENALTY ATTACHED TO BLASPHEMY IS TO BE ACQUIESCED IN BY THE PEOPLE OF THE LORD. The whole congregation in this case is called upon to repudiate the awful crime. Those who heard it are required to lay their hands on the blasphemer's head, to indicate that the guilt must be his own. They will not share it, and then the whole congregation are to be the executioners of the Divine decree. Now we are bound to entertain a similar and holy abhorrence of such a crime. We are most assuredly sinking in character if, through association with careless men, we come to regard blasphemy when indulged in as a light thing. The truth is, if we are making spiritual progress, we shall be advancing in the fear of his Name. Greater awe, not greater familiarity, will characterize us, until at length we shall see it to be just and right, if treason towards mere potentates on earth is regarded as a capital offence, much more ought treason against "the blessed and only Potentate" to be visited with death.

IV. LET US IN CONSEQUENCE ALL BOW AT THE NAME OF JESUS. To him hath the Father given a Name that is above every name, that at it every knee should bow (Phil. ii. 9, 10). Submitting reverently to him, we shall find in his Name that marvellous significance which was heralded before his birth (Matt. i. 21). As our Saviour from sin, he will show us how reasonable is the exhortation, "Let every one that nameth the Name of Christ depart from iniquity" (2 Tim. ii. 19). Baptized in his Name, as well as in the Name of the Father and of the Holy Ghost, we shall look to him for the fulfilment of the covenant promise therein implied.[1] Under the shadow of the Name and in the light of the face of God revealed in Jesus Christ, we shall be enabled to pass on reverently and peacefully towards our everlasting rest.—R. M. E.

Public justice secured by the law of retaliation. Ch. xxiv. 17—22; cf. Matt. v. 38—48; Rom. xii. 19—21. There is here presented to us, as a law upon which Israel was to act, the principle of retaliation. And yet we have seen in the moralities of ch. xix. 17, 18, an express denunciation of *revenge.* How are we to reconcile this retaliation commanded with the revenge which is forbidden? Evidently the retaliation is to be deliberate, in cool blood, without the fever-heat of vengeance.

Now, when we bear in mind the early age to which this law of retaliation was given, an age when the institution of public justice was rudimentary in character, then we can understand how very important a check it was on the lawlessness to which men are naturally tempted. Of course, when public justice has developed itself into a wide and vigilant system, the necessity for each man taking the law into his own hand ceases. Then it becomes a crime against law to usurp its functions; it only increases lawlessness to attempt for one's self what the organized state willingly undertakes for you.

[1] Cf. Tait's 'Thoughts for the Thoughtful,' pp. 186—195.

But in rude ages it is eminently desirable that savage spirits should contemplate as a dead certainty getting as much as they give.[1] Let us notice one or two points.

I. The law of retaliation, administered in a judicial spirit, was in the interests of justice and order. Its principle is a sound one. The criminal is to get exactly what he gave. It is only in this way that the nature of a crime can be driven home to a rude and tyrannical nature. If he has been cruel to a neighbour, let him taste the effect himself of the same amount of cruelty. A man who victimizes his neighbours will cease doing so if he finds that he is to be victimized in exactly the same fashion by public law. In fact, he comes to consider his own case as bound up most intimately with his neighbours', and, instead of indulging in cruelty, he by his better conduct ensures his personal peace.

And a distinct corollary of this law of retaliation is the penalty of murder (vers. 17, 21). If a man deliberately puts his brother out of life, it is an injury which admits of no repair, and so death becomes its just penalty.

II. The law of retaliation is in one respect a preparation for the golden rule. For the golden rule runs parallel to it. It is, so to speak, its glorious issue. "Therefore all things whatsoever ye would that men should do to you, do ye even so to them: for this is the Law and the prophets" (Matt. vii. 12). Yes, this very law of retaliation suggests to every thoughtful mind whether it would not be better to try the opposite plan, and do to others, not what we should be *afraid* they would do to us, but what we would *like* them to do to us. In other words, let us wisely win the good services of others, if we are to receive what we give, by doing all to them and for them that we would welcome ourselves.

And indeed, the reason why the golden rule does not prevail as widely as it might, is because *immediate* justice is not now executed as in the case of a law of retaliation it is. The return of kindness is often impeded by ingratitude, and men may do good to others for a long lifetime without receiving much thanks. But such an arrangement gives a field for faith and courage, such as a government of instantaneous justice could not secure. In truth, we should become mere mercenaries if the golden rule involved instantaneous returns. Now, however, we must rely on the wide range of providence, and believe that in the end it will prove wisest and best to have treated our neighbour as we would like to be treated ourselves.

III. In cultivating the spirit of love towards even our enemies, we are but following the footsteps of our Father in heaven. For while re-enforcing the courage of his people in rude ages by commanding retaliation, he was himself at the same time making his sun to shine on the evil and on the good, and sending rain upon the just and on the unjust (Matt. v. 45). He was not dealing with men after their sins, nor rewarding them according to their iniquities (Ps. ciii. 10). Not only in Nature, with its dignified refusal to be a respecter of persons, but also in his sacrificial worship, was God dealing with his enemies so as to make them his friends. He was pursuing even then the policy of overcoming evil by good (Rom. xii. 21). Such laws as retaliation, resting on inexorable justice, did something to *check* sin; but only love and goodness can overcome it. Hence the spirit of the old dispensation, while hostile to sin, as the outcome of a holy God must be, had an undertone of love and mercy. God, in fact, was practising all the time his own golden rule. He was doing by men what he wanted men to do by him. In some cases this succeeded, for this is the substance of the Divine appeal in the gospel of Christ, as it was the undertone of the preliminary law; in some cases it failed through the waywardness of men. Still, the golden rule is the spirit of the Divine administration, and will be till the present dispensation is finished. Then must the great Governor deal with the impenitent in the way of strictest justice, since they will not yield to his dying love. The rhythm of the ages will be maintained; if the wrath of man is not turned to praise by the exercise of love, it must be restrained by the exercise of the cool and deliberate infliction of deserved wrath.—R. M. E.

Vers. 10—23.—*Shelomith's son.* Here a narrative is introduced into the midst of a code of laws; but this is done as a preamble to enactments of whose publication the case was the occasion. We notice—

[1] Cf. Canon Mozley's 'Ruling Ideas in Early Ages,' pp. 180—221.

I. The crime of this son of Shelomith. 1. *It was blaspheming the God of Israel.* (1) We are not distinctly informed as to the particular form of this blasphemy. We are, however, told that this man, whose name is not given, was " the son of an Israelitish woman," that his father was an Egyptian, and that in striving with a man of Israel he blasphemed the sacred Name. It may hence be concluded that he angrily reflected upon the Divine equity in favouring the seed of Jacob. Anger is certainly implied in the words, " blasphemed the Name, and cursed." (2) Here was the very spirit of Satan, whose rebellion against God was probably excited by the honour he had put upon man. " Is thine eye evil because I am good ? " (3) Is not that hatred to God which is in the carnal mind of the very essence of this blasphemy ? Though the manifestations be restrained, the venom is still there. Let us beware how we entertain hard thoughts of God. 2. *Strife was its occasion.* (1) How little do men dream, when they enter into strife, where they may be carried by their passions (see Prov. xvii. 14)! The moral, therefore, is that it should be carefully avoided. (2) But how is this to be done? We must "*give* none offence." We must be willing to *suffer* wrong. The spirit (or temper) of Christ is gained through the indwelling of his (Divine) Spirit. 3. *Race was the origin of the strife.* (1) It appears to have been a contention between a pure Israelite and a mongrel. The father of Shelomith's son was probably one of the mixed multitude that came up with the Hebrews from Egypt. (2) Traced back another step, we find the origin in the marriage of Shelomith. Mixed marriages have ever been prolific in mischief. Of these sprang the monsters, viz. not so much in stature as in iniquity, who provoked the Deluge. (3) Even Dibri, the father of Shelomith, was, remotely, responsible for the blasphemy of her son, by consenting to her marriage with an alien. How careful we should be never to commit a wrong, since no man can tell how prolific it may be in mischief! The day of judgment will declare it.

II. The impeachment of the blasphemer. 1. *His witnesses arrested him.* (1) They were bound to do so. Had they allowed him to escape they would have been accomplices in his crime (see ch. xix. 17, margin). They might have brought down the wrath of God upon the nation. Witness how Achan troubled Israel (Josh. vii. 1), and how David also brought down a plague upon his people (2 Sam. xxiv. 15—17). (2) Happy is the nation whose sons are jealous for the honour of God (see Ps. lxix. 9). Happy is the nation whose sons are guardians of its morality. This is public spirit in perfection. 2. *They kept him in ward for the judgment of God.* (1) They brought his case before Moses (ver. 11). This was in accordance with Divine direction (see Exod. xviii. 22). They might have wreaked a summary vengeance, but they chose the more excellent way. " Judgment is of God " (Deut. i. 17); therefore judgment should be deliberate. (2) Moses accordingly appealed to God. Every cause must come ultimately before him. This should never be forgotten.

III. The judgment of the Lord. 1. *This had respect to the particular offender.* (1) He was to be carried without the camp, as an outcast from society and a person excommunicated from the Church. (2) There he was to die for his sin. The witnesses put their hands on his head. This was to clear themselves of all complicity in his guilt. His blood then ostensibly was upon his own head. (3) Stoning him was to be the mode of his punishment. The witnesses cast the first stone, and the congregation, by their representatives, followed, until he perished. Thus, as Henry says, in allusion to Ps. lxiv. 8, The tongue of the blasphemer fell heavily (see Deut. xvii. 7 ; John viii. 7). 2. *It had also respect to the community.* (1) This judgment was now made a law in Israel, as well for the stranger as for him that is born in the land. (2) It was also enacted that murder must be visited with death (vers. 17, 20). This was the incorporation in the Levitical code of the Noachian precept recorded in Gen. ix. 6. (3) The principle of compensation and retaliation was asserted (vers. 19, 20). In things judicial this principle still holds, though in matters of private wrong the gospel direction is that evil be suffered rather than revenged (see Matt. v. 38, 39 ; vii. 1, 2).—J. A. M.

Vers. 10—16, 23.—*A suggestive episode.* We have an affecting illustration in these verses of the truth that "The Law is not made for a righteous man, but for the lawless and disobedient, . . . for unholy and profane " (1 Tim. i. 9). The announcement of the Law is broken by the account of this transgression, and the transgression itself gives occasion for the enactment of other statutes (vers. 15—22). The story and the statutes suggest—

I. WHAT LASTING EVIL MAY ACCRUE FROM AN UNHOLY ALLIANCE. Had the Israelitish woman not married an Egyptian (ver. 10), it is morally certain that she would not have been called upon to part with her son under these tragic and terrible circumstances. She consulted her own fancy rather than the known will of Jehovah, and, long years afterwards, she bore her penalty in maternal grief. There is nothing fraught with more grave and enduring evils than an unwise, unholy alliance.

II. HOW LIKELY ONE FOLLY IS TO END IN ANOTHER. This son of the Israelitish woman strove with a man of Israel in the camp, and their strife led to blasphemy and cursing on the part of one of them. Strife led to profanity. Similarly, carelessness often ends in fraud, fraud in falsehood, indelicacy in impurity, occasional excess in habitual intemperance, anger in murder, etc.

III. HOW SERIOUS A SIN MAY RESIDE IN A FEW WRONG WORDS. (Ver. 16.) Probably the words in which Shelomith's son blasphemed were few in number. Words are but breath, impressions made on the air, we may say. Yet, simple though they be, they may (1) reveal a most foul and guilty state of soul, (2) work terrible mischief to other souls, (3) be heard with deep abhorrence by God and the good.

IV. HOW WISE A COURSE IS THE PATIENT ADMINISTRATION OF LAW. Had the crowd that gathered at the strife between these two men inflicted condign punishment on the transgressor, the event would have been regarded as an ordinary disturbance, and no moral effect would have been produced. Possibly the guilty man would have been pitied as a victim of the violence of a mob. But by the patient course pursued (vers. 11—15, 23) it was clearly seen by all that the man died because he had committed a grievous sin, and that whosoever followed him in his guilt must expect to suffer the same penalty he endured. Thus that which might have seemed nothing better than fatal exasperation was made to wear the true aspect of righteous vindication of law. It is always best to be patient in the infliction of punishment. Here as everywhere, but here especially, calmness is strength, passion is weakness. By restraining ourselves from hasty action we may restrain many others from the commission of sin.

V. HOW SAD A SERVICE SOME MEN ARE COMPELLED TO RENDER THEIR RACE. Some men serve their fellows involuntarily. They become beacons to warn all who approach from the danger they are running. Shelomith's son, by this evil deed of his, caused the enactment of ver. 16; and this weighty law, together with the impressive circumstance out of which it grew, undoubtedly produced a very deep and permanent impression on Israel. It materially contributed to the very striking result that no nation has been more reverent in its tone and spirit than the Jews. It is a sad reflection that a man should serve his race by suffering death as the penalty of his sin. We may be compelled, by overruling Omniscience, so to serve others. How much rather would the heavenly Father accept our willing service, and make use of our devout endeavour to bless our kind!—C.

Vers. 17—22.—*The holy Law of God.* These enactments, occasioned by the sin of the son of Shelomith, contain certain principles on which God founded his Law, and which he would have us introduce into our dealings and regulations now. These are—

I. THE SACREDNESS OF HUMAN LIFE. "He that killeth any man shall surely be put to death" (ver. 17). This is significantly repeated (ver. 21) We can hardly be said to have learnt this lesson yet, after eighteen centuries of Christian legislation. Here, however, is a statute which unmistakably and emphatically asserts it.

II. EQUITY. There is to be careful discrimination in awarding penalty (vers. 18—20). A man must suffer according to the injury he has done. Nothing is more destructive of the main purpose of law than undistinguishing, and therefore unrighteous, retribution, whether at the national tribunal, or in the school, or in the home; nothing more salutary than the calm, regulated equity which estimates degrees of guilt, and determines the fair penalty therefrom.

III. CONSIDERATENESS. Law is obliged to regard the general good, the welfare of the community at large, the result of action and of permission in the end and upon the whole. It therefore often bears severely on individual men. But it must not be inconsiderate. Where it can right one man that has been wronged it must do so. "He that killeth a beast, he shall restore it" (ver. 21).

IV. IMPARTIALITY. (Ver. 22.)

V. INSTRUCTIVENESS. Law should not only decide individual cases, and bring down appropriate penalty on individual transgressors; it should also, by its embodiment of Divine principles, be a most effective teacher of truth, a constant instructor in righteousness. The law of the land should be daily leading the nation to true conceptions of what is upright, moral, estimable. These few statutes contain that vital principle, the *supreme value of human* (as compared with animal) *nature*. If a man killed his fellow-man, he must die; if he killed a beast, he must restore it (vers. 17, 18, 21). There are too many who (1) treat themselves or (2) treat others as if there were nothing more in human nature than in the "beasts that perish." *How* much is a man better than a sheep? He is better by the immeasurable height of his intelligent, responsible, spiritual, immortal nature. Let us estimate our own worth, and recognize the preciousness, before God, of the meanest soul that walks by our side along the path of human life. We may add that we see here—

VI. ROOM FOR FURTHER REVELATION. Righteous law, applicable to all, vindicated by just administrators, without a trace of personal resentment, says, "an eye for an eye, a tooth for a tooth." But beside this righteous law, consistent with it while high above it, is the spirit of individual, generous forgiveness. Where duty to society does not demand it, let the spirit of retaliation, so natural to unrenewed humanity, give place to the spirit of magnanimity,—the spirit of Jesus Christ, the Great Teacher (Matt. v. 38—41), the Divine Exemplar (Luke xxiii. 34).—C.

Vers. 10—12.—*A blasphemer punished.* An incident is here inserted that explains part of the Law by pointing to its origin. It is a practical illustration that throws lurid light upon the possibility and consequences of transgression.

I. THE SIN. It is described as blasphemy. 1. *A sin of the tongue.* Not the light matter some deem it. The tongue can cut like a sword. We need to take heed to our ways, lest we sin with the tongue. The prayer befits us, "Set a watch, O Lord, before my mouth." A word quickly spoken may have lasting results. What a power for good or evil is placed within our reach! 2. *Its criminal character.* The Name of God is to be had in reverence. This man sinned against the third commandment. If it be treason to speak ill of the ruler, how much more to utter with contempt the Name of the King of kings! Lost to all sense of propriety must he be who can curse God. Far from this, his Name should not even be jestingly or frivolously mentioned, nor should he be called to witness in our casual remarks.

II. ITS CAUSES. 1. *The immediate cause was strife.* This rouses angry passions and leads to worse sin. The beginning of strife is as the letting out of water; none can foretell how far it will spread. Little, perhaps, did this man suspect that the quarrel would end in his speedy death. Let the rivulet of contention be checked, ere it develop into a torrent! Men heated by a dispute will give utterance to sentiments of which in calmer moments they would be ashamed. 2. *The remote cause was marriage with an unbeliever.* This man's mother had espoused an Egyptian, and the son would appear to have followed the religion of his father, for, wishing to taunt an Israelite, he reviled the Name of Israel's God. Imprudent alliances are a source of continual grief and disappointment. The mother had the pain of beholding her son put to death with every mark of ignominy. The advice of the Apostle Paul with respect to marrying an ungodly person is based on religious principle, and its worth is confirmed by the dictates of common sense and the facts of experience. It is not desirable that there should be a difference of opinion on matters of religion between the husband and the wife. The loss of the children is great when they are not trained in ways of piety by the hearty co-operation of their parents.

III. THE PUNISHMENT. It is not surprising that the people should have been so astounded at such wickedness that they requested Jehovah to instruct them concerning the penalty adequate to the offence. The punishment made known and inflicted was *severe*, revealing God's estimate of the enormity of the sin; *swift*, lest the conscience of the people now aroused should have time to slumber, and lest hope of a reprieve should in after-days lead to licence of language. It was *inflicted by the whole congregation*, to rid themselves of any guilt of tacit participation in the crime; the nation must avenge the insult perpetrated upon its covenant Head. The penalty was *not averted by ex-*

tenuating pleas of race or passion. *It gave occasion for the enactment of the law of retribution.* The *lex talionis* has a rude justice about it which appeals to the sentiment of uncivilized nations. King Bezek acknowledged its force (Judg. i. 7). This retribu-tion was allowed at first because of the hardness of men's hearts, but being permitted to run side by side with the law of love to one's neighbour and the stranger, the way was prepared for the Christian rule by which the waters of the former current are merged in the strength and beauty of the stream of love. Even under this dispensation, however, the law of love has its equitable as well as forgiving aspects.—S. R. A.

Vers. 10—23.—*The law of death.* Blasphemy, murder, wilful injury, whether by Israelite or stranger, judged and punished on the principle of compensation without mercy (cf. Isa. xii. ; Rom. xi.).

I. Here is the evil of a fallen nature and an apostate people set forth (see Rom. i., ii.). "All have sinned." Israel itself is defiled.

II. The contrast suggested between the law of death and the law of life (cf. Sermon on the Mount and Rom. vii., viii.). The true glory to the Name of Jehovah is not the death of the blasphemer, but the life of God's people. What the Law could not do, *i.e.* restore the injured, heal the wound, give back the life, is done by the grace of the gospel.

III. Historical illustrations of the insufficiency of the Law in the hands of a fallen race. Jesus accused of blasphemy. Stephen stoned. Paul treated as violator of the Law. Through the Jews and their defection the Name of Jehovah blasphemed in the world. The *lex talionis* no real protection either of the individual or society.—R.

EXPOSITION.

CHAPTER XXV.

The subject of the sacred seasons is taken up again in this chapter, after the parenthetical insertion of ch. xxiv. There remain the septennial festive season and that of the half-century—the sabbatical year and the jubilee.

The sabbatical year was instituted not for any supposed physical benefit accruing from it to the land, but, first, as serving for a link between the sabbath and the jubilee by means of the sacred number seven—the sabbatical year being the seventh year, and the jubilee being the year following the seven-times-seventh year; and secondly, and chiefly, as enforcing the lesson of the weekly sabbath in a manner that could not be overlooked, and symbolically teaching the universal application of the sabbatical law, even where physical needs were not concerned, and in that way suggesting the expectation of a rest to be hereafter attained by all God's creatures. The sabbatical year began with the commencement of the civil year, the 1st of Tisri, just before the autumn sowings, which were intermitted for one year. The ground was not tilled during this year (ver. 4). There was a release of debts (Deut. xv. 1—11), and there was to be

public reading of God's Law (Deut. xxxi. 10—13). During the previous six years the husbandmen had been well aware of the coming sabbatical year, and would have laid by in store accordingly, so as to support themselves and their families during that year. The release of debts inculcated mercy. The command that the Law should be publicly read showed that the intention of the institution was not that the year should be spent in idleness, but that the time saved from ordinary labour was to be given to devotional pursuits. The law of the sabbatical year was so hard of observance by an agricultural people, that it was seldom or never acted upon until the Captivity (see 2 Chron. xxxvi. 21). But after that time it seems to have been religiously kept (see Josephus, 'Ant.,' xi. 8, 6; xiv. 10, 6; xiv. 16, 2; xv. 1, 2; 1 Macc. vi. 49; Gal. iv. 10; Tacit., 'Hist.,' v. 2, 4).

The jubilee was a joyous year appointed to be observed every fifty years. The cycle of the sabbatical year and the jubilee touched without coalescing. The forty-ninth year was necessarily a sabbatical year, and the following year was the jubilee. It has appeared to some so difficult to believe that two years in which it was not allowable to engage in agricultural work should come together, that they have assumed that the sabbatical year itself, that is, the forty-ninth year, was the year of the jubilee. But this was clearly not the case. Twice in the century the land was to lie fallow for two years running—from September to the second September following—special preparations having, of course, been made by laying up a store of grain from the abundant harvest promised in the previous year (ver. 21), and foreign crops being, no doubt, imported to take the place of the usual home crops. In matter of fact, however, these two blank years seldom, if ever, occurred together; for as the sabbatical year was not observed before the Captivity, while there are indications of the existence of the jubilee (1 Kings xxi. 3; Isa. lxi. 1—3), so probably the jubilee ceased to be observed after the Captivity, when the sabbatical year was carefully kept. Supposing that they did come together, the second year in which labour was prohibited would end just in time for the seed to be sown for the next summer's harvest.

The jubilee affected both land and men. Land could only be sold for fifty years, its value immediately after a jubilee had passed being that of fifty harvests, or rather, deducting the sabbatical years and the fiftieth year, of forty-two harvests. If it were sold, it might be bought back by the original owner or any of his relations, counting the number of harvests remaining before the next jubilee, and buying out the previous purchaser with the sum of money thus estimated. No more effective plan could be well devised for preserving the various properties in the families to which they were at first assigned.

The other point chiefly affected by the law of the jubilee was slavery. In case a brother Israelite became poor, it was the duty of his richer brethren to help him, and to lend him money without interest, to set him up in the world again. But if this did not succeed, the poor man might sell himself as a slave, either to an Israelite or to a foreigner living in the land. In the former case it had been already enacted that his slavery was not to last beyond six years (Exod. xxi. 2). To this enactment it was now added that he must be also set free whenever the year of jubilee occurred.

If he became the slave of a non-Israelite, he must be set free, not as before on the seventh year of his slavery, but still at the jubilee. He had also preserved for him the right of being redeemed by any kinsman, the price paid for him being the wages which would be paid up to the next jubilee. In either case, he was to be treated without rigour, and it was the duty of the Israelite magistrate to see that no undue harshness was used by the foreign master. The principle is, as before, that as the land is God's land, not man's, so the Israelites were the slaves of God, not of man, and that if the position in which God placed them was allowed to be interfered with for a time, it was to be recovered every seventh, or at furthest every fiftieth, year. The possession of slaves was not forbidden—the world was not yet ready for such a prohibition. The Hebrews might purchase and own slaves of alien blood, but between Hebrew and Hebrew the institution of master and slave was practically abolished, and superseded (in most respects) by the relationship of master and servant.

Ver. 1.—**And the Lord spake unto Moses in mount Sinai.** The purpose of the words, *in Mount Sinai*, is not to distinguish the place in which the sabbatical law and the law of the jubilee were given from that in which the preceding laws were delivered. The words mean only, "in the Sinai district;" and they are employed because these laws form the conclusion of the series of laws given while the people were encamped under Mount Sinai. The law on vows is, it is true, added to them, but it is by way of appendix.

Vers. 2—7.—The sabbath of the seventh year could only be observed **when ye come into the land which I give you.** The habit of making no distinction in the seventh year during the whole of the life in the wilderness may have led to the neglect of the law after the settlement in Canaan. Another excuse for the neglect may have been a difficulty which would have presented itself of fixing the date from which to count up to the seventh year, as different parts of the land were conquered at different times. According to the law, from New Year's Day of the seventh year (the 1st of Tisri, which occurred about the middle of September) to the following New Year's Day, there was to be neither sowing nor pruning, reaping or gathering. The expression, **Neither shalt thou gather the grapes of thy vine undressed,** would be more literally rendered, *the grapes of thy Nazarite* *vine*, the vine with its unpruned tendrils, being likened to the Nazarite with his unshorn locks. As to sowing and reaping, an exception was made with respect to the barley sown and reaped for the Passover sheaf, and the wheat sown and reaped for the Pentecost loaves. The spontaneous fruits of the earth, and they were very large in the rich fields of the valleys and plains, were to be the property of all alike, whether the owners of the land or not, "that the poor of thy people might eat" (Exod. xxiii. 11). And what was left by man was to be food for the cattle and beasts of the field. The cessation of agricultural labours must have served, and may have been intended to serve, as an encouragement to mercantile pursuits, as well as to the study of the Divine Law (Deut. xxxi. 10—13). The Feast of Tabernacles of the seventh year was specially appointed by Moses as a day for reading the Law to the assembled people (Deut. xxxi. 10—13). And the Mishna appoints the following passages of Deuteronomy to be read on that day:—Deut. i. 1—6; vi. 4—8; xi. 13—22; xiv. 22; xv. 23; xvii. 14; xxvi. 12—19; xxvii., xxviii. ('Mish. Sotah.,' vii. 8). The other ordinance connected with the sabbatical year, the release of debts to the poor (Deut. xv. 1—6), was, like the fifth commandment, made of none effect by rabbinical traditions —notably by one which required a debtor, when his creditor said, " I remit," to insist that nevertheless he should accept payment. The moral purpose of the sabbath of the seventh year is well drawn out by Keil:— "In the sabbatical year the land which the Lord had given his people was to observe a period of holy rest and refreshment to its Lord and God, just as the congregation did on the sabbath day; and the hand of man was to be withheld from the fields and fruit gardens from working them that they might yield their produce for his use. The earth was to be sacred from the hand of man, exhausting its power for earthly purposes as his own property, and to enjoy the holy rest with which God had blessed the earth and all its productions after the Creation. From this, Israel, as the nation of God, was to learn, on the one hand, that although the earth was created for man, it was not merely created for him to draw out its power for his own use, but also to be holy to the Lord and participate in the blessed rest; and on the other hand, that the great purpose for which the congregation of the Lord existed did not consist in the uninterrupted tilling of the earth, connected with bitter labour in the sweat of the brow (Gen. iii. 17, 19), but in the peaceful enjoyment of the fruits of the earth, which the Lord their God had given them and would give them still, without the

labour of their hands, if they strove to keep his covenant and satisfy themselves with his grace."

Vers. 8, 9.—The word **jubile** (as it is always spelt in the Authorized Version) is taken from the Hebrew word *yovel*, and it came to mean a year of liberty (Ezek. xlvi. 17; Josephus, 'Ant.,' iii. 12, 3), because it freed men and lands from the obligations to which they would otherwise have been liable; but originally it signified no more than a cornet-blast, and thence the year of the cornet-blast. The way to find the jubilee year was to number seven sabbaths **of years,** that is, seven weeks of years (ch. xxii. 15), **seven times seven years; and the space of the seven sabbaths of years shall be unto thee forty and nine years:** then by a blast of the cornet (the word is inexactly rendered **trumpet) on the tenth day of the seventh month, in the day of atonement,** the approach of the jubilee in the following year was announced.

Ver. 10.—This verse contains a short statement of the two purposes of the jubilee: (1) to **proclaim liberty throughout all the land unto all the inhabitants thereof;** (2) **ye shall return every man unto his possession.**

Vers. 11, 12.—So far as the tillage of the land went, the jubilee year was to have the same effect as a sabbatical year.

Vers. 13—17.—The Israelites were only tenants of God. They might regard themselves as owners for fifty years, but at the end of every fifty years the land was to come back to him to whom the Lord had assigned it, or to his representative. It might be bought and sold on that understanding, the value of the purchase being found by reckoning the price of the harvests up to the next jubilee day; but in this period only "the years of the fruits" were to be counted, that is, the sabbatical years, in which there would be no harvests, were to be deducted. **Ye shall not therefore oppress** (or overreach) one another by demanding more for the land than would be its just value under the limitation of the jubilee law.

Vers. 18—22.—"Not only the year of jubilee, but the sabbatical year also, commenced in the autumn, when the farmers first began to sow for the coming year; so that the sowing was suspended from the autumn of the sixth year till the autumn of the seventh, and even till the autumn of the eighth whenever the jubilee year came round, in which case both sowing and reaping were omitted for two years in succession, and consequently the produce of the sixth year, which was harvested in the seventh month of that year, must have sufficed for three years, not merely till the sowing in the autumn of the eighth or fiftieth year, but till the harvest of the ninth or fifty-first year, as the Talmud and rabbins of every age have understood the law" (Keil). The question, **What shall we eat?** would present itself with double force when the sabbatical and the jubilee years came together. It and the answer to it therefore properly follow on the institution of the jubilee, instead of preceding it, as Ewald, Knobel, and others demand that it should do.

Vers. 23, 24.—**For the land is mine; for ye are strangers and sojourners with me.** Many incidental advantages, if some difficulties, arose from the jubilee law (which will be the more appreciated if we compare the evils resulting from slavery and the accumulation of land in a few hands, found in the history of Rome or any other ancient nation); but its essential features, so far as the land was concerned, was its inculcation of the lesson of the proprietorship of the Lord. Palestine was God's land: he divided it once for all in the time of Joshua among his people, and every fifty years he required that recourse should be had to that original division, in order that in each generation the people might feel themselves to be his tenants, not independent owners, *possessores*, not *domini*.

Vers. 25—28.—The right of redemption of land sold continued always alive, and might be exercised by the original owner or his kinsman. If not exercised, the owner returned into his possession at any rate in the jubilee year. If a man had to sell his land, he was bound to offer it to his nearest kinsman first (see Jer. xxxii. 7, 8).

Vers. 29—31.—Houses in walled cities are not subject to the law of restoration at the jubilee, as that law applies only to lands and to men; but houses in the country are subject to the law, as they are regarded only as appurtenances of the land. Houses in cities, being occupied by artisans and built by human industry, not originally assigned in the territorial division, are not considered in so strict a sense the property of the Lord as the soil is, and may be parted with more readily. Yet the owners, if obliged to part with them, are allowed a year's grace, during which they are to have the right of buying them back. The expression, within a **full year**, would be more literally rendered *during a fixed time*, that fixed time having just before been declared to be a year.

Vers. 32—34.—The houses of the Levites are, by an exception, subject to the law of jubilee. They constituted the share of the national property which was assigned to the tribe of Levi, and so far stood in the same relation to them as the land did to the other tribes. They therefore returned to the original possessor or his represen-

tative in the year of jubilee, and might at any earlier time be redeemed. The words, **Notwithstanding the cities of the Levites,** should rather be rendered, *But in respect to the cities of the Levites.* There is a difficulty also as to the translation of the clause, **And if a man purchase of the Levites,** for the word rendered *purchase* means elsewhere *redeem;* but here the Authorized Version would seem to be correct. The sense that it gives is that if any one bought a house of the Levites, he had to render it back in the year of jubilee, just as though it had been land. On the other hand, the land belonging to the Levites, in the suburbs of the Levitical cities, which was used for the pasturage of the flocks of the Levites, could not be sold except to a Levite, and therefore no question between the Levites and members of the other tribes could arise regarding it. The phrase, **the house that was sold, and the city of his possession,** must be understood, by a hendiadys, to mean, *the house that was sold in the city of his possession* (see Gesenius, 'Lex.,' *s.v.* ב i.b.).

Vers. 35—38.—Slavery. It is presumed that no Hebrew will become a slave except on the pressure of poverty, and this poverty his brethren are commanded to relieve; but foreseeing that either want of charity on the part of the rich or unthrift on the part of the poor would certainly bring about slavery, the legislator makes regulations so as to soften its character as far as possible. The literal translation of ver. 35 is as follows: **If thy brother becomes poor, and his hand faileth by thee, thou shalt lay hold of him; a stranger or a sojourner that he may live with thee.** The translation of the latter clause adopted by the Authorized Version, *yea, though he be a stranger, or a sojourner; that he may live with thee,* makes the duty of giving charitable support and loans of money to apply to the case of the stranger and sojourner as well as of the Israelite. The other and more probable rendering confines its application to native Israelites. *If thy brother becomes poor, and his hand faileth, thou shalt support him as a stranger or a sojourner,* that is, treat him with the forbearance shown to resident foreigners, to whose state he had reduced himself by the loss of his land. The command in ver. 36, **Take thou no usury of him, or increase,** does not bear upon the general question of taking interest for money when lent to wealthy men or companies for business purposes. It simply forbids the taking of interest or increase of a brother Israelite who had become poor. The history of Rome shows how much cruelty and revolution such an injunction may have prevented. The words, *or increase,* added to *usury,* forbid the exaction of any greater quantity of food or clothing (a method of evading the law against usury) than that which had been lent. The injunction was transgressed in the time of Nehemiah, when "he rebuked the nobles, and the rulers, and said unto them, Ye exact usury, every one of his brother. . . . Then held they their peace, and found nothing to answer" (Neh. v. 7, 8).

Vers. 39—42.—We see the way in which a poor Israelite might become a slave in the case of the sons of the widow whose oil was multiplied by Elisha. "Thy servant my husband is dead; (and thou knowest that thy servant did fear the Lord:) and the creditor is come to take unto him my two sons to be bondmen" (2 Kings iv. 1). And in the time of Nehemiah, "Some also there were that said, We have mortgaged our lands, vineyards, and houses, that we might buy corn, because of the dearth. . . . And, lo, we bring into bondage our sons and our daughters to be servants, and some of our daughters are brought unto bondage already: neither is it in our power to redeem them; for other men have our lands and vineyards" (Neh. v. 3—5). But the fact that an Israelite could not be kept in slavery for more than six years (Exod. xxi. 2), and that the period of his service had to be still shorter if the jubilee fell before the seventh year, and the further fact that at the time of the jubilee he would not only be free, but recover any ancestral property that he had forfeited, so that he might become once more on an equality with his master, would have made his position totally different from the hopeless, helpless state of the Greek or Roman slave, even without the positive command that he was to be treated, not as a bondservant: but as an hired servant, and as a sojourner. All alike, master and bondsman, were the slaves of God, and therefore not only were they, so far, on an equality one with another, but the master would be encroaching on the right of God if he claimed God's slaves for his own inalienably.

Ver. 43.—**Thou shalt not rule over him with rigour; but shalt fear thy God,** is paralleled by the New Testament injunction, "And, ye masters, do the same things unto them, forbearing threatening: knowing that your Master also is in heaven; neither is there respect of persons with him" (Eph. vi. 9).

Vers. 44—46.—Slavery is not forbidden in respect to non-Israelites. The world was not yet ready for it, as it was not ready in the days of St. Paul.

Vers. 47—55.—Rules are laid down for the case of an Israelite who has sold himself for a slave to a non-Israelite. In this case he is not set free at the end of six years, as he would be if his master were a countryman, but in other respects his treatment is to be like that of the man with an Israelite master. He may be redeemed by the value of his work down to the jubilee being paid by himself or his kinsman; he is to be set free when the jubilee comes at any rate; he is to be treated kindly while continuing in his master's service, and his countrymen are to see that no over-severity is used.

HOMILETICS.

Vers. 8—34.—The jubilee, being a year of deliverance and joy, came to be a type of the Messianic dispensation, and of the final deliverance and state of happiness which is still to come. "The Spirit of the Lord God is upon me; because the Lord hath anointed me to preach good tidings unto the meek; he hath sent me to bind up the brokenhearted, to proclaim liberty to the captives, and the opening of the prison to them that are bound; to proclaim the acceptable year of the Lord" (Isa. lxi. 1, 2). We have our Lord's authority for saying that these words bear spiritual reference to his ministry on earth (Luke iv. 21). They are partially fulfilled in his kingdom here, and will be fully accomplished at "the restitution of all things" (Acts iii. 21) in his kingdom hereafter, when his people shall "rest from their labours" and be delivered from the burden of their debts and emancipated for ever from slavery.

Vers. 35—55.—*The power of slavery was undermined, not at once destroyed, by the Bible.* I. IN THE OLD TESTAMENT. It is accepted as a fact, not denounced or approved, but recognized and gradually ameliorated. 1. Hebrew slaves are not to be treated with rigour (vers. 43, 53), but as hired servants. How different from the state of slaves in the workshops of Greece and Rome! 2. In the case of Hebrew slaves, the duration of slavery was not to be perpetual. At the end of six years every slave was to be restored to liberty, and at the end of fifty years at the utmost he was to be replaced in a social position which might equal his master's (vers. 28, 54).

II. In the New Testament. It is still accepted as a fact. But : 1. A principle is laid down, which, like leaven leavening the whole lump, could not but cause its destruction. "Ye masters . . . your Master also" (or, as it would be better translated, "your and their Master ") "is in heaven ; neither is there respect of persons with him" (Eph. vi. 9). "Ye call me Master and Lord : and ye say well ; for so I am. If I then, your Lord and Master, have washed your feet ; ye also ought to wash one another's feet. For I have given you an example, that ye should do as I have done to you" (John xiii. 13—15). "Art thou called being a servant (slave)? care not for it : but if thou mayest be made free, use it rather. For he that is called in the Lord, being a servant (slave), is the Lord's freeman : likewise also he that is called, being free, is Christ's servant (slave) " (1 Cor. vii. 21, 22). "There is neither . . . bond nor free : but Christ is all, and in all "(Col. iii. 11). 2. An example is given. St. Paul thus speaks of Onesimus, the runaway slave, now converted to Christianity : " I beseech thee for my son Onesimus, whom I have begotten in my bonds : . . . thou therefore receive him, that is, mine own bowels. . . . For perhaps he therefore departed for a season, that thou shouldest receive him for ever ; not now as a servant (slave), but above a servant (slave), a brother beloved, specially to me, but how much more unto thee, both in the flesh, and in the Lord? If thou count me therefore a partner, receive him as myself" (Philem. 10—17). Contrast the feeling entertained contemporaneously towards slaves in the Roman Empire. "Their growing power was sometimes restrained by legalized murder ; they were sold without remorse ; they were tortured and beaten and crucified without pity. Even Cicero apologizes to Atticus for being affected by the death of his slave" (Wordsworth, 'Church History,' ch. xxiii.).

III. Teaching in the second century. "We ought," says Clement of Alexandria, "to treat our slaves as ourselves. They are men as we are ; and there is the same God of bond and free ; and we ought not to punish our brethren when they sin, but to reprove them. Whatever we do to the lowest and meanest of Christ's brethren, we do to him" ('Pædag.,' p. 307, as quoted by Wordsworth).

IV. Slow but certain extinction of slavery. There was a long battle to be fought between the selfish and the Christian instinct ; but slavery could not coexist with Christianity, and wherever Christianity now stretches, slavery, though it may still linger here and there, is condemned by public sentiment and doomed to extinction.

HOMILIES BY VARIOUS AUTHORS.

The fallow year. Ch. xxv. 1—7 ; cf. Deut. xxxi. 10—13. We have here a ceremonial appendix to the fourth commandment. The land must have its sabbath as well as man, and so every seventh year was to be fallow year for the ground. The necessity of giving land rest is recognized still in agriculture. Continual cropping impoverishes a soil, and reduces it eventually to barrenness. This was one of the grave charges made by political economists against the slavery of North America, that, in consequence of the inefficiency of slave labour, the land was subjected to a monotonous process of cropping, and in consequence killed. The finest virgin soil was being reduced to wilderness, for the land was allowed neither variety nor rest.[1] This arrangement in Israel, therefore, was economically most wise. But "the sabbath of the fields " had a wider basis than this mere natural one. It was attended by most important religious results.

I. The fallow year proclaimed that the land belonged to the Lord. For if the fourth commandment really implies that the people, called from their own work to do God's work on God's day, belong to him, and so are under obligation to obey this call, in the very same way the claim that the land should rest proclaims that the land is his. What was thus claimed in Canaan is only part of a still wider claim ; for "the earth is the Lord's, and the fulness thereof ; the world, and they that dwell therein. For he hath founded it upon the seas, and established it upon the floods" (Ps. xxiv. 1, 2). The demand for "a sabbath of rest unto the land " is for "a sabbath for the

[1] Cf. Cairnes' ' Slave Power,' p. 56, etc.

Lord." He thus stamps the land as his, and had we the clear vision, we might see the "sign manual" of the Lord upon all the world.

II. THE FALLOW YEAR CHANGED AGRICULTURAL INTO PASTORAL LIFE. The people of necessity gave greater attention to the rearing and the tending of cattle. It is evident from ver. 7 that the care of the cattle and of the beasts of the field was specially contemplated by the arrangement. National life would become in consequence more *idyllic*. A wholesome change would thus be introduced every seventh year, and the people would morally be improved. The population would become more and more humane, and the whole country profit thereby.

Now, in pastoral countries there is of necessity more time for pensive meditation and thought. Pastoral life is in the interests of reflection. It is a providential aid thereto. Hence we see in the sabbatic year the condition supplied for greater thoughtfulness and reflection. If we compare the blank intellectual condition of agricultural labourers, ground down by ceaseless toil, with the thoughtful, poetic mood often met with among shepherds, we can have no difficulty in recognizing the great moral importance of a pastoral year.

III. THE FALLOW YEAR WAS A FINE EXERCISE FOR THE NATIONAL FAITH. For men would naturally ask, "What shall we eat the seventh year?" (ver. 20). And to this the Lord made answer, "Then I will command my blessing upon you in the sixth year, and it shall bring forth fruit for three years" (ver. 21). For a nation to prepare for this fallow year required great faith in God. The sixth year was a year of "great expectations;" they looked to God to provide for the coming year of rest, and thus were drawn up to an exercise of faith and hope of the most profitable description. Amid our multiplied methods of livelihood we are in danger of losing sight of the Divine hand altogether, and of living a low life of sight. And yet, by periodic returns of hard times and difficulties, the Lord is still calling on us for faith in him, to enable us to serve him. He still desires us to exercise this faith in him, that none of us shall ever suffer real loss in seeking to serve him. "So those who abstain from their labours upon the sabbath," says an old writer in this connection, "it shall never impoverish them, for the blessing of God upon the week-days shall supply all their wants; so the Lord promised, when they shall go up to Jerusalem to serve him at their feasts, that he would keep their land from the incursion of their enemies (Exod. xxxiv. 24). We see also (Josh. v. 1, 2), when they were circumcised, the Lord struck such a fear and terror into the hearts of the Canaanites, that they durst not touch them, as Simeon and Levi killed the Shechemites when they were newly circumcised. Never man yet got hurt in the service of God; he shall still find the Lord's protecting hand and blessing in his service."

IV. THE FALLOW YEAR BROUGHT INTO PROMINENCE THE GREAT TRUTH ABOUT THE BROTHERHOOD OF MAN. Although the land was to lie fallow, it gave much in the way of spontaneous growth. This became public and common property, so that servant, and maid, and hired servant, and stranger, as well as the rightful owner, "had all things common." In fact, there was, to adopt the modern phraseology, a "commune" established in Canaan so far as the produce of the sabbatic year was concerned. Was this not a recognition of the brotherhood of man, and of the obligation to make some provision for poorer brethren? It was thus the year of *charity*, when all alike sat at the table of the Divine bounty, and realized thereat their common relation.

It was a similar outcome of the religious spirit which occurred at Pentecost. Then "the multitude of them that believed were of one heart and of one soul: neither said any of them that ought of the things which he possessed was his own; but they had all things common" (Acts iv. 32). And although the Christian commune did not work well, but broke down speedily, it showed the true tendency of inspired men. The obligation under which they live to do their best for all about them, especially for those of the household of faith, is cheerfully and gladly recognized. And possibly, in the perfect world and sabbath of the spirit, this community of goods will be found workable, the selfish elements which now cause friction having entirely disappeared.

V. THE FALLOW YEAR AFFORDED SPECIAL FACILITIES FOR PROMOTING NATIONAL EDUCATION. It is evident from Deut. xxxi. 10—13 that the sabbatic year was to be a season of special study of the Law. The Feast of Tabernacles with which it began was to be devoted to the public reading of it. Not only the adults, male and female, but also the children, were to be instructed in it. So that the national desire might very properly find its expression in the words of the Psalm (cxix. 19), which celebrates the Divine Law, "I am a stranger in the earth : hide not thy commandments from me." A pilgrim people in extemporized tents applied themselves in the sabbatic year to the study of God's commandments.

Thus national education was promoted, and this education was of such a character that "the revival of religion" must have resulted if the sabbatic years had been faithfully kept. It would seem from such a passage as Jer. xxxiv. 14, however, that Israel was not careful about the sabbatic year, and the result was judgment without mercy (Jer. xxxiv. 17—22). The institution was most valuable, morally and spiritually, but it was disregarded by an apostatizing people, who came in consequence into an inheritance of judgment rather than of blessing.—R. M. E.

The jubilee. Ch. xxv. 8—55; cf. Isa. lxi. 1—13; Luke iv. 18, 19. We have here a further appendix to the fourth commandment. After seven sabbatic years there came another year, called the jubilee, which was also sabbatic, and during which there was to be a universal restitution. The trumpet was to be blown on the Day of Atonement, and the captives were then to be released, the unfortunate ones who had been compelled to part with their inheritance had it restored to them, and there was a general restoration of heart and of hope throughout the land. It was the year of liberty, of comfort, of restoration; in one word, it was every half-century a *bloodless revolution*, giving to the entire nation the opportunity of a new departure.

I. THE JUBILEE WAS PRE-EMINENTLY THE LORD'S, AND AS SUCH WAS A HALLOWED YEAR. The fallow year was a year of rest unto the land, the jubilee was a year of liberty and release unto the people, and, as the year which was reached after a series of seven sabbatic years, it was hallowed as no other year was hallowed, to the service of the Lord. His will ruled all the year, just as his will is pre-eminently regarded on the sabbath days. Now, the principle embodied in the jubilee was this: "All members of the community are the direct servants of Jehovah, not the servants of men, and they must therefore have an unfettered body and unencumbered estate, in order to live worthy of their vocation."[1] Hence God gave his people in the jubilee who had become "servants of men" through the pressure of the times, release from their bondage; he gave those of them who had disposed of their estates, which they could only dispose of until the jubilee, a new gift of their inheritance; he gave every exile from his home and family through the exigencies of the times, right to return to his family and begin life amid the old associations and without encumbrance. This was surely to show that his service is perfect freedom, and that when his will is done on earth as it ought to be, men shall have such social privileges and such adequate temporal provision as will make life an antepast of heaven!

The only exception to the law of restoration was the case of a house in a walled town, which, if not redeemed within a year, might become the inalienable inheritance of the buyer. It was only by some little possibility of this kind that the stranger could have any footing in the holy land at all. The growth of cities, and of the civilization which cities bring, was thus provided for. If every house as well as field reverted to its former owners, every jubilee would have witnessed an emigration of all but the descendants of the old proprietors, and business would have been brought to n utter standstill. We see in this exception the possibility of a foreign and advantageous element amid the native population.

II. THERE WAS A SLAVERY WHICH TERMINATED, AND A SLAVERY WHICH DID NOT TERMINATE, IN THE YEAR OF THE JUBILEE. The slavery which did terminate was that into which a Jewish debtor had entered, in order to give his service in lieu of the debt. In fact, slavery was the form that the bankruptcy laws took in Palestine. It would be well if some such system were engrafted on our own jurisprudence. A man who has got unfortunately into difficulties might thus honourably redeem his position and his character, instead of compromising both by availing himself of present legal facilities.

On the other hand, foreigners or natives of Canaan might become perpetual slaves to

---

[1] Ewald's 'Antiquities of Israel,' pp. 378, 379.

the Jews. In so doing, they shared in Jewish privileges, and had the advantage of Jewish training. This was compensation for the loss of their freedom. Besides, their considerate treatment was carefully secured by the Law of God. It was right, therefore, that it should thus be unmistakably exhibited that other nations were only "hewers of wood and drawers of water" to the Lord's own people. This was what slavery among the Jews embodied.

III. THE JUBILEE WAS THE TYPE OF GOSPEL TIMES. Our Lord appropriated the prophecy delivered by Isaiah, "The Spirit of the Lord God is upon me; because the Lord hath anointed me to preach good tidings unto the meek; he hath sent me to bind up the brokenhearted, to proclaim liberty to the captives, and the opening of the prison to them that are bound; to proclaim the acceptable year of the Lord" (Isa. lxi. 1, 2; cf. Luke iv. 18, 19). We are living consequently amid the glorious privileges of the Lord's acceptable year. The gospel, as preached to men, is the trumpet blown at the beginning of the jubilee. It is blown over the completed atoning sacrifice of Christ. It proclaims, therefore—

1. *The pardon of sin.* Sin constitutes the great debt, and as sin-burdened hearts feel, the pardon of sin is the great release. What a liberty forgiveness brings!

2. *The gospel proclaims freedom from the power of sin.* For if God gave us liberty to sin with impunity, it would be no real blessing. He gives us through Christ and his Spirit freedom from the dominion of sin. He takes away the love of sin, which is the real liberty.

3. *The gospel proclaims the sanctity of family life.* Just as in the jubilee broken family circles were restored again, and social enjoyments regained, so the gospel exalts the family as the unit, and sets its highest sanctions round the home.

4. *The gospel has wrought steadily towards the liberties of men.* For while there was no "servile war" proclaimed in the apostolic time, but seeds of liberty were left to fructify in the bosom of the race, we know they have sprung into vigorous being, and that it is pre-eminently to the force of gospel truth and principle the battle of freedom and its victory are due.

5. *And the gospel is the charter of all wise reform.* It might be shown that true progress and the bloodless revolutions of such countries as England and America are due to the force of gospel principles making their hallowed way among men. It is only so far as the will of God is regarded in the politics and policy of nations that true progress and needful revolutions shall be secured.

IV. THE JUBILEE IS ALSO THE TYPE OF THE EVERLASTING REST. "There remaineth," we are told, "a *sabbatism* to the people of God" (Heb. iv. 9). This jubilee of Creation is to be ushered in by the trump of God (1 Thess. iv. 16). And regarding the heavenly state, we may in this connection remark—

1. *That heaven will be an everlasting sabbath.* If the jubilee was a sabbath extending over a year, heaven is to be a sabbath extending over an eternity. All time, if such an element is recognized in eternity, will prove consecrated there.

2. *All wrongs shall then be righted.* All the burdens and injustices and sorrows which we endure here will give place in the jubilee of heaven to the utmost justice and the most scrupulous reward.

3. *The Divine family shall be complete.* The scattered children of God shall be restored to their rightful place in the great family circle, and the home-feeling shall be the heritage of all.

4. *And everlasting progress shall characterize the everlasting rest.* For if progress towards perfection is life's most real joy, we can see how heaven itself can afford a field for it. God's infinite nature and boundless operations will not be comprehended in a flash of intuition; but insight will be, let us thankfully believe, the steady growth of ages.—R. M. E.

Vers. 1—7, 18—22.—*The sabbatic year.* At the close of the original week the sabbath of the seventh day was given; that of the seventh year, on the entrance of the Hebrews into Canaan. The former was a memorial of creation; the latter, of redemption. These are intimately related. There are correspondences between the old creation and the new—the material and the spiritual. The grand effect of redemption will be the constitution of a new creation, in which the mundane system will participate.

I. THE SEVENTH YEAR WAS A "SABBATH OF THE LAND." Then : 1. *The soil re-mained untilled.* (1) In other years it was customary to sow the grain after the Feast of Ingathering, and the vines were pruned in the spring. While we are in this world the greater portion of our time should be occupied in its concerns. This is God's order. The thing in hand should be done with might. (2) In this year no seed was sown, and there was no dressing of vines. The affairs of this world must not engross all our time and care. (3) The sentiment of religion must be with us in our earthly business. Religion must limit the time it claims—the intensity with which it is pursued. Thus : 2. *The people were taught to trust God.* (1) They lived upon the natural productive-ness of the soil. But not without the blessing of God upon it. Natural productiveness without the blessing of God is a poor dependence. (2) With that blessing, such was the bounty of the sixth year that it carried the nation on to the harvest of the eighth (see vers. 21, 22). Thus miraculously was the fruit of three years brought forth in one. This was in perpetuity the miracle of the manna (Exod. xvi. 22 ; see also Matt. iv. 4). (3) What reply to this institution can those give who would convict Moses as an impostor? (see Exod. xxiii. 10, 11). No sensible man would have made such a law as this, unless he acted under Divine direction ; for the sixth year would have refuted his pretensions. Thus also: 3. *The people were taught to hope in God.* (1) Every re-currence of the sabbatic year reminded them of the period before sin entered, in which the earth of its natural strength brought forth plenty. (2) In it too they anticipated the period when, through the redemption of the gospel, the curse shall be lifted from the earth, and men shall be released from the burden of labour (see Gen. iii. 17 ; iv. 11, 12 ; v. 29 ; also Isa. lxv. 17—25 ; Rom. viii. 18—23 ; Rev. xxii. 3).

II. THEN THE FRUIT OF THE LORD'S LAND WAS FREE. 1. *The land is the Lord's.* (1) In this law he asserted his right as Landlord to impose conditions upon his people when he gave them possession of Canaan. All God's gifts carry conditions. This should ever be remembered. (2) God's laws will regulate the new heavens and earth. They will not then be contravened. Happy will that state be. By loyalty to the laws of God we should now anticipate that state as much as in us lies. 2. *This year the tenant shared his benefits with all comers.* (1) What fruit came spontaneously was free to the poor—free to the stranger—free to the cattle—free even to the wild animal. What a lesson of generosity! of public spirit! of kindness to animals! Consider here also the Divine philosophy of rights in property. (2) Note that the resolution of the primitive Christian Church to have all things in common was not without precedent (see Acts ii. 44). Also that in the light of this precedent we may discern their purpose ; and learn that when the Spirit shall be poured out upon all flesh, of which the baptism of the Pentecost was but an instalment, the consummation will be happy. (3) But how different are the theories of our socialists! Satan is an adept at setting up counterfeits. The idle vagabond has no objection to be the subject of love from others, if he can thereby live on their property. He would eat without working, in contra-vention of the apostolic rule (see 1 Thess. iv. 11, 12 ; 2 Thess. iii. 10). He has no con-ception of those spiritual blessings in connection with which alone communism is a happy possibility. (4) The feeding together of the cattle and wild animals points to the *universality* of the blessings of the gospel (see Isa. xi. 6—9 ; lvi. 7—9 ; Hos. ii. 18 ; Acts x. 11, 12). The feeding together of the stranger and poor Hebrew on the holding of the rich sets forth the *spirituality* of the gospel. These things will be blessedly realized in the sabbaths, viz. of the millennium, and of the heavenly world. 3. *There was a release from debts* (see Deut. xv. 1, 2). (1) The gospel truly is "the Lord's release." (2) This release will be perfected in the heavenly state.

III. THE LEISURE OF THIS YEAR WAS RELIGIOUSLY SPENT. 1. *The Law was publicly read* (see Deut. xxxi. 10, 11). (1) Our leisure should be largely given to the study of the Word of God. (2) Leisure should be made for this important duty. 2. *If not religiously used, leisure is fruitful in mischief.* (1) The want of a worthy aim is in itself a great mischief. The faculties suffer. (2) The want of a worthy aim implies the pursuit of that which demoralizes. We are constitutionally active. We cannot sleep away existence. (3) The curse of labour is a blessing in disguise. All God's curses crop up as blessings somewhere. This must be so, for he is essentially and everlastingly Good. Men who retire from business should give their leisure to Church work.—J. A. M.

Vers. 8—17.—*The jubilee.* The sabbath of the seventh day is commemorative of the rest of God after the work of creation, and anticipative of the rest in heaven for his people after the world's great week of toil and sorrow (see Heb. iii., iv.). The more to impress these things upon us, to keep alive our gratitude, and to stimulate our faith and hope, he also instituted the sabbaths of the Levitical system. Conspicuous amongst these are the grand sabbaths mentioned in this chapter, viz. that of the seventh year and that of the week of years. This last comes now under review; and we notice—

I. THE TIME OF THE JUBILEE. 1. *In its astronomical aspect.* (1) It was regulated by the sun. It was reckoned from the entrance of the children of Israel into Canaan, and recurred at the time of the autumnal harvest. (2) It was also regulated by the moon. It was counted from the tenth day of the first month, that being the month in which Israel crossed the Jordan. (3) It was itself an important factor in reconciling solar and lunar time. Forty-nine years is a soli-lunar cycle. The interval from the tenth day of the first month of the year to the tenth of the seventh month of the forty-ninth year is exactly six hundred lunations. The sabbaths are all worked in, as elements of intercalation, and the intercalations of the Levitical system are very superior to those of the Gregorian (see ' Dissertation Concerning the Sabbath; and a Sabbatical Era,' in the third volume of King's 'Morsels of Criticism'). Who but God could have instituted a system so scientifically perfect? (see Gen. i. 14). 2. *In its theological aspect.* (1) The jubilee dated from the great Day of Atonement. Some compute that the very year in which Christ suffered was the year of jubilee, and the last of the Levitical series. (2) Its provisions were typical of gospel mysteries. As the jubilee ended the yoke and burden of the slave, so the bringing in of the gospel released us from the yoke and burden even of the ceremonial Law itself. (3) When the gospel is received by faith, it introduces us into a spiritual rest from the burden and yoke of sin. (4) The rest of the soul in Christ is an earnest of the rest in heaven. This last also springs from the great atonement of Calvary.

II. THE PROCLAMATION OF THE JUBILEE. 1. *This foreshadowed the preaching of the gospel.* (1) It was by sound of trumpet. Some suppose that the jubilee had its name (יבל) from a particular sound of the trumpet. The word *jobel* (יבל) is used for a *trumpet* in Exod. xix. 13. The gospel should have a certain sound (see 1 Cor. xiv. 8). (2) The trumpet was sounded over the sacrifices. This foreshowed the connection between the great atonement of Christ and the blessings of salvation. The preaching of the gospel is the preaching of the cross. "The great liberty or redemption from thraldom, published under the gospel, could not take place till the great atonement—the sacrifice of the Lord Jesus—had been offered up" (Clarke). (3) The trumpet was sounded throughout the land (ver. 9). (*a*) If the land of Canaan be taken as a specimen of the world at large, then was this a prophecy of the proclamation of the gospel to the ends of the earth (Matt. xxviii. 19; Mark xvi. 16; Col. i. 23). (*b*) But if the land be taken in a restricted sense as applicable to the people of the Law in contradistinction to the heathen, then the teaching is that those only who renounce sin by repentance are concerned in the blessings of the gospel. 2. *The trumpet also suggests the judgment.* (1) The *jobel,* or *trumpet,* sounded at the giving of the Law (Exod. xix. 13). It called attention to the Law as the standard by which we shall be judged. The trumpet will sound at the last day, (*a*) to awaken the dead (1 Cor. xv. 52); (*b*) to summon all men to the tribunal. (2) The jubilee trumpet was the trumpet of a seventh period. There was the trumpet of the seventh day; again, of the seventh year; and now again, of the sabbath of a week of sabbatic periods. To these correspond the seventh of the seven great trumpets of the Apocalypse, which proclaims the judgment. (3) While to the wicked the trumpet of the judgment is a fearful alarm, to the good it is a joyful sound. If we sing of judgment we must also sing of mercy (Ps. ci. 1). The seventh trumpet heralds in the reign of peace.

III. THE BLESSINGS OF THE JUBILEE. 1. *It proclaimed a release.* (1) As to the person. The slave was released from the hand of his brother; from the hand of the stranger. Whom the Son maketh free is free indeed. (2) As to the land. Every man returned to his possession. Adam Clarke derives the word *jubilee* (יובל) from *hobil* (הוביל), to cause to bring back, because estates, etc., which had been alienated, were then brought back to their primitive owners. No true believer can be deprived of his share in the land of promise (see Eph. i. 14 ; Heb. xi. 9—14).   2. *It was a season of joy.* (1) The poor then rejoiced in plenty. In the sabbatic year the fruit of the Lord's land was free. In the year of jubilee every man returned to his possession. (2) The generous rejoiced in the prosperity of the poor. No doubt there were churls. Such persons are never to be envied; least of all in a season of rejoicing. Heaven would be hell to the churl. (3) The spectacle of blessedness periodically witnessed in sabbatic years and jubilees encouraged generous habits of thought, feeling, and action. Happy is the people whose God is the Lord.—J. A. M.

Vers. 23—34.—*Redemption.* This subject is intimately connected with that of the jubilee; and the redemption of the Law prefigured that of the gospel, which also stands intimately related to the glorious jubilee of the great future. In this light we have to consider—

I. The NATURE OF THE REDEMPTION. This we may view: 1. *In respect to the possession.* (1) Canaan may be taken as a specimen of the earth at large. The Hebrew word for that land (ארץ) is the term also for the whole world. In the largest sense the earth was given to mankind for an inheritance (Gen. i. 26—29 ; Ps. viii. 5—9 ; cxv. 16). If the Israelites were ever reminded that they had their possession of Canaan from God (ver. 23), we must never forget that we have nothing that we receive not (John iii. 27 ; 1 Cor. iv. 7 ; Jas. i. 17). (2) The Hebrews held their possession upon the tenure of faith and obedience (Deut i. 34—36 ; xxx. 15—20 ; Heb. iii. 18, 19). Such also is the tenure upon which the earth at large is held. And as the expulsion of Adam from Eden vividly brought home to him his forfeiture of right to the earth, so did the forfeiture of Canaan keep alive in the Israelite the remembrance of the consequences of the Fall. (3) The land of Canaan was not only a specimen of the earth at large, but also of a type of the new earth of the future. Eden also was a "like figure." Like the garden, Canaan was "the glory of all lands" (Deut. viii. 7—10 ; Ezek. xx. 6, 15). So in the institution of the law of redemption we have bodied forth the means by which we shall recover our interest in the earth (see Luke xxi. 28; Rom. viii. 23 ; Eph. i. 14 ; iv. 30). (4) While Satan is the god of this world, the true heir may be kept out of his inheritance, but his title cannot be ultimately defeated. This was one of the important lessons of the jubilee, and of the law of redemption (vers. 23, 24, 28; see also Eph. i. 4; Heb. xi. 9—14). (5) As the possessions of the Levites were inalienable (ver. 34), so the "kingdom of priests" shall for ever enjoy their possessions in the renovated earth (1 Pet. ii. 5; Rev. i. 6). We may view this subject: 2. *In respect to the person.* (1) By sin we have not only forfeited our right to Eden, to Canaan, to the old earth, to the new earth, but we have also become enslaved. The habit of evil is a chain of iron. The terror of death is formidable bondage. The tyranny of Satan is merciless. Bad enough to have our liberties sold to a fellow-man ; but to be sold over to this "stranger" from the infernal world is intolerable. (2) But there is redemption for the Hebrew slave. He may redeem himself if he have the means. His next of kin has the right of redemption (vers. 25, 26). He may be redeemed by his brother Hebrew (see Neh. v. 8). So to the truly penitent, who like the Hebrews are the people of the Law, there is the redemption of the gospel. (3) But the Law has no provision for the redemption of the stranger who cannot purchase freedom for himself. Yet might he be the subject of mercy. The gospel reaches those whom the Law discourages. The pagan slave might become a Jewish proselyte, and be released in accordance with the Law. So those who are furthest off may in true repentance be brought nigh to God. (4) But the mercy of the gospel has its limits. It may be forfeited by obstinacy. It may also be forfeited by neglect. A year only is allowed in which to redeem a house in a city (ver. 30). The house is a common figure for the people; and the interpretation of the year of recovery may be seen in Isa. lxi. 2; lxiii. 4 ; 2 Cor. vi. 2. If taken in time, the whole city of God may be redeemed ; but the period of probation missed, the case is hopeless. Consider—

II. The QUALIFICATIONS OF THE REDEEMER. 1. *A slave might redeem himself.* (1) That is, if it be in the power of his hand. Under favourable conditions of earning and saving, this might become possible. (2) But when the slave is the sinner and he is in bondage to the justice of God, this is impossible. Our deeds are sin. And the wages of sin is death. 2. *The near kinsman is the legal redeemer.* (1) This kinsman was a type of Christ. Bishop Patrick quotes a rabbi, who says, "This Redeemer is the Messiah, the Son of David." Job speaks of Messiah as his Redeemer (xix. 25). So is he elsewhere termed in Scripture (see Isa. lix. 20; Rom. xi. 26). (2) To be qualified to redeem, Jesus became our Kinsman by taking up our nature. As any Hebrew brother might become a redeemer, so Jesus, in our flesh, became "the brother of every man," that he might redeem. Job speaks of seeing his Redeemer *in his flesh,* or incarnate—for this I take to be the sense. (3) Every near kinsman may not have it in his power to become a *Goel* or Redeemer. No mere human being can give to God a ransom for his brother (Ps. xlix. 7). But Christ is a competent Redeemer, having in his Godhead all resources. (4) We can imitate Christ as redeemers of our brethren only by endeavouring instrumentally to recover them from the snares of Satan. (5) What a blessing is liberty! "Whom the Son maketh free is free indeed."—J. A. M.

Vers. 35—55.—*Justice and mercy.* The equity of the Mosaic laws has striking illustrations in the words now under review. We see it—

I. IN THE KINDNESS ENJOINED TOWARDS THE POOR. 1. *Their necessities are to be relieved.* (1) Though they be strangers. The stranger "with" the Hebrew, and so, subject to his law, is recognized as a brother (see vers. 35, 36). (2) Usury is not to be taken from the poor. "That thy brother may live." Rights of property must not override those of existence (Matt. vi. 25). "That thy brother may live *with thee.*" The hands of the poor are as necessary to the rich as is the wealth of the rich to the poor. 2. *The reasons for mercy are edifying.* (1) "I am the Lord your God." I stand in covenant relationship to you. I have a right to require this of thee. (2) I "brought thee out of the land of Egypt." The remembrance of thy miseries in Egypt should influence thee to consider those of the poor stranger by thee. (3) I "gave you the land of Canaan." Gratitude to me should move thee. I can yet more gloriously reward thy mercy in giving thee inheritance in the heavenly Canaan.

II. IN THE KINDNESS ENJOINED TOWARDS THE SLAVE. 1. *The Hebrew must show it.* (1) Not to his brother only, but also towards the stranger. (2) Yet there is a difference. The Hebrew slave goes out in the jubilee; but the power of a Hebrew master over the stranger is not then removed. This law prefigured the dominion which the righteous will have over the wicked in the morning, viz. of the resurrection (see Ps. xlix. 14). (3) The stranger, by becoming a proselyte, might claim the privilege of the Hebrew. So may the wicked, by repentance towards God and faith in the Lord Jesus, become a Christian, and enjoy the privileges of the righteous. 2. *The stranger must show it.* (1) The stranger is presumed to be not so merciful as the Hebrew. Privileges of grace should make men generous. (2) The cruelty of the wicked must be restrained by the laws of the good.

III. IN THE DETERMINATION OF THE RANSOM PRICE. In this determination: 1. *The rate of wages is an element.* The principles of hired service should be remembered by masters in the treatment of slaves. 2. *This rate was then multiplied into the years prospective to the jubilee.* (1) This determination of the rate was in favour of the slave; for if the law had not settled it, then it must be settled by agreement, in which case the master would be in a position to drive a hard bargain to the prejudice of the slave. Law should, for the same reason, control the claims of landlords where they prejudice the rights of their tenantry. (2) In this law there is equity also with respect to the master. Any difference in the value to him of a slave over that of a hired servant is compensated in the risk of life, in which, after the redemption, he has now no pecuniary concern.

IV. IN THE DIFFERENCE OF THE LAW RELATING TO A COUNTRY HOUSE AS COMPARED WITH A HOUSE IN A WALLED CITY. 1. *The country house returned to the owner of the land.* (1) This house is presumed to be simply a residence. The inconvenience of removal of residence is not formidable. (2) To a Christian the removal of residence from this world should not be formidable. 2. *The house in the walled city did not so return.* (1) Such a house may be presumed to be a place of business. In this case, establishment in a locality is often of great importance. Landlords should consider the interests of their tenants as well as their own. (2) But within the first twelve months after the sale of a house in a walled city, the owner had a power of redemption. This was before the business could be said to be *established.* It gave the seller an opportunity to repent of a bargain which may have been forced upon him by the pressure of a temporary necessity. (3) What a mercy that the sinner has space for repentance!—J. A. M.

Vers. 1—7.—*Divine discipline.* This was certainly one of the most striking institutions which God gave to Israel. It was, in a high degree, disciplinary. Rightly taken, it would engrave sacred truth on their minds more deeply and effectually than either word or rite. It was calculated—

I. To TEACH THEM THE TRUTH AS TO THE DIVINE OWNERSHIP. God claimed to be the One Proprietor of the land. He had given it to the nation by his direct guidance, and by his interposing power. To him it belonged, and those who occupied were to feel that they held everything at his good pleasure. What could more effectually and impressively teach this than the right which God reserved, to require them to do what he thought was best with the soil—to cultivate it or to leave it untilled? How difficult we find it to realize as we should that we hold everything as tenants at the Divine will; that we must be ready at his word to lay down that which we most regard as "our own;" that *we* are but "strangers and sojourners with God" (ver. 23)!

II. To INCULCATE MODERATION IN THE USE OF THAT WHICH THEY POSSESSED. Making haste to be rich, men too often exhaust themselves and the objects on which they work. How often is land impoverished by the incessant demand the agriculturist makes upon it! God demanded that the rich land he gave Israel should not be rendered infertile by their drawing immoderately on its virtue. He would have us use prudently, as those who look forward, the things which he puts in our power. The lesson particularly applies, in our time, to the use we make of our physical and mental powers; we should give these full measure of rest, a restorative sabbath, that they may serve us the better and the longer.

III. To ENCOURAGE A SENSE OF BROTHERHOOD AND KINDNESS OF HEART. (Vers. 6, 7.) Of that which was spontaneously produced all might freely partake. The land was for the nation, and not merely for those whose names were enrolled as proprietors. The husbandman was to be trained to see his neighbours, whatever their condition or relation to himself, gathering the fruits of his land. This sabbatic institution said practically to him, and says to us, "God has given the earth and all it bears to the many and not to the few, to all classes of the people: cause *all* to rejoice in the abundance of his gifts."

IV. To TEST THEIR MORAL AND RELIGIOUS DISPOSITION. 1. It would test their obedience. They would be under some temptation to make the ordinary use of their opportunity, and to secure a harvest by tillage. This word of the Lord *tried* them; the obedient regarded, the disobedient disregarded, his will. 2. It would also test their industrial virtues. Perhaps there was more room left for daily activity than some have imagined. "Each day would still present certain calls for labour in the management of household affairs, the superintendence or care of the cattle, the husbanding of the provisions laid up from preceding years, and the execution, perhaps, of improvements and repairs." Nevertheless, there must have been some temptation to abuse the long holiday. A wise man has said that nothing is so certain a criterion of character as the way in which men spend their leisure hours. The idle are tempted to vacancy or folly; the wise find an opportunity for (1) real recreation, for (2) self-improvement, for (3) service of others, for (4) the worship of God (see Deut. xxxi. 9—13).—C.

Vers. 8—55.—*Year of jubilee:* I. *A nation's joy.* On every fiftieth year of national life, as the sun went down on the great Day of Atonement, when the sins of the nation had been forgiven, and peace with God was once more assured, the sound of many trumpets ushered in the blessed year of jubilee. Then (1) the forfeited patrimony was restored to its rightful heir (vers. 10, 13, 28, 41); then (2) the bondsmen were free once more (vers. 10, 41—54); then (3) members of the same family, long separated, were reunited (vers. 10, 41); then (4) the ties which bound man to man throughout all classes and conditions of the nation were to be recognized and honoured (vers. 12—14, 17, 35, 36); then (5) the relation in which Israel stood to Jehovah was to be distinctly and peculiarly realized (vers. 17, 18, 23, 38, 55); and then (6) in holy joy the favoured nation was to be glad in the prosperity which came from God (ver. 19).

No nation now can expect to enjoy such an institution as this; we must learn to dispense with such miraculous arrangements as that which made the year of jubilee a possible thing to Israel (vers. 20—22). It is our national wisdom to bring about, by (1) wise and equal laws, and by (2) virtuous and godly lives, the happy estate in which the people of God found themselves when the trumpets of jubilee announced that a new era of liberty, sufficiency, piety, prosperity, had begun.

A nation may truly rejoice, and may feel that its jubilee is approaching, when it is attaining to: 1. Freedom from degrading poverty; the community not being constituted of a few wealthy men and a multitude of paupers, but being composed of those who earn an honourable livelihood by self-respectful industry, there being general, wide-spread prosperity. 2. The possession of liberty—individual and national, civil and religious; every cruel, degrading, injurious bond being broken, and all men being free to exercise their God-given faculties without hindrance or restraint. 3. Domestic well-being; purity, love, order in the household. 4. Piety; the recognition of indebtedness to God, and a full and deep understanding that we are, above all things, his servants. 5. Charity; a kind and generous regard to those who are "waxen poor and fallen into decay;" a ready hand to help the needy, and give them a new start in the race of life. Let a nation only be advancing in these elements of goodness and prosperity, and it may rejoice greatly in its inheritance, for then "God, even our own God, will bless it;" and though no trumpet sound the note of jubilee, then shall its "light break forth as the morning . . . and its righteousness shall go before it; and the glory of the Lord shall be its rereward" (Isa. lviii. 8).—C.

Vers. 8—55.—*Year of jubilee:* II. *The world's redemption.* The whole Christian era is one long year of jubilee. It is "the acceptable year of the Lord" (Luke iv. 19). That "acceptable year," the fiftieth year in the Jewish calendar, was a year of (1) emancipation (ver. 10); (2) readjustment of social relations (vers. 10, 39—41, 43, 54); (3) national regeneration (vers. 10, 13). The land rested a second year, and recovered any virtue it may have lost, and the old patrimonies reverted to the heirs of the original owners; (4) rest from cultivation (ver. 11); (5) abounding joy.

These, in a deeper, a spiritual sense, are the characteristics of the Christian era: 1. It is a time of *spiritual emancipation.* Sin is the slavery of the soul; "men are "holden with the cords of their sins" (Prov. v. 22). They are in the bondage of selfishness, or of worldliness, or of one or other (or more than one) of the vices, or of the fear of man, or of a foolish and frivolous procrastination. To accept Jesus Christ as Saviour of the soul and Lord of the life is to be released from these spiritual fetters. 2. *Social readjustment.* Christianity, indeed, effects no immediate revolution in the forms of social life. It does not say to the slave, "Escape from thy master" (1 Cor. vii. 20); it does not give directions as to the way in which human relations are to be organized. But it *infuses a new spirit* into the minds of men; it introduces those principles of righteousness and those feelings of considerateness which silently, but most effectually, "make all things new." It drops the seed of "charity" in the soil of human nature, and behold a goodly tree springs therefrom, the leaves of which are for the healing of the social sores of all the nations. 3. *Individual and national regeneration.* The soul that receives Jesus Christ as its Lord, and the nation that surrenders itself to his holy and beneficent rule, make an entirely new departure in their course. So great and radical is the change which is thereby effected, that the Truth himself speaks of it as a "regeneration" (John iii.). In Christ we are born again, or born from above. We enter on a new life, the life of faith, love, humility, zeal, holy service, godliness, anticipation of future blessedness. 4. *Rest of soul.* The rest of body enjoyed in the year of jubilee has its analogue in the rest of soul which we enjoy in the acceptable year of the Lord—rest from (1) a burdensome sense of condemnation; (2) self-reproach, remorse; (3) spiritual struggle and disquietude; (4) anxious, torturing fears. 5. *Joy in God.* In this "acceptable time" we have not only peace, but we also "joy in God through our Lord Jesus Christ" (Rom. v. 11). We are bidden to "rejoice in the Lord alway" (Phil. iv. 4); and though there may be found in the sorrows of others as well as in our own and in the difficulties and depressions that attend us here too much of cloud and shadow to feel that it is always jubilee-time with us in our home-ward journey, yet the felt presence of our Saviour, his unchanging friendship, the blessedness of doing his work, honouring his Name, and even hearing his holy will, the view of the heavenly land,—these will "put a new song into our mouth," a real gladness into our heart, the brightness and music of the "acceptable year" into our Christian life.—C.

Vers. 8—55.—*Year of jubilee*: III. *The blessed kingdom.* It may be thought that, while it is indeed true that the year of jubilee has a true counterpart in that dispensation of spiritual emancipation, social readjustment, regeneration, rest, joy, in which we stand; yet, on the other hand, there is so much of detraction in the sins and sorrows of the present time as to make the one but a very imperfect picture of the other. There is truth in this thought: it is only in a qualified sense that we can speak of the Christian era as a time of jubilee. Its perfect realization is yet to come; its true and glorious fulfilment awaits us, when the blessed kingdom of the Son of God shall have come in all its fulness and the latter-day glory shall appear; then there shall be—

1. *Emancipation* from all bondage. Every fetter shall be struck from the soul, as well as from the body, and we ourselves shall be free in all "the glorious liberty of the children of God."

2. *Restitution.* We shall recover the heritage forfeited by sin; the estate which our Father intended to bestow originally on all his human children will then revert to us, and we shall "return every man unto his possession" (ver. 13). We shall know by blessed experience what God designed for holy manhood.

3. *Regeneration.* So great and blessed will be the change, the new conditions under which we shall live, that we shall feel that a "new heaven and a new earth" have been created. God will have made "all things new" to us.

4. *Reunion.* We shall "return every man unto his family" (ver. 10). Parents and children, brothers and sisters, pastor and people, long-separated friends, will gather again in the same home, and "join inseparable hands" of holy, heavenly reunion.

5. *Reign of love.* If there be gradation, inferiority, rule, and service there, all "rigour" will be unknown (ver. 46). Our "brother will live with us" (vers. 35, 36) in love; all rule will be beneficent; all service sweet and cheerful.

6. *Perfect service of the Supreme.* "Unto me the children of Israel are servants; they are my servants" (ver. 55). There is no fairer promise in the Word of God concerning the future than this—"his servants shall serve him" (Rev. xxii. 3). Then shall we attain to the ideal of our humanity when, escaping from ourselves, we shall, in thought and feeling, in word and deed, consciously and unconsciously, be serving God in stainless, uninterrupted ministry. Then God will be "all in all."

7. *Rest and joy.* The toil and care of earth will be left behind, will be lost in the endless sabbath, and we shall "enter into rest." Only those happy activities will await us in which we shall engage with untiring energy and unfading joy.—C.

Vers. 1—7.—*The sabbatical year.* Rest of the land, as the physical source of blessings, as the consecrated portion of God's people.

I. THE NATURAL BASIS OF RELIGION. Creation. Providence. Moral government. "Man is one world, and hath another to attend him" (George Herbert). The ascent of the higher nature from the lower. The subordination of the material and temporary to the immaterial and eternal. Care of all life involved in the covenant of God with his people. The life of the vegetable world, the life of the animal world, viewed in their relation to higher purposes of God. Art is perfected only in the atmosphere of religion. Science, both theoretic and applied, requires to be pervaded with religious spirit, or becomes atheistic, worldly, and corrupt.

II. THE BLESSING OF GOD ON HIS PEOPLE. "A sabbath for the Lord," that he may rejoice with his children. 1. Material blessings promised: "All these things shall be added unto you;" "he careth for you;" "godliness hath the promise of the world which now is." 2. Rest in the Lord, over all the land, in all states and conditions, eventually in all men. The resting land typical of the Divine promise of a restored earth and regained paradise. The weekly sabbath enlarged. Time expanding to eternity. Special opportunities granted for the larger spiritual culture.—R.

Vers. 8—34.—*The year of jubilee.* Accumulation of sabbaths and sabbatical years;

climax of rest. Proclaimed on Day of Atonement. Outcome of the original covenant. Specially soul-stirring and delightful, "waked up the nation from the very centre of its moral being." "All estates and conditions of the people were permitted to feel the hallowed and refreshing influence of this most noble institution. The exile returned; the captive was emancipated; the debtor set free; each family opened its bosom to receive once more its long-lost members; each inheritance received back its exiled owner. The sound of the trumpet was the welcome and soul-thrilling signal for the captive to escape; for the slave to cast aside the chains of his bondage; for the man-slayer to return to his home; for the ruined and poverty-stricken to rise to the pos-session of that which had been forfeited. No sooner had the trumpet's thrice-welcome sound fallen upon the ear than the mighty tide of blessing rose majestically, and sent its refreshing undulations into the most remote corners of Jehovah's highly favoured land." Regard it (1) socially, (2) morally, (3) spiritually.

I. SOCIALLY. An example of wise and beneficent legislation. As: 1. Security against accumulation of property in the hands of the few, to the oppression of the many. 2. Relief to inevitable reverses of fortune. 3. Maintenance of family life and bonds of natural affection. 4. Destruction of slavery. 5. Promotion of equality of condition and opportunity. 6. Preservation of hopefulness and cheerfulness in society. 7. Avoid-ance of litigation and social strife.

II. MORALLY. An abiding support of the higher moral sentiments. 1. Benevolence and compassion. 2. Patriotism. 3. Personal liberty. 4. Moderation. 5. Brother-hood. 6. Industry.

III. SPIRITUALLY. A type of realized salvation by Divine grace. 1. Proclaimed on Day of Atonement; fruit of reconciliation with God. 2. Universality of the offered deliverance, independent of human merits. 3. Promise of restored human condition—the "meek inheriting the earth." 4. The jubilee of heaven—"glorious liberty of the children of God" (Rom. viii. 21; cf. Isa. lxvi. 12—23; Luke iv. 16—22; Rev. xi. 15; xiv. 6, 7; xxi.).—R.

Vers. 35—55.—*The law of personal servitude.* I. GENERAL PRINCIPLE, *love of our neighbour.* Servitude admitted in that early stage of the world, but limited and modified, and its extinction provided for in that principle of love and compassion which was seized and exalted by the gospel. God's method to subdue and extinguish effects of man's fall by the vital force of higher motive. Distinction between strangers and fellow-Israelite preserved the covenant, therefore the religion which taught love and saved the stranger.

II. LESSON OF UNSELFISHNESS AND UNWORLDLINESS. All servants of the Lord. All property his. The underlying facts of redemption, "bought with a price, there-fore glorify God," etc.—R.

Vers. 19—21.—*The sabbatical year.* All the Divine institutions are marked by practical wisdom, and doubtless subserved many purposes which are not distinctly mentioned in the Law. To celebrate a year of abstinence from agricultural labour must have benefited the ground itself, as well as tended to produce a spirit of brotherhood amongst all classes of the people. For in that year the natural uncultivated produce of the soil was free to be partaken of by the poorest. But we shall concern ourselves chiefly with the reasons given in the Law for the observance of the sabbatical year.

I. THE PROPRIETORSHIP OF THE LAND IS CLAIMED BY GOD. "The land is mine" (ver. 23). As proprietors occasionally shut up a path for a day in order to prevent its being claimed as public property, so God refuses every seventh year to let the Israelites do what they please with the land, in order to remind them of the fact that he is the real owner whose grace bestowed the tenancy on them. *Men are but stewards.* God's dominion is universal over their persons and possessions. Nothing that man is or has can be exempted from the need of consecration. *The conditions of tenancy must be complied with.* If the people were unwilling to observe the terms, let them quit their holding, and start somewhere for themselves. But where shall we procure aught by our own exertions apart from the favour of the Almighty? Our very existence is due to him. Useless, then, is it to quarrel with the lease of our premises.

II. MAN IS TAUGHT THAT HE HAS OTHER DUTIES THAN THAT OF PROVIDING FOR HIS

PHYSICAL WANTS. Work is the fundamental necessity, the burden laid upon us by the declaration, " In the sweat of thy face thou shalt eat bread." Mere idleness is disgraceful. Yet by this command of the text God asserts that *rest is a duty as well as toil.* The one does indeed fit us for the other. Recreation is by no means sinful, and that is a narrow, false view which deems it so. God's rest after the work of creation has for ever hallowed legitimate relaxation. *Rest from servile labour may be properly employed in holy service.* It was during this sabbatical year that the Law was to be read in the hearing of the entire people. Man does not find his noblest end in the industrial pursuit of his daily occupation. He is not always to be surveying the same span of earth. He may lift up his head, and rejoice in upward thoughts and wider prospects. *This world is not man's final home.* So we may without violence interpret the statement, " Ye are strangers and sojourners with me." It refers primarily to the placing of Israel in a land which did not belong to them, but it conveys a deeper lesson, one of pertinent application to modern circumstances. Many fancy that if they diligently attend to their business and pay their way, they do all that can be demanded of them. Such low-thoughted action is here rebuked.

III. TIMID FORETHOUGHT INQUIRES AS TO THE FEASIBILITY OF COMPLIANCE WITH THE ENACTMENT. " What shall we eat the seventh year ? " Man is expected to use his reason, and to anticipate the future. Ushered into the world the most helpless of animals, he is enabled to surround himself with ample might and resources. One harvest suffices to fill his granaries till they are replenished by the stores of another year. Is he to run in the teeth of prudence, and to neglect the usual tillage operations ? The requirement of the Law is superior to such scruples. It may seem unreasonable conduct, unbelief may suggest terrible eventualities, but if the will of God has been clearly expressed, the devout Israelite dares not falter. *There are many Divine precepts which appear to impose trying obligations upon the faith of God's people.* Some have feared to risk the loss involved in renouncing Sunday trading. Some have refused to sacrifice any portion of their time or profits to engage in religious work. The livelihood of themselves and families has been the one prominent object. Too often the necessary provision is rated too high, and luxuries are included among the essentials. There are others to whom the question suggests itself, " How can I compete with my rivals if I adhere to moral laws and discountenance all practices savouring of dishonesty ? To make a profession of Christianity may entail the loss of position and worldly esteem."

IV. GOD PROMISES THAT NOTHING SHALL BE LOST THROUGH OBEDIENCE TO HIS STATUTES. " I will command my blessing upon you." The sixth year shall bring forth fruit for three years. Of course, this supposes a supernatural association of conduct and prosperity which is not to be looked for in the ordinary course of providence. Yet *the promise of blessing upon the faithful is for every generation.* There is a full recompence guaranteed for all tribulation endured in the service of righteousness. Nor are the instances few in number where men have in modern times experienced the truth of the assertion that God withholds no good thing from them that walk uprightly, that the righteous are not forsaken, nor have their poor been obliged to beg for bread. Recently a Greek newspaper owned that since it had discontinued its Sunday issue, its profits had increased rather than diminished. This, at least, is certain, that he makes a good investment who takes shares in God's companies formed for righteous purposes. Such shall realize the double assurance of " safety " and " abundance " (ver. 19). Note our Lord's reply to Peter asking, " What shall we have then ? " Moses esteemed "the reproach of Christ greater riches than the treasures in Egypt." *Let the promises of God's Word scatter all doubt and hesitation !* His counsel may appear strange as it did to King Zedekiah (Jer. xxxviii. 20), but the result shall verify his wisdom. " What shall it profit a man, if he gain the whole world and lose his own soul ? " In keeping his commandments there is great reward. It is good for this life, and even better for the life to come.—S. R. A.

Ver. 42.—*Servants of God.* The Law contains other than ceremonial regulations. Many of its precepts are moral in the highest degree, and breathe the spirit of purest Christianity. Indeed, the Christian Church, with the relationship of its members, its benefits, and obligations, is clearly outlined in the nation of Israel ; rather, however, sad to say, in its constitution than in actual observance of its conditions.   Little alteration is needed to suit the injunctions of this passage to modern circumstances.

I. GOD'S SERVANTS ARE SO BY VIRTUE OF WHAT HE HAS DONE FOR THEM. "They are my servants which I brought forth out of the land of Egypt." Redemption from the iron furnace of affliction was the ground on which Jehovah continually claimed the Israelites as his own peculiar property. "I have broken the bonds of your yoke." So God gave his Son as the price of man's ransom from sin, and Christ is said to have purchased the Church of God with his own blood. Paul delighted to call himself a " bondservant " of Christ in the superscription of his Epistles. To the goodness of God the Israelites owed their preservation and their installation in a goodly land. *Gratitude constrains to faithful service.* We have but to review the past to notice numberless golden bands that attach us to the Redeemer. The matchless character of our God furnishes sufficient reason for executing his commands, but this character is best evidenced by a survey of the deeds of sovereign love that have made us what we are and placed us where we are.

II. GOD'S SERVICE PRECLUDES OUR BEING IN BONDAGE. We cannot serve two masters, and if we belong to God, others cannot claim absolute lordship over us. " They shall not be sold as bondmen," for this would signify that God's ownership is disputed. Only the foreigner can be treated as a slave without insulting Jehovah. *Slavery is thus really condemned,* though permitted with restrictions. The Law must not be too far in advance of the morality of those who are to keep it, lest it overshoot the mark and prove powerless to guide and instruct. What was granted in earliest ages may be altogether unpardonable in days of modern illumination and progress. We shall be judged according to the light we have to direct our steps. *The truth shines clearly forth that to serve God is truest freedom.* It accords with the noblest dictates of our nature ; reason and conscience glorify such obedience. Like the railway train, we fulfil our highest functions, not by deserting but by running upon the lines laid down for our advance. See the warnings addressed to Christians by Jesus Christ (Matt. viii. 34), Paul (Rom. vi. 16), and Peter (2 Pet. ii. 19). When we are actuated by the suggestions of the tempter, we rebel against God's authority and proclaim ourselves unworthy servants. And to seek to ensnare others or to induce them to act contrary to Divine instructions, is even worse than to have been brought into bondage ourselves. God will not brook these infractions of his majesty.

III. THE SERVANTS OF GOD ARE BOUND TO AVOID ALL HARSH TREATMENT OF ONE ANOTHER. Unjust dealing is reprobated. Bad in any case, it is peculiarly offensive here. The people of God are not to forget that they are brethren in the employment of the one master. "If that evil servant shall say in his heart, My Lord delayeth his coming, and shall begin to smite his fellow-servants, the lord of that servant shall come in a day when he looketh not for him," is the New Testament version of the command, " Thou shalt not rule over him with rigour ; but shalt fear thy God " (ver. 43). Christian brotherhood is not intended to upset the constitution of a society in a fruitless endeavour after social equalization. Distinction of rank and class is recognized by the Apostle Paul, and proper regard must be paid to those in authority. The servant is not to despise his master because the latter is a brother in Christ ; on the other hand, the masters are to forbear threatening, " knowing that both their Master and yours is in heaven " (Eph. vi. 9). It cannot be pleasing to Christ to see an unfair advantage taken of a brother Christian's hour of weakness. Such conduct virtually dishonours the Master whom we profess to serve, it offends " one of these little ones." And further, *fellow-servants should relieve each other's wants* (see ver. 35, and margin, " strengthen "). There is a " bond " of union between them, and love and regard for the Master must lead them to see that in giving to the poor they are lending unto the Lord. " One is your Master " (Instructor), "and all ye are brethren." To collect for the Church poor at the observance of the Lord's Supper is a happy recognition of this truth. Many are the vicissitudes of life that befal the most honest and industrious. Changes of fortune merit our sympathy, and the cloud is beautified with rainbow hues when the sun of brotherly love shines athwart its darkness. Another's fate may at any time become our own. How it will mitigate our grief to know that in our season of elevation and prosperity we were not unmindful of the woes of others ! " Blessed is he that considereth the poor : the Lord will deliver him in the time of trouble." " As we have opportunity, let us do good unto all men, especially unto them who are of the household of faith."—S. R. A.

PART V.

CONCLUDING EXHORTATION.

EXPOSITION.

CHAPTER XXVI.

THE first two verses of this chapter contain a prohibition of idolatry, and a command to observe the sabbath and to reverence God's sanctuary; that is, they repeat in summary the substance of the Israelites, religious duty, negative and positive, as comprised in the first table of the Decalogue. They form, therefore, a prologue to the remainder of the chapter, which solemnly announces : 1. The blessings which should result from obedience (vers. 3—13). 2. The curses which should follow disobedience (vers. 14—39). 3. The gracious treatment which would ensue on repentance (vers. 40—45).

Hitherto the Book of Leviticus has consisted of ceremonial and moral injunctions, with two historical passages interposed. In the present chapter it rises in its subject and its diction from legal precepts and a legal style to prediction and the style which became a prophet. We may trace in Joel (ii. 22—27) an intimate acquaintance on the part of the earliest prophet of Judah with this chapter. The first promise there, as here, is that of *rain*, and as here it is to be " *in due season*," so there it is " the former and the latter rain," that is, the regular autumn and spring rains. " *The land shall yield her increase, and the trees of the field shall yield their fruit*," appears in the prophet as, " the pastures of the wilderness do spring, for the tree beareth her fruit, the fig tree and the vine do yield their strength." The following clause, " *your threshing shall reach unto the vintage, and the vintage shall reach unto the sowing time*," as, " the floors shall be full of wheat, and the fats shall overflow with wine and oil ; " the next clause, " *ye shall eat your bread to the full, and dwell in your land safely*," as, " I will send you corn, and wine,

and oil, and ye shall be satisfied therewith," and " ye shall eat in plenty, and be satisfied ; " the clause, " *I will give peace in the land, and ye shall lie down, and none shall make you afraid*," as " I will no more make you a reproach among the heathen," and " my people shall never be ashamed ; " and the clause, " *I will rid evil creatures* [not *beasts*] *out of the land, neither shall the sword go through your land*," as, " I will remove far off from you the northern," and " I will restore to you the years that the locust hath eaten, the cankerworm, and the caterpiller, and the palmerworm, my great army which I sent among you."

The blessings and the curses rise one above the other in regular gradation : on the one side, rain, abundance, peace, deliverance, victory, increase in numbers, communion with God ; on the other side, (1) horror, wasting, and the burning fever, hostile spoiling of the fields, defeat, and causeless flight ; (2) the heaven iron, and the earth brass, failure of crops and fruits in spite of labour spent upon them ; (3) wild beasts for the destruction of cattle, children, and men, desolation of the highways ; (4) the sword, pestilence, and famine ; (5) cannibalism, overthrow of their heathen idols and of God's own house and worship, destruction of their cities, utter desolation of their lands, and their captivity among the heathen. And even yet the full measure of their misery is not accomplished, for while the land enjoys her sabbaths, the captives, if unrepentant, are to fall from one misery to another, till they pine away and are consumed. Each of these grades is described as being symbolically seven times worse, that is, incomparably worse, than that which has gone before. Because these plagues would come, and in fact did come, upon them as the immediate result of physical or moral causes that could be traced, they are none the less the effect of God's wrath upon his apostate people.

Confession of sin, recognition of God's providence in all that had happened to them, humility, and acquiescence in their punishment, would restore them to their forfeited covenant relation (vers. 40—45). Then God would "*not abhor them to destroy them utterly*," but would "*remember the covenant of their fathers*." Thus it was that God brought them back after the Babylonish Captivity; and thus it is that, upon their repentance, he replaces in a state of salvation Churches and individuals that have fallen away from him. In this way punishments become a blessing, and men are able to "*accept of them*," or *rejoice in them*, as the word might be rendered.

Ver. 1.—**Ye shall make you no idols nor graven image, neither rear you up a standing image, neither shall ye set up any image of stone in your land, to bow down unto it.** The word *idols* (*elilim*) means the "nothings" which the heathen substituted for the Lord God. The *graven image* (here meaning a carved wooden image), the *standing image* (meaning a sacred pillar), and the *image of stone* (that is, a sculptured stone idol), are the three forms of images under which adoration was paid, whether to the true God or to a false deity. The expression, *to bow down unto* (or *towards*) *it*, forbids worshipping before an image as well as worshipping an image.

Ver. 2.—**Ye shall keep my sabbaths, and reverence my sanctuary : I am the Lord.** These words are repeated textually from ch. xix. 30.

Ver. 3.—**If ye walk in my statutes.** The free will of man is recognized equally with God's controlling power.

Vers. 4—6.—These verses appear to have been in the mind, not of Joel only, as already pointed out, but of Ezekiel (xxxiv. 20 —31). In Leviticus we find, **Then I will give you rain in due season**; in Ezekiel, "And I will cause the shower to come down in his season; there shall be showers of blessing." In Leviticus, **And the land shall yield her increase, and the trees of the field shall yield their fruit**; in Ezekiel, "And the tree of the field shall yield her fruit, and the earth her increase." In Leviticus, Ye shall **dwell in your land safely**; in Ezekiel, "They shall dwell safely in the wilderness, and sleep in the woods." In Leviticus, **And I will give peace in the land, and ye shall lie down, and none shall make you afraid: and I will rid evil beasts out of the land, neither shall the sword go through your land**; in Ezekiel,

"And I will make with them a covenant of peace, and will cause the evil beasts to cease out of the land. . . . And they shall no more be a prey to the heathen, neither shall the beast of the land devour them; but they shall dwell safely, and none shall make them afraid." The promise, **Your threshing shall reach unto the vintage, and the vintage shall reach unto the sowing time**, is similar to that in the prophet Amos, "Behold, the days come, saith the Lord, that the plowman shall overtake the reaper, and the treader of grapes him that soweth seed" (ix. 13).

Ver. 8.—**And five of you shall chase an hundred.** Cf. Josh. xxiii. 10, "One man of you shall chase a thousand." For examples, see Judg. iii. 31; xv. 15; 1 Sam. xiv. 6—16; 2 Sam. xxiii. 8.

Ver. 10.—**Ye shall eat old store, and bring forth the old because of the new.** The provisions of the past year would be so abundant that they would have to be removed to make place for the new stores.

Ver. 11.—**And I will set my tabernacle among you.** This was fulfilled, spiritually, as shown to St. John in his vision of the new Jerusalem : "I heard a great voice out of heaven saying, Behold, the tabernacle of God is with men, and he will dwell with them, and they shall be his people, and God himself shall be with them, and be their God" (Rev. xxi. 3). **And my soul shall not abhor you.** The result of God's abhorrence being his rejection of those whom he abhors (see ch. xx. 23).

Ver. 12.—**And I will walk among you, and will be your God, and ye shall be my people.** These words are quoted by St. Paul as a ground of the holiness required of God's people (2 Cor. vi. 16).

Ver. 13.—**And I have broken the bands of your yoke.** This expression, used also in the parallel passage of Ezekiel above referred to (xxxiv. 27), and Jer. xxvii. 2 receives an illustration from the ancient method of harnessing oxen, still kept up in the East and South. *The band* means the straight piece of wood laid across the necks of the oxen, by which their heads are fastened together to keep them level with each other, and by which they are attached to the pole of the waggon. The single collars worn by horses in more northern countries have not the same oppressive effect.

Vers. 14—17.—Punishment in its first degree. **Terror, consumption,**—that is, *wasting* —and **the burning ague, that shall consume the eyes, and cause sorrow of heart :**—a proverbial expression for great distress (see 1 Sam. ii. 33)—and **ye shall sow your seed in vain, for your enemies shall eat it** (see Jer. v. 17, and Micah vi. 15, "Thou shalt sow, but thou shalt not reap; thou shalt tread the olives, but thou shalt not anoint thee with oil")... and ye shall be slain before your enemies (as took place often in their after history, see Judg. ii. 14; iii. 8; iv. 2); they that hate you shall reign— that is, *rule*—over you; and ye shall flee when none pursueth you.

Vers. 18—20.—Punishment in its second degree. I will make your heaven as iron, and your earth as brass; the result of no rain in a land scorched by the fiery Eastern sun. Your land shall not yield her increase, neither shall the trees of the land yield their fruits. Cf. 1 Kings viii. 35; Hag. i. 10, 11.

Vers. 21, 22.—Punishment in its third degree. I will also send wild beasts among you, which shall rob you of your children, and destroy your cattle, and make you few in number. So in the case of the Assyrians transported to Palestine, " At the beginning of their dwelling there, they feared not the Lord : therefore the Lord sent lions among them, which slew some of them" (2 Kings xvii. 25)—and your high ways shall be desolate. Cf. Judg. v. 6, " In the days of Shamgar the son of Anath, in the days of Jael, the highways were unoccupied, and the travellers walked through byways."

Vers. 23—26.—Punishment in its fourth degree. I will bring a sword upon you, that shall avenge the quarrel of my covenant: . . . I will send the pestilence among you; and ye shall be delivered into the hand of the enemy—that is, *ye shall go into captivity* . . . and ye shall eat, and not be satisfied. Cf. Ezek. v. 12, " A third part of thee shall die with pestilence, and with famine shall they be consumed in the midst of thee : and a third part shall fall by the sword round about thee; and I will scatter a third part into all the winds, and I will draw out a sword after them." The famine that is to come upon them is described as making ten women bake bread in one oven,—whereas in ordinary times one oven was only sufficient for one woman's baking—and they shall deliver you your bread again by weight; that is, the quantity baked will have to be weighed out in rations, before any one is allowed to take it. See 2 Kings vi. 25; Isa. iii. 1; Jer. xiv. 18; and as illustrative of the last point, Ezek. iv. 16, " Behold, I will break the staff of bread in Jerusalem: and they shall eat bread by weight, and with care; and they shall drink water by measure, and with astonishment."

Vers. 27—33.—Punishment in the fifth degree. Ye shall eat the flesh of your sons, and the flesh of your daughters shall ye eat. We find that this threat was fulfilled in Samaria (2 Kings vi. 28), and in Jerusalem at the time both of the earlier siege by the Chaldæans, and of the later siege by the

Romans (see Lam. ii. 20; iv. 10; Josephus, ' Bell. Jud.,' v. 9, 3; and the terrible case of Mary daughter of Eleazar, Josephus, ' Bell. Jud.' vi. 3, 4). And I will destroy your high places. By *high places* is meant the tops of hills or eminences chosen for worship, whether of Jehovah (see Judg. vi. 26; 1 Kings iii. 2; 2 Kings xii. 3; 1 Chron. xxi. 26), or of false gods. The high places intended here are the spots where the " sun-images " were erected (see 2 Chron. xiv. 5; Isa. xvii. 8; Ezek. vi. 4)—and cut down your images, and cast your carcases upon the carcases of your idols—that is, they should roll in the dust together. And I will make your cities waste —as Samaria and Jerusalem—and bring your sanctuaries unto desolation,—by the *sanctuaries*, which are to be desolated, is meant all the consecrated things: the holy of holies, the holy place, the court, the ark, the altar of incense, the altar of burnt sacrifice — and I will not smell the savour of your sweet odours — so in Jer. vi. 20, " To what purpose cometh there to me incense from Sheba, and the sweet cane from a far country? your burnt offerings are not acceptable, nor your sacrifices sweet" (cf. Isa. i. 11—15). And I will bring the land into desolation (cf. Jer. ix. 11): and your enemies which dwell therein shall be astonished at it (cf. Ezek. v. 15). And I will scatter you among the heathen, and will draw out a sword after you. See Jer. ix. 16, " I will scatter them also among the heathen, whom neither they nor their fathers have known: and I will send a sword after them, till I have consumed them."

Vers. 34, 35.—The land had not participated in the sins of its inhabitants. The latter had thought that, by the neglect of the sabbatical years, they had enriched themselves by the fruits of those years which would otherwise have been wasted. The result was that they lost the land altogether for a period equal to that during which it ought to have kept sabbath, and the land " as long as she lay desolate kept sabbath, to fulfil threescore and ten years" (2 Chron. xxxvi. 21). From the entrance into the holy land until the Babylonish Captivity there elapsed eight hundred and sixty-three years, in which time there ought to have been kept one hundred and twenty-three sabbatical years. As only seventy are made up by the duration of the Captivity, it may be concluded that fifty-three sabbatical years were observed by the Israelites; but this conclusion is very doubtful. It is more likely that seventy, being a multiple of the sacred number seven, was regarded as sufficient to purge all previous neglects, whatever they might have been.

Vers. 36—39. -- The final punishment.

Upon them that are left, that is, the sur-viving captives and exiles, I will send a faintness into their hearts,—so Ezek. xxi. 7, " And every heart shall melt, and all hands shall be feeble, and every spirit shall faint, and all knees shall be weak as water "— ... and the sound of a shaken (or *driven*) leaf shall chase them; ... and they shall fall, ... and ye shall perish among the heathen, and the land of your enemies shall eat you up. And they that are left of you shall pine away in their iniquity in your enemies' lands. This is the concluding threat. It is con-ditional in its nature, and the condition having been fulfilled, we may say with re-verence that it has been accomplished. Those of the ten tribes who did not find their way to Babylon, and so became ab-sorbed in the body which returned to Jeru-salem, have been *eaten up by the land of their enemies*, and have *pined away in their enemies' lands*. Neither they nor their descendants are to be found in any part of the globe, however much investigation may employ itself in searching for them. They have been absorbed by the populations among which they were scattered.

Vers. 40—45.—God's pardon will, even yet, as always, follow upon confession of sin and genuine repentance. They must re-cognize not only that they have sinned, but that their sufferings have been a punish-ment for those sins at God's hand. This will work in them humble acquiescence in God's doings, and then he will remember his covenant with Jacob, and also his cove-nant with Isaac, and also his covenant with Abraham, and for the sake of the covenant of their ancestors, he will not cast them away, neither will he abhor them, to destroy them utterly, and to break his cove-nant with them. Whether Jewish repent-ance has been or ever will be so full as to obtain this blessing, cannot be decided now. Perhaps it may be the case that all the blessings promised by Moses and by future prophets to repentant and restored Israel are to find their accomplishment in the spiritual Israel, the children of Abraham who is " the father of all them that believe " (Rom. iv. 11), seeing that "God is able of stones to raise up children unto Abraham " (Matt. iii. 9).

Ver. 46.—This is the closing paragraph of the Book of Leviticus; to which another chapter has been added, in the form of an appendix, on the subject of vows.

HOMILETICS.

Vers. 3—46.—*Promises and threatenings.* In this chapter the prophet looks forward, and declares how God would deal with his people; which should be according to the way in which they should act. In 2 Chron. xxxvi. 14—21, the chronicler looks back, and shows how God had dealt with them; which had been according to the way in which they had acted.

The promises and the threatenings are to the nation, not to individuals; and the prophetical assurance is that national obedience to God shall bring about national happiness and prosperity, and that disobedience shall cause the ruin of the nation. In spite of the rough, wild times of the Judges, and of the apostacy of Saul, the heart of the nation was on the whole loyal to Jehovah till the end of the days of Solomon. And till that time there was an upward growth in the flourishing estate of the people—their wealth, their power, their prosperity, their happiness. In the latter days of Solomon, outwardly glorious as they were, decay and corruption began. King and people were alike affected by the splendid despotism which one wielded and under which the other flourished in material prosperity. In that prosperity they forgot the source of it. The king himself pushed his tolerance for foreign habits into idolatry, " His wives turned away his heart after other gods: and his heart was not perfect with the Lord his God, as was the heart of David his father. . . . And the Lord was angry with Solomon, because his heart was turned from the Lord God of Israel " (1 Kings xi. 4—9). Like prince, like people; a general relaxation of moral fibre and religious zeal ensued through-out the kingdom. Its culminating point had been reached, and now there followed the rapid descent and fall which resulted from disobedience. The first step to ruin was the great schism, from the effects of which neither the northern nor the southern king-dom ever recovered. Then followed the various apostacies and punishments. In the southern kingdom, "Rehoboam forsook the Law of the Lord, and all Israel with him. And it came to pass, that in the fifth year of King Rehoboam, Shishak King of Egypt came up against Jerusalem, because they had transgressed against the Lord " (2 Chron. xii. 1, 2). Jehoram " walked in the way of the kings of Israel, like as did the house of

Ahab (for he had the daughter of Ahab to wife): and he wrought that which was evil in the eyes of the Lord. . . . In his days the Edomites revolted. . . . Moreover the Lord stirred up against Jehoram the spirit of the Philistines, and of the Arabians, that were near the Ethiopians: and they came up into Judah, and brake into it" (2 Chron. xxi. 6—17). In the latter days of Joash, "they left the house of the Lord God of their fathers, and served groves and idols: and wrath came upon Judah and Jerusalem for this their trespass. . . . And it came to pass at the end of the year, that the host of Syria came up . . . with a small company of men, and the Lord delivered a very great host into their hand, because they had forsaken the Lord God of their fathers" (2 Chron. xxiv. 18—24). In the reign of Amaziah, Jerusalem was taken by Joash King of Israel, because "Amaziah sought after the gods of Edom" (2 Chron. xxv. 14—24). Ahaz "made molten images for Baalim. . . . Wherefore the Lord his God delivered him into the hand of the King of Syria . . . and into the hand of the King of Israel" (2 Chron. xxviii. 2—5). At the beginning of the reign of Manasseh, "the Lord spake to Manasseh, and to his people: but they would not hearken. Wherefore the Lord brought upon them the captains of the host of the King of Assyria" (2 Chron. xxxiii. 10, 11). And at last, these partial chastisements having failed to bring about reformation, came the Babylonish Captivity. "The Lord God of their fathers sent to them by his messengers, rising up betimes, and sending; because he had compassion on his people, and on his dwelling place: but they mocked the messengers of God, and despised his words, and misused his prophets, until the wrath of the Lord arose against his people, till there was no remedy. Therefore he brought upon them the King of the Chaldees, who slew their young men with the sword in the house of their sanctuary, and had no compassion upon young man or maiden, old man, or him that stooped for age: he gave them all into his hand. . . . And them that had escaped from the sword carried he away to Babylon" (2 Chron. xxxvi. 15—20).

The transgressions of the northern kingdom were even greater than those of the southern kingdom, and their final punishment, therefore, fell upon them earlier. "For so it was, that the children of Israel had sinned against the Lord their God, . . . and walked in the statutes of the heathen, . . . for they served idols, whereof the Lord had said unto them, Ye shall not do this thing. . . . And they rejected his statutes, and his covenant that he made with their fathers. . . . Therefore the Lord was very angry, . . . and removed them out of his sight" (2 Kings xvii. 7—18). This occurred in the reign of Hoshea, and in the case of the ten tribes we find no symptoms of repentance under suffering. The two tribes produced a Daniel; and his prayer for the forgiveness of his people (Dan. ix. 3—19) illustrates the feelings of the better of his fellow-captives; and therefore, according to the promise of ch. xxvi. 40—42, God remembered his covenant with Jacob, and Isaac, and Abraham, and raised up Zerubbabel, Ezra, and Nehemiah to effect the restoration; while the ten tribes pined away in the land of their captivity. Thus Moses' prediction was fulfilled.

God deals with other nations as with Israel; but we have not the inspired record of his dealings. While Greece cultivated intellectual wisdom, she flourished; when she turned to sophistry, she perished. While Rome spread order and law throughout the globe, she grew in strength; when she submitted to the sway of arbitrary despots, she fell. What is England's mission in the world? To disseminate at once true religion and true liberty. As long as she does this, she will receive God's blessing. As soon as she fails to fulfil the purpose of her existence as a nation, she will be withdrawn from the scene, and another instrument raised up in her stead.

HOMILIES BY VARIOUS AUTHORS.

Temporal rewards and punishments. Ch. xxvi.; cf. Eccles. viii. 11; Isa. xlviii. 18; Matt. v. 44, 45; and 1 Tim. iv. 8. There is in this chapter a distinct assertion of moral government exercised over Israel. If they obeyed God's Law, he would grant them great temporal blessing; if they disobeyed, he would send them sore chastisement; but if after disobedience they became penitent, he would remember their fathers and his covenant with them, and receive their penitent seed into favour again. The whole question, consequently, of the "method of the Divine government" is hereby raised. And here let us remark—

I. GOD'S JUDGMENTS, WHETHER REWARDS OR PUNISHMENTS, WERE EXECUTED WITH BECOMING LEISURE AND DELIBERATION. It is along the lines of natural law, as distinguished from miracle, that he proposes to execute his decisions. If the people prove obedient, then they are to have (1) bountiful harvests; (2) national triumph and consequent peace; (3) riddance of the beasts of the field, so far as they would injure their crops; (4) great increase of the population; and (5) the enjoyment of religious ordinances. On the other hand, if the people prove disobedient, they are to have (1) sickness; (2) scarcity; (3) defeat; (4) devastation by wild beasts; (5) famine in its most fearful forms; and (6) a sabbatic desolation in the Lord's land.

Now, it is to the leisurely and deliberate element in the rewards and the punishments that we direct attention. If God chose to execute his sentences speedily, if obedience got its reward immediately, if disobedience got its punishment without one moment's delay,—then men would have no room for question, and no room for moral education and decision. Such a childish regulation would doubtless prevent a large amount of evil in the world, but it would keep men children always. It is a pitiable stage of education when the child insists on seeing its reward before it obeys, and requires the immediate "slap" to prevent disobedience. If men are to be trained morally, they must be asked to *take upon credit* God's promises and threatenings, and decide in the interval before he is pleased to act.

This leaves room for a large amount of evil. "Because sentence against an evil work is not executed speedily, therefore the heart of the sons of men is fully set in them to do evil" (Eccles. viii. 11). Men may say, because God does not show quickly his hand, that he may possibly not show it at all. Hence they sin and say, "The Lord shall not see, neither shall the God of Jacob regard it" (Ps. xciv. 7). The Lord's delay is interpreted as Divine indifference. This is one of the evils due to man's sinful heart exercising its freedom under a truly paternal government. Instead of God's goodness in the delay leading men to repentance, it is allowed to foster a hope that he will resign the reins of government altogether and sit indifferently by, while men do as they please. An instance of this tendency to misinterpretation is afforded by Professor Tyndall, in his 'Fragments of Science,' where he has the audacity to deduce from Matt. v. 45, "He maketh his sun to rise on the evil and on the good, and sendeth rain on the just and on the unjust," as the doctrine of the Master himself, that "the distribution of natural phenomena is not affected by moral or religious causes;"[1] whereas the context shows that the whole arrangement is prompted by love towards his enemies, that they may be induced to become his friends. Men get easily warped in their interpretations, and miss the point, or want to miss it.

On the other hand, God's delay in making good his promises and threatenings affords an opportunity for humiliation and faith. When men believe he will be as good and as severe as he says, then they humble themselves under his mighty hand, and supplicate his forgiveness. When also, as his forgiven ones, they try to the best of their ability to obey him, then the delay of the promised blessing enables them to cultivate the "patience of hope," and thus to complete their character. If, therefore, there are drawbacks through man's sin on the one side, there are vast advantages to human character on the other attending this arrangement.

II. GOD'S JUDGMENTS, EVEN WHEN EXECUTED, HAVE NOT THE AIR OF FINALITY ABOUT THEM. Notwithstanding the special pleading of Warburton and his followers about the temporal character of the Divine judgments among the Jews, and their consequent ignorance about a future life,[2] it is evident on the face of the judgments that they are not final. Little children perishing and eaten in the sieges (ver. 29) could not be regarded surely as a final judgment. Children suffering for their parents' sins could not be regarded as a final judgment. In truth, God's judgments among the Jews, like his judgments still, were imperfect, and designedly so. "For observe," says the Rev. Charles Wolfe, "if we found every man in this life received just what he deserved, and every evil work always brought swift punishment along with it, what should we naturally conclude? There is no future punishment in store. I see nothing

---

[1] Page 36 of 3rd edit.   [2] 'Divine Legation of Moses,' bk. v.

wanting; every man has already received the due reward of his works; everything is already complete, and, therefore, there is nothing to be done in the next world. Or if, on the other hand, there were no punishment visited upon sin at all in this world, we might be inclined to say, Tush, God hath forgotten; he never interferes amongst us; we have no proof of his hatred of sin, or of his determination to punish it; he is gone away far from us, and has left us to follow our own wills and imaginations. So that if sentences were either *perfectly* executed on earth, or *not executed at all*, we might have some reason for saying that there was a *chance* of none in a future world. But now it is *imperfectly* executed; just *so much done* as to say, 'You are watched; my eye is upon you; I neither slumber nor sleep; and my vengeance slumbereth not.' And yet, at the same time, there is *so little done*, that a man has to look into eternity for the accomplishment." [1]

III. GOD'S PROMISE TO THE PENITENT IMPLIES THAT THEY ARE NOT PARDONED SIMPLY ON THE GROUND OF THEIR PENITENCE. The Lord contemplates the Jewish defection as practically certain. At the same time, he holds out the hope of the penitent people being restored to favour (vers. 40—46). But it is surely significant that penitence is expressly shown not to be the *ground* of acceptance. Doubtless it is the *condition;* but were it the sole ground of acceptance, as it is confidently asserted to be,[2] it is not easy to see why in such a case as that now before us God would speak about remembering their fathers, and throwing the radiance, so to speak, of their obedience round about their children (vers. 42, 45). It is evident the penitents, even after they have been punished, cannot stand alone. And in truth, when the whole matter of acceptance is analyzed, it is seen to rest upon a *covenant of sacrifice.* The sacrifices of the covenant, as we have already seen, point unmistakably to a suffering Substitute, the glory of whose merits must encircle all accepted ones. In a word, we are led straight to Jesus, the Lamb of God, by whose blood we are redeemed and received into covenant relations. "Accepted in the Beloved," we are careful to "abstain from the very appearance of evil," and in the exercise of new obedience we find a triumphant power bestowed. When we hearken to his commandments our peace flows like a river, and our righteousness becomes resistless like the waves of the sea (Isa. xlviii. 18). We find that "godliness is profitable unto all things, having promise of the life that now is, and of that which is to come" (1 Tim. iv. 8).—R. M. E.

Vers. 1—13.—*The blessedness of the righteous.* In the words before us we have—

I. THE QUALITIES OF THE RIGHTEOUS DESCRIBED. These are: 1. *That they worship the true God.* (1) They make no idols. Graven images. Pillars to memorialize advantages supposed to be derived from false gods. Witness the votive offerings of the papists. They might not superstitiously worship such stones of memorial as Jacob set up to memorialize the blessings of Jehovah (see Gen. xxviii. 18; and comp. 2 Kings xviii. 4). The images of stone or "stones of picture" (see margin) would probably be statues. Note: men *make* their idols. (2) They respect Jehovah. He is the Maker of all things. He is himself uncreate. He is the Covenant Friend of the righteous. 2. *That they worship him truly.* (1) By keeping his sabbaths. *Memorials* of his works of creation and redemption. *Pledges* of the rest of heaven. (2) These are: weekly—monthly—yearly—septennial—in the jubilee. (3) By reverencing his sanctuary. The place of his presence, of his altar, of the congregation of his people. 3. *They serve him obediently.* (1) Walking in his statutes. This implies the study of his Word. (2) To keep his commandments also implies prayer for Divine grace.

II. THEIR BLESSEDNESS ASSURED. They have the promise of: 1. *Plenty.* (1) The elements were to be propitious to them. Seasonable rains. These are very important. They are here mentioned as representing all benign elemental influences—light, heat, electricity,—all which are essential. (2) The result then is abundance (ver. 5). Before they could have reaped and threshed out their *corn,* the *vintage* should be ready, and before they could have pressed out their wine, it would be time again to sow. (3) This was to prefigure the abundance of grace which should mark the times of the gospel (see Amos ix. 18). 2. *Security.* (1) From the hostility of the *elements.* No plague should invade them. (2) From the hostility of *men.* No warrior should invade them.

---

[1] Wolfe's 'Remains,' 6th edit., pp. 325, 326.   [2] Cf. Hutton's 'Essays,' vol. i. p. 372.

No robber should trouble them. (3) From the hostility of *animals*. Where population is reduced by wars and famines, beasts of prey prowl. (4) How the faithfulness of God has been verified in the history of his people! 3. *Victory*. (1) God puts the dread of them into their enemies. They fly before them. Witness the flight of the Syrians in the days of Elisha (2 Kings vii.). (2) He puts courage into their hearts. Witness the exploits of Gideon, of Samson, of Jonathan and his armour-bearer (1 Sam. xiv. 6, 12). 4. *Multiplication*. (1) This is a blessing of the covenant. It is a real strength to a nation. It is a real strength to a Church. (2) But outside the covenant mere numbers may prove a formidable evil. 5. *Divine favour*. (1) "I will have respect unto you." Contrast with this Heb. x. 38. (2) The token of the favour of God is his presence. (*a*) His tabernacle was amongst them in the wilderness. What miracles of mercy were shown to them then! (*b*) How glorious were the days of Solomon when the Shechinah entered the temple! (*c*) His tabernacle was set among his people in the presence of Jesus (John i. 14). But they did not know the blessedness of their day. (*d*) How blessed is the mystical incarnation of Christ in the believer! (John vi. 56; 2 Cor. vi. 16—18; vii. 1). (*e*) The glory of the tabernacle will culminate in the new heavens and earth (see Rev. xxi. 3).

All this blessedness was pledged in the emancipation from the bondage of Egypt (ver. 13). More fully in the redemption of the gospel typified thereby.—J. A. M.

Vers. 14—39.—*Prophetic maledictions.* The promises of God are prophecies of good; so are his threatening prophecies of evil. Prophecy, therefore, gives no countenance to fatalism, since it is made to depend upon conditions. God may, therefore, repent him of evils threatened, viz. when sinners repent of the sin that provoked him. So long as the Hebrews were faithful to their God, they found him faithful in mercy; when they rebelled, they found him no less faithful in judgment. What a commentary upon the verses before us is the history of the Israelites! Let us review—

I. THE JUDGMENTS DENOUNCED AGAINST THEM IN THEIR LAND. For their rebellion: 1. *They were to be visited with plagues.* (1) The plague of *terror*. This is the natural plague of a guilty conscience. The apprehension of formidable judgments. (2) Of *consumption*. This term expresses all chronic diseases. (3) Of *burning ague*. This describes those diseases which are more acute. (4) All these plagues are to "consume the eyes, and cause sorrow of heart." 2. *They were to suffer from invasion.* (1) The sword of the enemy was to consume them. How fearfully they suffered under the judges, under the kings, and afterwards! (2) The exactions of the tyrant were to distress them. When the invaders mastered them, how grievously were they oppressed! 3. *They were to encounter the anger of their God.* (1) The plague and the sword of the enemy could not otherwise have visited them. (2) But in the source itself there is the most formidable terror. "I will set my face against you." 4. *Their obstinacy was to bring upon them aggravated evils.* (1) The land was to become unfruitful. For the heaven was to be like iron, which might reflect the glare of heat, but could distil no rain or dew. (2) Wild beasts were to come among them. When the people become diminished by war and pestilence and famine, wild animals multiply and become formidable (see Numb. xxi. 6; 2 Kings xvii. 25; ii. 24; Ezek. v. 17). (3) It is a fearful thing to fall into the hands of the living God. Rather let us seek his mercy.

II. THOSE DENOUNCED AGAINST THEM IN THE LANDS OF THEIR CAPTIVITY. 1. *They were to be scattered amongst the heathen* (ver. 33). (1) Thus ten of the tribes were carried away by the Assyrians. (2) The two remaining tribes were afterwards removed by the Babylonians. (3) Some of these returned under Ezra and Nehemiah, and were ultimately carried away by the Romans. 2. *The sword was to follow them there.* (1) The sword of war. (2) The sword of persecution. So they suffered from pagans, from papists, from Mohammedans. 3. *They were to suffer astonishment* (vers. 36—39). (1) Faintness of heart, suspicion of danger where it existed not, susceptibility to panic. (2) Pining in terror. (3) Perishing through the rapacity of their enemies. 4. *Their sufferings were to be protracted.* (1) The land was to enjoy her sabbaths. Houbigant observes how literally this was fulfilled in the seventy years of the Babylonish Captivity. "From Saul to the Babylonish Captivity are numbered about four hundred and ninety years, during which period there were seventy sabbaths of years; for seven, multiplied by seventy, make four hundred and ninety. Now, the Babylonish Captivity lasted seventy years, and during that time the land of Israel rested. Therefore the land rested just as many years in the Babylonish Captivity as it should have rested sabbaths if the Jews had observed the law relative to the sabbaths of the land." (2) The longer term of "seven times" thrice repeated (vers. 21, 24, 28) is also notable. These are the "times of the Gentiles," during which Jerusalem is to be trodden down of them (Luke xxi. 24). 5. *Meanwhile their land was to lie desolate* (vers. 31—35). (1) Such has been its history, under the Romans, under the Saracens, under the Crusaders, under the Turks. (2) Who but God could have foreseen all this? How unreasonable is unbelief!—J. A. M.

Vers. 40—46.—*Hope for Israel.* The curses of this chapter have proved prophetic. So, may we infer, will the blessings prove. We may therefore hope to see the con-version of the Hebrews to Christ, their restoration to their ancient inheritance, and the sun of prosperity shining brightly upon them.

I. THEY WILL CONFESS THEIR SIN. 1. *Their personal iniquity.* (1) They will have many things to confess, as all sinners have. They will "humble their uncircum-cised heart" (see Jer. ix. 26; Rom. ii. 29). (2) In particular they will confess their capital sin in rejecting Christ. This crime filled up the measure of their fathers. 2. *The iniquity of their fathers.* (1) This was the same as their own. They will acknowledge themselves, not in pride, but in penitence, to be the children of their fathers. (2) Instead of attempting to extenuate their sin because of the example of their fathers, they will repent for the sin of their fathers as well as for their own. This is in accord-ance with the principle of the visitation of the iniquities of the fathers upon the children. 3. *The justice of God in their punishment.* (1) They acknowledge that they walked contrary to God (see Ezra ix.; Neh. i. 4; ix. 1, 2, 29; Dan. ix. 3, 4). (2) That he has therefore walked contrary to them. Afflictions do not spring out of the dust.

II. THEN GOD WILL REMEMBER HIS COVENANT. Therefore: 1. *He will not destroy them utterly.* (1) His providence will be over them. What else could have preserved them now for nineteen centuries amidst untoward circumstances? They are, notwith-standing their sufferings, as numerous to-day as they were in the zenith of their prosperity in the days of Solomon. (2) The remnant of them shall be saved. (3) How tender is the compassion of God! (Hos. xi. 8, 9). 2. *He will reinstate them in their land.* (1) He will remember his land. For in the covenant they are promised the land "for ever." (2) Remembering the land also implies that it will recover its ancient fruitfulness (see promises, vers. 4, 5, 10). (3) In that condition it will be the appropriate type and pledge of the heavenly country (see Isa. lxii. 4). 3. *He will make them a blessing in the earth.* (1) They will grow into a multitude. (2) They will rejoice in spiritual blessings. (3) The miracles of the Exodus from Egypt will be repeated. (4) The heathen will be startled into thoughtfulness (ver. 45). (5) The heathen will once more learn the way of salvation from the lips of Hebrews. 4. *In all this they are beloved for the fathers' sakes.* (1) This is distinctly stated (ver. 42; comp. Rom. xi. 28). (2) The patriarchs of the covenant are referred to in the order of ascent, viz. Jacob, Isaac, Abraham. Note: when the Jews in humility confess them-selves the children of their more recent sinful fathers, God will acknowledge them as the children of their earlier faithful ancestors. (3) It is an encouragement to faith that the memory of Divine mercy is far-reaching—everlasting.—J. A. M.

Ver. 1.—*Idolatry: our danger and our security.* Knowing, as we do, how wide-spread was the idolatry of the age and how terribly tempted were the children of Israel to fall under its fascination, we do not wonder either at the *repetition* or the *fulness* of this commandment. God made it quite clear to his people, and impressed the truth on their minds with strong emphasis, that they must not permit any visible image to come between themselves and him. He would sanction "no idol, nor graven image, nor pillar, nor figured stone" (marginal reading). Respecting idolatry we may do well to consider—

I. ITS NATURAL HISTORY. Men do not descend at once into the blind and blank idolatry with which we are familiar. 1. The first step downwards is when men take some object or construct some image which shall remind them of Deity, or stand for God, or be a sign and token of his presence, so that when they *see that* they shall *think of him.* This was the case with the "golden calf" which Aaron made. The people presented their offerings to it in connection with a "feast to the Lord" (Exod. xxxii. 5). It is too great a mental labour to realize God's presence by pure thought and meditation; men crave a visible object which shall remind them of the Supreme. 2. The next step—deep into the thick darkness—is to identify the Deity with the object which is the chosen sign of his presence; and the constant, inevitable accompaniment of this act is to multiply the number of divinities; for, as the visible images are many, the gods become many also to the popular imagination. However antecedently unlikely it may seem to us that men would commit such great folly as this, universal history compels us to believe that they have done so. Beginning with the demand for "a sign," men have "bowed down unto" and worshipped the image, the pillar, the figured stone. 3. Then follows mental, moral, spiritual degradation. The worshippers of idols have attributed to their gods their own infirmities and sins, and then their worship has reacted on their own character, and they have sunk to the lowest depths of abjectness of mind, vileness of spirit, grossness of life.

II. ITS ESSENTIAL ELEMENTS. We must not identify idolatry with those more shameless forms of it which historians and travellers have made known to us. These are its last and worst developments. But the idolatrous element is found where there is (1) a false association of God with an object with which he has nothing to do, as (in the case referred to) where the Israelites associated Jehovah in their thoughts with an image with which he had no connection whatever; or (2) a false trust in an object with which God is more or less connected. That was an idolatrous act on the part of the Israelites when they made sure of victory because the ark of God was in the camp (1 Sam. iv. 3—11). God had connected himself with the ark in an especial manner; but the Jews were trusting in *it* rather than in *him,* and they leant on a broken reed.

III. ITS APPEAL TO OURSELVES. Our danger is not from the grosser forms of idolatry, nor is it in the former of the two essential elements of it; it is in the latter of these. We are liable to trust idolatrously in that with which God is connected, but which has no virtue at all *in itself.* We are invited, and sometimes find ourselves tempted: 1. To imagine that a priest can bless us, independently of the truth which he teaches or the spiritual help which he renders us. 2. To suppose that we are nearer to God in sacred places, irrespective of the consideration whether we realize his presence and draw nigh to his Spirit. 3. To seek sanctity, or even salvation, in sacraments apart from the reverent thought and consecrated feeling which they should suggest or excite. This is an idolatrous delusion.

IV. THE PATH OF SAFETY. This is: 1. The avoidance of temptation. We must shun those Churches and services which would seduce us from spiritual purity. 2. The acceptance of the One Divine Mediator we have in Christ our Saviour. There is "one man we can adore without idolatry—the man Christ Jesus." 3. The use of our faculties for the worship of the Invisible. We *can* worship him who is a Spirit "in spirit and in truth." We can realize the presence of the infinite God; we can love him whom we have not seen (1 Pet. i. 8); we can walk the whole path of life conscious of a Divine Companion whose hand we cannot grasp, but who "leads us all our journey through." By a living faith, "our fellowship is with the Father, and with his Son Jesus Christ" (1 John i. 3).—C.

Vers. 3—13.—*Incentives to obedience.* Religion has the first claim upon us as the supreme obligation of the soul. We are bound to worship and honour God because we owe far more to him than to all other beings in the universe. The first and all-sufficient reason why we should "worship and bow down" before him, is in the fact that "he is our God"—that One from whom we come, in whom we live, from whom cometh down every good gift. But God condescends to urge us to obedience by presenting incentives to our minds. He wishes us to consider that he has made it infinitely remunerative for us to do so; that, by so doing, we become recipients of the largest blessings he can confer and we can receive. There is so much of contrast as well as comparison between the blessings of the old and the new dispensations, that we must divide our subject into two parts.

I. THE INCENTIVES WHICH GOD HELD OUT TO HIS ANCIENT PEOPLE. These were *importantly spiritual, but prominently temporal.* If they did but "walk in his statutes, and keep his commandments, and do them" (ver. 3), they might reckon on (1) fertility in the field (vers. 4, 5, 10); (2) sense of security from without and disturbance from within (safety and peace, vers. 5, 6); (3) victory in war (vers. 7, 8); (4) national growth (ver. 9); (5) God's presence with them (vers. 11, 12); (6) his pleasure in them (ver. 11); and (7) his guarantee of their liberty and self-respect (ver. 13).

II. THE PROMISES WHICH HE HAS MADE TO US. These are *partly temporal, but principally spiritual.* They include: 1. Sufficiency of worldly substance. God does *not* now say, "Serve me, and you shall be strong, wealthy, long-lived," but he does say, "Seek ye first the kingdom of God, . . . and all these things" (food, clothing, etc.) "shall be added unto you" (Matt. vi. 33). "Godliness has promise of the life that now is" (1 Tim. iv. 8). Those who are his children in Christ Jesus may reckon upon all needful support from his bountiful hand. 2. Consciousness of spiritual integrity. As God made his people to be delivered from the yoke and to "go upright" (ver. 13), so he makes those who have returned to him, and who have escaped from the yoke of sin, to "walk in uprightness of heart." Instead of shrinking in fear, bowing down with a depressing sense of wrong-doing, we have a happy consciousness of integrity of soul. We say with the psalmist, "As for me," etc. (Ps. xli. 12). 3. Sense of reconciliation with God. God promises peace and a sense of safety (vers. 5, 6) to those who seek his favour in Christ Jesus. Being justified by faith in him, we have peace with God; and we know that, whatever may be our circumstances, we are secure behind the shield of his almighty love. 4. Victory in the battle of life. If it be not wholly true that "our life is but a battle and a march," yet it is true that there is so much of spiritual struggle in it, from its beginning to its close, that we all understand only too well what is meant by "the battle of life." There are many foes with which to wrestle (Eph. vi. 12), and we need the invigorating power which only the Spirit of the Strong One can impart. If we are his, he will help us in the strife. "Our enemies will fall before us" (ver. 7; see 2 Cor. ii. 14 and Rom. viii. 37). 5. His presence with us and his pleasure in us. "God will set his tabernacle among us;" he "will walk among us" (vers. 11, 12). He will be "with us always," and his sustaining presence will uphold us in the darkest hour, in the most trying scene. "His soul will not abhor us" (ver. 11); he will take Divine pleasure in us; we shall be his children, his guests, his friends, his heirs. 6. An everlasting heritage in him. He will be our God (ver. 12). The sacred page does not speak of any duration; but that which is adumbrated in the Old Testament is revealed in the New. Jesus Christ has brought life and immortality *out into the light,* and we know that "him that overcometh will the Son of man make a pillar in the temple of his God, and he shall go no more out," etc. (Rev. iii. 12), and that "to him that overcometh will he grant to sit with him on his throne," etc. (Rev. iii. 21). The present and the future, the best of the one and the whole of the other, are the heritage of those who "know the will of God and do it." Surely it is the choice of the wise to "make haste and delay not to keep his commandments."—C.

Vers. 23, 24.—*Our God and ourselves.* The text suggests the question, How far does God's treatment of us depend on our attitude towards him? And the answer must be somewhat complex.

I. IN LARGE MEASURE, GOD'S TREATMENT OF US IS QUITE IRRESPECTIVE OF OUR CONDUCT TOWARD HIM. He has done much for us from the promptings of his own generous and beneficent nature. As the sun gives light because it *is* light, regardless of the objects on which it shines, so our God, who is a Sun (Ps. lxxxiv. 11), is sending forth beams of truth, love, beauty, happiness, because in him is all fulness, and from that abundance there must flow blessing and bounty on every hand (see Ps. ciii. 10, 11; Matt. v. 45).

II. IN LARGE MEASURE, GOD'S TREATMENT OF US DEPENDS ON OUR ATTITUDE TOWARD HIM. 1. Right feeling on our part is reciprocated with kind feeling on his. If we love him, he will love us and come to us (John xiv. 23). 2. Rebellious conduct on our part brings down adverse action on his part. If we "will walk contrary to him, he will walk contrary to us, and punish us for our sins." The greater part of this chapter (vers. 14 —39) is a terrible admonition that, if we provoke God by our wilful disobedience, we must expect to find his hand against us in all the paths of life, our growing iniquity meeting with his multiplying wrath and darkening retribution. 3. Repentant action on our part is met by returning favour on his (Jer. iii. 22; Joel ii. 12—14; Isa. xliv. 22; lv. 7). Let the prodigal son arise to return, and, "while yet a great way off," the heavenly Father will run to meet and to welcome him (Luke xv.).

III. GOD'S GOODNESS TO US WILL SEEM TO US TO VARY ACCORDING TO THE RECTITUDE OF OUR SOULS TOWARD HIM. As men seem to us to be just or unjust, kind or unkind, according to the position we occupy toward them, so also does the Father of spirits. "All the paths of the Lord are" (and are seen to be) "mercy and truth unto such as keep his covenant and his testimonies" (Ps. xxv. 10). But the ways of the Lord will seem "contrary" to the rebellious. With the merciful man God shows himself merciful; with the froward he shows himself froward (Ps. xviii. 26). The guilty will exclaim against the inequality of God's dealings (Ezek. xxxiii. 17). *He will seem* unjust because *they are* unholy, because their spirit is false and wrong (Matt. xx. 15). Those who fear God and love his Son their Saviour, join in the psalm of the Church on earth, "The Lord is righteous in all his ways, . . . his tender mercies are over all his works" (Ps. cxlv.); they anticipate the strain of the Church in heaven, "Just and true are thy ways, thou King of saints" (Rev. xv. 3).—C.

Vers. 14—39.—*Divine retribution.* The Divine Legislator of Israel knew well that he must contemplate disobedience as well as obedience to his laws. When he had intimated the fulness of the reward he would bestow on the faithful, he was compelled to pass on to "But if ye will not hearken unto me, and will not do," etc. It is sad to think that it did not *need* Divine prescience to foretell this issue. Human disobedience is too constantly occurring a factor in human history to require that: it may always be safely assumed. We have now to deal with God's treatment of it; and we see—

I. THAT GOD PUNISHES IT WITH VARIOUS EVILS. (Vers. 14—18.) God always says to us, "If ye will not do my commandments, I will set my face against you." To the Israelites he threatened specifically: (1) bodily sickness; (2) unprofitable labour; (3) defeat in battle; (4) subjection to a hated rule; (5) ignominious terror and flight. If we sin we must expect to suffer in mind, body, or estate. Guilt and misery are necessarily conjoined. Sin deserves to suffer: there needs no further explanation of suffering than that God's holy and righteous Law has been transgressed. Yet, while the Divine Lawgiver visits sin with retribution because it is *right* that it should receive this mark of his holy disapproval, it is also true—

II. THAT GOD'S PUNISHMENT IS MEANT TO BE REMEDIAL. "If ye will not yet for all this hearken unto me" (ver. 18). Then it is clear that these providential visitations would be meant to lead to a better spirit, to a disposition to hearken and to obey. God, when he punishes, not only does an act of righteous retribution, which his position as Supreme Judge demands of him, but he also does that which he desires shall lead to penitence and restoration. He smites us in one member that he may heal us altogether. He takes away a little that he may give very largely. He sends passing pain that he may give enduring joy. God's retributions are his "corrections," his paternal chastisements, his strong but kind admonitions. By them he lays his hand upon us and says to us, in tones we cannot fail to understand, "Repent and return, and be restored." But we learn from these verses—

III. THAT MAN TOO OFTEN REFUSES TO HEED THE DIVINE CORRECTION. "If ye will not yet for all this hearken" (ver. 18); "if ye will not hearken unto me" (ver. 21); "if ye will not be reformed by me by these things" (ver. 23). Often men do listen and learn and obey when God comes to them in sickness or in sorrow; but only too often they do not. They continue in or revert to their evil course, they fall again into crime, into vice, into unconcern, into indecision.

IV. THAT GOD LAYS A HEAVIER HAND ON PERSISTENT AND OBDURATE IMPENITENCE. He gave to his people fair and full warning of what they were to expect at his hand. They knew that obduracy on their part would entail gathering and growing evils, leading on and down to uttermost destruction. There would come the enmity of the elements, with consequent disaster in the field (vers. 19, 20); desolation and bereavement (ver. 22); pestilence and famine (vers. 25, 26); revolting and unnatural cruelties wrought among themselves (vers. 28, 29); exile and dispersion (ver. 33); terror of soul (vers. 36, 37); national destruction and impending extinction (vers. 38, 39). These solemn and fearful threatenings are, no doubt, directed against Israel, the specially instructed people. As God "exalted that land unto heaven" in privilege and opportunity, so he "brought it down to hell" in condemnation and doom. But when we remember with what retribution God visited the sins of the antediluvian world, of the cities of the plain, the Canaanites, the great cities of Babylon and Nineveh, and when we recall the sufferings and humiliations he has brought down on lands and cities in more modern times, we may conclude that those nations which will not learn when God speaks to them in wrath and in "his high displeasure" may look forward to a time of gathering disaster and final ruin.

God's retributive dealings with nations have their counterpart in his action toward individual lives. Men who sin and suffer, and who will not learn by the things they suffer, may take to heart the truth that God's manifested wrath will reach them here or will overtake them hereafter; they may well wish that it may arrive soon rather than late, for as time passes and as sin indurates and blinds the soul, there is the less likelihood that the sacred lesson will be learnt before death shuts the book of opportunity, and eternity opens that other book of judgment and award.—C.

Vers. 40—45.—*Sorrow unto salvation.* The chastisements of God, like the gospel of Jesus Christ, are either a savour of life unto life or of death unto death; they either make or mar; they may sanctify and save or they may leave the soul more bound in the bonds of sin than ever. It is only godly sorrow—sorrow regarded in a true light and treated in the way that God intended—that works repentance unto salvation; otherwise it works death (2 Cor. vii. 10). The right use of affliction is indicated in the text; there must be—

I. A SENSE OF ILL DESERT. The uncircumcised heart must be humbled (ver. 41). God seeks by his chastisements to break our pride, our haughtiness of heart, our sinful self-complacency. Until this is done nothing is done. When the soul is at ease in its iniquity, it is in a very "far country," a long way from God, truth, salvation. When trouble touches and pierces our complacency, filling the soul with a sense of its rebelliousness, as soon as the heart says, "I have sinned," a large part of the work of the correcting hand is wrought. Then necessarily and readily follows—

II. THE LANGUAGE OF CONFESSION. Directly the heart feels the lip speaks. Too often men use the language of penitence when the feeling is entirely absent. But he that searcheth the hearts makes due distinction between the words which are true and those which are false. There is nothing gained with God by adopting the language which we ought to be disposed to use, but which does not express our actual condition; everything unreal is offensive in his sight. But there is much gained by the simple, natural, heartfelt utterance of penitential feeling. "If they shall confess their iniquity," etc. (vers. 40—42). "With the mouth confession is made unto salvation" (Rom. x. 10). The spirit thus taught of God through his servant, sorrow, has now—

III. THE SUBJECT WILL. It "accepts of the punishment of its iniquity" (ver. 41). It says, "Surely it is meet to be said unto God, I have borne chastisement, I will not offend any more: that which I see not teach thou me," etc. (Job xxxiv. 31, 32). It is "in subjection unto the Father of spirits" (Heb. xii. 9). It submits to his guidance and surrenders itself to his will. And then comes—

IV. DIVINE RESTORATION. God "remembers his covenant" (vers. 42, 45). As he remembered the covenant he made with the ancestors of the children of Israel, and "did not abhor them" (ver. 44), but withdrew his anger from them, so he remembers his promise with us, sealed with a Saviour's blood, to pardon our sins and to restore our souls to his Divine favour. Yet there are—

V. LINGERING CONSEQUENCES OF SIN. With penitent Israel, toward whom God was extending his mercy, "the land also was to be left of them, and was to enjoy her sabbaths, while she lay desolate without them" (ver. 43). With us, when penitent and restored, when taken back into the family and kingdom of God, there are lingering consequences of sin which even Divine mercy does not, cannot remove—consequences in: (1) miserable memories which will visit the mind; (2) enfeebled faculty that must work in a lesser sphere with smaller influence; (3) diminished reputation among men; (4) abiding results in those who have been injured, and who are beyond the reach of our restoration, etc. While facing this solemn fact—a fact which makes sin seem to us the stern, sad, hurtful thing it is—we may nevertheless find a glad relief in recalling—

VI. THE BLESSED HOPE OF THE HOLY. There is a country where the penal consequences of sin will be so removed from sight and sense that to our consciousness they will exist no more. Sin and sorrow shall never cross the stream that "divides that heavenly land from ours;" they must always remain on this side of it. What will remain to us there is a remembrance that will enhance our joy—a recollection of sin that has been forgiven, and of sorrow that has been endured, both the one and the other magnifying the mercy of our crowned and exalted King.—C.

Vers. 3—8.—*Obedience and prosperity.* The connection between godly conduct and material good may not seem to us so close or so clearly discernible as that which is promised in these verses. Still, the heart of the promise remains, and instances have never been wanting to prove that "godliness is profitable unto all things, having promise of the life that now is, and of that which is to come." The prophecy of Amos (ix. 13)—evidently founded on this passage of the Law—refers to gospel times, and reminds us that the declarations of the text are capable of a spiritual application which invests them with deeper meaning and grander results.

I. THE PROPRIETY OF OBEDIENCE. 1. *Man is unfit to guide his own way.* "It is not in man that walketh to direct his steps." He is a creature swayed by passion, short-sighted, fallible in judgment. Nor can the united wisdom of the multitude secure the framing of a code free from prejudice and error. We may consult the instructions of Scripture as our unfailing chart; we may listen to its precepts as the helmsman does to the commands of the captain, assured that from his loftier position he can better determine the course the vessel ought to take. 2. *The Almighty possesses irresistible claims upon our obedience.* He is our Creator and Governor, Father and Benefactor. He has bestowed upon us all our earthly and our spiritual benefits, and in particular spared not his only Son for our sakes. Supremely wise and holy, we cannot without manifest incongruity refuse to follow his counsel and rule of life. We are rebels if we neglect his injunctions. To pick and choose which we will conform to is to assume presumptuous functions. 3. *The statutes are such as to commend themselves upon maturest reflection.* Any precept plainly contrary to reason or morality no will has power to enforce. But the hexaplar verdict of the psalmist will be pronounced by all who study the laws of God, "The statutes of the Lord are right," etc. (Ps. xix. 7—9). The teachings of Jesus Christ are a master-piece of skill, goodness, and purity. If universally adhered to, the world would become an Eden.

II. THE REWARD OF OBEDIENCE. 1. *Blessings are promised to the obedient. Plenty.* The ground shall be fertile, the fruit gathered in harvest shall more than suffice to carry the husbandman on to the next ingathering. The gospel does at any rate teach Christian stoicism, making a man contented with his lot, and he who has sufficient for his wants cannot complain. But in the spiritual region we may have a never-ceasing flow of gifts. For God is bountiful, and loves to grant richest graces unto his people. If only we are prepared to receive, the floodgates of his bounty will be opened. *Peace.* They shall dwell at home in safety, none causing terror. Strife amongst God's own people shall be unknown, the inestimable blessing of tranquillity shall diffuse its sweetness over the land. "Thou wilt keep him in perfect peace whose mind is stayed on thee." Calm of conscience is the peculiar privilege of the believer in Christ. Bodily suffering cannot destroy this peace. The testimony of a well-known minister on his death-bed recently was, "Within I have deep peace, though around is constant searching pain." *Victory,* if foes attempt to molest. The Christian life is a warfare, and this is quite consistent with the enjoyment of peace. It is an external sphere of conflict, the enemy is determined and active, "but thanks be to God, which giveth us the victory through our Lord Jesus Christ." The obedient soldiers are likeliest to come off conquerors when the general is skilled in strategy. And as Havelock's men, by their observance of moral rules, were ever prepared for duty, so are those who conform to the precepts of Christ certain of success in the struggle against sin. The association is much more intimate between obedience and spiritual triumph than that which is here promised in the Law. 2. *These blessings are eminently desirable.* It speaks a wise and gracious God to have made it so greatly men's interest to keep his laws. In any case we are bound to do what seems right, yet, if this conduct were not coincident with advantage, life would be a melancholy scene. Peace, plenty, and victory are just what the heart desiderates and men strive to attain. God will not offer what men contemn. It is true that the degraded may at first fail to appreciate the joys of prosperity and tranquillity, yet education is possible, and even brief reasoning must convince of the value of these inducements. 3. *The list is comprehensive.* There is material prosperity and moral good, and in the following verses religious satisfaction is promised—God dwelling in the midst of his people. Nothing that can add to man's real happiness is absent from the catalogue of pleasures to be participated in by the obedient.

III. GENERAL REFLECTIONS. 1. *There is nothing wrong in allowing ourselves to be influenced by the promise of rewards.* Man is compelled to anticipate; prudence is a virtue. All depends upon the character of the rewards. If they minister to base, ignoble lusts, then to be moved thereby is indicative of an evil state of mind. But if the blessings are legitimate and elevating, in accordance with principles implanted by our Maker, then the hope of obtaining them is a strong incitement to be cherished rather than checked. To impel men to a holy life by preaching the bliss and glory of heaven is surely allowable and to be commended. 2. *The worth of these rewards will be enhanced by a consideration of the misery of their opposites*—want, turmoil, and defeat. Such is the lot of those who follow their own devices, blindly hurrying to ruin. The prodigal imagined that he must see the world and leave his father's home in order to be happy, but he soon discovered his dire mistake. 3. *History proves God's faithfulness to his word.* As long as the Israelites kept the Law, their condition was one of security, development, and honour. Every age has testified to the fulfilment of Divine declarations, forcing from the sceptical an acknowledgment of " a power that makes for righteousness." Seeking first the kingdom of God and his righteousness, all other things have been added. On the other hand, it has been found hard to kick against the pricks. What Carlyle terms the " eternities " war against the evil-doer. As predictions have been fulfilled in the past, so we are confident that all the promises of God shall ultimately be realized in the experience of his faithful servants.—S. R. A.

Ver. 11.—*God dwelling amongst men.* All possible methods were employed to attach the Israelites to the Law. Solemnity of its promulgation, judgment executed on transgressors, enticing promises and terrifying threats. Chief among inducements to obedience was the promise of the text.

I. SETTING UP A TABERNACLE IMPLIES. 1. *Settled residences in the midst of the people.* This was more than an occasional appearance on the mountain-top or in the wilderness. A tent is, at least for a season, a fixed abode. The Almighty would never be far distant from his lieges as he had seemed to be in preceding years. 2. *Friendly, familiar intercourse with the people.* He condescended to their manner of life, inhabiting a home as they did, passing as it were from one to the other. This is expressed in ver. 12, " I will walk among you." Naught of pollution was suffered for the reason given in Deut. xxiii. 14, " The Lord thy God walketh in the midst of the camp." A special revelation of God is intimated, that he would be known, not as omnipresent in space, but as peculiarly present, interchanging visits with his people. 3. *The assurance of Divine blessing.* Guidance, assistance, forgiveness,—all are herein included. God would be always near to be entreated. At the tabernacle sacrifices could be offered to purge away defilement. " The heathen shall know that I the Lord do sanctify Israel, when my sanctuary shall be in the midst of them for evermore " (Ezek. xxxvii. 28), God's presence is superior to any of his works; if we have him, we have all good things guaranteed.

II. THE PEOPLE OF GOD MAY WELL WONDER THAT HE SHOULD DELIGHT IN THEM AND NOT VIEW THEM WITH ABHORRENCE. To abide with man would be impossible if disgust were continually uppermost in the mind of God. 1. *Consider man's sinfulness.* How repugnant to the pure and holy One of Israel is every thought of iniquity, much less its overt commission! How often must he be shocked at the sights and sounds that gratify sinful creatures? Peter, awakened to a sense of his unworthiness, cried out, " Depart from me, for I am a sinful man, O Lord." 2. *Consider man's imperfections,* his ignorance and frailty, his dulness of perception, his insensibility to refined and elevated tastes and emotions. If one nurtured in good society revolts at the idea of close communion with those inferior in the social scale, whose manner of life and habits of thinking are so different, how great must be the disparity between heaven and earth!

what a descent must God feel it to be to consort with creatures of such petty selfish aims and uncultured ways! Only real pitying love, a desire to benefit and raise these miserable objects, a vision of what it was possible for them to become by such fellowship with the Most High, could have invested men with sufficient interest in the eyes of God to permit him to dwell amongst them. If the people strive to fulfil the behests of the Law, much of their degradation will vanish, and be succeeded by integrity and righteousness, which shall gradually beautify their character and customs. "My soul shall not abhor you," if you honour my precepts by strict fidelity.

III. THE PROMISE VERIFIED. 1. *In the local habitation of God* at Shiloh and Jerusalem. There God placed his Name and exhibited his power and favour. 2. *In his personal manifestation in Christ Jesus.* "In him dwelleth all the fulness of the Godhead bodily." "The Word . . . dwelt among us." Then was answered the question, "Will God in very deed dwell with man upon the earth?" Christ sojourned like ourselves in a house of clay, mingling with men and women in their daily tasks, sat at the same table with publicans and sinners. 3. *In the presence of God spiritually* in the heart of the individual believer, in the Church of Christ as a whole, making it the temple of God, and in the various assemblies, small or great, of the saints. "Where two or three are gathered together in my Name, there am I in the midst of them." The grandest fulfilment will be when the Lord God Almighty shall himself constitute the temple in which they shall offer their worship and service. "He that sitteth on the throne shall dwell among (spread his tabernacle over) them." No more hungering nor thirsting, no death, sorrow, nor crying, when God shall thus absolutely completely draw near to his people.—S. R. A.

Vers. 1, 2.—*Command to maintain the public worship of Jehovah.* I. PURITY OF WORSHIP. No idols or images. 1. *Spirituality* of religion. 2. Dependence of man on *revelation.* The deistic position of natural religion untenable. 3. The worship of God should be the free and grateful remembrance of past benefits received, therefore the leading elements of it should be faith and praise, not, as in heathenism and corrupt Christian systems such as the Roman Catholic, the slavish subjection of man to the fear of Divine wrath and the mediation of priests.

II. CONSECRATION BOTH OF DAY AND PLACE. Sabbath and sanctuary. 1. As necessary on account of the weakness of our nature. We cannot keep the mind above the world unless we are separated at times altogether from it. 2. The rallying point of fellowship. In the communion of saints there is special spiritual help. 3. As maintaining the holy order of human life, giving distinction and eminence to the highest things, predicting the future rest, revealing the dependence of the bodily life on the life of the soul, and of the happiness of earthly toil on the blessing of God. 4. The Christian sabbath as based on the resurrection of Christ has a new form of obligation and a larger sphere of holy suggestion. It is not so much commanded as vitally connected with the whole strength of Christian motive.—R.

Vers. 3—39.—*Promises and threatenings.* Ver. 12, "And I will walk among you, and will be your God, and ye shall be my people."

I. The true law of human life. 1. Religion the upholding support of individual, social, national well-being. Natural laws subservient to higher ends. Ascending scale in the universe, the physical the basis of the psychical, the psychical of the moral, the moral of the spiritual. 2. The covenant relationship of God and man the only true form in which the ideas of religion can be realized and maintained. Personality of God, freedom of man. Interchange of confidence. Living communion. Support of prayer, which should embrace all wants and possibilities. 3. Illustration of the connection between providence and religion in the history both of individuals and nations. Importance of insisting on the truths contained in this chapter as against secularism and fanaticism and mysticism. Religion is objective as well as subjective. Tremendous fact that, notwithstanding both the promises and threatenings, Israel failed to keep the Law. Illustration of human fall and dependence on Divine grace.

II. Divine government. 1. Righteous. 2. Merciful. 3. Revealed in connection with a system of truth and actual promises appealing to faith. 4. Embracing those who know not God, as well as his people.—R.

Ver. 21.—*Threatenings.* I. Actually fulfilled in history of the Jews, especially at siege of Jerusalem, ᴀ.ᴅ. 70.

II. Illustrating the moral nature of man as connected with a moral government.

III. Taken in order of announcement after the promises, reminding us that God willeth not the death of a sinner. The brightness of the love on the background of righteousness.—R.

Vers. 40—46.—*The gracious invitation to repentance.* The covenant may be restored. Even in the midst of the declarations of Divine sovereignty and government, long-suffering mercy meets "the earliest and faintest breathings of a broken and penitent spirit."

I. Confirm by history (see Judges and Kings). The restoration from Babylon. All consummated in Messiah.

II. The free grace of God is the foundation of hope; "I am the Lord their God;" "I will remember;" "for all that I will not cast them away;" "of faith, that it might be by grace."

III. The forgiveness of God dependent on the fulfilment of declared conditions. "If they shall confess;" "if their uncircumcised heart be humbled." 1. Spirituality of religion maintained from the beginning. 2. The purpose and end of all Divine chastisements to produce an acceptable state of heart. 3. The true penitence was the true circumcision, in other words, it was a renewal of the covenant, therefore included faith and acceptance of the Divine revelation and ordinances. Repentance and faith are one in the higher light of the gospel, for they are both " *toward* " the covenant in Christ Jesus.—R.

APPENDIX.

EXPOSITION.

CHAPTER XXVII.

Tʜᴇ final chapter, attached to the book after the concluding exhortation, is a short treatise on persons (vers. 2—8), animals (vers. 9—13), houses (vers. 14, 15), lands (vers. 16—24), vowed to God; and on the commutation of vows.

A man might vow to the service of God whatever he had a right over, that is, himself, his wife, his children, his slaves, his beasts, his houses, his fields. In case persons were vowed, the rule was that they should be redeemed at a certain price, though occasionally the redemption was not made. Vowing a person to God thus, was, as a rule, no more than vowing so much money to the use of the sanctuary as was fixed as the price of the redemption of the person vowed. Yet there is a great difference between the two acts of vowing a person and vowing the correlative sum of money. A man in great danger or distress might devote himself (Gen. xxviii. 20) or another (Judg. xi. 30; 1 Sam. i. 11)

to God, when he never would have vowed money. Such vows were redeemable, and, as a rule, were redeemed, though there were some exceptions, as in the case of Samuel.

If beasts were vowed to the Lord (vers. 9—13), they could not be redeemed if they were such as could be sacrificed to him; if they were not such as could be sacrificed, they were to be valued by the priest, and either retained as a possession of the sanctuary, or, if the owner preferred it, redeemed by him at the price fixed and one-fifth additional.

If houses were vowed to the Lord (vers. 14, 15), they became the property of the sanctuary, unless they were redeemed at the valuation set upon them by the priest, with one-fifth additional.

If hereditary lands were vowed to the Lord (vers. 16—21), they became the possession of the sanctuary at the year of jubilee, unless they had been previously redeemed; redemption, however, was in this case the ordinary rule, and we do not hear of any accumulation of landed property in the hands of the priests from this source. In the case of a field which was not an hereditary possession, but a purchase, being vowed to the Lord (vers. 22—24), the commutation sum was paid down *"in that day,"* that is, on the spot in a lump sum, the land going back at the jubilee to the original owners from whom the temporary possession had been bought by the man who made the vow.

A section is added forbidding the firstborn of animals, things devoted, and tithes to be vowed, because they were already the Lord's; allowing the redemption of the firstborn of unclean animals, and of the tithes of corn and fruits, but prohibiting redemption in the case of sacrificial animals, of things devoted, and of the tithes of animals.

Ver. 2.—**When a man shall make a singular vow,**—literally, *when a man shall separate a vow*, that is, *make a special vow* (see Numb. vi. 2)—**the persons shall be for the Lord by thy estimation**; that is, when a man has vowed himself or another person to the Lord, the priest shall declare the amount at which the person vowed is to be redeemed.

Vers. 3—7.—The sum at which a man between twenty and sixty years of age was to be redeemed was fifty shekels, equal to £6 9s. 2d.; a woman, thirty shekels, or £3 17s. 6d.; a youth between five and twenty years of age, twenty shekels, or £2 11s. 8d.; a maiden between the same ages, ten shekels, or £1 5s. 10d.; a boy between one month and five years, five shekels, or 12s. 11d.; a girl between the same ages, three shekels, or 7s. 9d.; a man above sixty years, fifteen shekels, or £1 18s. 9d.; a woman of the same age, ten shekels, or £1 5s. 10d.

Ver. 8.—A discretion is left with the priest to lower these valuations in case the man who has made the vow is very poor. **According to his ability that vowed shall the priest value him.**

Vers. 9, 10.—In case a clean animal is vowed to the Lord, it is not to be exchanged for another on the plea of not being good enough or being too good for sacrifice. If any such attempt is made, both animals are to be given up and sacrificed, or, if blemished, added to the herd of the sanctuary.

Vers. 11—13.—An unclean animal, which might not be sacrificed, if vowed, was to be valued at a price fixed by the priest. If its original owner took it back again, he was to pay this price and one-fifth more than

the sum named; if he did not, it became the property of the sanctuary. The words, **the priest shall value it, whether it be good or bad,** should rather be rendered, *the priest shall estimate it between good and bad*, that is, at a moderate price, as though it were neither very good nor very bad. And so in the next verse.

Vers. 14, 15.—The rule as to the redemption of houses is the same as that regarding the redemption of unclean animals. The ordinary practice was to redeem.

Vers. 16—21.—In case **a man shall sanctify unto the Lord** some part **of a field of his possession,** that is, of his hereditary lands, the redemption price is fixed by the quantity of seed required for sowing it. If it requires a homer, or five bushels and a half, of barley seed to crop it, the redemption price is fifty shekels, or £6 9s. 2d., *plus* one-fifth, that is, £7 15s., supposing that the vow had been made in the year succeeding the jubilee; but if the vow was made at any time **after the jubile,** the value of the previous harvests was deducted from this sum. The amount does not seem to have been paid in a lump sum, but by annual instalments of one shekel and one-fifth of a shekel, equal to 3s. 1½d., each year. In case he had sold his interest in the field up to the approaching jubilee before making his vow, then no redemption was allowed; he paid nothing, but the field passed from him to the sanctuary at the jubilee.

Vers. 22—24.—The case of a man who shall **sanctify unto the Lord a field which he hath bought, which** is not **of the fields of his possession,** or *inheritance*, is necessarily different, because he was not the owner of the land, but only the possessor of it until the next jubilee. For this reason he had to pay the redemption price immediately **in that day,** the land, of course, reverting to the original owner at the jubilee.

Ver. 25.—The estimation is to be made **according to the shekel of the sanctuary,** that is, the shekel at its full value, before worn by use in traffic (see Exod. xxx. 13; Numb. iii. 47; xviii. 16).

Vers. 26—33.—The law of vows and their commutation is further declared in four subjects: (1) the firstborn of animals; (2) things already devoted; (3) tithes of the produce of the land; (4) tithes of the produce of the cattle.

Vers. 26—28.—The firstborn of animals were already the Lord's, and they could not, therefore, be vowed to him afresh; the sacrificial animals were to be offered in sacrifice (Exod. xiii. 15); the ass was to be redeemed by a sheep or be put to death (Exod. xiii. 13; xxxiv. 20); other unclean animals are to be either redeemed at the fixed price, *plus* one-fifth, or, if not redeemed, sold for the benefit of the sanctuary.

Vers. 28, 29.—Whatever is already *cherem* (a word here first used as a term well understood), that is, *devoted* to God, whether devoted for the purpose of destruction or of entire surrender to him, may be neither redeemed nor sold. Whether it be of man, like the Canaanites at Hormah (Numb. xxi. 2), or of beast, as the sheep and oxen of the Amalekites (1 Sam. xv. 21), or of the field, as referred to in ver. 21, or of other inanimate objects, as the cities of Hormah (Numb. xxi. 2), it is either to be put to death or given up without reserve or commutation to God's ministers. In the case of men they must be put to death. "This provision would have applied only to the devoting of those who were already manifestly under the ban of Jehovah—those guilty of such outrageous and flagrant violation of the fundamental law of the covenant that they manifestly came under the penalty of death. Such persons, instead of being tried and condemned, might be at once devoted and put to death" (Gardiner). "To this it may be added that the devotion by ban (*cherem*) of any object or person was not to be done by private persons, at their own will, but was performed by the civil magistrates, under known conditions and laws; *e.g.* the cities of idolaters, such as Jericho, were so devoted, and the inhabitants, by the command of God himself, who made his people to be the executioners of his judgments against inveterate idolatry (see Deut. xiii. 13; Josh. vi. 17)" (Wordsworth).

Vers. 30—32.—Tithes, like the *cherem*, are introduced as things well known. Abraham gave tithes to Melchizedek (Gen. xiv. 20; Heb. vii. 4). Jacob vowed the tenth to the Lord (Gen. xxviii. 22), whence we see that the practice of the payment of tithes was not of Mosaic institution, but immemorial. The duty was, however, commanded afresh for the Israelites. "I have given the children of Levi all the tenth in Israel for an inheritance, for their service which they serve, even the service of the tabernacle" (Numb. xviii. 21), and of this tithe they were to pay a tenth to the priests (Numb. xviii. 26). Being already the Lord's, the tithe of the corn and fruits could not be vowed to the Lord, but it could be redeemed, or commuted, by the owner paying one-fifth more than the price at which it was valued.

Vers. 32, 33.—The tithe of the cattle could neither be vowed nor redeemed. As the young oxen and sheep passed under the rod by which they were counted by the herdsman, the tenth animal was touched (the rod, according to tradition, having been dipped in red paint), and handed over to the Levites. There was to be no change made in the animals, nor was commutation allowed.

Ver. 34.—The final verse of the previous chapter is repeated after the further legislation on vows and on their commutation has been added, to show that it too makes part of the Sinaitic code.

HOMILETICS.

Vers. 1—34.—Vows are not instituted by the Mosaic legislation; they were already in existence as a habit of the Hebrew people, and they are only regulated by Moses. The principle on the subject of vows is that no one was bound to make a vow, but that when a vow was made, it must be observed by the payment of the thing vowed or its recognized commutation. Thus Deut. xxiii. 21, "When thou shalt vow a vow unto the Lord thy God, thou shalt not slack to pay it: for the Lord thy God will surely require it of thee; and it would be sin in thee. But if thou shalt forbear to vow, it shall be no sin in thee." And Numb. xxx. 2, "If a man vow a vow unto the Lord, or swear an oath to bind his soul with a bond; he shall not break his word, he shall do according to all that proceedeth out of his mouth." And Eccles. v. 5, "Better is it that thou shouldest not vow, than that thou shouldest vow and not pay."

I. OLD-TESTAMENT VOWS WERE PROMISES TO GOD TO GIVE UP TO HIM SOMETHING OF VALUE ON CONDITION OF DELIVERANCE IN DISTRESS OR HELP IN ATTAINING SOMETHING DESIRED. Examples: 1. Jacob's vow: "And Jacob vowed a vow, saying, If God will be with me, and will keep me in this way that I go, and will give me bread to eat, and raiment to put on, so that I come again to my father's house in peace; then shall the Lord be my God: and this stone, which I have set for a pillar, shall be God's house: and of all that thou shalt give me I will surely give the tenth unto thee" (Gen. xxviii. 20—22). 2. Jephthah's vow: "And Jephthah vowed a vow unto the Lord, and said, If thou shalt without fail deliver the children of Ammon into mine hands, then it shall be, that whatsoever cometh forth of the doors of my house to meet me, when I return in peace from the children of Ammon, shall surely be the Lord's, and (or) I will offer it up for a burnt offering" (Judg. xi. 30, 31). What Jephthah appeared to contemplate as likely to meet him was either a non-sacrificial animal, which would then be handed over to the sanctuary (ch. xxvii. 11—13), or a sacrificial animal, which would be offered up. His daughter came under the first head (ch. xxvii. 9, 10). 3. Hannah's vow: "And she vowed a vow, and said, O Lord of hosts, if thou wilt indeed look on the affliction of thine handmaid, and remember me, and not forget thine handmaid, but wilt give unto thine handmaid a man child, then I will give him unto the Lord all the days of his life, and there shall no razor come upon his head" (1 Sam. i. 11). 4. Absalom's pretended vow: "For thy servant vowed a vow while I abode at Geshur in Syria, saying, If the Lord shall bring me again indeed to Jerusalem, then I will serve the Lord (offer sacrifices in Hebron)" (2 Sam. xv. 8).

II. CHRISTIAN VOWS ARE PROMISES MADE TO GOD, DIFFERING FROM THE JEWISH VOW BY BEING INDEPENDENT OF ANY DELIVERANCE OR BENEFIT TO BE RECEIVED IN RETURN. Examples: 1. The baptismal vow, ratified and confirmed in Confirmation: "Wilt thou then obediently keep God's holy will and commandments, and walk in the same all the days of thy life? I will." "Do you here, in the presence of God, and of this congregation, renew the solemn promise and vow that was made in your name at your baptism; ratifying and confirming the same in your own person? I do" (Baptism and Confirmation Services). 2. The marriage vow: "Wilt thou have this woman to thy wedded wife, to live together after God's ordinance in the holy estate of matrimony?" "Wilt thou have this man to thy wedded husband, to live together after God's ordinance in the holy estate of matrimony?" "I will" (Form of Solemnization of Matrimony). 3. The ordination vow: "Will you then give your faithful diligence always so to minister the doctrine and sacraments, and the discipline of Christ, as the Lord hath commanded, and as this Church and realm hath received the same, according to the commandments of God?" "I will so do, by the help of the Lord" (The Ordering of Priests).

III. THE CONDITIONS UNDER WHICH VOWS AND OATHS ARE NOT, OR CEASE TO BE, OBLIGATORY. Jeremiah writes (iv. 2), "And thou shalt swear, The Lord liveth, in truth, in judgment, and in righteousness." Isaiah speaks of those "which swear by the Name of the Lord, and make mention of the God of Israel, but not in truth, nor in righteousness" (Isa. xlviii. 1). Accordingly, any oath or vow is void which was an unrighteous oath or vow when taken; and the sin of breaking it, though a sin, is less than that of keeping it. Therefore Herod ought not to have kept his oath to the daughter of Herodias (Matt. xiv. 9); and the observance of their oath by the forty conspirators who had bound themselves to kill Paul, would have been a sin on their part (Acts xxiii. 12—21). Further, a vow, as distinct from an oath or contract, ceases to be obligatory if the person concerned comes to regard it as unrighteous and wrong for him to fulfil with his changed mind or under changed circumstances. Thus, the vow taken at ordination to administer the sacraments in the form received by a special Church, is not binding if a man ceases on conscientious grounds to be a member of that Church, and the vow of celibacy taken by Luther and others, who have become reformers, no longer binds them when they have come to the conviction that the vow was unrighteous, and when they have rejected the discipline of their Church. The marriage vow, however, stands upon a different basis, because marriage is a contract, containing not only a vow to God, but also a promise to man, by the non-fulfilment of which wrong would be done.[1]

HOMILIES BY VARIOUS AUTHORS.

On keeping vows. Ch. xxvii.; cf. Eccles. v. 4, 5; Gen. xxviii. 20—22; xxxv. 1—7. We have in this apparent appendix to the book an interesting chapter about keeping vows. Religious enthusiasm may very properly express itself in the dedication either of one's self, or a relative in whose destiny we have a voice, or a beast, or a house, or finally a field. Such a sense of special obligation may be laid upon us that we feel

---

[1] The best treatise on this difficult subject is Bishop Sanderson's 'Seven Lectures Concerning the Obligation of Promissory Oaths,' delivered in Latin, at Oxford, and translated by the command of Charles I.

constrained to dedicate either a person, an animal, or a piece of property unto God. But it may be highly inconvenient for the priests to accept of the dedicated article at the tabernacle. It may be much more convenient to receive, in lieu thereof, its money equivalent, and so a scale of charges is here given, according to which the vow's value is to be estimated.

I. WE MUST DEDICATE IN THIS SPECIAL WAY ONLY WHAT LIES BEYOND THE LORD'S USUAL DUES. The tithes, the firstlings, and the Nazarites may be regarded as the Lord's ordinary dues. We have no right to "make a fuss" about what is lawfully his own. The margin beyond the tithe is broad enough from which to make our special vows without encroaching upon the tithe. Let the nine-tenths or the four-fifths, according as we regard a single or a double tithe the Jewish proportion in systematic giving, be the source from which we shall draw our special vows.

II. IT IS A GOOD THING TO GIVE OUR INCREASING GRATITUDE SUCH SPECIAL OUTLETS. For after all, the Lord has given us everything, and may demand all if he pleases. When he is so "modest in his demands"—if we may be allowed such an expression regarding his claim upon the tithes—it is surely becoming in us from time to time to give our hearts free play, and have persons or things specially set apart for him.

III. BUT WE MUST NOT BE RASH OR INCONSIDERATE IN OUR VOWS. Jephthah, for example, was most rash in his vow. So was Saul in the war with the Philistines, when he almost insisted on Jonathan dying because, in eating a little honey in the wood, he had in ignorance transgressed the vow of the inconsiderate king. We have no right to make "rash promises" to any one, much less to God.

IV. WHEN WE HAVE REGISTERED A SPECIAL VOW WE MUST KEEP IT SCRUPULOUSLY. There is a temptation to make liberal vows on condition of receiving certain blessings from God, and then to forget them when the blessing is received. Let us take in illustration the case of Jacob. When he was posting in hot haste towards Padan-aram for fear of the injured Esau, he spent a remarkable night at Bethel. God there gave him a reassuring vision. Sin, he saw, had not separated him altogether from heaven, but even a deceiver like himself might return penitently to God and rise on the rounds of a ladder of light into fellowship and peace. In this ecstasy he registers in the calm morning light a vow : " If God will be with me, and will keep me in this way that I go, and will give me bread to eat, and raiment to put on, so that I come again to my father's house in peace ; then shall the Lord be my God : and this stone, which I have set for a pillar, shall be God's house : and of all that thou shalt give me I will surely give the tenth unto thee " (Gen. xxviii. 20—22). Did Jacob keep his vow? Surely the moment he returns to Canaan he will make for Bethel, and set up his altar, and discharge his vow ? Nothing of the kind. He forgot all about it, and went to Succoth, and then to Shechem, and it was not till Dinah had been defiled, and members of his family were becoming idolaters, and God commanded him to go to Bethel and perform it, that the wily old patriarch was brought to a sense of his duty (Gen. xxxv. 1—7).

Let us, then, enter upon our vows calmly, deliberately, without any unseemly haste. Then, whatever it may cost, no matter how great the sacrifice, let us undertake it, and our whole religious life will rise to the occasion. The future life, into which we hope to enter, will be so completely dedicated to God's glory, that the distinction we must needs now make between ordinary and special vows shall be lost completely, for the enthusiasm which leads to such special vows now shall make them the ordinary rule for ever.—R. M. E.

Vers. 1—25.—*Singular vows.* The loving heart will ask not only what *must*, but what *may*, be done ; and the sacrifices offered in the flames of love are acceptable to God (2 Chron. vi. 8). These are the principles which underlie the laws concerning singular vows.

I. THE SINGULARITY LIES IN THE ELEMENT OF SEPARATION. 1. Hence the subject of the vow is styled a Nazarite. (1) From נזר, to separate, to consecrate (see Numb. vi. ; Judg. xiii. 5 ; 1 Sam. i. 11, 28). (2) Probably the prayer of Jabez was of the nature of a singular vow (1 Chron. iv. 10). Paul seems to have taken upon himself such a vow (see Acts xviii. 18). 2. *Jesus was a Nazarite in spirit.* (1) He was not a Nazarite in the letter (Matt. xi. 19). What a rebuke is here to the uncharitableness of certain extreme advocates of total abstinence ! (2) Yet in spirit was Jesus the Grand

Antitype of all those anciently separated to God. Hence his dwelling at Nazareth was in the order of providence, and in fulfilment of prophecy, viz. that he should be called a Nazarene (Matt. ii. 23). 3. *So are true Christians.* (1) The disciples of Jesus, who were first called "Christians" at Antioch, were also distinguished as "Nazarenes" (see Acts xi. 26; xxiv. 5). They do not appear to have refused either title. (2) Professors should strive to prove themselves worthy of both. All Christians, in their baptism and in their voluntary acceptance of Christ, are bound by sacred vows. (3) The true merit of our modern abstainers from intoxicants who are so for the glory of God, is that of the Nazarite.

II. THINGS MAY BE CONSECRATED AS WELL AS PERSONS. 1. *A beast might be the subject of a singular vow.* (1) The Law prescribes that should it be such as might be offered in sacrifice to God, it must not be exchanged (vers. 9, 10). The reason appears to be that in this case it must be looked upon as a type of Christ, and for him there can be no substitute. (2) But if unsuitable for sacrifice, then it becomes the priests'. In this case it became the subject of estimation, and from the value put upon it by the priest there is no appeal. This assumes that his valuation is just; and this certainly is true of his Great Antitype, who will be our Judge. 2. *A house may be the subject of a singular vow.* (1) By means of dedicated things the sanctuary came to be the depository of great treasure (1 Kings xv. 15). (2) The riches of the gospel are principally spiritual. The houses which enrich the Church are saintly families. 3. *A field might be the subject of a singular vow.* (1) The estimation of the land is by the quantity of seed sown in it, fifty shekels to the homer (ver. 16). But the estimation was modified with respect to the law of the jubilee. The values of all earthly things are influenced by their relation to things heavenly. (2) If the owner would redeem that he vowed to God, he must add a fifth to the estimated value. This was a general rule; and was instituted to discourage fickleness in relation to the service of God.— J. A. M.

Vers. 26—34.—*Devoted things.* The earlier part of this chapter is mainly concerned with things sanctified to God by vows.

I. DEVOTED THINGS DIFFER FROM THINGS SANCTIFIED. 1. *In that they may not be redeemed.* (1) Things sanctified might be redeemed. The laws of estimation proceeded upon the recognition of this principle. (2) But it is otherwise with things devoted (see vers. 6, 21, 28). They are in the category of things "most holy," which only may be touched by the priests. (3) Hence firstlings must not be sanctified (ver. 26). The reason is that they are already the property of God. They can neither be given to him nor redeemed from him. They were types of Christ, who is therefore called the "Firstfruits of every creature"—the Antitype of all the firstfruits. 2. *Persons when devoted were doomed to die.* (1) Such was the fate of the enemies of the Lord. The Canaanites as unfit to live were so devoted (see Exod. xxii. 19; Deut. xxv. 19; Josh. vi. 17; 1 Sam. xv. 3; 1 Kings xx. 42). (2) Here is no reference to human sacrifices, as some have imagined. It is a question of justice and judgment upon the wicked. (3) But by a rash vow the innocent may suffer. Thus through the adjuration of Saul Jonathan's life was imperilled (1 Sam. xiv.). Jephthah's vow compromised the life of his daughter (Judg. xi. 30, 31, 39). The reading in the margin (ver. 31) is preferable. Jephthah could not make a burnt offering of anything unsuited to that purpose, and whatever else came forth he vowed not to sanctify but to devote. (4) The severity of God upon those devoted for their wickedness should admonish sinners of the formidableness of his anger in the great day of his wrath.

II. THE LAW CONCERNING TITHES. 1. These are now formally required. (1) They were originally vowed to God (see Gen. xiv. 19; xxviii. 22). (2) The acts of the patriarchs bound their posterity. Hence Levi paid tithes to Melchizedek, being yet in the loins of Abraham (Heb. vii. 9, 10). (3) Therefore God now claims them (vers. 30, 32). (4) The spirit of this law is still binding upon the spiritual seed of Abraham (see 1 Cor. ix. 11; Gal. vi. 6). 2. *Things marked as tithes must not be exchanged.* (1) The expression, "passeth under the rod," is thus explained by the rabbins: "When a man was to give the tithe of his sheep or calves to God, he was to shut up the whole flock in one fold, in which there was one narrow door capable of letting out one at a time. The owner stood by the door with a rod in his hand, the end of which was dipped in vermilion or red ochre. The mothers of those lambs or calves stood without, and as the young ones passed out, when the tenth came he touched it with the colour, and this was received as the legitimate tithe." (2) Here note the vicarious principle. When the tenth was taken, nine went free. Christ is our Tenth (see Isa. vi. 13). (3) The tenth must not be exchanged for better or worse. Providence is presumed to have guided the rod. While Christ becomes the Substitute for mankind, no one can take his place.—J. A. M.

Vers. 1—33.—*Spontaneous devotion.* The relations between God and his ancient people were not so rigid as they are sometimes supposed to have been. It was not all enactment on the one hand, and obedience or disobedience on the other. We find illustration here—

I. THAT THE LAW OF GOD LEAVES AMPLE ROOM FOR THE PLAY OF SPONTANEOUS DEVOTION. Under the inspiring influence of some signal mercies, individual or national, the Israelite might devote to God either (1) a person (ver. 2), or (2) an animal (ver. 9), or (3) a house (ver. 14), or (4) a piece of land (ver. 16). This was to be a *singular* vow (ver. 2), the dedication of something over and above that which was, by law, already appropriated to the service of Jehovah (see vers. 26, 30). It was and is the will of our God that special favours received at his hand, or special influences wrought by his Spirit in our heart, should be marked by optional and exceptional services on our part. We may, when thus animated by gratitude for his kindness, or penetrated with a sense of his goodness and grace, freely and spontaneously bring to the altar of our Lord (1) our possessions, (2) our time and labour, (3) our children (whom we may surrender to his service in distant and dangerous scenes), (4) any precious thing which we are not bound to give, but which we voluntarily and joyfully lay at his feet.

II. THAT THE FORM OF OUR DEVOTION MAY CHANGE SO LONG AS THE SPIRIT OF IT IS RETAINED. The Israelite who vowed a " person " redeemed the vow by presenting money according to a nicely graduated scale (vers. 3—8); or he might redeem a beast by paying money equal to its estimated value, together with one-fifth part added thereto (ver. 13); so with a piece of land (ver. 19). In a similar way, we may resolve and may undertake to give ourselves or our possessions to some particular sacred cause, and there may arise conditions which render it undesirable or even impossible for us to complete our work. In such case our Lord does not hold us to a mere literal fulfilment; what he looks for, and should certainly receive at our hands, is some equivalent in which we *at least as freely* express our gratitude and devotion. The essential thing is to preserve the spirit of our piety, and also to maintain a good measure of its most suitable expression, whatever that, at any time, may be.

III. THAT WE MAY GO SO FAR IN THE WAY OF DEDICATION THAT IT IS NOT PERMISSIBLE TO RETIRE. The Jew under the Law might, as we have seen, redeem certain things at a certain point; but there was a point at which everything was irredeemable. No " devoted thing " could be redeemed (vers. 28, 29). A beast " devoted to the Lord " must be offered up; an enemy once " devoted " must be put to death. When this point is reached in Christian consecration must be left to each Christian conscience. But we may contend that withdrawal is seldom, if ever, allowable when (1) there has been a solemn and formal dedication of person or substance in the presence of Christ and his people; (2) an overt action has been taken which commits other people, and when our retirement would involve theirs also; (3) such withdrawal would bring dishonour on the sacred Name we bear. Under such conditions as these we must proceed at all risks and costs, and having vowed, we must " pay unto the Lord our God " (Ps. lxvi. 11).—C.

Vers. 3—7.—*The distinctions which remain.* A pious Hebrew might, under a sense of gratitude, or in an hour of spiritual elevation, dedicate something dear to himself unto Jehovah. It might be a person, or an animal, or a field. If the first of these, he or she was to be redeemed, and a table was drawn according to which the redemption was to be made. In this scale, we find the extremes of life, age and infancy, valued at the least sum, youth at more, and prime at the most; we find also woman placed lower in the list than man. These distinctions in the estimated value of human life may remind us—

I. THAT IN THE GOSPEL OF CHRIST THERE ARE NO DISTINCTIONS IN RESPECT OF

AGE, SEX, OR CLASS. Age is not less welcome because it is old, nor youth because it is young, nor poverty because it is poor, nor wealth because it is rich, to the Saviour of souls. Woman stands on the same ground with man, and her love and service count for as much in the Lord's esteem as his. "In Christ Jesus there is neither Jew nor Greek, there is neither bond nor free, there is neither male nor female" (Gal. iii. 28). There is no respect of persons with the God and Father of our Lord Jesus Christ.

II. THAT IN THE VALUE OF CHRISTIAN SERVICE SOME DISTINCTIONS MUST REMAIN. The kind of service we render our Lord differs at different periods of our life. Obviously that of the little child is distinct from that of the man in the maturity of his strength. The scale of redemption under the Law, as given in this passage, suggests : 1. That age, though of declining value, has its tribute to bring (ver. 7) ; it can bring its purity, its calmness, its caution, its contentedness, its patient waiting : " planted in the house of the Lord, . . . we shall still bring forth fruit in old age " (Ps. xcii. 13, 14). 2. That prime has the largest offering to lay on the altar of the Lord (ver. 3). Manhood brings its strength, its maturity, its experience, its learning, its vigour. 3. That youth is of great account in the estimate of God (ver. 5) ; it can bring to the service of Christ its eagerness, its ardour, its faith, its devotedness. 4. That childhood has its figure also in the Divine reckoning (ver. 6) ; it can bring its innocence, its trustfulness, its docility, its winsomeness, its obedience. We are thus reminded that, while there is no stage in our life when we are not heartily welcome to our Saviour, there is at each period some special work we can do, some peculiar service we can render him, and we may add that every offering of every kind is acceptable to him if it be presented in humility and with a willing mind.—C.

Ver. 34.—*The Law and the gospel.* 1. It may be rightly said that true religion is essentially the same everywhere and at all times. Whithersoever and whensoever we look, we shall find the same cardinal elements—the fear of God, the love of God, respect for our own spiritual nature, regard for the rights and claims of others, abstinence from that which is immoral, kindness and helpfulness, etc. 2. It may also be truly said that in the Law there was much more than many have supposed of those elements which are prominent in the gospel : more of spiritual freedom, of joy in God, of happy and sacred fellowship than we are apt to associate with "Mount Sinai," and "the commandments which the Lord commanded Moses." When, therefore, we draw a distinction between the Law and the gospel, it must be remembered that it is not without important qualifications ; that the Law had, in most cases, an aspect which was essentially Christian ; and that, similarly, the gospel in most cases has an aspect which is legal. With this in mind, we may draw the contrast—

I. THAT THE LAW WAS PREPARATORY AND PROPHETIC ; the gospel is final and in fulfilment of that which had been anticipated. This, especially, in regard to sacrifice and offering.

II. THAT THE LAW WAS PRECEPTIVE ; the gospel is suggestive. The one supplied a multitude of rules for the regulation of worship and of daily life, the other has few "commandments." Its positive precepts are small in number, but it lays down those principles and implants that spirit by which the right and the wrong course are suggested, to be pursued or shunned by the obedient heart.

III. THAT THE LAW WAS PROHIBITIVE ; the gospel is inspiring. Not wholly, but strikingly, in each case. The Law continually said imperatively, "Thou shalt not;" the gospel says encouragingly, "Wilt not thou?" The Law interdicted very many things, and an Israelite was obedient very much according to his conscientious avoidance of that which was forbidden. The gospel incites to feelings, words, actions of goodness, wisdom, grace, helpfulness ; and a Christian man is obedient and acceptable in proportion as he opens his heart to heavenly inspiration, and is stirred to be and do that which is noble and Christ-like.

IV. THAT THE LAW MADE ITS APPEAL TO HUMAN FEAR ; the gospel to human love. Jehovah was, indeed, presented often to the Hebrew as his Redeemer from bondage ; but, upon the whole, he was so revealed as, above everything, to strike the soul with profoundest reverence and awe. The Jew never ceased to hear the thunderings and see the lightnings of Sinai. The motto of the devout Israelite was this—"I fear God." In the gospel God is manifested in Jesus Christ, our Saviour, our Friend, our sympathizing

High Priest; and, while not without deepest reverence, we feel that "the love of God in Christ Jesus" is the spring and the strength of our devotion; it is the key to which the sacred music of our life is set.

V. THAT THE LAW HAD RESPECT TO EARTHLY LIFE; the gospel to the farthest future. The Law said, "Do this, and thou shalt live long in the land;" "do this, and the rains shall fall and the vines shall bear and the barns be full;" but the gospel says, "Do this—repent, believe, follow Christ; and while there shall be sufficiency of present food for present need, there shall be abounding grace in the heart, fruitfulness in the life, peace in death, and a long eternity of sinless service and unclouded joy in the presence of the King, in the home of God.—C.

Vers. 1—34.—*Vows and dues.* I. We find here a representation of the union of righteousness and grace in the kingdom of God. The sacredness of vows and dues; but the estimation, by the priest, *according to the ability* of him that made the vow. The Law makes its claim, but God provides against its rigour.

II. Comparison of the Law of God as given to his ancient people with the imperfect and cruel laws of merely human origin. Especially as to human sacrifices. The only human life which could be vowed to God was that which was already doomed by right of war or otherwise. The animal sacrifices, being strictly prescribed, excluded human sacrifice. The true religion is the only protection of human life. Those who profess enthusiasm of humanity, instead of and as a substitute for faith in Christ, have no security to offer that their inadequate theory of human obligation will extirpate cruelty and promote the happiness of the world.

III. The commutation of vows and dues pointed to the pitifulness of Jehovah, who, while upholding the inviolability of his Law, would yet provide for the weakness of man. "He knoweth our frame," etc. These glimpses of love in the midst of the thunders of Sinai were the promises of a revelation of the Divine nature in which love should predominate—a new covenant, which should take up into itself all that was enduring and Divine in the old. Underneath all the regulations of Leviticus lies the original promise of redemption, and through all the vail of the Mosaic economy shines the Shechinah glory of God manifest in the flesh—the Prophet, Priest, and King, who came, not to destroy the Law, but to fulfil it, and in whom all the promises of God are Yea and Amen.—R.

HOMILETICAL INDEX

TO

THE BOOK OF LEVITICUS

CHAPTER I.

THEME   PAGE

The Sacrificial System 4
The Burnt Offering... 5
Mediation 6
Entire Consecration, as Illustrated in
     the Burnt Offering 6
The Weakness of Man and the Grace
     of God 8
The Greatness of God 9
Our Reasonable Service 10
Sacrificature 12
The Burnt Sacrifice of the Herd ... 13
The Burnt Offering of the Flock and
     of the Fowls 14
God in Special Manifestation ... 15
The True End of Sacrifice—Entire
     Consecration to God 16
Principles of Spiritual Sacrifice ... 17
God's Pleasure in Man 18
The Law of Burnt Offerings ... 19
"Speak unto the children of Israel" 20
The Burnt Sacrifice 21
"And he shall put his hand upon the
     head," etc. 21
The Killing, Flaying, and Consuming
     of the Victim 22
The Offering from the Flocks ... 22
The Offering of Fowls 23

CHAPTER II.

The Meat Offering 25
Salt 26
Consecrated Life-work, as brought out
     in the Meat Offering 27

THEME   PAGE

Honouring God with our Firstfruits... 28
Mediate and Immediate Presentation 29
The Salt of the Covenant 30
The Offering of Daily Life ... 31
The *Minchah*, a Type of Christ ... 32
The Feast upon the *Minchah* ... 33
Notable Things 34
The *Minchah* of the Firstfruits ... 35
Our Recognition of the Hand of God
     in the Blessings of Life 36
Purity in Worship 37
Priest and People : Reciprocal Services 38
The Meat Offering 39
The Various Kinds of Meat Offerings 39

CHAPTER III.

The Peace Offering ... 41, 46, 49
Fellowship with God and Man as
     Illustrated in the Peace Offering ... 42
A General View of Offerings ... 44
Jehovah's Portion 45
The Peace Offering of the Flock ... 47
The Foundation of Fellowship with
     God 48
The Guarding of Sacred Feeling ... 48
"The fat that covereth the inwards" 51
"And Aaron's sons shall burn it," etc. 51
Varieties in the Offerings—Unity in
     the Sacrifice 52

CHAPTER IV.

The Sin Offering 55, 67
Atonement for the Penitent, as Illus-
     trated in the Sin Offering ... 55

THEME	PAGE
Unintentional Transgression ...	57
Atonement for Involuntary Transgression	58
Rites Essential to an Atonement ...	58
The Sin Offering for the Priest ...	59
The Sin Offering Viewed as Typical of the Sacrifice of Calvary	60
Sin Offering for the Congregation ...	61
Sin Offering of the Ruler and of any of the People	63
The Mind of God respecting the Sin of Man	64
Gradations in Guilt	65
Collective Guilt Unconsciously Incurred	66
Full Acceptance with God	66
Access for All: Comparison and Contrast	67
The High Priest's Burnt Offering ...	70
The Whole Congregation Sinners through Ignorance	70
A Ruler can Sin through Ignorance, and Requires Atonement ...	71
The Sins of the Common People ...	71

CHAPTER V.

Confession of the Sin Committed ...	73
Guilt Removed	74
The Trespass Offering ... 75, 80, 85	
Fidelity in Bearing Witness ...	76
Shunning the Impure	77
Redeeming Promises	77
Pardon Possible to All	78
Cases of Concealment of Knowledge and Ceremonial Uncleanness ...	79
Restitution as Inculcated in the Trespass Offering	80
Trespass Amended	82
Trespass in Sacrilege	82
Restitution to God	83
Unconscious Sin	84

CHAPTER VI.

Swearing Falsely	86
Repentance, Confession, Satisfaction, Absolution	86
Dishonesty Atoned for	86
Restitution	87
Human Ownership and Dishonesty ...	88
Sin a Germ as well as a Fruit ...	89
Trespasses done Wittingly ...	89
The Priests' Ritual	91

THEME	PAGE
Quench not the Spirit	91
The Ever-burning Fire	93
The Holiness of the Sin Offering ...	93
The Law of the Burnt Offering ...	94
The Law of the Meat Offering ...	95
The Law of the Sin Offering ...	96
Three Principles of Piety	97
"Fellowship with the Father" ...	98
Communicated Sanctity	98
Ministerial Function and Obligation	99
Instructions on the Offerings for the Priests	99
Meat Offering	100
Special Regulations as to the Sin Offering	100

CHAPTER VII.

That which is itself Unclean Makes whatever it Touches Unclean also	102
Ministerial Support ... 103, 113	
Fidelity to Precept Enforced ...	104
The Threefold Participation ...	105
The Law of the Trespass Offering ...	106
The Peace Offering of Thanksgiving	107
The Sanctity of the Service of God ...	108
The Service of the Oblation ...	109
Emphatic Truths; or Things God Lays Stress upon	110
The Kingdom of God: Lessons from the Heave Offering	110
Four Thoughts on Sacred Service ...	111
Divine and Human Severity ...	112
Three Features of Acceptable Service	112
The Peace Offerings and Thank Offerings	113
Instructions for the People on the Fat and on the Blood	114
The Wave Breast and the Heave Shoulder	114

CHAPTER VIII.

Priesthood	118
Priestly Consecration	120
The Installation of Aaron	122
The High Priesthood of Christ ...	123
The Triple Offering	124
The Baptism of Aaron and his Sons	125
The Holy Garments of Aaron ...	126
Levitical Anointings	128
The Vesting of the Priests and the Offerings for them	129
The Ram of Consecration	130

THEME	PAGE
A Time for Publicity	131
The Human and Divine Priesthood— Contrast	132
The Human and Divine Priesthood— Comparison	132
Spiritual Apparel	133
Equipment for Special Work ...	134
The Burden of the Lord	135
Public Inauguration of Divine Service	135
"And Moses brought Aaron and his sons," etc.	136
Aaron's Dress	136
Anointing	136
The Sacrifices of Consecration ...	137

CHAPTER IX.

Miraculous Confirmation of the New Polity	139
A Sign Expected and Received ...	140
The Glory of the Lord	141
The Eighth Day	142
Aaron's First Priestly Services ...	143
Appearing together before God ...	144
Sacrifice for Sin	145
The Priest at the Altar	146
Holy Invocation	147
The Manifested Presence	148
God's Glory Manifested in the Blessedness of His People	148

CHAPTER X.

The Sinfulness of Man Mars the Full Effect of the Good Purposes of God	150
Fire	151
Increase of Privilege Involves Increase of Danger	151
Counterfeit Fire	152
Submission in Bereavement ...	153
Disobedience Swiftly Punished ...	154
A Bereaved Parent	155
Restrictions and Infirmities of Religious Service	156
Nadab and Abihu	156
Sin and Penalty in Sacred Things ...	157
Strange Fire 158,	160
Self-Restraint and Utterance ...	159
That Priests are Teachers	162
Abstinence Enjoined	162
Sobriety in the Priesthood	163
The Eating of the Holy Things ...	164
Moses and Aaron: an Allegory ...	165
Wine and Worship	166

THEME	PAGE
Instruction as well as Sacrifice ...	166
The Spirit of Obedience	167
That which is Left to us	168
Ministers to be Examples of Purity ...	168

CHAPTER XI.

Meats Distinguished into Clean and Unclean 172, 176, 182, 183,	184
"Ye shall be holy; for I am holy"	173
The Religious Use of Nature ...	174
The Waters and their Inhabitants ...	177
Flying Creatures	178
Unclean Creeping and Dead Things	180
The Abominable Thing	181
Health a Duty as well as a Blessing	182
The Significance of Death	184
Sacred Separation	185
High Reasons for Holiness ...	185
Holiness and its Requirements ...	186
Holiness	187

CHAPTER XII.

The Purification of the Church ...	190
Born in Sin	191
The Statutes on Maternity ...	193
Woman under the Law and under the Gospel	194
Ceremonial Purifications	195

CHAPTER XIII.

Leprosy regarded as the Type of Sin	198
The Extrusion of the Leper from the Camp is a Type of Excommunication from the Christian Church ...	199
The Diagnosis of Sin as Illustrated in the Leprosy	200
Leprosy	202
The Priest's Adjudication	203
A Picture of Sin	204
The Chosen Type of Sin—	
(1) Its Individual Aspect ...	206
(2) Its Social Aspect	207
Conviction of Sin	208
Affections of the Mind	208
The Right and Duty of Excommunication	209
Purity of Garments	211
Impure Surroundings	**212**

CHAPTER XIV.

The Cleansing of the Leper Represents the Absolution of the Sinner ...	216

THEME	PAGE
The Cleansing of Sin as Illustrated in the Cleansing of the Leper ...	218
Restoration Suggestions	219
Readmission	220
Final Rites of Readmission ...	221
Divine Considerateness	222
Thorough Purification	223
The Cleansing of the Leper—	
(1) Ceremonies outside the Camp ...	224
(2) Ceremony in the Tabernacle ...	225
Uncleanness in Houses	228
Cleansing the Corrupt House ...	230
Leprosy in a House	230

CHAPTER XV.

THEME	PAGE
The Figure of the " woman which was diseased with an issue of blood twelve years"	232
Secret Sins	233
Uncleanness	234
Personal Purity	235

CHAPTER XVI.

THEME	PAGE
Union and Communion with God ...	244
The Annual Reiteration of the Purification made on the Day of Atonement	246
The Great Day of Atonement ...	246
A Sabbath of Rest	248
The Climax of Sacrificial Worship ...	248
The High Priest on the Day of Atonement	250
The Sacrifices on the Day of Atonement	251
The Day of Atonement ...	252, 254
A Solemn Ceremony	253
The Peril of Privilege	256
Type and Antitype—	
(1) The Priest	256
(2) The Offering	257
The Great Anniversary—Sacred Seasons	258
The Imperfect Ritual and the All-sufficient Sacrifice	259

CHAPTER XVII.

THEME	PAGE
Sacrifice is not in Itself Enough ...	262
The Eating of Blood Prohibited ...	264
Grace before Meat	264
Statutes concerning Blood	265
One Place of Sacrifice	266
Features of Christian Service ...	267

THEME	PAGE
Atoning Death	268
Sanctity of Animal Life	268
The Sanctity of the Atoning Blood ...	269

CHAPTER XVIII.

THEME	PAGE
The Restraints thrown about Marriage by God's Law	276
Unworldliness	278
Abominable Doings	280
Two Aspects of Sin	281
Life in Obedience	281
Impurity—its Extent and Source ...	282
The Penalty of Sin	283
Obedience Enjoined	284
Abominations Denounced	285

CHAPTER XIX.

THEME	PAGE
Morality has a Basis of its Own ...	290
The Laws of Submission	291
The Laws of Piety and of Faith ...	293
The Law of Kindness	294
Stealing is Forbidden by the Law of God and Man	294
" Ye shall not swear by my Name falsely "	295
Mingled Seed	297
Respect for Old Age	298
Moral Commandments have a Double Sanction	298
Religion and Superstition	298
" Honour to whom honour " ...	298
Considerateness	299
Integrity	300
Love—its Root and Fruit	301
Aids to Purity	302
The Range of Sin and the Rule of God	302
Three Helps to Spiritual Progress ...	303
Social Morality	303
Purity in Worship	305
Kindliness	306
Justice	307
Fidelity to God	307
The Fear of God	309
" Ye shall be holy," etc.	309
The Holy Law in the Holy Life ...	310

CHAPTER XX.

THEME	PAGE
The Difference between the Religious and the Secular Law	312
The Pursuit of Knowledge by Right Means	313
" Ye shall be holy unto me " ...	313

THEME	PAGE
Human Sacrifices	314
Sin at its Worst	315
Credulity and Faith	316
Sanctity — Demand, Inducement, Promise	317
The Unforgiven	317
God's Displeasure with Ourselves ...	318
Three Aspects of Human Life ...	319
Sin unto Death	320
Punishments Assigned to Presumptuous Sins	321

CHAPTER XXI.

The Marriage of the Clergy ...	323
Priestly Qualifications	323
Law of Holiness for the Priests ...	325
Distinctions and Degrees in Obligation	325
Unblemished Service	326
The Perfection of the Priesthood ...	327

CHAPTER XXII.

The Perfection Demanded in the Sacrificial Victims	330
Holiness of Priests and Sacrifices ...	330
Priestly Disqualifications	331
The Service of Abstention ...	332
The Guilt of Profanation	332
Characteristics of Acceptable Service	333
The Culture of Kindness	334
The Eating of the Holy Things ...	334
Laws of the Oblations	335

CHAPTER XXIII.

The Paschal Supper Observed by our Lord	341
The Offering of Rest: The Sabbath	343
The Sabbath	344
Aspects of the Sabbath	345
The Harvest Festivals	349
The Passover 350, 356
The Feast of the Firstfruits ...	351
The Pentecost	352
The Feast of Trumpets ... 353, 360, 368
The Annual Repentance—the Day of Atonement	354
The Pilgrim Spirit as Illustrated in the Feast of Tabernacles... ...	355
The Feast of Harvest	357
The Hebdomad	359
The Feast of Expiation	361
The Feast of Tabernacles ... 362, 368, 371
The Influence of Sacred Recollections	363

THEME	PAGE
Provision and Piety	364
Piety in Prosperity	365
The Summons of God	365
Joy before the Lord	366
The Festivals	367
The Passover and Feast of Unleavened Bread	367
The First Sheaf a Wave Offering of the Harvest	367
The Day of Pentecost	368
Religious Festivals	368
The Beginning of Harvest	369

CHAPTER XXIV.

Everlasting Light	374
The Weekly Offering	375
The Lighting of the Sanctuary ...	376
The Bread of the Presence... 377, 380
Ourselves as Lights	378
The Lesson of the Loaves	379
The Lights in the Sanctuary ...	380
The Candlestick	380
The Shewbread	382
The Crime of Blasphemy	386
Public Justice Secured by the Law of Retaliation	387
Shelomith's Son	388
A Suggestive Episode	389
The Holy Law of God	390
A Blasphemer Punished	391
The Law of Death	392

CHAPTER XXV.

The Power of Slavery	396
The Fallow Year	397
The Jubilee 399, 402
The Sabbatic Year ... 400, 407, 408
Redemption	403
Justice and Mercy	404
Divine Discipline...	405
Year of Jubilee—	
(1) A Nation's Joy ... 405, 407
(2) The World's Redemption ...	406
(3) The Blessed Kingdom ...	407
The Law of Personal Servitude ...	408
Servants of God	409

CHAPTER XXVI.

Promises and Threatenings ...	414
Temporal Rewards and Punishments	415
The Blessedness of the Righteous ...	417
Prophetic Maledictions	418

THEME	PAGE
Hope for Israel	419
Idolatry : Our Danger and our Security	419
Incentives to Obedience	420
Our God and Ourselves	421
Divine Retribution	422
Sorrow unto Salvation	423
Obedience and Prosperity	424
God Dwelling amongst Men ...	425
Command to Maintain the Public Worship of Jehovah	426
Promises and Threatenings ...	426
Threatenings	427

THEME	PAGE
The Gracious Invitation to Repentance	427

CHAPTER XXVII.

Vows	429
Keeping Vows	430
Singular Vows	431
Devoted Things	432
Spontaneous Devotion	433
The Distinctions which Remain ...	433
The Law and the Gospel	434
Vows and Dues	435

NUMBERS

INTRODUCTION BY

THOMAS WHITELAW

EXPOSITION AND HOMILETICS BY

R. WINTERBOTHAM

HOMILIES BY VARIOUS AUTHORS

W. BINNIE
E. S. PROUT

D. YOUNG
J. WAITE

INTRODUCTORY ESSAY ON

THE AUTHENTICITY AND AUTHORSHIP

OF

THE BOOK OF NUMBERS

BY

THE REV. THOMAS WHITELAW, M.A.

ITS AUTHENTICITY.

The general question of the historic credibility of the narrative contained in the first five books of the Hebrew Scriptures having already been considered in an Essay on the Authorship of the Pentateuch prefixed to the Genesis volume of the present series of Commentaries, attention needs now to be directed to such difficulties alone as are specifically associated with the Book of Numbers; and these it will be most convenient to investigate under the threefold subdivision of seeming chronological inaccuracies, so-called statistical errors, and alleged physical impossibilities.

a. Seeming Chronological Inaccuracies.

I. The second passover. On the ground that ch. ix. 1 appears to relate to a second celebration of the passover in the first month of the second year, while the census (ch. i. 1) was taken in the second month of the same year, Bleek declares it to be "most evidently conspicuous" that the unknown compiler of the history has here inadvertently perpetrated a grievous chronological blunder ('Introd.,' Vol. I. p. 249). It is, however, precarious to assert, in the absence of indication from the writer himself, that he clearly and deliberately designed, in every separate portion of his composition, to adhere strictly to the order of time. The circumstance "that the separate laws, as they were made known to Moses by Jehovah, and to the people by Moses, are interwoven in the history of the journeyings through the wilderness," while exceedingly valuable as a note of the historic credibility and Mosaic authorship of the entire narrative (vide infra, p. xx), does not justify the conclusion that Bleek desires it to carry—that "we should certainly expect that if Moses wrote the Pentateuch as it is now constructed, all the particulars would have been fitted together in a consecutive order and connection in accordance with the actual sequence of events." Not to mention that Bleek does not deem it necessary to insist upon the application of this criterion in determining the authenticity and genuineness of the synoptical Gospels of Matthew and Luke (*vide* ' Introd. to N. T.,' Vol. I. p. 280), it is certain with regard to Numbers that the account of the princes' offerings at the dedication of the altar (ch. vii.) does not occupy the place to which it is chronologically entitled, while it is doubtful if the instructions relating to the construction of silver trumpets (ch. x. 1—10) should not be assigned to an earlier period than immediately before the march, and yet, according to Bleek, this latter paragraph bears "in the highest measure the stamp of exactness, distinctness, and historic fidelity," while, with reference to the former, even Ewald would admit that the writer had derived his information from antique Mosaic fragments ('History of Israel,' Vol. II. p. 18). But the question still remains whether in point of fact the narrative has at this particular stage suffered, even inadvertently, a chronological dislocation. If the writer's purpose had been simply to chronicle the interesting circumstance that the anniversary of the exodus had been kept in the wilderness by a second celebration of the passover, then it must be conceded that at least it wears this aspect. A closer scrutiny of the passage, however, leads to a somewhat different conclusion. The historian, it is seen, is engaged in recording the transactions that occurred preparatory to departing from Sinai, and has arrived at that point where only two remain to be noted, viz., the observance of a supplementary or, as it is sometimes designated, a little passover, and the construction of silver trumpets for signal-giving on the desert march. Accordingly, with reference to the first, instead of writing down in so many words that certain parties performed a special paschal celebration on the fourteenth day of the second month, he details the circumstances out of which the necessity for such celebration arose, and the authority they had received for its observance, leaving it to be inferred by his readers that the Divine prescription with regard to the matter was not neglected, just as, in connection with the silver trumpets, instead of stating that they were manufactured as God had enjoined, he contents himself with simply engrossing in his narrative the order he had received for their construction. Thus, instead of being an "evident inaccuracy," the section about the passover has been introduced into the history on a principle at once perfectly lucid and readily intelligible.

II. THE THIRTY-SEVEN YEARS' CHASM. It is immaterial whether, with Bleek, Ewald, Colenso, Kuenen, and others, we regard the first month spoken of in ch. xx. 1 as the first month of the third year, or, with Gerlach, Lange, Kurtz, Keil, ' Speaker's Commentary,' &c., consider it to be the first month of the fortieth year—immaterial, that is to say, so far as the present argument is concerned. In the former case, a gap occurs in the history of over thirty-seven years concerning which the writer preserves unbroken silence, while in the latter the chronological break is scarcely less, though the silence is not so absolute—the rebellion of Korah and his company occurring in the interval. In either case the difficulty is pretty much the same, viz., to understand how, on the hypothesis of the Book of Numbers having been composed as a connected historical work, so long a series of years should have been passed over, if not without the least, yet with so little, information. "It is impossible," writes Bleek, "to imagine how a contemporary historian could have skipped so long a period with such seeming unconsciousness;" "it is hardly conceivable that, circumstanced as they were, nothing should have happened to them which deserved to be recorded as much as many other events described in the Pentateuch;" and accordingly he adds, "It follows that this gap can only be attributed to the want of completeness and accuracy of the history " (*vide* 'Introd. to the Old Test.,' Vol. I. p. 251). Bohlen, with much bolder ingenuity, blots the thirty-seven years out altogether, regarding the number forty of which the narrative speaks, especially when conjoined with the story of the whole generation perishing, as conclusive evidence of its mythical complexion. "The epico-traditional period of forty years was prescribed to the author of the Book of Numbers, and he does his best to fill it up with the few events which were at his command, even specifying the days and months when they occurred " ('Introd.,' Vol. I. p. 86; cf. Kuenen, 'The Religion of Israel,' Vol. I. p. 131). Ewald, with less audacity, ascribes it to an almost total obscuration of the national memory in the time of his Elohist concerning a dark period of their history which they were anxious to forget. "When the people were already established in Canaan, and looked back upon the long period of their wanderings in the desert after their exodus, undoubtedly the view became fixed among them that the time passed in the desert had been forty years—a round number, the adoption of which may be inferred from the Book of Origins. But when its author sought to assign to the several still remembered events of this long period their proper dates—their years, months, and days—we see at once how difficult it was even then to effect this in any historical sense." Accordingly, he explains that "all those events which could not belong to the close of the wanderings were placed in the first two years, and all the remainder in the last year of the forty," leaving the entire middle of these forty years "a completely blank space, of which nothing further is said than that the generation which came up from Egypt had to die in the desert for its backslidings, in order to make room for a better " ('History of Israel,' Vol. II. p. 186). And perhaps no better or more fascinating theory could be adopted for the solution of this singular phenomenon, if it were perfectly certain that the present narrative would resist every endeavour to regard it as contemporaneous history, and that on such an assumption the remarkable *lacuna* could not be reasonably accounted for. The hypothesis of Hävernick may indeed be dismissed as improbable and unsatisfactory, that "little transpired during that long space of time that was sufficiently remarkable and important to deserve mention, or of which even a remembrance was preserved " ('Introd. to Pent.,' § 27). Even the explanation offered by Kurtz scarcely commends itself as perfectly sufficient, that, "so far as the wanderings in the desert are concerned, nothing of a stationary (or retrograde) character was regarded as forming part of the history to be recorded, but only that which was *progressive*," and that "the thirty-seven years were not only stationary in their character,—years of detention, and therefore without a history,—but they were also years of dispersion " ('Hist. of Old Covenant,' Vol. III. p. 309). The true solution rather lies, we apprehend, in the direction of the thought hinted at by Gerlach, that "it is the manner of sacred history to relate only the events of most weight and consequence in the progress of the kingdom of God," or, as we should prefer to state it, to record events only in so far as they have a bearing on the kingdom of God, "and so it passes over in silence the long time which was spent in the wilderness by the generation destined to die there " ('Commentary on Numbers,' ch. xx.). So to speak, at Kadesh, in consequence of the people's unbelief and condemnation, the continuity of God's kingdom in Israel was interrupted, and was not again resumed till the old race, having perished for their sins, was supplanted by a new; and this view would seem to be countenanced by the remarkable coincidence, that almost immediately after the reassembling of the tribes at Kadesh, Miriam, probably the sole survivor of the doomed race, dies, and that soon after steps are taken, by the removal of

Aaron and the transference of his official garments to Eleazar his son, to complete
the renovation of the congregation by giving them a new high priest in room of
one who was rather a representative of the congregation that had disappeared.
Hence, if this be the proper light in which to regard the relation subsisting between
the old congregation and the new, it will supply an answer to the query why Moses
did not write the story of these years of wandering—which was simply because
the people were during that long interval no longer, *quâ* people, the congregation
of the Lord, though of course as individuals many of them may have found
salvation ; it will afford an explanation of why the rebellion of Korah and his
associates was inserted in the narrative—which was not simply to fill an otherwise
inconvenient gap, or because of its appallingly tragic character, but because Aaron,
having not yet been placed under the ban of exclusion from Canaan, though the
people were, might be said to belong to and represent God's kingdom on earth, so
that an invasion of his high priestly functions by unauthorised persons like Korah
and his companions had still a bearing on the history of the theocratic kingdom,
though the ordinary annals of the dying people had none ; and it will reply to
Kurtz's difficulty, that "the history does not break off immediately after the
rejection, but embraces several events, as well as several groups of laws, which
belong to the period subsequent to the rejection"—the events being of the character
just described, and the laws being either for the priests or the people *when they had
come into the land of their habitations*, i. e. for the new theocratic congregation.
Thus the thirty years' chasm does not invalidate, but rather marvellously authenticate, the history in which it occurs. It may be added that if the writing had
been, as Bohlen styles it, " a popular inventive legend," it is scarcely likely, if we
may judge from the apocryphal Gospels, that the writer would have left any gap
which the spirit of romance could have filled.

III. THE FORTIETH YEAR. The number and importance of the transactions
assigned to the brief interval of six months between Aaron's death, on " the first
day of the fifth month " of the fortieth year of the wanderings (ch. xxxiii. 38),
and the commencement of Moses' address, on the first day of the eleventh month
(Deut. i. 3), render it impossible, according to Kuenen ('The Religion of Israel,'
Vol. I. ch. ii. p. 131) and Colenso ('On the Pentateuch,' Part I. ch. xxii. pp. 144—
146), to maintain the historic credibility of at least this portion of the narrative.
But it is pertinent to observe in reply, (1) that it is not perfectly certain that all
the incidents reported in chs. xxi.—xxxvi. took place in the comparatively short
space referred to. The Aradite War, *e. g.*, though succeeding in the history the
account of Aaron's death at Mount Hor (ch. xxi. 1—3), is by competent expositors
(Kurtz, Keil, Lange, Gerlach, 'Speaker's Commentary'), and with much probability,
believed to have occurred before that event, at the commencement of the march
from Kadesh, or while the ambassadors were negotiating with the king of Edom
for a passage through his dominions ; and there is nothing in the narrative that
absolutely enjoins us to hold that every single transaction of which these chapters
speak was finished, and every word which they record uttered, before Moses began
his exhortation on the first day of the eleventh month (cf. ch. xxvii. 12 — 14
with Deut. xxxii. 48, and ch. xxxv. 9—34 with Deut. iv. 41). But even if it
were required to compress them all within the space of half a year, it might be
remarked, (2) that many of those occurrences for which successive periods are
somewhat arbitrarily demanded may easily enough have happened contemporaneously. For instance, the struggle with the king of Bashan, though, according to
Deut. iii. 4, 5, not at all a trifling skirmish, but a serious engagement which

resulted in the capture of "threescore cities fenced with high walls, gates, and bars, beside unwalled towns a great many," and which, according to Colenso, must have occupied at least a month, might well have been undertaken and concluded during the absence of the king of Moab's messengers, whose double journey to the Babylonian town of Pethor, on the great river Euphrates, a distance of 350 miles, which began after the slaughter of the Amorites, and before the attack on the Bashanite monarch (ch. xxii. 2), could scarcely have been completed in less than six weeks; and since the expedition against Midian in which Balaam lost his life did not employ more than 12,000 men (ch. xxxi. 3, 4), it will be difficult to show why many of the transactions reported as having taken place before the end of the tenth month may not have occurred during the progress of that event. Yet, if even this hypothesis be discarded, and it be deemed imperative that all the several incidents comprised in the history should find a place in distinct chronological succession within the limits of the six months specified, it still is competent to maintain, (3) that until we can determine precisely the rapidity with which events moved in the closing months of Israel's pilgrimage, it will be impossible to assert with anything like dogmatic certitude that a young and vigorous people, trained in the wilderness, inspired by a great national hope, and led, as it were, by God himself, would not have been able to carry them through in the time appointed.

b. So-called Statistical Errors.

I. The number of the fighting men. It appears from the record that on three several occasions,—in the third month of the first year after the exodus for the purpose of raising a poll tax (Exod. xxx. 11 sqq. ; cf. xxxvii. 25, 26), in the second month of the second year for the organisation of an army (ch. i. 3), and in the fortieth year, in the steppes of Moab, with a view to the prospective division of Canaan among the tribes (ch. xxvi. 4),—in accordance with Divine instructions, a formal registration of the male heads of the people from twenty years old and upward was effected, the result being that in each case the numbers were practically the same—603,550, 603,550, and 601,730 ; the Levites, who were reckoned separately, numbering 22,000 in the second census, and 23,000 in the third. In the correspondence between the third summation and the second, although not a single individual survived in the third that was numbered in the second except Caleb and Joshua, and although the tribe of Levi showed an increase of 300, it is unnecessary, with Bohlen, to detect an exemplification of the "inventive process," since it is almost certain that a fictitious writer would have either equated the two numbers precisely, or rendered the divergence between them more striking, and since it was clearly not impossible, considering the special mortality that is represented as having overtaken the old nation during the years of penal wandering, that the deaths should have been as many as the births, while, if we have regard to the Divine purpose of supplanting the adult congregation of unbelievers with a fresh population of desert-born warriors, inured to hardship and trained to confidence in God, there will appear a special fitness in arranging that the regenerated nation, in resuming, as it were, the interrupted thread of its history, should be of exactly the dimensions, or nearly so, of the community which had perished. The historic accuracy of the two lists, besides, receives authentication from the circumstance that, while the totals of both so nearly approximate, the difference being only 1820, considerable variations exist in the numbers of the individual tribes, as appears from the appended table, and that these can in no small degree be accounted for.

				At Sinai.				In the plains of Moab.
Reuben	...	...	...	46,500	...	...	...	43,730
Simeon	...	...	...	59,300	...	...	...	22,200
Gad	...	...	...	45,650	...	...	...	40,500
Judah	...	...	...	74,600	...	...	...	76,500
Issachar	...	...	...	54,400	...	...	...	64,300
Zebulun	...	...	...	57,400	...	...	...	60,500
Ephraim	...	...	...	40,500	...	...	...	32,500
Manasseh	...	...	...	32,200	...	...	...	52,700
Benjamin	...	...	...	35,400	...	...	...	45,600
Dan	...	...	...	62,700	...	...	...	64,400
Asher	...	...	...	41,500	...	...	...	53,400
Naphtali	...	...	...	53,400	...	...	...	45,400
Total				603,550				601,730

Thus Judah shows an increase in the second computation of 1900, which was amply sufficient to enable him to retain the precedence of his brethren, in accordance with the prophetic benediction pronounced upon him by his venerable ancestor (Gen. xlix. 8—12). The increase of Issachar was 9900, of Zebulun 3100, of Manasseh 20,900, of Benjamin 10,200, of Dan 1700, and of Asher 11,900; but not even the largest of these indicates a proportion which can be said to be absolutely unparalleled; and, considering the highly favourable circumstances under which the new race grew up in comparison with the enervating bondage of Egypt, it can hardly be required to show that it was by no means impossible. The principal difficulty attaching to the census lists is not to account for the increase of certain tribes, but satisfactorily to explain the decrease in others. Thus the diminution of Reuben amounted to 2770, and it is commonly supposed that its cause must be sought in the destruction of the Korahite company, Dathan and Abiram being distinguished members of this particular tribe (ch. xxvi. 9, 10). The extraordinary fall of 37,100 which Simeon exhibited has with much probability been ascribed to the plague which had recently cut off 24,000 persons, most of whom, it has been conjectured, were Simeonites—Zimri, whose wickedness "in the matter of Cozbi, the daughter of a prince of Midian," provoked the *jus zelotarum* of Phinehas, having been "a prince of a chief house among the Simeonites" (ch. xxv. 14). Then the remarkable paucity of numbers in the tribe of Levi, in the one census 22,000, and in the other 23,000, has been explained by considering "that this tribe sustained two heavy strokes," it being expressly mentioned that the sons of Aaron, Nadab and Abihu, died childless (ch. iii. 4), and "the stress put upon the fact that the children of Korah were not destroyed with their father" (ch. xxvi. 11) pointing directly "to the implied antithesis that after all many Levites did perish in the conspiracy of Korah" (Lange 'on Numbers,' p. 11); while if the rate of increase, 1000 persons, or less than five per cent., was small when compared with that of the other tribes, it has been shown that "in the interval between Moses and David their rate of increase was still below that of other tribes" (Keil 'on Numbers,' p. 9), so that the peculiarity here adverted to was at least not exceptional in the history of Levi. Thus the difficulties connected with the second and the third enumerations of the people may be regarded as completely vanishing on a little close examination; and the same will suffice to dispose of the objection that the numbers in the first and second censuses should have been exactly the same, which, it is alleged, could hardly have been the case, even in round numbers, considering that an interval of nine months had elapsed between them (Colenso ' on the Pent.,' Vol. I. ch. vii. p. 42). But without insisting on the fact that stationary communities, in respect of population, are by no means unknown in modern times, it may be legitimately urged either, (1) with Michaelis, Kurtz, and others, that there was no actual numbering at all on the occasion of the lifting of the poll tax, but that the real census was taken on making up the muster roll, the number yielded by it being employed without hesitation to indicate the amount raised by the tax, in consequence of the variation in the sum total being but trifling; or, (2) with Gerlach, Keil, 'Speaker's Commentary,' &c., that the second registration was not a fresh census in the strict sense of the term, but simply a classification of the results of the preceding enumeration by thousands, hundreds, and tens, in accordance with Jethro's suggestion; or, (3) with Lange, that the two censuses were really one, which, beginning with the view of lifting a tax and ending with the construction of an army, extended, like the census of David at a later period (2 Sam. xxiv. 8), over the entire space of nine months or a year.

II. THE NUMBER OF THE CONGREGATION. Accepting then what seems to be indisputable, that the census of the adult males reached the round sum of 600,000, and estimating the proportion of those adult males or persons in the prime of life and capable of bearing arms, to the rest of the population, in accordance with the somewhat precarious standard of modern statistics, as that of one to four or five, it may be safely concluded that the entire body of the people, or " the whole congregation," numbered between two and three millions. But neologic criticism professes itself at a loss to understand how in the course of 215 years the seventy souls that came into Egypt (Gen. xlvi. 26, 27; Deut. x. 22) could have developed into so formidable a community; how in the Arabian peninsula, which at the present moment is a scene of barrenness and desolation, scarcely capable of sustaining a population of over 5000, so vast a multitude could have subsisted for a period of forty years, and how, if the Israelites had been so large a nation in the Mosaic age, they should either have been so long in conquering the land of Canaan as the Books of Joshua, Judges, and 1 Samuel represent them to have been, or have found it possible to live alongside of the Canaanites within so limited a territory.

1. Colenso ('Pent.,' Vol. I. ch. xvii.), following Bohlen, declares the increase of seventy souls into two and a half millions in the space of 215 years, the interval between the descent into Egypt and the exodus from Egypt, to be open to serious difficulties, if not impossible (cf. Kuenen, 'The Religion of Israel,' Vol. I. ch. ii. p. 163); and it may be frankly conceded that if his principles of computation are correct, his conclusion cannot possibly be set aside. If in the 215 years there were only four descents, if the rate of increase was no greater in Egypt than it had been previously, i. e. four or five sons to a family, and if none but pure Israelites were recognised as forming part of the congregation, then it need not surprise one to learn that, "instead of 600,000 warriors in the prime of life, there could not have been 5000," that "if the numbers of all the males in the four generations be added together (which supposes that they were all living at the time of the exodus), they would only amount to 6311," and that, even with the addition of the children of the fifth generation, " the sum total of males of all generations could not, according to these data, have exceeded 28,465, instead of being 1,000,000." But none of the above assumptions can be regarded as established certainties. The first indeed appears to receive support from Exod. vi. 16, 18, 20, which seems to style Moses the great-grandson of Levi. But as Levi was at least forty years of age at the descent into Egypt, and had three sons before that event, we may reckon that

Kohath was born in his father's thirty-eighth year, and was accordingly two years of age when he was deported from the land of Canaan. But Kohath in turn married, say at thirty years of age, and had a son named Amram, who is represented as having begotten Moses, say at the age of forty. Adding twenty-eight (30—2) and forty and eighty as the age of Moses at the exodus, we can only make 148 years instead of 215, showing that between Levi and Moses there were more descents than four, and that the Amram of ver. 20, who was Moses' father, was not the son of Kohath spoken of in ver. 18, but a remote descendant of that individual. The accuracy of this calculation is further strikingly confirmed by a reference to the number of the Kohathites in the time of Moses, of whom the fourth part, or 2150 (men and boys), were Amramites (ch. iii. 27, 28); from which it follows, since Moses had only two sons, that he must have been possessed of brothers and nephews to the number of 2147, which is simply inconceivable (cf. Keil ' on Ex.,' vi. 27 ; Kurtz, ' Hist. of O. C.,' Vol. II. p. 144). Hence, instead of four descents for the increase of Israel, we may reasonably reckon seven, and in some instances, like that of Joshua, eight or nine (1 Chron. vii. 20—27); and this, without demanding any higher rate of increase than attended Jacob's sons in the first generation, would abundantly satisfy all the requirements of the case. Of the seventy souls who went down into Egypt, assuming that only Jacob's grandsons, fifty-one in number, were capable of further out-population, and that each of these had only four sons (Colenso allows four and a half), their increase may be thus represented :—

At the end of 1st 30 years			...	...	...	204	males.
,,	,,	2nd ,, ,,	...	...	...	816	,,
,,	,,	3rd ,, ,,	...	...	...	3,264	,,
,,	,,	4th ,, ,,	...	...	...	13,056	,,
,,	,,	5th ,, ,,	...	...	...	52,224	,,
,,	,,	6th ,, ,,	...	...	...	208,896	,,
,,	,,	7th ,, ,,	...	...	...	835,584	,,

That is, the 208,896 fathers of the sixth descent had at the close of the next thirty years, or immediately before the exodus, 835,584 sons, to whom if we add 64,416 surviving fathers and grandfathers we shall bring the total up to 900,000 males, the number requisite, according to Colenso, to give 600,000 fighting men above twenty years of age. It is true that in this calculation we have excluded the operation of the law of mortality among families, but then to counterbalance this we might warrantably have claimed a higher rate of increase than that adopted, since it is certain God had promised that the blessing of fruitfulness should attend Jacob's descendants in Egypt, and since we know that Pharaoh must have observed something unusual in the rapid multiplication of the Hebrews to cause him to promulgate his truculent decree. Thus, without resorting to the (somewhat doubtful) hypothesis of Kurtz (' Hist. of O. C.,' Vol. II. p. 149), that Jacob and his sons were accompanied into Egypt by men-servants and maid-servants, whose offspring were included in the family of Israel, there need be no difficulty in believing that the entire congregation of Israelites proper numbered between two and three million souls.

2. Nor was it likely that the question of finding sustenance for themselves and for their flocks and herds occasioned them as much anxiety as it has since done to rationalistic critics. Colenso, again following in the wake of Knobel and Bohlen, has declared it an absolute impossibility that such a mass of human beings with their cattle could obtain support for such a length of time as forty years from the

scanty vegetation of the desert. But (1) the story does not represent the Israelites as having been maintained exclusively by the natural produce of the wilderness, but, on the contrary, expressly claims that they enjoyed for themselves (and we may rest assured also for their cattle, if such was necessary) a miraculous supply both of meat and of drink; and (2) there is good reason for believing that the Arabian peninsula was considerably more fertile than it is to-day, that, in fact, there were resources in the country of which they might have availed themselves in cases where no special miraculous provision was granted; while (3) there are indications in the narrative itself that the flocks and herds were scattered far and wide during the sojourn in the desert, and so were able the more easily to obtain pasture. The first of these considerations may be disregarded by rationalising critics, but, unless a disbelief in the miraculous is to be postulated as a preliminary to historical research, intelligent and unprejudiced Bible students will find it impossible to ignore the circumstance that the entire narrative belongs to the region of the supernatural, that the writer explicitly asserts the intervention of causes which were supramundane in effecting Israel's guidance through the great and terrible wilderness, and that, as the Hebrew Psalmist expresses it, "man did eat angel's food." At the same time, while observing that the desert pilgrims were at special times and places provided with miraculous supplies, they will hardly fail to notice that nowhere does the narrative affirm that these were their sole support, or convey the impression that the region through which they passed was an immense plain of sand, or a bleak and sterile tract of bare and calcined rock. The passage adduced by Colenso to prove that the inhospitable desert was incapable of affording sustenance to the two millions of Israelites who passed through it, with their two millions of sheep and oxen, rather makes for the opposite contention (ch. xx. 2), since it relates to the beginning of the fortieth year, thereby showing that during all the previous thirty-nine years at least neither the people nor the animals had perished, and since it applies not to the whole extent of the Arabian peninsula, but to the most barren and desolate region of it, styled "the desert of Sin," now called the Wady-el-Arabah, situated between the land of Edom and the wilderness of Paran. And indeed a sufficient refutation of the sweeping statements of Knobel, Bohlen, Colenso, Kuenen, and others may be found in the fact, which is incontrovertible, that at the very period when the Israelites passed through it, it was the seat of several numerous and powerful nomadic tribes, like the Amalekites, with whom they warred at Rephidim, the Midianites, whom they encountered at Shittim, and the Kenites, who inhabited some parts of the same wilderness, "having their nest in the rock." Then there are grounds for believing that the scene of Israel's wanderings is not precisely the same to-day as it then was. "There is no doubt that the vegetation of the wâdys has considerably decreased. . . . If this be so, the greater abundance of vegetation would, as is well known, have furnished a greater abundance of water, and this again would react on the vegetation, from which the means of subsistence would be procured" (Stanley's 'Sinai and Palestine,' pp. 24, 25). Carl Ritter also thus sums up the circumstances which appear to him to warrant the inference that the Sinaitic peninsula was capable of providing sustenance for a more numerous population than it is presently able to maintain:—"There was, it is evident, in former times, a growth both of the larger sorts of trees and of smaller shrubs, of which we have no remnant; there was also a large number of plants which might contribute in part to the sustenance of Israel during the journey; there was a universally distributed agriculture, as we learn from the existence of mines, and from the oldest Egyptian habitations, as well as from the Christian monuments which are everywhere found—cloisters, hermitages, walls, gardens, and fountains; and, lastly, there is an evident possibility that there was a much greater supply of water in the wâdys, more abundant rain-storms, and the possibility of economising the supplies thus gained by a use of the same appliances which were common elsewhere in countries similarly situated and conditioned" ('Geography of Palestine,' Vol. I. p. 380. Clark's 'For. Theol. Lib.'). And of course the ability of the Israelites to procure support for themselves and their flocks would be largely increased if it was not imperative, as is often arbitrarily asserted, that they should keep constantly together, but if, on the contrary, it was permissible to disperse themselves abroad among the more fertile localities. Nor need this have been impossible though considerable bodies of armed men should have been required to guard them from the attacks of hostile tribes, since the entire army was 600,000 strong, and could easily have spared a few detachments for such a purpose had that been necessary. Of this, however, there is no evidence; and if Moses fed the flocks of Jethro in the Sinaitic desert for forty years without the presence of a military guard, it does not seem unreasonable to conclude that Moses' countrymen, especially when assisted by the mixed multitude (עֶרֶב, *plebs promiscua*, ἐπίμιξτος λαός, a swarm of foreigners, though by a slight change in the punctuation it might be made to mean inhabitants of the desert, or wandering Arabs or Bedaween, who had joined themselves to Israel on the eve of the exodus), might be competent in the same region and for the same number of years to feed their own. But without enlarging further on this controverted problem, it may be satisfactory to note that the general accuracy of the views here propounded is recognised by Ewald, who thus writes:—"We cannot, therefore, fail to see that then the peninsula must have supported a far more numerous population than now; in a condition of great privation and trial certainly, of which indeed in all the traditions there is frequent complaint, but still so that a frugal and laborious people would not absolutely perish if only they made the trials themselves the sources of warning and strength. From the present number of the inhabitants of a country which has, moreover, been utterly neglected by the human hand, no certain conclusion respecting its earlier state can be drawn; and that peninsula is not the only country from whose present scanty population we should never have guessed the former density of human life. . . . . This only we can perceive, although the country has not yet been thoroughly explored in all directions by intelligent Europeans, that it is by no means one vast sandy plain, . . . but shows clear indications of having been formerly much more extensively cultivated. Moreover, we cannot exactly know how far the various tribes may have straggled out from Kadesh to procure subsistence; for it is clear that Kadesh was only the resting-place of Moses and the tabernacle, and the meeting-place of the community on appointed days ('History of Israel,' Vol. II. p. 197).

3. The third difficulty in connection with the size of the congregation may be disposed of in a few sentences. That 600,000 soldiers should not have found the conquest of Canaan so hard a matter as the Biblical narrative represents might seem an obvious conclusion, were it not that it rests upon two unwarrantable assumptions: (1) that the Canaanites were neither numerous nor powerful, whereas they were both, having thirty-one kings, and possessing mamy towns (Josh. xii. 7—24); and (2) that the warfare in which Israel engaged was one in which victory was determined by purely military considerations, whereas the siege of Jericho (*ibid.* vi. 2) and the defeat at Ai (*ibid.* vii. 4) were witnesses to the contrary. But, in truth, the ease or difficulty of the conquest of Canaan is largely a matter of opinion, and it is at least in this connection interesting to note

that Kuenen objects to the historic credibility of the conquest on the ground that it was much too easily accomplished ('The Religion of Israel,' Vol. I. ch. ii. p. 131). As to the possibility of finding room in Canaan for two millions more of people than it had previously contained, it is sufficient to reply, (1) that in order to make room for them a pretty considerable removal of the earlier inhabitants was effected by means of the sword, and (2) that it is doubtful if the remaining Canaanitish population, though increased by the influx of three millions of Israelites, would be as large as the five millions of inhabitants that were contained in Palestine in the flourishing period of the Israelitish kingdom.

III. THE NUMBER OF THE FIRST-BORN. Rationalising critics appear to be unanimous in pitching upon this as an insuperable obstacle to the historical validity of the Mosaic narrative. It will accordingly be desirable to state the difficulty in their own words. "According to ch. i. 46 and ii. 32, the number of all the male Israelites from twenty years old and upwards was, without the Levites, 603,550. If, however, the number of the first-born of the male sex, reckoned from one month old and upwards, amounted only to a little over 22,000 (according to ch. iii.), the number of them from twenty years old and upward could only be reckoned at from about 11,000 to 14,000, and in that the first-born of the Levites would also be comprehended, so that from the rest of the tribes they would only amount to from about 10,000 to 13,000. According to this the proportion of the first-born males to the whole of the male Israelites would only be as one to forty-five. But this is a proportion that we cannot well think could have really existed" (Bleek, 'Introd. to Pent.,' Vol. I. p. 315). "At one time the number of men able to bear arms above twenty years of age is said to amount to 603,550, exclusive of the Levites ; soon afterwards, however, the number of the first-born males is set down at 22,273. A comparison of these two statements is sufficient to show the fictitious character of the whole census ; for from it we may deduce that every mother, taking one with another, must have brought into the world no less than forty-two male children ; or, in other words, that only one first-born child is to be allowed for every forty-two males" (Bohlen, 'Introd. to Pent.,' p. 113). The problem is stated in substantially equivalent terms by Vater 'on Numb. iii. 39,' Colenso 'on the Pent.,' Part I. ch. xiv., Kuenen in 'The Religion of Israel,' Vol. I. ch. ii. p. 172, and others ; and as thus presented it has met with various replies. 1. Michaelis has endeavoured to resolve it by supposing that polygamy extensively prevailed among the Israelites, and that only the first-born of the fathers were counted ('Laws of Moses,' ii. § 94) ; but, as Keil properly observes, "polygamy never prevailed among the Israelites or any other people with anything like the universality which this would suppose," and, besides, the expression "פֶּטֶר רֶחֶם" (ch. iii. 12) distinctly points to the first-born on the mother's side, in which case, as Kurtz remarks, "the existence of polygamy would only serve to render the difficulty perfectly colossal." 2. Hävernick has so far modified the above opinion as to hold that the first-born on the sides of both parents were alone reckoned, but this is a purely arbitrary assumption, and tends rather to increase than remove the perplexity. 3. Baumgarten has suggested that only the first-born under six years of age were numbered, adducing in support of this view that all above that age had been redeemed by partaking of the passover in Egypt, but such a sentiment has no foundation in anything contained in Scripture. 4. Kurtz has advanced a number of considerations which in his judgment afford an adequate explanation of the otherwise inexplicable fact :— (1) the rarity of polygamy, which lessened the proportion of the first-born ; but, on Kurtz's own theory that ch. iii. 12 points to the mother's first-born, the rarity or prevalence of polygamy has properly speaking no bearing whatever on the question; (2) the fruitfulness of Hebrew mothers, to which unquestionably some degree of weight must be attached; and (3) the exclusion of first-born sons who were not also the first-born of their mothers, or who were themselves heads of families, which, though controverted by Colenso, appears to be a step in the right direction. Every one, however, of the above solutions proceeds upon the assumption that the law relating to the sanctification of the first-born was intended to have a retrospective force, but exactly in the denial of this *ex post facto* operation of the Divine enactment lies the true solution of this *quæstio vexata*, which is given by— 5. Keil, after Vitringa, viz., that only the first-born were counted who had come into the world since the night of the exodus when the law was promulgated (Exod. xiii. 2), *i. e.* thirteen months before, so that, as has been aptly remarked, the real difficulty is not that the first-born were so few, but that they were so many; and yet the peculiar situation of Israel during those thirteen months abundantly provides the required explanation. "When the Israelites were groaning under the hard lash of the Egyptian task-masters, and then under the inhuman and cruel edict of Pharaoh, which commanded all the Hebrew boys to be put to death, the number of marriages no doubt diminished from year to year; but with the emancipation and the revival of the nation's hopes "there might very well," says Keil, "have been about 36,000 marriages contracted in a year, say from the time of the seventh plague, three months before the exodus, and about 37,600 children born by the second month of the second year after the exodus, 22,273 of them being boys."

c. Alleged Physical Impossibilities.

I. The duties of the priests. "The Book of Leviticus is chiefly occupied in giving directions to the priests for the proper discharge of the different duties of their office, and further directions are given in the Book of Numbers;" "and now let us ask, for all these multifarious duties, during the forty years' sojourn in the wilderness, ... how many priests were there? The answer is very simple. There were only three, Aaron (till his death) and his two sons, Eleazar and Ithamar. . . . Yet how was it possible that these two or three men should have discharged all these duties for such a vast multitude?" ('Colenso on the Pent.,' Part I. ch. xx.) The reply, like the objection, is very simple. 1. The Levitical laws, though given in the desert, were not designed to come into full operation there. This was obviously the case with the important legislation delivered during the period of penal wandering (ch. xv. 2). The terms also in which the passover was instituted bear that it was meant for Canaan (Exod. xiii. 5). At the time of the erection of the tabernacle it was contemplated that a few months would see them in the land of their inheritance. Hence there is no sound reason for supposing that the multifarious duties recorded in the Books of Leviticus and Numbers (at that time not composed) were performed by the priests. 2. In point of fact the Levitical laws were not observed in the wilderness in all their completeness. As much as this is testified by Moses in Deut. xii. 8. But, it is alleged, with reference to the second passover, it is absolutely certain that no part of the original ceremony was omitted. The phrase, "according to all the rites of it, and according to all the ceremonies thereof, shall ye keep it," precludes the idea of any departure from the statutory regulations; and how could three priests, it is asked, slaughter 150,000 lambs according to Colenso, 100,000 according to Kurtz, or even 50,000 according to Keil, and sprinkle their blood upon the altar in the short space of time allotted for that work? Keil thinks it might have been done, quoting an instance from Josephus ('Wars,' VI. ix. 3) in which the blood of 256,500 paschal lambs was sprinkled upon the altar in the time of the Emperor Nero; but since this second passover was entirely exceptional, and was not directly contemplated in the enactments which had been made in view of the people's settlement in Canaan, and since the statute forbidding the killing of the paschal lambs at any other place than the tabernacle (Deut. xvi. 2) had not yet been published, nay, since the terms of this statute appear rather to imply that up to the time of its publication, the fortieth year, they had been in the habit of slaughtering them elsewhere, it would seem as if the inference of Kurtz were correct—that the lambs were killed by the heads of families themselves, and the blood sprinkled on the door-posts; that, in short, the second year's passover was observed not upon the model of the future celebrations in Palestine, but upon that of the past celebration in Egypt; so that, even with regard to this, no undue exaction of strength would be required from Aaron and his sons. But even should we hold that the Levitical system was in operation in the wilderness with anything approaching to completeness, it must be borne in mind (3) that the Levites had been assigned to the priests for assistants in matters relating to the tabernacle, and that they were not strangers forbidden to come nigh on pain of death, as Colenso alleges, on the strength of ch. iii. 10, 38, but, as ch. i. 51 shows, persons who by their very office were under obligation to minister unto the tabernacle (ch. i. 47).

II. THE ASSEMBLING OF THE CONGREGATION. The objection here alluded to only needs to be stated to discover its absurdity. Interpreting the narrative with the severest, and let it be also said the *simplest*, literality, it supposes that two millions and a half of people were required to assemble at the door of the tabernacle, which according to exact arithmetical calculation was eighteen feet wide, which would allow nine full-grown men to stand in front of it, which, with eighteen inches between each rank, would necessitate a line of nearly twenty miles to bring all the adult males precisely in front of it, and a line of sixty miles if the old men, women, and children were included! "It is surely inconceivable," writes Colenso, "that such an enormous congregation should have been summoned expressly by Jehovah to attend for the purpose of witnessing a ceremony taking place in a tent eighteen paces long and six wide, which could only have been seen by a few standing at the door" ('On the Pent.,' Part I. ch. iv.). To this it might be amply sufficient to reply that there is one thing even more inconceivable, viz., that a person of intelligence could have proposed such a difficulty; but for further satisfaction it may be added that the expressions, "the whole assembly" (Exod. xii. 6; Numb. x. 3, 4), and "all the congregation" (ch. xvi. 19, 25), do not necessarily signify every individual member of the community, but, in perfect consistency with historical accuracy, may mean a portion, representative or otherwise, of the whole. The foolishness of insisting in every instance on the universal sense of the terms "all" and "whole" is recognised by Colenso himself, who, writing of ch. x. 3, 4, admits that "no one would suppose that *every individual* would be able to attend such a summons (to the tabernacle door), or would be expected to do so," and who accordingly limits the expressions, "all the congregation," and "the whole assembly," first to *the adult males in the prime of life*, and eventually to "the great body of the 603,550 warriors," *i. e.*, we presume, the major part of them. But if "all" may import something less than the whole, it will be difficult to adduce a cogent argument to show that the "all" may not sometimes be represented by a part. And indeed in the Book of Numbers itself there are not wanting hints of the representative character of the great congregational assembly, as when, in ch. i. 16, the princes of the tribes are designated " the renowned of the congregation," literally, the called men of the congregation, " because," adds Keil, " they were called to diets of the congregation, as representatives of the tribes, to regulate the affairs of the nation," an interpretation concurred in by the best authorities (cf. ch. xvi. 2).

III. THE MARCHING OF THE HOST. In the estimation of some the observance by two and a half millions of people of the marching orders prescribed for their journeyings seems a harder problem than even their subsistence in the wilderness. According to ch. ii., as subsequently modified by ch. x. 14—28, the camp of Judah, consisting of 186,400 soldiers, led the van. These were followed by the Gershonites and Merarites, 13,700 strong, accompanied by the tabernacle furniture on waggons. Next came the camp of Reuben, numbering 151,450 men of war. Behind these the Kohathites, 8600, kept the charge of the sanctuary. These were succeeded by the camp of Ephraim, containing 108,100 adult males; while the camp of Dan, with 157,600 warriors, brought up the rear. In each case the soldiers were accompanied by their families, so that, counting women and children, each of the four camps may be roughly estimated at half a million. Now, since the narrative does not permit us to think of anything but an orderly march, we must imagine, it is said, these four main divisions of half a million each falling into line and moving off the ground, not simultaneously, but in prearranged succession, so that, as the first camp would require at least four or five hours for its necessary evolutions, the day would practically be at an end before the last company had begun to move; after which we must further contemplate this long line of two and a half millions travelling, say ten or a dozen miles, and at the close of the day's journey re-forming, no matter where they halted, into a camp of exactly the dimensions of that from which in the morning they had broken up—all which, even with the help of a little miracle in the way of warding off sickness and imparting unusual vigour and intelligence to the people and their leaders, it is alleged is scarcely within the limits of physical possibility. And unquestionably, as thus represented, it must have been a problem for the Israelites to understand how they were to get away from the spot, since, if sixteen hours were demanded for the work of falling into line, it is doubtful if they could have been expected to do more for the day than fall out again and return to their square formations. But the manifest absurdity of this suffices to show that such a representation must be wholly incorrect; and indeed any interpretation of the marching orders which professes to exhibit their impracticability will be found as difficult to harmonise with the modern theory of a late authorship as with that of a Mosaic origin, since it is simply incredible that any writer possessed of intelligence would have inserted in his manuscript what by the supposition is so palpably impossible. The essential fallacy in the hypothesis is that each division waited before commencing its movements until those of its predecessor were completed, that the camp of Reuben, e. g., remained perfectly stationary till the last line in Judah's company was started, nay, till the Gershonites and Merarites had taken up position in Judah's rear. But obviously all the four divisions might have simultaneously commenced their preparations, by falling into line as far as practicable on the ground; and the work of doing so, it must not be forgotten, would be largely facilitated by the principle adopted in their several encampments, the men being arranged " by their generations, after their families, by the house of their fathers, according to the number of their names," i. e. by hundreds and fifties and tens; so that, even granting four or five hours for the completion of the movements of Judah, it does not follow that more than three or four hours additional would be required for similarly completing the movements of the other three divisions. Meantime Judah has been travelling, let us suppose, four hours at the rate of two or two and a half miles an hour, so that, after a journey of ten miles, he is ready for encampment, which consumes, we may conjecture, not more than four hours. Thus the entire day of Judah was divided into three equal portions of four hours each, the first of which was spent in breaking up and forming into line, the second in travelling, and the third in re-camping. As we have supposed the last line to be four hours later than Judah in starting, they would likewise be four hours later in arriving. And though darkness must have set in before the last travellers were quartered for the night, it is not likely that that would greatly impede their progress or interfere with their comfort, since, according to the story, Jehovah went before them in a pillar of cloud by day, and a pillar of fire by night. Of course in the above calculations we do not pretend to show how the march actually was accomplished, but simply to demonstrate that assertions as to its impossibility are extremely rash, and not such as would be made by any modern general of intelligence and capacity. Besides, it should be noted that, though the ideal order and method of marching are depicted by the historian, it is not necessary to assume, what certainly the historian does not assert, that these were in every minute particular carried out on the first trial with the same faultless precision that might have been exhibited by a highly-disciplined modern army, or that they themselves would display at a later period when practice had made perfection. On the contrary, it may be reasonably supposed that, during the fortnight which intervened between the construction of the camp and the marching of the host, the various sections of the army, under their captains of hundreds and fifties and tens, would be subjected to a sort of preparatory drill in anticipation of the general advance, and that though, in consequence of the numerous hitches that might naturally be expected to occur in an initial experiment on so great a scale, the first day's marching would almost certainly prove a serious affair, occupying a great many hours, and leaving them only a few miles from Sinai; yet, as the days went by, and frequent repetition imparted facility to their movements, these imperfections would gradually disappear, and the actual method of marching more nearly approach the ideal. Then, if it further be borne in mind that the narrative does not affirm that the work of reconstructing the camp was undertaken every night, thus involving the tedious labour of deploying into line each successive morning, which would certainly have involved an unnecessary expenditure of time and energy that might have been otherwise profitably consumed in journeying, but that only then was the tabernacle set up when, as at Kibroth-Hattaavah, they had reached a station where the multitude could conveniently rest—when this circumstance in addition is remembered, it will be seen that, attended though it must have been with much painful labour, the marching of the host need not by any means have been an insuperable difficulty, and much less a physical impossibility.

IV. THE VICTORY OVER MIDIAN. While dwelling largely and with much impressiveness upon the immoral aspects of this remarkable campaign, Colenso, after Bohlen, is particularly scandalised at the idea of 12,000 Israelites slaying *all* the male Midianites, capturing *all* their females and children, including 32,000 virgins, seizing *all* their cattle and flocks (72,000 oxen, 61,000 asses, 675,000 sheep), and *all* their goods, and burning *all* their cities and *all* their goodly castles, without the loss of a single man! (ch. xxxi. 49; 'On the Pentateuch,' Vol. I. ch. xxii.). De Wette regards this particular statement as proof conclusive of the mythical character of the narrative; but Tacitus ('Annals,' xiii. 39) records an instance in which, at the capture of a Parthian castle, the Romans slaughtered all their foes without losing a single man, and Strabo (xvi. 1128) mentions a battle in which 1000 Arabs were slain by only two Romans (*vide* Rosenmüller on Numb. **xxxi.** 49), while Hävernick affirms that the life of Saladin contains almost in the same words a like statement respecting the issue of a battle ('Introd.,' p. 330). Hence the extraordinary preservation which Israel enjoyed on this occasion, though owing more to Divine interposition than to the operation of natural causes, such as the non-military character of the Midianites and the suddenness of the attack to which they were exposed, can scarcely be held, on any principles of sound reasoning, to afford colourable pretext for impeaching the correctness of the narrative.

ITS AUTHORSHIP.

The authorship of the Book of Numbers may be regarded as practically settled by the previous question of its historic credibility. If no valid argument can be adduced for impugning the veracity of its contents, the inference is irresistible that it can only have proceeded from the pen of Moses. Yet it is alleged that the Book of Numbers presents features which can only be explained by the modern theory of its being, like the rest of the Pentateuch, a late compilation.

1. The alternating use of the Divine names, which forms so prominent a characteristic of the Book of Genesis, and which largely disappears in the Books of Exodus and Leviticus, reasserts itself, it is maintained (De Wette, 'Kritik der Israelitischen Geschichte,' p. 362), in the Book of Numbers, in particular in the section relating to Balaam and his prophecies (chs. xxii.—xxiv.), in such a way as to suggest the idea of composite authorship. Without anticipating what may be advanced in the body of the work on this important subject, it may suffice in this place to notice that the peculiarity attaching to Balaam's use of the Divine names, no less than that belonging to the historian's employment of them, admits of a perfectly intelligible explanation on the theory of the Mosaic authorship. Whatever view we adopt as to the character of Balaam,—whether, with Philo, Josephus, Origen, Augustine, Lyra, À Lapide, and others, we regard him as having been "*prophetam non Dei, sed diaboli*," an Oriental wizard who claimed to possess the gift of prophecy, קוֹסֵם, the Old Testament counterpart of Simon Magus in the primitive apostolic Church, or accept the view of Tertullian, Jerome, Deyling, Buddæus, &c., that he was a true prophet of God who fell through covetousness,—and whatever opinion we may entertain as to the source of his religious information,—whether, with Tholuck and Lange, we discover that in the primeval monotheism which still lingered in Mesopotamia, or, with Hengstenberg, find it in the report of God's dealings with Israel, which even then had penetrated as far east as the Euphrates, or, with Kurtz, Keil, and the 'Speaker's Commentary,' seek for it in both,—it seems apparent that Balaam professed to be a worshipper of Jehovah (ch. xxii. 8, 18); in which, as Kurtz correctly observes, the king of Midian could not fail to discern peculiarly welcome intelligence, for "if he succeeded in inducing *him* to curse the Israelites, their power, he thought, would be effectually broken" ('Hist. of O. C.,' Vol. III. p. 387). Hence it was specially fitting that he should use the term Jehovah as he does, whether conversing in plain prose with the Moabitish messengers, or pouring forth predictions in elevated strains of poetry, even though it should have been the case, as Keil suggests, that the Jehovah whom Balaam worshipped was "only Elohim, *i. e.* only a Divine Being, but not the God of Israel." Nor does it look a hard problem

to explain why in ch. xxii. 38 he should have discarded the favourite term Jehovah for the more general expression Elohim, since it was not at that moment his desire to emphasise the fact that Jehovah had declined to extend him the needful sanction to undertake the solicited mission, which indeed he had already done (ch. xxii. 13), but to repudiate the insinuation of the king of Moab that he had hesitated to comply with the invitation addressed to him simply through fear of not receiving a sufficient recompense, by representing that he had really been hindered, not through personal reluctance, but by Divine restraint, in which case, as Hengstenberg remarks, " even a member of the chosen people would have used Elohim." Then the mode in which the historian employs the terms is as little suggestive of a diverse authorship, but is possessed of a significance as remarkable and specific, as that in which they were employed by Balaam. In the first place, when recording the interview between Balaam and the elders, although the *Kosem* says Jehovah, he writes Elohim (ch. xxii. 9, 10, 12, 20). And even if we cannot unreservedly adopt the view of Hengstenberg, that the historian's design was " to determine Balaam's personal relation to God in opposition to his hypocritical pretensions" ('Authenticity and Genuineness of the Pentateuch,' Vol. I. p. 388), or believe with Baur that the writer meant to intimate "that the heathen seer did not stand at first in any connection whatever with the true God of Israel " ('Geschichte der alttestl. Weissagung,' i. p. 344), or affirm with Keil that it serves as an indication that " Balaam's original attitude towards Jehovah was a very imperfect one " ('Commentary on Numbers,' ch. xxii. 1), we may hold it as a perfectly adequate explanation that as yet there was no necessity to take the slightest cognisance of Balaam's relation to Jehovah, assumed or otherwise, but simply to draw attention to the fact that the Divine interposition solicited by Balaam was granted. At the same time we regard the preponderance of argument as lying on the side of Hengstenberg's interpretation of a contrast which, as he justly observes, is too remarkable and occurs too often to have been purely accidental, while we cannot attach a large degree of importance to the objection of Keil that such a view " sets up a chasm between Elohim and Jehovah, with which the fact that, according to ch. xxii. 22, the wrath of Elohim on account of Balaam's journey was manifested in the appearance of the angel of Jehovah is irreconcilable," since it rather seems to bridge over any such imaginary chasm by showing that the Elohim who was angered was not different from the Maleach Jehovah who accorded permission, but was in reality one and the self-same Being. And now if we inquire why from this point onward Jehovah is so frequently employed by the writer, it will be difficult to discover a more satisfactory reason than that supplied by Hengstenberg, that he designed "to point out how Jehovah, the God of Israel, overruled the whole transaction for his people's welfare, and how Balaam, who otherwise had no intercourse with him, was obliged, in this extraordinary juncture, to serve him as an instrument."

2. The narrative contains repetitions and variations which, in the estimation of the higher criticism, suggest a remodelling of the original documents by subsequent editorship, and a working up of different, and sometimes contradictory, accounts into the same writing. Bleek specifies as an example the account of the spies in chs. xiii. and xiv., in which he assigns ch. xiii. 1—xiv. 4, 10—25, 39—45 to the fundamental or Elohist writing, and the remainder (ch. xiv. 5—10, 26—38) to the revisionary labours of the Jehovist, the ground of this apportionment of the text being that ch. xiv. 10—25 declares that " of all the Israelites who had been witnesses of Jehovah's wonders in Egypt and the wilderness, and had so often

tempted him, not one should behold the promised land except Caleb," while ch. xiv. 26—38 affirms "that except Caleb and Joshua, all those previously numbered from twenty years old and upwards should perish in the wilderness, and that their children only, after a forty years' journeying through the wilderness, should arrive at the land of Canaan," the first statement agreeing with ch. xiii. 30, where Caleb quiets the people who were agitated through the report of the spies, and the second with ch. xiv. 6, where Joshua and Caleb do this ('Introd. to Old Testament,' Vol. I. § 119). The 'Speaker's Commentary' agrees with this opinion so far as to regard it as "likely that a later and independent, but not inconsistent, account has been interwoven with the earlier one," only it seems unable to determine which account was the original narrative, and which the interpolation; in the Introduction to Numbers, §§ 4, 7, saying, "The passages introducing the name of Joshua would seem to be the inserted ones," and in the exposition of ch. xiv. 24 assigning this distinction to those in which the name of Caleb only is mentioned. But there does not appear to be any urgent necessity for adopting the theory of combined accounts, either in the exaggerated form of Bleek or in the modified form of the 'Speaker's Commentary.' "The fact that Caleb only is mentioned in ch. xiii. 30, though, according to ch. xiv. 6, Joshua also stood by his side, may be explained on the simple ground that at first Caleb was the only one to speak and maintain the possibility of conquering Canaan" (Keil). Another instance commonly adduced in support of the idea of commingled documents is found in chs. xvi. and xvii., in which, according to Stähelin, De Wette, Bleek, and others of the rationalising school of criticism, the story belonging to the earliest narrative of the insurrection of Korah with his 250 Levites against the priestly power of Moses and Aaron has been mixed up with another tradition relating to the sedition of certain Reubenite princes against the civil authority of the law-giver in particular, ch. xvi. 12—15, 2 —34 being additions of the supplementer. But the hypothesis that there were originally two distinct rebellions and that the accounts of these have been incorporated into one narrative, does not necessarily militate against the idea of the Mosaic authorship of the writing, since the original narrative may have been subsequently expanded by its first composer so as to include the two accounts in one. Indeed if we suppose, what is not at all unlikely to have been the case, that the spirit of mutiny was abroad in the congregation, there might easily have been more than one distinct centre of insubordination; and this hypothesis, that the Reubenite princes with their followers acted in confederation with the Levite Korah and his company (cf. Ewald, 'History of Israel,' Vol. II. p. 179), will be found to go far to explain the seeming dislocation of the narrative, in which a distinction appears to be kept up between the priestly and the princely rebels. Other specimens might be given of the so-called repetitions and contradictions that exist in Numbers, such as ch. xiii. 16 compared with ch. xi. 28, ch. xiv. 45 compared with ch. xxi. 3, and ch. xxi. 13 with ch. xxxiii. 45 ff.; but, besides admitting of easy refutation, none of them are of such importance as to call for extended notice.

3. Once more, in common with the other portions of the Pentateuch, the Book of Numbers is believed to exhibit traces of a later authorship than that of Moses, in such like passages, e. g., as ch. xv. 32—36, which appears to intimate that at the time of its composition the children of Israel were no longer in the wilderness; ch. xx. 5, which suggests that they were then in Canaan; ch. xxi. 14, 15, 17, 18, 27—30, in which the writer alludes to certain archaic songs with which his readers were familiar; ch. xxiv. 7, which could not have been penned before the days of

the monarchy; and ch. xxiv. 17, 18, which clearly belongs to the time of David, when Idumea was conquered by Israel. But as the most of these have been examined in the Essay on the Authorship of the Pentateuch already referred to (*vide* 'Genesis,' Pulpit Commentary), it will be the less needful to subject them at present to separate consideration. It may suffice to remark that though unquestionably when thus brought together they appear to have a cumulative force of great value, yet the exact amount of importance to be attached to them depends upon whether they individually will bear the light of candid and impartial investigation, for if when separately taken they break down on examination, the nett result of even an infinite series of such examples will be *nil*, and it may with confidence be affirmed, as Keil and Hengstenberg have abundantly shown, that every one of the above so-called difficulties is capable of easy solution. Besides, to borrow an arrow from the quiver of an opponent, "he who relies upon the impression made by the whole, without interrogating the parts one by one, repudiates the first principles of all scientific research, and pays homage to superficiality" (Kuenen. 'The Religion of Israel,' vol. i. p. 11).

But now, on the other hand, the Book of Numbers possesses characteristics which point as unmistakably in the direction of a Mosaic authorship as the foregoing peculiarities are believed to speak in favour of a later origin.

1. The Book of Numbers contains several sections which in their existing shapes were either written by the hand of Moses or belong to the Mosaic age. Of these passages the following is the list prepared by Bleek ('Introduction to Old Testament,' Vol. I. § 118):—chs. i., ii., iii., iv.; vi. 22—27; x. 1—10; xix.; xxi. 14, 15, 17, 18, 27, 30; xxxiii. 1—49; with which in the main Ewald agrees, adding ch. x. 35, 36; xx. 14—22, as fragments "of the earliest accounts of the Mosaic times," at the same time guarding himself, with reference both to ch. xx. 14—22 and ch. xxxiii., by declining positively to affirm "that these catalogues were kept during the journey, or written down at once during its last year," though he admits that at a much later period they could not have been attempted ('History of Israel,' Vol. II. pp. 24, 26). *a*. The list of camping stations indeed distinctly claims to have been written by Moses (ch. xxxiii. 2), and though Bohlen ('Introduction to Genesis,' Vol. I. p. 88) professes to be able to detect in it everywhere traces of fiction, he may be said to stand alone in the possession of so remarkable a power of vision. The almost unanimous verdict of critical inquirers assigns this ancient catalogue of desert stations to Mosaic times for the simple reason that such a long series of names could not possibly have been retained in the memory for any lengthened period, and regards it as perfectly authentic because, as Ewald acknowledges, on examination it appears to be correct. *β*. With regard to the songs contained in ch. xxi., "it is so absolutely against all probability that they should be the production of a later age," writes Bleek, "that it has been acknowledged by De Wette that they are certainly derived from the Mosaic age;" and, again, "if we find here songs which bear indications of belonging to the Mosaic age, which, however, do not contain any reference at all to the circumstances of a later time, but are, on the contrary, full of features of individuality which are not otherwise intelligible, and are without meaning except in reference to circumstances in the time of Moses, it becomes highly probable that they were not only composed in the Mosaic age, but that they were then written down, and have come down to us from thence" ('Introduction to Old Testament,' Vol. I. § 79). *γ*. The legislation of ch. xix. bears upon the face of it that it was meant for a time when the people dwelt in camps

and tents (cf. vers. 3, 7, 9, 14), and could scarcely have been composed at a later period, when the circumstances of the people were so entirely altered as to render directions about camps and tents quite inapplicable. *δ.* Similarly, the ordinance relating to the silver trumpets (ch. x. 1—10), and the instructions bearing on the census and the arrangement of the camp (chs. i.—iv.), so unmistakably discover their connection with the desert, that no intelligent critic ever dreams of disputing that at least they belong to that early era; while—*ε.* That the high priestly benediction (ch. vi. 24—26) and the military order which was uttered at the marching and halting of the camp (ch. x. 35, 36) were also composed then seems impossible to deny, for, to use the words of Ewald, "in these antiquely simple but powerful and beautiful utterances there is nothing contrary to the age and spirit of Moses; the first poetically describes the peaceful, and the second the warlike, feelings of the community during that primeval age." If, therefore, these different portions of the present Book have descended from the age in which Moses lived, why should it be deemed imperative to search for another author to whom to ascribe their actual composition? And if it should appear, as on reflection it can hardly fail, that there is no such urgent necessity, may it not be regarded as creating at least presumptive evidence that the other sections of the Book have also proceeded from his pen?

2. The Book of Numbers bears evidence of having been composed in the desert by an eye-witness of, and participator in, the scenes and transactions he records. Here, of course, the argument will be more satisfactory if proof can be advanced from those parts of the Book whose Mosaic origin is commonly disputed; and to these alone, accordingly, attention will at present be directed. Now that the children of Israel were as yet sojourning in the Arabian peninsula, and had not settled in Canaan when this division of the Pentateuch was composed, may be inferred from the character of the legislation which it records, which always presupposes that the people "had not yet come into the land of their habitations," but were dwelling in camps and tents with the tabernacle in their midst (*vide* ch. v. 3. 4; vi. 10, 13; viii. 1; xv. 2; xviii. 2, 6, 21). It is on this principle that Bleek identifies the legislation in Leviticus as belonging to Mosaic times, and there can be no reason of a valid nature for refusing assent to the truth of this principle when applied in the same way to Numbers. Then, that the author must have been familiar with the desert is apparent from the accuracy of his geographical knowledge, which has not only in many of its details been verified by modern explorers, as, *e. g.*, Hebron (ch. xiii. 22) and Kadesh (*ibid.* ver. 26), but which strenuously resists all attempts at further identification except upon the hypothesis of its own correctness (cf. Lange 'on Numbers,' Introduction, p. 7); while the way in which the history and the legislation are commingled in the narrative—the history often affording the requisite basis for the legislation, and the legislation frequently springing naturally out of the circumstances described—renders it impossible that any but an actual participant in the events and transactions themselves could have written it (*vide* chs. v., ix., xxx., xxxvi.). "Evidently the alternations of historical and legislative portions reflect the order of actual transaction," and "this feature is exactly one which belongs to the work of a contemporary annalist" ('Speaker's Commentary,' Introduction to Numbers, § 4, (2)).

3. The Book of Numbers reveals an intimate acquaintance on the part of its author with Egyptian manners and customs, which at least harmonises with the idea that that author was Moses. (1) The trial by jealousy (ch. v. 11—35) may be compared with the tale of Setnau translated by Brugsch from a demotic manuscript

belonging probably to the third century B.C., but relating to the times of Rameses II., in which Ptah-nefer-Ka, having found the book which the god Thoth wrote with his own hand, copied it on a new piece of papyrus, dissolved it in water, and drank it, with the immediate result that "he knew all that it contained" (*vide* 'Records of the Past,' Vol. IV. p. 138). (2) The consecration of the Levites (ch. viii. 7) finds a counterpart in the ablutions of the Egyptian priests, who shaved their heads and bodies every third day, and spared no pains to promote the cleanliness of their persons, bathing twice a day and twice during the night, and performing a grand ceremony of purification preparatory to their periods of fasting, which sometimes lasted from seven to forty-two days, or even longer (*vide* Wilkinson's 'Ancient Egyptians,' Vol. I. p. 181). (3) The notion that contact with a dead body communicated uncleanness (ch. xix. 11) was not unknown to the Egyptians, who, according to Porphyry ('De Abst.,' ii. 50, quoted in 'Speaker's Commentary'), required their priests to shun graves, funerals, and funeral feasts. (4) The dainties referred to in ch. xi. 5, cucumbers, melons, leeks, onions, and garlick, were such as abounded in ancient Egypt (cf. Herodotus, ii. 93, 125; Hengstenberg's 'Egypt and the Books of Moses,' ch. vii. pp. 208—214; Wilkinson's 'Ancient Egyptians,' Vol. II. pp. 23 *sqq.*). (5) The antiquarian statement in ch. xiii. 22 about the age of Hebron indicates an acquaintance with Egyptian history which was less likely to have been possessed by a foreigner than by one who was native born. Now, although it cannot be maintained that these allusions to Egypt and its history demonstrate with mathematical certainty that Moses was the author of Numbers, it is yet a fair and legitimate inference that they are much more easily explained on that hypothesis than any other.

4. It may be noted that the Book of Numbers is not destitute of incidental and undesigned traces of having been composed in Mosaic times. (1) The mention of Arnon as the territorial boundary between Moab and the Amorites (ch. xxi. 13), though cited by Bohlen ('Introduction,' Vol. I. p. 70) as a geographical anachronism under the mistaken impression that David first constituted the Arnon the northern limit of Moab, is in reality an indication that the Amorites had not then been dispossessed by the two tribes and a half, or, in other words, that the clause was written while the Israelitish army was still upon the south bank of the river. (2) The circumstance that in ch. xxxiv. a larger extent of territory was assigned to Israel than they ever permanently occupied indirectly confirms the Mosaic authorship, since, as has been well remarked in the 'Speaker's Commentary,' "a historian of later times would hardly have ascribed to his people, without explanation or qualification, districts which in fact they did not possess," whereas "a romancer of such times, drawing an imaginary frontier, would certainly not have left out of it the renowned city of Damascus, especially after carrying his border line almost round this district, and in view of the fact that the city and its territory were in the dominions of David and Solomon, and afterwards of Jeroboam II." (Introduction, § 4). (3) The want of correspondence between the settlements of the two tribes and a half, as described in ch. xxxii. 34—42, and as actually held by them at a later period (Josh. xiii. 15—33), also points to a contemporary author, since a late writer would almost certainly have made the two to harmonise by constructing both passages in accordance with existing fact.

Thus the Book of Numbers, when fairly and dispassionately interrogated, not only does not support the modern hypothesis of its being a late compilation from pre-existing documents, some of which had descended from primitive times, but the majority of which were only the praiseworthy endeavours of subsequent ages to preserve the national traditions of the Beni-Israel from becoming extinct, but abundantly warrants the still popular belief, that while there is every probability that, like the rest of the Pentateuchal writings, it has been subjected to one or more revisions, and may even have suffered interpolation in unimportant passages, such as ch. xii. 3 (though this of course is not absolutely certain), yet in the main, and substantially as we still possess it, it proceeded as an original composition from the hand of Moses.

THE BOOK OF NUMBERS

INTRODUCTION.

THE Book of Numbers is a part of the Mosaic writings ordinarily called the Pentateuch. It would be more correct in a literary sense to say that it forms part of those records of the Beni-Israel which bring down the history of that peculiar people to the date of their victorious entry into their own land. The Book which follows is (on any theory as to its authorship) widely dissevered from the previous records in character and scope. The Book of Numbers forms the concluding fourth of a work of which the substantial unity and continuity cannot be reasonably questioned, and therefore very much which affects this Book is better treated of in an Introduction to the whole. The division, however, which separates Numbers from Leviticus is more marked than that which separates Leviticus from Exodus, or Exodus from Genesis. The narrative (which has been almost entirely suspended throughout the third Book) reappears in the fourth, and leads us on (with divers breaks and interruptions indeed) through the whole of that most important and distinctive period which we may call the fourth stage in the national life of the Beni-Israel. The first of these stages extends from the call of Abraham to the beginning of the sojourn in Egypt. The second includes the time of sojourning there. The third is the short but critical period of the exodus from Rameses to Mount Sinai, including the giving of the Law. The fourth reaches from Mount Sinai to the river Jordan, and coincides with the whole period of probation, preparation, failure, recovery. It will be noticed that our Book is the only one of the four which corresponds entirely to one of these stages ; it has therefore more real distinctness of character than any of the other three.

A. ON THE CONTENTS OF THE BOOK.

If we take the Book of Numbers as it stands, apart from any preconceived theories, and allow its contents to divide themselves into sections according to the actual character of their subject matter, we shall obtain, without any serious difference of opinion, the following result. Perhaps no book in the Bible falls more easily and naturally into its component parts.

SYNOPSIS OF NUMBERS.

Section I.—Preparations for the Great March.

CHAP.

1. i. 1—46 ... ... The first census of Israel.
2. i. 47—54 ... ... Special orders about the Levites.
3. ii. 1—34 ... ... Camping order of the tribes.
4. iii. 1—4 ... ... Notice of the priestly family.
5. iii. 5—51 ... ... Dedication of the Levites in lieu of the firstborn: their number, charge, and redemption.
6. iv. 1—49 ... ... Duties of the Levites on the march.

Section II.—Repetitions of and Additions to the Levitical Legislation.

1. v. 1—4 ... ... The exclusion of the unclean.
2. v. 5—10 ... ... Laws of recompense and of offerings.
3. v. 11—31 ... ... The trial of jealousy.
4. vi. 1—21 ... ... The Nazirite vow.
5. vi. 22—27 ... ... The formula of priestly benediction.

Section III.—Narrative of Events from the setting up of the Tabernacle to the Sentence of Exile at Kadesh.

1. vii. 1—88 ... ... Offerings of the princes at the dedication.
2. vii. 89 ... ... The voice in the sanctuary.
3. viii. 1—4 ... ... The lamps lighted in the tabernacle.
4. viii. 5—26 ... ... Consecration of the Levites.
5. ix. 1—14 ... ... The second passover, and the supplemental passover.
6. ix. 15—23 ... ... The cloud on the tabernacle.
7. x. 1—10 ... ... The silver trumpets.
8. x. 11—28 ... ... The start and order of march.
9. x. 29—32 ... ... The invitation to Hobab.
10. x. 33—36 ... ... The first journey.
11. xi. 1—3 ... ... Sin and chastisement at Taberah.
12. xi. 4—35 ... ... Sin and chastisement at Kibroth-hattaavah.
13. xii. 1—16 ... ... Sedition of Miriam and Aaron.
14. xiii. 1—33 ... ... Mission and report of the spies.
15. xiv. 1—45 ... ... Rebellion and rejection of the people.

Section IV.—Fragments of Levitical Legislation.

1. xv. 1—21 ... ... Law of offerings and first-fruits.
2. xv. 22—31 ... ... Law of trespass offerings, and of presumptuous sins.
3. xv. 32—36 ... ... Incident of the sabbath-breaker.
4. xv. 37—41 ... ... Law of fringes.

Section V.—Narrative of the Revolt against the Aaronic Priesthood.

1. xvi. 1—50 ... ... Rebellion of Korah and his confederates, and its suppression.
2. xvii. 1—13 ... ... The rod of Aaron which budded.

Section VI.—Further Additions to the Law.

1. xviii. 1—32 ... ... The charge and emoluments of priests and Levites.
2. xix. 1—22 ... ... Law of the red heifer, and the pollution of death.

SECTION VII.—NARRATIVE OF EVENTS DURING THE LAST JOURNEY.

CHAP.
1. xx. 1—13 ... ... The water of strife.
2. xx. 14—21 ... ... The insolence of Edom.
3. xx. 22—29 ... ... The death of Aaron.
4. xxi. 1—3 ... ... Episode of King Arad.
5. xxi. 4—9 ... ... Episode of the brazen serpent.
6. xxi. 10—32 ... ... Last marches and first victories.
7. xxi. 33—xxii. 1 ... ... Conquest of Og.

SECTION VIII.—STORY OF BALAAM.

1. xxii. 2—38 ... ... The coming of Balaam.
2. xxii. 39—xxiv. 25 ... The prophecies of Balaam.

SECTION IX.—NARRATIVE OF EVENTS IN THE PLAINS OF MOAB.

1. xxv. 1—18 ... ... Sin and atonement at Shittim.
2. xxvi. 1—65 ... ... Second census of Israel with a view to the allotment
                          of the land.
3. xxvii. 1—11 ... ... Suit of Zelophehad's daughters.
4. xxvii. 12—23 ... ... Supersession of Moses by Joshua.

SECTION X.—RECAPITULATIONS OF AND ADDITIONS TO THE LAW.

1. xxviii. 1—xxix. 40 ... The annual routine of sacrifice.
2. xxx. 1—16 ... ... Law of vows made by women.

SECTION XI.—NARRATIVE OF FURTHER EVENTS IN THE PLAINS OF MOAB.

1. xxxi. 1—54 ... ... Extirpation of Midian.
2. xxxii. 1—42 ... ... Settlement of the two and a half tribes.

SECTION XII.—THE ITINERARY.

xxxiii. 1—49 ... ... List of marches from Rameses to Jordan.

SECTION XIII.—FINAL INSTRUCTIONS IN VIEW OF THE CONQUEST OF CANAAN.

1. xxxiii. 50—56 ... ... The clearance of the holy land.
2. xxxiv. 1—15 ... ... Boundaries of the holy land.
3. xxxiv. 16—29 ... ... Allotment of the holy land.
4. xxxv. 1—8 ... ... Reservation of cities for the Levites.
5. xxxv. 9—34 ... ... The cities of refuge, and law of homicide.
6. xxxvi. 1—13 ... ... Law of the marriage of heiresses.

Other divisions than these may of course be founded upon considerations of chronology, or upon the wish to group together the historical and legislative portions in certain combinations; but these considerations are obviously foreign to the Book itself. While a general sequence is evidently observed, dates are almost entirely absent; and while it is very natural to trace a close connection between the facts of the narrative and the matter of the legislation, such connection (in the absence of any statement to substantiate it) must remain always uncertain, and often very precarious.

The contents, therefore, of this Book fall naturally into thirteen sections of very various length, clearly marked at their edges by the change either of subject matter or of literary character. Thus, e. g., no reader, however uneducated, could avoid noticing the abrupt transition from ch. xiv. to ch. xv. ; and thus again no reader who had any ear for literary style could fail to isolate in his own mind the story of Balaam from the narrative which precedes and follows it. Perhaps the only question which could be seriously raised on this subject is the propriety of treating the Itinerary as a separate section. The character, however, of the passage is so distinct, and it is so clearly separated from what follows by the formula of ch. xxxiii. 50, that there seems no alternative if we wish to follow the natural lines of division.

It will be seen that of the thirteen sections, eight are narrative, four are legislative, and one (the last) is of a mixed character.

B. On the Chronology of the Book.

The dates given in the Book itself are (excluding the date of the departure from Rameses, ch. xxxiii. 3) only four ; but the reference to the setting up of the tabernacle is equivalent to a fifth. We have, therefore, the following as fixed points in the narrative.

1. The dedication of the tabernacle, with the offering of the princes (vii. 1, 2) and the descent of the sacred cloud (ix. 15) ... ... 1st day of Abib in year 2.
2. The second passover (ix. 5) ... ... 14th day of Abib in year 2.
3. The census at Sinai (i. 1) ... ... 1st day of Zif in year 2.
4. The supplemental passover (ix. 11) ... ... 14th day of Zif in year 2.
5. The start for Canaan (x. 11) ... ... 20th day of Zif in year 2.
6. The death of Aaron (xxxiii. 38) ... ... 1st day of Ab in year 40.

There is, however, a note of time in this Book which is more important than any date, for in ch. xiv. an exile of forty years is denounced against the Beni-Israel ; and although it is not stated at what precise point the exile terminated, yet we may safely conclude that it was either at or very near the conclusion of this Book. If, therefore, we had no subsequent data to guide us, we should say that ch. i.—x. 10 covers a space of one month, twenty days ; ch. x. 11—xiv. a space which may be variously estimated from two months to four months ; ch. xv.—xx. 28 a space of very nearly thirty-eight years (of which the great bulk would coincide with chs. xv.—xix.); and the remainder a space of nearly two years. It is, however, stated in Deut. i. 3 that Moses began his last address to the people on the first day of the eleventh month of the fortieth year, i. e. exactly six months after the death of Aaron, and only five months after the departure from Mount Hor. This does no doubt crowd the events of the last period into a strangely brief space of time, and shortens the time of wandering from forty to thirty-eight and a half years. The latter difficulty, although not to be lightly passed over, is yet fairly met by the assumption that the Divine mercy (which ever loves to take hold on any excuse for leniency) was moved to include the time of wandering already spent in the term of punishment inflicted at Kadesh. The former difficulty is more serious, for it implies a hurry which does not appear upon the face of the narrative. We may, however, remember that a generation which had grown up in the desert, hardened to exposure, and inured to fatigue, would move with a swiftness and strike with a vigour altogether foreign to the nation which came out of Egypt. The actual distance traversed by the main bulk of the people (more than 200 miles) need not have occupied more than a month, and some of the operations recorded may have been carried on simultaneously. It will not, however, be forgotten that the difficulty arises from a comparison of two dates, neither of which is found in the main narrative of the Book of Numbers.

C. Of the Composition of the Book, and the Sequence of its Contents.

If we compare the table of contents with the table of dates, we shall see at once that the earlier portions of the narrative are out of chronological order, and we shall not find any sufficient reason assigned for this dislocation. On the contrary, closer examination will leave the greater certainty that ch. vii. and ch. viii. to ver. 4 (at least) connect themselves rather with Exod. xl. or Levit. ix. than with their present context. It appears, also, from the synopsis of the Book, that narrative alternates with legislation in such a way as cut it up into clearly marked sections. It is asserted that the legislative matter thus interspersed grows out of, and shows a natural connection with, the narrative. This is true in some cases, but in many more cases it is not true. *E. g.* it is at least plausible in the case of the law for the exclusion of the unclean which interrupts the narrative in ch. v. 1—4. But it is not even plausible with respect to the laws which follow to the end of ch. vi.; no ingenuity can show any special connection between the preparations for departure from Sinai and the trial of jealousy or the Nazirite vow. Again, it is possible to argue that the law which regulated the respective offices and emoluments of the priests and Levites finds its proper place after the record of Korah's rebellion; and also that the ordinance of the red heifer was historically connected with the sentence of death in the wilderness and the compulsory disuse of the ordinary routine of sacrifice. But it could hardly be seriously contended that the fragmentary enactments of ch. xv. or the regulations of ch. xxx. have the least apparent connection with their place in the record. It is not at all too much to say, with regard to the greater number of the laws in this Book, that their position is arbitrary as far as we can now see, and that the reasons assigned for their standing where they do are purely artificial. It does not follow that there were not actual reasons, unknown to us, why these laws should have been revealed at times corresponding to their position; nevertheless, the presumption which arises upon the face of the record is certainly this, that the legislative matter in this Book consists mainly of fragments of the Levitical legislation which have in some way become detached and have been interspersed through the narrative. One exception, however, is so obvious that it must be noted: the routine of sacrifice in chs. xxviii., xxix. is not a fragment, nor an isolated enactment; it is a recapitulation in a very complete form of the whole law so far as it applied to a distinct and important department of Jewish worship. As such it accords with its assigned position on the threshold of the promised land ; or it may even represent a later codification of the Mosaic legislation on the subject. Turning now to the narrative, we find that it is exceedingly uneven and intermittent in its character as a record. Three hundred and twenty-six verses are devoted to the arrangements and events of the fifty days which preceded the march from Sinai ; one hundred and fifty-five more contain the story of the few months which ended with the defeat at Kadesh ; to the next thirty-eight years belong only sixty-three verses, relating in detail a single episode without date or place ; the rest of the narrative, consisting of three hundred and sixty-one verses, relates to the last period, of little more than eleven months according to the accepted chronology. Even in this last portion, which is comparatively full, it is evident by a reference to the Itinerary that no notice is taken of many places where the camp was halted, and where no doubt incidents of greater or less interest occurred. The Book, therefore, does not profess to be a continuous narrative, but only to record certain incidents—some briefly, some at considerable length—of the journeys from Sinai to Kadesh, and from Kadesh to Jordan, together with a single episode from the long years between. But the narrative, broken as it is in chain of incident, is further broken in literary character. The questions which arise out of the story of Balaam are discussed in their proper place ; but it is impossible to believe (unless some very strong necessity can be shown for believing) that the section ch. xxii. 2—xxiv. has the same literary history as the rest of the Book. Inserted in the Book, and that in its proper place as to order of events, its distinctness is nevertheless evident, both from other considerations and especially from its rhetorical and dramatic character. It requires no knowledge of Hebrew, and no acquaintance with learned theories, to recognise in this section an epic (partly prose and partly verse) which may indeed have come from the same author as the narrative which surrounds it, but which must have had within that author's mind a wholly different origin and history. What is said of the story of Balaam may be said in a somewhat different sense of the archaic quotations in ch. xxi. Imbedded as these are in the story, they are on the face of them as plainly foreign as the erratics which the icebergs of a vanished age have left behind. But, more than this, the very presence of these quotations gives a peculiar character to the narrative in which they occur. It is hard to believe that the historian, e. g., of the exodus would stoop to cull these snatches of old song, which are for the most part devoid of any religious import; it is hard not to think that they are due to popular memory, and were repeated by many a camp-fire before they got written down by some unknown hand.

Looking, therefore, at the Book of Numbers simply as one of the sacred books of the Jews, we find that it presents the following features. It narrates a variety of incidents at the beginning and ending of the desert wanderings between Sinai and Jordan, and carries on the story of Israel (with one remarkable break) from the holy mount of consecration to the holy land of habitation. The narrative, however, incomplete as to matter, is also inconsecutive as to form; for it is interspersed with legislative matter which does not seem for the most part to have any special connection with its context, but would find its natural place among the laws of Leviticus. Moreover, while the main part of the narrative entirely harmonises in literary style and character with that of the previous books (at least from Gen. xi. 10 onwards), there are portions towards the end which bear internal evidence—the one less, the other more strongly—of a different origin. If we had no other data to go upon, we should probably come to the conclusion—1. That the materials used in compiling the Book were in the main from one hand, and that the same to which we owe both the previous history of the Beni-Israel and the Sinaitic legislation. 2. That the materials had existed in a somewhat fragmentary state, and had been arranged in their present order by some unknown hand. 3. That in one chapter at least some other material of a more popular kind had been drawn upon. 4. That in one case an entire section had been inserted, complete in itself, and of a character very distinct from the rest. These conclusions are, however, by no means so certain but that they may be set aside by sufficient arguments if such can be found.

D. On the Authorship of the Book.

It has been until lately assumed as a matter of course that the whole of this Book, together with the other four of the Pentateuch, was written by Moses. With regard to ch. xii. 3 alone, the obvious difficulty of ascribing such a statement to Moses himself has always led many to regard it as an interpolation by some later (sacred) writer. When we come to examine the evidence for the Mosaic authorship of the whole Book as it stands, it is astonishing how little it amounts to. There is not a single statement attached to the Book to show that it was written by Moses. There is indeed a statement in ch. xxxiii. 2 that "Moses wrote their goings out according to their journeys by the commandment of the Lord;" but this, so far from proving that Moses wrote the Book, somewhat strongly militates against it. For the statement in question is found in a section which is obviously distinct, and which has more the appearance of an appendix to the narrative than of an integral part of it. Moreover, it does not even apply to the Itinerary as it stands, but only to the bare list of marches upon which it is founded; the observations appended to some of the names (e. g. to Elim and to Mount Hor) are much more like the work of a later writer copying from the list left by Moses. If we found in an anonymous work a list of names inserted towards the end with the statement that the names had been written down by such and such a person (whose authority would be unquestioned), we should not certainly quote that statement in order to prove that that person wrote all the rest of the book. Supposing the statement to be true (and there seems no alternative between accepting it as true within the knowledge of the writer and rejecting it as a wilful falsehood), it simply assures us that Moses kept a written record of the marches, and that the Itinerary in question is based on that record. Turning to the external testimony as to authorship, we come to the evidence afforded by the opinion of the later Jews. No one doubts that they ascribed the whole Pentateuch to Moses, and comparatively few doubt that their tradition was substantially correct. But it is one thing to believe that an opinion handed down from an uninquiring age as to the authorship of a book was substantially correct, and quite another thing to believe that it was formally correct. That the Law was of Mosaic origin and authority may have been perfectly true for all practical religious purposes ; that the Law was written down verbatim as it stands by the hand of Moses may have been the very natural, but at the same time inaccurate, form in which a true belief presented itself to minds wholly innocent of literary criticism. To set the tradition of the later Jews against the strong internal evidence of the writings themselves is to exalt tradition (and that at its weakest point) at the expense of Scripture. It may be very true that if the Law was not really of Mosaic origin, the saints and prophets of old time were grievously deceived ; it may be quite false that any particular opinion current amongst them as to the precise character of the Mosaic authorship has any claim upon our acceptance. That "the Law was given by Moses" is a thing so constantly affirmed in the Scriptures that it can hardly be denied without overthrowing their authority ; that Moses wrote every word of Numbers as it stands is a literary opinion which naturally commended itself to an age of literary ignorance, but which every ensuing age is at liberty to revise or reject.

It is, however, argued that our Lord himself has testified to the truth of the ordinary Jewish tradition by using the name "Moses" as tantamount to the Mosaic books. This argument has more special reference to Deuteronomy, but the whole Pentateuch is included within its scope. It is answered—and the answer is apparently incontrovertible—that our Lord merely used the common language of the Jews, without meaning to guarantee the precise accuracy of the ideas on which that language was based. As a fact, the Pentateuch was known as "Moses," just as the Psalms were known as "David." No one, perhaps, would now contend that Ps. xcv. must of necessity be ascribed to David himself because it is cited as "David" in Heb. iv. 7 ; and few would maintain the like of Ps. cx., even though our Lord certainly assumed that "David" spake therein (Matt. xxii. 45). Both these psalms may have been David's own, and yet we need not feel ourselves tied up to that conclusion because the ordinary language and opinion of the Jews concerning them is followed in the New Testament. The common sense of the matter seems to be, that unless our Lord's judgment had been directly challenged on the subject, he could not have done otherwise than use the common terminology of the day. To do otherwise had been the part, not of a prophet, but of a pedant, which he assuredly never was. We may be sure that he always spake to people in their own language, and accepted their current ideas, unless those ideas involved some practical religious error. He took occasion, *e. g.*, to say that Moses did *not* give the manna from heaven (John vi. 32), and did *not* institute circumcision (*ibid.* vii. 22), for these exaggerations in the popular estimate of Moses were both false in themselves and might be known to be false; but to open up a literary controversy which would have been unintelligible and unpractical for that and many succeeding generations was wholly foreign to that Son of man who was in the truest sense the child of his own age and of his own people. To take an instructive instance from the region of physical science: it has actually been made a reproach against the sacred writers that they speak (as we do) of the sun rising and setting, whereas in truth it is the movements of the earth which cause the appearances in question. It does not occur to such critics to ask themselves how the sacred writers could have used in that age scientific language which even we cannot use in common conversation. That our Lord spake of the sun rising and setting, and not of the earth revolving on its axis from west to east, is a thing for which we have perhaps as much reason to be thankful as those who heard him. Similarly, that our Lord spake of Moses without hesitation or qualification as the author of the Pentateuch is a matter not of surprise, but of thankfulness to us all, however much modern investigation may have modified our conception of the Mosaic authorship. What could possibly be more alien from the revealed character of that adorable Son of man than a display either of scientific or of literary knowledge, foreign to the age, which had no bearing upon true religion or the saving of the world from sin?

External testimony, therefore, only seems to force upon us the conclusion that the substance of "the Law" (in some general sense) is of Mosaic origin; but it does not oblige us to believe that Moses wrote down either the legislative or narrative portions of our Book with his own hand. We are therefore left to internal evidence for the determination of all such questions. Now it must be at once conceded that internal evidence is extremely difficult to weigh, especially in writers so remote from our own age and our own literary canons. But a few points come out strongly from the study of the Book.

1. As already shown, its very form and character point to the probability of its having been compiled from documents previously existing, and put together for the most part very inartificially. Scarcely a trace appears of any attempt to soften down the abrupt transitions, to explain the obscurities, or to bridge over the gaps with which the Book abounds; its multiplicity of beginnings and endings is left to speak for itself.

2. The great bulk of the Book bears strong evidence to the truth of the ordinary belief that it was written by a contemporary, and that contemporary none other than Moses himself. If we look at the narrative, the curiously minute touches here and the equally curious obscurities there point alike to a writer who had lived through it all; a later writer would have had no motive

for inserting many of the details, and would have had strong motives for explaining many things which now arouse, without gratifying, our curiosity. The antiquarian information incidentally given about Hebron and Zoan (ch. xiii. 22) seems thoroughly incompatible with a later age than that of Moses, and points to one who had had access to the public archives of Egypt ; and the list of cheap delicacies in ch. xi. 5 is evidence of the same sort. The boundaries assigned to the promised land are indeed too obscure to be made the basis of much argument, but the one plain fact about them—that they exclude the trans-Jordanic territory—seems inconsistent with any subsequent period of Jewish national feeling. Until towards the close of the monarchy the regions of Gilead and Bashan were a part, and an integral part, of the land of Israel ; Jordan could only have been made the eastern frontier at a time when the self-willed choice of the two and a half tribes had not yet obliterated (so to speak) the original boundary of the promised possession. Moreover, the obvious want of coincidence between the settlements recorded in ch. xxxii. 34—38 and those afterwards held by these tribes tells strongly in favour of the contemporary origin of this record. If, on the other hand, we look at the legislation included in this Book, we have not indeed the same assurances, but we have the fact that very much of it is on the face of it designed for a wilderness life, and required to be adapted to the times of settled habitation : the camp and the tabernacle are constantly assumed, and directions given (as e. g. in ch. xix. 3, 4, 9) which could only be replaced by some equivalent ritual after the temple was set up. It is of course possible (though very improbable) that some later writer might have imagined himself to be living with the people in the wilderness, and have written accordingly ; but it is eminently unlikely that he would have succeeded in doing so without betraying himself many times. The religious fictions of a much later and more literary age, such as the Book of Judith, continually blunder, and if the Book of Tobit escapes the charge, it is because it restricts itself to domestic scenes. Against this strong internal evidence—all the stronger because it is difficult to reduce it to definite statement —there is really nothing to be set. The theory, which once seemed so plausible, that the use of the two Divine names, Jehovah and Elohim, pointed to a plurality of authors whose various contributions might be distinguished, has happily been long enough in the hands of its advocates to have reduced itself to absurdity. If there be any one left who is disposed to pursue this *ignis fatuus* of Old Testament criticism, it is not possible for soberness and common sense to follow him—he must chase his phantoms until he be weary, for he will always find some one more foolish than himself to give him a reason why " Jehovah " should stand here and " Elohim " there. The argument from the use of the word *nabi* (prophet —ch. xi. 29 ; xii. 6) seems to be founded on a misunderstanding of 1 Sam. ix. 9, and the few other exceptions which have been taken refer to passages which may well be interpolations. The conclusion, therefore, is strongly warranted that the bulk of the material contained in this Book is from the hand of a contemporary, and if so, from the hand of Moses himself, since no one else can even be suggested.

3. There is every reason to believe, and no necessity to deny, that interpolations were made either by the original compiler or by some later reviser. Instances will be found in ch. xii. 3; xiv. 25, and in ch. xv. 32—36. In the last case it may be reasonably contended that the incident is narrated in order to illustrate the sternness of the law against the presumptuous sinner, but the words "when the children of Israel were in the wilderness" seem to show conclusively that the illustration was interpolated by some one living in the land of Canaan. No one perhaps would have doubted this except under the strangely mistaken idea that it is an article of the Christian faith that Moses wrote every word of the Pentateuch. In chs. xiii., xiv., and xvi. there are signs not so much of interpolation, but of a revision of the narrative which has disturbed its sequence, and in the latter case has made it very obscure in parts. These phenomena would be accounted for if we could suppose that one who had himself been an actor in these scenes (such as Joshua) had altered and revised, not very skilfully, the record left behind by Moses. We have, however, no evidence to substantiate such a supposition. In ch. xxi. 1—3 we have an apparent example neither of interpolation nor of revision, but of accidental dislocation. The notice of King Arad and his defeat is evidently very ancient, but it is generally agreed that it is out of place where it stands; nevertheless, the displacement would seem to be older than the present form of the Itinerary, for the passing allusion in ch. xxxiii. 40 refers to the same event in the same geographical connection. The repetition of the genealogy of Aaron in ch. xxvi. 58—61 has all the appearance of an interpolation. The character of ch. xxxiii. 1—49 has been already discussed.

4. There remain two important passages on which objections have been founded against the Mosaic authorship of the Book. The one is the narrative of the march round Moab in ch. xxi., with its quotations of ancient songs and sayings. The objection indeed that no "book of the wars of the Lord" could have been then in existence is arbitrary, for we have no means of proving a negative of this kind. That written records were very rare in that age is really no reason for denying that Moses (who had received the highest education of the most civilised country in the then world) was able to write down memorials of his own time, or to make a collection of popular songs. But that Moses should have quoted from one of those songs, which could only just have been added to the collection, seems very unlikely; and this fact, together with the different character of the narrative in this part, may incline us to believe that the compiler here added to the (perhaps meagre) record left by Moses by drawing upon some of that popular lore, partly oral, partly written, which happened to illustrate his text. The other passage is the long and striking episode of Balaam, which has been already spoken of. There is no difficulty in supposing that this came from the hand of Moses, if we look upon it as an epic poem based upon

facts, although it is a matter of conjecture how he became acquainted with the facts. The possible explanation is suggested in the notes, and it is clear in any case that no subsequent Jewish writer would be in a better position than Moses himself in this respect, while to regard it as a mere effort of the imagination creates a host of difficulties greater than those it solves.

This part of the subject may be summed up by saying, that while the external evidence as to authorship is indecisive, and only obliges us to believe that "the Law" was given by Moses, the internal evidence is strong that the Book of Numbers, like the preceding books, is substantially from the hand of Moses. The objections urged against this conclusion are either in themselves captious and untenable, or are merely valid against particular passages. As to these, it may be fearlessly allowed that there are some interpolations by a later hand, that portions have been revised, that the various sections would seem to have existed separately, and to have been put together with little art, that some other material may have been worked into the narrative, and that some of the legislation may perhaps be rather a later codification of Mosaic ordinances than the original ordinances themselves.

E. On the Truth of the Book.

It may perhaps seem that in surrendering the traditional opinion that in all this Book we have the *ipsissima verba* written down by Moses, we have given up its veracity. Such an inference, however, would be quite arbitrary. Nothing turns upon the question whether Moses wrote a single word of Numbers, unless it be the list of marches, of which as much is expressly stated. There is no reason for asserting that Moses was inspired to write true history, and that Joshua, *e. g.*, was not. The Books of Joshua, Judges, and Ruth are received as true, although we do not know who wrote them, and the Book of Judges at any rate is apparently compiled from fragmentary records. Even in the New Testament we do not know who wrote the Epistle to the Hebrews; and we do know that there are passages in the Gospel of St. Mark (ch. xvi. 9—20) and in the Gospel of St. John (ch. viii. 1—11) which were not written by the evangelists to whom they have been traditionally assigned. The credibility of these writings (considered apart from the fact of their inspiration) turns mainly upon the question to whose authority the statements contained in them can be traced, and in a very minor degree to whose hand the present arrangement of them is due. As to the first, we have every reason to believe that the materials of the Book are substantially from Moses himself, whose knowledge and veracity are alike beyond suspicion. As to the second, we have only to acknowledge the same ignorance as in the case of the greater part of the Old Testament and of some part of the New Testament. It is, of course, open to any one to doubt or to deny the truth of these records, but in order to show reason for doing so he must not be content with pointing out some difference of style here, or some trace of a later hand there, but he must bring forward some clear instance of error, some undeniable self-contradiction, or some statement which is fairly incredible. The mere existence of a record so ancient and revered, and the unmistakable tone of simplicity and straightforwardness which characterises it, give it a *primâ facie* claim upon our acceptance until good cause can be shown to the contrary. If the early records of other nations are largely fabulous and incredible, no presumption passes over from them to a record which on the face of it presents such utterly different features. It remains to examine candidly the only objection of a serious nature (apart from the question of miracles, which it is useless to consider here) which has been brought against the substantial truth of this Book. It is urged that the figures set down as representing the numbers of Israel at the two censuses are incredible, because inconsistent, not only with the possibilities of life in the wilderness, but also with the directions given by Moses himself. This is in truth a very serious objection, and there is much to be said for it. It is quite true that a population of some 2,000,000 people, including a full proportion of women and children (for the males of that generation would be rather under than over the average), would under any ordinary circumstances seem unmanageable in a wild and difficult country. It is quite true (and this is much more to the point) that the narrative as a whole leaves a distinct impression upon the mind of a very much smaller total than the one given. It is sufficient to refer for proof to such passages as ch. x. 3—7, where the whole nation is supposed to be within hearing of the silver trumpet, and able to distinguish its calls ; ch. xiv., where the whole nation is represented as joining in the uproar, and therefore as included in the sentence ; ch. xvi., where a similar scene is described in connection with the revolt of Korah ; ch. xx. 11, where the whole thirsty multitude is represented as drinking (together with their cattle) of the one stream from the smitten rock ; ch. xxi. 9, where the brazen serpent on a standard may be seen, apparently, from every part of the camp. Each one of these instances, indeed, if taken by itself, may be shown to be far from conclusive ; but there is such a thing as cumulative evidence—the evidence which arises from a number of small and inconclusive testimonies all pointing the same way. Now it can hardly be denied that all these incidents raise in the mind a strong impression, which the entire narrative tends to confirm, that the numbers of Israel were much more moderate than those given. The difficulty, however, comes to a head in connection with the marching orders issued by Moses directly after the first census, and to that point we may confine our attention.

According to ch. ii. (as slightly modified afterwards—see on ch. x. 17) the eastern camps of Judah, Issachar, and Zebulun, containing more than 600,000 people, were to march first, and then the tabernacle was taken down and carried on waggons by the Gershonites and Merarites. After them marched the southern camps of Reuben, Gad, and Simeon, more than 500,000 strong; and behind them the Kohathites bore the sacred furniture; the other Levites were to put up the tabernacle against the Kohathites arrived. The remaining camps of the west and of the north followed with some 900,000 souls.

If we try to picture to ourselves a day's march between Sinai and Kadesh (for the marching orders were doubtless suspended then, and may never have been issued again), we have to think of 600,000 people at the first signal of departure striking their tents, forming into columns under their natural leaders, and setting forth in the direction taken by the cloudy pillar. We are not at liberty to suppose that they straggled far and wide over the face of the land, because it is evident that an orderly march is intended under the guidance of a single moving object. It is difficult to believe that a multitude so vast and so mixed could have moved off the ground in less than four or five hours at least, even if this was possible; but this was only one division out of four, and these were separated by some little interval, so that it would be already dark before the last division could possibly have fallen into the line of march. Now if we turn our eyes from the beginning to the end of the day's march, we see the journey arrested by the cloudy pillar; we see the first division of 600,000 souls turning to the right in order to take up camping ground towards the east; when these are out of the way we see the Levites arriving and setting up the tabernacle beside the cloudy pillar; then another division of half a million people come up and spread themselves on the south of the tabernacle across the onward track; behind the last of these come the Kohathites with the sacred furniture, and, passing through the midst of the southern camps, rejoin at last their brethren in order to place the holy things in the tabernacle; then follows a third division, some 360,000 strong, who march off to the left; and last of all the fourth division, which contains more than another half-million, has to make a circuit entirely round the eastern or western camps in order to take up its own quarters on the north. Undoubtedly the question forces itself on every one who permits himself to think about it, whether such orders and such numbers are compatible with one another. Even if we allow for the providential absence of all sickness and all death, it appears very doubtful whether the thing was within the limits of physical possibility. Again, we have to ask ourselves whether Moses would have separated the tabernacle from its sacred furniture on the march by half a million of people, who must (under any circumstances) have been many hours in getting out of the way. It may be said, and with some truth, that we scarcely know what may be done by vast multitudes animated by one spirit, habituated to rigid discipline, and (in this case) aided by many peculiar and indeed miraculous circumstances. Still there are physical limits of time and space which no energy and no discipline can overpass, and which no conceivable exercise of Divine power can set aside. It may be granted that 2,000,000 of Israelites might have wandered for years in the peninsula under the given conditions, and yet it may be denied that they could follow the marching orders issued at Sinai. Without attempting to solve this question, two considerations may be pointed out which affect its character. 1. No simple alteration of the text will set the figures in accord with the apparent requirements of the narrative. The total of 600,000 adult males is repeated again and again, from Exod. xii. 37 onwards; it is made up of a number of smaller totals, which are also given; and it is to some extent checked by comparison with the number of the "first-born" (whatever that may mean) and the number of Levites. 2. If the numbers recorded were given up as untrustworthy, it is certain that nothing else in the Book would be directly affected. The numbers stand quite apart, at least in this sense, that they have no value and no interest whatever of any moral or spiritual kind. Arithmetic enters into history, but it does not enter into religion. The same things have, from the point of view of religion, precisely the same value and the same meaning when done or suffered by one thousand which they would have had if done or suffered by ten thousand. If, then, any earnest student of Holy Writ should find himself unable to accept, as historically trustworthy, the numbers given in this Book, he is not therefore driven to discard the Book itself, fraught as it is with so many a message to his own soul. Rather than do this—rather than cast away, as if it had no existence, all that mass of positive, albeit indirect and often subtle, evidence which goes to substantiate the truth of the record—he would do well to put aside the question of mere numbers as one which, however perplexing, cannot be looked upon as vital. He may even hold that in some way the numbers may have been corrupted, and he may think it possible that the Divine providence which watches over the sacred writings has suffered them to be corrupted because mere numbers are of no moral or spiritual import. He may feel encouraged in this opinion by the apparently undeniable fact that the Holy Spirit who inspired St. Paul did not prevent him from misquoting a number out of this very Book (1 Cor. x. 8); for he cannot fail to perceive that the misquotation (supposing it to be one) does not make the slightest possible difference to those holy and important lessons which the Apostle was drawing from these records. It is not by any means affirmed by the present writer that the numbers in question *are* unhistoric; nor would he deny that their accuracy is maintained by far greater scholars and theologians than himself; he would only submit to the reader that the whole question, with all its attendant difficulties, may be calmly considered and argued on its own merits without involving anything which is really vital in our faith as concerning the word of God. We should surely have learnt little from the perplexities and victories of faith in the last forty years if we were not prepared for the possibility of admitting many modifications into our conception of inspiration without any fear lest inspiration should become to us less real, less full, less precious than it is.

The introduction to a single book is not the place to discuss the character of that inspiration which it shares with the other "God-inspired Scriptures." The present writer may, however, be excused if he points out once for all that the testimony of our Lord and of the Apostle Paul is clear and emphatic to the typical and prophetical character of the incidents here narrated. Such a reference as that in John iii. 14 and such a statement as that in 1 Cor. x. 4—11 cannot be explained away. Here then is the heart and kernel of the inspiration of the Book as recognised by our Lord, by his apostles, and by all his devout followers. They who live (or die) before us in these pages are τύποι ἡμῶν, types or patterns of ourselves; their outward history was the fore-shadow of our spiritual history, and its records were written for our behoof. Having this clue, and holding this as of faith, we shall not greatly err. The questions which arise may perplex, but may not shake us. And if a wider acquaintance with scientific criticism tend at first to unsettle our faith, yet, on the other hand, a wider acquaintance with experimental religion tends every day to strengthen our faith, by testifying to the marvellous and profound correspondence which exists between the sacred records of that long-vanished past and the ever-recurring problems and vicissitudes of Christian life.

LITERATURE ON NUMBERS.

A vast number of Commentaries may be consulted on the Book of Numbers, but as a rule they deal with it only as a portion of the Pentateuch. It is indeed so inseparably united to the Books which precede it that no scholar would make it the subject of a separate work.

It is therefore to works on the Pentateuch that the student must be referred, and amongst these the Commentary of Keil and Delitzsch (translated for Clark's Foreign Theological Library) may perhaps be mentioned as the most useful and available for careful interpretation and explanation of the text. The 'Speaker's Commentary,' and the smaller works which have followed in its wake, must be pronounced very inferior in thoroughness and general usefulness to the equally accessible standard German Commentaries. Ewald, Kurtz, and Hengstenberg, in their several works, have treated of the incidents and ordinances recorded in Numbers with considerable fulness from very varying standpoints; the last-named has also a lengthy mono-graph on the history of Balaam. For the homiletical treatment of the Book there is nothing so suggestive within a moderate compass as what may be found in the Bishop of Lincoln's Commentary.

It must be frankly acknowledged that the student who wishes to form an intelligent opinion on the many difficult questions which arise out of this portion of the sacred narrative will *not* find all these questions honestly faced or satisfactorily answered in any one of the existing Commentaries. He will, however, by combining what appears best in each, have before him the materials by means of which he may either form his judgment, or suspend it until in God's good time a clearer light shall shine.

THE

BOOK OF NUMBERS

EXPOSITION.

CHAPTER I.

THE CENSUS DIVINELY COMMANDED (vers. 1—16). Ver. 1.—**In the tabernacle of the congregation**—where the Lord spake with Moses "face to face" (Exod. xxxiii. 11), and where all the laws of Leviticus had been given (Levit. i. 1). **On the first day of the second month, in the second year.** On the first day of Zif (or Ijar); a year and a fortnight since the exodus, ten months and a half since their arrival at Sinai, and a month since the tabernacle had been set up.

Ver. 2.—**Take ye the sum of all the congregation.** The census here ordered had clearly been anticipated, as far as the numbers were concerned, by the results of the half-shekel poll-tax for the service of the sanctuary levied some time before on all adult males on pain of Divine displeasure (Exod. xxx. 11, *sq.*). Since all who were liable had paid that tax (Exod. xxxviii. 25, 26), it would only have been requisite to make slight corrections for death or coming of age during the interval. The totals, however, in the two cases being exactly the same, it is evident that no such corrections were made, and that the round numbers already obtained were accepted as sufficiently accurate for all practical purposes. **After their families.** This was to be a registration as well as a census. No doubt the lists and pedigrees collected at this time laid the foundation of that exact and careful genealogical lore which played so important a part both in the religious and in the secular history of the Jews down to the final dispersion. Every Jew had not only his national, but also (and often even more) his tribal and family, associations, traditions, and sympathies. Unity, but *not* uniformity, —unity in all deepest interests and highest purposes, combined with great variety of character, of tradition, and even of tendency, —was the ideal of the life of Israel. **The number of their names.** It is impossible to help thinking of the parallel expression in Acts i. 15, of the similarity in position of the two peoples, of the contrast between their numbers and apparent chances of success, of the more striking contrast between their actual achievements.

Ver. 3.—**By their armies.** Every citizen was a soldier. The military monarchies of mediæval or of modern days, with their universal obligation to service in the ranks, have (so far) but followed the example of ancient Israel.

Ver. 4.—**A man of every tribe.** The former census, which was for religious purposes only, was made with the assistance of the Levites. This, which was rather for political and military purposes, was supervised by the lay heads of the people.

Ver. 5.—**These are the names of the men.** The tribes are here mentioned (through their princes) very nearly in the order of their subsequent encampment—south, east, west, and north. Gad alone is displaced, in order that he may be classed with the other sons of the handmaids *after* the sons of the free women.

Ver. 7.—**Nahshon**—the brother-in-law of Aaron (Exod. vi. 23), and ancestor of David and of Jesus Christ (Matt. i. 4).

Ver. 10. — **Elishama** — grandfather of Joshua (1 Chron. vii. 26). All the rest are unnamed elsewhere.

Ver. 16.—**Heads of thousands.** Septuagint, *chiliarchs;* but the word is used for families (see Judges vi. 15), and, like all such words, it rapidly lost its numerical significance.

HOMILETICS.

Vers. 1—16.—*The numbering of God's people.* We have here, spiritually, the Church of God militant here on earth, " drawn up unto eternal life " (Acts xiii. 48), numbered and counted and ordered by the Great Captain of the Lord's host; man by man, soul by soul, to be his valiant soldiers and servants in the march and the conflict, and the manifold trials and temptations of this probation. Consider, therefore—

I. That this numbering of all his soldiers by name was MADE AT THE EXPRESS AND PARTICULAR COMMAND OF GOD, as it were for the Divine information; herein contrasting with that other numbering so sorely avenged under David, because made to feed his own pride. Even so the Lord is exceeding careful of the number of his own; one of the two sacred mottoes stamped upon his Church is, " The Lord knoweth them that are his " (2 Tim. ii. 19); " The Good Shepherd calleth his own sheep by name " (John x. 3); and every one of them is expressed by name in his book (Rev. iii. 5). We are " numbered " in the census of a great nation; every one of us is something stronger, holds his head somewhat higher, for the thought that he is numbered amongst the thirty millions of a great country, the ninety millions of a greater people. Are we also " numbered " among the innumerable and ever-victorious hosts of the Lord? Are we included in his census? If so, are we mindful of the condition? (2 Tim. ii. 3, 4). Are we tremblingly hopeful of the promise? (Rev. iii. 5).

II. That it was IN THE SECOND YEAR that they were thus numbered " by their armies : " first came the great deliverance unto Sinai, the mount of God; then came the teaching of the moral law; then came the instructions of outward religion; then —and not till then—the command to number into the ranks. Even so the soldiers of the cross are not called at once to arms; the deliverance came first of course, the decease, "the exodus" (Luke ix. 31) which he accomplished at Jerusalem; after that came to each the inculcation of the immutable laws of moral conduct; after that the ordinances of public and private worship; and *then* only, after such training, with such aids, is each believer numbered unto active service, and called, as it were, by name to approve himself as a trusty soldier of Jesus Christ.

III. That only those were "numbered," and entered, as it were, on the roll-call of the Lord, WHO WERE " ABLE TO GO FORTH TO WAR in Israel ; " all the others, the women and the children, &c., remained unspecified and unnoted. Even so *all* the Lord's people whose names are written in the Book of Life must be combatants. They need not indeed be men, but they must "quit" themselves "like men" (1 Cor. xvi. 13). They may be weak women, or even tender children, for such have shown themselves (and do show) to the full as valiant for Christ as any men. But they *must* be combatants, for that is the one condition on which we are received into that " multitude which no man can number " (but the Lord can), and the promise is "to him that overcometh," and to none other.

IV. That of these names in ver. 16, renowned amongst men and chosen of God to honour and dignity, ALL BUT TWO ARE TOTALLY UNKNOWN TO US, and those two only through their descendants. So in the Church, those that are the greatest with God are often the obscurest in the annals of men. As " Antipas " was expressly called (by a singular honour), " my faithful martyr " by Christ; yet is there no knowledge of him, not even a legend concerning him, in the Church.

HOMILIES BY VARIOUS AUTHORS.

Vers. 1, 2.—A HOMILY FOR THE CENSUS DAY. *The numbering of the people.* I. A FEW WORDS ABOUT THE CENSUS which is being taken to-day in every town, every hamlet, every remote habitation of the United Kingdom, from the English Channel to the seas that surge round the Shetland Islands. There are still some people—not many, let us hope—who have a scruple about filling up the census papers. They are haunted with an apprehension that there is something wrong, something dangerous, about the business. " Did not King David transgress in numbering the people ? Did he not by so doing bring God's wrath upon his kingdom ? Would that which brought guilt and sorrow on David be right or safe for us ? " What are we to say to these scrupulous persons ? I have not time to go into the questions that have been raised about the real nature of David's sin. One thing is plain : the evil lay not in the taking of a census, but in the intention of that particular census. David was a man of war. In his hands the kingdom was in danger of becoming a despotic and military monarchy, such as the nations of the world have had occasion to know too well. And there can be little doubt that the census he projected was meant to subserve the ends of such a monarchy. It was meant to be just such an instrument of oppression in Israel as William the Conqueror's *Domesday Book* was in England. The design of the compilation seems to have been, in both cases, very much the same. Anyhow, it is certain that the simple numbering of the people was not forbidden by the law of God. On the contrary, the Bible is dead against such a barbarous and hazardous style of national administration as is inevitable when the national governors are in the dark regarding the statistics of the people. The Israelites dealt largely in statistics ; to a surprising degree they anticipated the practice of the nineteenth century in this matter. At all the great turning-points in their history a census was taken. This Book of NUMBERS owes its name to the fact that it records two census-takings, one at the beginning, the other at the close, of the forty years' sojourn in the wilderness. So long as the Bible has a Book of Numbers in it, intelligent Bible readers will see in it an admonition to fill up their census papers with exactness and for conscience sake.

II. MEDITATIONS PROPER TO THE CENSUS DAY. The filling up of a census paper is, in itself, a piece of secular business. Yet I do not envy the man who can perform it without being visited with a touch of holy feeling. The setting down of the names of one's household brings up many tragic memories. The setting down one's own age, after a lapse of ten years—surely it summons us to count our days that we may apply our hearts to wisdom. It is not often observed that *the law of Moses prescribed a religious service for the occasion of a census-taking* (Exod. xxx. 11—16). This the children of Israel are to perform, " that there be no plague among them when thou numberest them." A measure may be right in itself, and yet may be apt to become to us an occasion of sin. When a nation is reckoning up the number of its sons, it will be apt to harbour proud confidence in their valour ; and proud confidence in man God will not bear. When Nebuchadnezzar begins to say, " Is not this great Babylon which I have built for the house of my kingdom ? "God's humbling stroke is near. On the census day the Israelites were to bring " every man a 'ransom for his soul.' " The act was as much as to say, " I am not worthy to be registered among the living in Israel, the holy nation, the kingdom of priests. I am a sinful man, O Lord ; but I believe that there is forgiveness with thee. Forgive me, therefore, O Lord reject me not. Remember me with the favour thou bearest unto thy people, that I may rejoice in the gladness of thy nation, and glory with thine inheritance." The ransom money required from every Israelite on the census day was a poll-tax of half a shekel. The rich paid no more, the poor paid no less. The law of Moses did not often impose this sort of tax ; for with a show of equality, it is the most unequal of taxes. Ordinarily the law invited princes to bring princely gifts, while it suffered the poor man's pair of turtle-doves to come up with acceptance on the altar. The poll-tax of the census day was altogether exceptional. Nor is it difficult to understand why the exception should have been made on this one occasion. It was very significant. Religion does not abrogate all social inequalities ; but the non-recognition of these in the atonement-money admonishes us that the inequalities which find place among men in regard to wealth, station, intellectual gifts, are as nothing in comparison with their essential equality as creatures made in the image of God. It admonishes us also that all who have obtained an inheritance among God's people are on one level with regard to their right to be there. " There is no difference ; for all have sinned, and all are justified freely." Yet another reflection. *The Lord keeps an exact register of his people.* There is a Book of Life in which are inscribed the names of all whom he has chosen, and caused to approach unto him, that they may dwell in his house. How true this is, the whole Scripture bears witness (see Exod. xxxii. 32 ; Isa. iv. 3 ; Ezek. xiii. 9 ; Luke x. 20 ; Phil. iv. 3 ; Heb. xii. 23 ; Rev. xiii. 8). We commonly think of this as a book which is shut and sealed. No man on earth can take it into his hand and read out the names inscribed in it. The Lord only knoweth them that are his; we may not sit in judgment on one another's state before God. All this is true. Yet the truth has another side: if the seventy are to rejoice because their names are written in heaven, it must be possible for them to ascertain the fact. A man may ascertain his own acceptance with God. Not only so. If the Apostle was confident regarding certain of the early Christians that their names were in the Book of Life, we also may, without prying into God's secrets, attain to a similar persuasion respecting such of our brethren as bear Christ's image, and abound in his work. Who bear Christ's image, and abound in his work—I use these words advisedly; they express the evidence which avails to prove that a given name is in the Book of Life. The census-table compiled by Moses contained only the names of such as were, by birth or adoption, the sons of Jacob. The Book of Life contains only the names of those whom God has "predestinated to the adoption of sons by Jesus Christ." To make sure that I am a son—that God has brought me home to himself by his Word and Spirit—this is the only way of making sure that my name has a place in the Lamb's Book of Life.—B.

Vers. 1–3.—*God commands a census.* I. THE PLACE AND TIME OF THE COMMAND. God spoke to Moses *in the wilderness of Sinai.* Many wildernesses, though uncultivated, were fertile and well watered, but the wilderness of Sinai was a desolate place. Moses calls it "the great and terrible wilderness, wherein were fiery serpents and scorpions and drought, where there was no water;" and, again, "a desert land, a waste howling wilderness" (see Stanley's 'Sinai and Palestine'). Very different from the riches of Egypt left behind, and the riches of Canaan lying before. But though a wilderness, the *tabernacle of the congregation* was there, made by God's appointment and direction, even down to its minutest arrangements and furniture. As long as the tabernacle in their midst was honoured, the people could dwell safely even in the wilderness.

II. THE PURPOSE OF THE NUMBERING. *To ascertain the strength of the people for war.* Canaan, towards which they were advancing, was in the possession of enemies, who appreciated all its riches, and would not relinquish them without a severe struggle. At the time of the census the Israelites had not brought on themselves the penalty of the forty years' wandering. The census was meant to be one preparation for immediate conquest, as the mission of the spies was another. There was everything to give them courage and strength of mind when they remembered that there were more than 600,000 fighting men amongst them. And as they counted up their resources for war, so we may be sure Christ would ever have his militant Church on earth to do the same. The tone of the New Testament is not less warlike than of the Old, our Canaanites being principalities and powers, the rulers of the darkness of this world, and spiritual wickedness in high places.

III. THE METHOD OF THE NUMBERING. The method was determined by the purpose. Note, first, *the exclusions. The women and the children were left out.* In counting the Levites the children were not left out. Every male from a month old was numbered, for theirs was a constant service, and even the youngest was looked on as in training for it. But when war is imminent we can only count on such as can be ready at once, those from twenty years old and upward. The Church of Christ still divisible in the same way—those who can fight, and those who cannot; the men who are strong, because of the solid food they take, and the babes who are still hanging on milk and spoon meat. *The Levites also were left out.* A numerical loss may yet be a real gain. The Israelites were strong in their 600,000 only as long as they served God, according to his statutes and commandments. For the Levites to go to battle meant that all would go to neglect and disorder in the tabernacle. God obeyed and honoured is God on our side, and who then can be against us? The man who keeps his fifty-two sabbaths every year for God has not lost them, and the weekly contribution set aside for God's cause is not wasted. Secondly, *the order* observed in the numbering. By each tribe and family the result would be more speedily and correctly arrived at. Nature, even under the curse of sin, has its order, and will help us, if we are observant of it, to do the work of grace in an orderly way. Though there is a limit at the one end of life, there is none mentioned *at the other*. A man is never too old to fight for God, directing and inspiring the stronger arm of younger men.   There is room for a Nestor as well as an Achilles, and Venice loved to keep the fame of

"Blind old Dandolo,
Th' octogenarian chief, Byzantium's conquering foe."

Thirdly, with all the information gained, there was much unknown. Those fit for fight by age could be counted up ; but what of disposition ? who could sift out the Korahs, Dathans, and Abirams, and the people whose hearts lingered after the flesh-pots of Egypt ?—Y.

Vers. 5—16.—*The men of renown who managed the census.* I. THEY ARE MERE NAMES TO US. Were we asked who Eliab was, we should say the eldest, envious, angry brother of David, not the census-taker for Zebulun ; or Gamaliel, he who stood up in the council, not the census-taker for Manasseh.   High as they may have been once, their position in human history is little better than oblivion.

"The long, proud tale of swelling fame
Dried to a brief and barren name."

II. Yet though mere names now, they WERE ONCE WELL KNOWN. Every child of Zebulun would be taught to look up to Eliab.

III. Though mere names to us, THEY DID A USEFUL WORK IN THEIR TIME. It would be no small satisfaction to them, if they looked at the thing rightly, to consider that they had been able to undertake for Moses such an important work as making sure of the fighting strength of each tribe.

IV. There was doubtless some appreciation of their services AT THE TIME, both by Moses and the sober-minded of the people.

V. But in any case GOD HAS MARKED WHAT THEY DID. He has the record of all the faithful and the holy who have only their names in human history, and the far greater part of them not even that.—Y.

Ver. 3.—"*From twenty years old and upward.*" By this census all the young men of Israel were urged to the consideration of a possible claim upon them. It is to the young men that a country looks when her integrity and liberties are in danger. Young men are wanted still to take a brave and intelligent part in the strife of the Church militant. "I have written unto you young men because ye are strong, and the word of God abideth in you, and ye have overcome the wicked one." So Paul to Timothy: "Endure hardness, as a good soldier of Jesus Christ." God's people have to deal with the Canaanites, Amorites, and all the rest of the hostile nations. Many iniquities are in possession of the earth. Old men, who have struggled against them and done something to diminish them, ask who will take up the sword and shield and go forth against the mighty. The word comes to us. "You are fit to fight. Will you fight ? " Young men dazzled with the visions of military glory, here is a campaign where not men are slaughtered, but the evils that ruin men. Our Lord, the Captain of our salvation, will richly equip us with weapons mighty for the pulling down of strongholds, the armour of righteousness on the right hand and the left.—Y.

EXPOSITION.

THE CENSUS TAKEN (vers. 17—46). Ver. 17.—These men. Designated by direct command of God ; yet probably the same, or some of the same, selected by Moses for obvious personal and social reasons a short time before (Exod. xviii. 25).

Ver. 18.—On the first day of the second month. The natural meaning is that the census was completed in one day. If so, the "census papers," the pedigrees and family lists, must have been ready beforehand.

Notice had in fact been given more than a month before, and the lists made up, when the poll-tax was paid.

Ver. 19.—As the Lord commanded Moses, so he numbered them. The usual note of absolute obedience to the Divine instructions ; but it serves to express the fundamental difference between this numbering and David's.

Ver. 21.—Forty and six thousand and five hundred. All the numbers (save of Gad only) are in unbroken hundreds. It might have been so arranged by miracle; but such an overruling would have no assignable object, and therefore it is far better to fall back on the obvious and natural explanation that the totals were approximate. If they were simply the poll-tax figures unaltered, it would be natural to suppose that the offerings were made up in fifty-shekel lots, and the offerers divided as nearly as possible into hundreds. For military purposes a certain number of supernumeraries would be convenient. In the one excepted case of Gad a half-hundred appears for some unexplained cause.

Ver. 24.—**Gad.** He is here ranked immediately after Reuben and Simeon, because he was placed with them in the encampment (see above, ver. 5).

Ver. 26.—**Judah.** The immense and disproportionate increase of Judah is no doubt a difficulty in itself; but it is quite in keeping with the character assigned to him in prophecy and the part played by him in history.

Ver. 32.—**Of the children of Joseph.** Both are numbered as separate tribes, but Ephraim already takes precedence, not as being larger, which is not considered in this list, but according to prophecy (Gen. xlviii. 5, 14).

Ver. 38.—**Of the children of Dan.** The enormous numerical increase in this tribe is the more remarkable because it is clearly intimated that Dan had but one son, Hushim or Shuham (Gen. xlvi. 23; Numb. xxvi.

42). It may, of course, be said that he had other sons not enumerated, but such an assumption is arbitrary and improbable in the face of the family genealogies in ch. xxvi. If he had any other sons, they did not leave any families behind them. But if the sojourning of the Israelites in Egypt was 430 years, according to the plain statement of Exod. xii. 40, even this increase is quite within possible, and even probable, limits, considering the peculiar circumstances and the known fecundity of the race. For if Hushim, who came into Egypt with his grandfather, had only three sons born to him within the next twenty-five years, and if his descendants doubled themselves every quarter of a century, which is not an uncommon rate of increase under certain circumstances, then his numbers would have fully reached 200,000 by the time of the exodus. Perhaps the most puzzling feature about the increase is the great inequality with which it was spread over the various tribes, a fact of which we cannot even suggest any explanation.

Ver. 46. — **Six hundred thousand and three thousand and five hundred and fifty.** See Exod. xxxviii. 26. As the adult male Levites numbered about 10,000, this represents an increase of 13,000 since the exodus. Some thousands had died through the Divine displeasure, but, on the other hand, the natural mortality may have ceased. It was evidently in the purpose of God that *all* who crossed the Red Sea should also enter their promised land.

HOMILETICS.

Vers. 17—46.—*God's army.* We have here, spiritually, the army of the living God numbered and arrayed unto the march and the victory. Consider, therefore—

That it would appear, as far as we can gather from the increase in numbers, that none had died since the exodus, save through disobedience and idolatry. Even so, none can perish or be lost from the vast army which has come through the Red Sea of the blood of Christ, save through their own disobedience, through departing in their heart from the living God, and making them other gods. The armies of God do not and cannot decrease by death, by violence, or accident: such things have no dominion over them; only sin can separate from the society of the elect, from the communion of saints.

HOMILIES BY VARIOUS AUTHORS.

Vers. 44—46.—*The two numberings in the wilderness.* The Bible abounds in statistics. The historical books, in particular, bristle with genealogies and census-tables. "Numbers" gets its name from the circumstance that it contains the tabulated results of two distinct numberings. The statistical chapters are commonly passed over in the consecutive reading of the Scripture, in the family, and in the Church. The wine of the kingdom does not flow from them freely; all the rather ought care to be taken to read and expound them occasionally. All Scripture is profitable; and the statistical chapters, hard and barren as they look, are no exception.

I. For one thing, these chapters serve admirably to ANCHOR THE RELIGION OF THE BIBLE ON THE FIRM GROUND OF HISTORY. The Lord Jesus was not a mythical character, not a mere play of glorious colour on a bank of unsubstantial vapour. He was the son of a daughter of David's house. His genealogy is extant; and a long chain of family registers, imbedded in the historical books of the Old Testament, afford the means of verifying it. The sacred writers are never afraid to descend from the region of moral and religious disquisition into the region of exact numbers, which can be sifted and weighed in the light of our modern statistical science. The importance of all this can hardly be exaggerated, especially for an age like the present, which so confidently calls in question the historical verity of the Scriptures. To come to these census chapters in Numbers. The critics laugh at the idea that a nation of two millions and more were led out of Egypt by Moses and sojourned in the wilderness for forty years. Objections formidable enough are brought forward ; but the objectors have to face the fact that the history, besides giving the round numbers, explain how they were made up. What is more; the details are found, on examination by men expert in statistics, to have such an air of reality that the ablest commentator (Knobel) of the Critical School, can think of no more feasible explanation than to suggest that some Levite must have laid his hands on the report of some real census, taken in a later age, and inserted it here in the Pentateuch. How writings so dishonestly compiled should have reached the high moral elevation of the Pentateuch, the critic has omitted to explain. He is certainly right in taking the chapters in Numbers for veritable census-tables.

II. NOR IS IT ONLY IN THIS GENERAL VIEW OF THEM THAT THESE STATISTICAL CHAPTERS ARE INSTRUCTIVE. The facts recorded (like all the authentic facts of God's providential government of men) are very suggestive. 1. Observe how unequally the several tribes have *multiplied*. Compare Judah and his 74,600 with Benjamin and his 35,400. All family histories and national histories are full of similar inequalities. There are great nations (France, Spain) in which the population is stationary or receding ; others, similarly situated, in which there is steady increase (Germany, Russia). In the course of two or three centuries, facts like these must powerfully affect the history of the world. What hopes with regard to the future are excited by observing that, as a rule, it is the Protestant nations that are multiplying, and replenishing the earth, and subduing it ! 2. How the blessing delivered by Jacob bears fruit after he has gone ; in Gen. xlix. two sons—Judah and Joseph—are honoured above the rest. (*a*) To *Judah* is assigned the primacy of honour and power forfeited by Reuben, the firstborn (vers. 8—12). How the fulfilment of this comes to light in the census at Sinai ! His tribe outnumbers all the others save one ; his tents occupy the place of honour in the camp, being pitched towards the rising of the sun ; his standard (the lion of the tribe of Judah) leads the van in the march ; in the captain of his host, Nahshon, the son of Amminadab, we recognise the ancestor of our Lord. (*b*) *Joseph*, the best-beloved of the twelve, was to be a fruitful vine, a fruitful bough by a well, whose branches run over the wall. His two sons were to become each a several tribe, " as Reuben and Simeon they shall be mine" (Gen. xlviii. 5, 6 ; xlix. 22—26). This also is exactly accomplished ; not only are Ephraim and Manasseh reckoned as two tribes, but each takes rank with the other tribes in respect both to honour and numbers. Contemplating these facts in the light of Jacob's blessing, we can perceive a moral purpose in them ; Joseph and Judah were the two who excelled in godliness and magnanimity. The faithful God keepeth covenant to a thousand generations (comp. Ps. ciii. 17). 3. How a family, which at one time promised well; may catch a blight and fade away. Mark the story of Simeon ; at Sinai he was one of the most populous of the tribes; thirty-eight years later he is much the smallest. From nearly 60,000 he has shrivelled into about 22,000 (comp. 1 Chron. iv. 27). This downward course went on after the conquest. Simeon's allotted inheritance was next to that of the tribe of Judah ; and ere many generations passed he seems to have been absorbed by his more energetic and prosperous brother. The statistics of the Bible, being the digested statement of facts in the Divine government of families and nations, are mines where those who choose to dig find much silver. " The works of the Lord are great, sought out of all them that have pleasure therein."—B.

EXPOSITION.

THE LEVITES (vers. 47—54). Ver. 47.—
Not numbered among them. They *were*
numbered (ch. iii. 39), but not among the
rest; their census was taken separately, and
on a different basis.

Ver. 48.—**Had spoken.** Rather, "spake,"
and so Septuagint. This was the formal
command to separate, although it had been
anticipated to a considerable extent. The
Levites had been marked out from the others
(1) as the tribesmen of Moses and Aaron,
(2) as the champions of Jehovah in the matter of the golden calf (Exod. xxxii. 26, *sq.*);
they had been already employed, or at least
designated, for religious services; and the
peculiarity of their future position in Israel
had been recognised in the Divine legislation
(Levit. xxv. 32, *sq.*), and in their not being
called upon to contribute to the capitation
for the sanctuary. In a word, this ordinance,
like so many others, did little more than give
a formal and direct sanction to a state of
things which had already come into play,
partly through natural causes, partly through
providential directions.

Ver. 51.—**The stranger.** The word appears to mean here any unauthorised person
(see ch. xvi. 40). This is the first intimation
given of the extreme and awful sanctity of
the tabernacle, as the tent of the Divine
Presence. It is, however, quite of a piece

with the anxious warnings against intrusion
upon the holy mount at the time of the
giving of the law (Exod. xix. 21, *sq.*). The
great necessity for Israel was that he should
understand and believe that *the Lord* before
whom he had trembled at Sinai was really
in the midst of him in all his travail and his
danger. This could only be impressed upon
his dull mind and hard heart by surrounding
the presence chamber of Jehovah with awful
sanctities and terrors. At a subsequent
period, when the religious reverence here
thrown around the tabernacle had been
transferred to, or rather concentrated upon,
the ark alone, Uzzah was actually smitten
for breaking this law (1 Chron. xiii. 10).
The tumult raised against St. Paul (Acts
xxi. 27, *sq.*) was justified by a supposed
violation of the same.

Ver. 53.—**That there be no wrath upon
the congregation**—that no man, not being
a Levite, intrude himself through ignorance
or presumption upon the sacredness of the
tabernacle, and so bring death upon himself,
and displeasure upon the people. **The Levites shall keep the charge of the tabernacle.** Out of this command grew the Levitical guard of the temple, which afterwards
played a considerable part in the history of
Israel (2 Kings xi.).

HOMILETICS.

Vers. 47—54.—*The servants of God.* We have here, spiritually, the multitude of
those who are specially devoted to the service and ministry of God, whoever they
may be, and whatever their labour for the body of Christ: that these have their own
duties and charges, and therewith their own immunities and liberties. Or we may
take it rather of all the people of God, *so far as* they rise to the higher religious
life, dying unto the world, and living unto Christ. Consider, therefore—

I. THAT THE LEVITES WERE NOT NUMBERED WITH THE REST, FOR THE ORDINARY
PURPOSES OF THE LIFE IN THE WILDERNESS. Those that are devoted to the service
of God, or addicted to the ministry of the saints, are to be mixed up as little as
possible in the entanglements of business, of politics, of society, and of all the transitory things which make up the life of the world.

II. That they were NOT NUMBERED among the other tribes, not in order that they
might be idle, or have less to do, but THAT THEY MIGHT THE BETTER DO THEIR OWN
WORK which the Lord assigned them. Even so, no one is marked off, or set apart,
that he may live on others, or look down on others, or enjoy more ease or more consideration than others; but only that he may be the more free to do the work which
the Lord hath appointed him.

III. THAT THE SUM OF THEIR LABOUR AND CHARGE WAS TO ATTEND UPON THE
TABERNACLE—to be in waiting upon the Divine presence in the midst of Israel. So
they who would give themselves to the work of Christ must set this before them
as the great object of it all: that he be glorified, and his spiritual presence be
cherished in the midst of his people. As in one sense, the true way to serve God is
to serve his people, so in another the true way to serve the people is to help them to
serve God. Nor is *their* work of least real value, who, having none opportunity of

benefiting their fellows directly, do yet assist by their practice and example to keep alive reverence and devotion amidst a careless world.

IV. That the encamping of the Levites was to be close round about the tabernacle. So those that are especially called to the service of God must have their dwelling very near him: they can only do more for him, on condition of living nearer to him. It is their one real privilege—if they know it—that, having their duties about holy things, and being free from many distractions common to others, they have opportunity of keeping closer to the holy one.

V. That no "stranger" might come nigh unto the tabernacle on pain of death. So can no profane person intrude upon Divine things except at deadly spiritual peril. That nearness to God which is life to the humble and meek is death to the presumptuous soul; that familiarity with holy things which is a source of growth in grace to the holy is hardening and destruction to the unholy. No "stranger" to the atoning love can venture upon the presence of the All-holy and live: every one that knows not God, and has not his love abiding in him, is a "stranger" in this sense.

VI. That very much of the Levites' work was laborious, tiresome, or trivial, yet it was all under the same awful sanctions, and invested with the same holy character. So, if any will be really devoted to the work of Christ, he must do that which falls to his lot, however humble outwardly, or apparently unspiritual; for the work is all one, and all *of* one, if only it be done *for* that one.

HOMILIES BY VARIOUS AUTHORS.

Vers. 47—54.—*The appointment of the Levites to be the sacred tribe.* This is the first of a series of passages in which the law regarding the Levites is delivered. These all occur in Numbers, excepting a very few which are found in Deuteronomy; and they must be read together if you would get a connected and complete view of the statutes relating to the sacred tribe. Read together, the several texts will be found to dovetail one into another. The first is quite general, merely intimating that the Levites were to be numbered and marshalled as a host by themselves, being wholly dedicated to the service of the sanctuary. The second, entitled "The generations" of the Levites, their Family Book, gives particulars regarding their divisions and several offices (chs. iii., iv.). The third describes how they were set apart to office by a solemn purification (ch. viii. 5). Subsequent passages contain (fourthly) the tragic story of Korah and his company (ch. xvi.), and (fifthly) the provision made for the Levites' honourable maintenance (chs. xviii., xxxv.). One who reads this series of passages with care will make a discovery of some value regarding the structure of these books of the Pentateuch. Because the several laws relating to one subject are not set down in one place, as they would be in our books, and are not arranged according to our ideas of order, it is confidently affirmed that they are set down without any order, and indeed that the Mosaic law is a somewhat random collection of documents diverse in date and character. This is certainly an error. The beautiful order discoverable in the ordinances regarding the Levites will be found to prevail in the ordinances—scattered as they may seem—on many other subjects.

I. This, being the earliest notice of the Levites as a separate and sacred tribe, invites us to review the story of their calling. The first step was taken when the Lord, ordaining in Israel a hereditary priesthood, nominated "Aaron the Levite" and his sons. Still, though Aaron the Levite was called, nothing was said regarding the rest of the tribe. But it was plain that one man and his two sons (the whole number of the Aaronites after the death of Nadab and Abihu) could not execute the priests' office for a great nation. Helpers they must have. Who more fit than their brethren of their own tribe? They were much the smallest of the tribes, so that their maintenance would not be too burdensome; and they had already distinguished themselves by their zeal for the Lord to such a degree as amounted to a virtual consecration to his service (see Exod. xxxii. 29). Accordingly, when the order was given to number and marshal the congregation, an exception was made in relation to the Levites. They were numbered by themselves, as a separated and sacred tribe. Recall the fact just noticed, that the Levites were fitted for their office before they were called to it. Their fitness was made manifest before a word was spoken regarding the honourable office in which it was to be exercised. The whole history of the Church is full of similar facts. When some great exigency arises calling for the services of men possessing special qualities of character or attainment, it is generally found that the Head of the Church has anticipated the occasion by raising up the men required. See for an illustrious example, Gal. i. 15, 16.

II. THE WORK APPOINTED TO THE LEVITES. It was "to keep the charge of the tabernacle" (ver. 53). They carried it; guarded it; did all the work of it except offering sacrifice, burning incense, and blessing the people. In a word, they, under the hand and oversight of the priests, attended to the "outward business of the house of God" (Neh. xi. 16). One cannot read this account of the Levites' work without being touched with a sense of the superiority of the Christian Church and its services over the tabernacle and the Levitical ministrations. To thoughtful and spiritually-minded men the Levitical ministrations must have been an intolerable burden. Barnabas the Levite would, without doubt, say Amen when he heard Peter's description of them as "a yoke which neither we nor our fathers were able to bear" (Acts xv. 10). It is right to remember that, as time passed, the yoke was much mitigated. If the Pentateuch gives no express commandment to the Levites except about the external business of the tabernacle, that simply confirms the antiquity of the Pentateuch. By King David they were invited to higher service as *singers* and even as *psalmists*. Jehoshaphat employed them largely as public teachers of the law throughout the cities of Judah (2 Chron. xvii. 8, 9). Moreover, the Levitical services as prescribed by Moses, although burdensome and unprofitable when compared with those of the New Testament Church, had a great purpose to serve both in prefiguring the truth to be afterwards revealed, and as an educational institute by which the people of God were prepared for the better time. It is a good thing to have a charge to keep in connection with Christ's Church, in any capacity, however humble. Better be a Levite to keep the door of the house of God than live without God in a palace.—B.

Vers. 45—50.—"*Differences of administrations*" *in the service of God.* The different departments of service appointed to the host of Israel and to the Levites remind us of similar diversities in national and Church life at present. I. THE SERVICE OF THE SWORD. II. THE SUPERIOR SERVICE OF THE SANCTUARY.

I. 1. The apparent strength of the Israelites was according to the number of its soldiers. So with a nation and its bread-winners, or with a Church and its active workers. The "mixed multitude" (representing hangers-on, idlers, grumblers; ch. xi. 4), not reckoned or "mustered": only true Israelites can be relied on. 2. Their aggregation by tribes illustrates the value of natural affinities in Christian work (vers. 18, 20, 22, &c.). This truth may be applied—(1) To Christian nationalities, whether of a European or Asiatic type: *e. g.* Chinese Churches should not be cast in English moulds. (2) To Christian denominations, which may work best as separate, yet allied denominations, each having its own methods and rallying round the standard of some special truth. We are reminded also of—3. The value of noble Church traditions. "The house of their fathers" had a special honour in the eyes of every patriotic Israelite. So with British Christians: *e. g.* attachment of Episcopalians to the Church of the Protestant martyrs, and of other Christians to the Churches of Puritan, Covenanting, Nonconforming, or Methodist ancestors (Ps. xxii. 4, 5; xxxiv. 4).

II. The Levites were not mustered as soldiers, but were active in another department of service. The ark and its ministries were symbols of the source of the nation's strength. Their valuable services are described as a "warfare" (ch. iv. 23, marg.). Just as in a nation, it is not the hand-workers only that are a source of strength and wealth, but thinkers, writers, lecturers, preachers also, so in a Church the least prominent may not be the least useful (Cf. 1 Cor. xii. 12—28). The Levites pitched nearest the tabernacle (vers. 52, 53), "that there be no wrath," &c. Simeons and Annas in the temple, invalids "dwelling in the secret place of the Most High," may not be "numbered" among the workers of the Church, but may have power with God and prevail as intercessors for their brethren.—P.

Ver. 52.—*Our position in the Church.* "And the children of Israel shall pitch their tents, every man by his own camp, and every man by his own standard, throughout their hosts."

I. UNITY WITHOUT UNIFORMITY. Reading the history of the Israelites, we are made to feel they were assuredly one nation, and yet just as assuredly twelve tribes. Everything was done to keep each tribe separate and yet all the tribes together. So, ever and anon, some new regulation came out to manifest afresh the unity, yet diversity, of Israel. Every man traced his genealogy back to a son of Jacob, and this itself showed him to be of the seed of Abraham. Jacob had a blessing for each of his children separately, a blessing meant to rest upon each tribe down through all its increase and vicissitudes. So here each tribe was numbered as well as the sum of the congregation. Each tribe had its place in resting and in marching; whether honourable or not was scarcely the question, seeing it was by express appointment of Jehovah. And as if to emphasise this separation, it was provided for in Canaan as well as in the wilderness.

II. THE TYPICAL SIGNIFICANCE OF THIS WITH RESPECT TO THE CHURCH. *There are diversities in the Church.* There is *one* Saviour and *one* gospel; but there were twelve apostles, each directly chosen of the Saviour. Consider the epistles: the individuality of the writers is as clear as their inspiration. So there is one Church, but many sects; and one might almost say God has ordered there should be many sects. There is probably no sect in evangelical Christendom but what, if it were possible to interrogate its founders, they would say, "We could do no other." God has honoured all the sects in turn. Princes in Israel and captains in the war against sin have sprung from all of them. We see in part and we prophesy in part; and we do not all see the same parts, and thus our prophecies differ. Must be faithful, each of us, to what we see of truth, keeping clear of all that is censorious with respect to those who, though they differ, are still our brethren. Diversity must belong to the imperfections of mankind. Imperfections in the regenerate even more manifest than in the unregenerate. *In all the diversity there is unity.* Tribe does not infringe on tribe; each man has his own camp, his own standard. But with all these separating regulations, there was a central power to unite. The tribes lay eastward, southward, westward, northward; but eastward, &c. of what? *The tabernacle.* Immediately around it were Aaron and the Levites in special charge, but the whole of Israel was also around it. So in all our diversities we are related to Christ. We cannot separate from one another as long as each is true to him. In all our divisions, even in our sometimes acrimonious disputings, it remains true—one Lord, one faith, one baptism. A family none the less a family though there be many differences among its members. The spirit of Christ is one that first of all produces *life*, and then leads us into *all the truth.* As all the tribes compose one nation, so all the sects one Church. We have all one God and Father, and the features of our celestial parentage will be revealed in each, however much there may be for a time to obscure. *This diversity as well as unity may extend to the heavenly state.* It may belong to heaven as well as earth. Diversity may belong to the perfection of the believer as well as his imperfection. The highest perfection may be that of harmony. This diversity is significantly hinted at in Rev. vii., where twelve thousand are sealed from each tribe. The twelve foundations in the New Jerusalem had each of them its own order of precious stones. Cherish both variety and unity as essential elements in the kingdom of God.—Y.

Ver. 54.—*Remarkable obedience.* "And the children of Israel did according to all that the Lord commanded Moses, so did they." We have here *a remarkable obedience*— very remarkable, as being found in a book marked with records of murmuring, disobedience, and rebellion. Whence the possibility of such a statement here?

I. THE OBEDIENCE WAS IN AN OUTWARD THING. If inward disposition had been demanded as well as outward action, we should hardly have heard such complete obedience spoken of. It is easier to make a pilgrimage to Rome or Jerusalem than to live for one hour in complete surrender to God.

II. THE OBEDIENCE WAS MADE AS EASY AS POSSIBLE. Jehovah told them not only the thing to be done, but the way in which to do it. Besides, something of the same kind had been done a little while before.

III. THERE WERE CERTAIN ENDS TO BE ATTAINED WHICH MADE THE WORK ATTRACTIVE. A certain carnal satisfaction in counting up the full warlike strength of the nation; also a sense of rivalry between tribe and tribe to see which was most numerous. Some commands of God, so far as the *letter* is concerned, may jump with our own inclination. It is further to be noticed that this remarkable obedience did not prevent an early and extensive disobedience in other ways. A command to number the people was not a sufficient test of obedience. Recollect one who said to Christ with respect to the commandments, " All these have I kept from my youth." He little knew a searching test was close at hand. It is possible to render outward service, and that in many ways, and for a long time, with an unchanged heart. The spirit that underlies every ordinance of God may be repugnant to our natural disposition (Matt. vii. 21—23). The practical warning is, that we should labour to make the outward things the fruit and manifestation of the inward. "These things ought ye to have done,"—the numbering, &c.,—" and not left the other undone"—the loving of the Lord with all the heart and soul and might.—Y.

EXPOSITION.

CHAPTER II.

THE ENCAMPING OF THE TRIBES (ch. ii.). Ver. 1.—**The Lord spake unto Moses and unto Aaron.** Probably when they had finished the census, and brought the results into the tabernacle.

Ver. 2.—**Shall pitch by his own standard.** We are not told how they had pitched hitherto; the tribal and family order now enforced was the natural order, but in the absence of precise directions would sometimes be departed from. **With the ensign.** Rather, " ensigns" (*othoth* in the plural). Each tribe, it would seem (see ver. 31), had its standard (*degel*), and each family in the tribe its ensign (*oth*). **Far off.** Rather, " over against," *i. e.* facing the tabernacle, with a certain space (perhaps 2000 cubits, Josh. iii. 4) between.

Ver. 3.—**On the east.** The van, the post of honour. The general direction indeed of their march was northwards, not eastwards; but nothing can obliterate the natural pre-eminence given to the east by the sunrise, the scattering of light upon the earth, the daily symbol of the day-spring from on high. **The standard of the camp of Judah.** Judah led the way not because he was the greatest in number, for the order of the tribes was not determined by this consideration, but because of his place in prophecy, and as the ancestor of the Messiah (Gen. xlix. 10). According to Aben Ezra and other Jewish expositors, the device upon the standard of Judah was a young lion, and this agrees with Rev. v. 5. The same authorities assign to Reuben a man, to Ephraim an ox (cf. Deut. xxxiii. 17), to Dan an eagle. If it were so, we should find in these banners the origin of the forms of the living creatures in the visions of Ezekiel and St. John (Ezek. i. 26; x. 1; Rev. iv. 4—6), unless, indeed, the devices on the standards were themselves taken from the symbolic forms of the

cherubim in the tabernacle, and these in their turn borrowed from the religious art of Egypt. But the tradition of the Jews is too fluctuating to carry any weight. The Targum of Palestine assigns to Judah the lion, but to Reuben a stag, to Ephraim a young man, and to Dan a basilisk serpent.

Ver. 5.—**Next unto him.** Whether the leading tribe occupied the centre or one extreme of its own side of the encampment is a matter of mere speculation.

Ver. 9.—**These shall first set forth.** No order to set forth had been given, but the necessity of doing so was understood, and is here anticipated, as in ch. i. 51.

Ver. 14.—**Reuel.** Probably an error of transcription for Deuel, which actually appears here in many MSS. The Septuagint, however, has Raguel (see ch. i. 14; vii. 42, &c.). The error is utterly unimportant, except as proving the possibility of errors in the sacred text.

Ver. 17.—**Then the tabernacle . . shall set forward.** Thus it was provided that, whether at rest or on the march, the Divine habitation should be exactly in the midst of Israel.

Ver. 24.—**All that were numbered of the camp of Ephraim.** All the descendants of Rachel, forming at this time the smallest of the four divisions, although destined to become very numerous. Their association in the camp was continued in the promised land, for the greater part of their territory was coterminous. Subsequently, however, the great division of the kingdom separated Benjamin for ever from his brethren. **In the third rank.** Immediately behind the tabernacle. This position is clearly alluded to in Ps. lxxx. 1, 2.

Ver. 25.—**The standard of . . Dan.** In the light of its subsequent history, it is remarkable that this tribe should at this time have been so prominent and so honoured. Dan is, so to speak, the Judas among the twelve. In history he ends by melting away into the heathen among whom he intruded himself. In the sacred writings he ends by being omitted altogether; he has no part in the new Jerusalem—perhaps on account of the idolatry connected with his name (see Judges xviii.; Rev. vii.).

Ver. 34.—**So they pitched.** The Targum of Palestine (which embodies the traditional learning of the Palestinian Jews of the 17th century) says that the camp covered a space of twelve square miles. Modern writers, starting from some measurements of the Roman camps given by Polybius, compute the necessary space at three or three and a half miles square. This would require the strictest discipline and economy of space, and makes no provision for cattle; but supposing that the women and children were closely packed, it might suffice. It is, however, evident that there would be very few places in the wilderness, if any, where more than three square miles of fairly level ground could be found. In the plains of Moab the desired room might perhaps have been found, but scarcely anywhere in the wilderness of Paran. We must conclude, therefore, that this order of encampment was an ideal order, beautiful indeed by reason of its faultless regularity and equality, but only to be attained in practice as circumstances should permit, more or less. Indeed, that the foursquare symmetry of the camp had an ideal meaning and significance more really, because more permanently, important than its actual realisation at the time, is evident from its recurrence again and again in the Apocalyptic writings (see Ezek. xlviii. 20, and especially Rev. xxi. 16). It is impossible to help seeing that the description of the heavenly Zion is that of a city, but of a city modelled upon the pattern of the camp in the wilderness. Here is one of those cases in which the spiritual significance of an order is of such importance that it matters comparatively little whether it *could* be literally carried out or not.

HOMILETICS.

Ch. ii. —*The camp of the Saints.* We have here, spiritually, the Church of God in its order and its beauty and its balanced proportion of parts; resting inwardly upon, and ranged outwardly around, the abiding presence of the Almighty, and thus prepared either to abide in harmony and safety, or to set forward without confusion and without fear. Consider, therefore, on a broad view of this chapter—

I. THAT THE ONE AND ONLY CENTRE OF THE WHOLE CAMP, of all its symmetry and all its order, WAS THE TABERNACLE OF GOD. About this were arranged in the inner lines of encampment the priests and Levites, in the outer lines the rest of Israel; the tent of the Presence was, as it were, the jewel of priceless worth, of which the camps of Levi formed the inner case, the other camps the outer casket. Even so the whole Church of God, in its broadest extent, is centred upon and drawn up about the spiritual presence of God in Christ, according to that which is written: "I will dwell in them, and walk in them." Whether for rest or for progress, for safety or success, all depends exclusively upon, all can be measured only with reference to, that Presence in the midst of her. She is herself, in the truest sense, the living shrine, the spiritual casket, which encloses and enfolds this Divine jewel. About this Presence—"over against" it, full in view of it, looking straight towards it, albeit separated yet by an uncrossed interval—all the tribes of God are drawn up, all of them near, all equally near, save that those are nearest who are specially devoted to the waiting upon that Presence.

II. That as the glory and beauty of the encampment depended as to its internal symmetry upon the presence of God in the midst of it, SO IT DEPENDED AS TO ITS OUTWARD PERFECTION UPON THE ORDERLY ARRANGEMENT AND HARMONY OF ITS PARTS. Every tribe and every family had its place, knew its place, kept its place, mutually supporting and supported by all the others. Even so God is not the author of confusion, but of peace, in all the Churches of the saints. Conflicting aims, rivalries, counter-workings, cannot be in the Divine ideal. Towards them that are without, in the face of the difficulties and hostilities of the Church's earthly pilgrimage, an absolute discipline, a perfect oneness of purpose, a universal walking by the same rule and minding the same thing, is an essential part of the truth as it is in Jesus (John xvii. 21, 22; 1 Cor. i. 10; Phil. ii. 2; iii. 16).

III. That this perfect order and discipline was not attained by ignoring or effacing the natural divisions and distinctions of the people, and by making of each individual an isolated unit before God ; but, on the contrary, BY RECOGNISING AND UTILISING HUMAN DIVISIONS. "Every man shall pitch by his own standard, with the ensign of their father's house." Even so within the common life of the Church of Christ there is room and use for many strong and lasting divergencies of Christian character and cast of thought due to national or social or educational distinctions. Variety embraced in unity is the law of the Spirit. There is a true sense in which all Christian truth and virtue are the proper heritage of each Christian soul, which each ought to possess ; but there is also a true sense in which the Christian virtues, and even the complemental truths of the Christian faith, are rather distributed among the various portions of the Church than equally spread over all, or perfectly combined in any one. If we would have a true conception of the *full* beauty and power of Christianity, we must embrace in one view all the ages of faith, we must have respect unto east and west and north and south alike. If our own sympathies are chiefly with one or other, there will be the more reason to give heed that we do not overlook the excellence most remote from our own. Dan and Simeon, whatever might be said or feared of them, had their place in the camp of God as well as Judah and Ephraim.

Consider, again, on a closer inspection of the camp—1. That it lay foursquare in twelve great divisions, with the tabernacle in the centre. And this arrangement is clearly of spiritual import, because it is carefully preserved in the prophetic visions of Ezekiel and St. John. The heavenly city, which is the camp of the saints, lieth foursquare, and the length is as large as the breadth (Rev. xx. 9 ; xxi. 16). And this seems to denote the absolute and unbroken equality, and the equal development in every direction, of the heavenly state, wherein it contrasts so strongly with the strange inequality and the one-sided character of all earthly good. The Church should lie foursquare because she should show an equal front, and have attained a like extension *in every direction*, in whatsoever way regarded. And notice here that the superior perfection of the gospel is shown herein, that the holy city not only lieth as a perfect square, but standeth as a perfect cube,—"the length and the breadth and the height of it are equal " (Rev. xxi. 16),—an impossibility bordering on the grotesque, in order to emphasise the entire absence of *anything* one-sided, unequal, or imperfect. Again, the holy city, like the camp of Israel, is laid out with careful respect unto the number twelve, because this is the full and perfect number of the tribes, and intimates that the Church is of all, and for all, who can in any wise be reckoned as the people of God. 2. That the foursquare arrangement of the camp was ideal, and could only be approximately realised in the wilderness through the evil necessity of things : the camps could not be pitched across rugged mountains or precipitous ravines, such as constantly lay in their way. Even so the ideal picture of the Church drawn in the New Testament has never been adequately realised, nor perhaps can be, amidst the confusions and contradictions of time. Her harmony and symmetry are grievously marred for want of room, and through the impracticable nature of men and circumstances. Nevertheless, the Divine ideal lives before her eyes and within her heart, and it is the unchanging hope of every faithful soul to behold it realised, sooner or later, in the good providence of God. In the mean time, when outward regularity was impossible, the one thing for each tribe to do was to pitch as near to the tabernacle, on its own side, as possible. Even so the practical wisdom and duty of every Church is to abide as near to God as it can according to the truth and order it has received ; the nearer to God, the closer to one another. 3. That, among the tribes, Judah held the van, and his standard led the way, on which was borne aloft "the lion of the tribe of Judah." Even so Christ—concerning whom "it is evident that our Lord sprang out of Juda " (Heb. vii. 14)—must always go before us in the way, and all the hosts of light must follow after him. 4. That Dan at this time was very large in numbers, and held an honourable place, and was a standard-bearer ; yet afterwards he dwindled, and left the place given him by Providence, and sought another for himself, and fell into idolatry, and was struck out at last from the list of the Israel of God. Even so it happens that some particular Church or some individual at one time shall stand high, and be a leader, and hold a place of command, yet afterwards shall swerve from the right way, and fall into some idolatry, and be cast out as evil at the last. But it is not necessary to seek to discover wickedness in the first estate because it is in the last ; as in Dan it is not possible to find any cause of wrath while he walked with the others in the wilderness; and even Judas must have been sincere at first, and was not discerned from the other eleven. 5. That at this time the children of Leah were all together, and that this union was apparently made sure for ever by their dwelling side by side in Canaan. Yet when the great division came, Ephraim and Manasseh went one way, Benjamin the other. Even so it often happens that those who have grown up together as brethren in the common enjoyment of spiritual blessings and practice of religious duties, are thereafter widely separated by some great sifting, and take opposite sides on some fundamental question.

HOMILIES BY VARIOUS AUTHORS.

Ch. ii.—*The muster at Sinai.* The children of Israel in the wilderness were a divinely-framed figure or parable of the Church of Christ. Devout readers of the story of the long march from Egypt to Canaan have always been haunted with such an irrepressible feeling of this figurative and spiritual intention, that traces of it are apparent in the familiar speech of all the Christian nations. Christians everywhere speak of redemption from bondage, the wilderness of this world, the wilderness journey, the heavenly manna, the "Rock of ages cleft for me," the land of promise, Pisgah views of the better land, the dark Jordan, the promised inheritance. The muster at Sinai is a chapter in the long parable; a chapter as replete as any with instruction regarding the Church of God.

I. THE CHURCH IS AN ARMY. The enumeration at Sinai was not an ordinary census. It took note only of such as were fit to bear arms. These opening chapters of Numbers are a muster-roll. The Church in this world is the Church militant. Christ is a Man of war (Ps. xlv. 3—5). Every true follower of Christ is called to be a soldier, and to fight a good fight. There is no place in Christ's host either for neutrals or non-combatants (Matt. xii. 30).

II. THE CHURCH IS AN ARMY ON THE MARCH. 1. Not settled in permanent quarters. The wilderness was not a place to build cities in or to plant vineyards. As little is the world a continuing city to Christ's saints. Compare "this tabernacle," 2 Cor. v. 1; 2 Pet. i. 14. We are passing travellers here. 2. Marching to an appointed place. In some sense all men—believers and unbelievers alike—are on the march. Compare the Anglo-Saxon prince's comparison of human life to the flight of the bird out of the dark night, through the lighted hall, and out by the opposite door into the darkness again. God's people are not only passers-by, but "strangers" here, who have in view a country beyond. Their back is toward Egypt, their face toward Canaan, and they are on the move from the one to the other.

> "We nightly pitch our moving tent
> A day's march nearer home."

III. THE CHURCH IS AN ARMY WITH BANNERS. Not a mob, but a marshalled host. Observe the order prescribed in this chapter for the encampment and for the march. This idea of the Church has often been abused to the support of ecclesiastical systems for which there is no warrant in the New Testament. The sort of organised unity proper to the Hebrew Church cannot be transferred to the Church Catholic. Still the idea is true and valuable. God is a God of order, and not of confusion. We believe in the communion of saints. Christians are not to fight every one for his own hand, or march every one by himself. It is a good and pleasant thing for brethren to come together and keep together.

IV. THE CHURCH IS AN ARMY OF WHICH GOD KEEPS A PERFECT ROLL. A good general would like to know, and Christ does know, every one of his men by name, and they are written in his book. When a soul is born again—born in Zion—the Lord registers the fact (Ps. lxxxvii. 6); and he continually remembers the person's name. "I am poor and needy, yet the Lord thinketh upon me."

V. THE CHURCH IS AN ARMY WHICH HAS THE LORD FOR ITS EVER-PRESENT LEADER AND COMMANDER. The ark of the covenant led the van on the march, and rested in the midst of the congregation when it encamped. "Go ye into all the world; . . . and, lo, I am with you alway."—B.

Vers. 1, 2.—*God's tabernacle in the midst of Israel's tents.* I. As THE SOURCE OF ORDER. Israel formed an armed encampment, not a mob. The place of each tribe was assigned by God, and thus was not a matter of caprice or partiality on the part of Moses (ver. 34). They were grouped according to their tribes and families. A post in the rearguard was as honourable as one in the van, because a matter of Divine appointment. Yet all "afar off," as a sign of the reverence due to their God. Apply this truth to the tribes, *i. e.* the visible Churches and denominations of the Israel of God. This may be illustrated from apostolic days, or from modern Church history. Each has a position, historical, geographical, social, assigned by the providence of God. Each tribe had some peculiarities (cf. Gen. xlix.), as each section of the Church has. And as there were, no doubt, reasons for the position allotted to every family, so the God of "order" and "peace" (1 Cor. xiv.) designed that every Church should fill its appointed place ("by its own standard," &c.), and, as part of the militant host, stand in orderly relations to himself and to the brotherhood. The same truth extends to individuals, the bounds of their habitation and the sphere of their service having been fixed by God.

II. As A CENTRE OF ATTRACTION. The doors of the tents probably faced the tabernacle. It was a centre of attraction—1. For guidance, through the high priest, and Moses, and the symbolic cloud (cf. Ps. xxv. 4, 5, 9, 15). 2. For pardon, through sacrifice. And God himself is the only hope of a sinful Church (Jer. xiv. 7—9 ; 2 Cor. v. 18, 19). 3. For purity, through the restraining and elevating influence of a holy God ever present in their midst (cf. Deut. xxiii. 14 with 2 Cor. vi. 16—vii. 1).

III. As A PLEDGE OF SAFETY, both when encamped (ver. 2) or on the march (ver. 17). So "God is in the midst" " of the tabernacles of the Most High," the homes of his people (cf. Deut. iv. 7, and Rom. viii. 31). He is in our midst as "a lion" to terrify our foes (Hos. xi. 10 ; see Acts v. 17—42), as a fire to enlighten and to protect (Isa. iv. 5), as "a man of war" to fight for us (Isa. xlix. 25, 26 ; Numb. xxiii. 21). This presence of God in our midst should inspire (1) confidence (Deut. xxxiii. 29), (2) reverence (Ps. lxxxix. 7), (3) joy (Ps. cxviii. 15), and should prepare us for the fulfilment of the promise in Rev. xxi. 3—7.—P.

Ch. ii.—*The discipline of God's army.* As the first chapter discovers the *size* of God's army, so the second discovers the *discipline* of it. Number is nothing without order and discipline. A handful of cavalry can scatter a mob. Discipline also *prevents rivalries.* If those about our Lord, in spite of all his teaching, asked, "Who shall be greatest in the kingdom of heaven?" then we may be sure there were many ambitious souls asking in the wilderness, "Who shall be greatest in Israel?" The discipline set before us in this chapter was particularly related to *the tabernacle.* In this connection the discipline may be regarded as intended to secure three things.

I. REVERENCE FOR THE SANCTUARY. They were to pitch the camp far off about the tabernacle. There was plenty of a superstitious and idolatrous spirit among the Israelites, but the reverence was wanting that comes from intelligent appreciation. But for a special injunction to the contrary, they would very likely have crowded round the tabernacle, as feeling nothing peculiar about the ark. This lesson of reverence had to be sharply taught again and again, *e. g.* to the Philistines and the men of Bethshemesh (1 Sam. v. and vi.), and to Uzzah (2 Sam. vi.). The fear of God is not only the beginning of wisdom, but also of security and spiritual conquests. It is a fearful thing to fall into the hands of the living God. The Israelites carried about with them something as awful as the mount that burned with fire. So in the Church of Christ there should be a deep habitual reverence for the Almighty. The death of Ananias and Sapphira is a lesson for all ages as to the danger of forgetting that God is strict to mark iniquity. Confidence is necessary, but in our boldest approaches there must be the deepest humility. If we waged our spiritual warfare with real reverence for the great Trinity above, there would be more success.

II. DEFENCE OF THE SANCTUARY. It was in the midst, alike in resting and in marching. Travellers in savage countries circle themselves with fire at night, to keep off the wild beasts. So the circling tribes were to be a defence to the tabernacle. The company of Judah marched in front, and Dan brought up the rear. Judah went from honour to honour among the tribes, until the honour culminated in the inn at

Bethlehem.   Reuben, though the eldest, was not put first.   " Unstable as water, thou shalt not excel."   He could do something, leaning on Judah ; not last, yet not competent to be first.   But exactly all the reasons why the tribes were arranged *thus, and not otherwise*, we cannot tell.   Jehovah had the sovereign disposal of the matter ; not therefore arbitrary, or without cause.   A commander does not give reasons for his strategy, though some of them may be afterwards discoverable.   God has given his people to defend the sanctuary still, to contend earnestly for the faith once for all delivered to the saints ; against the paganism of the old world, and all sorts of corruption in Christendom itself ; against the pride of science transgressing its borders.   We have to fight for an *open* Bible, free to every one caring to read it ; a *full* Bible, its truths not minimised or attenuated to suit the fancies of men ; a *pure* Bible, interpreted in its own light, and not confused with the distortions of later traditions.   The Scriptures are our tabernacle, and we must defend them as something solemnly put in our charge.

III. PROTECTION FROM THE SANCTUARY.   That which we defend protects us.   Peter, before the Council, asserted and acted his right to preach the gospel.   "We must obey God rather than men."   Defending what was committed to his charge, he also was defended when God delivered him from Herod's prison.   The unfaithful are the insecure.   When we are searching the Bible to defend it against the attacks of its enemies, we are multiplying comforts and defences for our own souls.   How many looking for arguments have also found balm and security !   The Lord would have Israel to understand that it was not because they were 600,000, but because he was their Leader, they were strong.   Let our protection come from God.   Protections of human device are like the experiments in modern naval construction.   A defence may be announced perfect, but some new weapon will make it worthless.   The shield of faith alone will quench all the fiery darts of the wicked one.   Compare 1 Cor. xiv. with this chapter, as showing the need both for order and discipline.—Y.

EXPOSITION.

CHAPTER III.

THE NUMBERS AND DUTIES OF THE LE-VITES ; THEIR SUBSTITUTION FOR THE FIRST-BORN (ch. iii.).   Ver. 1.—**These .. are the generations of Aaron and Moses**.   The word " generations" (*toledoth*) is used here in a peculiar and, so to speak, technical sense, with reference to what follows, as in Gen. ii. 4 ; vi. 9.   It marks a new departure, looking *down*, not *up*, the course of history.   Moses and Aaron were a beginning in themselves as the chosen heads of the chosen tribe :   Moses having the higher office, but one entirely personal to himself ; Aaron being the first of a long and eminent line of priests.   The actual genealogy, therefore, is that of Aaron, and he is placed first.   **In the day**.   Apparently the day mentioned in ch. i. 1 ; or it may be more general, as in Gen. ii. 4.

Ver. 3. — **Whom he consecrated**.   The "he" is impersonal ; the Septuagint has, " whose hands *they* filled."

Ver. 4.—**They had no children**.   If they had left sons, these would have succeeded to their office, and to the headship of the priestly line.   **In the sight of Aaron**.   In his lifetime (cf. Gen. xi. 28).   Septuagint, "with Aaron."   In the time of David the descendants of Eleazar were divided into sixteen courses, the descendants of Ithamar into eight (2 Chron. xxiv. 3).

Ver. 6.—**Bring the tribe of Levi near**. Not by any outward act of presentation, but by assigning to them solemnly the duties following.   The expression is often used of servants coming to receive orders from their masters.

Ver. 7.—**They shall keep his charge, and the charge of the whole congregation**. Septuagint, " shall keep his watches, and the watches of the children of Israel."   The Levites were to be the servants of Aaron on the one side, and of the whole congregation on the other, in the performance of their religious duties.   The complicated ceremonial now prescribed and set in use could not possibly be carried out by priests or people without the assistance of a large number of persons trained and devoted to the work. Compare St. Paul's words to the Corinthians (2 Cor. iv. 5), "Ourselves your servants for Jesus' sake."

Ver. 8.—**Instruments**.   Vessels and furniture.   Septuagint, σκεύη.   Vulgate, *vasa*.

Ver. 9. **They are wholly given unto him**. The word *nethunim* (wholly given) is emphatic here, and in ch. viii. 16.   As the whole house of Israel at large, so especially (for a reason which will presently appear) the tribe of Levi belonged absolutely to God ;

and he, as absolutely, made them over to Aaron and the priests for the service of his sanctuary. Cf. Eph. iv. 11, "*gave* some apostles," &c. The Levites, as gifts from God (*nethunim*) to their brethren the priests, must be distinguished from the *nethinim* or serfs of foreign extraction given by the congregation of the Levites to do their most menial work for them (Josh. ix. 27).

Ver. 10.—**The stranger that cometh nigh.** This constantly recurring formula has not always quite the same meaning: in ch. i. 51 it signified any one not of the tribe of Levi ; here it includes even the Levite who was not also a priest. The separation of the Levites for the ministry of the tabernacle was not to infringe in the least upon the exclusive rights of Aaron and his sons.

Ver. 12.—**I have taken the Levites.** The actual separation of Levi had been already anticipated (see ch. i. 47, 53), but the meaning and purpose of that separation is now formally declared. No reason, however, is assigned for the choice of this particular tribe. It is almost always assumed that their zeal in the matter of the golden calf was the ground of the preference shown to them now. But it may be doubted whether there was any "preference" in the matter at all. To Aaron and his seed an undoubted and important preference was shown, but the functions and position of the Levites were not such as to give them any pre-eminence, or to secure them any substantial advantage. They were tied down to the performance of routine duties, which demanded no intelligence, and gave scope for no ambitions. The one obvious reason why Levi was selected is to be found in the fact that he was by far the smallest in numbers among the tribes, being less than half the next smallest, Manasseh, and almost exactly balancing the first-born. A larger tribe could not have been spared, and would not have been needed, for the purpose in question. If any more recondite motive must be sought for the Divine selection, it must be found in the prophecy of Gen. xlix. 7. Levi as well as Simeon, though in a different way, was doomed never to raise his head as a united and powerful tribe among his brethren.

Ver. 13.—**Because all the first-born are mine** (see Exod. xiii. 2, and below on ver. 43). That the powers of heaven had a special claim upon the firstling of man or beast was probably one of the oldest religious ideas in the world, which it would be difficult to trace to any origin but in some primeval revelation. It branched out into many superstitions, of which the cruel cultus of Moloch was the worst. Among the tribes which preserved the patriarchal faith, it retained more or less of its primitive meaning in the assignment of sacrificial duties to the

eldest son. According to the Targums, the "young men of the children of Israel" sent by Moses to offer sacrifices before the consecration of Aaron (Exod. xxiv. 5) were first-born. Whatever ancient and latent claims, however, God may have had upon the first-born of Israel, they are here superseded by a special and recent claim founded upon their miraculous preservation when the first-born of the Egyptians were slain. All the first-born in that day became "anathema," devoted to God, for evil or for good, for death or for life. He, to whom belongs the whole harvest of human souls, came and claimed his first-fruits from the fields of Egypt. He took unto himself by death the first-born of the Egyptians ; he left for himself in life the first-born of the Israelites. For the convenience, however, of the people, and for the better and more regular discharge of the ministry, he was content to take the single small tribe of Levi in lieu of the first-born of all.

Ver. 12.—**Instead of all the first-born.** The Septuagint inserts here, "they shall be their ransom."

Ver. 13.—**Mine shall they be: I am the Lord.** Rather, "mine shall they be, mine, the Lord's."

Ver. 15.—**From a month old.** The first-born were to be redeemed "from a month old" (ch. xviii. 16).

Ver. 17.—**These were the sons of Levi.** These genealogical notices are inserted here in order to give completeness to the account of the Levites in the day of their dedication.

Ver. 23.—**Shall pitch.** These directions as to the position and duties of the Levitical families retain the form in which they were originally given. The way in which they are mixed up with direct narrative affords a striking proof of the inartificial character of these sacred writings. **Behind the tabernacle westward.** The tabernacle opened or looked eastward towards the sunrise.

Ver. 25.—**The charge of the sons of Gershon.** See ch. iv. 24—26.

Ver. 28.—**Eight thousand and six hundred.** The four families of the Kohathites, of which that of Amram was one, must have contained about 18,000 souls. Moses and Aaron were sons of Amram, and they seem to have had but two sons apiece at this time. If, therefore, the family of the Amramites was at all equal in numbers to the other three, they must have had more than 4000 brothers and sisters, nephews and nieces. It is urged in reply that Amram lived 137 years, and may have had many other children, and that the variations in the comparative rates of increase are so great and so unaccountable that it is useless to speculate upon them. There is, however, a more serious difficulty connected with the genealogy of Moses and

Aaron, as given here and elsewhere. If they were the great-grandchildren of Levi on their father's side, and his grandchildren on their mother's side, it is impossible to maintain the obvious meaning of Exod. xii. 40. Either the genealogy must be lengthened, or the time must be very much shortened for the sojourning in Egypt. The known and undoubted habit of the sacred writers to omit names in their genealogies, even in those which seem most precise, lessens the difficulty of the first alternative, whereas every consideration of numbers, including those in this passage, increases the difficulty of the second. To endeavour to avoid either alternative, and to force the apparent statements of Scripture into accord by assuming a multiplicity of unrecorded and improbable miracles at every turn (as, *e. g.*, that Jochebed, the mother of Moses, was restored to youth and beauty at an extreme old age), is to expose the holy writings to contempt. It is much more reverent to believe, either that the genealogies are very imperfect, or that the numbers in the text have been very considerably altered. Every consideration of particular examples, still more the general impression left by the whole narrative, favours the former as against the latter alternative.

Ver. 30.—**Elizaphan the son of Uzziel**—of the youngest branch. This may have aroused the jealousy of Korah, who represented an elder branch.

Ver. 32. — **Eleazar.** The priests were themselves Kohathites, and therefore their chief is here mentioned as having the oversight over the other overseers—*ipsos custodes custodiens*.

Ver. 38.—**Before the tabernacle toward the east, . . . Moses, and Aaron and his sons.** The most central and honourable place in the camp, and the most convenient for constant and direct access to the sanctuary. Moses held a wholly personal and exceptional position as king in Jeshurun (Deut. xxxiii. 5); Aaron was hereditary high priest. Between them they represented the union of royal and sacerdotal authority, which had many partial continuations in Jewish history, but was fully realised in Christ.

Ver. 39.—**Twenty and two thousand.** It is obvious that there is a discrepancy between this total and its three component numbers, which make 22,300. It is so obvious that it must have been innocent; no one deliberately falsifying or forging would have left so palpable a discrepancy on the face of the narrative. It may, therefore, have arisen from an error in transcription (the alteration of a single letter would suffice); or it may be due to the fact that, for some reason not stated, 300 were struck off the Levitical total for the purpose of this census. Such a reason was found by the Hebrew expositors, and has been accepted by some moderns, in the fact that the Levites were taken and counted instead of the first-born, and that, therefore, their own first-born would have to be excluded. There is nothing to be said against this explanation, except that no trace of it appears in a narrative otherwise very full and minute. The first-born of the Levites *may* have been just 300 (although the number is singularly small), and they *may* have been considered ineligible for the purpose of redeeming other first-born; but if so, why did not the sacred writer say so, instead of silently reducing the total of "all that were numbered of the Levites"?

Ver. 43.—**Twenty and two thousand two hundred and threescore and thirteen.** These were the first-born of the twelve tribes; but who were included under the designation "first-born" is a matter of grave dispute. The smallness of their number (not much above one per cent. of the whole population) has given rise to several conflicting theories, all of which seem to be artificial, arbitrary, and therefore unsatisfactory. It is urged by some that the expression "every male that openeth the womb" must be strictly pressed, and that there would be no "first-born" in those families (which form a considerable majority) in which either a girl was born first, or the eldest, being a boy, had died. It is further urged that only those first-born would be counted who were not themselves fathers of families. These considerations will indeed reduce the probable numbers very largely, but not to the required amount. Others, again, give an entirely different turn to the difficulty by urging that as the command in Exod. xiii. 1 was prospective only, so at this time only the first-born since the exodus were counted. This makes it necessary to assume an altogether unprecedented birth-rate during that short period. One other explanation strives to satisfy the arithmetical conditions of the problem by assuming that the whole of the Divine legislation in this matter was in reality directed against the worship of Moloch, and was designed to prevent the offering of first-born to him by redeeming them unto himself. As the rites of Moloch only demanded young children of tender age, only such were counted in this census. It may, indeed, be very probably concluded that their heavenly Father *did* claim these first-born, partly in order to save them from Moloch, because the people would thereafter be exposed to the fascination of that horrid superstition; but there is no proof whatever that they were acquainted with it at this time. These cruel rites, together with many other heathen abominations, are forbidden in Levit. xviii. 21 and Deut. xviii. 10, in view of the entry into Canaan, where they were practised. The prophet Amos, when he reproaches them with having "carried the tabernacle of" their "Moloch" even in the wilderness (Amos v. 26), absolves them by implication from any darker superstition ; and the highly rhetorical passage Ezek. xx. 26 seems to refer to the consequences of disobedience at a later date, and can hardly be pressed against the entire silence of the Pentateuch. Anyhow it does not seem possible, on the strength of a supposed intention on the part of God of which no trace appears in the text, to impose a narrow and arbitrary limit upon the plain command to number "all the first-born, from a month old and upward." If we turn from these speculations to the reason and ground of the matter as stated by God himself, it will appear much more simple. It was distinctly on the ground of their preservation from the destroying angel in Egypt that the first-born of Israel were claimed as God's *peculium* now (see ver. 13). The command in Exod. xiii. 1 was no doubt prospective, but the sanctification of the first-born was based upon the deliverance itself ; and this command was intended not to limit that sanctification for the present, but to continue it for the future. Now if we turn to Exod. xii. 29, 30, and ask who the first-born were whom the destroying angel cut off, we see plainly enough that they included the eldest son, being a child, in every house ; that every family lost one, and only one. On the one hand, Pharaoh himself was in all probability a first-born, but he was not in any personal danger, because he ranked and suffered as a father, not as a son. On the other hand, the majority of families in which the first-born was a daughter, or had died, did not therefore escape : "there was not a house where there was not one dead." Taking this as the only sure ground to go upon, we may conclude with some confidence that the first-born now claimed by God included all the eldest sons in the families of Israel who were not themselves the heads of houses. These were the destroyed in Egypt —these the redeemed in Israel. How they came to be so few in proportion is a matter in itself of extremely slight importance, and dependant, perhaps, upon causes of which no record was left.

Ver. 47. — **Five shekels apiece.** This amount had already been fixed (Levit. xxvii. 6, if indeed this chapter does not belong to a later period) as the commutation value of a male child under five years old who had been vowed unto the Lord. If the redeeming of the first-born by the Levites began with the eldest, those that were left over would all be within this age. **A shekel.** See Exod. xxx. 13.

Ver. 51.—**Gave the money . . . unto Aaron.** The Levites were given to Aaron in lieu of the first-born. As, however, their number fell somewhat short, the redemption money taken for the remainder was due to Aaron as compensation, and was doubtless applied to the support of the tabernacle worship.

HOMILETICS.

Ch. iii.—*The servants of God, and the Church of the First-born.* We may see in this chapter, spiritually, the obligation of the whole people to be the bond-servants of Jesus Christ, and the dedication, as their representatives in the outward and visible service of God, of such as are separated unto the Holy Spirit at his call. For the whole Church of Jesus Christ is the general assembly and Church of the first-born, and they are all wholly his by right of redemption, and are all priests unto God ; nevertheless, for convenience, and almost of necessity, their outward ministry and service in holy things is discharged by such as God's choice and their own aptness have marked out therefor.

Consider, therefore, WITH RESPECT TO THE LEVITES—

I. THAT THEY WERE "WHOLLY GIVEN" UNTO AARON, THE HIGH PRIEST. EVEN SO THEY THAT ARE DEVOTED UNTO SACRED MINISTRIES ARE "WHOLLY GIVEN" UNTO JESUS CHRIST, the great High Priest, and are placed at his disposal, that he may use their labours according to his will ; and this is the one simple consideration which must govern their life, unless they be rebellious.

II. That they were given unto Aaron "TO KEEP HIS CHARGE, AND THE CHARGE OF THE WHOLE CONGREGATION ; " *i. e.* TO ASSIST HIM AND TO ASSIST THEM IN THE DISCHARGE OF THEIR SEVERAL OFFICES AND DUTIES, so that they might be rendered aright to the well-pleasing of God. Even so it is in the deepest sense true (if rightly considered) that every one who has some special call is a partner partly in the work of Christ, partly in the duty of the Church ; he helps to carry on the one or to discharge the other (or both). The atonement indeed was made by Aaron—as by Christ—himself, alone ; but the outward and subordinate matters of his office he discharged by means of the Levites, and he could not otherwise have discharged them. Even so does Christ outwardly and visibly fulfil his manifold office upon earth by the mouths and by the hands of his servants. Thus, if any preach the word, he is doing the work of Christ our Prophet; if any minister to the sick, of Christ our Healer; if any feed his lambs, of Christ our Good Shepherd; if any rule over men for their good, of Christ our King. Even if any suffer in the spirit of Christ, he is filling up the yet unfilled measures of the afflictions of Christ (Col. i. 24), because it is appointed unto Christ to suffer, as once in himself, so now in his earthly members, until the cup be wholly drained (cf. Rev. i. 9; xiv. 12). So, on the other hand, every one that is devoted to some ministry is discharging the duty of all to all, and through all to God. The body of Christ, which is the Church, owes unto all her members spiritual and temporal care and tendance; unto God ceaseless worship, prayer, and praise. But as the natural body discharges many of its functions through separate members or organs, so does the body of Christ through individuals set apart thereunto.

Consider, again, WITH RESPECT TO THE FIRST-BORN—

I. THAT GOD CLAIMED, AS OF RIGHT, THE SERVICES OF ALL THE FIRST-BORN BECAUSE OF THEIR PRESERVATION THROUGH THE BLOOD OF THE (PASSOVER) LAMB IN EGYPT. Even so all who belong to "the general assembly and Church of the first-born," which are enrolled not in the lists of Aaron on earth, but in the book of God in heaven (Heb. xii. 23), i. e. all Christian people, so far as they understand their high calling, are claimed as his, and wholly his, by God; and this because he redeemed them by the precious blood of Christ (1 Cor. vi. 19, 20; Rom. xiv. 8; 1 Pet. i. 19, &c.). And notice that this " hallowing" of the first-born was a kind of death. All the first-born throughout the land of Egypt were " anathema "—a thing devoted. God had claimed them. If then these are saved from the destroyer by the death of the substituted lamb, they are still regarded as dead unto the old, the ordinary, life of men who are *sui juris*, as living only for God, and unto God. And this is precisely and unequivocally the position of all redeemed souls. Christ did not die that they should not die, but that their death should take a happy and blessed form, instead of one dark and terrible (2 Cor. v. 15; Col. iii. 3, &c.). Every soul, elect, first-born, redeemed, is hallowed and dedicated and marked as dead unto sin and self, alive only unto God.

II. THAT THE FIRST-BORN WERE NUMBERED BY NAME, EVEN TO THE LAST INDIVIDUAL; which does not seem to have been the case even with the Levites. Even so there is no one of his redeemed, first-born, that does not come into separate remembrance before God, because a soul hallowed by the precious blood is of priceless worth.

III. THAT THE ODD NUMBER of the first-born over and above those redeemed by the Levites HAD TO BE REDEEMED WITH A PRICE; for they were his, and he could by no means renounce his rights over any. Even so all the assembly of the first-born are the Lord's, and he cannot forego his claims over any one of them, neither can any one of them say, " It does not matter about *me*—*I* shall not signify—*I* need not be counted." The services of *all* are due to Christ, and God will have this acknowledged without any exception.

Consider, again, as incidentally appearing—1. That the whole matter begins with the genealogy of Aaron and Moses—the priest and the Ruler in Israel. Even so all questions of religion and devotion, however seemingly simple or entirely practical, do really begin with and from the " generations " of him who is both Priest and Ruler in Israel, of him who came forth out of Bethlehem, whose goings forth are from everlasting (Micah v. 2). And so do the Gospels begin with the human genealogy (Matthew, Luke), or the Divine (John), of the Anointed, or with the briefest summary of both (Mark—" the Son of God "). 2. That Nadab and Abihu, priests of the line of Aaron, who offered strange fire, had no children. Even so the solitary priesthood of Christ is ministered visibly in the Church, and there are that attempt to minister it presumptuously and falsely, as though it were their own; but these are spiritually barren, and leave no children in the faith, because the blessing and power of God is not with their ministry, and because human ambitions are " strange " to the gospel of love. 3. That Moses and Aaron camped on the east of the tabernacle, as the place at once most central and most near the Divine presence. Even so our King and Priest doth so abide as that he may ever appear in the presence of God for us (Heb. ix. 24), and yet may ever be in the midst of his Church (Matt. xxviii. 20; Rev. ii. 1).

HOMILIES BY VARIOUS AUTHORS.

Ch. iii.—*The families of Levi get their several commissions.* The third and fourth chapters of Numbers form a section by themselves, and of this section the opening verse is the descriptive title: THE GENERATIONS OF AARON AND MOSES. According to the idiom of the Bible, this means that the two chapters which follow constitute the Book of the Families of Levi (compare the titles of the several sections of Genesis, viz., ch. ii. 4; v. 1; vi. 9; x. 1; xi. 27, &c. ; also Matt. i. 1). The design of the book is to note the principal divisions of the tribe and allot to each its place and duties. Observe how the names of Aaron and Moses stand where we should have expected to find Levi's. The patriarch's fame has been quite eclipsed by that of his illustrious descendants, insomuch that here the tribe takes its title from them rather than from him. The book of the Levites is entitled the Book of Aaron and Moses.

I. IN THIS FAMILY BOOK THE PRE-EMINENCE IS GIVEN TO AARON. The name of Moses is inscribed in the title, but his family is otherwise of no note. The noble self-denial of Moses in this matter has been much commended, and with reason. He was superior to the ambition which seeks to build up a family at whatever cost to the nation. There is some reason to think that his sons were unworthy. Their mother was a Midianite, and seems to have had little sympathy with her husband's faith. It was otherwise with Aaron. His wife was a daughter of Amminadab, the prince of Judah and ancestor of our Lord (Exod. vi. 23). Her name was Elisheba ("a worshipper of God "); and as the name became a favourite one among the daughters of the priestly house (Luke i. 5), it may be presumed that she was worthy of the name, the first of all the saintly Elisabeths. The sons of Aaron and Elisabeth, being the heirs of the priesthood, took precedence of the other families of Levi, and occupied the place of honour in the camp. They, with Moses, pitched their tents in front of the tabernacle, towards the east (ver. 38). Note in passing how, at this early date, the two families which were to be pre-eminent for fifteen hundred years in respect of force of character, variety of services, and public honours are already marked out by the hand of God. On the march the prince of Judah leads the van (ch. i. 7; ii. 3, 9); in the encampment Aaron and his sons occupy the place of honour. In the family book of Levi the sons of Aaron and Elisabeth take precedence of all their brethren. Yet not so as to give any foothold in Israel to that sacerdotal pride which made the Brahmins of India and the priests of Egypt a sacred caste, and taught the people to bow before them as demigods. If Aaron and Elisabeth ever read this family register, their hearts did not swell with pride. The first sentences recall the tragedy of their house. Aaron's two eldest sons, with the oil of their consecration yet fresh upon them, sinned presumptuously, were smitten, and their names perished from Israel. Not even in the house of the godliest pair is grace hereditary. Aaron, the saint of God, and his saintly Elisabeth mourn over sons whom God has cut off in their sin. God will endure no rival in his house. His most honoured servants must be content to be only his servants, and the servants of all men for his sake. The Bible tolerates no hero worship. It tells the truth about the best of men, lovingly indeed, but without extenuation. In our family registers we are not bound by the same rule. We do not occupy the throne of judgment, and may bury domestic tragedies out of sight. But God is Judge, and his book, as it cannot err in its judgments, must speak without reserve, although the effect should be to "stain the pride of all glory" (Isa. xxiii. 9).

II. THE GREATER PART OF THIS FAMILY BOOK IS OCCUPIED WITH THE CENSUS OF THE LEVITICAL CLANS AND THE ALLOTMENT TO EACH OF ITS PLACE AND DUTIES. The particulars falling under this head do not call for special notice here. They concur with those related in the earlier chapters of this book in showing that the march of the tribes was performed with the most perfect order. Never was any great multitude more unlike a mob than the congregation in the wilderness. Moses in Egypt had shown himself a man "mighty in deeds" (Acts vii. 22). The tradition which makes him to have led victorious armies in his youth is probably true. Certainly the order laid down in Numbers for the march and the camp, for the nation in general and for the Levites in particular, shows everywhere the hand of the general accustomed to handle great bodies of men.—Care is taken to put on record *the reason for the separation of the Levites* to the service of the tabernacle. By primitive custom a certain sanctity was attributed to the first-born. The act of God in passing over the first-born of Israel in Egypt established an additional claim upon the first-born thenceforward (cf. Exod. xiii., also ch. xxii. 29, &c.). To have required the personal service of the eldest son of every house would have been inconvenient. Better let the tribe of Levi be substituted, and let them minister to Aaron their brother ; an arrangement facilitated by the circumstance that the Levites were nearly the same in number as the first-born. (The equation is not without its difficulties. But there is great doubt as to who exactly were meant by the "first-born." Till that is settled it is too soon to charge the narrative with error.) It was needful to state very distinctly the reason for the separation of a whole tribe to sacred service. The tribe thus separated had to be supported by their brethren, besides being disabled for doing their share of military and other public service. The Israelites would be unlike the rest of mankind if they did not, by and by, grudge such a great expenditure. They are to be reminded that the separation of the Levites was in liquidation of a prior claim, and took place by way of accommodation to their convenience. When money or service is asked for religious or charitable objects there are sure to be grumblers, and it is very expedient to fortify the demand with a clear statement of the reasons.—B.

Ver. 4.—"*Strange fire.*" There are various kinds of "fire" used in the service of God which, if not as hateful in his sight as that offered by Nadab and Abihu, are "strange." There is a fire which is appropriate and acceptable, because kindled by God ; all others are "strange fire, which he commanded not" (Levit. x. 1). *E. g.*—

I. ILLEGITIMATE ZEAL, as seen in every kind of persecution (see Luke ix. 51—56). Yet a writer on the origin of the Inquisition quotes the passage in justification of the burning of heretics : "Lo ! fire the punishment of heretics, for the Samaritans were the heretics of those times " (Prescott's 'Ferdinand and Isabella,' i. 319, *n.*). See Gal. iv. 18. But let the zeal run in the path marked out for it by Christ towards enemies (Matt. v. 44), backsliders (Gal. vi. 1), or heretics (James v. 19, 20).

II. UNAUTHORISED SERVICES ; whether offered by unauthorised persons, as Korah, who yet had the true fire (ch. xvi. 17, 18), or Saul (1 Sam. xiii. 9—14), or Uzziah (2 Chron. xxvi.) ; or by God's servants, but in ways alien to his mind (Illus., Uzzah, 1 Chron. xiii. 9, 10 ; xv. 13). Such are the "voluntary humility" and "neglecting of the body" condemned in Col. ii. 18—23, and all similar austerities. The fire God approves must be presented by accepted worshippers in an appointed way.

III. SUPERSTITIOUS DEVOTIONS. These may be presented through Christ "the way," and yet marred by ignorant fears of God, or unworthy fancies, or errors intertwined with God's truth in the many ways known to ancient or modern superstition (1 John iv. 18 ; v. 13—15).

IV. ARTIFICIAL EMOTION. We need never dread the emotion caused by God's own truth, used in legitimate ways. Truth is like solid fuel that ought to keep up a glowing heat, whether of alarm (Acts ii. 37 ; xxiv. 25) or of joy (Acts ii. 41). But emotion excited apart from the communication of appropriate truth may be disastrous ; or at best like a blaze of straw, soon leaving only blackness and ashes. All such "strange fire " tends to the injury, or even the destruction, of the offerers (John iv. 24). To worship God in truth we must ourselves be "accepted in the beloved," enlightened by the Holy Spirit, and must present spiritual sacrifices kindled by his own celestial fire of love.—P.

Ver. 4.—*A mortal sin.* "And Nadab and Abihu died before the Lord," &c.

I. WHO THEY WERE THAT COMMITTED THIS SIN. Sons of Aaron ; elder sons, in whom, therefore, a greater sense of thoughtfulness and responsibility might have been expected. They had also been duly anointed and consecrated. They could hardly plead ignorance and inexperience in the things of God. They had nothing else to do than attend to the tabernacle. They knew, or ought to have considered, that Jehovah had laid down instructions, even to the minutest points, as to what the priests were to do. It is a warning then to all who stand among peculiar privileges and enjoy greater light, *e. g.*, those who live in a household where there is piety at the head, and a continual regard in all things for the will of God (Matt. xi. 20—24).

II. THE SIN THEY COMMITTED. They offered strange fire before the Lord. The fire to be used was the holy fire ever burning upon the altar (Levit. vi. 13). To offer incense was to symbolise thanksgiving and supplication, and this, of all things, requires to be done in most careful conformity with Divine appointments. All offerings to God, to be worth anything, must be voluntary; yet even a voluntary offering may be an abomination before him when it is a random and reckless exercise of our own freedom. The highest of human actions is to do God's will with all our will, as seeing clearly that it is the right thing to do.

III. THE TERRIBLE CONSEQUENCE. It was truly a *mortal* sin, a sin which on the very commission of it was followed by death, like the taking of some swift-working poison. It was as dangerous for a careless priest to take up the tabernacle services as for a man to take naked lights about a powder magazine. The fire of the Lord was a hidden thing, yet in a moment its full energy might be revealed, either to bless or destroy (cf. Levit. ix. 24 with Levit. x. 2). But though the sin was a mortal sin, it was not in itself worse than other offences against which sentence is not executed speedily. All sin is mortal, though the deadly result be spread over long periods. This sin was punished promptly and terribly, as were some other sins in Israel, not because they were worse, but because the people, and particularly the Levites, needed a lesson in the most impressive way in which it could be given. The fire of the Lord went out against the *priests* here, but soon after it went out against the *people* (ch. xi. 1). "Except ye repent, ye shall all likewise perish."

Lessons:—*A worthy office may have an unworthy occupant.* There are a Nadab and Abihu here; there were a Hophni and Phinehas afterwards, and a Judas among the apostles. Anointing, consecration, imposition of hands may have official value, but God only can give the faculty of true inward service. We may bring strange fire before God when we bring zeal not according to knowledge. There may be great fire and intensity and activity with nothing of the baptism of the Holy Ghost and of fire. Consider the lamentations of Paul over his persecuting days. There is here another instance of the letter killing. In the Old Testament punishment predominated over reward, because disobedience predominated over obedience.—Y.

EXPOSITION.

CHAPTER IV.

THE DUTIES OF THE LEVITES (ch. iv.). Ver. 2.—**Take the sum of the sons of Kohath.** The Levites having been separated from the other tribes, the Kohathites are now to be separated from amongst the other Levites for the most honourable and sacred duties. To them the preference was given presumably because the priests were Kohathites.

Ver. 3.—**From thirty years old and upward.** The age at which they became liable for service was shortly after reduced to twenty-five (ch. viii. 24), and at a later period to twenty (1 Chron. xxiii. 27). In the wilderness a larger number of the men might be required to attend to their own camps, and their own families; but the explanation may probably be found in the unusually large proportion who were at this time between the ages of thirty and fifty. The Septuagint has altered thirty into twenty-five to make it agree with ch. viii. 24. Thirty years became among the Jews the perfect age at which a man attained to full maturity, and entered upon all his rights and duties (cf. Luke iii.

23). **Into the host.** Not the military ranks, but the *militia sacra* of the Lord. **To do the work.** Literally, "to war the warfare."

Ver. 4. — **About the most holy things.** Rather, "the most holy things:" *they* were the service of the Kohathites. So the Septuagint.

Ver. 5.—**The covering veil.** The curtain which hung before the holy of holies, afterwards known as "the veil of the temple" (Luke xxiii. 45).

Ver. 6.—**The covering of badgers' skins.** Probably of sea-cow skins (*tachash*), but see Exod. xxv. 5. The Targum of Palestine, and the Septuagint, both render it "a covering of hyacinthine skin." The later Jews would have no knowledge of the marine animals common on the shores of the Red Sea. **A cloth wholly of blue.** This was the distinctive outer, and therefore visible, covering of the *most* sacred thing, the ark.

Ver. 7.—**The dishes, and the spoons, and the bowls, and covers to cover withal.** Rather, "the plates, the bowls, the wine pitchers, and the chalices for pouring out," *i. e.* the drink offerings. The two first seem to have been used in the meat offering, the two last in the drink offering.

Ver. 8.—**Shall put in the staves thereof.** This formula is repeated alike with reference to the ark, the table, and the two altars. It would therefore be natural to suppose that the staves had all been taken out while the various coverings were put on. On the other hand, it is expressly directed in Exod. xxv. 15 that the staves of the ark shall "not be taken from it." Two explanations are possible. Either the former command does not contemplate the necessity of wrapping up the ark, and only applies to all times when it was at rest, or in movement; or else the latter direction only means, in the case of the ark, that the staves should be adjusted for the purpose of bearing.

Ver. 9.—**Snuff-dishes.** Some render this word "extinguishers," but it could hardly bear that meaning, since it also signifies censers in ch. xvi. 6, and fire-pans in Exod. xxvii. 3. They were evidently shallow metal pans available for many different purposes.

Ver. 10.—**Upon a bar**—i. e. a bearing-frame. Ἐπ' ἀναφορέων, Septuagint; "upon a rest," Targum of Palestine.

Ver. 12.—**All the instruments of ministry.** These do not seem to be, at any rate exclusively, the vessels pertaining to the golden altar. They are not packed up with it, but separately, in a blue cloth and a skin covering of their own. Probably they include all the vessels and utensils used inside the tabernacle which have not been previously mentioned.

Ver. 13.—**Take away the ashes.** This is omitted by the Septuagint. The Hebrew word for "ashes" is of somewhat doubtful meaning, being only used here and in Exod. xxvii. 3; Ps. xx. 3 (see margin). Being connected with the word "fat," it may perhaps mean the grease or dripping from the burnt offerings. The Targum of Palestine renders it "cinders." As the altar was hollow, and was filled with earth or stones when used, there would be no need to cleanse it from ashes; if this be the meaning of the word, the command would rather have been to collect the living embers before the altar was removed, in order to keep alive the sacred fire. That this fire was never allowed to go out may be looked upon as certain.

Ver. 15.—**These things are the burden of the sons of Kohath.** One thing which the Kohathites almost certainly had to carry is omitted here, possibly because it was carried without any cover at all, and was not regarded as of equal sanctity with the rest. Anyhow, the omission is very remarkable, and may have been accidental. It is supplied by the Septuagint and the Samaritan text in the following addition to ver. 14: "And they shall take a purple cloth, and cover the laver

and its foot, and they shall put it into a hyacinthine cover of skin, and put it on bars." The burdens of the Kohathites were six, not counting the laver and its foot: (1) the ark; (2) the table of shewbread; (3) the candelabrum; (4) the golden altar; (5) "instruments of ministry;" (6) the frame of the brazen altar.

Ver. 16.—**To the office of Eleazar, . . . oversight.** Septuagint, ἐπίσκοπος Ἐλεάζαρ . . : ἡ ἐπισκοπή. On him was laid the oversight of and the responsibility for all the material appliances of Divine worship, and in especial it devolved upon him to see to the oil, the incense, and the chrism, and the materials for the daily meat offering. No doubt it is intended, although not precisely expressed, that the Kohathites were specially under his orders.

Ver. 18.—**Cut ye not off the tribe of the families of the Kohathites.** The word tribe (shebet) is used in an unusual way here, not in the sense of tribus, but of stirps. Perhaps as Levi was himself a microcosm of all Israel, so his families ranked as tribes; and no doubt they remained more distinct than the families of any other tribe. The meaning of the command is plainly this, "Take care that the Kohathites are not cut off through any negligence or want of consideration on your part;" and the form of the command, "cut ye not off," conveyed most emphatically the warning, that if any mischief befell the Kohathites which the priests could have prevented, they would be responsible for it in the sight of God. No doubt, as a fact, the Kohathites would take their cue from the conduct of the priests: if they were irreverent and careless, the Levites would be the same, and would sooner or later presume, and, presuming, would die.

Ver. 19.—**Thus do unto them,** i. e. exactly as commanded in vers. 5—15.

Ver. 20.—**They shall not go in to see when the holy things are covered.** This translation is disputed. The word rendered "are covered" is the Piel infinitive from bala, to swallow, and so to destroy. It may signify the extreme rapidity with which the most holy things were hidden from sight and removed from touch, so as to become, as it were, non-existent for the time. So the Syriac, Arabic, Samaritan, and the Targums of Onkelos and Palestine. On the other hand, it may be a proverbial expression, "in a swallow, at a gulp," i. e. "for an instant," as in Job vii. 19. And so the Septuagint, ἐξάπινα, and most modern scholars. Whichever way, however, we take it, the phrase, "they shall not go in to see," seems to limit the prohibition under pain of death to the deliberate act of entering the tabernacle out of curiosity during the process of packing up the holy things. The case of the men of

Bethshemesh, therefore (1 Sam. vi. 19), does not fall within the letter of this law, although it does within its spirit. The command, thus limited, is no doubt an addition to the previous command not to touch, but it is altogether in keeping with it. If it was the will of God to hedge about these sacred symbols of his presence and his worship with an awful sanctity, it is obvious that he was as much bound to defend them against the irreverent prying of the eye as against the irreverent touch of the hand ; and the prying here prohibited would have been distinctly wilful and inexcusable.

Ver. 25.—**They shall bear the curtains,** &c. For these four coverings, of tapestry, of goats' hair, of rams' skins, and of sea-cow skin respectively, see Exod. xxvi. In addition to these, the Gershonites carried all the hangings belonging to the tabernacle and to the outer court, with the single exception of the "veil" which was wrapped round the ark.

Ver. 26.—**And their cords, and all the instruments of their service.** Taking this verse in connection with ver. 37, we must understand the word "their" as applying to the things mentioned in the previous verse. The Merarites carried the cords, &c. of the hangings of the court.

Ver. 28.—**Under the hand of Ithamar,** as also were the Merarites. He had been already engaged in overseeing the construction of the tabernacle (Exod. xxxviii. 21).

Ver. 31.—**This is the charge of their burden,** viz., all the solid parts of the fabric of the tabernacle and its court ; by far the heaviest burden, and so allotted to the largest number.

Ver. 32.—**By name ye shall reckon the instruments of the charge of their burden.** This injunction only occurs here. The Septuagint has "number them by name, and all the articles borne by them." Perhaps the solid parts of the fabric were numbered for convenience of setting up, and, therefore, were assigned each to its own bearer.

Ver. 48.—**Those that were numbered of them were eight thousand and five hundred and fourscore.** The census of each family is described in the same form of words with much particularity. No doubt it was carried out with extreme solicitude, as made for a purpose especially sacred and important. The results are remarkable in more ways than one. The following table presents the numbers in each family above one month, and between the ages of thirty and fifty.

Kohath,	8600	2750	per cent.	32
Gershon,	7500	2630	,, ,,	35
Merari,	6200	3200	,, ,,	51
	22,300	8580	,, ,,	38

The first conclusion which naturally arises from these figures is, that after all the numbering must have been made by tens, and not by individuals. As it was impossible that 3000 persons could be employed in carrying the various portions of the tabernacle, it may be that each group of ten undertook a unit of responsibility. The second consideration is, that the average of men between thirty and fifty in all Levi is higher than modern statistics show (it is said to be twenty-five per cent. now in the whole population), although not very materially. The third is, that this average is very unequally distributed, rising to a most remarkable proportion in the case of Merari. It is quite clear that something must have disturbed the relative numbers as between the Merarites and the other families. It has been suggested that the small number of male Levites generally, and the small number of male Kohathites, between thirty and fifty especially, may have been caused by heavy losses incurred in carrying out the Divine sentence upon the worshippers of the golden calf (Exod. xxxii.). But—1. The slow increase of Levi continued to be very observable down to the time of David ; while the other tribes grew from 600,000 to 1,300,000, he only increased to 38,000 (1 Chron. xxiii. 3). 2. The average of males over thirty is already higher among the Kohathites than might have been expected ; it is the largeness of the number, not the smallness, which needs to be explained. 3. It is Merari, and not Kohath, that is markedly distinguished from the other two : there is little difference between Kohath and Gershon. It is evident that something must have happened to the tribe of Levi, and in especial to the family of Merari, to reduce very greatly the number of births within the last thirty years. We do not know what the causes were, or why they should have pressed much more heavily on one tribe, or one family, than on another ; but it is easy to see that many such causes may have acted, and acted unequally, under the cruel tyranny of Pharaoh. The children may have been systematically slaughtered, or marriages may have largely ceased, while Moses was in the land of Midian. If this were generally the case, it would much diminish the estimated total of the nation, and still more the estimated difficulties of the march.

Ver. 49.—**Thus were they numbered of him.** Literally, "and his mustering." It may have the meaning given to it in the A. V. (and so the Septuagint and Targums), or it may be translated "mustered things," *i. e.* things assigned to him in the mustering, and read with the previous words, "Every one to his service, and to his burden, and his mustered things."

HOMILETICS.

Ch. iv.—*Duties of the Church militant.* In this chapter we have, spiritually, certain duties of the Church on the way to heaven in respect of faith and worship, and the spirit in which matters of religion ought to be conducted. Consider, therefore—

I. THAT THE DIVINE RULE IN THE CARE OF THE SANCTUARY WAS ONE OF DISTRIBUTION. Each family within the tribe, each group within the family, perhaps each individual in the group, had his own allotted "burden." Kohath did not interfere with Merari, nor did Merari come into collision with Gershon. Even so, in all religious and ecclesiastical labours, distribution is the rule of the gospel, the Holy Spirit dividing to each severally as he will (1 Cor. xii. *passim;* Eph. iv. 11—13). And note that this distribution was not made according to any superiority that we know of, but rather the reverse. Levi himself was by far the smallest of the twelve tribes, and Merari was by far the largest (for the purpose in hand) of the three families. Even so under the gospel no rules of human pre-eminence restrict the Divine distribution of gifts and offices ; rather, the first shall be last, and the last first.

II. THAT THE WHOLE FABRIC OF THE TABERNACLE HAD TO BE CONTINUALLY TAKEN TO PIECES AND RECONSTRUCTED, as the host moved on in its appointed path. Even so, in the onward progress of the Church of Christ, the outward form and frame of religion has to be constantly built up afresh with ceaseless labour. For each succeeding century, for each new generation that comes up, for each new nation added to the Church, the fabric of its faith and worship has to be built up from the beginning. If not, religion, like the tabernacle, would be left far behind, the empty monument of a forsaken faith.

III. THAT, ON THE OTHER HAND, THE FURNITURE OF THE TABERNACLE AND ITS CONSTITUENT PARTS, THOUGH PERPETUALLY BEING RECONSTRUCTED, YET REMAINED IDENTICALLY THE SAME. Nothing lost, nothing added. Even so the elements of our faith and worship must remain unchangeably the same from age to age ; nothing really old cast away, nothing really new introduced. " The faith once (for all) delivered to the saints." Worship primitive and apostolic. However fresh the putting together, the substance eternally the same.

IV. THAT WHILE THE WHOLE FABRIC WAS TO BE CARRIED WITH GREAT CARE AND REVERENCE, YET THE MOST SOLICITOUS CARE AND THE MOST PROFOUND REVERENCE WERE RESERVED FOR THOSE HOLY THINGS WHICH THE FABRIC ENSHRINED. Even so all that is any part of our religion, claiming any Divine authority, is to be handed down and carried on with care and with respect ; but it is the few central facts and truths of revelation upon which the loving veneration and extreme solicitude of Christian teachers and people must be concentrated.

V. THAT AMONGST THESE THE ARK WAS FIRST AND FOREMOST, having three coverings, and being distinguished outwardly also by its blue cloth. Even so it is the incarnation of God in Christ—the doctrine of Emmanuel, God with us—which is before all other things precious and holy, to be guarded with the most reverent and jealous care, to be distinguished openly with the most evident honour. And note (1) that as the mercy-seat, resting on the ark, and forming its lid, was carried whithersoever the ark went, and shared in all its honour, so the doctrine of propitiation and of God reconciled to men, resting as it does essentially upon the doctrine of Emmanuel—God with us—is carried ever with it, and honoured with it. And note (2) that as blue is the colour of heaven, so the blue outer covering of the ark (alone) may signify that the greatest effort of the Church's teachers should be so to present the doctrine of God in Christ before men that it may appear clad in heavenly love and beauty.

VI. THAT THE SHEW-BREAD WAS NOT ALLOWED TO FAIL FROM ITS TABLE EVEN DURING THE JOURNEY, but was carefully placed upon it and so carried, and thus answered to its name of " continual bread." Even so it is certain that the " living Bread which came down from heaven" must be with the Church as her " continual Bread " in all her marches. But it is more commonly considered that the shew-bread in its twelve loaves represents the whole people of God, in all its sections, as always present to the eye of God, and always remembered before him for good; in which case this would emphasise the truth that we must without any intermission be had in merciful remembrance before God, lest we die. And note (1) that as the shew-bread on the table was covered with a cloth of scarlet, which is the colour of atoning blood, this may signify that it is as covered by and, so to speak, seen through the precious blood of Christ that the Church in all her travail is remembered before God for good. And note (2) that as the ark and the table were more honoured in their coverings than the rest, though the ark most of all, this may intimate that the two doctrines of chiefest honour in the faith are those of Christ and of his Church, i. e. of God in Christ, and Christ in us; God present with us through Christ, and we present before God through Christ (John xvii. 20—23, 26).

VII. THAT THE SONS OF KOHATH WERE TO CARRY THOSE HOLY THINGS, BUT NEITHER TO TOUCH THEM NOR TO GO IN TO SEE THEM FOR AN INSTANT, LEST THEY SHOULD DIE. Even so the holy mysteries of the gospel are ever to be borne onwards, but neither to be handled with irreverent carelessness nor pried into with irreverent curiosity, else they become the savour of death rather than of life. It is indeed true that in Christ "the veil is taken away," and that now the gospel is openly declared to all nations; but it is also true, as to its central doctrines, that wilful irreverence and idle curiosity are visited with severer punishments, because purely spiritual, now than then. It is not possible that any one be saved by faith if he handle the faith with rude familiarity, as having nothing sacred for him, or with cold curiosity, as a matter of mere intellectual interest (cf. Matt. xxi. 44; Luke ii. 34; 2 Cor. ii. 16. Cf. also 1 Cor. xi. 29, 30).

VIII. THAT THE PRIESTS WERE CHARGED NOT TO " CUT OFF " THE KOHATHITES, i. e. NOT TO CAUSE THEIR DEATH BY GIVING THEM EXAMPLE OR OPPORTUNITY OF IRREVERENCE IN THEIR NECESSARY WORK ABOUT THE SACRED THINGS WHICH WOULD BE FATAL TO THEM. Even so an enormous responsibility is laid upon all who are set over others in the Lord, especially with respect to those who are necessarily brought into outward contact with religion. Those who, being *custodes* of sacred treasures, set an example of irreverence to those associated with them, or give them the impression of secret unbelief in what they preach or minister (an impression how quickly caught!), will be held responsible for any souls that may perish thereby. How miserably true that, "the nearer the Church, the further from God ; " that none are so hardened as those whose outward duties are concerned with the maintenance of public worship; that no families are so notoriously irreligious as those of Church dignitaries and other ministers of God! And this due not more to the subtle danger arising from familiarity with the forms of religion, than to the subtler danger arising from the irreverent and careless conduct and temper of the ministers of religion. How often do such, by their behaviour at home, or when off duty, leave an impression of unbelief or of indifference, which they do not really feel, upon their families, dependants, subordinates! How awful the responsibility of such an one! He has "cut off" souls which were most nearly in his charge from amongst the people of God. The poison-breath of his (it may be, heedless) irreverence has blighted their eternal future. And this holds true, in its measure, of fathers, masters, all who lead the religion of others. And note that as Aaron and his sons could only escape responsibility for any catastrophe among the Kohathites by doing exactly as the Lord commanded in the matter (see ver. 19), even so we can only escape responsibility for the loss of other souls by following *exactly* the Divine precepts; if *we* allow ourselves to deviate from them at all, others through our example will deviate from them more: we *are* our brothers' keepers to the uttermost reach of our example.

HOMILIES BY VARIOUS AUTHORS.

Vers. 1—4.—*None may bear the vessels of the Lord but Levites at their best.* From the giving of the law till the building of Solomon's temple, a space of about 500 years, the Lord at no time "dwelt in any house, but walked in a tent and in a tabernacle" (2 Sam. vii. 6). The sanctuary was a moving tent, and one principal part of the business of the Levites, the most honourable function assigned to them, was the carriage of it from place to place. Moses, who regulated so exactly the order of all the tribes, both for the march and the encampment, did not omit to appoint to every division of the Levites its duty in relation to the tabernacle and its holy furniture—what each was to carry, and in what order they were to pitch their tents. In this chapter of detailed regulations, special interest attaches to the law laid down regarding THE LEVITES' PERIOD OF SERVICE in carrying the tabernacle. It was from thirty years old till fifty (vers. 3, 23, 30). This must be taken along with chap. viii. 24, where the age for entering on service is fixed at twenty-five. The explanation of the seeming discrepancy, no doubt, is that the first five years were a kind of apprenticeship. Certain other sorts of work about the tabernacle the Levites might do between twenty-five and thirty, and these they might continue to do, so far as their strength served, long after fifty ; but except between thirty and fifty they might not bear the tabernacle and its vessels. When David gave to the ark a permanent abode at Jerusalem, and the service of the Levites was readjusted accordingly, the age for entering on duty was lowered to twenty, and at that point it thereafter stood (see 1 Chron. xxiii. 27 ; Ezra iii. 8). The principle underlying the law was still the same. The service of God, especially in its most sacred parts, requires and deserves the best of our years, our strength, our affections. His soul desires the first ripe fruit. There are three errors men are apt to fall into in this matter of service ; I refer more especially to official service. 1. *Some enter on it too young.* No hard and fast line can be drawn for all men and every service. One kind of service demands greater maturity than another, and one man ripens earlier than another. But the rule here prescribed to the Levites is a good one for the average of cases. To speak only of the Christian ministry: few men under twenty-five are ripe for it, and places of special trust would require a man of thirty. Undue haste is neither reverent nor safe. The first sermon of our blessed Lord was not preached till " he began to be about thirty years of age " (Luke iii. 23) ; a touching and most suggestive example. 2. *Some delay entering till they are too old.* This is most frequently seen in unofficial service. Many men, not destitute of piety, think it incumbent on them to give their prime so entirely to " business " that they have no time for anything else. Church work, home mission work, charity services, participation in these they look forward to as the employment of their leisure, after they shall have retired from business. That, at the best, is giving to the Lord not the first-fruits, but the gleanings. It will be found that, as a rule, it is not these tardy labourers whom God honours to be most useful. He honours those rather (thank God, they are many, and increasing in number) who consecrate to him a fair proportion of their strength when they are at their prime. 3. *Some do not know when it is time for them to resign.* The Levites' period of active service, whether it began at thirty, or twenty-five, or twenty, always ended at fifty. Not that the law thrust them out of the sanctuary when their term expired ; that would have been cruelty to men who loved the service. They might still frequent the sanctuary, and perform occasional offices (see ch. viii. 26). But after fifty they ceased to be on the regular staff. Here too the rule has to be applied to the Christian Church with discrimination. For services which are characteristically mental and spiritual, a man's prime certainly does not cease at fifty. Nevertheless, the principle at the root of the rule is of undying validity and importance. The Levites' maintenance did not cease at fifty ; and any Church system which does not make such provision as enables its ministers to retire when their strength fails is unscriptural and defective. On the other part, it is the duty and will be the wisdom of the Church's servants to seek retirement when they are no longer able to minister to the Lord with fresh vigour.—B.

Vers. 17—20.—*The Lord is to be served with fear.* " LEST THEY DIE : " that note of warning is often heard in the law. If any man or woman touched the flaming mount, it was death (Exod. xix. 12). It was death if the high priest entered into the holiest on any day but one, or on that day if he omitted to shroud the mercy-seat in a cloud of fragrant incense (Levit. xvi. 3—13). It was death if any son of Aaron transgressed the ritual, were it only by officiating in any other than the appointed garments (Exod. xxviii. 43). In the same strain, this law in Numbers makes it death for any common Levite to touch, or gaze upon, the holy things till the priest has packed them up in their thick wrappings (vers. 19, 20; cf. ch. i. 51 ; iii. 10). The example first of Nadab and Abihu, and afterwards of Korah and his company, showed that these threats were spoken in earnest. We cannot marvel that, after hearing and seeing all this, the people were smitten with terror, and cried out to Moses, "We perish, we perish, we all perish. Whosoever cometh anything near unto the tabernacle of the Lord shall die. Shall we be consumed with dying?" (Numb. xvii. 13).

I. THIS FEATURE OF THE LAW WILL HELP YOU TO UNDERSTAND THE DEPRECIATORY TERMS IN WHICH IT IS SO OFTEN MENTIONED IN THE NEW TESTAMENT, especially by the Apostle Paul. The law was "the ministration of death and of condemnation" (2 Cor. iii. 7, 9); it "worketh wrath" (Rom. iv. 15); it breathed a "spirit of bondage" and fear (Rom. viii. 15); it "gendered to bondage" (Gal. iv. 24); it was "an intolerable yoke" (Acts xv. 10). Not that the whole contents of the Pentateuch fell under this description. Much of promise was spoken in presence of the mountain of the law. But let the law be taken by itself, and let the gospel verities foreshadowed by its ritual be shut out from view, and does it not answer to the disparaging descriptions? It was full of wrath, condemnation, fear. No doubt there was an element of grace even in the covenant of Sinai. It was a benefit done to Israel when the Lord delivered to them the commandments, pitched his tabernacle among them, and suffered them to draw near under the conditions of the ritual. Nevertheless, the conditions were hard and terrible; we may well thank God for abolishing them. They are utterly abolished. The veil is rent from top to bottom; the yoke is broken; we have received the spirit of adoption, not the spirit of bondage again to fear; we have boldness to enter into the holiest.

II. NOTHING THAT HAS BEEN SAID IMPLIES THAT THE LEVITICAL LAW WAS REALLY UNWORTHY OF THE WISDOM OR THE GRACE OF GOD. For the time then present it was the best thing that could be. Certain truths of primary importance men were everywhere forgetting: among others, the holy majesty of God; that communion with God is to the soul of man the very breath of life; that man is a sinner for whom there is no remission, no access, without atonement. These lessons the law was meant and fitted to teach. These lessons it did teach, burning them into the conscience of the nation. The law was not the gospel, but it led forward to the gospel. A service beyond all price.

III. NOR HAS THE BENEFICENT OFFICE OF THE LAW CEASED WITH THE ADVENT OF THE BETTER TIME. Men are ready to abuse the grace of God, to give harbour to licentiousness on pretext of Christian liberty. If you doubt it, search well your own heart. What is the remedy? It is found sometimes in the rod of God's afflicting providence, sometimes in the searching discipline of the law. For the law, although in its letter abrogated, abides for ever in its substance. We are not bound—we are not at liberty —to slay sin offerings or burn incense. But we are bound to ruminate on the law of sacrifice and intercession. The Levitical ritual belongs in this sense to us as much as it ever belonged to the Jews. It admonishes us of the reverence due to God. A certain filial boldness he will welcome, but presumptuous trifling with his majesty and holiness he will not suffer. If we would be accepted, we must worship God with reverence and godly fear, for our God is still a consuming fire (Heb. xii. 29).—B.

Vers. 15—20.—*The perils of distinguished service.* The sons of Kohath had the most honourable of the duties assigned to the Levites, in being permitted to carry the sacred vessels of the tabernacle. But they were thus exposed to temptations and perils from which their less favoured brethren were exempt. To touch or even to see the holy things was death. Similar temptations, to those intrusted with distinguished service in God's Church, may arise from—

I. CURIOSITY. Illustrate from the sin of the men of Bethshemesh (1 Sam. vi.). Men brought by their duties into close contact with Divine mysteries may yield to the curiosity of unauthorised speculations to which ignorant and grovelling minds are not exposed (cf. Col. ii. 18). Illustrate from speculations on the Trinity, the incarnation, or the profitless inquiries of some of the schoolmen as to angels, &c. Caution applicable to theological speculations of to-day (Deut. xxix. 29).

II. THOUGHTLESSNESS. A thoughtless disregard of God's strict injunctions, by either a priest (vers. 18, 19) or a Kohathite, might have been fatal. So now those who have perpetually to deal with Divine things are in danger of irreverence from thoughtlessness. *E. g.* Christian ministers, who have to be constantly praying and preaching, as part of their service for God. Christians who have a reputation for saintliness above their brethren need special reverence, lest they should handle Divine things in a familiar, unauthorised manner. Apply to some habits of modern public worship tending to sad irreverence.

III. DISTRUST. Illustrate from the sin of Uzzah (2 Sam. vi. 6, 7). We are thus warned against using illegitimate means in support of the cause of God which *we* think to be in danger. Carnal methods must not be resorted to for the defence of spiritual truths. Some of the most devoted servants of Christ have profaned the ark of God, when they thought it in danger, by touching and propping it by supports God has never sanctioned. *E. g.* persecutions on behalf of *the truth of God*. Caution to those who now rely on worldly alliances and statesmanship on behalf of God's Church. From such perils we may be preserved by the spirit of (1) profound humility, at the privilege of being allowed to come so near and to deal with the mysteries of God (Eph. iii. 8; Heb. xii. 28, 29); (2) reverential obedience to every item of the instructions God has given us (1 Chron. xv. 12, 13; Ps. cxix. 128); (3) fearless trust in the Lord Jesus Christ, who has guarded his Church hitherto, is saving us, and who will protect his people and his truth by his own power to the end (2 Tim. iv. 18).—P.

Ch. iv.—*The Levites and the regulation of their duties.* One tribe has been set apart in lieu of the first-born of all Israel, and to this tribe is entrusted the service of the tabernacle. The nature and distribution of that service are now placed before us. Note—

I. THE REGARD FOR THE PRINCIPLE OF INHERITANCE. As the *tribes* had their appointed place around the tabernacle, so the *three great natural divisions* of the tribe of Levi had their appointed place in it. So in the service of the Church of Christ there must ever be something corresponding to this natural division in Levi. The great Head has given some apostles, some prophets, some evangelists, some pastors and teachers. There are always some Christians rather than others who may be taken as spiritual children of certain in the spiritual generation before them, those on whom the prophet's mantle may fall, as did that of Elijah on Elisha.

II. THE LIMITATIONS OF SERVICE. *No Levite could do the work of an anointed priest.* The Kohathites were to bear the things of the holy place, but they were not to see them or prepare them for removal. There was a gulf of difference between Aaron and the noblest of the Kohathites, though they belonged to the same tribe. So between Christ and even the best of his people. There is so much to link us to our Lord, so much to reveal him as walking about on the same level, that we cannot be too careful to remember the differences between our services, humble even the most honourable of them, and that glorious peculiar service where Christ is Priest and Atonement in one. *The limitations of age.* None under thirty, none over fifty. At twenty a man may have strength and courage for fighting (ch. i. 3), but ten years more must pass over his head before he is judged to have the sobriety and sedateness needed for tabernacle service. Then at fifty he retires. God has consideration for failing strength. The burdens of the tabernacle must be carried, therefore God provides that the bearers shall be strong. There were constantly fresh and, we may suppose, often eager accessions at the younger limit of the service. Jesus was about thirty when he entered on his public life (Luke iii. 23), and the Baptist would be about the same. Let these limitations of God be considered by all whom they concern. There are duties of manhood which youth has not the experience, nor age the strength, to perform.

III. THE SECURING OF PERSONAL SERVICE (vers. 19, 49). Only certain persons were fit to do the work, but all who were fit had some work to do. In the Church of Christ fitness for anything, clearly seen, distinctly felt, has in it the nature of a command. We need not fear that there will ever be too many persons engaged in the service of the true tabernacle. There were between eight and nine thousand at this first appointment, but the Lord's promise runs (Jer. xxxiii. 22), "As the host of heaven cannot be numbered, neither the sand of the sea measured, so I will multiply the Levites that minister unto me." We are all Levites now.

IV. THE WORK WAS ALL NECESSARY WORK. No doubt a certain honour attached to the Kohathites, but great risk went with it; and after all, the honour was more in the eyes of men than of God. All that is needful to be done for him is honourable. The least peg or cord was not to be left behind, any more than the ark itself. There should be a spirit of humble joy and gratitude in us that we are counted worthy to do anything for God. All are needed to make up the perfection of service. To the *complete* body the little finger is as needful as the complex and powerful brain. For the circulation of the blood the capillaries are as needful as the great arteries and veins. God calls for no superfluous work from us. He has no mere ornaments in the Church. If a thing is not of use, it is no ornament, however it be decorated.

Application : — Find your work and burden. Every one has his own burden (φορτίον) to bear. No one else then can carry your burden than you. Seek your place. Take the lowest one, then assuredly you will come in time to the right one. The lowest place in the tabernacle service is better than the highest among the ungodly (Ps. lxxxiv. 10).—Y.

INTERIOR SANCTITIES OF ISRAEL (CHS. V., VI.).

Ch. v. 1—4: REMOVAL OF THE UNCLEAN. Vers. 5—10: RESTITUTION OF TRESPASS. Vers. 11—31: JEALOUSY PURGED.

Ch. vi. 1—21: NAZIRITES DEDICATED. Vers. 22—27: BLESSING OF THE PEOPLE.

Whether these portions of the Divine legislation are connected with the surrounding narrative (1) by an order of time, as having been given at this point, or (2) by a harmony of subject, as completing on its inward side the perfection of the camp, or whether (3) their insertion here was in a sense accidental, and not now to be accounted for, must remain uncertain. Against (1) it must be observed that there is a decided break in the order of time at the beginning of ch. vii.; against (2) that a large part of the Levitical enactments might have been added here with an equal propriety.

EXPOSITION.

CHAPTER V.

THE UNCLEAN TO BE REMOVED (vers. 1—4). Ver. 2.—**Every leper.** The law of the leper had been given in great detail in Levit. xiii. and xiv., and it had been already ordered that he should be put out of the camp (Levit. xiii. 46, and cf. xiv. 3). **Every one that hath an issue.** These defilements are treated of in Levit. xv.; where, however, it is not expressly ordered that those so polluted should be put out of the camp. **Whosoever is defiled by the dead.** The fact of being thus defiled is recognised in Levit. xi. 24; xxi. 1, but the formal regulations concerning it are not given until ch. xix. 21. Probably the popular opinion and practice was sufficiently definite to explain the present command.

Ver. 3.—**That they defile not their camps, in the midst whereof I dwell.** Cleanliness, decency, and the anxious removal even of unwitting pollutions were things due to God

himself, and part of the awful reverence to be paid to his presence in the midst of Israel. It is of course easy to depreciate the value of such outward cleanness, as compared with inward; but when we consider the frightful prevalence of filthiness in Christian countries (1) of person and dress, (2) of talk, (3) of habit in respect of things not so much sinful as uncleanly, we may indeed acknowledge the heavenly wisdom of these regulations, and the incalculable value of the tone of mind engendered by them. With the Jews "cleanliness" was not "next to godliness," it was part of godliness.

Ver. 4.—**So did the children of Israel.** It is difficult to form any estimate of the numbers thus separated; if we may judge at all from the prevalence of such defilements (especially those under the second head) now, it must have seriously aggravated both the labour and the difficulty of the march. Here was a trial of their faith.

HOMILETICS.

Vers. 1—4.—*The necessity of putting away sin.* In this section we have, spiritually, the necessary sentence of banishment upon those defiled with sin, and the duty of separating them. Consider, therefore—

I. THAT NO LEPER MIGHT STAY IN THE CAMP OF ISRAEL; HE MUST BE "WITHOUT." Even so it is the necessary fate of the sinner, who is the true leper,—a fate which God himself, as we may reverently believe, cannot alter,—that he must be for ever separated from the company of all pure and holy beings (Heb. xii. 14; Rev. xxi. 27; xxii. 15). Until he is healed he may be *with*, but not *of*, the people of God; numbered with them indeed, and following the earthly fortunes of the Church, as the lepers in the wilderness; but really separated from them, and this the more profoundly because of the outward proximity. If a sinner could go to heaven as a sinner, even there he would be a banished man, beholding the joy of the saints from outside with a sense of difference, of farness, which would itself be hell.

II. THAT NO ONE UNCLEAN THROUGH ANY ISSUE MIGHT STAY IN THE CAMP OF ISRAEL. And this was more severe, because it was a much more common and much less dreadful case than leprosy, being in most cases neither very apparent nor very permanent; yet this also entailed banishment while it lasted. Even so all habits of sin, however little shocking to the natural mind, exclude the sinner until he be healed from the true fellowship of the saints. They are indeed "natural" enough to the fallen soul, as these issues are natural to our present body of humiliation, but they are not therefore harmless. One sinful habit, however common amongst men, would disqualify and unfit the soul for the companionship of heaven, and so would entail an inward and real exile even there. A habit of lying is one of the commonest outcomes of human life as it is; but "whatsoever . . maketh a lie" must be "without."

III. THAT NO ONE EVEN WHO HAD TOUCHED A DEAD BODY MIGHT STAY IN THE CAMP OF ISRAEL. The defilement of death passed over with the taint of it upon all that came in contact with the dead. Even so that contact, to which we are daily and hourly exposed, with those dead in trespasses and sins is enough to unfit us for fellowship with pure and holy beings. If only the taint, the subtle contagion, the imperceptible communication of spiritual death pass upon us, as it almost must in daily intercourse with the world, it separates *pro tanto* from the communion of saints. It must be purged by the daily prayer of repentance and supply of grace ere we can be at home and at one with the really holy. And note that these three forms of uncleanness—(1) leprosy, which was rare and dreadful; (2) issues, which are common and little noticed; (3) the taint of death, which was imperceptible save to God—represent in a descending scale the three forms of sin which separate from God and his saints, viz. (1) open and notorious wickedness; (2) sinful habits such as spring out of ordinary life, and are little regarded; (3) the subtle taint of spiritual death caught by careless contact with the evil world.

IV. THAT IT WAS THE DUTY OF ISRAEL—a duty to be discharged at cost of much inconvenience; a duty in which all must help, not sparing their own—TO PUT AWAY ALL WHO WERE KNOWN TO BE POLLUTED FROM THE CAMPS. Even so it is the *duty* of the Churches of Christ to separate open sinners from their communion, not only lest others be defiled, but lest God be offended (Matt. xviii. 17; 1 Cor. v. 2, 11, 13; 2 Thess. iii. 6). And note that many unclean may have remained in the camp, whose uncleanness was not suspected, or could not be proved; but if so, they alone were responsible. Even so there be very many evil men in the Church who cannot now be separated; but if the *principle* be zealously vindicated, the Church shall not suffer (Matt. xiii. 47, 49; 1 Cor. xi. 19; 2 Tim. ii. 20).

HOMILIES BY VARIOUS AUTHORS.

Vers. 1—4.—*The expulsion and restoration of the unclean.* The host has now been marshalled. The several tribes have taken the places allotted to them in relation to the tabernacle and to one another. They are about to set forth on the march from the wilderness of Sinai. Before the signal is given, certain final instructions for the regulation of the camp have yet to be delivered, and this about the removal of unclean persons is one of them. The general intention of it is intimated in the terms employed. The host is to be so ordered, both in the camp and on the march, as to make it a living picture of the Church, and the Church's relation to God. It is to be made manifest that he dwells and walks among the covenant people (Levit. xxvi. 11, 12), that he is of pure eyes, and cannot suffer evil to dwell with him. Accordingly, there must in no wise abide in the camp any man or woman that is unclean. Persons afflicted with uncleanness must be removed, and live outside of the sacred precinct. Such is the law here laid down.

I. IN ATTRIBUTING TO THIS LAW A RELIGIOUS INTENTION, I DO NOT FORGET THAT A LOWER AND MORE PROSAIC INTERPRETATION HAS SOMETIMES BEEN PUT ON IT. There are commentators who remind one of the man with the muck-rake in the 'Pilgrim's Progress.' They have no eye except for what is earthly. To them the removal of the unclean is simply a sanitary measure. I freely admit that there was a sanitary intention. The sequestering of lepers, the early and "extramural" burial of the dead—these are valuable sanitary provisions, and it is plain that this law would lead to them. But I need not wait to prove that the law looks higher, and that its paramount intention is moral and spiritual.

II. Passing on, therefore, to the RELIGIOUS INTENTION of this law, observe who exactly are excluded by it from the camp. They are of three sorts, viz., lepers, persons affected with issues of various kinds, and persons who had come in contact with the dead. This does not by any means exhaust the catalogue of defilements noted in the Levitical law. But these were the gravest. Only these three disabled from residence in the camp. My reason for calling attention to this point you will understand when I mention that these three uncleannesses, so prominent in the law of Moses, received the same kind of prominence in the gracious ministry of Christ. Read the story of the leper (Mark i. 41); of the woman with the issue of blood (Mark v. 27—30); of the raising of Jairus' daughter and the widow's son at Nain (Mark v. 41 and Luke vii. 14). In no one of these passages is the Levitical law named. Much the greater number of those who read or hear them fail to perceive that in Christ's mode of performing the miracles there was any reference to what the law had said about the defiling quality of the evils on which his gracious power was put forth. That there truly was a reference surely needs no proof. No Jew ever forgot what the penalty would be if he suffered himself to be in contact with a dead body, with a leper, with a person having an issue of blood. Certainly our Lord did not forget. Nor would it be doing justice to the truth to say that our Lord touched as he did, *notwithstanding* the defilement thereby contracted, and its troublesome consequences. He, of set purpose, sought occasion to put himself in contact with every one of the three causes of defilement noted in the law. Keeping this in mind, let us ask the meaning of the law. 1. *The general intention.* It was to be a memorial of the truth that our nature is deeply infected with sin, and that sin disables all in whom it is found for enjoying the fellowship of God here and hereafter. In this Levitical statute, I admit, the lesson is not taught explicitly. There was nothing morally wrong in any one of the three sources of defilement named. The teaching is by symbol—a kind of object lesson— and not the less impressive on that account. 2. *The meaning of the several symbols.* (1) Defilement by the dead. Why is this? Because death is the wages of sin (Gen. ii. 17; iii. 19). Compare the representation of death which pervades Ps. xc.— 'the prayer of Moses." (2) Defilement by leprosy. A touching symbol. It admonishes us that sin, besides being blameworthy and deserving of death, is a vile thing, to be loathed and recoiled from, as men loathe and recoil from a leper; contagious also, and apt to spread. (3) Of the third symbol I need say only this, that it reminds us that sin is an hereditary evil (Ps. li. 5). 3. *The relation of this law to Christ and his work.* That it has a relation has been already pointed out. The relation may be conceived of thus:—The law is the dark ground on which the redemptive work of Christ unfolds the brightness of its grace. Christ did not keep aloof from the evils which afflict our fallen nature, and which perpetually remind us how deep our fall has been. He took occasion to put himself in contact with them. He touched the leprous man. Not that leprosy was sweet to him; it was to him as loathsome as to any man in Palestine that day. Nevertheless, he touched the leprous man, and the leprosy fled before the power of that touch. Leprosy, wasting issues, death—these are the memorials and tokens of the sin that is the fatal heritage of our fallen race ; and one who would know our need of redemption cannot do better than meditate on them as they are set forth in the Levitical law. Leprosy, wasting issues, death—these evils our blessed Lord went up to in his ministry ; he touched them, and their flight the instant that they felt his touch gave, and continues still to give, assurance to men that he is indeed the Saviour. He can forgive sin ; he can make us clean ; he is the resurrection and the life.—B.

Vers. 1—4.—*The public exclusion of the unclean.* This law, like many others, in part a sanitary law ; but also educational in spiritual truth, and typical of eternal realities. Two truths taught :—

I. THE HOLINESS OF GOD. This lesson, so hard to the Israelites, was impressed on them in many ways, *e. g.*, sacred men ministering in sacred places, on sacred days, &c. This holy God dwelt in the midst of their tents, and walked among them (Levit. xxvi. 11, 12). The God of life and purity was utterly alien from death and impurity. Defilement, whether wilful or unavoidable, could not be tolerated in his presence. If the polluted are retained, God withdraws. Sin is "the abominable thing" which God hates. He is " of purer eyes than to behold evil" (Jer. xliv. 4 ; Hab. i. 13).

II. THE EXCOMMUNICATING POWER OF SIN. The consequences to the excluded Hebrews, though limited, were by no means light. They had to suffer loss of privileges, ceremonial and spiritual, and a sense of humiliation from the notoriety of their position. For the time they were out of communion with God and his people. Thus sin has an isolating power. Apart from an act of ecclesiastical excommunication or Divine judgment, its tendency is to separate us from the people of God through want of sympathy. We cease to enjoy their privileges even if not debarred from them. We lose self-respect when sin is exposed, if not before. We are out of communion with God, into whose presence we cannot truly come with sin indulged in our hearts (Ps. lxvi. 18 ; Ezek. xiv. 3). God's salvation is *from* sin, not *in* sin. No wonder, therefore, that the impure are sentenced—(1) to excommunication from the Church on earth (1 Cor. v. 9—13, &c.), (2) to exclusion from the Church in heaven (Rev. xxi. 27).—P.

Vers. 1—4.—*Things that defile.* The book up to this point is occupied with the counting and discipline of the people, both those for war and those for tabernacle service. Now the *cleansing* of the camp is to be attended to.

I. THE CLASSES WHO WERE DECLARED UNCLEAN. Certainly we must not be too curious in our inquiries here, or we may soon pass the verge of what is edifying. But there are some points of note with regard to all three classes. *The leper.* Why should he be declared unclean ? Perhaps as suffering from a more manifest disease than others, maybe a peculiarly offensive one, and one of the most difficult to cure. These are conjectures which give a little light, but the great reason for ceremonial uncleanness in the case of human beings, as in the case of lower animals, is to be found in Jehovah's positive injunction. Leprosy was thus to be one of the great types in the body of the defiling effect of sin upon the soul. It is clear that in the course of ages the idea got fixed in the Israelite mind that the cure of leprosy was to be considered as a cleansing. Jesus commanded his apostles to *heal* the sick, *cleanse* the lepers. The leper was not a common victim, but singled out to impress the fact that the ultimate cause which produces disease is a strange and polluting thing ; no necessary element in human nature, though now it be actually present in us all. *The person with an issue.* Thus uncleanness is connected with *birth* as well as with *death.* Whenever a child is born, a being is brought into the world, which certainly will add something to the evil in it, though possibly it may add much to the good. The saintliest of believers has had in him the possibilities of the worst of unbelievers. Human nature is truly the creation of God, fearfully and wonderfully made ; but there is also the fact of birth from sinful human parents to be remembered. This is a great mystery, to be delicately handled ; but the uncleanness here indicated may be taken as intended to remind parents how one generation transmits not only nature, but sinful nature, to another. *The person defiled by the dead.* There is great significance in being made unclean by the dead. Of all things in the world that manifest the effects of sin, this is the greatest—death. By sin came death. All lesser results lead up to this. A dead body, in one sense as sacred a thing as there is in the world, is yet also one of the most unclean. As long as there is life there is something to protest against the reign of sin, and resist it; but life being gone, sin riots and revels in the corruption of what was once fair and strong. The coffin and the gravestone hide, but they only hide. It was one of our Lord's most terrible words to the Pharisees to compare them to whited sepulchres.

II. THE LINE OF SEPARATION. There are large details in Leviticus respecting all these instances of uncleanness (chs. xii.—xv.). The line of separation was clearly marked, sternly enforced. To go out of the camp meant much personal inconvenience, perhaps pain—suffering added on to existing suffering. Imagine the mother tending her sick child, waiting its expiring breath, closing its eyes, composing its body, then compelled to go without the camp. This typical ceremonial uncleanness indicates the sharp *separation between good and bad men.* The word of God accords in all its references to this. There are two classes, and only two—the clean and the unclean, the sheep and the goats, the wheat and tares, the children of God and the children of wrath. It also indicates the *extent to which discipline can be carried in the Church of Christ on earth.* There are some offences so plain that the guilty may at once be cut off from outward communion. But there may be others quite as unworthy who yet do and must escape, because their life makes no crying scandal. Many a professed and long-continued adherent to the true Church is, nevertheless, as worldly, hard, and selfish as any of the ungodly. God reckons all such outside the camp. He alone has the knowledge and authority to reckon. Learn then the danger of all spiritual uncleanness. That so much was declared typically unclean, shows that spiritual uncleanness is a very great danger. The boundary between the Church and the world cannot be too strictly kept. Since we are all advancing to death, it is proof of the power of sin in our nature. We are *all* unclean with the worst of uncleanness. It only waits for us to feel all the evil, and the way is clear to the remedy (1 John i. 7—10).—Y.

EXPOSITION.

RESTITUTION TO BE MADE FOR TRESPASSES (vers. 5—10). Ver. 6.—**Shall commit any sin that men commit.** Literally, "[one] of all the transgressions of men," *i. e.* the wrongs current amongst men. **To do a trespass against the Lord.** This qualifies the former expression, and restricts its reference to the sins mentioned in Levit. vi. 2, 3, 5, viz., wrongs done to the property of another. Such wrongs, perhaps because they were considered legitimate as long as they were not found out, were taken up by the Lord himself as involving a trespass against his own righteousness.

Ver. 8.—**If the man have no kinsman.** No *goel*, or personal representative. This supposes that the wronged man himself is dead, and it is an addition to the law of restitution as given in Levit. vi., an addition clearly necessary to its completeness. The wrong-doer must in no case be the gainer by his own wrong, and if the trespass could not be "recompensed" to man, it must be "recompensed" to the Lord, who was as it were joint-plaintiff in the cause. **To the priest.** On the general principle that the priest was the visible representative of the invisible majesty.

Ver. 9.—**Every offering.** Hebrew, *terumah,* heave offering (Exod. xxix. 28). Septuagint, ἀπαρχή. Those offerings, or portions of offerings, which were not consumed on the altar, but "presented" at the altar. Having been offered, they were the property of the Lord, and were given by him to the priests.

Ver. 10.—**Every man's hallowed things.** Dedicatory offerings, such as first-fruits, not exactly of the nature of sacrifices. **His,** *i. e.* the priest's. **Whatsoever any man giveth the priest, it shall be his.** A general principle, including and confirming the previous rules; subject, of course, to the other and greater principle, that whatever the Lord claimed for himself by fire must first be consumed. These directions concerning the rights of the priests to offerings are very often repeated in various connections. There was probably a strong tendency amongst the people to cheat the priests of their dues, or to represent their claims as exorbitant. It is in the spirit of covetousness which underlies all such conduct that we are to find the connection between these two verses and the rest of the paragraph.

HOMILETICS.

Vers. 5—10.—*No fraud permitted by God.* We have here, as part of the moral law of God which changeth not, the duty of making confession of, and satisfaction for, any wrong done to another, and the duty of not withholding what is rightly theirs from the ministers of God. Consider, therefore—

I. THAT EVERY WRONG DONE TO ANOTHER IN RESPECT OF HIS PROPERTY WAS ASSUMED BY THE LORD AS A TRESPASS AGAINST HIMSELF. So now every wrong or fraud, and all cheating or sharp dealing, practised by one of us against another, is not merely an offence against man,—such as may be excused by the necessity of the times, or the custom of business, or the universal prevalence of such practices,—but is an outrage against the righteousness of God which he will never overlook. To such a man God himself is "the adversary" (Matt. v. 25); and if he be not repaid, then will he himself "repay" that man (Isa. lix. 18; Rom. xii. 19). He that hath cheated his neighbour of a penny hath gained unto himself an eternal and immeasurable loss, except he repent, confess, restore (Exod. xxxiv. 7; Isa. lxi. 8).

II. THAT EVERY ONE WHO HAD DONE SUCH WRONG MUST (1) CONFESS, (2) MAKE RESTITUTION. So now there is no true repentance for, and no real forgiveness of, such wrongs—from the least even to the greatest—unless they are (1) humbly acknowleged, (2) liberally made good (Luke xix. 8). Those wrongs (alas, how many!) which are never found out, which are not acknowledged through false shame, and not made good through covetousness, are like bullets lodged in the body, which will not cease to cause misery, disease, and death.

III. THAT IF THE WRONGED MAN WAS DEAD, AND HAD LEFT NO REPRESENTATIVE, THE TRESPASS MUST STILL BE RECOMPENSED TO THE LORD BY BEING PAID TO THE PRIEST. So now it is a certain maxim of Christian morality (as of law) that no man be a gainer by his own wrong. If he cannot repay to the person wronged, directly or indirectly, he is bound to make recompense to God by devoting it to some pious purpose. If a man has made a fortune by fraud, his repentance is vain unless he make over the whole of it to the good of his neighbours. This will not cleanse his conscience,—only the one Sacrifice can do that,—but without it his conscience cannot be cleansed.

IV. THAT GOD DID CAREFULLY INSIST THAT HIS PRIESTS SHOULD RECEIVE THEIR PORTION, and SHOULD NOT BE OVER-REACHED. Even so is the law of Christ (1 Cor. ix. 7—14; Gal. vi. 6; 1 Tim. v. 17, 18).

HOMILIES BY VARIOUS AUTHORS.

Vers. 5—10.—*Conscience money.* This precept is a continuation of the one laid down in the preceding verses, and, like it, admonishes the people regarding the purity which ought to prevail in a camp honoured with the presence of the Holy One. Since the Lord dwells in the midst of the camp, there must not abide in it anything that defileth—any leper, any one having an issue, any one who has been in contact with the dead. Nor is it bodily defilement only that entails this disability. The man "that doeth hurt to his neighbour" is unclean in God's sight. Fraud is as defiling as leprosy. Even if it is such as the criminal law cannot reach, God's eye sees it, and is offended with it; and the wrong-doer must regard himself as excluded from the camp till he has made restitution to his wronged neighbour, and brought a sacrifice of atonement to the Lord.

I. Keeping in view the scope of the law as I have described it, you will without difficulty master the particulars laid down, especially if you read along with it the law in Levit. vi. 1—7. It is essential to observe that this injunction is not a part of the criminal code. It is not laid down for the guidance of the judges, but for the guidance of a man's own conscience. The restitution enjoined is similar to that known among ourselves as CONSCIENCE MONEY. Take an example. A man finds a pruning-hook by the highway-side, evidently left there by mistake. He takes it home. "An excellent pruning-hook; the very thing I was in need of. I need not make a noise about the lucky find; I will keep it to myself." A few days after, the loser turns up, and makes inquiries about his hook. But the finder denies all knowledge of it, and it remains in his possession. Among us the criminal law would have something to say to this dishonest finder. The meshes of the Hebrew criminal code seem to have been wide enough to let him go. But the holy law of God speaks to his conscience. 1. He is to confess his fault. Even in matters belonging to the criminal law, the Jews laid great stress on confession. It was a maxim among them, that if a man brought an offering for his offence, but omitted to confess the evil he had done, his offering would not avail for atonement (cf. 1 John i. 9). 2. He is to make restitution to the person wronged. In the instance supposed the pruning-hook must be restored, or its equivalent in money, with one-fifth part added. This, let me observe in passing, shows that the trespass contemplated is not a trespass such as fell within the scope of the criminal law; for the restitution enjoined in the criminal law was much ampler. A thief restored double; a sheep-stealer fourfold; a cattle-lifter fivefold (Exod. xxii. 1—4). Mild penalties certainly, but more severe than the restitution enjoined here. 3. A ram is to be brought to the Lord as a trespass offering for atonement. 4. If the person who was wronged is dead, the restitution is to be made to the next heir,—the kinsman, or *goel* (ver. 8),—whom failing, it is to be made to the Lord in the person of the priest. In connection with this, the people are admonished that all gifts solemnly dedicated to the priest fall under the same rule as conscience money paid by way of compensation for fraud. Omission to pay them will defile the camp.

II. WHAT DOES THIS STATUTE OF CONSCIENCE MONEY TEACH US? 1. When a man does wrong to his neighbour he sins against God, and must crave God's pardon for the wrong. There have been religious systems—the old Greek and Roman paganism, for example—which completely disconnected religion from morality. A tendency in the same direction, who that knows himself has not caught a glimpse of in his own heart? Against that fatal divorce the whole word of God is a protest and warning. Read Psalm xv. 2. When a man does wrong to his neighbour he must make compensation to his neighbour. It will not do simply to confess the wrong to God, and beg his pardon. That is only one half of what the case demands. Satisfaction must be made to the person wronged. In many cases the civil magistrate will see to this. In many other cases the wrong-doing is of a kind which his sword cannot reach—fraudulent bankruptcies often elude the law. In all cases alike, God commands the person who has wronged his neighbour to repay him with increase. 3. The wrong-doer who omits to repay as required is admonished that he is an unclean person, whose presence defiles God's sanctuary. In God's sight the camp is defiled by the presence of a man who defrauds as much as by a leper. If you would see how deeply this aspect of the precept before us impressed itself on consciences in Israel, read Psalm xv., a psalm fitted surely to suggest alarm to those amongst us who in business habitually violate the golden rule, and yet claim a place in God's sanctuary. 4. In the complications of modern life it will happen far more frequently than in ancient Israel that satisfaction for fraud cannot be made directly to the parties defrauded. In this case the money is to be devoted to charitable and pious uses. To be sure, ill-gotten wealth is a very undesirable source of income for either Church or charity. I much doubt whether God honours it to do much good. But if the fraudulent person is truly penitent, and has done his best to make compensation to his victims, he may hope to escape the defilement and curse that cleave to dishonest gains by bestowing them where they may possibly do some good.—B.

Vers. 5—8.—*Confession and restitution.* These trespasses are explained and illustrated in Levit. vi. 1—7. In both passages provision is made for confession, restitution, interest, and atonement—in Leviticus the atonement being spoken of more fully than here. Notice that three parties are provided for in the directions given.

I. THE WRONG-DOER. The wrong-doer has done injury to himself as well as another. In one sense the injury is even greater. What we suffer from others, grievous and irritating as it may be at the time, need not be an abiding ill; but the injury we inflict on others is great spiritual danger to ourselves. Hence the man *truly* confessing the wrong he had done was proving himself in a better state of mind, no longer the victim of selfishness, and glorying in his shame, but showing an awakened conscience, and a repentance needing not to be repented of. Consider the benefit David got (Ps. li.). Confession, restitution, and atonement cleanse the bosom of a great deal of " perilous stuff." Restitution, though a loss in possessions, is a gain in peace. Reparation of a wrong done to a fellow-man is to be valued for the injured person's sake ; but it is a great deal more that the wrong-doer for his own sake has been brought right with God.

II. THE PERSON WRONGED. He is provided for as far as he can be provided for. To make reparation in all respects is indeed impossible. A wrong-doer, with all his efforts, cannot put things exactly as they were before. Still he must do what he can. Hence the provision to add a fifth over the principal. Doubtless a truly repentant trespasser would not stop even at that to show his sincerity in reparation. Zaccheus restored fourfold. Surely there are some injured persons to whom it would be a greater joy and a greater benefit to see their enemies altogether altered than if they had never been hurt by them at all. One great good, as concerned the person wronged, was that confession and restitution would do much to allay, and perhaps obliterate, the sense of injustice. " It is not what a man outwardly has or wants that constitutes the happiness or misery of him. It is the feeling of injustice that is insupportable to all men. The brutalest black African cannot bear that he should be used unjustly " (Carlyle). Again, injured persons themselves may be injurers. A sense of wrong suffered is not always effectual in hindering the sufferer from wronging others. So the confession and repentance of one might lead to the confession and repentance of another. Who knows the *total effect* produced on the persons to whom Zaccheus made his fourfold restitution ?

III. JEHOVAH HIMSELF. Acknowledgment and restitution were not enough without *atonement*. To injure a fellow-man is to rebel against the government of God, robbing him of some possible service from the person injured. The wrong-doer, from prickings of conscience, or mere uneasiness of mind, may make some reparation to his fellow-man, whom he can see ; but if he thinks he has then done all, he may find, from continued uneasiness, that something is yet unaccomplished. It is the greatest blot on sinful men, not that they are unjust to one another, but that they have come short of the glory of God. That glory must be restored, and God take the place of self, if human relations are to come right. There is no scheme of teaching or example that, acting on natural lines, will ever make men perfectly just to one another. Things must be put right with God, for of him, and through him, and to him are all things. Let no one, therefore, make confession and restitution here look large, and atonement be pushed into the corner as an unimportant detail. Just as the confession and restitution point forward to the pure and vigorous ethics of Jesus, so the slain animals point forward to him who takes away the sin of the world.—Y.

EXPOSITION.

THE TRIAL OF JEALOUSY (vers. 11—31). Ver. 12. — **If any man's wife . . . commit a trespass against him.** The adultery of the wife is here regarded only from a social point of view ; the injury to the husband, the destruction of his peace of mind, even by the bare suspicion, and the consequent troubling of Israel, is the thing dwelt upon. The punishment of adultery as a sin had been already prescribed (Levit. xx. 10).

Ver. 13.—**If it be hid.** Or, " if he be hid." This verse is explanatory of the former. **Taken with the manner.** The latter words are not in the Hebrew. It means no doubt " taken in the act " (cf. John viii. 4). Αὐτὴ μὴ ᾖ συνειλημμένη, Septuagint.

Ver. 14.—**And she be not defiled.** As far as the mischief here dealt with was con-

cerned, it was almost equally great whether the woman was guilty or not.

Ver. 15.—**He shall bring her offering for her.** קָרְבָּנָה, " her offering ;" עָלֶיהָ, " on her account." It was to be a meat offering—not connected on this occasion with any other sacrifice—of the fruits of the earth, symbolising the fruits of her guilty, or at least careless and suspicious, conduct. As of barley meal, not of fine wheat flour, it indicated her present low and vile estate (deserved or undeserved) ; as without incense or oil, it disclaimed for itself the sanctifying influences of God's grace and of prayer. Thus every detail of the offering, while it did not condemn the woman (for one found guilty could not have made any offering at all), yet represented her questionable repute and unquestionable dishonour, for even the unjust suspicion of the husband is a dishonour to the wife. **Barley meal.** In the days of Elisha half the price of fine flour (2 Kings vii. 1), and only eaten by the poor (Ezek. iv. 12 ; John vi. 9). **An offering of jealousy.** Literally, "of jealousies." מִנְחָת, an intensive plural. **An offering of memorial, bringing iniquity to remembrance.** Θυσία μνημοσίνου, Septuagint. An offering to bring the woman into judicial remembrance before the Lord, in order that her sin (if any) might be remembered with him, and be declared.

Ver. 16.—**Before the Lord.** Either at the brazen altar or at the door of the tabernacle.

Ver. 17.—**Holy water.** Probably from the laver which stood near the altar (Exod. xxx. 18). The expression is nowhere else used. The Septuagint has ὕδωρ καθαρὸν ζῶν, pure running water. **In an earthen vessel.** Cheap and coarse, like the offering. **Of the dust that is in the floor of the tabernacle.** This is the only place where the floor of the tabernacle is mentioned. As no directions were given concerning it, it was probably the bare earth cleared and stamped. The cedar floor of the temple was overlaid with gold (1 Kings vi. 16, 30). This use of the dust has been held to signify the fact (*a*) that man was made of dust, and must return to dust (Gen. iii. 19) ; or (*b*) that dust is the serpent's meat, *i. e.* that shame and disgust are the inevitable fruit of sin (Gen. iii. 14 ; Isa. lxv. 25). Of these, (*a*) is not appropriate to the matter in question, since mortality is common to all, and (*b*) is far too recondite to have been intended here. It is very unlikely that the spiritual meaning of Gen. iii. 14 was known to any of the Jews. A much simpler and more intelligible explanation is to be found in the obvious fact that the dust of the tabernacle was the only thing which belonged to the tabernacle, and which was, so to speak, impregnated with the awful holiness of him that dwelt therein, that could be mixed with water and drunk. For a similar reason the "sin" of the people, the golden calf, was ground to powder, and the people made to drink it (Exod. xxxii. 20). The idea conveyed to the dullest apprehension certainly was that with the holy dust Divine "virtue" had passed into the water—virtue which would give it supernatural efficacy to slay the guilty and to leave the guiltless unharmed.

Ver. 18. — **Uncover the woman's head.** In token that she had forfeited her glory by breaking, or seeming to have broken, her allegiance to her husband (1 Cor. xi. 5—10) ; perhaps also with some reference to the truth that "all things are naked and open to the eyes of him" with whom she had to do (Heb. iv. 13). **Put the offering of memorial in her hands.** That she herself might pre-

sent, as it were, the fruits of her life before God, and challenge investigation of them. **Bitter water.** It was not literally bitter, but it was so fraught with conviction and judgment as to bring bitter suffering on the guilty.

Ver. 19. — **If no man.** The oath presupposed her innocence. **With another instead of thy husband.** Hebrew, "under thy husband," *i. e.* as a wife subject to a husband (Ezek. xxiii. 5 ; Hos. iv. 12). Ὕπανδρος οὖσα, Septuagint. It was only as a *femme couverte* that she could commit *this* sin.

Ver. 21.—**Then the priest shall . . say unto the woman.** These words are parenthetical, just as in Matt. ix. 6. The latter part of the oath is called "an oath of cursing," because it contained the imprecations on the guilty. **To rot.** Hebrew, "to fall." Τὸν μηρόν σου διαπεπτωκότα, Septuagint. **To swell.** The Hebrew *zabeh* is not of quite certain meaning, but probably this.

Ver. 22.—**Into thy bowels.** Cf. Ps. cix. 18. Εἰς τὴν κοιλίαν σου, Septuagint. It has been thought that these symptoms belonged to some known disease, such as dropsy (Josephus, 'Ant.,' iii. 11, 6), or ovarian dropsy. But it is clear that the whole matter was outside the range of the known and of the natural. An innocent woman may suffer from dropsy, or any form of it ; but this was a wholly peculiar infliction by direct visitation of God. The principle which underlay the infliction was, however, clear : δι' ὧν γὰρ ἡ ἁμαρτία, διὰ τούτων ἡ τιμωρία—the organs of sin are the seat of the plague. **Amen, amen.** Doubled here, as in the Gospel of John. The woman was to accept (if she dared) the awful ordeal and appeal to God by this response ; if she dared not, she pronounced herself guilty.

Ver. 23. — **In a book.** On a roll. **Blot them out with the bitter water.** Rather, "wash them off into the bitter water," in order to transfer the venom of the curses to the water. Ἐξαλείψει . . . εἰς τὸ ὕδωρ, Septuagint. The writing on the scroll was to be washed off in the vessel of water. Of course the only actual consequence was that the ink was mixed with the water, but in the imagination of the people, and to the frightened conscience of a guilty woman, the curses were also held in solution in the water of trial. The direction was founded on a world-wide superstition, still prevalent in Africa, and indeed amongst most semi-barbarous peoples. In the 'Romance of Setnan,' translated by Brugsch. Bey, the scene of which is laid in the time of Rameses the Great, a magical formula written on a papyrus leaf is dissolved in water, and drunk with the effect of imparting all its secrets to him that drinks it. So in the present day, by a similar superstition, do sick Mahomedans swallow texts of the Koran ; and so in the middle ages the canonised Archbishop Edmund Rich (1240) on his death-bed washed a crucifix in water and drank it, saying, " Ye shall drink water from the wells of salvation."

Ver. 24.—**He shall cause the woman to drink.** This is said by anticipation, because she did not really drink it until after the offering (ver. 26).

Ver. 25.—**Offer it upon the altar.** According to the law of the *minchah* (Levit. ii.), only an handful was burnt as a "memorial" (Hebrew, *azkārāh*), the rest being "presented," and then laid at the side of the altar to be subsequently eaten by the priests. All this was done before the actual ordeal by drinking the water, in order that the woman might in the most solemn and complete way possible be brought face to face with the holiness of God. She stood before him as one of his own, yet as one suspected and abashed, courting the worst if guilty, claiming complete acquittal if innocent.

Ver. 27.—**Shall enter into her, and become bitter.** Rather, "as bitter," or "as bitterness," *i. e.* as producing bitter sufferings. **Shall be a curse,** *i. e.* shall be used as an example in the imprecations of the people.

Ver. 28.—**And shall conceive seed.** As a sign of the Divine favour ; to a Jewish woman the surest and most regarded (1 Sam. ii. 5 ; Ps. cxxvii. 3 ; Luke i. 58).

Ver. 29.—**This is the law of jealousies.** A law prescribed by God, and yet in substance borrowed from half civilised heathens ; a practice closely akin to yet prevalent superstitions, and yet receiving not only the toleration of Moses, but the direct sanction of God ; an ordeal which emphatically claimed to be infallibly operative through supernatural agencies, yet amongst other nations obviously lending itself to collusion and fraud, as does the trial by red water practised by the tribes of West Africa. In order to justify heavenly wisdom herein, we must frankly admit, to begin with—(1) That it was founded upon the superstitious notion that immaterial virtue can be imparted to physical elements. The holiness of the gathered dust and the awfulness of the written curses were both supposed to be held in solution by the water of jealousy. The record does not *say* as much, but the whole ordeal proceeds on this supposition, which would undoubtedly be the popular one. (2) That it was only fitted for a very rude and comparatively barbarous state

of society. The Talmud states that the use of it ceased forty years before the destruction of Jerusalem (if so, during our Lord's earthly lifetime) ; but it may be held certain that it ceased long before—indeed there is no recorded instance of its use. It was essentially an ordeal, although one Divinely regulated, and as such would have been morally impossible and highly undesirable in any age but one of blind and uninquiring faith. And we find the justification of it exactly in the fact that it was given to a generation which believed much and knew little ; which had a profound belief in magic, and no knowledge of natural philosophy. It was ever the wisdom of God, as revealed in the sacred volume, to take men as they were, and to utilise the superstitious notions which could not at once be destroyed, or the imperfect moral ideas which could not at once be reformed, by making them work for righteousness and peace. It is, above all, the wisdom of God not to destroy the imperfect, but to regulate it and restrain its abuses, and so impress it into his service, until he has educated his people for something higher. Everybody knows the extreme violence of jealousy amongst an uncivilised people, and the widespread misery and crime to which it leads. It may safely be affirmed that *any* ordeal which should leave no place for jealousy, because no room for uncertainty, would be a blessing to a people rude enough and ignorant enough to believe in it. Ordeals are established in a certain stage of civilisation because they are wanted, and are on the whole useful, as long as they remain in harmony with popular ideas. They are, however, always liable to two dangers. (1) They occasionally fail, and are known to have failed, and so fall into disrepute. (2) They always lend themselves readily to collusion or priestcraft. The trial of jealousy being adopted, as it was, into a system really Divine, and being based upon the knowledge and power of God himself, secured all the benefits of an ordeal and escaped all its dangers. It is probable enough that the awful side of it was never really called into play. No guilty woman would dare to challenge so directly a visitation so dreadful, as long as she retained any faith or any superstition. Before the time came when any Jewish woman had discarded both, the increasing facilities of divorce had provided another and easier escape from matrimonial troubles.

HOMILETICS.

Vers. 11—31.—*The sin of adultery.* We have here, in the letter, a piece of legislation altogether obsolete, because adapted to an age and to ideas utterly foreign to our own ; yet, in the spirit, we have, as part of the moral law of God which changeth not, the unspeakable abhorrence in which the sin of adultery is held with him, and the great displeasure with which he regards the mere suspicion of it. For this ordeal was not merely or primarily to punish guilt or to restore domestic peace but to remove sin and passion from before the eyes of God. Consider, therefore—

I. THAT GOD RESERVED HIS MOST AWFUL VISITATION OF OLD TIMES FOR SUCH ADULTERY AS HAD SUCCESSFULLY ESCAPED HUMAN OBSERVATION. So there is no sin which more surely destroys a nation or a class by kindling the wrath of God against it than adultery. So the Jews in the time of the later prophets (Jer. v. 8; Hos. iv. 2), and in the time of our Lord (John viii. 7; the Talmud, as above); so the upper classes in France before the Revolution; so perhaps our own to-day.

II. THAT GOD DID NOT APPOINT DIVORCE AS A REMEDY AGAINST CONJUGAL UNFAITH-FULNESS. For it is no remedy against the sin, but only against some of its painful consequences. The glosses and traditions of the Jewish lawyers made divorce easy and common, because they no longer believed in the righteousness of God or in the hatefulness of sin, as sin.

III. That nothing is more abhorrent from the will of God concerning us THAN THAT FIERCE JEALOUSY AND CRUEL SUSPICION SHOULD INVADE FAMILIES, and poison the purest source of human happiness. Both, therefore, sin greatly—the wife who gives the least ground for suspicion by levity or carelessness of conduct, the husband who nurses a spirit of jealousy, and does not try to bring it to the test of facts.

IV. That the sin of adultery was PUNISHED UNDER THE LAW WITH MISERABLE DEATH, WHEREAS CHRIST REFUSED TO AWARD ANY SECULAR PUNISHMENT TO IT (John viii. 11). And this is (1) because of the greater mercifulness of the gospel, calling men to repentance (Rom. ii. 4; 2 Pet. iii. 9); but also (2) because of the greater severity of the moral law now revealed, threatening eternal death to all adulterers (Gal. v. 19, 21; Heb. xiii. 4).

V. THAT THIS SPECIAL AND AWFUL PROVISION WAS MADE ONLY AGAINST THE SIN OF THE WIFE, because it is from *her* sin that jealousy and its consequent crimes do as a fact arise in rude communities. But under the more perfect law of Christ there is no difference made between the same sin in men and women, but rather the sin of the man is denounced because it is more lightly accounted by the world (Matt. v. 28; 1 Thess. iv. 6, "in *the* matter").

HOMILIES BY VARIOUS AUTHORS.

Vers. 11—31.—*The trial of jealousy.* Just previously, regulations are laid down with respect to offences in general. Here is an offence which needed to be dealt with in a special way, as being one where restitution was impossible. The offence also destroyed a relation of peculiar sacredness and importance, and the discovery of guilt was difficult, perhaps impossible of attainment, by ordinary lines of proof.

I. THE HUSBAND'S POSITION IS RECOGNISED. The spirit of jealousy is not condemned as in itself an evil passion. In it he might be angry and sin not. The spirit of jealousy could not be too much excited or too amply satisfied, if only the facts corresponded to his feelings. No mention is made of a similar ordeal for the husband to pass through if a spirit of jealousy were awakened in the wife, and so it may seem that more severity was meted out to the woman than the man. But the offence of an unfaithful husband, equally great of course as a sin, might not be equally dangerous as a crime. The principles of human law which compel men to graduate crime and punishment had to be remembered in the theocracy. An examination of the Mosaic laws against sexual impurity shows that they provided stringently for both sexes. The adulterer was punishable with death. A guilty wife in the discovery of her guilt dragged down her paramour (Levit. xx. 10).

II. THE WIFE'S POSITION IS RECOGNISED. To punish her more severely for a lapse of conjugal fidelity was really to honour her, showing that in one respect more was expected from her. It became every Israelite to walk circumspectly; it peculiarly became the Israelite matron. May we not say that the spirit of jealousy, though it might often be manifested on insufficient grounds, was nevertheless in itself a provision of God, through nature? The reputation of a wife is a very delicate thing, and was meant so to be. The tenth commandment specifies, "Thou shalt not covet thy neighbour's wife." Hence we may infer there was some temptation to men to commit this sin, and wives needed to be specially on their guard. The ordeal to which God called them, hard as it might seem, had a most honourable side. Let it not be said that Mosaic legislation showed the Oriental depreciation of woman. God was caring for her even then, but she had to partake of the severity of the law, even as, long after, represented by the woman taken in adultery, she shared in the clemency and tenderness of the gospel.

III. THE UNERRING DISCOVERY OF GUILT. God took the matter away out of the obscurities of circumstantial evidence. The very nature of the offence made it difficult for a suspicious husband to get beyond presumption. "The eye of the adulterer waiteth for the twilight" (Job xxiv. 15). But God called the accused wife among the solemnities of the tabernacle, and concealment and evasion thenceforth became impossible. Notice how the ordeal was painless in itself. There was no walking on burning ploughshares nor demand on physical endurance. It was independent also of anything like chance, as if the casting of a lot had been held to settle the matter. The bitter water was drunk, and God, who brings all secret things into judgment, showed the indubitable proof in the swollen body and the rotted thigh. Proof, sentence, and punishment were all in one.

IV. THE DISCOVERY, EQUALLY UNERRING, OF INNOCENCE. One wonders what the history of this ordeal was in practice; how often used, and with what results. We know not what terrible tragedies it may have prevented, what credulous Othello it may have restored to his peace of mind, what Desdemona it may have vindicated, and what Iago it may have overthrown in his villanous plots. "God shall bring forth thy righteousness as the light, and thy judgment as the noonday" (Ps. xxxvii. 6). There will be a final clearing of all the innocent, however many have been condemned at a human bar. The whole matter assumes its most significant aspect when we note how the apostasy of God's people is figured by gross and shameful breaches of the marriage vow (Ezek. xvi.). The doom of the adulterous wife foreshadows the doom of the backsliding believer.—Y.

EXPOSITION.

CHAPTER VI.

THE VOW OF THE NAZIRITE (vers. 1—21). *Note.*—The Hebrew *Nazir* has been written Nazarite in English under the mistaken impression that there is some connection between Nazir and Nazarene (Matt. ii. 23). A very little reflection will show that "the Nazarene" not only was no Nazir, but that he even took pains to let it be seen that he was not. John the Baptist was the Nazir of the New Testament, and in all outward things the contrast was strongly marked between them (Luke vii. 14, 33, 34; John ii. 2).

Ver. 2.—**Either man or woman.** It was not a little remarkable that women could be Nazirites, because, generally speaking, the religious condition of women under the law was so markedly inferior and so little considered. But this is altogether consistent with the true view of the Nazirite vow, viz., that it was an exceptional thing, outside the narrow pale of the law, giving scope and allowance to the free movements of the Spirit in individuals. In this too it stood on the same plane as the prophetic office, for which

room was left in the religious system of Moses, and which was designed to correct and supplement in its spiritual freedom the artificial routine of that system. As the prophetic office might be exercised by women, so the Nazirite vow might be taken by women. In either case we find a tribute to and a recognition of the Divine liberty of the Holy Ghost, and an anticipation of the time when the spirit of self-devotion should be poured out without distinction upon men and women. **Shall separate themselves to vow a vow of a Nazarite, to separate themselves unto the Lord.** Rather, "shall make a solemn vow, a Nazirite vow, to live consecrated unto the Lord." The two words translated "separate" are not the same. The first (from *pala*, to sever, to consecrate, to distinguish as exceptional) is of somewhat doubtful use here. In Judges xiii. 19 it appears to be used as an intensitive, "did wonderously," and the Septuagint has here μεγάλως εὔξηται εὐχήν. The other word (from נזר, to separate) is used in a general sense in Gen. xlix. 26; Deut. xxxiii. 16, or with the addition, "unto the Lord," as in Judges xiii. 5. It had, however, acquired a technical sense before this, as appears from Levit. xxv. 5, 11, where the undressed vines are called "Nazirites," as recalling the unshorn locks of those who had taken the vow. It is evident indeed, from the way in which the Nazirite vow is here spoken of, that it had been, perhaps long, familiar among the people. All that this commandment did was to recognise the practice, to regulate it minutely, and to adopt it into the religious code of Israel. Whence the custom was derived is wholly uncertain, for although the separate elements existed in many different quarters, yet the peculiar combination of them which made the law of the Nazirite is entirely peculiar. Vows of abstinence have, of course, been common among all religions. Mingled with much of superstition, self-will, and pride, they have sprung in the main from noble impulses and yearnings after a higher life, prompted by the Holy Spirit of God ; and it may be said with some confidence, that in spite of all reproaches (deserved or undeserved), such voluntary vows of abstinence have done more than anything else to save religion from becoming an unreal profession. Hair offerings, on the other hand, springing from a simple and natural sentiment, have been common enough amongst the heathen. Compare the sacred lock of Achilles ('Iliad,' xxiii. 142, *sqq.*), and the various use of the tonsure in pursuance of vows among the ancient Egyptians (Herod., ii. 65) and amongst modern Mahomedans and Christians. The physical fact on which all these hair offerings rest is that the hair is the only portion of oneself which can be conveniently detached and presented.

Ver. 3.—**Strong drink.** Hebrew, *shekār ;* σίκερα (Levit. x. 9 ; Luke i. 15). Any intoxicating drink, other than wine, including the beer of the Egyptians. **Vinegar.** Hebrew, *chamets.* It seems to have been freely used by the poorer people (Ruth ii. 14), and was, perhaps, a thin, sour wine ("vile potet acetum," Horat.). **Liquor of grapes.** A drink made by soaking grape-skins in water.

Ver. 4.—**From the kernels even to the husk,** or skin. Of grape-skins it is said that cakes were made which were considered a delicacy (Hos. iii. 1, mistranslated "flagons of wine "), but this is doubtful. The Septuagint has οἴνου ἀπὸ στεμφύλων ἕως γιγάρτου, "wine of grape-skins (the liquor of grapes mentioned before) even to the kernel." The expression is best understood as including anything and everything, however unlikely to be used, connected with the grape. It is clear that the abstinence of the Nazirite extended beyond what might possibly intoxicate to what was simply pleasant to the taste, like raisins, or refreshing, like *chamets.* The vine represented, by an easy parable, the tree of carnal delights, which yields to the appetite of men such a variety of satisfactions. So among the Romans the Flamen Dialis might not even touch a vine.

Ver. 5.—**There shall no razor come upon his head.** The meaning of this law is best understood from the case of Samson, whose strength was in his hair, and departed from him when his hair was cut. No doubt that strength was a more or less supernatural gift, and it went and came with his hair according to some supernatural law ; but it is clear that the connection was not merely arbitrary, but was founded on some generally received idea. To the Jew, differing in this from the shaven Egyptian and the short-haired Greek, the hair represented the virile powers of the adult, growing with its growth, and failing again with its decay. To use a simple analogy from nature, the uncropped locks of the Nazirite were like the mane of the male lion, a symbol of the fulness of his proper strength and life (cf. 2 Sam. xiv. 25, 26, and, for the disgrace of baldness, 2 Kings ii. 23). In later ages Western and Greek feeling on the subject prevailed over Eastern and Jewish, and a "Hebrew of the Hebrews" was able to argue that "even nature itself" teaches us "that if a man have long hair it is a shame unto him" (1 Cor. xi. 14). No doubt "nature itself" taught the Greek of Corinth that lesson ; but no doubt also "nature itself" taught the Jew of Palestine exactly the opposite lesson ; and the Apostle himself did not quite discard the earlier sentiment, for he too made a Nazirite vow, and suffered his hair to grow while it lasted (Acts xxi. 24). The meaning, therefore, of the law was that the whole fulness of the man's vitality was to be dedicated without any diminution to the Lord, as typified by the free growth of his hair. It has been conjectured that it was allowed to the Nazirite to "poll" (κείρασθαι) his hair during his vow, although not to "shave" it (ξυρᾶσθαι) ; and in this way the statement is explained that St. Paul "polled his head" (κειράμενος τὴν κεφαλὴν, Acts xviii. 18, compared with xxi. 24) in Cenchræa, because he had a vow. It is, however, quite evident that any permission to cut the hair is inconsistent with the whole intention of the commandment ; for if a man might "poll his head" when he pleased, he would not be distinguished from other men. If it was allowed in the Apostle's time, it is only another instance of the way in which the commandments of God were made of none effect by the traditions of men.

Ver. 7.—**He shall not make himself unclean for his father, or for his mother.** The same injunction had been given to the priests (Levit. xxi. 12)—"for the crown of the anointing oil of his God is upon him." A similar reason restrained the Nazirite. **Because the consecration of his God is upon his head,** *i. e.* because he wears the unshorn locks which are the outward sign of his separation unto God. The hair of the Nazirite was to him just what the diadem on the mitre was to the high priest, what the sacred chrism was to the sons of Aaron. Both of these are called by the word *nezer* (Exod. xxix. 6 ; Levit. xxi. 12), from the same root as *nazir*. It was thought by some of the Jewish doctors that in these three particulars—the untouched growth of the hair, the abstinence from the fruit of the vine (cf. Gen. ix. 20), and the seclusion from the dead—the separated life of the Nazirite reproduced the unfallen life of man in paradise. This may have had some foundation in fact, but the true explanation of the three rules is rather to be found in the spiritual truth they teach in a simple and forcible way. He who has a holy ambition to please God must (1) devote to God the whole forces of his being, undiminished by any wont and use of the world ; (2) abstain not only from pleasures which are actually dangerous, but from such as have any savour of moral evil about them ; (3) subordinate his most sacred private feelings to the great purpose of his life.

Ver. 9. **If any man die very suddenly by him.** עָלָיו, in his presence, or neighbourhood, so that, having hastened to his assistance, he found himself in contact with a corpse. This case is mentioned particularly, because it was the only one in which simple humanity or mere accident would be likely to infringe upon the vow. **In the day of his cleansing, on the seventh day.** This appears to be an anticipation of the law given below (ch. xix. 11) ; but that law may have only sanctioned the existing custom. **Shall he shave it.** Because "the consecration of his God upon his head" was desecrated by the pollution of death, it must, therefore, be made away with and begun over again.

Ver. 10.—**Two turtles, or two young pigeons.** The same offerings had been prescribed for those defiled by divers uncleannesses in Levit. xv. (cf. Levit. xii. 8).

Ver. 11.—**For that he sinned by the dead.** This is one of the cases in which the law seemed to teach plainly that an outward, accidental, and involuntary defilement was sin, and had need to be atoned for. The opposite principle was declared by our Lord (Mark vii. 18—23). The Septuagint has here the strange reading περὶ ὧν ἥμαρτε περὶ τῆς ψυχῆς. **Shall hallow his head.** By dedicating again to God the free growth of his hair.

Ver. 12.—**For a trespass offering.** Rather, "for a guilt offering." Hebrew, *asham* (see Levit. v.). The *asham* always implied guilt, even though it might be purely legal, and it was to be offered in this case in acknowledgment of the offence involved in the involuntary breach of vow. In the education of conscience, on anything lower than the

"perfect law of liberty," it was only possible to secure thoroughness and consistency at the cost of introducing much that was arbitrary and destined to pass away. Something similar must always be tolerated in the moral education of children. **The days that were before shall be lost.** Literally, "shall fall." Septuagint, ἄλογοι ἔσονται, "shall not be counted."

Ver. 13.—**When the days of his separation are fulfilled.** The original law contemplated only a vow for a certain period, longer or shorter. All the Nazirites, however, of whom we read in Scripture were lifelong Nazirites : Samson (Judges xiii. 5), Samuel (1 Sam. i. 11), John the Baptist (Luke i. 15). In all these cases, however, the vow was made for them before their birth. Hegesippus (in Euseb. ii. 23) tells us that James, the Lord's brother, was a Nazirite : "He did not drink wine nor strong drink, and no razor came on his head."

Ver. 14.—**He shall offer his offering.** This offering included all the four ordinary sacrifices—the sin offering, the burnt offering, the peace offering, and the meat offering. For the meaning of these see Levit. iv., i., iii., ii.

Ver. 15.—**A basket of unleavened bread . . . anointed with oil.** Required for every sacrifice of thanksgiving, as this was (Levit. vii. 12). **And their meat offering, and their drink offerings,** *i. e.* the gifts of meal, oil, and wine which belonged to burnt offerings and peace offerings (see below, ch. xv. 3, *sqq.*).

Ver. 18.—**Shall take the hair of the head of his separation, and shall put it in the fire which is under the sacrifice of the peace offerings.** It is not said, nor intended, that the hair was offered to God as a sacrifice. If so, it would have been burnt with the burnt offering which represented the self-dedication of the worshipper. It had been holy to the Lord, growing uncut all the days of the vow. The vow was now at an end ; the last solemn act of sacrifice, the peace offering, which completed all, and typified that fearless and thankful communion with God which is the end of all religion, was now going on ; it was fitting that the hair which must now be shorn, but could not be disposed of in any ordinary way, should be burnt upon the altar of God. **In the fire,** *i. e.* on the brazen altar. In later days it seems to have been done in a room assigned to the Nazirites in the court of the women : another deviation from the original law.

Ver. 19.—**The sodden shoulder,** or boiled shoulder ; the left. The right, or heave shoulder, was already the priest's, according to the general rule (Levit. vii. 32). That the other shoulder was also "waved" and accepted by God as his portion, to be consumed in his name by the priest, was a further token of the gracious acceptance of the self-dedication of the Nazirite, and of the fulness of eucharistic communion into which he had entered with his God.

Ver. 20.—**Shall wave them.** By putting his hands under the hands of the Nazirite. On the symbolism of this see Levit. vii. **Drink wine.** Perhaps at the sacrificial feast.

Ver. 21.—**This is the law of the Nazarite who hath vowed, and of his offering.** "And of" are not in the text. We should probably read, "This is the law of the Nazirite who

hath vowed his offering unto the Lord in accordance with his consecration," *i. e.* these are the offerings which, as a Nazirite, he is bound to make. **Beside that his hand shall get.** Literally, "grasp." If he can afford or can procure anything more as a free-will offering, he may well do so. In later days it became customary for richer people to defray for their poorer brethren the cost of their sacrifices (Josephus, 'Ant.,' xix. 6, 1; and cf. Acts xxi. 24).

HOMILETICS.

Vers. 1—21.—*Individual consecration to God.* In this section we have, spiritually, the consecration of the individual life to God as a reasonable, holy, and lively sacrifice (Rom. xii. 1). This consecration was the ideal for all Israel (Exod. xix. 6); but inasmuch as the people at large could not attain unto it fully, a tribe and a family were in varying degree "separated" unto the Lord. In order, however, that individuals might not be hindered from obeying the call to self-dedication as the Spirit moved them, the vow of the Nazirite was allowed, encouraged, and regulated. Consider, therefore—

I. THAT ANY INDIVIDUAL IN ISRAEL WHO WAS OF AGE TO TAKE A VOW MIGHT BECOME A NAZIRITE, WHETHER MAN OR WOMAN, WHETHER OF THE PRIESTHOOD OR OF THE PEOPLE. John the Baptist was a priest; Samuel a Levite; Samson of the tribe of Dan. Even so it is the fundamental character of the gospel that every individual Christian, without any distinction of male or female, clerical or lay, is free to obey the call of the Spirit to an individual consecration of self to God. All are indeed called to "die unto sin, and rise again unto righteousness;" unto all it is said, "Ye are dead, and your life is hid with Christ in God" (Col. iii. 3); but yet it is palpably true that individuals here and there are specially moved by the Spirit to realise this their consecration, to translate into practical life their professed detachment from the world and attachment unto God. And this action of the Spirit is perfectly free; none can say beforehand *who* may be moved to dedicate himself or herself to a life of entire self-sacrifice and of unlimited obedience.

II. THAT THE CHILD OF ISRAEL SO CALLED INWARDLY BY THE SPIRIT WAS PERMITTED AND ENCOURAGED TO TAKE A VOW. Yet this vow limited as to obligations and as to time, so as it should not become a snare. And it appears that a Christian apostle took a vow of the sort (Acts xviii. 18). Even so it would seem that religious vows are not now in themselves unlawful or displeasing, provided they be really free, and that there be provision for being discharged from them. And note that almost all the Nazirites of Scripture appear to have been lifelong Nazirites, we know not why. Probably it is the tendency of all vows to become perpetual, because there seems something arbitrary and incomplete in any self-devotion or self-denial which ends before life itself ends. Nevertheless, it is plain that the Divine command contemplated only vows for a specific time.

III. THAT THE FIRST OBLIGATION OF THE NAZIRITE WAS TO ABSTAIN FROM EVERYTHING PRODUCED BY, OR MADE FROM, THE VINE, HOWEVER HARMLESS. Even so, if any man will dedicate himself, according to his Christian liberty and the impulse of the Spirit, to the nearer following of Christ, he must renounce all the excitements of this world, all those stimulants of pleasure, gain, or ambition which intoxicate the mind and distract it from the service of God; and not only that which is plainly evil and confessedly dangerous, but also that which has any savour of evil, any suspicion of danger, about it. The wisdom of nim who would at any cost please God is not to walk as near the border line of things unlawful or unwise as possible, but rather to give them a clear berth, so as through no mischance he may be entangled therein; and this because of human weakness, whereby (1) we glide so easily from pleasures or cares lawful to the like unlawful, and (2) we find it so much easier to take a simple and decided line, even against ourselves, than a wavering and uncertain one

(Luke ix. 24; x. 42; xviii. 22; xxi. 34; 1 Cor. vi. 12; ix. 25, 27; 2 Tim. ii. 4; and cf. Matt. xix. 12; 1 Cor. vii. 32).

IV. THAT THE SECOND OBLIGATION OF THE NAZIRITE WAS TO DEDICATE THE FREE, UNTOUCHED GROWTH OF HIS HAIR TO THE LORD. Even so the servant of God must dedicate to him the whole forces of his nature, unrestrained and undiminished by any conventionalities of the world, by those customs and fashions of society which cramp and limit on every side the possibilities of usefulness and of power which are in man. The true servant of Christ, neither acknowledging the principles nor guided by the maxims of the world, must be content to be singular, to be wondered at, to be regarded as extreme (cf. Luke vii. 33; 2 Cor. xi., xii.; Gal. vi. 14; Phil. iii. 8). "Let your *moderation*" (Greek, τὸ ἐπιεικές, "forbearance") "be known unto all men" is a text much more often misquoted in the devil's service than quoted in Christ's.

V. THAT THE THIRD OBLIGATION OF THE NAZIRITE WAS NOT TO COME INTO CONTACT WITH DEATH, EVEN FOR HIS NEAREST RELATIONS. Even so the servant of God must cross his nearest earthly affections, and do violence to his most natural feelings, rather than expose himself to the contagion of spiritual death. Where this danger really exists may indeed be known only to God and to him; but where he knows it to exist he is bound to avoid it at any cost of affection or of appearance, so as he make it not a cloak for escaping duty (Matt. x. 35—37; Luke xiv. 26, 33; ix. 60—62; and cf. Matt. v. 29, 30; 1 Cor. v. 11; 2 Cor. vi. 14). Few have strength and vigour of soul to mix with impunity in the society of those spiritually dead; wisdom and loyalty alike demand that we avoid them except we can really do them good.

VI. THAT THE CASE OF THE NAZIRITE BEING UNAVOIDABLY DEFILED WITH DEATH WAS PROVIDED FOR, AND PROVISION MADE FOR HIS BEGINNING AFRESH. Even so God knows that in the confusions and mixtures of life it is hard indeed to escape altogether from the subtle contagion of spiritual deadness, which will often seize upon a soul most unexpectedly from unavoidable contact with others. No profession and no earnestness of self-devotion is a safeguard against this danger. But if it come to pass that the soul be thus defiled, and deadness come over it, all is not therefore lost, nor is its consecration at an end. It must offer the sacrifice of a contrite heart, and begin again with penitence and patience, not counting that which is behind, nor dwelling on its loss, but reaching forth after those things which lie before it (Ps. xxxvii. 24; Micah vii. 8; Phil. iii. 13, 14).

VII. THAT WHEN THE SELF-DEVOTION OF THE NAZIRITE WAS PERFECTED, IT STILL NEEDED TO BE COMMENDED UNTO GOD THROUGH THE FOURFOLD SACRIFICES OF THE LEVITICAL LAW. Even so our highest service and greatest self-denial is not acceptable to God except it be offered through and with the prevailing sacrifice of Christ. And inasmuch as one of these sacrifices was a sin offering, so is there need that the best of our best things should be purged from the sin which clings to them by the atoning death of Christ.

VIII. THAT THE HAIR, THE SYMBOL OF SEPARATION, WAS AT LAST TO BE PUT IN THE ALTAR FIRE UNDER THE PEACE OFFERING. Even so the good will, the earnest desire, the single purpose with which we have been enabled to serve God, is to be brought at last—when its work on earth is done—and simply laid upon the altar of the love of God, and of our thankful communion with him in peace through Christ; and this not as being anything worthy in itself, but only as being part of our gratitude to God.

IX. THAT ON THIS OCCASION, AND THIS ALONE, THE SECOND SHOULDER WAS ACCEPTED BY GOD AS HIS OWN PORTION FROM THE PEACE OFFERING. Even so it is undeniable that a more devoted life does infallibly lead to a greater acceptance with God and to a fuller communion in peace and thankfulness with him.

HOMILIES BY VARIOUS AUTHORS.

Vers. 1—21.—*Separated to the service of God* (the law of the Nazirite). This passage, barren and unpromising as it looks, is nevertheless invested with an undying interest by the circumstance that three of the most famous men in the sacred history belonged to the order whose rule is here prescribed. *Samson*, with all his faults, was a heroic character, and he was a Nazarite from his mother's womb. *Samuel*, his contemporary, was a hero of a purer and higher type, the earliest of the great prophets after Moses, and he too was a Nazarite, by his mother's consecration, before he was born. As Samuel was the first, *John the Baptist* was the last, of the old prophets, and he likewise was a Nazarite from his birth.

I. WHAT, THEN, WAS A NAZARITE? The term (more correctly written *Nazir,* or *Nazirite*) is a Hebrew one, and signifies *separated,* or *set apart.* In Israel there were three orders of men who may be said to have been separated to God's service. 1. The *priests.* Their office was hereditary. The separation attached to Aaron's house. The work to which they were separated was to offer sacrifice, to burn incense, and to bless the people. 2. The *prophets.* Their office was not hereditary. The true prophet was such by a Divine call addressed to him individually. His work was purely spiritual. He delivered to the people the word of the Lord. 3. The *Nazarites* proper. Their separation was neither hereditary, like the priests', nor necessarily by special Divine call, like the prophets'. It was by their own act, or that of their parents, and was sometimes spontaneous, sometimes by a more or less stringent Divine direction. Any free man or woman—any man or woman not under some prior obligation incompatible with it—could separate himself or herself by the Nazarite's vow. The separation might be either for a limited period or for life.

II. Regarding THE DUTIES PERTAINING TO THE ORDER, nothing is here laid down It is simply implied that the Nazarite was to show an example of pre-eminent devotedness to God. To judge by the lives of Samuel and John the Baptist, the Nazarite's devotedness was to be manifested in the best of all ways, namely, by a life of active labour in diffusing the knowledge and fear of the Lord. However, the law did not prescribe this. It simply put around the Nazarite's separation the hedge of legal recognition and ceremonial regulation. How the garden thus protected was to be filled—what flowers and fragrant herbs and fruit it was to yield—was left to be determined by the motions of God's free Spirit in the individual Nazarite's heart. Anyhow, the practical working of this kind of separation in Israel came to be such that it was looked upon as a sure sign that piety was flourishing when the Nazarites abounded (see Amos ii. 11, 12).

III. Turning to THE LAW AS LAID DOWN HERE IN NUMBERS, it is to be observed that the Nazarite's separation was to be expressed in three ways. 1. By entire abstinence not only from wine and strong drink, but from all the produce of the vine (vers. 3, 4). John Baptist came neither eating nor drinking. 2. By absolutely refusing to defile themselves for the dead (vers. 7—12). The rule was as absolute on this head for the Nazarite as for the high priest. Not even for father or mother, for wife or child, might he contract defilement. If by any chance he should come in contact with a dead body, the law demanded a sin offering for atonement and a burnt offering in token of renewed dedication, and his term of separation had to begin anew. 3. By letting the hair of the head grow unshorn (ver. 5; cf. 1 Cor. xi. 10, *marg.*). Every child remembers the seven locks of Samson's head. When the period of separation was expired, the head was shaved and certain prescribed offerings were presented, besides any free-will offering the person might choose to bring (vers. 13—21). As these last offerings were costly, it was not uncommon for wealthy persons to come forward and bear the Nazarites' charges (Acts xxi. 24).

IV. WHAT CONCERN HAVE WE WITH THIS LAW OF THE NAZARITE? Is any corresponding vow of separation to be in use under the New Testament? The Church of Rome, I need hardly say, founds on the Nazarite's vow an argument for her religious orders, so called—orders of men and women who are bound by oath to lifelong poverty, celibacy, and obedience. But there is no real correspondence between the two institutions. Not one of the three vows of the religious orders was included in the vow of the Nazarite. He could hold property; he was generally married; he submitted his conscience to no man's authority. No warrant can be extracted from this law for ensnaring consciences with the threefold vow. Yet it by no means follows that this Old Testament vow has no lesson for us. It furnishes a valuable analogy. The Apostle Paul evidently felt this, for he liked to think of himself as a man " separated unto the gospel of God " (Rom. i. 1), and to think of this separation as having taken place (like Samuel's and John Baptist's) before he was born (Gal. i. 15). This does not refer merely to his being separated to preach the word, for that was common to him with all ministers of the gospel; nor does it refer simply to his apostolate. It refers but to his special work as the great missionary apostle. There is room and need in the Christian Church not only for men separated by the authority and call of the Church to official service, but for men also who are moved to separate themselves to free and unofficial service. Robert Haldane of Airthrey was not an ordained minister, never held a pastoral charge, never administered the sacraments, yet he devoted his whole time and wealth to the cause of Christ. Selling Airthrey Castle, he purchased a mansion-house where he could live at less expense, and he thenceforward lived for the diffusion of true religion at home and abroad. Blessed be God, Mr. Haldane was not singular in this sort of separation. It answers exactly, under the Christian and spiritual dispensation, to the separation of the Nazarite under the law. Without doubt men and women separated thus to God will have a great part to play in the victorious progress of the kingdom of Christ. It should be the constant prayer of the Church that Christ would, of her young men, raise up not only prophets (he is doing that), but Nazarites also.—B.

Vers. 1—8.—*The temporary vow of the Nazarite symbolical of the lifelong vow of the Christian.* Though the Israelites had a priesthood, they were themselves " a kingdom of priests." Individual responsibility toward God was pressed upon their consciences in many ways; *e. g.* Deut. xxvi. 1—14, &c. And private persons might aspire to the honour of an especial priestly consecration. Since temporary vows were acceptable to God under the old covenant, they may be under the new covenant, if taken for a limited time and for Christian ends; *e. g.* celibacy or abstinence (cf. Acts xviii. 18; xxi. 6). But a higher form of vow is that of entire consecration *for life,* that we may be daily led by the Spirit of God, and live the life of faith on the Son of God. Our Nazarite state is to be lifelong. None can disallow the Christian's vow to Christ (cf. ch. xxx. 1—5 with Matt. x. 37). The consecration which we avow must be marked by three facts, of which we see symbols in this chapter— I. SELF-DENIAL (vers. 3, 4); II. VISIBLE PROFESSION (ver. 5); III. PERSONAL PURITY (vers. 6—8).

I. The priests had, when " on duty," to exercise the self-denial required of the Nazarite (Levit. x. 9). The kind of self-denial demanded is a significant testimony in favour of total abstinence (see Milton's words in ' Samson Agonistes:' " Oh, madness, to think use of strongest wines," &c.). Self-denial, in a wider sense, at any rate, always required of us, because we are always " on duty " (Matt. x. 38; Luke ix. 23 : John xii. 25).

II. The Nazarites' locks marked their separation. Our consecration must be marked not by tonsures or cowls, but by verbal avowals (Rom. x. 9, 10) and good works (Matt. v. 16; Phil. ii. 14—16), which shall excel those of men who make no profession to the supernatural life of the disciples of Christ (cf. Matt. v. 47, 48).

III. We are " called to be *saints,*" personally pure and separated from the world and its dead works (John xvii. 11—19; 2 Cor. vi. 17). Christ's claims on us are paramount (Luke ix. 59, 60) and perpetual (Rev. ii. 10). We cannot violate our pledges and go on as though our relations to Christ were unchanged, but must renew our vows (ver. 12; Ezek. xxxiii. 12, 13). When the period of the vow ended, the restraints were removed, but the honour remained. So will it be with us at death (John xii. 26, &c.).—P.

Ver. 2.—THE NAZARITE'S VOW. " When either man or woman shall separate themselves to vow a vow of a Nazarite," &c. Here we meet with the Nazarite's vow as something already in existence, and needing to be regulated. The fact that such regulations were necessary points to a class of persons, not perhaps very large, but likely to be permanent in Israel, who felt it laid upon them to be separate for a while from the common track of their neighbours. There are several instances of vows recorded in Scripture. A person might vow that if a certain wish were granted, a certain thing would be done in return; *e. g.* Hannah, Jephthah. Here we are on different ground. There is nothing like a bargaining with the Almighty. The Nazarite's vow is of a higher kind, and demands special consideration. It does not rise among such natural feelings as are common to all human breasts. The motive shows a class of men to whom the common level of their neighbours' thoughts concerning religion was quite insufficient.

I. Consider THE STATE FROM WHICH THE NAZARITE SEPARATED HIMSELF. The name signified the state—separation. The average of religious feeling and activity in the minds of the Israelites must have been very low. Jehovah for his purposes had constrained them into a special relation to him, but as for them, they had not with all their hearts chosen him in return. They were groaning over Egypt lost, and the perils, trials. and discomforts of the wilderness. They did not delight in the law of the Lord. They learned how to go through the routine of outward ceremonies, but that perfect law which converts the soul, rejoices the heart, and enlightens the eyes was foreign to all their sympathies.

II. Hence THE SEPARATION OF THOSE WHO SOUGHT A HOLIER AND SPIRITUAL LIFE. Some, at all events, out of the multitude at Sinai must have been impressed with its solemn circumstances, and with the claims which Jehovah made for himself in the first four commandments of the Decalogue. What contented their neighbours in the way of compliance with God's wishes fell far short of contenting them. Others had to be dragged. The wish of a Nazarite was, "I will run in the way of thy commandments, when thou hast enlarged my heart." Such were the true successors of Enoch, who walked with God, and Noah, who preached righteousness. Such men, in the ruling wish of their spirits, are set before us in the Psalms of David, where he expresses the heights and depths of personal religion as it was possible in the old dispensation. We may well believe there were thousands who could adopt and sing such, as the language of their experience. It was from men of the Nazarite spirit that prophets could be taken, burning with zeal for the Lord of hosts, and for justice and compassion among men. Note the connection of prophets and Nazarites, Amos ii. 11, 12.

III. THE NAZARITE THUS BECOMES A TYPE OF WHAT SHOULD EVER BE SOUGHT IN THE CHRISTIAN LIFE. It is easy enough to get into a routine, the omission of which would offend the conscience, yet the observance of which does nothing to bring the life nearer to God. We must not measure ourselves by the attainments and opinions of nominal adherents to the Church of Christ. It is no business of ours to judge them, but what satisfies them should not satisfy us. We must try to find out for ourselves in a satisfactory way what God would have us be and do, not falling in easily with what the crowd may profess to be his will. "What do ye more than others?" Avoid that fatal question which so completely, yet so unconsciously, reveals the unspirituality of the person who asks it—"Where's the harm?" (Rom. xii. 1, 2; Phil. iii. 12—15).—Y.

Vers. 3—21.—*The regulations for observance of the Nazarite's vow.* As a vow of separation, it was to be observed in as significant a way as possible. It was not only a separation in heart and sympathy, but it had its *signs*, which plainly indicated the separation to others. These regulations were also helpful to the Nazarite himself as remembrancers. We may conclude that not only the details of them, but the very substance, was of God's appointment. Thus security was taken that all should be in harmony with the great body of the law, and also give the greatest chance of profit to the Nazarite himself, and the greatest chance of instruction to the people.

I. REGULATIONS DURING THE CONTINUANCE OF THE VOW. 1. *Abstinence from the fruit of the vine.* It was to be a *rigorous* abstinence. This we may take to signify a protest in the most comprehensive way against all seeking of mere pleasure and comfort. The grape was the symbol of sensual delights. The spies brought back grapes of Eshcol more than any other produce to testify the riches of Canaan: this shows how much the Israelites thought of the fruit. There was, of course, no peculiar merit and advantage in abstaining from the grape itself. The abstinence was simply a sign indicating a desire to rise above the common pleasures of men. The Nazarites were not ascetics. They did not refrain from a good creature of God by way of penance. But in the grape there was the possibility of wine and strong drink, and the wine and strong drink were the testimony of the worldly soul that he loved to gratify his sensual nature, and cared not that his body should be so disciplined and restrained as to be the effectual minister of God. The appropriate joys of human life are not to be found among the powers that link us to the lower creation.

We are to look for them in communion with God and following Christ. Our joy is in the Holy Ghost. "Is any merry, let him sing Psalms." 2. *The unshorn head.* The Nazarite was not his own. Not even the least thing about his person was at his own disposal. He was not allowed to cast away even a thing so easily and painlessly separated as the hair, seemingly of so little consequence, and so quickly growing again. It was just because the hair seemed so little a thing that leaving it unshorn was so fit for a sign (Matt. v. 36; x. 30). So when we become Christ's we become his altogether. We must be faithful in that which is least. *All* of life is for him, though there are many things that, hastily considered, look as little important as the short light hairs clipped from the head. The unshorn head also *made a manifest difference in the sight of men.* Abstaining from the vine was only known at the social board; the unshorn head revealed the Nazarite to every one he met. It was an unostentatious challenge and rebuke to the more easy-going multitude. God had accepted the Nazarite, and stamped his acceptance by this simple, impressive regulation. 3. *The avoidance of the dead.* Death was uncleanness (ch. v. 2). The Nazarite as a consecrated one dare not touch the dead. "Separated for God, in whose presence death and corruption can have no place, the Nazarite must ever be found in the habitations and society of the living." Not even dead kindred may the Nazarite— man or woman—touch. What a striking reminder in ver. 7 of the requirements of Christ! (Luke xviii. 29, 30). He that would please God and rise to higher attainments in Divine things must subordinate all human kinship to higher claims. Christ divides the family against itself, and makes a man's foes those of his own household. The nearest kindred may be an obstacle to the regenerate, as still dead in trespasses and sins. "Let the dead bury their dead." A Nazarite in the observance of his vow was ever on the watch against all occasion of uncleanness, for the very least defilement compelled a fresh start from the beginning.

II. REGULATIONS FOR THE RETURN TO ORDINARY LIFE. This was to be done in a public, deliberate, and sacred way. Precisely ordained offerings had to be made before the Nazarite again put razor to his head or wine to his lips. These offerings doubtless had relation both to the period just expired and the freer life to be presently resumed. There was thanksgiving for the vow successfully observed, atonement for the sin that nevertheless had mingled in it, and something to express his purposes for the future. The freer life was still to find him a Nazarite in heart. To be nearer God for a time and then go away to a distance, to taste the pleasures of holiness for a season and then go back to pollution, such conduct would have made the vow a mockery and abomination. We must all be Nazarite in spirit, opposed to the world as resolutely as was the Baptist, but not, like him, fleeing to the wilderness. Our guide and example is Jesus himself, the holiest of all Nazarites, who kept himself unspotted even at the table of the glutton and wine-bibber. His prayer for us is not that we should be taken out of the world, but kept from the evil.—Y.

EXPOSITION.

THE PRIESTLY BENEDICTION (vers. 22—27). Ver. 22. — **The Lord spake unto Moses**. It is a matter of mere conjecture at what point of time this command was given. As it concerned the priests and their daily ministration, it would be natural to suppose that it was given at the time when the tabernacle service was set up, *i.e.* at the precise point fixed by the first verse of the following chapter. That the command was given to Moses, and to Moses alone, and that *after* the consecration of Aaron to the high priesthood, serves to bring out into clear relief the relative position of the two. Aaron and his sons alone, as the "official" representatives of the Lord, could bless in his name and put his name upon the people; but the formula of blessing was delivered to Aaron himself through Moses, as the "personal" representative of the Lord, the mediator of the old covenant. Ὁ νόμος . . διαταγεὶς . . ἐν χειρὶ μεσίτου (Gal. iii. 19). Our Lord is both the Moses (Acts iii. 22) and the Aaron (Heb. vi. 20) — ὁ μεσίτης and ὁ ἀρχιερεὺς — of this dispensation. Ver. 23.—**On this wise ye shall bless**. In Levit. ix. 22 it is recorded that Aaron blessed the people, first by himself from the brazen altar of sacrifice, and afterwards in conjunction with Moses, when they came out of the tabernacle; and that he might so bless the people is mentioned as one object of his consecration (Deut. xxi. 5; and cf. 1 Chron. xxiii. 13). Blessing in or with the name of the Supreme Being was an important part of all primitive religion, as appears from the case of Melchizedec and Abraham, of Isaac and his sons, of Jacob and Pharaoh. And this act of blessing was far from being a mere expression of good will, or from being a simple prayer ; for " without all contradiction the less is blessed of the greater " (Heb. vii. 7), *i. e.* the blessing must be given by one who stands nearer to God to one who stands less near. The name of God could not be used in blessing save by one who had some right to such use of it, whether as prophet, as priest, or as patriarch. For that name in which the blessing was given was not inoperative, but was mighty with untold spiritual efficacy where rightly used as the name of blessing. To Aaron and to his sons was now confided this use of the Divine name, that all Israel might know and might hear in their appointed words the voice of God himself. **Saying unto them.** The benediction here appointed consists of three clauses, each complete in itself, and each consisting of two members, the second of which seems to present the application and result in experience of the grace besought in the first. Both, therefore, in its form and its contents this benediction is one of the most profound and most fruitful of the Divine oracles ; and this indeed we might have expected, because (if we may venture to say so) God is never so entirely and absolutely himself as in blessing.

Vers. 24—26.—**The Lord, . . the Lord, . . the Lord.** Are we to see in this threefold use of the Divine name a shadowing forth of the Holy Trinity ? It is obvious that it cannot be proved, and that it would not even have suggested any such idea to the priest who gave, or to the people who received, the benediction. To them the threefold form merely added beauty and fulness to the blessing (cf. Eccles. iv. 12). But that is not the question. The real question is whether the Old Testament was written for our sakes (1 Cor. ix. 10 ; x. 11 ; 2 Tim. iii. 15, 16), and whether the God of the Jews was indeed the Father of our Lord Jesus Christ (John v. 17 ; viii. 54). If so, it is not possible for us to avoid seeing in this benediction a declaration of the threefold Being of God, and it is not possible to avoid believing that he meant us to see such a declaration, veiled indeed from the eyes of the Jew, but clear enough to the Christian. For a somewhat similar case compare Isa. vi. 3 ; Rev. iv. 8.

Ver. 25.—**The Lord make his face shine upon thee.** The "face" of God is his personality as turned towards man, or else turned away from him. His face hidden or turned away is despair and death (Deut. xxxi. 17, 18 ; Job xiii. 24) ; his face turned against man is destruction and death (Levit.

xvii. 10 ; Ps. xxxiv. 16) ; his face turned upon man in love and mercy is life and salvation (Ps. xxvii. 1 ; xliv. 3). It is to the soul of man what the blessed sun of heaven is to his body. **And be gracious unto thee.** Ἐλεήσαι σε, Septuagint. Be kind and beneficent to thee : the effect in and on the soul of the clear shining upon it of the face of God.

Ver. 26.—**The Lord lift up his countenance upon thee.** Ἐπάραι . . τὸ πρόσωπον αὐτοῦ ἐπὶ σέ, Septuagint. This clause seems to repeat the last in a somewhat stronger form, as implying more personal and individual attention from the Lord. His face shines upon all that love him, as the sun shines wherever no clouds intervene ; but his face is lifted up to that soul for which he has a more special regard. נָשָׂא פָנִים אֶל seems to mean the same thing as נָשָׂא עֵינַיִם or שִׂים (Gen. xliii. 29, ἀναβλέψας . . τοῖς ὀφθαλμοῖς αὐτοῦ ; xliv. 21). To lift up the eyes or the face upon any one is to look upon that one with peculiar and tender interest. **And give thee peace** (*shalom*). This peace, being the perfect fruit in experience of the grace which comes from God, forms the climax and conclusion of the benediction.

Ver. 27.—**They shall put my name upon the children of Israel.** The "name" of God is uniformly treated in Scripture as something very different from a mere arrangement of letters or an arbitrary vocal sound. All nations have had names for the Supreme Being, but there was nothing sacred about them, except from association. *The* name of God was not of man, nor from man, but of his own direct revelation (Exod. vi. 3), and was therefore of an unspeakable sanctity (Exod. xx. 7 ; xxxiii. 19). Like the "word" of God, it cannot be dissociated from God himself. It is in some sense an extension outwards, into the sphere of the created and sensible, of the ineffable virtues of the Godhead itself. · It stands in a real, though unassignable, relation to infinite goodness and power, and therefore it comes fraught with untold blessing (or perchance cursing) to those on whom it lights. Hence, to put the name of God—the covenant name—upon the people had a real meaning. No one could do it except by his express direction ; and when it was so done there was an invisible reality answering to the audible form ; with the name pronounced in blessing came the blessing itself, came the special providence and presence of God, to abide upon such at least as were worthy of it. It is a fact, the significance of which cannot be denied, that *the name* which was commanded to be put upon the people was lost, and irrecoverably lost, by the later Jews. Out of an exaggerated dread of possible profanation, they first disobeyed the command by substituting Adonai for that name outside the sanctuary; and finally, after the death of Simeon the Just, the priests ceased to pronounce that name at all, and therefore lost the tradition by which the pronunciation was fixed. Our method of spelling and pronouncing the name as Jehovah is merely conventional, and almost certainly incorrect. It would seem to be the more devout opinion that the name itself, as revealed by God and uttered by many generations of priests, was forfeited (like Paradise), was withdrawn, and ought not to be inquired after. **And I will bless them.** Here is the precise truth of all effectual benediction : *they* shall put my name; . . . *I* will bless. The outward form was ministered by the priests, the inward reality was of God and from God alone. It is observable that the form of blessing is expressed in the singular ; either (1) because all Israel was regarded as one, even as the first-born son of God (Exod. iv. 22, 23 ; Hos. xi. 1), or (2) because all real blessing must in truth be individual—a nation can only be blessed in its several members.

HOMILETICS.

Vers. 22—27.—*The Blessing of God Almighty.* In this benediction we have spiritually the love of God, and the grace of our Lord Jesus Christ, and the communion of the Holy Ghost, as imparted unto us in the kingdom of heaven, into which we are called, that we may inherit a blessing (2 Cor. xiii. 14 ; 1 Pet. iii. 9). Consider, therefore—

I. That all blessing in the Name was given by Aaron and his sons only, because they were the chosen representatives of God. Even so, all blessing in the Triune Name is given by Christ alone, the High Priest of our profession, and the only channel of blessing. All ministerial blessing is only the continuation made audible in times and places of that blessing which our Lord was pronouncing when he left the world (Luke xxiv. 50, 51), which blessing, as it was never finished upon earth, so it was taken up with him, and became eternal in the heavens, and is still the benediction wherewith his servants are blessed.

II. That to bless the people, as it was the peculiar privilege, so it was the bounden duty, of the priests, and that in which their office towards the people was, as it were, summed up (Deut. xxi. 5). Even so Jesus Christ was " sent to bless us " (Acts iii. 26), and " Benedictus benedicat " is the simplest and surest of all Christian prayers ; and it is the object and the office of such as are called in any wise to minister the priestly authority of Christ to bring home his benediction to the souls of men.

III. That the first clause of the blessing intimates the love of God the Father, through which we are preserved. For it is of his blessing that the whole world, and the race of men, and we ourselves have been kept from the destroyer, and held in life and plenty (Gen. i. 28 ; ix. 1 ; Acts xiv. 17 ; xvii. 28). And it is of his blessing that we have escaped the destruction which threatened our souls (Gen. ii. 17) ; and that because he had a favour unto us (Deut. vii. 8 ; x. 15), and because he had predestinated us in love (Ephes. i. 4, 5, ἐν ἀγάπῃ προορίσας ἡμᾶς), and because he is not willing that any should perish (2 Peter iii. 9).

IV. That the second clause intimates the love of God the Son whereby we have obtained, and do obtain, grace. For in the Incarnation of the Son the face of God is made to shine upon us, and that clearly and brightly, as the natural sun being risen shines upon the earth which lay in darkness or in twilight (Mal. iv. 2 ; Luke i. 78 ; John i. 14, 17 ; xiv. 9 ; 2 Cor. iii. 18 ; iv. 4, 6 ; Heb. i. 3). Thus Moses not being permitted to see the face of God, but only his back parts (Exod. xxxiii. 23), signified, that before the Incarnation the revelation of God in grace and truth could not be made.

V. That the third clause intimates the love of God the Holy Ghost, whereby we obtain peace through the fellowship of the Spirit. For the loving regard of God—his tender gaze upon the soul which he loves—is the coming forth of the Holy Spirit to abide upon and within that soul, bringing with him the life of the Incarnate Son (John xvi. 14, 15 ; 1 John v. 11), and the love of the Eternal Father (Rom. v. 5), and uniting us to both (1 John i. 3). And this life (Gal. ii. 20) and this love (Jude 21) are peace (Gal. v. 22 ; Rom. viii. 6 ; 1 John iv. 18) ; and peace is the ripened fruit and accomplished purpose of the gospel (Luke ii. 14; John xx. 19; Ephes. ii. 15).

VI. THAT THE PEOPLE OF ISRAEL WERE TO BEAR THE COVENANT NAME OF GOD, whereby he was revealed to them alone. Even so is the holy and awful and Triune Name of our God called down upon us (Matt. xxviii. 19, εἰς τὸ ὄνομα; James ii. 7, τὸ καλὸν ὄνομα τὸ ἐπικληθὲν ἐφ' ὑμᾶς), and we bear it as a most potent talisman to shield us from all harm, as a most precious jewel to be our secret joy and pride (Rev. ii. 7); cf. Ps. xci. 14; ix. 10, &c.). Note, that the name of the Holy Trinity is often apparently interchanged with the name of Jesus (Acts ii. 38; xix. 5), because in "Jesus" is the whole fulness of the Godhead (Col. ii. 9), and "Jesus" is the name under which the Divine Being is personally made known unto us, as under that now forgotten name to the Jews (Acts iii. 16; iv. 10). And note again, that amongst Israel, as amongst ourselves now, the sacred Name is put upon the people of God, yet so as it may pass away from them like the thin air, and leave no trace of sanctity behind: whereas in "him that overcometh" the Name shall be *written*, and that indelibly, because by Christ himself (Rev. iii. 12).

VII. THAT THE JEWS LOST THE HOLY NAME BECAUSE THEY USED IT NOT ARIGHT, FEARING TO MAKE IT KNOWN. Of that Name which wrought so many miracles (Isa. xxx. 27) nothing remains but four letters without any certain meaning, or any possible use. But the Name in which we trust can never be lost, because it is preached unto every creature under heaven (Acts xvii. 3; Phil. ii. 10), and its sweetness is everywhere diffused (Cant. i. 3). And so it is with all which that name means to us,—we keep it *for* ourselves exactly in proportion as we do not keep it *to* ourselves.

HOMILIES BY VARIOUS AUTHORS.

Vers. 22—27.—*The benediction.* So far as I have observed, the *blessing of the people* has less consideration bestowed upon it than any other of the stated ordinances of Divine service. It is seldom made the subject of discourse from the pulpit; divines seldom treat of it in their books; there is reason to fear that it seldom gets its due place in the minds and hearts of the people. The Benediction occurs in Scripture in several forms. Of these, two are in most frequent use in our Churches: the "Apostolic benediction" in 2 Cor. xiii. 14, and the "Aaronic benediction" in the text. Properly these are not two benedictions, but only two forms of one and the same. The benefits expressed are, in substance, the same. The principal difference is that the thrice-holy Name, and the benefits of God's salvation, are declared more plainly and articulately in the later than they could well be in the earlier form. There is nothing expressed in the apostolic benediction which was not implied in the Aaronic. "What mean ye by this service?" When our children ask this question, what are we to reply?

I. IT IS A PROCLAMATION OF THE NAME OF GOD. In blessing the people Aaron was to "put the name of the Lord upon the children of Israel" (ver. 27), thus constituting them his witnesses. Compare Micah iv. 5. This design is plain in the case of the apostolic form. Every time that form is used in the Church, it is as much as to say, Let all men know that the Name called upon in this place is the name of the Father Almighty, and of Jesus Christ his only-begotten Son, and of the Holy Ghost. The older form fulfilled the same purpose for the older time. There lurked in it a suggestion of the Trinity, to be brought to light in due time; and for the time then present, it loudly proclaimed at once the Unity and the personality of God—a proclamation sorely needing to be repeated in our time also. There is a philosophy walking abroad, which invites us to substitute for the living God, whose name is Love, an impersonal "tendency that makes for righteousness." It is the old Pagan substitution of nature for God. In opposition to it and to all similar error, the Aaronic benediction is a standing witness, that the God in whom all things live and move and subsist, is the LORD, a personal God, who can think upon us, and be gracious to us.

II. A DECLARATION OF THE BENEFITS GOD HAS LAID UP FOR THEM THAT SEEK HIM. If you would understand its true intention, you must bear in mind that the benediction is not spoken to men indiscriminately. It is for the Israel of God; for those on whom Christ's name is called, and who walk in his name. It is a solemn and authoritative declaration of the relation which subsists between him and them; and of the benefits flowing therefrom. 1. "*The Lord bless thee, and keep thee,*" q. d. The Lord is the keeper of Israel. He will care for thee. He will keep thy land and thine house; he will preserve thy going out and coming in, and will guard thy life; he will keep thy soul. He will deliver thy soul from death, thy feet from falling, thine eyes from tears. Compare Ps. cxxi., where the Church, opening its heart and drinking in the benediction, turns it into a song, "Jehovah Shomer." 2. "*The Lord make his face shine upon thee, and be gracious unto thee;*" q. d. There is grace in God's heart for thee. He has given proof of this times without number. To many a man stained with sin and utterly cast down, he has said, Live; has taken him by the hand, and brought him near, and made him glad with his loving countenance. The best commentary on this, also, is to be found in the Psalms. A glance at the references in the margin will show that the benediction—and especially this particular member of it—was welcomed in many hearts in Israel, and was responded to with peculiar ardour. From it the Church borrows the refrain of the eightieth psalm (vers. 3, 7, 19). Peculiar interest attaches to the form which the Church's response takes in Psalm lxvii.: "God ... bless us, and cause his face to shine upon us; that thy way may be known on earth, thy saving health among all nations: "q. d. Not for our own sakes alone do we beseech thee to make us glad with thy face, but that we, being sanctified and gladdened, may bear thy name to the nations who know thee not. 3. "*The Lord lift up his countenance upon thee, and give thee peace.*" Take this member and the foregoing, and what do they amount to but this, "Grace be to you, and peace from God the Father, and from our Lord Jesus Christ" (Rom. i. 7; 1 Cor. i. 3, &c. &c.). There is a look of God which fills with dismay, and makes men call to the mountains to hide them from his presence. But there is a look of God which fills the soul with peace. The Lord can, with a glance of his eye, say to the soul, " I am thy salvation: " he can so lift up his countenance upon us as to give us rest.

III. A CALLING DOWN OF GOD'S BLESSING ON THOSE WHO SEEK HIM. A Benediction is a Beatitude. It is also a Prayer. But it is more than either or both of these. To speak of the latter only, every benediction is a prayer, but every prayer is not a benediction. Into a benediction there enters an element of authority not found in every prayer. Joseph's sons may very well have prayed for Jacob; but we cannot fancy the lads putting their hands on the head of the venerable patriarch and blessing him. "Without all contradiction, the less is blessed of the better" (Heb. vii. 7). The case of Jacob may remind us, that it was not the priests only who blessed the congregation. Moses did it; David and Solomon did it; any aged saint may bless his younger brethren. So, also, the minister of the gospel, when the Lord calls him to preside in public worship, may bless the people in the name of the Lord, in the assured hope that the Lord will indeed bless them, and keep them, and give them his grace and peace.—B.

Vers. 22—27.—*The priestly blessing.* I. CERTAIN NOTEWORTHY POINTS IN REGARD TO THIS BLESSING. 1. One of the special duties of the priests was to be the medium of blessing (Deut. xxi. 5). The priests had much to do with slaughter and sacrifice; here we have a pleasant view of one of their higher functions. Yet to enter heartily into this duty required an elevation of character which the mechanical duties of the altar did not call for. Every servant of God who is faithful in that which is least may find opportunities for higher spiritual services (Matt. xiii. 12; xxv. 29). 2 The triple repetition of the name Jehovah was supposed by the Jews themselves to contain some mystery. At any rate it suggested that as there was in God an infinity of holiness that no one term could express (Isa. vi. 3), so God has for his people a fulness of blessing beyond what any single utterance of his favour would have suggested (cf. Exod. xxxiii. 19; xxxiv. 6, 7; Isa. lxiii. 7; Eph. ii. 4—10). To us the mystery is further revealed by the doctrine of the Trinity. For it is to be noted that in the New Testament that doctrine is always presented in some practical aspect, often in connection with privileges conferred by the triune "God of our salvation" (*e. g.* John xiv. 16, 17; 2 Cor. xiii. 14; Eph. ii. 18, &c.). 3. The Divine blessing, though uttered on the nation, was designed for each individual. The "thee" brings the blessing home to each house and heart. God, who has blessings full enough for the whole world, has an appropriate benediction for the neediest of his children (Ps. xl. 17). The sunlight is for the sake of the tiniest insect and seedling as well as for the whole human race; and God's blessing is for the sick child in the cottage as much as for "the holy Church throughout all the world" (Ps. xxv. 10; Rom. viii. 28). 4. This priestly benediction supplied or suggested the substance of many prayers and benedictions in later days. Echoes of it are heard repeatedly in the Book of Psalms (e. g. Ps. iv. 6; xxix. 11; xxxi. 16; lxvii. 1; lxxx. 3; cxxi.; cxxxiv.). As God's mercies are from everlasting to everlasting, and are "new every morning," so God's words of benediction are like germs of beauty and fruitfulness, reproducing themselves from generation to generation in new and precious forms. "The form of sound words" may be a valuable heritage in the Church of God.

II. THE PARTICULARS OF THE BLESSING. Each clause of the triple blessing contains a promise from God. Combining these, we find that the blessing includes these three favours: protection (ver. 24), pardon (ver. 25), peace (ver. 26). 1. *Protection.* "The blessing of God," says Calvin, "is the goodness of God in action, by which a supply of all good pours down to us from his favour, as from its only fountain." We can confidently commend ourselves, and all who are the "blessed of the Lord," to his keeping, both in regard to spiritual preservation (1 Thess. v. 23, 24) and temporal deliverances (Ps. xci. 11; Isa. xxvii. 3). Because our High Priest has offered the prayer (John xvii. 11), we may utter the doxology (2 Tim. iv. 18; Jude 24, 25). 2. *Pardon* (ver. 25). The face of the Lord represents the aspect which God bears towards man, whether of sunshine and favour (Ps. xxi. 6; xxxiv. 15; cxix. 135; Dan. ix. 17) or cloud and wrath (Exod. xiv. 24; Ps. xxxiv. 16; Levit. xvii. 10; xx. 3). The shining of God's countenance is an assurance that God will be gracious; its shining upon "thee" a pledge that we have received the grace and pardon we need (Ps. xxxi. 16; lxxx. 3). The little child feels the difference between the shining and the averted face of the mother, and the Christian cries, Ps. cxliii. 3, 7. If God grants us to hear "the joyful sound" of forgiveness, we "walk all day long in the light of his countenance." 3. *Peace* (ver. 26). The lifting up of God's countenance may suggest his active intervention to secure to us the blessing of peace. Illustrate, sun rising on the world, "with healing in its wings." Such looks from God will compensate for earthly privations (Ps. iv. 6, 7), and the expectation of them may sustain us in the night of trouble (Ps. xlii. 5). The Christian's peace is "the peace of God," "my peace," communicated by Divine power to the soul (John xiv. 27; xv. 11; Phil. iv. 6, 7). These prayers of blessing remind us that all the relations of life may be thus sanctified, and our warmest wishes breathed forth in the form of prayers: e. g. pastor for flock (Eph. vi. 23, 24; 2 Thess. iii. 16); Christian for fellow-worshipper (Ps. cxviii. 26; cxxxiv. 3); master for servants (Ruth ii. 4; 2 Sam. vi. 18, 20); friend for correspondent (2 Tim. iv. 22). But our words of blessing avail not unless God adds his "Amen," as he promises in ver. 27. Our benediction, whether of men or God, is only in words; God's blessing is in deeds. His blessing when pledged cannot be reversed (Gen. xxii. 15—18; Numb. xxiii. 19, 20). Spiritual blessings are part of the new covenant, which by faith we may enjoy for ourselves and invoke on others (Eph. i. 1—3, 15—19).—P.

Vers. 22—26.—*The benediction through the priests.* A beautiful and touching benediction, and more beautiful for the place in which we come upon it. It is found in the midst of stern commandments and restrictions, minute specifications of duty, dreadful punishments for disobedience and rebellion. How clearly it thus shows that all Jehovah was requiring and doing was for the people's good. Note—

I. THE VERBAL CHANNEL OF THIS BENEDICTION. Spoken through *Aaron and his sons.* It became an office of the priest as much as were any of the sacrifices. He was not only the way from men to God, but very tenderly from God to men. It was not a blessing to each tribe to be pronounced by its head, nor for each household to be spoken by the father, though doubtless in many families it was repeated, explained, and impressed. Aaron was the great *official* mediator between God and the people. Doubtless this benediction was to form a part in all solemn approaches of the priest to the people. It would come to them when in the discharge of sacred duties, at times of holy festival and Divine forgiveness. Others might utter idle, powerless good wishes, sinking with oft petition into mere politeness. The priest's words official, solemn, spoken from the tabernacle. Thus they expressed the permanent good will of God, in spite of all negligence and forgetfulness towards him. *We have a better Aaron*, seeing perfection was not by the Levitical priesthood. The life and work of Jesus give one long and various utterance of this benediction. He the Minister of the sanctuary and true tabernacle which the Lord pitched, and not man. God's good will to the *true Israel* is expressed in no doubtful, grudging way in Jesus. All that Aaron said to the people in respect of temporal blessings, Jesus says to the spiritual seed of Abraham in respect of spiritual blessings.

II. The elements of the benediction. 1. *As to the attitude of God.* (1) *He blesses*, which we may take to mean an expression of his favourable disposition, in the most general sense of the term. "Let it be an understood thing, O Israel, that God favours you." In the eyes not only of Israelites, but of other nations, it was a serious thing to be under the favour or frown of Deity. Favour meant the best of good, frown the worst of evil. Balak thought all his ends would be served if he could get Balaam *only to curse the Israelites*. Thus there would come on them in some mysterious but certain way an irresistible blight. (2) *He makes his face to shine.* The sun may and does bless even when not shining, but shining it speaks for itself. The Lord is *a sun as well as a shield*, a sight that is sweet, and a pleasant thing for the eyes to behold. The face of Jesus shone as the sun upon the mount of transfiguration. (3) *He lifts up his countenance.* What expressiveness there is in the face! The language of men's tongues was confounded at Babel, but the language of the countenance all Babel's confusion could not touch. The language of the face needs no interpreter. When we see the face of a fellow-man shining, and his countenance lifted on us, then we know he will help us if he can. Just so sure were the Israelites to be of God's interest in them. No intermediate voice was needed to maintain the reality of his good will. And we are to behold the glory of God in the face of Jesus. "He that hath seen me hath seen the Father." And he who has seen Jesus knows all the grace in those features, how his countenance is ever lifted on the unstable, wandering children of men. 2. *As to the communications which God makes.* (1) *He keeps* his people. *Security* the first of blessings to those who have much to lose. The rich man had increase of goods, and built bigger barns, but the barns could not keep him against death. Perhaps it is worthy of note that in Matt. vi. is the warning to keep our treasures *in heaven*. Not until we come to Matt. xiii. is the pearl of great price set before us. Insecurity was the mark of Eden. God's face shone, his countenance was lifted up on Adam and Eve, but he warned them there was danger in the midst of all their blessings. Perfect security belongs to the New Jerusalem. He who crept into Eden can never be found where entereth nothing that defileth or maketh a lie. (2) *He is gracious to them.* He *heaps* on them tokens of his favour, just as one friend heaps presents on another. If we see one person enjoying a great number of gifts from another, we judge that he is regarded with special interest. There are gifts to the evil and the good, the common attendants of nature, but there are special gifts for God's own people. Saved from Egypt, they might have been turned loose in the wilderness, but instead they were guided through into the promised land. (3) *He gives peace.* His lifted countenance and benignant eye speak reconciliation so soon as the atonement is offered and the fruits meet for repentance brought forth. If his people are at peace with him, in hearty and diligent obedience, what matter all other foes?

God's benediction then, thus considered, appears suitable to man's needs, and perfectly definite. Our trust and expectation should agree with what is a benediction to us through Christ, as much as it was to the Israelites through Aaron.—Y.

EXPOSITION.

CHAPTER VII.

THE OFFERINGS OF THE PRINCES (ch. vii.).
Ver. 1.—**On the day that Moses had fully
set up the tabernacle.** This expression, "on
the day" (Hebrew, בְּיוֹם ; Septuagint, ᾗ
ἡμέρᾳ), has given rise to considerable difficulty. Strictly speaking it should mean the
first day of the first month of the second year
(Exod. xl. 17); and so the Targum of Palestine,
"It was on the day which begins the month
Nisan." It is, however, quite clear from the
narrative itself, as well as from its position,
that the offerings were not actually made
until after the taking of the census and the
distribution of their respective duties to the
Levitical families, i. e. until the eve of the
departure from Sinai. Moreover, since the
same phrase, בְּיוֹם, occurs in ver. 10, it is
certain that it cannot apply to the actual
presentation of the offerings, which was spread
over twelve days (ver. 11). The majority,
therefore, of the commentators would read
בְּיוֹם here as in Gen. ii. 4, "at the time."
It is, however, impossible to admit that there
is any similarity whatever between the two
passages. In Gen. ii. 4 the context itself, as
well as the subject matter, oblige us to understand the phrase in the looser sense ; but
in a plain historical account such as the
present the obligation is all the other way.
Either the date here given is a mistake
(which, on any supposition, is most improbable), or it must be referred to the intention and inception of the princely offerings, the actual presentation being made at
the time indicated in the narrative, i. e. in
the first half of the second month. **And had
anointed it.** From Levit. viii. 10, as compared with Exod. xl. 35, it would rather appear
that Moses did not anoint the tabernacle on
the day it was set up, but on some subsequent
day. It is, however, a mistake to suppose
that the tabernacle and the holy things were
anointed through seven successive days : the
statement in Levit. viii. 33—35 refers only to
the consecration of the priests. Since the
anointing of the tabernacle was connected
with the setting of it up, as the last act of
one ceremonial, and was only unavoidably
postponed, there is nothing remarkable in
the two things being spoken of as if they had
taken place on one and the same day.
Ver. 2.—**The princes of Israel.** These are
the same men, and are called by the same
titles, as those Divinely nominated in ch. i.
4, *sq.* No doubt they were the heads of the
nations according to some established rules
of precedence before the exodus. **And were
over them that were numbered.** Hebrew,

"stood over." The most natural reference
is to the fact of their presiding over the
census, and so the Septuagint, οὗτοι οἱ παρεσ-
τηκότες ἐπὶ τῆς ἐπισκοπῆς. But it may mean
simply that they were the leaders of the
numbered hosts, and offered as their natural
representatives.

Ver. 3.—**They brought their offering before the Lord,** i. e. probably to the entrance
of the tabernacle. **Six covered wagons.** צַב
עֶגְלֹת. The meaning of the qualifying word
צַב is extremely doubtful. The Targums
render it as the A. V. On the other hand,
Gesenius and De Wette render it "litters,"
as the similar word צַבִּים in Isa. lxvi. 20
(where the Septuagint has ἐν λαμπήναις
ἡμιόνων). The reading of the Septuagint,
ἁμάξας λαμπηνίκας, is equally doubtful.
Λαμπήνη, itself probably a foreign word, is
explained by the Scholiasts as ἅμαξα βασιλικὴ,
or as ἅρμα σκεπαστὸν ; and Aquila has here
ἅμαξαι σκεπασταί, and the Vulgate *plaustra
tecta.* But Euseb. Emis. understands it as
meaning "two-wheeled vehicles." It is a
matter of little importance, but the nature
of the country itself and the small number
of oxen to each carriage point to the probability that they had no wheels, and were
carried by the oxen, one in front, and one
behind, by means of shafts, as is still the
case in parts of India.
Ver. 4.—**The Lord spake unto Moses.** The
Targum of Palestine here inserts the statement that Moses was not willing to receive
them. He may very well have doubted
whether God would sanction their use, as it
had not been commanded ; and it may be
that some delay, perhaps of several days,
occurred before he was able to accept them
and to assign them to their future uses. In
this, or some similar way, must be explained
the apparent discrepancy of time.
Ver. 5.—**Take it of them.** It was the first
absolutely voluntary offering made for the
service of God, and as such altogether acceptable. Former "free-will offerings" had been
at the least invited—this had not.
Ver. 8.—**Four wagons . . . he gave unto
the sons of Merari.** The heavy portions
of the fabric, which were intrusted to the
Merarites, especially required this means of
transport.
Ver. 9.—**Upon their shoulders.** For which
purpose poles or bearing-frames had been
provided, as implying more honour and care
than the use of carriages. The death of Uzzah
seems to have been the melancholy consequence of neglecting this rule (2 Sam. vi. 3,
7, as compared with 1 Chron. xv. 13).

Ver. 10.—**For dedicating of the altar.** The altar was "dedicated" in the sense of being consecrated, by the anointing with the sacred oil and with the blood of the appointed sacrifices (Levit. viii. 10, 15). But it could still be "dedicated" in another sense by the sacrificial gifts, freely offered for the purpose, of the people. No rules appear to have been made as to dedications, but there is an allusion in Deut. xx. 5 to the dedication of houses, which may have been accompanied with religious rites, and we know that as a fact the temple was dedicated by Solomon (2 Chron. vii. 5), and re-dedicated by the Maccabees (1 Macc. iv. 54, *sq.*), and the wall of Jerusalem was dedicated by Nehemiah (Neh. xii. 27, *sq.*). The Septuagint has here εἰς τὸν ἐγκαινισμὸν, as in 1 Macc. iv. 56, and cf. John x. 22. **Offered their offering before the altar.** This assuredly points to an offering made in common, and made at one time, viz., on the day when the altar was anointed. It may be that the twelve princes all came for the purpose of making their offerings on that day, the day they would naturally choose for the purpose ; but on account of the great number of other sacrifices, and the fewness of the priests, *their* offerings were postponed by the Divine command, and were actually received later. Thus in will and in meaning the offerings were made "on the day" of the consecration, but were publicly and solemnly received at some subsequent time.

Ver. 11. — **The Lord said unto Moses.** Doubtless in answer to his inquiry (see ver. 89), at the time when the princes desired to make their offerings. **Each prince on his day.** For more convenience and solemnity, that the sacrifices might not be hurried over, and that none might feel neglected.

Ver. 12.—**Nahshon.** The same appointed to act with Moses in the census, and to be captain of the children of Judah (ch. i. 7 ; ii. 3). The names of the other princes are to be found in the same passages, and their order in presenting is their order for the march. This seems to show that their offerings were actually made after the arrangement of the camps had been settled.

Ver. 13.—**His offering was.** And exactly the same was the offering of each of the rest. This was right and good, because it showed an equal zeal and thankfulness and forwardness to give unto the Lord, and it took away all occasion for jealousy or boasting. **One silver charger,** or dish. Hebrew, *kearah,* a deep vessel (Exod. xxv. 9). Septuagint, τρυβλίον (cf. Matt. xxvi. 23). **An hundred and thirty shekels**—weighing about as much as 325 shillings. **One silver bowl.** Hebrew, *mizrak,* from *zārak,* to scatter ; a bowl for pouring ; translated bason Exod. xxvii. 3. Septuagint, φιάλη (cf. Rev. v. 8 ; xv. 7).

After the shekel of the sanctuary. According to the standard weight kept in the tabernacle (see Exod. xxx. 13). It seems to have weighed about as much as half-a-crown. **Full of fine flour mingled with oil.** This was for a present meat offering to accompany the animal sacrifices, and also to intimate the future use of the vessels—the larger as a measure for the fine flour, the smaller as a measure for the oil.

Ver. 14.—**One spoon,** or small cup, with a handle. Hebrew, *kaph,* as in Exod. xxv. 29. Septuagint, θυίσκη. **Of ten shekels of gold**—weighing about as much as eleven and a half sovrans, but the value of the precious metals was much greater then. **Full of incense.** Both for a present incense offering, and as intimating the use of the cups.

Ver. 15.—**One young bullock, one ram, one lamb.** One of each kind that might be offered for a burnt offering (Levit. i. 2).

Ver. 16.—**One kid of the goats.** Literally, "one shaggy one." Hebrew, *sa'eer.* Septuagint, χίμαρον (see on Levit. iv. 23). It is noticeable that while the burnt offerings and peace offerings were multiplied, the sin offering remained a single victim.

Ver. 17.—**For a sacrifice of peace offerings.** See Levit. iii. 1, 6, 12. These were the most multiplied, as befitted an occasion of joy and of thankful communion with the God of Israel.

Ver. 23. — **This was the offering of Nethaneel the son of Zuar.** His offering, and that of all the rest, is described in exactly the same words and phrases, with the single minute exception, that in ver. 19 we have, "he offered for his offering," instead of "his offering was." Even the small peculiarity of omitting the word *shekels* from the statement of the weight of the silver chargers and the golden spoons appears throughout (cf. Gen. xx. 16). No doubt the record was copied or enlarged from some document written at the time, and its studied sameness reflects the careful and equal solemnity with which the offerings of the several princes were received.

Ver. 48.—**On the seventh day.** This did not necessarily fall on the sabbath ; but if the days of offering were consecutive, one of them must have done so, and the order of offering was the same as on other days.

Ver. 84.—**This was the dedication of the altar.** The sacrificial gifts for present sacrifice, and for the use of the altar, were its dedication.

Ver. 85.—**Two thousand and four hundred shekels.** In weight equal to about £300 of our money.

Ver. 86.—**An hundred and twenty shekels.** About £138. These values were not very great, nor was the number of the animals very large, as compared with the lavish, and perhaps extravagant, profusion displayed at the dedication of the temple and altar by Solomon ; but we may believe they were at least as acceptable. The verb substantive should be removed from these verses (86—88), which simply continue the totals of the offerings which formed the dedication.

Ver. 89.—**And when Moses was gone into the tabernacle of the congregation.** Rather, "the tent of meeting." Hebrew, *ohel moëd*, where God had promised to *meet* with him (Exod. xxv. 22). **To speak with him,** *i. e.* with God, as implied in the word "meeting." **He heard the voice of one speaking unto him.** Rather, "he heard the voice conversing with him," making itself audible to him. מִדַּבֵּר, part. Hithpael, as in Ezek. ii. 2. Here is a distinct statement of the supernatural fact that God spake to Moses with an audible human voice, and (no doubt) in the Hebrew language, from out the empty darkness behind the veil. In the fact, indeed, of God so speaking audibly there was nothing new (see Gen. iii. 8 ; xvii. 1, &c.), nor in the fact of his so speaking to Moses

(see Exod. iii. 4 and xxxiii. 9) ; but this records the fulfilment of that promise which was part of God's covenant with Israel, that he would at all times converse with Moses as their mediator from above the mercy-seat (see on Exod. xxv. 20—22, and cf. Deut. v. 23—28). **And he spake unto him,** *i. e.* God spake unto Moses: the voice made itself audible, and by the voice God himself spake unto him. It is quite obvious that this statement more properly belongs to an earlier period, viz., to that immediately succeeding the consecration of the tabernacle. On the day it was set up Moses was not able to enter it (Exod. xl. 35), but no doubt he did so very soon afterwards, and received from the mouth of the Lord, speaking in the holiest, all the commandments and ordinances recorded in Leviticus and in the beginning of this book. Perhaps the first communication made to him in this way concerned the offerings of the princes when first brought near (vers. 4, 11), and for that reason the statement may have been appended to the record of those offerings.

HOMILETICS.

Ch. vii.—*Acceptable offerings.* In this chapter we have, spiritually, the free-will offering, acceptable unto God, of what they have and what they are, by his people. Consider, therefore—

I. THAT THE OFFERINGS WERE CONNECTED IN TIME WITH THE DAY OF CONSECRATION, BUT WERE ACTUALLY PRESENTED LATER. Even so all Christian offerings, whether of ourselves or of our substance, date from the day when the altar of the cross was consecrated, and the mercy-seat sprinkled with the precious blood ; it is from that day they draw their inward inspiration and their meaning, but they are outwardly dispersed through many days (2 Cor. v. 14).

II. THAT THE COMMON OFFERING OF THE PRINCES WAS FOR THE EASIER ONWARD MOVEMENT OF THE SANCTUARY, the pattern, centre, and microcosm of the Church. Even so all the faithful are bound to give common help to further the onward progress of the Church in her ceaseless extension and her journey towards her consummation.

III. THAT ALL THE SEVERAL OFFERINGS OF THE PRINCES WERE RECEIVED WITH LIKE FAVOUR AND SOLEMNITY : that of Dan as much as that of Judah. Even so all equal offering or sacrifice on the part of Christian Churches or individuals is equally acceptable with God, and comes into the same remembrance with him. Only this equality is not now a material equality (as then), but is proportioned to advantages and opportunities (Mark xii. 43 ; Luke xii. 48 ; 2 Cor. viii. 12).

IV. THAT THE OFFERINGS WERE IN EACH CASE MINUTELY RECORDED, having evidently been entered in some roll kept in the sanctuary. Even so there is nothing, however trivial, done for God or given to him which shall ever be forgotten (Mal. iii. 16 ; Matt. x. 42 ; xxv. 40 ; Heb. vi. 10 ; xiii. 16).

V. THAT WHILE THE BURNT OFFERINGS AND (STILL MORE) THE PEACE OFFERINGS WERE MULTIPLIED, THE SIN OFFERING REMAINED (IN EACH CASE) BUT ONE. Even so it is open to all good people to multiply their self-oblations and their offerings of thankfulness and praise, but there is for each (and can be) but the one offering for sin, even he who was in himself the Lamb of God, and yet in respect of the sin which he assumed, and the curse he endured, was as it were "the shaggy one of the goats." Note that this word, *sa 'eer*, is translated "devil" (Levit. xvii. 7 ; 2 Chron. xi. 15), and "satyr" in Isa. xiii. 21 ; xxxiv. 14, being a most manifest type of Christ.

VI. That God spake unto Moses according to his promise, from above the mercy-seat (ἄνωϑεν τοῦ ἱλαστηρίου). Even so the Divine intercourse with man in Christ rests upon the incarnation and the atonement, of which the ark and the mercy-seat were the types. But note that whereas these holy things were but figures, God hath now spoken unto us plainly by his Son, whom he set forth as the propitiation through faith (ὃν προέϑετο ἱλαστήριον διὰ τῆς πίστεως). And note that then the voice spake out of the darkness behind the veil, but in Christ the veil is taken away, and heaven laid open, and God himself revealed and declared (Matt. xxvii. 51; John i. 18; 2 Cor. iii. 14; Heb. ix. 8).

VII. That whenever (as it would seem) Moses went in to speak unto God, he heard the Divine voice speaking to him. Even so as often as we go to God in Christ, having somewhat really to say to him, we shall not fail also to hear the Divine voice speaking unto us in answer.

HOMILIES BY VARIOUS AUTHORS.

Ch. vii.—*The princes and their princely offering.* Here is perhaps the longest chapter in all the Bible. What is it occupied with? It is, in effect, a List of Subscribers. Certain costly articles were wanted to complete the furnishing of the tabernacle. Twelve men of chief note in their respective tribes came forward, of their own accord, and offered to provide the articles. The offer was accepted; and in this chapter of God's word the Holy Spirit has inscribed, one by one, the names of the donors, together with an inventory of the articles which each of them brought. Some people affect to despise the piety which expresses itself in costly gifts to the Church of Christ, and deem Lists of Subscribers an exhibition of ostentatious vulgarity. But in this chapter there is the best of warrants for these despised features of our modern Christianity.

I. Observe the OCCASION of the gifts here commemorated. The Lord's tabernacle has been constructed, furnished, anointed, and (what is best of all) occupied by the King whose pavilion it was intended for. Yes; and the construction and furniture of this royal tent have been effected by the voluntary gifts of a willing people. The tabernacle and its furniture are completed according to the pattern shown to Moses on the mount. No necessary part is wanting. Still there is room for some supplementary gifts. Take two examples. 1. When the tabernacle was first dedicated there would no doubt be a golden spoon for Aaron's use when he burned incense at the golden altar. One such spoon was all that was strictly necessary. But it would occasionally happen that there would be more than one call to burn incense about the same time, and it was evidently unbecoming that in the palace of the King any worshipper should have to wait till the golden spoon was available. Hence the gift of the twelve golden spoons now presented by the princes. 2. The Levites have been appointed to bear the tabernacle and its furniture. They are able to do it; but not without difficulty, especially during the sojourn in the wilderness, where it is to be emphatically a moving tent. There was room, therefore, for a present of carriages and draught oxen. There are Christian congregations to whom this chapter teaches a much-needed lesson. The roll of their membership includes men of substance, yet they suffer the sanctuary to wear an aspect of threadbare penury and its services to be hunger-bitten. This ought not so to be.

II. The INVENTORY OF THE GIFTS. 1. Some were for the tabernacle in its wandering state. Six waggons were provided,—they seem to have been small covered chariots,—and a yoke of oxen was attached to each. These waggons were distributed among the Levitical families according to the nature and amount of the burdens which had been assigned them respectively. 2. Others were for the *handselling* of the tabernacle service. These consisted partly of gold and silver utensils for the stated service; partly of offerings to be presently consumed. The offerings included all the principal kinds in use under the law. There were burnt offerings, sin offerings, peace offerings. The first sort and the last were much the most numerous. It was a time when the congregation might well rejoice before the Lord—freely devoting themselves to him, and expatiating on the blessedness of communion with him. A time of spontaneous bountifulness in God's service is always a time of gladness. Yet even at such times we are not to forget that we are sinners. The sin offering may not be prominent in this chapter of gifts, yet it has a place in every one of the twelve lists of offerings. What has been said about the nature of the gifts will explain the circumstance that the presenting of them was spread over twelve days. The peace offerings far exceeded in number all the rest. While the sin offering in each case consisted of a solitary kid, and the burnt offering consisted of only three animals, a bullock, a ram, and a lamb, the animals included in the peace offering were no fewer than seventeen. Now the specialty of the peace offering was this, that the person who presented it thereafter feasted upon it with his friends before the Lord. It was a becoming arrangement, therefore, that the disposal of this offering should be spread over several days.

III. A word or two about THE MEN by whom the gifts were brought. They were the hereditary princes of the tribes—the princes of the congregation who had taken charge of the census. This deserves to be noted, for it explains a certain feature of the present gifts in which they differ from almost all other gifts recorded in Scripture. The rule laid down in the Bible for all ordinary cases is that every man is to give according as God hath prospered him. Here, on the contrary, the gifts of the princes are identical in number and value—doubtless by prior concert. There would be richer and poorer among the princes, yet they all give alike. It was not so at the erection of the tabernacle. On that occasion there was the utmost diversity : the mite of the poor widow was made as welcome as the rich man's ingot of gold. Although a man could bring no more than a handful of goat's hair, he was not denied the honour of having a share in the work. There are times for both sorts of giving. When a place of worship, where rich and poor are to meet together, is to be built, it would be wrong to exclude any from the subscription list, however poor. When a college of sacred learning is to be built or endowed, it may be the fittest plan to limit the subscription list to twelve or twenty " princes of the congregation " who are able to contribute every man his thousand or his five thousand pounds. It is a good omen for a nation when its "nobles put their necks to the work of the Lord." And it is good for the nobles themselves when they have the heart to do this. They who are honourable should show themselves serviceable. *Noblesse oblige.* When the nobles forget their duty in this respect, God will not long maintain their nobility.

IV. Does any hearer complain that we have been doing him wrong in preaching to-day from this chapter of the law—barren and secular (as he thinks)—instead of conducting him into the green pastures of the gospel ? Let such a hearer remember how Christ sat over against the treasury and marked what every one cast into it. That scene in the gospel and this chapter in the law—is not the scope of them the very same?—B.

Vers. 1—88.—*The free-will offering of the princes.* The completion of the tabernacle was celebrated by offerings of the princes, as representatives of the tribes. Lessons may be derived from two points noted, viz.—I. THEIR SPONTANEITY. II. THEIR UNIFORMITY.

I. 1. The princes had already given offerings towards the erection of the tabernacle (Exod. xxxv. 27, 28), and now they bring further offerings for its conveyance (ver. 3) and for its complete furnishing (vers. 10—17). The power and will to give are a " grace " bestowed (2 Cor. viii. 7), and the more we give the more of the grace of giving we may enjoy (Matt. xiii. 12). 2. If regarded simply as a duty, it was right that the princes should take the lead, as now it is a duty for men in authority and men of wealth, pastors and officers in Christ's Church, to be "zealous for good works." 3. But the chief excellence of these and similar gifts was the " willing mind " (2 Cor. viii. 12). Under the law of Moses much was left to spontaneity (cf. Exod. xxxv. 5 ; Levit. i. 3, &c.), how much more under the law of Christ (Matt. x. 8 ; 2 Cor. ix. 7). The absence of willinghood may change the fine gold into base metal in the sight of God.

II. 1. The uniformity of the gifts might possibly have been the result of fashion ; Nahshon, of the tribe of Judah, setting the fashion, and the other princes following it. The "fashion" of generous giving may well be set and followed, that the illiberal may be shamed out of their mean devices. But, 2. The uniformity here was probably the result of previous arrangement, and the sign of an honourable emulation. This God approves (Heb. x. 24), and St. Paul seeks to employ (2 Cor. viii. 1—7; ix. 1—5). With this object public benefactions (subscription-lists, &c.) are acceptable to God if the spirit of the precept (Matt. vi. 3, 4) is not violated. The details here published for posterity remind us that every particular of our gifts and services is recorded before God. *E. g.* a coin and its value, absolute and relative (Mark xii. 41—44). A jewel, a family heirloom, and how much it *cost* to give it up (2 Sam. xxiv. 15). 3. The uniformity was a sign that each tribe had an equal share in the altar and its blessings; even as different families, races, and individuals, have in the world-wide redemption of Christ (Rom. x. 11—13).—P.

Ver. 16.—*The universality of the sin offering.* The sin offering was one of the expiatory sacrifices of the law. We meet with it so often and under such varied circumstances that it bears a striking testimony (1) to the universality of sin, and (2) to the need of an absolute, world-wide, everlasting atonement. Classifying the references to the sin offering, we find various illustrations of this truth, fruitful of application to our need of the great offering for sin at all times, and under the manifold circumstances of private and public life. The sin offering was required, and presented—1. From one end of the year to the other, on every return of the new moon (ch. xxviii. 15). 2. On feasts as well as fasts; at the feasts of Pentecost, trumpets, and tabernacles (Levit. xxiii. 19; ch. xxix. 5, 16), as well as on the day of atonement (Levit. xvi.). 3. In connection with voluntary dedication, whether of gifts (ch. vii. 16), or of personal consecration, as of the Nazarite (ch. vi. 14). 4. At the consecration to sacred offices, as *e. g.* Aaron (Exod. xxix. 14), or the Levites (ch. viii. 5—12). 5. At the consecration of sacred things, *e. g.* the altar of incense (Exod. xxx. 10). A sin offering was presented every year for the sanctuary (Levit. xvi. 15, 16). 6. For sins of all classes of men; *e. g.* a priest, the whole congregation, a ruler, " one of the common people " (Levit. iv.). In these offerings there were gradations, according to position and privilege, or according to means (Levit. v. 6, 7). 7. For purification from unavoidable defilement, whether of leprosy (Levit. xiv. 22) or childbirth (Levit. xii. 6—8). 8. These offerings were for sins of omission or of ignorance, but not for presumptuous sins (Levit. v.; ch. xv. 22—31; Heb. x. 26, 27).—P.

Ver. 89.—*Intercourse with God.* The position of this verse, after vers. 1—88, is significant. But the words refer not to a single occasion, but to a continued privilege. The promise (Exod. xxv. 17—22) is now fulfilled, and Moses, as mediator, enjoys exceptional privileges even beyond the high priest, his brother (cf. Levit. xvi. 2 with text, and ch. xii. 6—8). We are reminded of a truth respecting all times of intercourse with God in prayer. When we speak to God, we ought to expect God to speak to us.

I. THE SOUL INQUIRING. Our privilege (Heb. x. 19—22) greater than that of Moses. Every place may be as " a tabernacle." (Gen. xxviii. 17; John iv. 23). Yet good to have some special place, consecrated by hallowed associations (Illus. 2 Sam. vii. 18; Dan. vi. 10; Matt. vi. 6; Acts i. 13). Then we go to " speak with " God, words which imply holy boldness and confidence. As Moses brought to God the burdens of his office and his own temptations and sins, so may we (cf. Ps. xxvii. 5; lxxiii. 16, 17; lxxvii. 1; Heb. iv. 16; James iv. 8).

II. GOD RESPONDING. "Then," &c.—perhaps sometimes even before Moses began to speak. So at times Isa. lxv. 24 fulfilled. See Esther v. 3. If we hear no voice from God at the first moment of approaching him, we ought not to be satisfied unless, while we are speaking to God, God speaks to us (Ps. xxviii. 1; xxxv. 3; cxliii. 7, 8). The response we desire and receive will be from the same spot as Moses' answer " from off the mercy-seat." To sinners, God in nature keeps silence: God on the throne of judgment is " a consuming fire; " God on the mercy-seat is " God in Christ," &c. (2 Cor. v. 19). Such manifestations and voices of God are earnests of further answers, if not immediate, yet certain (*e. g.* Matt. vii. 7; xxvi. 38—44; Acts x. 3—6; 2 Cor. xii. 8—10).—P.

Vers. 1—9.—*The waggons for the Levites.* This chapter describes two sets of gifts, one of waggons to help the Levites in transporting the tabernacle, the other for the dedication at the anointing of the altar. The first gift, when we look into it, is seen to be peculiarly beautiful and significant.

I. IT WAS VOLUNTARY. Jehovah had made no provision that these wagons should be got. The Levites had the bearing of the tabernacle assigned them, and there was nothing to show but they must use their own backs and hands for the purpose. What was essential had been pointed out. But this did not prevent voluntary additions where such did not contradict commands already given. There were men enough—at least, so it would seem—among the Gershonites and Merarites to have borne the heavy furniture. *God had not laid on them a work beyond their skill and strength.* We may conclude, therefore, that the gift of the waggons was an act of pure good will from these princes to the Levites. It was a fresh bond in the unity of the nation.

II. IT WAS SUITABLE. Many gifts of good will are mere ornaments. Sometimes they are white elephants. It is a great deal when a gift shows both a loving heart and a sound judgment. These wagons and oxen were just the thing to help. Probably there had been careful estimates, so as to secure a sufficient number. These waggons were well used (see ch. xxxiii.).

III. IT WAS A UNITED GIFT. Something to express the interest of all Israel in the Levites. The whole nation, in an indirect yet real way, had its part in the service of the tabernacle. It is a good thing to have many joined in a good work. It is better to have a hundred people interested in a hundred good institutions to the extent of a pound a piece, than one man in one institution to the extent of a hundred pounds. God sends down his clouds in the wide-scattering, tiny drops of rain.

IV. IT WAS DULY PROPORTIONATE. Each tribe had its share in the gift and its share in the credit. It was such a kind of gift that each tribe might reasonably give an equal share. It was the gift of all and the gift of each. The niggardliness of the individual should not be hidden away in the munificence of the community.

V. IT WAS ACCEPTED OF GOD. A contrast with the way in which he treated the rashness and presumption of Nadab and Abihu. God is glad to have us lighten burdens and help one another, when it does not lead to a mean shirking of personal duties. It was right for these princes to take care that the strength of the bearers of burdens should not be decayed (Neh. iv. 10). We see moreover a certain honour put upon the lower creation; it was an honour to be used for sacrifice, an honour to bear the tabernacle furniture.

VI. When accepted, THE GIFT WAS PROPORTIONED BY GOD. The *princes* gave, but *God* arranged. It was not fit that brute beasts should carry the vessels of the sanctuary, therefore the Kohathites could not avail themselves of the waggons. The Merarites, we may presume, had more to bear than the Gershonites, and they had more in the way of help. If even among these minute specifications of God's commands to Moses there was this room for voluntary gifts, how much more under the gospel. Where the Spirit of the Lord is, there is liberty, a great deal more liberty in giving than most believers avail themselves of.—Y.

Ver. 13.—*The shekel of the sanctuary.* Mentioned several times in Exodus, Leviticus, and Numbers. Was there a different standard for the sanctuary from that used in ordinary trade? or was the sanctuary shekel the standard to which all were supposed to conform? The very uncertainty teaches a lesson. One cannot err in being on the right side and taking the sanctuary shekel as a standard. The mention of this weight may be taken to illustrate the following line of thought. *The fixed standard of God as contrasted with the fluctuating standards of men.* We should have a fixed standard—

I. IN DEALING WITH GOD. His claims are first. He took the first born and the first fruit. The great exactness that was required in all offerings as to quality and quantity. These sacrifices, perfect after their fashion, were only valuable as symbolising the entire consecration and genuine penitence of those who brought them. *Worship* must be according to the shekel of the sanctuary. We must have a full sense of the reality of his existence, and adequate conceptions of all that belongs to his glory and sovereignty over creation. Also correct notions of *ourselves as worshippers*. Not with the humility of sinless angels who veil their faces, but as the polluted children of men, with their hands on their mouths, and their mouths in the dust. Our praise must be especially for his love, wisdom, and power in our redemption. *Our expectations from God* must be according to the shekel of the sanctuary. We must not lust for the comforts of Egypt. We must have expectations that correspond with the greatness of our redemption. Our Father in heaven treats us to an exhibition of the good and perfect gifts—be ours the desire for them. To look for temporal comforts is to look for trifles, things not promised, things that come without prayer and seeking, if we would only look for such things as God would have us seek. *Ask* for God's Spirit—you are then supplicating according to the shekel of the sanctuary. *Seek* for the kingdom of God and his righteousness—you are then seeking according to the shekel of the sanctuary. The sanctuary measure of expectation is in the Lord's prayer. *The daily conduct of life* must be according to the shekel of the sanctuary. Everything in which our voluntary powers are concerned should be done as for God. The world is hard to please, but even when it is pleased, it is with a low standard. We are careful when the eyes of men are upon us, for that means *reputation ;* let us be careful also when no human eye can see, for that means *character*. Each daily presentation of the living sacrifice should make that sacrifice holier, more acceptable to God.

II. IN DEALING WITH MEN. The Israelites were to do no unrighteousness in meteyard, in weight, or in measure. They were not to have divers weights and measures, great and small. Solomon tells us all the weights of the bag are the Lord's work. Amos spoke of the wickedness of the people who waited for the Sabbath to be gone that they might sell their corn, making the ephah small and the shekel great. The Almighty is just as particular about our work as our worship. Trade customs are no excuse in his sight. The eye that never misses anything or mistakes anything is on the weights and measures of all dishonest traffickers. God is just as angry when a man defrauds his neighbour as when he breaks the Sabbath. How many have been hindered in their religion, lost their peace of mind, and finally backslidden from the ways of God, because all was not right in their daily business. *Remember also all the other relations*. Commercial relations only a small part of human intercourse. Husband and wife, parents and children, brothers and sisters, friends and neighbours, rulers and subjects, debtor and creditor, rich and poor, well and sick, young and old, believer and unbeliever : the shekel of the sanctuary has its place in all such intercourse. We need then to live in continual watchfulness and prayer, to have everything agreeable to this standard. One set of principles we should have, and one only, got from the teaching and example of our Divine Master. We must deal with one another as God has dealt with us, he who so loved the world that he gave his only begotten Son to redeem it. The actions of the Almighty himself are weighed according to the shekel of the sanctuary.—Y.

EXPOSITION.

CHAPTER VIII.

THE LIGHTING OF THE LAMPS (vers. 1—4). Ver. 1.—**The Lord spake unto Moses.** It does not appear when. The attempt of modern commentators to find a real connection between this section and the offering of the princes or the consecration of the Levites is simply futile. Such connection may be imagined, but the same ingenuity would obviously be equally successful if this section had been inserted in any other place from Exod. xxxvii. to the end of this book. The more probable explanation will be given below.

Ver. 2.—**When thou lightest the lamps.** The command to light the lamps had been given generally (" they shall light the lamps thereof ") in Exod. xxv. 37, and the care of them had been specially confided to Aaron and his sons (" from evening to morning ") in Exod. xxvii. 21. The actual lighting of the lamps for the first time by Moses is recorded in Exod. xl. 25. In the face of these passages it is incredible that the lamps had not been regularly lighted by Aaron for more than a month before the offering of the princes. **The seven lamps shall give light over against the candlestick.** It is somewhat uncertain what this expression, here repeated from Exod. xxv. 37, means. The Targums give no explanation of it ; the Septuagint merely renders verbally, κατά πρόσωπον τῆς λυχνίας φωτιοῦσιν ; the Jewish expositors seem to have thought that the light was to be thrown inward towards the central shaft ; most modern commentators, with more probability, understand it to mean that the lamps were to be so placed as to throw their light across the tabernacle towards the north side.

Ver. 4.—**And this work of the candlestick.** For the meaning of the details here given see Exod. xxv. 31, *sq.* **According unto the pattern which the Lord had shewed Moses,**—viz., in the mount (see Exod. xxv. 40) — **so he made the candlestick.** This has been recorded in Exod. xxxvii. 17. The repetition of the statement in this place seems to be conclusive that these verses are out of their historical position, and that their insertion here is due to some fact connected with the original records with which we are not acquainted. It may be simply this, that these verses originally followed verse 89 of the previous chapter, and followed it still when it was inserted, for reasons already suggested, after the narrative of the offerings of the princes. Why, or how, such an admission should discredit the sacred narrative or imperil the truth of its inspiration it would be hard to say. The only thing really likely to imperil the sacred narrative is to persistently deny the obvious literary conclusions which arise from an honest consideration of the text.

HOMILETICS.

Vers. 1—4.—*The sacred lamps.* In this section we have, spiritually, the Divine concern that the light of revelation should be made to shine out and to illumine the whole Church of God by the ministers of his word. Consider, therefore—

I. THAT THE REPETITION HERE OF WHAT HAD BEEN SUFFICIENTLY DECLARED BEFORE SHOWS THE DIVINE CONCERN ON THE SUBJECT. Even so there is nothing which more concerns God than that the light of his revelation in Christ should be made to shine abroad strong and clear (Matt. xxviii. 19, 20 ; Mark xvi. 15 ; 1 Cor. ix. 16 ; 2 Cor. iv. 4—7).

II. THAT THE LAMPS WERE TO BE SO ARRANGED AS THAT THEIR LIGHT SHOULD BE THROWN RIGHT ACROSS THE HOLY PLACE, AND FALL UPON THE TABLE WITH ITS LOAVES. Even so the light of the gospel—without which the Church were in total darkness, as the holy place without the candelabrum—is to be so shed abroad as that it illumine the whole breadth of the Church, and fall especially upon the faithful, represented by the loaves of remembrance (John viii. 12 ; Acts xiii. 47 ; Eph. v. 14 ; 2 Pet. i. 19).

III. THAT AARON DID SO, AS COMMANDED, AND THE LAMPS DID SO SHINE. Even so the light of revelation has never ceased to shine out in the Church, and to illumine the faithful—even if not always very brightly—amidst all the changes of time, and the commotions of the world.

IV. THAT IT IS REPEATED HERE (AS IF VERY IMPORTANT) THAT THE CANDELABRUM WAS WHOLLY OF BEATEN WORK, AND WAS MADE AFTER THE PATTERN IN THE MOUNT. As made of beaten work, it was of human art and much labour ; as made after the pattern in the Mount, it was Divine in conception, and that even in detail. Exactly so is the Divine revelation which is the light of the Church on earth : in its outward presentation to the senses and the understanding of men it is beholden to human labour and elaboration ; but in its essence, its "idea," it is Divine, proceeding from the mind of God.

V. THAT IT IS SPECIALLY RECORDED THAT IT WAS ALL OF GOLD FROM THE CENTRAL SHAFT TO THE ORNAMENTAL FLOWERS. Even so the revelation of God, which giveth light (Ps. cxix. 105), is altogether pure and precious from the main stem of sacred history even to the lightest flowers of sacred poetry.

HOMILIES BY VARIOUS AUTHORS.

Vers. 1—4.—*The lamps of the sanctuary.* This passage is to be considered in connection with Rev. i. 9—20. Moses had revelations in Sinai even as John had in Patmos. Matt. v. 14—16 will serve for a link to connect the two passages.

I. THERE WAS A TIME TO LIGHT THE LAMPS. "When thou lightest the lamps." *Dressing* them was morning work: they were then ready for Aaron to light " at even"

(Exod. xxx. 7, 8). The light was symbolic only when it was clearly useful. By day no light was needed, but it was fitting that at night the holy place of him who is light and in whom is no darkness at all, should be well illuminated. Seven is said to be a number of perfection; if we take it so seven lamps would denote perfect illumination. Similarly the Churches of Christ are to be as lamps in a darkened world, that by their light the things of God may be discerned. The words to the seven Churches are thus words to every Church, admonishing it to tend and replenish the lamp that has been lighted at even.

II. THE LAMPS WERE TO BE LIGHTED OVER AGAINST THE CANDLESTICK. This, taken together with the reference in ver. 4 to the construction of the candlestick, seems to indicate that the candlestick with its richness and beauty was to be revealed by the lamps. Bezaleel and Aholiab had been specially endowed to make this and like elaborate work (Exod. xxxv. 30—35; xxxvii. 17—24). If the Churches then are as the lamps, we may take the candlestick to signify the doctrines, the promises, the duties, the revelations to be found in the word of God. Law and gospel are intermingled by prophet and apostle in a splendour and richness of which Bezaleel's work was a feeble type. The candlestick supports the lamps, which in turn reveal the candlestick. The truths of God's word are in charge of his Churches. They rest upon that word, and their lives, conspicuous for abiding purity and brightness, must recommend the word. The lamps must reveal that the candlestick holds them, and it must be made obvious that the candlestick is for this purpose.

III. IT WAS AARON WHO LIGHTED THESE LAMPS, and so it is from Christ the true Aaron that every Church gets its light. We cannot recommend God's word by anything save the holy, beautiful, benign life which his Son, by the Spirit, can create within us. Then, and only then, will our light so shine that men will glorify our Father who is in heaven.

IV. THE LAMPS REVEALED THE GLORY OF AARON'S OWN VESTURE—those holy garments which were for glory and beauty. Read carefully Exod. xxviii., and then consider that Aaron arrayed in all these splendours was the type of the true Intercessor afterwards to come. That is an unworthy Church which does not reveal much of Christ; which does not, by the shining of its life, attract attention more and more to the glories of his person. We cannot glorify our Father in heaven, unless by glorifying the Son whom he has sent.

Lessons : — 1. That which is useful may also be beautiful, and in its use its beauty will be revealed. 2. The candlestick was something permanent, made of gold, and not needing renewal. We have no occasion for a new, an altered, or an increased gospel; all required of us is to show it forth, by daily replenishings from the beaten oil of the sanctuary.—Y.

EXPOSITION.

THE HALLOWING OF THE LEVITES (vers. 5—23). Ver. 5. — **The Lord spake unto Moses.** At some time subsequent to the command given in ch. iii. 6—13, and no doubt before the passover.

Ver. 6.—**And cleanse them.** Before they actually entered upon their new duties they were to be solemnly hallowed. This hallowing, however, is not called קַדֵּשׁ, as is that of the priests (Exod. xxix. 1), but טַהֵר, cleansing. There was in their case no ceremonial washing, no vesting in sacred garments, no anointing with holy oil, or sprinkling with the blood of sacrifices. The Levites, in fact, remained simply representatives of the congregation, whereas the priests were representatives also of Christ.

Ver. 7.—**Sprinkle water of purifying upon them.** Rather, "water of sin," so called because it had to do with the removal of sin, just as "water of separation" (ch. xix. 9, 13) was that which delivered from the legal state of separation. It is not likely to have been prepared in the same manner as this latter (ch. xix. 9), both because of the great difference between the two cases, and because the ordinance of the red heifer belonged to a later period. Nor is it likely to have resembled that used for cleansing the leper, or the water of jealousy. But it is rash to conclude that, because we do not read any special directions for its preparation, it must, therefore, have been nothing but water from the laver which stood in the outer court. That water appears, indeed, to be called "holy water" in ch. v. 17, which is intelligible enough; but no probable reason can be shown why it should be called "sin water;" it would seem as reasonable to call the water which our Lord turned into wine "sin water," because it stood there "for the purifying of the Jews." It is better to say that we do not know, because it is not recorded, how this water was prepared, or how it corresponded to its name. The Levites who were to be sprinkled would seem to have included all the males, some twenty thousand in number; because it was *all* the males, and not only those between thirty and fifty, who were to be dedicated in place of the first-born. In any case it was, of course, impossible that Moses could have sprinkled them individually (see below on ver. 11). **Let them shave all their flesh.** Literally, "let them cause the razor to pass over their whole body." Some, distinguish between עָבַר תִּעַר here and גִלָּה in Levit. xiv. 8, 9, as though the latter meant a much more complete shaving off of the hair than the former; but this difference is doubtful; the fact that the whole body as well as the head was to be shaved implies that it was more than a mere cutting short of the hair. **Let them wash their clothes.** This was constantly enjoined on all the faithful as a preparation for any special religious service (see on Exod. xix. 10). **And so make themselves clean.** The shaving and washing had, no doubt, a symbolic significance, but their primary object was simply and obviously personal cleanliness; it is the hair and the clothes that chiefly harbour impurities, especially in a hot climate.

Ver. 8. — **Another young bullock shalt thou take for a sin offering.** The ordinary sin offering was a shaggy one of the goats (see on ch. vii. 16); but a bullock had been prescribed for the sin of the high priest, and for the sin of the congregation, in certain circumstances, and the analogy is followed here. It might seem as if the larger animal were meant to distinguish aggregate or collective guilt (see on Levit. iv. 3); but the scape-goat offered for the sin of the whole people makes against such a supposition.

Ver. 10.—**Before the Lord.** As in ch. v. 16, either near the brazen altar, or more probably before the entrance of the tabernacle. **And the children of Israel shall put their hands upon the Levites.** Presumably by means of their representatives, probably the tribe princes. This laying on of hands signified that the obligation to assist personally in the service of the sanctuary was transferred from the whole congregation to the Levites.

Ver. 11. — **And Aaron shall offer the Levites before the Lord for an offering.** Rather, "Aaron shall wave" them "for a wave offering" (Hebrew, *nuph*; see Exod. xxix. 24); and so in vers. 13, 15, and 21. This injunction seems conclusive that the whole ceremonial was to be symbolically performed, for the Levites could not possibly be waved in any literal sense. Some have supposed that they were marched up and down before the altar, forgetting that the court would scarcely afford standing room for 1000 people, while the Levites between thirty and fifty numbered more than 8000. It is certain that the Levites could only be brought before the Lord, could only be waved (howsoever that was done), could only lay their hands upon the bullocks, by representation. If we suppose, *e. g.*, that a hundred men of position and command among them entered the court as representatives of the tribe, then we can understand how the ceremonial here commanded might have been effectively carried out. **That they may execute the service of the Lord.** Literally, "that they may be to execute the service of the Lord." Their being waved made them over in a figure to the Lord to be wholly his, and to live only for his service, and at his command. But just as wave offerings were assigned by Divine permission to the use of the priests, so were the Levites given to Aaron and his sons for ever.

Ver. 12.—**Shall lay their hands upon the heads of the bullocks.** In token that they constituted these victims the ritual representatives and embodiments, the one of their sin, to be consumed and done away as by fire, the other of their life and strength, to be wholly offered unto God and accepted as by fire.

Ver. 13.—**And thou shalt set the Levites before Aaron.** This is not an additional command, but repeats in a slightly different form the previous orders. A similar repetition occurs in ver. 15 *b.*

Ver. 16.—**For they are wholly given unto me.** See ch. iii. 5—13, the substance of which is emphatically repeated here.

Ver. 19 *b.*—**To make an atonement for the children of Israel.** This is a remarkable expression, and throws light upon the nature of atonement. It is usually confined to purely sacerdotal ministrations, but it clearly has a somewhat different scope here. The idea that the Levites "made an atonement" by assisting the priests in the subordinate details of sacrifice hardly needs refutation: as well might the Gibeonites be said to "make an atonement" because they supplied the altar fire with wood. The real parallel to this is to be found in the case of Phinehas, of whom God testified that "he hath turned my wrath away from the children of Israel," and "made an atonement for the children of Israel" (ch. xxv. 11, 13). It is evident that Phinehas turned away the wrath of God not by offering any sacrifices, but by making the sin which aroused that wrath to cease: he made an atonement for the people by discharging for them that holy and bounden duty (of putting away sin) which the rest of them failed to perform. Similarly the Levites made an atonement not by offering sacrifice (which they could no more do than the children of Judah), but by rendering unto God those personal duties of attendance and service in his courts which *all* the people ought to have rendered had they only been fit. **That there be no plague among the children of Israel, when the children of Israel come nigh unto the sanctuary.** See ch. i. 53. The children of Israel were in this strait. As "an holy nation," they were all bound, and their first-born as redeemed from the destroyer were specially bound, to render certain religious duties to God. But if they had attempted to render them they would have erred through ignorance and foolishness, and so have incurred Divine wrath and punishment, when they came nigh unto the sanctuary. From this strait the substitution of the Levites delivered them.

Ver. 21. — **Were purified,** or "purified themselves." It refers not to the ceremonial sprinkling, but to the personal preparation prescribed.

Ver. 22.—**In the tabernacle of the congregation.** This can only mean that they went in after the holy things had been packed up in order to take the fabric to pieces; no one but the priests went into the tabernacle for any other purpose, or at any other time.

Ver. 24.—**From twenty and five years old and upward.** A short time before the minimum age had been fixed at thirty (ch. iv. 3). That direction, however, concerned the transport of the tabernacle and its belongings; this was a permanent regulation designed for the ordinary labours of the sanctuary at a time when the Levites would be scattered throughout their cities, and could only serve by courses. For the latter purpose many more would be required; and indeed they were found insufficient as it was in the latter days of David, when the wealth and devotion of the kingdom were fast increasing (see on 1 Chron. xxiii. 24—27). **To wait upon the service.** Literally, "to war the warfare;" the idea of the *militia sacra* is kept up.

Ver. 26.—**Shall minister . . . to keep the charge, and shall do no service.** The word "charge" (Hebrew, *mishmereth*) seems to signify the care of the furniture and belongings of the tabernacle, while "service" means the laborious work of transport, or of preparing sacrifice. The duties of the Levite over fifty were in fact honorary, given to him probably for his own sake, that he might have some place and post in the house of God. This careful provision for those who should attain the age of fifty shows that the commandment was designed for the promised land rather than for the wilderness.

HOMILETICS.

Vers. 5—23.—*The dedication of the Levites.* In this section we have the due preparation of those who are specially devoted to the service of God. Consider, therefore—

I. THAT BEFORE THEY COULD SERVE THEY MUST BE CLEANSED. Even so all that would do God service, or be useful to others in religious concerns, must first themselves be cleansed; because all that is human is unclean (Job xv. 14), and nothing that is unclean can do God service, for he requireth holiness in his servants (Prov. xx. 9; Ps. v. 5; Isa. lii. 11; Hab. i. 13; Matt. v. 48; xxii. 12).

II. THAT THIS CLEANSING WAS TWOFOLD, PARTLY WROUGHT UPON THEM, PARTLY WROUGHT BY THEM. Even so the cleansing which prepares for the service of God, and for his nearer presence, is twofold; partly it is done for us by the Mediator, partly by us through our own efforts (Ps. li. 7; 2 Cor. vii. 1).

III. THAT THE CLEANSING A PARTE DEI WAS BY SPRINKLING OF SIN WATER, THE EXACT NATURE OF WHICH IS DISPUTED. Even so every one that would belong to the kingdom of God must receive that washing of water and of the Holy Spirit, which is in its nature mysterious, and in definition controverted (Ezek. xxxvi. 25; John iii. 5; Acts xxii. 16; Heb. x. 22).

IV. THAT THE CLEANSING A PARTE SUA WAS BY SEDULOUSLY GETTING RID OF ANY POSSIBLE IMPURITY WHICH MIGHT ADHERE FROM WITHOUT. Even so he who would truly serve God must be not only careful, but conscious, and according to the ordinary standard extreme, to detach and remove from himself all those impurities of common life which so easily cling to us; to reform those private, social, and domestic habits, which sit as closely to us as our clothes, which seem as much a part of us as our hair, and which, as it were, absorb and retain the inherent sinfulness of our nature (1 John iii. 3; 2 Pet. iii. 14; James i. 21; iv. 8).

V. THAT FOR THE LEVITES WERE OFFERED FIRST A SIN OFFERING, AND A BURNT

OFFERING, FOR AN ATONEMENT. Even so no service, however able and laborious, is acceptable unto God except it have been sanctified through the sacrifice and self-sacrifice of Christ (Heb. x. 10).

VI. THAT THE CHILDREN OF ISRAEL LAID THEIR HANDS UPON THE LEVITES WHEN THEY WERE DEVOTED. Even so whatever labour be undertaken for the body of Christ, should receive recognition and sympathy from all members of the body, for all are concerned (1 Cor. xvi. 15, 16; Acts xiii. 3; xiv. 26; 1 Cor. xii. 26).

VII. THAT THE LEVITES WERE "WAVED." Even so all who would labour in holy things must present themselves as a living sacrifice to God, to be wholly his and no longer *suæ potestatis.* Those who do religious work, *because* they like it themselves, "have their reward;" but where the Pharisees had it, in this world only (Rom. xii. 1; 1 Cor. vi. 20; Gal. ii. 20).

VIII. THAT ONLY AFTER THEIR CLEANSING AND WAVING COULD THEY ENTER IN TO WAR THE WARFARE OF THE TABERNACLE. Even so, none can do real service to God unless they are wholly converted and have given themselves to him (Luke xxii. 32 *b.* ; Acts viii. 21; James i. 8; and cf. Judges vii. 4, 7).

IX. THAT AFTER THE FIFTIETH YEAR THEY WERE RELEASED FROM DOING SERVICE, BUT WERE STILL PERMITTED TO KEEP THE CHARGE. Even so it is part of the good-ness of God that no one should be held to do laborious work in the Church when he is old; but also part of his goodness that he should still keep such charge as is fitted to his years.

Note, *that the Levites are said to have made an atonement for the children of Israel.* —1. By taking upon themselves, in their separated but representative character, those religious obligations of the congregation (especially of the first-born) which they dared not attempt. 2. By performing such obligations rightly, which those could not have done. There is none of us that can do this, because we cannot even do our own duty, far less another's (Ps. xlix. 7; Luke xvii. 10; Gal. vi. 5) Where-fore this applies only unto Christ, by whom we have received the atonement (Rom. v. 11), and throws an important light upon that atonement. Consider, therefore— 1. Christ hath "made atonement" for us, as having undertaken for us those duties of a human life and ministry wholly and perfectly devoted and consecrated to the Father, which we for our unworthiness durst not even have attempted (Luke ii. 49; John iv. 34; vi. 38; Heb. x. 5—9; ix. 14). 2. Christ hath "made atonement" for us, as having lived that perfect life, and rendered that perfect ministry, which we never could have lived or rendered, and therefore never could have pleased God, nor satisfied his just and necessary requirements (Matt. iii. 17; xii. 18; xvii. 5; John xvii. 4; xix. 30; James iii. 2). 3. Christ hath "made atonement" for us, as having thus pleased God, as man, and as our separated and accepted representative, "the Son of man"—"the second man." 4. Christ hath saved us thereby from the sorrow which even in heaven itself (could we have got there) our want of will and want of power to serve God acceptably would have brought upon us (Ephes. i. 6), having appeared in our behalf in the presence of God with the offering of a perfect human life.

HOMILIES BY VARIOUS AUTHORS.

Ver. 14.—*The separation of the Levites; or an ordination service in the wilderness.* "Thus shalt thou separate the Levites from among the children of Israel: and the Levites shall be mine." There was a threefold reason why the Levites were separated from the rest of the nation and wholly dedicated to the Lord's service. In the first place, they were to stand instead of the first-born, whom the Lord had specially claimed for himself (vers. 16—18). It was judged expedient that to the service of the sanctuary one whole tribe should be dedicated, rather than individuals out of all the tribes. Secondly, the due serving of the tabernacle being much too burdensome for the single family of Aaron, their brethren of the tribe of Levi were appointed to help them. But there was a third and deeper reason. All the chosen people are the Lord's, and he claims their service. But all cannot, in person, serve him in the way of keeping the charge of the sanctuary. Some of them must be separated to this ministry. Official service is necessary under the gospel. Much more was it necessary under the law. Hence the separation of the Levites. When the time came for the Levites to enter on duty, they were set apart in a service, not so solemn indeed as the service on the occasion of Aaron's consecration, nevertheless highly impressive, and fitted to suggest many a lesson worthy to be laid to heart by us on similar occasions.

I. Let us begin by taking A GENERAL VIEW OF THIS ORDINATION SERVICE. The outstanding features were these. It took place at the door of the tabernacle and in presence of the whole congregation. The Levites being marched in, the congregation put their hands on them, *q. d.* : "We are thine, O Lord. Thou hast redeemed us and brought us out for thyself, to be to thee a kingdom and priests. With respect to the charge of this thy sanctuary, thou hast made choice of these our brethren to minister to thee in our stead. We freely give them up to thee, and renounce all the rightful claim we should otherwise have had upon their service in peace and war." This done, Aaron "offered " the Levites to the Lord as a " wave offering." Finally, Aaron in turn accepted the Levites as the Lord's gift to him, to aid him in the tabernacle. Who can fail to see the significance of all this? Besides suggesting (1) how fit it is that men who are entering on a life of official service in the Church should be solemnly set apart to their office and charge, it plainly teaches (2) that ordination to sacred office should take place in the face of the congregation. It ought not to be performed in a corner. The people are vitally interested, and have a right to be present. This is the rule, I believe, in all evangelical Churches. (3) When a man has been set apart to sacred service, at the instance of his brethren and in their presence, a relation is formed between him and them which involves reciprocal obligation. He is to lay out his strength in their service; and they are to charge themselves with his maintenance while he does so. The people of Israel having laid their hands on the Levites, were thenceforward to communicate with them in all good things (see Deut. xii. 19; xiv. 27). When Dr. Carey consented to go down into the pit of heathendom, it was only fair and just that the brethren at whose instance he went should "hold the rope," as he stipulated that they should.

II. BESIDES THESE MORE CATHOLIC AND SPIRITUAL SERVICES, THE LEVITES' ORDINATION WAS ACCOMPANIED WITH OTHERS PURELY CEREMONIAL. These were of three kinds. 1. *Lustral* (ver. 7). First, Aaron sprinkled the Levites with water of purifying—either that described ch. xix., or, more likely, spring-water, such as was used in the laver. Then the Levites, on their part, shaved off their hair and washed their clothes, *q. d.*: " Lord, we are not meet for thy house and service. Holiness becometh thine house. Thou art of purer eyes than to behold evil. And we are unclean. But thou canst make us clean. As thou hast sprinkled our persons with clean water, so do thou remove all filthiness from our hearts. And we, for our parts, are resolved by thy grace to put away the evils of our past lives and to follow after holiness henceforward." 2. *Expiatory* (vers. 8, 12). The Levites were to bring a sin offering for atonement; laying their hands upon it with confession of sin (see Levit. iv.). They were thus reminded of their guilt as well as impurity, and were encouraged to believe that there is forgiveness with God, on the ground of which they might hope to be accepted in their persons and service. 3. *Dedicatory.* The sin offering was to be followed by a burnt offering to signify that the Levites presented their whole persons to the Lord, a living sacrifice, to be employed in his service all their days. Blessed be God, we are rid of these burdensome and carnal rites. Care must be taken not to let anything like them creep again into the sanctuary. But the ideas they set forth—the great realities of purification, and pardon, and dedication—ought to be often present to our minds and hearts in the house of God.—B.

Vers. 12, and 19.—*An offering to God, needing for itself an atonement.* The tribe of Levi was set apart for God's service in the tabernacle in place of all the firstborn. Before they could enter on that service they needed a special call and consecration, including atoning sacrifices (vers. 5—12). Thus we are reminded of the obvious truth that, without a sacrifice for us, we can never ourselves be acceptable sacrifices to God. Illustrate from the position of Rom. xii. 1 in the Epistle, coming after the exposition of the mercies of God, including the atonement of Christ (Rom. iii.). But in ver. 19 the services of the Levites (or the Levites themselves) are said to be an atonement. The Levites were regarded as a vicarious offering to God (vers.

10, 11). In the wider sense of the word atonement, they are said to make (or to be) an atonement. ("The priests made an atonement by sacrifice; the Levites by attendance."—M. Henry.) Yet even this vicarious offering needs to be atoned for (ver. 12). Hence the lesson, that every human *saint* (separated to God, ver. 14), *service*, or *sacrifice* needs an atonement. This is needed for—1. All God's chosen servants, "a kind of first-fruits of his creatures." (Illustrate from 1 John i. 7—10; ii. 1, 2, and from John xiii. 10.) 2. All God's selected ministers (pastors, missionaries, &c.). Illustrate from Tertullian's request to his brethren: "Ye have sought, and ye have found; ye have knocked, and it is opened to you. Thus much I ask, that when you seek again, you remember me, Tertullian, a sinner;" or from W. Carey the missionary's selected epitaph—

> "A guilty, weak, and helpless worm,
> On thy kind arms I fall."

3. All the most sacred services of the most saintly men. Their prayers need to be prayed for; their tears to be washed from impurity; their gifts of gold to be refined from the dross of earthly motives. Though all Christians are priests unto God, their most solemn priestly acts need the blood of Christ to cleanse them from all sin.—P.

EXPOSITION.

CHAPTER IX.

THE PASSOVER AT SINAI (vers. 1—14). Ver. 1.—**In the first month of the second year.** Before the census, and all the other events recorded in this book, except in part the offerings of the princes (see ch. vii. 1). There was, however, an obvious reason for mentioning together the two passovers, the second of which immediately preceded the departure from Sinai.

Ver. 2.—**Let the children of Israel also keep the passover at his appointed season.** Septuagint, ποιείτωσαν τὸ πάσχα. Cf. Matt. xxvi. 18, ποιῶ τὸ πάσχα, and Luke xxii. 19, τοῦτο ποιεῖτε εἰς τὴν ἐμὴν ἀνάμνησιν. They may have been in doubt as to whether they were to keep it in the wilderness, and indeed they do not seem to have attempted to keep it again until they reached the promised land (see on Josh. v. 5, 6). The passover had indeed been made an "ordinance for ever," but only when they were come to the land which the Lord should give them (Exod. xii. 24, 25; xiii. 5). Apart, therefore, from express command, it would have been doubtful whether the feast should not at least be postponed. Inasmuch, however, as they had been detained at Sinai by Divine direction (albeit partly in consequence of their own idolatry, but for which they might already have been "at home"), it pleased God that they should not lack the blessing and support of the passover at its proper season.

Ver. 3.—**At even.** See on Exod. xii. 6. **According to all the rites of it, and according to all the ceremonies thereof.** This must be understood only of the essential rites and ceremonies of the passover, as mentioned below (vers. 11, 12). It is singular that no mention is made of the considerable departure which circumstances necessitated from the original institution. It was not possible, e. g., to strike the blood of the lamb upon the lintel and the side-posts of the doors, because in the wilderness they had no doors. In after ages this rite (which was of the essence of the institution) was represented by the sprinkling of the blood of the lambs on the altar (2 Chron. xxx. 16), but no command is on record which expressly authorised the change. In Levit. xvii. 3—6 there is indeed a general direction, applying apparently to all domestic animals slain for food, that they be brought to the tabernacle to be slain, and that the priest sprinkle the blood upon the altar; and in Deut. xvi. 5—7 there is an order that in future times the passover was only to be slain at the place which the Lord should choose. The actual practice in later ages seems to have been founded partly upon the command in Deuteronomy, which restricted the killing of the passover to Jerusalem (not, however, to the temple), and partly on the command in Leviticus, which really applied (at any rate in the letter) to the time of wandering only. As the celebration of the paschal feast had apparently been neglected from the time of Joshua until that of the later kings (Josh. v. 10; 2 Kings xxiii. 22), they were no doubt guided in the observance of it by the analogy of other sacrifices in the absence of express commands. It would, however, be an obvious source of error to assume that the practice of the age of Josiah or Hezekiah was the practice of the earliest passovers; so far as these necessarily differed from the original institution, it is absolutely uncertain how the difficulty was solved. Nothing perhaps better illustrates the mingled rigidity and elasticity of the Divine ordinances than the observance of the passover, in which so much of changed detail was united with so real and so unvarying a uniformity.

Ver. 5.—**And they kept the passover.** It is a question which inevitably arises here, how they obtained a sufficient number of lambs for the requirement of so many people, and how they were slain sacrificially within the appointed time. The first difficulty does not seem serious when we consider, (1) that kids were available as well as lambs (see on Exod. xii. 3) ; (2) that the desert tribes would have abundance of lambs and kids for sale at this season, and that the Israelites certainly had money ; (3) that in view of their speedy departure they would be disposed to kill off the young of their own flocks. The second difficulty is more serious, and would be insurmountable if we had to believe that the ritual of this passover was the same which afterwards prevailed. Josephus tells us ('Bell. Jud.,' vi. 9, 3) that in his day 256,000 lambs were slain and their blood sprinkled upon the altar within the three hours "between the evenings." At that time, according to the same authority, a lamb was shared by ten, and often by as many as twenty people. The number of males who would partake of the paschal meal in the wilderness may be set down as not more than 800,000. If the women partook of it at all (which is very doubtful ; cf. Exod. xii. 44, 48), they would doubtless content themselves with the scraps left by the men. Allowing twenty souls to each lamb, the number required would be not more than 40,000. It is obvious at once that the three priests could not possibly kill 40,000 lambs in three hours, much less sprinkle their blood upon the altar ; indeed the same may be said for 10,000, or even 5000, especially as they could not have acquired the extreme dexterity and despatch which long practice taught to the later priests. Nor is it satisfactory to reply that the priests did the work "out of the hand of the Levites" (2 Chron. xxx. 16), (1) because this passover took place before the Levites were formally separated for the service of God and of the priests (see ch. viii. 22) ; (2) because the smallness of the space about the altar would not allow of many people assisting ; (3) because the actual slaying and sprinkling, which was restricted to the priests (being distinctively sacrificial in nature), are the very things which we find impossible in the time. There are but two alternative conclusions, from one or other of which there is no honest escape : either (a) the numbers of the people are greatly exaggerated, or (b) the ritual of after days was not observed on this occasion. As to (a), see what is said on the whole question of numbers in the Introduction. As to (b), it must be borne in mind that no direction whatever had been given, as far as we know, either that the lambs must be slain by the priests only, or that their blood must be poured upon the altar. If the Jews were left to follow the original institution as nearly as possible, they would have killed the lambs themselves, and sprinkled the blood around the doors of their tents. It is true that according to the Levitical ritual, now recently put into use, all other animals slain in sacrifice (or indeed for food) must be slain at the tabernacle by the priest, and the blood sprinkled on the altar ; and it is true that this general rule was afterwards held especially binding in the case of the passover. But there is nothing to show that it was held binding then : the passover had been ordained before the establishment of the Levitical priesthood and law of sacrifice ; and it might very well have been considered that it retained its primal character unaffected by subsequent legislation, and that the priesthood of the people (in other rites transferred to Aaron and his sons) was recalled and revived in the case of this special rite. If this was the case both at this passover and at that under Joshua, it is easy enough to understand why the later practice was so entirely different ; the neglect or disuse of centuries obliterated the tradition of the passover, and when it was revived by the later kings, they naturally followed the analogy of all other sacrifices, and the apparently express command of Levit. xvii. 3—6. They could not indeed obey this command in their daily life, but they could and did obey it in the striking and typical case of the paschal feast.

Ver. 6.—**There were certain men.** It has been supposed by many that these men must have been Mishael and Elizaphan, who had recently (cf. Exod. xl. 17 ; Levit. ix. 1 ; x. 4) been defiled by burying their cousins Nadab and Abihu. This, however, is based upon the assumption that the totals given in Exod. xxxviii. 26 and in ch. i. 46 are really independent, and that therefore no one belonging to any other tribe than that of Levi had died in the interval. As that assumption is untenable (see above on ch. i. 46), so this "coincidence" falls to the ground. We know indeed that Mishael and Elizaphan were defiled at this time, and we do not know that any one else was ; but, on the other hand, the words "the dead body of a man" seem to point to a single corpse only. **Dead body.** Hebrew, *nephesh*, as in ch. v. 2 ; vi. 11, and other places. It is inexplicable how this word, which properly means "soul," should have come to be used of a corpse ; perhaps it is an additional testimony to the complete absence from Jewish teaching of any doctrine of an immortal spirit. The Septuagint uses ψύχη here.

Ver. 7.—**Wherefore are we kept back?** The direction to remove from the camp all that were defiled by the dead (ch., v. 2) had not apparently been given at this time, nor was there any express command that such should not partake of the passover, for Levit. vii. 20 may probably refer only to such uncleannesses as are mentioned in Levit. xv. 3; but that men were in fact considered as defiled by contact with the dead is clear from Levit. xxi. 1. The men, therefore, had reason for asking why they were excommunicated, and Moses for referring the matter to the Divine decision.

Ver. 10.—**If any man of you or of your posterity.** The particular case of these men is made the occasion for a general provision for all succeeding times. **Shall be unclean by reason of a dead body, or be in a journey.** It is somewhat strange that these two cases only were provided for: a man otherwise unclean (as, *e. g.*, in the case described Levit. xv. 13), even if actually recovered, was unable to take advantage of the little passover. Probably the real reason of it is to be found in this, that both the far journey and the burial of the dead would presumably be works of charity. **Afar off.** This word, רְחֹקָה, is one of ten in the Pentateuch distinguished in the Hebrew Bibles with *puncta extraordinaria*, for some unknown and probably trifling reasons. The Rabbins ruled that it meant a distance of fifteen miles or more from the temple at sunrise of the fourteenth of Abib.

Ver. 11. — **The fourteenth day of the second month.** The interval gave ample time to return from any ordinary journey, or to be purified from pollution of death. It was in the spirit of this command, though not in the letter of it, that Hezekiah acted (2 Chron. xxx. 2). And possibly it was in the spirit of this command that our Lord acted when he ate the passover by anticipation with his disciples twenty-four hours before the proper

time—at which time he was himself to be the Lamb slain. **With unleavened bread and bitter herbs.** These and the following directions are expressly added for fear lest any should think that the little passover might be celebrated with less solemnity and with less carefulness than the great passover.

Ver. 12.—**According to all the ordinances of the passover.** The later Jews held that this passover need only be kept for one day, and that leaven need not be put away from the house. But this was a clear departure from the original rule, for it was evidently intended that it should be in all respects a true passover, and in this case six clear days were allowed for the keeping of it (see on ch. x. 11).

Ver. 13.—**But the man that is clean, and is not in a journey.** This threat was added no doubt in order to prevent men from taking advantage of the permission to keep a supplemental passover in order to suit their own convenience or interest. Only two reasons could absolve a man from the absolute necessity of keeping the passover at the due season, and these reasons must be *bonâ fide*, and not pretended. **Because he brought not the offering of the Lord.** In the original institution the paschal lamb did not appear distinctly in the character of an offering made to God, although undoubtedly it was such. It was rather the eating of the lamb that was insisted upon, as placing the partaker in communion with the God and Church of Israel, and so in a state of salvation. But after the law of sacrifices had been elaborated, then the paschal lamb, though prior to them all, naturally took its place amongst them as the greatest of them all, and as uniting in itself the special beauties of all.

Ver. 14.—**Ye shall have one ordinance.** This is repeated from Exod. xii. 49 as a further warning not to tamper more than absolute necessity required with the unity, either in time or in circumstance, of the great national rite.

HOMILETICS.

Vers. 1—14.—*The paschal feast.* In the keeping of the passover we have, under the law, what the celebrating of the sacrament of the Lord's Supper is under the gospel; for it was the nature and use of *that* to show the Lord's death until he came the first time, as of *this* to show the Lord's death until he come the second time. Consider, therefore—

I. That it was the will of God, specially declared, that all Israel should be partakers thereof ere they left the holy mount of consecration and plunged into the desert of wanderings. Even so it is the will of God that all his people, when they have been taught of him, should be partakers of "that one bread," and thereby be brought into closer union with one another and with him for the journey of life (John vi. 56; Acts ii. 42; 1 Cor. x. 17).

II. That the Israelites kept that passover under difficulties, little dreaming that it was to be their last; for only Caleb and Joshua survived to take part in the next.   How often have faithful people made special effort to join in keeping the Christian passover, and it has proved to be their last! (Luke xxii. 15; 1 Cor. v. 7).

III. THAT THE PASSOVER WAS KEPT "ACCORDING TO ALL THE RITES OF IT," AND YET THERE WERE SOME RITES AND CEREMONIES WHICH MUST OF NECESSITY HAVE BEEN ALTERED; but this did not mar the Divinely-ordered uniformity.   Even so there be things in the Christian passover which have been altered, yet if the alteration have not been wilfully nor needlessly made, it leaves the religious identity of the rite untouched.

IV. THAT THE PASSOVER WAS EATEN IN THE WILDERNESS, AS IN EGYPT BEFORE, AND IN CANAAN AFTERWARDS (Josh. v. 10), ON THE EVE OF GREAT JOURNEYS AND BATTLES. Even so is the Christian made partaker of heavenly food that he may be stronger and braver for the journey and the conflict of life (cf. 1 Kings xix. 7).

V. THAT ONE DEFILED BY THE DEAD COULD NOT JOIN IN THE PASSOVER.   So he that hath suffered in soul by contact with the spiritually dead cannot be partaker of the Lord's Table until he be recovered from that contagion (cf. 1 Cor. x. 21; xi. 27—30).

VI. THAT THE UNCLEAN, AND THEY THAT WERE AFAR OFF, WERE NEVERTHELESS ADMITTED TO THE FELLOWSHIP OF THE PASSOVER AS SOON AS THEY WERE CLEANSED AND RETURNED.   Even so none need be banished from the communion of the body of Christ because he is unclean, for time is given him to be cleansed; nor because he is afar off, for time is given him to return (Mark i. 41; Luke xv. 20; James iv. 8); only the cleansing and the returning must be in due time, and not too late (Matt. xxv. 10 b.; Luke xiii. 25; 2 Cor. vi. 2).

VII. THAT TWO REASONS ONLY, AND THEY OF UNAVOIDABLE NECESSITY, WOULD ABSOLVE ANY ONE FROM THE DUTY OF KEEPING THE PASSOVER WITH ALL THE PEOPLE. Even so no light excuses, but only (1) compulsory absence or (2) unworthiness to approach, will avail any one who wilfully neglects the invitation of Christ to his feast (Luke xiv. 24; xxii. 19 b.; 1 Cor. xi. 25 b.).

VIII. THAT IT WAS AGAIN AND AGAIN DECLARED THAT THERE SHOULD BE "ONE ORDINANCE" ONLY FOR ALL FROM ALL QUARTERS AS CONCERNED THE PASSOVER, for it was the ordinance of unity.   Even so the sacrament of the Lord's Supper is above all things the sacrament of unity (1 Cor. x. 17), and therefore the manner of it is especially declared (1 Cor. xi. 23, and the three Gospels).

HOMILIES BY VARIOUS AUTHORS.

Vers. 6—14.—*A communicant in Israel, disabled by some mischance from eating the passover on the right day, may eat it a month after.*   The law here laid down is supplementary to the law of the passover set forth at large in Exod. xii.   The supplement, beside being of some interest in itself, is specially important on account of certain general principles relative to God's worship which come into view in it.

I. THE OCCASION WHICH LED TO THIS SUPPLEMENTARY DIRECTION.   From Exod. xii. 25 and xiii. 5 it may be inferred that the passover was not intended to be statedly observed till the tribes should have received their inheritance in Canaan; and the inference is confirmed by the circumstance that there seems to have been no celebration of the passover during the thirty-eight years between the departure from Sinai and the crossing of the Jordan.   For reasons not difficult to understand, the first anniversary of the night of deliverance, since it found the people still encamped at Sinai, was commanded to be observed.   Hence the charge vers. 1—5.   This, since it was, in some sense, the first of all the regular passovers, was ordained to be kept with great solemnity.   All the greater was the chagrin felt by certain men of Israel who, on account of a mischance which had befallen them, were disabled from taking part in the general solemnity.   A relative or neighbour had died on the eve of the feast.   They had not shirked the duty of laying out and burying the dead.   Thus they were ceremonially unclean, and might not eat the passover.   It seemed hard to be debarred from the joyous rite, especially since no blame attached to themselves in the matter.   Was there no remedy?   They brought the matter before Moses and Aaron; Moses brought it before the Lord, with the result to be presently described.

II. THE LAW FOR THOSE DISABLED IN PROVIDENCE FROM EATING THE PASSOVER IN THE

APPOINTED SEASON (vers. 10, 11).   1. The person disabled by uncleanness at the full moon of the first month might keep the feast at the full moon of the second.   This was not a perfect remedy.   The passover was a national solemnity.   It was a witness to the religious unity of the tribes.   It was designed at once to express and to foster the communion of the whole people in the faith and worship of the God of Abraham. These very attractive aspects of the ordinance failed to come into view when the passover was observed only by a few individuals, and on another than the appointed day.   However, there were other and more private aspects of the ordinance to which this did not apply, so that the permission to keep the passover in the second month was a valuable concession.   2. The concession was extended not only to persons defiled by the dead, but to all who might be defiled from any cause beyond their own control.   For example, if a man happened unavoidably to be on a distant journey on the fourteenth day of the first month, he might keep the passover at the next full moon.   3. The concession was expressly extended to the foreigner as well as to the born Israelite. It ought never to be forgotten that, although the passover was so emphatically a national feast, provision was carefully made, from the first, for the admission of foreigners to it (Exod. xii. 48, 49).   Let the foreigner accept circumcision, " he and all his," and he is entitled to sit down at the paschal table, as a communicant in the Hebrew Church, just as if he had been born in the land.   The Old Testament Church was not a missionary Church.   It was not enjoined to preach to the Gentiles and compel them to come in.   But if a Gentile desired to come in, he was to be made welcome. The law before us, besides presupposing the right of the proselyte to be admitted, emphatically declares the parity of right which was to be accorded him on his admission.   4. Care was to be taken not to abuse the concession.   Liberty is one thing ; license is another and very different thing ; yet history and daily experience bear witness that the two are apt to be confounded.   Many, when they hear liberty proclaimed, think that license is to reign.   See how carefully this is guarded against in the present instance.   In two ways :—(1) Wilful neglect to observe the passover in its appointed season was still to be deemed presumptuous sin (ver. 13)—a warning which the habitual neglecters of the Lord's Supper would do well to lay to heart. We, as evangelical Protestants, believe that participation in the Lord's Supper is not the indispensable means of communion in the body and blood of the Lord ; nevertheless, we hold that no man can habitually withdraw himself from the Lord's Supper without sin and loss.   (2) The supplementary passover was not, because supplementary, to be a passover of maimed rites (vers. 11, 12).   It was to be observed with all the rites ordained for the great festival of the first month.   With this law compare the history of Hezekiah's passover in 2 Chron. xxx.

III. THE PRINCIPLE WHICH LIES AT THE ROOT OF THIS LAW is this, namely, that rigid exactness in points of external order ought to be waived when adherence to it would hinder the edification of souls.   The same principle was laid down by our Lord in reference to the observance of the day of rest when he said, " The sabbath was made for man, and not man for the sabbath."   The principle must, of course, be used with discretion.   It was dutiful and expedient that the passover should be observed, not by every man when he pleased, but on the anniversary of the exodus, and by the whole congregation at once.   Nevertheless, this good rule was not to defraud of the passover those disabled from keeping it on the right day.   If this principle was so carefully recognised under the comparatively servile dispensation, much more ought it to prevail under the dispensation of evangelical liberty.   Points of external order are not to be despised, especially when they are such as have express warrant of Holy Scripture.   The wilful contempt of them may amount to presumptuous sin. Nevertheless, the edification of souls must ever be treated as the paramount consideration to which all else must yield.—B.

Vers. 1—14.—*The letter and the spirit of the law of the passover*.   We learn from this narrative certain lessons which may illustrate the relation of the letter to the spirit of Divine precepts on other subjects beside the passover.

I. THE LETTER OF THE LAW WAS STRINGENT.   The observance of the feast was binding, even under inconvenient circumstances (ver. 5), at fixed times (ver. 3), and with prescribed rites (ver. 3).   No trifling allowed (ver. 13).   Neglect of any one law may be fatal (James ii. 10). Yet this stringent law could be modified. It was flexible, because God was a paternal King, and not a despotic martinet. But God, alone could modify the law (ver. 8), or condone for its literal non-observance (*e. g.* 2 Chron. xxx. 15—20). Provision was made for disabilities arising from (1) uncleanness, contracted unavoidably, or in the path of duty (cf. Ps. ciii. 14); or (2) absence from home, for such journeys were not prohibited because the passover was near. To meet such cases—

II. THE SPIRIT OF THE LAW WAS BENEFICENT. Neglect was not sanctioned; *it never is.* Great care needed lest, while claiming liberty to set aside the letter of the law in favour of the spirit, we neglect the spirit also (apply, *e. g.*, to the sanctification of the Lord's day). But God provided a substitute for the literal observance (vers. 9—12).

Learn—1. The laws of Christ are not "grievous," but may not be trifled with. A difficulty in the way of observing some law may arise from *circumstances,* or *character.* Illustrate, the Lord's Supper. In the early history of some of the Polynesian missions, where no bread or "fruit of the vine" was to be had, the service was not neglected on account of these circumstances, but bread fruit and water, or other beverage, was used. If the hindrance to our observance should arise from any "uncleanness," we need not wait for a lengthened process of purification, but may apply to our cleansing High Priest at once (John xiii. 1—10). 2. Precepts that are called "positive" must not be neglected because moral precepts are observed. Illustrate from Matt. v. 23, 24 (cf. Matt. xxiii. 23; Deut. iv. 2; Ps. cxix. 128). Christ having redeemed us unto God by his blood, his law extends to every department of our life.—P.

Ver. 14.—*The beneficent aspect of the law of Moses towards foreigners.* Judaism, according to the "law given by Moses," was not the exclusive and repulsive system that many have imagined. The gate into Judaism, through circumcision, &c., may seem strait to us; but a thorough separation from the corrupt heathen world was a necessity and a blessing, just as the utter renunciation of Hinduism by breaking caste is now. Laws relating to strangers occupy no inconsiderable place in the legislation of Moses. These laws have a most beneficent aspect, which may suggest lessons regarding our duties as Christians towards aliens, whether of blood or creed. We find precepts recognising for the strangers—

I. EQUALITY BEFORE THE LAW. This is taught in our text and in several other passages (Exod. xii. 49; Levit. xxiv. 22; Numb. xv. 15, 16, 29). This is especially noticeable in regard to the laws of the sabbath (Exod. xx. 10; xxiii. 12; Deut. v. 14), and of the cities of refuge (Numb. xxxv. 15). Hence the Israelites were repeatedly warned against oppressing the stranger (Exod. xxii. 21; xxiii. 9), though he might be a hired servant, at the mercy of his employer (Deut. xxiv. 14, 15), or an Egyptian (Deut. xxiii. 7). In administering these laws strict impartiality is demanded of the judges (Deut. i. 16; xxiv. 17). Such equality is recognised under the laws of Christian England, but needs to be most carefully guarded. *E. g.* in our treatment of coolies or other coloured people in our colonies, foreign sailors in our ports, &c. Oppression of strangers one great crime before the fall of the Jewish monarchy (Ezek. xxii. 7, 29). Ill-treatment of non-Christian races outside its borders one of England's national crimes (Chinese opium traffic; some of our colonial wars, &c.).

II. A CLAIM ON BENEVOLENCE. Strangers were not only guarded from oppression, but commended to the love of the Israelites. See precepts in Levit. xix. 33, 34; Deut. x. 18, 19; Levit. xxv. 35, blossoming into the beautiful flower, "Thou shalt love *thy neighbour* as thyself," which our Lord plucks from its hiding-place in Leviticus and exhibits and enforces on the whole world. Hence follow the precepts requiring that gleanings be left for the strangers (Levit. xix. 10; xxiii. 22), and that they should be allowed to share "in every good thing" God bestowed on Israel (Deut. xiv. 29; xvi. 11, 14; xxvi. 11). God be praised for all the philanthropic agencies of England on behalf of foreigners. Let us see that our personal benefience is not limited by race or creed (Isa. lviii. 6—11, &c.).

III. INVITATIONS TO NATIONAL AND PERSONAL BLESSINGS. Gentiles were welcomed to all privileges of Judaism through conformity to its laws. They could enter into the covenant (Deut. xxix. 10—13), offer sacrifices (Levit. xxii. 18), and keep the passover (Exod. xii. 43—49 ; Numb. ix. 14). And it was required that they be instructed in the law of God (Deut. xxxi. 10—13, read in the light of Josh. viii. 33—35). Having all these privileges, they were liable to the same punishments as the Israelites (Levit. xvii. 8, 12, 15 ; xxiv. 16, &c.). We need not wonder that the adhesion and conversion of strangers was anticipated (1 Kings viii. 41—43 ; Isa. lvi. 3, &c.). Apply to the missionary work of the Church, which can speak to strangers of "a better covenant," "Christ our passover," "grace and truth by Jesus Christ."—P.

Vers. 1—5.—*A needed reminder.* When Jehovah ordered Moses to prepare the Israelites against the visit in which he smote the firstborn, he also said the day was to be kept as a feast through all their generations by an ordinance for ever. And now it was nearly twelve months since the great deliverance by which in haste and pressure Israel departed out of Egypt. The instructions (Exod. xii.) are plain enough; but God deemed it needful, as the anniversary time drew near, to give his people a special reminder. *Why was it needed?* 1. *Because much had happened in the interval.* At the time, many of the Israelites would say, "Surely we shall never forget this wonderful and terrible night!" But since then there had been the crossing of the Red Sea, and all the impressive dealings of God with his people at Sinai. One event retreats as another comes on. Men march forward into the future, and great events are soon lost to view, even as great mountains are upon a journey. 2. *Because the trials of the wilderness made many long for the comforts of Egypt.* They soon forgot the hardships of bondage. Less than two months was enough to make them wish they had died in Egypt, by the flesh-pots, where they had bread to the full (Exod. xvi.). What then of forgetting might not happen in twelve months ? Thus, by all the details of the memorial celebration, God would have them bring back to mind distinctly the extraordinary mercy of that night in which they left Egypt. 3. *Because an emphatic reminder helped to distinguish the passover from other great events.* The smiting of the firstborn was the decisive blow to Pharaoh. It liberated the Israelites from their thraldom. All previous chastisements led up to it, and the wonders of the Red Sea were the inevitable sequence. Above all, there was the great typical import of the passover. Christ our passover is slain for us (1 Cor. v. 7). What the passover was to the Israelites, the atoning death of Jesus is to us, an event which there is a solemn obligation on us to recollect and commemorate in a peculiar way. 4. *Because there was need of preparation and care in the celebration.* It was on the fourteenth day of the month at even that it was to be kept. It was in the first month of the second year that the Lord spoke to Moses. Hence we may suppose that he saw no signs of preparation, nothing to indicate that the people were being stirred by the thought of the glorious deliverance. This admonition of the Lord to Moses may be applied to such as, admitting the permanent obligation of the Lord's Supper, yet are negligent and irregular in practising the obligation. If the passover and the sprinkled blood of the lamb demanded a yearly memorial from Israel, even more does the sprinkled blood of Christ demand a regular commemoration. He seems to have provided for our naturally forgetful ways in saying, "Do this in remembrance of me."—Y.

Vers. 6—13.—*A difficulty removed.* I. THE DIFFICULTY STATED. Certain men, ceremonially unclean, could not partake of the passover (ch. v. 1—4). One ceremonial observance, therefore, might clash with another. No one could with certainty be clean at the passover time. Hence we see how all ceremonial is purely subordinate to higher considerations. If one ceremonial obligation could interfere with another, how clear that the claims of justice, mercy, and necessity, rise above ceremony altogether (Matt. xii. 1—8; xv. 1—6). The very existence of such a difficulty showed that rites and ceremonies were only for a time. The distinction of clean and unclean is gone now. There is no more uncleanness in the leper, in the mother with her new-born offspring, in the attendant on the dead. We have to guard against a deeper than ceremonial uncleanness. "Let a man examine himself, and so let him eat of that bread and drink of that cup" (Matt. xv. 18—20; 1 Cor. xi. 28; 2 Cor. vii. 1).

II. How THE DIFFICULTY WAS REMOVED. Moses is consulted, and he *consults God*. The example of Moses in this matter needs our study and imitation. God will leave none of his servants in doubt if they only truly seek to him, and lean not to their own understanding. In God's answer notice—1. *His appreciation of the difficulty.* Ceremonial uncleanness was a very serious thing, as being the type of the unclean heart. To keep these men back from the passover was not the act of ecclesiastical martinets, God himself being witness. 2. *The duty that cannot be done to-day may be done to-morrow.* We should take care that what has to be deferred is only deferred. Just because the passover was too sacred to be touched by unclean hands, it was too sacred to be passed over altogether. 3. *The removal of one difficulty gives an opportunity for removing another.* Ceremonial observances were regulated with regard to the claims of ordinary life. " If a man be in a journey afar off." He did not say that every man was bound to be home that day, at whatever cost. God makes allowance for the urgency of a man's private affairs. 4. *God's consideration for these real difficulties made the observance all the more important where such difficulties did not exist.* God listens to reasons ; he will see them, even when they are not expressed ; but mere excuses, in which men's lips are so fruitful, he cannot tolerate. If we are prevented from joining the assembly for worship, or approaching the Lord's table, let us be quite sure that our reason is sound, based in conscience and not in self-will, not a mere pretext for indolence and unspirituality. Where the heart is right towards God, and an obedient spirit towards all his commandments, he will take every difficulty away.—Y.

EXPOSITION.

THE SIGNALS OF GOD (vers. 15—23). Ver. 15.—**On the day that the tabernacle was reared up.** Here we are sent back again to *the* great day of Israel's sojourn at Sinai, when God took visible possession of his dwelling in the midst of them (Exod. xl. 34). Everything after that was but preparatory to the approaching departure, and therefore is narrated not in any order of time, but either as it referred back to the first day of the first month, or forward to the twentieth day of the second month. **The cloud covered the tabernacle, namely, the tent of the testimony**. The testimony was the decalogue written on the two tables of stone, and enshrined within the ark, the moral law which lay at the heart of Judaism. The tent of the testimony was the holy of holies in which the ark dwelt (see on ch. x. 11 ; xviii. 2). The exact meaning of the words מִשְׁכָּן לְאֹהֶל הָעֵדֻת is disputed, or rather the significance of the לְ with which the phrase "tent of the testimony" is appended to the word "tabernacle" (dwelling). Some take it as equivalent in construction to the genitive, "the dwelling of the tent of the testimony ;" in which case it would simply mean that the cloud covered the whole tabernacle, the *mishcan* which enveloped and enclosed the *ohel*, which again enshrined the ark and the testimony. Others take לְ here in the sense of "at" or "towards," and read, " covered the dwelling, towards the tent of the testimony," *i. e.* over that part of it in which the testimony was

kept. Apart from the strict grammatical question, the comparison of other passages cited (especially Exod. xl. 34) seems in favour of the first interpretation, and so apparently the Septuagint and the Targums.

Ver. 16.—**So it was alway.** This supernatural phenomenon was not transitory, like the glory-cloud *within* the tabernacle (Exod. xl. 35 ; cf. 1 Kings viii. 10), but permanent, as long at least as the Israelites were in the wilderness.

Ver. 17.—**When the cloud was taken up.** This verse and the following to the end of the chapter are an amplification of Exod. xl. 36—38 (cf. Exod. xiii. 21, 22 ; Neh. ix. 12 ; Ps. lxxviii. 14). It would appear from Exod. xiii. 21 that there was nothing new in the fact of the cloudy fiery pillar directing the movements of the host, but only in the fact of its resting on the tabernacle when in repose. **In the place where the cloud abode**, or "came down." שָׁכַן. As the tabernacle was taken all to pieces, and its portions widely separated on the march, the cloud could not rest upon it as a signal for halting. We must probably picture to ourselves the cloud rising to some considerable height when it was "taken up," so as to be visible for a great distance, and as settling down again over the spot where the tabernacle was to be set up. In this way the signals given by the cloud would be immediately perceived by a vast multitude.

Ver. 19.—**Tarried long.** Hebrew, אָרַךְ, " to prolong," *i. e.* the resting. The Septuagint has ἐφέλκηται .. ἡμέρας πλείους.

Ver. 20.—**And so it was**. Rather, "did it happen that." אֲשֶׁר וַיֵּשׁ, hypothetical clause introducing several other cases which actually occurred, and by which their perfect obedience was proved.

Ver. 21.—**From even unto the morning**. Allowing but a single night's rest.

Ver. 22.—**Or a year**. Rather, "days" (*yamin*): an undefined period (Gen. iv. 3; xl. 4), often equivalent to a year (Levit. xxv. 29). It is not known whether or on what occasion the Israelites actually remained in camp for a year. But it is evident that this passage must have been written after the wanderings were over, because it is a kind of retrospect of the whole period as regards one important feature of it. It may of course have been added here by the hand of Moses on the eve of entry upon the promised land: or it may have been added by a later hand, perhaps that of Ezra when he revised these books (see the Introduction).

HOMILETICS.

Vers. 15—23.—*Divine guidance*. In this section we have, spiritually, the Divine guidance of the faithful through the wilderness of this life. Consider, therefore—

I. THAT THE THEOPHANY, OR DIVINE APPEARANCE UPON THE TABERNACLE, WAS AS A CLOUD BY DAY AND AS FIRE BY NIGHT. Even so is the Lord unto his people both shelter and illumination,—shade that they faint not, light that they wander not astray (Ps. xxvii. 1; xxxvi. 9; cxxi. 5; Isa. xxv. 4; Matt. xi. 29; John viii. 12).

II. THAT THE CLOUD WAS UPON THE TABERNACLE OF WITNESS, WITHOUT, AND YET IN A MANNER CONNECTED WITH THE "TESTIMONY" ENGRAVEN UPON THE TABLES OF STONE. Even so the comfort and illumination of the faithful, albeit not of themselves but of God, are yet vitally connected with the law of holiness which is enshrined in their hearts (John xiv. 15, 23; Heb. xii. 14).

III. THAT THIS THEOPHANY WAS THE INFALLIBLE GUIDE TO THEIR MOVEMENTS, WHETHER TO REST OR TO ADVANCE. Even so the Lord himself, even God made manifest in Christ, is our only guide along the way to heaven (Ps. xlviii. 14; Luke i. 79; John xxi. 22 *b.*; 1 Thess. iii. 11).

IV. THAT THE BEHAVIOUR OF THE CLOUD WAS APPARENTLY ARBITRARY, SOMETIMES LINGERING LONG AS THOUGH IT HAD FORGOTTEN HOW TO MOVE, SOMETIMES HASTENING ON WITHOUT REST. Even so the Divine guidance, whether of the Church or of the individual, is often unintelligible and sometimes apparently perverse: how unequal are the advances of the Church, or of the soul, towards perfection (John xiii. 7): what need of (1) patience, and (2) preparedness (Luke ix. 59, *sq.*; xii. 36; xxi. 19; Eph. vi. 15; Rev. xiii. 10 *b.*).

V. THAT THE PEOPLE WERE STRICTLY OBEDIENT IN THIS, THAT THEY JOURNEYED NOT EXCEPT BY THE DIRECTION OF THE CLOUD, BECAUSE THEY FEARED TO BE WITHOUT IT. Even so the faithful will follow him that leadeth them as obediently as they can, because away from him and his guidance they would neither be able to endure, nor to progress (John vi. 68; x. 4; xiii. 37; xiv. 6).

VI. THAT WHEN ONCE, AND ONLY ONCE, THEY PRESUMED TO GO ON WHEN THE CLOUD BID THEM NOT, THEY MET DISASTROUS DEFEAT (ch. xiv. 44, 45). Even so if any will presume to go beyond the command and permission of his Lord (even in zeal) he will be overthrown of Satan (cf. Luke xxii. 55 *b. sq.*; 1 Cor. vii. 5 *b.*).

HOMILIES BY VARIOUS AUTHORS.

Vers. 15—23.—*The guiding pillar of cloud and flame*. This pillar served more purposes than one; but without doubt the purpose noted here by Moses himself was that principally intended. It was the signal by which the Lord guided the march of the tribes (Neh. ix. 12, 19; Ps. lxxviii. 14). Some such signal was absolutely necessary. To direct the march of a nation through the wilderness was no easy matter. When Alexander the Great led his army across the wide levels of Babylonia he caused a grating filled with a blazing fire to be borne aloft on a long pole, that its smoke might guide the march by day, and its fire by night. A similar device is constantly made use of by the caravans which make the pilgrimage to Mecca. The march of the tribes from Egypt had the Lord himself for its Guide, and the cloud of his presence showed the way. No feature of the long march has more deeply impressed itself on the imagination of the Church than this guiding pillar. It has been instinctively accepted as a sign in which we too may claim an interest. For are not we also, as truly as the Church in the wilderness, making the journey from the land of bondage to the promised rest? Is not our life a wilderness journey; a march along a path we never trod before? The forty years' wanderings being thus a parable of our life on earth, may we not warrantably see in the pillar of the cloud a token of certain happy conditions of the journey which it is the business of faith to apprehend?

I. Observe that the children of Israel had THEIR ROUTE DETERMINED FOR THEM. It was the hand of God which chalked out the strangely circuitous line of their march; which measured the several stages; which fixed upon the halting-places; and determined the length of the stay at each. "At the commandment of the Lord they rested, and at the commandment of the Lord they journeyed." No doubt there still remained large scope for the exercise of judgment on the part of leaders so familiar with the desert as Moses and Hobab. There were a thousand details to care for. But the general fact remains, and is noted with extreme care in the history, that—so far as regards the line of march and the successive stages—the ordering of the journey from first to last was by the Lord. It would not be difficult to prove that our route also is determined for us. God has determined our appointed times, and the bounds of our habitation (Acts xvii. 26). The mapping out of our lives is his doing. This, I say, is capable of proof. Yet I should imagine that, to such as have been reasonably careful to observe their own course, no formal array of evidence will be needed. They know how often their own plans and those of friends have been upset, and the whole circumstances of their lives arranged quite otherwise than they ever contemplated, and yet with a most wise and considerate regard for their good. What then? (1) Do not forget to give God the glory. Acknowledge his overruling hand (Ps. cvii. 43). Many forget to do this; and accordingly they learn nothing of his mind, even when his providence speaks most plainly. A thing dishonouring to God and entailing great loss to them. (2) Thankfully commit your way to him for the time to come.

II. The Lord not only determined the route of the tribes but gave them A VISIBLE SIGN of his guidance. Here, it may be supposed, the parallel fails, and we must resign ourselves to a more uncertain and precarious guidance than the tribes enjoyed. But it is not so. For the guiding pillar in the wilderness was meant for the comfort of the Church in all times. Remember the principle laid down by the apostle in 1 Cor. x. 11. The moving cloud was an "ensample" or type which did not cease to speak when it disappeared from view as the tribes entered the land. To faith it continues still to attest the Lord's presence and guiding wisdom. The Divine guidance was not more patent in the desert to the *sight* of the tribes than it is this day to the *faith* of the Church. "Thy rod and thy staff they comfort me." *Patent to faith!* That saying lays bare the difficulty of which we complain. A visible guide—every one can appreciate that. An invisible guide, discerned only by the mind, or rather by faith alone—that is too shadowy, intangible, precarious. So men are apt to judge. But without reason. Arduous our faith certainly is. But precarious, barren, impotent to sustain and comfort, it certainly is not. God's presence visible to the eye availed to guide and cheer the tribes in the wilderness; but God's presence seen by faith has availed much more to guide and cheer the Church of Christ these nineteen centuries. To walk by faith is the achievement of the Church's maturity. To walk by sight belonged to the Church's childhood. And we can trace all through the Scripture a gradual weaning of the Church from the one, and a gradual training of it to the other. In the wilderness the Church's weakness was comforted with the pillar of cloud and fire towering high in the sight of the whole camp: during the time of the first temple the cloud was seen only within the holy place: during the period of the second temple it was quite withdrawn. Yet Ezra and his company made the journey as safely as Moses and the tribes; and the glory of the latter house was greater than of the former. "He hath said, I will never leave thee; so that we may boldly say, I will not fear."—B.

Ver. 23.—*God's ceaseless providence a motive to prompt obedience.* God's presence with Israel was perpetual (Exod. iii. 12; xiii. 17—18). The sign of it in the cloud was given as soon, and was continued as long, as it was needed (Exod. xiii. 21, 22; xl. 38). God's active, providential presence was—I. A SOURCE OF SAFETY; II. A GROUND OF FAITH; and therefore, III. A MOTIVE TO OBEDIENCE.

I. The cloud (1) led them the safest way (Exod. xiii. 17). (2) Ensured protection from foes when near at hand (Exod. xiv. 19, 20, 24). (3) Gave light on the camp in moonless nights (Neh. ix. 19). (4) Was a pledge of safety to sinners, as it rested on the mercy-seat (Levit. xvi. 2). This visible cloud a symbol of protection by an invisible God (Isa. iv. 5). Illustrations, *bird* and young (Ruth ii. 12; Ps. xvii. 8; xci. 4). *Father* carrying his child by day (Deut. i. 31), and watching by him at night (Ps. cxxi). There is safety for sinners not away from God but in God (Ps. cxliii. 2, 9).

II. God showed himself in the cloud for the very purpose of guiding. He took the responsibility out of the hands of the people and Moses that they might have the privilege of trusting (Exod. xxxiii. 9—17; Deut. i. 33). Such a guiding presence we may enjoy by the aid of God's *written counsels, providential acts, and inward monitions* (Ps. xxv. 4, 5, 9, 14). See how these three are combined in the narrative (Acts viii. 26—35).

III. Ver. 23 is very emphatic. They obeyed even if at times the journey was very arduous (Numb. xxi. 4), or the halt very tedious (ver. 22), or the start was sudden, as when a midnight alarm of the trumpets was a sign that the cloud had begun to move (ver. 21). Hence we learn (1) not to take for granted that any place is our rest (Job xxix. 18; Micah ii. 10). (2) To be willing to go to the wilderness with God, rather than to stay in the choicest paradise without God. (3) To be willing to endure, at God's bidding, protracted toil or enforced inactivity. (4) To be ready at any time to strike our tent and go home. Thus waiting on God and waiting for God, we are safely led, and have the rest of trustful obedience (Ps. v. 11, 12; xlviii. 14; lxxxiv. 11, 12).—P.

Vers. 15—23.—*The cloud upon the tabernacle.* There is a fuller account of the rearing of the tabernacle and the descent of the cloud upon it in Exod. xl. Note—

I. THE CONNECTION OF THIS CLOUD WITH PAST EXPERIENCES. It is spoken of as "the cloud"—something, therefore, already known. It was known as associated with the glorious doings of Jehovah in the midst of the people. A remembrancer of the perilous march, with the Red Sea before and the Egyptians behind, when he who made his presence known by the pillar of cloud so gloriously delivered his people and overwhelmed their enemies (Exod. xiv. 19). A remembrancer of the provided manna, when, after God had promised it, the people looked toward the wilderness, and behold, the glory of the Lord appeared in the cloud (Exod. xvi. 10). A remembrancer, again, of the solemn waiting upon Jehovah's will at Sinai (Exod. xix. 9; xxiv. 15—18). Compare with these experiences under the law the great and abiding experience under the gospel. "The Word was made flesh, and dwelt among us (and we beheld his glory, the glory as of the only begotten of the Father) full of grace and truth" (John i. 14). He who afterwards tabernacled in the flesh, made his glory to rest on the tabernacle in the wilderness. When Jesus came, God showed his favour resting not only on the Israelites, but on all mankind.

II. THE CONNECTION OF THIS CLOUD WITH OBEYED COMMANDMENTS. The cloud that had hitherto rested on Sinai now came down on the tabernacle. This showed Jehovah's approval of the tabernacle. All had been fashioned according to the pattern in the mount. The tabernacle and the holy place, themselves made of perishable materials, were nevertheless typically perfect. They were not inspired by the invention of men, but by the revelation of God. God will give indubitable signs of approval when we are doing things according to his will. This tabernacle and its contents were the types of the truths, duties, and privileges of the gospel, and only as we receive the truths, practise the duties, and employ the privileges, shall we have the glory of God resting upon us. Until that time we come short of the glory of God. We may talk as we like about the glorious achievements of human thought, making our little clouds and fires about the earth, and calling them immortal and imperishable, but God will approve no man until his life is ordered in all things by the requirements of the gospel.

III. THE CLOUD SO APPEARING WAS A PROOF OF GOD'S FAVOUR, VISIBLE TO ALL AND APPRECIABLE BY THEM. All Israel could see the tabernacle and the cloud. God had told his people they were not to make any graven image, or likeness of any created thing, but they found the first and second commandments very hard to obey. They hankered after something they could see. The idolatries of Egypt had infected them, and even within sight of Sinai they made a golden calf, for which gross transgression the Lord terribly plagued them. Nevertheless, though there is no material or shape on earth fit to indicate Jehovah, he will minister to human weakness, remembering that we are dust, and he gives the glory-cloud for all to see. What a help to faith! What a warning to unbelief! What mercy amid severity! So God, whom no man hath seen or can see, becomes God manifest in the flesh. He who has seen the Son has seen the Father.

IV. THE CLOUD SO APPEARING, VARIED IN ITS APPEARANCE, ACCORDING TO HUMAN NECESSITY. There was a cloud by day, and the appearance of fire by night. We need not suppose any change in the cloud itself as day slipt into night, and night back again into day. As darkness fell upon the scene the fiery element in the cloud became more noticeable and valuable. So there is encouragement for wandering and bewildered souls. The darker life becomes, and the more perplexing our path, the more manifest becomes the presence of God. During the days of a man's content with natural possessions and resources, when the sunshine of nature is falling on his life, then the cloud of God's providence appears, but let the night of spiritual distress, the great difficulties of sin, and death, and eternity darken the soul, then the bright, conspicuous fires of grace at once appear.

V. THE CLOUD BY ITS MOVEMENTS BECAME AN INFALLIBLE GUIDE. Thus Jehovah showed that he, the invisible one, was the leader of the people. The resting and the moving cloud meant the resting and the moving people. It was ever with them to point the way. God's goodness does not pass away as the morning cloud and the early dew. The cloud said plainly, "Follow me." So Jesus says, "Follow me," reiterating, emphasizing, and illustrating the command. If we are ever to reach the rest that remaineth for the people of God, it must be by acting towards Jesus as the Israelites did towards the cloud in the wilderness (Deut. xxxii. 10—12; 2 Chron. v. 13; Ps. xliii. 3; Isa. iv. 5; xlix. 10).—Y.

EXPOSITION.

CHAPTER X.

THE SILVER TRUMPETS (vers. 1—10). Ver. 1.—**And the Lord spake.** The command to make the silver trumpets is introduced here, because one principal use of them was connected with the order of march. It does not necessarily follow that the command was actually given exactly at this time, or that all the different directions for use formed part of one communication. They may have been gathered together for convenience' sake. See the Introduction on this subject. It is, however, a mistake to suppose that this use of trumpets has been anticipated in Levit. xxv. 9, or elsewhere, for the "trumpets" there mentioned were altogether different in shape, as in material.

Ver. 2.—**Make thee two trumpets.** Hebrew, *khatsotserah.* From the testimony of Josephus, from the representation on the arch of Titus, and from a comparison of ancient Egyptian trumpets, it is clear that these trumpets were straight, long, and narrow, with an expanded mouth. The *shophār,* or trumpet of the Jubilee, on the other hand, was a buccina or cornet, either made of a ram's horn, or shaped like one. **Of a whole piece.** Rather, "of beaten work." Hebrew, *mikshah* (see on Exod. xxv. 18). Septuagint, ἐλατὰς ποιήσεις αὐτάς. Probably they were made of a single plate of silver beaten out into the required shape, which was very simple.

Ver. 3. — **When they shall blow with them,** i. e. with both of them. **All the assembly,** i. e. by their natural or customary representatives.

Ver. 5.—**When ye blow an alarm.** Hebrew, תְּרוּעָה. This seems to signify a continuous peal, easily distinguished, wherever audible, from the blowing in short, sharp tones (Hebrew, תָּקַע) mentioned below, ver. 7. The peal of alarm was to be blown—לְמַסְעֵיהֶם— "for their breaking up"—for that purpose, and no other. **The camps.** Only those on the east (Judah, with Issachar and Zebulun) and on the south (Reuben, with Simeon and Gad) are here mentioned. It may be that the silver trumpets themselves were carried with the sacred utensils after the southern camps, and that some other means were employed to start the remaining tribes ; or it may be that the omission is due to some accidental circumstance. The Septuagint inserts in ver. 6, "And ye shall sound a third alarm, and the camps which are pitched westwards shall move ; and ye shall sound a fourth alarm, and the camps which are pitched northwards shall move." No doubt this was the actual order of starting, however the signal was given.

Ver. 8.—**The sons of Aaron, the priests, shall blow.** It was natural that they should be made responsible for the custody and use of these trumpets, not because their sound represented the voice of God, but because they were used for religious purposes, and could only be safely kept in the sanctuary. **An ordinance for ever.** The accustomed formula for some sacred institution which was to have a permanent character and an eternal meaning (cf. Exod. xii. 24). The truth of these words cannot be exhausted by an actual use of 1500 years, followed by complete disuse for 1800 years. The "ordinance" of the silver trumpets must be perpetuated "for ever" in the gospel, or else the Divine word has failed.

Ver. 9.—**If ye go to war.** בּוֹא מִלְחָמָה, "come into war," or "be engaged," denoting actual hostilities. **In your land.** The practical use of the trumpets ceased with the years of wandering ; the ceremonial use was continued as long as the people dwelt in "their land ; " the spiritual use remains an "ordinance for ever," as long as the Church

is militant here on earth. That the use of the two silver trumpets was ceremonial, and not practical, after the conquest of Canaan is evident from the purpose and effect ascribed to that use. Whether in war or in worship, that purpose was *not* to convoke the people, nor to give signals to the host, *but* to put God in mind of his promises, and to invoke his covenanted grace. Indeed, *two* trumpets, as here prescribed, could not be otherwise than ceremonially used after the nation was spread abroad over the whole face of Canaan ; and there is no direction to make more than two such trumpets. The use of trumpets in subsequent times is indeed often mentioned both in war and in holy festivities, and it was undoubtedly founded upon this Divine ordinance ; but it was not in literal compliance with it, for the obvious reason that many trumpets were used instead of two only (see 1 Chron. xv. 24 ; 2 Chron. v. 12 ; Neh. xii. 35). In these passages (and probably in 2 Chron. xiii. 12) we have abundant evidence of one of those expansions and adaptations of the Mosaic ritual which were so freely made under the house of David. Ch. xxxi. 6, and (perhaps) 1 Chron. xvi. 6, and Ps. lxxxi. 3 may be quoted as pointing to the strict fulfilment of the law as it stands.

Ver. 10.—**In the day of your gladness.** Any day of national thanksgiving, celebrated with religious services, as the feast of the dedication (John x. 22) or of Purim (Esther ix. 19, *sqq.*). **In your solemn days.** מֹעֲדִים. The feasts appointed to be observed by the law (see chs. xxviii. and xxix.). **In the beginnings of your months.** New moon days (Ps. lxxxi. 3). Only the first day of the seventh month was properly a feast (Levit. xxiii. 24), but all were distinguished by special sacrifices (ch. xxviii. 11).

HOMILETICS.

Vers. 1—10.—*The sacred trumpets.* Spiritually we have in the two silver trumpets *the gospel in its twofold use*—(1) as preached to men, (2) as pleaded before God ; for that which is preached to men must also be pleaded by and for men. The substance of our faith is also the substance of our intercession. *Lex credendi, lex orandi.* "Our Father, . . . through Jesus Christ our Lord," is the norm at once of every true sermon, and of every right prayer. The death of Christ, *preached,* is the voice of God to start the faithful on their way to heaven ; the death of Christ, *shown,* is the voice of the faithful to put God in mind of his sure mercies, to bring themselves into remembrance before him. Consider, therefore—·

I. That THE SACRED TRUMPET MUST BE OF ONE WHOLE PIECE OF SILVER, NEITHER ALLOYED WITH BASER METAL, NOR MADE UP OF FRAGMENTS. The gospel which we preach or plead must be the whole faith, and the pure faith once delivered to the saints, neither alloyed with human inventions nor pieced together out of fragments and remnants of the Divine revelation. Human art and labour has no further place than in bringing the gospel—as the trumpet—into such a shape as that it can be effectually used, without adding aught to it, or diminishing aught from it.

II. That the PRIMARY USE OF THE SACRED TRUMPET was—(1) for summoning the people into the more immediate presence of God; (2) for ordering their march towards Canaan. The gospel is preached, on the one hand, to call men from their cares, and pleasures, and earthly ties, in order to present themselves for pardon and for blessing before him who is their covenanted God and King; on the other hand, to instruct men in an orderly Christian walk, seeking the kingdom, not as isolated individuals, but as members of one body, soldiers in one army, units in one vast and organised whole.

III. THAT A PLAIN DISTINCTION OF SOUND WAS TO BE MADE IN CALLING THE ASSEMBLY, AND IN ORDERING THE MARCH. The persuasions of the gospel, by which we call men to draw nigh unto God, must needs differ in sound and in tone from the precepts of the gospel by which we seek to direct their onward march; but both are equally sacred, and equally necessary to be observed.

IV. THAT THE SUBSEQUENT USE OF THE SACRED TRUMPETS WAS TO INVOKE, WITH HOLY AND CONSECRATED SOUND, THE DIVINE AID AGAINST THE FOE, THE DIVINE ACCEPT-ANCE UPON THE SACRED FEAST OR OFFERING: IN DANGER OR IN WORSHIP TO BRING HIS_OWN INTO REMEMBRANCE WITH THEIR GOD. The facts of the gospel which we preach, and whereby we "persuade men," the same do we plead; and thereby we "persuade God." All true prayer and intercession of the faithful for aid against spiritual enemies, for acceptance of spiritual sacrifices, is not only *founded upon* the gospel; it *is* the gospel, pleaded (whether in holy words or in holy rites) before high heaven; it is "the Lord's death" shown "until he come;" it is the sacred trumpet sounded in the ears of God prevailingly according to his command.

V. THAT THE USE OF THE TRUMPETS FOR THOSE PURPOSES WAS TO BE "AN ORDIN-ANCE FOR EVER." The calling of men to draw nigh unto God; the ordering of their onward walk; the cry to heaven for promised aid against our unseen foes; the plead-ing of the finished work of Christ wherein we trust, will never cease until there shall be no more time. Neither can the Church at large, nor can any faithful soul, dare to despise or to ignore any of these uses of the gospel trumpet; for they are of Divine and perpetual appointment.

HOMILIES BY VARIOUS AUTHORS.

Vers. 1—10.—*The silver trumpets.* The blowing of the silver trumpets by Aaron and his sons has generally been taken to denote the preaching of the gospel. But the interpretation is a mistaken one, and arises from confounding the trumpet of jubilee (Levit. xxv. 9; Luke iv. 16) with the silver trumpet. Although bearing the same name in the English Bible, these are quite different instruments, and are called by different Hebrew names. The former is the *shophar* or cornet, which, as its name implies, was of horn, or at least horn-shaped; whereas the latter, the *chatsotser*, was a long straight tube of silver with a bell-shaped mouth. The true intention of the silver trumpets is distinctly enough indicated in the law before us. They were to be to the children of Israel for a memorial before their God (ver. 10); the promise was that when the trumpets were blown, the people should be remembered before the Lord their God, and he would save them from their enemies (ver. 9). In other words, the blowing of the silver trumpets was a figure of PRAYER (cf. Acts x. 4). An exceed-ingly striking and suggestive figure it is.

I. IT PRESENTS CERTAIN ASPECTS OF PRAYER WHICH CAN HARDLY BE TOO MUCH REMEMBERED. For one thing, it admonishes us that *prayer ought to be an effectual fervent exercise* (James v. 16). A trumpet-tone is the opposite of a timid whisper. There is a clear determinate ring in the call of a silver trumpet. This is not meant to suggest that there ought to be loud and vehement speaking in prayer. But it does mean that we are to throw heart into our prayers and put forth our strength. The spirit of adoption *cries*, Abba Father (see 2 Chron. xiii. 14). When we call on God we ought to stir ourselves up to take hold of him (Isa. lxiv. 7.) More-over, the silver trumpet emits a *ringing, joyous sound*. In almost every instance in which the blowing of these trumpets is mentioned in Scripture, it is suggestive of gladness, hope, exultation. And ought not a note of gladness, hope, exultation to pervade our prayers? When we pray we are to use a certain holy boldness; we are to draw near; we are to speak in full assurance of faith. This, I confess, may be pressed too far. There was nothing of the trumpet-tone in the publican's prayer. There may be acceptable prayer in a sigh, in a cry of anguish, in the groaning of a prisoner. But it is not the will of God that his children's ordinary intercourse with him should be of that sort. They are to call on him with a gladsome confidence that he is able and ready to help them. And many of them do this. There are Christian people whose prayers are always rising into the ringing tones of the silver trumpet. I have spoken first of the general design or spiritual intention of this ordinance of the silver trumpets.

Let us now note THE PARTICULARS:—1. It belonged to the *priest's* office (ver. 8). It is not to be confounded with the Levitical service of song, instituted long after by David. 2. It served a variety of *secular* uses. Public assemblies were convened by the sounding of the trumpets, as they are convened among us by the ringing of bells (vers. 2, 3, 7). And they were the bugles by which military signals were given (vers. 4—6). That it was the priests who blew the trumpets on all such occasions reminds us that Israel was, in a special sense, "an holy nation;" and may also carry forward our minds to the time when "holiness to the Lord" will be written on the life of all Christian nations in all their relations. 3. The blowing of the silver trumpets found place chiefly in the service of the sanctuary. The particulars are noted in ver. 10, and are of uncommon interest for the Christian reader. (1) The trumpets were to be blown *over the sacrifices.* How this was done appears from the example related in 2 Chron. xxix. 26—28. The intention was as much as to say, "O thou that dwellest in the heavens, give ear to us when we cry; remember all our offerings and accept our burnt sacrifice. Grant us the wish of our heart, and fulfil all our counsel." (2) The sacrifices particularly named as to be thus signalised are *the burnt offering and the peace offering.* Not the sin offering. The omission can hardly have been accidental. When I have fallen into some notable sin, I am to humble myself before God with shame. The cry of the publican is what befits me, rather than trumpet-toned exultation. The sin offering is most acceptably presented without blowing of trumpets. As for the burnt offering, which denotes dedication; and the peace offering, which speaks of communion with God and of our communion with each other in the Lord; these are most acceptable when they are attended with gladness and thankful exultation in God. (3) The blowing of the silver trumpets was especially *to abound at the great solemnities.* That is to say, at the new moons, at the three great festivals, the "solemn days" of the Jewish year, and on all days of special gladness (cf. 2 Chron. v. 12; vii. 6; Ezra iii. 10; Neh. xii. 35). (4) Above all other solemn days, the first day of the seventh month was to be thus distinguished. The seventh month was that in which the Feast of Tabernacles happened—at the full moon, in the end of September or beginning of October, after the Lord had crowned the year with his goodness. The new moon of this month was the Feast of the Blowing of Trumpets (cf. Levit. xxiii. 24); and fitly ushered in the Feast of Ingathering, the most joyous of all the festivals of the year.—B.

Vers. 1—10.—*The use of the trumpets.* There is a manifest connection between the cloud and the trumpets. At Sinai there was "a thick cloud upon the mount, and the voice of the trumpet exceeding loud" (Exod. xix. 16). This seems to have been a miraculous sound, but Jehovah now orders Moses to have two silver trumpets made for permanent use. Thus trumpets as well as cloud were remembrancers of Sinai. God uses sound along with light to signify his will to his people; he appeals not only to their eyes, but also to their ears. Though the cloud was there they were not ever watching it. The longer it rested, the less conscious of its presence they became. Therefore God added the sound of the trumpets, a sudden, startling sound, to stop each one in his work, or raise him out of his sleep.

I. GOD TAKES SUFFICIENT MEANS TO CONVEY TO MEN ALL THAT IT IS NEEDFUL FOR THEM TO KNOW. Exactly where they would next pass, and how long stay there, and how long be in the wilderness, the Israelites knew not; but when the hour came for them to move, it was of the first importance that none should be in ignorance or doubt. So with regard to the practical matters of the gospel; we may take it as perfectly certain that difficulties with regard to salvation and Christian duty are in *us*, not in *God*. Men have eyes, yet see not; ears, yet hear not. They clamour for more light, more evidence, more signs. "If they hear not Moses and the prophets, neither will they be persuaded though one rose from the dead." And now they have also Christ and the apostles to listen to. All the great appeals and proclamations of the gospel have the trumpet sound in them; only men are so drenched and stupefied with the opiates of sin that the sound is as if it were not.

II. God could use the one agent to indicate many requirements. There were always the same two trumpets, but sounded in different ways for different purposes. There was one sound for the princes, and another for the people. The trumpet called them to the march, and in later days, when the marching was over, it called them to the battle. It had to do with great religious occasions, and times of special gladness, *e. g.* the jubilee year (Levit. xxv. 9). So there is one Spirit and diversity of opera· tions. There is the Spirit calling the attention of men by signs and wonders; there is the same Spirit breathing through the men who wrote book after book of the Scriptures. And now these Scriptures lie like a silent silver trumpet, till the same Spirit, breathing through them, makes them to teach, console, promise, warn, accord- ing to the need of the individual who listens. The trumpet of God gives no uncer- tain sound (1 Cor. xiv. 8). Paul trusted it with the most complete confidence in his missionary work (Acts xvi. 6—10). There is a trumpet sound telling us not only to do something for God, but exactly what to do. "He that hath ears to hear, let him hear."

III. The trumpet was for special occasions. It was not a daily sound. It indicated fresh departures, and was associated with great celebrations. Between the soundings there were intervals for the quiet practice of every day duties. It is good thus to have the ordinary and the extraordinary mingled in our life. It is an ill thing both for individuals and communities to be settled too long in the same circum- stances. Too much change is bad; but too much rest is worse. Times of quiet, plodding toil scarcely noticed, faithfulness in little things day after day—then the trumpet sounds and there is change and strife. But though the trumpet is there for special occasions, God has voices for every day to all who have the listening ear. (2 Chron. v. 12—14; Isa. xviii. 3; xxvii. 13; lviii. 1; Jer. iv. 5; vi. 1; xlii. 14; li. 27; Ezek. xxxiii. 1—6; Hosea viii. 1; Joel ii. 1; Amos iii. 6; Zeph. i. 16; Zech. ix. 14; Rev. i. 10.)—Y.

EXPOSITION.

The order of march from Sinai (vers. 11—28). Ver. 11.—**On the twentieth day of the second month.** This answered ap- proximately to our May 6th, when the spring verdure would still be on the land, but the heat of the day would already have become intense. We may well suppose that the departure would have taken place a month earlier, had it not been necessary to wait for the due celebration of the second or supple- mental passover (ch. ix. 11). As this march was, next to the actual exodus, *the* great trial of Israel's faith and obedience, it was most important that none should commence it otherwise than in full communion with their God and with one another. **The cloud was taken up.** For the first time since the taber- nacle had been reared up (Exod. xl. 34). This being the Divine signal for departure, the silver trumpets would immediately an- nounce the fact to all the hosts.

Ver. 12.—**Took their journeys.** Literally, "marched according to their journeys" (לְמַסְעֵיהֶם). Septuagint, ἐξῆραν σὺν ἀπαρ- τίαις αὐτῶν, set forward with their baggage. **And the cloud rested in the wilderness of**

Paran. Taken by itself this would seem to apply to the first resting of the cloud and the first halt of the host after break- ing up from "the wilderness of Sinai." It appears, however, from ch. xii. 16 that "the wilderness of Paran" was only reached after leaving Hazeroth at the end of three days' journey from Sinai, nor would a shorter space of time suffice to carry the host across the mountain barrier of the Jebel et-Tih, which forms the clearly-marked southern limit of the desert plateau of Paran (see next note). Some critics have arbitrarily extended the limits of "the wilderness of Paran" so as to include the sandy waste between Sinai and the Jebel et-Tih, and therefore the very first halting-place of Israel. This, however, is unnecessary as well as arbitrary; for (1) vers. 12, 13 are evidently in the nature of a sum- mary, and the same subject is confessedly taken up again in ver. 33, *sq. ;* and (2) the departure from Sinai is expressly said to have been for a "three days' journey" (ver. 33), which must mean that the march, although actually divided into three stages, was re- garded as a single journey, because it brought them to their immediate destination in the wilderness of Paran. Here then is a plain reason for the statement in this verse: the cloud *did* indeed rest twice between the two wildernesses, but only so as to allow of a night's repose, not so as to break the continuity of the march. "*The wilderness of Paran.*" Septuagint, ἐν τῇ ἐρήμῳ τοῦ φαράν. This geographical expression is nowhere exactly defined in Holy Scripture, and the name itself has disappeared; for in spite of the resemblance in sound (a resemblance here, as in so many cases, wholly delusive), it seems to have no connection whatever with the Wady Feiran, the fertile valley at the base of Serbal, or with the town which once shared the name. All the allusions, however, in the Old Testament to Paran point to a district so clearly marked out, so deeply stamped with its own characteristics, by nature, that no mistake is possible. This district is now called et-Tih, *i. e.* the wandering, and is still remembered in the traditions of the Arabs as the scene of the wanderings of the people of God. Little known, and never thoroughly explored, its main features are nevertheless unmistakable, and its boundaries sharply defined. Measuring about 150 miles in either direction, its southern frontier (now called the Jebel et-Tih) is divided by the broad sandy waste of er-Ramleh from the Sinaitic mountains and the Sinaitic peninsula properly so called; its northern mountain mass looks across the deep fissure of the Wady Murreh (or desert of Zin), some ten or fifteen miles broad, into er-Rachmah, the mountain of the Amorite, the southern extension of the plateau of Judah; on the east it falls abruptly down to the narrow beach of the Elanitic Gulf, and to the Arabah; on the west alone it sinks slowly into the sandy desert of Shur, which separates it from the Mediterranean and from Egypt. Et-Tih is itself divided into nearly equal halves by the Wady el Arish (or "river of Egypt"), which, rising on the northern slopes of the Jebel et-Tih, and running northwards through the whole plateau, turns off to the west and is lost in the desert of Shur. That the western half of the plateau went also under the name of Paran is evident from the history of Ishmael (see especially Gen. xxi. 21; xxv. 18), but it was through the eastern portion alone that the wanderings of the Israelites, so far as we can trace them, lay. This "wilderness of Paran" is indeed "a great and terrible wilderness" (Deut. i. 9), lacking for the most part the precipitous grandeur of the granite mountains of Sinai, but lacking also their fertile valleys and numerous streams. A bare limestone or sandstone plateau, crossed by low ranges of hills, seamed with innumerable dry water-courses, and interspersed with large patches of sand and gravel, is what now meets the eye of the traveller in this forsaken land. It is true that a good deal of rain falls at times, and that when it does fall vegetation appears with surprising rapidity and abundance; it is true also that the district has been persistently denuded of trees and shrubs for the sake of fuel. But whatever mitigations may have then existed, it is clear from the Bible itself that the country was then, as now, emphatically frightful (cf. Deut. i. 19; viii. 15; xxxii. 10; Jer. ii. 6). Something may be set, no doubt, to the account of rhetoric, and much may be allowed for variety of seasons. Even in Australia the very same district will appear at one time like the desolation of a thousand years, and in the very next year it will blossom as the rose. But at certain seasons at any rate et-Tih was (as it is) a "howling" wilderness, where the dreadful silence of a lifeless land was only broken by the nightly howling of unclean beasts who tracked the footsteps of the living in order to devour the carcases of the dead. Perhaps so bad a country has never been attempted by any army in modern days, even by the Russian troops in Central Asia.

Amongst the many Wadys which drain the uncertain rain-fall of the eastern half of et-Tih (and at the same time testify to a greater rain-fall in bygone ages), the most important is the Wady el Terafeh, which, also rising on the northern slopes of Jebel et-Tih, runs northwards and north-westwards, and finally opens into the Arabah. Towards its northern limit et-Tih changes its character for the worse. Here it rises into a precipitous quadrilateral of mountains, about forty miles square, not very lofty, but exceedingly steep and rugged, composed in great measure of dazzling masses of bare chalk or limestone, which glow as in a furnace beneath the summer sun. This mountain mass, now called the Azâzimat, or mountain country of the Azâzimeh, rising steeply from the rest of the plateau to the southward, is almost completely detached by deep depressions from the surrounding districts; at the north-west corner alone it is united by a short range of mountains with er-Rachmah, and so with the highlands of Southern Palestine. From this corner the Wady Murreh descends broad and deep towards the east, forking at the eastern extremity towards the Arabah on the south-east, and towards the Dead Sea on the north-east. The interior of this inaccessible country has yet to be really explored, and it is the scanty nature of our present knowledge concerning it which, more than anything else, prevents us from following with any certainty the march of the Israelites as recorded in this book.

Ver. 13. — **And they first took their**

journey. The meaning of this is somewhat doubtful. The Septuagint has ἐξῆραν πρῶτοι, the foremost set out; the Vulgate, *profecti sunt per turmas suas.* Perhaps it means, "they journeyed in the order of precedence" assigned to them by their marching orders in ch. ii.

Ver. 14.—**According to their armies.** In each camp, and under each of the four standards, there were three tribal hosts, each an army in itself.

Ver. 17.—**And the tabernacle was taken down.** That is, the fabric of it; the boards, curtains, and other heavy portions which were packed upon the six waggons provided for the purpose (ch. vii. 5—9). **And the sons of Gershon and the sons of Merari set forward.** Between the first and second divisions of the host. In ch. ii. it had been directed in general terms that "the tabernacle" should set forward with the camp of the Levites in the midst of the host, between the second and third divisions. At that time the duties of the several Levitical families had not been specified, and the orders for the taking down and transport of the tabernacle and its furniture had not been given in detail. It would be historically an error, and theologically a superstition, to imagine that Divine commands such as these had no elasticity, and left no room for adaptation, under the teaching of experience, or for the sake of obvious convenience. Whether the present modification was directly commanded by God himself, or whether it was made on the authority of Moses, does not here appear. There can be no question that subsequent theocratic rulers of Israel claimed and used a large liberty in modifying the Divinely-originated ritual and order. Compare the case of the passover, the arrangements of Solomon's temple as corresponding with those of the tabernacle, and even the use of the silver trumpets. The Septuagint has the future tense here, καθελοῦσι τὴν σκηνήν κ. τ. λ., as if to mark it as a fresh command.

Ver. 21.—**The sanctuary.** Rather, "the holy things." הַמִּקְדָּשׁ, equivalent to the קֹדֶשׁ הַקֳּדָשִׁים of ch. iv. 4. Septuagint, τὰ ἄγια. The sacred furniture mentioned in ch. iii. 31 (but cf. ver. 33). **The other did set up the tabernacle.** Literally, "they set up," but no doubt it means the Gershonites and Merarites, whose business it was.

Ver. 25.—**The rereward of all the camps.** Literally, "the collector," or "the gatherer," of all the camps." The word is applied by Isaiah to God himself (Isa. lii. 12; lviii. 8) as to him that "gathereth the outcasts of Israel." Dan may have been the collector of all the camps simply in the sense that his host closed in all the others from behind, and in pitching completed the full number.

Under any ordinary circumstances, however (see next note) the work of the rear-guard in collecting stragglers and in taking charge of such as had fainted by the way must have been arduous and important in the extreme.

Ver. 28.—**Thus were the journeyings.** Rather, "these were the journeyings," the marchings of the various hosts of which the nation was composed. The question may here be asked, which is considered more at large in the Introduction, how it was possible for a nation of more than two million souls, containing the usual proportion of aged people, women, and children, to march as here represented, in compact columns closely following one another, without straggling, without confusion, without incalculable suffering and loss of life. That the line of march was intended to be compact and unbroken is plain (amongst other things) from the directions given about the tabernacle. The fabric was sent on in advance with the evident intent that it should be reared up and ready to receive the holy things by the time they arrived. Yet between the fabric and the furniture there marched more than half a million of people (the camp of Reuben), all of whom had to reach the camping ground and turn off to the right before the Kohathites could rejoin their brethren. Now discipline and drill will do wonders in the way of ordering and expediting the movements even of vast multitudes, if they are thoroughly under control; the family organisation also of the tribes, and the long leisure which they had enjoyed at Sinai, gave every opportunity of perfecting the necessary discipline. But it is clear that no discipline could make such an arrangement as the one above mentioned feasible under the ordinary circumstances of human life. It would be absolutely necessary to eliminate all the casualties and all the sicknesses which would naturally clog and hinder the march of such a multitude, in order that it might be compressed within the required limits of time and space. Have we any ground for supposing that these casualties and sicknesses *were* eliminated? In answering this question we must clearly distinguish between the journey from Sinai to Kadesh, on the borders of Palestine, *which was a journey of only eleven days* (Deut. i. 2), and the subsequent wanderings of the people of Israel. It is the eleven days' journey only with which we are concerned, because it was for this journey only that provision was made and orders were given by the God of Israel. During the subsequent years of wandering and of excommunication, there can be no doubt that the marching orders fell into abeyance as entirely as the sacrificial system and the rite of circumcision itself. During these years the various camps may have scattered themselves abroad, marched, and halted very much as the circumstances of the day demanded. But that this was not and could not be the case during the short journey which *should* have landed them in Canaan is obvious from the whole tone, as well as from the particular details, of the commandments considered above. It is further to be borne in mind that the Divine promise and undertaking at the exodus was, impliedly if not explicitly, to bring the whole people, one and all, small and great, safely to their promised home. When the Psalmist asserts (Ps. cv. 37) that "there was not one feeble person among their tribes," he does not go beyond what is plainly intimated in the narrative. If of their cattle "not an hoof" must be left behind, lest the absolute character of the deliverance be marred, how much more necessary was it that not a soul be abandoned to Egyptian vengeance? And how could all depart unless all were providentially saved from sickness and infirmity? But the same necessity (the necessity of his own goodness) held good when the exodus was accomplished. God could not bring any individual in Israel out of Egypt only to perish in the wilderness, unless it were through his own default. He who had brought them *out* with so lavish a display of miraculous power was (we may say with reverence) bound also to bring them *in;* else they had been actual losers by obedience, and his word had not been kept to them. Under a covenant and a dispensation which assuredly did not look one hand's breadth beyond the present life, it must have seemed to be of the essence of the promise which they believed that not one of them should die or have to be left behind. And as the death or loss of one of God's people would have vitiated the temporal promise to *them*, so also it would have vitiated the eternal promise to *us*. For they were ensamples of us, and confessedly what was done for them was done at least as much for our sakes as for theirs. Now the promise of God is manifest unto every one that is included within his new covenant, viz., to bring him safely at last unto the heavenly Canaan, and that in spite of every danger, if only he do not draw back. The whole analogy, therefore, and the typical meaning of the exodus would be overthrown if any single Israelite who had crossed the Red Sea failed to enter into rest, save as the consequence of his own sin. We conclude, therefore, with some confidence that the ordinary incidents of mortality were providentially excluded from the present march, as from the previous interval; that none fell sick, none became helpless, none died a natural death. We know that the great difficulty of a sufficient supply of food was miraculously met; we know that in numberless respects the passage from Egypt to Canaan was hedged about with supernatural aids. Is there any difficulty in supposing that he who gave them bread to eat and water to drink, who led them by a cloudy and a fiery pillar, could also give them health and strength to "walk and not be weary"? Is it unreasonable to imagine that he who spake in his tender pity of the flight from Judæa to Pella, "Woe to them that are with child, and to them that give suck in those days," miraculously restrained for that season the natural increase of his people?

HOMILETICS.

Vers. 11—28.—*The journey home.* Spiritually, we have in this section *the Divinely-appointed order of the Church of God*, the ideal method of her journeying, towards the eternal rest. All the time which the children of Israel spent beneath the holy mount was to prepare them for a speedy and triumphant march by the shortest way into Canaan. All which we have learnt of the law of Christ, and in his school, is to fit us to make our way right onwards through the difficulties of this troublesome world to the home beyond; and this is the practical test of all we have acquired. Consider, therefore—

I. That the immediate march of Israel was out of the "wilderness of Sinai" into the "wilderness of Paran," from one desert to another. Even so is the onward course of the Church, or of the faithful soul, in this world. The only change is from one set of difficulties and hardships to another, from an unrest of one kind to an unrest of another kind. After the green level of Egypt, Sinai was awful, but Paran was worse. To the natural mind the difficulties which surround the beginning of a Christian life are terrible, but those which beset its middle course are mostly harder, because drearier, even if less striking. The young always think that when the special temptations of youth are past it will be an easy and simple matter to walk uprightly. In truth the whole of this life is a desert-journey, and we only remove from the awful precipices of Sinai to encounter the rugged and barren expanse of Paran. The hope which cheers and sustains lies beyond (Matt. x. 22; James i. 12).

II. That the children of Israel, as soon as the cloud removed, could not

STAY WHERE THEY WERE, BUT MUST SET FORTH THROUGH THE RUGGED WILDERNESS OF PARAN, IF THEY WERE EVER TO REACH CANAAN. Even so the Church cannot attain her rest by studying divinity or perfecting the definitions of morality or the appliances of worship ; it must walk in faith and righteousness amidst the endless contradictions of time. Even Mary cannot always sit at the Master's feet; the hour will come when he will be taken away, and when she must follow in the hard way of practical goodness and self-denial, if she would see him again.

III. THAT THE MARCHING ORDERS GIVEN BY GOD TO ISRAEL SEEM ON THE FACE OF THEM TO BE INCONSISTENT WITH THE ENORMOUS NUMBER OF THE PEOPLE ON THE ONE HAND, AND THE EXTREME DIFFICULTY OF THE COUNTRY ON THE OTHER ; there seems no room left for any physical incapacity, or for the least human failure. And these orders were in fact more or less departed from before long. The Divine ideal of the Christian life, whether as lived by the Church at large or by the individual soul, as drawn out in the New Testament, seems to be too high and too perfect to be possible in the face of the contradictions of the world and the perversities of human nature. It is apparently true that the infinite complications of modern life, and the infinite variety of human dispositions, have made the lofty purity and the unbroken unity of the gospel plan a thing practically unattainable in the Church.

IV. That the appointed ORDER OF MARCH WAS NOT IN FACT OBSERVED IN ITS ENTIRETY EXCEPT AT THE VERY FIRST, because sin and rebellion altered the face of things and made it impossible. The holy picture of the Christian community, drawn in Scripture, was only realised in the earliest days, and was soon made obsolete in many points by sin and unbelief.

V. That in spite of all apparent difficulties THE MARCH TO CANAAN WOULD HAVE BEEN ACCOMPLISHED WITHOUT A CHECK, without a loss, IF ONLY THE PEOPLE HAD OBEYED THE DIVINE COMMANDS, and relied upon the supernatural aid extended to them. Had Christians remained faithful, and responded to the heavenly graces promised to them, the Church would have gone on as it began, in spite of all difficulties ; the whole earth had been evangelised, the number of the elect accomplished, and the heavenly rest attained long (it may be) ere this.

VI. THAT THE GREAT SECRET, HUMANLY SPEAKING, OF THE ONWARD PROGRESS OF THE HOST WAS ORDER, in that every single person had his place and his work, and knew it. Without order carefully maintained that multitude had become an unmanageable mob, which could not have moved a mile or lived a day. Humanly speaking, *order*, discipline, due subordination, allotted division of labour, is the secret of the Church's success; and the absence—still more the contempt—of such order, is the obvious cause of the Church's failure.

VII. THAT THE GREAT SECRET, DIVINELY SPEAKING, OF ISRAEL'S SAFETY AND PROGRESS WAS THE FACT THAT THE LORD HIMSELF WAS IN THEIR MIDST when they rested, at their head when they marched, by the ark and by the cloud. In the deepest and truest sense the secret of our safety and of our victory is the supernatural presence of God with the Church and in the soul, by his incarnate Word and by his Spirit. *There* is at once the real bond of union, and the real source of strength. It may also be noted—1. That, as soon as their time of preparation was fulfilled, the cloud led Israel into the wilderness of Paran, to be tried by the manifold temptations of that way. Even so, when the preparation of Jesus for his work was finished, he was led up of the Spirit into the wilderness to be tempted of the devil. Israel, called out of Egypt, was a type of Christ (Matt. ii. 15), and the cloud was the symbol of the Divine Spirit. 2. That the fabric of the tabernacle was sent on in order to be set up in readiness to receive the ark and sacred vessels when they arrived. It is not always an idle nor a useless thing to set up the external formalities of religion in advance of the true spirit of worship, in faithful expectation that this too will come, and with it the promised blessing of God.

EXPOSITION.

THE INVITATION TO HOBAB (vers. 29—32). Ver. 29.—**Hobab, the son of Raguel** (or rather Reuel, of which Raguel is simply the Septuagint and Vulgate variation), **Moses' father-in-law.** It is not quite certain who this "Hobab" was. The name occurs only here and in Judges iv. 11. The older opinion, followed by the A. V., identified Hobab with Jethro, and Jethro with Reuel the "priest of Midian," and father of Zipporah, Moses' wife. It is, of course, no real objection to this opinion that Hobab is here called the "son of Reuel;" for the name may quite well have been an hereditary one, like Abimelech and so many others. Nor need the multiplicity of names given to one individual astonish us, for it is of frequent occurrence in the Old Testament, and not infrequent in the New. The father-in-law of Moses was a priest, holding (probably by right of birth) the patriarchal dignity of tribal priest, as Job did on a smaller, and Melchizedec on a larger, scale. He may very well, therefore, have had one or more "official" names in addition to his personal name. If this is accepted, then it may serve as one instance amongst many to remind us how extremely careless the inspired writers are about *names*—"careless" not in the sense of not caring whether they are right or wrong, but in the sense of not betraying and not feeling the least anxiety to avoid the appearance and suspicion of inaccuracy. Even in the lists of the twelve apostles we are forced to believe that "Judas the brother of James" is the same person as "Lebbæus" and "Thaddæus;" and it is a matter of endless discussion whether or no "Bartholomew" was the same as "Nathanael." On the face of it Scripture proclaims that it uses no arts, that it takes no pains to preserve an appearance of accuracy—that appearance which is so easily simulated for the purposes of falsehood. Holy Scripture may therefore fairly claim to be read without that captiousness, without that demand for minute carefulness and obvious consistency, which we rightly apply to one of our own histories. The modern historian avowedly tells his story as a witness does in the presence of a hostile counsel; the sacred historian tells his as a man does to the children round his knee. Surely such an obvious fact should disarm a good deal of the petty criticism which carps at the sacred narrative.

Many, however, will think that the balance of probability is against the older opinion. It is certain that the word translated "father-in-law" has no such definiteness either in the Hebrew or in the Septua-gint. It means simply a "marriage relation," and is even used by Zipporah of Moses himself (Exod. iv. 25, 26—Hebrew. The Septuagint avoids the word). It is just as likely to mean "brother-in-law" when applied to Hobab. As Moses was already eighty years old when Jethro is first mentioned (Exod. iii. 1), it may seem probable that his father-in-law was by that time dead, and succeeded in his priestly office by his eldest son. In that case Hobab would be a younger son of Reuel, and as such free to leave the home of his ancestors and to join himself to his sister's people.

Ver. 31.—**Forasmuch as thou knowest how we are to encamp in the wilderness, and thou mayest be to us instead of eyes.** It is an obvious conclusion, from the reasons here urged by Moses, that the many and wonderful promises of Divine guidance and Divine direction did *not* supersede in his eyes the use of all available human aids. It is not indeed easy to say *where* any room was left for the good offices and experience of Hobab; the cloud of the Divine Presence *seemed* to control absolutely the journeying and encamping of the people; yet if we really knew in detail the actual ordering of that wondrous march, we should doubtless find that the heavenly guidance did but give unity and certainty to all the wisdom, caution, and endeavour of its earthly leaders. Indeed if we recall to mind that the host is calculated at more than two millions of people, it is quite evident that even during the march to Kadesh (and much more in the long wanderings which followed) it must have been extremely difficult to keep the various divisions together. In the broken and difficult country which they were to traverse, which had been familiar to Hobab from his youth, there would be scope enough for all his ability as a guide. And it would seem that it was just this prospect of being really useful to the people of Israel that prevailed with Hobab. He must indeed have felt assured that a wonderful future awaited a nation whose past and present were, even within his own knowledge, so wonderful. But that alone could not move him to leave his own land and his own kindred, a thing so unspeakably repugnant to the feelings and traditions of his age and country. Doubtless to the child of the desert, whose life was a never-ending struggle with the dangers and vicissitudes of the wilderness, the land of promise, flowing with milk and honey, watered with the rain of heaven, seemed like the garden of Eden. Yet the offer of an heritage within that land moved him not so much, it would appear, as the claim upon his own good offices in helping the chosen people to reach their own abode. The Septuagint translation, or rather paraphrase, of this verse is, " Leave us not, forasmuch as thou wast with us in the wilderness, and thou shalt be an elder among us." This seems, on the one hand, to identify Hobab with Jethro ; on the other, to imply that he was shortly afterwards one of the seventy elders upon whom the spirit came. This, however, is not likely. Hobab does indeed seem to have gone with the people, but his descendants were not incorporated into Israel ; they were with them, but not of them.

Ver. 32.—**If thou go with us.** From Judges i. 16 we learn that the sons of Hobab joined themselves to the sons of Judah, and dwelt amongst them on the southern border of the land. Here is an " undesigned coincidence," albeit a slight one. Judah led the way on the march from Sinai to Canaan, and Hobab's duties as guide and scout would bring him more into contact with that tribe than with any other.

HOMILETICS.

Vers. 29—32.—*The friendly invitation.* Spiritually, we have here the voice of the saints calling to the wavering and undecided to cast in their lot with them, and to be partakers with them in those good things which God hath prepared for them that love him. Thereupon we have the voice of the wavering and undecided urging the ties and affections of this world as supreme. Then again the voice of the saints holding up the prospect at once of greater usefulness and of higher reward in the service of God. Finally (in the subsequent history), we have the assurance that these persuasions prevailed, and that these promises were made good. Consider—

I. THAT THE INVITATION WAS ADDRESSED TO HOBAB. This Hobab was—1. A child of the desert, a " Kenite," whose *home* was in the wild country outside the promised land : a country which had a certain wild freedom and a precarious abundance, but withal full of dangers, of drought, and of the shadow of death. 2. A child of a patriarchal family ; his father, " the priest of Midian," and a worshipper of the true God according to tradition. 3. A child of Reuel, " Moses' father-in-law," and therefore connected by family ties with Israel, and moreover an eye-witness to some extent of the power and mercy of the God of Israel. Hobab is the *child of this world*, whose *home* is amidst the precarious beauties and fading hopes of *time ;* who has a knowledge of God by tradition, and a knowledge of religion by observation, yet of both rather as belonging to others than to himself.

II. THAT THE INVITATION CAME FROM THE ISRAEL OF GOD. " Come with *us.*" From a people redeemed and separated, and sanctified, a " holy nation, a royal priesthood," whom God had chosen to be the peculiar instruments of his glory, the peculiar recipients of his bounty. The Israel of God are *we* who are indeed in this world, but not of it, having our true and certain home beyond the reach of chance and change. Note, that countless *individuals* amongst the tribes of Israel never reached that land, and never tried to—but the people, *as a people,* reached it ; even so, countless numbers of professing Christians will never get to heaven, and do not try to, but the Church of God, *as a Church*, will attain to eternal life. Therefore, " come with *us.*"

III. THAT THE INVITATION WAS TO GO WITH THEM, *i. e.,* 1. To be partner and partaker in their pilgrimage, their toils, and trials ; 2. To be partner and partaker in their promised home to which *they* were journeying, in the blessings unto which *they* were called. As God " would have all men to be saved," so is it the chiefest desire of our hearts that all around us (and especially those connected with us) should share our blessings and our hopes, should be partakers with us (if need be) of that " light affliction " which worketh an " eternal weight of glory" (cf. Rom. ix. 3 and x. 2).

IV. THAT THE INDUCEMENT WAS, " WE WILL DO THEE GOOD." Not of their own ability, or of their own abundance, but by communicating unto him the good things which God should bestow on them. We may fearlessly say to the child of this world, " *we* will do thee good." Christianity is not individualism, but we are called " in one body," and spiritual blessings flow chiefly in one way or another through human channels. As a fact men find peace, support, sympathy, consolation here— heaven hereafter—*in* the society of the faithful, not *out* of it (cf. Mark x. 30).

V. THAT THE HINDRANCE TO HIS GOING WAS THE PRIOR CLAIM OF AN EARTHLY HOME AND KINDRED. "To mine own land, and to my kindred." His own land, although not half so good as the promised land, was familiar and accustomed. So were his relations, although they could not do half so much for him as Moses and the elders of Israel. Even so *the* great hindrance to a really religious walk are to be found in the habits of life which are so familiar, and in the associates who have so much influence. Many find an insuperable difficulty in breaking with the evil or vain traditions of their home, their education, their "set" or class: they *would* go—but the bondage of custom is too strong for them (cf. Luke ix. 59—62; xiv. 25, 26).

VI. THAT THE FURTHER AND (AS IT SEEMS) THE PREVAILING INDUCEMENT WITH HIM TO GO WAS THE HELP HE MIGHT AFFORD, THE GOOD HE MIGHT DO. Perhaps it was after all as much for Hobab's sake as for the people's, that Moses suggested to him of how much use he might be; but no doubt his training and qualifications did fit him for this service, and he felt that it was so. Even so there is a nobler, and often more potent, incentive to a religious life than even the glory which is to come. The prospect of being really useful to others, of making the utmost of all their gifts and acquirements—and *that* in the service of the Most High—is the great ambition which we ought to set before the eyes of men. A worldly life is a wasted life; a religious life is (or at least may be, and ought to be) a life of unselfish activity; and this, of all prospects and attractions, has the strongest charm for each nobler soul (cf. Matt. iv. 19; Luke xix. 31, 34; Acts ix. 16; xxvi. 16—18). Consider, also—

VII. THAT HOBAB'S WORK AND SERVICE ON THE MARCH WERE NOT SUPERFLUOUS IF RENDERED, NOR YET ESSENTIAL IF DENIED. The supernatural guidance vouchsafed to Israel left plenty of room for his human skill and experience; but if Israel had been deprived of them, no doubt the supernatural guidance would somehow have sufficed. Even so there is room in the work of salvation of souls for all human effort and wisdom, however Divine a matter it appears; and yet if any man withhold his co-operation the work shall not therefore be really injured (cf. 1 Cor. i. 27, 28; iii. 7, 9).

HOMILIES BY VARIOUS AUTHORS.

Vers. 29—32.—*Hobab invited; or, the Church's call to them that are without.* This incident carries one back in thought to the day, one and forty years ago, when Moses, a fugitive from Egypt, arrived at the well in Midian, and there met with the daughter of Jethro. At the expiry of forty years the call of the Lord constrained Moses to forsake Midian, that he might be the leader of Israel; but it did not finally sever him from all connection with the house of his Midianite father-in-law. When Israel, on the march from Egypt, arrived at the border of the wilderness of Sinai, Jethro came out to meet him, and to welcome him. This done, he returned to his own house and sheep-walks. But his son Hobab stayed behind, and witnessed the giving of the law. When the march was about to be resumed, Hobab proposed to bid farewell to his sister and Moses. But Moses would not hear of it. Reminding Hobab of the inheritance awaiting Israel in the land of the Canaanites, he, in his own name, and in the name of the whole people, invited him to join himself to their company, and share in all the goodness which the Lord was about to do to them in fulfilment of his promise. This invitation, addressed by Moses and the congregation to one who did not belong to the seed of Jacob, is of no small interest historically. And its practical interest is still greater; for it exhibits a bright example of a desire which ought always to find place in the hearts of the faithful—the desire to allure into their fellowship "them that are without," whether these are the heathen abroad, or the careless and vicious at home. Viewing the text in this light, it presents three topics which claim consideration.

I. THE CHURCH'S PROFESSION OF FAITH AND HOPE. "We are journeying unto the place of which the Lord said, I will give it you. . . . The Lord hath spoken good concerning Israel." On the lips of Moses and the congregation this was really a profession and utterance of faith. From the day that God called Abraham, he and his seed were taught to expect Canaan as their inheritance; and it was faith's business to embrace the promise and look for its accomplishment. In the faith of this promise Abraham and Isaac and Jacob lived and died. In the faith of it Joseph, when he died, gave commandment concerning his bones. In the faith of it Moses forsook Pharaoh's house. In the faith of it he refused to cast in his lot with Jethro's Midianites, and called the son born to him in Midian Gershom, "a stranger there." In the faith of the same promise Israel was now resuming the march towards Canaan. It is no idle fancy which sees in all this a parable of the Christian faith and the Christian profession. We also look for an inheritance and rest. "We believe that we shall be saved." We have been begotten to a living hope by the resurrection of Christ. As truly as the tribes in the wilderness, we (unless we have believed in vain) have turned our backs upon Egypt, and have set our faces towards the better country. We are journeying. We are strangers and pilgrims. I admit that among professing Christians there are many who have no real hope of the kind described; many, also, whose hope is anything but bright and strong. Nevertheless, the world is certainly mistaken when it persuades itself that the Christian hope is an empty boast. There are tens of thousands whose lives are sustained and controlled by it continually.

II. THE CHURCH'S INVITATION TO THEM THAT ARE WITHOUT. "Come thou with us." The words remind us of a truth too often forgotten, namely, that even under the Old Testament the Church was by no means the exclusive body which some take it to have been. It had an open door and a welcome for all who desired to enter. In point of fact, a considerable proportion of those who constituted the Hebrew commonwealth at any given time were of Gentile descent. Moses did not act without warrant when he invited Hobab to come in—he and all his. At the same time it is to be remembered that the gospel Church is not to be contented with simply maintaining the attitude of the Old Testament Church towards them that are without. We are not only to keep an open door and make applicants welcome, we are to go forth and compel them to come in. Christ's Church is a missionary Church. A religious society which neglects this function—which refuses to obey the command to go and preach the gospel to every creature—lacks one of the notes of the Christian Church. We are to charge ourselves with the duty of sending the gospel to the far-off heathen. As for the careless and ungodly who are our neighbours, we are not only to send to them the word, but ought personally to invite them to come with us.

III. THE ARGUMENTS WITH WHICH THE INVITATION IS FORTIFIED. I refer especially to those urged by Moses and the congregation here. 1. It will be well for Hobab and his house if he will come (ver. 32). No doubt the man who follows Christ must be prepared to take up the cross—must be ready to suffer reproach, to encounter tribulation, to take in hand self-denying work. These things are not pleasant to flesh and blood. Yet after all, Wisdom's ways are the ways of pleasantness. Compared with the devil's yoke, the yoke of Christ is easy. Godliness has the promise of both worlds. Those who have given Christ's service a fair trial would not for the world change masters. 2. Hobab is to come, for the Lord hath need of him (vers. 30, 31). It seems that Moses' brother-in-law feared he might be an intruder and a burden. No such thing. A son of the desert would be of manifold service to the congregation in the desert. There is great wisdom in this argument. It is a great mistake to suppose that people seriously inquiring after salvation will attach themselves most readily to the Church which will give them nothing to do. The nobler sort will be attracted rather by the prospect of being serviceable. To sum up—the argument which will carry the greatest weight with unbelievers and despisers of God is that which utters itself in the Church's profession of its own faith and hope. A Church whose faith is weak and whose hope is dim will be found to have little power to rouse the careless and draw them into its fellowship. Men are most likely to be gained to Christ and the way of salvation by the Church whose members manifest by their words and lives the presence in their hearts of a bright and living hope of eternal life.—B.

Vers. 29—32.—*Moses and Hobab.* I. THE WONDERFUL CHANGES GOD MAKES IN HUMAN LIFE. What men do themselves, the history of self-made men, is often very astonishing, yet nothing to the history of God-made men. For forty years Moses had been a shepherd in this wilderness; as we may conjecture, an oft companion with Hobab in these very scenes. Suddenly he goes away to Egypt to visit his brethren, and in the course of a few months returns to the wilderness with over 600,000 fighting men, beside women and children. So in the Scriptures we find many other wonderful God-made changes in human life. Joseph leaving his brethren a slave— his brethren finding him again prime minister to Pharaoh. The lad David brought from the recluse pastoral scene to stand before armies and slay the dreaded foe of Israel. Jesus visiting Nazareth to be a wonderment and stumbling-block to those who had known him from infancy. Saul among the persecutors when he left Jerusalem—among the persecuted when he returns.

II. These wonderful changes may be exhibited so as to make others the subjects of them. Hobab had probably been much with Moses, for old acquaintance' sake, while the people of God were round about Sinai. The recollections of the past were comparatively fresh, and Moses had a natural interest in a kinsman. But now the time has come to move, and what must Hobab do ? The necessities of God's kingdom bring a separation sooner or later in all friendship, unless both parties are in the kingdom. It is the critical moment of Hobab's life, and he must decide at once. Not but what he might change his mind, and follow afterwards, only the chances were that it was now or never. Thus Hobab is the illustration of all who are asked and pressed to join the people of God. To such persons every narration of God's experienced grace to others brings a cordial invitation in the very telling of it. It is our own fault if we be mere spectators of the cloud, hearers of the trumpet. God had made most gracious provision for the stranger to come into Israel. No word could be more cordial and pressing than that of Moses here. It was not hatred of outsiders as outsiders, but as abominably wicked, that brought God's vengeance on them.

III. These wonderful changes may be exhibited without producing sympathy and appreciation. The reply of Hobab illustrates the natural man in his want of sympathy with spiritual struggles. "The natural man receiveth not the things of the Spirit of God." How many there have been of such spectators in every age, those who have seen some old companion suddenly borne away, come under the influence of new powers, and turn what is called fanatic and enthusiast ! The old ties are all broken, or, if any remain, there is no substance in them. Believer and unbeliever may continue to meet in the commerce of the world, but in closer relations they can meet no longer. When Pitt was told of the great religious change that had passed over Wilberforce, he suggested to his friend that he was out of spirits, and that company and conversation would be the best way of dissipating his impressions. Hobab was quite contented with his sheep in the desert. He did not want to be circumcised, and held in with such rigorous restrictions. Doubtless he had a warm place in his heart for Moses, but he could not say as Buxton once signed himself in a letter to J. J. Gurney, "Yours, in the threefold cord of taste, affection, and religion."—Y.

Ver. 29.—*A right feeling and a Christian invitation.* I. The feeling which should be in all Christian hearts. "We are journeying unto the place of which the Lord said, I will give it you." Thus our view of the future should be regulated as a future not of our achieving, but of God's giving. The end is definite and assured, however devious and tedious the way may be. The end is one not to be reached immediately ; the place which God will give us must be at a secure distance from spiritual Egypt, with its bondage and tyranny. The feeling which we entertain with respect to this place must be a confident one, and expressed in a manner corresponding. The feeling thus entertained and expressed must have all our actions in harmony with it. Our closest connections with earth should be as nothing more than the pegs of the Israelite tents, here to-day and gone to-morrow (John xiv. 1—3 ; xvii. 24 ; 2 Cor. v. 1—9 ; Heb. iv. 11 ; xi. 13—16 ; xii. 27 ; 1 Pet. i. 3, 4).

II. The invitation which should come from all Christian lips. "Come thou with us, and we will do thee good." Addressed to those who may think they have a true home among things seen and temporal, but who are as really without a home as is the Christian. If Christians are sure they are going onward to the true home chosen, secured, and enriched by God, what is more Christ-like than that they should ask their Hobab-neighbours to join their well-protected, well-provisioned caravan ?

If even now sweet influences from the rest that remaineth for the people of God possess our souls, these should be used to win others from the illusions of this passing scene.   What a blessed occupation to be drawing human spirits into that sphere of the unseen and eternal which alone gives them a fitting service here, and a true rest and reward hereafter !   The invitation must be a loving and constraining one.   To promise good to others, we must feel and show that we have got good ourselves. The invitation can only come when we ourselves feel that we are in the right way to the desired end.

III. THE REASON BY WHICH THE INVITATION IS ENFORCED.   "The Lord hath spoken good concerning Israel."   Concerning *Israel*.   Concerning other nations he had spoken ill for their idolatries and abominations.   Sodom was a witness to his consuming wrath, and his hand had been laid heavily on Egypt.   But concerning Israel he had spoken good in a large and loving way (Exod. iii. 6—8; vi. 6—8; xxiii. 20—33).   The stranger then must cease to be a stranger, and enter by circumcision of the heart into the spiritual Israel.   The force of the invitations does not depend on our sanguine anticipations.   Others are as well able to consider what the Lord has spoken as we are.   His word is the guarantee.   If even the Jewish nation, the typical Israel, has still to have prophecies fulfilled, how much more its antitype, the spiritual Israel, those who are Jews inwardly !   Consider for yourselves then all the good that God has spoken concerning Israel.—Y.

Ver. 31.—*A fresh appeal*.   Moses has failed in appealing to Hobab by a regard for his own best interests, but he has a second arrow in his quiver.   He will touch Hobab's sense of friendship, his manliness, anything that was chivalrous in him ; he will put him on his honour to render just the one service he was able to render. Note—

I. THE SERVICES WHICH THE WORLD CAN RENDER TO THE CHURCH.   We may fairly assume, considering Judges i. 16, that Hobab went with Moses after all (Matt. xxi. 29). He will help Moses the man, when he cares nothing for Moses the prophet of God. There may be a certain sense of duty even when there is none of sin and spiritual need, a certain power to help, even though the highest power be utterly lacking. The peculiar strength of the Church is in God ; when it does spiritual work with spiritual instruments ; but the world may also be tributary in its own way.   The wealth of the world is not a spiritual thing, but it has been helpful to the Church. Men of the world have neither the Christ-like love nor the self-denial to initiate enterprises, which, nevertheless, they will generously support.   In person they will do nothing ; in purse they will do much.   The printer who cares nothing for Christ, who to-day prints the scoffs and quibbles of an atheist, or some frivolous fiction, may to-morrow print a Bible, or a precious biography of some departed saint.   Places of worship have been built by men who had no religion in them.   Fishers' boats ferried Jesus across the lake of Galilee ; trading ships took Paul on his missionary journey ; and soldiers of Cæsar conveyed him to Rome, where for so long a time he had panted to preach the gospel.

II. THE HOLD WHICH THE CHURCH KEEPS ON THE WORLD.   Hobab said very bluntly he would not go with Moses ; but he had not thought of all the considerations that might be brought to bear upon him.   The grasp of Moses was firmer than he thought.   Let no worldly man despise what he deems the dreams and delusions of the Christian.   They may have a greater power on him in the end than at present he has any conception of.   Human friendships and old associations are part of the bait with which Christ furnishes his fishers of men.   Those who will not read the Scriptures for salvation, and who laugh at the schemes of doctrine drawn from them, yet find in the same Scriptures too much of poetry and interest to be slightingly passed by.   What a strange thing, too, to hear men, even in all their vehement denials of the supernatural, extolling Jesus of Nazareth, admiring his spirit, and recommending his ethics.   However they try, they cannot get away from him.   "I, if I be lifted up, will draw all men unto me."   We must not despair of unbelievers, even after many refusals (Luke xiii. 6—9).   In connection with Moses and Hobab, a reference to Tennyson's 'In Memoriam,' lxiii., "Dost thou look back on what hath been ?" &c., may be found homiletically helpful.—Y.

EXPOSITION.

THE ACTUAL DEPARTURE FROM SINAI (vers. 33—36). Ver. 33.—**And they departed.** These words mark the moment of actual departure, which has been anticipated in the general statement of ver. 12. It was one of the supreme moments in the life of Israel—one of those beginnings or "departures" which lead to untold gain or loss; it was, in fact, although they knew it not, the commencement of a march which for almost all of them should know no end except within a hasty grave. No doubt, during the months spent at Sinai, every preparation had been made for the onward journey; but none the less it was a stupendous enterprise to march that vast host, so largely composed of women and children, so little inured to such fatigue, and so impatient of such discipline, for three consecutive days into a wilderness. **Three days' journey.** This expression is apparently a general one, and not to be strictly pressed (cf. Gen. xxx. 36; Exod. iii. 18; xv. 22). At the same time it implies (1) that the host twice halted for the night during the journey, and (2) that the whole journey was regarded as one and in some sense as complete in itself. The *terminus ad quem* of this three days' journey is given us in ver. 12; it was to take them across the intervening belt of sand, and to land them fairly within the "wilderness of Paran." During this journey no doubt the march would be pushed on as steadily as possible, but it is not likely that it would cover so much as thirty miles. A modern army, unencumbered with non-combatants, does not make more than ten miles a day over difficult country, nor can cattle be driven faster than that. Even to accomplish that rate, and to keep the whole multitude together, as the narrative implies, required supernatural aid and strength. For the direction of the march see notes on ch. xiii. **The ark of the covenant of the Lord went before them.** It is obvious that what is apparently affirmed here is apparently at variance with ch. ii. 17 and ver. 21 of this chapter, which speak of the "holy things"—of which the ark was the most holy—as carried by the Kohathites in the very midst of the long line of march. Three opinions have been held on the subject. 1. That the ark was really carried with the other "holy things," and only "went before" metaphorically, as a general may be said to lead his troops, although he may not be actually in front of them; to which it is obvious to reply that if the ark did not actually precede the host, there was no possible way in which it could direct their movements; the cloud alone would be the visible expression of the Divine guidance. 2. That the "holy things" generally were ordered to be carried

in the midst of the host by the Kohathites, but that God reserved the place of the ark itself to his own immediate disposition. A general does not include himself in his own marching orders, however minute; and the ark was the outward symbol of God's own personal presence and guidance. It is, therefore, not at all surprising that the first intimation of the position of the ark on the march should be given at the moment when the march actually commenced. 3. That the usual place for the ark was no doubt with the sanctuary, as implied in the orders, but that *on this special occasion* the ark went to the front in consequence of some Divine intimation, just as it did at the crossing of Jordan and at the taking of Jericho. Certainly there is much reason in this view, considering how momentous and formidable was their first assay at marching from their temporary home towards that unknown land beyond the northern horizon. If the deep waters of Jordan might fright them, or the walls of Jericho defy them, well might they shrink from plunging into the broken, stony, and intractable country into which the ark and the cloud now led them. We shall probably think that either habitually or at least occasionally the ark *did* go before, and that the feet of them that bare it were supernaturally directed, either by the movements of the cloud, or by some more secret intimation, towards the destined place of rest. It is allowed by all that the cloud preceded and directed the march, and it would be strange indeed if these twin symbols of the Divine presence had been so far separated from one another; for the accustomed place of the cloud was above the tabernacle, *i. e.* above the ark, yet outside of the tabernacle, so as to be visible to all.

Ver. 34.—**The cloud of the Lord was upon them by day.** It would seem as if the cloud, which was luminous by night, dense and dark by day, spread itself upwards and backwards from over the ark, overshadowing the host as it followed—a refreshment at any rate to those who were near, perhaps to all, and a guiding beacon to those who were afar. To what extent the people at large were able to enjoy this shade amidst the burning heats of the desert we cannot possibly tell, but there is no doubt that it dwelt in the memory of the nation, and gave meaning to such expressions as the "shadow of the Almighty" (Ps. xci. 1), and "the shadow of a cloud" (Isa. xxv. 4, 5).

Ver. 35.—**When the ark set forward.** These words, taken in connection with the words "when it rested," in the following verse, confirm the belief that at this time (at any rate) the ark went before the host; for if it had remained in the midst, it would not have stirred until half the tribes had moved off, nor would it have halted until half the camp was pitched, whereas it is evident that its setting forward and standing still were the decisive moments of the day. They had, as it were, a sacramental character; they were visible signs, corresponding to invisible realities, as the movements of the hands on the dial correspond to the action of the machinery within. When the ark and the cloud set forward, it was the Almighty God going on before to victory; when the ark and the cloud rested, it was the all-merciful God returning to protect and cherish his own. This is clearly recognised in the morning and evening prayer of Moses. The typical and spiritual character of that setting forward and that resting could not well have been lost upon any religious mind—that God going before us is the certain and abiding pledge of final victory, that God returning to us is the only hope of present safety. **Rise up, Lord, and let thine enemies be scattered.** The sixty-eighth Psalm, which we have learnt to associate with the wonders of Pentecost and the triumphs of the Church on earth, seems to be an expansion of Moses' morning prayer.

Ver. 36.—**Return, O Lord, unto the many thousands** (literally, myriad thousands; see ch. i. 16) **of Israel.** שׁוּבָה being construed with the accusative is of somewhat doubtful interpretation. It may be as in the beautiful and familiar rendering of the A. V., than which nothing could be more obviously in harmony with the circumstances, and the feelings which gave rise to the prayer. Or it may be necessary to translate it by a transitive verb, and then it will be either, with many moderns, "*Restore*, O Lord, the myriad thousands of Israel," *i. e.* to ·their promised home; or, with the Septuagint, "*Convert*, O Lord (ἐπίστρεφε, Κύριε), the thousand myriads of Israel." If the ordinary reading be (as it appears) grammatically defensible, it is unquestionably to be preferred. Only Moses, as he looked upon that huge multitude covering the earth far and wide, could rightly feel how unutterably awful their position would be if on any day the cloud *were* to rise and melt into the evening sky instead of poising itself above the sanctuary of Israel. The Septuagint transposes ver. 34 from its proper place to the end of the chapter, apparently in order to keep together the verses which speak of the movements of the ark. Many Hebrew MSS. mark vers. 35, 36 with inverted nuns, ؟, but the explanations given are fanciful, and the meaning uncertain.

HOMILETICS.

Vers. 33—36.—*The heavenward march.* Spiritually, we have here the journey of the Church of God, or of the faithful soul, towards heaven under the guidance of the Saviour. For the ark, whereon rested the Shechinah, and in which was carried the law, is the type of Jesus, in whom dwelt the whole fulness of the Godhead bodily (cf. 2 Cor. iii. 18; iv. 6 *b.*; Col. ii. 9), and in whom as manifested to us is found the new law of love and liberty (Ps. xl. 8; cf. Mark xii. 30, 31; Rom. vii. 6; Jas. i. 25; 1 Pet. ii. 21 *b.*). Therefore we have here Jesus going before his own, (1) to guide them in the daily path, (2) to lead them to their rest when the journey is over (cf. John x. 4; xiv. 2). In the cloud, again, we have (it may be) the refreshment of the Holy Spirit ("another Comforter"), when we face the burden and heat of life. Lastly, we have the devout prayers of the faithful for the help of God in their spiritual warfare, for the presence of God with their souls. Consider, therefore, on vers. 33, 34—

I. THAT THE HOUR OF DEPARTURE FROM HOREB, SO LONG DELAYED, AND THE PLUNGE INTO THE STONY DESERT, SO OFTEN ANTICIPATED, CAME AT LAST. Many may have thought it would never really arrive, but it did; and in a few hours the mount, which had been the scene of such wondrous events, was hidden for ever from their eyes. Even so we cannot abide on the heights of contemplation (with Moses), or in the plains of instruction (with the people). There is a time to receive marching orders; there is a much longer and more trying time to march accordingly amidst hard trials and difficult undertakings—and this time will surely come to each and all (Matt. x. 38; Acts xiv. 22 *b.*; 2 Tim. ii. 12; iii. 12).

II. THAT THE ISRAELITES WERE NOT REQUIRED TO FIND THEIR OWN WAY, OR TRUST TO HUMAN GUIDANCE: THE ARK WENT BEFORE THEM. They only had to follow as best they might. Even so Jesus goes before his own; once for all, by his death, resurrection, and ascension; daily, by his example and encouragement. As he has gone before us all into heaven to prepare a "rest" for the people of God, so he goes before each weary soul in life and death to find out resting-places and places of refreshment for it (Ps. xxiii. 4; John viii. 12; xii. 26; xiv. 2, 6).

III. That the Israelites were in part shielded from the fierce and fatal heats of the desert march by the cloud which overshadowed them from above the ark. For that luminous cloud which rested permanently over the ark was spread over the following host when on the march. St. Paul says that the Jews were "baptized unto Moses *in the cloud* and in the sea" (1 Cor. x. 2), whence it appears that as the passage of the sea represented in a figure the baptism of water which separates outwardly unto Christ (the Moses of the better covenant), so did the over-hanging cloud with its moist coolness represent the baptism of the Spirit, which is an abiding refreshment to the faithful while (but only while) they follow Christ. And thus the old hymn, *Veni Sanctus Spiritus*—

> Thou of Comforters the best ;
> Thou the soul's most welcome guest ;
> *Sweet refreshment here below ;*
>
> In our labour rest most sweet.
> *Grateful coolness in the heat,*
> *Solace in the midst of woe.*

Even so, therefore, the overshadowing presence (cf. Luke i. 35) of the Holy Ghost is the blessed solace, comfort, and refreshment of the faithful in fiery trials, fierce temptations, and weary disappointments ; and this overshadowing Presence reaches us only from and through the glorified humanity of Jesus (our Ark), and only while we walk in faith and patience (cf. John vii. 39 ; xvi. 7 ; Rom. viii. 14 ; 1 John ii. 20 ; 1 Pet. iv. 14). Note, that the unrecorded sufferings and vexations of such a host on such a march must have been beyond description ; but this much appears, that the nearer they kept to the ark the more they were sheltered by the cloud : if any staid in camp, he had *no* shade. The more closely we follow Jesus, the more comfort of the Spirit shall we have amidst the unavoidable sorrows and sufferings of life. And note, that there are in the Old Testament very few symbols of the Holy Spirit, whereas there are an endless number of types of Christ—and this, no doubt, in accordance with the deep saying of John vii. 39 (οὔπω γὰρ ἦν πνεῦμα ἅγιον). When, therefore, we find one which is recognised in the New Testament, it is the more precious. Consider, again, on vers. 35, 36—

I. That every day of the march had for Moses its two supreme moments, of setting out and of settling down, and each had its own dangers and anxieties. Even so every day in a Christian's life has its morning and evening, its opening and closing ; its going forth to work, to business, to converse with the outer world, to manifold encounter with the strange, the unexpected, the difficult, perhaps the terrible ; its coming in to rest, to ease, to unguarded relaxation, to the little circle where self is paramount, where the individual is all important. These two points are the critical points in the Christian's daily life.

II. That Moses made his morning prayer for Divine defence and aid against the foe. He knew that many enemies were hovering round (like the Amalekites) who might attack them at any time, even when least expected, and might find them, humanly speaking, an easy prey. He prayed that *God* would undertake their cause, and put to flight their foes. Even so the faithful soul, looking forward to the active hours of the day, knows from sad experience that spiritual foes will dog its path to assail it by temptation and overthrow it by sin when least prepared. Therefore, before it ventures forth, it beseeches God to be its succour and defence against all the craft and subtlety of its foes.

III. That Moses made his evening prayer for the continuance of the Divine Presence in their midst. He knew that the people were helpless, and moreover stiff-necked and hard-hearted, and that mischief would breed in the camp as readily as it might meet them on the march, and that they must perish miserably if left to themselves. He prayed that God would stay with them, and be their worship, and remain the centre of their life *ab intra*, as well as their defence *ab extra*. Even so the Christian's evening prayer is, "Abide with us." The faithful soul, when it ceases from outward cares and is most thrown upon itself, feels most how lost would be its state without the abiding Presence and grace of God ; and then it beseeches him—whom it has more or less offended—to return to it, because without him it were empty, desolate, and destroyed. Note, that if we read with some, "Restore the many thousands of Israel," *i. e.* to their promised land, then it is the voice of the faithful, recognising at each pause in life that we are still strangers and wanderers here, and beseeching God to bring us to our true and only rest (cf. 2 Cor. v. 4 ; Phil. iii. 11 ; Rev. vi. 10, 11). And cf. the ancient prayer, "Beseeching thee shortly to accomplish the number of thine elect, and to hasten thy kingdom, that *we with all those* that are departed in the true faith of thy holy name, may have our perfect consummation and joy in thy eternal and everlasting glory." Or, if we read with the Septuagint, "convert the many thousands of Israel," then it is the voice of the faithful in the intervals of labour supplicating God for all who in any wise belong to the Israel of God, that the grace of a true and entire conversion—which is the one thing needful—may be granted unto them (cf. Luke xxii. 32 *b.* ; 2 Cor. xiii. 9 *b.* ; 1 Thess. iii. 10 *b.*).

HOMILIES BY VARIOUS AUTHORS.

Vers. 35, 36.—*The prayers at the moving and resting of the ark.* Here are two petitions—one as the cloud rose to point the way, the other as it settled down again to indicate the time for rest. The morning and the evening prayer cannot be the same ; there is one set of needs to be supplied during the day, and another during the night.

THE FIRST PETITION. It was fixed on the one thing needed, as the Israelites journeyed on into unknown territory. Moses needed not to pray for *guidance.* They were being guided, and had nothing to do but follow. Behind the ark and the cloud there was the evident duty of *obedience*, but what was there in front? Moses could make some guess from what he had already experienced. Before the Israelites had been three months out of Egypt, they were met by Amalek at Rephidim, blocking the way to Sinai. Moses, therefore, recognises the great likelihood of *more enemies in front*, now they have left Sinai. The great bulk of his followers doubtless thought more of the present than the future, and both present and future they wanted to be like the past in Egypt, full of good things for their sinful cravings. But Moses, with a different spirit, felt there were enemies in the way. Getting into Canaan meant not only journeying but fighting. It is a serious defect in us that we do not think enough of the spiritual enemies in front. There are examples to warn : Peter overrating natural courage ; Demas, overcome by the allurements of the present age. Notice that, *in its own way*, the New Testament is every whit as warlike in its spirit as the old (Matt. x. 34 ; Rom. vii. 23 ; 2 Cor. vii. 5 ; 2 Cor. x. 3—5 ; Eph. vi. 10—17 ; 1 Tim. i. 18 ; Heb. iv. 12 ; Rev. i. 16 : indeed the Revelation is full of spiritual war and conquest). These enemies in front are considered also as *God's enemies.* "*Thine* enemies." As men attack one another through their property, so God's enemies attack him through his people. God in the blessedness and security of his own nature is unassailable, but in the workings of his manifold creation the powers of evil may attack him, maintaining a long and bitter struggle ('Paradise Lost,' B. ii. 310—370). Do not think of these powers as aiming simply at our destruction. This is but a means to an end. There is a far sublimer and more encouraging view, that they are aiming to destroy the government of God. We never find out the purpose of a battle by looking at the conflicts of the private soldiers and inferior officers. We must come to the supreme authorities. It is they who inspire and direct everything. So there may be a struggle going on in the universe of which we, with our little horizon, can form but a feeble conception. Lastly, it is prayed that these enemies should be *decisively dealt with.* It is an awful thing to think of, but we must not shut our eyes to plain and solemn facts, that as we look backwards from this point to the beginning of the Scriptures, we find the Almighty, in three instances, acting against the iniquity of the world in a most decisive and comprehensive way. The deluge was a scattering, so was the destruction of Sodom, so was the overwhelming of Pharaoh and his hosts, which last great punitive act of God, Moses had seen with his own eyes, and celebrated with his own lips. There is enough to assure his people that he will make a final scattering in his own time.

THE SECOND PETITION. 1. It *was a welcome to the conqueror.* God was doing something for his people in conquest every day. We may be sure there was no day in all these long forty years but something was done to undermine the huge and threatening powers that opposed advancing Israel. As the huge tree is slowly hollowed and eaten away, leaving a mere shell to come down at last with a crash, so the strongholds of iniquity are effectually sapped, little by little. Jericho seemed to fall as in a day before the trumpet blasts of Israel ; in reality it had been nodding to its fall for years. So we may be constantly welcoming Jesus as the Captain of our salvation (Exod. xv. 2 ; Luke iv. 14, 15 ; Acts xiv. 26—28). 2. *It indicated the use to be made of the victory.* The enemies of God were scattered and dispossessed in order that his own people may come in and exercise a faithful stewardship for him. His victories open up regions which could not otherwise be attained. *E. g.* the risen Saviour, having triumphed over sin, death, and the grave, returned to his disciples in Galilee, telling them that all power was given to him in heaven and on earth, and thence he drew this consequence in the way of duty for them, that they were to go and disciple all nations, etc. (Matt. xxviii. 18—20). If the *risen Lord* be indeed with *us,* then, because he is risen, we, having still our fight with sin and death to accomplish, are nevertheless assured of ultimate victory.—Y.

EXPOSITION.

CHAPTER XI.

THE PLACE OF BURNING (vers. 1—3). Ver. 1.—**And when the people complained, it displeased the Lord.** There is no "when" in the original. It is literally, "And the people were as complainers evil in the ears of the Lord." This may be paraphrased as in the A. V. ; or it may be rendered as in the Septuagint, ἦν ὁ λαὸς γογγύζων πονηρὰ ἔναντι κυρίου (cf. 1 Cor. x. 10), where πονηρά means the wicked things they uttered in their discontent ; or the "evil" may mean the hardships they complained of. The Targums understand it in the same way as the Septuagint, and this seems to agree best with the context. As to the time and place of this complaining, the narrative seems to limit it within the three days' march from the wilderness of Sinai ; but it is not possible to fix it more precisely. It is sufficient that the very first incident in the great journey thought worthy of record was this sin and its punishment, and the natural conclusion is that it came to pass very shortly after the departure. As to the reason of the complaining, although it is not stated, and although there does not seem to have been any special cause of distress, we can hardly be mistaken about it. The fatigue and anxiety of the march, after a year's comparative idleness, the frightful nature of the country into which they were marching, and the unknown terrors of the way which lay before them, these were quite enough to shake their nerves and upset their minds. Such things could only be borne and faced in a spirit of faith and trustful dependence upon God and their appointed leaders, and that spirit they knew nothing of. Slavery, even when its outward pressure is past and

gone like a bad dream, leaves behind it above all things an incurable suspicion of, and a rooted disbelief in, others, which shows itself outwardly by blank ingratitude and persistent complaint of bad treatment. This is the well-known mental attitude of liberated slaves even towards their benefactors and liberators ; and in the case of Israel this temper extended to the King of Israel himself, whom they held responsible for all the privations and terrors of an apparently needless journey through a hideous waste. The Targum of Palestine says here, "There were wicked men of the people who, being discontent, devised and imagined evil before the Lord." The complaining, however, seems to have been general throughout the host, as the Psalmist more truly acknowledges (Ps. lxxviii. 17—22). **And the fire of the Lord burnt among them.** The "fire of the Lord" may mean one of three things. 1. Lightning, as apparently in Job i. 16 ; for lightning to the unscientific is the fiery bolt, even as thunder is the angry voice, of God (cf. 1 Sam. xii. 18, 19). 2. A miraculous outburst of flame from the Presence in the tabernacle, such as slew Nadab and Abihu (Levit. x. 2), and afterwards the 250 men who offered incense (ch. xvi. 35). 3. A miraculous descent of fire from heaven, as apparently in 2 Kings i. 10— 12 (cf. Rev. xiii. 13). Of these the second seems to be excluded by the fact that the conflagration was in the outskirts of the camp furthest removed from the tabernacle. If we suppose the fire to have been natural, we may further suppose that it set alight to the dry bushes and shrubs which abound in parts of the desert, and which blaze with great fury when the flame is driven by the wind. It is, however, at least as likely that a wholly supernatural visitation of God is here intended. What is most important to notice is this, that the punishment in this case followed hard and sore upon the sin, whereas before they came to Sinai the Lord had passed over similar murmurings without any chastisement (Exod. xv. 24 ; xvi. 2). The reason of this difference was twofold. In the first place, they had now had abundant opportunity to become acquainted with the power and goodness of the Lord, and had solemnly entered into covenant with him, and he had taken up his abode among them ; wherefore their responsibilities grew with their privileges, their dangers kept pace with their advantages. In the second place, they had while at Sinai committed an act of national apostasy (Exod. xxxii.), the punishment of which, although suspended (ver. 14), was only suspended (ver. 34), and was always capable of being revived ; Israel was plainly warned that he was under sentence, and that any disobedience would awake the terrors of the Lord against him. **And consumed . . . in the uttermost parts of the camp.** Probably setting fire to the outer line of tents, or some pitched outside the line, and consuming the people that were in them. The Targum of Palestine affirms that it "destroyed some of the wicked in the outskirts of the house of Dan, with whom was a graven image ;" but this attempt to shift the responsibility, and to alter the character of the sin, is clearly worthless, and only suggested by occurrences wholly unconnected with the present (see Judges xviii.).

Ver. 2.—**And the people cried unto Moses.** Fear brought them to their senses, and they knew that their only hope was in their mediator, who had already saved them by his intercession from a worse destruction (Exod. xxxii. 30—34). **The fire was quenched.** Rather, " went out." As its beginning was supernatural, or at least was so ordered as to appear so, its end also was due to the Divine intervention, not to human efforts.

Ver. 3.—**And he called the name of the place Taberah.** Or Tabeérah (תַּבְעֵרָה). This name does not occur in the list of stations in ch. xxxiii., which mentions nothing between Sinai and Kibroth-Hattaavah. It would seem probable, however, that the conflagration occurred while Israel was encamped, or else there could hardly have been a burning "in the end of the camp." We may therefore suppose either that Tabeérah was some spot in the immediate neighbourhood of Sinai whither the people gathered for their first long march ; or that it was one of the halting-places on the "three days' journey" not mentioned in the list, because that journey was considered as all one ; or that it was the same place afterwards called Kibroth-Hattaavah. There is nothing in the narrative to decide a question which is in itself unimportant. It is necessary to remember that where the ancient and local names derived from marked natural features were not available, such names as Tabeérah given to the halting-places of so vast a host must have had a very loose significance.

HOMILETICS.

Vers. 1—3.—*Wrath awaked and wrath appeased.* In this short passage we have, in a microcosm, the whole sad history of the Church. For the history of the Church, as it is glorious on the side of God and his faithfulness, so it is sad indeed on the side of man and his unfaithfulness. Here we may see trial followed at once by failure, temptation by sin ; failure and sin followed by fiery wrath. Yet wrath is never without mercy, for the fire is quenched by the voice of the mediator. Consider, therefore—

I. THAT THE VERY FIRST INCIDENT RECORDED BETWEEN SINAI AND CANAAN WAS SIN. There was no gradual descent ; it broke out all at once. So it was in the beginning—immediately after the creation, the fall ; and so it was in the second beginning of the race (Gen. ix. 21). Even so it is still : the first actual fact which meets us in the history of a soul on its way to heaven is some sin or failure on its part. It is the one thing which more than any other determines the character of *practical* religion, as distinguished from *theoretical* (James iii. 2 ; 1 John i. 8).

II. THAT THE ROOT OF THIS EVIL PLANT WAS TO BE FOUND IN THE NATURE OF THE PEOPLE, MADE CROOKED BY GENERATIONS OF SERVITUDE, AND NOT RADICALLY ALTERED BY THE DISCIPLINE OF A YEAR. Even so human nature, terribly corrupt as it is, is the nature of the elect too : it is indeed sanctified and improved by the operations of grace, but not superseded ; it remains human nature still, and as such is sure to assert itself. Therefore " regeneration," which signifies the renewal of this nature, is indeed bestowed in time (John iii. 5 ; Titus iii. 5), but is also reserved for eternity (Matt. xix. 28), in testimony that it is only partial here. One of the saddest, the most obvious, and yet most unlooked-for and perplexing of facts about regenerate humanity is the persistence within it of evil, whether proper to the age, the race, the family, or the individual (Rom. vii. 18—25).

III. THAT THE FRUIT OF THIS EVIL PLANT WAS THUS SUDDENLY RIPENED BY THE OUTWARD HARDSHIPS AND TRIALS OF THE MARCH. Encamped at comparative ease about Sinai, the tendency to sin lay dormant, the root seemed dead : a few days, a few hours perhaps, of scorching heat and unaccustomed toil, and the poison fruit was already matured, the whole camp was in rebellion against God. Even so there are evil dispositions latent in many (if not in all) of us which need but a little stress of circumstance to bring them into active play, to ripen them into open sin, and that with startling quickness, unless restrained by grace. The sudden falls of good men are only sudden because we do not see the strength of evil in them which is waiting its opportunity. Hence the absolute necessity of trial and conflict to test the worth of our religion (Matt. x. 22 ; 2 Tim. ii. 12 ; James i. 12 ; Rev. i. 9 ; ii. 11, &c. ; vii. 14).

IV. THAT THE FORM WHICH THEIR REBELLION TOOK WAS THAT OF COMPLAINING— there being indeed nothing that they could *do* under the circumstances. Even so the fruit of sinful feelings and desires is quite as often discontent as anything more active, because the more active forms of sin are so often out of our reach. An evil heart is the source of all sins, and the evil heart almost always shows itself in a state of inward discontent which finds vent in outward complaints. Hence the " unthank- ful " are next door to the " unholy " (2 Tim. iii. 2), and all one with the " evil " (Luke vi. 35). A discontented heart is a hot-bed of every kind of sin (cf. Mark xiv. 10 ; John xii. 4—6).

V. THAT THE ANGER OF THE LORD WAS MORE HOT AGAINST THEM, AND THEIR PUNISHMENT MORE SEVERE, THAN BEFORE THEY CAME TO SINAI. For they had received the law, and entered into the covenant, and had the worship and presence of God in the midst of them. Even so the more light and grace we have, the more awful will it be to sin against that light, in despite of that grace. So the sin of the Jew was worse than that of the heathen ; of the Christian than of the Jew ; of the Christian in an enlightened age than of the Christian in a dark age. What must be the wrath of God against the sins of an age and people such as this ! (Luke xii. 47, 48 ; John ix. 41 ; Rom. ii. 12 ; Heb. ii. 2, 3 ; x. 26—31).

VI. THAT THE PEOPLE IN THEIR FEAR CRIED TO MOSES. They dared not cry to God, by reason of their unworthiness, but they knew that if Moses prayed for them he would be heard, because he was their mediator (Gal. iii. 19, 20). Even so we, in our sin and our distress, are neither able nor worthy to pray to God save through the mediation of Jesus Christ. All prayer must be addressed, consciously or uncon- sciously, through him. Even the prayer of the heathen, who knows no mediator, will be heard *because* the Son of man receives his prayer and offers his own intercession with it. How presumptuous is it in Christian people to join in prayers which are *not* offered in the name, or through the mediation, of the one Mediator ! (John xiv. 14 ; 1 Tim. ii. 5 ; Heb. xii. 24, and cf. Rev. viii. 3). And note, that the Lord's Prayer may be objected to this doctrine of mediation. But it is to be noted—(1) that it was modelled on the synagogue prayers before the atonement ; (2) that as a Christian prayer, it is the prayer of Christ in us, in which we share by virtue of our sonship in him (John xx. 17 ; 1 John iii. 1).

VII. THAT THE PEOPLE CRIED TO MOSES ONLY. They did not resort to Aaron or to Miriam, because they were relations of Moses, or to Joshua, because he was an eminent servant of Moses, and had great influence with him ; for Moses only was their mediator. Even so Christian people must not "cry" to any but the one Mediator, if the fire of God's anger against sin is to be quenched. It is one thing to ask the prayers of a fellow-suppliant ; it is another and very different thing to address oneself to God under the protection, and through the mediation, of some favourite of Heaven (Heb. viii. 6 ; ix. 15 ; cf. Acts viii. 22—24).

VIII. THAT WHEN MOSES PRAYED, THE FIRE WENT OUT. No doubt in answer to the prayer. Even so the intercession of Christ quenches the flames of the Divine anger against sin. Not that the anger and the mercy of God are rival powers striving against one another : in eternity they act in perfect harmony ; nevertheless, in the sphere of time and space they display themselves separately, and in apparent antagonism. It pleased God that his anger against sin and rebellion should be visibly kindled by the complaints of the people ; that his mercy should be moved by the prayer of Moses. Thus was signified the eternal purpose of God to show mercy and forgiveness to all men through the atonement of Christ (Rom. viii. 34 ; Heb. vii. 25 ; ix. 24 ; 1 John ii. 1 ; cf. Luke xxiii. 34).

And consider again—1. *That the very next place after Sinai was Taberah—a burning.* Even so it is but one short journey without a break for sinful man from the revelation of the moral law to the fires of hell. The law is holy and good ; but sinful man cannot keep it, nor can God suffer it to be broken. Wherefore by the law came death ; after the law, condemnation ; behind the commandment, fiery wrath against the transgressors thereof. Thus also the moral law of Christ without his atonement (as some would have it) would only be worse condemnation—a Taberah without a Moses (Rom. iii. 20; v. 20 *a.* ; vii. 7—13 ; viii. 1—4). 2. *That Israel would have got no further than Taberah had they not had a mediator.* Even so burnings had been our everlasting portion, except Christ had delivered us (Isa. xxxiii. 14; Mark ix. 44, &c. ; 1 Thess. i. 10).

HOMILIES BY VARIOUS AUTHORS.

Vers. 1, 2.—*A summary view of sin and its remedy.* I. A CHAIN OF MORAL SEQUENCES, containing the following links:—1. The people's sin. The complaints probably various, as may be illustrated from other narratives. 2. Their sin noticed. " The Lord heard it," as he hears every idle word, and reads every sinful thought (see outline on ch. xii. 2). 3. This notice awakens God's anger. By the necessity of his nature, " God is angry with the wicked every day." 4. His anger flamed forth in visible judgments. " The fire of the Lord burned among them," for " our God is a consuming fire," either to purge us from our sins, or to destroy us in our sins. 5. These judgments are fatal, " and consumed them" (Ps. lxxvi. 7). For another chain of sequences cf. James i. 14, 15.

II. A CHAIN OF REMEDIAL BLESSINGS. 1. God's mercy tempers judgment. The fire only destroys " those in the utmost part of the camp" (Ps. ciii. 8—10). 2. The judgments inflicted humble the people, and lead them to appeal to Moses. Such judgments are blessings. Servants of God sought for by sinners, or even despisers, in the day of trouble (cf. Isa. lx. 14). 3. Moses, when appealed to, himself appeals to God. We disclaim all power as saviours, but look and point to the one Saviour (Ps. lx. 11 ; Acts iii. 12). 4. God appealed to in acceptable intercession, turns from the fierceness of his wrath (Ps. xcix. 6). And the High Priest of sinners, by a more costly mediation and a prevailing intercession, still interposes for sinners who " come unto God by him " (Rom. viii. 34 ; Heb. vii. 25).—P.

Vers. 1—9.—*Murmuring, lusting, and loathing.* We have here a very painful self-revelation. Through prophets and apostles, and especially through his Son, God has said many humiliating things of the children of men, but nothing more humiliating than by their own actions they have written down against themselves. Note—

I. A SPIRIT UNAFFECTED BY CHASTISEMENT. The people run away from pain, but do not cease from lust. They forget the blow of Jehovah almost before the wound is healed. Nor let us wonder at their stupidity, for this fire of God was only a more rapid and more manifest form of that fire of Divine chastisement which comes in some form to us all. We treat all pain as the Israelites did. As they cried to Moses, so we cry to our fellow-men, and make no mention of our sin against God. We never stop to think of the fire of God as having his anger in it, or a check upon us in our selfish career (Ps. lxxviii. ; Isa. i. 2—6 ; ix. 13 ; Jer. vii. 23—28).

II. A SPIRIT UNCHANGED BY BENEFITS. So far as any word or action here shows, they might have utterly forgotten everything God had done for them. They do recollect the manna, but only to grumble at it and despise it. God had indeed abounded toward them in grace and power, wisdom and prudence, yet not one of all his doings is remembered to his glory. What then of our state of mind in regard of the wonderful manifestations of God in Christ Jesus? We, even more than the Israelites, are the objects of God's gracious interposition. It seemed of no use to remind them of God the Deliverer and Provider. And so now, although Jesus is the Way, the Truth, and the Life, although he has conquered sin and death for all mankind, yet mankind is far more concerned about matters a long way less important. The truth was, the Israelites had not yet been delivered, in the highest sense of the word. The body was free, but the spirit was in bondage. Egypt had still a strong hold upon their hearts. Their experience there must have been a strange mixture of oppression and pampering. Compelled to make bricks without straw, and yet they had flesh to eat.

III. A SPIRIT THAT SOON FORGOT PAST GRIEVANCES. It was not so long ago that they had been sighing and crying by reason of their bondage (Exod. ii. 23). Then their lives were bitter, and all the flesh they got could not sweeten them. These past grievances were immeasurably greater than anything they had to complain of now. *Then* there was really no comfort in life at all—oppression and injustice gave wormwood flavour to everything; *now* they are but *minus some old comforts.* They have plenty to eat, and that of special miraculous food, by which God said to them at every meal, " Open thy mouth wide, and I will fill it." It was well for them even in the wilderness troubles that they were not as Egypt; for though Egypt might have flesh to eat, it was surely eaten amid many groans and sighs. The ten plagues and the destruction of Pharaoh and his army were a very serious set-off against the most savoury of creature comforts.

IV. A SPIRIT UTTERLY INSENSIBLE TO THE GLORIOUS VOCATION WHEREWITH GOD HAD CALLED THEM (Eph. iv. 1). What a difference is here revealed between Moses and the people! As Moses talks with Hobab, and lifts his prayer to God, all is expectancy, ardour, and exultation. No complaints of the manna, no hankerings after Egypt, come from that noble soul. But as for the people, Paul exactly describes them in Phil. iii. 18. Their end was destruction, their God was their belly, their glory was in their shame, they minded earthly things. Even though the ark rested on the many thousands of Israel, they are blind to the glory and profit coming from the presence of it. They will go anywhere if only they can get the lost delicacies of Egypt. Such a table as Milton represents the tempter spreading out before Jesus would just have been to their taste (' Paradise Regained,' ii. 337—365). Their cry is not that of natural hunger, but the passionate screaming of a pampered child. Plain living and high thinking, the Nazarite vow and the Nazarite aspiration, manna for the body and true bread of heaven for the spirit—with these things they had no sympathy.

Practical truths:—1. Let every pain that comes to us have its proper effect in the way of discipline. Thus that which otherwise will be loss is turned to substantial gain. 2. In the midst of the greatest privileges we may be near to the most subtle temptations. Where God is nearest, there Satan also may be most active. 3. We need a great work of God to bring us to a due appreciation of the spiritual blessings in heavenly places in Christ Jesus. It takes a great deal to make us see that godliness is profitable, having the promise of the life *that now is.*

> " Trouble is grudgingly and hardly brook'd,
> While life's sublimest joys are overlook'd."

4. Let the estimate of our wants and the provision for them be left to God. For us to live is Christ, and the highest occupation of life to seek the kingdom of God and his righteousness; then all other needed things will be added unto us. Never fear but God will give food convenient for us. *N. B.* John vi. gives a most instructive New Testament parallel to this passage.—Y.

EXPOSITION.

KIBROTH HATTAAVAH (vers. 4—35). Ver. 4.—**The mixed multitude.** Hebrew, *hasaphsuph*, the gathered ; the riff-raff, or rabble, which had followed the fortunes of Israel out of Egypt, where they had probably been strangers and slaves themselves. What the nature and the number and the fate of this rabble were is a matter of mere conjecture and of some perplexity. There does not seem any room for them in the regulations laid down for Israel, nor are they mentioned in any other place except at Exod. xii. 38. In Levit. xxiv. 10 we read of the son of an Israelitish woman by an Egyptian father, and this might lead us to conjecture that a great part of the "mixed multitude" was the off-spring of such left-handed alliances. These half-breeds, according to the general rule in such cases, would follow their mothers; they would be regarded with contempt by the Jews of pure blood, and would accompany the march as hangers-on of the various tribes with which they were connected. As to their fate, it may be probably concluded, from the reason of things and from the absence of any further notice of them, that they found their way back to the slavery and the indulg-ences of Egypt; they were bound by no such strong restraints and animated by no such national feelings as the true people of the Lord. **And the children of Israel also wept again.** This expression, again (Hebrew, שׁוּב, used adverbially), would seem to point to some former weeping, and this is generally found in the "murmuring" of which they had been guilty in the desert of Sin (Exod. xvi. 2, 3). This, however, is unsatisfactory for several reasons: first, because that occurrence was too remote, having been more than a year ago; second, because there is no men-tion of any "weeping" at that time; third, because the matter of complaint on the two occasions was really quite different: *then* they murmured faithlessly at the blank starv-ation which apparently stared them in the face; *now* they weep greedily at the absence of remembered luxuries. It is therefore much more likely that the expression has regard to the "complaining" which had just taken place at Tabeérah. It was indeed wonderful that the punishment then inflicted did not check the sin; wonderful that it burst out again in an aggravated form almost immediately. But such was the obstinacy of this people, that Divine vengeance, which only perhaps affected a few, and only lasted for a brief space, was not sufficient to silence their wicked clamour. **Who shall give us flesh to eat?** בָּשָׂר—Septuagint, κρέα—means flesh-meat generally. They had flocks and herds it is true, but they were no doubt care-fully preserved, and the increase of them would little more than suffice for sacrifice; no one would dream of slaughtering them for ordinary eating.

Ver. 5.—**We remember the fish, which we did eat in Egypt freely,** i. e. gratis. No doubt this was an exaggeration on the part of the murmurers, but it is attested by clas-sical writers that fish swarmed in the Nile waters, and cost next to nothing (Diod.

Sic., i. 36, 52; Herod., ii. 93; Strabo, xvii. p. 829). **Cucumbers.** קִשֻּׁאִים. Cucumbers of peculiar softness and flavour are spoken of by Egyptian travellers as *fructus in Egypto omnium vulgatissimus.* **Melons.** אֲבַטִּחִים. Water-melons, still called *battieh*, grow in Egypt, as in all hot, moist lands, like weeds, and are as much the luxury of the poorest as of the richest. **Leeks.** הֶחָצִיר. This word usually means grass (as in Ps. civ. 14), and may do so here, for the modern Egyptians eat a kind of field-clover freely. The Septu-agint, however, translates it by τὰ πράσα, leeks or chives, which agrees better with the context. Pliny (Nat. Hist. 19, 33) speaks of it as *"laudatissimus porrus in Egypto."* **Onions.** בְּצָלִים. **Garlic.** שׁוּמִים. These are men-tioned in the well-known passage of Herodotus (ii. 125) as forming the staple food of the workmen at the pyramids; these still form a large part of the diet of the labouring classes in Egypt, as in other Mediterranean coun-tries. If we look at these different articles of food together, so naturally and inartificially mentioned in this verse, we find a strong argument for the genuineness of the narra-tive. They are exactly the luxuries which an Egyptian labourer of that day would have cried out for, if deprived of them; they are *not* the luxuries which a Jew of Palestine would covet, or would even think of. The very words here used for the cucumber, the melon, and the garlic were probably Egyptian, for they may still be recognised in the com-mon names of those vegetables in Egypt.

Ver. 6.—**Our soul is dried away.** This exaggerated statement expressed their craving for the juicy and savoury food of which they had been thinking, and which was obviously unattainable in the wilderness. There is a physical craving in man for variety of diet, and especially for such condiments and flavours as he has been used to all his life, which makes the lack of them a real hard-ship. It is not necessary to condemn the Israelites for feeling very keenly the loss of their accustomed food, which is notoriously the one thing which the poorest classes are least able to bear; it is only necessary to condemn them for making this one loss of more account than all their gain. **There is nothing at all, beside this manna, before our eyes.** Rather, "we have nothing (אֵין כֹּל) except that our eye (falls) upon this manna." These graphic words speak of the longing looks which turned in every direction after the accustomed dainties, only to fall with disgust upon the inevitable manna. It was very ungrateful of them to speak disparag-ingly of the manna, which was good and wholesome food, and sufficient to keep them in health and strength; but it is useless to deny that manna only for people who had been accustomed to a rich and varied diet must have been exceedingly trying both to the palate and the stomach (cf. ch. xxi. 5).

Ver. 7.—**The manna was as coriander seed.** On the name and the nature of the manna see Exod. xvi. 31. It is commonly supposed that the brief description here inserted was intended to show the unreasonableness of the popular complaints. There is no trace whatever of any such purpose. So far as the description conveys fresh information, it was simply suggested by the occurrence of the word "manna," according to the artless style of the narrative. If any moral purpose must be assigned to this digression, it would rather be to suggest that the people had some real temptation to complain. It is often forgotten that, although the manna was supernatural, at least as to the amount and regularity of its supply, yet as an article of food it contained no supernatural elements. If we had to live upon nothing but cakes flavoured with honey or with olive oil, it is certain that we should soon find them pall upon our appetite. To the eye of the Psalmist the manna appeared as angels' food (Ps. lxxviii. 25) ; but then the Psalmist had not lived on manna every day for a year. We have to remember, in this as in many other cases, that the Israelites would not be "our ensamples" (τύποι ἡμῶν, 1 Cor. x. 6) if they had not succumbed to real temptations. **As the colour of bdellium.** See on Gen. ii. 12. As no one knows anything at all about bdellium, this adds nothing to our knowledge of the manna. The Septuagint has here εἶδος κρυστάλλου, "the appearance of ice," or perhaps " of hoar-frost." As it translates bdellium in Gen. ii. 12 by ἄνθραξ (carbuncle), it is probable that the comparison to ice here is due to some tradition about the manna. Taking this passage in connection with Exod. xvi. 31, we may reasonably conjecture that it was of an opalescent white, the same colour probably which is mentioned in connection with manna in Rev. ii. 17.

Ver. 8.—**And the people . . . ground it in mills.** This information as to the preparation of the manna is new. It may be supposed that at first the people ate it in its natural state, but that afterwards they found out how to prepare it in different ways for the sake of variety. Small handmills and mortars for the preparation of grain they would have brought with them from their Egyptian homes. **As the taste of fresh oil.** In Exod. xvi. 31 it is said to have tasted like wafers made with honey. Nothing is more impossible adequately to describe than a fresh taste. It is sufficient to note that the two things suggested by the taste of the manna, honey and oil, present the greatest possible contrast to the heavy or savoury food which they remembered in Egypt.

Ver. 9.—**And when the dew fell, . . . the manna fell upon it.** We know from Exod. xvi. 14 that when the dew evaporated in the morning it left a deposit of manna upon the ground ; we learn here that the manna fell upon the dew during the night. Now the dew is deposited in the cool of the night beneath a clear sky, when radiation of heat goes on uninterruptedly from the earth's surface ; it is clear, therefore, that the manna was let fall in some way beyond human experience from the upper air. What possible physical connection there could be between the dew and the manna we cannot tell. To the untaught mind, however, the dew seemed to come more directly than any other gift of nature from the clear sky which underlay the throne of God ; and thus the Jew was led to look upon the manna too as coming to him day by day direct from the storehouse of heaven (cf. Ps. lxxviii. 23, 24 ; cv. 40).

Ver. 10. — **Throughout their families.** Every family weeping by itself. Such was the contagion of evil, that every family was infected. Compare Zech. xii. 12 for a description of a weeping similar in character, although very different in its cause. **Every man in the door of his tent.** So that his wailing might be heard by all. So public and obtrusive a demonstration of grief must of course have been pre-arranged. They doubtless acted thus under the impression that if they made themselves sufficiently troublesome and disagreeable they would get all they wanted ; in this, as in much else, they behaved exactly like ill-trained children. **Moses also was displeased.** The word "also" clearly compares and unites his displeasure with that of God. The murmuring indeed of the people was directed against God, and against Moses as his minister. The invisible King and his visible viceroy could not be separated in the regard of the people, and their concerted exhibition of misery was intended primarily for the eye of the latter. It was, therefore, no wonder that such conduct roused the wrath of Moses, who had no right to be angry, as well as the wrath of God, who had every right to be angry. Moses sinned because he failed to restrain his temper within the exact limits of what befits the creature, and to distinguish carefully between a righteous indignation for God and an angry impatience with men. But he sinned under very sore provocation.

Ver. 11.—**Wherefore hast thou afflicted thy servant?** These passionate complaints were clearly wrong, because exaggerated. God had *not* thrown upon Moses the responsibility of getting the people safely into Canaan, or of providing flesh for them ; and apart from these exaggerations, it was a selfish and cowardly thing thus to dwell upon his own grievance, and to leave out of sight the grave dishonour done to God, and the awful danger incurred by the people. It was the more blameworthy in Moses because upon a former occasion he had taken upon him, with almost perilous boldness, to remonstrate with God, and to protest against the vengeance he threatened to inflict (Exod. xxxii. 11—13). In a word, Moses forgot himself and his duty as mediator, and in his indignation at the sin of the people committed the same sin himself. It is a strong note of genuineness that so grave (and yet so natural) a fault should be recorded with such obvious simplicity. Compare the cases of Elijah (1 Kings xix.) and of Jonah (ch. iv.).

Ver. 12.—**Carry them in thy bosom, as a nursing father.** Probably he meant to say that this was the part and the duty of God himself as the Creator and Father of Israel. Compare the reading, which is perhaps the correct one, in Acts xiii. 18: Τεσσαρακονταετῆ χρόνον ἐτροφοφόρησεν αὐτοὺς ἐν τῇ ἐρήμῳ.

Ver. 14.—**I am not able to bear all this people alone.** This complaint, while reasonable in itself, shows how unreasonable the rest of his words were. However many he might have had to share his responsibilities, he could not have provided flesh for the people, nor enabled them to live one day in the wilderness; this had never been laid upon him.

Ver. 15.—**Kill me, I pray thee, out of hand,** or "quite." Hebrew, הָרֹג, inf. abs. **And let me not see my wretchedness.** Let me not live to see the total failure of my hopes and efforts.

Ver. 16.—**And the Lord said unto Moses.** The Divine dignity and goodness of this answer, if not an absolutely conclusive testimony, are at least a very strong one, to the genuineness of this record. Of what god, except the Father of our Lord Jesus Christ, was it ever witnessed, or could it have been ever imagined, that he should answer the passionate injustice of his servant with such forbearance and kindness? The one thing in Moses' prayer which was reasonable he allowed at once; the rest he passed over without answer or reproof, as though it had never been uttered. **Gather unto me seventy men of the elders of Israel.** That the number seventy has a symbolic significance in Scripture will hardly be denied (cf. Exod. i. 5; Dan. ix. 2, 24; Luke x. 1), although it is probably futile to affix any precise meaning to it. Perhaps the leading idea of seventy is fulness, as that of twelve is symmetry (see on Exod. xv. 27). The later Jews believed that there were seventy nations in the world. There is no reason, except a reckless desire to confound the sacred narrative, to

identify this appointment with that narrated in Exod. xviii. 21, sq. and Deut. i. 9, sq. The circumstances and the purposes appear quite distinct: those were appointed to assist Moses in purely secular matters, to share his burden as a judge; these to assist him in religious matters, to support him as a mediator; those used the ordinary gifts of wisdom, discretion, and personal authority; these the extraordinary gifts of the Spirit. It is more reasonable to suppose that these seventy were the same men that went up into Mount Sinai with Moses, and saw the God of Israel, and ate of the consecrated meal of the covenant, about a year before. Unless there was some decisive reason against it, an elder who had been chosen for that high religious privilege could hardly fail to be chosen on this occasion also; an interview with God himself, so mysteriously and awfully significant, must surely have left an ineffaceable stamp of sanctity on any soul at all worthy of it. It would be natural to suppose that while the present selection was made de novo, the individuals selected were personally the same. Compare note on ch. i. 5, and for "the elders of Israel" see on Exod. iii. 16. **Whom thou knowest to be elders of the people, and officers over them.** On the officers (Hebrew, shoterim), an ancient order in the national organisation of Israel, continued from the days of bondage, see Exod. v. 6. The Targ. Pal. paraphrases the word shoterim by "who were set over them in Mizraim." The Septuagint has here πρεσβύτεροι τοῦ λαοῦ καὶ γραμματεῖς αὐτῶν, words so familiar to the reader of the Greek Gospels. The later Jews traced back their Sanhedrim, or grand council of seventy, to this appointment, and found their elders and scribes in this verse. There was, however, no further historical connection between the two bodies than this—that when the monarchy failed and prophecy died out, the ecclesiastical leaders of the Jews modelled their institutions upon, and adapted their titles to, this Divinely-ordered original.

Ver. 17.—**I will take of the spirit which is upon thee, and will put it upon them.** The Holy Spirit is one and indivisible. But in the language of Scripture "the Spirit" often stands for the charismata, or gifts of the Spirit, and in this sense is freely spoken of as belonging to this or that man. So the "spirit of Elijah" (2 Kings ii. 9, 15), which was transferred to Elisha, as it were, by bequest. It was not, therefore, the personal indwelling presence of the Holy Ghost in Moses which God caused him to share with the seventy elders, for that can in no case be a matter of transfer or of arrangement, but simply those charismata or extraordinary gifts of the Spirit which Moses had hitherto enjoyed alone as the prophet of Israel. It is strange that in the face of the clear teaching of St. Paul in 1 Cor. xii., xiii., and in view of such cases as those of Saul (1 Sam. x. 10; xix. 23) and David (1 Sam. xvi. 13), any difficulty should have been felt about this passage. **They shall bear the burden of the people with thee.** It does not appear how they were to do this, nor is there any record of their work. Their gifts, however, were spiritual, and we may probably assume that their usefulness lay in producing and maintaining a proper religious tone among the people. The real difficulty which stood in the way of Moses was not one of outward organisation or of government, for that had been amply provided for; it lay in the bad tone which prevailed among the people, and threatened to destroy at any moment the very foundations of their national hope and safety. We may see in these seventy not indeed a Sanhedrim to exercise authority and discipline, but the first commencement of that prophetic order which afterwards played so large a part in the religious history of Israel and of the early Christian Church—an order designed from the first to supplement by the freedom and originality of their ministry the more formal and unvarying offices of the priesthood. If this was the nature of their usefulness, it is not surprising that they are never mentioned again; and it is observable that a similar obscurity hangs over the activity of the prophets of the New Testament, who yet formed a most important part of the gospel *régime* (cf. 1 Cor. xiv. 29 —32; Eph. ii. 20).

Ver. 18.—**Sanctify yourselves against to-morrow.** By certain ablutions, and by avoidance of legal pollution (see Exod. xix. 10, 14, 15). The people were to prepare themselves as for some revelation of God's holiness and majesty. In truth it was for a revelation of his wrath, and of the bitter consequences of sin. There is about the words, as interpreted by the result, a depth of very terrible meaning; it was as though a traitor, unknowing of his doom, were bidden to a grand ceremonial on the morrow, which ceremonial should be his own execution. **For it was well with us in Egypt.** These false and wicked words, in which the base ingratitude of the people reached its highest pitch, are repeated to them in the message of God with a quiet sternness which gave no sign to their callous ears of the wrath they had aroused.

Ver. 20. — **But even a whole month.** There is some little difficulty about these words, because the Israelites do not seem to have made a long stay at Kibroth-Hattaavah, and the miraculous supply does not seem to have followed them. The words are words of stern irony and displeasure, and need not be literally pressed: it was enough that

animal food *was* given them in quantity sufficient to have gorged the whole nation for a month, if they had cared to go on eating it (see below on ver. 33).

Ver. 21.—**And Moses said.** Moses had not recovered from the impatient and despairing temper into which the ill-behaviour of the people had betrayed him. He could not really have doubted the Divine power to do this, after what he had seen in the desert of Sin (Exod. xvi. 13), but he spoke petulantly, and indeed insolently, out of the misery which was yet in his heart.

Ver. 22.—**Shall the flocks and herds be slain?** Which they had brought out of Egypt with them (see on Exod. xii. 32), and which no doubt were carefully husbanded, partly in order to supply them with milk and other produce, partly in order to maintain the sacrifices of the law. **All the fish of the sea.** A wild expression from which nothing can be fairly argued as to the present position of the camp.

Ver. 23.—**Is the Lord's hand waxed short?** So that it cannot reach far enough to fulfil his purposes. This simple and expressive figure of speech is adopted by Isaiah (ch. l. 2; lix. 1).

Ver. 24.—**Moses went out,** *i. e.* out of the tabernacle. It is not stated that he went into the tabernacle to bring his complaint before the Lord, but the narrative obviously implies that he did (see on ch. vii. 89).

Ver. 25.—**The Lord came down in a cloud,** *i. e.* in the cloud which was the symbol of his perpetual presence with them. At other times this cloud dwelt (שָׁכַן) above the tabernacle, soaring steadily above it in the clear air; but on certain occasions, for greater impressiveness, the cloud came down and filled the tabernacle, or at any rate the entrance of it, while Moses stood without (cf. ch. xii. 5 and Exod. xxxiii. 9; xl. 35). **Took of the spirit which was upon him.** Not certainly in anger, or by way of diminishing the fulness of the spirit which was in Moses, but in order that the seventy might participate, and be known to participate, in a gift originally and specially given to Moses. The whole intention of the ceremonial was to declare in the most unmistakable way that the gifts of the seventy were to be exercised only in union with and in subordination to the mediator of Israel. The Targums are substantially correct in their paraphrase: "The Lord *made enlargement* of the spirit that was upon him, and imparted to the seventy men, the elders." Theodoret very happily observes on this passage, "Just as a man who kindles a thousand flames from one does not lessen the first in communicating light to the others, so God did not diminish the grace imparted to Moses by the fact that he communicated of it to the seventy." **They prophesied.** The phenomenon here mentioned for the first time was no doubt an ecstatic utterance, not exactly beyond the control, but certainly beyond the origination, of those who prophesied. It must not be confounded with that state of calm, spiritual exaltation in which such men as Isaac and Jacob spake concerning things to come (Heb. xi. 20 ; cf. Gen. xxvii. 29 ; xlix. 28). The Hebrew יִתְנַבְּאוּ means literally "were caused to pour forth," and the fundamental idea is that those affected became for the time being vents for the audible utterance of thoughts and expressions which were not theirs, but the Holy Ghost's. Compare the thought in Job xxxii. 18—20, and the case of Saul and his messengers, as above. As to the matter of these prophesyings, we may probably conclude that they were of the same nature as the ecstatic utterances of the tongues on the day of Pentecost and afterwards ; not "prophecy" in the ordinary sense, but inspired glorification of God, and declaration of his wonderful works (Acts ii. 4, 11). **And did not cease.** Rather, " did not add," or "repeat." יָסָפוּ וְלֹא. Septuagint, καὶ οὐκ ἔτι προσέθεντο. The ecstatic utterance did not continue or reappear. The New Testament history no doubt supplies us with the explanation of this. The supernatural sign thus accorded was of little use in itself, and was of much danger, because it attracted to its exhibition an attention which was rather due to more inward and spiritual things. As a sign it was sufficient that it should be once unmistakably manifested before all the people. (cf. 1 Cor. xiv. 22 ; xiii. 8). The permanent *charisma* of the Holy Spirit which the seventy received and retained from this time forth was no doubt the ἀντιλήψις or κυβερνήσις of 1 Cor. xii. 28 ; the gift of "help" or " governance," not in temporal matters, but in the religious education and direction of the people.

Ver. 26.—**There remained two of the men in the camp.** No reason is here given why they did not accompany the rest to the tabernacle ; but as they did not thereby forfeit the gift designed for them, it is certain that some necessity or duty detained them. **They were of them that were written.** This incidental notice shows how usual the practice of writing was, at any rate with Moses, who was "learned in all the wisdom of the Egyptians" (Acts vii. 22). **And they prophesied in the camp.** As a sign that they too had received the *charisma* from the Lord. Seeing that it was the work of the Holy Spirit, there was of course nothing really more wonderful in their case than in the case of the others, but no doubt it seemed

so. That men in the camp, and away from the visible centre and scene of Divine manifestations, should be accessible to the heavenly afflatus was a vast astonishment to an ignorant people. We may compare the surprise felt by the Jewish Christians when the sign of tongues was shown among the Gentiles (Acts x. 45, 46).

Ver. 27.—**And there ran a young man.** Literally, "the young man,"—הַנַּעַר ; ὁ νεανίσκος, Septuagint,—by which some understand the young men of the camp collectively, but this is doubtful in grammar and unsatisfactory in sense. If this book was compiled from previous records, of which there are many apparent traces, we may suppose that the name of this young man was there given, but here for some reason omitted.

Ver. 28.—**Joshua the son of Nun.** See on Exod. xvii. 9. As before, he is called Joshua by anticipation. **One of his young men.** This implies that there were others who to some extent shared his duties towards Moses ; but that Joshua stood in a peculiar relation to his master is evident from Exod. xxiv. 13 and xxxii. 17, as well as from this passage itself. **My lord Moses, forbid them.** Probably he did not know that they had been enrolled, and he was naturally jealous for the honour of Moses—a jealousy which was not at all unnecessary, as the events of the next chapter proved. The prophesying of Eldad and Medad in the camp might well seem like the setting up of an independent authority, not in harmony with that of Moses.

Ver. 29.—**Enviest thou for my sake ?** In this answer speaks for once " the meekest of men." It was his sad fate that his position as representative of God obliged him to see repressed with terrible visitations any rebellion against his sole and absolute authority. But he was devoid of personal ambition at all times, and at this time weary and disgusted with the responsibility of ruling such a people. How much more for the glory of God, and for his own peace, would it be if not only these, but all the people, shared the gifts of the Spirit ! Mark ix. 38, 39 presents a partial, but still a striking, parallel.

Ver. 30.—**Moses gat him into the camp.** Although the tabernacle stood in the midst of the camp, yet it was practically separated from the tents of the other tribes by an open space and by the encampments of the Levites. There is, therefore, no ground for inferring from this and similar expressions that the record really belongs to a time when the tabernacle was pitched outside the camp.

Ver. 31.—**A wind from the Lord.** A wind Divinely sent for this purpose. In Ps. lxxviii. 26 it is said to have been a wind from the east and south, *i. e.* a wind blowing up the Red Sea and across the Gulf of

Akabah. **And brought quails from the sea.**
On the "quails" (Hebrew, *salvim*—probably
the common quail) see Exod. xvi. 13. The
Septuagint has in both places ἡ ὀρτυγομήτρα,
"the quail-mother," the sense of which is
uncertain. These birds, which migrate in
spring in vast numbers, came from the sea,
but it does not follow that the camp was
near the sea. They may have been following
up the Gulf of Akabah, and been swept far
inland by the violence of the gale. **Let them
fall by the camp.** Rather, "threw them down
on the camp." יִּטֹּשׁ עַל הַמַּחֲנֶה. Septuagint,
ἐπέβαλεν ἐπὶ τὴν παρεμβολήν. Either the
sudden cessation of the gale, or a violent
eddying of the wind, threw the exhausted
birds in myriads upon the camp (cf. Ps.
lxxviii. 21, 28). **Two cubits high upon the
face of the earth.** The word "high" is
not in the original, but it probably gives the
true meaning. The Septuagint, ὡσεὶ δίπηχυ
ἀπὸ τῆς γῆς, is somewhat uncertain. The
Targums assert that the quails "flew upon
the face of the ground, at a height of two
cubits ;" and this is followed by the Vulgate
("*volabant in aere duobus cubitis altitudine
super terram*") and by many commentators.
This idea, however, although suggested by
the actual habits of the bird, and adopted in
order to avoid the obvious difficulty of the
statement, is inconsistent with the expressions used here and in Ps. lxxviii. If the
birds were "thrown" upon the camp, or
"rained" upon it like sand, they could not
have been flying steadily forward a few feet
above the ground. It is certainly impossible
to take the statement literally, for such a
mass of birds would have been perfectly unmanageable ; but if we suppose that they
were drifted by the wind into heaps, which
in places reached the height of two cubits,
that will satisfy the exigencies of the text :
anything like a uniform depth would be the
last thing to be expected under the circumstances.

Ver. 32.—**And the people stood up . . .
next day.** A statement which shows us
how greedy the people were, and how in-
ordinately eager to supply themselves with
an abundance of animal food. They were so
afraid of losing any of the birds that they
stayed up all night in order to collect them ;
probably they only ceased gathering and
began to eat when the available supply was
spent. **Ten homers.** It is difficult to calculate the capacity of the homer, especially
as it may have varied from age to age. If
it contained ten ephahs, as seems to be implied in Ezek. xlv. 11, and if the estimate of
the Rabbinists (which is less than that of
Josephus) be correct that the ephah held nearly
four and a half gallons of liquid measure,
then half a million of men must have collected

more quails apiece than would have filled a
450 gallon tun. No doubt the total number
was something enormous, and far above anything that could have been supplied by
natural agencies. The gift of quails, like
that of manna, was one of the gifts of nature
proper to that region Divinely multiplied
and extended, so as to show forth in the
most striking way the boundless power
and beneficence of God. **They spread them
all abroad.** In order to dry them in the
sun, as the Egyptians used to do with fish
(Herod., ii. 77), and as the South Americans
do with beef. Flesh thus cured does not
need salt, which the Israelites would not
have in sufficient quantities.

Ver. 33.—**And while the flesh was yet
between their teeth, ere it was chewed.** If
this were taken in the most literal sense, it
would mean that no one of the people had
time to swallow a single morsel of the coveted
food ere he was stricken down by the Divine
visitation. We can scarcely imagine, however,
that such was the case in every single instance. It would indeed appear as if they
had with one consent postponed the enjoyment of eating the quails until they had
gathered as huge a quantity for future use
as possible ; as if in defiance and contempt
of the Divine warning that their greed would
turn to satiety and loathing (see vers. 19 and
32). If this were so, then the feast to which
they so eagerly looked forward would begin
throughout the camps on the second night,
and the visitation of God might well have
had the sudden and simultaneous character
attributed to it here and in Ps. lxxviii. 30,
31. At any rate the statement of the text
positively excludes the idea that they went
on eating quails for a whole month, according
to the promise (or threat) of ver. 20. There
was flesh enough to have secured the literal
fulfilment of that promise by gorging them
for a whole month ; but it is evident that
the Divine wrath anticipated any such tardy
revenges, and smote its victims in the very
moment of their keenest gratification. **The
Lord smote the people with a very great
plague.** Both ancients and moderns state
that the flesh of quails is unwholesome (cf.
Pliny, x. 23), but this appears to have no
very valid foundation. Unquestionably
quails eaten for a month by people unused
to a flesh diet would produce many and fatal
sicknesses ; but there is no room for any
such natural results here. Whatever form
the plague may have taken, it was as clearly
supernatural in its suddenness and intensity
as the supply of quails itself. We do not
know anything as to who were smitten, or
how many ; the Psalmist tells us that they
were "the fattest" and "the chosen" in
Israel, and we may naturally suppose that
those who had been foremost in the lusting

and the murmuring were foremost in the ruin which followed.

Ver. 34.—**Kibroth-Hattaavah.** The graves of greediness. Septuagint, Μνήματα τῆς ἐπιθυμίας. This name, like Tabeérah, was given to the place by the Israelites themselves in connection with their own history; the name, therefore, like the sad memory it enshrined, lived only in the sacred record. It is utterly uncertain where it lay, except that it was apparently the terminus of a three days' journey from Sinai, and in the desert of Paran. How long they stayed at Kibroth-Hattaavah is also quite uncertain. If the plague followed hard upon the coming of the quails, a few days would suffice for all the events recorded in this chapter, and we may well believe that the people would be only too glad to receive the signal of departure as soon as they had buried their unhappy brethren.

Ver. 35.—**And abode at Hazeroth.** Or, "were in Hazeroth." Septuagint, ἐγένετο ὁ λαὸς ἐν 'Ασηρώθ. Hazeroth, from חָצֵר,

to shut in, means "enclosures;" so named perhaps from some ancient stone enclosures erected by wandering tribes for their herds and flocks. It has been identified with Ain el Hadhera, a fountain eighteen hours north-east of Sinai, but on no satisfactory grounds beyond a partial resemblance of name. Assuming that the march lay in a northerly direction through the desert of Paran, the Israelites would naturally follow the road which leads across the southern mountain barrier of et Tih, and on by the Wady es-Zulakeh into the desert plateau. On this road there is a large fountain, with pasturage, at a place called el Ain, and another somewhat further at Bir ed-Themmed. One or other of these was probably the site of Hazeroth (cf. Stanley, 'Sinai,' p. 84). It is, however, entirely a matter of conjecture, and of little real interest. The progress of Israel which is of unfading importance to us is a moral and religious, and not a geographical, progress.

HOMILETICS.

Vers. 4—35.—*The sin of concupiscence, and its punishment.* We have in this section a Divine commentary, in dark and terrible characters, on the commandment, "Thou shalt not covet." And we know that the record was given to us "to the intent that we should not lust after evil things as they also lusted" (1 Cor. x. 6). We have also, intermingled with the dark record of sin and wrath, a beautiful picture of the long-suffering of God with the errors and impatience of his servant, and of the unfettered energy of his free Spirit. In all these things they were τύποι ἡμῶν, our examples. Consider, therefore—

I. THAT ALL THIS SIN AND MISERY BEGAN WITH "LUST," *i. e.* UNHALLOWED AND UNRESTRAINED DESIRE, which is indeed the inner source of all iniquity, because it is the will of the creature setting itself upon that which the Creator has forbidden or denied; hence it is the simplest and readiest way in which the creature can rebel against the Creator, for it is always possible, and indeed easy, to lust, and there is no one who is not tempted to it. Thus Eve lusted for the forbidden fruit, and brought death into the world. Even so St. James says, "Every man is tempted, when he is drawn away of his own lust, and is enticed. Then when lust hath conceived, it bringeth forth sin." And our Saviour, that all evil proceeds out of the heart, which is the seat of the emotions and desires. If, therefore, our desires were held in subjection to the will and word of God, there would be no sin in us; but as long as concupiscence is in us, it will assuredly draw us into evil (cf. Rom. vii. 7, 8, 11; Eph. ii. 3; 1 John ii. 16).

II. THAT THE FIRST EXPRESSION (AT ANY RATE) OF THIS UNHALLOWED DESIRE CAME FROM THE MIXED MULTITUDE—the aliens, or half-breeds, who had come with them, not from faith in God, but from inferior motives. Even so the low moral tone and the frequent enormities chargeable upon Christians are due in the first instance to those who are only nominally Christian, who have been attracted into the fellowship either by accident of birth or by worldly and unspiritual motives. It is the fate of every great and successful movement to carry away with it *many* who have (inwardly) no sympathy with it and no part in it. So it was with Israel, so with the Church of Christ, so with any religious revival. Here is the great danger of an established and fashionable Christianity; it numbers a multitude of nominal adherents, whose motives and desires are wholly unchastened, and who are always ready to set the worst example, and to encourage the most pernicious practices. Compare the "false brethren," 2 Cor. xi. 26.

III. THAT THE CHILDREN OF ISRAEL WERE CARRIED AWAY WITH IT, IN SPITE OF THE WARNING THEY HAD SO RECENTLY RECEIVED AT TABEERAH. No doubt it spread the more rapidly because, (1) it fell in with their own secret feelings, (2) it was recommended by considerations of friendship and relationship, (3) the voice of prudence is scarcely ever a match for the promptings of desire. Even so it is the most striking feature of sin in feeling or in act that it becomes an epidemic which only a very sound and vigorous spiritual state can resist. Compare the case of Judas and the other apostles (Matt. xxvi. 8, 9 ; John xii. 4, 5) ; compare St. Peter and the Judaisers (Gal. ii. 12, 13) ; compare the Corinthians (1 Cor. v. 1, 2, 6, 11) ; and the sins which each generation of Christians has committed or does commit in common—such as lying, duelling, swindling. There is no sin against which more fearful warnings and examples lie than that of covetousness ; yet there is none of which Christians are more generally guilty under stress of bad example and the low moral tone and degraded traditions of society, of trade, of business, &c. The warnings of the New Testament, though always fresh in the hearing and clear in the remembrance of Christian people, are absolutely in-effective as against the common promptings of evil desire.

IV. THAT WHAT THEY EVILLY DESIRED WAS NOT EVIL IN ITSELF. There was no harm in eating flesh, nor were any of the cheap luxuries they coveted objectionable in themselves. Even so we ever excuse ourselves for wanting, because what we want is not *forbidden*, but only *denied*. There is no harm (absolutely) in being rich, therefore we take no shame at covetousness. There is no harm (absolutely) in the pleasures of the flesh, therefore we are ready to excuse any indulgence in them. Christian morality is a law of liberty, unbound by formal rules, therefore we boldly strain that liberty to our immediate advantage, and fancy that the absence of pro-hibition is tantamount to actual allowance on the part of God.

V. THAT WHAT THEY DESIRED WAS WRONG, BECAUSE, (1) IT WAS SUPERFLUOUS, (2) BELONGED TO THE DAYS OF BONDAGE, (3) HAD BEEN WITHHELD BY GOD, WHO ALONE COULD GIVE IT. (1) Inasmuch as the food they had given them was nutritious, wholesome, and abundant for the short journey which lay before them. (2) Inas-much as the savoury and luscious things they wept for were peculiarly Egyptian, and went hand in hand (as they do still) with cruel oppression and degradation : it was the food of slavery. (3) Inasmuch as such things were clearly not to be expected in a wilderness such as God was leading them through. Even so sinful greed among Christians is known by the same three tokens. (1) It is a craving for superfluities. What God has given us (however little compared with our desires) is enough ; for it will suffice, if well used, to bring us to our home in health and strength (Philip. iv. 11 ; 1 Tim. vi. 6—8 ; Heb. xiii. 5). More than we have must be more than enough, for God is pledged to give us *that* (Matt. vi. 33, 34 ; Luke xii. 32 ; Rom. viii. 32). (2) It is a craving for things essentially connected with the bondage of sin and worldliness, from which we are escaped. Such luxuries as wealth, rank, or fashion can afford are (without being in themselves evil) so closely connected with evil that every earnest Christian must dread rather than covet them (Matt. vi. 19, 21, 31, 32 *a*. ; Luke vi. 24 ; xvi. 19, 25 ; James v. 1). (3) It is an open contempt of God's appointment, who *hath not* given us any inheritance here, and *hath* told us to expect tribulation, and to love poverty and reproach, because it is good for us (Luke vi. 20, 22 ; John xvi. 33 ; Acts xiv. 22 ; Rom. viii. 24 ; 2 Cor. iv. 18 ; 1 Tim. vi. 9 ; Heb. xiii. 14 ; James ii. 5).

VI. THAT THE UNRESTRAINED WEEPING OF THE PEOPLE FOR THE DAINTIES THEY COULD NOT HAVE WAS EXCEEDING HATEFUL IN THE SIGHT OF GOD. It did indeed make no account of all his mercies, but rather reproached him for bringing them out of Egypt and setting them free. It was as good as saying they wished he had never troubled himself about them. Even so the greed of Christians is an open reproach against him that loved them and gave himself for them, as though he had done nothing to earn their trust and gratitude, and had rather treated them unkindly. He who passionately desires earthly gains, or bitterly laments earthly losses, flings contempt upon the gifts of Heaven and reproach upon his God and Saviour. Wherefore it speaks of "the covetous, whom the Lord abhorreth" (Ps. x. 3 ; cf. Luke xii. 15 ; Eph. v. 3 ; Col. iii. 5 ; James iv. 3, 4).

VII. THAT THE LORD, IN ORDER TO PUNISH THE PEOPLE, GAVE THEM AN ABUNDANCE

OF WHAT THEY ASKED FOR.   Even so God punishes our greed by letting us have as much as we want of the coveted thing.   The covetous person is punished by ample wealth, the slothful by abundance of ease, the proud by success and flattery, the vain by large admiration, the sensual by unstinted gratification.   Thus the man punishes himself, the Lord providing him with the means of destruction.   Whether we like it or not, this *is* the law of Providence; and to us it is the justice of God. Compare the case of Pharaoh (Rom. ix. 17, 18); of the rich fool (Luke xii. 16); of Herod (Acts xii. 22).

VIII. THAT THE PEOPLE IN THEIR GREED LABOURED DAY AND NIGHT TO ACCUMU-LATE PRODIGIOUS QUANTITIES OF FOOD WHICH THEY NEVER ATE.   Even so do vain men labour and toil to lay up treasures upon earth, never resting as long as anything remains to be got—treasures which after all they shall never enjoy, and shall perhaps eternally regret (Matt. xix. 24; Luke xii. 21; xvi. 25; James v. 2; Rev. iii. 17).

IX. THAT THE PEOPLE, APART FROM ANY SUPERNATURAL INTERVENTION, WOULD HAVE SICKENED OF THE QUANTITY OF ANIMAL FOOD THEY THOUGHT TO EAT, AND FOUND IT "LOATHSOME."   Even so self-indulgence soon reaches its natural limits, even when left to itself, and provokes a natural reaction of disgust.   If this world were all, moderation, self-restraint, and contentment with a little would still make a happier life than luxury and dissipation.   The "roses and raptures of vice" which are sung by many poets, ancient and modern, do not only fade very quickly, but leave a very evil smell behind them.

X. THAT THE JUSTICE OF GOD LEFT NOT THE ISRAELITES TO THE SLOW REVENGE OF NATURAL SATIETY; hardly had they tasted the flesh ere the plague began among them.   Even so greed has its natural reaction of misery, even in the life of this world, but it has its Divine punishment in the soul.   "He gave them their request, but sent leanness into their *soul*," says the Psalmist (Ps. cvi. 15), revealing the spiritual truth which lay hid in this history.   There is a balance Divinely held be-tween the bodily life and that of the soul, so that if the first is full and fat and well-liking, the second is empty and lean and ill-favoured.   No man can cater greedily for his body without impoverishing his soul; no man can gratify eagerly his carnal appetites without incurring spiritual disease (Luke vi. 24—26).

XI. THAT ONE OF THE EARLIEST STATIONS ON THE WAY TO CANAAN WAS "THE GRAVES OF GREED," AND THAT THE NEXT WAS "ENCLOSURES."   Even so in the heaven-ward journey of the Church we soon come (alas, how soon!) to the graves of greed, to the dishonourable sepulchres of such as perished through love of money or of pleasure.   Behold the graves of Ananias, of Sapphira, of those who "slept" at Corinth (1 Cor. xi. 30), of "that woman Jezebel" (Rev. ii. 20), of Demas.   And after this we come to "enclosures"—long series of outward restrictions and regula-tions, some apostolic and some later, which mark a stage in the Church's journey, and testify to her efforts to maintain her moral purity (cf. 1 Cor. v. 9, 11; xi. 34 *b.*; 1 Tim. v. 9).   And what is true of the Church is true of many an individual member. As memory retraces the onward path, how soon come the "graves of greed," the sad memorials of passions sinfully indulged and sharply revenged! and after that the "enclosures"—the restraints and restrictions by which liberty was perforce abridged in order that sin and folly might be fenced out.

Consider, again, *with respect to the manna*—

I. THAT THE PEOPLE WERE REALLY TEMPTED TO WEARY OF THE SAMENESS AND INSIPIDITY OF THE MANNA, their staple food.   To a palate accustomed to the pungent condiments and varied delicacies of Egypt, it was a great trial to have nothing but manna for a year; no doubt it failed to satisfy the appetite, and cloyed upon the taste, in spite of its wholesome and nutritious qualities.   Even so it is a real trial to one who has known the excitements of sin and the dissipations of the world to satisfy himself with the spiritual joys and interests of religion, and we ought to recognise the fact that it is a real trial.   In many who have been recovered from a life of indulgence the craving for excitement is at times almost intolerable.   Nature itself, even when not depraved by long habit, longs for excitement and change, and wearies of the calm monotony of faith, hope, and charity.   Even the "sweetness" of the bread of life, which is at first as "honey" and as "fresh oil" to the starved and sickly soul, palls upon it after a while, and the old longings reassert themselves. How many tire of " angels' food " who took to it eagerly enough at first! (cf. 1 Tim. v. 11—13, 15; Rev. ii. 4).

II. That the manna was in form as "coriander seed," which we know; in colour as "bdellium," which we do not know. Even so there is about the true bread of heaven a mixture of the known and the unknown, of that which can be expressed, and of that which passes human understanding. The coriander seed is of common use, but the bdellium is of paradise (Gen. ii. 12). And so may we all know the beauty of Christ in part, but in part we shall never know until we see him as he is (cf. Rev. ii. 17, "hidden manna;" iii. 12, "my new name;" xix. 12).

III. That the people habitually prepared the manna for eating in various ways, as experience and their own preference guided them. Even so the manna of souls, although it does not need, yet it does not reject, the use of human means and art in order to present it acceptably to the spiritual needs of men. God has nowhere said that all men, of whatsoever habit of mind, must receive the word and sacrament of Christ in the simplest and barest form, or not at all; it is only needful that Christ, however received, be the sole and substantial sustenance of the soul (John vi. 50, 58; 1 Cor. iii. 11; Gal. i. 9; Philip. i. 18).

Consider, again, *with respect to Moses and the seventy*—

I. That the sin of the people led to a different sin in Moses. He would never have murmured at hardships, or have lusted; but he lost his temper, and spake unadvisedly with his lips. Even so sin constantly leads to sin, even where it has no direct influence, and other people's faults are often not less dangerous temptations to us because we abhor them. Thus a frivolous wife may make a soured husband; an unprincipled father a hard and stern child; a worldly clergyman a sarcastic and incredulous congregation (cf. Matt. xxiv. 12; Luke xviii. 11; Rom. ii. 22 *b.*).

II. That the temptation under which Moses fell was a peculiarly insidious one. His passionate anger with the people and disgust with his position as their leader might seem only a noble indignation against wrong. Even so many are tempted to feel nothing but scorn at "baptized heathenism," and impatience with the moral failures of the age, without due consideration either of the wise and loving purposes of God or of their own duties (Ps. xxxvii. 8; Jonah iv. 9; Eph. iv. 26, 27; James i. 19, 20).

III. That in his sorrow and resentment by reason of the wicked he was guilty of grave injustice and insolence against God. Even so we, if we are carried away by indignation against un-Christlike Christians, are in danger of sinning against God, who has borne with them, and bears with them still, and who has made us responsible *not* for their perfection, but only for our own, and has not given to any a greater burden than he is able to bear (Luke ix. 55, 56; 2 Cor. ii. 11; 2 Tim. ii. 21, 25, 26; 2 Pet. iii. 15).

IV. That Moses also erred by forming far too high an estimate of his own official importance and responsibility, as though he had been the real father of his people, whereas " one was their Father, which was in heaven." Even so it is very easy and natural for us, if we are in earnest, to exaggerate the importance of our work, and to mistake the nature of our responsibility in the Church. It is only God who by his one Spirit does all good work in the Church, and he will take care that it is done to his own mind; we are but instruments, who have no responsibility, save that of being "meet for the Master's use" (1 Cor. iii. 5; iv. 2; xii. 4—6).

V. That God was exceeding merciful to the sin of Moses, because it was of human infirmity, and because it was the petulant outbreak of a mind and heart over-charged with grief and failure. Even so did our Lord bear with his apostles, and will bear with all the errors and outbreaks of an honest heart (Ps. ciii. 13, 14; Luke xxii. 31—34, 61; John xx. 27).

VI. That God allowed the one complaint of Moses which was reasonable, and founded the prophetic order to assist in the religious direction of the people. Even so out of complaints and difficulties have arisen many permanent gifts of the Spirit to the Church, for in this as in other ways man's extremity is God's opportunity. Thus out of the murmuring of the Grecians arose the diaconate (Acts

vi. 1, 6); out of the troubles at Corinth the better regulation of the Agape and the Eucharist (1 Cor. xi. 17—34).

VII. That it was the Spirit which rested upon Moses which was communicated to the seventy, inasmuch as their prophetic office was to be held and exercised in unity with, and subordination to, the mediator of Israel. Even so it is the Spirit of Jesus which is the spirit of prophecy—the Spirit of Christ and from Christ which must rest upon every Christian teacher. The anointing which qualifies to speak Divine mysteries must be from him who was anointed the one Mediator and the only Prophet (John i. 16, 33; xvi. 13, 14, &c.).

VIII. That the anointing of the Spirit showed itself in the seventy by ecstatic utterance—a thing never recorded of Moses himself. Even so the first evidence of the outpouring of the Spirit of Christ upon the disciples was that they spake with tongues, which our Lord had never done; for all such manifestations are for a sign, and are no evidence of any superior greatness or holiness in the person so endowed. How often are mere "gifts" mistaken for intrinsic worth, and "the disciple" really esteemed "above his master," because he is *not* "as his master"! (John xiv. 12 *b*.; 1 Cor. xiii.).

IX. That the manifestation of the Spirit was independent of outward accidents, though not of outward order. The designation of the seventy was left to Moses, and Eldad and Medad were among the number selected; they were prevented from attending at the tabernacle, but they received the same gift as the others. Even so the gifts of the Spirit are not independent of ecclesiastical order, nor are they bestowed at random; but they are not restrained by anything unavoidable or accidental. It is the purpose of God which is operative, not the ceremonial, however authoritative. The Spirit of God is a free Spirit, even where he elects to act through certain channels (cf. Acts i. 26; xiii. 2; 1 Cor. xii. 11; 2 Cor. iii. 17).

X. That the jealousy of Joshua for his master was right in principle, although wrong in the particular application. It was impossible for him always to distinguish between a right and a wrong jealousy for the authority and supremacy of Moses. Even so jealousy for the sole pre-eminence of Christ is deeply rooted in all true Christian hearts, but it constantly shows itself in the most mistaken forms. The most opposite bigotries derive their strength from this principle in ignorant or prejudiced minds, and indeed the very best and wisest may often err in this matter. Good people do, as a fact, constantly denounce this or that as an interference with the prerogatives of Christ, when it is in truth only a carrying out of his work in his name. Since, however, the *principle* is right, we must bear with the wrong application of it; we must not be angry even with intolerance if it spring from genuine loyalty to the one Lord and only Mediator, Christ (cf. Mark ix. 38—40; 1 Cor. xii. 3 with Gal. v. 12; 2 John 10, 11; Jude 19).

XI. That Moses desired nothing so little as a monopoly of spiritual gifts. If he ever had been personally ambitious, a larger knowledge of his people and experience of his work had quite delivered him from it. Even so every true Christian teacher and leader, howsoever he may feel bound to magnify his office, will greatly long for the time when "all will be taught of God," and when all distinctions will be for ever abolished, save such as depend on personal nearness to God. How hateful is the idea that the flock should be kept in darkness in order that the shepherds may have a monopoly of influence! How happy were the pastor's charge if all were "spiritual"! (Jer. xxxi. 34; John vi. 45; 1 Cor. xiv. 5; iv. 8 *b*.; 1 Pet. v. 3; 1 John ii. 20, 27).

HOMILIES BY VARIOUS AUTHORS.

Vers. 16, 17, 24, 25.—*The seventy elders, and how they were fitted for their high office.* The murmuring of the people so soon after setting out on the march from Horeb reminded Moses again, very painfully, what a heavy burden had been laid upon him in the leadership of so great a multitude of people newly escaped from slavery. He complained to the Lord. His complaint was graciously heard. He was directed to gather around him a company of seventy elders, who might aid him with their counsel, and share his burden.

I. Regarding THE STATUS AND FUNCTIONS OF THIS COMPANY OF SEVENTY there have been many debates. Some have identified them with the Sanhedrim or Council of Seventy whom we meet with so often in the Gospels and the Acts. Passing by these questions, let us note the facts recorded in the text itself. What was wanted was not the appointment of ordinary rulers or judges. Every tribe had already a prince, a body of elders and officers, and rulers of tens and fifties and hundreds and thousands, who judged between man and man. What was wanted was a council to aid Moses with their advice and assistance in the administration of the national affairs. (Compare the Governors and Council in a British dependency.)

II. THE MANNER OF THE APPOINTMENT OF THE SEVENTY IS CAREFULLY DESCRIBED. 1. No one was appointed who was not *in public office already.* "Gather unto me seventy men, whom thou knowest to be the elders of the people, and officers over them;" *i. e.* they were not to be raw, inexperienced, untried men. Only those were eligible who had given proof of ability and faithfulness in the public service, either as elders or as officers (*i. e.* writers or scriveners—this is the literal meaning of the Hebrew *shoterim.* The reference is to professional scribes, the assessors of non-professional magistrates, such as the Hebrew elders were). This rule was a good one. No man should be raised at one bound to high office, either in Church or State. 2. They were *nominated by Moses.* In this respect the procedure was exceptional. There was far less of centralisation in the government of Israel than a modern and Western reader of the Bible is apt to think. To be sure, there were no representative bodies such as we are familiar with. Nevertheless, the government was truly popular. Even in Egypt the people were ruled, in the first instance, by their own elders—the heads of families and tribes; and this primitive system was continued in a more perfect form in Palestine. But although local government could be best administered by local magistrates, it was otherwise with the supreme and central government with which Moses was charged. A council such as he required could only be had by freely calling forth men of outstanding ability and approved wisdom. 3. They were *invested with office in the face of the congregation, and before the Lord.* In the face of the congregation, to remind them that they were to act for the public good, and not in pursuance of any private interest. Before the Lord, to remind them that "there is no power but of God;" their authority is from God, and is to be used as they shall answer to him. 4. They were *endowed from above with new gifts* to qualify them for their new office. When Moses gathered them before the tabernacle, "the Lord came down in a cloud, and spake unto him, and took of the spirit that was upon him, and gave it unto the seventy elders." This has been interpreted to mean that there was abstracted from Moses some part of the spirit by which he had hitherto been sustained. But that is certainly a perverse misinterpretation. Twenty lamps may be lighted from one lamp without diminishing its brightness (cf. 2 Kings ii. 9). God sendeth no man to warfare at his own charges. When he calls any man to public service, whether in Church or State, the man so called may, without doubting, ask and expect the wisdom, strength, courage which the service requires (James i. 5—8).

III. The most picturesque feature in the narrative is that which remains yet to be noticed—THE STRIKING SIGN BY WHICH NOTIFICATION WAS GIVEN THAT THE SEVENTY ELDERS HAD TRULY BEEN CALLED BY GOD AND WOULD BE COUNTENANCED BY HIM. "When the Spirit rested on them, they prophesied, and added no more" (such is the rendering now preferred by all the best translators). "They prophesied," that is, they spoke as men who were for the time lifted above themselves—as men under the influence of an irresistible power external to themselves. We may presume that what they did say would be of such a kind as to make it plain that the power acting upon them was Divine and heavenly. This prophesying was intended to signalise the inward gifts with which the newly-appointed elders were now being endowed. This is plain from the parallel case related in 1 Sam. x. The Lord in appointing Saul to be king over Israel promised to "be with him;" to "give him another heart," so that he should "be turned into another man." With the kingly office he was to get from the Lord the kingly mind. In token of this, the Spirit came upon him, and he prophesied (cf. Acts ii. 3, 4; x. 44—47). The impulse was only a transient one. "They prophesied, and added no more." The miracle, having served its purpose, ceased; but the spiritual endowment of which it was the token remained. This prophesying, if you consider it well, will be seen to be more than a token. Besides notifying the Lord's approval of the elders, and assuring them of help, it suggested much instruction regarding the principles which should regulate their administration. The tongues of fire and the rapturous speaking with tongues on the day of Pentecost, we know what that miracle meant. It admonished the disciples that the warfare of Christ's kingdom is to be accomplished not with the sword, but with the tongue; not with violence and bloodshed, but by the earnest and living manifestation of the truth. It was a lesson of the same kind which the Lord suggested by the miracle wrought on the seventy elders in front of the tabernacle. They were admonished that in their administration of affairs they ought to make use rather of wise and persuasive speech than of brute force. And is not this a lesson for us also? The time is not come yet—perhaps will never come in the present state—for rulers to lay aside the sword altogether. Violent men, if they will not listen to reason, must be restrained with violence. Nevertheless, even for civil rulers, the employment of force is the less honourable function of their office. Better to restrain and guide and govern men with wise, firm, persuasive words than with the sword.—B.

Vers. 26—30.—*Eldad and Medad; or, irregular prophesying.* This narrative brings up a subject which is at once of great practical importance and of great delicacy, on which men have been apt to run to extremes on the one side or the other. It will be our wisdom, therefore, to begin by weighing carefully the facts as they are set forth in the sacred narrative.

I. THE FACTS are, shortly, these:—Moses having complained that the leadership of the nation was a burden greater than he could bear, the Lord gave direction that a Council of Seventy should be associated with him in it. This was done. From among the acting elders and officers of the congregation Moses called out seventy and they were solemnly set apart to the new office, before the Lord and the congregation. This consecration-service (as it may be called) did not pass without a palpable token of the Divine approval, a palpable token that appropriate gifts would be forthcoming to the new rulers as they had been to Moses. When the Seventy were being set apart, the Spirit fell upon them, and they prophesied. While this was going on at the tent of meeting, a young man came running with the tidings that two men were prophesying in the camp. On inquiry it turned out that these were two of the seventy whom Moses had nominated for the council. For some reason or other they had not come forward with the rest to the tent of meeting. Notwithstanding of this, the Spirit had come on them in the camp exactly as he had come on their brethren, and they were prophesying. Clearly there was in this a breach of due order. Eldad and Medad ought to have presented themselves along with the rest. They were chargeable with an irregularity. Accordingly, Joshua, who is already the trusted "minister of Moses," suggests that they should be silenced. "My lord Moses, forbid them." But Moses is of another mind. Is it certain that Eldad and Medad are prophesying? If so, the hand of the Lord, we may presume, is in the matter. Spiritual gifts are not such cheap and common things that we can afford to throw them away. Possibly enough these prophets in the camp have failed to make due acknowledgment of me as the Divinely-appointed leader of the congregation. But let no man look with an evil eye on them for my sake. Would that the Spirit were put on all the people! I should rejoice to see my light outshone in such a general brightness!

II. WHAT HAVE THESE FACTS TO SAY TO US? What lesson do they teach? 1. At first sight it might seem as if they taught us to make light of office, solemn ordination to office, official service, and to attach importance only to the possession and exercise of gifts. But that certainly is not intended. The new council was not to consist of men simply obeying an internal call. No one was admissible without prior experience in office, and without election by Moses. And it was by Divine command that the sixty-eight were solemnly set apart before the Lord and the congregation. I need not prove that in the State it is the will of God that there should be magistrates, laws, and strict enforcement of the laws. In the Church there is, no doubt, a difference; for the Church has no coercive power. Its weapons are the truth and the tongue of fire, not the sword. Nevertheless, order is quite as necessary in the Church as in the State. "In all churches of the saints God is the author of peace, not of confusion," and all things are to be "done decently and in order" (1 Cor. xiv. 33—40). 2. The narrative admonishes us that office and order and official service, necessary as they may be, are not everything. They are not everything, even in the State, much less are they everything in the Church. The salvation and edification of souls will not go forward unless there is a continual ministration of the Spirit in gifts and in grace. That is a general lesson the facts teach. More particularly they admonish us that *we need not be surprised if it should occasionally happen that men who are walking irregularly give evidence of having been richly endowed with spiritual gifts.* I will not discuss the question, How such a thing can be ; how the God of order can, without contradicting himself, bestow his valuable gifts on men who do not quite conform to the good order of his house. For the fact is plain. Whether we can account for it or no, the fact is indubitable. Has not Christ raised up men like Pascal within the Romish communion ? Yet every Protestant believes that the Church of Rome has grievously erred both in respect to Church order, and in the weightiest points of faith and holiness. Do not suppose that these and similar facts are to be accounted for by alleging that Christendom has for a long while fallen away into anarchy. For facts of the same kind found place in connection with the personal ministry of Christ himself. The Twelve were Christ's apostles, and it was the duty of all disciples to follow with them. Did, therefore, Christ withhold his gifts from all save those in the apostles' company ? On the contrary, there was found an individual now and then who, though he followed not with the apostles, nevertheless both spoke in Christ's name, and spoke to such good purpose that devils were cast forth (cf. Mark ix. 38—40). 3. What, then, is the conclusion to which we are led ? "Quench not the Spirit : despise not prophesying." I do not say that it was the duty of Moses, or is our duty in similar circumstances, to go forth to Eldad and Medad, and identify ourselves with them in their work. That will depend on circumstances. Sometimes one cannot take part with the irregular prophets without concurring in what would for us be sin. Christ's command was not, Go and join yourselves to the man who is casting out devils in my name, irregularly. But it was, Forbid him not. Is a man really prophesying ? Is he casting out devils ? Is he setting forth the truth and doing good ? Then do not forbid him. Bring him, if you can, to a fuller knowledge of the truth, and to more regular courses, but do not look on him with jealous eyes, or try to put him down. If Christ is preached, whether it be in pretence or in truth, I therein do rejoice, yea, and will rejoice (Phil. i. 14—28).—B.

Vers. 4—15 ; 31—35.—*The complainers, and how God made answer to their complaints.* This eleventh of Numbers is a chapter of complainings. First, at Taberah, vague murmurings are heard throughout the camp. Then at Kibroth-hattaavah, a stage further on, the vague murmurings take shape in bitter complaint because of the fare to which the congregation was now confined. Manna ! nothing but manna ! While the people were harping on this grievance Moses also lifted up his voice in complaint. "Why has the Lord dealt so hardly with him as to lay on him the burden of so great a company ? Better kill him out of hand, and not let him see his wretchedness !" Consider this scene at Kibroth-hattaavah. It is not pleasant to look at, especially when one becomes aware that it is a glass in which are to be seen passages in one's own history which one would gladly forget. Scenes not pleasant may nevertheless be profitable.

I. THE COMPLAININGS OF THE PEOPLE. 1. Where the sin began. It was among "the mixed multitude." A great crowd of foreigners who had been neighbours to the Israelites in Egypt, came forth with them at the Exodus, moved some by one motive and some by another (Exod. xii. 38). It is instructive to observe that these were the first to break out into rebellious murmurs ; equally instructive to observe that the evil generated amongst them spread from them into the body of the people. Every community has its mixed multitude, its pariahs, its residuum. To the existence of this class men have been too willing to shut their eyes. I know no better sign of the present age than its wide-spread desire to take note of these masses, and if possible bring them to God. Were there no higher motive, self-preservation might well plead with men to labour in this work. When destitution and filth are suffered to generate typhus among the poor, the deadly infection will make its way into the palaces of the rich. So when sin is suffered to become rampant in one class the other classes will not long escape the contagion. 2. The matter of complaint was little to the credit of the complainers. So long as the congregation lay encamped in Horeb, the fare would be occasionally diversified with herbs and the like. In the wilderness of Paran there is only the manna. Certainly no just ground of complaint. The daily miracle ought rather to have moved to daily thanksgiving. But even of manna the people wearied. They craved greater variety. 3. How the complaint is answered (vers. 18—21, 31—33). The people demand flesh, and flesh is given them beyond their utmost thought. They get their desire, but not God's blessing with it. So it becomes to them a curse in the end. Such a plague followed the " shower of flesh " that the place has ever since borne the ghastly name of Kibroth-hattaavah, the graves of lust. It is an admonition to us not to give way to impatience on account of real or imagined hardships in our lot; above all, not to let our impatience hurry us into rebellious demands for a change. Many a time such demands are granted to the confusion of those who made them. Before leaving this story of the people's sin at Kibroth-hattaavah, let me caution you against supposing that it is a mere parable, a late fiction, not the history of a real transaction. It is at present the fashion in some quarters to get rid of the miracles of the Exodus and of the forty years in the wilderness, by denying the historical truth of the Pentateuch, and interpreting it as at best an allegory or parable. But the Spirit of God has been careful to leave on the narrative indubitable marks of historical verity to confound such interpretations. For example, in this narrative (1) observe the terms in which the people utter their complaint. "We remember the fish, . . cucumbers, melons, leeks, onions, garlic." Egypt all over! These are precisely the articles of food which were distinctively Egyptian. No one writing in Judah or Ephraim would ever have thought of putting such a bill of fare into the mouths of the complainers. (2) Observe the nature of the miracle by which the people were fed. A shower of quails. This is as characteristic of the Sinaitic peninsula as the bill of fare was of Egypt. It was spring when the congregation arrived at Kibroth-hattaavah ; at this season the quails "are annually in the habit of crossing the desert in countless myriads, flying very low, and often in the morning so utterly exhausted by their night's flight that they are slaughtered by the thousand " (Tristram). This chapter is history, not fable.

II. MOSES, TOO, WAS A COMPLAINER AT KIBROTH-HATTAAVAH (read vers. 11—15). His words are sufficiently bitter and impatient. There is in them no little sin ; yet they are not resented as the people's were. Moses is not taken at his word and smitten with a plague. On the contrary, the Lord comforts him with cheering words, and grants him a council of elders to alleviate the burden. This is the more worthy of notice, because it is by no means singular (see 1 Kings xix. 4). Do you ask, What can be the reason of this ? Why deal so gently with the complaints of Moses and Elijah, when the complaints of the congregation are so sharply punished ? The difference can be explained. Observe where and to whom Moses expressed the grief and weariness of his heart. It was not to the Egyptians from whom they had come out ; nor was it to the congregation of Israel. It was in the ear of God himself; he complains not *of* the Lord, but *to* the Lord—two very different sorts of complaint. A dutiful son may remonstrate with his father when the two are alone, but he will not cry out against his father to strangers. When the child of God has a complaint to make, it is to God he carries it. And complaints carried to God, even although there should be much impatience and unbelief at the root of them, will be listened to very graciously. The Lord, so great is his condescending love, would rather that we should pour out the griefs—even the unreasonable griefs—of our hearts, than that we should let them rankle in our bosoms.—B.

Ver. 10.—*The disastrous consequences of the sin of discontent.* Discontent springs from distrust. *Distrust* is a root-sin from which different kindred evils spring, such as *dis*content, *dis*satisfaction, *dis*gust, *dis*obedience, and other *dis*agreeable states of mind. But " those that know thy name," &c. (Ps. ix. 10 ; Lam. iii. 24). From these strange cairns in the wilderness,[1] "the graves of lust," we hear a voice (1 Cor. x. 6). I. THE DISCONTENT OF THE ISRAELITES. II. ITS DISASTROUS CONSEQUENCES.

I. 1. Its disgraceful origin: "the mixed multitude," "hangers-on," "riff-raff." The chosen people of God listened and sympathised with them rather than with Moses and God. Apply to worldlings grumbling about weather, homes, situations, incomes, &c. (Prov. i. 10; Rom. xii. 2; 2 Cor. vi. 14). 2. The gross ingratitude of it. They were dissatisfied with the manna, which was wholesome, abundant, and adapted to various uses (vers. 7—9), as though Hindoos should quarrel with their rice or the English with their wheat (1 Tim. vi. 8). They recollect certain casual sensual advantages of past bondage, but forget its cruelties and degradation (vers. 4—6). Why not remember the whips and fetters and infanticide? They think of suppers more than sufferings, of full stomachs rather than of famished souls. Let Christians beware of hankering after the indulgences of their old life (Prov. xxiii. 3; 1 John ii. 15). And they complain of temporary deprivations, though hastening to a home of permanent and abundant good. They were passing through "that great and terrible wilderness" (Paran) because it was the direct route to the promised land (Deut. i. 19; cf. 1 Pet. i. 13; ii. 11). 3. The aggravations of it. For they had seen God's power already (Exod. xvi. 13; Ps. lxxviii. 19, 20). And have not we? (cf. Ps. xxii. 4, 5, 9, 10). And they overlooked recent chastisement (ver. 1). God forbid that Isa. xxvi. 11 should be true of us, lest Prov. xxix. 1 should be also.

II. The disastrous results of their sin. 1. They angered Jehovah. Discontent in the guests of his bounty dishonours their generous host, as though Reuben had complained because Joseph gave more to Benjamin (Gen. xliii. 34). 2. They grieved Moses, and even infected him with their own desponding spirit (vers. 11—15; see sketch below). Note how sin may become epidemic, spreading from the mixed multitude to the Israelites, and thence to Moses, like a disease introduced by foreign sailors spreading to our homes and palaces. Beware of carrying infection (Illustration, Asaph, Ps. lxxiii. 11—15). 3. They got what they desired, but are ruined thereby. Moses' prayer for help is answered in mercy (vers. 16, 17); theirs for flesh, in judgment (vers. 18—20). They probably added gluttony to lust, and perished in the sight of plenty and at the moment of gratification (cf. Job xx. 22, 23; Ps. lxxviii. 30, 31).

Learn—1. Prayers of discontent may bring answers of destruction. *E. g.* Rachel demanding children, and the Israelites a king. Greater wealth but worse health (Eccles. vi. 1, 2); worldly prosperity, but leanness of soul (Ps. cvi. 15; 1 Tim. vi. 9; James iv. 4). 2. The blessedness of a contented trust (Philip. iv. 11—13; Heb. xiii. 5).—P.

Vers. 11—15.—*The sin of despondency in a servant of God.* Moses is infected by the people's sin of discontent, though in the milder form of despondency. The signs and effects of it are as follows:—

I. MOSES FORGETS THAT THE BURDENS OF RESPONSIBILITY AND THE AFFLICTIONS THEY BRING WITH THEM, INSTEAD OF BEING A SIGN THAT HE HAS "NOT FOUND FAVOUR" IN GOD'S SIGHT, ARE A PROOF OF THE HONOUR PUT UPON HIM. Illustration: a diplomatist or a general (*e. g.* Sir Garnet Wolseley) selected out of all the Queen's servants for some arduous enterprise. Christian wife honoured by God with the responsibilities and burdens of motherhood.

II. HE FORGETS THAT OUR DUTIES ARE NOT LIMITED BY OUR NATURAL RELATIONSHIPS (ver. 12). We are all "members of one another" (Rom. xiv. 7; Philip. ii. 4). All are in danger of a selfish disregard of those afar off (savage Caffres, idolatrous Hindoos), or even of those at our doors, not our own kindred, respecting whose spiritual welfare we may be selfishly indifferent or despondent.

III. HE SPEAKS AS THOUGH THE BURDEN WAS THROWN ENTIRELY ON HIMSELF. The questions in vers. 12, 13 are very unworthy of him. The cold fog of despondency chills him and obscures the light of God's presence which was promised to him (Exod. xxxiii. 14).

IV. HIS DESPONDENCY LEADS TO UNWORTHY REFLECTIONS ON GOD AND EXAGGERATED STATEMENTS ABOUT HIMSELF (vers. 13, 14). A smaller burden would have

---

[1] 'Our Work in Palestine,' pp. 284-6.

been too great for him "alone ; " a heavier not too great with God (cf. John xv. 5 ; Philip. iv. 13).

V. IT PROMPTS HIM TO A SINFUL PRAYER (ver. 15). Imagine that the prayer had been answered, and Moses had died on the spot ; what a humiliating end ! (cf. 1 Kings xix. 4).

Let us learn the lesson Ps. lvi. 3, and thus climb to the level of a still higher experience : " I will trust, and not be afraid " (Isa. xii. 2 ; xxvi. 3).—P.

Ver. 17.—*The communication of a spiritual endowment.* The endowment of the elders for official duties was—1. A Divine gift imparted by God himself (1 Cor. xii. 4—6 ; James i. 17). 2. Yet mediate, through Moses, who was the first to enjoy it, but was thankful to share it with men in sympathy with himself (cf. 1 Cor. iii. 21, 22 ; iv. 6, 7). 3. A means of relief to Moses and of blessing to the people. The communication did not impoverish Moses, but enriched him. He was like a lamp from which seventy other lamps were lit. The communication of the gift, like mercy, was twice blessed—to him that gives and him that takes. It relieved Moses and enriched the elders, yet not for their own advantage, but as a means of discharging their new and solemn trust. All "gifts," however received, are to be looked on as talents and trusts. The law of the stewardship is found in Rom. xii. 3—8 ; 1 Pet iv. 10, 11.

Learn—1. The value of every spiritual gift. Men should not envy the possessor of it, but thank God for him, since the gift is communicable. If there had been no inspired Moses, there would have been no inspired elders. An Elisha is the heir of an Elijah (2 Kings ii. 9, 10) ; a Timothy is the son of a Paul (2 Tim. i. 2, 6). 2. The privilege of being the medium of communicating a spiritual gift (Rom. i. 11 ; Phil. i. 6). 3. The importance of "coveting the best gifts " which God can bestow, without human intervention, through his beloved Son.—P.

Vers. 26—29.—*Largeness of heart.* The brevity of the narrative prevents us forming an adverse judgment of the conduct of Eldad and Medad, for we do not know their motive for remaining in the camp. It may have been ignorance of the call, or shrinking through timidity from a duty which, nevertheless, God would not allow them to escape. But the narrative is not too brief to enable us to see in Moses' words a fine illustration of largeness of heart. Note—

I. JOSHUA'S APPEAL. His love of order may have been offended. He feared lest the unity of the camp under the leadership of Moses should be disturbed. He was anxious for the honour of his master, and desired that political and ecclesiastical discipline should be not only really, but ostensibly, in his hands. The call of the seventy elders with prophetic powers was a new departure in the history of the theocracy, and now the prophesying of Eldad and Medad, apart, threatened still further apparently to derogate from the honours of Moses. Thus now narrow minds or small hearts may be fearful of that which is novel, and envious of those who take a course independent of established authorities and Church traditions, even though they "seem to have the Spirit of God." They may forbid, or at least "despise, prophesyings" which are not according to rule.

II. MOSES' REPLY. The only question with Moses is one not of place or method, but of reality. Are the prophesyings and the spirit "of God"? Largeness of heart cannot exempt us from this duty (1 Thess. v. 21 ; 1 John iv. 1—3). Moses could not recognise the falsehoods uttered in the tabernacle of Korah, though he rejoiced in the prophesyings of Eldad. Spurious charity is traitorous to truth ; true charity can only rejoice "in the truth " (1 Cor. xiii. 6). The lesson taught us is illustrated by various incidents in the New Testament. A large-hearted Christian will not be offended—1. If those who are clearly working in the name of Christ, and with the seal of his approval, do not follow with him (Mark ix. 38—40). 2. If their success seems to imperil the prosperity of his party or denomination (John iii. 26, &c.). 3. He will rejoice in the work, though unofficial and obscure men have originated it (Acts xi. 19—24). 4. He will not " envy," but delight, in the proclamation of the gospel, even if the motives of the preachers are marred by " envy and strife " (Philip. i. 15—18). Large-heartedness will " covet earnestly the best gifts " for others, whatever the consequences may be to ourselves.—P.

Ver. 4.—*The mixed multitude.* I. How CAME IT THERE? It left Egypt with them (Exod. xii. 38). It had been accumulating, one knows not how long, and in how many ways. Egypt had not been a very comfortable place even for the Egyptians just before the exodus. Ten plagues in swift succession and increasing severity would make many outside Israel to desire another abode. The tyranny of Pharaoh may have been grievous to many of his own people. Many would join departing Israel uninvited ; many also may have been asked by well-wishers and acquaintances, " Come with us, and we will do you good " (ch. x. 29). *So now there is a mixed multitude in the Church of Christ.* It cannot be kept out. The supreme relation among men is no doubt that of union in Christ, spiritual brotherhood, fellowship ever becoming more intimate and precious ; but the relations that arise out of nature, all domestic and social bonds in short, must also exert their influence during the earthly course of the Church. Who can tell what effect natural feelings have had in modifying, sometimes even in obscuring, the full force of Divine truth ? How hard it was to keep the first generation of Hebrew Christians from mixing the bondage of Judaism with the liberty which is in Christ ! Nor must we forget that in *every individual Christian* there is something of the spirit of the mixed multitude, the old man not yet dead, and struggling to keep his hold, even while the new man is growing in grace and in the knowledge of the Lord and Saviour Jesus Christ. Whatever precaution and strictness the Church may observe, it cannot keep the spirit of the world out.

II. THE DANGER FROM ITS PRESENCE. The mixed multitude began to lust, therein acting according to its nature. There was no covenant with it, no promise to it, no assurance of Canaan. It had no lot in the tabernacle, and what share it got of the manna was to be regarded as one in later days regarded the Saviour's boon to her : " The dogs eat of the crumbs which fall from their masters' table." Hence it was free to think without let or hindrance on the much-loved delicacies of Egypt. Just so there is a mixed multitude in and about the Church of Christ, which, with the spirit of the world dominant in its heart, soon makes the ways of the world to appear in its life. From many temptations you can escape by running away from the scene of them ; but what must you do if temptations beset you in the very paths of religion themselves ? This is the peculiar danger from the mixed multitude. When Jesus foils the third temptation in the wilderness, Satan departs from him for a season ; but what shall he do when Peter, the chosen, daily companion, in the impulse of his carnal heart, would turn him from the cross ? We know what Jesus did, but none the less was he exposed to the spirit of the mixed multitude then. Or what shall Paul do, intrepid enough against avowed enemies, when his friends at Cæsarea assail him in a way to break his heart (Acts xxi. 12, 13). There is a subtle, unconscious, unintended way in which the prophecy may be carried out that a man's foes shall be they of his own household. The mixed multitude may have been dangerous most of all in this, that it did not mean to be dangerous at all.

III. How TO GUARD AGAINST THE DANGER. There is but one way, and that to live more and more in pursuit of heavenly objects. The mixed multitude *will not alter in the objects of its love ;* when any of its number cease to do so, it is because they have passed over to join the true Israel. The change then must be in us—more of ardour and aspiration. Note Paul's counsel to Timothy : " Flee also youthful lusts : but follow (διώκε) righteousness, faith, charity, peace, with them that call on the Lord out of a pure heart " (2 Tim. ii. 22). The fleeing is not a *mere fleeing ;* it is a *pursuing ;* a fleeing because it is a pursuing. Many temptations will pant in vain after the ardour and simplicity in Christ Jesus of such a man as Paul (2 Cor. iv. 18 ; v. 14—17 ; Eph. iv. 17—24 ; Phil. i. 21—23 ; iii. 7—14). And even the subtlest temptations of the mixed multitude are turned gently aside, as by Jesus himself, when his mother and brethren desired to speak with him (Matt. xii. 46—50). We must not only say, but feel it, that the Father's business is the main thing. From the very depths of our hearts must rise the cry, almost a groaning that cannot be uttered, " *Thy will* be done on earth, as it is in heaven." *Thy will,* not the wishes of corrupted human affections, however strong and entangling the affections may be (1 Cor. v. 9, 10 ; vii. 10—16).—Y.

Vers. 10—15.—*The expostulation of Moses.* Jehovah and his servant Moses are very differently affected by this universal complaint of the Israelites. "The anger of the Lord was kindled greatly;" how it was expressed, we see later on. At present we have to consider the displeasure of Moses. God was made angry by the unbelief and ingratitude of the people, but Moses is chiefly concerned because of the great straits into which he himself is being brought. Hence his expostulation.

I. IT CONTAINS A CLEAR RECOGNITION OF DUTY. Duty may be perfectly clear, even when there is much perplexity as to how it is to be performed. Moses had no manner of doubt that God had put him in his present position. Intolerable was the burden and keen the pain, but they had not come through any ambition of his own, and this in itself made a great deal of difference. If Moses had led the Israelites into the wilderness for his own purposes, he could not have spoken in the way he did. From the intolerable burden there were two ways of escape, flight and death—death did suggest itself, but flight never. Moses even in his very complaining is nobler than Jonah running away. As we see him thus suffering this great pressure for the sins of the people, we cannot help thinking of Jesus in the garden, praying that, if possible, the cup might pass from him. So Paul tells us that, in addition to things from without, the care (μέριμνα) *of all the Churches* came upon him (2 Cor. xi. 28). It may be our duty, in the name of God, and at his clear command, to attempt what the world, following out its own order of thinking, calls impossible.

II. IT INDICATES A TOO FAVOURABLE ESTIMATE OF HUMAN NATURE, AS HAVING BEEN ENTERTAINED BY MOSES. He must have thought better of his followers and fellow-countrymen than they deserved. Not that he who had seen so much of them could possibly be blind to their faults; but we may well suppose that he expected too great a change from the influences of the sojourn near Sinai. He gave them credit, probably, for something of his own feeling, full of expectation and of joy in the abiding favour and protection of God. And now, when the reality appears in all its hideousness, there is a corresponding reaction. Unregenerate human nature must always be regarded with very moderate expectations. At its best it is a reed easily broken. How much higher than Moses is Jesus! He knew what was in man (Matt. vii. 13, 14; xiii. 13—15; xviii. 21—22; xxvi. 31—35; Mark xiv. 18—20). And what light he gave to his apostles on this subject, *e. g.* to Paul, who saw and declared so distinctly the weakness of law to do anything save expose and condemn. It is not possible for us to make too much allowance for the corruption and degradation of human nature through sin. Only thus shall we appreciate the change to be effected before men are what God would have them to be.

III. THE REACTION FROM THIS TOO FAVOURABLE ESTIMATE SHOWS ITSELF IN THE DESPAIRING LANGUAGE OF MOSES. He goes from one extreme to the other. Having thought too well of Israel he now speaks of them below the truth. They are but sucking children. The many thousands of Israel have been thrown like helpless infants on his hands. We see presently that seventy men out of this very multitude are found fit to assist him, but in his confusion and despair he cannot stop to think of anything but death. He saw only the cloud and not the silver lining. Life henceforth meant nothing but wretchedness, and God's greatest boon would be to take it away. He wanted to be in that refuge which Job sought after his calamities, where the wicked cease from troubling, and the weary are at rest (Job iii. the whole chapter). It is worth while again contrasting Moses under the law with the apostles under the gospel. When Moses feels the heavily-pressing burden, he loses his presence of mind and begins to talk of death. When the apostles have the murmurers coming to them, they at once in a calm and orderly way prepare to get assistance (Acts vi. 1—6).—Y.

Vers. 16, 17.—*The answer of God.* 1. *He does not openly and directly reprove the reckless language of his servant.* Both Moses and the people had sinned, but with such a difference that while God visits the people with immediate and condign punishment he stretches forth his hand to Moses, even as Jesus did to Peter sinking in the sea. God treated Moses here very much as he treated the complaining Elijah (1 Kings xix.). Moses was just the sort of man who might be trusted to rebuke himself, and bitterly repent all the unjust and unbelieving thoughts, which, upon this sudden temptation, had come into his mind. 2. *The first word of God tends to bring Moses to a calmer mind.* It sets before him something practical and not very difficult. Left to himself, he knows not how to begin dealing with this anarchy, especially with his own mind in such a distressed state. But it was a task quite within his reach, to pick out from a limited and probably well-known circle, seventy elders, official and experienced men. As he went through this work, he would be brought to feel, and not without a sense of shame, that he had been overtaken by panic. He has talked about sucking children; he now learns that there are at least seventy elders upon whose experience and influence he can lean. We soon find out, if we only listen to God, that temporal troubles are never so bad as they seem. 3. *The way in which this help was made as effectual as possible.* As God had given a certain spirit to Moses, so he would give it also to these seventy assistant elders. This was a reminder that he had not afflicted his servant and frowned upon him, as he so recklessly said (ver. 11). We often murmur and complain against Providence for neglecting us, when the real neglect is with ourselves in making a bad use of gifts bestowed. God never tells his people to do things beyond natural strength, without first assuring a sufficiency of power for the thing commanded. "I can do all things, through Christ who inwardly strengthens me," said Paul. There is further encouragement in God's promise here, as being an illustration of how the spirit is given without measure. There was not a certain limited manifestation to Moses, so that if others shared the spirit with him, he must have less. Neither his power nor his honour were one whit diminished. The question always is, What is the need of men in the sight of God? Then, according to that need, and never coming short of it, are the communications of his Holy Spirit. Moses, instead of being poorer, was really richer, for the spirit was working in a mind to which a precious experience had been added. 4. In the sight of these directions we are reminded how *Moses spoke out of a comparative inexperience of the burden.* Moses said there was nothing left for him but to die. The history tells us, that so far from dying, he had yet in him nearly forty years of honourable mediatorship between God and men. His proper word was, "I shall not die, but live, and declare the works of the Lord" (Ps. cxviii. 17). It is marvellous to think what some men have gone through in the way of difficulties, losses, and trials. Even the natural man has greater strength in the hour of trouble than at first he is conscious of—a great deal of trouble, when it is once fairly over, comes in the course of time to look a very small thing—and if we have God's strength, then we shall not merely endure tribulation, but glory in it. From these words of Moses and the practical gentle reply of God, learn one great lesson—how easy it is to exaggerate our difficulties and underrate our resources.—Y.

Vers. 18—20; 31—35.—*Self-will surfeited and punished.* I. GOD'S TREATMENT OF SELF-WILL. This is always to be well considered where instances of it are found in the Scriptures, because one of the great ends of God's dealings with us is to establish his holy, wise, and righteous will in place of our low, jealous, ignorant self-will. The way of parents dealing with children is to curb and restrain them at once; but children grow to be men, and what then? We cannot deal effectually with one another, for self-will is in all of us, and so far as temporal circumstances are concerned, it not unfrequently gets much of its own way. When we come to the discipline of the whole man, God only can effectually deal with self-will. He might curb him in at once, but such would not be discipline fit for a man. It might break the spirit, but it would do nothing to enlighten and change; we see here that God's treatment is to let people walk awhile in their own way. Self-will breaks out in complaints against the manna: self-will then shall have its desire, and what satisfaction it can get from the flesh for which it craves. Its mouth waters at the thought of the fish of Egypt; it shall have quails, which we may presume were an even greater delicacy. So when, in later years, Israel, in envy of surrounding nations, clamoured for a king, forgetting that the King of kings was theirs, God gave them their wish. The bulk of men will only learn by experience. The prodigal son must know the end of riotous living for himself. It is better to take God's word at the beginning and not sow to the flesh; but men shall have the opportunity if they choose. So God causes his wind to blow and the quails come, an exceeding great multitude (Ps. lxviii. 23—29).

II. GOD'S TEST OF SELF-CONTROL. He gives the quails, not for one day's luxury, but to be the food of a month. As nothing is said to the contrary, we must presume the manna was still continued. Indeed we can easily see the reason for its continuance. God in giving the quails, adds an express and solemn warning. They are to be taken with all their consequences. Sweet at first, they shall turn to objects of bitter loathing. They were given, not in complacency, but in anger, hence they had in them the efficacy of a test. Surely the whole of Israel was not rebellious and murmuring. There must have been men of the Nazarite spirit even then, and the question for them is : " Shall we go out after our wont and gather the manna (Exod. xvi.), or shall we, like the rest, gratify our appetites with these delicious quails? " Who can doubt that God was watching his own faithful ones, the Israelites indeed in whom there was no guile? There are doubtless many things in the world, the chief use of which is to test the disposition of man to obey God (Gen. ii. 16, 17). These quails were given, but there was no obligation to eat them. Every Israelite was free to refuse. A timely repentance, and another wind would have blown away the quails as rapidly as they came. There was a lesson if the people would learn it, from the submissive birds to the rebellious human beings.

III. GOD'S PENALTY FOR SELF-INDULGENCE. There is a seeming contradiction between vers. 19, 20, and ver. 33, but it is only seeming. God hastened his judgment and thereby really showed his mercy. As David chose the brief pestilence, and to fall into the hand of the Lord (2 Sam. xxiv.), so here God comes with an immediate and sweeping visitation. Besides, it is possible the people neglected the command to sanctify themselves, and thus further provoked the anger already stirred up ; when people get lust into their hearts all sense of law is apt to vanish. It was well the people should see clearly the close connection between disobedience and retribution. Thus did God show, even in these quails, the spirit of a good and perfect gift. Nothing in creation is a blessing in itself ; God must make it so, and he can easily in his anger turn it to a curse. God, in making the effect of eating the quails so conspicuous and sudden, still further illustrated by contrast the glory of the manna, for this manna was a beautiful type of the true bread that cometh from heaven. The people had never gathered the manna with such greed and application as they had gathered the quails. When a man breaks the law he is at once guilty, and the punishment, if it be deferred, is so as a matter of expediency, not of right. The lapse of time only makes the connection between sin and punishment less obvious, not at all less certain (Ps. cvi. 15 ; Gal. vi. 7—9).—Y.

Vers. 21—23.—*Deeper in unbelief.* I. MOSES IN HIS REPLY SHOWS AN IMPERFECT APPRECIATION OF WHAT GOD HAD SAID. 1. *As to God's purpose.* He had spoken in holy anger, promising flesh, but threatening retribution along with it. The threat is quite as emphatic as the promise, but somehow Moses does not heed. At Sinai, when the people made the golden calf, he was so oppressed with the sense of their great sin, and so solicitous for their pardon, as to beg if the pardon were not granted that he might himself be blotted out of God's book. Where was this anxiety now ? His great concern is, not how God may be propitiated and the people spared, but how the people may be propitiated and he himself spared. Contrast Moses here with Christ at all times. Think of the Son's never-failing remembrance of the Father's glory. The Son saw and appreciated all things the Father showed him ; hence the confidence with which we look to Christ for a revelation of all God's purposes concerning us, so far as it is right for us to know them. Jesus could ever go out and declare in fitting words and with proper emphasis all the will of God, for he had a perfect appreciation of that will himself. But how was Moses to go out and speak properly to the people when he himself had only half-heard, as it were, what God had said to him ? Doubtless he repeated the message of God in the very same words ; but one fears that while he made it quite clear to the people they should have flesh, he made it not quite so clear that God was sending it in anger. Let us ever get to the spirit of God's messages to us ; never content till their fulness of meaning has passed into our heart, so that something like the fulness of service may pass out of it again. 2. *As to God's power.* History repeats itself. Unbelief, natural ignorance of God, slowness of heart to take in what he has spoken,—these repeat themselves in their manner of receiving God's promises. Moses talks here as the disciples did at the feeding of the five thousand (Matt. xiv. 15). And yet, after all his wonderful experiences, there should not have been the slightest difficulty in receiving what God had said. Of all possible convictions, this should have rested on solid ground—that what God had promised he assuredly had power to perform. Is not this one of the great differences between God and men? Men promise and forget, or fall short ; God is always better than his promises, for they have to be spoken in defective human words, while they are fulfilled in complete Divine actions.

II. THE CAUSE OF THIS IMPERFECT APPRECIATION. Can we not detect, and especially in the light of his subsequent language, something like doubt, something like leaning upon creature supports instead of God, in the invitation which he gave to Hobab? If this be so, we wonder little at his language of bitter complaint and despair (vers. 11—15) ; and we wonder less that he so soon showed himself out of sympathy with the Divine purposes. The eye of faith had become dim ; self-preservation, escape from an intolerable burden, occupied his thoughts. Was it astonishing that, unbelief having found a temporary lodgment in the heart of the leader, the followers should have failed to take in *all* the purport of God's message? Learn from this how carefully spirituality of mind needs to be guarded. We must not be seduced into leaning upon men *instead of trusting in God.* Men may solace and encourage us as companions ; they are never to take the place of Providence. So neither are we to be terrified and paralysed by sudden and stupendous revelations of human wickedness. In the midst of them all we hear the one voice speaking, " Be still, and know that I am God."—Y.

Vers. 26—29.—*Foolish advice wisely rejected.* God fulfils his promise, and gives to these seventy men a spirit which doubtless brings them into more active sympathy with Moses, and takes away the carnal and selfish views which had prevailed in their minds. The difference between their present and former state was probably much like that between the state of the apostles after and before the day of Pentecost. They had a perspicacity, a power, a courage, a zeal, which did not belong to them before. As they prophesied, may we not suppose that Moses heard from them expressions quite new to his ears as coming from Israelite lips? And to make the occasion more memorable and significant, two of the seventy, who for some unexplained reason remained in the camp, nevertheless prophesied, as did those in the tabernacle. The intelligence was very quickly brought to Moses. Some of the Israelites would be greatly shocked by such an irregular proceeding, though perhaps they had seen nothing very censurable in the general cry of the people for flesh. Punctiliousness in ceremony and etiquette is often joined with laxity in things of moment (Matt. xxiii. 23). The reception of the news is followed by—

I. THE FOOLISH ADVICE OF JOSHUA. Foolish, *although given by a devoted friend.* Joshua would probably have died for Moses, but he could not, therefore, give him good counsel. Attachment itself has not unfrequently a blinding effect on the judgment. A stranger might advise more wisely. It is the *right* of friendship to offer advice, but it is often the *height* of friendship, the very bloom and delicacy of it, to refrain. We find similar instances (Matt. xvi. 21—23 ; Acts xxi. 12, 13). Foolish, because *evidently given without consideration.* The circumstances were quite novel to Joshua. The grounds on which he dashed out his advice were mere matters of hearsay. *There was enough to have made him cautious.* Eldad and Medad were among the chosen ones ; those present had been gifted with the spirit ; what more likely then upon consideration, what more worthy of reverent acceptance, than that the absentees should have been similarly visited? Advice, when it is given with full knowledge of circumstances and full consideration of them, may be indeed precious, the very salvation and security of a perplexed mind. Otherwise, the greater the ignorance the greater the mischief. Advice should mostly come in response to a request for it. Foolish, because *it concerned the status of Moses rather than the glory of God.* Much of the advice of friendship is vitiated, through shutting out all save personal considerations. One friend advises another as a counsel does his client, not that justice may be done, but that his client may gain his end. Joshua was considering how the reputation and influence of "his lord Moses" would be affected.

Foolish because it was given *to a man who was in no doubt*. Moses was rejoicing in escape from a heavy burden, and the visitation upon Eldad and Medad was the very thing still further to comfort him. The folly of the advice is crowned, as we observe *that it recommended an impossibility*. "Forbid them." Forbid what? That they should prophesy! As well forbid the branches not to sway with a strong wind as forbid men to prophesy when the Spirit comes upon them. Even Balaam could not help uttering the Lord's prophecies and blessing Israel from the very mouth that would fain, in its greed of filthy lucre, have uttered a curse.

II. This FOOLISH ADVICE WISELY REJECTED. 1. As to the *substance* of the rejection. Possibly if Moses had been a different kind of man, he might have said to himself, "There is something in what Joshua says." But he was not one of the *aut Cæsar aut nullus* order. Joshua, in his impetuous word, was concerned for his master's honour; the master himself was concerned about his grievous burden. Not even Joshua understood the bitter experiences through which Moses had lately passed. "Would that all the Lord's people were prophets!" Our measure before God does not depend on our standing among men. Moses would not have been one whit less esteemed in heaven if every other Israelite had been as spiritually-minded as himself. Joshua had been speaking to a man who, like Christian, had been toiling on with a weary weight on his back. He has just got rid of it, and "Forbid them" really meant, "Take the burden up again." 2. As to the *spirit* of the rejection. Moses shows here the meekness and gentleness with which he is so emphatically credited in the next chapter. Advice, when it cannot be taken, even when it is most foolish and meddlesome, should be pushed gently away; and if the spirit in which it has been given is evidently kind and generous, let the refusal be mingled with gratefulness. Joshua loved Moses, and Moses loved Joshua. "Enviest thou for my sake?" Thus Moses recognises the devotion and *bona fides* of his friend.—Y.

EXPOSITION.

CHAPTER XII.

The SEDITION AND PUNISHMENT OF MIRIAM (ch. xii.). Ver. 1.—**And Miriam and Aaron spake against Moses.** While the people were encamped at Hazeroth (see ver. 16), and therefore probably very soon after the events of the last chapter. That Miriam's was the moving spirit in the matter is sufficiently evident, (1) because her name stands first; (2) because the verb "spake" is in the feminine (תְּדַבֵּר, "and she said"); (3) because the ground of annoyance was a peculiarly feminine one, a *mésalliance;* (4) because Miriam alone was punished; (5) because Aaron never seems to have taken the lead in anything. He appears uniformly as a man of weak and pliable character, who was singularly open to influence from others, for good or for evil. Superior to his brother in certain gifts, he was as inferior to him in force of character as could well be. On the present occasion there can be little question that Aaron simply allowed himself to be drawn by his sister into an opposition with which he had little personal sympathy; a general discontent at the manifest inferiority of his position inclined him to take up her quarrel, and to echo her complaints. **Because of the Ethiopian woman whom he had married: for he had married an Ethiopian woman.** Hebrew, a Cushite woman. The descendants of Cush were distributed both in Africa (the Ethiopians proper) and in Asia (the southern Arabians, Babylonians, Ninevites, &c.). See Gen. x. Some have thought that this Ethiopian woman was none other than the Midianite Zipporah, who might have been called a Cushite in some loose sense by Miriam. The historian, however, would not have repeated in his own name a statement so inaccurate; nor is it at all likely that that marriage would have become a matter of contention after so many years. The natural supposition undoubtedly is that Moses (whether after the death of Zipporah, or during her lifetime, we cannot tell) had taken to himself a second wife of Hamite origin. Where he found her it is useless to conjecture; she may possibly have been one of the "mixed multitude" that went up out of Egypt. It is equally useless to attribute any moral or religious character to this marriage, of which Holy Scripture takes no direct notice, and which was evidently regarded by Moses as a matter of purely private concern to himself. In general we may say that the rulers of Israel attached neither political, social, nor religious significance to their marriages; and that neither law nor custom imposed any restraint upon their choice, so long as they did not ally themselves with the daughters of Canaan (see Exod. xxxiv. 16). It would be altogether beside the mark to suppose that Moses deliberately married a Cushite woman in order to set forth the essential fellowship between Jew and Gentile. It is true that such marriages as those of Joseph, of Salmon, of Solomon, and others undeniably became invested with spiritual importance and evangelical significance, in view of the growing narrowness of Jewish feeling, and of the coming in of a wider dispensation ; but such significance was wholly latent at the time. If, however, the choice of Moses is inexplicable, the opposition of Miriam is intelligible enough. She was a prophetess (Exod. xv. 20), and strongly imbued with those national and patriotic feelings which are never far removed from exclusiveness and pride of race. She had—to use modern words—led the Te Deum of the nation after the stupendous overthrow of the Egyptians. And now her brother, who stood at the head of the nation, had brought into his tent a Cushite woman, one of the dark-skinned race which seemed even lower in the religious scale than the Egyptians themselves. Such an alliance might easily seem to Miriam nothing better than an act of apostasy which would justify any possible opposition.

Ver. 2.—**And they said, Hath the Lord indeed spoken only by Moses ? hath he not spoken also by us ?** This is evidently not the "speaking against Moses" mentioned in the previous verse, for that is distinctly said to have been on the score of Moses' marriage. This is their justification of themselves for daring to dispute his judgment and arraign his proceedings ; a thing which clearly required justification. Moses himself, or more likely others for him, had remonstrated with them on the language they were using. They retorted that Moses had no monopoly of Divine communications ; Aaron also received the revelation of God by Urim and Thummim, and Miriam was a prophetess. They were acknowledged in a general sense as sharing with him the leadership of Israel (see Micah vi. 4) ; upon this they meant to found a claim to co-ordinate authority. They would have had perhaps all matters settled in a family council in which they should have had an equal voice. It was hard for them both to forget that Moses was only their younger brother : for Miriam that she had saved his life as an infant ; for Aaron that he had been as prominent as Moses in the original commission from God to the people. **And the Lord heard it.** In one sense he hears everything ; in another sense there are many things which he does not choose to hear, because he does not wish to take judicial notice of them. Thus he had not "heard" the passionate complaints of Moses himself a short time before, because his will was then to pardon, not to punish (cf. Isa. xlii. 19 ; Mal. iii. 16).

Ver. 3.—**Now the man Moses was very meek, above all the men which were upon the face of the earth.** For the Hebrew עָנָו the Septuagint has πραΰς here ; the Vulgate, *mitis*. The Targum Palestine has "bowed down in his mind," *i. e.* overwhelmed ("plagued," Luther). The ordinary version is undoubtedly right ; the object of the parenthesis was either to explain that there was no real ground for the hostility of Miriam and Aaron, or to show that the direct interference of the Lord himself was necessary for the protection of his servant. The verse bears a difficulty on its very face, because it speaks of Moses in terms which could hardly have been used by Moses of himself. Nor is this difficulty in the least degree diminished by the explanations which are offered by those who are determined to maintain at any cost the Mosaic authorship of every word in the Pentateuch. It is no doubt true to some extent that when a great and good man is writing of himself (and especially when he writes under the influence of the Holy Spirit), he can speak of himself with the same calm and simple truthfulness with which he would speak of any other. It is sufficient, however, to refer to the example of St. Paul to show that neither any height of spiritual privilege and authority, nor any intensity of Divine inspiration, obliterates the natural virtue of modesty, or allows a really humble man to praise himself without pain and shrinking. It is also to be observed that while St. Paul forces himself to speak of his privileges, distinctions, and sufferings, all of which were outward to himself, Moses would here be claiming for himself the possession of an inward virtue in greater measure than any other living soul. Surely it is not too much to say that if he did possess it in such measure, he could not possibly have been conscious that he did ; only One was thus conscious of his own ineffable superiority, and this very consciousness is one of the strongest arguments for believing that he was infinitely more than a mere man, howsoever good and exalted. There is but one theory that will make it morally possible for Moses to have written this verse, viz., that in writing he was a mere instrument, and not morally responsible for what he did write. Such a theory will find few upholders. But, further, it is necessary to prove not only that Moses might have made this statement, but also that he might have made it in this form. Granted that it was necessary to the narrative to point out that he was very meek ; it was *not* necessary to assert that he was absolutely the meekest man living. And if it was unnecessary, it was also unnatural. No good man would go out of his way to compare himself to his own advantage with all men upon the face of the earth.

The whole form of the sentence, indeed, as well as its position, proclaim it so clearly to be an addition by some later hand, that the question may be left to the common sense and knowledge of human nature of every reader; for the broad outlines of human character, morality, and virtue are the same in every age, and are not displaced by any accident of position, or even of inspiration. A slight examination of passages from other sacred writers, which are sometimes adduced as analogous, will serve to show how profound is the difference between what holy men *could* say of themselves and what they *could not* (cf. Dan. i. 19, 20; v. 11, 12; ix. 23; x. 11). On the question of the inspiration of this verse, supposing it to be an interpolation, and as to the probable author of it, see the Preface. As to the fact of Moses' meekness, we have no reason to doubt it, but we may legitimately look upon the form in which it is stated as one of those conventional hyperboles which are not uncommon even in the sacred writings (cf. Gen. vii. 19; John xxi. 25). And we cannot avoid perceiving that Moses' meekness was far from being perfect, and was marred by sinful impatience and passion on more than one recorded occasion.

Ver. 4.—**The Lord spake suddenly.** How he spake we cannot tell, but the word "suddenly" (Septuagint, παραχρῆμα) points to something unexpected and unusual. The voice seems to have come to the three in their tents before there was any thought in their minds of such an intervention. **Come out ye three,** *i. e.* out of the camp—probably the camp of Moses and Aaron, on the east of the tabernacle (see ch. iii. 38).

Ver. 5.—**The Lord came down in the pillar of the cloud.** The cloud which had been soaring above the tabernacle descended upon it (see ch. xi. 25 and xii. 10). **And stood in the door of the tabernacle.** It would seem most natural to understand by these words the entrance to the holy place itself, and this would manifestly accord best with the movements of the cloud, as here described; for the cloud seems to have sunk down upon the sacred tent in token that the Lord was in some special sense present within it. On the other hand, the phrase must certainly be understood to mean the entrance of the court, or sacred enclosure, in Levit. viii. 3, 31, 33, and probably in other places. As it is hardly possible that the phrase can have had both meanings, the latter must be preferred. **And they both came forth.** Not out of the sanctuary, into which Miriam could not have entered, but out of the enclosure. The wrath which lay upon them both, and the punishment which was about to be inflicted upon one, were sufficient reasons for calling them out of the holy ground.

Ver. 6.—**If there be a prophet among you**

I the Lord will make myself known. More probably "the Lord" belongs to the first clause: "If there be to you a prophet of the Lord, I will make myself known." So the Septuagint, ἐὰν γένηται προφήτης ὑμῶν Κυρίῳ, . . . γνωσθήσομαι. **In a vision.** Ἐν ὁράματι. An internal vision, in which the eyes (even if open) saw nothing, but the effects of vision were produced upon the sensorium by other and supernatural means (see, *e. g.*, Amos vii. 7, 8; Acts x. 11). **Speak unto him in a dream.** Rather, speak "in him"—בׄוֹ. The voice that spake to the prophet was an internal voice, causing no vibration of the outer air, but affecting only the inner and hidden seat of consciousness. It is not necessary to restrict the prophetic dream to the time of sleep; a waking state, resembling what we call day-dream, in which the external senses are quiescent, and the imagination is freed from its usual mental restraints, was perhaps the more usual mental condition at the time. Indeed the Divine communications made to Joseph (Matt. i. 20; ii. 13) and to the Magi (*ibid.* ch. ii. 12) are almost the only ones we read of as made during actual sleep, unless we include the case of Pilate's wife (*ibid.* ch. xxvii. 19); and none of these were prophets in the ordinary sense. Compare, however, Acts ii. 17 *b.*

Ver. 7.—**My servant Moses is not so.** No words could more clearly and sharply draw the distinction between Moses and the whole *laudabilis numerus* of the prophets. It is strange that, in the face of a statement so general and so emphatic, it should have been doubted whether it applied to such prophets as Isaiah or Daniel. It was exactly in "visions" and in "dreams," *i. e.* under the peculiar psychological conditions so-called, that these greatest of prophets received their revelations from heaven. The exceeding richness and wonder of some of these revelations did not alter the mode in which they were received, nor raise them out of the ordinary conditions of the *gradus propheticus.* As prophets of future things they were much greater than Moses, and their writings may be to us far more precious; but that does not concern the present question, which turns exclusively upon the relation between the Divine Giver and the human receiver of the revelation. If words mean anything, the assertion here is that Moses stood on an altogether different footing from the "prophet of the Lord" in respect of the communications which he received from the Lord. It is this essential superiority of position on the part of Moses which alone gives force and meaning to the important declarations of Deut. xviii. 15; John i. 21 *b.*; vi. 14; vii. 40, &c. Moses had *no* successor in his relations with God until that Son of man came, who was "in heaven" all the time he walked and spake on earth. **Who is faithful in all mine house.** נֶאֱמָן with בּ means to be proved, or attested, and so established (cf. 1 Sam. iii. 20 ; xxii. 14). The Septuagint gives the true sense, ἐν ὅλῳ τῷ οἴκῳ μου πιστός, and so it is quoted in the Epistle to the Hebrews (ch. iii. 2). The "house" of God, as the adjective "whole" shows, is not the tabernacle, but the house of Israel ; the word "house" standing for household, family, nation, as so often in the sacred writings (see Gen. xlvi. 27 ; Levit. x. 6 ; Heb. iii. 6).

Ver. 8.—**Mouth to mouth.** Equivalent to face to face in Exod. xxxiii. 11. What the exact facts of the case were it is not possible to know, scarcely to imagine ; but the words seem to imply a familiar speaking with an audible voice on the part of God, as distinguished from the internal voice, inaudible to the ear, with which he spake "in" the prophets. To assert that the revelations accorded to Moses were only subjective modifications of his own consciousness is to evacuate these strong words of any meaning whatever. **Apparently.** מַרְאָה (Septuagint ἐν εἴδει) is an accusative in apposition to what goes before by way (apparently) of further definition. It is the same word translated "vision" in ver. 6 ; but its meaning here must be determined by the expression "in riddles," which stands in antithesis to it. It was confessedly the case with most prophetic utterances that the language in which they were couched was quite as much intended to conceal as to express their full meaning ; but to Moses God spake without any such concealments. **The similitude of the Lord shall he behold.** תְּמוּנָה יְהוָֹה. Not the essential nature of God, which no man can see, but a form (wholly unknown and unimaginable to us) in which it pleased him to veil his glory. The Septuagint has τὴν δόξαν Κυρίου εἶδε, referring, apparently, to the vision promised in Exod. xxxiii. 22 ; and the Targum Palestine speaks here of the vision of the burning bush. The motive for this alteration is no doubt to be sought in a profound jealousy for the great truth declared in such texts as Deut. iv. 15 ; Isa. xl. 18, and afterwards in John i. 18 ; 1 Tim. vi. 16. But the statement in the text is a general one, and can only mean that Moses habitually in his intercourse with God had before his eyes some visible manifestation of the invisible God, which helped to make that intercourse at once more awfully real and more intensely blessed. Such manifestation to the sense of sight must be distinguished both from the visionary (or subjective) sight of God in human figure accorded to Ezekiel (ch. i. 26), to Isaiah (ch. vi. 1), to St. John (Rev. iv. 2, 3), and perhaps to others, and also from such theophanies in angel guise as are recorded in

Gen xxxii. 30 ; Judges xiii. 22, and elsewhere. On the other hand, the seventy elders seem to have seen the "Temunah" of the Lord upon that one occasion when they were called up into Mount Sinai (Exod. xxiv. 10, 11). **Wherefore then were ye not afraid to speak against my servant Moses?** No doubt it was the double fact of their relationship to Moses after the flesh, and of their sharing with him in certain spiritual gifts and prerogatives, which made them oblivious of the great distinction which lifted him above their rivalry, and should have lifted him above their contradiction. That contradiction, however, served to bring out in the clearest way the singular and unapproached position of the mediator of Israel; and it serves still to enable us to estimate aright the peculiar dignity of his legislation and his writings. The substance of prophetic teaching may be of deeper interest and of wider import than "the law," but this latter will still rank higher in the scale of inspiration, as having been more directly communicated from on high. Thus "the law" (as the Jews rightly taught) remained the body of Divine revelation until "that Prophet" came who was "like unto" Moses in the fact that he enjoyed constant, open, and direct communication with the Godhead.

Ver. 9.—**And he departed.** As a judge departs from his judgment-seat after trying and convicting evil-doers.

Ver. 10.—**The cloud departed from off the tabernacle.** During this awful interview the cloud of the Presence had rested on the tabernacle, as if it were the Divine chariot waiting for the King of Israel while he tarried within (cf. Ps. civ. 3 ; Isa. xix. 1 ; Rev. xi. 12). Now that his work is done he ascends his chariot again, and soars aloft above the host. **Miriam became leprous.** The Hebrews had become familiar with this terrible disease in Egypt. The Levitical legislation had made it more terrible by affixing to it the penalty of religious and social excommunication, and the stigma, as it were, of the Divine displeasure. Before this legislation Moses himself had been made partially and temporarily leprous, and that solely for a sign, and without any sense of punishment (Exod. iv. 6). In Miriam's case, however, as in all subsequent cases, the plague of leprosy was endued with moral as well as physical horror (cf. 2 Kings v. 27). **As snow.** This expression points to the perfect development of the disease, as contrasted with its earlier and less conspicuous stages. **Aaron looked upon Miriam.** If we ask why Aaron himself was not punished, the answer appears to be the same here as in the case of the golden calf. 1. He was not the leader in mischief, but only led into it through weakness. 2. He was, like many weak men, of an affectionate disposition (cf. Levit. x. 19), and suffered his own punishment in witnessing that of others. 3. He was God's high priest, and the office would have shared in the disgrace of the man.

Ver. 11.—**Aaron said unto Moses, Alas, my lord, I beseech thee.** Septuagint, δέομαι, Κύριε. In thus addressing his brother Aaron acknowledged his superior position, and tacitly abandoned all pretension to equality. **Lay not the sin upon us.** Aaron speaks to Moses almost as if he were praying to God, so completely does he recognise in his brother the representative of God (in a far higher sense than himself), who had power to bind and loose in the name and power of God. What Aaron really prays for is that the sin, which he frankly confesses, may not be imputed to them. The Levitical law had taught them to look upon sin as a burden, which in the nature of things the sinner must carry, but which by the goodness of God might be got rid of, or transferred to some one else (cf. Levit. iv. 4; xvi. 21; John i. 29).

Ver. 12.—**As one dead.** Rather, "as the dead thing," *i. e.* the still-born child, in which death and decay have anticipated life. Such was the frightful effect of leprosy in its last stages.

Ver. 13.—**Moses cried unto the Lord.** A much harder and prouder man than Moses was must needs have been melted into pity at the sight of his sister, and the terrible suggestion of Aaron. **Heal her now, O God, I beseech thee.** The "now" has no place here, unless it be merely to add force to the exclamation. Moses, although directly appealed to himself, can only appeal to God.

Ver. 14. — **The Lord said unto Moses.** Presumably in the tabernacle, whither Moses would have returned to supplicate God. **If her father had but spit in her face.** The "but" is superfluous, and obscures the sense; the act mentioned is referred to not as something trifling, but as something in its way very serious. The Septuagint renders it correctly εἰ ὁ πατὴρ . . . πτύων ἐνέπτυσεν. The Targums have, "if her father had corrected her." Probably they used this euphemism from a sense of a certain want of dignity and propriety in the orignal expression, considered as coming from the mouth of God. The act in question was, however, not uncommon in itself, and in significance clearly marked (see Deut. xxv. 9). It was the distinctive note of public disgrace inflicted by one who had a right to inflict it. In the case of a father, it meant that he was thoroughly ashamed of his child, and judged it best (which would be only in extreme cases) to put his child to shame before all the world. So public a disgrace would certainly be felt in patriarchal times as a most severe calamity, and entailed by ordinary custom (as we learn here) retirement and mourning for seven days at least. How much more, when her heavenly Father had been driven to inflict a public disgrace upon her for perverse behaviour, should the shame and the sorrow not be lightly put away, but patiently endured for a decent period ! (cf. Heb. xii. 9).

Ver. 15.—**Miriam was shut out from the camp seven days.** It does not say that Miriam was healed forthwith of her leprosy, but the presumption is to that effect. Not the punishment itself, but the shame of it, was to last according to the answer of God. Her case, therefore, would not fall under the law of ch. v. 2, or of Levit. xiii. 46, but would be analogous to that treated of in Levit. xiv. No doubt she had to submit to all the rites there prescribed, humiliating as they must have been to the prophetess and the sister of the law-giver ; and these rites involved exclusion from her tent for a period of seven days (Levit. xiv. 8). By God's command exclusion from her tent was made exclusion from the camp.

Ver. 16.—**In the wilderness of Paran.** It is somewhat strange that this note of place should be used a second time without explanation (see ch. x. 12, 33). Probably it is intended to mark the fact that they were still within the limits of Paran, although on the very verge of their promised land. In the list of stations given in ch. xxxiii. it is said (ver. 18), "They departed from Hazeroth, and pitched in Rithmah." This is with some probability identified with the Wady Redemât, which opens from the mountain mass of the Azazimât into the singular plain of Kudes, or Kadesh, the scene of the decisive events which followed.

HOMILETICS.

Ch. xii.—*The contradiction of sinners.* We have in this chapter, spiritually, the contradiction of the Jews against their brother after the flesh ; morally, the sin and punishment of jealousy and envy in high places. Consider, therefore—

I. That as Moses is the type of him who was the mediator of a better covenant, who was meek and lowly in heart ; so Aaron and Miriam, when arrayed against Moses, represent the Levitical priesthood at the time of our Lord, and the Jewish synagogue, in their carnal pride and exclusiveness.

Nor is this typical character arbitrary or unreal, for we may clearly see in them the same tendencies which afterwards ripened into utter blasphemy and Deicide.

II. THAT THE OFFENCE OF MOSES IN THE EYES OF MIRIAM WAS HIS HAVING ALLIED HIMSELF WITH A GENTILE WIFE OF A DESPISED RACE. Even so the crime of our Lord, in the sight of a narrow and bigoted Judaism, was that he went about to present unto himself a Gentile Church, of the dregs of the nations, to be his spouse (cf. Cant. i. 4—6; Luke xv. 28; Acts xxii. 21, 22; Eph. v. 25—32).

III. THAT MIRIAM AND AARON JUSTIFIED THEIR OPPOSITION TO MOSES BY DWELLING UPON THEIR OWN SPIRITUAL AUTHORITY. Even so the synagogue and priesthood of the Jews magnified themselves against the Lord's Christ and their own Messiah, on the ground that they themselves were commissioned of God (cf. John vii. 48; viii. 33; ix. 28, 29).

IV. THAT THEY WERE ABLE TO BE OBLIVIOUS OF HIS TRUE GREATNESS, BECAUSE HE WAS THEIR BROTHER, AND THEIR YOUNGER BROTHER. Even so Christ was despised by the Jews because he was (as it were) one of themselves, and because they seemed to be familiar with his antecedents and training (cf. Matt. xiii. 55—57; Luke iv. 22, 28; John vi. 42).

V. THAT MOSES DISPLAYED A MEEKNESS WHICH SEEMED MORE THAN HUMAN. Even so our Lord endured the contradiction of sinners with a meekness which *was* more than human (cf. Isa. xlii. 19; liii. 7; Matt. xi. 29; Heb. xii. 3; Jas. v. 6; 1 Pet. ii. 23).

VI. THAT GOD INTERVENED TO ADVANCE HIS FAITHFUL SERVANT TO BE ABOVE ALL PROPHETS, AND TO BE MUCH NEARER TO HIMSELF THAN MIRIAM AND AARON. Even so did God vindicate his holy servant Jesus against all the blasphemy of the Jews, and give him a name which is above every name (cf. Acts ii. 22—24, 32; iv. 10, 27, 30; Rom. i. 4; Phil. ii. 9; Heb. iii. 1—3).

VII. THAT GOD INTERFERED TO PUNISH MIRIAM WITH LEPROSY FOR HER PRIDE AND RANCOUR. Even so the synagogue of the Jews became the synagogue of Satan, and they themselves are in exile, political and religious, until they shall cry for mercy to their Brother, the one Mediator (Rom. xi. 25; 1 Thess. ii. 15, 16; Rev. ii. 9; iii. 9).

Consider again—

I. THAT THE SECRET CAUSE OF ALL THIS DISTURBANCE WAS PROBABLY MIRIAM'S JEALOUSY OF HER BROTHER'S WIFE. It is likely she hoped to have exercised a growing influence over him herself. Even so history and experience testify that personal jealousies and envies are at the root of very many of the disorders in churches and congregations (cf. 2 Cor. xii. 20; 1 Pet. ii. 1 b.).

II. THAT A COINCIDENT CAUSE WAS A SECRET DISSATISFACTION ON THE PART OF AARON AT THE INFERIORITY OF HIS OWN POSITION AND INFLUENCE AS COMPARED WITH HIS BROTHER'S. Even so ambition and lust of power have betrayed many a highly-gifted and perhaps really religious soul into making claims, and taking up a position derogatory to Christ, and inconsistent with his sole pre-eminence (cf. Col. ii. 19).

III. THAT THEY EXCUSED THEIR SEDITION UNDER THE PLEA (WHICH WAS TRUE IN ITSELF) THAT THEY TOO ENJOYED DIVINE FAVOURS AND PRIVILEGES. How often do men speak and act as if the fact of being spiritual (Gal. vi. 1), or of being called to some ministry, authorised them to ignore all distinctions, refuse all control, and give the rein to their own enmities and evil feelings.

IV. THAT MOSES TURNED A DEAF EAR TO THEIR INVECTIVES, BUT ALL THE MORE GOD TURNED A LISTENING EAR. MOSES WOULD NOT TAKE UP HIS OWN QUARREL, THERE-FORE GOD TOOK IT UP FOR HIM, AND GREATLY MAGNIFIED HIM. Even so they that will avenge themselves must be content with the results of their own efforts, and they that will fight their own battles must take their chance of victory; but they that will not avenge themselves, God will vindicate, and that gloriously. The meek shall inherit the earth, because at the present they are dispossessed of the earth (cf. Ps. lxxvi. 9; Isa. xi. 4; Matt. v. 5; Rom. xii. 19; Heb. x. 30).

V. THAT THE PUNISHMENT OF MIRIAM WAS THE MOST TERRIBLE OF DISEASES—A LIVING DEATH. A jealous spirit, stirring up dissensions, reckless of the souls for which Christ died, incurs awful guilt, and is in danger of hell-fire (cf. Matt. xviii. 7—9; 1 Tim. vi. 4; James iv. 5).

VI. THAT AARON CRIED HUMBLY TO THE BROTHER WHOM HE HAD SPOKEN AGAINST,

AND THAT BROTHER INTERCEDED FOR THEM, AND THUS AARON'S FAITH SAVED HIMSELF AND HIS SISTER. Even so the Lord Jesus is ever ready to intercede for his enemies ; much more for those whom he loves as brethren, when they cry to him, even if they have treated him ill (cf. Luke xxiii. 34 ; Rom. v. 8, 9 ; Heb. ii. 11, 12, and of the synagogue itself (Rom. xi. 26, 28 ; 2 Cor. iii. 16).

VII. THAT MIRIAM'S FAULT, ALTHOUGH FORGIVEN, WAS NOT TO BE LIGHTLY FORGOTTEN BY HERSELF OR THE PEOPLE ; SHE WAS TO BE ASHAMED FOR SEVEN DAYS. Even so it is not according to the will of God, nor for the edification of the Church, nor for the good of the sinner, that a sin which is also a scandal should be straightway smoothed over and forgotten, because it is acknowledged and forgiven. There is a natural impatience to be rid of the disagreeable consequences of sin in this life, which is purely selfish on the part of every one concerned, and is dishonouring to God. Shame is a holy discipline for those who have done wrong, and they should not be hastily removed from its sanctifying influences (cf. Ezek. xxxix. 26 ; 2 Cor. ii. 6 ; vii. 9—11).

VIII. THAT MIRIAM, PROPHETESS AS SHE WAS, AND SISTER OF THE LAWGIVER, HAD TO PASS THROUGH THE ORDINARY CEREMONIAL FOR THE CLEANSING OF LEPERS—A CEREMONIAL DESIGNED TO SET FORTH THE ATONEMENT OF CHRIST. Even so there is one only way to restoration for all sinners, however highly placed or gifted, and that through the sprinkling of the precious blood (cf. Levit. xiv. 2 ; Acts iv. 12 ; Rom. iii. 22, 23).

IX. THAT GOD WOULD NOT GIVE THE SIGNAL FOR DEPARTURE UNTIL MIRIAM WAS RESTORED. Even so God, who will have all men to be saved, waiteth long and delayeth the entry of the Church into her rest, lest any who will come in should be shut out (cf. Luke xviii. 7 *b*. ; 2 Pet. iii. 9, 15 ; Rev. vii. 3).

Consider also—THAT THE OPPOSITION OF HIS OWN ONLY LED TO THE SUPREME AND SOLITARY GREATNESS OF MOSES BEING MADE FAR MORE CLEAR THAN EVER, AND BEING PLACED BEYOND CAVIL OR MISTAKE. Even so the persecution of our Lord by the Jews only led to his being declared the Son of God with power ; and still more, the efforts of heretics to deny or to explain away his Divine glory, have only led to that glory being much more clearly defined, and much more devoutly believed than ever.

HOMILIES BY VARIOUS AUTHORS.

Vers. 1—6.—*The sedition of Miriam and Aaron.* Here is another sedition in Israel. What is worse, the sedition does not, at this time, originate among the mixed multitude, the pariahs of the camp. The authors of it are the two leading personages in the congregation, after Moses himself. Nor are they strangers to him, such as might be deemed his natural rivals ; they are his own kindred, his sister and brother.

I. THE STORY OF THE SEDITION was, in brief, this :—Moses was not the only member of the family of Amram whom the Lord had endowed with eminent gifts. Aaron, his elder brother, was a leading man among the Israelites before Moses received his call at Horeb. Miriam also was a woman of high and various gifts, both natural and gracious. She was a prophetess—the earliest recorded example of a woman endowed with the gift of prophecy—and she excelled also in song (Exod. xv. 20 ; Micah vi. 4). The eminent gifts of these two were not passed over. They found such recognition and scope, that next to Moses, Aaron and Miriam were the two most honoured and influential individuals in the camp. But they were not content with this. Moses was set in yet higher place, and this roused their jealousy. They could not bear to see another, one brought up in the same family, a younger brother too, elevated above them. Miriam could not brook the thought of being subject to the younger brother whose infancy she had tended, and whose ark of bulrushes she had been set to watch when their mother committed him to the unfeeling bosom of the Nile. "Hath the Lord indeed spoken only by Moses? hath he not spoken also by us ? " Envy is a root tenacious of life in the human heart. When some one whom you have known familiarly as your junior or inferior is raised above you in office or wealth, in gifts or grace, watch and pray, else you will be very apt to fall into Miriam's sin. I say *Miriam's* sin, for it is plain that the sedition originated with her. Not only is her name put first, but in the Hebrew the beginning of

the narrative runs thus: " Then she spake, even Miriam and Aaron, against Moses."
When there is envy in the heart, it will soon find occasion to break out.   Very
characteristically, the occasion in this instance was some misunderstanding about
Moses' wife.   She was not of the daughters of Israel.   Miriam affected to despise her
as an unclean person, and persuaded Aaron to do the same.   It was an instance of a
thing not rare in history, a family quarrel, a fit of ill-feeling between two sisters-in-
law, stirring up envy and strife between persons in high office, and troubling the
community.   There was something very petty in the conduct of Miriam and Aaron,
but it was not, therefore, a trifling offence.   When they were giving vent to their
envy " the Lord heard."

II. THE PUNISHMENT OF THE SEDITION.   It does not appear that Moses made any
complaint; he was the meekest of men, humble and patient.   All the rather does the
Highest take the defence of his servant in hand.   "Suddenly," *i. e.* in sharp displeasure, Miriam and the two brothers were commanded to present themselves before
the Lord, at the entrance of the tabernacle.   Whereupon,—1. *The Lord pronounced
a warm eulogy upon Moses.*   Observe the terms in which he is described, for there
is much more in them than is perceived at first.   " My servant Moses,"—"servant in
all mine house,"—"faithful in all mine house."   (1) Moses was " the servant of the
Lord," "the man of God," in a sense more ample than any other individual who ever
lived excepting only Christ himself; and one can perceive a tone of singular love in
the way in which the title is here used: " my servant Moses."   (2) The commission
of Moses extended to every part of the Lord's house, and in every department of his
service he showed fidelity.   As a prophet, he was more extensively employed and
more faithful than Miriam; as a priest, he was more honourable and faithful than
Aaron; and he was, moreover, king in Jeshurun, the valiant and faithful leader and
commander of the people.   These were facts, and Moses might well have appealed
to them in vindication of himself against the complainers.   But he did better to leave
the matter in the Lord's own hand (Ps. xxxvii. 5, 6).   2. Besides vindicating Moses
and rebuking his detractors, *the Lord put a mark of his displeasure on Miriam.*   The
ringleader in the sedition, she bears the brunt of the punishment.   She has affected
to abhor her sister-in-law as unclean; she is herself smitten with leprosy, a disease
loathsome in itself, and which entailed ceremonial defilement in the highest degree.
This done, the cloud of the Divine presence rose as suddenly as it had come down.
Miriam and Aaron stood before the tabernacle utterly confounded, till Aaron was fain
to humble himself before his brother, saying:—We have done foolishly, we have
sinned; forgive us, and do not let the sad affair go further; have pity on poor Miriam
especially; see how pitiable a sight she is.   " Like the dead thing of which the flesh is
half consumed when it cometh out of its mother's womb."   Moses was not the man to
resist so touching an appeal.   Miriam was healed; but she was shut out from the camp
as an unclean person for the space of a week, as the law prescribed.   The lesson lies
on the surface.   Do not give harbour to envy because of the welfare or honour of
your neighbour, rather " rejoice with them that do rejoice."   It is not always easy to
rejoice when some one younger, or of humbler birth than ourselves, is exalted above
us.   Nor is the difficulty lessened when the person exalted is of our own kindred.
Nevertheless envy must be cast forth.   The author of all gifts and honours is God.
To envy the receivers is to rebel against him and provoke his displeasure.   And
God's ordinary method in punishing envious pride is to inflict some peculiarly ignominious stroke.   When Miriam swells with pride she is smitten with leprosy.—B.

Vers. 6—8.—*The singular honour of Moses.*   The best commentary on these verses
is supplied by the comparison instituted between Moses and our blessed Lord in the
Epistle to the Hebrews (iii. 1—6).   The Hebrews are reminded that of all the
servants whom the Lord raised up to minister in the ancient Church, there was not one
who approached Moses, in respect either to the greatness and variety of the services
performed by him, or the greatness of the honours bestowed upon him.   Moses was
set over all God's house, and in this eminent station he was conspicuously faithful.
In these respects Moses was the most perfect figure of Christ.   Christ's priesthood
was foreshadowed by Melchisedec, his royalty by David and Solomon, his prophetical
office by Samuel and the goodly company of prophets who followed him.   But in

Moses all the three offices were foreshadowed at once. Of these two men, Moses and Christ, and of no other since the world began, could it be affirmed that they were "faithful in all the Lord's house." No doubt there was disparity as well as a resemblance. Both were servants. But Moses was a servant in a house which belonged to another, in a household of which he was only a member, whereas Christ is such a servant as is also a son, and serves in a household of which he is the Maker and Heir. This is true. Nevertheless it is profitable to forget occasionally the disparity of the two great mediators, and to fix attention on the resemblance between them, the points in which the honour of Christ the Great Prophet was prefigured by the singular honour of Moses. Hence the interest and value of this text in Numbers.

I. As a foil to bring out the singular honour of Moses, the Lord puts alongside of it the honour bestowed on other prophets. "Consider the prophets that have been or yet are among you. How has my will been made known to them?" Two ways are specified. 1. "*In a vision.*" There was a memorable example of this in the case of Abraham (Gen. xv.). Visions continued to be the vehicles of revelation during the whole course of the Old Testament history. Isaiah (vi., xiii., &c.), Jeremiah (i., &c.), Ezekiel and Daniel (everywhere). Peter's vision at Joppa is a familiar example of the same kind under the New Testament. 2. "*In a dream.*" This was a lower way of revelation. The stories of Pharaoh and Nebuchadnezzar remind us that the dreams (I do not say the interpretations of them) were not seldom vouchsafed to men who were strangers to God. We shall see immediately that these ways of making himself known to men through the prophets, were inferior to the ways in which the Lord was wont to reveal himself through Moses. But let us not so fix our attention on the points of difference as to lose sight of or forget the bright and glorious feature which they have in common. "I, the Lord, do make myself known in a vision, and do speak in a dream." For reasons we can only guess at, the Lord was pleased to suffer the nations to walk in their own ways. But in Israel he revealed himself. At sundry times and in divers manners he was pleased to speak to the fathers by the prophets. The Scriptures of the Old Testament are oracular. In them we inherit the most precious part of the patrimony of the ancient Church. For this was the chief advantage which the Jews had above the Gentiles, that "unto them were committed the oracles of God." It is our own fault if, in reading the Old Testament, we fail to hear everywhere the voice of God.

II. Over against the honour vouchsafed to all the prophets, the Lord sets forth the singular honour of Moses. It is denoted by the loving title by which the Lord here and elsewhere names him: "My servant Moses." "Were ye not afraid to speak against my servant Moses?" (vers. 7, 8; cf. Josh. i. 2; also Deut. xxxiv. 5). The word here translated "servant" is a word of honourable import; and in the singular and emphatic way in which it is applied by the Lord to Moses, it is applied by him to no other till we come to Christ himself (see Isa. lii. 13; liii. 11, &c.). The singular honour of Moses is indicated, moreover, by this, that he was called and enabled to do faithful service "in all God's house." Aaron served as a priest, Miriam as a prophetess, Joshua as a commander, each being intrusted with one department of service; Moses was employed in all. More particularly, Moses was singularly honoured in regard to the manner of the Divine communications granted to him. With him the Lord spoke "mouth to mouth," even apparently, *i. e.* visibly, and not in dark speeches, and he beheld the similitude of the Lord. 1. When prophets received communications in dreams and visions they were very much in a passive state, simply beholding and hearing, often unable to make out the meaning of what they saw and heard. Moses, on the contrary, was admitted as it were into the audience chamber, and the Lord spoke to him as a man speaks with his friend (cf. ch. vii. 89). 2. A few of the prophets, specially honoured, had visions of the Divine glory (Isa. vi., &c.). But in this respect Moses was honoured above all the rest (Exod. xxxiii., xxxiv.). In these respects he prefigured the great Prophet, the only begotten Son, who is in the bosom of the Father, knows the Father even as the Father knows him, and has fully declared him. It has seemed to some learned men a thing unlikely, a thing incredible, that the vast body of doctrine and law and divinely-inspired history contained in the last four books of the Pentateuch should have been delivered to the Church within one age, and chiefly by one man. But the thing will not seem strange to one who believes and duly considers the singular honour of Moses as described in this text, especially if it is read in connection with the similar testimony borne elsewhere to Christ. Moses, and the Prophet like unto Moses, stand by themselves in the history of Divine revelation in this respect, that each served "in all God's house;" each was commissioned to introduce the Church into a new dispensation, to deliver to the Church a system of doctrine and institutions. In harmony with this is the patent fact that, as at the bringing in of the gospel dispensation the stream of Holy Scripture expands into the four gospels, even so at the bringing in of the ancient dispensation the stream of Holy Scripture originated in the Books of the Law.—B.

Vers. 1—16.—*God the vindicator of his calumniated servants.* The serpent's trail was found in Eden, and "a devil" among the apostles. No wonder then at this narrative of strife in a godly family. We notice—

I. AN UNJUST INSINUATION. Neither Moses' marriage nor his conduct to his relatives (ver. 3) had given fair cause of provocation. If his wife had done so, the charge Aaron and Miriam brought against the man who chose her was utterly irrelevant (ver. 2). "The wife of Moses is mentioned, his superiority is shot at" (Bp. Hall). No wonder if the most conscientious and cautious are calumniated since false charges were brought against Moses, Job, Jeremiah, and Jesus Christ. The assault was aggravated because—1. It came from his nearest kindred (Ps. lv. 12—14; Jer. xii. 6). Miriam apparently began it, perhaps through a misunderstanding between the sisters-in-law, and drew Aaron into the plot (1 Tim. ii. 14). 2. Because it was in the form of an unjust insinuation that Moses claimed exclusive prophetic gifts (ver. 2; cf. Exod. xv. 20; Micah vi. 4).

II. A TRIUMPHANT VINDICATION. Moses apparently had taken no notice of the charge; perhaps acting on Agricola's rule, "*omnia scire, non omnia exsequi*" (cf. Ps xxxviii. 12—15; John viii. 50). But the Lord heard it and interposed. 1. The three are summoned before an impartial judge, but with what different feelings. 2. The calumniated servant of God is distinguished by special honours (vers. 6—8). 3. The murmurers are rebuked, and a humiliating punishment is inflicted on the chief offender. The punishment of Aaron, the accomplice, only less severe (through sympathy with his sister) than that of Miriam (Job xii. 16). 4. They are indebted for deliverance to the intercession of the man they have wronged. Illustration, Jeroboam (1 Kings xiii. 6; Job's friends, Job xlii. 7—10). Thus God will vindicate all his calumniated servants (Ps. xxxvii. 5, 6). Protection (Ps. xxxi. 20); peace (Prov. xvi. 7); honour (Isa. lx. 14; Rev. iii. 9); and final reward (Ps. xci. 14—16; and Rom. viii. 31). Such are the privileges of the faithful but maligned servants of God.—P.

Ver. 2.—*The Lord listening.* "And the Lord heard it." Compare with this the words, "And the Lord hearkened and heard" (Mal. iii. 16). We are thus reminded that God listens not only to take note of our sinful words, but to record every loving, faithful word, spoken of him or for him. What a proof of the omnipotence of God! Wonderful that he should attend to every prayer addressed to him. Still more so that he should listen to every word spoken not to him but to others. But at the same moment he can hear the brooks murmuring over their rocky beds, the trees clapping their hands, the floods lifting up their voice, the birds singing in the branches, the young lions roaring for their prey, and every sound of joy or cry of pain, every hymn of praise or word of falsehood issuing from human lips (Ps. cxxxix. 3, 4, 6). Without speaking of direct prayers we may seek illustrations of the truth that God listens to everything we say to one another, records it, passes his judgment on it, and lays it up in store as one of the materials of his future verdict on our lives. We may regard this truth—

I. AS AN ENCOURAGEMENT. As illustrations—1. Turn to the scene described in Mal. iii. 16. A few godly persons are trying to keep alive the flame of piety in a godless age (vers. 13—15). Apply to social means of grace for mutual edification. 2. See that Christian man on a lonely walk, courteously conversing with a stranger, and seeking to recommend Christ to him. The stranger may go away to pray or to scoff, but that is not all. God hears and records the words as one of the good deeds done in the body (2 Cor. v. 10). 3. A godly mother in the midst of daily duties, not only praying but soliloquising, as in Ps. lxii. 1, 2, 5—7. Whether or not she may say Ps. v. 1, God does "give ear," and the words are "acceptable" (Ps. xix. 14). 4. Sufferers lamenting; *e. g.* Hagar (Gen. xvi. 11); Ishmael (Gen. xxi. 17); Israel in Egypt (Exod. ii. 24); mourners in Zion (Isa. xxx. 19).

II. As a warning. The truth has its shady as well as its sunny side. We may apply to—1. The swearer's prayer, not intended for the ear of God, but reaching it. 2. Calumnies and backbitings, *e. g.* against Moses (vers. 1, 2), or other servants of God (cf. Zeph. ii. 8); perhaps disliked because their lives are a rebuke to others (cf. Ps. xciv. 4, 7, 8, 9; John xv. 18). 3. Impure words. The youth would be ashamed all day if his mother accidentally heard. But God heard. 4. Solitary words of repining or rebellion. Spoken in haste, they are soon regretted, and you say, "Well, at any rate nobody heard them." Stop and think again (ch. xi. 1; Ps. cxxxix. 7). The ear of God, like his eye, is in every place." Therefore Matt. xii. 37. This truth leads us by a single step to the heart of the gospel (Acts xx. 21). And if we say Ps. xvii. 3, God will hear that too, and give us strength to serve him with "righteous lips" and "joyful lips" (Ps. xix. 14).—P.

Vers. 1, 2.—*A hideous manifestation of pride.* Amid much obscurity we discern that family jealousies were the occasion of this outbreak. Some occasion certainly would have arisen, so we need not trouble ourselves whether this Cushite wife was Zipporah or a wife lately taken. There is room for much conjecture, and real need for none. Out of the heart cometh pride. Pride was in Miriam's heart; it must come out sooner or later. We specify Miriam, as she was evidently the principal transgressor. Aaron simply and easily followed where she led. Let us fix our attention on the hideous revelation of her pride.

I. It was A PRIDE THAT OVERWHELMED NATURAL AFFECTION. To whom in all Israel might Moses have more confidently looked for sympathy than his own sister? Especially if it were she who stood afar off, and watched the ark of bulrushes (Exod. ii. 4). It was an unworthy thing of a sister to hinder one on whom God had laid such great and anxious duties. But when self-esteem is once hurt, the wound soon inflames beyond all control; and even those on whom we are most dependent, and to whom we owe the most, are made to feel the grievous irritation of our spirits.

II. It was A PRIDE THAT MADE MIRIAM FORGET THE OBLIGATIONS OF HER OWN HONOURABLE OFFICE. She was a prophetess, even as Moses was a prophet. She does, indeed, in one sense recollect her office. "Hath the Lord not spoken also by us?" True; and this was the very reason why she should have been specially careful of what she said, even when the Lord was not speaking by her. *A prophet's tongue should be doubly guarded at all times.* Those who speak for God ought never to say anything out of their own thoughts incongruous with the Divine message. If Miriam and Aaron had ever been obliged to deal with Moses as once Paul had to deal with Peter, and withstand him to the face because he was to be blamed, then the prophet element in them would have been more glorious than ever. But here Miriam stoops from her high rank to give effect to a mean personal grudge.

III. It was PRIDE THAT PUT ON A PRETENCE OF BEING BADLY TREATED. It is very easy for the proud to persuade themselves that they have been badly treated. They are so much in their own thoughts that it becomes easy for them to believe that they are much in the thoughts of other people; and from this they can soon advance to the suspicion that there may be elaborate designs against them. Men will go step by step to great villainies, justifying themselves all the way. The scribes who sat in Moses' seat no doubt made their conspiracy against Jesus look very laudable to their own eyes. Miriam does not speak here with the arrogance of a straightforward, brutal, "I wish it, and it must be so." The iniquity of her heart sought to veil itself in a plausible plea for justice.

IV. It was the WORST OF ALL PRIDE, SPIRITUAL PRIDE. Pride of birth, of beauty, of wealth, of learning, all these are bad, often ridiculous; but spiritual pride is such a contradiction, such an amazing example of blindness, that we may well give it a pre-eminence among the evil fruits of the corrupt heart. It is the chief of all pride, most dangerous to the subject of it, and most insulting to God. Contrast Miriam with Mary, the mother of Jesus: the one all chafed and swelling within, who thinks the people should attend her as much as her brother; the other having the ornament of a meek and quiet spirit, humbly submissive to Gabriel's word, nothing doubting, yet prostrate in amazement that she should have been chosen as the mother of Messiah, sending forth her *Magnificat* like a lark soaring from its humble bed, singing its song, and straightway returning to the earth again. Or contrast her with Paul, saying, because he truly felt, that he was less than the least of all saints, an earthen vessel, the chief of sinners. Amid our greatest privileges we are still in the greatest danger if without a sense, habitually cherished, of our natural unworthiness. The more God sees fit to make of us, the more we should wonder that he is able to make so much out of so little.—·Y.

Ver. 3.—*A distinguished example of meekness.* This quality of meekness, for which Moses is here so much praised, is not without its signs earlier in the narrative of his connection with the Israelites; and as we look back in the light of this express declaration, the quality is very easily seen. Such a declaration was evidently needed here, and we may trace its insertion by some hand soon after as much to the control of inspiration as we trace the original narrative. The meekness of Moses is not only a foil to the pride of Miriam, but evidently had something to do with exciting her pride. She would not have gone so far with a different sort of man. She knew intuitively how far she could go with him, and that it was a very long way indeed. Therefore, to bring out all the significance of the occasion, it was needful to make special mention of the meekness of Moses. Notice *the emphatic way in which it is set forth.* "Meek above all the men which were upon the face of the earth." We talk of Moses as the meekest of men and Solomon as the wisest of men to indicate that the one was very meek indeed and the other very wise. Let us look then in the life and character of Moses to see how that eminent virtue was shown which ought also to be in all of us.

I. The meekness included A CONSCIOUSNESS OF NATURAL UNFITNESS FOR THE WORK TO WHICH GOD HAD CALLED HIM. A consciousness we may well believe to have been profound, abiding, and oftentimes oppressive. God meant it to be so. We know not what Moses was physically. He was a goodly child (Exod. ii. 2), but a mother's partiality may have had something to do with this judgment. In after years that may have been true of Moses which Paul pathetically observes was the opinion of some concerning himself—that in bodily presence he was weak and in speech contemptible. It may have been a wonder to many, as well as to himself, that God had chosen *him*. In that memorable interview with God at Horeb (Exod. iii.), the first word of Moses is, "Here am I;" but the second, "Who am I, ... that I should bring forth the children of Israel out of Egypt?" There was no jumping at eminence, no vainglorious grasping at the chance of fame. He had to be constrained along the path of God's appointment, not because of a disobedient spirit, but because of a low estimate of himself. He abounded in patriotism and sympathy for his oppressed brethren, but the work of deliverance seemed one for stronger hands than his. Perhaps there is nothing in the natural man more precious in the sight of God for the possibilities that come out of it than this consciousness of weakness. The work to be done is so great, and the man who is called to do it, even when he has stretched himself to his fullest extent, looks so small.

II. THIS SENSE OF WEAKNESS WOULD APPEAR IN ALL HIS INTERCOURSE WITH MEN. He was exposed continually to the risk of insult and reproach. The people vented their spleen and carnal irritation upon him, yet he did not make their words a matter of personal insult, as some leaders would undoubtedly have done. He felt only too keenly his own insufficiency, and how far short he fell of the high requirements of God. Although the particular hard things which men said about him might not be just, yet he felt that many hard things might justly be said, and so there was no inclination to fume and fret and stand upon his dignity when fault-finders began to speak. Even when Miriam joins the traducing herd he seems to bear it in silence. The dying Cæsar said, "*Et tu, Brute;*" but Moses, in this hour of his loneliness, when even his kindred forsake him, does not say, "And thou, Miriam." Each succeeding revelation of God made him humbler in his own spirit, and seemed to increase the distance between his created and corrupted life and the glory of the great I AM. If God were so gracious, forgiving, and bountiful to him (ch. xi.), why should not he be long-suffering and meekly tolerant with Miriam? (Matt. xviii. 23—35). We shall not blow ourselves out and strut before men if we only constantly recollect how defiled we are in the sight of God.

III. This meekness is especially to be noticed because of ITS CONNECTION WITH CERTAIN OTHER QUALITIES WHICH GOD LOVES. The more conscious Moses became of his natural weakness, the more God esteemed him. If meekness springs from the sense of weakness, yet it grows and becomes useful in association with the strength of God. Though Moses was meek, he was not a pliable man. Though meek, he none the less went right onward in the way of God's appointment. This meekness of his went along with *obedience to God*. He quietly listened to all his enemies said in the way of invective and slander, and still went on his way, with eye and ear and heart open to the will of God. He was like a tree, which, though it may bend and yield a little to the howling blast, yet keeps its hold firm on the soil. There was also a *never-failing sense of right*. Moses was one of those men—would that there were more of them in the world!—who had a deep feeling of sympathy with the weak and the oppressed. Meek as he was by nature, he slew the Egyptian who smote his Hebrew brother. There was also *courage* along with the meekness—courage of the highest sort, moral courage, daring to be laughed at, and to stand alone. These are the brave men who can do this, planting alone, if need be, the standard of some great cause; meek and humble, but dauntless in their meekness, confiding in him whose righteousness is like the great mountains. Look at the bravery of meek women for Christ. Then there was *persistency*. Is not this great part of the secret of the fulfilling of that beatitude, " Blessed are the meek, for they shall inherit the earth ? " The violent, the unjust, the greedy, may grasp the earth for a time, but it is the meek, the gentle, never irritating, yet never withdrawing, persistent, generation after generation, in the practice and application of spiritual truth, it is they who in the fulness of time will truly inherit the earth.—Y.

Vers. 4—15.—*The humbling of the proud and the exaltation of the meek. The humbling was evidently by the action of God himself.* The Lord heard Miriam and Aaron in the words of their pride, and even though Moses might bear these words in the silent composure of his magnanimity and meekness, it nevertheless became God to justify his servant, as God alone could effectually and signally justify. God notes all unjust and slanderous doings with respect to his people. He hears, even though the reviled ones themselves be ignorant. God then proceeds by one course of action to produce a double result—to humble Miriam and Aaron, Miriam in particular, and to exalt Moses. In what he did, notice that with all his anger and severity he yet *mingled much consideration for the transgressors.* We need not suppose that their words had been spoken to any considerable audience. More likely they were confined to the limits of the domestic circle. And so the Lord spake suddenly to the three persons concerned. Probably none but themselves knew why they were summoned. There was no reason for exposing a family quarrel to the gossip of the whole camp. The *sin* of Miriam need not be published abroad, though it was necessary, in order to teach her a lesson, that it should be condignly punished. So they were called to the door of the tabernacle, and there God addressed them from the pillar of cloud, with all its solemn associations. This word *suddenly* also suggests that when God does not visit *immediately* the iniquity of the transgressor upon him, it is from considerations of what we may call Divine expediency. He can come at once or later, but, at whatever time, he certainly will come. Consider now—

I. THE HUMBLING OF THE PROUD. This was done in two ways. 1. *By the plain distinction which God made between them and Moses.* It was perfectly true that, as they claimed, God had spoken by them, but he calls attention to the fact that it was his custom to speak to prophets by vision and by dream. There was no mouth to mouth conversation, no beholding of the similitude of the Lord. God can use all sorts of agencies for his communications to men. It needs not even a Miriam; he can speak warning from the mouth of an ass. But Moses was more than a prophet; prophet was only the part of which steward and general, visible representative of

God, was the whole. What a humbling hour for this proud woman to find that Jehovah himself had taken up the cause of her despised brother! It is probable that Moses himself had mentioned little of the details of his experiences of God; they were not things to talk much about; perhaps he could not have found the fit audience, even though few. Upon Miriam it would come like a thunderbolt to know how God esteemed the man whom she had allowed herself to scorn. So God will ever abase the proud by glorifying his own pious children whom they despise. Satan despises Job, says he is a mere lip worshipper, a man whose professions will not bear trial; he gets him down into the dust of bereavement, poverty, and disease; but in the end he has to see him a holier man, a more trustful and prosperous one than before. Miriam meant the downfall of Moses; she only helped to establish him more firmly on the rock. 2. *By the personal visitation on Miriam.* She became a leper. As her pride was hideous in the manifestation of it, so her punishment was hideous—a leprosy, loathsome and frightful beyond the common. We might expect this. A malignant outbreak in her bodily life corresponded with the malignity of the defilement in her spirit. As to Aaron, we may presume that his sacred office, and to some extent the fact that he was a tool, secured him from leprosy, but the visitation on his sister was punishment in itself. He felt the wind of the blow which struck her down. Proud souls, take warning by Miriam; you will at last become abhorrent to yourselves. Remember Herod (Acts xii. 21—23).

II. THE EXALTATION OF THE MEEK. This is a more inward and spiritual thing, and therefore not conspicuous in the same way as the humbling. It is something to be appreciated by spiritual discernment rather than natural. Besides, the full exaltation of the meek is not yet come. The resurrection and ascension of the Lord Jesus himself were arranged very quietly. But we cannot help noticing that from this sharp and trying scene Moses emerges with his character shining more beautifully than ever. He does nothing to forfeit the reputation with which he was credited, and everything to increase it. He acted like a man who had beheld the similitude of the Lord. Notice particularly the way in which he joins in with Aaron, interceding for his afflicted sister. This is the true exaltation: to be better and better in oneself, shining more because there is more light within to cast its mild radiance, as God would have it cast, alike upon the evil and the good, the just and the unjust (Ps. xxv. 9; lix. 12; Prov. xiii. 10; xvi. 18; xxix. 23; Dan. iv. 37; Matt. xxiii. 12; Gal. vi. 1—5; 2 Tim. ii. 24—26; 1 Pet. iii. 4; v. 6).—Y.

EXPOSITION.

CHAPTERS XIII., XIV.

THE REBELLION AT KADESH (chs. xiii., xiv.). Ver. 2.—**Send thou men, that they may search the land.** If this account of the mission of the spies be compared with that given in Deut. i. 20—25, it may be seen in a striking instance how entirely different a colour may be put upon the same circumstances by two inspired narratives. No one indeed will affirm that the two records are contradictory, or even inconsistent, and yet they leave an entirely different impression upon the mind; and no doubt were intended to. It is important to note that the Divine inspiration did not in the least prevent two sacred authors (cf. 2 Sam. xxiv. 1 with 1 Chron. xxi. 1), or even the same author at different times, from placing on record very distinct and even strongly contrasted aspects of the same facts, according to the point of view from which he was led to regard them. In Deut. i. Moses reminds the people that on

their arrival at Kadesh he had bidden them go up and take possession; that *they* had then proposed to send men before them to examine the land; that the proposal had pleased him so well that he had adopted it and acted upon it. It is unquestionably strange that facts so material should have been omitted in the historical Book of Numbers. It is, however, to be considered—1. That there is no contradiction between the two accounts. We may be certain from many a recorded example that Moses would not have acted on the popular suggestion without referring the matter to the Lord, and that it would be the Divine command (when given) which would really weigh with him. 2. That the recital in Deuteronomy is distinctly *ad populum*, and that therefore their part in the whole transaction is as strongly emphasised as is consistent with the truth of the facts. 3. That the narrative of Numbers is fragmentary, and does not profess to give a full account of matters, especially in such particulars as do not directly concern the Divine government and guidance of Israel. It is not, therefore, a serious difficulty that the record only begins here at the point when God adopted as his own what had been the demand of the people. If we ask why he so adopted it, the probable answer is that he knew what secret disaffection prompted it, and to what open rebellion it would lead. It was better that such disaffection should be allowed to ripen into rebellion before they entered their promised land. Miserable as the desert wandering might be, it was yet a discipline which prepared the nation for better things; whereas the invasion of Canaan without strong faith, courage, and self-restraint (such as they showed under Joshua) could but have ended in national disaster and destruction. **Of every tribe of their fathers shall ye send a man.** This was not part of the original proposition (Deut. i. 22), but was agreeable to the general practice in matters of national concern, and was no doubt commanded in order that the whole people might share in the interest and responsibility of this survey. **Every one a ruler among them.** This does not mean that they were to be the tribe princes (as the names show), for they would not be suitable in respect of age, nor could they be spared for this service. They were "heads of the children of Israel" (ver. 3), *i. e.* men of position and repute, but also no doubt comparatively young and active, as befitted a toilsome and hazardous excursion.

Ver. 4.—**These were their names.** None of these names occur elsewhere, except those of Caleb and Joshua. The order of the tribes is the same as in ch. i., except that Zebulun is separated from the other sons of Leah, and placed after Benjamin, while the two sons of Joseph are separated from one another. In ver. 11 "the tribe of Joseph" is explained to be "the tribe of Manasseh;" elsewhere it is either common to both, or confined to Ephraim (see Rev. vii. 8, and cf. Ezek. xxxvii. 16). No spy was sent for the tribe of Levi, because it was now understood to have no territorial claims upon the land of promise, and to stand altogether by itself in relation to the national hopes and duties.

Ver. 6.—**Caleb the son of Jephunneh.** In ch. xxxii. 12 he is called "the Kenezite" (הַקְּנִזִּי), which appears in Gen. xv. 19 as the name of one of the ancient races inhabiting the promised land. It is possible that Jephunneh may have been connected by descent or otherwise with this race; it is more likely that the similarity of name was accidental. The younger son of Jephunneh, the father of Othniel, was a Kenaz (קְנַז), and so was Caleb's grandson (see on Josh. xv. 17; 1 Chron. iv. 13, 15). Kenaz was also an Edomitish name.

Ver. 16.—**Moses called Oshea the son of Nun Jehoshua.** The change was from הוֹשֵׁעַ (Hoshea, help or salvation) to יְהוֹשֻׁעַ (Jehoshua —the same name with the first syllable of the sacred name prefixed, and one of the vowel points modified). It was afterwards contracted into יֵשׁוּעַ (Jeshua; cf. Neh. viii. 17), and has come to us in its current form through the Vulgate. The Septuagint has here ἐπωνόμασε . . τὸν Αὐσὴ . . Ἰησοῦν, and so the name appears in the New Testament. It is an obvious difficulty that Joshua has already been called by his new name at Exod. xvii. 9, and in every other place where he has been mentioned. In fact he is only once elsewhere called Hoshea, and that in a place (Deut. xxxii. 44) where we should certainly not have expected it. There are two ways of explaining the difficulty, such as it is. We may suppose that the change of name was really made at this time, as the narrative seems (on the face of it) to assert; and then the previous mentions of Joshua by his subsequent and more familiar name will be cases of that anticipation which is so common in Scripture (cf., *e. g.*, Matt. ix. 9 with Mark ii. 14). Or we may suppose, what is perhaps more in harmony with the course of Joshua's life, that the change had been already made at the time of the victory over Amalek. In that case the Vav consec. in וַיִּקְרָא (and . . called) must be referred to the order of thought, not of time, and a sufficient reason must be shown for the interpolation of the statement in this particular place. Such a reason may fairly be found in the probable fact that the names of the spies were copied out of the tribal registers, and that Joshua still appeared under his original name in those registers. As to the significance of the change, it is not easy to estimate it aright. On the one hand, the sacred syllable entered into so many of the Jewish names that it could not have seemed a very marked change; on the other hand, the fact that our Saviour received the same name because he was our Saviour throws a halo of glory about it which we cannot ignore. In the Divine providence Hoshea became Joshua because he was destined to be the temporal saviour of his people, and to lead them into their promised rest.

Ver. 17.—**Get you up this way southward.** Rather, "get you up there (זֶה) in the Negeb." The Negeb, meaning literally "the dryness," was the south-western district of Canaan, which bordered upon the desert, and partook more or less of its character. Except where springs existed, and irrigation could be carried out, it was unfit for settled habitation. See Josh. xv. 19; Judges i. 15, where the same word is used. **Go up into the mountain.** From the

Negeb they were to make their way into the mountain or hill country which formed the back-bone of Southern Palestine, from the Wady Murreh on the south to the plain of Esdraelon on the north. In after ages it formed the permanent centre of the Jewish race and Jewish power. Cf. Judges i. 9 where the three natural divisions of Southern Palestine are mentioned together : הָהָר (ἡ ὀρεινή), the mountain ; הַנֶּגֶב (ὁ Νότος), the steppe ; הַשְּׁפֵלָה (ἡ πεδινή), the maritime plain.

Ver. 18.—**Whether they be strong or weak, few or many.** It would appear that Moses was guilty of some indiscretion at least in giving these directions. Whether the people were strong or weak, many or few, should have been nothing to the Israelites. It was God that gave them the land ; they had only to take possession boldly.

Ver. 20.—**And what the land is.** It is impossible to suppose that Moses needed himself to be informed on such particulars as are here mentioned. The intercourse between Egypt and Palestine was comparatively easy and frequent (see on Gen. l. 7), and no educated Hebrew could have failed to make himself acquainted with the main features of his fathers' home. We may see in these instructions a confirmation of the statement in Deut. i., that it was at the desire of the people, and for *their* satisfaction, that the spies were sent. **The time of the first-ripe grapes.** The end of July : the regular vintage is a month or more later.

Ver. 21. — **From the wilderness of Zin.** The extreme southern boundary of the promised land (ch. xxxiv. 3, 4 ; Josh. xv. i. 3). There seems to be but one marked natural feature which could have been chosen for that purpose—the broad sandy depression called the Wady Murreh, which divides the mountain mass of the Azazimeh from the Rakhmah plateau, the southern extremity of the highlands of Judah. The plain of Kudes communicates with it at its upper or western end, and may be counted a part of it. **Unto Rehob, as men come to Hamath.** Septuagint, ἕως Ροὸβ εἰσπορευομένων Αἱμάθ. Hamath, now Hamah, was in Greek times Epiphaneia, on the Orontes, outside the limits of Jewish rule. The southern entrance to it lay between the ranges of Libanus and Antilibanus (see note on ch. xxxiv. 8). The Rehob here mentioned is not likely to have been either of the Rehobs in the territory of Asher (Josh. xix. 28—30), but the Beth-rehob further to the east, and near to where Dan-Laish was afterwards built (Judges xviii. 28). It lies on the route to Hamath, and was at one time a place of some importance in the possession of the Syrians (2 Sam. x. 6).

Ver. 22.—**And came unto Hebron.** This and the following details of their journey are appended to the general statement of ver. 21 in that inartificial style of narrative still common in the East. On the name Hebron, and the perplexities which it causes, see on Gen. xiii. 18 ; xxiii. 2. **Where Ahiman, Sheshai, and Talmai, the children of Anak, were.** יְלִידֵי הָעֲנָק, "Anak's progeny." Septuagint, γενεαὶ Ἐνάχ (as in ver. 28 and Josh. xv. 14 b.), means simply "descendants of Anak." The Beni-Anak (Beni-Anakim in Deut. i. 28 ; Anakim in Deut. ii. 10, &c.) were a tribe whose remote and perhaps legendary ancestor was Anak son of Arba (see on Josh. xiv. 15). These three chiefs of the Beni-Anak are said to have been expelled from Hebron fifty years later by Caleb (Josh. xv. 14 ; Judges i. 20). The gigantic size which the Anakim shared with the Emim and Rephaim, other remnants of the aboriginal inhabitants, may have been accompanied by remarkable longevity ; or they may have been quite young at the time of this visit ; or, finally, they may not have been individuals at all, but families or clans. **Now Hebron was built seven years before Zoan in Egypt.** Hebron was in existence at the time of Abraham. Zoan was Tanis, near the mouth of the eastern branch of the Nile (see on Ps. lxxviii. 12, 43). If it be true that the Pharaoh of the exodus had his royal residence at Zoan, Moses may have had access to the archives of the city, or he may have learnt the date of its foundation from the priests who gave him his Egyptian education. That there was any real connection between the two places is extremely problematical, nor is it possible to give any reason for the abrupt insertion here of a fragment of history so minute and in itself so unimportant. There is, however, no one but Moses to whom the statement can with any sort of likelihood be traced ; a later writer could have had no authority for making the statement, and no possible reason for inventing it.

Ver. 23.—**The brook of Eshcol.** Rather, "the valley of Eshcol," for it is not a land of brooks. Probably between Hebron and Jerusalem, where the grapes are still exceptionally fine, and the clusters of great size. **They bare it between two on a staff.** Not on account of its weight, but simply in order not to spoil it. Common sense dictates the like precaution still in like cases.

Ver. 24.—**The place was called the brook Eshcol, because of the cluster.** It is very probable that it was already known as the valley of Eshcol, from the friend of Abraham, who bore that name and lived in that neighbourhood (Gen. xiv. 13, 24). If so it is an admirable instance of the loose way in which etymologies are treated in the Old

Testament : what the place really received was not a new name, but a new signification to the old name ; but this appeared all one in the eyes of the sacred writer.

Ver. 25.—**They returned . . after forty days.** This is a period of time which constantly recurs in the sacred books (see on Exod. xxiv. 18). It points to the fact that their work was completely done, and the land thoroughly explored.

Ver. 26.—**To Kadesh** (see note at the end of ch. xiv.).

Ver. 27.—**It floweth with milk and honey.** According to the promise of God in his first message of deliverance to the people (see on Exod. iii. 8).

Ver. 28.—**Nevertheless.** כִּי אֶפֶס. "Only that." Septuagint, ἀλλ' ἢ ὅτι. **The people be strong.** Moses himself had directed their attention to this point, and now they dwell on it to the exclusion of everything else.

Ver. 29.—**The Amalekites.** These descendants of Esau (see on Gen. xxxvi. 12) formed wild roving bands, which (like the Bedouins of the present day) infested rather than inhabited the whole country between Judæa and Egypt, including the Negeb. They are not numbered among the inhabitants of Canaan proper. **The Canaanites dwell by the sea, and by the coast of Jordan.** It is not easy to say in what sense the word "Canaanites" is used here. At one time it is the name of one tribe amongst many, all descended from Canaan, the son of Ham, which dwelt in the land of promise ; at another time it is apparently synonymous with "Amorites," or rather includes both them and the allied tribes (cf. e. g. Judges i. 9). It is possible, though far from certain, that "Canaanites" in this place may mean "Phœnicians," since Sidon was the first-born of Canaan (Gen. x. 15), and the northern portion of the maritime plain was certainly in their possession, and probably the upper part of the Ghor, or coast of Jordan. It would appear that the Philistines had not at this time made themselves masters of the plain, although they dwelt in some parts of it (see on Exod. xiii. 17).

Ver. 30.　**Caleb stilled the people.** That Caleb alone is named here, whereas Joshua is elsewhere joined with him in the matter (as in ch. xiv. 6, 30), has been considered strange ; but it is not difficult to supply a probable explanation. Joshua was the special companion and minister of Moses, his *alter ego* in those things wherein he was employed : for that reason he may very well have given place to Caleb as a more impartial witness, and one more likely to be listened to in the present temper of the people ; for it is evident from Deut. i. that that temper had already declared itself for evil (see on ch. xiv. 24).

Ver. 31.—**For they are stronger than we.** In point of numbers the enormous superiority of the Israelites over any combination likely to oppose them must have been evident to the most cowardly. But the existence of numerous walled and fortified towns was (apart from Divine aid) an almost insuperable obstacle to a people wholly ignorant of artillery or of siege operations ; and the presence of giants was exceedingly terrifying in an age when battles were a series of personal encounters (cf. 1 Sam. xvii. 11, 24).

Ver. 32.—**A land that eateth up the inhabitants thereof.** This cannot mean that the people died of starvation, pestilence, or other natural causes, which would have been contrary to facts and to their own report. It must mean that the population was continually changing through internecine wars, and the incursions of fresh tribes from the surrounding wastes. The history of Palestine from first to last testifies to the constant presence of this d anger. The remarkable variation in the lists of tribes inhabiting Canaan may be thus accounted for. All the people . . are men of great stature, מִדּוֹת אַנְשֵׁי "men of measures." Septuagint, ἄνδρες ὑπερμήκεις. The "all" is an exaggeration very natural to men who had to justify the counsels of cowardice.

Ver. 33.—**The giants, the sons of Anak, which come of the giants,** עֲנָק מִן־הַנְּפִלִים אֶת־הַנְּפִילִים בְּנֵי. The Nephilim, Beni-Anak, of the Nephilim. The Septuagint has only τοὺς γίγαντας. The Nephilim are, without doubt, the primæval tyrants mentioned under that name in Gen. vi. 4. The renown of these sons of violence had come down from those dim ages, and the exaggerated fears of the spies saw them revived in the gigantic forms of the Beni-Anak. There is no certainty that the Nephilim had been giants, and no likelihood whatever that the Beni-Anak had any real connection with them. **As grasshoppers.** We have no means of judging of the actual size of these men, unless the height assigned to Goliath (six cubits and a span) be allowed to them. Probably men of this stature were quite exceptional even among the Anakim. The report of the spies was thoroughly false in effect, although founded on isolated facts.

Ch. xiv. 1.—**And the people wept that night.** As the spies repeated their dismal tidings, each to the leading men of his own tribe, and as the report was spread swiftly through the tents (cf. Deut. i. 27) with ever-increasing exaggerations, the lamentation became universal.

Ver. 2.—**Murmured against Moses and against Aaron** ; whom they probably suspected and accused of seeking their own personal ends. Here we may see the true reason why Joshua had not been put forward to advocate an immediate advance. The Septuagint has διεγόγγυζον (cf. 1 Cor. x. 10). **Would God we had died.** לּוּ־מָתְנוּ. Septuagint, ὄφελον ἀπεϑάνομεν. The A. V. is unnecessarily strong.

Ver. 3.—**Wherefore hath the Lord brought us.** Rather, "wherefore doth the Lord bring us." מֵבִיא. Septuagint, εἰσάγει. They were not actually in the land yet, but only on the threshold.

Ver. 4.—**Let us make a captain, and let us return into Egypt.** Although this was only proposed in the wildness of their distress, yet it was a height of rebellion to which they had never risen before. They had lamented that they had not died in Egypt, and they had wished themselves back in Egypt, but they had never proposed to take any overt steps towards returning thither. Nothing less than an entire and deliberate revolt was involved in the wish to elect a captain for themselves, for the angel of the covenant was the Captain of the Lord's host (Josh. v. 14, 15). The proposal to depose him, and to choose another in his place, marked the extremity of the despair, the unbelief, and the ingratitude of the people.

Ver. 5.—**Moses and Aaron fell on their faces.** After making ineffectual efforts to reason with the people, or rather with their leaders (Deut. i. 29—31). It was not, however, in this case an attitude of intercession, but the instinctive action of those who await in silent horror a catastrophe which they see to be inevitable; it testified to all who saw it that they were overwhelmed with shame and sorrow in view of the awful sin of the people, and of the terrible punishment which must follow.

Ver. 6.—**And Joshua.** In a last hopeless effort to bring the people to a better mind, or at least to deliver their own souls, there was no reason why Joshua should hold back any more. **Rent their clothes.** Another token of grief and horror practised from patriarchal times (cf. Gen. xxxvii. 29, 34; Job i. 20).

Ver. 8.—**If the Lord delight in us.** An expression used by Moses himself (Deut. x. 15). It did indeed place the whole matter in the only right light; all the doubt that could possibly exist was the doubt implied in that "if."

Ver. 9.—**They are bread for us.** "They are our food," i. e. we shall easily devour them (cf. ch. xxiv. 8; Ps. xiv. 4). Perhaps it has the further significance that their enemies would be an absolute advantage to them, because they would (however unwillingly) supply them with the necessaries of life. So apparently the Septuagint: μὴ φοβηϑῆτε τὸν λαὸν τῆς γῆς, ὅτι κατάβρωμα ὑμῖν ἐστιν. **Their defence is departed from them.** Literally, "their shadow," that which shielded them for a while from the fierce blast of Divine wrath. This "shadow" was not positively the Divine protection (as in Ps. xci. 1, and elsewhere), but negatively that Providence which left them a space wherein to walk in their own ways (cf. τὸ κατέχον of 2 Thess. ii. 6).

Ver. 10.—**Bade stone them with stones.** Angry people cannot endure the counsels of calm reason, and perhaps the hostility which they felt against Moses they were very ready to vent upon his "minister." **The glory of the Lord appeared . . before all the children of Israel.** At the moment when they were about to proceed to violence, the Divine glory filled the tabernacle, and flashed forth with a brilliancy which compelled their awe-struck attention.

Ver. 11.—**And the Lord said unto Moses,** who had, as we may suppose, risen and drawn nigh when the glory of the Lord appeared.

Ver. 12.—**And will make of thee a greater nation and mightier than they.** By electing Moses, in the place of Jacob, to be the founder and ancestor of the chosen race, God would still have made good his promises to Abraham, and would only have vindicated for himself the same freedom of choice which he had used in the case of Ishmael and of Esau. We cannot, however, regard this offer as embodying a deliberate intention, for we know that God did not really mean to cast off Israel; nor can we regard it as expressing the anger of the moment, for it is not of God to be hasty. We must understand it distinctly as intended to try the loyalty and charity of Moses, and to give him an opportunity of rising to the loftiest height of magnanimity, unselfishness, and courage. Moses would unquestionably have been less noble than he was if he had listened to the offer; it is therefore certain that the offer was only made in order that it might be refused (cf. Exod. xxxii. 10).

Ver. 13.—**And Moses said unto the Lord.** The words which follow are so confused, and the construction so dislocated, that they afford the strongest evidence that we have here the *ipsissima verba* of the mediator, disordered as they were in the moment of utterance by passionate earnestness and an agonising fear. Had Moses been ever so eloquent, a facility of speech at such a moment would have been alike unnatural and unlovely. What we can see in the words is this: that Moses had no thought for himself, and that it never occurred to him to entertain the tempting offer made to him by God; that he knew God too well, and (if we may say so) cared for God too much, to let him so compromise his honour among the nations, and so thwart his own purposes, without making one effort (however audacious) to turn his wrath aside. We can see that it is (as in Exod. xxxii. 11, 12, only much more boldly and abruptly) the thought of what the heathen would say which he wishes to thrust upon the Almighty ; but we cannot be sure of the right translation of the words. The most literal rendering would seem to be, " Both the Egyptians have heard (וְשָׁמְעוּ) that thou broughtest out this people from among them with thy might, and they have told it (וְאָמְרוּ) to the inhabitants of this land ; they have heard (שָׁמְעוּ, repeated) that thou, Lord, art amongst this people," &c. The Septuagint, however, translates the first verb by a future (καὶ ἀκούσεται Αἴγυπτος), and, as this gives a much clearer sense, it is followed by the Targum Palestine and most of the versions.

Ver. 16. —**Because the Lord was not able to bring this people into the land.** Moral or religious difficulties could not be comprehended by those heathen nations as standing in the way of God's purposes. Physical hindrances were the only ones they could understand ; and they would certainly infer that if he slew the Israelites in the wilderness, it could only be in order to cover his own defeat and failure before the rival deities of Palestine.

Ver. 17.—**And now, I beseech thee, let the power of my Lord be great.** Here the argument of Moses rises to a higher level ; he ventures to put God in mind of what he had himself declared to Moses in the fullest revelation which he had ever made of his own unchangeable character, viz., that of all Divine prerogatives, the most Divine was that of forgiving sins and showing mercy. **According as thou hast spoken.** See on Exod. xxxiv. 6, 7. The words are not quoted exactly as there given, but are substantially the same.

Ver. 19.—**From Egypt until now.** From the first passion of despair in Egypt itself (Exod. xiv. 11, 12), through the murmurings in the wilderness of Sin, and the apostasy of Mount Sinai, to the last rebellion at Kibroth-Hattaavah.

Ver. 20.—**I have pardoned.** Whatever necessary exceptions and qualifications might remain to be afterwards declared, the great fact that he forgave the nation, and that the nation should not die, is announced without delay and without reservation (cf. 2 Sam. xii. 13). **According to thy word.** Such power had God been pleased to give unto man, that at the intercession of the mediator a whole nation is delivered from imminent death and destruction.

Ver. 21.—**As truly as I live, all the earth shall be filled with the glory of the Lord.** Rather, "as truly as I live, and the glory of the Lord shall fill all the earth." Both clauses are dependent on וְאוּלָם, and the second is but the necessary correlative of the first.

Ver. 22.—**Because all those men.** The particle כִּי is not to be rendered "because ;" it simply introduces the substance of the oath : "As I live, .. all those men .. shall not see." So the Septuagint. **And have tempted me now these ten times.** It is not in the least necessary to press this expression, borrowed from the vague usage of men, literally. It is the language of indignation, meaning that the full measure of provocation had been received (cf. Gen. xxxi. 7 ; Job xix. 3). The recorded instances of national "temptations" cannot be made to reach the number ten.

Ver. 23.—**Surely they shall not see.** אִם־יִרְאוּ, "if they shall see," according to the usual' Hebrew idiom. Cf. Ps. cvii. 11 (Septuagint), Heb. iv. 3, ὡς ὤμοσα .. εἰ εἰσελεύσονται.

Ver. 24.—**My servant Caleb.** Caleb alone is mentioned here, as if he were the only exception to the sentence just passed upon the generation which came out of Egypt. Taken in connection with ch. xiii. 30, and in contrast with ch. xiv. 6, 30, 38, it has been supposed to point to the interweaving here of two narratives, from the one of which the name of Joshua was intentionally omitted (see the Introduction). The fact, however, is that Joshua is not the only, nor the most remarkable, exception to the general sentence which is not specified here. Moses and Aaron themselves were undoubtedly not included in that sentence at this time, although they afterwards came under the severity of it (see on Deut. i. 37). Eleazar, the priest, was one of those who entered with Joshua (Josh. xiv. 1), and it is vain to argue that he might have been under twenty at the time of the numbering (cf. ch. iv. 16). There is, indeed, every reason to believe that the whole tribe of Levi were excepted from the punishment, because they were not compromised in the guilt. They had no representative among the spies, nor were they called upon to go up and fight ; moreover, they had been steadily loyal to Moses since the matter of the golden calf. But if the exception of the Levites was taken for granted, and passed without mention, much more might the exception of Joshua. He did not stand by any means in the same position as Caleb and the other spies ; he was the "minister" and lieutenant of Moses, whose fortunes were obviously bound up, not with those of his tribe, but with those of his master. If Moses had accepted the Divine offer to make him the head of a new chosen race, no doubt Joshua would have been given to him. His subsequent separation as leader, not of Ephraim, but of Israel, was already anticipated in the singularity, at least, of his position. Caleb, on the other hand, was merely a chieftain of the tribe of Judah, with nothing to distinguish him from the mass of the people but his own good conduct. There is, therefore, nothing perplexing in the fact that Caleb alone is mentioned in this place, and nothing to warrant the assumption of a double narrative. **Another spirit.** The spirit which possessed and prompted Caleb was no doubt the Holy Spirit, just as the spirit which moved the rebellion was an evil spirit (Eph. ii. 2) ; but how far any such personality is here attributed to the "spirit" is hard to determine. **Hath followed me fully.** Literally, "fulfilled to walk behind me." Caleb treasured up this testimony with natural pride (cf. Josh. xiv. 8). **And his seed shall possess it,** *i. e.* a portion of it and in it. No mention is made here of any special heritage, nor is it clear from Josh. xiv. 6—13 that Caleb received any definite promise of Hebron. He spoke indeed of a promise made him, probably at this time, by Moses ; but that promise was a very general one. He asked for "this mountain, whereof the Lord spake in that day ;" but he may only have referred to the Divine command first to explore and then to occupy "the mountain," as the nearest portion of the promised land.

Ver. 25.—**Now the Amalekites and the Canaanites dwelt in the valley.** This parenthesis bears on the face of it several difficulties, both as to the meaning of the statement and as to its position in the text. 1. It has been stated just before (ch. xiii. 29) that the "Canaanites" dwelt by the sea, and in the Ghor, and it has been proposed by some to understand under this name the Phœnicians, because "Sidon" was the first-born of Canaan, and because they are known to have occupied the coast. But if "Canaanite" means "Phœnician" in ch. xiii. 29, it is difficult to maintain that it is here equivalent to "Amorite." Again, if "Canaanite" be taken in this vaguer sense, yet it is clear that the Amorites dwelt in "the mountain" (cf. *e. g.* ver. 45 with Deut. i. 44), and not in the lowlands. This has been got over by supposing that עֵמֶק may mean an upland vale, or plateau, such as that to which the Israelites presently ascended. It is, however, a straining of the word to assign such a meaning to it. It is rightly translated by the Septuagint ἐν τῇ κοιλάδι. And even if one looking down from above might call an upland plain by this name, yet certainly one looking up from below would not. If the word stands rightly in this place, בָּעֵמֶק must mean "in the Wady Murreh," the broad sandy strait which bounded the

"mountain of the Amorite" on the south. If so, we must conclude that not only the roving Amalekites, but also the Canaanites, or Amorites, had established themselves in some parts of the Wady. 2. It is scarcely credible that an observation of this sort, which would seem unusual and abrupt in any speech, should have formed a part of God's message to Moses. It has no apparent connection with the context. It does not (as often alleged) afford a reason for the command which follows ; it was not at all because enemies were already in possession before them that the Israelites had to turn their backs upon the promised land, but because God had withdrawn for the time his promised aid. If the "valley" be the Rakhmah plateau, they had always known that hostile tribes held it, and that they would have to conquer them. That the words are an interpolation, as the A. V. represents them, seems as certain as internal evidence can make it ; but by whom made, and with what intent, is a question which will probably never be answered. It may be worth while to hazard a conjecture that the interpolated words are really connected with what goes before, viz., the promise of inheritance to Caleb. Now that promise was fulfilled in the gift of Hebron to Caleb and his seed (Josh. xiv. 14). But we have express mention in Gen. xxxvii. 14 of the "vale of Hebron," and the same word, עֵמֶק, is used in the Hebrew. Is it not possible that this parenthesis was originally the gloss of one who had a special interest in the heritage of Caleb, and wished to note that at the time it was given to him "the vale" was occupied by two hostile peoples? **Into the wilderness,** *i. e.* the Sinaitic peninsula, as distinguished from Palestine on the one hand, and from Egypt on the other. **By the way of the Red Sea,** *i. e.* towards the Red Sea ; here apparently the Elanitic Gulf (cf. ch. xi. 31).

Ver. 26.—**And the Lord spake unto Moses and unto Aaron.** This communication is clearly by way of continuation and amplification of the sentence briefly pronounced above. It is markedly distinguished from the latter, as being (1) spoken to Aaron as well as to Moses ; (2) addressed through them to the people at large. The one was the Divine answer to the effectual pleading of the mediator ; the other the Divine reply to the rebellious cries of the people. The two are blended together in the narrative of Deut. i.

Ver. 27.—**How long shall I bear with this evil congregation, which murmur against me ?** Literally, "How long this evil congregation, that they murmur against me." Septuagint, ἕως τίνος τὴν συναγωγὴν τὴν πονηρὰν ταύτην ; The verb is supplied from the sense.

Ver. 29.—**All that were numbered of you,** **.. from twenty years old** (cf. ch. i. 18, 19, 47). All that had been enrolled as the soldiers of the Lord, to fight his battles and their own, but had refused, and had incurred the guilt of mutiny.

Ver. 30.—**Sware.** Literally, "lifted up my hand" (see on Gen. xiv. 22). **And Joshua the son of Nun.** The exception in favour of his "minister," Joshua, had been taken for granted in the brief answer of God to Moses ; in the fuller announcement of his purposes to the congregation it was natural that he too should be mentioned by name.

Ver. 33.—**Your children shall wander.** Literally, "shall pasture." רֹעִים. Septuagint, ἔσονται νεμόμενοι. It was not altogether a threat, for it implied that the Lord would be their Shepherd and would provide for their wants in their wanderings. **Forty years.** This period was made up by counting in the year and a half since the exodus. It was one of those many cases in which the word of God was fulfilled in the meaning and substance of it, but not in the letter. The delay which had already occurred was itself practically due to the same spirit of mutiny which had grown to a head at Kadesh ; it was therefore strictly equitable to count it as part of the punishment inflicted (see on Deut. ii. 14). **And bear your whoredoms.** "Whoredom" had been already used (Exod. xxxiv. 16) as a synonym for idolatry in its aspect of spiritual unfaithfulness, and there is no reason to depart from that well-marked meaning here. That the Jews were guilty of idolatry in the wilderness is distinctly asserted (cf. Acts vii. 42, 43) ; and these idolatrous practices, carried on no doubt in secret, must have been a sore trial to the generation which grew up amidst them (cf. Josh. xxiv. 14, 23).

Ver. 34.—**After the number of the days,** **.. each day for a year.** It is said, and truly, that the connection between the two periods was arbitrary, and that the apparent correspondence lay only upon the surface. Exactly for this reason it was the better fitted to fix itself in the mind of a nation incapable of following a deeper and more spiritual analogy of guilt and punishment. It served the purpose which God had in view, viz., to make them feel that the quantity as well as the quality of their punishment was entirely due to themselves ; and it needed no other justification. If God assigns reasons at all, he assigns such as can be understood by those to whom he speaks. **Ye shall know my breach of promise.** תְּנוּאָתִי. The noun only occurs elsewhere in Job xxxiii. 10, but the verb is found in ch. xxxii. 7 in the sense

of "discouraging," or "turning away" (Septuagint, ἰνατί διαστρέφετε). Here it must mean "my withdrawal," or "my turning aside, from you." They should know by sad experience that "with the froward" God will "show" himself "froward" (Ps. xviii. 26).

Ver. 37.—**Died by the plague before the Lord.** Septuagint, ἐν τῇ πληγῇ. "Plague" has here its older signification of "stroke," or visitation of God. We are not told what death they died, but it was sudden and exceptional enough to mark it as the direct consequence of their sinful conduct.

Ver. 40.—**Early in the morning.** Wishing to anticipate the retrograde movement commanded by God (ver. 25). **Into the top of the mountain.** What summit is here spoken of as the object of their enterprise is quite uncertain. Probably it was some ridge not far distant which seemed to them from below to be the height of land, but was itself commanded by loftier heights beyond. **For we have sinned.** The prospect of being taken at their own word, and being excluded from the land which lay so near, brought home to them a sense of their folly ; but their repentance merely consisted in a frantic effort to avoid the punishment which their sin had incurred.

Ver. 41.—**And Moses said,** *i. e.* had said, before they left the camp (cf. ver. 44, and Deut. i. 42).

Ver. 44.—**They presumed to go up.** This gives the sense very well : they were deaf to all persuasion or command to stay. Septuagint, διαβιασάμενοι, ἀνέβησαν. Thus they added to an evil distrust in the power of God an almost more evil trust in their own power. It does not seem correct to say that "unbelief" was the real cause of both errors —unbelief, firstly in God's promises, and secondly in his threats. It was rather one of those many cases in which men seek to atone for a fault on one side by rushing into as great a fault on the other side. They spoke brave words about the "place which the Lord hath promised," as though it were indeed obedience and trust which spurred them on, instead of presumption and selfishness. **The ark of the covenant of the Lord, and Moses, departed not out of the camp.** The plainest possible token that the Lord was not with them. With Moses remained no doubt all the Levites, and the silver trumpets, and Joshua, and perhaps the bulk of the people.

Ver. 45.—**The Amalekites came down, and the Canaanites.** See on Deut. i. 44. They came down from the summit of the mountain country, and drove the Israelites off the saddle, or lower level, to which they had ascended. **Discomfited them.** Septuagint, κατέκοψαν αὐτούς, "cut them up." **Unto**

Hormah. This mention of Hormah is extremely perplexing, especially when we find from Deut. i. 44 that it was "in Seir" (בְּשֵׂעִיר), which is the ordinary name for the territory of the Edomites. The name Hormah meets us again in ch. xxi. 3 (see the notes there), as having been bestowed by the Israelites upon the place where they destroyed the people of King Arad. If this be the same Hormah, it must be so named here by anticipation. It is, however, quite possible that it is another place altogether. Again, if the Seir of Deut. i. 44 be the country usually so called, we must suppose that the Edomites had at this time occupied a part of the Azazimeh, contiguous to the Wady Murreh, and westwards of the Arabah. We should then represent the Israelites to ourselves as being driven off the mountain, and across the Wady Murreh, and cut down in the mountains beyond, as far as a place called Hormah, perhaps from this very slaughter. Others have found Hormah (or Zephath, Judges i. 17) and Seir among the multitudinous names of past or present habitation in the south of Palestine ; the perplexing resemblances of which, coupled with the vagueness of the sacred narrative, lead to the rise of as many different theories as there are commentators. It must, however, be erroneous to represent this hasty incursion of the Israelites, without their leaders, and without their daily food from heaven, as a campaign in which they advanced for a considerable distance, and were only partially expelled at last. It is clear from this passage, and still more from the parallel passage in Deut. i., that the expedition was swiftly and ignominiously repelled and avenged. Compare the expression, "chased you as bees do."

NOTE TO CHAPTERS XIII., XIV. ON THE POSITION OF KADESH AND THE ROUTE TAKEN BY THE ISRAELITES.

The old name of Kadesh was En-mishpat (Gen. xiv. 7), or the "Well of Judgment." Its later and more familiar name was equivalent to "the sanctuary" or "holy place" (compare the Arabic name for Jerusalem, "El Kuds"). It is possible that it received this name from the long sojourn of the tabernacle in its neighbourhood (Deut. i. 46); but it is more likely that it possessed some character of sanctity from ancient times, a character which would very well harmonise with the fact that justice was administered there. It is evident that in order to obtain any clear and connected idea of the history of Israel between the departure from Sinai and the encampment upon the plains of Moab, it is above all necessary to fix approximately the position of this place, which for one generation was the most important place in the whole world. It was no doubt from the neighbourhood of Kadesh that the spies were sent, and it was certainly to Kadesh that they returned from searching the land (ch. xiii. 26). From Kadesh the first disastrous attempt was made to invade the country, and from thence again the final journey began which led the nation round the coasts of Edom to the plains of Moab. Thus Kadesh was of all places, next to Mount Sinai, the one associated with the most momentous events of those momentous years, marking at once the terminus of their first journey (which should have been their last), the beginning of their tedious wanderings, and the starting point of their final march. So far, however, from there being any certainty or agreement as to the site of Kadesh, we find two sites proposed widely separated from one another, each maintained and each assailed by powerful arguments, which divide between them the suffrages of geographers and commentators; and besides these there are others less powerfully supported.

The view adopted in the notes to this book is that of the travellers Rowland and Williams, and of the great majority of the German commentators: it is fully stated and minutely argued in Kurtz's 'History of the Old Covenant' (vol. iii. in Clark's 'Foreign Theol. Lib.'). According to these authorities Kadesh is to be recognised in the plain and fountain of Kudes, just within the north-west corner of the mountains of the Azazimeh (see note on ch. x. 12). This desert plain, some ten miles by six in extent, is screened from ordinary observation by the outer mountain walls of the Azazimat, which shut it off on the west from the desert road from Sinai to Hebron, on the north from the Wady Murreh. At the north-east of the plain is a bold and bare rock, a promontory of the northern mountain rampart, from the foot of which issues a copious spring, which begins by falling in cascades into the bed of a torrent, and ends by losing itself in the sands. Amongst the Wadys which open into the plain is one which bears the name of Redemat (see note on ch. xii. 16). It is uncertain whether there is any easy communication between this plain and the Wady Murreh, but there are several passes on the western side which lead by a slight circuit to the southern table-lands of Palestine.

The view adopted by the majority of English commentators is that of the traveller Robinson. According to these authorities Kadesh must be sought in the Arabah, the broad depression which runs northward from the head of the Elanitic Gulf until it meets the Ghor below the Dead Sea. By most of those who hold this view the site of Kadesh is placed at Ain-el-Weibeh, ten miles to the north of Mount Hor, and opposite the opening (from the east) of the Wady el Ghuweir, which affords the only easy passage through Edom to the north-west. Others, however, prefer Ain Hash, a few miles further north. The local peculiarities of either place are such as to satisfy the requirements of the narrative, although they would not by themselves have recalled the scenes with which Kadesh is associated.

Of other theories none perhaps need to be considered here, because none can reasonably enter into competition with the two already mentioned; they avoid none of the difficulties with which these are beset, while they incur others of their own. If, indeed, Rabbinical tradition (followed in this case by Jerome) were worth anything, it would decide the question in favour of Petra, the Aramaic name of which (Rekem) uniformly takes the place of Kadesh in the Syriac and Chaldee, and in the Talmud. Kadesh-Barnea in the Targums is Rekem-Geiah. Petra itself (of which the ancient name apparently was Selah (2 Kings xiv. 7), the very word used in ch. xx. 10, 11) stands in a gorge famous for its giant cliffs, still called the Wady Musa, concerning which the local tradition is that it was cleft by the rod of Moses. But apart from these resemblances of name, which are so fallacious, and these legends, which are so worthless, there is absolutely nothing to connect Kadesh with Petra; on the contrary, the position of Petra, far away from Palestine, on the skirts of Mount Hor, and in the heart of Edom, distinguish it sharply from the Kadesh of the Bible story. The two can only be identified on the supposition that the sacred narrative, as it stands, is mistaken and misleading.

In examining briefly the arguments by which the western and eastern sites respectively are maintained and assailed, it will be better to dismiss the evidence (such as it is) afforded by modern nomenclature, which is always open to grave suspicion, and is at best of very variable value. The Wady Retemât, e. g., is so named from the broom plant, which is very plentiful in the peninsula, and may have lent a similar name to many another place.

In favour of the western site, that of the so-called plain of Kudes, we have the following arguments in addition to the marked natural features which suggested the identification. 1. Previous mentions of Kadesh would certainly dispose us (in the absence of any indication that there was more than one place of that name) to look for it to the south of Palestine, and rather to the south-west than to the south-east. In Gen. xiv. 7 it is mentioned in connection with the "country of the Amalekites," which was apparently between Canaan and Egypt. In the same region we may place with more confidence the well of Hagar (Gen. xvi. 14), which is placed between "Kadesh and Bered." It is difficult to think that this Kadesh could possibly have been in the Arabah. Gerar, again, which was certainly near to Beersheba, is placed (Gen. xx. 1) "between Kadesh and Shur." These notices are indeed indefinite, but they certainly point to the western rather than to the eastern site. 2. Subsequent mentions of Kadesh point in the same direction. In ch. xxxiv. 4, 5 and Josh. xv. 3, 4 the southern frontier of Judah, which was also that of Canaan, is traced from the scorpion cliffs at the head of the Ghor to the Mediterranean (see note on the first passage). On this frontier Kadesh occurs in such a way that we should look for it not at one extremity, but somewhere about the middle of the line. The same is still more clearly the case in Ezek. xlvii. 19, where only three points are given on the southern frontier, of which Kadesh is the middle one. It is, again, very difficult to imagine that this Kadesh could have been in the Arabah. 3. It is a weaker argument, but still of some moment, that Kadesh is pointedly said to have been in the "wilderness of Paran" (ch. xii. 16; xiii. 3), and also to have been in or near the wilderness of Zin (ch. xiii. 21; xx. 1). But the eastern site of Kadesh far up the Arabah does not seem to answer to this double description nearly as well as the western. The plain of Kudes is strictly within the limits of that southern desert now called et-Tih, and yet it is quite close to the Wady Murreh, which with its sandy expansions towards the east may well have been the wilderness of Zin (see note on ch. xiii. 21).

In favour of the eastern site, the only argument of real weight is founded upon the repeated statement that Kadesh was close upon the territory of Edom. In ch. xx. 16, e.g., it is spoken of to the king of Edom as "a city in the uttermost of thy borders." But the only position in which the children of Israel would be at once on the borders of Canaan and on the borders of Edom as commonly understood, would be in the neighbourhood of Ain el-Weibeh, with the pass of es-Safâh on their left, and the Wady Ghuweir on their right, as they looked northwards. With this agrees the statement that they came to Kadesh "by the way of Mount Seir" (Deut. i. 2), and the fact that there is no station mentioned between Kadesh and Mount Hor (ch. xxxiii. 37), although the western site is seventy miles from that mountain.

The necessity indeed of placing Kadesh on the border of Edom must be conclusive in favour of the eastern site, if the common assumption is correct that the name and territory of Edom were bounded westwards by the Arabah. It is, however, contended, with some show of reason, that the kings of Edom had extended their authority at this time over the country of the Azazimeh as far as the plain of Kudes. There is, at any rate, nothing improbable in this, because this great mountain fastness is almost as sharply severed from Canaan as from Mount Seir, properly so called; and in fact it never appears to have been in possession of the Canaanites. When, however, the southern boundary line is traced in detail (ch. xxxiv. 3, 4; Josh. xv. 1, 2, 21), it is said to have extended עַל-יְדֵי, "on the sides," or אֶל-גְּבוּל, "to the borders," of Edom, and this expression can hardly be satisfied by the single point of contact at the south-east corner of Judah, especially when we consider the long list of cities which were on or near this border (Josh. xv. 21—32). Again, when the extreme southern and northern points of Joshua's conquest are mentioned (Josh. xi. 17; xii. 7), the former is "the bald mountain which goeth up Seir"—a natural feature which we look for in vain (for it cannot possibly be the low line of the scorpion cliffs), unless it be the northern rampart of the Azazimat. We have seen that the Hormah to which the Israelites were repelled on their first invasion is placed (Deut. i. 44) "in Seir," which can hardly be Mount Seir in its ordinary restricted sense. If the name Seir has to be sought anywhere outside of Edom proper, it would seem more natural to find it in the northern part of the wilderness of Paran, where it is said to be still common, than anywhere else. And if this extension of Edom can be established, there appears to be no further objection of any moment to the western site. Mount Hor would still be on the coast or edge of the land of Edom, because it would be the meeting-point of the two boundaries, the one striking westwards across the Arabah, the other southwards down the Arabah. The absence of any name between Kadesh and Hor is not conclusive, because the people certainly made journeys of several days without any regular halt (see note on ch. x. 33).

Upon the whole the question may fairly be stated thus :—

1. The general tenor of the narrative would lead us to suppose that the host of Israel had marched from Sinai through the midst of the desert of Paran, by the route which led most directly to the extreme south of Palestine ; and if they did this, they must have passed near to Rowland's Kadesh.

2. The natural features of this site, its position with regard to the desert of et-Tih and the Wady Murreh, its distance from Sinai (Deut. i. 2), and its proximity to the Negeb and the plateau of Rakhmah, seem to harmonise better with all that we read about Kadesh than the corresponding characteristics of the rival site.

3. The general effect of the various mentions of Kadesh, both before and after, is undeniably, though not decidedly, in favour of the western site.

4. The minor arguments which are urged on one side or the other may be allowed to balance one another, for it is certain that neither is free from difficulty.

5. The difficulty with respect to Edom is a very serious one, and with many will be decisive against Rowland's Kadesh.

6. What must turn the scale one way or the other is the independent evidence that the border of Edom extended at this time across the Arabah, and included the north-east portion of the desert of Paran, viz., the mountain mass which fronted the southern edge of Canaan. There is *some* evidence that this was the case, and it cannot be met by the simple assertion that the territory of Edom consisted only of Mount Seir, and that Mount Seir lay wholly to the east of the Arabah.

It is to be expected that travel and research in these regions now so inaccessible, and, after all said and written, so little known, will before long bring fresh and more decisive evidence to light. In the mean time that view is consistently maintained in these notes which, if it had apparently the greatest difficulty to surmount, yet receives the greatest amount of positive support from the general and incidental testimony of the Scripture record. One lesson emerges clearly from the obscurity involving this question, which appears to us so important to the understanding of God's holy word : the geography of the Bible must be of very small importance indeed as compared with its moral and religious teachings. These are not affected by any ignorance of localities and routes. The rebellion of Kadesh has exactly the same moral for us (Heb. iii. 19 ; iv. 11) whether Kadesh was in the Azazimat or the Arabah ; and the very uncertainty in which its site is involved may be designed to remind us that it is very easy to exaggerate the value of these outward details to the neglect of those inward teachings which alone are in the highest sense important.

HOMILETICS.

Chs. xiii., xiv.—*The revolt of Israel.* In these two chapters we have, as the writer to the Hebrews teaches us, a Divinely-recorded " example of unbelief " (Heb. iv. 11)—of that ἀπειθία which we cannot satisfactorily translate, because it is a *disbelief* which prompts and produces, and so appears in practice as, *disobedience;* of that ἀπειθία which is to the Christian's life exactly what the "evil heart of unbelief" (ἀπιστίας) is to the Christian's faith. The fall of Israel is "written," and fully written, "for our admonition," because the like temper and the like behaviour leads in us to the like misery and loss. Spiritually, therefore, we see the Israel of God—1. *Brought very nigh to the promised rest, almost within sight, and actually within taste.* 2. *Refusing to enter that rest through disbelief.* 3. *Sentenced to exile from the rest they would not enter.* 4. *Attempting (vainly) to enter that rest in their own unbidden and unblessed ways.* And subordinately to this great and striking lesson, we have other lessons and examples both of good and evil.

I. CONSIDER, THEREFORE, IN RESPECT OF THIS ὑποδείγμα ἀπειθείας—

1. *That the place where Israel now lay was "in the wilderness of Paran," "that great and terrible wilderness;" but it was also "in the wilderness of Zin," which was the southern frontier of Canaan; and therefore (wherever Kadesh may have been) the desert journey lay behind him, and his rest was close before him: only one steep climb and he would begin to enter into the land of promise.* Even so are we placed to-day. God has brought us with a mighty hand within reach of home; has led us by a way we knew not of; has given us a law and a worship; has fed us with heavenly food; has separated us (outwardly at least) from a perishing world. Rest lies before us: rest in this world from sin and self (Heb. iv. 10); in the next from sorrow and sadness too (Rev. xiv. 13). It is not far away, not out of reach; it only needs a little patient effort to make that rest our own.

2. *That it pleased God not only to tell the people about the land of promise, but to let them see its goodness, as it were, for themselves through the report of their own brethren, representative men whom he suffered to view the land.* Even so it is the good pleasure of God that, concerning the happiness of a holy life, we should have not only his promise, but the testimony of men also, even of our brethren. Yea, concerning the glories of the world to come, how great they are, we have the report of men to whom it hath been given to "go up thither," to see what "eye hath not seen," to hear "what ear hath not heard," even "unspeakable things" which could only be set forth to us in types and figures (2 Cor. xii. 2, 3, compared with Rom. viii. 18; Rev. iv. 1; xxi. 10, &c.).

3. *That the people at Kadesh not only heard the report of Canaan, but tasted of the fruits of it which the spies brought back; and they might know by these fruits how much pleasanter a land it was than Egypt itself, even apart from its slavery.* Even so it is given to us in Christ not only to hear by report, but to taste also of the good things of the world to come (Heb. vi. 4, 5). It is a fact of experience that we may partake to some extent, here and now, of delights which no more spring from the conditions of unregenerate human nature than those fruits could have grown in the desert of Paran—delights which are as superior to the luxuries of sin as the grapes of Eshcol to the pungent dainties of Egypt. Nothing can rob us of the consciousness that we have tasted them, and it is this which makes heaven so real to us, as Canaan to them.

4. *That none of the spies concealed from them the fact that the land which invited them had its grave difficulties, as well as its great attractions: milk and honey and fruit, and all good things, but many strong foes to be conquered first.* Even so it is not concealed by any that great obstacles and sore conflicts stand between the longing soul and the promised rest. If any represented the entry into the inheritance of the saints as an easy thing and unopposed, he would but contradict the Master himself (Mark viii. 34, 35; Luke xiii. 24; Rev. ii. 26, &c.) and his inspired servants (1 Cor. ix. 26, 27; Heb. iv. 1; James i. 3, 12; 2 Pet. i. 10, 11; 2 John 8; Jude 20, 21).

5. *That the obstacles which confronted Israel in the gigantic size and fortified cities of their foes were truly formidable, and to the military science of that day insuper-*

able. Even so the powers of evil which bar our upward way are indeed mighty, and that for two especial reasons: (1) as wielded and swayed by beings of superhuman origin and power (Eph. vi. 12); (2) as having entrenched themselves in the ancient and (as it were) invincible habits, customs, and tendencies of the human race (cf. 2 Cor. x. 4, 5). And note that while the former ground of hopelessness becomes less and less potent as faith shrinks within her deepest channels, so the second becomes more and more alarming. Those evil principles which nineteen centuries of Christianity have failed to expel from Christian society are indeed formidable hindrances.

6. *That the faithless among the spies led the people astray in two ways: (1) by exaggerating the real difficulties which existed, and (2) by ignoring the Divine aid they would have in overcoming them.* When they *did* enter they found no Nephilim, nor do their foes seem to have been as a rule superior in size to themselves. And God had brought them through far greater perils, and made them victors over far more formidable foes (cf. Exod. xiv. 15 b., 31). Even so the counsels of the natural man are doubly false: (1) as exaggerating the real difficulty of leading a life of holiness and attaining unto rest, raising up creatures of the imagination, and magnifying existing obstacles, to excuse cowardice and sloth; (2) as putting out of sight the fact that when God calls us to a certain thing he pledges himself to give us the strength we need (Exod. iii. 12; Deut. xxxiii. 25; 1 Cor. x. 13). The natural man would ever persuade us that heaven and peace are not attainable in the way which God points out as *the* way; that it is not possible in this or that position to lead a holy life, or to give up this or that sin, or to attain a real mastery over self—which is mere unbelief (2 Cor. xii. 9, 10; Phil. iv. 13; cf. 2 Kings vi. 16, 17).

7. *That the faithful among the spies (in whom was "another spirit") gave counsel, "Let us go up at once and possess it, for we are well able to overcome it."* And herein were three points: (1) to "go up," because the ascent, whether from the Arabah or the Wady Murreh, was necessarily steep; (2) to go up "at once," because delay would strengthen the hands of their enemies, and could only weaken theirs, as offending the Lord; (3) to go up at once, because the victory was assured to them if they did, with the help of God. Even so is the voice of the Spirit, and of all who are led by the Spirit, however full an acquaintance they may have with the dangers and difficulties of the spiritual life—(1) to go up, because it *is* an ascent, and must involve toil and fatigue (Acts xiv. 22); (2) to set out "at once," because any delay *may* be fatal (Heb. iii. 13; James iv. 13, 14), and *must* add to the difficulty; (3) to proceed with holy confidence, because, although we have to "overcome," and that by dint of doing and suffering, yet it is God who fighteth and God who getteth the victory in us (Rom. viii. 37; Philip. ii. 13; Col. i. 27).

8. *That the crisis of Israel's fate was come when they had to choose between these persuasions.* God had brought them to the very verge of Canaan, but they could not enter unless their will united itself to his will, unless they chose to go on in his name and strength. Their future was at that hour in their own hands, and they wrecked it because they did not trust God, because their faith was too weak to pass into obedience in the face of serious discouragement. Even so are our eternal fortunes placed (in a certain true sense) in our own hands. Holiness and heaven are set before us, brought within our reach in Christ; the "rest which remaineth" is ours, to be entered on now, to-day; and God calls upon us to enter, and encourages us by the voice and experience of those who have made trial of it. And it may be we will not go on; it is too hard—too much to encounter; too difficult—too many obstacles in the way. It may be we find the prospect so much less easy and encouraging than we had fancied. We will not make the effort, or undertake the risk, looking to Divine grace for success; and therefore we too cannot enter in because of unbelief. We must bear the evil consequences; we have ruined ourselves; we have shut ourselves out from happiness and heaven. And note that as this crisis (although in some sense often anticipated) only happened once to Israel in the wilderness, so does the true crisis in his spiritual fortunes happen only once (as far as we can see) in the lives of many men. There is a set time when they are called, in some unmistakable way, to make a bold and decisive advance in the spiritual life, which will leave them really masters of themselves, and so at rest. If, then, they shrink from taking it because it is hard, or because (as they say) they are not worthy or prepared for it

they forfeit the rest prepared for them, and doom themselves to a fruitless wandering in dry places.

9. *That the first fruit of that refusal to advance was mourning, the second murmuring, the third flat rebellion.* Even so when we, being called, shrink from going on unto perfection, the first consequence is that unhappiness which is both a symptom of disaffection to God and a part of it; the second is a complaining spirit, as though we had been ill-treated, and a readiness to put the blame on others, perhaps our best friends; the third is a desperate intention to throw off the yoke of religion altogether, and to return to the old licence of sin from which we had escaped.

10. *That the proposal to return to Egypt was as infeasible as it was wicked.* Had it been possible to get there, it is certain that even the poor luxuries of their former slavery would never have been given back to them. Even so the faint-hearted and faithless Christian can yet never be as the heathen, or even as the ungodly, again: for one thing, he knows enough of true happiness and freedom to find the yoke of open sin intolerable; for another, the pleasures of sin are departed for him: he may sin, and recklessly, but it will not have the zest it once had, when it was in a manner natural to him. The ungodly *do* enjoy the pleasures of sin, such as they are; the half-converted who draw back are of all men most miserable: they will not have Canaan, and they cannot have Egypt, and there is nothing for them but the wilderness (cf. Heb. x. 38, 39, in the true version).

11. *That the punishment which God inflicted upon the rebels was perpetual exile from the land which they would not enter.* Thus he simply took them at their own word (ch. xiv. 28); for though they had imagined the alternative of return to Egypt, that was impossible. Even so the sentence which Christ passes upon them that *will not* come to him is simply, "Depart from me" (Matt. xxv. 41). If men will not labour to enter into rest (Heb. iv. 11), there is no alternative before them but perpetual *unrest*, lasting as long as they last; and this is itself "the fire prepared for the devil and his angels," for this is the natural state of evil spirits apart from artificial and temporary disguises (Matt. xii. 43; cf. Isa. lvii. 20, 21).

And note that the ἀνύδροι τόποι and the ἀνάπαυσις of Matt. xii. 43 exactly correspond to the wilderness of Paran on the one hand, and to Canaan on the other (cf. Matt. xi. 29).

And note again, with regard to the punishment inflicted—1. That all who were numbered (and none other) were counted worthy of punishment, as having been enrolled for the military service of the Lord, but having mutinied. So will our sentence (if we incur it) be one passed not on aliens, or enemies, but on servants who have betrayed their trust, on soldiers who have disobeyed their orders and turned their backs upon their Captain (1 Cor. vii. 22; Col. iii. 24; 2 Tim. ii. 3, 4). 2. That only the adult generation, who were strong and able, were excluded; their little ones, whom they counted so helpless, and of whom they said they would be a prey, inherited the land. Even so in the kingdom of his grace the wise and prudent are left out, and the proud are scattered in the imagination of their hearts, whilst unto babes mysteries are revealed (cf. Matt. xviii. 3; xix. 14; 1 Cor. i. 26—28; 2 Cor. xii. 10). 3. That the years of exile were reckoned in exact accordance with the days of searching. So must there be a perfect correspondence between sin and its punishment—a correspondence which is not merely on the surface (as in their case), but lies deep down in the nature of man, so that sin works out its own revenges both in kind and in measure (cf. Luke xii. 47).

II. CONSIDER AGAIN, IN RESPECT OF THE VAIN ATTEMPT TO CONQUER CANAAN FOR THEMSELVES—

1. *That the people added to their former sin an opposite sin—despairing first, and presuming after.* Even so do many think to atone for the unbelief and sloth and disobedience of the past by a presumptuous reliance upon their own strength of character and of will for the future. So when one is compelled to acknowledge his irreligion and sin, he sets up to mend his life himself, saying, "*I* will," and "*I* have made up my mind," and "*I* am determined," being governed as much by self-will in running the way of God's commandments as before in refusing to run.

2. *That they sought to justify their attempt by a hasty acknowledgment of their*

sin, and by a presumptuous appropriation of God's promises, as though the land was theirs whenever and however they chose to take it. Even so do many put aside all genuine repentance and self-humiliation for their grievous sins, when those sins are brought home to them, speaking and acting as if a bare acknowledgment of sin (which cannot be avoided) replaced them at once in the favour of God, and gave them a sure title to all the blessings of the covenant.

3. *That they went against their foes without Moses, and without the ark,* as if they could do *without* Divine help to-day what yesterday they had despaired of doing *with* that help. Even so when men have discovered the folly of their sins by sharp experience, they will set to work to lead a good life and to overcome temptations without the means of grace, without the presence and aid of Jesus, without any ground of confidence that he is with them in their strife.

4. *That the result was speedy and disastrous defeat at the hands of their enemies.* Even so have all men fared who have tried to achieve holiness and heaven without the Divine aid carefully sought and constantly had (Heb. iv. 16; xii. 28).

III. Consider again, with respect to the spies and the land of promise—

1. *That the proposal to search the land did not at first proceed from God, but probably from a secret disaffection on the part of the people; nevertheless, he made it his own.* Even so there are many things in the Church of God which have their first origin in human defection from the obedience of faith, which yet, as not being wrong in themselves, God has adopted and made a part of that order of things which is our practical probation. A great part of Christian civilisation, *e. g.,* had its real origin in pride, ambition, or covetousness; nevertheless, it is certain that God has adopted it, and we could not go back from it without flying in the face of providence.

2. *That the change whereby Hoshea (help) became Jehoshua (God's help) was either made or declared at this time.* Even so when it is any question of finding the way to heaven, or making any report concerning it, no "help" is of any avail which is not clearly and avowedly "God's help" (Acts xxvi. 22).

3. *That the instructions given by Moses seem to have erred by directing attention too much to possible difficulties.* Even so it is a frequent error, and a natural one, in rulers of the Church that they direct attention too much to matters of worldly policy and to outward difficulties, and thereby encourage a spirit of cowardice and discouragement which they do not themselves share.

4. *That Hebron was older than Zoan.* Most likely they thought that Zoan, the residence of Pharaoh, was the oldest place in the world, but, as a fact, Hebron was seven years (a perfect number) older still. Even so we think and speak naturally of the present order of things as though it always had been, as though all the prestige of antiquity at any rate were on its side. In truth the country to which we go is infinitely older, having been prepared for us " before the foundation of the world."

5. *That the valley of Eshcol had a new meaning given to its name because of the famous cluster which they bare thence.* Even so many an old name in the Bible becomes instinct with new meaning through its association with the joys of the world to come (cf. Paradise, Zion, &c.); and so many a scene in our individual lives, being connected with some spiritual happiness.

6. *That the spies confirmed all that God had said of the land.* Even so those who have had visions of heaven, and those too among ourselves who have tasted of its sweetness and its gifts in a heavenly life on earth, must needs testify that all which God hath said of its blessedness is most true, and not exaggerated.

7. *That Caleb differed from the rest of the spies, and was the only reliable counsellor, in that he had " another spirit," and " fulfilled to walk after" the Lord.* Even so the faithful Christian, whom it is safe to follow, is known among the many faithless—(1) as being led by another spirit from that which sways the disaffected and disobedient (Rom. viii. 15; Eph. ii. 2); (2) as having not merely promised, or begun, or set out, but "fulfilled" to follow Christ in the way he went (1 Cor. xi. 1; Eph. v. 1; 1 Thess. i. 6).

8. *That the other spies died by the hand of God, as having turned their brethren away from Canaan.* Even so it is a fearful sin, and one that will be fearfully

avenged, to discourage the wavering, and to provide those that are disaffected with arguments and reasons against a religious life.

9. *That Joshua and Caleb lived on, sharing the present punishment, but not destroyed by it, because cheered with certain hope.* Even so in an evil age, amidst an unspiritual people, the faithful few must live sadly, but they live. The Lord knoweth them that are his, and they shall stand in their lot at the end of days (Jer. xlv. 5; Dan. xii. 13; Mal. iii. 16, 17; 2 Tim. ii. 19). And note, that the spies were specially directed to see "whether there be wood " in the holy land, or not; *i. e.* trees (Septuagint, δένδρα), which did not grow in the wilderness. It is especially told us that in the holy city there grows the tree of life (Rev. ii. 7)—yea, many trees of life, such as we vainly seek here (Ezek. xlvii. 12; Rev. xxii. 2). And note again, that in the bunch of grapes borne upon a staff the ancient commentators saw an image of Christ crucified. " Christus est botrus qui pependit in ligno " ('St. Aug. c. Faust.,' xii. 42). The two that bear are the two peoples, Jew and Gentile; they who go before see not what they carry; they who come after carry the same, and see what they carry.

IV. CONSIDER AGAIN, IN RESPECT TO THE LAST FRUITLESS APPEAL OF JOSHUA AND CALEB (ch. xiv. 6—9), that they urged very truly—

1. *That the land was exceeding good.* Even so is the land set before us, whether it be the life of holiness and devotion here, or the life of perfection beyond; it floweth with milk and honey, because all that is most wholesome and pleasant is to be had freely without money and without price.

2. *That the Lord would bring them in, if he delighted in them*—and there could be no doubt of that, after what he had done. Even so, if the Lord delight in us, as he has said and proved abundantly, he can surely give us victory and give us possessions, for his Spirit is able to sustain our weakness, and all things are his (Rom. viii. 26, 31, 37; 1 Cor. iii. 21, 22).

3. *That the one thing which could harm them was rebellion.* Even so the only thing which a Christian has to fear, the only thing which can keep him far from rest, out of heaven, is disaffection towards God. If he does not believe God's word; if he shrinks from really putting it to the test; if he will not in an actual case go forth in faith of his promised aid to overcome a temptation, to live down an evil habit, to practise a recognised virtue, then he sins through unbelief, and forfeits grace (Luke xii. 5; Heb. iv. 2; x. 23—26, 35, 36; Rev. ii. 5, 16; iii. 16).

4. *That their foes were not in fact formidable, but rather an advantage,* as providing them with sustenance. Even so there is nothing in temptation or in trial, apart from unfaithfulness in us, which need seriously stand in our way. Our enemies, natural or supernatural, are powerless against him in us. And when met as they should be, they are our greatest helps to holiness and heaven, for neither can be attained except by " overcoming." No one does so much for us as he who persecutes us, for he makes ours the eighth and highest beatitude, which we cannot have otherwise. No one helps us so fast to heaven as the devil himself, resisted, withstood, trampled down (Matt. v. 11, 12; Rom. viii. 28; 1 Pet. i. 7; iv. 13; James i. 2—4, 12).

5. *That fear was unreasonable, since the Lord was with them,* viz., in his ark and cloudy pillar. Even so our watchword is " Emmanuel," the Lord with us in the incarnation of the eternal Son. and in his perpetual presence with all and each of us, and in his assurance of our Father's love, and in his entire adoption of our interests as his own (Matt. xxviii. 20, *b.*; Luke xii. 32; John xiv. 1, 2; Heb. xiii. 6; Rev. vi. 2).

V. CONSIDER AGAIN, WITH RESPECT TO THE INTERCESSION OF MOSES AND THE ANSWER OF GOD—

1. *That the sin of the people and the wrath they incurred brought out the noblest trait in Moses' character.* In his perfect unselfishness, and in his ardour of intercession, he reached the true ideal of a mediator. Even so the fall and condemnation of the human race were the conditions (and necessary conditions, as far as we can see) of the manifestation of redeeming love and power in Christ. And as Israel is (in the long run) more ennobled by the heroism of Moses than it is disgraced by the cowardice of the people, so did humanity rise more in the righteousness of Christ than it fell in the vileness of Adam and the rest (Rom. v. 15, 17, 20).

2. *That God did not desire the sin of the people, but he so dealt with their sin as to bring out the singular goodness of his servant.* Even so it was not of God that man should fall into condemnation, but it was overruled by him for unspeakable good in the self-sacrifice of his dear Son (Rom. v. 8; Gal. ii. 20 *b.*; 1 John iv. 9, 10).

3. *That the offer made to Moses by God was intended to be refused, for it was a temptation to advance himself at the expense of the people.* Even so our Lord was " driven " into the wilderness by the Spirit to be tempted with the offer of all the kingdoms of the world (Matt. iv. 9 ; Mark i. 12, 13) ; and the temptation was often repeated (John vi. 15).

4. *That one element in the nobleness of Moses' character was his unconsciousness of his own unselfishness.* He did not even decline the tempting proposal, he only ignored it, as though it had never been made. And on subsequent occasions, while he often referred to his fault and punishment, he never alluded to his self-sacrifice (cf. Deut. i. 37, 38). Even so the true beauty of a Christian character is its simplicity, candour, and absence of self-conceit, such as we admire (and our Lord too) in children (Matt. xviii. 1—4 ; 1 Cor. xiii. 4 *b.*).

5. *That the effectual intercession of Moses was based on two arguments : that God would not destroy his own work begun ; that God would not belie his own character revealed.* Even so is all-prevailing Christian prayer based upon the same foundations : we plead with God his own work begun in us or others (Phil. i. 6, 20 ; cf. Job x. 3 ; Ps. cxxxviii. 8) ; we plead with him his eternal love and mercy declared in Christ, and extended to sinners in days past. And note that the work which God hath wrought for us is on an infinitely greater scale, and of infinitely greater moment and renown, than the exodus of Israel. The character also and mercy of God, which was revealed to Moses in a *name*, is manifested to us in the person of his Son.

6. *That God was very ready to pardon at the intercession of Moses, although his wrath was hot ;* and this partly because Moses showed a courage, a love, and an indifference to self which pleased God, but chiefly because as mediator he represented *the Mediator* who was to come (Ps. cvi. 23). Even so our Lord himself was heard for his devoutness (Heb. v. 7), his holiness (*ibid.* vii. 26), and his absolute self-sacrifice (*ibid.* ix. 14) ; and by virtue alike of what he was, and what he did, is the only Mediator between God and man (1 Tim. ii. 5 ; Heb. ix. 15).

7. *That God alone "pardoned," yet he pardoned " according to the word " of his servant Moses.* Even so in the highest sense " who can forgive sins but God only ? " (Mark ii. 7). Nevertheless, " God had given such power (*i. e.* authority) unto men," that the Divine pardon was bestowed on penitent sinners " according to the word " of Jesus (Matt. ix. 2, 6), and through him of his apostles (Matt. xviii. 18 ; John xx. 21—23 ; 2 Cor. ii. 10 ; cf. 2 Sam. xii. 13). Again, forgiveness of sin is no arbitrary thing, but bestowed only upon repentance and faith ; and *yet* it is bestowed " according to the word " of the humblest Christian (1 John v. 16 ; James v. 16 *b.*).

8. *That God's pardon did not cancel the temporal consequences of sin.* Israel, as Israel, was spared for a glorious future ; but the rebels as individuals were self-doomed to exile and destruction. Even so the pardoning love of God, although it saves the sinner, yet it does not abolish the natural consequence of his sin. Just as God's pardon to Israel allowed the young and innocent to grow up, while the old and stubborn died off, so in the renewed man the grace of God so quickens and strengthens the good that it gathers strength and courage while the evil dies slowly out. Nevertheless, the consequences of sin remain in body and mind, and even in soul. David never recovered his fall, either in outward fortunes (2 Sam. xii. 10) or in character (cf. 1 Kings i. 2 ; ii. 6, 9, &c.), or probably in peace of mind. Many Christians sin lightly, trusting always to repent and be forgiven, not knowing that every sin leaves some evil behind it.

HOMILIES BY VARIOUS AUTHORS.

Ch. xiii.—*The spies.* The tribes have at length reached the border of the promised land. Leaving the wilderness of Sinai, they have travelled northwards till they have reached Kadesh-barnea, a place situated in the Arabah, the long valley reaching from the Dead Sea to the Gulf of Akabah, and which may be said to be a prolongation of the Jordan valley southwards to the Red Sea. From Kadesh the people can see, rising before them towards the north-west, the steep ascent which leads into the hill country, the destined inheritance of the tribe of Judah. The march from Egypt, including the twelve months' sojourn in Horeb, has occupied only sixteen months; yet the tribes already stand on the threshold of the promised rest, and Moses is in high hopes that within a few weeks they will have taken possession of the long-expected inheritance. In this chapter we see the first appearance of the cloud which soon shrouded in darkness the fair prospect. Instead of going resolutely forward with the shining pillar of the Divine presence for their guide, the people desired to have the land "reported upon" by chosen men of their own company. These spies brought back a report which put the congregation in fear, and they refused to enter in. Observe—

I. WHERE THIS PROPOSAL TO SEND FORWARD SPIES ORIGINATED. Thirty-eight years later, Moses laid the blame of it on the people (Deut. i. 22). He adds, however, that "the saying pleased him well," and that it was agreed to without difficulty, so that the statement in the text which represents *the Lord* as directing the spies to be sent is quite consistent with the one in Deuteronomy. There was nothing in itself sinful in the people's proposal, and it received the Divine approval. Nevertheless, it was in the circumstances a doubtful project. It betrayed a lurking distrust of the Lord's promise and leadership. They wanted to see for themselves before committing themselves further. Prudence is without doubt a virtue. Before beginning to build our tower we are to count the cost (Luke xiv. 28). There are times when this needs to be earnestly preached. Men are apt to make great ventures for the world, rushing forward blindly enough. But let these same men be asked to venture much for God, they will be sufficiently cautious. They will sit down and count the cost; they will have the land diligently searched before invading it. Men do well to be prudent, provided only that they do not leave God's promise out of their calculations. Where God's command and promise are clearly given, the greatest boldness is the truest wisdom. When Paul received the command to pass over to Macedonia, and plant the Church of Christ in Europe, he did not send over Timothy and Luke to search out the land and see whether they and Silas and he were equal to the work. Had he done that, he never would have taken ship for Europe. Where God's command is clear, our wisdom is to venture upon great things for God, and to expect great things from God.

II. HOW THE PROPOSAL WAS CARRIED OUT. Twelve men were chosen, one for every tribe. These men, climbing the steep ascent from Kadesh, travelled through the thirsty south country (the *Negeb*) as far as to Hebron. From Hebron they went up by the brook Eshcol into the hill country, "the mountain of the Amorites," the long ridge midway between Jordan and the sea, which extends from the south country till it is lost among the roots of Lebanon. Every step in the journey opened up scenes of beauty and varied fruitfulness which must have delighted eyes accustomed only to the monotony of the Nile valley. It was a land flowing with milk and honey. The proof of its fertility they brought back with them. The cluster from Eshcol declared that the land was one worth fighting for. A trait this which has fixed itself for ever in the imagination of the Church. For are not these Eshcol grapes a figure of those foretastes of the Better Country which the Lord grants his people here in the wilderness? No doubt there was much to be said that was less promising. The country was exceedingly populous. The inhabitants belonged to many races, and everywhere there appeared tokens of highly-advanced civilisation. There had been great progress since Jacob went down to Egypt. There was much, therefore, to impress the spies with a sense of extreme difficulty in the task lying before the congregation. But the spies saw something which ought to have armed them against fear. They saw Hebron and that cave hard by which contained the bones of Abraham and Sarah, of Isaac and Rebekah, of Jacob and Leah; the cave where the progenitors of Israel were buried, in the sure and steadfast hope that the land would yet be the inheritance of their seed. They being dead were still speaking, and their testimony might well have put unbelief to shame.

III. THE TENOR AND EFFECT OF THE SPIES' REPORT. On one point the spies were unanimous. The land was good. Beyond that there was disagreement. 1. The *majority* kept harping on the difficulties they had discovered—the walled cities, the giants, the multitudes of people. They added, moreover, this, That the land ate up the inhabitants—a statement which probably refers to the circumstance (a remarkable one it is) that Palestine had been the meeting-place and battle-ground of many nations, where one nation had exterminated another. 2. The *minority* did not call in question the facts on which their brethren harped. But they set them in another light. Read ch. xiv. 7—9. And this suggests THE LESSON the story of the spies is fitted to teach. When God makes the way of duty plain, we must beware how we suffer our minds to dwell on the difficulties to be encountered. To do so will be apt simply to weaken our hands. " The fearful and unbelieving " have no portion in the heavenly city, but are shut out. Faith laughs at impossibilities, for it knows that in the Lord's strength it can do all things.—B.

Vers. 1—20.—*The mission of the spies.* I. THE ORIGIN OF THE MISSION. We know from Deut. i. 22 that this commandment of God followed on a resolution of the people. It was their wish that spies should go forth and tell them something of the way beforehand. And even Moses fell in with them. It would seem an easier thing to be meek than to take no thought for the morrow. Even Moses the servant of God must be taking up to-morrow's burdens before the time. How much better it would have been patiently and trustfully to wait upon the cloud and the trumpets! (ch. ix. 15—23 ; x. 1—10). But since the people's hearts are so, God sends the spies. The unfitness of Israel for immediate entrance into the promised land was showing itself more and more, and God sent these searchers, that in their searching both they and the people they represented might also be searched. May we not as it were detect a tone of rebuke and remonstrance in the words, " which I will give unto the children of Israel " ? The Israelites by demanding this mission were trying to guard themselves on a side that really needed no defence, while leaving themselves more and more exposed to all the perils of an unbelieving mind.

II. THE MEN WHO WERE SENT. Whether by choice of Moses or the people we are not told, but probably there was much careful consultation on the matter, *according to human wisdom.* Doubtless they seemed the best men for the purpose ; chosen for physical endurance, quickness of eye, tact in emergencies, and good judgment of the land and people. Yet some very important requisites were evidently not considered. Out of the twelve, only two were men of faith in God and deep convictions as to the destiny of Israel. A great deal depends on the sort of men we send in any enterprise for God. Believing and devout spirits can see prospects others cannot see, because they have resources which others have not. Perhaps in the whole nation there were not twelve men to be found of the right stamp in every particular, and even if they had been found, they might have failed in commanding popular confidence. We can easily imagine that Caleb and Joshua had not a very comfortable time with their colleagues, and that it was not a very easy matter to agree upon a report. But such as they were, they went forth. The people had come to depend on twelve limited minds like their own, each with its own way of looking at things, instead of on him who had already done such great things—the unchangeable One, the ample Providence, the sure Defence.

III. THE INFORMATION REQUIRED. Moses gives them their instructions (vers. 17—20), and they come from a man who is acting rather in accordance with the wishes of the people than in strict harmony with previous revelations from God. Had not God said to Moses, or ever the chains of Egypt were loosed, that he would bring his people into the land of the Canaanites, a land flowing with milk and honey, a land promised in solemn covenant to Abraham, Isaac, and Jacob, when as yet they were strangers in it? (Exod. iii. 17 ; vi. 3, 4). It was the people who, in their unbelief and carnal anxiety, wanted something in the way of human testimony. Let them, therefore, indicate such details of inquiry as in their opinion were necessary. They were like a suspicious buyer, who, not content with the word of the person from whom he makes his purchase, though he be a man of tried integrity, hunts round for all sorts of independent testimony, even from those who may have very doubtful capacity as witnesses. " A land flowing with milk and honey, is it ? See then if it be such a good land. See if the people appreciate its fertility by their cultivation of it. Observe the climate and the people themselves, if they be a strong, stalwart race, and numerous. Do they live peacefully among themselves, or in strongholds?" There was not a sentence in these instructions but threw some doubt on the wisdom, power, and faithfulness of Jehovah. When God sends out people to do such work as delights his heart, it is in a very different spirit; as he sent out the single stripling, unaccustomed to war, against the giant; as Jesus sent out the twelve on their gospel mission, encumbered with as few material resources as possible. The land to be searched was the land in which their honoured progenitors had lived; but there is no word to say, "Tell us of Bethel, and of the plain of Mamre, and the cave of Machpelah in Hebron." And to crown all, the result shows that they took all this trouble and waited these forty days for useless information. The fear of God is the beginning of wisdom.—Y.

Vers. 21—29.—*The search and the report.* I. THE SEARCH. The land passed over is indicated in a somewhat indefinite way. Contrast it with the definiteness of the tribal boundaries in Joshua (chs. xiii.—xix.). These were forty days of speculative and dangerous wandering, with no guiding cloud, though doubtless God protected them even when they felt not the protection; if for nothing else, for the sake of the faithful two who would yet serve his purposes and confirm his word. Forty days too of waiting in the wilderness of Paran—days, one may imagine, of much conjecture, full of apprehension to some, while by others many airy castles would be built, how soon to tremble at the first breath of God's approaching anger! Forty days was not much time to see even so small a land, geographically speaking, as Canaan. We know by our own land the ludicrous mistakes of travellers passing through it, and their sometimes serious mistakes; how they exalt exceptions into rules, and the eccentricities of the individual into the character and habits of the race. Live in a land, and then you shall report on it with the authority of experience. We have heard the story of the traveller who visited a Carthusian monastery in Italy. He admired the situation, and said to one of the monks, "What a fine residence!" "*Transeuntibus,*" was the sad, satiric reply. If we wish to know the fatness, the beauty, and the safety of the land in which God's people dwell, we must have something more than forty days of superficial rambling. It is not Saul, with eyesight lost, and waiting at Damascus, crushed in spirit, for Ananias, who shall tell us how Jesus is the Way, the Truth, and the Life; but rather such a one as Paul the aged, thirty years later, sounding from the fulness of his experience, "I know whom I have believed" (2 Tim. i. 12).

II. THE REPORT. After forty days they came back, bearing on a staff between two of them the cluster of grapes—bearing it thus, as some think, because of its weight; as others, that the fruit might keep its shapeliness and bloom. And, indeed, along with the pomegranates and figs, which were doubtless choice samples, this fruit was God's own beautiful testimony. Human messengers might differ and deceive, but these sweet silent messengers seemed to intimate that God had been making ready the land for his own people. So much for what the spies *brought in their hands.* But as to the *verbal report,* what a meagre thing it is! As to the quality of the land, they content themselves with saying, " Surely it floweth with milk and honey." Yes. God had said this very thing to Moses long before: it was the highest poetry of promise to speak thus; it was meant to excite large anticipations of something fertile and beautiful; but men who had been over the land for a personal inspection might have said something more prosaic and exact. Then as to the strong people, the walled towns, and the giants, God had indicated these very things as being in the future of his people, when he caused the fighting men to be numbered not long before. The report was meagre, we may well believe, because not otherwise could it have been unanimous. As long as they kept to certain bare facts, and did not proceed to advise, the spies could agree, and yet it very speedily appeared how hollow their agreement was. Caleb and Joshua had to strike out their own path, no longer wasting time in trying to sustain vain compromises.—Y.

Vers. 30—33.—*Conflicting counsels.* The report has been received, such as it is, and the next question comes: What shall be done? "Caleb stilled the people before Moses." This intimates the excitement and turbulence of their feeling. The chances are that a good deal of disparagement of Canaan had come to their ears, losing nothing as it passed from one tongue to another. Notice the *temporary effacement*, as it were, of Moses. It is Caleb who here takes the lead. Moses is nothing save as the mouth-piece of God, and the time is not quite ripe for God to speak. But Caleb, who, here as afterwards, shows himself a courageous man, prompt and ready, has formed his opinion, and at once expresses it; to be immediately followed by opinions just as decided in the opposite direction. We need not here so much to consider who was right and who wrong; God himself brings all out presently into the clearest of light. The great matter to be noticed is that the people were now exposed to conflicting counsels.

I. THESE CONFLICTING COUNSELS WERE THE CONSEQUENCE OF BACKSLIDING FROM GOD. The people had turned away from their true Guide, and the consequence of being in a wrong path very soon appears. God is *one*, and in his infinite wisdom and power can make all things work together for good to them that love him, and are called according to his purpose. But men are *many* and *diverse*, and if those who are called according to his purpose fall from the obedience which shows their love, how shall *they* make things work together for good? To God the scheme of human affairs is as a machine, complicated and intricate indeed, but well under control, and producing large results. To men it is, more or less, a maze of motions. They understand it a little in parts, but are hopelessly divided as to the meaning and service of the whole.

II. THE PREPONDERANCE IN THESE CONFLICTING COUNSELS WAS AGAINST THE COURSE WHICH GOD HAD ALREADY LAID OUT. God had promised the land, kept it before the people, and brought them to the very verge; yet ten out of twelve men—responsible men in the tribes, men who had journeyed through the land for forty days—declared that it was beyond the strength of Israel to obtain. What a satire on *vox populi vox Dei!* What a humbling revelation of the motives that work most powerfully in unregenerate human nature! How easy it is to exaggerate difficulties when one's heart is not in a work; to see, not everything that is to be seen, but only what the eye wants to see, and to see in a particular way! It is a part of spiritual prudence to reckon that, whatever strength there may be in mere numbers, in brute force and material appliances, they cannot be counted on in advancing the kingdom of God. With all these resources heaped up around them, craven spirits will still cry out that there is a lion in the way.

III. IT IS EVERYTHING TO RECOLLECT THAT THERE WERE CONFLICTING COUNSELS. Cowardice, carnality, and backsliding did not altogether get their own way. Things were bad enough, but after all Caleb and Joshua counted for a great deal on the other side. We must not only count men, but weigh them. There are times when it is no credit to men, when it says but little for their piety or their humanity, that they are found among majorities. It is the glory of God's cause on earth that it never loses its hold on at least a few. There is always a Caleb to fling to the wind considerations of base expediency.—Y.

Ch. xiv.—*They could not enter in because of unbelief.* Less than two years have passed since the congregation marched out of Egypt, yet already they stand at the threshold of the land of promise. Turning their gaze northward and westward from Kadesh, they see the hills which form the outworks of the famous and goodly mountain which is to be their inheritance. A crowd of joyous thoughts fill the hearts of Moses and the faithful at the sight. "Those hills belong to the land for which Abraham left his native country, and was content to be a sojourner all his days. They enclose the sepulchre in which the bones of the patriarchs were laid, in the sure hope that the land should yet be the inheritance of their seed. The promise has tarried long; it is now at the door. Ere the clusters of Eshcol shall have again ripened under the southern sun, the Canaanites will have been dispossessed, and we shall have been settled in their place." So Moses and the godly in Israel fondly thought. But they were doomed to disappointment. For thirty-eight years more the Canaanites were to dwell undisturbed. Moses and all the grown-up people were to die in the wilderness. How this came about the present chapter relates. The people refused to enter the land. The Lord took them at their word, and declared that they should not enter.

I. We see in this A SIGNAL INSTANCE OF A SORT OF FAILURE THAT IS NOT UN-COMMON.

> "There is a tide in the affairs of men
> Which, taken at the flood, leads on to fortune;
> Omitted, all the voyage of their life
> Is bound in shallows and in miseries."

This is a principle of God's government. He will open to men—to communities or individuals—a door leading straight to success. If they fail to discern their opportunity, or to take prompt advantage of it, the door is closed, and they are either shut out altogether, or enter after long delay and heavy toils. We must take the current when it serves. The Apostle Paul, himself an eminent example of the resolute promptitude he enjoins, used to say, " Redeem the time " (Eph. v. 16; Col. iv. 5), *i. e.* seize the occasion while it serves; lay hold on the opportunity. To know when to go forward is no small part of Christian wisdom; to go forward resolutely when the hour has come is no small part of Christian virtue.

II. More particularly, there is here A SIGNAL EXAMPLE OF UNBELIEF AND ITS WOEFUL FRUIT. In this instance the failure was not due merely to blindness or slackness; it sprang from disbelief of God's promise. " They could not enter in because of unbelief " (Heb. iii. 19). This is the Lord's account of the matter at the time. " How long will it be ere this people *believe* me, for all the signs which I have showed among them ? " (ver. 11). *Q. d.*, " Not only did I promise the land to their fathers, but to themselves I have showed great signs in Egypt, at the Red Sea, at Horeb, on the long march. After all this they might have believed my word; they might have trusted in me that, after having brought them so far, I would not now forsake them or fail to subdue the Canaanites before them. They do not believe my word; they do not trust me; hence their refusal to go forward." It is remarkable how exactly this fatal example of unbelief at the beginning of the Old Testament dispensation was repeated at its close. Read Heb. iii. 7—iv. 3. Among the many parallels with which history abounds, it would not be easy to find a parallel so close or instructive. When Christ came and the Spirit was given, the first offer of inheritance in the gospel Church was made to the Jews. The gospel was preached, " beginning at Jerusalem." The offer was not altogether fruitless. Thousands of Jews believed and thereupon entered into God's rest within the bosom of the Christian society. But, like Joshua and Caleb, they were in the minority. The great body of the people rejected Christ, and could not enter in because of unbelief. What was the consequence ? They were taken at their word. The doom was spoken : " They shall not enter into my rest." We believe, indeed, that the doom is not final. As the children of the unbelieving generation which fell in the wilderness entered Canaan under Joshua, so the Jews are one day to be saved. Still the doom has been a terrible one. For more than 1800 years the Jews have been pining in the wilderness. There is another view of the matter which comes home to every one to whom the gospel of the grace of God has been preached. Here is the lesson deduced in Ps. xcv. from the chapter in hand. " To-day, if you will hear his voice, harden not your heart." I can imagine that there may be amongst us some to whose hearts God has been speaking. He has taken you by the hand, has taught you something of the burden and foulness of sin, has made you sensible that worldly prosperity cannot give rest and satisfaction to the soul, has stirred in you desires after a worthier portion, has set before you Christ and his salvation. If this be so, do not let the matter remain undecided. Delays are dangerous. They provoke God's spirit. God has set before you an open door. It will not remain open for ever; it may not remain open long. When men will not hear Christ's invitation, " Come unto me, and I will give you rest," he does not go on repeating it for ever. He closes the door and says, " They shall not enter into my rest."—B.

Vers. 1—20.—*Moses standing in the breach, or the power of intercessory prayer.* The PRAYERS of the Bible open up a field of singularly interesting and instructive study. One thing particularly remarkable in them is that such a large proportion are intercessory. The earliest prayer of any length recorded in Scripture is that of

Abraham in Gen. xviii. It is an intercession for Sodom. It would seem that, while prayer of every kind is made welcome in heaven, a peculiarly gracious welcome is prepared for the prayers in which the petitioner forgets himself for the time, in the ardour of his desire for the good of others. It is in connection with the command to " pray one for another " that the assurance is given, " the effectual fervent prayer of a righteous man availeth much " (James v. 16). And one can perceive that the intercessory prayers of the Bible saints have been recorded in Scripture by the Holy Spirit with a peculiarly affectionate care. In this highest kind of prayer Moses excelled. During his long leadership of the people, dangers from without and murmurings from amongst the people themselves gave frequent occasion for deprecating God's wrath and invoking his help ; and Moses never failed to rise to such occasions. His intercessions are amongst the most instructive of any on record.

I. The occasion of the present prayer. The people have at length reached the threshold of the promised land ; but beyond the threshold they will not advance. Disbelieving the promise, they first insisted on sending spies ; and then, when the spies returned, they would hear only the bad report. They even proposed to stone Moses, choose a new leader, and go back to Egypt. They would not listen to Joshua and Caleb, and were only restrained by a threatening appearance of the Lord in the cloud above the tabernacle. So greatly was the wrath of God kindled, that he threatened to consume the congregation utterly, and raise up a more faithful people in their stead. " I will smite them ; I will disinherit them ; I will make of thee a greater nation and mightier than they." Moses may have been—I believe he was— unprepared for the incredible perversity of the present outbreak of rebellion ; but he was not unprepared for the threatening which it provoked. A similar outbreak had been followed with the same threatening at Sinai. And Moses did not fail to remember how, on that occasion, the threatened destruction had been averted by his intercession (Exod. xxxii. 7—14). So, now also, he with reverent boldness " stood before the Lord in the breach, to turn away his wrath, lest he should destroy them " (Ps. cvi. 23).

II. The prayer. It is summed up in one word, " *Pardon!* " (ver. 19). " Pardon, I beseech thee, the iniquity of this people." Forgive, yet this once, their perverse disobedience ; revoke the sentence pronounced against them ; fulfil thy promise by granting them the land.——I need not say more about this petition. The remarkable thing in the prayer is not what Moses asks, but the argument with which he enforces his request. First, *he pleads that the honour of God's great name is at stake.* The Lord had been pleased to put his name on the children of Israel. He had chosen them to be his special possession, making them the depositaries of his oracles and ordinances, and the witnesses for his truth. All this was now become matter of notoriety. In the mind of the nations round about the name of the Lord was identified with the seed of Abraham. Vers. 13—16, *q. d.*, " If the tribes perish here, the Egyptians will hear of it, and what will they think ? The signs wrought in their sight, both in Egypt and at the Red Sea, have taught them that thou, the God of Jacob, art the Most High, and that thou hast chosen Israel for thy people ; and the report of thy doings in Horeb, and by the way, have deepened the impression made by the Egyptian signs. Let not this salutary impression be effaced by discomfiture now. Let not Egypt from behind, and the Canaanites in front, shout in derision of thy great name."—I much fear that this argument does not usually find the place of prominence in our prayers that it finds here in Moses' prayer. The interest of God's name—his truth and cause—in the earth does not lie so near our hearts. Yet it certainly ought. " Hallowed be thy name " should get the place of honour in our prayers. More particularly, we ought to guard against everything which would bring reproach on true religion in the view of the outside world. Christians are to " walk in wisdom toward them that are without." There are still Egyptians and Canaanites watching to hear, and eager to spread, any report regarding the professed people of Christ which they think can be made use of to the disparagement of Divine truth and the Christian cause. Secondly, *Moses pleads the Lord's promise.* Along with vers. 17, 18 read Exod. xxxiv. 5—7. The reference cannot be mistaken. *Q. d.,* " Didst not thou show me thy glory in Horeb, and was not thy glory this, viz., that thou hast mercy ? Didst not thou declare to me that thy name is the Lord, the Lord God, merciful and gracious, forgiving iniquity and transgression? Into this name I will now run. In this name I take refuge. Remember thy word on which thou hast caused me to hope. Let thy name be now manifested in forgiving this people."——There is no encouragement in prayer to be compared with that which is got from the study of God's promises. "He hath said —therefore we may boldly say" (Heb. xiii. 5, 6). What God has promised to give, we may ask without wavering. Thirdly, *Moses pleads former mercies* (ver. 19). Next to the promise of God, the remembrance of former instances of kindness received in answer to prayer ministers encouragement to pray still, and not faint.—Such then was the prayer of Moses at Kadesh-barnea—the prayer which turned away the fatal sword of God's wrath from Israel. I am much inclined to think that instances of like success in prayer are not so rare as many suppose ; that, on the contrary, if an inspired historian were to write the annals of our families, churches, communities, it would be found that not seldom public judgments have been turned aside by the intervention of the Lord's hidden ones—his Noahs and Daniels and Jobs. When all secret things are brought to light, these intercessors will not fail to obtain recognition and reward.—B.

Vers. 3, 4.—*The sin and shame of apostasy.* The sin of the Israelites at this time is almost incredible. Their rash words (ver. 3) prompt to reckless resolutions (ver. 4), which, if not actually carried out, are laid to their charge (Neh. ix. 17). Their crime includes the following sins :—1. *Criminal forgetfulness,* as though the bondage of Egypt were better than warfare under "Jehovah Nissi" (Exod. xvii. 15). 2. *Gross ingratitude.* They imply that God has spared them and cared for them thus far in order to destroy them at last. 3. *Shameful distrust,* notwithstanding all the promises God has given, and the "signs" of his faithfulness he has shown (ver. 11). 4. *Obstinate disobedience*—a stubborn disregard of the word and will of their God. 5. *Utter madness.* In returning to Egypt they must part company with Moses their leader and Aaron their priest. They must abandon the ark and the altar. They could not expect the manna to feed them or the cloud to guide them. And if they ever reached Egypt, what a reception would meet them there! All these sins are seen in a still more glaring form in the shameful crime of apostasy from Christ. Such a "drawing" back to perdition implies a previous coming near to Christ, and an enjoyment of blessings analogous to the covenanted blessings of ancient Israel (Exod. xix. 3—6 ; xxiv. 4—8). In apostasy we see—1. Criminal forgetfulness of the bondage of evil habits, the burden of an uneasy conscience, the yearnings of unsatisfied desire, and all the other evils from which we looked to Christ to deliver us. How can it be "better to return" to these? 2. Gross ingratitude to God for all the blessings enjoyed during the Christian pilgrimage so far ; as though such a God could fail or forsake us, and not "perfect that which concerneth us," as all his previous blessings are a pledge that he will do (Ps. cxxxviii. 8 ; Rom. viii. 32). 3. Shameful distrust. "An evil heart of unbelief" is generally the primary cause of departing from God (Heb. iii. 12). Distrust makes us weak against temptations even of the grossest kind. We may lose courage amid foes or temptations which, but for shameful want of confidence in God, would have little power to alarm and divert us from the path of duty (cf. Ps. xxvii. 1—3 ; cxviii. 6—12, and, in contrast, 1 Sam. xxvii. 1). 4. Obstinate disobedience. For we are "under law to Christ ; " and "*his will* is our sanctification," our perseverance, our conflict and victory till we reach the heavenly Canaan (1 Thess. iv. 3 ; 1 Tim. vi. 11—14 ; Heb. iii. 14 ; vi. 12). 5. Utter madness ; for to "draw back" is to forfeit the fellowship of Christ's Church, the tokens of his favour, his promises, his consolations, and the good-will of God. To succeed is perdition (Heb. x. 26—39).—P.

Vers. 8, 9.—*With God on our side we are in the majority.* Caleb and Joshua here describe—

I. THE CONDITIONS ON WHICH WE MAY EXPECT GOD TO BE WITH US. 1. The unmerited good pleasure of God. "If the Lord delight in us." This is repeatedly mentioned as the origin of God's favour to the Israelites (Deut. iv. 37 ; vii. 7, 8, &c.) and to Christians (Eph. i. 3—6 ; 2 Tim. i. 9, &c.). Only provided that this good pleasure is not forfeited by obstinate disobedience or distrust. So that the second condition is—2. Obedience. "Only rebel not," &c. That generation sinned away the favour of God, though it could not annul his faithfulness. 3. Confidence in God. "Neither fear ye the people." To fear them was to distrust God (Isa. viii. 13, 14; Heb. xiii. 6, &c.).

II. THE CERTAIN SUCCESS OF THOSE WHO ENJOY THE HELP OF GOD. Caleb and Joshua express their confidence in various ways; *e. g.* in ch. xiii. 30 (*"veni, vidi, vici"*); ver. 8, "he will bring us in;" ver. 9, "bread for us," &c. The Canaanites dwelt in fortresses, but God, their strength, was departed from them. Israel dwelt in tents, but Prov. xviii. 10. Such confidence we may have, when opposed by foes, human or diabolical, however numerous or powerful. With God on our side we are in the majority (Illus. Exod. xiv. 13; 2 Kings vi. 16; 2 Chron. xiv. 11; xx. 12; xxxii. 7, 8; Ps. xlvi. 11; Rom. viii. 31, &c.). A good illustration may be found in a letter of the Prince of Orange after the fall of Haarlem, in which he says, "Before ever I took up the cause of the oppressed Christians in these provinces I had entered into a close alliance with the King of kings," &c. (Motley's 'Rise of the Dutch Republic,' Pt. III. ch. ix.).—P.

Vers. 11—19.—*Skilful intercession.* The crowning act of unbelief on the part of the Israelites at Kadesh brings God into their midst in righteous anger. He remonstrates (ver. 11) and threatens (ver. 12). God's foreknowledge of Moses' prayer did not prevent this apparently absolute threat. This need be no difficulty to us, unless we hold opinions about God which would make the government of free, moral beings by promises and threats impossible. For illustrations of Divine words or acts contingent on human actions see 2 Kings xx. 1—11; Luke xxiv. 28, 29; Acts xxvii. 22—24, 31. Moses stands in the breach, and skilfully urges two motives, suggested by—I. HIS ZEAL FOR THE HONOUR OF GOD. II. HIS FAITH IN THE MERCY OF GOD.

I. (vers. 13—16). The Egyptians would soon "make comedies out of the Church's tragedies." Our best pleas are founded on the prayer, "Hallowed be thy name." *E. g.* 1. In pleading for a highly-favoured but guilty nation. After all God has done for Britain and by it, may we not feel as though it would be a dishonour on the Christian name and a reflection on the Christian's God if we were altogether cast off. Our plea is Jer. x. 24, and our hope is Jer. xxx. 11. 2. In pleading for a fallen Christian. 3. Or for ourselves (Ps. lxxix. 9; Jer. xiv. 7, &c.). God feels the power of this motive (Deut. xxxii. 27; Ezek. xx. 9, 14). God is not, like some men, indifferent to his own reputation (Isa. xlviii. 11).

II. Note how skilfully Moses uses God's own declaration of his name in Exod. xxxiv. He appeals (1) to the *pure mercy* of God; (2) to the *past mercies* of God (Ps. xxv. 6, 7; li. 1; Isa. lv. 7, 8).—P.

Vers. 22, 23.—*A priceless privilege offered, refused, lost.* The lessons from the narrative of chs. xiii. and xiv. may be summed up as follows. We see here a priceless privilege—

I. OFFERED. It is Canaan, "the glory of all lands," the gift of the God of their fathers, who redeemed them from Egypt that he might bring them to a land of liberty and rest. The first report of the spies (ch. xiii. 27—29) is true in itself, but its style suggests faithless fears which infect the congregation (ch. xiii. 30). The exaggerated or false reports that are now given (ch. xiii. 31—33) increase the panic, but God's offer is still before them (2 Tim. ii. 12).

II. REFUSED. The shades of evening were gathering when the report of the spies was delivered. (Sketch the spread of the panic during the night, ch. xiv. 1.) In the morning the murmurings take a definite form (vers. 2—4). The cogent reasonings of Caleb and Joshua are in vain (vers. 6—9). They threaten to depose Moses, and to stone the faithful witnesses, and they deliberately reject the offer of God. Thus are sinners wont to believe lies and distrust true witnesses; to assent to fallacies and resist the soundest arguments; to neglect or persecute their best friends, and distrust and rebel against their Redeemer, God.

III. LOST. God interposes to protect his servants and sentence the rebels. Moses' intercession saves them from immediate destruction, but not from irremediable loss. There are limits to the power of intercessory prayer (Jer. xv. 1; 1 John v. 16). A new panic, another night of weeping (ver. 39). On the morrow a reaction, a revulsion of feeling, but not a repentance of heart (cf. 1 Sam. xv. 30). What was impossible yesterday is practicable to-day (ver. 40). But they go without the prayer of Moses (ch. x. 35) or the presence of God (ver. 44). The mountain pass is impregnable. It is too late. The offer is lost to that generation. Their opportunity has been sinned away. Defeat and death await them (Isa. xlii. 24, 25). These truths applicable—1. To the offer of spiritual conquests to the Church. The Church of Christ often on the borders of a land promised to our conquests. Unbelief suggests fears, our enemies' strength, our own weakness, &c. Gradually faith in our own power may depart, because faith in God is lost. While others are useful we may be ciphers in the Church. Special excitement, or the pricks of conscience, may incite us to make spasmodic efforts; but the faculty for Christian service may be wellnigh extirpated by disuse (Matt. xxv. 29). 2. To the offer of a present salvation to the sinner. Christian Calebs bring a good report of God's promised land of rest; but indecision or unbelief may forfeit it (Heb. iii. 19).—P.

Ver. 28.—*Fatal answers to faithless prayers.* The faithless prayer was heard by God when the people murmured (ver. 2). Now the answer comes to their own destruction. Apply to—1. Reckless transgressors, who brave the consequences of their sins. Illustration—Jews (Matt. xxvii. 25), who, however, soon, dreaded the answer (Acts v. 28; cf. Prov. i. 31). 2. The discontented. *E. g.* Rachel (Gen. xxx. 1; xxxv. 19); Hebrews lusting for flesh (ch. xi. 18—20), or desiring a king (1 Sam. viii. 6—22; Hosea xiii. 11; cf. Prov. xii. 13). 3. Profane swearers imprecating damnation and receiving it (Ps. lix. 12; lxiv. 8; Matt. xii. 36). 4. Distrustful servants of God, who, in haste, may proffer requests which, if granted, would leave a stain on their memories, if not actually fatal to their reputation. *E. g.* Moses (ch. xi. 15); Elijah (1 Kings xix. 4); Jonah (iv. 3). What thanks are due to God that in his mercy he does not always answer our prayers, implied or expressed! And how much we need the teaching and the spirit of Christ, that we may pray thoughtfully and trustfully, and that he may not have to say to us, "Ye know not what ye ask" (Mark x. 35—40).—P.

Vers. 1—3.—*A repentance to be repented of.* I. As WE CONSIDER HOW IT WAS CAUSED. 1. *By the fears of an all-devouring selfishness.* Selfishness swallowed up every other consideration. Their vexation was caused not by the stirrings of a guilty conscience, but by suffering and fleshly loss. All they wanted was the suffering taken away. There was not the slightest sign of shame and penitence and return to God with fruits meet for repentance. Self-will was as strong in this night of weeping as it had been in the day when they proposed to send the spies (Deut. i. 22). 2. *By a false report.* How many are terrified by representations of religion as far from the truth as what the spies said of Canaan! Even where there is nothing malevolent or base in purpose, the difficulties of religion may be set forth as if it were all the valley of the shadow of death from end to end, and heaven a mere peradventure at the last. These Israelites were given over to strong delusion that they should believe a lie. Selfishness was the source of all their weeping, and a false report brought it forth. Such views of religion, got upon such representations, will have to be changed, or there can be no real return to God, no real achievement of the rest of his people.

II. As WE CONSIDER HOW IT WAS EXPRESSED. 1. *In unjust complaints of their leaders.* Moses and Aaron were neither of them faultless, far from it, but their faults were such as God marked, and not rebellious men. These faults the people had no notion of, nor would it have mattered if they had. A Moses less faithful to God, more indulgent to their whims and caprices, would have suited them better. They blamed Moses when they should have praised him, and it was his highest glory that there was nothing about him they could praise. 2. *In frenzied references to themselves.* They speak as men with all judgment, self-control, and self-respect clean gone out of them. They were not in a state of mind to form a right estimate of anything whatever. "The mind must retain its full strength when engaged on such a work as repentance." 3. *Their rash reproaches against God.* There was but one thing they said of him that was true. He had indeed brought them into this land.

Certain it is that they could never have found their way so far themselves. But their present strait was none of his bringing. It had come through unbelief, cowardice, and lying. Men have low, miserable views of what is good for themselves, and the end is blasphemous language with respect to the all-loving, all-wise-God above. He knew far better than they how to protect their wives and children.

III. As we consider how the folly of it was exposed. Everything went contrary to their anticipations. The men who brought up the evil report died by the plague before the Lord. This was in itself a clear intimation of their wickedness in misleading the people. Caleb and Joshua stood out, vindicated both as wise counsellors and speakers of the truth. Canaan was all they had represented it to be, but this thankless, rebellious generation should have no personal experience of it. They were indeed to die in the wilderness, gradually dropping off for forty years, and the children whose impending fate they deplored, themselves entered the land of which their fathers had shown themselves unworthy. Forty years! Who can tell how many during that time may have sought carefully, with tears, and in due time found, a place of true repentance and godly sorrow? Not able to enter the earthly Canaan, any more than Moses, Aaron, or Miriam, they may still have found their part in the heavenly one.—Y.

Ver. 4.—*A vain proposition.* Very briefly and comprehensively put, with an appearance of decision and unanimity, but nevertheless utterly vain with respect to both matters mentioned in it.

I. The making of a captain. They could call a man a captain, but that would not make him one. The power of election may be a great privilege, but it is greater negatively than positively. No election can make a fool into a wise man, or a coward into a hero, any more than it can make the moon give the light of the sun, or thorns to produce grapes. Election may give a man opportunity only to show decisively that he is not able to use it. On the other hand, no election can give the most capable of men the power to do impossibilities. *Captains are not made in this way at all.* The true captain is he who, having been faithful in that which is least, finds his way on by natural attraction to that which is greater. He is not so much elected as recognised. There is much significance from this point of view in Christ's words: "Ye have not chosen me, but I have chosen you." The Israelites had rejected the word of the Lord and the leader he had chosen, and what wisdom was there in them to find a better leader for themselves? Even as God, for his own purposes, chooses men after his own heart, such as his penetrating, unerring eye sees can be trained and fashioned in the right way, so men make choice after their hearts only to show their folly and ignorance, and that oftentimes right speedily. The true election is to elect ourselves to follow the good, the true, the noble, and the wise, and only them so far as they are plainly following Christ (Heb. xii. 1—4).

II. The return to Egypt. The land they had been through and knew was even less accessible than the unvisited land of which they had such exaggerated fears. Where should they get provision without God to give them manna? and would not Egypt be even more hostile than Canaan? By this time the name Israel had become connected in the Egyptian mind with disaster of every sort. What sort of men then were these to talk of the welfare of wife and children when they proposed a step which would bring them into the direst destitution? Even while they spoke God was sustaining them and their families with bread from heaven. It was even from his manna that these rebels were made strong against him. Proud-hearted, vain, conceited man will propose the most silly ventures rather than submit to God. He is the last refuge, in more senses than one, of the perplexed. Anywhere, into any absurdity and refuge of lies, rather than give up the darling lusts of the heart, and face the necessities of true repentance. Every man is trying to return to Egypt who, having been disappointed in one earth-born hope, straightway proceeds to indulge another. It is poor work, when we find ourselves checked by difficulties in living a better life, to give up in despair. To make the future as the past is impossible; it must either be better or worse. God helps the man who steadily and strenuously keeps his face towards Canaan.—Y.

Ver. 5.—*A mute appeal.* I. THERE COMES A TIME WHEN ALL EXPOSTULATION WITH MEN IS VAIN, at all events the expostulation of certain people. Moses felt no word he could say would be of the slightest use. In vain you throw the pearls of truth and soberness before the swinish multitude, and it is the humbling testimony of history that only too often men get so embruted in their prejudices and passions as to be for all purposes of rational action little better than swine. Caleb and Joshua spoke, only to be threatened with stones. Moses and Aaron make no attempt to speak, but fall on their faces before all the assembly. What the seventy elders were about all this time we know not. When even Moses has to be silent it is little wonder their presence should count for nothing. We need to recollect this madness and perversity of men, this ease and rapidity with which human passion mounts to the violence of a hurricane. The reasonableness of human nature is far too frequently glorified. There was a time when Paul's converts in Galatia would have plucked out their eyes, and given them to him; yet as years pass on, and they listen to another gospel, which is not another, he has to mourn that he seems to have become their enemy because he tells them the truth (Gal. iv. 15, 16).

II. But when we can do nothing for men directly, WE MUST NOT, therefore, WAIT IN COMPLETE INACTION. Moses was obliged to be silent in words; not even to God does he seem to have spoken; but he fell to the ground in mute and humble appeal. There, prostrate before the tabernacle, were Moses and Aaron, the leader and the priest, brethren according to the flesh, united now by deep affliction, if a little while ago they were separated by envy. Nor was the lowly attitude simply an appeal to God; it might have effect on some *of the better sort among the multitude,* finding a way to the heart by the eye, which for the time was not open by the ear. Neither was the appeal simply *for the sake of Moses and Aaron.* The people had treated them badly, but this was a small matter compared with their treatment of God. How often we fume over injustice to ourselves, utterly forgetting the great world's huge and light-hearted negligence of him who made and redeemed it. Consider Martha, complaining so bitterly of Mary, while she herself was refusing the true hospitality to Jesus. A man with the mind of Christ Jesus in him will be always more affected by slights upon the Saviour than upon himself.

III. There is always then this one thing we can do in the turmoil of human affairs: we CAN RECOGNISE WITH DEEP HUMILITY THE AWFUL PRESENCE OF GOD. As we are driven into a sense of utter helplessness, let us think of him from whom, and by whom, and to whom are all things. It is only when we are humbled before him, and recollect his love and power in Christ, that we can be calm in the presence of the awful problems of human existence. How much better off was Moses in his extremity than the Israelites in theirs! They rejected Moses and the tabernacle to speak vain words about returning to Egypt; he, shut out as it were from service to them, found his sure refuge in prostration before God (Ps. xlvi. 1—3).—Y.

Vers. 6—10.—*Speaking out: a last appeal.* Moses is *silent* from necessity, his power with men in abeyance, and he waiting humbly upon God. Joshua and Caleb, who were not only men of a different spirit, but also very imperfectly acquainted with Moses' peculiar burden, *spoke out.* As it was well for Moses and Aaron to be silent, it was also well for Caleb and Joshua to speak out. Moses and Aaron were for the time separated, forsaken, and as it were condemned; but Caleb and Joshua are still in the multitude—Caleb indeed partly declared, and only waiting further opportunity to speak his mind fully on the subject. Now Joshua and he take their stand without any hesitation or chance of being mistaken. They had something to say which Moses could not say, for they had been through the land. Thus, when God's servant is compelled to be silent, friends arise to say what is right and just. Consider—

I. THE MANNER OF THE SPEAKERS. "They rent their clothes." This was the symbol of hearts rent with grief and astonishment because of impending disaster. To the Israelites their only hope appeared in retracing their steps. To Caleb and Joshua this was the summary and utter extinction of a great opportunity. The multitude looked on Canaan as worse than the grave, a scene of vain struggles and harassing privations. Caleb and Joshua looked on the multitude as threatening the unutterable folly of drawing back from certain and inestimable blessings when they lay within their reach. Therefore they accompanied their speech with an action that indicated the distress and laceration of their hearts. Truth may do such things naturally in the very vehemence and consistency of its onset. We do not read that the spies who brought up a slander on the land rent their clothes while they were telling their story. Hypocrisy must always be careful in its histrionics not to overdo the thing.

II. THE MATTER OF THEIR SPEECH. *They give the testimony of experience.* They had passed through the land to search it. Although they were only two against ten who told a different story, yet, strong in the consciousness of sincerity and competency, they declared what they had seen with their eyes, looked upon, and handled. Though their testimony would not have been enough for some purposes, yet it was quite enough to throw as a check in the way of revolted Israel. *They emphatically assert the goodness of the land.* It was a land to be desired, corresponding to all the promises made and the hopes cherished, worth all the struggling and self-denial that might be needed in order to attain it. *They show a devout recognition of Jehovah.* This alone might make their word, though only two, outweigh the exaggerations of the other ten. The recognition shows itself in two ways. 1. They avow the necessity of his favour. " If the Lord delight in us ; " that means, surely, " If we believe in the Lord." That which delights the Lord is to see men walking by faith, and not by sight, stepping forward into the darkness upon his clear command. Caleb and Joshua felt sure, from what they had seen of the fatness and beauty of Canaan, that God wished to delight in his people, if only they would allow it. 2. They avow the necessity of submission to God. Unbelief is not only separation, it is rebellion. This was the real danger of Israel—rebellion against God's appointments and restrictions. By their present conduct they were strengthening the nations of Canaan with more than all their walled cities, giants, and strong men could give them. *They show that the Canaanites are really very weak.* There is nothing more fallacious than outside show and casual inspection. The spies had brought some fruit, and doubtless tasted much more ; but how could they report adequately on defences which they could not examine in any accurate way ? They did not know how all these people were undermined and enervated by their wickedness. The very wealth of the land became a curse and corrupting influence to the idolaters who dwelt in it. Wicked nations in the midst of all their boasting and revelry are preparing their own destruction.

III. THE RESULTS OF THEIR SPEECH. 1. *The exasperation of the people reaches its highest pitch.* " All the congregation bade stone them with stones." This was the punishment which God had appointed for serious transgressions (Levit. xx. 2, 27 ; xxiv. 14 ; Numb. xv. 35 ; Deut. xiii. 10, &c.). And now the people adopt it, numbering Caleb and Joshua with transgressors against their sovereign will. If we speak the truth, all of it, and at the time when it should be spoken, we must be ready for the consequences. The two faithful witnesses would certainly have been stoned, as Zechariah long after (2 Chron. xxiv. 21), but—2. *God himself interfered.* "The glory of the Lord appeared," &c. In a moment, in the twinkling of an eye, the rebels were reduced to impotence. One can imagine the uplifted stone dropped, as if it had turned to a blazing coal. Israel may still be sullen and rebellious in *heart,* but its *hand* is in the power of God. He can rescue his servants from the power of their enemies, if that be most expedient. Caleb and Joshua still had much work to do. Or, as happened to Stephen, he can turn the unchecked fury of men into the agent of a quick and glorious dismission from the toils and perils of earthly service. In God's house the more manifest the faithfulness of the servant, the more manifest also the faithfulness of the Master.—Y.

Vers. 11, 12.—*The Lord breaks silence.* It was time now for the people to be silent. They had talked and acted enough of folly. The Lord asks certain questions, and follows them with certain propositions. We can hardly call them determinations, but rather suggestions of action, such as may be further modified, if modifying considerations can be introduced.

Ver. 11.—*God implies that it is useless to wait any longer.* It is not a question of whether he is long-suffering, but whether the long-suffering will answer any good

end. He had been engaged, as it were, in a solemn experiment with the liberated
Israelites, and the experiment was now complete. No further knowledge could be
gained, and no change in the direction of trust and obedience could be hoped for,
from longer waiting. To wait, therefore, was only to waste time and simulate long-
suffering. It must be plain to every one who will consider carefully, that the
Israelites had shown by their conduct the great distance that the calamity of human
nature's fall has placed between men and God. God knows the distance ; it is we
who deny it or trifle with it. This experiment with *one generation* was not for the
information of God himself, but to instruct and impress *all generations*. Israel,
unconsciously, was helping to lay a foundation in history for the great doctrine of
regeneration. "Except a man be born *again,* he cannot see the kingdom of God "
(John iii. 3). Here is a generation, *not born again,* but taken in *the ordinary course
of nature.* Nothing is done to alter *them,* but a complete change is made in their
circumstances. Liberated from the thraldom of oppressors, they are brought under
authority of the law of God, holy and just and good. That law follows them into
every hour of life. And the result of all proves that a man cannot by such strength
and disposition as nature gives him inherit the kingdom of God. This generation
was not fit even for the earthly Canaan. That land was no place for carnal minds
to indulge their own inclinations. The people were not fit, and the unfitness is now
perfectly clear. As they lift up the stones against Caleb and Joshua the experiment
is complete. Hence we see the language of God here is in perfect consistency with
all the Scripture that emphasises the fact of his long-suffering. It still remains a
duty of man, as it is an undoubted and gracious disposition of God, to forgive unto
seventy times seven. Recollect, further, that God was dealing *with these Israelites
as a whole.* What his relation was to each as a man, and not simply as an Israelite,
is hardly to be considered here. The great lesson of Jehovah's questionings in this
verse may be stated in the words of Jesus : "That which is born of the flesh is flesh,
and that which is born of the Spirit is spirit."

Ver. 12.—*God makes three propositions.* 1. *As to the fate of the unbelieving
nation.* "I will smite them with the pestilence." If Israel is to perish, it shall not
be at the hands of some other nation, which may thus glorify and exalt itself. The
occasion is one on which, if a blow is to be struck, it must be a *manifestly supernatural one,* even as in the Deluge or the destruction of Sodom. The destruction,
too, shall be sudden. The people shall not be left to wander and droop and die in
the wilderness. The disease which comes from sin and works out death shall have
its energy concentrated in one swift tremendous blow. 2. *As to the aspect in which
this visitation is to be regarded.* " I will disinherit them." God looked on Israel as
the legitimate and responsible heir to Canaan. It was considered as Abraham's land,
by a solemn covenant, even when he was a stranger in it (Gen. xii. 7 ; xiii. 14—17 ; xv.
7, 18—21 ; xvii. 8). The aspect of Canaan as an inheritance was still further confirmed in Isaac as the child of promise, and Jacob as acquirer of the birthright. But
in spite of all this, Israel obstinately refused to make ready for the great inheritance.
The heirs to high rank and great possessions in this world are watched with great
solicitude. Hereafter they will not only have great means for indulgence, but great
opportunities for good and evil. And sometimes a parent, with deep pain of heart,
will feel compelled to disinherit an unworthy son. This word "disinherit," rightly
considered, puts a tone of inexpressible sadness into this verse. Recollect that tone
as well as words, manner as well as matter, has to be considered in listening to any
judicial sentence of God. A sceptic talking with Dr. Channing reproached Jesus
Christ for what he called his angry denunciations in Matt. xi. 20—24. In answer,
Channing opened the New Testament, and read the passages referred to aloud. As
soon as he had finished, his hearer said, " Oh, if that was the tone in which he spoke,
it alters the case." 3. *As to the future of Moses.* " I will make of thee a greater
nation, and mightier than they." Here is the suggestion of another experiment.
Abraham was an eminent believer. Against all his shortcomings and infirmities in
other respects, and they are very plain, his faith stands out in relief, conspicuous,
almost colossal, one may say, in its manifestations. Nevertheless, his descendants
turned out utter unbelievers. Take away from them for a single moment the light
of things seen and temporal, and they become frantic and rebellious as a child left

alone in the dark. And now God seems to suggest that *possibly the seed of Moses may prove of a better sort.* Thus we have in the propositions of this verse what we may call alternative suggestions. They show what things might, conceivably, and not unjustly, have happened at this critical turning-point.—Y.

Vers. 13—19.—*Moses' view of the position.* God has presented some of the considerations which needed to be presented; Moses now presents others; and all taken together produce the decision actually arrived at. What God had said it was not for Moses to say, and so what Moses said it was not for God to say; nevertheless, all needed to be said.

I. NOTE THE CHARACTER IN WHICH MOSES CHIEFLY APPEARS. His first words indicate a concern for the reputation of Jehovah among the nations, and it would be wrong to suppose that this was not a matter of real concern, but it is evident the chief thought in his mind was how to secure mercy for rebellious Israel. *He is the intercessor.* All considerations he can appropriately urge are urged with the ingenuity of one who feels the calamity of others as his own. He is consistent here with past appearances on similar occasions.

II. NOTE THE CONSIDERATIONS WHICH HE URGES. 1. *He makes no attempt to extenuate the wickedness of the people.* He can say nothing by way of excuse. He does not plead as Abraham concerning Sodom, on the chance of a righteous remnant being found in the multitude. He does not distinctly plead for another trial, like the dresser in the vineyard (Luke xiii. 8, 9). The sin was fresh, patent, monstrous, coming as the climax of so much that had gone before. He does not attempt to make the sin of the people look less than the sin of the spies, but leaves all in its enormity. So we may say it is better for us not to go excusing self, when too often excuse but adds to existing sin. Our danger is to under-estimate our sin, to think of our sorrows and trials rather than our disobedience and ingratitude. God knows what may be said for us. At all times, and in all our transgressions, *he* remembers that we are dust. Let us rather aim to get a due sense of how much, how very much, needs to be done in us to make us holy and perfect. 2. *He makes God's reputation among surrounding nations a matter of great concern.* In God's government of the world, the consideration of his *real glory* is ever to be kept in view, and this of course is not dependent on what any man may think. Nevertheless, what men may think and say is by no means to be neglected. Whatever is done, some will criticise and jeer. Strange things have been said, and are said still, concerning the God revealed in the history of Israel. A monster of hideous attributes is conjured up and represented as the Deity of the Hebrews. Now as among men it is a consideration that their good should not be evil spoken of, if they can possibly arrange it otherwise, so, reverently be it said, a similar consideration may be present to God when he reveals himself in human affairs. What he said here asserted that there was *no need for further probation of these Israelites.* What Moses now suggests is that there was *no need to cut them down at once,* and good reason to do otherwise, so as to stop the mouth of Egypt and the nations of Canaan. 3. *One more act of mercy would be consistent with God's character.* God had said, upon the making of the two tables to replace the former two (Exod. xxxiv.), that though he could not treat iniquity as a trifle, and must ever stamp on it signs of the serious way in which he regarded it, yet he was a God merciful and gracious, and disposed to pardon. Moses now humbly reminds God of these words, and pleads an application of them to the present transgression. He does not seem to have meant much by the word *pardon;* it was simply that God might turn away the pestilence. Indeed, for anything more it was not in the power of Moses to ask. A full pardon, a full reconciliation to God, these demand, as a pre-requisite, full repentance. And so far Israel had made no sign. Perhaps the people were dumb and stupefied with terror. Other people may ask pardon for us in a certain sense, but such pardon as will be complete can only come from the cry of awakened, enlightened, and truly penitent souls.—Y.

Vers. 20—23.—*The ultimate decision.* I. THE EXTENT OF THE BOON WHICH GOD GRANTED. "I have pardoned according to thy word." God gave all that Moses asked, and all that in the light of his former words (vers. 11, 12), he could give. But what did it come to ? Nominally, it might be called a pardon ; in reality it came to no more than a reprieve. It did not put Israel where it was before. It was a boon, so far as it is a boon to a man condemned to die when he is told that his sentence is commuted to penal servitude for life. To him trembling under the shadow of the scaffold it may seem an inestimable mercy. So here Israel may have counted it the same to have been delivered from the pestilence. So a man will esteem recovery from a critical illness or the near chance of sudden death. Yet what has such a boon come to ? Death and the demands of eternity are only put off a little into the future. We have not escaped them ; we are pressed on towards them ; every day of life narrows the distance, and at any moment the distance may be swept altogether away.

II. God secures that he shall be glorified in the bestowing of the boon. "All the earth shall be filled with the glory of the Lord." As much as to assure Moses that he need not be in the least apprehensive. The nations of Canaan should have no cause for exultation, nothing to enable them to glorify their gods against Jehovah. They should have one pretext the less, if only one. There would be no chance to sneer at the swift destruction of Israel, as if it had come from one of the passionate and revengeful deities of Paganism. Still, if there was one pretext the less, there was only one. The removal of one pretext only opens up to the prejudiced and carnal mind the vision of another. The world will always have something to say against God, whithersoever the ways of his providence or his grace may tend. And so it is good for us to take the assurance he gave to Moses. All the earth, in a wider sense than Moses understood, shall be filled with the glory of God ; for not only the kingdom and the power are his, but also and emphatically the glory. There will come a day when the most ingenious and admired criticism of men on the ways of God will be shrivelled into everlasting oblivion before the full blaze of that glory.

III. He secures in particular that he shall be glorified in Israel. What Israel might think of him now it was spared was a matter of more immediate importance than what the nations might think. There was to be no opportunity for them to say, "This is a God who threatens, and yet when the pinch comes, the terrible blow is withdrawn." The people were to behold both his goodness and his severity. He magnifies their sin before the eyes of Moses, and there was the more need to do so when he was sparing the transgressors. The mere lapse of time neither diminishes the impression made by sin on God himself, nor the destructive power of it on the transgressor. Repented and forsaken sins are blotted out, but a recurrence of them, and that in a more flagrant way, brings them back, and illustrates what an inveterate and ingrained thing sin has become. When Whately was principal of St. Alban's Hall, he would sometimes say after some escapade of an undergraduate, "I pardon this as a first offence, and I do not wish to remember it. I will not unless you force me to do so. But recollect that if you commit a second, I must remember the first." So God had to call up everything from the beginning of his wonders in Egypt: on the one hand, all his glory and miracles, and impressive commands and promises; on the other hand, their persistent indifference, disobedience, and unbelief. Let them therefore understand, that even though they be spared, they cannot see Canaan. This is all the Lord says at present, but it is enough to secure that he shall be glorified in Israel.

IV. The great practical lesson to us is, that we should be very observant of the signs of God's presence with us, and promptly obedient to the God who is revealed in them. Of how many it may truly be said, that they travel through life unobservant of God's wonderful works to them, and tempting him many times ! What a terrible thought, that as the fate of this generation was fixed, though some of them lived well-nigh forty years after, so the fate of many may be fixed even before they die—probation ended, though earthly existence may continue ; dead even while they live ! While still in vigorous health of body, and active in all worldly concerns, the last faint trace of spiritual sensibility may have passed away. Doing perhaps what they reckon to be good, and what is good in a certain way, they nevertheless miss the great end of life, because faith in the Son and in the Father who sent him has never been allowed to enter their minds (Rom. ii., xi. 20—22).—Y.

Ver. 24.—*The promise to Caleb.* - God grants the prayer of Moses for the people, and makes clear how small a boon it is by notifying at the same time their necessary exclusion from Canaan. The smallness of the boon compared with the greatness of the loss is still further shown when he goes on to make the promise to Caleb. Consider—

I. How CLEAR SUCH A PROMISE MAKES THE REASON WHY GOD'S PROMISES SEEM SO OFTEN UNFULFILLED. Men do not supply the conditions requisite for their fulfilment. The same claims, promises, and warnings were laid before others as before Caleb; but when they were rebellious he was obedient, and the end of it is indicated here. The law of sowing and reaping, of cause and effect, is at work. Let Christians consider how many promises given for the guidance and comfort of present life are yet unfulfilled in their experience. The power and disposition of God are toward us, as toward the Israelites, but the rebellious hearts are many and the Calebs few (Eph. i. 19).

II. A BEAUTIFUL ILLUSTRATION OF SPECIAL PROVIDENCE. As we read on and learn that Caleb was to spend forty years in the wilderness before the fulfilment of the promise, then we discern how constantly he must have been under the eye of God, how surely provided for and protected. He had known much of danger already: something as a spy and something as a faithful witness, and the lifting of stones against him was perhaps but an earnest of further perils from his own countrymen. And yet, although his wanderings were to be long and dangerous, God, speaking with that assurance which becomes God only, promises Caleb an entrance into the land at last. Who can tell what hearts this very promise made more hostile, and what special interpositions may have been required to protect him?

III. THE REASONS FOR GOD'S GRACIOUS TREATMENT OF CALEB. "He was a man of another spirit." Of another spirit as to *his recollections of the past*. The others thought much of the past, but it was in a selfish and grovelling spirit. They hankered after the creature comforts and delicacies of Egypt, and continually bemoaned the simpler life of the wilderness. The ten misleading spies very likely took thoughts of Egypt into their inspection of Canaan, comparing it not with God's promises, but with what they recollected of the land they had left. On the other hand, Caleb's thoughts would run much on the bondage and oppression in Egypt. Humbly and devoutly observant of each wonderful work of God as it was being performed, he would have it more deeply impressed on his mind; and every time the thought returned there would be something of the power of a first impression. There would be the recollection also of God's forbearance and long-suffering with him in his own imperfect services. Of another spirit, consequently, as to *his conduct in the present*. To one who had learned to look on the past as he did, the present would appear in all its glory immeasurably better than the past. Hence, what made others mourn made him rejoice; while others were rebelling and hatching conspiracies, he was doing all he could to sustain Moses. May we not conjecture that he went on the search expedition not so much because he deemed it needful, as in order that one at least might bring back a faithful testimony? So let it be said of us that wherever the spirit of the world is manifested in greed, passion, false representation, or any other evil thing, we by our conduct in present circumstances, as they rise fresh and often unexpected day by day, show indeed another spirit. It is only by having the right spirit alive and strong within us that we shall be equal to the claims ever coming on Christ's servants. Of another spirit as to *his expectations in the future*. Every man who lives so that his present is better than his past has a growing assurance that the future will be better than the present. He who lives in the constant appreciation and enjoyment of fulfilled promises will consider the future as having in it the promises yet to be fulfilled. It would doubtless be a keen personal disappointment to Caleb when he found the people determined to retreat. He had known something of the future in the present when he visited the promised land, and joy would fill his thoughts at the prospect of speedy possession. A man of such a spirit as Caleb gives God the opportunity of accomplishing all his word. "He hath followed me fully." As fully, that is, as was possible for a sinful man in earthly conditions. God does not expect the service of glorified spirits during the life we live in the flesh. But wherever he finds diligence, caution, the spirit that says, "This one thing I do;" wherever he finds the loving heart, the giving hand, the bridled tongue, he is not slow to give approval. When the heart is fully set towards him, without division and without compulsion, he recognises such a state in the most emphatic language. Hence, in spite of great blots faithfully recorded, Abraham is called the friend of God (James ii. 23), and David the man after his own heart (1 Sam. xiii. 14). So Caleb is described as having followed God fully; not that he was a faultless man, but there was that in him which in due time would make all the outward the full and beautiful expression of the inward. God sees the fruit within the seed, and speaks accordingly. Compare Caleb with the unbelieving multitude, and the words will not appear one whit too strong. Note in conclusion that Caleb was now required *to exercise the high quality of patience.* He himself deserved immediate entrance, but he must wait while the unbelieving generation died away, and those who at present were only striplings and infants rose to take their place. He had to be patient, but his patience was the patience of hope. "It is good that a man should both hope and quietly wait for the salvation of the Lord" (Lam. iii. 26). Caleb had a spirit within him which could find the best things of Canaan even in the waste wilderness ('Paradise Regained,' i. 7).—Y.

Vers. 26—35.—*God's decision repeated as a message.* What God has already said to Moses by way of answer to his intercession is now amplified in a solemn message to the people. The punitive aspect of the decision is made to appear still more distinctly. Cf. vers. 11 and 27. In the first he asks how long the people mean to pursue their unbelieving conduct; in the second, how long shall he bear with them. The time has come for God himself to decide, and make his decision known in the clearest manner.

I. THIS GENERATION WAS NOT ALLOWED TO GO ITS OWN WAY. It was not to die at once, neither was it to enter the land; and perhaps some may then have anticipated dismissal altogether, like a disbanded army, that each might be free to take his own path. In reality, all was to go on as before, save that the promise was taken away. They were to continue in the wilderness, and die there. No relaxation is intimated as to the service of the tabernacle and the duties of the camp. We do not escape God's constraints because our hearts have rejected him. He spared Israel, but he did not let it go back to Egypt. Men may congratulate themselves on being free from the restrictions of a godly life, and talk wildly of those who shut themselves up in the service of Christ, yet they know very well that they are themselves under restraint. Anything like license and recklessness brings suffering on them very quickly. God takes care even now that if men will not serve him, neither shall they please themselves. The fruits of evil-doing sometimes ripen with wonderful rapidity.

II. IT WAS NOT LEFT TO ITS OWN RESOURCES. It is not expressly said that the manna would be continued, but doubtless all was continued that was not formally revoked. This doomed generation, which could neither go its own way, nor entirely in God's way, nevertheless had something to do for God which could be done by the ordinary provisions of nature. A generation mostly born in the wilderness had to be brought up to manhood. The lot was, therefore, to some extent mitigated by the continuance of family life, with all its affections, occupations, and enjoyments. In the course of time, as the first bitterness of their doom passed away, parents might even find a certain pleasure in the thought that their children would enjoy the land from which by their own folly they had been excluded.

III. NO ROOM WAS LEFT FOR A MORE HOPEFUL PROSPECT WITH RESPECT TO THEMSELVES. They had said in their haste, "Would God we had died in this wilderness!" (ver. 2). And now through their own folly what they hastily wished has become a necessity. All who had been numbered (ch. i.) are to die, as not being fit to fight the Lord's battles. No less than four times does the Lord refer to this doom, with variety of expression, which only makes more certain the identity of meaning. Are any of them saying that this very doom is a change of purpose, and therefore they may hope that in a short time God will gladden their ears with the words, "Arise, enter, and possess"? He closes the door against such a hope by giving the long term of forty years to exhaust the doomed generation. This stretch of time would bring even the youngest of them to be a man of sixty, and thus, though the wearing away might be very gradual, yet it would be none the less certain. The rule is made more express and rigorous by the very exceptions in Caleb and Joshua.

IV. THOUGH THEY THEMSELVES WERE DOOMED, CLEAR INDICATION IS GIVEN TO THEM THAT GOD'S PURPOSES WOULD BE ACCOMPLISHED. Forty years, and they would be gone! and what then? Why they themselves would be the instruments, and that to a large extent unconsciously, of fulfilling the very purpose which once they seemed to have imperilled. Their little ones God would bring into the land. "Your little ones, which ye said should be a prey." Men are fearful when they ought to be bold, and bold when they ought to be fearful. Israel was alarmed for its tender offspring, but not afraid to rebel against God, and treat his servants with contempt. And now God says that in the exercise of his providence and the carrying out of his extensive plans, these very children, these infants, helpless on the mother's breast, shall enter and conquer where their fathers were afraid to go. Another generation would arise, not knowing Egypt except at second hand, and which could not very well lust after things it had never tasted. The delay in accomplishing God's purposes was more apparent than real. The loss was chiefly a loss to the disobedient themselves. God can take the most adverse things, the most determined outbreaks of the wicked, and work them in with his own purposes.

V. AN ILLUSTRATION IS FURNISHED OF THE TRUTH THAT CHILDREN HAVE TO BEAR THE SINS OF THE PARENTS (ver. 33). A dreadful name, and only too frequent in his after-dealings with Israel, does the Lord give to these sins—"whoredoms" he calls them. The generations of men are so interwoven that the blow which falls on the parent cannot be entirely averted from the child. Not only was the punished generation unfit for entrance, but its children had to wait in consequence. The children born on this very day of sentence would be well on in manhood when they entered the land. Sinners should well consider how their sin includes others in its consequences. The Israelites thought they were doing a good thing for their little ones when they rebelled; but the real result was the detention of them forty years in the wilderness. If the fathers had been believing, they could have entered at once, and brought up their children in the land flowing with milk and honey. As it was, they had to nourish them in the wilderness, and on the manna they so much despised.

VI. THERE IS SOMETHING THROUGH ALL THESE FORTY YEARS TO REMIND THEM OF THEIR SIN AND ITS PUNISHMENT. As the unbelievers died off one by one, and as each succeeding year began, and whenever Caleb and Joshua appeared, there was something to remind of God's chastising hand.—Y.

Vers. 39—45.—*A confession contradicted in action.* The way of Israel seems now closed up. The way to Egypt is closed, and also the way to the promised land, where of late was fixed up the clear intimation, "This is the way, walk ye in it." There is now but one way open—to wander in this wilderness for forty years till all the rebels have passed away. The full measure of their doom is now before them, and as it appears in all its naked severity, it fills them with grief and consternation. Everything corroborates the word of Moses. The ten spies who brought up the slanderous report are lying plague-stricken corpses, while Caleb and Joshua stand among the living confessed by God himself as faithful and true witnesses. Nevertheless, in the midst of this utter collapse the people were not unprovided for as to their course of action (ver. 25). God had told Moses the direction into which to take them. But they cannot learn even so much obedience as this without being taught it in a terrible lesson.

I. WE HAVE A CONFESSION CONTRADICTED EVEN WHILE IT WAS BEING MADE. The confession is, "We have sinned." It is very easy to say this, and to say it meaning something by it, but in a great multitude of cases it is said with very little understanding of what sin really is. Pharaoh said at last, when he had been visited with seven plagues, "I have sinned this time: the Lord is righteous, and I and my people are wicked" (Exod. ix. 27); but as soon as the rain, hail, and thunders ceased at the intercession of Moses, he sinned yet more and hardened his heart. So with the Israelites here; it was not sin they felt, but suffering. If they had truly felt sin, they would have submitted at once to the decision of God and his direction for their present need (ver. 25). A mind filled with the sense of sin is filled also with the sense of God's authority. It is so impressed with its own sin and God's righteousness, that its first thought is how to end the dreadful alienation from God by reason of wicked works. It will at once attempt to bring disobedience to an end by prompt obedience in the nearest duties. But here the confession of sin is not even put first. They are occupied with self, its aims and disappointments, even while professing themselves humbled before God. What a proof that God judged them truly when he said that any further trial of their obedience was useless! They had forgotten that wisdom has to do with times and seasons. What was obedience yesterday may be disobedience to-day. They tried to open a door closed by him who shuts so that none can open. They said "We have sinned" in the same breath with the most audacious purpose of sin they could form. Learn from them how hard it is to have, not simply an adequate sense of sin, but a sense of sin at all. It is a dreadful thing to sin, and yet persistently deny it through failing to feel it (1 John i. 8, 10); it is also a dreadful thing to confess sin while the felt trouble is not sin, but mere fleshly vexation and pain. Read carefully Dan. ix. for a becoming confession of sin really felt.

II. A CONFESSION STILL FURTHER CONTRADICTED IN ACTION, EVEN AFTER THE CONTRADICTION HAS BEEN POINTED OUT. We have seen how the resolution to advance into Canaan made the confession of sin worthless. How worthless it was is made more evident by the *action* of the people. Notice that Moses takes not the slightest heed of their confession of sin, but aims direct at their wild resolution. What can be more urgent and more strongly fortified with reasons than his dissuasive words? He puts in the front, as the most proper thing to be put, that they are about to transgress the commandment of the Lord. Fresh from one transgression, and with its penalty pronounced, they yet rushed headlong into another. They are foolish enough to suppose that by an energetic effort they can release themselves from the penalty. Such a rebellious purpose must assuredly be frustrated. By so much as the *presence* of God would have been felt if they had gone onward at the right time, by just as much would his *absence* be felt now. As formerly they would have had a force far above nature against their enemies, now they have a force far below. But all that Moses can say is in vain. All their notion of sin was that they had not advanced into Canaan. They had such poor thoughts of God as to think that they could wipe the sin out by advancing with all energy now, forgetting that the sin lay in unbelief and disobedience. If by any chance they had got into Canaan, they would not have found it a promised land. God could and would have made it just as hard and unattractive as the wilderness they had left.

III. THE CONTRADICTION IS STILL FURTHER AGGRAVATED BY BREAKING AWAY FROM MOSES AND THE ARK. One can imagine that in their impetuosity all tribal order and discipline was lost. Possibly they had some commander; there may have been just enough cohesion to agree so far. But though a crowd may choose a commander, a commander cannot at will make a crowd into an army. The peculiarity of Israel was that its army was fixed and disciplined by Jehovah himself, and to break away from the ark, where his honour dwelt, was openly to despise it, as if it were nothing but common furniture. There was not only a rebellion of the people against its governor, but a mutiny of the army against its commander. Does it not almost seem as if a host of demons had gone into these men, carrying them headlong to destruction, even as they carried the swine down the steep place? Only a little while before, no argument, no appeal would have dragged them an inch against the Amalekites and the Canaanites, and now there is nothing can keep them back. Surely this crowns the illustrations of Israel's perversity, and makes it very wonderful that out of them, as concerning the flesh, the Christ should have sprung.

IV. THEIR DISCOMFITURE CAME AS A CERTAIN CONSEQUENCE. The enemy, we may conjecture, had been preparing for some time. Probably, as the Israelites sent spies into Canaan, so the Canaanites may have had spies in the wilderness. And so as Israel in this battle was at its very weakest, Canaan may have been at its strongest. Yet Israel would appear strong, advancing with furious onset, and bent on cancelling these dreadful forty years. Hence the enemy would exult in a great victory gained by their own powers, being ignorant that they owed it rather to the disobedience of Israel. The world is not strong in itself, as against those who truly confide in God, but its strength is enough and to spare when God's people fight against it with fleshly weapons. The best allies of God's enemies are oftentimes found among his professed friends.—Y.

PRELIMINARY NOTE TO CHAPTERS XV.—XIX.

A great break in the story of Israel occurs here. Perhaps in the whole history of the theocracy, from Abraham downwards, there is no such entire submergence of the chosen people to be noted. After the rebellion at Kadesh they disappear from view, and they only reappear at Kadesh again after an interval of thirty-eight years. Only one occurrence of any historical moment can be assigned to this period (ch. xvi.), and that is recorded without note of time or place, because its ecclesia-tical interest gave it an abiding value for all time. The sacred history of Israel in the wilderness may be compared to one of the streams of that wilderness. From its source it runs, if circumstances be favourable, full and free for a certain distance, and even spreads itself abroad upon the more level ground; here, however, it meets a thirstier soil and more scorching heat; it loses itself suddenly and entirely. If its course be followed with doubt and difficulty, a few small water-holes may be discovered, and perhaps in some exceptionally shaded and sheltered spot a permanent pool; only at the furthest end of the dried-up wady, near the great sea, the stream re-forms itself and flows on without interruption to its goal. The void in the record which thus divides in two the story of the exodus is explained readily and satisfactorily by the one fact that during all these years the history of Israel was actually in abeyance. For that history is the history of a theocracy, and in the higher sense it is the history of God's dealings with his own people, as he leads them on "from strength to strength," until "every one of them in Zion appeareth before God." Thus all the Old Testament from Gen. xii. (in which the history properly so called commences) to the end of Joshua has for its goal the entry into and conquest of the promised land; and thence again to 1 Kings x. and 2 Chron. ix. it leads up to the firm and full establishment of the temple and of the Lord's anointed in the place which he had chosen. But during the thirty-eight years this advance was absolutely suspended; the generation that excommunicated itself at Kadesh had thenceforth no part and no heritage in Israel; their lives were spared indeed at the time, but they had to die out and another generation had to take their place before the history of the theocracy could be resumed. Instead, therefore, of the blank causing perplexity or suspicion, it most strikingly corresponds with and confirms the whole tenor and purport of the Pentateuch, and the Old Testament in general. It was at Kadesh that the onward march of Israel, as Israel, was summarily suspended; it was from Kadesh that that march began once more after thirty-eight years; and the sacred narrative conforms itself with the utmost simplicity and naturalness to this fact.

The condition of the nation during this period of submergence is a matter of considerable interest. In endeavouring to picture it to ourselves, we are left to a few scattered statements, to some probable conclusions, and for the rest to mere conjecture. The most important of these statements are as follows:—

1. Deut. viii. 2—6; xxix. 5, 6. God did not wholly abandon them to themselves. He supplied them every day with manna, and also (no doubt) with water

when there was no natural supply (see on 1 Cor. x. 4). He provided them also with raiment and shoes, so that they had the " food and clothing " which are the actual necessaries of life.

2. Josh. v. 4—8. It may seem strange that no children were circumcised between Egypt and Canaan, considering the extreme importance assigned to the rite (see on Exod. iv. 24—26). If any children were born before the first arrival at Kadesh (see note on ch. x. 28), it is probable that their circumcision was postponed in view of a speedy settlement in the land of promise. After that time the general neglect of religious ordinances and the extreme uncertainty of their movements (ch. ix. 22) would sufficiently account for the general disuse of the rite. It is only reasonable to conclude that the passover also was omitted during all this period. Even if the material elements for its celebration could have been provided, it is hardly possible that the men who came out of Egypt only to die in that wilderness could have brought themselves to renew the memory, so bitter to them, of that great but fruitless deliverance. And with the passover we may probably conclude that the whole sacrificial system fell into abeyance, save so far as it might be maintained by the zeal of the Levites alone (see below on ch. xix.).

3. Ezek. xx. 10—26. This is a strong indictment against Israel in the wilderness, and all the more because the children are reproached in the same strain as the fathers. It is apparently to the former that the difficult verses 25 and 26 refer exclusively. If so, we have two facts of grave moment made known to us through the prophet. 1. That the Lord, by way of punishment, gave them statutes and judgment which were not good. 2. That they systematically offered their first-born to Moloch. It is only necessary here to point out that these statements occur in the course of an impassioned invective, and must therefore be taken as the extreme expression of one side only of a state of things which may have had other aspects.

4. Amos v. 25, 26; Acts vii. 42, 43. This again is a strong indictment. It is indeed contended that Amos v. 26 should be read in the present tense, and that St. Stephen was misled by an error of the Septuagint. This, however, introduces a much greater difficulty; and even apart from the quotation in the Acts, the ordinary reading is the more natural and probable (see note on ch. xiv. 33).

While, therefore, the general impression left upon us by these passages is dark indeed, it is hopeless to look for anything definite or precise as to the moral and religious condition of the people at this time. A similar obscurity hangs over their movements and proceedings. We have nothing to guide us except the probabilities of the case, and a list of stations which really tells us nothing. It is only reasonable to suppose that the marching orders issued at Sinai fell *ipso facto* into abeyance when the short, swift, decisive march for which they were designed came to an abrupt conclusion. We have no authority for supposing that the host held together during these years of wandering which had no aim but waste of time, and no end but death. The presumption is that they scattered themselves far and wide over the wilderness (itself of no great extent), just as present convenience dictated. Disease, and death, and all those other incidents revived in full force which make the simultaneous march in close array of two million people an impossibility. No doubt the head-quarters of the host and nation, Moses and Aaron, and the Levites generally, remained with the ark, and formed, wherever they might be, the visible and representative centre of the national life and worship. It is of the movements of this permanent centre, which contained in itself all that was really distinctive and abiding in Israel, that Moses speaks in ch. xxxiii., and elsewhere; and no doubt these movements were made in implicit obedience to the signals of God, given by the cloudy pillar (ch. ix. 21, 22). It is quite possible that while the ark removed from time to time, some portion of the people remained stationary at Kadesh, until the "whole congregation" (see on ch. xx. 1) was reassembled there once more. If this were the case, the peculiar phraseology of Deut. i. 46 as compared with the following verse may be satisfactorily explained.

EXPOSITION.

CHAPTER XV.

VARIOUS LAWS OF SACRIFICE (vers. 1—31). Ver. 1.—**The Lord spake unto Moses.** It must have been during the years of wandering, but within those limits it is impossible even to conjecture the probable date. There is no external evidence, and the internal evidence is wholly indecisive. Neither can it be reasonably maintained that these regulations were designed to revive the hope and sustain the faith of the rising generation. Incidentally they may have had some effect in that way, but it is evident that the primary object of their promulgation was simply to supply certain defects and omissions in the Levitical legislation. Why that legislation should have had the fragmentary and unfinished character which it so evidently bears, requiring to be supplemented, here by an isolated commandment, and there by oral tradition, is an interesting and difficult question ; but there can be no doubt as to the fact, and it is superfluous to look any further for the reason of the enactments here following.

Ver. 2.—**When ye be come into the land.** The same formula is used in Levit. xxiii. 10 concerning the wave-sheaf. It is only remarkable here because it tacitly assumes—(1) that the burnt offerings and sacrifices mentioned would not be offered any more in the wilderness ; (2) that the nation to which it was spoken would surely enter into Canaan at last.

Ver. 3.—**A burnt offering, or a sacrifice,** i. e. a whole burnt offering, or a slain offering. There should be a comma after the word "sacrifice." **In performing a vow, or in a free-will offering, or in your solemn feasts.** The burnt offering, or slain offering, might be offered in either of these three ways, in addition to the more ordinary sacrifices which do not come into question here.

Ver. 4.—**A meat offering.** See on Levit. ii. The command to add the meat offering in every such case had not been given before, but it had apparently been the practice (see Levit. xxiii. 18) in accordance with the law of the daily sacrifice given in Exod. xxix. 40, 41.

Ver. 5.—**A drink offering.** This is nowhere separately treated of in Leviticus, but it is mentioned along with the meat offering in the passages just referred to. Libations

are amongst the simplest and most universal of offerings to the unseen powers. **For one lamb.** בֶּכֶשׂ, lamb or kid.

Ver. 6.—**Or for a ram.** The meat and drink offerings were to be proportionate in amount to the size of the victim.

Ver. 8.—**Peace offerings.** The sacrifices made of free-will, or made on solemn feast-days, would commonly be peace offerings (see on Levit. vii.).

Ver. 9.—**Then shall he bring.** The rapid interchange of the second and third persons in these verses is awkward and perplexing. No doubt it is due to some sufficiently simple cause in the inditing of the original record, but we are not in a position even to guess at its nature. Meanwhile the broken construction remains as a witness to the faithfulness with which the record has been handed down.

Ver. 12.—**According to the number.** The strict proportion of the meat and drink offerings was to be carried out with respect to the numbers, as well as the individual value, of the sacrifices.

Ver. 13.—**All that are born of the country.** כָּל־הָאֶזְרָח, all the native born. Septuagint, πᾶς ὁ αὐτόχθων. The phrase is used no doubt from the point of view of a resident in Canaan ; but it was only to such residents that these ordinances applied. **These things.** The regulations just mentioned.

Ver. 14.—**A stranger.** Septuagint, προσήλυτος.

Ver. 15.—**One ordinance shall be both for you of the congregation,** &c. Rather, "As for the congregation (הַקָּהָל, construed absolutely), one law for you, and for the stranger that sojourneth, an eternal ordinance for your generations ; as with you so shall it be with the stranger before the Lord."

Ver. 17.—**And the Lord spake unto Moses.** Whether on the same or on some other occasion we cannot tell. The two enactments have the same supplemental and (humanly speaking) trivial character.

Ver. 19.—**When ye eat of the bread of the land.** A thing which the younger Israelites, few of whom had ever tasted bread, must have eagerly looked forward to (see on Josh. v. 11, 12). **An heave offering.** See on Exod. xxix. 27 ; Levit. vii. 14. The dedication of first-fruits had been ordered in general terms in Exod. xxii. 29 ; xxiii. 19.

Ver. 20.—**A cake of the first of your dough.** עֲרִסֹת, only used here and in the two passages which refer to this enactment (Neh. x. 37; Ezek. xliv. 30). It probably means whole meal coarsely ground, the first preparation of the new corn available for baking and eating. Septuagint has ἀπαρχὴ φυράματος, an expression used by St. Paul in Rom. xi. 16. **As . . the heave offering of the threshing floor, so shall ye heave it,** i. e. the offering of bread from the home was to be made in addition to the offering of ears or grains from the threshing-floor, and in the same manner. No doubt this latter offering was a very ancient (Gen. iv. 3) and general one, but it is not clearly described in the Law (see, however, Levit. ii. 14; xxiii. 10). All these heave offerings were the perquisite of the priest.

Ver. 22.—**And if ye have erred.** The absence of the usual formula, "and the Lord spake unto Moses," is singular, because what follows has reference not to the enactment just made, but to the whole Law. Perhaps it is a part of the thoroughly unscientific and inartificial character of the Mosaic legislation that a principle of extreme importance and wide application is appended to an insignificant matter of ceremonial. Provision is here made for the forgiveness of sins due to ignorance and oversight—a provision which was sorely needed, considering the great complexity of the Law, and the bad training they had for the accurate observance of it (Deut. xii. 8). A similar provision had been made in Levit. iv. The two, however, differ, inasmuch as *that* contemplates sins of commission, while *this* contemplates sins of omission.

Ver. 23.—**From the day that the Lord commanded, . . and henceforward among your generations.** Or, "thenceforward according to your generations." These words are obscure, because they point apparently to a much larger lapse of time since the first giving of the Law than had really occurred. It may be that they include the possibility of fresh revelations of the Divine will in the time to come.

Ver. 24.—**If ought be committed.** Rather, "if it be committed," i. e. the non-observance of "all these commandments." It cannot, however, be necessary to suppose that a falling away from the whole body of the Mosaic legislation is here intended; such an apostasy could not happen by oversight, and if it did, the remedy provided would seem much too slight for the occasion. The analogy of the provision which follows (ver.

27), and of the parallel provisions in Levit. iv. 2, 13, points clearly to the neglect of any one of the Divine commandments. **One young bullock for a burnt offering.** In the case of a sin of commission done ignorantly, the bullock was treated as a sin offering (Levit. iv. 14, 20), for in that case the expiation of guilt incurred is the prominent point in the atonement; in this case it is the necessity of a fresh self-dedication to the Lord. **According to the manner.** כַּמִּשְׁפָּט, according to the ordinance given above. **One kid of the goats for a sin offering.** This was no doubt offered first, because expiation must precede self-oblation, but the bullock is mentioned first as forming the principal part of the sacrifice. The kid was probably treated according to the regulations of Levit. iv.14, *sq.*

Ver. 26.—**Seeing all the people were in ignorance.** Literally, "because (*sc.* it happened) to the whole nation in ignorance." As the stranger was counted as of the nation for religious purposes, he shared both in its sin and in its forgiveness. There is no record of this atonement ever having been made, although there was abundant occasion for it; it may well be that it was intended only to stand on record against the Jews, and to point them to the one true expiation for their national as well as for their particular transgressions.

Ver. 27.—**And if any soul sin through ignorance.** No doubt by way of omission, as in the preceding case, and thus this regulation will be distinguished from that in Levit. iv. 27. In either case the ritual is apparently intended to be the same, although not so fully described here. In ver. 29 the benefit of the ordinance is extended to strangers; this was natural in a law which directly contemplates the residence of Israel in their permanent home.

Ver. 30.—**The soul that doeth . . presumptuously.** Literally, "with a high hand," i. e. defiantly. A similar phrase is used of God himself (Exod. xiii. 9). **The same reproacheth the Lord.** מְגַדֵּף, revileth. Septuagint, παροξυνεῖ. In Ezek. xx. 27 it is translated "blasphemeth." Perhaps "affronteth" would be better. He that deliberately broke the commandment of the Lord avowed himself his open enemy, and, as it were, challenged him to single combat. **Cut off.** See Gen. xvii. 14.

Ver. 31.—**His iniquity . . upon him.** עֲוֹנָה בָהּ, "its crime upon it," i. e. the sin of that soul must come upon it in punishment.

HOMILETICS.

Vers. 1—31.—*Ordinances of sacrifice.* The laws given in this section were to be " an ordinance for ever," but they have long ago come to an end as far as the literal observance of them is concerned ; it is certain, therefore, that they have an abiding spiritual fulfilment in the law of Christ. Consider, therefore—

1. That the two first of those laws were designed for the Israelites when they came into the land of their habitation ; they do not contemplate the period of wandering in the desert which was then going on. Even so a great part of the law of Christ is designed for that state of holy "joy and peace in believing," for that "rest" which is intended to be our habitation even now, and into which we do enter (Heb. iv. 3 *a.*), albeit imperfectly and uncertainly. Many of the counsels of our Lord and his apostles are manifestly out of all harmony with the ordinary lives of ordinary Christians, because they pertain to a state of detachment and self-conquest which we, through perversity or half-heartedness, have not attained (Matt. v. 29, 39, 40, 48 ; vi. 34 ; xvi. 25 ; xvii. 20 ; xix. 12, 21 ; xx. 26, 27 ; Luke vi. 35 ; xii. 33 ; Rom. xiv. 21 ; 1 Cor. v. 11 ; vi. 4, 7 ; vii. 29—31 ; Philip. ii. 5 ; 1 Tim. vi. 8, &c.). These are indeed addressed to all Christians ("speak unto the children of Israel "), not to a select few ; but they are addressed to them on the assumption that they have striven after and attained the higher life of the Spirit ("when ye be come," &c.). And this is the real answer to the mocking or uneasy spirit which reproaches the gospel of Christ with being visionary, and with having failed to realise itself in the actual life of Christendom. It is quite true that, as far as the present is concerned, the mind of Christ is not fulfilled in the great majority even of decent-living Christians, because they have not attained to rest, but are wandering still in the deserts of a divided allegiance, one half to God, the other to the world and self (1 Cor. ii. 14 ; iii. 3 ; Heb. xii. 5).

II. That the very giving of these laws involved the assurance that those who were to keep them should enter the holy land ("which I give you"). Even so the very fact that so much of the mind of Christ as yet unfulfilled in us has been plainly revealed in the gospel is a pledge to us that God has yet much to do for us and in us, and that he will do it (2 Cor. xiii. 9 ; Philip. i. 6, 9, 10). If it be true that the majority even of earnest Christian people never attain a thorough mastery over self, or an entire conformity to the will of God in this life, then it is certain that this will be wrought in them in the world of spirits beyond our ken ; for only this conformity willingly pursued and embraced is our rest (cf. Matt. xi. 28, 29 ; Heb. iv. 10).

III. That it was ordained that a meat and drink offering should always accompany the voluntary presentation of burnt or slain offerings. Now the burnt and slain offerings represented Christ in his atonement (1) as having in our name and stead offered himself in entire self-oblation to the Father (Heb. ix. 14 ; x. 9, 10), (2) as being the means of access to and communion with God to them that are justified (John vi. 57 ; Eph. ii. 14 *a.*, 18) ; moreover, the voluntary presentation of these sacrifices out of the ordinary routine signified a more personal and earnest pleading of that one Sacrifice by the faithful, as distinguished from that which is more formal and, as it were, obligatory. Again, the meat and drink offering represented the oblation of human labour and care co-operating with Divine grace, for the flour and the oil and the wine were all prepared from the gifts of nature with more or less of industry and skill. Even so, therefore, is it a part of the higher law of Christ, which many do not seem to attain unto, that the earnest pleading of, and reliance upon, and joy in the atonement of Christ shall be always accompanied with the offering of personal service, of good work done for Christ. This cannot truly take the place of the other, any more than the meat offering could supersede or precede the sacrifice ; but yet the other is for ever incomplete without it. The most lively faith and devout worship is not acceptable when unaccompanied by the willing tribute of good works (Titus iii. 8, 14 ; James ii. 17, 26 ; 2 Pet. i. 8).

IV. That this meat and drink offering was always and in every way to be proportionate to the burnt and slain offerings presented. Even so the tribute of our industry and zeal dedicated to God should bear a full proportion to our faith and joy in the atonement of Christ, and should still increase with the increase of these. Nothing is more painful than the entire disproportion often visible between a man's earnest and lively desire to appropriate by faith and devotion the merits of Christ's sacrifice, and the grudging reluctance with which he offers to God of his own time, means, and labour (Matt. vii. 21; xxv. 44, 45, compared with James ii. 16; 2 Cor. ix. 6; Heb. xiii. 16).

V. THAT IN THIS RESPECT THERE WAS TO BE ONE RULE FOR ALL, WHETHER NATIVE BORN OR STRANGER. Even so in the Church of Christ there is but one law of faith and works. There is indeed no "stranger" where all are brethren, but this very fact means among other things that there is no one having part and lot in the atonement of Christ who is relieved by any personal circumstances from the duty of helping together with the rest in the tribute of good works (Rev. xx. 12).

VI. THAT THE FIRST-FRUITS OF BREAD WERE TO BE OFFERED, AS WELL AS OF CORN, i. e. of food as prepared by human labour, as of food in its natural state (fruits of the earth). Even so everything which belongs to our life is to be sanctified by dedication to God, however much human art and labour have conspired to make it what it is. It is not only that which seems to come direct from the bountiful lap of nature which is to be thus acknowledged, but that also which through any process of industry has been adapted to our actual wants. The art and ingenuity and contrivance of man have gone wildly astray, and led to fearful abuses, just because they have not been dedicated to God and to pious uses (cf. Luke xi. 41; Rom. xi. 16; Rev. xxi. 24 b.).

VII. THAT PROPER SACRIFICES WERE APPOINTED, WITH PROMISE OF FORGIVENESS, FOR THE BREACH OF ANY OF THE COMMANDMENTS BY WAY OF OMISSION, such omission not being presumptuous. Even so it is certain under the gospel—1. That sins of omission are still sins, albeit done through neglect, or carelessness, or in ignorance. In nothing is Christian morality more lax than on this point. The double law of Christian charity requires an instructed and attentive mind, if it is to be fulfilled; the carelessness, therefore, of Christians as to how they discharge their positive duties towards God and man is distinctly sinful. 2. That such sins will find forgiveness. The far-reaching nature of our obligations as laid down in the New Testament, and the unending consequences of our most heedless acts and words, might well terrify us if it were not so (Matt. xii. 37; xviii. 6; xxv. 27, 45; James iii. 2; Rev. iii. 2).

VIII. THAT THE WHOLE DIVINE LEGISLATION WAS INCLUDED IN THE MOST COMPREHENSIVE LANGUAGE. Even so there is nothing discretionary, nothing permissive, about the laws of Christian morality. None may be overlooked or ignored from first to last without incurring guilt (Matt. v. 18, 19; James ii. 10; Rom. ii. 22 b.).

IX. THAT THE SACRIFICE FOR SINS OF OMISSION WAS A SIN OFFERING, BUT ALSO, AND MORE ESPECIALLY, A BURNT OFFERING. Even so sins of neglect of duty, of supineness and indifference, demand indeed to be expiated by the one offering made for sin, but also to be repaired by a fresh and entire self-dedication to the will and service of God. To acknowledge our past neglects without an earnest effort to fulfil our duty in future is a feeble and imperfect thing (Heb. xii. 12, 13; 1 Pet. i. 13; Rev. ii. 5). Note, that the law recognised the distinction between the guilt of the nation and the guilt of the individual, and both had their expiations. It is difficult to say whether there is now any "national" guilt, for Christianity does not recognise nations as such; modern nations correspond to the tribes of Israel, if to anything. But there is of course "collective" guilt, of which each must discharge himself by an individual repentance. The atonement for an individual sin of omission was the same as for one of commission.

X. THAT NO PROVISION WAS MADE UNDER THE LAW FOR THE PARDON OF A WILFUL SIN AGAINST GOD—A SIN OF DEFIANCE. Thus the law brought no satisfaction to the tender conscience, but rather conviction of sin, and longing for a better covenant. Herein is at once contrast and likeness: contrast, in that the gospel hath forgiveness for all sin and wickedness (Mark iii. 28; Acts xiii. 39; Rom. viii. 1; 1 John ii. 1); likeness, in that a marked distinction is made between sins against the light and other sins (Mark iii. 29; Luke xxiii. 34; John xix. 11; 1 Tim. i. 13; Heb. vi. 4;

x. 26 ; 1 John v. 16 b.). It is certain that (e. g.) one deliberate lie spoken deliberately, and of malice aforethought, may do more lasting injury to a soul, as far as we can judge, than a whole life of reckless, thoughtless, heedless vice. Compare the case of the Pharisees (Mark iii. 30) with that of the harlots (Luke vii. 37) and publicans (ibid. xix. 2), and that of Ananias and Sapphira with that of the sinful Corinthian.

HOMILIES BY VARIOUS AUTHORS.

Vers. 22—31.—*Presumptuous sins and sins of ignorance.* Some sins are more heinous in the sight of God than others ; more heinous in their own nature, or by reason of aggravating circumstances. The distinction is familiar to all. Murder is a sin more heinous in the sight of God and man than petty theft. Armed rebellion against just authority is a greater sin than heedless omission to pay due honour and courtesy to a superior in office. Yet old and familiar as the distinction is, it is one in connexion with which men have often fallen into mischievous error. Hence the value of texts like this in Numbers, which throw light upon it.

I. Observe HOW THE DISTINCTION BETWEEN GREATER AND LESSER SINS IS HERE STATED. 1. Some sins are described as *sins of ignorance.* The reference is to faults that are due to error or inadvertence. We all know, to our cost, how liable we are to these. Never a day passes but we omit duty and commit faults, either because we knew no better, or because we were " off our guard " and stumbled before we were aware. These are sins of infirmity, such as cleave to the best of men in the present life. 2. Other sins are *done presumptuously.* (Literally, " with a high hand.") The matter is one about which there is no dubiety ; the person knows well what is right and what is wrong ; knowing this, he deliberately and purposely does the wrong. He offends against light, conviction, conscience. This is presumptuous sin. I have said that the distinction between greater and lesser sins is old and familiar. Turning to any Roman Catholic book of devotion, you will find tables in which are enumerated respectively the "mortal sins" and the "venial sins." That is one way of describing the two classes. I very much prefer the terms employed here in God's word. And the superior wisdom of God is to be seen not only in the fitter terms employed, but also in the absence of any attempt, here or elsewhere in the Bible, to give a tabular enumeration of the sins belonging to either class. For one thing, a correct distribution is impossible. The same act which, in ordinary circumstances, one might deem trivial, may in other circumstances be a most heinous crime ; whereas what seems a heinous crime may be found to have been committed in circumstances so extenuating, that you hesitate to pronounce it a crime at all. Besides, the distribution, if it were possible to be made, could only do mischief. It is not good for men to be trying to find out how near they may go to the line which separates sins of infirmity from presumptuous sins, without actually passing over. The Bible refuses to give help in that sort of study. It indicates the quality which aggravates offences, so that we may learn to fear it and keep as far off from it as we can.

II. Observe THE LAW WHICH IS LAID DOWN WITH REFERENCE TO THE TWO KINDS OF SIN. 1. When the party—whether it be the congregation or an individual Israelite—who has sinned inadvertently becomes aware of the sin, *a sin-offering is to be presented with the accustomed rites, and the sin will be forgiven* (vers. 24, 25, 27, 28). The point to be noted here is, that however much the sin may have been due to mere ignorance or inadvertence, the law demanded satisfaction; that is to say, Transgression of God's law is transgression still, though done through mere heedlessness or error. Ignorance and heedlessness may extenuate, but they do not justify ; nor do they exempt from suffering the consequences of evil doing. Nor ought this to be deemed strange or harsh. The same principle prevails in human governments. A transgressor does not escape the penalties annexed to his acts because he did not know they were forbidden, or because he acted recklessly. It is a mischievous abuse of the distinction between sins, if occasion is taken from it to make light of any sin. Remember that all sin is, in its own nature, mortal. Paul persecuted "ignorantly and in unbelief ; " yet, for having persecuted, he reckoned himself the chief of sinners. 2. *As for the presumptuous transgressor, the law holde out to him no hope* (vers. 30, 31).   The reference, no doubt, is, in the first instance, to deliberate violations of the Mosaic constitution—the refusal to accept circumcision, or celebrate the Passover, or observe the Sabbatic rest.   For such offences no sacrifice was provided.   The person forfeited his place in the covenant society.   But this part of the law, like the former part, has an ultimate reference to offences considered as strictly moral.   It suggests lessons regarding all deliberate and presumptuous sins.   It is a most striking and significant fact, that for such sins the law of Moses provided no sacrifice.   What are we to make of this?   (1) It may remind us that there is such a thing as "a sin unto death," and for which "there remaineth no more sacrifice" (Heb. x. 26, 27; 1 John v. 16).   We believe, indeed, that no penitent, however heinous his sin, will be turned away from God's door unforgiven; but there are dark admonitory texts of Scripture, of which this in Numbers is one, which distinctly warn us that God's mercy will not be trifled with; that there is a point to which, if men go, in resisting the testimony of God's word and Spirit in their consciences, the Spirit will withdraw and give them over to hardness and impenitence.   (2) But there is a brighter side of the matter.   "By Christ all that believe are justified from all things, from which they could not be justified by the law of Moses" (Acts xiii. 39).   David's great crime was a "presumptuous sin."   The law prescribed no sacrifice for it.   The law could suggest to him no hope.   What then?   He remembered the name of the Lord which was enshrined in the Pentateuch side by side with the law (Exod. xxxiv. 6).   He confessed and was forgiven.—In Ps. xix. there occur a remarkable succession of meditations and prayers which, to all appearance, were suggested originally by this law in Numbers, and which may be taken as expressing the thoughts and exercises to which the study of it gave birth in the soul of David. At all events, they so perfectly indicate the practical use to be made of the law that they cannot be too earnestly commended to your consideration.   "*Who can understand his errors?*   (Who can make sure that he has noted, or can remember and confess his sins in this kind?)   *Cleanse thou me from secret faults.*"   "*Keep back thy servant also from presumptuous sins; let them not have dominion over me: then shall I be upright, and I shall be innocent from the great transgression.*"—B.

Vers. 15, 16.—*The impartiality of God.*   The treatment of foreigners among the Jews one sign of the impartiality of God.   For—1. They were all "of one blood" (Acts xvii. 26).   2. The Israelites were "strangers and sojourners with God" in his own land (Levit. xxv. 23), as we all are upon earth (1 Chron. xxix. 15; 1 Pet. ii. 11).   3. All are involved in sin.   The guilt of the favoured Israelites was greater than that of heathen strangers (Rom. ii. 6—12).   4. All are included in the one salvation (Rom. iii. 21—30).   For further illustrations see outline on ch. ix. 14.—P.

Vers. 30, 31.—*Presumptuous sins.*   I. THE GUILT OF PRESUMPTUOUS SINS.   The transgressor sinneth "with a high hand" (Heb.).   It is not easy exactly to define sins of presumption or deliberate disobedience, for which there was no expiation by sacrifice.   Some crimes involved capital punishment (Levit. xx. 1, 2, 10; Exod. xxi. 14; Deut. xvii. 12), or were followed by fatal judgments by God (Levit. xvii. 10; xx. 4—6).   The impossibillity of drawing up a complete schedule of wilful, presumptuous sins suggests a caution.   For their heinous guilt is described by the term "reproacheth the Lord," *i.e.* blasphemes God in word or act.   A presumptuous sinner reproaches God in four ways.   He acts as though (1) his commands were harsh; (2) his authority was of no account; (3) his favour was to be little prized; (4) his threats were to be still less feared (Deut. xxix. 19, 20).   Such guilt is aggravated under the law of the gospel, inasmuch as God's commands, authority, favour, and threats are invested with greater weight and sanctity through the revelation of his will and his love in Jesus Christ (Heb. ii. 1—3).
II. THE DANGER OF PRESUMPTUOUS SINS.   1. Under the law there was no sacrifice to expiate for such sins, but fatal punishment at the hand of man or of God himself. 2. Under the gospel a sacrifice even for wilful sin is provided.   But as "*the* condemnation" is for unbelief, the neglect of the Saviour and his sacrifice is the most terrible, though a most common presumptuous sin, for which "there remaineth no more sacrifice" (Heb. x. 26—29).   There is a sin "unto death," which "shall not

be forgiven," &c. (Matt. xii. 32; 1 John v. 16). 3. The difficulty of exactly deciding, either under the law or the gospel, what sins are beyond the power of expiation, and expose us to be "cut off," adds to their danger. All sins are like poisons, fatal if remedies are not applied. But if some are *certainly* fatal, and we know not which, what need for faith in the Physician, and prayer that we may be kept from all sins so as to be guarded from presumptuous sins among them (Ps. xix. 12—14).—P.

Vers. 1—16.—*God giving laws for the distant future.* I. HE TREATS THE FUTURE AS THE PRESENT. The people had been very near to a land of habitations, and to a time when the requirements of this passage would have been close upon them. That time is now moved int） a distant future; but it is equally certain to come, and the requirements are equally practical. The land of promise was Israel's inheritance, and to become its possession, even though Amalekite and Canaanite had just been victorious. God can speak of things that are not as if they were. And after so much gloom as the previous chapter presents, such a rebellious, unmanageable spirit and ominous outlook, there was need of something bright, such as we find in the state of things which these ordinances of offering imply.

II. HE POINTS TO A FUTURE FULL OF SATISFACTION TO THE PEOPLE. It will be approved by them as according with his prediction to Moses: "a good land and a large, a land flowing with milk and honey." They shall have cause for all manner of voluntary offerings over and above the necessary offerings for sin. Fulfilled desires would lead to the fulfilment of vows. The very mention of these sacrifices as possible indicated that Israel would be rich in flocks and herds, in corn and wine and oil. There would be reason for much gratitude in the heart, and consequent gifts of thanksgiving. And thus, in spite of all that may be a cause of despondency in the Christian's present outlook, there will yet be cause of thanksgiving to him. We must not judge the future from our present humiliation and almost vanished hopes, but from the greatness of God's power and purposes. He sees the rich, bright future of his people even when they do not.

III. HE COUNTS ON THE EXISTENCE OF A THANKFUL SPIRIT. There would be abundant cause for such a spirit, and so it was right to provide for any effects that might appear. In spite of all present murmuring and ingratitude, in spite of all sullen compliance with the compulsion to turn back into the wilderness, there would surely some day be a thankful spirit, a devout recognition of God in the midst of prosperity. Thus we may take it that there is something of prophecy, something of reasonable expectation, as well as of appointed duty in the commands here given. Just as the regulations for the Nazarite (ch. vi.) indicated an expectation that there would be much of the feeling leading men to the Nazarite vow, so here there is an expectation of much in the way of free-will offerings.

IV. These free-will offerings must be joined with offerings from the corn, the oil, and the wine TO MAKE ALL INTO ONE COMPLETE AND ACCEPTABLE SACRIFICE. The desire to do something acceptable to God needs to be directed by a knowledge of what is acceptable. The thankful soul will ever be glad to learn his will. No offering to him is worth anything unless it be a cheerful one; but the most cheerful gifts may be nullified for the want of other needed qualities. Hence there should ever be a careful pondering of God's will in all our offerings to him, so that they may be good and perfect according to the measure of human ability. When most of all we are free agents, then most of all should we look to be directed by necessary commandments from on high.

V. THE PROVISION FOR STRANGERS. The land of promise was to be attractive and beneficent to them as well as to Israel. They also would share in its advantages, and be stirred to a corresponding acknowledgment. Thus ever and anon does God raise his warning against all disposition to exclusiveness. He had the case of the stranger and proselyte ever before him. A word of hope this for Hobab, whose heart may have been cast down within him, when he saw how contemptuously Moses had been treated of late.—Y.

Vers. 17—21.—*An offering from the dough: domestic religion.* I. A DAILY OFFERING, or if not daily, so frequent as to be practically daily. God has spoken so far of free-will offerings, but here is one connected with such a frequent and necessary act as the eating of bread. There are occasions for free-will offerings when evident mercies and peculiar gains prompt to something special in the way of acknowledgment; but men are only too prone to forget the common and daily mercies which in reality are greatest of all. Where we abound in forgetting, God most abounds in reminding. The time of eating bread was an appointed opportunity for acknowledging his daily goodness. The manna was so evidently miraculous, that very little was needed to remind Israel how entirely it was produced without their intervention. It was not the sort of food they would have cultivated. They took it, not that they liked it, but it was the only thing to be got. But bread is a thing on which man spends much care. It goes through so many processes before it reaches his mouth that he easily exaggerates his share in the production of it. Sowing and reaping, grinding and baking, help to hide the good hand of God behind them. Hence the giving of the first from every piece of dough was a deliberate and frequent recognition of dependence on God for the bread in Canaan, as much as for the manna in the wilderness.

II. A DOMESTIC OFFERING. Thus religion was brought into the house to sanctify a common homely duty. There was something to excite the curiosity of children. It was an opportunity of explaining to them, from whose loving-kindness came their daily bread; teaching them lessons of dependence and gratitude in the seed-time and the harvest, by the mill and the oven. Contrast with this the melancholy picture by Jeremiah of the children gathering the wood, the fathers kindling the fire, and the women kneading dough to make cakes to the queen of heaven (Deut. xxviii. 5; Neh. x. 37; Ps. civ. 14, 15; Jer. vii. 18; Ezek. xliv. 30; Haggai i. 9).—Y.

Vers. 22—29.—*God shows himself strict and yet considerate.* I. THE SERIOUSNESS OF GOD'S EXPECTATIONS. God gave to Israel many and elaborate commandments, in the mode of obeying which he left nothing to personal discretion. Hence the work of obedience was often a difficult and always a careful one, and sometimes the people might be tempted to say, "Surely this minute and unvarying compliance in outward things cannot be seriously intended." But everything God commands has a reason, even though we see it not. God hides reasons in order that the obedience of faith may be complete. An Israelite quite conceivably might say, "Surely I am not expected to remember all these commandments in all their details." The answer is, that though the commandments might not all be remembered, yet every one of them was important. And so we find that God made it a dangerous, even a deadly thing, knowingly and wilfully to disobey them. He has high aims with respect to his people, far higher than they can at present appreciate, and this is the surest way of getting great results. He may seem to be imposing intolerable burdens, but he is really leading us onward in strength and capacity until we shall be able to bear the burdens. Hence the large demands which Christ also makes on his disciples. He came to *fulfil* the law. His people are not only to do more than others, but much more, and in many ways. Whatever be provided for in the way of pardon and expiation, the standard must not be lowered in the least. God has constituted man to reach great attainments, and he will enable him to reach them, if only the proper means be taken.

II. HIS REMEMBRANCE OF HUMAN INFIRMITY. It is no real contradiction, to them who will consider, that God meant his commandments to be kept, yet knew they would be oftentimes broken. As he was serious in giving the commandments, he wished the people to be serious in trying to keep them, and serious also in asking why they were not able to keep them. He provided for the commandments being broken. While serious in expectations, he was also considerate and encouraging. He who knows what his people will one day be able to do, knows full well how little they can do at present. He is really more considerate of feeble men than they are of each other. The parable of the servant forgiven of his master, yet refusing to forgive his fellow-servant, finds its application only too often in the difference between God's tender treatment of man, and man's harsh treatment of his fellow-man. God makes allowance for the difficulty of turning away from inveterate habits. He makes allowance for what we know by daily experience is a great infirmity of men, sheer forgetfulness. He considers how many suffer from defective instruction, bad example, and early orphanhood. He can say far more for us than with our utmost skill we can plead for ourselves. He knows all the difficulties we have in getting at the knowledge and practice of his truth. What comfort could we possibly have in the midst of all our differing sects, confessions, and ceremonies, did we not think of God looking kindly and patiently on the sins of ignorance, and remembering that we know only in part? It was Paul's great comfort to feel that the cruelties of his persecuting days had been committed ignorantly and in unbelief.

III. HIS STRICT REQUIREMENT OF EXPIATION. They were not allowed to say, "We knew it not; therefore it will not be required from us." Evil done in ignorance does not cease to be evil because done in ignorance. Whatever is commanded ought to be done, and if omitted there is loss somewhere in God's universe because of the omission. We must not plead ignorance of the commandment, for the reason of that ignorance lies with man, and not with God. It may not lie with the particular transgressor, but still it lies with man, and therefore the transgression must be confessed and atoned for; and when we humble ourselves in confession of sin committed and service omitted, there is need that we should dwell with much self-examination and seeking for light on the things that have been left undone through ignorance. What we have done that we ought not to have done is much more discoverable than what ought to have been done, yet has been left undone. Many conscientious, earnest, and enlightened Christians have been transgressors through ignorance. Prayer for the doing of God's will on earth as it is done in heaven must be accompanied by an incessant seeking for the knowledge of his will. Assuredly we suffer by our ignorance in this matter, even though, in a certain sense and to a certain extent, this ignorance cannot be helped. This provision here made for atonement, this prophecy, as it were, that many transgressions unconsciously committed would be discovered in due time, is a reminder to us how much we may still have to discover of God's will concerning us. Much as we may know, and much as we may do, there may be large fields of obedience where we have not taken a single step. The great essentials, of course, if we be Christians at all, we cannot be ignorant of, but it is quite possible to know them, yet be ignorant of other things God would also have us know. We are not to look for the laws of life in Scripture only; God has put there such things as are not to be found in nature and the dealings of his common providence. We must look for his will in every place where intimations of it are to be found, and be quick in discovering what has been revealed to others. Mark these words of Joseph Sturge:—"It seems to be the will of him who is infinite in wisdom that light upon great subjects should first arise, and be gradually spread through the faithfulness of individuals in acting up to their own convictions."—Y.

EXPOSITION.

THE SABBATH-BREAKER (vers. 32—36). Ver. 32. — **And while the children of Israel were in the wilderness.** It is maintained by some that these words were intended to mark the contrast between the previous laws, which were only to be observed when the people came into their own land, and the law of the sabbath, which was strictly enforced during the period of wandering. There is no doubt that such a distinction existed in fact, but there is no reason to find the intentional assertion of it in this expression. The simpler and more natural, and therefore more probable, explanation is, that the incident was recorded after the people had left the wilderness. At the same time, there is nothing unreasonable in ascribing the narrative to Moses himself if we suppose him to have written it at the end of his life, when the people were encamped in the steppes of Moab. It seems probable that the record of the incident was inserted here as an example of a "presumptuous" sin, and of its punishment. **A man that gathered sticks upon the sabbath day.** This was clearly presumptuous, because the prohibition to do any work for oneself on the sabbath had been made so clear, and was so constantly forced upon their attention by the failure of the manna on that day, that ignorance could not possibly be pleaded here.

Ver. 33.—**Unto all the congregation,** i. e. unto the council of elders, who were the congregation by representation (see on Exod. xviii. 25, 26).

Ver. 34. — **They put him in ward** (cf.

Levit. xxiv. 12), **because it was not declared what should be done to him.** This is perplexing, because the punishment of death had been decreed in Exod. xxxi. 14, 15, and xxxv. 2. It seems an evasion to say that although death had been decreed, the mode of death had not been fixed; for (1) it was clearly part of the Divine answer that the offence was really capital (see ver. 35 *a.*), and (2) it was understood that in such cases death was to be inflicted by stoning (see Levit. xx. 2; xxiv. 14; Josh. vii. 25; in the last case the command was to burn the delinquents with fire, yet it was rightly taken for granted that they were to be stoned to death first). There are only two explanations which are satisfactory because they are honest. 1. The incident may possibly have occurred between the first institution of the sabbath (Exod. xvi. 23, 29) and the decree of death to those that broke it. There is nothing in the record as it stands here to contradict such an assumption. 2. It is more likely that it occurred after the departure from Sinai, and that the hesitation in dealing with the criminal was due not to any real uncertainty as to the law, but to unwillingness to inflict so extreme and so (apparently)

disproportioned a punishment for such an offence without a further appeal. If it be said that such unwillingness to carry out a plain command would have been sinful, it is sufficient to answer that Moses and Aaron and the elders were human beings, and must have shrunk from visiting with a cruel death the trivial breach of a purely arbitrary commandment.

Ver. 35.—**Without the camp.** That it might not be defiled (cf. Acts vii. 58, and Heb. xiii. 12).

Ver. 36.—**And he died.** He was killed not for what he did, but for doing it presumptuously, in deliberate defiance of what he knew to be the will of God. If the covenant relation was to be maintained between God and Israel, the observance of the sabbath, which was an integral part of that covenant, must be enforced, and he who wilfully violated it must be cut off; and this consideration was of exceptional force in this case, as the first which had occurred, and as the one, therefore, which would govern all the rest (cf. Acts v. 5, 10). On the punishment of stoning see Levit. xx. 2; xxiv. 14; Acts vii. 58.

HOMILETICS.

Vers. 32 — 36. — *The Sabbath of God.* We have here a record which is both valuable in itself as revealing the mind of God, and also valuable indirectly as revealing the mind of man. The perversity of human nature, and the extreme subtleness of superstition, are remarkably exemplified in the popular treatment of this record. It has indeed made a deep impression upon men, but that impression has been almost wholly false, and has simply led to superstition. The story of the man who picked up sticks on the Sabbath appears in every Christian age, and every Christian land; but in all cases it is the act itself which is regarded as being so awful and so fearfully avenged. Yet even under the law the act itself was lawful in the priests, as our Lord points out (Matt. xii. 5), for the temple fire was supplied with wood; and under the gospel the law of the Sabbath, so far as it was outward and arbitrary, was totally repealed: it passed away like a shadow, leaving us face to face with the substance, the reality which it had obscured—viz., the eternal rest from sin and self which belongs to the kingdom of heaven (Rom. xiv. 5; Gal. iv. 10; Col. ii. 16; Heb. iv. 9, 10). We keep indeed the Lord's day because as a fact it has been kept from the first, and no one has a right to ignore the universal custom of Christians; but our Sabbath is a spiritual one, for it is that ceasing from our own works by virtue of unselfishness and self-devotion which, as it is the secret of "rest" in this life, so it will be the essence of "rest" in the life to come. It follows that the popular use of this story to enforce the outward observance of a legal Sabbath is simply and purely superstitious, and directly antagonistic to its true teaching. Consider therefore—

I. THAT WHILE ALMOST ALL OTHER ORDINANCES, EVEN CIRCUMCISION AND THE PASSOVER, FELL INTO DISUSE, THE SABBATH REMAINED FIXED, INVIOLABLE, AND ETERNAL. Even so while all outward things may change, while even sacraments themselves might fail, the true Sabbath of the soul can never alter, never cease to be observed and sought. To cease from our own works by a true unselfishness; to live for others by an active love; to find our rest in contemplating good and rejoicing in it; *that* is to rest from our labours *as God did from his,* and that is the law of the holy Sabbath which can never be altered. As long as God is God, and man is man, God can only set to us, and we can only set to ourselves, this law as the law of all laws to be observed for ever.

II. THAT THE VIOLATION OF THE SABBATH-LAW WAS NOT PARDONABLE. The sentence of death was confirmed, on special appeal, by God himself. Even so whatever directly violates the law of rest, and so destroys that rest, is fatal and deadly to the soul. For as this rest is the end of all religion, and is to be heaven itself, that which directly militates against it (and that is in the deepest sense selfishness) has never forgiveness, can never be overlooked or suffered to continue.

III. THAT THE ESSENCE OF THE MAN'S CRIME WAS NOT THAT HE GATHERED STICKS ON THE SABBATH, BUT THAT HE GATHERED THEM FOR HIMSELF. For the priests were guiltless, cleaving wood for the altar on the Sabbath; and though the Jews to this day will not make a fire on the Sabbath even to save a man's life, yet it is certain that our Lord would have commended it, and that from an Old Testament point of view (Mark ii. 26, 27; iii. 4). Even so the essence of all sin, and the cause of all wrath, is selfishness. Selfishness is the real and only Sabbath-breaker, because it alone disturbs that Divine rest which stands in conformity to the will of God (see on Gal. ii. 20; Col. iii. 3; 1 John iii. 21, 22, &c.).

IV. THAT THE DOOM OF THE SABBATH-BREAKER WAS STONING—A PUNISHMENT INFLICTED BY ALL, AND EXPRESSIVE OF UNIVERSAL CONDEMNATION. Even so the true punishment of sin is that it arrays against us both God and all good and holy beings. A selfish person would find neither sympathy nor allowance in heaven: his soul would fall, crushed beneath the weight of silent disapproval and unintended reproach. And so the only way to war against a sin of selfishness upon earth is to enlist the sympathies of all good people against it.

V. THAT THE END OF THE SABBATH-BREAKER WAS DEATH, ALTHOUGH IT WAS NOT IM-MEDIATELY EXECUTED. Even so spiritual death is the certain end of selfishness. Amidst the uncertainties of time indeed that death appears to be postponed; selfishness is quite consistent with some amount of religion. But the sentence of death against it is plain and irrevocable, and it will surely be carried out (Matt. x. 38, 39; xvi. 25; Luke xii. 21; Rom. viii. 6; Phil. ii. 4, 5, 21).

HOMILIES BY VARIOUS AUTHORS.

Vers. 30—36.—*The doom of the presumptuous illustrated by that of the Sabbath-breaker.* Disobedience to the commands of God is ranged under two classes. First, that which has just been considered, disobedience through ignorance; secondly, disobedience from presumption, a bold, conscious, reckless defiance of God and following out of the promptings of self. God indicates that such conduct must be met in a corresponding way. "That soul shall be cut off from among his people, ... utterly cut off." Notice that while God supposed the case of the whole people sinning ignorantly, he does not make a similar supposition with regard to presumptuous sin. Unanimity in an open and deliberate defiance of God seems to be impossible. It is only too possible, however, that single men should be guilty in this matter, and an illustration of presumptuous sin, from actual life, immediately follows. The people were to be left without excuse for saying that they were in any doubt as to this dangerous sin. Where death was the punishment, the offence could not be too clearly indicated. Let us consider then the doom of the presumptuous sinner, as illustrated by that of the Sabbath-breaker.

I. THE COMMANDMENT WITH RESPECT TO THE SABBATH HAD BEEN PUT IN PECULIAR PROMINENCE. It stands among those ten solemn announcements of God's will, with respect to which we may say that all other commandments existed for them. Surely to sin against any of these was to sin presumptuously. It is reckoned the business of all men to know all the laws under which they live—ignorance is not allowed for a plea,—but with respect to the ten commandments, special means had been taken to impress them on the minds and memories of the people. Even before the fourth commandment had been formally announced, the double provision of manna on the sixth day had helped to give a peculiar significance to the seventh. So it may be said, if we are disobedient in respect of those requirements mentioned repeatedly and held out prominently by Christ and his apostles, we are sinning presumptuously.

Who can deny that continued unbelief in the face of pressing requirements for faith is a presumptuous sin? Who can deny that where love and unselfish service are kept·back from God and men there is presumptuous sin? Such sins persisted in, against all light, instruction, warning, and appeal, will end in a cutting off from the people, a terrible exclusion from all those gracious rewards which come to the faithful and obedient. Presumptuous sins strike at the very foundation of the throne of God.

II. There was everything to call the attention of this transgressor in the fact that others were keeping the Sabbath. None could come into the Israelite camp and mistake the Sabbath for some other day, just as none could enter an English town on the day of rest and mistake it for a working day. When the man went out gathering sticks, there was something fresh at every step he took to remind him that he was transgressing a commandment of God; a dozen steps from his own door was enough for this. He went into sin with his eyes open and his selfish will determined to disobey God. Thus also there is presumptuous sin in despising those requirements of Christ which are not only plainly and repeatedly stated by him and his apostles, but carried out, from a sincere heart, in the daily practice of many who rejoice to call themselves his servants. Every Christian who by his life and the results of it shows that in his judgment certain requirements of Christ are all important, becomes thereby a witness to convict others of presumptuous sin. To act on the principle that faith in Christ is not absolutely necessary to salvation, righteousness, and eternal life, is to run counter to the life and emphatic confession of many in all generations of the Christian era. Every life in which Christ is manifested ruling and guiding is a fresh repetition of his great requirements, a fresh evidence of presumptuous sin on the part of those who neglect these requirements.

III. The sin appears all the greater from the act itself being so trifling. The first thought of many on reading the narrative may be, " What severity for such a little offence! " But the more it is looked at the greater the offence appears. There would have been more to say for the man if the temptation had come from some great thing. If a fortune or a kingdom had been in question, then there would have been some plausibly sufficient motive for a great transgression; but to break such a commandment, to run counter to the conduct of the whole camp for a handful of sticks, does it not show how proud-hearted the man was, how utterly careless of all and any of God's regulations? Such a man would have turned to idolatry and profanity on the one hand, or to theft and even murder on the other, at very slight provocation. It was a little thing for Esau to crave a mess of pottage, but it deservedly lost him his birthright when he valued it so little. Thus have men sinned against their Saviour for the paltriest trifles. Peter moves our sympathy when he denies Jesus, for life is dear when closely threatened, and we consider ourselves lest we also be tempted; but when Judas sells his master, and such a master, for thirty pieces of silver, how abominable the act appears! Yet men are constantly turning from Jesus on considerations as paltry and sordid. They will not be religious, because such continual carefulness is required in little things. This man sinned a great and daring sin against God; he was dragged in shame before the whole congregation, and then stoned outside the camp. And what had he by way of set-off? A few sticks. If it was a little thing to do, it was just as little a thing to be left undone. Small as it was, it showed the state of the man's heart, that corroding and hopeless leprosy within, which left no other course but to cut him off from the people.

IV. Thus we arrive at the full measure of the man's insult to the majesty of God. We see in what way he reproaches the Lord and despises his word. If this man had gone before Moses, when with the tables in his hands he came fresh from Sinai, and if he had heaped contumely on the messenger, and spat upon the tables, he could not have done more then to show contempt than he did by the gathering of those few sticks on the day which God had claimed for his own. Human governments, with all their imperfections, look upon deliberate defiance of their authority as a thing to be punished severely; what, then, must be done where there is a deliberate defiance of the authority of God? A terrible doom awaits those who despise and ridicule God's ordinances of right and wrong. Though it may not be swift and sudden, it will assuredly be certain and complete. Those who mourn their inability to keep the law of God are separated in his sight from those who contemn that law, far as the east is from the west. Be it ours to feel with David, " rivers of waters run down my eyes, because they keep not thy law " (Ps. cxix. 136), and not as the fool who says in his heart, There is no God (Ps. liii. 1 ; xix. 12—14).—Y.

Vers. 32—36.—*The law of the Sabbath : a solemn vindication.* I. THIS DOOM OF DEATH SHOWS THE IMPORTANCE OF THE SABBATH IN THE SIGHT OF GOD. 1. *There was need of something special to call attention to this point.* Those commandments which concerned himself directly he had to fence in a special way. Commandments against filial impiety, murder, adultery, theft, false witness, covetousness, these concerned man *directly*, and through him they concerned God ; man, therefore, might be trusted to help in vindicating these commands. But those against polytheism, idolatry, profanity, and Sabbath-breaking concerned God directly and man only indirectly. Man, therefore, might not perceive the hurt, even though it was real and most serious. Thus it became needful for God to deal in a specially stern and impressive way with the Sabbath-breaker. His people must be made to perceive and bear in mind that he meant the seventh day to be a holy day. It was as much sacrilege to spend it in common occupations as it was to defile the ark in the holy place. 2. *There was need to arrest the attention of such as kept the Sabbath in a negative rather than a positive way.* God gave the Sabbath, not for idleness, but for that most valuable of all rest which is gained in quiet, undisturbed communion with God, and meditation on all his wonderful works. Those who employed the Sabbath in solemn and devout approaches to the God of the covenant were delivered from temptation to break the Sabbath. Filled with the fulness of God, there would be no room for base, transgressing thoughts. But no commandment could bring the unwilling heart to God. It might do something to keep the work of the common day away from the hands ; it could do nothing to keep the thoughts of the common day out of the heart. The heart was to be sought ; it could not be forced, being in its nature beyond force. Many, therefore, would keep the day *negatively*, in utter idleness, and this idleness itself tended to disobedience. The doing of little things would seem practically the same as doing nothing. So men had to be taught, by terrible examples, not to trifle with holy things. If a man thoughtlessly touches things dangerous to physical life, his thoughtlessness will not deliver him from fatal consequences. If a man sports with poisons, or moves carelessly among machinery, he is very likely to lose his life; so men who trifled with the Sabbath were in great peril. Safety, progress, approval, blessedness, were for those who obeyed from the heart. But those who through heedlessness of the heart disobeyed with the hand had no right to complain when death outside the camp awaited them.

II. THIS SOLEMN VINDICATION HAS AN IMPORTANT BEARING ON THE CHRISTIAN DAY OF REST. This is not the place to take up even a fragment of the interminable discussion on the obligation of the Sabbath. But is not the very fact of such a discussion evidence that the lapse of the obligation is by no means a thing clearly and easily to be seen ? 1. *This solemn vindication hints to us that it is a prudent thing to be on the safe side.* Thus we may both escape great dangers and secure great blessings. To spend the day of rest just as we please is a claim, not of conscience, but of self-will. It cannot be pretended that ceasing from work one day in seven is a *hurt* to one's self or to the world. Practically, all Christians confess the need of a day of rest. If God so blessed one day in seven to those who knew him as he might be known in the obscurities and distances of the Jewish economy, is it not reasonable to expect that in the fuller light and nearer approach of God in Christ Jesus, a seventh day of rest, rightly used, may be the means of the greatest blessing. We are now under the perfect law of liberty ; and because it is a law of liberty it is all the more a law to the liberated soul. We use not our liberty for an occasion to the flesh ; we ought to use it for an occasion to the Spirit. God blessed and hallowed the seventh day, because in it he rested from his work of creation. What a propriety then in keeping the first day of the week, as that in which the Christian's Master rested from temptation, toil, and his victorious struggle with death and Hades ! 2. *This solemn vindication should make us considerate of all who are called by the ugly name of Sabbatarian.* No doubt with regard to the Sabbath there has been much of bigotry, ignorance, and of melancholy misinterpretations of the Scripture; but the weak brother who reads this narrative of the Sabbath-breaker's doom may well be excused if to stronger minds he seems ridiculously precise. Christ will deal with us as severely as his Father dealt with the Sabbath-breaker if we make one of his little ones to offend. It is necessary above all things to be safe. We must not confound the scrupulosity of the weak with the scrupulosity of the Pharisee. That, indeed, is always abominable—attending to little external things, and neglecting the weightier matters of the law. God's service, after all, whether on week day or Sunday, consists in the things we do rather than in those we refrain from doing. God, we may be sure, will take care that the day of rest is not narrowed out of harmony with the liberty of the gospel. As there were matters of necessity provided for under the law, so there is like provision under the gospel. A man of right spirit will not misinterpret the necessities. Jeremiah Horrocks, the young clergyman who first observed the transit of Venus, is said to have made his discovery on the Lord's Day, without allowing it in the least to interfere with his duties in the church. One of the most important principles of his steam-engine flashed into the mind of Watt as he was walking along Glasgow Green one Sunday morning. And it was one Sunday morning that Carey, entering his pulpit in India, received the new regulation prohibiting suttee. He at once sent for his pundit, and completed the translation into Bengalee before night.—Y.

EXPOSITION.

THE LAW OF TASSELS (vers. 37 — 41). Ver. 38.—**Bid them that they make them fringes.** צִיצִת, probably tassels. It seems to signify something flower-like and bright, like the blooms on a shrub ; the word צִיץ is applied to the shining plate of gold upon Aaron's head-band (Exod. xxviii. 36). In Jer. xlviii. 9 it seems to mean a wing, and in Ezek. viii. 3 צִיצִת is a lock of hair. The exact meaning must be gathered from the context, and on the whole that suggests a tassel rather than a fringe. The word גְּדִלִים, used in the parallel passage Deut. xxii. 12, seems to have this meaning. The Septuagint renders it by κράσπεδα, which is adopted in the Gospels (see on Matt. xxiii. 5). **In the borders of their garments.** Literally, " on the wings," ἐπὶ τὰ πτερύγια. The outer garment (בֶּגֶד here, כְּסוּת in Deut. xxii. 12) was worn like a plaid, so folded that the four corners were dependent, and on each of these corners was to be hung a tassel. It was also used as a coverlet by the poor (Exod. xxii. 27). **That they put upon the fringe of the borders a ribband of blue.** Rather, "that they put a string (or thread) of hyacinth-blue upon the tassel of the wing." Septuagint, κλῶσμα ὑακίνθινον. This may have been a blue string with which to fasten the tassel to the corner of the garment, as if it were the stalk on which this flower grew; or it may have been a prominent blue thread in the tassel itself. The later Jews seem to have understood it in this sense, and concerned themselves greatly with the symbolical arrangements of the blue and other threads,

and the method in which they were knotted together, so as to set forth the whole law with all its several commandments. The later Jews, however, have always contrived, with all their minute observance, to break the plain letter of the law : thus the modern *tālīth* is an under, and not an upper, garment.

Ver. 39.—**That ye may look upon it, and remember all the commandments.** It was indeed a minute and apparently trivial distinction, and yet such an one as would most surely strike the eye, and through the eye the mind. It was like the facings on a uniform which recall the fame and exploits of a famous regiment. The tasseled Hebrew was a marked man in other eyes, and in his own ; he could not pass himself off as one of the heathen ; he was perpetually reminded of the special relation in which he stood to the Lord, whose livery (so to speak)—or, to use another simile, whose colours—he wore. No doubt the sky-blue string or thread which was so prominent was meant to remind him of heaven, and of the God of heaven. **And that ye seek not after your own heart and your own eyes, after which ye use to go a whoring.** The office of the tassels was to promote a recollected spirit. As it was, their fickle minds were always ready to stray away towards any heathen follies which their restless eyes might light upon. The trivial but striking peculiarity of their dress should recall them to the thought that they were a peculiar people, holy to the Lord.

Ver. 41.—**I am the Lord your God.** This intensely solemn formula, here twice repeated, may serve to show how intimately the smallest observances of the Law were connected with the profoundest and most comforting of spiritual truths, if only observed in faith and true obedience. The whole of religion, theoretical and practical, lay in those words, and that whole was hung upon a tassel. It is further to be noted that this precept was given during the years of exile, and probably given as one which they *could* keep, and which would be helpful to them, at a time when almost all other distinctive observances were suspended.

HOMILETICS.

Vers. 37—41.— *A distinguishing mark of the faithful.* In the ordinance of the tassels we have at once the height and depth of the old dispensation—the most trivial of outward observances married to the deepest truths and greatest blessings of true religion. Spiritually we are to see here the distinctive marks of the faithful Christian which separate between him and the children of this world. Consider therefore—

I. THAT THE TASSELS WERE DESIGNED TO BE UNMISTAKEABLE MARKS OF DISTINCTION AND SEPARATION BETWEEN ISRAEL AND ALL OTHER PEOPLES; and that at a time when many other distinctions had fallen into abeyance. Even so it is exceeding necessary that the faithful disciple (who is the true Israelite) should not only be different, but be obviously different, from others; and this especially in an age when the old distinctions between the Church and the world are so greatly broken down. Nothing can be more abhorrent to God than a crypto-Christianity, which is ashamed of itself and endeavours to efface all visible distinctions between itself and the irreligion of the world. Christians were to be emphatically "a peculiar people," and if they seem "peculiar" to those who are not governed by Christian motives and principles, so much the better. It does not follow that they are right because they are unlike others, but at any rate they would not be right if they were like them (Rom. xii. 2; 2 Cor. vi. 14—18; Titus ii. 14; Heb. vii. 26; James iv. 4; 1 Pet. ii. 9).

II. THAT THE DISTINCTION HERE COMMANDED WAS TRIVIAL IN ITSELF, AND IN AFTER AGES TURNED TO SUPERSTITION AND ARROGANCE (Matt. xxiii. 5). Even so all external distinctions, however harmless and even venerable by association, have an unalterable tendency to substitute themselves for the inward differences which they symbolize. Consider the reproach which has overtaken the very name of "Christian"—a name so full of significance, warning, and encouragement—among heathens and Mahometans. And how little effect the high-sounding names of Christian bodies have had upon their lives, save indeed in fostering arrogance and self-righteousness. No external distinction is of any value unless it has a real correspondence to something inward and spiritual (Rom. ii. 29; xiv. 17; 1 Cor. viii. 8; Gal. vi. 15).

III. THAT THE TASSELS WERE INTENDED TO PRODUCE AND TO FOSTER A HABIT OF RE-COLLECTEDNESS, ESPECIALLY AMONG STRANGERS. The tasseled Hebrew was perpetually reminded that he shared in privileges, responsibilities, and dangers which the nations knew nothing of. Even so the faithful Christian has no greater or more necessary safeguard than a habit of recollectedness, and he is bound to cultivate it carefully by prayer and self-discipline. In the midst of innumerable entanglements, confusions, and perplexities, he has continually to call to mind whose he is and whom he serves. Mixing, conversing, dealing in every way with those whose aims, motives, and principles are avowedly worldly and selfish, he has to check himself at every turn by this recollection; and only thus can he escape from sin (Philip. ii. 15, 16; 1 Tim. vi. 1, 2; Titus ii. 8).

IV. THAT THE HYACINTHINE BLUE OF THE STRING, OR THREAD, WAS MEANT TO REMIND THE ISRAELITE OF HEAVEN, AND THE GOD OF HEAVEN (cf. the "jacinth" of Rev. ix. 17). Even so there must be in the faithful soul a perpetual remembrance of heaven as at once his home and goal; for it is this remembrance only mingling with all other thoughts which will keep him from the subtle greed and from the base attractions of earth (Philip. iii. 20; Heb. xii. 1, 2; 1 Pet. ii. 11; 2 Pet. iii. 12, 13). And note that this spirit of recollectedness in these two particulars, viz., whose we are, and whither we are bound, is the true and destinctive adornment of all faithful Christians, no matter in what diversity of outward circumstance they may be arrayed. And this, without the least ostentation or self-consciousness, will at once make them known to one another (cf. Mal. iii. 16), and mark them out for an instinctive wonder and admiration in the eyes of all who are seeking after God.

V. THAT THE ONE GREAT AND BLESSED TRUTH WHICH GAVE REALITY AND MEANING TO THIS DISTINCTION WAS, "I AM THE LORD YOUR GOD." Even so whatever may distinguish the faithful Christian from others has no other foundation than this, that God is *his* God—his in Christ, his in a sense which is beyond words or thought. It is not the fact that he is more righteous than others which any distinctive conduct or observance is meant to proclaim ; but simply that God has been more merciful to him, and has drawn him closer to himself in Christ (1 Cor. iii. 21—23 ; 1 John i. 3 ; 2 Pet. i. 4).

HOMILIES BY VARIOUS AUTHORS.

Vers. 37—41.—*The use and abuse of memorials.* This law is one of the many illustrations of the minute particulars prescribed by the laws of Moses. We find other illustrations in precepts respecting ploughing (Deut. xxii. 10), sowing (Deut. xxii. 9), reaping (Levit. xxiii. 22), threshing (Deut. xxv. 4), killing (Levit. xvii. 13), cooking (Exod. xxiii. 19), clothing (Deut. xxii. 11), &c. All these laws had certain moral or spiritual significations. The precept respecting the fringes teaches us—

I. THE VALUE OF MEMORIALS. 1. To remind us of spiritual truths. The peculiarity of the Jew's dress was a witness to him that he belonged to "a peculiar people" (Deut. xiv. 2) separated unto God. Possibly the blue colour (cf. Exod. xxviii. 31) was intended to remind him that he belonged to a kingdom of priests. 2. Such memorials are needed because of our treacherous memories, which, like sieves, may let pure water run away, but retain the sediment and rubbish. 3. And they are valuable for the sake of others. The Jews taught that even a blind man must wear the fringe, because others could see it. Strangers may be impressed by our memorial services, even if we are blind to their significance. Our children and their descendants may learn by them. Illustrations—Passover (Exod. xii. 24—27) ; altar and stones on Ebal and Gerizim (Deut. xxvii. 1—8 ; Josh. viii. 30—35). The Lord's Supper, by which we "show Christ's death till he come."

II. THE DANGER OF THEIR ABUSE. 1. Because of our inveterate tendency to exaggerate the importance of what is external. Hence fringes were "enlarged" (Matt. xxiii. 5) and phylacteries were invented (Deut. vi. 6—9). The simple supper of the Lord has been developed into the pompous ceremonies of the mass. 2. And thus to stop at the symbol and thereby prevent it. Illustrations—The serpent of brass idolised (2 Kings xviii. 4) ; the ark treated as a charm (1 Sam. iv. 3). 3. And by so doing to "come short" of the promise of salvation which is "in Christ Jesus," who is "the way, and the truth, and the life." Nevertheless, God does not take away symbolic memorials from us, but throws on us the responsibility of using "as not abusing" them.—P.

Vers. 37—40.—*The fringes: ever-present reminders.* I. A NEED TO BE PROVIDED FOR. These numerous and all-important commandments must, if such a thing is possible, be kept continually before the minds of the people. God has already provided for the need, in fact, by appointing an atonement for sins of ignorance. These would be very largely sins of forgetfulness, and so, as prevention is better than cure, it was desirable to guard against forgetfulness. Sins of ignorance, when committed, may be atoned for, but it is better, if such a thing can be, not to commit them at all. Hence God, knowing the natural forgetfulness of the human heart, and how many cares, pleasures, novelties, and objects of interest there are to draw it away from the consideration of his will, recognises a need to be provided for in a special way. The will of God, moreover, needed to be *constantly remembered.* It bears on all our conscious life, and through that in many unknown ways on the unconscious life beneath. There was no action of an Israelite's life but could be done in God's way or in his own. A moment's incaution, and he might step into some great transgression. The law through Moses was a thing of details, and to neglect the least detail was to impair the whole. Evidently *this need has still to be provided for.* The law through Christ for our life is also one needing to be constantly remembered. There is no moment when it does not stand before us in all its spirituality, and its searching for inward conformity. Nor can we pretend that our hearts are any better, any more in sympathy with God, than those in Israel of old. The human heart under Christ needs to be provided for just as much as under Moses. Thus we may be sure that if God saw the need then, he sees it equally now.

II. GOD'S PROVISION FOR THE NEED. *He provided something that should always be before the eye.* Fringes or tassels on the garments were ever-present remembrancers. Many times a day the wearer could not but cast his eye on this addition to his garment, and he was at once to recollect that it was something not added by his own fancy, but that he might ask himself the question, " Am I at this moment doing the will of God ? " Nor on his own garment only was the fringe of use ; every time his eye rested on the garments of others, similarly adorned, he was reminded to treat them in a just, godly, and brotherly fashion, as being also Israelites, holy and privileged as himself (Gal. vi. 10). And may we not say that we have reminders, so various, numerous, and increasing, as to the claims of God upon us, that they amount to something like a fringe on our garments ? There may be nothing of distinct Divine appointment in many of these reminders, but if they are such as naturally turn our attention to holy things, then the presence of them adds very much to our responsibility. Every Bible that we see ; every passage of Scripture set in other writing ; every church spire rising to the sky, or even the humblest building given to religious uses ; every known minister of religion, or indeed any one known to be a Christian ; every grave-yard and burial procession—these and many such have all in them something of the fringes. We cannot afford to despise any helps towards knowledge and obedience. *He provided the same memorial for all.* He did not count it sufficient there should be any memorial the individual might choose. There was to be no room for individual caprice. The memorial was a fringe, and it was always blue. Thus, while there are many things which *may be used* to remind us of God's will, there are some *especially designed for this end.* Those who accept the permanent obligation of the Lord's Supper are brought, on every observance of it, face to face with him whom only too easily we forget. " Do this in remembrance of me." But since all do not accept this obligation, and those who do meet in different ways and with varying frequency, we can hardly find here that which is to correspond in the gospel with the fringes in the law. Is there any one settled and definite thing which Christ gives us now the same for us all ? May we not answer from John xvi. 13 : " When he, the Spirit of truth, is come, he will guide you into all (the) truth " ? Where Moses gave commandments, Christ gave promises, which are only commandments in another form. We have now to do not with a body of positive precepts, to be understood and obeyed in our natural strength, but with a living and life-giving *Spirit*, and the more we have the life of that Spirit in us, the more we shall be preserved from errors in doctrine, and from omissions, exaggerations, and defects in duty. We are not now called to manufacture lifeless and merely typical observances according to a pattern. Obedience now is to be a growth ; and if there is heavenly, pure, and energetic life in us, then we shall not be lacking in strength, beauty, and fruitfulness. *What signification, if any, may there be in the colour ?* Perhaps it is not fanciful to suppose that it may have been chosen as having correspondence with the tint of the sky—something to help in turning the thoughts of the people away from earth to him who dwells on high. Tennyson reminds us (' In Memoriam,' li.) of

" The sinless years
That breathed beneath the Syrian blue."

III. THE LIMITED USE OF GOD'S PROVISION. It was as good a monitor as could be given in the circumstances, always moving about with the person who had to remember. But remembrance, even supposing it exact and opportune, would only reveal more and more the inevitable weakness in action. What could the fringes help in the doing ? Could they turn men from seeking after their own hearts and their own eyes ? By the law is the knowledge of sin (Rom. iii. 20). Hence the better their knowledge of the law in its requirements, and the more exact their remembrance, the more painful and depressing would be the consciousness of their own sin. The holier they became in outward compliances, the more would they feel their pollution and their separation of heart from God. If any one ever knew the value of the fringes, we should judge it to have been David, yet read Ps. cxix., and notice how he there gathers up his earnest longings for conformity with God's law, and not unfrequently seems to tread the verge of despair. We must have more than mere admonitions, however frequent and earnest, if we are to do God's will and be in truth holy before him. Hence we come back to that work of the Spirit of Christ, putting within us new life, and that love which is the best of all monitors. The fringe above all fringes, the riband made of heaven's own blue, is to have love in the heart. Love never forgets. It has its object ever in its thoughts—first in the morning, last at night, and flitting even through dreams. Fringes may recall words and outward ceremonies, but love discovers fresh applications and larger meanings. Love does with the mere words of commandment as the chemist does with material things, ever discovering in them new combinations, properties, and powers (John xiv. 23—26).—Y.

Ver. 41.—*God recalls a great deed and the purpose of it.* I. GOD RECALLS A GREAT DEED. " I brought you out of the land of Egypt." 1. *It was deliverance from a bitter bondage.* The Israelites had been making light of it of late, but in Egypt it was grievous indeed (Exod. i. 13, 14; ii. 23; iii. 7; vi. 9). So God, by the work of his incarnate Son, delivered the world from a bitter bondage. " Behold the Lamb of God which taketh away the sin of the whole world." The act of Divine power by which Jesus rose from the grave did not sweep away all difficulties and make life henceforth a path of roses. But it is a great deal to stand on this side, historically, of the sepulchre from which the stone was rolled away. The generations before the resurrection of Jesus were, as we may say, in Egypt, waiting deliverance. The world since that event stands, as it were, delivered. He who brought life and immortality to light destroyed him that had the power of death, that is, the devil, and delivered them who through fear of death were all their lifetime subject to bondage (Heb. ii. 14, 15). 2. *It was a deliverance worked out entirely by God.* "*I* brought you out, &c." There was no struggle against Pharaoh on the part of the people. We do not see the prisoner within conspiring with the deliverer outside. The bondage was so bitter, the subjection so complete, that the people were not moved to conspiracy and insurrection. We read constantly in history of servile and subject races winning their way to freedom through the bloody struggles of many generations, but these Israelites before Pharaoh were like oxen broken to the plough. They groaned, but they submitted. And in this Egyptian sort of bondage the world was fast before Christ came to deliver. Men groaned under the burdens of life; they were filled with the fruits of sin; they yielded at last to the grasp of death. All was accepted as a mysterious necessity; men did not protest and struggle against calamity and death. The deliverance is from Jesus, and in it we have no hand. " When we were yet without strength, in due time Christ died for the ungodly " (Rom. v. 6). A delivered world was even incredulous as to its deliverance. It could not believe that as by one man came sin and death, so by one also had come conquest over sin, death, and the devil. Thomas, the very disciple, doubts, and before long Paul has to write 1 Cor. xv. Jesus may say to the world for which he died and rose again, "*I* brought you out of spiritual Egypt." 3. *While the deliverance was being worked out, the Israelites were scarcely conscious of what was being done.* They saw the plagues, but only as wonders, stupendous physical calamities. They felt the grasp of Pharaoh alternately tightening and relaxing, but little did they comprehend of that great, significant struggle going on between Jehovah and Pharaoh. They waited, as the prize of victory waits on the athletes while they contend; it knows nothing of the energy and endurance it has evoked. And so it was and is in Christ's redeeming work. It is wonderful to notice how unconscious the world was of that great work which was transacted between Bethlehem and Jerusalem, between the cradle of Jesus and his opened grave. The world looked upon him, and to a large extent it still looks, in any light but the right one. Let us know him first then, and fully in all that the work means, as Deliverer from spiritual Egypt.

II. THE PURPOSE OF THIS GREAT DEED. "I brought you out of the land of Egypt to be your God." It is one thing for Israel to be brought out of Egypt; quite another for it to understand why it has been brought out. And so we find the people complaining of the wilderness quite as much as they had done of Egypt. Their expectations pointed in a direction opposite to God's purpose, and never could the wilderness become a better place than Egypt until they did appreciate God's purpose and make it their own. God did not bring them out as one might bring a man out of prison, and then say, "Go where you like." They were brought out of a bitter bondage to enter upon a reasonable service, otherwise the wilderness would prove only an exchange of suffering, not a release from it. In like manner we need to ask how the world may be made better by the redeeming work of Christ. The difference between the state of the world before the death of Christ and since does not look as great from certain points of view as one might expect. A countless host of those for whom he died and rose again nevertheless goes about in a bewilderment and unbelief equal to that of the Israelites in the wilderness. Christ died for us and rose again, that we, rising with him, might live not to ourselves, but to him (Rom. vi. 4, 10—13, indeed the whole chapter; xii. 1; xiv. 7—9; 1 Cor. iii. 22, 23; x. 31; 2 Cor. v. 15—18; x. 5; Eph. ii. 10; Philip. i. 20, 21; Col. iii. 1—3). Deliverance from Egypt is not equivalent to entrance into the promised land. The wilderness is a critical place for us, and all depends on what heed we take to this purpose of God. We must receive the gospel *in its integrity*. If the full purpose of God becomes our full purpose, then all will be right. Christ died for us not that we might just escape the penalty and power of sin, as something painful to ourselves, and know the luxury of a washed conscience; not that we might just pass into a perfect blessedness beyond the tomb; but that, becoming pure and blessed, we might engage in the service of God and set forth his glory. We must be pleased with what pleases him. The work of Christ brings us that highest of all joy, to serve God with a perfect heart and a willing mind.—Y.

VINDICATION OF THE AARONIC PRIESTHOOD (CHS. XVI., XVII.).

EXPOSITION.

CHAPTER XVI.

THE GAINSAYING OF KORAH (vers. 1—40). Ver. 1.—**Now Korah . . took men.** קֹרַח וַיִּקַּח. The word "took" stands alone at the head of the sentence in the singular number. This does not by itself confine its reference to Korah, because it may be taken as repeated after each of the other names; at the same time, the construction suggests that in its original form Korah alone was mentioned, and that the other names were afterwards added in order to include them in the same statement. The ellipsis after "took" (if it be one) may be filled up by "men," as in the A. V. and in most versions, or by "counsel," as in the Jerusalem Targum. The Septuagint has in place of וַיִּקַּח ἐλάλησε, representing apparently a different reading. Some commentators regard it as an anacoluthon for "took two hundred and fifty men, . . and rose up with them;" others, again, treat the "took" as a pleonasm, as in 2 Sam. xviii. 18 and elsewhere; but the change of number from וַיִּקַּח to וַיָּקֻמוּ makes it difficult. It seems best to say that the construction is broken and cannot be satisfactorily explained. Indeed there can be no question that the

whole narrative, like the construction of the opening verses, is very confused, and leaves on the mind the impression that it has been altered, not very skilfully, from its original form. The two parts of the tragedy, that concerning the company of Korah, and that concerning the Reubenites, although mingled in the narrative, do not adjust themselves in the mind, and the general effect is obscure. It is sufficient to point out here that no one can certainly tell what became of the ringleader himself, who was obviously the head and front of the whole business. Some are strenuously of opinion that he was swallowed up alive, others as strenuously that he was consumed with fire; but the simple fact is that his death is not recorded in this chapter at all, although he is assumed to have perished. The obscurity which hangs over this passage cannot be traced to any certain cause; the discrepancies and contradictions which have been discovered in it are due to mistake or misrepresentation; nor can any evil motive be plausibly assigned for the interpolation (if it be such) of that part of the story which concerns the Reubenites. If, for some reason unknown to us, an original narrative of Korah's rebellion was enlarged so as to include the simultaneous mutiny of the Reubenites and their fate ; and if, further, that en-largement was so unskilfully made as to leave considerable confusion in the narrative, wherein does that affect either its truth or its inspiration ? The supernatural influence which watched over the production of the sacred narrative certainly did not interfere with any of those natural causes which affected its composition, its style, its clear-ness or obscurity. **Korah, the son of Izhar, the son of Kohath, the son of Levi.** On the genealogy of the Levites see Exod. vi. 16—22, and above on ch. iii. 17—19. It is generally supposed that some generations are passed over in these genealogies. Korah be-longed to the same Kohathite sub-tribe as Moses and Aaron, and was related to them by some sort of cousinship ; his father (or ancestor) Izhar was the younger brother of Amram and the elder brother of Uzziel, whose descendant Elizaphan had been made chief of the Kohathites. **Dathan and Abiram, the sons of Eliab.** Eliab himself was apparently the only son of Pallu, the second son of Reuben (ch. xxvi. 5, 8). If the word " son " is to be literally understood in all these cases, then Korah, Dathan, and Abiram would all be great-great-grandsons of Jacob himself. **On, the son of Peleth.** It is one of the strange obscurities of this narrative that On, who appears here as a ring-leader, is never mentioned again either in this chapter or elsewhere. **Sons of Reuben.** Reubenites. The encampment of their tribe was on the south side of the tabernacle in the outer line (ch. ii. 10), while that of the Kohathites was on the same side in the inner line. Thus they were to some extent neighbours ; but see below on ver. 24.

Ver. 2.—**And they rose up before Moses.** It is suggested that the Reubenites were aggrieved because their father had been deprived of his birthright in favour of Judah, and that Korah was aggrieved be-cause the Uzzielites had been preferred in the person of Elizaphan to the Izharites (ch. iii. 30). These accusations have nothing whatever in the narrative to support them, and are suspicious because they are so easy and so sure to be made in such cases. In all ecclesiastical history the true reformer, as well as the heretic and the demagogue, has always been charged with being actuated by motives of disappointed ambition. Without these gratuitous suppositions there was quite enough to excite the anger and opposition of such discontented and insubordinate minds as are to be found in every community. **With certain of the children of Israel.** These were gathered from the tribes at large, as implied in the statement that Zelophehad a Manassite was not amongst them (ch. xxvii. 3). **Famous in the congregation.** Literally, " called men of the congregation." Septua-

gint, σύγκλητοι βουλῆς, representatives of the host in the great council (cf. ch. i. 16 ; xxvi. 9).

Ver. 3.—**They gathered themselves to-gether against Moses and against Aaron.** They had risen up before Moses, i. e. made a tumult in his presence, because they regarded him (and rightly) as the actual ruler of Israel in religious as well as in secular matters. At the same time, the attack of Korah and his company (with whom alone the narrative is really concerned here) was directed especially against the ecclesiastical rule which Moses exercised through his brother Aaron. **Ye take too much upon you.** רַב־לָכֶם, "much for you," probably in the sense of "enough for you" (cf. the use of רַב in Gen. xlv. 28), i. e. you have enjoyed power long enough ; so the Targum Palestine. It may, however, be taken with the following כִּי as meaning, "let it suffice you that all the congregation," &c. ; and so the Septuagint, ἐχέτω ὑμῖν ὅτι, κ. τ. λ. The Targum of Onkelos renders it in the same sense as the A. V. **All the congregation are holy, every one of them.** This was perfectly true, in a sense. There was a sanctity which pertained to Israel as a nation, in which all its members shared as distinguished from the nations around (Exod. xix. 6 ; Levit. xx. 26) ; there was a priest-hood which was inherent in all the sons of Israel, older and more indelible than that which was conferred on Aaron's line — a priesthood which, apart from special restric-tions, or in exceptional circumstances, might and did assert itself in priestly acts (Exod. xxiv. 5, and compare the cases of Samuel, Elijah, and others who offered sacrifice during the failure of the appointed priesthood). If Moses had taken the power to himself, or if he had (as they doubtless supposed) restricted active priestly functions to Aaron because he was his brother, and wholly under his influence, their contention would have been quite right. They erred, as most violent men do, not because they asserted what was false, but because they took for granted that the truth which they asserted was really in-consistent with the claims which they as-sailed. The congregation were all holy ; the sons of Israel were all priests ; that was true— but it was also true that by Divine command Israel could only exercise his corporate priest-hood outwardly through the one family which God had set apart for that purpose. The same God who has lodged in the body certain faculties and powers for the benefit of the body, has decreed that those faculties and powers can only be exercised through certain determinate organs, the very specialisation of which is both condition and result of a high organisation. **The congregation of the Lord.** There are two words for congregation in this verse: קָהָל here, and עֵדָה before. The former seems to be used in the more solemn sense, but they are for the most part indistinguishable, and certainly cannot be assigned to different authors.

Ver. 5.—**He spake unto Korah.** That Korah was the mainspring of the conspiracy is evident (cf. ver. 22; ch. xxvii. 3; Jude 11 *b*.). It may well be that his position as a prominent Levite and a relation of Moses gave him great influence with men of other tribes, and earned him a great name for disinterestedness and liberality in advocating the rights of all Israel, and in denouncing the exclusive claims and privileges by which he himself (as a Levite) was benefited. It is often assumed that Korah was secretly aiming at the high-priesthood, but of this, again, there is not a shadow of proof; his error was great enough, and his punishment sore enough, without casting upon him these unfounded accusations. It would be more in accordance with human nature if we supposed that Korah was in his way sincere; that he had really convinced himself, by dint of trying to convince others, that Moses and Aaron were usurpers; that he began his agitation without thought of advantage of himself; that, having gained a considerable following and much popular applause, the pride of leadership and the excitement of conflict led him on to the last extremity. **The Lord will show who are his.** אֶת־אֲשֶׁר־לוֹ, the meaning of which is defined by the following words, "whom he hath chosen." Moses refers the matter to the direct decision of the Lord; as that decision had originated the separate position of Aaron, that should also vindicate it.

Ver. 6. — **Take you censers.** מַחְתּוֹת. Septuagint, πυρεῖα. Translated "fire-pans" in Exod. xxvii. 3. From the number required, they must have been either household utensils used for carrying fire, or else they must have been made in some simple fashion for the occasion. The offering of incense was proposed by Moses as a test because it was a typically priestly function, to which the gravest importance was attached (Levit. x. 1; xvi. 12, 13), and because it was so very simply executed.

Ver. 7.—**Ye take too much upon you, ye sons of Levi.** רַב־לָכֶם, as in ver. 3. The exact meaning of this *tu quoque* is not apparent. Perhaps he would say that if he and Aaron were usurpers, the whole tribe of Levi were usurpers too.

Ver. 8. — **Hear, I pray you, ye sons of Levi.** No son of Levi is mentioned in the narrative except Korah, and this address itself passes into the second person singular (vers. 10, 11), as though Korah alone were personally guilty. It is possible enough that behind him was a considerable body of public opinion among the Levites more or less decidedly supporting him; but there is no need to impute any general disloyalty to them.

Ver. 9.—**Seemeth it a small thing to you.** Rather, "is it too little for you." מִכֶּם הַמְעַט.

Ver. 11.—**For which cause both thou and all thy company are gathered together.** It does not follow that Korah was seeking an exclusive dignity for himself, or for his tribe. His "company" apparently included representative men from all the tribes, or at least from many (see on ver. 2). They were seeking the priesthood because they affirmed it to be the common possession of all Israelites. **Against the Lord.** It was in *his* name that they appeared, and to some extent no doubt sincerely; but since they appeared to dispute an ordinance actually and historically made by God himself, it was indeed against him that they were gathered. **And what is Aaron, that ye murmur against him?** The construction is broken, as so often when we have the *ipsissima verba* of Moses, whose meekness did not enable him to speak calmly under provocation. The sentence runs, "For which cause thou and all thy company who are gathered against the Lord,—and Aaron, who is he, that ye murmur against him?" It was easy to represent the position of Aaron in an invidious light, as though they were assailing some personal sacerdotal pretensions; but in truth he was only a poor servant of God doing what he was bid.

Ver. 12.—**And Moses sent to call Dathan and Abiram.** The part really taken by these men in the agitation is very obscure. They were not of the two hundred and fifty, nor were they with them when they gathered together against Moses and Aaron—perhaps because they took no interest in ecclesiastical matters, and only resented the secular domination of Moses. Neither can we tell why Moses sent for them at this juncture, unless he suspected them of being in league with Korah (see below on ver. 24). **We will not come up,** *i. e.* to the tabernacle, as being spiritually the culminating point of the camp.

Ver. 13.—**Is it a small thing.** Rather, "is it too little," as in ver. 9. **A land that floweth with milk and honey.** A description applying by right to the land of promise (Exod. iii. 8; ch. xiii. 27), which they in their studied insolence applied to Egypt. **Except thou make thyself altogether a prince over us.** Literally, "that (כִּי) thou altogether lord it over us." The expression is strengthened in the original by the reduplication of the verb in the inf. abs., גַּם־הִשְׂתָּרֵר.

Ver. 14.—**Moreover thou hast not brought us.** According to the promises (they meant to say) by which he had induced them to leave their comfortable homes in Egypt (Exod. iv. 30, 31). **Wilt thou put out the eyes of these men?** *i. e.* wilt thou blind them to the utter failure of thy plans and promises? wilt thou throw dust in their eyes?

Ver. 15.—**And Moses was very wroth.** The bitter taunts of the Reubenites had just enough semblance of truth in them to make them very hard to bear, and especially the imputation of low personal ambition; but it is impossible to say that Moses did not err through anger. **Respect not thou their offering.** Cf. Gen. iv. 4. It is not quite clear what offering Moses meant, since they do not seem to have wished to offer incense. Probably it was equivalent to saying, Do not thou accept them when they approach thee; for such approach was always by sacrifice (cf. Ps. cix. 7). **I have not taken one ass from them.** Cf. 1 Sam. xii. 3. The ass was the least valuable of the ordinary live stock of those days (cf. Exod. xx. 17). The Septuagint has here οὐκ ἐπιθύμημα οὐδενὸς αὐτῶν εἴληφα, which is apparently an intentional paraphrase with a reference to the tenth commandment (οὐκ ἐπιθυμήσεις, κ. τ. λ.). **Neither have I hurt one of them.** As absolute ruler he might have made himself very burdensome to all, and very terrible to his personal enemies. Compare Samuel's description of the Eastern autocrat (1 Sam. viii. 11—17).

Ver. 16.—**And Moses said unto Korah.** After the interchange of messages with the Reubenites, Moses repeats his injunctions to Korah to be ready on the morrow to put his claims to the test, adding that Aaron too should be there, that the Lord might judge between them.

Ver. 18.—**Stood in the door of the tabernacle,** *i. e.* at the door of the court, so that they were visible from the space outside.

Ver. 19.—**And Korah gathered all the congregation against them.** It does not follow that the whole congregation was actively or deliberately on Korah's side. But a movement ostensibly in behalf of the many as against the few is sure to enlist a general, if not a deep, sympathy; nor is it to be supposed that Moses and Aaron could escape a large amount of unpopularity under the grievous circumstances of the time. The thoughtless multitude would have hailed their downfall with real though short-lived satisfaction. **The glory of the Lord appeared.** As before (ch. xiv. 10), filling the tabernacle probably, and flashing out before the eyes of all.

Ver. 21.—**That I may consume them in a moment.** Literally, "and I will consume them." The same thing must be said of this as of ch. xiv. 11, 12.

Ver. 22.—**O God, the God of the spirits of all flesh.** אֵל אֱלֹהֵי הָרוּחֹת לְכָל־בָּשָׂר. The *ruach* is the spirit of life which the Creator has imparted unto perishable flesh, and made it live. In some sense it belongs to beasts as well as to men (Eccles. iii. 19, 21); but in the common use of the word men only are thought of, as having received it by a special communication of a higher order (Gen. ii. 7; 1 Cor. xv. 45). Moses, therefore, really appeals to God, as the Author and Giver of that imperishable life-principle which is lodged in the mortal flesh of all men, not to destroy the works of his own hands, the creatures made in his own image. Here we have in its germ that idea of the universal fatherhood of God which remained undeveloped in Jewish thought until Judaism itself expanded into Christianity (cf. Isa. lxiii. 16; lxiv. 8, 9; Acts xvii. 26, 29). **Shall one man sin.** Rather, "the one man (הָאִישׁ) hath sinned," *i. e.* Korah, who had misled all the rest.

Ver. 23.—**The Lord spake unto Moses.** No direct answer was apparently vouchsafed to the remonstrance of Moses and Aaron, but it was tacitly allowed.

Ver. 24.—**Get you up from about the tabernacle of Korah, Dathan, and Abiram.** The word "tabernacle" (*mishcan*) is the same word which is so translated in ver. 9, but not the same which is used in vers. 18, 19; it properly signifies "dwelling-place." It is certainly the natural conclusion, from the use of this expression here and in ver. 27, that this *mishcan* was something different from the "tents" (אֹהָלֵי) mentioned in vers. 26, 27, and was some habitation common to the three rebels (see below on ver. 31). The Septuagint, in order to avoid the difficulty, omits the names of Dathan and Abiram, and has only ἀπὸ τῆς συναγωγῆς Κορέ.

Ver. 26.—**Touch nothing of theirs.** Because they, and all that belonged to them, were *anathema*, devoted to destruction. Compare the case of Achan (Josh. vii. 1).

Ver. 27.—**And Dathan and Abiram . . stood in the door of their tents.** To see what Moses would do. Nothing is said of Korah.

Ver. 28.—**For I have not done them of mine own mind.** Literally, "that not of my heart." כִּי־לֹא מִלִּבִּי. Septuagint, ὅτι οὐκ ἀπ' ἐμαυτοῦ.

Ver. 29.—**If they be visited after the visitation of all men.** פָּקַד is of somewhat doubtful meaning; it seems to answer to the ἐπίσκεψις and ἐπισκοπή of the Septuagint, and to our "oversight," or "visitation" (German, *heimsuchung*. Thus it may mean practically the providence of God for good, *i. e.* in the way of protection, or for evil, *i. e.* in the way of judgment. In either sense providence showed itself in no ordinary form towards these men.

Ver. 30.—**Make a new thing.** "Create a creation." בְּרִיאָה יִבְרָא. **Into the pit.** Rather, "into Sheol." שְׁאֹלָה. Septuagint, εἰς ᾅδου. Sheol is not "the pit," but Hades, the place of departed spirits (Gen. xxxvii. 35; xlii. 38), which is regarded, according to the general instinct of mankind, as being "under the earth" (cf. Philip. ii. 10 *b.*; Rev. v. 13). They were to go down "quick" into Sheol, because they were still alive at the moment that they were lost to sight for ever.

Ver. 31.—**The ground clave asunder that was under them.** As it sometimes does during an earthquake. In this case, however, the event was predicted, and wholly supernatural. The sequence of the narrative would lead us to suppose that the earth opened beneath the tents of Dathan and Abiram in the camp of Reuben. It is difficult to think of the gulf as extending so far as to involve the tent of Korah in the Kohathite lines in the same destruction, while there is nothing to suggest the idea that the earth opened in more than one place. It is true that the camps of the Reubenites and of the Kohathites were more or less contiguous; but when it is remembered that there were 46,500 adult males in the former, and 8600 males in the latter, and that a broad space must have been left between the two lines of encampment, it is obviously improbable that Korah's tent was in a practical sense "near" to those of Dathan and Abiram, unless indeed he had purposely removed it in order to be under the protection of his Reubenite partisans. It is very observable that not a word is said here as to the fate of Korah himself. It is implied in ver. 40 that he had perished, and it is apparently asserted in ch. xxvi. 10 that he was swallowed up with Dathan and Abiram (see the note there). On the other hand, Deut. xi. 6; Ps. cvi. 17 speak of the engulfing of the other two without any mention of Korah himself sharing their fate; and while "all the men that appertained unto Korah" perished, his own sons did not (ch. xxvi. 11). On these grounds it is held by most commentators that Korah died by fire among those who offered incense (ver. 35). This, however, is untenable, because "the two hundred and fifty men who offered incense" are distinctly mentioned as having been his partisans (ver. 2), and are always

counted exclusive of Korah himself. On the whole, while it is certain that the narrative is very obscure, and the question very doubtful, it seems most agreeable to all the testimonies of Holy Scripture to conclude — 1. That Korah had left his own place, and had some sort of dwelling (*mishcan*) either in common with Dathan and Abiram, or hard by their tents. 2. That the earth opened and swallowed up the *mishcan* of Korah, and the tents of Dathan and Abiram. 3. That Korah's men (see next verse) and their property were swallowed up with his *mishcan*, and (as far as we can tell) Korah himself also. If this be correct, then the much disputed heading of the chapter in the A. V. will be right after all.

Ver. 32.—**And their houses,** *i. e.* their families, as in ch. xviii. 13. **And all the men that appertained unto Korah.** Literally, "all the men who to Korah." Whether it means his dependants, or his special partisans, is uncertain. Perhaps some had clung to his fortunes in blind confidence when the rest gat up from his *mishcan*.

Ver. 34.—**At the cry of them.** לְקֹלָם, "at the noise of them;" at the mingled sound of their shrieks and of the natural convulsion amidst which they disappeared.

Ver. 35.—**There came out a fire from the Lord.** The fire probably flashed out from the sanctuary with the destructive force of lightning. **The two hundred and fifty men.** These had remained swinging their censers before the gate of the tabernacle while Moses and (presumably) Korah himself had gone to the camp of Reuben.

Ver. 37.—**Speak unto Eleazar.** This is the first time that any special duty is assigned to Eleazar, who was destined to succeed to the high-priesthood. We may suppose that he was sent instead of his father because the duty of gathering up the censers could hardly have been carried out without incurring legal defilement by contact with the dead. **Out of the burning.** Or, "out of the burnt." Septuagint, ἐκ μέσου τῶν κατακεκαυμένων. From amongst the charred and smouldering corpses. **Scatter thou the fire yonder; for they are hallowed.** The censers had been made holy even by that sacrilegious dedication, and must never revert to any common uses; for the same reason the live coals which still remained in them were to be emptied out in a separate place.

Ver. 38.—**These sinners against their own souls.** בְּנַפְשֹׁתָם, "against their own lives." The thought is not that they had ruined their souls, but that they had forfeited their lives. The Pentateuch does not contemplate any consequences of sin beyond physical death. The same phrase occurs in Prov. xx. 2. **For a covering of the altar.** The altar of burnt incense. The censers were no doubt brazen pans, and when beaten out would form plates which could be affixed to the boards of which the frame of the altar was composed.

Ver. 40.— **That he be not as Korah.** בְקֹרַח וְלֹא־יִחְיֶה. That he do not meet with the same fate as Korah.

HOMILETICS.

Vers. 1—40.—*The true and only Priesthood.* It is quite clear that the homiletic application of this passage turns upon a question which is strongly controverted—a question which it is alike impossible (save at the cost of honesty and truth) to shirk, or to take for granted one way or the other. That the rebellion of Korah was directed under specious pretences against a divinely-ordained priesthood vested in one man and his successors is of course undenied, but is of little interest or value apart from its application to our own times and circumstances. The practical question which immediately arises, and arises only to be disputed. is this, What priesthood now corresponds to that assailed in Aaron? It may no doubt be said that there is nothing which now answers to it, nothing of which *that* was a shadow and a type; that Judaism was a sacerdotal religion, but that Christianity is not. If that were true then Korah was after all right; his only error was that he held opinions in advance of his age. But apart from that, such a position simply robs both the incident and record of any value for ourselves, and is point-blank opposed to the Apostolic teaching in such places as 1 Cor. x. 11, and Jude 11. In the latter the "gainsaying of Korah" is specified as one of those typical acts of wickedness in which a virulent form of moral evil active in the days of the apostle had been anticipated both as to sin and punishment; the bad men of whom he speaks (vers. 4, 8, 10) had already met their doom in a figure when Korah and his company perished. It is clear that Holy Scripture recognises, both generally and specifically, a teaching value for Christian times in this record. The most useful and honest plan will therefore be to set forth the elements of the question impartially, and to leave them to the consideration of the reader. Some points will come out with sufficient clearness to command general (if not universal) assent; and others will at least be cleared of misleading arguments and false associations.

I. The first position which we can take up with authority and certainty is the positive position that THE PRIESTHOOD OF AARON AND HIS SONS WAS THE OLD TESTAMENT TYPE AND SHADOW OF THE PRIESTHOOD OF CHRIST CONFERRED UPON HIM IN HIS HUMAN NATURE AS THE SON OF MAN. This is argued and proved with many illustrations by the author of the Epistle to the Hebrews (see especially ch. v. 4, 5; vii. 11—28; viii. 1—4; x. 11—14, 21). The elaborate comparison of the two priesthoods, the old and the new, which was also infinitely older,—and especially the assertion that the Levitical priests were many only because death deposed them from office (ch. vii. 23), whilst Christ abideth for ever,—forbid us to regard any other priesthood than that of our Lord as the Christian analogue of the Jewish priesthood. As far as the type went Aaron lived on in all his priestly race, just as he had lived before in his chosen ancestor Abraham (Heb. vii. 10): there was but one Jewish high-priest, and unto him corresponds in the kingdom of heaven Jesus and Jesus alone. Herein all will be substantially agreed who loyally accept the testimony of Scripture, and herein (if it be clearly and devoutly held) is the real heart of the matter. and the sufficient safeguard against superstition.

II. The second position which we can take up on purely Scriptural grounds, and which is not fairly assailable, is the negative position THAT NO ARGUMENT AGAINST MINISTERIAL OR SACERDOTAL ASSUMPTIONS OR CLAIMS IS VALID WHICH IS BASED UPON THE HOLINESS AND PRIESTLY CHARACTER OF ALL THE FAITHFUL. It is perfectly clear that Korah and his company had both Scripture and fact on their side when they said that all the congregation were holy and all were priests. They erred in taking for granted that the priesthood of all Israelites was really inconsistent with the special priesthood of Aaron. As things were, it is certain that the universal priesthood of Israel could best express itself, best translate itself into worship, through the ministerial acts of Aaron and his sons. A spiritually-minded Jew, who recognised most deeply his own priestly calling in Israel, would most devoutly give thanks for the separation of the tribe of Levi and family of Aaron, because he would feel that no one benefited so much by that separation as himself; far from standing between him and the God of Israel, it enabled him to draw nigh to God in a multitude of ways otherwise impossible. He would indeed be able to argue from the histories of Gideon, of Samuel, of Elijah, and of others of the chosen race, that the priesthood of the ordinary Israelite, although usually dormant as to outward sacerdotal functions, was always capable of being called into play by Divine permission under stress of circumstances, and he would be prepared to understand the significance of such a passage as Rev. vii. 5—8, in which Levi takes his place again (and not at all a foremost place) among the tribes, the Holy Ghost thus signifying that in the world to come all such distinctions will be merged for ever in the common priesthood of the saved. But in the mean time there was nothing antagonistic, either in doctrine or in practice, between the truth which Korah asserted and that other truth which Korah assailed: the priesthood of the many was helped, not hindered, by the special priesthood of the few. It is therefore impossible honestly to use such texts as 1 Pet. ii. 9; Rev. i. 6, against the doctrine of a special Christian priesthood, because they only assert of Christians what the texts relied upon by Korah asserted of the Jews.

III. Abandoning the false line of argument just mentioned, we may yet so far develop the first position taken up as to maintain with confidence, THAT NO PRIESTHOOD CAN HAVE ANY EXISTENCE IN THE CHURCH OF CHRIST OTHER THAN THAT OF OUR LORD HIMSELF. This is made evident, not only by the exclusive way in which his priesthood is dwelt upon in the New Testament, but (what concerns us more in this place) by the whole analogy of the Old. Aaron alone had the priesthood, and the extreme malediction of God lighted upon all, even of the separated tribe, who dared to meddle with it; but Aaron was certainly the type of Christ Himself. Any priesthood which should claim to have any independent existence, even if it professed to draw its authority from Divine appointment, would be *ipso facto* in direct antagonism to the solitary prerogative of Jesus Christ. Hence it follows that the upholders, not the impugners, of such a priesthood would be "in the gainsaying of Korah." It follows also that there can be no direct analogy drawn between those who rose up against Moses and Aaron, and those who rise up against any earthly ministry; it will be shown that a true resemblance *may* be traced under certain conditions.

IV. Admitting these principles, which ought not to be controverted, we may bring the question to a practical issue as follows:—While there cannot be set over us any other priesthood than the only, immutable, and incommunicable priesthood of the Messiah, yet there is nothing in Holy Scripture to negative *à priori* the idea THAT OUR LORD (being withdrawn from sight and sense) MAY CHOOSE TO PERFORM PRIESTLY FUNCTIONS UPON EARTH VISIBLY AND AUDIBLY BY THE HAND AND MOUTH OF CHOSEN MEN; nor is there anything to negative *à priori* the further contention that those men were and are set apart in some special and exclusive way. Whether this be so is a matter of fact which must be decided upon the testimony, fairly and conscientiously weighed, of Scripture and of history. It depends upon the two historical questions. 1. Whether our Lord constituted the apostles his representatives for any priestly functions. 2. Whether the apostles transmitted such representation to others after them. In any case our Lord is the only priest, or rather has the only priesthood, although upon one view of the case he will execute some offices of his priesthood by means of visible human agents, in whom and through whom he himself speaks and acts. Without, therefore, entering upon any argument, we can safely conclude as to the Christian application of this passage. 1. That it must be directly referred to the everlasting priesthood of Christ, and to assaults upon it, or infringements of it. 2. That it may be in a secondary sense referred to a visible Christian priesthood, and to assaults upon it, on the supposition that such priesthood is in fact and in truth only the priesthood of Christ ministered in time and space by his appointment.

In point of fact there are many obvious and many subtle resemblances between the gainsaying of Korah and the popular contention against a Christian priesthood, or even against any Christian ministry, which no thoughtful student of Scripture can overlook. In the homiletics, however, which follow these are left to speak for themselves, and the deeper line of application will be followed. Consider, therefore—

I. THAT KORAH ON ONE SIDE, DATHAN AND ABIRAM ON THE OTHER, HAD HARDLY ANY-THING IN COMMON EXCEPT DISLIKE TO THE RULE OF MOSES, THE MEDIATOR OF ISRAEL AND KING IN JESHURUN (Deut. xxxiii. 5). *His* dislike was ecclesiastical, *theirs* was political ; but this common dislike made them allies, and gave them a "tabernacle" in common (ver. 27). Even so amongst the many who say, "We will not have this man to reign over us" (Luke xix. 14), there are to be found the most various dispositions, and the most distinct causes of complaint. As in the days of his earthly ministry (Mark iii. 6 ; xiv. 64, "all"), so now the opposition to him and to his sole governance is made up of the most heterogeneous, and at other times dissociate, elements.

II. THAT KORAH WAS HIMSELF A LEVITE OF SOME DISTINCTION, AND WAS THE SOUL OF THE CONSPIRACY. Even so it is hardly possible to find in history any grave assault upon the work or doctrine of Christ which has not been inspired by some one whose ecclesiastical position has given him both aptness and influence for this evil.

III. THAT KORAH REPRESENTED MOSES AND AARON IN AN INVIDIOUS LIGHT, AS MEN WHO KEPT THE PEOPLE IN SPIRITUAL SUBJECTION, AND DENIED TO THEM THEIR COMMON RIGHTS AS CHILDREN OF ISRAEL. Even so the constant clamour of unbelief is that Christianity is a system devised in the interests of tyranny and obscurantism in order to keep men in moral slavery, and to rob them of their freedom of thought, and to fetter their freedom of action.

IV. THAT KORAH ASSERTED TRUE FACTS AND APPEALED TO TRUE PRINCIPLES IN OP-POSITION TO WHAT HAD BEEN DIVINELY APPOINTED, AND WAS TO BE DIVINELY VINDI-CATED. Even so do men continually bring against the Truth himself facts which are undeniable, and principles which must be admitted. Herein is the real danger when war upon the Truth is waged with half-truths plausibly paraded as whole, with truths on one side confidently assumed to be fatal to the complemental truths on the other side. The liberty, *e. g.*, of private judgment is arrayed against the authority of inspiration ; the universal fatherhood of God against any distinction of the children of God, or necessity for the mediation of Christ ; the fact that we are all members of one body against any mutual subordination or distribution of functions amongst those members.

V. THAT KORAH WAS PROBABLY SINCERE IN SO FAR AS HE HAD PERSUADED HIMSELF THAT HE WAS RIGHT, otherwise he would hardly have ventured upon the fatal test. Even so the leaders of opposition to Christ are commonly sincere ; only vulgar intolerance brands them off-hand with hypocrisy or self-seeking. And this is their power, for men are led by personal regard and trust much more than by any ability to judge between rival systems. The only way to meet the sincerity and zeal of error is by showing a more transparent sincerity and a more ardent zeal on the side of truth (2 Cor. vi. 3—10 ; 1 Tim. iv. 12—16 ; Titus ii. 10).

VI. THAT WHEN MOSES HEARD THE INDICTMENT AGAINST HIMSELF AND AARON HE COULD BUT REFER IT TO THE DECISION OF THE LORD. The people were either actively or passively on the side of Korah, and argument had been unavailing. Even so when Christianity at large, or any system which we believe to be an integral part of Christianity, is assailed with popular and plausible arguments, there is really nothing to be done but to refer it to the arbitrament of God himself. Arguments convince only those that are convinced ; clamours only intensify prejudice ; mutual accusations only repel—Moses himself effected nothing by the angry words into which he was betrayed. And the arbitrament of God is unequivocally declared by our Lord to be the practical outcome of our religion in our lives (Matt. vii. 15, 20 ; John xiii. 35). That the test is not capable of easy or of immediate application, that it has to be applied broadly, and with many allowances for disturbing causes, is true ; but yet it is the test, and the only test, to which our Lord calls us. It is the test out of which Aaron, with all the weight of popular opinion against him, will ultimately come triumphant ; in which Korah, with all his sincerity and plausibility, will come to nothing. And note that while religious questions must be referred to the arbitrament of God, and that arbitrament is not always distinct or immediate in this world, there is a further decision which will be absolutely certain and conclusive. "Even to-morrow the Lord will show who are his," " for the day shall declare it " (1 Cor. iii. 13), and " it shall be revealed by fire," as it was with Korah's company. Woe unto them who cannot abide, whether personally or as to their work, the test of fire. Our God is still, as then, a consuming fire (Heb. xii. 29), and that fire burns and will burn against all falsity of teaching, as well as all unholiness of living (1 Cor. iii. 15; Heb. xii. 14). And note again that " even him whom he hath chosen will he cause to come near unto him ; " for although the election be not arbitrary, yet it *is* the election of grace, and not the personal worth or aptitude or desire, that does place any, or will place any hereafter, near unto God (cf. Mark iii. 13 ; x. 40; John xv. 16 ; Rom. viii. 28).

VII. THAT THE AMBITION OF KORAH WAS THE MORE TO BE BLAMED BECAUSE HE WAS HIMSELF A LEVITE, AND INTRUSTED WITH A SPECIAL MINISTRY IN HOLY THINGS. Even so is ambition or envy especially evil in a Christian man, forasmuch as he has an " unction " and an office in the body of Christ to which he cannot with all his zeal do justice, and which if faithfully used will bring him the highest possible reward (cf. Luke xxii. 26 ; 1 Cor. xii. 16, 22 ; 1 Pet. ii. 5 ; 1 John ii. 20, 27 ; Rev. iii. 21 ; vii. 14, *sq.*).

VIII. THAT THE PARTICULAR OFFENCE OF KORAH AND HIS COMPANY WAS THEIR DARING TO OFFER INCENSE, WHICH AARON ALONE MIGHT DO. The incense seems to have signified not simply " prayer," but rather the intercessory and prevailing prayer of the great High Priest and Mediator. Thus the " much incense " in Rev. viii. 3, 4, which is undoubtedly the intercession of Christ, is added *to* and rises *with* the prayers of all saints. Thus then the special sin reprobated in Korah is any interference with the mediatorial office of Christ, whether by endeavouring to draw near to God through other mediators, or without any mediator at all (cf. John xiv. 6 ; Gal. i. 8 ; 1 John ii. 1).

IX. THAT THE COMPANY OF KORAH (WHATEVER BECAME OF HIMSELF) DIED BY FIRE, THE ELEMENT IN WHICH THEY SINNED. Even so he that presumptuously meddles with holy things, not being holy himself, shall perish by that very nearness which he rashly courted. The hand that is really and entirely *wet* can be plunged into molten metal without injury, and so he who is covered with the robe of righteousness may be a ministering servant of the consuming Fire, and live ; but how great is the risk if the call be not clear (cf. Mark ix. 49 *a.*).

X. THAT THESE MEN WERE " SINNERS AGAINST THEIR OWN LIVES " IN TRUTH, AL-THOUGH THEY ONLY SEEMED TO BE VINDICATING THEIR JUST RIGHTS AGAINST USURPERS. Even so is every one that seeks his supposed rights not in the spirit of meekness and of personal self-abnegation, but in a spirit of pride, contradiction, and vain-glory. To contend for oneself—albeit sometimes necessary—is of all things most dangerous, lest even in gaining our cause we lose our souls (cf. Matt. xxiii. 12 ; 1 Cor. xiii. 5 ; Philip. ii. 5—7).

XI. THAT THEIR CENSERS WERE HALLOWED EVEN BY AN UNLAWFUL RELIGIOUS USE. Even so there is a kind of sanctity which attaches to every religious effort, however much it may be stained with pride or vitiated by error, and whatever ill results it may lead to, if it be made with sincerity. No such effort can be ignored as though it had not been made, nor cast out as wholly evil because not rightly made. Nothing which is done in the sacred name of religion (saving sheer hypocrisy) ought to be despised or neglected.

XII. THAT THE RESCUED CENSERS BECAME AN ADDITIONAL STRENGTH AND ORNAMENT TO THE ALTAR, AND A WARNING TO ALL GENERATIONS. Even so all assaults upon the faith and discipline of Christ are over-ruled for good, at the same time adding strength to some weak or neglected side of religion, and furnishing a warning against the mistakes and faults which misled their authors (cf. 1 Cor. xi. 19).

Consider again, *with respect to the Reubenites*—
I. THAT THEY WERE ANGRY WITH MOSES FOR WHAT WAS DUE TO THEIR OWN FAULT AND THE FAULT OF THE CONGREGATION. If they had not disobeyed they would have been in their own land by this time. Even so men are angry and impatient with the rule of Christ because it has not brought them peace or happiness, whereas this **is** wholly due to their own unfaithfulness. And so again men assail Christianity for

not having reformed the world and abolished all evils, whereas they themselves will not submit to the easy yoke and light burden of Christ.

II. THAT THEY FALSELY AND WICKEDLY SPAKE OF EGYPT IN TERMS ONLY APPLICABLE TO CANAAN. Even so do the enemies of Christ speak of a state of nature, and of the life of the natural man, unvexed by fear of hell or hope of heaven, as if *that* had been true happiness and peace, whereas they know that it is sheer misery and slavery (Rom. i. 28—32 ; vi. 20, 21 ; Eph. ii. 2, 3).

III. THAT THEY CHARGED MOSES WITH AMBITION AND SELF-SEEKING, AND WITH THROWING DUST IN THE EYES OF THE PEOPLE. Even so is Christianity commonly accounted (or at least described) by its open and more vulgar enemies as mere obscurantism intended to keep the people in darkness, and to make them an easy prey to designing men for power and profit (cf. 2 Cor. xi. 12, 20 ; xii. 16, &c.).

IV. THAT DATHAN AND ABIRAM, BEING OBDURATE, WERE SWALLOWED UP BY THE EARTH, because it was with their earthly lot that they were angry, and with their earthly ruler that they contended. Even so they that are of the earth earthy shall perish with the perishing world ; it is their punishment that they are "swallowed up" in gross material cares or pleasures, and have no lot nor part in the upper air of spiritual life (1 Cor. xv. 48 ; Phil. iii. 19, and compare the use of 'the earth" in the Apoc., as in ch. vii. 1 ; viii. 13).

Consider again, *with respect to the congregation at large—*

I. THAT THEY WERE IMPLICATED IN THE SIN, AND MIGHT HAVE BEEN INCLUDED IN THE PUNISHMENT, OF THESE MEN. Even so the pride and discontent which is active in a few is latent in the many, and brings danger and damage to the whole Church of Christ. The conventional restraints of Christianity prevent for the most part any open outbreak ; nevertheless, it may be said almost of the mass of nominally Christian people that they have "a revolting and a rebellious heart" (cf. 1 Cor. v. 6 ; 2 Tim. ii. 17 ; Heb. xii. 15).

II. THAT THEY WERE SAVED BECAUSE THEY GAT UP FROM THE TABERNACLE OF THESE MEN ON EVERY SIDE, AND TOUCHED NOTHING THAT BELONGED TO THEM. Even so our safety is to separate ourselves wholly from the fellowship or influence (in religious things) of such as oppose themselves to the paramount and absolute claims of Christ as Prophet, Priest, and King (Rom. xvi. 17 ; 1 Cor. x. 22 ; 2 Cor. vi. 14—17 ; Jude 22, 23).

HOMILIES BY VARIOUS AUTHORS.

Vers. 1—3.—*Korah's rebellion.* 1. *The ringleader and his policy.* Of all the seditious movements which embittered the heart of Moses and wrought trouble in Israel during the forty years' wanderings, the rebellion of Korah was by far the most formidable. The anxious tone of the narrative betrays a consciousness of this, and it is confirmed by the facts narrated. The other seditions were either confined to a few individuals, like the sedition of Miriam and Aaron, or, like the disturbances at Marah, and Kibroth-hataavah, and Kadesh, they were the confused movements of a crowd without definite aims, without leaders, without organisation. In this sedition of Korah there is not only a general ferment of rebellious feeling, but there is an organised conspiracy, with a resolute and able man at its head—a man who knows exactly what he would be at, and is consummately skilful in turning to account all the floating elements of discontent that exist in the congregation.

I. Let us begin by taking careful note of THE RINGLEADER. Korah was, like Moses and Aaron, of the tribe of Levi and family of Kohath. He was therefore a far-off cousin of the men against whom he rebelled. That Korah was the soul of the sedition is too plain to need proof. (Compare "the company of Korah," vers. 6, 16, 32 ; xxvi. 9, &c. ; "the gainsaying of Korah," Jude 11). His design is not difficult to fathom. He is a man of honourable rank. But being an ambitious man, he cannot rest so long as there is in the camp any one greater than himself. He looks with envious eye on his cousins Moses and Aaron. Moses, under God, is supreme in peace and war. As for Aaron, not only has he been invested with the exclusive right to offer sacrifice and burn incense before the Lord, but his family have been set apart to form a priestly *caste* in Israel. These honours did not come to the brothers by birthright, but by the special gift and appointment of the Lord. It would seem that Korah was of the elder branch of the family. He resolves to cast down both brothers from their high place. Thus far his intention is open and avowed. We need not hesitate to add that he means to vault into their place; but about this part of his intention he holds his peace for the present. So much for the man.

II. HIS POLICY. 1. *He begins by announcing a doctrine or principle.* As much as anything else in the sedition, this enables us to take the measure of Korah's genius for leadership. Movements which repose merely on brute force rarely achieve abiding results. Blood and iron are not all-sufficient. A true leader of men spares no pains to get hold of men's minds. He likes to give his followers a good watchword or rallying cry. When a nation gets thoroughly possessed with a great and sound principle, when some high and far-reaching doctrine seizes its heart, it is almost invincible. It is characteristic of Korah that he so far appreciates the importance of a great doctrine to rally round, that he casts about for some truth which may be made a handle of for his purpose. In the great oracle which was the first to be uttered at Sinai he thinks he sees what will serve admirably. "Ye shall be to me a kingdom of priests, and an holy nation" (Exod. xix. 6). Accordingly, he raises the cry of Equality and Fraternity ! Moses and Aaron have engrossed to themselves privileges which are the inalienable right of every Israelite. They have taken too much upon them, and must be stripped of their usurped honours. A cry of this sort has often been raised, in all sincerity, by men of excitable temperament. But Korah was no enthusiast. The principle that all Israelites are kings and priests, if it had been really inconsistent (as he pretended to think) with the rule of Moses and the priesthood of Aaron, would have been equally inconsistent with the rule which he coveted for himself. Still there can be little doubt that the cry Korah raised would gain him many supporters. 2. *He organises a band of conspirators.* By one means or another he succeeds in gathering around him no fewer than 250 accomplices. Nor were these obscure men. They all belonged to the ruling class. They are entitled (1) " princes of the assembly," *i. e.* chiefs of the congregation, natural leaders in their several tribes ; (2) "famous in the congregation," more correctly, "men summoned in the assembly," *i. e.* members of the national council ; (3) "men of renown," *i. e.* not nameless persons, but men of note among the people. Their names are not given, nor the tribes to which they belonged. Korah would take care to have all the tribes represented ; but probably the Levites and Reubenites would be most numerous. It was a formidable conspiracy. 3. He diligently *enlists into his company all the malcontents* of the congregation. An example is seen in the Reubenites. They had a grievance. Reuben was the first-born, and as such had certain rights of priority, according to immemorial custom. These rights have been ignored, or transferred to Judah and Ephraim. The Reubenites are Korah's neighbours in the camp. He has inflamed their discontents, and held out flattering hopes. So Dathan, Abiram, and their people join him in open revolt (vers. 12—14). 4. Korah does not confine his attentions to the two hundred and fifty leaders and their pronounced followers. *The whole camp is pervaded with his emissaries.* Things are in such a train that when the two hundred and fifty confront Moses and Aaron at the door of the tabernacle, Korah is able to " gather all the congregation " at the same time. He hopes to overawe Moses by this demonstration of popular sympathy.

We see here:—1. An example of fine abilities abused. What an admirable helper in the kingdom of God Korah might have been ! He might have been a second Joshua. Instead of that, he leads the wretched life of a conspirator, comes to a bad end, and leaves behind him an infamous name. The lust of power—the determination to be the greatest, has been the ruin of many a richly-gifted man. 2. An admonition to leaders in Church and State. There are leaders, not a few, who are such not of their own choice, but by the call of their brethren and by the clear appointment of Divine providence. It is natural and reasonable for them to expect the loyal support of the people. Certainly they are entitled to expect that they shall not be reviled and resisted, as if they had been ambitious and selfish usurpers. The example of Moses admonishes them not to be surprised if such reasonable expectations should be disappointed. A good conscience is an excellent companion under bitter reproach and opposition, but it will not always ward them off. Never was leader less ambitious, less selfish, than Moses; yet he could hardly have been treated worse if he had been another Korah.—B.

Vers. 4—35.—*Korah's rebellion.* 2. *How the rebellion was encountered and put down.* Moses was the meekest of men. There were circumstances of aggravation in the rebellion of Korah which would have exhausted the meekness of most men, but they failed to break down that of Moses. The much-enduring patience of the servant of the Lord never shone out more brightly than in the way in which he encountered the sedition of his bold, unscrupulous kinsman.

I. He carried the cause by appeal to the Most High. A proposal to this effect was made—1. To Korah and the two hundred and fifty chiefs of the conspiracy; vers. 5—7: *q. d.* "You challenge the legitimacy of my government and of Aaron's priesthood. You insinuate that we climbed so high by treading on the rights of our brethren. I might plead in reply that Aaron and I did not grasp at our present honours; they were thrust on us by the Lord. But let us refer the matter to the Lord's decision. Let him show who are his, who are holy, whom he hath chosen to draw near to him in his sanctuary. Take censers and present yourselves before the Lord to-morrow; I and Aaron will come likewise. Let the Lord answer by fire." Such is the proposal. To Moses the result is not doubtful. Yet his heart yearns over the misguided men. This comes out—(1) In his putting off the trial till next day. After a night's reflection they may perhaps repent. (2) In his remonstrance with those of the two hundred and fifty who were Levites (vers. 8—10). Their participation in the rebellion was peculiarly inexcusable. 2. To the Reubenites. Moses sent for them also; but they were not so bold as the two hundred and fifty, and refused to come. They sent back, instead, an insolent and reproachful reply (vers. 13, 14). Nevertheless, in their case also Moses refers the decision to the Lord (ver. 15): *q. d.* "They accuse me of playing the prince and tyrant over them, whereas I have never exacted from them an ordinary governor's dues. So far from defrauding them, I have not taken from them so much as an ass. The Lord judge between them and me, and respect not their offering."

II. The appeal was heard and judgment was pronounced. 1. We are not told how the two hundred and fifty passed the night. Some of them must have had misgivings. They could not fail to remember the tragic death of Nadab and Abihu when they drew near to the Lord with strange fire. But Korah suffered no flinching. He mustered them on the morrow. His emissaries too had been busy in the camp, for when the two hundred and fifty took their places they were surrounded with a vast congregation of eager and sympathizing spectators. This gathering it was hoped would at once confirm the resolution of the conspirators and overawe Moses and Aaron. Moses, on his part, having referred the matter to the Lord, left it in his hand; with what result need hardly be told. First the pillar of fire appeared in a way that struck dismay; and then, after a while, fire came forth and consumed Korah and his two hundred and fifty—"those sinners against their own souls." 2. The fate of the Reubenites presented features of a still more tragic interest (vers. 23—34). It was resolved that they should be made a signal example of Divine vengeance. But, in the first place, the congregation were charged to separate themselves from them (cf. Rev. xviii. 4). This might well have awakened fear, and led to repentance. But they were infatuated in their error. Instead of repenting and craving mercy, "they came out and stood in the door of their tents, and their wives, and their sons, and their little children." Oh these last words! What a harrowing scene they bring before the mind! Was it not enough that Dathan and Abiram and their sons should perish? Why should the women and unconscious children die? The sight is a harrowing one, but it is one that meets us every day. When a blaspheming wretch passes us on the road with his like-minded wife, and a string of little children at their heels, is not that Abiram over again, with his wife and little children? A sight not to be contemplated without fear and pity.—Read the terms in which Moses referred the decision in this case to the Lord, and the awful judgment that ensued, vers. 28—34. . . . One can hardly help commiserating the Reubenites more than the Levites. for the Levites, one would think, must have sinned against the clearer light. Yet the facts seem to show that the Reubenites were the more aggravated sinners, or at least that their families took part more entirely in their sin. This at least is certain, that while the families of the Reubenite rebels perished with them, the family of Korah survived. Centuries after this, the sons of Korah flourished in Judah, and did honourable service as psalmists (titles of Psalms xlii.—xlix., and lxxxiv.—lxxxviii.)

The story of Korah is an admonition to nations, and especially to churches, to "look diligently lest any root of bitterness springing up trouble them, and thereby many be defiled" (Heb. xii. 15). When a society provokes God's displeasure, he does not need to send against it some external foe; there are other and more humiliating forms of chastisement at his disposal. He may suffer some root of bitterness to spring up from within; he may suffer some one of its own children to be its scourge. A Korah will work more mischief in Israel than the Egyptians and the Amalekites put together can effect.—B.

Vers. 19—22, 41—50.—*Korah's rebellion.* 3. *How the congregation abetted the rebels, and were only saved through the intercession of Moses and Aaron.* Bold and crafty as Korah was, he could not have done so much mischief if elements of mischief had not been everywhere rife in the camp. Many things conspire to show that his policy was to inflame and turn to bad account discontents previously existing among the people. The existence of these discontents is not inexplicable. A crowd of bondmen are not to be transferred into a nation of reasonable free men all at once. Moreover, the circumstances of the congregation at Kadesh Barnea were not fitted to make the task of Moses an easy one. After having reached the threshold of Canaan, the people had been turned back and condemned to pass the rest of their days in the wilderness. To be sure they had no one but themselves to blame; but this did not mend the matter. The consciousness that the ditch into which a man has fallen is a ditch of his own digging does not always move a man to take his fall meekly. Penitent hearts may be silent under God's chastisement; but impenitent hearts blaspheme him the more for what they suffer. We need not marvel, therefore, that there were many in the congregation, besides his active coadjutors, who were ready to lend their countenance to Korah in his rebellion.

I. THE SYMPATHY OF THE PEOPLE WITH KORAH showed itself in various ways. 1. They did not rise and vindicate the government of Moses, as they ought to have done. 2. In the crisis of the rebellion they gathered together in front of the tabernacle to encourage Korah and his two hundred and fifty with their countenance. Probably enough they did this with light hearts. Individuals moving with a crowd are apt to lose the sense of personal responsibility. But we shall have to answer to God for what we do, none the less because many others are doing it along with us. In the case in hand the general countenance given to the rebels was so deeply resented by God that it had almost proved fatal to the whole nation. To swell with our voice the shouts of a popular assembly may seem a trifle; but if the shouts are directed against the maintainers of truth and righteousness, we cannot take part without sin and danger. 3. When the rebels died for their sin, the people charged Moses and Aaron with their blood (ver. 41). A fresh example of perversity which again had almost proved fatal to the whole nation.

II. It is a relief to turn from the perverse ungodliness of the people to THE MEEKNESS AND UNSELFISH ZEAL OF MOSES AND AARON. When the Reubenite rebels and the 250 conspirators perished, Moses did not utter a word in deprecation of their terrible doom. A signal example had become necessary. But when the whole people was threatened, he fell on his face and pleaded for it. This he did twice, he and Aaron. 1. When the people abetted Korah and his company before the tabernacle (ver. 22). Twice before Moses had been tempted to desert his office of intercessor, and to separate his fortunes from those of his brethren (cf. Exod. xxxii. 10—13; Numb. xiv. 12). On this third occasion, as on the two former, he refuses to do so. On the contrary, he intercedes with the energy of a man pleading for his own life. When sin abounds and judgments threaten, may the Lord always raise up among us intercessors like Moses and Aaron! 2. When the people charged him with the death of the rebels (ver. 41). This time his intercession took a new form. While the people were murmuring the plague was breaking out in the camp. How shall it be stayed ? Let Aaron show himself a true priest by making atonement for the people. There is no time for presenting a sin offering. Let him instead fill his censer with coals from the altar of sacrifice, and run in between the living and the dead, burning incense. It was a palpable token and demonstration of the Divine authority of the priesthood which the rebels had affected to condemn, that whereas the two hundred and fifty had by their incense-burning brought on themselves death, Aaron by his incense-burning warded off death, and that not only from himself but from the whole congregation.

General lessons:—1. The greatest storm of trial will not overthrow the man who makes God his strength. Moses begins, carries on, finishes his conflict against Korah with prayer (vers. 4, 22, 45). Hence his unfailing meekness. 2. General demonstrations of sympathy with men who are the champions of error and unrighteousness bring guilt on the community, are displeasing to God, and may be expected to bring down his chastisements. 3. Moses, in his meek endurance of obloquy and his successful intercession for those who assailed him with it, is the figure of our blessed Lord. He endured the contradiction of sinners against himself. He prayed, "Father, forgive them." And thousands of them were forgiven. Christ's priesthood which men despise, how often is it glorified in their salvation ! 4. The best answer that a Church or a ministry can give to men by whom their legitimacy is challenged or derided, is to bestir themselves like Aaron, standing between the dead and the living, and turning back the tide of destruction.—B.

Vers. 1—35.—*Envy and its bitter fruits.* I. A CONSPIRACY OF SLANDEROUS REBELS. 1. They begin by blowing up the flame of envy in one another's hearts. The vicinity of the Reubenites to the Kohathites in the camp gave opportunities for this. "Woe to the wicked man, and woe to his neighbour," is a Jewish saying perhaps derived from this incident. 2. Their sin the more serious because they were "men of renown." Influential sinners particularly dangerous. 3. Korah's sin especially grievous (1) because of his kinship to Moses, but chiefly (2) because of the honour already bestowed on him and his brethren (vers. 9, 10). Note the insatiableness of sin. 4. Their conduct condemns their motives also as bad. They envied the power or privileges, perhaps even the provision, made for the priests, as being somewhat better than that of the Levites. "Seekest thou great things for thyself? Seek them not." 5. They bring a false charge against Moses (ver. 3), which recoils on themselves (ver. 7). God had "lifted up" Moses ; they were seeking to lift up themselves. 6. They will not avail themselves of " space for repentance " till the morrow, when God will decide. They will not "sleep over it" with any advantage to themselves. 7. They are unmoved by the reminder that their murmuring is really against God (ver. 11). 8. They meet the friendly interposition of Moses by a fresh conspiracy of grievous falsehoods: of ambition (ver. 13), deception (ver. 14: "Wilt thou put out the eyes of these men ? "), and responsibility for the evils they had brought on them by their own sins (vers. 13, 14: "to kill us;" "thou hast not brought us," &c.). 9. They persist in the most audacious defiance of God till the very last. Sketch Korah and his company with their censers at the door of the tabernacle, while Dathan, Abiram, and their kindred are recklessly waiting the issue at the doors of their tents, in spite of the warning of ver. 26. This last act of sin one element also of their punishment.

II. A FEARFUL RETRIBUTION FROM AN ANGRY GOD. 1. The infatuation of the rebels one part of the judgment. The madness of hardened sinners their own guilt, but God's punishment (cf. Exod. iv. 21 ; 1 Kings xxii. 19—23 ; Acts xxviii. 23—27). 2. New, strange sins call for a new, "strange work" of judgment (vers. 31—33 ; Prov. xxix. 1). 3. Those who unbidden handled sacred fire in their censers perished by the fire of God. Learn hence the guilt and peril of murmuring against the appointments of God in regard to the methods of his government, or the means of acceptable approach to him through our Divine High Priest. Teachers and rulers in God's Church are to be honoured and followed (1 Thess. v. 12, 13 ; Heb. xiii. 17), and Christ is to be recognised as "the head of all principality and power" (Col. ii. 10), and the one and only medium of acceptance with God (Ps. ii. 12 ; John v. 22, 23 ; xiv. 6).—P.

Ver. 22.—" *The God of the spirits of all flesh.*" This name of God reminds us of some of the relations in which God stands to us his creatures, who are immortal spirits in mortal flesh. We select three, and speak of him—

I. As PROPRIETOR. "He *formeth* the spirit of man within him" (Zech. xii. 1). The verb used is applied to a potter or a smith, and reminds us that God has modelled the human spirit, with its varied powers, according to his own ideal (Ps. xxxiii. 15). Since he formed man in his own image, he is "the Father of spirits" in a sense in which he is not the Father of animals. Thus he is our Proprietor, who can say, "All souls are mine," who feels a deep interest in "the work of his own hands" (Ps. cxxxviii. 8), and who will use, according to his judgment, the spirits he has formed and variously endowed. See Moses' use of this truth in Numb. xxvii. 15—17.

II. As HEART-SEARCHER. Sin has broken into the natural relation of God to his creatures. He has to deal with them as sinners with various degrees of criminality. Hence need of discrimination which only the Creator and Searcher of hearts possesses. This truth used by Abraham (Gen. xviii. 23—33) and by Moses and Aaron (ver. 22). It is only the Heart-Searcher who can righteously adjust (1) the direct punishment of sin, which falls only on the guilty (Ezek. xviii. 1—32), and (2) the indirect consequences, which may fall on the innocent (Exod. xxxiv. 7), as on Dathan's children (vers. 27, 32). In this narrative we see (1) conditional preservation (ver. 24), (2) diverse judgments (vers. 32, 35, 49), (3) bereavements and dishonour to the survivors (ch. xxvii. 3). Faith in "God, the God of the spirits of all flesh," may keep us calm in the midst of judgments (Isa. lvii. 16).

III. As THE SAVIOUR. If God were not a Saviour there would soon be no "spirits of flesh" to be the God of (Mal. iii. 6). But God's salvation is for all flesh (2 Cor. v. 19 ; 1 Tim. ii. 6 ; 1 John ii. 2). If God is our Saviour, then we may delight in his proprietorship of us (Ps. cxix. 94 ; cxvi. 12 ; Isa. xliii. 1). And we can cheerfully accept any discipline which our Heart-Searcher sends (Heb. xii. 5—10) ; for "the God of my life" is also "the God of my salvation."—P.

Vers. 31—33.—*The destructiveness of sin.* Some things are very much dreaded because so destructive. *E. g.* locusts, war, pestilence. But there is nothing so destructive as sin. As "no man liveth," so no man sinneth, "to himself." Of Korah, as of Achan or of other transgressors, it may be said, "That man perished not alone in his iniquity" (Josh. xxii. 20). The destructive effects of sin are twofold—I. PERSONAL, II. SOCIAL.

I. PERSONAL : on the sinner himself, as in the case of Korah the Kohathite, honoured as one of the ministers of God's ark. Illustration—Infection, taken unawares, may not be suspected by friends, hardly by the victim ; but its effects (fever, eruption, &c.) will be seen by and by. Sin cannot always be kept secret (Isa. lix. 12 ; James i. 15). "*Evil* shall slay the wicked." If the consequences are not as fatal as in Korah's case, moral destruction is going on. As Alpine granite may be reduced by frost and damp to a kind of mould, so sin—some sins especially—seems to break up the moral nature and reduce it to ruins. From the personal consequences of sin *the destroyer* we can only be delivered by Christ *the Saviour* (Titus ii. 14).

II. SOCIAL : on others. In the case of Korah and his conspirators, sin was fatal to their families. So perhaps in the case of Achan (Josh. vii. 24—26 ; xxii. 20) ; if not, how terrible for them to see the husband, the father, killed, and to know that he had caused the loss of thirty-six men at Ai ! "Curses, like chickens, always come home to roost." We cannot sin with impunity to our family any more than Adam did. Sin propagates sin. It involves others, directly or indirectly, in its fatal consequences. Illustration—King Saul, and the catastrophe to both family and nation at Gilboa. Unrighteous statesmen. Men of high social position who are immoral or infidel. Each sinner a centre of contagion (Eccles. ix. 18). The fate of the children of Korah's company a warning to sinful parents. The children of the godless may be expected to become the parents of godless children, and thus the evil may be perpetuated from generation to generation. Mournful epitaph for a sinner's grave : "That man perished not alone in his iniquity." "But where sin abounded, grace did much more abound" (Rom. v. 20, 21 ; viii. 2, 3).—P.

Vers. 1—3.—*The rebellion of Korah. The conspirators and their pretext.* Here is now the sin of Miriam and Aaron (ch. xii.) on a larger scale. Aaron, who had been inveigled into troubling Moses, is now joined with Moses in suffering from the pride and envy of others.

I. THE CONSPIRATORS. They were men of position and influence. We come upon a different kind of grievance from that of the ignorant multitude. Korah and his band may have been comparatively free from lusting after the delicacies of Egypt. Different men, different temptations. Korah was a Kohathite, joined therefore in the honourable office of bearing the ark and the sanctuary furniture (Numb. iv. 1—20). The others belonged to the tribe of Reuben, the eldest son of Jacob, and with them were 250 of the leaders in the nation. A conspiracy of men of this sort was not so easily dealt with as an outbreak of the whole people. Korah was probably a man of deep, deliberate designs, able to bide his time, and watching as he had opportunity, to draw first one and then another into his schemes. Here was a set of men seeking great things for themselves (Jer. xlv. 5). They had got as far as they could get in the orderly and appointed way, but they wanted to be higher, and somehow or other Moses and Aaron blocked the way. These two men were a long way above the rest, and seemingly in an altogether different order of service, and thus the rebellious, envious spirit of Korah was excited. He was a man of the sort who would rather reign in hell than serve in heaven.

II. THE PRETEXT OF ATTACK. Conspirators against rightful authority like to have a pretext of something fair and just. Thus Miriam: "Hath the Lord not spoken also by us?" And thus Korah: "All the congregation are holy, every one of them." There was something in Korah's office to furnish temptation to an envious mind. As he was engaged in the service of the tabernacle he saw Aaron going where he dare not go, touching things which he dare not touch. He heard Moses coming forward with a message professedly from God, but it was a message from the invisible. No one saw this God with whom Moses professed to hold intercourse, and doubtless Korah concluded that the messages were presumptuous inventions of Moses himself. He considered the honours and privileges only of the leader and priest; he made no allowance for the burdens. Being a self-seeking, self-aggrandising man, he could see no higher feeling in others. He wanted to be at the top of the tree himself, and seeing Moses and Aaron there, he made sure they had got there by audacity and determination, and not by any appointment from God at all. "All the congregation are holy." This was a true statement, but an insufficient reason for attack. Thus the plea of all men being equal is put forth against those who hold high rank and great power. The outward eminence only is seen; the burdens of state, the ceaseless care, are all unknown. "Uneasy lies the head that wears a crown." Thus jealously Paul and Timothy were dealt with in the Church at Corinth, when they wished, not to have dominion over the faith of their brethren, but to be helpers of their joy (2 Cor. i. 24). Little did the schismatics dream of the Apostle's trials, crowned with the thorniest of all, the care ($\mu\epsilon\rho\iota\mu\nu\alpha$) of all the Churches (2 Cor. xi. 23—28). Moses would have rejoiced to take Korah's place, or even the lowest place in the camp, if God had not put him where he was. But of all this inner life of Moses, Korah knew and cared nothing. In his eyes Moses was a self-exalted man, to be immediately and irretrievably abased. "Do we not all wear the fringes, and look each of us on his own riband of blue? Did you not tell us yourself that these were to remind us of our holiness towards God. Why then should you 1 ave an access to God and consequent honour which are denied to us?" Thus these leaders of the people had yet to learn, as only bitter lessons would teach them, that they were under a theocracy. There was no room for a democracy, either real or pretended, in Israel. Nor is the Church of Christ now a democracy, though it is the fashion sometimes to speak of the democratic spirit in it. It does indeed make light of human distinctions, traditions, fashions, and prejudices, but only to put in place of them the authority of Christ. He has appointed his Church humbly and faithfully to execute his will. Professing Christians may indeed choose Church officials, but the real call and choice and guidance are of the Master himself.—Y.

Vers. 4—11.—*The reply of Moses to Korah.* I. KORAH'S QUESTION IS ONE FOR GOD TO ANSWER. It brings an accusation to which Moses had no answer in any language or conduct of his own. He was in a humbler way like Jesus before his enemies. When Jesus spoke of his relation to the Father, his complete dependence on the Father's will, and obedience to it, and of himself as the sole revealer of the Father, these enemies sneered and threatened; and no reply was effectual except that in which the Father glorified the Son by raising him from the dead. And even this was denied by those so enamoured of lies that it was impossible for them to receive the truth. Moses here could but wait an answer in some effectual and crushing way out of the great Invisible. Thus we have the impressive sight of a man who knows he is falsely accused and can wait serenely for the justifying word. If he had been guilty of self-seeking, as Korah was, and with the stain of it on his conscience, he could never have appealed in this way. It was not an empty call upon God, a mere rhetorical device. The challenge to Korah and his band is definite, and expresses a sure confidence in God as vindicator of his servants. "An honest cause fears not a trial, fears not a second trial, fears not a speedy trial." An innocent person needs do nothing in rashness, nor will he seek causes of evasion and delay. Let there be time for decent preparation, and on the morrow a decisive answer shall be given.

II. THE QUESTION SHALL BE ADDRESSED TO GOD IN THE MOST EXPLICIT WAY. By a solemn act he shall be questioned, and by a solemn act he shall answer. Let the people be effectually tested as to this holiness of which Korah makes so much. If even he and his band are holy before God as Aaron is, then let them attempt a part of Aaron's office (Exod. xxx. 1—9). If God accepts the service from them as from Aaron, then all that Korah says may be taken as true, and Aaron may retreat into obscurity and shame as a detected impostor. Moses was ready for the one test that should be complete. It is always open to us, if we do not believe statements made on authority, to try them for ourselves. If we do not believe that arsenic is poisonous, it is quite open to us to make the experiment on our own life. It may be a foolish experiment, but it is certainly a possible one. There was no fortified wall round the sanctuary. God did not put a guard of soldiers to keep defilers back. He himself was guard of his sanctuary. His own Divine energy resided in the holy things to avenge them against any polluted touch. Thus when men repudiate gospel truth and say, "Who is Christ, or who Paul, that we should be tied to square our future and control our hopes by their requirements?" God takes in hand the clearing of his Son and servants from all reproaches. There is nothing to prevent a man *trying* to please God apart from him who is appointed the Way, the Truth, and the Life, and to whom all power is given in heaven and on earth; but God in his own due time will make the trial manifest as ending in disastrous, ignominious failure. The more distinct and emphatic the challenge, the more distinct and emphatic shall the answer be.

III. MOSES SUGGESTS CERTAIN CONSIDERATIONS WHICH MAY LEAD TO A TIMELY RETREAT. Moses doubtless had a prophet's premonitions of the terrible doom into which this proud band was advancing; therefore he mentions things which Korah had neglected sufficiently to consider, and which would show him that God had been honouring him as well as Moses and Aaron. Korah belonged to a tribe specially separated to the service of God. If we complain of those who stand in a higher rank than ourselves, then those who are lower may complain of us in turn. All had been by God's appointment. The tribe of Levi had no more right to complain against Moses and Aaron than any other tribe had to complain against Levi. The God who arranged one body and many members arranged the whole body of Israel, so that every part should contribute in harmony to the whole, and receive good in return. The service of Korah was just as needful in its way as that of Moses and Aaron. Korah was clamouring for the priesthood: who then was to do Korah's work if he stepped into Aaron's shoes? Thus Moses made an appeal to whatever generous and public spirit was in him to think more seriously on the good of the whole. God could not allow any one to imperil the integrity of Israel. They were in a dangerous position, this band of rebels, yet they knew it not. It was the Lord they were gathered against, and not Moses and Aaron, and just in proportion to the greatness of their ignorance was the greatness of their peril. They had talked indeed as if it was the Lord's cause they were thinking of, but their real object, which seemed easily in their grasp, was to trample down Moses and Aaron and take their place. "What is Aaron, that ye murmur against him?" An earthen vessel is a very common, cheap, fragile thing. If it is nothing more than an earthen vessel, then you may in a moment, unhindered, dash it to pieces. But if God, to show the excellency of his power, has put his treasure in an earthen vessel, then it were safer for you to conspire against the best founded of human governments than to touch that earthen vessel with so much as your little finger.—Y.

Vers. 12—15.—*Dathan, Abiram, and Moses.* Dathan and Abiram seem to have been absent from the interview, as if to show their particular and utter contempt for Moses. It was a sort of crime against the new authority to have any dealings with him, to treat him with any civility. But Moses does not treat them as they treat him. It is good-to stoop to rebels even, and show them a way of being reconciled— a way all in vain, however, so far as these two were concerned. What contempt they had silently shown by their absence is now made clear in unmistakable words. A free vent is found for all the rage and scorn pent up in their hearts, and one can see a sort of sidelong rebuke to Korah for condescending to make any terms with such a deceiver.

I. THEIR CHARGE AGAINST MOSES. Notice how *all their complaints end with him.* There is no word concerning Jehovah. Korah, at any rate, made a pretence of thinking of God's glory, as if Moses were not merely injuring the people, but robbing God of their service. Dathan and Abiram talk like utter atheists, as if the promises were of Moses, and not of God, and as if the non-fulfilment came from the inability or malice of Moses, and not from the righteous indignation of God. God had said that he brought them out of Egypt to be their God. Dathan and Abiram leave God altogether out of the question. It is Moses who has brought them out of a land that might be counted one of milk and honey, as compared with the wilderness. That assertion of Jehovah's appointment, favour, and protection which Moses so rejoicingly made was to them nothing but the lying of tyrannous statecraft. Men who are themselves without perceptions of the Eternal, whose thoughts are wholly within the sphere of time and sense, are fond of speaking concerning such as walk in the light of the Eternal as if they must be either fools or knaves. It is possible that Dathan and Abiram had been so blinded by the god of this world as to have persuaded themselves they were the champions of a righteous cause. *The savage and heartless aims which they attribute to him.* How easy it is when one's heart is so inclined, to distort into hideousness the lineaments of the most noble characters! Vindictive minds are like those spherical mirrors which alter the shape of everything presented to them. Thus did Dathan and Abiram make it out that Moses had drawn them from comparative comfort and security, to trifle with them and knock them about hither and thither at his own caprice. How differently the same things look according to the point from which we view them! How we should be on our guard against the representations of wicked, self-seeking men! how slow to credit or even to consider any slander upon God's servants! They charge him, moreover, with drawing them into the wilderness by *specious promises*, made only to be broken, as if, finding he could not keep these promises, he had cunningly thrown the fault on a pretended deity behind. Men will look anywhere for the reasons of disappointment save in their own headstrong and self-regarding lives. *The infallible discernment which they claim for themselves.* "Do you think people have only eyes for what you would have them see?" What is harder than to get the Dathans and Abirams of the world out of the supercilious egotism in which they are entrenched? It is bad enough to have eyes and yet see not, to fail in discerning the great realities of the unseen and eternal, but it is even worse to see all sorts of horrors and iniquities that have no existence. There is a sort of people in the world who suspect everybody, and the better any one seems, the more for that very reason are they doubtful. Thus Jesus is held for a gluttonous man and a wine-bibber, one casting out demons by the prince of the demons; Paul is a pattern of duplicity; there is no real integrity among men, no real purity among women. The defiled minds of such pull down every other person, without hesitation, to their own level. There is no arguing with the man who believes that every face is nothing but a mask.

II. MOSES' INDIGNANT PROTEST. He does not address the slanderers, for where would have been the use? He makes a direct appeal to God: "Respect not their offering." Probably they were going to set up some sort of altar in their own tents, since they refused to come to the tabernacle; only to find out, as Cain did before, and many have done since, that will-worship (Col. ii. 23) has no acceptance with God. Even if their offering had been made by the strictest ceremonial rules, what would have been its chance of acceptance with him to whom lying lips are an abomination? "Lord, who shall abide in thy tabernacle?" (Ps. xv.). There is a claim here not only for the vindication of Aaron as the appointed priest, but of Moses also as the appointed leader, the faithful messenger, the pure channel of the pure command-ments and promises of God. The man who would teach the people righteousness must be clear of the faintest suspicion that robbery or oppression clings to his own garments. He must be far different from those rulers of after days whom Isaiah denounces (Isa. i. 10—15, 23). "Moses got more in his estate when he kept Jethro's flock than since he came to be king in Jeshurun."—Y.

Vers. 16—35.—*The destruction of Korah and his company.* I. THE APPLICATION OF THE TEST. 1. *Moses and Aaron put themselves on a perfect outward equality with the rest.* They humbled themselves that they might be exalted. Aaron, already chosen of the Lord, stands with his censer and incense in the midst of the company of rebels, as if he were but a candidate waiting for approval. Such is not the way of the dignitaries of the world. Their pomp and honour is mostly a mere conven-tion; strip them of their titles and gauds, and you would scarcely notice them in the street. But Aaron was the priest of God wherever he went, and howsoever he was surrounded. Therefore, without fear or shame, he could take the lowest place, sure that he would presently be addressed, "Come up hither." So Jesus was numbered with the transgressors, reduced to the level of criminals, crucified instead of Barabbas. Christians have often had to stand among the ranks of evil-doers, but in due time they have gone out from them, because they were not of them (1 Pet. ii. 19—23). 2. *Korah shows unquailing audacity to the last,* i. e. up to the appearing of the glory. The more the servants of God humbled themselves, the higher and more confident were his enemies in their pride. Korah was at his very highest before he fell. Aaron, whom he had so often seen going where he was forbidden, stands now on a level with the ordinary Levite; nay, more, he is as low as the other tribes. The con-gregation too has gathered round Korah in sympathy and expectation, for doubtless he has promised them such things as they love. And even as God had allowed rebellious Israel to go on even to the lifting of stones against Caleb and Joshua (ch. xiv. 10), so here he allows the pride of Korah to swell to its fullest extent. And hence God's people should ever gain confidence in the times when he seems to be inactive. We are not to be discouraged because the wicked go on from strength to strength. The Jews rejected Christ; they consulted to slay him; they seized him; they put him through an examination in their own court; they handed him to Pilate; he was mocked, scourged, crucified; yet God did not intervene. And who now does not see that all this time he was in process of answering the prayer, "Glorify thy Son, that thy Son also may glorify thee"? (John xvii. 1). Korah, rising, was lifting Moses and Aaron with him. He fell; they remained. 3. *The first expression of Divine wrath.* A general destruction is threatened, without mitigation or delay. And if we only consider, we shall see how fitting it was that the first word should be a menace of complete and terrible destruction. The holiness of God is a great reality, keenly sensitive to any sin. How much then was it outraged by such a daring attempt as that of Korah and his company! And the whole congregation had shown a sad alacrity in their support. Why, even we ourselves, when we hear of some great crime in which many are engaged, do not stop to make distinctions between princi-pals and accomplices. We feel that our first word must be one of utter abhorrence and condemnation with respect to all who had part in such great wickedness. It is only because we are so little sensitive to the evil of sin, that we find difficulty in understanding the menace of ver. 21. 4. *Moses and Aaron promptly intercede.* God has already shown what a distance separates them from the rest of the people. Now they proceed to show it themselves. It was the hour of exaltation and triumph but, like truly humble and holy men, they were occupied with intense pity for the great multitude suddenly exposed to the full wrath of God. Was there any in that great multitude who would thus have thought of *them* ? Their position towards God and men comes out in something like its completeness. If Moses had much on behalf of God to say to men, so he had much on behalf of men to say to God. And Jesus is put before us as the great High Priest. If the sinful Aaron could be touched with a feeling of the infirmities of his brethren, not less is the same true of the sinless Jesus. Amid the threatening penalties of sin, and with the growing consciousness of our own helplessness, we can look to him for intercessory services, even those which he came to earth specially to render. His Father, who is God of the spirits of all flesh, sent him not to destroy men's lives, but to save them (Luke ix. 56).

II. THE AWFUL PRACTICAL CONSEQUENCE. 1. *Korah, Dathan, and Abiram are devoted to destruction.* The intercession of Moses and Aaron, earnest and prevailing as it is, has a limit in the request and the result. "If any man see his brother sin a sin which is not unto death, he shall ask, and he shall give him life for them that sin not unto death. *There is a sin unto death: I do not say that he shall pray for it*" (1 John v. 16). The people are first of all included in menace with the three chief rebels that presently they may be separated from them. Leaders and followers are both guilty, but there are degrees in wickedness as in holiness. It is perhaps of great significance, if only we will consider that God in this manifestation of his wrath came not only with three separate punishments, but three different modes of punishment. He seems to shadow forth something of degrees of punishment in the eternal world. If the blind lead the blind, *both* shall fall into the pit ; but surely the woe of a deeper fall is to those presumptuous blind who drag others with them. Here were those who would not admit that Moses and Aaron had been Divinely separated for a peculiar service, and now in their towering pride they are separated for a peculiar doom. If they had not climbed so high they would not have fallen so far. 2. As we see the people falling away from Korah, we notice *what a feeble bond unites the wicked.* Only a few minutes ago the people were pressing admiringly on him as he bearded Moses in the very door of the tabernacle ; now they flee from him and the other two as if they infected the air with death. The bond that looks so firm is but a rope of sand. It will not hold when anything appears that looks like a peril to individual selfishness. We may be reminded indeed of "honour among thieves," but this at the most can only mean that wicked men may act together till the last, not that they may be trusted to do it. There is no such coherency possible amongst the wicked as amongst the good. They have no entirely common purpose ; each has his own advantage to seek, and so one may easily thwart all the rest. The Jews in the hour of their triumph over Jesus are chagrined by the inscription which obstinate Pilate puts on the cross. 3. Notice *the reference to the elders* in ver. 25. They had been appointed, seventy of them, to help Moses in the burden which had become so grievous (ch. xi.). Where then had they been all this time ? Men with the Spirit of God upon them should surely have sided boldly with Moses, even before the glory appeared. Perhaps indeed they were on his side ; and we must not infer too much from silence, else Caleb and Joshua would appear in a dubious light. But this much at all events may be said, that even though they were select and judicious men, and God took of the spirit that was upon Moses and put it upon them, all this was insufficient to help Moses in his extremest needs. We may take their appointment rather as an expression of regard and sympathy, something fitted to teach the elders themselves to be full of consideration and attention towards Moses. The great crowning needs of life cannot be met by human help, even when sanctified ; we must still, like Moses, fall on our faces before God. Not until God has appeared, vindicated his servant, and scattered the unfriendly crowd, do we hear that the elders of Israel followed him. 4. *The carrying out of the judgment on Korah, Dathan, and Abiram.* Moses announces that the mode of their death was to have great evidential value with respect to himself. Those who had been foremost as accusers and slanderers shall now be chief witnesses on his side, speaking more loudly for him in their death than ever they had spoken against him in their life. It had been their charge against Moses that he had assumed undue authority; therefore, to show how much he was in the secrets of the Divine government, he announces, not only that God himself would take in hand the execution of a righteous sentence, but would execute it in a way hitherto unheard of. And this very way Moses proceeds to indicate. What a point of faith he here reaches! what a perfect community of thought with God! for scarcely has he spoken when that happens which he said would happen, and in exactly the same way. Death and burial are included in the same act. No one was made unclean by these three men or any of their belongings.—Y.

EXPOSITION.

THE PLAGUE BEGUN AND AVERTED (vers. 41—50). Ver. 41.—**Ye have killed the people of the Lord.** They had in truth forfeited their own lives, and Moses and Aaron had no more part in their death than St. Peter had in the death of Ananias and Sapphira. But it was easy to represent the matter as a personal conflict between two parties, in which the one had triumphed by destroying the other. In speaking of Korah and his company as the "people of the Lord," they meant to say that their lives were as sacred as the lives of Moses and Aaron, and the crime of taking them as great; they did not know, or did not heed, that their own immunity was due to the intercession of those whom they thus charged with sacrilegious murder.

Ver. 42.—**The cloud covered it.** Not soaring above it, as usual, but lying close down upon it, to signify that the presence of the Lord had passed in some special sense into the tabernacle (see on ch. xii. 5, 10).

Ver. 45.—**Get you up.** הֵרֹמּוּ, from רָמַם. The command is substantially the same as that in ver. 21. Since it was not obeyed, we must conclude (as before) that it was not intended to be obeyed. **They fell on their faces.** In horror and dismay. No doubt they would have interceded (as in ver. 22), but that Moses perceived through some Divine intimation that wrath had gone forth, and that some more prevailing form of mediation than mere words must be sought.

Ver. 46.—**Take a censer.** Rather, "the censer," i. e. the proper censer of the high priest, which he used upon the great day of atonement (Levit. xvi. 12), and which is said in Heb. ix. 4 to have been of gold, and to have been kept in the most holy place. It is not, however, mentioned amongst the sacred furniture in the Levitical books. **And go quickly.** הוֹלֵךְ. Rather, "take it quickly." **And make an atonement for them.** There was no precedent for making an incense offering after this fashion, but it was on the analogy of the rite performed within the

tabernacle on the day of atonement (Levit. xvi.). Whether Moses received any intimation that the wrath might be thus averted, or whether it was the daring thought of a devoted heart when all else failed, it is impossible to say. As it had no precedent, so it never seems to have been repeated; nor is the name or idea of atonement anywhere else connected with the offering of incense apart from the shedding of blood.

Ver. 48.—**And he stood between the dead and the living.** If this is to be understood literally, as seems most consistent with the character of the narrative, then the plague must have been strictly local in its character, striking down its victims in one quarter before passing on to another; only thus could it be arrested by the actual interposition of Aaron with the smoking censer. **And the plague was stayed.** Thus was given to the people the most striking and public proof of the saving efficacy of that mediatorial and intercessory office which they had been ready to invade and to reject. Thus also was it shown that what in profane hands was a savour of death unto death, became when rightly and lawfully used a savour of life unto life.

Ver. 49.—**Fourteen thousand and seven hundred.** A very large number to have died in the course of a few minutes, as the narrative seems to imply. The plague was undoubtedly of a supernatural character, and cannot be considered as a pestilence or other natural visitation. **Beside them that died about the matter of Korah.** These were (1) the two hundred and fifty men who offered incense, (2) Dathan and Abiram, and their families, (3) probably Korah himself, (4) possibly some other partisans of Korah (see on ver. 32), making in all about 300 souls. Thus we get the round number of 15,000 as the total of those that perished on this occasion.

Ver. 50.—**And the plague was stayed.** Not only temporarily, while Aaron stood between the dead and the living, but finally and effectually.

HOMILETICS.

Vers. 41—50.—*The priestly atonement.* We see in this section the priesthood of the anointed at once exercised and vindicated in the fullest and highest sense by shielding from wrath and death those who were appointed to die on account of sin. The spiritual meaning so far and so plainly eclipses the literal that we might well suppose the passage to have been written in the light of the finished work of Christ; as it is, we cannot possibly refuse to read the "mind of the Spirit" testifying before of the atonement and intercession of our High Priest. Consider, therefore—

I. That wrath had gone forth against all Israel because of their active or passive participation in rebellion against the will and ordinance of God. Even so had wrath gone forth against all mankind, for that all were compromised (albeit not all to the same degree, or by the same deliberate choice) in sin and rebellion (Rom. v. 12, 14 ; xi. 32 ; Eph. ii. 3).

II. That Moses did not even attempt to pray at this time for Israel, because the sentence was gone forth, and even his prayer had been unavailing. Even so, however much the intercessions of righteous men may have been heard in other and lesser matters (James v. 16 b.), yet could not any human means avail to turn aside from us the sentence of death which follows upon sin (Gen. ii. 17 ; Ps. xlix. 7, 8 ; Rom. vi. 23 ; vii. 24). And note that as far as we can see even the incarnate Son had not saved us as Lawgiver and Ruler except his intercessions had been based upon his meritorious cross and passion. Moses must give place to Aaron here.

III. That the plague advanced all the while with frightful celerity. Even so sin and death made havoc of an evil world ere Christ came forth to stay the plague (Rom. i.; iii.; v.). And still, where it is not stayed, its progress is as rapid and as irresistible as ever. Thousands are daily swept away to destruction.

IV. That the fervent, self-sacrificing love of Moses for his people (who had opposed and rejected him) devised this new remedy, unknown before. Even so it was the infinite, self-abasing love of the eternal Son which devised the means of our salvation, albeit we had rebelled against him and cast off his dominion (Ps. ii. 2, 3, 12 ; Luke xix. 14 ; John iii. 16 ; Acts iii. 26 ; Rom. v. 8 ; 1 John iv. 10).

V. That this remedy was found in an incense offering (1) made by Aaron, (2) in the censer, (3) among the dying people. Even so the one Divine deliverance from eternal death is (1) in the high priestly intercession of Christ, (2) offered in the golden censer of his infinite merits, (3) offered "in the midst of the congregation," *i. e.* in our nature, wherein he lived and died, and in which he ever liveth to make intercession (Luke xxiii. 34 ; John xvii. 19, 20 ; Rom. v. 9, 10 ; Heb. ii. 12—17 ; vii. 24, 25 ; Rev. viii. 3, 4).

VI. That the incense was to be lighted with fire from off the altar of burnt offering, otherwise it had been as ineffectual for good as the offering of Nadab and Abihu (Levit. x. 1). Even so the intercessions of Christ whereby we live are not only offered as of his infinite merits, but as based upon his one perfect and sufficient sacrifice. It is fire from the altar of the cross which kindles and makes to ascend in fragrance his "much incense" before the throne. From another point of view it is the burning love which prompted and inspired his death which inspires and kindles his unceasing intercession for us.

VII. That Aaron ran into the camp to make an atonement for the people, regardless of any danger to himself. Even so our Lord hasted in his great zeal to expose himself to all danger in our midst in order to work out our salvation (Ps. xl. 10 ; Mark x. 32 ; Luke xii. 50).

VIII. That Aaron stood between the dead and the living—all on one side of him (as it should seem) dead, all on the other side alive, through his intervention. Even so our High Priest stands, and stands alone, between us and death. Nothing separates us from the eternally lost but the saving efficacy of his intercession ; had he not appeared upon the scene we too had perished. Moreover, he stands between the living and the dead in this sense, that all souls are divided by him and his cross into two lots, the living who accept, the dead who reject him. Thus he hung between the penitent and impenitent robbers, and thus he will place the goats and the sheep on the one side of him and on the other.

IX. THAT THE PLAGUE WAS STAYED BY AARON'S INTERPOSITION OF HIMSELF BETWEEN IT AND ITS VICTIMS. Even so Chr:st has averted death from us, and taken away its sting, by placing himself between it and us, by interposing between the wrath of Heaven and our souls (Rom. vii. 25 ; viii. 1). And so long as we are sheltered behind his atonement and intercession we are absolutely safe.

X. THAT AARON, AFTER MAKING AN ATONEMENT, RETURNED TO THE MOST HOLY PLACE WITH HIS CENSER (cf. Heb. ix. 4). Even so our Lord, after making atonement for us upon the cross, and breaking the empire of sin and death, returned to that heaven from which he came, leaving us free from the power of death.

XI. THAT THIS WAS THE GLORIOUS VINDICATION OF AARON'S PRIESTLY OFFICE, IN THAT IT BROUGHT LIFE AND DELIVERANCE TO THE VERY MEN WHO HAD DESPISED AND SLANDERED IT. How much better and more effectual than if a thousand Korahs had been slain by reason of it! Even so the true vindication of the priesthood of Christ, in whatsoever sense or by whomsoever assailed, is its marvellous and ever-living efficacy for the healing of sinners, and for their salvation from spiritual death. Those that are ready to strive against it to the uttermost to-day will know themselves beholden to it for life and liberty to-morrow. Whatever belongs to the priesthood of Christ must here, and here only, find its defence and confirmation, not in smiting down them that oppose themselves (which is of the law only), but in saving them from the fatal consequences of their own sin and blindness (which is of the gospel alone). Cf. Luke ix. 55, 56 ; John xii. 47 ; 2 Cor. x. 8 ; xiii. 10 ; Gal. i. 23 ; 1 Tim. ii. 4.

HOMILIES BY VARIOUS AUTHORS.

Vers. 41—50.—*The priesthood still further honoured and established.* I. THE PEOPLE REMAIN UNCHANGED IN HEART. They had been terrified for the moment, and fled to what they thought a safe distance, but by the morrow all their audacity has returned. It would seem as if men soon become accustomed to even the most terrible visitations of God ; and the more they see of his doings, the less able they are to understand them. There was a time when such destruction as they had gazed on would have taught them caution for more than a day, but now a day is quite sufficient to make them bolder than ever. The evidential value which Moses had pointed out in vers. 28—30 is quite lost upon them. Perverse minds disregard the clearest evidence. It may be a good thing for some purposes to multiply evidences of Christianity, but if the whole earth were filled with books written on the subject, many would remain unconvinced. The conduct of these people, so quickly murmuring again, may seem scarcely credible as we read it, yet are they in reality worse than unbelievers now ? If we also read of these things that happened to Israel of old, and are not in the least impressed by them, then what are we different in our folly and audacity ? The lapse of more than three thousand years has not made God less jealous of his ordinances, less able and determined to punish those who slight them. Fearful things are spoken of those who crucify the Son of God afresh and put him to an open shame. Instead of marvelling at Israel, we shall do well to see in it, as in a mirror, the perversity, blindness, and frivolity of the natural man everywhere. As Israel was, so are we, until and unless God puts within us a new and different life.

II. A STILL FURTHER RECOGNITION OF THE PRIESTLY OFFICE. One is not astonished to read that simultaneously with the gathering of the murmuring people, the glory of the Lord appeared again. Hitherto there has been some little interval, some time as it were for repentance, but now along with this high pitch of audacity, it is fitting that the revelation of the glory should be prompt, and prompt also the vindication of what God had but lately done. Once again he warns Moses and Aaron out of the way of death. And now what can Moses do, for his pleas are exhausted ? The people have gone on sinning, until at last the ingenuity of his pitying heart has nothing left to say. In this extremity he turns where all must turn at last, namely, to the atonement for sin which God has solemnly appointed. Probably in the first institution of the priestly office he did not comprehend all the power and blessing it could confer. He was now to know, and Israel with him, that atonement for sin, made through the appointed officer, had a most certain effect in destroying some, at least, of the consequences of sin. The atonement made under the law sets forth that more efficacious and searching atonement lying at the foundation of the gospel, but it was not, therefore, a mere form. It could not indeed cleanse the conscience or change the life, but it was effectual to keep back the plague that brought physical death. In the light of the honour which God here puts upon his priest, and the real effect produced by this offering for sin, how clearly we see the real effect that must come from the work of Jesus! If Aaron, the feeble, sinful type, could do so much, how much more we are bound to expect from Jesus, the sinless, perfect antitype!

III. THE SIGNIFICANCE OF AARON'S POSITION. He stood between the dead and the living. *What a quickly destructive power sin has!* The language indicates that Moses and Aaron were full of alacrity. Not a moment was lost in interposing the atoning service, but even so more than fourteen thousand of the people had already perished. The connection between sin and death is very close, and in such a visitation as this the closeness is made very clear. It may seem constantly contradicted, that in the day men eat of the forbidden fruit they shall surely die, but the contradiction is in appearance only. In the sinful act death is begun, and if God so chooses, its full power may be very quickly manifested. Thus when Aaron went in he found death had been before him, and he had to stand between the dead and the living. It was from the dead that the plague passed greedily on to the living, like the licking fire from the black ruins where it has done its work to the things still unconsumed. But the moment Aaron enters, the atonement begins to work. The very fact that so many had perished, and so rapidly, glorifies the efficacy of his intervention. Sin is then at once in check. It was a noble position for the priest to occupy, and we should think of it as occupied by Jesus. He indeed stands between the dead and the living. As we gaze upon those wrecked and ruined ones, fast settled in despair, and beyond any succour that we can discern, Christ stands between us and them to give assurance that with him there is power to deliver us from such a fate. It is his great and glorious power to deliver us from death by giving to us a new and higher life, and giving it more abundantly, that mortality may be *swallowed up* of life (2 Cor. v. 4).—Y.

EXPOSITION.

CHAPTER XVII.

AARON'S ROD THAT BUDDED (vers. 1—13). Ver. 1.—**And the Lord spake.** Presumably upon the same day, since the design was to prevent any recurrence of the sin and punishment described above.

Ver. 2.—**Take of every one of them a rod.** Literally, "take of them a rod, a rod," *i. e.* a rod apiece, in the way immediately particularised. מַטֶּה (Septuagint, ῥάβδον) is used for the staff of Judah (Gen. xxxviii. 18) and for the rod of Moses (Exod. iv. 2). It is also used in the sense of "tribe" (ch. i. 4, 16). Each tribe was but a branch, or rod, out of the stock of Israel, and, therefore, was most naturally represented by the rod cut from the tree. The words used for sceptre in Gen. xlix. 10, and in Ps. xlv. 7, and for rod in Isa. xi. 1, and elsewhere are different, but the same imagery underlies the use of all of them. **Of all their princes . . . twelve rods.** These princes must be those named in ch. ii. and vii. Since among these are to be found the tribe princes of Ephraim and Manasseh, standing upon a

perfect equality with the rest, it is evident that the twelve rods were exclusive of that of Aaron. The joining together of Ephraim and Manasseh in Deut. xxvii. 12 was a very different thing, because it could not raise any question as between the two.

Ver. 3.—**Thou shalt write Aaron's name upon the rod of Levi.** There was no tribe prince of Levi, and it is not probable that either of the three chiefs of the sub-tribes (ch. iii. 24, 30, 35) was called upon to bring a rod. This rod was, therefore, provided by Moses himself, and inscribed by him with the name of Aaron, who stood by Divine appointment (so recently and fearfully attested) above all his brethren. For the significance of the act cf. Ezek. xxxvii. 16—28. **For one rod . . for the head of the house of their fathers.** For Levi, therefore, there must be, not three rods inscribed with the names of the chiefs, but one only bearing the name of Aaron, as their common superior.

Ver. 4.—**The tabernacle of the congregation.** "The tent of meeting." See on Exod. xxx. 26. **Before the testimony,** *i. e.*

in front of the ark containing the two tables of the law (Exod. xxv. 21).

Ver. 5.—**Whom I shall choose.** For the special duty and service of the priesthood (cf. ch. xvi. 5). **I will make to cease.** מֵעָלַי הֵשַׁבֹּתִי. I will cause to sink so that they shall not rise again.

Ver. 6.—**And the rod of Aaron was among the rods.** As there was no prince from whom this rod could have come, and as there were twelve rods without it, this must mean that Moses did not keep Aaron's rod separate (which might have caused suspicion), but let it be seen amongst the others.

Ver. 7.—**Before the Lord,** i. e. in front of the ark. **In the tabernacle of witness.** "In the tent of the testimony." בְּאֹהֶל הָעֵדֻת.

Ver. 8. — **Was budded :** or "sprouted." פָּרַח. **And yielded almonds.** Rather, "matured almonds." This particular rod had been cut from an almond tree, and it would seem probable that it had on it shoots and flowers and fruit at once, so that the various stages of its natural growth were all exemplified together. The almond has its Hebrew name שָׁקֵד, "awake," from the well-known fact of its being the first of all trees to awake from the winter sleep of nature, and to herald the vernal resurrection with its conspicuous show of snow-white blossoms, which even anticipate the leaves (cf. Eccles. xii. 5). Thus the "rod of an almond-tree" (מַקֵּל שָׁקֵד) was shown to the prophet Jeremiah (Jer. i. 11) as the evident symbol of the vigilant haste with which the purposes of God were to be developed and matured. It is possible that all the tribe princes had official "rods" of the almond-tree to denote their watchful alacrity in duty, and that these were the rods which they brought to Moses. In any case the flowering and fruiting of Aaron's rod, while it was an unquestionable miracle (for if not a miracle, it could only have been a disgraceful imposture), was a σημεῖον in the true sense, i. e. a miracle which was also a parable. Aaron's rod could no more blossom and fruit by nature than any of the others, since it also had been severed from the living tree ; and so in Aaron himself was no more power or goodness than in the rest of Israel. But as the rod germin-

ated and matured its fruit by the power of God, supernaturally starting and accelerating the natural forces of vegetable life, even so in Aaron the grace of God was quick and fruitful to put forth, not the signs only and promise of spiritual gifts and energies, but the ripened fruits as well.

Ver. 9.—**And took every man his rod.** So that they saw for themselves that their rods remained dry and barren as they were by nature, while Aaron's had been made to live.

Ver. 10. — **Before the testimony.** By comparison with ver. 7 this should mean before the ark in which the "testimony" lay. In Heb. ix. 4, however, the rod is said to have been in the ark, although before Solomon's time it had disappeared (1 Kings viii. 9). We may suppose that after it had been inspected by the princes it was deposited for safer preservation and easier conveyance inside the sacred chest. **To be kept for a token against the rebels.** Rather, "against the rebellious," literally, "children of rebellion" (cf. Eph. ii. 2, 3). It could only serve as a token as long as it retained the evidences of having sprouted and fruited, either miraculously in a fresh state, or naturally in a withered state. As a fact, however, it does not appear that the lesson ever needed to be learnt again, and therefore we may suppose that the rod was left first to shrivel with age, and then to be lost through some accident.

Ver. 12.—**And the children of Israel spake unto Moses.** It is a mistake to unite these verses specially with the following chapter, for they clearly belong to the story of Korah's rebellion, although not particularly connected with the miracle of the rod. These are the last wailings of the great storm which had raged against Moses and Aaron, which had roared so loudly and angrily at its height, which was now sobbing itself out in the petulant despair of defeated and disheartened men, cowed indeed, but not convinced, fearful to offend, yet not loving to obey.

Ver. 13. — **Shall we be consumed with dying ?** It was a natural question, considering all that had happened ; and indeed it could only be answered in the affirmative, for their sentence was, "In this wilderness they shall be consumed" (ch. xiv. 35). But it was not in human nature that they should calmly accept their fate.

HOMILETICS.

Vers. 1—13.—*The sign of the true Priesthood.* In this chapter we have the testimony of God to the priesthood of his Anointed in a σημεῖον, a teaching miracle, setting forth the inner and hidden truths upon which the exclusive claims of that priesthood rest. The application, according to what has been set forth above, is governed by the saying, "*Aaronis virga refloruit in Christo.*" Consider, therefore—

I. That the "rod" was the natural symbol of each unit in the body

CORPORATE OF ISRAEL, and was therefore synonymous with "tribe;" for each tribe collectively, as represented by its prince, was one of the twelve branches which grew out of the one parent stem of Israel. Even so our Lord has said, "I am the Vine, ye are the branches;" and this holds good whether we regard the individual Christian as a unit in that collective whole which is Christ (1 Cor. xii. 12), or the particular Church as a unit in that same whole which is the body of Christ (1 Cor. xii. 27; Eph. i. 22, 23).

II. THAT THE ALMOND ROD HAD A SPECIAL SIGNIFICANCE FOR AARON, inasmuch as its name and character spake of vigilance and the attribute of preventing others both in promise and in performance. Even so it is the fitting emblem of the Rod out of the stem of Jesse, and the Branch which grew out of his roots; for that Branch was "beautiful and glorious" (Isa. iv. 2) when all the other trees in the garden of God (Ezek. xxxi. 9) stood dry and leafless, and there was no sign of any life stirring nor promise of any fruit coming. Then was he "awake," and showed the pure beauty of a perfect life before the eyes of men (Luke ii. 52; iii. 22). Even more in his resurrection was the almond rod his natural symbol; for then indeed he had been cut off from the stock of Israel, from the natural stem out of which he grew, and had been laid in the dust of death, and had seemed to be withered and lifeless; but on the third day he "awoke" early (Ps. cviii. 2), and became the first-fruits of them that slept, anticipating all expectation, and putting forth the glorious blossom of life and immortality (Cant. ii. 10—13).

III. THAT THE VISIBLE CONFIRMATION OF AARON'S PRIESTHOOD IN THE TYPE WAS THE BLOSSOMING AND FRUITING OF HIS ROD. Even so our Lord is commended unto us beyond all cavil as the High Priest of our profession in that his priesthood is ever adorned with the buds of hope, the blossoms of beauty, the ripened fruits of holy deeds, such as always and everywhere grow out of that priesthood as ministered among us, and testify to its enduring vitality and energy, whereas no such results follow any other guide and redeemer of souls. And note that what is true of the priesthood of Christ must be true, in a secondary sense, of all ministries of grace claiming rightly to be such. "By their fruits ye shall know them," or by their absence of fruit. If they really live and blossom into purity and beauty, and ripen the fruits of holy and devoted deeds, then are they attested by God to be ministries of grace indeed, standing in vital relation to the only priesthood of Christ. Moreover, since only Aaron's rod can blossom, it is certain that every true grace and beauty not of earth which is found in Christian souls and lives must be due to the fruitful energy of "Christ in us" through the Spirit.

IV. THAT THE CONTINUED VITALITY AND FRUITFULNESS OF THE ROD WAS NOT NATURAL, BUT WAS SIMPLY DUE TO GOD'S POWER FOLLOWING HIS ELECTION. Even so whatever energy for good is found in any Christian ministry, whatever grace in any means of grace, is assuredly not of nature, for there is no inherent power in any man or in any outward thing to communicate spiritual life or blessing. It is only the Divine grace, following the Divine choice of the agents and instruments of redeeming love, which can make them or their ministry of any real effect; it is not they who can produce any change for the better, but only the mighty power of God working in them and through them.

V. THAT THE BUDS, THE BLOSSOMS, AND THE FRUIT WOULD SEEM TO HAVE BEEN ON THE ROD ALL AT ONCE. Even so in the history and course of Christianity there was no slow progression towards the perfection of Christian character and action. The ripened fruits of holy living were put forth at once side by side with the promise of better things in some, and with the beauty of early piety in others. And so it is, wherever the powers of the world to come are at work, there may always be discerned, apparently from the first, the three stages of growth in Christ. What the energy of the Spirit seems to ripen at once in some happy souls seems to take him many years to bring to maturity in others, even if maturity be ever reached in this world. Nevertheless, the bud and the blossom are as impossible to mere nature as the fruit itself.

VI. THAT THE ROD WHICH BUDDED WAS LAID UP FOR A TOKEN AGAINST THE REBELLIOUS. Even so if men oppose themselves we have no other sign but this. Pilate asked our Lord, "What hast thou done?" and if he had but sought the answer which so many could have given him, he had not condemned the Lord of glory. "By their fruits ye shall know them," for thereby shall they be judged at the last day. Our good works then are the credentials of our creed and of our priesthood. The "doctrine" is (and must be) but a dry rod which savours only of rule and domination in the eyes of a natural man unless it be "adorned" with these fair blossoms, this substantial fruit.

VII. THAT THE OBJECT OF THE MIRACLE WAS ESPECIALLY TO CONVINCE THE PEOPLE FOR THEIR GOOD, LEST THEY SHOULD RUSH AGAIN UPON DESTRUCTION (ver. 10 *b*). Even so it is the will of God that the witness of good works and piety come abroad, and not that men "keep their religion to themselves," and within their own doors, in order that prejudice may be dispelled and souls attracted to their own salvation (Matt. v. 16; 1 Pet. ii. 12).

VIII. THAT THE SINFUL PEOPLE CHARGED UPON THE LAW OF GOD THE FATAL CONSEQUENCES OF THEIR OWN SIN, AND DESPAIRED WHEN THEY COULD NO LONGER REBEL. Even so do men complain bitterly of their misfortunes when they reap the fruits of their own wilful sin, and are filled with an amazed despair when they find that a man must really reap as he has sown.

IX. THAT THE TABERNACLE AND PRIESTHOOD, WHICH SHOULD HAVE BEEN A SAFETY AND DELIGHT, DID IN TRUTH BECOME A DANGER AND A FEAR, BECAUSE THE PEOPLE WERE CARNAL. Even so the very nearness of God to us in Christ and in his Church, which is the glory of the gospel (2 Cor. vi. 16), is fraught with fearful dangers to them that walk unworthy of the heavenly calling (Matt. xxi. 44; 2 Cor. ii. 15, 16).

HOMILIES BY VARIOUS AUTHORS.

Ver. 8.—*The budding of Aaron's rod.* The budding, blossoming, and fruit-bearing of the dry staff of office laid by Aaron in the tabernacle, significant—

I. AS A MIRACLE. It was an unmistakable sign of God's interposition (such a natural impossibility the occasion of an oath among the heathen: Homer's 'Iliad,' i. 233, and Virgil's 'Æneid,' xv. 206), as every miracle is,—on behalf of his servant Aaron, "disallowed indeed of men, but chosen of God,"—and in condemnation of "the rebels." Even if regarded as an arbitrary sign, it was none the less sufficient. God required that the miracles of Moses *per se* should be accepted both by the sympathetic Israelites and the reluctant Pharaoh (Exod. iv. 1—8). So too did our Lord (John xiv. 11; xv. 24). This miracle permanent so long as the rod existed. And all miracles, though transitory, of permanent value as proofs of the interposition of God (Exod. iii. 14).

II. AS A SYMBOL. 1. "The almond tree, as that which most quickly brings forth blossoms and beautiful fruit, is an emblem of the mighty power of the word of God, which is ever fresh and unfailing in its fulfilment" (Jer. i. 11, 12). 2. A sign of the permanent vitality of God's appointed priesthood as "an everlasting priesthood throughout their generations" (Exod. xl. 15). 3. A type of the miraculous attestation of the unchangeable priesthood of Christ. God, who "fulfils himself in many ways," about, hereafter, to replace the priesthood of Aaron by a Priest chosen by himself, after the order of Melchizedec. This priesthood attested by a resurrection (Acts xiii. 33; Heb. v. 9, 10), of which the resurrection of this dead tree was a type. And now that the risen Christ is in the holiest place, in the presence of God, his resurrection and reign in glory are signs to all murmurers of his appointment as the one High Priest and King, who "shall send forth the rod of his strength," and reign till all enemies are placed beneath his feet.—P.

Ver. 10.—*The two brethren and their rods.* I. The rod of Moses, a shepherd's staff, a commonplace instrument, changed by God's power into "the rod of God" (Exod. iv. 17), "the rod of his strength." (1) For the conviction of Moses himself (*ibid.* iv. 1—5); (2) for the punishment of the rebellious (*ibid.* vii. 20, &c.); (3) for the deliverance of God's servants from imminent danger (*ibid.* xiv. 16, 26); (4) for the supply of their most urgent wants (*ibid.* xvii. 5, 6); (5) for the conquest of their foes (*ibid.* xvii. 9—12). Thus God makes the weakest commonest things of the world "mighty through God" (1 Cor. i. 27 ; 2 Cor. x. 4). The rod of the lowly Jesus is "a rod of strength," or "of iron" (Ps. ii. 9 ; cx. 2 ; Isa. xi. 4).

II. The rod of Aaron, a tribal sceptre, a symbol of power, as the shepherd's staff was not. This symbol of authority used for remedial and spiritual purposes. (1) For the confutation of presumptuous upstarts ; (2) for the preservation of the tempted from further sin and consequent destruction (ver. 10) ; (3) for a type of the fruitfulness of every institution ordained and sustained by God. See further under ver. 8. Thus God makes his mightiest power the means of attaining spiritual ends for the welfare even of sinners. "Christ the power of God" is "the power of God unto salvation." The " Prince" is also the " Saviour" (Acts v. 31).—P.

Vers. 1—9.—*Aaron's rod that budded.* The priesthood of Aaron, as a solemn reality, and no mere arrogant pretence, had already been amply shown. It had been shown, however, in a way which left behind terrible associations. Those who impugned it had died by a sudden and fearful death. And though the priesthood appears differently when it becomes the means of staying death from the living, yet even this was not sufficient to glorify it before the eyes of the people. These illustrations of its validity had arisen from the urgent pressure of circumstances. If the people had not sinned against God by despising his ordinance, that ordinance would not have been manifested in such awful power. It becomes God now to glorify the priesthood by a new and independent testimony, the way of which had been prepared by the judgments they had lately seen and suffered.

I. AARON IS EQUALISED WITH THE REST. He had been equalised before in voluntary humility (ch. xvi. 16, 17). Now the thing is specially commanded. Aaron is taken as a simple member of the tribe of Levi, and Levi itself is considered as but one of the tribes of Israel. Thus to any one disposed to complain of Aaron exalting himself, God, as it were, gave for answer: "Aaron does not exalt himself; he is nothing more than any of you. Let there be a rod for each of the tribes, and nothing to make his better than the rest. It shall then be made manifest that whatever his power, his holiness, his honour, they do not come from anything inherent in himself as a simple Israelite." And so in a certain sense Jesus was equalised with men (Philip. ii. 6—8). He grew to manhood among the poor and lowly. He had been so like the rest of the simple Nazarenes in outward form, so unpretending, so little fitted to excite attention and wonderment, that his brethren did not believe in him. There was everything in him but sin to show his community with men. He became in all things like his brethren ; and one of the results of this full, demonstrative humanity is to make clear how highly God exalted him (Philip. ii. 9—11)

II. The objects taken to represent the tribes ONCE HAD LIFE IN THEM. They were not stones of the wilderness which God was about to turn into living, fruitful branches. The work was one of restoration, not of creation altogether fresh and original. But for sin, all these Israelites, Aaron included, would have been like branches, full of beautiful and fruitful life rejoicing in God's presence, instead of being, as they were, dead to him, alive to sin. These rods, were significant *for their past as well as their future.* The Israelites used these rods doubtless for some purpose to which dead wood could be put, and thinking nothing of the life that had once been in them. Dead wood is useful, but the state and service are low as compared with those of the living tree. So Israel was now in an utterly humiliated state, quite ignorant and careless as to the glory and joy of man's first unfallen days. These tribes were now as dead rods, but if all had gone according to the original purpose, they would have been as living, fruitful branches. It is part of the priestly office of Christ to bring back that which is lost, and to swallow up in a new and glorious creation the ruin that has befallen the old one.

III. Hence the CAPACITY OF RESTORATION is indicated to the people. Ask an Israelite if a rod, a dead, sapless, long-separated branch, shall live again, he will reply, "No." In one sense he is right, for such a thing is outside of his experience ; in another sense he is wrong, as not knowing the power of God. Aaron's rod alone lived, but it is plain that the same power which revived it could have acted on the rest with a like result. When Jesus was raised from the dead, this was an indication that all dead ones might come back to life. "Because I live, ye shall live also"

(John xiv. 19). The very descent of Aaron to an equality with the rest implied a possibility that they might ascend to an equality with him. The risen Saviour in the glory of his heavenly life is the first-born among many brethren. Aaron became different from the rest in order that by his difference he might draw the rest nearer to God. The rod budded for the benefit of the rods that remained dead.

IV. THERE IS AN ANTICIPATION OF THE SLOWER PROCESSES OF NATURE. Not only is dead wood restored to life, but the life rushes forward into fruit. In the Lord's hand the work of all seasons can be done in a night. Buds, blossoms, and fruit at the same time! What a fulness of life this indicates! By thus combining in one example three stages of plant life, God shows the power of the priest's office. There was not only promise, but performance. It would have been a work of God to show just peeping buds; but *the* work of God here is to show life in its fulness. It was the clamour of the people that nothing more than empty promise had been got out of Moses. They had lately learned that Aaron's office was full of worth by his protecting atonement as against the plague. Now in this budding, blossoming, fruit-bearing rod they see both promise and performance. He who makes the rod bud is thereby promising; he who makes it blossom is drawing onward in increased hope; but he who also makes it yield fruit shows that he can perform as well as promise. So may we think of Jesus. Consider the multitudes for whom and in whom his priestly work is being done. They are in different stages. With some the bud, with some the blossom, with some the ripened, fragrant fruit. It needed that all stages should be shown in the life of the typifying rod.

V. THE USUAL AIDS OF NATURE, THE AIDS COMMONLY COUNTED NECESSARY, ARE DISPENSED WITH. There is no planting of the rods in the soil, no exposure to the sunshine and the rain. God, who usually works through many combined ministries, and shows man the blessed fellow-worker with himself, finds it fitting here, for his glory, and for the full manifestation of the truth, to set all customary ministries on one side. If *usually* there are all these aids, it is because of what is fitting, not of what is indispensably needed. Nothing is needed but to lay the rods in the tabernacle, before the testimony. Thus we see *how far from any human choice, contrivance, or control* was the budding of this rod. The result was from God's secret power, and that alone. Thereby he invested Aaron and the ark and every priestly function with fresh importance. Henceforth we look upon Aaron not only as one who keeps back death from the living, but who has to do with the giving back of life to the dead. When this rod was formerly on the tree it did not live after this glorious fashion. There was life, but not in such exaltation and abundance. This rod was known henceforth not after its first life, but its second. So now we know Christ not after the flesh, but after the spirit; not according to those first works, in curing the sick, assuaging temporal sorrows, or even bringing back Lazarus to continue awhile longer his mortal life, but according to those second works by which he, the chosen and only mediatorial channel of them, saves, sanctifies, and perfects those who come to God through him. If this marvellous rod so glorified Aaron, and stopped the murmurings of the people, should it not have some effect, rightly and repeatedly considered, in glorifying Jesus, and bringing us closer to him in humble acceptance and faith. The murmuring of the Israelites was a great evil, but our neglect of that gracious Intercessor whom God has appointed is not one whit better.—Y.

EXPOSITION.

CHAPTER XVIII.

STATUS AND REVENUES OF PRIESTS AND LEVITES (vers. 1—32). Ver. 1.—**The Lord spake unto Aaron.** This clear and comprehensive instruction as to the position and support of the sons of Aaron on the one hand, and of the Levites on the other, may very naturally have been given in connection with the events just narrated. There is, however, no direct reference to those events, and it is quite possible that the only connection was one of subject-matter in the mind of the writer. That the regulations which follow were addressed to Aaron directly is a thing unusual, and indeed unexampled. The ever-recurring statement elsewhere is, "the Lord spake unto Moses," varied occasionally by "the Lord spake unto Moses and unto Aaron" (as in ch. ii. 1; iv. 1; xix. 1); but even where the communication refers to things wholly and peculiarly within the province of Aaron, it is usually made to Moses, and only through him to his brother (see *e. g.* ch. viii. 1—3). This change in the form of the message may point to a later date, *i. e.* to a time subsequent to the gainsaying of Korah, when the separate position of Aaron as the head of a priestly caste was more fully recognised than before, and he himself somewhat less under the shadow of his greater brother. **Thou and thy sons and thy father's house with thee shall bear the iniquity of the sanctuary.** Aaron's father's house, according to the analogy of ch. xvii. 2, 3, 6, was the sub-tribe of the Kohathites, and these had charge (to the exclusion of the other Levites) of the sanctuary, or rather sacred things (הַמִּקְדָּשׁ, as in ch. x. 21. Septuagint, τῶν ἁγίων). See on ch. iv. 15. This mention of the Kohathites in connection with the sanctuary is an incidental proof that these instructions were given in view of the wanderings in the wilderness, for after the settlement in Canaan no Levites (as such) came into contact with the sacred furniture. It is not easy to define exactly the meaning of "shall bear the iniquity (תִּשְׂאוּ אֶת־עֲוֹן) of the sanctuary." The general sense of the phrase is, "to be responsible for the iniquity," *i. e.* for anything which caused displeasure in the eyes of God, "in connection with the sacred things and the service of them;" hence it meant either to be responsible for such iniquity, as being held accountable for it, and having to endure the penalty, or as being permitted and enabled to take such accountability on oneself, and so discharge it from others. This double sense is exactly reflected in the Greek word αἴρειν, as applied to our Lord (John i. 29). The priests, therefore (and the Kohathites, so far as they had anything to do with the sanctuary), were responsible for all the unholiness attaching or accruing to it, not only by reason of all offences committed by themselves, but by reason of that imperfection which clung to them at the best, and made them unworthy to handle the things of God. In a further and deeper sense they might be said to be vicariously responsible for all the iniquity of all Israel, so far as the taint of it affected the very sanctuary (see on Exod. xxviii. 38; Levit. xvi. 16). **The iniquity of your priesthood.** The responsibility not only for all sinful acts of omission and commission in Divine service (such as those of Nadab and Abihu, and of Korah), but for all the inevitable failure of personal holiness on the part of those who ministered unto the Lord. This responsibility was emphatically recognised and provided for in the rites of the great day of atonement.

Ver. 2.—**Thy brethren also of the tribe of Levi.** The Levites generally, as distinguished from the Kohathites in particular (see on ch. iii.). **That they may be joined unto thee.** וְיִלָּווּ, a play upon the name Levi (see on Gen. xxix. 34). **But thou and thy sons with thee shall minister before the tabernacle of witness.** The Hebrew has only וְאַתָּה וּבָנֶיךָ אִתָּךְ, which may be rendered, "And thou and thy sons with thee (shall be)," &c., or more naturally read with what goes before, "that they may minister unto thee; both thee and thy sons with thee," &c. The Septuagint and the Targums appear to favour the former rendering, but it is not evident what distinction could be drawn between priests and Levites as to the mere fact of being before the tabernacle.

Ver. 3.—**They shall keep their charge, &c.** See on ch. iii. 7, 8. **That neither they, nor ye also, die.** This warning does not seem to refer to the danger of the Kohathites seeing the sacred things (ch. iv. 15), but of the other Levites coming near them; the further warning, "nor ye also," is added because if the carelessness or profanity of the priest led to sacrilege and death in the case of the Levite, it would be laid to his charge (cf. ch. iv. 18).

Ver. 4.—**A stranger.** זָר, *i. e.* one not a Levite, as in ch. i. 51.

Ver. 5.—**That there be no wrath any more upon the children of Israel.** As there had been in the case of Korah and his company, and of the many thousands who had fallen in consequence.

Ver. 6.—**I have taken your brethren the Levites.** See on ch. iii. 9; viii. 19.

Ver. 7.—**Shall keep your priests' office for everything of the altar, and within the vail.** That the Levites were made over to Aaron and his sons to relieve them of a great part of the mere routine and drudgery of their service was to be with them an additional and powerful motive for doing their priestly work so reverently and watchfully as to leave no excuse for sacrilegious intrusion. The altar (of burnt offering) and "that within the vail" (cf. Heb. vi. 19) were the two points between which the exclusive duties of the priesthood lay, including the service of the holy place. **A service of gift.** A service which was not to be regarded as a burden, or a misfortune, or as a natural heritage and accident of birth, but to be received and cherished as a favour accorded to them by the goodness of God.

Ver. 8.—**And the Lord spake unto Aaron.** The charge and responsibility of the priests having been declared, the provision for their maintenance is now to be set forth. **The charge.** מִשְׁמֶרֶת, as in ver. 5, &c.; but here it means "the keeping" for their own use (cf. Exod. xii. 6). **Mine heave offerings.** תְּרוּמֹתָי. The possessive pronoun marks the fact that these did not belong to the priest in the first instance, although they naturally came to be looked on as his perquisites (cf. 1 Sam. ii. 16), but were a gift to him from the Lord out of what the people had dedicated. The word *terumoth* must here be understood in its widest sense, as including everything which the Israelites dedicated or "lifted" of all their possessions, so far as these were not destroyed in the act of offering. **Of all the hallowed things.** The genitive of identity : "consisting of all the hallowed things." **By reason of the anointing.** Rather, "for a portion," לְמָשְׁחָה (see on Levit. vii. 35). The Septuagint has εἰς γέρας, "as an honour,' or *peculium*.

Ver. 9.—**Reserved from fire,** *i. e.* from the sacrificial altar. **Every oblation of theirs.** As specified in the following clauses. The burnt offering is not mentioned because it was wholly consumed, and only the skin fell to the priest. The sin offerings for the priest or for the congregation were also wholly consumed (Levit. iv. 12, 21), but the sin offerings of private individuals, although in no case partaken of by the offerers, were available for the priests (Levit. vi. 26), and this was the ordinary case.

Ver. 10.—**In the most holy place thou shalt eat it.** בְּקֹדֶשׁ הַקֳּדָשִׁים. Septuagint, ἐν τῷ ἀγίῳ τῶν ἀγίων. This expression is somewhat perplexing, because it stands commonly for the holy of holies (Exod. xxvi. 33). As it cannot possibly have that meaning here, two interpretations have been proposed. 1. That it means the court of the tabernacle, called "the holy place" in Levit. vi. 16, 26 ; vii. 6, and there specified as the only place in which the meat offerings, the sin offerings, and trespass offerings might be eaten. There is no reason why this court should not be called "most holy," as well as "holy ;" if it was "holy" with respect to the camp, or the holy city, it was "most holy" with respect to all without the camp, or without the gate. 2. That the expression does not mean "in the most holy place," but "amongst the most holy things," as it does in ch. iv. 4, and above in ver. 9. A distinction is clearly intended between the "most holy things," which only the priests and their sons might eat, and the "holy things," of which the rest of their families might partake also. It is difficult to decide between these renderings, although there can be no doubt that the "most holy" things were actually to be consumed within the tabernacle precincts.

Ver. 11.—**And this is thine.** Here begins a second list of holy gifts which might

be eaten at home by all members of the priestly families who were clean ; they included (1) all wave offerings, especially the wave breast and heave shoulder of the peace offerings ; (2) all first-fruits of every kind ; (3) all that was devoted ; (4) all the first-born, or their substitutes. The first and third must have been very variable in amount, but the second and fourth, if honestly rendered, must have brought in a vast amount both of produce and of revenue. **With all the wave offerings.** Rather, "in all the wave offerings," as in ver. 8.

Ver. 12.—**All the best.** Literally, "all the fat" (cf. Gen. xlv. 18).

Ver. 14.—**Everything devoted.** כָּל־חֵרֶם. Septuagint, πᾶν ἀνατεθεματισμένον, all deodands, or things vowed (see on Levit. xxvii. 28).

Ver. 16.—**From a month old.** Literally, "from the monthly child," as soon as they reach the age of one month. **According to thine estimation.** See on Levit. v. 15 ; xxvii. 2—7. It would seem that the priest was to make the valuation for the people, since each first-born or firstling was separately claimed by God, and had to be separately redeemed ; but at the same time, to prevent extortion, the sum which the priest might assess was fixed by God. **For the money of five shekels.** About seventeen shillings of our money (see ch. iii. 47). It is extremely difficult to estimate the number of first-born, but it is evident that in any case a large income must have accrued to the priests in this way. No value is here set upon the firstlings of unclean beasts; in the most usual case, that of the ass, the rule had been laid down in Exod. xiii. 13 ; and in other cases it was apparently left to the discretion of the priests, subject to the right of the owner, if he saw fit, to destroy the animal rather than pay for it (see Levit. xxvii. 27).

Ver. 17.—**But the firstling of a cow,** &c. Only those things which were not available for sacrifice could be redeemed ; the rest must be offered to him that claimed them. The first-born of men belonged partially to both classes : on the one hand, they could not be sacrificed, and therefore were redeemed with money ; on the other hand, they could be dedicated (being clean), and therefore had been exchanged for the Levites.

Ver. 18.—**The flesh of them shall be thine, as the wave breast and as the right shoulder are thine.** This is on the face of it inconsistent with the direction given in Deut. xv. 19, 20, that the flesh of the firstlings should be eaten by the offerers in the holy place (cf. also Deut. xii. 17, 18). Two explanations have been proposed. 1. That the firstlings were given to the priest in the same sense as the peace offerings, *i. e.* only as regarded the breast and shoulder, while the rest went to the offerer. This, however, does obvious violence to the language, and is not supported by the Septuagint. 2. That as the priest was bound to consume the firstlings with his family, and could not sell them, he would be certainly disposed to invite the offerer to join him in the sacred meal. This may have been usually the case, but it was entirely within the option of the the priest, and could scarcely be made the basis of a direct command, like that of Deut. xv. 19, still less of an indirect assumption, like that of Deut. xii. 17, 18, that the firstlings stood upon the same footing as free-will offerings and heave offerings. It is easier to suppose that the law was actually modified in this, as in some other particulars.

Ver. 19.—**All the heave offerings of the holy things.** Those, viz., enumerated from ver. 9. **It is a covenant of salt for ever.** Septuagint, διαϑήκη ἁλὸς αἰωνίου (cf. 2 Chron. xiii. 5). Salt was the natural emblem of that which is incorruptible; wherefore a binding alliance was (and still is) made by eating bread and salt together, and salt was always added to the sacrifices of the Lord (Levit. ii. 13 ; Mark ix. 49).

Ver. 20.—**Thou shalt have no inheritance in their land.** The priests had of necessity homes wherein to live when not on duty, but they had no territory of their own in the same sense as Jews of other tribes. **I am thy part and thine inheritance.** Septuagint, ἐγὼ μερίς σου καὶ κληρονομία σου. This is not to be explained away, as if it meant only that they were to live " of the altar." Just as the priests (and in a lesser sense all the Levites) were the special possession of the Lord, so the Lord was the special possession of the priests; and inasmuch as all the whole earth belonged to him, the portion of the priests was, potentially in all cases, actually for those who were capable of realising it, infinitely more desirable than any other portion. The spiritual meaning of the promise was so clearly felt that it was constantly claimed by the devout in Israel, irrespective of their ecclesiastical status (cf. Ps. xvi. 5 ; Lam. iii. 24, &c.).

Ver. 21.—**All the tenth.** The tithe of all fruits and flocks had been already claimed absolutely by the Lord (Levit. xxvii. 30, 32). It is probable indeed that the giving of tithes had been more or less a matter of obligation from time immemorial. Abraham had paid them on one memorable occasion (Gen. xiv. 20), and Jacob had vowed them on another (Gen. xxviii. 22). From this time forth, however, the tithes were formally assigned to the maintenance of the Levites, in return for their service.

Ver. 22.—**Lest they bear sin, and die.** לָשֵׂאת חֵטְא לָמוּת. Septuagint, λαβεῖν ἁμαρ-

τίαν ϑανατηφόρον. In the sense of incurring sin, and the consequent wrath and death.

Ver. 23.—**And they shall bear (יִשְׂאוּ) their iniquity.** The Levites were to take the responsibility of the general iniquity so far as approach to the tabernacle was concerned. **They have no inheritance.** Like the priests, they had homes and cities, and they had pasturages attached to these cities, but no separate territory.

Ver. 24.—**As an heave offering.** This means nothing more than an " offering" apparently. It is not to be supposed that any ritual was observed in the giving of tithes.

Ver. 25.—**And the Lord spake unto Moses.** This part of the instruction alone is addressed to Moses, probably because it determined a question as between priests and Levites to the advantage of the former, and therefore would not have come well from Aaron.

Ver. 26.—**Ye shall offer up an heave offering of it for the Lord, even a tenth part of the tithe.** Thus the principle of giving a tenth part of all to God was carried out consistently throughout the whole of his people.

Ver. 28.—**Ye shall give thereof the Lord's heave offering to Aaron the priest.** The Levites tithed the people, the priests tithed the Levites. At this time the other Israelites were nearly fifty times as numerous as the Levites, and therefore they would have been exceptionally well provided for. It must be remembered, however, that the Levites would naturally increase faster than the rest, not being exposed to the same dangers ; and still more that tithes are never paid at all fully or generally, even when of strict legal obligation. A glance along the history of Israel after the conquest will satisfy us that at no time could the people at large be trusted to pay their tithes, unless it were during the ascendancy of the Maccabees, and afterwards under the influence of the Pharisees (cf. Mal. iii. 9, 10). The Levites, indeed, appear in the history of Israel as the reverse of an opulent or influential class. It was no doubt much easier for the sons of Aaron to obtain their tithes from the Levites ; and as these were very numerous in proportion, and the tithes themselves were only a part of their revenues, the priests should have been, and in later times certainly were, sufficiently rich. If they were devout they no doubt spent much on the service of the altar and of the sanctuary.

Ver. 30.—**Thou shalt say unto them,** i. e. to the Levites. When they had dedicated their tithe of the best part, the rest was theirs exactly as if they had grown it and gathered it themselves.

Ver. 32.—**Ye shall bear no sin.** עֲלָיו

לֹא־תִשְׂאוּ. They would not incur any guilty responsibility by enjoying it as and where they pleased. **Neither shall ye pollute the holy things of the children of Israel, lest ye die.** This seems to be the true transla-tion, and it conveyed a final warning. See Levit. xxii. 2 for one very obvious way in which the Levites might pollute "holy things."

HOMILETICS.

Vers. 1—32.—*Responsibilities and privileges of God's servants.* We have in this chapter, spiritually, the status of those who are ἱερεῖς τῷ Θεῷ and δοῦλοι Ἰησοῦ Χριστοῦ, as being the inheritance of the Lord, and (in this world) "having nothing, and yet possessing all things." Much that has been considered under the head of chs. iii., iv., and viii. is applicable here. Consider, therefore—

I. THAT A HEAVY RESPONSIBILITY WEIGHED UPON PRIEST AND LEVITE IN RESPECT OF THE SANCTUARY, OF WHICH THEY HAD THE CHARGE AND THE HANDLING. Whatever pollution came upon it was chargeable upon them in the double sense, (1) that if due to them, they should suffer for it; (2) that whether due to them or not, they should be bound to purge it by atonement. Even so all the faithful in Christ Jesus are deeply responsible for all the shame, reproach, and disparagement which comes upon that temple which is themselves (Eph. ii. 22; 1 Tim. iii. 15; Heb. iii. 6), and that in the following senses:—1. So far as such evils may be due to their own sin or carelessness (Matt. xviii. 6, 7; Rom. xiv. 15, 16; 1 Cor. x. 32; 2 Cor. vi. 3; 1 Thess. v. 22). 2. So far as the evil can be undone or counteracted by their own piety and zeal (Matt. v. 16; Philip. ii. 15, 16; 1 Pet. ii. 12). 3. If this cannot be, then at least to this extent, that they bear it on their heart in sorrow and in prayer (Ezek. ix. 4; Dan. ix. 20; 1 Cor. xii. 25, 26; 2 Cor. xi. 29). Nothing is worse than the complacency with which Christians regard the scandals of religion, although such are often due in part to themselves, or might in part be cured by their own efforts, or should at least be a cause of inward grief and humiliation to them as members of Christ.

II. THAT A SIMILAR RESPONSIBILITY ATTACHED TO THE PRIESTHOOD IN RESPECT TO ALL FAULTS AND IMPERFECTIONS ATTENDING ITS EXERCISE. Even so it is no light or trivial thing to have received an unction from the Holy One, making us, in any sense of the words, priests unto God. There are no vain titles in the kingdom of heaven to gratify man's love of distinction; whatever we have is a dispensation committed unto us (1 Cor. ix. 17); any ministry ill discharged, made a scandal or offence, is ruin to the soul (1 Cor. iv. 2; Col. iv. 17; 1 Tim. iv. 16; Rev. iii. 2, 15, 16).

III. THAT THEY WERE UNDER SPECIAL RESPONSIBILITY TO WATCH THEIR WATCH AND OBSERVE THE DUTIES OF THEIR OFFICE ABOUT THE SANCTUARY AND THE ALTAR, lest wrath should come upon the people. Even so the custodians of Divine truth are under special obligation to guard most carefully and reverently the two doctrines of Jesus in heaven ("that within the vail," Heb. vi. 19, 20) and of Jesus upon the cross (*ibid.* ix. 14), lest, either being tampered with, damage should accrue to the souls of men.

IV. THAT THE OFFICE OF THE PRIESTS WAS "A SERVICE OF GIFT." Even so every office in the Church of God is a service, for there is no such thing as a sinecure in the kingdom of heaven; and it is a service of gift, because it is not a matter of earthly honour, or of pay, or of human choice, or even of personal aptness, but of free grace and gift on the part of God—a trust conferred, a bounty bestowed.

V. THAT THE PRIESTS "WERE PARTAKERS WITH THE ALTAR." Even so hath the Lord ordained, &c. (1 Cor. ix. 13, 14).

Consider again, *with respect to the Levites*—

I. THAT THEY WERE GIVEN TO AARON TO "WATCH HIS WATCH" AND "THE WATCH OF ALL THE TABERNACLE." Even so are we all the kindred of Christ given unto him to be his soldiers and servants to keep his watches, and to be the guardians of his spiritual house until he come again (Mark xiii. 35—37; 1 Cor. xvi. 13; Eph. v. 15; Rev. xvi. 15).

II. That while ever watchful and on the alert, they must not intrude upon the sacred things of the sanctuary, or the altar, on pain of death. Even so it is fatal presumption and loss of spiritual life when men leave their practical duties to "intrude" by vain speculation into "those things which they have not seen" in the heavenly state; or when they pry curiously into the unrevealed mysteries of the cross, "which things the angels desire to look into," yet forbear, because it is not given them to understand (Col. ii. 18; 1 Pet. i. 12).

Consider again, *with respect to Aaron and the people at large—*
I. That every oblation or offering of theirs was given to Aaron. Even so everything which the piety or gratitude of man freely offers to God has been made over to Christ, as the High Priest of our profession, by an indefeasible title (Matt. xi. 27 *a*.; xxviii. 18 *b*.; 1 Cor. iii. 23).
II. That the first and best (the fat) of everything was to be given to God and to Aaron. Even so ought every faithful person to dedicate the first and best of all he has (or is) to the Lord and his Christ. It is a fearful thing to put him off with the odds and ends of our time, the gleanings of our mind and thought, the stray coins of our wealth.
III. That everything under a ban—a vow, or curse—was given to Aaron. Even so does every soul devoted to destruction, every soul under the curse, belong to Christ, because he was made a curse for us, and devoted himself to death and wrath for our redemption; wherefore all souls are his, being given unto him of the Father for his portion.
IV. That all the people were to pay tithes to the Levites, and the Levites themselves to Aaron, and thus the principle was doubly maintained that a tenth part of all was due to God for the support of religion. Aaron did not pay tithes, because he was the figure of Christ himself. Even so all good Christian people are bound, not of necessity to give an exact and literal tenth, but certainly no less than that, unless they think that their obligation to God is less than that of the Jews. This may be enforced by the following considerations:—1. We are as much beholden for all we have to the mere bounty of Providence as the Jews. 2. We are in at least as much danger of covetousness as they. 3. We are much more in the practice of luxury and superfluity than they. 4. We are more distinctly called to a voluntary choice of (comparative) poverty than they (Matt. xiii. 22; xix. 23; 1 Tim. vi. 6—10). 5. There is more need of abundant offerings now than then, because we have all the world to evangelise, instead of a single temple with its services to maintain. 6. Our giving should be more ample, just because it is left to the holy impulse of faith and love. God has refrained from demanding a tenth in order that we might freely give —more (Mal. iii. 10; Matt. xxvi. 13; Acts ii. 45; xx. 35; Philem. 19, &c.).
V. That the Levites, having "heaved from the best" of all they received, were then to enjoy the remainder with a clear conscience. Even so the servants of Christ, when they have dedicated (and only when) the best of all they have—time, money, talents, opportunities, influence—to the direct service of Christ, may enjoy the good things which fall to them with singleness and gladness of heart (Luke xi. 41; Acts ii. 46; 1 Tim. vi. 18; and cf. 1 Kings xvii. 13 *sq.*).

Consider again, *with respect to priests and Levites—*
That they had no inheritance amongst the tribes, but the Lord was their portion and their inheritance. Even so hath the Lord given unto us no inheritance in this world, because he himself is ours, as we are his. We do indeed have (most of us) many things richly to enjoy, but these are not our own, as the world counts its good things its own, but are only lent for an uncertain season (Luke xvi. 11, 12—what we have here is "another man's," as distinguished from "our own"); and that we have anything at all is only of indulgence, not of right, nor of promise (Matt. xix. 21; Luke xii. 33; John xvi. 33; Acts xiv. 22 *b*.; James ii. 5); and, further, whatever we have we hold only on condition of giving it up at once, without complaint or astonishment, if called thereunto (Luke xiv. 26; Heb. x. 34; James i. 10; Rev. iii. 17; xii. 11). Nevertheless, we are not poor, though having nothing; but rich beyond compare, having the Pearl of great price, and the Treasure

(albeit "hid" for the present, Col. ii. 3), and the bright and morning Star (2 Pet. i. 19 *b.*), and in him all things indeed (1 Cor. iii. 21, 22; 2 Cor. iv. 18; Rev. iii. 20; cf. Gen. xv. 1 *b.* ; Ps. xvi. 5; lxxiii. 26, &c.).

Consider again, *with respect to sacrifice*—
THAT CERTAIN THINGS MOST HOLY MIGHT BE CONSUMED ONLY WITHIN THE SACRED PRECINCTS BY THE PRIESTS THEMSELVES ; OTHERS HOLY, BUT NOT SO HOLY, AT HOME BY ALL MEMBERS OF THE FAMILY. Even so there are things pertaining to the one sacrifice for sin with which none may intermeddle but the priest himself of the sacrifice; others which may be shared in common amongst all members of the family of Christ. Or, in another sense, there are aspects of the atonement which can only be made our own in a religious solitude and retirement, and which are profaned by being brought abroad ; others, again, which befit the common and social life of Christian people, always providing that no "uncleanness," *i. e.* no unrepented sin, hinder them from having part or lot therein.

HOMILIES BY VARIOUS AUTHORS.

Vers. 1—7.—*The responsibility of authority.* Recent assaults on the priesthood give occasion for a reaffirmation of its prerogatives. Lest this should tend unduly to elate the family of Aaron, the same Divine oracle which confirms to them their distinguished privileges insists on their grave responsibilities.
I. THE DISTINGUISHED PRIVILEGES OF THE PRIESTS. 1. The priest's office is described as "a service of gift," conferred by God himself (Heb. v. 4). 2. It was confined to the family of Aaron (ver. 2). 3. It had special duties into which not even the priests' kindred, the Levites, might intrude (ver. 3 ; ch. iv. 4—15). 4. The priests had authority over the Levites as their ministers (ver. 2), and over the people in a variety of ways: teachers (Levit. x. 11) ; mediators of blessing (ch. vi. 22—26 ; Deut. xxi. 5); judges (Deut. xvii. 8—13); sanitary officers (Levit. xiii., xiv.). 5. Provision was made for their daily wants, that they might "attend upon the Lord" without distraction (vers. 8—15). 6. They were thus, as mediators, the means of averting wrath from the nation (ver. 5).
II. THEIR GRAVE RESPONSIBILITIES. Lest Aaron's "pride" should "bud" (Ezek. vii. 10), even as his rod had, and the priests should be exalted above measure through the abundance of their privileges, they are reminded of some of their responsibilities. 1. The priests and their father's house (the Levites or Kohathites) had to "bear the iniquity of the sanctuary" (cf. Exod. xxviii. 38). Some errors might be atoned for, but they were responsible for any profanation of the tabernacle. 2. The priests alone had to "bear the iniquity of their priesthood." An annual atonement provided (Levit. xvi. 6), but not for such wilful transgressions as Nadab's, or for gross neglect (*e. g.* Levit. xxii. 9). 3. They had a responsibility in regard to the Levites, not to allow them to intrude into the priest's office, "that neither they *nor ye also* die" (ver. 3). 4. The neglect of these duties might be fatal to others as well as to themselves (vers. 3, 5).
These two truths admit of various applications. 1. *To Christian rulers*, to statesmen called to the duty of governing a country on Christian principles, but incurring tremendous responsibility thereby. Illustrate from the history of Jeroboam (cf. Jer. xlv. 5 ; Luke xii. 48). 2. *To Christian teachers* (1 Tim. iii. 1, yet James iii. 1). The burden of responsibility quite enough to account for the "*Nolo Episcopari.*" Yet where God calls to the honour he will give strength and grace for the burden.—P.

Ver. 20.—*God, the best inheritance.* The tribe of Levi was left out in the division of the land. Some of its members might have wished to be landowners rather than Levites. Yet their loss was a special privilege, for they were selected that they might "come nigh to God," and serve in his tabernacle. God who called them did not forget them. They received houses, gardens, pasture lands (ch. xxxv. 1—8), and tithes (ver. 21), and were commended to the care and sympathy of the nation (Deut. xii. 12, 14, 27—29). Just so, under the gospel, those called to give up their lives to the service of God, though they may not have even manses or glebes, are

provided for by God through the law of Christ (1 Cor. ix. 13, 14), and are commended
to the care of his people (Gal. vi. 6; 1 Thess. v. 12, 13).   Let no young Christians
who hear God's call to be pastors, evangelists, or missionaries hesitate to obey it.
They may have many trials and heart-aches, but they know God's word: "Them that
honour me I will honour."   Their experience may be that of the Apostle's (Luke
xxii. 35), for their Master's promise stands good (Matt. xix. 29).   But the privilege
of the Levites may be enjoyed by all God's servants who can say with David, "The
Lord is the portion of my inheritance."

I. THE CHRISTIAN'S INHERITANCE.   Wisdom is needed in choosing an earthly
inheritance or investing our "portion" of this world's goods.   It may be invested
in a freehold, embarked in a business venture, spent on one's own education, or
squandered in riotous living.   Much more is wisdom needed in regard to the soul's
inheritance.   Other portions allure some: modern idolatries, worldly wealth or ease
(Ps. xvii. 14; Isa. lvii. 6).   But the Christian, like a loyal Levite, prefers God without
the land to the land without God.   He has committed his soul entirely to God.   He
has no second spiritual portion to fall back upon if this should fail him.   Of this he
has no fear.   He has accepted God's offer to be his God and his portion, and he can
say 2 Tim. i. 12.

II. THE RESPONSIBILITIES AND PRIVILEGES OF HAVING SUCH AN INHERITANCE.   The
grave responsibilities of the Levites have their parallel in the entire consecration
needed from every Christian (Ps. cxix. 57; Titus ii. 14).   But we need not shrink
from our responsibilities when we remember our privileges.   The two things most
needed in our inheritance are *safety* and *sufficiency*.   1. *Safety*.   If God is our
portion, he himself is our security (Deut. xxxiii. 27).   When he invited us to take
him as our portion, it was because he took us as his inheritance (Deut. xxxii. 9; Isa.
xliii. 1; 1 Cor. iii. 23).

> "Be thou my God, and the whole world is mine.
>   Whilst thou art Sovereign, I'm secure;
>   I shall be rich till thou art poor;
>   For all I hope and all I fear, heaven, earth, and hell, are thine."

2. *Sufficiency*.   So was it with the Levites (ver. 21, &c.), David (Ps. xvi. 6), Jacob
(cf. Gen. xxviii. 21; xlviii. 15, 16), and so is it with all Christians.   In God they have
sufficiency for both spiritual wants (John i. 16; 1 Cor. iii. 21, 22; James iv. 6) and
temporal also (Ps. lxxxiv. 11, 12; Matt. vi. 33; Phil. iv. 19).

We can thus recommend God as the best portion for all.   1. A good portion for
the young, who, like those born heirs to an estate, are entitled to this inheritance if
they will claim it.   2. A good marriage portion.   Illustration—Ruth, who brought
Boaz an excellent portion (Ruth i. 16, 17; ii. 11, 12).   3. A good inheritance in
troublous times when banks and companies are failing.   None of these vicissitudes
in our inheritance (Deut. xxxii. 31).   4. A good inheritance in reserve (Lam. iii. 24).
That hope cannot be disappointed; the heirs of God know that "still there's more
to follow" (Ps. xxxi. 19).   5. A good inheritance on a dying bed.   Then all earthly
inheritance daily drop in value to the proprietor, and at last "flesh and heart fail."
But the Christian can say Ps. lxxiii. 26.   Because God has been the "portion of his
inheritance" he can add Ps. xvi. 8, 9, 11.—P.

Ver. 1.—*The iniquity of the sanctuary and priesthood.*   It is full of significance
that this provision for the iniquity of the sanctuary and priesthood stands first among
the regulations of this chapter.   Though God had separated Aaron, and in recent
transactions exalted and glorified him, he had not thereby made it an easy or certain
thing to serve in this office of priest as in all respects one was required to serve.
God had called Israel to be his own people, and honoured them, but they were very
perverse in all their ways.   It is therefore far from wonderful that Aaron and the
Levites, being of the same flesh and blood as rebellious Israel, should have fallen
short in the holy service to which they were appointed.   That rebellious spirit
Korah, who was a Kohathite, shows how much iniquity could attach to the sanctuary; and the iniquity of the priesthood is amply shown in Aaron's conduct when
he made the golden calf, and joined Miriam in her envious outbreak against Moses.

But even apart from such capital instances of transgression, we may be sure there was continual iniquity both in sanctuary and priesthood—things done too often in a formal, listless way, priest and Levite alike conscious that the heart was not always in the work. It was necessary to provide also for imperfections in the offerings. The animals without blemish were only relatively so, not blemished so far as the contributors knew, the very pick, doubtless, of the flocks and herds. There was sincerity of purpose, but there could not be completeness of knowledge. Hence we are led to consider—

I. The inevitable shortcomings in our holiest services. Considering how much we fall short even in our relations to men, how deficient in equity, benevolence, and gratitude, we may well feel that the iniquity of our religion must be a very large and serious matter indeed. In relation to God, how ignorant is the understanding, how dull the conscience, how languid are the affections! What formality and pre-occupation in the worship! how apt we are to turn it as far as we can into mere selfish pleasure, from music or eloquence! And when in the mercy of God we become more sensitive to his claims, more spiritually-minded, better able to estimate rightly this present evil world, then also we shall see our shortcomings in a clearer light. Faults that are not noticeable in the dim light of this world's ethics become not only manifest, but hideous and humiliating, when the light that lighteth every man coming into the world shines upon them. The holier we become, the humbler we become; the nearer we draw to God, the more conscious we are of the difference between him and us. We neither repent nor believe as we ought. Praise, prayer, meditation, good works, gospel efforts, all are seen to be not only imperfect, but lamentably so.

II. The peculiar dangers which beset those engaged in special service. The Levites, however reverently they might at first bear the ark and the holy vessels, would gradually and insensibly contract a sort of indifference. The burdens would become like other burdens, thoughtlessly and mechanically borne. It is no easy matter for such as have to exhibit God's truth to an indifferent world to keep above indifference themselves. All the more reason, therefore, that they should be on their guard. There must needs be iniquity both in priesthood and sanctuary, but woe either to Aaron or his sons, or any Kohathite who presumed on this as an excuse for relaxing from the strictest attention. Though we cannot attain entire perfection, we are bound to labour on, getting more and more out of mediocrity and formality. Remember the humility, caution, and self-distrust with which Paul invariably speaks of his own attainments, ever magnifying the grace of God, ever confessing his need of Divine support, and the instant failure and danger which come from its with-drawal. Formality in any special work which God may require from his people, say, the exposition and enforcement of his truth, is ruinous. Christian work can never come to appear impossible, but it must never cease to appear difficult. It must always require attention, concentration, self-denial, and patience. It was a saying of J. J. Gurney, "The ministry of the gospel is the only thing I know which practice never makes easy."

III. The diffusive, penetrative power of sin. It is not so much as assumed that iniquity of the sanctuary and priesthood could be guarded against. However much was done in this direction, something would be left undone, needing to be pro-vided for in the way of atonement. Sin is working in us and against us even when we are not conscious of it. It is a vain thing to make out that there is not much after all of sin in us, that it is a stage of weakness, ignorance, and imperfection out of which we shall naturally grow.—Y.

Vers. 2—7.—*Aaron and his helpers.* I. Aaron had many helpers. No less than a whole tribe of Israel, 22,000 in number (ch. iii. 39). And if it be said, "What work could be found about the tabernacle for so many?" the answer is given in the portioning out of the work among the three great divisions of the tribe. The Levites were not around Aaron like the embellishments of a court, merely to impress the vulgar mind. They were there for work—real, necessary, honourable, beneficial work. A great deal of it might seem humble, but it could not be done without. So notice how Jesus gathered helpers around himself. It was one of the earliest things he did. He gave them also great power, such as to heal diseases, raise dead persons, and cast out demons; that thus they might authenticate the gracious and momentous message with which he had intrusted them. And in the course of ages how the helpers have increased in numbers and in variety of service! Doubtless when Israel settled in Canaan, and the Levites became distributed over the land, it was found that they were not at all too numerous for the religious requirements of the people. Christ is the centre and the guide of an immense amount of spiritual industry; nevertheless, the cry goes out that many more hearts and hands might be engaged helping the Divine Saviour of men (John iv. 35—38). It will be a long time before the Church has occasion to complain, with respect to labourers together with God, that the supply exceeds the demand. The house-holder had work to be done in his vineyard even at the eleventh hour.

II. THESE HELPERS MUST BE DULY QUALIFIED. They must all be of the tribe of Levi. Levi was taken in place of the first-born of Israel, and when the first-born were numbered it was found that they somewhat exceeded the number of qualified persons among the Levites. But God did not make up the deficiency by taking from other tribes; he kept the tabernacle service within the limits of Levi, and provided for a ransom instead (ch. iii. 39—51). The service was thus to be a matter of inherit-ance. Aaron and his sons had their portion—Kohathite, Gershonite, Merarite, each had his own field of work, and was not to transgress it. Strangers were cautioned against putting unauthorised hands on the tabernacle. It was as real a violation of the sanctuary for a common Israelite to touch even a peg of the tabernacle as to intrude within the veil itself. So we should ever look with great jealousy and care-fulness on the qualifications for serving Jesus. There have been great hindrances, occasions for blasphemy, because unclean hands have not only meddled with holy things, but kept them long in charge. The service of Jesus should go down by spiritual inheritance. We take care in affairs of this world that there shall be due apprenticeship and preparation, ascertained fitness, the tools intrusted to those who can handle them, and surely there is equal if not greater need in the supremely important affairs of Christ's kingdom. Spiritual things should ever be in charge of those who have spiritual discernment.

III. THOSE QUALIFIED WERE THEREBY PLACED UNDER OBLIGATION TO SERVE. As the service was confined to Levi, so every Levite, not otherwise disqualified, had to take part in it. There was nothing else for a Levite to do than serve God in con-nection with the sanctuary. He had no land; he was a substitute for others in holy service, and therefore they had to provide him with the necessaries of life. Thus his way in life was made clear; there was no need to consult personal inclination, and no room for reasonable doubt. And so, generally speaking, what service God expects from us we may be sure he will signify in the clearest manner. If we allow per-sonal inclination to be the great prompter and decider, there is very little we shall do. Many there are whose personal inclinations lead them into some sort of connection with the Church of Christ, and keep them there, yet they never enter into anything like real service. They have a name to serve, yet are only idly busy. Personal inclination is a very small factor in Christian service, at least at the beginning, else Christ would not have been so urgent in his demands for self-denial. Not much, of course, can be done without love; but duty, the sense of what we ought to do, is to be the great power at the beginning. Those who have had the five talents from God may have to appear in his presence to be judged, conscious that not only have the talents been lost to him, but used so selfishly as rather to have gained five talents besides in worldly possessions, influence, and reputation. It is a monstrous sin to use God's property for the low, injurious aims of self. "Power," said John Foster, "to its very last particle, is duty."

IV. THOUGH THEY WERE HELPERS OF AARON, THEY COULD NOT BE HIS SUBSTITUTES. When the priest dies, it is not some experienced and sagacious Levite who can take his place; the priesthood is to be kept in the priest's own family. The hand cannot supply the place of the head. Take away the priest, and the head is gone. Aaron, if it had been necessary, could have stooped to do the humblest Levitical service, but not even the highest of the Kohathites could enter within the veil. And thus must the helpers of Christ ever look on him as separated by his nature and person to a work which no other human being can do.   He did indeed himself take up the work of the Baptist at one time, preaching repentance (Matt. iv. 17), and he also at times became his own apostle in proclaiming the gospel; but to his own peculiar work neither Baptist nor apostle could rise.   Whatever responsibility be laid on us, we are only helpers at best.   Let no admiration we feel for the achievements of the men famous in Church history allow us to forget that their work has been really Christian and beneficial just in proportion as they made themselves secondary and subordinate to Christ.   We do not sufficiently appreciate the service of any Christian, unless as we trace in it the sustaining and guiding power of Christ himself.   In the Church one generation goeth and another cometh, but Christ abideth for ever.—Y.

Vers. 8—20.—*The provision for the priests.*   Already, upon different occasions, something has been said as to parts of certain offerings being reserved for Aaron and his sons (Exod. xxix. 28, 31—33; Levit. ii. 3, 10; vi. 16—18, 26, 29, &c.), and now in this passage the whole question of how the priests were to be provided for is taken up and answered.   It was a fitting occasion, seeing that priestly duties had just been laid down, so exacting and exclusive in their demands.   When a man is called away from the ordinary business of life, where he is as it were naturally provided for by the fruits of his industry, it must always be an anxious question as to how he shall be supported.   If the priests, along with the holding of their priestly office, had been able to farm or trade there would have been no need to point out a special means of support.   But since the priest was to be wholly given to tabernacle service, it was right not only to assure him beforehand of the necessaries of life, but to point out to him something of the way in which they were to be provided.

I. THE SUPPORT OF THE PRIESTS WAS CLOSELY CONNECTED WITH THE FAITHFUL DISCHARGE OF THEIR OFFICE.   They were provided for in the very act of carrying out their priestly duties.   Forsaking the appointed service of God at his altar, they found themselves forsaken of his providence.   He might have continued for them some miraculous provision by manna or otherwise, if such a course had seemed fitting; but he rather arranged it that in faithful waiting upon the altar their support should come from day to day.   Faithfulness was required of them, first of all, in keeping the people instructed and reminded as to all the offerings required.   An omitted offering might mean an impoverished priest.   Faithfulness also was required in being continually at the altar.   It was the appointed place for the people to give and for the priest to receive.   There was no call for him to go on mendicant expeditions round the land, or lean upon the suggestions of his own prudence in order to make sure of daily bread.   When he went to the altar it was as to a table provided by the Lord himself.   So when God manifestly calls any of us to special service, our very faithfulness in the service will bring a sufficient supply for all our need.   If we leave the path of duty we leave the path of Providence.

II. THIS MODE OF PROVISION TENDED TO BIND PRIESTS AND PEOPLE CLOSER TOGETHER.   The priest, while in some respects separated from the people by an impassable barrier, was in others united by an indissoluble bond.   Standing before them as an anointed one, with awful and peculiar powers, treading unharmed where the first footstep of a common Israelite would have wrought instant death, he nevertheless appeared at the same time dependent for his bodily sustenance on the regular offerings of the people.   Thus the priest was manifested as one of themselves.   There was everything in this remarkable mingling of relations to keep the people from presumption and the priest from pride.   Their dependence on him was not more manifest than his dependence on them.   Thus, also, we observe in many and touching ways how dependent our Saviour was on those whom he came to save.   He threw himself, as no one ever before or since, on the hospitality of the world, manifesting that there were real needs of his humanity which he looked even to sinful men to supply.   And may we not well suppose that even in his glory Jesus is not only a giver to men, but a receiver from them?   May it not be that by our fidelity and diligence in respect of the living sacrifice we are ministering a very real satisfaction to the glorified Jesus?

III. As this provision required faithfulness in the discharge of duty, so also it required FAITH IN GOD.   If he had said he would provide manna or some direct miraculous gift, such an intimation would have been easier to receive than the one actually made. That which has to come to us indirectly, gives occasion for a greater trial of faith than what has to come directly. The food of these priests was to flow through a circuitous and, to judge by late experience, not very promising channel. Had not these very people, whose offerings were to support the priests, only lately shown their contempt for Aaron and unbelief as to the reality of his office? How then should they be the channels of God's providence? Thus the opportunity for faith comes in. Looking towards man, all is unlikely; looking through man to God, all appears certain and regular. God will make his own channels, in places we think unlikely, for those who put their trust in him. He knew that, stubborn and unsympathetic as the people now were, yet the day would come when their offerings might be looked for with a reasonable confidence. We are very poor judges by ourselves of what is likely or unlikely. The Divine arrangements, perplexing as they may appear on the surface, have in all cases a basis of knowledge and power which it is our wisdom humbly and gratefully to accept.

IV. This provision EVIDENTLY GUARDED AGAINST ANYTHING LIKE EXTORTION. The people themselves knew exactly how the priests were to be provided for. And this was no small matter, seeing that in course of time the holy priesthood became in the hands of arrogant and grasping men an occasion for priestcraft. Priests learned only too soon the power of an *ipse dixit* over superstitious and timid minds. But God does not allow the authority of an *ipse dixit* to any but himself. The priest was bound by a written and definite commandment which lay open to the perception of every one who had to do with him. All these offerings, of which he had a certain part, were to be presented in any case. They were not presented in order that he might be provided for, but, being presented, they gave occasion sufficiently to provide for him. The people were to feel that he was being supported by a reasonable service.

V. THERE WAS A GREAT OPPORTUNITY FOR PEOPLE TO GIVE IN A RIGHT SPIRIT. If any one had a grudging and fault-finding disposition there was certainly opportunity for him to exercise it. He could say, not without plausibility in the ears of like-minded men, that the priests were managing things very cleverly, so as to be provided for at the public expense. Misrepresentation is not a very difficult thing to achieve if certain considerations, and these alone, are brought into view. God's appointments for the support of the priesthood were a standing trial of the people's views with respect to it. Misrepresentations cannot be escaped, but woe to those who, without troubling fully and honestly to understand the thing of which they speak, are the authors of misrepresentations. The priesthood itself was a Divine, a necessary, and a beneficial institution, and every devout Israelite would count it a joy to support it, even though particular holders of the office might be very unworthy men. We must honour and support every Divine appointment, and that all the more if the persons appointed show themselves insensible to the duties laid upon them.—Y.

Ver. 19.—*A covenant of salt.* God has defined the provisions for the priesthood, and indicated in what certainty and sufficiency they would come. He also indicates the *permanency* of the supply. The things given would be given to Aaron and to his sons and daughters with him by a statute for ever. Everything was done to make and keep the priesthood separate, and prevent those who had it from being tempted into the ordinary business of life, by fear lest they should lack sufficient support. And still further to emphasise the solemnity of the pledge, God adds this peculiar and suggestive expression: "It is a covenant of salt for ever." Dr. Thomson, in 'The Land and the Book,' tells us that it is a habit still common among the Bedawîn, and probably coming from the remotest times, for host and guest to eat together. This is said to be *bread and salt* between them, and constitutes a pledge of protection, support, and fidelity even to death. Thus we may understand God saying to Aaron, and through him to the long succession of priests, "There is bread and salt between us." But we must also go back and consider Levit. ii. 13. All the meat offerings presented to God were to be seasoned with salt. When presented, a part was burnt,—as it were, eaten by God himself,—and the remainder he returns to the priest for his own use. Thus there are mutual pledges of fidelity. God is the guest of the priest, and the priest in turn the guest of God. In this way God lifted a social custom to a holy use. We cannot but notice in the second chapter of Leviticus that while some things are mentioned as constituents of the meat offering, viz., oil and frankincense, and others as excluded, viz., leaven and honey, a special emphasis is laid on the presence of salt. A special significance was to be indicated by that presence, and it agrees with this that when Ezra was going up from Babylon, furnished by Artaxerxes with all he might require for sacrifice, the salt is given without prescribing how much (ch. vii. 22). We must, however, look further back than social customs even, to find the reason why salt was present in this covenant. Social customs, could they be traced back, rise, some of them at least, out of religious ordinances. Why was *salt* chosen as the symbol? It is something to notice that salt gives flavour to that which is insipid. God's gifts may easily pall and become worthless if his presence is not associated with them; with the sense of that presence they cannot but be grateful. But the chief service of salt is to preserve that which is dead from decay. Salt will not bring back life, but it will hinder putrefaction. Under the old covenant God did not give life, though he was preparing to give it; but at the same time he did much to preserve the world, dead in trespasses and sins, from corpse decay, while he made ready in the fulness of time to bring back the dead to life. Thus the covenant with men through types and shadows was emphatically *a covenant of salt.* And the same may he said of the new covenant through the great reality in Christ Jesus. There is an element of salt in this covenant also. "Ye are the salt of the earth," said Christ to his disciples in the great and honourable burden of service which he laid on them. Indeed, what we call the old and the new covenant are really but shapes of that great covenant between God and man made in the very constitution of things. God, creating man in his own image, and planting within him certain powers and aspirations, is thereby recording the Divine articles in the covenant; and man also, by the manifestations of his nature, by his recognition of conscience, even by his idolatries and superstitions, and gropings after God, testifies to his part in the covenant. And in this covenant all true disciples are as the salt, the solemn, continuous pledge from God to the world that he does not look on it as beyond recovery. Be it the part of all disciples then to keep the savour of the salt that is in them. "Walk in wisdom towards them that are without, redeeming the time. Let your speech be alway with grace, seasoned with salt" (Col. iv. 5, 6). It rests with us to honour God's covenant of salt and make it more and more efficacious.—Y.

EXPOSITION.

CHAPTER XIX.

THE ASHES OF AN HEIFER SPRINKLING THE UNCLEAN (vers. 1—22). Ver. 1.—**And the Lord spake unto Moses and unto Aaron.** On the addition of the second name see on ch. xviii. 1. There is no note of time in connection with this chapter, but internal evidence points strongly to the supposition that it belongs to the early days of wandering after the ban. It belongs to a period when death had resumed his normal, and more than his normal, power over the children of Israel; when, having been for a short time expelled (except in a limited number of cases—see above on ch. x. 28), he had come back with frightful rigour to reign over a doomed generation. It belongs also, as it would seem, to a time when the daily, monthly, and even annual routine of sacrifice and purgation was suspended through poverty, distress, and disfavour with God. It tells of the mercy and

condescension which did not leave even the rebellious and excommunicate without some simple remedy, some easily-obtainable solace, for the one religious distress which must of necessity press upon them daily and hourly, not only as Israelites, but as children of the East, sharing the ordinary superstitions of the age. Through the valley of the shadow of death they were doomed at Kadesh to walk, while their fellows fell beside them one by one, until the reek and taint of death passed upon the whole congregation. Almost all nations have had, as is well known, an instinctive horror of death, which has everywhere demanded separation and purification on the part of those who have come in contact with it (Bähr, 'Symbolik,' ii. p. 466 *sq.*). And this religious horror had not been combated, but, on the contrary, fostered and deepened by the Mosaic legislation. The law everywhere encouraged the idea that sin and death were essentially connected, and that disease and death spread their infection in the spiritual as well as in the natural order of things. Life and death were the two opposite poles under the law, as under the gospel; but the eye of faith was fixed upon natural life and natural death, and was not trained to look beyond. It could never have occurred to a Jew to say, "*Dulce et decorum est pro patriâ mori.*" To die, however nobly, was not only to be cut off from God oneself, but to become a curse and a danger and a cause of religious defilement to those around. There is, therefore, a beautiful consistency between this enactment and the circumstances of the time on the one hand, between this enactment and the revealed character of God on the other hand. Although they were his covenant people no more, since they were under sentence of death, yet, like others, and more than others, they had religious horrors and religious fears—not very spiritual, perhaps, but very real to them; these horrors and fears cried to him piteously for relief, and that relief he was careful to give. They must die, but they need not suffer daily torment of death; they must not worship him in the splendid and perfect order of his appointed ritual, but they should at least have the rites which should make life tolerable to them. It appears to be a mistake to connect this ordinance especially with the plague which occurred after the rebellion of Korah. It was not an exceptional calamity, the effects of which might indeed be widespread, but would be soon over, which the people had to dread exceedingly; it was the daily mortality always going on in every camp under all circumstances. If only the elder generation died off in the wilderness, this alone would yield nearly 100 victims every day, and by each of these a considerable number of the survivors must have been defiled. Thus, in the absence of special provision, one of two things must have happened: either the unhappy people would have grown callous and indifferent to the awful presence of death; or, more probably, a dark cloud of religious horror and depression would have permanently enveloped them.

Ver. 2.—**This is the ordinance of the law.** חֻקַּת הַתּוֹרָה. Law-statute: an unusual combination only found elsewhere in ch. xxxi. 21, which also concerns legal purifications. **A red heifer.** This offering was obviously intended, apart from its symbolic significance, to be studiedly simple and cheap. In contradiction to the many and costly and ever-repeated sacrifices of the Sinaitic legislation, this was a single individual, a female, and of the most common description: red is the most ordinary colour of cattle, and a young heifer is of less value than any other beast of its kind. The ingenuity indeed

of the Jews heaped around the choice of this animal a multitude of precise requirements, and supplemented the prescribed ritual with many ceremonies, some of which are incorporated by the Targums with the sacred text; but even so they could not destroy the remarkable contrast between the simplicity of this offering and the elaborate complexity of those ordained at Sinai. Only six red heifers are said to have been needed during the whole of Jewish history, so far-reaching and so long-enduring were the uses and advantages of a single immolation. It is evident that this ordinance had for its distinguishing character oneness as opposed to multiplicity, simplicity contrasted with elaborateness. **Without spot, wherein is no blemish.** See on Levit. iv. 3. However little, comparatively speaking, the victim might cost them, it must yet be perfect of its kind. The later Jews held that three white hairs together on any part of the body made it unfit for the purpose. On the sex and colour of the offering see below. **Upon which never came yoke.** Cf. Deut. xxi. 3; 1 Sam. vi. 7. The imposition of the yoke, according to the common sentiment of all nations, was a species of degradation, and therefore inconsistent with the ideal of what was fit to be offered in this case. That the matter was wholly one of sentiment is nothing to the point: God doth not care for oxen of any kind, but he doth care that man should give him what is, whether in fact or in fancy, the best of its sort.

Ver. 3.—**Unto Eleazar the priest.** Possibly in order that Aaron himself might not be associated with death, even in this indirect way (see ver. 6). In after times, however, it was usually the high priest who officiated on this occasion, and therefore it is quite as likely that Eleazar was designated because he was already beginning to take the place of his father in his especial duties. **Without the camp.** The bodies of those animals which were offered for the sin of the congregation were always burnt outside the camp, the law thus testifying that sin and death had no proper place within the city of God. In this case, however, the whole sacrifice was performed outside the camp, and was only brought into relation with the national sanctuary by the sprinkling of the blood in that direction. Various symbolic reasons have been assigned to this fact, but none are satisfactory except the following:— 1. It served to intensify the conviction, which the whole of this ordinance was intended to bring home to the minds of men, that death was an awful thing, and that everything connected with it was wholly foreign to the presence and habitation of the living God. 2. It served to mark with more emphasis the contrast between this one offering, which was perhaps almost the only one they had in the wilderness, and those which ought to have been offered continually according to the Levitical ordinances. The red heifer stood quite outside the number of ordinary victims as demanded by the law, and therefore it was not slain at any hallowed altar, nor, necessarily, by any hallowed hand. 3. It served to prefigure in a wonderful and indeed startling way the sacrifice of Christ outside the gate. In later days the heifer was conducted upon a double tier of arches over the ravine of Kedron to the opposite slope of Olivet. **That he may bring her forth, . . and one shall slay her.** The nominative to both these verbs is alike unexpressed. Septuagint, καὶ ἐξάξουσιν . . καὶ σφάξουσιν. In the practice of later ages the high priest led her out, and another priest killed her in his presence, but it was not so commanded.

Ver. 4. –**And Eleazar . . shall . . sprinkle of her blood directly before** (אֶל־נֹכַח פְּנֵי) **the tabernacle.** By this act the death of the heifer became a sacrificial offering. The sprinkling in the direction of the sanctuary intimated that the offering was made to him that dwelt therein, and the "seven times" was the ordinary number of perfect performance (Levit. iv. 17, &c.).

Ver. 5.—**One shall burn the heifer.** See on Exod. xxix. 14. **And her blood.** In all other cases the blood was poured away beside the altar, because in the blood was the life, and the life was given to God in exchange for the life of the offerer. This great truth, which underlay all animal sacrifices, was represented in this case by the sprinkling towards the sanctuary. The rest of the blood was burnt with the carcase, either because outside the holy precincts there was no consecrated earth to receive the blood, or in order that the virtue of the blood might in a figure pass into the ashes and add to their efficacy.

Ver. 6.—**Cedar wood, and scarlet, and hyssop.** See on Levit. xiv. 4—6 for the significance of these things. The antiseptic and medicinal qualities of the cedar (*Juniperus oxycedrus*) and hyssop (probably *Capparis spinosa*) make their use readily intelligible ; the symbolism of the "scarlet" is much more obscure.

Ver. 7.—**The priest shall be unclean until the even,** *i. e.* the priest who superintended the sacrifice, and dipped his finger in the blood. Every one of these details was devised in order to express the intensely infectious character of death in its moral aspect. The very ashes, which were so widely potent for cleansing (ver. 10), and the cleansing water itself (ver. 19), made every one that touched them, even for the purifying of another, himself unclean. At the same time

the ashes, while, as it were, so redolent of death that they must be kept outside the camp, were most holy, and were to be laid up by a clean man in a clean place (ver. 9). These contradictions find their true explanation only when we consider them as foreshadowing the mysteries of the atonement.

Ver. 9.—**For a water of separation,** *i. e.* a water which should remedy the state of legal separation due to the defilement of death, just as in ch. viii. the water of purification from sin is called the water of sin.

Ver. 10.—**It shall be unto the children of Israel . . a statute for ever.** This may refer only to the former part of the verse, according to the analogy of ver. 21, or it may refer to the whole ordinance of the red heifer.

Ver. 11.—**Shall be unclean seven days.** The fact of defilement by contact with the dead had been mentioned before (Levit. xxi. 1 ; Numb. v. 2 ; vi. 6 ; ix. 6), and had no doubt been recognised as a religious pollution from ancient times ; but the exact period of consequent uncleanness is here definitely fixed.

Ver. 12.—**With it.** בּוֹ. *I. e.,* as the sense clearly demands, with the water of separation.

Ver. 13.—**Defileth the tabernacle of the Lord.** On the bearing of this remarkable announcement see Levit. xv. 31. The uncleanness of death was not simply a personal matter, it involved, if not duly purged, the whole congregation, and reached even to God himself, for its defilement spread to the sanctuary. **Cut off from Israel,** *i. e.* excommunicate on earth, and liable to the direct visitation of Heaven (cf. Gen. xvii. 14).

Ver. 14.—**This is the law.** הַתּוֹרָה. By this law the extent of the infection is rigidly defined, as its duration by the last. **In a tent.** This fixes the date of the law as given in the wilderness, but it leaves in some uncertainty the rule as to settled habitations. The Septuagint, however, has here ἐν οἰκίᾳ, and therefore it would appear that the law was transferred without modification from the tent to the house. In the case of large houses with many inhabitants, some relaxation of the strictness must have been found necessary.

Ver. 15.—**Which hath no covering bound upon it.** So the Septuagint (ὅσα οὐχὶ δεσμὸν καταδέδεται ἐπ' αὐτῷ), and this is the sense. In the Hebrew פָּתִיל, a string, stands in apposition to צָמִיד, a covering. If the vessel was open, its contents were polluted by the odour of death.

Ver. 16.—**One that is slain with a sword.** This would apply especially, it would seem, to the field of battle ; but the law must certainly have been relaxed in the case of soldiers. **Or a bone of a man, or a grave.** Thus the defilement was extended to the mouldering remains of humanity, and even to the tombs (μνήματα. Cf. Luke xi. 44) which held them.

Ver. 17.—**Running water.** Septuagint, ὕδωρ ζῶν (cf. Levit. xiv. 5 ; John iv. 10).

Ver. 18.—**Shall take hyssop.** See Exod. xii. 22, and cf. Ps. li. 7.

Ver. 19.—**On the third day, and on the seventh day.** The twice-repeated application of holy water marked the clinging nature of the pollution to be removed ; so also the repetition of the threat in the following verse marked the heinousness of the neglect to seek its removal.

Ver. 21.—**It shall be a perpetual statute.**

This formula usually emphasises something of solemn importance. In this case, as apparently above in ver. 10, the regulations thus enforced might seem of trifling moment. But the whole design of this ordinance, down to its minutest detail, was to stamp upon physical death a far-reaching power of defiling and separating from God, which extended even to the very means Divinely appointed as a remedy. The Jew, whose religious feelings were modelled upon this law, must have felt himself entangled in the meshes of a net so widely cast about him that he could hardly quite escape it by extreme caution and multiplied observances ; he might indeed exclaim, unless habit hardened him to it, " Who shall deliver me from the body of this death ? "

HOMILETICS.

Vers. 1 — 22. — *The remedy of death.* We have in this chapter, spiritually, death, and the remedy for death. Death is treated of not as the mere physical change which is the end of life, nor as the social and domestic loss which breaks so many hearts and causes so many tears to flow, but as the inseparable companion and, as it were, *alter ego* of sin, whose dark shadow does not merely blight, but pollutes, which shuts out not so much the light of life as the light of God. It is death, not as he is to the *dead*, but as he is to the *living*, and to them in their religious life. It is true that according to the letter it is physical death only which is spoken of, and the ceremonial uncleanness which ensued upon contact with it. It is true also that this uncleanness, so minutely regulated, and so held in abhorrence, was a matter of superstition. The last relics of religious feeling (or, upon another view, its first dawnings) in the lowest savages take the form of a superstitious dread of the lifeless remains of the departed and of their resting-place. There is in truth nothing in the touch of the dead which can infect or contaminate the living, or affect in the least their moral and spiritual condition. Nevertheless, most of the nations (and especially the Egyptians) elaborated the primitive superstition of their forefathers into a code of religious sentiment and observance which took a firm hold of the popular mind. It pleased God to adopt this primitive and widespread superstition (as in so many other cases) into his own Divine legislation, and to make it a vehicle of deep and important spiritual truths, and an instrument for preparing the national mind and conscience for the glorious revelation of life and incorruption through Christ. Only in the light of the gospel can the treatment of death in this chapter be edifying or indeed intelligible, for otherwise it were only the imposition of a ceremonial yoke, extremely burdensome in itself, and grounded upon a painful superstition. But it is sufficient to point out that death is only treated of in connection with its remedy, even as eternal death is only clearly revealed in that gospel which tells us of everlasting life. In this remedy for death we have one of the most remarkable types of the atonement, and of its application to the cleansing of individual souls, to be found in the Old Testament. The very exceptional character of the ordinance, and its isolation from the body of the Mosaic legislation ; the singular and apparently contradictory character of its details, as well as the great importance assigned to it both in the ordinance itself and in the practice of the Jews ; would have led us to look for some eminent and distinctive foreshadowings of the one Sacrifice once offered. The New Testament confirms this natural expectation, not indeed dwelling upon details, but ranking "the ashes of an heifer sprinkling the unclean" side by side with "the blood of bulls and of goats," as typifying the more prevailing expiation made by Christ. We have, therefore, in this ordinance Christ himself in the oneness of his election and sacrifice ; Christ in the perfectness, freedom, and gentleness of his untainted life ; Christ in many circumstances of his rejection and death ; Christ in the enduring effects of his expiation to do away the contagion and terror of spiritual death ; in a word, we have him who by dying overcame death, and delivered them who through fear of death were all their lifetime subject to bondage.   In drawing out this great type we may consider—1. The circumstances under which the ordinance was given.   2. The choice of the victim.   3. The manner of sacrifice.   4. The application of its cleansing virtue.

I. AS TO THE CIRCUMSTANCES OF TIME AND PLACE.   Consider—1. *That the ordinance of the red heifer was given not at Sinai, but in the wilderness of Paran,* the region of exile, of wandering ; the land of the shadow of death, which was but the ante-chamber of the tomb and of eternal darkness to that generation.   The whole Levitical system had been given in the wilderness, but in the wilderness as a land of liberty to serve God, and as the threshold of the promised land of life flowing with milk and honey.   Even so Christ was given to us when we lay in darkness and the shadow of death, living in a world whose prince was Satan, wherein was no rest, and wherefrom was no escape, save into the gloomier land beyond the grave.   2. *That it was given at a time when Israel lay under condemnation for rebellion, and under sentence of death ;* when death, who had been restrained for a season, was let loose upon them with multiplied terrors to prey upon them until they were consumed, filling the minds of them that lived with horror and despair.   Even so Christ was given unto a dying race, lying under the wrath of God for sin, and in perpetual bondage through certain fear of coming death.   Death was the universal tyrant whose terror sickened the boldest heart and saddened the uneasy mirth of the gayest. 3. *That it was given at a time when the routine of sacrifices and holy rites was abandoned,* partly as out of their power to maintain, partly as useless for such as were alienated from God and appointed to die.   How should men eat the passover who had but escaped from Egypt to perish miserably in a howling wilderness ?   Even so Christ was given to a race which had little belief and less comfort in its religious rites, Jewish or Gentile ; which knew itself alienated from God, excluded from heaven ; which had tried all outward and formal rites, and found that they could not deliver from the fear of death.   Even the Divinely-given, religious system of Moses had not a word to say about the life to come, could not whisper one syllable of comfort to the dying soul.

II. AS TO THE CHOICE OF VICTIM.   Consider—1. *That the victim was (so far as could possibly be) one, and one only ;* in striking contrast to the multiplicity and constant repetition (with its consequent difficulty and expense) of the ordinary sacrifices of the law.   One red heifer availed for centuries.   Only six are said to have been required during the whole of Jewish history ; for the smallest quantity of the ashes availed to impart the cleansing virtue to the holy water.   Had it indeed been possible to preserve the ashes from unavoidable waste, no second red heifer would ever have needed to be offered.   Even so the sacrifice of Christ is one, and only one, as opposed to all the offerings of the law ; and this because the availing power of it and the cleansing virtue of his atonement endure for ever, without the slightest loss of efficacy or possibility of being exhausted.   2. *That the victim was a heifer, not a male animal, as in almost all other cases.*   Even so we may believe with reverence that there was a distinctly feminine side to the character of Christ, a tenderness and gentleness which might have been counted weakness had it not been united with so much masculine force of command and energy of will.   And this was necessary to the perfect Man ; for whereas Eve was taken from out of Adam after his creation, this points to the subtraction from the ideal man of some elements of his nature, so that man and woman only represent between them a complete humanity. As, therefore, we ever find in the greatest men some strongly-marked feminine traits of character, so we may believe that in Christ, who was the second Adam, and (in a special sense) the seed of the woman, this feminine side of the perfect ideal was fully restored.   3. *That the victim was red.*   Even so our Lord, as touching his bodily nature, was of that common earth, which is red, from which Adam took his name.   Moreover, he was red in the blood of his passion, as the prophet testifies (Isa. lxiii. 1, 2 ; Rev. xix. 13).   4. *That it was without blemish.*   A matter about which the Jews took incredible pains, three hairs together of any but the one colour being held fatal to the choice.   Even so our Lord, even by the testimony of Jews and heathens, was without fault and irreproachable (John vii. 46 ; xviii. 23 ; xix. 4 ; 1 Pet. ii. 22). 5. *That no yoke had ever come upon it.* The innocent freedom of its young life had never been harshly bent to the purposes and plans of others. Even so our Lord was never under any yoke of constraint, nor was any other will ever imposed upon him. It is true that he made himself obedient to his Father in all things, to his earthly parents within their proper sphere, and to his enemies in his appointed sufferings ; but all this was purely voluntary, and it was of the essence of his perfect sacrifice that no constraint of any sort was ever put upon him. It was his own will which accepted the will of others, as shaping for him his life and destiny.

III. As to the manner of sacrifice. Consider—1. *That the red heifer was led outside the camp (or city) of God to die in an unhallowed place*—a thing absolutely singular, even among sacrifices for sin. Even so our Lord, by whose death we are restored to life, suffered without the gate (Heb. xiii. 12) ; partly because he was despised and rejected, but partly because he was an *anathema,* made a curse for us, concentrating upon himself all our sin and death ; partly also because he died not for that nation only (whose home and heritage was the holy city), but for the whole wide world beyond. 2. *That the heifer was delivered to the chief priest, and by him led forth to die, but slain by other hands before his face.* Even so our Lord was delivered unto Caiaphas and the Jewish priesthood, and by them was he brought unto his death ; but he was crucified by alien hands, not theirs,—God so over-ruling it (John xviii. 31),—yet in their presence, and with their sanction and desire. 3. *That the death of the heifer was not in appearance sacrificial, but became so when its blood was sprinkled towards the sanctuary by the finger of the priest.* Even so the death of Christ upon the cross was not made an atoning sacrifice by its outward incidents, or even by its extreme injustice, or by the hatred of the Truth which prompted it ; for then it had been only a murder, or a martyrdom, and not equal to many others in the cruelty shown or the suffering patiently endured ; but it became a true propitiatory sacrifice by virtue of the deliberate will and purpose of Christ, whereby he (being Priest as well as Victim) offered his sufferings and death in holy submission and with devout gladness to the Father. As the priest sprinkled of the blood with his own finger towards the sanctuary, and made it a sacrifice, so Christ, by his will to suffer for us and to be our atonement with God, imparted an intention or direction to his death which made it in the deepest sense a sacrifice (Luke xii. 50 ; John xvii. 19 ; Heb. ix. 14 ; x. 8—10). 4. *That the heifer was wholly consumed with fire,* as was the case with all sin offerings for the sins of many, as a thing wholly due unto God. Even so Christ was wholly given up by himself unto that God who is a consuming fire, a fire of wrath against sin, a fire of love towards the sinner. In this flame of Divine zeal against sin, of Divine zeal for souls, was Christ wholly consumed, nothing in him remaining indifferent, nothing escaping the agony and the cross (cf. John ii. 17). 5. *That, contrary to the universal rule, the blood of the heifer was not poured away, but was burnt with the carcase,* and so was represented in the ashes. Even so " the precious blood " of Christ which he shed for our redemption did not pass away ; the cleansing virtue of it and the abiding strength of it reman for ever in the means and ministries of grace which we owe to his atoning death. 6. *That cedar, hyssop, and scarlet were mingled in the burning.* Even so there are for ever mingled in the passion of Christ, never to be lost sight of if we would view it aright, these three elements : fragrance and incorruption, cleansing efficacy, martial and royal grandeur. If we omit any of these we do wrong to the full glory of the cross ; for these three belong to him, as the Prophet, the fragrance of whose holy teachings has filled the world ; as the Priest, who only can purge us with hyssop that we may be clean ; as the King, who never reigned more gloriously than on the tree (see Cant. iii. 11 ; Matt. xxvii. 28 ; Col. ii. 15). 7. *That the priest himself and the man that slew the heifer became unclean,* contrary to the usual rule. Even so the Jewish priesthood and the heathen soldiery who slew our Lord, albeit he died for them as well as for others, yet incurred a fearful guilt thereby (Acts ii. 23).

IV. As to the application of the expiation. Consider—1. *That the ashes were, so far as could be presented to the senses, the indestructible residue of the entire victim,* including its blood, after the sacrifice was completed. Even so the whole merits of

Christ—the entire value and efficacy of his self-sacrifice, of his life given for us, of all that he was, and did, and suffered—remain ever, and abide with us, and are available for our cleansing. 2. *That the ashes of the heifer were laid up, but not by the priest, or by any one concerned in its death, without the camp in a clean place.* Even so the merits of Christ and the efficacy of his sacrifice are preserved for ever; yet not in the Jerusalem below, nor by any agency of them that slew him; but he himself (see 4.) hath laid them up for the use of all nations in the Church which is "clean," as governed and sanctified by his Holy Spirit. 3. *That the ashes of the heifer when mixed with " living water " were made a purification for sin unto Israel to deliver them from the bondage of death.* Even so the merits of Christ and the virtue of his atonement are available for all, through the operation of the Holy Spirit (John iv. 10; vii. 38), to purify from all sin, and to set free from the power of death. 4. *That when any unclean person was to be purged, it must be done by " a clean person,"* not by any one having need of cleansing himself. Even so the cleansing efficacy of Christ's atonement must be applied to the sinful soul only by one that is clean, and not by any one under like condemnation with himself. And this "clean person" can only be Christ himself, who only is holy, harmless, and undefiled (Job xiv. 4; xv. 14; Rom. iii. 23; Gal. iii. 22) ; wherefore the sprinkling of purification from sin and death can only be effected by Christ himself. 5. *That the clean person did not apply the water for purification with his finger, as when the priest sprinkled the blood, but by means of hyssop, a lowly herb used as an aspergillum* (cf. Exod. xii. 22; 1 Kings iv. 33; Ps. li. 7). Even so it hath pleased the Lord to apply the cleansing virtue of his blood and passion to souls unclean not directly and personally, as he offered his sacrifice of himself to the Father, but through lowly means and ministries of grace, by means of which he himself is pleased to work (cf. John iv. 1, 2 ; xiii. 20; xx. 21—23 ; 1 Cor. x. 16 ; 2 Cor. ii. 10; iv. 7; Gal. iii. 27). 6. *That the unclean person was to be sprinkled on the third day and on the seventh day* ere he was wholly cleansed from the savour of death. Even so must the cleansing virtue of the atonement come unto us in the twofold power, (1) of the resurrection, wherein we rise from the death of sin unto the active life of righteousness ; (2) of the holy sabbath, wherein we rest from our own works by renouncing self and living for God and for our neighbour. The cleansing which has not this double moral aspect is not perfect—the savour of death is not taken away. Nor is the order inverted because the third day (of resurrection) comes before the seventh (of rest) ; for as a fact the activities of the new life in Christ do precede in the soul the cessation of the old life, which is the spiritual sabbath.

` CONSIDER, FURTHER, WITH RESPECT TO THE INFECTION OF DEATH — 1. *That the Jews were taught most emphatically and most minutely to regard death as a foul and horrible thing, the slightest contact with which alienated from God and banished from his worship.* Even so are we taught that death is the shadow of sin (Rom. v. 12) and the wages of sin (*ibid.* vi. 23), and the active enemy of Christ (1 Cor. xv. 26 ; Rev. vi. 8 ; xx. 14), and that the death of Christ was an awful mystery connected with his being made " sin " and " a curse " for us (Matt. xxvii. 46, and the Passion Psalms *passim*). Yet in the law the horror is concentrated upon physical death, whereas in the gospel it is removed from this and attached to the second death, of the soul (Matt. x. 28; Mark v. 39, 41 ; 1 Thess. iv. 14; Rev. ii. 11; xx. 6). 2. *That whoso came into contact, even indirectly, with the dead, or even entered a tent where any corpse lay, was unclean a whole seven days.* Far from being able to give any of his own life to the deceased, he himself was infected with his death. Even so are we powerless of ourselves to do good to the spiritually dead beside us, but rather are certain to catch from them the contagion of their death. None can live (naturally) among those that are dead in trespasses and sins without to some extent becoming like them. 3. *That this rule applied as much to the Levitical priests as to any other;* nay, the very high priest who superintended the sacrifice, and the man who applied the holy water, became themselves unclean. Even so there is none of us, whatever his office may be, or howsoever he may be occupied about religious things, that does not contract defilement from the dead world and the dead works which are around him. Our Lord alone could utterly disregard the infection of death, because in his inherent holiness he was proof against its infection. 4. *That there was no cleansing for those defiled with death but by means of the sprinkling of the ashes.* Even so there is no deliverance from the sentence and savour of death which hath passed upon us but through the sprinkling of the blood of Christ. 5. *That if any was not purified in the appointed way, he did not simply forego a great benefit to himself, he incurred the wrath of God as one that wantonly defiled his sanctuary.* Even so that Christian who will not seek cleansing for his uncleanness and the hallowing of the precious blood does not only sin against his own soul, remaining in alienation from his God ; he grieves the Spirit of God, and provokes him to anger, as one that despises his goodness, and mars by his state and example the sanctity of God's living temple, which is the Church (Matt. xxii. 11—13 ; John xiii. 8, 10, 11 ; 1 Cor. iii. 16, 17 ; Eph. ii. 20—22 ; Heb. x. 29).

HOMILIES BY VARIOUS AUTHORS.

Vers. 1—10, 17—19.—*Purge me with hyssop, and I shall be clean.* This law respecting the purification of one who has contracted uncleanness by contact with the dead must have been familiar to every Israelite. Death with impartial foot visits every house. No one can long remain a stranger to it. There is evidence, moreover, that this law did not fail to impress devout hearts, deepening in them the feeling of impurity before God and unfitness for his presence, and at the same time awakening the hope that there is in the grace of God a remedy for uncleanness. Hence David's prayer, " Purge me with hyssop, and I shall be clean." The law gives direction regarding—

I. THE PURIFYING ELEMENT. 1. It was water, *pure spring water* (ver. 17). A most natural symbol, much used in the Levitical lustrations, and which is still in use in the Christian Church. At the door of the sanctuary there is still a laver. In the sacrament of baptism Christ says to every candidate for admission into his house, " If I wash thee not, thou hast no part with me." 2. In the present instance *the ashes of a sin offering were mingled with the water.* A heifer was procured at the expense of the congregation,—red, unblemished, on which never yoke had come,— and it was slain as a sacrifice. The red heifer was a true sin offering. It is so named in vers. 9, 17 (Hebrew). But in several respects it differed remarkably from all the other sin offerings. Although the priest was to see it slain, and with his own finger sprinkled its blood toward the holy place, he was forbidden to slay it himself; it was slain not at the altar, but outside the camp, and the carcase was wholly consumed without being either flayed, or cleaned, or divided, or laid out in order. Besides, every one who took part in the sacrificial act was thereby rendered unclean ; for which reason Eleazar, not Aaron, was to do the priest's part—the high priest might not defile himself for any cause. The ashes of this singular offering were carefully preserved to be used to communicate purifying virtue to the water required for lustration from time to time. None of these details is without meaning, if we could only get at it. The points of chief importance are these :—(1) The sin offer- ing prefigured Christ in his offering himself without spot to God (Heb. ix. 14). The singular rule which forbade the slaying of the red heifer within the precinct of the camp, who does not see in it a prophecy of the fact that the Just One suffered the reproachful death of a malefactor without the gate of Jerusalem ? (Heb. xiii. 12, 13). (2) Without prior expiation there could be no purification, and, conversely, expiation being made, the way was open for purification. So when Christ had once offered himself without spot to God, provision was thereby made for purging our consciences. There is a cleansing virtue in the blood of Christ. The man who believes in Christ is not only pardoned, but is so purified in his conscience that he no longer shrinks in shame from the eye of God, but draws near with holy confidence.

II. THE PURIFYING RITE (vers. 17—19). Nothing could be more simple. A few particles of the ashes of the sin offering were put into a vessel of spring water ; this was sprinkled with a bunch of hyssop on the unclean person on the third day and again on the seventh, an act which any clean person could perform in any town ; by this act the uncleanness was removed. A simple rite, but not, therefore, optional. Wilful neglect was a presumptuous sin.

General lessons :—1. There is something in sin which unfits for the society of God.

One of the chief lessons of the ceremonial law. When the grace of God touches the heart, one of its first effects is to open the heart to feel this. "Lord, I am vile." As habits of personal cleanliness make a man loathe himself when he has been touched with filth, so the grace of God makes a man loathe himself for sin. 2. There is provision in Christ for making men clean. His blood purges the conscience from dead works to serve the living God. 3. Of this provision we must not omit to avail ourselves. Wilful neglect of the blood of sprinkling is presumptuous sin.—B.

Ver. 11.—*Defilement by contact with the dead.* The law of Moses was a yoke which neither the fathers of the nation nor their descendants were able to bear. It would be difficult to name any part of the law in regard to which Peter's saying was more applicable than it is to the regulations here laid down regarding defilement by the dead. They must have been not only irksome in a high degree, but trying to some of the purest and most tender of the natural affections.

I. For WHAT ARE THE PROVISIONS OF THE LAW? 1. Contact with a dead body rendered the person unclean, and so disabled him from enjoying the privileges of the sanctuary. Many an Israelite would, like Jacob, desire that a beloved son should be with him when he died, to hear his last words and put his hand upon his eyes. Many a Joseph would covet the honour of paying this last tribute of filial affection. Yet the son who closed his father's eyes found himself branded by the law as unclean, so that if it happened to be the passover time, he could not keep the feast. The same unwelcome disability befell any one who, walking in the field, came upon a dead body and did his duty by it as a good citizen. When a company of neighbours assembled to comfort some Martha or Mary whose brother had died, and to bear the mortal remains to the burial-place, this act of neighbourly kindness rendered every one of them unclean. Our Lord, when he entered the chamber of death in Jairus' house, and when he touched the bier at the gate of Nain, thereby took upon himself legal defilement and its consequences. Not only so; if a man happened to touch a grave or a human bone, he contracted defilement, and would have been chargeable with presumptuous sin, as a defiler of the sanctuary, if he had ventured thereafter to set foot within the house of the Lord. 2. The defilement consequent on contact with the dead was defilement of the graver sort. Many forms of defilement only disabled till sunset, and were removed by simply washing the person with water. Defilement by the dead lasted a whole week, and could be removed only by the sprinkling of the water of purification on the third and the seventh days: an irksome rule. 3. Hence all specially devoted persons in Israel were forbidden to pay the last offices of kindness to deceased friends. A priest might not defile himself for any except his nearest blood relations: his father, or mother, or brother, or unmarried sister. As for the high priest, he was forbidden to defile himself even for these. And the same stringent prohibition applied to the Nazarite also.

II. WHAT WAS THE REASON OF THIS REMARKABLE LAW? AND WHAT DOES IT TEACH US? 1. According to some it was simply a sanitary regulation. The suggestion is not to be wholly set aside. So long as this law was in force extramural interment must have been the rule. No city in Israel contained a crowded burial-ground, diffusing pestilence within its walls, nor was any synagogue made a place of interment. Much less did the Israelites ever revert to the Egyptian custom of giving a place within their houses to the embalmed bodies of deceased friends. In these respects the provisions of the Mosaic law anticipated by 3000 years the teaching of our modern sanitary science. However, this intention of the law was certainly not the principal one. 2. Another view of it is suggested by Heb. ix. 14: "The blood of Christ shall *purge your conscience from dead works* to serve the living God." Dead works are works which have in them no breath of spiritual life. Transgressions of God's law are dead works; so also are "duties" not animated with a loving regard for the glory of God. Such works are dead, and, being dead, defile the conscience, so that it needs to be purified by the blood of Christ. 3. But the chief reason of the law is, without doubt, to be sought in the principle that *death is the wages of sin.* This principle, taught so plainly in Rom. v. and 1 Cor. xv., was not unknown to the Old Testament Church. It is taught in the story of the Fall, and is implied in Ps. xc., "the prayer of Moses." The habit of making light of death—as if it were no evil at all, but rather the welcome riddance of the soul from a burdensome and unfit companion—was not learned from the word of God.   The Bible teaches us to regard the body as the fitting dwelling-place of the soul, and necessary to the completeness of our nature.   That separation of body and soul which takes place in death, it teaches us to regard as penal.   Death, accordingly, is the awful effect and memorial of sin, and contact with the dead causes defilement.   Blessed be God, the gospel invites us to look on a brighter scene.   If the law admonished men that the wages of sin is death, the gospel bears witness that God in Christ offers to us a gift of eternal life.   To say this is not to disparage the law.   Bright objects show best on a dark ground.   The gospel is appreciated rightly by those only who have laid to heart the teachings of the law.   Still it is not the dark ground that we are invited to gaze upon so much as the bright object to whose beauty it serves for a foil.   The relation between the law we have been considering and the grace of Christ is strikingly seen in the story of the raising of Jairus's daughter, and of the widow's son at Nain.   In both instances Christ was careful to touch the dead body; and in both instances the effect immediately wrought proclaimed the intention of the act.   From the dead there went out no real defiling influence on the Lord.   On the contrary, from him there went forth power to raise the dead.   In Christ grace reigns through righteousness unto life; he is the Conqueror of death.—B.

Vers. 1—22.—*The water of purification, and its lessons.*   The extreme difficulty of applying the details of this chapter to the spiritual truths of which they were a shadow forbids us attempting more than a general application of the narrative.

I. GREAT CARE WAS NEEDED IN PROVIDING THIS SIN OFFERING (for so it is called in vers. 9, 17).   There were precepts as to the victim's sex, age, colour, freedom from blemish, and from compulsory labour.   There were further minute requirements as to the method of killing and burning.   The animal, first killed as a sacrifice, was to be utterly consumed.   No ordinary pure water, but water impregnated with ashes, might serve as a medium of purification.   These typical facts are applicable to the means of purification provided in the gospel.   Christ was no ordinary sacrifice, but "without blemish," "separate from sinners," voluntary (John x. 18), appointed to death in a particular manner (*ibid.* xii. 32, 33); a complete sacrifice, vicarious, for all the congregation (1 Tim. ii. 6; 1 John ii. 2), in order that God might thus provide the means of complete purification (Heb. ix. 13, 14).

II. DEFILEMENT WAS INCURRED IN THE PURIFYING PROCESS.   This was shown in various ways.   The heifer was not killed before the altar, but outside the camp. The high priest was to have nothing to do with it, nor was even Eleazar to kill it himself.   The blood was not brought into the tabernacle, but sprinkled at a distance, in the direction of it.   The priest that sprinkled the blood and burnt the cedar wood was defiled.   The man that burned the carcase was defiled.   The man, ceremonially clean, who collected the ashes became unclean.   Even the "clean" man who sprinkled the unclean with the purifying water became himself unclean.   Thus God seeks by type and symbol, "line upon line," to impress on us the truth that sin is "exceeding sinful."   And we are reminded that even our sinless Priest and Sacrifice needed to be "made sin" for us in order that we might be cleansed from all unrighteousness and made "the righteousness of God in him."

III. THE PURIFICATION PROVIDED WAS IN PERPETUAL DEMAND.   "Deaths oft" compelled frequent contact with the dead.   A corpse, even a bone or a grave, was sufficient to cause defilement.   As death is the penalty of sin, in this way too God taught the defiling effect of sin, and therefore the need of perpetual purifications (Heb. x. 1, 2).   These are still needed even by Christians who have been justified and have exercised "repentance from dead works" (John xiii. 10; Heb. vi. 1).

Thus we learn—1. The fearfully polluting character of sin.   Its contagion spreads to all who are susceptible.   It exerts its baneful effects on that part of the creation incapable of guilt (Rom. viii. 20—22), and even on the sinless Son of God when he comes into contact with it as a Saviour (Isa. liii. 5, 6; 1 Pet. ii. 24, &c.).   2. The mysterious method of purification.   Some of these ceremonies are "hard to be understood," and we have some difficulty in knowing exactly how to apply them to the truths respecting spiritual purification in the gospel.   Just s in "the mystery of godliness " itself there are "secret things which belong unto the Lord our God." But we may be satisfied because the way of salvation is "the gospel *of God*," the Lamb slain is "the Lamb *of God*," the atonement is *God's* atonement. In the purification of our consciences "from dead works" we have the best proof of "the mystery of the gospel" (Eph. i. 8, 9 ; vi. 19) being "the power of God," &c. (Rom. i. 16). 3. Our entire dependence on this purification. The thoughtless touching of a dead man's bone defiled, and the man who neglected the water of purifying was "cut off." So with sinners, who should not dare to plead forgetfulness (Ps. xix. 12), but who may be cleansed from every sin. But without this cleansing they too will be "cut off" (1 John i. 7—10).—P.

Vers. 1—22.—*Defilement from the dead.* In the laws given to the Israelites there is much said concerning uncleanness. The ceremonial difference between the unclean and the clean sets forth the real difference between the sinful and the sinless. This difference was therefore as important in its way, and as much requiring attention, as that between the holy and the profane. In the Book of Leviticus a large section (chs. xi.—xv.) is exclusively occupied with regulations on the subject, pointing out how uncleanness was caused, and how to be removed—oftentimes very easily caused, but never easy, and often very tedious, to remove. It was a charge brought against the priests long after (Ezek. xxii. 26) that they showed no difference between the unclean and the clean. Already in this Book of Numbers one kind of defilement, that contracted by contact with the dead, has been referred to thrice (ch. v. 2 ; vi. 6—12 ; ix. 6—8). In the second of these instances the defilement came as a hindrance to the Nazarite in fulfilling his vow, and the manner of his cleansing was carefully indicated. Here in ch. xix. we come to a very elaborate provision for defilement by the dead in general. The immediate occasion of this provision may have been the sudden and simultaneous death of nearly 15,000 of the people, by which many were of necessity defiled, and placed in great difficulties as to their extrication from defilement. But whatever the occasion, the contents of this chapter show very impressively and suggestively the way in which God looks on death.

I. We gather from this chapter HOW UTTERLY OBNOXIOUS DEATH IS TO GOD. The person who has come in contact with it, however lightly or casually,—it may have been unconsciously,—is thereby unclean. Unlike the leper, he may feel no difference in himself, but he is unclean. Notice further why death is so obnoxious to God. It is the great and crowning consequence of sin in this world. Sin not only spoils life while it lasts, but brings it to a melancholy, painful, and in most cases premature end. Consider how much of human life, that might be so glorifying to God, so useful to man, and so happy in the experience of it, is nipped in the earliest bud. Doubtless God sees in death abominations of which we have hardly any sense at all. It is obnoxious to us as interfering with our plans, robbing us of our joys, and taking away the only thing that nature gives us, temporal life. We look at death too much as a cause. God would have us well to understand that its great power as a cause comes from what it is as an effect. In one sense we may say the uncleanness of leprosy was less offensive than that of death, for the power of sin was less evident in a disease of the living person than when life was altogether gone. Every instance of death is a fresh defiance, and apparently a successful one, of the ever-living God. Death seems to wait on every new-born child, saying, "Thou art mine."

II. WE SHOULD SO CORRECT OUR THOUGHTS THAT DEATH MAY BECOME OBNOXIOUS TO US IN THE SAME WAY AS IT IS TO GOD. Do not be contented to talk of death as coming through disease, accident, or old age. Behind all instruments look for the wielding hand of sin. Ask yourself if egress from this world would not be a very different sort of thing if man had continued unfallen. To a sinless nature, how gentle, painless, glorious, and exultant might be the process of exchanging the service of earth for the service of a still higher state! Death in its pain and gloom and disturbing consequences to survivors is something quite foreign to the original constitution of human nature. Only by learning to look on death as God by his own example would have us look, shall we find the true remedy against it, both in its actual power and in the terrors which the anticipation of it so often inspires.

III. Occasion is given for much humility and self-abhorrence as we consider the hold which sin has on our mortal bodies. The agonising appeal of sin-burdened humanity is, " O wretched man that I am! who shall deliver me from the body of this death ? " Every consideration should be welcomed which will make us feel more deeply and abidingly the dreadful power of sin, the impossibility of getting rid of all its consequences until we are passed out of the present life.   Does not a fair consideration of this ceremonial uncleanness for the dead body go far to settle the oft-debated point as to the possibility of complete holiness in this world ? How can there be complete holiness when this supreme effect of sin, temporal death, remains undestroyed?   What a thought for a devout Israelite, a man of the spirit of the Psalmist, that, solicitous as he might be all through life to keep in the way of God's commandments, nevertheless, when life had left the body, he would inevitably be the means of defilement to others !

IV. There is pointed out to us the true mode of triumph over death. Death can be conquered only in one way, by conquering sin.   He who destroys the *power of sin* in a human life destroys the *power of death*.   The raising of Lazarus was not so much a triumph over death as a humiliation of him who has the power of death, an intimation that the secret of his power was known and vulnerable. Lazarus was raised, but died again in the course of mortal nature, and only as he believed in Jesus to the attainment of eternal life did he gain the real triumph over death.   If then by any means our life here is becoming more and more free from sin, more abundant in holy service, then in the same proportion the hellish glory of death is dimmed.   The physical circumstances of death are not the chief thing to be considered, but what sort of future lies beyond.   If it is to be a continuance, improvement, and perfecting of the spiritual life of Christ's people here, then where is the triumph of death?   To have been transformed by the renewing of our minds, and to have found our chief occupation and delight in the affairs of the kingdom of heaven, may not indeed take away the terrors of death, but they do effectually destroy its power.

V. The very fact of death being so obnoxious to God should fill us with hope for its removal.   Is it not a great deal to know that what is peculiarly dreaded by us is peculiarly hateful to him?   Is there not a sort of assurance that God's wisdom and power will be steadily directed to the removal of what is so hateful?—Y.

We have now to notice the way in which this defilement was removed—by sprink-ling over the defiled person running water mingled with the ashes, prepared in a peculiar way, of a slain heifer.

I. The preparation was very elaborate.   It needed great care in its details, and was, therefore, very easily spoiled.   There has been much discussion, with little agreement, over the significance of many of the details, the truth being that there is not sufficient information for us to discern reasons which may have been clear enough to those who had to obey the command, though even to them the purpose of many details was doubtless utterly obscure, and even intentionally so.   What room is there for faith if we are to know the why and wherefore at every step?   One thing is certain, that if any detail had been neglected, the whole symbolic action would have failed.   The water would be sprinkled in vain.   God would intimate in no doubtful way that the defiled person remained defiled still.   So when we turn from the shadow to the substance, from the cleansing of the death-defiled body to that of the death-defiled person to whom the body belonged, we find Christ complying in the strictest manner with the minutest matters of detail ; and doing so, this indicated his equal compliance inwardly with every requirement of the law of God considered as having to do with the spirit.   Thrice we know did God intimate his satisfaction with his Son, as one who in all things was carrying out his purposes—twice in express terms (Matt. iii. 17; xvii. 5), and the third time implying the same thing not less signifi-cantly (John xii. 28).   Then also we are called to notice how many prophecies as to matters of detail, such as places, circumstances, &c., had to be fulfilled.   As in the preparing of the heifer the *commands* of God had to be accomplished, so in the preparing of Jesus for his great cleansing work the *prophecies* of God had to be accomplished.

II. The devoted animal was in a typical sense very peculiar. There is the selection of one kind of animal, one sex in that kind, one colour, all absence of blemish, and complete freedom from the yoke. May we not say that to find all these marks in one animal was indication of some special provision from on high? "It must be a red heifer, because of the rarity of the colour, that it might be the more remarkable. The Jews say, if but two hairs were black or white, it was unlawful." Whether this were so or not, we have in this remarkable typical animal a suggestion of him who in his person, works, claims, and influence is totally unlike any one else who has ever taken part in human affairs. As the heifer was without spot or blemish, so far as human eye could discern, so Jesus was faultless in the presence of God's glory. And just as the combination in the heifer of all that God required was a great help to the people in believing in the cleansing efficacy of the ashes, so we, regarding Jesus in all the peculiarities which centre and unite in him, may well apply ourselves with fresh confidence and gratitude to the blood that cleanseth from all sin.

III. The ashes were reserved for permanent use (ver. 9). It is of course an exaggeration to say that the ashes of this first heifer served for the cleansings of a thousand years, but doubtless they served a long time, thus sufficiently indicating the cleansing power that flows from him who died once for all. We stand in the succession to many generations who have applied themselves to the one fountain opened for sin and uncleanness. Where the earliest believers stood, submitting the impurity of their hearts to Jesus, we also stand, and the evident result to *them*, as seen in the record of their experience, may well give joy and assurance to *us*.

IV. Only, we must make like closeness and fidelity of application. Consider what was required from these death-defiled ones. For seven days they were unclean, and on the third day as well as the seventh they were to be sprinkled. To prepare the sprinkling agent was no light or easy matter, so that its virtue might be sure. But even when prepared it required repeated applications. Thus to be cleansed from sin requires a searching process, indicated in the New Testament by the baptism of the Holy Ghost and of fire. There must be a discerning of the thoughts and intents of the heart, and a rigorous, uncompromising dealing with them. Let none apply himself to the cleansing which Christ provides unless he is ready for a thorough examination of his nature, a disclosure of many deep-seated abominations, and a tearing away from his life of much that he has cherished and for a time may sadly miss.

V. There is no cleansing except in strict obedience to God's appointment. The defiled one could not invent a purification of his own, nor could he go on as if defilement were a harmless, evanescent trifle. He might indeed say, "What the worse am I for touching the dead?" judging by his own present feelings and ignorance of consequences. Nor might any immediate obvious difference appear between the defiled and the cleansed; nevertheless, there was a difference which God himself would make very plain and bitter in the event of persevering disobedience. So between the conscious and confessing sinner who, humbly believing, is being washed in the blood of Christ, and the careless, defiant sinner who neglects it as a mere imagination, there may seem little or nothing of difference. But the difference is that between heaven and hell, and God will make it clear in due time. Note the connection of the following passage with the whole chapter:—"If the ashes of an heifer sprinkling the unclean, sanctifieth to the purifying of the flesh: how much more shall the blood of Christ, who through the eternal Spirit offered himself without spot to God, purge your conscience from dead works to serve the living God?" (Heb. ix. 13, 14).—Y.

EXPOSITION.

CHAPTER XX.

The last march: from Kadesh to Hor (vers. 1—29). Ver. 1.—**Then came the children of Israel, even the whole congregation.** The latter words are emphatic here and in ver. 22, and seem intended to mark the period of reassembly after the dispersion of nearly thirty-eight years. Probably a portion of the tribes had visited Kadesh many times during those years, and perhaps it had never been wholly abandoned. **Into** the desert of Zin, *i. e.*, if the western site be maintained for Kadesh, the Wady Murreh. See the note on Kadesh. **In the first month.** In the month Abib (Nisan), the vernal month, when there was "much grass" (cf. John vi. 10) in places at other seasons desert, and when travelling was most easy. From comparison of ch. xiv. 33 ; xxxiii. 38 and the sequence of the narrative, it appears to have been the first month of the fortieth, and last, year of wandering. Then it was that they reassembled in the same neighbourhood from whence they had dispersed so long before (see the note before ch. xv.). **And the people abode** (יֵּשֶׁב. Septuagint, κατέμεινεν) **in Kadesh.** From the date given in ch. xxxiii. 38 it would seem that they remained three or four months in Kadesh on this occasion. This delay may have been occasioned partly by the mourning for Miriam (cf. ver. 29), and partly by the necessity of awaiting answers from Edom and from Moab (see on ver. 14). **And Miriam died there, and was buried.** Nothing could be more brief and formal than this mention of the death of one who had played a considerable part in Israel, and had perhaps wished to play a more considerable part. It can scarcely, however, be doubted that her death in the unlovely wilderness was a punishment like the death of her brothers. There is no reason whatever to suppose that she had any part in the rebellion of Kadesh, or that the sentence of death there pronounced included her ; she was indeed at this time advanced in years, but that would not in itself account for the fact that she died in exile ; it is, no doubt, to the arrogance and rebellion recorded in ch. xii. that we must look for the true explanation of her untimely end.

Ver. 2.—**There was no water.** There was a large natural spring at Kadesh, and during the time of their previous sojourn there no complaint of this sort seems to have arisen. At this time, however, the bulk of the encampment may have lain in a different direction (cf. ver. 1 with ch. xiii. 26), or the supply may have failed from temporary causes. In either case a total absence of water need not be imagined, but only an insufficient supply.

Ver. 3. — **And the people chode with Moses.** As their fathers had done in similar circumstances, as recorded in Exod. xvii. **Would God that we had died.** See on ch. xiv. 2. **When our brethren died before the Lord.** This is difficult, because the visitations of God at Kibroth-hattaavah (ch. xi. 34) and at Kadesh (ch. xiv. 37) had overtaken not their brethren, but their fathers, some thirty-eight years before. On the other hand, the daily mortality which had carried off their brethren is clearly excluded by the phrase, "before the Lord." It may be that

the rebellion of Korah happened towards the end of the period of wandering, and that the reference is to the plague which followed it ; or it may be that the formula of complaint had become stereotyped, as those of children often do, and was employed from time to time without variation and without definite reference. The latter supposition is strongly supported by the character of the words which follow.

Ver. 4. — **Why have ye brought up the congregation of the Lord into this wilderness ?** These words are almost exactly repeated from Exod. xvii. 3. They, and those which follow, are no doubt out of place if considered as expressing the feelings of the great bulk of the people, who had no knowledge of Egypt, and had grown up in the wilderness. But on such occasions it is always the few who put words into the mouths of the many, and the ringleaders in this gainsaying would naturally be the survivors of the elder generation, whose disposition was exactly the same as ever, and who had always shown a remarkable want of originality in their complaints.

Ver. 5.—**No place of seed.** Septuagint, τόπος οὗ οὐ σπείρεται. A place where there is no sowing, and therefore no harvest.

Ver. 6.—**They fell upon their faces.** See note on ch. xiv. 5.

Ver. 8.—**Take the rod.** The ῥάβδος, or staff of office, with which Moses and Aaron had worked wonders before Pharaoh (Exod. vii. 9 *sq.*), and with which Moses had smitten the rock in Rephidim (Exod. xvii. 6). This rod had not been mentioned, nor perhaps used, since then ; but we might certainly have supposed that the instrument of so many miracles would be reverently laid up in the tabernacle "before the Lord," and this we find from the next verse to have been the case. **Gather thou the assembly together,** *i. e.* by their representatives. **Speak ye unto the rock before their eyes.** The word used for the rock in this narrative is הַסֶּלַע instead of הַצּוּר, as in Exod. xvii. It does not seem that any certain distinction of meaning can be drawn between the words, which are obviously interchanged in Judges vi. 20, 21, and are both translated πέτρα by the Septuagint ; but the careful use of different terms in the two narratives serves to distinguish them, just as the use of κοφίνους and σπυρίδας by St. Mark (vi. 43 ; viii. 8, 19, 20) helps to distinguish the two miracles of feeding the multitude.

Ver. 10.—**Hear now, ye rebels.** הַמֹּרִים. Septuagint, οἱ ἀπειθεῖς. The verb is used in a similar sense of Moses and Aaron themselves in ver. 24. It has been suggested that this was the word really used by our Lord in Matt. v. 22, and translated μωρός. This, however, is extremely precarious, and is indeed to accuse the Evangelist of a blunder, for there is no real correspondence between the words. **Must we fetch you water.** Septuagint, μὴ . . ἐξάξομεν ὑμῖν ὕδωρ. And this is no doubt the sense. It has been rendered by some "Can we fetch you water," on the supposition that Moses really doubted the possibility of such a miracle, but this seems to be an entire mistake (see next note).

Ver. 12.—**Because ye believed me not, to sanctify me in the eyes of the children of Israel.** It is very important, and at the same time very difficult, to understand what the precise sin of Moses and Aaron was upon this occasion. That it was very serious is manifest from the punishment which is entailed. Aaron, indeed, does not appear in the narrative, save in his usual subordinate position as associated with his brother by the Divine mandate. It has been said that he might have checked the unadvised words of Moses, but that is wholly beside the mark. Aaron had obviously no control whatever over his far more able and energetic brother, and therefore could have no responsibility in that respect. We can only suppose that he inwardly assented to the language and conduct with which he was outwardly associated, and therefore shared the guilt. A less degree of sin was (so to speak) necessary in his cause, because he had on former occasions so greatly dishonoured his office ; and the anger of God against the sin of his ministers, although laid to sleep, is ever ready to awake upon the recurrence of a similar provocation. We may therefore dismiss him, and consider only the case of Moses. It is impossible to suppose that Moses actually doubted the power of God to supply the present need, for he held in his hand the very rod with which he had struck the rock in Rephidim, nor is there anything in his words or acts upon this occasion to imply any such disbelief. The language of ch. xi. 21, 22 may be cited on the other side, but that was spoken in passion, and spoken to God, and cannot be held as expressing an actual failure of faith. Nor do subsequent references point to unbelief as having been the sin of Moses (cf. ch. xxvii. 14 ; Deut. xxxii. 51 ; Ps. cvi. 33). Rather, they point to disobedience and indiscretion ; to such disloyal conduct and language as produced a bad impression upon the people, and did not place the Divine character before them in its true light. We must understand, therefore, that the want of belief with which Moses stood charged was not a want of faith in the power of God, but a want of obedience to the will of God, bearing in mind that the two faults of disbelief and disobedience are but two sides of one inward fact, and are perpetually confounded in the language of Scripture (compare the use of ἀπειθεῖν in the New

Testament). What then was the disobedience of Moses ? Here, again, the more obvious answer is insufficient. It is true that Moses struck the rock twice instead of (or perhaps in addition to) speaking to it ; but God had bid him take the rod, and he might naturally think he was meant to use it as before ; moreover, the people could not have known anything of the exact terms of the command, and would have thought no more of his striking the rock at Kadesh than at Rephidim ; but it was the fact of the bad impression made upon the people which was the ground of the Divine rebuke. We come back, therefore, to the simple conclusion expressed by the Psalmist (Ps. cvi. 32, 33), that Moses lost his temper, and in the irritation of the moment spoke and acted in such a way and in such a spirit as to dishonour his Master and to impair the good effect of the Divine beneficence. It is quite likely that the repeated striking of the rock was one sign of the anger to which Moses gave way, but we could hardly have attached any serious character to the act if it had stood alone. It is in the words of Moses, words in which he associated Aaron with himself, that we must find the explanation of the displeasure he incurred. That he called the people "rebels" was unseemly, not because it was untrue, or because it was an uncalled-for term of reproach, but because he himself was at that very moment a rebel, and disloyal in heart to his Master (cf. ver. 24). That he should say, "Must we fetch you water out of this rock?" showed how completely he was carried away. It is true that God had said to him, "Thou shalt bring forth to them water," and, "Thou shalt give the congregation . . drink" (compare this with Exod. xvii. 6), and it is probable that his own words were more or less consciously dictated by this remembrance ; but he knew very well that the Divine mandate afforded him no real justification ; that he and Aaron were the merest instruments in the hand of God ; that it was peculiarly necessary to keep this fact before the minds of the people ; nevertheless, his vexation and anger betrayed him into putting himself—a mere man, and a man too in a very bad temper—into the place of God before the eyes of the whole congregation. Moses had fallen at least once before (see on ch. xi. 11--15) into a similar error, one so natural to an angry mind ; but this was the first time that he had made his error public, and thereby dishonoured the Master whom it was his special duty to uphold and glorify. This was the sin, and if the punishment seem disproportionate, it must be remembered that the heinousness of a sin depends quite as much on the position of the sinner as upon its intrinsic enormity. **Ye shall not bring this** congregation into the land. That they should die in the wilderness was implied in this sentence, but was not strictly a part of the sentence itself. Moses, indeed, although he did not enter the land of promise in its narrower sense, yet he died within the inheritance of Israel. Since they had behaved unworthily of their high office as leaders of the people, therefore that office should be taken from them before the glorious end.

Ver. 13.—This is the·water of Meribah. or "water of strife." Septuagint, ὕδωρ ἀντιλογίας. The word "Meribah" appears, however, to form part of a proper name in Deut. xxxii. 51. A similar use of the word is recorded in Exod. xvii. 7. That the same name was more or less definitely attached to these two scenes is only another way of saying that there was a strong similarity between the two sets of associations. At the same time the differences are so marked in the narratives that they leave very distinct impressions upon the mind. And he was sanctified in them, i. e. he revealed there his holiness and power, and put to silence their evil murmurings against him. He was sanctified in them all the more abundantly because Moses and Aaron failed to sanctify him in the eyes of the people; but what they failed to do he brought to pass without their agency.

Ver. 14.—And Moses sent messengers from Kadesh unto the king of Edom. On the kings of Edom see on Gen. xxxvi. 31. It would seem probable from Exod. xv. 15 that the government was at that time (forty years before the present date) still in the hands of "dukes," and that the change had but recently taken place. It is stated in Judges xi. 17 that Moses sent messengers at this time with a like request to the king of Moab. We are not indeed obliged to suppose that Jephthah, living 300 years after, stated the facts correctly; but there is no particular reason to doubt it in this case. That no mention of it is made here would be sufficiently explained by the fact that the refusal of Edom made the answer of Moab of no practical moment. That Moses asked a passage through the territory of Edom implies that he had renounced the idea of invading Canaan from the south. This was not on account of any insuperable difficulties presented by the character of the country or of its inhabitants, for such did not exist; nor on account of any supposed presence of Egyptian troops in the south of Palestine; but simply on account of the fact that Israel had deliberately refused to take the straight road into their land, and were therefore condemned to follow a long and circuitous route ere they reached it on an altogether different side. The dangers and difficulties of the road they actually traversed were, humanly speaking, far greater than any they would have encountered in any other direction; but this was part of their necessary discipline. Thy brother Israel. This phrase recalled the history of Esau and Jacob, and of the brotherly kindness which the former had shown to the latter at a time when he had him in his power (Gen. xxxiii.). Thou knowest all the travel that hath befallen us. Moses assumed that Edom would take a fraternal interest in the fortunes of Israel. The parallel was singularly close between the position of Jacob when he met with Esau, and the present position of Israel; we may well suppose that Moses intended to make this felt without directly asserting it.

Ver. 16.—And sent an angel. It is probable, that Moses purposely used an expression which might be understood in various senses, because he could not explain to the king of Edom the true relation of the Lord to his people. At the same time it was in the deepest sense true (cf. Exod. xiv. 19; xxxii. 34), because it was the uncreated angel of the covenant, which was from God, and yet was God (cf. Gen. xxxii. 30; Josh. v. 15; vi. 2; Acts vii. 35), who was the real captain of the Lord's host. In Kadesh, a city in the uttermost of thy border. See note on Kadesh. It is clear that Kadesh itself was outside the territory of the king of Edom, although it lay close to the frontier.

Ver. 17.—Let us pass, I pray thee, through thy country. Moses desired to march through Seir eastwards and north-eastwards, so as to reach the country beyond Jordan. If the northern portion of the wilderness of Paran was at this time held by the king of Edom, it would be through this region that Israel would first seek to make their way from Kadesh to the Arabah; thence the broad and easy pass of the Wady Ghuweir would lead them through Mount Seir (properly so called) to the plains of Moab. Through the fields, or through the vineyards. These words attest the change for the worse in the condition of these regions. Even in the Wady Ghuweir, although springs and pasturage are abundant, fields and vineyards hardly exist. Neither will we drink, i. e., as appears from ver. 19, without obtaining leave and making payment. By the king's highway. דֶּרֶךְ הַמֶּלֶךְ. The state road used for military purposes.

Ver. 18.—And Edom said, . . Thou shalt not pass by me. This was the first of a series of hostile acts, prompted by vindictive jealousy, which brought down the wrath of God upon Edom (compare the prophecy of Obadiah). See, however, on Deut. ii. 29.

Ver. 19.—And the children of Israel said, i. e., probably, the messengers sent by Moses.

By the highway. בַּמְסִלָּה. The Septuagint

translates παρὰ τὸ ὄρος, but no doubt the word means a "high road" in the original sense of a raised causeway (cf. Isa. lvii. 14). Such a road is still called Derb es Sultan—Emperor-road. **I will only, without doing anything else, go through on my feet.** Rather, "It is nothing :" (רַק אֵין־דָּבָר. Septuagint, ἀλλὰ τὸ πρᾶγμα οὐδὲν ἐστι) "I will go through on my feet." They meant, "We do not ask for anything of value, only leave to pass through."

Ver. 22.—**And the children of Israel, even the whole congregation** (see note on ver. 1), **journeyed from Kadesh, and came unto Mount Hor.** If the narrative follows the order of time, we must suppose that the Edomites at once blocked the passes near to Kadesh, and thus compelled the Israelites to journey southwards for some distance until they were clear of the Azazimât; they would then turn eastwards again and make their way across the plateau of Paran to the Arabah at a point opposite Mount Hor. It is supposed by many, although it finds no support in the narrative itself, that the armed resistance offered by Edom is out of chronological order in ver. 20, and only occurred in fact when the Israelites had reached the neighbourhood of Mount Hor, and were preparing to ascend the Wady Ghuweir. On the name of Mount Hor (הָהָר הֹר) see on ch. xxxiv. 7, 8. There can be no doubt that tradition is right in identifying it with the Jebel Harun (mount of Aaron), a lofty and precipitous mountain rising between the Arabah and the site of Petra. On one of its two summits the tomb of Aaron is still shown, and although this is itself worthless as evidence, yet the character and position of the mountain are altogether in agreement with the legend.

Ver. 23.—**By the coast of the land of Edom.** Mount Hor was on the eastern side of the Arabah, which at this point certainly formed the frontier of Edom; but it was no doubt untenanted, owing to its bare and precipitous character, and therefore was not reckoned as the property of Edom. We may suppose that at this time the encampment stretched along the Arabah in front of the mountain (see on ch. xxxiii. 30; Deut. x. 6).

Ver. 24.—**Aaron shall be gathered unto his people.** On this expression see at Gen. xxv. 8.

Ver. 25.—**Bring them up unto Mount Hor.** It can scarcely be doubted that the object of this command was to produce a deeper effect upon the people. The whole multitude would be able to see the high priest, whose form had been so familiar to them as long as they could remember anything, slowly ascending the bare sides of the mountain; and they knew that he went up to die. The whole multitude would be able to see another and a younger man descending by the same path in the same priestly robes, and they knew that Aaron was dead, and that Eleazar was high priest in his room. Death is often most striking when least expected, but there are occasions (and this was one) when it gains in effect by being invested in a certain simple ceremonial.

Ver. 28.—**Moses stripped Aaron of his garments, and put them upon Eleazar his son.** This was done in token that the office was transferred; it was done out of sight, and far above, in token that the priesthood was perpetual, although the priest was mortal. **Aaron died there.** In this case, as in that of Miriam (ver. 1), and of Moses himself (Deut. xxxiv. 5), no details are given. God drew as it were a veil over a departure hence which could but be very sad, because it was in a special sense the wages of sin. We may perhaps conclude that Aaron died alone, and was buried, as Moses was, by God; otherwise Moses and Eleazar would have been unclean under the law of ch. xix. 11 (cf. also Levit. xxi. 11).

Ver. 29.—**They mourned for Aaron thirty days.** The Egyptians prolonged their mourning for seventy days (Gen. l. 3), but thirty days seems to have been the longest period allowed among the Israelites (cf. Deut. xxxiv. 8).

HOMILETICS.

Vers. 1—29.—*Sorrows and trials of the way.* We have in this chapter, spiritually, the final departure of the Church of God upon its last journey towards the promised land; and we have certain sad incidents of moral failure, of disappointment, and of death which marked the commencement of that journey.

I. CONSIDER, THEREFORE, WITH RESPECT TO THE POSITION OF ISRAEL—1. *That he was once more at Kadesh, not one step nearer home than he had been thirty-eight years before.* Because he had rebelled then his life had run to waste ever since, and been lost like the fountain of Kadesh in the sands, and only now, after such a lapse of time, and after so much suffering, did he find himself in a position to recommence the march then suspended. Even so it is with Churches which have reached a certain point, and then have rebelled against the voice of God. Their history runs to waste; they exist, but hardly live ; there is indeed a movement in them, but it has no definite aim, it leads no whither ; they do but return upon themselves. Only after a long time (if God have mercy upon them) do they find themselves once more in a position to start afresh, and not one step further forward than all those years, or cen turies, ago. Even so it is with individuals who will not go resolutely on when they are called. They are spent and wasted in movement to and fro which is not progress. After many years perhaps—perhaps after a whole lifetime—of wandering in dry places they find themselves once more at the very point to which they had attained, not one step nearer heaven than so long ago. 2. *That although Israel was once more at Kadesh, yet he was in a far worse position than on the former occasion.* *Then* he might have marched straight into Canaan, *now* he must reach it by a long and circuitous route. Even so with Churches and with individuals which have done despite to the Spirit of grace. By God's mercy their aimless wanderings may be ended, and they may take up the broken thread of spiritual progress ; but they can not take up the opportunities and possibilities which once were theirs. If their position be the same, *they* are not the same ; the effects of past faithlessness remain ; a far more weary course awaits them ere they attain to rest than if they had obeyed from the beginning. 3. *That Miriam died in Kadesh, and went not with them on the last march.* She was a " prophetess," and uttered inspired words of praise and thanksgiving (as Deborah, Hannah, and Mary), and was especially associated with the glorious triumph of the exodus (Exod. xv. 20—22). Even so the soul which has greatly erred and lost itself, and is at last recovered and sets its face Zionward, may not look to be cheered with songs of gladness and of triumph on its way, but must do without them. And note that Miriam, Aaron, Moses all died this year, a little before the entrance into Canaan under Joshua. The Fathers see in this a figure of the passing away of prophecy, the priesthood, and the law, and their giving place to Jesus. " Videtur mihi in Mariâ (Miriam) Prophetia mortua ; in Moyse et Aaron Legi et Sacerdotio Judæorum finis impositus, quod nec ipsi ad terram repromissionis transcendere valeant nec credentem populum de solitudine hujus mundi educere, nisi solus Jesus Deus Salvator."

II. WITH RESPECT TO THE WATERS OF STRIFE (see at Exod. xvii.). Consider—1. *That it was in Kadesh that this temptation befell the people, where they had apparently not experienced any want of water before.* Even so it often happens that great religious trials and deprivations are permitted to overtake us when and where we are least prepared to face them, and perhaps at the very moment when we hope to begin a new life and make a decided advance. 2. *That of all gifts which were necessary to their life, water was the one the absence of which was most terrible.* Conceive the suffering and terror of the multitude ! Even so it is the water from the Rock of Ages, the grace of Christ, upon which we daily and hourly depend in this evil world ; and there are moments when that grace threatens to fail us, and spiritual death stares us in the face (cf. 1 Cor. x. 4 ; xii. 13). 3. *That they should have trusted him who had followed them as a spiritual Rock, giving them both water and shade in a thirsty land ; but their temper and their very words were the same as forty years before.* Even so do we fail again and again under trial, as if all experience went for nothing, and as if fallen human nature were never going to be really altered in us for the better. Nothing is more striking than the way in which a man's behaviour under temptation repeats itself in spite of all that he has learnt. 4. *That the Lord did not show any displeasure with them, but gave them water at once,* knowing their sore necessity. Even so patient and long-suffering is he with us, however unreasonable and impatient we are, for he knoweth our feebleness, and our great need, and that we must die without his grace. 5. *That the Lord was angry (and declared it) with Moses because he spoke and acted impatiently and unworthily ;* for what he overlooked again and again in the ignorant and unstable people, that he could not pass over in the wise and powerful leader, who was to them the visible representative and mouthpiece of the invisible God. Even so the Lord will pass over a thousand errors and faults in the poor and ignorant and miserable more easily than one in him that has known him, and that has a ministry from him, and that stands to others in the place of leader and guide. It is a fearful thing by word or act to dishonour God or his gospel in the eyes of those who look up to us, and who will more or less consciously take their ideas of religion from our practice of it. 6. *That Moses erred because he lost his temper, and regarded the sinful murmuring of the people only as a trial and vexation to himself.* He had in fact nothing to complain of, for he was only an instrument in God's hand, and it was against God that they were sinning. Even so we, if we are angry when men do wrongly and foolishly, are sure to err greatly ; for anger can only see the bad conduct of others as an offence to itself, and so resent it, thereby placing self in the room of God, and presuming to judge and to condemn in his stead. 7. *That Moses spake unadvisedly with his lips in calling the people " rebels," because he was himself a rebel in heart.* He was indeed, considering his position and advantages, more disloyal to his Master at that moment than even they were. Even so when we sit in judgment on others, and call them by hard names, it often happens that we are in truth more unfaithful to our calling than even they. *Their* unfaithfulness may be of a kind to arouse our disgust and disdain, but *ours* may be in truth more heinous in the eyes of God. 8. *That he spake yet more unadvisedly in saying, " Must we fetch you water ?"* as though it were their power and goodness to which the supply of water was due. Even so it is a sore evil when the stewards of the manifold grace of God magnify themselves even in hasty words, and speak as if they were the authors instead of the mere dispensers of the gifts of God, and lead men to look to them instead of through them, and pass (as it were) the free grace and goodness of God through the discoloured medium of their own selfish tempers. 9. *That he erred also through wilfulness, in that he smote the rock twice instead of speaking to it*—an error trifling in itself, but betraying the irritation under which he acted, and suggesting that the copious supply was in some way due to his energy. Even so men often err greatly and do harm by acts in themselves inconsiderable which are prompted by impatience and self-will, as though the necessary supply of Divine grace and the blessings of the gospel were really dependent upon their efforts. If we are stewards of the grace of God at all, we have to act (1) with careful obedience towards him, (2) with quiet patience towards his people, knowing that the result lies altogether with him. 10. *That Moses was probably tempted to speak and act as he did because God had said to him, " Thou shalt bring forth to them water,"* &c. Even so we find our temptation to a self-asserting temper which dishonours God in the fact that God has really made the interests of religion (humanly speaking) dependent upon his servants' efforts. It is our trial to remember this as far as labour and earnestness are concerned, to forget it (or rather to remember the complemental truth) as far as personal feelings are concerned. 11. *That God did not withhold the stream because Moses acted wrongly.* Even so the blessings of the word and sacraments are not withheld from the souls of men because there is error and even disobedience in those that minister them. 12. *That God punished Moses and Aaron with personal exclusion from the promised land because they had failed to sanctify him in the eyes of the people ;* i. e. they had, as far as in them lay, obscured the revelation of the Divine power and goodness, and impaired the good effect of it upon the people. Even so God will certainly lay sin to the charge of all who, being in any way his representatives to others, have in anything dimmed the lustre of his beauty or distorted the features of his perfection in their eyes. Thus have all, even Moses, sinned and come short of the glory of God, so that none have wholly pleased him except Christ (Matt. iii. 17 ; xvii. 5 ; 2 Pet. i. 17) ; nor can any look for an entrance into rest save in Christ. 13. *That the Lord was sanctified in the children of Israel at Meribah, albeit his appointed servants failed to sanctify him.* Their sentence was perhaps the most effective possible revelation of his exceeding holiness. Even so the Lord will make his glory to be known and felt through his servants if they be faithful, but without them if they be faithless. He will be sanctified in us to our great reward in the one case, to our shame and sorrow in the other.

III. CONSIDER FURTHER, WITH RESPECT TO THE ERROR OF MOSES—1. *That he was now very old, in his hundred and twentieth year.* An irritable and hasty temper is the special temptation of old age. 2. *That he had shown the same temper on at least one previous occasion* (ch. xi.), *and had then been betrayed into the use of unseemly and untrue language,* which ought to have been a warning to him. There is nothing which people have more need to watch very carefully than their temper, for there is nothing that grows upon a man more certainly than bad temper. 3. *That God had been very forbearing with him on that occasion, but on this was very strict;* the reason no doubt being that then Moses uttered his unreasonable and passionate complaints only in the ear of God, whereas now his angry insolence was vented upon the people.   If we address ourselves directly to God he will receive graciously even the outpourings of a disordered and embittered mind, and we shall find relief; if we reserve our angry temper for our neighbours—much more for those committed to our keeping—God will be sore displeased at us for *their* sakes.   Art thou angry? Go and complain to God (cf. Ps. lxxvii. 3, P. B. V.).

IV. Consider, with respect to the conduct of Edom — 1. *That Israel had reason to expect no friendly treatment from Edom, because of the bad conduct of Jacob towards Esau,* which had left an angry and jealous spirit in the minds of his descendants against Israel.   The quarrels and injuries of individuals bear evil fruit in years to come, and in after generations, and that especially among brethren, whether in blood or in religion. 2. *That, nevertheless, Israel addressed Edom as his brother, and bespoke his friendly sympathy and help.*   We are bound to treat others as our brethren, and to approach them as such, and to bespeak their sympathy in our religious interests, until we are actually repulsed. 3. *That Israel did not claim any right, as the chosen people of God, to be served by Edom, or to take anything of him without payment,* but only asked the ordinary courtesy due to a friendly people.   In addressing ourselves to others in matters of this world we must be careful to ask and to expect only what is strictly fair and reasonable from their point of view, and not to claim any exceptional regard or deference because we are more highly-favoured than they. 4. *That when Israel found himself rudely denied and opposed, he did not attempt to avenge himself, but turned away from Edom.*   If we meet with opposition and hostility where we looked for help and sympathy, it is useless to complain, and wicked to bear malice; the only thing is to turn away from such, and leave them to God and to themselves. 5. *That the hostile conduct of Edom was not forgotten of God, but in due time (not being amended) was punished.* It is a great sin, out of personal (or collective) jealousy and dislike, to cast obstacles in the path of others, or to refuse them such friendly assistance as they seek of us.

V. Consider, with respect to the death of Aaron — 1. *That it testified to the infirmity of human nature at its greatest.*   Aaron had been invested with a sacred character, and to that generation (which had not known his origin) must have seemed an awful being, almost more than man; yet he died, and was not. 2. *That it testified to the inherent imperfection of the Levitical priesthood, in that Aaron could not continue by reason of death,* so that the continuance of the office depended upon natural succession, which must some day fail—and has failed. 3. *That it testified to the exceeding sinfulness of sin.*   For one little sin, and one to which he was merely accessory, the high priest must die without even beholding the land so long sought, and now so nearly found. 4. *That the demise of Aaron in that lonely mountain, in a foreign land, testified to the mysterious and typical character of his office.* The anointed of the Lord, although, as being man and sinful, he must die, yet not as other men die, but in a vast far solitude alone with God. 5. *That the transfer of the priestly robes from Aaron to Eleazar testified that the priesthood was abiding, and would abide until it vested in One who should live for ever.*   Therefore was it effected out of sight of the people, and far above them, in order that no gap or interval might be perceptible to them. 6. *That the mourning for Aaron during thirty days testified that, with all his faults, he was yet honoured as a great leader in Israel;* and perhaps this too, that Aaron as a man was not so swallowed up in Aaron as a priest but that his personal loss was duly felt and lamented.

HOMILIES BY VARIOUS AUTHORS.

Ver. 12.—*The sin of Moses.* There must have been something in this sin of Moses at the crag in Kadesh very unworthy of his high place, and very displeasing to God.   The sharpness of the Lord's reprimand and the severity of the punishment make this sufficiently clear.   By Moses himself the punishment was felt to be severe.

And no marvel. For eighty long years he had waited and laboured for the fulfil-ment of the promise. During the last thirty-seven of these he had been cheering himself with the hope that he, along with Joshua and Caleb, and the men of the younger generation, would be suffered to take possession of the land. This lay so near his heart that, after learning that he was not to set foot within the promised rest, he laboured hard to get the sentence reversed (Deut. iii. 25).

I. What then was Moses' sin ? Two circumstances are obvious on the face of the story. 1. Moses, being directed *to speak to* the rock that it might give forth its water, *smote it* instead with the rod of God which was in his hand ; and this he did not once only, but twice. 2. He spoke to the people, not with meekness and calm authority, but in heat and bitterness. "Ye rebels, must we fetch you water out of this rock ?" Thus he "spake unadvisedly with his lips" (Ps. cvi. 33). It is not difficult to understand how Moses should have so far forgotten himself on this occa-sion. Let the facts be weighed. The servant of the Lord is now 120 years old. The generation which sinned thirty-seven years ago, and was condemned to die in the wilderness, is nearly all gone. Moses is mortified to find that the new generation is infected with a touch of the same impatient unbelief which wrought in their fathers so much mischief. No sooner are they at a loss for water than they rise against Moses with rebellious murmurings. For once he loses command of him-self. On all former occasions of the kind his *meekness* was unshaken ; he either held his peace, or prayed for the rebels, or at most called on the Lord to be his Wit-ness and Judge. Now he breaks out into bitter chidings. At the root of this there was a secret failure of faith. "Ye believed me not,"—did not thoroughly rely on my faithfulness and power,—"to sanctify me in the eyes of the children of Israel" (ver. 12). His former meekness had been the fruit of faith. He had been thoroughly persuaded that the Lord who was with him could accomplish all he had promised, and therefore he faced every difficulty with calm and patient resolution. Now a touch of unbelief bred in him hastiness and bitterness of spirit.

II. Lessons. 1. The failings of good men may be culpable in God's sight and dis-pleasing to him out of all proportion to the degree of blameworthiness they present to our eye. So far is it from being true (as many seem to think) that believers' sins are no sins at all, and need give no concern, that, on the contrary, the Lord dislikes the stain of sin most when it is seen in his dear children. The case of Moses is not singular. Sins which the Lord overlooks in other men he will occasionally put some mark of special displeasure upon, when they are committed by one who is eminent for holiness and honourable service. It is, no doubt, a just instinct which leads all right-thinking people to be blind to the failings of good men who have been signally useful in their day. But if the good men become indulgent to their own faults they are likely to be rudely awakened to a sense of their error. The better a man is, his sins may be the more dishonouring to God. A spot hardly visible on the coat of a labouring man, may be glaringly offensive on the shining raiment of a throned king. 2. The sins we are least inclined to may nevertheless be the sins which will bring us to the bitterest grief. Every man has his weak side. There are sins to which our natural disposition or the circumstances of our up-bringing lay us peculiarly open ; and it is without doubt a good rule to be specially on our guard in relation to these sins. Yet the rule must not be applied too rigidly. When Dum-barton Rock was taken, it was not by assailing the fortifications thrown up to protect its one weak side, but by scaling it at a point where the precipitous height seemed to render defence or guard unnecessary. Job was the most patient of men, yet he sinned through impatience. Peter was courageous, yet he fell through cowardice. Moses was the meekest of men, yet he fell through bitterness of spirit. We have need to guard well not our weak points only, but the points also at which we deem ourselves to be strong.—B.

Ver. 23—29.—*The death of Aaron.* The fortieth year of the Wanderings, remark-able in so many other respects, was remarkable also for this, that it witnessed the removal of the three great children of Amram, who had been the leaders of the nation from the time that the Lord began to plague the Egyptians till the day that the host removed from the camping-ground at Kadesh. Of the three, Miriam, seemingly the eldest, was the first to be removed. She died, and was buried at Kadesh, in the beginning of the year. Aaron, the elder of the brothers, followed in the fifth month. Lastly, Moses died at the end of the year. The surpassing fame of Moses has thrown that of Miriam and Aaron into the shade. Nevertheless, they were eminent both for sanctity and public usefulness. It was not the least of the Lord's benefits that they, as well as Moses, were spared to the people during so many years.

I. THE TERMS IN WHICH THE DEATH OF AARON IS FORETOLD (ver. 23). Moses is the first to hear of the coming event; and there is something of wrath, or at least of displeasure, against both him and Aaron in the way in which it is announced: "Ye shall not enter the land, because ye rebelled against my word at Meribah." But the displeasure is only, as it were, a passing frown. There is in the words much more of loving kindness and tender mercy. Not only is the saintly high priest forewarned of his approaching departure, but this is done in terms at once most kindly in tone and strongly suggestive of hope regarding the future life. "Aaron shall be gathered unto his people." Christian readers have always, as by a kind of instinct, taken this to mean that Aaron, upon his departure from this world, was to pass into the company of those who were his relatives in the truest and tenderest kindred—the patriarchs who had died in faith before him, the congregation of the righteous beyond the grave. The interpretation is distasteful to certain critics, who have persuaded themselves that in the Mosaic age the views and hopes of the best of men were bounded by the grave. It is easy to cite texts which seem to countenance that low estimate of the views which God had opened up to the early saints of the patriarchal and Mosaic times. But after all it is no better than a paradox, as hard to reconcile with historical fact as with the instinctive perceptions of devout readers of God's word. It is a familiar fact that the Egyptians, among whom Moses and Aaron were brought up, not only believed that men survive the dissolution of the body, but occupied their minds exceedingly about the other world. In the absence of clear and explicit statements to the contrary, we must suppose that Moses and Aaron knew at least as much as the Egyptians, and looked for a continued conscious existence after death. But we are not left to surmise. What can this "gathered unto his people" mean? It cannot mean "buried in the sepulchre where the ashes of his kindred lie," for in that sense neither Aaron nor Moses was ever gathered to his people. Each was buried in a solitary grave. Nor can it mean merely "gathered to the mighty congregation of the dead" (although that also would imply continued existence after death), for the phrase is used in Scripture regarding none but the righteous (Gen. xxv. 8, 17; xxxv. 29; xlix. 33, &c.). What then do we gather from this intimation? 1. There is, beyond the grave, a congregation of the righteous, where those who die in faith shall enjoy the congenial society of their own people—men and women like-minded with themselves. Surely a most comfortable thought! A great change has no doubt taken place in the view presented to faith of the future life ever since our blessed Lord rose and ascended. The ancient conception of the heavenly life has been thrown into the shade by the conception of it as being "for ever with the Lord." Yet the ancient conception has lost nothing either of its truth or of its power to comfort. A new source of comfort has now been added, but the old one has not been superseded. We who believe in Christ look forward not only to "the coming of our Lord Jesus Christ," but to "our gathering together unto him" (2 Thess. ii. 1). 2. Into the congregation of the righteous God is careful to gather his people when they die. They are not driven away into darkness—dismissed like Judas to their own place. They are gathered; they are taken home: *with care,* that none be lost; *with loving kindness* also, that they may not fear.

II. THE CIRCUMSTANCES OF AARON'S DEPARTURE. 1. He was divested of his office and robes before he died, and they were transferred to Eleazar in his sight. The priest was to die, but the priesthood was to live. The priesthood was entailed in Aaron's house, but the entail had not yet been confirmed by long transmission. To prevent any attempt to alter the succession, the transference took place while Aaron was yet alive. Probably there was an eye also to Aaron's comfort. It would be a satisfaction to him to see his son invested with office before he died. 2. Aaron's death and burial took place on Mount Hor. This was, in the first instance, designed for publicity. Eleazar was to be high priest to the congregation. It was due to them that his investiture should take place in their sight (cf. ch. xxvii. 22). Ordination to a public office ought to take place in public. This particular mountain was chosen because from it Aaron's eye might descry the southern outskirts of the land of promise. Moses and Aaron were forbidden to enter it; but to each there was vouchsafed a distant prospect of it before he died.

REFLECTION. In this life good and evil are inextricably conjoined. Within the same town, in the same street, in the same congregation, in the same family, there are to be found believers and unbelievers, just and unjust, children of God and children of the wicked one. But hereafter there will come a great severance—lamentable separations, joyous reunions. The haters of God will be taken from among the just, and be dismissed to their own place. The lovers of God will be gathered to their own people, and sit down with Abraham, and Isaac, and Jacob in the kingdom. This being so, it behoves me to ask myself the question, Who are my people? What is the people whose likeness I bear, whose company is to me congenial, whose tastes I share?—B.

Ver. 12. — *The great sin of disobedience even under palliating circumstances.* There are various ways in which we may show that sin is "exceeding sinful:" *e. g.* the character of God; the precepts of his ceremonial and moral law; the words and work of the Lord Jesus Christ. Not the least impressive proof of God's estimate of sin is God's chastisement of his sinning children. Confining ourselves to the conduct of Moses, we note—

I. THE NATURE OF MOSES' SIN. It is described in ver. 12, but is not easy to analyse. 1. Its root appears to have been a temporary failure of faith, indicated by the words "must we," or, "shall we bring you water," &c. In spite of the promise (ver. 8), he expresse: uncertainty as to whether such rebels will be gratified. Unbelief is infectious, and needs a robust faith to resist it. Like a powerful electric current, only a strong non-conductor can arrest its course. Apply to Christians fearing they must fail in their labours because of unbelief in others (cf. Matt. xvii. 17, 20). This distrust led to further faults, such as—2. Haste of temper. Words, acts, and manner indicated this. May it not have been that because of his distrust, at the first blow, the water did not flow forth? Or was it that both blows were given in great haste? "He that believeth shall not make haste." 3. Disregard of instructions in striking when merely told to speak (cf. Deut. iv. 2; xii. 32; Prov. xxx. 5, 6). 4. The appearance, at least, of assuming too much honour to himself and Aaron, and thus failing to "sanctify" God before the people (Ps. cvi. 33). Distrustful or disobedient thoughts, when shut up, like rebels, within the citadel of the heart, do mischief enough and give a world of trouble; but if they sally forth in the form of words they may cause public injury and lead to consequences some of which may be irreparable. Combining the resolution of Ps. xxxix. 1 with the prayer of Ps. cxli. 3, we may be safe. Yet in considering Moses' sin we may see—

II. THE PALLIATIONS OF IT. 1. Great provocations from the rebels, who, after all the lessons of the past, inherited and perpetuated their fathers' sins (cf. Exod. xvi. 3; xvii. 3; Numb. xi. 5). 2. His first public offence. He was "very meek" (ch. xii. 3), and he needed to be. Now for the first time his meekness failed him. 3. His sin was very brief—a temporary failure of faith, causing a passing gust of anger, yet soon over; he was not "greatly moved" (Ps. lxii. 2). 4. It led to no public evil consequences appreciable by the congregation. But though we may see in our own sins or the sins of others many circumstances that seem to palliate the offence, we must not expect to escape chastisement if we reflect on—

III. MOSES' PUNISHMENT. Moses had one cherished desire of his life, that, having led the people through the wilderness, he might conduct them into the promised land. Illustrate this from the scene graphically suggested to our imagination in Deut. iii. 23—27. True, the punishment was only for this life, and, like many other of God's fatherly chastisements, was overruled for his child's good in sparing him from future conflicts (cf. 1 Cor. ii. 32). But still it was a punishment, reminding us of the great sin of disobedience even under palliating circumstances. And the penalty may be more serious. Illustrate from the case of the disobedient prophet deceived at Bethel (1 Kings xiii.); or from some case we may have known of a life blighted through one sin of haste or disobedience in word or act. The favour of God brings with it great privileges, but imposes on us grave responsibilities (cf. Amos iii. 2; Luke xii. 47; 1 Pet. iv. 17). What need for the confession and the prayer, Ps. xix. 12—14!—P.

Ver. 28.—*The death of Aaron:*—"*Mercy and judgment.*" This chapter begins with the death of Miriam and ends with Aaron's decease. No chapter of any length in the history even of a godly family without death in it. In every believer's death there is a blending of judgment and mercy. In this case we see—

I. JUDGMENT. Aaron's death was—1. A chastisement (ver. 24; Rom. v. 12; viii. 10). 2. A deprivation (ver. 26). His garments were taken off because his priesthood was taken away. So with the most sacred and honourable office of the Christian (Heb. vii. 23; 2 Pet. i. 13—15). 3. A severance. The aged Moses loses the last companion of his early days. 4. A grief to many (ver. 29).

II. MERCY; indicated in Aaron's death by such facts as these. It was, 1. A calm departure, not a sudden judgment. He was not "cut off from," but "gathered unto, his people." 2. A release from the toils of life in the wilderness and the contradiction of sinners. 3. A gentle dismission from the responsibilities of office. 4. A transference of his duties and honours to a beloved son. He saw the robes and the office of the priesthood intrusted to Eleazar. 5. A promotion to the higher service of a sinless world; from the mount of communion to the heavenly Mount Zion.—P.

Ver. 1.—*The abiding in Kadesh and the death of Miriam.* 1. *The abiding in Kadesh.* This was a return to the district occupied at the time when God pronounced the doom of wandering for forty years on the people (ch. xiii. 26). We know also that the return took place as this long period was drawing to a close. There had been, so to speak, a profitless and melancholy wandering in a circle. We have but little information concerning this period, and what we have seems to have been given for the purpose of showing now rigorously God carried out the sentence. Ch. xxxiii. tells us of the various halting-places, as if to impress us with the fact that Israel had not been allowed to go out of the wilderness. We are told of the rebellion of Korah and the giving of certain laws, but there is nothing to indicate progress. Probably, as has been suggested, there was more or less of dispersion during the forty years. God was waiting for an obstacle to be taken out of the way. In the Scriptures we do not find anything recorded unless as it bears on the advancement of the kingdom of God. Much of what the world calls history is after all mere trifling, and it is our wisdom and profit to notice not only what God has revealed, but also what he has concealed. This generation of the Israelites was thus a type of the many profitless lives that are lived in every generation. After a period of wandering and toil they come back to where they started from. There is nothing to show for all the years of weary work. Sadder still, there are many who come to be looked on as obstacles; their life stands in the way of human improvement and advance, and little or nothing can be done till they go. The return to Kadesh was like some great sign that a long and rigorous winter is drawing to its close. 2. *The death of Miriam.* There is a certain fitness in following up the regulations of ch. xix. with a record of death and burial. Death had dogged these Israelites all through their wanderings. There was perhaps no halting-place but what might have had this sentence joined with it: "Such a one died there and was buried there." Why then is the death of Miriam singled out for special mention? In the first place, she was a person of distinction by her office as prophetess, particularly as she was not only a prophetess, but sister to the two chief men in Israel. Then, being so, it is very noticeable that none of the three, so eminent in their life, were allowed to enter the promised land. There is mystery in their calling, mystery in the services they are called to render, and mystery in the seeming thwarting of all their hopes. One feels the hand of God is in all this. Man proposes, and reckons with something like certainty, but God disposes in a very different fashion. Miriam had sinned a great sin (ch. xii.), but was it not a long while ago? She has lived on through all these wanderings, having seen many younger than herself falling on every hand. May she not then hope to live a little longer, and see the promised land before she dies? Perhaps such thoughts were in the aged woman's mind, perhaps many a time she had wept bitterly over her pride and envy in the past; but God's determinations cannot be set aside, and even when the earthly Canaan is again coming in sight, that sight is not for her. There was no way for Miriam, any more than the rest of us, to escape that suffering and loss *in this world* which so often come from wrong-doing. As to her possible part in the better country, there is necessary silence here. It is Christ who brought life and immortality to light. The great thing to be noticed is that Miriam died in Kadesh, was buried there, and consequently failed of entrance into the earthly Canaan.—Y.

Vers. 2—13.—*The gift of water at Meribah.* I. THE COMPLAINT OF THE PEOPLE. 1. It was occasioned by *a pressing and reasonable want.* "There was no water for the congregation." The people were often discontented without cause, but here was a real strait. Experience shows that many so-called necessities, instead of being necessities, are even injurious. Life might be made more simple and frugal with no loss, but rather increase, of the highest joys of life. But if we are to live here at all there are some things necessary. The bread and the water must be sure. 2. *There was no apparent supply for the want.* We may presume that for the most part Israel had found water, even in the wilderness, without much difficulty. Unobserved and unappreciated, God may have opened up many fountains before the Israelites approached. Hence when they came to Kadesh and found the rocks dry, they hastily judged there was no water. We are very dependent on customary outward signs. 3. *Past experience of similar circumstances should have led to calm faith and expectation.* God had made sweet for them the bitter waters of Marah, and directly after brought them to Elim with its ample supply (Exod. xv. 23—27). And when they came to Rephidim, and found no water, Moses by command of God smote the rock in Horeb (Exod. xvii.). But then the rising generation had not been sufficiently instructed in these things, and impressed with the goodness of God. How should unbelieving and forgetting fathers make believing and mindful children? If we would only base our expectations on what God has done in the past, we should look in vain for occasion of fear and doubt. After Jesus had fed one multitude, the disciples had yet to ask with respect to another, "Whence should we have so much bread in the wilderness, as to fill so great a multitude?" (Matt. xv. 33). Consider also Matt. xvi. 5—10. We continually, and in the most perverse way, confine our views of what is possible within the limitations of our own natural powers. To God the wilderness is as the fruitful field, and the fruitful field as the wilderness. He can make the earth whatever pleases him (Ps. cvii. 33—39). 4. *The complaints of the people were not confined to the urgent need.* They do not approach Moses with a simple, humble plea for water. They had not considered why they had been brought to *Kadesh,* and that in the plans of God they were bound to come again into that district, whether water was there or not. First of all they utter *an impious, hasty wish,* though if it had been taken seriously they would have complained bitterly. Men are apt to say they wish they were dead when really their circumstances are more endurable than those of many who have learned, like the apostle, in whatsoever state they are, therewith to be content. A discontented heart makes a reckless tongue. The expression was used thoughtlessly enough, just as many take God's name in vain, hardly conscious of what they are saying. Next they advance to *an unjust reproach.* Forty years of Divine chastisements, sharp and severe, had taught them nothing. They could see nothing more than that Moses and Aaron were leading the people about at their own will. How easy it is through our ignorance of the unseen God to attribute to the men whom we do see a power immensely beyond their resources. The people came back to Kadesh as they left it, blind, ungrateful, inconsiderate as ever. Moses and Aaron, sorrowing for their dead sister, have once again to listen to accusations which long ago had been answered by God himself. The reproach is mingled with *vain regrets, still surviving all these years of chastisement.* There could not now be many survivors of the generation that had come out of Egypt, yet, doubtless, all the while Egypt had been so often mentioned as to have deeply infected the minds of the younger generation. Garrulous old people, who might so easily have inspired their children by telling them of God's dealings with Pharaoh in Egypt and at the Red Sea, and of all his goodness in the wilderness, were rather poisoning and prejudicing their hearts with recollections of carnal comforts and delicacies which seemed hopelessly lost. Instead of pointing out that the wilderness with all its hardships was a place of Divine manifestations, they could only see that it was no place of seeds, or figs, or vines, or pomegranates. *The mention of water*, coming in at the last, seems almost an after-thought, as much as to say, "Even if we had water, there would none the less be ground for great complaints."

II. GOD'S ANSWER TO THE COMPLAINT. 1. The people speak against Moses and Aaron, who thereupon make their usual resort to God. Beforetime when his glory appeared in response to their appeal it was the herald of destruction (ch. xiv. 10; xvi. 19, 42); but now there is no threatening of destruction. Even in the midst of their murmuring and ingratitude *God recognises their real need.* Thus as we consider the work of God in Christ Jesus we find a similar recognition. Men came to Jesus with all sorts of selfish complaints; but while they found in him a pitying listener, there was no disposition to deal with them according to their complaints. God did not give to Israel at Kadesh, figs, vines, and pomegranates, but he gave water speedily and abundantly. It is made a charge against the Divine providence and government, and sometimes a ground for denying the reality of such things, that men are so unequally supplied with temporal possessions. But all this falls to the ground if only we notice how prompt, how effectual, God is in meeting real necessities. *It is he who is to judge of these.* There is no absolute necessity even for the bread that perisheth, but there is need, whether here or elsewhere, to be free from sin, to have that spiritual food, that bread and water of eternal life, which Jesus himself has spoken of so largely and attractively in the Gospel of John. Thus while the Jews went on wickedly complaining against Christ, showing more and more their ignorance and selfishness, he, on the other hand, went on in the midst of all, revealing, expounding, setting forth in the clear light of his matchless teaching the supreme want of men and his own adequate supply for it. We must cease clamouring for the figs, vines, and pomegranates, and be more athirst for that water of which if one drink he shall never thirst again. God will not supply everything we think to be wants. But let a man come to himself and discern his real needs, and God, like the father to the prodigal son, will run to meet him with an ample supply. 2. *God makes the supply from an unlikely source.* Moses was to speak to the rock before their eyes, the one nearest them at the time. There was no searching about among the hills if haply some natural reservoir might be found which a touch could open in all its fulness to the panting crowd. There was water in the rock before them, requiring nothing more than the word of God through his servant Moses. We must consider what happened as if Moses had completely carried out his instructions. Thus in many things connected with our salvation we are directed to unlikely places and unlikely methods. Who expects the King of the Jews to be born in Bethlehem? Why not in Jerusalem? Can any good thing come out of Nazareth? Shall one look for the food of a multitude among five loaves and two small fishes? Shall one look for an apostle of the Gentiles in Paul, the fierce and persecuting Jew? God makes a messenger out of the child Samuel, and a champion out of the stripling David. God delights in finding everything he needs where we can find little or nothing. We may be nearest help when to our natural judgment we may seem farthest from it. 3. There is thus *a warning against all hasty judgments.* We who are so utterly weak, so constantly in need of help, should be very slow to say, "Neither is there any water to drink." Let us bear in mind how ignorant we are of the Scriptures and the power of God. God will not leave his own true children unsupplied with any needful thing. He will choose the right time, and way, and form. It is the besetting sin of far too many minds to form conclusions not only when there is lack of sufficient information, but when there is no need of present conclusion at all. "Wait on the Lord, be of good courage, and he shall strengthen thine heart." Do not say in haste and ignorance that there is no strength to be got anywhere.—Y.

Vers. 10—12.—*The sin of Moses and Aaron.* It was the sin of men who had been specially chosen, long occupied, often approved, and greatly honoured as servants of God. If *they*, being what they were, fell so easily, how important it is for *us* earnestly to consider the sin by which they fell! It is another proof of the hold which sin has on our nature, and of the need that we should walk warily, and look for snares at every step. Consider—

I. How the sin was committed. 1. *It was a sin of inattention.* If there was anything which Moses and Aaron should have learned after forty years of service, it was that God's commandments required constant attention and exact obedience. They had a long experience of One who gave details as well as general instructions. Moreover, it was not the first time Moses had been charged to bring water from the rock. At Rephidim God said to him, "Thou shalt smite the rock" (Exod. xvii. 6). At Kadesh he says, "Speak to the rock." The very difference should have been enough to bring the command distinctly before him. Notice then what serious results simple inattention may bring; we know that thousands of lives have been lost by it. Furthermore, how many have failed in the attainment of salvation and spiritual blessedness through nothing more than lack of attention! They have not run greedily in the way of sin, but simply gone through a decent, reputable life, neglecting the way of salvation. In the things of God attention is required as a regular habit, not only that we may escape loss, but secure real advantage. The more attention there is, the more advantage there will be. 2. *It was the inattention of men whose very experience had made them habitually careful.* Whatever Moses and Aaron may have been by nature, they had been trained to faithfulness in little things. It has not perhaps been sufficiently noticed how diligent and exact Moses must have been in his apprehension of all that God revealed to him. When we think how easy misunderstandings are, how easy it is to get wrong impressions and be confused among details, then we feel how very carefully Moses must have listened. Aaron also in his priestly service was a man of detail. 3. *Hence there must have been some extraordinary disturbing cause to throw them out of their usual carefulness.* What this was we can hardly make out with certainty. In the murmuring and repining of the people there was nothing new either as to spirit or language. Moses had listened to the same sort of attack before, and through it all kept his meekness and feeling of personal unworthiness. But as the last straw breaks the camel's back, so even the patience of Moses became at last exhausted. The weight of years and cares united were telling on him. He was now Moses the aged, and though we are assured that when he died his eye was not dim, nor his natural force abated, yet we must not so take these words as to free him from every infirmity of age. It was a very hard thing for a man after forty years of service, through all which he had kept the consciousness of a heart true to God and to Israel, to have the people still meet him with the old ingratitude and the old slanders. Thus it was that he went into the presence of God with a mind preoccupied, thinking a great deal more about the rebellious spirit of the people than about the glory of his Master. There is no safety but in keeping God *first in our thoughts.* We must be like the house founded on the rock, *never* disconnected from it. The nature of the foundation may seem to matter little in calm weather, but the foundation and our connection with it are everything when the tempest comes. Let a believer wear the *whole* armour of God, and he is invincible, but let him lay it aside for a single moment, and the waiting, watching enemy may inflict a painful, serious, humiliating wound, even if it be not a mortal one.

II. In what the sin consisted. 1. *In a want of faith.* "Because ye believed me not." God says nothing about inattention or irritation, but goes at once to the root of the matter. Moses had failed in faith; not altogether, of course, for the very fact that he took the rod and approached the rock shows some faith and some spirit of obedience; but still faith must have been lacking, and to a very serious extent. It has been suggested that, seeing the spirit of the people, Moses was after all in doubt whether another long term of wanderings might not be in store for them. The one clear thing is that God ascribes the sin with its serious consequences to unbelief. Outwardly nothing appears but inattention and irritation; inwardly there is an unbelieving heart. Perhaps even Moses himself may have been startled to hear such a charge, and utterly unconscious that his faith was seriously imperilled. Had he been charged with inattention irritation, want of strict obedience, these were only too plain; but want of faith! Nothing but the clear word of God could make that credible. The lesson to us is that an impaired faith may be the cause of many of our spiritual troubles. We, worse than Moses, may be habitually inattentive and irritable, and afflicted with the sad consciousness that the habits are becoming more and more fixed. To treat them by direct effort is only to mitigate the symptoms of a deep disease, but to get into a truly believing state of mind, to have faith, and to have it more abundantly, will soon weaken and ultimately destroy these harassing spiritual infirmities. 2. *In a consequent failure to sanctify God in the eyes of the people.* The unbelief of Moses was not only a loss to him personally, but those who were out of the way already it led still further out of the way. All eyes were looking to Moses; his fall was not that of some obscure man. Furthermore, he made God's action appear stern and wrathful just at the very time when it was intended to be specially gracious. For forty years the people had been under God's displeasure. Now the gloomy cloud was breaking, the time for entrance into Canaan drawing near, and at the very place where God had once appeared in wrath he evidently intends now to appear in grace and mercy. But the conduct of Moses and Aaron spoils all this beautiful revelation. It was a strange reversal of what had hitherto happened. We no longer see God threatening wrath, and Moses offering ingenious pleas for mercy, but God is now gracious, overlooking a time of ignorance, and Moses, whom one would have expected to see radiant with benignity and satisfaction, goes to the very extreme of denunciation. The grace of the benefit was utterly spoiled. It seemed as if God threw down a supply for the people's need, as a churlish hand might fling a loaf at a beggar. We must labour to live as Christ would have us live, so that men may glorify God in us, and find no occasion to blaspheme; following in the footsteps of him who was able to say, "I have glorified thee on the earth: I have finished the work which thou gavest me to do" (John xvii. 4).

III. THE WAY IN WHICH THE SIN WAS PUNISHED. Those who fail to sanctify God before the people, and make his glory to appear, must in turn bear humiliation before the people. This was not a private intimation to Moses and Aaron, so that only they knew the reason why they were to die before entrance on the promised land. The publication of the doom was needed. Moses himself at the beginning of Deuteronomy (ch. i. 37) seems to make some allusion to this doom upon him: "The Lord was angry with me for your sakes, saying, Thou also shalt not go in thither;" though certainly there is some difficulty arising from the blending of these words with the general doom on the Israelites forty years before. Anyway it is plain that the people knew Moses was to die with the doomed generation. His death happening as it did was a kind of blotting out of all that seemed harsh in the giving of the water. It was an impressive reminder to all future generations of what God had meant to be done. We must not exaggerate this penalty beyond its proper extent and purpose. To the people it would seem very great, and to Moses also at that time it would seem great. But, at the worst, it was only a temporal deprivation. Moses lost the earthly Canaan, but the better land he did not lose. Who was it that appeared in glory to Jesus on the mount? This very Moses, with whom God for a time dealt so sternly. The greatest of temporal losses, the one that now brings most pain, and seems as if it never could be made up, will look a very little thing from among the attainments of eternity. What shall it hurt a man if he lose the whole world and gain a place in the inheritance of the saints in light? Learn, lastly, that none can humiliate us or bring us into loss but ourselves. It may not be our own fault if we are ridiculed; it is always our own fault if we are ridiculous. Moses had suffered many things from the people in the way of scorn and threatening, but through all these things he moves with unimpaired hopes and possessions. It is his own unbelief that brings this bitter disappointment. One traitor within the gates is more dangerous than all the army outside.—Y.

Vers. 14—21.—*The claim of kinship rejected.* I. THE CLAIM. 1. It is the claim of *a kinsman,* even a brother. The message is not from Moses, but "thy brother Israel," who was also a twin-brother. The long intervening space of years seems to fade away, and with it the hosts of the Israelites and Edomites. Jacob and Esau stand before us, as on the morning of reconciliation, after the wrestling at Peniel

(Gen. xxxiii.). The descendants had passed through very different experiences, and were now in very different positions; but Moses felt that this common ancestry constituted a claim which he might reasonably plead. So wherever the · believer travels, though he cannot put in the claim of grace upon the unbeliever, he may put in the claim of nature. "God hath made of one blood all nations of men," said the Jew Paul to the Gentiles of Athens. The changes of grace transform the ties of nature, but do not destroy them. Believers must always do their best to keep hold of unbelievers by virtue of their common humanity. Israel must remind Edom of brotherhood, not only that Israel may profit by the tie, but may also have the chance of profiting Edom (1 Cor. vii. 12—16). 2. It is the claim *of a kinsman in need.* We are not told exactly how the request came to be made. God commanded the people to pass through the coasts of Edom (Deut. ii. 4), and the presumption is that Moses discovered on approach that the way through Edom would be the most direct and convenient to the land of Canaan. One gets the impression that the people were now allowed to make their way to Canaan with what speed they could, as if to make contrast with the penal delay which God had so long and sternly imposed. If Edom had been willing, Israel might have got to Jordan all the sooner. And so the Church of Christ, in its onward rush, has had to plead with the world, its brother, for toleration and free passage, freedom to speak and act according to conviction. Our chief resort, and always our last one, is to God himself, but there are some ways in which the world can help. Paul counted it part of his advantage, as an apostle, that he could plead for justice, protection, and free course as a Roman before Roman tribunals. 3. It is the claim of *a kinsman who had been through very peculiar experiences.* The great need of Israel was that it wanted to get home again. The plea is the plea of an exile, who has been in a strange land for a long time, and amid cruel oppressors. Further, the experiences had been peculiar not only in respect of the cruelty of men, but also of *the goodness of God.* He had sent an angel to deliver and guide. More indication Moses could not give, because it would not have been understood. So peculiar had these experiences been that Edom *had heard something of them.* The presumption is that all through the past Edom had known something of Israel's history, and Israel something of Edom's. The histories of the Church and the world intermingle. The world cannot but know such experiences of the Church as are perceptible to the eye of sense. "This thing was not done in a corner," said Paul to the incredulous Festus. The course of the Church has been one of sufferings, marvels and mysteries, interpositions and favours of God, which are not to be concealed in any appeals which are to be made to the world. "He hath not dealt so with any nation" (Ps. cxlvii. 20). "Blessed is the nation whose God is the Lord; and the people whom he hath chosen for his own inheritance" (Ps. xxxiii. 12). 4. *It asks comparatively little, and promises much in return.* The request throws great light on Moses' own character, and shows clearly how far he was from reckless ambition. It was an honest request, founded in truth, and Moses made it as one quite reasonable and safe for Edom to grant. The people of God have but little to ask the world for themselves, if it will but let them go through quietly and peaceably. They want none of this world's goods and pleasures, and are ready to assure it that these will remain untouched. There is nothing in the shape of a holy city, a new Jerusalem, among this world's possessions. It is a grand assurance to give, that no one in the world will be the worse for the true Christians who pass through it. Moses might even have said, "Let us through, and a blessing will rest upon you." Wherever the Christian goes, he not simply refrains from evil, but does positive good. "Ye are the salt of the earth; ye are the light of the world."

II. THE REJECTION OF THE CLAIM. 1. *It was rejected without giving reasons.* There is no answer but that of the "much people" and the drawn sword. This in general has been the method by which the world has met the Church when pleading for toleration, liberty of conscience, liberty to serve God according to his will. The world in its pride will not stoop to understand or calmly consider what the Church may feel it needful to ask. It gets its brute force ready at once, whether in coarser or more refined forms, for those who have different purposes and sympathies (Acts iv. 3, 17, 18; v. 18, 40; vii. 57, 58; ix. 1, 2; xiv. 5, 19, &c.). 2. *Though no reasons were given, yet Edom had them, strong and potent, in its heart.* It is not always easy or decent to avow reasons for action; beside which, Edom felt that promptitude in action was required. Moses had sent a message which called up all the past, not only what he wished called up, but many things he would rather not have brought to mind. The name of Esau's brother was Jacob as well as Israel, and both names were connected with disturbing recollections to the Edomites. "Thou knowest," said Moses. But his way of presenting the facts, and that alone, could not be confidingly accepted by Edom. A great deal of ugly and disquieting news must have filtered through with respect to this great host of fighting men. The great difficulty Moses had in keeping them in order was probably not unknown to surrounding peoples. Thus the Edomites would feel in their hearts that the pledges of Moses were but as broken reeds to rely on. How could he be responsible for the orderliness and honesty of such a host, a host with such a suspicious history? The world has ever had its instinctive fears of the Church. It hears of certain promises and prophecies, and interprets these against its own present security. Herod, trembling for his throne, slays the infants of Bethlehem to make sure of it. The world, loving its own and thinking there is nothing like it, ignorantly supposes that its possessions must stand esteemed by the Church in the same way. Edom, in its suspicious spirit, looked on Israel much as the Jews in Thessalonica on Paul and Silas: "These that have turned the world upside down are come hither also." The Church says, "I am thy friend, O world, thy brother; I will not harm thee;" but the world thinks it well to be on the safe side, and give no chance of harm, if it can prevent it. 3. *The refusal of Edom emphasises the peculiar destiny of Israel.* Moses said that Israel wanted nothing of all Edom's treasures. Its treasures were elsewhere, and it pressed onward to possess them. Nevertheless, the treasures of Edom would not have been without temptation, and Edom, unconsciously, spares Israel a trial of its steadfastness. The true people of God have reason to be thankful even for the intolerance of the world. The delays and toils of circuitous roads, where mountains and hills are not yet brought low, nor the crooked made straight, and the rough ways smooth, may have more advantages than in the midst of present discomforts we dream of. The temporal prosperity of its members has not been the boon to the Church that many think. The great boon is to have God continually impressing on our minds that this is not our home. "I gave our brethren a solemn caution not to love the world, neither the things of the world. This will be their grand danger. As they are industrious and frugal, they must needs increase in goods. This appears already in London, Bristol, and most other trading towns. Those who are in business have increased in substance seven-fold, some of them twenty, yea, a hundred-fold. What need then have these of the strongest warnings, lest they be entangled therein and perish!" ('Wesley's Journal,' iii. 139).—Y.

Vers. 22—29.—*The death of Aaron.* The chapter, beginning with the death of the sister, closes with the death of the brother, and Moses, in the midst of many official anxieties, is further smitten with great personal bereavement. But not a word of his feeling appears. This is a history of the children of Israel, and the death of Aaron is recorded here not because of Aaron the man, but because of Aaron the priest. The whole solemn event, peculiarly dignified in the transaction of it, is peculiarly dignified also in the record of it. He who had been specially holy to God during his life passes away in circumstances accordant with the dignity and holiness of his office.

I. HIS DEATH, NEVERTHELESS, IS A PENAL ONE. All the holiness of the office cannot obliterate, it cannot even condone, the sin of the man. Great as his privileges had been, and great as the power shown when he stood successfully between the living and the dead, the difference between him and his brethren was only in *office*, not in *nature*. The people were to be impressed with the fact that the priest was not only a great chosen mediator, but a sinful brother. He died, not in the seclusion and privacy of a tent, but upon the mountain, in sight of all the congregation. His part in the sin of Meribah, subordinate as that part seemed, could not be passed over. The sin of omission is as serious as the sin of commission. God had spoken the command in the ears of both the brothers, and what Moses failed to recollect or attend to, Aaron should have supplied from his own knowledge. Thus holy, faithful, and honourable as his life might rightly be called, his sin at the hour cf death is brought right into the foreground. We justly magnify the lives of God's servants, and point with satisfaction to the serenity and expectancy that mark their closing days, and often their closing hour itself, but never let us forget what sin has had to do in bringing them where they are. It is because of Christ that his people die peacefully, but it is because of sin that they have to die at all. He surely dies the calmest who, forgetting his own good works, casts himself, more conscious than ever of his sin, on the mercy of God and the redeeming work of Christ.

II. Though penal, it was tranquil ; we may even say it was hopeful. A great deal—more than we can fathom—may be hidden in that expression, " gathered unto his people." If Aaron did not receive the promise, it was because he could not be made perfect without us (Heb. xi. 39, 40). The man who presumptuously neglected the passover was to be cut off from among his people (ch. ix. 13 ; xv. 30) ; Korah and his companions perished from among the congregation ; but Aaron was gathered to his people. Doubtless he went up in repentance, faith, obedience, and deep humility to face the great mystery. Though he had sinned at Meribah, disobedience to God and self-seeking were not the chosen and beloved principles in his life. It is a dreadful thing to die in sin, but to the repentant sinner, showing his repentance in sufficient and appropriate fruits, and steadfastly believing in Christ, how can death be dreadful? Many who have lived in long bondage to the fear of death have been wonderfully relieved and calmed as the dreaded hour drew nigh.

> "Many shapes
> Of Death, and many are the ways that lead
> To his grim cave, all dismal ; yet to sense
> More terrible at th' entrance than within."

III. The continuity of holy service is provided for. Among the kingdoms of this world the cry is, "The king is dead—long live the king." The departing king keeps his authority and pomp to the last breath. But here while Aaron is still alive, before death can stain those rich and holy garments with its hated touch, they are taken from the father and assumed by the son. Consider this transfer of office thus made, in the light of ch. xix. It was not on Aaron's part a spontaneous abdication,—that he could not make,—but a further significant hint how abominable death is to God. It is not the priest who dies, but the sinful man. There in the sight of all the people it was signified that though they had lost the man, never for a moment had they lost the priest. There was nothing Aaron had done which Eleazar could not do as well. Aaron personally does not seem to have been a very remarkable man ; if anything, wanting in individuality, and easily led. Do not let us look with apprehension when those who seem to be pillars are giving way. The word of Jesus should reassure our doubts, and make us utterly ashamed of them. "Lo, I am with you alway, even to the end of the world."—Y.

THE LAST MARCH : FROM MOUNT HOR TO JORDAN (CH. XXI.—XXII. 1).

EXPOSITION.

CHAPTER XXI.

Episode of the king of Arad (vers. 1—3). Ver. 1.—**And when king Arad the Canaanite, which dwelt in the south, heard tell.** Rather, "And the Canaanite, the king of Arad, which dwelt in the Negeb, heard tell." It is possible that Arad was the name of the king (it occurs as the name of a man, 1 Chron. viii. 15), but it was almost certainly the name of his place. The "king of Arad" is mentioned in Josh. xii. 14, and "the Negeb of Arad" in Judges i.

16. From the context of these passages it is evident that it was situated in the southernmost district of what was afterwards the territory of Judah. According to Eusebius, it stood twenty Roman miles to the south of Hebron, and its site has been found by modern travellers at Tel-Arad, a low hill in this direction. On the Negeb see note on ch. xiii. 17. **By the way of the spies.** דֶּרֶךְ הָאֲתָרִים. Septuagint, ὁδὸν 'Αθαρείν. The translation is very uncertain ; atharim may be a proper name, as the Septuagint seems to suppose, or it may be an unusual

plural formed from תוּר, equivalent to הַתָּרִים, "spies," as the Chaldee, Samaritan, and most of the versions take it; or it may be simply the plural from אַתָר, a place, used with some local meaning which made it practically a proper name. If the rendering of the A. V. be correct, "the way of the spies" must have been the route by which they ascended to Hebron through the Negeb (ch. xiii. 17, 22), and the king of Arad must have anticipated an invasion in that direction, and sought to forestall it. **And took some of them prisoners.** This would seem to show that he fell upon them unawares, and cut off some detached parties. Nothing is said of any disobedience on the part of Israel to account for defeat in battle.

Ver. 2.—**And Israel vowed a vow.** On these vows, and on things "devoted" or "banned" (חֵרֶם—ἀνάθεμα), see on Levit. xxvii. 28, and on the moral character of such wholesale slaughters see on ch. xxxi. If it was right to destroy the Canaanites at all, no fault can be found with the vow; it merely did for that military proceeding what national feeling and discipline does for the far more bloody exigencies of modern warfare, removing it from the sphere of private hatred, revenge, and cupidity, and placing it upon a higher level. The patriot soldier of these days feels himself to be a mere instrument in the hands of the rulers of his people to maintain their rights or avenge their wrongs. The Israelite could not have this feeling, which was foreign to his time and place in history, but he could feel that he was a mere instrument in the hands of God to perform *his* will upon *his* enemies. In either case a most important advantage is secured; the soldier does not slay in order to gratify his own hatred, or in order to satisfy his own cupidity. It is quite true that such vows as are here mentioned would certainly in a more advanced stage of civilisation be abused to throw a cloak of religion over frightful enormities; but it does not in the least follow that they were not permitted and even encouraged by God in an age to which they were natural, and under circumstances in which they were beneficial.

Ver. 3.—**They utterly destroyed them and their cities.** Rather, "they banned (יַחֲרֵם— ἀναθεμάτισεν) them and their cities." No doubt the banning implies here their utter destruction, because it is not the vow before the battle, but the carrying of it out after the victory, which is here spoken of. **And he called the name of the place Hormah.** Rather, "the name of the place was called (impersonal use of the transitive) Charmah." חָרְמָה. Septuagint, 'Ανάθεμα. It is not very clear what place received this name at this time. It does not appear to have been

Arad itself, as would have seemed most natural, because Arad and Hormah are mentioned side by side in Josh. xii. 14. It is identified with Zephath in Judges i. 17. It may have been the place where the victory was won which gave all the cities of Arad to destruction. Whether it was the Hormah mentioned in ch. xiv. 45 is very doubtful (see note there). The nomenclature of the Jews, especially as to places, and most especially as to places with which their own connection was passing or broken, was vague and confused in the extreme, and nothing can be more unsatisfactory than arguments which turn upon the shifting names of places long ago perished and forgotten. It must be added that the three verses which narrate the chastisement of this Canaanite chieftain have caused immense embarrassment to commentators. If the incident is narrated in its proper order of time, it must have happened during the stay of the Israelites under Mount Hor, when they had finally left the neighbourhood of the Negeb, and were separated from the king of Arad by many days' march, and by a most impracticable country. It is therefore generally supposed that the narrative is out of place, and that it really belongs to the time when Israel was gathered together for the second time at Kadesh, and when his reappearance there in force might well have given rise to the report that he was about to invade Canaan from that side. This is unsatisfactory, because no plausible reason can be assigned for the insertion of the notice where it stands, both here and in ch. xxxiii. 40. To say that Moses wished to bring it into juxtaposition with the victories recorded in the latter part of the chapter, from which it is separated by the incident of the fiery serpents, and the brief record of many journeys, is to confess that no explanation can be invented which has the least show of reason. If the narrative be displaced, the displacement must simply be due to accident or interpolation. Again, it would seem quite inconsistent with the position and plans of Israel since the rebellion of Kadesh that any invasion and conquest, even temporary, of any part of Canaan should be made at this time, and that especially if the attack was not made until Israel was lying in the Arabah on his way round the land of Edom. It is therefore supposed by some that the vow only was made at this time, and the ban suspended over the place, and that it was only carried out as part of the general conquest under Joshua; that, in fact, the fulfilment of the vow is narrated in Josh. xii. 14; Judges i. 16, 17. This, however, throws the narrative as it stands into confusion and discredit, for the ban and the destruction become a mockery and an unreality if nothing more was done to the towns of the king of Arad than was done at the same time to the towns of all his neighbours. It would be more reverent to reject the story as an error or a falsehood than to empty it of the meaning which it was obviously intended to convey. We are certainly meant to understand that the vow was there and then accepted by God, and was there and then carried into effect by Israel ; the towns of Arad were depopulated and destroyed as far as lay in their power, although they may have been immediately reoccupied. There are only two theories which are worth considering. 1. The narrative *may* really be displaced, for what cause we do not know. If so, it would be more satisfactory to refer it, not to the time of the second encampment at Kadesh, but to the time of the first, during the absence of the spies in Canaan. It is probable that their entry was known, as was the case with Joshua's spies (Josh. ii. 2) ; and nothing could be more likely than that the king of Arad, suspecting what would follow, should attempt to anticipate invasion by attack. If it were so it might help to account for the rash confidence shown by the people afterwards (ch. xiv. 40), for the mention of Hormah (ch. xiv. 45), and for the reappearance of kings of Hormah and of Arad in the days of Joshua. 2. The narrative *may* after all be in place. That the Israelites lay for thirty days under Mount Hor is certain, and they may have been longer. During this period they could not get pasture for their cattle on the side of Edom, and they may have wandered far and wide in search of it. It may have been but a comparatively small band which approached the Negeb near enough to be attacked, and which, by the help of God, was enabled to defeat the king of Arad, and to lay waste his towns. It had certainly been no great feat for all Israel to overthrow a border chieftain who could not possibly have brought 5000 men into the field.

HOMILETICS.

Vers. 1—3.— *Victory won, and followed up.* In this brief narrative of three verses we have by anticipation almost the whole spiritual teaching of the Book of Joshua ; we have, namely, the struggle and the victory of the soldier of Christ over his spiritual foes, and the consequent duty which he has to perform. Consider, therefore—

I. THAT THE FEAR AND THE ANGER OF THE CANAANITE WERE KINDLED BY THE NEWS THAT ISRAEL WAS COMING BY THE WAY OF THE SPIES, *i. e.* were following in the steps of those that had gone before into the land of promise. Even so the rage of Satan and of all evil spirits is stirred against us because he knows that we follow in the way which leads to heaven, and because it is his ardent desire to keep us out, if he can and while he can. If the Canaanite had perceived that Israel had rebelled and turned his back on the land of promise, he would never have troubled to come forth and attack him. Satan makes no direct assault on those whom he sees to be walking contrary to God and to rest.

II. THAT HE ATTACKED ISRAEL SUDDENLY AND UNEXPECTEDLY, AND WITH SOME SUCCESS. Most likely they were scattered abroad in search of pasture when he fell upon them, and made them prisoners. Even so the assaults of our spiritual foes are secretly prepared and suddenly delivered at moments when we are off our guard, and many a one falls a victim, at least for a while. The enemy goeth about indeed as a roaring lion, but the lion does not roar at the moment that he springs upon his prey, nor does Satan give any signal of his worst temptations.

III. THAT HE MADE SOME OF THEM PRISONERS, which seems to have been his object— perhaps that they might serve as hostages. Even so the enemy of souls desires to make prisoners who may not only be held in miserable bondage themselves, but may give him control and influence over their brethren.

IV. THAT ISRAEL DID NOT ATTEMPT TO MEET THE CANAANITES AS ORDINARY FOES, BUT VOWED TO TREAT THEM AS GOD'S ENEMIES, AND TO EXTERMINATE THEM ACCORDINGLY. Even so the right way and the only way to overcome the temptations and sins, the evil habits, passions, and tempers, which assail us (and often too successfully) on the way to heaven, is to regard them as God's enemies, as hateful to him, and to smite them accordingly without remorse, weariness, or thought of self. Many are vexed and annoyed with follies and tempers which get the better of them, and they contend against them on the ground of that vexation, wishing to get the mastery over them, and yet not caring to go to extremities against them. But the faithful soul will solemnly resolve, as before God and for *his* sake, to make an utter end at any cost of the sins which have prevailed against them, and so dishonoured him.

V. THAT GOD ACCEPTED THAT VOW AND GAVE THEM THE VICTORY OVER THE CANAANITES. Even so if we regard and face our spiritual enemies in the true light, as God's enemies, to be relentlessly exterminated, God will give us strength and power to have victory and to triumph over them, and it may be to set our captive brethren free also (2 Tim. ii. 26).

VI. THAT THE ISRAELITES PROCEEDED TO FULFIL THEIR VOW, although, as all the spoil was *anathema,* they had nothing to gain themselves but labour and loss of time. Even so will the good soldier of Christ not cease his most earnest efforts until he has quite destroyed (so far as may be in this life) the evil habits and evil tempers over which God has given him victory. The majority of Christian people are too lazy and selfish to do this; they will strive to overcome a known sin or bad habit; but when it has been (as they think) overcome they have not sufficient zeal to pursue it into its last lurking-places and exterminate it. As long as it does not actively trouble them they are content, and so the remnants remain to the dishonour of God and to their own future loss and danger. How few Christians radically get rid even of a single fault!

VII. THAT THE PLACE WAS CALLED HORMAH—ANATHEMA: a perpetual reminder that the enemies of God are under a ban, and should be exterminated; a sacred *delenda est Carthago.* Even so it is ever impressed upon the soldier of Christ that there can be no truce between him and sin, or even between him and selfish indifference. "If any man love not the Lord Jesus Christ, let him be anathema"—a Hormah, a thing devoted, a being with whom no compromise can be made and no amity knit until that indifference of his which is so hateful to God be abolished for ever.

EXPOSITION.

THE FIERY SERPENTS (vers. 4—9). Ver. 4.—**They journeyed from Mount Hor.** It appears from comparison of ch. xxxiii. 38 and ch. xx. 29 that their departure was not earlier than the beginning of the sixth month of the fortieth year. This season would be one of the hottest and most trying for marching. **By the way of the Red Sea,** *i. e.* down the Arabah, towards Ezion-geber, at the head of the Elanitic Gulf. Septuagint, ὁδὸν ἐπὶ θάλασσαν ἐρυθρᾶν. Not far from this place they would reach the end of the Edomitish territory, and turn eastwards and northwards up the Wady el Ithm towards the steppes of Moab. **Discouraged.** Literally, "shortened" or "straitened," as in Exod. vi. 9. Septuagint, ὠλιγοψύχησεν ὁ λαός. **Because of the way.** The Arabah is a stony, sandy, almost barren plain shut in by mountain walls on either side, and subject to sand-storms. It was not only, however, merely the heat and drought and ruggedness of the route which depressed them, but the fact that they were marching directly away from Canaan, and knew not how they were ever to reach it.

Ver. 5.—**There is no bread, neither is there any water.** The one of these statements was no doubt as much and as little true as the other. There was no ordinary supply of either; but as they had bread given to them from heaven, so they had water from the rock, otherwise they could not possibly have existed. **Our soul loatheth this light bread.** קָלֹקֵל, a stronger form than קָל, from

קָלַל. Septuagint, διακένῳ. They meant to say, as their fathers had (ch. xi. 6), that it was unsavoury and unsubstantial in comparison with the heavy and succulent diet of Egypt (see note on ch. xx. 3).

Ver. 6.—**Fiery serpents.** נְחָשִׁים שְׂרָפִים. *Nachash* is the ordinary word for serpent. The word *saraph,* which seems to mean "burning one," stands (by itself) for a serpent in ver. 8, and also in Isa. xiv. 29; xxx. 6. In Isa. vi. 2, 6 it stands for one of the symbolic beings (seraphim) of the prophet's vision. The only idea common to the two meanings (otherwise so distinct) must be that of brilliance and metallic lustre. It is commonly assumed that the "fiery" serpents were so called because of the burning pain and inflammation caused by the bite, after the analogy of the πρηστῆρες and καύσωνες of Dioscorus and Ælian. But is hardly possible that Isaiah should have used the same word in such wholly dissimilar senses, and it is clear from comparison with Ezekiel's vision of the cherubim (Ezek. i. 7) that the *saraph* of Isa. vi. 2 was so called from the burnished lustre of his appearance. Even our Lord himself is described in the Apocalypse as having in the highest degree this appearance of glowing brass (Rev. i. 15; ii. 18). It is further clear that the *saraph* was so named from his colour, not his venom, because when Moses was ordered to make a *saraph* he made a serpent of brass (or rather copper), with the evident intent of imitating as closely as possible the appearance of the venomous reptile. We may conclude then with some confidence that these serpents were of a fiery red colour, resembling in this respect certain very deadly snakes in Australia, which are known as "copper snakes." Travellers speak of some such pests as still abounding in the region of the Arabah, but it is quite uncertain whether the fiery serpents of that special visitation can be identified with any existing species.

Ver. 7.—**Pray unto the Lord.** This is the first and only (recorded) occasion on which the people directly asked for the intercession of Moses (cf., however, ch. xi. 2), although Pharaoh had done so several times, and never in vain.

Ver. 8.—**Make thee a fiery serpent.** A *saraph.* The Septuagint, not understanding the meaning of *saraph*, has simply ὄφιν (cf. John iii. 14). **Set it upon a pole.** נֵס. Septuagint, σήμειον. Vulgate, *signum*. The same word is better translated "ensign" in such passages as Isa. xi. 10; "banner" in

such as Ps. lx. 4; "standard" in such as Jer. li. 27. The "pole" may have been the tallest and most conspicuous of those military standards which were planted (probably on some elevation) as rallying points for the various camps; or it may have been one loftier still, made for the occasion.

Ver. 9.—**When he beheld the serpent** (נָחָשׁ in all three places of this verse) **of brass, he lived.** The record is brief and simple in the extreme, and tells nothing but the bare facts. The author of the Book of Wisdom understood the true bearing of those facts when he called the brazen serpent a σύμβολον σωτηρίας (ch. xvi. 6), and when he wrote ὁ ἐπιστραφεὶς οὐ διὰ τὸ θεωρούμενον (the thing he looked at) ἐσώζετο, ἀλλὰ διὰ σὲ τὸν πάντων σωτῆρα. At an earlier day Hezekiah had estimated the σύμβολον σωτηρίας at its true value, as being in itself worthless, and under certain circumstances mischievous (see on 2 Kings xviii. 4).

HOMILETICS.

Vers. 4—9.—*Sin and the Saviour.* The type of the brazen serpent lifted up in the wilderness is the only one which our Lord directly claims for himself as a type of his own crucifixion. No one can doubt that many other types, hardly less wonderful and instructive, exist; but this one will always have a certain pre-eminence of regard, because our Lord in his own words applied it to himself. Spiritually, therefore, we have in this passage Christ lifted up upon the cross in the likeness of sinful flesh in order to save from the deadly virus of sin and from eternal death all those who will raise the eye of faith to him. There is much else, but all subordinate to this. Taking the type as a whole, we may divide it under the four heads of discouragement, complaint, destruction, salvation.

I. THE DISCOURAGEMENT WHICH GAVE RISE TO COMPLAINING, AND SO LED TO THE RAVAGES OF SIN. Consider—1. *That the Israelites were discouraged, or straitened in soul, because of the way,* and this was the beginning of all that suffering and death. Even so are we often and often discouraged because of the way to heaven, the way of life by which it pleases God to lead us, and which seems so hard, so weary, so interminable, so unendurable at times. It is "because of the way" that all our distresses and discouragements arise. The "end" is well enough; who would not seek it? but the way is weary indeed! 2. *That this discouragement was not only because of the hardships of the road, although they were great, but especially because it did not seem to be leading them to Canaan at all*—rather away from it. Even so we are, many of us, discouraged grievously, not only because the way in which we walk is so hard and painful, and demands so much self-denial, but especially because we seem to make no progress in it; we do not feel that we are any nearer to the promised rest; the cross is as heavy as ever, but the crown does not show any more bright; rather we seem to be getting further and ever further from that repose of mind and soul to which we had looked forward. 3. *That their discouragement because of the way was aggravated by the fact that the evil was due to the unkindness of their brother Edom,* who forced them to march round by the Arabah. Even so very many of our discouragements and difficulties arise from the unkindness, the opposition, even the hostility in religious matters, of those who are most nearly related to or most closely connected with us. Often they seem to hold the passes through which lies our way to rest, and they deliberately block them against us.

II. THE COMPLAINING IN WHICH THEIR DISCOURAGEMENT FOUND VENT. Consider— 1. *That they complained of Moses and of God instead of reproaching themselves, as they should have done.* Even so when we are suffering, as we must expect sometimes to suffer, from religious depression and discouragement we are in great danger of murmuring against God and of complaining of our lot. If it were, as it ought to be,

> " our *chief* complaint
> That our love is weak and faint,"

we should soon cease to have cause to complain. 2. *That they spoke contemptuously of the manna.* Even so are we tempted at times of weariness to think slightingly and ungratefully of the spiritual food which God has provided for us, as though it not only palled upon us by reason of sameness, but failed to satisfy us by reason of its unsubstantial character. We demand something more coarse, more exciting.

III. THE DESTRUCTION IN WHICH THEIR SINFUL MURMURING INVOLVED THEM. Consider—1. *That fiery serpents came among them.* Even so it is when men lose heart and faith, and complain of their lot (*i. e.* of God's providence), and contemn their religious privileges, that they are especially in danger of falling a prey to deadly sins which war against the soul. A heart discouraged and an angry mind are Satan's grand opportunities, for they mean God alienated and his grace forfeited. 2. *That the serpents bit them, and their bite was fatal,* for much people died. Even so do sins—not mere sin in the abstract, but definite and particular sins—fasten upon unhappy souls and instil a poison into them which works death; for the life of the soul is union with God, and this union is broken up by the action of sin upon the soul, so that it *must* die if the poison be not cast out. And many do die, as we see.

IV. THE SALVATION WHICH GOD PROVIDED. Consider—1. *That the perishing people cried to Moses to pray for them,* for he was their mediator. Even so the cries of men yearning to be delivered from their sins, and from the death which follows sin, have always reached the Father through the intercession of the one Mediator, even though they knew him not. 2. *That a " saraph " was ordained to heal the deadly bites of the " seraphim."* Even so our Lord was made in the likeness of sinful flesh, —of that sinful flesh in which the deadly poison of sin existed,—and took that very form which in every other case was full of sin (Rom. viii. 3 ; 2 Cor. v. 21 ; 1 Pet. ii. 22—24). 3. *That Moses made the serpent of brass in order to resemble the fiery serpents in appearance.* Even so our Lord was so thoroughly human, and in the eyes of men so like to sinners, that he was freely suspected, loudly accused, and finally condemned as a sinner. 4. *That the brazen serpent, however much a saraph in form and colour, had no poison in it.* Even so our Lord, though truly and perfectly human, was without sin, neither was any guile found in his mouth. 5. *That the brazen serpent was lifted up upon a standard;* no doubt in order that all eyes might be drawn to the "symbol of salvation." Even so our Lord was lifted up upon the cross, which is an ensign unto the nations, the standard of the Lord's host, and the sign (*signum—σήμειον*) of the Son of man ; and he was lifted up to draw all men unto him by the startling character and persuasive attraction of that elevation. 6. *That whoever looked at the brazen serpent was healed of the bite of the serpent.* Even so every one that beholdeth Christ crucified with the eye of faith is healed of the deadly wound inflicted upon him by the old serpent, and "hath everlasting life." Moreover, as they died of the bite of some particular serpent, and were healed of *that* bite, so do we suffer from the effects of some particular sin or sins, and from these —their power and poison—we must be and may be healed. Christ is evidently set forth before us crucified that we may be saved from our besetting sin, whatever it may be ; and it is to that end that we must look to him. 7. *That everybody within sight of the standard might have been healed, but only those who looked were healed.* Even so there is in the cross of Christ healing full and free for all sinners to whom the knowledge of the cross may come, but as a fact only those are healed who fix upon the Saviour the gaze of faith. 8. *That it was not the " symbol of salvation," but the power and goodness of God acting through it, which saved the people.* Even so it is not anything formal or material in the sacrifice of Calvary, neither is it any definitions or dogmas about that sacrifice, but it is the saving grace of God in Christ and in him crucified, which delivers from the terror and virus of sin. Notice further—(1) *That it does not say that those who beheld the serpent were relieved of all pain and suffering from their bites, only that they "lived."* Even so those who are saved through faith in Christ crucified are not therefore saved from the sad and bitter consequences of their sins in this world, but the promise is they shall "not perish, but have everlasting life." (2) *That it does not say that the serpents were taken away,* as it does in the case of the plagues of Egypt. They may have continued to infest the camp as long as they travelled through that region, and the brazen serpent may have been daily lifted up. Even so the Divine remedy appointed for sin has not taken away sin out of the world. Sins will beset us still and war against our souls, and as long as we journey through this wilderness we shall need to look for healing to the cross (1 John i. 10; ii. 1).

HOMILIES BY VARIOUS AUTHORS.

Ver. 4.—*The discouragements of the way.* The circumstances of the Israelites suggest some of the discouragements of Christian pilgrims. These may arise from—

I. THE DIRECTION OF THE WAY. It led away from Canaan; it was apparently a retreat. Our circumstances may seem to be drawing us further and further from God and heaven; but if we are in God's way it must lead right at last. Illustrate from Exod. xiii. 17, 18, and cf. Ps. xxv. 4, 5, 10.

II. THE LENGTH OF THE WAY. It might have been shorter, through Edom instead of round it; but it would have been a way of war, on which God's blessing would not have rested. The length avoided loss. Our short cuts may be perilous; *e. g.* David (1 Sam. xxvii. 1), Jeroboam (1 Kings xii. 26—30).

III. THE ROUGHNESS OF THE WAY. Among rocky mountain defiles and treacherous foes. Portions of our pilgrimage are among the green pastures of peace; but others over hills of difficulty, intricate paths, and rugged mountain passes, and amidst powers of darkness that tempt us to despair. Illustrate Jeremiah in his trying and unpopular mission (Jer. xii. 5, 6; xv. 10—21).

IV. THE COMPANIONSHIPS OF THE WAY. Some of our comrades are complainers, and may infect us; others laggards, and tempt us to sloth; others apostates, who turn back and bring an evil report of the way beyond us (like Bunyan's Timorous and Mistrust). But God may be our companion to the end of the way (Ps. xlviii. 14; lxxiii. 24).

V. THE PROVISIONS OF THE WAY (ver. 5). This a discouragement of their own seeking, and most culpable. Applicable to those who are dissatisfied with the truth provided as spiritual food for the pilgrimage (its quality, or quantity, or the means of imparting it, as though God must be expected to satisfy every intellectual whim). Applicable also to those who distrust the providence and promises of God in regard to temporal supplies. Our only safe course is to "walk in" (Col. ii. 6) Christ, "the Way."—P.

Vers. 6—9.—*The brazen serpent as a type of Christ.* If this narrative was a bare record of facts, it would supply precious lessons respecting sin and salvation; but being one of the typical histories, applied by the Saviour to himself, it has in itself "no glory in this respect, by reason of the glory which excelleth." It was a type, not through the discernment of men, but by the preordination of God. Among the analogies the following may be suggested, from which such truths may be selected as will best further the object for which the subject is used in the pulpit. 1. The origin of the evil in the camp and in the world was the same sin. 2. The fiery serpents apt "ministers" (2 Cor. xi. 15) of "the old serpent," and so sufferings and death the natural work of Satan, who "was a murderer from the beginning," and who hath "the power of death" (Rom. vi. 23; Heb. ii. 14). 3. The devil could have no power to injure "except it were given him from above." "The Lord sent the serpents" (cf. Isa. xlv. 7; Amos iii. 6; 1 Cor. v. 5; 1 Tim. i. 20). 4. The helplessness of the sufferers the same. A new life needed in each case. But neither herbs, nor cordials, nor caustics, nor charms could expel the poison from the blood. And neither reformation, nor tears, nor services, nor ceremonies can avert the consequences of sin. 5. The remedy of Divine appointment. "*God* sent forth his Son" (Rom. viii. 32; Gal. iv. 4, 5; cf. Wisdom. xvi. 6, 7, 12). 6. In both cases a resemblance between the destroyer and the deliverer. The brazen serpent a deliverer in the likeness of the destroyer; Christ a Saviour in the likeness of the sinner (Rom. viii. 3). But the serpent was without venom, and Christ without sin. 7. Deliverance was provided not by words, but by deeds. The Son of man, like the serpent, lifted up. 8. In both cases a declaration of God's plan follows its appointment. Moses proclaimed to the camp the heaven-sent remedy, and "we preach Christ crucified." 9. An appropriation of God's offer required: "when he looketh," "whosoever believeth." Salvation limited to those who trust. 10. No obvious connection between the means and the result. The serpent and the cross "foolishness" to the scoffer. 11. Saving faith impossible without "godly sorrow working repentance" (cf. ver. 7; Acts xx. 21; 1 John i. 9). 12. The offer of salvation made to all, and the effect of faith alike in all. Cf. ver. 9 and the world-embracing "whosoever."—P.

Vers. 4, 5.—*A hard bit of the road.* "The soul of the people was much discouraged because of the way."

I. THE ACTUAL REASON FOR DISCOURAGEMENT. Discouragement and trouble of mind because of the difficulties of life is of course very common, but a great deal depends on where the difficulties come from. Here we are plainly told the discouragement arose *because of the way.* 1. *It appears to have been a bad bit of the road in itself.* None of the way over which the Israelites had travelled since they left Egypt could be called easy. They had begun with a strange experience, marching through the depths of the sea, and ever since they had wandered in the wilderness in a solitary way; they found no city to dwell in. For forty years they had been accustomed to wilderness life, but the district through which they were now passing is, by the description of travellers, desolate and repellent in an extraordinary degree. So the course of the Christian, all the way through, is subject to external difficulties and hardships, and the more faithful he is, the more these may abound, and at certain stages they may be so increased and intensified as to become well nigh intolerable. Discouraged by different things at different times, there may come a time to us, as to Israel, when we shall be especially discouraged *because of the way.* 2. *It came as a sort of rebuff after God had given them special encouragement.* For forty years they had been under chastisement, a doomed, dying, hopeless generation, but recently God had brought them back to Kadesh, and made the dry, forbidding rock to pour forth plenteously for the thirst of man and beast. Man is easily lifted up by anything that satisfies his senses, and gives him a visible support, and when it subsides he is correspondingly depressed. The desolate district through which the people passed probably looked all the worse because of the hopes which had been excited in them at Meribah. 3. *It was particularly vexatious because they had been turned out of a more direct way.* They were *compassing* the land of Edom, because brother Edom, of whom Israel expected kinder things, had closed the way *through* his land with a drawn sword. Even though the road had been pleasanter in itself, the very fact that it was circuitous was enough to cause some annoyance.

II. THIS ACTUAL REASON WAS NOT SUFFICIENT. It was natural enough, to some extent excusable, but not a reason worthy of the people of God. 1. *It pointed to purely external difficulties.* It was by no fault of Israel that it found itself in this cheerless and starving place. Canaan was not a land easy to get into, and the Israelites had been shut up to this road, difficult as it was. We dishonour God greatly when we are discouraged by difficulties rising entirely outside of ourselves. The less of help and comfort we can discern with the eyes of sense, the more we should discern those unfailing comforts and resources which come through a childlike dependence upon God. The Israelites wanted a Habakkuk among them to say, "Though the fig tree shall not blossom, neither shall fruit be in the vines; the labour of the olive shall fail, and the fields yield no meat; the flock shall be cut off from the fold, and there shall be no herd in the stalls: yet I will rejoice in the Lord, I will joy in the God of my salvation." 2. *There was a negligent and ungrateful omission to consider reasons for encouragement.* Even if the way was hard, it was a mercy there was a way at all. The way through Edom, direct and easy as it looked, might have proved both tedious and perilous in the end. God knows the way of the righteous, even when the righteous himself scarcely knows it. Bad as the way was, it is called the way of the Red Sea, and the very sight of those memorable waters should have brought to mind, and kept in mind, an unparalleled instance of God's guiding and delivering power. 3. *The discouragement because of the way prevented other and weightier reasons for discouragement from being felt.* The state of the heart within should have caused far more depression and anxiety than the state of the world without. We know the people themselves were in a bad state of heart, for the words of murmuring prove it. Whatever hopes the gushing waters of Meribah had raised were carnal, and found no sympathy with God. There are two states of heart on which we may be sure he looks with approval. (1) When his people, in spite of the way, surrounded by poverty, sickness, and all the circumstances of a cold, unsympathetic world, are nevertheless courageous, trustful, grateful, cheerful. (2) When his people, with everything in their circumstances pleasant and attractive, are nevertheless utterly cast down because of the proofs they daily get of the power of inbred sin. To trust *God*, in spite of the badness of the way, and to distrust and abhor *self*, in spite of the comforts of the way—be it our care to attain and preserve these states of mind as long as they are needed.

Robert Hall has a sermon on ver. 4.—Y.

Vers. 6—9.—*Destruction and salvation through the serpent.* Each time the people break into open sin there is something new in the treatment of them. Now God gives the fruition of their desires ; they are surfeited with quails, and perish with the delicate morsels in their mouths (ch. xi.). Again he makes as if at one sudden, comprehensive blow he would sweep away the whole nation (ch. xiv. 12). Yet again we read of the fifteen thousand who perished in different ways at the gainsaying of Korah (ch. xvi.). Then there is a complete change of treatment, and though the people murmured bitterly at Meribah, God is gracious to *them*, and visits *Moses* and *Aaron* in wrath. Thus we advance to consider this present outbreak of sin, which is treated in a novel and very peculiar way, and one very profitable indeed to consider.

I. DESTRUCTION THROUGH THE SERPENT. 1. It was *through* the serpent. *The Lord* sent the fiery serpents. It is said that the district abounds in serpents which would be well described by the word *fiery*. But the Israelites were not allowed to consider the serpents as one of the perils of the district, into which they had fallen by some kind of chance. *The Lord sent the serpents.* Because the people ceased to trust in him, he delivered them to one of the dangers of the way (Deut. xxxii. 24 ; Job xxvi. 13 ; Jer. viii. 17 ; Amos ix. 3). 2. *The serpent rather than another mode of destruction was chosen.* God in his wrath does not take the first weapon that comes to hand. If destruction, simply and only destruction, had been in view, doubtless there were other deadly creatures in the wilderness which might have served the purpose. But it is not enough for the people to die ; the *way* in which they die is also significant. Their thoughts are turned back to the very beginning and fountain of human troubles, to Eden before it was lost, and to the serpent who led our first parents into the ways of sin and death. As the serpent had to do with bringing sin into the world, so he is shown as having to do with the punishment of it. 3. *The destruction is represented as being in many cases complete.* " Much people of Israel died." Probably some of the few aged still surviving and doomed to die in the wilderness (ch. xiv. 29) perished thus, confirmed in their rebellious spirit beyond remedy. Many of those bitten by a serpent toss awhile in pain, looking vaguely for a remedy, but, being ignorant of the original cause of their suffering, and not understanding that *God* has sent the serpent, they do not find the remedy, and then they die. 4. *But in other cases the destruction is incomplete.* The bite of the serpent, with its effects, sets before us that gnawing consciousness of misery which comes to so many, and which no art of man can conjure away. *Why were some bitten and others not ?* He who can answer that question can answer another— why some can go through life light-hearted, never having the weight of a wasted life on their consciences, never made miserable by anything save physical pain or disappointed selfishness, and happy at once if the pain and disappointment cease ;

while others so soon have the serpent poisoning their consciousness and filling them
with a deep sense of the failure, sadness, and misery of natural human life.   There
are some who seem to have triple armour against the serpent-bite.   Of the bitten
ones, many had been no worse in their unbelief than some who remained unbitten.
It is part of the mystery of life that it is not the worst man who is obviously in all
cases the suffering one.   Then of those who were bitten, *some went on to death,
others sought if there might be some means of deliverance.*   Many would give themselves up to fatalism and despair.   Many do so still.   The question for the miserable
in conscience is, " Will you go on allowing the misery of the serpent-bite to eat out
all that is salvable in you, or will you do as some of Israel wisely and promptly did
in their sore distress, namely, turn to God ?   Only he who sent the serpents can take
the venom of their bite away.

II. SALVATION THROUGH THE SERPENT.   1. *The cry for salvation contained in
ver.* 7.   There is a show of repentance here, but *we must not make too much of it.*
The people had talked in the same humble fashion before, saying they had sinned,
yet soon showing that they did not understand what sin was (ch. xiv. 40) ; though
perhaps the expression in ver. 5 should be particularly noted—" the people spake
against God."   Hitherto their wrath had been vented on the visible Moses and Aaron.
It is something that even in their murmurings they at last seem distinctly to recognise God as having a hand in the disposition of their course.   And so now they put
in the confession, " We have spoken against the Lord."   This may have had more
to do with the peculiar way in which God treated them than at first appears.
Whether their repentance is good for anything will be seen if they bring forth such
fruit of repentance as they will presently have the opportunity of manifesting.   Note
also *the connection of the healing with the request of the people.*   If they had gone on
in silent endurance they might all in course of time have died.   Their confession of
sin told the truth, whether they felt all that truth or not.   The serpent-bite was
connected *with their sin.*   Observe also their approach to God *through a mediator,*
one whose services they had often proved, yet often slighted, in the past.   They come
to Moses for a greater service than they have yet any conception of.   Thus we are
encouraged to make Jesus the Mediator of spiritual salvation and blessing, by considering how often, while upon earth, he was the Mediator of salvation and blessing
in earthly things.   The God who is infinite in power and unfailing in love, and who
gave through Jesus the *lesser blessings to some,* waits also to give through Jesus the
greater blessings to all.   2. As the destruction was *through* the serpent, so the
salvation also.   *God* sent the fiery serpents, and also the serpent of brass.   There
was nothing in it to save if Moses had made it as Aaron made the golden calf.   It
had not the efficacy of some natural balm.   A bit of brass it was to begin with, and
to a bit of brass in the course of ages it returned (2 Kings xviii. 4).   So Jesus
expressly tells us that in all his gradual approach to the cross he was carrying out
his Father's will.   All the process by which he was prepared to be lifted up was a
process appointed by the Father.   It was his meat and drink, that which really and
truly sustained him, and entered as it were into his very existence, to do his Father's
will and finish his work.   When the brazen serpent was finished, fixed and lifted on
the pole, this act found its antitype in that hour when Jesus said, " It is finished."
All was finished then according to the pattern which God himself had indicated in
the wilderness.   3. As destruction was through *a serpent,* salvation also was through
a serpent.   " He was made sin for us who knew no sin."   Jesus was lifted on the
cross amid the execration and contempt of well-nigh all Jerusalem.   In its esteem
he was worse than Barabbas.   To judge by the way the people spoke and acted, the
consummation of all villanies was gathered up in him.   It was a great insult, and so
considered in the first days of the gospel, to proclaim him of all persons as Saviour
of men.   And so when Moses lifted up the brazen serpent it may have been received
indignantly by some.   " Do you wish to mock us with the sight of our tormentor ? "
When we look at Jesus in his saving relation to us, we are brought closer than ever
to our own sins, and indeed to the sin of the whole world.   We see him, the sinless
One, under a curse, as having died on the tree, manifestly under a curse, groaning
forth as the Father's face passes into the shade, " My God, my God, why hast thou
forsaken me ? "   Forsaken of God, the holy One, forsaken of unfaithful and terror-

stricken servants, hated by the world, we may well say that the semblance of the serpent sets him forth. 4. And yet it was *the semblance* only. By the way men treated him, he appeared to be judged as a destroyer and deceiver, but we know that in himself he was harmless. 5. *There is the prominence of the saving object.* The serpent was set upon a pole. We may suppose that it was as central and prominent an object as the tabernacle itself. It was to be placed where all could see, for there were many in the camp, and the bitten ones were everywhere around. And what Moses did for the brazen serpent, God himself, in the marvellous arrangements of the gospel, has done for *the crucified Jesus.* It is not apostles, evangelists, theologians who have pushed forward the doctrine of the cross; Jesus himself put it in the forefront in that very discourse which contains the deepest things of God concerning our salvation (John iii. 14). No one saw him rise from the dead; thousands saw him, or had the opportunity of seeing him, on the cross. We can no more keep the cross in obscurity than we can keep the sun from rising. 6. *The pure element of faith is brought in.* Contrast the mode of God's treatment here with that employed when Aaron with his smoking censer stood between the living and the dead (ch. xvi. 47). On that occasion nothing was asked from the people. Aaron with his censer was the means of sparing even the unconscious. The mercy then was the mercy of *sparing;* now through the serpent it is the mercy of *saving.* The serpent was of no use to those who did not look. A man may long be spared in unbelief, but in unbelief he cannot possibly be saved. It is a great advance from sparing to saving. Thus the faith required was put in sharp contrast with past unbelief, which had been so sadly conspicuous and ruinous, gaining its last triumph a little while before in the fall of Moses and Aaron (ch. xx. 12). The people were shut up to pure faith. If once in their great pain and peril they began to doubt how a brazen image of a serpent should save, then they were lost. If there had been anything in the image itself to save, there would have been no room for faith to work. If one serpent-bitten person had been healed without looking, that would have proved faith no necessity. But only those who looked were healed; all who looked were healed; and those who refused to look perished. Thus Jesus early began inviting a needy world to look to him with a spirit full of faith and expectation, and the more he seemed to a critical world incapable and presumptuous, the more he asked for faith. "After that, in the wisdom of God, the world by wisdom knew not God, it pleased God by the foolishness of preaching to save them that believe" (1 Cor. i. 21). 7. *The salvation depends on the disposition of the person to be saved.* Man fell with his eyes open and in spite of a solemn commandment and warning. And every man must be saved with his eyes open, turning himself intelligently, wholly, and grate-fully towards the Saviour. There is everything to help the sinner if he will only turn. Some there might be in Israel who seemed too far gone even to turn their eyes, but doubtless God recognised the genuine turning of the heart. Though the eyes of sense beheld not the serpent, the eyes of the heart beheld, and this was enough for healing. It was very helpful to be assured that there was one mode of healing, and only one, for only one was needed. It is only while we are cleaving to our sins that we find distraction and perplexity. There was distraction, anxiety, and fear in abundance as long as the Israelite lived in momentary terror of the fatal bite; but with the lifted serpent there came not only healing, but composure. God in sending his Son has not distracted us by a complication of possible modes of salvation.—Y.

EXPOSITION.

THE END OF JOURNEYS, THE BEGINNING OF VICTORIES (ver. 10—ch. xxii. 1). Ver. 10.—**The children of Israel set forward, and pitched in Oboth.** In the list of ch. xxxiii. there occur two other stations, Zalmonah and Phunon, between Mount Hor and Oboth. Phunon may be the Pinon of Gen. xxxvi. 41, but it is a mere conjecture.

All we can conclude with any certainty is that the Israelites passed round the southern end of the mountains of Edom by the Wady el Ithm, and then marched north-wards along the eastern border of Edom by the route now followed between Mekka and Damascus. On this side the mountains are far less precipitous and defensible than on the other, and this circumstance must have abated the insolence of the Edomites. Moreover, they must now have seen enough of Israel to know that, while immensely formidable in number and discipline, he had no hostile designs against them. It is therefore not surprising to find from Deut. ii. 6 that on this side the mountaineers supplied Israel with bread and water, just as they supply the pilgrim caravans at the present day. That they exacted payment for what they supplied was perfectly reasonable : no one could expect a poor people to feed a nation of two million souls, however nearly related, for nothing. Oboth has been identified with the modern halting-place of el-Ahsa, on the pilgrim route above mentioned, on the ground of supposed similarity in the meaning of the names ; but the true rendering of Oboth is doubtful (see on Levit. xix. 31), and, apart from that, any such similarity of meaning is too vague and slight a ground for any argument to be built upon.

Ver. 11.—**And pitched at Ije-abarim**. Ije (עִיֵּי), or Ijm (עִיִּים), as it is called in ch. xxxiii. 45, signifies "heaps" or "ruins." Abarim is a word of somewhat doubtful meaning, best rendered "ridges" or "ranges." It was apparently applied to the whole of Peræa in later times (cf. Jer. xxii. 20, "passages"), but in the Pentateuch is confined elsewhere to the ranges facing Jericho. These "ruinous heaps of the ranges" lay to the east of Moab, along the desert side of which Israel was now marching, still going northwards : they cannot be identified.

Ver. 12.—**Pitched in the valley of Zared**. Rather, "in the brook of Zered." בְּנַחַל זָרֶד. Perhaps the upper part of the Wady Kerek, which flows westwards into the Salt Sea (see on Deut. ii. 13).

Ver. 13.—**Pitched on the other side of Arnon**. The Arnon was without doubt the stream or torrent now known as the Wady Môjeb, which breaks its way down to the Salt Sea through a precipitous ravine. It must have been in the upper part of its course, in the desert uplands, that the Israelites crossed it ; and this both because the passage lower down is extremely difficult, and also because they were keeping well to the eastward of Moabitish territory up to this point. It is not certain which side of the stream is intended by "the other side," because the force of these expressions depends as often upon the point of view of the writer as of the reader. It would appear from Deut. ii. 26 that Israel remained at this spot until the embassage to Sihon had returned. **That cometh out of the coasts of the Amorites**, *i. e.* the Arnon, or perhaps one of its confluents which comes down from the northeast. **For Arnon is the border of Moab**. It

was at that time the boundary (see on ver. 26).

Ver. 14. — **Wherefore**, *i. e.* because the Amorites had wrested from Moab all to the north of Arnon. **In the book of the wars of the Lord**. Nothing is known of this book but what appears here. If it should seem strange that a book of this description should be already in existence, we must remember that amongst the multitude of Israel there must in the nature of things have been some "poets" in the then acceptation of the word. Some songs there must have been, and those songs would be mainly inspired by the excitement and triumph of the final marches. The first flush of a new national life achieving its first victories over the national foe always finds expression in songs and odes. It is abundantly evident from the foregoing narrative that writing of some sort was in common use at least among the leaders of Israel (see on ch. xi. 26), and they would not have thought it beneath them to collect these spontaneous effusions of a nation just awaking to the poetry of its own existence. The archaic character of the fragments preserved in this chapter, which makes them sound so foreign to our ears, is a strong testimony to their genuineness. It is hardly credible that any one of a later generation should have cared either to compose or to quote snatches of song which, like dried flowers, have lost everything but scientific value in being detached from the soil which gave them birth. **What he did in the Red Sea, and in the brooks of Arnon**. Rather, "Vaheb in whirlwind, and the brooks of Arnon." The strophe as cited here has neither nominative nor verb, and the sense can only be conjecturally restored. וָהֵב is almost certainly a proper name, although of an unknown place. בְּסוּפָה is also considered by many as the name of a locality "in Suphah ;" it occurs, however, in Nahum i. 3 in the sense given above, and indeed it is not at all a rare word in Job, Proverbs, and the Prophets ; it seems best, therefore, to give it the same meaning here.

Ver. 15.—**And at the stream of the brooks**. Rather, "and the pouring (וְאֶשֶׁד) of the brooks," *i. e.* the slope of the watershed. **Ar**. עָר is an archaic form of עִיר, a city. The same place is called Ar Moab in ver. 28. It was situate on the Arnon somewhat lower down than where the Israelites crossed its "brooks." The peculiarity of the site, "in the midst of the river" (Josh. xiii. 9, cf. Deut. ii. 36), and extensive ruins, have enabled travellers to identify the spot on which it stood at the junction of the Môjeb (Arnon) and Lejum (Nahaliel, ver. 19). It is uncertain whether the Greeks gave the name of Areopolis, as Jerome asserts, to Ar, but in later times it was Rabbah, a town many miles further south in the heart of Moab which bore this name. Ar was at this period the boundary town of Moab, and as such was respected by the Israelites (Deut. ii. 9, 29).

Ver. 16.—**And from thence . . . to Beer.** A well ; so named, no doubt, from the circumstance here recorded. That they were told to dig for water instead of receiving it from the rock showed the end to be at hand, and the transition shortly to be made from miraculous to natural supplies.

Ver. 17.—**Then Israel sang this song.** This song of the well may be taken from the same collection of odes, but more probably is quoted from memory. It is remarkable for the spirit of joyousness which breathes in it, so different from the complaining, desponding tone of the past.

Ver. 18.—**By the direction of the lawgiver.** בְּמִחֹקֵק. Literally, "by the lawgiver," or, as some prefer, "with the sceptre." The meaning of *michokek* is disputed (see on Gen. xlix. 10), but in either case the meaning must be practically as in the A. V. It speaks of the alacrity with which the leaders of Israel, Moses himself amongst them, began the work even with the insignia of their office. **And from the wilderness . . . to Mattanah.** Beer was still in the desert country eastward of the cultivated belt : from thence they crossed, still on the north of Arnon, and probably leaving it somewhat to the south, into a more settled country.

Ver. 19.—**And from Mattanah to Nahaliel.** The latter name, which means "the brook of God," seems to be still retained by the Encheileh, one of the northern affluents of the Wady Môjeb. **From Nahaliel to Bamoth.** Bamoth simply means "heights" or "high places," and was therefore a frequent name. This Bamoth may be the same as the Bamoth-Baal of ch. xxii. 41; Josh. xiii. 17, but it is uncertain. A Beth-Bamoth is mentioned on the Moabite stone.

Ver. 20.—**And from Bamoth in the valley, that is in the country of Moab, to the top of Pisgah.** The original runs simply thus : "And from Bamoth—the valley which in the field—Moab—the top—Pisgah." It may therefore be read, "And from the heights to the valley that is in the field of Moab, viz., the top of Pisgah." The "field" of Moab (Septuagint, ἐν τῷ πεδίῳ) was no doubt the open, treeless expanse north of Arnon, drained by the Wady Waleh, which had formerly belonged to Moab. Pisgah ("the ridge") was a part of the Abarim ranges west of Heshbon, from the summit of which the first view is gained of the valley of Jordan and the hills of Palestine (cf. ch. xxxiii. 47; Deut. iii. 27 ; xxxiv. 1). **Which**

looketh toward Jeshimon. Jeshimon, or "the waste," seems to mean here that desert plain on the north-east side of the Salt Sea now called the Ghor el Belka, which included in its barren desolation the southernmost portion of the Jordan valley.

Ver. 21. —**And Israel sent messengers unto Sihon.** The narrative here returns to the point of time when the Israelites first reached the Upper Arnon, the boundary stream of the kingdom of Sihon (see on ver. 13, and cf. Deut. ii. 24—37). The list of stations in the preceding verses may probably have been copied out of some official record ; it may be considered as marking the movements of the tabernacle with Eleazar and the Levites and the mass of the non-combatant population. In the mean time the armies of Israel were engaged in victorious enterprises which took them far afield. **King of the Amorites.** The Amorites were not akin to the Hebrews, as the Edomites, Moabites, and Ammonites were, who all claimed descent from Terah. They were of the Canaanitish stock (Gen. **x.** 16), and indeed the name Amorite often appears as synonymous with Canaanite in its larger sense (Deut. i. 7, 19, 27, &c.). If at one time they are mentioned side by side with five or six other tribes of the same stock (Exod. xxxiv. 11), yet at another they seem to be so much the representative race that "the Amorite" stands for the inhabitants of Canaan in general whom Israel was commissioned to oust on account of his iniquity (Gen. xv. 16). It is not, therefore, possible to draw any certain distinction between the Amorites of Sihon's kingdom and the mass of the Canaanites on the other side Jordan. Both Sihon and his people appear as intruders in this region, having come down perhaps from the northern parts of Palestine, and having but recently (it would seem) wrested from the king of Moab all his territory north of Arnon. It was the fact of the Amorites being found here which led to the conquest and settlement of the trans-Jordanic territory. That territory was not apparently included in the original gift (compare ch. xxxiv. 2—12 with Gen. **x.** 19 and xv. 19—21), but since the Amorite had possessed himself of it, it must pass with all the rest of his habitation to the chosen people.

Ver. 22.—**Let me pass through thy land.** Cf. ch. xx. 17. Israel was not commanded to spare the Amorites, indeed he was under orders to smite them (Deut. ii. 24), but that did not prevent his approaching them in the first instance with words of peace. If Sihon had hearkened, no doubt Israel would have passed directly on to Jordan, and he would at least have been spared for the present.

Ver. 23. —**And he came to Jahaz, or** Jahzah, a place of which we know nothing.

Ver. 24.—**And Israel smote him with the edge of the sword.** This was the first time that generation had seen war, if we except the uncertain episode of the king of Arad, and they could have had no weapons but such as their fathers had brought out of Egypt. It was, therefore, a critical moment in their history when they met the forces of Sihon, confident from their recent victory over Moab. We may suppose that Joshua was their military leader now, as before and after. **From Arnon unto Jabbok.** The Jabbok, which formed the boundary of Sihon on the north towards the kingdom of Og, and on the east towards the Ammonites, is the modern Zerka: it runs in a large curve northeast, north-west, and west, until it falls into Jordan, forty-five miles north of the mouth of the Arnon. **Even unto the children of Ammon: for the border of the children of Ammon was strong.** This is perhaps intended to explain rather why the Amorites had not extended their conquests any further than why the Israelites made no attempt to cross the border of Ammon; they had another and more sufficient reason (see Deut. ii. 19). Rabbah of Ammon, which stood upon the right (here the eastern) bank of the Upper Jabbok, was an extremely strong place which effectually protected the country behind it, even until the reign of David (see on 2 Sam. xi., xii.).

Ver. 25.—**And Israel dwelt in all the cities of the Amorites.** The territory overrun at this time was about fifty miles north and south, by nearly thirty east and west. It was not permanently occupied until a somewhat later period (ch. xxxii. 33); but we may suppose that the flocks and herds, with sufficient forces to guard them, spread themselves at once over the broad pasture lands. **Heshbon, and all the villages thereof.** Literally, "the daughters thereof." By a similar figure we speak of a "mother city." Heshbon occupied a central position in the kingdom of Sihon, half way between Arnon and Jabbok, and about eighteen miles eastward of the point where Jordan falls into the Salt Lake; it stood on a table-land nearly 3000 feet above the sea, and had been made his city (*i. e.* his capital) by Sihon at the time of his victories over Moab.

Ver. 26.—**All his land.** This is qualified by what follows: "even unto Arnon" (cf. Judges xi. 13—19).

Ver. 27.—**They that speak in proverbs.** הַמֹּשְׁלִים. Septuagint, *οἱ αἰνιγματισταί.* A class of persons well marked among the Hebrews, as perhaps in all ancient countries. It was their gift, and almost their profession, to express in the sententious, antistrophic poetry of the age such thoughts or such facts as took hold of men's minds. At a time when there was little difference between poetry and rhetoric, and when the distinction was hardly drawn between the inventive faculty of man and the Divine afflatus, it is not surprising to find the word *mashal* applied to the rhapsody of Balaam (ch. xxiii. 7), to the "taunting song" of Isaiah (xiv. 4), to the "riddle" of Ezekiel (xvii. 2), as well as to the collection of earthly and heavenly wisdom in the Book of Proverbs. That which follows is a taunting song, most like to the one cited from Isaiah, the archaic character of which is marked by its strongly antithetic form and abrupt transitions, as well as by the peculiarity of some of the words. **Come to Heshbon.** This may be ironically addressed to the Amorites, lately so victorious, now so overthrown; or, possibly, it may be intended to express the jubilation of the Amorites themselves in the day of their pride.

Ver. 28.—**There is a fire gone out of Heshbon.** This must refer to the war-fire which the Amorites kindled from Heshbon when they made it the capital of the new kingdom. Ar Moab and the (northern) heights of Arnon were the furthest points to which their victory extended.

Ver. 29.—**O people of Chemosh.** עַם־כְּמוֹשׁ. Chemosh was the national god of the Moabites (1 Kings xi. 7; Jer. xlviii. 7), and also to some extent of the Ammonites (Judges xi. 24). It is generally agreed that the name is derived from the root כבש, to subdue, and thus will have substantially the same meaning as Milcom, Molech, and Baal; indeed it appears probable that there was a strong family likeness among the idolatries of Palestine, and that the various names represented different attributes of one supreme being rather than different divinities. Thus Baal and Ashtaroth (Judg. ii. 13) represented for the Zidonians the masculine and feminine elements respectively in the Divine energy. Baal himself was plural (Baalim, 1 Kings xviii. 18) in form, and either male or female (ἡ βάαλ in Hosea ii. 8; Rom. xi. 4). In the inscription on the Moabite stone a god "Ashtar-Chemosh" is mentioned, and thus Chemosh is identified with the male deity of Phœnicia (Ashtar being the masculine form of Ashtoreth), while, on the other hand, it was almost certainly the same divinity who was worshipped under another name, and with other rites, as Baal-Peor (see on ch. xxv. 3). On the coins of Areopolis Chemosh appears as a god of war armed, with fire-torches by his side. Human sacrifices were offered to him (2 Kings iii. 26, 27), as to Baal and to Moloch. **He hath given his sons,** *i. e.* Chemosh, who could not save his own votaries, nor the children of his people.

Ver. 30.—**We have shot at them.** וַנִּירָם.
A poetical word of somewhat doubtful meaning. It is generally supposed to be a verbal form (first person plural imperf. Kal), from
יָרָה, with an unusual suffix (cf. יִלְבָּשָׁם for
וִלְבָּשָׁם in Exod. xxix. 30). יָרָה has the primary meaning "to shoot at," the secondary, "to overthrow," as in Exod. xv. 4. Others, however, derive the word from ארה, a root supposed to mean "burn." **Even unto Dibon.** See on ch. xxxii. 34. The site of Nophah, perhaps the Nobah of Judges viii. 11, is unknown. **Which reacheth unto Medeba.** The reading is uncertain here as well as the meaning. The received text has
אֲשֶׁר עַד־מֵידְבָא, which gives no meaning, but the circle over the *resh* marks it as suspicious. The Septuagint (πῦρ ἐπὶ Mωάβ) and the Samaritan evidently read אֵשׁ, and this has been generally followed: "we have wasted even unto Nophah,—with fire unto Medeba." Medeba, of which the ruins are still known by the same name, lay five or six miles south-south-east of Heshbon. It was a fortress in the time of David (1 Chron. xix. 7) and of Omri, as appears from the Moabite stone.

Ver. 32.—**Jaazer.** Perhaps the present es-Szîr, some way to the north of Heshbon (see on Jer. xlviii. 32). This victory completed the conquest of Sihon's kingdom.

Ver. 33.—**They turned and went up by the way of Bashan.** The brevity of the narrative does not allow us to know who went upon this expedition, or why they went. It may have been only the detachment which had reconnoitred and taken Jaazer, and they may have found themselves threatened by the forces of Og, and so led on to further conquests beyond the Jabbok. **Og the king of Bashan.** Og was himself of the aboriginal giant race which had left so many remnants, or at least so many memories, in these regions (see on Deut. ii. 10—12, 20—23 ; Josh. xii. 4 ; xiii. 12) ; but he is classed with Sihon as a king of the Amorites (Josh. ii. 10) because his people were chiefly at least of that race. Bashan itself comprised the plain now known as Jaulan and Haulan beyond the Jarmuk (now Mandhur), the largest affluent of the Jordan, which joins it

a few miles below the lake of Tiberias. The kingdom of Og, however, extended over the northern and larger part of Gilead, a much more fertile territory than Bashan proper (see on Deut. iii. 1—17). **At Edrei.** Probably the modern Edhra'ah, or Der'a, situate on a branch of the Jarmuk, some twenty-four miles from Bozrah. The ancient city lies buried beneath the modern village, and was built, like the other cities of Bashan, in the most massive style of architecture. The cities of Og were so strong that the Israelites could not have dispossessed him by any might of their own if he had abode behind his walls. Either confidence in his warlike prowess or some more mysterious cause (see on Josh. xxiv. 12) impelled him to leave his fortifications, and give battle to the Israelites to his own utter defeat.

Ver. 34.—**Fear him not.** He might well have been formidable, not only on account of his size (cf. Deut. i. 28 ; iii. 11 ; 1 Sam. xvii. 11), but from the formidable nature of those walled cities which are still a wonder to all that see them.

Ver. 35.—**So they smote him.** Acting under the direct commands of God, they exterminated the Amorites of the northern as they had of the southern kingdom.

Ch. xxii. 1.—**And the children of Israel set forward.** Not necessarily after the defeats of Sihon and Og ; it is quite as likely that this last journey was made while the armies were away on their northern conquests. **And pitched in the plains of Moab.** The Arboth Moab, or steppes of Moab, were those portions of the Jordan valley which had belonged to Moab perhaps as far north as the Jabbok. In this sultry depression, below the level of the sea, there are tracts of fertile and well-watered land amidst prevailing barrenness (see on ch. xxxiii. 49). **On this side Jordan by Jericho.** Rather, "beyond the Jordan of Jericho," לְיַרְדֵּן יְרֵחוֹ
מֵעֵבֶר. On the phrase, "beyond the Jordan" ("Peræa"), which is used indifferently of both sides, the one by a conventional, the other by a natural, use, see on Deut. i. 1. The Jordan of Jericho is the river in that part of its course where it flows past the district of Jericho.

HOMILETICS.

Ver. 10—ch. xxii. 1.—*Progress and triumph.* In this passage, which has a very distinctive character, we have, spiritually, the rapid progress of the soul towards rest, and the first great triumphs given to it over its spiritual foes, after that, by the power of the cross through faith in him that was lifted up, the soul has been delivered from the deadly venom of the sins which did beset it. There is a time when the soul hangs between death and life ; there is a time when, this crisis past, it speeds onward with unexpected ease and **victory** towards its goal in the full assurance (πληροφορία, as under full sail) of faith. Consider, therefore, with respect to *these last journeys*—

I. THAT AFTER THE LIFTING UP OF THE BRAZEN SERPENT THE PROGRESS OF ISRAEL WAS SURPRISINGLY RAPID AND UNINTERRUPTED; most markedly so if compared with the tedious turnings and returnings of the time before. This journey from Mount Hor to Pisgah occupied at most five months, as compared with the thirty-nine and a half years wasted theretofore. Even so it is with the progress of the soul towards the heavenly rest. Until Christ has been lifted up, and the poison of sin overcome through the steadfast gaze of faith in him, there can be no real progress, only a drifting to and fro in the wilderness. But after that, no matter how difficult the road, or how many the foes, the soul goes forward swift and unhindered to the haven where it would be.

II. THAT AFTER THE BRAZEN SERPENT WE HEAR OF NO MORE COMPLAININGS OR REBELLIONS, BUT, ON THE CONTRARY, WE CATCH THE ECHOES OF A GLAD ALACRITY AND OF A CHEERFUL COURAGE. Even so the soul that has not mastered the lesson nor known the healing of the cross is always unhappy, sure to complain, and ready to despair; but when this is past it is of another spirit, joyful through hope, patient through faith, obedient through love.

III. THAT AS THE JOURNEY DREW TO AN END ISRAEL WAS ENCOURAGED TO USE HIS OWN EFFORTS TO SUPPLY HIS NEEDS. He bought bread and water of the Edomites, and dug for water at Beer, and probably helped himself to some extent to the provisions of the conquered Amorites. Even so the soul which is trained by grace for glory is encouraged more and more to co-operate with grace and to "work out its own salvation" not because it can do without supernatural grace, but because God is pleased to give his grace according to its efforts.

IV. THAT THE FIRST SONG OF ISRAEL AFTER THE TRIUMPH OF THE EXODUS, FORTY YEARS BEFORE, WAS OVER THE DIGGING OF A WELL, by which God was to give them water. Even so our work of faith, and that labour which looks for blessing from God, is the only condition of gladness and of spiritual songs. And note that this labour was shared by all, the very nobles beginning the work with their staves of office. Thus it is labour in a good cause which unites us all, and it is the union of all that promotes a glad alacrity.

Consider again, with respect to *these first victories*—

I. THAT THE CONQUESTS BEYOND JORDAN WERE NOT PART, SO TO SPEAK, OF GOD'S ORIGINAL PLAN FOR ISRAEL. If Moab had been still in possession to the south of Jabbok, and Ammon to the north, then Israel would have passed straight through and over Jordan; it was the fact of Sihon having extruded the Moabites which led to these conquests of Israel. Even so it is often the case that the triumphs of Christian principle and Christian faith are forced upon us, as it were, by the action, and the evil action, of others, under the providence of God. The soul that would pass quietly on its way to heaven is driven to victories of faith great and lasting by the unexpected obstacles in its way.

II. THAT EVEN SIHON WAS APPROACHED WITH WORDS OF PEACE, IF HE WOULD HAVE HAD PEACE. Even so it becomes us to live peaceably with all men, even with the profane and accursed, if it be possible. He that forces on a conflict with evil men or evil passion, even if that conflict be indeed inevitable, may thereby forfeit the grace of God. Courtesy and forbearance before the encounter are the best pledges for courage and success in the encounter.

III. THAT SIHON, ALTHOUGH CONQUEROR OF MOAB, AND MUCH MORE FORMIDABLE THAN THE CANAANITES WHOM ISRAEL HAD FEARED AT KADESH, FELL EASILY BECAUSE ISRAEL FOUGHT IN FAITH. There is no adversary that can really offer any effectual opposition to our onward march if assailed in the strength of Christ with a cheerful courage.

IV. THAT OG THE KING OF BASHAN WAS MUCH MORE FORMIDABLE EVEN THAN SIHON, YET HE SEEMS TO HAVE FALLEN YET MORE EASILY, judging from the brief notice of the conquest. Even so when once we have overcome a difficulty or conquered an evil habit in the strength of faith, other conquests open out before us readily and naturally which we should not have dared to contemplate before. It is most true in religion that "nothing succeeds like success."

V. THAT THE EASY OVERTHROW OF SIHON AND OG WAS PROVIDENTIALLY ORDERED BY GOD FOR THE PURPOSE OF ENCOURAGING AND ANIMATING ISRAEL FOR THE GREAT WORK OF CONQUEST IN CANAAN PROPER (see Ps. cxxxvi. 17—22). Even so to the faithful soul that fears the great strife against sin, God is often pleased to give some anticipatory victories of singular moment in order to inspire it with a dauntless confidence in him.

VI. THAT WHEN ISRAEL REACHED CANAAN PROPER HE WAS ALREADY POSSESSED OF A LARGE AND VALUABLE TERRITORY, which God had enabled him to win by his own sword. Even so when the soul shall reach its heavenly rest it will not only enter into its reward, but it will, as it were, take a part of its reward with it, gained already on this side the river. Thus it is said of the dead that "their works do follow them;" and thus the apostles were bidden to bring of the fish which they had caught to add to that heavenly meal (John xxi. 9, 10). What we have achieved by the grace of God here will be part of our reward there.

Consider once more, with respect to the *well of Beer*—

I. THAT A WELL WAS A PERPETUAL SOURCE OF COMFORT AND CENTRE OF BLESSING; hence so many of the events of Scripture are connected with wells. Even so in the gospel there are wells of salvation (Isa. xii. 3), from which a man may draw with joy; nor only so, but he shall have a well of life in himself which shall never fail (John iv. 14; vii. 38).

II. THAT TO THIS WELL MOSES WAS TO GATHER THE PEOPLE; GOD WAS TO GIVE THEM WATER. Even so in the Church of God it is the part of human leaders to gather the people together, to direct their search, to combine their efforts; but it is the part of God, and of God only, to give the spiritual blessing and refreshment. So too, in another sense, Moses in the Pentateuch gathers the people to a well, a well full of Divine consolation and knowledge, and God will give them water if they seek in faith.

III. THAT ISRAEL SANG OVER THE WELL, OR RATHER OVER THE PLACE WHERE GOD PROMISED THEM WATER. Even so it is ours to sing and make melody in our hearts, and to encourage ourselves and others with spiritual songs, while we seek and labour for the sure mercies of God.

IV. THAT THE PRINCES AND NOBLES DIGGED THE WELL. Even so that God only gives spiritual blessings does not dispense with, but, on the contrary, requires and encourages, earnest effort on our part. In a settled and ordinary religious state the fountains of salvation must not be expected to gush in a moment from the rock, but must be dug for in wells. So too they that are most eminent in the Church of God must be foremost in labour for this purpose.

V. THAT THEY DUG BY THE DIRECTION OF THE LAWGIVER. If they had dug where fancy or even their own experience guided them, they had not found water. Even so when we seek the supply of grace and of the Spirit of God we must seek it by the direction of the one Lawgiver (Matt. vii. 29; James iv. 12), in implicit obedience to him.

VI. THAT THE NOBLES AND PRINCES DUG THE WELL WITH THEIR STAVES, the insignia of their office. Even so in the Church of God, if men will labour for the common good, it must be according to the station which God hath given them. If they have received authority, they must use authority; if they bear a commission, they must not be ashamed of it. It may be easier to act merely as one of the throng; it does not follow it is right.

HOMILIES BY VARIOUS AUTHORS.

Vers. 10—35.—*A period of unbroken progress.* The lifted serpent and the spirit of faith excited among the people produce not only the immediate and direct effect of healing; certain other encouraging effects are not obscurely indicated in the remainder of the chapter. The events recorded must have extended over some considerable time, and they took the Israelites into very trying circumstances, but there is not a word of failure, murmuring, or Divine displeasure. The narrative is all the other way, and in this surely there must be some typical significance. Look-ing to the lifted serpent made a great difference. All things had become new; there was alacrity, success, gladness, hitherto lacking—a spirit and conduct altogether different. So Paul, speaking of those who are justified by faith, and have peace with God, through our Lord Jesus Christ, goes on to indicate for them a course of satisfaction and triumph, which is in things spiritual what the course of Israel, as recorded in the remainder of this chapter, was in things typical and temporal (Rom. v.).

I. THEY ADVANCE UP TO A CERTAIN POINT WITHOUT HINDRANCE OF ANY SORT. We hear nothing more of this difficult and depressing way which had troubled them so much. Nothing is spoken of as arresting their progress till they come to the top of Pisgah. God takes them right onward to the place where afterward he showed Moses the promised land, and the hindrance which comes there is *from outside them-selves*. It is not the lusting and murmuring of the people that come in the way, nor is it a craven fear of the enemy, nor the ambition and envy of a Korah. It is the enemy himself who comes in the way, and of course he must be expected, and may be amply prepared for.

II. DURING THE ADVANCE THERE WAS MUCH SATISFACTION AND JOY. It was a *negative* blessing, and much to be thankful for, to have no murmurings and discords. It was a *positive* blessing, and even more to be thankful for, to take part in such a scene as that at Beer. How different from Marah, Rephidim, and Meribah, where God's mercy came amid complainings! from Meribah especially, where the mercy was accompanied with judgments on the leaders of the people. Here, unsolicited, God gives water; he makes the princes and nobles of the people his fellow-workers; and, above all, the voices so long used in murmuring now sounded forth the sweet song of praise. The Lord indeed put a new song in their mouth. There had been a sad want of music before. There had been loud rejoicings indeed at the Red Sea, but that was a long while ago. It was something new for the people to sing as they did here. Where there is saving faith in the heart, joy surely follows, and praise springs to the lip.

III. ISRAEL MAKES A COMPLETE CONQUEST OF THE FIRST ENEMY HE MEETS. Israel did not want Sihon to be an enemy. He offered to go through his land, as through Edom, a harmless and speedy traveller. If the world will block the way of the Church, it must suffer the inevitable consequence. Sihon, emboldened doubtless by the knowledge of Israel's turning away from Edom, presumed that he would prove an easy prey. But Sihon neither knew why Israel turned away nor how strong Israel now was. The people were no longer discouraged because of the way, though they were contending not against the adversities of nature, but against the united forces of Sihon struggling for the very existence of their land.

IV. THERE IS AN OCCUPATION OF THE ENEMY'S TERRITORY (vers. 25, 31). "Israel dwelt in the land of the Amorites." There was thus an earnest of the rest and possession of Canaan, a foretaste of city and settled life that must have been very inspiring to people so long wandering, and having no dwelling more substantial than the tent.

V. THERE IS CONTINUED VICTORY. The second hindrance disappears after the first. Og, king of Bashan, last of the giants (Deut. iii. 11), fared no better for all his strength than Sihon. It was not some peculiar weakness of Sihon that overthrew him. All enemies of God, however different in resource they may appear when they measure themselves among themselves, are alike to those who march in the strength of God. The power by which the Christian conquers one foe will enable him to conquer all. And yet because Og did *look* more formidable than Sihon, God gave his people special encouragement in meeting him (ver. 34). God remembers that even the most faithful and ardent of his people cannot get entirely above the deceitfulness of outward appearances.

VI. THERE IS GREAT ENERGY IN DESTROYING WHAT IS EVIL. Israel asks and is refused a way through the land of brother Edom, and then quietly turns aside to seek another way. By and by he asks Sihon for a peaceful way through his land, and is again refused, whereupon he conquers and occupies the land. But Og did not wait to be asked, perhaps would not have been asked if he had waited. It was a case of presumptuous opposition in spite of the warning fall of Sihon. And what made Og's opposition especially evil, *looked at typically*, was that he interposed the last barrier before reaching Jordan. Having conquered him, Israel was free to go right on and pitch "in the plains of Moab, on this side Jordan, by Jericho." Og, therefore, is the type of evil fighting desperately in its last stronghold. And similarly the destroying energy of Israel seems to show how utterly evil will be smitten by the believer, when he meets it even at the verge of Jordan. Thus we have a cheering record of unbroken progress from the time the people looked to the lifted serpent to the time when they entered on the plains of Moab.—Y.

PRELIMINARY NOTE TO CHAPTER XXII. 2—XXIV.

That this section of the Book of Numbers has a character to a great extent peculiar and isolated is evident upon the face of it. The arguments indeed derived from its language and style to prove that it is by a different hand from the rest of the Book are obviously too slight and doubtful to be of any weight; there does not seem to be any more diversity in this respect than the difference of subject matter would lead us to expect. The peculiarity, however, of this section is evident from the fact that these three chapters, confessedly so important and interesting in themselves, might be taken away without leaving any perceptible void. From ch. xxii. 1 the narrative is continued in ch. xxv., apparently without a break, and in that chapter there is no mention of Balaam. It is only in ch. xxxi. (vers. 8, 16) that two passing allusions are made to him: in the one his death is noted without comment; in the other we are made acquainted for the first time with a fact which throws a most important light upon his character and career, of which no hint is given in the section before us. Thus it is evident that the story of Balaam's coming and prophecies, although imbedded in the narrative (and that in the right place as to order of time), is not structurally connected with it, but forms an episode by itself. If we now take this section, which is thus isolated and self-contained, we shall not fail to see at once that its literary character is strikingly peculiar. It is to all intents and purposes a sacred drama wherein characters and events of the highest interest are handled with consummate art. No one can be insensible to this, whatever construction he may or may not put upon it. Probably the story of Balaam was never made the subject of a miracle play, because the character of the chief actor is too subtle for the crude intelligence of the age of miracle plays. But if the sacred drama were ever reintroduced, it is certain that no more effective play could be found than that of Balaam and Balak. The extraordinary skill with which the strangely complex character of the wizard prophet is drawn out; the felicity with which it is contrasted with the rude simplicity of Balak; the picturesque grandeur of the scenery and incident; and the art with which the story leads up by successive stages to the final and complete triumph of God and of Israel, are worthy, from a merely artistic point of view, of the greatest of dramatic poets.

There is no such minute drawing out of an isolated character by means of speech and incident to be found in the Old Testament, unless it be in the Book of Job, the dramatic form of which serves to give point to the comparison; but few would fail to see that the much more subtle character of Balaam is far more distinctly indicated than that of Job. Balaam is emphatically a "study," and must have been intended to be so. Yet it must be remembered that it is only to modern eyes that this part of the varied truth and wisdom of Holy Scripture has become manifest. To the Jew

Balaam was interesting only as a great foe, greatly baffled; as a sorcerer whose ghostly power and craft was broken and turned backward by the God of Israel (Deut. xxiii. 5; Josh. xiii. 22; xxiv. 10; Micah vi. 5). To the Christian of the first age he was only interesting as the Scriptural type of the subtlest and most dangerous kind of enemy whom the Church of God had to dread—the enemy who united spiritual pretensions with persuasions to vice (Rev. ii. 14). To the more critical intellects of later ages, such even as Augustine and Jerome, he was altogether a puzzle; the one regarding him as *prophetam diaboli*, whose religion was a mere cloak for covetousness; the other as *prophetam Dei*, whose fall was like unto the fall of the old prophet of Bethel. The two parallel allusions to his character in 2 Pet. ii. 15, 16; Jude 11 do not take us any further, merely turning upon the covetousness which was his most obvious fault. Unquestionably, however, Balaam is most interesting to us, not from any of these points of view, but as a study drawn by an inspired hand of a strangely but most naturally mixed character, the broad features of which are constantly being reproduced, in the same unhallowed union, in men of all lands and ages. This is undeniably one of the instances (not perhaps very numerous) in which the more trained and educated intelligence of modern days has a distinct advantage over the simpler faith and intenser piety of the first ages. · The conflict, or rather the compromise, in Balaam between true religion and superstitious imposture, between an actual Divine inspiration and the practice of heathen sorceries, between devotion to God and devotion to money, was an unintelligible puzzle to men of old. To those who have grasped the character of a Louis XI., of a Luther, or of an Oliver Cromwell, or have gauged the mixture of highest and lowest in the religious movements of modern history, the wonder is, not that such an one should have been, but that such an one should have been so simply and yet so skilfully depicted.

Two questions arise pre-eminently out of the story of Balaam which our want of knowledge forbids us to answer otherwise than doubtfully.

I. Whence did Balaam derive his knowledge of the true God, and how far did it extend? Was he, as some have argued, a heathen sorcerer who took to invoking Jehovah because circumstances led him to believe that the cause of Jehovah was likely to be the winning cause? and did the God whom he invoked in this mercenary spirit (after the fashion of the sons of Sceva) take advantage of the fact to obtain an ascendancy over his mind, and to compel his unwilling obedie...e? Such an assumption seems at once unnatural and unnecessary. It is hardly conceivable that God should have bestowed a true prophetic gift upon one who stood in such a relation to him. Moreover, the kind of ascendancy which the word of God had over the mind of Balaam is not one which springs from calculation, or from a mere intellectual persuasion. The man who lives before us in these chapters has not only a considerable knowledge of, but a very large amount of faith in, the one true God; he walks with God; he sees him that is invisible; the presence of God, and God's direct concern about his doings are as familiar and unquestioned elements of his every-day life as they were of Abraham's. In a word (whatever difficulties a shallow theology may find in the fact), he has religious faith in God, a faith which is naturally strong, and has been further intensified by special revelations of the unseen; and this faith is the basis and condition of his prophetic gift. Balaam's religion, therefore, on this side was neither an hypocrisy nor an assumption; it was a real conviction which had grown up with him and formed part of his inner self. It is true that in Josh. xiii. 22 he is called a soothsayer (*kosem*), a name of reproach and

infamy among the Jews (cf. 1 Sam. xv. 23, "witchcraft;" Jer. xiv. 14, "divination");
but no one doubts that he played for gain the part of a soothsayer, employing with
more or less of inward unbelief and contempt the arts of heathen sorcery; and it was
quite natural that Joshua should recognise only the lower and more obvious side of
his enemy's character.

It remains then to consider how Balaam, living in Mesopotamia, could have had so
considerable a knowledge of the true God; and the only satisfactory answer is this,
that such knowledge had never disappeared from that region. Every glimpse which
is afforded us of the descendants of Nahor in their Mesopotamian home confirms the
belief that they were substantially at one with the chosen family in religious feeling
and religious speech. Bethuel and Laban acknowledged the same God, and called
him by the same name as Isaac and Jacob (Gen. xxiv. 50; xxxi. 49). No doubt
idolatrous practices prevailed in their household (Gen. xxxi. 19; xxxv. 2; Josh.
xxiv. 2), but that, however dangerous, was not fatal to the existence of the true faith
amongst them, any more than is the existence of a similar cultus amongst Christians.
Centuries had indeed passed away since the days of Laban, and during those centuries we may well conclude that the common people had developed the idolatrous
practices of their fathers, until they wholly obscured the worship of the one true
God. But the lapse of years and the change of popular belief make little difference to the secret and higher teaching of countries like the Mesopotamia of that age,
which is intensely conservative both for good and evil. Men like Balaam, who
probably had an hereditary claim to his position as a seer, remained purely mono-
theistic in creed, and in their hearts called only upon the God of all the earth, the
God of Abraham and of Nahor, of Melchizedec and of Job, of Laban and of Jacob.
If we knew enough of the religious history of that land, it is possible that we might
be able to point to a tolerably complete succession of gifted (in many cases Divinely-
gifted) men, servants and worshippers of the one true God, down to the Magi who
first hailed the rising of the bright and morning Star.

There is connected with this question another of much narrower interest which
causes great perplexity. Balaam (and indeed Balak too) freely uses the sacred name
by which God had revealed himself as the God of Israel (see on Exod. vi. 2, 3).
There are two views of this matter, one or other of which is tolerably certain, and
for both of which much may be said: either the sacred name was widely known
and used beyond the limits of Israel, or else the sacred historian must have freely
put it into the mouths of people who actually used some other name. There are
also two views both of which may be summarily rejected, because their own advocates have reduced them to absolute absurdity: the one is, that the use of the two
names Elohim and Jehovah shows a difference of authorship; the other, that they are
employed by the same author with variety of sense—Elohim (God) being the God
of nature, Jehovah (the Lord) the God of grace. It is no doubt true that there are
passages where the sole use, or the pointed use, of one or other of these names does
really point to a diversity either of authorship or of meaning; but it is abundantly
clear that in the general narrative of Scripture, including these chapters, not the
least distinction whatever can be drawn between the use of Elohim and Jehovah
which will stand the simplest test of common sense; the same ingenuity which
explains the occurrence of Elohim instead of Jehovah in any particular sentence
would find an explanation quite as satisfactory if it were Jehovah instead of
Elohim.

II. Whence did Moses obtain his knowledge of the incidents here recorded, many of which must have been known to Balaam alone? Was it directly, by revelation; or from some memorials left by Balaam himself?

The former supposition, once generally held, is as generally abandoned now, because it is perceived that inspiration over-ruled and utilised for Divine purposes, but did not supersede, natural sources of information. The latter supposition is rendered more probable by these considerations:—1. That a man of Balaam's character and training would be very likely to put on record the remarkable things which had happened to himself. Such men who habitually lead a double life are often keenly alive to their own errors, and are singularly frank in writing themselves down for the benefit of posterity. 2. That Balaam was slain among the Midianites, and that his effects must have fallen into the hands of the victors. On the other hand, it is inconceivable that Balaam, being what he was, should have written these chapters at all as they stand; the moral and religious intent of the story is too evident in itself, and is too evidently governed by Jewish faith and feeling. It may be allowable to put it before the reader as an opinion which may or may not be true, but which is quite compatible with profound belief in the inspired truth of this part of God's word, that Moses, having obtained the facts in the way above indicated, was moved to work them up into the dramatic form in which they now appear—a form which undoubtedly brings out the character of the actors, the struggle between light and darkness, and the final triumph of light, with much more force (and therefore much more truth) than anything else could. If it be objected that this gives a fictitious character to the narrative, it may be replied that when the imagination is called into exercise to present actual facts, existing characters, and prophecies really uttered in a striking light,—and that under the over-ruling guidance of the Divine Spirit,—the result cannot be called fictitious in any bad or unworthy sense. If it be added that such a theory attributes to this section a character different from the rest of the Book, it may be allowed at once. The episode of Balaam and Balak is obviously, as to literary form, distinct from and strongly contrasted with the narrative which precedes and follows.

It has been made a question as to the language in which Balaam and his companions spoke and wrote. The discovery of the Moabite stone has made it certain that the language of the Moabites, and in all probability of the other races descended from Abraham and Lot, was practically the same as the language of the Jews. Balaam's own tongue may have been Aramaic, but amongst his western friends and patrons he would no doubt be perfectly ready to speak as they spoke.

EXPOSITION.

CHAPTER XXII.

THE COMING OF BALAAM (vers. 2—40). Ver. 2.—**Balak the son of Zippor.** The name Balak is connected with a word "to make waste," and "Zippor" is a small bird. Balak was, as is presently explained, the king of Moab at this time, but not the king from whom Sihon had wrested so much of his territory (ch. xxi. 26). He seems to be mentioned by name on a papyrus in the British Museum (see Brugsch, 'Geogr. In-schr.,' ii. p. 32). The later Jews made him out to have been a Midianite, but this is nothing but the merest conjecture.

Ver. 3.—**Moab was sore afraid of the people.** While the Israelites had moved along their eastern and north-eastern border, the Moabites supplied them with provisions (Deut. ii. 29), desiring, no doubt, to be rid of them, but not disdaining to make some profit by their presence. But after the sudden defeat and overthrow of their own Amorite conquerors, their terror and uneasiness forced them to take some action, although they dared not commence open hostilities.

Ver. 4.—**Moab said unto the elders of Midian.** The Midianites were descended from Abraham and Keturah (Gen. xxv. 2,

4), and were thus more nearly of kin to Israel than to Moab. They lived a semi-nomadic life on the steppes to the east of Moab and Ammon (cf. Gen. xxxvi. 35), supporting themselves partly by grazing, and partly by the caravan trade (Gen. xxxvii. 28). Their institutions were no doubt patriarchal, like those of the modern Bedawin, and the "elders" were the sheiks of their tribes. **As the ox licketh up the grass of the field.** The strong, scythe-like sweep of the ox's tongue was a simile admirable in itself, and most suitable to pastoral Moab and Midian.

Ver. 5.—**He sent messengers therefore.** It appears from ver. 7 that Balak acted for Midian as well as for Moab; as the Midianites were but a weak people, they may have placed themselves more or less under the protection of Balak. **Unto Balaam the son of Beor.** בִּלְעָם (Bileam: our common form is from the Septuagint and New Testament, Βαλαάμ) is derived either from בָּלַע, to destroy or devour, and עַם, the people; or simply from בָּלַע, with the terminal syllable םָ־, "the destroyer." The former derivation receives some support from Rev. ii. 14, 15, where "Nicolaitans" are thought by many to be a Greek form of "Balaamites" (Νικόλαος, from νικάω and λαός). Beor (בְּעוֹר) has a similar signification, from בָּעַר, to burn, or consume. Both names have probable reference to the supposed effect of their maledictions, for successful cursing was an hereditary profession in many lands, as it still is in some. Beor appears in 2 Pet. ii. 15 as Bosor, which is called a Chaldeeism, but the origin of the change is really unknown. A "Bela son of Beor" is named in Gen. xxxvi. 32 as reigning in Edom, but the coincidence is of no importance: kings and magicians have always loved to give themselves names of fear, and their vocabulary was not extensive. **To Pethor, which is by the river of the land of the children of his people.** Rather, "which is on the river," i. e. the great river Euphrates, "in the land of the children of his people," i. e. in his native land. The situation of Pethor (Septuagint, Φαθουρά) is unknown. **Here is a people come out of Egypt.** Forty years had passed since their fathers had left Egypt. Yet Balak's words expressed a great truth, for this people was no wandering desert tribe, but for all intents the same great organised nation which had spoiled Egypt, and left Pharaoh's host dead behind them.

They abide over against me. מִמֻּלִי. Septuagint, ἐχόμενός μου. This would hardly have been said when Israel was encamped thirty miles north of Arnon, opposite to Jericho. The two embassies to Balaam must

have occupied some time, and in the mean while Israel would have gone further on his way. We may naturally conclude that the first message was sent immediately after the defeat of Sihon, at a time when Israel was encamped very near the border of Moab.

Ver. 6.—**I wot that he whom thou blessest is blessed, and he whom thou cursest is cursed.** This was the language of flattery intended to secure the prophet's services. No doubt, however, Balak, like other heathens, had a profound though capricious belief in the real effect of curses and anathemas pronounced by men who had private intercourse and influence with the unseen powers. That error, like most superstitions, was the perversion of a truth; there are both benedictions and censures which, uttered by human lips, carry with them the sanction and enforcement of Heaven. The error of antiquity lay in ignorance or forgetfulness that, as water cannot rise higher than its source, so neither blessing nor cursing can possibly take any effect beyond the will and purpose of the Father of our souls. Balaam knew this, but it was perhaps his misfortune to have been trained from childhood to maintain his position and his wealth by trading upon the superstitions of his neighbours.

Ver. 7.—**With the rewards of divination.** קְסָמִים, "soothsayings." Septuagint, τὰ μαντεῖα. Here the soothsayer's wages, which St. Peter aptly calls the wages of unrighteousness. The ease with which, among ignorant and superstitious people, a prophet might become a hired soothsayer is apparent even from the case of Samuel (1 Sam. ix. 6—8). That it should be thought proper to resort to the man of God for information about some lost property, and much more that it should be thought necessary to pay him a fee for the exercise of his supernatural powers, shows, not indeed that Samuel was a soothsayer, for he was a man of rare integrity and independence, but, that Samuel was but little distinguished from a soothsayer in the popular estimation. If Samuel had learnt to care more for money than for righteousness, he might very easily have become just what Balaam became.

Ver. 8.—**Lodge here this night.** It was therefore in the night, in a dream or in a vision (cf. Gen. xx. 3; ch. xii. 6; Job iv. 15, 16), that Balaam expected to receive some communication from God. If he had received none he would no doubt have felt himself free to go.

Ver. 15.—**More, and more honourable than they.** Balak rightly judged that Balaam was not really unwilling to come, and that it was only needful to ply him with more flattery and larger promises. The heathens united a firm belief in the powers of the seer with a very shrewd appreciation of the motives and character of the seer. Compare the saying of Sophocles ('Antig.,' 1055), τὸ μαντικὸν γὰρ πᾶν φιλάργυρον γένος.

Ver. 18.—**I cannot go beyond the word of the Lord my God.** Balaam's faith was paramount within its own sphere of operation. It did not control his wishes; it did not secure the heart obedience which God loves; but it did secure, and that absolutely, outward obedience to every positive command of God, however irksome; and Balaam never made any secret of this.

Ver. 22.—**And God's anger was kindled because he went,** or, "that he was going." כִּי־הוֹלֵךְ הוּא. Septuagint, ὅτι ἐπορεύϑη αὐτός. There can be no question that the ordinary translation is right, and that God was angry with Balaam for going at all on such an errand. It is true that God had given him permission to go, but that very permission was a judicial act whereby God punished the covetous and disobedient longings of Balaam in allowing him to have his own way. God's anger is kindled by sin, and it was not less truly sin which prompted Balaam to go because he had succeeded in obtaining formal leave to go. **The angel of the Lord stood in the way.** The same angel of the covenant apparently of whom Moses had spoken to the Edomites (see on ch. xx. 16).

For an adversary against him. לְשָׂטָן לוֹ. Septuagint, διαβαλεῖν αὐτόν. Not so much because Balaam was rushing upon his own destruction as because he was going to fight with curses, if possible, against the Israel of God (cf. 2 Kings vi. 17; Ps. xxxiv. 7).

Ver. 23.—**And the ass saw the angel of the Lord.** This was clearly part of the miracle, the σημεῖον which was to exhibit in such a striking manner the stupidity and blindness of the most brilliant and gifted intellect when clouded by greed and selfishness. It is nothing to the point that the lower animals have a quicker perception of some natural phenomena than men, for this was not a natural phenomenon; it is nothing to the point that the lower animals are credited by some with possessing "the second sight," for all that belongs to the fantastic and legendary. If the ass saw the angel, it was because the Lord opened her eyes then, as he did her mouth afterwards.

Ver. 25.—**She thrust herself unto the wall.** Apparently in order to pass the angel beyond the reach of his sword; when this was clearly impossible she fell down.

Ver. 28.—**And the Lord opened the mouth of the ass.** On the face of it this expression would seem decisive that an audible human voice proceeded from the ass's mouth, as St. Peter beyond doubt believed: ὑποζύγιον ἄφωνον ἐν ἀνϑρώπου φωνῇ φϑεγξάμενον. It

is truly said, however, that a passing illusion of this kind, while it testifies that the Apostle understood the words, like all his contemporaries, in their most natural and simple sense, does not oblige us to hold the same view; if he was mistaken in this matter, it does not at all affect the inspired truth of his teaching. Two theories, therefore, have been proposed in order to avoid the difficulties of the ordinary belief, while vindicating the reality of the occurrence. It has been held by some that the whole affair took place in a trance, and resembled St. Peter's vision of the sheet let down from heaven (Acts x. 10), which we rightly conceive to have been purely subjective. This is open to the obvious and apparently fatal objection that no hint is given of any state of trance or ecstasy, and that, on the contrary, the wording of the narrative as given to us is inconsistent with such a thing. In ver. 31 Balaam's eyes are said to have been opened so that he saw the angel; but to have the eyes open so that the (ordinarily) invisible became visible, and the (otherwise) inaudible became audible, was precisely the condition of which Balaam speaks (ch. xxiv. 3, 4) as that of trance. According to the narrative, therefore, Balaam was in an ecstasy, if at all, after the speaking of the ass, and not before. By others it has been put forward, somewhat confusedly, that although Balaam was in his ordinary senses, he did not really hear a human voice, but that the "cries" of the ass became intelligible to his mind; and it is noted that as an augur he had been accustomed to assign meanings to the cries of animals. If instead of "cries" we read "brayings," for the ass is endowed by nature with no other capacity of voice, being indeed one of the dumbest of "dumb" animals, we have the matter more fairly before us. To most people it would appear more incredible that the brayings of an ass should convey these rational questions to the mind of its rider than that the beast should have spoken outright with a man's voice. It would indeed seem much more satisfactory to regard the story, if we cannot accept it as literally true, as a parable which Balaam wrote against himself, and which Moses simply incorporated in the narrative; we should at least preserve in this way the immense moral and spiritual value of the story, without the necessity of placing nonnatural constructions upon its simple statements. Supposing the miracle to have really occurred, it must always be observed that the words put into the ass's mouth do nothing more than express such feelings as a docile and intelligent animal of her kind would have actually felt. That domestic animals, and especially such as have been long in the service of man, feel surprise, indignation, and grief in the presence of injustice and ill-treatment is abundantly certain. In many well-authenticated cases they have done things in order to express these feelings which seemed as much beyond their "irrational" nature as if they had spoken. We constantly say of a dog or a horse that he can do everything but speak, and why should it seem incredible that God, who has given the dumb beast so close an approximation to human feeling and reason, should for once have given it human voice? With respect to Balaam's companions, their presence need not cause any difficulty. The princes of Midian and Moab had probably gone on to announce the coming of Balaam; his servants would naturally follow him at some little distance, unless he summoned them to his side. It is very likely too that Balaam was wont to carry on conversations with himself, or with imaginary beings, as he rode along, and this circumstance would account for any sound of voices which reached the ears of others.

Ver. 29.—**And Balaam said unto the ass.** That Balaam should answer the ass without expressing any astonishment is certainly more marvellous than that the ass should speak to him. It must, however, in fairness be considered—1. That Balaam was a prophet. He was accustomed to hear Divine voices speaking to him when no man was near. He had a large and unquestioning faith, and a peculiar familiarity with the unseen. 2. Balaam was a sorcerer. It was part of his profession to show signs and wonders such as even now in those countries confound the most experienced and sceptical beholders. It is likely that he had often made dumb animals speak in order to bewilder others. He must indeed have been conscious to some extent of imposture, but he would not draw any sharp line in his own mind between the marvels which really happened to him and the marvels he displayed to others. Both as prophet and as sorcerer, he must have lived, more than any other even of that age, in an atmosphere of the supernatural. If, therefore, this portent was really given, it was certainly given to the very man of all that ever lived to whom it was most suitable. Just as one cannot imagine the miracle of the stater (Matt. xvii. 27) happening to any one of less simple and childlike faith than St. Peter, so one could not think of the ass as speaking to any one in the Bible but the wizard prophet, for whom—both on his good and on his bad side—the boundary lines between the natural and supernatural were almost obliterated. 3. Balaam was at this moment intensely angry, and nothing blunts the edge of natural surprise so much as rage. Things which afterwards, when calmly recollected, cause the utmost astonishment, notoriously produce no effect at the moment upon a mind which is thoroughly exasperated.

Ver. 31.—**The Lord opened the eyes of Balaam, and he saw the angel.** As on other occasions, the angel was not perceptible to ordinary sight, but only to eyes in some way quickened and purged by the Divine operation. This explains the fact that Balaam's companions would appear to have seen nothing (cf. Acts ix. 7).

Ver. 32.—**Because thy way is perverse.** יָרַט, an uncommon word, which seems to mean "leading headlong," i. e. to destruction.

Ver. 33.—**Unless . . surely.** כִּי - - - אוּלַי. It is somewhat doubtful whether this phrase can be translated as in the Septuagint (εἰ μὴ . . νῦν οὖν) and in all the versions; but even if the construction of the sentence be broken, this is no doubt the meaning of it. **And saved her alive.** Compare the case of the ass of the disobedient prophet in 1 Kings xiii. 24. It is plainly a righteous thing with God that obedience and faithfulness should be respected, and in some sense rewarded, even in an ass.

Ver. 35.—**Go with the men.** It may be asked to what purpose the angel appeared, if Balaam was to proceed just the same. The answer is that the angel was not a warning, but a destroying, angel, a visible embodiment of the anger of God which burnt against Balaam for his perversity. The angel would have slain Balaam, as the lion slew the disobedient prophet, but that God in his mercy permitted the fidelity and wisdom of the ass to save her master from the immediate consequences of his folly. If Balaam had had a mind capable of instruction, he would indeed have gone on as he was bidden, but in a very different spirit and with very different designs.

Ver. 36. — **Unto a city of Moab**, or, "unto Ir-Moab" (אֶל־עִיר מוֹאָב), probably the same as the Ar mentioned in ch. xxi. 15 as the boundary town of Moab at that time.

Ver. 39. — **Kirjath-huzoth.** "City of streets." Identified by some with the ruins of Shîhân, not far from the supposed site of Ar.

Ver. 40.—**Balak offered oxen and sheep.** Probably these sacrifices were offered not to Chemosh, but to the Lord, in whose name Balaam always spoke. Indeed the known fact that Balaam was a prophet of the Lord was no doubt one of Balak's chief reasons for wishing to obtain his services. Balak shared the common opinion of antiquity, that the various national deities were enabled by circumstances past human understanding to do sometimes more, sometimes less, for their special votaries. He perceived that the God of Israel was likely, as things stood, to carry all before him ; but he thought that he might by judicious management be won over, at least to some extent, to desert the cause of Israel and to favour that of Moab. To this end he "retained" at great cost the services of Balaam, the prophet of the Lord, and to this end he was willing to offer any number of sacrifices. Even the resolute and self-reliant Romans believed in the wisdom of such a policy. Thus Pliny quotes ancient authors as affirming "in oppugnationibus ante omnia solitum a Romanis sacrdotibus evocari Deum, cujus in tutelâ id oppidum esset, promittique illi eundem aut ampliorem apud Romanos cultum," and he adds, "durat in Pontificum disciplinâ id sacrum, constatque ideo occultatum, in cujus Dei tutela Roma esset, ne qui hostium simili modo agerent." **And sent,** *i e.* portions of the sacrificial meats.

HOMILETICS.

Vers. 2—40.—*The way of Balaam.* In this section we have some of the profoundest and most subtle, as well as some of the most practical, moral and religious teachings of the Old Testament. In order to draw them out fully we may consider—I. The character and position of Balaam with regard to God and man ; II. The policy of Balak in sending for Balaam ; III. The conduct of Balaam when asked and urged to come to Balak ; IV. The incidents, natural and supernatural, of Balaam's coming.

I. THE CHARACTER OF BALAAM, AND HIS POSITION WITH REGARD TO GOD AND MAN. Consider under this head—1. *That Balaam had a true knowledge of the most high God.* He was not in any sense a heathen as far as his intellectual perception of Divine things went. And it was not merely Elohim, the God of nature and creation, whom he knew and revered, but distinctly Jehovah, the God of Israel and of grace. Speculatively he knew as much of God as Abraham or Job. 2. *That Balaam had an unquestioning faith in the one true God.* Whatever difficulties it may create, it is obviously true that Balaam walked very much by faith, and not by sight. The invisible God, the will of God, the power of God, the direct concern of God with his doings, were all realities to Balaam, strong realities. God was not a *name* to him, nor a theological expression, but the daily companion of his daily life. 3. *That Balaam had an undoubted prophetic gift from God.* He was not an ordinary servant of the true God ; he held as it were a very high official position in the service of God. He enjoyed frequent and direct intercourse with him ; he expected to receive supernatural intimations of the Divine will ; he professed to speak, and he did speak, words of inspired prophecy far beyond his own origination. 4. *That at the same time Balaam's heart was given not to God, but to covetousness.* He loved the wages of unrighteousness. Not perhaps in the lowest sense. He may have valued influence, power, consideration even more than mere money ; but money was necessary to all these. 5. *That Balaam was a soothsayer.* He practised magical arts and sought for auguries. He traded on the superstitions of the heathen, and even sought to prostitute his prophetic powers to excite astonishment, obtain power, and make money. He hired himself out to curse the enemies of those who employed him. And note that Balaam's fall in this respect was accountable enough ; for we may naturally conclude (1) that Balaam had an hereditary position as seer which it was his interest to keep up at any cost ; (2) that the ignorant people put strong pressure upon him to play the soothsayer. How easily Samuel might have become the same if he had been covetous ! How constant is the temptation to abuse spiritual powers in order at once to gratify others and to exalt oneself ! (cf. 1 Sam. ix. 6—8 ; Jer. v. 31)

II. THE POLICY OF BALAK, AND HIS ERROR. Consider under this head—1. *That Balak was afraid of Israel,* because he was mighty, and had overthrown the Amorites. Yet he had no cause to fear, for Israel had not touched him, and did not mean to. Men are afraid of the Church of God because it is a great power in the world, albeit it is a power for good, and not for evil. 2. *That Balak was afraid of the God of Israel.* He rightly judged that Israel's success was due to his God ; but he wrongly thought that the Lord was but a national deity who was victorious at present, but might be turned aside or bought off. 3. *That Balak put his trust in Balaam because he was a prophet of the Lord, and might be expected to use his influence to change the purposes of the Lord ;* perhaps even to counterwork those purposes. How often do people seek the aid of religion *against* God ! How often do they seek for religious support and solace in doing what they must know is contrary to the moral law of God ! 4. *That Balak professed, and no doubt felt, a profound belief in the efficacy of Balaam's benedictions and maledictions, even as against the people of Balaam's God.* Here was the very essence of superstition, to suppose that anything whatsoever can have any spiritual efficacy contrary to, or apart from, the will of God; most of all, that the word of God, as officially employed by his ministers, can be made to work counter to the declared mind of God. As though Peter could ban whom Christ hath blessed. Yet note that Balak's superstition was the depraving of a great truth. Balaam had no doubt authority to censure or to bless in the name of God ; and his censures or blessings would have had validity if pronounced with a single eye to the glory of God and the good of souls, and in clear dependence upon the higher knowledge and necessary ratification of Heaven. 5. *That Balak sought to obtain supernatural aid from Balaam by means of flatteries, gifts, and promises ;* and thought, no doubt, to buy over the powers of the world to come. He rightly gauged the *character* of the man ; he was utterly deceived as to the worth of his alliance. How often do shrewd and worldly men make the same mistake ! Because they see through the selfishness and worldliness of the human ministers of religion, they fancy they can command the services, and employ in their own behalf the powers, of religion itself.

III. THE COMING OF BALAAM. Consider under this head—1. *That Balaam was solicited to come for a purpose which he must have felt sure was wrong.* To curse any people was an awful thing, and only to be done with sorrow if commanded by God. To curse Israel, of whose history Balaam was not ignorant, was on the face of it treason towards God. When men are invited to lend their aid in opposing or destroying others, how careful should they be to make sure that such hostile action is a matter of duty ; for we are called unto blessing (1 Pet. iii. 9). 2. *That Balaam was tempted through his love of money and of good things.* A true-hearted prophet would have been ashamed to receive gifts and promises for the use of his spiritual powers, and he would have vehemently suspected such as offered them, even with flattery and deference. If anything appeals all the more to our cupidity and promises advantage in this world, we ought all the more to turn against it, unless it is irresistibly proved to be right. With what just scorn does the world regard the universal propensity of religious people to exercise their gifts and throw their influence where and as *it pays the best !* 3. *That Balaam was forbidden to go, for the plain and unalterable reason that he could not possibly do what he was wanted to do without flying in the face of God.* If he went, he must either act dishonourably towards Balak by taking his money for nought, or he must act treasonably towards God by cursing his people. And this was perfectly clear to Balaam. The moral law of God is plain enough in its broad outlines, and if men loved righteousness more than gain they would have little practical difficulty. 4. *That Balaam's outward conduct was consistently conscientious.* He would not go without leave ; he refused to go when forbidden ; when allowed to go, he repeatedly protested that he could and would say nothing but what God told him to say. And no doubt his protestations were sincere. He had no intention of rebelling against God ; it was a fixed principle with him that God must be obeyed. 5. *That Balaam's inward desire was to go if possible, because it promised honour and gain to himself.* He obeyed God, but he obeyed grudgingly ; he obeyed God, but he gave him clearly to understand that he wished it might be otherwise ; he respected the definite command not to go, but he paid no heed to the reason given—because Israel was not to be cursed. The only obedience which God really cares for is obedience from the heart (Rom. vi. 17 ; Ephes. vi. 6). How many are strict in not violating the moral law (as they understand it), but *not* in order to please God, *not* because they love the will of God ! To how many are the commandments of God formal barriers which they do not overleap only because they dare not ! But for such these barriers are sooner or later done away, that they may have their own way. 6. *That Balaam did not get credit for the conscientiousness he did possess.* He said that God refused to give him leave, which was true, although not expressed in a proper spirit, whereas the messengers reported that he refused to come ; and Balak believed that he only wanted more pressing. So it is with men who do what is right, yet not from the true motive; they do not get credit even for the good that is in them; they are always tempted afresh, because they are felt to be open to temptation; the world sees that their heart is with it, and puts their hesitation down to mere self-interest. There is no safety for the man whose heart is not on the side of God. 7. *That Balaam, when he referred the matter again to God (as if it were still open), was allowed to go.* This is the very essence of tempting God—to cast about for ways and means to follow our own will and compass our own ends without open disobedience. How many treat the rule of God as a disagreeable restraint which must indeed be respected, but may be thankfully avoided if possible! Such men find themselves able to go with a clear conscience into circumstances of temptation which are presently fatal to them. If thou hast once had a clear intimation of what is right, cleave to it with all thy heart, else shalt thou be led into a snare. 8. *That Balaam's going, though permitted, was controlled;* and this not in his own interest (for he should not have gone), but in the interest of Israel. When men *will* go into evil they are judicially permitted to go, and the law of God ceases so far to constrain their conscience; but the consequences of their inward disobedience are over-ruled that they may not be disastrous to God's own people.

IV. THE JOURNEY OF BALAAM. Consider under this head—1. *That God was angry with Balaam for going, although he had given him leave to go.* For it was sin which made Balaam wish to go if possible; and it was his wish to go on an evil errand for gain which obtained him leave to go. Even so if men are inwardly desirous to do what is wrong, God will suffer them to persuade themselves that it is not actually wrong, and they will go on with a clear conscience; but God will be angry with them all the same. How many very religious people find it permissible to walk in very crooked ways for the sake of gain, and are yet resolute not to do a wrong thing! But God is angry with them, and they have forfeited his grace already. 2. *That the destroying angel stood in the way as an adversary to him.* Even so destruction awaits us in every way wherein greed leads us contrary to the will of God. God himself is an adversary to us (Matt. v. 25), and is ready at any moment to fall upon us and cut us asunder. It is useless to say that we have *done* nothing wrong; if our motives be corrupt, the sword of Divine justice is drawn against us. 3. *That Balaam saw not the angel, but the ass did;* and this although Balaam was a "seer," and prided himself on "having his eyes open," and on being familiar with the unseen things of God. Even so the "religious" and "spiritual" man, who has great "experiences," and yet is secretly led by greed and self-interest, is often much blinder than the most carnal and unenlightened to perceive that he is rushing upon destruction; the most stupid person has often a clearer perception of moral facts and situations than the most gifted, if this be blinded by sin. 4. *That the ass by her fidelity and instinct of self-preservation saved her master.* Even so are men, wise in their own eyes, often indebted to the most despised and neglected agencies for preservation from the consequences of their blind folly. 5. *That Balaam was enraged with the ass, and ill-treated her.* Even so foolish men are often very angry with the very circumstances or persons which are really saving them from destruction. 6. *That the ass was Divinely permitted to rebuke her master, and to teach him a lesson if he would learn it;* for she had been faithful, and docile, and had never played him false ever since she had been his; while he had been and was unfaithful, obstinate, and disloyal to his Master in heaven. Even so do the very beasts teach us many a lesson by their conduct; and those whom we account in some sense worse than the beasts—the heathen, and men who have no religion at all—will often put us to shame by the strong virtues which they display where we perhaps fail. 7. *That then Balaam saw and knew his danger.* Even so do men complacently walk in the road which leads to destruction, and have not the least idea of it, but are angry with any that thwart them, until some sudden influence opens their eyes to their awful danger. 8. *That he offered then to go back, if necessary, and acknowledged that he had done wrong (perhaps sincerely), but was not permitted to go back.* Even so when men have, as it were, insisted upon taking a line which is unwise, dangerous, and wrong, it is often impossible for them to turn back. They are committed to it, and God's providence compels them to go on with it, even though it brings awful peril to their souls; for God is a jealous God, and the judicial consequences of our own (albeit inward and disguised) disobedience cannot be got rid of in a moment. 9. *That he was met by Balak with honour and ceremony and religious rites*; and no doubt all that happened by the way faded like a dream from his mind. Even so when men walk after their own covetousness they may receive the most solemn and (at the time) impressive warnings, but amidst the converse of the world, and the honour received of men, and the outward ceremonies even of religion, these warnings have no lasting effect, and are as though they had never happened.

Consider again, as to the broad lessons to be drawn from Balaam's character and history—1. *That there may be in a man high spiritual gifts with out real goodness.* Balaam was a veritable prophet, and had in a remarkable degree the faculty both of understanding the hidden things of God and of announcing them to men. Yet, as in the case of Saul (1 Sam. x. 11 ; xix. 24) and Caiaphas (John xi. 51), his prophetic gifts were not accompanied by sanctification of life. Even so many in all ages and lands have great spiritual gifts of understanding, of interpretation, of eloquence, &c., whereby others are greatly advantaged, but they remain evil themselves. 2. *That a man may have a true and strong religious faith, and yet that faith shall not save him, because it does not affect his heart.* That Balaam had a strong faith in the Lord God is evident ; on the intellectual side it was as strong as Abraham's ; he walked with God as truly as any in the sense of being constantly conscious and mindful of God's presence and concern with him. No definition of religious faith could be framed with honesty which should exclude Balaam and include Abraham. Yet he was not saved, because his faith, although it largely mingled with his thoughts and greatly influenced his actions, did not govern his affections. Even so it is useless, however usual and convenient, to deny that many men have strong religious convictions and persuasions—in a word, have religious faith—who are not saved by it, but fall into deadly sins and become castaway. This is not a matter of theology so much as of facts ; the combination of strong religious feelings, and of power to realise the unseen, with deep moral alienation from God, is by no means uncommon. 3. *That a man may do much and sacrifice much in order to obey God without receiving any reward.* Balaam repeatedly crossed his own inclinations, and forewent much honour and emolument from Balak, from a conscientious motive ; and yet he was all the time on the verge of destruction, and was miserably slain at last. Even so many men do much they do not like, and give up much they do like, because they feel they ought to; and yet they have no reward for it either here or hereafter, because their self-restraint is grounded on some lower motive than love of God and the desire to please him. 4. *That a man's conduct may be to all appearance irreproachable, and yet be displeasing to God.* No one could have found distinct fault with any one step in Balaam's proceedings ; each could be singly justified as permissible ; yet the whole provoked the Lord to anger, because it was secretly swayed by greed. Even so many men are careful, and to ordinary eyes irreproachable, in their doings, because no act is by itself without justification ; yet their whole life is hateful because its governing motive is selfishness, not love. It is not enough to be able to justify each step as we take it, neither will a mere resolve to keep straight with God insure his favour. 5. *That a man may have profound religious insight, and yet be very blind to his own state.* Balaam justly prided himself upon his intelligent and spiritual religion as compared with the follies and mummeries of the heathen around, yet he was more blind than his own beast to the palpable destruction on which he was running. Even so many of those who are most enlightened, and most removed from ignorance and superstition, are most blind to their own entire moral failure, and to the terrible danger they are in. They, *e. g.*, who most denounce idolatry are often utterly blind to the fact that their whole lives are dominated by covetousness, *which is idolatry.*

Consider again, with respect to the miracle of the dumb beast speaking with human voice—1. *That the lower animals, of which we reck so little, save as a matter of gain, have often great virtues by which they teach us many a lesson.* How much more faithful are they to us than we to our Master ! It is their pride and study to observe and follow, almost to anticipate, the least indication of our will. How inferior are we in that respect! 2. *That God is not insensible to their virtues, as we very generally are, but at times at least gives them a certain recompense of reward* (see on ver. 33). Since they seem to have no future state, it is a duty laid upon us to remember and reward their fidelity in this world. 3. *That to be enraged with dumb animals when their conduct vexes us is sin and folly.* Sin, because we have no right to be angry except with sin (Jonah iv. 4); folly, because they are less in the wrong with us than we are with God; sin and folly, because such anger surely blinds the mind and leaves us a prey to temptation. 4. *That God delights to choose " the foolish things of the world to confound the wise," and " things which are despised" and " things which are not "* (as the intelligible voice of an ass) *" to bring to nought things that are."* Even so are we often rebuked and reproved in our madness by things most contemned and familiar, by those whom we regard as brutish and senseless, and standing upon a lower level than ourselves.

HOMILIES BY VARIOUS AUTHORS.

Vers. 5, 6.—*Balaam's greatness and fall.* Balaam's character and history have supplied materials for many theological and ethical studies. His character and conduct, though somewhat perplexing, are not more so than those of many around us, and are full of instruction and warning. At present we confine ourselves to two points:—I. BALAAM'S LOFTY POSITION AND PRIVILEGES. II. THE SECRET OF BALAAM'S HUMILIATING FALL.

I. (1) He had a knowledge of the true God. Among the heathens of Mesopotamia he retains a knowledge of the God revealed " from the creation of the world." (Compare the cases of Melchizedec and Job.) He was like the evening star, showing in which direction the sun of truth had set (Rom. i. 21), and reflecting some of its light. His knowledge may be illustrated by his lofty utterances respecting God and his people; *e. g.* ch. xxiii. 10, 19; and according to some interpreters, ch. vi. 8. (2) He enjoyed the gift of inspiration by God. Though there were no Scriptures, God was not left without witnesses, and among them was Balaam "the prophet" (2 Pet. ii. 16). He expected Divine communications, and was not disappointed. No wonder then that (3) he enjoyed wide-spread fame. It extended hundreds of miles away, to Moab and Midian, whence more than once an embassy crossed the desert with such flattering words as those in ver. 6. Yet we know that Balaam was a bad man who came to a bad end. Thus we have lessons of warning for ourselves, who have a fuller knowledge of God than Balaam, and may enjoy gifts, if not as brilliant, yet more useful than his. All of these may avail nothing for our salvation, but may be perverted to the worst ends. Illustrations:—Hymenæus and Alexander, the companions of St. Paul (1 Tim. i. 19, 20); Judas, the apostle of Jesus Christ (cf. Matt. vii. 21—23; xi. 23; 1 Cor. xiii. 1, 2).

II. Balaam's name mentioned in the New Testament only three times, and each time it is covered with reproach (2 Pet. ii. 15; Jude 11; Rev. ii. 14). His root sin was the ancient, inveterate vice of human nature, selfishness. He knew God, but did not love him, for " he loved the wages of unrighteousness." He did not follow the Divine voice, but "followed after" reward. God taught him sublime truths; he "taught Balak" base arts of seduction. His selfishness was shown in—(1) Ambition. There was nothing of the self-forgetfulness of such prophets as Elijah, Elisha, Jeremiah, or Balaam's contemporary, Moses. He is esteemed as a great man, and he takes good care he shall be so esteemed. He knows divination has no power with God, but to magnify himself among the heathens of Moab, he resorts to it. He constantly aspires to the " very great honour " to which Balak offers to promote him (cf. Ps. cxxxi. 1—3; Jer. xlv. 5). (2) Covetousness. He would be rich, and therefore fell into temptation, &c. (1 Tim. vi. 9; 2 Pet. ii. 15). His words were fair (ver. 18), yet suspicious, like those of a venal voter boasting his incorruptibility. Balaam coveted the offered honour and wealth. How could he gain them while God was keeping him back? Two ways were possible. He might get God to change his mind. He wanted to get permission from God to do what was at present a sin. He might have known from the first, as he says (ch. xxiii. 19). But he struggles to conquer God, as though the fact was *not* that God *cannot* change, but that God *will not* change. Hence his repeated changes of place and new sacrifices. At length it was clear that this way was closed against him. He is constrained to bless Israel again and again. At the close of the narrative (ch. xxiv. 10—24) he seems to be taking his place boldly as an ally of the people of God. But it was only a temporary impulse, not a true conversion. Greedy for the wages of unrighteousness, he allies himself with hell. ("*Flectere si nequeo superos, Acheronta movebo.*") What a contrast between his fair promises (ver. 18) and this wicked deed! The reason is that in trying to "bend" God he was miserably perverting himself (like a weak tool used to move a great weight), while seeking permission to sin he was growing less sensitive to sin (see next Homily). Learn then from the fall of this great and gifted prophet to what a depth of infamy selfishness, that mother of sins, and its offspring, ambition and covetousness, may lead us. Warned by the selfishness of Balaam, may we copy the unselfishness of Christ (Rom. xv. 3 ; Philip. ii. 3—8).—P.

Ver. 13.—*Balaam, an illustration of systematic resistance of conscience.* The final fall of Balaam was not sudden. A process of deterioration had been going on, the first clear sign of which is in the text. In trying to change God's will he had been changing himself for the worse (see Homily on vers. 5, 6). We can trace his resistance of conscience step by step. 1. When the first embassy came, his knowledge of God and of Israel's history should probably have led to a decisive refusal. But if we assume that he needed direction, it is clear that the rewards of divination made him anxious to go. Not that he had a desire to curse Israel ; he would just as soon have blessed them for reward. Yet he had no intention then to disobey. If a prophet could have shown him that evening his future career, he might have shrunk in loathing from the self that was to be. The will of God is declared (ver. 12), and the struggle between conscience and covetousness begins. At first conscience prevails, but the form of refusal (ver. 13) indicates double-mindedness. In contrast to Joseph (Gen. xxxix. 9), Balaam lays himself open to fresh temptations. If we give Satan a hesitating "No," instead of a "Get thee behind me," he will understand that we would like to sin, but dare not, and will try us with more honourable embassies and costlier gifts. 2. The ambassadors leave, but lingering regrets keep the fire of covetousness smouldering in Balaam's heart. It flames up afresh on the arrival of the second embassy (vers. 16, 17). Fair professions (ver. 18) reveal his weakness, for what "more" (ver. 19) could he want God to say unless it was to give him permission to sin ? God gives him leave *not to sin,* but *to go.* (Illustrate this act by similar Divine proceedings : *e. g.* allowing the Israelites, under protest, to elect a king ; a wild youth receiving reluctantly permission to carry out his determination to go to sea.) 3. Balaam went, and God is angry, not because he went, but because he went with a wicked purpose. When he found the ways of transgressors hard, and offers to return (ver. 34), God knows that he would only carry his body back to Pethor, and leave his heart hankering after the rewards of Balak. May we not suppose that if he had shown real repentance in the future, and heartily entered into the Divine purposes, though he lost Balak's rewards, he would have received God's blessing ? But he ran greedily after reward, and found, as sinners still find, under God's providence, that it is hard to retrace false steps. Therefore, "enter not," &c. (Prov. iv. 15). 4. Balaam meets with a flattering reception, yet renews his good professions (ver. 38). He means them, for he still hopes to gain God's consent to his purpose. His use of enchantments to impose on the heathen is one sign of unconscientiousness. His first attempt to curse is a failure (ch. xxiii. 7—10), but the struggle with conscience and God is not abandoned. ("No sun or star so bright," &c., Keble's 'Christian Year,' Second Sunday after Easter.) Three times he persists in this "madness," trying to change or circumvent the will of God. At length he *seems* to give up the struggle, but is probably only "making a virtue of a necessity ; " at the best it is but a passing impulse, followed by a relapse, and by the infamous act by which he clutched his wages and brought God's curse on Israel (ch. xxv.). He thus shows that he has renounced God, has entered thoroughly into Balak's schemes, and even outstripped him in wickedness. His perverted conscience does not keep him even from such unutterable baseness. His triumph is brief, and his "end is destruction" (ch. xxxi. 8; Ps. xxxiv. 21). Learn from this the guilt and danger of resisting and thus corrupting conscience. (Explain process of this corruption, and note natural analogies to a conscience dulled by persistence in sin.) To try and bribe conscience is like seeking permission to sin. (Illustrate by story of Glaucus inquiring at the oracle of Delphi whether he might keep stolen money— Herodotus, vi. 86.) Conscience, like a railway signal-lamp, is intended to warn against danger or direct in the path of safety. If through negligence the lamp is put out or shows a wrong light, the consequences may be fatal (Isa. v. 20; Matt. vi. 23). A healthy conscience accuses of sin and warns of danger only that it may be a minister to lead us to Christ.—P.

Vers. 15—17.—*The importunity and impudence of the tempter.* Such appeals as Balak sent to Balaam are constantly addressed to us, in word or substance, by human tempters, and through them by the infernal tempter. The honour offered is represented as "very great," and as essential, and the promises are as vast as we can desire (" whatsoever," &c., ver. 17; Luke iv. 6, 7). Though at first the tempter may be resisted, and may depart "for a season" (cf. ver. 14), yet his solicitations may be renewed in a more alluring form than at first, with this appeal, "Let nothing," &c. (ver. 16). Neither (1) conscience. Away with childish scruples in a man of the world who has to see to his own interests. Nor (2) considerations of mercy to others. Balaam was required to curse and, if possible, ruin a nation that had done him no harm. Selfishness is bidden to make any sacrifice at its shrine. *E. g.* ambitious rulers, dishonest traders or trustees, heartless seducers. Nor (3) the will of God; for who can be sure whether God has really revealed his will, or will enforce it (Gen. iii. 1—5). Nor (4) the grace of our Lord Jesus Christ in dying that he might save from the ruin of sin; for though you sin, grace will abound. Nor (5) the fear of judgment; for after all the threats of judgment may be old wives' fables, or you may make all right before you die. Thus speaks the tempter, bidding us make riches and honour "the prize of our calling," and overleap or break down every barrier that God has set up to hinder us from ruining ourselves and others. (Illustrate from the case of Judas, and the barriers he broke through at the call of Satan, and contrast the impregnability of Jesus Christ when offered the wealth and honour of the world.) Christ himself, the motives supplied by his cross when applied by his Spirit, are the greatest hindrances to keep us from yielding to the tempter.—P.

Ver. 32.—*On cruelty to animals.* In ver. 28 we are reminded of the silent protest of the brute creation against the cruelty of men. From ver. 32 ("Wherefore hast thou smitten thine ass these three times?") we may learn that this protest is heeded and supported by God. Cruelty of all kinds is one of the foulest of the works of the flesh, opposed to the character of God and to the instincts of humanity. Cruelty to animals is especially hateful, because of I. THE WRONG DONE TO THE CREATURES; II. THE EFFECTS ON OURSELVES.

I. 1. They are our inferiors, therefore magnanimity and sympathy should protect them. 2. They are often helpless to defend themselves; cruelty is then unutterably mean. 3. Some of these animals are part of our property, and of great value to us, though absolutely within our power. 4. If they are not "wont to do so" when they provoke us, some good reason may exist which we should seek to discover. There-fore—5. When tempted to harshness, short of cruelty, it is our duty to consider whether they need it, and in this sense deserve it. For—6. Past misconduct of ourselves or of others may have occasioned their present obstinacy, through timidity or some other cause. 7. Animals suffer too much already, directly or indirectly, through men's sins (war, famines, &c.) without the addition of gratuitous cruelties. 8. No future life for them is revealed, so that we have the more reason for not making them miserable in this life.

II. 1. It fosters a despotic habit of mind, as though might and right were identical. 2. It hardens the heart and tends to nurture cruelty to men as well as brutes. *E. g.* the child Nero delighting in killing flies. 3. It still further alienates us from the mind of Christ, the character of "the Father of mercies." 4. It is a sign of unrighteousness (Prov. xii. 10), against which God's wrath is revealed, and from which we need to be saved by Christ (Rom. i. 18; 1 John i. 9).—P.

Vers. 2—4.—*Moab takes alarm.* I. AN INTERESTED OBSERVER OF AN IMPORTANT ACTION. "Balak saw all that Israel had done to the Amorites." *The thing was worth observing in itself*, that this great host of people, coming with but little notice, having no land of its own, no visible basis of operations, no military renown, should yet have crushed into ruin such powerful kings as Sihon and Og. It was not merely the conquest of one army by another; there was something decisive and very significant about the conquest. Just as in profane history some battles, such as Marathon and Salamis, Waterloo and Trafalgar, stand out like towering mountains because of the great issues connected with them, so these victories of Israel over Sihon and Og are for all generations of God's people to consider. Balak of course was interested as a neighbour, but we, living thousands of miles from the scene of these events, and thousands of years after them, should be not less interested. They concern us just as much as they concerned Balak. Distant as they are from us in time, they have to do very practically with our interests and the yet unaccomplished purposes of the ever-living God. We are too observant of trifles, the gossip of the passing day, the mere froth on the waves of time. *The thing also pressed for notice.* The Amorites were Moab's neighbours, and Moab had been conquered by them. If Israel then had conquered the conqueror, there was need for *prompt action.* So long as Israel was far away, wandering in the wilderness, with no aim in its course that could be ascertained,—that course aimless rather, so far as others could make out,—there was no feeling of alarm. But now, with Israel in its very borders, Moab feels *it must do something.* Yet the pressure was not of the right sort. Moab was driven to consider its position not because of dangers within, not because of idolatry and unrighteousness (ch. xxv.), nor that it might become a pure and noble-minded nation, but because of the selfish fear that another people close to its territory might prove hostile and destructive. Thus we allow considerations to press on us which should not have the slightest force. Where our minds should be well-nigh indifferent they are yielding and sensitive; and where they should be yielding and sensitive, indifference too often possesses them. When Jesus fed the multitude, the action pressed for notice not because the multitude appreciated the spiritual significance of the action, but they eat of the loaves and were filled. Balak did well when he noticed the victories of Israel, but very ill when he noticed them simply as bearing on the safety of his kingdom.

II. THE CONSEQUENT DISQUIETUDE OF MOAB. The Amorites had conquered Moab, but Israel had conquered the Amorites. The presumption then was that Israel, having the power, would as a matter of course advance to treat Moab in the same fashion; just as an Alexander or Napoleon goes from one conquered territory to conquer the next; just as a fire spreads from one burning house to its neighbour. It was therefore *excusable* for Moab to be sore afraid; but though excusable, it was *not reasonable.* The alarm came from knowledge of some things, mixed with ignorance of things more important. The alarm then was *groundless.* General as that alarm was, Moab had really nothing to fear. Its way of reasoning was utterly erroneous. If Moab had known the internal history of Israel half as well as it knew the present external appearance and recent triumphs, it would not have been alarmed because of the children of Israel, and because they were many. The children of Israel had been commanded to cherish other purposes than those of conquering Moab, and the mind of their leader was occupied with things far nobler than military success. Besides, as God had remembered the kinship of Israel and Edom, so he remembered that of Israel and Moab (Deut. ii. 9). Moab was afraid of the people *because they were many.* What a revelation of their craven and abject spirit in the past he would have had if he had seen them threatening to stone Caleb and Joshua (ch. xiv.). And though they were many, he would have seen that all their numbers availed nothing for success when God was not with them (ch. xiv. 40—45).

III. MOAB'S CONCLUSION WITH REGARD TO HIS OWN RESOURCES. He could no more resist Israel than the grass of the field resist the mouth of the ox. This expresses his complete distrust of his own resources, and was a prudent conclusion, even if humiliating, as far as it went, and always supposing that Israel wished to play the part of the ox. The fall of Sihon had taught nothing to Og, the self-confident giant, but the fall of Sihon, and next the fall of Og, had taught Moab this at least, that in the battle-field he could do nothing against Israel. If a man refuses to go in the right path, it is not, therefore, a matter of little consequence which of the wrong paths he chooses. One may take him swiftly in the dark to the precipice; another, also downward, may afford more time and occasions for retrieval. It was a wrong, blind, useless course to send for Balaam, but at all events it was not so immediately destructive, as to rush recklessly into the field of battle against Israel.—Y.

Vers. 5, 6.—*Balak's message to Balaam.* War being useless, what shall Balak do? In his mind there were only two alternatives, either to fight or to send for Balaam. And yet there was a better course, had he thought of it, viz., to approach Israel peacefully. But prejudice, a fixed persuasion that Israel was his enemy, dominated his mind. We do very foolish things through allowing traditional conceptions to rule us. That Israel was the enemy of Moab was an assumption with not the smallest basis of experience. Many of the oppositions and difficulties of life arise from assuming that those who have the opportunity to injure are likely to use the opportunity. He who will show himself friendly may find friends and allies where he least expects them. We must do our best in dubious positions to make sure that we have exhausted the possibilities of action. Balak then sends a message to Balaam. Notice—

I. A TESTIMONY TO THE POWER OF RELIGION. Balak cannot find sufficient resources in nature, therefore he seeks above nature. When men, who in their selfishness and unspirituality are furthest from God, find themselves in extremity, it is then precisely that they are seen turning to a power higher than their own (1 Sam. xxviii.). Man has a clinging nature, and if he cannot lay hold of the truth as it is in Jesus, he must find some substitute. Balak did not know God as Moses knew him; he knew nothing of his spiritual perfections and holy purposes. But still he recognised the God of Israel as really existent, as a mighty potentate; he felt that Balaam had some power with him; and thus even in his ignorance he believes. It is a long, long way to pure atheism, and surely it must be a dreary and difficult one. May not the question be fairly raised whether there are any consistent atheists, those whose practice agrees even approximately with their theory? There are men without God in the world, *i. e.* lacking conscious and happy connection with the God and Father of our Lord Jesus Christ; but even so they may bear testimony unthinkingly to their need of him. The witnesses to the power of religion are not only many, but of all sorts, giving testimony often when they least suspect it.

II. A TESTIMONY TO THE EMPTINESS OF IDOLATRY. Balak had a god of his own, probably more than one, and doubtless he would have felt very uncomfortable in omitting the worship of them; but he did not trust in his gods. He may have sacrificed to them on this very occasion with great profusion and scrupulosity, but he did not trust them. Though they were near at hand, he felt more hope from Balaam far away; and yet if there was any good in his gods, this was the very time to prove it and receive it. There is a Nemesis for all idolatry. The idols of Moab were put to shame before the God of Israel, and that by the very man who was bound to be their champion. It does not need always for a Dagon to fall in the presence of the ark. There are other ways of dishonouring idols than casting them to the moles and the bats. They may have shame written across their brows, even while they stand on the pedestal of honour. Thus we see also *an exposure of formalism.* Balak's great need strips the mask off his religion, and underneath we see, not living organs, but dead machinery. And bear in mind, formalism in serving the true God is just as certain to come to shame as formalism in serving an idol. The principle is the same, whatever deity be formally acknowledged.

III. AFTER ALL, THE RESORT TO BALAAM WAS A VERY PRECARIOUS ONE, even supposing Balaam had all the power with which Balak credited him. For Pethor was a long way off, and the dreaded, victorious Israelites were close at hand. Balaam did not live in the next street. While you are sending from Land's End for the celebrated London physician, the patient's life is steadily ebbing away. That is no sufficient help in our supreme necessities which has to be brought over land and sea. "Say not in thine heart, Who shall ascend into heaven? (that is, to bring Christ down from above:) or, Who shall descend into the deep? (that is, to bring up Christ again from the dead). The word is nigh thee, even in thy mouth, and in thy heart " (Rom. x. 6—8). Go into thy closet ; retreat into the seclusion and security of thine own heart, and meet the mighty Guide and Helper there. The God of Israel went about with his people. Jesus did not say, " Wheresoever I am, there my people are to gather together," but, " Where two or three are gathered together in my name, there am I in the midst of them."

> " God attributes to place
> No sanctity, if none be thither brought
> By men who there frequent, or therein dwell."

IV. A MAN MAY BE IGNORANT OF THINGS LYING NEAREST HIM AND UNSPEAKABLY IMPORTANT, while he abounds in useless knowledge of things far away. Balak knew not the needs of his own heart, the real power of Israel, the disposition of Israel's God to him, the possibilities of friendship which lay within those tents on which he looked with so much apprehension. But somehow he had got to know concerning Balaam in far-away Pethor. How much useless, deceiving, pretentious knowledge we may accumulate with infinite labour, and at the time feeling great certainty of its value. " Knowledge comes, but wisdom lingers." It is of great moment in a world where so much is to be known, and yet so little can be acquired, not to miss acquiring the right things. Said Dr. Arnold, " If one might wish for impossibilities, I might then wish that my children might be well versed in physical science, but in due subordination to the fulness and freshness of their knowledge on moral subjects. This, however, I believe cannot be ; and physical science, if studied at all, seems too great to be studied ἐν παρέργῳ. Wherefore, rather than have it the principal thing in my son's mind, I would gladly have him think that the sun went round the earth, and that the stars were so many spangles set in the bright blue firmament." Thus also the great discoverer Faraday in his old age—" My worldly faculties are slipping away, day by day. Happy is it for all of us that the true good lies not in them. As they ebb, may they leave us as little children, trusting in the Father of mercies and accepting his unspeakable gift ! "

V. THE MESSAGE WAS VERY FLATTERING TO BALAAM. Kings have much to do with courtiers, and all the delicate preparations of flattery must be well known to them. Balak made Balaam to understand that it was not for a trifle he had summoned him, for a service that could be rendered by a second-rate soothsáyer. The people he so dreaded had come out from Egypt, that home of strength in those days, that populous and wealthy land, and by no means lacking in reputed wise men, sorcerers and magicians. They had come in great numbers : " behold, they cover the face of the earth ; " and they were in close proximity and apparently settled condition : " they abide over against me." There is the willing confession by Balak of his own inability, and his evident faith in Balaam's power to cast a fatal paralysis over all the energy of Israel. Now all this must have been very pleasant for Balaam to hear, sweeter maybe than the jingle of the rewards of divination. Thus did the temptation to Balaam, already only too open to temptation, begin. His carnal mind was appealed to in many ways. The rewards of divination were only a part of the expected wages of unrighteousness. " Pride goeth before destruction, and an naughty spirit before a fall " (Prov. xvi. 18).

VI. BALAK HAD MORE FAITH IN FALSEHOOD THAN ISRAEL FOR A LONG TIME HAD SHOWN TOWARDS TRUTH. The conduct of Balak in sending so far, in casting the fortunes of his kingdom with such simplicity on what was utterly false, should put us to shame, who have the opportunity of resorting at all times to well ascertained and established truth. Balak had only a Balaam to seek, such an ignoble and doubleminded man as appears in the sequel ; not a Moses, who could have told him truly, not only how the blessing and the curse really come, but how to secure the one and escape the other.—Y.

Vers. 7—14.—*The first visit to Balaam.* I. BALAK'S NOTION OF WHAT WOULD BE MOST ACCEPTABLE TO BALAAM. It is all a matter of money, Balak thinks. " Every man has his price," and the poor man who cannot pay it must go to the wall. Not that we are to suppose Balaam a specially greedy man, but it has been the mark of false religions and all corruptions of the true service of God that priests and prophets have been greedy after money. They promise spiritual things and make large demands for carnal things; the more they get the more they promise, and the more they get the more they want. "The priests teach for hire, and the prophets divine for money" (Micah iii. 11). Simon Magus must have known well the greed of his tribe when he offered money to Simon Peter. It is the mark of a true bishop that he is not greedy of *filthy* lucre (1 Tim. iii. 3). Jesus sent forth his disciples to make a *free gift* in healing the sick, cleansing the lepers, raising the dead, and casting out devils. "*Freely* ye have received, *freely* give." "Ho, every one that thirsteth, come ye to the waters, and he that hath no money; come ye, buy, and eat; yea, come, buy wine and milk without money and without price" (Isa. lv. 1).

II. BALAAM'S RECEPTION OF THE MESSENGERS. *He cannot give a prompt answer.* We are certainly very much in the dark concerning Balaam's past life and present position. If he knew anything of Israel's true character and God's purpose concerning Israel, then, of course, there was not the smallest excuse for delay. But even supposing him ignorant in this respect, was there any excuse for delay to an upright man? Did not Balak's wish at once suggest the answer an upright man would have given? Blessing and cursing are great realities, not mere priestly fictions (Deut. xxvii., xxviii.), but they can never become mere matters of money. "The curse causeless shall not come." He who deserves blessing cannot be cursed, nor he who deserves cursing, blessed. God's sovereignty, mysterious enough in its operations, is never arbitrary. An upright man would have felt it was no use pretending to consult God with a bribe in his hand. The bribe vitiated the spirit of his prayer, and prevented a proper reception of the answer. There are certain propositions which upright men do not need to sleep or deliberate over. The answer should follow the request like the instantaneous rebound of a ball. Balak did not send asking advice in general terms, or that Balaam should do the best he could, but he pointed out a certain, well-defined road which no upright man could possibly take. If we acquit the prophet of dishonesty and evasion in this plea of delay, we can only do it by convicting him of great darkness in his own spirit and great ignorance of God.

III. THE INTERPOSITION OF GOD. God does not seem to have waited for any request from Balaam. While the prophet is considering all the honour and emolument that may come to him out of this affair, God comes to him with the prompt and sobering question, "What men are these with thee?" All the depths of this question we cannot penetrate, but at all events it was enough to prepare the prophet, one would think, for an unfavourable answer. And may we not also assume that it was expressive of a desire to extricate him when he had only taken one or two steps into temptation? As to Balak's request, God settles everything with a brief, a very brief, but sufficient utterance: "The people are blessed." And blessed beyond all doubt they had been of late, not in word only, but in deed. Note that *God does not send any message of reassurance to Balak.* There is guidance for Balaam, security for Israel, but for Balak only blank denial. If Balak had come in the right spirit to Balaam, and Balaam in the right spirit to God, then the messengers might have gone back cheerful, and welcome to their expectant master. But what begins badly ends worse. He who sets himself in opposition to God's people cannot expect to hear comfortable words from God. If we are to hear such words, we must approach him in the right spirit. We must not seek good for ourselves by a *selfish* infringement on the good of others. It was one thing for Israel, under the leadership of God, to attack the wicked Amorites; quite another for Moab, on a mere peradventure, to attack Israel.

IV. BALAAM'S ANSWER TO THE MESSENGERS. He does not repeat what the Lord said; thus advancing further in the revelation of his corrupt heart. Why not have told them plainly these words: "Thou shalt not curse the people, for they are blessed"? Simply because it was not pleasant to say such words with the flattering message of Balak still tickling his ears. It was not true then that whom he blessed was blessed, and whom he cursed was cursed; but to have told Moab so would have been to publish his humiliation far and wide, and hurt his repute as a great sooth-sayer. Yet how much better it would have been for Balaam as a man, and a man who had been brought in some respects so near to God, if he had told the whole truth. It would perhaps have saved a second embassy to him. Men are looking to the main chance even when among the solemn things of God, and fresh from hearing his voice. Balaam first of all, in speaking to God, omits from the message of Balak, saying nothing of his own reputation in the eyes of the Moabitish king, suspecting very shrewdly that this would be offensive to God. Then he omits again in his answer to the messengers, and, to make all complete, they omit still more in their report to Balak. There is nothing in their word to show that *God had said anything in the matter*. This is what is called diplomacy ; not telling a lie, but only leaving out something of the truth, as being of no practical importance. It is a great blessing that there are *Scriptures* for us all to read. Philosophers and preachers may leave out part of the truth, or colour and distort it to suit their own prejudices, but they cannot get over the written word. Out of their own mouths they may be contradicted when they read one thing out of the Scriptures and say another as the fruit of their own lips.—Y.

Vers. 15—21.—*The second visit.* I. THE RESULT OF MUTILATED ANSWERS. 1. *As concerns Balak.* Balaam does not tell the first messengers all that God had spoken to him ; they do not tell Balak all that Balaam had spoken to them. The consequence is that he comes to a wrong conclusion, and really he had no information by which to come to a right one. His thoughts on the subject may be supposed to have run thus :—" All the difficulty lies with Balaam. He took the night to think the matter over, and concluded it was not worth his while on such poor considerations to undertake so serious a journey. My messengers and rewards have not sufficiently impressed him with the rank of Moab." In Balak's mind it is *all a question of degree*, and so he sends more princes, and more honourable than before. And possibly, if these had been unsuccessful, as a last resort he would have gone himself. Thus poor Balak, in the quagmire of misunderstanding already, was led still deeper into it. The great end was to get Balaam's curse into operation, and there was nothing to shake his faith in the possibility of this end being gained. Between God and Balak there were interposed a self-seeking Balaam, and, to say the least, messengers who were careless, if nothing more. *Ours is a more secure position.* We come to God through a Christ, not through a Balaam ; enlightened by a Spirit who teaches us the proper needs of sinful men, and shows us our real danger. 2. *As concerns Balaam.* Whether he thought that by his first answer he had finally disposed of the request, or wanted time to consider if it should be preferred again, we cannot make sure. His first answer had to be given very much on the spur of the moment. If it had been a truthful answer, one not only with the lips, but with the whole countenance, and the whole man speaking all God had said, he would not have been troubled again. But now he has to deal with more princes, and more honourable than before. He sees precisely why *they* have been sent, and as he listens to their urgent and obsequious words and comprehensive promises, he understands exactly what is expected of him. His proper answer even now was to say that he could not go on any consideration. But there was no spirit and courage of repentance in him. His reply, with all its seeming emphasis, is very evasive and ambiguous. It looks strong to say, " If Balak would give me his house full of silver and gold," and to speak of God as " the Lord *my God*," but after all he leaves the messengers in the dark as to what the word of the Lord was, though he knew it well. He pretends that it is needful to wait another night for what the Lord might say. This time it is a *mere pretence*, beyond any doubt. Perhaps he reckons that he will have nothing to do but wait till the morning, and then repeat to the second messengers what he had said to the first. How startled then he must have been, not only to get another revelation of God, but *a totally different direction !* And yet, when we consider, we see that he could not get the same answer as before. Balaam does not stand where he did at the time of the previous answer. He is a worse man ; he has yielded to temptation from which God would have preserved him, and now, with open and greedy heart, he is in the midst of greater temptation still. He had daringly neglected God's previous word, and *would assuredly neglect it again if he got the opportunity.* Why then should God repeat the word ? Balaam will still suppress the fact that he cannot curse Israel, seeing they are blessed. What was the needful word yesterday may become useless to-day. The possible of one hour becomes the impossible of the next. Jesus says, "Watch and pray, that ye enter not into temptation;" but that does not prevent him saying very soon afterwards, "Sleep on now, and take your rest. . . . *Rise, let us be going.*" The father has not changed because the child whom he commands in one way to-day he commands in another to-morrow. Different actions outwardly may reveal the same character and advance the same purpose. The appearance of contradiction in God's dealing arises from our hasty thinking, not because there is any reality corresponding to the appearance. God was speaking, as we more and more clearly see, both for the real good of Balaam and the safety and blessedness of his own people.

II. THE WORLD'S CONFIDENCE IN THE ATTRACTIVENESS OF ITS REWARDS. The world never has any doubt but what it can make its possessions fascinating to every man, and appeal successfully to his affections and sympathies. Weak as the world is, it never loses its self-confidence. Though Balak's throne is in peril, he brags of the honours he can confer on Balaam; and when he sends the second message, he does not change the considerations, but simply increases them to the utmost. So, to take the other side, the world is equally confident in *the terrifying power of its penalties.* Nebuchadnezzar, sorely troubled about his forgotten dream, does not for all that forget to play the despot. He menaces the astrologers, threatening them with a dreadful death, in right royal style. It must be acknowledged also that the result only too often shows that *the confidence is justified.* We cannot guard too carefully against the world, alike in its attractions and its threats; and he does this best who is filled with a purer love and a worthier fear than anything in the world can inspire.

III. BALAK'S ALARM HAD NOT BEEN LOST NOR LESSENED BY THE LAPSE OF TIME. "These Israelites are not going to steal away my suspicions by their quietude. The less they look my way, the more sure I am they mean ultimate mischief." And yet what was Israel doing all this time of going to Balaam and returning and going again? Why, while Balak is in all this fret and stir, Israel is steadily preparing for the promised land. Whatever God's enemies may do in plot and counsel, let it not hinder our advance. Enemies outside cannot hinder, if only we, whom God has called and guided, lay aside every weight, and the sin which doth so easily beset us.—Y.

Vers. 22—35.—*The angel, the prophet, and the ass.* I. WE MUST LOOK NOT ONLY AT THE LETTER OF GOD'S COMMANDS, BUT THE SPIRIT OF THEM. "If the men come to call thee, rise up, and go with them" (ver. 20). "God's anger was kindled because he went" (ver. 22). It has been said indeed that God was angry not because he went, but with something that happened on the journey; and to support this view grammatical considerations are urged, from the participle being used instead of the finite verb ('Keil and Delitzsch on the Pentateuch,' iii. 168. Clark's Translations). It is further urged, as a consequence of this construction, that the encounter with the angel took place not at the outset of the journey, but rather towards its close. All this may be true, but there is no distinct affirmation of it in the narrative and it is not necessary to assume it *for reconciling purposes.* There is no difficulty in admitting that God was displeased with Balaam because he went at all. We must not go by *words* simply. There is something, even in communications between men, which cannot be put into words. And just as the Spirit makes intercession for us with groanings which cannot be uttered, so there are communications of the answering God which can be put in no human tongue. The obedient heart will distinguish between the permissive and the imperative, between the concession to human weakness and the call to holy duty. Those who want to be right with God, to attend to his will rather than their own desires, will never lift a permission into a command Our interpretations of God's words are a searching test of our spiritual state. How many jump at them to excuse self-indulgence, but conveniently ignore equally prominent words that call for self-denial. The word telling Balaam that he might go to Balak was not like the call to Abram to get out of his country and away from his kindred to a land *which the Lord would show him;* nor like the sending of Moses to Pharaoh, and Jonah to Nineveh.

II. BALAAM WAS GOING ON THIS EXPEDITION EVIDENTLY FULL OF THE DESIRES OF HIS OWN HEART. All, so far as he could see, was pointing in the way he wanted. He could plead God's permission, which was a very comfortable, not to say a necessary, beginning to one who was a prophet. As he rode along, his heart filled with expectation of the future—riches, honours, fame, power—an ample share in the kingdoms of this world and the glory of them. God's permission may have seemed to the infatuated man a *clear indication of further favours.* If he allowed Balaam to have his own way in one thing, why not in others? Thus he had in view the possibility of exercising an extraordinary power, one that would make him famed and dreaded far and wide. It is something to make a man's heart swell when he can wield the immense forces of *nature,* say in the strength of a disciplined army, or of some huge steam-engine. But Balaam had in view the possibility of wielding forces *above nature,* cursing Israel so that its strength might utterly melt away. What wonder God was angry with him, seeing he had desires in his heart which could only be satisfied by accomplishing the ruin of the chosen race! Not that he deliberately desired their destruction; but selfishness in its blind absorption destroys with little scruple all that comes in its way. There is some parallel between Balaam and Paul, all the more striking because it extends only a little way. Paul set out for Damascus, like Balaam for Moab, his fanatical heart brimful of darling projects. Hence in both instances we see *special, extraordinary, and unfailing methods adopted to check the men and bring them to consideration.* Men who are in the ordinary paths of sin may be dealt with by ordinary methods, peculiar indeed to each individual, yet never rising above the ordinary experiences of humanity. But Balaam and Paul, being extraordinary transgressors, were dealt with by extraordinary methods. We do not expect sinners to be met by angels now, or to hear human speech from brute beasts. Still we may have this much in common with Balaam and Paul, that we may be so absorbed in our own things, so utterly careless of God, Christ, salvation, and eternity, as to require sharp, sudden, accumulated agencies to stir up our attention. It takes a great deal to bring some men to themselves.

III THE PROCESS ADOPTED TO MAKE BALAAM FULLY CONSCIOUS OF THE WRATH OF GOD. 1. *The presence of an angel in front.* Why an angel? Why not communicate with Balaam as before? The answer is that Balaam did not appreciate such communications. He heard them indeed, but they did not lay hold of his conscience, they did not secure his obedience, they did not even make him think seriously of his danger. Hence the appearance of a visible sign in the angel—one who should equally speak the word of God *and be seen as he spoke.* We know that persons were greatly terrified and impressed by the visits of angels (Judges xiii.). Men can go about the world delighting in sin, unconscious that all the time they are in the presence of God himself, but let them see what seems an apparition from another world, and they tremble like the aspen. The disciples in their earlier, carnal-hearted days were not much affected by the holiness and spiritual beauty of their Master's life; but what an impression he made when they saw him walking on the sea! They thought it was an apparition. *So soon as Balaam perceived the presence of the angel* it brought him up at once. "He bowed down his head, and fell flat on his face." God makes use of visible agents to prepare results in the sphere of the invisible. And not only did an angel appear, *but he was right in front,* signifying that he was there to meet with Balaam. He had also *his sword drawn.* There was significance in meeting a messenger bearing a sword, but the drawing of the sword, even without a single word spoken, was the clearest possible intimation of opposition. The way of transgressors may be hard in more senses than one. How many persevere in the ways of sin in spite of urgent, repeated warnings and entreaties, everything short of physical force, from those who love and pity them! Such at all events cannot say that no one has cared for their souls. 2. *The extraordinary means by which God made Balaam to notice the angel.* Balaam would not attend to the warnings of an invisible God presented to the eye within, therefore a visible angel was sent to appeal through the eye without to the eye within. But though the angel was in front with the drawn sword, Balaam did not see him. *How then shall he be made to see him?* God, as his custom is, takes the weak things of the world to confound the mighty. He opens the mouth of the prophet's ass. Ridiculous! say the men who will have no miracles, no admission of the supernatural; and ludicrous as well as ridiculous, seeing that it is an ass, of all animals, which is chosen to speak. But that is only because we associate Balaam with the despised and buffeted animal which the word "ass" recalls to us. We may be sure that a man of Balaam's dignity would have a beast to carry him such as became his dignity. And as to the absurdity of an animal uttering human speech, it is no harder to believe that God should here have opened the mouth of the ass, than that he should afterwards have opened the mouth of Balaam, *being such a man as he was*, to utter glorious predictions concerning the people whom it was in his heart to curse. If we were allowed to think of things as being either easy or difficult to God, we might say that it was more difficult for him to control the mouth of a carnal-minded man like Balaam than the mouth of a brute beast. It is not pretended that he changed the intellect and gave the ass human thoughts along with human speech. The words were the words of a man, but the thoughts were the thoughts of an ass. *Balaam himself was not astonished to hear it speak.* He was too much exasperated with the strange stubbornness of an animal hitherto so docile and serviceable, to notice the still stranger power with which it had been so suddenly endowed. Observe, again, *how naturally all leads up to the speaking of the ass.* The ass is not brought specially on the scene, as the angel was. Balaam saddles the ass, and takes the road on it in his customary way. At first there is nothing miraculous. The ass sees the angel, and turns aside into the field; there is nothing strange in that. Coming to the path of the vineyards, and still seeing the angel, it crushes Balaam's foot against the wall; there is nothing strange in that. Still advancing into the narrow place, and still seeing the angel, it sinks to the ground; there is nothing strange in that. The ass was in a strait before and behind, on the right side and on the left. Thus its speaking is prepared for as a climax. Accept the statement that the ass spoke, and all the previous narrative leads beautifully up to it. Deny the statement, and the chief virtue of the narrative is lost. 3. *Let us not fail to notice this instance of the lower creation recognising God's messenger.* The question of course suggests itself, Who was this angel? one of the unnamed host, or the Son of God himself in his old covenant guise? If the latter, then he who while in human flesh signified his will to the stormy sea might well signify his warning presence to the ass. Not that the ass knew the angel as a human being could; but even as the lower creation is sensible in its own way of the presence of man, so the ass might be sensible in its own way of the presence of the angel. We argue concerning the lower animals far more from ignorance and carelessly-accepted tradition than from real and discerning knowledge. We know positively nothing as to what sort of consciousness underlies the phenomena of their existence. We know wherein they are not like us, but what they are in themselves we cannot know. 4. *Every Balaam has his ass*, i. e. every man who has the spirit and conduct of Balaam in him may expect to be pulled up at last in like manner. What God made the ass to his master, that God makes their consciences to many. For a long time the ass had only been of ordinary and commonly-accepted use. Balaam had ridden on it ever since it was his, a long time we may conclude, and doubtless rejoiced in having so convenient and trustworthy a servant. And thus many find their consciences as little troublesome, as constantly agreeable, as the ass was to Balaam. Some sort of conscience they must have, but it amounts to nothing more than taking care to keep a reputation for honesty and respectability. They find such a conscience useful in its way, just as Balaam found his ass when out on soothsaying business. But even as the ass sees the angel, so *conscience begins to waken to nobler uses.* One gets out of the little world of mere give and take, business customs and local habits. Something suggests that we are in the wrong road, pulls us up for a moment, tries to turn us aside. In reality God is beginning to close with us for our own good. At first there is latitude, opportunity of evasion. We go a little further, and God comes closer. Onward still! and at last the soul cannot escape. Blessed is that man, blessed in his opportunity at all events, whose conscience, once the humble instrument of his baser self, is thoroughly roused so that it will not allow him further with its consent in his chosen and accustomed way. The crisis comes, and the question is, "Will you from the heart obey the Divine command, come in subjection to the angel of God, or go on greedily in the way of unrighteousness, which you have been so clearly shown is also the way of destruction ? "

IV. THE EXTENT TO WHICH THE PROCESS IS SUCCESSFUL. 1. *Balaam is enlightened at last, but after all only partially enlightened.* At last, and only when forced to it, does he become aware of the angel's presence. And now he is quick enough and humble enough to recognise that presence, but not with the quickness and humility of a full repentance. *The Lord opened the eyes of Balaam*, even as he opened the eyes of the ass, but the opening left his disposition and wishes unchanged, even as it left the ass-nature unchanged. He saw the angel, the drawn sword, his danger at the moment, and the danger he had been in before ; but his folly, his duplicity, his covetousness, his spiritual danger he did not see. Then when his eyes were opened, and at the same time his ears unstopped, the angel goes on to speak to him such words as might bring him to a right state of mind. Nothing was left undone that could be done. The angel shows him plainly in what danger he had been from the first swerving of the ass, and how the ass was perhaps more aware of the master's danger and solicitous for his safety than was the master himself. Nothing but the sagacity and fidelity of the ass had saved his life. The ass was more faithful to its master than the master had been to God. 2. *Hence, the enlightenment being partial, the confession is inadequate, indeed worthless.* " I have sinned." There are no more complaints against the ass ; there is no extenuation with the lip ; so far all is satisfactory. What is said is all right so far as it goes. The mischief is in what is left unsaid, because unthought. Balaam should have asked himself, " How is it that though my ass saw the angel, I did not ? " His confession was lacking in that he did not say, " I have sinned because my heart has not been right. I have sinned in going on an expedition to glorify and enrich myself. I will turn back at once." The only thing of real use and worth in God's sight is a voluntary turning from the ways of sin. When the younger son came to himself, he did not say, " I will go back to my father *if he wishes me to go, if he will not let me stop where I am*," but definitely, " I will arise and go," &c. Therefore, in spite of the angel's presence, the drawn sword, the thrice intimation through the ass, in spite of all the words to make all plain, *Balaam goes on.* He may indeed plead God's permission, but this plea will avail him nothing. For himself it matters little now, seeing he is not one whit changed in heart, whether he goes forward or backward ; any path that he takes is *downward.* If he returns to Pethor, it will not be to a life of true repentance. He is the same low-minded man wherever he is, and it matters little to himself whether he is destroyed in Pethor or in Moab. Let him then go forward into Moab, so that in his further descent and ultimate destruction he may at the same time be used for the glory of God. Even if he refuses a willing obedience, God may get gain out of him by an unwilling one.—Y.

Vers. 36—38.—*Balaam and Balak meet at last.* I. BALAK'S SOLICITUDE TO CONCILIATE BALAAM AND SHOW HIM HONOUR. Balak does not yet know what unhealed wounds may be in the prophet's pride, or whether that pride has been sufficiently pleased by the dignity of the second deputation and the extent of the promises it has made. He does all he can, therefore, to minister to Balaam's vanity. The children of this world are wiser in their generation than the children of light. They will leave nothing undone to gain their ends ; they will creep to reach them, if they cannot reach them standing erect. Balak goes to meet the prophet at the utmost border of his land. It is a dangerous thing to offend the powerful ones of this world ; they must be kept in good humour. How different from the spirit in which God would have us approach him or any one whom he may send ! If he sends to bless us, it is because of our need ; he is not a man, that he should be kept in a favourable disposition by our flatteries and fawnings. We need to remember this. Cornelius had a sincere desire to serve God, but very mistaken apprehensions in some respects of what God required, seeing how he fell before Peter's feet and worshipped him. Let us take heed lest in our anxiety to offer God what we think he wants we are found utterly insensible as to what he really wants. We cannot be too solicitous to please God, if only we are doing it according to his will ; we cannot be too solicitous to conciliate men, if only we are doing it for their good. There is nothing degrading or unmanly, nothing that compels cringing or obsequiousness, in the service of God. When we bow before the grandees and plutocrats of the world and watch their wishes as a dog the eyes of its master, then we are reptiles, not men. We must be all things to all men only when it will save them, not simply to advantage ourselves.

II. BALAAM AND BALAK MEET, IN SPITE OF ALL THE HINDRANCES PUT IN THE WAY. Balak of course has his own notion of these hindrances; he thinks they lay in Balaam's waiting for a sufficient inducement; and very likely he congratulates himself on his insight, his knowledge of the world, his pertinacity, his choice of agents, and of the right sort of bait to attract Balaam. Yet after all Balak had not the slightest idea of what great hindrances he had overcome. If he had known of God's interferences, he might have been prouder than ever; that is, if the knowledge of these interferences had not changed his pride to alarm. Balak's earnest sending had been more potent and fascinating than, in his greeting to Balaam, he unwittingly supposed. It had outweighed the direct commands of God, the mission of the angel, the influence of a very peculiar miracle and a very narrow escape from death. How much there must have been in Balaam's greedy heart to draw him on when even mighty and unusual obstacles like these could only stay him for a moment! Balak drew him because in his heart there was something to be drawn; and they came together as streams that, rising miles apart, and winding much through intervening lands, yet meet at last because each pursues its natural course. All the obstacles put in our way to perdition will not save us if we are bent on the carnal attractions to be found in that way. Drawing is a mutual thing. There was nothing in Balaam's heart to be drawn towards God. The hugest magnet will do no more than the least to attract another body to it unless in that body there is something to be attracted.

III. THE MEETING, AFTER ALL, DOES NOT SEEM A SATISFACTORY ONE. One would have thought that, after overcoming so many hindrances, these two kindred spirits would have met each other with cordial congratulations. But instead of this being so, Balak must show himself a little hurt with what he thinks Balaam's want of confidence in his word and prerogative as king. And though Balaam's difficulty has not lain in these things, he cannot explain the misunderstanding; he has to hear that word "wherefore" as if he heard it not. "Lo, I am come unto thee," that must be sufficient. And as to Balak's expectations, he can only fall back upon the old misleading generalities; he cannot meet the king with the open, eager, joyous countenance of one who sees success within his grasp. Balak, he sees, has more confidence in him than he can possibly have in himself, considering the strange things he has experienced since he set out on his journey. It is not even the proverbial slip between the cup and the lip that he has to prepare for. It is not the probability of success with the possibility of failure, but the strong probability of failure with just the possibility of success. "Have I now any power at all to say anything? the word that God putteth in my mouth, that shall I speak." Not that we are to suppose Balak was unduly taken aback by such a want of ardour and sympathy in Balaam. Very likely he thought it was nothing more than a proper professional deference to Jehovah, and that in the event all would be right; just as men say "God willing" and "please God" when they are in the midst of schemes where God's will and pleasure are never thought of at all.—Y.

Vers. 13, 14.—*Balaam—the summons.* The story of Balaam is full of contrarieties. The pure faith and worship of Jehovah is seen coming into strange contact with the superstitions of heathenism; and as regards the personal character of Balaam, utterly discordant moral elements are seen struggling together in the same breast. The chief interest of the story centres in the moral phenomenon presented by the man himself—"that strange mixture of a man," as Bishop Newton well calls him. He was a heathen soothsayer, and yet had some real knowledge of God. He was under the influence of sordid passions, and yet was in personal converse with the Spirit of truth, and received from him, at least for the time, a real prophetic gift. He had no part or lot with the chosen people, but rather with their worst enemies, and yet his "eyes were opened," and he had very lofty conceptions of Israel's dignity and blessedness. His history has its clearly-marked stages. In this first stage we have the summons that came to him from Balak, and the answer he was constrained to send back to it. Note here—

I. HEATHEN FAITH IN THE UNSEEN. Balak in the extremity of his fear sends beyond the limits of his own people, into distant Mesopotamia, to secure the help of one supposed to be endowed with supernatural gifts, in special relation to the invisible powers, able to "curse and to bless" (ver. 6). A striking illustration of that blind instinct of human nature by virtue of which it believes ever in the interposition of Deity in the world's affairs. All idolatrous rites, oracles, divinations, incantations, sacerdotal benedictions and maledictions, rest ultimately on this basis. It is this makes the sway of the priest and the supposed "prophet of the Invisible" so mighty in every land and age. Christianity teaches us to lay hold on the substantial truth that underlies these distorted forms of superstition. It enlightens this blind instinct; reveals the righteous "God that judgeth in the earth;" leads humanity to Him who is at once its "Prophet, Priest, and King."

II. THE WITNESS FOR GOD THAT MAY BE FOUND IN THE SOUL OF A DEPRAVED MAN, even of one whose inward dispositions and whole habit of life are most opposed to his will. Balaam practised an art that was "an abomination unto the Lord" (Deut. xviii. 12), and his way was altogether "perverse" (ver. 32), and yet God was near to him. God spoke to him, and put the spirit of prophecy into his heart, and a word into his mouth. He "heard the words and saw the vision of the Almighty." Whether his knowledge of God was the result of dim traditions of a purer faith handed down from his forefathers, or of influences that had spread in his own time into the land of his birth, we at least see how scattered rays of Divine light then penetrated the deep darkness of heathendom. So now God is often nearer to men than we or they themselves suppose. He does not leave himself without a witness, even in the most ignorant and vile. The light in them is never totally extinguished. They have their gleams of higher thought, their touches of nobler, purer feeling. Conscience rebukes their practical perversity, and the Spirit strives with them to lead them into a better way. When God is absolutely silent in a man's soul, all hope of guiding him by outward persuasions into the path of righteousness is gone.

III. THE PROSTITUTION OF NOBLE POWERS TO BASE USES. Here is a man whose widespread fame was the result, probably, to a great extent of real genius. His native capacity—mental insight, influence over men, poetic gift—was the secret of this fame. Like Simon Magus, he "bewitched the people," so that they all "gave heed to him, from the least unto the greatest, saying, This man is the great power of God." But these extraordinary powers are perverted to the furtherance of an unhallowed cause; he makes them the servants of his own base ambition and desire for gain. "He loved the wages of unrighteousness." It was in his heart to obey the behest of Balak and secure the offered prize. There is a tone of disappointment in the words, "The Lord refuseth to give me leave to go with you." He lets "I dare not" wait upon "I would." And notwithstanding all his poetic inspiration and his passing raptures of devout and pious feeling,

"Yet in the prophet's soul the dreams of avarice stay."

How full is all human history of examples of the waste of noble faculties, the prostitution to evil uses of God-given powers! The darkest deeds have ever been done and the deepest miseries inflicted on the world by those who were most fitted by nature to yield effective service to the cause of truth and righteousness, and to confer blessings on mankind. And it is generally some one base affection—the lust of the flesh, self-love, avarice, an imperious will, &c.—that turns the rich tide of their life in a false direction. As the spreading sails of a ship only hasten its destruction when the helm fails, so is it with the noblest faculties of a man when he has lost the guidance of a righteous purpose.

IV. THE DIVINE RESTRAINT OF MAN'S LIBERTY TO DO EVIL. "And God said, Thou shalt not go with them," &c. The spell of a higher Power is over him. In a sense contrary to that of Paul the Apostle, he "cannot do the thing that he would." So are wicked men often made to feel that there is after all a will stronger than their will; that, free as they seem to be, some invisible hand is holding them in check, limiting their range of action, thwarting their purposes, compelling them to do the very thing they would fain avoid, turning their curses into blessings, so that in the end they serve the cause they meant to destroy. The hope of the world lies in the absolute mastery of the Will that is "holy, and just, and good" over all conceivable opposing forms of human and Satanic power.—W.

Vers. 31—35.—*Balaam—the arrest.* The secret willingness of Balaam to yield to the solicitations of Balak, seen at first in the tone of his answer, "The Lord refuseth," &c., was still more manifest in his parleying with the second appeal. Though he felt the resistless force of the Divine restraint, yet he delayed the return of the messengers for the night in hope of getting a reversal of the sentence (vers. 18, 19). No wonder God's anger was kindled against him, and that, though permission was at last given him to go, he was made in this startling way to feel that he was in the hands of a Power that would not be mocked. Whatever view we take of the strange incidents of this narrative, whether as objective realities, or as the visions of a trance, the moral lessons remain substantially the same. Three features of Balaam's conduct are specially prominent.

I. HIS CRUEL ANGER. His rough treatment of the dumb ass is marked with reprobation. It was both itself evil and the symptom of a hidden evil. 1. We may believe that the secret unrest of his conscience had a great deal to do with this outburst of anger. Note the subtle connection that often exists between certain unusual phases of conduct and the hidden workings of the heart. Jonah's anger at the withering of the gourd was but one of the signs of his general want of sympathy with the Divine proceedure. Balaam, perhaps, was not a cruel man, but the sense of wrong within and the feeling that he was doing wrong betrayed itself even in this form of behaviour. Conscience made him a coward, and cowardice is always cruel. If it had not been for the "madness" of his passion, he might have judged, as a diviner, that the unwillingness of the beast to pursue her journey counselled him to return ; but when a man's heart is not right with God, resentment is often roused against that which is meant to turn him into a better way. "Am I become your enemy because I tell you the truth?" (Gal. iv. 16). 2. It illustrates the sad subjection of the inferior creatures to the curse of moral evil. "The creature was made subject to vanity, not willingly." "The whole creation groaneth," &c. We think it strange that the dumb ass should "speak with man's voice, and rebuke the prophet's madness," but, to the ear that can hear it, such a voice is continually going forth from all the innocent creatures that suffer the cruel consequences of man's abuse. Well may St. Paul represent them as "waiting with earnest expectation for the manifestation of the sons of God" (Rom. viii. 19, 22).

II. HIS BLIND INFATUATION. It is deeply significant that he should not have seen the angel. Even the poor dumb creature that he rode saw more than he did. It was his moral perversity, the frenzy of his carnal ambition, that was the true cause of the dulness of his spiritual vision. Note—1. Sin blinds men to the things that it is most needful for them to apprehend and know. Mental blindness often, not always, has a moral cause. "This people's heart is waxed gross, and their ears are dull of hearing," &c. (Matt. xiii. 15). The highest spiritual truths, realities of the spirit world, tokens of the Divine presence and working, eternal moral laws, sacred responsibilities of life, &c.—all these are darkly hidden from him whose heart is "thoroughly set in him to do evil." 2. Even animal instinct is a safer guide than the moral sense of a bad man. It effectually warns of danger, and prompts to the pursuit of the good nature requires. It is to the animal a sufficient law. But when the "spirit in man, the inspiration of the Almighty that giveth him understanding," the sovereignty of reason and conscience, is overborne by base fleshly lust, man sinks lower than the brutes that perish. Their obedience to the law of their being puts him to shame. Though they "speak not with man's voice," their silent wisdom "rebukes him for his iniquity." "If the light that is in thee be darkness," &c. (Matt. vi. 23).

III. HIS HELPLESSNESS. This is seen—1. In his abject submission. "He bowed down his head, and fell flat on his face," saying, "I have sinned;" "now, therefore, if it displease thee, I will get me back again." He must have known from the beginning that his obstinate self-will was displeasing to God, but now that the consequences of it stare him in the face he is filled with alarm. There are those who grieve over their sin only when it is found out. It is not the evil itself they dread, but only its discovery and punishment. Fear often makes men repent and reform when there is no genuine abhorrence of wrong-doing. 2. In the Divine compulsion under which he is placed to pursue his journey. "Go with the men," &c. He would fain draw back, but it is too late now; he must do the work and bear the testimony that God has determined for him. When men are bent upon that which is evil, God often allows them to become entangled in circumstances of danger from which there is no escape, that "they may eat of the fruit of their own way, and be filled with their own devices" (Prov. i. 31).—W.

EXPOSITION.

BALAAM'S PROPHECIES (ch. xxii. 41—xxiv.). Ch. xxii. 41.—**The high places of Baal**, or "Bamoth-Baal." Perhaps the Bamoth mentioned in ch. xxi. 19, 20. This is, however, by no means certain, because high places were no doubt numerous, and that Bamoth would seem to have been too far from the present camp of Israel. In any case they crossed the Arnon, and ran some risk by adventuring themselves on hostile territory. **That thence he might see the utmost part of the people.** According to the quasi-sacramental character attributed to the cursing of a seer, it was held necessary that the subject of the curse should be in view. Balak desired to attain this object with as little risk as possible, and therefore he took Balaam first of all to these heights, whence a distant and partial view of Israel might be had.

Ch. xxiii. 1.—**Build me here seven altars.** According to the common opinion of the heathen, it was necessary to propitiate with sacrifices the God with whom they had to do, and if possible to secure his favourable consideration on their side. The number seven was especially connected with the revelation of the true God, the Creator of the world, and was probably observed here for this reason. The sacrifices were offered no doubt to Jehovah.

Ver. 3.—**Peradventure the Lord will come to meet me.** It might be concluded from ch. xxiv. 1 that Balaam went only to look for "auguries," i. e. for such natural signs in the flight of birds and the like as the heathen were wont to observe as manifestations of the favour or disfavour of God, the success or failure of enterprises. It seems clear that it was his practice to do so, either as having some faith himself in such uncertainties, or as stooping to usual heathen arts which he inwardly despised. But from the fact that God met him (we know not how), and that such supernatural communication was not unexpected, we may conclude that Balaam's words meant more for himself than the mere observance of auguries, whatever they may have meant for Balak. **To an high place.** Rather, "to a bald place" (שְׁפִי—compare the meaning of "Calvary"),

from which the immediate prospect was uninterrupted.

Ver. 4.—**I have prepared seven altars.** Balaam, acting for the king of Moab, his heathen patron, in this difficult business, points out to God that he had given him the full quota of sacrifices to begin with. It was implied in this reminder that God would naturally feel disposed to do something for Balaam in return.

Ver. 7.—**Took up his parable.** מָשָׁל (cf. ch. xxi. 27). Balaam's utterances were in the highest degree poetical, according to the antithetic form of the poetry of that day, which delighted in sustained parallelisms, in lofty figures, and in abrupt turns. The "_mashal_" of Balaam resembled the "burden" of the later prophets in this, that it was not a discourse uttered to men, but a thing revealed in him of which he had to deliver himself as best he might in such words as came to him. His inward eye was fixed on this revelation, and he gave utterance to it without consideration of those who heard. **Aram**, i. e. Aram-Naharaim, or Mesopotamia (cf. Gen. xxix. 1; Deut. xxiii. 4). **Defy**, or "threaten," i. e. with the wrath of Heaven. **Jacob.** The use of this name as the poetical equivalent of Israel shows that Balaam was familiar with the story of the patriarch, and understood his relation to the people before him.

Ver. 9.—**The people shall dwell alone, and shall not be reckoned.** Rather, "It is a people that dwelleth apart, and is not numbered." It was not the outward isolation on which his eye was fixed, for that indeed was only temporary and accidental, but the religious and moral separateness of Israel as the chosen people of God, which was the very secret of their national greatness.

Ver. 10.—**The fourth part of Israel.** אֶת־רֹבַע is so rendered by the Targums, as alluding to the four great camps into which the host was divided. The Septuagint has δήμους, apparently from an incorrect reading. The Samaritan and the older versions, followed by the Vulgate, render it "progeny," but this meaning is conjectural, and there seems no sufficient reason to depart from the common translation. **Let me die the death** of the righteous. The word "righteous" is in the plural (יְשָׁרִים, δικαίων): it may refer either to the Israelites as a holy nation, living and dying in the favour of God ; or to the patriarchs, such as Abraham, the promises made to whom, in faith of which they died, were already so gloriously fulfilled. If the former reference was intended, Balaam must have had a much fuller and happier knowledge of "life and immortality" than the Israelites themselves, to whom death was dreadful, all the more that it ended a life protected and blessed by God (cf. *e. g.* Ps. lxxxviii. 10—12 ; Isa. xxxviii. 18, 19). It is hardly credible that so singular an anticipation of purely Christian feeling should really be found in the mouth of a prophet of that day, for it is clear that the words, however much inspired, did express the actual emotion of Balaam at the moment. It is therefore more consistent with the facts and probabilities of the case to suppose that Balaam referred to righteous Abraham (cf. Isa. xli. 2) and his immediate descendants, and wished that when he came to die he might have as sure a hope as they had enjoyed that God would bless and multiply their seed, and make their name to be glorious in the earth. Let my last end be like his. אַחֲרִית (last end) is the same word translated "latter days" and "latter end" in ch. xxiv. 14, 20. It means the last state of a people or of a man as represented in his offspring ; the sense is not incorrectly expressed by the Septuagint, γένοιτο τὸ σπέρμα μου ὡς τὸ σπέρμα τούτων.

Ver. 13.—Come . . unto another place. Balak attributed the miscarriage of his enterprise thus far to something inauspicious in the locality. Thou shalt see but the utmost part of them. אֶפֶס קָצֵהוּ תִרְאֶה. Both the meaning of the nouns and the tense of the verb are disputed. By some "*ephes katsehu*" (the end of the last of them) is held equivalent to "the whole of them," which seems to contradict the next clause even if defensible in itself. The ordinary rendering is favoured by the Septuagint (ἀλλ᾿ ἢ μέρος τι αὐτοῦ ὄψει) and by the Targums. On the other hand, some would read the verb in the present tense, and understand Balak's words to refer to the place they were leaving. This is in accordance with the statement in ch. xxii. 41, and it would certainly seem as if Balak and Balaam moved each time nearer to that encampment which was for different reasons the centre of attraction to them both.

Ver. 14.—The field of Zophim, *i. e.* of the watchers. Probably a well-known outlook. To the top of Pisgah. They followed apparently on the track of their enemies (see on ch. xxi. 20).

Ver. 15.—While I meet the Lord yonder. Rather, "and I will go and meet thus." וְאָנֹכִי אִקָּרֶה כֹּה. Balaam does not say whom or what he is going to meet, but from the use of the same term in ch. xxiv. 1 it is evident that he employed the language of soothsayers looking for auguries. He may have spoken vaguely on purpose, because he was in truth acting a part with Balak.

Ver. 20.—I have received commandment to bless. The word "commandment" is not wanted here. Balaam had received, not instructions, but an inward revelation of the Divine will which he could not contravene.

Ver. 21.—He hath not beheld iniquity in Jacob. The subject of this and the parallel clause is left indefinite. If it is God, according to the A. V., then it means that God in his mercy shut his eyes to the evil which did exist in individuals, and for his own sake would not impute it to the chosen nation. If it be impersonal, according to the Septuagint and the Targums, "one does not behold iniquity," &c., then it means that the iniquity was not flagrant, was not left to gather head and volume until it brought down destruction. Perverseness. Rather, "suffering" (עָמָל. Septuagint, πόνος), the natural consequence of sin. Compare the use of the two words in Ps. x. 7 ; xc. 10. The shout of a king is among them. The "shout" (תְּרוּעָה) is the jubilation of the nation with which it acclaims its victor king (cf. 1 Sam. iv. 5, 6). In Levit. xxiii. 24 ; Ps. xlvii. 5 it is used of the sounding of the sacred trumpets.

Ver. 22.—God. אֵל, and also at the end of the next verse, and four times in the next chapter (vers. 4, 8, 16, 23). The use seems to be poetic, and no particular signification can be attached to it. Brought them, or, perhaps, "is leading them." So the Septuagint : Θεὸς ὁ ἐξαγαγὼν αὐτόν. Unicorn. Hebrew, רְאֵם. It is uniformly rendered μονοκέρως by the Septuagint, under the mistaken notion that the rhinoceros was intended. It is evident, however, from Deut. xxxiii. 17 and other passages that the reem had two horns, and that its horns were its most prominent feature. It would also appear from Job xxxix. 9—12 and Isa. xxxiv. 7 that, while itself untameable, it was allied to species employed in husbandry. The reem may therefore have been the aurochs or urus, now extinct, but which formerly had so large a range in the forests of the old world. There is some doubt, however, whether the urus existed in those days in Syria, and it may have been a wild buffalo, or some kindred animal of the bovine genus, whose size, fierceness, and length of horn made it a wonder and a fear.

Ver. 23.—**Enchantment,** נַחַשׁ. Rather, "augury." Septuagint, οἰωνισμός. See on Levit. xix. 26, where the practice is forbidden to Israel. **Against Jacob,** or, "in Jacob," as the marginal reading, and this is favoured by the Septuagint and the Targums, and is equally true and striking. It was the proud peculiarity of Israel that he trusted not to any magic arts or superstitious rites, uncertain in themselves, and always leading to imposture, but to the direction and favour of the Almighty. **Divination.** קֶסֶם. Septuagint, μαντεία. The art of the soothsayer. **According to this time it shall be said of Jacob and of Israel.** Rather, "in season," *i.e.* in God's good time, "it shall be said to Jacob and to Israel." **What hath God wrought!** or, "what God doeth." The meaning seems to be that augury and divination were useless and vain in the case of Israel, because God himself declared and would declare his mighty acts in behalf of his people, and that by no uncertain vaticination, but by open declaration.

Ver. 24.—**As a great lion.** לָבִיא, generally translated "old lion," as in Gen. xlix. 9. By some it is rendered lioness (cf. Job iv. 11; Nahum ii. 12). **As a young lion.** אֲרִי, the ordinary term for a lion without further distinction. It is altogether fantastic to suppose that Balaam had just seen a lion coming up from the ghor of Jordan, and that this "omen" inspired his "*mashal.*" The rising of a lion from its covert was one of the most common of the more striking phenomena of nature in those regions, and the imagery it afforded was in constant use; but in truth it is evident that these similes are borrowed from Jacob's dying prophecy concerning Judah (Gen. xlix. 9), in which the word "prey" (Hebrew, טֶרֶף, a torn thing) is also found. Balaam was acquainted with that prophecy, as he was with the promises made to Abraham (cf. ver. 10 with Gen. xiii. 16; xxviii. 14).

Ver. 27.—**I will bring thee unto another place.** At first (ver. 25) Balak had in his vexation desired to stop the mouth of Balaam, but afterwards he thought it wiser to make yet another attempt to change the mind of God; as a heathen, he still thought that this might be done by dint of importunity and renewed sacrifices.

Ver. 28.—**Unto the top of Peor.** On the meaning of Peor see on ch. xxv. 3. This Peor was a summit of the Abarim ranges northwards from Pisgah, and nearer to the Israelites. The adjacent village, Beth-Peor, was near the place of Moses' burial (Deut. xxxiv. 6). From the phrase used in Deut. iii. 29; iv. 46, with which the testimony of Eusebius agrees, it must have lain almost opposite Jericho on the heights behind the

Arboth Moab. From Peor, therefore, the whole encampment, in all its length and breadth, would lie beneath their gaze. **Jeshimon.** See on ch. xxi. 20.

Ch. xxiv. 1.—**As at other times,** or, "as (he had done) time after time." Septuagint, κατὰ τὸ εἰωθός. **To seek for enchantments.** Rather, "for the meeting with auguries." לִקְרַאת נְחָשִׁים. Septuagint, εἰς συνάντησιν τοῖς οἰωνοῖς. *Nachashim,* as in ch. xxiii. 23, is not enchantments in the sense of magical practices, but definitely auguries, *i. e.* omens and signs in the natural world observed and interpreted according to an artificial system as manifesting the purposes of God. As one of the commonest and worst of heathen practices, it was forbidden to Israel (Levit. xix. 26; Deut. xviii. 10) and held up to reprobation, as in 2 Kings xvii. 17; xxi. 6; 2 Chron. xxxiii. 6. **Toward the wilderness.** הַמִּדְבָּר. Not "Jeshimon," but apparently the Arboth Moab in which Israel was encamped, and which were for the most part desert as compared with the country around.

Ver. 2.—**The spirit of God came upon him.** This seems to intimate a higher state of inspiration than the expression, "God put a word into his mouth" (ch. xxiii. 5, 16).

Ver. 3.—**Balaam . . hath said.** Rather, "the utterance of Balaam." נְאֻם is constantly used, as in ch. xiv. 28, for a Divine utterance, *effatum Dei,* but it does not by itself, apart from the context, claim a superhuman origin. **The man whose eyes are open.** הַגֶּבֶר שְׁתֻם הָעָיִן. The authorities are divided between the rendering in the text and the opposite rendering given in the margin. סָתַם is used in Dan. viii. 26, and שָׁתַם in Lam. iii. 8, in the sense of "shut;" but, on the other hand, a passage in the Mishnah distinctly uses שׁתם and סתם in opposite senses. The Vulgate, on the one hand, has *obturatus;* the Septuagint, on the other, has ὁ ἀληθινῶς ὁρῶν, and this is the sense given by the Targums. Strange to say, it makes no real difference whether we read "open" or "shut," because in any case it was the inward vision that was quickened, while the outward senses were closed.

Ver. 4.—**Falling into a trance.** Rather, "falling down." *Qui cadit,* Vulgate. The case of Saul, who "fell down naked all that day" (1 Sam. xix. 24), overcome by the illapse of the Spirit, affords the best comparison. Physically, it would seem to have been a kind of catalepsy, in which the senses were closed to outward things, and the eyes open but unseeing. The word for "open" in this verse is the ordinary one, not that used in ver. 3.

Ver. 6.—**As the valleys,** or, "as the torrents" (נְחָלִים), which pour down in parallel courses from the upper slopes. **As gardens by the river's side.** The river (נָהָר, as in ch. xxii. 5) means the Euphrates. Balaam combines the pleasant imagery of his own cultivated land with that of the wilder scene amidst which he now stood. **As the trees of lign aloes.** אֲהָלִים. Aloe trees, such as grew in the further east, where Balaam had perhaps seen them. **Which the Lord hath planted,** or, "the Lord's planting," a poetical way of describing their beauty and rarity (cf. Ps. i. 3; civ. 16).

Ver. 7.—**He shall pour the water,** or, "the water shall overflow." **Out of his buckets.** דָּלְיָו is the dual, "his two buckets." The image, familiar enough to one who lived in an irrigated land, is of one carrying two buckets on the ends of a pole which are so full as to run over as he goes. **And his seed . . in many waters.** It is uncertain in what sense the word "seed" is used. It may be an image as simple as the last, of seed sown either by or actually upon many waters (cf. Eccles. xi. 1), and so securing a plentiful and safe return ; or it may stand for the seed, i. e. the posterity, of Israel, which should grow up amidst many blessings (Isa. xliv. 4). The former seems most in keeping here. **His king shall be higher than Agag.** Rather, "let his king be higher than Agag." The name Agag (אֲגַג, the fiery one) does not occur again except as the name of the king of Amalek whom Saul conquered and Samuel slew (1 Sam. xv.) ; yet it may safely be assumed that it was the official title of all the kings of Amalek, resembling in this "Abimelech" and "Pharaoh." Here it seems to stand for the dynasty and the nation of the Amalekites, and there is no reason to suppose that any reference was intended to any particular individual or event in the distant future. The "king" of Israel here spoken of is certainly not Saul or any other of the kings, but God himself in his character as temporal Ruler of Israel ; and the "kingdom" is the kingdom of heaven as set forth by way of anticipation in the polity and order of the chosen race. As a fact, Israel had afterwards a visible king who overthrew Agag, but their having such a king was alien to the mind of God, and due to a distinct falling away from national faith, and therefore could find no place in this prophecy.

Ver. 8.—**And shall break their bones.** יְגָרֵם (cf. Ezek. xxiii. 34) seems to mean "crush" or "smash." The Septuagint has ἐκμυελιεῖ, "shall suck out," i. e. the marrow, but the word does not seem to bear this meaning. **Pierce them through with his**

arrows, or, "dash in pieces his arrows," i. e. the arrows shot at him. הִצָּיו יִמְחָץ. The difficulty is the possessive suffix to "arrows," which is in the singular ; otherwise this rendering gives a much better sense, and more in keeping with the rest of the passage. The image in Balaam's mind is evidently that of a terrible wild beast devouring his enemies, stamping them underfoot, and dashing to pieces in his fury the arrows or darts which they vainly launch against him (compare the imagery in Dan. vii. 7).

Ver. 9.—**A lion.** אֲרִי. **A great lion.** לָבִיא. See on ch. xxiii. 24, and Gen. xlix. 9. **Blessed is he that blesseth thee,** &c. In these words Balaam seems to refer to the terms of Balak's first message (ch. xxii. 6). Far from being affected by blessings and cursings from without, Israel was itself a source of blessing or cursing to others according as they treated him.

Ver. 12.—**Spake I not also.** This was altogether true. Balaam had enough of the true prophet about him not only to act with strict fidelity, as far as the letter of the command went, but also to behave with great dignity towards Balak.

Ver. 14.—**I will advertise thee.** אִיעָצְךָ has properly the meaning "advise" (Septuagint, συμβουλεύσω), but it seems to have here the same subordinate sense of giving information which "advise" has with us. The Vulgate here has followed the surmise of the Jewish commentators, who saw nothing in Balaam but the arch-enemy of their race, and has actually altered the text into "dabo consilium quid populus tuus populo huic faciat" (cf. ch. xxxi. 16).

Ver. 16.—**Knew the knowledge of the Most High.** Septuagint, ἐπιστάμενος ἐπιστήμην παρὰ Ὑψίστου. This expression alone distinguishes this introduction of Balaam's *mashal* from the former one (vers. 3, 4), but it is difficult to say that it really adds anything to our understanding of his mental state. If we ask when Balaam had received the revelation which he now proceeds to communicate, it would seem most natural to reply that it was made known to him when "the Spirit of God came upon him," and that Balak's anger had interrupted him in the midst of his *mashal*, or possibly he had kept it back, as too distasteful to his patron, until he saw that he had nothing more to expect from that quarter.

Ver. 17.—**I shall see him, but not now : I shall behold him, but not nigh.** Rather, "I see him, but not now : I behold him, but not near" (אֲשׁוּרֶנּוּ . . . אֶרְאֶנּוּ exactly as in ch. xxiii. 9). Balaam does not mean to say that he expected himself to see at any future time the mysterious Being of whom he speaks, who is identical with the "Star" and the "Sceptre" of the following clauses; he speaks wholly as a prophet, and means that his inner gaze is fixed upon such an one, with full assurance that he exists in the counsels of God, but with clear recognition of the fact that his actual coming is yet in the far future. **There shall come a Star out of Jacob.** Septuagint, ἀνατελεῖ ἄστρον. It may quite as well be rendered by the present; Balaam simply utters what passes before his inward vision. The star is a natural and common poetic symbol of an illustrious, or, as we say, "brilliant," personage, and as such recurs many times in Scripture (cf. Job xxxviii. 7; Isa. xiv. 12; Dan. viii. 10; Matt. xxiv. 29; Philip. ii. 15; Rev. i. 20; ii. 28). The celebrated Jewish fanatic called himself Bar-cochab, "son of the Star," in allusion to this prophecy. **A Sceptre shall rise out of Israel.** This further defines the "star" as a ruler of men, for the sceptre is used in that sense in the dying prophecy of Jacob (Gen. xlix. 10), with which Balaam was evidently acquainted. Accordingly the Septuagint has here ἀναστήσεται ἄνϑρωπος. **Shall smite the corners of Moab.** Rather, "the two corners" (dual), or "the two sides of Moab," i. e. shall crush Moab on either side. **And destroy all the children of Sheth.** In Jer. xlviii. 45, where this prophecy is in a manner quoted, the word קַרְקַר (qarqar, destroy) is altered into קָדְקֹד (quadqod, crown of the head). This raises a very curious and interesting question as to the use made by the prophets of the earlier Scriptures, but it gives no authority for an alteration of the text. The expression בְּנֵי־שֵׁת has been variously rendered. The Jewish commentators, followed by the Septuagint (πάντας υἱοὺς Σήϑ) and the older versions, understand it to mean the sons of Seth, the son of Adam, i. e. all mankind. Many modern commentators, however, take שֵׁת as a contraction of שְׁאֵת (Lam. iii. 47—"desolation"), and read "sons of confusion," as equivalent to the unruly neighbours and relations of Israel. This, however, is extremely dubious in itself, for שֵׁת nowhere occurs in this sense, and derives no support from Jer. xlviii. 45. It is true that בְּנֵי שֵׁת is there replaced by בְּנֵי שָׁאוֹן, "sons of tumult," but then this very verse affords the clearest evidence that the prophet felt no hesitation in altering the text of Scripture to suit his own inspired purpose. If it be true that קַרְקַר will not bear the meaning given to it in the Targums of "reign over," still there is no insuperable difficulty in the common rendering. Jewish prophecy, from beginning to end, contemplated the Messiah as the Conqueror, the Subduer, and even the Destroyer of all the heathen, i. e. of all who were not Jews. It is only in the New Testament that the iron sceptre with which he was to dash in pieces the heathen (Ps. ii. 9) becomes the pastoral staff wherewith he shepherds them (Rev. ii. 27—ποιμανεῖ, after the Septuagint, which has here misread the text). The prophecy was that Messiah should destroy the heathen; the fulfilment that he destroyed not them, but their heathenism (cf. e g. Ps. cxlix. 6—9 with James v. 20).

Ver. 18.—**Seir also shall be a possession for his enemies.** Seir (Gen. xxxii. 3), or Mount Seir (Gen. xxxvi. 8), was the old name, still retained as an alternative, of Edom. It is uncertain whether the rendering " for his (i. e. Edom's) enemies" is correct. The Hebrew is simply אֹיְבָיו, which may stand in apposition to Edom and Seir, "his enemies," i. e. the enemies of Israel. So the Septuagint, Ἠσαῦ ὁ ἐχϑρὸς αὐτοῦ. **Shall do valiantly,** or, "shall be prosperous" (cf. Deut. viii. 17; Ruth iv. 11).

Ver. 19.—**Shall come he that shall have dominion.** וְיֵרְדְּ. Literally, "one shall rule," the subject being indefinite. **Of the city.** מֵעִיר; not apparently out of any city in particular, but "out of any hostile city." The expression implies not only conquest, but total destruction of the foe.

Ver. 20.—**He looked on Amalek.** This looking must have been an inward vision, because the haunts of the Amalekites were far away (see on Gen. xxxvi. 12; Exod. xvii. 8; Numb. xiv. 25, 45). **The first of the nations.** Amalek was in no sense a leading nation, nor was it a very ancient nation. It was indeed the very first of the nations to attack Israel, but it is a most arbitrary treatment of the words to understand them in that sense. The prophet Amos (vi. 1) uses the same expression of the Jewish aristocracy of his day. As it was in no better position than Amalek to claim it in any true sense, we can but suppose that in either case there is a reference to the vainglorious vauntings of the people threatened; it would be quite in keeping with the Bedawin character if Amalek gave himself out to be "the first of nations."

Ver. 21.—**He looked on the Kenites.** This mashal is excessively obscure, for both the subject of it and the drift of it are disputed. On the one hand, the Kenites are mentioned among the Canaanitish tribes that were to be dispossessed, in Gen. xv. 19; on the other, they are identified with the Midianitish tribe to which Hobab and Raguel belonged, in Judges i. 16, and apparently in 1 Sam. xv. 6 (see on ch. x. 29). It has been supposed that the friendly Kenites had by this time left the camp of Israel and established themselves by conquest in the south of Canaan, and even that they had occupied the territory and taken the name of the original Kenites of Gen. xv. 19. This, however, is a mere conjecture, and a very improbable one. That a weak tribe like that of Hobab should have done what Israel had not dared to do, and settled themselves by force of arms in Southern Palestine, and, further, that they should be already known by the name of those whom they had destroyed, is extremely unlikely, and is inconsistent with the statement in Judges i. 16. **And thou puttest thy nest in a rock.** Rather, " and thy nest laid (שִׂים) upon a rock." We do not know where the Kenites dwelt, and therefore we cannot tell whether this expression is to be understood literally or figuratively. If the Canaanitish tribe is here spoken of, it is very likely they had their residence in some strong mountain fastness, but if the Midianitish tribe, then there is no reason to suppose that they had crossed the Jordan at all. In that case the "nest" must be wholly figurative, and must refer to that strong confidence which they placed in the protection of the God of Israel.

Ver. 22.—**Nevertheless the Kenite shall be wasted.** כִּי אִם־יִהְיֶה לְבָעֵר קָיִן. Rather, " Kain shall surely not be wasted." כִּי־אִם is of doubtful meaning, but it seems here to have the force of a negative question equivalent to a negation. Kain is mentioned in Josh. xv. 57 as one of the towns of Judah, but there is little reason to suppose that an insignificant village is here mentioned by name. Probably "Kain" stands for the tribe-father, and is simply the poetical equivalent of Kenite. **Until.** עַד־מָה. There is some uncertainty about these two particles, which are sometimes rendered "how long?" In the sense of "until" they are said to be an Aramaism, but this is doubtful.

Ver. 23.—**When God doeth this.** Literally, "from the settling of it by God." מִשֻּׂמוֹ אֵל, i. e. when God shall bring these terrible things to pass. Septuagint, ὅταν θῇ ταῦτα ὁ θεός. This exclamation refers to the woe which he is about to pronounce, which involved his own people also.

Ver. 24.—**Chittim.** Cyprus (see on Gen. x. 4). The "isles of Chittim" are mentioned by Jeremiah (ii. 10) and by Ezekiel (xxvii. 6) in the sense apparently of the western islands generally, while in Dan. xi. 30 "the ships of Chittim" may have an even wider reference.

Indeed the Targum of Palestine makes mention of Italy here, and the Vulgate actually translates "venient in trieribus de Italiâ." There is, however, no reason to suppose that Balaam knew or spoke of anything further than Cyprus. It was "from the side of" (מִיַד) Cyprus that the ships of his vision came down upon the Phœnician coasts, wherever their original starting-point may have been. **Shall afflict,** or, " shall bring low." The same word is used of the oppression of Israel in Egypt (Gen. xv. 13). **Eber.** The Septuagint has here Ἑβραίους, and is followed by the Peschito and the Vulgate. It is not likely, however, that Balaam would have substituted " Eber " for the "Jacob" and " Israel " which he had previously used. The Targum of Onkelos paraphrases " Eber " by "beyond the Euphrates," and that of Palestine has "all the sons of Eber." From Gen. x. 21 it would appear that "the children of Eber" were the same as the Shemites; Asshur, therefore, was himself included in Eber, but is separately mentioned on account of his fame and power. **And he also shall perish for ever.** The subject of this prophecy is left in obscurity. It is difficult on grammatical grounds to refer it to Asshur, and it does not seem appropriate to " Eber." It may mean that the unnamed conquering race which should overthrow the Asian monarchies should itself come to an end for evermore ; or it may be that Balaam added these words while he beheld with dismay the coming destruction of his own Shemitic race, and their final subjugation by more warlike powers. It must be remembered that the Greek empire, although overthrown, did not by any means "perish for ever" in the same sense as the previous empires of the East.

Ver. 25. — **And returned to his place.** יָשָׁב לִמְקוֹ. It is doubtful whether this expression, which is used in Gen. xviii. 33 and in other places, implies that Balaam returned to his home on the Euphrates. If he did he must have retraced his steps almost immediately, because he was slain among the Midianites shortly after (ch. xxxi. 8). The phrase, however, may merely mean that he set off homewards, and is not inconsistent with the supposition that he went no further on his way than the head-quarters of the Midianites. It is not difficult to understand the infatuation which would keep him within reach of a people so strange and terrible.

NOTE ON THE PROPHECIES OF BALAAM.

That the prophecies of Balaam have a Messianic character, and are only to be fully understood in a Christian sense, seems to lie upon the face of them. The Targums of Onkelos and Palestine make mention of King Meshiha here, and the great mass of Christian interpretation has uniformly followed in the track of Jewish tradition. It is of course possible to get rid of the prophetic element altogether by assuming that the utterances of Balaam were either composed or largely interpolated after the events to which they seem to refer. It would be necessary in this case to bring their real date down to the period of the Macedonian conquests, and much later still if the Greek empire also was to "perish for ever." The difficulty and arbitrary character of such an assumption becomes the more evident the more it is considered ; nor does it seem consistent with the form into which the predictions are cast. A patriotic Jew looking *back* from the days of Alexander or his successors would not call the great Eastern power by the name of Asshur, because two subsequent empires had arisen in the place of Assyria proper. But that Balaam, looking *forward* down the dim vista of the future, should see Asshur, and only Asshur, is in perfect keeping with what we know of prophetic perspective,—the further off the events descried by inward vision, the more extreme the foreshortening,—according to which law it is well known that the first and second advents of Christ are inextricably blended in almost every case.

If we accept the prophecies as genuine, it is, again, only possible to reject the Messianic element by assuming that no Jewish prophecy overleaps the narrow limits of Jewish history. The mysterious Being whom Balaam descries in the undated future, who is the King of Israel, and whom he identifies with the Shiloh of Jacob's dying prophecy, and who is to bring to nought all nations of the world, cannot be David, although David may anticipate him in many ways ; still less, as the reference to Agag, Amalek, and the Kenites might for a moment incline us to believe, can it be Saul. At the same time, while the Messianic element in the prophecy cannot reasonably be ignored, it is obvious that it does not by any means exist by itself; it is so mixed up with what is purely local and temporal in the relations between Israel and the petty tribes which surrounded and envied him, that it is impossible to isolate it or to exhibit it in any clear and definite form. The Messiah indeed appears, as it were, upon the stage in a mysterious and remote grandeur ; but he appears with a slaughter weapon in his hand, crushing such enemies of Israel as were then and there formidable, and exterminating the very fugitives from the overthrow. Even where the vision loses for once its local colouring in one way, so that the King of Israel deals with all the sons of men, yet it retains it in another, for he deals with them in wrath and destruction, not in love and blessing. There is here so little akin to the true ideal, that we are readily tempted to say that Christ is not here at all, but only Saul or David, or the Jewish monarchy personified in the ruthlessness of its consolidated power. But if we know anything of the genius of prophecy, it is exactly this, that the future and the grand and the heavenly is seen through a medium of the present and the paltry and the earthly. The Messianic element almost always occurs in connection with some crisis in the outward history of the chosen people ; it is inextricably mixed up with what is purely local in interest, and often with what is distinctly imperfect in morality. To the Jew—and to Balaam also, however unwillingly, as the servant of Jehovah— the cause of Israel was the cause of God ; he could not discern between them. "Our country, right or wrong," was an impossible sentiment to him, because he could not conceive of his country being wrong ; he knew nothing of moral victories, or the triumphs of defeat or of suffering; he could not think of God's kingdom as asserting itself in any other way than in the overthrow, or (better still) the annihilation, of Moab, Edom, Assyria, Babylon, Rome, the whole world which was not Israel. The sufferings of the vanquished, the horrors of sacked cities, the agonies of desolated homes, were nothing to him; nothing, unless it were joy—joy that the kingdom of God should be exalted in the earth, joy that the reign of wickedness should be broken.

All these feelings belonged to a most imperfect morality and we rightly look upon them with horror, because we have (albeit as yet very imperfectly) conformed our sentiments to a higher standard. But it was the very condition of the old dispensation that God adopted the then moral code, such as it was, and hallowed it with religious sanctions, and gave it a strong direction God-ward, and so educated his own for something higher. Hence it is wholly natural and consistent to find this early vision of the Messiah, the heaven-sent King of Israel, introduced in connection with the fall of the petty pastoral state of Moab. To Balaam, standing where he did in time and place, and all the more because his personal desires went with Moab as against Israel, Moab stood forth as the representative kingdom of darkness, Israel as the kingdom of light. Through that strong, definite, narrow, and essentially imperfect, but not untrue, conviction of his he saw the Messiah, and he saw him crushing Moab first, and then trampling down all the rest of a hostile world. That no one would have been more utterly astonished if he had beheld the Messiah as he was, is certain; but that is not at all inconsistent with the belief that he really prophesied concerning him. That he should put all enemies under his feet was what Balaam truly saw; but he saw it and gave utterance to it according to the ideas and imagery of which his mind was full. God ever reveals the supernatural through the natural, the heavenly through the earthly, the future through the present.

It remains to consider briefly the temporal fulfilments of Balaam's prophecies.

Moab was not apparently seriously attacked until the time of David, when it was vanquished, and a great part of the inhabitants slaughtered (2 Sam. viii. 2). In the division of the kingdom it fell to the share of Israel, with the other lands beyond Jordan, but the vicissitudes of the northern monarchy gave it opportunities to rebel, of which it successfully availed itself after the death of Ahab (2 Kings i. 1). Only in the time of John Hyrcanus (B.C. 129) was it finally subdued, and ceased to have an independent existence.

Edom was also conquered for the first time by David, and the people as far as possible exterminated (1 Kings xi. 15, 16). Nevertheless, it was able to shake off the yoke under Joram (2 Kings viii. 20), and, although defeated, was never again subdued (see on Gen. xxvii. 40). The prophecies against Edom were indeed taken up again and again by the prophets (e. g. Obadiah), but we must hold that they were never adequately fulfilled, unless we look for a spiritual realisation not in wrath, but in mercy. The later Jews themselves came to regard " Edom " as a Scriptural synonym for all who hated and oppressed them.

Amalek was very thoroughly overthrown by Saul, acting under the directions of Samuel (1 Sam. xv. 7, 8), and never appears to have regained any national existence. Certain bands of Amalekites were smitten by David, and others at a later period in the reign of Hezekiah by the men of Simeon (1 Chron. iv. 39—43).

The prophecy concerning the Kenites presents, as noted above, great difficulty, because it is impossible to know certainly whether the older Kenites of Genesis or the later Kenites of 1 Samuel are intended. In either case, however, it must be acknowledged that sacred history throws no light whatever on the fulfilment of the prophecy; we know nothing at all as to the fate of this small clan. No doubt it ultimately shared the lot of all the inhabitants of Palestine, with the exception of Judah and Jerusalem, and was transplanted by one of the Assyrian generals to some far-off spot, where its very existence as a separate people was lost.

The "ships from the side of Cyprus" clearly enough represent in the vision of Balaam invaders from over the western seas, as opposed to previous conquerors from over the eastern deserts and mountains. That the invasion of Alexander the Great was not actually made by the way of Cyprus is nothing to the point. It was never any part of spiritual illumination to extend geographical knowledge. To Balaam's mind the only open way from the remote and unknown western lands was the waterway by the sides of Cyprus, and accordingly he saw the hostile fleets gliding down beneath the lee of those sheltering coasts towards the harbours of Phœnicia. Doubtless the ships which Balaam saw were rigged as ships were rigged in Balaam's time, and not as in the time of Alexander. But the rigging, like the route, belonged to the local and personal medium through which the prophecy came, not to the prophecy itself. As a fact it remains true that a maritime power from the West, whose home was beyond Cyprus, did overwhelm the older power which stood in the place and inherited the empire of Assyria. Whether the subsequent ruin of this maritime power also is part of the prophecy must remain doubtful.

HOMILETICS.

Ver. 41—ch. xxiv.—*Balaam and his prophecies.* The prophecies of Balaam were the utterances of a bad man deeply penetrated by religious ideas, and inspired for certain purposes by the Spirit of God; hence it is evident that many deep moral and spiritual lessons may be learnt from them, apart from their evidential value as prophecies. Consider, therefore, with respect to *the moral character and conduct of Balaam*—

I. That Balak and Balaam thought to move the God of Israel by importunity, or perhaps to get the better of him by contrivance; hence Balak repeatedly shifted his ground and brought Balaam to another point of view. Even so do ungodly men imagine that the immutable decrees of right and wrong may somehow be changed in their favour if they use sufficient perseverance and address. By putting moral questions in many different lights, by getting their outward or inward adviser to look at them from diverse points of view, they think to make right wrong, and wrong right. With what insensate perseverance, *e. g.*, do religious people strive, by perpetually shifting their ground, to force the Almighty to sanction in their case that covetousness which he has so unmistakably condemned.

II. That Balaam clearly hinted to the Almighty that, as he had procured much honour for him from Balak, he was expected to do what was possible in the matter for him. Even so do men who are in truth irreligious, although often seeming very much the reverse, give the Almighty to understand (indirectly and unavowedly, but unmistakably) that they have done much, laid out much, given up much for his honour and glory, and that they naturally look for some equivalent. To serve God for nought (Job i. 9) does not enter into the thoughts of selfish people; to them godliness is a source of gain (1 Tim. vi. 5), if not here, then hereafter.

III. That Balaam was moved to wish he might die the death of the righteous, but was not disposed to live the life of the righteous; hence his wish was as futile as the mirage of the desert, and was signally reversed by the actual character of his end. Even so do evil men continually desire the rewards of goodness, which they cannot but admire, but they will not submit to the discipline of goodness. A sentimental appreciation of virtue and piety is worse than useless by itself.

IV. That Balaam received no reward from Balak because he had not cursed Israel, and none from God because he had wished to curse him. Even so it is with men whose religious feelings restrain, but do not direct, their lives. They miss the rewards of this world because they are outwardly conscientious, and the rewards of the next world because they are inwardly covetous.

V. That Balaam returned to his place, *i. e.* he went back, as it seemed, to his old home and his old life on the banks of Euphrates; in truth "he went to his own place" (Acts i. 25), for he rushed blindly on destruction, and received the recompense of death.

Consider again, with respect to *the sayings of Balaam*—

I. That it is not possible to curse whom God hath not cursed. There is in fact but one curse which there is any reason to dread, and that is "Depart from me." Any malediction of men, unless it be merely the echo of this upon earth, spoken with authority, does but fall harmless, or else recoil upon him that utters it.

II. That the singular glory of Israel was his separateness—a separateness which was outwardly marked by a sharp line of distinction from other peoples, but was founded upon an inward and distinctive holiness of life and worship. Even so is the glory of the Church of Christ and of each faithful soul to be "separate from sinners," as was Christ. And this separation must needs be outwardly marked in many ways and in many cases (1 Cor. v. 11; 2 Cor. vi. 17); but its essence is an inward divergence of motive, of character, and of condition before God. To be "even as others" is to be the "children of wrath" (Ephes. ii. 3); to be Christians is to be "a peculiar people" (Titus ii. 14). If men cannot bear to be peculiar, they need not look to be blessed; if they must adopt the fashions of this world, they must be content to share its end (Gal. i. 4; 2 Tim. iv. 10; 1 John ii. 15—17).

III. That the death of the righteous is blessed and an object of desire in a far higher sense than Balaam was able to comprehend. It may appear to the foolish that the life of the righteous is full of sadness, but none can fail to see that his death is full of immortality, that he is in peace by reason of a good conscience, and in hope of glory by reason of the sure mercies of God.

IV. That the latter end of the righteous is more blessed and desirable than his death; for this is to live again, and to live for ever, and to inherit eternity of bliss in exchange for a few short years of strife and patience.

V. That it is not possible for man to reverse the benedictions which God has pronounced upon his people. This has been tried by Balaam, and by very many since, but to no effect. The blessings which we are called to inherit, as set forth in the New Testament, will certainly hold good in every age and under all circumstances. No matter what the world may say, or we be tempted to think, the "poor" and the "meek" and the "merciful" and the "persecuted for righteousness' sake" will always be "blessed," in spite of all appearances to the contrary.

VI. That God doth not behold iniquity in his people. Not that it doth not exist (as it existed then in Israel), but because it is not imputed to them that repent and believe in Christ Jesus. God doth not behold sin in the faithful soul, because he regards it not in its own nakedness, but as clothed with the righteousness of Christ, which admits not any spot or stain (Gal. iii. 27; Philip. iii. 9; Rev. iii. 18). And this non-imputation of sin is not arbitrary now (as it was to a great degree in the case of Israel), because it is founded upon a real and living union with Christ as the source of holiness. There is a *spiritual* unity of life with him (John iii. 5; vi. 57; xv. 4; Gal. ii. 20; Ephes. v. 30), and there is a consequent *moral* unity of life with him (Col. iii. 3; 1 John ii. 6; iii. 3; iv. 17, &c.), which is only slowly and partially attained in this life; but it hath pleased God for the sake of the spiritual unity to regard the moral unity as though it were already achieved, and therefore he imputeth not sin to them that "walk in the light" (1 John i. 7).

VII. That if the Lord our God be with us, then the shout of a king is among us, *i. e.* the joyful acclamation of them that welcome the King who never fails to lead them to victory. And this is one note of the faithful, that they rejoice in their King (Ps. cxlix. 2, 5, 6; Matt. xxi. 9; Philip. iv. 4), and that gladness is ever found in their hearts (Rom. xiv. 17) and praise in their mouths (Acts xvi. 25; Heb. xiii. 15; 1 Pet. ii. 9; and cf. Eph. v. 18—20).

VIII. That no magical influence can be brought to bear against the righteous. If they fear God they need not fear any one else (Luke xii. 4, 5; Rom. viii. 38, 39). Superstitious fears are unworthy of a Christian. But note that, according to the other rendering of ch. xxiii. 23, the spiritual meaning is that the faithful have no need of, and no resort to, any such uncertain and unauthorised pryings into the unseen and unrevealed as superstition and irreligion do ever favour. Here is a warning against all the arts of so-called " spiritualism," which (if it be not wholly an imposture) is rank heathenism and abominable to God.   If the gospel be true, then we have all the light we need for our present path, and we have the assurance of all the light we could desire in our future home (John viii. 12 ; 1 Cor. xiii. 12 ; 1 John iii. 2).

IX. THAT THE CAMP OF ISRAEL WAS LOVELY IN THE EYES OF THE PROPHET NOT SO MUCH BY REASON OF ITS SIZE, AS BECAUSE OF THE ORDER AND METHOD WITH WHICH IT WAS LAID OUT—like the cultivated gardens of the East.   Even so is the order Divinely imparted to the Church its chiefest beauty.   It is not its mere size, in which indeed it is inferior to some false religions, but its unity in the midst of variety, its coherence side by side with manifold distinctions, which stamps it as a thing of heavenly origin and growth.   The highest art of the gardener is to allow to each tree the fullest liberty of individual growth, while arranging them for mutual protection and for beauty of effect ; even so is the art of the Divine Husbandman (John xv. 1) with the trees which he hath planted in his garden.

X. THAT THE FUTURE PROSPERITY OF ISRAEL WAS SPOKEN OF BY BALAAM UNDER TWO FIGURES—OF OVERFLOWING BUCKETS USED IN IRRIGATION, AND OF SEED SOWN BY MANY WATERS.   Even so the prosperity of the Church has a twofold character : it stands partly in the diligent and ample watering of that which is already sprung up, which is her pastoral work ; partly in the widespread sowing by many waters, far and near, which is her missionary work.

XI. THAT THE CHURCH OF GOD IS NOT AFFECTED BY THE BLESSING OR CURSING, THE GOOD OR EVIL WILL OF MEN, BUT, ON THE CONTRARY, IS THE SOURCE OF BLESSING OR CURSING TO THEM ; according as they treat her, so must they fare themselves.   For since Christ hath loved her and given himself for her (Ephes. v. 25), his interests and hers are all one, and howsoever we act towards the Church, he taketh it unto himself (cf. Matt. xxv. 40, 45).

Consider again, with respect to *the enterprise of Balaam*—

I. THAT BALAAM WAS HIRED TO CURSE ISRAEL, BUT WAS CONSTRAINED TO BLESS HIM ALTOGETHER (cf. Deut. xxiii. 5 ; Josh. xxiv. 10 ; Micah vi. 5).   Even so all the efforts of the world to cast infamy and odium upon the Church are turned backward, unless indeed she is untrue to herself.   No weapon is forged against her more terrible than the interested enmity of gifted and intellectual men, which often promises to succeed where brute force is powerless ; but even this cannot prosper.   It is often the policy of the world to assail religion by religious influences, but God overrules this also.   Gifts which are truly of his giving cannot be really turned against him or his.

II. THAT GOD'S PURPOSES AND PRONOUNCEMENTS CONCERNING HIS CHURCH ARE ETERNAL AND IMMUTABLE, SINCE HE CANNOT DENY HIMSELF, NOR GO BACK FROM HIS WORD.   The future of his Church is perfectly safe and absolutely unassailable, because it depends not on any human counsel or constancy, but upon the eternal predestination and changeless will of God.

Consider again, with respect to *that which Balaam spake by the Spirit of God*—

I. THAT BALAAM HAD A VISION OF CHRIST HIMSELF, *i. e.* of a mysterious Being, a King of Israel, exalted and extolled, and very high, whom the Jews believed, and we know, to be the Christ.   Even so all true prophecy looks on, more or less consciously, to him in whom all the promises of God are Amen (2 Cor. i. 20), and in whom all the gifts of God to men are concentrated.   The spirit of prophecy is the testimony of Jesus (Rev. xix. 10), because there was nothing else really worth prophesying.

II. THAT BALAAM SAW HIM UNDER THE EMBLEMS OF A STAR AND OF A SCEPTRE. Even so the Lord is both a luminary (Luke ii. 32 ; 2 Pet. i. 19 ; Rev xxii. 16) and a ruler (Luke i. 33 ; Heb. i. 8 ; Rev. xii. 5) for ever.

III. THAT BALAAM SAW HIM AS A DESTROYER, CRUSHING THE ENEMIES OF GOD AND OF HIS PEOPLE.   And this is at first sight strange, because he came not to destroy men's lives, but to save them.   But as it is quite naturally explained from a moral point of view when we take into account the moral ideas of Balaam's age, so it is found perfectly true in a spiritual sense when we consider what the work of Christ really is.   For that work is indeed a work of destruction : he came to destroy the works of the devil (1 John iii. 8) ; he came to destroy—not men, but—all that is sinful in men ; not the enemies of God (for God has no enemies among men), but all in men which is inimical to him and to his truth.   Hence he is ever represented as a destroyer in the Apocalypse, which reverts to the imagery of the Old Testament (Rev. vi. 2 ; xix. 11, 13, 15, &c.).   And this aspect of his work, which is true and necessary, and is jealously guarded as his in Holy Scripture, ought not to be set aside or obscured by the gentler and pleasanter aspects of his reign.   That he must put all enemies under his feet is the first law of his kingdom, and must somehow or other be brought to pass in us, as in others.

IV. That Balaam saw (according to his day) the enemies of the Church of God under the semblance of Moabites, Edomites, Amalekites, Kenites, and Assyrians. And these may . be interpreted in a spiritual sense as typifying the different forms in which a common hostility to the truth of Christ displays itself. In Moab we may see the hostility of cunning, which fears an open contest, but enlists the intellect and craft of others on its side ; in Edom the hostility of insolent opposition, which loses no opportunity of inflicting annoyance and injury ; in Amalek we may see vainglorious anger, which resents pretensions greater than its own, and rushes upon a hopeless conflict ; in the Kenites we may see confidence in earthly strength, and in a lodgment so naturally strong as to defy all assaults ; in Asshur we have the embodiment of brute force brutally used.   If, however, the Kenites were the friends, not the foes, of Israel, then we may see in them how vain is the self-confidence even of religious people in any advantages of position or circumstance. The Kenites are not known to have provoked God, as Israel did, and their abode was peculiarly inaccessible and defensible ; nevertheless, they too fell victims to Assyria, at the very time perhaps when Hezekiah and Jerusalem escaped.

V. That Balaam was struck with fear when he foresaw these destructions extending even to his own people.   Who shall live ?   In the crash of these great contending world-powers who could hope to escape ?   How much more may evil men fear " when God doeth this " which he hath so clearly foretold !   And not evil men only, but all who are not in the truest sense of the Israel of God (1 Pet. i. 17 ; iv. 17, 18 ; 2 Pet. iii. 11).

HOMILIES BY VARIOUS AUTHORS.

Ver. 8.—*The safety of all who enjoy the blessing of God.*   God's " defiance " the signal of destruction ; God's " curse," fatal.   But if protected from these we are safe, for " the curse causeless cannot come."   We are safe from—1. Malicious designs.   *E. g.* Balaam's wish to curse ; the plot of the Jews to stone Paul at Iconium (Acts xiv. 5), and to assassinate him at Jerusalem (Acts xxiii.).   2. Words of execration.   *E. g.* Shimei (2 Sam. xvi.) ; the blasphemies spoken against Christ, and the libels uttered against his people (Matt. x. 24—26).   3. Witchcraft and divination.   In reply to all such foolish fears let it suffice to say, " I believe in God " (Isa. viii. 13, 14 ; 1 Pet. iii. 13).   4. Assaults and all violence.   *E. g.* the various attempts to seize or kill Jesus Christ when " his hour was not yet come."   When the hour for suffering " as a Christian " is come, " let him glorify God " (1 Pet. iv. 12—16).   Such calamities are not " curses " from God, and God can change all other curses into blessings, as in the case of Balaam (Deut. xxiii. 5).   5. Every kind of persecution (Rom. viii. 35—39).   The devil's curse is a *telum imbelle ;* his defiance an empty threat.   The objects of God's care are invincible, if not invulnerable (Isa. liv. 17).—P.

Ver. 19.—*The unchangeable faithfulness of God.*   Two truths are suggested in contrast.   I. It is natural to men to change their mind and break their word. 1. They repent. *i. e.* they change their mind, frequently, hastily, because of ignorance, or short-sightedness, or prejudice, or narrow-mindedness.   Picture a man, fickle, irresolute, and therefore "unstable" (James i. 8). When he does not repent it may be a sign of obstinacy rather than of laudable firmness (Jer. viii. 6). 2. They lie. Children of Satan (John viii. 44), often trained from childhood in ways of false-hood (Ps. lviii. 3), they help to undermine the foundations of society (Isa. lix. 13—15), and to tempt truthful men to universal distrust (Ps. cxvi. 11). Such men are apt to think that God is like themselves, changeable and unfaithful. They project an image of themselves, like idolaters, and call it God (Ps. cxv. 8). *E. g.* Balak (vers. 13, 27), and Balaam himself at first (ch. xxii. 8, 19).

II. IT IS "IMPOSSIBLE FOR GOD TO LIE." Some of God's threats and promises are conditional, though in form they may seem absolute. *E. g.* Numb. xiv. 11, 12; Ezek. xxxiii. 12—20. But others are fixed and absolute. We see this in—1 Threats. *E. g.* exclusion of Hebrews from Canaan (ch. xiv. 20—22); Saul's loss of the kingdom (1 Sam. xv. 22—29); exclusion of the impure from heaven (Heb. xii. 14; Rev. xxi. 27). Hence learn the folly of those who hope that God may change his mind, while theirs is unchanged; that God may repent instead of themselves. (Illustrate from Simon Magus, who desired to escape God's wrath while he gave no hint of abandoning his sins—Acts viii. 24.) 2. Promises. *E. g.* (1) To Abraham, hundreds of years before (Gen. xii. 1—3). Therefore Balaam says, vers. 19, 20. So we may trace the effects of the promise down to the latest of the Old Testament prophets (Mal. iii. 6) and the greatest of the Christian apostles (Rom. xi. 28, 29). (2) To believers in Christ. Because with God there is "no variableness," &c., there-fore we have "strong consolation," &c. (Heb. vi. 18, 19; James i. 17), and hope of the fulness of "eternal life, which God, who cannot lie, promised," &c. (Matt. xxiv. 35; Titus i. 2). (3) To suppliants who claim God's promises. God can as soon cease to exist as refuse to "make good" any promise claimed with faith through Jesus Christ our Lord.—P.

Ver. 39—ch. xxiii. 12.—*The first prophecy.* I. THE NECESSARY PREPARATIONS. 1. *The sacrifices.* Balak and Balaam, however different their thoughts in other respects, were agreed as to the necessity of the sacrifices, if the desired curse were to be put in the prophet's mouth. And so there was abundance of sacrificing. Balak first makes spon-taneous offerings, and then such as were specified by Balaam. They felt that God was not to be approached in an irregular way or with empty hands. As Balak thought of Balaam, so he thought of God. The prophet was to be bought with riches and honours, and God was to be bought with sacrifices of slain beasts. Here then is this common element in the practice of two men so different in other respects. It is in Aram and Moab alike. The tradition of Abel's accepted offering has come down far and wide, so that both men are found feeling that such sacrifices were in some way acceptable to God. But the faith and spirit of Abel could not be transmitted along with the knowledge of his outward act. These men did not understand that these sacrifices were worthless in themselves. God is a Spirit, and cannot eat the flesh of bulls and drink the blood of goats. Shedding of blood was for the remission of sins, and these men neither felt sin, confessed it, nor desired the removal of it. 2. *The sight of the people to be cursed.* The king took the prophet into the high places of Baal, that he might see the utmost part of the people. Very likely Balak himself had not seldom stood there, and gone down again each time more alarmed than ever. Balaam must now see these dreadful people, to satisfy himself that it was neither a trifling nor a needless work he had been called to do; to see how close at hand they were, and to be impressed with the necessity of making the curse potent, speedy, and sure. Added to which, Balak probably believed that, for the curse to operate, Balaam's eyes must rest on the people. Lane in his 'Modern Egyptians' tells us how dreaded is the evil eye. Here then Balaam looked on these people in something of their wide extent. What an opportunity for better thoughts if the spirit that brings them had been in his heart! How he might have said, "Have I been called then to blast this mighty host, who have now lain so long in such close neighbourhood to Balak, yet harmed him not?" 3. *The prophet has his own special preparations.* While Balak attends to the sacrifices, Balaam retires to his secret enchantments (ch. xxiv. 1) in some high, solitary place. God did choose that his servants should go into such places to meet with him alone, but how differently

Balaam looks here from Moses going up into Sinai, or Elijah when he went his day's journey into the wilderness, or Ezekiel when he heard the Lord say, " Arise, go forth into the plain, and I will there talk to thee " (Ezek. iii. 22) ; above all, from Jesus, in those solitary, refreshing, blessed hours of which we have some hints in the Gospels ! How far this retirement was sincere, how far it was meant to deceive Balak, and how far it was mere habit, we cannot tell. The conscience that is well-nigh dead to practical righteousness, to justice, compassion, and truth, may yet be in an everlasting fidget with superstitious fear.

II. THE UNEXPECTED RESULT. 1. *To Balaam.* The whole of what happened may not have been unexpected. The meeting with God he certainly would be prepared for. He had met with God only too often of late, and not at all to his peace of mind and the furtherance of his wishes. We may conclude that God allowed him to go through with his enchantments, else he would hardly have gone to repeat them a second time (cf. ch. xxiii. 15 and xxiv. 1). And perhaps the very fact that there was no interruption to his enchantments may have lifted his mind in hope that God was at last going to be propitious. If so it was but higher exaltation in order to deeper abasement. God meets with him, puts a word in his mouth, and commands him thus to speak with Balak. Are we to understand that by having the word put into his mouth, Balaam there and then had all the prophecy clearly before his mind, so that he could consider every word he had presently to utter ? Possibly so. And it is possible also that as he went back to Balak he considered how he could trim this prophecy, as previously he had trimmed the commands of God. And now comes something for which, with all his assertions of only being able to speak the word God put in his mouth, *Balaam was probably quite unprepared.* He gets no chance of exerting his skill to trim and soften down unacceptable words. God assumes perfect control of those rebellious, lying lips. God, who opened the mouth of an ass and made it utter human speech, now opens the mouth of one whose heart was ready to deceive and curse, and makes that mouth to utter truth and blessing. 2. *To Balak.* The words of the prophecy must have been utterly unexpected by him. He had counted with all confidence on getting what he wanted. Not a shadow of doubt had crossed his mind as to Balaam's power to curse and his own power to buy that power. Hardly a more impressive instance could be found of a man given over to strong delusion, to believe a lie. Counting on the curse as both attainable and efficacious, he now finds to his amazement, horror, and perplexity that Balaam cannot even speak the words of cursing ; for doubtless when the Lord took possession of Balaam's mouth he took possession also of eyes, expression, tone, gesture, so that there would be no incongruity between the words and the way in which they were uttered.

III. THE PROPHECY ITSELF. 1. *A clear statement of how these two men come to be standing together.* Balak brings Balaam all this long way in order to curse Jacob and defy Israel. The object of all these messages and these smoking sacrifices is stated in naked and brief simplicity. There is no reference to motives, inducements, difficulties. The simple historical fact is given without any note or comment ; the request of Balaam mentioned, in order that it may be clearly contrasted with the reason why it is refused. 2. *Balaam is forced into a humiliating confession.* What he had so long concealed, as dangerous to his reputation, he must now publish from the high places of Baal. And notice that he confines himself to saying that the required curse and defiance are impracticable. No more is put into his mouth than he is able truthfully to say. Glorious as this prophecy is, one might imagine it being made more glorious still by the mingling with it of a penitent, candid confession of wrong-doing. He might have said, " Balak hath brought me," &c., and surely God would not have sealed his lips if it had been in his heart to add, " I bitterly repent that I came." He might have said, " How can I curse whom God hath not cursed ? and indeed I discovered this long ago, but pride and policy kept the discovery confined within my own breast." And so we see how, while God kept Balaam from uttering falsehood, and forced him to utter sufficient truth, yet Balaam *the man* remained the same. He says no more than he is obliged to say, but it is quite enough ; with his own lips he publishes his incapacity to the world. 3. *The very place of speaking becomes subservient to the purpose of God.* We may presume that Balak well knew he was taking Balaam to the most favourable view-point.   It was thought to be the best place for cursing, and from what Balaam now sees and says it would seem to be a very fit place for blessing.   4. And now, as Balaam looks from the top of the rocks and from the hills, *what does he see?*   He may have been struck even already, and at that distance, and before he began the prophecy, with the outward peculiarities of Israel.   Some peculiarities of Israel could only be known by a close and detailed inspection; others, *e. g.* the arrangement of the camp around the tabernacle, were best known by a sort of bird's-eye view.   An intimate knowledge of London is only to be gained by going from street to street and building to building, but one thus gaining a very intimate knowledge of London would yet be without such an impression of it as is to be got from the top of St. Paul's.   As Balaam looks down from the tops of the rocks he sees enough for the present purposes of God.   He sees enough to indicate the *separation* and the *vast numerical force of Israel*.   It was not needful here to speak of more.   The immediate purpose of the prophecy was served if it deterred Balak from further folly.   A great deal more might have been said of Israel, and was said afterwards.   In one sense this was an introductory prophecy, followed up by fuller revelations in later ones; in another sense it stands by itself. The others would not have been spoken if the first had proved sufficient.   Passing over the concluding wish of Balaam, " Let me die the death of the righteous, and let my last end be like his ! " which demands to be considered by itself, we note—5. *The state of suspense in which the prophecy leaves Balak as to his own position.*   It would have been so easy to introduce a reassuring word—one which, if it did not actually take away Balak's alarm, would at all events have been fitted to do so.   But the king's request had something so peremptory and dictatorial about it that God's answer is confined to a refusal.   He might have explained that Israel was now busy with its own internal affairs, and would soon, according to his purpose, cross Jordan, and that in the mean time, if Balak would show himself friendly, there was nothing in Israel to make it his foe.   But Balak had so acted that the great thing to be done was to impress him with a deep sense of the strength and security of Israel.   If we prefer unreasonable and arrogant requests, we must expect to receive answers which, if we were uneasy before, will leave us more uneasy still.   God must go on speaking and acting so as to shake the ground under all selfishness.—Y.

Ver. 10.—" *Let me die the death of the righteous, and let my last end be like his !* " *The secret of Israel's prosperity.*   This certainly appears an extraordinary wish when we bear in mind the position and character of the man who uttered it.   Any one taking these words on his lips, and thereby making them his own, would inevitably direct our attention to his life, and compel us to consider what he might be doing to make the wish a reality.   From the time of his first entrance on the scene Balaam unconsciously reveals his *character*.   He could not by any stretch of the word be described as a good man; the whole narrative is little but an illustration of his duplicity, selfishness, vanity, greed of gain and glory, and utter disregard of the plain commandments of God.   The *position* of Balaam at this particular time is also to be remembered.   He has been called to curse, twice pressed to make a long journey for this special purpose; he has offered sacrifices and sought enchantments to secure it; and yet he not only fails to curse, but, more than that, is compelled to bless; and, last of all, to crown the reversal of what had been so carefully prepared for, he is heard expressing an emphatic wish that he himself might be found among this blessed people.

I. CONSIDER FOR A MOMENT THESE WORDS OF BALAAM DISCONNECTED FROM ALL THEIR ORIGINAL CIRCUMSTANCES.   Consider them as placed before some one who knew neither the character nor position of Balaam as the speaker, nor the position of Israel as the nation referred to.   Let him know simply that these words were spoken once upon a time, and ask him to imagine for himself the scene in which they might be *fitly spoken*.   Whither then would his thought be turned?   Would it not be to some aged believer, gradually sinking to rest, with the experience that as the outward man decayed, the inward man was renewed from day to day, and with the conviction that to be absent from the body was to be present with the Lord; looking forward from time into eternity, according to the familiar illustration, as being " but a going from one room into another." Such would be the view suggested by the term "righteous," and the person expressing the wish would seem to be some studious, susceptible observer, with frequent opportunities for observation, who had been impressed by the reality and the superlative worth of the experience on which he had gazed. Then let such a one as we have supposed be confronted *with these original circumstances.* How perplexed he would be when told that the words were spoken *by* such a man as Balaam appears in the narrative, and *of* a people that had done such things as are recorded in the Book of Numbers! These words, looked at in a particular light, might be taken as indicating deep spiritual convictions and earnest, faithful life on the part of whoever speaks them. But we are bound to look at them now in the light of Balaam's character, and in the light also of Israel's past career.

II. CONSIDER THE ACTUAL EXTENT OF BALAAM'S WISH. He wishes to die the death of the righteous. Do not be misled by the prominence of the word "righteous" into supposing that for its own sake Balaam cared about righteousness. It was not righteousness that he desired, but what he saw to be the pleasant, enviable effects of righteousness. He cared nothing about the cause if only he could get the effects. He loved the vine because it produced grapes, and the fig-tree because it produced figs, but if he could have got grapes from thorns and figs from thistles, he would have loved thorns and thistles just as well. *We have God revealing to an ungodly man as much as an ungodly man can perceive of the blessedness of the righteous.* Balaam was entirely out of sympathy with the purposes of God. He showed by the best of all evidence that he would have nothing to do with righteousness as a state of heart, habit of conduct, and standard in all dealings with God and men. But though Balaam did not appreciate the need of righteousness, he did appreciate happiness, and that very warmly, in his own carnal way. He saw in Israel everything a man could desire. To have Balaam uttering this wish was as emphatic a way as any God could have taken to show Balak his favour to Israel. Not only from the top of the rocks does the prophet see the separated and multitudinous people, which in itself was enough to drive Balak to unfavourable inferences, but so desirable does the state of the people appear, that Balaam cannot help wishing it were his own. God had told him at first "the people are blessed," and now, as soon as he sees them, God also makes the greatness of the blessedness sufficiently manifest even to his carnal and obscured heart.

III. THUS WE SEE THE DEEP IMPRESSION WHICH THE BLESSED LIFE OF GOD'S PEOPLE IS CAPABLE OF MAKING ON THE UNGODLY. Those who as yet have no sympathy with righteousness may have a keen desire for security, joy, and peace, and a keen perception of the fact that these somehow belong to real believers in Christ. It is a characteristic of the Scriptures, and a very notable and important one, that many of the appeals found in it are to what seem comparatively low motives. Has it not indeed been made a charge against Christian ethics that they make so much of rewards and punishments? But surely this is the very wisdom of God to draw men by inducements suitable to their low and miserable state, to promise joy to the joyless, peace to the distracted, security to the fearful, life to the dying. Certainly Christ the Saviour can do nothing for us as long as we remain impenitent, unbelieving, and unreconciled, but in his mercy he speaks first of all in the most general and sympathetic terms concerning our needs. The most comprehensive invitation the Saviour ever gave runs thus: "Come unto me, all ye that labour and are heavy laden, and I will give you rest." Not a word there of conviction of sin, wrath of God, need of righteousness, need of saving faith! Is it by accident that the first psalm begins with a reference to happiness? The sermon on the mount starts with this as the very beginning of Christ's teaching: "Men are unhappy; how can they find and keep blessedness, real happiness?" Suppose a man who has no experimental knowledge of the saving power of Christ, reading through the promises of the New Testament and the actual experiences therein recorded; suppose him to see that if words count for anything, godliness is indeed profitable for the life that now is. Would it be anything strange for such a man to say, "If righteousness brings such effects as these, then let *me* die the death of the righteous"? Appealing to high motives alone would be all very well if those appealed to were unfallen spirits or perfected saints; but men being what they are, God does not esteem it too great a condescension to draw them to himself by the promise of blessedness, high, peculiar, rich, and lasting.

IV. GOD GIVES HERE THROUGH BALAAM A CLEAR INDICATION OF HOW THIS DESIRABLE BLESSEDNESS COMES. Israel is not only the happy people, but the righteous people. Righteousness brings the happiness, and is the condition and the guarantee of its continuance. Wherever there is righteousness there is an ever-living and ever-fruitful cause of blessedness. The presence of this righteousness as essential is still more clearly indicated in the next prophecy: "God hath not beheld iniquity in Jacob." That is the great difference between Israel and Moab. Moab is not without its possessions and treasures, its carnal satisfactions; Moab has much that it thinks worth fighting for; it has honours and rewards to offer Balaam such as have brought him all this way to utter, if he can, a curse against Israel. But Moab is not righteous, and the sight of its happiness will never provoke such a wish as Balaam's here.

V. THIS BRINGS US TO CONSIDER THE PECULIAR WAY IN WHICH THE WISH IS EXPRESSED. "Let me *die the death* of the righteous, and let *my last end* be like his!" This is as comprehensive a way as was possible at the time of stating the blessedness of the righteous. Life and immortality were not yet brought to light. To die the death of the righteous was a very emphatic way of indicating the present life of the righteous in all its possible extent. No matter how long that life may stretch, it is one to be desired. "The righteous goes on as far as I can see him," Balaam seems to say, "and comes to no harm." The blessedness of God's people, if only they observe the requisite conditions, is a continuous, unbroken experience; not an alternation of oases and deserts. The fluctuations in that blessedness, the flowing and ebbing tides, come from defects in ourselves. Where there is the fulness of faith, prayer, and humility there surely will be the fulness of blessedness also. Then also, when we consider what Christ has shown us by his own experience of *what lies beyond death;* when we consider his own personal triumph, and the definite, unhesitating way in which a blessed resurrection is assured to his followers, and an inheritance incorruptible, undefiled, and that fadeth not away, we see *a great prophetic importance* in this particular mode of expression: "Let me die the death." Balaam's wish in the very form of it, so peculiar, and we may even say at first so startling, expressed far more than he had any possible conception of. Death stands crowning with one hand the temporal life of the righteous, and with the other opening to him the pure fulness of eternity.

VI. It is very important to notice that by the reference to Israel as the righteous AN UNERRING INDICATION IS GIVEN AS TO WHERE RIGHTEOUSNESS IS TO BE FOUND. Not they who call themselves righteous, but whom God calls righteous, are the people whose death one may desire to die. The true Israelite is he who fulfils the law and the prophets, as he is called to do and made competent to do by the fulness of that Holy Spirit which is given to every one who asks for him. "If ye know these things, happy are ye if ye do them." There is a worthless and deceiving righteousness which excludes from the kingdom of heaven, though the scribes and Pharisees, its possessors, make much of it. There is also a righteousness to be hungered and thirsted after (Matt. v.). We must be careful in this matter, lest we spend money for that which is not bread, and labour for that which satisfieth not (Isa. lv. 2). God hath not beheld iniquity in Jacob, for where he beholds iniquity the seed of Jacob is assuredly absent. Those who have learned the corruption and deception, the necessary ignorance and incapacity, of the unrenewed heart, and thereby been impelled to seek and enabled to find renewal, life and light from on high, and holy principles and purposes for their future course, they are the righteous. Israel born of the flesh exists but as the type. We must not limit our view by him. "Think not to say within yourselves, We have Abraham to our father: for I say unto you, that God is able of these stones to raise up children unto Abraham" (Matt. iii. 9).—Y.

Vers. 13—26.—*The second prophecy. Balak's state of mind.* Balaam has cursed where he was expected to bless, he has said things very hard to listen to and keep presence of mind, but Balak has not by any means lost faith in Balaam and his resources. He rather takes the blame to himself than to Balaam. If there be wrath in his heart with the speaker, who, instead of cursing Israel, has blessed it altogether, he manages to conceal the wrath. He cannot afford to quarrel with Balaam, the only known resource he has. He suggests, therefore, as the great cause of failure that the place of cursing has been badly chosen. Remove the cause, and the effect will disappear. Let the prophet come away from the top of the rocks to where his mind will not be filled with the presence of this bewildering multitude; and Balaam, whatever his private thoughts, consents to the experiment. It is the way of the blind, deluded world; all reasons for failure are accepted and acted on save the right one. Balak cannot yet see, will not see for a while, perhaps will never really see, that there is no place on earth where such requests can be granted. He is showing himself now, as Balaam had done before, unsatisfied with the *first intimation*. Balaam had been told plainly at the very first that Israel was blessed, yet here he is dabbling in superstitions, in enchantments and divinations, with no clear perception of the nature and character of God. Thus, all the narrative through, we see what egregious and scarcely credible blunders men make when they are left to themselves to make discoveries of God. What a proof that revelation in all the large extent of its Scriptural fulness is absolutely indispensable! God must not only give us the truth concerning himself, and the proper relation of men to him, but must also open our hearts and our eyes, and give us light whereby we may see the truth already given. How constantly we should remember the inevitable ignorance of those to whom gospel truth, light, and perceptive power have not yet penetrated! Take pity on them and help them—such darkened minds—as you think of Balak stumbling from one blunder to another, from one discredited resource to another, from one disappointment to another, only to find at last that all his schemes are vanity. And now we advance *to consider the second prophecy*. It is not only spoken in Balak's hearing, but is a direct appeal to himself. We are to imagine Balak standing with strained and eager look, already full of excitement and expectation, before ever a word is spoken. But this is not enough; he must be solemnly exhorted to attention. "Things are about to be said directly concerning you, and it may be that when you have heard them, and allowed them to have full effect on your mind, you will cease from these foolish attacks on the established purpose and counsel of Jehovah." That this call upon Balak for attention was not a superfluous one is shown by the fact, that after hearing the prophecy he nevertheless made a third attempt, modified indeed, but still such as to show that he had not taken in the prophecy to anything like its full extent. We know how the Scriptures abound in expressions of which "He that hath ears to hear, let him hear," and "Verily, verily, I say unto you," are representative. Such expressions do not make truth any truer, but they do throw on us a great responsibility, and involve us in unquestionable blame for neglect of the things which belong to our salvation.

I. THE PROPHECY BEGINS BY CORRECTING BALAK'S FATAL MISAPPREHENSIONS CONCERNING GOD. Balak having failed the first time he tried Balaam, succeeded the second; having failed the first time he tries Jehovah, it is natural for him to think he may succeed the second. Hitherto he has known only the idols of Moab, and these of course only in such aspects as the priests presented them. As the priests were, so were the gods; and Balak, having experienced Balaam's final compliance, might excusably argue from Balaam to that Being whom he took to be Balaam's God. And now there falls out of a holier sphere some unexpected and much-needed knowledge for poor Balak, whose chief experience had been of equivocating, vacillating, unstable men. "God is not what you think him to be; he is true and steadfast, neither changing his purposes nor failing in them." Notice the way in which this all-important statement is put. God puts himself in contrast with his fallen, unfaithful, and disgraced creature, man. "God is not a man;" and, as if to emphasise this matter, he speaks the word of truth concerning his own truth through lying lips. "Men change their minds, and therefore break their words; they lie because they repent." What a hint then for us all to change from deceitful hearts to sincere ones, from lying lips to truthful ones, from vain purposes that must some day be relinquished, engendered as they are in our own selfishness and folly, to such purposes as are inspired by the unchanging God himself! Changing thus, we shall get into a state partaking somewhat of God's own steadfastness; or, rather, the only change will be from good to better and better to best. Man may become such that it shall no longer be his reproach that he lies, either carelessly, ignorantly, or maliciously, and repents, playing the weathercock to every wind that blows. God, we may be sure, desires the day to come when, instead of finding in man this awful and humiliating contrast to himself, he will rather be able to say, "Man is now true, clear from all belief in lies, from all deception and evasion, and steadfast in all the ways of right-eousness, holiness, and love.

II. THE PROPHECY GOES ON TO REVEAL STILL MORE OF ISRAEL'S STRENGTH. The unchangeable God, having purposed to bless Israel, must go on blessing them. He does it in word continually through the great official channel (ch. vi. 22—27), and now it is Balaam's lot (strange expositor of the Divine goodness!) to show clearly that the blessing of God is anything but a nominal or a secondary one. Much has been done to show this in the first prophecy, but a great deal more is done in the second. God has not only put Israel by themselves and made them into this vast multitude, which was a great deal to do, for Jacob's posterity is likened to the dust in number; but now through Balaam he shows *quality* as well as *quantity*. The people are not only separated outwardly and visibly, but separated still more by some great peculiarity in their inward life. Their vast numbers are but the most easily perceptible result of the vigorous, abundant vitality within. When Balaam got his first glance from the top of the rocks he saw the most obvious fruit of Israel's peculiar relation to God. Now in the second survey he comes as it were nearer, and sees the root and trunk and branches, the sap and substance whence these fruits take their origin. 1. *There is the righteousness of the people.* God, who searches into all secrets, and to whom the darkness and the light are both alike, has beheld no iniquity in Jacob, no wrong in Israel; that is to say, putting the thing plainly, there was no iniquity in Jacob. And though it seems a strange thing to say, considering God's late dealings with the people, we feel at once that it must not only be true, but very important, or it would not be put so prominently forward. God looks upon the ideal Israel which lies yet undeveloped in the midst of all the unbelief and carnality of the present generation. Though at the present moment any dozen Israelites might be as debased as any dozen Moabites, yet in Israel there was a seed of holiness, a sure beginning of the perfect and the blessed, which was not to be found anywhere in Moab. God, bear in mind, sees what we cannot see. God is not a man, that he should lie; neither is he a man that his eye should be stopped by the surface and first appearance of things. Jesus sought a solid ground for the future of his saving work in the world, and he found it not amidst the world's wisdom, but.where we assuredly should never have looked—among the stumbling, ignorant disciples whom he gathered in Galilee. Looking with other eyes than men, and where proud men never look, he finds what they never find. 2. *There is the presence of God with them,* and that not only as God, but as King. "When you attack Israel, O Balak, you attack the kingdom of God. You, the king of Moab, appeal to the King of Israel to curse his own people." His sanctuary is also his throne, and where he is worshipped, there he also rules. Every act of worship is also an expression of loyalty. Balak described Israel as a people come out of Egypt (ch. xxii. 5); he is now to learn that they came because they were brought; because that very God brought them whose curse he had so laboriously and patiently sought to invoke. "Does it stand to reason, O Balak, that God can have brought them so far now to leave them for the sake of your sacrifices and Balaam's enchantments?" Thus also we may gather that as God in all the fulness of his being, Father, Son, and Spirit, has so long given his indubitable presence to his Church, he will assuredly for this very reason continue it to the end. God indeed looks on that Church in its actual coldness, indolence, and carnality,—and the Israel of God to-day is quite as far away from the fulness of its privileges, the perfection of its faith, and the exactness of its service as was Israel in the wilderness,—but he regards the ideal still. It is through the believers in Christ alone, the spiritual children of the faithful Abraham, that the nations are to be truly blessed. The ideal believer is the ideal man. Where the faithful

and true God finds germs of faithfulness and truth in man, there he will abide and
never depart. 3. *There is strength for all required service and toil.* "He hath as it
were the strength of the unicorn (or buffalo)." "Much increase is by the strength of
the ox" (Prov. xiv. 4), but an animal stronger even than the ordinary ox is needed to
set forth the extent of Israel's advantages. We may take it that the figure here is
intended to set forth strength pure and simple. Israel will have power to do whatever the course of events may bring to be done. It is strong *to do God's work* as
long as it is left to the peaceful pursuit of that work, and it is also strong *to make a
complete defence* whenever it may be attacked. "Rouse Israel by your attacks, and
the force that has hitherto been used for internal progress will become a wall against
you ; and not only so, but you may be swept away in the rush of the roused and
maddened unicorn." There is thus a warning to Balak not to provoke. It is when
the Church has been provoked by persecution that her true strength has been shown
to the world. What a mockery of this world's boasted resources, when all its persuasions, cajoleries, threats, and torments have failed to shake the faith of humble
believers ! It can burn, but it cannot convert. It is marvellous, the strength, energy,
and patience which God has bestowed on some of his servants. Paul toiling on
among infirmities and persecutions is a proverb ; but, to come nearer home, consider
John Wesley, hardly ever out of the saddle except when he was in the pulpit, amply
furnished for all the weariness of travel and the work of incessant preaching till
long past his eightieth year ; and in matters of defence so wonderfully strengthened
with the strength of the unicorn that he passed unharmed through all physical perils
and social opposition. It is one of the most remarkable of all his remarkable
experiences that he could say in his seventy-fourth year, "I have travelled all roads
by day and by night these forty years, and never was interrupted yet." 4. *God
gives his people certain, authoritative, regular knowledge as to his will and favour.*
He does not leave them to auguries and divination. These things indeed were not
only useless, but forbidden (Levit. xix. 26). Whatever he has to say he says through
appointed and recognised channels, and confirms and illustrates it by suitable acts.
There was place and need for lawgivers, prophets, and priests in Israel, but no room
for men like Balaam, augurs, magicians, and priestcraft in general. Enchantments
and divination had been the mainstay of Balak's hope, and though Balaam's experience
may have prevented him from trusting so fully in them, he nevertheless considered
them a very important element in propitiating Jehovah. *Man's ways of reaching
God are all vanity.* God himself has to come down and lay a way very clearly
marked and strictly prescribed. In that way, and in that alone, there is certainty and
sufficiency of knowledge, safety, and blessedness of life. "The law of his God is in
his heart; none of his steps shall slide " (Ps. xxxvii. 31).

III. THE PROPHECY CLOSES BY INDICATING HOW THERE WILL BE IN ISRAEL THE SPIRIT
OF DESTRUCTION AND THE STRENGTH TO DESTROY. Israel has not only the strength
of the buffalo, but the spirit and propensities of the lion. This is the first intimation
of threatening. The prophecy closes with, as it were, a growl and menace from the
lion of the tribe of Judah. Up to this time God has told Balak to go round about
Zion and tell the towers thereof, and mark well her bulwarks (Ps. xlviii. 12, 13), that
he might see how God's ideal people are invulnerable to all enemies. But now the
defensive is suddenly turned into the offensive. Israel is a lion. We know from the
frequent references to the lion in the Old Testament that this figure must have been
a very impressive one to Balak. In Isaiah's prophecy concerning Moab we find
these words: "I will bring lions upon him that escapeth of Moab" (Isa. xv. 9). The
roar, the spring, the resistless attack, the sudden and complete collapse of the victim,
all rise to our minds the moment this majestic animal is mentioned. The idea of
defence scarcely enters into our minds in connection with the lion. His resources
are those of attack. What shall Balak do if he has to meet a foe whose strength is
that of the unicorn, and whose ardour is that of the lion ? The figure, remember, is
suitable to the occasion. There is a time to compare the people of God to the sheep
whom the shepherd leads out and in, and gathers within the protecting fold, but
there is also a time to compare them to the restless lion, seeking for his prey, and not
lying down till he drinks its blood. The Church of Christ is *a destroying institution,*
and this part of its work must not be concealed and softened down to suit the preju-

dices of the world. The claws of the lion must not be clipped when it is dealing with vested interests and established iniquities. As it is not the way of the lion to make compromises with its prey, so neither must we make compromises with any evil. We have nothing to do with evil, save, in the name of the God of righteousness, to destroy it as soon as we can. *Nor need there be any fear of carrying the comparison too far.* He who has taken in the meaning of those words, " Be wise as serpents, and harmless as doves," will well understand how to be ardent, enthusiastic, uncompromising, almost fierce and lion-like, against monster evils, yet at the same time gentle as the lamb, pitiful as God himself, towards the men whose hearts have been hardened and their consciences blinded by the way in which their temporal interests have become intimately mixed with wrong. Wilberforce was one of the most gentle, affectionate, and considerate of men, always on the alert to say a word or write a letter for the spiritual good of others, yet his greatest work took the form of destroying evil. For many long years he had to look in the sight of the world a combatant more than anything else. When the slave trade was abolished in 1807 it is reported of him that he asked his friend Thornton, " What shall we abolish next? " a playful question, of course, but capable of a very serious meaning. No sooner does one great evil vanish from the scene than another becomes conspicuous. Evil seems continually growing as well as good. It is perhaps not without significance that so many associations clamouring for the attention of good and patriotic men have in the names of them such words as these: " *abolition*," " *repression*," " *prevention*." It must needs be so, even to the end. The devil well knows how to make the selfish interests of one half the world dependent on the sufferings and miseries of the other half.—Y.

Ver. 27—Ch. xxiv. 14.—*The third prophecy.* I. THE CIRCUMSTANCES IN WHICH IT WAS UTTERED. 1. *With regard to Balak.* After hearing the second prophecy, and especially its menacing conclusion, he is naturally much irritated. It is bad enough to have been disappointed even once, but kings like worse to have threatening added to disappointment, and at first Balak makes as if he would have nothing more said on the subject, one way or another. If Balaam cannot curse the people, neither shall he bless them. But becoming a little calmer, Balak determines to try a third time, and from a still different place ; so little did he heed the solemn assertion of God's unchangeable purposes to which his attention had been specially called. The conduct of Balak is a warning to us to keep our hearts right at all times with regard to the reception of Divine truth. Truths stated very clearly and emphatically, and in critical circumstances, may yet be utterly neglected. That which is necessary to be known will, we may be quite sure, have a clearness corresponding to the necessity. However clear and simple statements are in themselves, they must needs be as idle breath if we refuse to give humble and diligent attention to them. 2. *With regard to Balaam.* He no longer goes out seeking for enchantments, although he still clings to the inevitable sacrifices. This forsaking of the enchantments and clinging to the sacrifices, is it not a sort of testimony out of the very depths and obscurities of heathenism that God cannot be approached without something in the way of vicarious suffering? *Balaam saw that it pleased the Lord to bless Israel.* It had taken him a long time and caused him a great deal of trouble to see this, and yet the sequel proves (ch. xxxi. 8, 16) that, after all, seeing, he did not perceive, and hearing, he did not understand. Nevertheless, at this time he saw sufficient to convince him how vain were Balak's hopes of a curse from Jehovah. If Israel was to be overthrown, it was not in that way. Observe that in uttering this prophecy *Balaam is thrown into a higher state of receptivity than before.* When Balak refused to be satisfied with the first prophecy, he got a second one, specially addressed to himself, and fuller ; more indicative of Israel's resources, varied, ample, and unfailing as they were for every possible need. But now he does not so much get a prophecy fuller in itself ; it is rather a clearer proof that Balaam is indeed employed by God as a prophet. He is thrown into an ecstatic state. His eyes are closed to the outward world, but the mind's eye is opened, and a picture, first beautiful, and then terrible, is presented to his vision. We see from this *how much God can do in controlling the powers of carnal and unsympathising men.* God not only puts his own words into

Balaam's lying lips, but he makes him see such visions as were customarily confined to men who were spiritually fit for them. Balaam doubtless, looking away into the distance of time from the present encampment of Israel in Moab to their future life in Canaan, would rather have seen ruin, confusion, and desolation—something to rejoice the heart of his employer, and bring to himself the promised rewards. But he could only see what God showed him. If then God held this ungodly Balaam in such control, *what may not his power be over those who submit to him with all their hearts?* There is a sort of proportion in the matter. As the unwilling Balaam is to the completely submissive believer, so what God did to Balaam is to what God will do for such a believer. The more you give to God for working on, the more, by consequence, he will give to you in return. Yield yourselves to God, that he may not only work through you by his mighty power, but in you and for you according to the purpose of his love and the riches of his grace. The sad reflection is that Balaam allowed himself to be an evidence of the power, but not the grace ; allowed God's blessings to go through him, yet, in spite of his own expressed wish, made no attempt to keep blessings for himself.

II. THE PROPHECY ITSELF. Here are set before us two pictures, as it were, a beautiful one and a terrible one. *Picture the first.* A spectator in an ordinary state of mind, looking down with his natural vision on the Israelite camp, sees long ranges of tents, set in four divisions, and at a reverent distance from the tabernacle in the midst of them. The people dwelt " not in stately palaces, but in coarse and homely tents, and those, no doubt, sadly weather-beaten." But Balaam in his ecstasy, when the Spirit of God came upon him, looked upon a more attractive and inspiring scene. What he gazed upon at first was indeed these rows of tents, but, just as if in a dissolving view, they faded away before his eyes, and in place of them, valleys, gardens by the river-side, aloes of Jehovah's planting, and cedars beside the waters were spread out before him. Everything is suggestive of quiet, steady prosperity, of fruitfulness, peace, and beauty. This is the internal life of the Church of Christ, when his people are living to the extent of their privileges. This is the difference between the external appearance and the inward life and experience. Just at that moment when the lot of the Christian looks least attractive to the casual and uninstructed glance, it may be rich in all the great elements of true blessedness. The position of the Christian in this world is not seldom like that of the kernel within the shell : outside, the rough, repulsive, unpromising shell ; inside, the precious kernel, with " the promise and potency " in it of a tree like that from which it was taken. " Eye hath not seen, nor ear heard, neither have entered into the heart of man, the things which God hath prepared for them that love him. *But God hath revealed them unto us by his Spirit* " (1 Cor. ii. 9, 10). And thus it is here. It was not possible for Balaam to describe the blessed circumstances of Israel in direct language. He had to fall back on the comparison to certain visible things, such things as would raise in the mind of a dweller in Moab or Canaan, or anywhere round about, a picture of the highest satisfaction and success. *Picture the second.* The first picture is beautiful, and very beautiful ; it is Eden raised in the waste wilderness. The second picture is terrible, and very terrible ; yet what else could be expected ? If Balak will go on presumptuously defying the sacred and beloved people of God, undeterred by the menaces to which he has already listened, then those menaces must be repeated with all the force and thoroughness of expression that can be thrown into them. The sudden transition from such a peaceful, beautiful scene as goes before heightens the effect, and probably was meant to do so. *On one side is Israel engaged in tilling the garden,* the work to which man was set apart in the first days of innocence, watering his far-spread crops and enjoying his fragrant aloes and his cedars; *on the other side is Israel the Destroyer,* emphatically the Destroyer. The qualities of no one animal, however destructive, are sufficiently expressive to set him forth. Fierce, furious, strong, resistless as the lion is, the lion by himself is not enough to show forth Israel, and you must add the unicorn ; and there you are invited to gaze on this unicorn-lion, strong in power, thorough in execution, leaving not one of his enemies unsubdued and undestroyed. Let Balak well understand that Israel, under the good hand of God, is climbing to the highest eminence among the nations. The repetition of the references to the unicorn and the lion shows how important the references are, and how needful it is to let the mind of the Christian dwell encouragingly on them.   Balak sets forth the intolerant and suspicious spirit of the world in all its kingdoms; and the world does not heed prophecies; it does not take them to heart, else it would cease to be the world. These prophecies, though they were first spoken by a *Balaam* and listened to by a *Balak*, were meant in due course to reach, guide, assure, and comfort Israel.   If there are times when we are tempted to fear the world, with its designs, its resources, and the might of its fascinating spirit, then we shall do well to recollect that, by a double and enlarged assurance, God reckons his Church to have the strength of the unicorn and the spirit of the lion, utterly to subdue and destroy all those kingdoms of the world which, to keep up the figure, are considered as the natural prey of the Church.—Y.

Vers. 7—10.—*Balaam—the first parable.*   The word " parable " is used here in a somewhat peculiar sense.   It is not, as in the New Testament, a fictitious narrative embodying and enforcing some moral truth, but a " dark saying," a mystic prophecy cast in the form of figurative poetic language, a prophecy that partakes of the nature of allegory.   In these ecstatic utterances the impulse of Balaam's better nature overmasters his more sordid passion, and a true prophetic spirit from God takes the place of the false Satanic spirit of heathen divination.   The thoughts respecting Israel to which Balaam gives utterance in this first parable are deeply true of the redeemed people of God in every age.

I. THEIR SPECIAL PRIVILEGE AS OBJECTS OF THE DIVINE FAVOUR.   " How shall I curse," &c.   Balak had faith in Balaam's incantations.   " I wot that he whom thou blessest," &c. (ch. xxii. 6).   But he himself knew well that there was an arbitrament of human interests and destinies infinitely higher than his.   God has absolute sovereignty for good or ill over all our human conditions.   There is no real blessing where his benediction does not rest, nor need any curse be dreaded by those who live beneath his smile.   " If God be for us," &c. (Rom. viii. 31).   No alternative so momentous as this—the favour or the disfavour of God.   Note, respecting the Divine favour, that—1. *It is determined by spiritual character.*   Not an arbitrary, capricious bestowment.   It is for us to supply the conditions.   We must " be reconciled to God " if we would know the benediction of his smile.   God is " for " those who are *for him.*   The cloud in which his glory dwells gives light to those who are in spiritual accord with him, but is darkness and confusion to his foes.   2. *It is neither indicated nor disproved by the outward experiences of life.*   External conditions are no criterion of the state of the soul and its Divine relations.   The wicked may " have all that heart can wish " of the good of this life, and their very " prosperity may slay them; " while it is often true that " whom the Lord loveth he chasteneth " with sorest tribulations, and those tribulations " work out for them a far more exceeding and eternal weight of glory."   We judge very falsely if we suppose that spiritual experiences must needs be reflected in outward conditions.   3. *It is the source of the purest joy of which the soul of a man is capable.*   This is true blessedness—to walk consciously in the light of God's countenance.   " His favour is life," his loving kindness " better than life."   This was the pure joy of the well-beloved Son—the abiding sense of the Father's approval.   Have this joy in you, and you may defy the disturbing influences of life and the bitterest maledictions of a hostile world.

II. THEIR SEPARATENESS.   " Lo, the people shall dwell alone," &c. (ver. 9).   The Jews were an elect people (" Ye shall be a peculiar treasure unto me above all people"—Exod. xix. 5), chosen and separated, not as monopolising the Divine regard, but as the instruments of a Divine purpose.   They were called to be witnesses for God among the nations,—the majesty of his Being, the sanctity of his claims, the method of his government, &c.,—and to be the channels of boundless blessing to the world.   The same grand distinction belongs to all whom Christ has redeemed from among men.   " Ye are a chosen generation," &c. (1 Pet. ii. 9).   He says to all his followers, " Ye are not of the world," &c. (John xv. 19; xvii. 16, 17).   This separation is—1. *Not circumstantial, but moral;* lying not in the renunciation of any human interest or the rending of any natural human tie, but in distinctive qualities of spiritual character and life.   In moral elevation and spiritual dignity only are they called to " dwell alone."   2. *Not for the world's deprivation, but for its benefit.*

Not to withdraw from it powers that might better be consecrated to its service, but to bring to bear upon it, in the cause of righteousness, an energy higher and diviner than its own.

III. Their multiplicity. "Who can count the dust," &c. The promise given to Abraham is gloriously fulfilled in God's spiritual Israel. "Thy seed shall be as the dust of the earth," &c. (Gen. xxviii. 14). This indicates at once the grandeur of the Divine purpose and the diffusive power of the Divine life in men. On both these grounds their numbers will surely multiply till they "cover the face of all the earth." Little as we may be able to forecast the future, we know that the question, "Are there few that be saved?" will find its triumphant answer in "the great multitude which no man can number, of all nations," &c. (Rev. vii. 9).

IV. The blessedness of their end. "Let me die the death," &c. We gather from this not only Balaam's faith in the intrinsic worth of righteousness, but also in the happy issue to which a righteous life in this world must lead as regards the life to come. Why this wish if he had no faith in a glorious immortality and in righteousness as the path to it? There is an instinct in the soul even of a bad man that leads to this conclusion, and his secret convictions and wishes will often bear witness to a diviner good of which his whole moral life is the practical denial. You must be numbered with the righteous now if you would find your place with them hereafter, and live their life if you would die their death.—W.

Ver. 23.—*Balaam—the second parable.* We may look upon Balaam here as representing the Satanic powers that have ever been plotting and working against the kingdom of God among men, and as the unwilling prophet of their ultimate defeat. The spell of a higher Power is over him, and he cannot do the thing that he would. Looking down from "the high places of Baal" upon the tents of Israel spread out over the plain beneath, he is constrained in spite of himself to utter only predictions of good. His magic arts are utterly baffled in presence of the Divinity that overshadows that strange people. It is a picture of what is going on through all the ages. In the triumphant host approaching the borders of the land of promise we see the ransomed Church moving on to its glorious destination, its heavenly rest; the kingdom that Christ has founded among men consummating itself, "covering the face of the whole earth." And in the failure of his enchantments we see the impotence of the devices of the powers of darkness to arrest its progress. The Satanic working has assumed different forms.

I. Persecution. The followers of Christ soon verified his prophetic word: "In the world ye shall have tribulation." The infant Church was nursed and cradled in the storms. It no sooner began to put forth its new-born energies than it found the forces of earth and hell arrayed against it. But what was the result? The first outbreak of hostility only brought to the minds of those feeble men, with a meaning undiscovered before, the triumphant words (Ps. ii.), "Why do the heathen rage," &c. It drove them nearer to the Divine Fountain of strength. It made them doubly bold (Acts iv. 23, 30). Scattered abroad, they "went everywhere preaching the word, and the hand of the Lord was with them." A prophecy was thus given of the way in which persecution would always serve the cause it meant to destroy, and God would "make the wrath of man to praise him." Ecclesiastical authority has leagued itself with the tyrannous powers of the world in this repressive work. The sanctions of religion have been invoked for the destruction of the truth. But ever to the same issue. Whatever form it takes, the persecuting spirit is always essentially Satanic; there is nothing Divine in it. And it always defeats its own end. "The blood of the martyrs is the seed of the Church." The fire that has swept over the field, consuming the growth of one year, has only enriched it and made it more prolific the next. The kingdom of Christ has rooted itself in the earth, and its Divine energies have been developed by reason of the storms that have raged against it. Not only has "no weapon formed against it prospered," but the weapon has generally recoiled on the head of him who wielded it. The Satanic enchantments have been foiled just when they seemed to reach the climax of their success, and the curses of a hostile world have turned to blessings.

II. Corrupting influences within the pale of the Church itself. Christianity has suffered far more from foes within than ever it did from foes without. Christ has been wounded most "in the house of his friends." Read the history of the first three or four centuries of the Christian era if you would know to what an extent the hand of man may mar the fair and glorious work of God. They tell how Christian doctrine, worship, polity, social life gradually lost their original simplicity and purity. The traditions of Judaism, heathen philosophies and mythologies, the fascinations of a vain world, the basest impulses of our nature, all played their part in the corrupting process. The human element overbore and thrust aside the Divine, till it seemed as if Satan, baffled in the use of the extraneous persecuting powers, were about to triumph by the subtler forces of corruption and decay. But God has never left his Church to *itself* any more than to the will of its adversaries. In the darkest times and under the most desperate conditions the leaven of a higher life has been secretly working. Nothing is more wonderful than the way in which the interests of Christ's kingdom have been preserved, not only in spite of, but often through, the instrumentality of events and institutions that in themselves were contrary to its spirit and its laws. What are many of our modern agitations but the struggles of the religious life to cast off the fetters that long have bound it, to shake itself from the dust of ages, symptoms of the *vis vitæ* by which nature throws off disease. Even the retrograde movements that sometimes alarm us will be found by and by to have conspired to the same end. And when the Church shall " awake, and put on her beautiful garments" of simple truth and love and power, when "the Spirit is poured out upon her from on high," then shall it be seen how utterly even these subtler Satanic "enchantments" have failed to arrest her progress towards the dominion of the earth.

III. The assaults of unbelief. The intellectual force of the world in some of its most princely and commanding forms has ever set itself in deadly antagonism to the Church of Christ. Far be it from us to say that all who hold or teach anti-Christian doctrine are consciously inspired by the spirit of evil. But beneath the fairest aspects of aggressive unbelief we discern the Satanic aim to darken the glory that shines from heaven on human souls. It is given to " the mystery of iniquity" to pervert the genius, the learning, even the very mental integrity and honest purpose of men to its own false uses. But have these forces of unbelief ever gained a substantial victory? One would suppose, from what is often said on their side, that they were victorious along the whole line. Is it really so? Is there any one stronghold of revealed truth that they have stormed and taken? In all the battles that have been fought on the field of Christian doctrine, has any ground really been lost? Have any of the "standards" fallen? Is Christianity in any sense a defeated or even damaged cause? Nay, we rather believe that "the foolishness of God is wiser than men," and "the weakness of God is stronger than men." The camp of Israel need fear no hostile "enchantment," for "the Lord their God is with them, and the shout of a king is among them."—W.

Vers. 10—14.—*Balak relinquishes his project.* He sees now clearly that there is no chance of prevailing over Israel by means of a curse, and that any further appeal to the prophet would only bring words more galling to his pride and more menacing to his position, if indeed such words could be found. Considerations of policy and prudence need no longer restrain him in speaking out all his mind to the prophet.

I. Balak's treatment of his unsuccessful accomplice. 1. *An outbreak of selfish wrath.* Balaam indeed did not deserve much sympathy, seeing how he had played into Balak's hands from the very beginning. But if he had deserved sympathy ever so much, he would not have met with it. Balak has eyes, heart, and recollection for nothing but his own disappointment. He has no real sympathetic regard for Balaam, no consideration for one who is far from home, and whose professional reputation all around will be sadly damaged by this failure on a critical occasion. Wicked men in the hour of disaster show small consideration for their accomplices. Those in whose hearts the temptation of some great reward for evil-doing is beginning to prevail should consider that if they fail they will meet with scant mercy or excuse. When the Balaks of the world get a Balaam into their hands, they look on him just as a tool. If the tool does its work as they want it, well and good ; keep it carefully for further use ; but if it turns out a failure, fling it without more ado on the dunghill. Balak acts here towards Balaam just as he might be expected to act. 2. *He lays the whole blame on Balaam.* He does not consider that the evil purposes of his own heart must needs be frustrated. Three prophecies, full of solemn and weighty matter, uttered in his hearing, have not made him in the slightest degree conscious of the folly and iniquity of his project. He sees indeed that the project must fail, but is blind as a bat to the real reason of the failure. All that he has heard concerning Jehovah, his character, his past dealings with Israel, and his purposes for them, has not impressed him one whit, save with the fact that somehow, he cannot get his own way. His curse project has ended in a huge, humiliating, exasperating failure, and Balaam must bear the blame of it. Wicked men cannot be got to give Heaven credit for all its timely and irresistible interferences with their darling schemes. The fault in Balak's angry eye rested with Balaam, and with him alone. "The Lord hath kept thee back from honour." A true word indeed, but not applicable in the way in which Balak intended it. The Lord had kept Balaam back from honour, but not from the paltry honour which Balak would have conferred on him. The lesson for us is, that whenever any selfish plan of ours fails, we should not, like this blind, besotted king, go laying blame elsewhere, as if it would exonerate ourselves. Balaam of course was to blame, grievously to blame, a great deal more than Balak, seeing he sinned against greater light. But we must not let the grievous and conspicuous faults of others cast our own into the shade. We are at the best very poor judges of the transgressions of our fellow-men. When we fail in anything, it is far the wisest, kindest, and most profitable course to give diligent heed to such causes of failure as are in our own heart. Whatever disappointments may come to us in life, we shall never fail in anything of real importance if only *we keep our own hearts right with God.*

II. BALAK'S VAIN ATTEMPT TO GET PROMPT RIDDANCE OF THE PROPHET. He thinks it is enough to say, "Stop." But as he was not able to make Balaam speak what he wanted and when he wanted, so neither is he able to make Balaam cease when the Lord's message is on his lips. God opened Balaam's mouth, and it is not for Balak to close it. Before Balak is left, his impotence shall be manifested in the completest possible way. He had been the thoughtless and unwitting means of turning on the stream of glorious prophecy, and now he finds he cannot stop that stream at will. Jehovah did not seek this occasion, but when it is furnished he deems it well to avail himself of it to the full. And now Balak finds that, whether he will or not, he must listen to the doom of his own people, expressly and clearly announced. Learn that when you begin the headstrong course of making everything on earth—and perhaps, after Balak's fashion, in heaven as well—subservient to self, you cannot stop whenever the consequences begin to get troublesome. Balak said, "Let my will be done, not because it is right, but because it is mine," and he was not contented with a refusal, once or even twice. He must have it a third time, and then he finds that the choice is no longer under his control. Let us choose wisely while we are able to choose.—Y.

Vers. 15—25.—*The Star out of Jacob and the Sceptre out of Israel.* The final prophecy, unsolicited by Balak, which indeed he would have been glad to stop, goes far beyond the concerns of his kingdom and his reign. It stretches over an ever-widening extent of space and time. As long as there is any Moab kind of nation to be destroyed, Israel must continue to prevail. The kingdoms of this world not only will become the kingdoms of our Lord and of his Christ, but no other conclusion is easily conceivable. The power by which Israel conquers one enemy enables it to conquer all; and the disposition which leads it against one enemy must lead it against all. It will again and again be attacked, and must defend where it is attacked. It must expand by the ever-strengthening life within. The more it grows, the more room it will require, until at last the kingdoms of the world become its own. Notice—

I. THE ADVANCE IN THIS PROPHECY UPON THE PRECEDING ONE, AS SHOWN BY THE DIFFERENT FIGURE EMPLOYED. The lion destroys, and that most effectually, but he can do nothing more than destroy. The horse or the ox will draw the cart, and thus serve constructive purposes. Even the tiniest bird can build its compact and symmetrical nest, but the lion can do nothing save destroy. You may cage it and curb its savage propensities a little, but it is not tamed; the lion-nature is there, and the smallest taste of blood will cause it to burst forth in all its fury. The lion being thus a destroyer, and nothing but a destroyer, it is needful to present Israel as able to do more—able to destroy in order that there may be room for the construction of something more worthy to endure. It does not become God to stay the current of prophecy with a menace of dreadful destruction as the last word, and so he makes Balaam to speak of the star and the sceptre. The lion, as it rages about, can make a solitude; it can take away wickedness by taking away all wicked men; but a solitude is not a kingdom. The true kingdom of God is only gained when he gets willing hearts. The destruction which is spoken of with such energy and almost fierceness of illustration is for the purpose of completely taking away the evil out of human society, so that only the good may remain to serve and glorify the Maker of mankind.

II. THE SIGNIFICANCE OF THE STAR, AS INDICATING THE METHOD IN WHICH GOD WILL WORK TO CONQUER EVIL AND ESTABLISH GOOD. The star, it is said, is mentioned here as the symbol of governing power, according to the astrological notions of antiquity. It is further said that the joining of the sceptre with the star shows that authority and supremacy are the main things to be indicated by the mention of the star. Certainly the prophecy is full of the idea of supremacy and authority; but if this idea was the only thing to be considered, the mention of the sceptre would be enough. The star is a symbol of power, but it is also a symbol of many great realities besides. Let us ask not only why the sceptre is joined with the star, but why the star is joined with the sceptre. *The very first thing that a star indicates is light.* God will establish his rule by sending the Star out of Jacob to rise in the darkness. Christ, the fulfilment of the star, has come a light into the world, a rival to existent lights, and destined to outshine them all. He is a light ever protesting against the darkness, not comprehended by it, not swallowed up and lost in it. Rejoice in this, that the Star out of Jacob is inaccessible to the meddling of those who hate its inconvenient revelations. Christ comes to destroy, and at the same time to construct by letting light in upon all dark, idolatrous chambers and all self-deceiving hearts. The light is from him who knows what is in man, his wickedness, his weakness, and his wants. He brings reality where others only bring appearance. He brings truth where they, even in their very sincerity, bring error. There is no room for a Balaam in his kingdom. The Demas who makes a few steps within soon retreats from a light far too trying for the darkness of his heart. Notice, further, that *the light of the star is in some respects more significant of the work of Christ than would be the light of the sun.* We must have a figure which will keep before us both the light and the darkness. To us, individually, Christ may be as the sun (and may he be!), filling our hearts with light. We know, alas, that he is far from being a sun to many. Their light is still darkness, but the Star of Bethlehem shines in the firmament, waiting for the hour when in humility they may betake themselves to it. After all the search for truth, and whatever knowledge may be gained, there is still the sense of incompleteness; the knowledge stops with the intellect; it does not find its way to enlighten and comfort the whole heart. We can by no means dispense with the Star out of Jacob, the Star that shines from every page of the Scriptures.

III. THE SIGNIFICANCE OF THE SCEPTRE, AS INDICATING THE REALITY OF THE DOMINION. The sceptre is that of Christ's truth, wielded with all the power of God's Holy Spirit. We must have much assurance, not only of the illumination that comes from Christ, but of the consequent actual illumination in accepting human hearts. We must ever be ready in our approaches to God to say, "Thine is the kingdom *and the power.* Thine is not only the *rightful* authority, but also the *actual* authority." What is a more offensive sight than a merely nominal submission to Christ? How soon it becomes evident to the discerning eye that there is an utter want of harmony! Those who are really Christ's subjects soon justify their loyalty by the commotion they make among the accepted customs and traditions of the world. There is a sense in which they may covet often to hear the word, "They that have turned the world upside down have come hither also." As we read the Acts of the Apostles, we feel that there was not only a new teaching being diffused among men, but, above all things, *a new power*. It was not only fresh thought they brought to men, but a new and gladdening life.

IV. THE SIGNIFICANCE OF THE MANY NATIONS REFERRED TO, AS INDICATING THE EXTENT AND COMPLETENESS OF THE DOMINION. The details connected with each nation have of course their peculiar significance, but the significance of the details is not quite so clear as that of the great common element which runs through them all. All the details point forward to a time when the Star out of Jacob shall outshine the star out of every other nation, when the Sceptre out of Israel shall break every other sceptre. The kingdoms of the world are to fall—the kingdoms of mammon, of pleasure, of unbelief in Christ, of science falsely so called, of rationalism, of atheism, of individual self-assertion. These are kingdoms that now stretch their authority far and wide, in all continents, and in all ranks of men, and many are subjects of more than one of the kingdoms. In the kingdoms of this world it is largely true that there is neither Jew nor Greek, bond nor free, male nor female. The Star out of Jacob then has a large work to do in subduing and transforming the many and mighty kingdoms of this world. And all the glorious burden of prophecy heaves and swells with the emphatic assurance that he will do it. The day is to come when we shall all learn that to be king over one's own nature is more than to sway the most populous and wealthy territory among men. Then indeed will the description, " King of kings, and Lord of lords," fully apply, when God in Christ Jesus reigns over kings and lords such as these. The cry concerning man will no longer be,

" Lord of himself, that heritage of woe ! "

but, lord of a heritage reclaimed, purified, and made docile by the work of Jesus as he inspires in the breast every loving, righteous, and truthful motive.—Y.

Vers. 1—9.—*Balaam—the third parable.* This passage marks the period at which Balaam becomes finally convinced that it is vain for him to attempt to satisfy Balak, or to carry out the baser promptings of his own heart. He confesses his defeat, gives up his enchantments, " sets his face towards the wilderness " where the camp of Israel lay, and utters the words that God puts into his mouth. But still his spirit is not subdued, for, as we learn from ver. 14, instead of casting in his lot, as he might have done, with the chosen nation, he resolves in spite of all to go back to his own people and his old ways. Combining these two features of his case, we see how a man may " approve the right and follow the wrong." It affords a striking example of (1) true convictions followed by (2) a false and fatal determination.

I. TRUE CONVICTIONS. Though it was by the constraint of a higher Power that Balaam uttered these words of benediction, we must regard them also as being, to a great extent, the result of his own intuitions, symptoms of the struggling of better thought and feeling within him. He was not the mere senseless medium of the spirit of prophecy. Unwillingly, but not altogether unwittingly, was he made the organ of a Divine inspiration. A bad man may utter words that are good and true, and may often be compelled by the force of outward testimony, or of the inward witness of his own conscience, to do honour to that in others which condemns himself. There are chiefly three characteristics here which find their higher counterpart in the spiritual Israel, and which her enemies, like Balaam, have often been constrained to confess. 1. *Beauty.* " How goodly are thy tents, O Jacob ! " Rich valleys, smiling gardens, lign-aloes and cedars planted beside the water-courses, are, to the poetic imagination of the seer, the fitting images of their goodly array. But what is the beauty that captivates the eye compared with that which appeals to the sensibility of the soul ? All outward forms of loveliness are but the shadow and reflection of the Diviner beauties of holiness, the spiritual glory of truth, purity, goodness—the " adorning of the hidden man of the heart in that which is not corruptible." The richest Oriental imagery can but feebly represent the changing phases of this beauty. And many a man has felt the charm of it, and yet been utterly destitute of that sympathy of spirit that would move him to make it his own. It compels his admiration, but does not win his love. 2. *World-wide fruitfulness.* " He shall pour the water out of his buckets," &c.—the image of abundant, far-reaching beneficence. The promise to

Abraham was fulfilled: "In thy seed shall all the nations of the earth be blessed" (Gen. xxii. 16, 17). The benefits the seed of Abraham conferred upon the human race did but foreshadow those of Christianity. It is the "light of the world," the "salt of the earth," carrying the stream of a new life over all lands, diffusing a healing influence through all the waters. Its adversaries know this, and are often constrained in spite of themselves to acknowledge it. They are themselves living witnesses to its truth, for they owe to Christianity the very culture, the spiritual force, the social advantages, the literary facilities, &c., that they turn as weapons against it. 3. *Victorious power.* The triumphant way in which God led forth his people out of Egypt was prophetic of the power that should always overshadow them and dwell among them; often a latent, slumbering strength like that of a crouching or sleeping lion, but irresistible when once it rouses itself to withstand their foes. Such power dwells ever in the redeemed Church. "God is in the midst of her," &c. (Ps. xlvi. 5). "The weapons of our warfare," &c. (2 Cor. x. 4). Nothing so strong and invincible as truth and goodness. The light must triumph over the darkness. The kingdom of Christ is a "kingdom that cannot be moved," and many a man whose heart has had no kind of sympathy with the cause of that kingdom has been unable to suppress the secret conviction that it will surely win its way, till it shall have vanquished all its enemies and covered the face of the whole earth.

II. A FALSE AND FATAL DETERMINATION. "And now, behold, I go unto my people" (ver. 14). He returns to his former ways, plunges again into the darkness and foulness of idolatrous Mesopotamia, having first, it would appear, counselled Balak as to how he might corrupt with carnal fascinations the people whom it was vain for him to "curse" (see ch. xxxi. 16; Rev. ii. 14), and at last is slain with the sword among the Midianites (ch. xxxi. 8; Josh. xiii. 22). Learn—1. How powerless are the clearest perceptions of the truth in the case of one whose heart is thoroughly set in him to do evil. There are those who "hold the truth in unrighteousness" (Rom. i. 18). "They profess that they know God, but in works they deny him" (Titus i. 16). 2. How there is often a deeper fall into the degradation of sin when such an one has been uplifted for a while by the vision and the dream of a better life. "The last state of that man is worse than the first" (Matt. xii. 45). "For it had been better for them not to have known the way of righteousness," &c. (2 Pet. ii. 21, 22).—W.

Ver. 17.—*Balaam—the fourth parable.* Balaam appears before us here as one who "seeing, sees not." His "eyes are open," but he has no real vision of the eternal truth of things. He has a "knowledge of the Most High," but not that which consists in living sympathy with his character and will and law. He recognises the blessedness of the ransomed people, but has no personal share in that blessedness. He discerns the bright visions of the future, the rising of Jacob's Star, the gleam of the royal Sceptre that shall rule the world, the coming of the world's redeeming Lord, but he sees him only from afar. Not "now," not "nigh," does he behold him; not with a vivid, quickening, self-appropriating consciousness; not as the light, the hope, the life, the eternal joy of his own soul. It is a moral portraiture, a type of spiritual condition and personal character, with which we are only too familiar. The faith of many is thus destitute of efficient saving power. "It is dead, being alone." Their religious perceptions are thus divorced from religious life. They have just such a formal, ideal acquaintance with God, without any of that immediate personal fellowship with him which renews their moral nature after his likeness. They walk in the embrace of his presence, but their "eyes are holden that they should not know him." So near is He, and yet so far; so clearly revealed, and yet so darkly hidden; so familiar, and yet so strange.

I. This is seen in THE INSENSIBILITY OF MEN TO THE DIVINER MEANING OF NATURE. The material universe exists for spiritual ends. God has surrounded his intelligent creatures with all the affluence and glory of it in order to reveal himself to them and attract their thought and affection to himself. "The invisible things of him from the beginning of the world are clearly seen," &c. (Rom. i. 20). But how dead are men often to Divine impressions! They hear no voice and feel no influence from God coming to them through his works. They know none but the lower uses of nature, and never dream of entering through it into communion with Him who inspires it with the energy of his presence. Tribes whose life is nursed and cradled in the fairest regions of the earth are often mentally the darkest and morally the most depraved. The worst forms of heathenism have been found in those parts of the world where the Creator has most lavished the tokens of his glorious beneficence. The sweet associations of rural and pastoral life in a Christian land like ours are connected less than we should expect them to be with quickness of spiritual perception and tenderness of spiritual sensibility. Stranger still that men whose souls are most keenly alive to all the beauty of the world, and with whom it is an all-absorbing passion to search out its wonders and drink in its poetic inspirations, should fail, as they so often do, to discern in it a living God. Physical science is to many as a gorgeous veil that darkly hides him, rather than the glass through which the beams of his glory fall upon them, the radiant pathway by which they climb up to his throne. Their eyes are wondrously "open;" they have a "knowledge of the Most High" in the forms and modes of his working such as few attain to; "visions of the Almighty" in the glorious heavens above and the teeming earth beneath pass continually before them, and yet they see and feel and know him not. How different such a case from that of Job: "O that I knew where I might find him !" &c. (Job xxiii. 1—10). *There* you have the passionate outbreathing of a soul that is hungering and thirsting after a God that "hideth himself." *Here* you have God urging, pressing upon men the signals and proofs of his presence without effect. There is no blindness darker and sadder than that of those who boast that their "eyes are open," and yet, in a glorious world like this, can find no living God.

II. It is seen in THE INDISPOSITION OF MEN TO RECOGNISE THE VOICE OF GOD IN HOLY SCRIPTURE. To know that the Bible is a revelation of truth from God, and to know God as he reveals himself in the Bible, are two widely different things. There are those to whom revelation is as a Divine voice uttered long ago, but "not now;" a voice coming down to them through the ages as in distant echo, but not instant and near. To them these old records may be sacred, venerable, worthy to be preserved and defended, but in no sense are they a channel of direct personal communication between the living God and our living souls; "inspired" once, but not instinct with the spirit of inspiration now. No wonder the word is powerless and fruitless under such conditions. It is of no use to tell men that the Scriptures are "inspired" if they don't *feel God to be in them,* dealing as a personal Spirit with their spirits to draw them into fellowship with himself. A new kind of consciousness is awakened, a new order of effects produced, when once a man begins to feel that the written word is the living voice of God to his own soul. He cannot despise it then. It carries with it an authority that needs no extraneous authority to support it—the true "demonstration of the Spirit." Apart from this, the soul in presence of all these Divine revelations is like one under the influence of some powerful anæsthetic, receiving impressions on the outward sense of all that is going on around him, but conscious of nothing. The "eyes are open," but there is no living, spiritual realisation. "They seeing, see not, and hearing, hear not, neither do they understand" (Matt. xiii. 13; John xii. 40; 2 Cor. iv. 3, 4).

III. It is seen in THE PURELY IDEAL RELATION IN WHICH MEN TOO OFTEN STAND TOWARDS CHRIST. By multitudes Christ is seen, as it were, "afar off." He is to them but as the vision of a dream, a vague, distant abstraction, a mere historic figure, the central actor in a tragical historic drama. They have never entered into any kind of personal relation with him, have never bowed before him in heart-broken penitence, adoring wonder, childlike trustfulness, grateful, self-surrendering love. "Virtue" has never gone forth out of him to heal the disease of their souls, because they have not yet "touched him." There is a wide distinction between the knowledge that comes by mere hearsay and that which comes by personal converse, between a distant vision and the living "touch." Though faith be in great part blind and unintelligent, yet if there is the quick sensibility of life in it, it is better than all the clear, unclouded vision of an eye that is no real inlet to the soul. There is a *future* manifestation of Christ. "Behold, he cometh with clouds; and every eye shall see him" (Rev. i. 7). What shall be the relation in which we stand towards him then? There are those whose eyes will then be opened as they never were before. Shall it be only to have them closed again in everlasting night, "consumed with the brightness of his appearing"? You must be in living fellowship with Christ now if you would look with joy upon him when he comes in his "power and great glory."—W.

EXPOSITION.

CHAPTER XXV.

THE SIN OF ISRAEL AND ATONEMENT OF PHINEHAS (vers. 1—18). Ver. 1.—**Abode in Shittim.** For a considerable time; from their first arrival in the Arboth Moab until the crossing of the Jordan. Shittim is the shortened form of Abel-Shittim, "Field of Acacias" (ch. xxxiii. 49). It seems to have been the northernmost part of the last encampment of Israel on that side Jordan, and the head-quarters of the host (Josh. ii. 1; iii. 1). **Began to commit whoredom with the daughters of Moab.** This commencement of sin seems to have been made by Israel without special provocation. The very victories won, and the comparative ease and affluence now enjoyed, after long marches and hardships, may well have predisposed them to this sin, for which they now for the first time found abundant opportunity.

Ver. 2.—**And they called,** *i. e.* the women of Moab, encouraged to do so by the licentious intercourse which had sprung up. Without such encouragement it is difficult to suppose that they would have ventured on such a step. **And the people did eat.** Gluttony added its seductions to lust. No doubt this generation were as weary of the manna and as eager for other and heavier food as their fathers had been (see on ch. xi. 4; xxi. 5).

Ver. 3.—**Israel joined himself unto Baal-Peor.** This is a technical phrase, repeated in ver. 5, and quoted in Ps. cvi. 28, expressing the quasi-sacramental union into which they entered with the heathen deity by partaking of his sacrificial meats and by sharing in his impure rites (cf. Hosea ix. 10 and the argument of St. Paul in 1 Cor. x.). There can be little doubt that Peor (פְּעוֹר, from פָּעַר, to open) has the sense of *aperiens, in usu obsceno,* and that it was the distinguishing name of Baal or Chemosh when worshipped as the god of reproduction with the abominable rites proper to this cultus. For a notice of the same thing in the last days of Israel see Hosea iv. 14, and for the practice of Babylonian and (to some degree) Egyptian women, see Herodotus, i. 199; ii. 60). The Septuagint has here ἐτελέσθη τῷ Βεελφεγώρ, "was consecrated," or "initiated," unto Baal-Peor, which admirably expressed the sense.

Ver. 4.—**The Lord said unto Moses.** It seems strange that so fearful an apostasy had gone so far without interference on the part of Moses. He may have been absent from the camp on account of the wars with the Amorite kings; or he may have trusted to the chiefs to see that due order and discipline was maintained in the camps. **Take all the heads of the people,** *i. e.* the chiefs, who ought to have prevented, and might have prevented, this monstrous irregularity, but who seem, if we may judge from the case of Zimri, to have countenanced it. The mere neglect of duty in so gross a case was reason enough for summary execution. **Hang them up before the Lord.** Either by way of impalement or by way of crucifixion, both of which were familiar modes of punishment. In this case the guilty persons were probably slain first, and exposed afterwards. The hanging up was not ordered on account of its cruelty, nor merely for the sake of publicity ("against the sun"), but in order to show that the victims were devoted to the wrath of God against sin (cf. Deut. xxi. 23; 2 Sam. xxi. 2—6). The Septuagint has here παραδειγμάτισον αὐτούς. Cf. Heb. vi. 6, where this word is coupled with "crucify." There is no authority for referring the "them" (אוֹתָם) to the guilty persons instead of to the heads of the people, as is done by the Targums and by many commentators.

Ver. 5.—**The judges of Israel.** אֶל-שֹׁפְטֵי. This is the first place where "the judges" are mentioned by this name (cf. Deut. i. 16; Judges ii. 16), but the verb is freely used in Exod. xviii. in describing the functions of the officers appointed at Sinai. **Every one his men.** The men who were under his particular jurisdiction. This command given by Moses is not to be confounded with the previous command given to Moses to hang up all the chiefs. Moses only could deal with the chief, but it was within the power and the province of the judges to deal with ordinary offenders. It does not, however, appear how far either of these commands was put in practice.

Ver. 6.—**A Midianitish woman.** Rather, "the Midianitish woman." אֶת-הַמִּדְיָנִית. Septuagint, τὴν Μαδιανίτην. The writer deals with an incident only too notorious, and which by the peculiar aggravation of its circumstances had fixed itself deeply in the popular memory. This is the first mention of the Midianites in connection with this affair, and it prepares us to learn without surprise that they were in reality the authors of this mischief. **All the congregation, . . who were weeping.** According to the loose sense in which this expression is used throughout the Pentateuch, it evidently means that those who truly represented the nation, not only as a political, but also as a religious community, were gathered in this distress before the presence of their invisible King. They wept on account of the wrath of God provoked ; probably also on account of the wrath of God already gone forth in the form of a pestilence.

Ver. 7.—**Phinehas, the son of Eleazar.** See on Exod. vi. 25. He seems to have been the only son of Eleazar, and his natural successor in the office of high priest.

Ver. 8.—**Into the tent.** אֶל־הַקֻּבָּה. Septuagint, εἰς τὴν κάμινον. The word signifies an arched recess (cf. the Arabic "alcove," from the same root, and the Latin *fornix*), and means probably the inner division which served as the women's room in the larger tents of the wealthier Israelites. There is no sufficient ground for supposing that a special place had been erected for this evil purpose ; if it had been, it would surely have been destroyed. **Through her belly.** אֶל־קֳבָתָהּ. Septuagint, διὰ τῆς μήτρας αὐτῆς. **So the plague was stayed.** No plague has been mentioned, but the narrative evidently deals with an episode the details of which were very fresh in the memory of all, and is extremely concise. That a plague would follow such an apostasy might be certainly expected from the previous experiences at Kibroth-hattaavah, at Kadesh, and after the rebellion of Korah.

Ver. 9.—**Were twenty and four thousand.** "Fell in one day three and twenty thousand," says St. Paul (1 Cor. x. 8). As the Septuagint does not deviate here from the Hebrew, the Apostle must have followed some Rabbinical tradition. It is possible enough that the odd thousand died on some other day than the one of which he speaks, or they may have died by the hands of the judges, and not by the plague.

Ver. 10.—**The Lord spake unto Moses, saying.** On the Divine commendation here bestowed upon the act of Phinehas see the note at the end of the chapter. In the Hebrew Bible a new section begins here.

Ver. 11.—**While he was zealous for my sake.** Rather, "while he was zealous with my zeal" (אֶת־קִנְאָתִי. Septuagint, ἐν τῷ ζηλῶσαί μου τὸν ζῆλον, where μου stands emphatically before ζῆλον). **In my jealousy.** Rather, "in my zeal;" the same word is used.

Ver. 14.—**Now the name of the Israelite.** These details as to names seem to have been added as an after-thought, for they would naturally have been given in ver. 11, where the man and the woman are first mentioned. The woman's name is given again in ver. 18, as if for the first time. We may probably conclude that vers. 14, 15 were inserted into the narrative either by the hand of Moses himself at a later date, or possibly by some subsequent hand. **Zimri.** This was not an uncommon name, but the individual who bears it here is not elsewhere mentioned.

Ver. 15.—**Head over a people, and of a chief house in Midian.** Rather, "head of tribes (אֻמּוֹת, for the use of which cf. Gen. xxv. 16) of a father's house in Midian." It seems to mean that several clans descended from one tribe-father looked up to Zur as their head. In ch. xxxi. 8 he is called one of the five "kings" of Midian. That the daughter of such a man should have been selected, and should have been willing, to play such a part throws a strong light upon the studied character and the peculiar danger of the seduction.

Ver. 17.—**Vex the Midianites.** The Moabites, although the evil began with them, were passed over ; perhaps because they were still protected by the Divine injunction (Deut. ii. 9) not to meddle with them ; more probably because their sin had not the same studied and deliberate character as the sin of the Midianites. We may think of the women of Moab as merely indulging their individual passions after their wonted manner, but of the women of Midian as employed by their rulers, on the advice of Balaam, in a deliberate plot to entangle the Israelites in heathen rites and heathen sins which would alienate from them the favour of God.

NOTE ON THE ZEAL OF PHINEHAS.

The act of Phinehas, the son of Eleazar, in slaying Zimri and Cozbi is one of the most memorable in the Old Testament; not so much, however, in itself, as in the commendation bestowed upon it by God. It is unquestionably surprising at first sight that an act of unauthorised zeal, which might so readily be made (as indeed it was made) the excuse for deeds of murderous fanaticism, should be commended in the strongest terms by the Almighty ; that an act of summary vengeance, which we find it somewhat hard to justify on moral grounds, should be made in a peculiar sense and in a special degree the pattern of the great atonement wrought by the Saviour of mankind ; but this aspect of the deed in the eyes of God by its very unexpectedness draws our attention to it, and obliges us to consider wherein its distinctive religious character and excellence lay.

It is necessary in the first place to point out that the act of Phinehas did really receive stronger testimony from God than any other act done *proprio motu* in the Old Testament. What he did was not done officially (for he held no office), nor was it done by command (for the offenders were not under his jurisdiction as judge), nor in fulfilment of any revealed law or duty (for no blame would have attached to him if he had let it alone), and yet it had the same effect in staying the plague as the act of Aaron when he stood between the living and the dead with the hallowed fire in his hand (see on ch. xvi. 46—48). Of both it is said that " he made an atonement for the people," and so far they both appear as having power with God to turn away his wrath and stay his avenging hand. But the atonement made by Aaron was official, for he was the anointed high priest, and, being made with incense from the sanctuary, it was made in accordance with and upon the strength of a ceremonial law laid down by God whereby he had bound himself to exercise his Divine right of pardon. The act of Phinehas, on the contrary, had no legal or ritual value ; there is no power of atonement in the blood of sinners, nor had the death of 24,000 guilty people had any effect in turning away the wrath of God from them that survived. It remains, therefore, a startling truth that the deed of Phinehas is the only act neither official nor commanded, but originating in the impulses of the actor himself, to which the power of atoning for sin is ascribed in the Old Testament : for although in 2 Sam. xxi. 3 David speaks of making an atonement by giving up seven of Saul's sons, it is evident from the context that the " atonement " was made to the Gibeonites, and not directly to the Lord. Again, the act of Phinehas merited the highest reward from God, a reward which was promised to him in the most absolute terms. Because he had done this thing he should have God's covenant of peace, he and his seed after him, even the covenant of an everlasting priesthood. This promise must mean that he and his seed should have power with God for ever to make peace between heaven and earth, and to make reconciliation for the sins of the people ; and, meaning this, it is a republication in favour of Phinehas, and in more absolute terms, of the covenant made with Levi as represented by Aaron (see on Mal. ii. 4, 5). Nor is this all. In Ps. cvi. 31 it is said of his deed that " it was counted unto him for righteousness unto all generations for evermore." This word "counted" or "imputed " is the same (חשׁב) which is used of Abraham in Gen. xv. 6, and the very words of the Septuagint here (ἐλογίσθη αὐτῷ εἰς δικαιοσύνην) are applied to the obedience of Abraham in James ii. 23. It appears then that righteousness was imputed to Phinehas, as to the father of the faithful, with this distinction, that to Phinehas it was imputed as an everlasting righteousness, which is not said of Abraham. Now if we compare the two, it must be evident that the act of Phinehas was not, like Abraham's, an act of self-sacrificing obedience, nor in any special sense an act of faith. While both acted under the sense of duty, the following of duty in Abraham's case put the greatest possible strain upon all the natural impulses of mind and heart ; in the case of Phinehas it altogether coincided with the impulses of his own will. If faith was imputed to Abraham for righteousness, it is clear that zeal was imputed to Phinehas for righteousness for evermore.

This being so, it is necessary in the second place to point out that the act in question (like that of Abraham in sacrificing his son) was distinctly one of moral virtue according to the standard then Divinely allowed. An act which was in itself wrong, or of doubtful rectitude, could not form the ground for such praise and promise, even supposing that they really looked far beyond the act itself. Now it is clear (1) that under no circumstances would a similar act be justifiable now ; (2) that no precedent could be established by it then. The Jews indeed feigned a "zealot-right," examples of which they saw (amongst others) in the act of Samuel slaying Agag (1 Sam. xv. 33), of Mattathias slaying the idolatrous Jew and the king's commissioner (1 Macc. ii. 24—26), of the Sanhedrim slaying St. Stephen. But the last-mentioned case is evidence enough that in the absence of distinct Divine guidance zeal is sure to degenerate into fanaticism, or rather that it is impossible to distinguish zeal from fanaticism. Every such act must of necessity stand upon its own merits, for it can only be justified by the coexistence of two conditions which are alike beyond human certainty : (1) that the deed is itself in accordance with the will of God ; (2) that the doing of it is inspired by motives absolutely pure. That Christ came to save men's lives, and that God would have all men to repent, has made for us the primary condition impossible, and therefore the act of Phinehas would be immoral now. No one may take life unless he has the mandate of the State for doing so. But it was not so then ; God was the King of Israel, and the foes of Israel were the foes of God, with whom there could be no peace or amity as long as they threatened the very existence of God's people and worship. The Israelite who indulged in sinful intercourse with a heathen was a rebel against his King and a traitor to his country ; he became *ipso facto* an "outlaw," to slay whom was the bounden duty of every true patriot. If it be said that this view of things belongs to an inferior code of morality, which ignored the universal brotherhood of men and Fatherhood of God, that is admitted at once. The elder revelation founded itself plainly and avowedly upon the moral law as then universally held (and by no means supplanted yet by the higher law of Christ), that men were to love their brethren and hate their enemies. To complain that the act of Phinehas was moral in a Jewish and not in a Christian sense is only to find fault with God for suffering a confessedly imperfect and preparatory morality to do its work until the fulness of time was come.

While, therefore, we recognise the act of Phinehas as one determined, in its outward form, by the imperfect morality of the dispensation under which he lived, it is necessary to look below the act to the spirit which animated it for its permanent value and significance. That spirit is clearly defined by the testimony of God—"while he was zealous with *my* zeal." The excellence of Phinehas was, that he was filled with a zeal which was itself Divine against sin, and that he acted fearlessly and promptly (whilst others apparently hesitated even when commanded) under the impulse of that zeal ; in other words, what pleased God so greatly was to see his own hatred of sin, and his own desire to make it to cease, reflected in the mind and expressed in the deed of one who acted upon righteous impulse, not under any command or constraint.

It is impossible, in the third place, not to see that this record throws a flood of light upon the doctrine of the atonement ; for the act of Phinehas stands, in some respects, upon a higher level than all the types and shadows of the cross which had gone before ; being neither an act of submission to a definite command, like the sacrifice of Isaac, nor a piece of ordered ritual, like the sending forth of the goat for Azazel ;

but a spontaneous deed, having a moral value of its own. Partly at least for the sake of what it was, not merely what it showed in a figure, it was accepted as an atonement for the sin of Israel (which was very gross), and was imputed to its author for an everlasting righteousness. Phinehas, therefore, in one very important sense, would seem to bear a stronger resemblance to our Lord in his atoning work than any other person in the Old Testament. It may therefore be submitted that we must seek the truest ground of the atonement wrought by Christ not in the simple fact of the passion and death of the God-man, nor in the greatness or value of his sufferings as such; but in that zeal for God, that Divine indignation against sin as the opposite of God, that consuming desire to cause it to cease, which first animated the life of the Redeemer, and then informed his death. Phinehas in his measure, and according to his lights, was governed by the same Spirit, and surrendered himself to the prompting of the same Spirit, by which Christ offered himself without spot unto God. And that Spirit was the Spirit of a consuming zeal, wherein our Lord hastened with an entire eagerness of purpose (Luke xii. 50; John ii. 17; xii. 27, 28, &c.) to "condemn sin in the flesh" and so to glorify God, and to accomplish the object of his mission (Rom. viii. 3), not by the summary execution of individual sinners, but after an infinitely higher fashion, by the sacrifice of himself as the representative of the whole sinful race.

Lastly, it must be noted that as the act of Phinehas enables us, almost more than anything else, to enter into the nature of our Lord's atonement, so it is only in the light of that atonement that we can justify to ourselves either the strength of the Divine commendation accorded to Phinehas, or the vastness of the promises made to him. For the deed was after all an act of violence, and a dangerous precedent, humanly speaking; and, on the other hand, the covenant of peace given to him and to his seed, even the covenant of an everlasting priesthood, failed to give any peace at all, save in a very broken and partial manner, and did not even continue in the keeping of his family. As the house of Eleazar was the elder of the two descended from Aaron, it would have been only natural that the high priestly dignity should remain with its members; as a fact, however, it passed to the house of Ithamar from the days of Eli until Solomon, for political reasons, deposed Abiathar in favour of Zadok; and it was lost for ever with the final fall of Jerusalem. As in so many cases, therefore, we have to acknowledge that the act of Phinehas was accepted as an atonement for the sake of that truer atonement which (in a remarkable sense) it anticipated; and that the promises given to Phinehas were only partially intended and partially fulfilled for him, while the true and eternal fulfilment was reserved for him of whom Phinehas was a figure. To Christ, in whom was combined an entire zeal against sin and an entire love for the sinner, was indeed given God's covenant of peace and an everlasting priesthood.

HOMILETICS.

Vers. 1—18.—*Sin, zeal, and atonement.* We have in this chapter the sin of man and the righteousness of God set before us in the most striking light; the virulence of the one, and the triumph of the other through the zeal of God's servant. We may contemplate here—I. The seductions of the flesh and of the devil, and the apostasy to which they lead; II. The insolence of sin when allowed to gain a head; III. The zeal against sin which pleases God and obtains favour; IV. In a figure, the atonement wrought by God's holy servant Jesus.

I. Consider, therefore, with respect to THE APOSTASY OF ISRAEL—1. *That it was due to two things — their own licentiousness, and the craft of Balaam taking advantage of it.* They knew not indeed that Balaam had any part in it, but *we* know that the instigation came from him. Even so there is the same double origination of all grave fallings away from God and grace. A man is drawn away of his own lust (James i. 14), and enticed by the lust of the flesh and of the eyes (1 John ii. 16); but beneath and behind all these temptations is the craft of an evil will counter-working the grace and purpose of God (Ephes. vi. 11, 16; 1 Pet. v. 8). And note that Balaam could not harm them by his curses or magical practices, but only by taking advantage of their evil concupiscence. So has our adversary no power against us, save through our own sins. 2. *That the sin of Israel began with idleness, and the reaction from toil and victory, which encouraged them to give the rein to wandering desires.* Even so the most dangerous moments, morally speaking, in a Christian's life are those intervals of comparative inactivity and apparent safety when dangers seem to be surmounted, foes overcome, and toils left behind. 3. *That the danger of Israel against which they had been so strongly warned now beset them, viz., the danger of too friendly intercourse with people whose religion and morality were altogether inferior to that of Israel.* Even so the great and constant danger of Christian people—especially of such as mix much with others—lies in intercourse with a world which does not acknowledge the laws of God, and in the almost inevitable lowering of the moral and religious tone which follows. 4. *That the first fatal step was indulgence in carnal pleasures*—an indulgence such as was now for the first time thrown in their way. And this is still the frequent source of apostasy; a snare into which the most unlikely persons constantly fall when it is suddenly presented to them. How many of the greatest, intellectually, and most promising, spiritually, have fallen through lust! how many deem themselves absolutely above it simply because the temptation has never yet come in their way! 5. *That fellowship in sin led directly to fellowship in idolatry:* the two things being mutually intermixed in the abominations of those days. Even so it is impossible to take part in the sinful indulgences of the flesh and of the world without denying God and committing treason against him. Immorality is not simply evil in the sight of God, it is an outrage upon him, and a direct renunciation of our allegiance to him. The first Christians rightly regarded Venus and Bacchus as devils. Fleshly sin involves a quasi-sacramental union with the enemy of God (1 Cor. vi. 13—20; x. 21, 22; and cf. Ps. lxxiii. 27; Acts xv. 20; 1 Tim. v. 11). 6. *That the wrath of God burnt especially against the heads of the people, because they had permitted these iniquities to go on, and had perhaps encouraged them.* Even so their sin is greatest and their punishment will be sorest who fail to use their position and authority to discourage vice; much more if they countenance it by their example. 7. *That the sentence of death was pronounced upon all who were joined to Baal-Peor.* It is not the will of God that sin as such should now be punished by the magistrate, but none the less is the sentence of eternal death gone forth against all who through sinful indulgence have made themselves over to the prince of this world (Rom. i. 18, 32; vi. 23; Ephes. v. 5; Rev. xix. 20; xxi. 8). 8. *That the judges of Israel were commanded to execute judgment, not indiscriminately, but each upon such as he was responsible for.* Even so is every Christian held bound to extirpate by all needful violence his own sins and sinful inclinations which cleave unto iniquity and do dishonour to God. For each one of us is responsible for all that is within him, and not for others, save by example and admonition (Rom. viii. 13; 1 Cor. ix. 27; Gal. vi. 5; Ephes. v. 11; Col. iii. 5, where "mortify" is simply "put to death").

II. Consider again, with respect to THE SIN OF ZIMRI—1. *That the bad example and negligence of the chiefs went further in encouraging this evil than the declared wrath of God in discouraging it.* It would have been impossible for such a thing to have occurred if the leaders of Israel had been doing their duty. Even so in a society nominally Christian the bad example of its leaders has much more effect than all the denunciations of Scripture. Nothing is more remarkable than the extreme insolence with which the worst vices are ever ready to assert themselves, and to flaunt their vileness in the face of day, if they find encouragement, or even toleration, with those that lead opinion and set the fashion. Worse sins than that of Zimri, such as adultery, and murder (in the form of duelling), have been and are practised without shame and without rebuke by those who claim the name and privilege of Christians. 2. *That the rank of the two offenders no doubt increased their presumption, as shielding them from punishment.* Even so in the Churches of Christ it has ever been the rich and the great who have dragged down the moral law and outraged the holiness of their calling, because they seemed to be beyond the reach of discipline or correction in this world. 3. *That their sin was intensified by contrast with the penitential sorrow and the trouble all around them.* Even so does the reckless sin of abandoned people assume a darker hue in the sight of God and of good men, because it shows itself side by side with all the sorrow and the pain, the penitence and supplication, which that very sin has worked in unnumbered souls. There is not a city in Christendom where that scene of sin and weeping in the camp of Israel is not ever being reproduced in full sight of God, if not of men. 4. *That the sin of Zimri was, and is, revolting to everybody, not, however, because it was really worse than numberless other such acts, but only because it asserted itself in its naked hideousness.* Even so the most revolting crimes which all men cry out upon are not really worse than those which are committed every day ; it is only that circumstances have robbed them of the disguises and concealments beneath which men hide their ordinary sins.

III. Consider again, with respect to THE ZEAL OF PHINEHAS—1. *That it was well-pleasing in the sight of God because it was a zeal for God, and against sin.* Even such must be the character of all true religious zeal ; it must have no lesser or meaner inspiring motive than the pure desire that God may be glorified and sin may be destroyed. It is this zeal, and nothing else, which puts the creature at once on the side of the Creator, and produces an active harmony of will and purpose between God and man. How little religious zeal has this pure character ! Hence, although it achieves much,—builds churches, wins converts, gains all its ends on earth,—yet it does not obtain any commendation or reward from God. 2. *That it stood in strong contrast to the supineness of the chiefs, and even apparently of Moses ; they (at best) only mourned, Phinehas acted.* True zeal is always rare, and most rare in high places. It is so much easier to deplore the existence of evils than to throw oneself into active contention against them. The enthusiasms and reforms which have purged the Church of its grosser moral corruptions have never come from its leaders. 3. *That it was all the more acceptable with God because it was spontaneous, 'and not official.* Even so the zeal which pleases God is that which is not paid for directly or indirectly, and which is not prompted by any human expectations, and does not wait for any advantages of position. How often do men tacitly agree to leave zeal for religion and morality to their official exponents, as if it were a professional matter to seek the glory of God and the triumph of righteousness ! 4. *That it merited the favour of Heaven because it was unhesitating and unabashed.* No one else perhaps would have "followed" when and where Phinehas followed. Even so a genuine religious zeal does not hesitate to seek its ends by painful courses, and such as natural feeling and ordinary sentiment shrinks from. Zeal knows no shame except the shame of doing wrong or of suffering wrong to be done if it can be helped. 5. *That the act of Phinehas was commended because it was (1) according to the will of God, and (2) inspired by zeal for God unmixed with lower motives.* According to the law of Israel, as then understood and sanctioned by God, it was right that these sinners should die, and right that any private person in Israel should execute judgment upon them if the rulers hesitated ; and Phinehas had no private ends to gain or malice to gratify by what he did. Even such is the ultimate test of every act of religious zeal, by which it must be weighed in the last account. If a thing be right in itself, according to the revealed will of God, yet if it be done from any motive but the highest, it has no reward hereafter, because it seeks its reward here. 6. *That the act of Phinehas was one which was right then, but would be wrong now,* because the present dispensation is built upon eternal, not upon temporal, sanctions. Yet is his zeal and ours all one in its essence : we must put to death the deeds of the flesh by the arms of righteousness ; every man must be a Phinehas to his own lusts in act—to others in word and example only (cf. 2 Cor. vii. 11).

IV. Consider lastly, with respect to PHINEHAS AS A FIGURE OF CHRIST IN HIS ATONEMENT—1. *That the act of Phinehas was accepted as an atonement because it was inspired by a pure zeal for God and against sin, without regard of self.* And this was the moral element, the controlling motive power, in the life and death of Christ, which made it infinitely precious in the eyes of God, and infinitely available for the remission of sins. 2. *That God had sought for such an atonement before and it had not been given* (see ver. 4: "Hang them up, . . . that the fierce anger of the Lord may be turned away from Israel "). And God had looked in vain among the children of men for any that should have perfect sympathy with his own hatred of sin, and perfect self-devotion in seeking to destroy it (cf. Isa. liii. 11, "my righteous servant;" lxiii. 4, 5; Matt. iii. 17, &c.). 3. *That Phinehas "satisfied" the wrath of God against sin, inasmuch as he gave expression in the most open and public way to the real mind of God in respect of sin.* And our Lord did not merely regard sin with the eyes of God, but he manifested unto all the world in the very highest sense the righteousness of God as arrayed against the sinfulness of sin. Beholding the carcases of those sinners, Israel awoke from his evil dream to a consciousness of what such lust really was. Gazing upon the dead face of him that was made sin for us, we realise what the hatefulness and hideousness of sin truly is. 4. *That Phinehas condemned sin in the flesh by the death—since nothing less would suffice—of the sinners.* And God condemned sin in the flesh not by inflicting death, but by sending his only-begotten to suffer death in the name and in the place of that sinful race with which he had wholly identified himself. 5. *That Phinehas, having displayed and vindicated the righteousness of God, delivered the rest of Israel from the plague.* Even so our Lord, having condemned sin by his own death, through death destroyed the power of death, and delivered his brethren from the fear of death. 6. *That Phinehas received for his zeal God's covenant of peace, and the promise of an everlasting priesthood.* And our Lord, for that he made atonement for the sins of the world, and reconciled in one life and death the holiness and the love of God, became himself our peace (Ephes. ii. 14), and was made a priest for ever after the order of Melchizedec (Heb. v. 9, 10). 7. *That Phinehas could not abide because of death, nor his seed because of infirmity and change;* wherefore the promise could not be permanently made good to him. But Christ abideth for ever, for ever the same, eternal inheritor of all the promises made to all holy men (Heb. vii. 24; xiii. 8, &c.). See the note above.

HOMILIES BY VARIOUS AUTHORS.

Vers. 10—13.—*A terrible atonement.* We see in this narrative—

I. THE NATION WHICH GOD HAD BLESSED, CURSED THROUGH ITS OWN SINS. The Israelites, impregnable against the curses of Balaam, succumb to his wiles. We discover parts of a plot. In the foreground are women (true daughters of Eve the tempter), alluring feasts, flatteries, idolatries. In the background we discern the malignant face of the covetous Balaam (ch. xxxi. 16; Rev. ii. 14), and behind him his master the devil. Learn to discriminate the seen and unseen agents of temptation (Ephes. vi. 12), and to guard against the devices of our diabolical foe (2 Cor. ii. 11; xi. 14, 15). Sin did what Balaam could not do. The wrath of God, the plague on the thousands of Israelites, the execution of the ringleaders, follow in quick succession. Note the destructiveness of sin. Of every sinner it may be said as of Achan, "That man perished not alone in his iniquity." The guilt of the nation reached its climax in the shamelessness and audacity of the sin of Zimri. While shame, one of the precious relics of paradise, survives, there is more hope of restoration, but when shame is gone, sin is ripe for judgment (Jer. v. 7—9; vi. 15). If God's wrath had continued to burn, the whole nation must have perished.

II. THE WRATH REMOVED BY A TERRIBLE ATONEMENT. 1. The essence of it was not an outward act, but a state of heart. It was Phinehas' zeal for God which made the act possible and acceptable. Just so in the atonement, of a very different character, made by the Lord Jesus Christ, the essence of it was the zeal for the will of God which prompted the obedience unto death, the offering of the body of Christ once for all (Heb. x. 5—10). 2. The form of the atonement was a terrible manifestation of the righteousness of God in the prompt punishment of the two audacious transgressors. They expiated their crime by their lives. Phinehas' conduct, being inspired by godly zeal, is justified by God himself. Instead of being treated as a crime, it is regarded as a covering over of the nation's sin. Where that sin reached its climax, there it received such sudden retribution as to stamp it as an abominable thing which God hates. Zimri and his paramour are branded with eternal infamy, while Phinehas is rewarded by "the covenant of an everlasting priesthood." We learn thus that there is more than one way of making an atonement to God. In both cases it is by the manifestation of the righteousness of God (Rom. iii. 21, 25), but in different ways. 1. By his holy wrath flaming forth against sin, whether immediately (e. g. Josh. vii. 11, 12) or through the zeal of a man of God. The weeping of the people was not an atonement, for it did not *manifest* the righteousness of God as the act of Phinehas did. 2. By his righteous grace allowing another to interpose on behalf of sinners, to do or to suffer whatever God sees needful for a manifestation of his righteousness in the covering over of sin. Thus Moses (Exod. xxxii. 30—33) and Paul (Rom. ix. 3) were willing to have made atonement, if possible. Thus the sinless Son of God did atone (Rom. iii. 21—26), and sin is covered not by the destruction of the sinner, but by the righteous pardon of penitents trusting the atonement of Christ.—P.

Vers. 1—5.—*Moab finds a more effective weapon.* In spite of all his efforts and confident expectations, Balak fails in bringing down Jehovah's curse on Israel. But what cannot be accomplished in the way Balak proposes now gives fair promise of being speedily accomplished in another way. While Israel abode in Shittim the people began to commit whoredom with the daughters of Moab.

I. ISRAEL, FULLY AWARE OF SOME DANGERS, IS EQUALLY REGARDLESS OF MUCH GREATER ONES. Israel having been refused passage through Edom, and having also had to fight its way through the strong opposing forces of Sihon and Og, came at last into the plains of Moab, doubtless expecting a similar conflict with Balak. While he was looking for Israel to attack him, Israel would be wondering why he left it unmolested. And while Balak is waiting for the expected curse, Moab puts on a peaceful, harmless appearance. What was more natural than that Israel should enter into neighbourly intercourse? The nearness of the two peoples gave every facility for this. There must also have been a great charm in seeing fresh faces and hearing unaccustomed voices. As day followed day without any signs of hostility, Israelite and Moabite would mingle more freely together. *If Balak had followed the example of Sihon and Og, it would have been far better for Israel.* The worst enemies are those who, on their first approach, put on the smiling face and give the salutation of peace. We know what to do with the open enemy, who bears his hostility in his countenance; but what shall we do with him who comes insidiously, to degrade, corrupt, and utterly pervert the life within; and this by a very slow process, of which the victim at the beginning must not be conscious at all, and indeed as little conscious as possible until it is too late for escape? Puritanism, so much condemned, laughed at, and satirised, is really the only safety of God's people. Go with the courage which he inspires into any den of lions, into any physical peril whatsoever, remembering what Jesus has said: "Whosoever shall seek to save his life shall lose it; and whosoever shall lose his life shall preserve it" (Luke xvii. 33); but refrain with equal courage from everything that is mere pleasure, mere comfort of the flesh, for in doing so you may keep clear from some temptations in a world which is crowded with them. Remember that to go in the way of one temptation is *to go in the way of more than one, perhaps of many.* Israel got conversing with the daughters of Moab, and this led to whoredom, which assuredly was bad enough; but worse remained, for whoredom led on to idolatry, and idolatry to the manifested wrath of God. The devil was delighted when he saw the sons of Israel, God's own chosen and beloved race, of whom such glorious things had been spoken in prophecy, in abominable intercourse with the daughters of Moab; still more delighted when he saw the bowings to Moab's gods; and his delight was crowned when 24,000 died in the plague. One cannot enter a grocer's shop now-a-days without noticing how many things are hermetically sealed, in order to be kept free from taint. The very smallest crevice would be fatal. We cannot indeed be hermetically sealed—that would be to go out of the world, and Christ's prayer is, not that we should be taken from the world, but kept from the wicked one. But surely we shall not be slow in seconding Christ's prayer and effort with our prayer and effort. We must live in this world as knowing how corruptible we are, and that ceaseless vigilance is the price of spiritual safety.

II. BALAK, FULLY PERSUADED OF THE POWER OF ONE WEAPON, IS UTTERLY UNCONSCIOUS OF THE GREATER POWER OF ANOTHER. Balak, sending all this long way for Balaam, was utterly ignorant of a resource lying close at hand, which probably began to operate even while his negotiations with Balaam were in progress. The world is not conscious of *its greatest resources against the Church ;* it does its greatest damage unwittingly. Balaam certainly seems to have had something to do with bringing out to its full extent this power of the daughters of Moab (ch. xxxi. 16), but it must have been already in action, revealing to him something of the disposition of the Israelites, before he guessed what could be done with it towards utterly destroying them. The world inflicts much spiritual mischief simply by doing its own things in its own way—pursuing, with energy and vivacity, its godless, mammon-worshipping, pleasure-loving path, and thus drawing towards it God's people, never sufficiently heedful of their steps, never sufficiently looking away from the world to Jesus. *It is in the resources which the world does not consider that we are to look for the greatest dangers.* Balak was simply counting the fighting men of Moab ; the women he considered of no consequence. The world, it would seem, is given to despise its own weak ones as much as it despises the weak ones of the Church. God takes weak ones to do his work, but he takes them consciously, deliberately, and with well-ascertained ends, serviceable to the good of his people and the glory of his name. The world also has weak ones to do its work, but it knows not all they do or can do. The lustful daughters of Moab were more dangerous than a corps of Amazons, for they led Israel into idolatry, and that was even worse than if Israel's prime and strength had been stretched dead on some bloody field. Women have done untold and peculiar service in the Church ; and what they have done is but a small part of their possible service, if they would only all waken to their powers and opportunities, and if they were only allowed to make full proof of them. The *ill* that these daughters of Moab did is the measure of the great good that truly Christian women may accomplish. Notice that all the daughters of Moab were not as these mentioned here. There was one daughter of Moab, not so many generations after, of a very different spirit—Ruth, the great-grandmother of David.—Y.

Vers. 6—15.—*Zeal for God: the result and reward of it.* I. ZEAL FOR GOD. 1. *The occasion on which it was shown.* The people were passing through great suffering, as is evident from the mention of the weeping crowd before the tabernacle, and the great number who perished in the plague (ver. 9)—a number much exceeding that in the great visitation of wrath after the rebellion of Korah. God himself had sentenced the leaders of the people to a peculiar and shameful death. The people had sinned, it would seem, even beyond their usual transgressions, and now they are being smitten in a way utterly to terrify and abase them. Yet Zimri, a man of high rank in Israel, and Cozbi, a woman of corresponding rank among her own people, choose this moment to commit a most audacious and shameless act in the presence of weeping Israel. 2. *The person who showed this zeal.* Phinehas, son of Eleazar the priest, and the man who in due time would become priest himself. He might have said, "Is it laid on me more than on any one else to become executioner of Heaven's wrath on this daring couple ? " or, " Doubtless the Lord will signify his will concerning them." But holy indignation becomes his guide, and he rightly judges that this is an instance of presumptuous sin deserving immediate and terrible retribution. He shows here the true spirit of the servant of God in an office such as that for which he was in training. Those who had to do with the tabernacle as closely as the Aaronic family thereby professed to be nearer God than others. And if their service was anything more than a hollow form, then when the honour of Jehovah was peculiarly in question it was to be expected that his true servants would be correspondingly indignant. What would be thought of an ambassador who should listen cool, unmoved, and unresenting to the greatest insults upon the nation from which he had come ? The act of Phinehas was not that of a common Israelite ; there was not merely indignation because of Zimri's callous indifference to the sufferings and sorrows of his brethren ; he was zealous for the Lord. It was *daring, shameless sin* which provoked his wrath; it was as if he looked to heaven in going forth and said, "Against thee, thee only have they sinned." To be easily tolerant in the presence of great sins shows a heart far from right towards God. Mere cynical observations on the frailties and eccentricities of fallen human nature do not fall with good grace from the lips of the Christian, however much they may consist with the conduct of a man of the world. 3. *The way in which the zeal was shown.* A violent and extreme measure certainly, but we are not allowed to judge it. God has taken judgment out of our hands by unmistakably indicating his approval. We must distinguish between the spirit of the act and the outward mode of its commission. If the spirit and essence of the act be right, then the mode is a secondary matter. The mode largely depends on the times. Criminals were punished in England only a few centuries ago in ways which would not be tolerated now. What is wanted is that we should emulate the zeal of Phinehas without imitating the expression of it. One might almost say, better run a javelin through sinners than have that easy-going toleration for sins which some show who call themselves godly. If God is worth serving at all, he is worth serving with zeal. Zeal according to knowledge must be as free from mock-charity and humility on the one hand as from bigotry on the other. The more men there are in the Church of the stamp of Phinehas the better. There are even harder things to be done now-a-days than to thrust javelins through shameless fornicators. It needs a pure and fervent zeal to take one's stand with the few, or even alone, against all sorts of worldly principles and practices prevailing in what ought to be God's kingdom through Christ Jesus. When Paul withstood Peter to the face because he was to be blamed, he did something quite as hard as if he had run a javelin through him.

II. THE RESULT. The plague was stayed. A strange difference in method, is it not, from that adopted on the occasion when Moses commanded Aaron to take the censer and stand in the midst of the congregation, making atonement for them? (ch. xvi. 46). Why was not something of this sort done now? Did Moses feel that it would be of no use, or was his tongue mysteriously stayed from the command? It is plain that Jehovah felt his honour was seriously in question. The people had actually bowed before idols. The chosen race is disintegrating within sight of the promised land. The patriotism of the theocracy is dead. The shout of a king (ch. xxiii. 21) is not met by the answering shout of confiding and grateful subjects. They have utterly forgotten that God is a jealous God (Exod. xx. 5). Stay! there is one man at least, and he, be it marked, in the priestly succession, who does show an adequate jealousy against these idols, so suddenly and ungratefully exalted over against Jehovah. It is the act of only one man; but the act of one man rightly moved, full of holy indignation, energy, and heroism, is enough to stem Jehovah's wrath. Mark, it is not said that Phinehas did this *in order to stop the plague.* The narrative is evidently intended to convey the impression that what he did was in holy indignation at the slight put upon Jehovah. But a righteous action is never wanting in good results. The zeal of Phinehas for Jehovah stood as an atonement for the monstrous disobedience of Israel.

III. THE REWARD. *The result was in itself a reward.* To a man of the stamp of Phinehas it must surely have been no small joy to see the plague stayed. May we not presume that even the leaders escaped their doom, as in a most comprehensive amnesty? *But there is a specified reward beside.* Phinehas has shown his fitness to wear Aaron's robes; nay, in a sense he has worn them, seeing he has made atonement. The real reward for every one faithful to his present opportunity is to enlarge his opportunity and give him more and higher service. He who has the joy of faithfulness in present and perhaps humble duties cannot have a greater joy than that of faithfulness in all of larger and more conspicuous service that may come before him. Our Lord himself, being zealous for his Father on earth (which the formal and professed custodians of the Divine honour were not), cleansing his Father's house from profane and even unrighteous uses, was advanced to still higher service in the glorious opportunities belonging to a place at God's right hand. Among men there is lamentable waste, humiliating and ridiculous failure, because men are so seldom proportioned to the offices they fill. The fit man in the great multitude of instances does not seem to get his chance. *But in God's service every one really gets his chance.* Phinehas got his chance here. Everything depended on himself. The act was the outcome of his honest, fiery, devoted, godly heart. He had not to go to his father or to Moses, saying, "Think you I should do this thing?" If there is zeal in us, occasion will not be lacking. Phinehas had been required to show *the zeal of the destroyer,* and it proved to be also *the zeal of the preserver.* We have to be zealous for a God who is not only righteous and holy, and jealous of rivalry from any other god whatsoever, but also loving, and who desires not the death of a sinner. The zeal that can do nothing but protest, denounce, and destroy, God will never approve or reward. The becoming, fruitful, and praiseworthy zeal under the gospel is that which, following in the train of Paul, is all things to all men in order to save some.—Y.

EXPOSITION.

CHAPTER XXVI.

The second mustering (vers. 1—65). Ver. 1.—It came to pass after the plague. This plague was the last event which seriously diminished the numbers of the Israelites; perhaps it was the last event which diminished them at all, for it seems to be throughout implied that none died except through their own fault. It is often supposed that this plague carried off the last survivors of the generation condemned at Kadesh (see ver. 64); but this is opposed to the statement in Deut. ii. 14, 15, and is essentially improbable. The victims of the plague would surely be those who had joined themselves to Baal-Peor; and these again would surely be the younger, not the older, men in Israel. It is part of the moral of the story that these offenders deprived themselves, not merely of a few remaining days, but of many years of happy rest which might have been theirs.

Ver. 2.—Take the sum of all the congregation. This was certainly not commanded with a view to the war against Midian, which was of no military importance, and was actually prosecuted with no more than 12,000 men (ch. xxxi. 5). A general command to "vex the Midianites" had indeed been given (ch. xxv. 17) on the principle of just retribution (cf. 2 Thess. i. 6), but no attempt seems to have been made to act upon it until a more specific order was issued (ch. xxxi. 2). In any case the present mustering has to do with something far more important, viz., with the approaching settlement of the people in its own territory. This is clear from the instructions given in vers. 52—56, and from the distribution of the tribes into families. From twenty years. See on ch. i. 3.

Ver. 3.—Spake with them, *i. e.* no doubt with the responsible chiefs, who must have assisted in this census, as in the previous one (ch. i. 4), although the fact is not mentioned.

Ver. 4.—Take the sum of the people. These words are not in the text, but are borrowed from ver. 2. Nothing is set down in the original but the brief instruction given to the census-takers—"from twenty years old and upward, as on the former occasion." And the children of Israel which went forth out of the land of Egypt. This is the punctuation of the Targums and most of the versions. The Septuagint, however, detaches these words from the previous sentence and makes them a general heading for the catalogue which follows. It may be objected to this that the people now numbered did not come out of Egypt, a full half having been born in the wilderness, but see on ch. xxiii. 22; xxiv. 8.

Ver. 5.—The children of Reuben. The four names here registered as distinguishing families within the tribe of Reuben agree with the lists given in Gen. xlvi. 9; Exod. vi. 14; 1 Chron. v. 3.

Ver. 7.—These . . the families of the Reubenites. The mustering according to families (מִשְׁפָּחֹת — Septuagint, δῆμοι) was the distinguishing feature of this census, because it was preparatory to a territorial settlement in Canaan, in which the unity of the family should be preserved as well as the unity of the tribe.

Ver. 8.—And the sons of Pallu. This particular genealogy is added because of the special interest which attached to the fate of certain members of the family. The plural "sons" is to be explained here not from the fact (which has nothing to do with it) that several grandsons are afterwards mentioned, but from the fact that וּבְנֵי ("and the sons") was the conventional heading of a family list, and was written down by the transcriber before he noticed that only one name followed.

Ver. 10.—Swallowed them up together with Korah. יִתְּבְלַע אֹתָם וְאֶת־קֹרַח. Septuagint, κατέπιεν αὐτοὺς καὶ Κορέ. This distinct statement, which is not modified in the Targums, seems decisive as to the fate of Korah. If indeed it were quite certain from the detailed narrative in ch. xvi. that Korah perished with his own company, and not with the Reubenites, then it might be deemed necessary to force this statement into accordance with that certainty ; but it is nowhere stated, or even clearly implied, that he perished by fire, and therefore there is no excuse for doing violence to the obvious meaning of this verse. Korah, Dathan, and Abiram were swallowed up, we are told, at the same time that Korah's company were consumed by fire ; that is a clear statement, and cannot be set aside by any supposed necessity for avenging the sacrilegious ambition of Korah by the element of fire. **And they became a sign.** The Hebrew נס properly means a banner or ensign, and is unusual in this sense. It exactly corresponds, however, to the Greek σήμειον, and has no doubt the same secondary signification — a something made conspicuous in order to attract attention and enforce a warning (cf. ch. xvi. 30, 38).

Ver. 11.—**The children of Korah died not.** The confused nature of the narrative in ch. xvi. is well exemplified by this statement ; we should certainly have supposed from ch. xvi. 32 that Korah's sons had perished with him, if we were not here told to the contrary. The sons of Korah are frequently mentioned among the Levites, and Samuel himself would seem to have been of them (see on 1 Chron. vi. 22, 28, 33—38, and titles to Ps. xlii., lxxxviii., &c.) ; it is, however, slightly doubtful whether the Kohathite Korah of 1 Chron. vi. 22, the ancestor of Samuel, is the same as the Izharite Korah, the ancestor of Heman, in 1 Chron. vi. 38.

Ver. 12.—**The sons of Simeon.** As in Gen. xlvi. 10 ; Exod. vi. 15, with the omission of Ohad, who may not have founded any family. In such cases it is no doubt possible that there were children, but that for some reason they failed to hold together, and became attached to other families. In 1 Chron. iv. 24 the sons of Simeon appear as Nemuel, Jamin, Jarib, Zerah, and Shaul. In Genesis and Exodus the first appears as Jemuel. These minute variations are only important as showing that Divine inspiration did not preserve the sacred records from errors of transcription.

Ver. 15.—**The children of Gad.** Cf. Gen. xlvi. 16, the only other enumeration of the sons of Gad.

Ver. 20.—**The sons of Judah after their families.** The Beni-Judah, or "men of Judah," according to their sub-tribal divisions, are clearly distinguished from the "sons of Judah" as individuals, two of whom are mentioned in the previous verse. Of the families of Judah, three were named after sons, two after grandsons. As the Pharzites remained a distinct family apart from the Hamulites and Hezronites, it may be sup-

posed that Pharez had other sons not mentioned here, or in Gen. xlvi. 12, or in 1 Chron. ii. 3, 4, 5.

Ver. 23.—**The sons of Issachar.** As in Gen. xlvi. 13 ; 1 Chron. vii. 1, except that in Genesis we have Job instead of Jashub ; the two names, however, appear to have the same meaning.

Ver. 26.—**The sons of Zebulun.** As in Gen. xlvi. 14.

Ver. 29.—**The sons of Manasseh.** There is considerable difficulty about the families of this tribe, because they are not recorded in Genesis, while the details preserved in 1 Chron. vii. 14 — 17 are so obscure and fragmentary as to be extremely perplexing. According to the present enumeration there were eight families in Manasseh, one named after his son Machir, one after his grandson Gilead, and the rest after his great-grandsons. The list given in Josh. xvii. 1, 2 agrees with this, except that the Machirites and the Gileadites are apparently identified. It appears from the genealogy in 1 Chron. vii. that the mother of Machir was a stranger from Aram, the country of Laban. This may perhaps account for the fact that Machir's son received the name of Gilead, for Gilead was the border land between Aram and Canaan ; it more probably explains the subsequent allotment of territory in that direction to the Machirites (ch. xxxii. 40). Gilead appears again as a proper name in Judges xi. 2.

Ver. 33.—**Zelophehad . . had no sons, but daughters.** This is mentioned here because the case was to come prominently before the lawgiver and the nation (cf. ch. xxvii. 1 ; xxxvi. 1 ; 1 Chron. vii. 15).

Ver. 35.—**The sons of Ephraim.** These formed but four families, three named after sons, one after a grandson. In 1 Chron. vii. 21 two other sons of Ephraim are mentioned who were killed in their father's lifetime, and a third, Beriah, who was the ancestor of Joshua. He does not seem to have founded a separate family, possibly because he was so very much younger than his brothers.

Ver. 38.—**The sons of Benjamin.** These formed seven families, five named after sons, two after grandsons. The list in Gen. xlvi. 21 contains three names here omitted, and the rest are much changed in form. There is still more divergence between these and the longer genealogies found in 1 Chron. vii. 6—12 ; viii. 1—5 sq. It is possible that the family of Becher (Genesis), who had nine sons (1 Chron.), went under another name, because there was a family of Becherites in Ephraim (ver. 35) ; and similarly the family of the Ephraimite Beriah (1 Chron.) may have ceded its name in favour of the Asherite family of Beriites (ver. 44). But it must be acknowledged that the various genealogies of Benjamin cannot be reconciled as they stand.

Ver. 42.—**The sons of Dan.** These all formed but one family, named after Shuham (elsewhere Hushim), the only son of Dan that is mentioned. It is possible that Dan had other children, whose descendants were incorporated with the Shuhamites.

Ver. 44.—**The children of Asher.** Of these three families were named after sons, two after grandsons. In Gen. xlvi. 17; 1 Chron. vii. 30, 31 a sixth name occurs,

Ishuah, or Isuah. It is possible that its similarity to the following name of Isui or Ishui led to its accidental omission; but if the family continued to exist in Israel, such an omission could scarcely be overlooked.

Ver. 48.—**The sons of Naphtali.** As in Gen. xlvi. 24; 1 Chron. vii. 13.

Ver. 51.—**These were the numbered of the children of Israel.** The results of this census as compared with the former may be tabulated thus:—

Tribe.	No. of families.	First Census.	Second Census.	Decrease.	Increase.
Reuben.	4	46,500	43,730	6 p. c.	
Simeon.	5	59,300	22,200	63 ,,	
Gad.	7	45,650	40,500	11 ,,	
Judah.	5	74,600	76,500	.. ..	2½ p. c.
Issachar.	4	54,400	64,300	.. ..	18 ,,
Zebulun.	3	57,400	60,500	.. ..	5½ ,,
Ephraim.	4	40,500	32,500	20 ,,	
Manasseh.	8	32,200	52,700	.. ..	63 ,,
Benjamin.	7	35,400	45,600	.. ..	29 ,,
Dan.	1	62,700	64,400	.. ..	2½ ,,
Asher.	5	41,500	53,400	.. ..	28 ,,
Naphtali.	4	53,400	45,400	15 ,,	
		603,550	601,730		

It is evident that the numbers were taken by centuries, as before, although an odd thirty appears now in the return for Reuben, as an odd fifty appeared then in the return for Gad. It has been proposed to explain this on the ground of their both being pastoral tribes; but if the members of these tribes were more scattered than the rest, it would be just in their case that we should expect to find round numbers. The one fact which these figures establish in a startling way is, that while the nation as a whole remained nearly stationary in point of numbers, the various tribes show a most unexpected variation. Manasseh, e. g., has increased his population 63 per cent. in spite of the fact that there is not one man left of sixty years of age, while Simeon has decreased in the same proportion. There is indeed little difficulty in accounting for diminishing numbers amidst so many hardships, and after so many plagues. The fact that Zimri belonged to the tribe of Simeon, and that this tribe was omitted soon after from the blessing of Moses (Deut. xxxiii.), may easily lead to the conclusion that Simeon was more than any other tribe involved in the sin of Baal-Peor and the punishment which followed. But when we compare, e. g., the twin tribes of Ephraim and Manasseh, concerning whom nothing distinctive is either stated or hinted, whether bad or good; and when we find that the one has decreased 20 per cent. and the other increased 63 per cent. during the same interval, and under the same general circum-

stances, we cannot even guess at the causes which must have been at work to produce so striking a difference. It is evident that each tribe had its own history apart from the general history of the nation—a history which had the most important results for its own members, but of which we know almost nothing. It is observable, however, that all the tribes under the leadership of Judah increased, whilst all those in the camp of Reuben decreased.

Ver. 53.—**According to the number of the names.** The intention clearly was that the extent of the territory assigned to each tribe, and called by its name (ver. 55, b.), should be regulated according to its numbers at the discretion of the rulers.

Ver. 55.—**Notwithstanding the land shall be divided by lot.** This can only be reconciled with the preceding order by assuming that the lot was to determine the situation of the territory, the actual boundaries being left to the discretion of the rulers. Recourse was had as far as possible to the lot in order to refer the matter directly to God, of whose will and gift they held the land (cf. Prov. xvi. 33; Acts i. 26). The lot would also remove any suspicion that the more numerous tribes, such as Judah or Dan, were unfairly favoured (ver. 56).

Ver. 58.—**These are the families of the Levites.** The three Levitical sub-tribes have been named in the preceding verse, and the present enumeration of families is an independent one. The Libnites were Gershonites (ch. iii. 21), the Hebronites and Korathites (or Korahites) were Kohathites (ch. iii. 19 ; xvi. 1), the Mahlites and Mushites were Merarites (ch. iii. 33). Two other families, the Shimites (ch. iii. 21) and the Uzzielites (ch. iii. 27 ; 1 Chron. xxvi. 23, and cf. Exod. vi. 22 ; 1 Chron. xxiv. 24, 25), are omitted here, perhaps because the list is imperfect (see, however, the note on ver. 62).

Ver. 59.—**Jochebed, the daughter of Levi, whom her mother bare to Levi in Egypt.** Rather, "whom she (אֹתָהּ) bare." The missing subject is usually supplied, as in the A. V., and there certainly seems no more difficulty in doing so here than in 1 Kings i. 6. Some critics take " Atha " as a proper name—" whom Atha bare ; " others render "who was born ; " this, however, like the Septuagint, ἣ ἔτεκε τούτους τῷ Λευί, requires a change of reading. Perhaps the text is imperfect. The statement here made, whatever difficulties it creates, is in entire agreement with Exod. vi. 20 ; 1 Chron. xxiii. 6, 12, 13, and other passages. If two Amrams, the later of whom lived some 200 years after the earlier, have been confused (as we seem driven to believe), the confusion is consist-

ently maintained through all the extant records (see the note on ch. iii. 28).

Ver. 62.—**Those that were numbered of them.** We have here again a round number (23,000), showing an increase of 1000 since the former census. It is evident that the males of Levi were not counted by anything less than hundreds, and probable that they were counted by thousands (see note on ch. iii. 29). The smallness of the increase in a tribe which was excepted from the general doom at Kadesh, and which in other ways was so favourably situated, seems to point to some considerable losses. It is possible that portions of the tribe suffered severely for their share in the rebellion of Korah ; if so, the families of the Shimites and of the Uzzielites may have been so much reduced as to be merged in the remaining families.

Ver. 65.—**There was not left a man of them.** This had been known to be practically the case before they left the wilderness, properly so called (Deut. ii. 14, 15), but it was now ascertained for certain. For the necessary exceptions to the statement see note on ch. xiv. 24.

HOMILETICS.

Vers. 1—65.—*The final numbering of the elect.* Both the numberings of the children of Israel are to be spiritually interpreted of that knowledge which God has of his elect, and of their inscription in the registers of life. The people of God are to him as his flock is to the shepherd ; he knows his sheep, and ca'leth his own sheep by name, and leadeth them out to the journey, or leadeth them in to rest. Again, the people of God are to him as his army is to the captain ; they are drawn up (τεταγμένοι, Acts xiii. 48) and set in array unto eternal life, every one in his proper place, so that each may act most to his own advantage, and to the advantage of all. "The Lord knoweth them that are his" (2 Tim. ii. 19), according to the saying, "I know thee by name " (Exod. xxxiii. 17 ; cf. Isa. xliii. 1), and, " I will not blot out his name out of the book of life " (Rev. iii. 5 ; cf. Philip. iv. 3). But as the numberings of Israel were two, and a great distinction between them, so God's knowledge of his elect has a double character, which is in some important respects strongly contrasted. The first numbering (see the homiletic notes on ch. i.) was for that march which was to prove a fiery trial to all, and did in fact involve the destruction of most, albeit entirely through their own default ; the second numbering was for the actual entry into and possession of their long-promised rest. In like manner there is a twofold election on the part of God, according to which his people are counted his indeed, and are personally known to him. There is the election unto grace, whereby we have been called out of darkness, and made the soldiers of the cross, and assigned our place in the " one body " (Col. iii. 15), to share in its privileges and trials, its strifes and consolations ; there is also the election unto glory, whereby, when the probation is past and the temptation overcome, we are numbered unto eternal life and inheritance among the saints. On this distinction hangs all the teaching of this chapter. Consider, therefore, with respect to *this mustering as a whole*—

I. THAT THERE SHOULD HAVE BEEN BUT ONE CENSUS TAKEN, SINCE ALL WHO WERE NUMBERED AT SINAI WERE NUMBERED FOR VICTORY AND FOR SPEEDY INHERITANCE IN CANAAN. That a second muster was needful at all was entirely due to the rebellion at Kadesh, and the subsequent rejection of that generation. Even so there is in the will of God concerning us, as declared at large in the gospel, but one election and one enrolling in the ranks of salvation. All who are called to grace are designed for glory ; none are enlisted under the cross but may, and should, attain the crown ; the Christian name and calling is not a mockery in any case. That there is a double election, that names may be blotted out of the book of life, that it is not possible to maintain a consistent scheme of salvation on the ground of the Divine predestination alone, is all due, and only due, to the sin and cowardice of men, which does not indeed cancel the election or impair the glory of God's Church, but does alter the personal composition of that Church.

II. THAT AS A FACT NOT ONE (ORDINARY) NAME REMAINED IN THE SECOND MUSTER WHICH BELONGED TO THE FIRST. Even so there is not in any case an assurance that those who are called to grace will persevere unto glory. Not all indeed *will*, but all *may*, be lost through their own rebellion. The two lists, of the baptised and of the finally saved, *ought* (in a true sense) to be coincident ; as a fact they will no doubt be startlingly dissimilar.

III. THAT THOSE FORMERLY ENROLLED DISAPPEARED ONE BY ONE, ACCORDING TO THE DECLARATION OF GOD, BECAUSE THEY HAD REFUSED AT KADESH TO ENTER INTO REST. Even so if men fall out of the number of such as are being saved (οἱ σωζόμενοι, Acts ii. 47), it is simply because they have refused to enter upon their lot, and have counted themselves unworthy of, or unequal to, the attainment of eternal life.

IV. THAT, NEVERTHELESS, SOME NAMES WERE FOUND IN BOTH LISTS ; as those of Caleb, Joshua, Eleazar, and presumably many of the Levites. Even so it is abundantly evident, not only from the testimony of Scripture, but from the example of our brethren, that nothing in our probation need be fatal to our hopes, if only we be true to God and to ourselves. And note that here is one of the great contrasts between that dispensation and ours, that whereas only two individuals out of the twelve tribes obtained inheritance at the last, there will be of us " a great multitude whom no man can number." Nevertheless, we have the same warning (cf. Luke xiii. 23, 24).

V. THAT IN EACH CASE THE MUSTERING WAS LIMITED TO THE SAME CLASS OF MEN, VIZ., SUCH AS WERE FIT TO BEAR ARMS. Even so there is no difference between election to grace and to glory as far as the position and character of the individual is concerned. The two states are so far one, even when looked at from the side of man, that whoso is called to the one needs nothing more to be ready for the other ; he only needs to remain what he is, a soldier of Christ, in order to be crowned (cf. Rev. ii. 7, &c.).

VI. THAT THE TOTAL NUMBER OF ALL ISRAEL REMAINED PRACTICALLY STATIONARY ; so that as many entered after all as had refused at Kadesh. Even so God will have his kingdom filled (Luke xiv. 21—23), and his calling is without repentance (Rom. xi. 29) ; so that if some fall short of salvation, others will be found to take their place. And note that the long waiting of Israel in the wilderness was due to the necessity of an evil generation dying out, and another growing up to equal it in numbers. It may be that the long and unexpected tarrying of Christ is due to a like necessity ; that the number of the elect is slowly filled up amidst the defection and unworthiness of so many.

VII. THAT THE VARIOUS TRIBES OF ISRAEL SHOWED A REMARKABLE VARIATION ; some showing a great increase, others a decrease quite as great. Even so while the Church of Christ as a whole maintains, it may be, its position relative to the rest of the world, how great has been the variation in size and importance of various branches of the Church ! Think, *e. g.*, what the Greek-speaking Churches were at one time, and how they are now reduced ; and, on the other hand, to what relative importance have the English-speaking Churches grown from small beginnings.

VIII. THAT IN ONE CASE WE CAN TRACE THE CAUSE OF DECLINE WITH SOME ASSURANCE. Simeon, the tribe of Zimri, omitted in the blessing of Moses, must have joined himself more especially to Baal-Peor. Even so the one thing which we can unhesitatingly assign as the fruitful cause of loss of spiritual life and decay of Churches is immorality. Doubtless purity of doctrine is most potent for good, but impurity of life is still more potent for evil. That Church will train fewest souls for heaven which gives most place to those fleshly lusts which war against the soul. And note that this census was taken " after the plague " which followed on the harlotry of Baal-Peor ; for the thousands who perished then were not of them that were doomed at Kadesh (see Deut. ii. 14), but of those who would have inherited Canaan in a few months. So it is "after the plague" of fleshly sin and of its ruinous effects that the servants of God are numbered for eternal life. "The pure in heart shall see God" (cf. Gal. v. 19—21 ; Ephes. v. 5 ; Rev. xxii. 15).

IX. THAT IN ANOTHER CASE WE CAN DISCERN A POSSIBLE REASON FOR DECAY, IN THAT ALL THE TRIBES UNDER THE LEADERSHIP OF REUBEN FELL OFF IN NUMBERS (Reuben, Simeon, Gad). This may point to the unhappy effects of bad example, and the contagious nature of a turbulent and self-willed spirit in religious matters.

X. THAT, ON THE CONTRARY, ALL THE CAMPS WHICH WERE UNDER THE STANDARD OF JUDAH INCREASED (Judah, Issachar, Zebulun). For to Judah, as having the birth-right, appertained now the promise, "In thee and in thy seed shall all nations be blessed." Thus for the sake of Jesus, who sprang from the tribe of Judah, the companions of Judah were blessed long ago ; and this no doubt because his character and example were more or less in accordance with the dignity of his position.

XI. THAT AFTER ALL THE CAUSES OF INCREASE OR DECLINE ARE FOR THE MOST PART UNKNOWN, AND LIE BENEATH THE SURFACE OF THE SACRED RECORD. How little do we know of the inner history of Ephraim and Manasseh, which has left no trace in the narrative, and yet had such important effects in their comparative prosperity! Even so how little do we know of the real life of Churches ; how little can we estimate those forces which determine their spiritual growth or decadence !

XII. THAT NOTHING BROUGHT TO LIGHT THE GREAT DIFFERENCES BETWEEN THE TRIBES EXCEPT THE MUSTERING ON THE VERGE OF JORDAN. Even so nothing can really test the comparative excellence, the success or failure, of a Church, except the verdict of "that day," and the numbers then found worthy to stand before the Son of man.

Consider also, with respect to *the Levites*—
THAT THEY HAD INCREASED, BUT NOT NEARLY SO MUCH AS THEY SHOULD HAVE DONE, CONSIDERING THEIR IMMUNITIES AND PRIVILEGES. Four tribes, although under the condemnation of Kadesh, had prospered more than they. Even so it is certain that no situation of vantage, ecclesiastical or religious, delivers us from spiritual loss, or really makes religious progress easier. Many who have fewer advantages and greater difficulties, many even who have at some time fallen under greater condemnation, will nevertheless outstrip us in the heavenly race.

Consider again, with respect to *the inheritance of each tribe in Canaan*—
I. THAT ITS SITUATION WAS TO BE DECIDED BY LOT, *i. e.* BY DIVINE DISPOSITION, APART FROM HUMAN CHOICE OR FAVOUR. Even so our "place in heaven" will be allotted to us by God himself, being predestinated for us according to his infinite wisdom, without any respect of persons.

II. THAT ITS BOUNDARIES WERE TO BE DETERMINED BY ESTIMATION OF THE SIZE AND NEEDS OF EACH. Even so our "place in heaven" will be our own, not only as given to us of God's free grace, but as being exactly suited for us, and precisely adapted to our measure of spiritual growth.

Consider again, with respect to *the sins of Korah*—
THAT THEY DID NOT PERISH WITH THEIR FATHER (NOT BEING OF HIS "COMPANY"), BUT LIVED TO FOUND AN HONOURABLE AND USEFUL FAMILY IN ISRAEL. Even so God does not visit the sins of the fathers upon the children, unless the children also "hate him." It is a thing pleasing to God when the children retrieve the forfeited honour of their father's name by their good works. How often does the Church of God find its ornaments and supports amongst the children of its greatest enemies !

HOMILIES BY VARIOUS AUTHORS.

Vers. 52—56.—*The lot is to decide where every tribe shall receive its inheritance.*
Seventy years ago a party of emigrants from the Scottish border found themselves at the entrance of the valley in South Africa which had been assigned for their settlement. The patriarch of the party, gazing wistfully on the goal of their long wanderings, gave vent to the feeling of his heart in the exclamation, And this at length is the lot of our inheritance ! A sure instinct taught him to see, in the pro-

vidential ordering of the momentous turning-point in life which he and his companions had now reached, the same thoughtful and wise Hand which appointed to the tribes under Joshua their inheritance in the promised land ; and the language of the Old Testament history rose naturally to his lips.

I. To do justice to this aspect of Divine providence, it is of consequence to consider well WHAT AN IMPORTANT BUSINESS IS THE ORDERING OF THE LOCALITY IN WHICH MEN ARE TO PASS THEIR DAYS. The complexion of a nation's life and the tenor of its history are exceedingly affected by the sort of locality where it has its seat. A nation whose lot is fixed in the impenetrable depths of Africa, how different its history must necessarily be from that of a nation which has received for inheritance a sea-girt land, like Greece or Italy, Great Britain or Scandinavia ! The one is sequestered from all quickening intercourse, and is likely to sleep on in a semi-torpid state ; the other lies open to the influence of every tide of foreign thought and sentiment. Now it was precisely this question of *locality* which was determined for the tribes by lot. It is a mistake to suppose that the lot determined everything. The division of the country was to proceed on the principle that the extent of territory bestowed on the respective tribes was to be proportioned to the number of names in each (vers. 53, 54). A glance at the map will show how carefully this was attended to. The number of acres which fell to the lot of " little Benjamin " was much smaller than the number embraced in the inheritance of " the mighty tribe of Ephraim." The business of thus apportioning to every tribe a domain corresponding to the number of its families was devolved on a Commission of Twelve, under the oversight of Eleazar and Joshua (ch. xxxiv. 16—29). But before these commissioners could make the apportionment, it had first to be determined *whereabouts* each tribe was to be planted ; and this was done by lot. The Lord reserved to himself the business of determining the bounds of his people's habitation. And, I repeat, this was a momentous determination. If Judah, instead of occupying the inland hills and valleys of the south, had received for its inheritance the lot of Simeon, on the coast of the Mediterranean, and in the way of the Gentiles, how different the course of its history would have been !

II. CONSIDER THE PROVIDENCE OF GOD IN THIS MATTER OF ORDERING THE BOUNDS OF MEN'S HABITATIONS. It is not the tribes of Israel only about whose bounds Divine providence is exercised. Read Deut. xxxii. 8 and Acts xvii. 26. But although God " from the place of his habitation looketh upon all the inhabitants of the earth," it is equally evident from the Scripture that his providence occupies itself very specially about the affairs of his chosen people, and particularly about the ordering of their lot. 1. *How true this is* might be shown by many clear testimonies of Holy Scripture. At present it may be sufficient to remind you of the testimony borne by daily experience. When you left school you had in your mind many projects and resolves about the future—where you would settle, and what you would do. Have these stood? Have they not rather, in nine cases out of ten, been quite overruled ? You proposed, but God disposed. Your portion has fallen to you by lot. 2 This being so, *it is surely your duty to consider God's hand and providence in the matter.* " The lot is cast into the lap ; but the whole disposing thereof is of the Lord " (Prov. xvi. 33). Here again experience says Amen to God's word. The man must have been blind indeed who has never perceived the hand of a special providence prospering or frustrating his purposes, and ordering his lot far better than he could himself have ordered it. 3. Due consideration of God's hand will move the soul to *trust his providence.* Abraham, being told of a country which he should afterwards receive for inheritance, went out trustfully, although he knew not whither he went. This we also are to do ; it is the proper fruit and demonstration of our faith. And as we are to go forward in faith ourselves, so we are in faith to send forth into the world those most dear to us. We need not doubt that in answer to the prayer of faith the Lord will appoint to them a suitable lot, and give them cause to sing, " The lines are fallen unto me in pleasant places ; yea, I have a goodly heritage " (Ps. xvi. 6).—B.

Vers. 1—62.—*The second census.* I. THE PURPOSE OF IT. 1. *The number of those able to go to war in Israel had still to be ascertained.* Though the people are now reposing in unaccustomed and grateful quietude, with the promised Canaan just over against them, it is being impressed upon them in many ways that they must win it by conquest. The children, while inheriting the promises given to their fathers, inherit at the same time the services which the fathers had been found incompetent and unworthy to render. We may gather from this repeated census that God would have his people in every generation to count up their strength for conflict. It is only too easy to depreciate and forget our spiritual resources, and think them less than they are. Even a man like Elijah professed himself left alone, when the Lord knew there were still in Israel seven thousand who had not bowed to Baal. Those going forward into life must be made ready, so far as the advice and arrangements of others can make them ready, both for the certain conflict peculiar to each person, and for a part in the great battle against darkness and wrong which goes on through every age, under the leadership of Christ himself. 2. *Possession of the land had to be prepared for* (vers. 52—56). The conflict will be a great, an arduous, and a taxing one, but it will assuredly end in victory. God's command to prepare for war brings as its logical and cheering sequence the command to prepare for possession. God is able to make regulations for the future, which, if men were spontaneously to make them for themselves, would savour of braggadocio (ch. xv. 2).

II. THE EXACT TIME AT WHICH IT WAS MADE. *It was after the plague.* We may presume that Israel had been to some extent purified by this visitation, although the plague was doubtless no respecter of persons, but involved innocent and guilty in one common temporal suffering, according to the fixed law of our fallen nature that the sins of the fathers are visited on the children. The dreadful result which the infecting idolatries of Moab had brought upon Israel was indeed a very impressive intimation that the full strength of the people was required. Those numbered in the army by reason of fit age were to see to it, and examine their hearts, and become as fit as possible in all other respects.

III. THE METHOD. *Still the same as before, by tribes.* There had been many changes, losses, and sad disturbances during this time of wandering and severity, but each tribe had kept itself distinct. They were still ranged in the same order round the tabernacle, and regarding it from the same point of view. So if we take a period, say of forty years, in the course of Christ's Church, we shall find the sects at the beginning of the period still existent at the end of it. The men who looked at truth from a certain point of view at the beginning have their spiritual successors who look at truth from the same point of view. The differences, the marked, emphasised, and pertinacious differences, found amongst believers are not so much between truth and error as between different aspects of the same external object.

IV. THE RESULT. It must have been anxiously waited for, not only to see the grand total, but the relative position of each tribe. The result shows somewhat fewer in number, but, as we have suggested, they were possibly purer in quality. Some tribes have increased, others decreased. In Simeon there is a most extraordinary falling away, but still it was quite within truth to say that *for practical purposes* the number had not diminished. Yes; but if Israel had not been passing through a temporary curse there ought to have been, and probably would have been, a marked and exhilarating increase. But instead of increase there is a slight decrease. Things had not been going lately as they did in Egypt, when " the children of Israel were fruitful, and increased abundantly, and multiplied, and waxed exceeding mighty; and the land was filled with them " (Exod. i. 7). Certainly if one goes by the actual state of the people, there is but little room for Balaam's cheering words concerning the dust of Jacob and the fourth part of Israel (ch. xxiii. 10). In the light of this second census the whole narrative is seen to harmonise in a most subtle way. If Israel were under a curse these forty years, if there were a real suspending of God's favour and of the previous communications of his energy, it is just what might be expected that at the end of the period the people would be found no further forward than at the beginning—600,000 when they left Sinai, 600,000 still when they reach Jordan.—Y.

Vers. 64, 65.—*A generation gone.* Certain things strike us in examining this second census and comparing it with the former one at Sinai: *e. g.* the difference as to numbers; the fluctuations of the tribes, some increasing, others decreasing; in particular, the extraordinary decrease in Simeon arrests attention. But all these are passed over as not needing notice. There is one thing, however, to which attention is specially called, and indeed it must have been kept in view all the census through, namely, that not one of those numbered in the previous census was now alive. Those counted now had not been counted before.

I. ATTENTION IS CALLED TO A FULFILLED PREDICTION. It deserves special attention as a very remarkable, exact, and early fulfilment of prediction. Most of God's predictions for Israel worked on to their fulfilment slowly and imperceptibly through many generations; some in the highest sense of them are still incomplete; but here was a prediction concerning the present, moving to its fulfilment under the very eyes of many whom in their turn it would also include. Surely it must often have been talked of in the tents of Israel. And here was another purpose that the census served —to show clearly and impressively that the prediction had been fulfilled. The fulfilment had its dark side and its bright one. It was an impressive proof that what penalties God attaches to sin he can accomplish to their full extent. All had perished save Caleb and Joshua. Things had happened *exactly as God said they would*, the people themselves being witnesses. "If any one numbered in the previous census is still alive, save Caleb and Joshua, let him step forward," Moses and Eleazar might have said. But they were all silent in the mystery of a peculiar death. Rightly looked at, it was very comforting and inspiring for Israel to go into Canaan with such a wonderful proof of God's power in their minds. He who had so manifestly fulfilled such a peculiar prediction might be confidently expected to keep his word in all others.

II. THE COMPLETENESS OF THE DIVINE CONTROL OVER THE TERM OF HUMAN LIFE. What God did in the particular instance of this generation he can do in any and every generation, with any and every one of the children of men. We talk very grandly sometimes of the value of a sound constitution, the prudence of attending to the laws of health, and taking such means as may preserve life to a ripe old age. But while these considerations are indeed not to be neglected, God's will also must be taken into account, as at least *a possible* regulating force in the term of every human life. He may have some weighty reason of his own for shortening or lengthening, which will nullify alike the prudence of some and the recklessness of others. It is not competent for us to say that he does actually interfere in every instance, as he so plainly did with the men of this doomed generation; it is enough for us to feel that he has power to do it. We have here but one out of many evidences to be found in the Scriptures that God has death completely under restraint. He can keep us back from its grasp as long as may seem good to him. He can also allow us to fall into its grasp, if thereby his own purposes will be better served. They are much more important than the devices and desires which arise out of our selfish, ignorant, and unexperienced hearts.

III. THE SPECIAL INTERVENTION IN THIS INSTANCE SUGGESTS THAT, AS A GENERAL RULE, NATURE IS LEFT TO ITS OWN COURSE. Every one entering this world is left to the play of what, for want of a better term, may be called the forces of nature. So much of natural vitality and energy, so much power of assimilation and growth, so much, sometimes good and sometimes bad, by way of inheritance from parents, and, over and above what may be peculiar, the taint of that depravity which is the common calamity of the children of men—these are the elements with which we have to do our best. And might we not hope, if only the obstacles were taken away which arise from ignorance, error, prejudice, sensuality, and slavery to base appetites of every sort, that the term of human life would be extended far beyond what it is in the great majority of instances? Should it not be reckoned the normal state of things, the state of things according to God's own wish, for those who come into the world as infants to go out of it as old men? The reason why so many do not should be made a matter of urgent, light-seeking, personal inquiry. It is a very misleading thing to speak, and without any real authority to do so, of God calling people away; particularly infants and children, who furnish such a large and melancholy proportion of the world's mortality. We foreclose many questions of the greatest moment by a traditional, thought-benumbing fatalism, a seemingly pious, yet really impious, profession of submission to the will of God. The will of God would sooner be complied with in this ignorant, purblind world if Christians, who pray that God's will may be done on earth as in heaven, would only set themselves to discover what the will of God really is. Surely it is a strange and horrible thing that, without some plain reason such as we find in 2 Sam. xii. 14, many infants should breathe their little lives so quickly away ; and it is all the more horrible when they thus die in spite of the solicitude and patient care of a loving mother. Where love abounds, wisdom may yet be lacking. A world wiser to consider the laws of nature and self-denyingly to obey them would be a less anguished and sorrowing world. Mothers would not so often be sharing Rachel's bitter lot, weeping for her children and refusing to be comforted.

IV. THE EXTENSION OF GOD'S WRATH OVER THIS LONG PERIOD ESPECIALLY MARKS IT OUT AS WRATH AGAINST UNRIGHTEOUSNESS (Rom. i. 18). God is not a man, that he should be carried away in sudden bursts of passion, and need the exhortation, "Let not the sun go down upon your wrath." For forty years he went patiently through the vineyard, cutting down the cumberers of the ground. Sudden as were the flamings out of the Divine wrath on Israel, it was because Israel was as dry, susceptible fuel to the flame. Wherever there is unrighteousness of men there must be wrath of God. In the deliberate, steady fulfilling of God's wrath on the doomed generation we see a most sublime contrast with the caprice, uncertainty, and partiality of human passion.

V. THERE IS A VERY EMPHATIC ASSURANCE OF GOD'S INTEREST IN ISRAEL INDIVIDUALLY. Each man who thus died had the eye of the Lord on him as an individual. And though he suffered temporal death as a necessary consequence of belonging to the doomed generation, yet the very same watchful care of God which acted with severity in one way was equally available to act with mercy in another. The doom which fell upon the Israelite as Israelite was quite compatible with mercy to the Israelite as a man. Let us in the midst of our need, in the midst of our difficulties in finding a way to God, lay hold of every assurance we can get, and especially in the Scriptures, as to the reality of God's dealings with individuals. There is special record in the Scriptures of his dealings with some, but of many there is of necessity no such record. Here there is clear evidence of God's dealings, individually, with more than 600,000 men in forty years. That period was given for every one of them to pass from the earth, so that at the end of it there was not a survivor to enter the promised land, save the two men who had been singled out for preservation. *And God is dealing with every individual now*, and by his goodness would lead him to repentance. What is wanted in return is that every individual thus appealed to, when he meets the angel of repentance in the way, should have dealings with God such as may end in the full reception of eternal life and increased glory to the fulness of the Divine Trinity.—Y.

EXPOSITION.

CHAPTER XXVII.

THE DAUGHTERS OF ZELOPHEHAD (vers. 1—11). Ver. 1.—**The daughters of Zelophehad.** The genealogy here given agrees with those in ch. xxvi. 29—33 and in Josh. xvii. 3. These women would appear to have been in the eighth generation from Jacob, which hardly accords with the 470 years required by the narrative ; some links, however, may have been dropped.

Ver. 2.—**By the door of the tabernacle of the congregation,** *i. e.* evidently by the entrance of the sacred enclosure. Here, in the void space, in the midst of the camp, and close to the presence-chamber of God, the princes (*i. e.* the tribe princes who were

engaged upon the census) and the representatives of the congregation assembled for the transaction of business and for the hearing of any matters that were brought before them.

Ver. 3.—**He was not in the company of them that gathered themselves together against the Lord.** He had not been amongst the two hundred and fifty who gathered themselves together in support of Korah's pretensions. It does not appear why they should have thought it necessary to make this statement, unless they felt that the fact of his having died without sons might raise suspicion against him as one who had greatly provoked the wrath of God. **But died in his own sin.** This cannot mean that Zelophehad was one of those who died in the wilderness in consequence of the rebellion at Kadesh (see the next note). Apparently his daughters meant to acknowledge that they had no complaint against the Divine justice because of their father's death, but only against the law because of the unnecessary hardship which it inflicted upon them.

Ver. 4.—**Give unto us . . a possession among the brethren of our father.** The daughters of Zelophehad did not ask for any share of what had been their father's, but they asked that the lands which would have been assigned to their father in the settlement of Canaan might still be assigned to them, so that their father's name might attach to those lands, and be handed down with them. The request assumes that the "brethren" of Zelophehad would receive an inheritance in the promised land, either personally or as represented by their sons; hence it seems clear that Zelophehad was not of the elder generation, which had forfeited all their rights and expectations in Canaan, but of the younger, to whom the inheritance was transferred (ch. xiv. 29—32). This is confirmed by the consideration that these women were not married until some time after this (ch. xxxvi. 11; cf. Josh. xvii. 3, 4), and must, therefore, according to the almost invariable custom, have been quite young at this time. It is reasonable to suppose that the heads of separate families to whom the land was distributed would be at this time men of from forty-five to sixty years of age, comprising the elder half of the generation which grew up in the wilderness. Zelophehad would have been among these, but that he was cut off, perhaps in the plague of serpents, or in the plague of the Arboth Moab, and left only unmarried girls to represent him.

Ver. 5.—**Moses brought their cause before the Lord.** Presumably by going into the tabernacle with this matter upon his mind, and awaiting the revelation of the Divine will (cf. Exod. xviii. 19 ; ch. xii. 8).

Ver. 8.—**If a man die, and have no son.** On this particular case a general rule of much wider incidence was founded. The Mosaic law of succession followed the same lines as the feudal law of Europe, equally disallowing disposition by will, and discouraging, if not disallowing, alienation by grant. Upon the land was to rest the whole social fabric of Israel, and all that was valued and permanent in family life and feeling was to be tied as it were to the landed inheritance. Hence the land was in every case so to pass that the name and fame, the privilege and duty, of the deceased owner might be as far as possible perpetuated. **Unto his daughter.** Not for her maintenance, but in order that her husband might represent her father. In most cases he would take her name, and be counted as one of her father's family. This had no doubt already become customary among the Jews, as among almost all nations. Compare the cases of Sheshan and Jarha (1 Chron. ii. 34, 35), of Jair (ch. xxxii. 41), and subsequently of the Levitical "sons of Barzillai" (Ezra ii. 61). The question, however, would only become of public importance at the time when Israel became a nation of landed proprietors.

Ver. 11.—**A statute of judgment.** מִשְׁפַּט לְחֻקַּת. Septuagint, δικαίωμα κρίσεως. A statute determining a legal right.

HOMILETICS.

Vers. 1—11.—*The certainty of the promised inheritance.* The case of Zelophehad's daughters is no doubt in keeping with that favourable consideration of women, as capable of claiming rights and holding a position of their own, which certainly distinguished the Mosaic legislation, and affected for good the Jewish character. But the one thing which we may spiritually discern here is the security of the heavenly inheritance and the faithfulness with which it is Divinely reserved for them that have received the promise. Zelophehad died, and that through sin, but since he was not of the disinherited, therefore his name did not cease, neither was his portion taken away from among the people of the Lord. Consider, therefore—

I. THAT ZELOPHEHAD, AS ONE OF THE YOUNGER GENERATION, HAD A PROMISE OF AN INHERITANCE IN CANAAN TO BE HIS (*i. e.* HIS FAMILY'S) FOR EVER. Even so we, in that we belong to "this generation" (cf. St. Matt. xxiv. 34), which has received the promise of eternal life, and a kingdom which cannot be moved (Heb. xii. 28), are without question heirs of salvation, and look forward to a portion amongst the faithful.

II. THAT ZELOPHEHAD HIMSELF DIED IN THE WILDERNESS, AND THAT BY REASON OF SOME SIN WE KNOW NOT WHAT. Even so we die without having received the promised glory; in all probability we shall all so die; and death is the wages of sin, and the body is turned to corruption because of sin.

III. THAT THE DEATH OF ZELOPHEHAD SEEMED TO BAR HIS CLAIM TO ANY IN-

HERITANCE AMONGST HIS BRETHREN, SEEING HE HAD NO SON TO TAKE HIS PLACE AND NAME. Even so death seems at first sight, and in the eyes of the unwise, to cut off hope and to separate from the living, and to deprive those that "are not" of the reward to which they looked. And this was thought to be the case even by them that believed in the first days (1 Thess. iv. 13, *sq.*).

IV. THAT BY THE WILL OF GOD, HIS NAME AND INHERITANCE WERE PRESERVED IN ISRAEL BY MEANS OF HIS DAUGHTERS. Even so, neither death nor failure in this world will be permitted to deprive us of that inheritance in a better world which the mercy of God reserves for us, not because we have deserved it, but because he has promised it.

Consider again, with respect to *the daughters of Zelophehad*—

I. THAT THEY RECEIVED THE REWARD OF FAITH, IN THAT THEY DOUBTED NOT THAT THE LORD'S PEOPLE WOULD RECEIVE EVERY MAN HIS PORTION IN THE LAND OF PROMISE; although they were yet on the other side of Jordan. It is in perfect faith of the fulfilment of God's promises that we must so ask as to receive.

II. THAT THEY RECEIVED THE REWARD OF COURAGE, IN THAT THEY BEING WOMEN WITHOUT ANY NATURAL PROTECTOR, BROUGHT THEIR CAUSE OPENLY BEFORE MOSES, AND SO BEFORE GOD. It is with boldness, not confounded by our own weakness, that we are to make our requests known unto God (Eph. iii. 12; Heb. x. 19), assured that no one is unimportant with him, and no cause disregarded by him.

HOMILIES BY VARIOUS AUTHORS.

Vers. 1—11.—*The disabilities of sex.* I. THE POSSIBLE INJUSTICE CONSEQUENT ON A STRICT ADHERENCE TO SOCIAL TRADITIONS. Try to imagine how this appeal of the daughters of Zelophehad arises. Canaan is now very near, the borders of it visible across the flood; and God has just told Moses the great general principles on which it is to be allotted. Thus the minds of the people are naturally filled with the thoughts of the inheritance. They can no longer complain of being in desolate places. There was good land even before they crossed Jordan (ch. xxxii.), and so Canaan was looked forward to with great expectations. In such circumstances, every family would be on the look-out to anticipate and assert its share. The disciples after they had heard Jesus discoursing so frequently and earnestly on the coming kingdom of heaven, fell to in hot rivalry as to who should be greatest in the kingdom. So here we may well suppose that the sons of Hepher were only too ready to reckon the daughters of their brother Zelophehad as outside any right to the land that would fall to Hepher's children. Natural relations are only too easily trampled on in the greed of gain. Disputes over the division of property breed and sustain deadly quarrels among kindred (Luke xii. 13). Very possibly the brothers of Zelophehad told their nieces that they had no claim to inherit, it being the settled custom that inheritances were to go to sons. Let them be satisfied with marriage into some other family. But the daughters felt pride in their father's name. They do not claim great things for him, feeling that such a claim would not accord with the lot of one who belonged to the doomed generation; but at all events they can say that he died in his own sin; he was free from the taint of that great rebellion which left so deep an impression on Israel's mind. Why then should his name perish from among his family, because he had no son? The answer which we are led to infer is very simple; very worldly also, it is true, but all the more conceivable because of that, "We cleave to our customs; we cannot even give way to feelings which are so creditable to daughters." This perhaps openly—then in their own hearts they would add, "They are only women; they can do nothing."

II. A BOLD REVOLT AGAINST THE ARTIFICIAL DISABILITIES OF SEX. We have imagined an actual refusal to let these women share in the possession. But even if it were not actual, they have a shrewd idea of what will happen, and come appealing to Moses, in the most public manner, so that they may have his weighty authority to settle the matter before he goes. They were but women, yet they had all a man's decision and courage—and more than belongs to most men—to break away from all conventional notions rather than tamely submit to injustice. Paul's disapproval of women speaking in the churches was of course very good as pointing out a general rule, but probably he would have allowed, on a prudent occasion for allowing it, that it was a rule not without exceptions. He may have reckoned it well at the time, for reasons drawn from the state of a particular church, to make the injunctions express and decided. *Who were to speak for these women, if not they themselves?* When the down-trodden find no sufficient advocate among spectators, it is time for them to raise their own voices. *Is it not plain that these women were the best judges of their own position?* So in the pressure of modern social life, is it not very inconsistent with the maintenance of liberty and truth, to hinder women from asserting their claims in whatever way they deem best? They may indeed be unfit for many fields of labour which they profess their fitness and anxiety to occupy, but at all events let them discover the unfitness for themselves. Has it not been said beforehand of many achieved and glorious facts that they were impossible of attainment? Modern history abounds with such disgraced predictions. Paul said, " Let every man be fully persuaded in his own mind," which is surely every whit as needful and every whit as serviceable for the woman as the man.

III. THE ACTION OF THESE WOMEN WAS JUSTIFIED BY THE RESULT. God approves their action, as they gain from him the authoritative laying down of a general principle, applied indeed to property, but surely of equal application to all disabilities of sex which arise in other ways than from the impassable limits of nature. God has written for the woman, in her own nature, certain laws she must not transgress, but he never gave man the right to construe these laws, certainly not after the domineering fashion he so frequently adopts. It is undoubtedly true that God made the woman for the man ; human nature finds here its completeness, derives hence the means of its continuance, and that diversity of personality and character which constitute so much of the peculiar riches of humanity. But man is not therefore to settle the woman's sphere with his strong and irresponsible hand. Is it not a thing almost certain that many disabilities of sex have arisen through man being from the first the stronger? In the days when might made right—

> He took advantage of his strength to be
> First in the field.

There is a parallel between much in man's treatment of woman and his treatment of the Sabbath. Christ had to free the Sabbath, in his day, from Pharisees. It had been so fettered up by opinionated, obstinate clingers to the traditions of the fathers, as to have become useless for its original purposes, a burden and a terror more than anything else. He freed it by the great declaration that the Sabbath was made for man, and now we have those who rush to the other extreme, and quote his words for purposes utterly alien from his own. So there are the two extremes in judging the place of woman and the scope of her life and service. Some, blindly wedded to custom, would shut woman up in strict limitations, which though not as degrading as those of a Turkish harem, are quite as unjust and injurious in their own way. Others there are who seem inclined to claim for women more than nature in its utmost kindliness will ever yield. Women, who know their own nature best, can be the only true judges, ever under the guidance of God himself, as to the capabilities of their sex. Paul pleading for oneness in Christ Jesus, says, that in relation to him, as there is neither Jew nor Greek, bond nor free, so there is neither male nor female. The woman is on the same level as the man in the sight of Christ. To Christ she is directly responsible, bound to serve him with the fulness of her powers. Hence to take the highest ground, that of allegiance to Christ, it is unfaithfulness to him to put even the smallest obstacles in the way of women acting as their own hearts tell them they may best serve their Master.

IV. WE SEE A GOD OF EQUITY SHOWING HIS DISREGARD FOR MERE LEGAL RIGHTS. Nowhere is it shown more clearly than in the Scriptures that law is one thing and equity another. How should a world ignorant of the righteousness of God, and full of the selfish and domineering, make laws such as he will sanction and uphold ? " We have law with us," the uncles may have said. Possibly so ; but not the law of him who spoke from Sinai. Any law of men which contradicts the law of love to God, and love to the neighbour, is doomed in the very making of it. And is it not a blessed thing that such laws get broken and ultimately destroyed by the energy of an expanding life which cannot be contained within them? (Matt. ix. 10—13; xii. 1—13; xv. 1—20; xix. 3—9; xxii. 34—40; Rom. xiv. 5; Gal. iii. 28).—Y.

Ver. 3.—*The man who died in his own sin.* I. A PLEA FOR FAVOURABLE CONSIDERATION. The daughters of Zelophehad felt that if he had been numbered among the conspirators with Korah, it would have been very difficult for them to stand forward and make this claim. It is one of the saddest things in a world of sad things that the innocent children of guilty parents are made to inherit the shame of the parental offence. The parental name, instead of being one of the sweetest sounds to fall upon their ears, becomes one of the most hideous and torturing. Not seldom they are looked upon with suspicion, and though it be admitted they cannot help the parents' crime, yet they begin life with a millstone round their necks. The words of these women, *meant only as a plea for themselves,* inflicted at the same time a blow, none the less severe because unconsciously given, on any children of Korah (ch. xxvi. 11) or of his confederates who might be present. Not that it made any real difference to the principle of the matter in question, whether Zelophehad died in his own sin or as partaker in a huge rebellion, but it did make a difference in the spirit with which these women presented their case. The fact that they were women did not make them afraid to go into the face of the whole congregation, but if they had been children of Korah, the chances are that a sense of shame would have compelled them to suffer wrong. What an admonition to those who stand among temptations to some shameless and heinous deed to ponder well the consequent stain and difficulty that may come to their innocent progeny! That the sins of the fathers are visited on the children is a fact apparent in nature, but society heartily accepts the principle, and only too often works it out in the most unsparing fashion.

II. IT WAS THE RIGHT SPIRIT OF APPROACH TO GOD IN THE CIRCUMSTANCES. Zelophehad belonged to the doomed generation. He may indeed have been a better man than most, but a census had just been taken which revealed the fact that there was not a single survivor of the generation; and it was not the time to say more in way of commendation than that Zelophehad died in his own sin. A deferential humble recollection of the holiness of Jehovah we may well believe to have marked the present approach of these women. He would hardly have connected the assertion of a general principle with their request if there had been anything unseemly or insolent in the manner of it. We shall do well not to claim too much for men in the way of commendation, when we are thinking of them in relation to God. We must neither abase them too low nor exalt them too high, but preserve the golden mean of a loving, charitable, and Christian appreciation. How offensive in the hearing of God many eulogies of men must sound, where not only superlative is piled on superlative, but altogether erroneous principles of judgment are adopted. There is a time and a need to praise devoted servants of God, and to maintain their reputation for fidelity, zeal, and spiritual success, but never let it be forgotten that the very best of men, to say the least of him, dies in his own sin. That will be largely his own consciousness. Whatever his services may have been, it is in the grace, wisdom, and ample preparedness of God in Christ Jesus that he will find his only hope. It only needs a little thought to see the impropriety of praising men, because they are laden with the free gifts of God's grace, and at the very time when the suitability of those gifts is especially made manifest. Any sort of praise of human excellence and service which even for a moment pushes into the background the universal depravity of man and the universal necessity of God's grace and mercy, is thereby self-condemned.

III. THOUGH A MAN DIE IN HIS OWN SIN ONLY, YET THAT IS ENOUGH TO WORK IRREPARABLE MISCHIEF. It was well to be able to say of Zelophehad that he had kept out of Korah's conspiracy, but it was a poor thing to say, if there was nothing better behind. Out of negations, nothing but negations will ever come. It is of no avail to keep out of ten thousand wrong ways, unless we take the one right way. The sum of human duty is to leave undone all the things which ought to be left undone, *and to do all the things which ought to be done.* Your own sin, small as it may seem in your present consciousness, is enough to bring death. The mustardseed of inborn alienation from God will grow to a mighty and everlasting curse if you do not stop it in time. Those who have passed through untold agonies because of conviction of sin, once laughed at sin as a little thing. They did not dream it would give them such trouble, and drive them about incessantly till they got the question answered, "What must I do to be saved?" Sin sleeps in most, as far as the peculiar consciousness of it is concerned, but when it wakes it will prove itself a giant. Look at the analogy in physical life. A man says that he is full of health and vigour, and he looks it; he even gets complimented upon it. Suddenly, in the midst of these compliments, he is stricken down with a fierce disease, and a few days number him among the dead. Why? The real disease was in him already, even with all his consciousness of health. There must have been something in his body to give the outward cause a hold. Our present consciousness is no criterion of our spiritual state. The word of God in the Scriptures, humbly apprehended and obeyed, is the only safe guide to follow.

IV. THOUGH A MAN MUST NEEDS DIE IN HIS OWN SIN, HE MAY ALSO DIE IN THE FULNESS OF CHRIST'S SALVATION FROM SIN. The end of life, with all its gloom, with all its manifestations of despair, callousness, and self-righteousness in some, is in others an occasion to manifest in great beauty the power of God in the spirits of men. One must die in his own sin, yet he may also experience the cleansing of that blood which takes away all sin. One must die in his own sin, yet this very necessity may also lead to dying in the faith of Jesus, in the hope of glory, and in the arms of infinite love.

V. WE SHOULD AIM THAT NOTHING WORSE THAN DYING IN OUR OWN SIN MAY BE SAID OF US. It is bad enough that sin should be dominant, even without compelling us to leave the ordinary paths of life; those reckoned, among men, useful and harmless. It is bad enough to feel that in us there are the possibilities of the most abandoned and reckless, of the worst of tyrants, sensualists, and desperadoes; only lacking such temptations, associations, and opportunities, as may make the possible actual. Be it ours, if we cannot show a spotless record, if we cannot claim a personality that started from innocence, at all events to show as little of harm to the world as possible. We cannot keep out of Zelophehad's company; let us keep out of Korah's. There is a medium between being a Pharisee and a profligate.—Y.

EXPOSITION.

MOSES AND JOSHUA (vers. 12—23). Ver. 12.—**And the Lord said unto Moses.** It is impossible to determine the exact place of this announcement in the order of events narrated. It would appear from ch. xxxi. 1 that the war with the Midianites occurred later, and certainly the address to the people and to Joshua in Deut. xxxi. 1—8 presupposes the formal appointment here recorded; but the chronology of the concluding chapters of Numbers is evidently very uncertain; they may, or may not, be arranged in order of time. We may with good reason suppose that the summons to die was only separated from its fulfilment by the brief interval necessary to complete what work was yet unfinished (such as the punishment of the Midianites and the provisional settlement of the trans-Jordanic country) before the river was crossed. **Into this Mount Abarim.** See on ch. xxxiii. 47; Deut. xxxii. 49 sq., where this command is recited more in detail. Abarim was apparently the range behind the Arboth Moab, the northern portion of which opposite to Jericho was called Pisgah (ch. xxi. 20; Deut. iii. 27), and the highest

point Nebo (Deut. xxxii. 49; xxxiv. 1), after the name of a neighbouring town (ch. xxxiii. 47). **And see the land.** Moses had already been told that he should not enter the promised land (ch. xx. 12), yet he is allowed the consolation of seeing it with his eyes before his death. It would seem from Deut. iii. 25—27 that this favour was accorded him in answer to his prayer.

Ver. 14.—**For ye rebelled against my commandment.** Rather, "as ye rebelled." The same word, בַּאֲשֶׁר, quomodo, is used here as in the previous clause. **That is the water of Meribah in Kadesh in the wilderness of Zin.** These words have all the appearance of an explanatory gloss intended to make the reference more plain to the reader or hearer. It is impossible to suppose that they formed part of the Divine message; nor does it seem probable that Moses would have added them to the narrative as it stands, because, in view of ch. xx. 13, no necessity for explanation existed. It is quite possible that both ch. xx. 13 and the present clause are subsequent additions to the text intended to clear up an obvious confusion between the "strife" at Rephidim (Exod. xvii. 7) and that at Kadesh.

Ver. 15.—**And Moses spake unto the Lord.** The behaviour of Moses as here recorded (see, however, on Deut. iii. 23 *sq.*, which seems to throw a somewhat different light upon the matter) was singularly and touchingly disinterested. For himself not even a word of complaint at his punishment, which must have seemed, thus close at hand, more inexplicably severe than ever; all his thoughts and his prayers for the people—that one might take *his* place, and reap for himself and Israel the reward of all *his* toil and patience.

Ver. 17.—**Which may go out before them, and which may go in before them.** A comparison with the words of Moses in Deut. xxxi. 2, and of Caleb in Josh. xiv. 11, shows that the going out and coming in refer to the vigorous prosecution of daily business, and the fatigues of active service. **Which may lead them out, and which may bring them in.** The underlying image is that of a shepherd and his flock, which suggests itself so naturally to all that have the care and governance of men (cf. John x. 3, 4, 16). **As sheep which have no shepherd.** And are, therefore, helpless, bewildered, scattered, lost, and devoured. The image is frequent in Scripture (cf. 1 Kings xxii. 17 ; Ezek. xxxiv. 5 ; Zech. x. 2; Matt. ix. 36). The words of the Septuagint are ὡσεὶ πρόβατα οἷς οὐκ ἔστι ποιμήν.

Ver. 18.—**Take thee Joshua.** Joshua was now for the first time designated at the request of Moses as his successor; he had, however, been clearly marked out for that office by his position as one of the two favoured survivors of the elder generation, and as the "minister" and confidant of Moses. In regard of the first he had no equal but Caleb, in regard of the second he stood quite alone. **A man in whom is the spirit.** רוּחַ here, although without the definite article, can only mean the Holy Spirit, as in ch. xi. 25 *sq.* **Lay thine hand upon him.** According to Deut. xxxiv. 9, this was to be done in order that Joshua might receive with the imposition of hands a spiritual gift (*charisma*) of wisdom for the discharge of his high office. It would appear also from the next paragraph that it was

done as an outward and public token of the committal of authority to Joshua as the successor of Moses.

Ver. 19.—**Give him a charge.** צִוִּיתָה. Septuagint, ἐντελῇ αὐτῷ. Command or instruct him as to his duties.

Ver. 20.—**Put some of thine honour upon him,** or, "some of thy dignity" (מֵהוֹדְךָ). Septuagint, δώσεις τῆς δόξης σου ἐπ' αὐτόν.

Ver. 21.—**He shall stand before Eleazar the priest.** This points to the essential difference between Moses and Joshua, and all who came after until the "Prophet like unto" Moses was raised up. Moses was as much above the priests as he was above the tribe princes; but Joshua was only the civil and military head of the nation, and was as much subordinate to the high priest in one way as the high priest was subordinate to him in another. In after times no doubt the political headship quite overpowered and overshadowed the ecclesiastical, but this does not seem to have been so intended, or to have been the case in Eleazar's lifetime. **Who shall ask counsel for him after the judgment of Urim before the Lord.** Rather, "who shall inquire for him in the judgment of Urim." בְּמִשְׁפַּט הָאוּרִים. Septuagint, τὴν κρίσιν τῶν δήλων. The Urim of this passage and of 1 Sam. xxviii. 6 seems identical with the Urim and Thummim of Exod. xxviii. 30 ; Levit. viii. 8. What it actually was, and how it was used in consulting God, is not told us in Scripture, and has left no reliable trace in the tradition of the Jews; it must, therefore, remain for ever an insoluble mystery. It does not appear that Moses ever sought the judgment of Urim, for he possessed more direct means of ascertaining the will of God; nor does it seem ever to have been resorted to after the time of David, for the "more sure word of prophecy" superseded it. Its real use, therefore, belonged to the dark ages of Israel, after the light of Moses had set, and before the light of the prophets had arisen. **At his word.** Literally, "after his mouth," *i. e.* according to the decision of Eleazar, given after consulting God by means of the Urim (cf. Josh. ix. 14 ; Judges i. 1).

Ver. 23.—**And gave him a charge.** This charge is nowhere recorded, for it cannot possibly be identified with the passing words of exhortation in Deut. xxxi. 7.

HOMILETICS.

Vers. 12—23.—*The outward failure and inward victory of Moses.* In this section we have two things very plainly: spiritually, we have the weakness of the law, and its inability to do what only Jesus can do for his people: morally, we have the beauty of an uncomplaining submission to the chastening hand of God, and of gladly seeing others reap where we have sown; succeed where we have failed. Consider, therefore—

I. That Moses must not lead the people into the promised land because
of the proved imperfection of his character. It can hardly indeed be supposed
that Joshua was in himself more perfect, or on the whole more dear to God, than
Moses: but Joshua was not known to have failed distinctly and publicly as Moses
was at Meribah; therefore he seemed to answer to the Divine ideal, to the requirement of perfect holiness, better than Moses. Even so the law made nothing perfect, accomplished nothing fully, because it was known and felt to be imperfect. As
applied to the guidance and training of human life for a better world it broke down.
Therefore it must be set aside in favour of something more perfect: its glory must
be done away before the glory that excelleth (2 Cor. iii. 10; Heb. vii. 18, 19;
x. 1, &c.).

II. That Moses was not permitted to cross the Jordan: so much of the
inheritance of Israel as lay on the wilderness side of Jordan, he might enter and
settle, but he must not cross the river. Even so it was not possible for the law to
enter in any wise upon the life to come, the land which is very far off, beyond the
stream of Death. This was its limitation imposed upon it by God, by reason of its
weakness, that it dealt only with this life, and with such religious sanctions, joys,
and consolations, as lie upon this side the grave exclusively. Immortal life was
without the province of the law, and could only be entered in Jesus (John i. 17;
xi. 25; 2 Tim. i. 10).

III. That Moses was permitted to see the land ere he departed. Even so
the law, which brought men to the very confines of the kingdom of heaven, but
could not bring them in (cf. Matt. xi. 11), had yet within itself a clear vision of the
fulfilment of its own hopes. The Song of Simeon and the Voice of the Baptist are
the dying testimony of the law, seeing the salvation of God to which it had led
through many a weary year, and so content to pass away without enjoying it (Luke
ii. 29, 30; John iii. 29—31, and cf. Heb. xi. 13; John viii. 56).

IV. That Moses craved of God a successor to himself who should do what
he could not do. Even so the law through all its voices craved for one, and
demanded one of God, who should really save, who should indeed open that kingdom of heaven to which itself was too feeble to enter.

V. That God designated Joshua ('Ιησοῦς) to take up and to fulfil the work of
Moses. Even so, what the law could not do, in that it was weak through the flesh,
that hath God accomplished by his holy servant Jesus (Acts xiii. 39; Rom. viii. 3).

VI. That Moses instituted Joshua to his office before the people, and
declared his work to him. Even so was Jesus proclaimed beforehand to all the
faithful by the law which pointed him out as the Captain of our salvation; and our
Lord himself, in his human nature, learnt from the law what himself should be and
do and suffer (Luke xxiv. 26, 27; John xix. 28; cf. Matt. xxvi. 54; Acts xiii. 27;
xvii. 3; xxvi. 23; xxviii. 22).

Consider again, with respect to *the conduct of Moses at this time,* wherein he is
not a foil to one greater, but a pattern to all the servants of God —

I. That his punishment seemed very bitter at this time: much more so
surely than when first announced, because *then* the land was far off, *now* it was very
nigh; *then* there was yet hope that the Lord would repent him of his sternness, *now*
the decree was palpably final and irrevocable. After so many additional toils, and
after so many happy anticipations of victory, to find that the sentence of exclusion
still held good must have been bitter indeed!

II. That his punishment was in fact inexplicable to himself, and to all,
at that time—for the explanation was not to come for many centuries. It
is only in the glory of the Mount of Transfiguration that we can understand or justify
the apparent severity with which Moses was treated. His sentence was "exemplary," for the sake of the people, in order to show in the most striking instance that
God requireth a perfect holiness, and a sinless Mediator. But for himself, as (on the
whole) a most faithful servant, the sentence was in fact reversed; the wrath was
swallowed up in mercy. Moses died outside the promised land, but his body was
preserved from corruption by the power of God (cf. Deut. xxxiv. 6 with Jude 9),
and in that body he did actually stand within the inheritance of Israel and talk with

Jesus of the decease (ἔξοδον) which he should accomplish at Jerusalem (Luke ix. 31, &c.). *And note,* that in Moses and Joshua we may clearly see the distinction between the Divine treatment of men as *types* and as *individuals.* Moses, *e. g.,*was made in his own time to yield to Joshua, to die in exile while Joshua led on to victory and home; and that obviously because Moses represented the weakness of the law, Joshua the power of the gospel. We, however, with the New Testament in our hands, have no difficulty in seeing that as individual servants of God, Moses is more honoured and more greatly rewarded than Joshua; for God is *not* extreme to mark what is done amiss by those who in the main serve him nobly, unselfishly, and patiently; nor is it in truth a righteous thing with God for one sin of temper to confiscate the rewards of many years of devotion. As a *type* Joshua stands higher because he was unblamed : as a *man* Moses is more dear to God, because his work was far more hard, his position more discouraging, and his lot less happy, than that of Joshua, and he himself not less faithful.

III. THAT MOSES DID NOT COMPLAIN OR REBEL. We know indeed from his own mouth (Deut. iii. 24), that he privately besought the Lord to let him go over; but when the Lord refused him (for the time present) he submitted without a word of complaint. Here was Moses' meekness (ch. xii. 3) ; not that he was not sometimes provoked so that he forgot himself; but that he habitually humbled himself to bear meekly even what seemed most hard.

IV. THAT HIS HABITUAL UNSELFISHNESS SHOWED ITSELF IN CONCERN FOR HIS PEOPLE WHEN HE WAS GONE. He did not harp upon his own fate, or brood upon his own sorrow, but thought only of the people, what should become of them.

V. THAT IN HIS UNSELFISH CONCERN FOR THEM HE WAS WILLING AND ANXIOUS THAT ANOTHER SHOULD BE PLACED OVER THEM IN HIS STEAD. And this showed the highest generosity of mind, because even very noble and otherwise unselfish people constantly betray jealousy and displeasure at the thought of others taking their place. To one who had wielded absolute power for forty years, it might well have seemed impossible to ask for a successor.

VI. THAT IN HIS LOYALTY TO THE KING OF ISRAEL HE GLADLY DEVOLVED HIS OWN DIGNITY UPON ONE WHO HAD BEEN HIS OWN SERVANT, AND OF ANOTHER TRIBE. Moses made no effort to advance his sons, as even Samuel did (1 Sam. viii. 1), nor had they any name or pre-eminence in Israel; nor did he show the least jealousy of Joshua, although he had been his own minister and (humanly speaking) owed everything to him.

Consider, again, with respect to *Joshua as a figure of our Lord*—

I. THAT HE WAS TO SUPERSEDE MOSES. (See above, and cf. Matt. v. 17; Acts vi. 14; Heb. iii. 3.)

II. THAT HE WAS APPOINTED IN ANSWER TO THE PRAYER THAT GOD WOULD " SET A MAN OVER THE CONGREGATION." Even so the Lord is that Son of man whom God hath ordained to be the Head of the Church, the human arbiter of human destinies, the human pattern and guide of all believers (Acts ii. 36 ; x. 42 ; Heb. ii. 16—18 ; Eph. i. 22, 23).

III. THAT HE WAS TO GO OUT AND TO GO IN BEFORE HIS PEOPLE; *i. e.* he was to lead an active and busy life in their sight and in their behalf. Even so our Lord fulfilled his ministry before the eyes of all the people, not in solitary meditation nor in calm retirement, but in a ceaseless activity of labour for the bodies and souls of men (Luke ii. 49 ; John iv. 34 ; ix. 4 ; xviii. 20 ; Acts x. 38).

IV. THAT HE WAS TO LEAD HIS PEOPLE OUT, AND TO BRING THEM IN, as a shepherd does his flock. Even so our Lord goes before his own in all things whether in life or in death, leading them out of the uncertain wilderness of this world, bringing them in to the unchangeable rest of the world to come (Ps. xxiii. 4 ; John x. 3, *sq.;* 1 Pet. ii. 21 ; Rev. i. 18).

V. THAT HE WAS TO BE A SHEPHERD TO THEM THAT HAD OTHERWISE BEEN SHEPHERD-LESS (Ezek. xxxiv. 23 ; Matt. ix. 36 ; Heb. xiii. 20 ; 1 Peter v. 4 ; Rev. vii. 17). *But note,* whereas Joshua was to stand before Eleazar, and seek counsel and command through him, our Saviour is both Captain and Priest of his people, and knoweth of himself the will of the Father (Matt. xı. 27 ; John i. 18 ; x. 15), and is the Shepherd and Overseer of souls as well as bodies (1 Pet. ii. 25).

HOMILIES BY VARIOUS AUTHORS.

Vers. 12—14.—*God's word to his dying servant.* The death of Moses was as singular as his life had been. The *scene* of it, a mountain-top, where he might be alone with God and yet have a wide prospect of the promised land; the *manner* of it, not by gradual failure of natural strength, but while he was still able to breast the steep mountain side; the *mystery* of it, such that no man knew where he was buried. Yet underneath this singularity there was much that is often seen in the departure of God's servants, and which we shall find it profitable to contemplate.

I. THE LORD REMINDS HIS DYING SERVANT OF HIS SIN (ver. 14). Dying thoughts are serious thoughts, and it would be strange if they did not often turn on the falls and shortcomings of the past life. Thoughts about sin are of two kinds:—1. There may be the recollection of sin without any knowledge of forgiveness. It was not so that Moses remembered Meribah. The remembrance of unforgiven sin banishes peace. The soul cannot bear to look back, for the past is full of shapes of terror; it cannot bear to look up, for it sees there the face of an offended God; it cannot bear to look forward, for the future is peopled with unknown terrors. 2. There may be the recollection of sin and at the same time an assured persuasion of forgiveness. This is by no means inconsistent with peace. Not that, even thus, the remembrance of sin is pleasant. Moses is put in mind of Meribah to keep him humble. Sin remembered cannot but cause shame; yet it is quite compatible with great peace of mind. Not only so, there is a calm and soul-filling peace which is the fruit of forgiveness, and diffuses itself most abundantly when the soul expatiates on the remembrance at once of its own sin and the Lord's forgiving grace. "Bless the Lord, oh my soul, who forgiveth all thine iniquities."

II. THE LORD COMFORTS HIS SERVANT IN THE PROSPECT OF DEPARTURE. 1. By giving him a sight of the good in store for the Church. It is remarkable how often saints who have spent their strength on some great Christian enterprise, and earnestly desired to see it accomplished before their departure, have been denied this gratification. Moses did not cross the Jordan; David did not see the Temple, nor Daniel the Return, nor John the Baptist the manifestation of Christ's glory. Yet to all those saints there was granted some such view as that which gladdened the eye of Moses on Nebo. He who knows the hearts knew how dear to Moses' heart was the good of Israel. It is an excellent token of grace in the heart when the prospect of good days in store for the Church and cause of God is a cordial in one's last sickness. 2. By telling him of the good and congenial society that awaits him in the other world. "Thy people." When we die we go to God. The ascension of Christ in our nature has filled heaven for us with such a blaze of fresh light that we must ever think of heaven chiefly as a "being with the Lord." Yet it is a precious thought, and full of comfort, that those who fall asleep in Jesus are gathered to their people, their true kindred. Moses goes to be with Abraham and Isaac and Jacob, with Joseph, with Miriam and Aaron.—B.

Vers. 18—20.—*The appointment of Joshua to be Moses' successor.* Moses, after having been the leader of his people for forty years, is at length to get his discharge. Nothing has yet been determined regarding a successor. The point is, on every account, too important to be left open till the present leader has passed away. A change of leadership, always hazardous, is especially hazardous when the army is in the field and the enemy is on the watch. If the Divine wisdom judged it necessary that Eleazar should be invested with the high priesthood before Aaron died, much more is it necessary that, before Moses lays down the sceptre, a successor should be appointed and placed in command. We are now to see how this was done. The story, besides its intrinsic interest, which is not small, is interesting, moreover, on this account, that the mode of procedure prescribed and followed in this case furnished precedents which continue to be observed amongst us down to the present day. Three topics claim notice.

I. AT WHOSE INSTANCE THIS APPOINTMENT TOOK PLACE. It was Moses who sued for a successor. It was not the people who urged on the business, nor was it necessary to overcome the reluctance of the present leader by a Divine command. No sooner does Moses receive notice to demit than he prays for a successor, and begs that his eyes may see him before he dies. His experience of the government makes him dread the dangers of an interregnum. "Sheep without a shepherd," such would the tribes be without a leader; unable to keep order among themselves, and exposed to every enemy. It betokened great nobility of soul in Moses that this was the thought uppermost in his mind on hearing that his hour was come. The paramount feeling of his heart was concern for the honour of the Lord and the good of Israel after his decease. Some men cannot endure the sight of a successor; Moses earnestly desired to see his successor before he died. Such being his desire, see where he carries it. *"Let the Lord set a man over the congregation."* From the Lord he had received his commission at the bush; from the Lord he sues for a successor. Moses was emphatically the "servant of the Lord;" and none but the Lord has authority to nominate the heir to so high an office. Moses has another reason for turning Godwards at this time. None but the Lord knows the fittest man, or can furnish him with the wisdom and valour the office will crave. He is *"the God of the spirits of all flesh."* He made men's souls, and he knows them. He admits them into intimacy with himself. He is their Saviour and Portion. When the Church, or any part of it, finds itself in want of a man fit to be intrusted with some office of high responsibility, or to be sent forth on some peculiarly difficult mission, this is the quarter to which it must turn. The God of the spirits of all flesh can furnish them with the man they want; He, and no other.

II. ON WHOM THE APPOINTMENT WAS BESTOWED. "Joshua the son of Nun, a man in whom is the spirit." Joshua was no stranger to Moses; he had been "Moses' minister from his youth" (ch. xi. 28), and known to him as a man every way fitted to be his successor. He must have thought of him; yet he did not presume to suggest his name; he waited to hear what the Lord would speak. N.B. When Moses was about to die and a successor was sought, it turned out that the Lord had anticipated the want. The successor of Moses was in training for forty years before Moses died. This happens oftener than many suppose.

III. THE MANNER OF THE INVESTITURE. 1. Joshua was presented to the congregation in a public assembly. To be sure, he owed his appointment to Divine nomination, not to popular election. He was, like Moses, the Lord's vicegerent. Nevertheless, the people were acknowledged in the appointment. They were to be Joshua's subjects, but not his slaves. Accordingly, it was judged only fair and right that they should be informed publicly of the appointment; that they should witness the investiture and hear the charge (cf. ch. xx. 27). 2. Moses laid his hands upon him. This is the earliest example in Scripture of a rite of investiture which was afterwards much in use, which was transferred by the apostles to the New Testament Church, and is the familiar custom of the Churches of Christ still. The terms in which it is here enjoined place the intention of it in a clear light. (1) It denoted the investiture of Joshua with the office of leader and commander in succession to Moses. "Thou shalt put some of thine honour upon him, that all the congregation may be obedient" (ver. 20). Not *all* his honour; for Moses was set over all God's house, and in that respect had no successor; but *part* of his honour, particularly that part in virtue of which he was captain of the host of Israel (cf. Acts vi. 6; xiii. 3). (2) It denoted also the bestowment on Joshua of the gifts appropriate to his new office. Not that Joshua was, till now, without valour or wisdom. During his long apprenticeship of forty years he had given abundant evidence of a rich dowry of these virtues. But the laying on of the hands of Moses by Divine command was a token and pledge that a double portion of his master's spirit would be thenceforward bestowed, to strengthen him to take up his master's task and carry it forward to completion. The pledge was redeemed. "Joshua was full of the spirit of wisdom, for Moses had laid his hands upon him" (Deut. xxxiv. 9; cf. 1 Tim. iv. 14). 3. Moses gave him a charge. The scope and substance of the charge are recorded in Deut. iii. 28 and xxxi. 7, 8. The design of this part of the service was twofold. On the one hand, Moses faithfully expounded the duties belonging to the office with which he was now invested. He certified him that it was no idle dignity he was now entering upon, but an arduous work. And this was done not within a tent, or in some solitary place, but publicly, and before all the congregation, that they as well as Joshua might hear. On the other hand, Moses laboured to strengthen his successor's heart. No man was so well able to comfort Joshua as Moses was. The Lord in calling Moses at the bush had given him the promise, "Surely I will be with thee." He had kept the promise. Moses was able to testify that when God calls a man to any duty, he will be with him in the discharge of the duty ; so that the most timid man may well be strong and of a good courage in the work the Lord has given him to do.—B.

Vers. 12, 13.—*The alleviations of death.* Death a penalty even in the adopted family of God, though turned into a blessing to the believer. Some of the alleviations of the penalty suggested by this command to Moses. Through faith in Christ we may enjoy—

I. A CLEAR VIEW OF THE GLORIOUS FUTURE OF THE CHURCH. As Moses saw the land, not yet possessed, but already "given," so may faith anticipate the goodly heritage of the future. Illustrate Joseph's death-bed (Gen. l. 24) ; David's anticipations of an age of glory under Solomon ; the bright glimpses of the future with which nearly every one of the minor prophets concludes.

II. A RELEASE FROM THE GRAVE RESPONSIBILITIES OF THAT FUTURE. Moses was spared from the wars of the Lord in the conquest of Canaan. And Christians, though willing, like the aged Dr. Lyman Beecher, to " enlist again in a minute," "to begin life over again, and work once more" ('Autobiography,' ii. 552), are spared from the conflicts of the "perilous times " of the future.

III. AN ASSURANCE THAT THE WORK OF GOD WILL BE EFFICIENTLY CARRIED ON WITHOUT US. Not even a Moses is essential to the Church of God ; Joshua will do the work as well.

IV. AN ADMITTANCE TO THE COMPANY OF THE PIOUS DEAD. " *Thy people*," who died in faith, and now live with God. With brighter hopes than any heathens, or even than Moses, we may say, "I go to the majority."

V. A PEACEFUL DEPARTURE SUCH AS OTHER LOVED ONES HAVE EXPERIENCED. "As Aaron thy brother was gathered." We have seen " the end of their course " (Heb. xiii. 7), and may expect grace for dying hours such as they enjoyed.—P.

Vers. 18—21.—*The qualifications for the public service of God.* Some of these are illustrated in the case of Joshua.

I. THE INDWELLING OF THE SPIRIT OF GOD (ver. 18). This obvious from the past history of Joshua, especially at Kadesh (chs. xiii., xiv.). Union with Christ through faith, attested by his Holy Spirit, essential for us.

II. A CLEAR CONVICTION OF DUTY. We need the assurance of a mission, " a charge " (ver. 19), whether addressed from without or heard in the secret of the soul.

III. A PROVIDENTIAL APPOINTMENT. " Lay thine hand upon him." Not every impulse is to be taken for a Divine " charge," lest we should run without being sent (cf. Ps. xxv. 4, 5 ; cxliii. 8).

IV. THE CONFIDENCE OF THE PEOPLE OF GOD (ver. 20 ; cf. 1 Tim. iii. 7). In carrying on our work we may need the cheerful co-operation, or even " obedience " (ver. 20), which confidence in our character and commission inspires.

V. CEASELESS COMMUNION WITH AND DIRECTION FROM GOD (ver. 21). For the welfare of a "congregation " or of a nation may depend on the instructions given, or assumed to be given, in God's name.—P.

Vers. 12—23.—*Preparing for the end.* God has kept in view this solemn departure of Moses, even from the time of sentence on him for his transgression. The heights of Abarim were visible to God from Meribah. And now Israel lies at their base, the work of Moses is done, and God intimates the immediate preparations for his departure. God had already said to him that after taking vengeance on the Midianites he should be gathered to his people (ch. xxxi. 2). (Evidently the events of ch. xxxi. are earlier in time than those of ch. xxvii. 12—23.)

I. THE PLACE OF DEPARTURE IS ALSO THE PLACE OF A GLORIOUS VISION. The eyes of the dying leader closed upon the sight of the land which the Lord had given to the children of Israel. We may be sure that God directed the feet of Moses to the one spot where there was the most suggestive view of Canaan. Not of necessity the view of greatest geographical extent, but probably one that would sufficiently indicate the variety of surface and products, showing also something of the populous cities. There would be everything to impress on Moses a most decided and cheering contrast with the wilderness. There might be no place even in the promised land itself where he could get a better view for the purpose. He may have climbed to different heights during the sojourn of the people in Moab, and seen many things to gladden his heart, yet never found just the Abarim point of view, until God signified it to him. There are many points of wide and spirit-filling view to which we may come in our excursions through the high lands of Scriptural truth and privilege, but we must wait for God himself to give us the great Abarim point of view. Many a Moabite shepherd had wandered on those heights, and seen with the outward eye the same landscape as Moses; but it needed a Moses, with a long-instructed, experienced, and privileged heart, to see what the Lord would show him. Balaam was driven from one height to another by the unsatisfied Balak, yet from them all *even he*, the man of carnal and corrupt mind, saw something glorious. What then must not Moses have seen, being so different a man from Balaam, and looking from God's own chosen point of view?

II. IT IS ALSO THE PLACE FOR CHEERING ANTICIPATIONS OF THE EARTHLY FUTURE OF GOD'S PEOPLE. Moses is to see with his own eyes that the land was worth forty years' waiting and suffering for. The object stands revealed before him as worthy of the effort. And though the earthly future of Israel is not to be his future, yet how could he look upon it otherwise than with as much interest and solicitude as if it were his own? Certainly that future was assured, as far as promise could assure it, and all the tenor of experience in the past. Whatever the circumstances of Moses' death, they could not materially affect the course of the people, seeing the ever-loving, all-comprehending God had them in charge. But it became God—it was a sign of loving care for a faithful servant—that Moses should die as he did. Quite conceivably he might have died in the gloom caused by some fresh aberration of the people, or at the best in the ordinary circumstances of daily life, with nothing more to mark his departure than if he were one of the most obscure persons in the camp. But God orders all things so that he shall depart where and when his mind may be filled with great joy because of Israel's coming years in Canaan. It happened not to him, as it has happened often in great crises of human affairs, that the leader has been suddenly called away with the feeling in his heart, "After me the deluge." None indeed knew better than Moses that Canaan would have its own difficulties. From the wilderness to Canaan was in many things only an exchange of difficulties, but still Canaan had things the wilderness never had, never could have, else it would not have been the promised land. Moses looks down on Canaan, and he sees not only the land, but a Joshua, with 600,000 fighting men under him, a tabernacle, an ark of the covenant, institutions in a measure consolidated by the daily attention of forty years.

III. THE SIMILAR ASSURANCES WE MAY HAVE AS TO THE FUTURE OF GOD'S WORK IN THE WORLD. We have things which our fathers had not—instruments, opportunities, liberties, and successes which were denied to them. Yet they saw the bright day coming; its first streaks fell on their dying faces; and they rejoiced even in what they could not share. Aged and bone-weary Israelites who died just as the people were leaving Egypt would nevertheless rejoice with all their hearts in the deliverance of their children. And Moses, who had been born an exile, who had lived forty years among strangers in Egypt, forty years more in the second exile of Midian, and forty years in the wilderness, was just the man to appreciate the satisfactions which were coming to his brethren at last. Thus we should learn to rejoice with all our hearts in the advent of possessions and privileges which have come too late for us individually to share. It is not enough languidly to say that things will be better for the next generation than they are for the present; it should be our joy to live and work as Moses did for the attainment of this. Let all our life be a slow climbing of Abarim, then our closing days will be rewarded with Abarim's view. It was the glory and joy of Moses that while he looked from the top of the mount, Israel was in the plain beneath. They were not far away in the wilderness of Sinai or, worse still, in the brick-yards of Egypt. Moses had brought them with him, or rather God had brought him and them together. All humble, unselfish, and God-respecting hearts, who work through evil report and good report to make the world better, will assuredly have something of the reward of Moses from the top of Abarim. As concerns the greatest treasures of the kingdom of God, it matters not in what generation we live. It was better to be a believing Israelite in the wilderness, even though he died there, than an unbelieving one in Canaan. It will be better in the judgment for the man of two thousand years ago who looked forward longingly for the Messiah than for the man of to-day who looks back carelessly on the cross. The resources and revelations of eternity will equalise the disparities of time. All the same it will be no small matter if those who have taken part in guiding a generation through the wilderness see the earthly Canaan on which it is entering before they are gathered to their people. Each generation should leave to the next more of Canaan and less of the wilderness. Each generation, though it enters in some sort upon a Canaan, should leave it as only a wilderness compared with the brighter Canaan that is to follow. Let our confident, determined cry ever be, *Out of Christ there is no hope for the world.* Out of Christ the generations of men must become more and more corrupt, and give more hold for the pessimist with his dismal creed. But equally our cry must be, *In Christ there is no room even for despondency, let alone despair.* Black as the outlook remains on a world's sins and sorrows, the God who showed Canaan to Moses from Abarim holds his resources undiminished still (Matt. xxviii. 20 ; Rom. viii. 28 ; xi. 33—36 ; xv. 19, 29 ; 1 Cor. xv. 58 ; 2 Cor. i. 20).—Y.

Vers. 15—17.—*The solicitude of Moses for the helpless flock.* I. THE FIGURE UNDER WHICH MOSES INDICATES ISRAEL. He speaks of them as a flock of sheep, thus venturing on a meek reference to the quality of his own past services. He speaks like a man who had been long preparing, even before Meribah, for an emergency such as this. He knew he could not live always, and he saw no sufficiently hopeful change in Israel. He had to deal with the sheep-nature in them from the first, and that nature was in them still in undiminished vitality. They would, he implies, be as helpless in Canaan as in the wilderness. He had not yet got the view from Abarim, but that view would only deepen his thankfulness that God had given the people a shepherd. For the more impressive the view, and the more there was revealed of rich and abundant pasture, the more evident it would become that the sheep needed guidance in order to make full use of the pasture. Passing from the wilderness into Canaan, while it vastly enlarges the sheep-privileges, does not in itself change the sheep-nature. *The need remains in equal force both for guidance and protection.* Where the privileges are greater, there, consequently, the possessions will be greater ; there also there will be more to attack, more danger of attack, and more need of defence. And in like manner how helpless we are of ourselves among the vast resources and promises which belong to God's grace in Christ Jesus. Unless we have some one to guide and strengthen, and show us the meaning and power of Divine truth, we are as helpless as an infant would be with a steam-engine. Weak and strong are relative terms. Sheep are strong enough in certain ways—strong to rebel against wholesome restraints and break through them, but not strong enough to repel the dangers which come when the restraints are broken through. Moses had only too often seen Israel hanging together like sheep, going in troops after some headstrong Korah, while men of the Caleb and Joshua order were almost to be counted on one's fingers.

II. THE PEOPLE BEING SUCH, A SHEPHERD WAS A MANIFEST NECESSITY. Given sheep, it does not take much reasoning to infer a shepherd. Moses had been a shepherd himself, both literally and figuratively, and his experience of the sheep in Midian doubtless sharpened his sense of the analogy as he gazed on the human sheep whom he had led for forty years. A man unfamiliar with pastoral life might indeed talk in a general way of the fallen children of men as sheep ; but it needed a Moses to speak of the shepherd's work with such minuteness and sympathetic interest as he shows here. The shepherd is to go out before the sheep. With him rests the responsibility of choosing the place of pasture. And he must lead the sheep. He must go before them, and not too far before them, or he cannot truly lead. He leads them out to find pasture, and he leads them in to insure security. The Good Shepherd is in himself the guarantee both for nourishment and security, and the sheep follow him, as if to show that the real nourishments and securities of religion must come by a voluntary acceptance. There is much difference between being drawn and driven. The sheep following the shepherd is not like the ox dragging the plough and quickened by its master's goad. There are times indeed when, like the ox, we must be driven and chastised, but the greatest results can only be gained when we are drawn like the sheep. In the lives of God's people there is a very instructive mingling of freedom and constraint. Let us add, that in thinking of the responsibility of the shepherd for the providing of pasture it must not be forgotten how soon the manna ceased when Canaan was entered (Josh. v. 12). The people then needed guiding into a forethought and industry from which, in the presence of the daily manna, they had long been free.

III. It is manifest that nothing but a Divine appointment was adequate to meet this necessity. *Popular election was certainly not available.* The sheep would make a poor business of it if they had to choose a shepherd. Popular government is less objectionable than the rule of despots, but it has its own delusions, its own narrow aims. The natural man is the natural man, circumscribed by the limits of time, and sense, and natural discernment, whether he be noble or peasant. The follies and cruelties of democracy have caused as sad, humiliating pages to be written in the history of the world as the follies and cruelties of any despot whatever. The man who says *vox populi, vox Dei* speaks error none the less because he speaks out of a generous, enthusiastic heart. Never till the voice of Christ becomes the willing and gladsome voice of the people can *vox populi, vox Dei* be the truth. Equally plain is it that *the choice of Moses was not available.* He feels that the thing can only be done in entire submission to God. Moses himself, in the day of his first call, had spoken very depreciatingly of his own qualifications. Yet not only had God chosen him, but also proved the choice was right. The event had shown that he was the leader after God's own heart. What a thing if he had turned out like Saul; but that he could not do, he was so completely the choice of God. It was not for Moses then, who had gone so tremblingly from Midian to Egypt, to say, "Who is fittest man for shepherd now?" Moses felt well able to estimate the qualifications of a leader; but who best supplied those qualifications was a question which none but the all-searching, all-knowing God could answer. God had not only seen fitness in Moses, but he had seen fitness *in Moses only;* for we must ever believe that in each generation, and for each emergency, he takes the very fittest man among the thousands of Israel. God had chosen at the departure from Egypt; God also shall choose at the entrance into Canaan.

IV. Notice the suggestive and appropriate way in which God is addressed. "The God of the spirits of all flesh." It is God who breathes in the breath of life, sustains and controls it, and can fix the time of its cessation. Speaking to God in this way, there is thus *an expression of humble personal submission.* Moses cannot choose the time of death, any more than he has been able to choose anything else. God had shielded the faint and delicate breath of the infant as it lay in the flags by the river's brink, and now he calls upon the old man of a hundred and twenty years, who has passed through such a difficult and oft-endangered course, to yield that breath up. There is also in this mode of address *a clear recognition of how it is that God may be looked to for the choice of a leader.* God has but lately proved his knowledge of individual men by his complete control over those dying in the wilderness (ch. xxvi. 64, 65). He who assuredly knows the hearts of all the 600,000 lately counted can say who of them is fittest to be leader. God knows *who is nearest to him as a follower.* There is no fear but the sheep will recognise those whom God appoints. In spite of all the difficulties of Moses, in spite of rebellions and curses, in spite of the crumbling away of a whole generation, the nation is still there. Moses can say, on the verge of Jordan and at the foot of Abarim, "Here am I and the flock that was given me." But all this achievement only glorified God the more, that God who had chosen Moses and hedged up his way. Any other leader than the one God had chosen could never have got out of Egypt. Any other leader than the one God will now choose cannot get across Jordan.—Y.

Vers. 18—23.—*The solicitude relieved by the appointment of Joshua.* God makes an immediate, gracious, and full compliance with the request of Moses. It is a welcome sight when the will of God runs forward as it were to meet the wishes of man. God has so often to reveal himself refusing and thwarting the wishes of men, or at all events complying with them only in part. This request must have been expected, and the command to go up into Abarim prepared the way for it to be made.

I. THE QUALIFICATION OF JOSHUA. "A man in whom is the spirit;" a spirit doubtless such as was bestowed on the seventy elders, of whom, in all probability, Joshua was one (ch. xi.). Having the spirit was the one indispensable thing. Nothing of such work as Joshua had to do could be done without it. There are diversities of operations, but they are all the operations of those in whom there are special and necessary endowments for the work they have to do. *Others beside Joshua had some of the qualifications he possessed, but, lacking the spirit, they might as well have lacked everything.* What, for instance, was there to prevent Caleb from being leader? Like Joshua, he had been one of the spies, and seen Canaan before. He strikes us as being even a bolder and more resolute man than Joshua; but courage, fidelity, the following of God rather than man, while these are the qualities that make *martyrs*, they are not enough to make *leaders.* A Christian might make an excellent figure at the stake who would be nowhere as the guide of the flock. It is beautiful to feel that Caleb continued his simple-hearted devotion to the cause of Israel. Joshua and he seem to have continued the best of friends (Josh. xiv.). Whether a man is a leader or not should not affect our judgment of him in his whole humanity. Let us esteem most those who are best. It is a foolish question to ask who is greatest in the kingdom of heaven, for every one may conceivably have such excellence of spiritual qualities as may put him in the first place. We may conclude then that, good and true man as Caleb was, *he lacked the particular spirit which Joshua possessed.* Notice, again, that some who certainly had the spirit as well as Joshua *lacked other qualifications.* For one thing, Joshua had been long and intimately connected with Moses. It is interesting to notice how many things were done to give Moses pleasure in this departing hour. His death before crossing Jordan is a necessity; there is no way to obviate it; but really as we read of it we have hard work to connect the usual gloom of death with the event. The view that he gets, the compliance with his request, and the choice of one who had been long his faithful and affectionate companion, all these things made the cup of the dying Moses run over. It was *euthanasia* indeed. The friendship of Joshua with Moses may have had a very great deal to do with the appointment. Those who choose the *company* of the good and remain steadfast in it are likely to gain such positions as may enable them to transmit the *influence* of the good. Passing over the immediate circumstances of the appointment, which were such as to impress deeply both the shepherd and the sheep, and remain in the shepherd's mind, at all events, till his latest hour, we notice—

II. THE GREAT RULE FOR THE SHEPHERD'S GUIDANCE. God was not about to visit Joshua as he did Moses. Moses stood in lonely and awful eminence as the prophet with whom God spoke face to face (ch. xii. 8; Deut. xxxiv. 10). Such a mode of revelation was needed for the work Moses was called to do. The work in the wilderness was a peculiarly critical one. In one sense we may say it was even more important than the work in Canaan. Given your *foundation*, which may require great toil and great destruction of existing things if you are to get down to the rock; given your *materials*, which have to be accumulated with much searching, discernment, and exactitude; given, above all things, your *design*, in which even the least thing is to have vital connection with the great principles—given all these, and then the chief thing required is a competent, honest, and industrious builder. Moses was the man who gets to the foundation, gathers the material, and furnishes the design; Joshua, the subordinate, to come in afterwards and by simple-hearted, plodding, tenacious fidelity to complete the construction of what was intrusted to him. There was no need for God to visit Joshua as he did Moses. The signs of the Urim were quite sufficient, and therefore nothing more was given. Notice also that the priest became thus associated with the leader, to confirm his position when right, and to check him in case he showed signs of going wrong. If Joshua had gone anywhere else than to the intimations of Urim, the resort itself would have been sufficient to condemn him. God took care of Moses in all the directions he had to give by immediately and most abundantly strengthening and supporting him. And so Joshua here was wonderfully helped by the Urim. Any one who refused obedience to him must have been resolutely opposed to truth, for who could deny intimations plainly palpable to the senses? Thus we are helped by the thought of what the Urim was to Joshua in our consideration as to the authority of the New Testament Scriptures over Christians. It is sometimes asked why inspiration should be held to stop with the canon of Scripture. An equally pertinent question is to ask why it should continue. God alone is the judge as to the modes of revelation, and the duration of those modes. It is out of the sovereignty and wisdom of him whose ways are unsearchable that he dealt with Moses after one fashion, and with Joshua after another. And it is by a practical reference to the same sovereignty and wisdom that we shall account for the difference between the New Testament Scriptures and even the most copious and esteemed of the earlier post-apostolic writings. We have our Urim in the great principles of the New Testament.

III. THE CHOICE WAS JUSTIFIED BY THE RESULT. The Book of Joshua is a very remarkable one for this peculiarity, which it shares with the Book of Daniel, that there is no record of any stumbling on the part of its leading character. Joshua is always alert, obedient to God, jealous of God's honour, and keeping the great end in view. There is sin recorded in the Book and a dilatory spirit, but Joshua himself appears in striking contrast to this. And so it always has been and always will be; he whom God chooses will justify the choice. The successful leaders whom God has given his people in the past are an ample assurance that he will continue to provide them.—Y.

EXPOSITION.

CHAPTERS XXVIII., XXIX.

THE ROUTINE OF SACRIFICIAL OFFERINGS (chs. xxviii., xxix.). Ver. 1.—**The Lord spake unto Moses**. It is impossible to say with any assurance whether the law of offerings contained in these two chapters was really given to Moses shortly before his death, or whether it was ever given in this connected and completed form. It is obvious that the formula with which the section opens might be used with equal propriety to introduce a digest of the law on this subject compiled by Moses himself, or by some subsequent editor of his writings from a number of scattered regulations, written or oral, which had Divine authority. It is indeed quite true that this routine of sacrifice was only suitable for times of settled habitation in the promised land, and therefore there is a certain propriety in its introduction here on the eve of the entry into Canaan. But it must be remembered, on the other hand, that the same thing holds true of very much of the legislation given at Mount Sinai, and avowedly of that comprised in ch. xv. (see ver. 2), which yet appears from its position to have been given before the rebellion of Korah in the wilderness. It is indeed plain that the ritual, festal, and sacrificial system, both as elaborated in Leviticus and as supplemented in Numbers, presupposed throughout an almost immediate settlement in Canaan. It is also plain that a system so elaborate, and entailing so much care and expense, could hardly have come into regular use during the conquest, or for some time after. It cannot, therefore, be said with any special force that the present section finds its natural place here. All we can affirm is that the system itself was of Divine origin, and dated in substance from the days of Moses. In any case, therefore, it is rightly introduced with the usual formula which attests that it came from God, and came through Moses. It must be noted that a great variety of observances which were zealously followed by the Jews of later ages find no place here. Compare, e. g., the ceremonial pouring of water during the feast of tabernacles, to which allusion is made by the prophet Isaiah (xii. 3) and our Lord (John vii. 37, 38).

Ver. 2. — **My offering, and my bread**. Literally, "my *korban*, my bread." The general term *korban* (anything offered to God : cf. ch. vii. 3 ; Mark vii. 11) is here restricted by the words which follow to the meat offering. "Bread" (לֶחֶם) is translated "food" in Levit. iii. 11, 16 (see the note there). **Sweet savour**. רֵיחַ. Septuagint, εἰς ὀσμὴν εὐωδίας (see on Gen. viii. 21 ; Levit. iii. 16 ; Ephes. v. 2).

Ver. 3.—**This is the offering made by fire.** The daily offering prescribed at Exod. xxix. 38—42, and which had presumably never been intermitted since, is specified again here because it formed the foundation of the whole sacrificial system. Whatever else was offered was in addition to it, not in lieu of it. The sabbath and festival use of the Jews was developed out of the ferial use, and rested upon it. Hence in a connected republication of the law of offering it could not be omitted. **Without spot.** תְּמִימִם. Septuagint, ἀμώμους. This necessary qualification had not been expressed in the original ordinance, but in respect of other sacrifices had been continually required (see on Exod. xii. 5; Levit. i. 3; ch. xix. 2; Heb. ix. 14; 1 Pet. i. 19).

Ver. 7.—**In the holy place.** בַּקֹּדֶשׁ. Septuagint, ἐν τῷ ἁγίῳ. Josephus paraphrases this by περὶ τὸν βωμόν ('Ant.,' iii. 10), and so the Targum of Onkelos; Jonathan and the Targum of Palestine render, "from the vessels of the sanctuary." The former would seem to be the real meaning of the original. There is nowhere any specific direction as to the ritual of the drink offering (see on Levit. xxiii. and ch. xv. 7, 10), nor is it certain whether it was poured at the foot of the altar (as apparently stated in Ecclus. l. 15) or poured upon the flesh of the sacrifice on the altar (as seems to be implied in Philip. ii. 17). **The strong wine.** שֵׁכָר. Septuagint, σίκερα. The Targums render it "old wine," because the drink offering was in every other instance ordered to be made with wine (Exod. xxix. 40, &c.). *Shecar*, however, was not wine, but strong drink other than wine (such as we call "spirits"), and it is invariably used in that sense in contradistinction to wine (see on Levit. x. 9; ch. vi. 3, &c.). It can only be supposed that the difficulty of procuring wine in the wilderness had caused the coarser and commoner liquor to be substituted for it. It is certainly remarkable that the mention of *shecar* should be retained at a time when wine must have been easily obtainable, and was about to become abundant (Deut. viii. 8). As it would seem impossible that *shecar* should have been substituted for wine after the settlement in Canaan, its mention here may be accepted as evidence of the wilderness-origin of this particular ordinance. The quantity ordained (about a quart for each lamb) was very considerable.

Ver. 9.—**And on the sabbath day.** The special offering for the sabbath is ordered here for the first time. It does not say when the two lambs were to be slain, but in practice it was immediately after the morning sacrifice of the day.

Ver. 10. — **The burnt offering of every sabbath.** Literally, "the sabbath burnt offering for its sabbath."

Ver. 11. — **In the beginnings of your months.** The new-moon offering also is here enjoined for the first time, the festival itself having only been incidentally mentioned in ch. x. 10. There can be no doubt that this (unlike the sabbath) was a nature-festival, observed more or less by all nations. As such it did not require to be instituted, but only to be regulated and sanctified in order that it might not lend itself to idolatry, as it did among the heathen (cf. Deut. iv. 19; Job xxxi. 26, 27; Jer. vii. 18; viii. 2). The new-moon feast, depending upon no calendar but that of the sky, and more clearly marked in that than any other recurring period, was certain to fix itself deeply in the social and religious habits of a simple pastoral or agricultural people. Accordingly we find it incidentally mentioned as a day of social gathering (1 Sam. xx. 5), and as a day for religious instruction (2 Kings iv. 23). From the latter passage, and from such passages as Isa. lxvi. 23; Ezek. xlvi. 1; Amos viii. 5, it is evident that the feast of the new moon became to the month exactly what the sabbath was to the week—a day of rest and of worship (see also Judith viii. 6).

Ver. 15.—**One kid of the goats.** "One hairy one (שָׂעִיר) of the she goats (עֵז)." See on ch. vii. 16. This was probably offered first in order, according to the usual analogy of such sacrifices (Exod. xxix. 10—14). There is no authority for supposing that this sin offering superseded the one mentioned in ch. xv. 24 *sq.* *This* was essentially part of the customary routine of sacrifice; *that* was essentially occasional, and proper to some unforeseen contingency. It is likely enough that the national conscience would in fact content itself with the first, but it does not in the least follow that such was the intention of the legislator.

Ver. 17.—**In the fifteenth day of this month is the feast.** The fourteenth day of Abib, or Nisan, the day of the passover proper, was not a feast, but a fast ending with the sacred meal of the evening. Only the ordinary daily sacrifice was offered on this day. **Unleavened bread.** מַצּוֹת (*mattsoth*). Septuagint, ἄζυμα, unleavened cakes.

Ver. 18.—**In the first day,** *i. e.* on the fifteenth (see on Exod. xii. 16; Levit. xxiii. 7).

Ver. 19.—**Ye shall offer a sacrifice.** This offering, the same for each day of Mattsoth as for the feast of the new moon, had not been prescribed before, and almost certainly not observed at the one passover kept in the wilderness (ch. ix. 5).

Ver. 23.—**Ye shall offer these beside the**

burnt offering in the morning, *i. e.* in addition to, and immediately after, the usual morning sacrifice. Even when it is not expressly stated, the presumption is that all the sacrifices here treated of were cumulative. Thus the sabbath of the passover (John xix. 31) would have the proper sacrifices (1) of the day, (2) of the sabbath, (3) of the feast of Mattsoth, comprising two bullocks, one ram, eleven lambs, with their meat offerings and drink offerings.

Ver. 26.—**In the day of the first-fruits.** The feast of weeks, or day of Pentecost (Levit. xxiii. 15—21).

Ver. 27.—**Ye shall offer the burnt offering.** The festal sacrifice here prescribed is exactly the same as for the days of Mattsoth and for the feast of the new moon. It is not the same as that prescribed for the same day in Levit. xxiii., and it is difficult to determine whether it was meant to supersede the previous ordinance, or to be distinct and additional. The fact that no notice is taken of the sacrifice already ordered would seem to point to the former conclusion ; but the further fact that no mention is made of the offering of wave-loaves, with which the sacrifices in Leviticus were distinctively connected, seems to show that the two lists were independent (cf. Josephus, 'Ant.,' iii. 10, 6). The fact seems to be that throughout this section no sacrifices are mentioned save such as formed a part of the system which is here for the first time elaborated.

Ch. xxix. 1.—**In the seventh month, on the first day of the month.** The month Ethanim had been already specially set apart for holy purposes beyond all other months (Levit. xxiii. 23 *sq.*).

Ver. 2.—**Ye shall offer a burnt offering.** Such an offering had been commanded (Levit. xxiii. 25), but not specified. It comprised one bullock less than the new moon offering, but the reason of the difference is wholly unknown, unless it were in view of the large number of bullocks required at the feast of tabernacles.

Ver. 7.—**On the tenth day.** The great day of atonement (Levit. xvi. 29 ; xxiii. 27 *sq.*).

Ver. 12.—**On the fifteenth day.** The first day of the feast of tabernacles, which commenced at sunset on the fourteenth (Levit. xxiii. 35).

Ver. 13.—**Ye shall offer a burnt offering.** This also was ordered, but not prescribed, in Levit. xxiii. As it was the feast of the ingathering, when God had crowned the year with his goodness, and filled the hearts of men with food and gladness, so it was celebrated with the greatest profusion of burnt offerings, especially of the largest and costliest kind. **Thirteen young bullocks.** The number of bullocks was so arranged as to be one less each day, to be seven on the seventh and last day, and to make up seventy altogether. Thus the sacred number was studiously emphasised, and the slow fading of festal joy into the ordinary gladness of a grateful life was set forth. It seems quite fanciful to trace any connection with the waning of the moon. The observance of the heavenly bodies, although sanctioned in the case of the new moon feast, was not further encouraged for obvious reasons.

Ver. 35.—**On the eighth day.** On the twenty-second day of Ethanim (see on Levit. xxiii. 36). The offering here specified returns to the smaller number ordered for the first and tenth days of this month. The feast of tabernacles ended with sundown on this day.

Ver. 39.—**These things shall ye do,** or " sacrifice." תַּעֲשׂוּ. Septuagint, ταῦτα ποιήσετε (cf. Luke xxii. 19). **Beside your vows, and your free-will offerings.** These are treated of in Levit. xxii. 18 *sq.* ; ch. xv. 3 *sq.* The words which follow are dependent upon this clause. All the offerings commanded in these chapters amounted to 1071 lambs, 113 bullocks, 37 rams, 30 goats, in the lunar year, together with 112 bushels of flour, more than 370 gallons of oil, and about 340 gallons of wine, supposing that the drink offering was proportionate throughout.

HOMILETICS.

Chs. xxviii., xxix.—*The perfect system of sacrifice.* We have in this section the round of sacrifice—daily, weekly, monthly, and annual—drawn out in all its completeness and in all its symmetry. There were indeed other sacrifices ordained, such as those of the goat for Azazel and of the red heifer, which find no place here ; but these were essentially (as it would seem) of an exceptional nature, and stood out against the unvarying background of the sacrificial routine here depicted. No longer left to be gathered from scattered enactments, it is here ordained as a system, pervaded and inspired by certain definite and abiding principles. That those principles were not read into a fortuitous assemblage of ancient rites by the pious ingenuity of a later and more self-conscious age, but underlay those rites from the beginning, and determined their character and mutual relation, can hardly be doubted by any one who believes the system to have been of Divine origination ; and this, again, can hardly be doubted by any one who recognises the profound congruity between the sacrificial system of Moses and the sacrificial aspect of Christianity. It is this congruity which gives a living interest, because an abiding truth, to the sacrifices of the law. They were not merely shadows to amuse the childhood of the world ; they were shadows of coming realities, the most tremendous and of the profoundest moment. It is true that the inspired writers of the New Testament dwell rather on the contrast than on the correspondence between the sacrifice of Christ and the sacrifices of the law ; but they do so just because they took the correspondence for granted, not because they ignored it. The correspondence, in fact, was so obvious and so strong that it was necessary to emphasise the points of contrast, lest they should be overlooked. He that magnifies the substance above the shadow does not thereby deny that the shadow owes both its existence and its form to the substance. If we follow up the Pauline image of body and shadow (Col. ii. 17, where the reference is to this very round of festivals), we shall get at the truth of the matter. The relation of the shadow to the body is not one of simple resemblance, even of outline (except in one particular position), but it is one of certain correspondence. Given the position of the light, and the form of the surface on which the shadow falls, the shadow itself can be precisely determined from the outline of the body, and *vice versâ*. Now the light in our case is the twilight of the Divine revelation as it veiled its brightness to shine in part upon a darkened world ; the surface on which it shone was formed by the crude religious ideas and half-barbarous morals of the chosen race—a race whose hearts were hard, and whose eyes were dim, and whose rugged nature of necessity distorted any spiritual truth which came to them. Such was the light shining upon such a surface ; the body was " of Christ," *i. e.* was the solid and enduring fulness of his salvation ; and the shadow which it threw before was the sacrifical system of the Jews. We should therefore expect from analogy to find (1) a general and unmistakable resemblance ; (2) a failure of resemblance in parts and proportions, a likeness mingled with distortion, as in the shadows cast upon a rugged slope by the rising sun. This is exactly what we do find, comparing the substance of the gospel with the shadows of the law. No human art could have constructed the Christian scheme from the fore-shadows which it threw, because no human skill could have allowed for the peculiarities of the Jewish dispensation. But, on the other hand, we can trace along the entire outline of the substance a correspondence to the shadow which cannot be due to chance. It is of course possible to admit the fact of this analogy, and to explain it by the assumption that Christianity itself was the creation of minds saturated with Jewish ideas, and habituated to the Jewish system of sacrifices. But if this had been the case, the correspondence had surely been more direct, and much less oblique than it is, much less subtle in parts and less unequal as a whole. It would seem as much beyond the practical powers of man to translate the types of the law into the substantial and consistent beauty of the gospel, as to reduce the irregularity and distortion of a shadow to the regular symmetry of the unseen human form. We have, therefore, in accordance with apostolic teaching, to regard the daily offerings, the sabbaths, the new moons, the sacred months and annual festivals of the Jews, as so many shadows which are of interest only as they in part resemble, and therefore in part illustrate, the body, the reality, which belongs to Christ, and so to us. Consider, therefore, with respect to *this system as a whole*—

I. THAT IT WAS DESIGNED TO CONSECRATE WITH BURNT OFFERINGS AND OBLATIONS THE WHOLE ROUND OF THE JEWISH CALENDAR. It formed a complete system, combining variety with regularity, under which every day by itself, every week in its seventh day, every month in its first day, every year in its seventh month and in its great festivals, was consecrated by the shedding of blood, by the acknowledgment that their lives were forfeit, by vicarious death, and by vicarious dedication of self to God. Even such is the pervading meaning and purpose of Christianity ; that our whole life from end to end should be consecrated to God by the blood of Christ, offered for us on the one hand, and on the other dedicated to God by a voluntary and perfect self-surrender. As the Jewish year was hallowed by an endless round of sacrifice, so the Christian life is sanctified by a never-exhausted self-sacrifice—the self-sacrifice of Christ wrought *for* us on the cross, the self-sacrifice of Christ wrought *in* us by his Spirit.

II. That the whole system rested upon the daily sacrifice, which was never omitted, to which all other sacrifices were superadded. Not even the triumph of the passover or the affliction of the day of atonement affected the daily sacrifice. Even so in Christ does all religious life rest upon the hallowing of each day, as it comes and goes, by the blood of the Lamb. Whatever special observance may be given to sacred days and seasons, or reserved for times of special grace, yet such only is true religion which is daily renewed and daily practised. And note that the daily use taking precedence of all additional observances testified even to the Jews of the underlying equality of all days as holy to the Lord. Since each day was essentially sacred, it followed that all distinctions of days were arbitrary and transitory. And this was undoubtedly what St. Paul desired to see realised in the Church of Christ (Rom. xiv. 5, 6; Gal. iv. 10, &c.).

III. That upon the daily use a sabbatic use was raised up with extreme care; not only the seventh day of every week, but also the seventh month of every year, being made festal and marked by special sacrifices. This was in truth arbitrary to the Jewish apprehension, although it was mystically connected with the relation between God and the world (Exod. xx. 11), and historically associated with the deliverance from Egypt (Deut. v. 15); but it served to keep the Jew in mind of, and bring him into connection with, an order of things above and beyond the labour and gain and profit and loss of this world. Even so, while the sacredness of the sabbatic number (in days or months or years) is vanished in Christ, yet the meaning of the number, the sabbath or rest of the soul in God, the rest from sin, from self, and from sorrow, is the dominant idea which we find in Christ first and last. This is his first invitation (Matt. xi. 28), and this his last promise (Rev. iii. 21).

IV. That to the daily and sabbatic use was added the new moon festival with great honour in the way of sacrifices; and this although the festival was one of natural, and not of sacred, origin. This may have been partly from a wise caution lest superstition should usurp what religion left unoccupied, but more because the God of grace is the God of nature, and he who made the Church made the moon to rule the night. Even so it is the will of God that all natural turning-points and periods in our lives should be consecrated by religion and hallowed with the blood of Christ; for our whole body, soul, and spirit are his. Religion does not war against nature, but takes nature under her patronage. Whatever springs naturally out of our physical and social life (not being evil of itself) may be and should be connected with religious sanctions, and adorned with holy gladness as before God.

V. That to the daily, sabbatic, and new moon use was added the observance of the three festivals which were associated at once with the facts of past deliverance and of present plenty. For the passover itself, which was mainly a commemoration, also marked the first beginning of the harvest; and the feast of weeks, which was essentially a harvest festival, recalled also the giving of the law on Mount Sinai. Even so in Christ, besides the other elements of religion, the sanctification of daily life, the hallowing of natural changes and outward events, the ceaseless seeking for rest in God, there must be found prominently the devout and grateful celebration of the great triumphs of redemption in the past, and of the abounding blessings of grace in the present. And note that none of these may be absent without grievous loss. The new moon feasts, which *seemed* so wholly secular, and would not keep time with the sabbaths of Divine obligation, were as much honoured as the days of passover. And so a religion which does not blend itself with and twine itself about the secular joys and interests of our natural life is wanting in a most important point, and is not perfect before God.

Consider again, with respect to *the ordered sacrifices*—

I. That the daily offering, which never varied, was one lamb. Even so the Lamb of God is the one sacrifice, εἰς τὸ διηνεκές, by which each day is sanctified—a continual burnt offering acceptable to God.

II. That the lamb was offered both morning and evening. Even so the Lamb of God was in a manner doubly offered: in purpose and will "from the foundation of the world" (Rev. xiii. 8), but in outward act only "in these last days" (Heb. i. 2), *i. e.* in the morning and the evening of the world.

III. THAT WHILE OTHER SACRIFICES WERE MOSTLY CONFINED TO THE MORNING HOURS, THE DAILY LAMB WAS OFFERED AT MORN AND EVE. Even so each day of life is to be sanctified by prayer at its opening and its close—prayer which is based upon the sacrifice of Christ.

IV. THAT THE LAMB, ALBEIT THE SUBSTANCE OF THE SACRIFICE, WAS NEVER PRESENTED WITHOUT ITS ACCOMPANYING MEAT AND DRINK OFFERINGS; and these considerable in quantity and value. Even so, while we plead the sacrifice of Christ, which alone is meritorious, we must offer with it the tribute of good works, such as are the result and outcome (like the flour and oil and wine) of human toil and industry making the most of Divine gifts; "for with such sacrifices," when sanctified and sustained by the one offering, "God is well pleased" (Heb. xiii. 16). See above on ch. xv. And note that the flour, the oil, and the wine, which made up the meat and drink offerings, may be typical of Christian labour, Christian suffering (cf. Gethsemane, the oil-press), and Christian gladness respectively (see on Ps. iv. 7; civ. 15; Zech. ix. 17).

V. THAT THE SPECIAL OFFERING FOR THE SABBATH MORN WAS ALSO THE SACRIFICE OF A LAMB, ONLY DOUBLED. Even so there is nothing in the devotions of the Lord's day different from those of any other day, save that we are to seek God through Christ with redoubled ardour.

VI. THAT THE NEW MOON FEAST CALLED FOR A LARGER NUMBER OF BURNT OFFERINGS THAN THE ORDINARY DAY OR THE SABBATH. Even so days of natural joy and festivity need to be more carefully and earnestly dedicated to God by supplication and by self-surrender than days of secular work or of religious rest.

VII. THAT A SIN OFFERING WAS ADDED TO THIS FEAST, AS WELL AS TO THE GREAT FEASTS OF THE SUMMER SEASON. Even so there is almost always sin in times of excitement—not only of secular excitement, but of religious excitement too. There is always occasion in them to seek forgiveness for sins of ignorance and negligence.

VIII. THAT THE FEAST OF TABERNACLES IN THE AUTUMN WAS ELEVATED BY A SPECIALLY ELABORATE RITUAL ABOVE ALL OTHER FEASTS; possibly because it foreshadowed the incarnation (see on John i. 14), but probably because it marked the consummation of the year, and so was typical of the gathering together in one of all things in Christ, and of the fulness of joy in heaven (Acts iii. 21; Ephes. i. 10; 2 Thess. ii. 1; Rev. xiv. 15, compared with xv. 3). Even so, whatever glories and gifts the gospel has for the present, its chiefest blessings are reserved for the end of all things.

IX. THAT THE CEREMONIAL OF THE FEAST OF TABERNACLES WAS ORDERED ON A SLOWLY DECREASING SCALE THROUGHOUT. Even so the law itself, like all things transitory and preparatory, was in its nature evanescent and doomed to dwindle. So again are all things ordered in the predestination of God, that the sabbatic number ("on the seventh day seven") may be finally fulfilled in the rest of heaven.

X. THAT IN ALL THESE SACRIFICES GOD SPAKE OF "MY OFFERING" AND "MY BREAD FOR MY SACRIFICES." Even so all our devotions and our worship are not ours, but God's. They are his because due to him; his because of his own do we give unto him; ours only because we are privileged to render them unto him. Here is the rebuke of all pride and self-esteem in what we offer unto God. "Nemo suum offert Deo, sed quod offert, Domini est cui reddit quæ sua sunt" (Origen). On the typical significance of the three feasts see on Exod. xii., and above, ch. ix.; Exod. xxiii.; Levit. xxiii.; Deut. xvi.

HOMILIES BY VARIOUS AUTHORS.

Vers. 3—8.—*The lessons of the daily burnt offering.* In verses 1 and 2 we have a general statement respecting offerings to God, reminding us (1) of the paramount claims of God (note repetition of "my" and "me"), and (2) the promptness and punctuality needed in meeting those claims ("in their due season"). Then follow directions as to the most frequent of these offerings—the daily burnt offering, which suggests lessons derived from—I. ITS CHARACTER; II. ITS CONTINUANCE.

I. It consisted of two parts: (1) a lamb, a bleeding sacrifice; (2) a meat and drink offering, flour, &c., bloodless; but the whole was to be burned before God. We see here—1. Expiation. This we need every morning, for we awake and leave our beds *sinful*, and requiring an atonement that we may be able to present acceptable service during the day. And we need it every evening that daily sins may be forgiven, and that we may rest at peace with God, "clean every whit" (John xiii. 10). 2. Dedication. In the burnt offering, as distinguished from the trespass offering, expiation by blood-shedding is taken for granted, but the burning, as the symbol of entire surrender to God, is the culminating point. The various parts of the burnt offering may be regarded as typical of our surrender to God of all the varied powers and gifts he has bestowed. (Illustrate from Rom. xii.) As Christ presented himself in complete sacrifice to God, so should we (Ephes. v. 2, &c.).

II. "A continual burnt offering" (ver. 3). So constant must the Christian's self-surrender be. With each morning comes the summons "*Sursum corda*," and the appeal, Rom. xii. 1. Evening brings rest from earthly toil, but no cessation from a renewed, continual dedication to God. We should desire no exemption from this continual offering of ourselves when we remember the motives to it. 1. We ourselves and all we have are God's. 2. We have enjoyed expiation through the perfect sacrifice of Christ. The law of the daily offering is urged because "ordained in Mount Sinai" (ver. 6). The law of Christian self-sacrifice was published by deed, and not by word, at Calvary (1 Pet. ii. 24; iii. 18). 3. Such sacrifice is pleasing, a sweet savour unto God "the Lord" (ver. 6). 4. Such acts insure Divine manifestations. See Exod. xxix. 38—43, which suggests that the neglect of the daily offering would interrupt communion with God. 5. Thus complete self-surrender brings us into the fullest sympathy with God, and thus into the most perfect liberty (Ps. cxix. 45; John viii. 36, &c.).—P.

Vers. 1—8.—*The daily offering.* I. THE PROPRIETY OF THE DAILY OFFERING. All the offerings were to be made in their due season, and every day that passed over the head of the Israelite people was a due season to make offerings to Jehovah in connection with the daily manifestations of his goodness. As what might be called the ordinary and common gifts of God came day by day, so it was appropriate for Israel to make ordinary and common offerings day by day. We must remind ourselves continually of the unfailing goodness of God. Whatever the special mercies in each individual life, there are certain great common mercies for us all, always something, in acknowledging which every one can join. We know that to God the mere offering was nothing, apart from the state of mind in which it was made. God gave the form, and it was required of the people that they should fill it with the spirit of acceptance, appreciation, and gratitude. We have, indeed, no command for daily offering now, no stipulation of times and seasons; but how shall we utter the petition, "Give us *this day* our daily bread," unless we feel that the bread is a daily gift? This one petition implies that petition, and therefore all the constituents of prayer, must belong to our life every day. There must be the feeling that although the actual production of the bread is spread over a long time, we have to take it in daily portions; and our physical constitution is in itself the witness to the daily duty of making an offering to God in return. We can store up grain for months, for the seven years of famine if need be, but we cannot store up thus the strength of our own bodies. Man is not a hibernating animal. "Give us this day our daily bread" implies daily strength to work for it, daily power within to assimilate it when eaten. And since spiritual supplies and strength are meant to be received in like fashion, an acknowledgment of these should be a principal thing in our daily offering. Considerations drawn from the thought of God's daily gifts, both for natural life and spiritual life, should be beautifully blended in our daily approaches to him. Notice that these daily offerings were appropriately mentioned here at a time *when the camp relation* (ch. ii.) *was about to be dissolved.* Israel was soon to be distributed, not only from Dan to Beersheba, but on both sides of Jordan. Hence the daily offering would be very serviceable in helping to manifest the unity of the people, and to preserve the feeling of it. It was also especially needful to be reminded of this national duty of daily offering after the humiliating apostasy to idols while Israel abode in Shittim (ch. **xxv.**). The only guarantee against the soul lapsing into idolatrous offerings is to be continually engaging in hearty and intelligent offerings to God.

II. IT MUST BE A MORNING AND EVENING OFFERING. To make a daily offering was not enough. Israel was not left to its own will as *to the time of day* for the offering. The sustaining of life is indeed going on all day long, by the secret and unfailing power of God, and the recognition of this power is always meet at any hour of day or night. But the day has its own peculiar blessings, and also the night, and they are to be made special in our thoughts, as they are made special in our experience. The dawn and the twilight bring each their own associations. In the morning we look back on the rest, the sleep, and the protection of the night, and forward into the work, the duties, the burdens, and the needs of the day. Similarly evening will have its appropriate retrospect and anticipation. That is no true thanksgiving which does not discriminate, marking the difference between thanksgivings which may be offered at any hour, and those which are peculiar to the morning and evening. The very recollection of the gradual regular changes in the time of sunrise and sunset should impart an ever-freshening sense of the faithfulness of God, and of how orderly and exact all his arrangements are.

III. THE CONSTITUENTS OF THE OFFERING. The lambs, the flour, the oil, the wine. *These were parts of the actual product of Israelite industry.* In presenting the lamb there was the thought that Israel had shepherded it, had watched over the little creature from the day of its birth, and taken all care to obtain the unblemished yearling for the burnt offering. All the shepherd's thoughtfulness, vigilance, and courage are represented in the offering. And mark, *these*, not as the qualities of one man, but of all Israel. The service of the particular man is merged in the shepherd-service of Israel as a whole. So with the offering of the flour; in it there is the work of the ploughman, the sower, the reaper, the miller. The oil is there because the labour of the olive has not failed, and the wine because men have obeyed the command, "Go work to-day in my vineyard." In presenting so much of the result of its work, Israel was thereby presenting part of the work itself. But these offerings were not only the result of work, *they were also the sustenance of Israel, and the preparation for future work.* The lambs, the flour, the oil, the wine were taken out of the present food store of Israel. The Israelites were therefore presenting part of their own life. If these things had not been taken for offerings they would soon have entered into the physical constitution of the people. The acceptability of the offering lay to a great extent in this, that it was from Israel's daily ordinary food. There would have been no propriety in making an offering from occasional luxuries. *The significance of the unblemished lamb thus becomes obvious.* The lamb for God was to be unblemished; but surely this was a hint that all the food of Israel was to be unblemished, as far as this could be attained. The presumption was that if Israel would only give due attention, there would be much of the unblemished and the satisfying in all the products of the soil. We are largely what we eat, and unblemished nutriment tends to produce unblemished life. The constituents of this offering further remind us of *the great demand on us as Christians.* It is the weighty and frequent admonition of Paul that we are to present our bodies to God as a living sacrifice. The offering is no longer one of dead animals, grain, &c., mere constituents of the body, and still outside of it. We are to offer the body itself, made holy and acceptable to God. We must so live then, we must so eat and drink, we must so order habit and conduct, that all the streams from the outside world which flow into us may contribute to the health, purity, and effective service of the whole man. Let everything be tested according to its ability to make us better Christians, and therefore better men. In relation to this great offering which is asked from us, let us ponder earnestly these typical offerings of ancient Israel, and set ourselves to fulfil the law connected with them. Here almost more than anywhere else let it be true of us that we are advancing

> "From shadowy types to truth, from flesh to spirit,
> From imposition of strict laws to free
> Acceptance of large grace, from servile fear
> To filial, works of law to works of faith."

Let life be an offering to God, and it will be hallowed, beautified, and glorified as it cannot otherwise be.—Y.

Vers. 9, 10.—*The sabbath offering.* I. THE LESSON OF THE SPECIAL OFFERING. Special blessings belonged to the sabbath, over and above those of the ordinary day, and it became a duty to recognise them. The sabbath offerings represented what Israel had gained by the rest of the sabbath. We make our gains not only by the food we eat and the work we do, but also by the intervals of rest in the midst of labour. Moreover, by this offering God indicated that the sabbath was to have its own appropriate occupation. Most emphatically, by 'precept (Exod. xx. 10), and by punitive example (ch. xv. 32—36), God had commanded to Israel the cessation from ordinary work. Here he indicates that the most effectual way of providing for cessation is to find a holy work to do. We cannot be too earnest in finding such a positive use of the day of rest as will please God and promote our own spiritual advancement. Surely, in the judgment, many who have reckoned themselves Christians will be convicted of a sore misuse of the weekly opportunity. We may be very precise and even punctilious in our abstentions, but what will this avail by itself? The mind that is not earnestly and comfortably occupied with Divine things will assuredly be occupied in thinking of things that belong to the ordinary day. As it is now, instead of the Sunday casting its brightness on the week-day, the week-day 'too often casts its shadow on the Sunday. God is able to make the appropriate occupation of his day, if we enter on it in a right spirit, a joy all the day long. In the world, and through the week, we have to deal with all sorts of men. There is the strain, the discord, and the suspicion that must belong to all human relations in this mixed and sinful state. The week-day is the world's day, wherein we cannot get away from the world. The Lord's day ought to be what the name suggests, the day for us to feel that we have not only to do with the hard conditions of a selfish world, but with One in heaven, who is most considerate, and most able to satisfy us with all good things.

II. THE LESSON OF THE DAILY OFFERING WHICH WAS NOT TO BE OMITTED. The sabbath, in respect of God's gifts and dealings in nature, was the same as an ordinary day, and therefore had to be acknowledged as such. So far as God's operations in nature are concerned all goes on without a break, Sunday and week-day alike. The sun rises as on other days, the clouds gather and the rain falls, the rivers run, and the tides flow and ebb. It is as true, Sunday as week-day, that in God we live and move and have our being. The great difference is that while God in nature is making all to go on just as usual, man, if he be in harmony with the will of God in Christ Jesus, is resting from his toils. God needs not rest in the sense in which we need it. He rested from the exercise of his creative energy, but not because of exhaustion. We, who have to eat our bread in the sweat of our face till we return to the ground, need that regular and frequent interval of rest which he has so graciously provided. And thus, coming as we sometimes do to the close of the week, utterly spent and exhausted, ready to welcome the brief respite from toil, we have the joy of recollecting, as we see God continuing on the sabbath his work in the natural world, that he is indeed the everlasting God, the Lord, the Creator of the ends of the earth, he who fainteth not, neither is weary. "He giveth power to the faint; and to them that have no might he increaseth strength" (Isa. xl. 28—31).—Y.

Vers. 11—15.—*The offering at the new moon.* Here the services rendered to man by God in nature are once again linked in with the duties of religion. As God required offerings in the morning and evening of every day, so on the day when the new moon fell there was an *additional* and largely increased offering. Why should such special notice be taken of this occasion?

I. THE MOON IS OUR OWN SATELLITE AND PECULIAR SERVANT. It has evidently been given for our special benefit. The sun serves us with our share, as it does the other planets that circle round it, but the moon is peculiarly ours. When, therefore, it had passed through all its phases, it was well to mark the renewal of service by a special offering. If it be said that Israel was not aware of this nice distinction between the services of the sun and moon, the distinction is nevertheless real, was known then to God, and is known now to us. The commandments of God took into consideration not only what was known at the time of their announcement, but what would be further discovered in the progress of human inquiry. We can see a propriety in this ordinance of the monthly offering, as we think of the peculiar relation which the moon alone of all the heavenly bodies sustains to our earth.

II. THE MOON IS AN EMBLEM OF APPARENT CHANGE AND YET REAL STEADFASTNESS. Thus it is an emblem of the way in which God's dealings appear often to us. The Unchanging One looks like a changing one, and it takes all our faith to be sure of his faithfulness. We talk of the waxing and the waning moon, but we know that the moon itself remains the same, that the change of appearance arises from change of position, and depends on how it catches the light of the sun. When we do see it, we see the same face always turned towards us, and mysterious as its movements are to the ignorant and the savage, they are nevertheless so regular that all can be predicted beforehand. The moon therefore is a peculiar and suggestive emblem of constancy, if we look on it aright. Juliet, indeed, in her love-sick prattle says,

> O, swear not by the moon, the inconstant moon,
> That monthly changes in her circled orb.

But appearance is one thing and reality is another, and we are reminded of one who found a very different emblematic value in the moon when he said, "They shall fear thee as long as the sun and moon endure, throughout all generations." The faithfulness of God is the same, even when his face is hidden, and when his mercy, like the waning moon, seems to diminish before our very eyes. The mysterious hindrances, sorrows, and gloomy peculiarities of our present life would be largely cleared up, if we only knew as much of the wheels within wheels of God's moral government, as we do of the wheels within wheels in the motions and relations of the heavenly bodies.

III. THE CONNECTION OF THE MOON WITH THE MONTH IS ALSO TO BE BORNE IN MIND. Spring, summer, autumn, winter, are. after all, vague terms. We mark the changing phenomena of the year far more accurately by the months than by the longer seasons. We speak of blustering March, showery April, chill October, drear December, and may we not suppose that the Israelites had somewhat of the same way of thinking with regard to their months?—each month with its own character and making its own contribution to the fulness of the year (Deut. xvii. 3; xxxiii. 14; 1 Sam. xx. 5; 2 Kings iv. 23; Ps. lxxxi. 1—4; lxxxix. 37; Isa. xxx. 26; lx. 20; Gal. iv. 10; Rev. xxii. 2).—Y.

Vers. 16—25.—*The feast at the passover time.* I. IT WAS A REMINDER OF HOW SERIOUSLY GOD'S GIFTS TO THE ISRAELITES HAD BEEN INTERFERED WITH. There was the gift of the day with its morning and evening, the gift of the new moon, and probably we shall not do wrong in concluding that the patriarchs understood and appreciated much of the blessing of the Sabbath. But what were these to the Israelites amid the bitterness of their bondage in Egypt? Pharaoh had taken the choice gifts of God and distorted them into agents of the most exquisite pain. Instead of having a heart for the morning and evening sacrifice, they were in a state such as Moses indicated might occur to them again in the event of disobedience (Deut. xxviii. 67). Their morning cry might justly have been, "Would God it were even!" and their evening cry, "Would God it were morning!" In Egypt they had not materials enough for daily work, let alone holy service. Thus we have a forcible illustration of the way in which spiritual evil has embittered all God's natural gifts. In the use of them, they get turned away from his intentions so as to serve the selfish purposes of some, and cause perhaps the life-long privations and miseries of others. We must indeed be thankful for what God gives, even when it is interfered with, for the gift shows the disposition of the giver, and it is a good thing for us to be at all times assured of this. But then we must also carefully mark how much there is in human society to intercept, distort, and even as it were transmute these loving and suitable gifts of God. The very abundance of the blessings which God is disposed to bestow, should lead us to view with much alarm, with deep and abiding concern, the obstacles which lie in the way of a complete and profitable reception of the blessings.

II. It was a reminder of how completely God had taken the obstacles out of the way. The week of unleavened bread was a period for joyous commemoration of the deliverance from Egypt; and by their offerings Israel recognised that the deliverance was entirely by the act of God. Israel did nothing but walk out of the prison-door when it was opened. This was an inestimable blessing, to be a free nation, even although a nation whose territory had yet to be gained. Liberty leads to all other blessings. We cannot rejoice too much in the spiritual liberty which Christ has achieved for the children of men. We are bound to commemorate it in fitting ways; ways adequate to glorify God, and to impress us more and more with the magnitude of the blessing we have gained. As to the particular mode of commemoration, every Christian must judge for himself, as in the sight of God, with respect to the due season (ver. 2). Easter has come as a matter of fact to have special associations and special value for many. They feel that they have proved the worth of the season in their own experience, and can amply justify the observing of it. Those of us who live outside the traditions, the habits of thinking, and the peculiar spirit fostered by the observance of an ecclesiastical year, can hardly claim to be competent judges of the value of such times and seasons. But mark one thing. *No observance can be worth calling such unless it commemorates an actual, personal deliverance.* God not only put his strong hand on the gaoler Pharaoh, but drew forth the captive Israel. When Christ our passover was sacrificed for the children of men, he brought them into a new relation to God, one of possible reconciliation to him, and possible liberty for the whole man. How far the reconciliation and liberty shall be actual depends on our personal repentance and faith.

III. The particular commemorative value of the unleavened bread. The people leaving Egypt were not allowed to finish the preparing of their bread according to their wont. They were hastened out of the land at a moment's notice. And it was not God who did this, as when the angels hastened Lot out of Sodom. The Israelites were thrust out *by the Egyptians themselves.* The gaoler himself was found a fellow-labourer with the liberator. Thus the unleavened bread becomes an impressive reminder of the complete rupture which God makes between his people and their spiritual enemies. As there could be no mistake about the effect which was produced in Egypt by the death of the first-born, so there can be no mistake about the efficacy of the blow which God in Christ Jesus has dealt on our great spiritual adversary. That our Saviour in his own person, and for himself, has completely conquered sin, is a fact which we cannot dwell upon too much, as full of hope for ourselves and for a sinful and miserable world.

IV. Note the season of the year in which this feast was observed. It happened in the first month of the year, made the first month on account of this very deliverance. How devoutly would the true Israelite look upon the beginning of this month! Hail! new moon which brings near the season for celebrating the deliverance from Egypt. Who can doubt that such a soul as Simeon kept the days of unleavened bread in the very spirit of them, living as he did in those dark humiliating times, which were Egypt over again, when the land of his fathers was captive, and the temple of his God neglected by its own custodians? It is the most fitting time to recollect the sure mercies of the past when we need a renewal and perhaps an increase of them.

V. The continual obligation of the daily offering. The bondage in Egypt embittered the gifts of God, yet even then a patient and willing soul would find something to be thankful for. And when liberty came, if right thoughts came with it, the gifts of God becoming available for use would inspire special thankfulness for the mercy that had made them so. How much God's daily blessings should be heightened and sweetened in our esteem by the larger use which we can make of them as believers in Christ! We must not under-value common, daily mercies even in the presence of God's unspeakable gift. He who is the brightness of the Father's glory casts something of that brightness on every gift of the Father's love. That is no right appreciation of God's mercy in Christ Jesus which does not lead us to a better appreciation of every other mercy. God, whose presence and power we are called to observe in the redemption of the world, would have us to see the same presence and power wherever we have faculties to see them. To go from the cross, with the meaning of it and the spirit of it filling our minds, and in such a mood to receive the common mercies of God as one by one they come to us, will fill them with a new power. Henceforth they will minister, not only to the wants of flesh and blood, but to our growth in grace and meetness for glory.—Y.

Vers. 26—31.—*The feast of the first-fruits.* I. A RECOGNITION OF THE ANNUAL SUPPLY OF FOOD FROM GOD. The day of the first-fruits was the day for bringing " a new meat offering unto the Lord " (ver. 26). This meat offering was to consist of two wave loaves made of fine flour (Levit. xxiii. 17). Hence by this an indication was given that the chief constituent of the daily meat offering would not be lacking during the following twelve months. Corn is appropriately singled out above all the fruits of the earth as furnishing the staple of man's food. Other things, even the oil and the wine, are to be counted as luxuries in comparison. The prominence here given to bread accords with our Lord's teaching, when he tells us to pray not for *daily food in general*, but for the daily *bread*. It was a good thing thus to mark in a special way the completion of the corn harvest, that which had been " sown in the field," and not to wait and merely include it when the labours of the year had been gathered in (Exod. xxiii. 16). God's mercy in the daily bread flows out of his mercy in the annual harvest. We are called upon to behold him, year after year, filling the storehouse whence day by day he draws and distributes the daily supply. As we behold the annual harvest we can join the appreciative souls of the world in thanking God for the *production* of bread. And then in the daily offering we equally thank him for the *distribution* of what has been produced.

II. A RECOGNITION OF GOD'S EFFECTUAL BLESSING ON HUMAN INDUSTRY. How much in the way of combined effort is suggested by the sight of a tiny grain of corn ! What mighty forces are represented there—heat, light, air, moisture, soil— all acting on a living germ ! And not only these. That grain also represents human industry, forethought, attention, patience, all crowned with the blessing of God (1 Cor. iii. 6). And if we look upon the grain now, we see the light of modern science brought to bear upon its growth and increase in addition to all the other necessary effort. We may be quite sure that God will bless all honest, intelligent, and sedulous effort to increase the fruits of the earth. After all these centuries, man hardly yet seems to appreciate the scope of that command, "Subdue the earth" (Gen. i. 28). Man has rather learnt to replenish the earth with those who use it as a vantage ground whereon to subdue and devour one another.

III. To a Christian the feast of the first-fruits must ever bring to mind THE ALL-IMPORTANT EVENT WHICH HAPPENED AT THE FIRST PENTECOST AFTER THE ASCENSION OF CHRIST. There was doubtless some weighty reason for choosing the time when the day of Pentecost was fully come as the time when the disciples were to be all filled with the Holy Ghost. There was a close connection, we know, between the Passover feast and the Pentecost feast. A complete week of weeks, a perfect period, intervened between that day of the Passover feast when a sheaf of the harvest first-fruits was waved before the Lord (Levit. xxiii.), and the day of Pentecost, when the full meat offering was presented. Thus in this interval the harvest was gathered in, and then by the Pentecostal service it was signified that in the strength of the food which he had gathered man could go on for another year. And as God chose the Passover season, when the great deliverance from Egypt was celebrated, for that death and resurrection of Christ whereby he delivers his people from guilt, and spiritual bondage, and helplessness, so he chose Pentecost for the entrance of that Holy Spirit who makes the deliverance to be followed by such unspeakable positive consequences. The risen Saviour gives liberty to those who believe in him, and then he gives the Holy Spirit, that the right of liberty may not be a barren gift. What is even a free man without daily food ? What advantage is it to a man if you liberate him from prison merely to turn him into a sandy desert ? The forgiven sinner with his awakened spirit and new needs has the evident fulness of God's Spirit to which he may continually apply himself. God availed himself of the place which Pentecost naturally held in the minds of the disciples to teach them a great lesson. Hebrew Christians were not likely to give up their old times and seasons, and so the Passover feast was still further glorified by the recollection of Jesus dying for them, and the Pentecost feast by the recollection of how the Spirit had been poured upon all flesh. It is very certain that we do not sufficiently appreciate the practical significance of that memorable Pentecost. It ought to stand in our minds side by side with that other memorable day when the Word that became flesh first breathed at Bethlehem the air of this sin-tainted world. Is it not a matter of the greatest significance that after Pentecost the Holy Spirit of God was among men as he was not before? What a blessing, and yet what a responsibility, to feel that thus and then he came, and, as he came, still remains!—Y.

Vers. 7, 12.—*A solemn fast and a joyous feast.* Lessons may be drawn from the dates and the order of these two annual solemnities, viz., (1) the day of atonement, on the tenth day of the seventh month; (2) the feast of tabernacles, on the fifteenth day of the same month. I. God's order is first an atonement; secondly, a festival. The expiation of the nation's sins on the most solemn day of the year was God's preparation for the most joyous season of the year (cf. Levit. xxv. 9—the trumpet of Jubilee was sounded on the day of atonement). The world's great atonement must precede the world's feast of tabernacles. The feast of tabernacles was—1. A commemoration of the nation's low estate during its life in the wilderness. The booths ordered probably lest they should, in their prosperity, forget the lowliness of their past condition (Deut. viii. 2—18). 2. A thanksgiving for harvest blessings ("feast of ingathering," Exod. xxiii. 16). We too may "keep the feast" (1 Cor. v. 8) of the Christian life as—(1) A grateful commemoration of the low estate out of which God called us. (Illustrate from Deut. xxvi. 1—11; cf. Ps. xl. 1—3; Ephes. ii. 4—7.) (2) A joyous feast of ingathering of spiritual harvest, of blessings for ourselves and others through the atonement of Christ (Ephes. i. 3, 7—13; 1 Pet. i. 3—5). II. The knowledge of personal reconciliation with God prepares for the joys of life. Each Israelite who was penitently confiding in God's mercy could appropriate the blessings of the day of atonement (cf. Rom. v. 1, 11; Gal. ii. 20). (Illustrate from 2 Chron. xxix. 27.) An accepted sacrifice brings songs to the offerer's lips. Humiliation precedes exaltation in Christ (Philip. ii. 7—11) and in Christians (Luke i. 52; John xvi. 20; James iv. 10). Those who "sow in tears" of genuine humiliation and "afflicting of the soul" on the tenth day shall "reap in joy" on the fifteenth. Many seek to reverse this order; e. g. Isa. xxii. 12, 13. III. Days of rejoicing are yet to be days of sacrifice. More sacrifices were offered at the feast of tabernacles than at either of the other great festivals. So the joys of life and the greater joys of salvation are to be the occasion of the more entire dedication of ourselves to God, and of cheerful service to others (Neh. viii. 9—12; Heb. xiii. 10—16).—P.

Ch. xxix.—*The offerings of the seventh month.* I. CONSIDER THE INCREASE IN THE OFFERINGS DURING THIS MONTH. There was the customary morning and evening offering for every day; the customary offering at the beginning of the month; and an additional offering, as if to signify that it was the beginning of a more than ordinary month. There would also be the appointed offerings on the sabbaths of the month. The tenth day of the month brought the great day of atonement, when there was to be much affliction of soul because of sin. Then, to crown all, there were the eight days of the feast of tabernacles, when an unusual quantity of offerings were presented. We may therefore consider the seventh month as being, conspicuously, a month devoted in Israel to the service of God. II. CONSIDER THE LESSONS WE ARE TAUGHT BY THIS MONTH OF SPECIAL SERVICE. 1. *Note that it was at the season of the year when the fruits were all gathered in.* "The feast of ingathering, which is in the end of the year, when thou hast gathered in thy labours out of the field" (Exod. xxiii. 16). There was thus a time of leisure—not the commanded leisure of the sabbath, but the natural leisure of the man who has finished his year's work. There is an interval between gathering the fruits of one year and preparing for the fruits of the next. *What is to be done with this time?* The answer is, *Man's leisure must be used for God.* Let there be a month largely occupied with special national approach to God. And, depend upon it, something similar is expected from us. There is nothing in which the lot of men is less equal than in the amount of leisure time which they have at their disposal. One man has to labour long hours and hardly finds a holiday all the year round, while another has abundant leisure. What an awful responsibility for the rich and selfish triflers who lounge away their lives in a world where so much may be done for the miserable and the needy! How he spends his leisure is one of the great tests of a man. Where his heart is, there he will go, when for a few hours he is slipped out of harness. If we are God's at all, all our time is God's. If our hearts are right with him, our greatest joy will be in our religion, and we shall hail, we shall grasp, every opportunity of increasing our knowledge of God, of the Scriptures, and of how to render that service to Christ which is so plainly expected from us. The spirit in which an Israelite entered on this festal month would be a great test of him altogether. 2. *If God requires a service out of the common, he will furnish sufficient opportunity for it.* God did not institute these services simply to fill up a leisure month. They had to be rendered at some time or other, and he selected a season when all the details of them could be most conveniently carried out. If God requires any service from us, we may be sure that he will make the duty of that service clear to conscience. It is not allowed to any of us to say, " I have no time for this service, no opportunity for it, therefore I cannot do it." The method of God is to put a service clearly before us, and then tell us to trust him for the making of a way. He will not allow us to plead want of time and opportunity, any more than he allowed Moses to plead want of ability (Exod. iv. 11, 12). Here is the reason why faithful and obedient spirits have been so successful. God has said " Go," and they have gone, when there seemed no way more than a single step ahead. Wherever God finds a real believer he makes a way for him, like that royal road to which the Baptist referred (Luke iii. 4, 5). We see here how the events of the ecclesiastical year are gathered and arranged. When the Israelites first received these commandments to make offerings, receiving them as they did at different times, they may have said to themselves, " How can we possibly get through so much ? " But here they are all put in order, and it is seen that there is a time for everything, and that everything can be done in its time. The lesser service prepares for the greater. God does well continually to ask his servants for more, because he is ever making them able to give more. 3. *The day of temporal fulness is the day of spiritual danger.* It is not only that the time of leisure is the time of temptation; there is a peculiar temptation in the leisure because it follows on worldly success. In such circumstances men are tempted to think of their own industry and skill more than of the needful blessing of God. Not without reason did the great day of atonement stand in this month. Everything is good which will force upon a man, in the midst of his worldly prosperity, a sense of the presence and claims of God. When Israel had a good harvest, the time of leisure that followed would be a time of great anxiety to many as to how they might most profitably dispose of the harvest. It is oftentimes the rich man who is in danger of having the least leisure; when his riches lie in capital, the use of which he must watch continually.—Y.

EXPOSITION.

CHAPTER XXX.

OF VOWS MADE BY WOMEN (vers. 1—16). Ver. 1.—**And Moses spake unto the heads of the tribes.** The regulations here laid down about vows follow with a certain propriety upon those concerning the ordinary routine of sacrifices (see ver. 39 of last chapter), but we cannot conclude with any assurance that they were actually given at this particular period. It would appear upon the face of it that we have in Levit. xxvii. and in this chapter two fragments of Mosaic legislation dealing with the same subject, but, for some reason which it is useless to attempt to discover, widely separated in the inspired record. Nor does there seem to be any valid reason for explaining away the apparently fragmentary and dislocated character of these two sections (see the Introduction). The statement, peculiar to this passage, that these instructions were issued to the " heads of the tribes " itself serves to differentiate it from all the rest of the " statutes " given by Moses, and suggests that this chapter was inserted either by some other hand or from a different source. There is no reason what-ever for supposing that the "heads of the tribes" were more interested in these particular regulations than in many others which concerned the social life of the people (such as that treated of in ch. v. 5—31) which were declared in the ordinary way unto "the children of Israel" at large.

Ver. 2.—**If a man vow a vow.** נֶדֶר, a vow, is commonly said to be distinctively a positive vow, a promise to render something unto the Lord. This, however, cannot be strictly maintained, because the Nazarite vow was *neder*, and that was essentially a vow of abstinence. To say that the vow of the Nazarite was of a positive character because he had to let his hair grow "unto the Lord" is a mere evasion. It is, however, probable that *neder*, when it occurs (as in this passage) in connection with *issar*, does take on the narrower signification of a positive vow. **Swear an oath to bind his soul with a bond.** Literally, "to bind a bond upon his soul." אִסָּר, a bond, which occurs only in this chapter, is considered to be a restrictive obligation, a vow of abstinence. It would appear that the *issar* was always undertaken upon oath, whereas the *neder* (as in the case of the Nazarite) did not of necessity require it. **He shall not break his word.** This was the general principle with respect to vows, and, as here laid down, it was in accordance with the universal religious feeling of mankind. Whatever crimes may have claimed the sanction of this sentiment, whatever exceptions and safeguards a clearer revelation and a better knowledge of God may have established, yet the principle remained that whatsoever a man had promised unto the Lord, that he must fulfil. Iphigenia in Aulis, Jephthah's daughter in Gilead, proclaim to what horrid extremities any one religious principle, unchecked by other co-ordinate principles, may lead; but they also proclaim how deep and true this religious principle must have been which could so over-ride the natural feelings of men not cruel nor depraved.

Ver. 3.—**If a woman vow a vow.** The fragmentary nature of this section appears from the fact that, after laying down the general principle of the sacredness of vows, it proceeds to qualify it in three special cases only of vows made by women under authority. That vows made by boys were irreversible is exceedingly unlikely; and indeed it is obvious that many cases must have occurred, neither mentioned here nor in Levit. xxvii., in which the obligation could not stand absolute. **In her father's house in her youth.** Case first, of a girl in her father's house, who had no property of her own, and whose personal services were due to her father.

Ver. 5.—**If her father disallow her.** It appears from the previous verse that the disallowance must be spoken, and not mental only. If the vow had been made before witnesses, no doubt the father's veto must be pronounced before witnesses also.

Ver. 6.—**If she had at all a husband.** Literally, "if being she be to an husband." Septuagint, ἐὰν γενομένη γένηται ἀνδρί. Case second, of a married or betrothed woman. As far as the legal status of the woman was concerned, there was little difference under Jewish law whether she were married or only betrothed. In either case she was accounted as belonging to her husband, with all that she had (cf. Deut. xxii. 23, 24; Matt. i. 19, 20). **When she vowed.** Rather, "and her vows be upon her." Septuagint, καὶ αἱ εὐχαὶ αὐτῆς ἐπ᾿ αὐτῇ. The vows might have been made before her betrothal, and not disallowed by her father; yet upon her coming under the power of her husband he had an absolute right to dissolve the obligation of them; otherwise it is evident that he might suffer loss through an act of which he had no notice. **Or uttered ought out of her lips.** Rather, "or the rash utterance of her lips." The word מִבְטָא, which is not found elsewhere (cf. Ps. cvi. 33), seems to have this meaning. Such a vow made by a young girl as would be disallowed by her husband when he knew of it would presumably be a "rash utterance."

Ver. 9.—**Every vow of a widow, and of her that is divorced.** This is not one of the cases treated of in this section (see ver. 16), but is only mentioned in order to point out that it falls under the general principle laid down in ver. 2.

Ver. 10.—**If she vowed in her husband's house.** Case third, of a married woman living with her husband. The husband had naturally the same absolute authority to allow or disallow all such vows as the father had in the case of his unmarried daughter. The only difference is that the responsibility of the husband is expressed in stronger terms than that of the father, because in the nature of things the husband has a closer interest in and control over the proceedings of his wife than the father has over those of the daughter.

Ver. 13.—**Oath to afflict the soul.** No doubt by fasting or by other kinds of abstinence. The expression is especially used in connection with the rigorous fast of the day of atonement (Levit. xvi. 29; Numb. xxix. 7; and cf. Isa. lviii. 5; 1 Cor. vii. 5).

Ver. 15.—**Then he shall bear her iniquity,** i. e. if he tacitly allowed the vow in the first instance, and afterwards forbad its fulfilment, the guilt which such breach of promise involved should rest upon him. For the nature and expiation of such guilt see on Levit. v.

HOMILETICS.

Vers. 1 — 16. — *Vows unto the Lord.* This section, although fragmentary, yet reveals to us with great clearness the Divine mind concerning one important portion of practical religion. It lays down directly the principle that vows to God were lawful and binding. It lays down indirectly the limitation (although it only applies it to the case of women not *sui juris*) that no vows to God were valid without the consent of the lawful guardian, if such there were. It implies the general rule that no vows are binding to the damage of any who are not parties to the vow; and this is itself a part of the yet wider principle that God is not served nor honoured by anything which involves the injury or dishonour of man. In applying the teaching of this chapter there is indeed the serious preliminary difficulty of deciding whether vows are lawful at all under the Christian dispensation. Inasmuch as no direct utterance can be found in the New Testament upon the subject, it can only be argued upon broad principles of the gospel, and will probably for ever continue to be decided in different ways by different people. It will be truly said upon one side that by virtue of our Christian baptism and profession our whole self is dedicate unto God, to live a life of entire holiness, such as leaves no room for further and self-imposed limitations and restrictions. On the other side it will be truly replied that although in principle all that we have and are is " not our own," but "bought with a price," and only held in trust by us for the glory of God and the good of men, yet in practice there are many different degrees of self-renunciation between which a good Christian is often called in effect to make his choice, and that his vow may be simply his answer to the inward voice which bids him (in this sense) " go up higher." It will be said, again, and truly said, that the law of Christ is essentially a law of liberty, and therefore inconsistent with the constraint of vows; that as soon as a man crosses his natural will, not because his higher will deliberately embraces pain for the sake of God, but because he is bound by a vow, his service ceases to be free and ceases to be acceptable. On the other side it will be said, and truly said, that just because we are under the law of liberty, therefore we are at liberty to use whatever helps Christian experience finds to be for practical advantage in the hard conflict with self; the law of liberty will no more strip the weakling of the defensive armour which gives him confidence than compel the strong man to hamper himself with it. Once more, it will be said that the Christian service is "reasonable," *i. e.* one which continually approves itself to the honest intelligence of him that renders it; but since it may happen to any to have his convictions altered by growing knowledge or greater experience, it is not fit that the conduct of any be permanently restrained by vows. And this is to a certain extent unanswerable. No vow could oblige a Christian to act contrary to his matured convictions of what was really best for him, and so for God. If, *e. g.*, one who had vowed celibacy came to feel in himself the truth of 1 Cor. vii. 9, he would be a better Christian in breaking than in keeping his vow; for we are not under the law, which rigorously enforces the letter, but under the Spirit, who loves only that which makes for true holiness. It may, however, be truly urged that while no vow ought to be held absolutely binding upon a conscience which repudiates it, yet many vows may be taken with all practical assurance that the conscience never will repudiate them. One thing of course is certain; all vows (at least of abstinence) stand upon the same footing in principle, however various an aspect they may wear in practice. A vow, *e. g.*, of total abstinence from intoxicating liquors is in principle exactly as defensible or as indefensible as a vow of perpetual celibacy; nor can an attempt to defend one while condemning the other be absolved from the charge of hypocrisy. This being the doubtful state of the argument, of which the true Christian casuist can only say, " Let every man be fully persuaded in his own mind," it remains to treat of vows in that sense in which they are allowed by all, viz., as promises made by the soul to God, whether fortified or not by some outward ceremonial, whether made in response to the more general persuasions of the gospel, or the more secret drawings of the Holy Spirit. Consider, therefore—

I. THAT A MAN MUST NOT BREAK HIS WORD UNTO GOD. If a man is obliged in honour (and wherever practicable in law too) to keep his promise to his brother man; if an honest man (even among savages), having given his word to his neighbour, may not disappoint him, though it were to his own hindrance (Ps. xv. 4); if God himself have vouchsafed to make promises to man (and with an oath too—Heb. vi. 17, 18), which promises he for his part will most surely keep and perform, how much more is man bound to keep his promise made to God!

II. THAT A PROMISE MADE TO GOD IN SICKNESS OR DISTRESS MAY NOT BE DEPARTED FROM IN HEALTH AND PROSPERITY. No doubt most vows were made under stress of some calamity or need, as Jacob's (Gen. xxviii. 20), Hannah's (1 Sam. i. 11), and others (cf. Ps. lxvi. 13; lxxvi. 11). Yet how often do men treat their God with such indignity! (1 Cor. x. 22).

III. THAT A RESOLUTION DELIBERATELY FORMED AND OFFERED UNTO GOD IS QUITE AS SACRED AS THOUGH MADE WITH AN OATH. For an oath is on the part of God a condescension which has no meaning for him (Heb. vi. 17), on the part of man a device to overawe his own sinful weakness, but it adds nothing to the real sacredness of the vow. How many vows have we taken upon ourselves, either openly or secretly! They are all as binding on us as though we had imprecated the most frightful penalties upon our failure to observe them. The punishment of Ananias and Sapphira was intended to mark the extreme malediction of such as secretly withhold from God what of themselves or of their own they have deliberately dedicated to his service.

IV. THAT NO PROMISE CAN BE MADE TO GOD IN DEROGATION OF THE JUST RIGHTS OF ANOTHER OVER US. God can never be served with that upon which another has a rightful claim, nor honoured by anything which involves dishonour of another. Only that which is really ours to give can we give unto God. If it be unworthy to offer unto the Lord of that which doth cost us nothing (2 Sam. xxiv. 24), it is unjust to offer unto the Lord of that which doth cost another something.

V. THAT IN PARTICULAR A DAUGHTER'S PRIMARY DUTY IS TO HER PARENT, A WIFE'S TO HER HUSBAND. Only what lies beyond the sphere of their legitimate claims can she sacrifice in the name of religion.

VI. THAT THE " RASH UTTERANCE OF THE LIPS " IS NOT HELD BINDING BY THE LORD. Since he utterly rejects any service which is not truly willing, and since he is infinitely above taking advantage of the folly of man, it is mere obstinacy, not religion, which leads a man to abide by what he has ignorantly and rashly said that he will do.

VII. THAT A FATHER OR A HUSBAND MAY NOT PLAY FAST AND LOOSE WITH THE RELIGIOUS PRACTICES OF THOSE DEPENDENT UPON HIM, NEITHER DISALLOW ONE DAY WHAT HE ALLOWED THE DAY BEFORE. It is given to them to exercise control even in religious matters, but not to exercise it capriciously. It is a fearful responsibility to cross the devout purposes of God's servants from any but the purest motives, and for any but the weightiest reasons.

VIII. THAT IF WE, THROUGH NEGLIGENCE OR CAPRICE, DISTURB THE SPIRITUAL LIFE, AND HINDER THE HEAVENLY DESIRES OF THOSE DEPENDENT ON US, WE MUST BEAR THEIR INIQUITY. We do not know indeed *how* such responsibility will be apportioned at the day of judgment, but we do know that God will exact vengeance for every injury done to souls, and especially for injury done to such as are committed to our care (Matt. xviii. 6).

HOMILIES BY VARIOUS AUTHORS.

Vers. 1, 2.—*The solemn obligation of the vow.* I. NOTICE THE ABSENCE OF ANY REFERENCE TO THE SUBJECT MATTER OF THE VOW. Moses does not say anything as to certain vows being right and certain others being wrong. This was not needed, and would only have taken away from the sharp and clear announcement that a vow once made was not to be lightly esteemed. Even the exemptions from obligation which Moses mentions in the remainder of the chapter are those caused not by anything unlawful in the subject matter of the vow, but by the fact that it proceeded from one who was not a sufficiently free agent to make a vow. It was quite evident that a vow must not contradict any commandment of God, nor infringe any right of other men. It must lie within the proper province of a man's own free will; it must concern such things as he can really control. This was what gave the vow its virtue and significance. Certain things were commanded, with respect to which there was no choice but obedience; and outside of these there was still a large field, where the Israelite was left to his own control. What use he would make of this freedom was of course a test of his own disposition. That he must keep clearly within his own freedom was a thing that needed no insisting upon.

II. CONSIDER THE NECESSITY THERE WAS FOR IMPRESSING ON THE ISRAELITES THE SOLEMN OBLIGATION OF THEIR VOWS. *How came the Israelite to make a vow?* We must recollect that in those days there was a general and practical belief in the power of supernatural beings to give help to men. The Israelites, only too often found unbelievers in Jehovah, were not, therefore, wanting in religious feeling. When they lost faith in the God of Israel, the lapse was not into atheism, but into idolatry. And thus when their hearts were strongly set on some object, not only did they put forth the effort of self and solicit the aid of others, but especially the aid of Jehovah. And as they sought the aid of their fellow-men under the promise of a recompense, so they sought the aid of Jehovah under a similar promise. Under the influence of strong desires and highly excited feelings all sorts of vows would be made by the Israelites, and some of them, probably, very difficult to carry out. Doubtless there were Israelites not a few with somewhat of Balak's spirit in them. They felt how real was the power of Jehovah, and, being as little acquainted with his character as Balak was, they concluded that his power could be secured on the promise of some sufficient consideration in return. Among an unspiritual people whose minds were filled with a mixture of selfishness and superstition, vows would take the aspect of a commercial transaction. So much indispensable help from God, and, as the price of it, a corresponding return from man. And as the help of God would be felt to require a much greater return than the help of man, so the vow would undertake something beyond the ordinary range of attainment. May we not conclude that the petition connected with the vow was oftentimes answered, and that God for his own wise purposes did give people the desires of their own hearts, even as he did to Hannah? If so, we see at once the difficulty that would often arise in fulfilling the vow. We know how the desire of a man's heart, once accomplished, is often felt to be unworthy of the effort and expenditure. Thus there would be a strong temptation to neglect the fulfilling of the vow if it could be safely managed. *It was an invisible God who had to be dealt with;* and ready enough as the Israelite might be to believe in Jehovah as long as it was for self-advantage, the faith in him and the fear of him would begin to wax feeble when it was a question of meeting what had proved a profitless engagement. A vow to an idol was really a vow to be paid to avaricious and watchful priests. A promise made to a fellow-man he may be trusted to exact. But what is a vow to the invisible God? "I may neglect it with impunity," is the thought in the Israelite's heart (Ps. l. 21; lxxiii. 11). But the impunity was a delusion. God had marked the vow only too carefully; and it was less harm for a man to go with some heavy burden and great hindrance hanging about him all the days of his life, than that the sanctity of the vow or oath should be slighted in the smallest degree.

III. CONSIDER HOW THE PRINCIPLES THAT UNDERLIE THIS INJUNCTION ARE TO BE CARRIED OUT BY CHRISTIANS. We are passed into an age when vows are not commonly made. Most of those whose thoughts are filled with the desires of their own hearts do not believe in the power of God to help them. And Christians ought to be free from such desires. It is their part to pray the prayer of the Collect for the fourth Sunday after Easter: "Grant unto thy people that they may love the thing which thou commandest, and desire that which thou dost promise." But though modern Christians may not have the same inducements to make vows as ancient Israelites, still there are certain principles and duties underlying this injunction of Moses which deserve our careful regard. 1. *Consider well the great projects and ruling views of your life.* Let the prayer of the above Collect be uttered on every Sunday and week-day throughout the year. Enter only on such undertakings as not merely accord with God's will, but spring from it. Nothing really accords with God's will save what springs from it. The sooner we discover that the most practicable life and the most blessed one is that of being not our own masters, but what the apostles learned to be, servants of the Lord Jesus Christ (Rom. i. 1 ; Philip. i. 1 ; James i. 1 ; 2 Pet. i. 1 ; Rev. i. 1), the better it will be for us. We shall not then enter upon undertakings which we lack the skill, the resources, and perhaps the heart to finish. This very injunction of Moses is a suggestion of the difficulties which come from a wrong choice. Under the power of excitement and in the ignorance of inexperience we may enter into engagements which afterwards become the burden and curse of life. 2. *Consider wherein the evil of a broken vow really consists.* Do not suppose that God considers it worse to violate a vow or an oath than to violate any other promise. Truth for the sake of truth is a sacred thing in the eyes of God. Who can doubt that in his sight the affirmation, now happily allowed in courts of justice, is as binding as any oath what-soever? Not but what a solemn appeal to the universal presence and all-seeing eye of Almighty God, if made *voluntarily*, and with evident conviction, earnestness, and sincerity in the mode of expression, is of great service in pressing home the truth. Witness the force of such an appeal in the writings of Paul. The evil has been in forcing the oath on all men irrespective of their disposition. No forced oath will make the liar really truthful ; and no forced oath can make the truthful man any-thing more than truthful. Administering oaths to a man of veracity is like holding a candle to make the sun shine. As has been truly said, the compelled oath makes the ignorant and superstitious to think that there are two kinds of truth, and that it is harmless to say, free from an oath, what it would be very wicked to say under it. 3. *Consider what deliberation is required in entering on the obligations of the Christian profession.* Here are promises which it is right to make ; yet they must be made with due caution, circumspection, and inquiry. Christ would have us avoid with equal care the perils of haste and procrastination. We cannot begin too soon seriously to consider the claims of God upon us, but we are warned against hastily plunging into obligations which before long may be altogether too much for our worldly hearts. It is only too evident that many are led into a profession of religion, either in a fit of excitement which cannot be sustained, and which, indeed, would be of no use if it could be sustained, or by an insufficient consideration of all that a profession of religion includes. Our Lord stops us at the very beginning with an earnest entreaty to measure well what we are about, and understand exactly what it is that he asks. We must not mistake his demands and claims, and put some notion of our own in place of them (Matt. vii. 21—29 ; xvi. 24—26 ; Luke ix. 57, 58 ; xiv. 25, 35 ; John vi. 44). 4. *Consider the great peril of being unfaithful to the knowledge of what is right.* It is a dreadful thing to fall away from truth when it is done in the light of knowledge, and in spite of the prickings of conscience. A broken promise, whether to God or man, broken not through infirmity, but of set and selfish purpose, is in God's eye a great transgression. No doubt in many infractions of promise there are complications and difficulties, pros and cons, which prevent every one save the all-searching God himself from determining the real character of the action. We need not make estimates of particular cases unless we are compelled. Let us keep our own hearts with all diligence, and labour to be on the side of self-denial and a good conscience rather than on that of carnal inclinations. God has made his yea and amen felt in Christ Jesus. So may Christ Jesus be able to make his yea and amen felt in the sincerity, simplicity, and straightforwardness of the lives of his people.—Y.

Vers. 3—16.—*The head of the household honoured and cautioned.* The command contained in this section of the chapter secures a double result. 1. By specifying certain exceptions to the validity of the vow, it makes that validity all the more manifest where the exceptions do not obtain. Stating exceptions to a rule is only another way of stating the rule itself. 2. These exceptions relate to the interests of the household, to the preservation of its integrity, and, to this end, of the rights and authority of the person whom God has placed at its head. Moreover, that which secures the right of the father and the husband equally secures the interests of the daughter and the wife. Consider—

I. WHAT THIS COMMAND IMPLIED WITH RESPECT TO THE HEAD OF THE HOUSEHOLD.

Let us take the relation of the father and daughter, similar things being true, *mutatis mutandis*, with respect to the husband and wife. 1. *This command honoured parental authority.* God had laid a solemn injunction on children to honour father and mother, and we see here how careful he was to honour the parental relation himself. He puts everything in the shape of a vow, everything which the daughter was otherwise free to choose, under the father's control. He requires no reason to be given; the simple veto is enough, if only it be uttered at the appointed time. The father had a responsibility which the daughter had not, and it was fitting that God should give the father all possible help in meeting that responsibility. 2. *This command required much watchfulness on the part of the father.* To act rightly here demanded the whole compass of paternal duty. The father was not allowed to say that his daughter's vow was no business of his. He himself might not be a vowing sort of person, and therefore under no temptation to neglect a vow he was not likely to make. But even if indifferent to vows himself, he was bound to be interested in his daughter's welfare, and do his best to keep her from future difficulties. Her limited life hid many difficulties from her eyes. It was not for a father to expose himself in later days to reproach from the lips of his own daughter. It was not for him to run the risk of hearing her say, " Why did not your larger knowledge and experience shelter me from difficulties which my inexperience could not possibly anticipate ? " 3. *This command required much consideration on the part of the father.* He must not let the vow pass without notice, and when he noticed it must be with proper consideration. While it was within his right to stop the vow, he might in stopping it be doing a very unfatherly thing, a thing very hurtful to the religious life of his daughter. As God had honoured him and undertaken to help him in his fatherly relation, he must honour that relation himself. That relation from which God expects so much must be prepared to yield much in the way of care and consideration. The father may think too much of his own wishes, too little of his daughter's needs, and too little of the will of God. The vow of the daughter might be a rightful, helpful, and exemplary one, a vow of the Nazarite indeed (ch. vi. 2). It was not enough, therefore, for the father to fall back on the mere assertion of authority. It is a serious thing to offend one of the little ones—a serious thing for any one to do; but how unspeakably serious when the hand which casts down the stumbling-block is that of a father! 4. *This command required, in order to be fully complied with, sympathy with the voluntary spirit in religion.* A father who felt that the services of religion consisted chiefly in exact external conformity with certain rules for worship and conduct would be very likely to stop his daughter's vow as mere whimsicality. But religion must go beyond obedience to verbal commands; it must aim at something more than can be put into even the most exact and expressive of them. Commands are nothing more than finger-posts; and the joys of hope and preparation during the journey are directed towards something lying beyond the last of the finger-posts. The father who would act rightly by all possible wishes of his children must be one who comprehends that experience of John : " We love him because he first loved us " (1 John iv. 19). He must be one who feels that love can never be satisfied with mere beaten tracks and conventional grooves. He must be such a one as appreciates the act of the woman who poured the precious ointment on the head of Jesus. If he be a man of the Judas spirit, grudging what he reckons waste, he is sure to go wrong. He will check his children when he ought to encourage them, and encourage when he ought to check. If God opens their eyes he will do his best to close them again, so that the blind father may go on leading the blind children, till at last both fall into the pit.

II. WHAT THIS COMMAND IMPLIED WITH RESPECT TO THE DAUGHTER AND THE WIFE. 1. *Their right to make a vow was itself secured.* The command did not say that daughter and wife were to make no vow at all. They were as free *to make a vow* as any man in all Israel; and if it had not been for more important considerations connected with the household, they would also have been free to keep the vow. God would have us to understand that inferior and mutilated duties or privileges are no necessary consequence of a subordinate position. 2. *A gentle and patient submission was recommended on the part of the daughter and the wife.* The right to propose the vow being secured to every woman, it was no fault of hers, and would be counted no blame, if the father or husband cancelled it. The Nazarite vow might be thwarted in the very freshness of it, but the spirit of zeal which produced it needed not to grow languid. We cannot be hindered in the attainment of any good, save by our own negligence. God will meet us amid all restraints which untoward circumstances may impose upon us. The claims rising out of natural relations and the present needs of human society are imperative while they last, and must be respected. But they will not last for ever. "In the resurrection they neither marry nor are given in marriage" (Matt. xxii. 30).—Y.

EXPOSITION.

CHAPTER XXXI.

EXTERMINATION OF THE MIDIANITES (vers. 1—54). Ver. 1. — **The Lord spake unto Moses.** The command to "vex the Midianites, and smite them," had been given before (ch. xxv. 17), but how long before we cannot tell. Possibly the interval had been purposely allowed in order that the attack when it was made might be sudden and unexpected. From the fact that no resistance would seem to have been made to the Israelitish detachment, and that an enormous amount of plunder was secured, we may probably conclude that the Midianites had thought all danger past.

Ver. 2.—**Avenge the children of Israel of the Midianites.** The war was to be distinctly one of vengeance on the part of Israel. On the grave moral question which arises out of this war, and of the manner in which it was carried on, see the note at the end of the chapter. **Afterward shalt thou be gathered unto thy people.** It is quite possible that Moses himself had been reluctant to order the expedition against Midian, either because it involved so much bloodshed, or, more probably, because he foresaw the difficulty which actually arose about the women of Midian. If so, he was here reminded that his place was to obey, and that his work on earth was not done so long as the Midianites remained unpunished.

Ver. 3. — **Avenge the Lord of Midian.** God, speaking to Moses, had commanded a war of vengeance; Moses, speaking to the people, is careful to command a war of religious vengeance. In seducing the people of the Lord the Midianites had insulted and injured the majesty of God himself. On the question why Midian only, and not Moab also, was punished see on ch. xxv. 17. It is to be remembered that, however hateful the sins of licentiousness and idolatry may be, they have never aroused by themselves the exterminating wrath of God. Midian was smitten because he had deliberately used these sins as weapons wherewith to take the life of Israel.

Ver. 5.—**There were delivered,** or "levied." יִמָּסְרוּ. Septuagint, ἐξηρίθμησαν. The Hebrew word is only used here and in

ver. 16 (see note there), and in these two places not in the same sense. The context, however, leaves little or no doubt as to the meaning which it must bear.

Ver. 6.—**And Phinehas the son of Eleazar.** The high priest himself could not leave the camp and the sanctuary, because of his duties, and because of the risk of being defiled (see ver. 19); but his son, who was already marked out as his successor, could act as his representative (see on ch. xvi. 37). In after times the Messiah Milchama ("Sacerdos unctus ad bellum," alluded to in Deut. xx. 2) who accompanied the army to the field was a recognised member of the Jewish hierarchy. Phinehas was of course specially marked out by his zeal for the present duty, but we may suppose that he would have gone in any case. **With the holy instruments, and the trumpets.** Septuagint, καὶ τὰ σκεύη τὰ ἅγια, καὶ αἱ σάλπιγγες. The word "instruments" (כְּלֵי) is the same more usually translated "vessel," as in ch. iii. 31, and is apparently to be understood of the sacred furniture of the tabernacle. It is difficult to understand what "holy vessels" could have accompanied an expedition of this sort, unless it were the ark itself. The Israelites were accustomed at all critical times to be preceded by the ark (ch. x. 33; Josh. iii. 14; vi. 8), and the narrative of 1 Sam. iv. 3 sq. shows plainly that, long after the settlement at Shiloh, no scruples existed against bringing it forth against the foes of Israel and of God. Indeed there is a resemblance in the circumstances between that case and this which is all the more striking because of the contrast in the result. Most modern commentators, unwilling to believe that the ark left the camp (but cf. ch. xiv. 44), identify the "holy instruments" with "the trumpets;" this, however, is plainly to do violence to the grammar, which is perfectly simple, and is contrary to the Septuagint and the Targums. The Targum of Palestine paraphrases "holy instruments" by Urim and Thummim; these, however, as far as we can gather, seem to have been in the exclusive possession of the high priest.

Ver. 8.—**They slew the kings of Midian, beside the rest of them that were slain.** This is more accurately rendered by the Septuagint, τοὺς βασιλεῖς . . ἀπέκτειναν ἅμα τοῖς τραυματίαις αὐτῶν : "they put to death (הָרַג) the kings, in addition to those who fell in battle" (from חָלַל, to pierce, or wound). These five kings, who are mentioned here as having been slain in cold blood after the battle, are said in Josh. xiii. 21 to have been vassals (נְסִיכֵי) of the Amoritish king Sihon, and to have dwelt "in the country." From this it has been concluded by some that the Midianites at this time destroyed included only certain tribes which had settled down within the territory afterwards assigned to Reuben, and had become tributary to Sihon. This would account for the fact that the present victory was so easy and so complete, and also for the otherwise inexplicable fact that the Midianites appear again as a formidable power some two centuries later. **Zur.** The father of Cozbi (ch. xxv. 15). **Balaam also . . they slew with the sword.** Not in battle, but, as the context implies, by way of judicial execution (see on ch. xxiv. 25 ; Josh. xiii. 22).

Ver. 10.—**Their goodly castles.** טִירֹתָם. Septuagint, ἐπαύλεις. . This word, which occurs only here and in Gen. xxv. 16, no doubt signifies the pastoral villages, constructed partly of rude stone walls, partly of goats-hair cloth, which the nomadic tribes of that country have used from time immemorial. Probably these were the proper habitations of the Midianites ; the "cities" would have belonged to the previous inhabitants of the land.

Ver. 11.—**The spoil.** הַשָּׁלָל. Septuagint, τὴν προνομήν. The booty in goods. **The prey.** הַמַּלְקוֹחַ. Septuagint, τὰ σκῦλα. The booty in live-stock, here including the women and children, who are distinguished as "captives" (שְׁבִי) in the next verse.

Ver. 14.—**Officers of the host.** Literally, "inspectors." Septuagint, τοῖς ἐπισκόποις τῆς δυνάμεως.

Ver. 16.—**To commit trespass.** לִמְסָר־מַעַל. See on ver. 5. The word מסר seems to be used here much as the English word "levy" is used in such a phrase as "levying" war against a person.

Ver. 18.—**Keep alive for yourselves,** i. e. for domestic slaves in the first instance. Subsequently no doubt many of them became inferior wives of their masters, or were married to their sons. Infants were probably put to death with their mothers.

Ver. 19.—**Do ye abide without the camp.** In this case at any rate the law of ch. xix. 11 sq. was to be strictly enforced. **And your captives,** i. e. the women children who were spared. No peculiar rites are here prescribed for the reception of these children of idolaters

into the holy nation with which they were to be incorporated beyond the usual lustration with the water of separation. In after times they would have been baptized.

Ver. 20.—**Purify all your raiment, and all that is made.** Literally, "every vessel" (כְּלִי). This was in accordance with the principle laid down in ch. xix. that everything which had come into contact with a corpse needed purifying.

Ver. 21.—**And Eleazar the priest said, . . This is the ordinance of the law** (חֻקַּת הַתּוֹרָה, "law-statute," as in ch. xix. 2) **which the Lord commanded Moses.** There is something peculiar in this expression which points to the probability, either that this paragraph (vers. 21—24) was added after the death of Moses, or that "the law" was already beginning, even in the lifetime of Moses, to assume the position which it afterwards held—that, viz., of a fixed code to be interpreted and applied by the living authority of the priesthood. This is the earliest instance of the high priest declaring to the people what the law of God as delivered to Moses was, and then applying and enlarging that law to meet the present circumstances. It is no doubt possible that Eleazar referred the matter to Moses, but it would seem on the face of the narrative that he spoke on his own authority as high priest. When we compare the ceremonial of the later Jews, so precisely and minutely ordered for every conceivable contingency, with the Mosaic legislation itself, it is evident that the process of authoritative amplification must have been going on from the first; but it is certainly strange to find that process begun while Moses himself was alive and active.

Ver. 22.—**The brass.** Rather, "copper." The six metals here mentioned were those commonly known to the ancients, and in particular to the Egyptians and Phœnicians.

Ver. 23.—**Ye shall make it go through the fire.** This was an addition to the general law of lustration in ch. xix. founded on the obvious fact that water does not cleanse metals, while fire does. The spoils of the Midianites required purification, not only as being tainted with death, but as having been heathen property.

Ver. 26.—**Take the sum of the prey.** No notice is taken here of the spoil (see on ver. 11), but only of the captured children and cattle. **And the chief fathers.** Perhaps אָבוֹת (fathers) stands here for בֵּית־אָבוֹת (fathers' houses). So the Septuagint, οἱ ἄρχοντες τῶν πατριῶν.

Ver. 27.—**Divide the prey into two parts.** This division was founded roughly upon the equity of the case ; on the one hand, all Israel had suffered from Midian ; on the other, only the twelve thousand had risked their lives to smite Midian. For the application of a like principle to other cases see Josh. xxii. 8; 1 Sam. xxx. 24; 2 Macc. viii. 28, 30.

Ver. 29.—**An heave offering unto the Lord.** Septuagint, τὰς ἀπαρχὰς Κυρίου. The Hebrew word רוּם (to lift) from which *terumah* is derived, had practically lost its literal significance, just as the English word has in the phrase "to lift cattle;" hence *terumah* often means simply that which is set aside as an offering. No doubt the offering levied on the portion of the warriors was in the nature of tithe for the benefit of Eleazar and the priests.

Ver. 30.—**One portion of fifty.** Two per cent. of the prey. This probably corresponded very closely to the number of Levites as compared with the twelve tribes, and would tend to show that God intended the Levites to be neither better nor worse off than their neighbours.

Ver. 32.—**The booty, being the rest of the prey.** Rather, "the prey (הַמַּלְקוֹחַ, see on ver. 11), to wit, the rest of the booty" (הַבַּז, as in ch. xiv. 3, 31). Septuagint, τὸ πλεόνασμα τῆς προνομῆς, *i. e.* what actually remained to be divided. The numbers given are obviously round numbers, such as the Israelites seem always to have employed in enumeration. The immense quantity of cattle captured was in accordance with the habits of the Midianites in the days of Gideon (Judges vi. 5) and of their modern representatives to-day.

Ver. 49.—**There lacketh not one man of us.** The officers naturally regarded this as a very wonderful circumstance; and so indeed it was, whether Midian made any resistance or not. It was, however, in strict keeping with the promises of that temporal dispensation. It would have been no satisfaction to the Israelite who fell upon the threshold of the promised land to know that victory remained with his comrades. His was not the courage of modern soldiers, who fling away their lives in blind confidence that some advantage will accrue thereby to the army at large ; rather, he fought under the conviction that to each, as well as to all, life and victory were pledged upon condition of obedience and courage. In this case no one was found unfaithful, and therefore no one was allowed to fall.

Ver. 50.—**What every man hath gotten.** The whole, apparently, of their booty in golden ornaments was given up as a thank offering, and in addition to this was all that the soldiers had taken and kept. The abundance of costly ornaments among a race of nomads living in squalid tents and hovels may excite surprise; but it is still the case (under circumstances far less favourable to the amassing of such wealth) among the Bedawin and kindred tribes (see also on Judges viii. 24—26). **Chains.** אֶצְעָדָה. Septuagint, χλιδῶνα. Clasps for the arm, as in 2 Sam. i. 10. **Tablets.** כּוּמָז. Probably golden balls or beads hung round the neck (see on Exod. xxxv. 22). A different word is used in Isa. iii. 20.

Ver. 52.—**Sixteen thousand seven hundred and fifty shekels.** If the shekel of weight be taken as ·66 of an ounce, the offering will have amounted to more than 11,000 ounces of gold, worth now about £40,000. If, according to other estimates, the golden shekel was worth 30s., the value of the offering will have been some £25,000.

Ver. 54.—**Brought it into the tabernacle of the congregation.** It is not said what was done with this enormous quantity of gold, which must have been a cause of anxiety as well as of pride to the priests. It may have formed a fund for the support of the tabernacle services during the long years of neglect which followed the conquest, or it may have been drawn upon for national purposes. **A memorial.** To bring them into favourable remembrance with the Lord. For this sense of זִכָּרוֹן (Septuagint, μνημόσυνον) cf. Exod. xxviii. 12, 29.

NOTE ON THE EXTERMINATION OF THE MIDIANITES.

The grave moral difficulty presented by the treatment of their enemies by the Israelites, under the sanction or even direct command of God, is here presented in its gravest form. It will be best first to state the proceedings in all their ugliness ; then to reject the false excuses made for them ; and lastly, to justify (if possible) the Divine sanction accorded to them.

I. That the Midianites had injured Israel is clear ; as also that they had done so deliberately, craftily, and successfully, under the advice of Balaam. They had so acted as if *e. g.* a modern nation were to pour its opium into the ports of a dreaded neighbour in time of peace, not simply for the sake of gain (which is base enough), but with deliberate intent to ruin the morals and destroy the manhood of the nation. Such a course of action, if proved, would be held to justify any reprisals possible within the limits of legitimate war; Christian nations have avenged far less weighty injuries by bloody wars in this very century. Midian, therefore, was attacked by a detachment of the Israelites, and for some reason seems to have been unable either to fight or to fly. Thereupon all the men (*i. e.* all who bore arms) were slain; the towns and hamlets were destroyed; the women, children, and cattle driven off as booty. So far the Israelites had but followed the ordinary customs of war, with this great exception in their favour, that they offered (as is evident from the narrative) no violence to the women. Upon their return to the camp Moses was greatly displeased at the fact of the Midianitish women having been brought in, and gave orders that all the male children and all the women who were not virgins were to be slain. The inspection necessary to determine the latter point was left presumably to the soldiers. The Targum of Palestine indeed inserts a fable concerning some miraculous, or rather magical, test which was used to decide the question in each individual case. But this is simply a fable invented to avoid a disagreeable conclusion; both soldiers and captives were unclean, and were kept apart; and the narrative clearly implies that there was no communication between them and the people at large until long after the slaughter was over. To put the matter boldly, we have to face the fact that, under Moses' directions, 12,000 soldiers had to deal with perhaps 50,000 women, first by ascertaining that they were not virgins, and then by killing them in cold blood. It is a small additional horror that a multitude of infants must have perished directly or indirectly with their mothers.

II. It is commonly urged in vindication of this massacre that the war was God's war, and that God had a perfect right to exterminate a most guilty people. This is true in a sense. If God had been pleased to visit the Midianites with pestilence, famine, or hordes of savages worse than themselves, no one would have charged him with injustice. All who believe in an over-ruling Providence believe that in one way or other God has provided that great wickedness in a nation shall be greatly punished. But that is beside the question altogether; the difficulty is, not that the Midianites were exterminated, but that they were exterminated in an inhuman manner by the Israelites. If they had been so many swine the work would have been revolting; being men, women, and children, with all the ineffaceable beauty, interest, and hope of our common humanity upon them, the very soul sickens to think upon the cruel details of their slaughter. An ordinarily good man, sharing the feelings which do honour to the present century, would certainly have flung down his sword and braved all wrath human or Divine, rather than go on with so hateful a work; and there is not surely any Christian teacher who would not say that he acted quite rightly; if such orders proceeded from God's undoubted representative to-day, it would be necessary deliberately to disobey them.

It is urged again that the question at issue really was, "whether an obscene and debasing idolatry should undermine the foundations of human society," or whether an awful judgment should at once stamp out the sinners, and brand the sin for ever. But no such question was at issue. There were obscene and debasing idolatries in abundance round about Israel, but no effort was made to exterminate them; the Moabites in particular seem to have been just as licentious as the Midianites at this time (see ch. xxv. 1—3), and certainly were quite as idolatrous, and yet they were passed by. Indeed the argument shows an entire failure, so to speak, in moral perspective. Harlotry and idolatry are great sins, but there is no reason to believe that God deals with them otherwise than he does with other sins. It was no part of the Divine intention concerning Israel that he should go about as a knight-errant avenging "obscene idolatries." Many a nation just as immoral as Midian rose to greatness, and displayed some valuable virtues, and (it is to be presumed) did some good work in God's world in preparation for the fulness of time. Harlotry and idolatry prevail to a frightful extent in Great Britain; but any attempt to pursue them with pains and penalties would be scouted by the conscience of the nation as Pharisaical. The fact is (and it is so obvious that it ought not to have been overlooked) that Midian was overthrown, not because he was given over to an "obscene idolatry," wherein he was probably neither much better nor much worse than his neighbours; but because he had made an unprovoked, crafty, and successful attack upon God's people, and had brought thousands of them to a shameful death. The motive which prompted the attack upon them was not horror of their sins, nor fear of their contamination, but vengeance; Midian was smitten avowedly "to avenge the children of Israel" (ver. 2) who had fallen through Baal-peor, and at the same time "to avenge the Lord" (ver. 3), who had been obliged to slay his own people.

III. The true justification of these proceedings—which we should now call, and justly call, atrocities—divides itself into two parts. In the first place, we have to deal only with the fact that an expedition was sent by Divine command, to smite the Midianites. Now, this does indeed open up a very difficult moral question, but it does not involve any special difficulty of its own. It is certain that wars of revenge were freely sanctioned under the Old Testament dispensation (see on Exod. xvii. 14—16; 1 Sam. xv. 2, 3). It is practically conceded that they are permitted by the New Testament dispensation. At any rate Christian nations habitually wage wars of revenge even against half-armed savages, and many of those who counsel or carry on such wars are men of really religious character. It is possible that if the principles of the New Testament take a deeper hold upon the national conscience, all such wars will be regarded as crimes. This means simply, that in regard to war the moral sentiment of religious people has changed, and is changing very materially from age to age. Even a bad man will shrink from doing to-day what a good man would have done without the least scruple some centuries ago; and (if the world last) a bad man will be able sincerely to denounce some centuries hence what a good man can bring himself to do with a clear conscience to-day. Now it has been pointed out again and again that when God assumed the Jews to be his peculiar people, he assumed them not only in the social and political stage, but in the moral stage also, which belonged to their place in the world and in history. Just as God adopted, as King of Israel, the social and political ideas which then prevailed, and made the best of them; in like manner he adopted the moral ideas then current, and made the best of them, so restraining them in one direction, and so enforcing them in another, and so bringing them all under the influence of religious sanctions, as to prepare the way for the bringing in of a higher morality. What God did for the Jews was not to teach them the precepts of a lofty and perfect morality, which was indeed only possible in connection with the revelation of his Son, but to teach them to act in all things from religious motives, and with direct reference to his good pleasure. Accordingly God himself, especially in the earlier part of their history as a nation, undertook to guide their vengeance, and taught them to look upon wars of vengeance (since their conscience freely sanctioned them) as waged for his honour and glory, not their own. If this seem to any one unworthy of the Divine Being, let him consider for a moment, that on no other condition was the Old Testament dispensation possible. If God was to be the Head of a nation among nations, he must regulate all its affairs, personal, social, and national. We escape the difficulty, and wage wars of vengeance, and commit other acts of doubtful morality, without compromising our religion, because our religion is strictly personal, and our wars are strictly national. But the Old Testament dispensation was emphatically temporal and national ; all responsibility for all public acts devolved upon the King of Israel himself. It was absolutely necessary, then, either that God should reveal Christian morality without Christ (which is as though one should have heat without the sun, or a poem without a poet) ; or that he should sanction the morality then current in its best form, and teach men to walk bravely and devoutly according to the light of their own conscience. That light was dim enough in some ways, but it was slowly growing clearer through the gradual revelation which God made of himself ; and even now it is growing clearer, and still while religion remains fundamentally the same, morality is distinctly advancing, and good people are learning to abhor to-day what they did in the faith and fear of God but yesterday. Take, e. g., that saying, "Vengeance is mine, I will repay." For the Jew it meant that in waging wars of vengeance he fought as the Lord's soldier and not as in a private quarrel. For the Christian of the present day it means that revenge of private injuries is to be left altogether to the just judgment of the last day. To the Christian of some future age it will mean that all revenge for injuries and humiliations, private or public, individual or national, must be left to the justice of him who ordereth all things in this world or the world to come. Each has a different standard of morality ; yet each, even in doing what another will abhor, may claim the Divine sanction, for each acts truly and religiously according to his lights.

This being so, it is only necessary further to point out that the slaying of all the men whom they could get at was the ordinary custom of war in those days, when no distinction could be drawn between combatants and non-combatants. The practice of war in this respect is entirely determined by the sentiment of the age, and is always in the nature of a compromise between the desire to kill and the desire to spare. As these two desires can never be reconciled, they divide the field between them with a curious inconsistency. The first is satisfied by the ever-increasing destructiveness of war ; the second is gratified by the alleviations which strict discipline and skilled assistance can procure for the vanquished and the wounded. Whether ancient or modern wars really left the larger tale of misery behind them is a matter of great doubt ; but at any rate the custom of war sanctioned the slaughter of all the combatants, i. e. of all the men, at that time ; and if war is to be waged at all, it must be allowed to follow the ordinary practice.

In the second place, however, we have to deal with horrors of an exceptional character, in the subsequent slaughter of the women and boys. Now it is to be observed that the orders for this slaughter proceeded from Moses alone. According to the narrative of vers. 13 sq., Moses went out of the camp, and on perceiving the state of the case, gave instructions at once while his anger was hot. It is possible that he sought for Divine guidance, but it does not appear that he did, but rather that he acted upon his own judgment, and under the ordinary guidance of his own conscience. We have not, therefore, to face the difficulty of a direct command from God, but only the difficulty of a holy man, full of heavenly wisdom, having ordered a butchery so abhorrent to our modern feelings. Let it then in all fairness be observed—1. That Moses was not responsible for the presence of these captives. They ought either to have been killed, or left in their own land ; it was either the cupidity or the mistaken pity of the soldiers which brought them there. 2. That Moses could not tolerate their presence in the host. It seems a vile thing to kill a woman, but it was the women more than the men of Midian of whom they had just reason to be afraid. In justice to the men, in fairness to the wives, of Israel, it was simply impossible to let them loose upon the camp. Again, it seems cowardly to slay a helpless child; yet to suffer a generation of Midianites to grow up under the roofs of Israel would have been madness and worse, for it would have been to court a great and perhaps fatal national disaster. For the sake of Israel the captive women and children must be got rid of, and this could only be done either by slaughtering the women and boys, or by taking them back to their desolated homes to perish of hunger and disease. Of the two courses Moses certainly chose the more merciful. The nation was exterminated; the girls only were spared because they were harmless then, and likely to remain harmless; distributed through the households of Israel, without parents or brothers to keep alive the national sentiment, they would rapidly be absorbed in the people of the Lord; within a few weeks these girls of Midian would be happier, and certainly their future prospects would be brighter, than if they had remained unmolested at home.

The charge, therefore, which remains against Moses is, that he ordered the slaughter in cold blood of many thousands of women and children, not unnecessarily nor wantonly, but for reasons which were in themselves very weighty. It is of course an axiom of modern times that we do not wage war against women and children. But this, while partly due to Christian feeling, is partly due to the conviction that they are not formidable. If in any war the women of the enemy habitually attempted to poison, and often did poison, our soldiers, they would probably meet with scant mercy. In blockading a fortified city a modern army deliberately starves to death a great many women and children; and if they seek to escape they are sent back to starve, and to induce the garrison to surrender by the spectacle of their sufferings. If this is justified (as no doubt it is if war is to be prosecuted at all) by the plea of necessity, Moses' plea of necessity must be heard also. He deliberately thought it better that these women and boys should be slaughtered than that the future of Israel should be gravely imperilled. In these days, indeed, he would be wrong in coming to that conclusion, and his name would be justly branded with infamy. It would be unquestionably better to incur any loss, rather than outrage in so violent a manner the Christian sentiment of pity and tenderness towards the young, the innocent, the helpless; it would be better to run any risk than to brutalise the soldiery by the execution of such an order. So slowly do sentiments of mercy establish themselves in the hearts of mankind, and so unspeakably valuable are they when established, that he would be a traitor against humanity and against God who should on any pretence outrage any one of them. But there was no such sentiment to outrage in the time of Moses; none thought it wrong to slay captive women and children if any necessity demanded their lives. It was an axiom of war that a captive belonged absolutely to his captor, and might be put to death, or sold as a slave, or held to ransom, as pleased him best, without any scruple of conscience. Moses, therefore sharing as he certainly did the sentiments of his age, was morally free to act for the best, without any thought whether it was cruel or not; and God did not interfere with his decision because it was cruel, any more than he did with the similar decision of other good men who warred, and slew, and spared not before the coming of Christ, and indeed since that coming too. Finally, if the method of separation was odious, it was still the only way possible under the circumstances of separating the harmless from the harmful, and of clearing mercy towards the captives from danger to the captors. And here again a proceeding could be sanctioned without sin then which perhaps no necessity could excuse now, because the sentiment of modesty which it would violate did not exist then, or rather did not exist in the same form.

HOMILETICS.

Vers. 1—54.—*The extermination of sinful lusts.* The religious value of this chapter for Christian people must be based upon a "spiritual" interpretation; otherwise it can but excite abhorrence, and can only serve the negative purpose of showing by contrast with that darkness how fair is the light which now shineth. But "all these things," says St. Paul, writing of the events which followed the exodus (1 Cor. x. 11), "were written for our admonition;" and "all Scripture God-inspired is profitable" for some directly religious purpose. Those who reject all "spiritual" application (albeit directly sanctioned by apostolic example—1 Cor. ix. 10; Gal. iv. 24, &c.) must in honesty deny that such a chapter as this is "profitable" for anything except to afford some data for the science of comparative morality, an object valuable in itself, but certainly not worthy of Divine inspiration. If there be here nothing for immortal souls beyond the details of a horrid slaughter and of an enormous booty, it might better be omitted at once from the Bible. But if the hosts of Midian represent in an "allegory" the "fleshly lusts which war against the soul," then may Samson's riddle be found true—"Out of the eater came forth meat, and out of the strong came forth sweetness" (Judges xiv. 14); and a passage which has given occasion to many fierce and dangerous invectives against religion may yield store of food and refreshment for the souls of the wise. Having, therefore, this clue in our hands to guide us through these dark paths, slippery with blood of slaughtered infants, and ringing with the cries of frantic women, we may see at once a profound meaning in the broad and apparently unwarrantable distinction drawn between Moab and Midian. As to fleshly sin, there was nothing to choose between them; yet Midian only was smitten, because he alone had practised with design against the life of Israel. Even so it is against "fleshly lusts which war against the soul," *i. e.* which are prepared and used by a malignant will to alienate the soul from God, and so to destroy it—it is against such that Christianity denounces bitter and implacable war. Against "fleshly lusts," as they exist among the heathen, springing out of the mere wantonness of natural life untrained to any higher aim than present enjoyment, Christianity (rightly understood) has no vindictive sternness. It may look with sadness upon a melancholy degradation; it may avoid with anxiety a most perilous contamination; but it neither condemns, nor seeks to repress, save by the gentle force of a better example and a higher teaching. Consider, therefore, with regard to *the Midianites*—

I. THAT GOD HIMSELF PRESSED ON THE WAR WITH MIDIAN TO THE BITTER END, and that although there did not seem any present danger to Israel from that quarter. Even so in his holy word God ever urges us to wage an implacable war with the lusts of the flesh, and not to be content because we are not presently assailed by them, but to exterminate them wholly. Nothing is more striking than the urgency and the breadth of these exhortations. The Scripture assumes that all classes of believers (however respectable in outward life and position) have need to strive earnestly against their passions (Gal. v. 17—24; Col. iii. 5, and parallel passages). And note that subsequent events fully justified the slaughter then made of Midian (Judges vi., vii., viii.). We have, and shall have, but too good reason to know that fleshly sins are always a formidable danger.

II. THAT MOSES MUST FINISH THE DESTRUCTION OF MIDIAN ERE HE BE CALLED TO HIS REST, AND ERE ISRAEL MAY CROSS THE JORDAN. Even so the moral law, the wrath of God against sin declared by Moses, must remain in force until sin be destroyed in our mortal members. When the lusts of the flesh are wholly mortified, then, and only then, shall there be "no law," but only grace and love and heaven close at hand (Gal. v. 23; 1 Tim. i. 9, &c.).

III. THAT WAR WITH MIDIAN WAS COMMANDED OF GOD IN ORDER TO "AVENGE THE CHILDREN OF ISRAEL," BUT OF MOSES IN ORDER TO "AVENGE THE LORD." Even so has

God commanded us to strive against hurtful lusts because they "drown men in perdition" (1 Tim. vi. 9), and have caused incalculable loss of those who should have had inheritance with us; but we on our part fight against these sins because they dishonour God, and destroy the souls for which Christ died. And both these motives are in effect one, and unite to make our warfare a holy war, albeit a war of vengeance, in which no mercy may be shown.

IV. THAT THE WAR WITH MIDIAN WAS DISTINCTLY ONE OF VENGEANCE FOR INJURIES INFLICTED ON THEMSELVES AND ON THE LORD. Even so in the strife of the Christian against carnal sin there is a true element of revenge, and abundant room for holy indignation, and even for sharp reprisals; albeit these are all directed against that in himself which is hateful to a man's better self and to God (1 Cor. ix. 27; 2 Cor. vii. 11; Rom. viii. 13).

V. THAT IF ONLY 12,000 ACTUALLY WENT TO THE WAR, ALL ISRAEL WENT BY REPRESENTATION—1000 FROM EACH TRIBE. So the conflict against sin may be in a few only conspicuous and acute, yet these only represent what is going on secretly more or less in the hearts and lives of Christian people generally. The stress of fight may fall on some, but all are called to fight.

VI. THAT TO THIS WAR ISRAEL WAS ACCOMPANIED BY THE PRIEST (Phinehas—see on ch. xxv.), THE SACRED TRUMPETS, AND, AS IT SHOULD SEEM, THE ARK ITSELF. Even so the Christian warfare against sin is guided, sanctified, and cheered by the High Priest himself of our profession (Heb. ii. 18; xii. 2; Rev. iii. 4, 5), and by the stirring tones of the gospel, and by the glorious mystery of the incarnation itself— God with us, the All-holy tabernacled in our flesh, Christ in us, the hope of glory hereafter and the sweet constraint unto purity now.

VII. THAT ALL THE MEN OF MIDIAN WERE SLAIN, TOGETHER WITH THEIR KINGS. Even so it is the destiny of the Church at large, and may be our individual happiness, to overthrow and destroy all hurtful lusts, however strong and active, which are in enmity with the law of God. So also their princes, "the world-rulers of this darkness," shall not stand before us, but shall perish (1 Cor. xv. 25; Ephes. v. 27; vi. 12, &c.).

VIII. THAT THE SOLDIERS ERRED IN SPARING SUCH AS SEEMED WEAK AND HARMLESS, AND MIGHT BE SAFELY TURNED TO PROFIT. The women were in fact more dangerous than the men; the boys would become as dangerous as their fathers. Even so do we err in setting our faces strongly against certain sins which are accounted disgraceful, while we tolerate others because they seem comparatively harmless, or even profitable. This is exactly what civilisation does: it puts down very thoroughly the ruder vices of mankind, but it spares the softer vices, partly because it feels no repugnance to them, partly because they actually make for wealth. But these softer vices are even more fatal to morality, because more insidious and more fascinating; and these sins which seem to add to the general wealth are preparing a disastrous future for the nation. The moral law of the gospel bids us wage an equal war with all sins without exception, and takes no account whether they are offensive or inoffensive, hateful or pleasant, to the natural man, to public opinion, or to the sentiment of the age.

IX. THAT MOSES COMMANDED ALL TO BE SLAIN EXCEPT THE YOUNG GIRLS, WHO BY REASON OF THEIR YOUTH AND INNOCENCE MIGHT SAFELY BE DISTRIBUTED THROUGH THE HOUSEHOLDS OF ISRAEL. Even so all passions which belong to the lower and conquered nature of man must be "mortified" and exterminated, except such as can be safely and thoroughly absorbed in the sanctified life. This is the only test. Whatever natural desires can be taken up into the Christian life without remaining as a foreign element (and therefore a source of danger) within it may be spared, and ought to be welcomed, but no others. All the rest must at any cost be got rid of (Matt. xix. 12; Mark ix. 43—49; Rom. viii. 13; 1 Cor. ix. 27; Ephes. iv. 22; Col. iii. 5).

X. THAT ALL THE REST OF THE SPOIL MUST BE PURIFIED EITHER BY FIRE OR WATER, OR BOTH, BEFORE IT COULD COME INTO THE CAMP. Even so whatever is to be brought over (and it is indeed very much) from the natural life of passion into the sanctified life of grace must be purged by the cleansing virtue of the atonement (the water of separation: see on ch. xix.), and by the baptism of the Holy Spirit (see on Matt. iii.

11). Nothing which has been contaminated with sin can be turned to Christian uses unless it is first sanctified according to its nature. But, subject to this purifying, all that is not in itself sinful may be adapted to Christian ends, and used by Christian people.

Consider again, with respect to *the booty taken*—

I. THAT IT WAS VERY GREAT, AND GREATLY ENRICHED THE PEOPLE. Even so there is more spiritual gain to be made by attacking and destroying sins than by anything else. Churches and souls would never need to complain of spiritual poverty if they busied themselves in waging zealous and unsparing war against the sins within their own reach, within themselves.

II. THAT ALL SHARED IN THE SPOIL, BUT THOSE THAT WARRED HAD BY FAR THE LARGER SHARE INDIVIDUALLY. Even so it is for the profit and edification of all that sins should be successfully assailed; but those who bear the brunt of temptation and strive against sin even "unto blood" have by far the greater reward in themselves. Let this be our Christian ambition, to earn the higher prizes of "him that overcometh" (Mark x. 29, 30; 1 Tim. i. 18; 2 Tim. ii. 4, 5; Heb. xii. 4).

III. THAT AMONGST THE SPOIL THERE WERE A MULTITUDE OF HUMAN BEINGS, AND THESE PROBABLY THE MOST VALUABLE PART OF IT. Even so in the Christian warfare against sin there are a multitude of souls rescued from slavery, and these of priceless worth, beyond all other rewards which we could ask or think of. The girls of Midian seemed to be delivered into slavery; they were in fact delivered from a horrible slavery, and made free in the only way which was then possible. So are those souls which are brought into the service and strictness of Christ made free by the truth (Luke v. 10; John viii. 32, 34, 36; 2 Cor. i. 14; Philip. iv. 1; James v. 20).

IV. THAT THE LORD'S PORTION AND THE PORTION OF HIS MINISTERS WAS EXACTED BEFORE THE SPOIL MIGHT BE APPROPRIATED. Even so, whatever is allowed to Christian use which has belonged to a sinful world, God and his Church have a first claim upon it. It is only through the sanctifying influences of grace that Christian people can freely and safely enjoy the many comforts and luxuries and profits which else they must have forsworn. It is but right that these should first of all be willingly taxed for the glory of God among men, and for the support of all outward ministries of grace (Luke xi. 41).

Consider again, with regard to *Balaam's death*—

I. THAT HE FELL AT LAST WHERE HE HAD NO REASON TO APPREHEND DANGER. Israel had passed by these tribes of Midian, and Balaam no doubt believed that all present danger from them was over. Even so vengeance overtakes the wicked at the moment when he is least afraid, and when justice seems to have forgotten him.

II. THAT HE FELL BY THE SWORD OF ISRAEL, *i. e.* BY THE HAND OF THOSE WHO HAD BEEN THE VICTIMS OF HIS GUILE. Even so it is a just thing with God that evil men and seducers should receive their punishment through those whom they have wronged.

III. THAT BALAAM, THE ENCHANTER AND TEMPTER OF ISRAEL, FELL WITHOUT A STRUGGLE WHEN THE PRINCES OF MIDIAN HAD BEEN SLAIN. Even so the tempter himself, the arch-enemy of souls, will (as far as we are concerned) come utterly to an end as soon as we have overcome the allurements to sin which he uses against us (Rom. xvi. 20).

Consider again, with regard to *the offering of the officers*—

I. THAT NOT ONE HAD FALLEN IN THE RANKS OF ISRAEL—a thing clearly beyond expectation in any ordinary expedition. Even so there is no reason why any should fall or fail in the warfare against fleshly lusts. For the promise of victory is not to all in general, or to the Church at large only, but to each soul in particular that will earnestly strive. And victory over sin implies eternal life (Ezek. xviii. 23; Amos ix. 9; Micah vii. 8; Mal. iii. 17; 1 Cor. x. 13, &c.).

II. THAT THE OFFICERS FELT THAT THIS IMMUNITY WAS DUE TO THE SPECIAL PROVIDENCE OF GOD. Even so that we escape from sin and death, that we come unhurt through so many perils to the soul, is not of our strength, but of God's assistance, and to him all the glory is due (Isa. xl. 29; 2 Cor. xii. 9; Philip. iv. 13; 2 Tim. iv. 17, 18, &c.).

III. THAT THEY OWED A GREAT DEBT OF GRATITUDE TO GOD FOR THE PRESERVATION OF THOSE WHO HAD BEEN COMMITTED TO THEIR CHARGE (literally, "in their hand"). Even so we ought to feel and to show great gratitude to God for the spiritual safety of such as are put in our charge, whether as children or otherwise. According to our responsibility for them, and our sorrow if they were lost, so should be our thankfulness if the good hand of God be upon them to keep them in the way of life (Philip. i. 3; 1 Thess. i. 2, 3, &c.).

IV. THAT THEY SHOWED THEIR GRATITUDE BY THE SPECIAL DEDICATION TO GOD'S SERVICE OF THOSE PRECIOUS THINGS WITH WHICH THAT WARFARE HAD ENRICHED THEM. Even so when we and ours come unscathed out of the temptations of the world and of the flesh, we may well dedicate to God in some special way all the costly gifts of knowledge, of sympathy, of spiritual power and freedom which come of temptation and trial bravely overcome.

And note that the numbering of the men who had been to the war, and the offering of the golden spoil, may be interpreted of the last day. 1. That not one true soldier of Christ shall be missing then (John x. 28, 29; Philip. i. 6; Rev. vii. 3, 4 compared with xiv. 1). 2. That all the precious gifts yielded by human life amid strife and danger shall be brought into the holy city of God, to the glory of God (Rev. xxi. 24, 26). 3. That every one that overcometh shall be the better and the richer for his warfare against sin (see ver. 53).

HOMILIES BY VARIOUS AUTHORS.

Vers. 1—54.—*The lion and his prey.* In two of his prophecies Balaam had been compelled to speak of Israel as the lion (ch. xxiii. 24; xxiv. 9). We now behold, in the destruction of Midian, the rousing of the lion-spirit. Something of it had been seen already in the conduct of Phinehas (ch. xxv.), and now there is a manifestation on a larger scale in the achievement of these 12,000 men.

I. THE COMPLETENESS OF THE DESTRUCTION. All the males of Midian were slain, and the five kings are particularly mentioned as being among them. The women and their little ones were taken captive. The whole of their property was turned into spoil, and how large that spoil was we learn from the latter part of the chapter. Their cities and goodly castles were all burnt. And might not this seem destruction enough? Apparently not; for we read that Moses was wroth because the women had been spared, and they, as well as all the males of the little ones, had to be added to the slain. Thus the impression left upon us, and evidently intended to be left, is that of utter and merciless extermination. None were left to continue the race of Midian.

II. THE INSPIRATION OF THIS DREADFUL BLOW WAS EVIDENTLY FROM GOD. It was undertaken at his command, and not only so, but laid on Moses as his last great service before his departure.

> "Old age hath yet his honour and his toil;
> Death closes all: but something ere the end,
> Some work of noble note, may yet be done."

Midian did not lie in the way of advancing Israel, as did the hosts of Sihon and Og. In one sense Israel had to turn out of its way in order to inflict this blow. We need to keep distinctly before our minds that God gave special command and made special preparation for it. The motive of this act is not to be found in the vindictive spirit of a half-savage people. The wrongs which, by natural disposition, they would have burned to avenge were not such as those inflicted by Midian. In truth there is no occasion either for blame anywhere, or for attempt at palliation. We must read this dreadful record in a spirit of humble submission to the authority of God, who sees need for temporal destruction where we may fail to see it.

III. That this blow came from God is made still clearer as we consider how HIS POWER GAVE THE BLOW ITS EFFICACY. *Observe how small a part of the whole army was required*—about a fiftieth. There is no mention of a selected company to engage against Sihon and Og, but now this small force is enough to crush the whole of Midian. If Israel had gone forth of its own accord, it would have made the result as sure as possible by taking a far larger force than actually went. But where God is not present he can turn mere numbers into loss rather than gain. It was an occasion for the excellency of the Divine power to be manifested. *No actual leader is mentioned.* Moses sent them forth, and on their return he went out to meet them, but they evidently lacked what inspiration his presence and counsel might give them in the field. Phinehas went with them, but he was in charge of the holy instruments and trumpets. We are made to feel that the invisible Jehovah himself was leader, not only directing the attack, but also providing sufficient defence; for when the officers came to count up the army on its return, they were able to say, "There lacketh not one man of us."

IV. THE REASON FOR THIS DREADFUL DESTRUCTION IS FOUND IN THE PECULIAR INJURY WHICH MIDIAN HAD DONE TO ISRAEL (ch. xxv. 16—18). It must needs be that offences come, but woe to the Midianites through whom they come! Although they were not a very difficult people to defeat and destroy in battle, they had been very powerful to tempt Israel into idolatry. A thing which is comparatively easy to deal with in one way is impossible to deal with in another. Israel could annihilate Midian, and do something in that way to secure safety, but there was no chance of safety in having friendly intercourse with Midian. It had to be dealt with as a people saturated with the infecting corruptions of idolatry. Everything had to bend to the interests of Israel, as both typifying and cradling the Church of the future. For the sake of Israel God plagued and spoiled the tyrannous Egyptians; for the sake of Israel he made one whole generation of its own people to perish in the wilderness. What wonder then that for the sake of Israel he utterly destroyed the Midianite tempters! When a fire is extending it may be necessary to pull down other buildings to stop it— many buildings perhaps, as Evelyn tells us was the case in arresting the great fire of London. There is something very significant in the following sentence from his diary:—"This some stout seamen proposed early enough to have saved nearly the whole city, but this some tenacious and avaricious men, aldermen, &c., would not permit, because their houses must have been of the first." There may have to be a great deal of temporal destruction to make sure of eternal salvation.—Y.

Vers. 8, 16.—*The death of Balaam.* I. HOW CLEAR IT IS MADE THAT BALAAM DID NOT DIE THE DEATH OF THE RIGHTEOUS! He was slain among those who were slain by the vengeance of God. He might, of course, have died in circumstances more peaceful and less indicative of his wickedness, and yet died the death of the wicked all the same. But now the manner of his end is left in no doubt. He had not only suffered himself to be drawn into opposition to the people of God, he had not only been disobedient to God himself, but it seems that he had been the chief provoking agent in bringing destruction on a portion of the present generation of Israel. Moreover, the very people whom he thought to help he had unconsciously led to their own ruin. He certainly could not have done all this if he had not found the materials ready to hand—actual idolatry in Midian, and the spirit of lust and idolatry in Israel. But it was he who saw with a sort of Satanic quickness all that could be done with the material. A man cannot cause an explosion unless he has explosive substances to deal with, but we reckon him responsible who applies the exploding agent. One sinner not only destroyeth much good, but, as we see here, produceth much evil. Wicked men should learn from the history of Balaam that they may do a great deal more harm than they are conscious of. How much better it is to be on the other side, striving to draw men, even though it be with few apparent results, into the paths of purity, self-denial, and love!

II. FROM THE CHARACTER OF BALAAM WE SEE HOW REAL AND DESPERATE SPIRITUAL INSENSIBILITY MAY BE. Rightly considered, the whole conduct of Balaam is a great deal more perplexing than is the speaking of his ass. There we have to do just with the momentary occupation of the vocal organs of a brute by the speech of a human being. For a moment or two the ass was honoured beyond its natural faculties. But here is a man, raised above other men in many respects, acting in a way most humiliating to humanity.   Favoured again and again with light which came to him in different ways, he remained in gross darkness with respect to the character of God as a whole.   He saw not the folly, the absurdity, of the path in which he was treading.   *The conduct of Balaam in the essential principles of it has often been repeated, and is being repeated still.*   We are all spiritually blind unless God be pleased to open our eyes.   Seeing the things of God by the light of nature, and judging of them by natural reason, we come to some strange and impotent conclusions.   Balaam's indifference to the interferences of God is not one whit more marvellous than the unmoved, matter-of-fact way in which we can bear to have truths presented to our minds which, if they concern us to any extent, concern us more than all outward circumstances taken together.   It is easy to say as one reads of Balaam, "What a fool! what an enigma! what a bundle of contradictions! what a mixture in his life of unwilling obedience to God and most obstinate persistence in his own path!"   Take care lest it be said to one thus speaking, "Thou art the man."   There is not a man of the world living in a land of open Bibles but whose conduct might be so described as to appear quite as perplexing as that of Balaam here.

III.   A MAN MAY ENJOY GREAT PRIVILEGES, AND YET BE RUINED AT LAST.   A seeing man may be quite safe in a dangerous path, and on the darkest night, with a little lamp, if it is enough to show him where his feet are to be placed.   But a blind man will fall into the pit by noonday.   A firmament radiant with a score of suns would avail nothing to such a one.   A man may live in a land of Bibles, churches, and every conceivable variety of gospel ministrations, and yet die, after a long contact with all these, knowing nothing of his own state as a sinner, or of the power of Christ as a Saviour.   Another man, in the midst of Africa, with no more than a torn leaf of the New Testament, might come to know the one thing needful, and be effectually led to repentance, faith, salvation, and eternal life.   Privileges, as we call them, are nothing in themselves; all depends on how they are received.   It was the same seed that was sown in the four different kinds of ground.   One seed sown in the good ground will bring forth more than a cartload scattered by the wayside.

IV.   BALAAM KNEW JUST ENOUGH OF THE TRUTH TO MISLEAD HIM, NOT ENOUGH TO LEAD HIM RIGHT.   He apprehended the real power of Jehovah without apprehending his character as a whole.   He had made the discovery that if Israel fell away into the worship of any other god, it would be very severely dealt with.   Doubtless he had found his way into some intercourse with the Israelites, and been made acquainted with their past history, particularly with the commandment of God at Sinai against idolatry, and the sufferings which came upon the people because of the golden calf.   But he did not know that in the midst of the most faithless and apostate of generations there would still be preserved a faithful seed; he did not reckon on the energetic and efficacious zeal of a Phinehas.   And thus the great mischief to many arises not so much from total indifference to God as from misleading conceptions of him.   It is only too easy for us to miss the full view which a sinner ought to have of God, and remain all our lifetime with erroneous and most limited conceptions.   Some make too much of God's anger with sin, forgetting his love, his mercy, his patience, his revelation of himself as a Father; others make too much of his mercy, forgetting his unyielding righteousness, and the need of a radical change in man—a change in his motives, purposes, sympathies, and delights.   Nothing is more perilous than to see so much of one side of the Divine character as not to see the rest.   We must see it as it is revealed in Scripture.   There the living God moves before us in his actions.   We see his actions, and they cannot be understood unless as the harmonious outflow of all his character.—Y.

Vers. 25—47.—*The distribution of the spoils.*   I.   GOD TAKES THE DISTRIBUTION INTO HIS OWN HANDS.   The victory was his, and it was for him to arrange the spoils as might best serve his own purposes.   It was the only effectual way of blighting in the bud all discord and jealousy.   It was also the means of teaching important lessons to all in the community who were willing to learn.   It helped to manifest afresh the unity of Israel.   Those who had gone to the war had gone as representatives of the whole of Israel, hence it was for the whole of Israel to share in the spoil.   While part was away, avenging the Lord of Midian, another part stayed at home, also serving God in its own way, and looking after the interests of those who were absent. We must not get into the way of looking at one part of the community as more necessary than another. It was not for the army to say, "What would Israel have done in taking vengeance on Midian but for us?" seeing that God had made it plain how he was working in and through the army. Nor was it for the people who stayed at home to say, "What right have twelve thousand men to half the spoils?" The twelve thousand were not looked at in themselves; they stood for Israel militant. All Israel gained a real blessing by this expedition, and the chief gain to them was in so far as they were effectually warned against the perils of idolatry. Whatever there might be in the way of improved perception of truth and duty and the Divine character was far more than all the spoil. God did not send them against Midian for the sake of the spoil, but for the sake of vengeance.

II. THE SPECIAL TRIBUTE TO THE LEVITES. It was very appropriate that this should be strictly exacted, after all the service which Phinehas had rendered. The tribe of Levi had done its part in a way which could not be mistaken. Upon this great occasion, when so much had to be distributed, God taught the lesson that distribution should be made according to the needs of men. The Levites had need not only to be supported, but well supported. The work they had to do, in the reality, the extent, the continuity, and the minuteness of it, had been lately indicated in more ways than one. Consider all the Levitical service that was involved in the offerings mentioned in chs. xxviii. and xxix. It was becoming more and more clear that Levi must be set apart and properly maintained; for thus only could there be regularity and efficiency in the service of God.

III. BALAAM'S ASS WAS PROBABLY AMONG THE ASSES THAT WERE TAKEN (ver. 34). It is pleasant to imagine that it may have found its way into the Lord's tribute, and that the animal which had so long borne a wicked man faithfully, would now with equal faithfulness be able to bear perhaps Eleazar himself. We need much of the spirit of obedience to God to use rightly that vast multitude of the brute creation which God has put under our control. How pitiable to see the horse carefully trained for war, and, as one might almost think, taught to cherish feelings which by nature are alien to it! May we not well wish for the day when not only the sword of the dragoon shall be turned to the ploughshare, but the horse on which he rides shall draw that share along? Think how the horse and other animals are degraded by the occasions for gambling which they furnish. Think of all the cruel field-sports in which man finds such pleasure. When he leaves the pleasures which are appropriate to his nature, what a tyrannous and hideous monster he may become! Man in all his life should be drawing nearer to God, and, rising higher himself, should raise all creation with him. Whereas he is drawn downward, and in his willing descent he degrades even the lower creation.—Y.

EXPOSITION.

CHAPTER XXXII.

THE TWO AND A HALF TRIBES BEYOND JORDAN (vers. 1—42). Ver. 1.—**The children of Reuben and the children of Gad.** Reuben and Gad had both been camped on the same (southern) side of the tabernacle, but had not apparently been neighbours, since Simeon intervened on the march (see on ch. ii. 10—14). Simeon, however, was at this time enfeebled and disgraced, and was not likely to assert himself in any way. The "great multitude of cattle" belonging to the two tribes probably point to pastoral habits of long standing, since the cattle of the Amorites and Midianites would be equally divided among all. **The land of Jazer.** Jazer, or

Jaazer, probably stood near the northern source of the Wâdy Hesbân, which enters the Jordan not far from its mouth. The "land of Jazer" would seem to mean the Mishor, or plateau, of Heshbon, over which the Israelites had passed on their way to the plains of Moab (see on Deut. iii. 10, "all the cities of the Mishor"). **The land of Gilead.** Gilead as the name of a district only previously occurs in Gen. xxxvii. 25. It is used with a considerable latitude of meaning in this and the following books. In its widest sense it stands for the whole territory to the east of Jordan (see on vers. 26, 29), including even the rugged, volcanic districts of Bashan (Deut. xxxiv. 1; 1 Chron. v. 16); but more properly it denoted the lands on both sides the Jabbok, from the Wâdy Hesbân on the south, to the Yermuk and lake of Tiberias on the north, now known as the provinces of Belka and Jebel Ajlun. These lands are by no means uniformly flat, as the name "Mount Gilead" testifies, but include mountains and hills covered with fine open forests of oak (cf. 2 Sam. xviii. 8, 9) as well as rolling downs and treeless plains. The soil is almost everywhere of great fertility, and the water supply, although very scanty in summer, is sufficient if carefully husbanded. Even now these provinces produce great store of grain, and are depastured by vast flocks of sheep. In Roman times, as the innumerable ruins testify, they were filled with a large and opulent population. Indeed there could be no comparison in point of agricultural and pastoral value between these open and fertile lands and the broken, stony country of Southern Palestine. If they ever enjoy again the blessing of a strong government and continuous peace they will again justify the choice of Reuben and Gad. **A place for cattle.** מָקוֹם (Septuagint, τόπος) is used here in the broader sense of district (cf. Gen. i. 9), and is equivalent to אֶרֶץ in ver. 4.

Ver. 3.—**Ataroth.** As to the nine places here mentioned, see on vers. 34—38. They all lie to the south of Gilead, properly so called, within a comparatively short distance of the route by which the main body of the Israelites had advanced. Probably the cattle which followed the host were still grazing under guard around these places, and it was very natural that tribes which had hitherto lived closely crowded together should not at first contemplate spreading themselves very far afield.

Ver. 5.—**Bring us not over Jordan.** The two tribes have been charged on the strength of these words with "shameless selfishness," but there is nothing to justify such an accusation. If they thought at all of the effect of their request upon their brethren, it is quite likely that they intended to do them a kindness by leaving them more room on the other side Jordan; and indeed Canaan proper was all too strait for such a population. Whether they were *wise* in wishing to stay in the wider and more attractive lands which they had seen is another matter. They knew that the God of Israel had designed to plant his people between Jordan and the sea, and they certainly risked a partial severance from his promises and his protection by remaining where they did. The subsequent history of the trans-Jordanic tribes is a melancholy commentary on the real unwisdom of their choice. Yet it would have been difficult for them to know that they were wrong, except by an instinct of faith which no Israelites perhaps at that time possessed.

Ver. 6.—**Shall your brethren go to war, and shall ye sit here?** Moses had good cause to feel great anxiety about the entry into Canaan proper. Once already the faith and courage of the people had failed them on the very threshold of the promised land, and a slight discouragement might bring about a similar calamity. Hence he spoke with a degree of sharpness which does not appear to have been deserved.

Ver. 7.—**Discourage.** The verb נוּא, translated "discourage" here and in ver. 9, is of somewhat doubtful meaning. The Septuagint renders it by διαστρέφω, and perhaps the sense is, "Why do ye draw away the heart?" *i. e.* render it averse from going over.

Ver. 8.—**Thus did your fathers.** It is impossible not to see that this mode of address is in striking contrast to that used in the Book of Deuteronomy (*e. g.* in ch. i. 22, 27 ; v. 3, 23). At the same time it is obviously the more natural, and the more in accordance with facts, because there was not a man left of all those who had rebelled at Kadesh. **At Kadesh-Barnea.** This mode of writing the name forms a link between the closing chapters of Numbers (here and in ch. xxxiv. 4) and the two following books. In Deuteronomy it occurs four times, and "Kadesh" twice. In Joshua "Kadesh-Barnea" occurs exclusively. In the later books "Kadesh" only is used, as in Genesis and in the previous chapters of Numbers. The meaning of the combination is uncertain, and the etymology of "Barnea" altogether obscure. It may be an old name attaching to the place before it became known as a sanctuary. The Septuagint has Κάδης τοῦ Βαρνή in one place, as though it were the name of a man.

Ver. 9.—**When they went up,** *i. e.* no doubt the spies, although the word is not expressed. Moses, indeed, in the heat of his displeasure, seemed to charge their "fathers" generally with the wickedness of ten men. No further proof is needed to show that Moses was often disposed to speak unadvisedly with his lips.

Ver. 11.—**That came up out of Egypt, from twenty years old and upward.** Here is another instance of the haste and inaccuracy with which Moses spoke. The Divine sentence of exclusion had been pronounced upon all who were numbered at Sinai as being then over twenty (ch. xiv. 29).

Ver. 12.—**The Kenezite.** See on chap. xiii. 6.

Ver. 14.—**An increase of sinful men.** תַּרְבּוּת is rendered by the Septuagint σύντριμμα, which properly means a contusion or fracture ; but it is probably equivalent to "brood," used in a contemptuous sense. The strong language of Moses was not justified by the reality, although it was excused by the appearance, of the case.

Ver. 15.—He will yet again leave them in the wilderness. Properly speaking, Israel had already emerged from the wilderness; but until they had fairly made good their possession of Canaan, their desert wanderings could not be considered at an end.

Ver. 16.—Sheep-folds. גִּדְרֹת צֹאן. These were rude enclosures built of loose stones piled on one another, into which the flocks were driven at night for safety.

Ver. 17.—We ourselves will go ready armed. Rather, "we will equip ourselves in haste." נֵחָלֵץ חֻשִׁים. They meant that they would not delay the forward movement of Israel, but would hasten to erect the necessary buildings, and to array themselves for war.

Ver. 19.—On yonder side Jordan. לַיַּרְדֵּן מֵעֵבֶר. Septuagint, ἀπὸ τοῦ πέραν τοῦ Ἰορδάνου. This phrase is here used in what is apparently its more natural sense, as it would be used by one dwelling in the plains of Moab (see on ch. xxii. 1, and on next verse). **Or forward.** וָהָלְאָה. Septuagint, καὶ ἐπέκεινα, i. e. onwards towards the west and south and north, as the tide of conquest might flow. **Our inheritance is fallen to us on this side Jordan eastward.** It does not appear on what ground they spoke so confidently. They do not seem to have received any Divine intimation that their lot was to be on the east of Jordan, but rather to have been guided by their own preference. If so, they cannot be acquitted of a certain presumptuous wilfulness in action, and of a certain want of honesty in speech. The phrase here rendered "on this side Jordan" (מֵעֵבֶר הַיַּרְדֵּן) cannot be distinguished grammatically from that which bears an opposite signification in the preceding verse. In itself it is perfectly ambiguous without some qualifying word or phrase, and it is very difficult to know what the ordinary use of it was in the time of Moses. In later ages, no doubt, it came to mean simply the trans-Jordanic territory, or Peræa, without reference to the position of the speaker. The difficulty here is to decide whether the expression, as further defined by " eastward," would actually have been used at that time and in that place, or whether the expression is due to a writer living on the west of Jordan. All we can say is, that the awkward use of the phrase in two opposite meanings, with words of clearer definition added, points more or less strongly towards a probability that the passage as it stands was written or revised at a later date.

Ver. 20.—Before the Lord. Perhaps in a quasi-local sense, as the vanguard of the host before the sacred symbols of the Lord's presence (see on ch. x. 21, and Josh. vi. 9). But since the same expression (לִפְנֵי יְהוָֹה) is twice used in a much vaguer sense in ver. 22, it is more probable that it only means " in the Lord's service," or "beneath his eye."

Ver. 23.—Be sure your sin will find you out. Or rather, "ye will know your sin " (וּדְעוּ חַטַּאתְכֶם) "which shall find you out" (for מָצָא cf. Gen. xliv. 16). So in effect the Septuagint: γνώσεσθε τὴν ἁμαρτίαν ὑμῶν, ὅταν ὑμᾶς καταλάβῃ τὰ κακά. When they had cause to rue their folly, then they would recognise their sin.

Ver. 26.—In the cities of Gilead. The name is used here in a vague sense for all the central and southern trans-Jordanic districts.

Ver. 28.—Moses commanded. See on ch. xxxiv. 17, 18 ; Josh. i. 13 ff. ; xxii. 1 ff.

Ver. 33.—And unto half the tribe of Manasseh. As no mention has been previously made of this tribe in this connection, we are left to conjecture why it should, contrary to all analogy, have been divided at all, and why the one half should have received the remote regions of Northern Gilead and Bashan. That the tribe was divided at all can only be explained by the pre-existence of some schism in its ranks, the probable origin and nature of which are discussed in the notes on vers. 39, 41. The enormous increase in the tribal numbers during the wanderings (see on ch. xxvi. 34) may have made the division more advisable, and the adventurous and independent character of the Machirites may have rendered it almost a necessity. They had not apparently preferred any request to Moses, but since the trans-Jordanic territory was to be occupied, Moses probably prevented a grave difficulty by recognising their claim to the conquests they had made.

Ver. 34.—The children of Gad built, i. e., no doubt, they put these places in some habitable and defensible state of repair until they should return. **Dibon.** Now Dhibân, four miles north of Arnon. It is called Dibon-gad in ch. xxxiii. 45, 46, but it is doubtful whether there is any allusion to its present occupation, since " Gad " was a common affix in the languages of Canaan (cf. Josh. xi. 17). Dibon was subsequently assigned to Reuben (Josh. xiii. 9), but was recovered by Moab, and became one of his strongholds (cf Isa. xv. 2 ; Jer. xlviii. 18, 22). The Moabite stone was found here. **Ataroth.** Now Attârûs, seven miles from Dibon. **Aroer.** Not the Aroer before Rabbath (Josh. xiii. 25), but the Aroer by the brink of Arnon (Deut. ii. 36 ; Josh. xiii. 16).

Ver. 35. — **Atroth, Shophan.** Rather, "Atroth - Shophan," another Ataroth, the site of which is unknown. **Jaazer.** See on ver. 1. **Jogbehah.** Now perhaps Jebeiha, to the north of Jaazer (cf. Judges viii. 11). All these places were only temporarily occupied by the Gadites, and fell to Reuben in the subsequent division.

Ver. 36.—**Beth-nimrah and Beth-haran.** Supposed to be the present Nimrûn and Beit-haran in the plains of Moab, beside the Jordan, and in the immediate neighbourhood of the Israelitish camp. The latter would seem to have fallen subsequently to Reuben. **Fenced cities, and folds for sheep.** There should be no stop between these two clauses. All these places were "built" for the double purpose of affording protection to the families and to the flocks of the tribe.

Ver. 37.—**The children of Reuben.** Reuben had, at the time of the last census, been greater in number than Gad, and had been his leader on the march. He now begins to take that secondary position which was always to be his. Of the towns which he now occupied, the Moabites recovered many, while the most important of all (Heshbon) had to be surrendered to the Levites. He was indeed compensated with the southern settlements of the Gadites as far as the Wady Hesbân, but even so his limits were very straitened as compared with those of Gad and of half Manasseh. **Heshbon.** Cf. ch. xxi. 25. In Josh. xxi. 39; 1 Chron. vi. 81, Heshbon is spoken of as belonging to Gad. This can only be explained on the supposition that the temporary settlements of the two tribes were really intermixed, and that Heshbon, as the old capital of that region, was jointly occupied. In after times it, too, together with Elealeh and Kirjathaim, Nebo, Baal-meon, and Sibmah, all fell into the hands of Moab (Isa. xv. 2, 4; xvi. 8; Jer. xlviii. 22, 23).

Ver. 38.—**Baal-meon.** Called Beon in ver. 3, Beth-meon in Jer. xlviii. 23, Beth-Baal-meon in Josh. xiii. 17. **Their names being changed.** מוּסַבֹּת שֵׁם, "with change of name," dependent on the verb "built." The Septuagint has περικεκυκλωμένας (Symmachus, περιτετευχισμένας), apparently reading שׁוּר for שֵׁם, but without authority. It is possible that the Beon of ver. 3 may be an instance of this attempt to change names, many of which were connected with idolatry. The attempt failed, but both the attempt itself and its failure were very characteristic of the partial and feeble hold which Israel had on this territory. **Gave other names to the cities which they builded.** Literally, "they called by names the names of the towns;" a round-about expression correctly paraphrased by the A. V.

Ver. 39.—**The children of Machir.** The relation of the Beni-Machir to the tribe of Manasseh is obscure, because all the Manassites were descended from Machir. In the absence of any direct information, we can only guess at the nature of the tie which united the Beni-Machir as a family, and kept them distinct from the other Manassite families. It is evident from their history that they formed a sub-tribe powerful enough to have a name of their own in Israel (cf. ver. 40 and Judges v. 14, and see note on ver. 41). **Went to Gilead.** This would seem to refer to the expedition briefly recorded in ch. xxi. 33. It is mentioned here out of place, in the simple historical style of the Pentateuch, because the gift of Gilead to Machir grew out of its conquest by Machir. The name Gilead is again used in a very vague sense, for the territory actually allotted to Machir was rather in Bashan than in Gilead proper.

Ver. 40.—**And he dwelt therein.** This expression does not necessarily look beyond the lifetime of Moses, although it would be more naturally taken as doing so. In ch. xx. 1 יֵשֶׁב is used of the "abiding" of Israel at Kadesh.

Ver. 41.—**Jair the son of Manasseh.** This hero of Manasseh is mentioned here for the first time; in Deut. iii. 14 his conquests are somewhat more fully described. His genealogy, which is instructive and suggestive, is given here.

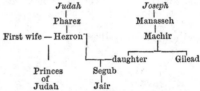

It will be seen that Segub, the father of Jair, was a Machirite in the female line only. His father Hezron, according to 1 Chron. ii. 21, married the daughter of Manasseh in his old age, when his elder sons were probably already fathers of families. It may probably be conjectured also that Manasseh, who must have inherited exceptional wealth (cf. Gen. xlviii. 17), and had but one grandson, left a large portion to his grand-daughter, the young wife of Hezron. It was therefore very natural that Segub should have attached himself to the fortunes of his mother's tribe. Is it not also very probable that Machir had other daughters (cf. Gen. l. 23), who also inherited large portions from their grandfather, and whose husbands were willing enough to enter into a family which had apparently brighter prospects than any others? If so, it would account at once for the existence of a large family of Machirites not descended from

Gilead, and not on the most friendly terms with the rest of the tribe. It is quite possible that many of the more adventurous spirits amongst the tribe of Judah joined themselves to a family whose reputation and exploits they might naturally claim as their own (see on Josh. xix. 34). **The small towns thereof,** or, "their villages." Septuagint, τὰς ἐπαύλεις αὐτῶν, *i. e.* the hamlets of the Amorites who dwelt in Argob (Deut. iii. 14), the modern district of el Lejja, on the north-western waters of the Yermuk or Hieromax. **And called them Havoth-jair.** חַוֹּת יָאִיר. Septuagint, τὰς ἐπαύλεις 'Ιαίρ, and so the Targums. The word *chavvoth* only occurs in this connection, and is supposed by some to be the plural of חַוָּה, "life." There does not, however, seem to be anything except the very doubtful analogy of certain German names in favour of the rendering "Jair's lives." It is more likely the corruption of some more ancient name. There is some discrepancy in subsequent references to the Chavvoth-jair. According to 1 Chron. ii. 22, Jair had twenty-three towns in Gilead; from Judges x. 4 it appears that the sons of the later Jair had thirty cities "in the land of Gilead" which went under the name of Chavvoth-jair; while in Josh. xiii. 30 "all the Chavvoth-jair which are in Bashan" are reckoned at sixty. The plausible, though not wholly satisfactory, explanation is, that the conquests of Nobah came to be subsequently included in those of his more famous contemporary, and the vague name of Chavvoth-jair extended to all the towns in that part of Gilead, and of Bashan too (see notes on the passages cited).

Ver. 42.—**Nobah.** As this chieftain is nowhere else named, we may probably conclude that he was one of the companions of Jair, holding a position more or less subordinate to him. **Kenath.** The modern Kenawât, on the western slope of the Jebel Haurân, the most easterly point ever occupied by the Israelites. It is apparently the Nobah mentioned in Judges viii. 11, but it has reverted (like so many others) to its old name. In spite of the uncertainties which hang over the conquest of this north-eastern territory, there is something very characteristic in the part played by the Machirite leaders. That they acted with an independent vigour bordering on audacity, that they showed great personal prowess, and had great personal authority with the humbler members of their family, and held something like the position of feudal superiors among them, is evident from the way in which they are spoken of. And this is quite in keeping with the character of the Manassites in after times. The "governors" who came at the call of Barak, Gideon, the greatest of the warrior-judges, and probably Jephthah also ("the Gileadite"), as well as the younger Jair, maintained the warlike and impetuous character of their race. If "Elijah the Tishbite" was really from this region (although this is extremely doubtful), we should find in him the characteristic daring and self-reliance of Machir transmuted into their spiritual equivalents.

HOMILETICS.

Vers. 1—42.—*The mistaken choice.* In this chapter we have, spiritually, the choice of those who do not (on the one hand) wish to sever themselves from the people of God, nor to desert their brethren, but who are (on the other hand) greatly disinclined to go the whole length to which the word of God would lead them, and are determined to abide in the middle ground between the Church and the world. And this choice is set before us both on its worse side, in that it is at once presumptuous and foolish, albeit not unnatural; and on its better side, as being consistent with a large measure of really good and honest principle. The whole spiritual value of the chapter turns upon the lesson thus taught. Consider, therefore—

I. THAT THE CHILDREN OF REUBEN AND GAD DESIRED TO STAY YON-SIDE OF JORDAN BECAUSE IT SUITED THEM; *i. e.* because (1) they had much cattle, (2) for which the rolling downs and plateaus of that region were admirably adapted, whereas (3) it would be a difficult matter to transport their scattered flocks and herds across the tangled valley and deep stream of Jordan, and (4) the straiter limits of Canaan proper seemed unsuited to pastoral wealth. Even so a multitude of Christians hang back from going all lengths with Christ because (1) they have much wealth of this world, (2) for the enjoyment of which a manner of life only partially limited and restrained by strict Christian principle is on the face of it very suitable, while (3) there is a manifest difficulty about introducing this wealth into a strictly religious life, and (4) an evident incongruity between the requisite attention to such wealth and the restraints and demands of such a life.

II. That these two tribes were undoubtedly intended, like the rest, to find their inheritance in Canaan proper. For this, and not the land beyond Jordan, was the land which the Lord had sworn to give to Abraham, Isaac, and Jacob ; this was the land of the seven nations, the promised land, of which the land of Jaazer and Gilead formed no integral part, but only as it were a vestibule, an outlier, an *annexe*. These did indeed belong to the Holy Land, but were distinctly less holy than the rest. Even so it is the will of God that all Christians should press on unto perfection, *i. e.* to the perfect life of faith and duty spoken of in the New Testament. This is distinctly what God hath called them to, for it is to this that he hath attached his blessings and promises. Nevertheless there is in practice a vast tract of Christian living which is as clearly distinct from this as it is inferior to it ; which lies outside of it in the strict sense, but yet in a wide sense is certainly united to it.

III. That nature itself justified the Divine wisdom in calling the people into Canaan proper. For this Holy Land is separated from all other lands by remarkable geographical features, especially by the deep cleft of Jordan from the children of the east ; whereas the trans-Jordanic territory was wholly exposed to a multitude of heathen and hostile neighbours towards the east, and south, and north. Even so it is a matter which needs no discussion that a strict Christian life is by the very laws of human nature fenced from innumerable dangers and assaults to which a half-and-half religion lies completely open. Nothing indeed is more practically helpless, or at least more utterly unsafe, than the Christian life of a half-converted man.

IV. That the history of Israel supplies a melancholy commentary on the unwisdom of their choice. The very places mentioned as the first settlements of Reuben all fell into the hands of the Moabites, with some of those of Gad. Amidst the uncertainties which overhang their history we can make out that these regions were a continual battle-field, never attained a settled prosperity, and were finally conquered before the rest. Even so all experience sets forth the sad results of such a life as is a compromise between the claims of religion and of the world. It is always and of necessity the first to go ; the powers of evil strike upon it first, and with the greatest strength. In the day of temptation, when those who live most near to God can hardly stand, what chance is there (humanly speaking) for the half-hearted and half-converted ?

V. That the choice of Reuben and Gad was after all very natural. Unquestionably the open lands which they had seen were then (as they are now) much more fertile and pleasant than the stony limestone ridges of Southern Palestine ; and the deep, sullen stream of Jordan was a formidable obstacle. Even so there is to the natural man something very attractive about the comparative freedom of a life which claims the promises of Christ, and yet is not altogether constrained by his demands. To cross the gloomy-looking gulf of an entire conversion, and to be cooped within the apparently uninviting limits of a consecrated life, *is* repugnant to much that exists in all of us, and that reigns supreme in many of us.

VI. That their choice really showed a want of faith. For they knew that God had attached his promises to the land beyond Jordan, and they knew that the ark of God was going across, and that the chosen site of God's presence would be on the other side, yet they deliberately risked the danger of being (to some real extent) separated from the presence and promises and protection of their Holy One. Even so when men settle down in a half-and-half Christianity, it is because they have no strong faith in the promises, and no great longing for the presence of God ; they do not disbelieve or despise these, but they are in practice less concerned about them than about temporal advantages.

VII. That their choice also showed a blindness to their actual dangers. Had they foreseen the swarms of enemies to whose assaults they would remain exposed, and realised their comparatively defenceless position, they would surely have petitioned to go over Jordan too. Even so men remain half converted with a light heart because they under-estimate their danger, and over-estimate their strength. Conscious that they intend what is right, they are content to abide far from the succours of Divine grace, at once more exposed to temptation and less able to resist it than more earnest Christians.

VIII. That the two tribes which asked, and the half tribe which seems to have taken without asking, obtained their inheritance where they wished to have it ; and they were not cast out of the chosen people, nor treated with disdain. Even so a great multitude of Christians remain distinctly and deliberately below the level and outside the pale (so to speak) of the true Christian life as portrayed in the Gospels and Epistles. Their life and conversation is in fact governed half by the gospel, and half by the precepts and fashions of the world. Yet they are Christians, and, however great their danger and unsatisfactory their position, they are not and cannot be separated from the Church of God.

Consider more particularly, as to *the petition of the two tribes*—
I. That it was partly positive—"let this land be given unto thy servants;" partly negative—"bring us not over this Jordan." Here we have the attraction of a life of apparent freedom and enjoyment, the repulsion of a concentrated effort, and of a life apparently limited and uninteresting.
II. That the conquests already made might seem the natural conclusion of their long journeying and waiting. Why should they go further and perhaps fare worse? Here we have the secret of much imperfect religious life. Many stop far short of a thorough-going obedience because they have advanced far enough to feel themselves safe from judgment, and at rest from stings of conscience, and inheritors of the kingdom of heaven ; and they have no mind (because they see no necessity) to go any further in the onward path.
III. That the two tribes, because they had determined to remain where they were, assumed that they had Divine authority to do so : "Our inheritance is fallen to us on this side Jordan." Here we have that confidence which Christian people constantly express, that *they* are not called to "go on unto perfection." Other people have their own vocation, but it is given unto them to lead a life less strict and less devout because business, or society, or their own disposition requires it, *i. e.* because they choose to.

Consider again, as to *Moses' treatment of their petition*—
I. That he judged them harshly and unfairly, as if they had been wilful rebels against God and cowardly betrayers of their brethren, which was not at all the case. Even so those who have the interests of God's kingdom very much at heart are always tempted to judge too harshly those who show a want of earnestness and of forwardness, and to cast them out as unprincipled ; whereas in fact there is often very much to thank God for in their character and conduct.
II. That having thus put himself in the wrong, he could not take up the true ground of remonstrance, *i. e.* the injury they would entail upon themselves. Even so to condemn imperfect Christians altogether is to prevent any effective appeal to their own highest interests and truest ambitions.
III. That what Moses did exact was an assurance that they would not abandon nor weaken their brethren pressing on. Even so we have a right to require that those who are not willing themselves to go all lengths with Christ shall at least not hinder nor discourage those who are willing and are trying. Here is the crying evil and sin of our degenerate Christianity, that it not only falls short of the gospel standard, but practically sets up a standard of its own, and utterly discourages any attempt to rise above it ; and this is certainly that wickedness against God and man which Moses mistakenly charged on the two tribes.
IV. That the evident policy of Moses was to unite the tribes which remained beyond Jordan by as many ties as possible to the rest. Even so it is our wisdom to unite all Christian people, especially those who are lukewarm, in common enterprises for good, and in common labours for the Church, so that they may not be more separated from one another than is unavoidable.

Consider again, on the words, "bring us not over this Jordan"—1. That "this Jordan" is the accepted figure of the narrow stream of death, which divides us from the promised land wherein God dwelleth. 2. That the trans-Jordanic territory represents the less perfect holiness of life *here* as contrasted with the more perfect holiness of life *there*. 3. That this saying, therefore, represents the shrinking which so many feel from that death which is the gate of true life, and their desire to remain amid the familiar and congenial scenes of this world. 4. That this saying, although very natural (since this life is sweet, and death awful, and the land beyond unknown), is certainly due to a want of faith (since the kingdom prepared for us is there, not here), and betrays a certain presumption, since as long as we live here we are in danger of separation from God. 5. That we justify the saying on the ground that life *here* is holy (as indeed it is), not sufficiently remembering that life *there* is holier, and that we are only here on the march with a view to crossing Jordan and reaching the true rest. 6. That however good may be the land on this side, "Jerusalem," the place which God hath chosen, the centre of Israel's life and happiness, is beyond Jordan. "Absent from the body," "present with the Lord."

Consider again, on the words, "be sure your sin will find you out"—1. That it is indeed true, as the heathen witnessed in many remarkable ways. "Nemesis" is a fact. 2. That it is not what Moses meant to say; rather, "Ye will recognise your sin when it overtakes you." 3. That men fail to recognise their sin at the time; often, that it is a sin at all; generally, how great a sin it is in deed. 4. Then when it overtakes them in its consequences, then they see it in its true light. The awfulness of sin is not due to its awful consequences, but it is manifested by them. 5. That the particular sin against which Moses warned them was the sin of selfishly deserting their brethren, and thereby discouraging and enfeebling them. And this is a sin as great as it is common, the disastrous consequences of which are most sadly evident.

Consider again, with respect to *the "cities" which the children of Reuben and Gad "built"*—

I. THAT AT THE TIME, AS COMPARED WITH THE TENTS AND BOOTHS OF THE WILDERNESS, THEY SEEMED NO DOUBT TO BE IMPORTANT AND PERMANENT SETTLEMENTS, BUT THEY PROVED TO BE VERY TEMPORARY. Even so there is nothing fixed or abiding in any religious life short of that perfect life unto which we are called. It is not only the "fashion of this world," but "the fashion" of the "religious world," which passeth away, because it is in truth only partly and provisionally Christian.

II. THAT IN AFTER DAYS THEY MOSTLY FELL INTO THE HANDS OF THE CRUEL AND IDOLATROUS MOAB, AND RESUMED THEIR OLD HEATHEN NAMES. Even so a manner of life which is not distinctly Christian, albeit lived by Christians, is for ever slipping back into practical heathenism, and reverting to the evil and sinful conditions from which it seemed to have been rescued.

III. THAT THE CURSE OF REUBEN (Gen. xlix. 4) BEGAN NOW TO BE FULFILLED THROUGH UNHAPPY CIRCUMSTANCES WHICH WERE YET ENTIRELY OF HIS OWN SEEKING. It was he that settled himself close upon the frontier of Moab, where he could not have peace or prosperity for any length of time. Even so that incapacity to excel in anything which seems to cling to some Christian people like a curse is after all due to their own precipitate unwisdom in placing themselves at a permanent disadvantage for the sake of immediate gain or ease.

Consider once more, with respect to *Machir*—

I. THAT THEY SEEM TO HAVE ACTED INDEPENDENTLY OF MOSES, AND TO HAVE TAKEN THEIR OWN WAY. Even so there are those in the Church whose great natural abilities and singular daring lead them to act without much reference to the law of Christ, and yet it is not easy to condemn them, or to refuse their aid.

II. THAT THEY DID LITTLE GOOD TO THEMSELVES BY CONQUESTS SO REMOTE, BUT THEY DID MUCH GOOD IN MANY WAYS TO ISRAEL. Even so these irregular champions of the Church gain little spiritual profit to themselves, but they are often the means of manifold gain unto their brethren at large.

HOMILIES BY VARIOUS AUTHORS.

Ver. 23.—" *Be sure your sin will find you out.*" These words, though ultimately true of every sin, are spoken of actions which, going forth from us, perform their mischievous errands, but will come home again, bringing retribution with them. The Eastern proverb is true of crimes as well as curses: " Curses, like chickens, always come home to roost." God urges this truth as one out of many motives for strengthening us against allurements to sin. Sinners indulge vague hopes of impunity; they act as though they said, "The Lord shall not see," &c. (Ps. xciv. 7). But they cannot escape from sin. Lapse of time will not annihilate sin; careful concealment will not hide it up; mere repentance will not avert all its consequences. Nor will death screen from detection. We cannot escape from our sins—

I. BY LAPSE OF TIME. " Sin is the transgression of the law." It is a disturbing element, like a poison in the blood, or an error in a calculation as to the course of a ship. It is useless to say, " Let bygones be bygones " (cf. Ps. l. 21, 22 and Eccles. viii. 11). There is no " statute of limitations" in regard to the debt of sin. Illustrations: —Lot going to live in Sodom, and reaping domestic ruin years afterwards; Adoni-bezek (Judges i. 5—7); Saul's " bloody house " (2 Sam. xxi. 1).

II. CAREFUL CONCEALMENT. A sin may appear to be safely buried (like a murdered corpse), and grass may grow on the grave; but a resurrection awaits it. No immunity, because no concealment from God. In the law of Moses certain secret sins are mentioned which, through the ignorance or connivance of the judges, might escape punishment (Levit. xvii. 10; xx. 1—6, &c.); but God himself threatens to be the executioner. Conscience may at last make further concealment impossible. (Confessions of murderers.) A sinner should stand in awe of himself and dread the spy within him. Or a strange combination of circumstances may bring the sin to light when detection seemed almost impossible. Illustration:—Dr. Doune finding a nail in a skull dug up in his churchyard. Apply Eccles. x. 20 to the greater danger of sinning against God (Job xx. 27; Eccles. xii. 14).

III. BY REPENTANCE. The penitent who trusts in Christ is forgiven; but a sin when committed may have put in motion a series of temporal results from which no subsequent repentance may be able wholly to deliver us; *e. g.* habits of dissipation, or single acts of passion or of falsehood. Illustrations:—Jacob's receiving in the course of his life " the fruit of his doings" after having wronged Esau and deceived Isaac; David, pardoned, yet followed by the consequences of his sin (2 Sam. xii. 10—14). Thus God would make us wary of sin, as of a mad dog, or a poison that may lurk long in the system (Matt. vii. 2). God's caution signals against sin.

IV. BY DEATH. After death, in the fullest sense, sin must find the transgressor out. There is a fearful contrast suggested by the benediction in Rev. xiv. 13: " Cursed are the dead that die in their sins; for they have no rest from their transgressions, but their guilt follows them." Think of being found out in that world where the prospect is of " eternal sin " (Mark iii. 29). The only true salvation is from sin itself, assured to us through repentance and faith (Matt. i. 21; Titus ii. 14).—P.

Vers. 1—5.—*A bird in the hand worth two in the bush.* This common proverb, so limited in the scope of its application, and so liable to be misused by timid and selfish people, is clearly illustrated in the conduct of these two tribes. Doubtless it is a sound principle to hold a small certainty rather than run the bare chance of a large possibility. But principles are nothing unless we rightly apply them, and the children of Reuben and Gad were forsaking the most certain and enduring of all precious things, and leaning to their own frail understanding. It is a poor exchange to leave the path of Divine providence for that of purblind human prudence.

CONSIDER HERE THE MISTAKEN PRACTICAL NOTIONS BY WHICH REUBEN AND GAD WERE LED INTO THIS REQUEST. 1. *An exaggerated estimate of the importance of temporal possessions.* Reuben and Gad had a great multitude of cattle; the lands of Jazer and Gilead were places for cattle; and so the way is straight to the conclusion that these lands were the proper habitation of these tribes. It is the man of the world's view that the place which is good for one's property must be good for oneself, seeing that a man's abundance is in the things he possesses. The thought of the cattle so filled the minds of the two tribes that they could give no weight whatever to any other consideration. How hardly shall they that have riches enter the kingdom of heaven ! That faith which is the substance of *things hoped for* and the evidence of *things not seen* finds no room to grow in a neart choked up with the care of this world and the deceitfulness of riches. At this time, indeed, Reuben and Gad had many cattle, but it by no means followed that they would always have cattle. Job had many cattle, but in a few hours Sabeans and Chaldeans swept them all away. Consider well the thoughts that filled the mind of Lot (Gen. xiii. 10), as illustrating the foolish, partial, and short-sighted views of the children of Reuben and Gad. *The Dead Sea was no great distance from these very lands of Jazer and Gilead.* 2. *They acted on the presumption that a man is himself the best judge of his own interests.* They did not stop to consider that if God had meant this territory for them, he would have indicated his meaning in unmistakable fashion. He had made no sign, and this was in itself a proof that he judged their true home to be on the Canaan side of Jordan. It is the highest wisdom of man to wait, in simplicity and humility, on the *indispensable* directions of the All-Wise ; even as the mariner finds his position by looking heavenward, and by the aid of the compass confidently finds his path across pathless waters. In an unfamiliar place you can gain no knowledge of the points of the compass by the minutest consideration of terrestrial circumstances, but get a glimpse of the sun and know the time of day, and the information is yours at once. The heavens declare the glory of God in this, that they never mislead us ; and the God who made them is like them in ministering to the needs of our spirits. We cannot do without him. Instinct, so kind, so all-helpful to the brute, does little or nothing for us. God made us so that he might guide us with his eye. The great bulk of men act as these children of Reuben and Gad acted. The way of God, with all its real advantages, is yet so unpromising to the carnal eye that few there be who find it. 3. *Especially they had forgotten that the purposes of God were to be the great rule of life to them.* The great multitude of cattle was not theirs, but his. If they had made this proposition with a sense of stewardship in their minds, the proposition might have been not only excusable, but laudable. But the sense of stewardship was the very furthest of all feelings from their hearts. It is a late, a hard, and perhaps always an imperfect discovery, that a man only gains his right position when he manifests the glory of God. The earth is the Lord's and the fulness thereof. These people had not risen to the thought of Canaan as being the very best land *simply because it was God's choice.* Their minds were not full of Canaan, but of their own cattle. A great deal depends on our conception of heaven. If we think of it as the place and state where God is all in all, where law and life exactly correspond, and Christ is glorified in the perfection of all his people, then heaven is begun already. Caleb and Joshua had been waiting forty years for the promised land, yet in a certain sense it had been theirs all the time. It was not simple habitation that made Canaan a promised land, else the Canaanites would have been as blessed as the true Israel. Rightful possession, honest spiritual inheritance, these constituted the full and abiding enjoyment of Canaan.—Y.

Vers. 6—15.—*A thorough exposure of a selfish proposition.* I. MOSES APPEALS TO THE SENSE OF SHAME. They had been one nation until now. The suffering of one tribe had been the suffering of all. They had marched in company and fought in company ; but now, when Reuben and Gad see what seems the main chance, they say, " We have found what we want, we need go no further." Often the only way of treating selfishness is to make it thoroughly ashamed of itself. If there is no loving sympathy in the heart to be appealed to, we must do our best by appealing to a sense of decency ; we must ask the selfish, if they have nothing else to think of, to think a little of their own reputation. It was a very humiliating thing, if only Reuben and Gad had been able to see it, that Moses here made no appeal to high motives. He did not say, " Consider well, for your own sakes, what you propose to do ; consider whether you are not seeking a mere present, external, paltry gain, and paving the way for a tremendous loss hereafter." He might so have spoken, but what would the answer have been? " We are ready to take the risk of that." And so he leaves unasked and undetermined the whole question of what Reuben and Gad's own interest might be. That came up again in due time, as it was bound to do (Josh. xxii.). But there was a question bearing on the welfare of Israel which could not be postponed, and Moses sets it before the two tribes in a very direct way, neither repressing his just indignation nor softening his language. If men persist in taking a course which is hurtful to the real welfare of others, they must be whipped out of it by the readiest available means. There are only too many in the world who will do anything they can get others submissively to tolerate. Seemingly having no conscience of their own to speak of, they are dependent on the indignant, unsparing remonstrances of others. These remonstrances have to supply the place of conscience as best they can.

II. HE POINTS OUT A PROBABLE PERIL TO THE NATION. When an army is advancing to the attack, it is a serious thing if a sixth part of the whole shows signs of desertion and of want of interest in the desired victory. From patriots Reuben and Gad had sunk all at once into mere mercenaries. They had gone with the nation only as long as it seemed their interest to go. They could, without the slightest compunction, leave a great gap in the order of the camp round the tabernacle. They did not stop to consider how their desertion would affect the arrangements of the whole camp. Lukewarm, unspiritual, and self-indulgent Christians—if the name may be allowed where such qualities prevail—little think of the continual hindrances and discouragements they bring to struggling brethren. The Christian life is hard enough when there is the outside world to contend with, but how peculiar and how difficult to surmount are the perils that come from false brethren! Note how Moses bases his fear of this peril *on an actual experience*. If the words of the ten craven-hearted spies drove the whole of Israel into rebellion, and doomed a whole generation to die in the wilderness, then how great a danger was to be feared from the desertion of two whole tribes!

III. HE PLAINLY FIXES THE RISK OF THIS PERIL AND THE RESPONSIBILITY FOR IT UPON REUBEN AND GAD. It was not open to them to say, " All these gloomy chances that you foreshadow depend on the other tribes. They need not be discouraged. Canaan is just as attractive now as it was before. Our staying here can really make no difference." It is both cowardly and unavailing to try and escape responsibility by insisting on the personal responsibility of others. It is of no use to say that we do not wish others to look on us as leaders. We know that men will do it whether we wish it or not, and the very fact of this knowledge fixes on us a responsibility which we cannot escape. God makes use of this very disposition to follow which is found in human nature for his own gracious purposes. Jesus says, " Follow me." And those who follow him find that some at least become followers of them. If the way in which we are going is a way into which others may be drawn to their ruin, then the way is at once condemned. No amount of individual prosperity, pleasure, and ease can compensate the destruction of others who have perished in a path which they never would have entered but for us. Offences must needs come, but the caution and the appeal remain: " Woe be to him through whom the offence comes." Better for every beast in the herds to perish in Jordan than for the obscurest in all Israel to be prevented from getting into Canaan.—Y.

Vers. 16—32.—*The final arrangement*. I. REUBEN AND GAD DO NOT RESENT THE LANGUAGE OF MOSES. This is all the more noticeable because the language is so strong and humiliating. They seem to admit that his reproaches, his warnings, and his predictions had been only too clearly justified by their conduct. Learn from this that when there is occasion to express righteous anger, one must not begin to take counsel with the shallow maxims of worldly prudence. There is need in the service of God for great common sense, for far more of it than usually finds exercise, but there is no common sense where courage, straightforwardness, and the manly assertion of all Christian principles are absent. It is a very foolish thing to use strong language just by way of liberating the effervescence of the soul. But when strong language is deserved and the occasion demands the utterance of it, then do not spare. Moses might have said to himself, " This is a very ticklish state of affairs; if I do not humour these people they will certainly act according to their desire, whether I consent or not." Some leaders and so-called skilful managers and tacticians would have humoured Reuben and Gad at such a crisis as this. But it was not for Moses to humour anybody, or trifle with men who were trifling with God. And he had his immediate reward. "They came near unto him" (ver. 16). You can see them almost cringing before Moses, fawning upon him in their eagerness to get their requests. His eye has pierced into their mean hearts, and they know it. They have not one word of defence to offer, not one protest against being so hardly dealt with. Learn then from the example of Moses here, and of Paul on more than one occasion, how to speak out when silence, or, what is worse, delicate picking and choosing of words, involves unfaithfulness to God. We must never be coarse, vindictive, abusive, or spiteful; but if we have a genuine concern for the good of men and the glory of God, he will put as it were his own word into our lips, so controlling language, tone, and features that it will be what his word always is, a discerner of the thoughts and intents of the heart.

II. But though they do not resent the rebuke of Moses, they hold to their original purpose. So confident are they that they call this much-coveted land their inheritance. They cannot but feel the probing force of what Moses has said, but they are also quick to notice what he has omitted to say. If they had put their thoughts into speech they would have run somewhat like this: "He has been a shepherd himself, a practical man in flocks and herds, and of course he knows nicely that these lands for which we ask are just the place for our cattle. We shall hold to our choice, though it may involve a little more trouble and delay than we could have wished." Even when men are made to smart under a just, unanswerable rebuke they keep to their darling projects. They do not believe in their hearts, even though Christ says it, that one cannot serve God and mammon. Reuben and Gad mean to try the experiment of living east of Jordan, and yet keeping their place in the unity and the privileges of Israel.

III. They propose a rash and difficult compromise. The more we consider what they undertook to do, the more also we see their short-sighted policy. Mark *their overweening self-confidence.* They cannot risk the chance—which was indeed no chance at all, but a Divine certainty—of finding suitable pastures in Canaan, but they are quite willing to risk their families and flocks in fenced cities of the land they had chosen. Yet on their own admission fenced cities were no adequate security. The fighting men among them were going across Jordan to help in conquering a land where, as had been reported to their fathers, the cities were walled and very great (ch. xiii. 28). There appears in their resolution a curious mixture of reasonable faith and rash self-confidence. They have learned enough to assure them that Canaan will be conquered, and they are quite ready to believe that in some unaccountable way their own dearest possessions will also be safe. Yet they did not really know how long they were to be absent. It seems to have been several years before they were allowed to return, and when they did return it was not with the unmingled self-congratulations which might have been expected. He who would learn how disastrous their choice turned out in the end must carefully consider Josh. xxii. Most assuredly, whatever Reuben and Gad gained in pastures they more than lost in their permanent isolation from their brethren.—Y.

Ver. 23.—*The eyes of the sinner opened at last.* "Be sure your sin will find you out."

I. These words imply the possibility of sin being committed. The particular danger in this instance was of breaking a promise. These words of Moses certainly imply a humiliating estimate of the persons addressed, but it must be admitted that the estimate was justified by past experience. Moses cannot quickly accept the promise, for he knows well how hastily and recklessly it is made. There was no occasion to cast any doubt on the sincerity of their words, or to attribute to them a deliberate purpose of deception. But there was everything in impending circumstances to lead them into a broken promise. The promise itself was hastily made. It was made not for its own sake, but under a kind of compulsion, in order to get hold of a much-coveted possession. The fulfilment of it was beset, as Moses well knew, with difficult conditions, ever tending to increase in difficulty. Moses himself would not be with them across the Jordan, and when he had vanished from the scene, who else was to enforce with equal energy and authority the promise he had extorted? Moreover, the promise had been made on behalf of a heterogeneous crowd. Some of the better sort might be inclined to persevere in keeping it; others might only too readily make it an excuse that their leaders had promised without sufficiently consulting them. The great bulk had already shown themselves to be steeped in selfishness; were they likely then to stick at desertion, if only it could be managed with safety? It is a needful thing, even though it be a painful and humiliating one, *to assert, as Moses did here, the weakness of human nature.* When we form purposes which in themselves show the corruption and depravity of the human heart, we must not complain if we are dealt with in a humiliating fashion. And in our expectations from others we must ever make ready to meet with broken promises. Recollecting our own infirmities, we shall not be surprised at the many and sad consequences which come from the infirmities of our brethren. We should never feel insulted when any one gives us a word of caution against effusive and extravagant promises. He is the wisest Christian who, while he promises least in the hearing of his fellow-men, is ever striving to carry out in practice, and to its fullest extent, all that his heart would lead him to perform.

II. THESE WORDS ALSO AFFIRM THE CERTAINTY THAT IF SIN IS COMMITTED THE SINNER WILL AT LAST BE MADE FULLY CONSCIOUS OF HIS SIN. There was much, as we have seen, to lead Reuben and Gad to break their promise. In addition to what has already been mentioned, there was this as a possible consideration—that they might be able to break the promise with impunity. Indeed, from this solemn warning of Moses we may infer that he looked upon some such thought as likely to gain dominion in their minds. When the time of difficulty and sore temptation came they might argue thus: "If we do return, who is to mark our return or hinder it? The other tribes (perhaps hard beset in their conflict with the Canaanites) can do nothing against us. Moses is gone." They may have had it in their thoughts, after making the promise, that it would be enough to cross the river, wish their brethren God-speed, and then return. "They will understand our position, and not be so hard on us as Moses is. If they are willing that we should just go across, and then return, what can there be to make complaint about?" But Moses evidently meant them to keep their promise to the full. To break it was not only unbrotherly and ungrateful to the other tribes who had done so much for them; it was, he says with great emphasis, a sin against God, and in due time it would come back to them revealed as such, with all its dreadful consequences. 1. *We have a timely warning to those who are entering the paths of sin.* As it is true that God would have those who in their young enthusiasm and devotion propose to enter his service to consider well what it is that he asks, so it is equally true that he would have those who are beginning a life of sin to consider well what the end will be. These are the words of an *old and long-observant man, one who had lived unusually near to God.* They are spoken out of the fulness of his experience. He had seen sin revealed in all its enormity, and punished with the utmost severity. There must needs be in this world thousands of undetected crimes, thousands of accused persons acquitted not because they are innocent, but for lack of legal evidence. These failures come from the infirmities of men; but be sure of this, that they are failures only so far as men are concerned; not one evil-doer can escape God, though he may enjoy the pleasures and immunities of sin for a season. Sin may seem not to find men out while they are here, but it will be time enough by and by. Men must not despise the goodness and forbearance and long-suffering of God as if he were heedless of all their doings. The dresser of the vineyard who begged another year's reprieve for the fruitless fig-tree had marked its fruitlessness and anticipated its doom just as much as the man who owned the vineyard. We cannot too often recollect that the eye of God is on every unprofitable tree. The axe is laid to its roots, ready for use, if the use be compelled. 2. *We have here a great comfort and stay to the people of God.* The foolish, wicked man, making his proud and careless advances, says, "Doth God see?" Our answer, made not so much to him as to our own hearts, is, "God does see." He sees every sinner in his course, his doom, *and the opening of his eyes at last.* How many there are in the world whom we feel sure to be wrong! We cannot, try as we may, feel anything else; we cannot but believe them to be villains at heart, veneered and varnished up with a show of religion and goodness to impose on the simple-minded. But to give free utterance to our thoughts would be counted uncharitable and censorious, and assuming to be better than other men. What a comfort then to feel that what we cannot do God will do at last! The wolf will be utterly stripped of all his sheep's clothing, after all his gormandising and the warm, snug life he has lived so long; he will stand revealed in his true character, and become a gaunt, starving creature with all his opportunities of rapacity gone. "Found out at last" will be written on all those vain pretenders to a good and honourable life who at present fume and bluster and look unspeakably grieved when any of their actions are questioned in the slightest degree. And this, recollect, will be the crown of all other discoveries, that *the sin of sinners will be made clear and unquestionable in their own eyes.* 3. The practical lesson for you, O sinner, is, that *instead of waiting for sin to find you out, you should try with all energy and expedition to find sin out.* You know that though the Scriptures are full of references to it, there are, nevertheless, the greatest misapprehensions with respect to it. What a terrible thing it is to mock God by an outward and conventional confession of sin, and then go away to sin as much as before! It is one thing to join the customary crowd in saying, "We have sinned;" quite another to have an individual, searching, agonising experience such as we find in Ps. li. Find out what sin is, its reality, its magnitude, and how it stands behind all secondary causes of misery, almost as a great first cause. Find it out as dwelling deep-seated in your own heart, baneful beyond all imagination, spoiling the present life, and threatening the life to come.

Before passing from the consideration of this request from these two tribes, it is very noticeable that they kept their promise. When the time came for them to return to Jazer and Gilead, Joshua spoke to them in a very complimentary way (Josh. xxii.). Did this fulfilment show that the word of Moses had been constantly in their minds? Possibly his word had weight with some, but in all probability the miraculous discovery of Achan's guilt, and his terrible doom, had much more connection with the persistence of Reuben and Gad in keeping their promise. They doubtless saw very clearly that steady and patient obedience was the only way of escaping something like Achan's fate.—Y.

Ver. 42.—*Nobah—the man and the place.* This proceeding on the part of Nobah suggests a good deal of speculation as to the character, purposes, and actual achievements of the man. Concerning the children of Reuben, we are simply told in general terms that they gave names to the cities they builded (ver. 38). Jair, the son of Manasseh, gave to the small towns of Gilead the name of Havoth-Jair, which seems to be a general indication of them as being the property of Jair. Then in the last verse of the chapter we come to a kind of climax as we read that Nobah boldly called by his own name the district he had gained. What did he mean by this? Perhaps it was *for the sake of a fancied security.* The rigorous, inexorable demands of Moses were going to take him away, he knew not how long, and he may have reckoned that giving his name to his property before he went would be an excellent plan to guard himself against covetous and unscrupulous neighbours. How suspicious of one another selfish people are! When we busy ourselves laying up treasures on earth instead of in heaven, we have to use all sorts of schemes and devices in order to gain a security which in the end proves to be no security at all. Or Nobah may have been a man *full of personal ambition.* David tells us, in strains half-pitying, half-despising, of those infatuated, purse-proud grandees who call their lands after their own names (Ps. xlix. 11). From this we may infer that Nobah was not alone in his folly. Very possibly the name took root and lasted for generations; but even supposing it did, who in after days would trouble himself concerning the man Nobah? Calling a town or a street after a man will do nothing to preserve his memory if the man himself has been nothing more than a plutocrat. But if the man himself, by deeds and character, becomes memorable and glorious, then his birth-place and dwelling-place, however mean they otherwise may be, share in the glory of the man. How many obscure hamlets have thus become dignified in history, and chief among them stand Bethlehem, the little one among the thousands of Judah, and Nazareth, the mean, secluded village in the highlands of Galilee. "This place, dearest to the Christian heart of all on earth except Jerusalem, is not mentioned in the Old Testament, nor even by Josephus, who was himself on every side of it, and names the villages all about it, but seems yet totally ignorant of its existence."—Y.

EXPOSITION.

CHAPTER XXXIII.

ITINERARY OF THE WANDERINGS (vers. 1—49). Ver. 1.—**These are the journeys.** The Hebrew word מַסְעֵי is rendered σταϑμοί by the Septuagint, which means "stages" or "stations." It is, however, quite rightly translated "journeys," for it is the act of setting out and marching from such a place to such another which the word properly denotes (cf. Gen. xiii. 3; Deut. x. 11). Ver. 2.—**And Moses wrote their goings out** (מוֹצָא. Septuagint, ἀπάρσεις) accord-ing to their journeys by the commandment of the Lord. The latter clause (עַל־פִּי יְהֹוָה) may be taken as equivalent to an adjective qualifying the noun "goings out," signify-ing only that their marches were made under the orders of God himself. It is more natural to read it with the verb "wrote;" and in that case we have a direct assertion that Moses wrote this list of marches himself by command of God, doubtless as a memorial not only of historical interest, but of deep religious significance, as showing how Israel had been led by him who is faithful and true—faithful in keeping his promise, true in fulfilling his word for good or for evil. The direct statement that Moses wrote this list himself is strongly corroborated by internal evidence, and has been accepted as substan-tially true by the most destructive critics. No conceivable inducement could have ex-isted to invent a list of marches which only partially corresponds with the historical ac-count, and can only with difficulty be recon-ciled with it—a list which contains many names nowhere else occurring, and having no associations for the later Israelites. Whether the statement thus introduced tells in favour of the Mosaic authorship (as usually accepted) of the rest of the Book is a very different matter, on which see the Introduction. Ver. 3.—**They departed from Rameses.** Hebrew, Raemses. See on Exod. i. 11; xii. 37. The brief description here given of the departure from Egypt touches upon every material circumstance as related at large in Exod. xi., xii. **In the sight of all the Egyptians.** The journey was begun by night (Exod. xii. 42), but was of course con-tinued on the following day. Ver. 4.—**Buried all their first-born, which the Lord had smitten among them.** Liter-

ally, "were burying (Septuagint, ἔϑαπτον) those whom the Lord had smitten among them, viz., all the first-born." The fact that the Egyptians were so universally employed about the funeral rites of their first-born—rites to which they paid such extreme atten-tion—seems to be mentioned here as supply-ing one reason at least why the Israelites began their outward march without oppo-sition. It is in perfect accordance with what we know of the Egyptians, that all other passions and interests should give place for the time to the necessary care for the departed. **Upon their gods also the Lord executed judgments.** See on Exod. xii. 12, and cf. Isa. xix. 1. The false deities of Egypt, having no existence except in the imagin-ations of men, could only be affected within the sphere of those imaginations, i. e. by being made contemptible in the eyes of those who feared them. Ver. 6.—**Etham.** See on Exod. xiii. 20. Ver. 7.—**Pi-hahiroth.** Hebrew, "Hahi-roth," without the prefix. See on Exod. xiv. 2. Ver. 8.—**In the wilderness of Etham.** This is called the wilderness of Shur in Exod. xv. 22, nor is it easy to explain the occurrence of the name Etham in this con-nection, for the Etham mentioned in ver. 6 lay on the other side of the Red Sea. We do not, however, know what physical changes have taken place since that time, and it is quite possible that at Etham there may have been a ford, or some other easy means of communication, so that the strip of desert along the opposite shore came to be known as the wilderness of Etham. Ver. 9.—**Elim.** See on Exod. xv. 27. Ver. 10.—**Encamped by the Red Sea.** This encampment, like those at Dophkah and at Alush (ver. 13), is not mentioned in the narrative of Exodus. The phrase-ology, however, used in Exod. xvi. 1; xvii. 1 leaves abundant room for intermediate halting-places, at which it is to be presumed that nothing very noteworthy happened Nothing whatever is known of these three stations. Ver. 15.—**The wilderness of Sinai.** See on Exod. xix. 1. Ver. 17.—**Kibroth-hattaavah . . Haze-roth.** See on ch. xi. 34, 35. Ver. 18.—**Rithmah.** Comparing this verse with ch. xii. 16 and xiii. 26, it would appear as if Rithmah were the station "in the wilderness of Paran" from which the spies went up, and to which they returned—a station subsequently known by the name of Kadesh. There are two difficulties in the way of this identification. In the first place we should then only have three names of stations between Sinai and the southern border of Palestine, on what is at least eleven days' journey. This is, however, confessedly the case in the historical narrative, and it admits of explanation. We know that the first journey was a three days' journey (ch. x. 33), and the others may have been longer still, through a country which presented no facilities for encamping, and possessed no variety of natural features. In the second place, Rithmah is not Kadesh, and cannot be connected with Kadesh except through a doubtful identification with the Wady Retemât in the neighbourhood of Ain Kudes (see note at end of ch. xiii.). It is, however, evident from ch. xii. 16, as compared with ch. xiii. 26, that Kadesh was not the name originally given to the encampment "in the wilderness of Paran." It seems to have got that name—perhaps owing to some popular feeling with respect to an ancient sanctuary, perhaps owing to some partial shifting of the camp—during the absence of the spies. Rithmah, therefore, may well have been the official name (so to speak) originally given to the encampment, but subsequently superseded by the more famous name of Kadesh; this would explain both its non-appearance in the narrative of Numbers, and its appearance in the Itinerary here.

Ver. 19.—**Rimmon-parez.** The latter part of the name is the same as *parats* or *perets,* which commonly signifies a breaking out of Divine anger. This place may possibly have been the scene of the events related in chs. xvi., xvii., but the Targum of Palestine connects them with Kehelathah.

Ver. 20.—**Libnah.** Hebrew לִבְנָה ("whiteness") may perhaps be the same as the Laban (לָבָן, "white") mentioned in Deut. i. 1. So many places, however, in that region are distinguished by the dazzling whiteness of their limestone cliffs that the identification is quite uncertain. The site of this, as of the next eight stations, is indeed utterly unknown; and the guesses which are founded on the partial and probably accidental similarity of some modern names (themselves differently pronounced by different travellers) are utterly worthless. Of these eight names, Kehelathah and Makheloth seem to be derived from קָהַל, "an assembling," and thus give some slight support to the supposition that during the thirty-eight years the people were scattered abroad, and only assembled from time to time in one place. Rissah is variously interpreted "heap of ruins," or "dew;" Shapher means "fair," or "splendid;" Haradah, or Charadah, is "terror," or "trembling" (cf. 1 Sam. xiv. 15); Tahath is a "going down," or "depression;" Tarah is "turning," or "delay;" Mithcah signifies "sweetness," and may be compared (in an opposite sense) to Marah.

Ver. 30.—**Hashmonah.** This is possibly the Heshmon of Josh. xv. 27, since this was one of the "uttermost cities . . toward the coast of Edom, southward." The name, however ("fruitfulness"), was probably common on the edge of the desert. **Moseroth.** This is simply the plural form of Moserah ("chastisement"), and is no doubt the place so called in Deut. x. 6 (see note at end of chapter).

Ver. 31.—**Bene-Jaakan.** The full name is given in Deut. x. 6 as Beeroth-beni-Jaakan, "the wells of the children of Jaakan." Jaakan, or Akan, was a grandson of Seir, the legendary tribe father of the Horites of Mount Seir (Gen. xxxvi. 20, 27; 1 Chron. i. 42). The wells of the Beni-Jaakan may well have retained their name long after their original owners had been dispossessed; or a remnant of the tribe may have held together until this time.

Ver. 32.—**Hor-ha-gidgad.** The MSS. and Versions are divided between Chor ("cave") and Hor ("summit," or "mountain"). Gidgad is no doubt the Gudgodah of Deut. x. 7.

Ver. 33.—**Jotbathah.** The meaning of this name, which is apparently "excellent," is explained by the note in Deut. x. 7 "Jotbath, a land of rivers of waters." It would be difficult to find such a land now in the neighbourhood of the Arabah, but there are still running streams in some of the wadys which open into the Arabah towards its southern end.

Ver. 34.—**Ebronah,** or "Abronah," a "beach," or "passage," called "the Fords" by the Targum of Palestine. It is conjectured that it lay below Ezion-geber, just opposite to Elath, with which place it may have been connected by a ford at low tide, but this is quite uncertain.

Ver. 35.—**Ezion-gaber,** or rather "Etsiongeber," the "giant's backbone." This can hardly be other than the place mentioned in 1 Kings ix. 26; 2 Chron. viii. 17 as the harbour of King Solomon's merchant navy. At this later date it was at the head of the navigable waters of the Elanitic Gulf, but considerable changes have taken place in the shore line since the age of Solomon, and no doubt similar changes took place before. It was known to, and at times occupied by, the Egyptians, and the wretched village which occupies the site is still called Aszium by the

Arabs. The name itself would seem to be due to some peculiar rock formation—probably the serrated crest either of a neighbouring mountain or of a half-submerged reef.

Ver. 36.—**The wilderness of Zin, which is Kadesh.** See on ch. xx. 1.

Ver. 37.—**Mount Hor.** See on ch. xx. 22.

Ver. 38.—**In the fortieth year, . . in the first day of the fifth month.** This is the only place where the date of Aaron's death is given. It is in strict accordance with the Divine intimation that Israel was to wander forty years in the wilderness (ch. xiv. 33, 34), that period being understood, according to the usual mercy of God, which shortens the days of evil, to include the time already spent in the wilderness.

Ver. 39.—**An hundred and twenty and three years old.** He had been eighty-three years old when he first stood before Pharaoh, forty years before (Exod. vii. 7).

Ver. 40. —**And king Arad . . heard of the coming.** See on ch. xxi. 1. The introduction of this notice, for which there seems no motive, and which has no assignable connection with the context, is extremely perplexing. It is not simply a fragment which has slipped in by what we call accident (like Deut. x. 6, 7), for the longer statement in ch. xxi. 1—3 occupies the same position in the historical narrative immediately after the death of Aaron. It is difficult to suppose that Moses wrote this verse and left it as it stands ; it would rather seem as if a later hand had begun to copy out a statement from some earlier document—in which it had itself perhaps become misplaced—and had not gone on with it.

Ver. 41.—**Zalmonah.** This place is not elsewhere mentioned, and cannot be identified. Either this or Punon may be the encampment where the brazen serpent was set up ; according to the Targum of Palestine it was the latter.

Ver. 42. —**Punon.** Perhaps connected with the Pinon of Gen. xxxvi. 41. The Septuagint has Φινώ, and it is identified by Eusebius and Jerome with Phæno, a place between Petra and Zoar where convicts were sent to labour in the mines. Probably, however, the march of the Israelites lay further to the east, inasmuch as they scrupulously abstained from trespassing upon Edom.

Ver. 44.—**Oboth, . . Ije-abarim.** See on ch. xxi. 11.

Ver. 45.—**Dibon-gad.** This encampment may have been the same as that previously called by the name of Nahaliel or Bamoth (ch. xxi. 19, and see on xxxiii. 34). Several stages are here passed over in the Itinerary. At a time when the conquest and partial occupation of large districts was going on, it would be hard to say what regular stages were made by the host as such (see note at end of chapter).

Ver. 46. —**Almon-diblathaim.** Probably the same as the Beth-diblathaim mentioned in Jer. xlviii. 22 as a Moabitish town contiguous to Dibon, Nebo, and Kiriathaim. The name, which signifies "hiding-place of the two circles" or "cakes," was doubtless due either to some local legend, or more probably to the fanciful interpretation of some peculiar feature in the landscape.

Ver. 47. —**The mountains of Abarim, before Nebo.** The same locality is called "the top of Pisgah, which looketh toward the waste," in ch. xxi. 20 (see note there, and at ch. xxvii. 12). Nebo is the name of a town here, as in ch. xxxii. 3, 38, and in the later books ; in Deut. (xxxii. 49 ; xxxiv. 1) it is the name of the mountain, here included in the general designation Abarim.

Ver. 48.—**In the plains of Moab.** See on ch. xxii. 1.

Ver. 49.—**From Beth-jesimoth even unto Abel-shittim.** Beth-jesimoth, "house of the wastes," must have been very near the point where Jordan empties itself into the Dead Sea, on the verge of the salt desert which bounds that sea on the east. It formed the boundary of Sihon's kingdom at the south-west corner. Abel-shittim, "meadow of acacias," is better known by the abbreviated name "Shittim" (ch. xxv. 1 ; Micah vi. 5). Its exact site cannot be recovered, but the Talmud states that it was twelve miles north of the Jordan mouth. Probably the centre of the camp was opposite to the great fords, and the road leading to Jericho.

NOTE ON THE TWO LISTS OF STATIONS BETWEEN EGYPT AND THE JORDAN.

There can be no question that the chief interest of the Itinerary here given is due to its literary character as a document containing elements at least of extreme and unquestioned antiquity.   At the same time it is a matter of some importance to compare it with the history as given at large in Exodus and Numbers, and to note carefully the points of contact and divergence.   It is evident at first sight that no pains have been taken to make the two lists of stages agree, each list containing several names which the other lacks, and (in some cases) each having a name of its own for what appears to be the same place.   With respect to the latter point, the explanation usually given seems quite natural and satisfactory : the names were in many cases given by the Israelites themselves, and in others were derived from some small local peculiarity, or belonged to insignificant hamlets, so that the same encampment may very well have received one name in the official record of the movements of the tabernacle, and retained another in the popular recollection of the march.   With respect to the former point, it may fairly be argued that the narrative only records as a rule the names of places where something memorable occurred, and indeed does not always mention the place even then, while the Itinerary is simply concerned with the consecutive encampments as such.   It would be more correct to say that the narrative is essentially fragmentary, and does not purport to record more than certain incidents of the wanderings.

We have, therefore, no difficulty in understanding why the Itinerary gives us the names of three stations between Egypt and Mount Sinai not mentioned in Exodus. There is much more difficulty with the ensuing notices, because the name of Kadesh only occurs once in the list, whereas it is absolutely necessary, in order to bring the narrative into any chronological sequence, to assume (what the narrative itself pretty clearly intimates) that there were two encampments at Kadesh, separated by an interval of more than thirty-eight years.   It has accordingly been very generally agreed that the Rithmah of the Itinerary is identical with the nameless station " in the wilderness of Paran," afterwards called Kadesh in the narrative.   This is of course an assumption which has only probabilities to support it, but it may fairly be said that there is nothing against it.   The *retem*, or broom, is so common that it must have given a name to many different spots—a name too common, and possessing too few associations, to stand its ground in popular remembrance against any rival name (see note on ver. 18).   It has been argued by some that the whole of the twenty-one stages enumerated in vers. 16—35 were made on the one journey from Sinai to Kadesh ; and as far as the mere number goes there is nothing improbable in the supposition ; the " eleven days " of Deut. i. 2 are no doubt the days of ordinary travellers, not of women and children, flocks and herds.   It is true that the supposition is commonly connected with a theory which throws the whole historical narrative into confusion, viz., that Israel spent only two years intead of forty in the wilderness ; but that need not cause its rejection, for the whole thirty-eight may be intercalated between ver. 36 and ver. 37 of the Itinerary, and we could explain a total silence concerning the wanderings of those years better than we can the mention of (only) seventeen stations.   The only serious difficulty is presented by the name Ezion-geber, which it is very difficult not to identify with the place of that name, so well known afterwards, at the head of the Elanitic Gulf ; for it is impossible to find the last stage towards Kadesh at a spot as near to Sinai as to any of the supposed sites of Kadesh.

It is of course possible that more than one place was known as the "giant's back-bone;" but, on the other hand, the fact that at Moseroth Israel was near Mount Hor, and that they made five marches thence to Ezion-geber, is quite in accordance with the site usually assigned to it. It must remain, therefore, an unsettled point as to which nothing more can be said than that a balance of probabilities is in favour of the identification of Rithmah with the first encampment at Kadesh. Proceeding on this assumption, we have thereafter eleven names of stations concerning which nothing is known, and nothing can be with any profit conjectured. Then come four others which are evidently the same as those mentioned in Deut. x. 6, 7. That this latter passage is a fragment which has come into its present position (humanly speaking) by some accident of transcription does not admit of serious debate; but it is evidently a fragment of some ancient document, possibly of the very Itinerary of which we have only an abbreviation here. Comparing the two, we are met at once with the difficulty that Aaron is said to have died and been buried at Moserah, whereas, according to the narrative and the Itinerary, he died on Mount Hor during the last journey from Kadesh. This is not unnaturally explained by assuming that the official name of the encampment under, or opposite to, Mount Hor, from which Aaron ascended the mountain to die, was Moserah or Moseroth, and that the Israelites were twice encamped there—once on their way to Ezion-geber and back to Kadesh, and again on the last march round Edom, to which the fragment in Deut. refers. There remain, however, unexplained the singular facts—1. That the station where Aaron died is called Moserah in Deut. x. 6, whereas it is called Mount Hor not only in the narrative, but in the Itinerary, which nevertheless does give the name Moseroth to this very station when occupied on a previous occasion. 2. That the fragment gives Bene-Jaakan, Moseroth, Gudgod, and Jotbath as stages on the last journey, whereas the Itinerary gives them (the order of the first two being inverted) as stages on a previous journey, and gives other names for the encampments of the last journey. There is no doubt room for all four, and more besides, between Mount Hor and Oboth; but it cannot be denied that there is an appearance of error either in the fragment or in the Itinerary.

A further objection has been made to the statement that Israel marched from Ezion-geber to Kadesh, both on the score of distance and of the apparent absurdity of returning to Kadesh only to retrace their steps once more. It is replied (1) that the return to Kadesh for the final move may have been hurried, and no regular encampment pitched; (2) that when Israel returned to Kadesh it was still in expectation of entering Canaan "by the way of the spies," and in ignorance that they would have to treat with Edom for a passage—much more that they would have to come down the Arabah once again.

Lastly, with respect to the names which occur after Ije-abarim, we have again an almost total want of coincidence with this peculiarity, that the narrative gives seven names where the Itinerary only gives three. It must, however, be remembered that the whole distance from the brook of Arnon, where the Israelites crossed it, to the Arboth Moab is only thirty miles in a straight line. Over this short distance it is quite likely that the armies of Israel moved in lines more or less parallel, the tabernacle probably only shifting its place as the general advance made it desirable. That the two accounts are based on different documents, or drawn from different sources, is likely enough; but both may nevertheless be equally correct. If (as regards the last march) one record was kept by Eleazar, and another by Joshua, the apparent disagreement may be readily explained.

HOMILETICS.

Vers. 1—49.—*The journey home.* We have here a brief summary of the stages by which Israel travelled onwards from Egypt to Canaan ; spiritually, therefore, we have an epitome of the Church's progress, or of the progress of a soul, through this world to the world to come. Hence it follows that all the lessons, encouragements, and warnings which belong to these forty years weave themselves about this Itinerary, which might to the careless eye seem a bare list of names. " Per has (mansiones) currit verus Hebræus, qui de terrâ transire festinat ad cœlum," says Jerome. And in this connection it can hardly be an accident that as there are forty-two stations in this list, so there are forty-two generations in the first Gospel from Abraham (the starting-point of the faithful) to Christ (in whom they find rest). And, again, it may be more than a coincidence that the woman in the Apocalypse who represents the Church militant (Rev. xii.) was in the wilderness forty-two months. In all three cases (as certainly in the last) it is likely that the number forty-two was designedly chosen because it is $12 \times 3\frac{1}{2}$, and $3\frac{1}{2}$, or the half of 7, is the number which expresses trial, probation, and imperfection. Consider, therefore—

I. THAT THIS ITINERARY WAS WRITTEN " BY THE COMMANDMENT OF THE LORD," NO DOUBT AS A MEMORIAL UNTO THE CHILDREN OF ISRAEL OF THEIR TRIALS AND OF HIS FAITHFULNESS. Even so it is the will of God that every Church and every soul should keep in memory the stages of its own spiritual progress, for these are full of holy memories and needful lessons, all being eloquent of our own insufficiency and of his goodness. No one, being in plenty and at rest, should ever forget the straitness and the trial through which the good hand of God hath led him.

II. THAT THE TWO ENDS OF THIS ITINERARY ARE PLAINLY FIXED, THE ONE IN THE GLORIOUS DELIVERANCE FROM EGYPT "AFTER THE PASSOVER," THE OTHER ON THE VERGE OF JORDAN IN FULL VIEW OF CANAAN. Even so all spiritual life histories begin with the redemption from bondage through the blood of the Lamb, and end with the sure hope of immortality on the verge of the river of death.

III. THAT THE INTERMEDIATE STAGES ARE TO A GREAT EXTENT UNCERTAIN, SOME QUITE UNKNOWN, AND OTHERS MATTER OF DISPUTE. Even so, while we know whence all Christian progress leads men at the first, and whither it brings men at the last, yet the intermediate course (sometimes a very long one) is for the most part strangely indiscernible, its points of contact with the outer world having little meaning or interest save for the travellers themselves. Just as maps help us little to follow the forty-two stages, so do religious theories give us small assistance in tracing the actual course of a soul through the trials and perplexities of real life.

IV. THAT WITH EXCEPTION OF THE BEGINNING AND THE END, THE ONLY FIXED POINTS IN THE ITINERARY ARE SINAI, KADESH, AND HOR—WHERE THE LAW WAS GIVEN, WHERE PROGRESS WAS RESUMED AFTER LONG DRIFTING TO AND FRO, WHERE AARON DIED. Even so there are in the history of most souls these three conspicuous epochs to be noted : (1) where the obligation to obey the higher law of God's will came upon them ; (2) where after much drawing back and consequent failure a new call to advance was heard ; (3) where the old outward associations, upon which they had all along leaned, failed them, and yet left them none the weaker.

V. THAT THE FEW NOTES OF EVENTS APPENDED TO CERTAIN NAMES OF PLACES (ELIM, REPHIDIM, HOR) SEEM TO BE SELECTED ARBITRARILY. Some other places certainly had, and many others probably had, more interesting associations for the Israelites. Even so it is not only or chiefly those passages which attract attention and secure comment in the history of a Church or of a soul which are of deep interest and profound importance to itself ; names and facts which have no associations for others may for it be full of the deepest meaning.

And note that all the stations named in this list have their own signification in the Hebrew, but the spiritual teaching founded on such signification is too arbitrary and fanciful to be seriously dealt with.

HOMILIES BY VARIOUS AUTHORS.

Vers. 1—49.—*The journeyings of the Israelites.* Reading through this record, which looks, on the first appearance of it, much like a page from a gazetteer, we are made to feel—

I. How LITTLE WE SHOULD KNOW OF THE EXPERIENCES OF ISRAEL IN THEIR WANDERINGS IF WE HAD BEEN TOLD NO MORE THAN THIS. A period of forty years has to be covered ; and though by one kind of narration it takes four books, full of solemnity and variety, abounding in matters of stirring interest, and often going into the minutest detail, in order to indicate sufficiently the events of the period, yet by another kind of narration the period can be comprised in forty-nine short verses. All the way through these verses it is assumed that a particular aspect of the course of Israel is being presented, and that a full, edifying, and satisfying narrative is to be sought elsewhere. Consider what great omissions there are. We do indeed see something of the manner of starting, but even here there is hardly anything to explain how Israel came to leave Egypt. It is said that they passed through the midst of the sea, but nothing is said of the wonderful and glorious manner in which the passage was effected. There is nothing of all the law-giving at Sinai; nothing of the tabernacle, the ark, the offerings, and the priestly office ; nothing of the great manna mercies ; nothing even of the cloud and trumpets, though they had so much to do with the journeys ; nothing of the rebellion which was the great cause of this long wandering. If it was a mere record of places we could better understand it, but there are just enough of additional matters introduced to perplex us as to why some are inserted and others omitted. How clear it becomes, in the light of an artless record like this, that we shall err if we allow ourselves to look too constantly on the books of the Old Testament as being the literature, the classic literature, of the Hebrews! That they are literature is of course true, but it is so small a part of the truth concerning them, that if we allow it to become too prominent, it will hide much more important truth. Moses was evidently not a man to care about the niceties and elaborations so dear to fastidious writers. His hands were too full of guiding and governing. If what he wrote was written in a way to glorify God, that was sufficient. We find in the Pentateuch not history, but the rough, yet authentic and unspeakably precious, materials of history. A man with the requisite interest and knowledge may analyse, select, and combine these materials into a history from his own point of view, but thanks be to God that he took a meek, humble, and unselfish Moses, who had no views of his own to assert, and who thought of no *monumentum ære perennius*, and made him his pen to write something a great deal more important than the history of any nation, namely, the dealings of God with his own typical people, and through them with the world at large.

II. Though this is such a brief and apparently artless record, little more than a copy of names from a map, yet HOW MUCH IT WOULD TELL US, EVEN IF WE HAD BEEN TOLD NO MORE. If this were but the sole surviving fragment of the four books, it would nevertheless indicate the presence of God, and that in very remarkable ways. It would indicate *the authority of Jehovah over Israel.* Moses and Aaron are spoken of as the leaders of Israel (ver. 1), yet only leaders under God ; for Moses wrote this very record at the commandment of God (ver. 2), and Aaron went up into Mount Hor to die at the commandment of God (ver. 38). We should also learn something of *the punitive power of God.* We should feel ourselves in the presence of some terrible sin, some terrible suffering, and some crowning blow which had come upon Egypt. We should learn that God was *able to vindicate his majesty and glory against the arrogance of idolatry* (ver. 4). We should learn that human life was at the sovereign disposal of God, for he controls the death of the first-born and the death of Aaron. And from what we thus plainly see of God's presence in certain places, we might infer that he was also in the places where we see him not. We might infer that if he was in the midst of the Israelites when they left Egypt, and in their midst forty years after, then he must have been with them all the time between. Thus, though in these forty-nine verses we are told nothing whatever, in *a plain, direct way, of human character*, we are yet brought face to face with very suggestive intimations concerning *the character of God.* From the human point of view the record is indeed a very barren one; but this only helps to show how when man becomes scarcely visible, unless as a mere wanderer, the glory of God shines brilliantly as ever.

III. We have thus tried to imagine this passage as being the sole surviving fragment of the four books which deal with the wanderings. But we know in reality that it is only a sort of appendix to the record of notable and solemn proceedings already given. It may even seem as if it would not have been much missed if it had been left out. As we think over it, however, we become conscious that A DISTINCT AND PECULIAR IMPRESSION IS BEING PRODUCED ON OUR MINDS. Reading through the Book of Numbers, we wander with Israel from the day they leave Sinai down to the day they enter the plains of Moab by Jordan; and now in this passage we are all at once lifted as it were into an exceeding high mountain, and get a bird's-eye view of *the wandering, shifting life of Israel during these forty years.* It is well to be brought face to face with something that will remind us of the shifting character of human life. Even the lives that seem most stationary, as far as local circumstances are concerned, are full of change. It is not because a man is born, lives, and dies in one locality, perhaps even in one house, that his life is to be reckoned a settled one. Wherever we are, however rooted and grounded in appearance, we see one generation going and another coming, ourselves being a part of what we see. Here, in the record of these journeyings, was something true *for all Israel;* Moses and Aaron were brought down to the same level with the humblest of their followers. There are certain necessary outlines of change in the course of every human being who lives to the allotted term—birth, unconscious infancy, the common influences of childhood, the time to choose a temporal occupation, the day when father dies and when mother dies, the dropping away of kindred, companions, and friends, and so on till death comes at last. There is so much of life lived and so much of biography written under the fascinating glamour of mere mundane interests, that it is a good thing to go where, along with God himself, we may look down on the changing scenes of earth from the dwarfing and humbling heights of eternity. There is a time to listen to the botanist and the expert in vegetable physiology, while they discourse to us on the wonders of the leaf; there is a time to see what the painter can do with it, and what the poet; but from all these we must turn at last to God's own Isaiah, and hear him drawing out the great final lesson, " We all do fade as a leaf."—Y.

EXPOSITION.

THE CLEARANCE, THE BOUNDARIES, AND THE ALLOTMENT OF CANAAN (ch. xxxiii. 50—xxxiv. 29). Ver. 50.—**And the Lord spake.** It is quite obvious that a new section begins here, closely connected, not with the Itinerary which precedes it, but with the delimitation which follows. The formula which introduces the present command is repeated in ch. xxxv. 1, and again in the last verse of ch. xxxvi., thus giving a character of its own to this concluding portion of the Book, and to some extent isolating it from the rest.

Ver. 51.— **When ye are passed over Jordan.** Previous legislation had anticipated the time when they should have come into their own land (cf. ch. xv. 2; Levit. xxiii. 10), but now the crossing of the river is spoken of as the last step on their journey home.

Ver. 52.—**Ye shall drive out.** The Hebrew word (from יָרַשׁ) is the same which is translated " dispossess " in the next verse. The Septuagint has in both cases ἀπολεῖτε,

supplying (like the A. V.) the word "inhabitants" in ver. 53. The Hebrew word, however, seems to have much the same sense as the English phrase " clear out," and is, therefore, equally applied to the land and the occupants of it. No doubt it implies extermination as a necessary condition of the clearance. **Their pictures.** מַשְׂכִּיֹּתָם. Septuagint, τὰς σκοπιὰς αὐτῶν (their outlooks, or high places). The Targums of Onkelos and Palestine have " the houses of their worship;" the Targum of Jerusalem has "their idols." The same word occurs in Levit. xxvi. 1, in the phrase אֶבֶן מַשְׂכִּית, which is usually rendered "a stone image," *i. e.* a stone shaped into some likeness of man. If so, מַשְׂכִּית by itself has probably the same meaning; at any rate it can hardly be " a picture," nor is there the least evidence that the art of painting was at all practised among the rude tribes of Canaan. The same word, *maskith,* is indeed found in Ezek. viii. 12 in connection with " gravings " (from חָקַק ; cf. Isa. xxii. 16 ; xlix. 16 with Ezek. iv. 1 ; xxiii. 14) on a wall ; but even this belonged to a very different age. **Their molten images.** צַלְמֵי מַסֵּכֹתָם, "images cast of brass." Septuagint, τὰ εἴδωλα τὰ χονευτά. The word *tselem* is only elsewhere used in the Pentateuch for that "likeness" which is reproduced in Divine creation (Gen. i. 26, 27 ; ix. 6) or in human generation (Gen. v. 3) ; in the later books, however (especially in Daniel), it is freely used for idols. On "*massekah*" see on Exod. xxxii. 4 ; Isa. xxx. 22. **Their high places.** בָּמוֹתָם. See on Levit. xxvi. 30. The Septuagint translates Bamoth in both places by στῆλαι, and of course it was not the high places themselves, which were simply certain prominent elevations, but the monuments (of whatever kind) which superstition had erected upon them, which were to be plucked down. As a fact, it would seem that the Jews, instead of obeying this command, appropriated the Bamoth to their own religious uses (cf. 1 Sam. ix. 12 ; 1 Kings iii. 2 ; Ps. lxxviii. 58, &c.). The natural result was, as in all similar cases, that not only the Bamoth, but very many of the superstitions and idolatries connected with them, were taken over into the service of the Lord.

Ver. 53.—**I have given you the land.** "The earth is the Lord's," and no one, therefore, can dispute his right in the abstract to evict any of his tenants and to put others in possession. But while the whole earth was the Lord's, it is clear that he assumed a special relation towards the land of Canaan, as to which he chose to exercise directly the rights and duties of landlord (see on Deut. xxii. 8 for a small but striking instance). The first duty of a landlord is to see that the occupancy of his property is not abused for illegal or immoral ends ; and this duty excuses, because it necessitates, eviction under certain circumstances. It is not, therefore, necessary to argue that the Canaanites were more infamous than many others ; it is enough to remember that God had assumed towards the land which they occupied (apparently by conquest) a relation which did not allow him to overlook their enormities, as he might those of other nations (see on Exod. xxiii. 23—33; xxxiv. 11—17, and cf. Acts xiv. 16; xvii. 30). It was (if we like to put it so) the misfortune of the Canaanites that they alone of "all nations" could not be suffered to "walk in their own ways," because they had settled in a land which the Lord had chosen to administer directly as his own earthly kingdom.

Ver. 54.—**Ye shall divide the land by lot.** These directions are repeated in substance from ch. xxvi. 53—56. **Every man's inheritance.** Not only the tribe, but the family and the household, was to receive its special inheritance by lot; no doubt in such a way that the final settlement of the country would correspond with the blood relationships of the settlers.

Ver. 55. — **If ye will not drive out the inhabitants.** As was in fact the case (Judges i.). The warning is here given for the first time, because the danger was now near at hand, and had indeed already shown itself in the matter of the Midianitish women and children. **Pricks in your eyes, and thorns in your sides.** Natural symbols of dangerous annoyances. Possibly the thickets which fringe the Jordan supplied them with present examples. In Josh. xxiii. 13 we have "*scourges* in your sides, and thorns in your eyes," which sounds somewhat more artificial. In Judges ii. 3, where this warning is quoted, the figure is not expressed at all: "they shall be in your sides."

Ver. 56.—**I shall do unto you as I thought to do unto them,** *i. e.* I shall execute by other hands upon you the sentence of dispossession which ye shall have refused to execute upon the Canaanites. The threat (although in fact fulfilled) does not necessarily involve any prophecy, since to settle down among the remnants of the heathen was a course of action which would obviously and for many reasons commend itself to the Israelites. Indolence and cowardice were consulted by such a policy as much as the natural feelings of pity towards vanquished and apparently harmless foes. The command to extirpate was certainly justified in this case (if it could be in any) by the unhappy consequences of its neglect. Israel being what he was, and so little severed in anything but religion from the ancient heathen, his only chance of future happiness lay in keeping himself from any contact with them. On the morality of the command itself, see on the passages referred to, and on the slaughter of the Midianites. As a fact, the extirpation of the conquered did not offend the moral sense of the Jews then any more than it did that of our heathen Saxon ancestors. Where both races could not dwell in security, it was a matter of course that the weaker was destroyed. Such a command was therefore justified at that time by the end to be attained, because it was not contrary to the moral law as then revealed, or to the moral sense as then educated. Being in itself a lawful proceeding, it was made a religious proceeding, and taken out of the category of selfish violence by being made a direct command of God.

Ch. xxxiv. 2.—**Into the land of Canaan.** Canaan has here its proper signification as the land (roughly speaking) between Jordan and the sea (so in ch. xxxii. 32 ; Josh. xxii. 11, 32). Nor is there any clear instance of its including the trans-Jordanic territories. In the prophets the word reverts to its proper (etymological) meaning, as the "flat country" along the Mediterranean coast (cf. Isa. xix. 18; Zeph. ii. 5; Matt. xv. 22). **This is the land that shall fall unto you.** These words should not be placed in a parenthesis; it is a simple statement in the tautological style so common in these books. **With the coasts thereof,** or, "according to its boundaries," *i. e.* within the limits which nature and the Divine decree had set to the land of Canaan.

Ver. 3.—**Then your south quarter.** Rather, "and your south side." **From the wilderness of Zin along by the coast of Edom.** This general preliminary definition of the southern frontier marks the "wilderness of Zin" as its chief natural feature, and asserts that this wilderness rested "upon the sides" (עַל־יְדֵי) of Edom. The wilderness of Zin can scarcely be anything else than the Wady Murreh, with more or less of the barren hills which rise to the south of it, for this wady undoubtedly forms the natural southern boundary of Canaan. All travellers agree both as to the remarkable character of the depression itself and as to the contrast between its northern and southern mountain walls. To the south lies the inhospitable and uncultivatable desert; to the north the often arid and treeless, but still partially green and habitable, plateau of Southern Palestine. The expression, "on the sides of Edom," can only mean that beyond the Wady Murreh lay territory belonging to Edom, the Mount Seir of Deut. i. 2, the Seir of Deut. i. 44; it does not seem possible that Edom proper, which lay to the east of the Arabah, and which barely marched at all with the land of Canaan, should be intended here (see on Josh. xv. 1, and the note on the site of Kadesh). **And your south border.** This begins a fresh paragraph, in which the southern boundary, already roughly fixed, is described in greater detail. **Shall be the utmost coast of the salt sea eastward.** Rather, "shall be from the extremity (מִקְצֵה) of the salt sea eastward" (cf. Josh. xv. 2). The easternmost point in this boundary was to be fixed at the southernmost extremity of the Salt Sea.

Ver. 4.—**Shall turn from the south to the ascent of Akrabbim.** It is not at all clear what מִנֶּגֶב לְמַעֲלֵה can mean in this sentence. The A. V., which follows the Septuagint and the Targums, does not seem to give any sense, while the rendering, "to the south side of the ascent," does not seem grammatically defensible. Moreover, it is quite uncertain where the "ascent of Akrabbim," *i. e.* the "Scorpion-pass," or "Scorpion-stairs," is to be placed. Some travellers

have recognised both place and name in a precipitous road which ascends the northern cliffs towards the western end of the Wady Murreh, and which the Arabs call Nakb Kareb; others would make the ascent to be the steep pass of es Sufah, over which runs the road from Petra to Hebron; others, again, identify the Scorpion-stairs with the row of white cliffs which obliquely cross and close in the Ghor, some miles south of the Salt Sea, and separate it from the higher level of the Arabah. None of these identifications are satisfactory, although the first and last have more to be said in their favour than the second. Possibly the ascent of Akrabbim may have been only the Wady Fikreh, along which the natural frontier would run from the point of the Salt Sea into the Wady Murreh. **Pass on to Zin.** It is only here and in Josh. xv. 3 that the name Zin stands by itself; it may have been some place in the broadest part of the Wady Murreh which gave its name to the neighbouring wilderness. **From the south to Kadesh-barnea.** Here again we have the expression מִנֶּגֶב לְ, of which we do not know the exact force. But if Kadesh was in the neighbourhood of the present Ain Kudes, then it may be understood that the frontier, after reaching the western end of the Wady Murreh, made a *détour* to the south so as to include Kadesh, as a place of peculiarly sacred memory in the annals of Israel. It is indeed very difficult, with this description of the southern frontier of Canaan before us, to believe that Kadesh was in the immediate neighbourhood of the Arabah, where many commentators place it; for if that were the case, then the boundary line has not yet made any progress at all towards the west, and the only points given on the actual southern boundary are the two unknown places which follow. **Hazar-addar.** In Josh. xv. 3 this double name is apparently divided into the two names of Hezron and Addar, but possibly the latter only is the place intended here. A Karkaa is also mentioned there, which is equally unknown with the rest.

Ver. 5.—**The river of Egypt**, or "brook (נַחַל) of Egypt." Septuagint, χειμά ῥοῦν Αἰγύπτου. It was a winter torrent which drained the greater part of the western half of the northern desert of the Sinaitic peninsula. It was, however, only in its lower course, where a single channel receives the intermittent outflow of many wadys, that it was known as the "brook of Egypt," because it formed the well-marked boundary between Egypt and Canaan (cf. 2 Chron. vii. 8, and Isa. xxvii. 12, where the Septuagint has ἕως Ῥινοκορούρων, from the name of the frontier fort, Rhinocorura, afterwards built there). So far as we are able to follow the line drawn in these verses, it would appear to have held a course somewhat to the south of west for about half its length, then to have made a southerly deflection to Kadesh, and from thence to have struck north-west until it reached the sea, almost in the same latitude as the point from which it started.

Ver. 6.—**And as for the western border.** The Hebrew word for "west" (יָם) is simply that for "sea," because the Jews in their own land always had the sea on their west. Thus the verse reads literally, "And the sea boundary shall be to you the great sea and boundary; this shall be to you the sea boundary." It would seem very unlikely that the Jews familiarly used the word "*yam*" for "west" after a residence of several centuries in a country where the sun set not over the sea, but over the desert. Nothing can of course be proved from the use of the word here, but it cannot be overlooked as one small indication that the language of this passage at any rate is the language of an age subsequent to the conquest of Canaan (see on Exod. x. 19; xxvi. 22, and ch. ii. 18) The line of coast from the brook of Egypt to the Leontes was upwards of 160 miles in length.

Ver. 7.—**Ye shall point out for you,** *i. e.* ye shall observe and make for, in tracing the boundary. Septuagint, καταμετρήσετε . . παρά. **Mount Hor.** Not of course the Mount Hor on which Aaron died, but another far to the north, probably in Lebanon. The Hebrew הֹר הָהָר, which the Septuagint had rendered Ὤρ τὸ ὄρος in ch. xx., it renders here τὸ ὄρος τὸ ὄρος, taking הֹר as simply another form of הָר, as it probably is. Hor Ha-har is therefore equivalent to the English "Mount Mountain;" and just as there are many "Avon rivers" on the English maps, so there were probably many mountains locally known among the Jews as Hor Ha-har. We do not know what peak this was, although it must have been one clearly distinguishable from the sea. There is, however, no reason whatever for supposing (contrary to the analogy of all such names, and of the other Mount Hor) that it included the whole range of Lebanon proper.

Ver. 8.—**From Mount Hor ye shall point out your border unto the entrance of Hamath.** Literally, "from Mount Hor point out (תְּתָאוּ, as in the previous verse) to come to Hamath," which seems to mean, "from Mount Hor strike a line for the entrance to Hamath." The real difficulty lies in the expression לְבֹא חֲמָת, which the Septuagint renders εἰσπορευομένου εἰς Ἐμάθ, "as men enter into Hamath." The same expression occurs in ch. xiii. 21, and is similarly ren-

dered by the Septuagint. A comparison with Judges iii. 3 and other passages will show that "l'bo Chamath" had a definite geographical meaning as the accepted name of a locality in the extreme north of Canaan. When we come to inquire where "the entrance to Hamath" was, we have nothing to guide us except the natural features of the country. Hamath itself, afterwards Epiphaneia on the Orontes, lay far beyond the extremest range of Jewish settlement; nor does it appear that it was ever conquered by the greatest of the Jewish kings. The Hamath in which Solomon built store-cities (2 Chron. viii. 4), and the Hamath which Jeroboam II. "recovered" for Israel (2 Kings xiv. 28), was not the city, but the kingdom (or part of the kingdom), of that name. We do not know how far south the territory of Hamath may have extended, but it is quite likely that it included at times the whole upper valley of the Leontes (now the Litâny). The "entrance to Hamath" then must be looked for at some point, distinctly marked by the natural features of the country, where the traveller from Palestine would enter the territory of Hamath. This point has been usually fixed at the pass through which the Orontes breaks out of its upper valley between Lebanon and anti-Lebanon into the open plain of Hamath. This point, however, is more than sixty miles north of Damascus (which confessedly never belonged to Israel), and nearly a hundred miles north-north-west from Dan. It would require some amount of positive evidence to make it even probable that the whole of the long and narrow valley between Lebanon and anti-Lebanon, widening towards the north, and separated by mountainous and difficult country from the actual settlements of the Jews, was yet Divinely designated as part of their inheritance. No such positive evidence exists, and therefore we are perfectly free to look for "the entrance to Hamath" much further to the south. It is evident that the ordinary road from the land of Canaan or from the cities of Phœnicia to Hamath must have struck the valley of the Leontes, have ascended that river to its sources, and crossed the watershed to the upper stream of Orontes. The whole of this road, until it reached the pass already spoken of leading down to the Emesa of after days, and so to Hamath, lay through a narrow valley of which the narrowest part is at the southern end of the modern district of el Bekáa, almost in a straight line between Sidon and Mount Hermon. Here the two ranges approach most nearly to the bed of the Litâny (Leontes), forming a natural gate by which the traveller to Hamath must needs have entered from the south. Here then, very nearly in lat. 33° 30', we may reasonably place the "entrance to Hamath" so often spoken of, and so escape the necessity of imagining an artificial and impracticable frontier for the northern boundary of the promised land. **Zedad.** Identified by some with the present village of Sadad or Sudad, to the south-east of Emesa (Hums); but this identification, which is at best very problematic, is wholly out of the question if the argument of the preceding note be accepted.

Ver. 9.—**Ziphron.** A town called Sibraim is mentioned by Ezekiel (xlvii. 16) as lying on the boundary between Damascus and Hamath, and there is a modern village of Zifrân about forty miles north-east of Damascus, but there is no probable ground for supposing that either of these are the Ziphron of this verse. **Hazar-enan,** *i. e.* "fountain court." There are of course many places in and about the Lebanon and anti-Lebanon ranges to which such a name would be suitable, but we have no means of identifying it with any one of them. It must be confessed that this "north border" of Israel is extremely obscure, because we are not told whence it started, nor can we fix, except by conjecture, one single point upon it. A certain amount of light is thrown upon the subject by the description of the tribal boundaries and possessions as given in Josh. xix., and by the enumeration of places left unconquered in Josh. xiii. and Judges iii. The most northerly of the tribes were Asher and Naphtali, and it does not appear that their allotted territory extended beyond the lower valley of the Leontes where it makes its sharp turn towards the west. It is true that a portion of the tribe of Dan afterwards occupied a district further north, but Dan-Laish itself, which was the extreme of Jewish settlement in this direction, as Beersheba in the other, was southward of Mount Hermon. The passage in Josh. xiii. 4—6 does indeed go to prove that the Israelites never occupied all their intended territory in this direction, but as far as we can tell the line of promised conquest did not extend further north than Zidon and Mount Hermon. "All Lebanon toward the sunrising" cannot well mean the whole range from south to north, but all the mountain country lying to the east of Zidon. One other passage promises to throw additional light upon the question, viz., the ideal delimitation of the Holy Land in Ezek. xlvii. ; and here it is true that we find a northern frontier (vers. 15—17) apparently far beyond the line of actual settlement, and yet containing two names at least (Zedad and Hazar-enan) which appear in the present list. It is, however, quite uncertain whether the prophet is describing any possible boundary line at all, or whether he is only mentioning (humanly speaking at random) certain points in the far north ; his very object

would seem to be to picture an enlarged Canaan extending beyond its utmost historical limits. Even if it should be thought that these passages require a frontier further to the north than the one advocated above, it will yet be impossible to carry it to the northern end of the valley between Lebanon and anti-Lebanon. For in that case the northern frontier will not be a northern frontier at all, but will actually descend from the "entrance of Hamath" in a southerly or south-westerly direction, and distinctly form part of the eastern boundary.

Ver. 11.—**Shepham** is unknown. **Riblah** cannot possibly be the Riblah in the land of Hamath (Jer. xxxix. 5), now apparently Ribleh on the Orontes. This one example will serve to show how delusive are these identifications with modern places. Even if Ribleh represents *an* ancient Riblah, it is not *the* Riblah which is mentioned here. **On the east side of Ain,** *i. e.* of the fountain. The Targums here imply that this Ain was the source of Jordan below Mount Hermon, and that would agree extremely well with what follows. The Septuagint has ἐπὶ πηγάς, and there is in fact more than one fountain from which this head-water of Jordan takes its rise. Immediately before the Septuagint has Βηλά where we read Riblah. It has been supposed that the word was originally Ἀρβηλά, a transliteration of "Har-bel," the mountain of Bel or Baal, identical with the Harbaal-Hermon (our Mount Hermon) of Judges iii. 3. The Hebrew הָרִבְלָה being differently pointed, and the final ה taken as the suffix of direction, we get הָר־בֵל; but this is extremely precarious. **Shall reach unto the side of the sea of Chinnereth eastward.** Literally, "shall strike (מָחָה) the shoulder of the sea," &c. The line does not seem to have descended the stream from its source, but to have kept to the east, and so to have struck the lake of Galilee at its north-eastern corner. From this point it simply followed the water-way down to the Salt Sea. The lands beyond Jordan were not reckoned as within the sacred limits.

Ver. 15. — **On this side Jordan near Jericho.** Literally, "on the side (מֵעֵבֶר) of the Jordan of Jericho." It was not of course true that the territory which they had received lay eastward of Jericho, but it was the case that the tribe leaders had there asked and received permission to occupy that territory, and it was in this direction that the temporary settlements of Reuben and Gad lay, perhaps also those of half Manasseh.

Ver. 17.—**Eleazar the priest, and Joshua the son of Nun.** As the ecclesiastical and military heads respectively of the theocracy (see on ch. xxxii. 28).

se
Ver. 18. — **One prince of every tribe.** This was arranged no doubt in order to insure fairness in fixing the boundaries between the tribes, which had to be done after the situation of the tribe was determined by lot ; the further subdivision of the tribal territory was probably left to be managed by the chiefs of the tribe itself. Of these tribe princes (see on ch. xiii. 1 ; Josh. xiv. 1), Caleb is the only one whose name is known to us, and he had acted in a somewhat similar capacity forty years before. This may of itself account for the tribe of Judah being named first in the list, especially as Reuben was not represented ; but the order in which the other names follow is certainly remark-able. Taken in pairs (Judah and Simeon, Manasseh and Ephraim, &c.), they advance regularly from south to north, according to their subsequent position on the map. Differing as this arrangement does so markedly from any previously adopted, it is impossible to suppose that it is accidental. We must conclude either that a coincidence so apparently trivial was Divinely prearranged, or that the arrangement of the names is due to a later hand than that of Moses.

Ver. 20. — **Shemuel.** This is the same name as Samuel. Of the rest, every one except the last occurs elsewhere in the Old Testament as the name of some other Israelit

HOMILETICS.

Ch. xxxiii. 50—xxxiv. 29.—*The Holy Land.* In this section we have, spiritually, the promised inheritance of the saints, the kingdom of heaven, with the conditions under which it is to be received and enjoyed. No one can overlook the correspondence (which is fundamental and far-reaching) between *their* "holy land" and ours ; between that "rest" which awaited *them* in Canaan, and that "rest" into which we do now enter. The kingdom of heaven is the spiritual antitype of Canaan. But that kingdom is (practically considered) twofold : it is heaven, or rather rest in heaven, only reached by crossing the stream of death ; it is also (and in the Scripture much more often) the rest of the new life in Christ, which yet is neither absolute nor independent of our continued striving against sin (cf. Matt. v. 3, "theirs *is* the kingdom ;" Luke xvii. 21 *b*. ; Rom. xiv. 17 ; Col. iii. 3 ; Heb. iv. 3 *a*.). To this latter aspect (the kingdom as a spiritual and moral *state*) belong the lessons of this section, for the most part. Consider, therefore—

I. THAT THE ONE GREAT DUTY OF ISRAEL IN TAKING POSSESSION OF HIS OWN LAND WAS WHOLLY TO DISPOSSESS THE NATIVES, AS BEING ENEMIES OF GOD AND OF HIS WORSHIP. Even so the one condition on which we inherit that kingdom which (in its present aspect) is righteousness, peace, and joy in the Holy Ghost, is that we put to death the deeds of the flesh, and crucify the old man, and wage a war of extermination against all the sinful affections which have made their home in our human life.

II. THAT ISRAEL WAS FURTHER REQUIRED TO ABOLISH ALL THEIR MONUMENTS OF IDOLATRY, HOWEVER PLEASING AND INTERESTING. Even so all the devices and imaginations of the natural man, however attractive, which are contrary to the sole worship and service of the living God must be wholly, and without exception, destroyed.

III. THAT THE COMMAND TO EXTERMINATE SEEMED HARD, AND WAS UNGRATEFUL (NO DOUBT) TO MOST IN ISRAEL. Why be so extreme ? Why not enough to conquer, without extirpating ? Why not enough to possess the best of the land, without labouring to clear all the corners ? What harm could feeble remnants of heathen do ? could they not even make them useful ? Even so it seems hard that Christian people may make no compromise with, and show no toleration for, what is sinful and selfish in human life. Why need we be perfect ? Shall nothing be allowed to the old Adam ? May we never be content ? If leading on the whole a Christian life, why weary ourselves about small points of moral excellence ? Many things not exactly right may be very useful ; may they not be turned to account ?

IV. THAT AS A FACT THE COMMAND TO EXTIRPATE WAS NOT OBEYED. Many were left unmolested out of indolence and cowardice when the first rush of conquest was passed ; many were spared out of unwillingness to go to extremes with them. Even so most Christian people leave considerable portions of their own lives (which God hath given them for a prey, Jer. xlv. 5) under the dominion of passions, emotions, motives which are not Christian. They overcome the tyrannies of sin, but leave the remnants of sin unsubdued ; in other words, they subdue their evil passions and desires, but shrink from destroying them. *E. g.*, how few have their *temper* entirely under control! Thus the kingdom of heaven is never truly theirs, because of the sins which they have been too indolent or too self-confident to dislodge.

V. THAT AS A FACT THE OTHER COMMAND WAS NOT OBEYED WHOLLY; SOMETIMES GRAVEN IMAGES WERE SERVED, SOMETIMES HIGH PLACES TURNED TO THE WORSHIP OF THE LORD, TO THE GREAT DETRIMENT AND DANGER OF THE TRUE FAITH. Even so the vain devices and perverted imaginations of the natural man have not been discarded by the servants of Christ in many cases; too often they have been either *adopted* in their blank disloyalty to Christ (as, *e. g.*, that "covetousness which *is* idolatry"), or else *adapted* to religious ends (as many forms of will-worship, material and mental) to the detriment of that singleness of eye and heart which God requires.

VI. THAT THE REMNANTS OF THE HEATHEN, IF SPARED, WERE TO BECOME PRICKS AND THORNS (*i. e.* CONSTANT AND DANGEROUS ANNOYANCES) TO THEM, AND WOULD VEX THEM. Even so if we leave the remnants of sin in the new life which God has given us to lead, these will surely become a continual source of unhappiness and danger. This is why most Christians are more or less restless, dissatisfied, uneven in temper, uncertain in behaviour, having little "peace" and less "joy in the Holy Ghost." It is simply that they have not obeyed the call to make a clearance of old bad habits and evil tempers; do not recognise the sinfulness of little sins; think it does not matter; will not take the trouble necessary to hunt them down; have learnt by experience to tolerate them. No *more* than this, but no *less*. They can never be made happy save through patient, prayerful toil to root the remnants of sin out of their hearts and lives.

VII. THAT THE END OF SUCH UNFAITHFULNESS, IF NOT AMENDED, WAS TO BE EXPATRIATION. Both races could not dwell in the land; if Israel would not drive out the heathen, he must be driven out himself. Even so if Christian people will not labour by grace to take complete possession in God's name of their own lives, the end will be that they will lose them altogether. Either grace must make a full end of our sins, or our sins will make an end of grace, because God will withdraw it. There may not be any wilful toleration of moral evil in ourselves, nor urging of excuses for its continuance.

Consider again, with respect to *Canaan*—

I. THAT ISRAEL WAS TO POSSESS IT, BECAUSE GOD HAD GIVEN IT TO THEM; IT WAS HIS, AND HE CHOSE TO DO SO; NO SUCH TITLE WAS EVER GRANTED TO ANY PEOPLE. Even so we are to take possession (by patient well-doing) of the kingdom of heaven, not because it can be earned, but because God hath freely given it to us, whom he hath chosen. This kingdom, therefore, whether as within us or as above us, is ours by a most absolute and indefeasible title.

II. THAT THE GRANT OF CANAAN TO ISRAEL IMPLIED ALL NECESSARY SUCCOUR IN CONQUERING AND OCCUPYING IT, else had the name of God been disgraced. Even so the fact that God hath given to us the kingdom of heaven is pledge positive that we shall receive strength to overcome every hindrance and obstacle, if we be faithful.

III. THAT THE DIVISION OF THE LAND WAS SO ORDERED THAT EQUALITY SHOULD AS FAR AS POSSIBLE BE PRESERVED, AND FAVOURITISM MADE IMPOSSIBLE. Even so God hath so ordered his kingdom that none has cause to envy other, and none can complain of partiality; since all shall inherit heaven alike, and yet heaven itself shall be diverse according to the growth of each in grace (cf. Matt. xx. 13—15 and 23 with Luke xix. 15—19 and Matt. xxv. 21—23).

IV. THAT THE HOLY LAND WAS DELIMITED BEFORE THEY ENTERED, BUT THE BOUNDARIES ARE TO A CONSIDERABLE EXTENT UNKNOWN. Even so the kingdom of heaven is defined and described in manifold ways in the word of God, and yet it is hard to know how far it extends, and where the boundary runs between that which is of nature and that which is of grace. And as those frontiers could only be traced by such as were locally familiar with the places named, so the extent of the kingdom can only be known by such as are familiar by experience with every part of it.

V. THAT THE LIMITS MARKED DOWN WERE APPARENTLY THE NATURAL LIMITS OF CANAAN, WITHOUT ANY RESERVATIONS (such as Philistia, Phœnicia, &c.). Even so

God hath given to us to possess the whole life of man which may be lived in holiness, according to the utmost possible expansion of our human nature in all its fulness.

VI. THAT THE LAND ACTUALLY OCCUPIED BY ISRAEL WAS BOTH LARGER AND SMALLER THAN THAT DELIMITED; not reaching so far from south to north, yet not so strait from west to east, Even so it is certain that Christian life, as lived, does not agree with the ideal in the New Testament. It does not reach so far, not attain its full measure, in one way, while it occupies additional space in another way. And as the additional breadth gained by the trans-Jordanic settlement, while not commanded, was yet (it seems) allowed of God, so the unexpected developments of Christianity (as in the way of civilisation, with its varied gifts), although quite outside anything to be gathered from the New Testament, must yet be held allowed of God.

VII. THAT KADESH, OF FAMOUS MEMORY, WAS SPECIALLY INCLUDED IN THE SOUTHERN FRONTIER. Even so the experiences of our pilgrimage—the "sanctuaries" of our trial time—will be part of our eternal inheritance; nothing "holy" will be lost to us.

VIII. THAT THE LAND WAS ALLOTTED TO THE PEOPLE BY ELEAZAR THEIR PRIEST AND JOSHUA THEIR CAPTAIN. Even so our inheritance is in all particulars assigned to us by him who is at once the High Priest of our profession and the Captain of our salvation.

IX. THAT TOGETHER WITH THEM THERE ACTED PRINCES FROM EACH TRIBE, THAT JUSTICE MIGHT BE MANIFESTLY DONE TO ALL. Even so it would appear that in the judgment of the last day respect will be had even to human ideas of justice; and, moreover, that in some way not yet explained men will themselves act as assessors in that judgment (see 1 Pet. iv. 6, where κατὰ ἄνθρωπον seems to mean " in accordance with human ideas [of justice];" and 1 Cor. vi. 2, 3, which seems clearly to refer to the final judgment).

And note that the order of the tribes as here given is very different from any previous list; for two are absent, and the precedence of the rest is determined after a peculiar law by their subsequent position in the Holy Land. So the Divine order in which Churches or individuals stand is different from any founded on earthly or visible considerations, being in accordance with God's foreknowledge of their heavenly place.

HOMILIES BY VARIOUS AUTHORS.

Vers. 50—56.—*No compromise with idolatry.* I. THE COMMAND GIVEN. The Israelites were to be delivered from complicity with the immoral idolatry of Canaan by such extreme measures as these. 1. The idolaters were to be utterly driven out, and in some cases exterminated. On no account were covenants to be made with them (Exod. xxxiv. 12—17). 2. The idols were to be broken to pieces; even the precious metals on them were not to be spared (Exod. xxiii. 24, 30—33; Deut. vii. 25, 26). 3. The high places, groves, altars, pillars, &c. were to be destroyed (Exod. xxxiv. 13; Deut. xii. 2, 3). 4. Works of art, "pictures," &c., were doomed if tainted by idolatry. 5. The very names of the idols were to be consigned to oblivion, and all curious antiquarian inquiries as to the idolatries of the land were discouraged (Deut. xii. 3, 30, 31). Our missionaries have had to urge similar precepts on converts from heathenism; *e. g.* in Polynesia. And these precepts suggest applications to all Christians who have "escaped the pollutions of the world" and its spiritual idolatries, but who are still surrounded by them. No "covenants" are to be made with men of the world which would compromise the servants of Christ, or mar their testimony against the evil deeds of the world (2 Cor. vi. 14; Ephes. v. 11). Apply to marriages with the ungodly, and to other close alliances of interest. Illustrate from Jehoshaphat's history (2 Kings viii. 18; 2 Chron. xviii. 1; xix. 2). Even things lawful in themselves may have to be abandoned; whether money, in order to conquer "covetousness, which is idolatry" (illustrate Mark x. 21), or pleasures which may have associations of evil clinging to them (1 Cor. vi. 12), or even past helps to devotion—*e. g.* 2 Kings xviii. 4, Popish images, &c. To look back with strong desire even towards things elegant and attractive in themselves, but infected *to us* by the spirit of worldliness, may be fatal (Luke xvii. 32; 2 Cor. vi. 17). The Church of God has the duty of possessing the whole land, "the world" (1 Cor. iii. 22); but to do this they must "dispossess the inhabitants," *i. e.* they must make no compromise with the spirit of the men of the world. Worldliness is a *spirit* rather than a course of outward conduct. We must "use the world as not abusing it."

II. The motives urged. 1. The peril of perpetual unrest (ver. 55). Just so if Christians seek to make compromises with the sins and idolatries of the world they are called to overcome (1 John v. 4), and become subject to its maxims and fashions, there can be no true rest. The joy of entire obedience can never be known (Ps. xix. 11). Compromise is perpetual conflict, with the conviction of being on the losing side. We are wounded in the tenderest part ("pricks in our eyes") and vexed in the secret chamber of conscience ("thorns in our sides"). 2. The peril of being regarded as "conformed to the world," and therefore treated as "enemies of God" (ver. 56; Ps. cvi. 34—42; Rom. xii. 2; Philip. iii. 18, 19; James iv. 4; 2 Pet. ii. 20—22). From such guilty compromises we may be delivered through Christ—through his atonement (Gal. i. 4), intercession (John xvii. 15), examp e (*ibid.* xvi. 33; xvii. 16), and Spirit (Rom. viii. 2; 1 Cor. ii. 12).—P.

Vers. 50—56.—*How to deal with the Canaanites: an urgent warning.* It is assumed here that Israel will conquer the Canaanites; probably by this time the people had grown to somewhat of confidence, by reason of their recent successes over Sihon, Og, and Midian. But it was a thing of the first importance, when the victory was gained, to follow it up in the right way. Victories have been gained, and then worse than lost by want of wisdom to use them aright. Here we have a plain, strict, and severe command concerning the very first thing to be done upon the defeat of the Canaanites. They themselves were to be driven from the land, and all the instruments of idolatry utterly destroyed. The need of this command will be clearly seen if we consider—

I. The great object which was before the mind of God in giving the command. This is alluded to in ver. 54. Canaan was ever under the eye of God as being the destined inheritance of Israel; it had been counted as such even from the time of Abraham. The sadness of the threat against Israel in the day of its apostasy lay in this, that it was a threat of disinheriting (ch. xiv. 12). And that which had been so long preparing for Israel, which even while the Canaanites were dwelling in it had been under the peculiar supervision of God, was become at last an inheritance of great value. It was to be cultivated to the full, and would then richly repay for all the cultivation. Such interest did God show in giving this land to the Israelites in all its fulness, that he was about to portion it by lot. Each tribe in particular was to feel that the place of its habitation had been chosen by God. Hence the need of leaving no precaution unemployed *to make this favoured land secure.* It must be guarded from every kind of danger, however remote, improbable, and practically innocuous it may seem. If Israel lost this inheritance, there was no other place for it, no other possession on which it could advance with the certainty of conquest and, what was even more important, with the consciousness of being engaged in a righteous cause. In Canaan, as long as it kept its allegiance to God, Israel was the rightful possessor; but everywhere else it was a lawless, unblessed invader. That which is of inestimable value, and which once gone cannot be replaced, must first of all be founded in security and surrounded with the same. "If the foundations be destroyed, what can the righteous do?" (Ps. xi. 3). The security of the people was threatened by all that threatened the honour of God. And it was a distinct dishonour to his name to allow idolaters to remain in the land openly to practise their vicious and degrading rites. Moreover, there was every chance that the people themselves would be subtly and gradually drawn to idolatry. Recollect all these perils, and then you will see good reason why God made a stringent demand for such a sweeping treatment of the Canaanites. The cause of a world's redemption was bound up with the safety of Israel's inheritance. And *we also have an inheritance* (Matt. xix. 29; xxv. 34; Acts xx. 32; xxvi. 18; Rom. viii. 17; Gal. iii. 29; Ephes. i. 11, 14; iii. 6; 1 Pet. i. 4) far transcending that Canaan which was so much in the eyes of the Israelites. If it is worth anything at all, it is worth everything; worth all the self-denial, perseverance, complete submission to God, and patient waiting which are necessary for the attaining of it. We must not leave unexpelled from our life or undestroyed from our circumstances anything that may imperil the inheritance. Walk with no companion, engage in no business, cultivate no taste or recreation, if there be in them the slightest chance of peril to the inheritance. It is a glorious thing to conquer temptation in actual conflict, but it is better still so to watch and pray as not to enter into temptation at all.

II. THE GREAT TEMPTATION ON THE PART OF ISRAEL TO REST SATISFIED WITH AN IMPERFECT CONQUEST. Not of course that Israel thought it imperfect. Israel was anxious in its own way to have the conquest and possession complete. But God alone had the requisite wisdom and foresight to direct the people into real security. There were many temptations to what he knew was a premature cessation of hostilities. *The Canaanites would in due time make attempts at compromises and partial surrenders*, even as Pharaoh had made like attempts when his people were smitten by the plagues. There was the temptation that came from *the weariness of long waiting.* A complete expulsion involved much delay. We are tempted even in the affairs of this life to premature conclusions through sheer impatience. We want to pluck the fruit long before it is ripe. Moreover, the Israelites, many of them at least, would wish *to make slaves of the Canaanites.* They were not entering Canaan with the steward-feeling in their hearts. The promise was sufficiently fulfilled in their estimate when they got the land to do as they liked with it. The tribes crossing Jordan had the same carnal views concerning their possession as Reuben and Gad concerning the land which they had chosen. There was the temptation coming from self-confidence ; that of supposing *an enemy enfeebled to be practically the same as an enemy destroyed.* There might be the temptation also to show *a human, ignorant, undiscerning pity, as contrasted with a Divinely wise severity.* Such utter expulsion as God demanded could easily be made to look unreasonable, and indeed nothing better than sheer tyranny. It takes much patient inquiry to discover that what may be kind on the surface is cruel underneath ; kind at the present, cruel in the future ; kind to the few, cruel to the many ; kind for time, utterly ruinous for eternity. There was no reasonable pity in leaving those who were utterly corrupt to become the plentiful sources of idolatrous infection to the people of Jehovah. There was also the temptation that came from *a very imperfect sympathy with the purposes of God.* During their wanderings the Israelites had shown again and again their lack of apprehension and appreciation with respect to Jehovah. What then of hearty aversion from idolatry could be expected when its subtle perils came upon them ? Only those who were filled with an abiding sense of the holiness and majesty of God could estimate the dangers of idolatry and take the precautions needful to guard against them.

III. THE EARNEST WARNING IN WHICH GOD SPECIFIES THE RESULTS OF NEGLIGENCE. 1. *The earlier result* (ver. 55). These Canaanites, however fairly they speak, and with whatever leniency they be treated, will turn out pricks and thorns in the end. "Those which ye let remain of them." One, even though he be a child, and seem easily moulded to other ends, may be the cause of measureless mischief. A *little* leaven leavens the whole lump. Behold how great a mass of matter a tiny flame will kindle. A Canaanite, a real Canaanite, worshipping his idols, must be a bad man. Just as a true, believing connection with God leads into all purity and virtue, so a grovelling before idols makes a man vicious ; and not only vicious, but the viciousness is upon a sort of principle and rule. Those who change the glory of the incorruptible God into an image made like to corruptible man, and birds, and four-footed beasts, and creeping things, change at the same time much besides. It is one of the unspeakable miseries of idolatry that it changes vices into virtues, and idolaters do the most wicked things for conscience' sake. Hence the Canaanite could not but hurt the Israelite ; it was his very nature so to do. He might undertake allegiance and amity, but by the very necessity of the case he must prove in the end a prick in the eye and a thorn in the side. Therefore let Israel uproot with a timely and unsparing severity all that would end in pricks and thorns. Study the nature of things in their germs. Stop evil if you can at the very beginning. Consider, in connection with this expulsion of the Canaanites and the dangers of idolatry, the whole of the first chapter of Romans. 2. *The later result* (ver. 56). Leave the

Canaanites unexpelled, and the end will be the expulsion of Israel. "To him that knoweth to do good, and doeth it not, to him it is sin" (James iv. 17). In the light of this threatening, how clearly it is seen that what made the Canaanites so offensive in the sight of God was their idolatry! For centuries they had been pursuing their hideous practices in that very land where a holy and righteous God had revealed himself to Abraham, Isaac, and Jacob. And if the Israelites by a disobedient leniency fell into idolatry, their state would be even sadder and more dishonourable than that of Canaan, because the fall would be from such privileges. Note that God placed this expulsion of the Canaanites as a work of obedience for the people to perform. If they failed in obedience he would not by some miracle expel the Canaanites himself. "*As I thought to do unto them.*" The land in itself was no more than any other land on the face of the earth. It was the people—the holy people of God—who sanctified the land, and not the land the people. And if they disobeyed God in the presence of all these idols, with their associated abominations, then the holy became unholy, and the Canaanites might as well stay there as remove anywhere else (Prov. viii. 20, 21; xx. 21; Eccles. vii. 11; Rev. xxi. 7).—Y.

Vers. 1—15.—*The Lord appoints boundaries for the promised land.* I. CONSIDER THESE BOUNDARIES ACCORDING TO THE EXTENT OF WHAT THEY INCLUDED. The territory was a very limited one, geographically speaking. The promised land, intended to typify the large privileges of the believer, and the heavenly and everlasting inheritance, was not a continent, nor even a considerable part of a continent. The Lord would teach Israel, and through them all his people, the difference between bigness and greatness, between quantity and quality, between mere superficial extent and the inexhaustible wealth that comes out of a really good ground. A square mile in the land that the Lord hath blessed is better than all the sands of Sahara. There was no legitimate room in Israel for men of Alexander's spirit, weeping because there were no more worlds to conquer. The scene that God thus mapped out was large enough to give impressive and beautiful illustrations of his ways, and to bring peace, prosperity, and happiness worthy of bearing such names to all who received his will in the fulness of it. Though only a limited territory, it was for that reason all the more compact; and at a very short notice the whole nation could gather to any point for purposes of worship or defence. Outsiders, who did not know how blessed was the nation whose God was the Lord, might count the land only a little one among the thousands of the whole earth. All depends on what we mean when we speak of the lives of certain people as limited, poor, narrow, and unprivileged. Such words may only reveal our ignorance, our erroneous principles of judgment, and not the real state of affairs. It should ever be part of the brightest radiance of God's glory in the eyes of his people that he can welcome the poor and the lowly to his choicest blessings and to the sweetest pleasures he can confer upon the human heart. Their poverty and lowliness do not unfit them for these things. Paul, who had to work with his own hands, and who said that having food and raiment he was therewith content, was also able to say, "O the depth of the riches both of the wisdom and knowledge of God!" (Rom. xi. 33). No lord of broad acres ne, no partaker of luxurious repose among intellectual pleasures, but still he knew of the peace that passeth all understanding, the joy that is unspeakable and full of glory, and something of the breadth, and length, and depth, and height of that love of Christ which passeth knowledge. We had need be very sure of our competency before we begin to pronounce judgment on the compass and depth of a true believer's life.

II. CONSIDER THE EXACTNESS OF THESE BOUNDARIES. The country was carefully defined. and could give no occasion for boundary disputes. And all Christians have a carefully-defined life marked out for them. Even external circumstances are more under our control than at first seems to be the case. Many such circumstances indeed we cannot control, but many also depend on the spirit in which we regard the will of God. For instance, it could hardly be said that God marked out their territory for Reuben and Gad. For his own wise purposes he allowed their choice, but it was no true choice of his. If we have only a thoroughly trustful spirit, a spirit of stewardship towards God, we may all have the profit and comfort of feeling that we are working within the channels and limits that he would choose for our life. Social station makes no difference in this respect. The path of a pious king is just as strictly fixed as that of the humblest of his subjects. The farthest planet that circles round the sun has its path just as much marked out as the nearest one, though it travels a far longer distance.

III. CONSIDER THE EFFICACY THESE BOUNDARIES WERE MEANT TO HAVE IN THE WAY OF EXCLUSION. We see God clearly providing one necessary part in the means whereby to drive out and dispossess the Canaanites. He fixed the line beyond which they were to be driven, and within which they were not allowed to return and dwell. The lines between the Church and the world are not to be tampered with by such as value all that is most precious in spiritual possessions. Let the world have its own principles and assert them in its own field of action and in its own way. Let the men of the world act as men of the world, and transmit their much-belauded policy of life from generation to generation of such as believe in their principles. They go by what men are and by what they cynically assume men must be, for they do devoutly believe the fact that what is born of the flesh is flesh, even though they can make nothing of Christ's reference to the fact. But let us ever claim and preserve a place, and earnestly defend it, where the supercilious egotism of worldly wisdom shall find no entrance. Let our territory be fenced round with "Thus saith the Lord," and let us watch with a jealous vigilance the slightest encroachment on it. We also believe that what is born of the flesh is flesh, and that we must go by what men are ; but then we regard in addition what men ought to be, and recollect that what is born of the spirit is spirit. Blessed is he who feels marked out in his own heart the boundary which Paul specifies when he says, "The flesh lusteth against the Spirit, and the Spirit against the flesh" (Gal. v. 17) ; Canaanite against Israelite, and Israelite against Canaanite. It availed a man nothing to live within Israelite borders if he had a Canaanite heart. Of old idolaters were rigorously excluded from a certain well-marked territory, and the typical significance of this is that idolatries themselves must be driven out of the regenerate heart, and kept out of it by all the armour of righteousness on the right hand and on the left.

IV. CONSIDER THE SPECIAL SIGNIFICANCE OF THE WESTERN BORDER (ver. 6). The great sea was there, the open pathway of nations, the symbol, and to a large extent the avenue, of Israel's connection with the whole world. For though Israel had destroyed Amorite and Midianite, and was laid under command to drive out the Canaanite, yet in the seed of Abraham all families of the earth were to be blessed. From Canaan there was a path of blessing by a landward way to many lands beside, but by sea there was a way to every island also. Consider the place in respect of Christian privileges and influences which the island England occupies among the nations. The seaward aspect of Israel suggests to us the blessings that we, and indeed many peoples beside, have gained from her. Notice also *the element of reference to the sea which this seaward boundary of Canaan has brought into the Scriptures.* The Scriptures were written by men who felt the power of the ocean. Men within reach of the sea could then hear the whole of nature praise God. They could not only say, "Let the heavens rejoice, and let the earth be glad," but also, "Let the sea roar, and the fulness thereof" (Ps. xcvi. 11). How could David have given Ps. civ. its completeness without a sight of the sea ? And thus we find Haggai contrasting the great elements, first of the heavens and the earth, and then of the sea and the dry land (Hag. ii. 6). It helped David to think of the omnipresence of God, as he imagined himself dwelling in the uttermost parts of the sea, and feeling even there that mighty grasp guarding and sustaining him (Ps. cxxxix. 9, 10). And it served also to remind men how in after days the Lord would famish all the gods of the earth, and men would worship him, every one from his place, even all the isles of the heathen (Zeph. ii. 11). Truly it was by no accident, but by a deep and gracious design, that the land of promise had the great sea for one of its borders.—Y.

EXPOSITION.

CHAPTER XXXV.

THE LEVITICAL CITIES, AND CITIES OF REFUGE, AND LAWS AS TO HOMICIDE (vers. 1—34). Ver. 1.—**And the Lord spake.** Cf. ch. xxxiii. 50 ; xxxvi. 13.

Ver. 2.—**That they give unto the Levites . . . cities to dwell in.** This legislation forms the natural sequel and complement of the Divine decrees already promulgated concerning the Levites. Separated from the rest of the tribes from the time of the first census (ch. i. 49), excluded from any tribal inheritance (ch. xviii. 20), but endowed with tithes and offerings for their maintenance (ch. xviii. 21, &c.), it was also necessary that they should be provided with homes for themselves and their cattle. They might indeed have been left to exist as they could, and where they could, upon the provision made for them in the law. But, on the one hand, that provision was itself precarious, depending as it did upon the piety and good feeling of the people (which must often have been found wanting : cf. Neh. xiii. 10 ; Mal. iii. 8, 9) ; and, on the other, it is evident that the Levites were intended, as far as their family and social life was concerned, to share the ordinary comforts and enjoyments of Israelites. Nothing could have been more foreign to the Mosaic ideal than a ministry celibate, ascetic, and detached from this world's wealth, such as readily enough sprang up (whether intended or not) under the teaching of the gospel (cf. Luke x. 4 ; xii. 33 ; Acts xx. 34, 35 ; 1 Cor. vii. 7, 25, 26 ; ix. 18, 27 ; 2 Cor. vi. 10 ; 2 Tim. ii. 4). **Suburbs.** The Hebrew word מִגְרָשׁ undoubtedly means here a pasture, or a paddock, an enclosed place outside the town into which the cattle were driven by day to feed. It is possible that the A. V. may have used the word "suburbs" in that sense. To keep cattle to some extent was not only a universal custom, but was well-nigh a necessity of life in that age.

Ver. 3.—**For their cattle.** לִבְהֶמְתָּם, "for their great cattle," i. e. oxen, camels, and any other beasts of draught or burden. **For their goods.** "For their possessions," which in this connection would mean their ordinary "live stock," chiefly sheep and goats ; the word itself (לִרְכֻשָׁם) is indeterminate. **For all their beasts.** לְכָל-חַיָּתָם, an expression which apparently only sums up what has previously been mentioned.

Ver. 5.—**Ye shall measure from without the city** (מִחוּץ לָעִיר)—ἔξω τῆς πόλεως) . . . **two thousand cubits.** These directions are

very obscure. Some have held that the country for 1000 cubits beyond the walls was reserved for pasture (according to ver. 4), and for another 1000 cubits for fields and vineyards, so that the Levitical lands extended 2000 cubits in all directions. This is reasonable in itself, since 2000 cubits is only half a mile, and rather more than a square mile of land would not seem too much for pastures, gardens, &c. for a town with at least 1000 inhabitants. The smallest tribe territories seem to have comprised some 300 square miles of country ; and if we take the Levitical towns as averaging 1000 cubits square, their forty-eight cities would only give them seventy-three square miles of territory. There is, however, no notice of anything being given to the Levites except their "suburbs," so that this explanation must be at best very doubtful. Others have argued for a plan according to which each outer boundary, drawn at 1000 cubits' distance from the wall, would measure 2000 cubits, plus the length of the town wall ; but this is far too artificial, and could only be considered possible as long as it was confined to a paper sketch, for it presupposes that each city lay four-square, and faced the four points of the compass. If the first explanation be untenable, the only alternative sufficiently simple and natural is to suppose that, in order to avoid irregularities of measurement, each outer boundary was to be drawn at an approximate distance of 1000 cubits from the wall, and each of an approximate length of 2000 cubits ; at the angles the lines would have to be joined as best they might. In Levit. xxv. 32—34 certain regulations are inserted in favour of the Levites. Their houses might be redeemed at any time, and not only within the full year allowed to others ; moreover, they returned to them (contrary to the general rule) at the year of Jubilee. Their property in the "suburbs" they could not sell at all, for it was inalienable. It is difficult to believe that these regulations were really made at Mount Sinai, presupposing, as they do, the legislation of this chapter ; but if they were actually made at this time, on the eve of the conquest, it is easy to see why they were subsequently inserted in the chapter which deals generally with the powers of sale and redemption.

Ver. 6.—**And among the cities.** Rather, "and the cities." וְאֵת הֶעָרִים—καὶ τὰς πόλεις. The construction is broken, or rather is continuous throughout vers. 6—8, the accusative being repeated. **Six cities for refuge.** See below on ver. 11.

Ver. 7.—**Forty and eight cities.** The

Levites numbered nearly 50,000 souls (see on ch. xxvi. 62), so that each Levitical city would have an average population of about 1000 to start with. There seems no sufficient reason for supposing that they shared their towns with men of the surrounding tribe. Even if the provision made for their habitation was excessive at first (which does not appear), yet their rate of increase should have been exceptionally high, inasmuch as they were not liable to military service. It is possible that mystical reasons led to the selection of the number forty-eight (12 × 4, both typical of universality), but it is at least equally probable that it was determined by the actual numbers of the tribe.

Ver. 8.—**And the cities which ye shall give shall be,** &c. Rather, " And as to the cities which ye shall give from the possession of the children of Israel, from the many ye shall multiply, and from the few ye shall decrease." What seems to be a general rule of proportionate giving is laid down here, but it was not carried out, and it is not easy to see how it could have been. From the large combined territory of Judah and Simeon nine cities were indeed surrendered (Josh. xxi.), but all the rest, great and small, gave up four apiece, except Naphtali, which gave up three only. As the territory of Naphtali was apparently large in proportion to its numbers, this was probably for no other reason than that the tribe stood last on the list. **Every one.** Hebrew, שׁיאִ. It was in fact each tribe that surrendered so many cities, but since the tribal inheritance was the joint property of all the tribesmen, every man felt that he was a party to the gift. No doubt it was the Divine intention to foster in the tribes as far as possible this local feeling of interest and property in the Levites who dwelt among them (compare the expression "*their* scribes and Pharisees" in Luke v. 30). The dispersion of the Levites (however mysteriously connected with the prophecy of Gen. xlix. 5—7) was obviously designed to form a bond of unity for all Israel by diffusing the knowledge and love of the national religion, and by keeping up a constant communication between the future capital and all the provinces. According to the Divine ideal Israel as a whole was "the election" (ἡ ἐκλογή) from all the earth, the Levites were the ἐκλογή of Israel, and the priests the ἐκλογή of Levi. The priestly family was at present too small to be influential, but the Levites were numerous enough to have leavened the whole nation if they had walked worthy of their calling. They were gathered together in towns of their own, partly no doubt in order to avoid disputes, but partly that they might have a better opportunity of setting forth the true ideal of what Jewish life should be.

Ver. 11.—**Ye shall appoint you cities to be cities of refuge for you.** God had already announced that he would appoint a place whither one guilty of unpremeditated manslaughter might flee for safety (Exod. xxi. 13). The expression there used does not point to more than one "place," but it is not inconsistent with several. Probably the right of sanctuary has been recognised from the earliest times in which any local appropriation of places to sacred purposes has been made. It is an instinct of religion to look upon one who has escaped into a sacred enclosure as being under the personal protection of the presiding deity. It is certain that the right was largely recognised in Egypt, where the priestly caste was so powerful and ambitious; and this is no doubt the reason (humanly speaking) for the promise in Exod. xxi. 13, and for the command in the following verse. Inasmuch as the whole of Canaan was the Lord's, any places within it might be endowed with rights of sanctuary, but it was obviously suitable that they should be Levitical cities; the Divine prerogative of mercy could nowhere be better exercised, nor would any citizens be better qualified to pronounce and to uphold the rightful decision in each case.

Ver. 12.—**From the avenger.** Hebrew, לאֵֹּג. Septuagint, ὁ ἀγχιστεύων τὸ αἷμα. In all other passages (twelve in number) where the word occurs in this sense it is qualified by the addition "of blood." Standing by itself, it is everywhere else translated "kinsman," or (more properly) "redeemer," and is constantly applied in that sense to God our Saviour (Job xix. 25; Isa. lxiii. 16 &c.). The two ideas, however, which seem to us so distinct, and even so opposed, are in their origin one. To the men of the primitive age, when public justice was not, and when might was right, the only protector was one who could and would avenge them of their wrongs, and by avenging prevent their repetition. This champion of the injured individual, or rather family,—for rights and wrongs were thought of as belonging to families rather than to individuals,—was their goel, who had their peace, their safety, above all, their honour, in his charge. For no sentiments spring up quicker, and none exercise a more tyrannous sway, than the sentiment of honour, which in its various and often strangely distorted forms has always perhaps outweighed all other considerations in the minds of men. Now the earliest form in which the sentiment of honour asserted itself was in the blood-feud. If one member of a family was slain, an intolerable shame and sense of contumely rested upon the family until blood had been avenged by blood, until "satisfaction" had been done by the death of the manslayer. He who freed the family from this intolerable pain and humiliation—who enabled it to hold up its head, and to breathe freely once more—was the goel; and in the natural order of things he was the nearest "kinsman" of the slain who could and would take the duty upon him. To these natural feelings was added in many cases a religious sentiment which regarded homicide as a sin against the higher Powers for which they too demanded the blood of the guilty. Such was the feeling among the Greeks, and probably among the Egyptians, while among the Hebrews it could plead Divine sanction, given in the most comprehensive terms: "Your blood of your lives will I require, at the hand of every beast will I require it; and at the hand of man; . . . whoso sheddeth man's blood, by man shall his blood be shed" (Gen. ix. 5, 6). The moral difficulties of this proclamation need not here be considered; it is enough to take note that the Divine law itself recognised the duty as well as the lawfulness of private blood-revenge when public justice could not be depended on. The goel, therefore, was not merely the natural champion of his family, nor only the deliverer who satisfied the imperious demands of an artificial code of honour; he was a minister of God, in whose patient efforts to hunt down his victim the thirst for vengeance was to some extent at least superseded by, or rather transmuted into, the longing to glorify God (compare the difficult case of Rev. vi. 10). It was not merely human feelings of great reach and tenacity which were outraged by the immunity of the manslayer; it was still more the justice of God which received a grievous wound. Just because, however, God had made the cause of the slain man his own, and had sanctioned the avenging mission of the goel, he could therefore regulate the course of vengeance so as to make it run as even as possible with true justice. It was not indeed possible to distinguish *ab initio* between the homicide which deserved and that which did not deserve capital punishment. Such distinction, difficult under any circumstances, was impossible when vengeance was in private hands. But while the goel could not be restrained from immediate pursuit unhindered by investigation or compunction (lest his whole usefulness be paralysed), the manslayer might have opportunity to escape, and to be sheltered under the Divine mercy until he could establish (if that were possible) his innocence. No better instance can be found of the way in which the King of Israel adopted the sentiments and institutions of a semi-barbarous age, added to them the

sanctions of religion, and so modified them as to secure the maximum of practical good consistent with the social state and moral feelings of the people. No doubt many an individual was overtaken and slain by the goel who did not deserve to die according to our ideas; but where perfection was unattainable, this error was far less dangerous to that age than the opposite error of diminishing the sanctity of human life and the awfulness of Divine justice. **The congregation.** Hebrew, עֵדָה. This word is used frequently from Exod. xii. 3 to the end of this chapter, and again in Joshua and the last two chapters of Judges. It is not found in Deuteronomy, nor often in the later books. In every case apparently *eydah* signifies the whole nation as gathered together, *e. g.* as represented by all who had an acknowledged right to appear, for of course 600,000 men could not gather together in any one place. The force of the word may be understood by reference to its use in Judges xx. 1; xxi. 10, 13, 16. Another word (קָהָל) is also used, less frequently in Leviticus and Numbers, but more frequently in the later books, for the general assembly of the people of Israel. No distinction of meaning can be drawn between the two words, and it cannot, therefore, be maintained that the "congregation" of this verse means the local elders of Josh. xx. 4. The regulations there laid down are not inconsistent with the present law, but are quite independent of it. They refer to a preliminary hearing of the case as stated by the fugitive alone in order to determine his right to shelter in the mean time; which right, if accorded, was without prejudice to the future judgment of the "congregation" on the whole facts of the case (see below on ver. 25).

Ver. 13.—**Six cities.** See on Deut. xix. 8, 9, where three more are apparently ordered to be set aside upon a certain contingency.

Ver. 14.—**Ye shall give three cities on this side Jordan.** According to Deut. iv. 41—43, Moses himself severed these three cities, Bezer of the Reubenites, Ramoth of the Gadites, and Golan of the Manassites. Those verses, however, seem to be an evident interpolation where they stand, and are hardly consistent with previous statements if taken literally. It is tolerably clear that the two tribes had only formed temporary settlements hitherto, and that their boundaries were not defined as yet; also that the Levitical cities (to which the cities of refuge were to belong) were not separated until after the conquest. It is likely that Deut. iv. 41—43 is a fragment, the real meaning of which is that Moses ordered the severance of three cities on that side Jordan as cities of refuge, for which purposes the three cities mentioned were afterwards selected.

Ver. 16.—**With an instrument of iron.** There is no reasonable doubt that בַּרְזֶל has here (as elsewhere) its proper meaning of iron. The expression must be held to include both weapons and other instruments; the former may have been mostly made of bronze, but where iron is used at all it is sure to be employed in war.

Ver. 17.—**With throwing a stone, wherewith he may die.** Literally, "with a stone of the hand, by which one may die," *i. e.* a stone which is suitable for striking or throwing, and apt to inflict a mortal wound.

Ver. 18.—**A hand weapon of wood.** A club, or other such formidable instrument.

Ver. 19.—**When he meeteth him,** *i. e.* outside a city of refuge.

Ver. 20.—**But if.** Rather, "and if" (וְאִם). The consideration of wilful murder is continued in these two verses, although chiefly with reference to the motive. It is to be understood that the deliberate intent was present in the former cases, and a new case is added, viz., if he smite him with his fist with fatal consequences.

Ver. 22.—**Without enmity, . . . without laying of wait.** These expressions seem intended to limit mercy to cases of pure accident, such as that quoted in Deut. xix. 5. Neither provocation nor any other "extenuating circumstances" are taken into account, nor what we now speak of as absence of premeditation. The want of these finer distinctions, as well as the short and simple list of fatal injuries given, show the rudeness of the age for which these regulations were made.

Ver. 25.—**The congregation** (עֵדָה) **shall restore him to the city of his refuge.** It is perfectly plain from this (and from Josh. xx. 6) that the general assembly of all Israel was to summon both homicide and avenger before them with their witnesses, and, if they found the accused innocent, were to send him back under safe escort to the city in which he had taken refuge. **He shall abide in it unto the death of the high priest.** No doubt his family might join him in his exile, and his life might be fairly happy as well as safe within certain narrow limits; but under ordinary circumstances he must forfeit much and risk more by his enforced absence from home and land. It is not easy to see why the death of the high priest should have set the fugitive free from the law of vengeance, except as foreshadowing the death of Christ. No similar significance is anywhere else attributed to the death of the high priest; and it was rather in its unbroken continuance than in its recurring interruption that the priesthood of Aaron typified that of the Redeemer. To see anything of a vicarious or

satisfactory character in the death of the high priest seems to be introducing an element quite foreign to the symbolism of the Old Testament. The stress, however, which is laid upon the fact of his decease (cf. ver. 28), and the solemn notice of his having been anointed with the holy oil, seem to point unmistakably to something in his official and consecrated character which made it right that the rigour of the law should die with him. What the Jubile was to the debtor who had lost his property, that the death of the high priest was to the homicide who had lost his liberty. If it was the case, as commonly believed, that all blood feuds were absolutely terminated by the death of the high priest, might this not be because the high priest, as chief minister of the law of God, was himself the goel of the whole nation? When he died all processes of vengeance lapsed, because they had really been commenced in his name.

Ver. 26.—**Without the border of the city,** *i. e.* no doubt beyond its "suburbs."

Ver. 30.—**By the mouth of witnesses,** *i. e.* of two at least (cf. Deut. xvii. 6).

Ver. 31.— **Ye shall take no satisfaction for the life of a murderer.** The passion for vengeance is both bad and good, and is therefore to be carefully purified and restrained; but when the desire for vengeance can be appeased by a money payment, it has become wholly bad, and is only a despicable form of covetousness which insults the justice it pretends to invoke. Such payments or "ransoms" are permitted by the Koran, and have been common among most semi-civilised peoples, notably amongst our old English ancestors.

Ver. 32.—**That he should come again to dwell in the land.** No one might buy off the enmity of the avenger before the appointed time, for that would give an unjust advantage to wealth, and would make the whole matter mercenary and vulgar.

Ver. 33.—**The land cannot be cleansed.** Literally, "there is no expiation (יְכֻפַּר) for the land." Septuagint, οὐχ ἐξιλασθήσεται ἡ γῆ. By these expressions the Lord places the sin of murder in its true light, as a sin against himself. The land, his land, is defiled with the blood of the slain, and nothing can do away with the guilt which cleaves to it but the strict execution of Divine justice upon the murderer. Money might satisfy the relatives of the slain, but cannot satisfy his Maker.

Ver. 34.— **For I the Lord dwell among the children of Israel.** Therefore the murderer's hand is raised against me; the blood of the slain is ever before my eyes, its cry for vengeance ever in my ears (cf. Gen. iv. 10; Matt. xxiii. 35; Rev. vi. 10).

HOMILETICS.

Vers. 1—34.—*The dwelling of the faithful: the Redeemer: the sanctity of life.*
There are in this chapter three things closely connected historically, and therefore
closely consecutive in the narrative, but distinct in their spiritual application. We
have, therefore, separately to consider—I. THE PROVISION WHICH GOD MAKES FOR HIS
OWN, AND THEIR DISPERSION ; II. THE REFUGE SET BEFORE HIM THAT IS GUILTY OF
BLOOD ; III. THE SANCTITY OF LIFE.

I. In the regulations made for the habitation of the Levites and their cattle we
have some sort of precedent for religious endowments ; but this precedent loses all
value in argument when we consider that the old dispensation was essentially temporal, which ours is not; moreover, the Levites do *not* correspond to the clergy,
but rather to the inner circle of the faithful, who are more emphatically the
" salt of the earth." Consider, therefore, as to the habitation of the Levites—
1. *That it was the will of God to disperse them as widely as possible throughout
Israel*—a thing which might have been looked upon as a punishment to them
(Gen. xlix. 7), but was really for the common good. Even so it is his will that
his own, who are more especially his own, should be scattered far and wide among
the mass of imperfect or nominal Christians ; not gathered together in one corner
of Christendom, but everywhere found as the few among the many. And note that
this is the very law of "salt," which must be scattered and diffused to exercise
its antiseptic functions. 2. *That the Levites, although dispersed, yet lived in communities*, and this no doubt that they might set forth the life of holiness according
to the law. Even so there is, beside the law of dispersion, a counter-law of aggregation for "the spiritual," which makes mightily for holiness. For Christianity is a
life, and life is complex, and therefore can only be lived by many who agree. There
should be centres of high religious influence everywhere, but those centres should be
strong. 3. *That the allotments of the Levites, though sufficient, were far from being
extensive*, on any understanding of the text. Even so, for those who would be an
example to Christ's flock, sufficiency is the rule, and nothing more (1 Tim. vi. 8).
God does not *design* poverty for his own (Luke xii. 31), unless voluntarily embraced
(*ibid.* ver. 33), but assuredly not wealth (*ibid.* vi. 24). 4. *That the object aimed at
in the allotment of their cities was to give each tribe, and even each tribesman, a personal and local interest in the Levites.* Even so it is the will of God that those who
specially follow after him should be identified as strongly as possible with those
around them, in order that these may love and reverence them. Every Christian
land has its "saints," by whom it is the more edified in that it feels them to be
specially its own.

Consider also, mystically—1. *That the Levitical cities numbered forty-eight,* i. e.
12 × 4—the first being the symbol of the universal (apostolic—see Rev. xxi. 14)
Church, the second of the whole earth (Matt. viii. 11 ; Rev. xxi. 13), the whole signifying diffusion throughout the world. Even so the religious life is universal in all
parts of the Church of God, even in those which seem to us most remote. 2. *That
the enclosures round the Levitical cities measured the same every way—lay foursquare
as far as possible.* Even so it is the ideal of the religious life that it be not one-
sided, or unequal, but attain its full development in all directions ; if not it must
be *starved* to some extent.

II. The law of refuge from the goel is one of the most striking, and yet difficult,
of the foreshadowings of the gospel. It is complicated, in the spiritual interpretation,
by the fact that Christ is the Victim with whose blood our hands are stained, and our
only Refuge, while he is also typified as Redeemer by the goel, and as Messiah
by the anointed priest. Consider, however—1. *That the law presupposed and provided for a state of blood-guiltiness, which brought after it the sentence of death* (Gen.
ix. 6). Even so the gospel presupposes that all have sinned, and have become guilty
of the death of Christ, who died for our sins, and have incurred the sentence of
eternal death. David said, " Deliver me from blood-guiltiness " (Ps. li. 14), but he
had already incurred it (2 Sam. xii. 9) ; and so have we (cf. Heb. vi. 6 ; x. 29). 2.
That it provided for such blood-guiltiness as was unwittingly incurred. Even so
Christ's excuse for us is that we " know not what we do " (Luke xxiii. 24), and our

hope is that we have not wilfully and deliberately preferred sin as such (Acts iii. 17 ; 1 Tim. i. 13).   3. *That it presupposed that the avenger was on foot to take the life of the manslayer.*   Even so the gospel testifies by its very offers of mercy that the Divine justice is surely gone forth with the edict of death against every soul that hath sinned, and that it is a mere matter of time when that justice shall overtake the sinner (Gen. iii. 3 ; Ezek. xviii. 4 ; Rom. iii. 9, 19, &c.).   4. *That it pleased God to open a door of safety to the fugitive without staying the avenger.*   For the mission of the goel was very needful for that age, and yet it was the will of God to spare the unwitting homicide.   Even so it has pleased God in a wonderful manner to provide a refuge for the sinner without compromising the Divine justice.   The wrath of God against sin and the necessary punishment of sin are declared by the very means which bring salvation to the sinner (Rom. iii. 26, &c.).   5. *That this refuge was so distributed in six cities, three on each side Jordan, that it was everywhere accessible.*   Even so the sinner's refuge in Jesus Christ is everywhere and by all accessible, if they will without delay flee into it (Heb. vi. 18, &c.).   And note that whereas almost all other religious privilege and promise was concentrated at Jerusalem, this refuge was distributed to all quarters of Jewish settlement, intimating that salvation in Christ is attainable wherever men call upon his name (Rom. ix. 33, &c.).   6. *That in order to be safe the manslayer must flee to the city of refuge, which was a Levitical city (not a solitary post or a mere sanctuary), and there must take up his abode among the Levites.*   Even so the sinner who desires to escape from the sentence of Divine justice must flee for refuge unto Christ to take hold on his merits ; but in doing so he does *ipso facto* find a home in the society of the truly faithful, and in that society he will abide.   The life of one that is escaped from wrath is *not* a solitary walk with God, but a dwelling in a populous city (Acts ii. 42 ; Col. iii. 15 ; Heb. xii. 22, 23 ; cf. Ps. xxxi. 21, &c.).   7. *That the manslayer must never stir outside his refuge at risk of his life ;* if he did, the goel was at liberty to slay him. Even so the sinner must never quit his refuge in Christ for one hour, lest he perish ; neither may he (which is part of the same thing) withdraw from the society of the faithful, for that is his (outward) protection.   At whatever risk and loss of things temporal, he must abide under the shelter of the atonement.

Consider again, with respect to the death of the high priest, and the staying of blood-feuds—1. That the high priest typified Christ, not in that he died by virtue of individual mortality, but in that he lived by virtue of official immortality (see on ch. xx. 28 ; Heb. vii. 24, 25) ; wherefore it is contrary to the whole analogy of Scripture to attribute any power of atonement to the death of the high priest.   2. That the high priest was not only the mediator and intercessor for Israel, but was also the chief minister of the law of God, and therefore the avenger of all iniquity against Israel, especially of all blood-guiltiness ; in a word, he represented Divine justice as well as Divine compassion.   3. That the death of the high priest, which set the escaped manslayer free from all constraints and restrictions, must be taken to represent the passing away (as far as we are concerned) of the law of God as directed against sin.   But this will only be when sin itself shall have wholly ceased, *i. e.* at the resurrection of the just ; *then,* and only *then,* will all restraints, all constraints, all necessities for sacrifice and renunciation, all penalties for forsaking the society of the faithful, be for ever abolished as no longer needful.

Consider also, in connection with this—1. That the word *goel* is translated avenger, kinsman, and redeemer ; the same personage sustaining in fact all these characters, and that by a natural law due to the circumstances of the age.   2. That our Lord is unquestionably our Goel, in that he is our Kinsman, who has made himself our nearest blood relation, and in that he is our Redeemer, who hath redeemed for us our forfeited possession in the kingdom of heaven.   3. That he is also our Goel in that he is in readiness to avenge as Judge all wrongs done unto the temporal or spiritual lives of his own.   This is indeed little considered, but is certainly true, since he alone wields all power in heaven and in earth (see Matt. xxviii. 18 ; Heb. iv. 12, 13, where the "Word of God" is evidently the personal Word ; Luke xviii. 7 ; 2 Thess. i. 6 ; Rev. vi. 10 ; xix. 2, &c.).   4. That the work and office of Christ as Avenger and Defender of his own will cease and determine with the final end of all wickedness, and then he will be Goel no longer in this sense (see 1 Cor. xv. 24—28 compared with Rev. vii. 17, &c.). And this change, whereby the Avenger will be wholly swallowed up in the Kinsman and Redeemer, seems to be symbolised by the death of the high priest (see above).

III. The laws of manslaughter here declared have rather a moral than a spiritual value. The one thing which they uphold as a principle is the sanctity of human life, and the duty of inflicting capital punishment for murder, as laid down in Gen. ix. It is difficult to see that this duty is less under the gospel, because the bringing in of the gospel has not changed the fundamental relations of man to his Maker as based upon creation ; rather it would seem to have added to the sanctity of human life by adding to the ties which knit that life to the life of God (cf. Acts ix. 4, 5 ; 1 Cor. vi. 15 ; 2 Pet. i. 4). Whatever may be held, however, as touching the duties of civil governors, we may consider—1. That the sin against God involved in murder is enormous, and this guilt is incurred by every one that hateth his brother (1 John iii. 15). 2. That the guilt of murder lay before God in the intention to kill, wherefore murders also proceed out of the heart (Mark vii. 21). 3. That it was laid upon the congregation to show by prompt and righteous procedure that they had no sympathy with the murderer. 4. That in the absence of such vindication of justice the land was polluted with blood in the eyes of God, who dwelt therein. 5. That there is a crime which is murder, but is worse than any killing of the body, *i. e.* the destroying of the soul by leading it into sin. 6. That it is laid upon all the faithful to show their horror and detestation of this crime by their treatment of seducers and tempters (1 Cor. v. 11 ; Ephes. v. 11 ; 2 Tim. ii. 21 ; 2 John 11). 7. That indulgence and sympathy extended to destroyers of souls that have not repented brings down the wrath of God upon a Church, and makes it hateful in his eyes (see Isa. i. 21, &c.). 8. That this sinful indulgence of seducers is excused by human considerations, in forgetfulness that God is in the midst of his people, and that every sin so lightly excused or ignored stares him in the face (2 Cor. vi. 16 ; Rev. ii. 1). 9. That if the blood of Abel cried to him from the ground, and if the land of Canaan could not be cleansed from the blood of its slain, how much more will he be moved by that destruction of immortal souls which is wrought by the wicked lives and solicitations of bad Christians !

HOMILIES BY VARIOUS AUTHORS.

Vers. 1—8.—*The Levites to be distributed in certain cities throughout the whole land.* Unlike the other tribes, the Levites were to have no inheritance in the land. The names of Judah, Ephraim, Manasseh, Reuben figure on the map of Palestine, each giving name to a province or county of its own ; but the map knows no tribe of Levi. The Lord was the inheritance of this tribe. For their subsistence the Levites were to depend partly on the tithe, partly on certain dues and perquisites, supplemented by the free-will offerings of the faithful. But although they were landless, it was never the Lord's will that they should be houseless. A vagabond ministry could not have failed to be a scandalous ministry. Accordingly, the law here provides dwellings for the sacred tribe in forty-eight Levitical cities.

I. In this law TWO POINTS CLAIM NOTICE. 1. That the forty-eight cities, although denominated "Levitical cities," *were not devoted exclusively to members of this tribe.* For example, Hebron, which was perhaps the most noted of the forty-eight, being the city of refuge for what was afterwards the whole kingdom of Judah, formed part of the inheritance of Caleb the Kenezite (Josh. xiv. 14). Doubtless many families of Judah would also be found among the residents ; for the city belonged to Judah. What the Levites obtained was not, in any instance, exclusive possession of the city, but certain houses within the walls, and certain pasture grounds ("glebe lands") adjoining. The houses and glebes thus set apart became the inalienable inheritance of the respective Levitical families. They were as strictly entailed as the *lands* which constituted the patrimony of the other families in Israel. If at any time they were sold for debt, they reverted to the family at the Jubilee. 2. *The Levitical cities were scattered up and down the whole country.* The arrangement was a remarkable one. At first sight, indeed, it looks awkward and unnatural. For were not the Levites set apart to do the service of the sanctuary ? Would it not have been more convenient to have had them located where they would have been within easy reach of the sanctuary? In the ideal arrangement sketched in Ezekiel's vision, the Levitical families are seen located in the vicinity of Jerusalem. The circumstance that the law ordained an arrangement so different was meant, I cannot doubt, to suggest to the Levites that they had other duties to discharge in Israel besides doing the service of the sanctuary. It was the will of God that they should, in their several districts, be the stated teachers of the people in the Divine law (Deut. xxxiii. 10; Mal. ii. 4—8). This office and calling of the Levites being so honourable, it has often been thought strange that their dispersion throughout Israel should have been predicted by Jacob as a curse upon the tribe for their father's sin (Gen. xlix. 7). In itself it was honourable; nevertheless the words of the patriarch were fulfilled in the end. When the ten tribes revolted from the house of David, they fell away also from the sanctuary; and the Levites dwelling within those tribes had to choose between forfeiting their cities or being cut off from the sanctuary. In either case they found how bitter it was to be divided in Jacob and scattered in Israel.

II. WHAT MAY WE LEARN FROM THIS LAW? 1. It has been usual to see in the distribution of the Levites over the whole land *a type and prelude of the arrangement which, in Christendom, assigns to every parish and every congregation its own pastor.* The apostles "ordained elders in every city." Ministers of the gospel are not to be massed together in the great cities, but to be scattered everywhere, so that no family in God's Israel may be beyond reach of one "at whose mouth they may seek the law." Of the institutions which have co-operated to make society what it is in the Christian nations, it would not be easy to name one which has been more influential for good than this. 2. The arrangement may be regarded as representing *the principle according to which the lot of Christ's people in this world is ordered.* The faithful do not live apart from other men in towns and provinces of their own. Separation from the world, in this literal sense, has been often the dream of Christian reformers, and not seldom have societies been organised for the purpose of realising it. But the well-meant schemes have in every case failed. They were bound to fail, for they ran counter to our Lord's great prayer and rule: "I pray not that thou shouldest take them out of the world, but that thou shouldest keep them from the evil" (John xvii. 15). Nor is the reason of the rule doubtful. Christ's people are the salt of the earth; and salt, to do its work, must be mingled with that which it is to preserve. The godly must be content to have ungodly persons, more or fewer, for neighbours so long as they abide in this world. An unmixed "congregation of the righteous" belongs to the felicities of the world to come. But if Christ's people are like the Levites in regard to dispersion, they are like them also in respect to the provision made for their brotherly communion. As the Levites dwelt in their cities with other Levites, so Christians are to be gathered into Churches for mutual comfort and for common work. "We believe in the communion of saints."—B.

Vers. 9—29.—*The manslayer and the cities of refuge.* The law of sanctuary, as it is here laid down, never fails to remind the devout reader of the refuge which God's mercy has provided in Christ for those who, by their sin, have exposed themselves to the vengeance of the law. This way of regarding the matter can be thoroughly justified. At the same time it is well to bear in mind that the law was framed, in the first instance, for a humbler purpose.

I. THE ORDINANCE OF THE CITY OF REFUGE CONSIDERED AS A PART OF THE MOSAIC CRIMINAL LAW. In primitive and barbarous states of society the execution of vengeance for murder was devolved by ancient custom on the next kinsman of the murdered man. The *goël*, the redeemer and kinsman, was also the avenger of blood. The custom is sufficiently harsh and barbarous, and gives rise to blood-feuds and untold miseries. Yet, for the states of society in which it originated, it cannot be dispensed with. There are at this day tribes without number, especially in the East, in which the sanctity of human life is guarded only by fear of the avenger of blood. Accordingly, the law of Moses does not abolish the custom; the next kinsman was still held bound to take vengeance for blood. The aim of the Mosaic jurisprudence was to conserve what was good in the ancient custom, and at the same time to impose such a check upon it as would prevent its abuse. This twofold design was accomplished in the following way:—1. *Certain cities were made sanctuary cities* (Exod. xxi. 13). The avenger of blood might pursue the manslayer to the gate of the city of refuge ; might kill him, if he could, before reaching the gate; but at the gate he had to halt and sheathe his sword. 2. Although the gate of the city of refuge was open to every manslayer, *the city did not suffer the wilful murderer to laugh at the sword of justice.* It gave provisional protection to all, but only to save them from the blind and indiscriminating anger of the avenger of blood. The refugees were sheltered only till they had stood a regular trial (ver. 12). If it should be proved to the satisfaction of the congregation that the accused person had been guilty of murder, he was to be delivered up to the avenger of blood to be killed. 3. *If, on the contrary, it should be found that the manslayer meant no harm, that it was a case of accidental homicide, the city of refuge was to afford him inviolable sanctuary.* The law did not (as with us) suffer him to go home free. Accidental homicide is often the result of carelessness. To teach men not to trifle with the sanctity of life, the manslayer, although no murderer, had to confine himself to the city of his refuge. But so long as his abode within its walls he was safe.

II. THE ORDINANCE OF THE CITY OF REFUGE CONSIDERED AS A TYPE. That it had a typical reference might be gathered (were there nothing else) from the direction that the manslayer was to continue in the sanctuary city " until the death of the high priest ; " a meaningless provision if the statute had been only a piece of criminal law. Considered as a type, the ordinance represents—1. *Our condition as sinners.* We are exposed to the vengeance of God's law, and the stroke may fall upon us at any moment. A condition in which there can be no solid peace. 2. *What Christ is to those who are found in him.* He is their High Priest, whose life is the security for their life ; who "is able to save to the uttermost, seeing he ever liveth " (Heb. vii. 25). And he is their Refuge, insomuch that for them the one thing needful is that they be found in him (Rom. viii. 1, 38, 39 ; Philip. iii. 8, 9). 3. *How we may obtain the salvation which is in Christ.* It is by fleeing into him for refuge and thereafter abiding in him continually. In him we are safe, out of him we are lost. This way of salvation is such as renders inexcusable those who neglect it. The cities of refuge were so distributed that no manslayer had far to run before reaching one. There were three on each side of Jordan ; of the three, in each case, one lay near the north border, one near the south border, and one in the middle. Every city was the natural centre of its province and accessible from every side. They were so situated that no fugitive required to cross either a river or a mountain chain before reaching his refuge. How strikingly is all this realised in Christ our refuge !—B.

Vers. 30—34.— *Why the murderer must be put to death.* This passage brings up a subject not often discussed in the pulpit. Yet it surely is a subject which comes home to the business of us all. In a country like ours the administration of justice, the execution of vengeance on evil-doers, is a duty in which every one has to bear a part. We may not all be officers of justice, but we must all act as informers, or witnesses, or jurymen. It is of high importance, therefore, that every member of the community should be well instructed regarding the principles which lie at the foundation of the criminal law, and, in particular, should know why and on what authority the community lays hold upon evil-doers and inflicts on them the punishment of their crimes.

I. Observe THE OCCASION of the statute here delivered. It is an appendix to the law regarding the cities of refuge. That law was designed to shield the involuntary homicide from the avenger of blood. The intention was good ; but good intentions do not always prevent dangerous mistakes. It often happens that good men in labouring to cast out one evil open the door to a greater evil. A follower of John Howard may so press the duty of humanity towards prisoners as to deprive the prison of its deterrent power. So in Israel there was a danger that the care taken to restrain the avenger of blood from touching the involuntary manslayer might have the effect of deadening the public sense of the enormity of murder, and weakening men's resentment against the murderer. The design of the statute before us is to prevent so mischievous a result.

II. What then are THE PROVISIONS OF THE STATUTE ? 1. *The ancient law which condemned the murderer to death is solemnly reaffirmed* (ver. 30 ; compare with vers. 16—21 and Gen. ix. 6). To be sure, the extreme penalty ought not to be executed without extreme circumspection. The unsupported testimony of one witness is not to be held sufficient to sustain a charge of murder. Nevertheless, if there is sufficient evidence, the sword must strike, the murderer must not be suffered to go free. 2. *The death penalty may not be commuted into a fine* (ver. 31). In regard to this point the Mosaic law differs from many, perhaps from most other primitive codes ; for they suffered the murderer to compound with the kinsmen of his victim by paying a fine in cattle or in money. The law of Moses suffered no such composition. The murderer must be put to death. Even the restraint to which the law subjected the involuntary manslayer was not suffered to be relaxed by a money payment. In all cases affecting the sanctity of life pecuniary compositions are utterly forbidden.

III. THE REASON OF THIS STATUTE is carefully explained (vers. 33, 34). The reason lies in these three principles :—1. "*Blood defileth the land*" (cf. Ps. cvi. 38). That sin defiles the sinner, that murder especially defiles the conscience of the murderer— these are facts patent to all. It is not so often observed that crime perpetrated in a city defiles the whole city. The whole community has a share in the guilt. Hence the remarkable law laid down in Deut. xxi. 1—9 for the expiation of an uncertain murder. 2. *The proper expiation of murder is by the death of the murderer.* "The land cannot be cleansed of the blood that is shed therein but by the blood of him that shed it." Justice is satisfied, the honour of the law vindicated, when the murderer is put to death, and not otherwise. To accept a pecuniary satisfaction for blood is simply to pollute the land. 3. In this whole matter *the paramount consideration ought to be the honour of God.* Murder is criminal beyond all other offences, because it is the defacement of the image of God in man. Murder must not go unavenged, because it defiles the land before God.——Let these principles be carefully weighed. They set in a clear light the true and adequate reason for inflicting punishment on evil-doers. The true reason is neither the reformation of the criminal (for the sword must strike although there should be no hope of reformation) nor the protection of society. These are important objects, and not to be overlooked ; but the proper reason of punishment is the vindication of righteousness, the executing of vengeance on the man who doeth evil (Rom. xiii. 4).

IV. In conclusion, DOES NOT ALL THIS SHED WELCOME LIGHT ON THE ATONEMENT OF OUR BLESSED LORD? The death of Christ for our sins accomplished many great and precious purposes. It was an affecting proof of his sympathy with us. It was a revelation of the Father's love. But these purposes do not contain the proper and adequate reason of our Lord's sufferings. He died for our sins. It was necessary that our sins should be cleansed, that expiation or atonement should be made for them. (N.B. It is the same Hebrew word, commonly translated *atonement* elsewhere in the Old Testament, which in this passage is translated *cleansing* in the text and *expiation* in the margin.) They might have been expiated in our blood. But, blessed be God, his mercy has found out another way. By a blessed exchange Christ has become sin for us ; he has borne our sins and made atonement for them. This was the end of his sufferings—to satisfy the justice of the Father for our sins, so that his righteousness might not be dishonoured although we should go free.—B.

Vers. 9—34.—*The cities of refuge.* The laws in regard to the cities of refuge and manslaughter suggest truths on the following subjects. We see in them—

I. A TOLERATION OF WHAT GOD NEITHER HAS APPOINTED NOR APPROVES. The old custom of blood-avenging by the *goel*, though open to grave abuses, was not altogether proscribed. The laws given by God to Moses were not always absolutely the best, though, relatively to the state of the people, the best they could endure. Other illustrations are found in the laws relating to divorce, polygamy, and slavery. These examples of a wise conservatism suggest lessons for parents, who have to "overlook" (Acts xvii. 30) the times of ignorance of their children, and for missionaries, who may have for a time to tolerate inevitable evils in converts whose consciences are not yet trained. As God dealt with the Jews during their childhood as a nation, so does he in mercy deal with his sinful children during their education in this life (Ps. xix. 12 ; cxxx. 3, 4).

II. An education by means of the customs of the past. God tolerated the old custom, but not in its entirety. He modified it, and thus carried on the education of the nation. On the one hand, the cities of refuge were not like the *asyla* of the Greeks and Romans, for wilful murderers were led forth from them to justice (ver. 30). On the other hand, the homicide by accident was safe under certain conditions (vers. 12, 25—28). So too now God discriminates between wilful sins (Heb. x. 26—31, 38, 39) and sins of ignorance and imprudence, which may bring after them serious disabilities, but do not doom to destruction.

III. A prefiguration of spiritual truth in the future. The cities of refuge, if not strictly a type, are an illustration of Christ, the sinner's refuge. The rules prescribed by Jews in regard to the road being kept in good condition, finger-posts being provided, &c., suggest various applications. 1. The cities of refuge were near every portion of the land, and Christ is within reach of every one of us. 2. The way was to be made plain; and the word of the truth of the gospel is plain, so that "he that readeth it may run" straight to the refuge. 3. Every manslayer, native or foreign, received the shelter of the refuge; and sinners of every degree of guilt and every nation have no safety except in Christ. 4. Within the city, and "in Christ," there is no condemnation. 5. To quit the refuge, and to "go away" from Christ, is to meet destruction. 6. A murderer had but the appearance of safety within the city, and the wilful sinner can find no shelter from the wrath of God even when professing to believe in Christ.—P.

Vers. 1—8.—*God provides places for the Levites to dwell in.* God had laid upon the tribe of Levi many and onerous services, such as gave full occupation for their time (chs. i., iii., iv., viii., xxviii., xxix.); he had also made abundant provision for their support in the matter of food (ch. xviii.); it remained that he should give a clear indication of where they were to find a place of abode in Canaan. If their particular place of settlement was important to the other tribes, it was surely of peculiar importance to the tribe which in a representative aspect stood nearer to God than any of the rest. Levi, with all its solemn responsibilities, would assuredly not have been tolerated in such an assertion of self-will as came from Reuben and Gad. As we examine the mode of settlement indicated in this passage, we perceive how *God points out the golden mean between too much concentration and too much diffusion.*

I. The Levites were so settled as to avoid the great evils consequent on undue concentration. They might have had the tabernacle fixed up in a certain tribal allotment of their own, and then what would have happened? Those living at a distance from the territory of Levi would have been debarred from many privileges belonging to those in immediate proximity. God is no respecter of persons. He did all that was possible to put every tribe in Israel in a position of religious equality. The proportion of land and the proportion of Levitical service was to be according to the needs of each tribe. 1. Thus, *by a judicious diffusion, the unity of the nation was promoted.* Different circumstances require different means for the same end. While the Israelites were encamped in the wilderness, the tribe of Levi was all together, in the midst of the camp, and immediately around the tabernacle. But when the Israelites became distributed in Canaan, the Levites were distributed also, thus acting still as a principle of unity, although in a different way. And this distribution had been made all the more necessary since two tribes and a half had chosen to dwell on the east of Jordan. That the Israelites themselves were not supremely conscious of the need of unity had been shown only too clearly by the conduct of Reuben and Gad. Much more was wanted than to lie side by side within the same borders. A mere geographical unity was a mockery, a delusion, and a snare. 2. This judicious diffusion also helped in *promoting the knowledge of all that needed to be known in Israel.* The Levites were privileged to become—and the privilege was a very high one—the guides, instructors, counsellors, and monitors of the people. That which God had made known to Moses needed to be brought down very patiently and carefully to individual, private, daily life. The Levites had ample opportunities to explain the commandments of God and the significance of the types, the rites and ceremonies, and the great historic commemorations. And as the history of Israel grew, there grew with it opportunities to stimulate and warn by pointing out the mingled glory and shame of the nation's career, and the lessons to be learnt from considering the men who had been conspicuous in that career (2 Chron. xxxv. 3). But these opportunities of instruction only came because God had sufficiently distributed the instructors throughout the land. If a house is to be fully lighted up there must be a light in every room. Those who are already instructed must be where they can firmly lay hold of the ignorant, for the ignorant in the things of God need not only to be instructed, but first of all thoroughly wakened out of sleep. 3. *This diffusion also indicated the service which all Israel was to render to the world.* What Levi was to Israel, that Israel was to become to all mankind. Levi was diffused through the whole nation, and only kept its individuality as a tribe in proportion as it kept its fidelity to God. Other tribes were distinguished by their territory; Levi by being specially engaged in the holy service of the tabernacle and the temple. Thus what a benefit has been produced—more real perhaps than exactly appreciated—by the dispersion of Israel among all nations to bear their own peculiar, solemn, and pathetic testimony to Israel's God, and to the historic verity of the Old Testament! Thus also does God make his own gracious and comprehensive arrangements to diffuse believers in his Son throughout the world, according to the spiritual needs of the world. In one sense they are rigorously separated from the world, even as Israel was by the hard and fast lines of the national borders; in another sense they are meant to be so diffused that wherever there is a dark place, there the light of the truth as it is in Jesus may brightly shine. The gospel is debtor to all nations and all ranks, to both sexes and to all ages. We find the true Israelite in every society where a man has any right to be at all: among the highest and the lowest; in Parliaments, in courts of justice, in commerce, in literature, in science, and in art.

II. CARE WAS ALSO TAKEN IN THE SETTLEMENT OF THE LEVITES THAT THE NECESSARY DIFFUSION SHOULD NOT BE PUSHED TOO FAR. They were to be distributed through all Israel, but not according to the free choice of the individual Levite. Forty-eight cities, with sufficient accompanying land, were set apart for them. Thus, by fixing a limit of diffusion, God conferred a benefit both on them and on the whole people. Those who are engaged in a special work of such incalculable importance as the work of the Levites was, need to be where they can frequently counsel, comfort, and encourage one another. It was not good for the Levites to be alone. To be isolated was in itself a sore temptation. And though the work of God is only truly done where there is individual consecration, energy, and initiative, yet he is not a wise Christian who sets lightly by the advantage he gains from frequent recourse to those like-minded with himself. A certain measure of coherence among the Levites was needed for a healthy and profitable state of the official life. You shall have a fire blazing brightly in the grate, and if you leave it so it will go on for a long time giving out its flame, heat, and light. But take the pieces of coal and range them separately on the hearth, and very quickly the glowing fragments will become a dull red and soon die out altogether. The limits which God fixes are wise and loving limits; he ever keeps us from all the dangers of extremes. The Levites were neither to be too much separated from the people nor too much mingled with them.—Y.

Vers. 9—34.—*The cities of refuge.* We in our modern English life have an experience of the stability of social order, of general submission to a national law, and of confidence in the strict administration of justice, which causes this provision for the cities of refuge to come on us in a very unexpected way. We are not unprepared to read the other announcements which come at the close of this Book— *e. g.* the strict injunction to expel the Canaanites, the allotment of the inheritance, and the Divine marking out of the boundaries of the land; but this appointment of the cities of refuge is like a great light suddenly lighted up to reveal to us the peculiar social state of Israel.

I. We are brought face to face with A TIME WHEN THERE WAS NO GENERAL AND SECURE ADMINISTRATION OF JUSTICE. God had to make provision here for a strong feeling which had evidently grown up through many centuries. This provision pointed back to those unsocial days when the only effectual avengers of murder were the kinsmen of the slain person. The punishment of the murderer had come to be regarded as a family duty, because no one else would concern himself with it. And in the course of time what had begun in necessity ended in a conventional sense of honour, and of the obligations of kinship, which there was no way of escaping. Private revenge, whatever its abuses, whatever the dark instigations to it in the heart of the avenger, was in a certain sense imperatively necessary when there was no efficient public tribunal of justice. Thus we see how much of the barbaric element still remained in Israel. It is a matter of common agreement among us that a man must not take the law into his own hands, but in ancient Israel every man seems to have done it without the slightest hesitation.

II. We have here another illustration of THE ALLOWANCE THAT WAS MADE FOR HARDNESS OF HEART ON THE PART OF ISRAEL. When the Pharisees came to our Lord, tempting him with a question concerning divorce, he replied, "Moses because of the hardness of your hearts suffered you to put away your wives" (Matt. xix. 8). So here we may say that Moses, because of the hardness of heart in Israel, provided these cities of refuge. It was no manner of use to tell the *goel*, the blood avenger, not to pursue the manslayer. If he had neglected to do so he would have rested under heavy reproach all the days of his life. Moses knew well how deeply fixed was this institution of blood revenge. Had he not himself, in his patriotic zeal, taken the law into his own hand some eighty years before, and slain the Egyptian? God might indeed have forbidden this blood revenge altogether, but the command would have been a dead letter. He did a more efficacious thing in providing these cities of refuge. The existence of them was incompatible with the continuance in undiminished vigour of the practice of blood revenge. By appointing them God recognised the necessity out of which the practice had arisen. He allowed all that might be good and conscientious in the motive of the avenger. If the person pursued were really guilty of wilful murder, he could not escape; the city of refuge was no refuge for him. The line between murder and accidental homicide was very plainly drawn. Under such a system as God had established in Israel he could not but protect the unfortunate man who was fleeing from a passionate, unreasoning pursuer, and secure for him a fair inquiry. Everything was done to secure the best interests of all. God could not but honour his own solemn and exalted command, "Thou shalt not kill."

III. An illustration also of THE UNDESERVED CALAMITIES WHICH MAY COME UPON A MAN IN A WORLD WHERE SIN REIGNS EVEN UNTO DEATH. One man slaying another unwittingly deserves our deepest pity and sympathy. We have heard of those to whom such a misfortune had come having to walk softly all the days of their life because of the unintended act. They could not get it out of their minds. Yet here, in addition to possible grief of heart, there was a serious, a long, perhaps a life-long, disadvantage. The homicide, however really innocent he might be, had to flee for his life and stay in the city of refuge till the death of the high priest. Thus we have another proof of the manifold power which death has to disturb the world. These inconveniences to the manslayer could not all at once be removed. We live in a world where we not only may in a spirit of love bear one another's burdens, but some of them we must bear as a matter of necessity. The unwitting homicide had to bear the consequences of his fellow-man being mortal. Yet at the same time we are made to see how God was surely advancing to break the power of death. The lot of the manslayer was greatly mended by the institution of these cities of refuge. We may well believe that in the course of time their character became so recognised that this particular obligation of the *goel* would fall into disuse; the nation would come to accept the security, the superiority, and the rightness of public justice.

IV. Consider the points in connection with the institution of cities of refuge which show THE RESPECT FOR HUMAN LIFE WHICH GOD WAS SEEKING TO TEACH THE PEOPLE. The path of Israel from Egypt to Canaan had indeed been marked by much of violent death. The overwhelming of Pharaoh's army, all the sudden visitations of Divine wrath upon Israel, the slaying in battle of the Amalekites, Amorites, and Midianites—these had made God to seem as if he were continually girt with the horrid instruments of the executioner. But for all these acts, dreadful as they were, there was a reason—a Divine, and therefore sufficient, reason. Whatever was done was done judicially. If the circumstances and times of the Israelites are taken into account, sufficient cause will appear for the frequency with which God had recourse to violent death in the carrying out of his punitive purposes. Then, with respect to murder, it was the feeling of the time that a murderer must not be suffered to live. Putting the murderer to death was the only effectual way in those semi-savage times of teaching respect for life. Respect for life was taught to the avenger by putting the city of refuge between him and the unwitting homicide. Respect for life was taught also by the inconvenience, to say the least of it, to which the homicide was put. It was taught by the requiring of more than one witness to establish a capital charge. *And we also need more respect for human life than we often show.* We should not take it so recklessly and exultingly in war; we should not take it under an insufficient plea of necessity on the gallows. There is a lamentable way of speaking of the brutal and hardened members of society, the class from which murderers so often come, as if they were little better than vermin. Many seem to think that it is a matter of no great consequence whether a man be hanged or not. True, he has to die at last; but surely there is a great difference between death when it comes in spite of the attempts of physician and attendants to ward it off, and when it comes by our deliberate infliction of it. We have all sorts of institutions and instruments to defend life by land and by sea; we have one hideous instrument, the gallows, to take it away. And as we see God advancing men, by the appointment of these cities of refuge, from the "wild justice" of private revenge to a calm reliance on public justice, so we may hope that the spirit of love and the spirit of Christ will more and more prevail amongst us, till at last the gallows will be banished, if not into utter oblivion, at all events into antiquarian obscurity.

V. Consider how these cities of refuge were to be Levitical cities. It was fitting that the Levites should have charge of these cities, since the Levites belonged to no tribe in particular, but to the whole nation. They were removed from the temptation which would otherwise have come, if the city of refuge had belonged to the same tribe as the blood avenger. Unless the city of refuge was made really efficacious, it was no city of refuge at all. Giving Levi the charge of these cities also prevented jealousies between tribes. It conferred too on the homicide certain privileges he might not otherwise have had; he gained opportunities of Levitical instruction. God can make his own abiding compensations to those who fall into calamity by no fault of their own. None can really hurt us but ourselves in that which is inward, permanent, and of real importance.

VI. Consider how the death of the high priest affected the position of the unwitting manslayer. He was then free from any further disability and need of confinement. The death of the high priest had a great expiatory effect. According to the value of the types, he was holier than all the unblemished beasts, and his death counted for very much indeed in its cleansing efficacy. Thus we see, by this reference to the death of the high priest, how God regarded his own honour as a holy God. Blood defiled the land, even when spilt unwittingly, and nothing less than the death of the high priest could cleanse away the stain. Nothing less could do it, but this did it quite sufficiently.—Y.

EXPOSITION.

CHAPTER XXXVI.

THE MARRIAGE OF HEIRESSES (vers. 1—13). Ver. 1.—**The chief fathers.** The same phrase is more correctly translated in Exod. vi. 25 "heads of the fathers." It is, however, probable that הָאָבֹ֣ת (fathers) is a contraction for בֵּית־הָאָבֹות (fathers' houses). The fathers' house was the next recognised and familiar division below the *mishpachah* (family). Probably the fathers' house included originally all the descendants of a living ancestor, who formed the bond of union between them; but this union no doubt survived in many cases the death of the common ancestor, whose authority would then devolve upon the oldest efficient member of the house. **The families of the children of Gilead.** "The *mishpachoth* of the Beni-Gilead" certainly did not include the Machirites, who were somewhat sharply distinguished from the other Manassites (see above on ch. xxvi. 29; xxxii. 39 ff.); it is even doubtful whether they included the Gileadites proper, who took their name (and perhaps traced their descent) from Gilead, but not from his sons. It may be confidently assumed that the Machirites, who had received an extensive and remote territory beyond Jordan, had nothing whatever to do with this application. It was the other section of the tribe, the *mishpachoth* of the six sons of Gilead, who were yet to receive inheritance by lot in Canaan proper, to whom the matter appeared so serious that they came to Moses about it.

Ver. 2.—**My lord.** אֲדֹנִי. The singular form is constantly used in Hebrew, as in other languages, together with the plural personal pronoun (see at Gen. xxiii. 6). The deference now paid to Moses (cf. ch. xxxii. 25, 27) is in marked contrast to the treatment he had received from the former generation. Only Aaron (and that under the influence of terror—Exod. xxxii. 22 ; ch. xii. 11) and Joshua (ch. xi. 28) had addressed him as Adoni before.

Ver. 3.—**Whereunto they are received.** Literally, as in the margin, " unto whom (לָהֶם referring to the men of the tribe) they shall be."

Ver. 4.—**When the jubile of the children of Israel shall be.** It is remarkable that this is the only reference by name to the Jubile (יוֹבֵל *jubeel;* not jubilee, which is the vulgar form of the same word derived from the Latin *jubilæus*) to be found in the Scriptures. Some allusions more or less doubtful have been pointed out in the prophets, but the only one which seems incontrovertible is in Ezek. xlvi. 17, and belongs to the ideal *régime* of that vision. Jeremiah's right of redemption over the lands of his family was probably due to the fact that they were priestly lands (Josh. xxi. 18 ; Jer. i. 1 ; xxxii. 7—9), and as such incapable of permanent alienation. It is, therefore, doubtful whether the Jubile was ever actually observed, although the principle upon which it rested, the equity of redemption which no Israelite could divest himself of, was undoubtedly acknowledged (see notes on Levit. xxv.). **Then shall their inheritance be put unto the inheritance of the tribe whereunto they are received.** It is again remarkable that the one explicit reference to the Jubile should be only to an indirect consequence of its practical working. The Jubile could not really transfer the property of the heiress to her husband's tribe, but it would in effect confirm that transfer, and make it permanent. In practice no property would be considered to have finally changed hands until the year of Jubile, when an extensive re-settlement took place, and when all titles not successfully challenged would be considered as confirmed. Since the title of the heiress's children could not be challenged, and since any intermediate disposition of the

land must then determine, the Jubile would seem to effect the transfer of which it compelled the recognition. It is, however, none the less strange that the Manassites should have laid such stress upon the practical effects of a piece of legislation which had never yet come into use. It seems to point to the conclusion that the same thing had been customary among them in their Egyptian homes, and that they were acquainted, at least by tradition, with its actual working.

Ver. 5.—**The tribe of the sons of Joseph.** "The tribe (*matteh*) of the Beni-Joseph." There were two, or rather in effect three, tribes of the Beni-Joseph ; Moses referred, of course, to the one which had come before him.

Ver. 6.—**Only to the family of the tribe of their father shall they marry.** The direction is not altogether plain, since the tribe (*matteh*) contained several families (*mishpachoth*), and in this case one or more of the families were widely separated from the rest. Probably the words are to be read, " only to the tribe-family of their father," *i. e.* only into that *mishpachah* of Manasseh to which their father had belonged. Practically, therefore, they were restricted to the family of the Hepherites (ch. xxvi. 32, 33). This is made almost certain when we remember that the territory of the "family" was to be apportioned within the tribe in the same way, and with the same regard to relationship, as the territory of the tribe within the nation (see on ch. xxxiii. 54).

Ver. 7.—**Every one . . shall keep himself to the inheritance of the tribe of his fathers.** This was to be the general rule which governed all such questions. Every Israelite had his own share in the inheritance of his tribe, and with that he was to be content, and not seek to intrude on other tribes. Accordingly the decision in the case of the daughters of Zelophehad is extended to all similar cases.

Ver. 11.—**Mahlah, &c.** It is a curious instance of the inartificial character of the sacred records that these five names, which have not the least interest in themselves, are repeated thrice in this Book, and once in Joshua (xvii. 3). It is evident that the case made a deep impression upon the mind of the nation at the time. **Their father's brothers' sons.** The Hebrew word דּוֹד is always translated "father's brother," or "uncle ;" and that seems to be its ordinary meaning, although in Jer. xxxii. 12 it stands for uncle's son. There is no reason to depart from the customary reading here. No doubt the daughters of Zelophehad acted according to the spirit as well as the letter of the law, and married the nearest male relatives who were open to their choice. The Septuagint has τοῖς ἀνεψιοῖς αὐτῶν.

Ver. 13.—**The commandments.** הַמִּצְוֹת.
This is one of the words which recur so continually in Deuteronomy and in Ps. cxix. It is found four times in ch. xv., and in a few other passages of the earlier books, including Levit. xxvii. 34. **The judgments.** הַמִּשְׁפָּטִים.
A similar formula is found at the conclusion of Leviticus (xxvi. 46), where, however, "the commandments" represents a different word (הַחֻקִּים), and a third term, "the laws" (הַתּוֹרֹת), is added. It is difficult to say confidently what is included under the "these" of this verse. Comparing it with ch. xxxiii. 50, it would seem that it only referred to the final regulations and enactments of the last four chapters; but as we have no reason to believe that the later sections of the Book are arranged in any methodical order, we cannot limit its scope to those, or deny that

it may include the laws of chs. xxviii.—xxx. For a similar reason we cannot say that the use of this concluding formula excludes the possibility of further large additions having been subsequently made to the Divine legislation in the same place and by the same person, as recorded in the Book of Deuteronomy. All we can say is, that the Book of Numbers knows nothing about any such additions, and concludes in such sort as to make it a matter of surprise that such additions are afterwards met with. The continuity, which so clearly binds together the main bulk of the four books of Moses, ends with this verse. This fact does not of course decide any question which arises concerning the fifth book; it merely leaves all such questions to be determined on their own merits.

HOMILETICS.

Vers. 1—13.—*The sure inheritance.* The decision here recorded, and expanded into a general law, was wholly intended to preserve to each tribe and each family its own inheritance in the land of promise inviolate and undisturbed. Spiritually it can but point to the inheritance "incorruptible and undefiled, and that fadeth not away" (1 Pet. i. 4), for which we look. That there was any special intention in connection with this law to preserve intact the inheritance of Judah, or that it has any bearing on the tribal relationship of the earthly parents of the Divine child, is extremely unlikely. It would certainly appear that Mary had no patrimony, even if she had no brothers. Consider, therefore—

I. THAT THE OBJECT OF THE DIVINE LEGISLATION WAS BY ALL MEANS TO PRESERVE TO EACH ISRAELITE HIS FULL INHERITANCE IN CANAAN. Even so the final end of the dispensation of the gospel is that every one of the elect may obtain for ever that fulness of joy and of life which is prepared for him; to this end all things are made to work together.

II. THAT IN ORDER TO SECURE THIS, NOT ONLY THE INDIVIDUAL POSSESSION, BUT ALSO THE JOINT INTEREST OF EACH IN THE TERRITORY OF HIS TRIBE WAS JEALOUSLY GUARDED FROM INVASION. Even so there will, no doubt, in the future reward be many elements of common as well as of individual happiness, and some of these common to those who have lived and suffered together as members of the same particular Church; these also will be preserved inviolable. Whatever special graces have been developed in the common Christianity of any Church will doubtless be reflected in the immortal state.

III. THAT EACH INDIVIDUAL WAS TO KEEP TO HIS OWN LOT, AND NOT SEEK AFTER ANY ALIEN INHERITANCE. Even so every one of us should cultivate the grace given him, and seek the reward set before him, not coveting the gifts which belong to others, not aspiring to the glory to which he is not called.

IV. THAT EACH TRIBE WAS, IN LIKE MANNER, TO KEEP TO ITS OWN INHERITANCE, AND NOT TO INTRUDE UPON ITS NEIGHBOURS. Even so the different branches of Christ's Church, so far as they by the will of God divide the field between them, are strictly forbidden to invade one another's heritage.

V. THAT THIS WAS SECURED EVEN AT SOME COST OF LIBERTY OF CHOICE ON THE PART OF INDIVIDUALS. Even so the necessity of not intruding upon the portion of others must and does involve considerable self-restraint, and the sacrifice perhaps of cherished desires, on the part of individual members of the Church.

And note that this case so carefully recorded appears trivial, and unworthy of the space it occupies in Holy Writ. Nevertheless, it was not trivial, because it involved a most important principle, and because it was settled by an act of perfect obedience.   And note again that the operation of the Jubile, which was so graciously designed for all Israelites, threatened in this case to aggravate an evil, which, however, was averted by Divine provision.   There may be cases in which even the grace of the gospel may threaten hardship to some ; but if there are, God will find a remedy.

It would not be right to press the example of Zelophehad's daughters in a social sense, but we may draw the general moral lesson—1. That if any have exceptional opportunity of bestowing advantage on others, they should not consult their own fancy nor make an arbitrary choice, but be guided by the general good of all.   2. That none should put themselves forward in order to secure exceptional advantage, but let it fall to those for whom God has designed it.

HOMILETICAL INDEX

TO

THE BOOK OF NUMBERS

—◇—

CHAPTER I.

THEME	PAGE
The Numbering of God's People ...	2
The Numbering of the People ...	2
God commands a Census	4
The Men of Renown who managed the Census	5
"From twenty years old and upward"	5
God's Army	6
The Two Numberings in the Wilderness	6
The Servants of God	8
The Appointment of the Levites to be the Sacred Tribe	9
"Differences of Administrations" in the Service of God	10
Our Position in the Church ...	11
Remarkable Obedience	11

CHAPTER II.

The Camp of the Saints	13
The Muster at Sinai	15
God's Tabernacle in the midst of Israel's Tents	16
The Discipline of God's Army ...	16

CHAPTER III.

The Servants of God, and the Church of the First-born	20
The Families of Levi get their several Commissions	22
"Strange Fire"	23
A Mortal Sin	23

CHAPTER IV.

Duties of the Church Militant ...	27
None may bear the Vessels of the Lord but Levites at their best	28
The Lord is to be served with Fear ...	29
The Perils of Distinguished Service ...	30
The Levites and the Regulation of their Duties	31

CHAPTER V.

THEME	PAGE
The Necessity of putting away Sin ...	33
The Expulsion and Restoration of the Unclean	33
The Public Exclusion of the Unclean	35
Things that Defile	35
No Fraud permitted by God ...	37
Conscience Money	37
Confession and Restitution	38
The Sin of Adultery	41
The Trial of Jealousy	42

CHAPTER VI.

Individual Consecration to God ...	46
Separated to the Service of God ...	47
The Temporary Vow of the Nazarite symbolical of the Lifelong Vow of the Christian	49
The Nazarite's Vow	49
The Regulations for Observance of the Nazarite's Vow	50
The Blessing of God Almighty ...	53
The Benediction	54
The Priestly Blessing	55
The Benediction through the Priests	56

CHAPTER VII.

Acceptable Offerings	60
The Princes and their Princely Offering	61
The Free-will Offering of the Princes	62
The Universality of the Sin Offering ...	63
Intercourse with God	63
The Waggons for the Levites ...	64
The Shekel of the Sanctuary ...	64

CHAPTER VIII.

The Sacred Lamps	66
The Lamps of the Sanctuary ...	66
The Dedication of the Levites ...	69

THEME	PAGE
The Separation of the Levites; or an Ordination Service in the Wilderness	70
An Offering to God, needing for itself an Atonement	71

CHAPTER IX.

THEME	PAGE
The Paschal Feast	74
A Communicant in Israel, disabled by some Mischance from eating the Passover on the right Day, may eat it a Month after	75
The Letter and the Spirit of the Law of the Passover	76
The Beneficent Aspect of the Law of Moses towards Foreigners	77
A Needed Reminder	78
A Difficulty removed	78
Divine Guidance	80
The Guiding Pillar of Cloud and Flame	80
God's Ceaseless Providence a Motive to Prompt Obedience	82
The Cloud upon the Tabernacle	82

CHAPTER X.

THEME	PAGE
The Sacred Trumpets	84
The Silver Trumpets	85
The Use of the Trumpets	86
The Journey Home	90
The Friendly Invitation	93
Hobab Invited; or, the Church's Call to them that are without	94
Moses and Hobab	95
A Right Feeling and a Christian Invitation	96
A Fresh Appeal	97
The Heavenward March	99
The Prayers at the Moving and Resting of the Ark	101

CHAPTER XI.

THEME	PAGE
Wrath awaked and Wrath appeased	103
A Summary View of Sin and its Remedy	105
Murmuring, Lusting, and Loathing	105
The Sin of Concupiscence, and its Punishment	113
The Seventy Elders, and how they were fitted for their High Office	117
Eldad and Medad; or, Irregular Prophesying	119
The Complainers, and how God made Answer to their Complaints	120

THEME	PAGE
The Disastrous Consequences of the Sin of Discontent	121
The Sin of Despondency in a Servant of God	122
The Communication of a Spiritual Endowment	123
Largeness of Heart	123
The Mixed Multitude	124
The Expostulation of Moses	125
The Answer of God	125
Self-will Surfeited and Punished	126
Deeper in Unbelief	127
Foolish Advice wisely rejected	128

CHAPTER XII.

THEME	PAGE
The Contradiction of Sinners	135
The Sedition of Miriam and Aaron	135
The Singular Honour of Moses	136
God the Vindicator of his Calumniated Servants	138
The Lord listening	138
A Hideous Manifestation of Pride	139
A Distinguished Example of Meekness	140
The Humbling of the Proud and the Exaltation of the Meek	141

CHAPTERS XIII., XIV.

THEME	PAGE
The Revolt of Israel	154
The Spies	159
The Mission of the Spies	161
The Search and the Report	162
Conflicting Counsels	162
They could not enter in because of Unbelief	163
Moses standing in the Breach, or the Power of Intercessory Prayer	164
The Sin and Shame of Apostasy	166
With God on our Side we are in the Majority	166
Skilful Intercession	167
A Priceless Privilege Offered, Refused, Lost	167
Fatal Answers to Faithless Prayers	168
A Repentance to be Repented of	168
A Vain Proposition	169
A Mute Appeal	170
Speaking Out: a Last Appeal	170
The Lord breaks Silence	171
Moses' View of the Position	173
The Ultimate Decision	173
The Promise to Caleb	175
God's Decision repeated as a Message	176
A Confession contradicted in Action	177

CHAPTER XV.

THEME	PAGE
Ordinances of Sacrifice	183
Presumptuous Sins and Sins of Ignorance	185
The Impartiality of God	186
Presumptuous Sins	186
God giving Laws for the Distant Future	187
An Offering from the Dough : Domestic Religion	187
God shows Himself Strict and yet Considerate	188
The Sabbath of God	190
The Doom of the Presumptuous illustrated by that of the Sabbath-breaker	191
The Law of the Sabbath : a Solemn Vindication	193
A Distinguishing Mark of the Faithful	195
The Use and Abuse of Memorials ...	196
The Fringes : Ever-present Reminders	196
God recalls a Great Deed and the Purpose of it	198

CHAPTER XVI.

The true and only Priesthood ...	204
Korah's Rebellion 208, 210, 211	
Envy and its Bitter Fruits	212
" The God of the spirits of all flesh "	213
The Destructiveness of Sin	213
The Rebellion of Korah. The Conspirators and their Pretext ...	214
The Reply of Moses to Korah ...	214
Dathan, Abiram, and Moses ...	216
The Destruction of Korah and his Company	217
The Priestly Atonement	220
The Priesthood still further Honoured and Established	221

CHAPTER XVII.

The Sign of the True Priesthood ...	223
The Budding of Aaron's Rod ...	225
The Two Brethren and their Rods ...	225
Aaron's Rod that Budded	226

CHAPTER XVIII.

Responsibilities and Privileges of God's Servants	231
The Responsibility of Authority ...	233
God, the Best Inheritance	233
The Iniquity of the Sanctuary and Priesthood	234
Aaron and his Helpers	235
The Provision for the Priests ...	237
A Covenant of Salt	238

CHAPTER XIX.

THEME	PAGE
The Remedy of Death	242
Purge me with Hyssop, and I shall be Clean	246
Defilement by Contact with the Dead	247
The Water of Purification, and its Lessons	248
Defilement from the Dead	249

CHAPTER XX.

Sorrows and Trials of the Way ...	255
The Sin of Moses	258
The Death of Aaron	259
The great Sin of Disobedience even under Palliating Circumstances ...	261
The Death of Aaron :—" Mercy and Judgment "	262
The Abiding in Kadesh and the Death of Miriam	262
The Gift of Water at Meribah ...	263
The Sin of Moses and Aaron ...	264
The Claim of Kinship rejected ...	266
The Death of Aaron	268

CHAPTER XXI.

Victory won, and followed up ...	271
Sin and the Saviour	273
The Discouragements of the Way ...	275
The Brazen Serpent as a Type of Christ	275
A hard bit of the Road	276
Destruction and Salvation through the Serpent	277
Progress and Triumph	283
A Period of Unbroken Progress ...	285

CHAPTER XXII.

The Way of Balaam	294
Balaam's Greatness and Fall ...	298
Balaam, an Illustration of Systematic Resistance of Conscience	299
The Importunity and Impudence of the Tempter	300
On Cruelty to Animals	300
Moab takes Alarm	301
Balak's Message to Balaam	302
The First Visit to Balaam	303
The Second Visit	305
The Angel, the Prophet, and the Ass	306
Balaam and Balak meet at last ..	309
Balaam—the Summons	310
Balaam—the Arrest	312

CHAPTERS XXIII., XXIV.

Balaam and his Prophecies 321

THEME	PAGE
The Safety of all who enjoy the Blessing of God...	324
The Unchangeable Faithfulness of God	324
The First Prophecy	325
"Let me die the death of the righteous, and let my last end be like his!"	327
The Second Prophecy	329
The Third Prophecy	333
Balaam—the First Parable ...	335
Balaam—the Second Parable	336
Balak relinquishes his Project	337
The Star out of Jacob and the Sceptre out of Israel	338
Balaam—the Third Parable...	340
Balaam—the Fourth Parable	341

CHAPTER XXV.

Sin, Zeal, and Atonement	347
A Terrible Atonement	350
Moab finds a more Effective Weapon...	351
Zeal for God: the Result and Reward of it	352

CHAPTER XXVI.

The Final Numbering of the Elect	357
The Lot is to decide where every Tribe shall receive its Inheritance	359
The Second Census	360
A Generation gone	361

CHAPTER XXVII.

The Certainty of the Promised Inheritance	364
The Disabilities of Sex	365
The Man who Died in his own Sin	367
The Outward Failure and Inward Victory of Moses	369
God's Word to His Dying Servant	372
The Appointment of Joshua to be Moses' Successor	372
The Alleviations of Death	374
The Qualifications for the Public Service of God	374
Preparing for the End	374
The Solicitude of Moses for the Helpless Flock	376
The Solicitude relieved by the Appointment of Joshua	378

CHAPTERS XXVIII., XXIX.

The Perfect System of Sacrifice	381
The Lessons of the Daily Burnt Offering	384
The Daily Offering	385

THEME	PAGE
The Sabbath Offering	387
The Offering at the New Moon	387
The Feast at the Passover Time	388
The Feast of the First-Fruits	390
A Solemn Fast and a Joyous Feast	391
The Offerings of the Seventh Month	391

CHAPTER XXX.

Vows unto the Lord	394
The solemn Obligation of the Vow	395
The Head of the Household honoured and cautioned	397

CHAPTER XXXI.

The Extermination of Sinful Lusts	406
The Lion and his Prey	409
The Death of Balaam	410
The Distribution of the Spoils	411

CHAPTER XXXII.

The mistaken Choice	416
"Be sure your sin will find you out"	420
A Bird in the Hand worth two in the Bush	420
A thorough Exposure of a Selfish Proposition	421
The final Arrangement	422
The Eyes of the Sinner opened at last	423
Nobah—the Man and the Place	425

CHAPTERS XXXIII., XXXIV.

The Journey Home	431
The Journeyings of the Israelites	432
The Holy Land	438
No Compromise with Idolatry	440
How to deal with the Canaanites: an Urgent Warning	441
The Lord appoints Boundaries for the Promised Land	443

CHAPTER XXXV.

The Dwelling of the Faithful: the Redeemer: the Sanctity of Life	449
The Levites to be distributed in certain Cities throughout the whole Land	451
The Manslayer and the Cities of Refuge	452
Why the Murderer must be put to Death	453
The Cities of Refuge	454, 456
God provides Places for the Levites to dwell in	455

CHAPTER XXXVI.

| The sure Inheritance | 460 |